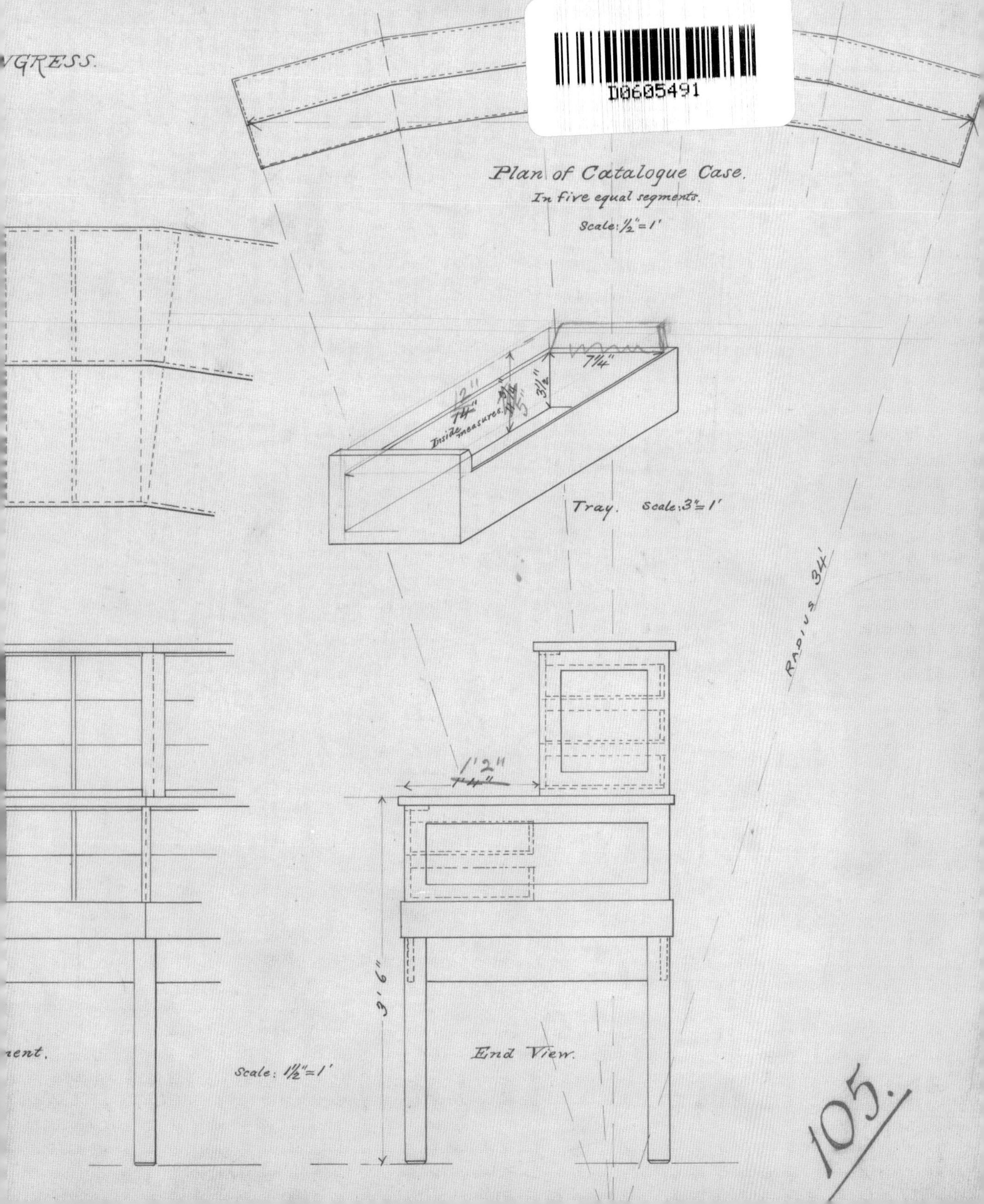
NGRESS.
Plan of Catalogue Case.
In five equal segments.
Scale: 1/2"=1'
7 1/4"
1'2"
14"
Inside measures.
3 1/4"
Tray. Scale: 3"=1'
RADIUS 34'
1'2"
1'4"
3' 6"
ment.
Scale: 1 1/2"=1'
End View.
105.

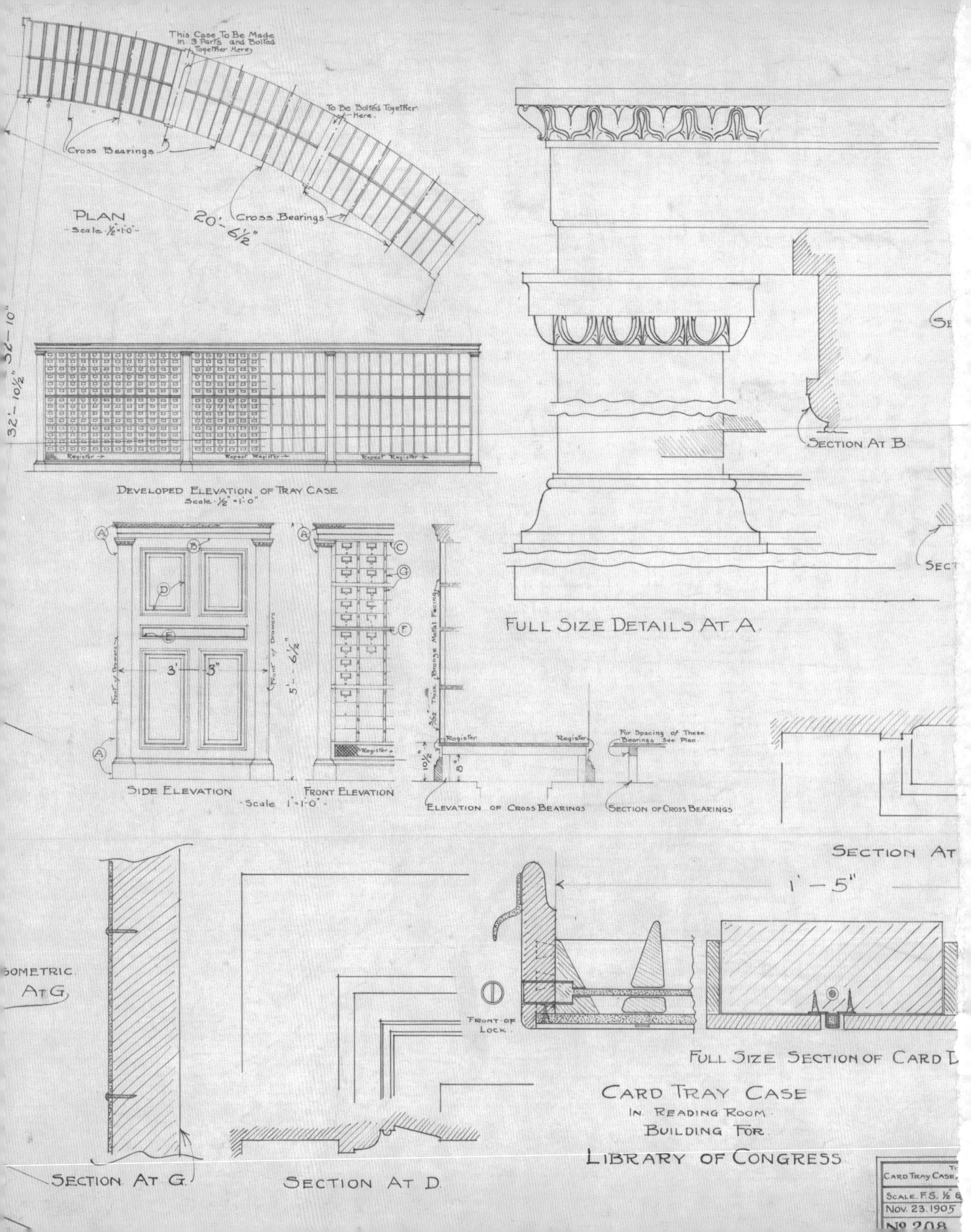
This Case To Be Made In 3 Parts and Bolted Together Here
To Be Bolted Together Here
Cross Bearings
Cross Bearings
PLAN
Scale 1/2"=1'-0"
20'-6 1/2"
32'-10 1/2"
32'-10"
Register
Repeat Register
Repeat Register
DEVELOPED ELEVATION OF TRAY CASE
Scale 1/2"=1'-0"
A
B
C
D
E
F
G
Front of Drawers
Front of Drawers
3'-3"
5'-6 1/2"
3/32" Thick Bronze Metal Facing
Register
Register
Register
For Spacing of These Bearings See Plan
10 1/2"
8"
SIDE ELEVATION
FRONT ELEVATION
Scale 1"=1'-0"
ELEVATION OF CROSS BEARINGS
SECTION OF CROSS BEARINGS
SECTION AT B
FULL SIZE DETAILS AT A.
SECTION AT
1'-5"
ISOMETRIC AT G
Front of Lock
FULL SIZE SECTION OF CARD D
CARD TRAY CASE
IN READING ROOM
BUILDING FOR
LIBRARY OF CONGRESS
SECTION AT G.
SECTION AT D.
CARD TRAY CASE,
SCALE F.S. 1/2"
NOV. 23. 1905
Nº 208

Truman, 1924– In cold blood.

(*Motion picture*) Columbia Pictures Corp.,

sd. b&w. 35 mm.

he book of the same title by Truman Capote.
irector, and screenplay, Richard Brooks; music, Quincy
or of photography, Conrad Hall; film editor, Peter Zin-
Robert Blake, Scott Wilson, John Forsythe, Paul Stew-
, O'Loughlin, Jeff Corey.
A semi-documentary about the actual and senseless
a Kansas family, tracing, as nearly as possible, the
o criminals from the time they initiate a robbery and
e until their deaths by hanging.

and criminals—Kansas. 2. Murder—Kansas. I.
an, 1924– In cold blood. II. Columbia Pictures

364.1
~~791.43~~ 75-707817

Official only

ongress 70 [2] F

DO NOT DISCARD

bz 37

Lee, Harper.

√√ **Work cat.** (first novel)

No conflict

To kill a mo
bird.

CG MAY 23 1960

0165–No. 7—(12/7/53)

1956–
GV863
B3

nin, 1706–1790.
nanac ... New York & Bosto
[1900] / 2 p. l., 132 p., 1 l., facsim
m. (By) Benjamin Franklin.
~~oor Richard's almanack for 1756 appended.~~
~~company, New York, N. Y. 1900, class A, no. 28328. N~~
~~1900.~~
ie border. Selections from Fra
reduction of the almanack for
title: Poor Richard improved: be
Ephemeris ... for
1756 ... By Richard Saunders. Ph

2d.Off.Cs

(Copyright 1900 a 2832
1756

Revised

Temporary En

~~Berry, Walter M.~~

"Baseball dope for 1909". [Bo

1909.

In progress. Additions
on shelflist.

For full entry see
Catalogue for the Public

(5)

1780–1851.
om original
Audubon ...
e author, 1827–
99½ cm.

†

MARC/IC

; v. 2, 1831–34;
See next card.

E185
.5
.D81

1.
1868–1963

Du Bois, William Edward Burghardt

The souls of black folk; essays and
sketches, by W. E. Burghardt Du Bois.
Chicago, A. C. McClurg & co., 1903.
viii p., 1 l., 264 p., 1 l. 21½ cm.
Contents: Of our spiritual strivings.—
Of the dawn of freedom.—Of Mr. Booker T.
Washington and others.—Of the meaning of
progress.—Of the wings of Atalanta.—Of
the training of black men.—Of the black

3-11173

PZ7
.A935
Li
5

Copy
Worn–retain

A
M

The Card Catalog

Books, Cards, and Literary Treasures

The Library of Congress

Foreword by Carla Hayden

LIBRARY OF CONGRESS

CHRONICLE BOOKS
SAN FRANCISCO

Published in association with the Library of Congress

Library of Congress Cataloging-in-Publication Data

Names: Library of Congress.
Title: The card catalog : books, cards, and literary treasures / the Library of Congress.
Description: San Francisco : Chronicle Books, [2017] | Includes bibliographical references and index.
Identifiers: LCCN 2016017476 | ISBN 9781452145402
Subjects: LCSH: Library of Congress—History. | Library of Congress—Catalogs—History. | Card catalogs—United States--History. | Catalog cards—United States—History. | Library catalogs—History. | Cataloging—History. | Classification—Books—History.
Classification: LCC Z733.U6 C36 2017 | DDC 025.3/13—dc23 LC record available at https://lccn.loc.gov/2016017476

Manufactured in China

MIX
Paper from responsible sources
FSC www.fsc.org FSC™ C008047

Design by Brooke Johnson
Typeset in Poynter Old Style, Benton Sans, and Prestige Elite
Front of case: Photograph by Shawn Miller

10 9 8 7 6 5 4 3 2 1

Chronicle Books LLC
680 Second Street
San Francisco, California 94107
www.chroniclebooks.com

frontispiece

Main Reading Room, Library of Congress, circa 1930s. Photograph by Jack Delano.

ends

Architectural drawings for miscellaneous fixtures, equipment, and finishes ("furniture") and alterations to the Library of Congress. 1893-1940.

Contents

Foreword

One of my first assignments when I began my library career was to file Library of Congress card catalog sets into a wooden case in a storefront branch of the Chicago Public Library. The importance of accuracy and the responsibility of the card catalog was impressed upon me.

For the better part of the twentieth century, the card catalog stood as the gateway to the wonders of a library's collection. Now it is celebrated in this new book from the Library of Congress. *The Card Catalog* reflects an important, if unheralded, aspect of our national library—the profound impact of the catalog in organizing the Library's vast holdings and the role of cooperative cataloging in helping isolated rural libraries serve their communities and larger libraries refine their collections.

As Librarian of Congress, I appreciate the daunting challenges my predecessors faced in leading the world's largest library, from former Librarian Herbert Putnam's bold leadership in developing a system for distributing standardized cards to libraries nationwide to Henriette Avram's extraordinary new technology that ushered in the modern age of the online catalog. How fortunate the Library of Congress was and is to have such a tireless and dedicated staff to carry out the different functions that make it one of the pillars of our democracy. I am honored to have the opportunity to build on the legacy and accomplishments of my predecessors as we continue to extend the sense of ownership and pride in our national treasures to all Americans.

Just as the card catalog afforded Putnam the opportunity to provide easy access to the Library's boundless resources, the tradition continues as digitization makes ever more items accessible to the public. Since the Library's establishment in 1800, with a collection of 740 volumes and only three maps, it has grown into a diverse collection of more than 162 million items, including more than 38 million cataloged books and other print materials in 470 languages. The public is welcome to visit the Library of Congress in Washington, D.C., or online at www.loc.gov as we strive to ensure that all citizens can fully and freely access information, pursue knowledge, and make use of our shared cultural heritage.

—CARLA HAYDEN
Librarian of Congress

People working at desks in the Main Reading Room of the Library of Congress, circa 1940.

Introduction

Wandering the stacks at the Library of Congress can be as overwhelming as it is inspiring. Drifting through the maze of bookshelves evokes images of Argentine writer Jorge Luis Borges's fictional Library of Babel—a seemingly infinite labyrinth of books. Being surrounded by the collected memory of the human race is a reminder of the intrinsic desire for both knowledge and organization. Ever since the emergence of the written word, humans have scribbled down myths, stories, histories, and natural observations and worked tirelessly to gather and protect these fragments of a shared past.

Evolving alongside, in the shadows of the written word, was one of the most versatile and durable technologies in history: the library catalog—a road map for navigating this wilderness of books. The humble yet powerful card catalog progressed slowly and, like countless other important inventions, owes its existence to a number of brilliant thinkers, as well as to the twists and turns of history. From the peculiar and idiosyncratic methods of ancient libraries to far more intricate, comprehensive modern attempts, library catalogs are a tangible example of humanity's effort to establish and preserve the possibility of order.

Assembled in handsome oak cabinets, the card catalog once framed the palatial Main Reading Room at the Library of Congress. It has now fallen to the exigencies of modern life, replaced by the flickering screens of the online computer catalog. One would need to venture farther into the stacks to find the Main Card Catalog. Opening a drawer and flipping through the well-worn cards, many handwritten and filled with marginalia containing valuable information not to be found in an Internet search, leaves one with a sense of awe at how catalogers distilled so much information onto simple 3-by-5-inch index cards—cards that still sit neatly filed, waiting to reveal the treasures hidden in the hundreds of miles of Library stacks on Capitol Hill.

—PETER DEVEREAUX

Writer-Editor, The Library of Congress

Main Reading Room, Library of Congress, circa 1950.

THEOLOGI
THEOLOGI
THEOLOGI
THEOLOGI
THEOLOGI
THEOLOGI
LITERATORES
LITERATORES
PHILOSOPHI
PHILOSOPHI
MATHEMATICI

Chapter 1

Origins of the Card Catalog

Cuneiforms to Playing Cards

CATALOGS OF CLAY

The origin of the card catalog goes back to the cradle of civilization nestled in the fertile ground between the Tigris and Euphrates rivers. About 3000 B.C., the Sumerians, who flourished in Mesopotamia (present-day Iraq), used ordinary reeds as styli to make impressions on wet clay. In doing so, they devised what is considered the first writing system. This system, called cuneiform, was initially used by bureaucrats to keep records of daily economic activity and was consigned to a modest group of scribes. As cuneiform gradually grew more refined over the millennia, scribes used it to engrave Sumerian oral literary works onto clay tablets. Excavations beginning in the late nineteenth century uncovered thousands of these tablets—filled with epic poems, hymns, fables, and myths.

One tablet, found near the Sumerian city of Nippur and dated around 2000 B.C., was clearly identified as a library catalog by renowned Sumerian history and language expert S. N. Kramer. At just 2½ by 1½ in (6.5 by 4 cm), the tablet foreshadowed the use of small index cards in cataloging, and it was divided into two columns listing the titles of sixty-two literary works. Among these titles was the oldest surviving piece of Western literature, *The Epic of Gilgamesh*, which predates Homer's *Iliad* and *Odyssey* by more than fifteen hundred years. The epic poem follows the adventures of the legendary king of Uruk through fierce battles and tender moments of friendship and grief as he attempts to make sense of his life.

Bill of sale, Sumerian cuneiform tablet, 2200-1900 B.C.

The logical idea of using a tablet for cataloging purposes parallels other clerical applications, such as accounting and documentation.

previous spread

Die Bibliothek der Universität Leyden La bibliothèque de l'université de Leyde. Jan Cornelis Woudanus, circa 1570-1615.

THE LIBRARY OF ALEXANDRIA'S GREAT CATALOG—THE *PINAKES*

From Pythagoras to Euclid, Homer to Sophocles, and Plato to Aristotle, the scholars, poets, playwrights, and philosophers of ancient Greece profoundly influenced Western civilization. Much of Western science, literature, and philosophy—and the methods used to organize them—can trace their roots to this period of antiquity.

Macedonian king Alexander the Great conquered Greece and much of the known world in the third century B.C. In the wake of his conquests, the most dynamic hubs of Greek culture could be found outside of Greece. On the Nile Delta he planned a monument to Greek cultural supremacy, the Library of Alexandria, the greatest library of antiquity. The library would attempt to encompass a universal scope never before seen, and was destined to become the intellectual center of the Mediterranean.

As no archaeological evidence remains, what this library looked like can only be gleaned from hints found in a few written accounts. The collection did not consist of books but rather scrolls. When Alexandria was founded in the fourth century B.C., the written word had moved on from the sturdy clay tablets to a fragile form of paper called papyrus. Papyrus was made from reeds found along the Nile and was fairly simple and cheap to produce but difficult to preserve over time. After the composition was complete, the papyrus was rolled over a peg and precariously stacked in piles.

It is in this library, dedicated to arts, intellectual exploration, and the advancement of science, that one finds the true precursor to the card catalog. As the scrolls began to pile up, the library staff faced a challenging job, for unlike modern books, the scrolls had no title page, table of contents, or index. In many cases the scrolls did not even list an author, and longer works, such as the plays of Sophocles or Euripides, would often take up

Hermann Göll, *Die Weisen und Gelehrten des Alterthums*, 2nd edition. Leipzig (Otto Spamer), 1876.

Artist rendering of the interior of the Library of Alexandria.

many scrolls with no indication as to their proper order. Alexandria's first librarian, Zenodotus, attempted to put this mass of scrolls in order. The scrolls were inventoried and then organized alphabetically, with a tag affixed to the end of each scroll indicating the author, title, and subject. These three categories came to define the traditional card catalog and are still the cornerstone of library cataloging.

With some semblance of structure applied to the collection, the Greek poet and scholar Callimachus was chosen to devise a way to provide reliable access to the scrolls. His cataloging and classification of the papyrus scrolls made him one of the most important figures in library history. Around 250 B.C., he compiled his *Pinakes*, or *Tables of Those Who Were Outstanding in Every Phase of Culture, and Their Writings—in 120 Books*. The *Pinakes* functioned as both a bibliography and an aid to finding the most important Greek works held by the Library of Alexandria.

The *Pinakes* was arguably the first time anyone compiled a sophisticated list of authors and their works. From the surviving fragments, scholars have deduced that Callimachus divided the scrolls into separate classes, such as poetry, philosophy, and law, and then further subdivided them into a narrower range of subjects or genres. Within each class, the scrolls were arranged alphabetically by author. While this seems obvious to anyone who has ever browsed a bookstore or library, it was groundbreaking in its day. In the *Pinakes*, Callimachus also included data on the scroll itself, such as the total number of lines and, perhaps most important for scholars, the opening words of individual scrolls. This cataloging feature continued through to the catalog cards of the nineteenth century, where in many instances the opening lines of a book would fill the front and back of a card.

Callimachus created the *Pinakes* during a time when Greek scholarship focused on gathering and compiling the creative works of the past. Encyclopedias, anthologies, dictionaries, and other curatorial endeavors begin to surface in this period. With the *Pinakes*, Callimachus was attempting to both list the holdings of important Greek works and provide the bibliographic details that would help readers find a particular work. In doing so, he is regarded as having invented the tools used by modern catalogers.

The fate of this ambitious library is obscured by historical myths as Greek supremacy gave way to Roman dominance. Legend has it, however, that the library and its collection were burned when Alexandria was

Alexander the Great has Homer's books buried under Darius's tomb. Engraving by Marcantonio Raimondi, circa 1480-1534; after a fresco in *grisaille* in the *Stanza della Segnatura*, the Vatican, by Raphael.

Alexander the Great treasured Homer's works, and legend has it that he slept with a dagger and Aristotle's personal copy of the Iliad.

besieged by Julius Caesar in 48 B.C. Although the library suffered some damage during the battle, its demise was probably gradual and much less dramatic. As the Roman Empire expanded across the Mediterranean, the center of culture and intellectual life shifted to Rome, and the rise of Christianity brought with it a suspicion of secular knowledge and the "pagan" scrolls held in the library. Most historians agree that the decline of the Great Library of Alexandria was due to what endangers libraries of the present day—general indifference and bureaucratic neglect.

CATALOGS OF THE FAR AND MIDDLE EAST

As ancient libraries were destroyed and abandoned over the centuries, the catalogs that survived came to be studied by new generations of librarians. In 213 B.C., during the Qin dynasty, the first emperor of a unified China reportedly ordered the burning of ancient texts, including the Confucian classics along with other philosophical and historical works, in an attempt to suppress nonconforming ideas. A few select copies, however, were gathered and preserved in the imperial library.

After the collapse of the Qin dynasty, Emperor Ch'eng Ti of the succeeding Han dynasty directed a historian and government official, Liu Xiang, to assemble a catalog of what remained. Scholars have noted that because this was a government-sponsored project with an agenda of its own, the resulting interpretive catalog enshrined certain philosophical and literary works, creating an official canon. The likely motivation behind this effort was to reconstitute a particular cultural heritage by creating an ideologically driven catalog, thereby compelling the reader to view the library's collection in a particular social and political context.

Although some governments sought to establish intellectual authority by injecting an ideological slant to library catalogs, other catalogs were created on a more personal level that freely and creatively organized books in an attempt to provide insight into the wider world. In A.D. 987, a Muslim bookseller, Ibn al-Nadim, created a somewhat chaotic but exhaustive

Thirteenth-century manuscript of Sharh fusul Abiqrat (The aphorisms of Hippocrates).

Manuscript copied on March 24, 1497, al-Adwiyah al-marufah al-mustamalah (Known and used medications).

Although both of these examples were created after al-Nadim's catalog was compiled, they are representative of the secular works found in the Fihrist.

bibliographic record of Arabic literature and translated works from other cultures. He collected thousands of slips of paper concerning authors, their biographical data, and the titles of their works, eventually compiling them into a book that came to be called *Fihrist*, or "Catalog."

An incredibly original and unique catalog, the *Fihrist* lists authors and details of their lives and works while offering candid assessments of their literary value. Along with religion, customs, and science as subjects, al-Nadim dealt with obscure facets of medieval Islamic history, including works on superstition, magic, entertainment, and other, often vulgar, topics. In the pages of the *Fihrist*, great poems and historical works from Persia, Babylonia, and Byzantium sit side by side with mundane titles and the bizarre, obscene prose of "jesters and clowns." Because the *Fihrist* was not tied to a single collection or library, al-Nadim had the freedom to be as selective as he wished, creating an inclusive cultural catalog of his time.

MEDIEVAL LIBRARIES, MOVABLE TYPE, AND GESSNER'S SCHEME

Throughout the Middle Ages, many European libraries were cloistered places that reflected the austerity of the Roman Catholic Church. The monastic libraries were shuttered to the general public, and books were literally chained to desks or shelves. The catalogs, in turn, were idiosyncratically devised by the person responsible for keeping track of a particular library's holdings. There was little reason for a custodian to be concerned about arranging his library in accordance with another's. Although monastic libraries were not particularly inviting, they served as a refuge for Western cultural heritage as the calamity of the plague ravaged outside.

As Europe plodded through the Dark Ages, the first of two major developments profoundly affected the book, the library, and, eventually, the card catalog. In the fourth to sixth centuries, the book transitioned from scroll to codex. Compared to the awkward and impractical scroll, the codex, which held smaller sheets of paper bound together on one side, had several advantages. It was compact and its pages could be inscribed on both sides, allowing it to hold twice as much text as a scroll. Along with its ease of handling and storage, the codex made cross-referencing possible. The ability to locate specific passages quickly by page number or to bookmark them for later reference changed the nature of scholarship forever.

The second radical innovation occurred during the Renaissance, when Johannes Gutenberg figured out how to cast individual letters from metal

J. W. Alexander, *Evolution of the Book*. "The Printing Press," 1897.

A mural in the Library of Congress, Jefferson Building, depicts a man working the press as Johannes Gutenberg and another man examine a proof sheet.

in the mid-fifteenth century. This "movable type" could then be assembled into words, covered in an oil-based ink, and affixed to a printing press in order to turn out identical pages. What would have taken scribes years to produce by hand could now be completed in a fraction of the time. The printing press took hold quickly and books proliferated across Europe, feeding an increasingly literate population.

The advent of the printing press caused an explosion in secular publishing that libraries could no longer ignore, and with it came uniformity in the layout and design of books. Title pages, tables of contents, and other conventional elements started to appear in the front pages of books. It now was possible to pick up a book and very quickly identify the title, author, publisher, place of publication, and in some cases even subject matter.

As it applied to cataloging, this standardization of information was a game changer. The capricious arrangements of medieval libraries no longer made sense. As the culture of the Renaissance suffused Europe, the rise in literacy brought about an increasing demand for books. A few libraries responded by opening their doors to the public, but for the average citizen these massive collections of books remained inaccessible. As creativity and scholarship reached new heights, libraries struggled to keep up. The staggering number of books that were printed in the first century of Gutenberg's press was unexpected, and a new vision for libraries was desperately needed if any order was to be brought to them.

Swiss naturalist and bibliographer Conrad Gessner brought cataloging into the modern era with his ambitious attempt at compiling a list of all Latin, Greek, and Hebrew books in print. Gessner spent years traveling around Europe, visiting libraries and collecting booksellers' and publishers' lists. Rather than copying the important information from these lists, he cut out what he wanted with scissors and arranged the slips of paper however he liked. He even thought to store these slips of bibliographic information in boxes for later use, a precursor to the modern catalog cabinets that would not become the standard for another three hundred years. In 1545, the first volume of his *Bibliotheca Universalis*, "The Universal Library," was published and comprised an alphabetical listing of writers and their works, with the authors' surnames inverted, something unheard of in its day. Three years later he produced the innovative *Pandectae*, probably the first classified subject catalog that complements an author catalog, making cross-referencing possible. He also created a system of numbers that corresponded to his bibliography, thus creating the first author/subject catalog, a system that was not implemented by the professional library community until the late nineteenth century.

Critical reaction to the power of the printing press was not unlike some responses to the Internet some 550 years later. Each caused a segment of society to panic as a new phenomenon became ubiquitous seemingly overnight. Prominent Renaissance-era intellectuals worried that newly printed books threatened the authority of the classics and would hinder serious scholarship. Dutch social critic Desiderius Erasmus complained, "Is there anywhere exempt from these swarms of new books? Even if taken out, one at a time, they offered something worth knowing, the very mass of them would be a serious impediment to learning." René Descartes quipped that there were "so many useless things and confusion heaped in such large volumes that it would take longer to read those books than we have to live in this life." (Substitute the word "websites" for "books" and those sentiments could be repurposed by critics of the Internet. Gessner's *Bibliotheca Universalis* is also reminiscent of the quixotic attempts a few libraries made to catalog the Internet in the 1990s. Most notably, the search engine Yahoo! aspired to create a hierarchical index of websites. The user-driven search engine, pioneered by Google, quickly rendered obsolete the jumbled Internet directories.)

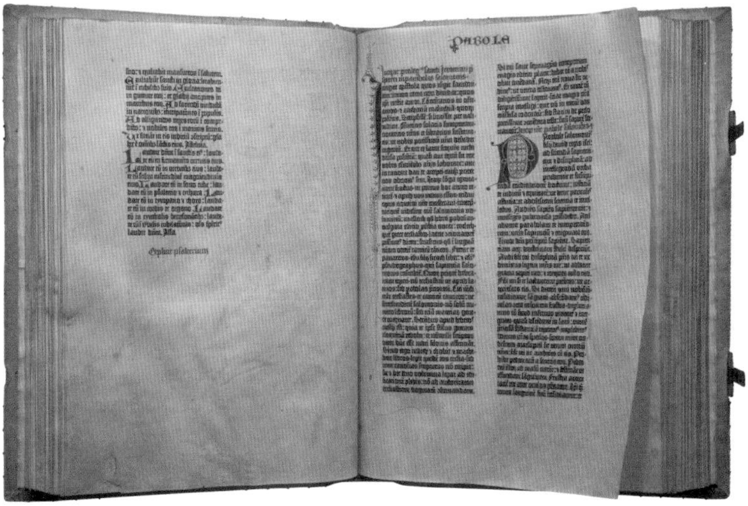

Biblia latina (Latin Bible), Library of Congress. Printed in Mainz. Johannes Gutenberg, 1455.

This Bible, with its noble Gothic type richly impressed on the page, is recognized as a masterpiece of fine printing and craftsmanship. It is all the more remarkable because it was undoubtedly one of the first books to emerge from Gutenberg's new press. This copy is printed entirely on vellum, a fine parchment made from animal skin, and is one of only three perfect vellum copies known to exist.

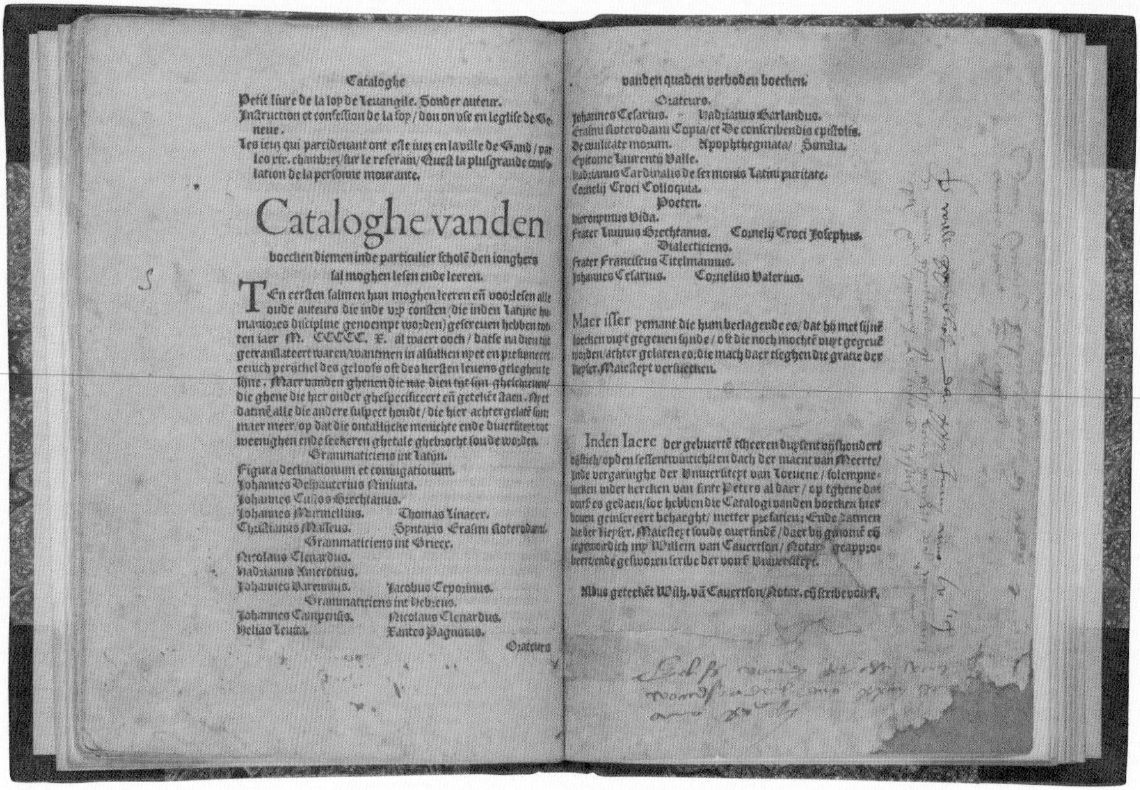

Index Librorvm Prohibitorvm. Catholic Church, 1558.

The rediscovery of ancient Greek literature and history was the driving force in the early Renaissance, and the resulting abundance of new humanistic works unnerved the Catholic Church. The church moved quickly to blacklist certain titles and created an *Index of Prohibited Books* it found heretical, seditious, or scandalous. Subsequent editions included major works by Machiavelli, John Calvin, Voltaire, and Johannes Kepler. The indexes were not officially abolished until 1966.

VIVE LA REVOLUTION . . . AND CARD CATALOGS

Throughout most of the seventeenth and eighteenth centuries, national and university libraries continued experimenting with the feasibility of different cataloging techniques, with relatively few innovations. Ironically, it wasn't until France descended headlong into the chaos of the French Revolution in 1789 that there was a concerted effort to codify cataloging rules and settle on a uniform format that would eventually lead to the standard index card.

At the time, France was on the verge of bankruptcy, and in an effort to relieve the financial crisis, the National Constituent Assembly—the ever-changing government then in power—issued a series of decrees that placed all church assets at the disposal of the nation. The intention was to seize the libraries and sell off the books. However, once it was pointed out that book sales would hardly offset the national deficit, it was decided that the confiscated collections would instead be the foundation for a new system of public libraries.

In May 1791, a handful of men with bibliographic experience, led by librarian Barthélemy Mercier, prepared basic instructions for local officials all over the country to assist others in cataloging their libraries. The genius

Dix Août 1792. Siege et prise du Chateau des Tuileries Paris. Chez Aubert, 1804.

France's revolutionary government seized all property, including library holdings.

of the French Cataloging Code of 1791 was in its brevity, its simplicity, and, most importantly, its medium. The method relied on playing cards, which then were blank on one side. The cataloging novice roped into service would write down the book's title, author, and date, underlining pertinent information. The use of playing cards was an especially astute choice: they could be purchased throughout France, were sturdy and roughly the same size no matter what brand, and could easily be interfiled. Within three years, some 1.2 million cards, representing more than 3 million volumes, were sent to overwhelmed offices in Paris. Once the cards were sorted, the results were mixed, as cataloging participants still all too often managed to botch their assignment. This should not be surprising considering that the project involved requiring inept local governments, already embroiled in a violent revolution, to catalog vast ecclesiastic libraries. Although the ambitious cataloging project did not result in the formation of a national catalog, it did demonstrate the potential of utilizing a uniform format.

In the end, it was the leader of another revolution across the Atlantic Ocean who would slowly build a library that would ultimately establish the archetype of all card catalogs.

French playing cards used to catalog books, eighteenth century. Courtesy of Larry T. Nix.

Deuces and aces were reserved for the longest titles, as those cards had the most space on which to write.

14389
.chap. .608.
le triomphe de S.
joachim et de saincte
anne par nôtre maitre
f. charles véron prieur
des ermites de S. augustin
en tournay. tournay
a. quinqué 1624.
in 16. veau.
paris. d'artois
Le Grand (Antoine)
Lond. J. Martyn 1680
4°. 1001
orat.

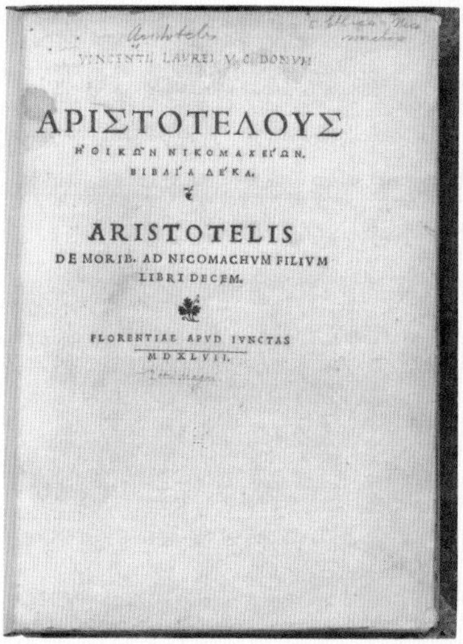
VINCENTII LAVREI V. C. DONVM
ΑΡΙΣΤΟΤΕΛΟΥΣ
ΗΘΙΚΩΝ ΝΙΚΟΜΑΧΕΙΩΝ.
ΒΙΒΛΙΑ ΔΕΚΑ.
ARISTOTELIS
DE MORIB. AD NICOMACHVM FILIVM
LIBRI DECEM.
FLORENTIAE APVD IVNCTAS
M D X L V I I.

ΑΡΙΣΤΟΤΕΛΟΥΣ ΗΘΙΚΩΝ
ΝΙΚΟΜΑΧΕΙΩΝ.
ΤΟ Θ'.
ΝΙΚΟΜΑΧΕΙΩΝ ΤΟ Θ'.
Aristo. Ethi.

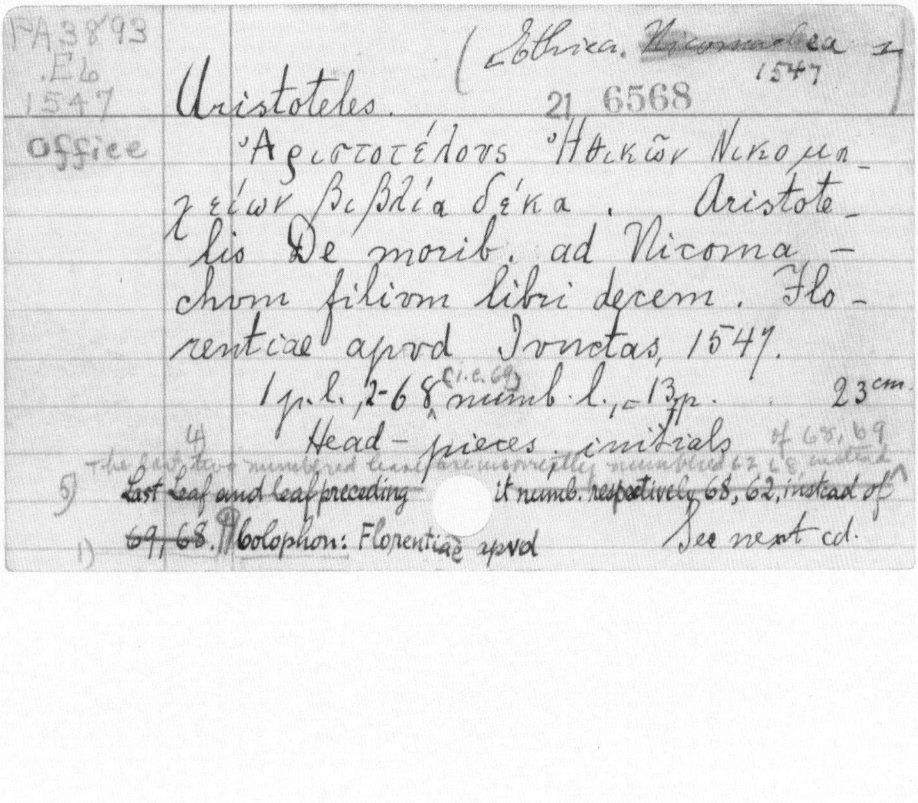
PA3893 .E6 1547

Office

Aristoteles. (Ethica. Nicomachea 1547) 21 6568

Ἀριστοτέλους Ἠθικῶν Νικομαχείων βιβλία δέκα. Aristotelis De morib. ad Nicomachum filium libri decem. Florentiae apud Iunctas, 1547.

1 p.l., 2-68 (i.e. 69) numb. l., 13 p. 23cm.

4 Head-pieces, initials

The last two numbered leaves are incorrectly numbered 62, 68 instead of 68, 69

5) Last leaf and leaf preceding it numb. respectively 68, 62, instead of 69, 68. ¶ Colophon: Florentiae apud

1) See next cd.

Aristotle, *Aristotelous Ethikōn Nikomacheiōn Biblia deka*, 1547.

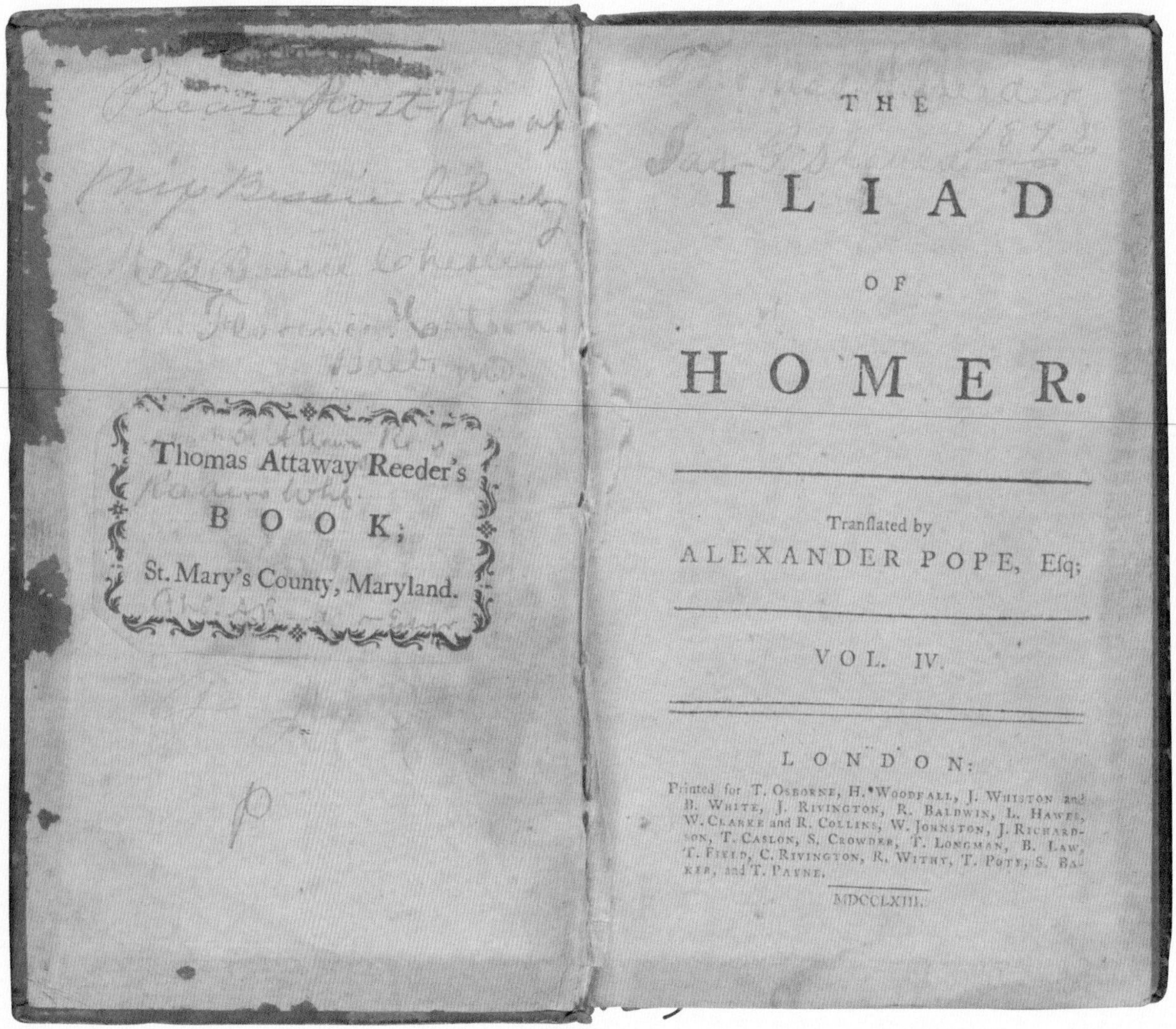
Thomas Attaway Reeder's
BOOK;
St. Mary's County, Maryland.
THE
ILIAD
OF
HOMER.
Translated by
ALEXANDER POPE, Esq;
VOL. IV.
LONDON:
Printed for T. Osborne, H. Woodfall, J. Whiston and B. White, J. Rivington, R. Baldwin, L. Hawes, W. Clarke and R. Collins, W. Johnston, J. Richardson, T. Caslon, S. Crowder, T. Longman, B. Law, T. Field, C. Rivington, R. Withy, T. Pote, S. Baker, and T. Payne.
MDCCLXIII.

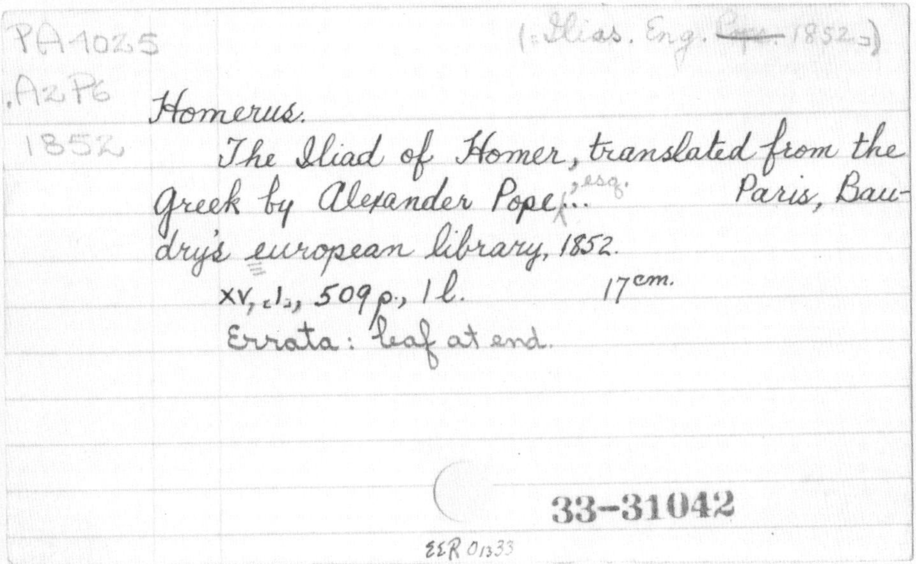

PA1025
.A2P6
1852

(Ilias. Eng. ~~Pope~~ 1852)

Homerus.

The Iliad of Homer, translated from the greek by Alexander Pope, esq. ... Paris, Baudry's european library, 1852.

xv, [1], 509 p., 1 l. 17cm.

Errata: leaf at end.

33-31042

EER 01333

Homer, *Iliad*. Baudry's European Library, Paris, 1872. Alexander Pope translation.

The card featured here is for the 1852 edition of Alexander Pope's famous translation of the Iliad, a translation that was praised by Samuel Johnson as "a performance which no age or nation could hope to equal."

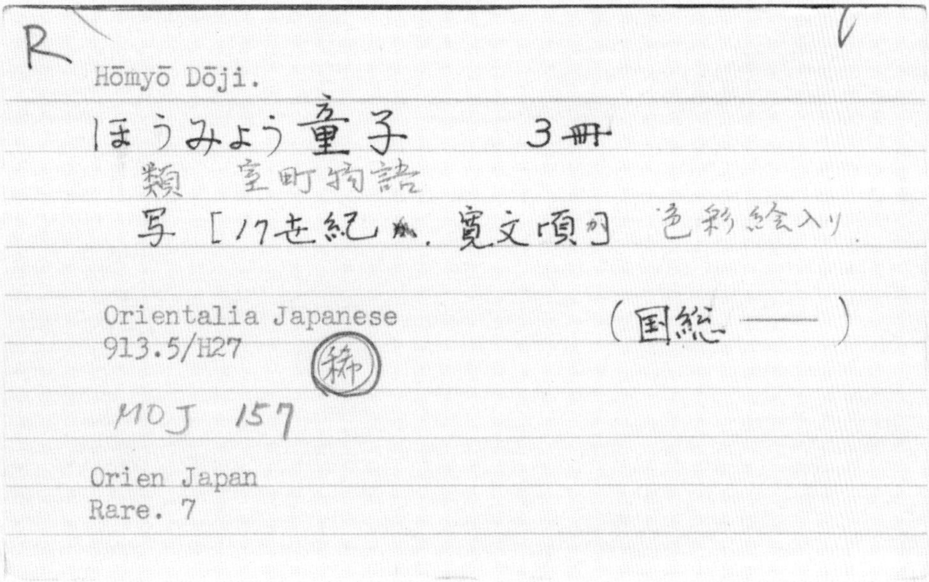
R

Hōmyō Dōji.

ほうみよう童子　3冊

類　室町物語

写 [17世紀か. 寛文頃カ]　色彩絵入り

Orientalia Japanese　(国総 ——)

913.5/H27　(稀)

MOJ 157

Orien Japan

Rare. 7

Hōmyō Dōji. Japan, circa eighteenth century. [Author/creator unknown]

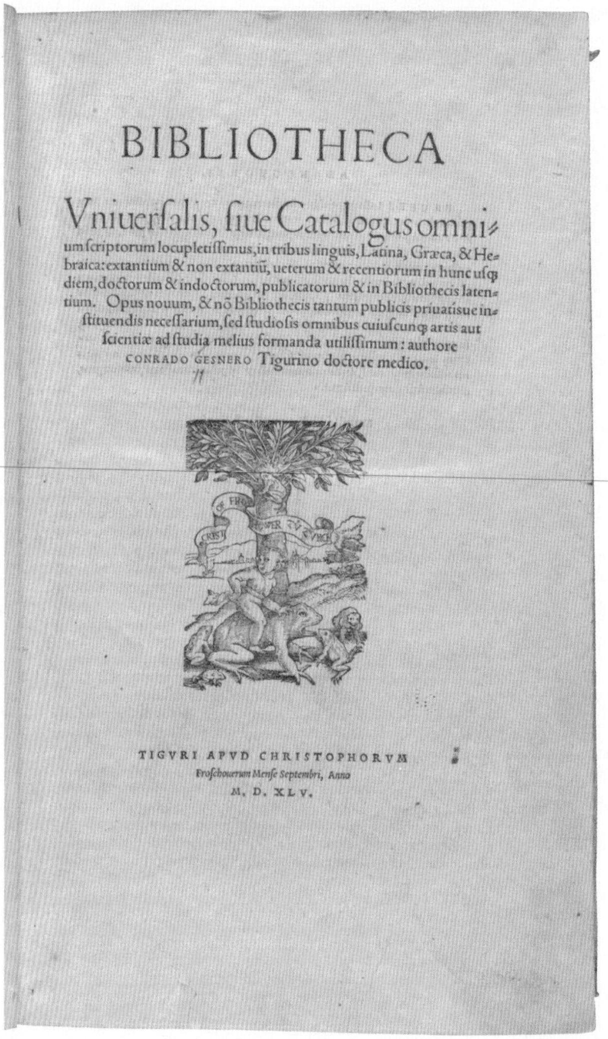

BIBLIOTHECA

Vniuerſalis, ſiue Catalogus omni-
um ſcriptorum locupletiſſimus, in tribus linguis, Latina, Græca, & Hebraica: extantium & non extantiũ, ueterum & recentiorum in hunc uſq;
diem, doctorum & indoctorum, publicatorum & in Bibliothecis latentium. Opus nouum, & nõ Bibliothecis tantum publicis priuatiſue in-
ſtituendis neceſſarium, ſed ſtudioſis omnibus cuiuſcunq; artis aut
ſcientiæ ad ſtudia melius formanda utiliſſimum: authore
CONRADO GESNERO Tigurino doctore medico.

TIGVRI APVD CHRISTOPHORVM
Froſchouerum Menſe Septembri, Anno
M. D. XLV.

Conrad Gessner, *Bibliotheca Universalis* . . . Tigvri, 1545-1555.

Some books required multiple catalog cards to completely describe the contents of the work. There are eight cards for this edition of Gessner's Bibliotheca.

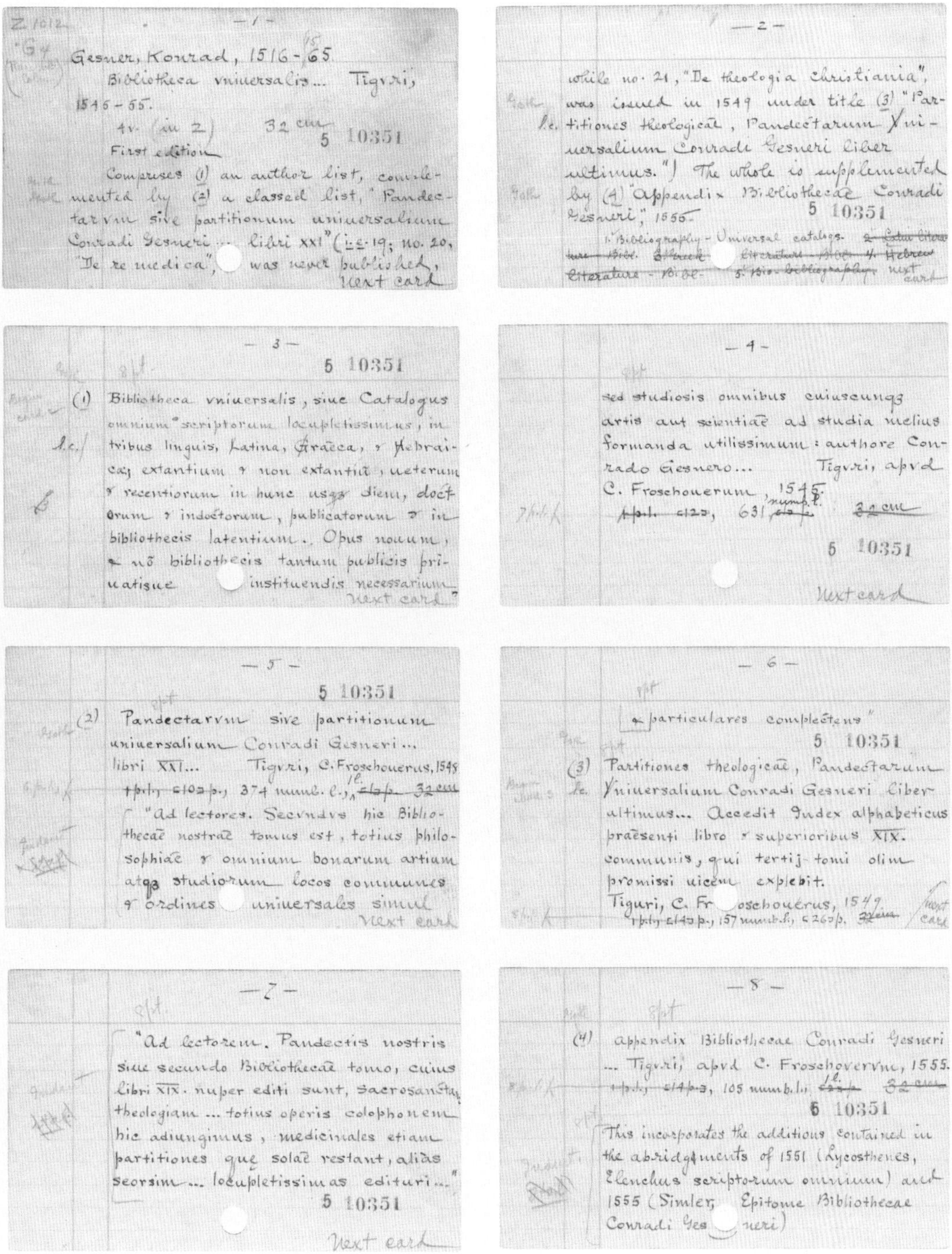

— 1 —

Z 1012 G4

Gesner, Konrad, 1516–65

Bibliotheca vniuersalis... Tigvri, 1545–55.

4v. (in 2) 32 cm 5 10351

First edition

Compuses (1) an author list, complemented by (2) a classed list, "Pandectarvm sive partitionum universalium Conradi Gesneri ... libri XXI" (i.e. 19; no. 20, "De re medica", was never published,

Next card

— 2 —

while no. 21, "De theologia christiania", was issued in 1549 under title (3) "Partitiones theologicae, Pandectarum Vniuersalium Conradi Gesneri liber ultimus.") The whole is supplemented by (4) "Appendix Bibliothecae Conradi Gesneri," 1555. 5 10351

1. Bibliography - Universal catalogs. ~~2. Latin literature - Bibl. 3. Greek literature - Bibl. 4. Hebrew literature - Bibl.~~ 5. Bio-bibliography. next card

— 3 —

5 10351

(1) Bibliotheca vniuersalis, siue Catalogus omnium scriptorum locupletissimus, in tribus linguis, Latina, Graeca, & Hebraica; extantium & non extantium, ueterum & recentiorum in hunc usq; diem, doctorum & indoctorum, publicatorum & in bibliothecis latentium. Opus nouum, & nō bibliothecis tantum publicis priuatisue instituendis necessarium

Next card

— 4 —

sed studiosis omnibus cuiuscunq; artis aut scientiae ad studia melius formanda utilissimum: authore Conrado Gesnero... Tigvri, apvd C. Froschouerum, 1545.

~~4 p.l. c120,~~ 631 numb. l. ~~c1 p.~~ 32 cm

5 10351

Next card

— 5 —

5 10351

(2) Pandectarvm sive partitionum universalium Conradi Gesneri ... libri XXI... Tigvri, C. Froschouerus, 1548

~~4 p.l., c102 p.,~~ 374 numb. l., ~~c1 p.~~ 32 cm

"Ad lectores. Secvndvs hic Bibliothecae nostrae tomus est, totius philosophiae & omnium bonarum artium atq; studiorum locos communes & ordines universales simul

Next card

— 6 —

& particulares complectens"

5 10351

(3) Partitiones theologicae, Pandectarum Vniuersalium Conradi Gesneri liber ultimus... Accedit Index alphabeticus praesenti libro & superioribus XIX. communis, qui tertij tomi olim promissi uicem explebit.

Tiguri, C. Froschouerus, 1549.

~~1 p.l., c140 p.,~~ 157 numb. l., ~~c26 p.~~ ~~32 cm~~

Next card

— 7 —

"Ad lectorem. Pandectis nostris siue secundo Bibliothecae tomo, cuius libri XIX. nuper editi sunt, sacrosanctaq; theologiam ... totius operis colophonem hic adiungimus, medicinales etiam partitiones quae solae restant, aliās seorsim ... locupletissimas edituri..."

5 10351

Next card

— 8 —

(4) Appendix Bibliothecae Conradi Gesneri ... Tigvri, apvd C. Froschovervm, 1555.

~~1 p.l., c14 p.,~~ 105 numb. l., ~~c1 p.~~ 32 cm

5 10351

This incorporates the additions contained in the abridgements of 1551 (Lycosthenes, Elenchus scriptorum omnium) and 1555 (Simler, Epitome Bibliothecae Conradi Gesneri)

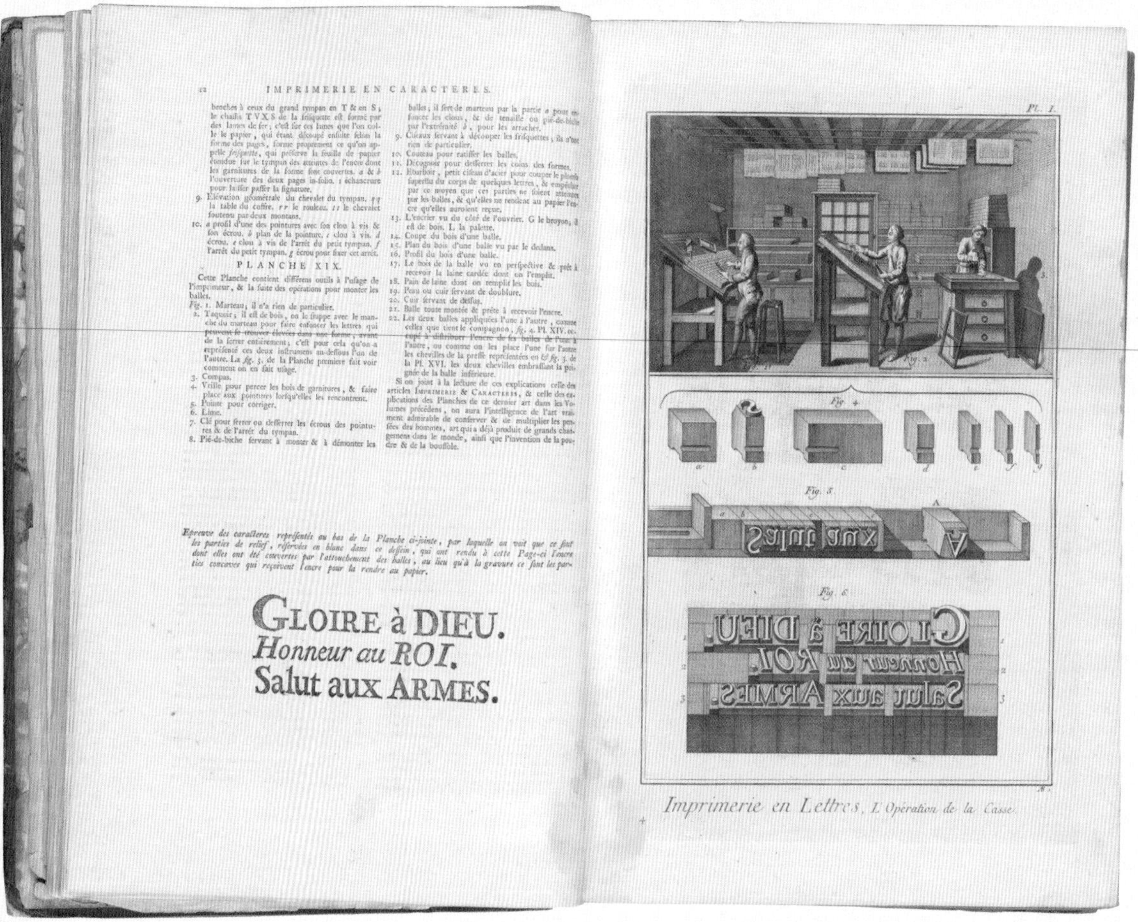
IMPRIMERIE EN CARACTERES.
PLANCHE XIX.
GLOIRE à DIEU.
Honneur au ROI.
Salut aux ARMES.
Pl. I.
Imprimerie en Lettres, L'Opération de la Casse.

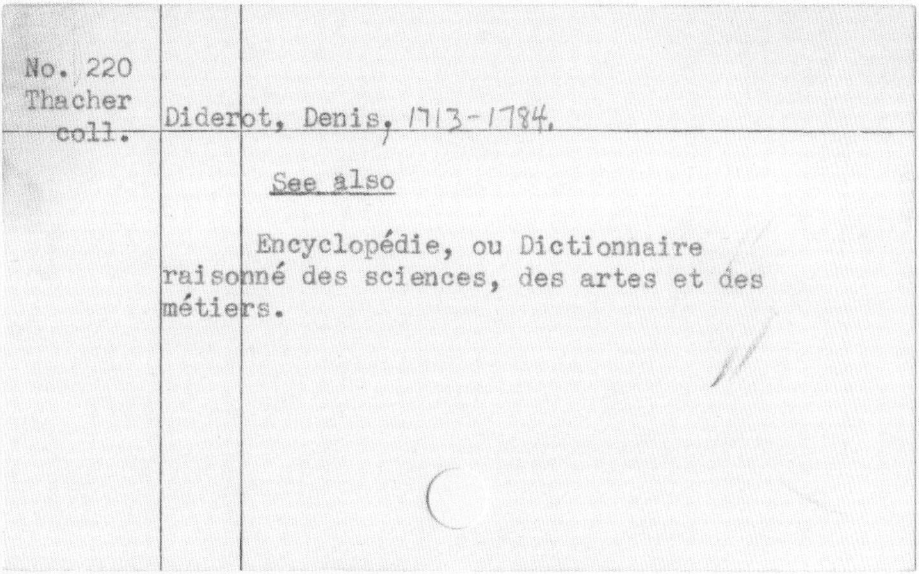

No. 220
Thacher
coll.

Diderot, Denis, 1713-1784.

See also

Encyclopédie, ou Dictionnaire raisonné des sciences, des artes et des métiers.

Denis Diderot, *Encyclopédie, ou, Dictionnaire raisonné des sciences, des artes et des métiers, par unesociété de gens de lettres.* Printed in Paris, Antoine-Claude Briasson, 1751-1765.

This illustration from the large folio volumes of Diderot's impressive Encyclopédie, *an exemplary work of the Enlightenment, demonstrates what a labor-intensive process printing was. Each letter was set by hand and paper was put under the press one sheet at a time.*

To the Reader.
This Figure, that thou here seest put,
It was for gentle Shakespeare cut;
Wherein the Grauer had a strife
with Nature, to out-doo the life:
O, could he but haue drawne his wit
As well in brasse, as he hath hit
His face; the Print would then surpasse
All, that was euer writ in brasse.
But, since he cannot, Reader, looke
Not on his Picture, but his Booke.
B. I.
Mr. WILLIAM
SHAKESPEARES
COMEDIES,
HISTORIES, &
TRAGEDIES.
Published according to the True Originall Copies.
LONDON
Printed by Isaac Iaggard, and Ed. Blount. 1623.
A CATALOGVE
of the seuerall Comedies, Histories, and Tragedies contained in this Volume.
COMEDIES.
HISTORIES.
TRAGEDIES.

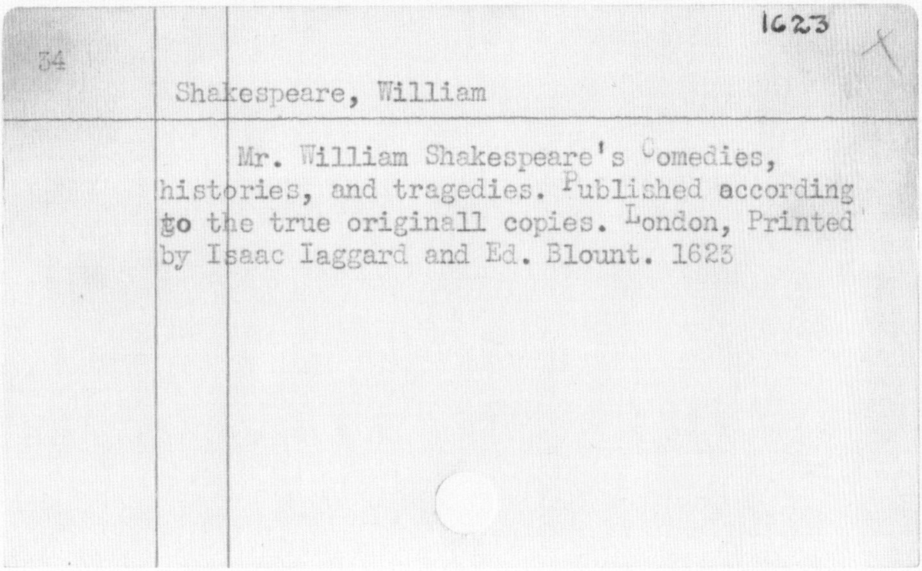

34

1623

Shakespeare, William

Mr. William Shakespeare's Comedies, histories, and tragedies. Published according to the true originall copies. London, Printed by Isaac Iaggard and Ed. Blount. 1623

Mr. William Shakespeares Comedies, Histories & Tragedies: Published according to the True Originall Copies. Printed by Isaac Jaggard and Ed. Blount, London, 1623.

The First Folio, as this edition is referred to, has been called "the most intrinsically valuable book in English."

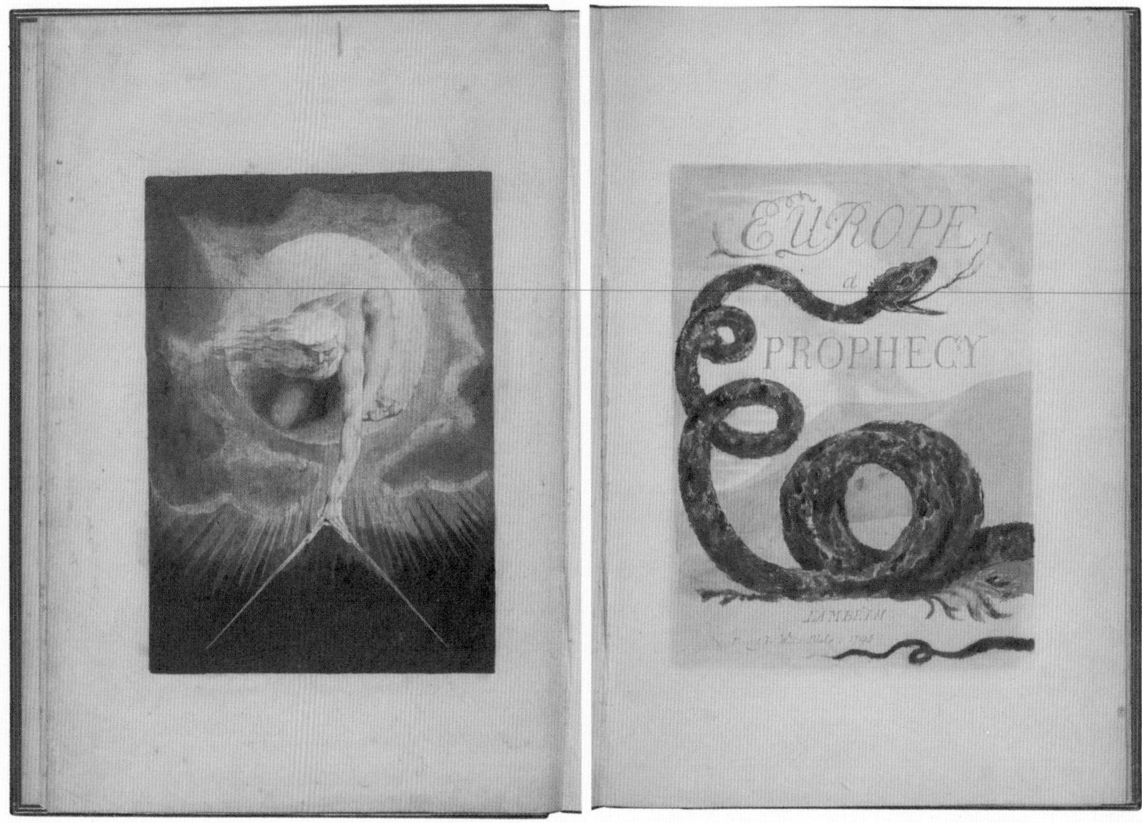
EUROPE
a
PROPHECY

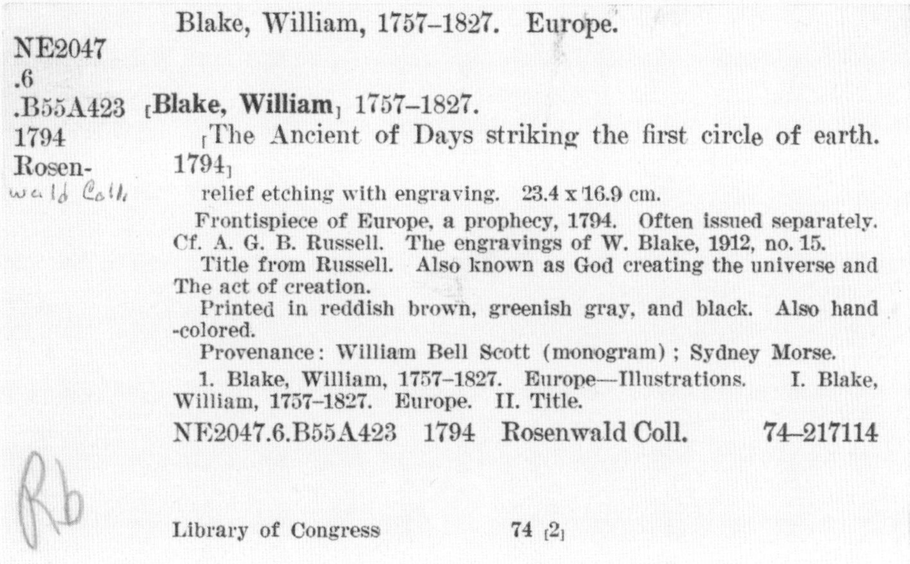

Blake, William, 1757–1827. Europe.

NE2047
.6
.B55A423
1794
Rosen-
wald Coll.

[Blake, William] 1757–1827.

[The Ancient of Days striking the first circle of earth. 1794]

relief etching with engraving. 23.4 x 16.9 cm.

Frontispiece of Europe, a prophecy, 1794. Often issued separately. Cf. A. G. B. Russell. The engravings of W. Blake, 1912, no. 15.

Title from Russell. Also known as God creating the universe and The act of creation.

Printed in reddish brown, greenish gray, and black. Also hand -colored.

Provenance: William Bell Scott (monogram); Sydney Morse.

1. Blake, William, 1757–1827. Europe—Illustrations. I. Blake, William, 1757–1827. Europe. II. Title.

NE2047.6.B55A423 1794 Rosenwald Coll. 74–217114

Rb

Library of Congress 74 [2]

William Blake, "The Ancient of Days," frontispiece to *Europe a Prophecy*, 1794.

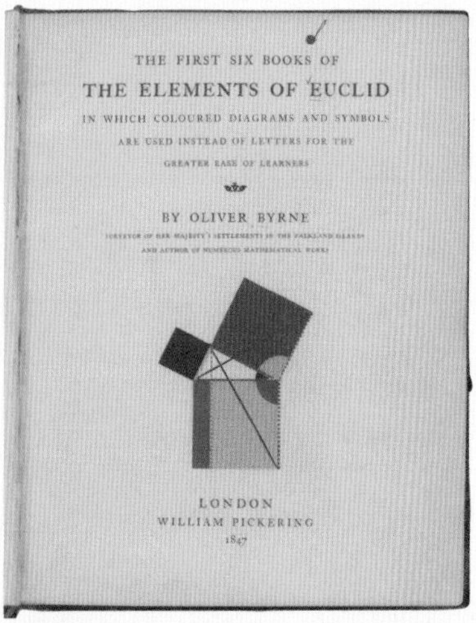
THE FIRST SIX BOOKS OF
THE ELEMENTS OF EUCLID
IN WHICH COLOURED DIAGRAMS AND SYMBOLS
ARE USED INSTEAD OF LETTERS FOR THE
GREATER EASE OF LEARNERS
BY OLIVER BYRNE
LONDON
WILLIAM PICKERING
1847

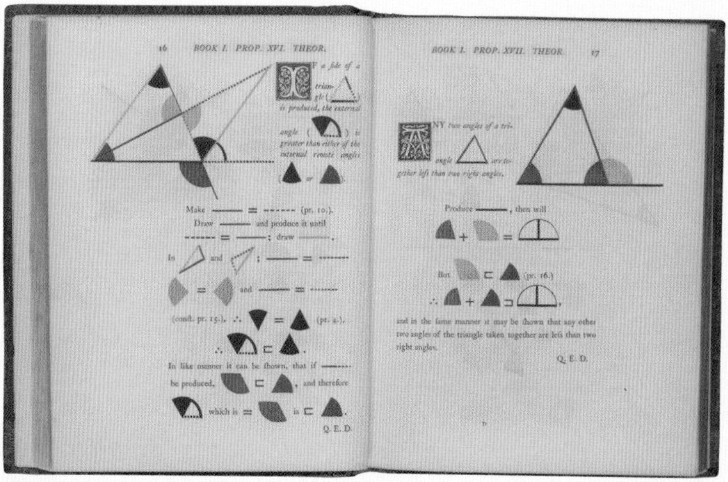
16 BOOK I. PROP. XVI. THEOR.
BOOK I. PROP. XVII. THEOR. 17
Q. E. D.
Q. E. D.

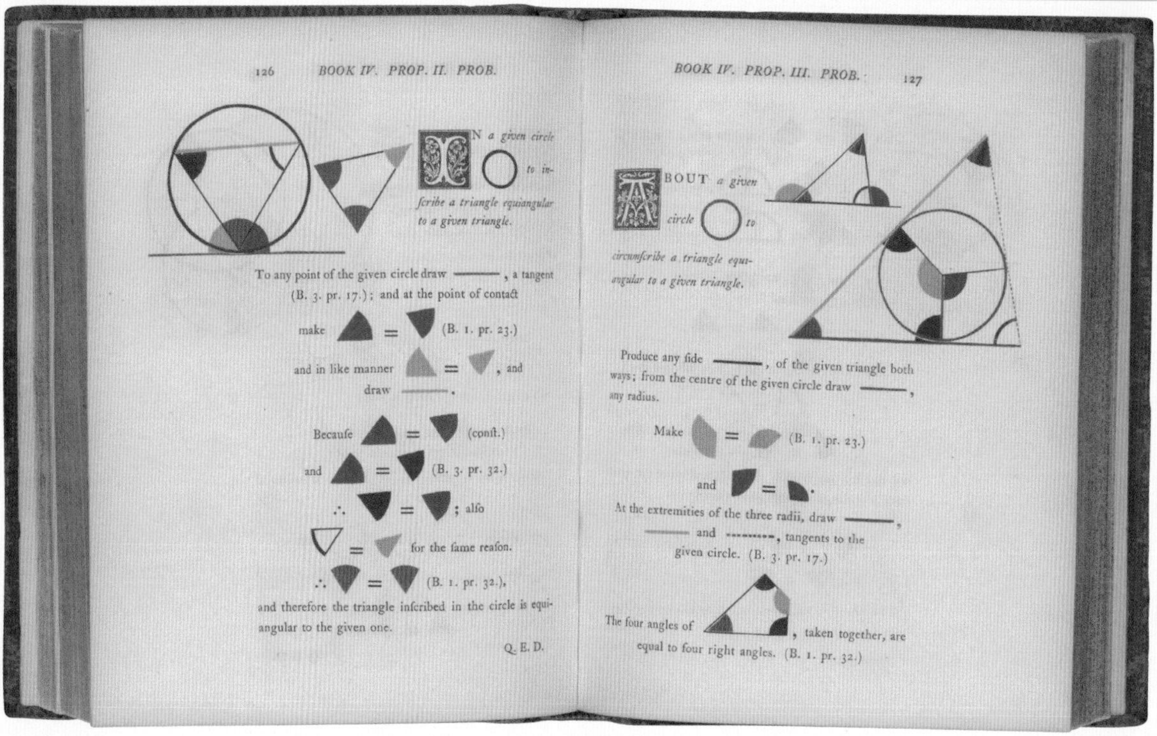
126 BOOK IV. PROP. II. PROB.
N a given circle
to inscribe a triangle equiangular
to a given triangle.
To any point of the given circle draw ———, a tangent
(B. 3. pr. 17.); and at the point of contact
make = (B. 1. pr. 23.)
and in like manner = , and
draw ——.
Because = (const.)
and = (B. 3. pr. 32.)
∴ = ; also
= for the same reason.
∴ = (B. 1. pr. 32.),
and therefore the triangle inscribed in the circle is equiangular to the given one.
Q. E. D.
BOOK IV. PROP. III. PROB. 127
BOUT a given
circle to
circumscribe a triangle equiangular to a given triangle.
Produce any side ———, of the given triangle both
ways; from the centre of the given circle draw ———,
any radius.
Make = (B. 1. pr. 23.)
and = .
At the extremities of the three radii, draw ———,
——— and ---------, tangents to the
given circle. (B. 3. pr. 17.)
The four angles of , taken together, are
equal to four right angles. (B. 1. pr. 32.)

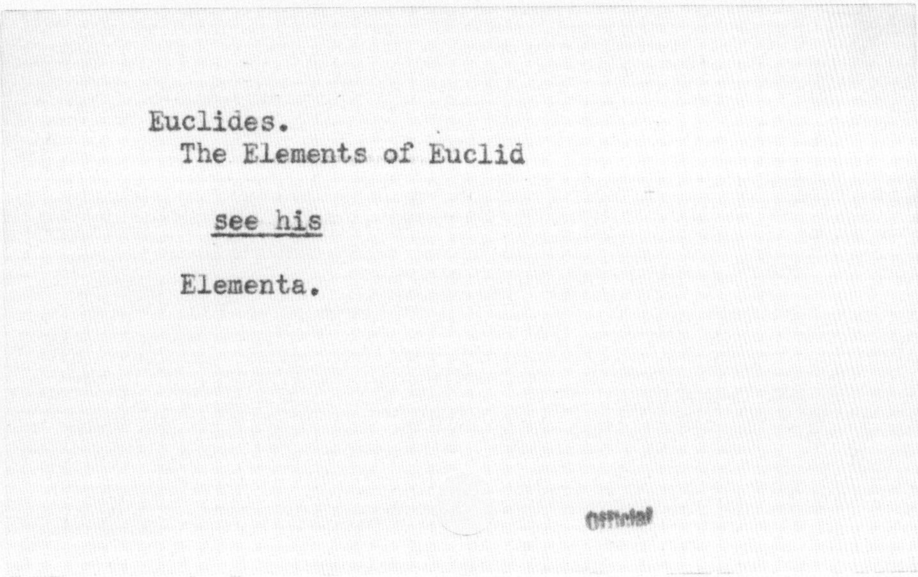

Euclides.
The Elements of Euclid

see his

Elementa.

Official

Oliver Byrne, *The First Six Books of the Elements of Euclid*. London, William Pickering, 1847.

ESOPVS

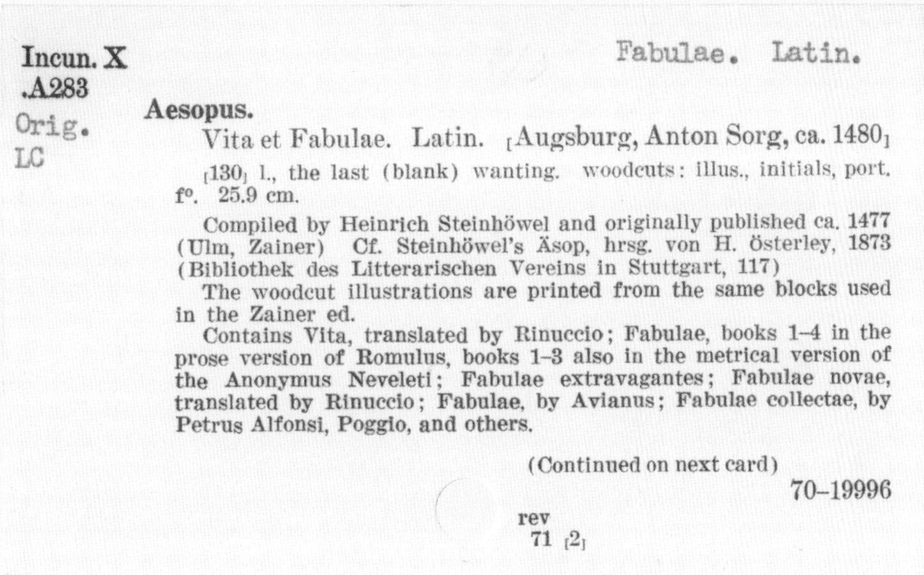

Incun. X
.A283
Orig.
LC

Fabulae. Latin.

Aesopus.

Vita et Fabulae. Latin. [Augsburg, Anton Sorg, ca. 1480]

[130] l., the last (blank) wanting. woodcuts: illus., initials, port. f°. 25.9 cm.

Compiled by Heinrich Steinhöwel and originally published ca. 1477 (Ulm, Zainer) Cf. Steinhöwel's Äsop, hrsg. von H. Österley, 1873 (Bibliothek des Litterarischen Vereins in Stuttgart, 117)

The woodcut illustrations are printed from the same blocks used in the Zainer ed.

Contains Vita, translated by Rinuccio; Fabulae, books 1–4 in the prose version of Romulus, books 1–3 also in the metrical version of the Anonymus Neveleti; Fabulae extravagantes; Fabulae novae, translated by Rinuccio; Fabulae, by Avianus; Fabulae collectae, by Petrus Alfonsi, Poggio, and others.

(Continued on next card)

70–19996

rev
71 [2]

Aesop, *Vita et Fabulae (Aesop's Fables)*. Augsburg, Germany, Anton Sorg, circa 1480.

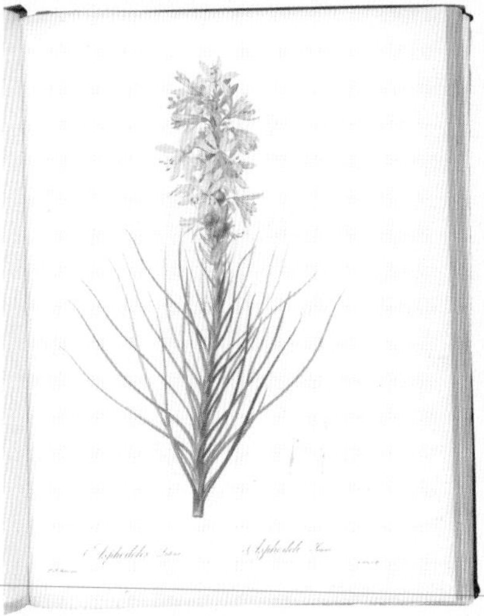

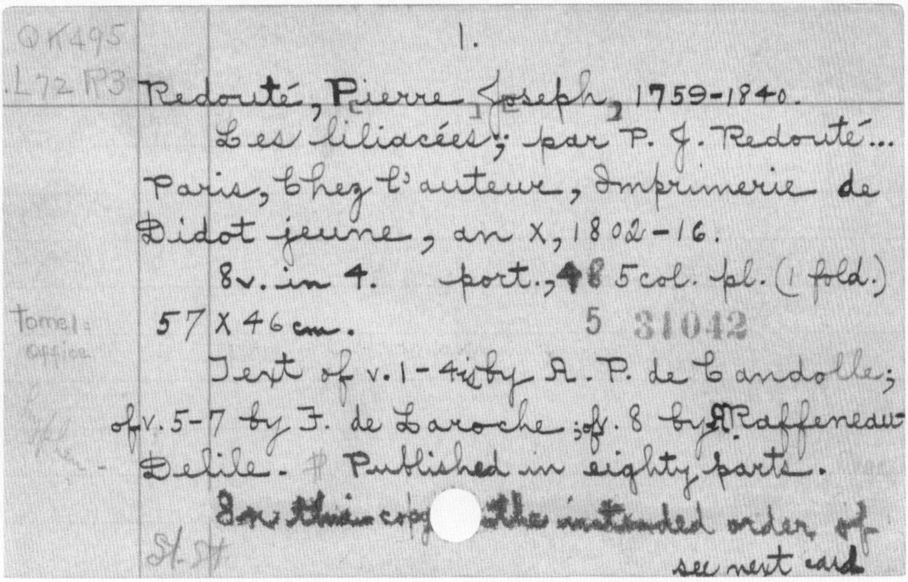

QK495
.L72 R3

1.

Redouté, P[ierre] J[oseph], 1759-1840.
Les liliacées; par P. J. Redouté...
Paris, chez l'auteur, Imprimerie de Didot jeune, an X, 1802-16.
8 v. in 4. port., 485 col. pl. (1 fold.)
57 X 46 cm. 5 31042
Text of v.1-4 by A. P. de Candolle; of v.5-7 by F. de Laroche; of v.8 by A. Raffeneau-Delile. # Published in eighty parts.
For this copy the intended order of
see next card

Tome 1: office

Pierre-Joseph Redouté, *Les Liliacées*. Paris, Didot Jeune, 1802-1816.

RECEIVED of the Librarian of Congress, the following books, which I pro[mise]
forfeit and pay twice the value thereof; as also one do[llar]

When delivered	When received	Folio—three weeks	Value dollars	Quarto—two weeks	Va[lue] Dol[lars]
11th 1819.					
6. 1820	14 Jany 1820				
14 ″	24 ″ ″				
15 ″	″ ″				
24 ″	Feby 3 ″				
″	4th ″				
1 ″	5 ″				
″	10 ″ ″				
0 ″	14 ″ ″			✓ Donatus Roman Antiq	
1 ″	15 ″ ″				
5 ″	17 ″ ″				
1 ″	22 ″ ″				
2 ″	29 ″ ″				
1 ″	14 March ″				
	″ ″				
4 ″	22 ″ ″				
3 ″	4 apl ″				
7 ″	″ ″ ″				
″					
24 ″	26 ″ ″				
26 ″					

RECEIVED of the Librarian of Congress, the following books, which I pro[mise]
forfeit and pay twice the value thereof; as also one do[llar]

When delivered	When received	Folio—three weeks	Value dollars	Quarto—two weeks	Va[lue] Dol[lars]

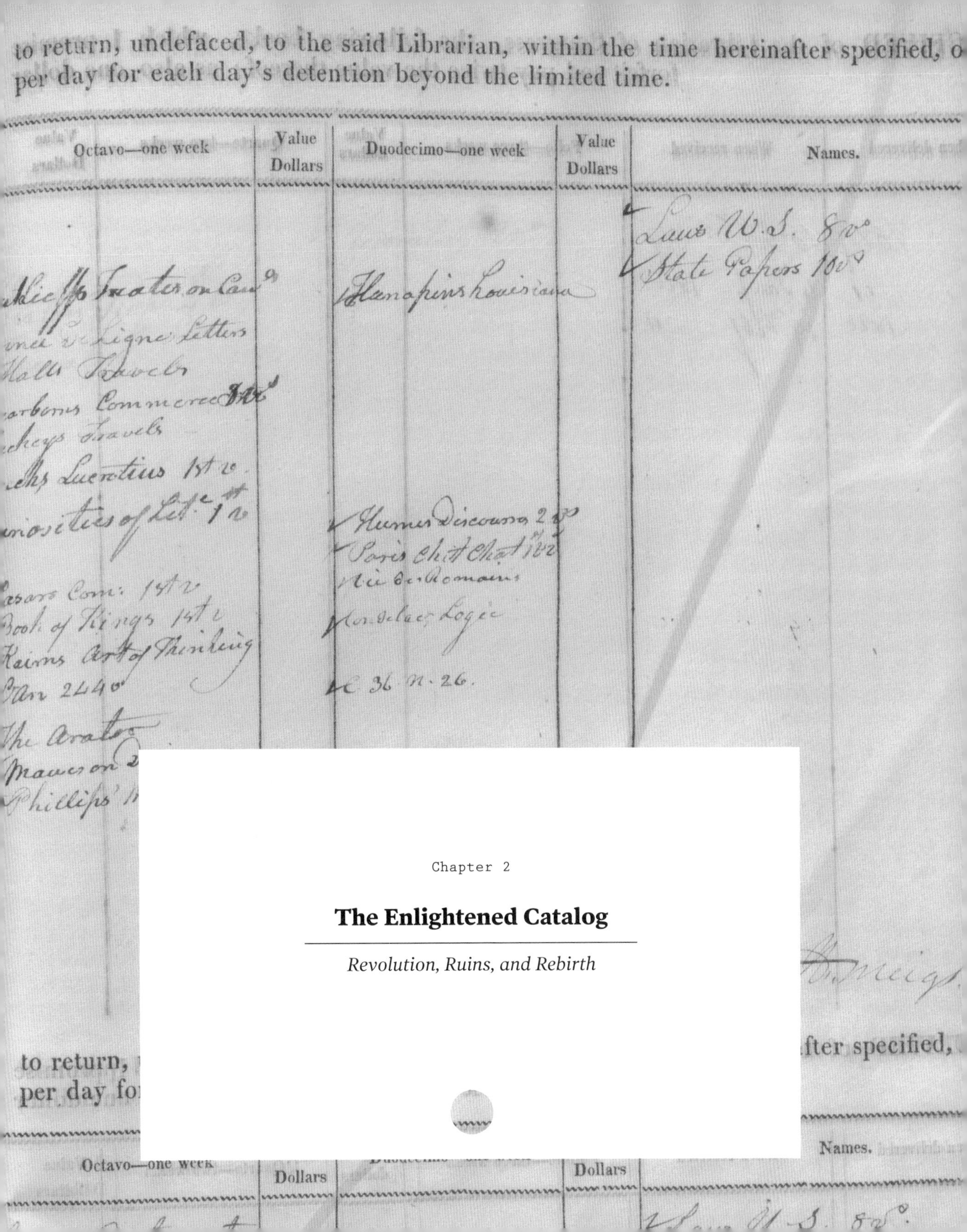

to return, undefaced, to the said Librarian, within the time hereinafter specified, o
per day for each day's detention beyond the limited time.

Octavo—one week	Value Dollars	Duodecimo—one week	Value Dollars	Names.
				Laws U.S. 8vo
				State Papers 10vo
Treaties on Can[illegible]		Hennepins Louisiana		
[illegible] Letters				
Halls Travels				
[illegible] Commerce				
[illegible] Travels				
[illegible] Lucretius 1st v.				
Curiosities of Lit. 1st v		Humes Discourses 2 v		
		Paris Chit Chat 1st v		
Caesars Com: 1st v		[illegible]		
Book of Kings 1st v		[illegible] Logic		
Rains Art of Thinking				
[illegible] 2440		C 36 N. 26.		
The Orator				
[illegible]				
Phillips' [illegible]				

Chapter 2

The Enlightened Catalog

Revolution, Ruins, and Rebirth

ELEVEN HAIR TRUNKS AND A CASE FOR THE MAPS

In the fall of 1774, as a crisis that would ultimately explode into the Revolutionary War was escalating between Great Britain and its thirteen American colonies, delegates from each colony met in Philadelphia for the First Continental Congress. Shared outrage at the harassing laws and regulations the British imposed in response to the Boston Tea Party brought the delegates together on the first floor of the newly built Carpenters' Hall. On the second floor, just above the delegates, resided Benjamin Franklin's Library Company of Philadelphia, America's first successful lending library and one of its oldest cultural institutions.

As they delineated their positions and drafted a response to King George III, the delegates had access to the library, often consulting its collection of works on political theory, history, law, and philosophy. After the war, John Adams suggested in a letter to Thomas Jefferson that the real revolution was in the arguments and exchange of ideas presented in newspaper editorials and pamphlets that so effectively swayed public opinion even before the first shots were fired at Lexington and Concord.

The Revolutionary War was in its final stages in 1782 when a young delegate from Virginia, James Madison, grasping the importance of books in the fledgling republic, drafted an impressive list of titles he felt Congress should procure. Madison's list, though not acted upon, contained renowned political treatises and classics of Greek philosophy—works reflecting the ideas and convictions that would soon be embodied in the new nation's Constitution. Private libraries, along with the Library Company of Philadelphia, served as the de facto Library of Congress until the seat of the United States government finally moved to a new federal city. It was this move to the marshes of the Potomac River between Maryland and Virginia that necessitated the creation of a new library.

When Congress was preparing to move in the spring of 1800, Washington, D.C., was hardly a bustling metropolis. French immigrant Pierre Charles L'Enfant's plan for the capital envisioned transforming low-lying farms, forests, and tidal flats into a grand city filled with imposing neoclassical architecture. But after receiving reports of blighted, unfinished buildings along muddy, rutted streets, Congress took action. On April 24, 1800, President John Adams signed an appropriations bill that provided funding for "footways," or sidewalks, throughout the city as well as for the

previous spread

Record of Books Drawn by Members of Congress for 1815.

purchase of furniture for the empty Capitol building. Five thousand dollars was tacked on to the bill "for the purchase of such books as may be necessary for the use of Congress and such a catalogue as shall be furnished by a joint committee of both houses of Congress to be appointed for that purpose." With that, the Library of Congress was established.

The committee appointed to oversee the creation of the new Library moved swiftly to compile a "want list" of books and maps they felt Congress must have. The details of how this original list was compiled are murky, but it is likely that the chairmen of the committee, William Bingham and Robert Waln, both Philadelphians, consulted the Library Company and referred to its catalog. It is also reasonable to assume that the well-known book collector and future president from Virginia, Thomas Jefferson, had some input in selecting appropriate volumes. Selected titles included an impressive assortment of classic works on history, law, economics, geography, and politics.

Books in early nineteenth-century America were expensive and difficult to find, and most had to be imported from Europe. In June 1800, Congress placed its hefty order with the prestigious London book dealers Cadell and Davies, one of the few firms that could handle such a large transaction.

Cadell and Davies "instantly set about executing the order in the best manner" and within five months obtained and packed 728 volumes and three maps into eleven hair trunks and arranged for their shipment on the *American*, which departed for Baltimore on December 11. Along with a bill of lading for £489 and an invoice, which offered Congress a discount for "prompt payment," Cadell and Davies sent a short note explaining the "advanced prices" of some of the books due to their rarity.

As Congress settled into its new home in the Capitol building that winter, clerks unpacked the eleven trunks and set up the Library. The joint committee had the handwritten invoice and cover letter from Cadell and Davies printed into an eight-page pamphlet that included each book title along with the sale price. This booklist constitutes the first printed catalog of the Library of Congress. It may seem peculiar that book prices were listed, but because the Library represented such a significant investment for the newly established country, Congressmen could only check books out by signing a note promising to return them—or pay for them in full.

William Russell Birch, *A view of the Capitol of Washington before It Was Burnt Down by the British.* Watercolor, circa 1800.

This view shows the only section of the U.S. Capitol that had been completed when the federal government moved to Washington in 1800. Workmen are still cutting stones in the left foreground, and the city can be seen in the distance on the right.

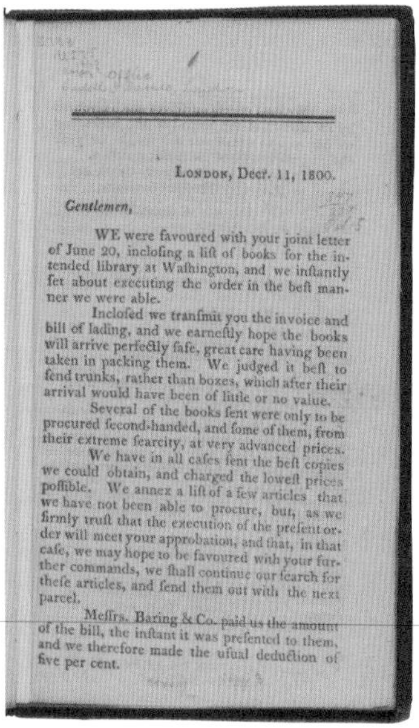

LONDON, Decr. 11, 1800.

Gentlemen,

WE were favoured with your joint letter of June 20, incloſing a liſt of books for the intended library at Waſhington, and we inſtantly ſet about executing the order in the beſt manner we were able.

Incloſed we tranſmit you the invoice and bill of lading, and we earneſtly hope the books will arrive perfectly ſafe, great care having been taken in packing them. We judged it beſt to ſend trunks, rather than boxes, which after their arrival would have been of little or no value.

Several of the books ſent were only to be procured ſecond-handed, and ſome of them, from their extreme ſcarcity, at very advanced prices.

We have in all caſes ſent the beſt copies we could obtain, and charged the loweſt prices poſſible. We annex a liſt of a few articles that we have not been able to procure, but, as we firmly truſt that the execution of the preſent order will meet your approbation, and that, in that caſe, we may hope to be favoured with your further commands, we ſhall continue our ſearch for theſe articles, and ſend them out with the next parcel.

Meſſrs. Baring & Co. paid us the amount of the bill, the inſtant it was preſented to them, and we therefore made the uſual deduction of five per cent.

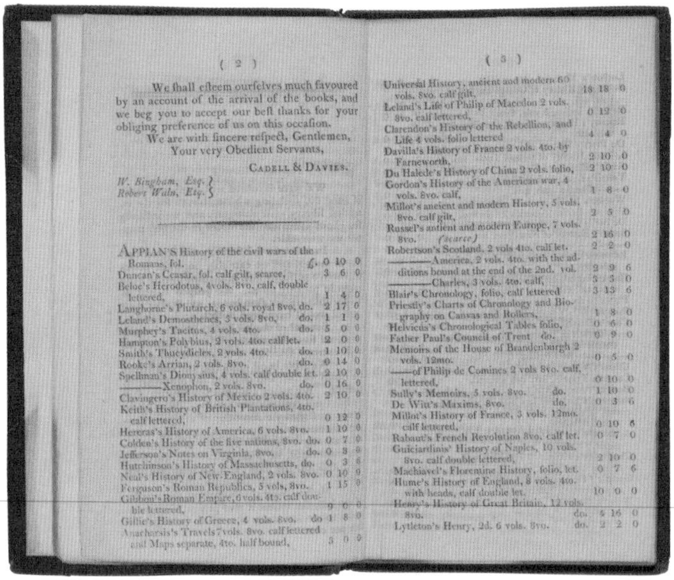

(2)

We ſhall eſteem ourſelves much favoured by an account of the arrival of the books, and we beg you to accept our beſt thanks for your obliging preference of us on this occaſion.

We are with ſincere reſpect, Gentlemen,
Your very Obedient Servants,

CADELL & DAVIES.

W. Bingham, Esq.
Robert Waln, Esq.

APPIAN'S History of the civil wars of the Romans, fol.	£. 0	10	0
Duncan's Cæsar, fol. calf gilt, scarce,	3	6	0
Beloe's Herodotus, 4vols. 8vo. calf, double lettered,	1	4	0
Langhorne's Plutarch, 6 vols. royal 8vo. do.	2	17	0
Leland's Demosthenes, 3 vols. 8vo. do.	1	1	0
Murphey's Tacitus, 4 vols. 4to. do.	5	0	0
Hampton's Polybius, 2 vols. 4to. calf let.	2	0	0
Smith's Thucydicles, 2 vols. 4to. do.	1	10	0
Rooke's Arrian, 2 vols. 8vo. do.	0	14	0
Spelman's Dionysius, 4 vols. calf double let.	2	10	0
———Xenophon, 2 vols. 8vo. do.	0	16	0
Clavingero's History of Mexico 2 vols. 4to.	2	10	0
Keith's History of British Plantations, 4to. calf lettered,	0	12	0
Hereras's History of America, 6 vols. 8vo.	1	10	0
Colden's History of the five nations, 8vo. do.	0	7	0
Jefferson's Notes on Virginia, 8vo. do.	0	3	0
Hutchinson's History of Massachusetts, do.	0	3	6
Neal's History of New-England, 2 vols. 8vo.	0	10	0
Ferguson's Roman Republics, 5 vols, 8vo.	1	15	0
Gibbon's Roman Empire, 6 vols. 4to. calf double lettered,	9	0	0
Gillie's History of Greece, 4 vols. 8vo. do	1	8	0
Anacharsis's Travels 7 vols. 8vo. calf lettered and Maps separate, 4to. half bound,	5	0	0

(3)

Universal History, ancient and modern 60 vols. 8vo. calf gilt,	18	18	0
Leland's Life of Philip of Macedon 2 vols. 8vo. calf lettered,	0	12	0
Clarendon's History of the Rebellion, and Life 4 vols. folio lettered	4	4	0
Davilla's History of France 2 vols. 4to. by Farneworth,	2	10	0
Du Halede's History of China 2 vols. folio,	2	10	0
Gordon's History of the American war, 4 vols. 8vo. calf,	1	8	0
Millot's ancient and modern History, 5 vols. 8vo. calf gilt,	2	5	0
Russel's antient and modern Europe, 7 vols. 8vo. *(scarce)*	2	16	0
Robertson's Scotland. 2 vols 4to. calf let.	2	2	0
———America, 2 vols. 4to. with the additions bound at the end of the 2nd. vol.	2	9	6
———Charles, 3 vols. 4to. calf,	3	3	0
Blair's Chronology, folio, calf lettered	3	13	6
Priestly's Charts of Chronology and Biography on Canvas and Rollers,	1	8	0
Helvicus's Chronological Tables folio,	0	6	0
Father Paul's Council of Trent do.	0	9	0
Memoirs of the House of Brandenburgh 2 vols. 12mo.	0	5	0
——of Philip de Comines 2 vols 8vo. calf, lettered,	0	10	0
Sully's Memoirs, 5 vols. 8vo. do.	1	10	0
De Witt's Maxims, 8vo. do.	0	3	6
Millot's History of France, 3 vols. 12mo. calf lettered,	0	10	6
Rabaut's French Revolution 8vo. calf let.	0	7	0
Guiciardinis' History of Naples, 10 vols. 8vo. calf double lettered,	2	10	0
Machiavel's Florentine History, folio, let.	0	7	6
Hume's History of England, 8 vols. 4to. with heads, calf double let.	10	0	0
Henry's History of Great Britain, 12 vols. 8vo. do.	4	16	0
Lytleton's Henry, 2d. 6 vols. 8vo. do.	2	2	0

Letter from Cadell & Davies, London booksellers, addressed to W. Bingham, esq., and Robert Waln, esq., 1800.

An invoice for the first consignment of books that the Library of Congress purchased with its $5,000 appropriation, approved on April 24, 1800.

THE WAR OF 1812, A BOOK BURNING, AND A NEW LIBRARY

As the British fleet sailed up the Pawtuxet River on August 22, 1814, to attack a vulnerable Washington, D.C., an intrepid J. T. Frost frantically searched the deserted capital for a carriage he could use to secure the Library's collection, which now numbered some 3,000 volumes. The newly appointed assistant Librarian of Congress was left in sole charge of the Library and was determined to try and save it. The rest of the congressional staff had either fled or been called into military service and nearly all of the carts and wagons had been seized by the army, and civilians were using the rest to escape.

Frost and another clerk, Samuel Burch, desperately tried to commandeer a carriage, but managed only to obtain a single cart. They hastily loaded up records, papers, and books and hid them out in the countryside. They courageously moved as many loads as possible, but on finding the British army amassed just outside the city, they abandoned any further efforts to save the Library.

Facing no resistance, the British marched into Washington on August 24 and, in an emphatic display (possibly in retaliation for the destruction American forces had brought on York, now Toronto, the previous spring), torched the White House, the Capitol, and most other government

U.S. Capitol after burning by the British, George Munger, artist, 1814.

The remains of the U.S. Capitol after the British burned it on August 24, 1814.

buildings. It was said that British soldiers used the books in the Library of Congress as kindling.

When the dust settled over the Capitol ruins, an exasperated Congress found widespread support for restoring their demolished Library. Sympathetic British newspapers declared its destruction egregious and comparisons were made to the burning of the Great Library of Alexandria. The act of vandalism even led the commander of British forces, General Ross, to remark, "Had I known it in time the books most certainly should have been saved."

When news of the fire reached former U.S. president Thomas Jefferson, he wrote to a friend in Washington offering to sell his personal library to Congress. At the time, Jefferson's book collection was the country's largest library in private hands. Jefferson's penchant for good wine and the continual construction and remodeling of his Monticello estate, among other things, had left him deeply in debt. The proposed sale would alleviate his financial difficulties and more than double the number of titles that had been in the Library of Congress. While both President James Madison and Secretary of State James Monroe regarded Jefferson's offer favorably, partisan politics led many Congressmen to oppose the deal. For others it was a matter of cost or an objection to the collection's subject matter, as some

Thomas Jefferson's Library Exhibit, courtesy of David Sharpe Studio.

The Library has reassembled all but about 300 titles that were in Jefferson's original library in an exhibition titled "Thomas Jefferson's Library." The display preserved Jefferson's original organizational scheme, which Jefferson described as "sometimes analytical, sometimes chronological, and sometimes a combination of both."

Letter from Thomas Jefferson to Samuel Harrison Smith, May 8, 1815.

After shipping his library to Washington, D.C., Jefferson reported to Smith, founder of the National Intelligencer, *"Our tenth and last wagon load of books goes off today . . . and an interesting treasure is added to your city . . . unquestionably the choicest collection of books in the U.S. and I hope it will not be without some general effect on the literature of the country."*

of Jefferson's books were said to have an "atheistically, irreligious, and immoral tendency." And some thought his collection was too arcane, literary, and philosophical. Jefferson, however, knew that his comprehensive library would prove especially helpful to legislators, noting that "there is, in fact, no subject to which a Member of Congress may not have occasion to refer."

After a lively debate on January 30, 1815, Congress passed a bill—by a margin of just ten votes—to purchase 6,487 volumes from Thomas Jefferson for $23,950. That spring the new Librarian, George Watterston, wrote Jefferson asking him to pack the books exactly as they had been displayed on his shelves. Jefferson replied, "You will receive my library arranged very perfectly in the order observed in the catalogue, which I have sent with it." Unlike the original Library's booklist of 1802, Jefferson's catalog endeavored to categorize all knowledge, and it stands as a unique, intimate document that reveals the breadth of his interests.

Jefferson adapted his cataloging scheme from Sir Francis Bacon's classification system that started with three main categories: Memory, Reason, and Imagination, later modified by Jefferson to History, Philosophy, and Fine Arts. These three categories are broken down further into forty-four distinct subject "chapters" that fully encompass the entire collection. Jefferson's catalog can be viewed as part of a continuum traced back to Bacon and even further to Aristotle and the *Pinakes*, which sought to classify realms of knowledge rather than just books. The order was analytical and also playful at times, reflecting the relationships that emerged between titles. For example, Jefferson's section on Geography is arranged chronologically and at times directionally. In the first instance, books on Lewis and Clark (new at the time) would begin a section and books on Spanish exploration of the New World would end it. In the latter instance, sections listed titles moving from north to south. After reviewing it, Watterston felt the catalog was too esoteric, so he simplified it by listing titles alphabetically within each chapter.

The Jefferson purchase instantly broadened the scope of the collection and introduced literature and poetry, previously excluded from the Library of Congress. Throughout the first half of the nineteenth century, the Library continued to grow in both stature and reputation. However, the catalog woefully failed to keep up. The Library produced a new bound catalog every ten years, which was doomed to obsolescence as soon as it

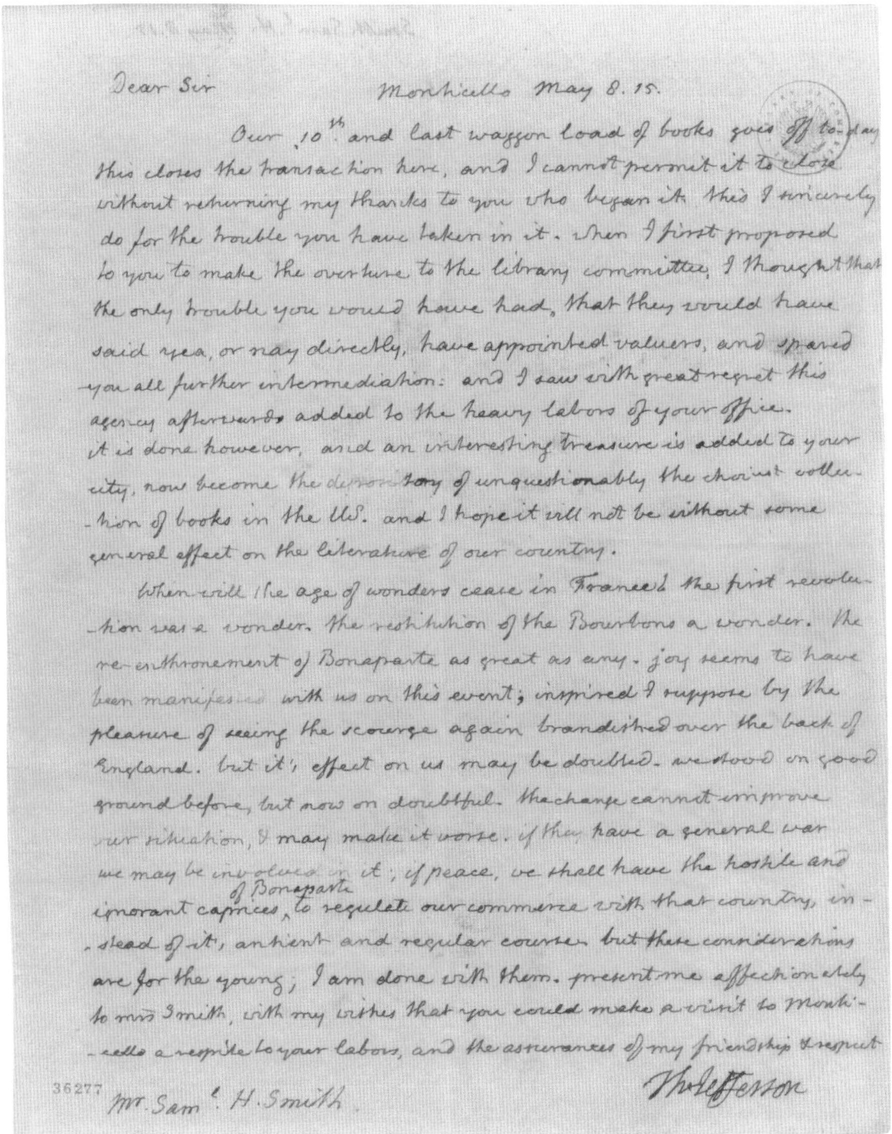
Dear Sir Monticello May 8. 15.

Our 10th and last waggon load of books goes off to-day this closes the transaction here, and I cannot permit it to close without returning my thanks to you who began it. this I sincerely do for the trouble you have taken in it. when I first proposed to you to make the overture to the library committee, I thought that the only trouble you would have had, that they would have said yea, or nay directly, have appointed valuers, and spared you all further intermediation: and I saw with great regret this agency afterwards added to the heavy labors of your office. it is done however, and an interesting treasure is added to your city, now become the depository of unquestionably the choicest collection of books in the US. and I hope it will not be without some general effect on the literature of our country.

When will the age of wonders cease in France? the first revolution was a wonder. the restitution of the Bourbons a wonder. the re-enthronement of Bonaparte as great as any. joy seems to have been manifested with us on this event; inspired I suppose by the pleasure of seeing the scourge again brandished over the back of England. but it's effect on us may be doubted. we stood on good ground before, but now on doubtful. the change cannot improve our situation, & may make it worse. if they have a general war we may be involved in it; if peace, we shall have the hostile and ignorant caprices of Bonaparte, to regulate our commerce with that country, instead of it's antient and regular course. but these considerations are for the young; I am done with them. present me affectionately to mrs Smith, with my wishes that you could make a visit to Monticello a respite to your labors, and the assurances of my friendship & respect

Th: Jefferson

36277 Mr. Saml. H. Smith

was printed. Criticism of the catalog and the cumbersome supplemental indexes, which continued to use Jefferson's system, began to mount from outside the Library—where key innovations in cataloging were beginning to take shape.

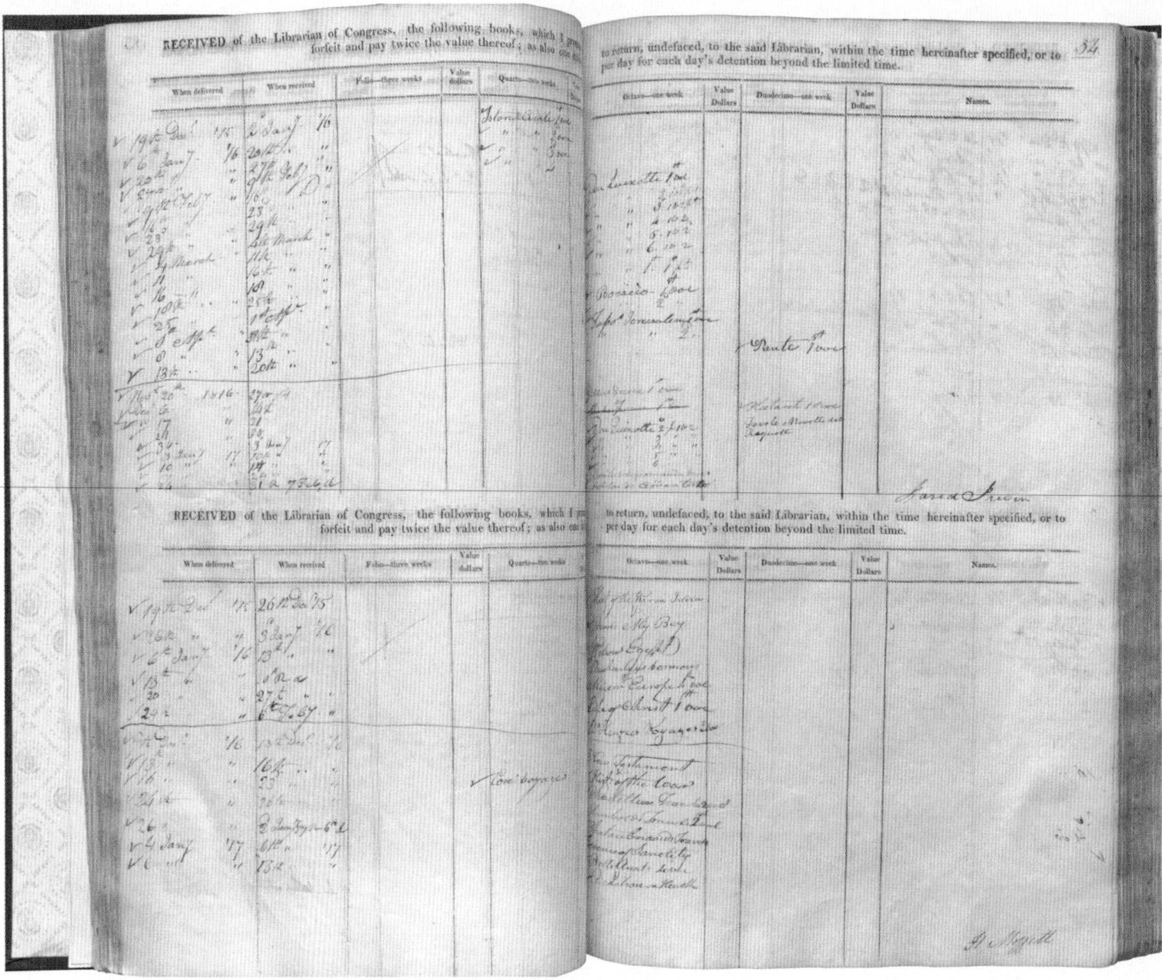

Record of Books Drawn by Members of Congress for 1815.

This record documents the titles members of Congress requested, when the books were checked out, and when they were returned. Members were charged a late fee of a dollar a day if the book was late.

Ledgers offer a fascinating look at the erudite reading habits of Congress and some U.S. presidents. The range in subject matter was eclectic—from politics, philosophy, and science to poetry and literature.

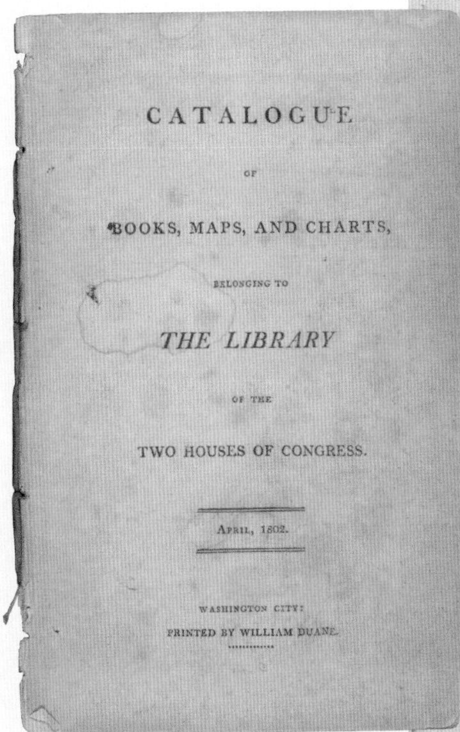
CATALOGUE

OF

BOOKS, MAPS, AND CHARTS,

BELONGING TO

THE LIBRARY

OF THE

TWO HOUSES OF CONGRESS.

APRIL, 1802.

WASHINGTON CITY:

PRINTED BY WILLIAM DUANE.

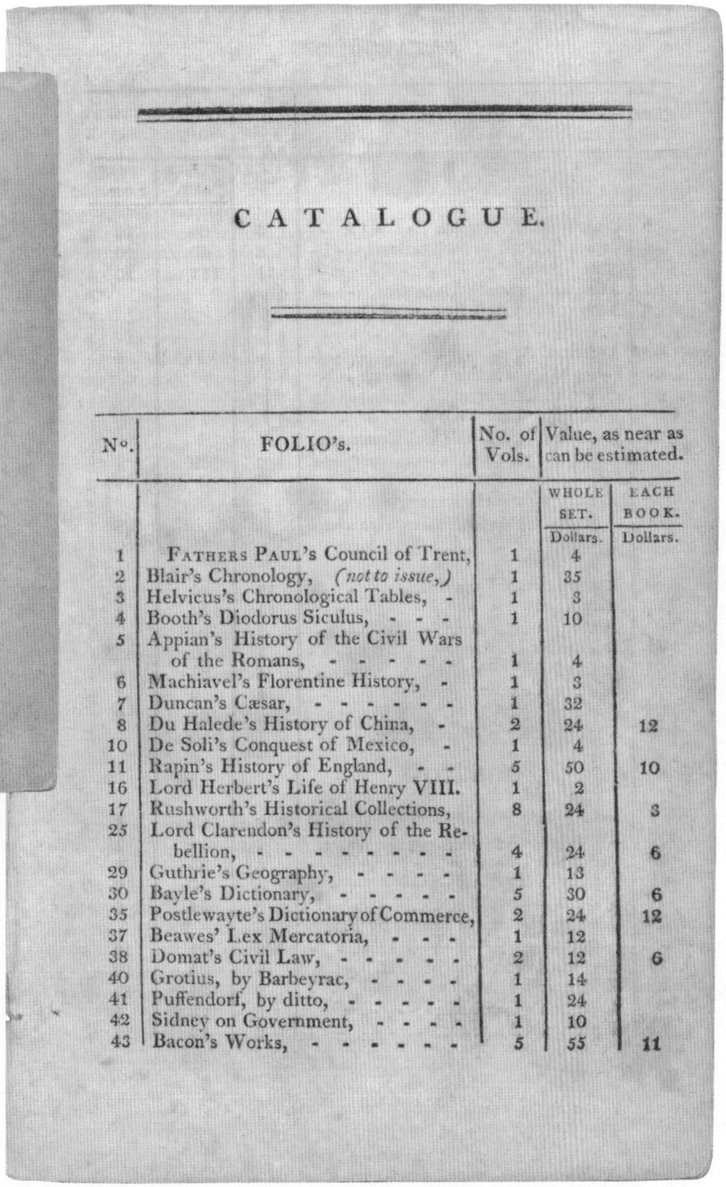
CATALOGUE.

N°.	FOLIO's.	No. of Vols.	Value, as near as can be estimated. WHOLE SET. Dollars.	EACH BOOK. Dollars.
1	FATHERS PAUL's Council of Trent,	1	4	
2	Blair's Chronology, *(not to issue,)*	1	35	
3	Helvicus's Chronological Tables, -	1	3	
4	Booth's Diodorus Siculus, - - -	1	10	
5	Appian's History of the Civil Wars of the Romans, - - - - -	1	4	
6	Machiavel's Florentine History, -	1	3	
7	Duncan's Cæsar, - - - - - -	1	32	
8	Du Halede's History of China, -	2	24	12
10	De Soli's Conquest of Mexico, -	1	4	
11	Rapin's History of England, - -	5	50	10
16	Lord Herbert's Life of Henry VIII.	1	2	
17	Rushworth's Historical Collections,	8	24	3
25	Lord Clarendon's History of the Rebellion, - - - - - - - -	4	24	6
29	Guthrie's Geography, - - - -	1	13	
30	Bayle's Dictionary, - - - - -	5	30	6
35	Postlewayte's Dictionary of Commerce,	2	24	12
37	Beawes' Lex Mercatoria, - - -	1	12	
38	Domat's Civil Law, - - - - -	2	12	6
40	Grotius, by Barbeyrac, - - - -	1	14	
41	Puffendorf, by ditto, - - - - -	1	24	
42	Sidney on Government, - - - -	1	10	
43	Bacon's Works, - - - - - -	5	55	11

Catalogue of Books, Maps, and Charts, Belonging to the Library of the Two Houses of Congress. Washington City. Printed by William Duane, April 1802.

This core foundation of Library of Congress books did not survive for long; the entire collection of 728 volumes from London went up in flames just twelve years later.

Trist Catalogue of the Library of Thomas Jefferson, 1823.

When Librarian of Congress George Watterston issued a printed catalog of Jefferson's collection in 1815, Jefferson was not happy with how Watterston had rearranged his books. Eight years later, Jefferson edited a copy of the 1815 catalog to indicate his original arrangement. He then asked Nicholas Trist, his future grandson-in-law, to copy out a clean new manuscript version of the catalog. This catalog was eventually donated to the Library of Congress in 1917. Its true purpose and value, however, remained unknown for decades because the label on its cover erroneously identified it as a University of Virginia library catalog.

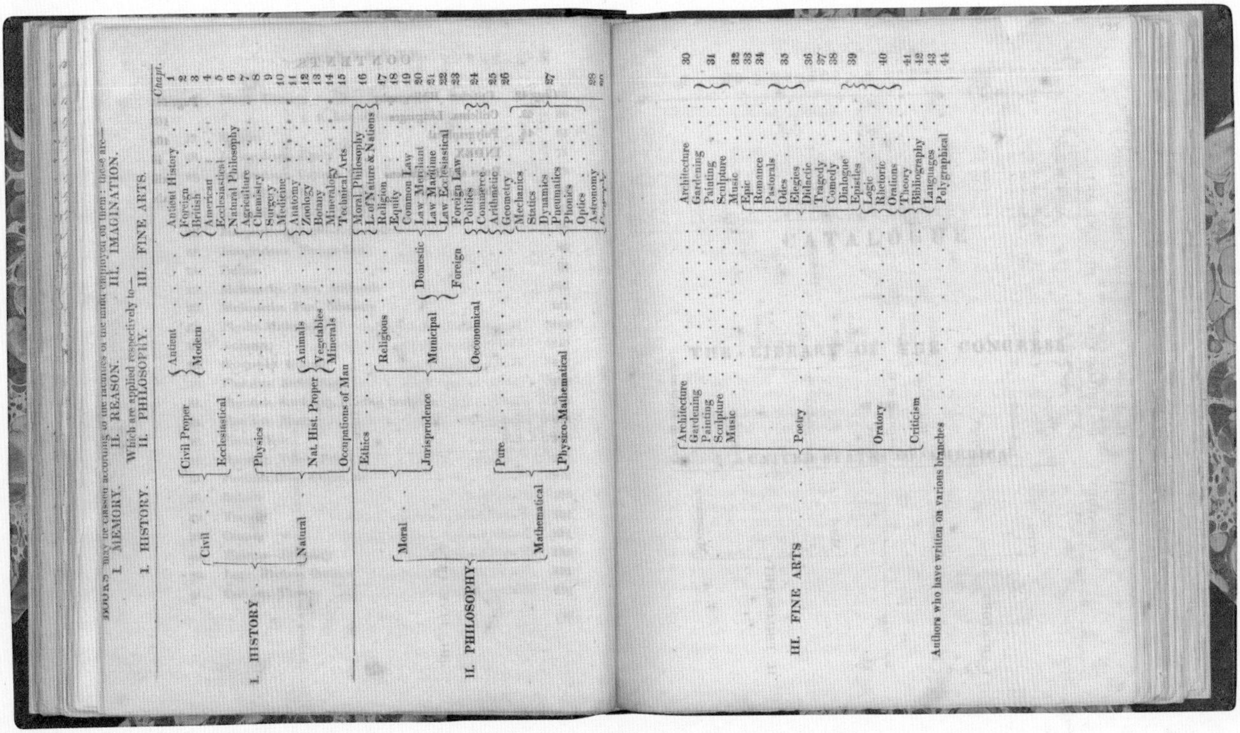

Catalogue of the Library of the United States: to Which is Annexed, a Copious Index, Alphabetically Arranged. Washington, U.S. Congress, 1815.

Jefferson preferred to arrange his books by subject. He chose Science, Memory (History), Reason (Philosophy), and Imagination (Fine Arts) as the main categories.

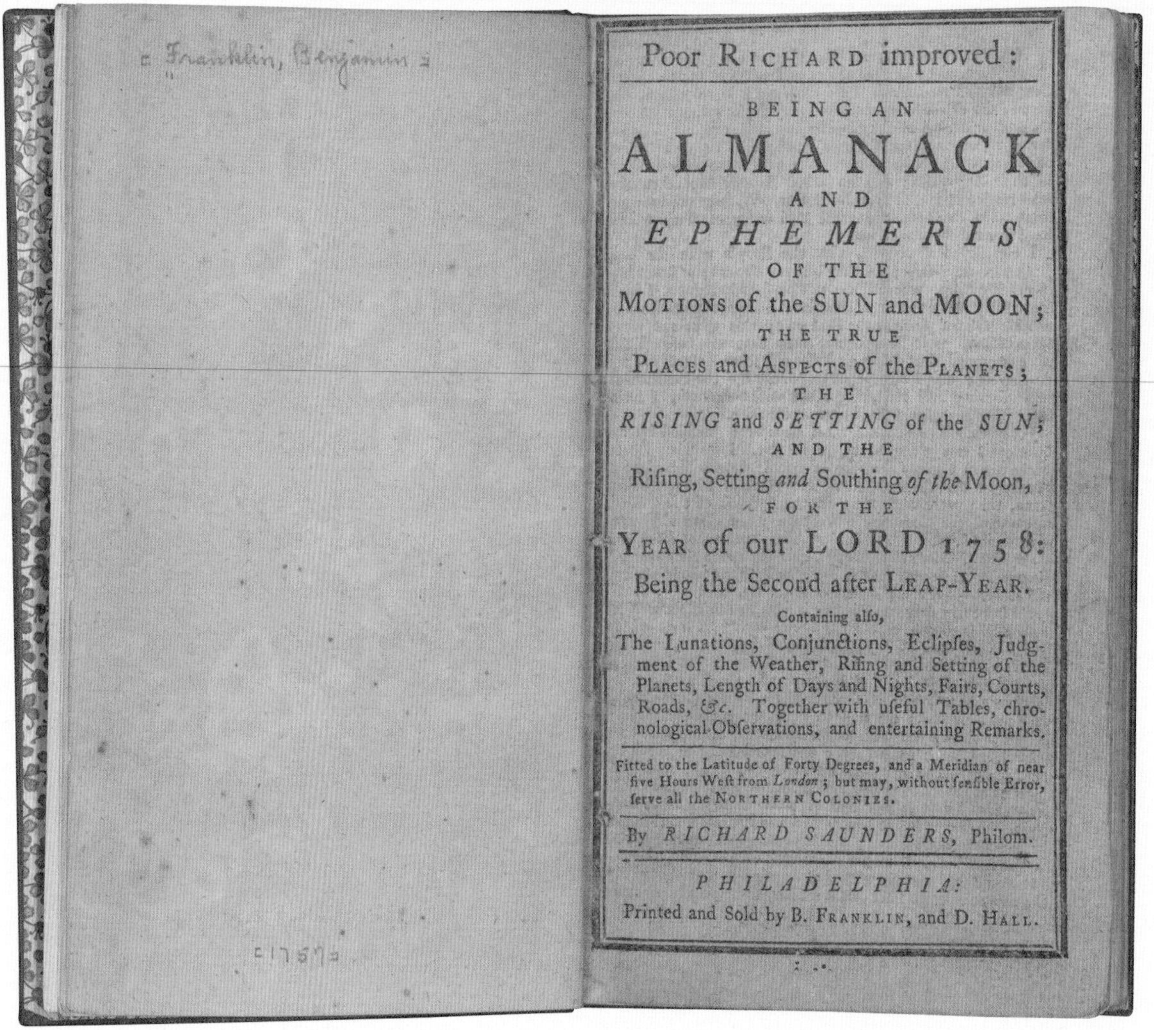
[Franklin, Benjamin]

[1757]

Poor RICHARD improved:

BEING AN

ALMANACK

AND

EPHEMERIS

OF THE

MOTIONS of the SUN and MOON;

THE TRUE

PLACES and ASPECTS of the PLANETS;

THE

RISING and *SETTING* of the *SUN*;

AND THE

Rising, Setting *and* Southing *of the* Moon,

FOR THE

YEAR of our LORD 1758:

Being the Second after LEAP-YEAR.

Containing also,

The Lunations, Conjunctions, Eclipses, Judgment of the Weather, Rising and Setting of the Planets, Length of Days and Nights, Fairs, Courts, Roads, *&c.* Together with useful Tables, chronological Observations, and entertaining Remarks.

Fitted to the Latitude of Forty Degrees, and a Meridian of near five Hours West from *London*; but may, without sensible Error, serve all the NORTHERN COLONIES.

By *RICHARD SAUNDERS*, Philom.

PHILADELPHIA:

Printed and Sold by B. FRANKLIN, and D. HALL.

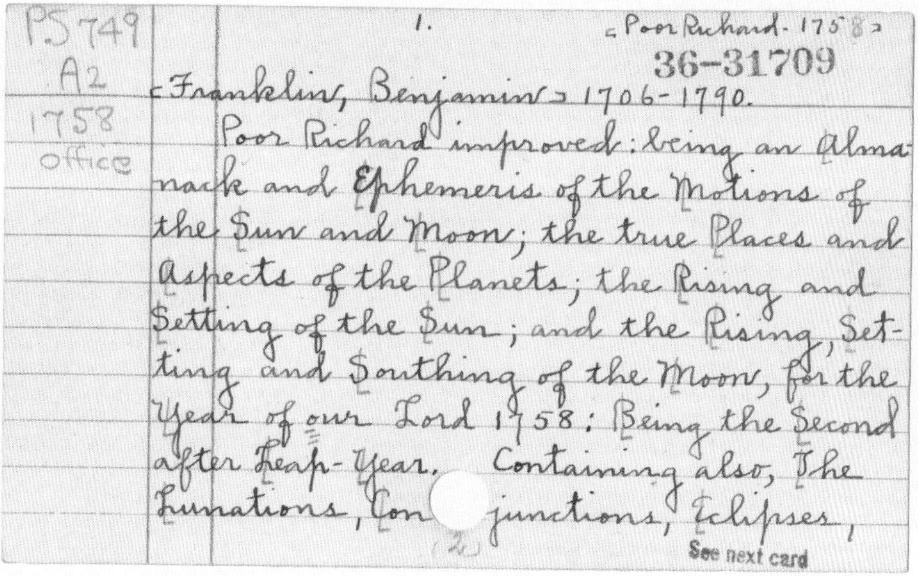
PS749
A2
1758
office

1.

[Poor Richard. 1758]

36-31709

[Franklin, Benjamin] 1706-1790.

Poor Richard improved: being an Almanack and Ephemeris of the Motions of the Sun and Moon; the true Places and Aspects of the Planets; the Rising and Setting of the Sun; and the Rising, Setting and Southing of the Moon, for the Year of our Lord 1758: Being the Second after Leap-Year. Containing also, The Lunations, Conjunctions, Eclipses,

(2)

See next card

Benjamin Franklin, *Poor Richard Improved: Being an Almanack . . . For the Year of Our Lord 1758.* Philadelphia, Franklin and Hall, 1757.

"In 1732 I first published my Almanack, under the name of Richard Saunders; it was continu'd by me about 25 Years, commonly call'd Poor Richard's Almanack. I endeavor'd to make it both entertaining and useful, and it accordingly came to be in such Demand that I reap'd considerable Profit from it, vending annually near ten Thousand. . . . I consider'd it as a proper Vehicle for conveying Instruction among the common People, who bought scarcely any other Books. I therefore filled all the little Spaces that occur'd between the Remarkable Days in the Calendar with Proverbial Sentences, chiefly such as inculcated Industry and Frugality, as the Means of procuring Wealth and thereby securing Virtue, it being more difficult for a Man in Want to act always honestly, as (to use here one of those Proverbs) it is hard for an empty Sack to stand upright." —Autobiography of Benjamin Franklin

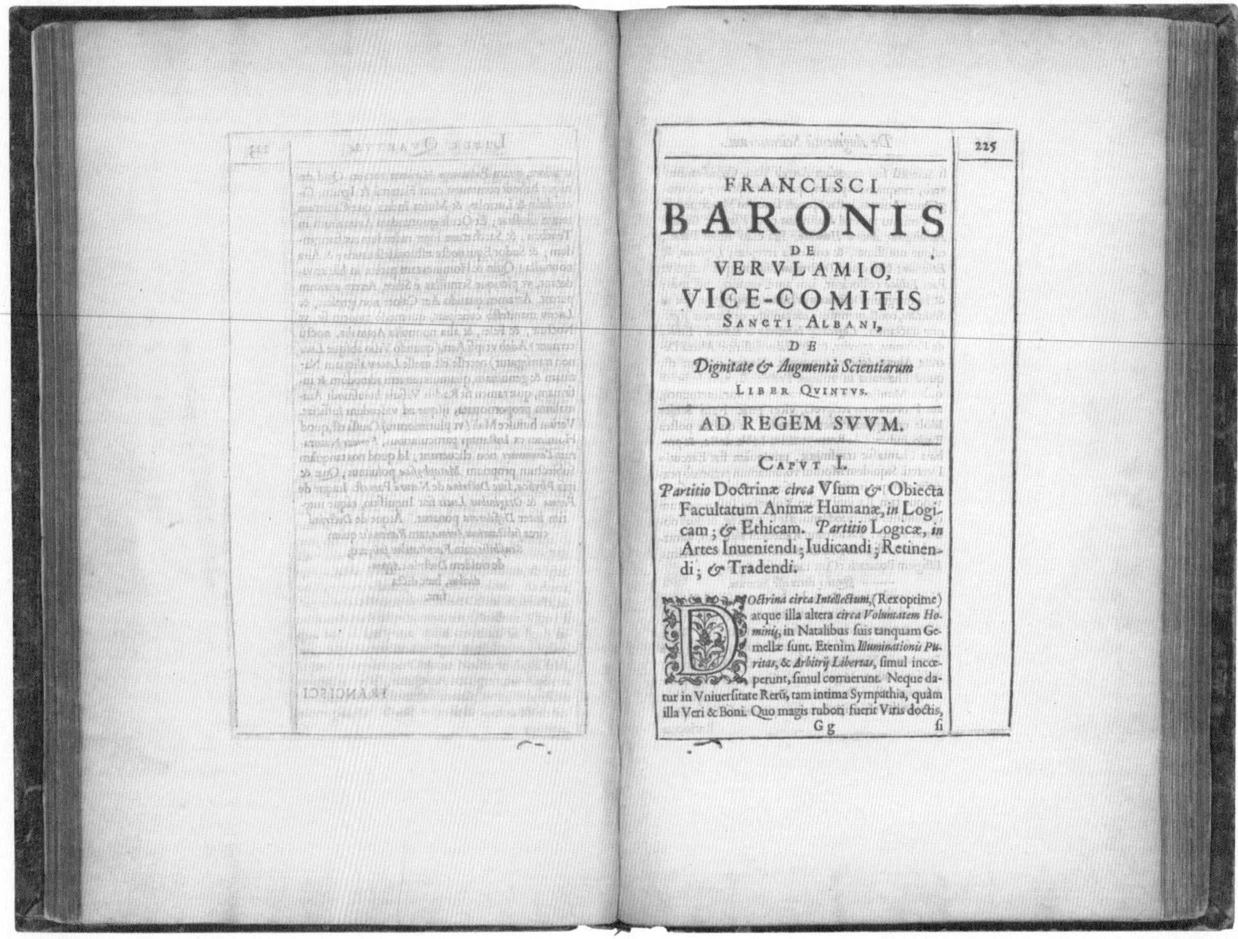
225
FRANCISCI
BARONIS
DE
VERVLAMIO,
VICE-COMITIS
Sancti Albani,
DE
Dignitate & Augmentis Scientiarum
Liber Qvintvs.
AD REGEM SVVM.
Capvt I.
Partitio Doctrinæ circa Vsum & Obiecta Facultatum Animæ Humanæ, in Logicam; & Ethicam. Partitio Logicæ, in Artes Inueniendi; Iudicandi; Retinendi; & Tradendi.
DOctrina circa Intellectum, (Rex optime) atque illa altera circa Voluntatem Hominis, in Natalibus suis tanquam Gemellæ sunt. Etenim Illuminationis Puritas, & Arbitrij Libertas, simul incœperunt, simul corruerunt. Neque datur in Vniuersitate Rerũ, tam intima Sympathia, quàm illa Veri & Boni. Quo magis rubori fuerit Viris doctis,
Gg si

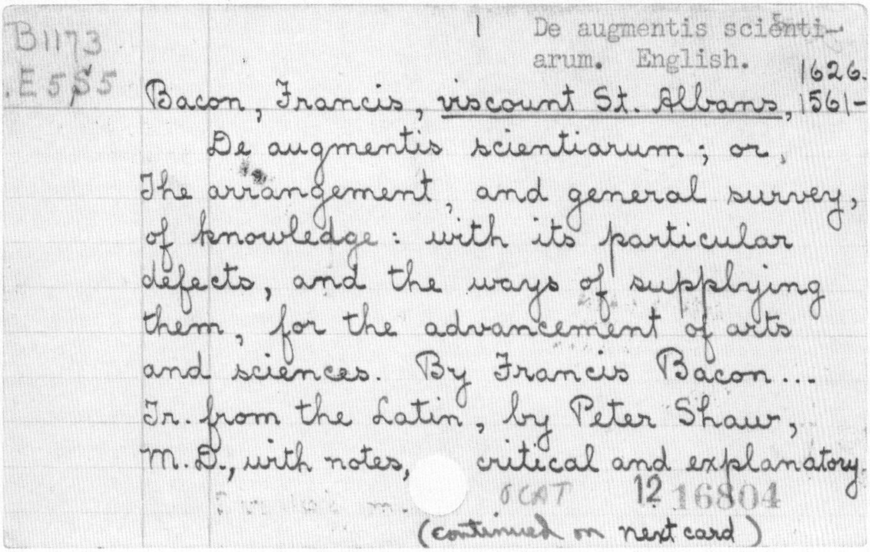

B1173
.E5S5

1 De augmentis scienti-
arum. English.

Bacon, Francis, viscount St. Albans, 1561-1626.
De augmentis scientiarum; or,
The arrangement, and general survey,
of knowledge: with its particular
defects, and the ways of supplying
them, for the advancement of arts
and sciences. By Francis Bacon...
Tr. from the Latin, by Peter Shaw,
M.D., with notes, critical and explanatory.

6CAT 12 16804

(continued on next card)

Francis Bacon, *De dignitate et augmentis scientiarum libri IX.* Londini, In officina loannis Haviland, 1623.

Bacon, a scientist, philosopher, and overall brilliant Renaissance man, greatly influenced Thomas Jefferson and inspired the organizational scheme he devised for his library.

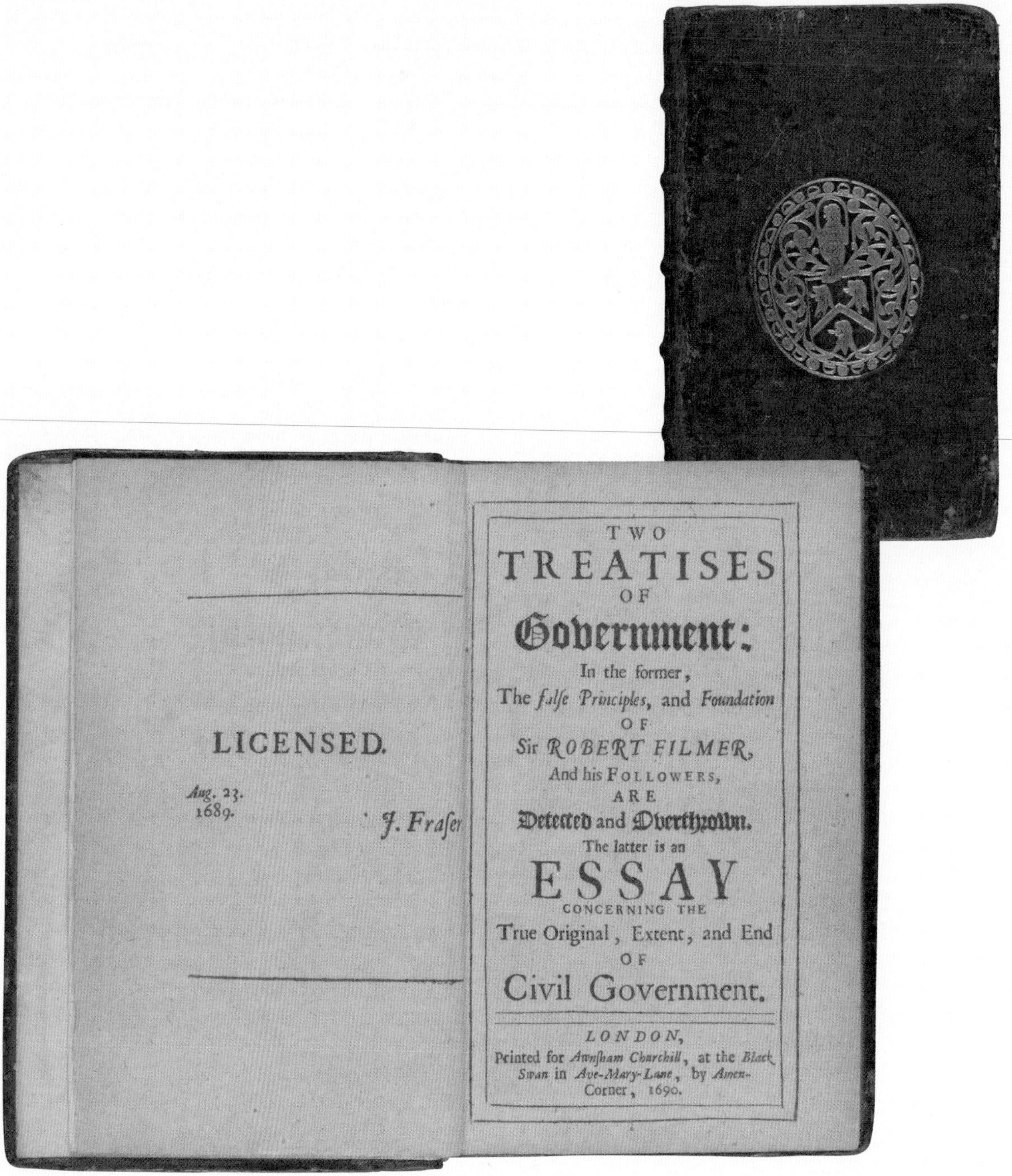
LICENSED.
Aug. 23.
1689.
J. Fraser
TWO
TREATISES
OF
Government:
In the former,
The false Principles, and Foundation
OF
Sir ROBERT FILMER,
And his FOLLOWERS,
ARE
Detected and Overthrown.
The latter is an
ESSAY
CONCERNING THE
True Original, Extent, and End
OF
Civil Government.
LONDON,
Printed for Awnsham Churchill, at the Black Swan in Ave-Mary-Lane, by Amen-Corner, 1690.

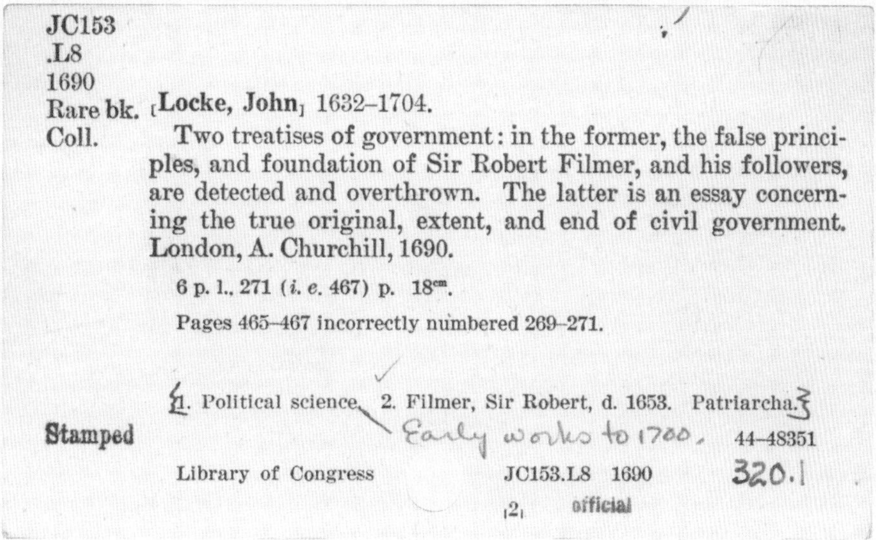

JC153
.L8
1690
Rare bk. [Locke, John] 1632–1704.
Coll.

Two treatises of government: in the former, the false principles, and foundation of Sir Robert Filmer, and his followers, are detected and overthrown. The latter is an essay concerning the true original, extent, and end of civil government. London, A. Churchill, 1690.

6 p. l., 271 (*i. e.* 467) p. 18cm.

Pages 465–467 incorrectly numbered 269–271.

1. Political science. 2. Filmer, Sir Robert, d. 1653. Patriarcha.

Stamped — Early works to 1700. — 44-48351

Library of Congress — JC153.L8 1690 — 320.1

[2] official

John Locke, *Two Treatises of Government*. London, A. Churchill, 1690.

The Founding Fathers never claimed their political theories of a liberal democracy were original. They readily acknowledged a debt to European Enlightenment writers such as Locke.

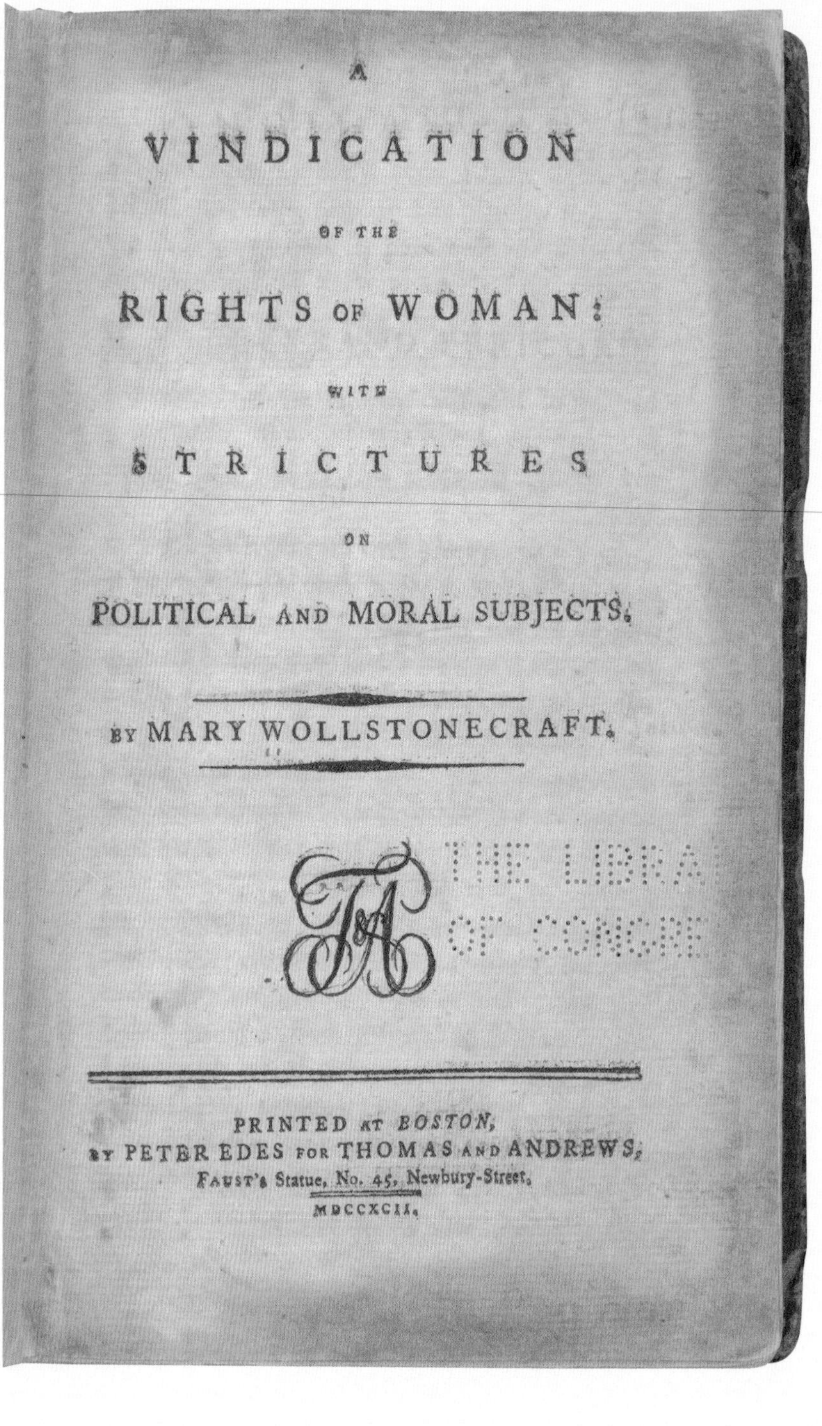

A
VINDICATION
OF THE
RIGHTS OF WOMAN:
WITH
STRICTURES
ON
POLITICAL AND MORAL SUBJECTS.

BY MARY WOLLSTONECRAFT.

THE LIBRA[RY]
OF CONGRE[SS]

PRINTED AT *BOSTON*,
BY PETER EDES FOR THOMAS AND ANDREWS,
FAUST's Statue, No. 45, Newbury-Street.
MDCCXCII.

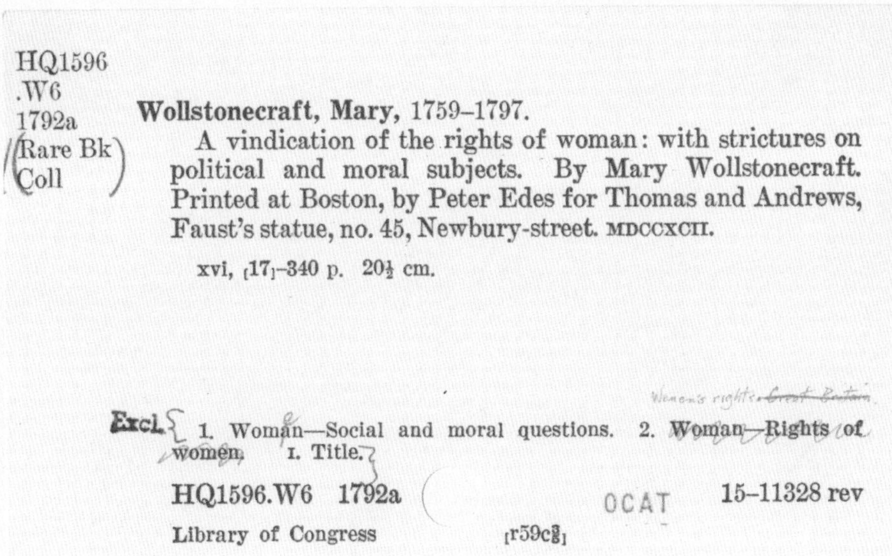

HQ1596
.W6
1792a
(Rare Bk
Coll)

Wollstonecraft, Mary, 1759–1797.

A vindication of the rights of woman: with strictures on political and moral subjects. By Mary Wollstonecraft. Printed at Boston, by Peter Edes for Thomas and Andrews, Faust's statue, no. 45, Newbury-street. MDCCXCII.

xvi, [17]–340 p. 20½ cm.

Women's rights. ~~Great Britain~~

Excl. 1. Woman—Social and moral questions. 2. ~~Woman—Rights of women.~~ I. Title.

HQ1596.W6 1792a OCAT 15-11328 rev

Library of Congress [r59c8]

Mary Wollstonecraft, *A Vindication of the Rights of Woman, with Strictures on Political and Moral Subjects*. Boston, P. Edes, 1792.

Wollstonecraft's book is considered a literary cornerstone in the struggle for women's rights. She clearly stated the need for raising the status of women and inspired women on both sides of the Atlantic to action.

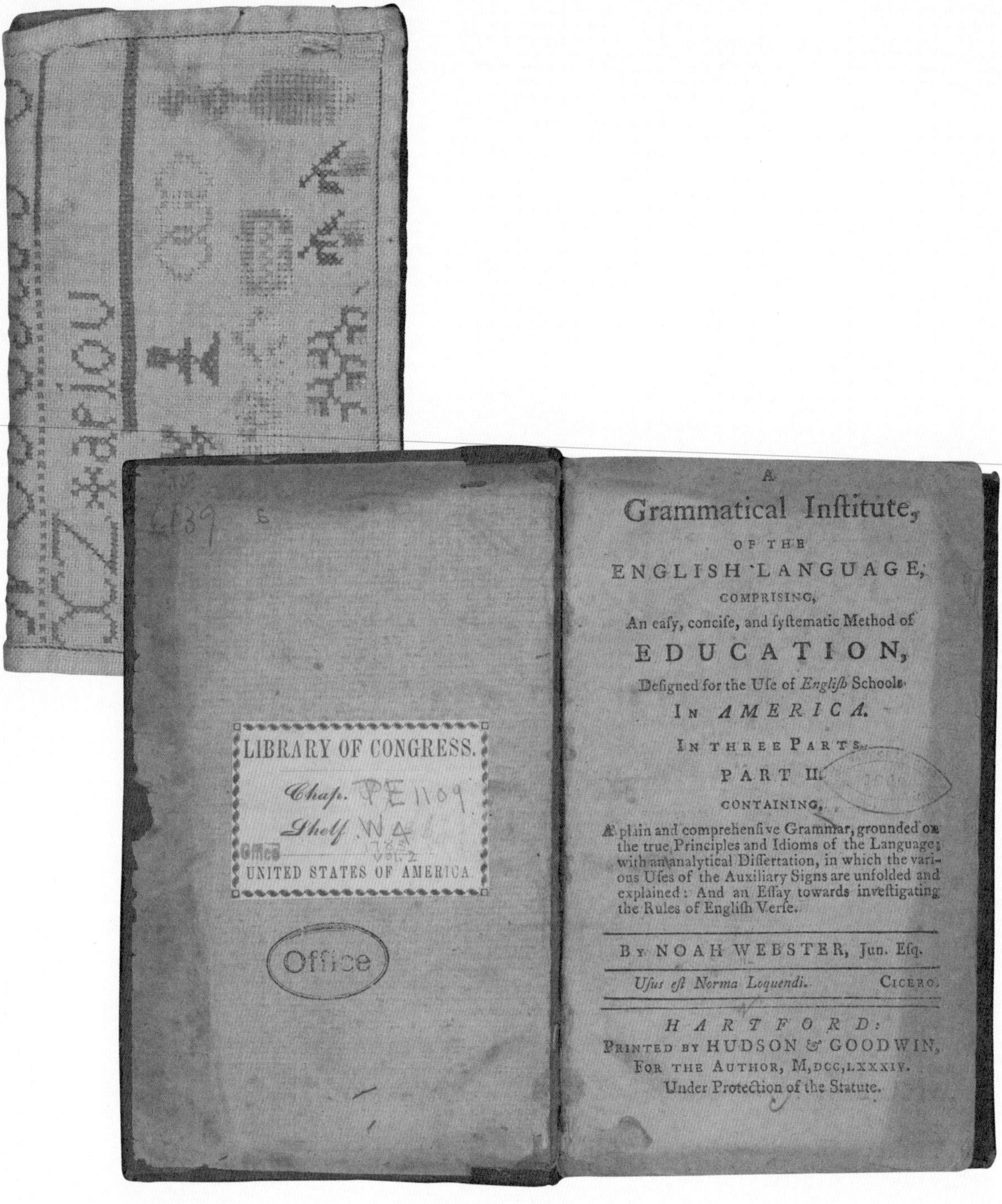
LIBRARY OF CONGRESS.
Chap. PE1109
Shelf W4
Office
UNITED STATES OF AMERICA.
Office
A
Grammatical Institute,
OF THE
ENGLISH LANGUAGE,
COMPRISING,
An easy, concise, and systematic Method of
EDUCATION,
Designed for the Use of English Schools
IN AMERICA.
IN THREE PARTS.
PART II.
CONTAINING,
A plain and comprehensive Grammar, grounded on the true Principles and Idioms of the Language; with an analytical Dissertation, in which the various Uses of the Auxiliary Signs are unfolded and explained: And an Essay towards investigating the Rules of English Verse.
BY NOAH WEBSTER, Jun. Esq.
Usus est Norma Loquendi. CICERO.
HARTFORD:
PRINTED BY HUDSON & GOODWIN,
FOR THE AUTHOR, M,DCC,LXXXIV.
Under Protection of the Statute.

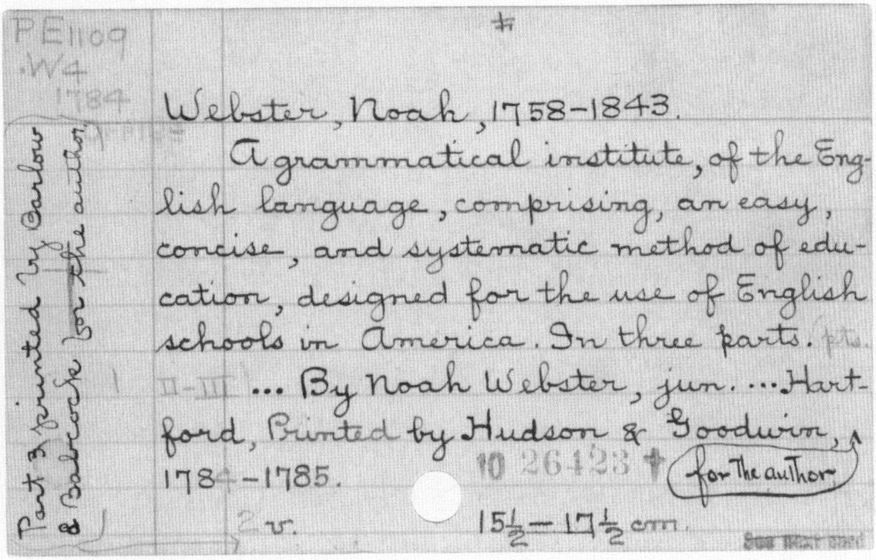

PE1109
.W4
1784

Webster, Noah, 1758-1843.
A grammatical institute, of the English language, comprising, an easy, concise, and systematic method of education, designed for the use of English schools in America. In three parts. pts. II-III ... By Noah Webster, jun. ... Hartford, Printed by Hudson & Goodwin, for the author 1784-1785.

10 26423 †

2 v. 15½–17½ cm.

Part 3 printed by Barlow & Babcock for the author

See next card

Noah Webster, *A Grammatical Institute, of the English Language*. Hartford, Hudson & Goodwin, 1784.

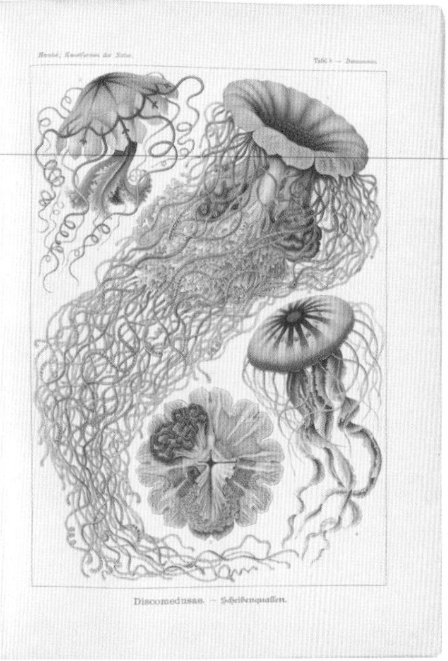
Discomedusae. — Scheibenquallen.

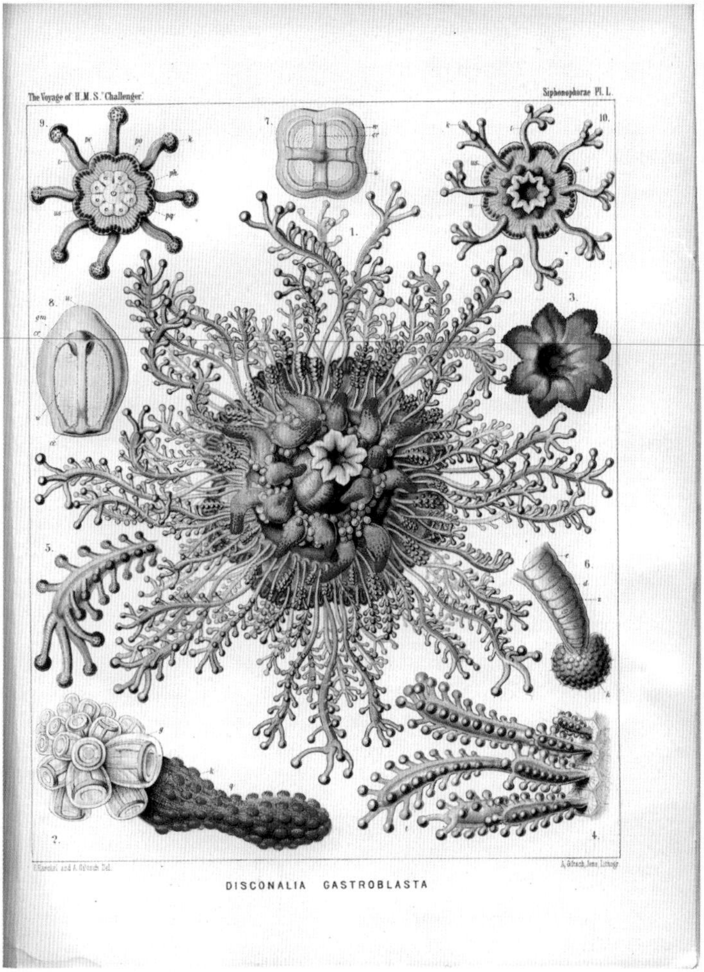
The Voyage of H.M.S. "Challenger."
Siphonophorae Pl. L.
DISCONALIA GASTROBLASTA

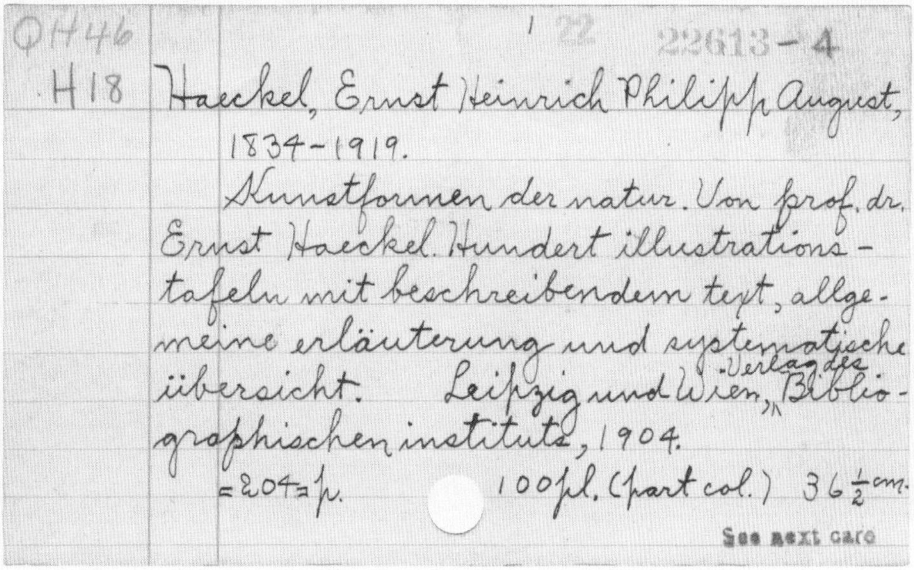

QH46
H18

22613-4

Haeckel, Ernst Heinrich Philipp August, 1834-1919.

Kunstformen der natur. Von prof. dr. Ernst Haeckel. Hundert illustrations-tafeln mit beschreibendem text, allgemeine erläuterung und systematische übersicht. Leipzig und Wien, Verlag des Bibliographischen instituts, 1904.

=204= p. 100 pl. (part col.) 36½ cm.

See next card

Lithograph by Adolf Giltsch after a sketch by Ernst Haeckel. Dr. Ernst Haeckel, *Kunstformen der Natur.* Leipzig und Wien, Verlag des Bibliographischen Instituts, 1904.

10 GENESIS, I. *ver.* 1, 2.

In the Beginning יהוה created

the and the

And the Earth was without Form and void, and Darkneſs was upon the Face of the Deep ; and the

of God moved upon the

In the Beginning *God* created the *Heaven* and the *Earth*. And the Earth was without Form and void, and Darkneſs was upon the Face of the Deep ; and the *Spirit* of God moved upon the *Waters*.

2 ESDRAS VI. *ver.* 45. 11

On the fourth Day

the Lord

commanded that the

ſhould ſhine, the give her

and that the ſhould be in Order. And gave them a Charge to do Service unto Man that was to be made.

On the fourth day the Lord commanded that the *Sun* ſhould ſhine, the *Moon* give her *Light*, and that the *Stars* ſhould be in Order. And gave them a Charge to do Service unto Man that was to be made.

2

BS560 1788 <Rare Bk Coll : Am Imp>

Bible. English. Authorized. Selections. 1788.
* A curious hieroglyphick Bible, or, Select passages in the Old and New Testaments, represented with emblematical figures, for the amusement of youth : designed chiefly to familiarize tender age, in a pleasing and diverting manner, with early ideas of the Holy Scriptures : to which are subjoined, a short account of the lives of the Evangelists, and other pieces / illustrated with nearly five hundred cuts. -- The first Worcester edition. -- [Worcester] : Printed at Worcester,

CONTINUED ON NEXT CARD 82-466849

Isaiah Thomas, *A Curious Hieroglyphick Bible*. Worcester, Massachusetts, 1788.

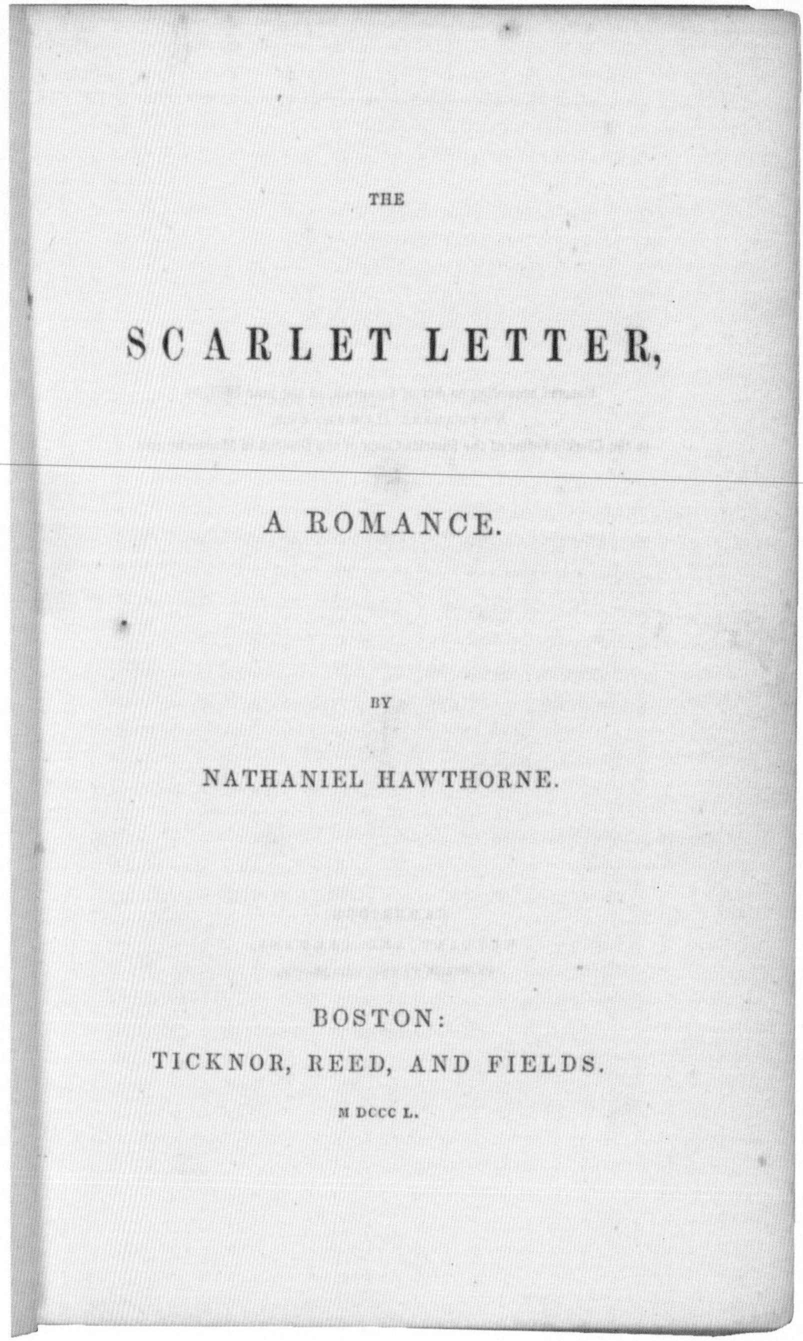

THE

SCARLET LETTER,

A ROMANCE.

BY

NATHANIEL HAWTHORNE.

BOSTON:

TICKNOR, REED, AND FIELDS.

M DCCC L.

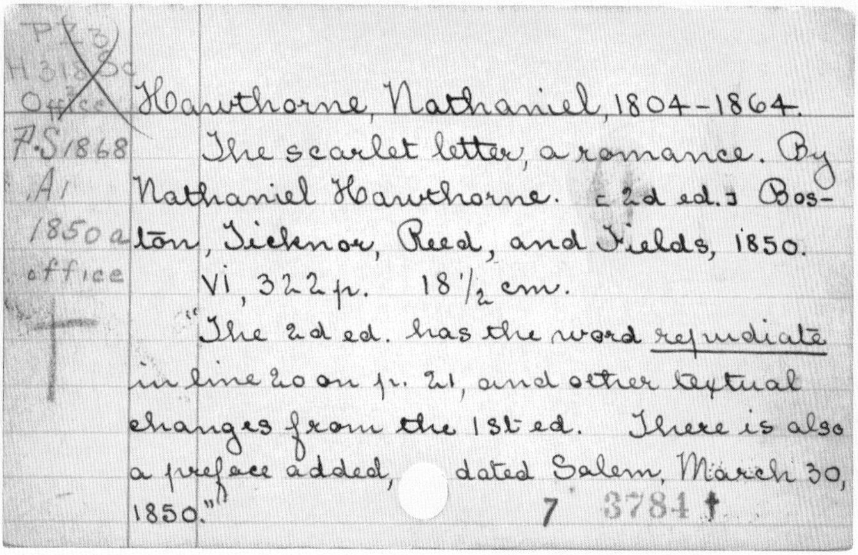

PZ3 H318Sc Office

PS1868 .A1 1850a office

Hawthorne, Nathaniel, 1804-1864.

The scarlet letter, a romance. By Nathaniel Hawthorne. [2d ed.] Boston, Ticknor, Reed, and Fields, 1850.

vi, 322 p. 18½ cm.

"The 2d ed. has the word repudiate in line 20 on p. 21, and other textual changes from the 1st ed. There is also a preface added, dated Salem, March 30, 1850."

7 3784 †

Nathaniel Hawthorne, *The Scarlet Letter, a Romance*. Boston, Ticknor, Reed, and Fields, 1850.

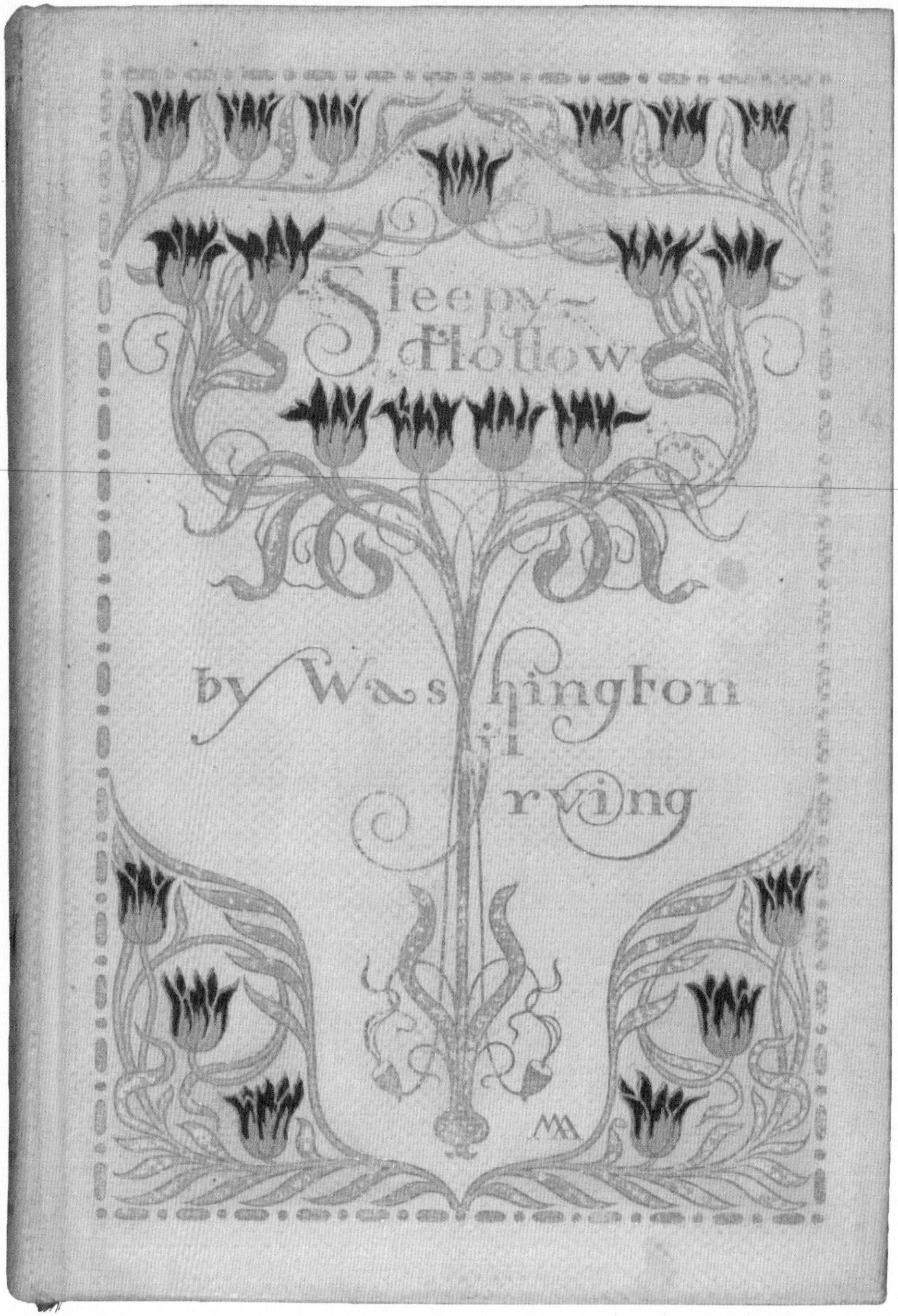
Sleepy Hollow
by Washington Irving
MA

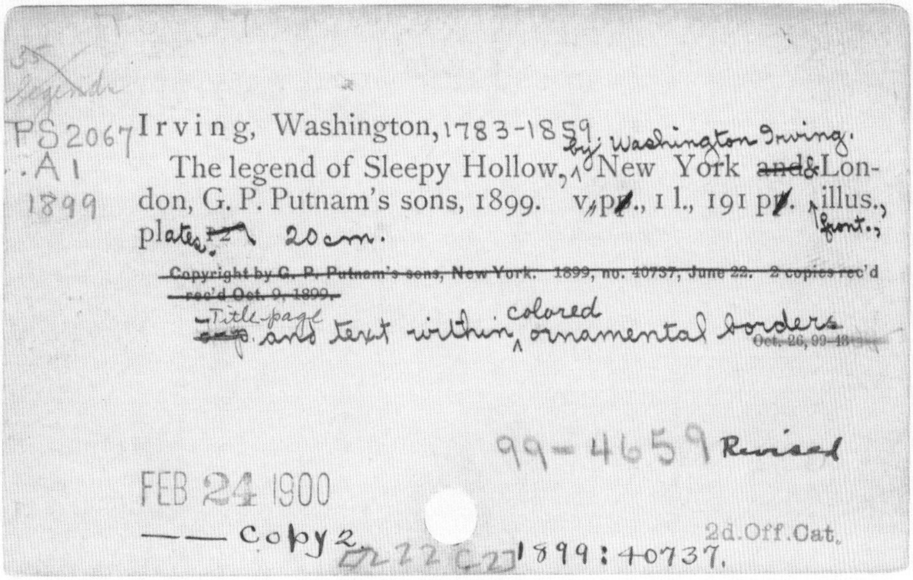

35
legends
PS2067 Irving, Washington, 1783-1859
.A1 The legend of Sleepy Hollow, by Washington Irving. New York and & London, G. P. Putnam's sons, 1899. v, p., 1 l., 191 p. front., illus., plates 20 cm.
1899
~~Copyright by G. P. Putnam's sons, New York. 1899, no. 40737, June 22. 2 copies rec'd rec'd Oct. 9, 1899.~~
Title-page and text within colored ornamental borders
~~Oct. 26, 99-18~~
99-4659 Revised
FEB 24 1900
—— Copy 2 22C22 1899: 40737.
2d.Off.Cat.

Washington Irving, *The Legend of Sleepy Hollow.* New York & London, G. P. Putnam's Sons, 1899.

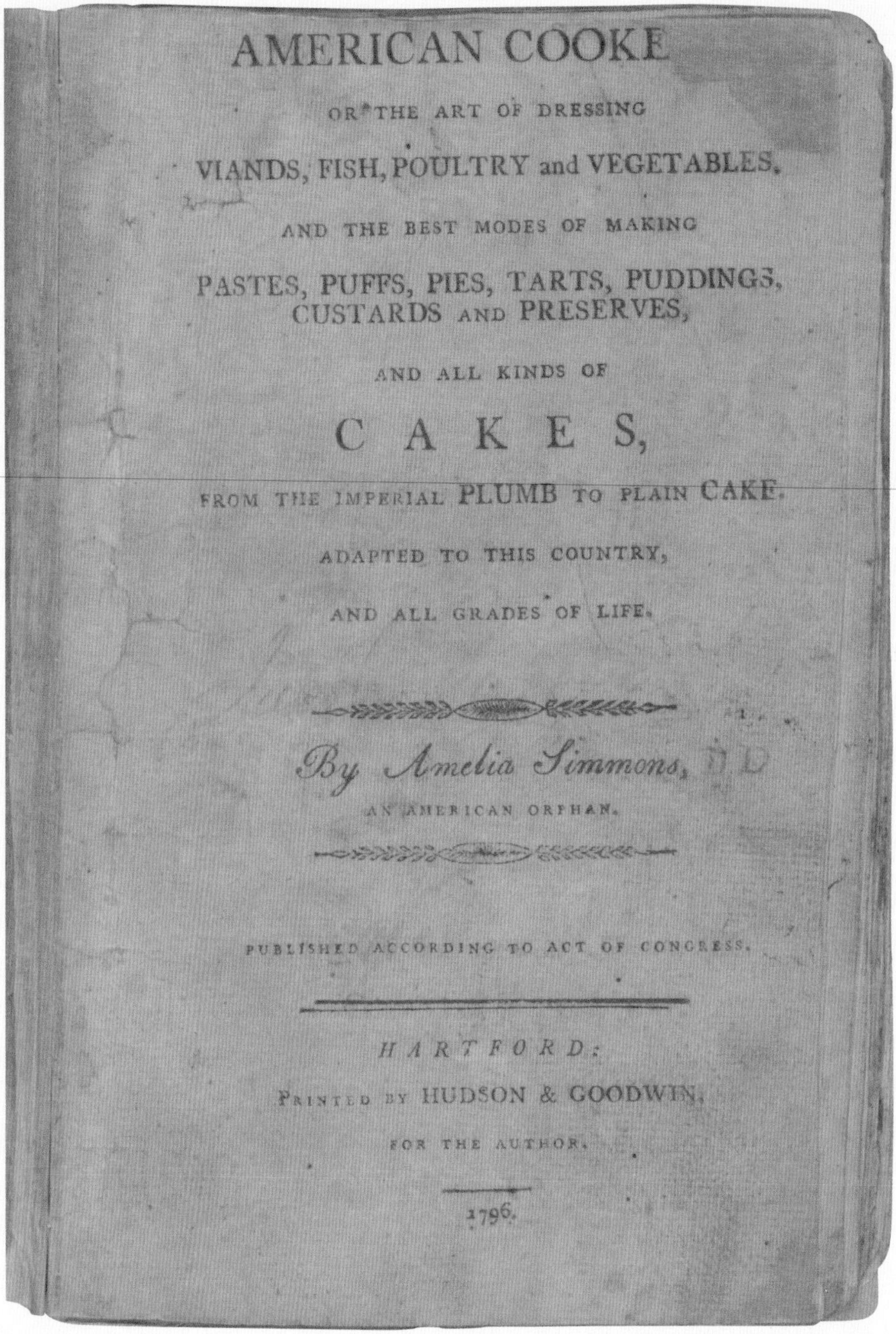
AMERICAN COOKE

OR THE ART OF DRESSING

VIANDS, FISH, POULTRY and VEGETABLES,

AND THE BEST MODES OF MAKING

PASTES, PUFFS, PIES, TARTS, PUDDINGS, CUSTARDS AND PRESERVES,

AND ALL KINDS OF

CAKES,

FROM THE IMPERIAL PLUMB TO PLAIN CAKE.

ADAPTED TO THIS COUNTRY,

AND ALL GRADES OF LIFE.

By Amelia Simmons,

AN AMERICAN ORPHAN.

PUBLISHED ACCORDING TO ACT OF CONGRESS.

HARTFORD:

PRINTED BY HUDSON & GOODWIN,

FOR THE AUTHOR.

1796.

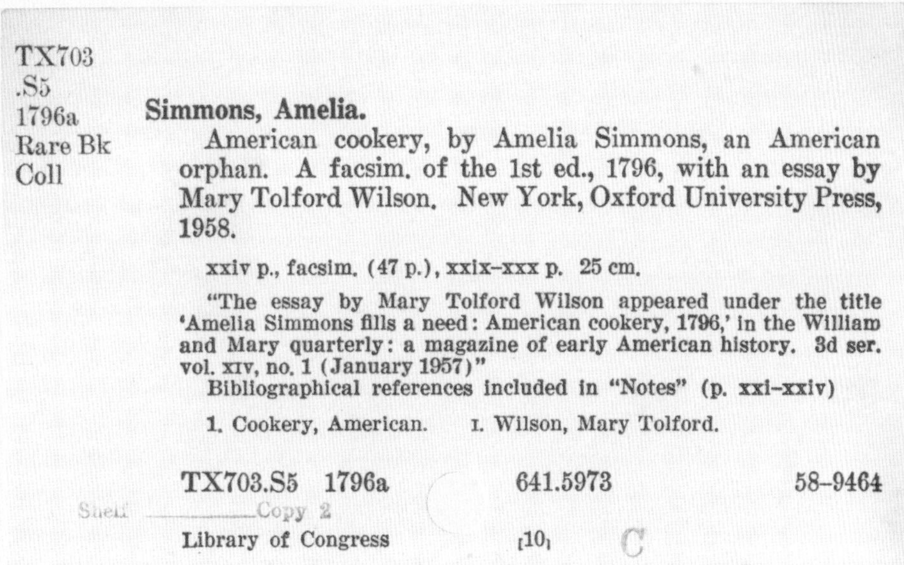

TX703
.S5
1796a
Rare Bk
Coll

Simmons, Amelia.

American cookery, by Amelia Simmons, an American orphan. A facsim. of the 1st ed., 1796, with an essay by Mary Tolford Wilson. New York, Oxford University Press, 1958.

xxiv p., facsim. (47 p.), xxix–xxx p. 25 cm.

"The essay by Mary Tolford Wilson appeared under the title 'Amelia Simmons fills a need: American cookery, 1796,' in the William and Mary quarterly: a magazine of early American history. 3d ser. vol. xiv, no. 1 (January 1957)"

Bibliographical references included in "Notes" (p. xxi–xxiv)

1. Cookery, American. I. Wilson, Mary Tolford.

TX703.S5 1796a 641.5973 58–9464

Shelf ________Copy 2

Library of Congress [10] C

Amelia Simmons, *American Cookery*. Hartford, Hudson & Goodwin, 1796.

The card is for a later facsimile of the first edition.

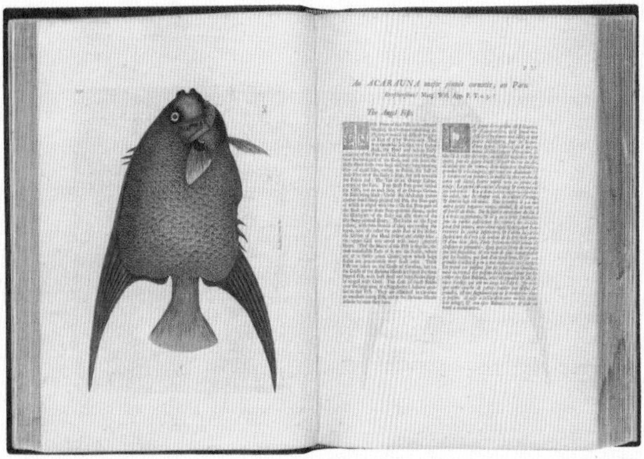
The Angel Fish.

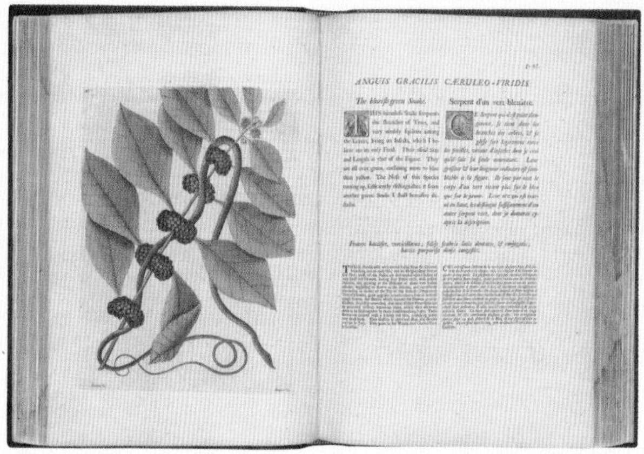
ANGUIS GRACILIS CÆRULEO-VIRIDIS
The blueish green Snake.
Serpent d'un vert bleuâtre.

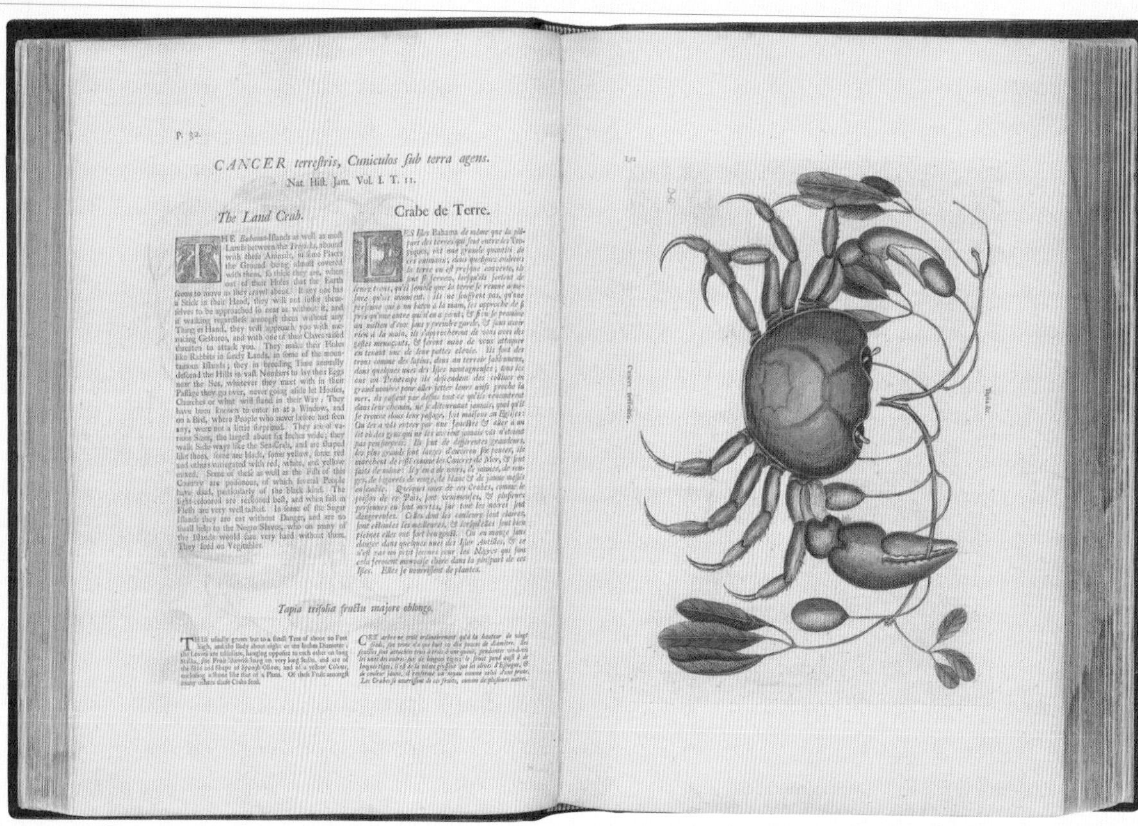
CANCER terrestris, Cuniculos sub terra agens.
Nat. Hist. Jam. Vol. I. T. 11.
The Land Crab.
Crabe de Terre.
Tapia trifolia fructu majore oblongo.

QH41
.C29
(Rare Bk.
Coll.)

Catesby, Mark, 1683–1749.

Histoire natvrelle de la Caroline, la Floride et les isles Bahama, contenant les desseins des oiseavx, animavx &c., et en particvlier des arbres, des forets, arbrisseavx et avtres plantes, avec vne carte novvelle des pais dont il s'agist. A Nvremberg, Chez les heritiers de Seligmann, 1770.

[88] p. fold. col. map. 40 cm.

Translation of the introductory chapter (entitled An account of Carolina and the Bahama Islands) of v. 2 of The natural history of Carolina.

— Southern States —

1. Natural history ~~—~~ Pre-Linnean works. ~~2. Natural history — Southern States.~~ ~~3.~~ 2. Natural history—Bahamas. — Pre-Linnean works. I. Title.

QH41.C29 8–31093 rev

Library of Congress [r68b2]

Mark Catesby, *Histoire Naturelle de la Caroline, la Floride et les isles Bahama*. A Nuremberg, Chez les Héritiers de Seligmann, 1770.

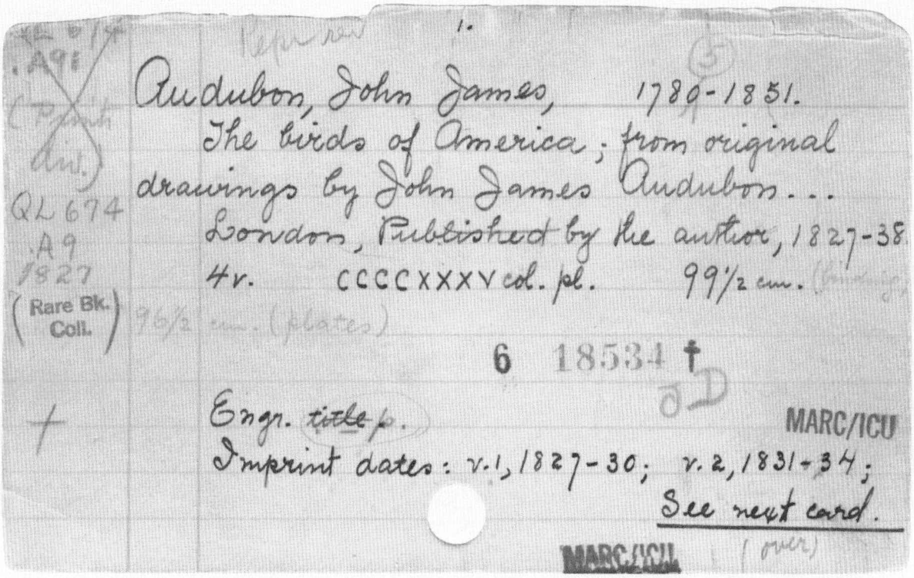

QL 674
.A9
1827
(Rare Bk. Coll.)

Audubon, John James, 1780-1851.
The birds of America; from original drawings by John James Audubon...
London, Published by the author, 1827-38.
4v. CCCCXXXV col. pl. 99 1/2 cm.
96 1/2 cm. (plates)

6 18534 †

Engr. title p.
MARC/ICU
Imprint dates: v.1, 1827-30; v.2, 1831-34;
See next card.
MARC/ICU
(over)

John James Audubon, *The Birds of America; from Original Drawings*. London, published by the author, 1827-1838.

John Silva Meehan was the Librarian during the fire of 1851; he noted the Library's copy "was saved and uninjured" and pointed out it was "one of the best; it having been selected for us by Mr. Audubon and bound in the most substantial manner for us under his own care and supervision."

Four-tray cabinet

Cat. no.
2314 Outside size, $8\frac{7}{8}$ in. high, $13\frac{1}{8}$ in. wide, $13\frac{3}{8}$ in. deep. Capacity 4400 lightweight, 3400 medium weight, or 2600 heavyweight cards,

Interior lock, additional
Pilaster lock, additional

No. 2314

Six-tray cabinet

Cat. no.
2316 Outside size, $12\frac{7}{8}$ in. high, $13\frac{1}{8}$ in. wide, $13\frac{3}{8}$ in. deep. Capacity 6600 lightweight, 5100 medium weight, or 3900 heavyweight cards,

Interior lock, additional
Pilaster lock, additional

No. 2316

Nine-tray cabinet

Cat. no.
2319 Outside size, $12\frac{7}{8}$ in. high, $19\frac{1}{2}$ in. wide, $13\frac{3}{8}$ in. deep. Capacity 9900 lightweight, 7650 medium weight, or 5850 heavyweight cards,

Lock, controlling all trays, additional

No. 2319

Twelve-tray cabinet

Cat. no.
23112 Outside size, $15\frac{3}{4}$ in. high, 20 in. wide, $15\frac{3}{4}$ in. deep. Capacity 16,800 lightweight, 12,975 medium weight, or 11,125 heavyweight cards,

Lock, controlling all trays, additional
2381 Swivel base, $27\frac{1}{4}$ in. high, additional

23812 Leg base, 26 in. high, additional

No. 23112

No. 23115 with no. 2381 swivel base

15-tray cabinet on swivel-top base

Cat. no.	
23115	Outside size 19⅜ in. high, 20 in. wide, 15¾ in. deep. Capacity 21,000 lightweight, 16,225 medium weight, or 13,925 heavyweight cards
	Lock, controlling all trays, additional
2381	Swivel base, 27¼ in. high, additional
23812	Leg base, 26 in. high, additional
23615	Pedestal base, 26 in. high, additional

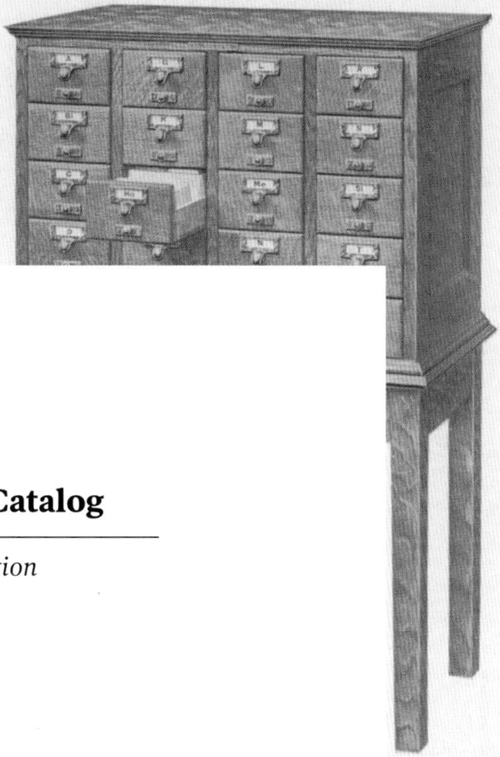

2C

Cat. n

2312

238

2382

2362

Chapter 3

Constructing a Catalog

The 3-by-5 Solution

THE CARD CATALOG TAKES SHAPE

In a stuffy, austerely furnished room in New York City in September 1853, the librarian of the recently established Smithsonian Institution, Charles Coffin Jewett, took the podium to address representatives from forty-seven libraries in the United States. Arguably the most distinguished librarian in the country, Jewett was the obvious choice to lead this first convention of librarians. During the three-day meeting, he presented a plan outlining the future of the library catalog, the key feature of which was to "form a general catalogue of all the books in the country, with reference to the libraries where each might be found."

Jewett's ambitious cataloging ideas and his steadfast desire to transform the Smithsonian into a national library ruffled feathers and eventually led to his dismissal less than a year later, but his vision of a national library with a central catalog was prophetic. The shift from the bound, expensive, and quickly outdated library catalogs was inevitable, but early attempts to create standard and efficient systems were riddled with competing views and numerous false starts.

Charles Coffin Jewett, circa 1860.

As chief librarian at the Smithsonian Institution and the Boston Public Library, Jewett helped elevate librarianship to a respected profession. His influential support of both public and academic libraries paved the way for later leaders like Melvil Dewey and Herbert Putnam and set the stage for centralized cataloging and the establishment of a national library.

previous spread

Supply catalog from the Library Bureau.

In the halls of two venerable institutions, Harvard and the Boston Athenaeum, cataloging efforts began to coalesce as the medium and method came together to provide a new, versatile gateway to a library's collection. Harvard's assistant librarian, Ezra Abbot, is credited with creating the first modern card catalog designed for readers. When Abbot introduced his catalog in the early 1860s, the "paper slip," or card catalog, was being used in Europe and a few American libraries, but the bound catalog was still prevalent. What made Abbot's card catalog special was that it was designed to be used by the patron—most other catalogs at the time were only handled by library staff. Anyone who has ever opened a drawer and fingered through the cards within to locate a book can appreciate this indelible aspect of the card catalog. The flexibility of adding or deleting cards to accurately and immediately reflect a library's holdings was groundbreaking when compared to the intractable bound catalog the card catalog was destined to supplant.

Abbot's associate in this project was Charles Ammi Cutter, who at age thirty-one became the librarian at the opulent Boston Athenaeum in 1868. Cutter immediately set about modernizing the Athenaeum's catalog and created an expansive new scheme that would later help establish the basis for the Library of Congress Classification system. It was also Cutter who

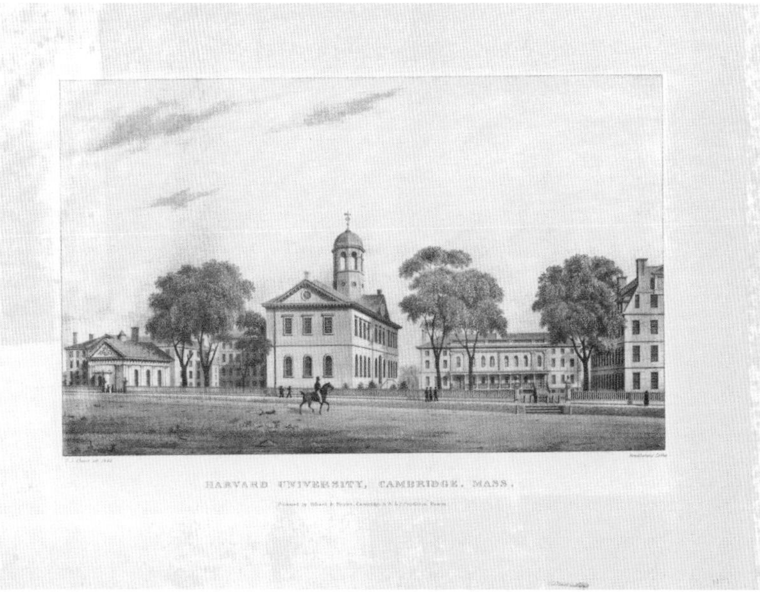

Harvard University, Cambridge, Massachusetts.

In addition to the card catalog, Charles Ammi Cutter introduced several long-lasting customs during his time at Harvard, including the glued pocket on the inside of a book's rear cover where a card was inserted indicating loan status.

insisted catalogs must give information concerning the author, title, and subject of a work—an approach that continues to stand as the primary access point to any book, website, or other searchable resource. Although Cutter's cataloging rules were adopted by many libraries, he is overshadowed by his occasional rival, a man whose name became synonymous with libraries and catalogs everywhere.

THE LIBRARY BUREAU

Melville Louis Kossuth Dewey was two years old when Charles Jewett chaired the 1853 conference that kicked off a movement culminating with the codification of a cataloging system at the end of the century. Keenly interested in organizing and simplifying things at a young age, he shortened his first name to Melvil, dropped his middle names altogether, and, briefly, even spelled his last name as "Dui." While still an undergraduate at Amherst, Dewey was obsessed with bringing order to the school's library, and he recounted that while daydreaming during a long lecture one day, "without hearing a word, my mind absorbed in the vital problem, the solution flasht over me so that I jumpt in my seat and came very near shouting 'Eureka!'"

Dewey's revolutionary approach to cataloging was a library classification system based on a controlled vocabulary of subject headings, represented

Wood engraving of Melvil Dewey, *Harper's Weekly*, September 26, 1896.

by numerical values that could be subdivided further by decimals. Thus was born the Dewey Decimal Classification, a system that borrowed generously from Bacon, Jewett, and Cutter and attempted to encapsulate all knowledge in ten distinct classes. It immediately caught on and expanded Dewey's influence within the library community. In hindsight there is no denying the impact his system had on libraries, but throughout his career Dewey remained a complicated figure, heralded as both a reformer and a genius in the library world, while at the same time being regarded as brash, stubborn, and difficult to work with.

The Centennial International Exhibition of 1876, the first major World's Fair held in the United States, opened on May 10 in Philadelphia. The country hoped the fair would improve its image in the international community, as the years following the Civil War were marred by political scandal, racial turmoil, and ineffectual governance. The sprawling exhibition halls showcased rising American industrial power in more than 30,000 exhibits. Some one hundred librarians met there as well and, encouraged by Dewey and Cutter, among others, signed on as charter members of a new national organization, the American Library Association (ALA). The first issue of its official house publication, the *Library Journal*, made clear that the most pressing issues facing libraries were the lack of a standardized catalog and an agency to administer a centralized catalog.

Responding to the standardization matter, the ALA formed a committee that quickly recommended using the 2-by-5-in (5-by-12-cm) cards as at Harvard and the Boston Athenaeum. However, in the same report, the committee also suggested that a larger card, approximately 3 by 5 in (7.5 by 12 cm), would be preferable. By the end of the nineteenth century, the bigger card won out, due mainly to the fact that the 3-by-5-in (7.5-by-12-cm) card was already the "postal size" used for postcards.

Dewey saw well beyond the importance of standardized cards and sought to outfit virtually all facets of library operations. To this end he established a Supplies Department as part of the ALA, later to become a stand-alone company renamed the Library Bureau. In one of its early distribution catalogs, the bureau pointed out that "no other business had been organized with the definite purpose of supplying libraries." With a focus on machine-cut index cards and the trays and cabinets to contain them, the Library Bureau became a veritable furniture store, selling tables, chairs, shelves, and display cases, as well as date stamps, newspaper holders, hole

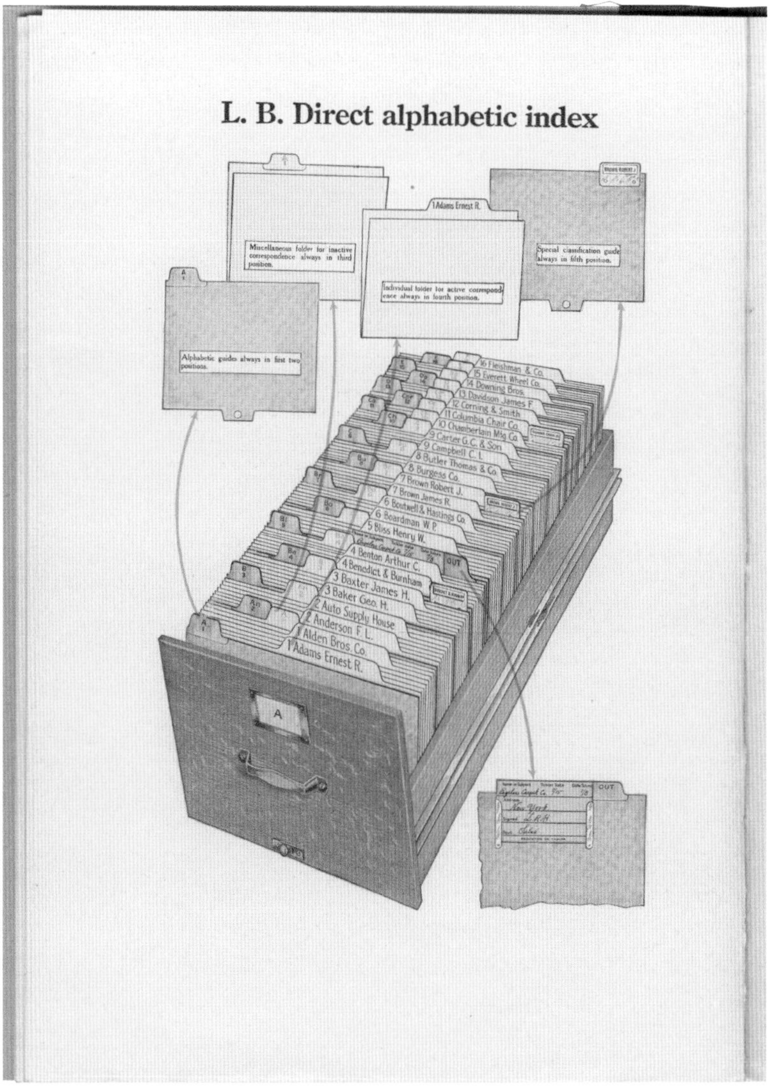

Supply catalog from the Library Bureau, 1897-1920.

With his success in supplying catalog cards and furniture to libraries, Dewey expanded his company's client list to include banks, insurance companies, railroads, and other industries.

punchers, paperweights, and virtually anything else a library could possibly need. With this one-stop shopping service, Dewey left an enduring mark on libraries across the country. Uniformity spread from library to library, a hallmark of which became the classic sturdy oak furniture found in many public and university libraries.

For Dewey, and the ALA, establishing standards for index cards was only half the battle. With the ever-growing number of public and university

Supply catalogs from the Library Bureau, 1897-1920.

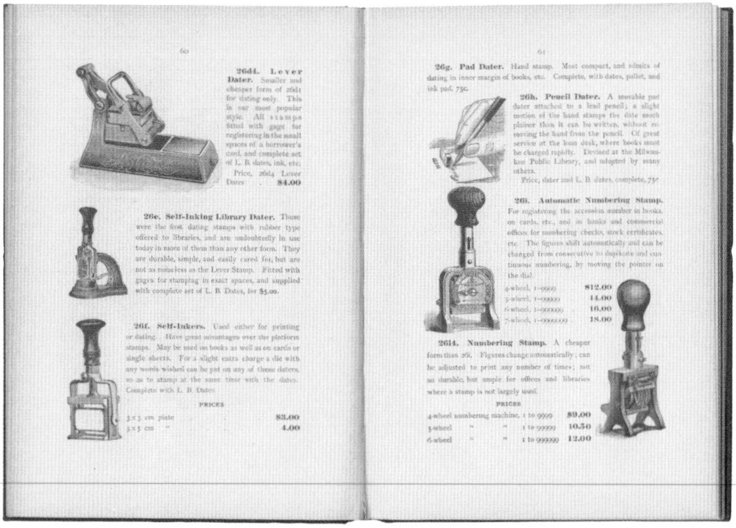

60

26d4. Lever Dater. Smaller and cheaper form of 26d1 for dating only. This is our most popular style. All stamps fitted with gage for registering in the small spaces of a borrower's card, and complete set of L. B. dates, ink, etc.

Price, 26d4 Lever Dater . **$4.00**

26e. Self-Inking Library Dater. These were the first dating stamps with rubber type offered to libraries, and are undoubtedly in use today in more of them than any other form. They are durable, simple, and easily cared for, but are not as noiseless as the Lever Stamp. Fitted with gages for stamping in exact spaces, and supplied with complete set of L. B. Dates, for **$5.00.**

26f. Self-Inkers. Used either for printing or dating. Have great advantages over the platform stamps. May be used on books as well as on cards or single sheets. For a slight extra charge a die with any words wished can be put on any of these daters, so as to stamp at the same time with the dates. Complete with L. B. Dates.

PRICES

3×3 cm plate	**$3.00**
3×5 cm "	**4.00**

61

26g. Pad Dater. Hand stamp. Most compact, and admits of dating in inner margin of books, etc. Complete, with dates, pallet, and ink pad, 75c.

26h. Pencil Dater. A movable pad dater attached to a lead pencil; a slight motion of the hand stamps the date much plainer than it can be written, without removing the hand from the pencil. Of great service at the loan desk, where books must be charged rapidly. Devised at the Milwaukee Public Library, and adopted by many others.

Price, dater and L. B. dates, complete, 75c

26i. Automatic Numbering Stamp. For registering the accession number in books, on cards, etc., and in banks and commercial offices for numbering checks, stock certificates, etc. The figures shift automatically and can be changed from consecutive to duplicate and continuous numbering, by moving the pointer on the dial.

4-wheel, 1-9999	**$12.00**
5-wheel, 1-99999	**14.00**
6-wheel, 1-999999	**16.00**
7-wheel, 1-9999999	**18.00**

26i1. Numbering Stamp. A cheaper form than 26i. Figures change automatically; can be adjusted to print any number of times; not so durable, but ample for offices and libraries where a stamp is not largely used.

PRICES

4-wheel numbering machine,	1 to 9999	**$9.00**
5-wheel " "	1 to 99999	**10.50**
6-wheel " "	1 to 999999	**12.00**

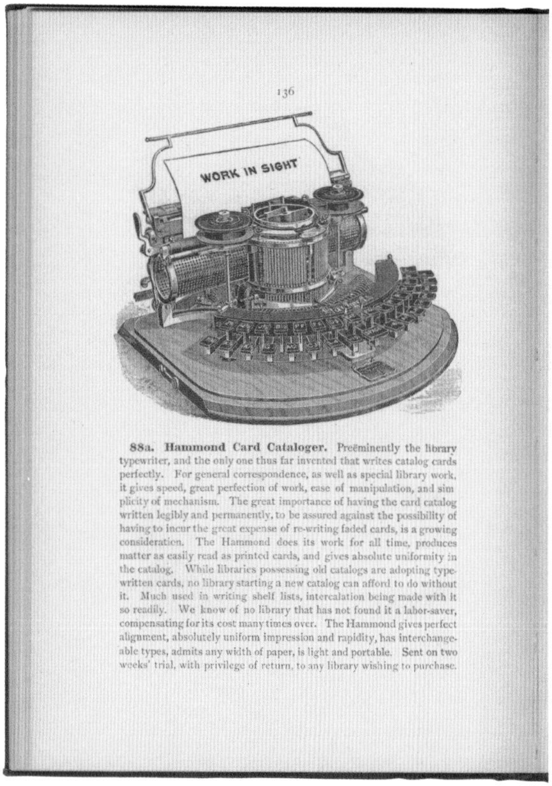

136

88a. Hammond Card Cataloger. Preëminently the library typewriter, and the only one thus far invented that writes catalog cards perfectly. For general correspondence, as well as special library work, it gives speed, great perfection of work, ease of manipulation, and simplicity of mechanism. The great importance of having the card catalog written legibly and permanently, to be assured against the possibility of having to incur the great expense of re-writing faded cards, is a growing consideration. The Hammond does its work for all time, produces matter as easily read as printed cards, and gives absolute uniformity in the catalog. While libraries possessing old catalogs are adopting typewritten cards, no library starting a new catalog can afford to do without it. Much used in writing shelf lists, intercalation being made with it so readily. We know of no library that has not found it a labor-saver, compensating for its cost many times over. The Hammond gives perfect alignment, absolutely uniform impression and rapidity, has interchangeable types, admits any width of paper, is light and portable. Sent on two weeks' trial, with privilege of return, to any library wishing to purchase.

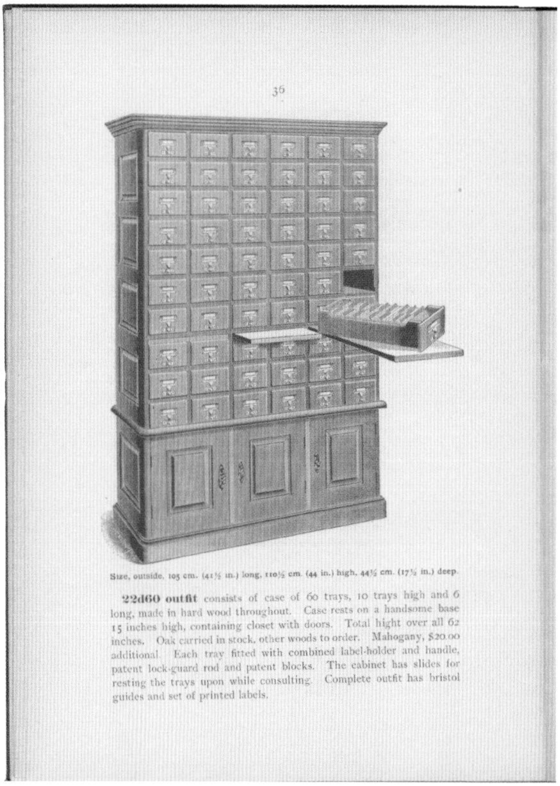

36

Size, outside, 105 cm. (41½ in.) long, 110½ cm. (44 in.) high, 44½ cm. (17½ in.) deep.

22d60 outfit consists of case of 60 trays, 10 trays high and 6 long, made in hard wood throughout. Case rests on a handsome base 15 inches high, containing closet with doors. Total hight over all 62 inches. Oak carried in stock, other woods to order. Mahogany, $20.00 additional. Each tray fitted with combined label-holder and handle, patent lock-guard rod and patent blocks. The cabinet has slides for resting the trays upon while consulting. Complete outfit has bristol guides and set of printed labels.

libraries across the United States, he fervently pursued the cherished dream of a cooperative cataloging agency that would issue cards from a centralized location. In the 1870s, there was already some discussion within the library community in favor of the Library of Congress taking on this leadership role. The notion was brought to the attention of the Librarian of Congress, Ainsworth Rand Spofford, a former Cincinnati bookseller and journalist. Spofford respectfully acknowledged Dewey's appeals, but it is highly unlikely he ever seriously considered leading a national cataloging effort. His relationship with the ALA was polite yet restrained, and he was reluctant to participate in ALA functions and conferences because he did not envision a collaborative role for the institution.

Spofford was busy shepherding an evolving institution through extensive changes while reshaping it into a great "national library." Taking control of catalog cards would have to wait. As Library of Congress historian John Cole wrote, "For the most part, Spofford operated quite independently from the American library movement and the American Library Association itself. The primary reason was, quite simply, that he did not have the time to participate. . . . Spofford's independence from other libraries and librarians was accentuated by his idea of a national library as well as by his personal temperament. He believed the Library should be, essentially, a comprehensive accumulation of the nation's literature, the American equivalent of the British Museum and the other great national libraries of Europe. He did not view it as a focal point for cooperative library activities and was not inclined to leadership in that direction."

A clearly frustrated Dewey, stymied by the Librarian's reticence, turned to his friends in the publishing industry, namely Frederick Leypoldt and Richard Rogers Bowker of *Publishers Weekly*. The plan was to goad publishers into working with Charles Cutter on cataloging their own books through the insertion of a paper slip containing the bibliographic information that could be used by libraries. The response from libraries was tepid. They viewed the scheme with skepticism and doubted it would provide the final answer to their cataloging needs. And following a few more halting attempts at collaboration between the Library Bureau and the publishing industry, Dewey was still left searching for the answer to a question he posed in one of his early editorials in the *Library Journal*— "Is it practicable for the Library of Congress to catalogue for the whole country?" "Practicable" or not, the Librarian of Congress had other plans.

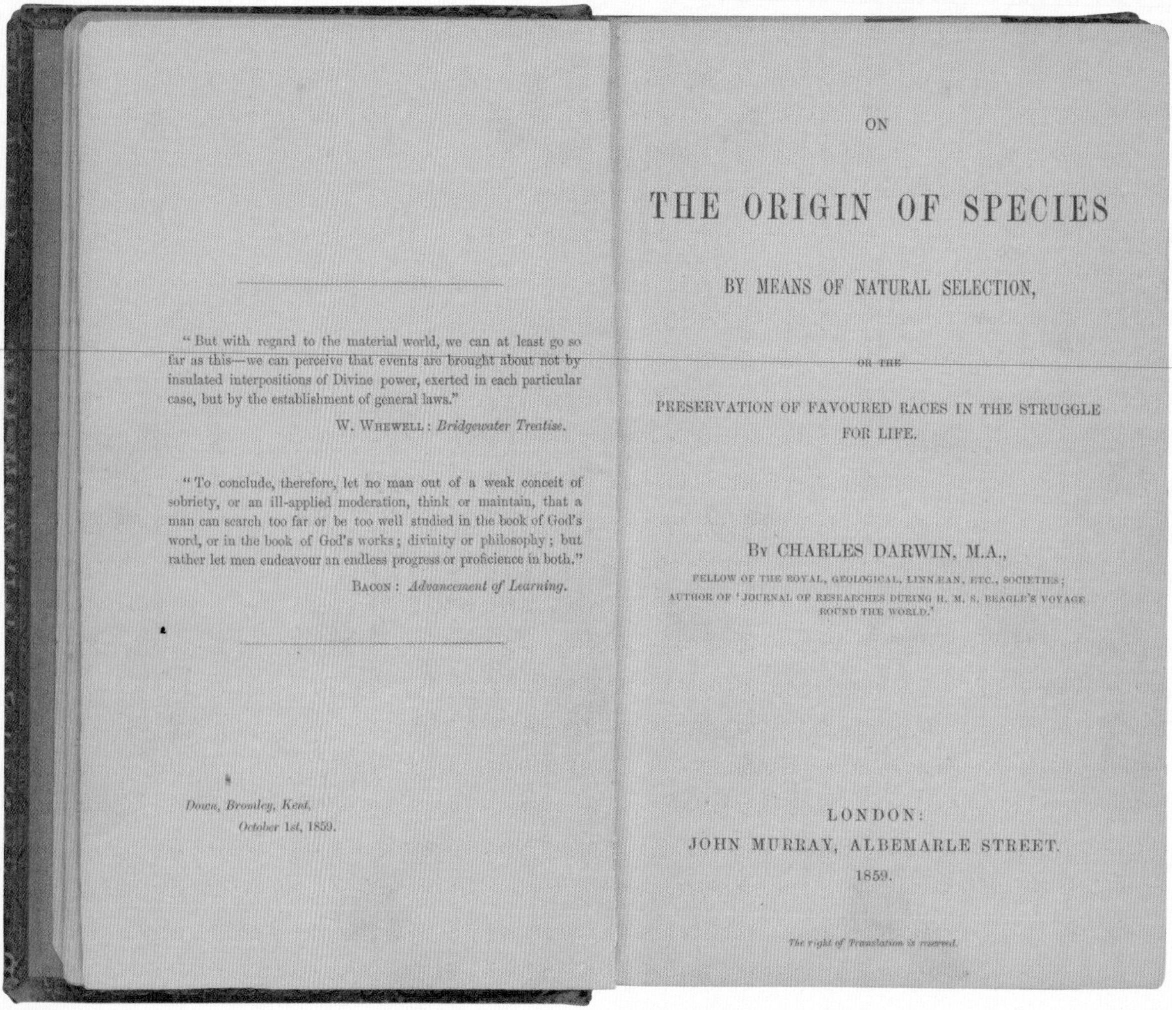

"But with regard to the material world, we can at least go so far as this—we can perceive that events are brought about not by insulated interpositions of Divine power, exerted in each particular case, but by the establishment of general laws."

W. WHEWELL: *Bridgewater Treatise.*

"To conclude, therefore, let no man out of a weak conceit of sobriety, or an ill-applied moderation, think or maintain, that a man can search too far or be too well studied in the book of God's word, or in the book of God's works; divinity or philosophy; but rather let men endeavour an endless progress or proficience in both."

BACON: *Advancement of Learning.*

Down, Bromley, Kent,
October 1st, 1859.

ON

THE ORIGIN OF SPECIES

BY MEANS OF NATURAL SELECTION,

OR THE

PRESERVATION OF FAVOURED RACES IN THE STRUGGLE FOR LIFE.

BY CHARLES DARWIN, M.A.,

FELLOW OF THE ROYAL, GEOLOGICAL, LINNÆAN, ETC., SOCIETIES;
AUTHOR OF 'JOURNAL OF RESEARCHES DURING H. M. S. BEAGLE'S VOYAGE ROUND THE WORLD.'

LONDON:
JOHN MURRAY, ALBEMARLE STREET.
1859.

The right of Translation is reserved.

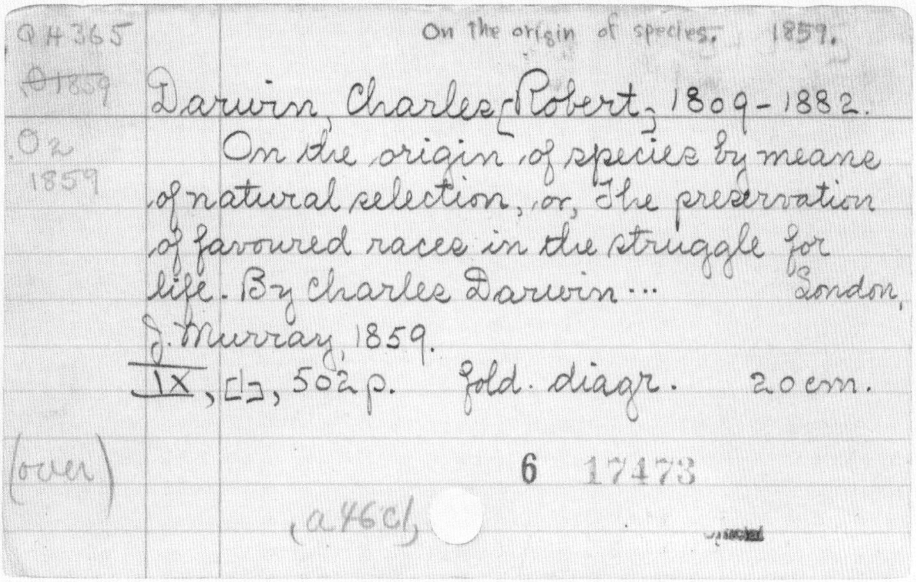

QH365
~~Q1859~~
Q2
1859

On the origin of species. 1859.

Darwin, Charles [Robert], 1809-1882.
On the origin of species by means of natural selection, or, The preservation of favoured races in the struggle for life. By Charles Darwin ... London, J. Murray, 1859.
ix, [1], 502 p. fold. diagr. 20 cm.

(over) 6 17473

Charles Darwin, *On the Origin of Species by Means of Natural Selection*. London, John Murray, 1859.

TO THE FRATERNITY
BASE BALL POLKA
COMPOSED BY JAS. M. GOODMAN.
PHILADELPHIA
PUBLISHED BY C.F. ESCHER 108 NTH SECOND ST.
Plain 3½
6 Lith

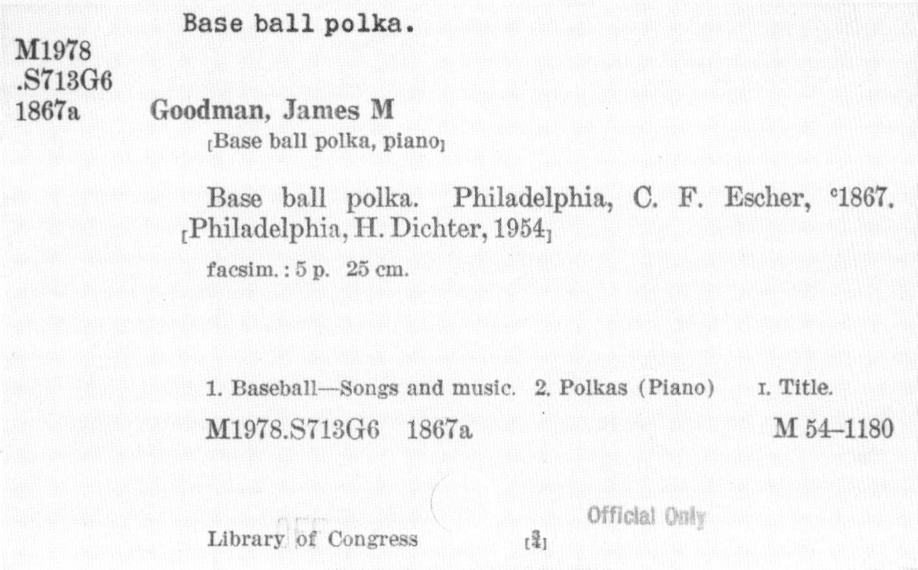

Base ball polka.

M1978
.S713G6
1867a **Goodman, James M**

[Base ball polka, piano]

Base ball polka. Philadelphia, C. F. Escher, ©1867. [Philadelphia, H. Dichter, 1954]

facsim. : 5 p. 25 cm.

1. Baseball—Songs and music. 2. Polkas (Piano) I. Title.

M1978.S713G6 1867a M 54–1180

Official Only

Library of Congress [3/4]

Jas. M. Goodman, *Base Ball Polka*. Philadelphia, C. F. Escher, 1867.

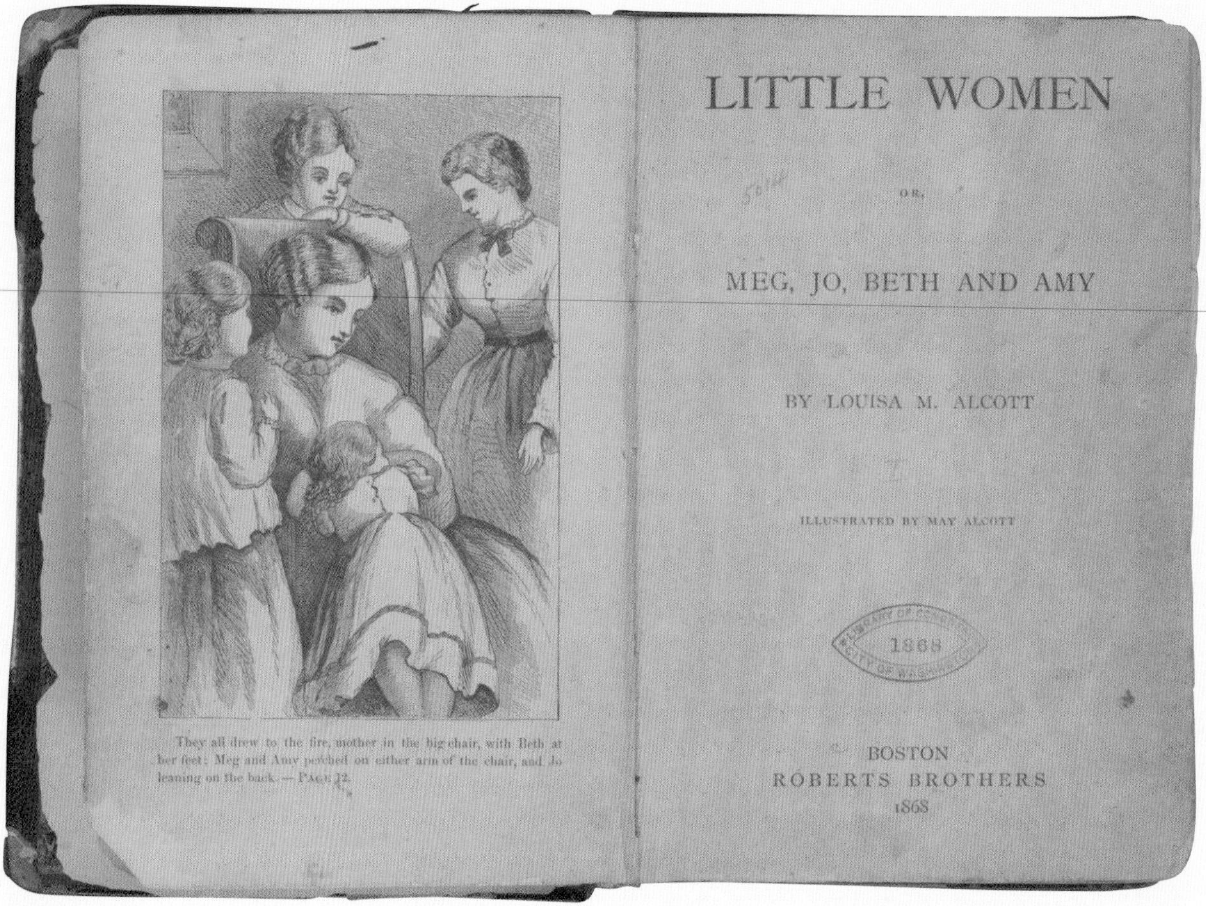
They all drew to the fire, mother in the big chair, with Beth at her feet; Meg and Amy perched on either arm of the chair, and Jo leaning on the back. — Page 12.
LITTLE WOMEN
OR,
MEG, JO, BETH AND AMY
BY LOUISA M. ALCOTT
ILLUSTRATED BY MAY ALCOTT
1868
BOSTON
ROBERTS BROTHERS
1868

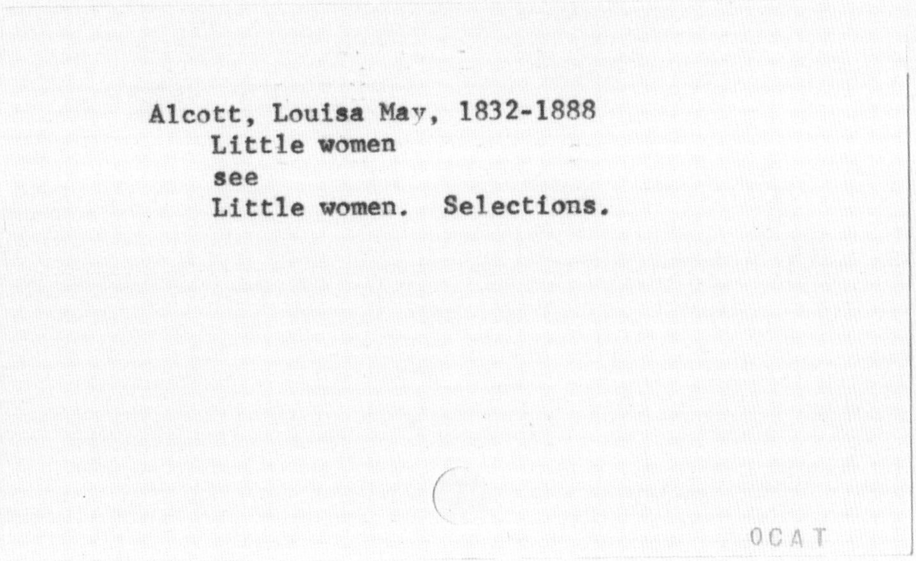
Alcott, Louisa May, 1832-1888
Little women
see
Little women. Selections.

OCAT

Louisa M. Alcott, *Little Women or, Meg, Jo, Beth and Amy.* Boston, Roberts Brothers, 1868.

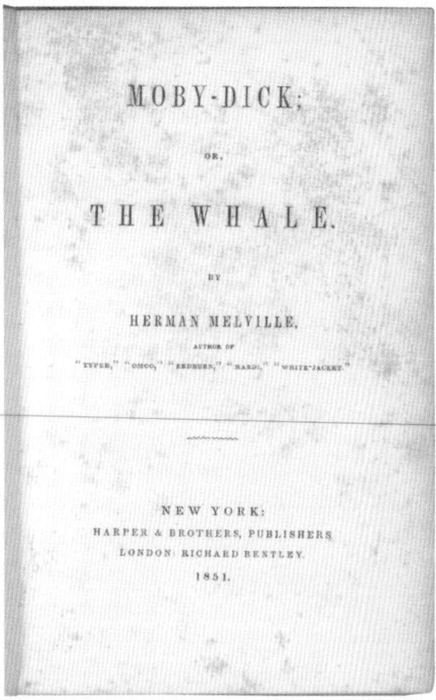

MOBY-DICK;

OR,

THE WHALE.

BY

HERMAN MELVILLE,

AUTHOR OF

"TYPEE," "OMOO," "REDBURN," "MARDI," "WHITE-JACKET."

NEW YORK:
HARPER & BROTHERS, PUBLISHERS.
LONDON: RICHARD BENTLEY.
1851.

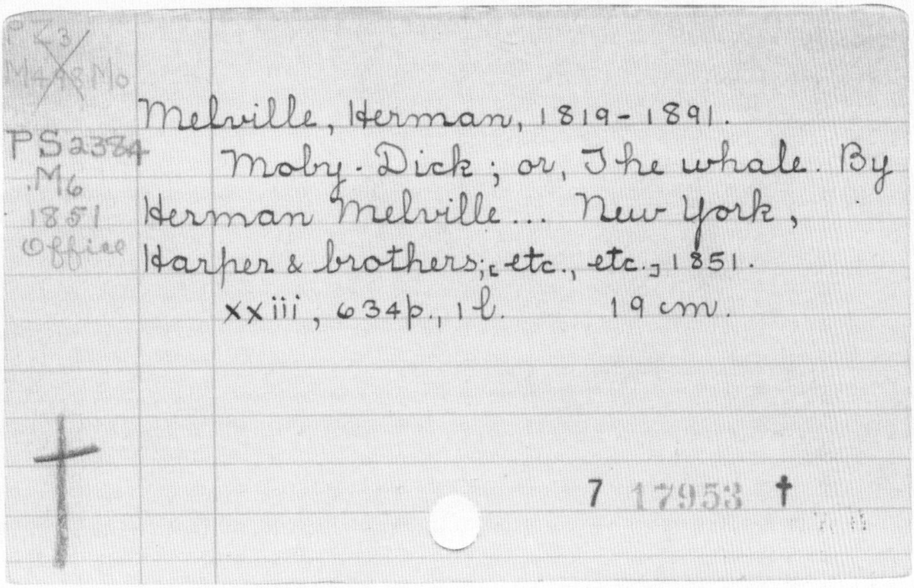

Herman Melville, *Moby-Dick; or, the Whale*. New York, Harper & Brothers; London, Richard Bentley, 1851.

·POEMS·
·Emily·Dickinson·

Dickinson, Emily, 1830-1886.
Fourteen poems
<u>see her</u>
Poems.

OCAT

Emily Dickinson, *Poems*.
Edited by Mabel Loomis Todd
and T. W. Higginson. Boston,
Roberts Brothers, 1890.

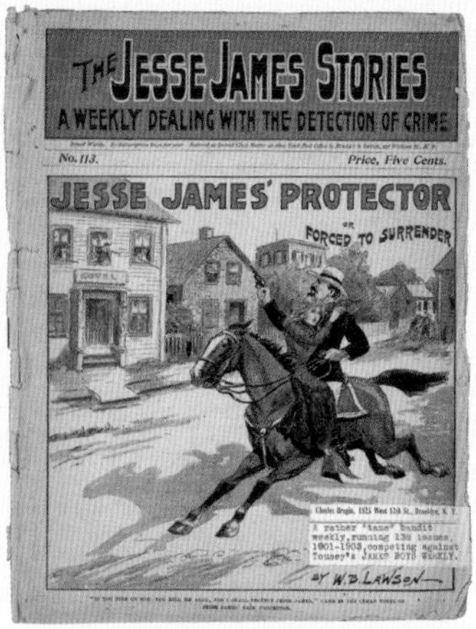

THE JESSE JAMES STORIES
A WEEKLY DEALING WITH THE DETECTION OF CRIME
No. 113.
Price, Five Cents.
JESSE JAMES' PROTECTOR
OR, FORCED TO SURRENDER
BY W. B. LAWSON

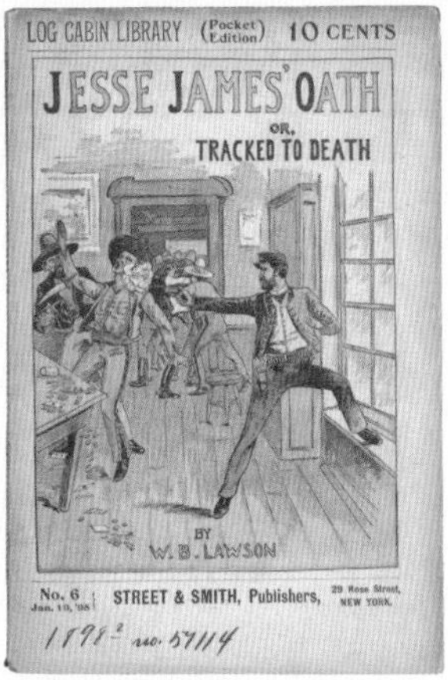

LOG CABIN LIBRARY (Pocket Edition) 10 CENTS
JESSE JAMES' OATH
OR, TRACKED TO DEATH
BY W. B. LAWSON
No. 6
STREET & SMITH, Publishers,
29 Rose Street, NEW YORK.

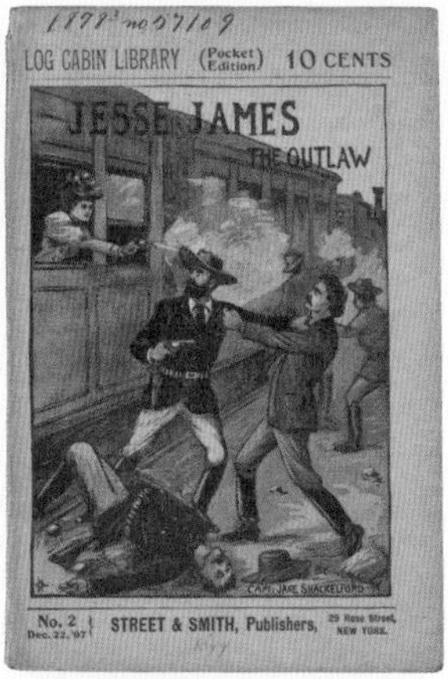

LOG CABIN LIBRARY (Pocket Edition) 10 CENTS
JESSE JAMES THE OUTLAW
No. 2
Dec. 22, '97
STREET & SMITH, Publishers,
29 Rose Street, NEW YORK.

THE BUFFALO BILL STORIES
A WEEKLY PUBLICATION
DEVOTED TO BORDER HISTORY
No. 243
NEW YORK, JANUARY 6, 1906.
Price, Five Cents
BUFFALO BILL'S SPECIAL SERVICE
OR, THE DEATH DANCE OF THE APACHES
BY THE AUTHOR OF "BUFFALO BILL"

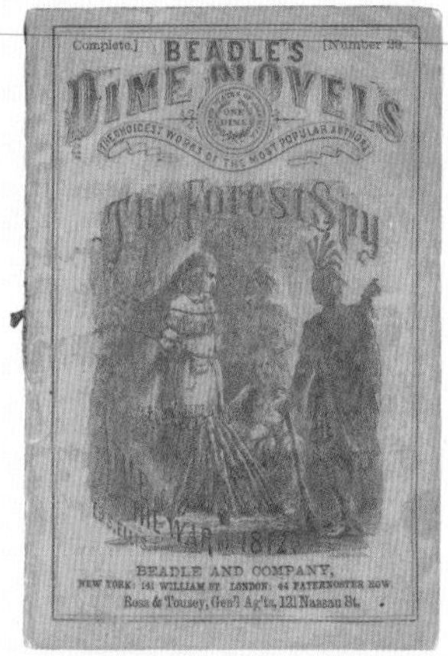

BEADLE'S DIME NOVELS
The Forest Spy
BEADLE AND COMPANY,

BEADLE'S DIME NOVELS
THE PARTISAN SPY.
BEADLE AND COMPANY, 98 WILLIAM STREET NEW YORK.
Albany News Company, Albany, N. Y.

The WAR Library
STORIES OF ADVENTURE IN THE WAR FOR THE UNION.
PRISON PEN; OR, DEAD LINE AT ANDERSONVILLE

ROUGH RIDER WEEKLY
THE BEST WILD WEST STORIES PUBLISHED
No. 170
Price, Five Cents
KING OF THE WILD WEST'S CATTLE-WAR
OR, Stella's Bout with the Rival Ranchers
BY NED TAYLOR.

Nº 27
IMPORTANT NOTICE!
5 CENTS
ARMY AND NAVY
THE MONARCH OF JUVENILE PUBLICATIONS
STREET & SMITH, Publishers, New York.
DECEMBER 18, 1897.

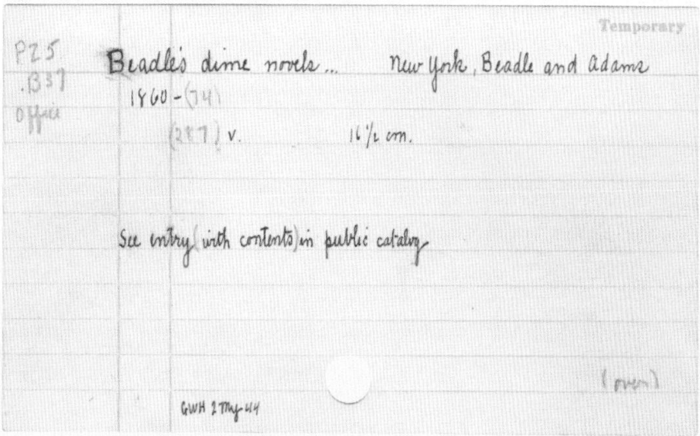

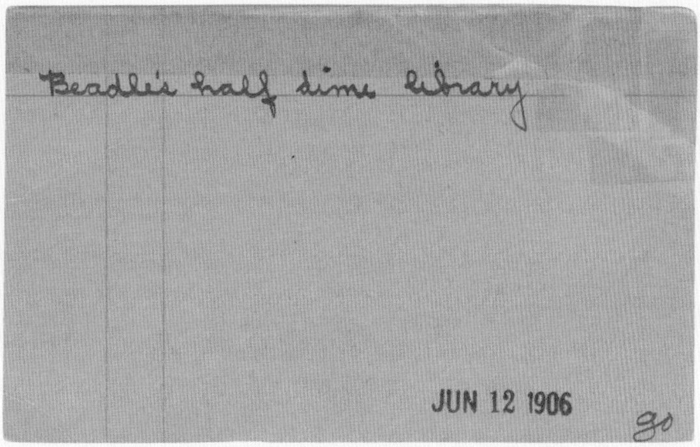

Library of Congress Dime Novel Collection

The dime novel publishing phenomenon, which first appeared in 1860, provided Americans with a wealth of popular fiction in a regular series at a fixed, inexpensive price. Early dime novels, first printed in orange wrapper papers, were patriotic—and often nationalistic—tales of encounters between Native Americans and backwoods settlers. In the 1870s, detective adventures, society romances, and rags-to-riches stories were introduced, and by the mid-1890s, bold color covers depicting scenes of bloodshed and courageous feats appealed to a mostly adolescent audience. Through copyright deposit, the Library of Congress accumulated a dime novel collection of nearly 40,000 titles from 280 different series. The prolific publishing houses of Beadle & Adams, Frank Tousey, and Street & Smith are well represented.

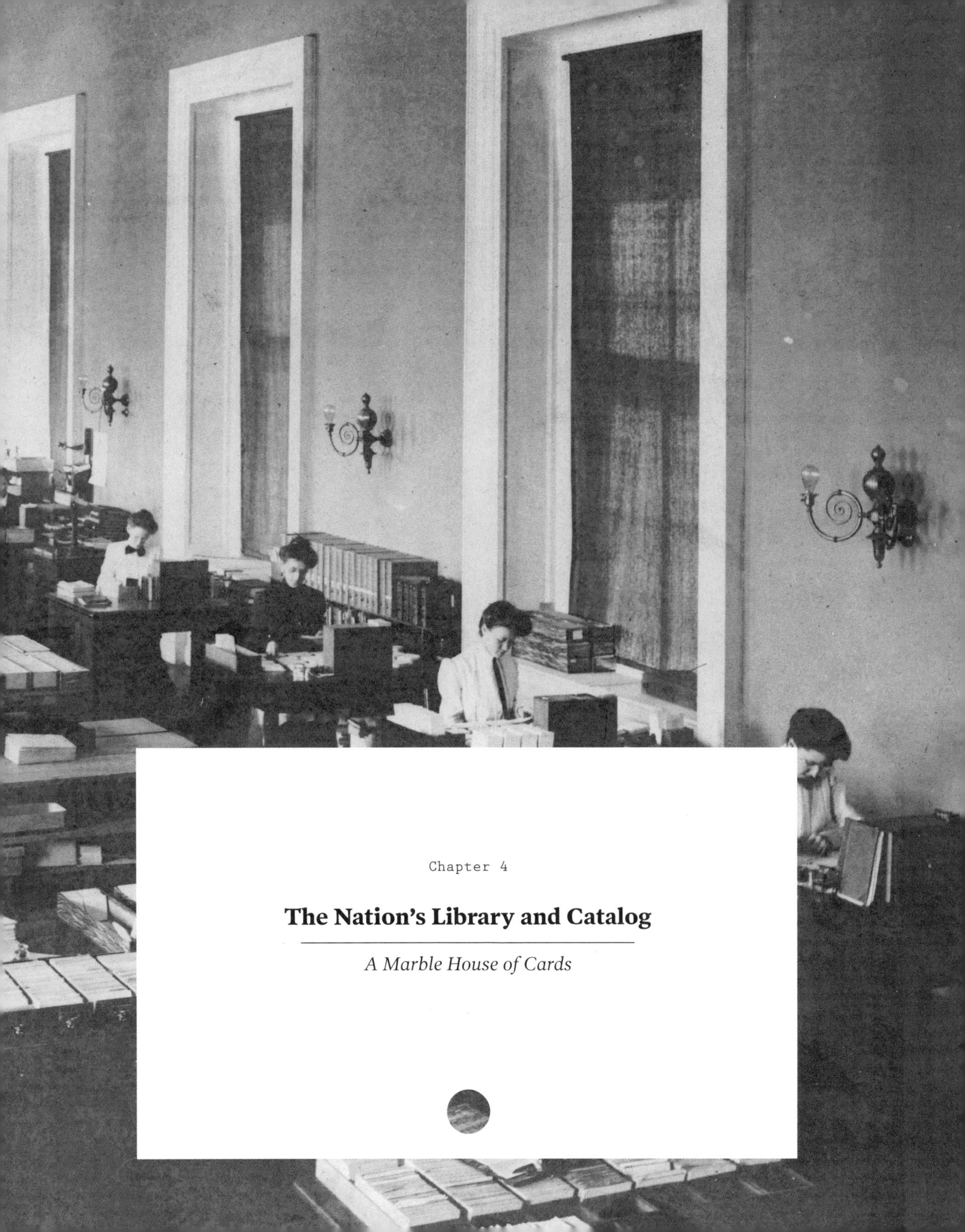

Chapter 4

The Nation's Library and Catalog

A Marble House of Cards

CHAOS IN THE CAPITOL

Meanwhile, by the mid-nineteenth century, as Charles Jewett was promoting the Smithsonian Library as the national library, the Library of Congress was questioning its own identity. Senator James A. Pearce, the chairman of the joint congressional committee that oversaw the Library in the 1840s, viewed it primarily as a legislative resource for Congress. A plantation-owning aristocrat and Southern sympathizer from Maryland, Pearce was determined to keep the Library's collections neutral by excluding controversial or partisan works. Purposefully omitting certain titles was becoming increasingly difficult and politically charged as the country began to awaken to the terrible truths of slavery as found in works by Frederick Douglass, Henry David Thoreau, and Harriet Beecher Stowe.

It was at this critical juncture that the Library met with even greater travails. On Christmas Eve in 1851, a faulty chimney flue ignited a fire that destroyed more than half of the Library's 55,000 books and nearly two-thirds of Jefferson's collection. As the Library once again picked up the smoldering pieces, it was an opportunity to think about its purpose and role in national life. What books should be acquired? How should they be cataloged? Who would be allowed access to the reading room?

Librarian of Congress Ainsworth Rand Spofford, 1825-1908.

Spofford's approach to cataloging and managing the Library's collections was much more idiosyncratic than emerging trends in librarianship dictated. In his view, "The organization of the library is a subjective one, and not governed by any Procrustean system of classification. I think that the best system in classifying a library is that which produces a book in the shortest time to one who wants it. I would ride over all rules that interfere with that promptitude of service."

previous spread

People working in the card distribution room of the Card Division, circa 1900-1920.

Librarian and historian David Mearns (1899–1981) summed up the situation following the fire: "Nothing was right. Everything was at loose ends. The Library had reached a new and strange and unpleasant level of despair." When the Southern states seceded in 1860 and the country descended into civil war, the future of the troubled congressional library was as uncertain as the fate of the nation.

On New Year's Eve in 1864, as the Confederacy was on the brink of defeat, President Lincoln appointed assistant Librarian Ainsworth Rand Spofford as the sixth Librarian of Congress. With a staff of just seven and a collection of 82,000 books, Spofford already envisioned the congressional library as the nation's library. The timing was fortuitous, as the immediate legacy of the Civil War was a dramatic expansion of the federal government. Spofford took full advantage of the situation, petitioning Congress early in his tenure for more funds to increase the Library's holdings and presidential approval to transfer the Smithsonian Institution Library (some 40,000 volumes) to the Library of Congress.

The massive Smithsonian acquisition, however, wasn't the most notable collection-building feat of Spofford's tenure. He recognized the value that copyright deposits could have in expanding the collection and argued for the centralization of all U.S. copyright registrations at the Library of Congress. It was a boon for the Library when Congress passed the Copyright Act of 1870 requiring two copies of every book, map, print, photograph, sheet music, periodical, and other material submitted for copyright be sent to the Library of Congress.

With the parallel expansion of federal agencies across Washington and a favorable political climate, Spofford established a cordial relationship with Congress, allowing him to further his vision of a national library. His dedication and photographic memory became legendary in the halls of the Capitol as congressmen routinely asked for his help writing their speeches and checking their facts. Although a printed catalog existed, the true gateway to the books of the Library of Congress was Spofford himself. His knowledge of the collection was both astonishing and essential, as the catalog could not keep up with the massive influx of books resulting from the new copyright deposits.

At the end of Spofford's first decade as Librarian in 1876, the same year the ALA was founded, the Library in the Capitol building was inundated with books and the collection tripled in size to more than 300,000 volumes. Visitors described seeing Spofford weaving in and out among the

Reproduction of watercolor by W. Bengough, 1897.

This scene of cluttered chaos shows the Library of Congress when it was located in the fireproof "iron room" at the U.S. Capitol. The Librarian, Ainsworth Rand Spofford, is standing at the right and the man on the left holding a lamp is David Hutcheson, assistant Librarian.

Interior of the old Congressional Library, U.S. Capitol building. Circa nineteenth century.

From the 1897 Annual Report*: "The Library was so congested, books were heaped up in so many crevices and out-of-the-way corners, down in the crypt, hidden in darkness from access of observation, that obtaining a volume, and especially, one out of the range of general reading, was a question of time and patience. Frequently, it depended upon the phenomenal memory of the distinguished Librarian."*

labyrinths of books piled up to the ceiling. Anticipating that the Library would quickly outgrow its modest confines in the Capitol, Spofford advised Congress that without more space he would soon "be presiding over the greatest chaos in America."

TEN FIRST STREET

A move was already long overdue when Spofford began urging Congress to fund a new building. In an impassioned speech supporting Spofford, Senator Justin Morrill of Vermont argued, "We must either reduce the Library to the stinted and specific wants of Congress alone, or permit it to advance to national importance, and give it room equal to the culture, wants, and resources of a great people. The higher education of our common country demands that this institution shall not be crippled for lack of room."

Congress was persuaded. In 1887, fourteen years after a design competition for a new Library was announced, the pale gray granite edifice began to rise across the street from the Capitol, at Ten First Street. John L. Smithmeyer and Paul J. Pelz's Italian Renaissance design was originally "void of lavish ornamentation" and followed Spofford's request for a circular reading room at the center. Once the architects realized they were going to be well under budget, they added flourishes and elaborate detailing to the building that was destined to parallel the great museums and libraries of Europe.

Hundreds of artists, craftsmen, sculptors, masons, steamfitters, plumbers, and carpenters collaborated on the construction. Marble from Tennessee, Italy, France, and North Africa covered some of the twenty-four million red bricks that formed the interior. The walls were adorned with frescoes and mosaics steeped in allegorical meaning and symbolic of the branches of knowledge. The grand new Library, ornate and lavishly decorated, was nevertheless intended as a working library whose primary purpose was to safely guard the collections within. The cast-iron and steel book stacks were divided into nine tiers meant to support and organize the growing collection. The intricately designed maze of shelves, alcoves, and corridors that radiate from the rotunda of the octagonal main reading room were known to confuse tourists and staff alike. During construction, a reporter who had been granted access to the site became lost in the labyrinth of book stacks, and after wandering aimlessly for hours, finally stumbled across a worker who guided him out.

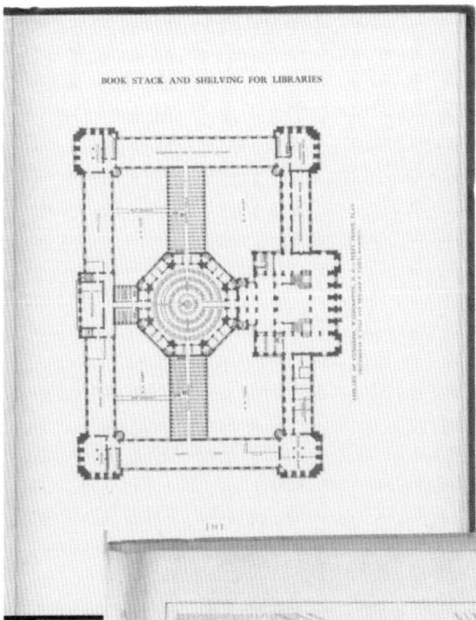

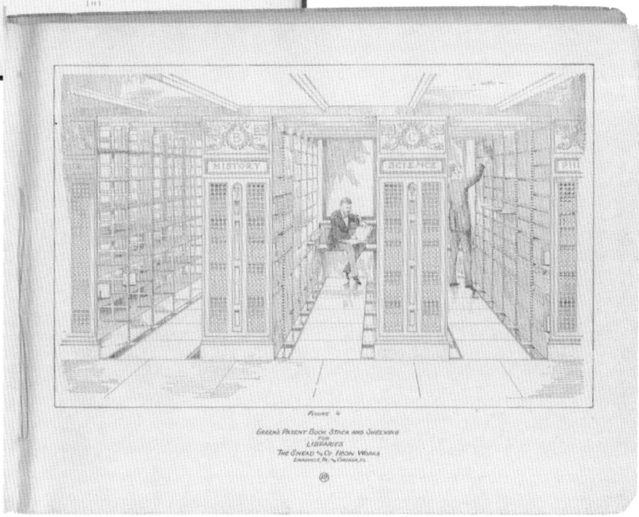

Blueprints and plans for the stacks and shelving in the Library of Congress (1895-1908).

As building superintendent and engineer, Bernard R. Green oversaw all phases of construction. He also prepared the drawings for the book stacks and shelves of the new Library, and his designs garnered much praise throughout the library community.

View of Library construction with the U.S. Capitol in the background, October 18, 1890.

This picture was taken a few months after the cornerstone was laid. In describing the new Library's exterior, Spofford reported that "the solid massiveness of the granite walls is relieved not only by the numerous windows, with their casings treated in high relief, but by foliated carvings beneath the cornices and pediments."

View from the Capitol of the Library of Congress, early 1900s.

When President McKinley addressed Congress in 1897, he remarked, "The Library building provided for by the act of Congress approved April 15, 1886, has been completed and opened to the public. It should be a matter of congratulation that through the foresight and munificence of Congress the nation possesses this noble treasure-house of knowledge. It is earnestly to be hoped that, having done so much toward the cause of education, Congress will continue to develop the Library in every phase of research, to the end that it may be not only one of the most magnificent, but among the richest, and most useful libraries in the world."

On a rainy November morning in 1897 the new Library of Congress opened its doors to the public, ahead of schedule and under budget. Readers entering the Main Reading Room approached the glossy wooden reference desk and gazed up in awe 175 ft (53 m) to the dome replete with murals, stained glass, imposing statuary, and ornamental arches. While the beauty and grandeur of the new Library was widely recognized by the public, the transition from congressional library to national library was hardly complete. As noted in the 1897 *Report of the Librarian*, "A library without a catalog is as a ship without a rudder." The Library had its new building, but with inadequate cataloging and more material pouring in daily, the newly christened ship required a much stronger rudder.

FACING CONGRESS

With the resplendent and nearly completed Library sitting squarely across the street from the Capitol (and connected by tunnel under First Street), Congress paid closer attention to its organization and inner workings. A year before the Library officially opened, Congress held hearings to discuss what exactly they had spent $6.2 million on. Spofford, along with Dewey and other prominent library figures, was called on to testify. It was not lost on Dewey, president of the ALA, that this would be an opportune time to argue directly before Congress in favor of centralized cataloging. Historically, the independent-minded Spofford was not inclined to collaborate with the ALA on standards.

Spofford's approach to librarianship, however, was exactly what Dewey and ALA leaders had grumbled about during the new building's construction. This younger generation of librarians was horrified at the lack of uniformity and cataloging at the Library during Spofford's tenure, and they were not impressed with his claim that the Library's organization was "a subjective one." They strongly believed that Spofford was out of touch with the "modern developments of library organization and practice."

During the hearings on Capitol Hill, Spofford's testimony revealed a more complicated picture. When pressed by Congress, he admitted that the author card catalog was the only access point to the collection, and that it was perhaps faster to browse the shelves to find a particular book than consult the antiquated catalog. But Spofford, aware of the system's shortcomings as far back as 1866, had been up front about his concerns. He knew that the catalog, including a subject catalog, had "advanced less rapidly than was intended" due in part to a small staff of only forty-two people that was preoccupied with the incessant flow of new material.

When it was Dewey's turn to testify, he declared that "the first great requisite of the new Library will be a well-made catalog." Dewey's dream of a national institution managing the distribution of standardized catalog cards was imminent. While he was cautious not to disparage Spofford directly, as Cole notes, he seized the opportunity to "exert [his] influence in the reorganization that obviously would take place once that spacious, modern structure was occupied." Pointing out that Harvard and the Boston Athenaeum catalogs were now "universally kept on cards," Dewey's strident testimony clearly presented the case for a standard author, title, and subject card catalog that could be distributed to libraries across the country.

The next witness called to testify, Herbert Putnam, was the head of the Boston Public Library, the country's largest public library at that time. With his compact frame and push-broom mustache, Putnam had a polite and reserved manner that stood in contrast to Dewey's more pugnacious style, but he endorsed the need for change at the new Library, including a standardized card catalog. Putnam, an experienced administrator,

Photograph shows interior view of hall with piles of copyright deposit materials on the floor, 1898.

Herbert Putnam, 1900.

During his testimony to Congress, Herbert Putnam described his conception of what the new Library ought to be: "This should be a library, the foremost library in the United States—a national library—that is to say, the largest library in the United States and a library which stands foremost as a model and example of assisting forward the work of scholarship in the United States."

acknowledged that Spofford was hampered by his small staff and testified that the Library should have a significantly larger cataloging division.

President William McKinley relieved Spofford of his duties less than a year after the hearings and only a few months before the new Library opened. As a replacement, he tapped his old friend, John Russell Young, a former diplomat and journalist, who had extensively covered the Civil War. Young's tenure, however, was brief. He died in office after serving less than two years, yet will always be associated with the Library's inaugural year and the cumbersome task of moving the entire collection across First Street. Young also appointed J. C. M. Hanson and Charles Martel, two men familiar with modern library practices, to lead the newly expanded cataloging division.

In two official annual reports to Congress, Young prudently referred to the catalog as "in arrears" and "somewhat in abeyance." The indefatigable duo of Hanson and Martel confronted a collection of more than 800,000 books, hardly any of which had been cataloged by subject. Hanson later wrote that, when faced with this incredible undertaking, "there were no printed or written rules, no definitive verbal instructions . . . apparently, it would be the part of wisdom to cut loose from the old catalogue altogether, and the sooner the better. It was, therefore, decided to begin an entirely new catalogue, on standard-size cards, 7 x 12 cm."

STARTING FROM SCRATCH

The main catalogue of the Library is to be on cards. —LC Annual Report 1901

The stage was set for standardized catalog cards when Herbert Putnam succeeded Young as Librarian in April of 1899. Hanson and Martel had fastidiously laid the groundwork and created a new classification system inspired by Cutter and Dewey's schemes, and they integrated a new system of subject headings that would eventually become known as Library of Congress Subject Headings, or LCSH.

Putnam quickly understood the challenges Hanson and Martel had been struggling with. The old system, inherited from Thomas Jefferson and based on Bacon's sixteenth-century conception of the forty classes of knowledge, was not expansive enough to handle the variety of books that were brought over from the Capitol, let alone what was to arrive in the coming years. Consider the number of inventions and new branches of scholarship that had emerged since Jefferson sold his collection to Congress in 1815. There had been no electric light, photography, or basketball, among hundreds of other subjects, when Jefferson prepared his 1815 catalog. Putnam was direct in his assessment of the existing Library catalog: "It is meager, rigid, inelastic, and unsuited to a library of a million volumes. The entire library must be reclassified."

In his first year as Librarian, Putnam worked not only to get his own house in order by re-cataloging every book to make the Library's collection more accessible to the public, but he also responded to calls for help from outside the Library. University and public libraries strongly urged the Library of Congress to make copies of their catalog cards available nationwide. Balancing the need for a new card catalog for the Main Reading Room and the sale and distribution of those same cards was a vast and complex undertaking. Fortunately, the newly expanded cataloging division was already one step ahead of Putnam, working with the Government Printing Office (GPO) to have new catalog cards printed based on the latest classification scheme.

The following winter, with its own dedicated branch of GPO nestled in the basement of the Library and equipped with new linotype machines, the Library began to crank out new cards at a rate of 225 titles a day and nearly

The Government Printing Office facility in the Library of Congress basement where catalog cards were printed, 1901.

Advertisement for the Remington Standard Typewriter from the April 1901 issue of *Library Journal*.

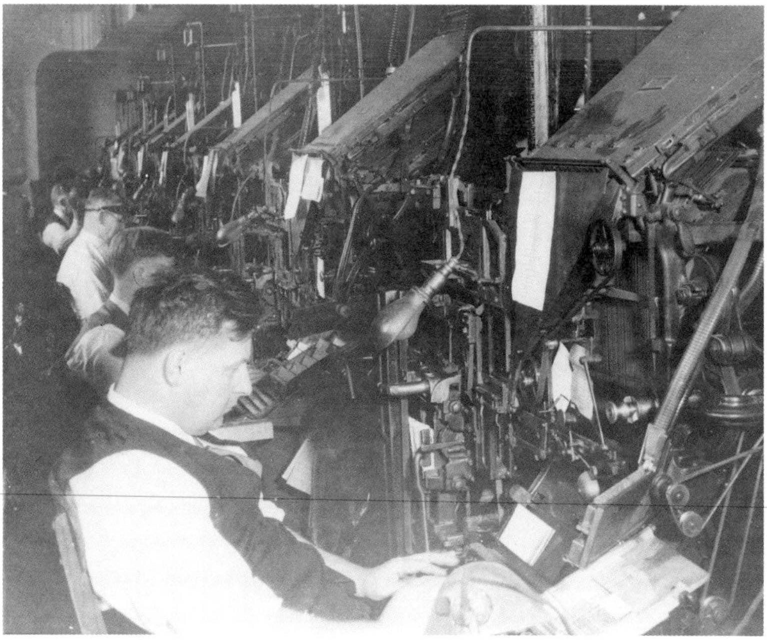

Men working at linotype machines in the Card Division Printing Office, between 1900 and 1920.

As catalogers moved away from preparing handwritten cards, clerks and their typewriters entered information on the cards. But once the Library began using linotype machines, the speed and efficiency in producing cards greatly increased. Linotype was widely used in printing newspapers, magazines, and broadsides.

70,000 a year. The titles were printed on sheets of the best linen ledger stock, forty cards to a sheet. They were then cut in the bindery to the 3-by-5-in (7.5-by-12-cm) index size and hole-punched at the bottom for the guard rods. Upstairs, the cataloging division was increased to more than seventy employees who worked long, hard hours doing the tedious work of classifying, proofing, revising, sorting, and filing the cards.

UNIVERSAL IN SCOPE, NATIONAL IN SERVICE

By the turn of the twentieth century, the boom in American publishing paralleled the growth and expansion of both public and university libraries. Staff at these institutions were becoming increasingly frustrated by the duplication of work occurring every day in their field: a book was published, libraries bought it, and then thousands of librarians nationwide each examined and cataloged the same book. Putnam spent the summer of 1901 crisscrossing the country getting a handle on the mood and needs of librarians. After conferring with the ALA and other library associations, he returned to Washington and informed President Theodore Roosevelt that the library community was looking to the Library of Congress for leadership in cataloging, noting, "American instinct and habit revolt against

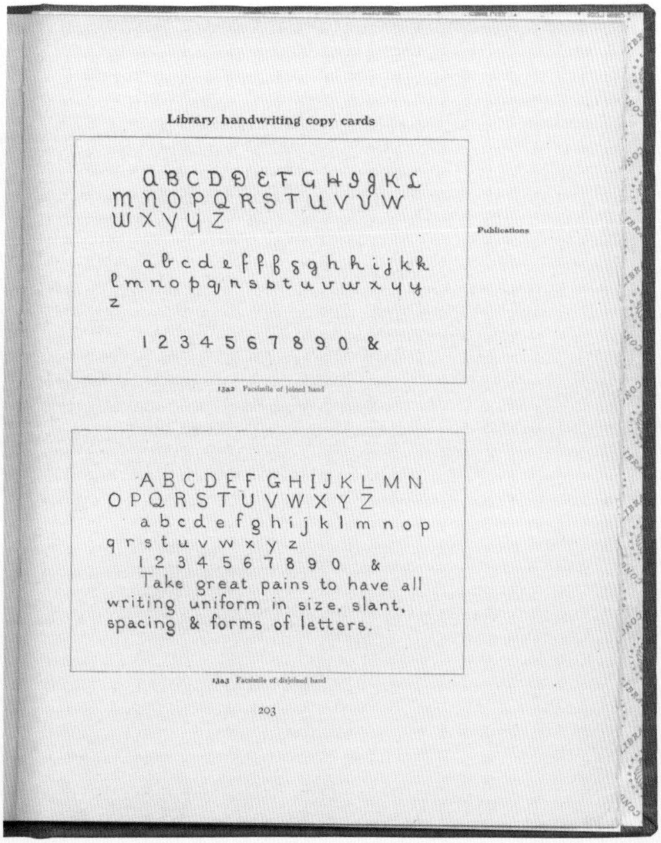

Library handwriting copy cards

ABCDEFGHIJKL
MNOPQRSTUVVW
WXYZ

abcdefffsghhijkk
lmnopqrsstuvwxyy
z

1 2 3 4 5 6 7 8 9 0 &

13a2 Facsimile of joined hand

ABCDEFGHIJKLMN
OPQRSTUVWXYZ
abcdefghijklmnop
qrstuvwxyz
1 2 3 4 5 6 7 8 9 0 &
Take great pains to have all
writing uniform in size, slant,
spacing & forms of letters.

13a3 Facsimile of disjoined hand

203

Publications

Supply Catalog from the Library Bureau, 1902.

Before the widespread use of typed or printed catalog cards, the respectable library relied on trained staff to produce cards written in "Library Hand," a script taught at library schools to ensure legibility and a standard appearance, which had been developed by Melvil Dewey and Thomas Edison. "In all that follows, beauty, speed and all other requirements have been considered as secondary to legibility," noted the *New York State Library School Handbook* in 1903. Some leeway was permitted as long as each library remained true to its chosen style "and all assistants [are] required to follow it." The script was characterized by rounded letters, usually in an upright form, and "if one cannot write exactly perpendicularly a slight backward slope is more legible than forward . . . Many library hands otherwise excellent are ruined by . . . having varying slants." Small letters were to be 2 mm high, capital letters twice that size, and there were specific rules for treating particular letters. Library hand courses also emphasized the proper equipment required for writing out cards and the posture one had to assume while doing so, such as allowing "the round muscle of the forearm [to] rest lightly on the desk away from the body to secure a free arm movement."

Workers in the Card Division, Library of Congress, 1900.

multiplication of brain effort and outlay where a multiplication of results can be achieved by machinery. [Cataloging] appears to be a case where it may."

On October 28, 1901, more than half a century after Jewett suggested the federal government centralize the printing and distribution of catalog cards, Putnam mailed a circular to more than four hundred libraries announcing the sale of its printed catalog cards. "The Library of Congress is now prepared to furnish a copy or copies of any of the catalogue cards which it is currently printing," he wrote. Libraries found the offer very appealing, given the Library of Congress's authoritative cataloging system. It was an enormous undertaking to classify and print just one card for each book for a collection that now numbered over one million volumes, let alone produce and dispense thousands of duplicate cards. To ensure that the Card Division was up to the job, Putnam put Charles Harris Hastings in charge of the new service. Hastings's dogged work ethic was essential to the program's success. "It is impossible to conceive of the Library's card distribution service surviving in its early years without his day-to-day supervision," said Paul Edlund, who was later chief of the Cataloging Distribution Service Division. "He was the card distribution service."

When the news broke that the Library would be selling their cards, Dewey and the library community were elated. In an address given at the 1901 ALA conference, Dewey told his audience, "You remember that when the Pacific railroad was built, and as the ends came together to make the connection, a great celebration was held through the country, a thrill that the work was at last done; and I feel today, now that we hear in this able report that printed catalog cards are really to be undertaken at the National Library, that what we have waited for [for] over twenty years, and what we have been dreaming about has come to pass at last."

The card service was an immediate success, providing either complete sets or individual cards to thousands of public libraries at cost plus 10 percent. Anyone who ever thumbed through the cards at a local public library probably referred to many that came from the Library of Congress. The operation grew exponentially over the years and at its peak in 1969, approximately seventy-nine million cards were printed and distributed annually. Coincidentally, this was the same year the Library introduced Machine-Readable Cataloging (MARC), which eventually would supplant the card catalog. The card service lasted nearly a century, with the last cards produced and distributed in 1997.

Although the Library of Congress is frequently—and erroneously—credited with the invention of the card catalog, it was ironically one of the last major libraries to embrace it. Nevertheless, its innovative classification system and mass distribution of catalog cards made it the standard-bearer, allowing smaller libraries in the farthest corners of the country to possess the same quality catalog as the greatest libraries in the world.

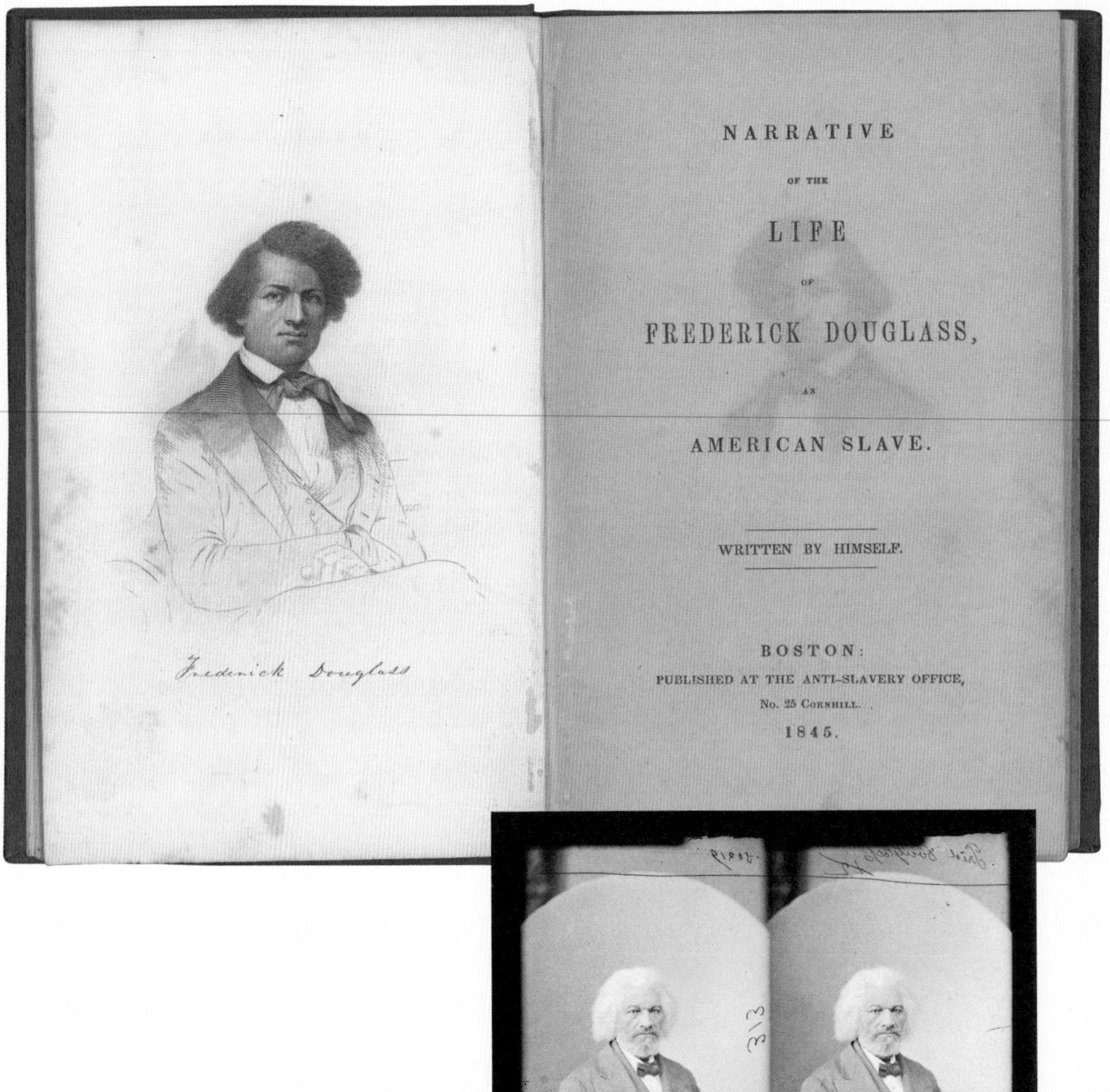
NARRATIVE
OF THE
LIFE
OF
FREDERICK DOUGLASS,
AN
AMERICAN SLAVE.
WRITTEN BY HIMSELF.
BOSTON:
PUBLISHED AT THE ANTI-SLAVERY OFFICE,
No. 25 CORNHILL.
1845.
Frederick Douglass

E449
.D751
E449
.D746

Douglass, Frederick, 1817?-1895.

Narrative of the life of Frederick Douglass, an American slave. Written by himself. Boston, Pub. at the Anti-slavery office, 1845.

xvi, 125 p. front. (port.) 17cm.

Preface signed: Wm. Lloyd Garrison.

excl. ~~stamp~~ 1. Slavery in the U. S.—Maryland. } stamp I. Garrison, William Lloyd, 1805-1879. [Name originally: Frederick Augustus Washington Bailey] 14-3386

Library of Congress E449.D737 Second Official

Frederick Douglass, *Narrative of the Life of Frederick Douglass, an American Slave*. Boston, Anti-slavery Office, 1845.

Frederick Douglass, glass negative, 1860-1880.

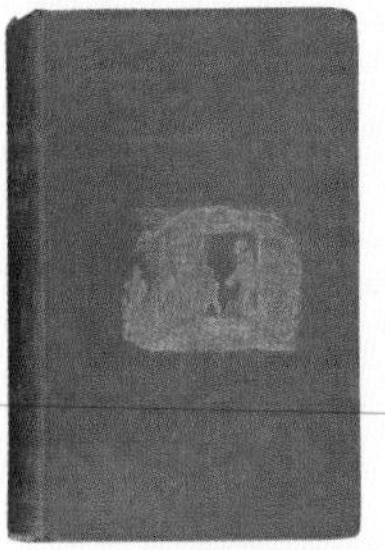

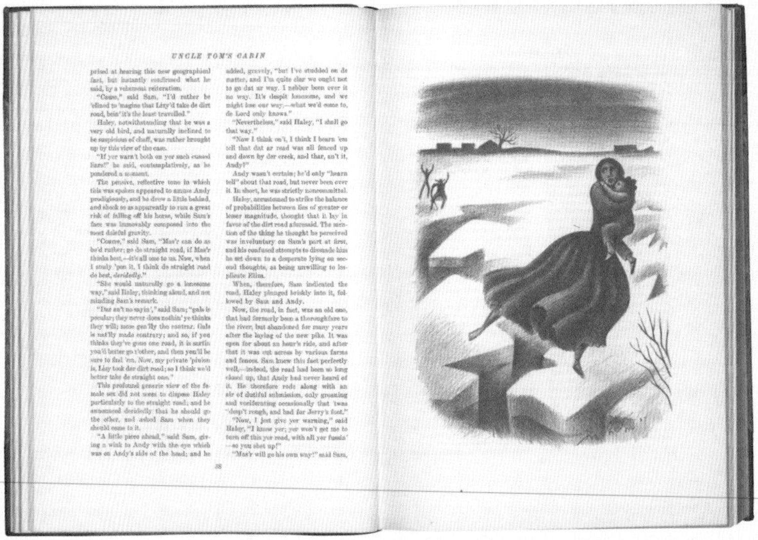

UNCLE TOM'S CABIN

prised at hearing this new geographical fact, but instantly confirmed what he said, by a vehement reiteration.

"Cause," said Sam, "I'd rather be 'clined to 'magine that Lizy'd take de dirt road, bein' it's the least travelled."

Haley, notwithstanding that he was a very old bird, and naturally inclined to be suspicious of chaff, was rather brought up by this view of the case.

"If yer warn't both on yer such cussed liars!" he said, contemplatively, as he pondered a moment.

The pensive, reflective tone in which this was spoken appeared to amuse Andy prodigiously, and he drew a little behind, and shook so as apparently to run a great risk of falling off his horse, while Sam's face was immovably composed into the most doleful gravity.

"Course," said Sam, "Mas'r can do as he'd ruther; go de straight road, if Mas'r thinks best,—it's all one to us. Now, when I study 'pon it, I think de straight road de best, *decidedly*."

"She would naturally go a lonesome way," said Haley, thinking aloud, and not minding Sam's remark.

"Dar an't no sayin'," said Sam; "gals is pecular; they never does nothin' ye thinks they will; mose gen'lly the contrar. Gals is nat'lly made contrary; and so, if you thinks they've gone one road, it is sartin you'd better go t'other, and then you'll be sure to find 'em. Now, my private 'pinion is, Lizy took der dirt road; so I think we'd better take de straight one."

This profound generic view of the female sex did not seem to dispose Haley particularly to the straight road; and he announced decidedly that he should go the other, and asked Sam when they should come to it.

"A little piece ahead," said Sam, giving a wink to Andy with the eye which was on Andy's side of the head; and he added, gravely, "but I've studded on de matter, and I'm quite clar we ought not to go dat ar way. I nebber been over it no way. It's despit lonesome, and we might lose our way,—what we'd come to, de Lord only knows."

"Nevertheless," said Haley, "I shall go that way."

"Now I think on't, I think I hearn 'em tell that dat ar road was all fenced up and down by der creek, and thar, an't it, Andy?"

Andy wasn't certain; he'd only "hearn tell" about that road, but never been over it. In short, he was strictly noncommittal.

Haley, accustomed to strike the balance of probabilities between lies of greater or lesser magnitude, thought that it lay in favor of the dirt road aforesaid. The mention of the thing he thought he perceived was involuntary on Sam's part at first, and his confused attempts to dissuade him he set down to a desperate lying on second thoughts, as being unwilling to implicate Eliza.

When, therefore, Sam indicated the road, Haley plunged briskly into it, followed by Sam and Andy.

Now, the road, in fact, was an old one, that had formerly been a thoroughfare to the river, but abandoned for many years after the laying of the new pike. It was open for about an hour's ride, and after that it was cut across by various farms and fences. Sam knew this fact perfectly well,—indeed, the road had been so long closed up, that Andy had never heard of it. He therefore rode along with an air of dutiful submission, only groaning and vociferating occasionally that 'twas "desp't rough, and bad for Jerry's foot."

"Now, I jest give yer warning," said Haley, "I know yer; yer won't get me to turn off this yer road, with all yer fussin' —so you shet up!"

"Mas'r will go his own way!" said Sam,

38

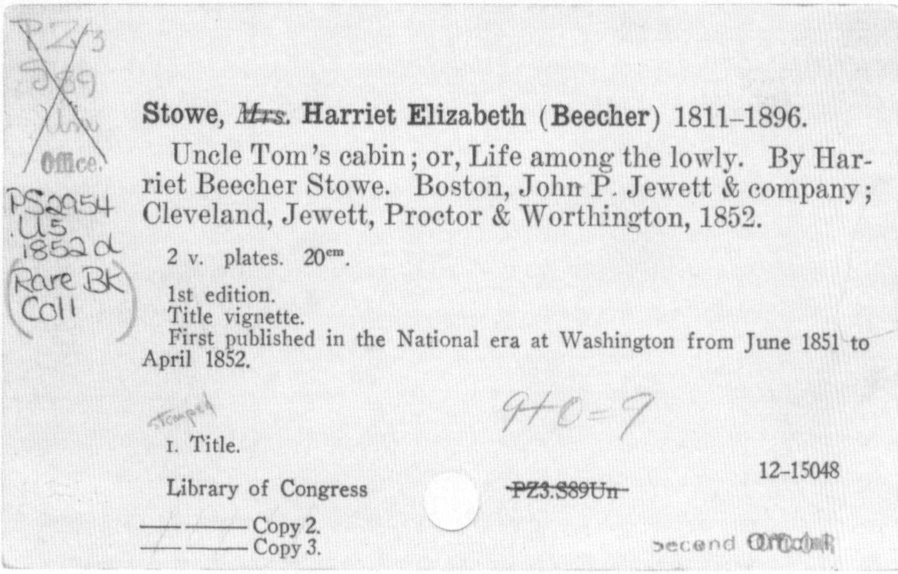
PS2954
.U5
1852d
Rare BK
Coll

Stowe, ~~Mrs.~~ Harriet Elizabeth (Beecher) 1811–1896.

Uncle Tom's cabin; or, Life among the lowly. By Harriet Beecher Stowe. Boston, John P. Jewett & company; Cleveland, Jewett, Proctor & Worthington, 1852.

2 v. plates. 20cm.

1st edition.
Title vignette.
First published in the National era at Washington from June 1851 to April 1852.

I. Title.

Library of Congress ~~PZ3.S89Un~~ 12–15048

——— Copy 2.
——— Copy 3.

second Office

Harriet Beecher Stowe, *Uncle Tom's Cabin; or, Life Among the Lowly*. Boston, John P. Jewett & Co., 1852.

Uncle Tom's Cabin, Cleveland, Ohio: W. J. Morgan & Co. lithographer, 1881.

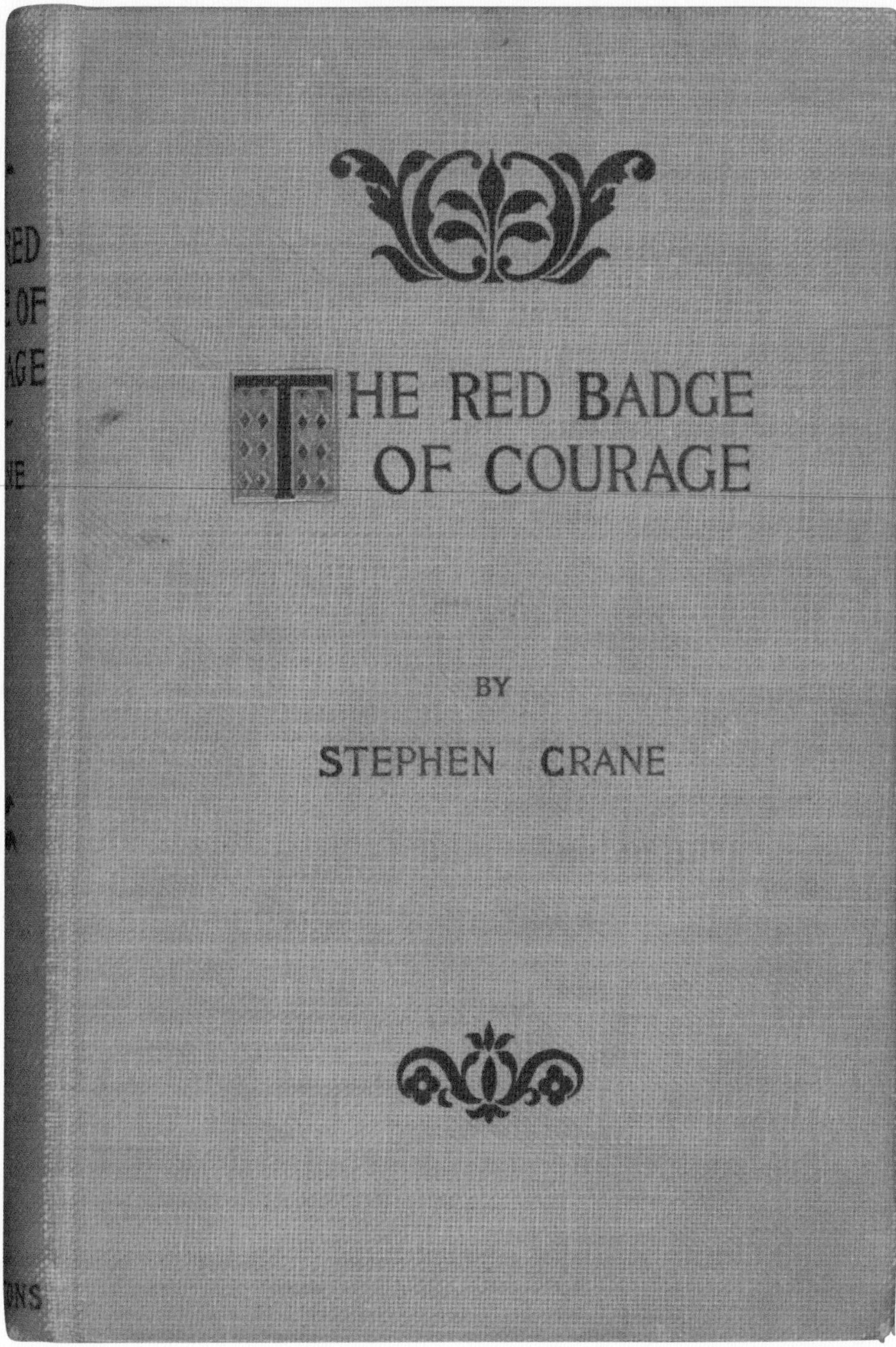
THE RED BADGE
OF COURAGE
BY
STEPHEN CRANE

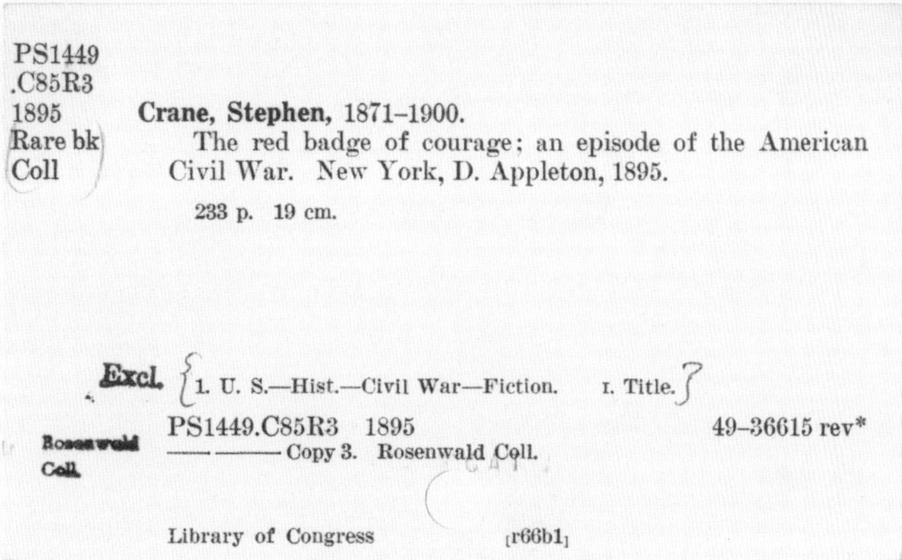

PS1449
.C85R3
1895 **Crane, Stephen,** 1871–1900.
Rare bk The red badge of courage; an episode of the American
Coll Civil War. New York, D. Appleton, 1895.

233 p. 19 cm.

Excl. {1. U. S.—Hist.—Civil War—Fiction. I. Title.}

Rosenwald Coll. PS1449.C85R3 1895 49–36615 rev*
——— ——— Copy 3. Rosenwald Coll.

Library of Congress [r66b1]

Stephen Crane, *The Red Badge of Courage*. New York, D. Appleton and Co., 1895.

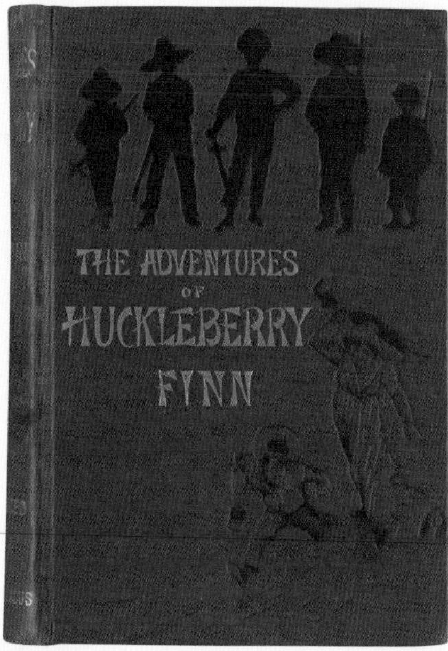
THE ADVENTURES
OF
HUCKLEBERRY
FINN

E.W. Kemble
1884
HUCKLEBERRY FINN.

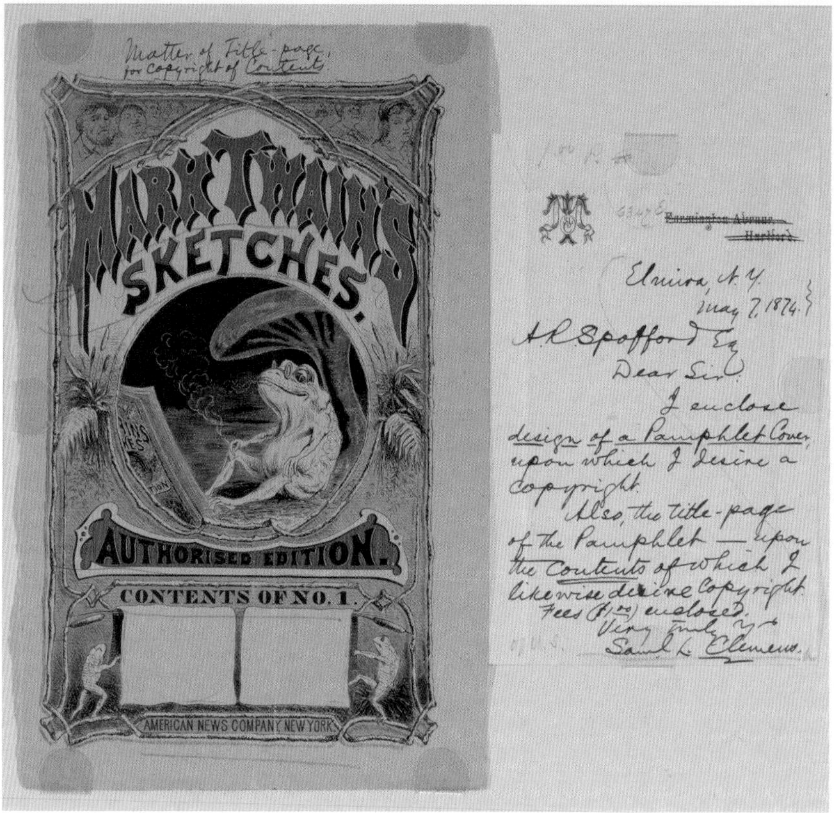
Matter of Title-page,
for Copyright of Content.
MARK TWAIN'S
SKETCHES.
AUTHORISED EDITION.
CONTENTS OF NO. 1.
AMERICAN NEWS COMPANY, NEW YORK.
Elmira, N.Y.
May 7, 1874.
A. R. Spofford Esq
Dear Sir:
I enclose
design of a Pamphlet Cover,
upon which I desire a
copyright.
Also, the title-page
of the Pamphlet — upon
the Contents of which I
likewise desire copyright.
Fees ($1.00) enclosed.
Very truly yrs
Saml L. Clemens.

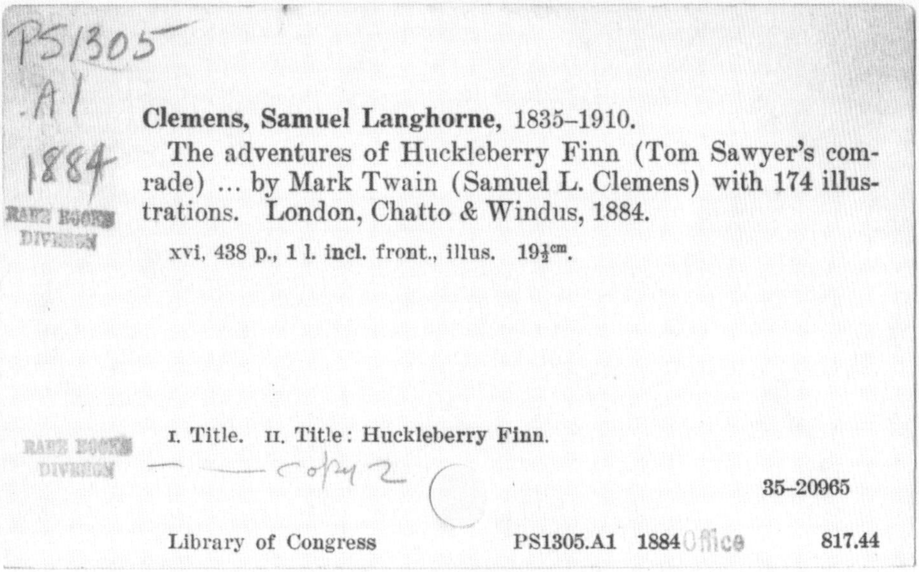

PS1305
.A1
1884

RARE BOOKS DIVISION

Clemens, Samuel Langhorne, 1835–1910.

The adventures of Huckleberry Finn (Tom Sawyer's comrade) ... by Mark Twain (Samuel L. Clemens) with 174 illustrations. London, Chatto & Windus, 1884.

xvi, 438 p., 1 l. incl. front., illus. 19½cm.

I. Title. II. Title: Huckleberry Finn.

RARE BOOKS DIVISION

— copy 2

35-20965

Library of Congress PS1305.A1 1884 Office 817.44

clockwise from top left

Mark Twain, *The Adventures of Huckleberry Finn*. London, Chatto & Windus, 1884.

Mark Twain, *The Adventures of Huckleberry Finn*. New York, Charles L. Webster & Co., 1885.

Letter from Samuel Clemens to Librarian of Congress Ainsworth Rand Spofford requesting a copyright for his pamphlet, May 7, 1874.

Pamphlet for which Samuel Clemens (Mark Twain) sought a copyright from the Library of Congress.

Mark Twain, *New York World-Telegram & Sun* Collection, 1907.

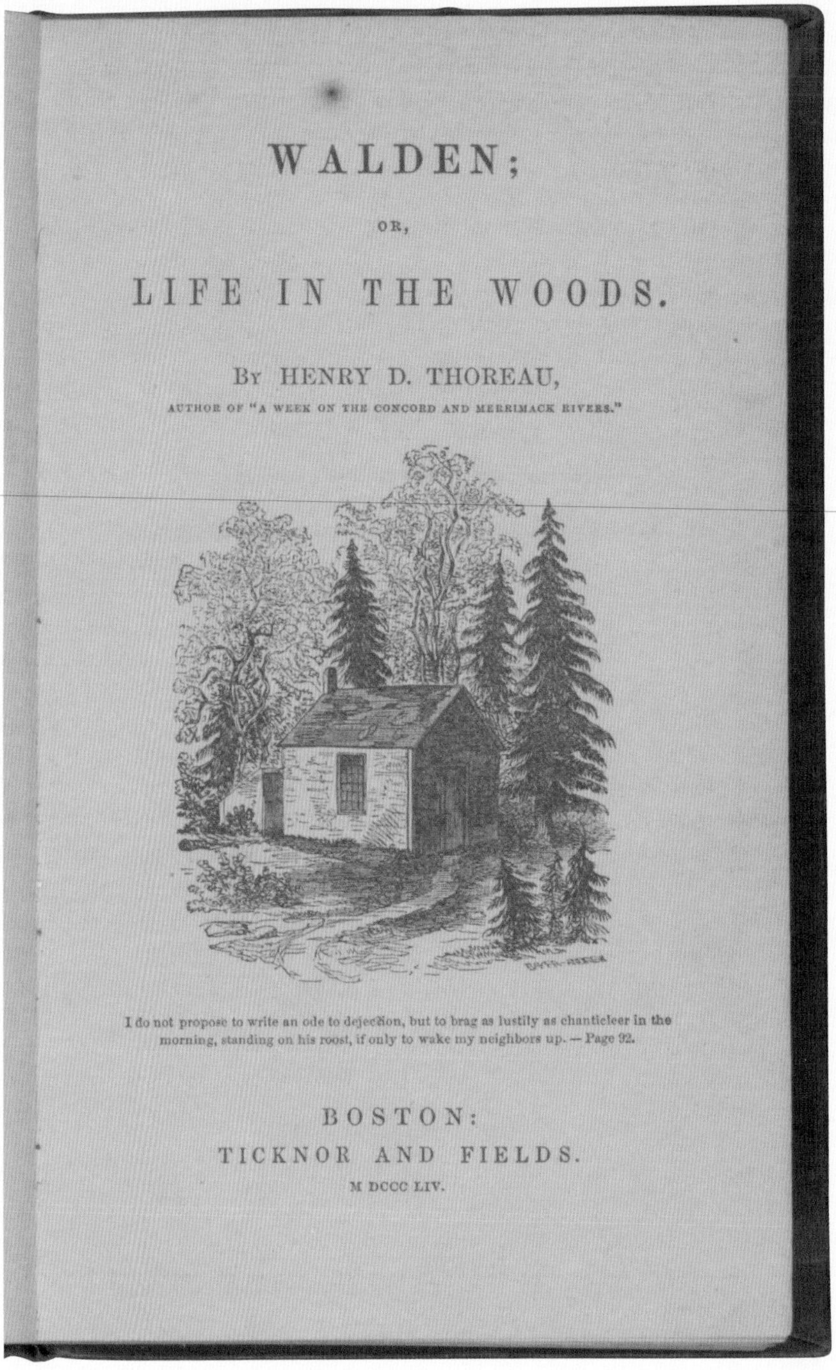

WALDEN;

OR,

LIFE IN THE WOODS.

BY HENRY D. THOREAU,

AUTHOR OF "A WEEK ON THE CONCORD AND MERRIMACK RIVERS."

I do not propose to write an ode to dejection, but to brag as lustily as chanticleer in the morning, standing on his roost, if only to wake my neighbors up. — Page 92.

BOSTON:

TICKNOR AND FIELDS.

M DCCC LIV.

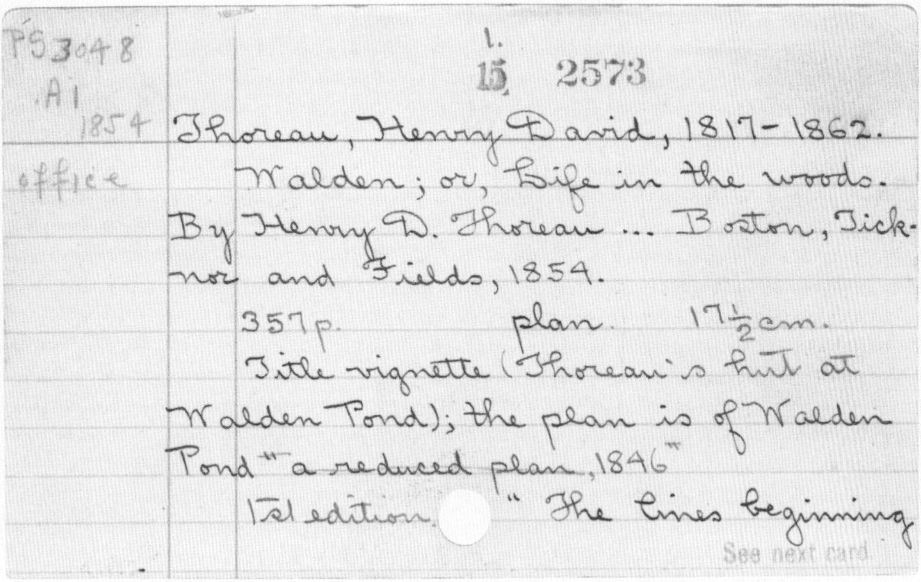

PS3048
.A1
1854
office

1.
15 2573

Thoreau, Henry David, 1817-1862.
Walden; or, Life in the woods. By Henry D. Thoreau ... Boston, Tick-nor and Fields, 1854.
357p. plan. 17 1/2 cm.
Title vignette (Thoreau's hut at Walden Pond); the plan is of Walden Pond "a reduced plan, 1846"
1st edition. "The lines beginning

See next card

Henry D. Thoreau, *Walden; or, Life in the Woods*. Boston, Ticknor and Fields, 1854.

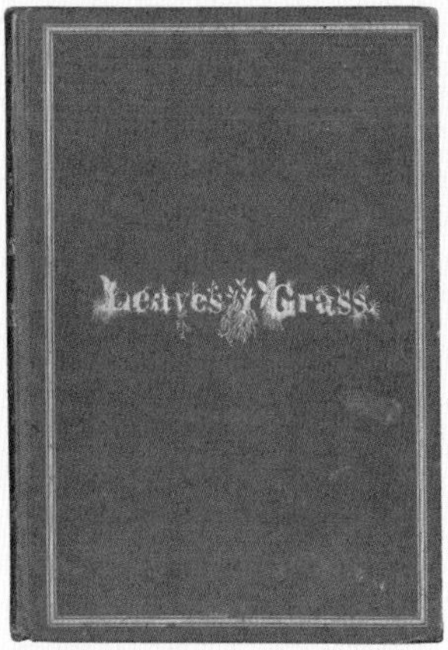

Leaves

of

Grass.

Brooklyn, New York:

1855.

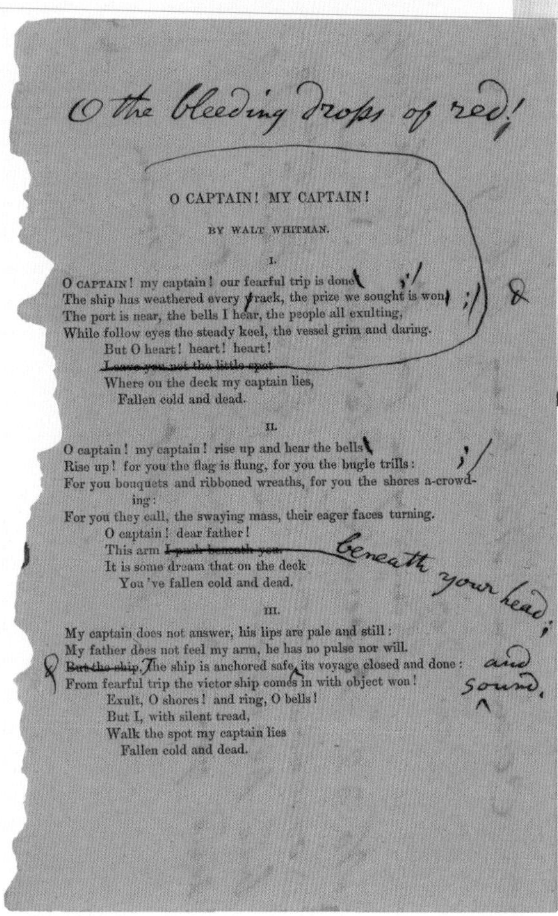

O the bleeding drops of red!

O CAPTAIN! MY CAPTAIN!

BY WALT WHITMAN.

I.

O CAPTAIN! my captain! our fearful trip is done ;/
The ship has weathered every wrack, the prize we sought is won ;/ &
The port is near, the bells I hear, the people all exulting,
While follow eyes the steady keel, the vessel grim and daring.
But O heart! heart! heart!
~~Leave you not the little spot~~
Where on the deck my captain lies,
Fallen cold and dead.

II.

O captain! my captain! rise up and hear the bells ;/
Rise up! for you the flag is flung, for you the bugle trills:
For you bouquets and ribboned wreaths, for you the shores a-crowding:
For you they call, the swaying mass, their eager faces turning.
O captain! dear father!
This arm ~~I push beneath you~~ beneath your head;
It is some dream that on the deck
You've fallen cold and dead.

III.

My captain does not answer, his lips are pale and still:
My father does not feel my arm, he has no pulse nor will.
& ~~But the ship,~~ The ship is anchored safe, its voyage closed and done: and sound.
From fearful trip the victor ship comes in with object won!
Exult, O shores! and ring, O bells!
But I, with silent tread,
Walk the spot my captain lies
Fallen cold and dead.

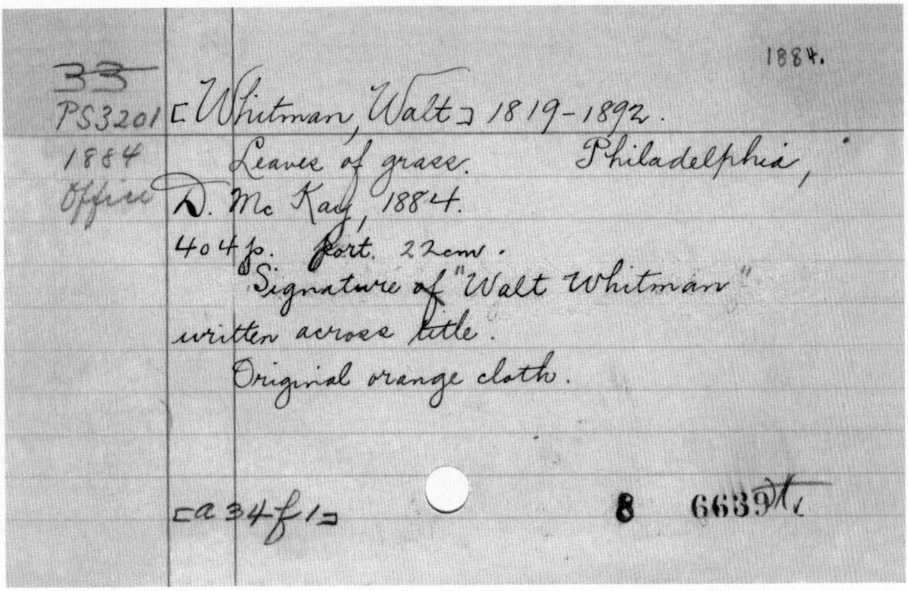

~~33~~

PS3201 [Whitman, Walt] 1819-1892. 1884.

1884 Leaves of grass. Philadelphia,

Office D. McKay, 1884.

404 p. port. 22cm.

Signature of "Walt Whitman" written across title.

Original orange cloth.

[a34f1] 8 6639

Walt Whitman, *Leaves of Grass*. Brooklyn, New York, 1855.

Walt Whitman, glass negative, circa 1860-1865.

"O Captain! My Captain!" Proof sheet with corrections in ink, 1888.

The Library of Congress houses the largest archival collection of Walt Whitman materials in the world. When Whitman noticed several errors in one edition of "O Captain! My Captain!" he mailed the page to the publishers with his corrections marked in ink.

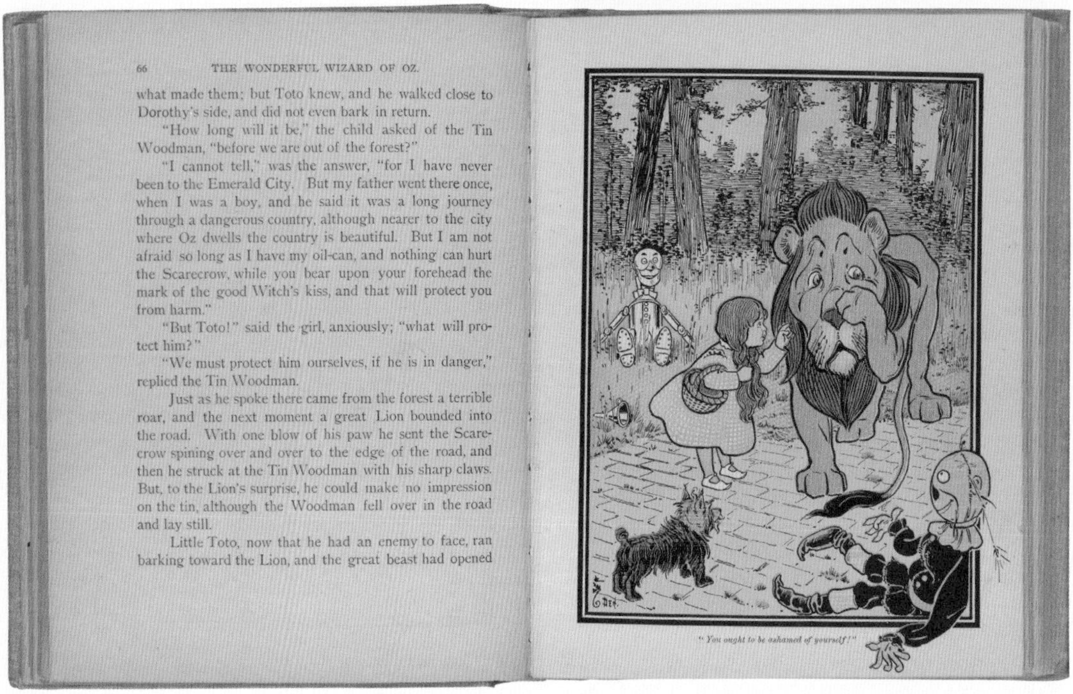
66 THE WONDERFUL WIZARD OF OZ.

what made them; but Toto knew, and he walked close to Dorothy's side, and did not even bark in return.

"How long will it be," the child asked of the Tin Woodman, "before we are out of the forest?"

"I cannot tell," was the answer, "for I have never been to the Emerald City. But my father went there once, when I was a boy, and he said it was a long journey through a dangerous country, although nearer to the city where Oz dwells the country is beautiful. But I am not afraid so long as I have my oil-can, and nothing can hurt the Scarecrow, while you bear upon your forehead the mark of the good Witch's kiss, and that will protect you from harm."

"But Toto!" said the girl, anxiously; "what will protect him?"

"We must protect him ourselves, if he is in danger," replied the Tin Woodman.

Just as he spoke there came from the forest a terrible roar, and the next moment a great Lion bounded into the road. With one blow of his paw he sent the Scarecrow spining over and over to the edge of the road, and then he struck at the Tin Woodman with his sharp claws. But, to the Lion's surprise, he could make no impression on the tin, although the Woodman fell over in the road and lay still.

Little Toto, now that he had an enemy to face, ran barking toward the Lion, and the great beast had opened

"You ought to be ashamed of yourself!"

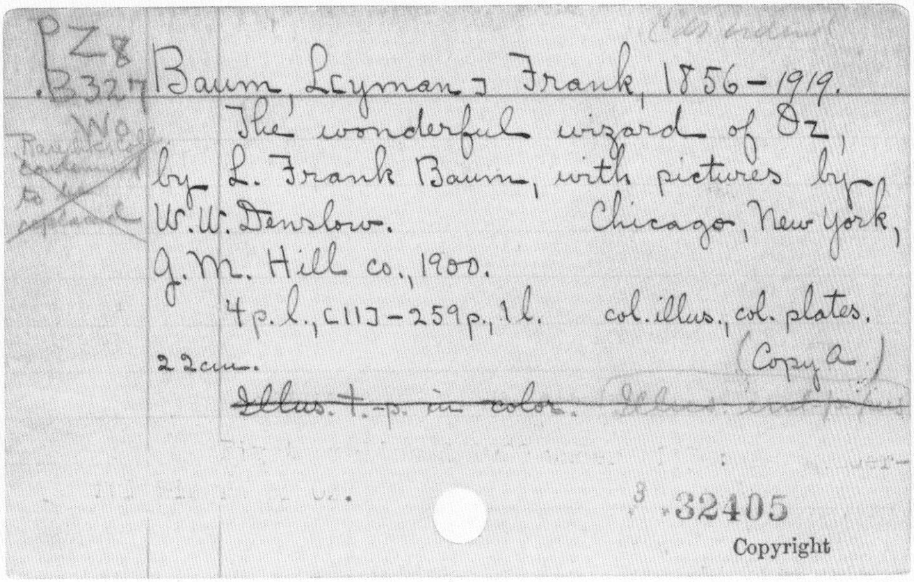
PZ8
.B327
Wo

Baum, L[yman] Frank, 1856-1919.
The wonderful wizard of Oz, by L. Frank Baum, with pictures by W. W. Denslow. Chicago, New York, G. M. Hill co., 1900.
4 p. l., [11]-259 p., 1 l. col. illus., col. plates. 22 cm. (Copy a.)
~~Illus. t.-p. in color.~~

32405
Copyright

L. Frank Baum, *The Wonderful Wizard of Oz*. Chicago & New York, Geo. M. Hill Co., circa 1899.

WILLIAM TELL
TOLD AGAIN
BY P G WODEHOUSE
ILLUSTRATED
BY
PHILIP DADD

PZ8
.1
.W82
Wi
1904
<Rare
Bk
Coll>
Juvenile
Coll.

Wodehouse, P. G. (Pelham Grenville), 1881-1975.
William Tell told again / by P.G. Wodehouse ; with illustrations in colour by Philip Dadd, described in verse by John W. Houghton. — London : Adam and Charles Black, 1904.

vii, 105 p., [1], xv leaves of plates : col. ill. ; 23 cm.

1. Tell, Wilhelm—Legends. I. Dadd, Philip. II. Title.

PZ8.1.W82 Wi 1904 84-255413
AACR 2 MARC

Library of Congress

P. G. Wodehouse, *William Tell Told Again*. London, Adam and Charles Black, 1904.

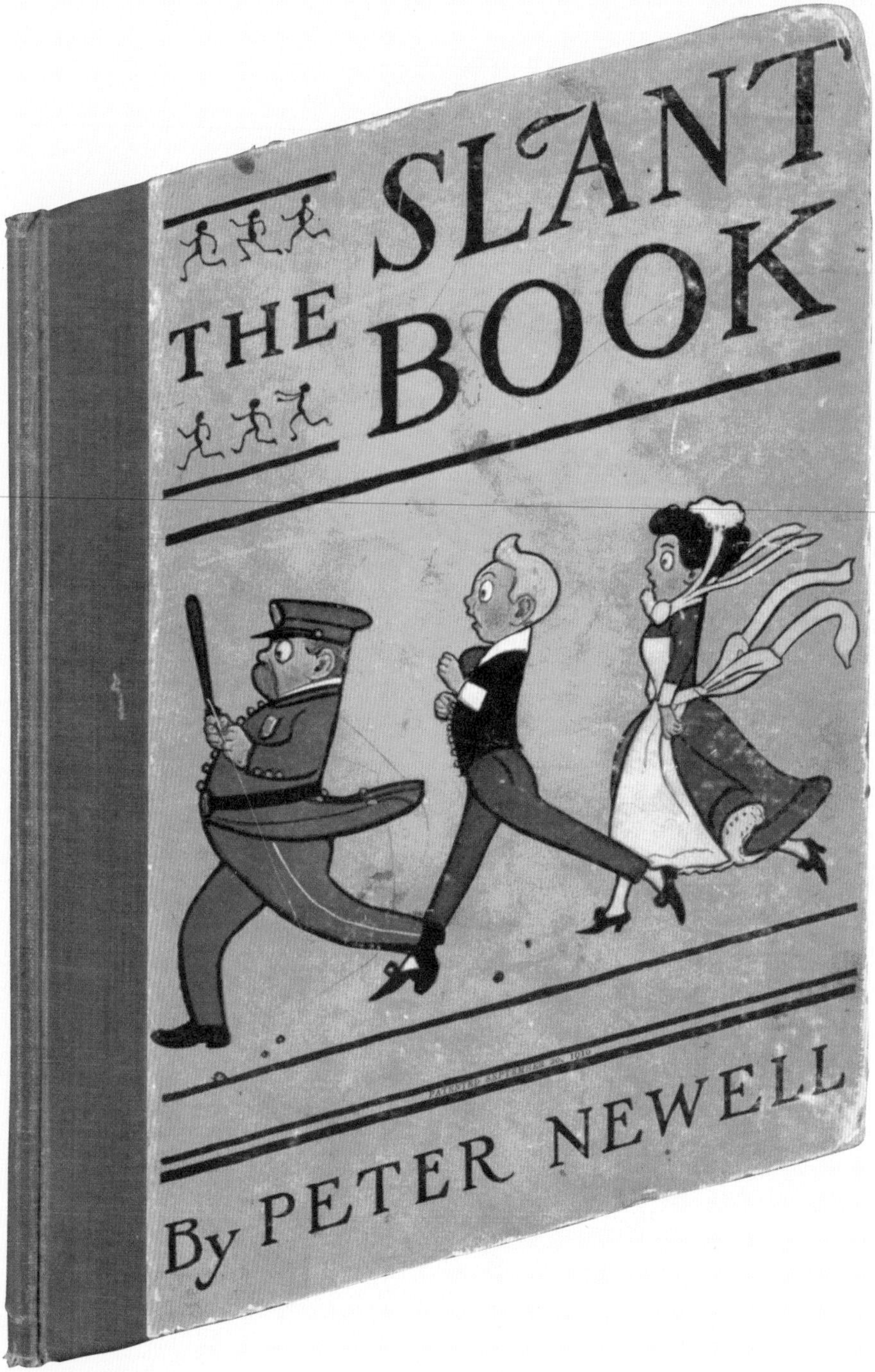
THE
SLANT
BOOK
By PETER NEWELL

Juvenile
Coll
1910 **Newell, Peter,** 1862–

The slant book, by Peter Newell ... New York, Harper & brothers [1910]

[47] p. col. illus. 22½ x 17½ᶜᵐ. $0.75

Illus. t.-p.

10–25818

Library of Congress

© Nov. 3, 1910; 2c. Nov. 4, 1910; A 275187; Harper & bros., N. Y., N. Y.

Peter Newell, *The Slant Book*. New York, Harper & Brothers, 1910.

THE CALL
of THE WILD
BY
JACK LONDON

JACK LONDON

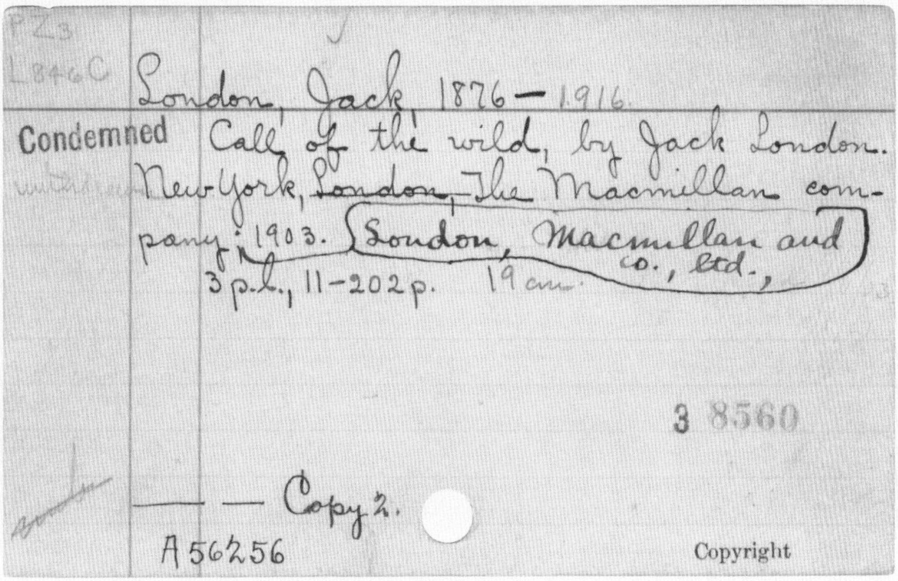

PZ3
L846C

London, Jack 1876— 1916.

Condemned

Call of the wild, by Jack London. New York, ~~London,~~ The Macmillan company, 1903. London, Macmillan and co., ltd.,
3 p.l., 11-202 p. 19 cm.

3 8560

— — Copy 2.

A56256

Copyright

Jack London, Bain News Service, year unknown.

Jack London, *The Call of the Wild*. New York, Macmillian Co., 1903.

THE EXPERT
AT THE
CARD TABLE
Over 100
Illustrations

HOUDINI
ÉDITÉ
PAR
PUBLIÉ
DANS
PATHÉ
L'ORDRE PUBLIC
LE MAÎTRE DU MYSTÈRE
GRAND ROMAN CINÉMA

© HOUDINI.
1914.
Dietz
N.Y.

BRIGHT-WITS
PRINCE
OF
MOGADORE

Ex Libris
Houdini
Class.
Book.
THE BEQUEST OF
HARRY HOUDINI

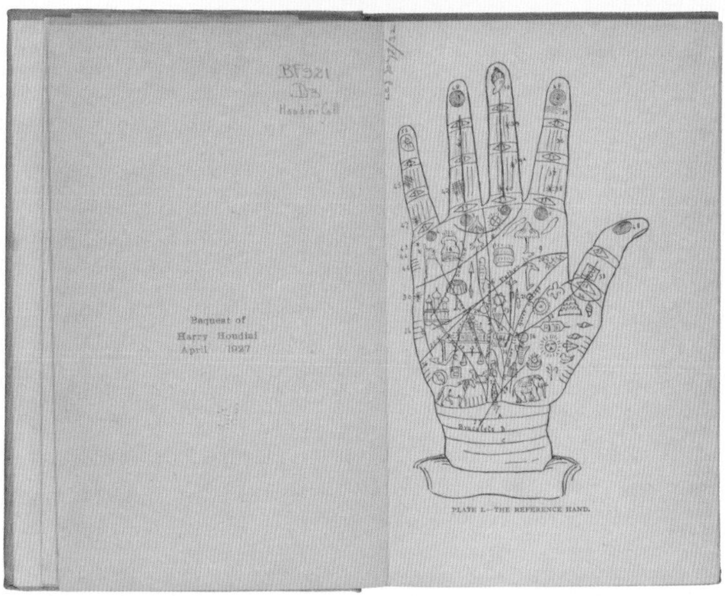
BF921
Bequest of
Harry Houdini
April 1927
PLATE I.—THE REFERENCE HAND.

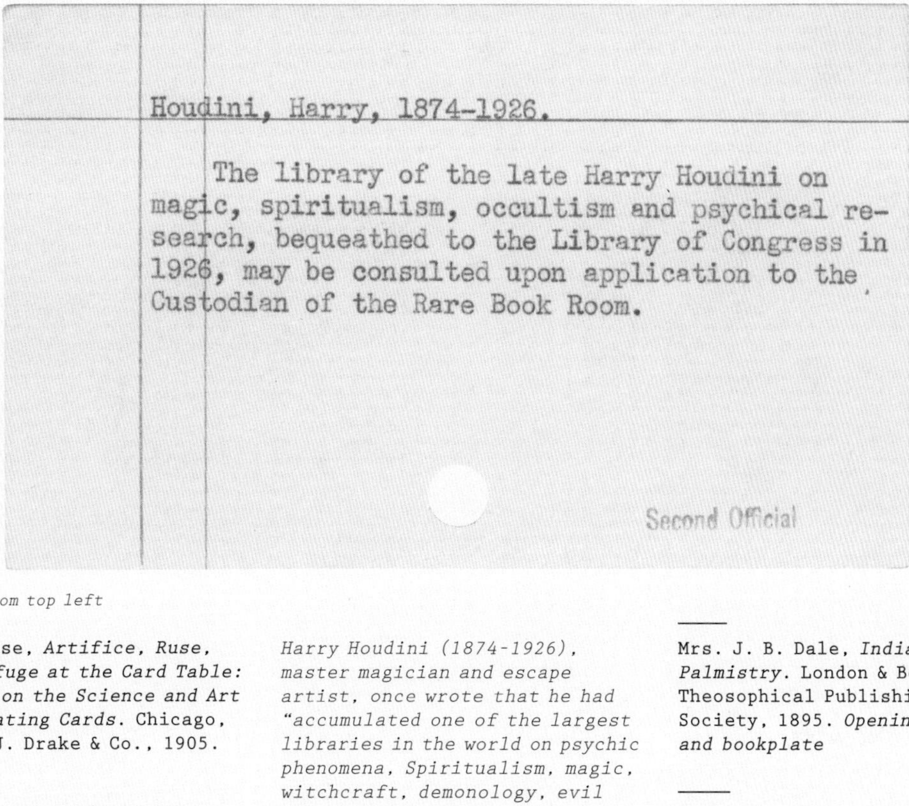

Houdini, Harry, 1874-1926.

The library of the late Harry Houdini on magic, spiritualism, occultism and psychical research, bequeathed to the Library of Congress in 1926, may be consulted upon application to the Custodian of the Rare Book Room.

Second Official

clockwise from top left

S. W. Erdnase, *Artifice, Ruse, and Subterfuge at the Card Table: A Treatise on the Science and Art of Manipulating Cards*. Chicago, Frederick J. Drake & Co., 1905.

Houdini—le maître du mystère, Paris, Daude Frères, 1910.

Harry Houdini stepping into a crate that will be lowered into New York Harbor as part of an escape stunt on July 7, 1912. Dietz, New York.

Harry Houdini (1874-1926), master magician and escape artist, once wrote that he had "accumulated one of the largest libraries in the world on psychic phenomena, Spiritualism, magic, witchcraft, demonology, evil spirits, etc., some of the material going back as far as 1489." In 1927, through Houdini's bequest, the Library of Congress received 3,988 volumes from his personal collection.

Mrs. J. B. Dale, *Indian Palmistry*. London & Benares, Theosophical Publishing Society, 1895. *Opening spread and bookplate*

Burren Loughlin, *Bright-Wits, Prince of Mogadore*. New York & Boston, H. M. Caldwell Co., 1909.

center

Stone walls and chains do not make a prison, photography by Lasky Corporation, 1898.

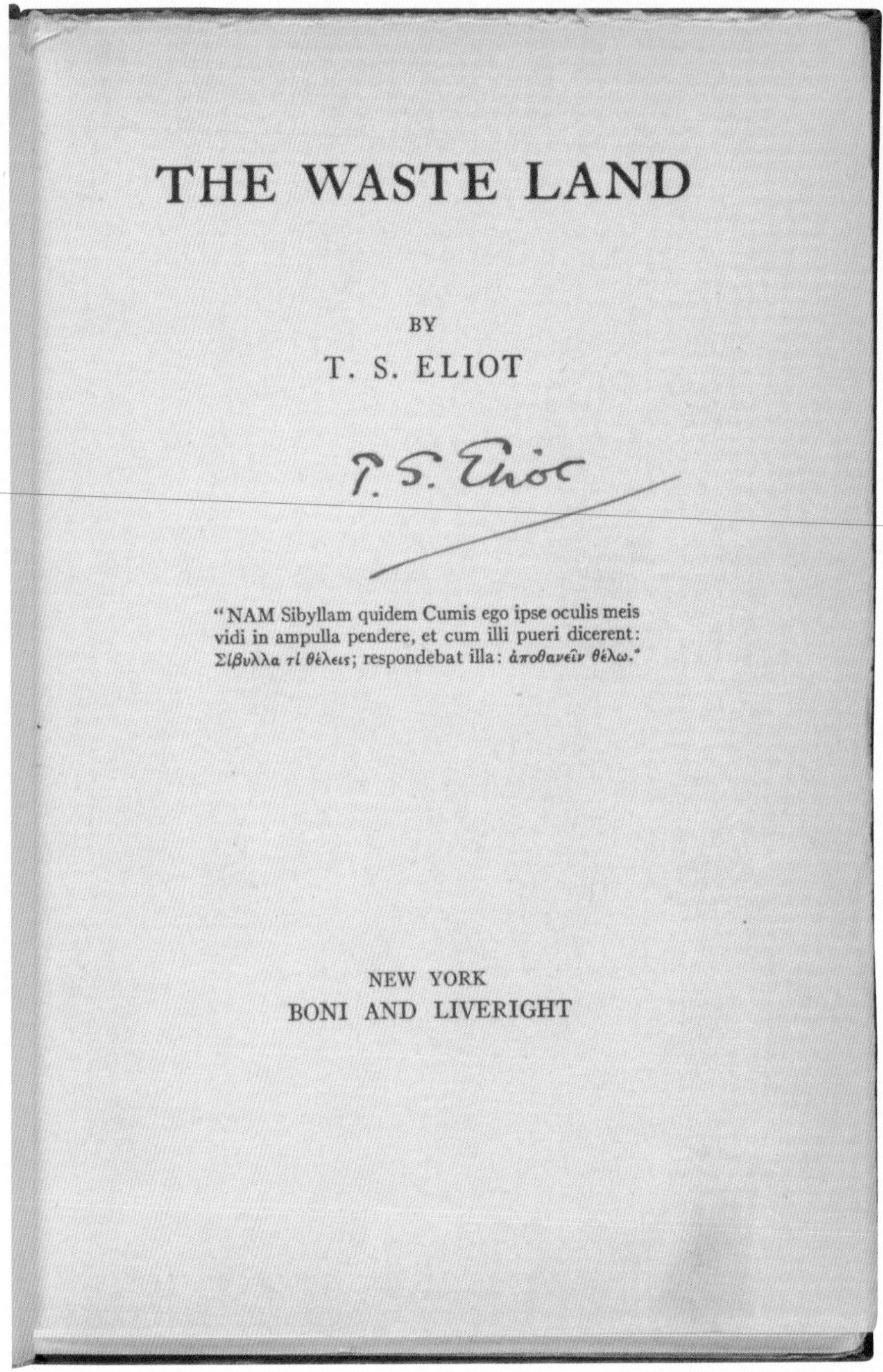

THE WASTE LAND

BY

T. S. ELIOT

T. S. Eliot

"NAM Sibyllam quidem Cumis ego ipse oculis meis vidi in ampulla pendere, et cum illi pueri dicerent: Σίβυλλα τί θέλεις; respondebat illa: ἀποθανεῖν θέλω."

NEW YORK
BONI AND LIVERIGHT

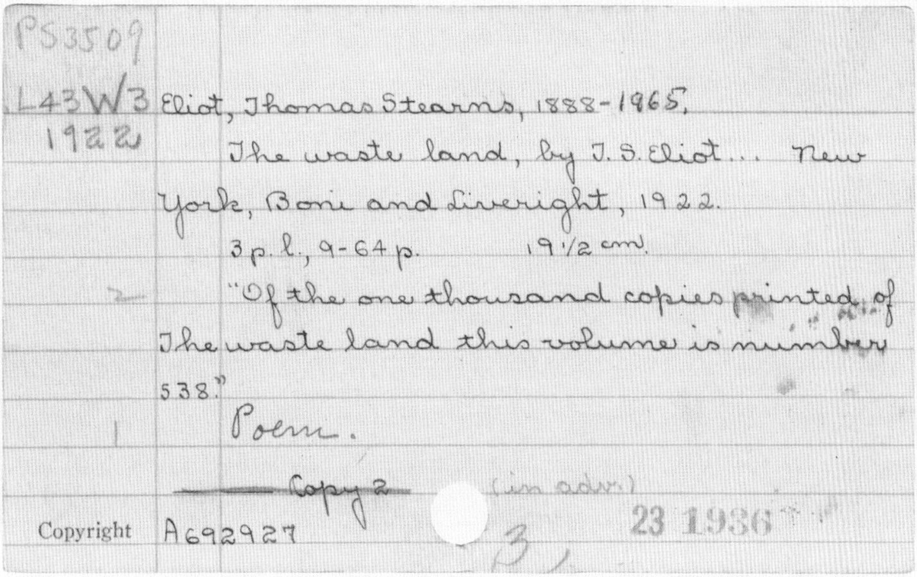

PS3509
L43W3 Eliot, Thomas Stearns, 1888-1965.
1922 The waste land, by T. S. Eliot ... New York, Boni and Liveright, 1922.
3 p. l., 9-64 p. 19 1/2 cm.
"Of the one thousand copies printed of The waste land this volume is number 538."
Poem.
Copy 2 (in adv.)
Copyright A692927 23 1936
3

T. S. Eliot, *The Waste Land*. New York, Boni and Liveright, 1922.

Eliot signed the Library of Congress copy of the first edition of The Waste Land, *widely considered to be one of the most influential poetic works of the twentieth century.*

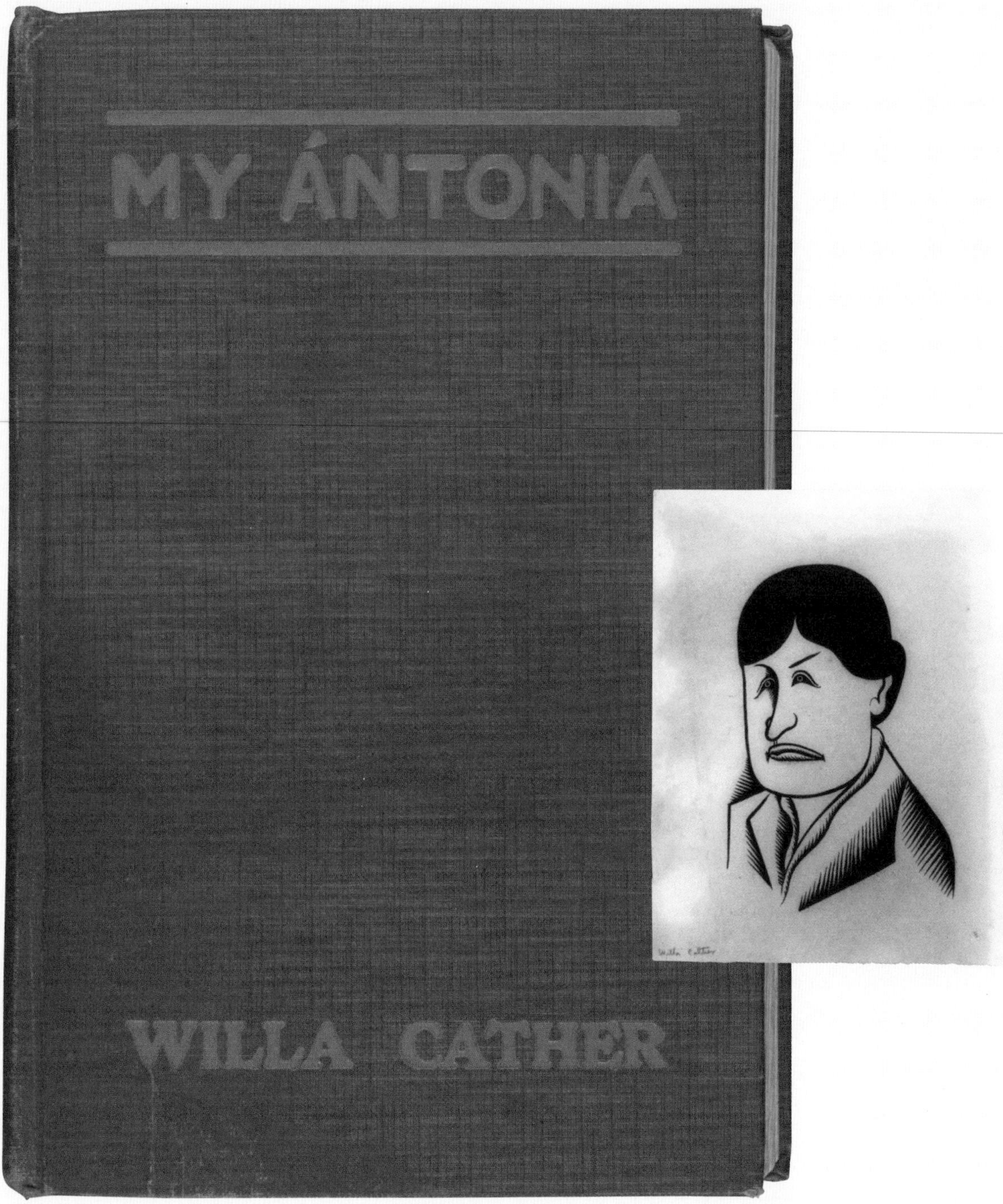
MY ÁNTONIA
WILLA CATHER

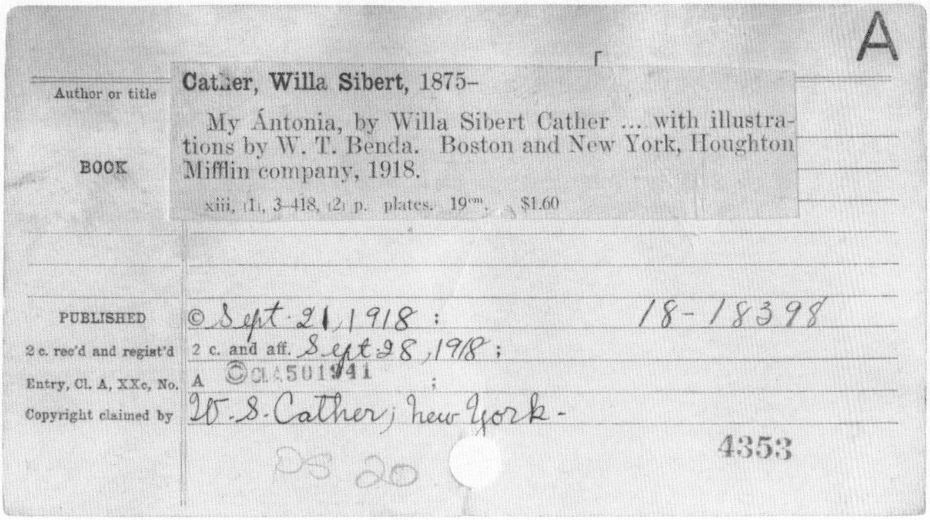

A

Author or title — Cather, Willa Sibert, 1875–

My Ántonia, by Willa Sibert Cather ... with illustrations by W. T. Benda. Boston and New York, Houghton Mifflin company, 1918.

xiii, [1], 3–418, [2] p. plates. 19cm. $1.60

BOOK

PUBLISHED © Sept. 21, 1918 : 18-18398

2 c. rec'd and regist'd 2 c. and aff. Sept 28, 1918 ;

Entry, Cl. A, XXc, No. A ©Cl.A501941 ;

Copyright claimed by W. S. Cather; New York-

4353

DS 20

Willa Cather, *My Ántonia*.
Boston, New York, Houghton
Mifflin Co., 1918.

Drawing by Miguel Covarrubias,
1925.

ULYSSES
BY
JAMES JOYCE

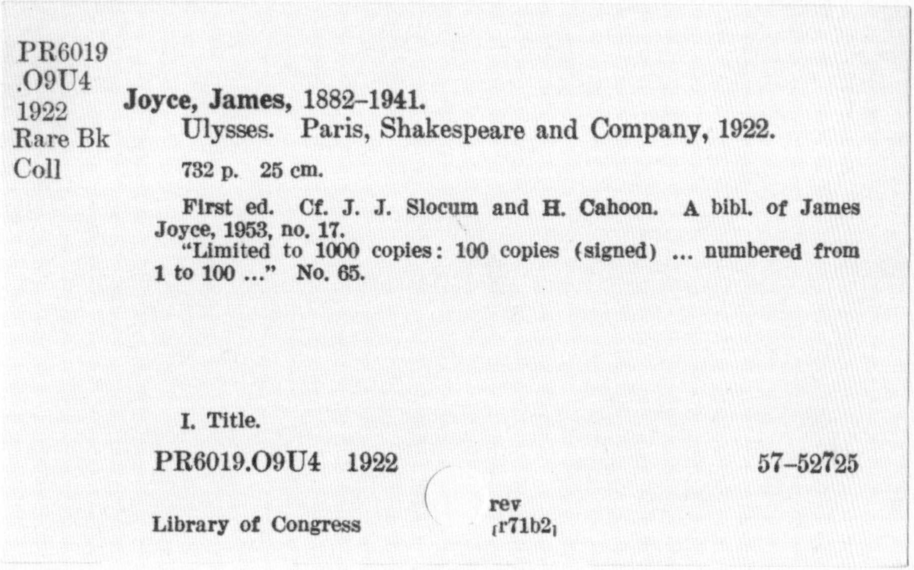

PR6019
.O9U4
1922
Rare Bk
Coll

Joyce, James, 1882–1941.
Ulysses. Paris, Shakespeare and Company, 1922.

732 p. 25 cm.

First ed. Cf. J. J. Slocum and H. Cahoon. A bibl. of James Joyce, 1953, no. 17.
"Limited to 1000 copies: 100 copies (signed) ... numbered from 1 to 100 ..." No. 65.

I. Title.

PR6019.O9U4 1922 57–52725

Library of Congress rev
[r71b2]

James Joyce, *Ulysses*. Paris, Shakespeare and Company, 1922.

This rare first edition was limited to 1,000 copies. The first hundred were signed and printed on handmade Dutch paper. The Library has number sixty-five.

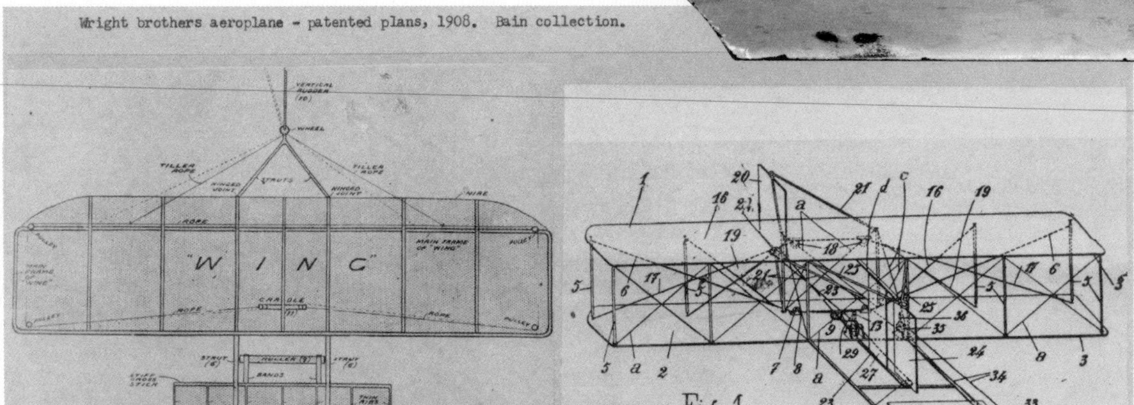

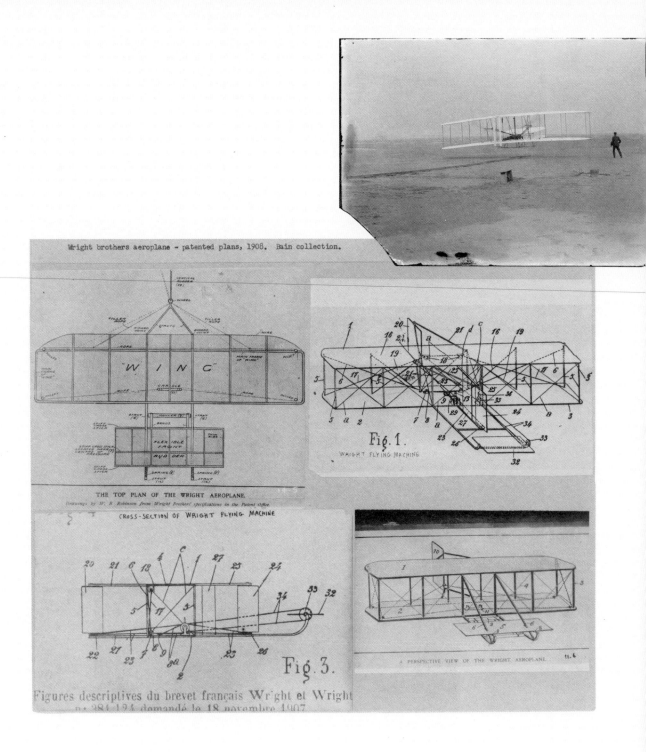

Wright brothers aeroplane - patented plans, 1908. Bain collection.

THE TOP PLAN OF THE WRIGHT AEROPLANE.

Drawings by W. B. Robinson from Wright Brothers' specifications in the Patent Office.

WRIGHT FLYING MACHINE

CROSS-SECTION OF WRIGHT FLYING MACHINE

Figures descriptives du brevet français Wright et Wright n° 384 124 demandé le 18 novembre 1907

A PERSPECTIVE VIEW OF THE WRIGHT AEROPLANE.

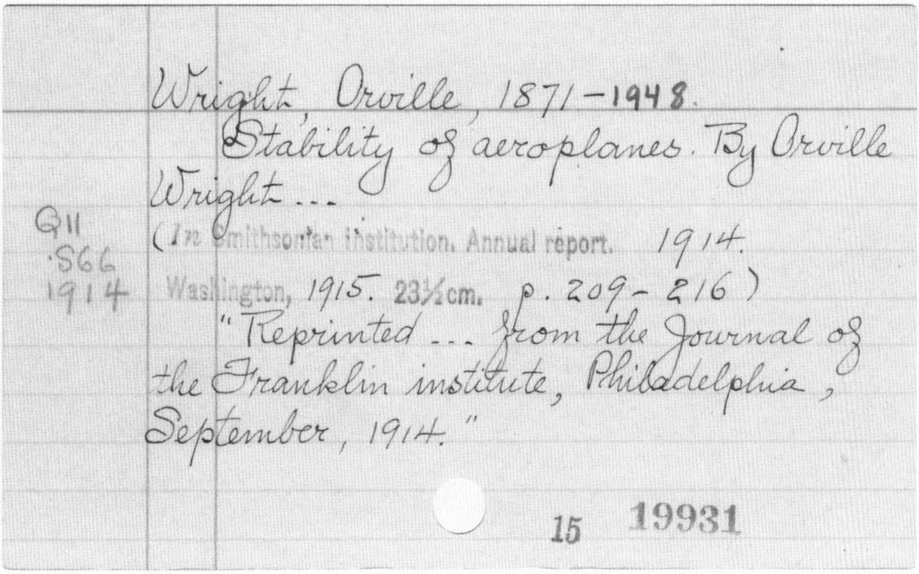

Q11
.S66
1914

Wright, Orville, 1871-1948.
Stability of aeroplanes. By Orville Wright ...
(*In* Smithsonian institution. Annual report. 1914. Washington, 1915. 23½cm. p. 209-216)
"Reprinted ... from the Journal of the Franklin institute, Philadelphia, September, 1914."

15 19931

First flight, 120 feet in 12 seconds, 10:35 a.m.; Kitty Hawk, North Carolina.

Wright brothers aeroplane, patented plans, 1908.

Wilbur and Orville Wright's papers at the Library of Congress include more than 10,000 items documenting the brothers' lives and their invention of the airplane. The collection includes diaries and notebooks, correspondence, scrapbooks, and drawings, largely from 1900 to 1940, as well as the Wrights' collection of 303 glass-plate photographic negatives.

FIRE EXTINGUISHER

Chapter 5

The Rise and Fall of the Card Catalog

Analog to Automation

AN EGALITARIAN EFFORT

The new Cataloging Distribution Service, along with the establishment of the interlibrary loan system, amounted to a major shift for the Library of Congress, solidifying its broader role in the library community. As the Library entered the twentieth century, it was no longer a cloistered legal library for Congress, or simply a vast, static warehouse of books acquired through copyright deposit. The interlibrary loan program, which allowed books to circulate outside of the Library, made some congressmen nervous, but Putnam defended this initiative. He pointed out that "a book used, is after all, fulfilling a higher mission than a book which is merely being preserved for possible future use." He boasted that the Library had now lent books, "as far east as Maine, as far west as California, and as far south as Texas."

But it was the Library's card catalog, and its distribution, that marked Putnam's crowning achievement. The cataloging service experienced modest growth in the early years, and was self-supporting by 1905 as revenues grew more than 100 percent from the previous year. With hundreds of new subscribers, many of which were smaller public libraries, the sale of cards became an important component in maintaining the service. Even as Charles Hastings and his eleven employees were swamped with orders, he

Library of Congress Card Division, 1919.

John Dana, a librarian in Newark, New Jersey, informed Putnam that "one of the greatest benefits of your printed cards has come and will continue to come from the fact that the general use of them brings together all the libraries that take from them."

previous spread

Library of Congress Data Processing Office, 1964.

echoed the Librarian in noting that "the value of the card distribution work to American libraries cannot be measured in dollars and cents. The general level of library catalogues is being raised throughout the country."

At its conference in 1906, the ALA had thrown its weight behind the Cataloging Distribution Service, urging members to "buy all catalog cards, if possible, from the Library of Congress." Later that year, the *Library Journal* stated that the service was "proving of very great value to libraries throughout the country, and that the usefulness of the cards is bound to increase and become more diversified as time goes on." However, *Library Journal* also expressed a prescient concern for the future: "Architects have not as yet given much attention to the demands of the catalog, in planning library buildings; but it is apparent that these demands are considerable, and that the growing use of cards means a steadily increasing requirement of storage space."

The premonition was ominously similar to Spofford's warning to Congress more than twenty years earlier, when he worried that the old Library in the Capitol was rapidly running out of space for its collection. Could the sheer number of catalog cards lead to a similar dilemma? The new Library was built with the bigger collection of books in mind, but the on-site card catalog and the distribution program were now growing

Location of Union Catalog in 1927
on sorting deck (deck 27) of the
stack of the Library of Congress.

Union catalogers at work, 1927.

The Union Catalog is perhaps the most comprehensive and unique of the various catalogs used at the Library of Congress. The idea for a shared catalog of publications held in American libraries took shape in 1901 when the Library agreed to exchange cards with the Boston Public Library, Harvard College Library, and the New York Public Library. The intention was to have a complete record of books in American libraries to assist researchers in finding the materials they needed.

by leaps and bounds too. In the early 1900s, the Library added numerous steel storage cases for the cards that were sold to other libraries. Stacked three stories high, this addition forced the cataloging staff to carry the boxes of new cards up to the narrow catwalks amid intolerable temperatures, as the staggering inventory of index cards towered above them. By 1916, the Library could no longer mince words, admitting in its annual report that "the expansion of the card catalogue is a subject of concern requiring immediate attention."

DROWNING IN CARDS

Improvements in printing technology led to enormous growth in the publishing industry, helping to both fuel an increase in literacy and feed the rising number of public libraries, which demanded ever more catalog cards. By the 1920s, the Library's card distribution division was overwhelmed: the rooms where the cards were sorted, packaged, and stored recalled the dwellings of the infamous New York hoarders Homer and Langley Collyer. In the Annual Report for 1925, Superintendent of the Reading Room Frederick William Ashley worried about "the space-consuming growth of the public card catalogue." Ashley suggested, ironically, to those who championed cards over book catalogs, that the solution might lie in "printing in book form large portions of the card and removing from the public catalogue the corresponding card entries." Most university and major public libraries were also facing a severe shortage of space as card catalogs devoured more square footage.

Fremont Rider, a scholar and inventor who studied under Dewey, estimated that some larger university libraries were doubling in size every sixteen years, a forecast that painted quite a grim picture of the future. In 1938, Rider penned an article for *Library Journal* titled "The Possibility of Discarding the Card Catalog," observing that "it is exactly when an organism seems to have reached perfection that the seeds of its decay begin to germinate." Conceding that the card catalog was well established and had no competition, Rider went on to list several drawbacks, including "continuous cost of filing, the physical bulk, and the awkwardness in use."

The sheer size of the catalog was the most obvious problem. However, internal reports at the Library in the 1950s also pointed to issues with misfiled or missing cards and worn or illegible cards. Clerical mistakes could essentially negate the existence of a book in the collection, as a misfiled or

erroneous heading on a card would make the title impossible to find. From the viewpoint of twenty-first-century "paperless offices," where massive databases can be manipulated with a click of a single button, it is hard to fathom just how rigorous and complex the job of managing, sorting, and filing millions of cards was. Adroit catalogers at the Library tackled both the dramatic growth and the intractable filing problems, but the proposed costly solutions failed to garner much administrative support. It seemed as if the plan was to tread water until a new comprehensive solution presented itself.

Library of Congress Card Division, circa 1940.

The tedious and demanding work of sorting and filing thousands of new catalog cards could be overwhelming. The clerks charged with filing cards were given weekly quotas, and rumor has it that those who failed to complete the task occasionally dumped their cards down the elevator shafts.

J. Edgar Hoover, December 22, 1924.

"I'm going to show her my old card catalog system at the Library of Congress," the future director of the Federal Bureau of Investigation (played by Leonardo DiCaprio) tells a fellow agent in the film *J. Edgar* (2011), explaining how he will impress his date that evening. J. Edgar Hoover did not invent the card catalog, but he was certainly inspired by it. Beginning in 1913, Hoover, then a college student, spent four years as a messenger and clerk in the Library's Order Division, where he had the opportunity to occasionally work in the Cataloging Division located next door. He would later write that his job "gave me an excellent foundation for my work in the FBI where it has been necessary to collate information and evidence." In 1921, when Hoover reorganized the Bureau's filing system, he implemented the Library's concept of cross-references within the card catalog. The card index system that made it possible to find a particular book among millions of titles also made it possible for Hoover to find people, organizations, and cases amid mountains of crime files—and to hide information in plain sight by creating cards with misleading key terms. Within three years, he and his staff produced more than 450,000 cards.

THE MARCH TO MARC

Just as the card catalog was emerging as the definitive system for libraries in the late nineteenth century, a curious editorial ran in the December 1893 issue of *Library Journal*: "The question recurs, of course, whether the card catalog is, after all, the final form of the library catalog, and whether, having reached the millennium of the card catalog, we shall not have to begin over again on an improved system. The critic of the card catalog might say that the printed card is only a new stone for the pavement of a very much over-paved region." Given that cataloging standards were finally in place and the card catalog was fast becoming a fixture in most university and public libraries, the question of whether it was just another momentary step toward a better method must have seemed absurd. However, as history had already demonstrated, the lead-up to the card catalog saw many competing visions and a wide array of cataloging approaches, most of which did not endure.

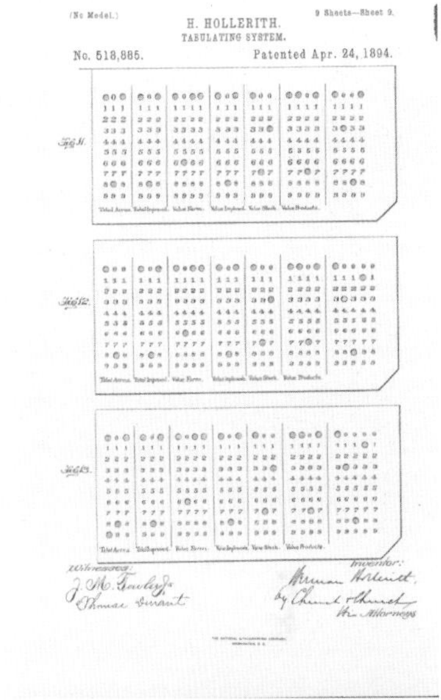

As it turned out, less than a century after the widespread advance of the card catalog, an alternate technology, also based on index cards, ultimately did replace it. In the 1880s, while Dewey and others were debating the size of the cards, another American inventor was using cards in a different way—for both storing and *processing* information. Herman Hollerith is generally considered the father of modern automatic computation and is credited with building the first punched card tabulating machine, the precursor to the modern personal computer.

Patent drawing for the first computer punch card. Herman Hollerith Paper, 1894.

Woman using a Hollerith pantographic card-punching machine, circa 1915.

Hollerith's cards were 3 by 7 in (7.5 by 18 cm) instead of 3 by 5 in (7.5 by 12 cm) and did not use words or numbers; rather, the cards were encrypted with data using a series of discretely punched holes arranged in different patterns. Harnessing the recent availability of electricity, the punched cards were placed into a tabulating machine that automatically read and sorted the cards. This technology was utilized for the 1890 U.S. Census, which allowed the federal government to report results within weeks instead of years. Hollerith was well on his way to forming his own concern, the Tabulating Machine Company, which eventually consolidated with others to form the Computing-Tabulating-Recording Company. In 1924, the name was formally changed to International Business Machines Corporation, better known as IBM.

There were a few scattered instances of libraries around the country using punched cards for cataloging, but by 1940 the Library of Congress had determined that the necessary equipment to operate a massive punched-card catalog was not yet available. Instead, the Library used punched cards for fiscal records, to generate serials listings, to track book circulation and prepare overdue notices, and, ironically, to compile information on how visitors used the regular card catalog. Throughout the 1950s, Library staff experimented with various technologies, including a hybrid punched-card catalog, in which half the card contained typewritten information and the other half coded data. There was even an experiment, in the Library's Navy Research Section, "in the application of television to the remote searching of catalog cards and the transmission of documents."

By the 1950s, as the main card catalog at the Library of Congress surged to more than nine million cards crammed into 10,500 trays, the administration kept a watchful eye on nascent computer technology as a possible solution to the looming catalog crisis. About the same time, the handful of computer companies that existed were making major innovations and had moved away from the punched-card system, advancing to vacuum tubes and magnetic tapes. Seeing new possibilities for cataloging and storing data, Librarian of Congress Lawrence Quincy Mumford established the Committee on Mechanized Information Retrieval in January 1958. In the years that followed, and with the approval of Congress, the Library purchased an IBM 1401, a small-scale computer system the size of a Volkswagen bus. The committee also recommended establishing a group to both design and implement the procedures required to automate the catalog. Unfortunately, there were few computer programmers around. The early ones were usually mathematicians, including one Henriette D. Avram, who joined the Library of Congress in 1965.

Avram hastily evaluated the card catalog and devised the first automated cataloging system in the world, known as Machine-Readable Cataloging (MARC). Launched in January 1966, MARC attempted to both convert and manipulate the data stored on a catalog card. Representatives from sixteen libraries were invited to participate in its development, and the collaboration yielded approximately 50,000 machine-readable records containing information for English-language books. Stored on magnetic tape, these catalog records, which incorporated the standard classification scheme, could be searched at a computer terminal. The days of the paper card catalog were now numbered.

Center: Henriette D. Avram (1919-2006).

MARC was quickly recognized as an international standard and libraries began to look at the feasibility of converting their existing catalogs. Avram noted that the herculean task of converting the cards to the new automated system would not be easy. By 1976, however, the first computer terminal for public use was installed in the Library of Congress Main Reading Room. Other libraries across the country soon followed suit and welcomed the newfangled technology as they considered phasing out their own card catalogs. On December 31, 1980, the last new cards were filed in the Main Reading Room's card catalog and at that point, it was declared "frozen"—no additional cards were ever added.

At the time, the idea of closing a library's card catalog was perceived as both startling and bold, and there were numerous glitches to overcome and major issues to consider, such as how to convert millions of handwritten and typeset cards to the new system. Even though a level of hesitation remained, libraries were left with a difficult decision: invest in an automated future or stay mired in the past. Younger library patrons in the 1990s who caught a glimpse, or even used, the "frozen" card catalogs that for a time stood side by side with the new computer terminals, may not have understood the reluctance many had in letting go of what scholar Markus Krajewski called the "paper machines."

When the twelfth Librarian of Congress, Daniel J. Boorstin, was appointed in 1975, he remarked on the amazing transition that was well under way. "Within the last century . . . and especially within the last few decades, this Library has come to bear vivid witness, in quite new ways, to the power of the Machine. The output of printing presses has been multiplying. The items which our Library receives in a single day are more than five times the whole numbers of volumes purchased from Thomas Jefferson in 1815. Now, by a lucky coincidence, the electronic computer makes it possible for us to keep track of our gargantuan collections. Dr. Mumford, my distinguished predecessor, ushered our great Library into the age of automation, and so has helped us from being buried under our own treasures."

CARDS AS ART

Once the New York Public Library and other large university libraries physically removed their catalogs in the 1980s, a subsequent domino effect was triggered. In the majority of libraries nationwide, as the Online Public Access Catalog (OPAC) replaced the old cards, these relics were cast into the dustbin. Many librarians were both tired of the cumbersome old card catalog and relished the opportunity to work with a new technology. Some libraries made a spectacle of removing their card catalog by holding a mock funeral, as at a public library in Danbury, Connecticut. Others found even more creative ways to say good-bye. A library in Maryland tied its cards to helium balloons and spectators gathered to watch them float away. Most libraries were more dispassionate and simply tossed millions of cards into dumpsters, then sensibly auctioned off the oak drawers and cabinets, perhaps indifferent to the irony that the containers now outvalued the cards they had once held. However, for those card systems that remained, the catastrophic avalanche of catalog cards predicted by Fremont Rider and others never occurred. One can wander into some libraries and still find the sturdy cabinets faithfully standing against a far wall, like a stalwart old friend.

There have been other instances where unwanted cards have been rescued from the landfill. A notable example involves one of the original and arguably most renowned card catalogs—the card catalog from Harvard University's Widener Library. On hearing that Harvard was abandoning its card catalog, Thomas Johnston, an artist based in the Pacific Northwest, secured a large portion of it. "I thought [the cards], as raw material, were so loaded with content that something interesting could be done with them," Johnston explained. "As a printmaker, I was fascinated by the idea of a large number of similarly sized and shaped things, as repeated components, and that each one was a unique contribution of an individual. I thought at minimum, an attempt should be made to save them from destruction, and perhaps someone may have a great idea for a project. As artifacts, they continue to be exciting to look through, to realize the creative activity, research, and information that each card represents, and further, how each card has played a role in advancing knowledge." Johnston has been in conversation with other artists about using them in a collaborative art project.

In the discussions about what to do with an old card catalog, the human aspect of the cards' creation is an oft-heard refrain. This is especially true of the old handwritten cards, wherein slight variations in the prescribed "library hand" reveal the personal touch brought to each card. Such a notion has contributed to the phenomenon of dormant card catalogs being appropriated for art projects. At Emory University, people were invited to create art out of the salvaged catalog cards. Various students, staff, faculty, and members of the community have colored and painted on the cards. "The card catalog itself should draw interest from viewers," says exhibitions manager Kathy Dixson. "For most of today's students, it's a curiosity. For those of us who remember searching through card catalogs, this 'artifact' is a touchstone to memories from our past."

Farther up the East Coast, at Massachusetts's Greenfield Community College, librarian Hope Schneider sought to preserve and celebrate catalog cards in a different way. After the library decided to remove the

Card catalog in Widener Library at Harvard, Cambridge, Massachusetts, 1915.

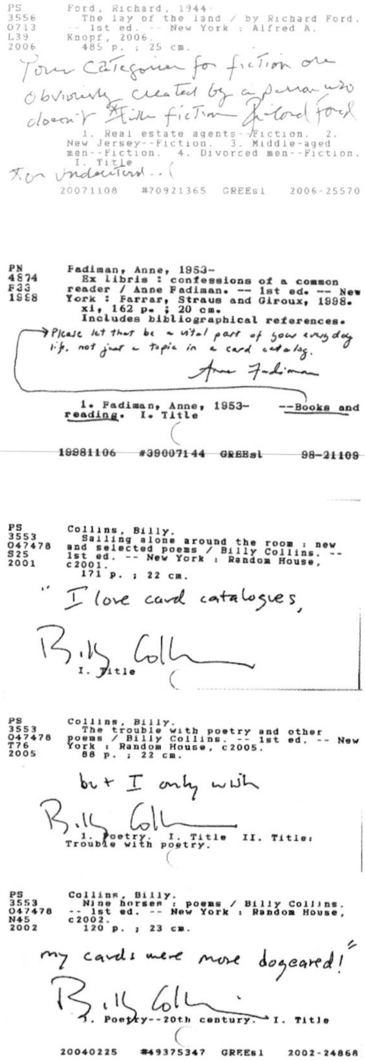
PS 3556 O713 L39 2006
Ford, Richard, 1944-
The lay of the land / by Richard Ford. -- 1st ed. -- New York : Alfred A. Knopf, 2006.
485 p. ; 25 cm.
Your categories for fiction are obviously created by a person who doesn't like fiction Richard Ford
1. Real estate agents--Fiction. 2. New Jersey--Fiction. 3. Middle-aged men--Fiction. 4. Divorced men--Fiction. I. Title
20071108 #70921365 GREEsl 2006-25570

PN 4874 F33 1998
Fadiman, Anne, 1953-
Ex libris : confessions of a common reader / Anne Fadiman. -- 1st ed. -- New York : Farrar, Straus and Giroux, 1998.
xi, 162 p. ; 20 cm.
Includes bibliographical references.
Please let that be a vital part of your every day life, not just a topic in a card catalog.
Anne Fadiman
1. Fadiman, Anne, 1953- --Books and reading. I. Title
19981106 #39007144 GREEsl 98-21109

PS 3553 O47478 S25 2001
Collins, Billy.
Sailing alone around the room : new and selected poems / Billy Collins. -- 1st ed. -- New York : Random House, c2001.
171 p. ; 22 cm.
"I love card catalogues,
Billy Collins
I. Title

PS 3553 O47478 T76 2005
Collins, Billy.
The trouble with poetry and other poems / Billy Collins. -- 1st ed. -- New York : Random House, c2005.
88 p. ; 22 cm.
but I only wish
Billy Collins
1. Poetry. I. Title II. Title: Trouble with poetry.

PS 3553 O47478 N45 2002
Collins, Billy.
Nine horses : poems / Billy Collins. -- 1st ed. -- New York : Random House, c2002.
120 p. ; 23 cm.
my cards were more dogeared!"
Billy Collins
1. Poetry--20th century. I. Title
20040225 #49375347 GREEsl 2002-24868

Cards courtesy of Hope Schneider, Greenfield Community College.

card catalog, she mailed the cards to various authors whose works were represented on them, asking if they would sign and return them for a library display. She received a variety of responses; some authors simply autographed their cards while others added short notes about card catalogs or simply bemoaned their fate. Former U.S. Poet Laureate Billy Collins jotted a poem across his cards: "I love card catalogues / but I only wish / my cards were more dog eared!" Novelist and poet Wendell Berry's candid response revealed the strong feelings the card catalog can evoke as he declined to participate and wrote back, "I refuse to cooperate in any way in the destruction of the card catalogues, which I think is a mistake, a loss, a sorrow."

Schneider notes that most of the responses she received "were heartfelt, passionate, and witty." Common threads conveyed "the importance of libraries for our collective culture, and the act of reading itself." Another former Poet Laureate, Rita Dove, signed her card with the message "Reading brings the world into your heart," while Pulitzer Prize–winner Annie Proulx, reflecting on the end of an era, wrote that she "regrets the loss of serendipitous discovery and the thrill of the chase" the cards once brought. Celebrated children's author Norton Juster, who wrote *The Phantom Tollbooth*, expressed what generations of children may have felt searching for their next adventure in a drawer of cards: "As a kid the card catalog was always my 'rabbit hole'—I am sorry to see it disappear."

In her letters to authors Schneider wrote, "We have salvaged some of the cards, and would like to create a display of these venerable and tactile guideposts to literature since many of our students have never used or seen an actual card from a card catalog. And perhaps it will prompt them to go to the stacks to find some of these books and read them, which is the whole point of it all in the first place." Even when the cards are stripped out of their cozy wooden drawers, scribbled on, and mounted on walls, they might end up steering another generation of readers to the books they once represented.

CUTTING THE GORDIAN KNOT

The people who built the card catalog at the Library of Congress were both dedicated and focused, and as a result, they created something exceptional. Former Smithsonian Institution historian Dr. Stanley Goldberg stressed the importance of the card catalog just as computers were beginning to edge them out in the 1980s. "The structure of the card catalog did not emerge overnight," Goldberg noted. "Its architecture was undoubtedly shaped by decades of the shared experience of users, reference librarians, and catalogers."

In the 1980s, a private firm converted the Library's cards to the new electronic format by hand, keyed in manually rather than scanned, and because of human error, a good deal of information failed to make it into the new system. Dr. Thomas Mann, a reference librarian in the Main Reading Room, was present during the transition and recalled, "These retrospective records are often not as complete or accurate as those created by the Library." In the early days of the online catalog, patrons were notified that the catalog records "are being edited to comply with current cataloging standards and to reflect contemporary language and usage." Part of the need for editing had to do with obsolete subject headings; for example, the word *aeroplanes* was replaced by *airplanes*. And while many problems like this were caught and corrected, others were lost in translating English to binary code.

It was suggested at one point, not long after the advent of computers, that the card catalog at the Library should be removed to free up space. However, Dr. Mann and others argued persuasively that the catalog had ongoing value to Library administration and to Congress. As a result, unlike other significant catalogs that met their demise, the Library of Congress catalog was saved for the most part. In one defense put forth, the catalog was referred to as "a sprawling record that is surely the mother of all catalogs. Trashing this unique historical document is simply unthinkable." A former Library rare book cataloger said that the cards held a "gold mine of information," often added by hand over the years, that helped correct the online records.

Library of Congress catalogers themselves claim that the original cataloging contains crucial evidence about older editions and can also prove an invaluable resource in cataloging new material. As Dr. Mann explained, "The Library did not retain its card catalog because anyone was sentimental about the texture of the cards and the smell of the wood. In short, the information contained in the Main Card Catalog—and not found anywhere else—continues to be needed in many instances for efficient access to the Library's millions of pre-1968 volumes because much of the needed information on the cards did not make the transition to the online catalog." There are also a handful of smaller, functioning card catalogs scattered across the Library of Congress that are dedicated to specific special collections, like the Library's architecture drawings or fine prints. These cards contain information beyond the reach of the online catalog and are essential to accessing these unique visual materials.

The prodigious effort that went into painstakingly creating and maintaining the Library's Main Card Catalog over the years is evident in drawer after drawer. The durable oak drawers still hold the well-handled and smudged cards, with worn-down edges revealing a book's popularity or importance, ready as ever to guide new readers to that unfamiliar title they did not even know they were looking for. At the twilight of the card catalog in 1976, Paul Edlund wrote, "Few libraries have been untouched by the work done by Library staff members over the years; it would be difficult to walk into a library anywhere in the United States and be unable to find one of these physical byproducts of the intellectual efforts of the cataloging staff of the Library of Congress."

In 1975, representatives from the Library of Congress and other large university and public libraries gathered in Chicago for the Association of Research Libraries' meeting to discuss the future of the card catalog. MARC was declared a runaway success and the card catalog sadly referred to as an albatross around the Library's neck. Alluding to the complexities of converting the old cards to a MARC record, one participant suggested that the time had come to cut "the Gordian knot that ties the present and future to the past." In Greek mythology, an oracle claimed that whoever was able to untie an intricate knot tied by King Gordius would become the next ruler of Asia. Alexander the Great, unable to untie the knot, became impatient and swiftly cut it with his sword. The idiom is now meant to express an intractable problem solved with quick, resolute action. Certainly many libraries took such action in tossing their cards, and one would probably be hard-pressed to find a leader in the library community who truly regrets cutting this Gordian knot.

The online catalog is clearly a more practical and efficient way to access the vast holdings at a library, but this does not diminish the legacy of the card catalog or discount its enduring utility. It stands next to the other edifying triumphs of civilization, like the printing press and the book. The card catalog was functional yet flawed, an astonishing innovation destined from the start to collapse under its own weight. In 1994, author Nicholson Baker wrote a eulogy of sorts in *The New Yorker*, extolling the intrinsic worth of the card catalog and concluding that, "the real reason to keep card catalogues is simply that they hold the irreplaceable intelligence of the librarians who worked on them." He suggested that resisting a quick disposal of the card catalog was a noble cause allowing for a more thoughtful course to take hold, especially when the appearance of obsolescence can sometimes be deceiving.

The card catalog lives on as both a nostalgic relic that continues to elicit positive feelings about libraries and books and as a vital resource to researchers and catalogers at the Library of Congress. Former Library cataloger John Rather once said the card catalog "is a living organism and, as a living organism, it is subject to growth, to change, and to deterioration," but the cards appear to have some life left in them. In the Library of Congress Main Reading Room the surviving rows of drawers stand as a tangible vestige of how important the collections are, but also as a reminder that change is both imminent and inescapable.

The passing of the card catalog follows the arc of so many other innovations. Just as quills are no longer pressed into wet clay, or molten lead injected into a mold to form type, 3-by-5-in (7.5-by-12-cm) index cards are no longer printed to represent humanity's collective knowledge. The efforts chronicled here represent a testament to the continual grasping and the ongoing struggle for order and clarity in a chaotic world. Throughout the ages, organizing systems were revised and adapted as the pace of information accelerated and new technologies provided more precise access to ever-larger collections. Whatever the future holds, the basic tenet of the card catalog will endure in new systems yet to come, and they will owe a debt to the ingenuity that preceded them.

Reference librarian Dr. Thomas Mann at the central desk in the Main Reading Room, 1985.

As computers eclipsed the card catalog, some scholars lamented its demise. In a 1985 issue of The New Yorker, *historian Barbara Tuchman wrote, "For me the card catalogue has been a companion all my working life. To leave it is like leaving the house one was brought up in."*

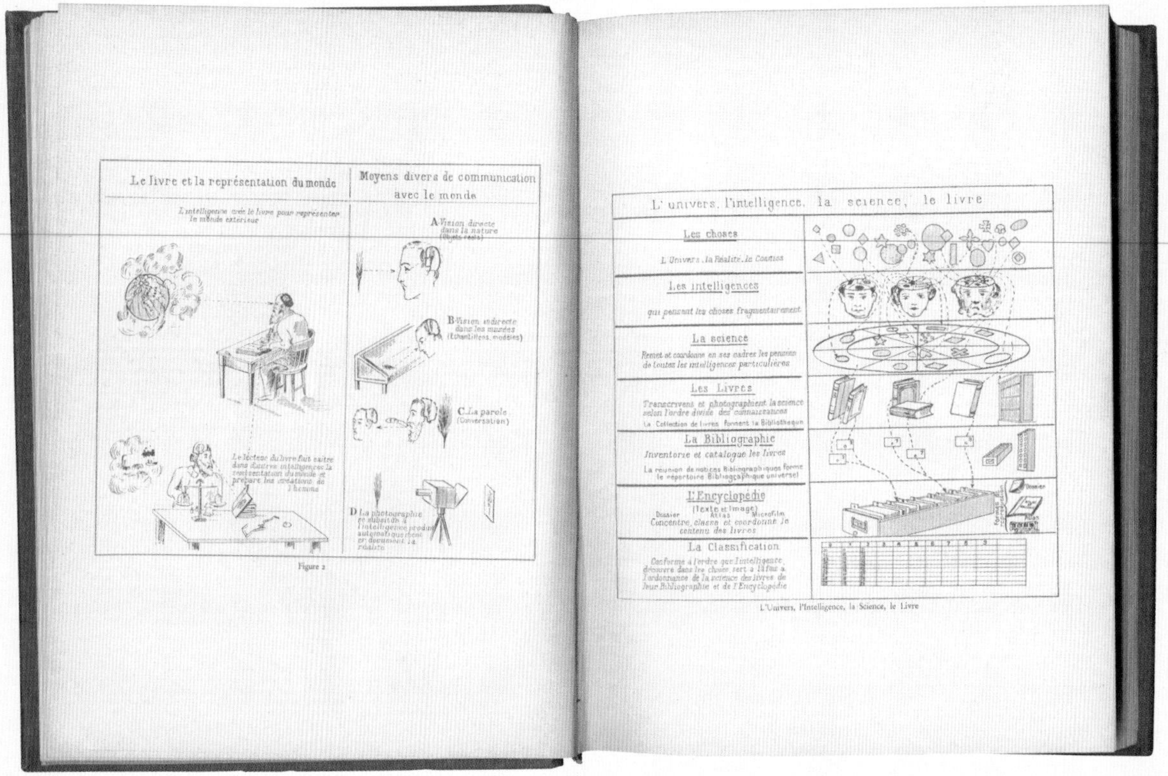

Paul Otlet, *Traité de documentation: le livre sur le livre, théorie et pratique*. Brussels, 1934.

Henriette Avram's work in developing MARC (Machine-Readable Cataloging) during the 1960s enabled discrete bits of structured data to be encoded and transmitted across long distances, an important advancement in the birth of the Internet. But the Internet also owes its existence, in part, to those who came even earlier and envisioned and implemented standardized index card catalogs. Paul Otlet was one of those visionaries. Born in Belgium in 1868, Otlet, a lawyer, was fascinated by bibliographic techniques and the potential for organizing information using standard index cards. Although he operated on the periphery of the library community and was drawn to various classification schemes, he developed an idea of bringing together the entire world's knowledge into a searchable system. Around the turn of the twentieth century, Otlet, along with international lawyer and

Otlet, Paul, 1868– 1944.

Traité de documentation: le livre sur le livre, théorie et pratique; par Paul Otlet ... Bruxelles, Editiones Mundaneum, 1934.

431, [12], viii p. illus. 26cm.

Page numbered 373bis. ("Annexe. Errata: (Page omise)") follows p. 431.
"Commencé d'imprimer 1932."

1. Bibliography—Theory, methods, etc. 2. Library science. I. Title. II. Title: Le livre sur le livre.

35-18377

Library of Congress Z1001.O88 NGS905

[2] Second Official 010

future Nobel Peace Prize-winner Henri La Fontaine, began to build an archive of facts on millions of 3-by-5-in (7.5-by-12-cm) index cards. They called this collection the Mundaneum*—a virtual analog Internet that users could search. This staggering collection of classified world knowledge was housed in Brussels until 1940, when Nazi Germany invaded Belgium and destroyed part of the* Mundaneum*.*

Otlet imagined a time when information could be disseminated across disparate populations, summing up his prescient vision in 1934: "Everything in the universe, and everything of man, would be registered at a distance as it was produced. In this way a moving image of the world will be established, a true mirror of his memory. From a distance, everyone will be able to read text, enlarged and limited to the desired subject, projected on an individual screen. In this way, everyone from his armchair will be able to contemplate creation in its entirety or in certain of its parts."

THE

SOULS OF BLACK FOLK

ESSAYS AND SKETCHES

BY

W. E. BURGHARDT DU BOIS

SIXTEENTH EDITION

CHICAGO
A. C. McCLURG & CO.
1928

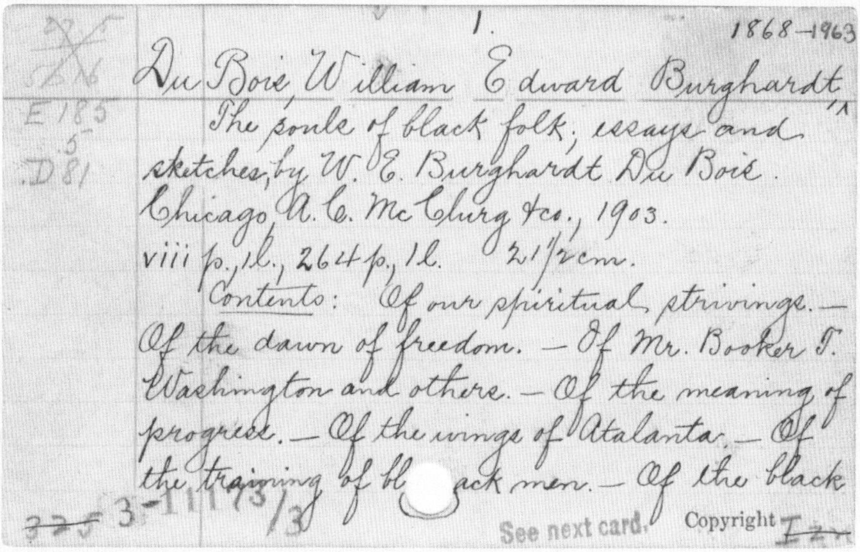

E185 .5 .D81

1. 1868–1963

Du Bois, William Edward Burghardt,

The souls of black folk; essays and sketches, by W. E. Burghardt Du Bois. Chicago, A. C. McClurg & co., 1903.

viii p., 1 l., 264 p., 1 l. 21½ cm.

Contents: Of our spiritual strivings.—Of the dawn of freedom.—Of Mr. Booker T. Washington and others.—Of the meaning of progress.—Of the wings of Atalanta.—Of the training of black men.—Of the black

3-11173/3

See next card. Copyright

W. E. Burghardt Du Bois, *The Souls of Black Folk: Essays and Sketches*. Chicago, A. C. McClurg & Co., 1928.

W. E. B. Du Bois, circa 1920-1930.

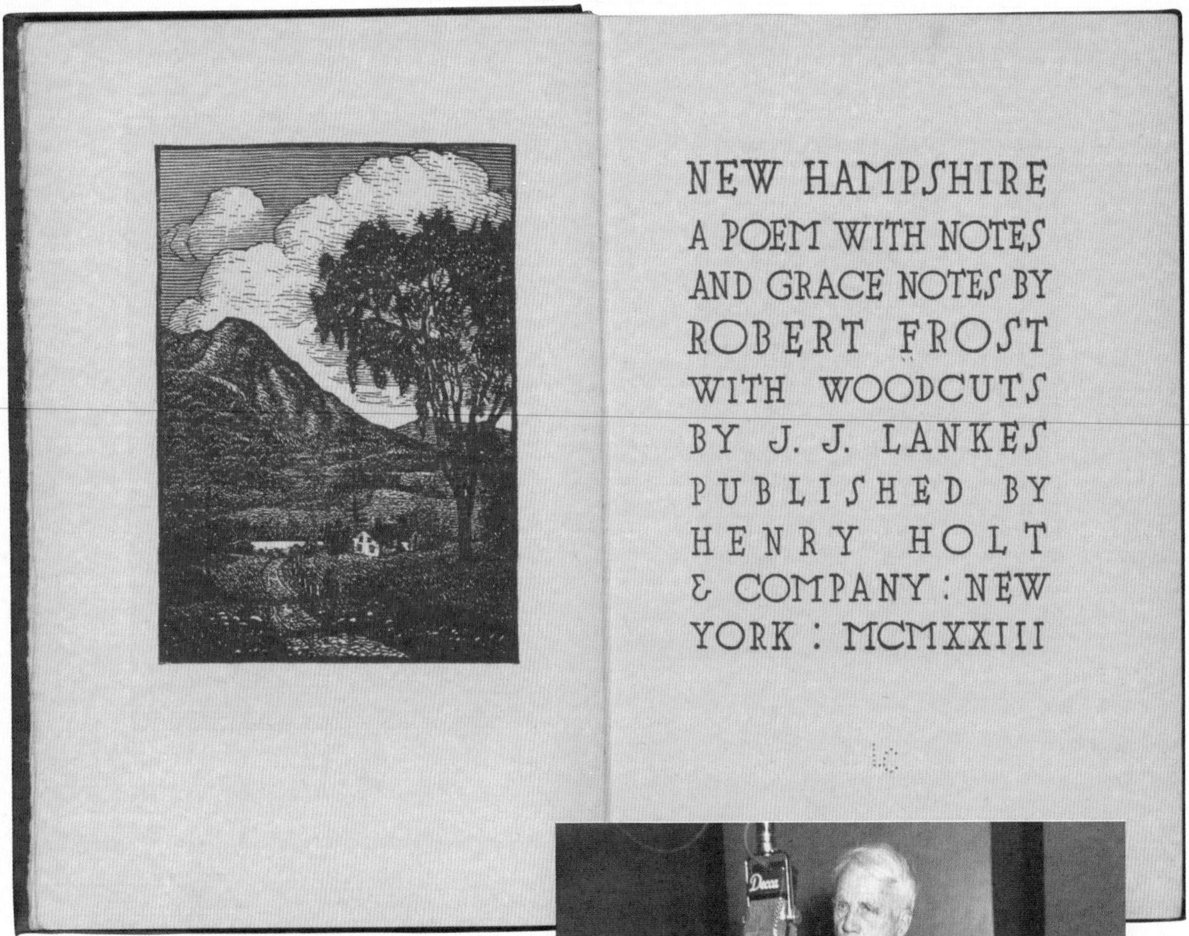

NEW HAMPSHIRE
A POEM WITH NOTES
AND GRACE NOTES BY
ROBERT FROST
WITH WOODCUTS
BY J. J. LANKES
PUBLISHED BY
HENRY HOLT
& COMPANY : NEW
YORK : MCMXXIII

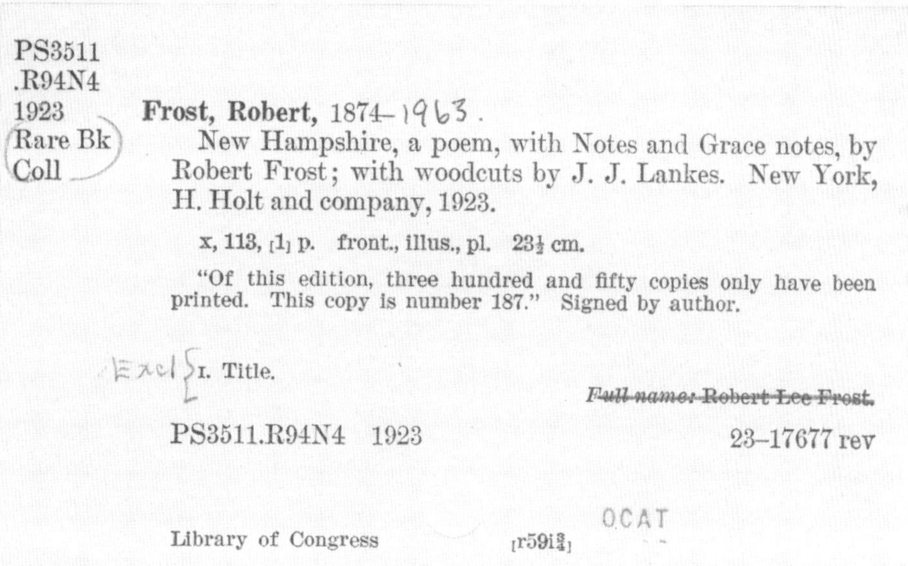

PS3511
.R94N4
1923
Rare Bk
Coll

Frost, Robert, 1874–1963.

New Hampshire, a poem, with Notes and Grace notes, by Robert Frost; with woodcuts by J. J. Lankes. New York, H. Holt and company, 1923.

x, 113, [1] p. front., illus., pl. 23½ cm.

"Of this edition, three hundred and fifty copies only have been printed. This copy is number 187." Signed by author.

Excl { I. Title.

~~Full name: Robert Lee Frost.~~

PS3511.R94N4 1923 23–17677 rev

Library of Congress [r59i⅔] OCAT

Robert Frost, *New Hampshire*. Henry Holt & Co., 1923.

Robert Frost speaking into a microphone at Decca Studios. Photograph by Warren Rothschild, New York, New York, October 31, 1951.

Librarian of Congress Lawrence Quincy Mumford named Robert Frost the twelfth Consultant in Poetry to the Library of Congress in 1958. One of the best-known and most beloved American poets of the twentieth century, Frost won the Pulitzer Prize for New Hampshire *in 1923.*

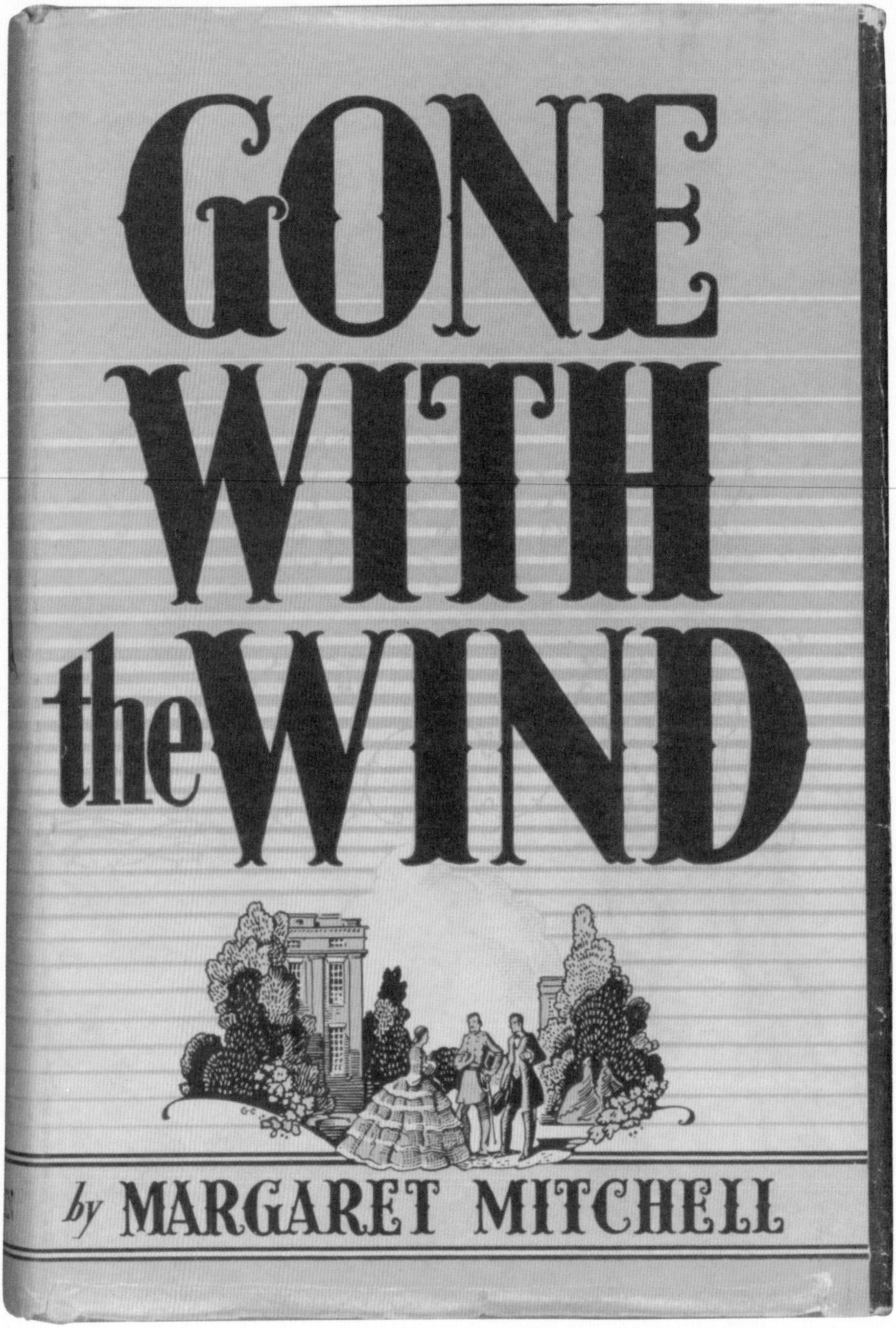
GONE WITH the WIND
by MARGARET MITCHELL

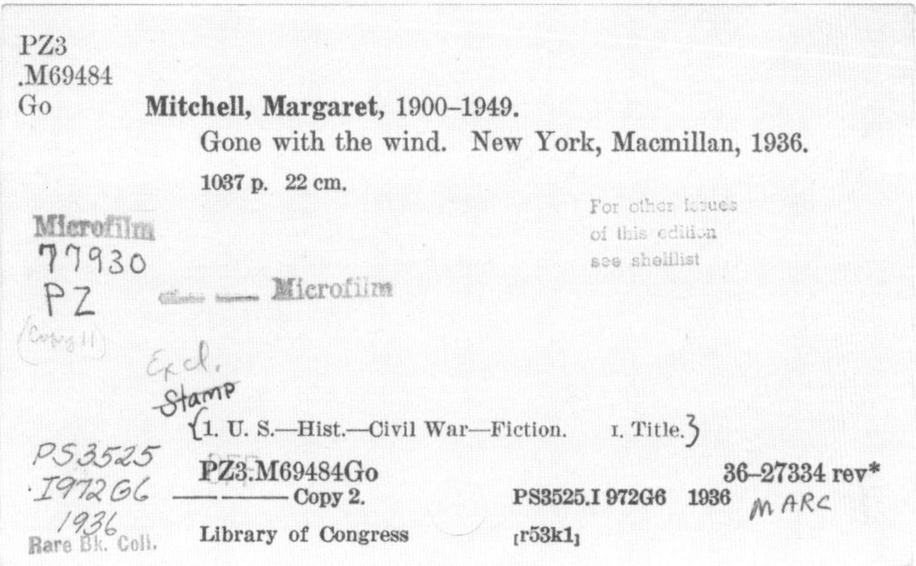
PZ3
.M69484
Go **Mitchell, Margaret,** 1900–1949.

Gone with the wind. New York, Macmillan, 1936.

1037 p. 22 cm.

Microfilm
77930
PZ

—— Microfilm

For other issues
of this edition
see shelflist

(Copy 1)

Excl.
Stamp

{1. U. S.—Hist.—Civil War—Fiction. I. Title.}

PS3525
.I972G6
1936
Rare Bk. Coll.

PZ3.M69484Go **36–27334 rev***

—— —— **Copy 2.** **PS3525.I 972G6 1936** MARC

Library of Congress **[r53k1]**

Margaret Mitchell, *Gone With the Wind.* New York, Macmillan, 1936.

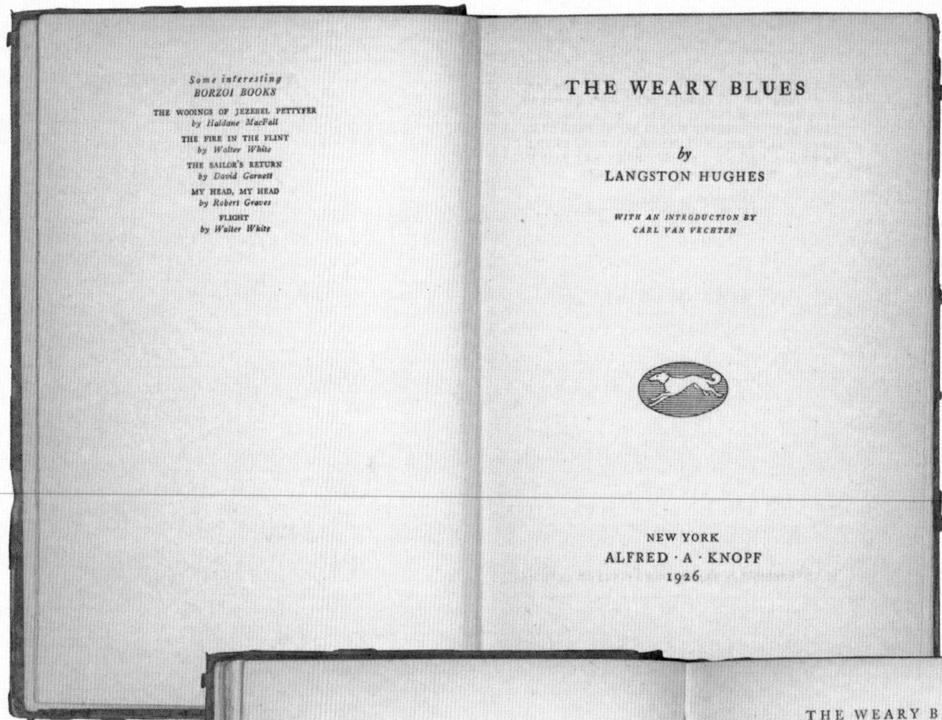

Some interesting
BORZOI BOOKS

THE WOOINGS OF JEZEBEL PETTYFER
by Haldane MacFall

THE FIRE IN THE FLINT
by Walter White

THE SAILOR'S RETURN
by David Garnett

MY HEAD, MY HEAD
by Robert Graves

FLIGHT
by Walter White

THE WEARY BLUES

by
LANGSTON HUGHES

WITH AN INTRODUCTION BY
CARL VAN VECHTEN

NEW YORK
ALFRED · A · KNOPF
1926

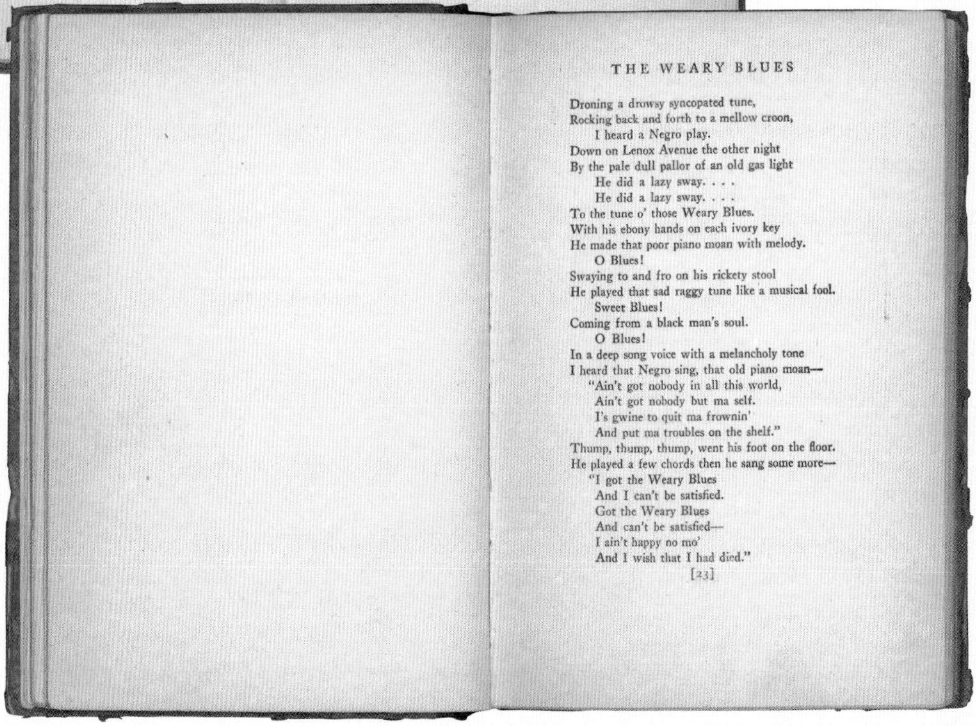

THE WEARY BLUES

Droning a drowsy syncopated tune,
Rocking back and forth to a mellow croon,
    I heard a Negro play.
Down on Lenox Avenue the other night
By the pale dull pallor of an old gas light
    He did a lazy sway. . . .
    He did a lazy sway. . . .
To the tune o' those Weary Blues.
With his ebony hands on each ivory key
He made that poor piano moan with melody.
    O Blues!
Swaying to and fro on his rickety stool
He played that sad raggy tune like a musical fool.
    Sweet Blues!
Coming from a black man's soul.
    O Blues!
In a deep song voice with a melancholy tone
I heard that Negro sing, that old piano moan—
    "Ain't got nobody in all this world,
    Ain't got nobody but ma self.
    I's gwine to quit ma frownin'
    And put ma troubles on the shelf."
Thump, thump, thump, went his foot on the floor.
He played a few chords then he sang some more—
    "I got the Weary Blues
    And I can't be satisfied.
    Got the Weary Blues
    And can't be satisfied—
    I ain't happy no mo'
    And I wish that I had died."

[23]

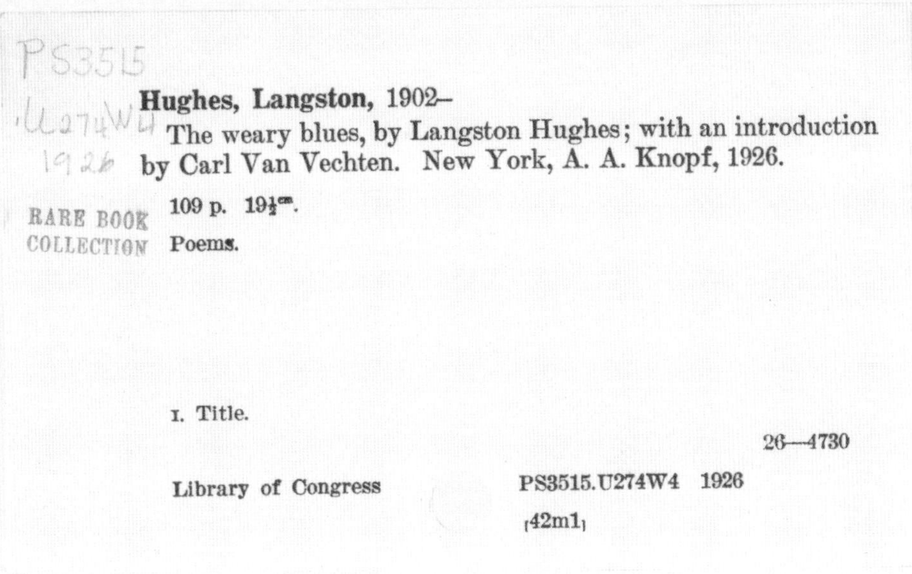

PS3515
.U274W4
1926

RARE BOOK
COLLECTION

Hughes, Langston, 1902–
The weary blues, by Langston Hughes; with an introduction by Carl Van Vechten. New York, A. A. Knopf, 1926.

109 p. 19½cm.

Poems.

I. Title.

26—4730

Library of Congress PS3515.U274W4 1926

[42m1]

Langston Hughes, *The Weary Blues*. New York, Alfred A. Knopf, 1926.

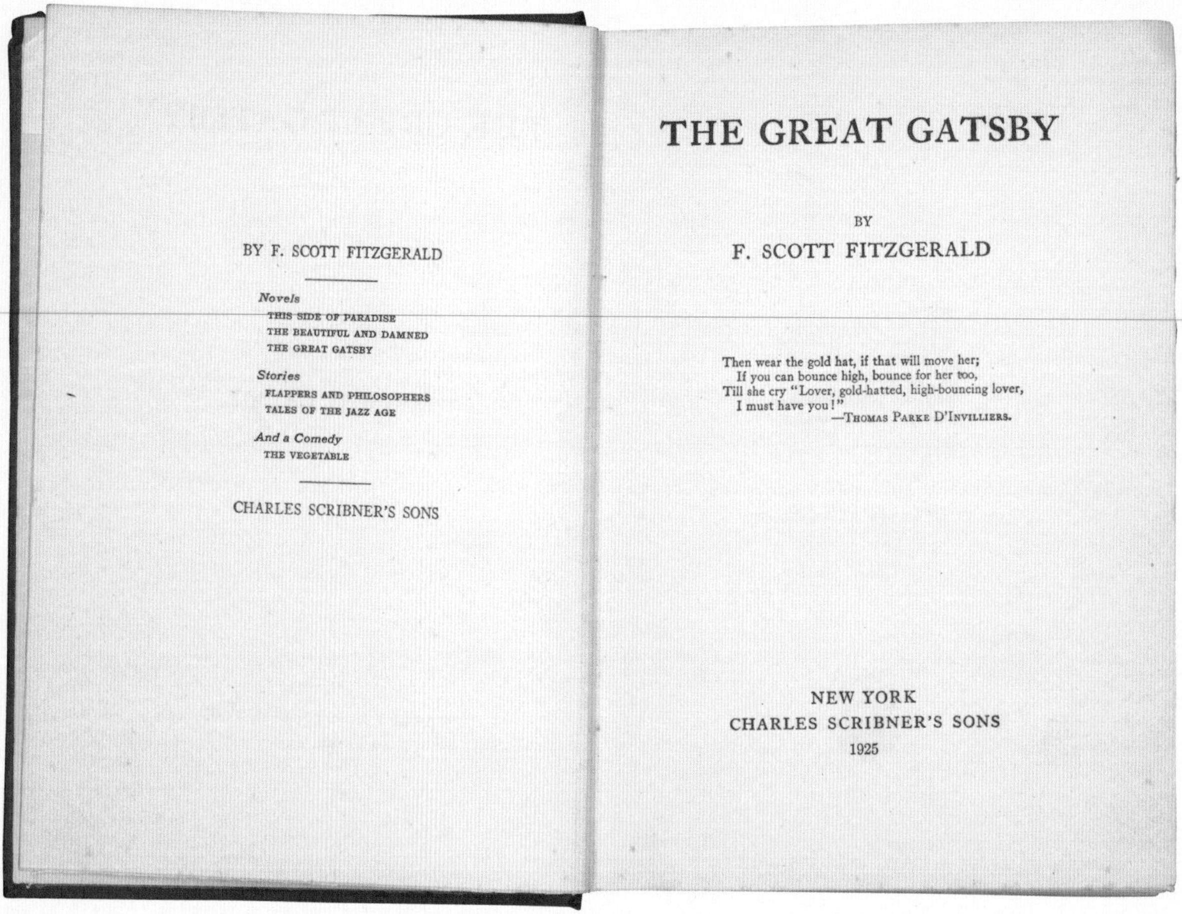

BY F. SCOTT FITZGERALD

Novels

THIS SIDE OF PARADISE
THE BEAUTIFUL AND DAMNED
THE GREAT GATSBY

Stories

FLAPPERS AND PHILOSOPHERS
TALES OF THE JAZZ AGE

And a Comedy

THE VEGETABLE

CHARLES SCRIBNER'S SONS

THE GREAT GATSBY

BY

F. SCOTT FITZGERALD

Then wear the gold hat, if that will move her;
If you can bounce high, bounce for her too,
Till she cry "Lover, gold-hatted, high-bouncing lover,
I must have you!"
—THOMAS PARKE D'INVILLIERS.

NEW YORK
CHARLES SCRIBNER'S SONS
1925

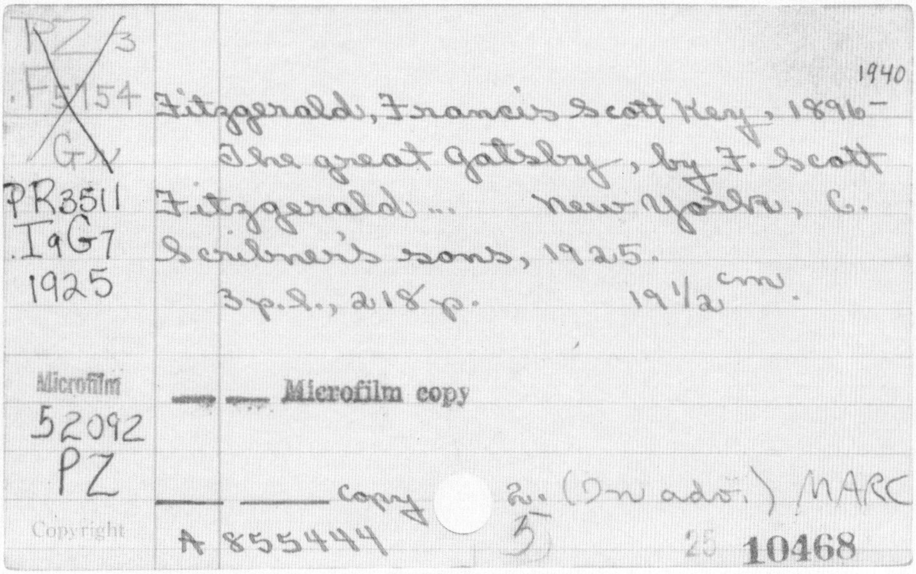

PZ3 .F5754 G

1940

Fitzgerald, Francis Scott Key, 1896–
The great Gatsby, by F. Scott Fitzgerald ... New York, C. Scribner's sons, 1925.
3 p. l., 218 p. 19½ cm.

PR3511 .I9G7 1925

Microfilm 52092 PZ — Microfilm copy

Copyright — copy 2. (On adv.) MARC

A 855444 5 25 10468

F. Scott Fitzgerald, *The Great Gatsby*. New York, C. Scribner's Sons, 1925.

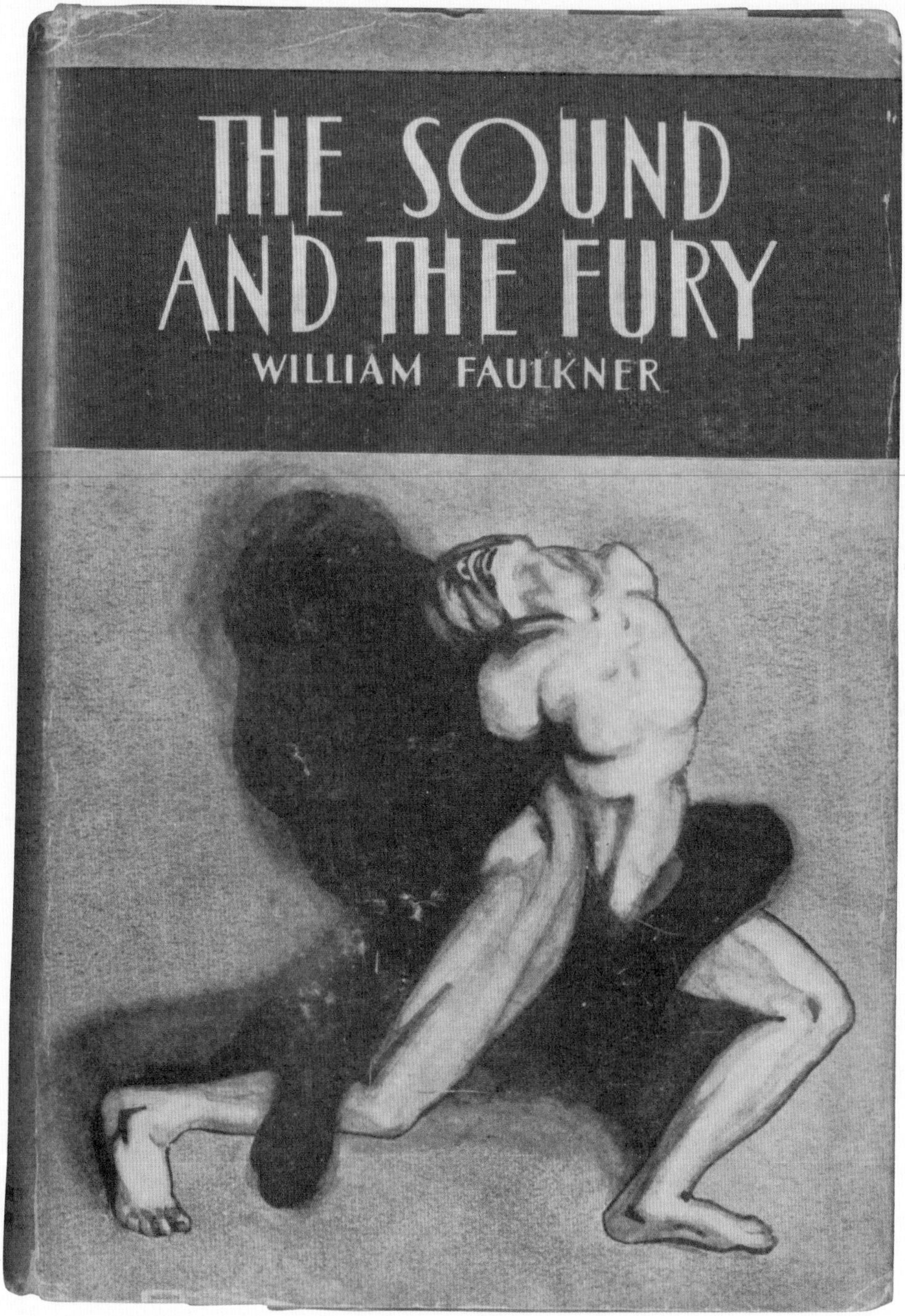
THE SOUND
AND THE FURY
WILLIAM FAULKNER

Sound and the fury. Selections.
Sound recording. 197-

Faulkner, William, 1897–1962.

William Faulkner reads a selection from his novel: The sound and the fury—Dilsey. [Sound recording] Listening Library AA 3336. [197–?]

on side 2 of 1 disc. 33⅓ rpm. mono. 12 in.

With: Faulkner, W. William Faulkner reads selections from his novel: Light in August.
Descriptive notes on container.

I. Title.

[PS3511.A86] 76–741057

OCAT

Library of Congress 76 MN

William Faulkner, *The Sound and the Fury*. J. Cape and H. Smith, 1929.

This card is for a vinyl record of The Sound and the Fury *as read by William Faulkner. The Library's Motion Picture, Broadcasting and Recorded Sound Division houses the largest and most comprehensive collections of American and foreign-produced films, television broadcasts, sound recordings, and radio broadcasts in the world.*

THE JOY OF COOKING

by

Mrs. IRMA S. ROMBAUER

A Compilation of Reliable
Recipes with a Casual
Culinary Chat

Illustrations by

MARION ROMBAUER BECKER

THE BOBBS-MERRILL COMPANY
Publishers
INDIANAPOLIS NEW YORK

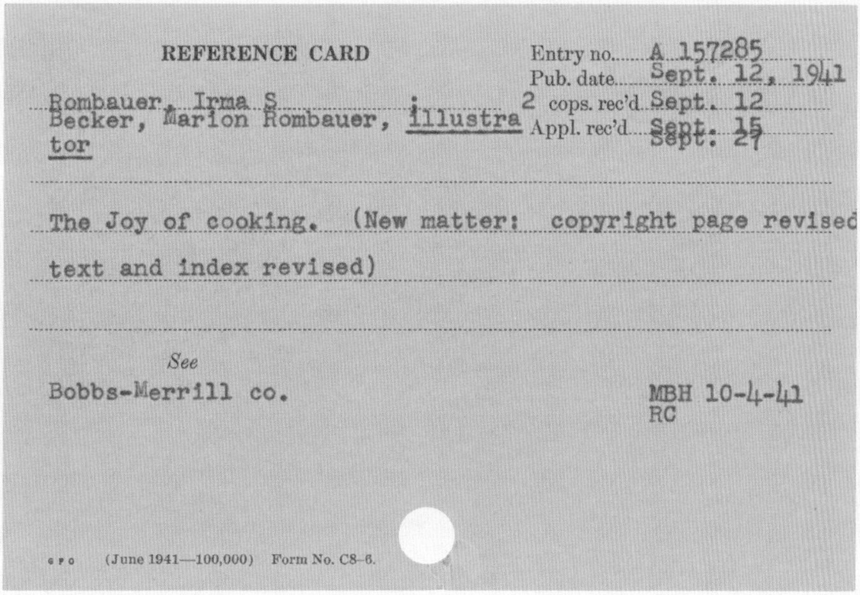

REFERENCE CARD

Entry no. A 157285
Pub. date Sept. 12, 1941
2 cops. rec'd Sept. 12
Appl. rec'd Sept. 15
Sept. 27

Rombauer, Irma S :
Becker, Marion Rombauer, illustrator

The Joy of cooking. (New matter: copyright page revised text and index revised)

See
Bobbs-Merrill co.

MBH 10-4-41
RC

GPO (June 1941—100,000) Form No. C8-6.

Irma S. Rombauer, *The Joy of Cooking*. Indianapolis, Indiana, Bobbs-Merrill Co., 1941.

THEIR EYES
WERE WATCHING GOD
A NOVEL
ZORA N· HURSTON

Hurston, Zora Neale.
Their eyes were watching God; a novel, by Zora Neale Hurston. Philadelphia, London, J. B. Lippincott company [©1937]

Microfilm

286 p. 21cm.

76651
PZ

Microfilm

I. Title.

37–18658

Library of Congress PZ3.H9457Th

——— Copy 2.

DN 357

Copyright A 108603 [3] Second Official

Zora N. Hurston, *Their Eyes Were Watching God: A Novel.* Philadelphia, J. B. Lippincott Co., 1937.

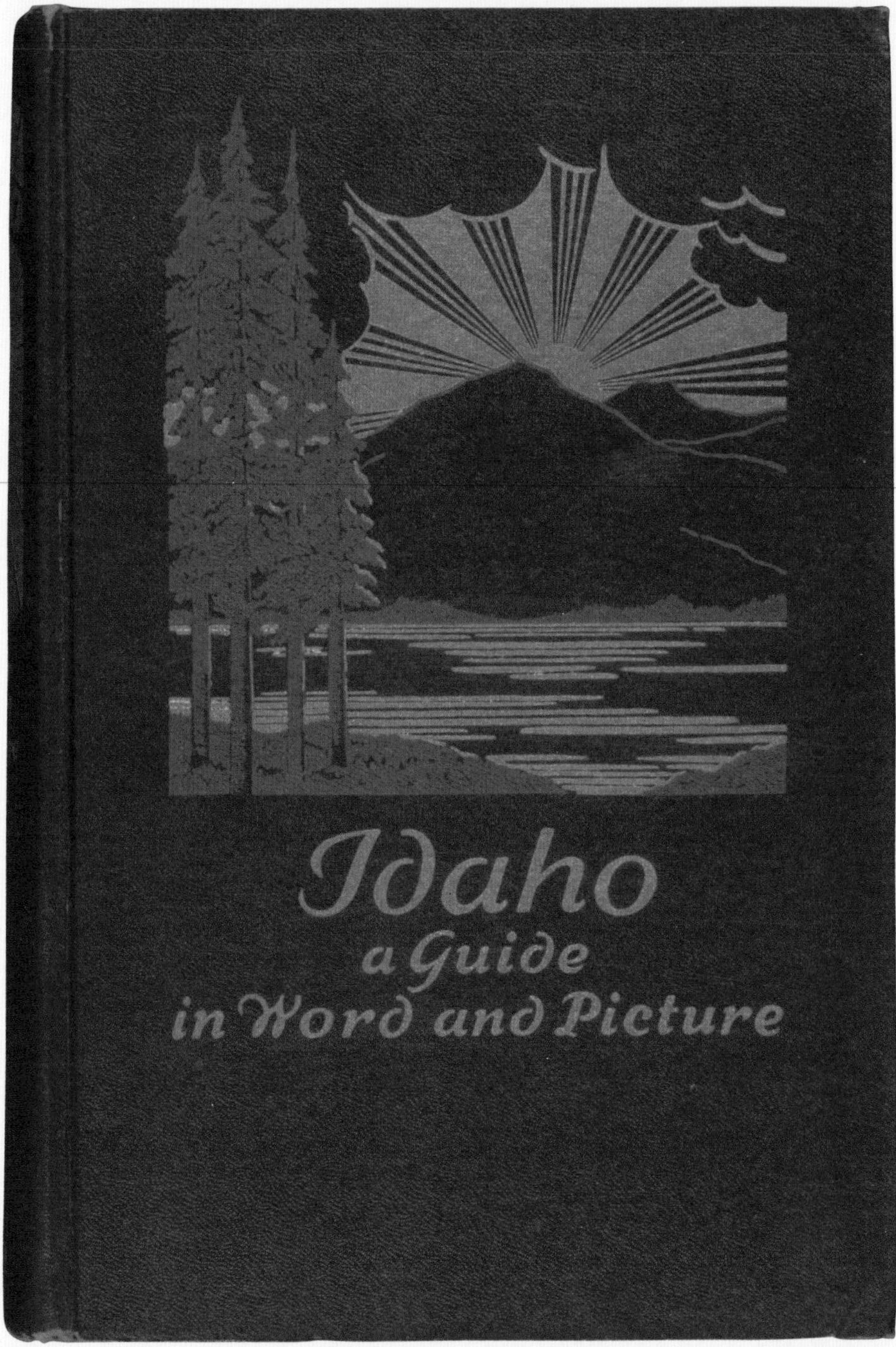
Idaho
a Guide
in Word and Picture

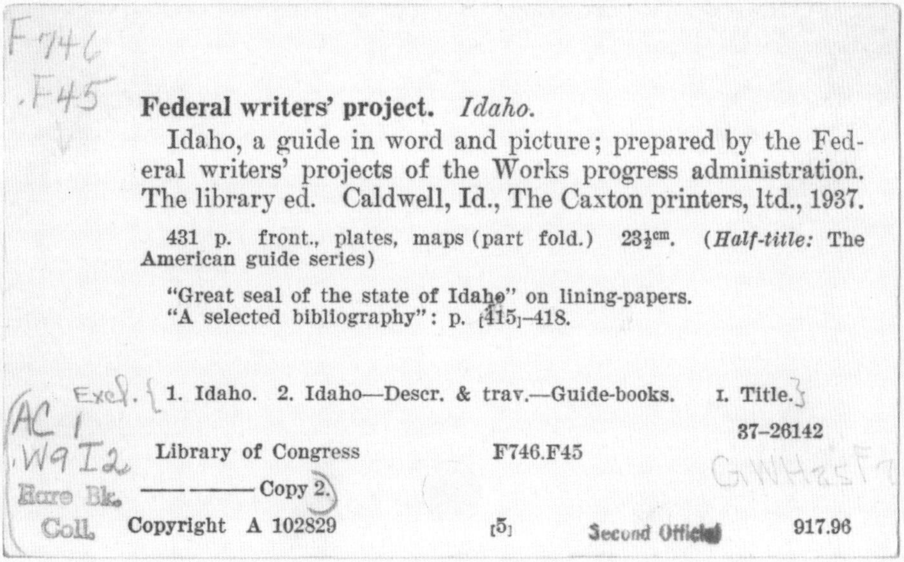

F746
.F45

Federal writers' project. *Idaho.*

Idaho, a guide in word and picture; prepared by the Federal writers' projects of the Works progress administration. The library ed. Caldwell, Id., The Caxton printers, ltd., 1937.

431 p. front., plates, maps (part fold.) 23½cm. (*Half-title:* The American guide series)

"Great seal of the state of Idaho" on lining-papers.
"A selected bibliography": p. [415]–418.

Excl. {1. Idaho. 2. Idaho—Descr. & trav.—Guide-books. I. Title.}

37-26142

AC 1 .W9 I2 Library of Congress F746.F45

Rare Bk. Coll. ——— Copy 2.

Copyright A 102829 [5] Second Official 917.96

Federal Writers' Project, *Idaho: A Guide in Word and Picture*, 1937.

THE
GRAPES of WRATH
John Steinbeck

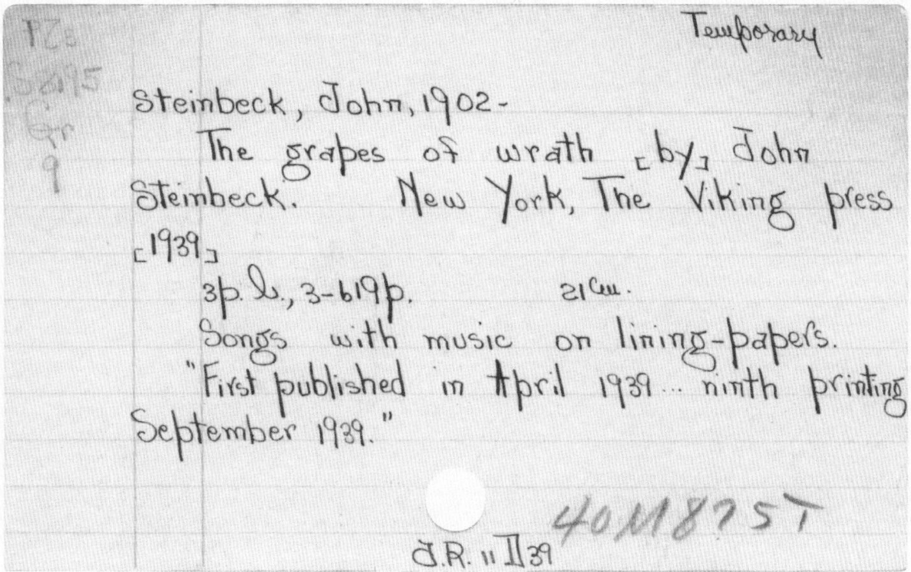

PZ3
.S8195
Gr
9

Temporary

Steinbeck, John, 1902-
The grapes of wrath [by] John Steinbeck. New York, The Viking press [1939]
3 p. l., 3-619 p. 21 cm.
Songs with music on lining-papers.
"First published in April 1939 ... ninth printing September 1939."

40M875T
J.R. 11 II 39

John Steinbeck, *The Grapes of Wrath*. New York, Viking, 1939.

Carol M. Highsmith, *Weed Patch Camp*, 2013.

The "rescue camp" for distressed migrant workers who fled the Dust Bowl during the Great Depression was also referred to as the Sunset Camp and was officially known as the Arvin Federal Government Camp. Author John Steinbeck called it "Weed Patch Camp" in his novel, The Grapes of Wrath.

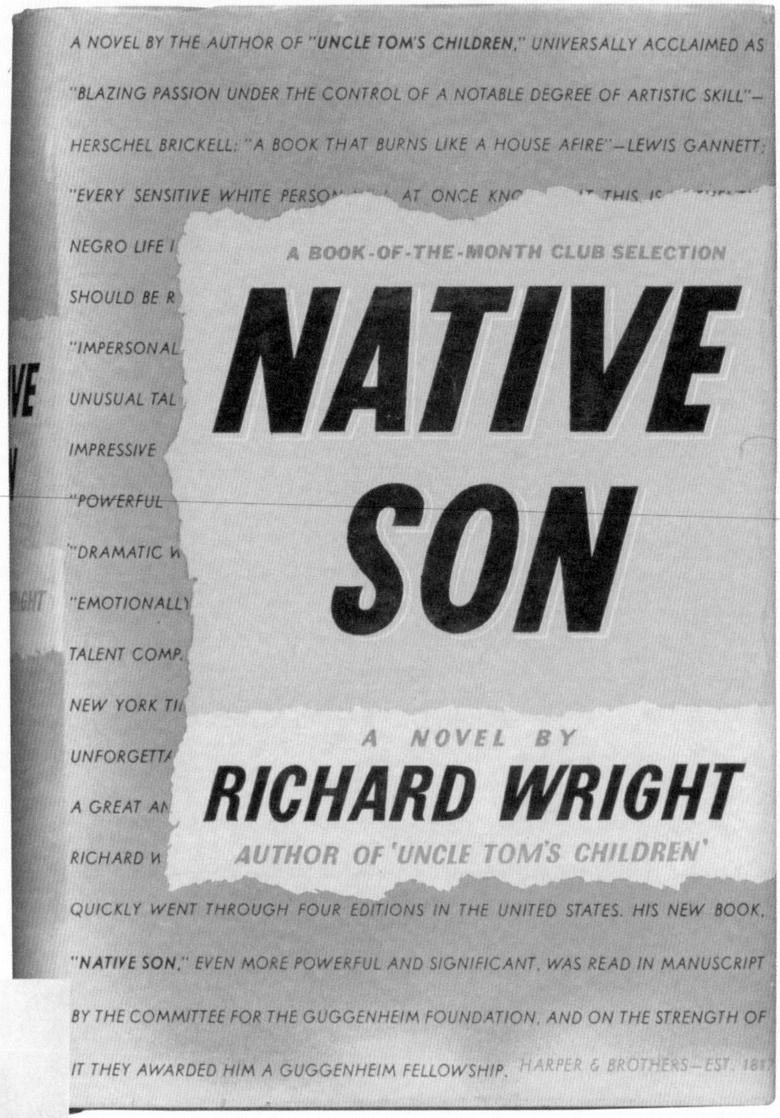
A NOVEL BY THE AUTHOR OF "UNCLE TOM'S CHILDREN," UNIVERSALLY ACCLAIMED AS
"BLAZING PASSION UNDER THE CONTROL OF A NOTABLE DEGREE OF ARTISTIC SKILL"—
HERSCHEL BRICKELL; "A BOOK THAT BURNS LIKE A HOUSE AFIRE"—LEWIS GANNETT;
A BOOK-OF-THE-MONTH CLUB SELECTION
NATIVE SON
A NOVEL BY
RICHARD WRIGHT
AUTHOR OF 'UNCLE TOM'S CHILDREN'
QUICKLY WENT THROUGH FOUR EDITIONS IN THE UNITED STATES. HIS NEW BOOK,
"NATIVE SON," EVEN MORE POWERFUL AND SIGNIFICANT, WAS READ IN MANUSCRIPT
BY THE COMMITTEE FOR THE GUGGENHEIM FOUNDATION, AND ON THE STRENGTH OF
IT THEY AWARDED HIM A GUGGENHEIM FELLOWSHIP.

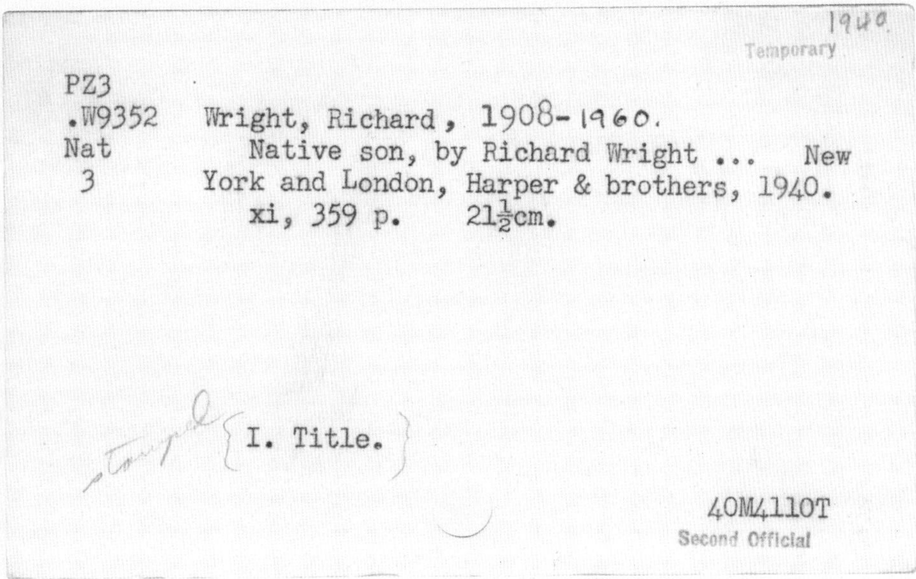

1940
Temporary

PZ3
.W9352 Wright, Richard, 1908-1960.
Nat Native son, by Richard Wright ... New
3 York and London, Harper & brothers, 1940.
xi, 359 p. 21½cm.

stamped {I. Title.}

40M4110T
Second Official

Richard Wright, *Native Son.*
New York and London, Harper &
Brothers, 1940.

Richard Wright, 1945.

FOR WHOM
THE BELL
TOLLS
Ernest
Hemingway

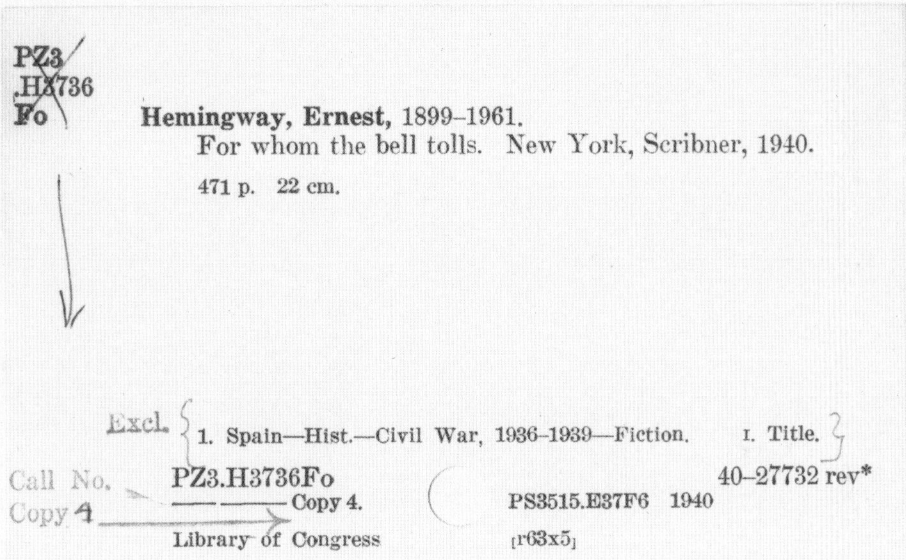

PZ3
.H3736
Fo

Hemingway, Ernest, 1899–1961.
For whom the bell tolls. New York, Scribner, 1940.
471 p. 22 cm.

Excl. 1. Spain—Hist.—Civil War, 1936–1939—Fiction. I. Title.

Call No. PZ3.H3736Fo 40–27732 rev*
Copy 4 Copy 4. PS3515.E37F6 1940
Library of Congress [r63x5]

Ernest Hemingway, *For Whom the Bell Tolls*. New York, Scribner, 1940.

Ernest Hemingway posed with Capt. Joe Russell of Key West beside hanging marlin or sail-fish, probably in Florida, circa 1930s.

A TREE GROWS IN BROOKLYN
A NOVEL
by BETTY SMITH
HARPER & BROTHERS · ESTABLISHED 1817

~~PZ3~~
~~.S64335~~ **Smith, Betty**, 1904-
~~Tr~~ A tree grows in Brooklyn, a novel by Betty Smith. New
PS3537 York, London, Harper & brothers [1943]
.M2895T7 3 p. l., 3-443, [1] p. 21 cm.
1943 "First edition."
copy 7
Finkel-
stein
Coll.

I. Title.

PZ3.S64335 Tr 43-12149
MARC

Library of Congress

Betty Smith, *A Tree Grows in Brooklyn*. New York, London, Harper & Brothers, 1943.

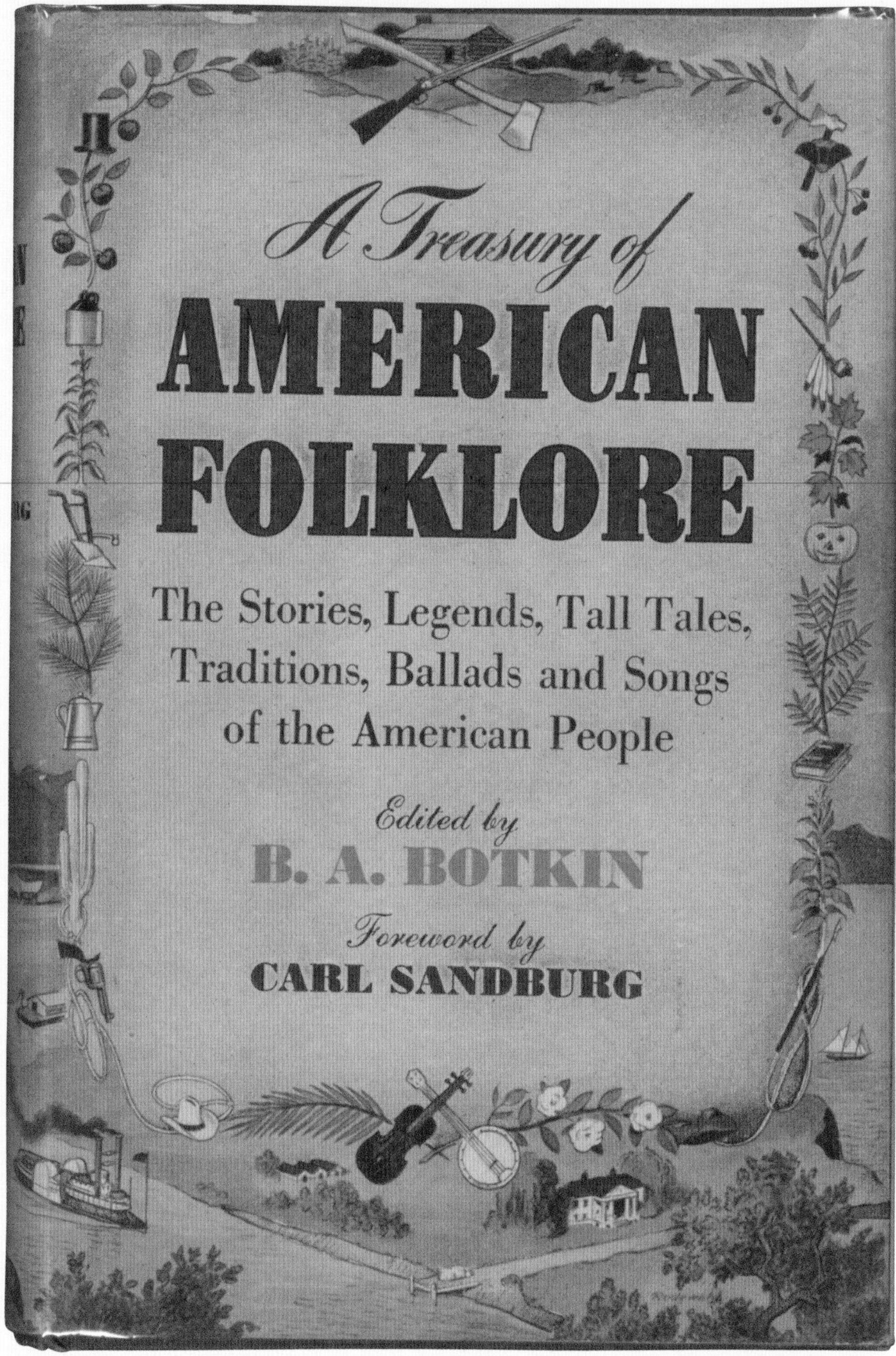
A Treasury of
AMERICAN
FOLKLORE
The Stories, Legends, Tall Tales, Traditions, Ballads and Songs of the American People
Edited by
B. A. BOTKIN
Foreword by
CARL SANDBURG

Botkin, Benjamin Albert, 1901- *comp.* Anglo-American ballads. [*Phonodisc*] (Card 2)

CONTENTS.—The golden willow tree.—The rambling boy.—The two brothers.—The four Marys.—The two sisters.—Lord Thomas and fair Ellender.—Bolakins (Lamkin).—The three babes.—Sanford Parney.—Claude Allen.

1. Ballads, American. 2. Folk-songs, American. I. U. S. Library of Congress. Archive of American Folk Song. II. U. S. Library of Congress. Recording Laboratory. III. Title. (Series)

R 53-567 rev

Library of Congress [r68d2]

B. A. Botkin, editor, *A Treasury of American Folklore: The Stories, Legends, Tall Tales, Traditions, Ballads and Songs of the American People*, illustrations by Andrew Wyeth. New York, Crown Publishers, 1944.

Botkin was a pioneering folklorist, and according to historian Jerrold Hirsch, "He attempted to formulate an approach to the study of American folklore that took into account the nation's different regions, races and classes and showed the interrelationship between folk, popular and high culture." He was head of the Library of Congress's Archive of American Folksong between 1943 and 1945 and previously served as national folklore editor of the Federal Writers' Project (1938-1939), a program of President Franklin Roosevelt's New Deal during the Depression.

This card is for a vinyl record edited by Botkin that was recorded in Kentucky, North Carolina, and Virginia by noted folklorist Alan Lomax.

The Member
OF THE
Wedding
Carson McCullers

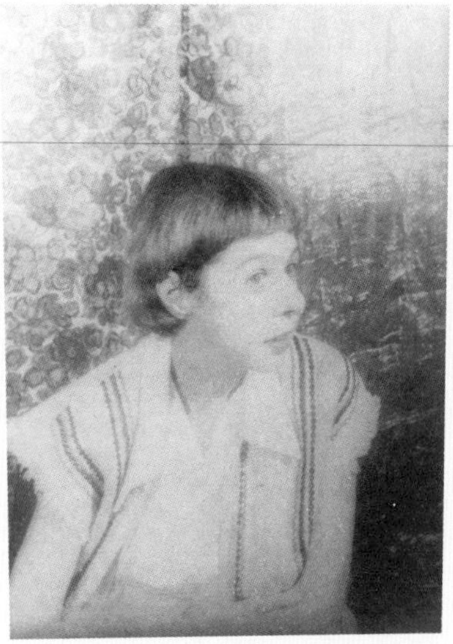

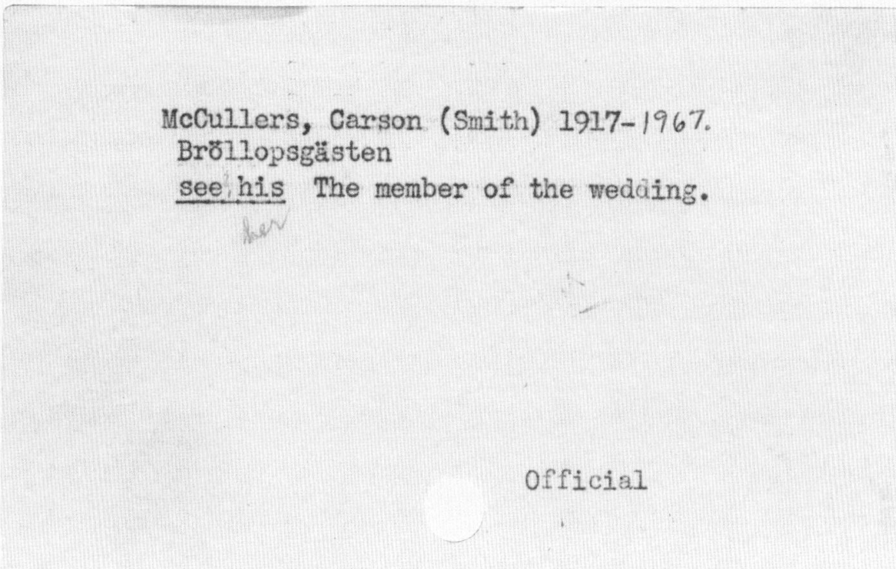
McCullers, Carson (Smith) 1917-1967.
Bröllopsgästen
see his The member of the wedding.
her

Official

Carson McCullers, *The Member of the Wedding*. Boston, Houghton Mifflin Co., 1946.

Photograph by Carl Van Vechten, 1959.

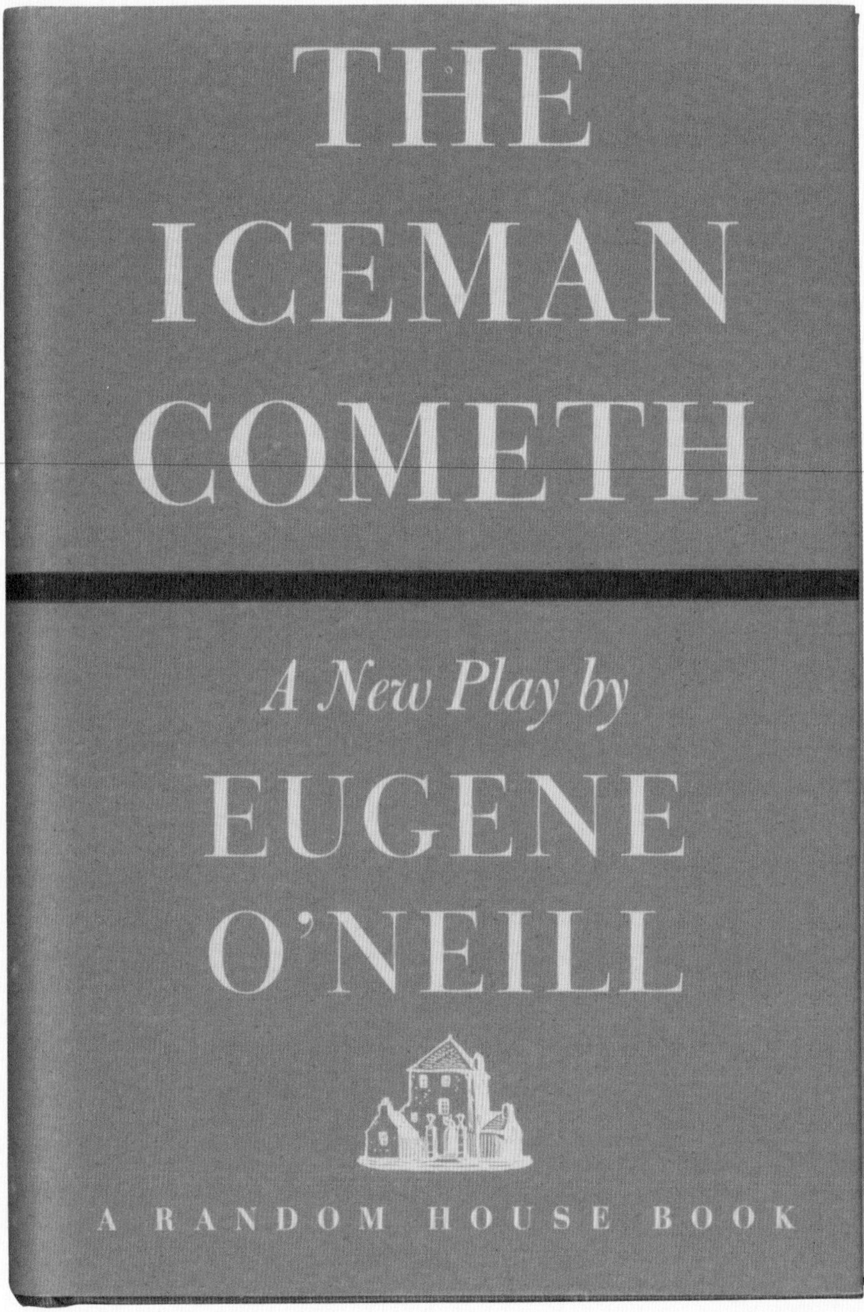
THE
ICEMAN
COMETH
A New Play by
EUGENE
O'NEILL
A RANDOM HOUSE BOOK

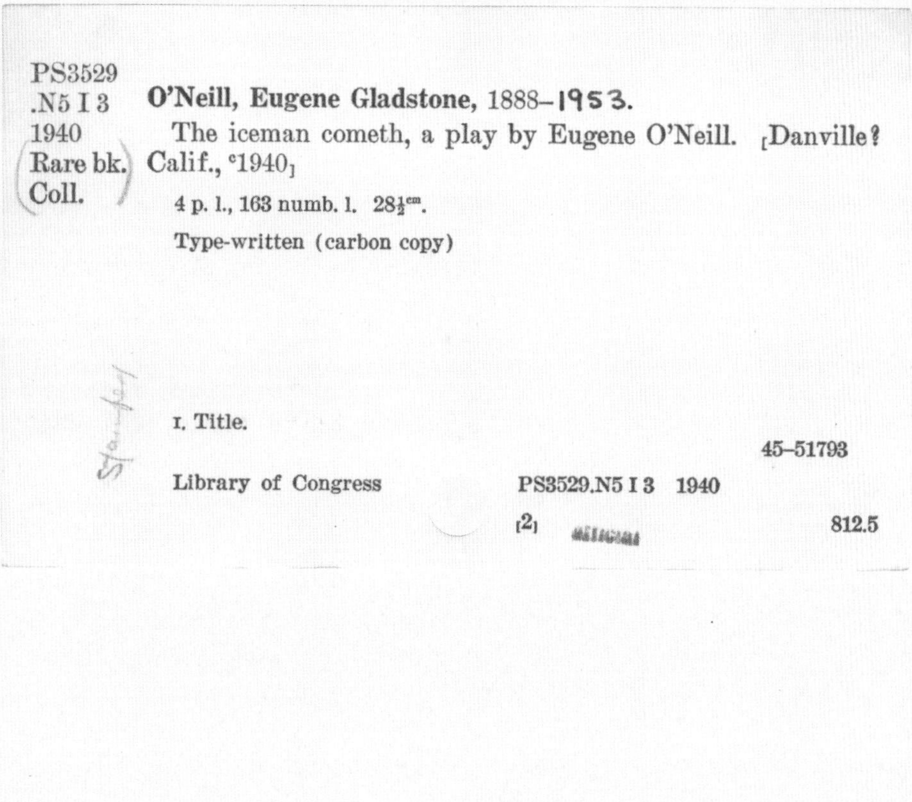

PS3529
.N5 I 3 **O'Neill, Eugene Gladstone,** 1888–1953.
1940 The iceman cometh, a play by Eugene O'Neill. [Danville?
(Rare bk. Calif., ©1940]
Coll.)

4 p. l., 163 numb. l. 28½cm.

Type-written (carbon copy)

I. Title.

45-51793

Library of Congress PS3529.N5 I 3 1940

[2] 812.5

Eugene O'Neill, *The Iceman Cometh.* New York, Random House, 1940.

There was an Old Person of Cromer, who stood on one leg to read Homer,
When he found he grew stiff he jumped over the cliff,
Which concluded that person of Cromer.
63

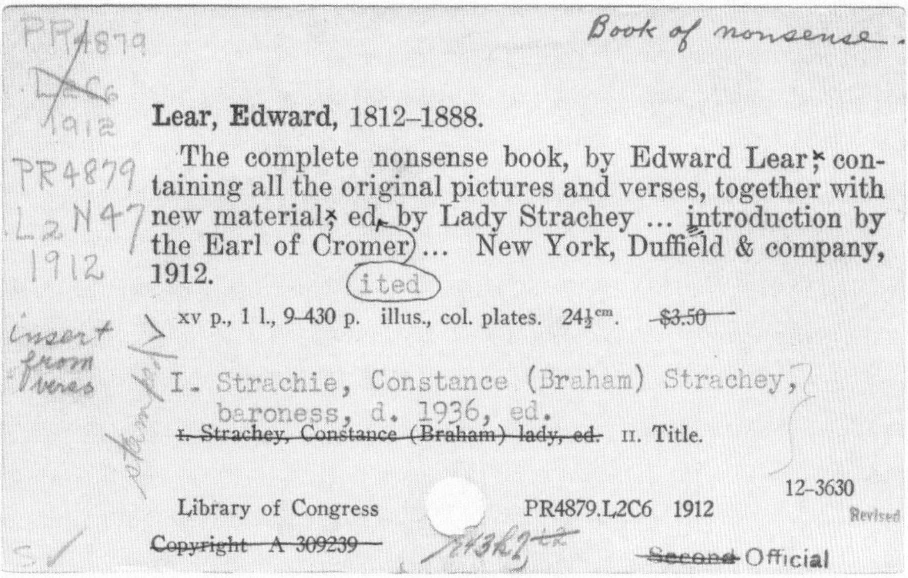

Book of nonsense.

~~PR4879 L2C6 1912~~

PR4879 .L2N47 1912

Lear, Edward, 1812–1888.

The complete nonsense book, by Edward Lear; containing all the original pictures and verses, together with new material; ed. by Lady Strachey ... introduction by the Earl of Cromer ... New York, Duffield & company, 1912.

(ited)

insert from verso

xv p., 1 l., 9–430 p. illus., col. plates. 24½cm. ~~$3.50~~

I. Strachie, Constance (Braham) Strachey, baroness, d. 1936, ed.

~~I. Strachey, Constance (Braham) lady, ed.~~ II. Title.

12–3630

Library of Congress PR4879.L2C6 1912 Revised

~~Copyright A 309239~~ ~~Second~~ Official

Edward Lear, *A Book of Nonsense. 1866.*

This card is for a later edition of Lear's popular children's book filled with his limericks, rhymes, and humorous illustrations.

The Catcher in the Rye
J. D. SALINGER

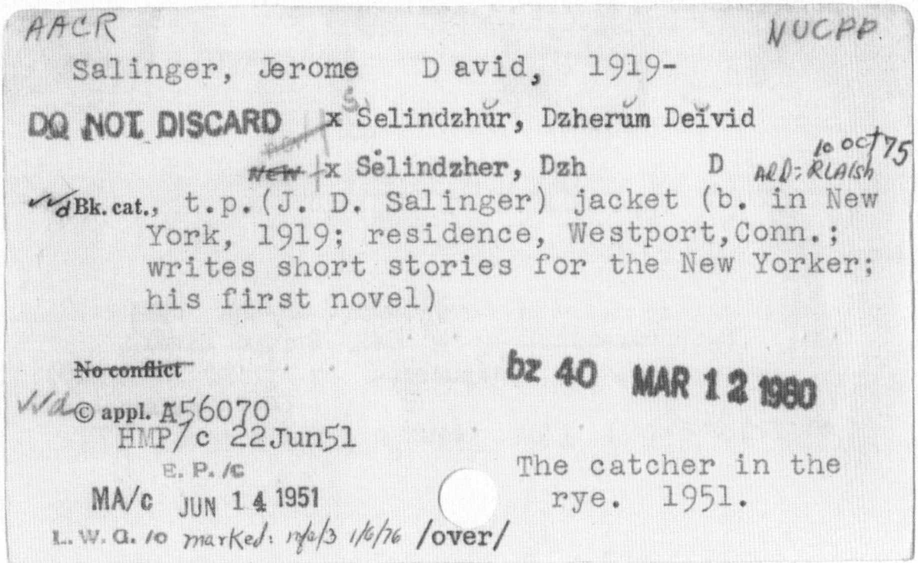
AACR NUCPP

Salinger, Jerome David, 1919-

DO NOT DISCARD x Selindzhur, Dzherum Deivid

~~New~~ x Selindzher, Dzh D 10 oct 75 ARD: RLAish

Bk. cat., t.p. (J. D. Salinger) jacket (b. in New York, 1919; residence, Westport, Conn.; writes short stories for the New Yorker; his first novel)

~~No conflict~~ bz 40 MAR 12 1980

© appl. A56070
HMP/c 22Jun51
E. P. /c
MA/c JUN 14 1951

The catcher in the rye. 1951.

L. W. Q. 10 marked: 1/6/76 /over/

J. D. Salinger, *The Catcher in the Rye*. London, Hamish Hamilton, 1951.

INVISIBLE
MAN
A NOVEL
BY RALPH ELLISON
A RANDOM HOUSE BOOK

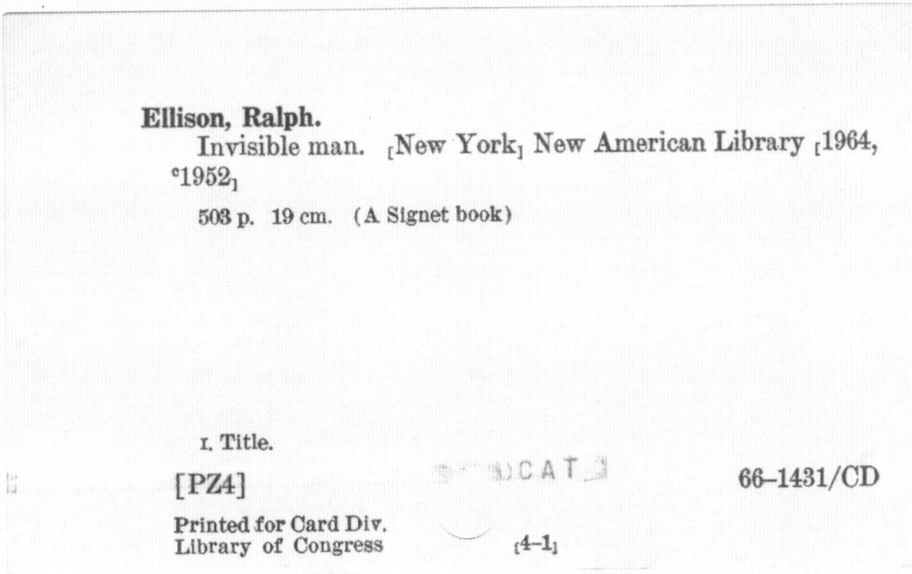
Ellison, Ralph.
Invisible man. [New York] New American Library [1964, ©1952]
503 p. 19 cm. (A Signet book)

I. Title.

[PZ4] 66–1431/CD

Printed for Card Div.
Library of Congress [4–1]

Ralph Ellison, *Invisible Man: A Novel*. New York, Random House, 1952.

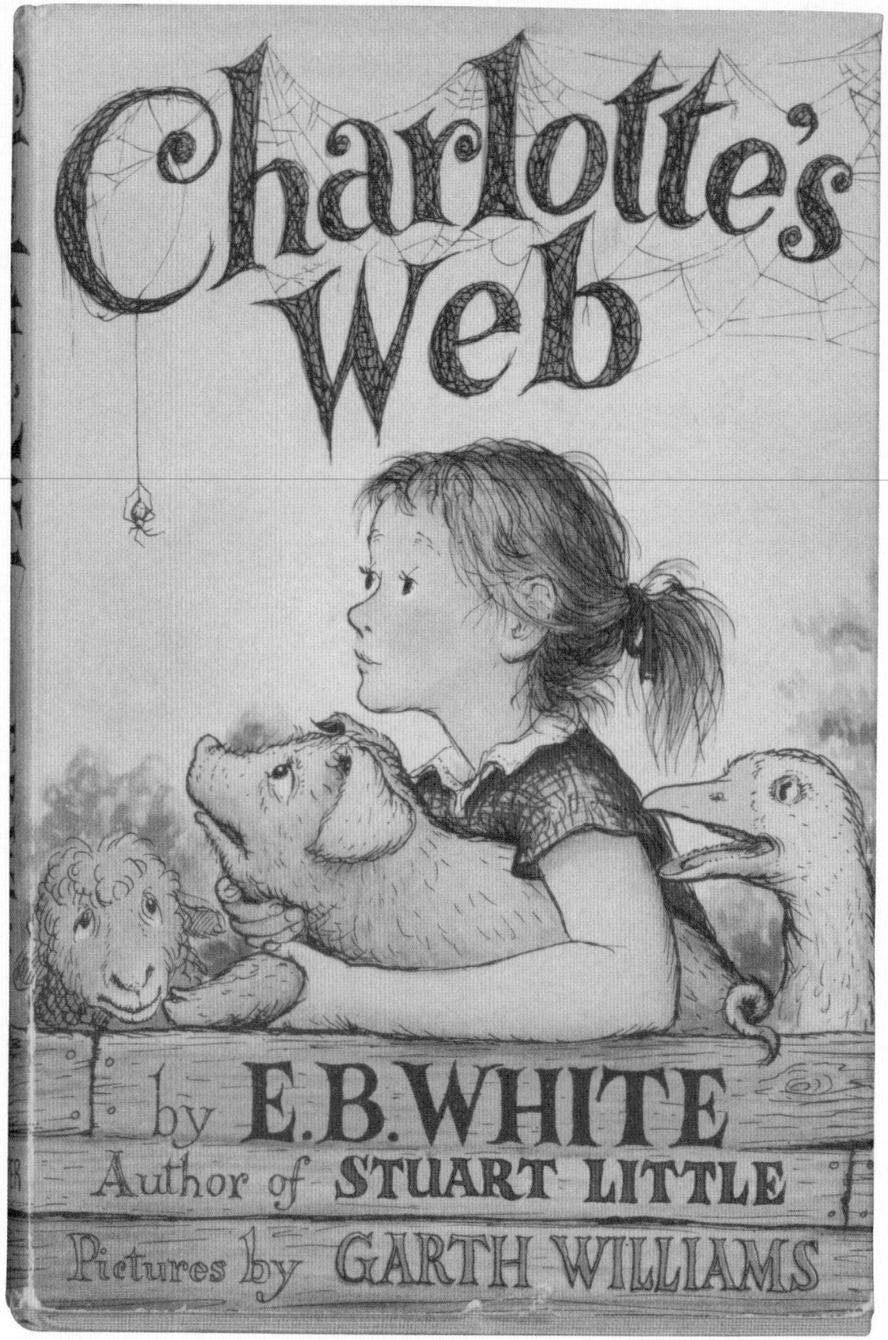
Charlotte's Web
by E.B. WHITE
Author of STUART LITTLE
Pictures by GARTH WILLIAMS

PZ 7
.W58277 **White, Elwyn Brooks,** 1899–
Ch
copy 2
Juv. coll.
Rare Books
Division

Charlotte's web. Pictures by Garth Williams. [1st ed.] New York, Harper [1952]

184 p. illus. 21 cm.

I. Title.

PZ7.W58277Ch 52–9760 ‡

Library of Congress [10]

E. B. White, *Charlotte's Web*, illustrations by Garth Williams. New York, Harper, 1952.

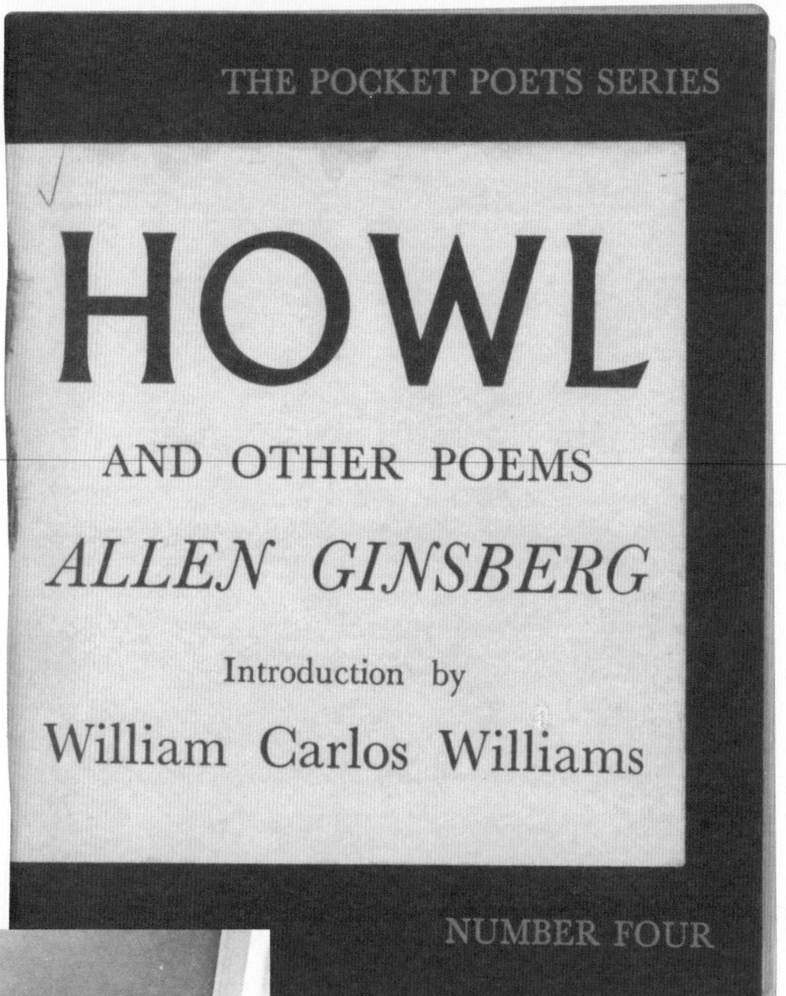
THE POCKET POETS SERIES
HOWL
AND OTHER POEMS
ALLEN GINSBERG
Introduction by
William Carlos Williams
NUMBER FOUR

PS3513
.I74H6
Rare Bk Coll

Ginsberg, Allen, 1926-

Howl, and other poems. San Francisco, City Lights Pocket Bookshop [1956]

44 p. 16 cm. (The Pocket poets series, no. 4)

Rare Bk Coll

---- ------Copy 2.

I. Title.

PS3513.I74H6 811.5 56-8587

MARC

Library of Congress Lim

Allen Ginsberg, *Howl and Other Poems.* San Francisco, City Lights Pocket Bookshop, 1956.

Bob Dylan with guitar and Allen Ginsberg. Photograph by Douglas R. Gilbert, June 15, 1964.

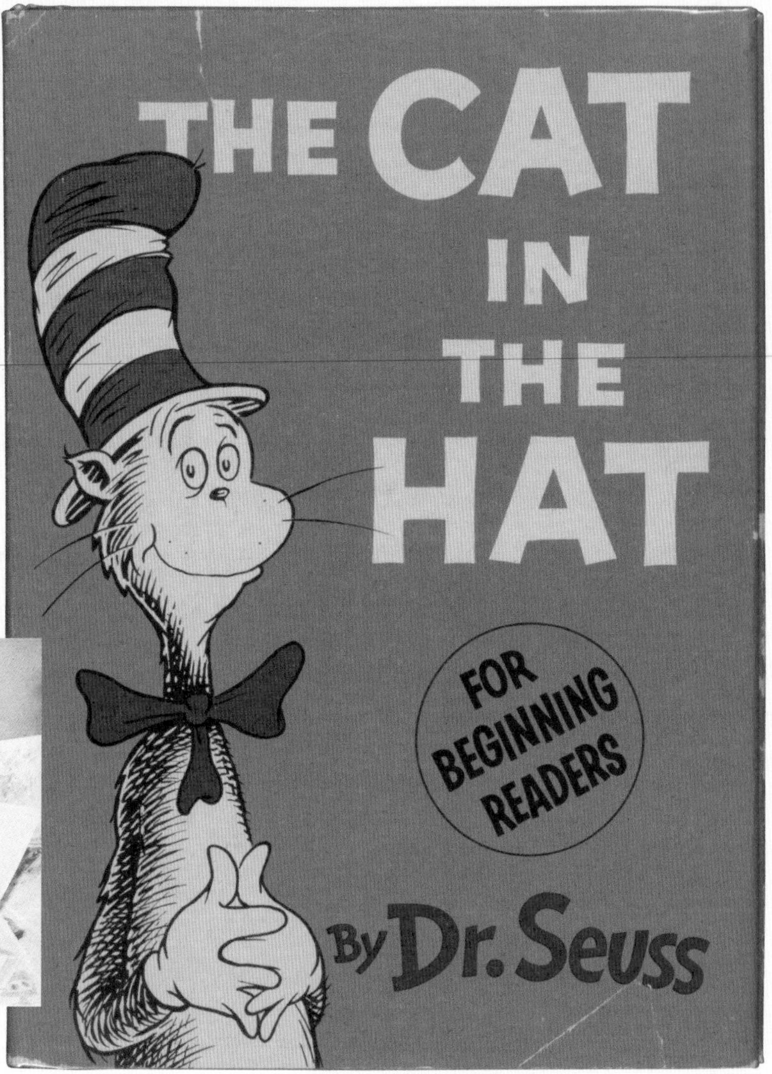
THE CAT
IN
THE
HAT
FOR BEGINNING READERS
By Dr. Seuss

Geisel, Theodor Seuss, 1904-

see also

Seuss, Dr.

Theodor Geisel ("Dr. Seuss"), *The Cat in the Hat*. New York, Random House, 1957.

Dr. Seuss (Theodor Geisel) at work on a drawing of the Grinch. Al Ravenna, photographer for *World Telegram & Sun*, 1957.

a novel
by Jack Kerouac
ON THE ROAD

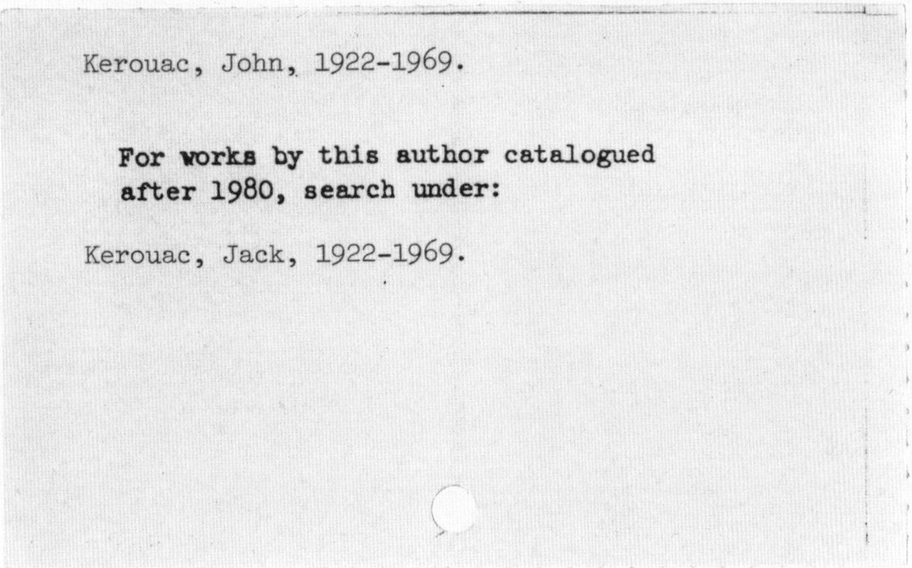

Kerouac, John, 1922-1969.

For works by this author catalogued after 1980, search under:

Kerouac, Jack, 1922-1969.

Jack Kerouac, *On the Road*. New York, Viking Press, 1957.

TO KILL A
Mockingbird
A NOVEL BY
HARPER LEE

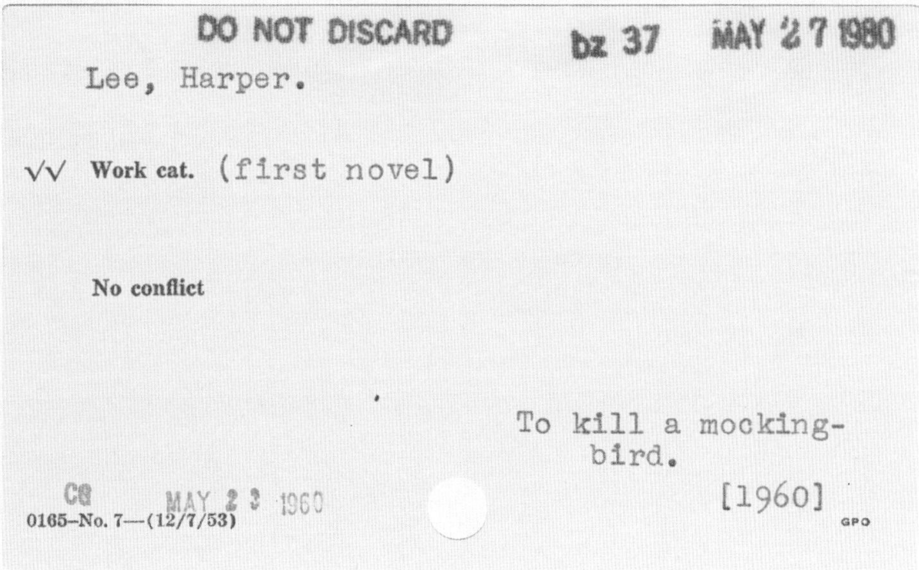

DO NOT DISCARD   bz 37   MAY 27 1980

Lee, Harper.

√√ **Work cat.** (first novel)

No conflict

To kill a mocking-
bird.

[1960]

CG   MAY 23 1960
0165–No. 7—(12/7/53)   GPO

Harper Lee, *To Kill a Mockingbird*. Philadelphia & New York, J. B. Lippincott Co., 1960.

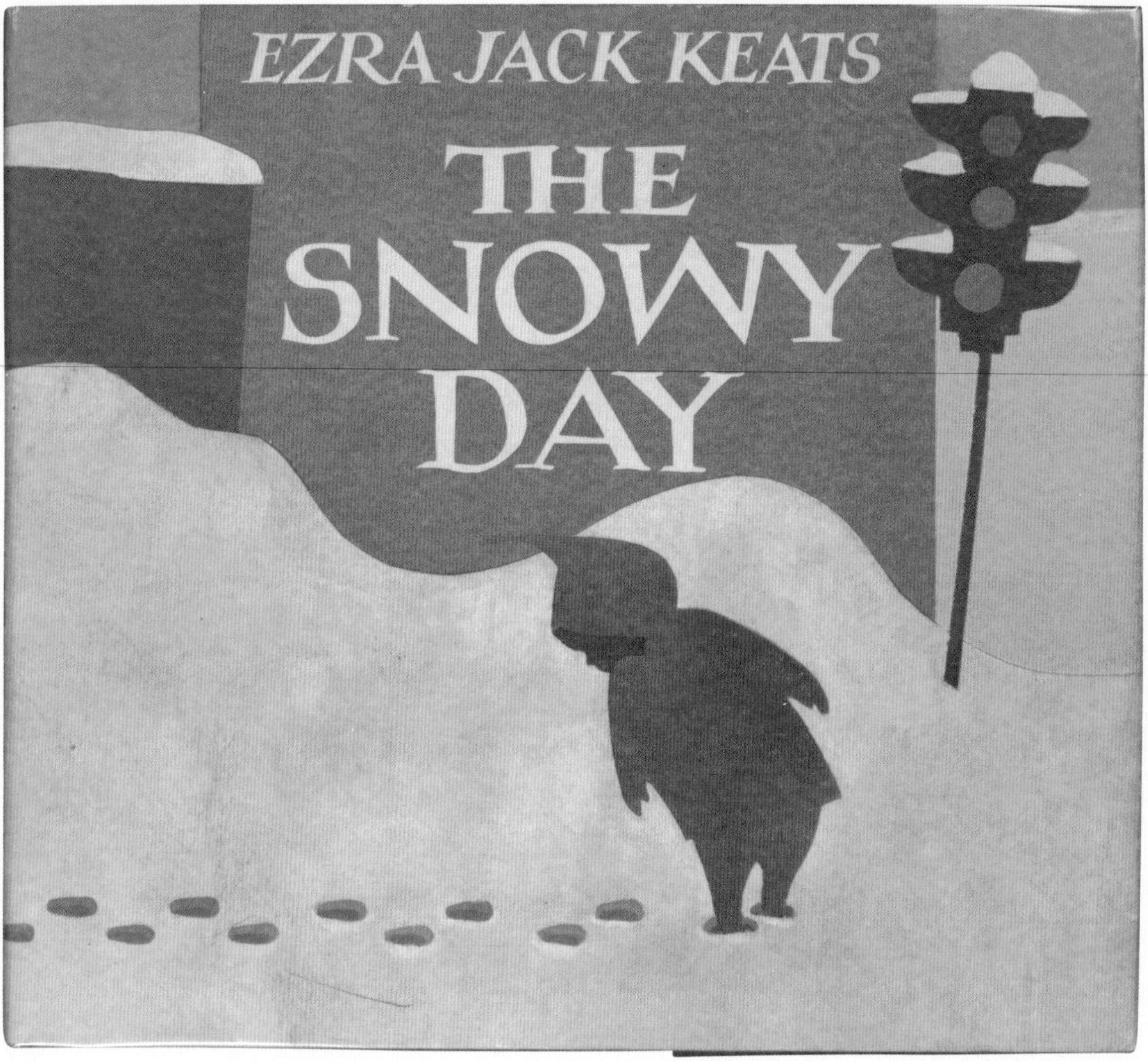
EZRA JACK KEATS
THE SNOWY DAY

PZ7
.K2253
Sn
Copy 2
Juv.
Coll.
1962

Keats, Ezra Jack.
The snowy day. New York, Viking Press [1962]
32 p. illus. 21 x 24 cm.

I. Title.

PZ7.K2253Sn 62—15441 ‡

Library of Congress [a63f7]

Ezra Jack Keats, *The Snowy Day*.
New York, Viking Press, 1962.

WHERE THE WILD THINGS ARE
STORY AND PICTURES BY MAURICE SENDAK
HARPER

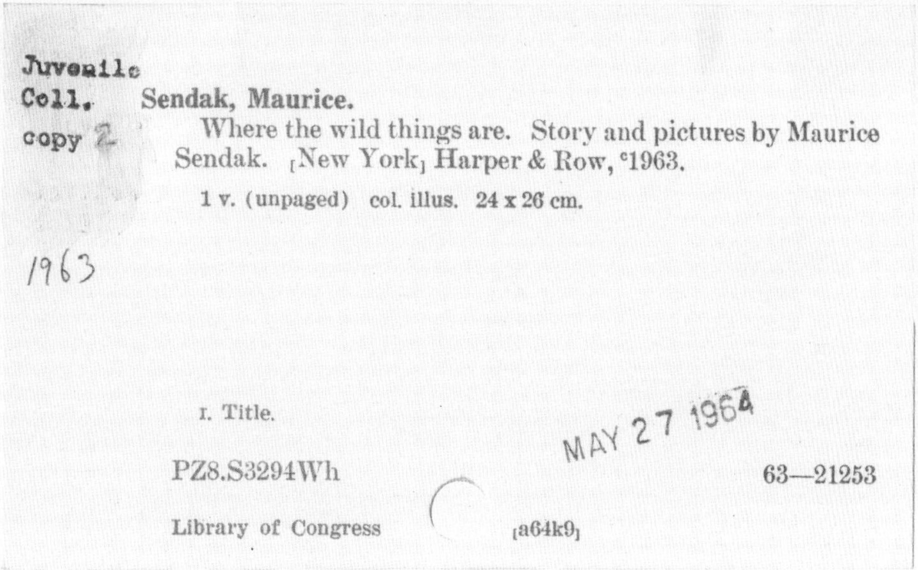

Juvenile
Coll. Sendak, Maurice.
copy 2 Where the wild things are. Story and pictures by Maurice Sendak. [New York] Harper & Row, c1963.

1 v. (unpaged) col. illus. 24 x 26 cm.

1963

I. Title.

MAY 27 1964

PZ8.S3294Wh 63—21253

Library of Congress [a64k9]

Maurice Sendak, *Where the Wild Things Are*. New York, Harper & Row, 1963.

The Fire
Next
Time
James
Baldwin

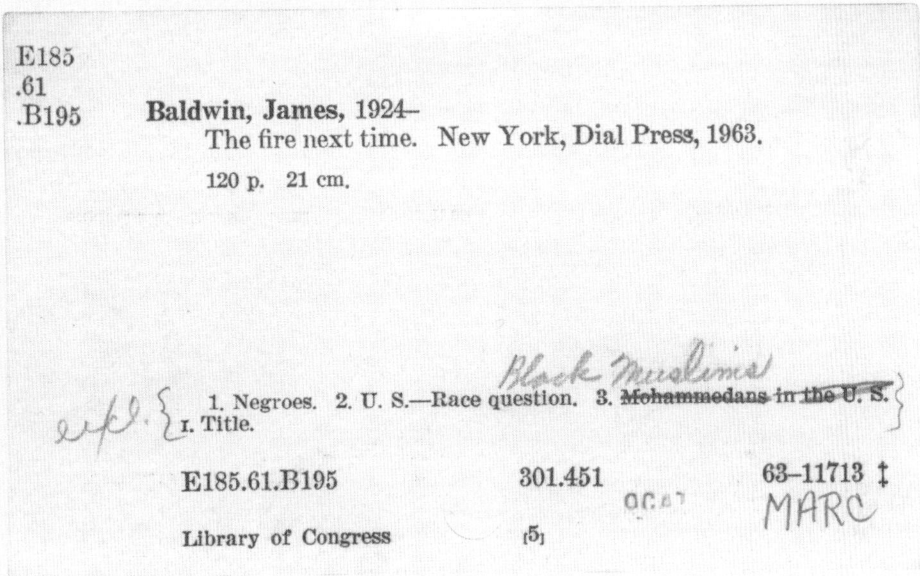

E185
.61
.B195 **Baldwin, James, 1924–**
The fire next time. New York, Dial Press, 1963.

120 p. 21 cm.

expl. { 1. Negroes. 2. U. S.—Race question. 3. ~~Mohammedans in the U. S.~~ Black Muslims }
{ I. Title.

E185.61.B195 301.451 63–11713 ‡

OC.A7 MARC

Library of Congress [5]

James Baldwin, *The Fire Next Time*. New York, Dial Press, 1963.

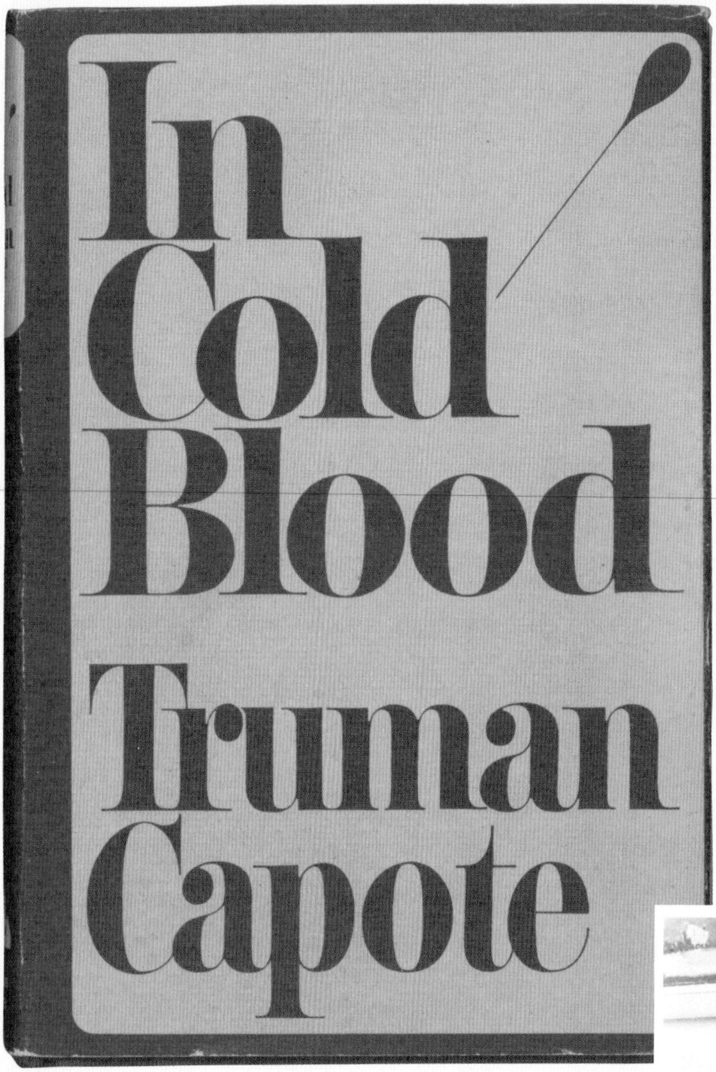
In
Cold
Blood
Truman
Capote

Truman Capote in an informal moment during the filming of a program about him for National Educational Television's "U.S.A.: The Novel." The program airs ______ at ______ on Channel ______. (Photograph by Bruce Davidson).

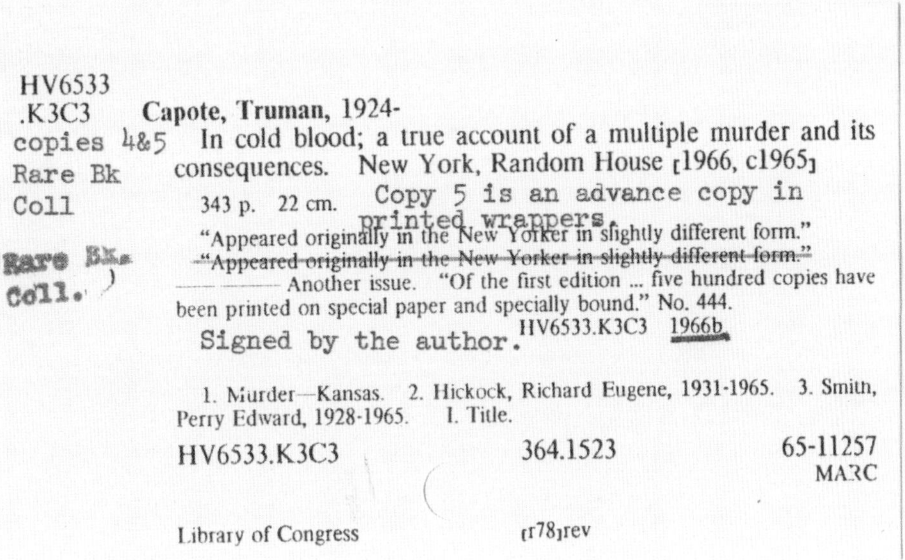

HV6533
.K3C3 **Capote, Truman, 1924-**
copies 4&5 In cold blood; a true account of a multiple murder and its
Rare Bk consequences. New York, Random House [1966, c1965]
Coll 343 p. 22 cm. Copy 5 is an advance copy in printed wrappers.
"Appeared originally in the New Yorker in slightly different form."
~~"Appeared originally in the New Yorker in slightly different form."~~
Rare Bk. Coll. ——— Another issue. "Of the first edition ... five hundred copies have been printed on special paper and specially bound." No. 444.
Signed by the author. HV6533.K3C3 1966b

1. Murder—Kansas. 2. Hickock, Richard Eugene, 1931-1965. 3. Smith, Perry Edward, 1928-1965. I. Title.

HV6533.K3C3 364.1523 65-11257
MARC

Library of Congress [r78]rev

Truman Capote, *In Cold Blood*.
New York, Random House, 1965.

Truman Capote holding first edition, Bruce Davidson photographer, 1966.

BURY MY HEART AT WOUNDED KNEE
An Indian History of the American West
by DEE BROWN
HOLT, RINEHART & WINSTON
New York Chicago San Francisco

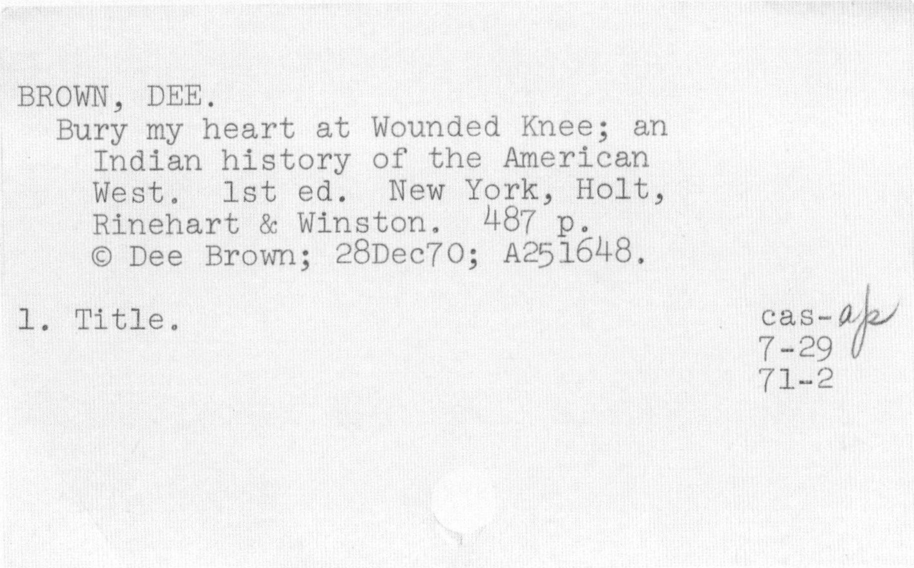
BROWN, DEE.
Bury my heart at Wounded Knee; an Indian history of the American West. 1st ed. New York, Holt, Rinehart & Winston. 487 p.
© Dee Brown; 28Dec70; A251648.

1. Title.

cas-ap
7-29
71-2

Dee Brown, *Bury My Heart at Wounded Knee.* New York, Holt, Rinehart & Winston, 1970.

Acknowledgments

Many of the talented people working at the Library of Congress helped me in the completion of this book. First and foremost I would like to thank my colleagues in the Library's Publishing Office for their constant encouragement, steadfast support, and diligent editing: Becky Brasington Clark, Peggy Wagner, Susan Reyburn, Athena Angelos, Aimee Hess, and Jake Jacobs. Additional thanks to Keith Shovlin and interns Ashley Thieme and Lea Harrison.

Thanks to all the curators and librarians who assisted me in navigating the collections at the Library. In particular, I'm grateful for the help I received from Mark Dimunation, Eric Frazier, Maphon Ashmon, and Jamie Roberts in the Rare Books and Special Collection Division; Cheryl Fox, Jeff Flannery, Lewis Wyman, and Bruce Kirby in the Manuscripts Division; and Kristi Finefield in the Prints and Photographs Division.

For the wonderful photographs of the Library and its collections I would like to acknowledge Shawn Miller, Domenic Sergi, Chris Pohlhaus, Jade Curtis, Ronnie Hawkins, Mark Manivong, Alan Haley, and Cheryl Regan.

John Y. Cole and Thomas Mann shared their vast knowledge of the Library's history with me and were forthcoming with advice throughout the writing of this book.

And special thanks to our partners at Chronicle Books: Rachel Hiles, who managed the project; Brooke Johnson for the design; and Christina Amini for her vision and enthusiasm early on in making this book possible.

Above all, a debt of gratitude is owed to the legions of nameless Library staff from the old Card and Cataloging Divisions whose painstaking efforts created the catalog cards featured in this book.

—PETER DEVEREAUX

Select Bibliography

Battles, Matthew. *Library: An Unquiet History*. New York: W. W. Norton, 2003.

Cole, John Y. *For Congress and the Nation: A Chronological History of the Library of Congress*. Washington, D.C.: Library of Congress, 1979.

Edlund, Paul. *A Monster and a Miracle: The Cataloging Distribution Service of the Library of Congress, 1901–1976*. Reprinted from the October 1976 issue of *The Quarterly Journal of The Library of Congress*. Washington, D.C.: Library of Congress, 1978.

Goodrum, Charles A., and Helen W. Dalrymple. *The Library of Congress, Second Edition*. Boulder: Westview Press, 1982.

Johnston, William Dawson. *History of the Library of Congress: Volume I, 1800–1864*. Washington, D.C.: Library of Congress, 1904.

Krajewski, Markus. *Paper Machines: About Cards & Catalogs, 1548–1929*. Translated by Peter Krapp. Cambridge: MIT Press, 2011.

Mearns, David C. *The Story Up to Now: The Library of Congress, 1800–1946*. Washington, D.C.: Library of Congress, 1947.

Ostrowski, Carl. *Books, Maps, and Politics: A Cultural History of the Library of Congress, 1783–1861*. Amherst: University of Massachusetts Press, 2004.

Rosenberg, Jane Aikin. *The Nation's Great Library: Herbert Putnam and the Library of Congress, 1899–1939*. Chicago: University of Illinois Press, 1993.

Wright, Alex. *Cataloging the World: Paul Otlet and the Birth of the Information Age*. New York: Oxford University Press, 2014.

Image Credits

The images are from the collection of the Library of Congress. The following list provides the reproduction numbers of those images from the Library's Prints and Photograph Division or notes the custodial division it is from. The images of book covers and interiors are from the Library's Rare Book and Special Collections Division unless otherwise noted.

Front Matter
1: LC-USZ62-100400; 8: LC-USP6-2891-A

Chapter 1
10, 11: LC-DIG-ds-06510; 12: African and Middle Eastern Division; 13: General Collections; 15: LC-USZ62-76398; 16: African and Middle Eastern Division; 18: LC-USZ62-104445; 19: Rare Book and Special Collections Division; 28: Asian Division

Chapter 2
44, 45: Manuscript Division; 47: LC-DIG-ppmsca-22593; 48: Rare Book and Special Collections Division; 49: LC-DIG-ppmsca-23076; 51: Manuscript Division

Chapter 3
80-81: General Collections; 82: LC-USZ62-128407; 83: LC-DIG-pga-07839; 84: LC-USZ62-40188; 85: General Collections; 86: General Collections; 96: LC-USZ62-90564

Chapter 4
100, 101: LC-USZ62-118630; 102: LC-USZ62-44185; 103: LC-DIG-ppmsca-17588; 104: LC-USZ62-1819; 105: Top, Middle; General Collection. Bottom; LC-DIG-ds-03840; 106: LC-USZC4-12221; 107: LC-USZ62-38245; 108: LC-USZ62-6012; 109: LC-USZ62-88135; 110: Left; LC-USZ62-59880 Right; LC-USZ62-118629; 111: General Collections; 112: LC-USZ62-118631; 114: LC-DIG-cwpbh-05089; 116: LC-USZC4-1298; 120: Left; LC-USZ62-112065 Right; Manuscript Division; 124: Left; Manuscript Division Right; LC-DIG-cwpbh-00752; 132: LC-DIG-ggbain-00675; 134: Top, Middle; LC-USZC4-1950 Bottom, Middle; LC-USZC2-3784 Right; LC-DIG-ppmsca-23992; 138: LC-USZ62-94310; 142: Top; LC-DIG-ppprs-00626 Bottom; LC-USZ62-127779

Chapter 5
144, 145: Manuscript Division; 146: LC-USZ62-60729; 147: Rare Book and Special Collections Division; 149: LC-DIG-ppmsca-31614; 150: LC-USZ62-92411; 151: Top; Manuscript Division Bottom; LC-DIG-hec-29778; 153: Manuscript Division; 154: LC-DIG-ppmsca-15424; 159: LC-USP6-9814-36; 162: LC-USZ62-123822; 164: LC-DIG-ds-05209; 180: LC-DIG-highsm-24208; 182: LC-USZ62-112318; 184: LC-USZ62-102481; 190: LC-USZ62-130115; 202: LOOK - Job 64-1887, frame 2; 204: LC-USZ62-124309; 216: LC-USZ62-119331

Index

LEONARDO

Maria Costantino

PRC

This edition first published in 2001 by
PRC Publishing
The Chrysalis Building
Bramley Road, London W10 6SP

An imprint of Chrysalis Books Group plc

ISBN 1 85648 677 X

Printed and bound in China

PAGE 1: *Self-Portrait,* c.1516, Palazzo Reale, Turin.

PAGE 2: *Mona Lisa,* detail, c.1505-13, Musée du Louvre, Paris.

BELOW: *A Long-stemmed Plant,* c.1505-08, pen and ink over black chalk, 8⅝ × 9 inches, (21.2 × 23 cm), Windsor Castle, Royal Library 12429. © 1994 Her Majesty The Queen.

Contents

CHAPTER 1

Florence, 1452–82

Despite the fact that only about a dozen paintings can be attributed to him with any certainty, Leonardo da Vinci is remembered as one of the greatest artists of the Renaissance. Much of what has been written about Leonardo stemmed initially from the writings of Giorgio Vasari (1511-74), whose *Le Vite dei pittori, sculteri et architetti italiani* was written some fifty years after Leonardo's death. Vasari began his biography by saying:

> Occasionally heaven sends us someone
> who is not only human but divine . . .

Subsequent biographies, particularly those written in the nineteenth-century milieu of Romanticism, or following Freudian psychoanalytical tendencies in the twentieth century, have all added to the 'legend' of Leonardo. In his own time Leonardo was appreciated by a mere handful of his contemporaries.

In 1452, in a small village called Anchiano near to the Tuscan town of Vinci, Leonardo was born to Ser Piero – the 'Ser' before his name denoted the traditional family occupation of notary – and a woman variously called Chateria or Caterina. Caterina's origins are unclear but she seems to have been regarded in rather a low light; in the same year that Leonardo was born, his father married another woman, Albiera di Giovanni Amadori. Ser Piero was in fact to marry four times, and had eleven other children by his third and fourth wives. By the time these children were born, Leonardo was already in his early twenties. In the municipal archive in Florence the documentary evidence (discovered only in 1930 by Emil Moeller) of Leonardo's birth reads: 'Born a grandson, son of Ser Piero, my son on the 15th of April.' This notice was written by grandfather Antonio and confirmed that Leonardo was accepted as a member of the family. The entry continues with a list of the people present at Leonardo's baptism, evidence that he was also accepted by the community as a Christian and a member of the Catholic Church. It has been said that Antonio hedged his bets: many of those present at the baptism were either tenants on his land or in some way in debt to him.

Nevertheless Leonardo was brought up by his mother Caterina for the first four years of his life, until she herself married a local man, Attacabrigi di Piero del Vacca, who was by trade a kiln builder. Leonardo then moved into the grander house in Vinci belonging to his father, where he grew up as an only child since his father's first two wives bore him no children. These facts have been deduced by historians from the fact that grandfather Antonio first registered Leonardo as a dependent living with the family in his income tax return for 1457.

Antonio died in 1469, when Leonardo was aged about 16 or 17, and the family moved to another house in Vinci. They also rented the ground floor of a house in the Piazza di San Firenze, close to the Bargello, or prison, in Florence. Leonardo's father was now notary to the Signoria, the ruling council of Florence. According to Vasari, it was because Ser Piero was a friend of Andrea di Cione, better known to us as Andrea del Verrocchio (c.1435-88), that Leonardo entered his studio. Verrocchio was Florence's leading painter, goldsmith and sculptor, famed for his exquisite craftsmanship.

It was the usual practice at this time for boys to be appointed to a *bottegha* or workshop after their preliminary schooling had been completed around the age of 13. Apprenticeships lasted around six years with the newcomer progressing from pupil, cleaning brushes, preparing pigments and generally fetching and carrying, to assistant, who had learnt all the techniques and tricks of the trade from his master and was able to take a hand in painting commissions where the contract between the master and client allowed.

LEFT: *Baptism of Christ*, detail of an angel's head, believed to be by Leonardo, Andrea del Verrocchio, c.1473-78, Galleria degli Uffizi, Florence.

ABOVE: Lorenzo di Credi (1459-1537), *Adoration of the Shepherds*, oil on wood, 88⅙ × 77⅙ inches (224 × 196 cm), Galleria dègli Uffizi, Florence. A pupil in Verrochio's workshop at the same time as Leonardo, Lorenzo's style follows very closely that of his master.

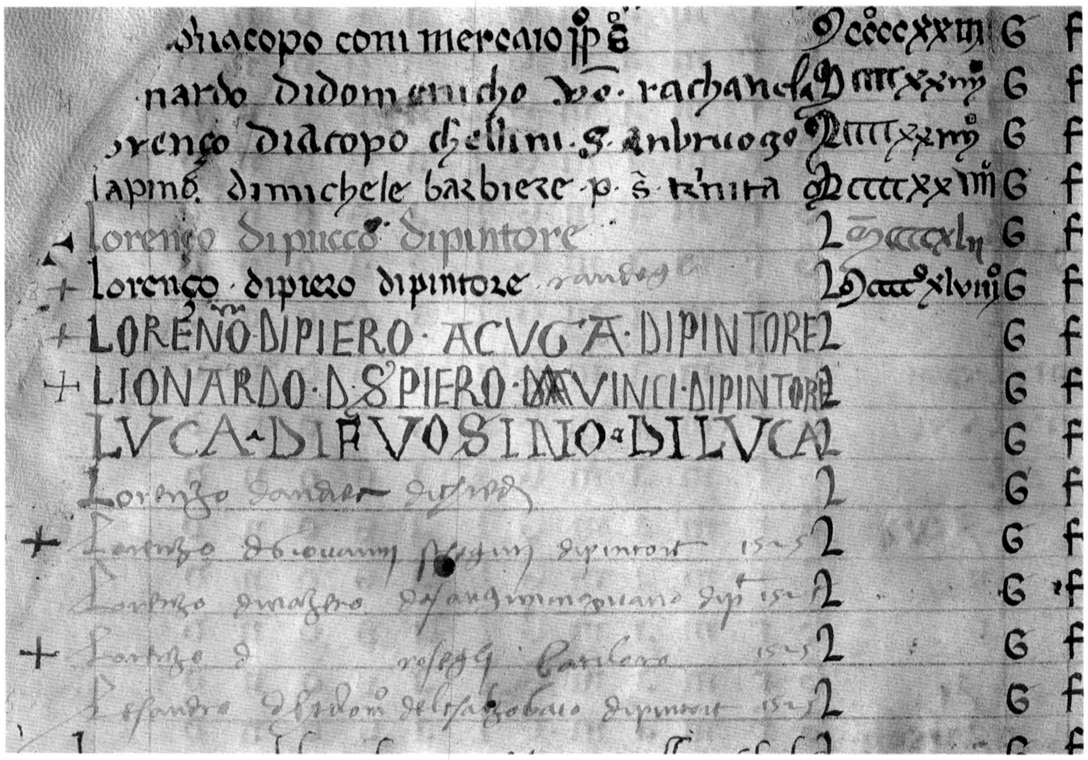

RIGHT: Leonardo's registration as a painter with the Guild of St. Luke, recorded in 1472.

Legend would have it that Leonardo was some 'boy-genius'. In fact, however, his schooling was modest and he was largely self-taught. He himself was acutely aware that he was 'unlettered': unable, that is, to write in Ciceronian prose, and because of this difficulty with Latin, Leonardo's reading, initially at least, was largely confined to works translated into Tuscan Italian. This deprived him of access to the new Humanistic works written in Latin at the educated courts of Italy. Instead, Leonardo compensated for his academic shortcomings by relying on his own sensory experiences.

Rather than the usual six years in Verrocchio's studio, Leonardo remained with his master for nine years. During the 1470s he would have been training and working alongside a number of other young assistants: Pietro Perugino (c.1450-1523), Lorenzo di Credi (1459-1537), Domenico Ghirlandaio (1449-94), Francesco Botticini (1446-97) and Cosimo Rosselli (1439-1507). Verrocchio's studio in Florence was rivaled in its output and talent only by the bottegha run by the brothers Pietro and Ambrosio Pollaiuolo. In all the studios at this time the atmosphere and methods of production were dominated by a communal spirit. A work of art was not yet regarded as the expression of a single personality, and during this period Verrocchio's workshops turned out a variety of work which Leonardo probably had a hand in producing.

By 1472 Leonardo's name was inscribed on the roll of the Guild of St Luke as a painter: 'Leonardo di Ser Piero da Vinci dipintore.' He was then just 20 years old and, having paid his guild fees, he was entitled to set up his own independent workshop. The guilds acted in a manner similar to trades unions: they were responsible for guidelines for training within each profession, whether law, medicine or the arts. Only when a student had completed the set period for his instruction and had mastered the various skills could he join the guild. Leonardo, however, chose to spend at least four more years with his master, during which time he was responsible for a number of projects. As well as probably taking part in arranging pageants for Lorenzo de' Medici and Giuliano de' Medici in 1469 and 1475, Leonardo was also involved in the arrangements for the festivities to welcome Galeazzo Maria Sforza, Duke of Milan, to Florence in 1471. It is also believed that Leonardo was asked to paint a watercolor cartoon for a tapestry representing the *Fall in Paradise*, to be woven in Flanders as a gift for the King of Portugal. It seems, however, that the tapestry never reached the weaving stage.

In addition to two paintings of the Virgin attributed to Leonardo, the *Benois Madonna* and the *Madonna and Child with a Vase of Flowers*, which are believed to date from this period in Verrocchio's workshop, Leonardo no doubt assisted his master with a number of other works

BELOW: Leonardo's earliest dated drawing, from 5 August 1473, depicts the valley of the Arno. It demonstrates his early interest in the forces of nature and his already accomplished drawing style. Galleria degli Uffizi, Florence.

then in hand: the gilded copper ball for the lantern over the dome of the Cathedral in 1471; the tomb of Piero de' Medici for the sacristy of the Medici church of San Lorenzo in 1472, and the bronze *David* for the town hall in 1476, for which many believe Leonardo was the model. According to Vasari, Leonardo was working with Verrocchio on *The Baptism of Christ* for the church of San Salvi when, as the story goes, Verrocchio saw his young assistant's work and promptly gave up painting because Leonardo was more capable than he was. It is more likely that, in such a busy commercial workshop, the master was able safely to entrust painting commissions to his assistant, while he himself concentrated on the more public and profitable sculptural commissions.

The Baptism of Christ is traditionally accepted as Leonardo's earliest surviving painted work. From the same period (August 1473) is his earliest dated drawing, a landscape depicting the valley of the river Arno. These two works are in fact related: a study of the drawing, particularly the background features of the mountains and lakes with their atmospherically rendered aerial perspective, leaves no doubt that Leonardo was responsible for the background painting in *The Baptism of Christ*. This is especially evident when the background features are compared with other natural features in the painting, such as the palm tree on the left and the rocks in the right foreground, which are painted in a much more conventional manner. Vasari records that Leonardo worked on the painting but, even without documentary evidence, a comparison of the two angels suggests that they were painted by two different hands, and the left-hand one is accepted as by Leonardo. Nevertheless, the monks of San Salvi appear not to have noticed any discernible differences and the painting passed into their hands.

With the *Benois Madonna*, Leonardo found a formula that he was to apply again in the figure of the Virgin in the Louvre *Virgin and Child with St Anne* (page 80) about 30 years later, and that was to be influential on a number of later artists. The Virgin's body is placed in a three-quarter view to the right, with the right leg extended forward and the left bent back to support the figure of the Christ Child. The figures are solidly modeled, as is the drapery which billows

ABOVE: Andrea del Verrocchio (1435-88), *Baptism of Christ* c.1473-78, oil on wood, 69⅝ × 59½ inches (177 × 151 cm), Galleria degli Uffizi, Florence. This work was painted for the monastery of San Salvi. The figure of the left-hand angel is generally accepted as Leonardo's earliest surviving painted work.

LEFT: *Benois Madonna*, c.1478, oil on wood panel, 18⅞ × 12¼ inches (48 × 31 cm), Hermitage Museum, St Petersburg.

ABOVE LEFT: *Madonna and Child with a Cat*, c.1478, pen and ink, 5³⁄₁₆ × 3¾ inches (13.2 × 9.5 cm), Courtesy of the Trustees of the British Museum, London.

ABOVE RIGHT: *Madonna and Child with a Cat*, c.1478, pen, ink and wash, 5³⁄₁₆ × 3¾ inches (13.2 × 9.5 cm), Courtesy of the Trustees of the British Museum, London. These two drawings are the recto and verso of a single sheet of paper. The outline of the right-hand drawing has been pressed through from the left-hand one, using a stylus, and then inked and washed in. These two drawings may have been preparatory studies for the *Benois Madonna*.

out from the Virgin's hips. The overall effect is enhanced by the strong light which falls from the top left to the bottom right across the figures, with a subsidiary soft light brought in from the window in the background. Preliminary drawings – the *Madonna and Child with a Cat* drawings could well be early studies – as well as other drawings of the period show that achieving this sense of volume was one of Leonardo's chief aims.

A second painting, the *Madonna and Child with a Vase of Flowers*, is sometimes associated with the 'finished' Madonna which Leonardo listed as one of his works in an inventory of his possessions in 1482, when he left Florence for Milan. There is, however, no consensus that this painting is in fact by Leonardo. It could be that Leonardo began it but that it was completed by a fellow pupil such as Lorenzo di Credi. As we shall see, it was not unusual for Leonardo to leave works unfinished.

While Leonardo's part in painting the *Baptism of Christ* has been accepted since around 1510, it was only in 1869 that the painting of the *Annunciation* was finally attributed to him. The painting came from the monastery of San Bartolomeo at Monteolivieto near Florence and was originally ascribed to Ghirlandaio, a con-

ABOVE: School of Verrocchio, *Madonna and Child with a Pomegranate*, c.1470-75, oil on wood panel, 6⅛ × 5 inches (15.7 × 12.8 cm), National Gallery of Art, Washington, Samuel R. Kress Collection. Characteristic of the 'Verrocchio style', the Virgin has a calm, static pose and her eyes are downcast. These elements were often copied by Verrocchio's pupils.

RIGHT: *Madonna and Child with a Vase of Flowers*, c.1475, oil on wood panel, 24½ × 18¾ inches (62 × 47.5 cm), Alte Pinakothek, Munich. This painting is sometimes associated with the 'finished' Madonna listed in Leonardo's inventory in 1482. While Leonardo may have begun the painting, Lorenzo di Credi may possibly have completed it.

ABOVE: *Annunciation*, c.1473, oil on wood panel, 38⅜ × 85½ inches (98 × 217 cm), Galleria degli Uffizi, Florence. Now accepted as by Leonardo, this painting was only attributed to him in 1869.

temporary of Leonardo's and a fellow apprentice in Verrocchio's studio. Another theory has it that the *Annunciation* was begun by Ghirlandaio and completed by Leonardo, although this thesis is somewhat contradicted by the existence of a drawing by Leonardo of the right sleeve of the angel, complete with the fluttering ribbon. In addition there are two other drawings which are related, but differ in too many small details for them to be considered as direct studies for the painting. One of these is the finished drawing of *A Lily* such as the one held by the archangel. The other is a study of drapery similar to that worn by the Virgin. The drapery drawing is an example of the studies which Leonardo continued to make throughout his career, and which Vasari describes as having been taken from clay models draped in plaster-soaked cloths.

The subject of the painting is the annunciation to the Virgin by the Angel Gabriel of her unique destiny, as detailed in Luke I, 26-38. The figures are set in the enclosed courtyard garden of a Florentine villa. Again certain features seem to have been drawn from the works of Verrocchio, in particular the base of the lectern, which recalls Verrocchio's decoration of the Medici tomb in San Lorenzo, and the rigid perspective of the building and pavement, which is also to be found in Verrocchio's *Madonna and Child* of 1468, now in the National Gallery of Scotland. The landscape background, however, is Leonardoesque, with its

misty mountains and lakes stretching into infinity. This background looks forward to both the *Madonna of the Rocks* (pages 40, 44) and the *Mona Lisa* (page 97), while the flower-strewn garden is a foretaste of the vegetation in the *Leda* (pages 95-99). The treatment of the plantlife in the *Annunciation* also reflects Leonardo's interest in botany; the inventory of items in his possession which he made around 1482 states that he had drawings of 'many flowers from nature'. It also serves to remind us of the volume of Leonardo's works that have been lost, since the bulk of his surviving botanical studies are related to the years 1508 and after, when he was working on the *Leda* theme.

The *Annunciation* can be dated by Vincian scholars, from the evidence of style and from the style of its associated drawings, to around 1473, and it must be assumed that Leonardo began work on the *Portrait of Ginevra de' Benci* soon after this date. Such portraits of Florentine women were frequently commissioned on the occasion of their marriage, and we know from documentary evidence that Ginevra was married to Luigi di Bernardo Niccolini in January 1474. However doubt has always surrounded this painting, which only came to light in 1733 in the collection of the Prince of Liechtenstein. Vasari describes Leonardo painting a portrait of Ginevra after his return to Florence, between 1500 and 1506, but by this time Ginevra would have been in her forties and the portrait is of a much younger woman. Nevertheless the painting is very accomplished, especially when compared to the *Annunciation*. Recent research has identified the device on the reverse of the panel as the personal seal of Bernardo Bembo, the Venetian ambassador to Florence in 1475-76 and 1478-80. The close but platonic relationship between Ginevra and Bembo has long been recognized, and was even celebrated in its day by the poets Alessandro Braccesi and Christoforo Landino. While there is no definite proof linking Leonardo and Bembo (supposing Bembo to be the commissioner of the portrait), Bembo was in fact a friend of Lorenzo de' Medici, one of Verrocchio's major patrons. It is not therefore impossible that the Venetian ambassador commissioned the portrait via the studio.

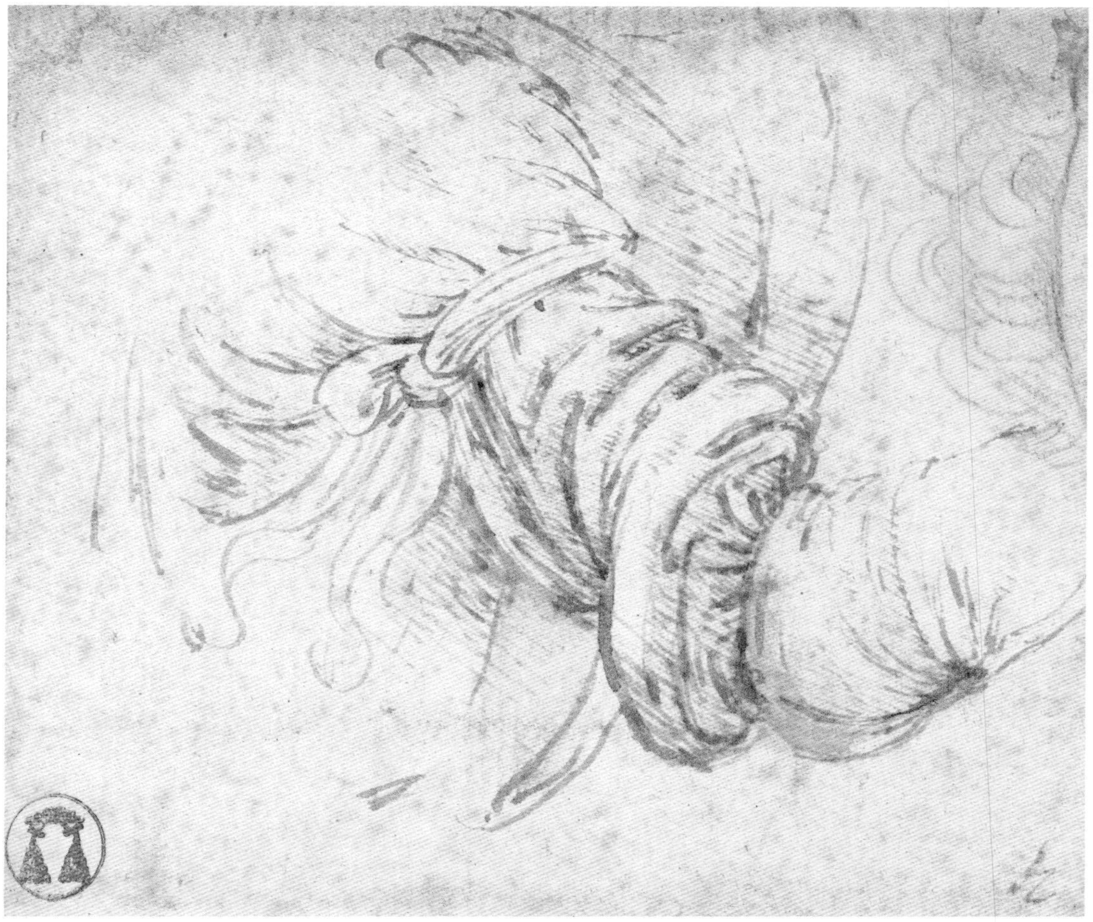

LEFT: *Study of a Sleeve*, c.1473, pen and brown ink, 3¼ × 3⅝ inches (8.2 × 9.3 cm), Courtesy of the Governing Body, Christ Church, Oxford. This drawing is almost certainly a preparatory study for the right sleeve of the angel in the *Annunciation* (pages 16-17).

BELOW: *Study of the Drapery of a Figure Kneeling to the Right*, c.1473, Cabinet des Dessins, Musée du Louvre, Paris. Leonardo made studies of drapery throughout his career and Vasari mentions that many were drawn from clay models draped in plaster-soaked cloths.

RIGHT: *A Lily*, c.1475, pen, ink and brown wash over black, heightened with white, the outlines pricked for transfer, 12⅜ × 7 inches (31.4 × 17.7 cm), Windsor Castle, Royal Library 12418. © 1994 Her Majesty The Queen. The earliest surviving plant drawing by Leonardo is of the Madonna Lily. It cannot be identified as the direct model for the lily held by the angel in the *Annunciation* because it differs in too many details. It is likely that this pricked drawing was used in another, now lost, painting. Notice also the faint geometrical drawing; this may relate to a perspective projection like that for the *Adoration of the Magi* (pages 30-31).

ABOVE: *Portrait of Ginevra de' Benci*, c.1476, oil on wood panel, 15¼ × 14½ inches (38.8 × 36.7 cm), National Gallery of Art, Washington, Ailsa Mellon Bruce Fund. This portrait only came to light in 1733 in the collection of the Prince of Liechtenstein.

RIGHT: Andrea del Verrocchio (c.1435-1488), *Madonna and Child*, c.1469, oil on wood panel, 42 × 30 inches (106.7 × 76.3 cm), National Gallery of Scotland, Edinburgh. As well as the 'sweet calm' of the Virgin often emulated by Verrocchio's pupils, the precisely worked out perspective of the background and pavement reveal that Leonardo's studies, such as those for the *Adoration of the Magi*, also have their precedent in Verrocchio's work.

AN·M·CCCCLXXXX QVO PVL
CHERRIMA CIVITAS OPIBVS VICTO
RIIS ARTIBVS AEDIFICIIS QVE NO
BILIS COPIA SALVBRITATE PACE
PERFRVEBATVR

PREVIOUS PAGES: Domenico Ghirlandaio (1449-94), *Apparition of the Angel to Zacharius*, 1485-90. This biblical scene also shows many of the most important members of fifteenth-century Florentine society.

BELOW: A fifteenth-century view of a Florentine garden; the garden was of great financial and symbolic value to Renaissance Florentines. In one of his manuscripts Leonardo mentions the Medici gardens where Lorenzo 'Il Magnifico' established the world's first academy of art.

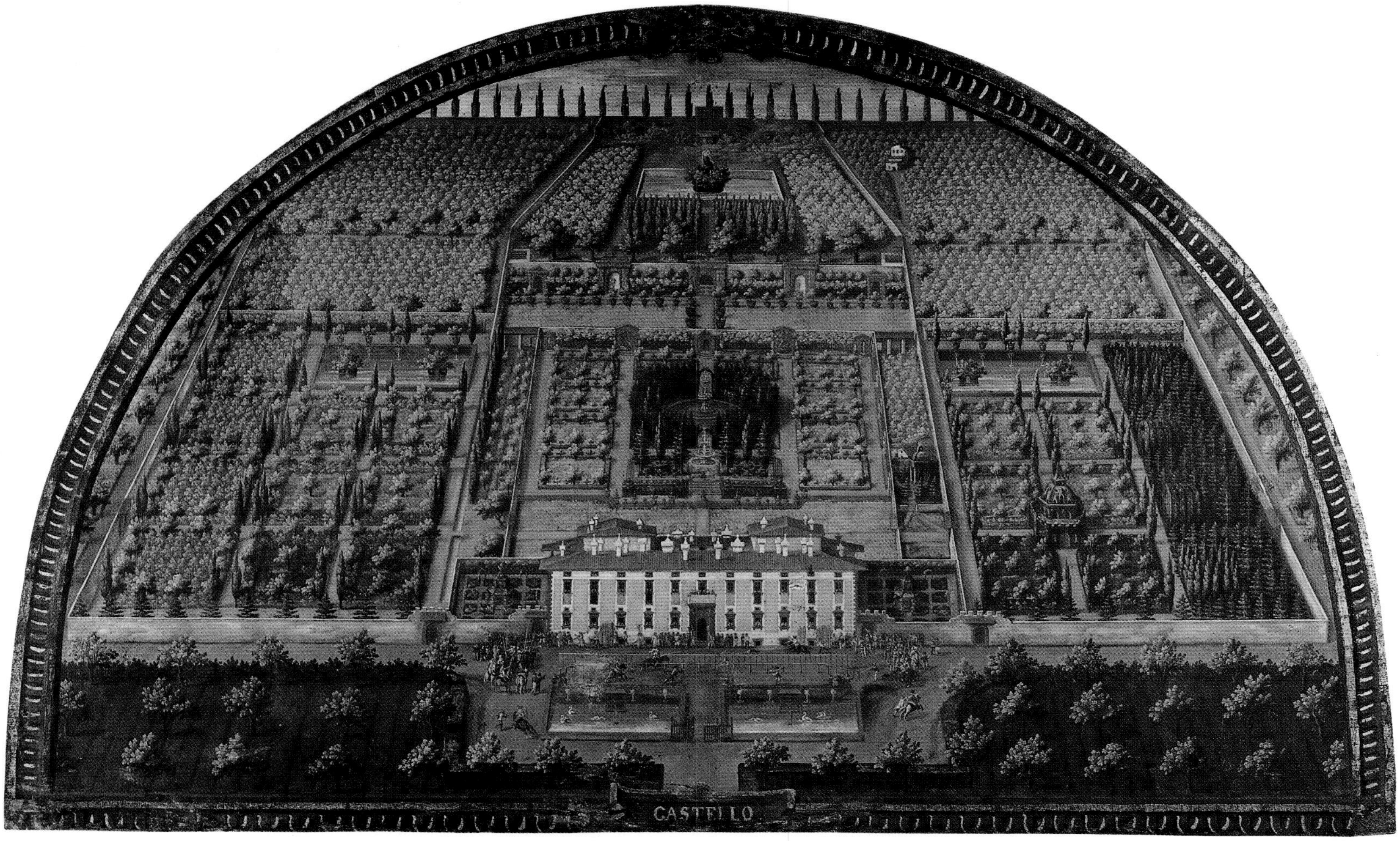

Andrea Corsali to Giuliano de' Medici about some people called *Guzzati*, who refused to eat food that contained blood and who had agreed among themselves not to do harm to any living thing, as Corsali wrote: 'Just like our Leonardo da Vinci.'

In 1477 Leonardo left Verrocchio's studio and began working independently. Florence at that time represented all that was modern in fifteenth-century Italy and was governed by the top political family, the Medici, whose banking network throughout Europe lent money to other top political families. On the basis of loans of money by the Medici, Edward IV of England (1442-83) won his battles against Henry VI and the Lancastrians and successfully laid the foundations for the Tudor state. Maximilian I (1459-1519), the Holy Roman Emperor, and his wife Margaret of Burgundy also borrowed heavily – so heavily that they broke the Bruges branch of the Medici bank.

Although the Medici were technically private citizens in Florence, during Leonardo's lifetime their influence was at its height; there was hardly anyone in power in Christendom who had not received or was looking forward to financial support from the Medici family. The Medici also contributed considerably to the artistic, literary and philosophical life of the city. Under Cosimo de' Medici, Lorenzo's grandfather, an ecumenical council had been held in Florence in 1438 for the union of the Greek Orthodox and Roman Catholic churches. Although the union did not take place, many Greeks found their way to Florence, bringing with them manuscripts and ideas that were new to western Europe. Cosimo himself financed several trips for scholars to search out treasures from Greece and the Levant.

The courts of Italy in the late fifteenth and early sixteenth centuries were not always peaceful places of artistic and scholarly activity, however, but were more akin to warring feudal cities. The prince of the court, whether pope, cardinal or duke, as well as being able to attract to his court those in search of his favors

BELOW: Filippino Lippi (1457-1504), *Adoration of the Magi*, 1496, tempera on wood panel, 101½ × 95⅝ inches (258 × 243 cm), Galleria degli Uffizi, Florence. The commission for an altarpiece for the chapel of San Bernardo in the Palazzo Vecchio was originally awarded to Piero Pollaiuolo in December 1477. Seventeen days later the job was transferred to Leonardo, whose *Adoration of the Shepherds* may have been a study. It seems Leonardo abandoned the project soon afterwards and left for Milan, and the commission passed to Domenico Ghirlandaio. In the end, the final altarpiece was painted by Lippi.

LEFT: A co-conspirator in the Pazzi plot to kill Lorenzo and Guiliano de' Medici in 1478, Bernardo Baroncelli was publicly executed in 1479, along with his wife. In this drawing Leonardo showed Baroncelli hanging from the noose, and at the top of the page carefully noted details of his clothing.

and patronage, could also call on his infinite resources to repel his enemies. The most powerful court in fifteenth-century Italy was that at Milan under the Sforza family. This was followed in power and prestige by the Papal court in Rome, the court at Ferrara under the d'Este family, and the court at Mantua under the rule of the Gonzaga. In Milan the Sforza residence was not a large villa but a castle in the middle of the city: a walled fortress capable of withstanding wars, revolution and riots. In addition to its defensive moat, the Castello Sforzesco boasted 62 drawbridges and, by 1500, could call upon an army of between 800 and 1200 mercenary troops armed with some 1800 machines of war. It is not surprising that alliances with the Sforza family, through treaties and marriages of convenience, were assiduously sought by other ruling families.

The smaller Florentine court of the Medici under Lorenzo 'Il Magnifico' was dominated by Neoplatonic thought. Lorenzo himself was a poet and philosopher, as well as the founder of the world's first academy of art. According to Anonimo Gaddiano in his *Codex Magliabechiano*, Leonardo was set to work in the gardens of the Piazza San Marco where the academy was to be established. In a note on a sheet of calculations and a drawing of a pair of scales, Leonardo mentions the gardens and the work on which he may have been employed:

The Labors of Hercules for Piero F.Ginori.
The Gardens of the Medici.

Despite Medici rule, Florence was still nominally a republic and Florentine artists continued to operate the time-honored system of payment for goods produced or services rendered. Leonardo appears to have been ill-suited to this business-like atmosphere. In the nine years after his registration with the guild of St Luke, he produced very little saleable material.

ABOVE: A posthumous portrait of Lorenzo 'Il Magnifico' de' Medici, the effective ruler of Florence for 23 years. Although Lorenzo was a patron of artists, writers and philosophers, there is no definite proof of any direct patronage of Leonardo.

LEFT: *Adoration of the Magi*, 1481, oil on wood panel, 96⅞ × 95⅝ inches (246 × 243 cm), Galleria degli Uffizi, Florence. Leonardo's first large group painting was this unfinished altarpiece commissioned by the monks of San Donato a Scopeto in Florence. The painting was left unfinished when Leonardo left for Milan in 1481-82.

From the minutes of the Florentine executive council, the Signoria, we learn that a commission for an altarpiece for the chapel of San Bernardo in the Palazzo Vecchio was awarded to Piero Pollaiuolo on 24 December 1477. Seventeen days later, the commission was re-awarded to Leonardo. On 16 March 1478, Leonardo received the first payment of 25 florins and began work, but the altarpiece was not far advanced when Leonardo abandoned work on it altogether. In May 1483, a resolution passed by the Signoria transferred the project once again, this time to Domenico Ghirlandaio. The final altarpiece, dating from 1485, is in fact the work of a fourth artist, Filippino Lippi. It has been suggested that a drawing of *The Adoration of the Shepherds* may have been a study for Leonardo's initial effort. His inability to work to deadlines, or even to complete commissions, was to dog him throughout his career.

In the same year that Leonardo was awarded the San Bernardo commission, Florence was rocked by a conspiracy that eventually dragged the Republic into war and nearly bankrupted the city. The 1478 Pazzi conspiracy involved the Archbishop of Pisa, a mercenary soldier called Montesecco, two priests and the Pope himself, among others. Lorenzo de' Medici had incurred the wrath of the Pontiff by refusing him a loan to buy the town of Imola. Lorenzo had in fact had his eye on the territory for himself, and gave instructions to Francesco de' Pazzi, who was the head of the Pazzi bank in Rome, not to advance the money to Pope Sixtus IV. Pazzi saw his chance to damage the Medicis' standing with the Pope and to advance his own position, however, and instead of following Lorenzo's orders, himself offered the Pope most of the money. The Pope promptly transferred his account from the Medici to the Pazzi bank. Meanwhile Jacopo Pazzi, Francesco's uncle (who lived up to the family name: Pazzi is a corrupt form of 'mad' or 'crazy' and Jacopo was known

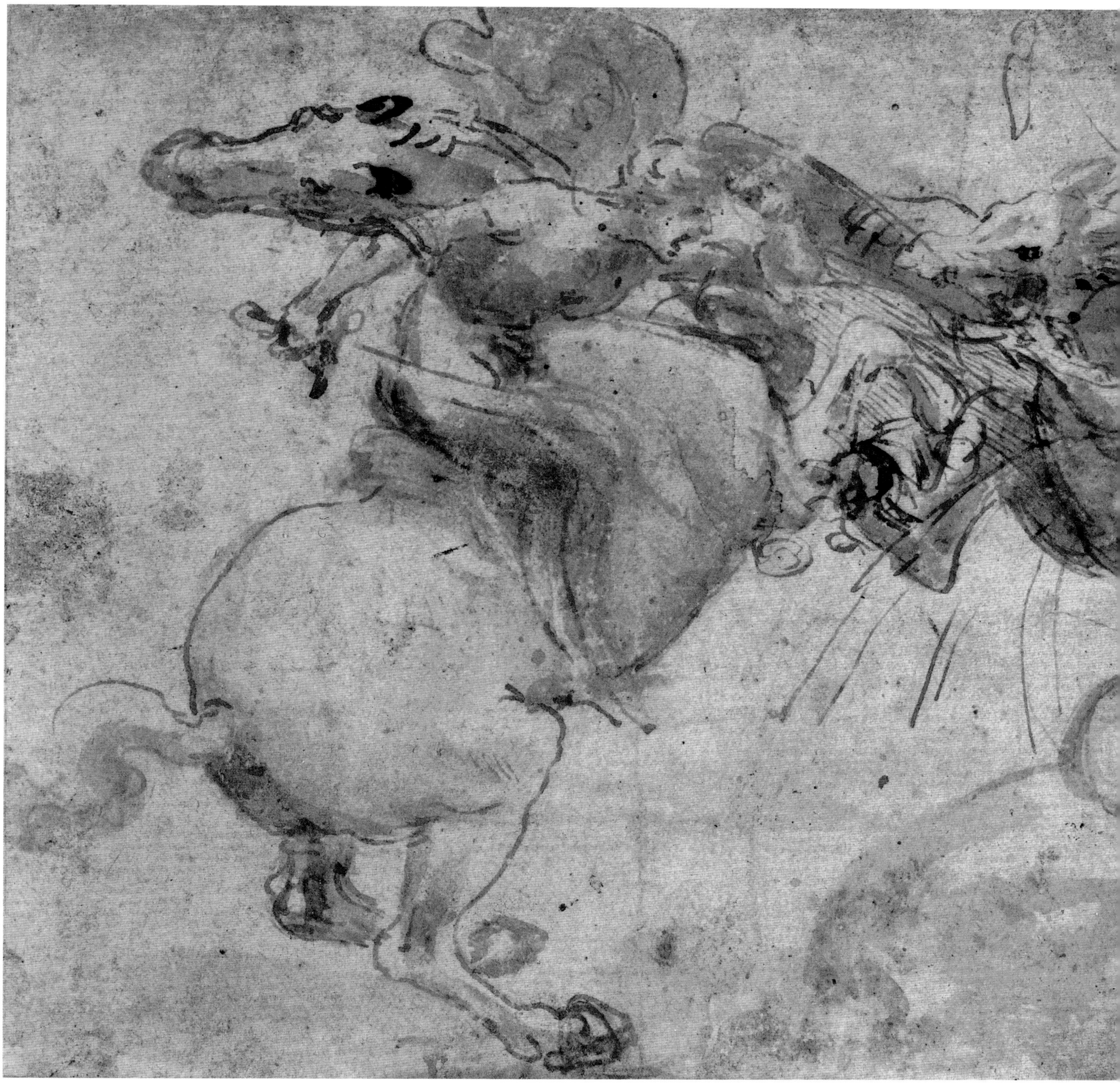

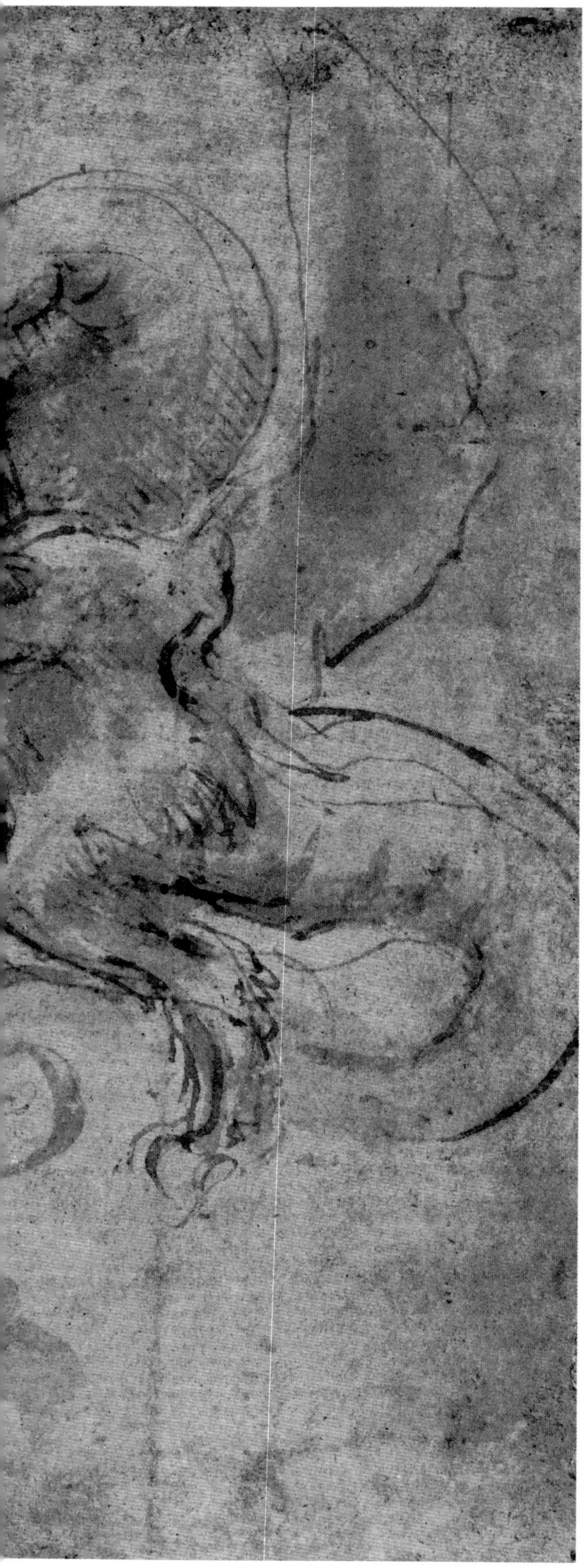

LEFT: *Battle Between Horsemen and a Dragon*, c.1481, pen ink and wash, 5½ × 7½ inches (13.9 × 19 cm), courtesy of the Trustees of the British Museum, London. While many of the elements in the *Adoration of the Magi* were designed to serve as symbolic devices, more difficult to understand are the battling figures in the background. These appear to have begun life in this drawing, which demonstrates Leonardo's interest in depicting mythical beasts. The horsemen are also a foretaste of his interest in equine compositions demonstrated in *The Battle of Anghiari* some 20 years later.

A blue coat lined with fur of fox's breasts.
Black hose.
Bernardo di Bandino Baroncelli.

On the day of the conspiracy Leonardo had gone about the city and drawn people's excited faces. It was said that, throughout his career, he would follow a man with an interesting face through the streets, to get his portrait down on paper.

Leonardo's inability to fulfil his contractual obligations was already well known and in March 1481, when a commission for the *Adoration of the Magi* was awarded to him, the friars at the monastery of San Donato a Scopeto drew up a complicated contract pinning Leonardo down to a strict timetable. Even this contract failed to impel Leonardo to work and the commission was eventually awarded to Filippino Lippi. Leonardo's first large group painting, the unfinished *Adoration of the Magi* gives us a foretaste of the large and complex later works, such as *The Last Supper* (pages 66-67) and the *Battle of Anghiari* (page 90-91). It is also the earliest of his paintings which can be identified with a specific commission. In 1475 a saddler had made an endowment to the monastery, to provide a painting for the high altar and a dowry for his grand-daughter. Leonardo's father (who conveniently was the notary to the monastery and so it may have been through him that Leonardo was awarded the commission in the first place) drew up the contract, which required that the painting be delivered within 24 months with the possibility of an extension of a further six months. Shortly after the contract was agreed and signed, early in 1481, the monks advanced Leonardo money to buy paints. In July he requested another 28 florins, and between July and September the monks also provided him with firewood, wheat and wine; on 28 September 1481, three monks delivered a barrel of wine to Leonardo's house. Unfortunately for the monks – and for the saddler's grand-daughter, who never got her dowry because of the complicated contract – Leonardo never completed

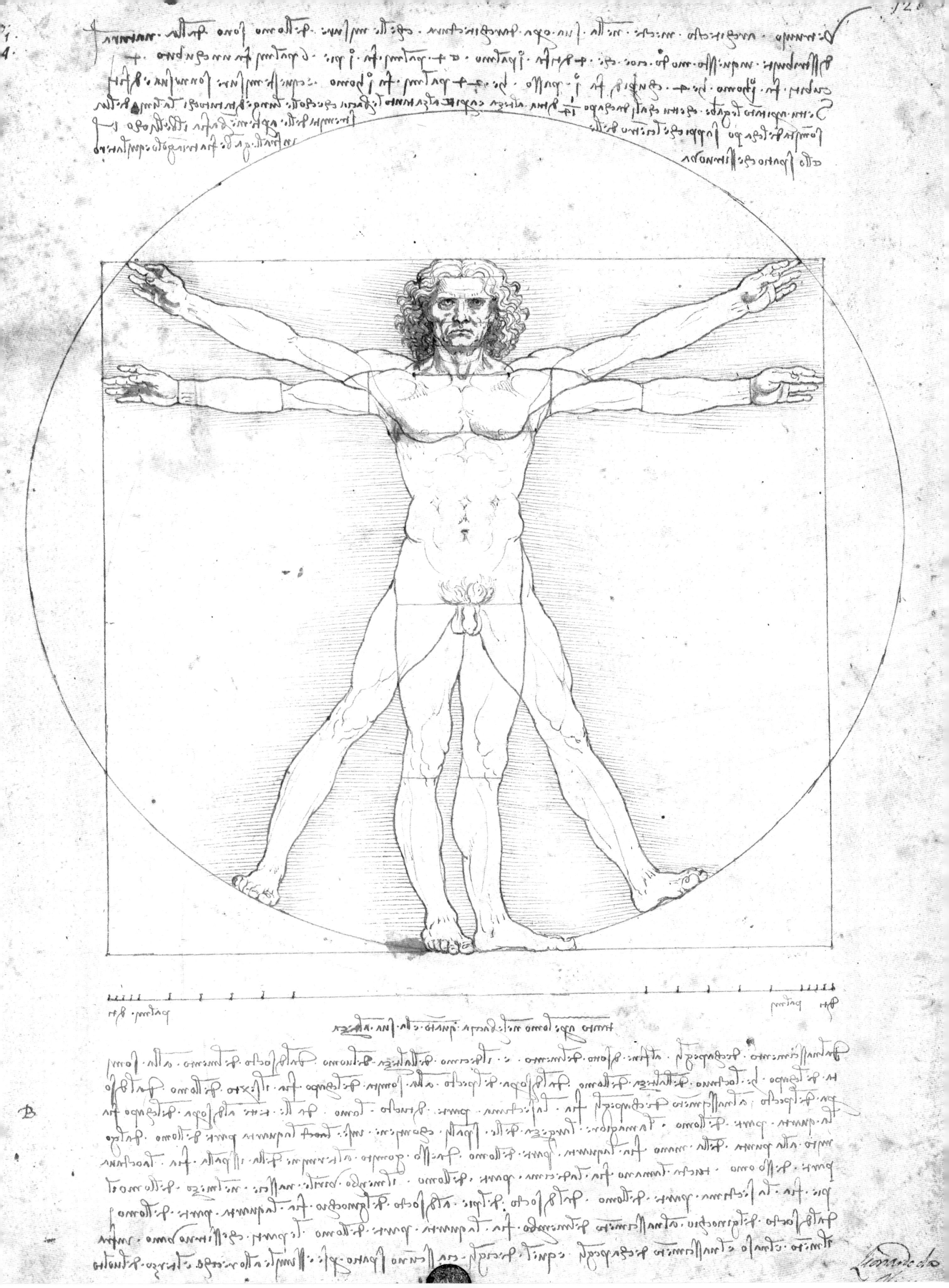

CHAPTER 2
Milan, 1482–99

Toward the end of 1481 Leonardo left Florence. Some say it was his restless spirit that drove him on to Milan, others cite his apparent lack of recognition by Lorenzo de' Medici. Since the attempt on Lorenzo's life, the Medici had been in political difficulties and had little time to devote to artistic matters; Lorenzo had been excommunicated by the Pope (for the killing of the Archbishop of Pisa) and the expected war had materialized, with Pisa and Naples allied against him. Florence, which depended on trade for its survival, was facing a severe financial crisis with its road and sea routes cut off. The Pope demanded that Lorenzo give himself up and leave Florence. In a desperate attempt to save himself, Lorenzo traveled in secret to see King Ferrante of Naples and threatened him with an onslaught by the Turks. Ferrante agreed to peace in February 1480. When the Pope threatened war later in that year, the Turks besieged Otranto, possibly at Lorenzo's request, and the Pope was forced to back down.

Later in 1481, Pope Sixtus IV summoned to Rome the finest artists in Tuscany to decorate the Vatican. Following new discussions with the Medici, Botticelli, Ghirlandaio, Signorelli, Perugino and Pintoricchio were summoned to Rome, but not Leonardo. Lorenzo had not entirely overlooked Leonardo, however; in 1478, during Ludovico Sforza's visit to Florence, Lorenzo is said to have recommended Leonardo to the duke as the artist most capable of undertaking the monument that Sforza was planning to erect as a tribute to his father Francesco Sforza. It is possible that Leonardo was in fact sent to Milan by the Medici as an emissary with the gift of a lute, for it seems that, when he left Florence, Leonardo was accompanied by a renowned sixteen-year-old lutenist, Atalante Migliarotti.

It was essential that the Medici remained on good terms with the court of Ludovico, 'Il Moro' (the Moor – so called because of his dark complexion and equally dark character). The rightful duke was in fact Gian Galeazzo Sforza, who was only thirteen years old. Il Moro, Duke of Bari, was virtual ruler of Milan, with serious designs on ruling all of Italy. In Milan, Il Moro was attempting to create the strongest and finest court in Europe. One of the great trade centers, Milan was ideally situated on the plain of Lombardy and the Artiglio canal. Furthermore Ludovico was able to exploit Milan's proximity to its political ally, France. At any time Il Moro could call upon the King of France to use his forces against any Italian city that threatened either Milan or Ludovico's plans.

Unlike his master Verrocchio, Leonardo enjoyed little direct Medici patronage. Furthermore the Florentine court could never offer the kind of patronage enjoyed by artists, writers and musicians at the courts of Milan, Mantua or Ferrara. It seems that Leonardo had an eye for opportunity; he wrote a letter of introduction to Ludovico Sforza listing his abilities and attainments and stating that he had plans for portable bridges, ramming devices, for cannon, catapults and armored cars. Only at the end of his letter did Leonardo assure Il Moro that he could also:

> Execute sculpture in marble, bronze or clay and also painting, in which my works will stand comparison with that of anyone else, whoever he may be.

Leonardo also added that he could undertake the bronze equestrian statue of Ludovico's father. We can assume that Leonardo was well aware of the opportunities afforded by the court at Milan but where exactly he gained all this technical knowledge and skill is uncertain, as is the date of his letter. There are indeed gaps in the chronology of his life between 1482 and 1487 and it has even been suggested that he visited the Near East where Kait Bey, the Sultan of Egypt, was engaged in warfare. In his notebooks there are letters to the Sultan and to the Devatdor of Syria which suggest official duties while in the employ of the Sultan in Armenia. There are also some drawings of rock formations near Mount Taurus and a sketch map of Armenia, but it is possible that these were taken from contemporary books.

The first definite proof we have of his being in Milan comes from 1483. A contract of 25 April, 1483, came not from Ludovico Sforza but from a religious brotherhood. The contract, between Leonardo and the brothers Evangelista and Giovanni Ambrogio da Predis, was drawn up and signed by Prior Bartolomeo Scorlione, Giovanni Sant'Angelo and the members of the Confraternity of the Immaculate Conception. The commission was for an altarpiece with an elaborately carved frame for the brotherhood's chapel in the church of San Francesco Grande in Milan. Leonardo and the da Predis brothers were to supply not only a central panel on the theme of 'Our Lady with Her Son', but also the wing panels, along with the painted and gilded decorative framework.

LEFT: *Human Figure in a Circle, Illustrating Proportion,* 1485-90, pen and ink, 13½ × 9⅝ inches (34.3 × 24.5 cm), Accademia, Venice. The Roman architect Vitruvius formalized, in his treatise *On Architecture,* the Greek canon for the p oportions of the human figure, which were revived during the Renaissance. This drawing by Leonardo was reproduced in an edition of Vitruvius' book published in 1511, in order to illustrate the concept that a well-proportioned body with feet together and arms outstretched can be inscribed in a square, while the same body spreadeagled occupies a circle described around the navel.

LEFT: *Madonna of the Rocks*, c.1483, oil on wood, transferred to canvas, 78⅜ × 48 inches (199 × 122 cm), Musée de Louvre, Paris. This painting formed the central panel in the altarpiece commissioned in 1483 from Leonardo and the da Predis brothers by the Confraternity of the Immaculate Conception in Milan. It is possible that the panel was sold privately when the brotherhood refused to pay the painters a further fee. In order to fulfil the terms of the contract, it appears that Leonardo painted a second version, now in the National Gallery in London.

ABOVE: Detail of the angel's head from the *Madonna of the Rocks*.

All did not go well with this commission and two versions exist of the *Madonna of the Rocks*, one in the Louvre in Paris, the other in the National Gallery in London. The contract for the commissioned named Leonardo as *maestro* over the da Predis brothers and stated that the fee was set at 800 Imperial Lire (200 ducats), the initial sum of 100 lire to be paid on 1 May 1483, with the balance in monthly instalments of 40 lire beginning in July. The final payment was to be made in January or February of 1485 when, on completion, the three brothers would be entitled to a bonus to be determined by the Brotherhood. The contract further stipulated that the altarpiece was to be completed no later than the Feast of the Immaculate Conception (8 December) 1485.

The subject of the central panel to be painted by 'the Florentine' was to be of the Virgin and Child with a group of angels and two prophets. On each of the wing panels there were to be four angels singing or playing musical instruments. These wing panels were entrusted to Ambrogio, while Evangelista undertook the gilding, coloring and retouching. The wooden retable into which the entire painting was to fit was contracted out and was carved by Giacomo de Mairo. In the end the decoration of the frame alone was to use up the entire 800 lire fee and, although they had completed the project, Leonardo and Ambrogio had to

LEFT: Detail of the head of the Virgin from the Louvre *Madonna of the Rocks*.

ABOVE: *Head of a Young Woman*, attributed to Leonardo, 1480's?, drawing on board, 10⅝ × 8¼ (27 × 21 cm), National Gallery, Parma.

petition the Duke of Milan in 1493 or 1494 for an additional payment, since technically they had only received the initial payment of 100 lire between them. This claim was dismissed, however, as was their request that Leonardo's central panel be sold, although it is possible that the central panel was in fact sold and that the second version of the central panel was begun as a replacement in the 1490s.

In 1503 Ambrogio appealed again, this time to the King of France, but by this time Leonardo was no longer in Milan and the case was once again deferred. Then on 27 April 1506 the altarpiece was judged to be unfinished – this must have been the second version of the central panel – and, despite his absence from Milan, Leonardo was ordered to complete the painting within two years. For

LEFT: *Madonna of the Rocks*, c.1506, oil on wood panel, 74⅝ × 47¼ inches (189.5 × 120 cm), Courtesy of the Trustees of the National Gallery, London. This is believed to be the second, later, version of the central panel of the altarpiece made for the Confraternity of the Immaculate Conception in Milan.

ABOVE: Detail of flowers from the London *Madonna of the Rocks*. Begun in the 1490s, this painting was completed by Leonardo and possibly Ambrogio da Predis or some other hand, who may have been responsible for minor details such as these flowers.

this work Leonardo was to receive 200 lire. Finally, on 18 August 1508, nearly 13 years late, the altarpiece was in place in San Francesco Grande.

Whatever the reasons for the two versions of the *Madonna of the Rocks*, the paintings are interesting in that neither version illustrates a specific incident in the Gospels and both are therefore open to a variety of interpretations. It is possible that the paintings show an incident popularized in the fifteenth century by the theologian Pietro Cavalca, relating to a meeting between the infants St John and Christ when the Holy Family were fleeing to Egypt. Certain elements do support this thesis: the angel could be the Angel Uriel, who was reputed to be the protector of the child-hermit St John. There are also symbols that prefigure the Baptism, such as the pool of water in the foreground, and the Crucifixion, such as the sharp leaves of the iris which may allude to the 'swords of sorrow' which pierced the Virgin's heart.

The *Madonna* is, however, more than just an illustration of a story. In the fifteenth century, the cult of the Virgin was at its strongest and the doctrine of her own Immaculate Conception – for Christ to have been entirely immaculate, the Virgin must herself have been born of a virgin mother – was particularly popular. Not only are the symbols of the Vir-

BELOW: *Bust of an Infant in Profile to the Left*, c.1506, red chalk, 4 × 4 inches (10 × 10 cm), Windsor Castle, Royal Library 12519. (c) 1994 Her Majesty The Queen.

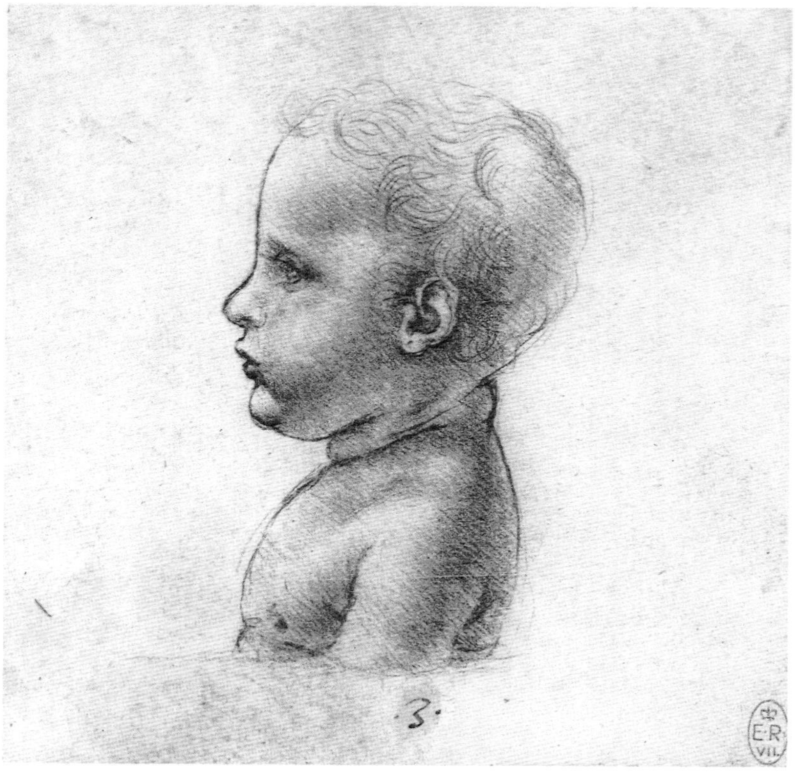

gin apparent in the paintings, for example the palm tree, but the *Song of Songs* was also a popular source of Marian iconography:

O my dove, in the cleft of the rocks,
in the covert of the cliff,
let me see your face.

It has been suggested that in these lines of verse lie the origins of the rocky landscape setting of the figures.

Furthermore, the *Madonna of the Rocks* was the earliest expression of a theory of painting that Leonardo was to explain in some detail in his notebooks. Briefly, Leonardo's thesis was that, in shadow, the individual quality of colors is lost; where an object is in shadow, it should not be differentiated from other objects of different colors. Only in bright light is the true color of an object seen. The result of this approach can be clearly seen in the *Madonna of the Rocks*, where it is tone rather than color that determines the three-dimensionality and relief of the painting.

While Leonardo worked sporadically on one or other version of the *Madonna of the Rocks* throughout the 1480s and 1490s, he was also busy with other projects. From the early period in Milan, around 1482 or 1483, date two paintings. One is the unfinished *Portrait of a Musician*, believed to represent Franchino Gaffurio, court musician, composer and music theorist at the Sforza court, and the only extant portrait of a male subject by Leonardo. The second painting, *Lady with an Ermine*, is a portrait of Cecilia Gallerani, one of Ludovico Sforza's mistresses. As well as being a writer and poet herself, Cecilia was a patron of the arts in her own right. She was Il Moro's mistress for some ten years until her marriage in 1491. Il Moro's court poet Bernardo Bellincioni described how, in Leonardo's portrait, Cecilia appears not to speak but to be listening. This accurately describes the attitude of the sitter as she turns to her left to listen to an unseen speaker. This gesture of turning, and more specifically of turning to look over the shoulder, is one that Leonardo used increasingly to enhance the dynamics and movement of his paintings, and complements the swirling movements he used to depict forms, beginning with the drawings for the *Madonna and Child with Cat* (page 13) and culminating in the Deluge drawings from c.1513 (page 100).

A third painting, known as *La Belle Feronnière*, dating from c.1485, has often been suggested as the work not of Leonardo but of his pupil Giovanni Antonio Boltraffio (1467-1516). Further complicating matters is the name *La Belle Feronnière*; this was the nickname given to a mistress of Henri II of France, and the name seems to have been erroneously given to this painting. As well as the portrait of Cecilia Gallerani, however, Leonardo is known to have painted a portrait of another of Ludovico Sforza's mistresses; Lucrezia Crivelli succeeded Cecilia in the 1490s and it is possible the painting is of her likeness.

RIGHT: Detail of the Christ Child from the London *Madonna of the Rocks*.

LEFT: *Portrait of a Musician*, c.1485, oil on wood panel, 17 × 12¼ inches (43 × 31 cm), Pinacoteca Ambrosiana, Milan. Possibly a portrait of Franchino Gaffurio (1451-1522), composer and musician to the Sforza court at Milan, this painting is Leonardo's only surviving secular representation of a male subject.

ABOVE: *Lady with an Ermine (Cecilia Gallerani)*, c.1485, oil on wood panel, 21¼ × 15⅜ inches (54 × 39 cm), Czartoryski Museum, Kraków. Cecilia was Ludovico Sforza's mistress for some ten years until her marriage in 1491. The ermine she holds functions both as a symbol of purity and as a pun on her name; in Greek the ermine is 'galay'.

LEFT: *La Belle Ferronière*, c.1495, oil on wood panel, 24¾ × 17¾ inches (63 × 45 cm), Musée du Louvre, Paris. It has been suggested that this painting is not the work of Leonardo but is in fact by one of his pupils, Giovanni Boltraffio (1467-1516). Doubt also surrounds the identity of the sitter, who has been variously identified as Lucrezia Crivelli (Sforza's mistress in the 1490s) and La Belle Ferronière, a mistress of Henri II of France.

ABOVE: Verrocchio's Colleoni Monument in Venice. This work by his master may well have influenced Leonardo's own conception of the Sforza and Trivulzio equestrian statues.

These were not the only projects to occupy Leonardo in the early part of his stay in Milan. Around 1483 he began work on a bronze equestrian statue of Francesco Sforza, a project that would occupy him for 16 years. During his apprenticeship to Verrocchio, Leonardo had assisted his master on the Colleone monument in Venice and so the job of designing, casting and erecting the bronze horseman in Milan fell to the Florentine 'engineer'. As part of his campaign to establish his claims as Duke of Milan and to aggrandize the Sforza clan in general, Ludovico planned the monument to celebrate his father Francesco, who had been the first Sforza to rule the city. In his introductory letter to Ludovico, Leonardo had said that he could undertake the work on the bronze, but the first real indication we have of his actually working on the project comes in a letter of 1489 from the Florentine ambassador to Lorenzo de' Medici, in which he expressed his doubts about Leonardo's capabilities and asked

RIGHT: *Study of a Horseman on a Rearing Horse*, c.1490, silverpoint on blue prepared paper, Windsor Castle, Royal Library 12357. © 1994 Her Majesty The Queen. This is almost certainly an early study for the Sforza Monument.

BELOW: This sixteenth-century bronze *Rearing Horse*, height 8⅝ inches (22 cm), relates to Leonardo's early studies for the Sforza monument.

FAR RIGHT: *A Horse in Profile to the Right and Its Forelegs*, c.1497, silverpoint on blue prepared paper, 8½ × 6¼ inches (21.4 × 16 cm), Windsor Castle, Royal Library 12321. © Her Majesty The Queen. As well as studying horses for their anatomy and proportions, Leonardo made a number of sketches from life as preliminary studies for the Sforza equestrian statue.

Lorenzo to recommend an alternative Florentine sculptor to do the work. Perhaps Leonardo was taking too long on the project, or maybe in the Ambassador's eyes he simply required technical assistance.

Leonardo's original ideas, judging from surviving drawings, seem to have been for a rearing horse, but by 1490 the decision was taken to portray a walking horse. Leonardo's own notes reveal that

he made a great number of studies from life of some of Il Moro's horses and, throughout his career, he was to seek out the underlying proportions in his studies of plants, animals and humans. The final pose he adopted was of a high-stepping horse with one front leg raised, a pose similar to the equestrian statue of Marcus Aurelius in Rome. No doubt such classical allusions would have been highly attractive to the Sforza clan.

Ludovico Sforza was not a patient man, however; he wrote to Leonardo that the statue must be completed by November 1493 as he wanted it as a showpiece at the wedding of his illegitimate daughter Bianca to the Emperor Maximilian (whose first wife Margaret had died leaving huge debts, crippling the Medici bank in Bruges). Leonardo replied that while he could not guarantee the bronze, he could promise a clay model, three times life size (about 56 feet from hoof to the top of Francesco's head). Surprisingly he managed to keep his word, and the clay statue was erected in the courtyard of the Castello Sforzesco and was ceremonially unveiled during the wedding celebrations. This clay model was as far as the project was ever to get.

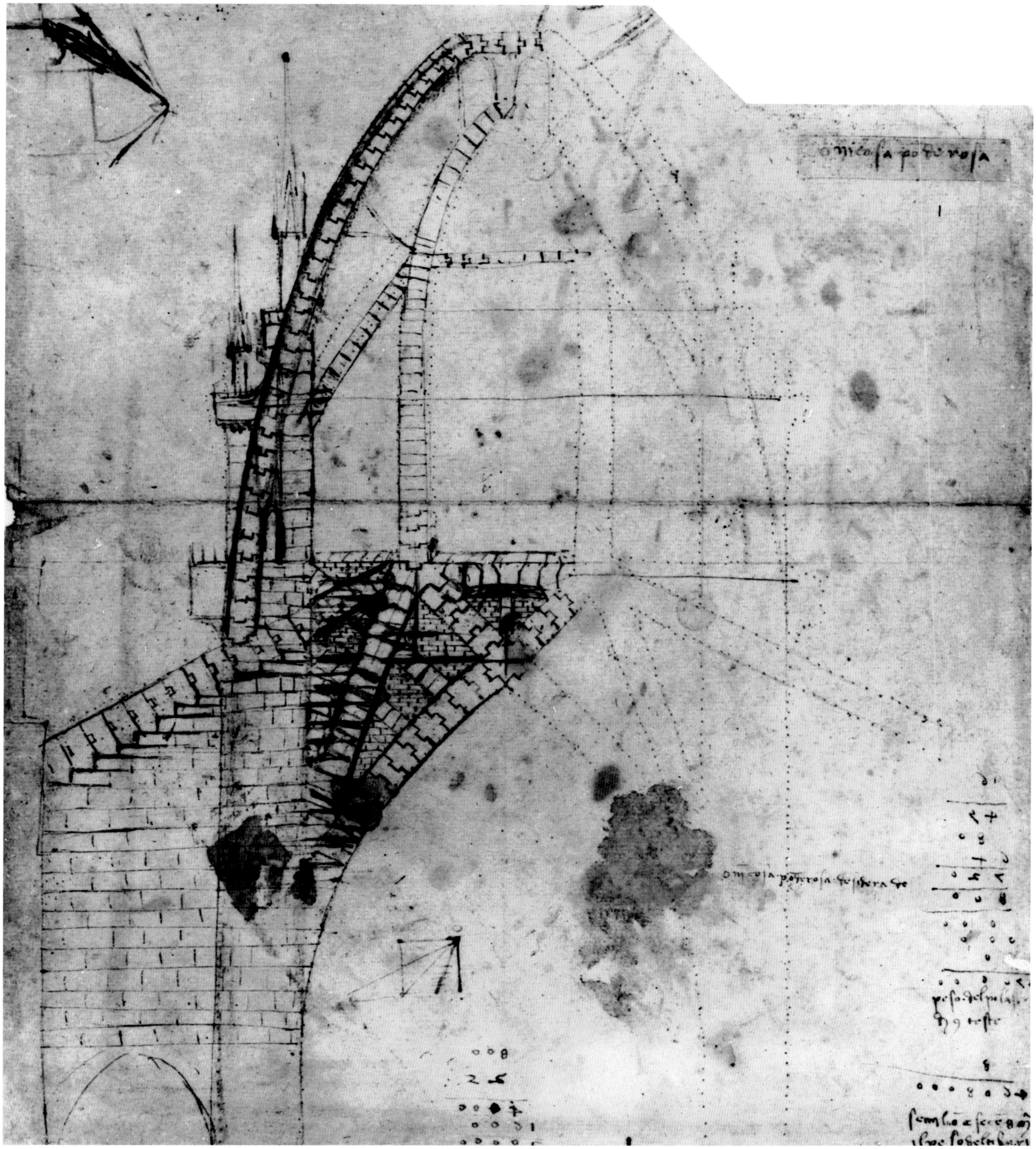

Other projects that occupied Leonardo in Milan included the construction of a model for the *triburio*, the central cupola planned for the dome of Milan Cathedral, for which a number of drawings exist. Ludovico also sent Leonardo to Pavia to restore the Sforza-Visconti castle. In the town that had been home to the poet Petrarch and to the explorer Christopher Columbus, Leonardo wrote his notes on optics which would, after his death, be turned into a treatise. Here he worked on the camera obscura to demonstrate his theory that all vision was determined by the angle at which light fell upon the eye.

Leonardo also proved to be adept at planning masques and devising stage machines for court occasions. For the wedding of Gian Galeazzo Sforza to Isabella of Aragon, scheduled for early 1489, Leonardo devised a portico covered in greenery to be erected in the castle courtyard: the countryside brought safely inside the Sforza Castle walls! A series of planned marriages serving to cement Milan's political alliances culminated in 1491 with Ludovico's own marriage to Beatrice d'Este, the sister of the aesthete Isabella who had herself married into the

LEFT: *Study for the Triburio of Milan Cathedral*, c.1487, pen and ink, Biblioteca Ambrosiana, Milan. Between 1487 and 1488 Leonardo was working on a model for the *triburio*, or central cupola, planned for the dome of Milan Cathedral. Along with a wooden model, Leonardo submitted a letter to the works department in which he compared the building in need of repairs to a sick body and the architect to a doctor.

BELOW: *A Scythed Chariot, Armored Vehicle and a Partisan*, c.1485-88, pen, ink and wash, 6⅞ × 9⅝ inches (17.3 × 24.6 cm), courtesy of the Trustees of the British Museum, London. One of Leonardo's most famous designs for machines of war, this shows two views of the armored vehicle, one without its roof, the other complete with gun barrels projecting outward.

Gonzaga family who ruled Mantua. To celebrate the union of Il Moro and Beatrice, Leonardo staged a pageant sponsored by Galeazzo di Sanseverino (Ludovico's son-in-law and a captain in the Milanese army).

Leonardo seems to have found favor with Ludovico for this type of work, but it appears from his notebooks that Leonardo had projects in mind that should have been of greater interest to the Duke. In 1485 he had produced his first designs for a flying machine, recommending in his notebooks that for safety's sake the test flight should be carried out over water. The same year he watched the eclipse of the sun and devised a method of observing such phenomena without injuring the eye. When Leonardo wrote to Ludovico offering his services and writing of his many talents, the list of skills which he offered included 30 of a technical nature and only three artistic. In an age of transition from the crossbow to the cannon, Leonardo has left us a wealth of designs for machines and weapons, as well as maps and studies of human anatomy. It appears, however, that Ludovico Sforza chose not to make use of any of Leonardo's 'inventions'. In his letter Leonardo claimed he could make cannons and mortars that were both beautiful and different from those already in use. The chief limitations of Renaissance firearms were their slow rate of fire and their inaccuracy. One of Leonardo's solutions was to devise a series of light cannon or *scoppietti* in a fan pattern. He seems to have had a particu-

22

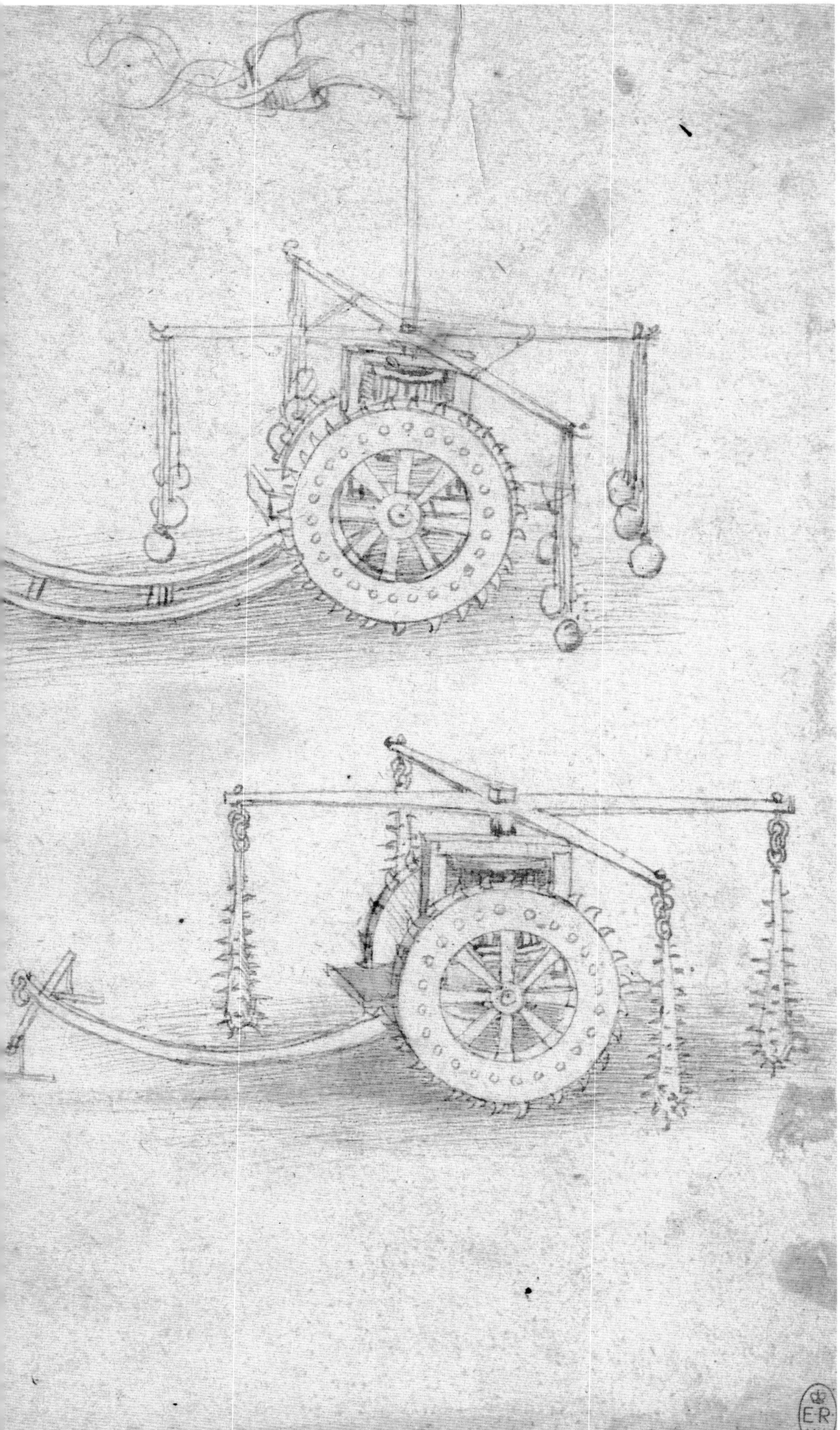

LEFT: *A Chariot Armed with Flails, an Archer with a Shield and a Horseman with Three Lances*, c.1485-88, pen, ink and wash, 7⅞ × 11 inches (20 × 20.7 cm), Windsor Castle, Royal Library 12563. © 1994 Her Majesty The Queen. Leonardo appears to have had a particular interest in designs which multiplied a single force. This sketch, made about a year after he arrived in Milan, shows a horseman with three lances, two of which are attached to the saddle.

lar interest in designs that multiplied a single force; almost 10 years after he had arrived in Milan he made a sketch depicting a mounted warrior carrying not one but three lances, two of which were attached to the rider's saddle.

The most famous of Leonardo's 'war machine' drawings is the *Scythed Chariot, Armored Vehicle and a Partisan* from c.1487. The scythed chariot was probably inspired by descriptions of antique war machines, such as the one reputedly driven by the Celtic leader Queen Boudicca. The drawing shows two views of the armored tank. One, like a turtle rolled on to its back, shows the arrangement inside designed to carry eight men. The other view, with its roof in place and guns poking out, is completed with a cloud of dust which Leonardo claimed was useful for breaking up enemy ranks.

Leonardo's designs for weapons can be divided into three broad categories: catapults (ballista) like the *Giant Crossbow on Wheels* of c.1485-88; cannon, like the drawing of *A Large Cannon being Raised on to a Gun Carriage (Artillery Park)* (c.1485-88), the various water-borne mortars and those with explosive, shrapnel-spreading projectiles; and muskets (arquebus), the matchlock-firing mechanisms for which are described in drawings from 1495. The demand for increased fire power led Leonardo to even grander schemes, such as the design for a treadmill-powered crossbow, a sort of huge machine gun where the archer is perched inside a big treadmill, which is turned by the foot power of soldiers placed on the outer rim of the wheel for added leverage. These soldiers are hopefully protected from enemy fire by a pivoted shield of wooden planks. For a man who professed a hatred of war, guns and artillery were to be a constant area of study for Leonardo.

Little escaped Leonardo's observation, no matter how mundane. In addition to weapons of war he turned his hand to devising labor-saving devices like the *De-*

RIGHT: *A Large Cannon Being Raised on to a Gun Carriage (Artillery Park)*, c.1485-88, pen and ink, 9⅞ × 7¼ inches (25 × 18.3 cm), Windsor Castle Royal Library 12647. © 1994 Her Majesty The Queen. A fusion of fact and imagination: teams of naked men struggle to haul an enormous cannon barrel by means of ropes, pulleys and winches. When this drawing was made, Leonardo was also studying the problems involved in casting his huge bronze equestrian monument. Ironically, the bronze earmarked for that project was eventually used in gun barrels.

BELOW: *A Giant Crossbow on Wheels*, c.1485-88, pen, ink and wash, 7⅞ × 10⅝ inches (20.2 × 27.25 cm), Bibilioteca Ambrosiana, Milan. This huge ballista has some advanced design features, including a laminated bow for extra flexibility and a worm and gear mechanism for drawing back the bow, which is shown in detail in the right-hand corner. The two left-hand drawings are designs for the release mechanism; the upper drawing shows a spring device operated by a hammer blow, while the lower one shows a lever action device.

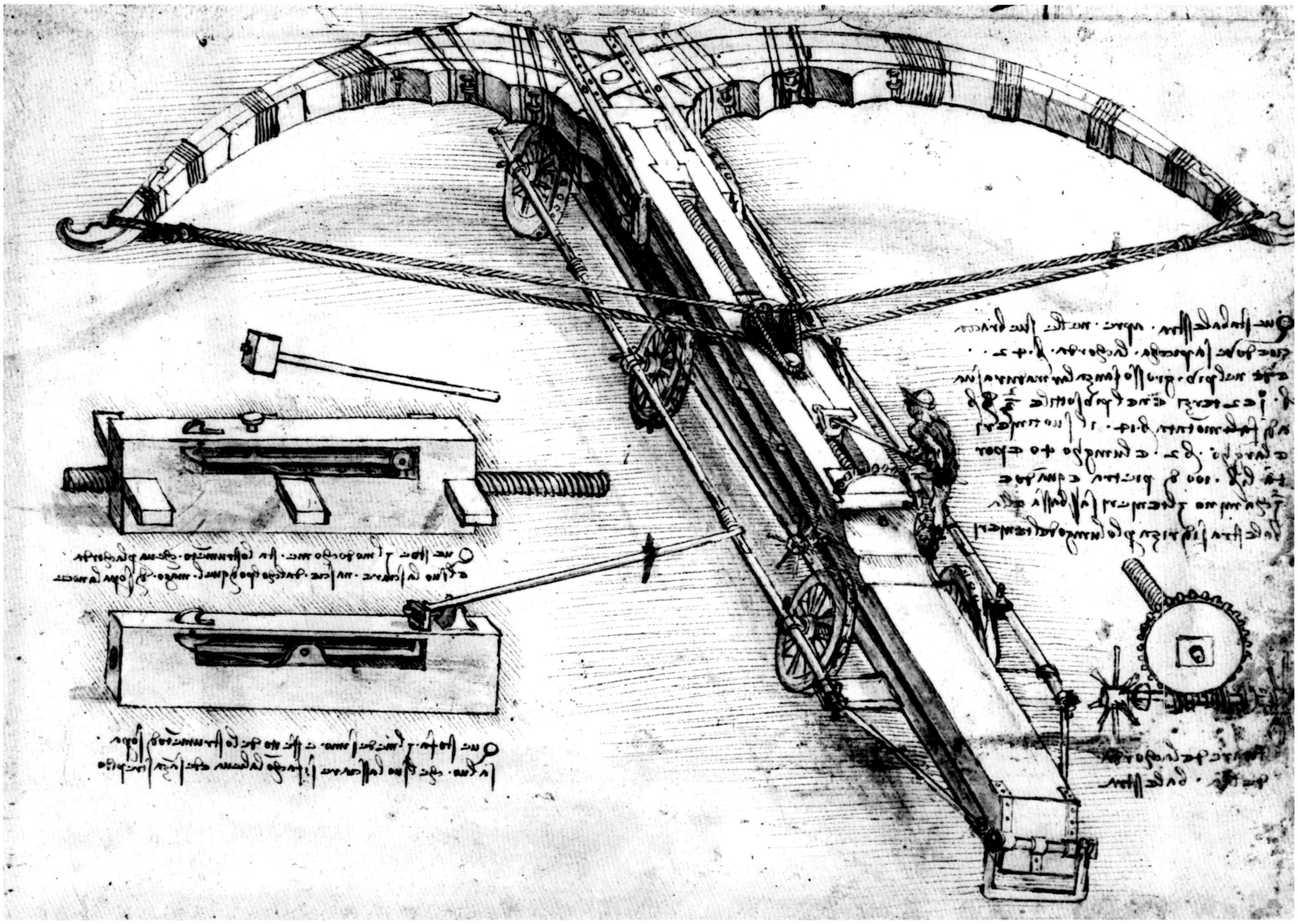

sign for a Napping Machine for producing a constant level of nap on cloth, thereby replacing tedious handwork with a mechanized process. One of his earliest designs was for a file or rasp marker, a machine designed to strike the teeth of the file evenly on the face of metal blanks. Once started, the machine required no human intervention apart from re-cranking the weight to its start position. There are also drawings in which Leonardo studied the problem of translating rotary motion into reciprocating or piston-like action and vice versa; he designed a windlass for lifting heavy loads. In this drawing Leonardo shows us two views of the device, one assembled, the other an exploded view of the mechanism. Another drawing shows a machine for boring holes; until the late seventeenth century, when cast iron piping began to be used for water mains, logs with holes bored through their centers served this function. What is inventive about Leonardo's machine is the set of adjustable chucks which would ensure that the axis of the logs remained in the center of the machine, whatever the diameter of the logs.

Although the most grandiose schemes and designs never left Leonardo's notebooks, he did understand fully the impact that such machines and technology would have on society. He expressed some of the resulting fears in his *Prophecies*, riddles devised to be solved at court parties. In the guise of clever word games,

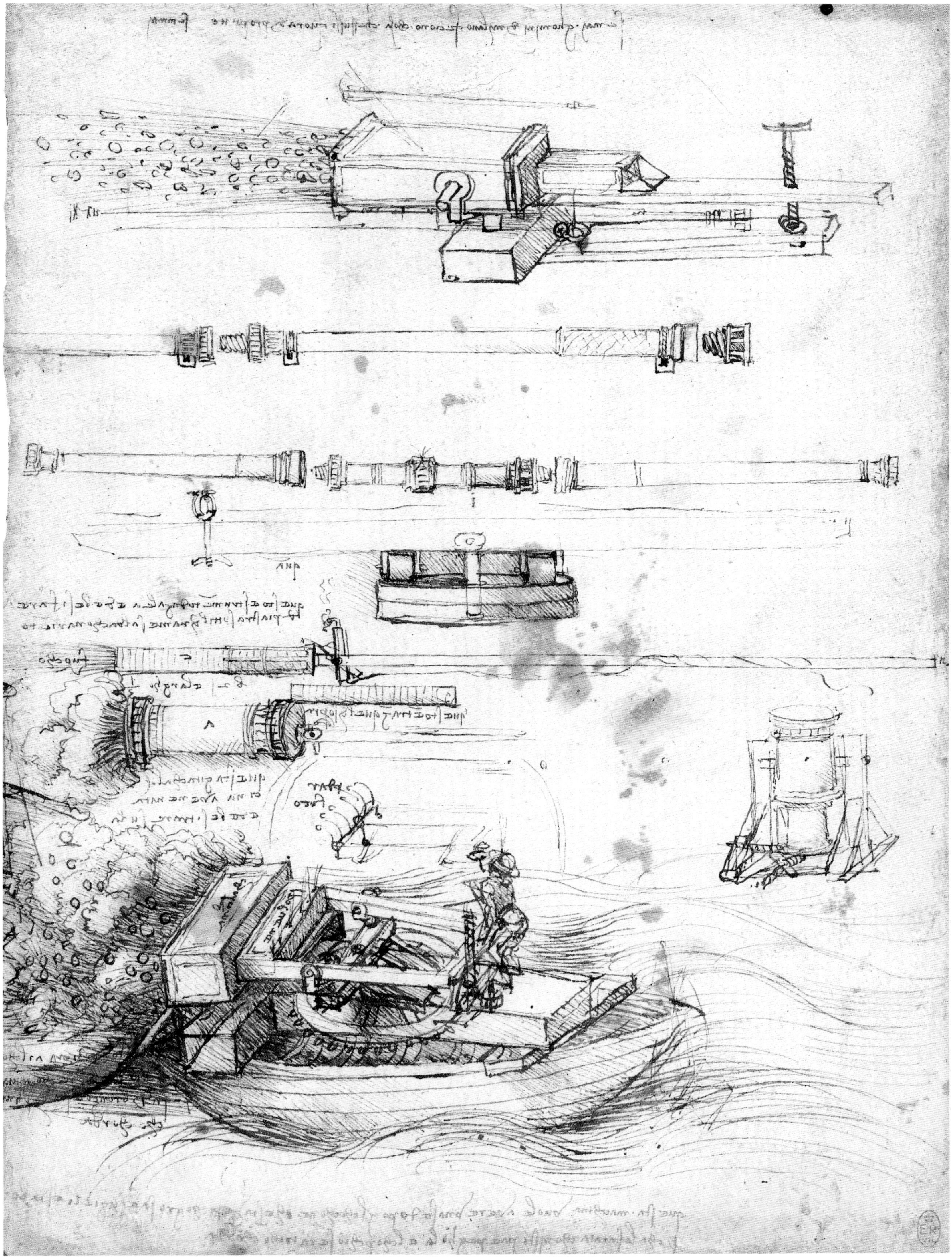

LEFT: *Studies of Mortars, One Firing from a Boat and of Cannon*, c.1485-88, pen and ink, 11⅛ × 8⅝ inches (28.2 × 20.5 cm), Windsor Castle Royal Library 12652r. © 1994 Her Majesty The Queen. These drawings support the claims that Leonardo made in his letter of introduction to Ludovico Sforza that he could make both offensive and defensive weapons, for land or sea. The cannon at the top was designed to hurl small stones or to shoot salvos of 'Greek fire' – incendiary shells. At the foot of the drawing, the cannon is shown mounted on to a boat. At the very top of the page are the words in Leonardo's mirror handwriting: 'If ever the men of Milan did anything which was beyond the requirements or never' – words generally interpreted as frustration with his Milanese employers' unwillingness to put any of his ideas into action.

BELOW: *Treadmill-powered Crossbow*, c.1485-88, Biblioteca Ambrosiana, Milan. The archer is suspended out of range of enemy fire in the middle of the huge treadmill, which is turned by the footpower of soldiers on the outer rim, who in turn are protected by the pivoted shield of wooden planks.

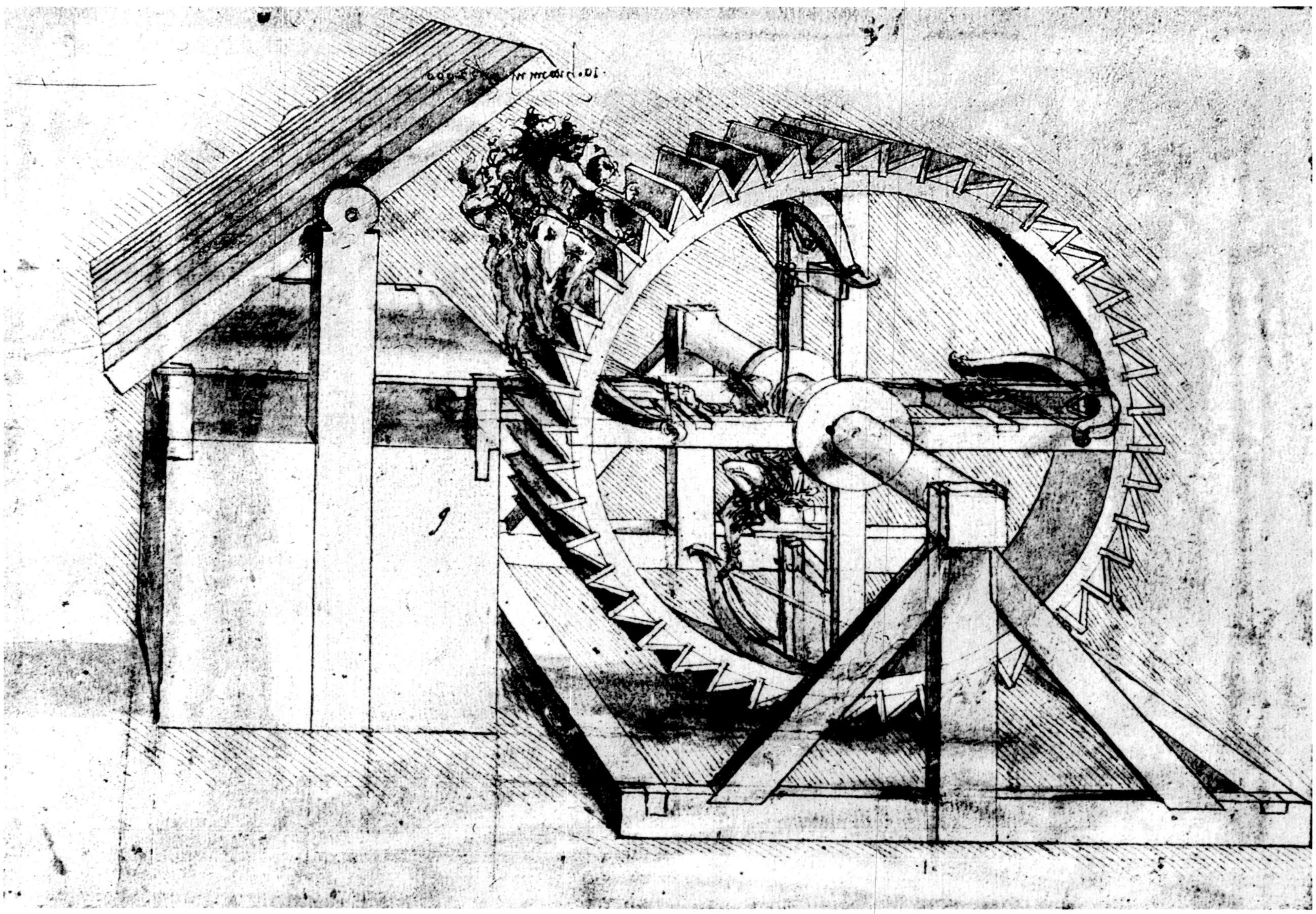

Leonardo not only pointed out the problems of his own era but commented on humanity in general, comments that regrettably hold true five hundred years later:

Creatures will be seen upon the earth who will always be fighting one another . . . there will be no bounds to their malice, by their fierce limbs a great number of trees of the immense forest of the world shall be laid to the ground.

The outbreak of plague in Milan in 1483 and again in 1486 may have inspired Leonardo to draw up his plans for the remodeling of the city. His plans called for a city built on two levels: the lower streets were set aside for use by carts, animals and the lower classes of citizens, while the upper level was to be a promenade with hanging gardens for the pleasure of the wealthy and noble. Archways and unobstructed views of the sky provided light and ventilation to the lower level, and every hundred meters or so a staircase connected the two levels. Leonardo had also observed that the Milanese were in the habit of leaving their garbage in corners; to overcome this, he planned his staircases as spirals! All of these schemes, including weapons, machines, underground sewage systems, running water supplies, a clean air project for Milan for circulating fresh air by windmills and many others, were dismissed by Ludovico Sforza. Furthermore the Duke failed at times to pay Leonardo the money due to him for other commissions, but was content for Leonardo to

BELOW: *The Firing Mechanism of a Gun*, c.1485-88, Codex Madrid I. f.18v, Biblioteca Nacional, Madrid. These drawings show Leonardo's ideas for improving the matchlock-firing mechanism of a gun. The mechanism shown simultaneously opens the powder chamber and sets fire to the touch hole.

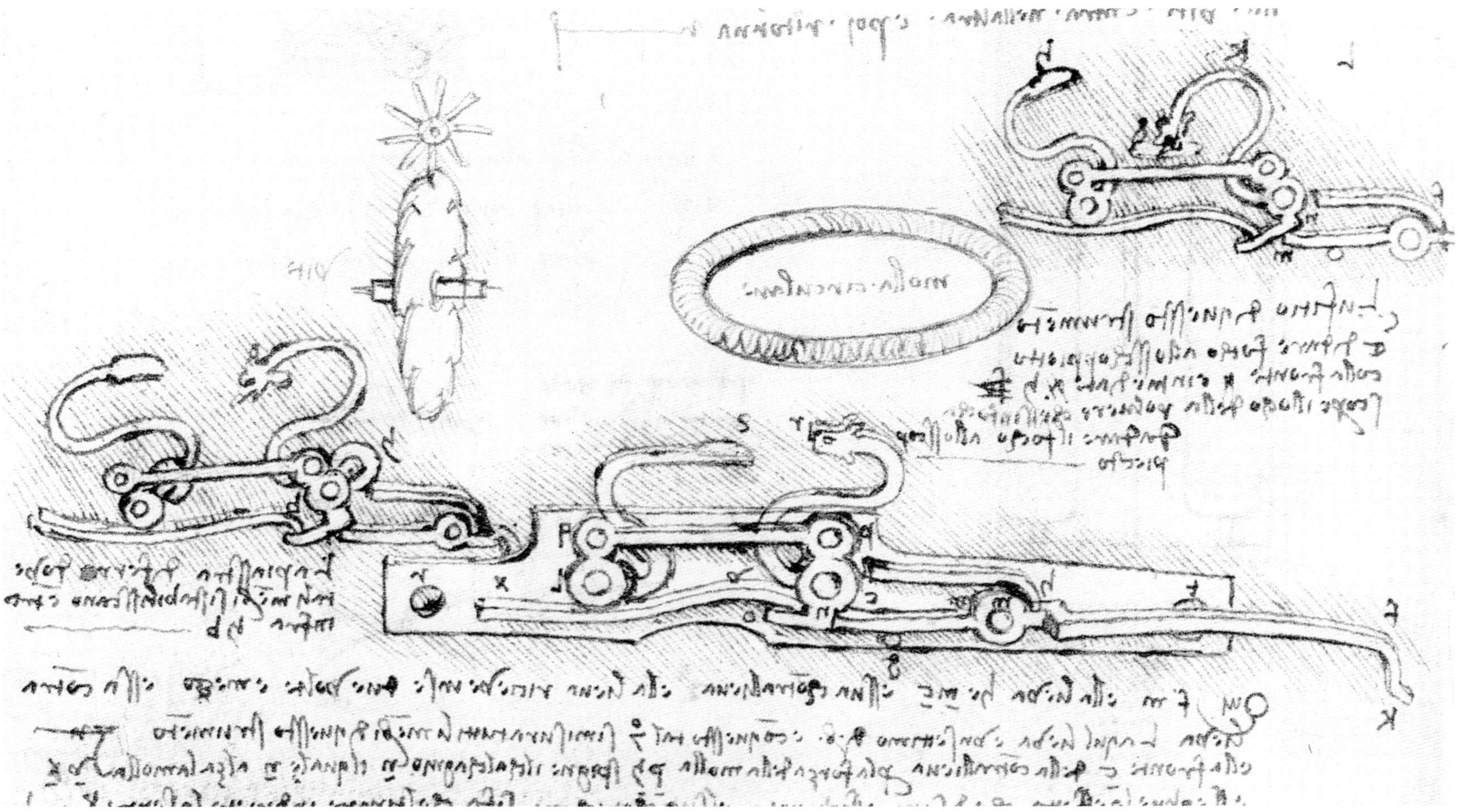

design his pageants and courtly diversions.

Ludovico did, however,have more immediate concerns. When he sent his niece Bianca off with a dowry of 400,000 ducats to marry the Emperor Maximilian – money the Emperor badly needed – Ludovico was buying Imperial protection. He had heard that his sister-in-law Isabella d'Este in Mantua was urging her grandfather the King of Naples to challenge Ludovico's right to the dukedom of Milan. In a counter-move, Ludovico contacted the French king Charles VIII and promised him support for his own claim to Naples. Ludovico began to arm, and the bronze that had been set aside for the casting of the equestrian statue of his father was now diverted to Ludovico's father-in-law Ercole d'Este in Ferrara, where it was made into cannons. Things were looking pretty bleak for Il Moro: few trusted him and he was already suspected of plotting to kill his nephew Gian Galeazzo, the rightful duke. While the French king was grateful for the support in claiming Naples, Ludovico did not realize that his French ally also had his eye on the throne of Milan. By October 1494, Gian Galeazzo was dead. Undaunted by the ensuing rumors of murder, Ludovico proclaimed himself Duke of Milan and continued with his magnificent patronage of the arts. In charge of court culture was Leonardo.

In 1491 Ludovico had sent Leonardo to divert the River Ticino from its natural course in order to irrigate the surrounding fields. There Leonardo met the nobleman Giovanni Melzi, who had a villa at Vaprio on the River Adda. Leonardo soon became one of Melzi's household and is believed to have completed *The Madonna of the Rocks* (page 40) while staying at Melzi's villa.

Ludovico, who took great care in promoting cultural life, did not neglect his own spiritual well-being. For some time he had been asking Leonardo to paint a *Last Supper* for the Dominican monastery in Milan, Santa Maria delle Grazie, which Ludovico had adopted as his 'court church'. The first notes on the design of the painting in Leonardo's manuscripts are dated between 1494 and 1495. At Ludovico's instruction, the east end of the church was reconstructed during the 1490s by Donato Bramante (1444-1514), later to be the architect of St Peter's in Rome. Using a plan similar to those

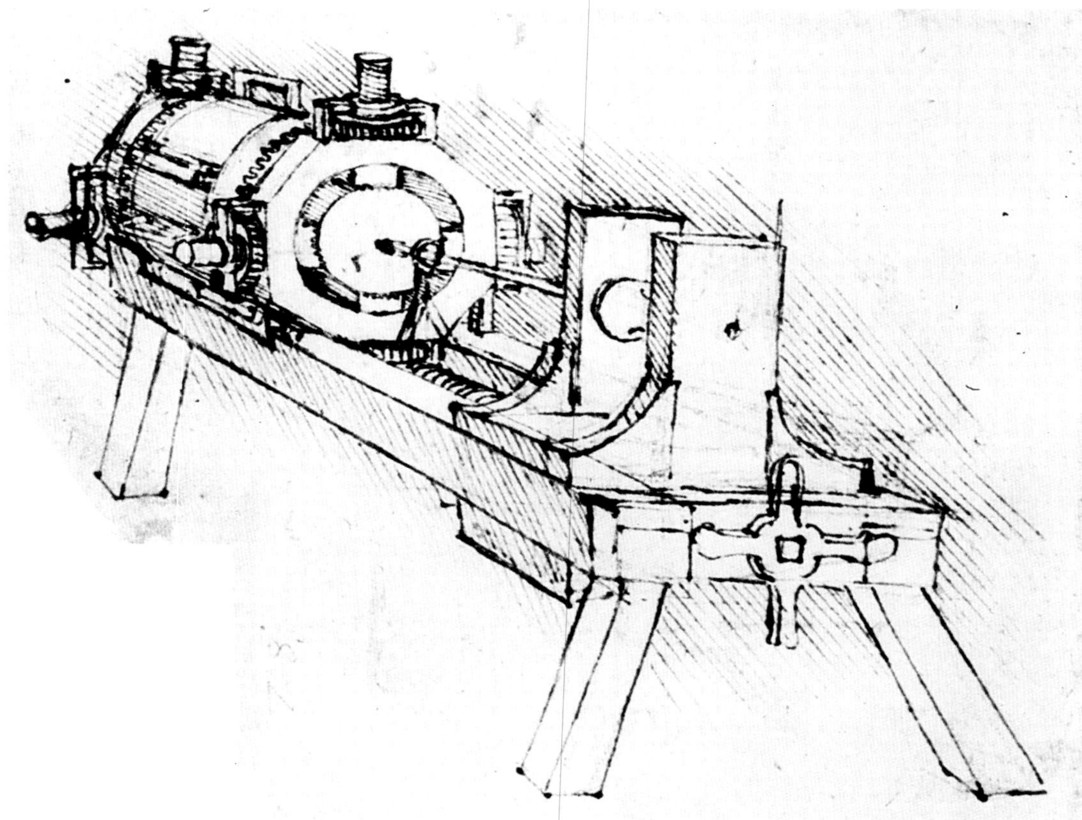

RIGHT: Resembling a modern lathe, this machine was devised for drilling wooden water pipes, which were widely used until the introduction of lead and, later, cast iron piping. A set of adjustable chucks ensures the drill bores precisely through the center of the log, no matter what its diameter. Biblioteca Ambrosiana, Milan.

BELOW: *Design for a Napping Machine*, c.1497, pen and ink, Biblioteca Ambrosiana, Milan. The tedious job of cutting the excess hair from the surface of newly woven cloth with hand-held shears could have been replaced altogether by this machine. As well as saving both time and labor costs, the machine would have produced a constant level of nap.

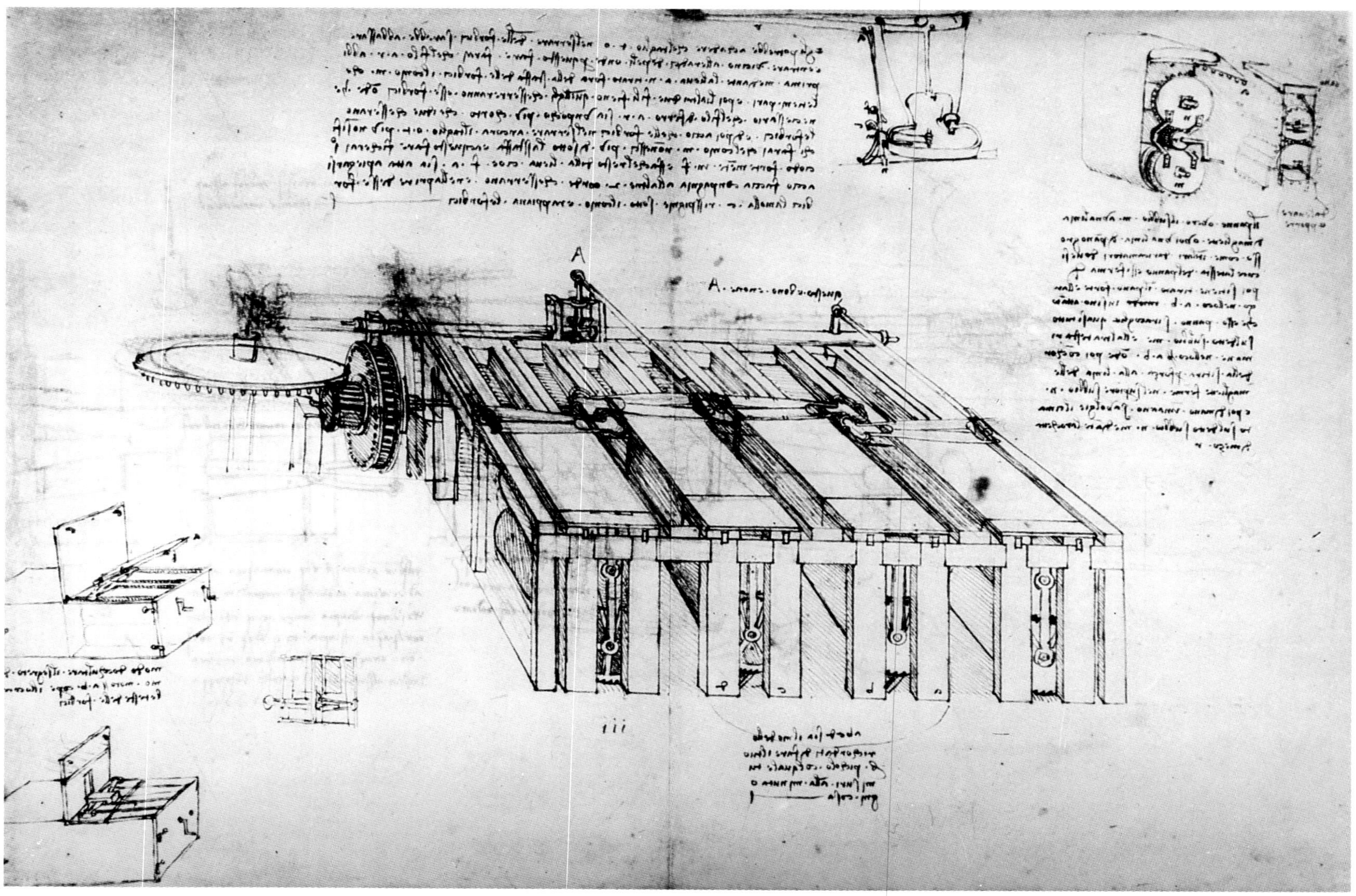

RIGHT: *Two Designs for a Domed Church with Surrounding Cupolas*, c.1488-89, pen and ink, 9 × 6¼ inches (23 × 16 cm), Bibliothèque de l'Institut de France, Paris. Centralized church designs were particularly favored by Renaissance architects and theorists because of their classical origins. This drawing dates from the period when Leonardo was involved in the project for the domed crossing for Milan Cathedral.

BELOW: *Design for a Multi-leveled Town*, c.1488, pen and ink, Bibliothèque de l'Institut de France, Paris. The outbreak of plague in Milan in 1483 may have inspired Leonardo to draw up plans for a remodeled city. His plan called for streets on two levels, the lower ones for carts and lower class citizens, the upper levels for hanging gardens and promenades for the noble Milanese. Every hundred meters or so a spiral staircase would link the two levels, and archways would provide light and ventilation to the lower streets.

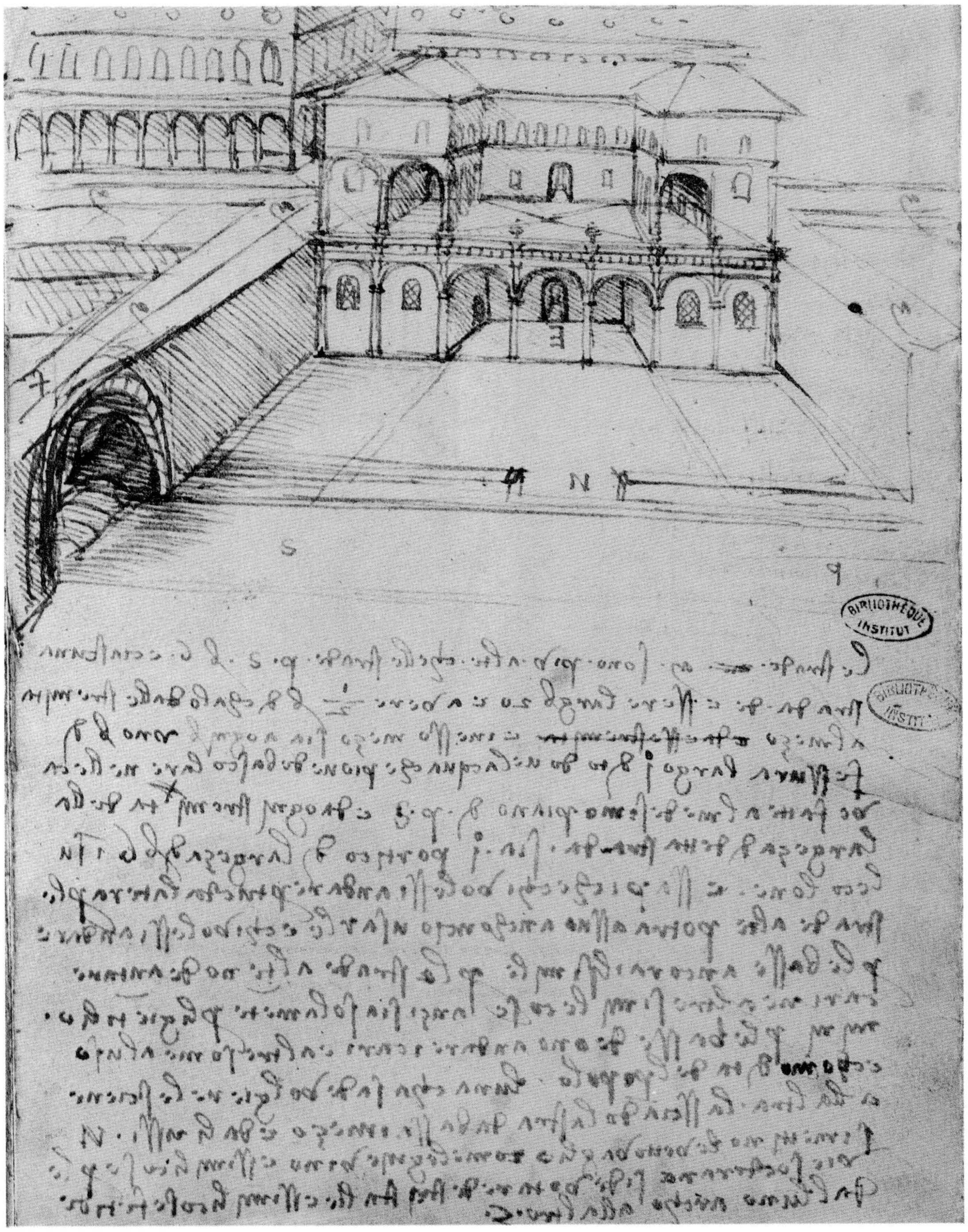

which Leonardo had worked out in 1488-89 in his notebooks for centrally planned churches, Bramante constructed a massive centralized space based on simple geometric forms. Ludovico intended the church as a family mausoleum and a dynastical memorial to the Sforzas. Piously, every Tuesday and Thursday, Ludovico dined in the refectory with the abbot and it was for the end wall of this room, facing the abbot's table, that he commissioned the *Last Supper*. Leonardo began working on the painting in 1496.

As the painting developed it created astonishment; the poet Boccaccio's brother, Matteo Bandello, who was receiving instruction at the monastery where his uncle was a prior, wrote a unique contemporary description of Leonardo at work on the *Last Supper* in 1497:

Many a time I have seen Leonardo go early in the morning to work on the platform before the *Last Supper*; and there he would stay from sunrise to darkness, never laying down the brush . . . Then three or four days would pass without his touching the work, yet each day he would spend several hours examining it and criticizing the figures to himself. I have also seen him, as the caprice or fancy took him, set out at midday from the Corte Vecchia, where he was at work on the clay model of the colossal horse, and go straight to the Grazie; on having mounted the scaffolding take up his brush and add one or two more touches to one of the figures and then abruptly part and go elsewhere.

This description offers us an insight into Leonardo's working method and how he could be distracted during periods of contemplation. the *Last Supper* was Leonardo's first wall painting and, because of the large scale and the nature of the wall surface, it was not practicable for him to work in oil paints, which would have allowed him to make alterations as he went along. The *buon fresco* method with which he would have

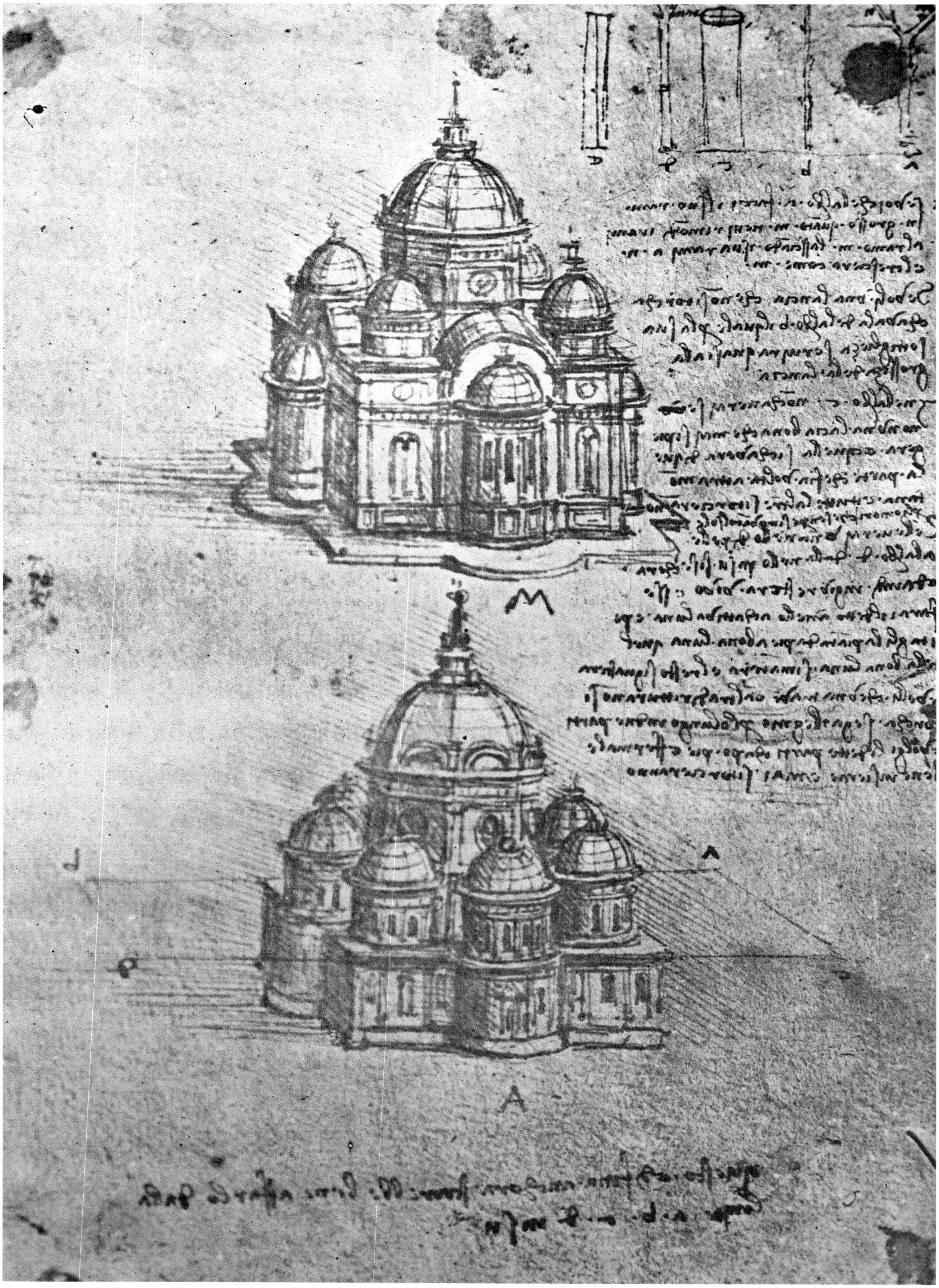

PREVIOUS PAGES: *Last Supper*, 1495-97, tempera on gesso, pitch and mastic, 15 feet 1 inch × 28 feet 10½ inches (460 × 880 cm), S Maria delle Grazie, Milan.

LEFT: Detail from the *Last Supper* showing, from the left, St Peter, Judas (in front) and St John and revealing the extent to which the painting has suffered from decay.

been familiar from his early years in Florence, although the most obvious choice for largescale wall paintings, allowed no changes to be made and was unsuitable from an artistic point of view. Leonardo therefore developed his own medium of tempera on stone. This required a strong base of gesso, pitch and mastic to seal the wall against damp and to provide an even ground for the paint. Unfortunately this medium proved unstable and, as a result, the paint began to detach from the ground within a few years of completion.

By 1556, when Vasari visited the monastery, the *Last Supper* had decayed so extensively that he described the painting as no more than a 'mass of blobs'. Apart from the 'natural' decay, further damage was to occur. The first damage was caused when a doorway was cut through the lower part of the table cloth in 1652 and, although this was subsequently filled in, the damage is still clearly visible. Throughout the eighteenth and nineteenth centuries, restoration attempts were made. The first of these was undertaken in 1726 by Michelangelo Bellotti, who mistakenly believed that Leonardo had worked in oils and therefore retouched the areas laid bare by paint loss and gave the finished restoration a heavy coat of oil varnish. Unfortunately, Bellotti did not take account of the humidity, one of the main problems that had caused much of the original decay.

In 1770 a second painter, Giuseppi Mazza, was called in by the monks. In addition to scraping off Bellotti's retouching, Mazza seems to have repainted more extensively than required. A third scheme in 1821 by Stefano Barezzi attempted to move the entire painting to a more stable environment. Barezzi had been very successful in detaching frescoes in one piece. These consist of two substantial layers of plaster, the *intonaco*, a rough base later applied to a wall on to which a sketch of the painting would be

LEFT: Detail from the *Last Supper* showing, from the left, Christ, St Thomas (with raised finger; his peculiar chin is in fact the result of a failed restoration work), St James the Greater and St Philip.

made, and the *arriccio*, a much finer layer applied over the *intonaco* in *giornate*, sections which corresponded to a day's work. In *buon fresco* the *arriccio* plaster would be painted on while still wet. Because the two layers were different textures, it was quite easy to separate one layer from the other. Leonardo's technique on the *Last Supper* was quite different, however, and the unfortunate Barezzi only discovered this after he had managed to damage a sizeable portion of the tablecloth and one of Christ's hands.

Over-zealous painter-restorers have not been the only culprits; Milan's strategic importance in European affairs saw the city frequently involved in wars. In 1796 Napoleon's troops entered the city and, despite his personal orders to the contrary, the refectory was used as a barn, arsenal and billet for troops and prisoners. The worst damage, however, occurred quite recently, in August 1943, when the roof and one of the supporting walls of the refectory were completely destroyed by a bomb. Fortunately a steel framework filled with sandbags had been erected beforehand to protect the painting. Modern science has yet to halt the decay still being caused by humidity, but until it decays completely, the *Last Supper* can still be seen in the setting for which it was intended.

The painting does seem to have been jinxed right from the start. In the New Year of 1497, Beatrice d'Este, the pregnant wife of Ludovico Sforza, was celebrating by dancing and drinking. The next day she miscarried and was dead. For many superstitious Milanese, her death and Leonardo's *Last Supper* were linked. In the early stages of the development of the painting scheme, the *Last Supper* had accompanied a *Crucifixion* by Montorfano, which included donor portraits of Ludovico, Beatrice and their two children. This painting was subsequently painted over and Beatrice's death was seen as a portent of evil things to come for the Sforzas and for Milan.

By the time Leonardo painted the *Cenacolo* or *Last Supper*, it was already a commonplace subject for wall paintings in the refectories of monasteries. Traditionally it formed one of the many scenes in fresco cycles of Christ's life, but by the middle of the fifteenth century, the Last Supper had become popular as an individual scene. Leonardo would have seen many of these *Cenacoli* in his youth, in particular Taddeo Gaddi's version of 1350 in the monastery of Santa Croce in Florence and Andrea del Castagno's version of 1450 in San Apollonia. Both of these show the room in which the last supper is taking place. In another example, this time by Leonardo's fellow student in Verrocchio's workshop, Domenico Ghirlandaio, in the monastery of Ognissanti in Florence, the room is represented as though it were an extension of the actual room on the wall of which the painting had been made. It is this approach that Leonardo also adopted in his *Last Supper*.

The composition of the *Last Supper* is less simple than it seems. The symmetrical disposition of the disciples on either side of Christ could have been boring. The setting too is unreservedly symmetrical, with its three windows, the center one framing Christ's head. Yet there is little that is bland about the arrangement of the disciples themselves. They are arranged in two groups of three on either side of Christ. In the first group to the left are Bartholomew, James the Less and Andrew. The next group comprises Judas, Peter and John. To the right of Christ are Thomas, with his finger raised, James the Elder, with outstretched arms, and Philip. The outside group comprises Simon, Jude and Matthew, who sweeps around them in disbelief. Because of the compositional restraint, the viewer's attention is concentrated on the reactions of the disciples to the news that one of them will betray Christ. In quiet calm contrast, Christ gestures to the bread and wine.

ABOVE AND RIGHT: The decorative scheme of the ceiling and part of the lower walls of the Sala delle Asse in the Castello Sforzesco in Milan. This work was only re-discovered at the end of the nineteenth century and has also been heavily restored. Nevertheless, the interest in natural forms and the intertwining of the foliage are typically Leonardoesque features.

so many of his projects, Isabella's portrait never materialized. All that remains is a badly damaged drawing which may or may not be by Leonardo. It is pricked for transfer and shows Isabella's head in profile, with her body turned toward the viewer and her hands folded in front of her, a formula familiar to us from Leonardo's earlier female portraits.

By March 1500 Leonardo was on the move again, this time to Venice. La Serenissima then (as now) was in her glory. The Venetian Republic was probably the richest in all Italy, with an empire stretching down the Dalmation coast and including the island of Crete. The city's own small population of around 200,000 was augmented by nearly two million 'colonial' subjects. During the fifteenth century Venice had also produced some of the most magnificent art and architecture in Europe and had nursed ambitions for greater land-based power. Had the Church been less powerful and influential, Venice might have dominated much of northern Italy. But above all else, Venice was 'foreign'. Surrounded by the impenetrable moat of the lagoon, which was navigable only by those who knew the safe routes through it, the Venetians were by nature suspicious of outsiders. A small army of private agents spied on newcomers and laws forbade Venetians to entertain foreigners in their homes. Leonardo, as a Florentine and thus a foreigner, would have found it very difficult indeed to find a patron in Venice to match Ludovico Sforza. He would instead have to earn his living, something he was not very good at doing.

The Turkish threat to Venice was one area that Leonardo appeared to try and exploit. The Battle of Lepanto in August 1499 had broken Turkish sea power, but Venice still feared an attack on the city by land. A fragment of a draft letter to the governing council of Venice details Leonardo's travels through the area under threat, the Isonza valley in Friuli, to the north of Venice, and outlines his scheme to flood the area as a defensive measure. Other plans that he outlined involved designs for mine ships, ramming vessels and a submarine, all part of a system for destroying the Turkish fleet. Leonardo overlooked two things, however: firstly his schemes were costly, and secondly Venice already had a fleet and an arsenal which was a closed shop to outsiders, jobs being passed from father to son, and to the ideas of outsiders. The Venetian council did not even officially record Leonardo's visit to the city.

Nevertheless while he was there he seems to have become friendly with a number of people, including the printer Aldous and Cardinal Grimani, whose collection of Flemish paintings and Greek marble of *Leda* Leonardo saw and possibly sketched. He also met the Comte de Ligny, who offered him a position in France. This offer Leonardo turned down – at least for the time being – and one month after his arrival, he was on his way back to Florence.

RIGHT: *Isabella d'Este*, 1500, black chalk heightened with red chalk, 24¾ × 18½ inches (63 x 46 cm), Cabinet des Dessins, Musée du Louvre, Paris. Believed to have been made during Leonardo's brief stay at Isabella's court at Mantua in 1500, this drawing is pricked for transfer but the final finished painted version was never undertaken.

CHAPTER 3

Florence 1499–1506

During Leonardo's 18-year absence, the political and artistic climate of Florence had changed considerably. The Medici were no longer in power; following a few unsuccessful attempts to govern the city-state, Lorenzo de' Medici's son had drowned in the river Garigliano during military action. Medici rule had been replaced by a republic under the leadership of their most hated enemy, the stern, fanatical Dominican friar Girolamo Savonarola, who supervised a puritan regime in the bankrupt city. Even Botticelli became a supporter and destroyed all his early works, while Pico della Mirandola abandoned Neoplatonism and Boccaccio's books were burnt. Some of Leonardo's old friends were still alive but many of those who had made Florence the artistic and philosophical center of Europe were dead: Ficino, Poliziano, Mirandola, the Pollaiuolo brothers, Domenico Ghirlandaio and above all, his old master Verrocchio.

It is possible that Leonardo was planning only an extended visit to Florence. In December 1499 he had lodged a letter of exchange for six hundred gold florins with the monastery of Santa Maria Novella in Florence. On his arrival in the city he cashed fifty of the florins; the transaction was dated 25 April 1500. With the Medici court dispersed, Leonardo had little chance of finding a new patron or attracting many commissions. Fortunately, Leonardo's father was now the procurator of the Servite monastery of the Annunciation, where the monks had already commissioned Filippino Lippi to complete two paintings for the high altar of their church. While Vasari tells us that Lippi happily gave up the commission to Leonardo, it is more likely that Ser Piero used his influence to get the commission transferred to his son.

FACING PAGE: Detail of the head of the Virgin from the *Virgin and Child with St Anne and St John the Baptist* (page 84).

BELOW: A view of Florence by Leonardo's biographer, Giorgio Vasari, depicting the seige which led to the collapse of republican rule in the city in 1530. The city center is dominated by Brunelleschi's dome of the cathedral.

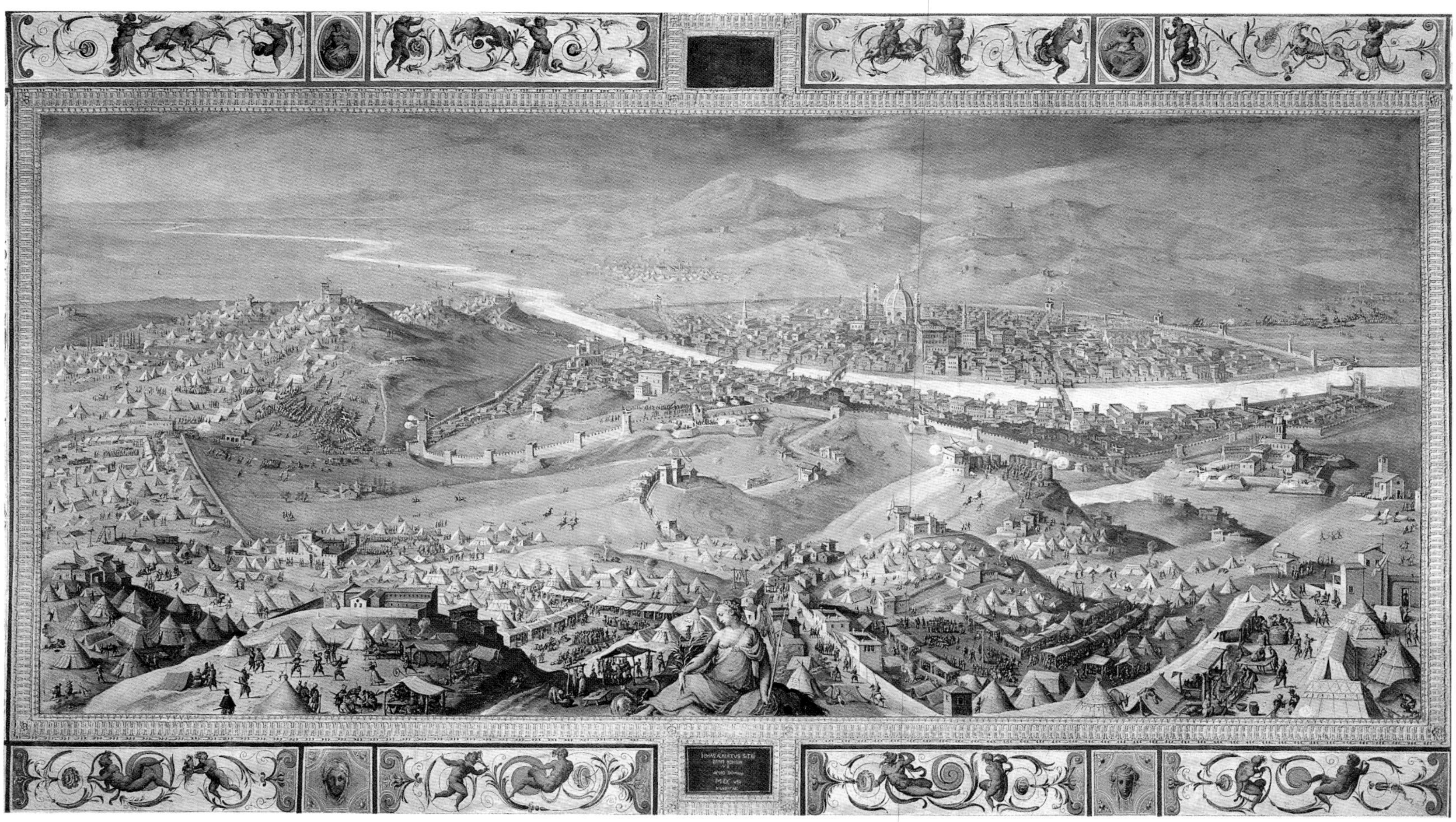

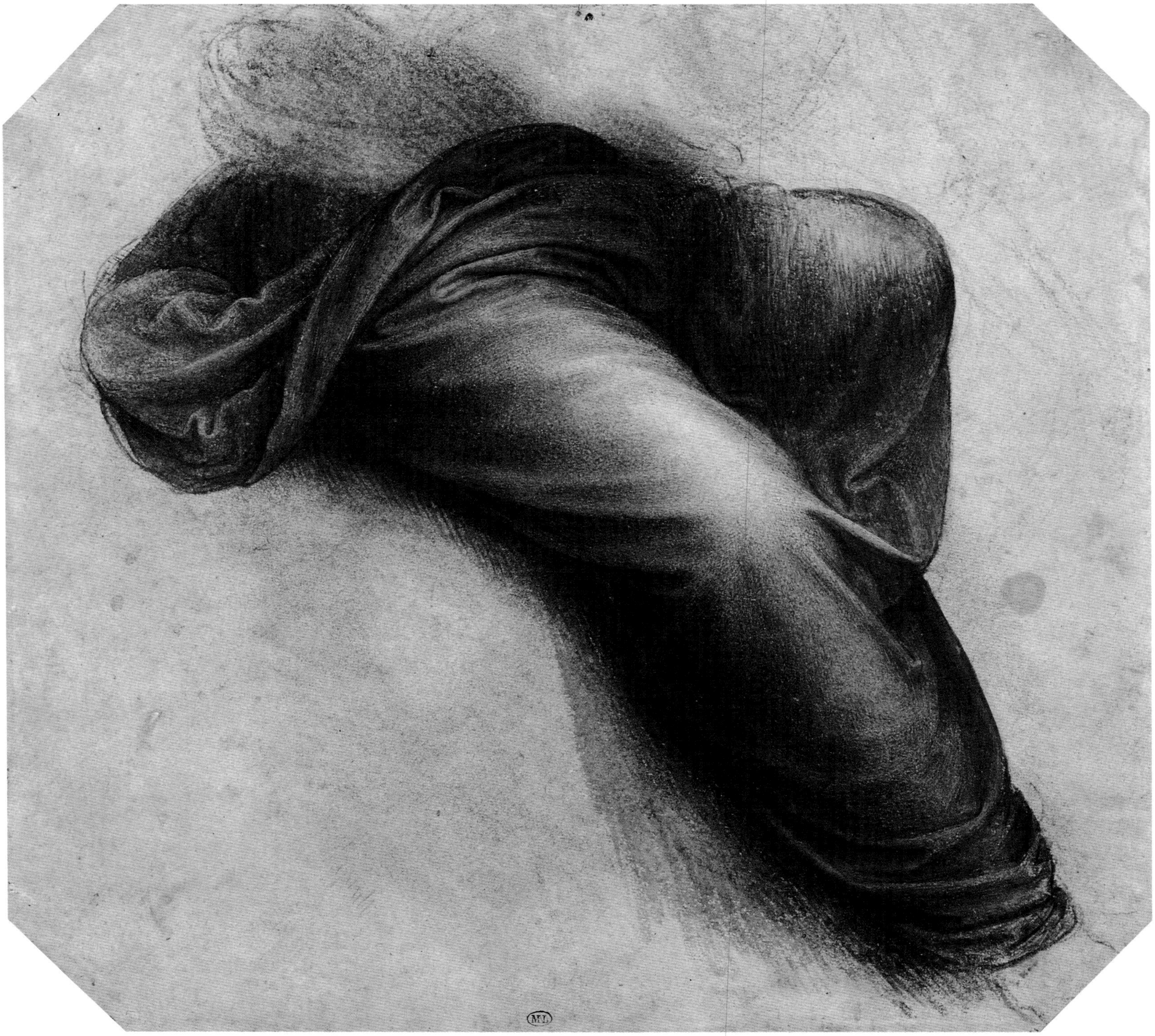

ABOVE: *Study of Drapery for the Virgin in the Virgin and Child with St Anne and a Lamb*, c.1508, black chalk and black wash heightened with white, 9 × 9⅝ inches (23 x 24.5 cm), Cabinet des Dessins, Musée du Louvre, Paris.

LEFT: *Virgin and Child with St Anne and a Lamb*, c.1508, oil on wood panel, 66⅛ × 44 inches (168 × 112 cm), Musée du Louvre, Paris.

In September 1500 Leonardo was hard at work, but not on the altarpiece. Isabella d'Este had written to Fra Pietro da Novellara, the Vicar-General of the Florentine Carmelites, in April 1501 enquiring about Leonardo's activities – no doubt she wanted to know when she was going to receive the finished portrait based on the cartoon – and asking Fra Pietro to persuade Leonardo to 'do a little Madonna, devout and sweet as is his wont.' Fra Pietro replied that as far as he knew, all Leonardo had done since his return to Florence was a study for the *Virgin and Child with St Anne* for the Servite monastery. Evidently Leonardo was spending much of his time studying geometry.

There are several cartoons and studies of the *Virgin and Child with St Anne*, at Windsor Castle, in the Louvre, in the Accademia in Venice and in the British Museum. The unfinished oil painting in the Louvre, *Virgin and Child with St Anne and a Lamb*, is usually dated around 1508-1510 but there is disagreement about Fra Pietro's description of the cartoon that he saw. He described the figures as turned to the left but it is unclear whether he meant his left or the sitter's left. He also described St Anne as preventing her daughter from discouraging the Christ Child as he grasps the lamb. The lamb is the sacrificial animal and the symbol of Christ's Passion, and St Anne's action of restraint thus signifies that the Church did not want to prevent the Passion. Matters are further complicated by the existence of a largescale cartoon, the *Virgin and Child with St Anne and St John the Baptist* in the National Gallery, London, which Vasari described and on which he said Leonardo was working as the basis for the altarpiece in

BELOW: *Study for the Virgin's Sleeve and Hand* for the *Virgin and Child with St Anne and a Lamb*, c.1508, black and red chalk, pen and ink, with washes of black, 3⅜ × 6¹¹⁄₁₆ inches (8.6 × 17 cm), Windsor Castle, Royal Library 12532. © 1994 Her Majesty The Queen.

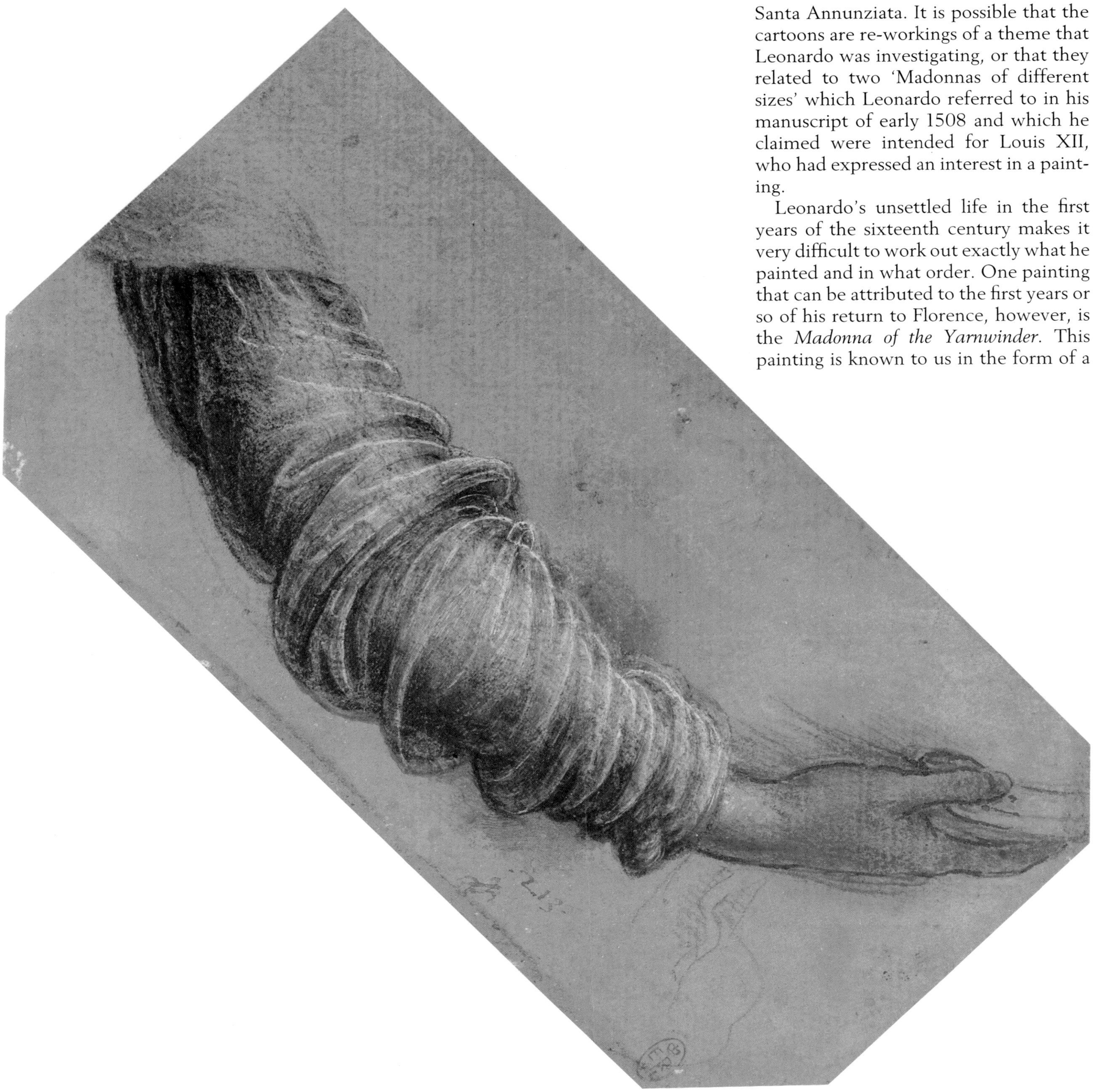

Santa Annunziata. It is possible that the cartoons are re-workings of a theme that Leonardo was investigating, or that they related to two 'Madonnas of different sizes' which Leonardo referred to in his manuscript of early 1508 and which he claimed were intended for Louis XII, who had expressed an interest in a painting.

Leonardo's unsettled life in the first years of the sixteenth century makes it very difficult to work out exactly what he painted and in what order. One painting that can be attributed to the first years or so of his return to Florence, however, is the *Madonna of the Yarnwinder.* This painting is known to us in the form of a

BELOW: *Studies for the Christ Child* in the *Virgin and Child with St Anne and a Lamb*, c.1505, red chalk, 11 × 8⅝ inches (28 × 22 cm), Galleria dell' Accademia, Venice.

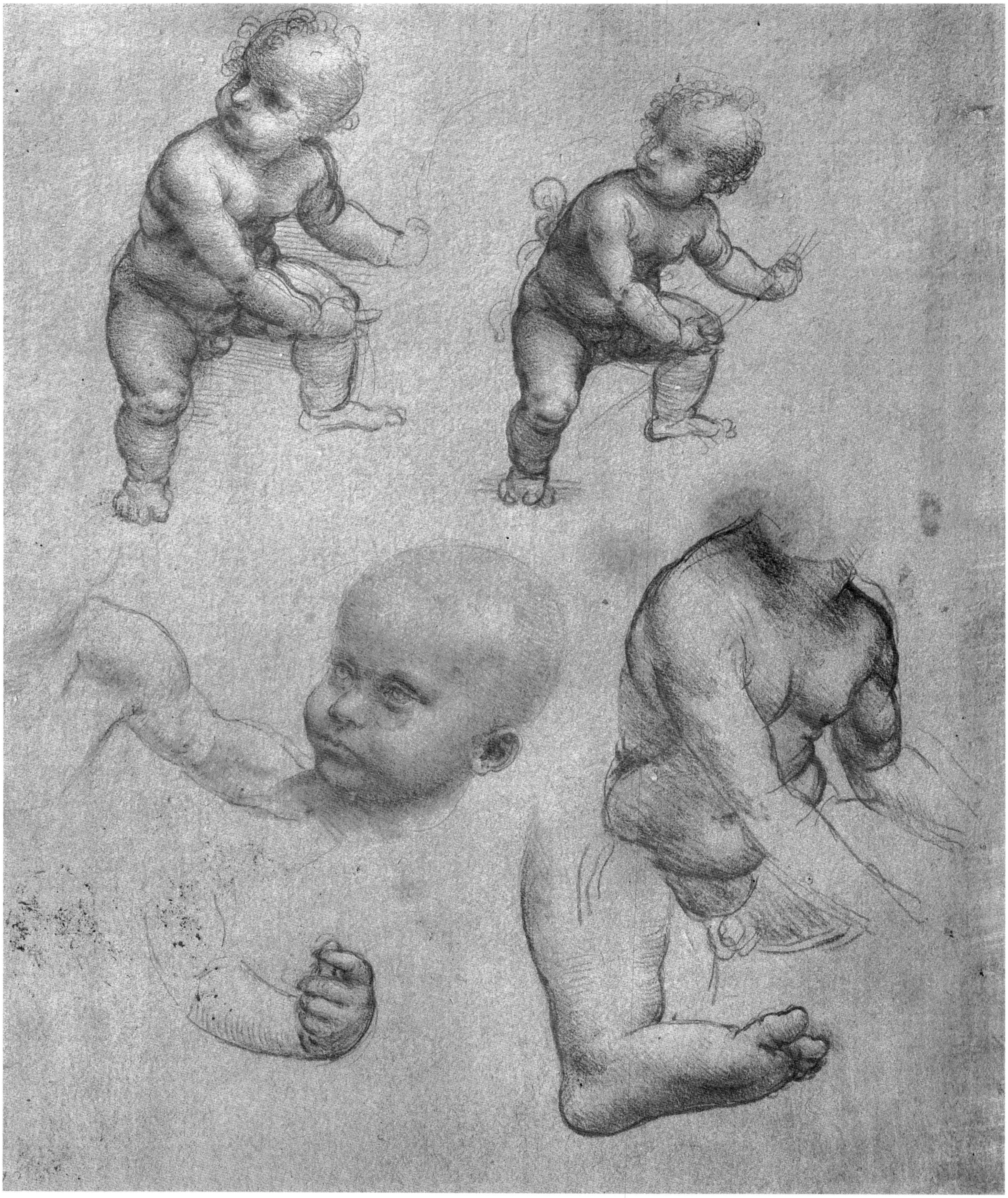

LEFT: *Virgin and Child with St Anne and St John the Baptist*, c.1505, 54¾ × 39¾ inches (139 × 101 cm), charcoal on brown paper heightened with white, National Gallery, London.

RIGHT: *Study for the Virgin and Child with St Anne*, c.1500-1505, pen, ink and wash over black chalk, 10¼ × 7¾ inches (26 × 19.7 cm), courtesy of the Trustees of the British Museum, London.

BELOW: Details of the heads of Christ (left) and St Anne (right) from the *Virgin and Child with St Anne and St John the Baptist*.

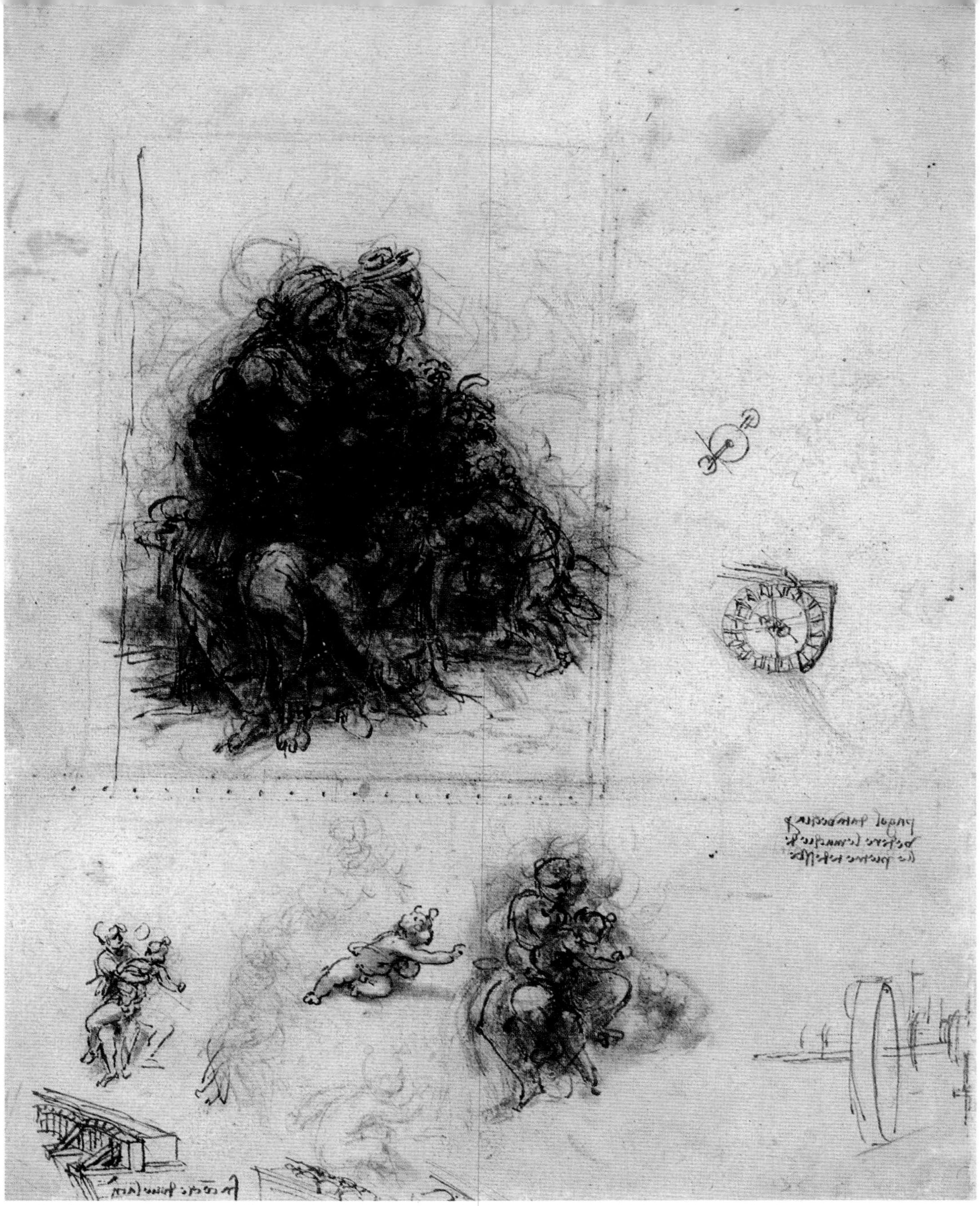

number of copies, the best of which Leonardo may well have had a hand in painting. It also conforms to the description of a small painting mentioned in Fra Pietro's letter to Isabella d'Este as having been executed for Florimund Robertet, Secretary of State to Louis XII of France. Fra Pietro describes how the Virgin is intent on spinning yarn but the child, whose feet rest on a basket of flax, takes hold of the yarnwinder and gazes intently at the four spokes which form the shape of a cross.

The records show that in July 1501 Leonardo signed a receipt for the rent of his vineyard outside Milan, and that Manfredo di Manfredi came to see him

LEFT: *The Madonna of the Yarnwinder*, c.1501, oil on wood panel, 18¼ × 14¼ inches (46.4 × 36.2 cm), in the Collection of the Duke of Buccleuch and Queensberry KT, Drumlanrig Castle, Dumfriesshire. This painting is believed to have been produced for Florimund Robertet, Secretary of State to Louis XII of France. It conforms to a description by Fra Pietro da Novellarra in a letter to Isabella d'Este.

BELOW: *Bird's Eye View of Part of Tuscany*, c.1502-03, pen, ink and watercolor, 10⅞ × 15⅞ inches (27.5 × 40.1 cm), Windsor Castle Royal Library 12683. © 1944 Her Majesty The Queen. This map is believed to have been made for Leonardo's patron Cesare Borgia.

on Isabella d'Este's behalf. Despite her request, Leonardo neither returned to the court at Mantua, nor painted anything for the Duchess. In the following year, 1502, Leonardo was asked by Francesco Malatesta to appraise four jeweled vases that had once belonged to the Medici family and which were now being offered for sale. At this time Leonardo had found himself a new patron, Cesare Borgia, who employed him as his architect and chief engineer.

Cesare Borgia, like Ludovico Sforza, dreamed of ruling all Italy; his motto read 'Either Caesar or Nothing'. His father, Pope Alexander VI, had made his son the Marshal of the Papal Troops and appointed him Duke of Romagna, thereby ousting the legitimate rulers of the area in the name of the Catholic Church. Florence was subdued by its powerful neighbor and a treaty named Cesare as 'Condottiere' of the Florentine Republic, a title that carried with it a handsome annual income of 30,000 gold ducats.

Borgia, with a mix of Arab and Castillian blood in his veins (and suffering from syphillis), had a reputation for intelligence, a foul temper and odd behavior; he went to bed in the morning, breakfasted at four in the afternoon and walked about all day wearing a mask. His driving political ambitions also made him capable of murder; in his personal retinue Cesare maintained the services of a hired assassin called Grifonetto. He dispatched Paolo Orini and the Pope's favorite, Perrotta, and executed his own governor of Romagna, Don Ramiro del Lorqua, officially for being an extortionist but actually because he fell in love with Cesare's sister Lucrezia (herself no angel) who had just married. Later Cesare was to murder his brother-in-law as well.

RIGHT: *View of Chiana and Arezzo*, c.1500, black chalk, Windsor Castle Royal Library 12682. © 1994 Her Majesty The Queen. This map, possibly made for Cesare Borgia, appears to have been drawn from the air. In fact it was created using an imaginary perspective, combined with earlier views and studies that Leonardo had made of the region.

BELOW: *Plan of Imola*, c.1502, pen, ink and watercolor, 17⅓ × 23⅔ inches (44 × 60.2 cm), Windsor Castle Royal Library 12284. © 1994 Her Majesty The Queen. Using a horizontally mounted and graduated surveying disc – possibly an astrolabe – Leonardo was able to record the radial angles of important features of the city when viewed from a high central vantage point. Faintly visible in places are the 64 equally spaced radiating lines, eight of which are drawn in bold and labeled according to the 'wind rose' – north, north-east, east and so on. In the map, every detail is color co-ordinated; the houses are pink, public squares are yellow and the streets are white.

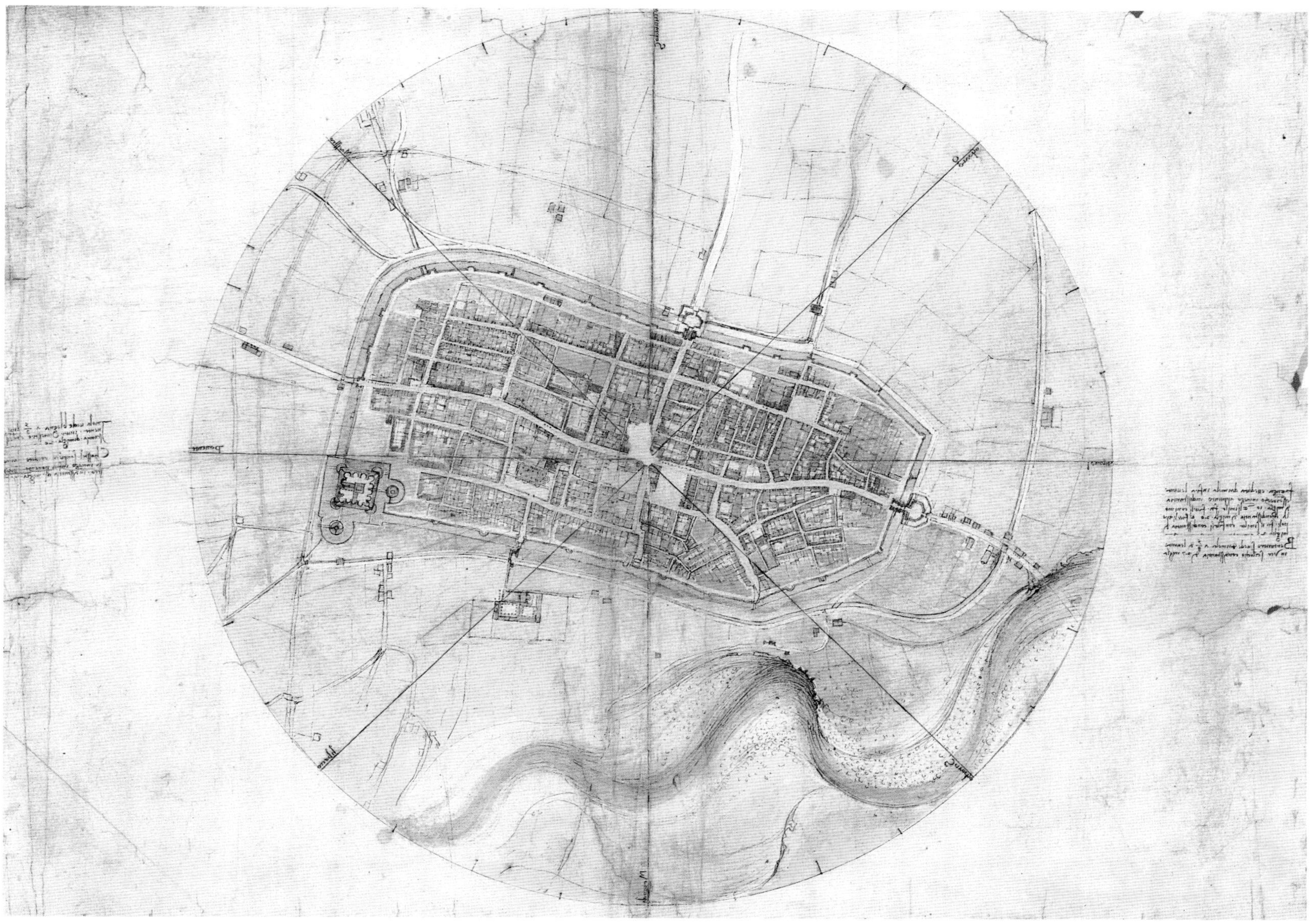

Busy creating his kingdom – the duchies of Faenza, Imola, Rimini, Pesaro and Urbino had already surrendered to him – Cesare was set to invade Umbria. Leonardo accompanied him on his military campaigns, producing maps and surveys. Cesare's chargé d'affaires, whose task as political observer was to report on the general situation, was Niccolò Macchiavelli, the first writer to develop a theory and program of political realism. His book *The Prince*, the main character of which was based on his employer, was a sort of handbook on how to be successful in politics.

In the summer of 1502 Leonardo accompanied Cesare on his conquering mission through Emilia and the Marches, operating as the chief inspector of military buildings. Manuscript L in the Bibliothèque Nationale in Paris is Leonardo's diary of the journey and in it he records the stops in the region between Imola, Cesena, Rimini, Urbino and Pesaro. Apart from some sketches for the docks at Porto Cesenatico, we do not have any further insight into Leonardo's official activities. He did, however, draw up the area of Borgia's military operations; part of a map of Tuscany and Romagna was made for Cesare, as was the magnificent circular *Plan of Imola* dated around 1502, an immensely accurate and beautiful plan in which every detail is pinpointed and color-coded. The houses are in pink, public squares in yellow, the streets in white. The castle is at the lower left and is surrounded by the blue moat. The notes at either side of the

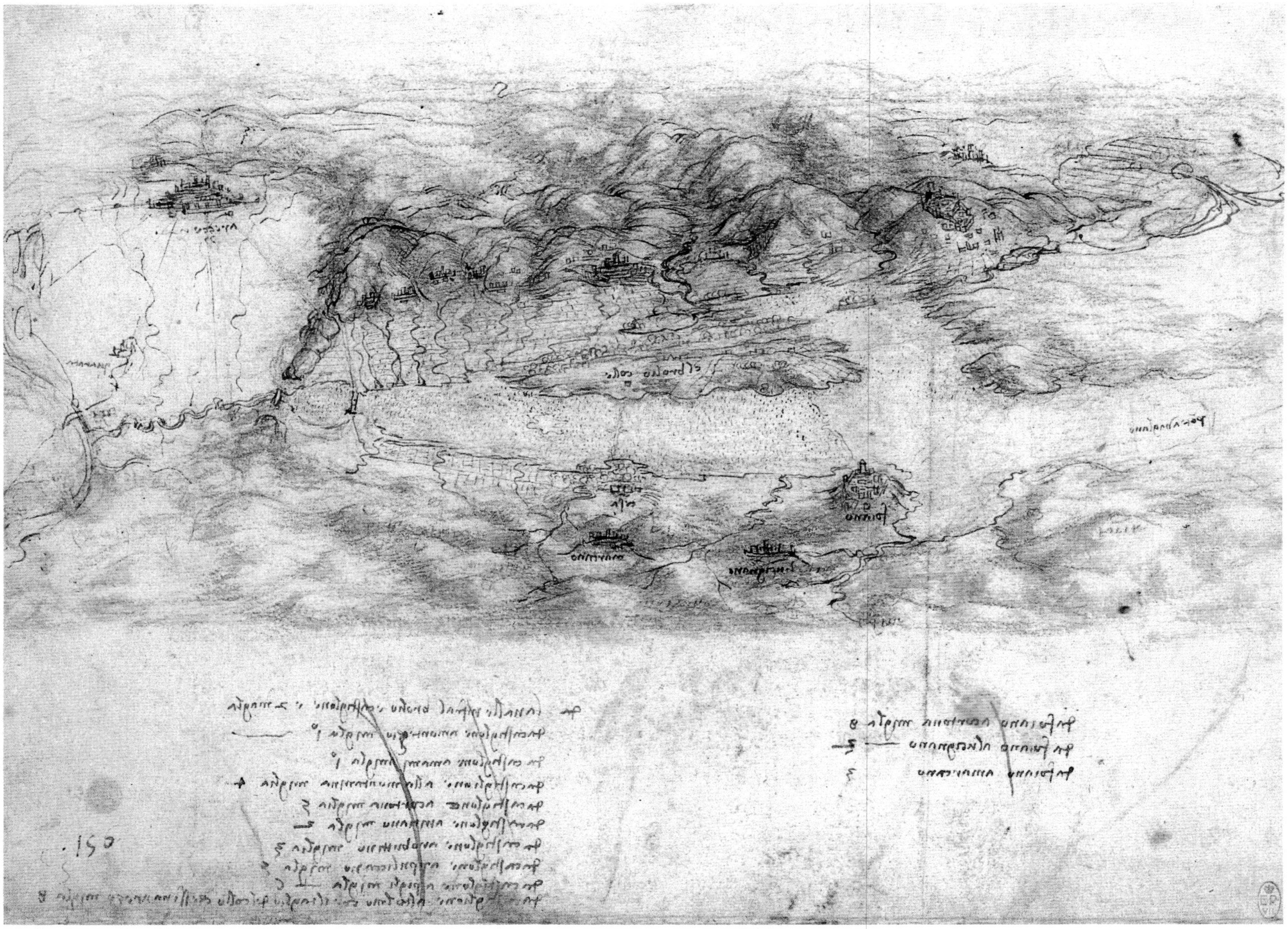

plan, written very neatly but nevertheless in Leonardo's famous 'mirror handwriting' (from left to right with the letter forms reversed) refer to the geography, distance and bearings of Bologna and other cities of strategic importance or interest to Borgia.

From remarks he made in Manuscript L, we also learn that Leonardo visited the area of Piombino, part of Borgia's dominion at the northern end of the Tyrrhenian Sea. Iron ore from the island of Elba was unloaded in Piombino's fortified harbor, but the port was more important politically since the city occupied the central point between the bordering territories of the Papal States in the south, Lombardy and Genoa to the north, and Florence to the east. Following a long seige in 1501 Borgia succeeded in wresting Piombino from its ruler Jacopo IV Appiani. In 1502 Leonardo also made the map showing Arezzo and the valley of the Chiana, using an imaginary perspective that gives the illusion of an aerial view. But by the spring of 1503 Leonardo had given up his position with Borgia and returned to Florence. Pope Alexander VI had died and Cesare, back in Rome after an officers' rebellion against him, also fell ill – some say from poison – but he rallied after being immersed in the steaming entrails of a mule. According to Macchiavelli, it was only because of his father's death and his own ill-health that Cesare was prevented from extending his rule throughout Italy. Ironically, had Cesare decided to launch a campaign against Tuscany, Florence might well have fallen, precisely because of Leonardo's map-making skills and the strategic engineering plans he had made for the Duke.

In Florence, Savonarola had been excommunicated and subsequently tried and burnt at the stake, but the system of government he had introduced, consisting of a chamber of 3000 enfranchized citizens, was to continue until 1512. This large council, the Signoria, needed a suitably large and magnificent meeting hall. In 1495 Antonio da Sangallo the Elder had designed a vast hall 178 feet long, 77 feet wide and 60 feet high. Having ousted the Medici, the new ruling Council needed to demonstrate its legitimacy and, hopefully, its expected longevity; the council hall became the vehicle for a decorative scheme demonstrating the virtues and achievements of republican power.

Filippino Lippi was commissioned to produce an altarpiece, depicting St Anne accompanied by numerous saints who all had particular associations with Florence. Some time in the fall of 1503, Leonardo was commissioned to execute a larger wall painting depicting a scene from the *Battle of Anghiari*, while the young Michelangelo was asked to produce an accompanying scene of the *Battle of Cascina*. Both battles were famous Florentine victories; Michelangelo's subject showed an episode in the war against Pisa when bathing Florentine soldiers were ambushed and rushed for the weapons they had left on the river bank, while Leonardo's was the 1440 triumph over Milanese mercenaries.

Like so many of Leonardo's paintings, *The Battle of Anghiari* was never completed and what he did complete had been lost by around 1560. Although no original contract for the commission survives, we know that on 24 October 1503, Leonardo was given the keys to a large room in Santa Maria Novella in which to produce a full-size cartoon for the painting. By the time the contract was signed, around May 1504, he had been supplied with paper, other drawing materials, and scaffolding. Records show that the contract was witnessed by Macchiavelli, who, clearly aware of Leonardo's reputa-

RIGHT: Copy of the fight for the standard from the center of the *Battle of Anghiari*, c.1550, oil on wood panel, 6 × 8⅜ inches (15.1 × 21.3 cm), Palazzo Vecchio, Florence. One of the copies of Leonardo's painting, which was lost by 1560 when Giorgio Vasari frescoed the Sala del Consiglio.

BELOW: *Studies for the Central and Left Groups of the Battle of Anghiari*, c.1503-04, pen and ink, 5¾ × 6 inches (14.5 × 15.2 cm), Galleria dell' Accademia, Venice.

tion for not working to deadlines, stipulated that the cartoon must be complete by February 1505 or, failing that, Leonardo should have started painting the part of the cartoon that had been finished. If the latter was the case, the deadline would be extended.

Throughout 1504 and on past the deadline of February 1505, Leonardo continued to receive supplies for making whitewash, flour for sticking the cartoon to the wall, wall plaster, Greek pitch, linseed oil and Venetian sponges. These materials suggest that he intended to paint the pitch over the smoother plaster base as a ground for oil-based paint. Much to the chagrin of the mayor of Florence, Piero Soderini, however, work on the *Battle of Anghiari* was abandoned in May 1506. Boards were erected to protect the painting in 1513, and several

copies were made of it before it finally disappeared under Vasari's frescoes in 1560. It is only from these copies and some preparatory drawings that we know something about this lost work.

Leonardo's work on the *Battle of Anghiari* was no doubt interrupted by other pressing needs. In 1503 the Republic of Florence had once again embarked on a new campaign against its old enemy Pisa and between 24 and 26 July 1503 Leonardo was in the Florentine camp, where plans were being laid to divert the river Arno and cut off Pisa's access to the sea, thus starving the city into submission. One of the chief promoters of this scheme was the Florentine war minister, Macchiavelli. Leonardo must have had some knowledge of this plan, but whether he was actually involved in its implementation remains in doubt. In

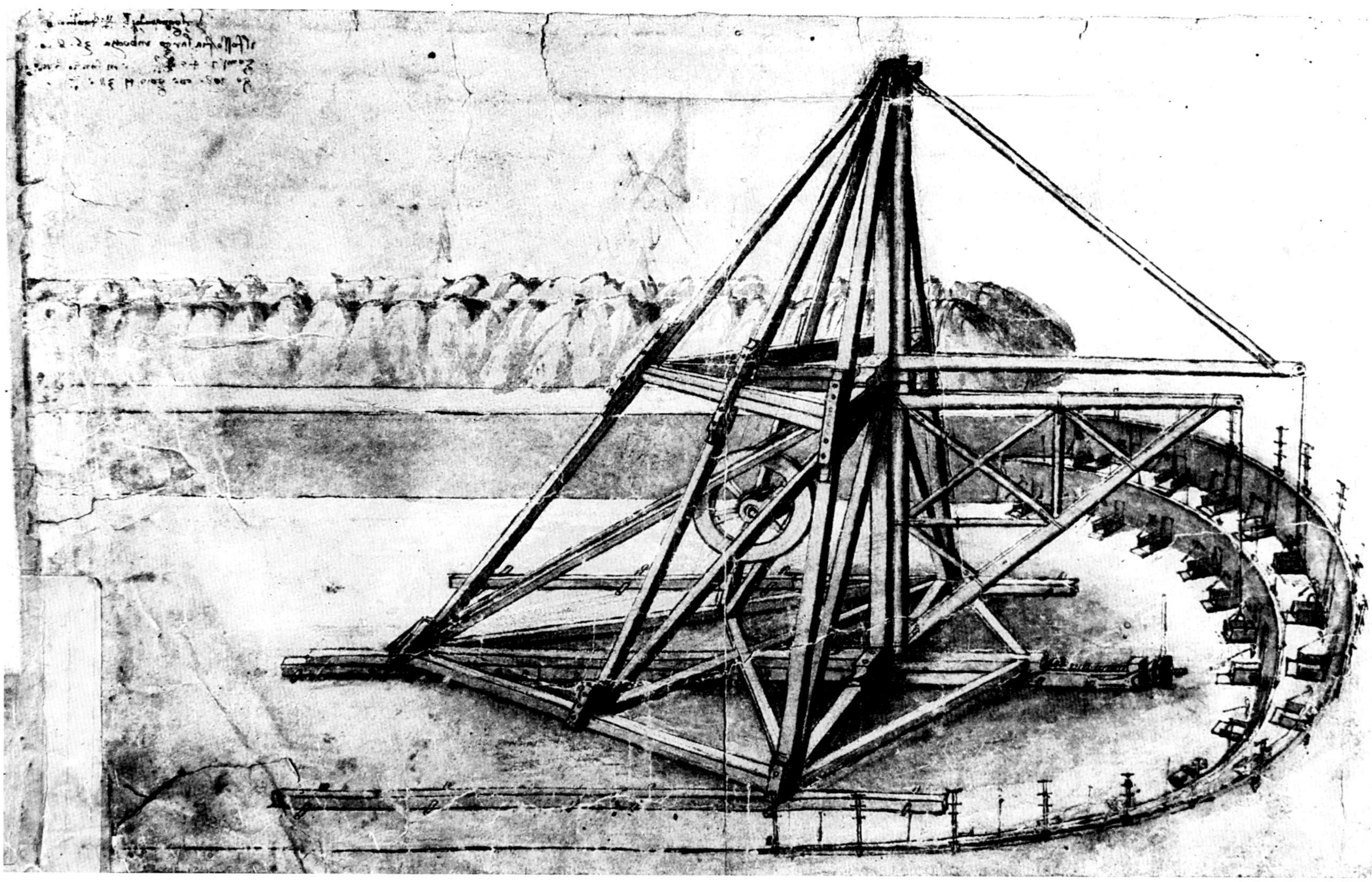

ABOVE: A huge treadmill-powered digging machine designed by Leonardo, possibly in conjunction with his schemes to canalize the river Arno between Florence and the sea.

July 1503, at the order of the Council, Leonardo set off to inspect the trench-digging on the project. For well over a year the Arno plan was in action but the cost of manpower – which had been underestimated at 2000 men completing the work in 20 days – and the technical problems of securing the canal walls against collapse led to the scheme being abandoned in October 1504.

Leonardo himself had for many years had a strong interest in diverting the Arno, not for military purposes, but to make the river navigable between Florence and Pisa and thereby increase the volume of trade in Tuscany. He drew up maps showing the course of the river and schemes for its canalization on several occasions. Aware of the manpower required to effect such a scheme, Leonardo also designed a huge treadmill-powered digging machine.

When the plan to cut Pisa off from the sea collapsed (along with much of the canal itself), military activities were temporarily halted. The Signoria recalled its troops and instead planned to isolate Pisa through political channels. In 1504 Macchiavelli went to Piombino to treat with Jacopo IV Appiani, who had returned to power in the city after Borgia's fall. Macchiavelli had to win back Jacopo's trust and confidence in Florence – in 1499 Jacopo had been passed over in favor of Borgia for the position of Condottiere – in order to win his neutrality regarding Florence's hostilities with Pisa and Siena. Neutrality toward Pisa was easy; Jacopo still bore a grudge against the city for having ousted his family four generations earlier. In order to woo him into neutrality toward Siena, Leonardo was sent to Piombino in the fall of 1504 to advise Jacopo on fortifications for the city – a scheme Leonardo had originally devised for Cesare Borgia!

This information is of relatively recent origin, made available by the 're-discovery' of the Madrid Codices. These had been erroneously catalogued and then recorded as missing, but were found in 1965 on the shelves of the national Library in Madrid. In the Madrid Codex II, Leonardo drew up plans for the reconstruction of the harbor with a breakwater similar to ones devised by Francesco di Giorgio in his *Treatise of Architecture, Engineering and Military Art*, a copy of which Leonardo owned. From Giorgio, Leonardo also 'borrowed' schemes for citadels with rounded towers and thick inclined walls, well suited to deflecting mortar bombardments. In his sketches of fortresses, Leonardo also drew in cannons on top of the walls; he was one of the first military architects to do so. Many of his sketches also show cannons in towers and diagrams which plot the line of fire. Although it is not known whether any actual construction was carried out at Piombino, the tower of the main gate of the city is still known today as 'Leonardo's Tower'.

Despite his efforts, Leonardo found himself out of favor with the Florentines: he had failed to complete *The Battle of Anghiari*; and the plan for diverting the Arno had drained the treasury and some of the collapsed canal had flooded, causing a swampland and resulting in an outbreak of malaria which claimed the lives of many Florentines. In addition Leonardo had led a somewhat 'aristocratic' lifestyle in a very puritan city, and to cap it all his father died in 1504 and he became entangled in a lawsuit with his step-brothers over shares in the family property. Leonardo stood accused of betraying Florence by his earlier association with Borgia and of practicing magic, an accusation no doubt fueled by further allegations of homosexuality. At this time, only Isabella d'Este continued to offer her support but, for reasons known only to Leonardo, he chose to avoid her. When Isabella visited Florence, Leonardo went into hiding in Fiesole!

BELOW: *Head of a Man Shouting,* c.1505, red chalk, 9 × 7⅓ inches (22.7 × 18.6 cm), Museum of Fine Arts, Budapest. This drawing is a preparatory study for the unfinished, and now lost, painting of the *Battle of Anghiari*.

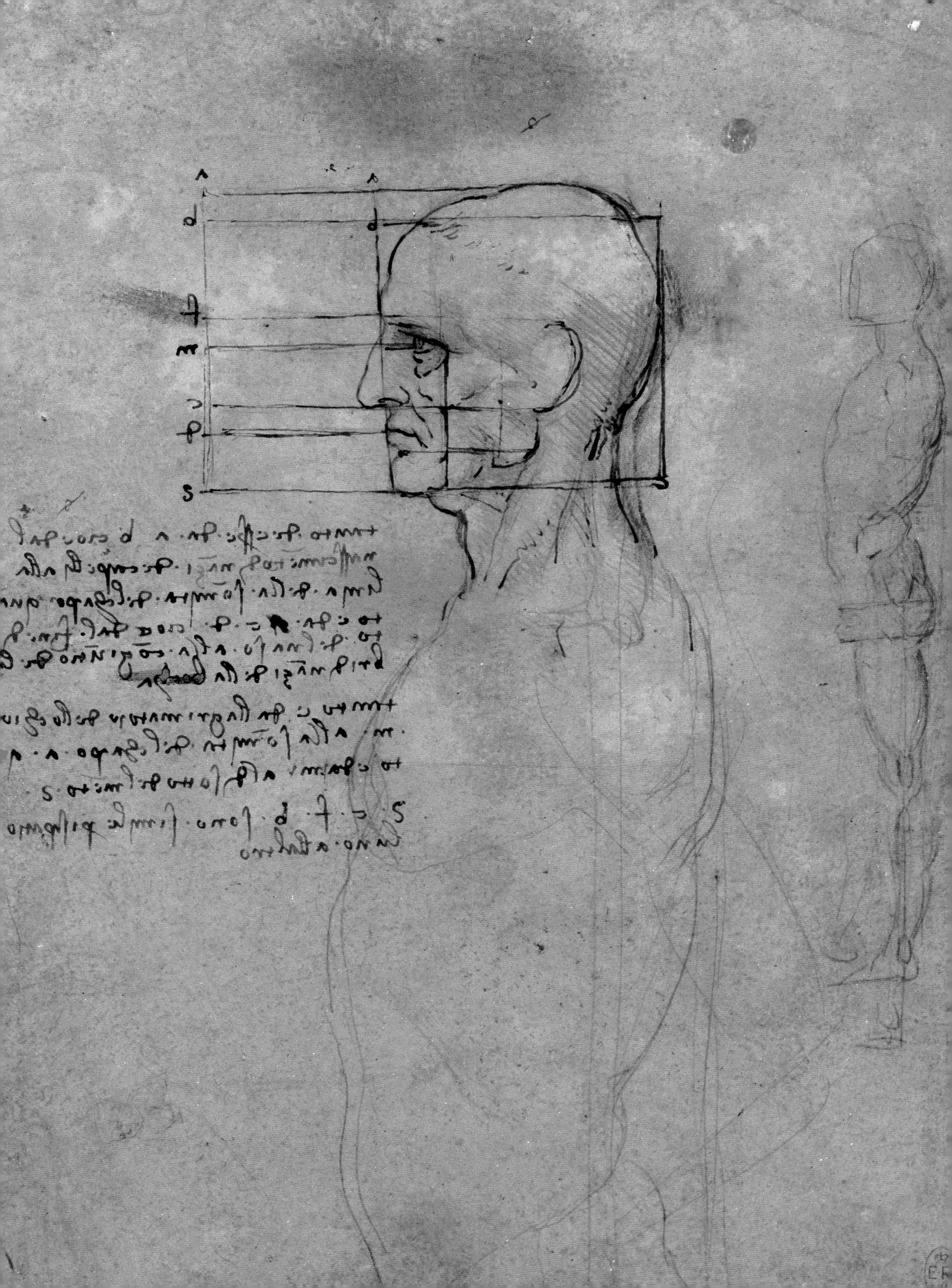

CHAPTER 4
Rome and France, 1506–19

In the spring of 1506, at the request of Charles d'Amboise, Lord of Clairmont-sur-Loire, and Governor of Milan in the name of Charles XII, Leonardo was back in that city. He had been granted three months leave by the Signoria, but he returned to Florence only in the fall of 1507 to end the legal battle with his family and to settle with the friars of San Francesco over the disputed commission for the *Madonna of the Rocks*. Once all litigation was complete, he returned to the French court at Milan, where he stayed until 1512. Joining him in Milan as his pupils were Francesco Melzi (the son of his old friend from Vaprio), Giovanni Boltraffio and Gian Giacomo Caprotti do Ornone, nick-named 'Salai' or 'little devil'. Salai had been part of Leonardo's 'household' since 1491 and was employed as a household servant and occasional model. Beautiful (according to Vasari), obstinate, greedy, a liar and a thief, Salai was also a talented artist and a faithful companion to Leonardo, staying with his master until he died. In Milan Salai was known as the painter Andrea Salaino.

On 27 May 1507 Louis XII made his official entry into Milan, and once again it fell to Leonardo to devise the official celebrations. According to Vasari he designed a vast lion 'which came forward several paces and then opened its breast which was full of lilies.'

FAR LEFT: *The Proportions of the Human Head*, silverpoint on blue prepared paper, $8\frac{3}{4} \times 6$ inches (21.3 × 15.3 cm), Windsor Castle Royal Library 12601. © 1994 Her Majesty The Queen. In his measured drawings Leonardo was attempting to divine the fundamental rules of proportion in nature, and as such these drawings are often much closer to his mathematical studies than to his anatomical drawings.

BELOW: Detail of the hands of the *Mona Lisa*.

LEFT: *Study for the Kneeling Leda*, c.1504, pen, bister and wash over black chalk, 6¼ × 5½ inches (16 × 13.9 cm), Devonshire Collection, Chatsworth House, Derbyshire, reproduced by courtesy of the Trustees of the Chatsworth Settlement.

RIGHT: *Mona Lisa*, c.1505-13, oil on wood panel, 30 × 20⅞ inches (77 × 58 cm), Musée du Louvre, Paris. It was Vasari who identified the sitter here as Madonna Lisa, the wife of Francesco di Bartolomeo di Zanobi del Giacondo, thereby giving this painting its name. Ironically, Vasari was describing a painting he had never even seen. It is possible that the portrait is of the Duchess of Burgundy, the wife of Louis XII of France; whoever she is, the painting must surely be the most famous portrait in the history of western art.

For some years Leonardo had also been working on what was to become the most famous portrait in the history of painting, the *Mona Lisa*. Mona or Madonna Lisa Gheraditi was identified by Vasari as the model. She came from a noble Neapolitan family and in 1495, aged about 17 or 18, she married a Florentine silk merchant, Francesco di Bartolomeo di Zanobi del Giacondo (hence the painting's other title *La Giaconda*). Francesco was about 20 years older than Lisa. She was his second wife, his first, Camilla Rucellai (whose family were also traders in silk) having died in childbirth.

It is very likely that Vasari's identification was based on a misinterpretation, as Anonimo Gaddiano recorded that Leonardo painted Francesco del Giacondo and not his wife. Other inconclusive evidence in documents of various dates has linked the woman in the painting with both Isabella d'Este (which seems unlikely given Leonardo's efforts to avoid her) and the Duchess of Burgundy, the wife of Louis XII. Since Louis was in effect Leonardo's patron, this thesis is not unreasonable. Whoever the portrait represents, Leonardo spent around four years on it. He took the portrait with him to Milan and it is unlikely that any money passed between him and Giacondo, which suggests that the *Mona Lisa* may not have been a commission at all, but a single painting in which Leonardo worked out all that he had been trying to achieve in his portraits of women, including those of angels, saints and Madonnas.

The presentation and setting of the figure in the *Mona Lisa* is highly original and, although the panel has been trimmed at the sides, we can see enough of the balustrade to recognize that the figure is seated on a balcony with a landscape vista behind her. Such an image was almost totally unprecedented in Florentine portraiture. Even Leonardo's previous female portraits, such as those of Cecilia Gallerani and Ginevra de' Benci, had no such background, or just a glimpse, as through a small window, of such a scene. In the *Mona Lisa* the background is no longer merely a decorative backdrop. The treatment of the figure and the landscape are a reflexion of Leonardo's twin areas of study in the early years of the sixteenth century, the anatomy of the human body, and the movement and development of landscapes through geological and meteorological changes. The twisting flow of drapery and head veil echoes the action of the flowing water, while the spiralling curls of her hair are reflected in the pattern of the waterfall. But the reason for the *Mona Lisa*'s fame rests less on this novelty than on the famous 'Giaconda Smile'. The key to the painting's success is the very ambiguity of her expression, and the question of whether or not Mona Lisa is smiling. Whatever our interpretation, we remain transfixed by her gaze.

At this time Leonardo was working on some of the finest botanical drawings ever produced. The majority of the extant studies are related to the years 1508 and after, when Leonardo seems to have been working on the *Mona Lisa* and on variations on the theme of Leda and the Swan, depicting a standing Leda and a kneeling Leda. The story of Leda tells how Jupiter, disguised as a swan, fathered four children: Castor, Pollux, Clytemnestra and Helen, who were all hatched from eggs. The painting of *Leda* is known only from drawings and from sixteenth-century copies of the work. The earliest studies for the painting date from around 1504 (the same time that Leonardo was working on the *Battle of Anghiari*). These, and subsequent studies up to around 1506, developed the theme of Leda kneeling with one arm around the swan. The kneeling Leda had classical precedents in a type of kneeling Venus. Some time around 1507-8 Leonardo transformed Leda into a standing figure and we can assume that this pose became the basis for the painting, since the best copies of the work use this format.

The Rotterdam *Leda* includes a drawing of the plant *Sparganum erectum*, which is also seen in the study *Flowering Rushes*. In the Chatsworth *Leda*, a highly finished drawing of the kneeling Leda, Leonardo included both this elegant marsh plant and a spiraling plant, *Ornithogalum umbrellatum*, at Leda's feet. The study of this plant, the *Star of Bethlehem*,

LEFT: School of Leonardo, *Leda*, oil on wood panel, 38 × 29 inches (96.5 × 73.7 cm), Collection of the Earl of Pembroke, Wilton House Trust, Salisbury, Wiltshire. Most of the finest copies of Leonardo's *Leda* depict a standing figure, so we can assume that after making studies of a kneeling Leda (page 95), Leonardo settled on this scheme.

ABOVE: *A Star of Bethlehem and Other Plants*, c.1505-08, red chalk, pen and ink, 7¾ × 6 inches (19.8 × 16 cm), Windsor Castle Royal Library 12424. © 1994 Her Majesty The Queen. Possibly Leonardo's most famous botanical study, this is a highly finished drawing of the same plant that appears at Leda's feet in the Chatsworth *Leda* (page 95) and to the bottom right in the Pembroke *Leda* (left).

in red chalk, pen and ink, is probably Leonardo's best known botanical drawing, as well as being the most spectacular; there are in fact three different species of plant depicted on this page. It has been suggested by botanists that in its leaf formation the 'star of Bethlehem' does not have such a pronounced spiral arrangement. Its appearance was most likely due to Leonardo's method of observation and analysis, which, as in some of his anatomical studies, tended to result in an emphasis on the underlying structure of things and the patterns that these structures produced. Nevertheless, while he was aware of the iconography of plants and flowers in paintings, Leonardo also ensured that any plant life appeared in its proper 'ecological' setting; while the plants and flowers carry symbolic meaning, they are also true to nature.

The spiraling form that is evident in the ringlets of the *Mona Lisa* and in the drawing of the *Star of Bethlehem*, and the energies embodied in such spirals, were an area of interest to which Leonardo often returned. We can see them in his studies of water, in cloud formations, in the *Deluge* drawings, and in the braided hair of the *Leda* herself. The sheer number of drawings of landscapes and plants testifies to the passionate interest with which Leonardo observed nature. In addition to recording the slight variations within families of trees, Leonardo laid the basis for a theory of landscape in his *Treatise on Painting*. For Leonardo a landscape, as a work of art, had to be not merely decorative but also to correspond to something actual and true. His manuscripts reveal his interest in the changing appearance of trees under different lighting conditions, as well as in their growth patterns, and he excelled, in both his paintings and drawings, in modeling forms by gradations of light and dark.

Some of the botanical studies are also related to architectural forms, such as arches and vaults. The grass *Coix Lachryma-Jobi* was a relatively new plant to Europe when Leonardo made his study of it, *A Long-stemmed Plant*, and we can see a similar shape in his studies for churches and in the *triburio* for Milan Cathedral. At the same time this study of grass also explores the theme of reproduction that can be seen in other drawings of seeding, flowering and fruiting plants. Some of the drawings which at first sight appear to be purely botanical

ABOVE: *Deluge*, c.1513, black chalk, 6½ × 8¼ inches (16.3 × 21 cm), Windsor Castle Royal Library 12378. © 1994 Her Majesty The Queen. The spiralling forms evident in Leonardo's studies of braided hair and plant forms appear again in his cloud and water formations.

RIGHT: *Studies of Water Formations*, c.1507-09, pen and ink, 11½ × 8 inches (29 × 20.2 cm), Windsor Castle Royal Library 12660v. © 1994 Her Majesty The Queen.

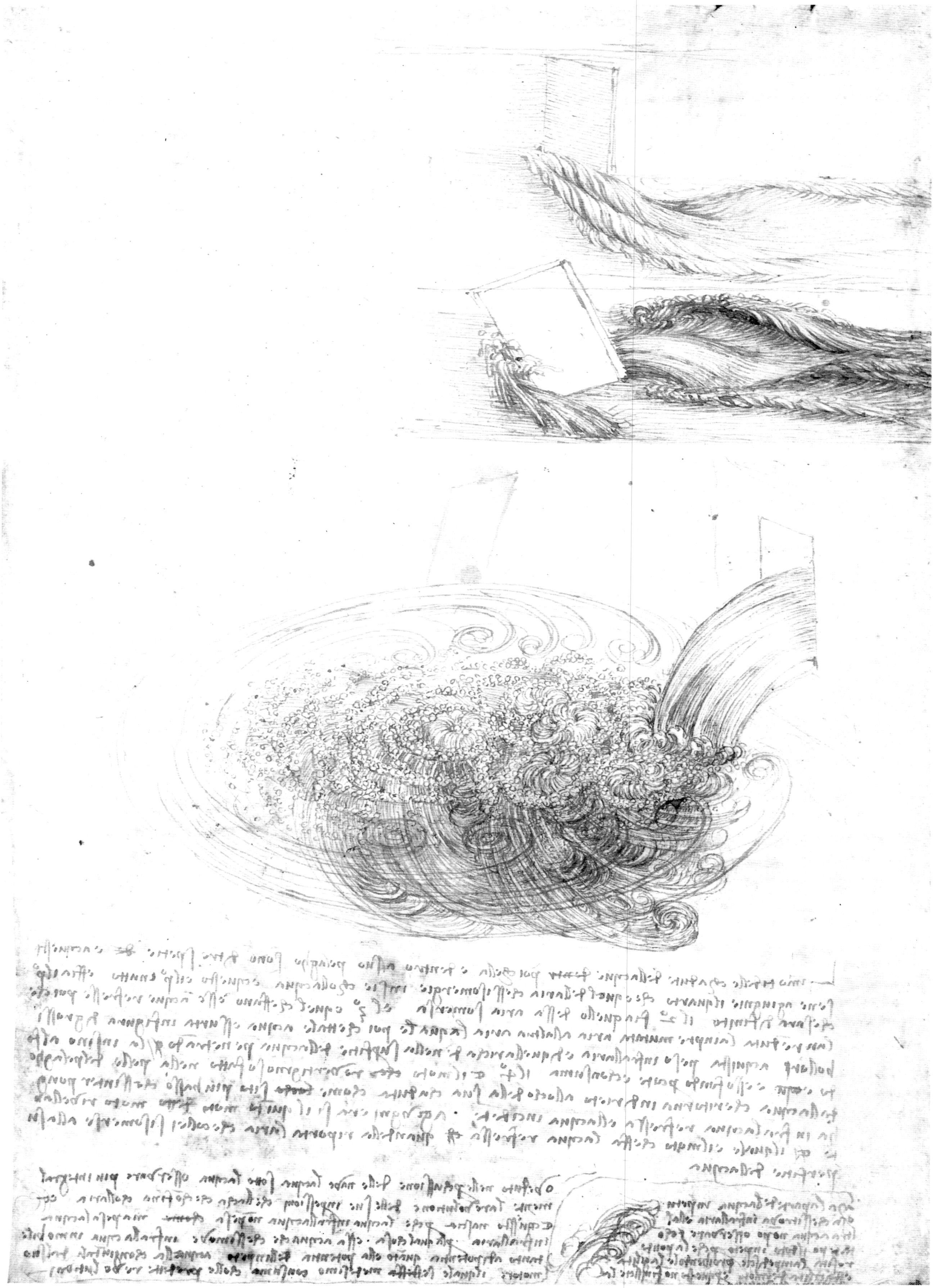

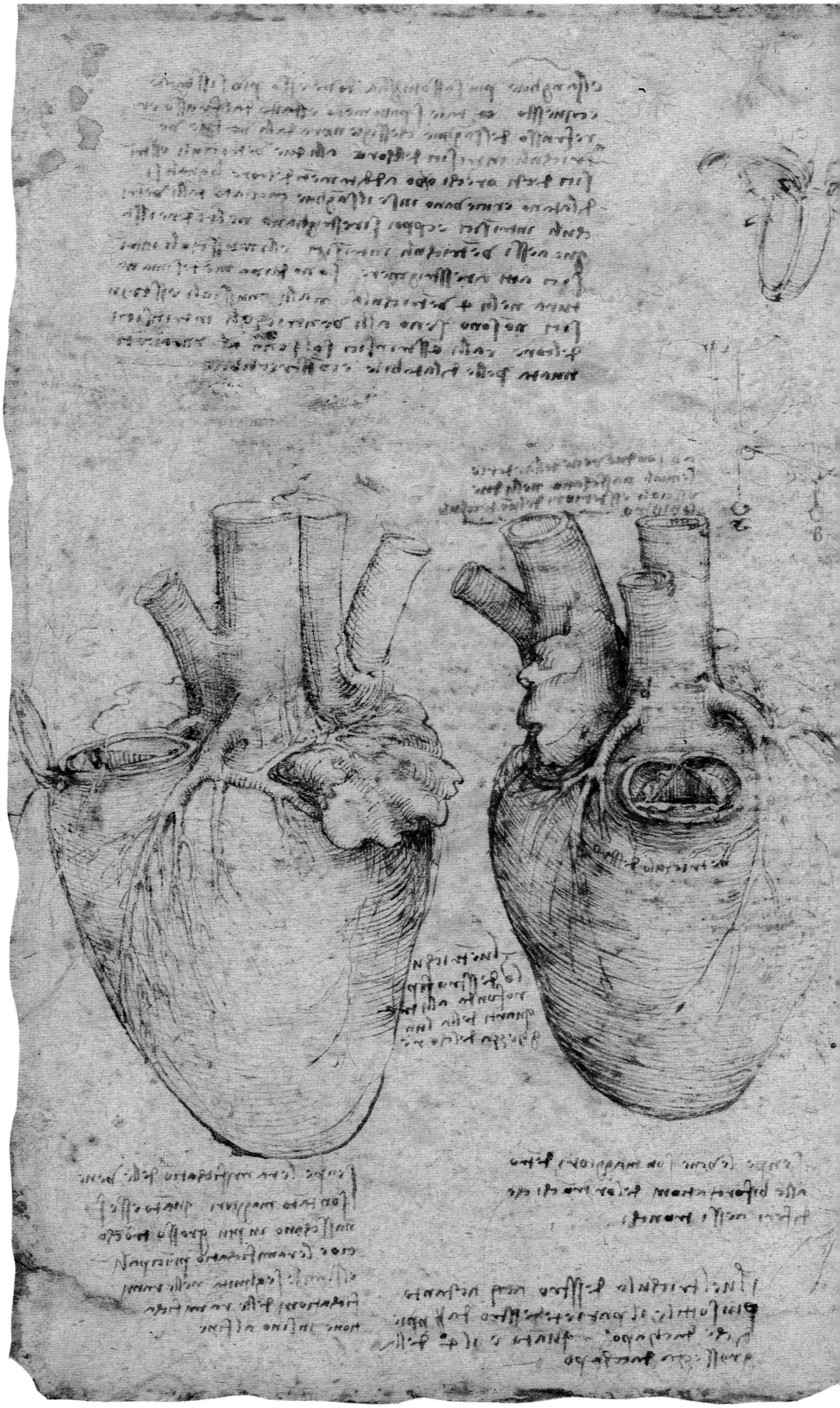

RIGHT: *Drawings of the Heart*, c.1513, pen and ink on blue paper, Windsor Castle Royal Library 19074r. © 1994 Her Majesty The Queen. The circulatory system was described in detail by Leonardo in over 50 drawings of the heart. Early drawings show it with two ventricals while later studies, no doubt informed by his dissections, show the four chambers of the heart in minute detail, but Leonardo did not fully understand the connection between the circulation of the blood and the pumping action of the heart itself.

studies are in fact related to motifs that appear in paintings. *Oak Leaves with Acorns and Dyer's Greenwood* comes from a group of studies in the Royal Collection at Windsor related to the lost *Leda* painting. The oak also appears as a motif in the lunette garlands of *The Last Supper* and in *St John-Bacchus*.

The large number of different studies of plants gives credence to the belief that Leonardo was planning a book on the subject. Had he produced one, it would have been the first of its kind, since the notes that accompany the drawings make no mention of any medicinal properties the plants have. Instead of producing a traditional 'herbal', he was studying and drawing plants in the manner of a true botanist, revealing the qualities of each plant for no other purpose than that of understanding its structure, growth, flowering and reproductive patterns.

Both *Leda* and the *Mona Lisa* represent ideas that Leonardo had formulated earlier in Florence. While there he was deeply involved in anatomical and geological studies, which were then worked on over a number of years up to and even perhaps after 1516, when he left Italy for France. The first date in Leonardo's notebooks on the subject of anatomy comes from April 1489; presumably he was undertaking illegal dissections, a practice strictly forbidden by papal decree. It is possible that rumors of this secret work were spread abroad in Florence, leading to the accusations of his being a heretic and of 'making magic'.

The majority of Leonardo's anatomical drawings, including the famous studies of the heart and of embryoes, were in fact carried out during the second period in Milan, between 1506 and 1513. These studies gained impetus from a particular dissection that had taken place in Florence in the winter of 1507-8, carried out on the body of an old man, the 'centenarian'. Leonardo believed that the old man's death was brought about by the failure of the blood to maintain a supply

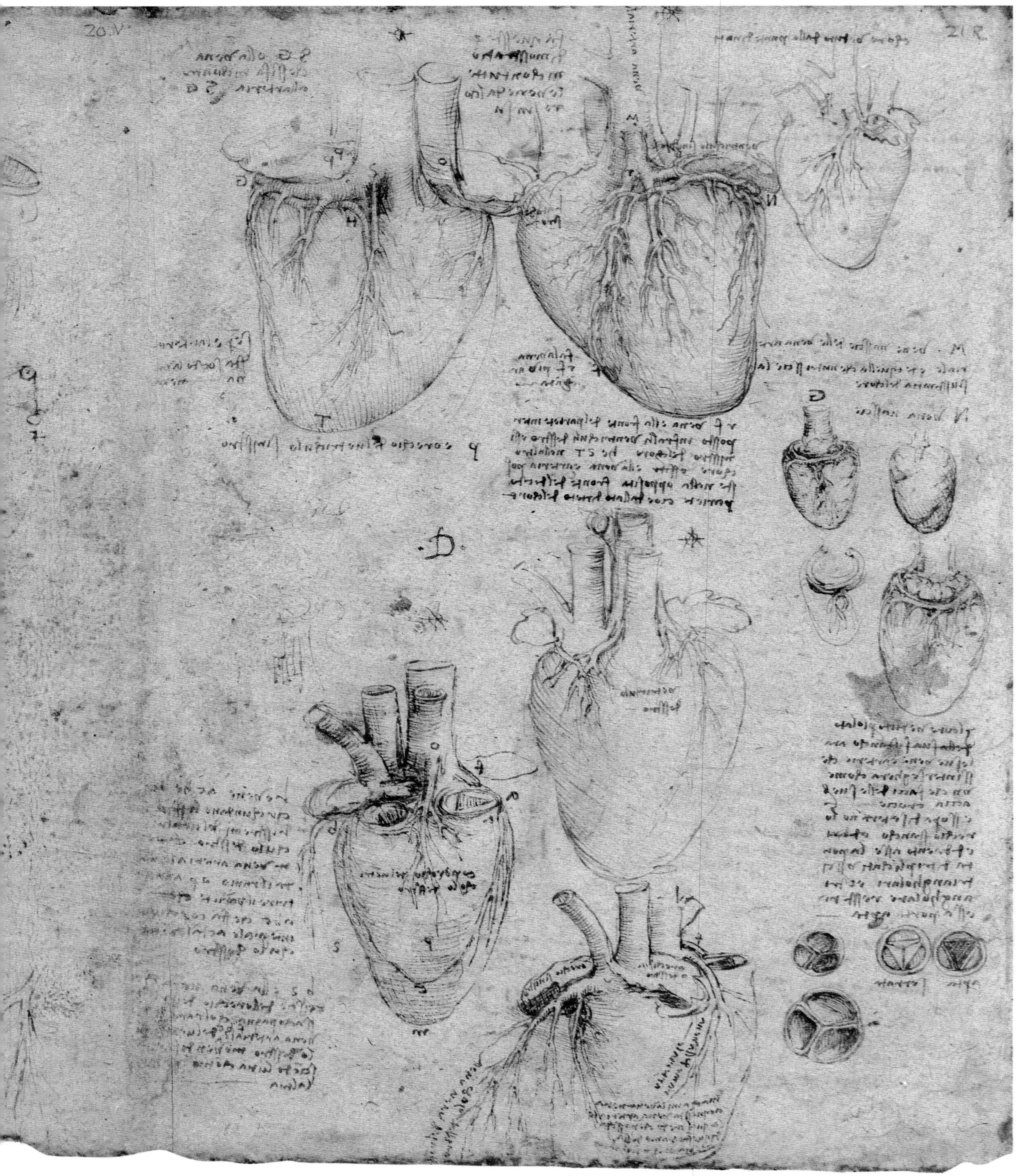

RIGHT: *Study of the Vulva*, c.1513, pen and ink, Windsor Castle Royal Library 190995. © 1994. Majesty The Queen.

FAR RIGHT: *Dissection of the Principal Organs of a Woman*, c.1510, pen, ink and wash over black chalk, 18½ × 13 inches (47 × 32.8 cm), Windsor Castle Royal Library 12281r. © 1994 Her Majesty The Queen. In the accompanying notes to this drawing, Leonardo wrote of a planned series of works, beginning with a study of the formation of the child in the womb, and followed by a discussion of digestion, reproduction and the blood vessels, as well as the cycles of life and death within the human body.

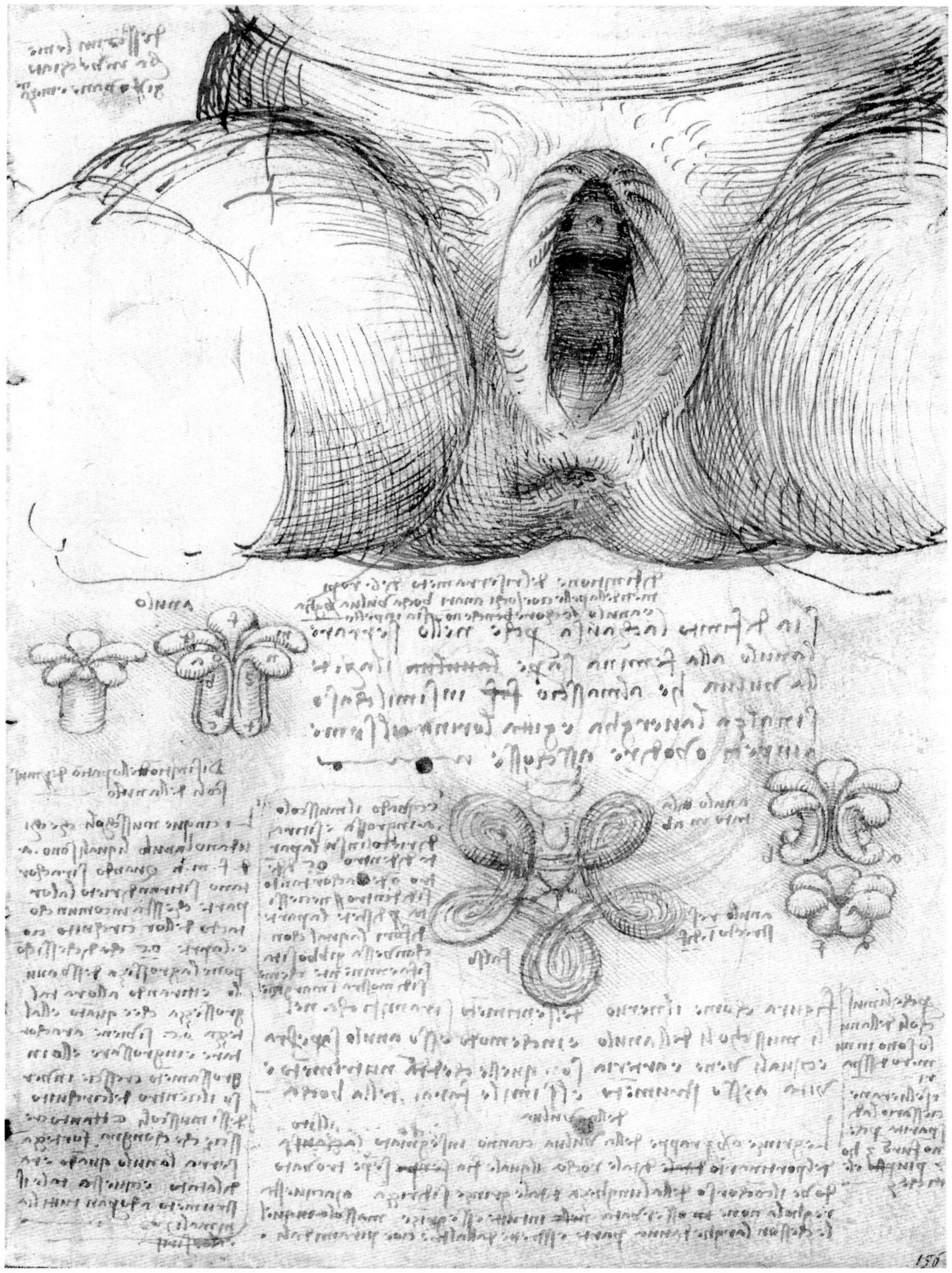

of life-giving humors to the parts of the body. In an analogy with the earth and the landscape, Leonardo saw the old man's channels as silted up and no longer able to irrigate the body. The 'irrigation' system of the human body was examined by Leonardo in his *Dissection of the Principal Organs of a Woman*, dating from c.1507, in which some forms appear in section, some are transparent, while others are shown three-dimensionally. Some organs, including the liver, spleen, kidneys and bronchial tubes, demonstrate the knowledge Leonardo had gained from dissections, while others, such as the heart and womb, are conceptualized.

From a note accompanying a drawing of a foot and lower leg, it appears that Leonardo was hoping to complete all his studies of human anatomy in the winter of 1510. He was convinced that his true task as an investigator was to explain each detail of the human body on the basis of its function. Thus the bones and muscles were conceived as perfect mechanical designs: small and economical, yet capable of many complex movements.

In the last decade of his life, particularly when he was in Rome in 1513, where he was given a dispensation allowing him to continue his studies in anatomy using cadavers (possibly because the papal authorities were convinced that he was searching for the 'seat of the soul'), Leonardo concentrated his studies on two fundamental areas: the heart and the embryo. He was the first to draw the uterine artery and the vascular system of the cervix and vagina, as well as the single-chambered uterus at a time when it was generally believed to be made up of several compartments. This was the explanation given for the mysteries of twin births and litters. Furthermore, Leonardo was the first to describe the fetus *in utero*, correctly tethered by the umbilical cord. The circulatory system was described in detail, often lavishly, in over 50 drawings of the heart. For Leonardo the circulation of blood in the heart, the flow of sap in plants and of waters in the earth were all analogous processes. Leonardo planned an unrealized treatise on anatomy like his *Treatise on Painting*; although he observed the human body with an anatomist's eye, he was neither surgeon nor physician but a painter. For Leonardo, the knowledge of anatomy was not in itself enough; the artist had to penetrate deeper in order to express the human spirit. The body for Leonardo was the physical expression of the spirit; as a painter he could only give expression to this spirit by understanding and 'reconstructing' the body.

One project that occupied Leonardo for a much shorter period of time was for the Trivulzio Monument. In 1504 the Milanese condottiere Giovanni Giacomo Trivulzio had assigned 4000 ducats to pay for a monumental tomb to be erected in his honor in the church of San Navarro. This commission seems to have offered Leonardo some compensation for the destruction of his masterpiece-never-to-be, the equestrian statue of Francesco Sforza. He toyed with the idea of a rearing horse, but the scheme he seems to have settled on was for a walking horse mounted on a canopy, over an effigy of Trivulzio on a coffin. Once again, however, the *Trivulzio Monument* was never completed; Trivulzio was not on good terms with Charles d'Amboise, the Governor of Milan, and was forced to flee to Naples. After Charles's death in 1511, Trivulzio returned to Milan and Leonardo's drawing of that date suggests that he hoped that the project might be resumed, but presumably the funds Trivulzio had set aside for were put to some other use. Most likely they were swallowed up in Milan's preparations against hostilities on its eastern borders.

When Pope Alexander VI had died in 1503, he had been succeeded (after the

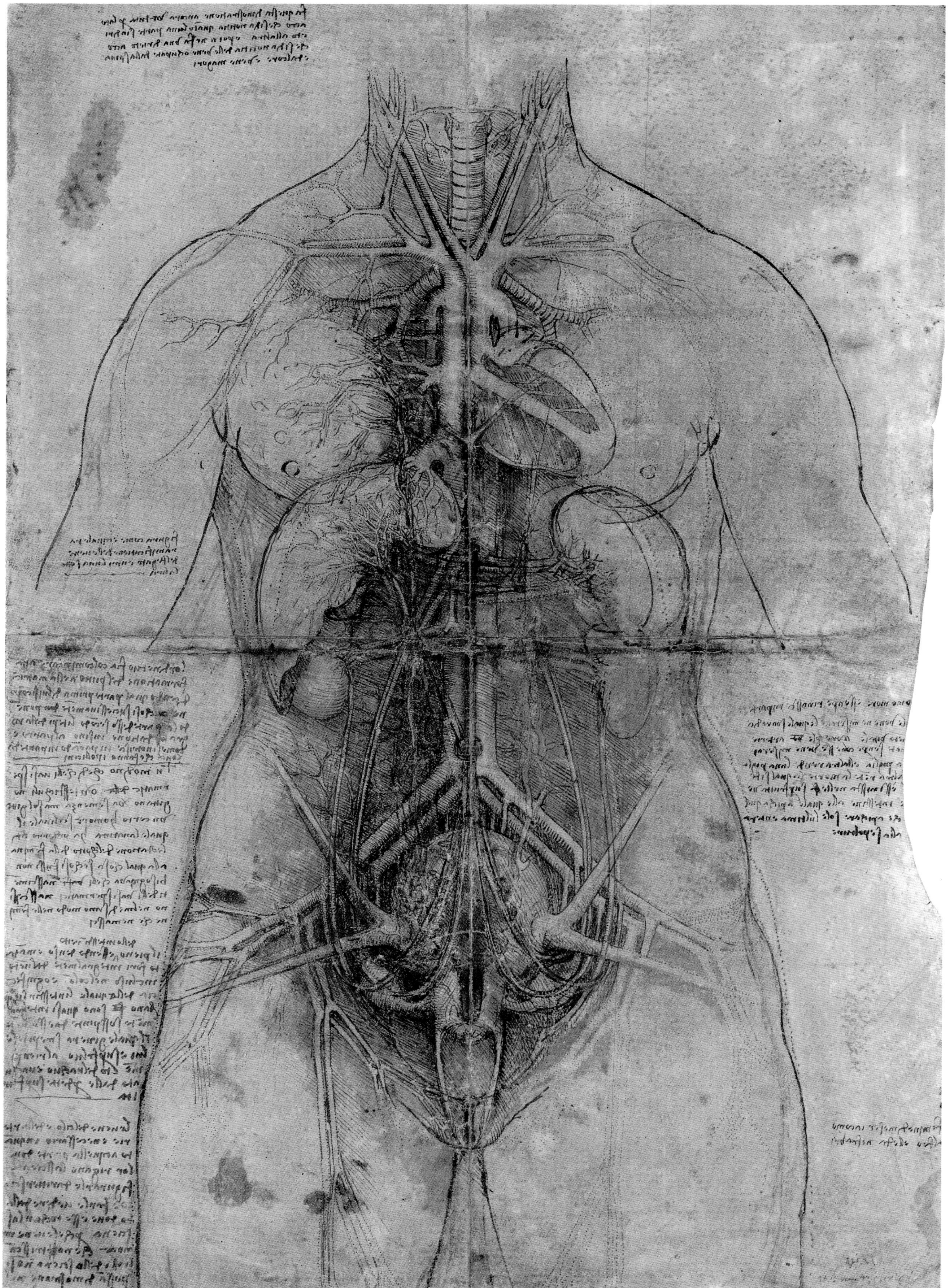

RIGHT: *Study for the Trivulzio Monument*, c.1511, pen, ink and red chalk, 8½ × 6⅝ inches (21.7 × 16.9 cm), Windsor Castle Royal Library 12356r. © 1994 Her Majesty The Queen.

FAR RIGHT: *St John the Baptist*, c.1509, oil on wood panel, 27⅛ × 22½ inches (69 × 57 cm), Musée du Louvre, Paris.

brief papacy of Pius II) by Julius II, and Cesare Borgia had found himself cut off from the papal treasury and opposed to Julius, who was a longtime enemy of the Borgias. As Cesare's Romagna dukedom fell apart, Venice was on hand to pick up the spoils. But since the land now claimed by Venice technically belonged to Rome, Julius, in preparation for war on Venice, entered into an alliance with the Emperor Maximilian and Louis XII of France. As pressure on Venice mounted, she ceded some of the lands formerly held by the Borgias but refused to give up others. Despite backing by Swiss and Romagna mercenaries, Venice was swiftly relieved of Trieste, Gorizia, Pordenone, Fiume and further territories in Hungary. At this point Julius and Maximilian successfully fostered anti-Venetian sentiments in Europe, and the result was the League of Cambrai, December 1508, which allied all major western powers against Venice.

In a sudden reversal of policy, however, in which Louis XII was now seen as the great enemy, Pope Julius resolved to rid Italy of the French through a coalition, the Holy League of 1511, which allied the Pope with Venice and Spain, with additional resources supplied by the English and Swiss. In 1512 Massimiliano Sforza, son of Ludovico Il Moro, entered Milan with the Pope, the Emperor and the Venetians and finally expelled the French.

Leonardo was in a tricky position: he would not be very popular with Massimiliano, since he had fled Milan and Ludovico at the first sign of trouble. Fortunately for him, a bloodless revolution in Florence had returned Lorenzo II de' Medici as head of state, and the following year Giovanni de' Medici was hailed as Pope Leo X and his brother Giulano became Prince of Florence. On 24 September 1513 Leonardo and his companions Salai and Francesco Melzi were on their way to Rome.

Once in the Eternal City, Leonardo was lodged in the Belvedere, the summer palace at the top of the Vatican hill. Also in Rome were Bramante, Raphael, and Michelangelo, all of whom seemed to be the preferred artists, since papal commissions for Leonardo were few. Rumors were being spread again that Leonardo was a sorcerer, rumors fueled, no doubt, by stories of night-time dissections. Of the commissions he did receive, one which interested Leonardo greatly was the project for draining the Pontine marshes around Rome. By transforming the Afonte river into a controled canal system, the marshes could be drained and the land reclaimed for much needed building land.

When the Pope finally awarded Leonardo a painting commission, he noted that he never expected the work to be completed. Leo X had learnt (according to Vasari) that Leonardo was experimenting with a varnish and he is said to have commented that Leonardo would never get any painting done because he was too busy thinking about the end of the project before he had even started!

The only surviving painting which seems, on the strength of a drawing relating to it, to belong entirely to the period after Leonardo left Florence in 1508 is *St John the Baptist*. The effects of age must surely play a part in the overall darkness of this painting, but this is merely an exaggeration of the original effect. The three-dimensionality of the figure is achieved by its being brightly lit against a dark background. This chiaroscuro effect is present to a greater or lesser degree in all of Leonardo's paintings, but in this instance it is used to underline St John's message, with the crucifix and the gesture of the raised finger found so often in Leonardo's paintings from *The Adoration of the Magi* onward.

It is difficult to determine what paintings Leonardo was working on after 1510, apart from presumably continuing work on the *Mona Lisa* and *Leda*. Some red chalk drawings from 1510 and after may be studies for a 'Christ, a Demicorps' being recorded as being at Fontainebleau in 1642. Several versions of the *Salvator Mundi*, a hieratic figure of Christ with a globe in one hand and the other raised, must be copies of the painting for which these drawings are preliminary studies.

RIGHT: *Study for a Sleeve* for the lost painting *Salvator Mundi*, c.1510-15, red chalk on red prepared surface with touches of white, 8⅝ × 5½ inches (22 × 13.9 cm), Windsor Castle Royal Library 12524. © 1994 Her Majesty The Queen.

FAR RIGHT: *St John-Bacchus*, c.1513, oil on wood panel, 69⅝ × 45¼ inches (177 × 115 cm), Musée du Louvre, Paris. Believed to be mostly the work of one of Leonardo's pupils, this painting is nevertheless very closely related to Leonardo's red chalk preparatory drawing.

At least partly by Leonardo, though largely by one of his pupils is the *St John-Bacchus*, a painting based closely on a red chalk drawing by Leonardo formerly in the mountain monastery at Varese. The drawing is of a seated St John figure, and the transformation of the figure in the painting to Bacchus, for reasons we can only speculate on, was achieved by merely adding the crown of vine leaves and the leopard skin.

The year 1515 proved to be yet another turning point for Leonardo, as it did for most of Italy. The first day of the year brought him the news of the death of the French king Louis XII. Succeeding him, Francis I set out to regain the Duchy of Milan for France. Allied with the Venetians, Francis quickly gained control of Genoa and defeated the combined forces of Maximilian, Ferdinand of Spain, Massimiliano Sforza, the Swiss cantons and Pope Leo X. In September 1515, against cavalry, artillery and some 20,000 Swiss pikemen, Francis was the victor at the Battle of Marignano. On 14 December 1515, Francis and Leo held secret discussions in Bologna and, according to statements in the Vatican archives which show that he was paid 33 ducats for expenses, Leonardo was in the Pope's retinue. It was in Bologna that Leonardo was probably introduced to the French king, who would have been familiar with the French court at Milan and his work for Charles d'Amboise.

Following Giuliano de' Medici's death in 1516, Leonardo realized that he had again lost a possible patron and looked with disdain on the prospect of working for the Pope. Francis offered Leonardo a pension and a small chateau at Cloux, near Amboise on the Loire river, and Leonardo entered France with the title 'Foremost Painter and Engineer and Architect to the King of France and Technician of the State.' Once again Leonardo was a celebrity adored by the French court, whose king is said to have visited him in his studio.

Leonardo, at the age of 65, was crippled with rheumatism and was suffering from the effects of a stroke. While he continued to devise pageants (there are designs for spectacular animals, such as dragons), canal systems, and even a royal residence, drawn up between 1516 and 1518 and planned as the Queen Mother's residence at Romorantin, Leonardo was unable to paint.

After a hard winter, and in declining health, Leonardo dictated his last will and testament to a royal notary at Amboise on 23 April 1519. To his student and friend Francesco Melzi he bequeathed his books, his instruments and the remaining portion of his pension. To a servant, Batista, he left half his Milanese vineyard, and to the ever faithful Salai he left the other half. To the poor of the parish of Saint Lazarre he left 70 *soldi*. On 2 May 1519 Leonardo da Vinci died, as one story has it, in the arms of the French king. Although certainly groundless, this has contributed to the tangled web of myth that has surrounded and embellished the few known facts of Leonardo's life. In August 1519 he was buried in the monastery of Saint Florentine in Amboise. In his life he had never settled and, ironically, in death Amboise was not to be his final resting place; Leonardo's mortal remains were scattered during the French Wars of Religion.

Index

Page numbers in *italics* refer to illustrations

DENVER MEN AND WOMEN AMONG TITANIC PASSENGERS

Mrs. J. J. Brown and Hugh Rood Known to Have Been on the Boat.

Relatives of Other Tourists Fearful That They Were on Wrecked Ship.

(Continued From Page One.)

heights. For several years past he has been living in Tucson, Ariz.

After her removal from Aspen Mrs. Brown maintained an elaborate home at 1340 Pennsylvania street, in this city. She entertained lavishly, but if the chronicles of Denver's social elect are correct, her wealth did not carry her into the most sacred circles of society.

IN EAST TWO YEARS.

For two years she has been living either in the East or in Europe, and from all accounts, she has found society of New York and European centers more receptive than that of Denver.

On January 25 last Mrs. Brown sailed from New York for Paris as a member of the John Jacob Astor party, en route for a winter in northern Africa. She was with the same party when it returned to Paris and later to England, homeward bound.

Lawrence Brown, the only son, came into some prominence a year ago when he applied for and was given a position as mucker in a mine at Cripple Creek. The young man married in Kansas City some time before, but despite the wealth of his parents was given to understand that for a few years, at least, he would have to "make good" by shifting for himself. He is now living in the Northwest.

Mrs. Brown's maiden name was Tobin. The family came to Colorado from Hannibal, Mo., during the boom days of mining in this state. Her sister attained social prominence, although not in a similar way. She married a title and is now the Baroness Von Ritzenstein, making her home in Portland.

Hugh R. Rood's name appears among those taken from the ship and a letter received by Mrs. Crawford Hill a few days ago from Mrs. Rood indicated that she, also, would be a passenger.

IN EUROPE TWO MONTHS.

Mrs. Rood was in London when she wrote Mrs. Hill. She said that she and her husband would be sailing for home soon. The letter, however, did not mention the ship on which they expected to sail or the probable date of their departure.

The Roods left Denver two months ago for Europe. Their departure followed the ending of an unusual suit filed in the district court against Mrs. Rood by Egbert W. Reed, and his wife. The Reeds live at 1040 Humboldt and the Roods at 1022 Humboldt. The Roods' residence is known as Stoiberhof and is surrounded by a high stone wall. The Reeds charged in their suit that the Stoiberhof wall extended on their property for an inch. The court ordered the wall removed, but the Reeds declined to allow the Rood workmen to trespass on their lawn while removing the wall. A decree was signed which made certain agreements obligatory before the wall should be removed and the suit was allowed to end with the agreements being made. The Reeds removed to California and the Roods went to Europe.

Mr. and Mrs. Rood spend most of their time in Denver. Mrs. Rood, who was formerly Mrs. Stoiber, is well known in Denver society. Mrs. Crawford Hill was in correspondence with her while she and her husband were traveling in Europe. They expected to be in Denver within a few weeks.

MRS. J. J. BROWN OF DENVER
Prominent Society Woman, Who Is Believed to Have Been on Steamer Titanic When the Vessel Struck an Iceberg in Mid-Ocean Last Night.

$12,000 DAMAGE TO OIL DERRICKS

Of Twenty-One in Boulder Field, Only Six Are Left Standing.

(Special to The Times.)

BOULDER, Colo., April 15.—Damage which is etimated at between $12,000 and $15,000 was done in the oil fields east of this city last Saturday by the windstorm. Of the twenty-one derricks at various wells in thef ield only six are now standing. The Inland Oil company, a subsidiary of the Standard company, lost nine derricks. The Boulder-Greeley company lost three, and three others belonging to individuals and smaller companies were also blown down. In addition to the damage to derricks the wind played havoc with the boiler houses, engine houses and oil tanks.

AVIATOR IN AUTO CRASH.

NEWTON, Mass., April 15.—Harry N. Atwood, the aviator, his parents and Miss Hilda Norman were all injured late last night when their automobile collided with a street car. The aviator was driving.

FIRE DAMAGES $200,000.

CHARLESTON W. Va., April 15.—Fire of unknown origin wiped out a large part of Beckley, W. Va., county seat of Raleigh county, early today causing a loss of more than $200,000. The fire swept the business section.

English Lad Wounded In Mexico Tells Experiences of Exciting Life

Stirring adventures on sea and land, war, romance and danger have crowded into the globe-trotting life of George Holland, the 17-year-old English boy who was shot in a bloody battle between Mexican federalists and insurrectos in the north of Mexico, and who finally landed in the county hospital at Denver on Saturday after a sensational escape from Mexico and months of wandering.

Unable to read or write, young Holland gained a remarkable education through his desire for travel. He has ridden before the masts, beaten his way a la tramp half around the world and has visited nearly every state in the Union. It was love for adventure which prompted him to weary of his uneventful life with his sister in Tucson, Ariz., and run away to Mexico over a year ago.

Forced to become an insurrecto or tramp sixty miles through the desert after being captured on a rebel train, Holland fought for six months under Orozco against the federalists.

He tells a graphic and thrilling story of the burning or houses, killing of women and children, and ferocious cruelty of the Mexicans. He says that the Mexicans have no knowledge of the science of war, but they face death with a fierce and stoical indifference. According to him, it was through the organized warefare of the American and Indians who joined the insurrecto forces rebels won their victories.

Finally wounded in a sharp encounter between the federalists and insurrectos, young Holland was carried to the river bank and his wound dressed. Then began the sensational escape, leaving behind a track of burning houses, pillaged for food. He and his two companions hid in the tall Mexican grasses by night and tramped miles and miles by day, holding up the farmers at the point of a gun and binding them to trees to obtain their food. He says that if Uncle Sam intercedes with American forces all the Americans in Mexico will be murdered.

This taste of battle has destroyed Holland's love for the life of a soldier, but his ambition now is to become a sailor and rise to the rank of captain. He will remain in Denver after his painful wound is healed, with the Bowdens of 1044 Lipan street, who were friends of the Holland family years ago in the county of Cornwall, England.

Among other adventures George Holland was a stowaway on John D. Rockefeller's oil ship sailing to Nova Scotia two years ago, and after two days in hiding without food or water he appeared on deck and was given work as a common sailor boy. He has had no trace of his sister and her husband for a year and a half, and does not know where they are now living.

He is as sharp as a whip, shrewd and intelligent, and now hopes to earn enough money to continue his neglected "book learning." He admits that his earlier school days were spent in playing hooky among the hills of Cornwall. He came to America three years ago, and since then has wandered about the country, to Australia and Old Mexico. His bullet wound will be examined today by X-ray to determine the exact nature of the wound.

HAVE YOU EVER NOTICED?

(Copyright, 1912, by John T. McCutcheon.)

"AW, WE DONT WANT HIM ALONG"
"IF WE LET YOU COME WILL YOU PROMISE NOT TO CRY"
"YES, I PROMISE"
That when little brother is allowed to go out with the older boys—
He can be knocked down, stamped on—
"I'D A CAUGHT THAT BALL IF IT HADN'T A BEEN FER HIM"
and thrown over without—
ever uttering a whimper.
BUT
Just let him fall down when mamma's sympathetic ear is near—
and you will hear him wail to beat the band.

ABANDONED AUTO, CONTAINING RIFLE, CLEW TO MURDER

LYNN, Mass., April 15.—An abandoned automobile, containing a Winchester rifle which the police believe was used in the murder of George E. Marsh, millionaire soap manufacturer, was discovered by the Boston police in a field near the Charles river bank today.

The police have traced the number on the abandoned machine and they declare that the license was that held by a man who came to Lynn from Stockton, Cal., and rented a room at 10 School street from Mrs. Maud York. The man had used the automobile for a week.

Chief of Police Thomas M. Burckes announced today that the man for whom Lynn inspectors are seeking in Maine and New York state and whom they wish to question in regard to the murder of George E. Marsh, the wealthy soap manufacturer, is W. A. Dorr, a motor cycle dealer of Stockton, Cal.

STOCKTON, Cal., April 15.—The police here are seeking the whereabouts of William Dorr, for whom a warrant charging murder was issued today at Lynn, Mass.

Dorr, who is a motor cycle dealer, left here on March 14 without making any explanation of his destination. He is a nephew of Miss Orpha Marsh, who lives here. She issued a statement declaring: "I am shocked to learn that the name of my nephew has been connected with the Lynn, Mass., murder, but I am satisfied that he is innocent. I do not know where he went, but I believe he left because of trouble he had had with his fiancee."

The murdered soap manufacturer was executor of the estate of the late James Marsh of Stockton, who was the foster father of Miss Marsh. The latter said that Dorr knew that George Marsh had not sent any remittances to Stockton recently.

WHEAT JUMPS UP, DOWN AND UP OVER 4-CENT RANGE; WAR TIME SCENES ACTED

Trading Reaches Magnitude of Days of Civil Strife and Prices Vacillate With Amazing Rapidity; Record Highest Mark Hit.

CHICAGO, April 15.—Buyers and sellers alike were whipsawed today in wheat. The market swiftly whirled up, then down, and up again over a range of nearly 4 cents.

Trading reached a magnitude seldom equalled except in war times.

The news which had the greatest influence on the bull side of the market was from a crop expert who had previously been disposed to minimize the effect of supposed winter killing in the soft winter states. Today, he telegraphed from Decatur, Ill., that between there and Mattoon, Ill., practically all wheat was dead; that the fields were perfectly bare and would have to be planted to oats and corn.

CHICAGO RECORDS HIGHEST PRICE.

On the other hand the bears pointed out that at Liverpool and elsewhere prices had not risen in anything like the degree recorded in Chicago and that according to conservative standards it was too early fully to determine the damage.

May wheat spun in astonishing fashion over a limit of prices bounded by 107½ below to 107½ on top. In less than a single quarter of an hour both levels were reached, but there was no stability at either, nor at any point between. The greater persistency was shown perhaps in the return of the market to the upper plane.

Statements which attracted much notice were that there was not one good field from Plymouth, Ind., to Logansport and that where drill rows showed at all, it was only as brown stubble. In La Preble, Montgomery and Clark counties, Ohio, it was asserted that out of fifty-two farms examined, thirty-four were entirely dead, eight that might make seed back and ten that would grade 60 per cent. Numerous damage reports also were received from Nebraska.

In consequence the market veered more strongly to the bull side and hit as hight as $1.11½ for May and $1.07¾ and $1.07⅞ for July, gains of more than 1½c above the topmost figures of Saturday.

Before the session ended May wheat surpassed all previous records on the bulge and sold as high as $1.11¾, making the extreme range between the top and bottom prices today 4¼c. The close was nervous and ragged, with May at $1.11 and July at $1.06@1.06⅛, showing a net advance of 1⅛c to 1¼ piled up in addition to the rise of 10c a bushel scored last week.

Heretofore they have largely confined themselves to spring wheat. Reports from the agricultural districts show that on account of the lateness of the season there will be less spring wheat and more oats and barley planted than usual.

$100,000 MADE BY DENVER INVESTORS ON WHEAT JUMP

Local Speculators Profit by Letters Mailed From Commission Houses.

Denver investors made between $75,000 and $100,000 through local commission houses as a result of the exciting advance in the price of May wheat on the Chicago Board of Tarde Saturday. The market continued choppy today, but the local speculators withdrew after their stroke of good luck and were not active. The movement among the Denver speculators resulted from letters sent out several days ago by the commission houses urging their customers to buy.

The advance in the market price of wheat in Chicago reflected on the local prices of the grain without reference to its speculative features. Local quotation on wheat today was $1.57 per 100 pounds, or 95 cents a bushel. These prices represent the amounts paid to farmers. They are based on the Chicago quotations and are 30 cents a hundred higher than a year ago.

The Colorado Milling and Elevator company, the largest buyer of wheat in Colorado, says that the winter wheat crop in this state was normal up to last Friday. The reports do not show yet what effect Saturday's windstorm had on the crop. It is too early yet to predict what acreage of spring wheat will be planted on account of the delay in planting the crop occasioned by the recent heavy snowstorms.

No reliable estimates have been made on the winter crop in the state, as it has only been in recent years that the farmers have been planting winter crops.

RUEF PETITIONS FOR DISMISSAL OF 80 INDICTMENTS

SAN FRANCISCO, Cal., April 15.—Abraham Ruef, serving a term in San Quentin prison for bribery, filed a petition in the district court of appeals today for a writ of mandate ordering the dismissal of the eighty remaining indictments pending against Ruef in the superior court.

Ruef's attorneys allege in the petition that on many of the indictments their client has not been arraigned, and that both District Attorney Fickert and former District Attorney Langdon had declared that the prosecution could not possibly convict on the evidence at hand.

The proceeding begun today is the same as that instituted in behalf of the indicted officials of the United Railways company, which resulted in an order by the appellate court for the immediate dismissal of the indictments.

National Delegates and Their Choices

REPUBLICAN.

STATE—	Total	Taft	Roosevelt	Cummins	La Follette
Alabama	24	22	..	..	..
Alaska	2	2	..	..	..
Colorado	12	8	..	..	..
District of Columbia	2	2	..	..	..
Florida	12	12	..	..	..
Georgia	28	26	..	..	..
Illinois	58	2	56	..	..
Indiana	30	20	8	..	..
Iowa	26	8	..	4	..
Kentucky	26	23	3	..	..
Louisiana	20	8	..	..	..
Maine	12	..	12	..	..
Michigan	30	18	4	..	..
Mississippi	20	20	..	..	..
Missouri	36	10	8	..	..
New Mexico	8	1	16	..	..
North Carolina	24	8	16	..	..
New York	90	83	7	..	..
North Dakota	10	..	..	..	10
Ohio	48	2	..	..	..
Oklahoma	20	2	67	..	..
Pennsylvania	76	2	74	..	..
Philippines	2	2	..	..	..
South Carolina	18	16	..	..	..
Tennessee	24	16	..	..	..
Vermont	8	6	2	..	..
Virginia	24	24	..	..	..
Wisconsin	26	..	..	..	26
Totals	..	353	201	4	36

Of the delegates credited to Taft, Roosevelt men announce they will contest 164.

DEMOCRATIC.

STATE—	Total	Clark	Wilson	Burke	Marshall	Harmon
Alaska	6	..	..	..	..	3
Illinois	58	58	..	..	..	..
Indiana	30	..	..	..	30	..
Kansas	20	20	..	..	..	..
Maine	12	1	5	..	..	4
Missouri	36	36	..	..	..	..
North Dakota	10	..	..	10	..	..
Oklahoma	20	10	10	..	..	..
Pennsylvonia	76	2	74	..	..	..
Wisconsin	26	6	19	..	..	..
Totals	..	133	108	10	30	7

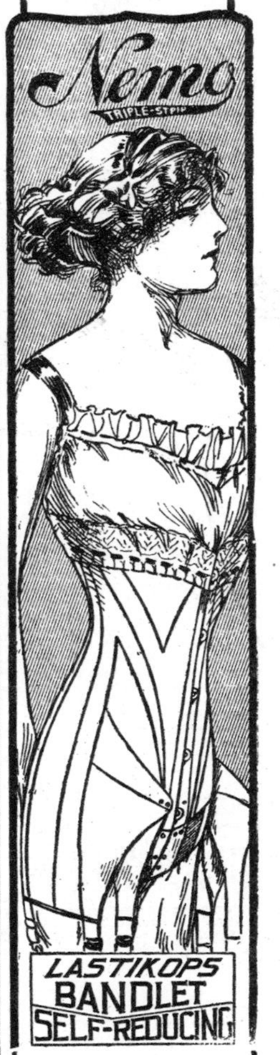

THE WEATHER.
Showers tonight or on Tuesday; warmer tonight.

THE BROOKLYN DAILY EAGLE

Complete Stock Market

LAST EDITION. Volume 72A No. 105 ★ NEW YORK CITY, MONDAY, APRIL 15, 1912. ★ 28 PAGES THREE CENTS.

MGR. P. J. McNAMARA VICAR GENERAL, DEAD

Was Rector of St. Joseph's Church, Pacific Street for Many Years.

BISHOP'S RIGHT-HAND MAN.

Born in Ireland 68 Years Ago, He Had Labored Nearly All His Life in Brooklyn.

The Right Rev. Patrick Joseph McNamara, senior vicar general of the Roman Catholic Diocese of Brooklyn, and rector of St. Joseph's Church, Pacific street near Vanderbilt avenue, died at 9 o'clock last night, at St. Catherine's Infirmary, Amityville, L. I., in the 68th year of his age. The cause of death was uraemia, following Bright's disease. The patient laspsed into unconsciousness at noon on Saturday and remained in that condition until his death. The funeral arrangements will be made this afternoon after a consultation between Bishop McDonnell and the Rev. Thomas J. Leonard, the acting rector of St. Joseph's. It is probable that the funeral will be held on Thursday morning, and that Bishop McDonnell will preside. The body will undoubtedly lie in state in the church for at least one full day before the funeral.

While Mgr. McNamara had been ailing for a long time, his illness did not assume an acute form until about three months ago, when after partially recovering from a slight attack, he insisted upon going to the church to attend to his duties. In going from the rectory to the church he slipped on the ice, receiving a painful injury that brought on a relapse, from which he never rallied.

About three weeks ago his physician, Dr. Sylvester J. McNamara, decided that a change of air and scene might benefit his patient, who was also his cousin, and accordingly he was transferred to the infirmary at Amityville, where everything possible was done to restore him to health, without effect.

The remains were brought in from Amityville today, and arrived at the rectory in Pacific street shortly after noon, in charge of Father Leonard.

The first alarm concerning the health of Mgr. McNamara was felt in August, 1910, when he went to St. Joseph's Sanitarium, in Monticello, N. Y. where he remained for several weeks. Once or twice he was reported to be dying, but the rumors proved to have no foundation, and on September 5 his parishioners were again delighted to see him back attending to his work.

Made Long Visit to Ireland for the Purpose of Gaining Health.

On the morning of June 17 of last year, accompanied by the Rev. Thomas S. O'Reilly, Mgr. McNamara sailed for his boyhood home in Ireland, where he remained until the end of September. He was accompanied on the return trip by his brother, Canon John McNamara of Bodyke, County Clare, who remained here on a visit with him for several weeks.

On the evening of October 1 a reception was tendered to their pastor by the people of St. Joseph's at the parish hall. An address was delivered by Supreme Court Justice Kelly, in which the work of the venerable priest was reviewed at ength. On October .. a dinner was tendered to Mgr. McNamara at the Brooklyn Club by his fellow officers of the Orphan Asylum Society, and at the time he appeared to be in fair health.

As an illustration of Mgr. McNamara's disinclination to show or pomp of any sort, his refusal to allow any demonstration in honor of his fortioth anniversary in the priesthood may be mentioned. Though all sorts of pressure was brought to bear upon him he firmly refused to allow any demonstration. The way in which the date, which was July 1, 1910, was signalized, was by the presentation of bouquets by the school children. His principal reason for refusing to sanction a celebration, was that the parishioners were at the time contributing to the erection of the new church, which will cost $250,000, and he did not wish to burden them with any further expense.

Long before his fatal illness, Mgr. McNamara had made arrangements for the building of the splendid new church, the cornerstone of which will be laid next Sunday. The fund for the work is in hand, as the late pastor did not believe in saddling a parish with a heavy debt. Other big improvements that he had in mind for the benefit of his 10,000 parishioners were a new school and other buildings to replace those that have outlived their usefulness.

As Senior Vicar General, Mgr. McNamara was the right-hand man of Bishop McDonnell, and during the absences of the Bishop, the work of administering the diocese had rested upon his shoulders.

Mgr. McNamara is survived by two brothers, the Rev. Canon John of Ireland, and Michael of Minneapolis; one sister.

Continued on Page 3.

RIGHT REV. MGR. PATRICK J. McNAMARA.

Senior Vicar General of Brooklyn Diocese and Rector of St. Joseph's Church, Who Died Last Night.

COLLISION.

Will Mr. Taft sympathize with the Titanic's passengers? He knows how it feels to strike an iceberg!

HONOR ROLL PUPILS.

The Eagle will print tomorrow the names of the Honor Roll Pupils in the Brooklyn Public Schools for the month of March. There will be about 12,000 names. Get The Eagle.

RESIDENTS SUE CITY.

Bay Ridge Property Owners Angry at Flooding of Cellars.

The work of raising the grade of Sixty-sixth street, between Fifth and Sixth avenues, has worked hardships on the residents of houses in the block, according to tenants in these buildings, which are detached frame houses. Water drains off the new grade into cellars, the tenants declare, and the value of property is depreciated, while the influx of water is a menace to health.

Mrs. Sadie Henner, living at 559 Sixty-sixth street, said today that she had brought suit against the city through her attorney, David G. McConnell, of 302 Broadway, Manhattan, as a result of damage done by water in her cellar. Mrs. Henner said that the grade of her yard conforms with the grade of the street as provided on the town map of New Utrecht, and that the city had no right to raise the street level in the way it has done.

Other residents who complain of damage are Thomas Pizzao, of 561 Sixty-sixth street, and Henry Fesse of 533 Sixty-first street.

HYDE CASE IN HIGHER COURT.

Argument on Habeas Corpus Writ Heard by Appellate Division.

District Attorney Whitman argued before the Appellate Division this afternoon that Justice Woodward had no right to make the Hyde habeas corpus writ returnable before himself. The argument was made on the motion to force the former City Chamberlain to trial this month before Judge Davis in New York County, on the indictment for bribery.

Mr. Whitman asserted that while Judge Woodward had the right to sign the writ, he should have sent it for hearing before a New York County justice. He asked that the judges prohibit Judge Woodward from going any further in the case.

Lawyers Coudert and Steuer, the former representing Judge Woodward and the latter Hyde, insisted that the decisions of the Appellate Division in this county, especially in the Patrick case, gave Justice Woodward the right to hear the merits of the habeas corpus.

At the conclusion of the argument decision was reserved.

500 POUNDS OF BUTTER SEIZED

Taken From Steamer by U. S. Marshals—Said to Contain Glucose.

United States marshals have seized 500 pounds of butter alleged to contain glucose tnd to be unfit for eating purposes, on board the Coamo of the New York and Porto Rica line, following the tip received from the Federal authorities in Washington that such a shipment was about to be made.

United States Assistant District Attorney Allen filed an information and libel in the United States District Court and the clerk, Percy Gilkes, issued a monition. If the butter is not claimed, it will be destroyed by the Board of Health, which today destroyed three barels of dry eggs seized recently by United States marshals.

GAYNOR RAPS BARNES.

Says Conditions in Albany Would Cause an Uprising Here.

Mayor Gaynor in an address to the Lutheran Ministers Association at the West Twenty-third street Y. M. C. A. Building, in Manhattan, said:

"What Mr. Barnes of Albany says of wide open conditions here don't interest me much and if things here were as they were in Albany there would be an uprising here. Not a political leader has had any influence with me in making appointments. I have had no quarrel with the political leaders. There was no need to quarrel. It would do no good."

TITANIC PASSENGERS SAFE ON CARPATHIA; DAMAGED STEAMSHIP REPORTED SINKING

From 800 to 1,200 Persons Already Transshipped to Cunarder in Boats.

OTHER SHIPS NEAR BY

Sea Is Smooth and Weather Calm, and Transfer Is Made Deftly.

ALL BELIEVED TO BE SAFE

Virginian Is Bringing the Leviathan Which Hit an Iceberg Into Port.

THE WHITE STAR LINER TITANIC.

Halifax, April 15—The Canadian Government Marine Agency here at 4.15 p.m. (correct) received a wireless dispatch that the Titanic is sinking. The message came via the cable ship Minia, off Cape Race. It said that the steamers towing the Titanic were endeavoring to get her into shoal water near Cape Race for the purpose of beaching her.

Wireless dispatches up to noon today showed that the passengers of the monster White Star liner Titanic, which struck an iceberg off the New Foundland coast last night, were being transferred aboard the steamer Carpathia, a Cunarder, which left New York April 13 for Naples.

Already twenty boatloads of the Titanic's passengers have been transferred aboard the Carpathia, and allowing forty to sixty people as the capacity of each lifeboat, some 800 or 1,200 people already have been transferred from the damaged liner to the Carpathia.

Other Steamers Close at Hand.

Another liner, the Parisian, of the Allan Company, which sailed from Glasgow for Halifax on April 6, is already close at hand and assisting in the work of rescue.

The Baltic and Virginian also are near the scene, and the Olympic apparently is near at hand, as the wireless information concerning the transfer comes from Captain Haddock of the Olympic.

The latest reports indicate that the transfer of passengers is being carried on successfully and deftly.

The sea is smooth and the weather calm.

It is probable that all of the passengers of the Titanic are safe.

Virginian Has the Titanic in Tow.

Montreal, April 15—The local office of Horton Davidson, one of the Titanic passengers, has received the following wireless message:

"All passengers are safe and Titanic taken in tow by the Virginian."

The officials of the Allan Line said at noon that they were without information and did not expect to hear from the Virginian until she got near Halifax. They added that now her wireless apparatus out of touch with land.

The Montreal Star today says that an unofficial dispatch from Halifax stated that word had been received there that the Titanic was still afloat and was making her way slowly toward Halifax.

Passengers Expected at Halifax Tomorrow.

The passengers of the Titanic, it is understood at the White Star offices here, will be taken to Halifax. The damaged liner will proceed to that port and there unship her passengers' luggage.

Manager Mitchell of the White Star offices left for Halifax today to attend to the despatch of passengers tomorrow, when it is expected they will arrive.

New Haven, Conn., April 15—The operating offices of the New York, New Haven and Hartford Railroad Company have been notified that the passengers of the Titanic will be landed at Halifax. There will be about 600 passengers requiring transportation to New York by sleeping cars, and some 800 by ordinary coaches.

Captain E. J. Smith,
Commander of the Titanic.

This will require the carrying out of the task of running five or more through trains from Halifax to New York. The supply of sleeping coaches will be drawn from the New England roads, the Canadian Pacific and probably to some extent from the New York Central.

The main arrangements for the special trains will be made by officials of the Maine Central Railroad, who are now planning for the routing, which will be either by the way of Boston or via the Nashua and Worcester line.

Meager News During Forenoon After Midnight Dispatch.

The first news that the giant liner Titanic, bound for New York on her maiden voyage across the Atlantic, had struck an iceberg off the banks of Newfoundland, was received in this city shortly after midnight this morning.

The message, sent out from the Titanic's wireless operator and caught at Cape Race, stated that immediate assistance was needed.

The accident occurred at 10:25 o'clock last night. Two hours later the ship's wireless apparatus, which had been working so badly as to permit of only intermittent and fragmentary messages, failed completely.

The last words sent by the operator told that the vessel was apparently doomed, "sinking by the head," and that the women passengers were being rushed into the lifeboats. A reassuring feature was that the weather was calm and clear and help only a few hours away.

After that there came no more messages from the Titanic herself. Throughout the morning hours wireless stations within range of the Titanic's position were endeavoring to get in touch with her. Anxious persons in Brooklyn could learn but little, and there was a continual flow of telephone inquiries into The Eagle offices.

The Titanic's first "S. O. S." message was received by the Allan liner Virginian, which, according to the position given by the Titanic's operator, was not more than 170 miles away. The captain of the Virginian at once started his boat at full steam for the scene of the disaster, announcing to his brother officer on the bridge of the Titanic that the Virginian should reach him by 10 o'clock this morning.

The Titanic's accident happened in latitude 41.46 north, longitude 50.14 west. This point is about 1,150 miles due east of New York City and 450 miles south of the Cape Race, Newfoundland, wireless station. All the messages from the ship were relayed to the Cape Race wireless station by the Virginian and forwarded by the Marconi Company to New York City. The Titanic's twin ship, Olympic, which left New York last week, was also in direct communication with the sinking boat from a point about 300 miles away and started at once for the scene.

The Titanic is commanded by Captain Smith, who was on the bridge of the big Olympic when that boat collided with the British cruiser Hawke last September. The Titanic carries 1,470 passengers, of whom 318 are in the first cabin and 262 in the second cabin.

White Star Officials Completely in the Dark.

Officials of the White Star Line in New York received no word this morning, other that from the press dispatches, of the reported accident to the Titanic. They were unable to understand why they had not received some direct dispatch from the Titanic. The following statement was made by one of the officers of the company:

"Twelve hours have passed since the collision was reported to have taken place, and we have heard nothing o fthe accident. It is most strange that the Titanic's sister ship, Olympic, which has a wireless aparatus of sufficient strength to send a message across the Atlantic, has sent us nothing.

"The Olympic left here last Saturday, and this morning is 360 miles away from the Titanic. The Olympic should be alongside of the Titanic at 2 o'clock this afternoon. The Olympic has been notified o fthe reported accident.

Vice Presidet P. A. S. Franklin of the International Merchant Marine, the highest official of the White Star Line here, was one of the first to be notified of the reported disaster, but it was only through the Associated Press that he learned of it, and for hours thereafter he could only express his astonishment at the news and his doubt that such a large and thoroughly protected ship as the Titanic could be in danger at sea.

Upon hearing the first reports, he spoke reassuringly, declaring that only eight or ten hours before the White Star officers had received a wireless, giving the liner's position. He was sure that if she had met with any accident he would have heard from her promptly.

"We are absolutely satisfied that even if she was in collision with an iceberg, she is in no danger," he said. "With her numerous water-tight compartments she is absolutely unsinkable, and it makes no difference what she hits. The report should not cause any serious anxiety."

When the more serious news came from Cape Ruce a little later, Mr. Franklin expressed the utmost astonishment, but he still qualified his statement with the hope that he repors were no rue. He doubted that they could be correct.

Mr. Franklin then gave out the following statement:

"We place absolute confidence in the Titanic. We believe the boat is absolutely unsinkable and although she may have sunk at the head, or bow, we know that the boat would remain on the water. We do not attach any significance to the fact that there are no Marconi messages being received from the boat. We think it denotes nothing but the fact that the boat is in communication with other steamers, for she may have gotten off all the messages she wanted to send. We are not at all worried about the loss of the ship, but we are extremely sorry for the annoyance, and inconvenience to our passengers, and the traveling public. You can make our views as forceful as you like regarding the capabilities of the ship to withstand any exterior damage. We figure the Virginian of the Allan Line will be alongside the Titanic by 10 o'clock, and we figure the Olympic of the White Star Line will be with the Titanic at 3 p.m. and the Baltic an hour later."

Mr. Franklin also sent the following wireless message to Captain E. S. Smith, the Titanic's commander:

"Anxiously awaiting information; full particulars; probable disposition of passengers."

Steamship Men Startled by News of Collision.

It was difficult for even mariners to interpret the situation from the Maconi despatches. They could not understand why it should be necessary to take off any passengers if the liner were sinking at the bow, unless her captain felt that the watertight compartments would give way.

Steamship men characteirzed the disaster as "the most startling news which has come in from the sea since the advent of wireless telegraphy."

THE TITANIC, LARGEST STEAMSHIP IN THE WORLD.

Gross register	46,328 tons
Displacement	66,000 tons
Length over all	882 ft. 6 in
Breadth over all	92 ft. 6 in.
Breadth of boat deck	94 ft.
Height from bottom of keel to boat deck	97 ft. 4 in.
Height from bottom of keel to top of captain's house	105 ft. 7 in.
Height of funnels above casing	72 ft.
Height of funnels over boat deck	81 ft. 6 in.
Distance from top of funnel to keel	175 ft.
Number of steel decks	11
Number of watertight bulkheads	15

$5,000,000 IN DIAMONDS; $5,000,000 INSURANCE

London, April 15—The Titanic was insured at Lloyds for $5,000,000.

No definite information is obtainable as to the amount of valuables on board, but it is generally understood that the vessel took diamonds of great value, consigned to dealers, whose estimated value is as high as $5,000,000, but this is admittedly largely conjecture. She also took a large amount of bonds.

The first heard of the acident was about 1 o'clock this morning when a bulletin from Montreal stated that the Allan line officers there had received a wireless from Captain Gambell of their steamer Virginian, stating that the Titanic was calling for assistance after a collision with an iceberg. The Virginian's captain added that he was heading his boat for the Titanic, whose position was said to be about 350 miles south of Cape Race, N. F.

Immediate inquiry by the Associated Press in an urgent dispatch to the Marconi station at Cape Race., was answered soon afterward in the following words:

"At 10:25 last night the steamship Titanic called 'C. D. Q.' and reported having struck an iceberg. The steamer said that immediate assistance was required. Half an hour afterwards another message came reporting that they were sinking by the head and that women were being put off in the lifeboat.

"The weather was calm and clear," the Titanic's wireless operator reported and he gave the position of the vessel as 41:46 north latitude and 50:14 west longitude. The Marconi station at Capt Race notified the Allan liner Virginian, the captain of which immediately advised that he was proceeding for the scene of the disaster.

"The Virginian at midnight was about 170 miles distant from the Titanic and expected to reach that vessel about 10 a.m. Monday.

"The Olympic at midnight was in latitude 40:32 north and longitude 61.18 west. She was in direct communication with the Titanic and is now making all haste toward her. The steamship Baltic also reported herself as about 200 miles east of the Titanic at 1:15 a.m., and making all possible speed toward her.

"The last signals from the Titanic were heard by the Virginian at 12:27 a.m. The wireless operator on the Virginian says these signals were blurred and ended abruptly."

Certain Titanic Cannot Be Sunk, Says Franklin.

At 11 o'clock Vice President Franklin called in the reporters to say that no information had come up to that time, to the White Star office in this city, either from the Titanic or the Virginian, but that he was more firmly convinced then than he was earlier in the day that no loss of life would result.

"I am absolutely certain," he said "that the Titanic cannot be sunk. She has fifteen bulkheads and not enough of them can be smashed at once to sink the vessel.

"I feel certain that only a question of determining the best course is confronting the captain. It may be he will transfer his passengers, some of them to the Virginian and let the Virginian hurry them ashore at Halifax and then come back to the Titanic, or he may wish the Virginian to stand by and tow the Titanic in. It will depend largely on the state of the weather, which now is fine. It will take longer to land the passengers at Halifax, of course, if the captain decides to be towed in rather than have the passengers transferred and I am sure that is the only problem confronting him.

"I want to say again I feel sure there will be no loss of life."

Inquiries began to pour into the offices of the company early in the day regarding the safety of the passengers, but all who asked were informed that the liner was in no immediate danger. Persons gathered in the offices in little clusters, but no fears were expressed for the safety of friends and relatives who were on board the damaged ship.

A second message was received from Captain Haddock of the liner Olympic, which stated that the steamers Parisian and Carpathia have reached the Titanic and that twenty boat loads of passengers have been transferred from the disabled vessel to the Carpathia.

Later information received at this city was to the effect that a wireless message had been received at Cape Race saying that the Virginian of the Allan Line had taken the Titanic in tow.

At the offices of the companies it was said that with four ships at hand, all possible danger of loss of life was averted.

2,200 ON TITANIC WHEN SHE HIT BERG

Karl Behr, Mrs. Swift, Wyckoff Vanderhoef and Mrs. Harder Brooklyn Passengers.

MANY NOTABLES ABOARD.

Majority of Persons on the Leviathan Americans—First and Second Class List.

Among the passengers on the Titanic were Mr. and Mrs. George A. Harder, who were married in Brooklyn on January 9 last. The wedding was a society event. Mrs. Harder is a niece of William N. Dykman, the well-known Brooklyn lawyer.

The Harders went to Europe on their wedding trip immediately after the ceremony and were returning on the Titanic when the big ship ran into the iceberg.

Colonel John Jacob Astor and his bride, who are returning from a honeymoon in Egypt [illegible] Europe were [illegible] Alfred Gwynne Vanderbilt. Other well-known persons among the passengers are:

Many Notables Among the Passengers.

Major Archibald Butt, military aid to President Taft; Charles M. Hays, president of the Grand Trunk Railroad; Mrs. Hays and daughter; Jacques Futrelle, the author, and wife; Benjamin Guggenheim, Henry B. Harris, the theatrical man, and wife; William T. Stead, the London editor; F. D. Millet, the artist; J. G. Weidener, Philadelphia traction magnate; Washington Roebling, 2d, a descendant of the engineer who built the Brooklyn Bridge; the Rev. J. Stuart Holden, who, on April 21, will begin a mission in St. Ann's Church, and the Countess Rothes, Mr. and Mrs. Isador Straus, Mr. and Mrs. Emil Taussig, Mr. and Mrs. J. B. Thayer, Mrs. J. Stuart White, Mr. and Mrs. H. J. Allison, Mrs. Aubert, Mrs. Cardoza, Mr. and Mrs. W. E. Carter, Mr. and Mrs. Herbert Chaffess, Mr. and Mrs. Mark Fortune, Mr. and Mrs. W. D. Douglas, Mr. and Mrs. Henry Harper, Mrs. E. D. Appleton, Norman C. Craig, M. P.; Mr. and Mrs. Washington Dodge, William C. Dulles, Colonel Archibald Gracie, Mr. and Mrs. Frederick M. Hoyt, Fletcher Fellowes, Lambert Williams Adolphe Saalfield, J. Clinch Smith, Mr. and Mrs. Frederick Speddin, Clarence Moore and Robert W. Daniel.

Other Brooklynites on the Titanic were Karl Behr, the famous international tennis expert, who played in England for the Davis Cup on two occasions; Mrs. Frederick Joel Swift of 171 Arlington avenue and Wyckoff Vanderhoef, secretary of the Williamsburg City Fire Insurance Company, and a cousin of George W. Chauncey, president of the Mechanics Bank. With the crew of 860 there were more than 2,200 souls aboard the great ship.

Among the other figures of Manhattan social life and interest in the Titanic's first cabin were Mr. and Mrs. Henry Sleeper Harper of 21 Madison avenue (Miss Myra Haxtun that was), J. Clinch Smith, who spends much of his time abroad, and who married Miss Bertha Luddington Barnes; the Countess of Rothes, Mr. and Mrs. F. M. Warren, Howard B. Case, Miss E. M. Eustis, Mr. and Mrs. F. N. Hoyt, Mr. and Mrs. Max Frolicher Stehli, Mr. and Mrs. George D. Wick, Walter Chamberlain Porter, Mr. and Mrs. R. L. Beckwith, Walter M. Clark, Miss Alice Newell, Mr. and Mrs. Frank P. Wood, Wyckoff Vanderhoef, Mrs. W. B. Stephenson.

lCarence Moore is also registered among the first cabin passengers. He is one of the best-known society men in Washington, master of hounds at the Chevy Chase Club, among other distinctions. He married a daughter of Swift, the beef packer, and they have a handsome home at Pride's Crossing, Mass., and a big house in Washington.

First-class Passenger List.

The first-class passenger list follows:

A

Miss E. W. Allen.
H. J. Allison, wife, daughter, son, maid and nurse.
Miss E. Adams.
Harry Anderson.
Miss Cornelia I. Andrews
Thomas Andrews.
Mrs. E. D. Appleton.
Raymond Artaga-Veytia.
Colonel John Jacob Astor, wife, man servant and maid.
Mrs. N. Aubert and maid.

B

O. H. Barkworth.
J. Bauman.
Mrs. James Baxter.
Quigg Baxter.
T. Beattie.
R. T. Beckwith and wife.
Karl H. Behr.

D. H. Bishop and wife.
M. Bjornstrom.
Stephen Weart Blackwell.
Henry Blank.
Miss Caroline Bonnell.
Lily Bonnell.
J. J. Borebank.
Miss Bowen.
Elsie Bowerman.
John B. Brady.
E. Brandeis.
George Brayton.
Dr. Arthur Jackson Brew.
Mrs. J. J. Brown.
Mrs. J. M. Brown.
Mrs. S. W. Bucknell and maid.
Major Archibald Butt.

C

E. P. Calderhead.
Mrs. Churchill Cardell.
Mrs. J. W. M. Cardeza and maid.
T. D. M. Cardeza and man servant.
Frank Carlson.
T. M. Curran.
J. P. Curran.
William E. Carter, wife and maid.
Lucille Carter.
Master Carter.
Howard B. Case.
Mr. and Mrs. T. W. Cavendish and maid.
Mr. and Mrs. Herbert F. Chaffee.
Mr. and Mrs. N. C. Chambers.
Miss Gladys Cherry.
Paul Chevro.
Mrs. E. M. Chibnall.
Robert Chisholm.
Mr. and Mrs. Walter M. Clark.
George Quincy Clifford.
E. P. Colley.
Mrs. A. T. Compton.
Miss S. W. Compton.
A. T. Compton, jr.
Mrs. R. C. Cornell.
John B. Crafton.
Mr. and Mrs. Edward G. Crosby and daughter.
Mr. and Mrs. John Bradley Cummings.

D

P. D. Daly.
Robert W. Daniel.
Mr. and Mrs. Thornton Davidson.
Mrs. B. Devilliers.
Mr. and Mrs. A. A. Dick.
Mr. and Mrs. Washington Dodge and son.
Mrs. F. C. Douglas.
Mr. and Mrs. W. Douglas and maid.
William O. Dulles.

E

Mrs. Boulton Earnshew.
Miss Caroline Endres.
Miss E. M. Eustis.
Mrs. A. F. L. Eganheim.

F

J. I. Flynn.
B. L. Foreman.
Mr. and Mrs. Mark Fortune and three daughters and son.
T. P. Franklin.
T. G. Frauenthal.
Dr. and Mrs. Henry Frauenthal.
Miss Marguerite Frolicher.
Mr. and Mrs. J. Futrelle.

G

Arthur Gee.
Mrs. L. Gibson.
Miss D. Gibson.
Mr. and Mrs. E. L. Goldenberg.
Mrs. E. L. Goldenberg.
George B. Goldeschmidt.
Colonel Archibald Gracie.
Mr. Graham.
Mrs. William Graham.
Miss Margaret E. Graham.
W. B. Greenfield.
Victor Giglio.
Benjamin Guggenheim.

H

Mr. and Mrs. George A. Harder.
Mr. and Mrs. Henry Sleeper Harper and man servant.
Mr. and Mrs. Henry B. Harris.
W. H. Harrison.

PROMINENT PASSENGERS ON THE TITANIC.

Colonel John Jacob Astor.

Mrs. John Jacob Astor.

Alfred G. Vanderbilt.

Isidor Straus.

Major Archibald Butt.

Washington A. Roebling.

H. Haven.
W. J. Hawksford.
Mr. and Mrs. Charles M. Hays, daughter and maid.
Christopher Head.
W. F. Host.
Herbert Henry Hilliard.
W. E. Hopkins.
Mrs. Ida S. Hippach.
Miss Jean Hippach.
Mrs. John C. Hogeboom.
Mr. and Mrs. A. O. Helverson.
Mr. and Mrs. Frederick M. Hoyt.
Nina Harper.
Anna Hamalainer and infant.
Mr. Hoffmann and two children.
Elizabeth Hocking.
Nellie Hocking.
George Hocking.
Martha Hietuner.
Henry P. Hodges.

I

Miss A. E. Isham.
Mrs. Ismay and man servant.

J

Birnbaum Jakob.
C. C. Jones.
H. F. Julian.
Clifford Jeffert.
Ernest Jeffery.
Sidney S. Jacobsohn.
Amy F. Jacobsohn.

K

Edward A. Kent.
Mr. and Mrs. F. R. Kenyon.
Mr. and Mrs. E. N. Kimball.
Herman Klaber.

L

William S. Lambert.
Mrs. A. Leader.
E. G. Lewy.
Mrs. Ernest H. Lines.
Mrs. Mary C. Lines.
Mrs. J. Lindstroom.
Milton C. Long.
J. H. Loring.
Miss Gretchen F. Longley.

M

Miss Georgetta Alexander Madill.
J. E. Maguire.
Pierre Marechal.
Mr. and Mrs. D. W. Marvin.
T. McCaffry.
Timothy J. McCarthy.
J. R. McGough.
A. Melody.
Mr. and Mrs. Edgar J. Meyer.
Hugh Rood.
Frank D. Millet.
Dr. W. E. Minehan, wife and daughter.
H. Markland Molsem.
Clarence Moore and man servant.
Mr. Morgan, wife and maid.

N

Charles Natsch.
A. W. Newell.
Miss Alice Newell.
Miss Madeline Newell.
Miss Helen Newsom.
A. S. Nicholson.

O

E. C. Ostby.
Miss Helen R. Ostby.
S. Ovies.

P

M. H. W. Parr.
Austin Partner.
V. Payne.
Thomas Pears and wife.
Victor Penasce, wife and maid.
Major Arthur Peuchen.
Walter Chamberlain Porter.
Mrs. Thomas Potter, jr.

R

Jenkheer Reuchlinjg.
George Rheims.
Mrs. Edward S. Robert and maid.
W. A. Roebling, 2d.
C. Rolmano.
Miss Rosenbaum.
J. Hugo Ross.
Countess Rothes and maid.
M. Rothschild and wife.
Alfred Rowe.
Arthur Ryerson, wife, maid, two daughters and son.

S

Adolph Saalfeld.
A. L. Salomon.
Mr. Schabert.
Frederick Seward.
Miss E. W. Schutes.
Mr. Silverthorne.
William B. Silvey and wife.
Colonel Alfonso Simmonius, president of the Swiss Bank Verein.
William T. Sloper.
John M. Smart.
J. Clinch Smith.
R. W. Smith.
John Snyder and wife.
Frederick O. Spedden, wife, son and maid nurse.
W. A. Spenser, wife and maid.
Dr. Max Stahelin.
W. T. Stead.
Max Frolicher Stehli and wife.
C. E. H. E. Stengel and wife.
Mrs. W. B. Stephenson.
A. A. Stewart.
Mrs. George M. Stone and maid.
Isador Straus, wife, man servant and maid.
Frederick Sutton.
Mrs. Frederick Joels Swift.

T

Emil Taussig and wife.
Ruth Taussig.
E. S. Taylor and wife.
J. B. Thayer, wife and maid.
J. B. Thayer, jr.
G. Thorne and wife.
G. M. Tucker, jr.

U

Mr. Uruchurtu.

V

Wyckoff Vanderhoef.

W

W. Anderson Walker.
F. M. Warren and wife.
J. Weir.
M. J. White.
Percival W. White.
Richard F. White, wife, maid and man servant.
George D. Wyck and wife.
Miss Mary Wyck.
George D. Widener, wife man servant and maid.
Harry Widener.
Miss Constance Willard.
Duane Williams.
N. M. Williams, jr.
Hugh Woolner.
George Wright.

Y

Miss Marie Young.

SECOND CLASS PASSENGERS.

London, April 15—The list of the second-class passengers on board the Titanic is as follows:

A

William Angle and wife, John Ashby, Samson Abelson, Hana Abelson, Edgar Andrew.

B

Lilian Bentham, Ada R. Balls, Kate Biss, Robert J. Bateman, Lawrence Beesley, Mrs. A. O. Beiker and three children, Reginald Butler, Edward Beane, Ethel Beane, H. J. Beauchamp, Jose de Brito, the Rev. Thomas R. D. Byles, Mr. Bambridge, Solomon Bowenur, Mildred Brown, Percy Baily, W. Hull Botsford, William Berreman, Carl Bryhl, Dagmar Bryhl, Karolina Bystrom, Frederick J. Banfield.

C

Erik Colender, R. C. Coleridge, Harvey Collyer, Marjorie Collyer, Irene C. Corbett, Mrs. C. P. Corey, John H. Chapman, Elizabeth Chapman, Rev. Ernst C. Carter, Lillian Carter, Alice Christy, Julia Christy, Charles V. Clarke, Ada Maria Clarke, Clear Cameron, Stuart Collet, Charles Chapman, William Carbines, Harry Cotterill, Albert F. Caldwell, Sylvia Caldwell, Alden G. Caldwell.

D

Baron von Drachstedt, Sebastiani de Carlo, Herbert Denbury, James V. Drew, Lulu Drew, Marshall Drew, Agnes Davis, John M. Davis, Florentina Duran, A. Duran, Percy Deacon, Charles Davies, William Dibden, Mary Davis, William J. Donton, Ada Doling, Elsie Doling, Lena N. Def.

F

Stanley Fox, Arnenj Fahlstrom, Harry Faunthorpe, Lizzie Faunthorpe, Charles Fillbrook, Annie Fjunk, Joseph Fynney.

G

Alfred Gaskell, William Gillespie, Ethel Garside, William Gilbert, Harry Gale, S. Gale, John Gill, Ralph Giles, Hans K. Givard, Samuel Greenberg, Fred Giles, Edgar Giles, Lawrence Gavey.

H

Mary D. Howlett, Walter Harris, Geo. Harris, Samuel Herman, Jane Herman, Kate Herman, Alice Herman, Stephen Hold, Annie Hold, George Hunt, Leonard Hickman, Stanley Hickman, Ambrose Hood, Benjamin Howard, Ellen T. Howard, Benjamin Hart, Esther Hart, Eva Hart, John Harper.

J

Stephen Jenkin, Dr. J. C. Jenkins, John D. Jarvis.

K

S. Kantor and wife, Daniel Keane, Nora A. Kane, the Rev. Charles Kirkland, F. Karnes, F. Kelly, John Henrik Kvillner.

L

Rene Learnot, John Linjan, Robert W. N. Leyson, Joseph Labroche and wife, Simonne Laroche, Louise Laroche, J. J. Lamb, Jessie Leitch, Amelia Lamore.
Alice Louch, R. F. Levy, Bertha Lehman, William Lahtigen and wife.

M

Emilio Masgiavacchi, Mr. Marshall, Mrs. Marshall, Ernest Moraweck, Noel Malachard, James McCrie, Elizabetth Mellinger and child, Joseph Mantvilia, Frank H. Maybury, Thomas F. Myles, Mary Mack, Thomas Moudd, Henry Mitchell, A. Mallet and wife, Master A. Mallet, W. J. Mathews, Peter McKane, William Mellers, August Meyer, Jacob Milling.

N

Joseph Nicholls, Robert D. Norman, Elizabeth Nye, Nicolas Nasser and wife, L. Nesson.

O

Richard Otter, Thomas Oxenham.

P

Robert Phillips, Alice Phillips, Dr. Alfred Paine, Frederick Pengelly, Emilio Pallas, Julian Padro, Clifford Parker, Mrs. L. Parish, Martin Ponzeli, Emilio Portaluppi, Frank Pulsaum.

Q

Jane Quick, Vera W. Quick, Phyllis Quick.

R

Peter H. Renouf, Lillie Rebouf, Lucy Ridsdale, Harry Rogers, Emily Rugg, Emile Richard, Selina Rogers, David Reaves, Miss E. Reynolds, Emily Richards, William Richards, George Richards.

S

George Sweet, Ernest A. Sjostedt, Augustus Smith, Maude Sincock, Richard J. Siemer, Marion Smith, Hayden Sobey, Philip J. Stokes, H. M. Slayter, F. W. Sedgwick, Percival Saharp, Anna Sinkkonen, S. Ward Stanton, George Swane, L. Manita Shelley, Lillie Silven, M. E. I. Strant.

T

Miss E. Trout, William J. Turpin, Dorothy Turpin, Ellen Tooney, Moses A. Tronpiansky, Mrs. A. T. Tervan.

V

James Veale.

W

Mrs. George Wilkinson, Ada C. Wilkinson, William J. Ware, Leopold Weisz, Matilda Weisz, Edward Wheadon, John James Ware, Florence L. Ware, Sussie Webber, Charles Wilhelm, Marion Wright, Bessie Watt, Bertha Watt, E. Arthur West, Ada West, Conance West, Barbara West, Edwin Wheeler, Mrs. Addie Wells, Miss J. Wells, Ralph Wells, Nellie Walcroft, C. Williams.

Y

Miss H. Yodis.

There were also 740 third class passengers on board.

DIX WAS TO SAIL ON TITANIC.

Albany, April 15—Governor and Mrs. Dix had engaged passage on the Titanic, and expected to sail for Europe on Saturday. The Governor may have to change his plans because of the accident to the steamship.

TITANIC AS LONG AS FOUR BLOCKS

200 Feet Higher, if Stood on End, Than Tallest Building in New York.

LIKE A LUXURIOUS CLUB.

Capable of Carrying 3,500 Passengers and a Crew of 860 Men.

In the Titanic and Olympic the White Star line has built the largest and most luxurious ships in the world. They are the same size. When the Titanic was launched last May in the River Laffan, Belfast, it was estimated that when she was ready for her first voyage she would represent an outlay of $10,000,000. J. Pierpont Morgan was among those who witnessed the launching.

The Titanic is longer than four city blocks and more than 200 feet higher, should she be stood on end, than the tallest building in New York. She is 882½ feet long, 92 feet in the beam and 94 feet deep. There are twelve decks. She has 45,000 tons register and 66,000 tons displacement.

A crew of 860 officers and men are required to operate this huge ship and she is capable of carrying 3,500 passengers.

The Titanic in comfort and luxury is more like an exclusive hotel or club than a steamship. There are elevators running up and down its nine stories; the stairways are wide with heavy balustrades. Besides the great saloons and restaurants there is a miniature theater, squash and tennis courts, swimming pools and Turkish baths, magnificently furnished music rooms, smoking rooms, card rooms, and on the top deck is a miniature golf links.

An average of 21 knots an hour is the speed of the Titanic. She is a stanchly built vessel.

The leviathan Titanic narrowly escaped serious disaster at the very outset of her maiden voyage last Wednesday. As the Titanic swept from her berth at Southampton she sucked the water between herself and the quay to which the steamship New York was tied, so that the hawsers holding the American liner snapped like cotton thread.

The passengers on the Titanic saw the New York drifting stern first toward them. The engines of the Titanic were reversed and the tugs Vulcan and Neptune raced to the New York and tried to drag her back to the quay. There was little space between the New York's stern and the side of the Titanic when the New York was caught by the tugs. The Titanic then slipped from her berth and proceeded on her first and eventful voyage. Captain Smith, the commander of the Titanic, was in command of the Titanic's sister ship Olympic at the time of her collision with the cruiser, Hawke, in the Solent, last September.

London, April 15—A member of a prominent firm of underwriters when informed of the disaster to the Titanic said:

"Even if the Titanic reaches port her owners will have to calculate on a loss of at least $750,000, but if she becomes a total loss it will be an extremely serious matter.

The vessel cost $10,000,000 to build. Her hull is valued for insurance purposes at $5,000,000. Then there are all sorts of miscellaneous matters to be taken into accounts for disbursements and for passage money and freights paid in advance, as well as for stores, baggage and other things.

"I do not suppose the owners are covered to the extent of more than $7,250,000, or at the utmost $7,500,000."

The news of the wreck received here is all coming from New York, with the exception of one message received at 2 a.m., from Lloyds' signal station at Cape Race giving only the first details, stating that she had struck an iceberg and was in a sinking condition and that the transfer of the passengers had begun at once.

The passengers who embarked on the Titanic, at Cherbourg, comprised 142 first class, 30 second and about 90 third class.

Belfast, April 15—A representative of Harland & Wolff, the constructors of the Titanic, interviewed today, said that if the Titanic were sinking, the collision must have been of great force.

The plating of the vessel, he said, was of the heaviest caliber, and even if it was pierced, any two of her compartments could be filled without imperiling the safety of the ship.

ICE FIELDS IN STEAMER LANE.

Serious Menace of the Bergs Reported by Other Steamers.

The presence of an unusually large number of icebergs in the paht of trans-Atlantic liners was indicated by wireless last week.

Twelve hours before the news of the Titanic's accident reached the world, the serious menace of the icebergs was pointed out by the arrival here of the Cunard line steamer Carmania, which reported having dodged twenty-five big bergs, some of them more than 250 feet high.

The Carmania reported that the French steamship Niagara had had a worse experience, having bumped into two small bergs which punched holes in her hull. The Niagara had this experience on Thursday, and unless she has greatly reduced speed, she should reach port some time today. The Titanic undoubtedly ran into this same ice bank.

Liverpool, April 15—The Canadian Pacific Steamship Company's liner Empress of Britain, which left St. John, N. B., on April 5, arrived here today and reports having encountered an icefield of a hundred miles in extent when three days out from Halifax.

MAIN STAIRCASE OF THE TITANIC.

GUARDS AT CONVENTION

Police Break in Doors for Hearstites—Militia Inside on Order Secured by Sullivan Men.

Chicago, April 15—Exciting scenes that were predicted for the Democratic County Convention today at the Seventh Regiment Armory materialized. Within the armory 100 members of the Illinois National Guard remained throughout the night. Outside, a cordon of 250 police was drawn. Scores of deputy sheriffs were ready to reinforce the police.

At noon County Judge Owens appeared at the armory and demanded that the doors be opened. On being refused he ordered the police to break in the doors. Assistant Chief of Police Scheuttler with an axe, battered down the doors and the Hearst-Harrison delegates who had been waiting outside filed into the armory.

On the orders of their officers the militiamen inside offered no resistance and the delegates proceeded to their seats.

While the doors were broken down, some one turned in an alarm of fire. Firemen who responded found nothing to do and returned to their quarters.

Both the militiamen and the police were backed by court orders. The guardsmen were upheld by a restraining order issued by Judge M. L. McKinley last night against the ruling of County Judge John E. Owens, who appointed Election Commissioner Czarnecki, a Republican, to organize the convention.

The battle for control of the convention is waged on one side by the Roger Sullivan forces and on the other by the Hearst-Harrison followers.

"Upon advice of my attorney I have decided to ignore Judge McKinley's order," said Sheriff Michael Zimmer. "I will act as if the order had never been issued and will follow the instructions of County Judge Owens."

BOROUGH BANK CONFERENCE.

Superintendent Van Tuyl and Mahoney Discuss Collection of Debts.

Jeremiah T. Mahoney, who was the chief inquisitor into the affairs of the defunct Borough Bank of Brooklyn, and Banking Superintendent George C. Van Tuyl, jr., are in conference this afternoon concerning Borough Bank affairs. The subject of further public investigation was not discussed, as they consider that it is now up to District Attorney Cropsey to take care of that end through Grand Jury proceedings. The principal thing that is now interesting Mr. Mahoney and Superintendent Van Tuyl is the status of the civil cases which have been started to collect outstanding debts due the wrecked banking institution.

Vincent Leibell, who has been assisting Mr. Mahoney in the case, this afternoon said:

"Mr. Cropsey now has all the testimony we have dug up, and also the report of Mr. Mahoney, in his office. We think that the next move should be from him. He can bring an investigation before the Grand Jury if he sees fit. We have received no word that he has undertaken such action as yet. He acknowledged the receipt of the report and evidence, but beyond that we have not had an inkling of his plans."

PALMER ESTATE $153,161.86.

Tax Appraiser Reports on Property of Hancock Street Physician.

Dr. A. Judson Palmer of 90 Hancock street, who died December 26, 1911, left an estate of $153,161.86, according to a report filed by Transfer Tax Appraiser Wentz in the office of Surrogate Ketcham. The house at 90 Hancock street is valued at $10,000, and the total amount of real property owned by the physician was $69,925.

During her life the widow, Mrs. Maria D. Palmer, gets the use of the house, and an annual income of $3,000. The residue of the income is divided equally between two daughters, Anna D. Palmer of 90 Hancock street, and Mrs. Phoebe V. S. Pierson of the same address, and the widow and children of George H. Palmer of 99 Herkimer street, who died before his father.

CYRUS B. GALE HURT.

Theater Manager Injured in Mixup With Trolley.

Cyrus B. Gale, manager of the Oxford Theater, Flatbush avenue and State street, was hit by a trolley car on Flatbush avenue at State street about noon today, and was painfully injured about the back and hip. It is not known just how the accident happened, but it is believed Mr. Gale was bewildered while attempting to cross the street.

Dr. Thomas S. Ellis of 447 State street, his physician, said over the 'phone that he could not tell for two or three days just the extent of his patient's injuries, but it is apparent that he is badly hurt and in much pain. Dr. Ellis feared that Mr. Gale might be injured internally.

WILLIAM E. LAMBERTON DEAD.

William Edward Lamberton, aged 42 years, died at his home, 462 Rugby road, yesterday after an illness of two months. He was a lifelong resident of Brooklyn and leaves his father, Edward L. Lamberton, two brothers, and a sister. Funeral services and interment will be at Westfield, N. J., in Fair View Cemetery, tomorrow.

ARREST DETECTIVES ON ASSAULT CHARGE

Simmonetti and Raynor Haled to Court, Then Suspended From Force.

MAN SAYS THEY STRUCK HIM.

John Agoglia Declares He Was Attacked by Sleuths in Saloon Without Provocation.

Paul Simmonetti, one of the best known men in the detective bureau, and Valentine Raynor, also a detective, were arrested today at Police Headquatrers by Lieutenants Fay and Duane, charged with assault in the third degree on John Agoglia, an undertaker, of 168 Twenty-first street. They were arraigned before Magistrate Voorhees in the Fifth avenue court this afternoon.

The assault is alleged to have occurred in the saloon of Louis Apenta, at Twenty-fourth street and Fifth avenue, Sunday morning, at 2 o'clock. Agoglia has a black eye and a split lip.

Simmonetti and Raynor were suspended from the force at 12:45 today until the charges against them are cleared up. Both detectives denied to reporters that they were in the Apenta saloon.

According to the story told by Agoglia he was drinking with friends in the saloon and Simmonetti and Raynor were there with a woman. Without provocation, Agoglia asserts, Simmonetti struck him in the mouth, splitting one of his lips.

Shortly afterward when Agoglia started to go home, he says the two detectives met him and asked him if he was going to "spueal" on them. Still without cause, Agoglia says, Raynor struck him in the eye. He went back into the saloon and the detectives followed. Agoglia says that William McDonald of 129 Prospect avenue, asked the Detectives why they had struck Agoglia and McDonald was asked if he wanted some of the same treatment. One of the detectives is alleged to have stuck a gun in McDonald's face.

Agoglia says he knows no reason for the assault. About a month ago a tenant in a house owned by Agoglia's father received a Black Hand letter demanding $500. Agoglia called up the police and Simmonetti and another detective were assigned to the case.

Simmonetti is 33 years old and lives at 638 Forty-fourth street. He has been on the police force twelve years and a detective six years. Raynor is 29, and has been a detective four years. He lives at 725 Fiftieth street. Both are second grade detectives.

Simmonetti has made a name for himself because of his work on Black Hand cases.

FLUSHING MAN SHOT.

William Sands in Serious Condition. Thomas Hudnell Arrested.

William Sands, 37 years old, who lives at 56 Kamia street, Flushing, is in the Flushing Hospital suffering with two pistol shot wounds alleged to have been inflicted by Thomas Hudnell of the same address. It is believed Sands will die.

The shooting is the result of a quarrel said to have taken place this morning between the two men over what Hudnell claimed were encroachments on his part otf the house by Sands. Hudnell leased part of the house to Sands and said that Sands was using more than his share.

It is alleged that in the heat of the argument Hudnell shot Sands twice, once near the heart and once in the foot.

Hudnell was arrested. He says that it was done in self defense.

EUGENE GERARD DEAD.

Eugene Gerard, one of the best known business men of the Bushwick section, and who had a cigar store at 957 Broadway for twenty-five years, died Saturday of apoplexy in the 47th year of his age, at his home, 18 Suydam place, where funeral services will be held this evening at 8 o'clock. The Rev. J. G. Hehr of the First German Presbyterian Church, will officiate. The interment will be in Evergreens Cemetery. Mr. Gerard was a member of Brooklyn Lodge, B. P. O. Elks, Merchants Lodge, F. and A. M.; the Arion Singing Society, the Brooklyn Shengerbund, the Wallabout Merchants Association, Gramercy Council, R. A., and was a Chapter Mason, a Knight Templar and a member of the Mystic Shrine. He leaves a widow, Katherine Battenfeld, a mother, Marion, widow of Anthony Gerard, a sister, Eugenia, and a brother, Ernest.

CHILD BADLY SCALDED.

Max Edelman, a child of 2½ years, who was just learning to walk, pulled a kettle of boiling water down over himself in his home at 559 Graham avenue yesterday. He was badly scalded about the arms and body. An ambulance took him away to the Williamsburg Hospital.

MR. CRANE ACCEPTS CALL.

The Rev. Arthur Crane, pastor of Lefferts Park Baptist Church, has accepted the call, recently extended, to the First Baptist Church in Newport, R. I. He will assume his duties on May 5.

UNITED STATES DISTRICT COURT.

Common law term, April 16, Van Vechter Veeder, J.:

11..Harry Cohen vs. Colgate & Co. and Pennsylvania Railroad Company.
2..Catherine Bewe vs. International Mercantile Marine Co.

DR. SULLIVAN WINS NEWBERY HOUSE

Court Decides Deed to Old Friend for St. Mark's Avenue Residence Valid.

NEWBERYS MUST GET OUT.

They Contested Validity of Transfer in Court, Though Physician Paid Taxes and Interest.

Justice Marean of the Supreme Court decided today that Dr. John F. Sullivan of 74 McDonough street has a valid deed to the residence of his former friend, John W. Newbery at 875 St. Mark's avenue, and he directed that possession of the house be turned over to Michael Schaffner of 847 Park place, who has bought the house from Dr. Sullivan.

The Newberys are well-known in Brooklyn society, and the house in question was the scene of a fashionable wedding reception a few weeks ago, when Miss Violet Von L. Newbery was married to Herbert I. Losee of Hempstead, L. I. The question of the ownership of the house was then pending in the Supreme Court.

The house which Mr. Newbery claims to have cost over $40,000 to build, was held in the name of Mrs. Newbery, and over a year ago it was turned over to Dr. Sullivan as security for money that he had advanced to pay the interest on a mortgage. Though holding a deed to the house and paying all the taxes, Dr. Sullivan testified that he allowed the Newberys to remain in the house, free of all expense.

When Dr. Sullivan transferred the house to Mr. Schaffner, the attorney for the purchaser called on the Newberys and demanded that they either pay rent or move out. He found only Mrs. Newbery home and in telling Dr. Sullivan about it later in a letter, her husband claimed that his wife had been insulted.

"If I had been home," he wrote, "I would have put him out of the house."

On the ground that the deed was only a temporary trust deed, which Dr. Sullivan would return as soon as his claims were paid, Mrs. Newbery started a suit against the physician, asking that the court declare the deed invalid. It is this Justice Marean has declined to do.

"It is suits like these that tend to discourage acts of friendship," was the dry comment of the judge at the conclusion of the case. He also stated that he would have been inclined to dismiss the suit on the testimony of the plaintiff and her husband. There was no evidence that the deed had not been given in good faith, the court ruled.

When the Newberys declined to give up the house Edward Lyons was appointed receiver for the property, and that matter is still pending before the Appellate Division.

MRS. F. J. SWIFT ABOARD

Victim of "Polite Burglar" on the Titanic.

Mrs. Frederick Joel Swift, well known in the Arlington section of East New York, chiefly because of her church and charity activities, and also as president of the Fortnightly Library Club of the Twenty-sixth Ward, was aboard the Titanic. The widow of a former builder, Mrs. Swift has done much traveling since the death of her husband, and on this trip went to the Azores before striking for the Continent. On March 12 she registered at The Eagle Paris Bureau.

Mrs. Swift lived in a handsome residence on the Highland Boulevard, and was negotiating with a purchaser for the sale of the property. She has been a widow since 1907, and has made her home in East New York since then. Her husband, who was an ordained minister of the Presbyterian Church, but who never had a parish, became well to do as a builder and in real estate operations. He was active in these dealings in East New York, White Plains and Newburgh.

For a time he was superintendent of the Arlington Avenue Presbyterian Sunday school, and also an officer of that church. Mrs. Swift is prominent in the Ladies Aid Society of the church, and is very popular. She organized, together with two or three other women, the Fortnightly Library Club, and as president of the organization has seen it grow into a successful club.

In November of last year Mrs. Swift was a victim of one of the most sensational burglaries ever known in Brooklyn. The thief, Edwin Jones, aged 24, appeared in Mrs. Swift's room one night, bedecked with a boutonniere and holding a lighted candle. When Mrs. Swift awoke the burglar politely said, "Pray, excuse me." He then disappeared, and with him went rugs, silver and other loot. Later he telephoned Mrs. Swift, declaring he was sorry, and wished to return the goods, without being arrested. Mrs. Swift kindheartedly gave the promise, but the police thought better of the matter, and he was arested. Mrs. Swift later declared she believed the man to be irresponsible.

SHOOTS DOG; HITS CHILD.

Patrolman Harry Luce of Traffic Squad D, who is chauffeur for Deputy Commissioner Walsh, wso told this morning that a small dog had just been run over by an auto truck in front of 82 Smith street, a few steps from local police headquarters on State street. He found the dog in agony, and, drawing his revolver, fired two shots at it to end its misery. The second shot went through the dog's head, struck the sidewalk and bounded across the street. Lena Levine, aged 12 years, whose father keeps a grocery store at 68 Smith street, on her way to school, had stopped to watch the proceedings. The half-spent bullet struck Lena on the right side of the neck, inflicting an ugly cut.

She screamed, and Luce, having dispatched the dog, took her to police headquarters and had an ambulance sent for. Surgeon Coakley came from the Holy Family Hospital and found that the injury to the child was superficial. He dressed her wound and she was able to go home.

INDEX

To Classified Advertisements in Today's Eagle.

*Indicates Supplement.

THE NEW YORK HERALD.

NEW YORK, MONDAY, APRIL 15, 1912.—EIGHTEEN PAGES.—BY THE NEW YORK HERALD COMPANY. PRICE THREE CENTS.

The New Titanic Hit by Iceberg, Appeals for Aid, Says Wireless Report

THE WHITE STAR LINE STEAMSHIP TITANIC.

The Virginian Notifies Allan Line and Rushes to Damaged Vessel.

WHITE STAR SHIP SENT APPEAL TO ALL

Just Off Cape Race When Collision Occurred, According to the Reports.

ALL DETAILS ARE LACKING

Allan Line Officers Ask Their Steamship for More Information in Order to Send Aid.

MONTREAL, Que., Sunday.—The New White Star line steamship Titanic is reported in advices received here late to-night to have struck an iceberg.

The news was received at the Allan line offices here in a wireless message from the captain of the steamship Virginian, of that line. It was stated that the Virginian had been in wireless communication with the Titanic, that she had reported being in collision with an iceberg and asked for assistance.

The Virginian reported that she was on her way to the Titanic.

The Virginian steamed from Halifax this morning and at the time the wireless was sent she is reckoned to have been about abeam of Cape Race. She has 900 passengers on board, but can accommodate 900 more of the Titanic's passengers should their removal be necessary.

The message from the Virginian's captain was ent by wireless to Cape Race and from thence by cable to Halifax and then by wire to Montreal. The Allan line officials here expect to hear further news at any moment.

CAPT. E. J. SMITH.

THE NIAGARA RAMMED BY ICE ON THE BANKS

Wireless Call Sends the Carmania on Three Hour Search for French Line Steamship.

The full significance of the reports of dangerous ice in the vicinity of the Newfoundland banks, which have reached this city in brief wireless messages during the last week, was understood clearly for the first time yesterday, when the Carmania, of the Cunard line arrived at this port fresh from an encounter with drifting icebergs and floes, and with word that the Niagara, of the French line, had been rammed by the pack and had been stove in below her water line in two places.

The Niagara is proceeding toward this port without assistance and was reported near Fire Island late last night. Her exact position was not given. It is presumed that she is leaking, but that whatever water she is making is confined to one compartment of her hull and that her pumps have it under control. But the belief that her commander must have entertained the fear of losing her at one time in his battle against the ice, is justified in the words of a wireless message entreating assistance received on board the Carmania last Thursday and on receipt of which the Carmania altered her course to seek the French steamship, and gave up the search only when a second message brought the assurance that the Niagara's pumps were keeping her bottom clear.

The Carmania did not come in sight of the Niagara at any time during three hours in which she steamed toward her through the ice fields. But she spoke to two other vessels, one a French bark and the other a small fishing schooner, both of which lay packed in the ice with all sail in and their hulls deadened with collision mats. Both had wooden hulls and were riding comfortably, because they were not trying to make headway. They signalled that they were in no danger, but the fisherman flew the information that he had been fast in the ice for a week.

Passengers Count 25 Icebergs.

The description of the icebergs and floes through which the Carmania steamed for four hours, as recounted by some of her passengers yesterday, compares with the records of the days of sail, before the era of steam. Twenty-five icebergs, many of them of monster size, were counted by passengers from the Carmania's boat deck. Captain Dow, her commander, said yesterday that from his position on the bridge, seventy feet above water line, he saw iceberg after iceberg in almost unbroken army, extending clear to one horizon, the north. The field ice was without a lane of water anywhere and covered the ocean from rim to rim.

It was at noon last Thursday when a cold sting in the air first gave intimation that the Carmania must be coming into the neighborhood of ice. There was none to be seen, but the thermometer sagged rapidly and a sharp lookout was kept from bridge and forecastle head. In half an hour the Carmania ran into fog so dense that it was like a wall, and by one o'clock she was set at half speed, when small cakes of ice came nibbling at her bows. By half-past one the ice was crowding fast about her and at two, when her speed had been so reduced that her engines were barely turning, she was surrounded by it. Then suddenly the fog tore away and revealed a spectacle that left crew and passengers speechless.

On every hand, gleaming in the sun, towered great peaks and plateaus of solid white. The heavy swell of the sea smote at their bases and spouted in mounds of foam. On every hand the steamship was encompassed by the pack. With the muffling fog gone, the grinding of the cakes rose in a sullen roar. Far away the passengers could see the two sailing vessels, their hulls and spars picked out in black against the interminable white. The Carmania steamed cautiously along for an hour. Then her progress was stayed by a wireless call for help.

The Niagara's Urgent Appeal.

The message was short, but urgent, and stated that the Niagara had been rammed and was leaking. Captain Dow had entered the ice in latitude 41.58, longitude 50.20. In her wireless message the Niagara gave her position as about twenty miles to the south and east of where the Carmania was. Captain Dow at once altered his course so as to send his vessel in a circle in the general direction of where the Niagara lay. He knew that the Niagara had left Havre on April 4. She carries no first class passengers. Captain Dow ordered his wireless operator to inquire how many immigrant passengers were aboard her, but the message was not answered. It is thought possible that in the Niagara's battle with the ice her wireless apparatus may have been put out of order.

Captain Dow made what speed he dared in the general direction of the Niagara for two hours. In steaming his new course he passed close to each of the sailing vessels that had been in the offing, and his passengers crowded the rail, thinking that he intended taking their crews off. This belief was stimulated for a while when both the sailing craft broke out signals, but when the Carmania proceeded, keeping well clear of either vessel, curiosity rose high. The passengers learned finally that they were being taken in the direction of the Niagara and that she had sent in a call for help.

Holding his course well to the south of east, Captain Dow finally ran out of the ice three hours after he had received the Niagara's call. Once in the open water he hauled his course east again, but at four o'clock changed it a point south again on receiving a second message from the Niagara. This time he was informed that her damage was slighter than had been at first suspected, but that she had had two holes driven in her hull. The message added that her pumps were keeping her clear of water and that she would be able to proceed to this port without aid.

Passengers on board the Carmania yesterday described some of the icebergs they had seen as towering five hundred feet in the air. At no time was the Carmania or her passengers in any danger.

MEXICO WARNED IT MUST PROTECT AMERICAN LIVES

Mr. Taft Serves Sharp Notice on Madero and Rebel Chief.

DEATH OF FOUNTAIN IS CALLED MURDER

Violations of Civilized Warfare Must Stop, Message Says, and Foreign Property Be Guarded.

NATION HELD RESPONSIBLE

Communication Tells of Resentment Here of Wanton Acts and Calls Attention to Heavy Penalties.

HERALD BUREAU, No. 1,502 H STREET, N. W., WASHINGTON, D. C., Sunday.

President Taft served formal notice to-night on the Mexican government and the rebels alike that the taking of American lives and the destruction of American property in Mexico must stop.

The increasing dangers to which all Americans in Mexico are being subjected, coupled with the reports of the last few hours, have made determined action necessary, and the first step taken to-night is the reassertion in considerate but unmistakably clear language that the United States expects and demands that American life and property in Mexico be justly and adequately protected.

This demand is in the form of a long telegram from Huntington Wilson, acting Secretary of State, to Henry Lane Wilson, the American Ambassador at Mexico City. Here is the telegram:—

"You will immediately communicate the following to the Minister of Foreign Affairs:—'The enormous destruction, constantly increasing, of valuable American properties in the course of the present unfortunate disturbances, the taking of American life contrary to the principles governing such matters among all civilized nations, the increasing dangers to which all American citizens in Mexico are subjected and the seemingly possible indefinite continuance of this unfortunate situation compel the government of the United States to give notice that it expects, and must demand, that American life and property within the Republic of Mexico be justly and adequately protected, and that this government must hold Mexico and the Mexican people responsible for all wanton or illegal acts sacrificing or endangering American life or damaging American property or interests there situated.

Warns Mexico of Penalty.

"'Meanwhile it should be apparent to all sections of the Mexican people that those who spread baseless rumors or provoke just resentment by attacks upon Americans or other foreign persons or property are working against the best interests and the honor of their country, for which the United States is known to hold, and in the present grave situation is manifesting, the greatest and most sincere friendship, and are seeking for their own selfish ends to burden the future of their countrymen with heavy obligations of enormous damages for their wrongful acts.

"'How strongly the government of the United States deprecates even the very few cases of participation by its citizens in the present insurrectionary disturbances is well known to the people of Mexico and was shown by the President's proclamation of March 2 and the various other acts of this government looking to the same end.

"'The government of the United States must insist and demand that American citizens who may be taken prisoners, whether by one party or the other, as participants in the present insurrectionary disturbances shall be dealt with in accordance with the broad principles of equitable justice and humanity as well as in accordance with the principles of international law which may be involved, and to which the people of Mexico have given their assent and adherence in numerous international agreements.

"'This government must hold the Mexican people strictly responsible for any departure from such principles.

"'Notwithstanding press reports that certain Mexican officers have announced a contrary policy, the government of the United States has every confidence in the disposition of the government of Mexico in the premises and must request that appropriate instructions be immediately issued to the proper military officers and officials in the sense indicated.'

"Letcher reports receiving a letter from Orozco which states that in view of the non-recognition of the belligerency on the part of the United States the insurrectionary heads would refuse to recognize consular representatives of the United States, and that henceforth he should not address the military leader of the insurrection on behalf of this government.

"The department is sending Letcher a copy of the above quoted instructions, and is directing him to deliver a copy to Orozco, with the statement that it sets forth the attitude which must be assumed by this government, and directing him to make further representations, as follows:—

"'The government and people of the United States have viewed with grave concern the practical murder under the positive order of one of your chief lieutenants of an American citizen who is reported to have been taken prisoner during or at the end of a regular engagement, the prisoner said to have been dressed in regular uniform and obviously one of the regular forces of the established government of Mexico.

"'The government of the United States must insist, insofar as the treatment of American citizens taken prisoners by whatever force is concerned, that the rules and principles accepted by civilized nations as controlling their actions in time of war shall be followed and observed, and the government of the United States must give notice that any deviation from such a course (and, indeed, any maltreatment of any American citizen will be deeply resented by the American government and people) must be fully answered for by the Mexican people, thus tending to difficulties and obligations which it is to the interest of all true Mexican patriots, as it is the desire of the United States, to avoid.'

"You will also call this to the attention of the Minister for Foreign Affairs and will at the same time point out that the press reports received here state that General Villa has threatened that if Orozco murders American citizens taken prisoners from the federals he will retaliate by murdering American citizens taken prisoners from the rebels. You will, while pointing out the utter inhumanity of such action, call attention to the fact that retaliation, if it be invoked by the federal forces, should certainly never be used against American citizens."

Balloon Novice Lost in Clouds

Bag Shoots Up Fifteen Thousand Feet After Losing Three Men and Ballast.

COSSONAY, Sunday.—The Swiss Aero Club's balloon St. Gothard is somewhere above the clouds carrying a man who never before made an ascent. The balloon was returning from a flight to-day with a pilot and three passengers. During an attempt to land the basket was blown against a rock by a heavy gust and the pilot and two of the passengers, together with twelve sacks of sand, were thrown out. Thus lightened, the balloon shot up to a height of 15,000 feet and whirled away with the third passenger, who is totally ignorant of ballooning.

THRONGS GO TO SEE KIDNAPPED BABY

Ruth Fleischman Receives Many Visitors at Parents' Home—Girl Abductor Quiet in Bellevue.

Annie Boyorsky, the girl who abducted the Fleischman baby Thursday and was found on the street with the child Saturday evening, spent a quiet day in the psychopathic ward of Bellevue Hospital yesterday. She is under observation regarding her mental condition. She probably will be held for five days and then will be taken before a Magistrate to be either discharged or committed to some institution. Thus far the physicians regard the girl as mentally defective, suffering from an hallucination.

Throngs of visitors crowded the apartment of Abraham Fleischman, at No. 1,437 Madison avenue, yesterday to see the baby that had been kidnapped. Neither Mrs. Fleischman nor the baby seemed any the worse for their experience yesterday. The baby, Ruth, is going on the stage. One of Mrs. Fleischman's relatives is a member of a stock company, and the manager of the company proposes to have a sketch written based upon the kidnapping incident, with Ruth as the star performer.

Carl Roseleaf, who found Ruth, has received a new suit of clothes from Mr. Fleischman as a reward. He wants a job now.

FIVE CHILDREN DIE FROM EATING FISH

Only One Left of a Family of Six—Father and Mother Both Escape Serious Consequences.

[SPECIAL DESPATCH TO THE HERALD.]

HALIFAX, N. S., Sunday.—Eating spoiled herring killed five of the six children of Patrick Magee, a farmer, near Montague, Prince Edward Island. Their sixth child was away from home and thus escaped the fatal meal. The father and mother, who also ate of the fish, suffered no serious consequences.

Two hours after eating the fish the children were taken violently ill. A physician was summoned, but could do nothing to save the children, the last two dying yesterday morning.

MR. T. SHAW SAFE ILL.

Stricken with Pneumonia in Newport Villa—Wife an Invalid, Too.

[SPECIAL DESPATCH TO THE HERALD.]

NEWPORT, R. I., Sunday.—Mr. T. Shaw Safe has been stricken with pneumonia at Ocean Lawn, his villa here. He recently returned from a visit to Panama and he was soon taken ill. His physicians said to-day he was doing well as could be expected.

Mrs. Safe is still ill with nervous trouble and just now there is a large corps of nurses at Ocean Lawn.

ROCKEFELLER AID AT FIRE.

Pocantico Hills Company Rushed to Aid of Eastview Neighbor, Whose House Is Burning.

[SPECIAL DESPATCH TO THE HERALD.]

TARRYTOWN, N. Y., Sunday.—John D. Rockefeller helped his neighbor James Butler at Eastview this morning when Mr. Butler's cottage caught fire from the kitchen range. He sent his fire company from Pocantico Hills when the alarm was given and the firemen did good work. The only fire department at Eastview is that at the county almshouse, and the men were unable to cope with the blaze.

Mr. Rockefeller's company was soon dashing down the hill behind one of Mr. Rockefeller's teams. Assistance was called from Elmsford and Tarrytown also, but by the time outside help arrived the blaze was under control. The damage amounted to $3,000.

HURLED AT BAND, STONE KILLS BABY IN MOTHER'S ARMS

Missle Thrown in Street Fight Crushes Skull of Two-Year-Old Boy.

POLICE RESCUE SLAYER FROM ANGRY CROWD

Mrs. James De Lane, Finding Her Infant Dead, Cries Out for Vengeance.

KILLING WAS AN ACCIDENT

Frank C. Baker Declares He Was Defending Himself from Attack by a Band of Young Foreigners.

Mrs. James De Lane, of Lawn avenue, Ozone Park, returned to her home last night with a dead baby in her arms. The two-year-old child had been killed by a stone thrown by Frank C. Baker, twenty-two years old, a steamfitter, of No. 1,326 Wyckoff avenue. He is locked up in the Jamaica police station, charged with homicide.

Baker said he was walking in Ocean avenue, when he saw a dozen young men coming toward him. One of them said:—"That's the fellow." Baker said he started to run, turned after a block, when he came to a pile of stones, and decided he would face his pursuers.

He says he saw knives in the hands of some of the men, while others put their hands in their hip pockets.

Just then Mrs. DeLane, with her baby, James, in her arms, turned into Ocean avenue. Believing the men were fooling, as they were not talking in English, she walked past them.

Baker stood his ground and when he saw the foreigners did not retreat he threw stones at them from the pile, which served as a protection from the missiles thrown by his assailants.

One stone after another whizzed passed the heads of the band, and still they walked toward Baker. He became frghtened and desperate, picked up a larger stone and threw it with all his strength.

Killed in Mother's Arms.

The stone struck the baby on the head, killing the boy instantly. The mother screamed when she saw that her baby's skull was crushed. Her cries brought several persons from the neighboring houses.

"That's the man. He has killed my baby!" she screamed.

The crowd set upon Baker and beat him with canes and umbrellas and with fists. Women were even more vengeful than the men. Baker begged for mercy, but the crowd would not listen to him, while the mother of the dead child cried out against him.

Some one thought of summoning an ambulance, and Dr. Tierney, of St. Mary's Hospital, examined the baby and told Mrs. De Lane her child was dead.

The reserves from Ozone Park police station fought their way through the crowd and rescued Baker.

Meanwhile Mrs. DeLane sat on the curb of the sidewalk weeping over her dead child. Women gathered about her and called to the baby to awake and not worry his mother.

But Jimmy did not wake up and the women tried to console the hysterical mother while the surgeon went to dress Baker's injuries. The young man's head was cut and his body was covered with bruises.

Calls It Accident.

"I did not do it purposely," he said. "It's all a horrible mistake. I'm just as sorry as any one here. I wish I had let those fellows get me rather than have this happen."

Baker could hardly walk when the patrol wagon arrived to take him to the police station. "I feel deeply sorry for that poor woman," he said.

Baker said he never before had seen any of the band who threatened him and could not give any reason why they should want to attack him.

DR. CLEMONS' BODY IS WASHED ASHORE

Cat's-eye Ring Aids Identification of Duck Shooter Who Was Lost in Great South Bay.

Captain David Van Nostrand, of the Short Beach Live Saving Station on Fire Island, yesterday found the body of Dr. Carl A. Clemons, of No. 175 West Seventy-second street, Manhattan, who was one of a duck shooting party of three men who were lost in January last in Great South Bay.

Dr. Clemons, who was a member of the brokerage firm of Carpenter, Clemons & McClave, of No. 67 Exchange place, was accompanied on the duck shooting trip by Edmund S. Bailey, also a broker, of No. 247 Fifth avenue, and Captain Thomas Veltman, of Bay Shore. The three men left for Mr. Bailey's shooting place on Fire Island on January 10, when Great South Bay was choked with ice.

Two days later the launch Rosalie, which they had been using, was picked up in the bay. For weeks fishermen searched for traces of the three men. Dr. Clemons' body is the first evidence that has been obtained of their fate. While the search was being made Mrs. Clemons and Mrs. Bailey spent days at Bay Shore waiting for information and offered a reward of $1,000 for the finding of the three men.

Mrs. Clemons went with Mrs. Bailey and Mr. Carpender to Seaford, where they identified the body by the heavy shooting suit and a diamond catseye ring worn by Dr. Clemons.

CALLS ENGLAND HAPPY.

Patrick Francis Murphy, Arriving by the Carmania, Says That Country Is Safe and Sane.

The United States and England are the two most prosperous and happy countries in the world, according to Patrick Francis Murphy, who arrived yesterday on board the Carmania of the Cunard line.

Mr. Murphy was mightily impressed, he said, with the striking coal miners in England, whom he imagines capable of keeping their tempers in any possible situation.

"England, next to the United States," he said, "is the safest and sanest country under the sun. There is so much money there and so much work for willing men that the strike or any other situation amounts to no more than a Presidential election in this country."

TEACHERS TO TOUR GERMANY.

Every State To Be Represented in Party to Go in July.

Twenty-five additional teachers, most of them women, registered last week with the committee of the National German American School Teachers' Association to go on its tour of Germany this summer. Every State will be represented by one or more tutors when the Grosser Kurfuerst, of the North German Lloyd line, which has been chartered for the trip, leaves New York on July 2 for Hamburg.

Hamburg, Bremen, Cologne, Wiesbaden, Heidelberg, Mannheim, Stuttgart, Cassel, Eisenach, Leipsic, Jena and other points of interest will be visited, and later the teachers will gather at the Niederwald, a famous national monument overlooking the Rhine, where five thousand members of German singing societies will take part in a musical festival.

CHANNEL LIGHT IS READY.

Range Lamp at Hampton Court To Be Used First Time To-Night.

The new Ambrose Channel light, which has just been completed at Hampton Court, Staten Island, will be lighted for the first time to-night. It is a white light of the fixed order and is of a power sufficient to make it visible on clear nights for thirty-one miles.

It is intended solely as a range light for vessels entering Ambrose Channel. It will shine at the top of a brick tower on an elevation three hundred feet above the sea.

TAKE NEGRO PIANIST ON MURDER CHARGE

Detectives Cause Surprise in Richmond by Arresting Professor Scotty, a Popular Entertainer.

Professor Scotty, a negro pianist, who has made money and fame as a musical entertainer in Richmond, Va., will leave that city at noon to-day in company with Detectives Joseph J. Ryan and Michael Meyers, of the East Eighty-eighth street station, and will be arraigned on his arrival here on a charge of having murdered Wong See and Wang Tue, at No. 56 West 135th street, on May 18, 1910.

Deputy Police Commissioner Dougherty, who announced the arrest last night, said that Detective Ryan, who has been working on the case for months, reports that Professor Scotty was well dressed, wore diamonds, had plenty of money, and, as evidence of his standing, was giving piano recitals in the Barton Heights High School for Girls, in the suburbs of Richmond. To the New York police Professor Scotty is known as Nathaniel J. Motley. Mr. Dougherty declares that after stabbing the two Chinese in a quarrel over the price of food, he fled to New Rochelle, thence to New Haven, Newark, N. J.; Henderson, N. C., and finally located in Richmond, where he has lived for the last fourteen months.

Charley Young, a Chinese who kept the restaurant after the previous owners were murdered, was found dead in the place last September, his skull having been crushed with a hatchet.

MOON AND VENUS NEIGHBORS.

Will Be Close Together To-Night, but Their Visit Will Be Visible Only in Florida and Georgia.

WASHINGTON, D. C., Sunday.—Venus and the moon will be close together to-morrow night, almost at what the astronomers call an occultation, but it will be visible only in parts of Florida and Georgia. If the weather is clear enough on a line drawn from Texas through Arkansas, Ohio and New York, however, Venus may be seen about eight minutes from the edge of the moon.

Astronomers at the Naval Observatory here say there will not be an absolute occultation.

On Wednesday there will be an eclipse of the sun, visible only in the eastern part of the United States. The New England States, except a part of Connecticut and New York, will be the only part of the United States in which the eclipse will be visible completely.

TAFT SAVES 11 DELEGATES IN KEYSTONE STATE

Later Returns from Five of the Outlying Counties Are in the President's Favor.

MR. ROOSEVELT'S STRENGTH NOW 53

State Convention and Twelve at Large Also in His Power.

SOME TAFT MEN WAVER

Five May Be Lost to the President When National Convention Reaches Balloting.

MR. WILSON HAS 74 VOTES

Only Few Scattering Delegates to the Democratic Meeting Are for Speaker Clark or Governor Harmon.

How Delegates Line Up to Date

Republican.

Based on theory that Mr. Roosevelt got 53 and President Taft 11 of the 64 delegates elected Saturday in Pennsylvania.

President Taft	345
Mr. Roosevelt	169
Senator La Follette	36
Senator Cummins	4
Unclassified	4
Number delegates in Republican National Convention	1,078
Necessary to nominate (majority)	540
Needed to give Mr. Taft a majority	195
Needed to give Mr. Roosevelt a majority	371
Yet to be elected	522

Democratic.

Speaker Clark	131
Governor Wilson	96
Governor Marshall	30
Governor Burke, No. D.	10
Governor Harmon	6
Unclassified (including all of New York)	101
Number delegates in Democratic National Convention	1,094
Necessary to nominate (two-thirds)	729
Yet to be elected	720

[SPECIAL DESPATCH TO THE HERALD.]

PHILADELPHIA, Pa., Sunday.—More complete returns of yesterday's State-wide primaries accentuate Theodore Roosevelt's victory over President Taft. He has made almost a clean sweep. In the fight for delegates to the national Convention Mr. Roosevelt has won 53 and President Taft 11, according to the latest figures, but of the Taft delegates three in Philadelphia and two in the Ninth district (Lancaster county) are half hearted and may turn in for Mr. Roosevelt at any time. This would leave President Taft but five of the 64 delegates elected yesterday. The Roosevelt men will also control the State Convention and will be able to name the twelve delegates at large, who will be selected May 1.

Latest returns from the Seventh Congressional district, composed of Delaware and Chester counties, show that President Taft gained one of the two national delegates. The other Taft nominee, T. Larry Eyre, a dyed in the wool organization man and one of Senator Penrose's lieutenants, was badly defeated.

In the Twentieth district, composed of York and Adams counties, Grier Hersh, for Mr. Taft, split with the Roosevelt candidate.

Governor Woodrow Wilson, of New Jersey, had an easy time of it in winning seventy-four of the seventy-six delegates to the Baltimore Convention. At present there are two democratic State organizations in Pennsylvania, and each has indorsed the New Jersey Governor for President. Two delegates were elected who favor Champ Clark.

Defeat for Senator Penrose.

Mr. Roosevelt's victory means the crushing defeat of Senator Boies Penrose, the manager of the Taft campaign, and an entirely new alignment of the forces which control the State. It eliminates Senator Penrose as the dominant figure in Pennsylvania politics and casts the toga of authority upon the shoulders of State Senator William Flinn, of Pittsburg.

As matters stand now the President can be accredited with winning only the First, Second, Third and half the Fifth district (all in Philadelphia); half of the Seventh, the Ninth (Lancaster) and half of the Twentieth, while Mr. Roosevelt has to his credit all the delegates from the other twenty-six Congressional districts, which are composed of the sixty-three counties outside Lancaster, Delaware, Chester and Philadelphia.

State Senator Edwin H. Vare, republican organization leader of South Philadelphia, will throw his support to Mr. Roosevelt, it is believed, in the Republican National Convention and in the Republican State Convention that meets on May 1. This means that the one time Recorder of Deeds, William S. Vare; the Receiver of Taxes, Hugh Black, and the President of Select Council, Harry C. Ransley,

WHAT'S THE MATTER WITH OUR BALL TEAMS?

Unsettled Tuesday, Wednesday fair and cooler; moderate southerly winds, becoming variable.

Average temperature yesterday 54
Average temperature for corresponding date last year..53
Average temperature for corresponding date last thirty-three years 48

New York American

EDITION FOR GREATER NEW YORK.

THE TWENTIETH CENTURY NEWSPAPER

NEW YORK AMERICAN. Published by Star Company, at 232-238 William st. President, S. S. Carvalho; Treasurer, Bradford Merrill; Secretary, Caleb Van Hamm; address, 238 William st. Main Advertising Office, 1 Park pl., cor. B'way.

No. 10,499. Copyright, 1912, by the Star Company. Registered in U. S. Patent Office. TUESDAY, APRIL 16, 1912. 16 PAGES PRICE ONE CENT in Greater New York and Jersey City. | Elsewhere TWO CENTS.

J. J. ASTOR LOST ON TITANIC

1.500 TO 1.800 DEAD

John Jacob Astor was among the passengers who went down with the ship, according to a wireless dispatch received by Bradstreets last night from the liner Olympic. Mrs. Astor was saved and is being brought to shore by the Carpathia.

The Wireless Operator at Cape Race, Newfoundland, Flashes: "Eighteen Hundred Lives Have Been Lost in the Wreck of the Titanic."

The Titanic as she rammed the iceberg. Drawn from the wireless reports of the disaster.

Vice-President P. A. S. Franklin, of the White Star Line, said:

"We have heard the rumor from Halifax that the three steamers—the Virginian, Parisian and Carpahia—stood by the Titanic.

"We have received a wireless from Captain Haddock, of the Olympic, that the Titantic went down at 2.20 a. m.

"We have also heard indirectly that the Carpathia has 675 survivors aboard.

"The total passengers and crew on the Titanic numbered 2,000.

"It is very difficult to say whether the Virginian and the Parisian have any survivors aboard until we get a direct report. We have asked for that report from our Halifax agent and from others.

Carpathia Proceeding Directly to New York

"The Carpathia is proceeding direct to New York. We very much fear there has been a serious loss of life. But it is impossible at this time to assure ourselves that the other steamers have or

Continued on Page 2.

More than 1,500 persons, passengers and crew, perished yesterday when the "unsinkable" Titanic, the $10,000,000 White Star liner, went to the bottom of the sea.

So report the steamers which, in answer to the Titanic's wireless shrieks for help, "Hurry! hurry!" rushed to her aid. There is little hope that the dread report is not true.

Of the 2,200 souls who were aboard the once mighty ship 675 were saved.

As The New York American told yesterday, the Titanic, the largest, most luxurious—vaunted as the safest—steamer that ever sailed the seas, collided with an iceberg at 10:45 P. M., Sunday, in about latitude 41.46 North and longitude 50.14 West.

That is, the ill-fated boat was about 1,200 miles east of Sandy Hook and about 900 miles southeast of Halifax, N. S.

Twentieth Century Triumph in Ship Building

The Titanic was the Twentieth Century triumph of shipbuilding. Yet,

Latest Authentic Bulletins From The Titanic

Halifax, April 16.—The steamer Parisian bucked heavy ice looking for wrecke victims. No rafts or bodies sighted. Weather very cold and exposure itself probably would kill.

New York, April 16.—Leyland line officials instruct steamer California to steam immediately to spot where Titanic went down and remain to offer aid until coal supply becomes short.

Southampton, England, April 16.—Town stunned by Titanic disaster. Every member of crew lived here.

London, April 16.—Crowds around White Star offices unmanageable. Late comers cannot get within blocks of bulletins. Flags at half mast.

Washington, April 16.—House of representatives adopts resolution extending sympathy to relatives of Titanic's victims.

St. Johns, N. F., April 16.—Messages from the Carpathia say all boats launched by Titanic are accounted for. Only Carpathia's passengers survived wreck.

London, April 16.—Premier Asquith expresses sympathy of Great Britain in connection with Titanic holocaust.

Halifax, April 16.—Parisian and Virginian have no Titanic survvors on board. Both vessels proceeding on way.

Montreal, April 16.—Violent thunderstorms spreading east. Little hope for any Titanic victims who may be on rafts or in boats.

Washington, April 16.—Senator Guggenheim of Colorado, in telephone consultation with the White Star line office in New York, was unable to learn the fate of his brother, Benjamin Guggenheim, reputed one of the wealthiest men in the world.

So far as known his wife did not accompany him.

"So fleet the works of men back to the earth again ancient and holy things fade like a dream."
—KINGSLEY

Wreck In Figures

Known survivors of Titanic wreck	868
Unaccounted for, probably drowned	1,350
Women and children in first and second cabins	230
Number of third-class passengers	740
Titanic sank east of New York, miles	1,200
Steamer bringing survivors to port	Carpathia
Due to arrive in New York city	Thursday

The Circulation of THE DENVER POST Yesterday Was 61,957

THE DENVER POST

TWO CENTS BY NEWSBOYS. FIVE CENTS ON TRAINS. DENVER, COLORADO, TUESDAY, APRIL 16, 1912.—18 PAGES. 3D EDITION.

Loss Represented by the Titanic

Approximate toll of human lives	1,235
Value of vessel	$10,000,000
Bonds carried on board	5,000,000
Value of jewels carried by women	5,000,000
Estimated value of cargo	1,250,000
Baggage and mail value	2,000,000
Diamonds consigned to jewelers	5,000,000
Loss from probable damage suits	5,000,000
Total	$23,250,000

1,300 PERISH WHEN TITANIC SINKS; 866 KNOWN TO BE RESCUED

WIVES DRAGGED FROM HUSBANDS TO SAFETY

Scantily-Clad Women and Children Floating in Open Boats in Sea of Ice Watch Ship Go Down With Loved Ones and Friends Aboard.

BRAVERY OF THOSE FACING CERTAIN DEATH MAKES CHAPTER IN HISTORY

Wireless From Carpathia Says Ship Will Arrive in New York Thursday With Those Safe--List Is Confusing.

New York, April 16.—Approximately 1,350 persons, passengers and crew, perished yesterday when the "unsinkable Titanic," the $10,000,000 White Star liner, went to the bottom of the sea.

So report the steamers, which, in answer to the Titanic's wireless shrieks for help, "Hurry! Hurry! Hurry!" rushed to her aid.

This means the wreck is the greatest maritime disaster of modern times.

There is little hope that the dread report is not true.

Of the 2,200 souls who were aboard the once mighty ship 868 were saved, and are en route to Boston or New York.

Another report, hardly credited, is that 1,800 lives were lost.

The Titanic, the most luxurious, most vaunted as the safest steamer that ever sailed the seas, collided with an iceberg at 10:45 p. m. Sunday in about latitude 41.46 north and longitude 50.14 west.

That is, the ill-fated boat was about 1,200 miles east of Sandy Hook and about 900 miles southeast of Halifax, N. S.

Niagara Narrowly Escaped Destruction.

Captain Rostron of the steamer Carpathia sent a wireless message to Charles P. Sumner, general agent of the Cunard line, this morning, saying the Carpathia, with 800 survivors of the Titanic on board, was proceeding slowly toward New York through a field of ice.

The Carpathia will arrive at New York Thursday night, according to a wireless dispatch received by Collector Loeb at Washington.

Customs regulations will be waived and the landing of everybody facilitated.

Hope clung desperately to the belief that the steamers Virginian and Parisian of the Allan line might have picked up survivors in addition to those on the Carpathia, but this was dispelled when the Sable island wireless station reported that the Parisian had no survivors,

DENVER'S BUSINESS DISTRICT BELOW BROADWAY LOOKING DOWN FROM THE STATE CAPITOL DOME, SHOWING HOW THE GIANT LINER TITANIC WOULD APPEAR IF IT WERE TO BE PLACED ON BROADWAY. THE BOW OF THE BIG SHIP WOULD BE PLACED AT THE CURBING OF THE PIONEER FOUNTAIN, THE STERN WOULD BE LOCATED AT THE SEVENTEENTH AND BROADWAY CORNER OF THE BROWN PALACE HOTEL, A DISTANCE OF 880 FEET.

BULLETIN.

Halifax, N. S., April 16.—The Allan line steamer Parisian reports via Sable island that she has no passengers from the Titanic on board. The Parisian has just come in touch with the Sable island wireless station. One message reads:

"The Marconi station at Sable island has been in communication with the Parisian and the ship has no passengers from the Titanic."

The other message reads: "No Titanic passengers are on Virginian."

and when the offices of the Allan line in Montreal issued a statement that the captain of the Virginian had sent them a wireless message saying he had "arrived at the scene of disaster too late to be of service."

The Virginian has proceeded on her way for Europe.

The Carpathia is coming in slowly to New York. All hope for details of the tragedy and its effects are centered on this ship. She will be in wireless communication with Sable island tonight, with Nantucket on Thursday and will reach New York some time Thursday night.

Alfred G. Vanderbilt in London.

London, New York and Paris are grief stricken, and overwhelmed by the news of the disaster. Tearful crowds of relatives and friends of passengers on board the Titanic thronged all three of the steamship offices, waiting hour after hour for news that more often than not meant bereavement and sorrow.

People in Paris and London went to bed last night in the belief that all the passengers on board the Titanic had been saved; this morning brought the appalling truth.

Of the survivors on board the Carpathia by far the larger number are women and children.

Many men of prominence on two continents are among the miss-

(Continued on Page 2—Col. 1)

Kings of Finance; Captains of Industry; World-Famed Men Who Went Down in Titanic

COL. JOHN JACOB ASTOR, worth probably $150,000,000; heir of famous house of Astor; was returning with bride from Egypt.
BENJAMIN GUGGENHEIM, fifth of seven sons of Meyer Guggenheim, founder of American Smelting & Refining company; worth about $95,000,000.
GEORGE D. WIDENER, son of P. A. B. Widener, Philadelphia traction king; fortune estimated at $50,000,000.
ISIDOR STRAUS, New York merchant and philanthropist; director in many banks; fortune estimated at $50,000,000.
COL. GEORGE WASHINGTON ROEBLING, son of builder of Brooklyn bridge; president John A. Roebling Sons Co.; fortune placed at $25,000,000.
CLARENCE MOORE, son-in-law of E. C. Swift, packer.
THOMAS PEARS, Pittsburg steel manufacturer.
WALTER D. DOUGLAS, multimillionaire manufacturer of Minneapolis.
W. T. STEAD, journalist.
PERCIVAL W. WHITE, Massachusetts cotton manufacturer.
H. MARKLAND MOLSON, banker of Canada.
THORNTON DAVIDSON, broker of Montreal.
H. J. ALLISON, financier of Montreal.
J. BRADY, president of Pomeroy, Wash., state bank.
MARK FORTUNE, Winnipeg capitalist.
HUGO ROSS, Winnipeg politician.
T. O. C. CAFFRY, Vancouver banker, are all reported wealthy.

BULLETIN.

Montreal, April 16.—The weather signal station on the Gulf of St. Lawrence reported today that heavy fogs lay off Nova Scotia and that a violent thunderstorm broke in that neighborhood last night and is traveling eastward. It was said that such conditions left little hope for the rescue of any survivors of the Titanic that might still be adrift in rafts or boats.

The Allan line issues the following: "We are in receipt of Marconi message via Cape Race from Captain Gambell of the Virginian stating that he arrived on the scene of the disaster too late to be of service and is proceeding on his voyage to Liverpool."

The Titanic's Final Voyage

Left Southampton on Wednesday, April 10, on her maiden trip.

Narrowly escaped collision with liner New York before leaving port, when smaller vessel was dragged from her moorings by the suction of the new liner.

Proceeded at top speed for New York until she struck huge iceberg at 10:25 Sunday night 450 miles south of Cape Race.

Flashed wireless "S. O. S." as water flooded through hole in her forward plates.

Distress signal first picked up by the Allen line steamer Virginian and later by the Carpathia, the Baltic and the Parisian and several other vessels, which were too far away, however, to reach the vessel in time to render assistance.

At 12:17 Monday morning the Titanic's wireless station was silenced. Message stating that the ship was sinking and the women were being taken off in small boats ended abruptly.

Information given out Monday afternoon stated all the passengers had been taken off and the liner was being towed to Halifax.

This information discredited by a wireless message from liner Carpathia stating that Titanic had gone down w rd except about 866.

BULLETIN.

New York, April 16.—The White Star line announced officially at 11 o'clock they had received positive news the number of survivors on the Carpathia was 868. This dispatc the Olympic, which, it is understood, is tion with the Carpathia.

The oak leviathan whose huge ribs make
Their play creator, the vain title take
Of lord of these, and arbiter of war—
These are thy toys, and as the snowy flake
They melt into thy yeast of waves which mar
Alike the armada's pride or spoils of Trafalgar.
—*From Apostrophe to the Ocean by Byron.*

H. R. ROOD AND MRS. BROWN CERTAINLY SAILED ON TITANIC

Denver Society Woman Wrote Nieces of Her Intention to Sail for Home--Friends Hope for News of Her Safety.

That Hugh R. Rood and Mrs. J. J. Brown of Denver were aboard the ill-fated Titanic, as reported, is considered practically certain by friends here who have been kept informed of their recent movements.

The firm of McBeth & May, attorneys for Mrs. Lena Stoiber Rood, wife of Hugh R. Rood, received a letter from her last Saturday from London, dated April 3, in which their client stated that her husband had completed his arrangements for sailing for home April 10 on the Titanic, but that she would remain in London for several weeks.

The attorneys and acquaintances of the Roods are deeply concerned, having no reason to doubt that the wealthy Denverite was listed among the passengers of the vessel whose maiden voyage ended at the bottom of the sea.

Mrs. Susan McManus of 1420 Clarkson street, with whom Florence and Helen Tobin, the two young nieces of Mrs. J. J. Brown, have made their home during their aunt's absence from Denver, says that the girls received a letter from Mrs. Brown from London last Saturday, in which she said she was preparing to sail for home, probably on the Titanic.

The letter was written to convey her approval of her nieces' accompanying Mrs. McManus to Europe, it being their plan to make the trip at once, sailing on the Virginian's first voyage out of Montreal. The Virginian is one of the vessels which went to the rescue of the Titanic.

GIVE UP VOYAGE AND WAIT FOR NEWS.

The news of the disaster has so distressed Mrs. McManus and the Misses Tobin that they will do nothing toward carrying out their own plans until definite news is received regarding Mrs. Brown.

The Denver society woman is the most heavily insured woman in Colorado, carrying insurance amounting to $125,000 on her life.

Whether her daughter, Helen, who has been in school in Paris, joined or intended to join her mother on the home voyage, is not known.

Lawrence Brown, son of Mrs. J. J. Brown, who left the Cripple Creek mines—where, despite his millionaire parentage, he worked for some time as a "mucker"—and went to Oregon some months ago, is still in the Northwest. His wife has recently been visiting in Idaho Springs, but is now in Denver for a few days.

There is much anxiety among the Denver officers of the American Smelting and Refining company concerning the fate of Benjamin Guggenheim, brother of Senator Simon Guggenheim, who was a passenger on the wrecked Titanic. At noon today they had not heard from Senator Guggenheim at Washington or from the New York offices of the company.

BENJAMIN GUGGENHEIM ONCE COLORADO MAN.

In 1883 Benjamin Guggenheim was se out from the East to assist in the m agement of the A. Y. Minnie mine Leadville which his father. Meyer

(Continued on Page 4—Col.

The sea remembers nothing; it is feline. It licks your feet—its huge flanks purr very pleasantly for you, but it will crack your bones and eat you, for all that, and wipe the crimsoned foam from its jaws as if nothing had happened.—Holmes: "The Autocrat of the Breakfast Table."

WRECK OF TITANIC GREATEST DISASTER OF MARINE HISTORY

LIST OF DEAD INCLUDES NOTABLE MEN OF AFFAIRS

Parisian and Virginian Send Messages That They Arrived Too Late to Pick Up Any Survivors.

(Continued From Page One.)

ing. No word has been received of Col. John Jacob Astor; his wife, however, has been saved. Alfred G. Vanderbilt was not on board the Titanic, as first reported. He is in London. Isidor Straus, the New York millionaire merchant and philanthropist, who was on board, has not been reported among the survivors.

Incoming steamships from Europe which have been held up down the bay by fog for the last twenty-four hours or more, all report having passed many large icebergs and ice fields near where the Titanic was lost.

The Red Star liner Lapland from Antwerp and Dover reports she passed large and small icebergs near longitude 49.50 and latitude 42, and that the ice fields extended as far as the eye could reach.

The steamer Niagara said that on April 10, in latitude 44.07 and longitude 50.40 she saw many icebergs followed by an ice field and that the liner steamed around the field until 3 o'clock the following afternoon.

While steaming through the ice fields the wash of the sea hurled a large block of flintlike ice against the port bow of the Niagara and perforated one plate.

The Titanic was the twentieth century triumph of ship building. Yet, as always, when puny man's mightiest work is brought into collision with nature's forces, she crumpled up when she struck the iceberg.

But she struggled for her life and for the lives of those on board her.

At 2:20 a. m. she went to her last resting place, sank by the head after four hours; slowly, slowly, most of her thirty water-tight compartments bursting under the pressure that no human-made titan could resist.

Most of those saved were women and children. The splendid rule of the sea prevailed—women and children first!

Bravery Shown by Men Passengers.

These women and children in boats, into which ice floes crunched, were picked up by the Cunard steamer Carpathia.

In the Titanic's cabins were 230 women and children, but it is not known how many there were among the 740 third class passengers.

In the first cabin there were 128 women and fifteen children, and in the second cabin seventy-nine women and eight children.

It was the Titanic's maiden voyage. Many wealthy people were on board.

No braver or more experienced sailor ever trod a ship's bridge, his friends say, than Captain Smith of the Titanic; never would he desert the sinking vessel.

Late complete messages tell of great bravery on the part of the men passengers. There was a minimum of disorder. John Jacob Astor, who, with his bride, was returning from their long honeymoon abroad, saw his bride placed in a lifeboat and taken safely away. Colonel Astor was drowned.

The work of getting the lifeboats away, the work of allaying the fears of the great crowd of passengers as much as possible, the work of keeping the pumps in operation and the engines throbbing—these tasks and countless others were directed by Captain Smith, the venerable commander of the Titanic, and before her advent the commander of the Olympic, who displayed almost superhuman power of mind and body as the world's most horrible sea disaster crowned his long and honorable service on the high seas.

While it seems most of the women and children were rescued, they suffered intensely. The boats that bore them were tossed in ice-covered waters and driven here and there, wide apart.

Marine architects and men prominent in naval construction today voiced the opinion that the number of lifeboats carried by the Titanic was inadequate and added that had the number of lifeboats been compatible with the human cargo, many more lives would have been saved.

P. S. A. Franklin, vice president of the International Marine company, stated that he was unable to tell the number of lifeboats on the Titanic, but he said that her sister ship, the Olympic, carried sixteen.

The rescue ship Carpathia, with the hundreds saved from the sea, is expected to arrive here by Thursday. It may be, however, that the Carpathia will put in at Boston.

Those taken from the lifeboats by the Carpathia are mostly first cabin passengers. It is reported that other vessels which sped to the Titanic's aid, among them the Virginian and the Parisian, also have passengers of the Titanic aboard.

585 Women and Children Aboard.

At the White Star offices it was stated that of the 325 first-cabin passengers on the Titanic, 128 were women and fifteen children. The second cabin, 285 passengers, included seventy-nine women and eight children, and in the steerage the complement of 710 was divided almost equally, it is believed, between women and men, with a small percentage of children.

Local officials of the White Star line refused to make any comment on a statement of Naval Constructor David W. Taylor that the bulkheads of the Titanic were of improper construction.

"Do you believe that Captain Smith went down with the ship?" Vice President Franklin was asked.

He replied that, knowing Captain Smith as he has for many years, and being familiar with his record as a seaman, he is certain that if any passengers in the Titanic were drowned, Captain Smith remained on board assisting in the rescue and went down with the ship while at his post of duty.

In addition to a valuable shipment of diamonds aboard the Titanic, it is said that among almost priceless jewels carried by the passengers are pearls belonging to an American woman, valued at $600,000. The steamer also carried a large amount in bonds and a very valuable registered mail.

"Loss 1,800 souls," was the text of the message to White Star officials here from the Olympic, the wrecked vessel's sister ship.

It is hoped and believed here that this is an error, unless the Titanic had more passengers on board. She carried about 2,200 persons, including passengers and crew. Deducting 868, the known saved, would indicate a loss of more than 1,300 persons.

It is feared that not one of the Titanic's passenger list of distinguished and wealthy men is alive. It is not believed that a man of the crew of the Titanic is alive to tell the tale of the epochal sea terror.

...rpathia Found Only Wreckage.

...s mute evidence of the disaster that overwhelmed the Titanic on her maiden trip is the comment of the captain of the Carpathia in a wireless message received tonight:

"We found only a sea covered with wreckage and debris."

The Carpathia's captain also said he had picked up the survivors in the boats and had sheltered them on board. They will be landed at either New York or Boston some time Thursday or Friday. The Carpathia also gave the full extent of the disaster by saying that the Titanic had gone to the bottom at 2:20 Monday morning.

A hundred vessels of all descriptions made for the scene of the disaster at top speed in the faint hope that some of the survivors may yet be saved. But it seems a forlorn hope. The giant boat racing for America in an attempt to delight its distinguished passengers with a trip that would startle the world, hit the iceberg with terrific force. The impact was sufficient to tear great seams in the vessel's prow and open one or more of the vessel's water-tight compartments.

Fighting a losing battle, the pride of the maritime world went to her doom in water two miles deep.

At every wireless station on the Atlantic coast from New York to Cape Race wireless operators bend over their instruments feeling for the pulsations of the marvelous Hertzian waves that will bring further details of the catastrophe.

Extra men are on duty, spurred on by hundreds of telegrams from all parts of the world for some intelligence of those on board. During the afternoon and as far into the night as midnight, tiny bits of news filtered in over the wonderful mechanism, but after that there was silence.

Rescued Were Thinly Clad.

A wireless dispatch received early today at Boston, which was relayed by the Olympic from the Carpathia, stated that the Carpathia had 868 of the Titanic's passengers on board, mostly women and children, concluding with the words:

"Grave fears are felt for the safety of the balance of the passengers and the crew."

A wireless dispatch from Cape Race, N. F., telling of the sinking also gave the information that the steamship Californian was remaining and searching the vicinity of the disaster.

That the Virginian may have some of the shipwrecked passengers of the Titanic on board was indicated in a telegram received here from St. Johns at 2:15 this morning, which stated that she would bring to St. Johns such survivovrs as she "may rescue."

Inasmuch as the Virginian was bound for Liverpool she would hardly return to the Newfoundland port unless for humanitarian reasons.

The brief wireless dispatches received so far show that the passengers and crew passed through thrilling experiences from the very moment that the Titanic crashed into the iceberg in the dead of night until the Carpathia, several hours later, reached the scene and rescued the survivors from lifeboats floating in a sea of ice.

The collision occurred at a time when most of the passengers had retired or were about to go to bed. The shock of the collision sent many of the passengers to the decks partly dressed. A wireless dispatch came through Camperdown, N. S., saying that the passengers were ordered to the lifeboats at once and that many were scantily clad as they took their places in the boats. This would indicate that the Titanic's condition was such that no time could be spared to return to staterooms for additional clothes.

Although rated as one of the most able commanders since the advvent of the modern steamship, Captain Smith's career recently had been marred with ill luck. He was in command of the Titanic's sister ship Olympic when that vessel was in collision with the British cruiser Hawke. Exonerated of all blame for this occurrence, he was placed in charge of the Titanic, only to graze disaster when his new charge fouled the New York in the Solent after leaving Southampton on her maiden voyage, which ended so disastrously. He had been in the line's employ more than thirty years and his first important command was the Majestic.

Captain Smith Has Had Ill Luck.

Although 868 persons are reported to be on the Carpathia, it is apparent that all of them are not passengers, for it was necessary for members of the Titanic's crew to man the lifeboats which set out from the sinking liner. How many of the crew were assigned to each boat is a matter of conjecture.

Gradually the names of the rescued began to come by way of Cape Race from the Carpathia and were posted. There were some who scanned the lists and turned away with faces showing hopes realized, but many who came were disappointed.

Repeated calls were made for information regarding Major Archibald Butt, President Taft's military aide, who is returning from abroad. President Taft telegraphed the company and was promised immediate word if anything of a definite nature was received.

Members of the Guggenheim and Straus families had representatives at the White Star offices in anticipation of definite word concerning Isador Straus and Benjamin Guggenheim. These names were not in the survivors' list received up to 8:30 o'clock.

Numerous inquiries were received regarding the fate of Henry B. Harris, the theatrical manager, and his wife. The list shows that Mrs. Harris had been saved.

A cablegram from London received at the steamship offices concerning the fate of Sir Cosmo and Lady Duff-Gordon remained unanswered until this morning, when it was definitely ascertained they were among the rescued Titanic passengers now on board the Carpathia.

Long distance telephone calls came from Philadelphia inquiring for the many society folks from that city aboard the Titanic. The name of Mrs. George D. Widener of Elkins Park was posted as among those on board the Carpathia. The names of her husband and her son, Harry Elkins Widener, did not appear.

Titanic's Insurance of $10,000,000 Will Be Paid by Lloyd's

The loss of $10,000,000 entailed by the sinking of the Titanic will doubtless be paid entirely by the 1,000 or more marine insurance underwriters who compose what is known to the world as "Lloyd's of London." Lloyd's of London is the recognized clearing house for ship ratings and for ship insurance. It is the stamp of the association that fixes the insurability of vessels, and to be "A-1 at Lloyd's" means to stand at the top in superiority.

Its history goes back more than 200 years, when Edwin Lloyd kept a coffee house near the London Tower. Here men who were willing to gamble on the safe return of ships sent to foreign ports gathered because Lloyd specialized in the latest news of vessels and their comings and goings. Until 1873, when Lloyd's was incorporated by act of parliament, the underwriters met in various places, as the growth in membership necessitated securing larger quarters, and the dingy little coffee house of its birth sheltered it only a few years.

Today to be elected a member of the corporation one's character must stand a searching investigation, £5,000 must be deposited against risks incurred, and an annual fee of £21 must be paid. The amount now on deposit is in excess of $15,000,000 when translated from English pounds to American dollars. Stations are maintained in every part of the world for reporting shipping news, and its rules for shipping insurance have been adopted by every marine insurance company in the world.

Insurance of every kind can be had from members of the association. Nothing is too much of a gamble not to find takers. Kubelik, the violinist, carries insurance on each of his fingers, so that if he should be totally disabled his benefits would amount to $235,000. De Pachmann, Paderewski and practically all of the world-famed pianists, have their salary earning digits and thumbs insured at Lloyd's. When Edward was crowned and later when King George's coronation meant fortunes to hotelmen and shopkeepers, it was Lloyd's of London who insured the tradesmen that the event would come off as scheduled and thus protected them against losses.

From the birth of twins to insurance against rain on a big league opening game Lloyd's of London will take a chance. But it is in connection with ship insurance that the corporation is best known. The $10,000,090 cost of the Titanic was posted duly at Lloyd's, and underwriters signified what part of the risk they cared to assume. It was parceled out among the members, and each subscription is guaranteed by the deposit fund of $25,000 in our money which the association holds for the subscriber. Divided as it is, the loss of the newest of trans-Atlantic liners will not fall heavily on any one man or firm, and today, tomorrow and continuously thereafter, Lloyd's of London will wager you immunity from los... on any proposition you care to sub...

TEI...
TO TF...
Best r...

How the Titanic Would Look If Placed on End in Arapahoe Street, Denver

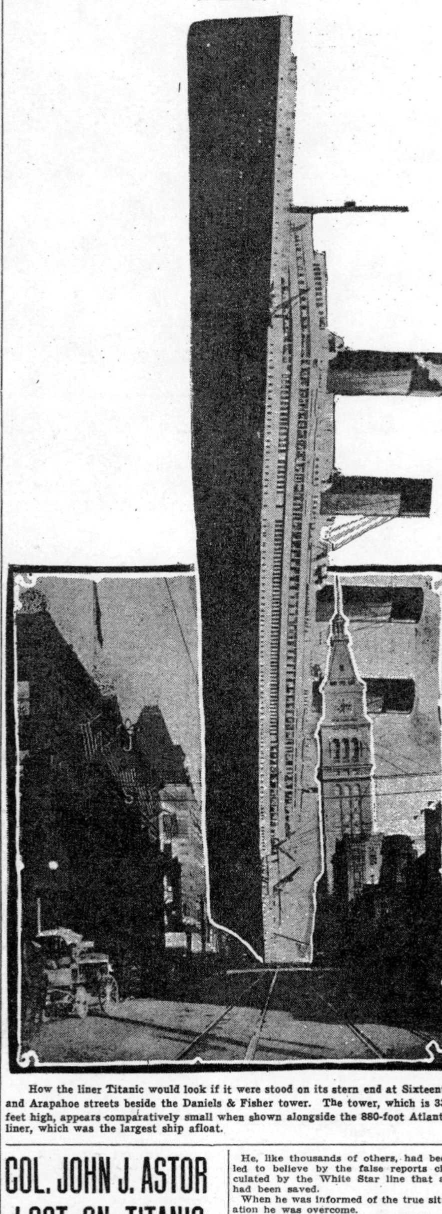

How the liner Titanic would look if it were stood on its stern end at Sixteenth and Arapahoe streets beside the Daniels & Fisher tower. The tower, which is 330 feet high, appears comparatively small when shown alongside the 880-foot Atlantic liner, which was the largest ship afloat.

COL. JOHN J. ASTOR LOST ON TITANIC; HIS WIFE SAVED

Father-in-Law Overcome When He Is Informed of the Tragedy.

NO WORD FROM OTHERS

Several Passengers Rush Wireless Messages to Allay Fears of Relatives.

New York, April 16.—The Bradstreet Commercial agency has given out a telegram received from the Olympic, sister ship of the Titanic, saying that Col. John Jacob Astor was among the hundreds who lost their lives in the catastrophe; that his body had been recovered and that his wife was safe on the Carpathia.

Shortly before 10 o'clock last night Vincent Astor, the only son, rushed into the offices of the White Star line at 9 Broadway seeking news.

"Have you heard from your father?" he was asked.

"Nothing except what I have read in the newspapers," he replied, his voice tremulous with emotion. Then the 19-year-old son of the millionaire turned away and left the steamship company's offices. He had rushed to New York on the fastest train leaving Boston, where he is a student at Harvard, as soon as rumors that his father was one of the victims of the awful sea horror had reached his ears. When he returned to the cool night air of the street tears were streaming from his eyes. He was accompanied by A. Biddle of Philadelphia.

ASTOR'S FATHER-IN-LAW OVERCOME BY NEWS.

W. F. Force, the father-in-la... Jo... Jacob Astor, said he had ... message from his daugh... ...r husband, was on th...

He, like thousands of others, had been led to believe by the false reports circulated by the White Star line that all had been saved.

When he was informed of the true situation he was overcome.

"Oh, my God, don't tell me that. Where do you get that report from? It isn't true, it can't be true," he exclaimed in a choking voice.

Relatives of Mr. and Mrs. Isidor Straus, also passengers on the Titanic, waited in vain all day for some message from the couple. Believing that their parents had been picked up by one of the rescue ships, Herbert Straus and his sister, Mrs. Alfred Hess, left tonight for Halifax to meet their parents.

Despite the fact that several of the passengers on the ship were able to rush wireless messages to their relatives here telling of their safety, no word has been received from Edgar J. Meyer of 158 West Eighty-sixth street and his wife. Mrs. Meyer is the daughter of Andrew Saks, head of Saks & Co., who died in this city a week ago last Sunday. The Meyers left this city on Feb. 28 for a trip through Europe, but were suddenly called home through the death of Mr. Saks.

Another family from which nothing has been heard is that of Emil Taussig of 777 West End avenue. Mr. Taussig, his wife and 17-year-old daughter, Ruth, were returning on the Titanic after spending the winter abroad.

Howard Cardeza of 210 Riverside Drive haunted the White Star offices all day for some news of his sister-in-law, Mrs. J. W. M. Cardeza of Philadelphia. With Mrs. Cardeza was her son.

STAR LINE OFFICIAL ISSUES A STATEMENT.

Vice President Franklin of the White Star line said last night:

"We have a report from Halifax that three steamers, the Virginian, Parisian and Carpathia, stood by the Titanic. We have received a wireless from Captain Haddock of the Olympic that the Titanic went down at 2:20 a. m. We have also heard indirectly that the Carpathia has 675 survivors aboard. The total passengers and crew on the Titanic numbered 2,000. It is very difficult to say whether the Virginian and the Parisian have any survivors aboard until we get a direct report. We have asked for that report from our Halifax agent and from others.

"The Carpathia is proceeding direct to New York. We very much fear there has been a serious loss of life. But it is impossible at this time to assure ourselves that the steamers have or have not other survivors aboard.

"The Titanic carried a sufficient number of lifeboats to get all her passengers off within four hours and we are very hopeful that both the Virginian and the Parisian have passengers on board. The situation, however, is very serious. It looks like a horrible loss of life.

"The Titanic was supposed by experts to be unsinkable. She was insured, but not fully. Her value was nearly $10,000,000. There is no rule of the sea, but it is customary in cases of this kind for the women to be saved first. Even the women in the steerage would be taken off before the men passengers of the first and second cabin. This does not, however, apply to the women employes of the boat.

"It is certain that the Titanic went down before the arrival of the Carpathia. The survivors aboard the Carpathia were picked up from lifeboats. I hardly think that any of the lifeboats would have been lost through the suction when the ship went down. I am certain that if anyone went down with the ship, Captain Smith was the man.

"The Carpathia will arrive at this port late Thursday night or early Friday morning."

TITANIC WRECK ECLIPSES FORMER OCEAN TRAGEDIES

Destruction of Norge With 750 People Held Record Until Great Liner Was Sunk by Iceberg.

The frightful loss of life when the Titanic sank off Cape Race displaces from first place in marine disasters the death toll of the Danish steamer Norge, which was destroyed on Rockall reef, 290 miles west of the Scottish coast, the night of June 29, 1904. Out of 774 on board, passengers and crew, 750 died when the ship went to pieces on the rocks, or later in struggles to reach shore or safety.

The reef was known to navigators and charted. No explanation was ever made, and the captain went down with his ship. It is presumed that the craft became helpless in the swift current which races through the islets and hidden rocks at this point on the coast of Scotland, and that the Norge got out of her course so far that it was impossible to put her about in time to save her. The life preservers proved defective, the life boats were smashed when the ship went to pieces, and an improvised raft carried the survivors.

In 1893 the greatest disaster of the English navy in times of peace was chronicled when the battleship Camperdown rammed the cruiser Victoria in the English channel during official maneuvers, sending the latter to the bottom with a loss of 360 men and officers. On Nov. 23, 1873, the White Star line lost the Atlantic, then one of the crack vessels of the fleet, which was wrecked off the coast of Nova Scotia with a loss of 547 human lives. March 17, 1891, the Anchor line steamer Utopia collided with the British steamer Anson off Gibraltar and sank. Of the crew and passengers 574 went down with the ship.

BURGOYNE DISASTER AMONG GREATEST TRAGEDIES.

The collision of the La Burgoyne of the French line and the Cromartyshire, an English tramp freighter, July 4, 1898, almost at the entrance to New York harbor, was one of the big tragedies of the sea, and fatalities totaled 571. It was made memorable as one of the few wrecks where women and children have had to battle with men passengers and with the ship's crew to get to the life boats.

February of 1907 chronicled two disasters, each with loss of life. On our own coast the Joy line steamer Larchmont from New York to Providence was struck off Block island by the three-masted coal schooner, Harry Knowleton, the night of the 12th. The steamer was leaking badly when the schooner's prow was backed from a gaping hole in the starboard side, and the captain tried to beach the ship on Block island. Before reaching shore the vessel sank and 150 passengers and crew went to the bottom with her.

On the 21st of the same month the Rotterdam mail steamer, Berlin, from England to Rotterdam, was wrecked at the entrance to the River Maas off the Hook of Holland. She struck at 6 a. m. and was pounded to pieces by heavy seas, which prevented tugs and lifeboats effecting a rescue of passengers. On the first night but one passenger, an Englishman, was believed to have been saved out of 140 persons on board. Later nine others were picked up, clinging to rigging and spars.

PACIFIC COAST HAS OWN HISTORY OF DISASTER.

The Pacific coast has shared in the disasters of the sea. The steamer Valencia, Captain Johnson, of the Pacific Coast line, was lost with 119 lives when the ship went on the rocks on the west coast of Vancouver island while trying to make the Straits of Juan de Fuca the night of Jan. 23, 1906. For three days the Valencia had been fighting its way up the coast in a terrific storm from the South Pacific. Added to other difficulties was a dense fog, and wrong calculations sent the craft on a reef. The Valencia was backed away, but the holes made by the submerged jagged rocks caused her to fill rapidly, and before help could reach her the inflowing flood carried the vessel to the bottom with nearly all on board.

The west coast of Vancouver is to the Pacific what the Newfoundland coast is to the Atlantic. Icebergs do not haunt its shoreline or lanes of ocean travel, but it is none the less a graveyard of ships, and more than 700 lives have been lost in the last fifty years because of its reefs and the gales that blow ships upon them.

Another Pacific tragedy was the sinking of the Columbia off the Mendocino coast the night of July 20, 1907. Signals unheard or disregarded in a fog resulted in the steam schooner San Pedro ramming the passenger carrier while the latter was out of the course for freighters. Helms were frantically put about, but before the Columbia could clear her bows were stoved in and before her captain could make the Shelter cove beach for which he steered, the incoming flood carried the craft below. Of a passenger list of 189 and a crew of sixty, the saved numbered all but seventy.

Among the important marine disasters recorded are:

1866, January 11—Steamer London, on her way to Melbourne, foundered in the bay of Biscay; 220 lives lost.

1867, October 29—Royal Mail steamers Rhone and Wye and about fifty other vessels driven ashore and wrecked at St. Thomas, West Indies, by a hurricane; about 1,000 lives lost.

1873, January 22—British steamer Northfleet sunk in collision off Dungeness; 300 lives lost.

1873, November 23—White Star liner Atlantic wrecked off Nova Scotia; 547 lives lost.

1874, December 26—Emigrant vessel Cespatrick took fire and sank off Auckland; 476 lives lost.

1878, March 24—British training ship Eurydice, a frigate, foundered near the Isle of Wight; 300 lives lost.

1878, September 3—British iron steamer Princess Alice sunk in collision in Thames river; 700 lives lost.

1878, December 18—French steamer Byzantin sunk in collision in the Dardanelles with the British steamer Rinaldo. 210 lives lost.

1880, January 31—British training ship Atlanta left Bermuda with 290 men and was never heard from.

1887, January 29—Steamer Kapunda in collision with bark Ada Melore off coast of Brazil; 300 lives lost.

1887, November 15—British steamer Wah Young caught fire between Canton and Hong Kong; 400 lives lost.

1890, February 17—British steamer Duburg wrecked in the China sea; 400 lives lost.

1890, September 19—Turkish frigate Ertogrul foundered off Japan; 540 lives lost.

1891, March 17—Anchor liner Utopia in collision with British steamer Anson off Gibraltar and sunk; 574 lives lost.

1892, January 13—Steamer Namehow wrecked in China sea; 414 lives lost.

1895, January 30—German steamer Elbe sunk in collision with British steamer Crathie in North sea; 335 lives lost.

1895, March 11—Spanish cruiser Reina Regenta foundered in the Atlantic at entrance to the Mediterranean; 400 lives lost.

1898, July 4—French line steamer La Bourgoyne in collision with British sailing vessel Cromartyhire; 571 lives lost.

1898, February 15—United States battleship Maine blown up in Havana harbor, 260 lives lost.

1898—Klondike gold steamship Clara Nevada, sank Lynn canal, Alaska; 110 drowned.

1901, February 12—City of Rio de Janeiro, Pacific Mail Steamship company, sank at entrance to San Francisco bay. 122 lives lost.

1904, June 29—Steamer Norge wrecked on Rockall reef in the North Atlantic; nearly 600 lives lost.

1904, June 15—General Slocum excursion steamboat took fire going through Hell Gate, East river; more than 1,000 lives lost.

1906, Jan. 21—Brazilian battleship Aquidaban sunk near Rio Janeiro by an explosion of the powder magazines; 212 lives lost.

1906, Jan. 27—Steamship Valencia, off Vancouver island; 117 lost.

1906, Aug. 4—Italian emigrant ship Sirio struck a rock off Cape Palos; 300 lives lost.

1907, July 20—American steamers Columbia and San Pedro collided on the California coast; 86 lives lost.

1908, March 23—Japanese steamer Mutsu Maru sunk in collision near Hakodate; 300 lives lost.

1908, April 30—Japanese trraining cruiser Matsu Shima sunk off the Pescadores owing to an explosion; 200 lives lost.

1909, Jan. 24—Collision between the Italian steamer Florida and the White Star liner Republic about 170 miles east of New York during a fog; large number of lives were saved by arrival of steamer Baltic, which received the "C. Q. D." or distress signal sent up by wireless by the Republic operator, Jan. 22; the Republic sank while being towed; six lives lost.

1909, Aug. 1—British steamer Waratah, from Sydney via Port Natal for London; last heard from leaving Port Natal on July 26; 300 lives lost.

1911, Sept. 25—French battleship Liberte sunk by explosion in Toulon harbor; 233 lives lost.

Titanic May Have Had Lifeboats to Accommodate 1,171

Washington, April 16.—A quick report from the White Star lin on the number of lifeboats and life rafts carried by the Titanic has been telegraphed for by Supervising Inspector Uhler of the government steamboat inspection service.

The federal steamship inspection service was awaiting the arrival of the Titanic for examination to see that she complied with the English law with regard to life and other equipment. If the vessel had been of American register it would have been obliged to have life boats or life rafts containing 23,470 cubic feet or accommodations for 2,347 persons.

New York, April 16.—Statistical information of the life-saving apparatus of the Olympic, sister ship of the Titanic, was given out today by the bureau of inspection of steam vessels. Figures for the Titanic are not available, but as the ships are almost identical in size, it is not likely that their equipment materially differs.

The Olympic has sixteen lifeboats and four rafts, calculated to accommodate 1,171 persons. This means about one-third of the total number of passengers and crew together can be accommodated. It is said at the bureau that no ship is required to have sufficient boat room to accommodate all its complete passenger and crew list.

The Olympic carries 3,455 life preservers and 48 life buoys, and these equipments are made in compliance with the regulations of the British board of trade. The United States bureau has no power except to see that each steamer meets the requirements of its home governmnt.

Young Heiress of St. Louis Saved

St. Louis, April 16.—Miss Georgette Madill, reported among the saved in the Titanic disaster, is one of the city's youngest heiresses. She is 15 years old. By an order of court a year ago she was awarded an annual "pin money" allowance of $7,500 to pay for her clothing and education until she became of age.

Miss Madill is the principal heir of Judge George A. Madill, who was for several years president of the Union Trust company in this city. She went to Europe in January of last year with her mother, Mrs. Edward Robert, and her cousin, Miss Elizabeth Allen.

It is estimated that the income from the estate of which Miss Madill is heir is not less than $50,000.

RELATIVES IN AGONY OF FEAR BESIEGE THE WHITE STAR OFFICES

COL. ASTOR'S DEATH BROKEN TO SON AND FATHER-IN-LAW

Latest Lists of the Dead, the Missing and Those Who Were Rescued.

Several Passengers Send Wireless Messages to Allay Suspense of Families--Bulletins Eagerly Read by Throngs.

London, April 16.—The news of the loss of the steamship Titanic and the probable drowning of more than a thousand of her passengers, overwhelmed London today. Those who had friends among the passengers or crew had gone to their homes last night after a day spent in eager inquiry, relieved and reassured by the late evening dispatches, which declared that the vessel was still afloat and proceeding to Halifax.

Londoners were sure all was well, until the authentic tidings came this morning of the disaster that had overwhelmed the great ship. The news, published in a few late editions of the morning newspapers and in early editions of the evening newspapers, spread rapidly, consternation resulting. This was particularly true at Lloyds'.

Throughout the morning the crowds which besieged the newspaper offices and the headquarters of the White Star line increased in size.

PITIFUL SCENES IN CROWDS ON STREETS.

Pitiful scenes were witnessed as women and children, unable to get information as to relatives or friends, left the crowds with tear-stained faces.

Officials of the White Star line had little to offer them beyond dispatches identical with those cabled to the newspapers from New York. These were to the effect that a considerable number of rescued passengers were aboard the Carpathia and that a few more might have been picked up by the Virginian.

The announcement that the steamship Californian was remaining in the vicinity of the wreck also gave hope that some more survivors might be found. The list of rescued began trickling into the newspaper offices during the morning, cabled from New York. Every name was eagerly scanned by waiting thousands of people, the list bringing joy to some, dismay to others.

Lrd Ashburton and Norman C. Craig, member of parliament, whose names appeared in some of the published lists of first cabin passengers, did not sail on the Titanic. Lord Ashburton is on his way to America on another steamer.

The family of J. Bruce Ismay, managing director of the White Star line, received no direct news from him, but the appearance of his name in the list of rescued posted by the papers brought great relief to his friends and relatives.

ONE MESSAGE READ "ALL WELL."

A wireless dispatch received today by the firm of Pears, soap makers, and timed 1:20 yesterday, said merely, "All well." It was unsigned, but was believed to be from Thomas Pears, who, with his wife, was among the Titanic's passengers. It came via the liner Potsdam, but there was no indication as to where it was originally sent from. It may have been dispatched before the Titanic sank, but nevertheless it gave welcome relief to the family, who believe that Mr. Pears is aboard one of the steamers which reached the scene of the disaster yesterday.

The underwriters at Lloyds were staggered at the news, but it is declared that the insurance on the lost vessel is so evenly distributed that none of the underwriters is likely to be hard hit.

LOSS NOW PUT AT $12,500,000.

When they reopened this morning a little business was done at 90 guineas, but the rate quickly was raised to 95, which is known as a "total loss' rate. The exact amount of property loss was hard to ascertain. Underwriters said they could not say accurately what securities were on board. It was estimated, however, that with the cargo the Titanic would represent a value of approximately $12,500,000. Of this total $750,000 was retained by the White Star company at its own risk and the balance was placed on the insurance market in London, Liverpool, Hamburg and elsewhere.

The loss sustained is the largest on record in connection with one "bottom."

The officials of the White Star company say that so far as they know every passenger whose name appeared on the lists cabled to New York yesterday sailed on board the Titanic. There may, they say, have been a few who changed their minds at the last moment, but at the offices up to the present no cancellations from or additions to the passenger list have been heard of.

THE WRECK OF THE TITANIC BY COLLIDING WITH AN ICEBERG AS DRAWN FROM TELEGRAPHIC DESCRIPTION OF THE DISASTER BY ARTIST PAUL GREGG OF THE POST. THE PICTURE SHOWS THE BOW OF THE BIG VESSEL STRIKING THE ICEBERG. THE SMALLER PICTURES AT THE BOTTOM SHOW COL. JOHN JACOB ASTOR BIDDING GOODBY TO HIS WIFE AS SHE WAS TAKEN ABOARD ONE OF THE LIFEBOATS, AND ALSO A BOATLOAD OF SURVIVORS DRIFTING IN THE OCEAN.

Survivors List Sent From the Carpathia

Much Difficulty Experienced in Getting Names by Wireless Which Do Not Agree With Advance List.

Cape Race, N. F., April 16.—The steamship Carpathia, which is believed to have on board all the survivors of the Titanic disaster, started early today to send by wireless to this station the list of the Titanic's survivors.

Great difficulty was experienced in getting many of the names correctly, and more than a score of names as made out here did not appear on the Titanic's original passenger list, but it is believed many of these were passengers who had booked at the last moment.

The receipt of the list of the first cabin survivors required more than six hours' effort. So far as the names check up correctly, the following saloon passengers of the Titanic are safe on board the Carpathia:

Anderson, Harry.
Andreus, Miss K. T.
Allen, Miss E. W.
Appleton, Mrs. E. W.
Astor, Mrs. John Jacob, and maid.
Arthur, Mrs.
Barkworth, A. S.
Baxter, Mrs. James.
Brayton, George A.
Beckwith, Mr. and Mrs. R. T.
Behr, Karl H.
Bishop, Mr. and Mrs. D. H.
Blank, Henry.
Bonnell, Miss Caroline.
Bowen, Miss G. C.
Bowerman, Miss Elsie.
Brown, Mrs. J. M.
Brown, Mrs. J. J.
Calderhead, E. P.
Chibnoll, Mrs. E. B.
Cardell, Mrs. Churchill.
Cardeza, Mrs. J. W.
Cardeza, Thomas.
Carter, Miss Lucille.
Carter, Mrs. William E.
Carter, Master William.
Case, Howard B.
Cavendish, Mrs. Turrell W., and maid.
Chaffee, Mrs. H. F.
Chambers, Mr. and Mrs. N. C.
Cherry, Miss Gladys.
Chevro, Paul.
Cornell, Miss R. G.
Crosby, Miss.
Daniel, W.
Davidson, Mrs. Thornton.
Devilliers. Mrs. B.
Douglas, R. D.
Dick, Mr. and Mrs. A. A.
Dodge, Mr. and Mrs. Washington, and son.
Douglas, Mrs. F. C.
Douglas, Mrs. Walter.
Ellis, Miss Eustia.
Earnshaw, Mrs. B.
Endres, Miss Caroline.
Flynn, J. F.
Frauenthal, Dr. Henry and wife.
Frauenthal, Mr. and Mrs. T. G.
Fortune, Mrs. Mark.
Fortune, Miss Lucille.
Frolicher, Miss Margaret.
Futrelle, Mrs. Jacques.
Fortune, Miss Alice.
Gibson, Mrs. Leonard.
Gibson, Miss Dorothy.
Goldenburg, Mrs. Samuel.
Goldenburg, Miss Ella.
Gordon, Sir and Lady Cosmo Duff.
Gracie, Col. Archibald.
Graham, Mr.
Graham, Mrs. William.
Graham, Miss Margaret E.
Greenefield, Mrs. Lee D.
Greenefield, William B.
Haraner, Henry.
Harder, Mr. and Mrs. George A.
Harper, Henry S. and man servant.
Harper, Mrs. Henry S.
Hawksford, Henry.
Hays, Mrs. Charles M., and daughter Margaret.
Harris, Mrs. Henry B.
Hippach, Miss Jean.
Hogeboom, Mrs. John C.
Hoyt, Mr. and Mrs. F. M.
Ismay, J. Bruce.
Keuyon, Mrs. F. R.
Kimball, Mr. and Mrs. E. N.
Leader, Mrs. A. F.
Lines, Mrs. Ernest.
Lines, Miss Mary C.
Lindstrom, Mrs. J.
Longley, Miss J. F.
Madill, Miss Gorgietti A.
Marschal, Pierce.
Millet, F. D.
Marvin, Mrs. D. W.
Minnihan, Mrs. W. E.
Minnihan, Miss Daisy.
Newell, Miss Madeline.
Newell, Miss Marjorie.
Newsom, Miss Helen.
Ostby, E. C.
Ostby, Miss Helen R.
Omond, Mr. Fiennad.
Puechen, Major Arthur.
Potter, Mrs. Thomas J.
Rheims, Mrs. George.
Robert, Mrs. Edward S.
Rogerson, J. N.
Rolmano, C.
Rosenbaum, Miss Edith.
Rogerson family.
Rothschild, Mrs. Martin.
Rothes, Countess of.
Sealfeld, Adolpe.
Salaman, Abraham.
Schabert, Mrs. Paul.
Schutes, Mrs. S. W.
Seward, Frederick.
Silvey, Mrs. William D.
Shedden, Mr. and Mrs. F. O
Simonius, Col. Alfonso.
Sloper, William T.
Snyder, Mr. and Mrs. John.
Spencer, Mrs. W. E., and maid.
Stepelin, Dr. Max.
Stengel, Mr. and Mrs. C. E. H.
Stone, Mrs. George M.
Swift, Mrs. Frederick Joel.
Thayer, J. B.
Taussig, Miss Ruth.
Taylor, Mr. and Mrs. E. Z.
Tucker, Gilbert M.
Warren, Mrs. F. M.
Williams, P. M. Jr.
White, Mrs. J. Stuart.
Wick, Miss Mary.
Widener, Mrs. George D., and maid.
Davis, Miss Mary.
Doling, Mrs. Ada.
Doling, Miss Elsie.
Faunthrope, E.
Garside, Miss Ethel.
Hewlett, Miss Mary D.
Harris, George.
Herman, Mrs. Jane.
Herman, Miss Kate.
Herman, Miss Alice.
Hold, Miss Annie.
Hart, Mrs. Esther.
Hart, Miss Eva.
Harper, Miss Nina.
Hamalainer, Anna, and son.
Hocking, Mrs. Elizabeth.
Hocking, Miss Nellie.
Jacobsohn, Mrs. Amy.
Keane, Miss Nora.
Kelly, Miss Fannie.
Lareche, Miss Louise.
Leitch, Miss Jessie W.
Lamore, Mrs.
Lehman, Miss Bertha.
Mellinger, Mrs. Elizabeth, and child.
Louch, Mrs. Alice.
Mallet, Mrs. A.
Mallet, Master Andrero.
Nye, Mrs. Elizabeth.
Philipps, Miss Alice.
Pailas, Emilio.
Padro, Julian.
Parish, Mrs. L.
Portaluppi, Mrs. Emilio.
Quick, Mrs. Jane O.
Quick, Miss Phyllis O.
Quick, Miss Wennie O.
Rebouf, Mrs. Lillie.
Ridsdale, Miss Lucy.
Rugg, Miss Emily.
Richard, Mr. and Mrs. Emile, and son.
Sincock, Miss Maude.
Smith, Mrs. Marion.
Trout, Miss Edna S.
Weisz, Mrs. Matilda.
Webber, Miss Susan.
Wright, Miss Marion.
Watt, Miss Bessie.
Watt, Miss Bertha.
West, Mrs., and two children.
Wells, Mrs. Addie.
Wells, Miss J.
Wells, Ralph.
Williams, Charles.

List of survivors whose names do not appear on the original sailing list probably includes a large number of those who took the ship at Cherbourg:

Bassina, Miss A.
Burns, Mrs. G. M.
Casebere, Miss D. D.
Chamdasen, Mrs. Victorine.
Daniel, Miss Sarah.
Desette, Miss.
Drauchensted, Alfred.
Emock, Philip.
Fleigheim, Miss Anterete.
Francatelli, Miss.
Googht, James.
Helversen, Mrs. A. O.
Homer, Henry R.
Mamy, Miss Ruberta.
Melicard, Madam.
Lavory, Miss Bertha.
Lesneur, Gustave J.
Panhart, Miss Nanette.
Renago, Mrs. Mamam J.
Ranelt, Miss Appie.
Seerepeca, Miss Augusta.
Steffanson, H. B.
Segesser, Miss Emma.
Smith, Mrs. P. P.
Slayton, Miss Hilda.
Shadell, Robert Douglas.
Smith, Mrs. Lucien P.
Ward, Miss Emma.
Thor, Miss Ella.
Tucker, Mrs., and maid.
Thayer, Mr. and Mrs. J. B.
Willard, Miss Constance.
Woolner, Hugh.
Young, Miss Marie.
Hippach, Mrs. Ida S.
Clark, Mrs. Walter.
Cummings, Mrs. John B.
Silverthorne, R. Spencer.
Brown, Edith.
Brown, T. S. W.
Cahries, William E.
Carmaccion, Renardo M.
Driscoll, Miss B.
Formery, Miss Elein.
Gerroa, Mrs. Margy I.
Healy, Miss Norah.
Hansen, Mrs. Jennie.
Hososons, Massefame.
McGowan, Miss Annie.
McDearmott, Miss Letitia.
Mare, Mrs. Florence.
Pensky, Miss Rossi.
Skeliery, Mrs. W. N.
Trout, Mrs. Jessie.

Wireless version:
Abbott, Mrs. Rose; probable meaning Mrs. N. Aubert.
Bessette, Miss.
Bucknell, Mrs. William.
Middle, Olivia.
Barrett, Karl.
Haussig, Mile.

Cape Race, N. F., April 16.—The names of the rescued cabin passengers, so far as they check up with the Titanic's published list, are:

Angle, William
Abelson, Hanna
Biss, Miss Kate
Beane, Edward
Beane, Miss Ethel
Bryhl, Miss Dagmar
Bystrom, Miss Karolina
Collyer, Mrs. Charlotte
Collyer, Miss Marjorie
Christy, Miss Alice
Christy, Miss Julia
Clark, Mrs. Ada Maria
Cameron, Miss
Collett, Mrs. Stuart
Caldwell, Albert F.
Caldwell, Mrs. Sylvia
Caldwell, Alden G.
Drew, Mrs. Lulu
Davis, Miss Agnes
Davis, John M.
Duran, Florentina
Duran, Ascuncion

W. H. HARRISON NOT ABOARD THE TITANIC

Clorado Springs, Colo., April 16.—In a dispatch just received from London it is stated that Joseph Harrison's cousin, W. H. Harrison of Philadelphia, did not sail in the Titanic.

2d-Class Passengers Aboard the Titanic Who Are Missing

London, April 16.—Second-class passengers on board the Titanic missing:

William Angle and wife.
John Ashby.
Samson Ableson.
Edgar Andrew.
Lillian Bentham.
Ada R. Balls.
Kate Bliss.
Robert J. Bateman.
Lawrence Beesley.
Mrs. A. O. Belker and three children.
Reginald Butler.
H. J. Beauchamp.
Jose de Brito.
Rev. Thomas R. D. Byles.
Mr. Bambridge.
Solomon Bowenur.
Mildred Brown
Percy Bailly.
W. Hall Botsford.
William Berrman.
Carl Bryhl.
Frederick J. Banfield.
Erik Collender.
R. C. Coleridge.
Harvey Collyer.
Irene C. Corbett.
Mrs. C. P. Corey.
John H. Chapman.
Elizabeth Chapman.
Rev. Ernest C. Carter.
Charles V. Clarke.
Olear Cameron.
Erik Collander.
Charles Chapman.
William Carbines.
Harry Cotterill.
Baron Von Drachstedt.
Sebastiani de Carlo.
Herbert Denbury.
James V. Drew.
Marshall Drew.
John M. Davis.
Percy E. Deacon.
Charles Davies.
William Dibden.
William J. Denton.
Lena N. DeF.
Stanley Fox.
Arnej Fahlstrom.
Harry Faunthorpe.
Lizzie Faunthorpe.
Charles Fillbrook.
Annie Fjunk.
Joseph Fynney.
Alfred Gaskell.
William Gillespie.
William Gilbert.
Harry Gale.
S. Gale.
John Gill.
Ralph Giles.
Hans K. Givard.
Samuel Greenberg.
Fred Giles.
Edgar Giles.
Lawrence Gavey.
Walter Harris.
Samuel Herman.
Alice Herman.
Stephen Hold.
George Hunt.
Leonard Hickman.
Stanley Hickman.
Ambrose Hood.
Benjamin Howard.
Ellen T. Howard.
Benjamin Hart.
Joseph Harper
Mr. Hoffman and two childen
George Hocking
Henry P. Hodges
Martha Hiltuner
Bertha Ilott
Clifford Jeffert
Ernest Jeffert
Sidney S. Jacobsohn
Stephen Jenkins
Dr. J. G. Jenkins
John D. Jarvis
S. Kantor and wife
Daniel Keane
Rev. Charles Kirkland
F. Karnes
John Henrik Kvillner
Rene Learnot
John L. Injan
Robert W. N. Leyson
Joseph Laroche and wife
Simonne Laroche
J. J. Lambe
Charles Louch
R. F. Levy.
William Lahtigan and wife.
Emilio Masgiavacchi.
Mr. Marshall.
Mrs. Marshall.
Ernest Morawreck.
Noel Malachard.
James McCrie.
Joseph Mantvila.
Frank H. Mayberry.
Thomas F. Myles.
Mary Mack.
Thomas Moudd.
Henry Mitchell.
A. Mallet.
W. J. Matthews.
Peter McKane.
William Mellers.
August Meyer.
Jacob Milling.
Joseph Nicholls.
Robert D. Norman.
Nicholas Masser and wife.
L. Nosson.
Richard Otter.
Thomas Oxenham.
Robert Phillips.
Dr. Alfred Paine.
Frederick Pengelly.
Clifford Parker.
Martin Ponezell.
Frank Pulsaum.
Vera W. Quick.
Peter H. Renouf.
Harry Rogers.
Selina Rogers.
David Reeves.
Miss E. Reynolds.
William Richards and son.
George Sweet.
Ernest A. Sjostedt.
Augustus Smith.
Richard J. Slemer.
Haydon Sobey.
Philip J. Stokes.
H. M. Slayter.
F. W. Sedgwick.
Percival Sharp.
Anna Sinkkonen.
S. Ward Stanton.
George Swane.
L. Manta Shelley.
Lillie Silven.
M. E. I. Strant.
William J. Turpin.
Dorothy Turpin.
Ellen Tooney.
Moses A. Troopiansky.
Mrs. A. T. Tervan.
James Veale.
Mrs. George Wilkinson.
Ada C. Wilkinson.
William J. Ware.
Leopold Weisz.
Edward Wheadon.
John James Ware.
Florence L. Ware.
Charles Wilhelm.
E. Arthur West.
Edwin Wheeler.
Miss J. Wells.
Ralph Wells.
Nellie Walcroft.
C. Williams.
Miss H. Yodis.

There were 740 third-class passengers on board.

The Ill Bread.

Five-year-old Johnnie was dining out in company with an auntie. He quietly ate what was given him until he tasted the bread, then he frankly announced:

"Auntie, this bread isn't good."

"Hush! Johnnie, that is ill bred," admonished auntie. Johnnie subsided, but when he reached home and mother asked him what good things he had had to eat he surprised them with: "Oh, we had jelly and meat and ice cream, but I didn't like the ill bread."—National Monthly.

His Honor at Stake.

"Young man, how do you expect to marry my daughter if you are in debt?"

"Why, sir, in my opinion, it's the only square thing to do. The longer I am engaged to her the worse off I will be."—Life.

Seven Men on Titanic Worth $420,000,000

Combined Wealth of First-Class Passengers on Ill-Fated Vessel Placed at $1,000,000,000.

New York, April 16.—Wealth aggregating something like half a billion dollars is represented by seven of the passengers on the Titanic. If calamity befell only a few of these seven it would materially affect vast business enterprises in the United States and England. The seven are:

Col. John Jacob Astor	$150,000,000
J. Bruce Ismay	40,000,000
Col. Washington Robeling	25,000,000
Isidor Straus	50,000,000
George D. Widener	50,000,000
Benjamin Guggenheim	95,000,000
J. B. Thayer	10,000,000
Total	$420,000,000

If the fortunes of the first-class passengers alone were placed together they would easily make $1,000,000,000.

Foremost among the passengers in point of wealth is Col. John Jacob Astor, who was returning to New York with his bride, formerly Miss Madeline Force. Colonel Astor's holdings may amount to $150,000,000. Besides attending to his realty in this country he is connected with many corporations.

Next in financial importance comes Benjamin Guggenheim. Mr. Guggenheim is in the American Smelting Securities company, the great mining corporation which was founded by his father, Meyer Guggenheim.

George D. Widener is connected with the Widener-Elkins traction syndicate of Philadelphia. He is one of two sons of P. A. B. Widener. George D. Widener's fortune is estimated at $50,000,000.

John B. Thayer, second vice president of the Pennsylvania railroad, another passenger, was accompanied by his wife and a young son.

Mrs. T. W. Cavendish, whose name appears on the list of passengers on the Titanic. is the daughter of Henry Siegel of this city.

The deepest anxiety as to the safety of herself, her husband and their two infant children, kept the Siegel household in a state of alarm.

Miss Siegel's marriage to Tyrell William Cavendish, scion of a noted English family, took place in 1906. The bride was presented at court, where her beauty attracted much attention.

She was on her way home to visit her parents in this city.

Baltimore, April 16.—Alfred G. Vanderbilt was not on board the Titanic. Capt. Isaac E. Emerson, the father of Mrs. Vanderbilt, who was formerly Mrs. Smith Hollins McKim, received a message from Mr. Vanderbilt in London stating that he and his wife were well and had not started for America.

Paris, April 16.—News of the Titanic disaster has caused the utmost excitement here, especially in the American colony, many of whose residents had friends on board the ill-fated vessel. Great throngs congregated in the streets for the latest bulletins of the wreck.

Nearly 300 of the Titanic's passengers went aboard at Cherbourg. Col. John Jacob Astor engaged passage here, as did also Mr. and Mrs. George W. Widener and Mrs. J. W. M. Cardeza and T. D. M. Cardeza. The latter engaged the most expensive suit on the vessel, paying $3,000

The White Star office was besieged today by weeping women, several of whom had sons on board. Among these was Mrs. William Dulles, who collapsed.

There is hardly a hotel here at which relatives of passengers are not staying and these are waiting anxiously for definite news.

It has been established that Lady Duff-Gordon, who is known in Paris as "Lucille," the name under which she conducts her dressmaking business, sailed on board the Titanic with her husband, Sir Cosmo Edmund Duff-Gordon. They appear on the official passenger list as Mr. Morgan and wife.

Robert Bacon, United States ambassador to France, with his wife and daughter, had planned to sail on the Titanic, but the delay in the arrival of Myron T. Herrick, his successor, caused Mr. Bacon to postpone his departure.

Halifax, N. S., April 16.—It is definitely known that, Charles M. Hays, president of the Grand Trunk railway, with his wife and daughter and H. Marklind Molson of the Montreal banking house bearing his name, were among the passengers on the Titanic.

SPRINGS MAN BUYS EDNA GOODRICH'S CAR

Colorado Springs, Colo., April 16.—A. W. Marksheffel, the automobile dealer of Colorado Springs, has purchased the $17,000 automobile presented by Nat Goodwin, the actor, to Edna Goodrich, the last of his many wives, who sold the car to a Detroit dealer after her divorce from Goodwin.

The automobile is a regular hotel on wheels. It contains a wash basin, a small bath tub, ice box, electric lights, two sleeping berths and a small kitchen. The body is constructed of the finest mahogany. The sides are entirely of glass and there is a set of copper screens to be used on warm days, when the glass is removed. All of the curtains are of silk. The hooks for the curtains are of hand-carved ivory. The car seats nine persons and is equipped with a fifty-horse power motor and has a 140-inch wheel base.

TITANIC HAD ROOM FOR 3,000 PERSONS WITHOUT CROWDING

This More Than Population of Alamosa, or Sterling or Montrose.

SHIP 882 FEET LONG

Set on End It Would Look Down on Highest Three Spires in Denver Combined.

Specifications of the Titanic—the bare figures that describe its capacity, its length, its breadth, the size of its staterooms, etc.—give, after all, a scant idea of the enormous proportions of the latest ocean-going monster.

But when one stops to consider that the entire population of the town of Alamosa or of Sterling or of Montrose or of Rocky Ford or of Lamar could have been carried on board it, and that more than the number of persons who call the thriving town of Delta home could have been accommodated, a suggestion of its magnitude is conveyed.

The Titanic could take care of 3,000 persons comfortably. Montrose and Rocky Ford exceed that number by a few hundred, Sterling and Alamosa just touch it, according to the last government census. In the Titanic's steerage the population of Aspen or of Central City could easily be cared for, and in the saloon as many persons as Akron or Fort Lupton claims.

And if the great ship had been set squarely in the middle of Sixteenth street, its stem resting at Lawrence street, the stern would have been found somewhere in the neighborhood of the alley between Champa and Curtis streets. The blocks along Sixteenth street measure 266 feet, with eight feet additional for street intersections, and the Titanic's length was 882 feet and 6 inches.

Set on end, the Titanic would have looked down on the combined heights of the Daniels & Fisher tower (330 feet), the Immaculate Conception cathedral spires (225 feet) and the capitol dome (272 feet). They aggregate but 827 feet, and the Titanic measured more than 882.

The main promenade deck had an unbroken sweep of 190 yards on either side of the ship. Its single-berth rooms were larger than the bedrooms in the average flat, and its two-berth cabins as large as the living rooms in comfortably built homes.

Over the boat deck the Titanic spanned 92 feet 6 inches. It boasted fifteen water-tight bulkheads to divide the great vessel. These the ship builders said would make the boat unsinkable even though half her compartments should be filled with water. These bulkheads are steel partitions, both transverse and longitudinal, which divide a vessel into a number of water-tight compartments and lessen the danger of foundering when the ship is breached.

The Titanic was equipped with swimming pool, squash racket court, gymnasium and Turkish baths.

Its cost, in the neighborhood of $7,500,000, is equal to twice that of duplicating the First National Bank building, the Equitable building, the Foster building, the Central Savings Bank building, the Daniels & Fisher addition and the Tramway building.

Scarcity of Boats on Titanic Was Put Before Parliament

New York, April 16.—The disaster to the Titanic brings to the minds of those who were in London last summer the spirited debate which took place in the British parliament when an effort was made to compel the White Star line to provide more life boats on the two new mammoth ships, the Olympic and Titanic.

Horatio Bottomley, representing the South Hackney district, a London division, asked the president of the Board of Trade whether the boat capacity of the Olympic, which was then about to make her maiden voyage, was sufficient to take care of all the passengers and crew in the event of an accident.

The reply Bottomley received was that the White Star line had complied with the existing laws, although it was pointed out that those laws were antiquated and dealt with ships up to 10,000 tonnage.

They never have been revised to meet the construction of the mammoth ships. Bottomley pointed out that if the White Star complied with the laws the Olympic could only handle about 600 persons in its lifeboats.

The resolution was pigeonholed.

Archibald C. Butt's Fate Sad News to President's Staff

Washington, April 16.—News of the Titanic disaster spread sorrow over official Washington. The report is especially distressing on account of the fate of Maj. Archibald Butt, the president's military aide, who was aboard the vessel returning from Europe.

Major Butt's trip to Europe was partly an official mission in that he bore a message to the pope from President Taft thanking his holiness for creating three American cardinals.

Major Butt had achieved greater popularity than any of his predecessors in the capacity of military aide to the president. He came to Washington from the South as a newspaper correspondent and was a favorite with the McKinley, Roosevelt and Taft administrations. He served in the war with Spain and at its conclusion was appointed to the regular army as a commissioned officer by President McKinley. He served as military aide to President Roosevelt and was retained in that position by President Taft, whose constant companion he has been since. Recently he was raised from the rank of captain to that of major.

Disappearance of Naronic Recalled

New York, April 16.—In the melancholy roll of marine tragedies, that which overtook the Titanic is the first on record wherein a conspicuous vessel has met disaster on her maiden voyage.

The nearest approach to such an unfortunate fate was the cruise of the Naronic, which belonged to the same line. She went to the port of missing ships on her second voyage. Carrying about 300 all told, she steamed out of this port on her return trip nearly twenty years ago, and since then there has never been a word as to how she met her fate.

SOME OF THE FAMOUS MEN WHO ARE BELIEVED TO HAVE DROWNED

(1)

(2)

(3)

(4)

(5)

(6)

(7)

(8)

1—Charles M. Hays, general manager Grand Trunk railroad system.
2—J. B. Ismay, head of the steamship combine.
3—Isidor Strauss, millionaire and New York philanthropist.
4—William T. Stead, world-famous English journalist.
5—W. A. Roebling, who built the Brooklyn bridge.
6—John B. Thayer, vice president of the Pennsylvania railroad.
7—Benjamin Guggenheim, brother of Senator Guggenheim.
8—Henry B. Harris, theatrical manager.

EXPERTS DISAGREE AS TO CAUSE OF TITANIC SINKING

Most Think Impact on Iceberg Shattered Ship's Safety Devices.

Washington, April 16.—The chaplains of both houses of congress mentioned the Titanic disaster in their invocations today. Chaplain Peirce in the senate referred to the "sore distress of our people and the sad fate that has overtaken our brethren on the great deep," andd asked Divine comfort. Chaplain Couden in the house prayed for more stringent laws for the protection of travelers by land or sea, as well as for those exposed to fire and flood.

Captain Charles A. McAllister expressed the belief that the mass which sent the Titanic to the bottom of the ocean was a salt water iceberg and not a plar berg of glacial formation. He pointed out that the ratio of ice above water in such an iceberg was only one-ninth of its bulk.

George Uhler, inspector general of the federal steamboat inspection service, said he believed the Titanic plunged into the iceberg with such momentum that the impact buckled her to pieces. The vessel in all probability, he added, ran over a submerged end of the berg, which ripped open her bottom; that her safety compartments thus qquickly filled and the vessel became a helpless mass of twisted steel wedged in a mountain of ice.

One of the engineer officers declared the weak point in the ship's design was a long central passageway running from the fire rooms forward to the collision bulkhead. At the fore end of this was a ladder whereby the firemen ascended from the fire rooms to their quarters on an upper deck.

It was his theory that the force of the collision started the plates at the end of this passage and that the great rush of water prevented the closing of the door in the bulkhead leading into the fire rooms. With the fire rooms filled, in addition to the bow compartments smashed by the blow against the ice, the ship would not have retained sufficient floative power to insure safety.

Springs People Had Relatives on Board the Titanic

Colorado Springs, Colo., April 16.—J. B. Thayer, president of the Pennsylvania railroads and a cousin of Mrs. Charles L. Tutt of Solorado Springs, was a passenger on the Titanic, as was also Milton C. Long, brother of Mrs. C. H. Standard of Broadmoor, who is in the East.

Several other passengers were well known in Colorado Springs, among them being A. W. Newell, Miss Alice Newell and Miss Madeline Newell, all of New York, who have spent several summer seasons in Colorado Springs.

Joseph Harrison of Broadmoore has a cousin, W. H. Harrison of Philadelphia, who was returning on the Titanic and also a number of close friends, among who were: Mr. and Mrs. J. B. Fair and son, G. M. Tucker Jr., and Mr. and Mrs. William E. Parker, son and daughter, and others.

"Anonymous" Wants to Know.

If a thing of beauty
Is ALWAYS a joy,
Why does grandma rejoice
When the baby's a boy?
—Chicago Tribune.

Rescued Women Had Thrilling Experience

Lifeboat Passengers Scantily Clad, Floated Helplessly Among Icebergs--Winter Most Severe in History.

New York, April 16.—Messages filtering through here indicate that the passengers in the lifeboats from the Titanic had thrilling experiences.

Huge quantities of field ice covered the ocean and the boat steerers had to guide their craft with the greatest care. In some cases the ice was so heavy that the boats could not force their way through it and as a result many of them became widely separated.

Many of the passengers in the lifeboats were scantily clad, having been hurried from their berths in the dead of night and ordered into the boats.

The prevalence of icebergs on the Grand Banks, N. F., this spring is due to the exceptional severity of the recent winter, which was the worst perhaps in the history of Newfoundland and Labrador. From mid-December up to the present time intense frost and incessant storms have prevailed.

20 SAILING VESSELS GONE DOWN THIS WINTER.

These conditions caused the ice forming in every harbor along Labrador and northern Newfoundland to become unusually thick, and as the severe winds tore the masses from the coast, these immense crystal mountains were flung widespread over the ocean and carried south by the current from the polar regions, which, meeting the gulf stream, cause the constant fogs which so greatly menace shipping.

Never in the history of Newfoundland has there been a winter so disastrous to steam and sail vessels since November. No less than twenty sailing crafts, from 100 to 300 tons burden, have gone to the bottom, seven of them carrying their whole crews down, as well as some sixty-three passengers. The crews of the remainder were rescued from the sinking hulks in the nick of time. Two steamers also sunk with all hands.

The first was the steamer Kampfiore, coal laden from Sydney, which, it is believed, was crushed by ice in the February blizzard off Cope Race and sank with her eighteen men. The second was the Erna, a 3,000-ton liner purchased in England and remodeled for use in the seal fisheries. She is now forty-eight days out from Glasgow with fifty-one people, and all hope of her survival is abandoned.

Besides this, the present season has been the severest in the annals of the island's seal fisheries. The sealing fleet this year comprised twenty-three steamers, from 500 to 3,000 tons, and all report ice conditions worse than ever before. As a result the seal catch this season will be only about 170,000, against 330,000 last year.

SEVERE WEATHER RUINED THE SEAL FISHING.

The steamers Bellaventure, Bonaventure, Florizel and Sagona, four of the finest in the fleet, had to return practically empty because their propellers were smashed off, and today the Labrador returned in a similar plight. Others of the fleet sustained sundry damages through being crushed amid the floes.

All incoming steamers report immense quantities of ice scattered over the Northern Atlantic, and so numerous and widespread have been the floes in the St. Lawrence that the steamship travel of the island has been seriously crippled the whole winter. Three Furness line steamers were so badly damaged by ice that as each in turn arrived in England she had to be docked for repairs, and the company has had to charter outside ships to continue the service. The northeast coast of Newfoundland has been icebound since early in January, coastwise traveling being practically impossible. Owing to similar conditions the Donaldson liner Tritonia, which was drydocked at Glasgow last winter and remodelled at a cost of $60,000 to serve as an ice breaker to enable the Harmsworths to get pulp and paper shipments out of their spring port at Botwood, found the ice so immensely heavy that she was thirty days making thirty miles up the Exploits inlet in Notre Dame bay to Botwood harbor, and only succeeded in getting there by the lavish use of dynamite. When she arrived on March 1, she was without coal to return and is still there with the inlet frozen solid.

FISHING FIELD DANGEROUS PLACE NOW.

Behind her, waiting for the spring freshets to break up the floes and admit a collier to supply her with fuel for the return voyage to England, is the Reid company's powerful new ice-breaker Bruce, which made her maiden trip in February and has been battling with the floes between Newfoundland and Cape Breton since and has suffered such damage—though she is the finest of her class in the world—that she will require extensive repairs in dry dock next month, when the vanishing of the ice will enable an unsheathed steamer to take her place.

Because of the prevalence of ice this winter the operations of the American, Canadian and Newfoundland fishing vessels on the Grand banks have been greatly hampered, while the fresh stream trawlers have found it impossible to operate at all.

The immense floes are dispersed over the whole ocean where these fishing smacks cruise and form the greatest menace to their success. The changing winds often bring in immense infields crashing together, jeopardizing fishing boats in their vicinity and when ice prevails on the Grand banks, as it has this winter fishing vessels are obliged to give the area a wide berth.

COL. ASTOR'S DEATH ON HONEYMOON IS SHOCK TO COUNTRY

Was Most Popular Millionaire With All Classes in New York.

SPANISH WAR VETERAN

Divorce From Ava Willing and Marriage to Madeline Force Food for Gossips.

New York, April 16.—Col. John Jacob Astor and his young bride, formerly Madeline Force, departed from New York Jan. 25 last for Europe to complete their honeymoon.

The millionaire drowned in the Titanic disaster was the fourth of the direct line to bear the Christian name of the founder of the family. He would have been 48 years old had he lived until July 13 next. Graduating at Harvard in the class of 1888 with the degree of B. S., Colonel Astor soon thereafter took his place as head of the family in America and conservator of the enormous Astor estate, the lowest estimate of which places its value at $150,000,000. Some estimates of the value of the total Astor wealth are as high as $450,000,000.

In 1891 Colonel Astor married Ava Willing, a reigning belle of Philadelphia. Society was shocked when a divorce was granted Mrs. Astor on Nov. 9, 1909. All the papers in the case were sealed and have not yet been made public.

RECENT MARRIAGE CAUSED NATIONAL STIR.

Colonel Astor's marriage to Madeline Force, the 20-year-old daughter of Mr. and Mrs. William H. Force, created a national sensation. In the decree of divorce given to the first wife the husband was forbidden to remarry in this state. For that reason the wedding occurred at Newport. Clergymen of the Episcopalian church, of which Colonel Astor is a communicant, led by the Rev. Dr. Richmond of Philadelphia, raised a hue and cry against the marriage ceremony being performed by a minister of that denomination because of an article of the Episcopalian faith which forbids the remarriage of a divorced person at fault. As a result difficulty was experienced in securing a regularly ordained minister to officiate. The marriage rite was performed by Rev. Dr. Joseph Lambert, pastor of the Elmwood Congregational church of Providence, R. I. A few weeks ago New York society was interested in a rumor that the Astors were returning from Europe in expectation of the birth of another heir to the Astor estate.

Only two children were born of his marriage with his first wife, a son, Vincent, now 19, and a daughter, Muriel, aged 10 years. Justice Mills' decree gave to the divorced wife custody of the little daughter and custody of Vincent to the father.

No millionaire by inheritance was as popular with all classes of New Yorkers as was Colonel Astor. A long-limbed, keen-faced man, elegant and quiet in manner, he mingled freely with all sorts and conditions of people.

ASTOR SERVED IN SPANISH WAR.

He manifested a lively interest in every public matter. He obtained his military title originally by serving on the staff of Governor Levi P. Morton as colonel. At the outbreak of the war with Spain Colonel Astor bought and equipped a mountain battery at an expense of $100,000 which he presented to the United States and which was used in the Porto Rican campaign. President McKinley commissioned him as a lieutenant colonel. In this rank he assisted Major General Breckenridge, inspector general of the army, in the inspection of the troops in camp at Chickamauga park, Ga.

Afterward he served on the staff of Maj.-Gen. Shafter and served throughout the Santiago campaign, being present at the surrender of the Spanish forces.

Although giving close attention to the management of the immense Astor estate, Colonel Astor's activities were not confined to that successful endeavor. A great reader of books, he also essayed authorship, publishing in 1890 "A Journey In Other Worlds," etc. He was also an inventor of merit. Among his inventions that have proved successful are a bicycle brake, a pneumatic road improver and an improved turbine engine.

Colonel Astor's reported death tonight recalled an accident to his yacht, the Nourmahal, near Fort Adams, R. I., August 16, 1905. For nine hours the big steamer was on the reef and although the pounding waters threatened momentarily to tear the ship to pieces, Colonel Astor personally took command of the crew and got the Nourmahal safely off.

Colonel Astor displayed his real attitude toward life in an article he contributed several years ago to the Strand magazine of London.

In his introduction he wrote:

"I have often had occasion to remember a remark made by the American sculptor, Hiram Powers, at his studio in Florence, 'Wealth is nothing.'

"And I recall these words because they represent pre-eminently the characteristic and distinctive opinion of a large proportion of the original American colonists and their descendants."

Colonel Astor was the hero of another ocean scare two years ago. He and his son Vincent aboard the Noma were caught in a terrific hurricane in the Caribbean sea. For days their yacht could not be located, although even the government sent fast dispatch boats in search of them. When it was thought that all on board the Astor yacht had been lost and the search was about to be abandoned, the Noma steamed into Jacksonville, Fla.

Mrs. T. Potter Jr. on the Way Home With Her Daughter

Philadelphia, April 16.—Mrs. Thomas Potter Jr., wife of the late Colonel Potter, a well known officer of the Pennsylvania National Guard, was on her way home on the Titanic from a tour of the Holy Land with her daughter, Mrs. Boulton E. Ernshaw.

Mrs. Potter is a sister-in-law of William Potter, president of the board of trustees of Jefferson Medical college and former United States ambassador to Italy. Her son is Wilson Potter, the well known athlete and member of the Racquet club.

Mr. and Mrs. Arthur Reyerson, who were also passengers aboard the Titanic, were on their way home to the funeral of their son, Arthur L. Reyerson, who was killed, with a friend, John Lewis Hoffman, in an automobile accident Easter Monday. Following the receipt of a cablegram telling of the accident to their son, the Reyersons caught the first steamer home, which happened to be the Titanic.

Says I to myself,
The Post is the paper to buy.

TWO PROMINENT WOMEN SAVED TWO MEN WHO WERE DROWNED

Mrs. J. J. Astor, who was rescued.

John Jacob Astor, who is believed to be dead.

Mrs. J. J. Brown of Denver, who is reported safe.

Maj. Archibald Butt, aid to President Taft, reported missing.

DISASTERS AT SEA BEAR WITNESS TO DEEDS OF HEROES

Man Who Faces Bullets in Heat of Battle Has Relatively Easy Task.

BRAVELY MEET DEATH

History Full of Accounts of Courage When Men Have Faced Doom Unmoved.

It is to histories of marine disasters that we turn for examples of supreme courage and bravery, the greatest that can be displayed by man in the face of danger. The soldier comes in frequently for his share of praise, when he rushes forward under fire to plant a flag on the enemy's ramparts, but what of the man who stands by at attention, listening to the strains of the national anthem, while the ship on which he stands sinks slowly into a watery grave?

As Kipling has put it in "Soldier and Sailor, Too:"

"To take your chance in the thick of a rush with firing all about,
Is nothing so bad when you've cover at 'and, an' leave an' liking to shout;
But to stand and be still to the Birkenhead drill is a damned tough bullet to chew."

The Birkenhead was a British troop ship which struck on a rock off Simon's bay, South Africa, in 1852. This was the danger point between the Cape of Good Hope and Cape Agulhas. Before the men were really aware of what was happening the ship had struck and was sinking. There was only time to summon all hands on deck, and with the crew of 700 men standing at attention, the boat sank swiftly. Only 184 of the crew were rescued.

THREE VESSELS SANK IN SAMOAN DISASTER.

In the Samoan disaster, which occurred in 1889, when six or seven warships were badly damaged in a sudden hurricane and three vessels sank, heroism of a rare type marked the numerous disasters. The harbor of Apia, at Samoa, is formed by a circular chain of coral reefs about a mile in circumference. There is one narrow outlet, barely wide enough to admit of a ship's passage. Into this small space seven ponderous men-of-war were crowded when a terrific hurricane broke forth on an afternoon in February. Unable to withstand the fury of the gale, the warships were tossed about, colliding with one another and finally being thrown upon the reefs. The Vandalia, an American boat, was one of the first to suffer. Colliding with the British Calliope, its bowsprit and figurehead were carried away and the boat beached on a reef. The men of the crew hung in the rigging until the following afternoon, when they were rescued by the Trenton, which bore down upon them after having hre side ripped by the Olga, a German warship.

As the Trenton drifted down on the Vandalia, although the Vandalia crew had been hanging for more than twenty-four hours to the rigging, the men found courage to lift their voices in greeting. "Three cheers for the Trenton!" they cried, faintly, and the sailors on the Trenton, despite the fact that they might be dashed to pieces at once by the collision with the hulk of the Vandalia, returned the cheer heartily. "Three cheers for the Vandalia!" and the band struck up the "Star Spangled Banner."

A few minutes later the Trenton was beached and life lines sent out to the Vandalia crew, the last man being hauled on board as the hulk of the Vandalia sank entirely from view.

HEROES OF THE MAINE REFUSED TO LEAVE SHIP.

The bravery of the officers and men of the fated Maine, who refused to leave the ship after the explosion, is well known. The first word of the disaster following the roar and shock of the explosion, was brought to Commander Sigsbee by a private, who bumped into his commanding officer as the latter was groping his way forward to learn the cause of the trouble.

"Beg pardon, sir," said Private Anthony, "I have the honor to report that the ship is sinking. The exact time of the explosion was 9:40, sir."

There was no excitement, no scurrying here and there, as the commander reached the forward deck. Boats were being lowered at the command of the officers, but only to rescue the wounded and drowning men who were shouting for help from the bay and not to save themselves.

Not until the life boats returned alongside and reported that all the men had been picked up was there a move among the survivors to leave the ship. Even then there was extreme politeness among the officers, not only to the commander, but to each other. Sigsbee claimed it as his privilege to be the last to leave the Maine. Even as Kipling said:

"We're most of us liars; we're 'alf of us thieves, an' the rest are as rank as can be,
But once in a while we can finish in style (which I 'ope won't 'appen to me.")

Heavily Charged.

Judge—What's the prisoned charged with?

Policeman—It acts like dynamite, y' honor, but I think it's just whisky.—Satire.

RICH DENVERITES CERTAINLY SAILED ABOARD TITANIC

(Continued From Page One.)

genheim of New York, had purchased. The son was then a young man just out of college, but he displayed so much knowledge of minerals and mining and such excellent managerial ability that in 1888 he was placed in charge of the Philadelphia Smelting and Refining company's works at Pueblo.

In this capacity he served the Guggenheim interests some six years and was then transferred to the East, where he took charge of the Perth Amboy refinery. After the Guggenheim interests were merged with those of the American Smelting and Refining company Benjamin Guggenheim relinquished active connection with the company and went into a number of other enterprises, the principal one being the International Steam Pump company, which he organized and of which he was president.

Mr. Guggenheim's friends say that he was a man of great business ability and of exceptionally fine qualities as a citizen and a man, and they are much distressed at the possibility that evil has befallen him.

DENVER WOMAN AWAITS NEWS OF UNCLE.

Mrs. John Kelley, of 838 Twenty-eighth street, is anxiously awaiting news of an uncle, P. J. Ryan, of Chicago, who, she has reason to believe, was aboard the steamship Titanic. Mr. Ryan, who is a retired business man, went to Europe two months ago. According to letters which have been received from him he was planning on reaching Chicago before the first of May. As he was to return by way of Cherbourg, stopping afterwards in New York city, Mrs. Kelley believes that he may have been aboard the Titanic.

WERE THE REPORTS OF OFFICERS MERE FAKES TO DECEIVE PUBLIC?

New York, April 16.—The Press, in an editorial this morning, says:

"Vast tragedies, far distant across stretches of the sea, with natural mystery and human deception intervening, do more than baffle fair criticism of a horror; they serve to outrage all the senses.

"No more agonizing cruelty can be inflicted upon the multitudes whose hearts are bursting for the truth about the disaster to the Titanic than to conspire to keep them in ignorance of the worst that is known by those responsible for authentic information; for only by knowing the worst can there be separated out the best providence has saved from the ghastly whole for the solace of some of those straining their thoughts to the watery graves hundreds of miles off Cape Race.

"Yet if those who have appeared to play the part of withholding dreadful truths which could only be postponed for the moment, not smothered forever, have struck a more maddening anguish into so many souls ashore, one must try to judge them as more pitifully weak in their failure of duty than wittingly cruel.

"Panic by officers here ashore gives a shuddering suggestion of what a panic could do afloat among those who were expected to hold thousands of lives in brave and competent charge. Yet with our faith in the noble calling of men of the sea, we must believe that, whoever was to blame for the wreck, there was better conduct on the decks of the doomed ship than in her home office.

"And even for these latter officers we must hope that the baseless reports which were given out yesterday afternoon to assure the anxious world that the wrecked passengers were all removed in safety and the ship itself, stanch even as a wreck, was in tow for port, were not fakes or deliberate invention, but that the company's officers had clutched at any rumor as at a straw that might encourage themselves in their misery.

"As for those hundreds adrift on the sea or sunken in its depths at such a time with such confusion and conflict of news and rumors one can only pray God's mercy on all."

"Away All Boats!" Order That Strikes Terror to Hearts Of All Aboard Ship and Means Lowering of Life Boats

That Cry Brings Passengers and Crew to the Deck.

Given Only When All Other Avenues of Safety Are Closed.

(By ELIZABETH KELLY.)

"Away all boats!"

It is the fearsome cry that is understood by every man in the steamship's crew from captain to messboy.

It is the signal for the manning of the lifeboats—the cry that, penetrating the bowels of the ship, calls the stoker from him grimy employment to make of him a hero.

Fraught with a sickening terror alike to the "old salt" and to the novice in marine service is the warning that the time for cool heads is at hand.

The first thing that the sailor learns when he enters the employ of the steamship lines is that "Away all boats" means that the little life-saving craft, which repose quiescently on the deck when danger is remote, must be lowered and manned after the women and the children among the passengers have been given preliminary assistance toward safety.

Authorities on seamanship agree that, while great brains have been diverted into channels leading toward the adoption of safety devices to make less hazardous ocean travel, comparatively little has been done toward systematic rescue work in the wake of disaster.

Very far from solution is the problem of saving human lives aboard a ship that is doomed. The nearest approach to it is the "lifeboat drill," a maneuver in which every member of the ship's crew has to be familiar before the maiden voyage is attempted.

In the building of ships master minds have figured the minimizing of danger from collision and fire, the two arch foes of seamanship.

Fire has been more successfully conquered than its twin antagonist.

GRIM SPECTER OF ICEBERGS HOVERS.

Every seaman knows that over ocean travel in the late spring and early summer hangs the grim specter of the iceberg.

Especially in the Atlantic steamer routes in summer is the iceberg a dread monster. The warm breath of spring loosens it from its frozen moorings and it is set adrift to do what havoc it may.

More dreaded by the seaman's skill is the iceberg of the late spring than is the storm and hurricane of the fall and winter.

It is the nightmare when fog is dense and impenetrable blackness stretches on all sides.

While the water-tight bulkhead is the invention that has been counted on by ship constructors to save from death the passengers confided to the ender mercies of the sea-going monster, its importance is almost trivial compared to the stress laid upon the lifeboat drill.

The bulkheads are steel partitions, transverse and longitudinal, which divide a vessel into a number of water-tight compartments, so that, when the ship is breached, the danger of foundering is lessened. The comfartment which has given way may be completely cut off from the rest of the vessel by water-tight doors. Neglect of these doors has crippled the efficiency of the device in some cases.

DRILL OF SHIP'S CREW MOST IMPORTANT.

However, with that precaution for the preservation of life, has gone hand in hand of late years the importance of the drill of the ship's crew.

Every man when he enters the ship's service is given a number. He knows his number and he knows the number of the lifeboat to which his number corresponds.

When "Away all boats" sounds there is no confusion among the crew. Cool headedness is demanded of the men. They pass test after test to make sure that their nerves are as of steel. Then when the ttime for action comes each man knows the location of the boat to which he is called. He finds it quickly, lowers it expeditiously, helps overboard the women and the children first, and then takes to it himself that it may be successfully piloted to safety. There is an unwritten law among marines that, in case of catastrophe, the women and children must be the first of the passengers helped to safety. Around the unwillingness of loyal women to leave husbands, fathers and brothers in such an extremity, romance after romance has been written. Many have refused to accept the proffered assistance because it meantt separation from loved ones.

Occasionally have been related instances of men who selfishly rushed forward ttoward the lifeboats—men who were the first to don the life-preservers, but in Anglo-Saxon histtory these instances have been rare.

DOES NOT MEAN ABSOLUTE SAFETY.

The filling of the lifeboats does not mean actual and absolute safety. Writers on seamanship have given much thought to the approach of the rescuing vessel. The officer in charge of the rescue boat has to decide for himself how best to proceed in the establishment of communication with the doomed ship. It is out of the question, say these writers, to go alongside to windward, and, if the rescue boat goes alongside to leeward, not only is there risk of being stove by the wreckage which is likely to be found floating under the quarter, but much more danger of being unable to get clear of the side again.

At no time may the rescue boat be alongside the wreck because of a tendency on the part of the vessel, in which the palpitant engines have been silenced, to drift to leeward, sometimes at remarkable speed.

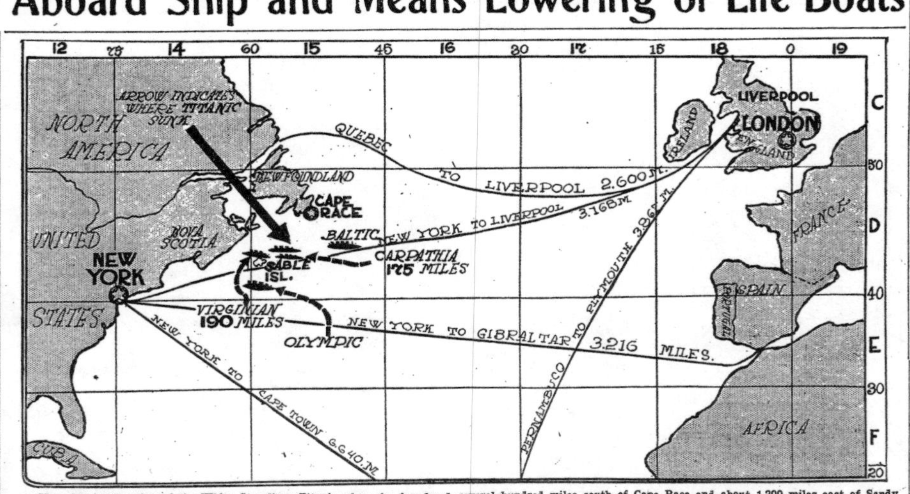

Map showing location of the White Star liner Titanic when she foundered several hundred miles south of Cape Race and about 1,200 miles east of Sandy Hook. At the time the wireless operator on the Titanic sent out the weird sputter "S. O. S.," the steamer Carpathia was the nearest of all vessels and proceeded under full steam to the rescue. The Carpathia is now proceeding to New York with 866 survivors, and will arrive there Thursday. The steamer was approximately 175 miles from the Titanic at the time the latter collided with an iceberg. The Virginian, Baltic and Olympic also were relatively close to the scene of the disaster and assisted the Carpathia in rescue work. Arrow indicates spot where Titanic went down, approximately midway between Cape Race and Sable island, off the Newfoundland coast.

Some idea of the giant size of the berg may be gained by comparing it with the government patrol steamer seen through the arch.

ICEBERGS ALWAYS HAVE BEEN MOST DANGEROUS SEA PERIL

With Seven-eighths of Bulk Submerged Bergs Cause More Marine Disasters Than Any Other Agency.

From the day when the Vikings first pushed their frail crafts across the Atlantic, to the present epoch of such liners as the Titanic, Mauretania and the Olympic, icebergs have been among the most fatal and mysterious perils of the sea. The hardy New England mariner, who has scant fear of gale or breakers, grows anxious when a sudden drop in temperature warns him that his vessel is nearing a mountain of floating ice.

Wrecks without number are due to icebergs. Their human victims are counted by thousands. In collision with their huge bulk the mightiest floating fortress is as fragile as a fishing smack.

Every year the Atlantic coast is bombarded from the frozen north with thousands of bergs, great and small. An iceberg is a fragment of a glacier, which has broken off as the result of the ocean waves melting the ice near the surface, leaving the upper portions unsupported. Most of the icebergs that menace Atlantic commerce have their origin in Greenland, which is covered with a coat of ice, forming a series of glaciers. The Arctic snows, frozen by pressure and alternate warm and cold weather, form a solid mass, which is forced, inch by inch, toward the sea. From the borders of these glaciers icebergs are broken off, swept down the coast by the Labrador current, and finally melted by the Gulf stream.

PEARY NARROWLY ESCAPED FALLING BERG.

From the time the berg, still attached to the parent glacier, projects over the sea until it finally disappears in the warm currents of the southern Atlantic coast it is a source of trouble to the mariner. The most foolhardy ship captain fears to venture near the edge of a glacier, lest a falling berg shatter his ship, or the waves caused by the plunge of a mass of ice into the sea swamp the vessel. Robert E. Peary, in his account of his North pole voyage, tells that his vessel escaped annhilation by a margin of a few inches when an iceberg plunged from a nearby ledge of glacier.

In 1857 an iceberg was sighted off the eastern edge of the Grand Banks, and frozen into the ice were seen two large, three-masted sailing vessels. Mariners believed them to be the Erebus and the Terror, the vessels which took Franklin and his party to their death in the Arctic regions. The theory was that the ships had been abandoned, then snowed in, and in time had become imbedded in a glacier, to be broken off years later as part of a huge iceberg. But no shipmaster would venture near enough to examine the vessels closely and the berg floated down the coast and finally broke up, while the ships which might have furnished the key to one of the most tragic riddles of the North were allowed to sink to their grave in the Atlantic.

BERG WHICH WRECKED TITANIC UNUSUAL SHAPE.

One of the greatest elements of danger in icebergs is the fact that they float with only one-eighth of their bulk above the surface. As to the shape of the submerged portion, a ship captain can make no guess. His only means of safety is to give the floating terror as wide a berth as possible. It is within reason to conjecture that the berg which sank the Titanic may have been of unusual shape below the surface and that the ship struck when the pilot thought he was well outside the danger zone.

The largest berg ever seen in Northern waters was sighted off Newfoundland in 1892. It was nine miles long, 200 feet high and 1,000 yards wide. Figuring the submerged portion as seven times this bulk, one may gain a conception of the vast size of some of these masses of ice. The highest berg ever seen was calculated to be 836 feet from water line to summit.

In 1894 a berg was sighted with five dead men near its summit. A cave had been hollowed out of the ice, and a beaten path could be seen. It is supposed that the five unfortunates had been shipwrecked on the iceberg and had perished of cold and hunger.

An iceberg floating with one-eighth of its bulk above water.

Marine history is full of tales of wrecks by icebergs. In 1856 the Tempest went down with 150 persons on board, after ramming a berg. In 1868 two fine passenger liners, the United Kingdom and the Hibernia, went to the bottom, carrying respectively 180 and 156 persons to death. The Colombo was sunk in 1857 with seventy-four men, and in 1875 the Ismalia went down with fifty-two souls aboard.

One of the three vessels sunk by bergs in 1881 was named the Titania—a name strangely similar to that of the Titanic, in view of the fate of the last named vessel thirty-one years later.

Twelve Iceberg Wrecks in 50 Years

Icebergs, such as the one that sank the Titanic, are one of three sources of peril to vessels navigating the North Atlantic. The others are fog and derelicts. The iceberg menace has been greater this spring than in recent years.

In the last fifty years there have been twelve disasters for which icebergs were responsible. A majority occurred off Newfoundland and the Grand Banks, near the Titanic's grave. The list includes:

SHIP LOST.	PLACE.	YEAR.	LIVES LOST.
Canadian	Mid-Atlantic	1863	45
Immigrant ship	Off Cape Race	1864	158
Vicksburg	Off Cape Race	1869	65
Warrior	Grand Banks	1878	29
North Star	Cabot Straits	1881	67
Medway	Off Newfoundland	1887	29
Valliant	Grand Banks	1897	70
Snowbird	Cape Race	1898	6
Endymion	Grand Banks	1900	8
Islander	Off Alaska	1901	67
Albatross	Mid-Atlantic	1903	22
Titanic	Off Cape Race	1912	1,234

7,000,000 PIECES OF MAIL AT THE BOTTOM

New York, April 16.—Postmaster Edward M. Morgan said today that the Titanic had on board 3,500 sacks of mail. It is not likely, he said, they were saved.

As the standard ocean mail bag holds about 2,000 letters, it is estimated that 7,000,000 pieces of mail matter have been lost.

Questions as to Identity

Cape Race, April 16.—The following are some of the names of survivors in question through faults in transmission:

WIRELESS VERSION.	PROBABLE MEANING.
Becker, Mrs. Allen. Miss Ruth. Miss Mary. Master Richard.	Undoubtedly the same as given in sailing list under names "Mrs. A. O. Beiker and three children."
Juliet, Mr. LaRoche. Mr. LaRoche, Simone.	Mrs. Joseph LaRoche and Simone LaRoche.
Link Kanca, Miss Anna.	Mrs. William Lahtigen.
Marshall, Miss Kate.	Mrs. Marshall.
Mange, Mr. Paula.	May be Mrs. William Angle.
Malcroft, Mrs. Millie.	Miss Nellie Walcroft.
Melloss, J. N.	May be William Mellers.
Naseraell, Mrs. Adelia.	Mrs. Nicholas Nisser.
Oxenham, Percy J.	Thomas Oxenham.
Rogers, Miss Eliza.	Selina Regers.
Silwana, Miss Synly.	Lillie Silven

Simon Guggenheim Can Get No News of Brother's Fate

Washington, D. C., April 16.—No definite word has been received by Senator Simon Guggenheim of Colorado regarding the safety of his younger brother, Benjamin Guggenheim, a passenger on the ill-fated steamship Titanic.

Late this morning Senator Guggenheim received a message through a brokerage house to the effect that 318 of the 350 first-cabin passengers were saved and while he has not been able tto get confirmation of the statement, it has revived his hope that his brother is alive.

Senator Guggenheim telegraphed to the offices of the steamship company for information about his brother. In reply he received the following: "Making inquiries about Benjamin Guggenheim. Have heard nothing. As soon as we hear will notify you."

How Binns, Wireless Operator, Saved 700 Lives on "Republic"

Jack Binns, the wireless operator on the White Star liner Republic, who sent out the call "C. Q. D." which brought aid to the ship and saved the lives of 700 passengers, gave an example of heroic conduct, devotion to to duty and alertness of mind under the most adverse circumstances that made his name a household word.

Apart from this he performed a service to humanity by clearly demonstrating the practical use of wireless telegraphy that resulted in the enforced installation of the wireless telegraph on all passenger steamers. Not many months before the collision of the eastbound White Star liner Republic and the Italian steamer Florida in January, 1909, a well-known expert in maritime matters declared that the wireless telegraph was of no value as a life saver.

Although this opinion was generally accepted, when the disaster occurred, Jack Binns, the young wireless operator, nothing daunted, sat among the ruins of his tiny coop and kept his hand upon the key.

He felt the ship settling beneath him, he saw the crew busy at the boats, and the officers commanding to quietness and order the terror-stricken passengers.

It was an alarming message and the wireless operators along the coast read from it the distressing story of how in the impenetrable fog the Republic had been rammed by an unknown ship and was sinking with all on board.

This message was followed by a long and distressing pause before the wireless of the Republic spoke again. But that fragmentary message from the sinking ship had brought to life every station along the coast, and the young operator sat at his post crying out the words of encouragement and messages of hope that came from all directions.

These messages, which charged the fog-ladened air, brought about the greatest achievement in the history of electricity and robbed history of another awful havoc at sea.

In the pursuit of his profession, Jack Binns has become much interested in the question of safety on the sea and has written many articles giving a comprehensive account of what has been accomplished in that direction.

When questioned regarding his heroism on board the Republic, Jack Binns replied: "Why, I didn't do anything." But the grateful passengers and crew take pleasure in telling over and over the story of how Jack Binns' heroism, resourcefulness and presence of mind, in the hour of danger, combined with the once-doubted invention of Marconi, saved the lives of more than 700 passengers and the crew of the ill-fated Republic.

It was his wireless signals and the aid of submarine bells that guided the rescuing steamer through the fog to the sinking ship, and enabled them to locate the Florida, the disabled ship which had dealt the death blow to the Republic.

WILLIAM T. STEAD,
Noted London editor and correspondent of several American papers. He was aboard the Titanic for a visit to the United States.

Ship's Whole Side Was Torn Away Is Designer's Belief

London, April 16.—Alexander Carlisle, designer of both the Titanic and Olympic, said today:

"I never thought there was such a thing as an unsinkable ship. When the news first came that the Titanic was sinking by the head I thought likely she would reach port. The fact that she sank within four hours after the impact with the ice indicates that her side was torn out."

One of the best known London representatives of the Standard Oil company, W. H. Harrison, failed to sail on the Titanic as he had intended. He is the father of the former second secretary of the United States embassy in London, Leland Harrison, now secretary of embassy at Bogota, Colombia.

Mr. and Mrs. Isador Straus had not intended to sail on the Titanic, but reached a sudden determination to take the new liner and caught the boat train at the last minute.

The message received by the parents of J. A. Phillips, the wireless operator on the Titanic, last night, stating "making slowly for Halifax. Practically unsinkable. Don't worry," was sent by an uncle of the operator, in London, to Godalming, where the father lives, and the parents assumed it had come from their son as it was signed "Phillips."

The trans-Atlantic lines have agreed, in consequence of the reports as to ice in the Atlantic, to cross longitude 47 in latitude 40.10 eastbound, beginning today, and longitude 47, latitude 41 westbound, beginning April 25.

'Atlantic's Graveyard,' Name Given the Coast

Many Vessels Reported 'Missing' Have Been Wrecked by Icebergs Off Shore of Newfoundland.

Off the coast of Newfoundland and along the ice-imperiled lanes of ocean travel, where the big bergs divert to the east with the current, is the "Graveyard of the Atlantic"—the port of missing ships. Until 1897, when the water highway was moved several hundred miles to the south to escape the menace of the floating ice mountains, crafts posted as missing in maritime exchanges, known to have been bound to destinations taking them into the danger zone, were credited to the toll taken from this source of marine disasters.

Liners, freighters, whalers and fishing craft by scores were each year sacrificed to the icebergs above and below the ocean's surface. Of most of them no trace ever was obtained; no survivor came back to tell of the manner in which ship, crew and passengers went to destruction and death.

In 1841 the steamer President, bound from New York to Liverpool with 120 people on board, disappeared forever.

The City of Glasgow, from Liverpool to Philadelphia, with 480 persons aboard, steamed into the path of the deadly bergs from Labrador and farther north in March, 1854, and was never reported.

In February, 1856, the steamer Pacific, from Liverpool to New York, went to the Atlantic graveyard with 185 passengers and crew.

The City of Boston, from that port to Liverpool, sailed outwardbound in May, 1870, and then was heard of no more, nor did any of its human freight of 191 souls ever return with a message of the catastrophe.

In February, 1892, the White Star liner Naronic, from the Mersey to New York; in the same month in 1896, the State of Georgia, out of Aberdeen; in February, 1899, the Alleghany from New York to Dover; in February, 1902, the Huronian from Liverpool to St. Johns—all these and others were posted "missing" where seamen congregate for news of past due ships, and no word ever came of them. They were marked down to the credit of the iceberg.

No record has been kept of whalers and fishing boats that have gone down off the Newfoundland shore line. It is the hazard of the game—the frightful fear of the womankind who are left behind when the men "go down to the sea in ships."

To few has it been given to face death from one of these perilous towering floes and tell the experience, yet such luck befell the passengers and crew of the Portia, out of Southampton to New York, in June, 1893. When off the Newfoundland coast the lookout sighted a monster berg 200 feet high and running lengthwise for 800 feet. The ship was well to the southward and would easily have passed without collision.

Passengers pleaded with the captain to run them in closer to the splendid spectacle. Several who had cameras wanted pictures, others were curious, and the captain good naturedly agreed. The craft approached within several hundred feet—a safe distance, as the skilled navigator thought. Then came the jeopardy of the gigantic mass often hidden under the water that furnishes the stability to the bergs and permits them to sail grandly along without careening or toppling.

A report like a gunshot was heard from the berg. There was a succession of snapping and grinding. From the keel of the Portia to the topmost masthead there was a shudder, then a violent jar, and the big vessel was lifted high in the air, cradled and rocked in a fragment of the mountain. If ever death looked squarely into faces of victims, the grim reaper stared at the passengers of the Portia. There was nothing to be done; the outcome was in the hands of the gods, and prayer and prayer only offered escape.

Then, following the cleavage made when the mighty ice island was rent, came a huge wave that caught the Portia gently and launched her stern first into the water—bruised, shaken, slightly damaged, but navigable and able to make port. It was the chance in the million, and the list of missing ships that did not get that chance indicates how rarely it comes.

In April, 1897, the French liner Valiant, from its home port to St. Pierre, Miquelon, with seventy-four men aboard, was hurled against an iceberg 120 miles from the coast of Newfoundland. The craft went to pieces like a bundle of boards and but four lived on a hastily built raft until picked up.

Ships Evei Menaced by Icebergs and Fog

No Vessel, However Staunchly Built, Likely to Withstand Plunge Against Wallof Ice.

New York, April 16.—The speed at which the Titanic was traveling when she shattered herself against the iceberg will perhaps not be known until the first of her survivors reach port. Whatever her rate of progress, however, ship builders here and abroad must admit that while the modern steamship may defy wind and weather, ice and fog remain an ever present element of danger.

No ship, they point out, no matter how staunchly built nor how many water-tight bulkheads protect her, may plunge headlong against a wall of ice without grave results. The general opinion is that the Ttanic's equipment was put to an extraordinary test which no vessel could have withstood.

"Under ordinary circumstances these watertight compartments will preserve a ship from sinking," said A. L. Hopkins, vice president of the Newport News Shipbuilding and Dry Dock company in New York. "But smashing into an iceberg could produce shattering effects that would render a ship helpless beyond the protection of any design yet known. In fore and after collisions, where the compartments are punctured, the lowering of either end of the ship produces an increased strain on the other compartments."

Granting that only the forward bulkhead of the Titanic had been crumpled by the impact with the iceberg, Mr. Hopkins was inclined to think that the relative buoyancy of the remaining compartments would have been sufficient to save the vessel.

Inasmuch as he was not familiar with the relative division of the Titanic's compartments he could not estimate how many compartments must have given way under the impact of the collision.

Robert Stocker, naval constructor of the Brooklyn navy yard, says:

"In the case of the Titanic I am inclined to think that her sinking was due to the effect of grounding rather than to the impact of collision. Frequently a ship strikes what is known as 'pinnacle rock,' ripping open her keel. The iceberg against which the Titanic smashed her bow may have had some such submerged projection which did additional damage to the keel. If the forward bulkheads of the vessel had held after the impact which smashed the bow, it certainly seems that the relative buoyancy of the remaining compartments would have been sufficient to keep the ship afloat.

"I am compelled to believe that a great many of her compartments must have been punctured or sprung."

Lewis Nixon, the eminent naval architect, is inclined to think the Titanic was either traveling at full speed or perhaps crashed into a berg so tremendous that there was practically no give.

"If the Titanic hit one of those great ice masses," said Mr. Nixon, "it is likely she struck one that had no more give than a rock. Under these circumstances something had to give way, and as the iceberg did not, the great ship had to crumple up. It is conceivable that an impact of this sort might have buckled her longitudinal plates from end to end shearing off and starting rivets and opening up the water-tight compartments throughout the length of the vessel."

For many years steamship men have asserted that the safest place to be on is a well equipped ocean liner. In proportion to the number carried the statistics show there is less loss of life and less chance of injury on board a modern liner than there is in any other means of transportation. Fleets come and go from New York and other ports with the regularity of the tides, and those carrying mails maintain a schedule which almost equals in punctuality that of railway mail trains.

Trans-Atlantic steamers travel in well defined routes, known as "steamship lanes," the westbound and the eastbound. This reduces to a minimum the chances of collision with another. But icebergs and derelicts have no respect for these rules and float into the paths or wallow across them to be a dire menace in time of fog or very thick weather. There is no way to give warning until too late. Out of a smother of a fog a pallid shape may be glimpsed over the bows, to be followed a half minute later by the crash of the bows against the mass of ice.

ICEBERGS 200 FEET HIGH AND 450 MILES IN AREA FLOAT IN OCEAN

New York, April 16.—Capt. J. P. Barker of the Lord's liner, Lord Cromer, which arrived in South Brooklyn a week ago from England, today gave a graphic description of the ice field his vessel encountered during the last week in March which almost sent the ship to the bottom.

"It was on March 27 that we ran into the ice pack. For 450 miles we could see nothing but ice. We were just in the position the Titanic was when she foundered. On all sides of us loomed the huge masses of ice. Finally we were caught so that we could not move one way or the other and were compelled to drift with the floe. It was on March 31 that we eventually loosened ourselves. We turned due south into safer seas.

"During her imprisonment among the icebergs sixty plates on the port side were bent and more than 200 rivets torn loose.

"I have been among icebergs, but those I saw last month were the largest. Some were 200 feet high and looked like church steeples. Scattered all over them were carcasses of seals. A few of the bergs were so large that I am sure they must have been anchored to the bottom of the ocean.

"Those bergs, which could be seen, were not the ones we feared. It was those which were submerged. I believe that the Titanic must have collided with one of the submerged floes."

Captain Barker said that he thinks the Titanic disaster will compel steamships to choose a more southerly course during this time of the year. Each year, Captain Barker said, the ice packs are becoming more numerous in the North Atlantic.

TITANIC CREW NOT DRILLED SUFFICIENTLY FOR DISASTER

Lieut. C. S. Ripley of Denver, Survivor of Many Shipwrecks, Says Men Were Probably Panic-Stricken.

(By LOUISE SCHER.)

Lieut. Charles S. Ripley, one of the survivors of the great Samoan disaster of 1889, when the U. S. S. Vandalia went to pieces off the reefs at Apia and foundered, drowning 275 naval officers and men, this morning gave a few reasons why he thought that the Titanic should not have gone down with only 866 lives saved.

"It seems to me that the sinking of the Titanic was not necessary," said he. "I cannot understand why the vessel did not have her bulkhead closed. In these days ships are made with compartments so that one part can be closed if a hole is made in the hull. They are absolutely water tight. Thus, if the boat struck in the bow the other compartments could

CAPT. C. J. SMITH,
Of the Titanic, who went down with his boat.

be closed, keeping out the water. It is almost impossible to sink a ship these days if the crew is a good one. It has been the custom, though, of different lines to hire, before they sail, 200 or 300 scrubs or stokies absolutely unused to any sort of discipline whatever.

CREW PROBABLY LOST HEADS.

It is most probable that this was the case in point when the Titanic's crew was about to take orders. They probably lost their heads and were vomited out of the passages like so many black-faced life-hungry savages ready to kill even a child or woman if a chance offered itself to save themselves.

"I have been, perhaps, in as many wrecks as any man living. Altogether I have been in seven or eight. My experience though on one of Uncle Sam's ships has been that in time of fire or wreck the men like one man worked right along at pumps until everything was saved or all hope was gone.

"The typhoon during the Samoan disaster, when the Vandalia went to pieces, lasted forty-eight hours. Seventy-five men escaped, but they were all injured and most of them died. The storm started early in the day, all day she raged, and we couldn't hold our anchors and she was beaten to pieces. I cannot remember many of my own sensations when I realized that we were going down. I only remember that after the day had spent itself and it was 9 o'clock at night I found myself clinging to a broken topmast with nine sailors.

"We were a mile from shore. Shunting back and forth we made for the shore. I was the only man who reached land. The others were beaten off the mast by the waves.

"This, perhaps, until this present wreck, was the greatest disaster at sea that the world ever knew. Ships without number were lost, but chief among them the German ship.

HELPED TAKE CREW OFF.

"Once, during a cruise on the Atlantic, I remember we were given a distress signal from a coast cargo steamer, which was carrying a big cargo of gasoline and provisions. When we reached her the crew had nearly all departed in small boats. We went to her assistance, but it was impossible to stop the explosion of the gasoline. The reason that I remember this particular wreck so distinctly was the fact that there was one woman aboard and, in the mad rush and fright, the poor thing was treated as a man—made to take her chance as did the rest of the crew. Until our ship came she had not been taken off.

"It's rather a peculiar thing, but in matters of this kind there is supposed to be an unwritten law that a man must stand aside and give the weaker sex a chance. As a rule, this is followed to the letter, especially among trained men. But there are times when a man forgets he is a gentleman and fights like any beast for the thing God gave him—life"

Lieutenant Ripley has the distinction of having been crowned the crown prince of Samoa by the natives of that island.

During the past seven years he has made his home in Denver and the vicinity. Since his retirement from the navy Lieutenant Ripley has been engaged in the mining business. He is the owner of large mines near Georgetown.

SAYS TITANIC WAS MISHANDLED.

Dr. E. Stone of the marine corps, stationed in Denver, gave some very excellent reasons as to why the Titanic had been probably mishandled and mismanaged.

"As far as my knowledge of liners in relationship to battleships is concerned, I can see no reason for the Titanic having such a large number of passengers. Good ships these days are built exactly alike—with numerous air-tight compartments. They have a contrivance on the bridge which by pulling a lever they can close every compartment on the ship. If the hole isn't too big they can keep afloat for any length of time.

"According to reports, the Titanic kept afloat four hours. It is remarkable that in that length of time every passenger was not put safely in a lifeboat.

"Eight hundred people can be lowered on a battleship to safety in less than one-half hour after the signal is given to abandon ship. The Titanic had three times this number with three or four good hours. No, I cannot understand how so many lives could possibly be lost and as most of the passengers were women, it seems more than astonishing."

NINETEEN INJURED WHEN ROCK ISLAND FLYER IS DITCHED

Westbound Passenger Train No. 7 Meets With Accident West of Pueblo.

Pueblo, Colo., April 16.—A broken angle bar on a blind switch at Cuba, a flag station eleven miles north of Pueblo on the D. & R. G., caused the wreck yesterday afternoon of westbound Rock Island passenger train No. 7, known as the Rocky Mountain Limited, and the injuring of nineteen persons, three of whom are in a serious condition. The engine and mail car passed over the switch in safety, but the day coach, in which all of those injured were riding, was thrown into the ditch, turning over several times. The Rock Island uses the D. & R. G. tracks between Colorado Springs and Pueblo.

Nine of the injured belong to one family, that of Robert Grier of Ogden, Utah.

Mr. and Mrs. Grier are among the seriously injured and one child is also seriously injured.

The injured:

Alfred Miller, Monte Vista, Colo., internal injuries; serious.

Robert E. Grier, Ogden, Utah, cut on head, neck and shoulders sprained; serious.

Mamie Grier, Ogden, Utah, legs injured, contusions on back and head; serious.

Minnie Grier, Ogden, Utah, bruises on left side and head.

Susie Grier, Ogden, Utah, broken arm and left leg bruised.

Bertha May Grier, Ogden, Utah, internal injuries, cuts on head and body.

Mrs. Margaret Grier, Ogden, Utah, breast, back and right side smashed, right shoulder sprained; serious.

Ardalia Grier, Ogden, head and back bruised, left leg broken.

Thomas Grier, Ogden, neck hurt.

Jackson Grier, Ogden, cut about head, right leg injured.

Maggie Grier, hurt about head, back and breast; serious.

Felix Risser, New York city, right side bruised and crushed, left leg and shoulder sprained.

James Hargis, Pueblo, hips hurt.

Mrs. James Hargis, Pueblo, breast and back hurt, internal injuries.

Alice Hargis, Pueblo, bruises and cuts about head and face.

Alma S. Hargis, Pueblo, back sprained, left arm broken.

Mrs. Lizzie Diller, Dysart, Iowa, head cut, left hand cut.

R. U. Walton, Lees Summit, Mo., cut about head and back; serious.

J. W. Cochran, Lees Summit, Mo., cut and briused on arms and legs.

None of the injured is likely to die.

The accident occurred at the end of a steel and cement bridge where the embankment is from thirty to forty feet high. The Pullman sleeper was derailed, but remained upright on the track at the end of the bridge.

JAILED ON CHARGE MADE BY COUNTESS, SEEKS VINDICATION

Another chapter has been published in the life of Countess von Richthofen in the third divlion of the district court, presided over by Judge Greeley W. Whitford. J. B. Thompson, a druggist who served a term of four months in the county jail on the charge of having obtained $1,500 from the countess on false pretenses, and free from further molestation from the countess, after having gone Eat and raised money from friends to vindicate himself, now claims that he was wrongfully imprisoned and asks for a new hearing in the case.

It was in 1907, in the month of September, that the countess claims that Thompson obtained her money. When released he disappeared and was not heard from until Monday, when hecame before Judge Whitford and filed a motion to have the judgment set aside. He says that he obtained the money honestly, but when sued by the countess he had not a penny to employ counsel and could not appear and defend himself. As a result he went to jail.

"But now I have the money to carry the matter through the courts to the end, and will go the route," he says, and prays the court for an opportunity to show his innocence.

Moses' Choice.

On being asked which manner of death he thought was preferable, being killed in a railroad wreck or drowned, Moses, the colored servant, propmtly replied:

"Railroad wreck."

We asked him why he preferred railroad wreck and he made the following rejoinder:

"If you is killed on de railroad, dar yo' is, but if you is drowned in de ribber, whar is yo'?"—National Monthly.

'SPRING MAID' JOYOUSNESS DAMPENED AT BROADWAY THEATER BY NEWS OF DISASTER

MIZZE HAJOS,
Sketched by the Well Known Post Artist, Keszthelyi.

Brieux Play on the Mating of the Physically Unfit Discussed in Lectures--The Orpheum Offering.

AFTER the first act of "The Spring Maid"—given before a packed house at the Broadway last night—the boys could be heard in the street outside crying "extra."

The awful news those late editions contained, the fearful disaster at sea, was quickly communicated to the pleasure seekers within the door, and a pall seemed to hang over the audience for the rest of the evening.

But the people had heard the first act of the pretty musical comedy. They had listened to the soothing plaintive melody of "Day Dreams" and the gaiety of "Two Little Bees," had also seen the diminutive prima donna at her best.

They had then really seen and heard all there was to "The Spring Maid," for after that bright and catchy first act, the music, the business and action of the play, drops into rather ordinary vaudeville.

If it were not for the opening numbers the Rheinhardt comedy would never have been heard of. They are the three swallows that make the spring. The composer certainly makes the most of them. He repeats, rearranges and improves for later consumption, and, with the aid of Robert Hood Bowers, who is introduced with a fetching interpolation, the melodies are made to do frequent duty for nearly three hours.

Somehow the graceful music, the dainty costumes, the clever Marion staging, did not seem to quite reach the point of complete success last evening.

Even Mizzi Hajos seemed changed from the bubbling, bouyant, youthful personality which flashed across the Broadway stage at the opening of the season that August night of last year.

It seemed as though the arduous eight months of travel and work had made her artificial, and robbed her of that individual magnetic effervescence, that was such a wonderful joy when she first came over from light-hearted Buda Pesth. ..

It is only natural it should.

And yet the little Hungarian is rounder and plumper than when she appeared last summer; is losing nothing in avoirdupois if she is in daintiness and sparkle, making some of us wonder last evening if it was really she that was on the stage.

First impressions, however, are always the most delightful.

Those who have never heard "The Spring Maid" nor seen Hajos, will be charmed by it. Those who have seen and heard it, may marvel why they do not enjoy its repetition as greatly as they expected. Last November the present writer saw it done in London by one of the most expensive companies that could be gathered together. It nevertheless seemed rather flat when compared with the Denver production of the preding August. London, however, wouldn't have it in any event, it proving one of the season's most brilliant failures over there.

The company last night showed some slight signs of wear and tear. The acting becomes parrot-like, but the beauty of the production and its fine color scheme is well kept up.

The new member of the organization is Charles McNaughton, comedian, who makes much of the fantastic sketch, "Othello." He has the troubles of the wandering Thespian and he retails them with a grim comicality. When his company deserts him and he insists upon presenting the tragedy a fellow-sufferer exclaims, "You cannot present a play without actors!" the tragedian replies, "Why not. It has been done, done frequently."

McNaughton is decidedly clever in his work, as is Raffael as the elderly prince, who masquerades as a woman. Raffael recalls the ancient days and nights when he was the husband of Betinna Girard and was to musical comedy what handsome Jack Mason was to the emotional drama.

* * * *

BRIEUX PLAY "MATERNITY."

Emma Goldman lectured last night on the Brieux play "Maternity."

Brieux, although one of the French immortals, is not well known to the English speaking people, his plays having been banished by the British censor.

He is an advanced thinker, of course, and holds to the doctrine, that marriage between the physically unfit is monstrous; that better race suicide than an overflow of infected children. His play "Maternity" presents this idea with terribly grim effect, and Miss Goldman last night, to an audience that by no means filled East Turner hall, discussed the Brieux viewpoint, with vigor, eloquence and intelligence, commending it, naturally.

The idea is much older than the French academician, but as long as nature lasts, as sentiment and human love exists, men and women will marry without thought of possible hereditary or immediate taint in their blood.

However, that the idea is taking hold of the public mind, is evidenced in the recent declaration of many prominent clergymen and judges in the United States not to perform the marriage service between couples unless they are personally competent, are not tubercular or afflicted with hereditary disease.

Common sense tells us that a sound race is the need of the world, that the mating of the physically unfit means generations of misery and incomparable distress.

A warning voice on this subject is not to be regarded then as something unmentionable, but as necessary and healthful instinct. One of the important uses of art is the betterment of mankind. Why not, in this case? Why taboo? Why discuss it only in the alleys or under one's breath?

75 SAN LUIS VALLEY MEN COMING TO DENVER

The business men and representatives of the various commercial organizations in the San Luis valley will arrive in Denver Friday morning and during the two days which they will stay will tell the people of Denver about the wonderful resources of their fertile valley. Between 50 and 75 boosters are expected and will be the guests of the Denver Chamber of Commerce at their luncheon Friday noon in the Savoy hotel.

F. D. Stanley, a prominent lawyer of Alamosa and member of the Business Men's club of the city, will be the principal speaker of the day. He will tell of the growth of that section of the state in the past ten years and of its close association to Denver.

Representatives will be here from LaJara, Antonito, Monte Vista and other San Luis valley towns.

TRAMWAY DEFIES RIGHTS OF PUBLIC, COMMITTEE SAYS

Chamber Investigating Board Urges Court Action to Enforce Fair Play.

CAN'T REDUCE FARES

Transfer Rule Violates Franchise and Cannot Be Imposed If Passengers Protest.

After a week of deliberation the subcommittee of the legal committee of the chamber of commerce finished its report on the Tramway situation this morning. The legal committee will draft a report tonight, which will be submitted to the chamber at its meeting in the Traffic club Wednesday evening.

The subcommittee was composed of W. F. Robinson, chairman, A. J. Bryant and Edward E. Stimson. The report is the result of the resolution introduced in the chamber two weeks ago by W. P. Daniels, calling for an investigation of the franchise of the Tramwy company, to determine whether or not the company has authority to refuse to issue transfers except at the moment the fare is paid.

The committee came to the conclusion that the Tramway is enforcing rules on the traveling public which are entirely uncalled for, and which have been abolished through the courts in several of the largest cities in the United States. It recommends, however, that legal action be taken aginst the company instead of passing an ordinance ,as the original resolution proposed.

REPORT TO COMMITTTEE WRITTEN BY ROBINSON.

Mr. Robinson's decision, as is stated in the report to the legal committee, is in part as follows:

"Section 7 of the franchise provides that the company may make and enforce proper and reasonable rules, regulations and conditions for the transfer of passengers. While the company has the right to make and enforce proper and reasonable rules, it has no right to arrogate to itself the sole right to interpret what is proper and reasonable. The issuance of what is commonly known as a transfer to a passenger wishing to be transferred would seem to be a reasonable rule. It has been held by using the words 'continuous passage,' it is reasonable to impose a time limit within which the transfer may be used."

PASSENGERS HAVE RIGHTS UNDER FRANCHISE.

In discussing the rule made by the company which requires a passenger to ask for a transfer at the time he pays his fare, the committee speaks of the possibility that a large number of persons might ask for a transfer at the same time. The report says:

"It would nott appear, however, that it would be necessary, to obviate this last mentioned difficulty, that the rule should be so drastic as to require the passenger to give up a right he has under the franchise so long before he is called upon to exercise that right. This is true especially of a passenger who has several lines over which he may reach his destination.

"It is well known that when there are several lines over which a destination may be reached the cars on these lines do not run very often. Hence, the passenger wishes to waitt until he is almost at the transfer point before he desires to declare upon which he wishes to proceed, desiring to take a transfer to the one which will save him the most time.

"That also leads to the qquestion of whether or not it is a reasonable rule that the passenger shall declare which line he wishes to proceed upon. He has a right under the franchise to be transferred from one to the other of the intersecting lines for a continuous passage. It would seem that that right might fairly be to more than one line, and it would therefore seem that the regulation requiring a passenger to name the line is not necessarily a reasonable rule, but is a limitation of his rights under the franchise.

OPE NTRANSFERS NEEDED FOR BEST SERVICE.

"Certainly if the rule required a passenger to declare at the time he pays his fare that he expects a continuous passage to his destination, the full right of the franchise ought to be extended to him and the transfer issued to the other intersecting lines. In other words, the transfer ought under such a rule to be what is known as an open transfer.

"Another question arises that is no included in the resolution, and that is whether or not the company has the right to make a rule prohibiting the issuance of a transfer upon a transfer. From the reading of the transfer it is doubtful if that rule is a reasonable interpretation of the rights of the passenger. Reading the entire section, it seems that it is intended that the passenger shall be carried from one portion of the cityt to another, except such portions as are adjacent to that reached by the line from which the transfer is sought. For instance, a person living at Twelfth and Columbine, desiring to go to Park Hill, boards a Thirteenth avenue car, whic hcarriees him to Madison, and is transferred the Madison car and is refused a transfer from the Madison to the Park Hill line going east. It is true that Park Hill could be reached by the passenger taking the Thirteenth avenue line in the opposite direction and coming into the city and going out over the Park Hill line, consuming probably not less than forty-five minutees of time. It is very doubtful in deed if such a rule to not issue a transfer in such a case could be upheld as reasonable.

REASONABLE RULES ARE ALOWED BY LAW.

"In the franchise we find that the city has given to the Tramway company the right to make proper and reasonable rules for the transfer of passengers. It is the right of the city to contest the question of whether or not the rules made by the company are proper and reasonable. This could be done by a legal proceeding. An individual passenger has the right to institute such a suit. There ought to be, if there is not already, some department of the city government that would take such matters up with the company and if satisfactory results be not obtained, bring suit in the name of the city restraining the company from enforcing any unreasonable and improper rules. It is important that some action be taken at this time.

"Another argument in favor of not requiring the passenger to demand a transfer at the time of paying his fare is the custom that prevailed at the time the franchise was granted. It appears to be certain that either an open transfer must be given or the passenger has the right to a transfer at any time prior to reaching the transfer point.

"As to the third question mentioned in the resolution, it is provided in section 6 of the franchise that the Tramway company shall be entitled to receive 5 cents and no more for a single passage on any line of the company's railway We do not believe that it is within the power of the city by ordinance or otherwise to limit the fare below 5 cents This is supported by numerous authorities

"Having expressed these views, no ordinance is prepared to submit herewith. An ordinance making rules does not seem necessary. An ordinance defining the department of the city government that would look after this and simlar matters, of course, is always in order."

AUTO GIVES PROOF AGAINST MURDERER

W. A. Dow, Believed to Have Killed George Marsh, Left Trail in Garage.

Lynn, Mass., April 16.—A warrant calling for the arrest of William A. Dorr, alias William A. Dow, on the charge of murdering George E. Marsh, has been sworn out by Chief of Police Burckes.

This followed his announcement that the police were seeking Dorr in connection with the finding of the body of the wealthy soap manufacturer beside a boulevard in West Lynn last Friday. Dorr's home is in Stockton, Cal.

The police located in a Boston garage an automobile thought to be the one in which Marsh's body was taken to the spot where it was found. They learned that the car had been abandoned, partly disabled, in Stanhope street. In the car were found a .22 caliber automatic rifle and a box partly filled with cartridges.

Chief Burckes made public a telegram sent him by Chief Briare of Stockton, which read:

"Find William Augustine Dorr. Left here March 14 mysteriously. Since he left here he went to see his sister in Maine. Thirty years, five, eight. Occupation, clerk. If found trace his movements. Has $1,800 in currency. He would benefit by death of George E. Marsh. Expert with automobiles and motorcycles."

SCHOOLMARM WAYLAYS CRITICISING EDITOR

Center, Colo., April 16.—Mrs. T. E. Henry, a teacher in the Center schools, did not like the criticism printed in the Center Post-Dispatch by Editor John D. Wehrle, so she waylaid him yesterday noon and attempted to adminster corporal punishment. Wehrle decided that discretion was the better part of valor and made a run for his office, while Mrs. Henry picked up and threw several stones at him, all of which missed their mark.

MAN FOUND DEAD, BULLET IN BRAIN; SUICIDE OR MURDER?

Death of Otto G. Seaman Shrouded in Mystery; No Motive Is Traced.

CRIME PUZZLES HIS WIFE

Can't Imagine Why Husband Killed Himself, If He Really Died by Own Hand.

Mystery surrounds the death of Otto G. Seaman, 38, a telegraph operator in the employ of the Colorado & Southern Railway company, whose corpse, with a bullet hole in the head, was discovered early this morning in a vacant lot on Eudora street, between Colfax and Fourteenth avenues.

All appearances indicate that Seaman committed suicide, but there exists an absolute lack of motive, as far as his family and friends are aware. He had been dead several hours when Thomas Waters, 1465 Fairfax street, who was sprinkling the lawn in front of his residence, looked across the prairie in the direction of Eudora street and saw the body.

Seaman had been working at Fort Collins and arrived in Denver Monday af-

O. G. SEAMAN,
A telegraph operator, who was found dead with a bullet through his head.

ternoon at 5:40, but his wife, who lives at 2816 Lafayette street, was unaware of his presence in the city until she received word of his death. Shortly before 6 o'clock Monday evening he called at the offices of the Colorado & Southern and drew the wages due him, $29. Between that hour and the time at which his corpse was found the authorities have been unable to trace his movements.

WATCH AND MONEY SAFE.

His watch, other jewelry and $25 in cash were found on his person, together with a letter addressed to Gamble Shields of 1140 Bannock street, which, when opened, was found to contain only the information that Seaman intended coming to Denver to take a position with the Western Union Telegraph company. The letter was written while Seaman still was in Fort Collins.

When found Seaman was lying on his back, with his overcoat wrapped tightly around him and a .32-caliber revolver clutched in his hand. Patrolman Frank Campbell was sent out from police headquarters to investigate and notified Seaman's wife. The body was removed to the morgue.

Mrs. Seaman last heard from her husband Sunday afternoon, when he telephoned from Fort Collins, informing her that he had secured a position in Denver and would be here Tuesday morning Mrs. Seaman had made all preparations to join him in Fort Collins, even to shipping part of her household goods. She was waiting for his arrival when the patrolman called with news of his death.

CAN'T UNDERSTAND DEATH.

"I cannot understand it," said Mrs. Seaman. "When I talked to him over the telephone he was cheerful and apparently in the best of health. The only motive I can assign for his suicide—if suicide it was—is that he had an attack of heart disease, from which he frequently suffered, and that it left him in a despondent frame of mind."

Seaman had been a resident of Denver for twelve years. For several years he was engaged as manager of the art department of the Colorado Interstate Fair and Exposition. His father is a resident of Atlantic, Iowa.

BELT UNABLE TO STAY OUT OF JAIL

Released From Charge of Taking $129, Is Arrested for Larceny of $65.

Fred A. Belt, former judge of the kangaroo court in "south lower" of the county jail, was presented with the most highly prized Christmas present that could be given him, Dec. 23 last. Judge Allen, sitting in the criminal division of the district court, gave him his freedom.

He had been convicted of embezzling $129 of the funds of the Schwarzchild & Sulzberger Meat Packing company, by whom he was employed, receiving a sentence of from one year to fifteen months in the penitentiary. Belt had won the friendship of Chief Deputy Sheriff Washington Rinker and other attaches of the West Side court, who interceded in Belt's behalf and Judge Allen suspended sentence.

Belt is back in south lower again, but not as judge of the kangaroo court. He was arrested after a few months' freedom and charged with operating a confidence game and grand larceny. The complaining witness is Kathryn James, 1616 Court place, who charges that Dec. 24, the day after he had secured his freedom, Belt defrauded her out of $65. Belt will be tried on the charge next Monday.

Red Wing Daily Republican.

VOLUME XXVII. NO. 158. RED WING, MINNESOTA, TUESDAY EVENING, APRIL 16, 1912. PRICE TWO CENTS.

SUFFERING INTENSE AND LOSS OF LIFE APPALING IN OCEAN DISASTER

SEA SWALLOWS TITANIC AND 1500 MEN ON BOARD; WOMEN, CHILDREN SAFE

BY UNITED PRESS:

Cape Race, April 16.—Unparalleled in the history of sea disasters were the scenes on board the Titanic, the White Star liner on her initial trip, when she sank at 3 o'clock Monday morning after striking icebergs at 10:30 Sunday night. Eight hundred and sixty-six women and children in twenty modern life-boats were put off the sinking vessel and were floating on a calm sea amid cakes of ice that surrounded the great vessel, at a safe distance from it.

The remaining men, passengers and crew of 800, numbering altogether 1,492, went down into the depths of the sea when the crushed plates and bulkhead let in the water faster than the pumps could throw it out.

The last wild scene on board the vessel will probably never be known for all are apparently dead who were witnesses to it, including Captain Smith, commander of the White Star liner. Whether the crew stood at their posts bravely or fought with passengers for life-rafts and life preservers will remain unwritten.

Monday morning's wreck and loss of the Titanic with nearly 1,500 men on board is the greatest disaster known in modern marine history. It was particularly so, because of the large number of prominent and wealthy people on the boat. But meagre reports show that the women and children were sent to the boats first, regardless of whether they were rich or poor, prominent or laborers.

In the darkness of the night there were wives and mothers of those who sank in ignorance of their fate although they were not far distant from them. Details of this part of the tragedy will not be known until the Carpathia arrives here with the 866 survivors. It is thought that nearly all the passengers were asleep when the crash came at 10:30 Sunday night. Many of the women and children were hurried to the boats in their night clothes and must have suffered terribly for eight hours during which they were in the small life-boats before they were rescued by the Carpathia.

Although a dozen steamers, summoned by wireless when the tragedy occurred, rushed to the scene with all possible speed, they all, with the exception of the Carpathia, arrived too late. As stated by Captain Gambell of the Virginian only the wreckage of the Titanic was found when they reached the place of the catastrophe.

The Carpathia will reach New York with the survivors late Thursday or on Friday morning. There is a slight hope yet of saving a few on life-rafts.

BY UNITED PRESS:

LONDON GREATLY STIRRED.

BY UNITED PRESS:

London, April 16.—Tearful, excited crowds stand about the White Star line offices demanding information which is not given. Dignified business men and nobility rub elbows with laborers, and many denounce the officers of the company for the reports yesterday that all were saved. All ships and many buildings are draped with flags at half staff. In parliament speeches were made today lauding the men for sending the women and children in boats and remaining to face death.

VIRGINIAN RESCUED NONE.

BY UNITED PRESS:

Montreal, April 16.—Captain Gambell of the Virginian reports to the agent here by wireless that his rescue trip was fruitless. "We arrived too late to rescue any one," he says, "and we are now proceeding to Liverpool." This means that the only ones saved were in the boats picked up by the Carpathia, 866 in all.

DO NOT BELIEVE REPORT.

BY UNITED PRESS:

Boston, April 16.—Officials of the Allan line do not believe the report that their steamer Virginian has 400 survivors on board. The Virginian cannot be reached by wireless. A telegram from Sable Island says that no victims were rescued by the Parisian.

THE TITANIC, THE LARGEST STEAMSHIP IN THE WORLD

PROBABLE DEATH LIST, 1,492.

BY UNITED PRESS:

New York, April 16.—Because of a variance between official and unofficial reports, it is impossible to say at all how many passengers were saved, and how many lost. With 866 on the Carpathia, the death list will be 1,492, if all the rest are lost, for the Titanic carried 2,358 passengers and crew when she sailed.

CONGRESS TO TAKE ACTION.

BY UNITED PRESS:

Washington, April 16.—Congress will pass a measure giving ample life-saving facilities on ocean liners. This may be expected as a result of the Titanic disaster, according to Congressman Alexander, chairman of the marine and fisheries committee in the house of representatives. Both houses of congress today unanimously adopted resolutions of sympathy for relatives of the victims of the Titanic disaster.

CROWDS THRONG WHITE STAR OFFICE

By United Press:

New York, April 16.—Utterly stunned by the disaster thousands of men, women and children are storming the offices of the White Star steamship line for information but little is received.

The officials content themselves with saying that there has been a horrible loss of life but they still hope for the best.

The Cunard line gave out a wireless this morning saying that the Carpathia had rescued 800 passengers and is slowly proceeding to New York through fields of ice.

The steamer officials are suppressing wireless reports. Relatives of the missing charge the company with not only suppressing facts but with sending out cheering reports yesterday when they knew better.

A list of the rescued women and children has been given out by the White Star officials sent by wireless by the captain of the Olympic. The list includes six hundred names. The story of the disaster, how the women and children were placed in the boats during the night, and how they suffered for eight hours before the other steamers came and the Titanic foundered with the crew and men passengers on board, has not been given out by the White Star people.

By United Press:

Boston, April 16.—The Charleston navy yard station has received a wireless dispatch which says "six hundred and fifty women and children who are on board the liner Carpathia, are the only ones saved from the Titanic. The others went down with the ship. The other rescue ships failed to find any more Titanic passengers." This wireless message was relayed by two ships which caught it off Cape Cod at 5 o'clock this morning, repeated twice clearly.

MRS. ASTOR AMONG RESCUED.

By United Press:

New York, April 16.—A wireless from the Carpathia says Mrs. John Jacob Astor was saved from the wreck. Her husband may be lost.

TITANIC CRUSHED BY BIG ICEBERG

Prof. Lenherts of State "U." Says Iceberg Must Have Been One of Largest.

Special to The Republican:

St. Paul, April 16.—Edward M. Lenherts, professor of geography and geology at the University of Minnesota, said that an iceberg large enough to sink a ship like the Titanic must have been one of the very largest type met with. He believed that the exposed part must have been as big as the state capitol. This is of course only about one-tenth the size of the entire iceberg, since they float nine-tenths submerged and one-tenth above water.

He said that large icebergs, especially when they are in the vicinity of the ice floes from which they break off, are usually shrouded with a heavy fog, which makes them of vastly greater danger to navigation. The ice floes, he said, rarely get south of Nova Scotia, but the bergs which break off frequently are seen far to the south.

WILLIAM T. STEAD.

Famous London editor among those who lost their lives in the disaster.

MAJOR ARCHIBALD BUTT.

Military aid to the president, believed to be among those lost on the Titanic.

Most Notable of Marine Disasters

1857—Central America sank; 400 lives lost.

1858—Pennsylvania exploded below Memphis; loss of life 539.

1860—Lady Elgin sank in Lake Michigan; 287 lives lost.

1863—Anglo-Saxon wrecked off Cape Race; 209 lives lost.

1866—Evening Star foundered while between New York and New Orleans; 250 lives lost.

1873—Ville du Havre sinks in mid-ocean; 230 lives lost.

1873—White Star line Atlantic sank off Halifax; 546 lives lost.

1890—Steamship Shanghai is burned; 300 lost.

Steamship Utsoria sunk in collision; 563 lives lost.

1892 Steamship Nanchwo foundered; 563 lives lost.

1895—British warship Victoria sunk; 560 lives lost.

1895—North German Lloyd Elbe lost; 330 perished.

1898—French steamer La Burgoyne sunk in collision; 560 lost.

1904—Steamer Norge wrecked on reef; 750 lost.

1904—General Slocum burned; 958 lives lost.

1904—Steamer Schesien sank in collision; 300 lives lost.

1909—Steamer Republic sank; 6 lives lost.

1910—British steamer Lowsky sank in collision; 230 lives lost.

1911—Liberte, French battleship sunk by explosion; 235 lives lost.

ABOARD LINER ON WAY HERE

BROTHER OF GUSTAF SELANDER OF THIS CITY TOOK PASSAGE ON TITANIC.

LOST WITH OTHERS

Coming From Sweden to Make His Home in Red Wing—Wrote That He Would Sail on Titanic and Arrive in This City the Last of This Week.—Others Feared For.

It is probable that among those who went down on the ill-fated liner Titanic on Monday morning is Carl Selander, a brother of Gustaf Selander, 1906 Main street.

A few weeks ago Mr. Selander purchased a third class ticket from Gust Lillyblad and forwarded it to his brother, Carl, living at Halmstad, Sweden. It was the young man's intention to come over to America and make Red Wing his home.

A short time since Gustaf Selander received a letter from his brother, Carl, that he had the ticket and expected to sail on the Titanic and arrive in Red Wing this week. If he carried out his plans he probably is numbered among those who went down with the vessel. He was 24 years old and unmarried. He was also a nephew of Andrew Selander and of Mrs. Gustaf Holmer.

A letter was received this morning by relatives from Mr. Selander, stating that he would leave Malmo, Sweden, April 6, for Southampton to take passage on the Titanic, April 10 for America.

A telegram was sent to Lieut. Fred Holmer, who is stationed at New York harbor this morning acquainting him with the facts and requesting him to get what information he could as to the whereabouts of Mr. Selander.

Red Wing friends of Miss Anna Heiberg of Minneapolis are also concerned about her. She had been visiting in Norway but was to leave Europe for New York the latter part of the week. The date she named for starting home in a recent letter written to friends here, was last Saturday. If she did not change her mind, she took some other steamer. It is probable that she is not included among the Titanic passengers.

Four Editions Issued Today

The Republican issued the following editions today:
- Pierce County Edition, 6 a. m.
- City Extra Edition, 7 a. m.
- Rural Morning Edition, 9 a. m.
- Regular City Edition, 4:30 p. m.

TITANIC, THE TITON OF THE OCEAN, FINDS WATERY GRAVE ON FIRST TRIP. OVER 1,400 PEOPLE ARE DROWNED

WHITE STAR LINER STRIKES AN ICEBERG, WHILE GOING AT FULL SPEED AT 1:25 MONDAY MORNING AND GOES DOWN IN LESS THAN AN HOUR.

WOMEN AND CHILDREN WERE SAVED

But Many Wealthy and Prominent Men Are Lost, Among Them Col. John Jacob Astor, Maj. Archibald Butt, Isidore Straus, George D. Widener, J. Bruce Ismay, Benjamin Guggenheim, Col. Washington Roebling, J. B. Thayer, the Artist Millet and Many Others.

(Early dispatches of disaster. Today's developments will be found on page 1).

New York, April 16.—The White Star liner Titanic, the world's greatest steamship has gone down some 500 miles off Cape Race, with 630 of her 1,300 passengers and her full crew of 860 men on board. That the greatest catastrophe in marine history has occurred to a vessel of their line is admitted by the officials of the White Star Steamship company in New York. The liner Carpathia, the first vessel to come within sight of the Titanic, rescued all the Titanic's life boats in which were 670 persons most of them women and children. Many women and children, however, have perished.

When the Carpathia reached the ill-fated vessel no sign of life was to be seen anywhere, the mountainous ocean swells giving much evidence to the stupendous disaster. Early reports stated that all the passengers and the crew of the Titanic had been taken off by the Allen liner's Virginian and the Parisian, and the Carpathia, but wireless message received here discredit these reports in every detail. No hope is held out at the offices of the White Star line that any man on board has survived to tell the story of the final sinking of the levithian, although some of the women in the boats may have witnessed the sinking. Only by a miracle, it is pointed out, could any person who stood by the ship escape the great vessel's powerful suction as she sank to the bottom. The Titanic carried the most notable list of passengers ever borne across the Atlantic by one vessel. Homecoming American tourist postponed their sailing weeks ago so as to ride the new wonder of the season on her maiden voyage.

Dispatches state that the Titanic went down at 2:20 o'clock Monday morning. The delay in the transmission of the news is attributed to the fact that all dispatches have been subject to difficult relays.

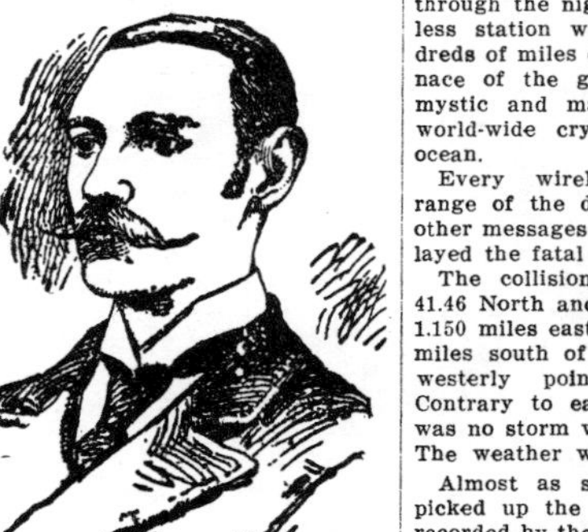

John Jacob Astor.

The collision of the Titanic with an iceberg is now known to have been a headon crash that occurred while the liner was proceeding little less than her best speed. She was a day ahead of her schedule and it is considered probable that an attempt to make a record-breaking voyage was the hope of her crew when she entered the ice field.

Her forward plates were completely wrecked. A gaping wound opening below her water line and letting the water into her forward compartments. In the meantime the lifeboats were manned and into them were placed as many of the women and children as they could hold. The boats were put off while there was yet some hope of saving the Titanic afloat until wireless could summon help. Later and more conservative estimates tell of great bravery on the part of the men passengers. There was a minimum of disorder. John Jacob Astor, who, with his bride, was returning from their long honeymoon abroad, saw his bride placed in a life boat safely away. Col. Astor was drowned. The work of getting the life-boats away, the work of allaying the fears of the great crowd of passengers as much as possible, the work of keeping the pumps in operation and the engines throbbing—these tasks and countless others were directed by Captain Smith, the venerable commander of the Titanic, and before her advent the commander of the Olympic who displayed almost superhuman power of mind and body at the world's most horrible sea disaster, crowned his long and honorable service on the high seas.

A wireless message from the Virginia states that the occupants of the small boats which she picked up have been transferred to the Carpathia which is proceeding to New York.

The Titanic struck the iceberg at 1:25 Sunday night and floundered at 2:20 Monday morning.

At daybreak the Carpathia arrived on the scene and her passengers and crew brought the small boats with their precious human cargo into New York.

The boats which rushed to the Titanic's aid found only the scattered life boats and a dismal scene of wreckage.

"Sinking by the head and women are being rushed into the life boats," were the last words that sputtered into the wireless room of the Virginian from the Titanic. All through the night and until her wireless station was silenced over hundreds of miles of seas from the antennace of the giant liner flashed the mystic and magic "S. O. S." the world-wide cry of distress on the ocean.

Every wireless operator within range of the doomed vessel dropped other messages to locate and many relayed the fatal message to the world.

The collision occurred in latitude 41.46 North and longitude 50.14 West, 1.150 miles east of New York and 450 miles south of Cape Race, the most westerly point of Newfoundland. Contrary to earlier dispatches there was no storm when the vessel struck. The weather was clear and calm.

Almost as soon as the Virginian picked up the distress signal it was recorded by the operator on the Olympic, the Titanic's sister ship, and next to her the largest vessel afloat. This was at midnight. At that hour the Olympic was 200 miles from New York enroute to Southampton.

The Baltic, famous for her rescue of passengers of the steamer Republic and for her Jack Binns, who sat aloft and braved death to summon help—was the next ship to pick up the brief story of the Titanic's plight.

She was on her way from New York to Liverpool but turned about and nu on full speed toward the Titanic's position. The Parisian, according to her messages reached the flotilla of rescue ships shortly after the Baltic.

A wireless message from Captain Haddock confirmed the fears of the White Star Line officials that all but the 670 women and children who escaped in the small boat from the $10,000,000 steamship had perished. A part of this message was witheld, but enough was divulged to make certain an appalling account of the catastrophe. Not until Captain Haddock flashed "Horrible disaster—all but 670 lost," would the White Star officials believe the largest ship ever launched had gone down on her maiden voyage. The scene in the White Star Line offices was pitiful. Brought to a realization of the stupenduous wreck—the complete destruction of the fruit of their dreams—gray haired men—many of them veteran seamen, wept.

MRS. JOHN JACOB ASTOR.

FACTS ABOUT THE TITANIC.

The largest vessel afloat.

On her maiden voyage. Was due in New York Tuesday, April 16.

Left Southampton April 10.

Forty-six thousand three hundred twenty-eight tons register.

Displacement, 66,000 tons.

Total length, 882 feet 6 inches.

Breadth, 92 feet 6 inches.

One hundred and seventy-five feet from the keel to the top of smoke-stack.

Eleven decks, with accommodations for 4,000 persons, including passengers and crew.

Two regal suites on the Titanic cost $4,350 per trip, occupants having private promenade deck.

Titanic was nearly four times as large as the Kaiser Wilhelm der Grosse, which, 10 years ago, was one of the largest, finest and fastest boats in service.

Officers of Titanic were: Captain, E. J. Smith; surgeon, W. F. N O'Loughlin; assistant surgeon, J. E Simpson; purser, H. W. McElroy; second purser, R. L. Brocker; chief steward, A. Lattimer.

TO REACH HOME FRIDAY.

Rescued Passengers Will Not Be Landed at Halifax.

New York, April 16.—Vice President Franklin positively refused to give out the full text of the message received from Captain Haddock, of the Olympic, reporting the sinking of the Titanic. This attitude led to the belief that the message told of loss of life, which the company desired to confirm before making public.

Mr. Franklin said Captain Haddock's message was brief and "neglected to say that all the crew had been saved."

It is said that the Carpathia had six or seven hundred of the Titanic's passengers aboard, including all of the first cabin, and that the vessel should reach New York Friday morning. No information had been received from the Virginian or Parisian at the White Star line offices, although it was said to "be known" that many of the Titanic passengers were on these vessels.

Mr. Franklin said he had cancelled arrangements for the special trains which they had planned to send to Halifax to bring the rescued passengers to this city by rail, as it was believed that the boats which had Titanic passengers aboard would steam direct for New York.

LIES TWO MILES DOWN.

No Hope of Salvage From Wreck of the Titanic.

Halifax.—The death bed of the $10,000,000 steamer Titanic is two miles at least below the surface of the sea.

About 500 miles from Halifax and about 70 miles south of the Grand Banks is where the Titanic is believed to have gone down.

This location is midway between Sable Island and Cape Race.

FIRST CABIN PASSENGER LIST.

MOST OF THE MEN ARE PROBABLY LOST; MOST OF THE WOMEN AND CHILDREN ARE SAVED.

London, April 16.—The first-class passenger list of the steamship Titanic includes 318 names, among whom are the following:

Miss E. W. Allen.
Miss E. Adams.
H. J. Allison, wife, daughter and son.
Harry Anderson.
Miss Cornelia I. Andrews.
Thomas Andrews.
Mrs. E. D. Appleton.
Raymond Artaga-Veita.
Col. John Jacob Astor and wife.
Mrs. N. Aubert.
O. H. Barkworth.
J. Baumann.
Mrs. James Baxter.
Quigg Baxter.
T. Beattie.
R. T. Beckwith and wife.
K. H. Behr.
D. H. Bishop and wife.
H. Bjornstrom.
Stephen Wear Blackwell.
Henry Blank.
Miss Caroline Bonnell.
J. J. Borebank.
Miss Bowen. Elsie Bowerman.
John E. Brady. E. B. Brandeis.
George Brayton.
Dr. Arthur Jackson Brew.
Mrs. J. J. Brown.
Mrs. J. M. Brown.
Mrs. S. W. Bucknell.
Maj. Archibald Butt.
E. P. Calderhead.
Mrs. Churchill Cardell.
Mrs. J. W. M Cardeza.
T. D. M. Cardeza.
Frank Carlson.
F. M. Carran.
J. P. Carran.
Wm. E. Carter and wife.
Master Carter. Lucille Carter.
Howard B. Chase.
T. W. Cavendish and wife.
Herbert F. Cahhee and wife.
N. C. Chambers and wife.
Miss Gladys Cherry.
Paul Chevre.
Mrs. E. M. Chibnall.
Robert Chisholm.
Walter M. Clark and wife.
George Quincy Clifford.
E. P. Colley.
Mrs. A. T. Compton.
Mrs. S. W. Compton.
A. T. Compton, Jr.
Mrs. R. C. Cornell.
John B. Crafton.
Edward G. Crosby, wife and daughter.
John Bradley Cummings and wife.
Robert W. Danie P. D. Daly.
Thornton Davidson and wife.
Mrs. R. Devilliers.
A. A. Dick and wife.
Washington Dodge, wife and son.
Mrs. F. Douglas.
M. W. Douglas and wife of Minneapolis.
William O. Dulles.
Mrs. Boulton Earnshew.
Miss Caroline Endres.
Miss E. M. Eustis.
Mrs. A. F. L. Eganheim.
B. L. Foreman. J. I. Flynn.
Mark Fortune, wife, three daughters and son.
T. G. Frauenthal. T. P. Franklin.
Dr. Henry Frauenthal and wife.
Miss Marguerite Frolicher.
J. Futrelle and wife.
Arthur Gee.
Mrs. L. Gibson.
Mrs. D. Gibson.
E. L. Goldenberg and wife.
George B. Goleschmidt.
Col. Archibald Gracie.
Mr. Graham.
Mrs. Wm. Graham.
Miss Margaret E. Graham.
Mrs. L. D. Greenfield.
W. B. Greenfield.
Victor Giglio.
Benjamin Guggenheim.
George A. Harder and wife.
Henry Sleeper Harper and wife.
Henry B. Harris and wife.
W. H. Harrison.
H. Haven.
W. J. Hawksford.
Charles M. Hays, wife and daughter.
Christopher Head.
W. F. Hest.
Herbert Henry Hilliard.
W. E. Hopkins.
Mrs. Ida S. Hippach.
Miss Jean Hippach.
Mrs. John C. Hoogeboom.
A. O. Holverson and wife.
Frederick M. Hoyt and wife.
Miss A. E. Icham.
Mrs. Ismay.
Birnbaum Jakob.
C. C. Jones.
H. F. Julian.
Edward A. Kent.
F. R. Kenyon and wife.
E. N. Kimball and wife.
Herman Klaber.
Wm. S. Lambert.
Mrs. A. Leader.
E. G. Lewis.
Mrs. Ernest H. Lines.
Miss Mary C. Lines.
Mrs. J. Lindstroom.
Milton C. Long.
J. H. Loring.
Mrs. Gretchen F. Longley.
Miss Georgetta Alexandra Madill.
J. E. Maguire.
Pierre Marochal.
D. W. Marvin and wife.
T. McCaffry.
Timothy J. McCarthy.
Timothy J. McCarthy.
J. R. McGough.
A. Melody.
Edgar J. Meyer and wife.
Frank D. Millet, the artist.
Dr. W. E. Minahan, wife and daughter.
H. Markland Molsom.
Clarence Moore.
Mr. Morgan and wife.
Charles Natsch.
A. W. Newell.
Miss Alice Newell.
Miss Madeline Newell.
Miss Helen Newsom.
A. S. Nicholson.
E. O. Ostby.
Miss Helen R. Ostby.
S. Ovies.
M. H. W. Parr.
Austin Partner.
V. Payne.
Thomas Pears and wife.
Victor Penasco and wife.
Maj. Arthur Peuchen.
Walter Chamberlain Porter.
Mrs. Thomas Potter, Jr.
Jonkheer Reuchlijg.
George Rheims.
Mrs. Edward S. Robert.
W. A. Roebling II.
C. Rolmans.
Hugh Rood.
Miss Rosenbaum.
J. Hugo Ross.
Countess Rothes.
M. Rothschild and wife.
Alfred Rowe.
Arthur Ryerson, wife, two daughters and son.
Adolph Saalfeld.
A. L. Saloman.
Mr. Schabert.
Frederick Seward.
Miss E. W. Schutes.
Mr. Silverthorne.
William B. Silvey and wife.
Colonel Alfonso Simonius.
Wm. T. Sloper.
John M. Smart.
R. W. Smith. J. Clinch Smith.
John Snyder and wife of Minneapolis.
Frederick O. Spedden, wife and son.
W. A. Spenser and wife.
Dr. Max Stahelin.
W. T. Stead.
Max Frolicher Stehli and wife.
C. E. H. Stengel and wife.
Mrs. W. B. Stephenson.
A. A. Stewart.
Mrs. George M. Stone.
Isidor Straus and wife.
Frederick Sutton.
Mrs. Frederick Joel Swift.
Emil Taussig and wife.
E. S. Taylor and wife.
J. B. Thayer and wife.
J. B. Thayer, Jr. Ruth Taussig.
J. Thorne and wife.
Mr. Uruchurtu. G. M. Tucker, Jr.
Wyckoff Vanderhoef.
W. Anderson Walker.
F. M. Warren and wife.
J. Wier. M. J. White.
Percival W. White.
Richard F. White and wife.
George D. Wick and wife.
Miss Mary Wick.
George D. Widener and wife.
Harry Widener. Duane Williams.
George Wright. Hugh Woolner.
Miss Constance Willard.
N. M. Williams, Jr.
Miss Marie Young.

THESE ARE POSITIVELY KNOWN TO BE SAVED.

Cape Race.—Following is a partial list of the first-class passengers who were rescued from the Titanic:

Mrs. Edward W. Appleton.
Mrs. Rose Abbott.
Miss G. M. Burns.
Miss D. D. Cassebero.
Miss Mary Clines.
Mrs. Singrid Lindstrem.
Miss Georgetta Amadill.
Mrs. Tucker and maid.
Mrs. J. B. Thayer.
Mrs. J. Stewart White.
Miss Marie Young.
Mrs. Thomas Potter, Jr.
Mrs. Edna S. Roberts.
Mrs. William M. Clarke.
Mrs. B. Chibinace.
Miss E. G. Crossbie.
Miss H. E. Crosbie.
Miss Jean Hippach.
Mrs. Henry B. Harris.
Mrs. Alexander Halverson.
Miss Margaret Hays.
Mr. and Mrs. Ed Kimberley.
Miss G. F. Longley.
Miss A. F. Leader.
Miss Bertha Lavory.
Mrs. Ernest Lives.
Mrs. Susan P. Rodgerson.
Mrs. Emily B. Rodgerson.
Mrs. Arthur Rodgerson.
Master Allison and nurse.
Miss K. T. Andrews.
Miss Ninette Panhart.
Miss E. W. Allen.
Mr. and Mrs. D. W. Bishop.
Mrs. James Baxter.
Mr. George A. Bayton.
Mrs. J. M. Brown.
Miss G. C. Brown.
Mr. and Mrs. R. L. Beckwith.
Countess of Rothes.
Mr. C. R. Olmane.
Mr. and Mrs. L. Henry.
Mrs. W. A. Hooper.
Mr. Miles J. Flynn.
Miss Alice Fortune.
Mrs. Hilda Slayter.
Mrs. Robert Douglas.
Miss Lucile Carter.
Mrs. Florence Mare.
Miss Alice Phillips.
Mrs. Paula Munge.
Mrs. P. Smith. Mrs. Braham.
Miss C. Bonnell. F. A. Kenyman.
William Carter. Miss Roberts.
Miss A. Basing. Mr. H. Blank.
J. B. Thayer, Jr. Miss Anna Ward
H. Woolner. Rich M. William
Madam Melicard Gustav J. Lesuer
Bruce Ismay.
Mrs. Jacob P. — Miss Cummins.
Miss Rosie —— Miss Phyllis O.
Mrs. Jane —— Miss Bertha ——
(The last four names were missed.)

MANY RICH MEN ON BOARD

COL. ASTOR HEADS LIST WITH $150,000,000.

Benjamin Guggenheim Followed, With $95,000,000—Interests Many and Varied.

FORTUNES ABOARD THE TITANIC.	
Col. John Jacob Astor....	$150,000,000
Isidor Straus	50,000,000
George D. Widener	50,000,000
J. Bruce Ismay	40,000,000
Benjamin Guggenheim	95,000,000
Col. Washington Roebling	25,000,000
J. B. Thayer	10,000,000
Total	$520,000,000

New York, April 16.—Wealth aggregating something like half a billion dollars is represented by ten of the passengers on the Titanic. If calamity befell only a few of these ten, it would materially affect vast business enterprises in the United States and England. Foremost among the passengers in point of wealth is Colonel John Jacob Astor, who was returning to New York with his bride, formerly Miss Madeline Force. Colonel Astor's holdings may amount to $150,000,000 and he is connected with nearly a score of corporations, besides attending to his realty interests.

Next in financial importance, come Benjamin Guggenheim and George D. Widener. Mr. Guggenheim is in the American Smelting securities company, the great mining corporation, which was founded by his father, Meyer Guggenheim. He is connected with the following corporations: Blake and Knowles Steam Pump Works, president and director; the Henry R. Worthington company, president and director; International Steam Pump company, president and director; the Laidlaw-Dunn-Gordon company, president and director; Power and Mining Machinery company, president and director.

MRS. GEORGE D. WIDENER.
Wife of Philadelphia Millionaire

George D. Widener is connected with the Widener-Elkins traction syndicate of Philadelphia. He is one of two sons of P. A. B. Widener. George D. Widener's fortune is estimated at $50,000,000.

Colonel Washington Roebling, builder of the Brooklyn bridge, is president and director of the John A. Roeblings Sons company. His fortune amounts to about $25,000,000.

Isidor Straus is one of the best known merchants in the world and is worth about $50,000,000. Mr. Straus is connected with the following organizations: R. H. Macy & Company, L. Straus & Sons, Abraham & Straus, the Birbeck Investment Savings and Loan company, vice president and trustee; the Educational Alliance, president and director; Hanover National bank, director; Second National bank, director.

J. Bruce Ismay is president of the International Mercantile Marine company and is one of the founders of that big organization. It was Mr. Ismay and J. P. Morgan who consolidated American and British steamship lines. It also was Mr. Ismay who conceived the idea of building the Titanic. He is worth probably $50,000,000.

John B. Thayer is vice president of the Pennsylvania railroad. His son J. B. Thayer, Jr., who was on the Titanic with his parents, formerly was a noted fullback on the University of Pennsylvania football team. Young Thayer was known as one of the best fullbacks that ever played on a college team.

If the fortunes of all the first class passengers were placed together they would make easily $1,000,000,000, while the fortunes of the ten richest of them would aggregate $500,000,000.

PASSENGERS SUFFER.

Remain in Life Boats Eight Hours Before Rescued.

New York.—Those who were saved after the Titanic disaster have gone through hardships of exposure and peril which may have left many of them in a serious condition. A dispatch given out at the White Star offices said that those rescued by the Carpathia were picked up from lifeboats at 10:30 o'clock Monday morning, eight hours after the Titanic sunk.

Mrs. Astor Saved.

New York.—According to best information here, Col. John Jacob Astor is among the lost, but his bride, who was Miss Madeline Force, a daughter of Frank Force, is saved. Mrs. Astor was reported to be in a delicate condition.

EXTRA THE BROOKLYN DAILY EAGLE EXTRA

'4 PAGES. Volume 72A No. 106 ★ NEW YORK CITY, TUESDAY, APRIL 16, 1912. ★ THREE CENTS.

1,234 TITANIC DEAD LATEST REVISED ESTIMATE; 866 SURVIVORS ARE ON THE STEAMER CARPATHIA

List of Survivors Who Are Aboard Carpathia Received by Wireless.

BROOKLYNITES IN LIST

Karl Behr, Mrs. F. J. Swift and Mr. and Mrs. Harder Saved.

CAPE RACE, N. F., April 16—The steamship Carpathia, which is believed to have on board all the survivors of the Titanic disaster, started early today to send by wireless to this station the list of the Titanic's survivors. Great difficulty was experienced in getting many of the names correctly, and more than a score of names as made out here did not appear at all on the Titanic's original passenger list, but it is believed that many of these were passengers who had booked passage at the last moment. The receipt of the list of the first cabin survivors required nearly six hours effort.

The list of survivors as it appears at offices of the White Star Line in Manhattan, shows that the following saloon passengers of the Titanic are safe on board the Carpathia:

A

ABBOTT, Mrs. Rose
ANDERSON, Harry
ALLEN, Miss E. W.
APPLETON, Mrs. E. W.
ASTOR, Mrs. John Jacob, and maid
ALLISON, Master, and Nurse.
ANDREWS, Miss K. T.
AMADILL, Miss Georgietta
ABALSON, Anna
ANGLE, William
ARDEN, George

B

BARKWORTH, A. H.
BAXTER, Mrs. James
BRAYTON, George A.
BECKWITH, Mr. and Mrs R. T.
BEHR, Karl H.
BISHOP, Mr. and Mrs. D. H.
BLANK, Henry
BONNELL, Miss Caroline
BOWEN, Miss G. C.
BOWERMAN, Miss Elsie
BROWN, Mrs. J. J.
BUCKWELL, Mrs. William
BURNS, Mrs. G. M.
BALLS, Ada
BISHOP, Mr. and Mrs. A. H.
BROWN, Miss Edith
BROWN, T. W. S.
BEALE, Edward
BEANE, Mrs. Ethel
BUYHL, Mrs. Dogman
BYSTRONE, Mrs. Caroline
BRAHAM, Mrs.
BARRETT, Carl
BESSETLE, Miss
BATHWORTH, M.

C

CALDERHEAD, E. P.
CARDELL, Mrs. Churchill
CARDEZA, Mrs. J. W.
CARDEZA, Thomas
CARTER, Miss Lucille
CARTER, Mrs. William E.
CARTER, Master William
CASE, Howard B.
CAVENDISH, Mrs. Turrell W., and maid.
CHAFEE, Mrs. H. F.
CHAMBERS, Mr. and Mrs. M. C.
CHERRY, Miss Gladys
CHEVRO, Paul
CROSBY, Mrs. E. G.
CROSBY, Miss
CARTER, W. E.
CARTER, Master William
CHANDASON, Mrs. Victoria
CLINES, Miss Mary
CUMMINGS, Mrs. John B.
CASSEBERE, Miss D. D.
CLARKE, Mrs. Walter
CUMMINGS, Miss
CHIBNOLL, Mrs. E. B.

D

DANIEL, Robert W.
DAVIDSON, Mrs. Thornton
DEVILLIERS, Mrs. B.
DICK, Mr. and Mrs. A. A.
DODGE, Mr. and Mrs. Washington and son.
DOUGLAS, Mrs. Fred C.
DOUGLAS, Mrs. Walter
DESSETT, Miss
DANIEL, Miss Sarah
DRAUCHENSTED, Alfred
DANZER, Mrs. Mary
DURANTE, Leonora A.

E

EMOCK, Philip
ELLIS, Miss
EARNSHAW, Mrs. Brulton
ENDRES, Miss Caroline

F

FLYNN, J. L.
FORTUNE, Mrs. Mark, Miss Lucille, Miss Alice.
FRAUENTHAL, Dr. H. and Mrs.
FRAUENTHAL, Mr. and Mrs. T. G.
FROLICHER, Miss Margaret
FUTRELLE, Mrs. Jacques E.
FLEGHEIM, Miss Antonette
FRANCATELLI, Miss
FAIR, J. B., Sr.
FAIR, J. B., Jr.
FANTINI, Mrs. Mark
FRAZENTHAL, H. W.
FRAZENTHAL, Mrs. F.

G

GIBSON, Mrs. Leonard
GIBSON, Miss Dorothy
GOLDENBURG, Mrs. Samuel
GOLDENBURG, Miss Ella
GORDON, Sir and Lady Cosmo Duff
GRACIE, Colonel Archibald
GRAHAM, Mr.
GRAHAM, Mrs. William
GRAHAM, Miss Margaret E.
GREENFIELD, Mrs. Lee D.
GREENFIELD, William B.
GOOGHT, James
GENOVESE, Argene

H

HARANER, Henry
HARDER, Mr. and Mrs. George A.
HARPER, Henry S. and man servant.
HARPER, Mrs. Henry S.
HAWKSFORD, Henry J.
HAYS, Mrs. Charles M., and daughter Margaret.
HARRIS, Mrs. Henry B.
HIPPACH, Miss Jean
HOGEBOOM, Mrs. John C.
HOYT, Mr. and Mrs. Fred M.
HIPPACH, Miss Ida
HALVORSEN, Mrs. Alex
HENRY, Mr. and Mrs. L.
HOOPER, Mrs. W. A.
HOMER, Henry R.
HASSIG, Miles
HAREN, H.

I

ISMAY, J. Bruce

J

JANE, Mrs.

O

OSTBY, E C.
OSTBY, Miss Helen R.
OMOND, Fiennad
O'CONNELL, Miss Robert (Probably Mrs. R. C. Cornell)
OLIVIA, Mlle.

P

PEUCHEN, Major Arthur
POTTER, Mrs. Thomas, Jr.
PANHART, Mrs. Ninnette
PHILIPS, Miss Alice
PASSINA, Miss A.
PIRRIE, Mr.

R

RHEIMS, Mrs. George
ROBERT, Mrs. Edward S.
ROLMANO, C.
ROSENBAUM, Miss Edith
ROTHSCHILD, Mrs. Martin
ROTHES, Countess of
RANELT, Miss Appie
ROGERSON, John (Probably Ryerson)
RENAGO, Miss M. J.
ROGERSON, Mrs. Susan P.
ROGERSON, Miss Emily B.
ROGERSON, Mrs. Arthur
ROBERTS, Miss
ROBERTS, Mrs.
RYERSON, Mrs. Arthur
RYERSON, Miss Emily B.

S

SAALFIELD, Adolphe
SOLOMON, Abraham
SCHABERT, Mrs. Paul
STEWARD, Frederick
SILVEY, Mrs. William D.
SIMONIUS, Colonel Alfonso
SLOPER, William T.
SNYDER, Mr. and Mrs. John
SPENCER, Mrs. W. A., and maid.
STEHELIN, Dr. Max
STENGEL, Mr. and Mrs. C. E. H. E.
STONE, Mrs. George M.
SWIFT, Mrs. Frederick Joel
STEFFASON, H. B.
SEGESSER, Miss Emma
SHUTTER, Mrs. (Probably Miss E. W. Schuter)
SPEDDEN, Mr. and Mrs. J. O.
SIMONIUS, Colonel Alfonzo
SMITH, Mrs. Lucien T.
STEPHENSON, Mrs. Walter P.
SLAYTER, Mrs. Hilda
SMITH, Mrs. P.
SMITH, Mrs. P. P.
SLAYTON, Miss Hilda
SHEDDELL, Robert Douglas
STOCKLIELIN, Mr. and Mrs. Max

WILLIAM T. STEAD.

Noted Journalist, Founder of Review of Reveiws, Who Was Probably Lost on the Titanic.

CARPATHIA HERE FRIDAY.

The 866 survivors of the ill-fated Titanic who are now on board the steamship Carpathia steaming to this city, are not expected to arrive before Friday morning. The Carpathia is a thirteen-knot liner and it was estimated early today that it would take her from 75 to 80 hours to reach port.

MR. ISMAY SAFE.

Managing Director of White Star Line Among the Survivors.

Joseph Bruce Ismay, the chairman and managing director of the White Star Line, was among the men who survived the tragic first voyage of the Titanic.

As president of the International Mercantile Marine Company he has been prominently identified with marine and mercantile interests in the United States and he started on the Titanic's maiden voyage with assurances of an almost royal welcome on this side of the ocean as one of the most prominent ship owners in the world.

Mr. Ismay was born in Liverpool on December 12, 1862, and he was educated at Elstree and Harrow. His father was Thomas Henry Ismay, of Dawpool, Cheshire, England. In 1888 he married Julia Florence Schieffelin, daughter of George R. Schieffelin, of this city. They have two sons and two daughters. His residence is at 15 Hill street, Sandheys, Mossley Hill, Liverpool. He has been a member of the Reform Club of that city, and a prominent clubman in London.

Mr. Ismay's father had a rapid rise from builder's apprentice in the shipyards to president of the White Star Line. At his death he had a fortune of nearly $6,500,000. His early life gave him an opportunity to study the ships in the old picturesque Cumberland port at Maryport and in the early fifties he entered the firm of Imrie, Tomlinson & Co., as an apprentice.

Mr. Ismay's father worked his way to the front until in 1867, when

Karl Behr,
Brooklyn Tennis Player Who Is Among the Survivors.

the managing owner of the White Star line, retired, he was in a position to take over the smart fleet of clippers which then composed the line. His policies were followed by his son, who was responsible for the competition in large and speedy vessels which resulted in the latest addition to the fleet, the building of the Titanic, now at the bottom of the ocean.

PRAYERS FOR PASSENGERS.

Men and Religion Conference Offers Supplications for Those on Titanic.

Prayers for the safety of the passengers aboard the Titanic were said yesterday at the af[illegible] conference of the Men and Religion Forward Movement in this city.

William T. Stead, the journalist, and the Rev. J. Seward Holden of London, who were among the Titanic's passengers, were on their way here to make addresses before the conference.

ABELSON, Hanna.
BALLS, Ada R.
BISS, Miss Kate.
BEANE, Edward.
BEANE, Miss Ethel.
BRYHL, Miss Dagmar.
BYSTROM, Mrs. Karolina.
COLLYER, Mrs. Charlotte.
COLLYER, Miss Marjorie.
CHRISTY, Mrs. Alice.
CHRISTY, Miss Julia.
CLARKE, Mrs. Ada Maria.
CAMERON, Miss.
COLLETT, Mrs. Stuart.
CALDWELL, Albert F.
CALDWELL, Mrs. Sylvia.
CALDWELL, Alden G.
DREW, Mrs. Lulu.
DAVIS, Miss Agnes.
DAVIS, John M.
DURAN, Florentina.
DURAN, Ascuncion.
DAVIS, Miss Mary.
DOLING, Mrs. Ada.
DOLING, Miss Elsie.
FAUNTHROPE, Mrs. Lizzie.
GARSIDE, Miss Ethel.
HEWLETT, Mrs. Mary D.
HARRIS, George.
HERMAN, Mrs. Jane.
HERMAN, Miss Kate.
HERMAN, Miss Alice.
HOLD, Miss Annie.
HART, Mrs. Esther.
HART, Miss Eva.
HARPER, MISS Nina.
HAMALAINER, Anna, and son.
HOCKING, Mrs. Elizabeth.
HOCKING, Miss Nellie.
JACOBSOHN, Mrs. Amy.
KEANE, Miss Nora.
KELLY, Miss Fannie.
LAROCHE, Miss Louise.
LEITCH, Miss Jessie W.
LAMORE, Mrs.
LOUCH, Mrs. Alice.
LEHMAN, Miss Bertha.
MELLINGER, Mrs. Elizabeth, and child.
MALLET, Mrs. A.
MALLET, Master Andrero.
NYE, Mrs. Elizabeth.
PHILIPPS, Miss Alice.
PALLAS, Emilio.
PADRO, Julian.
PARISH, Mrs. L.
PORTALUPPI, Mrs. Emilio.
QUICK, Mrs. Jane O.
QUICK, Miss Wennie O.
QUICK, Miss Phyllis O.
REBOUF, Mrs. Lillie.
RIDSDALE, Mrs. Lucy.
RUGG, Miss Emily.
RICHARD, Mr. and Mrs. Emile, and son.
SINCOCK, Miss Maude.
SMITH, Mrs. Marion.
TROUT, Miss Edina S.
WEISZ, Mrs. Matilda.
WEBBER, Miss Susan.
WRIGHT, Miss Marion.
WATT, Miss Bessie.
WATT, Miss Behtra.
WEST, Mrs., and two children.
WELLS, Mrs. Addie.
WELLS, Miss J.
WELLS, Ralph.
WILLIAMS, Charles.

ISIDOR STRAUS.

Member of the Firm of Abraham & Straus, Who Is Not Reported as a Survivor.

K

KIMBERLEY, Mr. and Mrs. E. M. (Probably E. M. Kimball)
KENYMAN, F. A.
KENCHEN, Miss Emilie

L

LEADER, Mrs. A. F.
LINES, Mrs. Ernest
LINES, Miss Mary C.
LONGLEY, Miss G. F.
LAVORY, Miss Bertha
LINDSTROM, Mrs. Singrid
LESNEUR, Gustave J.

M

MADILL, Miss Georgietta A.
MARSCHAL, Pierre
MARVIN, Mrs. D. W.
MINNIHAN, Mrs. W. E.
MINNIHAN, Miss Daisy
MARWIN, Mrs. D. W.
MAIMY, Miss Ruberta
MILE, Mr. (Probably Frank D. Millet)
MORE, Mrs. Florence
MUNGE, Mrs. Paula
MELICARD, Mme.

N

NEWELL, Miss Madeline
NEWELL, Miss Marjorie
NEWSOM, Miss Helen

SECKER, Miss Emma
STEFFANS, H. B.
SERREPCA, Miss Augusta
SILVERTHORN, R. L.

T

THAYER, J. B.
TAUSSIG, Miss Ruth
TAYLOR, Mr. and Mrs. E. Z.
TUCKER, Gilbert M.
THAR, Miss Ella
TUCKER, Mrs., and maid.
THAYER, Mrs. J. B., Jr.
TURNEY, J.

W

WARNER, Mrs. F. M.
WHITE, Mrs. J. Stuart
WICKS, Miss Mary
WIDENER, Mrs. Geo. D. and maid.
WILSON, Miss Helen A.
WILLARD, Miss Constance
WOOLMER, Frederick
WARD, Miss Anna
WILLIAM, Richard M.
WASHINGTON, M.

Y

YOUNG, Miss Marie

Cape Race, N. F., April 16—The names of the rescued second cabin passengers, so far as they check up with the Titanic's published list, are as follows:

ANGLE, William.

Rescued Passengers of the Ill-Fated Leviathan Drifted in Life Boats For Many Hours Before Succor Came.

MRS. J. J. ASTOR AMONG RESCUED

Hope That the Virginian Now En Route to St. Johns, N. F., Possibly Has Additional Survivors on Board

Steamship Carpathia, via Cape Race, N. F., April 16—Captain Rostron sent the following wireless dispatch to The Associated Press this morning:

"Titanic struck iceberg, sunk Monday 3 A.M., 41.46 north latitude, 50.14 west longitude; Carpathia picked up many passengers, proceeding New York."

Captain Rostron also sent in a wireless message to Charles P. Sumner, general agent of the Cunard Line here this morning giving the information that the Carpathia with 800 survivors of the Titanic on board was proceeding slowly toward New York through a field of ice.

These pinacles of fact concerning the world's greatest steamship disaster—the sinking at 2:20 a. m., Monday, of the great White Star liner Titanic off the banks of Newfoundland—stood out prominently early today as sifted from the wireless reports:

Revised estimate loss of life, 1,254 souls.

The $10,000,000 steamship, with cargo and jewels worth perhaps $10,000,000 more, a total loss.

Mrs. John Jacob Astor (nee Miss Force of Brooklyn) has been saved.

Major Archibald Butt, President Taft's aid, is still unaccounted for, as are many other persons of international importance. J. Bruce Ismay, president of the International Mercantile Marine, owners of the White Star Line, is among the survivors, as is his wife.

866 SURVIVORS ON THE CARPATHIA.

Wireless reports say the Cunarder Carpathia has on board 866 survivors, the total thus far accounted for. She is steaming for New York and should arrive on Friday.

The rescued passengers drifted in lifeboats for many hours before succor came.

Wireless messages to St. Johns, N.F., report the Allan Line Virginian en route there, possibly with additional survivors on board. That she carries survivors had not been confirmed at daybreak this morning, nor had confirmation been found that her sister ship, the Parisian, had aided in the rescue work, as was reported yesterday.

Of the foregoing summarized reports concerning the awful tragedy in the ice fields of the Atlantic, two were fraught with hope as the day dawned. The first was that the rescue ship Carpathia carried nearly 900 survivors, as against 675 reported to be on board yesterday. The second was the message saying that the Virginian might have others on board whose safety would cut the list of dead.

Captain E. J. Smith, commander of the Titanic, probably went to his grave with his ill-fated vessel without once being able to communicate direct with the agents of his line. Aside from the C Q D sent by his wireless operator, not one word from him was received up to the time the Titanic sank bow foremost into the ocean.

Women Saved First.

The presumption is that he met death at his post as a gallant skipper should. That he and his crew enforced rigidly the unwritten law of the sea—women and children first—is plainly indicated by the preponderance of women among the partial list of survivors that the wireless has given.

Although rated as one of the most able commanders since the advent of the modern steamship, Captain Smith's career had been recently marred with ill-luck. He was in command of the Titanic's sister ship Olympic when that vessel was in collision with the British cruiser Hawke. Exonerated of all blame for this occurrence, he was placed in charge of the Titanic, when his new charge fouled the steamship New York in the Solent after leaving Southampton on her maiden voyage, which has ended so disastrously. He had been in the line's employ for more than thirty years, and his first important command was the Majestic.

Although 866 souls are reported to be on the Carpathia, it is apparent that all of them are not passengers, for it was necessary for members of the Titanic's crew to man the lifeboats which set out from the sinking liner's sides. How many of the crew were assigned to each boat under the conditions prevailing is a matter of conjecture.

A similarly unsettled matter is the percentage of first-class passengers among those saved. While the names of survivors obtained are largely those of saloon passengers, the rule "women first" should apply equally to the second cabin and steerage, a regulation which may have cost the life of many prominent men above decks. It is natural also that the names of the more obscure survivors would be slower in reaching land.

Hysterical Crowds Seek News of Disaster.

False news and false hopes and an international belief that the palatial Titanic was practically unsinkable followed the slowly unfolding accounts of her loss in a way without precedent. Eager crowds in a dozen cities in the United States besieged bulletin boards when it became known that the giant liner had really sunk with terrible loss of life, and in New York City hysterical men and women crowded into the White Star Line offices seeking news of relatives. Vincent Astor, Colonel Astor's son, spent the entire night waiting for some wireless tidings of his father, alternately visiting the White Star Line headquarters and the newspaper offices.

The speed at which the Titanic was

traveling when she shattered herself against the iceberg perhaps will not be known until the first of her survivors reaches port.

Whatever her rate of progress, however, shipbuilders here and abroad must admit that while the modern steamship may defy the wind and weather, ice and fog remain an ever-present element of danger. No ship, they point out, no matter how stanchly built nor how many watertight bulkheads protect her, may plunge headlong against a wall of ice without grave results. The general opinion is that the Titanic's equipment was put to an extraordinary test which no vessel could have withstood.

Shattering Effects of Smashing Into an Iceberg.

"Under ordinary circumstances these watertight compartments will preserve a ship from sinking," said A. L. Hopkins, vice president of the Newport News Shipbuilding and Drydock Company, in New York, "but smashing into an iceberg could produce shattering effects that would render a ship helpless beyond the protection of any design yet known. In fore and after collisions where the compartments are punctured the lowering of either end of the ship produces an increased strain on the other compartments."

Granting that only the forward bulkhead of the Titanic had been crumpled by the impact with the iceberg, Mr. Hopkins was inclined to think that the relative buoyancy of the remaining compartments would have been sufficient to save the vessel. Inasmuch as he was not familiar with the relative division of the Titanic's compartments he could not estimate how many compartments must have given way under the impact of the collision.

Naval Constructor Believes Titanic Struck Submerged Projection.

Robert Stocker, naval constructor of the Brooklyn Navy Yard, said: "In the case of the Titanic I am inclined to think that her sinking was due to the effect of grounding rather than to the impact of collision. Frequently a ship strikes what is known as a 'pinnacle rock,' ripping open her keel. The iceberg against which the Titanic smashed her bow may have had some such submerged projection which did additional damage to the keel. If the forward bulkheads of the vessel had held after the impact which smashed the bow, it certainly seems that the relative buoyancy of the remaining compartments would have been sufficient to keep the ship afloat. I am compelled to believe that a great many of her compartments must have been punctured or sprung."

Lewis Nixon, the eminent naval architect, is inclined to think the Titanic was either traveling at full speed or perhaps the crash into a berg was so tremendous that there was practically no give.

"If the Titanic hit one of those great ice masses," said Mr. Nixon, "it is likely that she struck one that had no more give than a rock. Under these circumstances something had to give way, and, as the iceberg did not, the great ship had to crumple up. It is conceivable that an impact of this sort might have buckled her longitudinal plates from end to end, shearing off and starting rivets and opening up the watertight compartments throughout the length of the vessel."

For many years steamship men have asserted that the safest place to be is on a well-equipped ocean liner. In proportion to the number carried, the statistics show that there is less loss of life and less chance of injury on board a modern liner than there is in any other means of transportation. Fleets come and go from New York and other ports with the regularity of the tides, and those carrying mails maintain a schedule which almost equals in punctuality that of the railway mail trains.

Icebergs in the Steamship Lanes.

Trans-atlantic steamers travel in well-defined routes, known as "steamship lanes," the westbound and the eastbound. This reduces to a minimum the chances of collision with one another. But icebergs and derelicts have no respect for these rules and float into the paths or wallow across them to be a dire menace in time of fog or very thick weather. There is no way to give warning until too late. Out of a smother of a fog a pallid shape may be glimpsed over the bows, to be followed a half minute later by the crash of the bows against the mass of ice.

Worst Disaster in History, Says Old Seaman.

"It is a holocaust," once he choked out; "the worst in history."

He said that the senior captain of the White Star fleet was a kindly, humorous, grave man, watchful from long sailing of the sudden and treacherous seas; gentle to those under him, but strict in the hour of duty. He could not think of any conceivable explanation today for the terrible disaster which struck the merchant captain down at the close of one of the longest and most successful careers in the merchant service. Thought simply stood baffled before the terrible disaster.

White Star Line Had Four Captain Smiths in Its Service.

All in all, before the wreck of Monday there were four Captain Smiths in the service of the White Star Line. One was the man who went down with his ship. The others were Captain John N. Smith, Captain William Smith and Captain Harry Smith. The old employe of the line recalled an incident today which showed the senior captain's ease of manner and humor.

The three captains of the line were standing in a group one day, when Captain John N. Smith, the dockmaster, stepped up in a new, shining uniform. Captain Edward Smith, the senior captain, doffed his hat and called aloud:

"We are the captains, but here is the Admiral Smith of the White Star line and his Majesty's service."

[illegible] men at the White Star line today add their word of praise to the [illegible] went down to the grave of ships off the Newfoundland coast and of the [illegible] men of the merchant com[illegible] the old, tried captain, there is no shadow of doubt, no possibility of question.

FAMOUS MEN AMONG ROSTER OF LOST

More Notables Wiped Out Than in Any Previous Catastrophe of History.

TWO NATIONS ARE MOURNING.

Colonel Astor, Isidor Straus, H. B. Harris, Benjamin Guggenheim, William Stead and Many More.

Never in the history of the known world has a death roster of an accident, on either sea or land, contained even a tithe of the names that will make the Titanic disaster a thing to shudder over for all time to come.

Frantic relatives of persons of world-wide fame are today either plunged in an abyss of mourning in the practical certainty of the loss of their dear ones, or waiting with an almost groundless hope for what news the sea wil give up in the next few hours.

There are obituaries in the columns today of the newspapers the civilized world over, of men famous in every profession and in every walk of life.

The list of the persons on board the ill-fated Titanic contains the names of prominent personages from many lands as well as those of lesser significance in world history, but of great importance in their own circles. In New England there will be mourning in many cities, Boston furnishing a heavy quota of victims. East and West, North and South, in the United States, the death toll will be heavy. England and France, too, are represented in the list with some of their favorite sons.

The blow wil fall heaviest, however, upon New York City's financial and social circles—if some later word from off New Foundland does not mitigate the terrible news of this early morning.

A leading figure is Colonel John Jacob Astor, long a leader in social circles, scion of the famous Astor familyy and identified with the financial activities of the Metropolis for years.

Then, too, there is Renry B. Harris, one of the powers of the theatrical world; Isidor Straus, merchant and philanthropist; Benjamin Guggenheim, copper king; Frederick M. Hoyt, broker and yachtsman, and Major Butt, President Taft's aid. England's contribution is made up partly of William T. Stead, noted author, and one of the principal stockholders in the company which owned the Titanic.

WILLIAM T. STEAD.

William T. Stead, author, director, advocate of international peace, an investigator of psychic phenomena and well known in America because of his frequent visits to this country, has been famous throughout the world for years because of his writings.

Born at Embleton, England, July 5, 1849, the son of a Congregational minister, he was educated in Silcoats School, Wakefield, and was apprenticed in a mercantile office on leaving the school at the age of 14. He soon left business for journalism, becoming the editor of the Northern Echo, published at Darlington, at the age of 22.

Nine years later, in 1880, Mr. Stead was an assistant editor of the Pall Mall Gazette. He was promoted to the chair of editor in 1883 and two years afterward served three months in prison because of a political article he had written on the "Maiden Tribute."

The fame which he had achieved because of these various activities was considerably increased in 1890 and 1891, when he founded The Review of Reviews in England and the Review of Reviews in this country, the former coming first. From this work Mr. Stead went to Australia, where the Australasian Review of Reviews was also established by him.

Mr. Stead's repute as an enthusiastic worker for international peace began in 1898, after he had visited the Czar. He edited a weekly which he called "War Against War," did wonderful work at The Hague Peace Conference, and published many articles inveighing against the Boer War.

Mr. Stead's activities as a journalist were chiefly directed along magazine lines for many years, but his contributions to daily newspapers in the reporting of events of international prominence made his name known to practically everyone in the United States. On one of his visits to this country, in 1893, he published an article "If Christ Came to Chicago," that caused him to be spoken of in the remotest hamlets of America.

Significant tribute to Mr. Stead's genius as a writer has been given in this very disaster that has probably cost his life. After the ill-fated Titanic had sunk and while the world was still ignorant of the vessel's fate, the wireless bore message after message from several newspapers destined for Mr. Stead asking him to write an exclusive story of the disaster. But even while the wireless pulsed its call through the air, Mr. Stead had gone from the world.

MAJOR ARCHIBALD BUTT.

Major Archibald Willingham Butt, President Taft's Military Aid, was born in Georgia forty-one years ago. Before the Spanish War he had been in Washington correspondent of several Southern newspapers. At one time he was first secretary of the United States Legation in the City of Mexico. His army experience began by his selection as an officer of one of the new volounteer regiments to go to the Philippines. On his return from the Philippines he was given a commission in the regular army and went to Cuba with the forces to help the reconstruction of the new republic. President Roosevelt afterward made Major Butt one of his personal aids.

Major Butt was a bachelor living in splendid but quiet style in Washington. He was one of the most popular officers in the army. His presence on the Titanic was due to the fact that he was just returning from a visit to Rome, where he went to see the Pope and King Victor Emmanuel. Undoubtedly sent there as a personal messenger from President Taft, he is supposed to have been bearing an important message from Pope Pius to the President.

Many are the stories of Major Butt's popularity. Among his proudest possessions was a gorgeous cloak given him by President Diaz of Mexico. This was before he entered the army and even before he was a newspaper correspondent in Washington and was with the legation in the City of Mexico. His interest in Mexican life soon attracted President Diaz and the two became fast friends. When Butt was leaving the Mexican capital, President Diaz gave him the cloak, which is a brilliant affair of red, purple and gold. When President Taft visited in the fall of 1909, it was noted that

MADELEINE FORCE ASTOR.

Bride of Colonel John Jacob Astor. She Is Among the Survivors and Husband Is Probably Lost.

"Archie" Butt was the sole companion of Diaz and President Taft on their horseback rides.

While with President Roosevelt as his aid there were none of the physical stunts carried off by his illustrious superior that Major Butt did not participate in. He made the famous ride to Warrenton and back in one afternoon. At the White House receptions, Major Butt was adept at the art of reducing the work of the President to a minimum. He is said to have remembered and introduced 2,800 persons in one hour.

The recent trip of Major Butt to Rome is a record of note to his personal popularity. He was most cordially received by the Pontiff and after presenting an autograph letter from President Taft was engaged in conversation by the Pope, who recalled with pleasure the friendly intercourse between the Holy See and Mr. Taft as far back as 1902 when Mr. Taft, then Civil Governor of the Philippines, went to Rome to negotiate the question of the Friars lands in the Philippines.

ISIDOR STRAUS.

Isidor Straus, who, with Mrs. Straus, was on the Titanic, was one of the most famous merchants of his time. He was born in Rhenish Bavaria on February 6, 1845, and came to this country with his father, settling in Talbotton, Ga., in 1852, where he obtained a common school education, supplementing the same with a classical course at Collingsworth Institute.

At 16 years of age he was a volunteer in the Confederate Army, finding out, however, that at that time the officers of the army did not have sufficient guns to arm its men and wanted no boys. At the close of the war the family came to New York and organized the firm of L. Straus & Son to deal in earthenware. From the start the firm was successful, and branched out into porcelains and china, each son, as he became of age, being taken into the firm. From that time on the firm of L. Straus & Sons grew in reputation until its name was known throughout the business world.

It was in 1874 that the firm took charge of the china and glassware department of R. H. Macy & Co., and after the death of Mr. Macy the firm continued to devote itself to this part of the Macy business. In 1888 the brothers, Isidor and Nathan, entered the firm, and under the new management the business of the department store reached a high degree of development.

Mr. Straus was a member of the firm of Abraham & Straus, of which the late Abraham Abraham was for years the head. In connection with their department stores the Straus brothers have cut-glass factories in Germany, Switzerland and France.

The brothers of Isidor, Oscar and Nathan, have to as great a degree been in the public eye for years. The former was for many years Ambassador to Turkey, and a cabinet officer under President Roosevelt, while the philanthropies of Nathan, particularly in supplying pure milk for sick babies of the poor, has had worldwide attention. All the brothers have served the city in various honorary capacities.

It was when Mr. Cleveland became a presidential possibility that Isidor Straus began to take an active interest in politics, and when Mr. Cleveland was selected to a second term, Mr. Straus was prominently mentioned as Postmaster General. He refused to accept the post, however, but he was later elected to Congress and was a member of the Ways and Means Committee, being greatly interested in tariff legislation.

In almost every charitable and philanthropic institution in the city Mr. Straus appears as a supporter, and generally an active manager or director. He was also a director in several banking and financial institutions, among which are the Hanover National Bank, the New York County National Bank and the Birbeck Savings and Loan Company. He is vice president of the Chamber of Commerce and Board of Trade and vice president of the J. Hood Wright Memorial Hospital.

BENJAMIN GUGGENHEIM.

Benjamin Guggenheim, one of the most active of the family of that name, which has become so widely known because of the tremendous scope of its interests in the world of mines and mining, was born in Philadelphia, October 26, 1865. He was the fifth of the seven sons of Meyer Guggenheim, founder of the house of M. Guggenheim & Sons, who came to America from Switzerland in 1848. Benjamin Guggenheim married Miss Floretta Seligman, a daughter of James Seligman, the banker of Manhattan. There are three daughters.

To Benjamin Guggenheim is said to belong the credit of having turned the attention of his father and brothers to the smelting industry, where they soon became the dominant factor. This followed a visit to Leadville, Col., made by Benjamin when he was twenty years old, he having been designated by his father to take charge of the elder Guggenheim's interests in a mine there. A short time afterward Benjamin suggested to his father the building of a smelting plant at Pueblo, Col. The plant was established after much urging on the part of the young enthusiast, and he was placed at its head. This was the real foundation of the enormous fortune now represented by the Guggenheim interests. The original smelting plant was followed by others at Aguascalientes and Monterey, Mexico, and by an immense refining plant at Perth Amboy, N. J. Benjamin Guggenheim took charge of the works at Perth Amboy and managed them for several years. Then came the consolidation of the smelting industries here into the American Smelting and Refining Company —Smelters, on the stock market today—and the Guggenheims were its ruling factors.

Subsequent to the organization of "Smelters," Benjamin Guggenheim retired from business for a few years, taking a well-earned rest in Europe. When he returned to this country he established a company for the manufacture of mining machinery at Milwaukee, Wis., in 1903. Three years later this was merged with the International Steam Pump Company. He became chairman of the executive committee of the concern, serving in that capacity until he was made its president, in 1909. The company has seven great plants in this country and one in England. Its plant at Harrison, N. J., is enormous. More than 10,000 workmen are employed by the company in its various shops.

Senator Simon Guggenheim, of Colorado, is a brother.

FRANCI DAVIS MILLET.

Franci Davis Millet, artist, author and former newspaper correspondent, lived at 6 East Twenty-third street, Manhattan, and maintained a residence also on Broadway, Worcestershire, England. He was born in Mattapoisett, Mass., on November 3, 1846. He enlisted as a drummer in the Sixtieth Massachusetts Volunteers at the age of 18 years, and saw active service, within the year being promoted to acting assistant contract surgeon, Army of the Potomac.

After the war young Millet entered Harvard, where he was graduated in 1869, receiving an A.M. degree three years later. During the succeeding years he was secretary to the Massachusetts Commission to the Vienna Exposition, correspondent for the New York Herald, the London Daily News and the London Graphic during the Russo-Turkish war, director of decorations and then director of functions at the Chicago World's Fair, special correspondent of the London Times and Harper's Weekly at Manila during the Government's troubles in the Philippines; chairman of the United States Niagara Falls Commission, chairman of the advisory committee of the National Museum, secretary of the American Academy in Rome and of the American Federation of Arts, vice president of the Municipal Art Commission of this city, United States Commissioner-General to the Tokyo Exposition, and during this career received medals of honor from many societies and several Governments.

He was a member of the National Institute of Arts and Letters, the Society of Painters in Oil Colors, the G. A. R., and honorary member of the American Institute of Architects. He was the author of one or two fiction books and of fact tales based upon his own adventures. He married Elizabeth Greeley Merrill of Boston, March 11, 1879.

HENRY B. HARRIS.

News only of the death of Charles Frohman, Marc Klaw or Abraham Erlanger, among the men identified with the theatrical syndicate, would have caused a greater sensation in the theatrical profession than the tidings that Henry B. Harris was among the fated victims of the Titanic disaster.

Among the syndicate allies Henry B. Harris has been possibly the most active of the younger managers. His productions during the last ten years have been numerous, and for the most part worthy contributions to contemporary dramatic effort.

Mr. Harris in the past few years has directed the destinies of a number of popular stars, including Robert Edeson, Rose Stahl, Helen Ware and others.

His principal producing theater in New York has been the Hudson Theater, where both his own attractions and those of other syndicate managers have been presented. During the early part of the present season Mr. Harris added to his interests the former Hackett Theater, on West Forty-second street, which he renamed the Harris, and at which the opening attraction was a Harris attraction, Rose Stahl in the new Charles Klein play, "Maggie Pepper."

Mr. Harris won a tremendous success as the producer of Charles Klein's play, "The Lion and the Mouse," that was one of the pioneer productions in the list of plays dealing with "big business" and the conditions affecting the alliance between corporate wealth and politics.

Earlier in his career Mr. Harris, who was the son of William Harris, also a well-known theatrical manager, directed theaters in other cities, and was for a considerable period connected with the famous old Howard Athaneum in Boston. He later became a partner in the firm of Rich & Harris, that produced a number of plays on the circuit of medium-priced theaters.

"The Climbers," in which Amelia Bingham and a star cast appeared at the Bijou Theater, Manhattan, a few years ago, gave Mr. Harris his first firm foothold in the metropolis, and he soon after became manager of Robert Edeson, the Brooklyn actor, whom he launched as a popular and successful star. It was in 1903 that he acquired the Hudson Theater, in West Forty-fourth street.

Mr. Harris was born in St. Louis, in 1866, and his father, William Harris, now associated with Klaw & Erlanger, early identified himself with the theatrical syndicate, in which field Henry B. Harris remained.

Mr. Harris was president of the National Producing Managers of America and a director of the Theater Managers Association of Greater New York. He also was a member of the Friars and other organizations of theatrical people.

JACQUES FUTRELLE.

Jacques Futrelle, chiefly known for his authorship of "The Thinking Machine," a fantastic novel of wide popularity, amused and delighted large audiences in this country for nearly a decade with his unusual stories. Born in Pike County, Georgia, April 9, 1875, he was in newspaper work from 1890 to 1902, chiefly in Richmond, Va. He broke from this to embark as a theatrical manager, but returned to journalism in 1906, becoming a member of the staff of the Boston American. He had meanwhile done some short stories, but was not especially known as a writer until the publication of "The Chase of the Golden Plate," in 1906.

Mr. Futrelle was firmly established as a writer of fiction a short time later when "The Thinking Machine" was brought out. From this time on he also published many short stories in a number of the best known American magazines. His long stories of the type of "The Thinking Machine" are "The Simple Case of Susan," "The Thinking Machine on the Case," "Elusive Isabel," and "The Diamond Master."

Mrs. Futrelle, who was with her husband on the Titanic, also became known as a writer last year when she published "The Secretary for Frivilous Affairs." The two writers lived at Scituate, Mass., where Mr. Futrelle had an estate which he called "The Stepping Stones."

CHARLES MELVILLE HAYS.

Charles Melville Hays was president of the Grand Trunk and Grand Trunk Railway companies and was one of the most brilliant railroad men on the North American continent. His rise was meteoric. Born in 1856, at the age of 17 Charles Hays got his first job, which was a clerkship in the St. Louis office of a Pacific Coast railroad, at $40 a month.

At 21 he was secretary to the general manager of the Missouri Pacific and St. Louis, at $100 a month. At 28 he was private secretary to the general manager of the Wabash system, at $200 a month. At 29 he was general manager of this system at $12,000 a year.

At 33 he reorganized this system. At 40 he became general manager of the Grand Trunk at $25,000 a year. At 43 his salary was increased to $35,000. In 1900, at the age 44, he was made president of the Southern Pacific, at $55,000 a year, succeeding the late C. P. Huntington.

Meanwhile he had organized the Central Vermont Railway Company, supervised the completion of the Victoria Jubilee double span railroad bridge across the St. Lawrence River at Montreal; supervised the completion of the single span street arch bridge across the Niagara River at Niagara Falls; had double-tracked the Grand Trunk nearly the entire distance between Montreal and Chicago, and had held directorships and other offices in the Chicago and Western Indiana Belt Railway of Chicago, the Detroit Union Railway and Station Company, the Keokuk Union Station Company and other lines.

Sir Wilfred Laurier at a dinner of the Canadian Club in Manhattan once said of Mr. Hays:

"He is beyond question the greatest railroad genius in Canada. As an executive genius he ranks second only to the late Edward H. Harriman."

Mr. Hays lived at 27 Ontario avenue, Montreal.

WASHINGTON A. ROEBLING.

Washington A. Roebling, second, 31 years old, is known especially to Brooklynites because of the name he bears. He is of the third generation of the family which was so largely responsible for the successful construction of the Brooklyn Bridge.

He is a son of Charles G. Roebling, president of the John A. Roebling Sons Company of Trenton, N. J., the concern being formed about the name of the engineer who built the Brooklyn Bridge cables.

Young Roebling was one of the managers of the Mercer Automobile Works of Trenton, founded by the Roeblings. He had been known, also, as an automobile race driver. He had been touring in Italy and France in an automobile, with a friend, Stephen Blackwell, also of Trenton, prior to sailing on the Titanic.

FROM OTHER CITIES

Philadelphia, April 16—Among the passengers on the Titanic were some of the most prominent residents of this city. George D. Widener, a son of P. A. B. Widener, the traction magnate, and himself a widely known financier and sportsman, was returning with his wife and son from Europe, where they had gone for the purpose of purchasing a bridal trousseau for their daughter.

John B. Thayer, second vice president of the Pennsylvania Railroad, was accompanied by his wife and a young son.

Mr. and Mrs. Arthur Ryerson, their two daughters and a son, were returning to attend the funeral of another son, Arthur L. Ryerson, a Yale student who was killed in an automobile accident last week.

T. D. M. Cardeza, a wealthy sportsman and big game hunter, and his mother, Mrs. J. W. M. Cardeza, of Germantown, are widely known here.

Other passengers who are well known in society here and in New York are: William C. Dulles, whose country home is in Goshen, N. Y.; William E. Carter, who was accompanied by his wife and two children; Mrs. Thomas Potter, jr., and her daughter, Mrs. Boulton Earnshaw.

C. Duane Williams and his son, Richard Norris Williams, from Geneva, Switzerland, were on their way to visit relatives in this city.

Robert W. Daniel, a member of a banking firm here, made his home in the Southern Club.

San Francisco, April 16—Dr. Washington Dodge of this city, whose name appears on the passenger list of the Titanic, together with his wife and child, is widely known as an authority on taxation.

Walter N. Clark is the son of J. Ross Clark, vice president of the San Pedro, Los Angeles and Salt Lake Railroad.

Youngstown, O., April 16—Mr. and Mrs. George D. Wick and their daughter, Miss Natalie; Miss Caroline Bonnell and Miss Lily Bonnell, Birkdale, England, her cousin, were among the Titanic's passengers. The Wicks and Bonnells are among the wealthiest people of Youngstown.

Portland, Ore., April 16—F. H. Warren and wife, named in the Titanic's passenger list, live here. Mr. Warren is millionaire president of a packing company.

Herman Klaber, passenger, is a millionaire hop grower of Portland.

Minneapolis, Minn., April 16—Walter D. Douglas of Minneapolis, who, with his wife, was aboard the steamer Titanic, is a multi-millionaire and, with his brother, is owner of what is said to be one of the largest starch manufactories in the world at Cedar Rapids, Ia.

Mr. and Mrs. John Pillsbury Snyder, prominent in Minneapolis, who left here in January on their honeymoon trip to Europe, also were returning on the Titanic.

Pasadena, Cal., April 16—Countess Rothes, in the Titanic's passenger list, was on her way to Pasadena to spend the coming summer with her husband, Norman Evelyn Leslie, nineteenth Earl of Rothes and representative here for Scotland. He is now in New York, having left here a week ago to meet his wife there.

Brunswick, Me., April 16—Percival W. White, a Massachusetts cotton manufacturer, who was a passenger on the Titanic, makes his home in this town. Friends here say that he is accompanied by his son, Richard F. White, a senior at Bowdoin College, and not by Percival W. White, jr., as was first reported. No word has been heard from Mr. White since the accident to the liner.

Buffalo, N. Y., April 16—Edward A. Kent, whose name appears in the passenger list of the Titanic was one of the leading architects of this city. He had offices in Ellicott Square and lived at the Buffalo Club.

Rochester, N. Y., April 16—It is believed that three residents of the city were passengers on the Titanic: Howard B. Case of Ascot, England, who went from this city ten years ago as London manager for the Vacuum Oil Company; Stanley Fox, traveling man for a Rochester machine company, who sent a letter to the firm several days ago, saying he would sail on the Titanic, and Miss Lily Duncan, who was visiting abroad.

Troy, April 16—Among the passengers on the Titanic were A. O. Helverson of this city, foreign representative of Cluett, Peabody & Co., the collar manufacturers of Troy. Mrs. Helverson accompanied him and they were on their way to this country for a visit.

Cluett, Peabody & Co. received a telegram yesterday purporting to be a wireless from Mr. Helverson, stating that the Titanic had been disabled but was being towed to Cape Race. The wireless was sent to the New York office of the firm and was relayed to this city.

Chicago, April 16—Chicago was represented on the Titanic's passenger list by E. G. Lewy, member of the firm of Lewy Bros., jewelers.

The Moores had been visiting Europe with Ira Nelson Morris and family. The Morrises returned here last week.

St. Louis, April 16—Miss Georgette Madill, reported among the saved in the Titanic disaster, is one of the city's youngest heiresses. She is 15 years old. By an order of court a year ago she was awarded an annual "pin money" allowance of $7,500 to pay for her clothing and education until she became of age.

Miss Madill is the principal heir of Judge George A. Madill, who is a prominent banker of this city.

Cincinnati, O., April 16—Mrs. George M. Stone, mentioned in the list of the survivors of the Titanic, is from this city. She had been visiting a daughter in Cairo, Egypt, for the last year.

Detroit, Mich., April 16—George Floyd Eitemiller of this city was returning on the Titanic after a three months trip in Europe as the representative of a Cincinnati automobile company. He is a son of George Eitemiller, who for many years was wire chief at Pittsburg for the Western Union Telegraph Company.

Morgantown, W. Va., April 16—Mr. and Mrs. Lucian Smith of this city were passengers on the Titanic. They were completing a honeymoon trip around the world. Mrs. Smith is a daughter of Congressman Hughes of West Virginia.

Providence, R. I., April 16—Four Providence residents are known to have been passengers on the ill-fated Titanic. They include E. C. Ostby and his daughter, Helen, who were returning from a tour of Egypt; James Lamb, a theatrical man, who had been on a three months tour abroad, and Harry Sullivan, who was coming to make his home with his father in this city. Relatives have received no word from any of them.

Seattle, Wash., April 16—Hughes R. Rood, vice president and general manager of the Pacific Creosotin Company, whose name appears in the list of the Titanic's passengers, is a wealthy resident of this city who with his wife had been spending the winter on the Continent.

Mrs. Rood and her maid were to sail later.

Victoria, B. C., April 16—E. P. Coley of Victoria, who was among the passengers on the Titanic, is a land surveyor employed by the British Columbia government.

HOPE FOR MORE SURVIVORS

According to the last report from Captain Rostron of the Carpathia, there are about 800 survivors of the Titanic on board, which would show that 481 persons had been saved whose names had not been sent in by wireless.

Another wireless dated at sea from the Carpathia gave the information that Bruce Ismay, managing director of the White Star Line, has directed the Carpathia to turn to New York.

GRIEF IN PARIS

Paris, April 16—The American colony in Paris was plunged into profound grief this morning by the definite news of the stupendous loss of life caused by the wreck of the Titanic.

Hundreds of the permanent American residents and of the American tourists staying at the hotels had relatives on board.

All went to sleep last night comforted with the assurances cabled here that all had been saved, and it was only when they received their newspapers this morning that they learned the terrible toll of fatalities.

The White Star office was besieged by weeping women, several of whom had sons on board. Among these was Mrs. William Dulles, who left the office in a state of collapse supported by her friends.

There is hardly a leading hotel in Paris at which relatives of some of the passengers are not stopping, and these are waiting anxiously for any scrap of definite news.

It has been definitely established that Lady Duff-Gordon, who is known in Paris as "Lucille," in consequence of the name she has adopted in order to conduct her dressmaking business, sailed on board the Titanic with her husband, Sir Cosmo Edmund Duff-Gordon. They appear on the official list as Mr. Morgan and wife.

Robert Bacon, United States Ambassador to France, with his wife and daughter, had until a week ago planned to sail on board the Titanic, but in view of the delay in the arrival of Myron T. Herrick, his successor, Mr. Bacon decided to postpone his departure and to leave by the French liner France, on Saturday next.

Mrs. G. T. Levis and Miss A. K. Eastman, both of New York, now staying at the Hotel Meurice had engaged first class passages on the Titanic, but at the last moment transferred to the Olympic, sailing on April 24.

Among those in the second cabin who engaged their passages at the last moment at Cherbourg were Mrs. Irvan and Miss Lahman.

CAPTAIN WENT DOWN WITH SHIP, IS NEWS

"As It Should Be and as He Would Have Had It;" Says Friend.

HAD SPLENDID RECORD.

Captain Edward J. Smith Ranked All Commanders in Line's Service, Says Veteran Associate.

"The news is that Captain Smith went down with the ship. That is as it should be. It is as he would have had it. He would have gone mad had he lived. There was never a finer or more high-minded man sailed the sea."

This statement was made to The Eagle today by Captain John N. Smith, who is employed by the White Star Line, though in a minor capacity. But Captain John Smith was a sailing ship captain thirty years ago, under the merchant firm that gave Captain Edward J. Smith, commander of the ill-fated Titanic, his first command. He has had a life-long acquaintance with the man who was in charge of the ship that was lost.

"What could have caused the disaster?" Captain Smith was asked.

"God, only knows," he replied. "Captain Smith ranked all men in the service, and he ranked them because of carefulness, prudence, skill and long and valuable service.

Calls Icebergs Thugs of the Sea.

"The icebergs are the thugs of the sea. No man, no matter how careful, is safe from them."

The Captain Smith who talked today and the Captain Smith who has found his own tomb and the resting place of his brave ship up in that graveyard of the Atlantic coast off Cape Race and the Newfoundland banks, were captains together thirty years ago or more, under the firm of Rathbone & Co. of Liverpool. That was in the day of the gulls of the sea, the big sailing ships.

Captain Smith recalled those days this morning. His weather-marked rough face grew almost ashen under its burned in tan as he spoke of his old friend. His lips trembled and three times he wiped tears from his eyes of which no sailor need have been ashamed.

"It is terrible; terrible," he said, brokenly, as the picture of the disaster rose in his mind's eye.

He recalled, he said, the day that Captain Smith was given command of the great liner, the Olympic.

"He came down to the pier," he said, "and clapped his hand on my shoulder. 'Captain,' he said, 'they are making brave boats these days, and here I am in charge of the bravest of them, but there will never be boats like the sailing ships we used to take out of Liverpool. Those were the clippers that made old England the queen of the seas.' "

And the captain of the great line of steamers, the speaker went on, never felt the thrill on the bridge of one of the great floating palaces he had known as a rising sailor on the square-rigged ship.

Captain John Smith could not talk today of the accident itself. He bowed his head and choked back the tears. He is every inch a seaman, with the spirit of responsibility that has made the Anglo-Saxon seaman go to death without flinching in ten thousand battles with the great deep.

Titanic's Commander Had Never Had Serious Wreck Before.

Captain Smith until he took charge of the Titanic had never been in a serious wreck. He used to say that he had followed the sea all of his life and found it an uneventful career. He made this statement in 1907, when he came to these shores in charge of the Adriatic, on her maiden trip. He was a great believer in the art of the modern shipbuilder and contended that any decisive tragedy was practically impossible to one of the big, new liners. He said in 1907: "I will say I cannot imagine a condition which would cause one of the great new boats to founder. I cannot conceive of any vital disaster happening to the Adriatic. Modern shipbuilding has gone beyond that."

The first misfortune came into Captain Smith's life but recently. That was when the great Olympic, sister ship of the Titanic, was rammed by the British cruiser Hawke, off the Isle of Wight, on September 20, 1911. A great hole was stove into her steel ribs, and she was forced to put back to Southampton. The Hawke, even more badly damaged, put over to Portsmouth for repairs. The Hawke was at first blamed for the accident, but the British Court of Admiralty, after a long investigation, decided that her commander was blameless in the matter, inasmuch as his ship had been drawn out of its course and toward the Olympic by the tremendous suction of the Olympic's engines and the swish of water alongside her as she passed.

In February last, on her way over here, the Olympic, under Captain Smith, suffered another accident, when she lost a propeller blade at sea. She was able to complete her journey here, nevertheless, under her own steam.

But that no man fully knows the ways of the sea today's baffling tragedy proves. It almost seems as though the sea had trained this man, all through his uneventful career, for the supreme tragedy of modern sea-faring: had lulled him to sleep to find a tomb in the Atlantic's graveyard of great ships.

Captain Smith Planned to Retire After Bringing Titanic Out.

Captain Smith had announced to friends that after he had brought out the Titanic he was to retire for good and all from service on the sea. He said he had rounded out his time and he was going to take a rest. He would have retired with the highest honors which could have been accorded a merchant captain of his day.

Today shipping men recalled the fact that the White Star Line had gone in the face of the convention of the seas in giving the Titanic to Captain Smith. Sailors all said that after the commander's accident when in charge of the Olympic he should not have been sent out again by the firm. The fact that the firm did send the captain out again, and place him in charge of the greatest ship in the service, is taken to be full proof they did not think the Olympic accident due to his carelessness.

FREDERICK M. HOYT.

Frederick M. Hoyt, the prominent broker and yachtsman, was aboard the Titanic with his wife. Mr. Hoyt's offices are at 45 Broadway and his city home at 112 East Seventy-third street, Manhattan.

He has a beautiful summer home at Stamford, Conn. Few New Yorkers were as well known in yachting circles.

In 1900 he bought the yacht Isolde and spent his honeymoon, in 1906, aboard the yacht. Mrs. Hoyt was Miss Jane Ann Forby of Amsterdam, N. Y. Mr. Hoyt was commodore of the Larchmont Yacht Club in 1901 and he belonged to the Yale, Racquette and New York Yacht clubs, besides.

1500 DROWNED

EXTRA BOSTON AMERICAN EXTRA

VOL. 9—No. 27. BOSTON, TUESDAY, APRIL 16, 1912. Registered in U. S. Patent Office. ONE CENT.

LINER TITANIC SINKS; 866 PASSENGERS SAVED

NEW YORK, APRIL 16—BETWEEN 1200 AND 1500 PERSONS, PASSENGERS AND CREW, PERISHED WHEN THE "UNSINKABLE" TITANIC, THE $10,000,000 WHITE STAR LINER, WENT TO THE BOTTOM OF THE SEA, SO REPORT THE STEAMERS WHICH, IN ANSWER TO THE TITANIC'S WIRELESS CALLS FOR HELP, RUSHED TO HER AID. THERE IS LITTLE HOPE THAT THE DREAD REPORT IS NOT TRUE.

OF THE 2,200 SOULS WHO WERE ABOARD THE ONCE MIGHTY SHIP, BUT 866 WERE SAVED.

THE TITANIC, THE LARGEST, MOST LUXURIOUS—VAUNTED AS THE SAFEST—STEAMER THAT EVER SAILED THE SEAS, COLLIDED WITH AN ICEBERG AT 10:45 P. M. SUNDAY, IN ABOUT LATITUDE 41:46 NORTH, AND LONGITUDE 50:14 WEST. THAT IS, THE ILL-FATED BOAT WAS ABOUT 1200 MILES EAST OF SANDY HOOK AND ABOUT 900 MILES SOUTHEAST OF HALIFAX, N. S. SHE SANK AT 2.20 A. M. MONDAY.

WIRELESS STATION, CAMPERDOWN, N. S., APRIL 16.—MESSAGES FILTERING THROUGH HERE INDICATE THAT THE PASSENGERS IN THE LIFEBOATS FROM THE TITANIC HAD THRILLING EXPERIENCES:

"IN SEVERAL CASES THE ICE WAS SO HEAVY THAT THE BOATS COULD NOT FORCE THEIR WAY THROUGH IT. AS A RESULT MANY OF THEM BECAME WIDELY SEPARATED."

"MANY OF THE PASSENGERS IN THE LIFEBOATS WERE SCANTILY CLAD, HAVING BEEN HURRIED OUT OF THEIR BERTHS IN THE DEAD OF NIGHT AND ORDERED INTO THE BOATS."

"THE TRANSFER OF THE PASSENGERS TO THE LIFEBOATS WAS ATTENDED BY MUCH EXCITEMENT AND PANIC. WHILE IT IS IMPOSSIBLE TO FORM ANY ESTIMATE OF THE LOSS OF LIFE, IT IS BELIEVED THAT IT WILL BE ENORMOUS."

NEW YORK, April 16.—Most of those saved from the Titanic were women and children; the splendid rule of the sea prevailed, "women and children first."

These women and children, in boats against which ice floes crunched, were picked up by the Cunard steamer Carpathia.

Should it prove that no other vessel piked up any passengers of the sinking liner, this might mean that few of the men on board had been saved, as the proportion of women and children among the passengers was large. The same facts would likewise spell the doom of practically the entire crew.

230 WOMEN AND CHILDREN IN CABINS

In the cabins were 230 women and children, but it is not known how many there were among the 740 third-class passengers.

It was the Titanic's maiden voyage.

Wealthy persons who cross the ocean, often like to boast "I was on this or that steamer's firstrip across."

Many waited for the Titanic. Some of them were Mr. and Mrs. John Jacob Astor, Major Archibald Butt, military aide to President Taft; Charles M. Hays, president of the Grand Trunk Pacific of Canada, his wife and daughter; W. T. Stead, writer and correspondent of the Hearst newspapers; Benjamin Guggenheim, of the millionaire copper family; F. D. Millet, the artist, and J. G. Widener of Philadelphia; Mr. and Mrs. Isador Straus, J. B. Thayer, vice-president of the Pennsylvania Railroad, Henry B. Harris, the

SURVIVORS OF LINER TITANIC AS RECEIVED BY THE COMPANY

NEW YORK, April 16.—The following list of first-class passengers taken from the Titanic was recelvd at the White Star Line offices from Captain Haddock of the Olympia early today.

Harry Anderson.
Mrs. Edward W. Appleton.
Mrs. Rose Abbott.
Miss B. L. Burns.
Mrs. D. D. Cassibere.
Mrs. William M. Clark.
Mrs. B. Chaibinace.
Miss E. G. Crosbie.
Miss H. Rosebie.
Miss Jeane Hipack.
Mrs. L. V. B. Harry.
Mrs. Alexander Halverson.
Miss Margaret Bays.
Mr. and Mrs. Edward Kimberly.
Probably E. N. Kimball, Jr., of Boston.
F. A. Kenneyman.
Miss Elihu Kenchen.
Mrs. A. F. Leader.
Miss G. E. Langley.
Miss Bertha Lavory.
Mrs. Ernest L. Lines.
Miss Mary C. Lines.
Miss Margaret Lindstrom.
Gustav J. Lesleur.
Miss Georgetta Ara Amarill.
Mrs. Malcard.
Mrs. Tucker and maid.
Mrs. J. B. Thayer.
J. B. Thayer, Jr.
Henry Woomer.
Ella Ward.
Richard L. Williams.
Mrs. F. M. Warmer.
Miss Helen A. Wilson.
Miss Willard.
Mary Wioks.
Mrs. George Davidson and maid.
Mrs. J. Stewart White.
Mary Young.
Mrs. Thomas Potter, Jr.
Mrs. Edna S. Roberts.
Countess Rothes.
C. Rolmane.
Mrs. Susan B. Rogerson.
Wiley B. Rogerson.
Mrs. Arthur Rogerson.
Master Allison Rogerson and nurse.
Miss Kate T. Andrews.
Miss Nanette Panhart.
E. W. Allen.
T. D. Bishop.
H. Brank.
Miss A. Bassina.
Mrs. James Baxter.
George A. Baynton.
Miss C. Bonnell.
Mrs. J. M. Brown.
Miss G. C. Bowen.
Mr. and Mrs. B. L. Beckwith.
Thomas Wyle.
W. G. Hooper.
Alice Failure.
Miss Roberts.
Lucille Carter.
Mrs. Pinnings.
Allan Douglas.
Mr. and Mrs. M. L. Henry.
Mrs. W. A. Hooper.
J. Flynn.
Miss Emily Ryerson.
Master Allison Ryerson.
Miss Panhardt.
Mr. and Mrs. T. Bishop.
Miss A. Bassina.
Miss E. W. Allan.
Mrs. R. Douglass.
Miss Hilda Slya.
Mrs. P. Smith.
Miss J. M. Brown, Acton, Mass.
Mrs. James Baxter.
Miss Caroline Bonnell.
Mrs. George Brayton.
Miss A. Bassina.
Mrs. H. Blank.
Mrs. Ernest Lines.
Miss Bertha Lanery.
Mrs. Esther Ryerson.

theatrical manager and Mrs. Harris, and Colonel Washington Roebling, builder of the Brooklyn Bridge.

Besides, there were wealthy people from half a dozen other cities.

Colonel John Jacob Astor's private secretary sorrowfully said that he had given Colonel Astor up for lost. He, a yachtsman, would be the last man to leave a sinking vessel after seeing his wife and the other women in the boats.

SURVIVORS SUFFERED GREATLY

Nor is there more expectation that Captain Smith, of the Titanic, commodore of the White Star Line, has survived. As the company built larger ships Captain Smith has been promoted to the command of one after another, from the Olympic to the Titanic, for example. No braver or more experienced sailor ever trod a ship's bridge, his friends say; never would he desert the sinking Titanic.

Mrs. Cornelius Vanderbilt received a cablegram from Alfred G. Vanderbilt, her son, saying he had not sailed on the Titanic and was safe in London. This announcement was made at the Vanderbilt home.

While it seems most of the women and children were rescued, they suffered intensely. The boats that bore them were tossed in ice-covered waters and driven here and there wide apart. It is briefly but graphically told to the AMERICAN from the Marconi wireless station at Camperdown, N. S.

No hope is held out at the office of the White Star Line that a soul has survived to tell the story of th actual sinking of the leviathan.

Only by a miracle, it is pointed out, could any person who stood by the ship escape the great vessel's powerful suction as she sank to the bottom.

The Titanic carried the most notable list of passengers ever borne across the Atlantic by one vessel. Home-coming American tourists arranged their sailings weeks ago so as to ride the new wonder of the seas on her maiden voyage.

The collision of the Titanic with an iceberg is now known to have been

JOHN JACOB ASTOR AMONG LOST

a head-on crash that occured while the liner was proceeding at little less than her best speed. She was a day ahead of her schedule and it is considered probable that an attempt to make a record-breaking voyage was the hope of her crew when she entered the ice fields.

Her forward plates were completely wrecked, a gaping wound opening below her waterline and letting the water into her forward compartments. Her powerful pumps fought an even battle with the onrushing water for hours, but it was a losing battle.

In the meantime the life-boats were manned and into them were placed as many of the women and children as they could hold. These boats were put off while there was yet some hope of holding the leviathan afloat, until her wireless messages could bring help.

MEN SHOW BRAVERY.

Later and more comprehensive messages tell of great bravery on the part of the men passengers. There was a minimum of disorder.

John Jacob Astor, who, with his bride, was returning from their long honeymoon abroad, placed his bride in a lifeboat, saw her safely away, and then lent his assistance to getting the other women and children into the boats.

The work of getting the lifeboats away, the work of allaying the fears of the great crowd of passengers as much as possible, the work of keeping the pumps in operation and the engines throbbing—these tasks and countless others were directed by Captain Smith, the venerable commander of the Titanic, and, before her advent, the commander of the Olympic, who displayed almost superhuman power of mind and body as the world's most horrible sea disaster closed his long and honorable career on the high seas.

A wireless message from the Virginian states that the occupants of the small boats which she picked up have been transferred to the Carpathia, which is proceeding to New York.

Wire "S. O. S." Signal.

All through the night and until her wireless station was silenced over hundreds of miles of sea, from the antenna of the giant liner flashed the mystic and magic "S. O. S." the world's wide cry of distress on the ocean. Every wireless operator within range of the maimed vessel dropped her other messages to locate her, and meantime relayed the fatal three dots, three dashes and three dots to the world.

The collision occurred in latitude 41.46 north and longitude 50.14 west, 1,150 miles east of New York, and 450 miles south of Cape Race, the most westerly point of Newfoundland. Contrary to early surmises, there was no fog when the vessel struck—the weather was clear and the sea was calm. Almost as soon as the Virginian picked up the distress signal, as recorded by the operator on the Olympic, the Titanic's sister ship and next to her the largest vessel afloat. This was at midnight. At that hour the Olympic was 200 miles from New York enroute to Southampton.

The Olympic forged ahead under full steam, but tonight's wireless dispatches indicate that she reached the scene too late to be of any assistance.

Baltic to the Rescue.

The Baltic, famous for her rescue of the passengers of the steamer Republic when Jack Binns sat aloft and braved death to summon help, was the next ship to pick up the brief story of the Titanic's plight. She was on her way from New York to Liverpool, but turned about and put on full speed toward the Titanic's position.

The Parisian, according to her messages, reached the flotilla of rescuers shortly after the Baltic.

Not until Captain Haddock flashed "Horrible disaster" would the White Star officials believe that the mightiest ship ever launched had gone down on her maiden voyage.

The scene in the White Star offices tonight was pitiable. Brought to a realization of the stupendous wreck—the complete destruction of the fruit of their dreams—gray haired men, many of them veteran seamen, wept.

Vice-President P. A. S. Franklin of the White Star line said: "We have heard the rumor from Halifax that three steamers, the Virginian, Parisian and Carpathia stood by the Titanic. We have received a wireless from Captain Haddock of the Olympic that the Titanic went down at 2:30 A. M. We have also heard indifferently that the Titanic's list numbered 2,000. It is very difficult to say whether the Virginian and the Parisian have any survivors aboard until we get a report. We have asked for that report from our Halifax agents and from others.

"The Carpathia is proceeding direct to New York. W every much fear there has been a serious loss of life. But it is impossible at this time to assure ourselves that the other steamships have or have not survivors on board.

Not Fully Insured.

"The Titanic carried a sufficient number of lifeboats to get all her passengers off within four hours, and we are very hopeful that both the Virgian and the Parisian have passengers on board.

"The situation, however, is very serious. It looks like a horrible loss of life. The Titanic was supposed by experts to be unsinkable. She was insured, but not fully. Her value was between $7,500,000 and $8,000,000. Mr. Franklin said that Captain Haddock of the Olympic in his wireless dispatch did not make a report concerning the loss of life on board the Titanic."

Vice-President Franklin refuses to give out the full text of the message which he received from Captain Haddock of the Olympic, reporting the sinking of the Titanic. This attitude led to the belief that the message intimated a loss of life which the company desired to confirm before spreading alarm.

Mr. Franklin said that Captain Haddock's message was very brief and neglected to say all the crew had been saved.

The Allan line offices in Montreal announced the Virginian had re-transferred the passengers which she took from the Titanic to the Carpathia shortly after receiving them. This change was made because the Carpathia was bound for New York, while the Virginian was eastbound with mails.

A wireless message at Halifax at 10:52 o'clock last night from one of the vessels which went to the aid of the Titanic, said the loss of life on the Titanic would reach 1,800.

At 11 o'clock last night Vice-President Franklin issued the following statement at the White Star offices, No. 9 Broadway:

"Women First."

"We have received absolutely no definite news within the last two hours. The Virginian and the Parisian were not due alongside the Titanic until 10 A. M.

"There is no rule of the sea, but it is customary in cases of this kind for the women to be saved first. Even the women in the steerage would be taken off before the men passengers of the first and second cabin. This, however, does not apply to the women employes of the boat.

"We are hopeful of hearing from the Virginian and Parisian shortly. They both have low-powered wireless apparatus which carries only three hundred miles. It is certain that the Titanic went down before the arrival of the Carpathia.

"The survivors aboard the Carpathia were picked up from life boats. There were sufficient life boats on the Titanic to take off all the passengers. I hardly think that any of the life boats would have been lost through the suction when the ship went down.

"I am certain that if any one went down with the ship, Captain Smith was the man. We have no definite news of any single survivor.

"We have Marconied to every possible direction in an effort to obtain a list of the survivors. The Carpathia will arrive at New York late Thursday night or early Friday morning."

Late last night the steamship company's offices were besieged by a throng of persons who demanded word from loved ones aboard the ship. The officials, however, were unable to give assuring messages.

Astor's Son Weeps.

About half past ten o'clock, Vincent Astor, son of Colonel John Jacob Astor, accompanied by Mr. Dobbin, Colonel Astor's secretary, and Nicholas Biddle, young Astor's cousin, sped to the White Star offices in a touring car. They rushed to the offices of Vice-President Franklin and begged for information. Just what the young millionaire was told is not known, but when he reappeared on the street he was weeping.

He had only a short time before abandoned his trip to Halifax to meet his father. Mr. Franklin denied he informed the young man of the probable death of his parent. He did tell him, however, that all the women were taken off the sinking ship first.

Another caller at the office was the secretary of Mr. Isidor Straus. He learned nothing. The secretary said Jesse Straus, a son, was on the America, coming from Europe.

DORCHESTER MAN IS BELIEVED TO BE LOST; FAMILY PROSTRATED

Timothy J. McCarthy, passenger aboard the Titanic, was making his twenty-second voyage across the Atlantic and had been on the continent since last February as the purchasing agent of the Jordan Marsh Company. His home is at No. 52 Nelson street, Dorchester. He is married and has five children, Annie, age twenty-two; Mildred, age twenty; Justin, age seventeen; Edmund, age fifteen, and Brendan, age ten.

Mrs. McCarthy was prostrated when told of the disaster. A score of neighbors and relatives called at the residence and inquired for further information.

Mr. McCarthy is about fifty-one years old and has been in the employ of the Jordan Marsh Company since boyhood, rising from an inferior position to that of buyer of the stationery department. He was in the habit of visiting Europe annually and purchasing thousands of dollars' worth of goods.

The circulation of the AMERICAN is 300,000 more than its next highest competitor and 100,000 more than all the other evening papers of Boston combined.

TOLL OF 1,500 LIVES AND $22,000,000 IN WRECK

The loss represented by the sinking of the Titanic:

Probably 1,800

Value of the vessel, $10,000,000.

Value of jewels carried by women passengers, $5,000,000.

Baggage and mail, $2,000,000.

Loss from probable litigation and indemnities $5,000,000.

Left Southampton on Wednesday, April 10, on her maiden trip. Narrowly escaped collision with liner New York before leaving port when the small vessel was dragged from her moorings by the suction of the new liner.

Proceeded at top speed for New York until she struck huge iceberg at 10:25 Sunday night, 450 miles south of Cape Race.

Flashed wireless "S. O. S." as water flooded through hole in her forward plates.

Distress signal first picked up by the Allan Line steamer Virginian, and later by the Carpathia, the Baltic and the Parisian and several other vessels which were too far away to reach the vessel in time to render assistance.

Message stating the ship was sinking and the women were being taken off in small boats ended abruptly.

Information given out Monday afternoon stated all passengers had been taken off and the liner was being towed to Halifax.

This information discredited by a wireless message received in New York at 8:55 from liner Carpathia stating that Titanic had gone down with all on board, except 670 women and children.

At 9 o'clock officials of White Star Line in New York gave out message from Captain Haddock of the Olympic confirming the report of the great catastrophe. The disaster has been since confirmed from several sources.

It is probably the greatest disaster of modern times.

FEW MEN ARE AMONG RESCUED

John Jacob Astor Among Missing; His Bride Reported to Have Been Rescued.

The represntation of Boston and New England people among the passengers aboard the Titanic is comparatively small for this time of the year, but the list bears the names of some well-known people.

President E. N. Kimball, of the Hallett & Davis Piano Company and his wife were aboard, also President Arthur W. Newell of the Fourth National Bank, and his two daughters, Madeline and Marjorie, who were touring Europe. The Kimball's and Newells were among the saloon passengers on the fated ship and their names di not appear upon the incomplete list of passengers saved. Mrs. Newell is in New York, having left her Lexington home to meet her husband and daughters upon their arrival in that city.

One of the first of the names among the saved aboard the Carpathia is that of Mrs. J. M. Brown, of East Acton, whose two sons, Murray and Robert, left their home yesterday, one going to New York and the other to Halifax, not knowing where the rescue boat would land. At the time they left Boston they did not

John Jacob Astor and his bride. Colonel Astor has been given up by his family as among those who sank with the Titanic.

know whether their mother had been saved.

Others on the passenger ilst from New England were E. C. Ostby, the Providence, R. I., jeweler, and his daughter, Helen Ostby.

Maxwell Norman, the well-nown clubman of Boston and the North Shore, is saved by having, by force of an urgent business engagement, being detained, to sail alter on the Oceanic. He changed his mind so late that his name apeared on the Titanic sailing list.

Brockton People Aboard.

Brockton is interested in the fate of John E. Maguire, a salesman of the Dunbar Pattern Company and George Q. Clifford of the Belcher Last Company of Stoughton; Walter C. Potter, a last manufacturer of Worcester, is also on the passenger list.

wife, of Scituate, were two of the widely known passengers which the steamship much popular fiction, including "The Thinking Machine," and his wife is also a writer of note. The Futrelles, who are popular ony," and who were coming there for the Summer, had spent the Winter in Italy. They had made especial efforts to catch the Titantic.

George Q. Clifford, president of the Belcher Last Company of Stoughton, was another passenger. He was returning from a two months' tour of England, Germany, Russia, France and Austria.

He is one of the town's leading business men, the company being the town's largest industry and the world's largest last factory. Mr. Clifford has a wife and daughter living in Stoughton.

Miss Elizabeth M. Eustis of No. 1020 Beacon street, Brokline, who was also a passenger, was accompanied by her sister, Mrs. Walter B. Stephenson of Haverford, Pa. They left New York on the Cunarder Caronia about eight weeks ago and sailed to Mediterranean ports. For two or three weeks Eustic and her sister toured southern Europe, then going to Cherbourg. From there they started homeward on the Titanic.

Percival W. White, of Whichendon, accompanied by his son Richard, and the latter's wife, went aboard on the Olympic for the express purpose of making the trip on the maiden voyage of the new Titanic. Mr. White, who is a member of the firm of Nelson D. White & Son, cotton manufacturers, has a penchant for maiden voyages and laid his plans for the trip as soon as the date of sailing was announced. This is his thirtieth trip.

Like McCarthy, H. H. Hilliard of No. 40 Hichborn street, righton, was an old and trusted employe of the Jordan Marsh Company. The two were traveling together after an extended buying trip through Europe. They left for Europe February 13. Hilliard is married and has a married daughter, Mrs. Leon G. Chase of Somerville.

Others From Boston.

Mr and Mrs. Clarence Moore of Washington have resided on the North Shore in summer, their home being "Swiftmore," one of the show places at Pride's Crossing. Mrs. Moore was Miss Mabelle F. Swift, daughter of the late E. C. Swift. Their home is at No. 1746 Massachusetts avenue, Washington, where Mrs. Moore has been during her husband's absence abroad. He went to Europe about a month ago.

John Bradley Cumings is a Boston man and formerly was connected with the Boston office of Estabrook & Co. About ten years ago he went to New York for that firm and later entered the brokerage business for himself. He and Mrs. Cumings went abroad six weeks ago. Mrs. Cumings was Miss Florence B. Thayer.

Although a New York girl, Miss Gretchen N. Longley, one of the Titanic's passengers, was well known in social circles of Boston. Only two years ago she was one of the graduates at the fashionable Quincy Mansion schol for girls, Wollaston. At the schol yesterday the girls who had known her and the teachers under whom she studied expressed anxiety at her fate.

PASSENGERS SAVED ARE MOSTLY WOMEN AND CHILDREN—FEW OF CREW LEFT.

Her home was in Hudson, N. Y. At the close of her school career, arrangements were made for her to complete her education by a trip abroad. She was returning from a five months' stay in Europe.

Walter C. Porter, who is included in teh list of first cabin passengers, is a Worcester man, and connected with the Porter Last Company of that city, founded by his father. He has always been prominent in the Lakeside Boat Club of that city. Mr. Porter was returning from a brief European trip.

State street circles were made especially anxious for news of President Newell of the Fourth National bank, with his two daughters.

In this city Mr. Newell is widely known, being one of its most prominent business men. He is a leading citizen at Lexington ad his daughters stand high in society there.

Mr. Newell ad his daughters also visited the Holy Land and stopped at several cities in Egypt. He was in continental Europe only a few days. Great anxiety for sis safety was manifested last night by the officials with whom Mr. Newell is associated at the bank.

Mr. and Mrs. Kimball sailed from New York March 6 on the Cedric, en route for the Mediterranean, wher they intended to take a rest for some time. Among the places visited were Naples, Italy, Switzerland, France and England. Frequent postcards have been received at the office telling of their continued good health and enjoyment of the trip, while one of the latest received mentioned their contemplated return on the maiden voyage of the Titanic. Mr. Kimball is about forty years old and lives at 859 Beacon street. He is a member of the Boston Athletic Association and other clubs.

H. B. Harris, Theatrical Man, Aboard.

Henry B. Harris, the theatrical manager, Titantic, is known as one of the most popular men in his profession, and Boston's theatrical circles were shocked when the news of his possible death was received.

Mr. Harris was born in St. Louis December 1, 1866, the son of William Harris, of Rich & Harris. He received his early education in thes chools of his native city, but when a young lad the family moved to Boston, where his father at that time was manager of the Howard Athenaeum. Young "Harry" broke into the game when only fourteen, and under the able tutelage of his father, made rapid strides in the theatrical profession.

His first big exploit as manager was with May Irwin, and later he became manager of Pete Daly, Lily Langtry, Amelia Bingham, and was the first to recognize the histrionic ability of Robert Edeson. Recently he has been conneeted with "The Country Boy," of which he was the original producer, and "The Talker," a New York success. Rose Stahl and Elsie Ferguson have also been under his management during the past few seasons. Three of theg reatest successes of the past decade have been produced by Mr. Harris. They are: "The Lion and the Mouse," "The Traveling Salesman" and "The Third Degree."

He has been manager of the Hudson, the Forty-second Street and the Fulton theaters in New York for several years, and has also been president of the Henry B. Harris Co., National Producing Managers of America; director of the Association Metropolis Theater Co., and of the Theater Managers' Association of Greater New York; treasurer of the Actors' Fund of America, and trustee of the Hebrew Infant Asylum of New York. He is a member of the Lambs' Club and Green Room Club of New York.

He was married to Miss Irene R. Wallach of Washington on October 22, 1898. The couple have had no children.

A Massachusetts man aboard was Frank D. Millet, an artist with an international reputation. He was born in Mattapoisett, went out during the Civil War as a drummer boy and was graduated later from Harvard University.

His brother, Josiah B. Millet, is a Boston man and the president of a music-publishing firm in this city. The two brothers were planning to meet in New York next Sunday.

LINER'S SURVIVORS SUFFER MUCH

NEW YORK, April 16.—Bad luck has come to Captain E. J. Smith, commander of the Titanic and commodore of the White Star Line, after forty years on the sea, during which time he worked up from apprentice to commander of the largest steamship in the world.

During all this time, up to last September, when his steamer, the Olympic, then, as now, with the sinking of the Titanic, the queen steamship of the world, crashed into the British cruiser Hawke, he did not figure in a single disaster.

Since then, however, misfortune has come thick and fast, for in February the Olympic struck what is believed to have been a submerged wreck and lost a blade from one of her propellers, which made it necessary to put her in dry dock, and last Wednesday the Titanic, in leaving Southampton on her maiden voyage, narrowly missed colliding with the New York of the American Line, which had been pulled from her anchorage by suction from the new ocean giant.

Retained His Command.

It was undoubtedly because of Captain Smith's previous fine career that the officers of the White Star Line retained him in its service after the mishaps to the Olympic, thus violating a deep sea tradition that has been more rigorously maintained by the British merchant marine than by any other nation. The rule has been almost invariably among steamship companies to dispense with the officers in command of vessels that have met with disaster.

One reason for this is the insistence of the insurance companies. Lloyds keeps in its London office the records of all marine officers, so that when a man is put in command of a vessel his whole career can be immediately inspected.

Much interest attaches to the fate that now awaits Captain Smith if he has survived. If proved at fault in the collision of the Titanic with an iceberg—and this will depend in great measure on the degree of vigilance used after the delicate instruments all vessels now carry warned of the vessel's proximity to ice—he may not only be deprived of his command, but also of his certificate, which will force him to give up the sea.

Are Extremely Strict.

A few steamship companies, among them the North German Lloyd, have shown leniency toward officers whose previous records were good and have given them a second chance, provided the vessel had not been a total loss. The question arises: Has Captain Smith already had his second chance, and would he be given a third? The White Star Line has been among the strictest of the British companies in this regard, as is evidenced in the fate of Captain Inman Sealby, who commanded the Republic when she sank in collision with the Italian line steamship Florida, on January 23, 1909. No blame was attached to Captain Sealby for faulty navigation or bad seamanship in handling the vessel, and in all his sea career he had been with the White Star, without figuring in a wreck. Nevertheless, he was dismissed, after going to the University of Michigan to study admiralty law.

Began Career in 1869.

Captain Smith began his sea career in 1869, when he shipped as apprentice on the Senator Weber, an American clipper purchased by Gibson & Co. of Liverpool. In 1876 he got a commission as fourth officer of the square-rigger Lizzie Fennel, and in 1890 was appointed fourth officer of the old steamship Celtic of the White Star Line, which subsequently was sold to the Thingvalla Company and renamed the America. He attained the rank of captain in 1887, when he took command of the old Republic, later going to the old Baltic. Next he was in command of the old freighter Cufic and then of the Runic. Afterward he went to the old Adriatic, then the Celtic, Brittanic and Coplic in the Australian trade.

It was in 1892 that the White Star Line bestowed its first great honor on Captain Smith, when it made him commander of its best steamship, the Majestic, on Mediterranean voyages. Since that time he has commanded every large steamship of the White Star Line on her initial trip. When he was put in command of the Titanic it was reported that he would retire after he had conducted her across the Atlantic and back, but the White Star officials afterward announced that he would have charge of the Titanic until the company built a larger and finer steamship.

Captain Smith had the utmost confidence in the safety of the ocean giants that are now being constructed. In 1907, when he came to New York in command of the Adriatic on her maiden trip, he said: "Shipbuilding is such a perfect art nowadays that absolute disaster, involving the passengers, is inconceivable. Whatever happens, there will be time enough before the vessel sinks to save the life of every person on board. I will go a bit further. I will say that I cannot imagine any condition that would cause the vessel to founder. Modern shipbuilding has gone beyond that.

"When anyone asks me how I can best describe my experiences of nearly forty years at sea I merely say uneventful. In all my experience I have never been in an accident worth speaking of."

An officer of the Adriatic who heard part of Captain Smith's remarks put in: "Don't forget when you write of the captain's uneventful life to put in that it is the great captain who doesn't let things happen."

Last December, on arriving at New York with the Olympic, a banquet was given to Captain Smith at the Metropolitan Club, and among the guests were General Stewart L. Woodford, Chauncey M. Depew, W. H. Truesdale and W. A. Nash.

Among the marine officers who have been dismissed in the past were Captain Wright of the Norse King, who, with 2,504 passengers on board, went ashore on the Island of Zanta in April, 1893. The Norse King was cruising along seven miles from shore when a deputation of women passengers begged him to go nearer, so that they might see the picturesque village. He obliged them and his vessel crashed into a reef. The passengers lived three weeks on Zanta, living on dried currants, figs, wild pig and goats' cheese. The Norse King was a total loss, and Captain Wright had his certificate suspended for a year.

Captain LeHorn ended his career by letting his vessel, the China, crash into a reef off Perim Island, in the Red Sea in 1897, while he was enjoying a birthday dinner provided by Lady Brassey, one of the passengers. He ignored notes sent down by the second officer, asking that the course be changed. This disaster led to an order forbidding officers to associate with passengers, which caused 400 officers to resign.

AMERICAN GETS WIRELESS NEWS IN NEW YORK OFFICE

MARCONI STATION, WANAMAKER STORE, New York, April 16.—The wireless office of the Wanamaker stores at Broadway and Eighth streets, conducted jointly by John Wanamaker and the Marconi Wireless Telegraph Company, were converted into a branch office of the Hearst newspapers.

"Jack" Binns, the hero of the Republic-Florida disaster, when he shot to the world the wireless "C. Q. D." and saved the lives of over 2,000 passengers and crew, took charge.

The office was directed by David Sarnoff, manager of this station, assisted by J. H. Hughes, an expert Marconi operator. With every bit of energy at their command the men stood by their work and fired scores of messages and caught many concerning the wreck. From all over the coast line and far into the interior, even to Chicago, appeals for news of the disaster were heaped upon the temporary office.

The Wanamaker Marconi office is located on the roof of the famous department store and is one of the most powerful along the Atlantic seaboard. Through all the pandemonium of wireless conversation and confusion which prevailed, this station managed to pick up direct communication with Siasconsett, Sagaponack, Cape Cod, Hatteras, Sable Island and many other stations along the coast.

Faint signals were heard from the Olympic, but owing to the terrible confusion and disruption of static conditions, Mr. Hughes was unable to pick up the strands of direct communication. Other New York offices were unable to report any communication at all with the Olympic. Here are some of the wireless messages picked up:

CAPE RACE, Newfoundland, April 15.—The latest advices from the Olympic state she is in the zone of disaster. Olympic confirms that steamship Carpathia reported the position last reported by the Titanic as 41:46 N. and 50:14 West about daybreak.

CAPE RACE, N. F., April 15, 9:55 p. m. Orders to cancel the special train for passengers for Halifax to New York, we are now informed, means that the Carpathia is headed direct for New York.

Bringing in Survivors.

HALIFAX, N. S., April 15.—Orders have been countermanded for the special train to convey the surviving Titanic passengers to New York. It is believed here that the Carpathia, carrying the surviving members of the crew and passengers is trying to make either New York or Boston.

HOW THE WIRELESS HAS RESCUED MANY IN OCEAN DISASTERS

These are some of the rescues made through the instrumentality of wireless:

The White Star line steamship Republic, sunk off Nantucket on January 23, 1909, by the Italian liner Florida. The Republic had just left New York and was going through a thick fog. Jack Binns made famous the "C. Q. D." call, and about 1,000 persons were saved and brought to port on the Baltic.

Cunard liner Slavonia, wrecked off the Azores. This was on June 10 of last year. Again the "C. Q. D." was sent out and two steamers were brought to the aid of the wrecked vessel.

200 Taken Off.

City of Racine, of the Goodrich line, in June, 1909, while on her way from Chicago to Milwaukee, broke her propeller off Waukegan. Wireless brought the steamers Chicago and Christopher Columbus. The former took off her 200 passengers and the latter towed her to Chicago.

Arapahoe, of the Clyde line, New York for Charleston, broke her shaft on August 11, 1909, when twenty-one miles southwest of Diamond Shoals. She anchored until the Iroquois of the same line came in answer to the wireless call and towed her to port.

Steamship Ohio foundered off the Alaskan coast on August 17, 1909. Wireless Operator George E. Eccles stuck to his key until he lost his life. His "S. O. S." call brought help and the 150 passengers and most of the crew were saved.

Kentucky, sunk on February 4, 1910, off Hatteras. She was bound from New York for San Francisco. The wireless brought help, and those on board were transferred to the Mallory liner Alamo just before the steamer sank.

The Maine Steamship Company's steamer Horatio Hull was sunk off Handkerchief Shoal, near Nantucket, in collision with the H. F. Dimock of the Metropolitan line. This was on March 10, 1909. Wireless brought timely aid.

Thirty-two Saved.

Brewster, from Jamaica, went to the bottom in a gale near Hatteras. The wireless operator on the Diamond Shoal sent out an appeal for help, which resulted in the rescue of the men, thirty-two in all, by the life-savers. This was on November 29, 1909.

Puritan of the Graham & Morton line lost her rudder in a winter storm on Lake Michigan. Twenty-three hours after the accident she was met by a tug sent out in reply to the wireless "danger" call, and towed to Chicago. This happened in November.

Nueces of the Mallory line went ashore on French Reef, the Florida coast, in December, 1909. Wireless brought the government steamer Osceola to her assistance.

Iroquois, bound from New York to Charleston in December, lost her rudder. Wireless brought several steamships to her assistance, and she was towed to Charleston.

Respond to S. O. S.

Algonquin, Boston for Galveston, broke her shaft in a December blizzard off the North Carolina coast. The "S. O. S." call brought another vessel of the Clyde line, and she was brought to port in safety.

Antilles of the Southern Pacific Company went ashore sear Key West in October. She was bound from New Orleans to New York. Vessel and those on board saved by wireless appeal.

WRECKAGE LEFT OF TITANIC

GIANT OF SEAS PLUNGES AT POINT WHERE OCEAN IS TWO MILES DEEP

NEW YORK, April 16.—Vice-President Franklin of the White Star Line positively refused to give out the full text of the message which he received from Captain Haddock of the Olympic, reporting the sinking of the Titanic. This attitude led to the belief that the message hinted a loss of life which the company desired to confirm before spreading alarm.

Mr. Franklin said that Captain Haddock's message was very brief and neglected to say that all the crew were saved. It said that the Carpathia had 600 or 700 of the Titanic's passengers aboard, including all of the saloon passengers, and that the vessel should reach New York Friday morning.

No information had been received from the Virginian or Parisian at the White Star Line offices, although it was said to be "known" that many of the Titanic passengers were on board these vessels.

Vice-President Franklin said that he had cancelled arrangements for the special trian which they had planned to send to Halifax to bring the rescued passengers to this city by rail as it was believed that the boats which had Titanic passengers aboard would steam direct for New York.

Mr. Franklin continued: "As far as we know it has been rumored from Halifax that three steamers have passengers on board, namely, the Virginian, the Carpathia and Parisian. Now, we have heard from Captain Haddock that the Titanic sunk at 2:20 yesterday morning. We have also learned from him that the Carpathia had 675 survivors on board. It is very difficult to learn if the Virginian and the Parisian have any survivors on board. We have asked Captain Haddock and our agent at Halifax to ascertain if there are any passengers aboard the two steamships."

Mr. Franklin said there were sufficient lifeboats to take all the passengers from the Titanic. He said he was confident when he made the statement that "the Titanic was unsinkable" that the steamship was safe and that there would be no loss of life. The first definite news received came in the message from Captain Haddock, he said, and was given to the Press at once.

Mr. Franklin at 8:40 conceded that there had been "a horrible loss of life." He said that he had no information to disprove the press report from Cape Race to the effect that only 675 of the passengers and crew had been rescued.

He said that the monetary loss could not be estimated, although he intimated that it would run into millions.

"We can replace the money," he added, "but not the lives."

The text of the message received from Captain H. J. Haddock of the Olympic as made public by Mr. Franklin reads:

"At 2:20 a. m. Titanic foundered. Carpathia proceeding to New York with passengers."

One of Mr. Franklin's assistants, in announcing earlier that the Titanic had gone down, said that the Carpathia was proceeding to New York "with survivors."

MANY PASSENGERS ON WRECKED LINER FROM PHILADELPHIA

PHILADELPHIA, April 16.—Among the passengers on the ill-fated Titanic were some of the most prominent residents of this city. George D. Widener, a son of P. A. B. Widener, the traction magnate, and himself a widely known financier and sportsman, was returning with his wife and son from Europe, where they went to buy a bridal trousseau for their daughter.

John B. Thayer, second vice-president of the Pennsylvania Railroad, was another prominent passenger. He was accompanied by his wife and a young son.

Mr. and Mrs. Arthur Ryerson, their two daughters and a son were returning to attend the funeral of another son, Arthur L. Ryerson, a Yale student, who was killed in an automobile accident last week.

T. D. M. Cardeza, a wealthy sportsman and big game hunter, and his mother, Mrs. J. W. M. Cardeza of Germantown are also widely known her.

Other pasengers who are well known her and in New York are: William C. Dulles, whose countr yhome is in Goshen, N. Y.; William E. Carter, who was accompanied by his wife and two children; Mrs. Thomas Potter, Jr., and her daughter, Mrs. Boulton Earnshaw.

C. Duane Wiliams and his son, Richard Norris Williams, from Geneva, Switzer land, were on their way to visit relatives in this city.

Robert W. Daniel, a member of a bank ing firm here, made his home at the Southern Club.

RESCUE REPORT BY VIRGINIAN AS UNCONFIRMED

MONTREAL, April 16.—The two Allan line steamships Virginian and Parisian, toward the scene of the disaster, to the Titantic, had not reported to the company's headquarters here late last night any definite news of what they had done.

wireless to the effect that she rescued a number of passengers and then transferred them to the Carpathia was not confirmed. The general passenger agent of the line, George Hannah, thinks the Virginian arrived too late to be of any assistance, and being a mail boat she proceeded on her voyage. he may not be in touch with the world until she nears the Irish coast.

Mr. Hannah thinks, however, that the Parisian may have arrived in time to be of assistance to the Titantic. If she did, he thinks she would probably have spent possible, saved some.

CARMANIA NEAR BIG ICE FIELDS ON TRIP ACROSS

NEW YORK, April 16.—J. W. Welsford, a Liverpool shipowner, who has just reached New York on the liner Carmania, gave an interesting account of the ice fields the ship encountered off the grand banks on Thursday.

"I have crossed the ocean nearly a hundred times," he said, "but never before have I seen ice so far south and in such a great body.

"An interesting feature of the field," he continued, "was the fact that the sea, although presenting a surface like glass, was mountainous. A thick fog necessitated frequent stops and when the fog temporarily lifted bergs were discernable off both port and starboard.

The most impressive features were the numerous 'growlers"—large bergs that had melted on top until almost awash by the sea. In bad or failing lights they were extremely difficult to discern, and very dangerous because of the great quantity of ice below the waterline.

"The Carmania, after spending most of the day trying to navigate a passage through the field, decided to put about. Thus she made a passage to the south and avoided further damage."

TAFT ANXIOUS OVER SAFETY OF AIDE, MAJ. BUTT

WASHINGTON, April 16.—President Taft was anxious today for news of his aide, Major Archibald W. Butt, one of the four Washington folk on the Titanic. The President had frequent inquiries made at newspaper offices and the steamship agency.

No word has been received at the homes of Frank D. Millett, the artist; Col. Archibald Gracie or Clarence Moore, the three other Washingtonians aboard.

TITANIC CARRIED FOREIGN MAIL FOR PORT OF BOSTON

Postal officials are anxious over the accident to the White Star liner, Titanic, because a large amount of Boston mail is on the liner. An effort was made to ascertain how much mail for Boston was on the steamer, but this was impossible as no word was sent in advance of the steamer's sailing from England.

Superintendent of Mails Reed at the central postoffice stated that he expected the Titanic would carry considerable of the foreign mail destined for this port. He communicated with Foreman Barrett of the foreign division, but was unable to get even an approximate estimate of how large the Boston mail on the liner is.

The mail for Boston will in all probability be many days late in reaching here it is is saved.

J. G. PHILLIPS WAS WIRELESS-MAN ON STRICKEN TITANIC

NEW YORK, April 16.—The wireless operator on the Titanic, who sent out the "S. O. S." message when she struck the iceberg, is J. G. Phillips, formerly employed as a wireless operator on James Gordon Bennett's yacht. Later, he worked on the steamship Oceanic, from which he was transferred to the new Titanic.

HEAVY LOSS ON VALUABLES AND MAILS CARRIED DOWN WITH ICE BERG-BATTERED CAFT

Mrs. Cornelius Vanderbilt has received a cablegram from Alfred G. Vanderbilt, her son, saying that he did not sail on the Titanic, but is safe in London.

This announcement was made at the Vanterbilt home.

JACK BINNS TELLS HOW WIRELESS MAN SENDS S. O. S. CALLS

By JACK BINNS.

(Wireless operator on the ill-fated steamer Republic and the hero of the first disaster in which the wireless prevented loss of life).

NEW YORK, April 16.—That there has been an appalling loss of life with the sinking of the liner Titanic was not due to the failure of her wireless, for her operator stuck to his post until he had flashed the Marconi distress signal to all the world. This signal was "S. O. S.," meaning "Save Our Souls."

After the distress that befell the Republic the "C. Q. D.," made famous by that catastrophe, was abandoned on account of the confusion caused by its incessant use by amateur wireless operators. When the "S. O. S." goes out every ship within receiving distance is instantly alert.

The Titanic's equipment enabled her to reach every ship within a radius of 3,000 miles, under good atmospheric conditions. The "S. O. S." goes out in three dots, three dashes, three dots, in the International code, which was used by Operator Phillips on the Titanic.

If transmitted in American Morse code the flash would be three dots, two dots with a space between, three dots.

The operator receives this call through his headgear in a faint cracking, not unlike a stock ticker's sound.

"The sinking ship is 200 miles away," signals the operator to the officer's bridge of the ship from which aid is sought. Signals are flashed to the engine room, forced draught is put to the engines, the propellers turn with every ounce of the engines' power behind them and the race to save lives is on.

HUNT IN NEW YORK FOR DORR

The warrants for the arrest of William A. Dorr, of Stockton, Calif., and of an alleged accomplice, for whom a warrant was asked under the name of John Doe, in connection with the murder of George E. Marsh, the wealthy soap manufacturer, have been sent to New York, where the most vigorous search for the two men is being pushed. It is believed that Dorr went to New York.

The finding of the autoombile bought by Dorr and identified by half a dozen witnesses as the machine connected with the crime, together with the discovery of Marsh's cane and hat, have done much to aid the police in their search.

However, there are still gaps and inconsistencies in the testimony which the police are unable to bridge.

The cane was found before Marsh was supposed to have been last seen. This makes necessary a new theory as to the time of the murder, and must either discredit the story of those who declared they saw Marsh on the evening of Thursday at 6 o'clock or else that of the finedr of the cane.

$2,500 in Rewards.

The sum of $2,500 is now offered for the arrest and conviction of the murderer. The AMERICAN offered $1,000 for exclusive information that would lead to his arrest and conviction. Arthur E. Marsh has come forward with another $1,000, and the city of Lynn offered $500 reward.

Napoleon Des Rosier, a carpenter of No. 444 Lawnsdale avenue, East Saugus, who found on Thursday afternoon an automobile cap and walking stick which was later identified by Caleb Marsh as belonging to his brother George, said:

"I was coming down the boulevard from the Point of Pines where we are putting up some houses when I saw the cap and the cane lying in the middle of the road about half way between the Lynnway Club and the drawbridge. It was tehn 4:50, as nearly as I can estimate; the cap lay some twenty-five feet near the point than the stick.

WORST SEA TRAGEDY IN HISTORY

WHITE STAR LINE OFFICIALS NOW ADMIT "HORRIBLE DISASTER"—SHIP SANK MONDAY

NEW YORK, April 16.—More than 1,500 persons, it is feared, sank to their death when the mammoth Titanic went to the bottom off the Newfoundland Banks.

Of the nearly 2,200 persons on board the giant liner, some of them of world-wide prominence, only 675 are known to have been saved.

Accepting the early estimates of the fatality list as accurate, the disaster is the greatest in the modern marine history of the world.

Nearest approaching it in magnitude were the loss of the steamer Atlantic in 1873, when 574 lives were lost, and that of La Bourgogne in 1898, with a list of fatalities of 571.

Should it prove that other liner notable the Allan liners, Parisian and Virginian, known to have been in the vicinity of the Titanic, picked up others of her passengers, the extent of the calamity may fortunately be greatly reduced. This hope still remains.

Last Hope Gone.

News of sinking of the liner and the consequent loss of life reached New York with a much greater shock because hope had been buoyed up all day by reports that the steamship, although badly damaged, was not in a sinking condition and that all her passengers had been safely taken off.

The messages were mostly ounofficial, however, and none came direct from the liner, so that a lurking fear remained of possible bad tidings to come.

Finally there came flashing over the wires from Cape Race, within 400 miles of which, in the treacherous region of the Newfoundland Banks, the huge liner struck the berg, that at 2:20 o'clock Monday morning, three hours and fifty-five minutes after receiving her death blow, the Titanic sank.

The news came from the steamer Carpathia and it was relayed by the White Star Liner Olympic. It revealed that by the time the Capathia, outward bound from New York, and racing for the Titanic on a wireless call, reached the scene, the ill-starred vessel had disappeared.

Found Fleet of Lifeboats.

Left on the surface, however, were lifeboats from the Titanic, and in them, as appears from the meager reports received up to a late hour, were some 675 survivors of the disaster.

For the rest, the scene at the Carpathia came was one of desolation. All that remained of the $10,000,000 floating palace, on which nearly 1,400 passengers were luxuriously traveling to this side of the Atlantic, were bits of wreckage.

The biggest ship in the world had gone down, snuffing out in her downward plunge, it appeared, hundreds of human lives.

A significant line in the dispatch from Cape Race was the statement that of those women and children.

hould no other vessel have picked up any other passengers of the sinking steamer it may mean thta few of the men on board were saved, for the proporition of women larged.

All of Crew Lost.

This would almost certainly mean the loss of practically the entire crew of 860.

In the two saloons were 230 women and children, but it is not known how many passengers.

In the first saloon there were 128 women women and 8 children.

Notable persons, travelers on the Titanic, whose fate was in doubt in the lack of definite advices as to the identity of the survivors, were Mr. and Mrs. John Jacob Astor; Major Archibald Butt, aid to President Taft; Charles M. Hayes, president of the Grand Trunk Pacific of Canada, his wife and daughter; W. T. Stead; Benjamin Guggenheim; F. D. Millet, the artist, and J. C. Widener of Philadelphia; Mr. and Mrs. Isidor Straus; J. B. Thayer, vice-president of the Pennsylvania Railroad; J. Bruce Ismay; Henry B. Harris, the theatrical manager, and Mrs. Harris, and Colonel Washington Roebling, builder of the Brooklyn Bridge.

A ray of hope appeared in a message to New York from the operator at the Marconi wireless station at Sable Island, nea rthe scene of the disaster.

To an inquiry regarding the delivery of wireless messages to the passengers of the Titanic he replied that it was difficult to deliver them "as the passengers are believed to be dispersed among several vessels."

Hope in Other Vessels.

Even this faint indication that other vessels than the Carpathia had picked up survivors was eagerly seized upon by thousands of friends of those who set sail on her for this country.

The White Star line officers endeavored vainly to get further word from the Olympic about the Titanic.

The company was trying to get into wireless communication with the Carpathia and filed a message asking that if possible the entire list of the names of the 675 survivors said to be on board the Carpathia be sent by wireless.

Such a list, Vice-President Franklin believes, is of the utmost importance, for hope was waning among the White Star Line officials that any others than these 675 persons had survived.

Amid confusion at the offices the situation was studied as calmly as possible.

Passengers From Boston And Vicinity on Titanic

Mrs. John Murray Brown of Belmont and Acton.

George L. Clifford of Stoughton, president Belcher Last Company.

Miss Elizabeth M. Eustis of No. 1020 Beacon street, Brookline.

Mrs. Walter B. Stephenson, formerly Miss Martha Eustis of Brookline.

Mr. and Mrs. Jacques Futrelle of Scituate.

E. N. Kimball, Jr., of No. 857 Beacon street, Boston, president of the Hallet & Davis Piano Company.

Mrs. Kimball, wife of E. N. Kimball, Jr.

Herbert H. Hilliard of Brighton, buyer for Jordan Marsh Company.

Miss Gretchen N. Longley, formerly of Quincy Mansion School.

John F. Maguire of Brockton, salesman for Dunbar Pattern Company.

Timothy J. McCarthy of Dorchester, buyer for Jordan Marsh Company.

Frank D. Millet, the artist, formerly of Mattapoisett and Boston.

A. W. Newell of Lexington, president of Fourth National Bank of Boston.

Misses Alice and Madeline Newell of Lexington.

Walter Porter of Worcester.

Percival W. White of Boston and Winchendon.

Percival W. White, Jr., of Boston and Winchendon.

Milton C. Long of Springfield.

Mr. Franklin figured that, notwithstanding his fervent hope to the contrary, the Allan Line steamers Virginian and Persian could hardly have reached the scene of the disaster in time to have been of assistance.

When the Virginian first reported her receipt of the startling signal "S. O. S.," she said she was not likely to be able to reach the Titanic 'till nearly eight hours after the Titanic is now known to have sunk.

It was equally doubted that the Parisian could have reached the scene in time.

Mr. Franklin said that from his knowledge of Captain Smith's bravery and heroism on other occasions, the veteran navigator must have stuck to his bridge and gone down to his death.

Olympic Still Far Away.

There was discussion as to whether all the male passengers had sacrificed opportunity to save themselves by giving women and children the first cahnce at the boats.

"There is no rule of the sea," said Mr. Franklin, "which requires such a sacrifice. It is a rule of courtesy on land, as well as sea, that gallant men have often observed in time of disaster."

It was generally true, he added, taht men made this vital sacrifice at sea to the women of the steerage as well as those of wealthier class in the first and second saloons.

The White Star Line officers reckoned from their data that the Olympic was forty miles from the scene of the Titanic's loss when she sent the news of it.

At that hour the Carpathia was estimated as 1,080 miles east of Sandy Hook.

By midnight Bowling Green, in front of the White Star Line offices, was the parking place of a large number of automobiles of prominent residents of the city, who had driven odwn-town for first-hand information. Wealth rubbed elbows with poverty and democracy in the crowd which besieged the steamship line officials, and both classes were in deep grief. There were many instances of fashionably gowned women going into hysterics when the hopeful reports of the afternoon were blasted by the news that only 675 persons had probably been saved.

Vincent Astor, only son of Colonel John Jacob Astor, accompanied by A. J. Biddle of Philadelphia and Colonel Astor's secretary, were among the crowd at the offices, and left with tears in their eyes after a talk with Vice-President Franklin.

Relatives of Isidor Straus and of a number of other prominent passengers had similar talks with Mr. Franklin and came away equally dejected. Police reserves had to be called to several sections of the city tonight to govern the crowds which congregated around newspaper bulletin boards for news of the Titanic. The disaster stunned the gay Broadway district, for many of those who poured out of the theatres had friends on the steamer. The newspaper district was crowded till long after midnight.

SHACKLETON TELLS HOW ICEBERGS MAY BE DETECTED AT SEA

Special Cable to Boston American.

LONDON, April 15.—Sir Ernest Shackleton makes the following statement concerning the North Atlantic icebergs prevalent at this season of the year and how they may be detected by ships:

"Northern bergs are formed of land and ice carved from land glaciers in the Winter time. There is a general break-up of ice in pring and the danger zone consists not only of the actual icebergs but the great floes of ce that come drifting down until they eventually meet in the Gulf stream."

Speaking of the detection of icebergs Sir Ernest said:

"The usual method is to take the temperature of the water every half hour. An iceberg of the North Pole region has seven pasts below water to one part above."

TITANIC VALUED AT $10,000,000; INSURED FOR ONLY $5,000,000

LONDON, April 16.—The insured value of the Titanic is $5,000,000, while her real value is estimated at nearer $10,000,000. Of the insured value the White Star liner ran the risk of the first $750,000 of damage, the underwriters only meeting any claim in excess of that amount.

The cargo is understood to be worth $1,250,000. Of the $5,000,000 at risk in the open insurance market, three-quarters is held in London and the remainder in Liverpool, with some aid from Hamburg.

All the baggage and mails and valuables of passengers was insured privately. The original rate of insurance on the vessel at Lloyds was $3.75 on $500.

When the news of the disaster came, the rate immediately jumped to $300 per $500.

So far as known, there was no specie on board the ship, although a large number of valuable postal packages were carried.

There were 3,418 mail bags aboard the Titanic when she left Southampton. It is stated the proportion of registered packets carried was heavier than usual. There were no parcels. The letters addressed to Canada consisted of the usual midweek mail from North and South America and islands in the Pacific.

Much of the Titanic's cargo was destined for New York stores, and comprised expensive laces from Calais, the finest silks from the far East, an immense consignment of cotton material from Manchester and in addition there was a considerable stock of wines.

The man who sent the fateful "S. O. S." wireless call for help is John George Phillips, of Godalming, in Surrey. Marconi officials say he is one of the most trusted and efficient men in their employ.

He was twenty-six years of age and had been with them six years. He had operated wireless stations all over the world on many famous vessels. His equipment on the Titanic possessed a range of 500 miles under all conditions.

LAST HOME EDITION
If Your Paper Is Not Delivered on Time Call Champa 1200.

The Denver Times

FOUNDED AUGUST 1, 1870.

LAST HOME EDITION
WEATHER FORECAST.
Tonight Generally Fair; Wednesday Fair With Rising Temperature.

VOL. 42: NO. 70. TUESDAY EVENING, APRIL 16, 1912. TWENTY PAGES. PRICE 2 CENTS On streets. On trains 5 cents.

1,492 GO DOWN WITH TITANIC

RARE HEROISM OF BRAVE MEN OF AMERICA AND ENGLAND AS GIANT TITANIC FOUNDERS UNPARALLELED IN HISTORY OF DISASTERS

All Hope That Fewer Lives Were Lost Is Abandoned When Allan Liners Report 'No Survivors;' 'Women First' Was Rule; Men Representing $500,000,000 Lost; Heroism Touching

IN BITTER COLD AND FEARSOME DARK LINER'S PASSENGERS SEE DEATH APPROACH; ONLY 866 ESCAPE; HOPE FOR OTHERS FADES

Kings of Finance Smile at Death as They Stand Back to Let Poor Women Be Saved From Ice-Killed Ship.

Darkness Redoubles Horrors of Black Night as Half-Clad Passengers Are Told That There Is No Hope and Women and Children Alone Can Escape Alive.

CAPE RACE, N. F., April 16.—Unparalleled in history—the scenes that accompanied the foundering of the Titanic on the ice-strewn banks of Newfoundland were marked by intense suffering and rare heroism, according to the few disjointed and fragmentary messages that have been picked up by the wireless operators along the coast.

It was a night of black terror. Sunday had been cloudy and foggy, but the great liner had been steadily held on her course. Precautions were taken to guard against accident, but it seemed certain today that it was necessary to keep considerable headway on the giant vessel so that she would remain manageable.

The smash came at 10:25 Sunday night. Many of the passengers were undoubtedly in their beds at the time, but all must have been routed out immediately, as Captain Smith was too experienced a navigator to overlook any precaution or to fail to realize that the force of the collision had inflicted a mortal wound, despite the confident assertions he had made many times that the Titanic was unsinkable.

DARKNESS DOUBLES HORROR.

It was a black night—the thick, muggy atmosphere so peculiar to the banks—and the darkness redoubled the horrors of the ocean. The ship's company, assembled on the great decks of the floating hotel which was so soon to become the grave of many of their number, could have had little time to make their toilet.

Many of the passengers must have been garbed as they came from slumber, carrying only the wraps hastily caught up in the moments that followed.

Signals were burned, rockets sent up, as the wireless snapped out its frantic appeals for help, while the warders began the work of getting the big boats over the side and filled with their precious human freight.

It appeared today that there was no need for the order, "Women and children first," but that the men stood aside and pushed their women folk to the boat decks, where the lifeboats weer being filled as quickly as possible. Wives and sisters in tears, with the last kisses of husbands and brothers on their lips, were marshaled to their places, while the wounded giant staggered and sunk lower with every lurch of the sea.

LIFEBOATS INSUFFICIENT.

It must have been apparent from the outset that there was little hope for many of that company. Although she carried the maximum of liferafts and lifeboats, they were cruelly insufficient for that great company which a few hours previously had been so cheerful and happy at the prospect of soon reaching their journey's end. The staggering of the wounded monster and the gradual sinking by the head must have indicated to all that the end was certain.

Passengers were buoyed up by the hope that assistance was coming up as fast as ships that had picked up the urgent appeal for aid could be sent through the water. But the officers could have entertained no such hope.

They knew, from the messages received, that no vessel could reach them before daylight, and, with the water making in the holds faster than it could be checked by the pumps, they must have realized that only floating wreckage and the filled lifeboats and rafts would greet the rescuers.

So they carefully filled the boats, lowered them into the water and ordered them to row far enough away so that the whirlpool suction that would follow the final plunge of the Titanic would not swamp them. Th 455 life preservers were dealt out and the forty-eight life buoys placed where they could be used, but it was realized that after the final analysis these would be of little use, and those on board when the great plunge came were certain of death.

WOMEN'S REASON TOTTERS.

The small boats, bobbing like corks on the water amidst the floating ice, it was believed, witnessed the final plunge of the vessel to her grave, two miles below the surface.

It seemed certain today that they had rowed in company as far off as possible, but the swirling waters must have brought home at least to the crew that the vessel had gone down.

The waiting in the dark and cold may have cost the reason of many of the women.

It was believed today that the fact that the Carpathia, which was the first on the scene, started direct to New York as soon as she had taken the unfortunates from the lifeboats, indicated that many of the survivors were in a very bad way. She carried only one doctor, and his best efforts were needed to save the reason of the women, who realized that many of them were now alone in the world.

SUPREME COURT DECIDES ELECTION CASE AGAINST THE CITIZENS' PARTY

The supreme court at 1 o'clock this afternoon gave notice that it had reached a decision in the case involving the appointment of election judges for the coming municipal election.

The court sustained the decision of Judge Greeley W. Whitford, which was to the effect that the election cosmmission must name judges from lists presented by the chairmen of the two political parties casting the highest vote for governor at the last election, namely, the Democratic and Republican. This

(Continued on Page Two, Column One.)

THE OPERATOR.

STEAMER OFFICES SCENE OF BLASTED HOPES AS TEAR-FILLED EYES SCAN RESCUE LIST

Fashionably-Gowned Women Go Into Hysterics Upon Hearing Loved Ones Lost.

NEW YORK, April 16.—From midnight on Bowling Green, in front of the White Star line offices, was the parking place of a large number of automobiles of prominent residents of the city, who had driven down town for first-hand information from the Titanic. Wealth and society rubbed elbows with poverty in the crowd that besieged the steamship line officials and both classes were in deep grief.

Fashionably gowned women went into hysterics when the hopeful reports of the afternoon were blasted with the news that probably only 675 persons had been saved.

Vincent Actor, only son of Colonel John Jacob Astor, and A. J. Biddle of Philadelphia and Colonel Astor's secretary, were among the crowd at the offices and left with tears in their eyes after fifteen minutes' conference with Vice President Franklin.

Relatives of Isador Straus and of a number of other prominent passengers had similar conferences with Mr. Franklin and came away with the same dejection.

Gradually the names of the rescued began to come by way of Cape Race from the Carpathia and were posted. There were some who scanned the lists and turned away with faces showing hopes realized, but many who came were disappointed.

Repeated calls were made for information regarding Major Archibald Butt, President Taft's military aide, who is returning from abroad. President Taft telegraphed the company and was promised immediate word if anything of a definite nature was received.

MRS. ASTOR RESCUED.

Vincent Astor remained up through the night, trying to learn the fate of his father. Word came that Mrs. Astor, his step-mother, and her maid, were safe aboard the Carpathia.

Members of the Guggenheim and Straus families had representatives at the White Star offices in anticipation of definite word concerning Isador Straus and Benjamin Guggenheim. These names were not in the survivors' list received up to 8:30 o'clock this morning.

Numerous inquiries were received regarding the fate of Henry B. Harris, the theatrical manager, and his wife. The list shows that Mrs. Harris had been saved.

A cablegram from London received at the steamship offices concerning the fate of Sir Cosmo and Lady Duff-Gordon, remained unanswered until this morning, when it was definitely ascertained they were among the rescued Titanic passengers now on board the Carpathia.

MANY FROM PHILADELPHIA.

Long distance telephone calls came from Philadelphia inquiring for the many society folks from that city aboard the Titanic. The name of Mrs. George D. Widener of Elkins Park was posted as among those on board the Carpathia. The names of her husband and her son, Harry Elkins Widener, did not appear.

T. W. Cavendish of England, with his American wife, who is the daughter of Henry Siegel, the New York merchant, were first cabin passengers.

Christopher Head, London, is a barrister and son of the senior member of the firm of Lloyds, underwriters.

Mrs. Edward S. Robert is from St. Louis, as also are Miss E. W. Allen and Theophile Papin Jr. Mr. Papin is noted as an art connoisseur.

CANADIAN PASSENGERS.

Among noted Canadian passengers were H. Markland Molson, a banker; Mr. and Mrs. Thornton Davidson, Mrs. James Baxter, Q. Baxter, H. J. Allison and Mrs. Allison of Montreal; Major Arthur Penchen of the Queen's Own rifles, Toronto; Mrs. Mark Fortune and Mrs. Graham of Winnipeg.

Mr. Davidson is a member of the Montreal stock exchange and a son of Justice Davidson. His wife is a daughter of President Hays of the Grand Trunk railway, who, with Mrs. Hays and Miss Hays, also were passengers. Quigg Baxter is a well-known hockey player.

Paul Chevre, the well-known French sculptor, who made the Champlain monument, was in the first cabin on his way to Canada to complete the Mercier monument. Mr. Allison is a well-known Montreal financier.

Mr. and Mrs. William E. Carter and their children, Lucille and William, reside near Bryn Mawr. James Clinch Smith, a brother-in-law of the late Stanford White, is well known in New York society circles. He married Miss Bertha Barnes of Chicago.

PORTLAND, Ore., April 16.—F. M. Warren and wife, named in the Titanic's passenger list, live here. Mr. Warren is millionaire president of a packing company. Herman Klaber, passenger, is a millionaire hop grower of Portland.

SAN FRANCISCO, Cal., April 16.—Dr. Washington Dodge, whose name ap-

(Continued on Page Three, Column One.)

One Denver Man Believed Dead and Others Numbered Among the Saved.

WOMEN FIRST LAW RIGIDLY ENFORCED ON SINKING SHIP

These pinnacles of fact concerning the world's greatest steamship disaster—the sinking at 2:20 a. m. Monday of the great White Star liner Titanic off the banks of Newfoundland—stood out prominent today, as sifted from the wireless reports:

Revised estimates loss of life, 1,492 souls.

The $10,000,000 steamship, with cargo and jewels worth perhaps $10,000,000 more, a total loss.

No mention among the survivors of Colonel John Jacob Astor. Hih bride, who was Miss Force of New York, has been saved.

Major Archibald W. Butt, President Taft's aide, is still unaccounted for, as are many other persons of international importance.

J. Bruce Ismay, president of the Inter-

(Continued on Page Six, Column One.)

Liferafts Too Few and Husbands Bid Wives Farewell Forever; "Women First," Is Rule Followed.

Carpathia, With Survivors Aboard, Mostly Women and Children, Due Tomorrow; Narratives of Sea's Greatest Catastrophe Awaited With Interest.

NEW YORK, April 16.—Hope for the safety of passengers of the ill-fated Titanic, which foundered early Monday morning off the grand banks of Newfoundland, other than those reported by wireless from the Curnarder Carpathia, en route to this city, was practically abandoned this afternoon. Latest reports placed only 866 persons, and they chiefly women and children, on the Carpathia, while even the officials of the White Star line admitted there was practically no hope for the remaining 1,492 of the ship's company of 2,358 souls.

That all would have had a chance of safety had there been lifeboats and rafts enough was the general belief of navigators. But the liner, newest and greatest of transatlantic ships, carried only twenty large, modern lifeboats, and they were loaded to the gunwales with the women and children, who, in accordance with the unwritten law of the sea, had been put over the side first.

COLONEL ASTOR BELIEVED LOST.

Most of the men were missing. Colonel John Jacob Astor, Major Archie Butt, President Taft's aide; Benjamin Guggenheim, Jacques Futrelle, William T. Stead, F. D. Millet, Henry B. Harris—all of the well-known personages who had taken passage on the gala day of the Titanic's departure from her home port, were not included in the list of those reported saved.

The inference was that they had remained on the ship and gone to the bottom with her, a sacrifice to the custom which fails to compel enough boats and rafts on ocean steamers to take off every one on board.

Up to noon there had been a faint, glittering hope that, in addition to the Carpathia, other vessels that had rushed to the scene on receipt of the wireless appeal for aid had been in time to make rescues. Rumor had the Allan liner Virignian taking off some.

But this hope faded when Captain Gambell wirelessed his agents that he reached the scene too late.

"NONE LEFT TO RESCUE."

"There was none left to rescue, and I am proceeding on my voyage," was the melancholy word sent, and with it crumbled the hopes of the White Star agents here who had said this was the best chance of cutting down the death list.

Vice President Franklin of the White Star line, stunned by the magnitude of the disaster, said, soon after noon, that the Carpathia would reach this city with the survivors late Thursday, or early on Friday.

He said that he believed the Olympic was standing by the scene of the wreck, combing the sea, while acting as a wireless relay station to Cape Race. This, however, he carefully explained, was conjecture. He said that the California, of the Anchor line, was also searching for survivors, but that he had no direct word from her.

One scant hope that was clung to by the line officials that there might be survivors unaccounted for, came from the deduction that the steamer had drifted some thirty-four miles between the time she struck and the time she sank. There was a chance that some of the lifeboats or the liferafts that were lowered first might have drifted away and not been reached by the Carpathia.

Although admittedly only a straw, it was clung to by those having relatives whose names were not included in the list of the survivors which was sent to this city.

WOMEN AND CHILDREN FIRST.

That most of the women and children were in the boats picked up by the Carpathia was believed by marine experts here to indicate positively that the iron discipline of the merchant marine was maintained to the last. Captain Smith, of course, his friends say, went down with his ship.

Reports from the sations along the Nova Scotia coast say that the weather off shore today was foggy and that there was a heavy thunder storm last night which traveled eastward. The weather conditions, it was frankly stated, left little hope for the rescue of any survivors that might still be afloat.

The wireless people admitted they were unable to get messages to any of the steamers in the vicinity. They said that they had been unable to pick up the Carpathia, although they had many messages for the survivors who were on board. They said, however, that they were trying to reach her by a system of relays and hoped to do so, if not today, then tonight, when atmospheric conditions would be better for wireless telegraphing.

SCENES ARE HEARTRENDING.

The scenes at the offices of the White Star line were heartrending in the extreme. Millionaires and wives of millionaires importuned the officials to do something, but to all the one reply was made: "We have done all we can. Money can do no more."

One to whom this reply was made was Mrs. Benjamin Guggenheim, wife of the smelter king, was among the missing. She told Vice President Franklin that she was prepared to spend any amount to charter steamers to go to the rescue, but he gently told her that this would be of no avail.

"We spared no expense to get ships to the rescue," he said. "Vessels are standing by and searching for survivors. All we can do is to hope for the best."

That the stories of the half-frozen survivors will eclipse anything in fiction is certain from the brief and disjointed information that was available here from the wireless sources. The collision occurred in the deepest darkness and after many of the passengers had retired for the night.

(Continued on Page Five, Column One.)

DISASTER THROWS ALL COUNTRY IN MOURNING

HARDLY A TOWN IN UNITED STATES WITHOUT ITS DEAD

Wealth and Poverty Rub Elbows Awaiting Word From Wrecked Steamer.

(Continued From Page One.)

pears on the passenger list of the Titanic, together with those of his wife and child, is widely known as an authority on taxation. His mother expressed a doubt today that he had taken passage on the Titanic.

NEW YORK, April 16.—The following are among the most notable men on the Titanic believed to have perished:

Benjamin Guggenheim, capitalist, brother to United States Senator Guggenheim of Colorado.
John Jacob Astor, capitalist.
Major Archibald Butt, aide to President Taft.
William T. Stead, journalist.
F. D. Millet, artist.
Isador Straus, silk importer.
Henry B. Harris, theatrical manager.
Colonel Washington Roebling, Brooklyn bridge builder.
J. G. Widener, capitalist.
Clarence Moore, well-known Chicago sportsman, son-in-law of E. C. Swift.
Frederick M. Hoyt, New York yachtsman.
Dr. Washington Dodge, San Francisco author.
Paul Chevre, noted French sculptor.
Jacques Futrelle, short story writer.
Charles M. Hays, railroad president.

ST. LOUIS, April 16.—Miss Georgette Madill, reported among the saved in the Titanic disaster, is one of the city's youngest heiresses. She is 15 years old. By an order of court a year ago she was awarded an annual "pin money" allowance of $7,500 to pay for her clothing and education until she became of age.

ANNUAL INCOME $50,000.

Miss Madill is the principal heir of Judge George A. Madill, who was for several years president of the Union Trust company in this city. She went to Europe in January of last year with her mother, Mrs. Edward Robert, and her cousin, Miss Elizabeth Allen. It is estimated that the income from the estate of which Miss Madill is heir is not less than $50,000.

LOS ANGELES, Cal., April 16.—Walter M. Clark of the Titanic's passenger list is the son of J. Ross Cark, vice president of the San Pedro, Los Angeles & Salt Lake railroad. Clark, with his wife, was returning home from a trip abroad.

PASADENA, Cal., April 16.—Countess Rothes, in the Titanic's passenger list, was on her way to Pasadena to spend the coming summer with her husband, Norman Evelyn Leslie, nineteenth Earl of Rothes, and representative peer for Scotland. He is now in New York, having left here a week ago to meet his wife there.

NEW YORK, April 16.—Mrs. Cornelius Vanderbilt, mother of Alfred Gwynne Vanderbilt, announces that her son, who was reported on board the Titanic, still was in London.

OMAHA, Neb., April 16.—Emil Brandeis, a member of the mercantile firm of J. L. Brandeis & Sons, and a millionaire, was on the Titanic.

PROVIDENCE, R. I., April 16.—Four Providence persons are known to have been passengers on the ill-fated Titanic. They include F. C. Ostby and his daughter, Helen, who were returning from a tour of Egypt; James Lamb, a theatrical man, who had been on a three months' tour abroad, and Harry Sullivan.

MONTREAL, April 16.—A wireless message received here says that Charles M. Hayes, president of the Grand Trunk railway, is among the survivors aboard the Carpathia. His wife and daughter already had been reported saved.

ST. PAUL, Minn., April 16.—Mr. and Mrs. H. F. Chafee of Amenia, N. D., were undoubtedly among the passengers of the Titanic.

CHICAGO, April 16.—Three Chicagoans are known to have been on the Titanic. They are Clarence Moore and man servant and Erwin G. Lewey. Mrs. Moore formerly was Miss Mabel Swift, daughter of E. C. Swift, the packer. Lewey is a member of the Lewey Bros. company, jewelry.

MINNEAPOLIS, Minn., April 16.—Walter D. Douglas of Minneapolis, who with his wife was aboard the Titanic, is a multimillionaire, and his brother is owner of what is aid to be one of the largest starch manufactories in the world, at Cedar Rapids, Iowa.

ON HONEYMOON TRIP.

Mr. and Mrs. John Pillsbury Snyder, prominent in Minneapolis, who left here in January on their honeymoon trip to Europe, also were returning on the Titanic.

CHEHALIS, Wash., April 16.—Harry D. Aldis of Chehalis said today that his parents were passengers on the Titanic. They were coming to Chehalis to make their home with their son.

MORGANTOWN, W. Va., April 16.—Mr. and Mrs. Lucian Smith of this city were passengers on the Titanic. They were completing a honeymoon trip around the world.

ROCHESTER, N. Y., April 16.—It is believed that three residents of this city were passengers on the Titanic: Howard B. Case of Ascot, England, who went from this city ten years ago as London manager for an oil company; Stanley Fox, traveling man for a Rochester machine company, and Miss Lily Duncan, who was visiting abroad.

TROY, N. Y., April 16.—Among the passengers on the Titanic was A. O. Helverson of this city, foreign representative of Cluett, Peabody & Co. Mrs. Helverson accompanied him and they were on their way to this country for a visit.

SAVED BY HER HUSBAND'S HEROISM

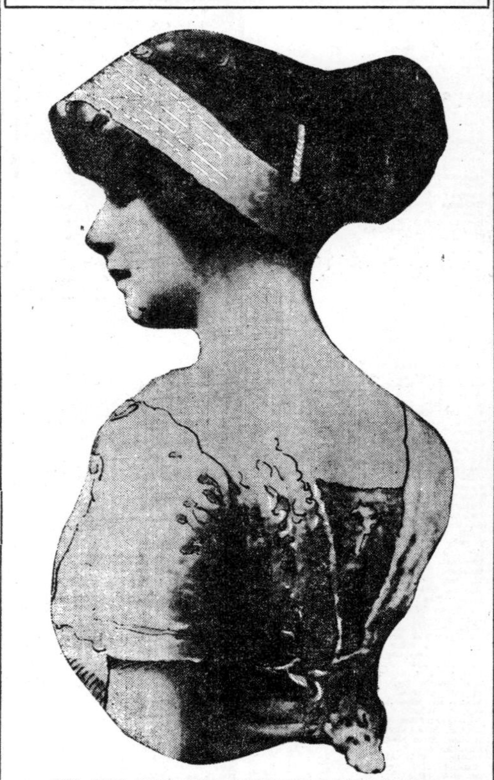

MRS. JOHN JACOB ASTOR, FORMERLY MADELINE FORCE
Whose Millionaire Husband Is Reported to Have Heroically Given Her a Chance for Life While He Himself Went to a Watery Grave.

BUFFALO, N. Y., April 16.—Edward A. Kent, whose name appears in the passenger list of the Titanic, was one of the leading architects of this city.

CONGRESSMAN'S DAUGHTER.

Mrs. Smith is a daughter of Congressman Hughes of West Virginia.

POMEROY, Wash., April 16.—J. Brady, a passenger on the Titanic, was president of the Pomeroy State bank. He had been visiting Europe with a party of friends, including several from Spokane.

VICTORIA, B. C., April 16.—E. P. Colley of Victoria, on the Titanic, is a land surveyor, employed by the British Columbia government.

YOUNGSTOWN. Ohio, April 16.—Mr. and Mrs. George D. Wick and their daughter, Miss Natalie; Miss Caroline Bonnell and Miss Lily Bonnell, Birkdale, England, her cousins, were among the Titanic's passengers. The Wicks and Bonnells are among the most wealthy people of Youngstown.

DETROIT, Mich., April 16.—George Floyd Eitemiller of this city was returning on the Titanic after a three months' trip in Europe as the representative of a Cincinnati automobile company. He is a son of George M. Eitemiller, who for many years was wire chief at Pittsburg for the Western Union Telegraph company.

LONDON, April 16.—Canadians on board the Titanic included Mark Fortune, a capitalist of Winnipeg; Hugh Ross, son of the late A. W. Ross of Winnipeg, a politician, and T. O. C. Caffry, the Western superintendent of the Union bank of Vancouver.

NEW YORK, April 16.—One of the most serious errors in the wireless list of survivors appears to be in the listing of four members of the "Rogerson" family. No such name appears in the passenger list.

ON FUNERAL JOURNEY.

It is believed these are the Ryersons of Philadelphia, who were bound home to attend the funeral of Arthur Ryerson Jr., who was killed in an automobile accident recently.

NEW YORK, Ajril 16.—Seldom in the history of navigation has a steamer carried so many noted persons as thronged the Titanic on her maiden trip. Hardly any of the noted passengers were saved, according to the meager advices available.

Colonel John Jacob Astor, direct male head of the famous Astor family, ranks as the largest individual land owner, so far as values are concerned, in America.

POWER IN THEATRICALS.

Henry B. Harris is a power in the theatrical world, a native of St. Louis and an official in various managerial associations.

Isador Straus is a brother of Nathan and Oscar S. Straus and New York's most prominent Hebrew merchant.

William Stead, noted author and for years editor of the Review of Reviews, was en route for a brief tour of the United States.

Charles Melville Hayes, president of the Grand Trunk railroad, considered one of the most brilliant railroad officials, was returning from a business trip in England.

Benjamin Guggenheim, fifth of the seven sons of Meyer Guggenheim, has for years been in charge of the Guggenheim mining interests.

Frank D. Millet, a noted artist and traveler, was returning from a trip to Italy, where he was at the head of the American academy at Rome.

PROMINENT SPORTSMAN.

Clarence Moore, one of Washington's most prominent society men and sportsmen, was returning from England, where, as master of the Chevy Chase hunt of Washington, he had purchased a new pack of hounds.

Major Archibald W. Butt, military aide to President Taft, had been abroad on a vacation.

Jacques Futrelle, the writer of fiction, had been on a pleasure trip with his wife.

J. Bruce Ismay, president of the International Mercantile Marine company, which controls the White Star line, was also on board.

Half a Billion Dollars Wealth of First Cabin

At Least Six Men on Board Whose Fortunes Are in Tens of Millions.

NEW YORK, April 16.—Untold wealth was represented among the passengers of the Titanic, there being on board at least six men each of whose fortunes might be reckoned in tens of millions of dollars. A rough estimate of the total wealh represented in the first-class passenger list would reach over $500,000,000.

JOHN JACOB ASTOR.

The wealthiest of the list is Colonel John Jacob Astor, head of the famous house whose name he bears, who is reputed to be worth $150,000,000. Mr. Astor was returning from a tour of Egypt with his bride, who was Miss Madeline Force, whom he married in Providence on September 9.

BENJAMIN GUGGENHEIM.

Benjamin Guggenheim, probably next in financial importance, is the fifth of the seven sons of Meyer Guggenheim, who founded the American Smelting and Refining company, the great mining corporation, and s a director of many corporation, and is a director of many corSteam Pump company, of which he is president. His fortune is estimated at $95,000,000. His wife is the daughter of James Seligman, the New York banker.

GEORGE D. WIDENER.

George D. Widener is the son of P. A. B. Widener, the Philadelphia traction king, whose fortune is estimated at $50,000,000.

ISADOR STRAUSS.

Isador Strauss, one of New York's most prominent dry goods merchants and notable for his philanthropies, has a fortune estimated at $50,000,000. He is a director in various banks, trust companies and charitable institutions.

J. BRUCE ISMAY.

J. Bruce Ismay, president and one of the founders of the International Mercantile Marine, who has always made it a custom to be a passenger on the maiden trip of every new ship built by the company, is said to be worth $40,000,000. It was Mr. Ismay who, with J. P. Morgan, consolidated American and British steamship lines under the International Mercantile Marine's control.

Colonel Washington Roebling, son of the builder of the Brooklyn bridge, president and director of John A. Roebling Sons' company, is credited with a fortune of $25,000,000.

Among others of reputed wealth who were on board are J. B. Thayer, vice president of the Pennsylvania railroad; Clarence Moore, a well-known sportsman, whose wife was Miss Mabel Swift, daughter of E. C. Swift, the Chicago meat packer, and Charles M. Hays, president of the Grand Trunk Pacific and vice president and general manager of the Grand Trunk railway of Canada.

Other persons of note on the first cabin list are W. T. Stead, writer, journalist and war correspondent; Jacques Futrelle, the short story writer; Frederick M. Hoyt, a well-known New York yachtsman; Dr. Washington Dodge of San Francisco, Henry Sleeper-Harper, grandson of John Wesley Harper, one of the founders of Harper Bros.' publishing house; William E. Carter of Philadelphia and Newport, and Thomas Pears, a Pittsburg steel manufacturer.

MRS. J. J. BROWN IS SAFE; HUGH R. ROOD PERISHED, IS BELIEF

Latest advices indicate that Hugh R. Rood of Denver perished when the steamship Titanic went down and that Mrs. J. J. Brown, who also was a passenger, was rescued. Mrs. Stocker-Rood is not believed to have been on the vessel in the light of later developments, while Helen Brown, daughter of Mrs. Brown, is believed to have remained in Paris to pursue her studies and thereby to have escaped the harrowing experiences of the disaster.

Rood's name does not appear in any of the lists of those who were rescued, and his friends here have little hope that he escaped death. Letters received by friends of Mrs. Rood show that it was not her intention to sail with her husband, but to come later, and unless there was a change in her plans she was not on the Titanic. Mrs. Forbes Ricard, wife of a well-known mining man, who resides at 2449 East Fourteenth avenue, had a letter from Mrs. Rood written several days before the Titanic sailed. In this letter she said it was her intention to remain a while longer, but that her husband was coming home. She changed her plans at the last moment and concluded to spend the summer in England with friends. A dispatch from Seattle says that Mr. Rood, who was vice president and general manager of the Pacific Creosoting company, had sailed, but that Mrs. Rood remained in England.

Miss Helen Brown decided just before her mother sailed that she would remain in Paris and continue her studies. That change in her plans probably saved her from being one of the victims of the disaster. Mrs. E. P. Hershey of 1345 Grant street received a letter from Miss Brown a few days ago. It was written in Paris the latter part of March and made no mention of coming to America. The letter told of her pleasant visit with her mother during their tour of Egypt and i nit she spoke of resuming her studies. Mrs. Lawrence Brown also received a letter from Miss Brown along the same lines and these led to the conclusion that she decided not to come to America with her mother and therefore was not on the Titanic when it struck the iceberg.

Loss of Millions Above Boat Cost, $10,000,000

NEW YORK, April 16.—The Titanic was insured at Lloyds for $5,000,000 and it was said here that the International Mercantile Marine company also carried a surplus fund for insurance purposes which could be applied to the loss.

The cost of building the great liner has been estimated at $10,000,000, although Vice President Franklin of the White Star line insists that her value was not over $8,000,000.

The total monetary loss caused by the sinking of the ship, however, is certain to run to many millions more, but the total amount cannot be conjectured.

It is generally understood she had aboard diamonds of great value, estimated as high as $5,000,000, and also a large amount of bonds.

The amount of freight carried was comparatively small, for the size of the ship, and according to a White Star official its value would not reach over $500,000.

The Titanic carried 3,424 bags of mail of unknown value, which it is hardly likely was saved.

It is said that among almost priceless jewels carried by the passengers are pearls belonging to an American woman valued at $600,000.

GRAVE OF TITANIC TWO MILES UNDER SEA SURFACE

HALIFAX, N. S., April 16.—The deathbed of the Titanic and of probably many who must have been dragged down with her, is two miles below the surface of the sea.

The calculation was made by an official of the government marine departmen, who finds that depth on the marine chart at a point about 500 miles from Halifax and about seventy miles south of the Grand banks where he believes the Titanic went down.

MISSED SHIP; ESCAPED DISASTER

—Photo by Kirkland.

MISS HELEN BROWN, DENVER SOCIETY GIRL
Who Had Booked Passage on the Titanic, but Changed Her Mind at the Last Moment and Remained in Europe. Miss Brown's Mother, Mrs. J. J. Brown, Was on the Steamer.

Wireless Record in Rescues From Ocean Disasters

CHICAGO, April 16.—Triumphs of the wireless in rescues from shipwreck:

January 23, 1909, 1,650 passengers and the crew of the Republic, saved by wireless after collision in fog with the Florida. Jack Binns, wireless operator on the Republic, won fame by heroic conduct. Wrecked vessel rescued by the Baltic of the White Star line.

September 9, 1910, thirty-three persons, rescued by Car Ferry summoned by wireless to wrecked Pere Marquette. Car ferry steamer No. 18, off Sheboygan, Wis. Two passengers and thirty-one officers and crew drowned.

July 29, 1911, Canadian training ship Niobe assisted in response to wireless signals of distress when wrecked off Yarmouth, N. S.

August 30, 1911, twelve passengers of the steamship Lexington rescued from wrecked vessel off Hunting Island, through wireless messages sent by 16-year-old Jack Sheets.

The loss of life on the Titanic doubtless would have been much larger but for the wireless appeals for aid.

On the Titanic the wireless operator who flashed "S. O. S." when she struck the iceberg, was J. G. Phillips, formerly employed as wireless operator on James Gordon Bennett's yacht. Later he worked on the steamship Oceanic, from which he was transferred to the new Titanic.

All steamships of consequence are required to be equipped with the wireless, which only a few years ago seemed a fanciful dream. By an act of congress passed June 24, 1910, all ocean-going steamers carrying fifty passengers or more are required to have wireless apparatus capable of transmitting messages at least 100 miles. The Canadian law is applied to all passenger ships.

If you want to get the news—
BUY THE TIMES.

LISTS OF THOSE RESCUED FROM THE LOST TITANIC

WIRELESS FLASHES CHEERING NEWS TO SOME; NAMES ONLY

Few Men Mentioned as Roll of Survivors Comes Through the Atmosphere.

CAPE RACE, N. F., April 16.—The steamship Carpathia, which is believed to have on board all the survivors of the Titanic disaster, started early today to send by wireless to this station the list of the Titanic's survivors.

Great difficulty was experienced in getting many of the names correctly and more than a score of names as made out here did not appear at all on the Titanic's original passenger list, but it is believed many of these were passengers, who had booked at the last moment. The receipts of the list of the first cabin survivors required more than six hours' effort. So far as the names check up correctly, the following saloon passengers have been saved:

Appleton, Mrs. Edward W.
Abbott, Mrs. Rose.
Burns, Miss G. M.
Cassebero, Miss D. D.
Clarke, Mrs. William H.
Chibinace, Mrs. B.
Crossbie, Miss E. G.
Crossbie, Miss H. E.
Hippach, Miss Jean.
Harris, Mrs. Henry B. (wireless version Mrs. Y. B. Harris).
Stephenson, Mrs. P.
Carter, W. E.
Ostby, Mrs.
Bessette, Miss.
Bucknell, Mrs. William.
Middle, Olivia.
Barrett, Karl.
Sheddell, Robert Douglas.
Haussig, Mlle.
Halverson, Mrs. Alex.
Hays, Miss Margaret.
Ismay, Bruce.
Kimberley, Mr. and Mrs. Ed.
Kenyman, F. A.
Kenchen, Miss Emile.
Longtry, Miss G. F.
Leader, Miss A. F.
Lavery, Miss Bertha.
Lives, Mrs. Ernest.
Rogerson, Mrs. Susan P.
Rogerson, Miss Arthur.
Rogerson, Miss Emily B.
Allison, Master, and nurse.
Andrews, Miss K. T.
Panhart, Miss Ninette.
Allen, Miss E. W.
Bishop, Mr. and Mrs. D.
Blank, H.
Basins, Miss A.
Baxter, Mrs. James.
Bayton, George A.
Bonnell, Miss C.
Brown, Mrs. J. M.
Bowen, Miss G. C.
Beckwith, Mr. and Mrs. R. L.
Countess of Rothes.
Olmane, C. R.
———, Mrs. Jacob P. (word missed).

(The above list was received by wireless at Cape Race station from the steamer Carpathia.)

Clines, Miss Mary.
Lindstrem, Mrs. Sigrid.
Lesneur, Gustav J.
Amadill, Miss Georgetta.
Meilcard, Mme.
Tucker, Mrs. and maid.
Thayer, Mrs. J. B.
Thayer, J. B. Jr.
Woolmer, H.
Ward, Miss Anna.
Williams Rich M.
White, Mrs. J. Steward.
Young, Miss Marie.
Potter, Mrs. Thomas Jr.
Roberts, Mrs. Edna S.
Rougias, Mrs. Robert.
Slayter, Miss Hilda.
Smith, Mrs. P.
Braham, Mrs.
Carter, Miss Lucille.
Carter, William.
Roberts, Miss.
Cummins, Miss.
Mare, Mrs. Florence.
Phillips, Miss Alice P.
Munge, Mrs. Paule.
———, Miss Rosie.
———, Mrs. Jane.
———, Miss Phyllise.
———, Miss Bertha.

(Last names were missed.)

(Mistakes were due to the hurried wireless transmission and relays.)

Andrews, Miss K. T., probably Miss Cornelia J.
Chibinace, Mrs. B., Mrs. E. B. Chibinall.
Douglas, Robert D., Mr. or Mrs. W. O. Douglass, or Mrs. F. C. Douglass.
Ellis, Miss, may be Miss Eustis.
Kenchia, Miss Emile, possibly Mrs. F. R. Kenyon.
Kimberly, Mr. and Mrs. E. D., possibly Mr. and Mrs. E. N. Kimball.
Kenniman, F. A., probably Mr. or Mrs. F. R. Kenyon.
Lindstrom, Sigrid, probably Mrs. J. Lindstrom.
Mile, probably Frank D. Millet.
Rogerson, J. N.
Arthur, Mrs.
Mrs. Emily B.
Miss Susan P.
Allison, Master, and maid of Philadelphia, practically certain this is Ryerson family.
Shutter, Miss D., probably Mrs. E. W. Schutes.
Spedden, Mr. and Mrs. J. J., probably Mr. and Mrs. Frederick O. Spedden.
Williams, Rich N., probably P. M. Williams Jr.
O'Connell, Mrs. Robert, probably Mrs. R. G. Cornell.

List of survivors whose names do not appear on the original sailing list, probably includes a large number of those who took the ship at Cherbourg:

Bassina, Miss A.
Burns, Mrs. G. M.
Casebere, Miss D. D.
Chamdasen, Mrs. Victorine.
Daniel, Miss Sarah.
Desette, Miss.
Drauchensted, Alfred.
Emock, Philip.
Fleigheim, Miss Anterete.
Francatelli, Miss.
Googht, James.
Halversen, Mrs. A. O.
Homer, Henry R.
Mamy, Miss Ruberta.
Meilcard, Mme.
Lavory, Miss Bertha.
Lesneur, Gustave J.
Panhart, Miss Nanette.
Renago, Mrs. Mamam J.
Raneit, Miss Apple.
Seerepeca, Miss Augusta.
Steffanson, H. B.
Segesser, Miss Emma.
Smith, Mrs. P. P.
Slayton, Miss Hilda.
Shadell, Robert Douglas.
Smith, Mrs. Lucian P.
Ward, Miss Emma.
Thor, Miss Ella.
Tucker, Mrs., and maid.
Newell, Miss Marjorie.
Newsom, Miss Helen.
Ostby, E. C.
Ostby, Miss Helen E.
Omond, Mr. Fiennad.
Puechen, Major Arthur.
Potter, Mrs. Thomas J.
Rheims, Mrs. George.
Robert, Mrs. Edward S.
Rolmano, C.
Rosenbaum, Miss Edith.
Rothschild, Mrs. Martin.
Rothes, Countess of.
Saalfeld, Adolphe.
Schabert, Mrs. Paul.
Seward, Frederick.
Silvey, Mrs. William D.
Simonius, Colonel Alfonso.
Sloper, William T.
Snyder, Mr. and Mrs. John.
Stepelin, Dr. Max.
Stone, Mrs. George M.
Swift, Mrs. Frederick Joel.
Thayer, J. B.
Taussig, Miss Ruth.
Taylor, Mr. and Mrs. E. Z.
Tucker, Gilbert M.
Warren, Mrs. F. M.
White, Mrs. J. Stuart.
Wick, Miss Mary.
Wildence, Mrs. George D. and maid.
Frolicher, Miss Margaret.
Futrelle, Mrs. Jacques E.

MRS. J. J. BROWN
Wealthy Denver Woman and Globe Trotter, Who Is Reported Among Those Saved From the Titanic.
(Copyright, 1912, by the Associated Literary Press.)

Gracie, Colonel Archibald.
Graham, Mrs. William.
Graham, Miss Margaret E.
Graham, Mr.
Carter, Miss Lucille.
Carter, Master William.
Cardell, Mrs. Churchill.
Calderhead, Mr. E. P.
Chandason, Mrs. Victorine.
O'Connell, Mrs. Robert (probably Mrs. R. C. Cornell).
Chaffee, Mrs. H. F.
Cardoza, Mr. Thomas.
Cardoza, Mrs. J. W.
Cummings, Mrs. J. B.
Washington, Mrs.
Swift, Mrs. Frederick Joel.
Schabert, Mrs. Paul.
Spedden, Mr. and Mrs. J. O.
Stahelin, Max.
Smith, Mrs. Lucian T.
Stephenson, Mrs. Walter P.
Solomon, Abraham.
Silvey, Mrs. William B.
Spencer, Mrs. W. A., and maid.
Sheddell, Robert Douglass.
Snyder, Mr. and Mrs. John.
Saalfield, Mr. Adolph.
Silverthorn, R. S.
Serepeca, Miss Augusta.
Haussig, Mlle.
Thayer, Mr. and Mrs. J. B.
Willard, Miss Constance.
Woolner, Hugh.
Young, Miss Marie.
Hippach, Mrs. Ida S.
Clark, Mrs. Walter.
Cummings, Mrs. John B.
Silverthorne, R. Spencer (some question as to identity).

Wireless version:

Abbott, Mrs. Rose, probably meaning Mrs. N. Aubert.
Anderson, Harry.
Allen, Miss E. W.
Appleton, Mrs. E. W.
Astor, Mrs. John Jacob, and maid.
Barkworth A. S.
Baxter, Mrs. James.
Brayton George A.
Beckwith, Mr. and Mrs. R. T.
Behr, Karl H.
Bishop, Mr. and Mrs. D. H.
Blank Henry.
Bonnell, Miss Caroline.
Bowen, Miss G. C.
Bowerman, Miss Elsie.
Brown, Mrs. J. M.
Brown, Mrs. J. J.
Calderhead, E. P.
Chase, Howard B.
Cavendish, Mrs. Turrell, and maid.
Chaffee Mrs. H. F.
Chambers Mr. and Mrs. N. C.
Cherry, Miss Gladys.
Chevre, Paul.
Crosby, Miss.
Daniel, W.
Davidson, Mrs. Thornton.
Devilliers, Mrs. B.
Dick, Mr. and Mrs. A. A.
Dodge, Mr. and Mrs. Washington, and son.
Douglas, Mrs. Fred C.
Douglas, Mrs. Walter.
Flynn, J. F.
Fortune, Mrs. Mark.
Fortune, Miss Lucille.
Fortune, Miss Alice.
Frauenthal, Dr. and Mrs. Henry.
Frauenthal, Mr. and Mrs. T. G.
Frolicher, Miss Margaret.
Gibson, Mrs. Leonard.
Gibson, Mrs. Dorothy.
Goldenburg, Mrs. Samuel.
Goldenburg, Miss Ella.
Gordon, Sir and Lady Cosmo Duff.
Gracie, Colonel Archibald.
Graham, Mr.
Graham, Mrs. William.
Graham, Miss Margaret E.
Greenefield, Mrs. Lee D.
Greenefield, William B.
Haraner, Henry.
Harder, Mr. and Mrs. George A.
Harper, Henry S., and manservant.
Harper, Mrs. Henry S.
Hawksford, Henry.
Hays, Mrs. Charles M., and daughter, Margaret.
Harris, Mrs. Henry B.
Hippach, Miss Jean.
Hogeboom, Mrs. John C.
Hoyt, Mr. and Mrs. Fred.
Ismay, J. Bruce.
Leader, Mrs. A. F.
Lines, Mrs. Ernest.
Lines, Miss Mary C.
Longley, Miss G. F.
Madill, Miss Gorgietta A.
Marschal, Pierce.
Marvin, Mrs. D. W.
Minnihan, Mrs. W. E.
Minnihan, Miss Daisy.
Newell, Miss Madeline.
Newell, Miss Marjorie.
Henry, Mr. and Mrs. L.
Hooper, Mrs. W. A.
Nile, Mr.
Flynn, Mr. J.
Fortune, Miss Alice.
Rosenbaum, Miss Edith.
Rheims, Mrs. George.
Stone, Mrs. George M.
Segesser, Miss Emma.
Seaward, Mr. Frederick.
Shutter, Miss E. W.
Slooper, William T.
Behr, Mrs. Carl H.
Dessette, Miss.
Bucknell, Mrs. William.
Barkworth, Mrs. A. H.
Steffasen, Mr. H. B.
Bowerman, Mrs. Elsie E.
Marvin, Mrs. D. W.
Emoch, Mr. Philip.
Geoght, Mr. James.
Maimy, Miss Ruberta.
Marschal, Mr. Pierre.
Minahan, Mrs. W. E.
Ranelt, Miss Apple.
Taussig, Miss Ruth.
Thor, Miss Ella.
Taylor, Mr. and Mrs. E. Z.
Tucker, Gilbert M.
Thayer, Mr. J. B.
Rogerson, Mr. John (probably Ryerson).
Newell, Miss Madelcine.
Newell, Mrs. Marjorie.
Newsom, Mrs. Helen W.
Omond, Mr. Flennad.
Ostby, Mr. B. C.
Ostby, Miss Helen R.
Renago, Mrs. Mamam J.
Olivia, Middle.

List of survivors whose names do not appear on the original sailing list:

Brown, Edith.
Brown, T. S. W.
Cahries, William E.
Carmaccion, Renardo M.
Driscoll, Miss B.
Formery, Miss Elein.
Gerros, Mrs. Margy I.
Healy, Miss Norah.
Hansen, Mrs. Jennie.
Hososons, Massefame.
McGowan, Miss Annie.
McDearmott, Miss Letitia.
Mare, Mrs. Florence.
Pansky, Miss Rossi.
Skeliery, Mrs. W. N.
Trout, Mrs. Jessie.
Bentham, Miss Lillian.

Captain of Olympic Reports Names of Rescued Tourists

NEW YORK, April 16.—The following list of survivors was sent by wireless by Captain Haddock of the Olympic to the White Star line offices:

Appleton, Mrs. Edward W.
Anderson, Harry.
Abbott, Mrs. Rose.
Burns, Mrs. G. M.
Cassebere, Mrs. D. D.
Clarke, Mrs. William.
Chibinace, Mrs. D.
Crossbie, Miss E. G.
Crossbie, Miss H. E.
Huppuch, Miss Jean.
Harris, Mrs. L. Y. B.
Halverson, Mrs. Alexander.
Hays, Miss Margaret.
Kimberly, Mr. and Mrs. Ed.
Kennyman, F. A.
Kenchen, Miss Emile.
Longley, Miss M. F.
Leader, Mrs. A. F.
Lavery, Miss Betha.
Lives, Miss Ernest.
Clines, Miss Mary.
Lindstrom, Mrs. Singrid.
Lesneur, Gustav J.
Amadill, Miss Giorgette.
Meilcard, Madam.
Tucker, Mrs., and maid.
Thayer, Mrs. J. B.
Thayer Jr., J. B.
Woolner, Henry.
Ward, Miss Anna.
Williams, Richard M.
Warner, Mrs. P. M.
Wilson, Miss Helen A.
Willard, Miss.
Wicks, Miss Mary.
Widener, Mrs. George D.
White, Mrs. G. Stuart.
Young, Miss Marie.
Potter Jr., Mrs. Thomas.
Roberts, Mrs. Edna S.
Rothes, Countess of.
Rolmane, C.
Rogerson, Mrs. Susan P.
Rogerson, Miss Emily B.
Rogerson, Mrs. Arthur.
Allison, Master and nurse.
Andrews, Miss K. T.
Panhart, Miss Ninette.
Allen, Miss E. W.
Bishop, Mr. and Mrs.
Blank, Mr.
Bassina, Miss A.
Baxter, Mrs. James.
Bayton, Miss George A.
Bonnell, Miss C.
Brown, Mrs. J. M.
Bowen, Miss G. C.
Beckwith, Mr. and Mrs. R. L.
Barratt, Carl B.
Bissett, Miss.
Becknell, Mrs. William.
Steffanson, Mrs. H. B.
Bowerman, Miss E.
BROWN, MRS. J. J.
Martin (or Marvin), Mrs. D. W.
Emmerk, Philip.
Googht, James.
Maimy, Miss Ruberta.
Pirie, Mr.
Marshall, Mr.
Ninhan, Mrs.
Ninanhan, Mrs. Daisy.
Newell, Mrs. Madelin.
Newell, Mrs. Marjorie.
Newson, Mrs. Helen W.
Ormond, Fionnam.
Ostby, E. C.
Ostby, Miss Helen.
Olivia, Miss Middie.
Renago, Mrs. M. J.
Piernault (or Raneit), Miss A. P.
Taussig, Miss Ruth.
Thor, Miss Ella.
Peuchen, Major Arthur.
Taylor, E. Z.
Taylor, Mrs. E.
Tucker, Gilbert.
Thayer, J. B.
Rogerson, John.
Rotschild, Mrs. Lord.
Rosenbaum, Miss Edith.
Heims, Mrs. George R.
Stone, Miss George N.
Ziegresser, Miss Emma.
Steward, Fred.
Shutter, Miss.
Loper, William T.
Swift, Fred Joel.
Scoabel, Paul.
Spedden, Mr. and Mrs. J. O.
Sheddel, Robert Douglas.
Snyder, Mr. and Mrs. John.
Sorefeira, Miss Augusta.
Spencer, R.
Thern, Silver.
Simonius, Alphonsine.
Smith, Lucien P.
Stephens, Mrs. Walter P.
Solemon, Abraham.
Silber, Mrs. William B.
Stengel, Mr. and Mrs. L. E. Helery.
Spencer, Mrs. W. A., and maid.
Taussig (or Haussig), Mlle.
Flynn, John.
Fortune, Miss Mabel.
Fortune, Miss Alice.
Fortune, Miss.
Fautini, Mrs. Mark.
Fraventhal, Henry W.
Fraventhal, Mrs.
Forchlicher, Mrs. Margaret.
Futrelle, Mrs. Jacques E.
Gracie, Colonel Arthur.
Graham, Mrs. William.
Graham, Miss.
Graham, Mr.
Carter, Miss Lucie E.
Carter, Master William.
Cander, Mrs. Churchill.
Colderhead, N. P.
O'Connell, Robert.
Cavendish, Mrs. Turrence, and maid.
Chaffee, Mrs. H. L.
Cardesea, Thomas.
Cardesea, Mrs. J. W.
Cummings, Mrs. J.
Washington, Mr.
Gordon, Sir and Lady Cosmo Duff.
Douglas, Fred C.
Gibson, Miss Dorothy.
Goldenburg, Mrs. Samuel.
Goldenburg, Miss Ella.
Greenfield, Mrs. Lee.
Dodge, Mrs. Washington.
Astor, Mrs. John Jacob, and maid.
Gibson, Mrs. Leonard.
Dogiboom, Mrs. I. C.
Hawksfort, W. J.
Harper, Henry, and valet.
Homer, Henry.
Hoyt, Mr. and Mrs. Fred M.
Harder, George.
Harder, Mrs.
Hayes, Mrs. Charles M.
Hipack, Mrs. Ida S.
Chiver, Paul.

ISADOR STRAUS
New York Millionaire, Reported Among the Drowned on the Titanic.

VINCENT ASTOR
Son of John Jacob Astor, Who, if His Father Was Lost on the Titanic, Will Inherit Many Millions and Become Head of the House.

Cherry, Miss Gladys.
Chambers, Mr. and Mrs. V. C.
Carter, Mr. and Mrs. W. E.
Devisiliet, Mme.
Daniel, Robert W.
Davidson, Mrs. Thornton.
Douglas, Walter.
Daniel, Mrs. Sarah.
Drachensted, Alfred.
Endres, Mrs. Caroline.
Ellis, Miss.
Earnshaw, Miss Belton.
Francalli, Miss.
Fiegenheim, Miss Antoinette.
Abelson, Anna.
Angel, William.
Durant, Leonera Asunsion.
Genovese, Argene.
Brown, Miss Edith.
Ball, Miss Ada.
Beale, Edward.
Deane, Mrs. Ethel.
Buyhl, Miss Dagnan.
Bystrom, Mrs. Caroline.

Bass, Miss K.
Christie, M. J.
Clark, Mrs. Ada.
Collier, Miss Marjorie.
Coldwell, Mrs. Sylvana.
Cameron, Miss.
Davis, Miss Mary.
Doling, Mrs. Ada.
Drew, Mrs. Lulu.
Davies, John.
Portalupp, Mrs. Emilie.
Faunthre, Mrs. Elizabeth.
Hart, Mrs. Esther.
Hearman, Mrs. Jane (?).
Healy, Mrs. Nora.
Hanson, Miss Jennie.
Hasons, M.
Herring, Eliza.
Richards, Miss Emily.
Richards, W. E., Jr.
Hamalanian, W.
Pedro, Julian.
Kelly, Miss Fannie.
Lehman, Miss Bertha.
Somine, Mrs. L.
Leach, Jessie W.
Lauch, Mrs. Alexander.
Mallett, Mme.
Marshall, Miss Kate.
McDearmont, Miss Leila.
Nye, Mrs. Elizabeth.
Oxenham, Percy J.
Becker, Miss Ruth.
Becker, Richard.
Pensky, Miss Rosie.
Mangi, Miss Paula.
O'Quick, Miss Winnie.
Rogers, Miss Eliza.
Didedale, Mrs. Lucy.
Ranouf, Mrs. Lizzie.
Skelley, Mrs. William.
Linnkanca, Miss Anna.
Formery, Miss Elaine.
Watt, Miss Bessie.
West, Mrs., and two children.
Moore, Mrs. Florence.
Webber, Miss Susan.
Wells, Mrs. A.
Wells, Mr.
Bentham, Miss Tellian.
Christy, Mrs. Alice.
Collier, Mrs. Stuart.
Collier, Mrs. Charlotte.
Caldwell, Albert.
Caldwell, Allan.
Davidson, Miss Mary.
Doling, Elsie.
Driscoll, B.
Davies, Miss Agnes.
Palli, Sig. Emilio.
Duvant, Miss Florentine.
Gurside, Miss Mabel.
Hartent, Miss Eva.
Harper, Miss Nancy.
Hewlet, Miss Marie.
Harris, George.
Hold, Miss Annie.
Hocking, Miss Nellie.
Richards, Mr.
Jackson, Mrs. Amy.
Gerrcia, Mrs. Mary.
Keen, Miss Nora.
Lawche, Miss Juliet.
Laroche, Miss Louise.
Lenore, Mrs. Elizabeth.
Mullingtere, Mrs. Elizabeth, and child.
Metelli, Andrie.
McGowan, Miss Anne.
Mellot, John.
Naseraeli, Miss Adelia.
Becker, Mrs. Allen.
Becker, Miss Mary.
Parsch, Mrs. L.
Phillips, Miss Alice.
O'Quick, Mrs. Jane.
O'Quick, Miss Phyllis.
Encarimo, Benardo.
Ruy, Miss Emile.
Smith, Mrs. Marion.
Silvana, Miss Sylvia.
Trout, Mrs. Jessie.
Williams, Charles.
Charles, William E.
Croft, Miss Miller M.
Wright, Miss Marion.
Watt, Miss Bertha.
Wells, Miss.

BRUNSWICK, Maine, April 16.—Percival W. White, a Massachusetts cotton manufacturer, who was a passenger on the Titanic, makes his home in this town. Friends here say he is accompanied by his son, Richard F. White, a senior at Bowdoin college, and not by Percival W. White Jr., as first reported.

Explanations of Names Confused by Wireless

CAPE RACE, N. F., April 16.—Survivors whose names are in doubt:

WIRELESS VERSION.	PROBABLE MEANING.
Becker, Mrs. Allen, Miss Ruth, Miss Mary, Master Richard.	Undoubtedly the same as given in sailing list under names "Mrs. A. O. Beiker and three children."
Juliet, Mr. Laroche.	Mrs. Joseph La Roche and
Mr. La Roche, Simone.	Simone La Roche.
Link Kanca, Miss Anna.	Mrs. William Lahtigan.
Marshall, Miss Kate.	Mrs. Marshall.
Mange, Mr. Paula.	May be Mrs. William Angle.
Malcroft, Mrs. Millie.	Miss Nellie Walcroft.
Melloss, J. N.	May be William Mellers.
Naserall, Mrs. Adelia.	Mrs. Nicholas Nisser.
Oxenham, Percy J.	Thomas Oxenham.
Rogers, Miss Eliza.	Selina Rogers.
Silwana, Miss Synly.	Lillie Silven.

Survivors Among Passengers From Second-Cabin List

CAPE RACE, N. F., April 16.—The names of the rescued second-cabin passengers, so far as they check up with the Titanic's published list, are:

Angle, William.
Aleison, Hanna.
Bell, Ada P.
Bliss, Miss Kate.
Beane, Edward.
Beane, Miss Ethel.
Bryhl, Miss Dagmar.
Bystrom, Miss Karolina.
Collyer, Mrs. Charlotte.
Collyer, Miss Marjorie.
Christy, Miss Alice.
Christy, Miss Julia.
Clark, Mrs. Ada Maria.
Cameron, Miss.
Collett, Mrs. Stuart.
Caldwell, Albert F.
Caldwell, Mrs. Sylvia.
Caldwell, Alden G.
Drew, Mrs. Lulu.
Davis, Miss Agnes.
Davis, John M.
Duran, Florentina.
Duran, Ascuncion.
Davis, Miss Mary.
Doling, Mrs. Ada.
Doling, Miss Elsie.
Faunthrope, E.
Garside, Miss Ethel.
Hewlett, Miss Mary D.
Harris, George.
Herman, Mrs. Jane.
Herman, Miss Kate.
Herman, Miss Alice.
Hold, Miss Annie.
Hart, Mrs. Esther.
Hart, Miss Eva.
Harper, Miss Nina.
Hamalainer, Anna, and son.
Hocking, Mrs. Elizabeth.
Hocking, Miss Nellie.
Jacobsohn, Mrs. Amy.
Keane, Miss Nora.
Kelly, Miss Fannie.
Lareche, Miss Louise.
Leitch, Miss Jessie W.
Lamore, Mrs.
Lehman, Miss Bertha.
Mellinger, Mrs. Elizabeth and child.
Louch, Mrs. Alice.
Mallet, Mrs. A.
Mallet, Master Andrero.
Nye, Mrs. Elizabeth.
Phillips, Miss Alice.
Pallas, Emilio.
Padro, Julian.
Parish, Mrs. L.
Portaluppi, Mrs. Emilio.
Quick, Mrs. Jane O.
Quick, Miss Phyllis O.
Quick, Miss Wennie O.
Rebouf, Mrs. Lillie.
Ridsdale, Miss Lucy.
Rugg, Miss Emily.
Richard, Mr. and Mrs. Emile and son.
Sincock, Miss Maude.
Smith, Mrs. Marion.
Trout, Miss Edna S.
Weisz, Mrs. Matilda.
Webber, Miss Susan.
Wright, Miss Marion.
Watt, Miss Bessie.
Watt, Miss Bertha.
West, Mrs., and two children.
Wells, Mrs. Addie.
Wells, Miss J.
Wells, Ralph.
Williams, Charles.
Trout, Miss Edna S.

Mrs. J. J. Astor Named Among the Survivors

NEW YORK April 16.—At 7 o'clock this morning the White Star company received a Marconigram from the Carpathia stating that among the survivors on board were Mrs. John Jacob Astor and maid.

In sending this word to Vincent Astor, her stepson, the agents of the line said:

"We hope that we will be able before long to tell you that your father is safe."

When an explanation of this enigmatic statement was demanded the company officials said that they had nothing tangible on which to base it.

"We are hoping for the best," they said.

Privately the line officials said they feared that Astor and all of the noted men on board went down with the steamer. They could figure out no way that they might have escaped.

WASHINGTON A. ROEBLING
Wealthy Wire Manufacturer, Listed Among the Titanic's Dead.

MRS. LENA ALLAN STOIBER-ROOD
Denver Woman, Whose Husband, Hugh Rood, Is Reported Among Those Lost With the Titanic.

List of Second-Class Passengers on Wrecked Ship

LONDON, April 16.—The list of second-class passengers on board the Titanic is as follows:

Angle, William, and wife.
Ashby, John.
Ableson, Samson.
Abelson, Hanna.
Andrew, Edgar.
Bentham, Lillian.
Balls, Ada E.
Bliss, Kate.
Bateman, Robert J.
Beesley, Lawrence.
Beiker, Mrs. A. O., and three children.
Butler, Reginald.
Beane, Edward.
Beane, Ethel.
Beauchamp, H. J.
Brito, Jose de.
Byles, Rev. Thomas R. D.
Bambridge, Mr.
Bowenur, Solomon.
Brown, Mildred.
Baily, Percy.
Botsford, W. Hall.
Berrman, William.
Bryhl, Carl.
Bryhl, Dagmar.
Bystrom, Karolina.
Banfield, Frederick J.
Collender, Erik.
Coleridge, R. C.
Collyer, Harvey.
Collyer, Charlotte.
Collyer, Marjorie.
Corbett, Irene C.
Corey, Mrs. C. P.
Chapman, John H.
Chapman, Elizabeth.
Carter, Rev. Ernest C.
Christy, Alice.
Christy, Julia.
Clarke, Charles V.
Clarke, Ada Maria.
Cameron, Olcar.
Collander, Erik.
Collett, Stuart.
Chapman, Charles.
Carbines, William.
Cotterill, Harry.
Caldwell, Albert F.
Caldwell, Sylvia.
Caldwell, Allen G.
Drachstedt, Baron von.
Carlo, Sebastiani de.
Denbury, Herbert.
Drew, James V.
Drew, Lulu.
Drew, Marshall.
Davis, Agnes.
Davis, John M.
Duran, Florentina.
Duran, A.
Deacon, Percy E.
Davies, Charles.
Dibden, William.
Davis, Mary.
Denton, William J.
Doling, Ada.
Doling, Elsie.
DeF., Lena.
Fox, Stanley.
Fahlstrom, Arnej.
Faunthorpe, Harry.
Faunthorpe, Lizzie.
Fillbrook, Charles.
Fjunk, Annie.
Fynney, Joseph.
Gaskell, Alfred.
Gillespie, William.
Garside, Ethel.
Gilbert, William.
Gale, Harry.
Gale, S.
Gill, John.
Giles, Ralph.
Givard, Hans K.
Greenberg, Samuel.
Giles, Fred.
Giles, Edgar.
Gavey, Lawrence.
Hewlett, Mary D.
Harris, Walter.
Harris, George.
Herman, George.
Herman, Samuel.
Herman, Jane.
Herman, Kate.
Hold, Stephen.
Hold, Annie.
Hunt, George.
Hickman, Leonard.
Hickman, Stanley.
Hood, Ambrose.
Howard, Benjamin.
Howard, Ellen T.
Hart, Benjamin.
Hart, Esther.
Hart, Eva.
Harper, Joseph.
Harper, Nina.
Hamalainer, Anna, and infant.
Hoffman, Mr., and two children.
Hocking, Elizabeth.
Hocking, Nellie.
Hocking, George.
Hodges, Henry P.
Hiltuner, Martha.
Ilott, Bertha.
Jeffert, Clifford.
Jeffert, Ernest.
Jacobsohn, Siney S.
Jacobsohn, Amy F.
Jenkins, Stephen.
Jenkins, Dr. J. G.
Kantor, S., and wife.
Keane, Daniel.
Kano, Nora A.
Kirkland, Rev. Charles.
Karnes, F.
Kelly, F.
Kviliner, John Henrik.
Learnot, Rena.
Injan, John L.
Leyson, Robert W. N.
Laroche, Joseph, and wife.
Laroche, Simonne.
Laroche, Louise.
Lambe, J. J.
Leitch, Jessie.
Lamore, Amelia.
Louch, Charles.
Louch, Alice.
Levy, R. F.
Lehman, Bertha.
Lahtigen, William, and wife.
Masgiavacchi, Emilio.
Marshall, Mr.
Marshall, Mrs.
Morawreck, Ernest.
Malachard, Noel.
McCrie, James.
Mellinger, Elizabeth, and child.
Mantvila, Joseph.
Maybery, Frank H.
Myles, Thomas F.
Mack, Mary.
Moudd, Thomas.

NO DISTINCTIONS OF WEALTH OR CLASS IN FACE OF DEATH

Titled Ladies and Second Cabin Passengers Given Equal Opportunities.

Mitchell, Henry.
Mallet, A., and wife.
Mallet, Master A.
Matthews, W. J.
McKane, Peter.
Mellers, William.
Meyer, August.
Milling, Jacob.
Nicholls, Joseph.
Norman, Robert D.
Nye, Elizabeth.
Masser, Nicholas, and wife.
Nosson, L.
Otter, Richard.
Oxenham, Thomas.
Phillips, Robert.
Phillips, Alice.
Paine, Dr. Alfred.
Pengally, Frederick.
Pallas, Emilio.
Padro, Julian.
Parker, Clifford.
Parish, Mrs. L.
Ponezell, Martin.
Portaluppi, Midio.
Pulsaum, Frank.
Quick, Jane.
Quick, Vera W.
Quick, Phyllis.
Renouf, Peter H.
Rebouf, Lillie.
Ridsdale, Lucy.
Rogers, Harry.
Rugg, Emily.
Richard, Emile.
Rogers, Selina.
Reeves, David.
Reynolds, Miss E.
Richards, Emily.
Richards, William.
Richards, George.
Sweet, George.
Sjostedt, Ernest A.
Smith, Augustus.
Sincock, Maude.
Siemer, Richard J.
Smith, Marion.
Sobey, Hayden.
Stokes, Philip J.
Slayter, H. M.
Sedgwick, F. W.
Saharp, Percival.
Sinkkonen, Anna.
Stanton, S. Ward.
Swane, George.
Shelley, L. Mannta.
Silven, Lillie.
Strant, M. E. I.
Trout, Miss E.
Turpin, William J.
Turpin, Dorothy.
Tooney, Ellen.
Troopiansky, Moses A.
Tervan, Mrs. A. T.
Veale, James.
Wilkinson, Mrs. George.
Wilkinson, Ada C.
William J. Ware.
Weisz, Leopold.
Weisz, Matilda.
Wheadon, Edward.
Ware, John James.
Ware, Florence L.
Webber, Susie.
Wilhelm, Charles.
Wright, Marion.
Watt, Bessie.
Watt, Bertha.
West, E. Arthur.
West, Ada.
West, Constance.
West, Barbara.
Wheeler, Edwin.
Wells, Mrs. Addie.
Wells, Miss J.
Wells, Ralph.
Walcroft, Nellie.
Williams, C.
Yedis, Miss H.

There were 740 third-class passengers on board.

Mrs. Guggenheim Hysterical Over Loss of Mate

NEW YORK, April 16.—The futility of money in the face of the appalling tragedy that overtook the victims of the wreck was exemplified in the case of Mrs. Benjamin Guggenheim, whose millionaire husband was one of the missing. She importuned everyone she could reach, semi-hysterically demanding that something be done.

"For God's sake, do something," she demanded of Vice President Franklin. "If there is any chance, do not let expense be spared.

"Can't you hire steamboats and rush them to the scene? There may be some boats still afloat and there may be men and women clinging to the wreckage," she pleaded.

She was assured that word had been sent to every steamer in the vicinity to comb the seas and see what they could do.

WASHINGTON, April 16.—Senator Guggenheim, in telephone consultation with the White Star line office in New York, was unable to learn the fate of his brother, Benjamn Guggenheim, reputed one of the wealthiest men in the world.

Icebergs One of Three Perils to Atlantic Liners

NEW YORK, April 16.—Icebergs, such as the one that sank the Titanic, are one of three sources of peril to vessels navigating the north Atlantic. The others are fog and derelicts. The iceberg menace has been greater this spring than in recent years.

In the last fifty years there have been twelve disasters for which icebergs were responsible. A majority occurred off Newfoundland and the Grand Banks, near the Titanic's grave. The list includes:

SHIP—Place.	Year.	Lives Lost.
Canadian, midatlantic	1863	45
Immigrant ship, off Cape Race	1864	158
Vicksburg, off Cape Race	1869	65
Warrior, Grand Banks	1878	29
North Star, Cabot straits	1881	67
Medway, off Newfoundland	1887	29
Vaillant, Grand Banks	1897	70
Snowbird, Cape Race	1898	6
Endymion, Grand Banks	1900	8
Islander, off Alaska	1901	67
Albatross, midatlantic	1903	22
Titanic, off Cape Race	1912	1,234

The drift of ice this spring has been farther south than for years. Vessels arriving here and abroad have reported ice fields extending far down into the southern track, and skipper have told of being shut in by ice as far as they could see on every side of the horizon.

The size of the bergs which have been encountered recently varies greatly, but according to reliable reports bergs reaching from sixty to one hundred feet to the top of its walls, with pinnacles and spires extending to a height of 250 feet or more, have not been unusual. Below the water some of thees giant bergs extend to probably 800 feet.

WOMEN ON SHIP SEE DEATH TAKE LOVED ONES

WHISPER FAREWELL AS TITANIC SINKS FOR FINAL PLUNGE

(Continued from page six.)

The crashing of steel upon solid ice must have struck terror to the ears of the ship's company and forecasted the horrors that were soon to come. There must have been the rush to the decks, with the few wraps hastily picked up in the mad flight, only to get the word immediately that the ship was wounded to death and that there was no chance of all being saved.

DEATH STANDS AND WAITS.

I nthe midst of an ice field, tossing and tumbling in the strong swell that never is absent from the grand banks, and with the bitter, piercing atmosphere cutting, tender flesh to the bone, men and women faced the end.

There must have been sad farewells. Loved ones were parted forever. Husbands embraced their wives and their babies for the last time, and then the stalwart began the work of putting the great boats—their number cruelly few—over the side.

The ice fields must have been very heavy. Other vessels just into port, both here and on the other side, describe the fields as almost solid and it is certain that the greatest care must have been taken on the launching of the boats so that they were not overturned.

DID WOMEN SEE END?

Whether or not the unfortunate women and children in the boats witnessed the final plunge of the wounded leviathian as she staggered to the bottom, carrying with her their nearest and dearest, will not be known until they tell their stories here. It is likely that they did, however, as the lights of the great floating hotel probably remained unextinguished utnil the final plunge.

The women and children, it sems certain, suffered greatly while the frail boats in which they had taken refuge tossed like corks on the surface of the water. It was long after daylight when the Carpathia finally arrived, only to find the score of heavily laden boats and the floating wreckage.

The Titanic was gone forever.

Tidings of Horror Told in Briefest Word by Wireless

Message Says 866 Only Titanic Survivors, Aboard Carpathia, En Route to New York.

NEW YORK, April 16.—The tidings that the Titanic had sunk came in a brief wireless dispatch to Cape Race, N. F., shortly after 7 o'clock last night from the White Star liner Olympic, which reported that the Titanic had foundered at about 2:20 Monday morning in latitude 41:16 north and longitude 50:14 west.

The message added that the steamship Carpathia, then on her way to Naples, had reached the scene of the wreck at daybreak and found only boats and wreckage and that all the Titanic's boats were accounted for and "about 675 souls saved, crew and passengers, latter nearly all women and children."

This news was confirmed shortly afterward by officials of the White Star line here, who announced that the Olympic had sent them a wireless dispatch that the Titanic had sunk.

A wireless dispatch received early today at Boston, which was relayed by the Olympic from the Carpathia, stated that the Carpathia had 866 of the Titanic's passengers on board, mostly women and children, concluding with the words:

"Grave fears are felt for the safety of the balance of the passengers and the crew."

SEARCH FOR SURVIVORS.

The wireless dispatch from Cape Race, N. F., telling of the sinking, also gave the information that the steamship Californian was remaining and searching the vicinity of the disaster.

The brief wireless dispatches received so far show that the passengers and crew passed through thrilling experiences from the very moment that the monster Titanic crashed into the iceberg in the dead of night until the Carpathia, several hours later, reached the scene and rescued the survivors from lifeboats floating in a sea of ice.

PASSENGERS IN BED.

The collision occurred at a time when most of the passengers had retired or were about to go to bed. The shock of the collision sent many of the passengers to the decks partly dressed. A wireless dispatch came through Camperdown, N. S., saying that the passengers were ordered to the lifeboats at once and that many were scantily clad as they took their places in the boats. This would indicate that the Titanic's condition was such that no time could be spared to return to staterooms for additional clothes.

Danger still confronted even those who were so fortunate as to be put aboard the lifeboats. Huge quantities of field ice covered the ocean, a wireless dispatch says, and in the darkness the crews had to guide their boats with the greatest care to prevent being jammed and overturned. The ice was so heavy that the lifeboats could not force their way through it and as a result the boats became widely separated. The air was biting cold and the chill that rose from the ice floes caused the passengers to hover close together to keep warm. All through the night the lifeboats bobbed helplessly between the shifting cakes of ice, while the survivors prayed for dawn to come.

Shortly after 2 o'clock the sinking Titanic made her great dive into the sea, carrying hundreds of persons to death.

Daylight came and with it arrived the Cunarder Carpathia, which found only the score of lifeboats, filled with crew and passengers, floating helplessly about the vicinity where the Titanic had passed under the waves.

SYMPATHY EXPRESSED.

WASHINGTON, April 16.—The house of epresentatves unanimously adopted a resolution today extending sympathy to the relatives of those who met their death in teh disaster of the Titanic.

HOW THE TITANIC, WOUNDED LEVIATHAN OF THE SEAS, PLUNGED BOW DOWNWARD TO THE BOTTOM OF THE ATLANTIC WITH 1,500 PEOPLE

Company's Officers Besieged by Those Who Lost Relatives

Officials Admit They Held Back Worst News For Many Hours.

NEW YORK, April 16.—Utterly stunned by the weight of the terrible disaster that followed the loss of the giant liner Titanic on her maiden voyage, New York halted today.

It was hard to realize that the latest creation of marine architecture, the great steamship which only yesterday, when news that she had been in collision was received, was proudly branded by her owners as "unsinkable," now lay below the waters of the Atlantic off the banks of Newfoundland and had carried with her much of the flower of American and British manhood.

Not since the ill-fated French liner Bourgoyne was rammed and sent to the bottom with all of her company by the great iron freighter Cromarthshire on July 2, 1898, have such scenes been witnessed as were enacted at the offices of the White Star line on lower Broadway throughout the night and today.

Men, women and children, many hysterical and weeping, stormed the offices and vainly begged for some word of comfort regarding the fate of their loved ones.

FEARS ARE UNALLAYED.

Few got any satisfaction. For the great majority all that the company would say was that there had been loss of life, but they were hoping for the best.

To relatives of noted passengers a private audience was granted, and it was quietly whispered that the outlook was most serious. But even they did not get all of the facts which the company had in its possession.

For some inexplicable reason the White Star line had steadily refrained from making public facts in its possession and apparently it was able to muzzle the wireless, as messages sent direct to ships on the scene were held up, while not a single word was permitted to penetrate from the fogbound banks of Newfoundland, where the worst tragedy of recent years was being enacted.

Charges were freely made by relatives of the missing tnat the company not alone withheld news of the disaster, but that it was responsible for the messages of comfort received yesterday saying all of the passengers had been rescued and the disabled liner was being towed to port. But the officials refused explanation.

They admitted they had known for some hours before they made public announcement that the Titanic had foundered, but they defended their action by saying that until Captain Haddock of the Olympic confirmed the reports they had not felt justified in alarming the people of the nation.

When the first announcement was made last night that the Titanic had sunk and that there was "probable loss of life," the offices of the line were immediately besieged by anxious men and women, all waiting for a word of comfort or assurance. To all the statement was made that the Titanic had foundered and that there was loss of life, but that no names were then available.

The word reached many while they were in the theaters and the restaurants and soon great automobiles and vehicles of all descriptions were rolling up to the offices and discharging their freight of anxious humanity, and soon the offices were crowded and the line had extended far out into the street.

ASTOR'S SON ARRIVES.

Among the first to reach the offices of the line was Vincent Astor, only son of Colonel John Jacob Astor. He was worried, but hopeful, when he arrived, and was admitted to the private offices of Vice President Franklin.

He was accompanied by A. J. Biddle and the representative of the Astor estate. Half an hour later the young man emerged weeping bitterly, was assisted into his automobile and taken home.

Sylvester Byrnes private secretary of Isidor Straus, another victim, remained at the office of the line all night, hoping against hope that Straus might have been saved. He went home at 8:30 saying that there was no doubt that his employer, with all the other noted men on board, had perished.

Other relatives of the missing soon arrived, and it was anounced the list of survivors would be made public as soon as possible.

LIST SLOW IN COMING.

The work of compiling this was slow, as the list had to be sent to the Olympic, which then sent it to another ship, which sent it to the wireless station at Siasconset, Mass., and from there it came into this city over the land lines. But before they would give the list out the line officials verified it.

It was seen at once that there had been no class distinction, but the women of the steerage had been cared for in the same manner as their more fortunate sisters of the first-class and second-class. The women had been taken off and the men remained to die, and even in their deep sorrow it was plain that most of those who heard the sad news were proud to know this fact.

The officers of the line were seemingly stupefied by the news. Only once did Vice President Franklin flash and flare up, and that was when he was told that it was reported and generally credited that the company had withheld its news of the disaster and muzzled the wireless so that reinsurance might be secured.

He said: "That is an absolute lie, and those who make the statement know they lie. We did not admit the Titanic was sunk until we were absolutely assured it was a fact. We are doing all we can to find out who were saved and who lost."

When Franklin was asked why the company gave out the wireless which it said that it had received from the Olympic yesterday saying that all of the Titantic's passengers were safely on board the Carparthia, he refused to reply.

Besides the personal appeals for news the offices were deluged with frantic appeals by long-distance telephone and telegraph. To all the same reply was made, that as soon as the actual facts were known the news would be made public.

It was accepted everywhere from the start that Captain E. J. Smith, admiral of the White Star fleet, went down with his ship. For forty years he had been a navigator and for more than twenty a master of ocean ships.

His first accident came last fall when, as master of the Olympic, he was on the bridge when that sister ship of the Titanic was smashed by the British cruiser Hawke.

NOTHING TO LIVE FOR.

Then at the outset of his work as commander of the Titanic he had encountered an accident when he just missed destroying the steamer New York by failing to shut off his engines when passing her berth at the Southampton docks.

His friends said there could be nothing for the veteran to live for after losing the Titanic. The very fact that he had failed to "sense" the icebergs would always have been held against him and the men who knew him best said he would hardly have lived to come to port even though he had saved his passengers.

Alfred G. Vanderbilt, at first supposed to have been lost, cabled his relatives here that he did not sail.

Agent Charles P. Sumner of the Cunard line gave out the following today which he said was an "unrelayed message" from Captain Rostron of the steamer Carpathia:

"The Titanic struck an iceberg at an early hour today. The Carpathia has picked up a number of survivors and expects to proceed to New York. We are at present in a field of ice. We have about 800 survivors aboard."

LONDON, April 16.—The managers of the White Star line here are still hoping against hope that other survivors of the Titanic disaster may have been picked up by vessels that rushed to the scene besides the Cartathia. They admitted, however, that the chance was slight. The Titanic and her valuable cargo, among which were diamonds valued at $5,000,000, can never be recovered.

Steamers Cruise Ice Fields in Vain Hunting Survivors

Parisian and Virginian Wireless, "We Were Too Late to Rescue Anyone.

HALIFAX, N S., April 16.—The Sable island wireless reports:

"We are now in communication with the Parisian. She has no Titanic passengers on board."

The Parisian steamed through much heavy field ice looking for passengers from the Titanic. No life rafts or bodies were sighted among the floating wreckage, which covered a large area.

The Parisian reports that the weather was cold and that even if all persons had been on the wreckage they would in all probability have perished from exposure before they could have been picked up. The Parisian is expected here tomorrow morning.

MONTREAL, April 16.—The last faint hope that more of the passengers and crew of the Titanic might have been saved went glimmering today when Captain Gambell of the Virginian reported to his agents here that his rescue trip had been fruitless.

"We arrived too late to rescue any one," says Gambell "and we are proceeding to Liverpool."

This was accepted here as meaning that the only persons saved were those taken from the lifeboats by the Carpathia.

ST. JOHNS, N. F., April 16.—Messages from Cape Race seem to indicate that a large majority of the men who were on the Titanic went down with the ship.

Messages from the Carpathia state

MILLIONAIRES GIVE LIVES THAT WOMEN MAY BE RESCUED

that all of the boats launched by the Titanic have been accounted for. The boats were filled largely with women and children, but had sufficient members of the Titanic's crew to guide them. The belief was general here that all who survived the wreck are on the Carpathia.

The cable steamer Minia, which left St. Pierre, Miq., yesterday, is supposed to be near the scene of the disaster, but little hope is entertained that she would find any of the Titanic's people.

WASHINGTON, April 16.—Gloom prevailed in the White house today as hope went glimmering with the receipt of dispatches of the Titanic catastrophe.

President Taft, deeply touched, kept in communication with the White Star officers in New York, endeavoring to "get just a word" concerning Major Archibald Butt, his military aide and companion, who, it is feared, was numbered among the hundreds who went to death in the sinking of the Titanic.

The tragedy of the Titanic was felt in the house and indirect reference was made to the sea horror by the Rev. Henry N. Couden, the blind chaplain of the house, in his prayer opening the session. The Rev. Mr. Couden prayed for more stringent laws for the protection of those whose work or travel exposed them to dangers.

MONTREAL, April 16.—The weather signal station on the Gulf of St. Lawrence reported today that heavy fogs lay off Nova Scotia and that a violent thunderstorm broke in that neighborhood last night and is traveling eastward. It was said that such conditions left little hope for the rescue of any survivors of the Titanic that might still be adrift in rafts or boats.

Nearby Steamer Urged to Rush to Grave of Titanic

NEW York, April 16.—Officials of the Marconi company said today that they had been trying to communicate with the steamships Megantic, Minewaska and Vaderland, all outward bound and which appear to be in a position to get into communication with the Carpathia.

The California, of the Leyland line, appears to be near the scene of the wreck today. The Leyland line officials have asked the Marconi company to send the necessary orders to the California to steam immediately to the point where the Titanic went down and remain there until relieved or her coal supply became short and to render what aid she could.

GREAT FIELDS OF ICE AROUND TITANIC GRAVE

NEW YORK, April 16.—Incoming steamships from Europe, which have been held up down the bay by fog for the last twenty-four hours or more, all report having passed many large icebergs and ice fields near where the Titanic was lost.

The Red Star liner Lapland, from Antwerp and Dover, reports she passed large and small icebergs near longitude 49.50 and latitude 42 and that the ice fields extended as far as the eye could reach.

The steamer Niagara said that on April 10, in latitude 44.07 and longitude 50.40, she saw many icebergs, followed by an ice field, and that the liner steamed around the field until 3 o'clock the following afternoon.

While steaming through the ice fields the wash of the sea hurled a large block of flint-like ice against the port bow of the Niagara and perforated one plate.

If you want to get the news—
BUY THE TIMES.

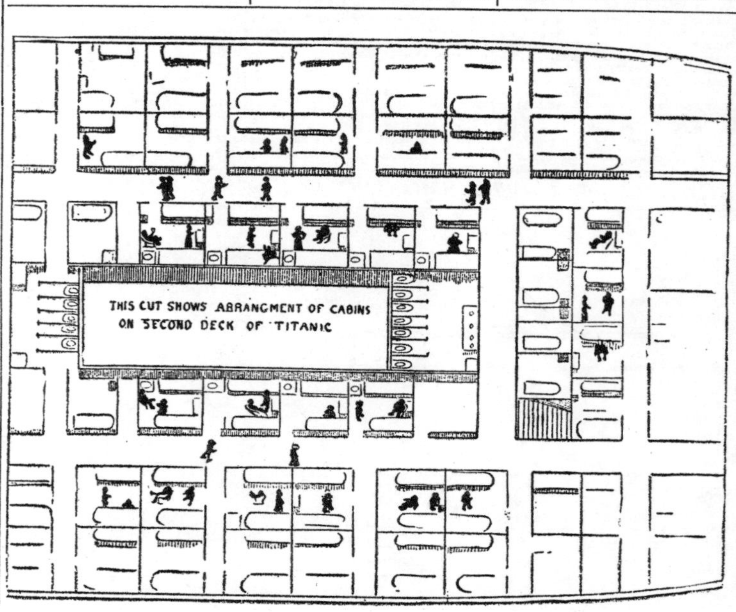

THIS CUT SHOWS ARRANGMENT OF CABINS ON SECOND DECK OF TITANIC

MEN VALUE THEIR LIVES LIGHTLY TO SAVE WOMEN

ANCIENT SEA LAW RIGIDLY ENFORCED BY CAPTAIN SMITH

Commander of Titanic Goes to Death on Bridge of Ill-Fated Ship.

(Continued From Page One.)

national Mercantile Marine, owners of the White Star line, is among the survivors, as is his wife.

Wireless reports say Cunard liner Carpathia has on board 866 survivors, the total thus far accounted for. She is steaming for New York and should arrive on Friday. The rescued pessengers drifted in lifeboats for many hours before succor came.

Captain E. J. Smith, commander of the Titanic, probably went to his grave with his ill-fated vessel without once being able to communicate direct with the agents of his line. Aside from the "C. Q. D" sent by his wireless operator, not one word from him was received up to the time the Titanic sank. The presumption is that he met death at his post as a gallant skipper should. That he and his crew enforced rigidly the unwritten law of the sea—women and children first—is plainly indicated by the preponderance of women among the partial list of survivors that the wireless has given.

CAREER OF ILL LUCK.

Although rated as one of the most able commanders since the advent of the modern steamship, Captain Smith's career recently had been marred with ill luck. He was in command of the Titanic's sister ship, Olmypic, when that vessel was in collision with the British cruiser Hawke.

Exonerated of all blame for this occurrence, he was placed in charge of the Titanic, only to graze disaster when his new charge fouled the steamship New York in the Solent after leaving Southampton on her maiden voyage, which has ended so disastrously. He had been in the line's employ more than thirty years and his first important command was the Majestic.

Although 866 persons are reported to be on the Carpathia, it is apparent that all of them are not passengers, for it was necessary for members of the Titanic's crew to man the lifeboats which set out from the sinking liner. How many of the crew were assigned to each boat is a matter of conjecture.

A similarly unsettled matter is the percentage of first-class passengers among those saved. While the names of survivors obtained are largely those of saloon passengers, the rule, "Women first," should apply equally to the second cabin and steerage, a regulation which may have cost the life of many prominent men above decks. It is natural also that the names of the more obscure survivors would be slower in reaching land.

FALSE NEWS, FALSE HOPES.

False news and false hopes and an international belief that the palatial Titanic was practically unsinkable followed the slowly unfolding accounts of her loss in a way without precedent. Eager crowds in a dozen cities in the United States besieged bulletin boards when it became known that the giant liner had really sunk, with terrible loss of life, and in New York city well-known men and women crowded into the White Star line offices seeking news of relatives.

The speed at which the Titanic was traveling when she shattered herself against the iceberg will perhaps not be known until the first of her survivors reach port. Whatever her rate of progress, however, ship builders here and abroad must admit that, while the modern steamship may defy wind and weather, ice and fog remain an ever present element of danger. No ship, they point out, no matter how stanchly built nor how many water-tight bulkheads protect her, may plunge headlong against a wall of ice without grave results. The general opinion is that the Titanic's equipment was put to an extraordinary test which no vessel could have withstood.

"Under ordinary circumstances those water-tight compartments will preserve a ship from sinking," said A. L. Hopkins, vice president of the Newport News Shipbuilding and Dry Dock company, in New York.

"But smashing into an iceberg could produce shattering effects that would render a ship helpless beyond the protection of any design yet known. In fore and after collisions where the compartments are punctured, the lowering of either end of the ship produces an increased strain on the other compartments."

SMASHED TO SECTIONS.

Granting that only the forward bukhead of the Titanic had been crumpled by the impact with the iceberg, Mr. Hopkins was inclined to think that the relative buoyancy of the remaining compartments would have been sufficient to save the vessel.

SKETCHED FROM TELEGRAPHIC DISPATCHES, SHOWING TITANIC COLLIDING WITH ICEBERG

Inasmuch as he was not familiar with the relative division of the Titanic's compartments, he coud not estimate how many compartments must have given way under the impact of the collision.

Robert Stocker, naval constructor of the Brooklyn navy yard, says:

"In the case of the Titanic I am inclined to think that her sinking was due to the effect of grounding, rather than to the impact of collision. Frequently a ship strikes what is known as a 'pinnacle rock,' ripping open her keel. The iceberg against which the Titanic smashed her bow may have had some such submerged projection, which did additional damage to the keel. If the forward bulkheads of the vessel had held after the impact which smashed the bow, it certainly seems that the relative buoyancy of the remaining compartments should have been sufficient to keep the ship afloat. I am compelled to believe that a great many of her compartments must have been punctured or sprung."

Lewis Nixon, the eminent naval architect, is inclined to think the Titanic was either traveling at full speed or perhaps crashed into a berg so tremendous that there was practically no give.

"If the Titanic hit one of those great ice masses," said Mr. Nixon, "it is likely she struck one that had no more give than a rock. Under these circumstances something had to give way, and as the iceberg did not, the great ship had to crumple up. It is conceivable that an impact of this sort might have buckled her longitudinal plates from end to end, shearing off and starting rivets and opening up the water tight compartments throughout the length of the vessel."

RISK ON WATER SMALL.

For many years steamship men have asserted that the safest place to be on is a well-equipped ocean liner. Proportional to the number carried, statistics show there is less loss of life and less chance of injury on board a modern liner than there is in any other means of transportation. Fleets come and go from New York and other ports with the regularity of the tides and those carrying mails maintain a schedule which almost equals in punctuality that of railway mail trains.

Transatlantic steamers travel in well-defined routes, known as "steamship lanes," the westbound and the eastbound. This reduces to a minimum the chances of collision with one another. But icebergs and derelicts have no respect for these rules and float into the paths or wallow across them, to be a dire menace in time of fog or very thick weather. There is no way to give warning until too late. Out of the smother of a fog a pallid shape may be glimpsed over the bows, to be followed a half minute later by the crash of the bows against the mass of ice.

After the first desperate calls of the Titanic for help had been sent flying through space and brought steamers for hundreds of miles around speeding to the scene, what seems to have been an impenetrable wall of silence was raised between the coast and the steamer. The giant liner went to her fate without so much as a whisper of what must have been the scenes of terrible tragedy enacted on her decks.

In the lack of even a line from a survivor imagination pauses before even trying to conjecture what passed as the inevitable became known and it was seen that of the more than 2,000 human lives with which she was freighted there could be hope of saving, as it appears, far less than half.

Other than the news last evening that 866 persons, largely women and children, had been rescued from the liner's boats by the Cunarder Carpathia, several hours passed without a word as to the fate of the rest of those on board at the time of the fateful crash.

Along the entire Atlantic coast wireless instruments were attuned to catch from any source the slightest whisper of hope that possibly one of the many steamships which rushed to the assistance of the Titanic bore other survivors. But from none of the ships reported to be at or near the scene of what, viewed in the light of probabilities, may be recorded as the world's greatest marine horror, came the slightest syllable of encouragement to the anxiously waiting world.

Early last night there was hope that any moment might bring word of cheer. But anxiety deepened and many friends and relatives of those who sailed on the Titanic began to despair as hours passed and the night grew old without word from either of the Allan liners Persian or Virginian, believed to be, with the exception of the Carpathia, the vessels nearest the Titanic's ocean burial place when she disappeared.

As the Titanic sank before 3 o'clock in the morning and it was not hoped that the Virginian could reach the scene before 10 a. m. at the earliest, while the Persian was said to be some distance farther away it was feared even by the White Star officials, trying their best to calculate accurately, that they would not have reached the scene in time to be of service.

The steamer Virginian was finally heard from at 2:15 o'clock this morning. She did not report the presence of any survivors on board, the message from her stating that she would bring to St. Johns N. F., such survivors as she "may rescue."

The Titanic herself lies buried two

TITANIC'S DISASTER TOPS ALL HORRORS OF LOSSES AT SEA

miles beneath the ocean surface midway between Sable island and Cape Race. Her position when she struck the iceberg was given as latitude 41.46 N., longitude 50.14 W.

According to the Carpathia's advices the liner, which struck the iceberg at 10:25 o'clcok Sunday night, sank at 2:20 o'clock Monday morning, nearly four hours later, in latitude 41.16, longitude 50.14, or not more than half a degree south of the point where the collision occurred. It seems improbable from this that the liner, after the accident, made much headway under her own steam.

Liner Co. Officers Bitterly Assailed for Deceptions

Was Suppression of Vital News of Titanic's Loss Mere Fake to Trick Public?

NEW YORK, April 16.—The Press, in an editorial this morning, says:

"Vast tragedies, far distant across stretches of the sea, with natural mystery and human deception intervening, do more than baffle fair criticism of a horror; they serve to outrage all the senses.

"No more agonizing cruelty can be inflicted upon the multitudes whose hearts are bursting for the truth about the disaster to the Titanic than to conspire to keep them in ignorance of the worst that is known by those responsible for authentic information; for only by knowing the worst can there be separated out the best providence has saved from the ghastly whole for the solace of some of those straining their thoughts to the watery graves hundreds of miles off Cape Race.

"Yet if those who have appeared to play the part of withholding dreadful truths which could only be postponed for the moment, not smothered forever, have struck a more maddening anguish into so many souls ashore, one must try to judge them as more pitifully weak in their failure of duty than wittingly cruel.

"Panic by officers here ashore gives a shuddering suggestion of what a panic could do afloat among those who were expected to hold thousands of lives in brave and competent charge. Yet with our faith in the noble calling of men of the sea, we must believe that, whoever was to blame for the wreck, there was better conduct on the decks of the doomed ship than in her home office.

"And even for these latter officers we must hope that the baseless reports which were given out yesterday afternoon to assure the anxious world that the wrecked passengers were all removed in safety and the ship itself, stanch even as a wreck, was in tow for port, were not fakes or deliberate invention, but that the company's officers had clutched at any rumor as at a straw that might encourage themselves in their misery.

"As for those hundreds adrift on the sea or sunken in its depths at such a time with such confusion and conflict of news and rumors one can only pray God's mercy on all."

DISASTER WILL CAUSE CONGRESS TO ENACT NEW LAWS GOVERNING LINERS

WASHINGTON, April 16.—Congressional action to assure adequate lifesaving facilities on ocean liners may be expected as a result of the Titanic disaster, according to Chairman Alexander (Dem., Mo.), chairman of the house merchant marine and fisheries committee.

The committee, according to Chairman Alexander, will take up the vexing question of American jurisdiction over foreign-owned transatlantic vessels sailing under foreign flags and will endeavor to find a way to enforce proper regulations. The regulation of steamship wireless apparatus will also be taken up.

PASSAGE ENGAGED, BUT THEY DID NOT EMBARK

SOUTHAMPTON, England, April 16.—The following passengers whose names were on the list of the Titanic did not embark:

First-Class—E. A. Melody, M. J. White, ——— Schabert.

Second-Class—Dr. J. C. Jenkins, Mrs. G. Wilkinson, Ada Wilkinson.

ST. JOHNS, N. F., April 16.—All hope that any of the passengers or crew of the Titanic, other than those on the Carpathia, was alive, was abandoned this afternoon. All the steamers which have been cruising near the disaster have continued their voyages.

UPPER PROMENADE DECK S. S. TITANIC, SHOWING VERANDA, PALM COURTS, SMOKING, LOUNGING, READING AND WRITING ROOMS

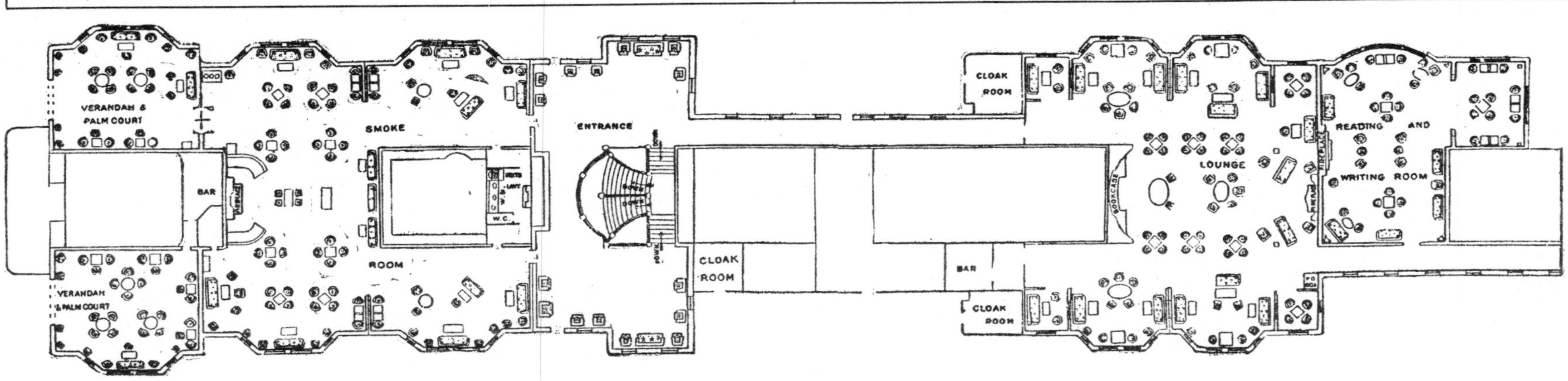

TRIUMPHS OF MAN PROVEN EMPTY BY FORCES OF NATURE

Much Boasted Conquest of the Sea Becomes Dream When Iceberg Cruches.

(BY DANIEL DILLON JR.)

The magnitude of yesterday's sea disaster, when the steamer Titanic went to an ocean grave after its collision with a huge iceberg, is literally incomprehensible; the one inkling we get of it comes from the sorrowful perusal of the list of the dead.

Only a seafaring man or a traveler of the arctic regions is able to appreciate the deadly peril with which an iceberg incessantly threatens a steamer treading the northern waters of the Atlantic. Ever since the earliest days of sailing vessels the fear of colliding with one of these floating islands of ice that come creeping southward each year from the Greenland glaciers has haunted the minds of mariners.

And today in the vaunted heyday of man's scientific conquest of nature and her laws there has not yet been devised any contrivance either to detect their presence or to nullify their danger. The peal of bells, the shrill of the siren, the boom of buoys and the wonder of the wireless has served to rob the fog of its terror, the shoals and jutting rocks of their danger, have made the dread of ships colliding in the night a thing of the past; but nothing has yet been discovered or conceived that can afford ample protection to the most powerful of vessels when it invades the kingdom of the iceberg.

There seems to be something studiedly sinister in the manner in which nature set the stage for this catastrophe. The Titanic had been christened "The Queen of the Sea;" was boastfully referred to as the final triumph of mind over matter. Even the cool, calculating designers said she could encounter and weather any disaster. As one of them put it, "She can telescope her stem or drive in her forefoot, but her bulkheads will always keep her afloat."

And while each little man was slapping his little brother on the back and vauntingly parading his conquests, far i nthe stillness of the frozen North nature was unleashing one of her Sampsons to do combat with man. One can almost see the launching of Neptune's servitor as it slid in ominous silence from its mooring at Greenland and began to move forward to the battle front. For daysit slipped through the deep with the deadly noiselessness of a water panther and the dynamic imprisoned force of a thunderbolt. It disdained foes of a meaner mettle and moved forward to lock horns with the champion of the waves.

And out there on the great stage of an unbounded horizon and a star-lit sky, the two forces met. The attendant shock of battle would baffle a Homer. All we know is that the hulk of inanimate matter shook itself like some confusing bear and then moved on out into the great bosom of the Atlantic to die a peaceful death under a summer sun; that the mind directed mass shivered in travail, strove gallantly to revive and then in death, sank to a fathoms deep grave, on the wreck-strewn floor of the Atlantic.

The Titanic was a floating city of 2,170 people, the iceberg must have been tremendous as only one-seventh of the size of one of these ice worlds appears above the surface of the water. It is as if the city of Golden has been hurled against the sides of mount Zion.

The danger that an ocean-going steamer has to encounter off the banks of New Foundland has never been underestimated and in 1897 the large steamship companies abandoned their northern and more direct route, which skirted the banks and selected a more southern and longer one simply because of frowning menace which threatened from icebergs.

Maritime history teems with the number of disasters that have attended the warfare of the iceberg upon the ship masters of the world. The government has endeavored in every way to offset the danger of them and charts of the sea denoting their location and their probable drift are made annually. Ships immediately report the appearance of one, and every vessel is warned of it and yet in the face of these precautions each year sees some disaster either in a greater or smaller degree blamed to them.

It is not the visible bergs, beautiful either in their dazzling whiteness or turquoise and beryl tints, that afford the great danger, but it is the black submerged mountains like the one the Titanic encountered that prove unvanquishable. There is no way to detect them, save at times the air becomes colder, the temperature drops and the old-fashioned tar opines that he can "smell them." But these premonitions prove ineffective, and while never before has such a fearful calamity happened, there have been innumerable smaller ones to trage the forcefulness of this danger.

But though man was vanquished by nature, there is something so heroic in his defeat that even in reading the story of the loss one feels proud to be classed with such martyrs as these men who knowingly went to their death rather than allow a single woman or child aboard to meet t similar fate. "Only the women and children were saved," succinctly tells a story of heroism that rivals the tales of the early Christians for fortitude and nobleness.

TITANIC ON STOCKS JUST PREVIOUS TO LAUNCHING, SHOWING IMMENSE SIZE OF VESSEL

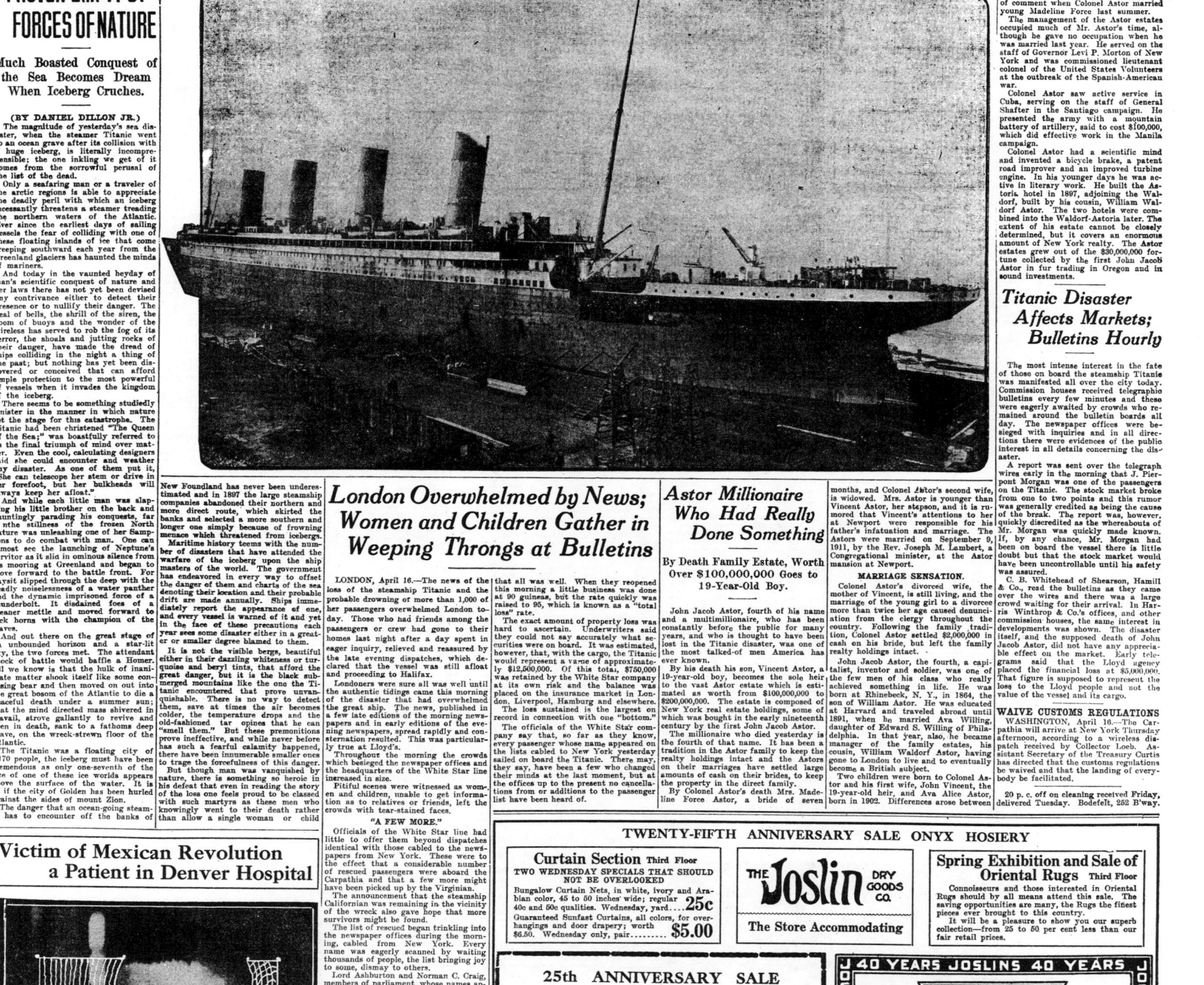

London Overwhelmed by News; Women and Children Gather in Weeping Throngs at Bulletins

LONDON, April 16.—The news of the loss of the steamship Titanic and the probable drowning of more than 1,000 of her passengers overwhelmed London today. Those who had friends among the passengers or crew had gone to their homes last night after a day spent in eager inquiry, relieved and reassured by the late evening dispatches, which declared that the vessel was still afloat and proceeding to Halifax.

Londoners were sure all was well until the authentic tidings came this morning of the disaster that had overwhelmed the great ship. The news, published in a few late editions of the morning newspapers and in early editions of the evening newspapers, spread rapidly and consternation resulted. This was particularly true at Lloyd's.

Throughout the morning the crowds which besieged the newspaper offices and the headquarters of the White Star line increased in size.

Pitiful scenes were witnessed as women and children, unable to get information as to relatives or friends, left the crowds with tear-stained faces.

"A FEW MORE."

Officials of the White Star line had little to offer them beyond dispatches identical with those cabled to the newspapers from New York. These were to the effect that a considerable number of rescued passengers were aboard the Carpathia and that a few more might have been picked up by the Virginian.

The announcement that the steamship Californian was remaining in the vicinity of the wreck also gave hope that more survivors might be found.

The list of rescued began trinkling into the newspaper offices during the morning, cabled from New York. Every name was eagerly scanned by waiting thousands of people, the list bringing joy to some, dismay to others.

Lord Ashburton and Norman C. Craig, members of parliament, whose names appeared in some of the published lists of first cabin passengers, did not sail on the Titanic. Lord Ashburton is on his way to America on another steamer.

The family of J. Bruce Ismay, managing director of the White Star line, received no direct news from him, but the appearance of his name in the list of rescued posted by the papers brought great relief to his friends and relatives.

A wireless dispatch received today by the firm of Pears, soapmakers, and timed 1:20 yesterday, said merely, "All well." It was unsigned, but was believed to be from Thomas Pears, who with his wife was among the Titanic's passengers. It came via the liner Potsdam, but there was no indication as to where it was originally sent from. It may have been dispatched before the Titanic sank, but nevertheless it gave welcome relief to the family, who believe that Mr. Pears is aboard one of the steamers which reached the scene of the disaster yesterday.

The underwriters at Lloyds were staggered at the news, but it is declared that the insurance on the lost vessel is so evenly distributed that none of the underwriters is likely to be hard hit. The reassuring cable dispatches received yesterday had sent the reinsurance rate down to 25 guineas per cent and the underwriters closed up at night hopeful that all was well. When they reopened this morning a little business was done at 90 guineas, but the rate quickly was raised to 95, which is known as a "total loss" rate.

The exact amount of property loss was hard to ascertain. Underwriters said they could not say accurately what securities were on board. It was estimated, however, that, with the cargo, the Titanic would represent a value of approximately $12,500,000. Of this total, $750,000 was retained by the White Star company at its own risk and the balance was placed on the insurance market in London, Liverpool, Hamburg and elsewhere.

The loss sustained is the largest on record in connection with one "bottom."

The officials of the White Star company say that, so far as they know, every passenger whose name appeared on the lists cabled to New York yesterday sailed on board the Titanic. There may, they say, have been a few who changed their minds at the last moment, but at the offices up to the present no cancellations from or additions to the passenger list have been heard of.

MESSAGE FROM THE DEAD.

LONDON, April 16.—The parents of J. A. Phillips, the wireless operator aboard the Titanic, received last night this wireless message from him:

"Making slowly for Halifax. Practically unsinkable. Don't worry."

GOVERNMENT INVESTIGATING

WASHINGTON, April 16.—A quick report from the White Star line on the number of lifeboats and liferafts carried by the Titanic has been telegraphed for by Supervising Inspector Uhler of the government steamboat inspection service.

Astor Millionaire Who Had Really Done Something

By Death Family Estate, Worth Over $100,000,000 Goes to 19-Year-Old Boy.

John Jacob Astor, fourth of his name and a multimillionaire, who has been constantly before the public for many years, and who is thought to have been lost in the Titanic disaster, was one of the most talked-of men America has ever known.

By his death his son, Vincent Astor, a 19-year-old boy, becomes the sole heir to the vast Astor estate which is estimated as worth from $100,000,000 to $200,000,000. The estate is composed of New York real estate holdings, some of which was bought in the early nineteenth century by the first John Jacob Astor.

The millionaire who died yesterday is the fourth of that name. It has been a tradition in the Astor family to keep the realty holdings intact and the Astors on their marriages have settled large amounts of cash on their brides, to keep the property in the direct family.

By Colonel Astor's death Mrs. Madeline Force Astor, a bride of seven months, and Colonel Astor's second wife, is widowed. Mrs. Astor is younger than Vincent Astor, her stepson, and it is rumored that Vincent's attentions to her at Newport were responsible for his father's infatuation and marriage. The Astors were married on September 9, 1911, by the Rev. Joseph M. Lambert, a Congregational minister, at the Astor mansion at Newport.

MARRIAGE SENSATION.

Colonel Astor's divorced wife, the mother of Vincent, is still living, and the marriage of the young girl to a divorcee more than twice her age caused denunciation from the clergy throughout the country. Following the family tradition, Colonel Astor settled $2,000,000 in cash on his bride, but left the family realty holdings intact.

John Jacob Astor, the fourth, a capitalist, inventor and soldier, was one of the few men of his class who really achieved something in life. He was born at Rhinebeck, N. Y., in 1864, the son of William Astor. He was educated at Harvard and traveled abroad until 1891, when he married Ava Willing, daughter of Edward S. Willing of Philadelphia. In that year, also, he became manager of the family estates, his cousin, William Waldorf Astor, having gone to London to live and to eventually become a British subject.

Two children were born to Colonel Astor and his first wife, John Vincent, the 19-year-old heir, and Ava Alice Astor, born in 1902. Differences arose between the couple and in 1909 Mrs. Astor obtained a divorce decree in a secret suit. Mrs. Ava Willing Astor since then has spent her time partly at Newport and New York and partly abroad. She is famous as a beautiful woman. It was this divorce which created such a storm of comment when Colonel Astor married young Madeline Force last summer.

The management of the Astor estates occupied much of Mr. Astor's time, although he gave no occupation when he was married last year. He served on the staff of Governor Levi P. Morton of New York and was commissioned lieutenant colonel of the United States Volunteers at the outbreak of the Spanish-American war.

Colonel Astor saw active service in Cuba, serving on the staff of General Shafter in the Santiago campaign. He presented the army with a mountain battery of artillery, said to cost $100,000, which did effective work in the Manila campaign.

Colonel Astor had a scientific mind and invented a bicycle brake, a patent road improver and an improved turbine engine. In his younger days he was active in literary work. He built the Astoria hotel in 1897, adjoining the Waldorf, built by his cousin, William Waldorf Astor. The two hotels were combined into the Waldorf-Astoria later. The extent of his estate cannot be closely determined, but it covers an enormous amount of New York realty. The Astor estates grew out of the $30,000,000 fortune collected by the first John Jacob Astor in fur trading in Oregon and in sound investments.

Titanic Disaster Affects Markets; Bulletins Hourly

The most intense interest in the fate of those on board the steamship Titanic was manifested all over the city today. Commission houses received telegraphic bulletins every few minutes and these were eagerly awaited by crowds who remained around the bulletin boards all day. The newspaper offices were besieged with inquiries and in all directions there were evidences of the public interest in all details concerning the disaster.

A report was sent over the telegraph wires early in the morning that J. Pierpont Morgan was one of the passengers on the Titanic. The stock market broke from one to two points and this rumor was generally credited as being the cause of the break. The report was, however, quickly discredited as the whereabouts of Mr. Morgan was quickly made known. If, by any chance, Mr. Morgan had been on board the vessel there is little doubt but that the stock market would have been uncontrollable until his safety was assured.

C. B. Whitehead of Shearson, Hamill & Co., read the bulletins as they came over the wires and there was a large crowd waiting for their arrival. In Harris Winthrop & Co.'s offices, and other commission houses, the same interest in developments was shown. The disaster itself, and the supposed death of John Jacob Astor, did not have any appreciable effect on the market. Early telegrams said that the Lloyd agency placed the financial loss at $5,000,000. That figure is supposed to represent the loss to the Lloyd people and not the value of the vessel and its cargo.

WAIVE CUSTOMS REGULATIONS

WASHINGTON, April 16.—The Carpathia will arrive at New York Thursday afternoon, according to a wireless dispatch received by Collector Loeb. Assistant Secretary of the Treasury Curtis has directed that the customs regulations be waived and that the landing of everybody be facilitated.

Victim of Mexican Revolution a Patient in Denver Hospital

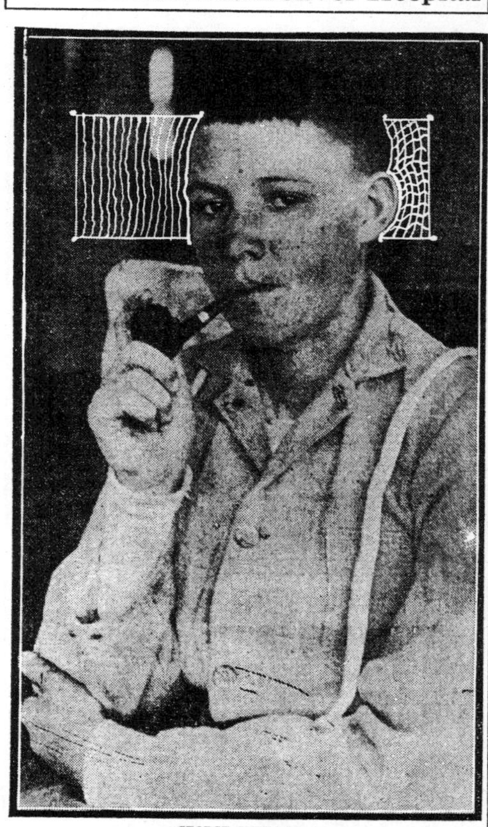

GEORGE HOLLAND

Seventeen-Year-Old English Boy, Who Is in County Hospital Suffering From Bullet Wound Sustained in Mexican Revolution.

BILLION DOLLARS IN HOLDINGS OF MEN ON TITANIC LIST

Kings and Princes of Financial World Among Those Reported Lost.

The wealth represented by the persons whose names appear on the first-class passenger list of the liner Titanic could pay the debts of all the states of the Union and still leave enough to pay the debts of the majority of the principal cities of the United States.

The initial estimate of the wealth represented aboard the vessel was in excess of a half-billion of dollars. A survey of the complete list of first-class passengers shows that, either through actual possession or through family connections, the wealth represented exceeds a billion dollars.

It is doubtful if ever before in the history of transatlantic travel have there been gathered together on a single steamship so many persons of distinction and wealth as those who on Sunday night and Monday morning figured in the most awful tragedy yet recorded of the sea. Judged from the standpoint of wealth and by comparative numbers, there have been few gatherings on land or sea surpassing this.

The wealth represented by the first-class passengers of the Titanic would have paid more than half the combined debts of all the states, cities and counties in the United States on the basis of the figures compiled by the government bureau of census in 1906.

With the exception of the North Atlantic division of states—which includes New York, Pennsylvania and Massachusetts—it would have more than paid the combined public debts of all states, cities and counties in the country.

The combined debts of all states, cities and counties in the United States, as published by the census bureau six years ago, was $1,864,195,826. The Titanic's first-class passenger list represented in wealth more than half this sum.

ASTOR THE WEALTHIEST.

John Jacob Astor, the greatest land owner in America, heads the list in point of wealth. The first half-dozen on the list represent nearly a half-billion of dollars, or but little less than enough to pay the combined debts of Ohio, Indiana, Illinois, Michigan, Minnesota, Wisconsin, Iowa, Missouri, North Dakota, Nebraska and Kansas.

The wealth of these six men is estimated in the following figures:

John Jacob Astor	$150,000,000
Benjamin Guggenheim	95,000,000
George D. Widener	50,000,000
Isador Straus	50,000,000
J. Bruce Ismay	40,000,000
Colonel Washington Roebling	25,000,000
	$410,000,000

John B. Thayer, second vice president of the Pennsylvania railroad, whose wealth is estimated at not less than $10,000,000, follows this list. In Clarence Moore of Chicago the Swift millions are represented, as Moore was the son-in-law of E. C. Swift. The long list of first-class passengers shows names representing in many cases millions expressed by two figures and many other fortunes ranging well above the $1,000,000 mark.

GUGGENHEIM VERY RICH.

Benjamin Guggenheim, a brother of Senator Guggenheim of Colorado, was president of the International Steam Pump company, and with the other members of his family was identified with the American Smelting Securities company and other Guggenheim enterprises, including the American Smelting and Refining company.

Isador Straus, a silk importer, was also identified with his brothers, Nathan and Oscar Straus, in R. H. Macy & Co. of New York, proprietors of one of the largest department stores in the world.

George D. Widener, son of the Philadelphia traction king, was connected with the Widener-Elkins traction syndicate.

J. Bruce Ismay, who is reported among the rescued, is a steamship builder and one of the owners of the White Star line.

Colonel Washington Roebling, builder of the Brooklyn bridge, was president of the John A. Roebling Sons' company of Trenton, N. J., manufacturers of steel, iron and wire.

Denver contributed its share of millions as represented by the first-class passenger list of the Titanic. In the person of Mrs. J. J. Brown there was represented the fortune, estimated at several millions, made by James J. Brown in the Aspen mines. H. R. Rood, who is believed to be lost, represented other Denver millions that came from Colorado mines.

Charles M. Hays, president of the Grand Trunk Pacific railroad, although not a resident, is well known in Denver railroad circles. His fortune is estimated in the millions.

FROM BOSTON FAMILY.

J. H. Loring is believed to be of the millionaire Loring family of Boston.

Omaha was represented among the millionaires aboard the Titanic in Emil Brandeis of J. L. Brandeis & Sons, one of the largest mercantile houses in the West.

Emil Taussig, many times a millionaire, is a member of the St. Louis Bridge company, one of the largest construction companies in the country. He was also interested in St. Louis banks and terminals.

Henry B. Harris, president of Henry B. Harris & Co., national producing managers of America, and known through the theatrical world, was a millionaire.

Edward B. Crosby was a member of the millionaire Crosby family of New York.

HEAD OF SWISS BANK.

Colonel Alfonso Simonius, a European millionaire aboard the Titanic, was president of the Swiss Bankveerin.

Miss Georgette Madill, one of the passengers reported saved, is a St. Louis heiress. Although only 15 years old, she came into prominence a year ago when, by order of the court, she was given an annual allowance of $7,500 for "pin money" until she became of age. She is principal heir to the estate of Judge George A. Madill.

F. M. Warren is a millionaire packer of Portland, Ore. Herman Klaber of the same city is a millionaire hop grower.

Included in the same long list of notables representing wealth counted in millions were Walter M. Clark, son of J. Ross Clark, vice president of the San Pedro, Los Angeles & Salt Lake railroad; T. W. Cavendish of England and his wife, the latter a daughter of Henry Siegel, millionaire New York merchant; Christopher Head, son of the senior member of the firm of Lloyds, underwriters of London; F. T. Ostby of Providence, R. I.; T. M. D. Cardeza, who was occupying a $3,000 suite on the Titanic.

Beethoven's love affair with the Countess Guicciardi has been made the subject of a Swedish novel, "Quasi, Una Fantasia;" the book will be issued in English form by Sturgis & Walton company.

TITANIC'S SALOON DECK, SHOWING ARRANGEMENT OF DINING AND RECEPTION ROOMS

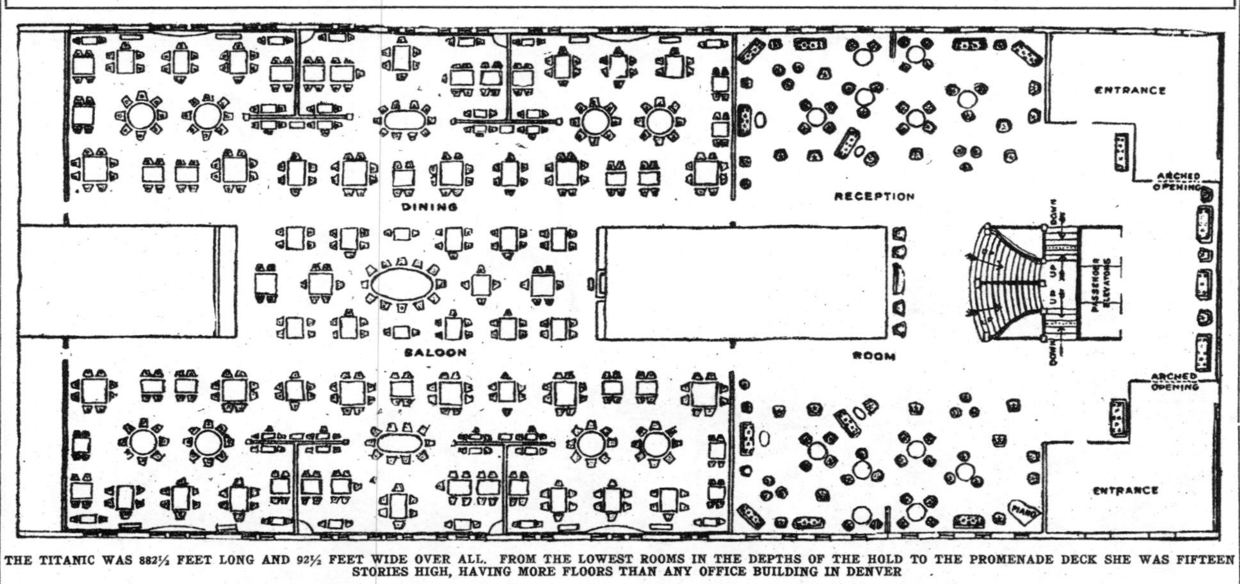

THE TITANIC WAS 882½ FEET LONG AND 92½ FEET WIDE OVER ALL. FROM THE LOWEST ROOMS IN THE DEPTHS OF THE HOLD TO THE PROMENADE DECK SHE WAS FIFTEEN STORIES HIGH, HAVING MORE FLOORS THAN ANY OFFICE BUILDING IN DENVER

Titanic Disaster Tops All in List of Losses at Sea

Appalling Catastrophe to the World's Biggest Ship Claims Greatest Number of Dead.

NEW YORK, April 16.—Among the important marine disasters recorded are:

1866, January 11—Steamer London on her way to Melbourne, foundered in the Bay of Biscay; 220 lives lost.

1867, October 29—Royal Mail steamers Rhone and Wye and about fifty other vessels driven ashore and wrecked at St. Thomas, West Indies, by a hurricane; about 1,000 lives lost.

1873, January 22—British steamer Northfleet sunk in collision off Dungeness; 300 lives lost.

1873, November 23—White Star liner Atlantic wrecked off Nova Scotia; 547 lives lost.

1874, December 26—Emigrant vessel Cespatrick took fire and sank off Auckland; 476 lives lost.

1878, March 24—British training ship Eurydice, a frigate, foundered near the Isle of Wight; 300 lives lost.

1878, September 3—British iron steamer Princess Alice sunk in collision in Thames river; 700 lives lost.

1878, December 18—French steamer Byzantin sunk in collision in the Dardanelles with the British steamer Rinaldo; 210 lives lost.

1880, January 31—British training ship Atlanta left Bermuda with 290 men and was never heard from.

1887, January 29—Steamer Kapunda in collision with bark Ada Melore off coast of Brazil; 300 lives lost.

1887, November 15—British steamer Wah Young caught fire between Canton and Hongkong; 400 lives lost.

1890, February 17—British steamer Duburg wrecked in the China sea; 400 lives lost.

1890, September 19—Turkish frigate Ertogrul foundered off Japan; 540 lives lost.

1891, March 17—Anchor liner Utopia in collision with British steamer Anson off Gibraltar and sunk; 574 lives lost.

1892, January 13—Steamer Namehow wrecked in China sea; 414 lives lost.

1894, June 25—Steamer Norge wrecked on rock reef in the North Atlantic; nearly 600 lives lost.

1895, January 30—German steamer Elbe sunk in collision with British steamer Crathie in North sea; 335 lives lost.

1895, March 11—Spanish cruiser Reina Regenta foundered in the Atlantic at entrance to the Mediterranean; 400 lives lost.

1898, February 15—United States battleship Maine blown up in Havana harbor; 260 lives lost.

1898, July 4—French line steamer La Bourgogne in collision with British sailing vessel Cromartyshire; 571 lives lost.

1898—Klondike gold steamship Clara Nevada, sank Lynn canal, Alaska; 110 drowned.

1901 February 22—City of Rio de Janeiro, Pacific Mail Steamship company, sunk at entrance to San Francisco bay; 122 lives lost.

1904, June 15—General Slocum, excursion steamboat, took fire going through Hell Gate, East river; more than 1,000 lives lost.

1906, January 21—Brazilian battleship Aquidaban sunk near Rio Janeiro by an explosion of the powder magazines; 212 lives lost.

1906, January 27—Steamship Valencia, wrecked on Cape Beale, Vancouver island, B. C.; 117 lives lost.

1906, August 4—Italian emigrant ship Sirio struck a rock off Cape Palos; 350 lives lost.

1907, July 20—American steamers Columbia and San Pedro collided on the California coast; 86 lives lost.

1908, March 23—Japanese steamer Mutsu maru sunk in collision near Hakodate; 300 lives lost.

1908, April 30—Japanese training Mutsu Maru sunk in collision near Hakodores owing to an explosion; 200 lives lost.

1909, January 24—Collision between the Italian steamer Florida and the White Star liner Republic, about 170 miles east of New York, during a fog; a large number of lives were saved by the arrival of the steamer Baltic, which received the "C. Q. D." sent up by wireless by the Republic operator; the Republic sank while being towed; six lives lost.

1909, August 1—British steamer Waratah, from Sydney via Port Natal for London, last heard from leaving Port Natal on January 26; 300 lives lost.

1911, September 25—French battleship Liberte sunk by explosion in Toulon harbor; 233 lives lost.

Titanic Struck and Sunk, Brief Word of Wireless

866 Survivors Picked Up From Lifeboats Where Leviathan of Deep Sank.

STEAMSHIP CARPATHIA (Via Cape Race, N. F.), April 16.—Captain Rostron of the Carpathia sent the following wireless dispatch to the Associated Press this morning:

"Titanic struck iceberg; sunk Monday, 3 a. m., 41.46 north latitude, 50.14 west longitude. Carpathia picked up many passengers, proceeding New York."

NEW YORK, April 16.—Accepting early estimates of the fatality list as accurate, the disaster is the greatest in marine history. Nearest approaching it in magnitude were the disasters to the steamer Atlantic in 1873, when 547 lives were lost, and the La Bourgoyne in 1898, with a fatality list of 571.

Shortly after 7 o'clock last night there came flashing over the wires from Cape Race, within 400 miles of which the liner had struck the iceberg, word that at 2:20 o'clock Monday morning, three hours and fifty-five minutes after receiving her death blow, the Titanic had sunk.

The news came from the steamer Carpathia, relayed by the White Star liner Olympic, and revealed that by the time the Carpathia, outward bound from New York, and racing for the Titanic on a wireless call, reached the scene, the doomed vessel had sunk.

Left on the surface, however, were lifeboats from the Titanic and in them it appears were 866 survivors of the disaster. These, according to advices, the Carpathia picked up and is now on her way with them to New York.

For the rest, the scene as the Carpathia came up was one of desolation. All that remained of the $10,000,000 floating palace on which nearly 1,400 passengers had been voyaging luxuriously to this side of the Atlantic, were bits of wreckage. The biggest ship in the world had gone down, snuffing out in her downward plunge, it appeared, hundreds of human lives.

A significant line in the Cape Race dispatch was the announcement that of those saved by the Carpathia, nearly all were women and children.

Should it prove that no other vessel picked up any passengers of the sinking liner, this might mean that few of the men had been saved, as the proportion of women and children among the passengers was large. The same facts would likewise spell the doom of practically the entire crew of 800.

In the cabins were 230 women and children, but it is not known how many there were among the 740 third-class passengers.

In the first cabin there were 128 women and fifteen children and in the second cabin seventy-nine women and eight children.

Republic Captain Tells How Titanic Went to Bottom

Sealby, Now Law Student, Believes Ship Struck Iceberg Glancing Blow.

ANN ARBOR, Mich., April 16.—Captain Innman Sealby of the ill-fated Republic of the White Star line at the time it was rammed and sunk by the steamer Florida, and who is now a senior law student at the University of Michigan, expressed no surprise this morning that a steamer like the Titanic had gone to the bottom after having struck an iceberg.

Captain Sealby spent twenty-five years on the large steamers of the Atlantic before leaving to take up his studies here and is thoroughly conversant with the dangers.

"The most dangerous thing that a captain of a large steamer has to contend with are icebergs," said the captain. "The reason for this is because they so closely resemble water.

"The reason boats like the Titanic could sink even though Mr. Franklin says it could be half full of water and still float, is probably because the ship struck the iceberg a glancing blow and then later scraped alongside, breaking in most of the bulkheads. There is no danger of losing a large boat if it strikes head-on. The most it could do in that case would be to cave in fifty or 100 feet of the bow.

"This has been an unusual winter in the north Atlantic and the ice commences to come down early. There are in the Atlantic what are called north and south tracks. The steamers travel the north track until about April 15."

Horrible and Hopeless, Cries Company Head

NEW YORK, April 16.—At 8:20 Vice President Franklin of the White Star line emerged from his private office and said that the line was absolutely without authentic information other than what it had already made public. He was well night hysterical, and said:

"This is a horrible, horrible disaster. We have no further authentic information regarding the wreck other than some of the survivors are on the Carpathia coming here. Whether the Virginian managed to rescue any more, we don't know.

"We are trying our best to get some information. I have asked Montreal by ling-distance telephone to tell me whether the Virginian is coming back. If she is there is hope, as she was eastbound and would not put back unless she had some of our rescued passengers on board.

"I admit it is a forlorn hope, but it is the only hope we have. We will probably not hear further from the Olympic until she reaches the other side. It is terrible! Terrible! Terrible!"

Author Who Was Jailed for Article on the Titanic

Wliam T. Stead, famous on two continents as an editor and author, was on his way to America on a brief trip on board the Titanic. Mr. Stead was a noted fighter, having used his virile pen to good effect in decrying certain conditions of which he disapproved.

His "Maiden Tribute of Modern Babylon," written in 1885, landed him in prison for three months. The work exposed outrages which the law permitted upon women and children. In spite of his prison sentence the work was successful, for it was followed by remedial legislation.

He was born at Embleton, England, in 1849, his father being a Congregational minister there. After a short schooling he was in business for eight years of his youth. In 1871 he became editor of the Northern Echo. He secured a place on the Pall Mall Gazette in 1880 and became its editor in 1883. In 1890 he founded the Review of Reviews followed the next year by the American Review of Reviews, and the Australasian Review of Reviews three years later.

While editor of the Pall Mall Gazette he introduced American newspaper ideas into England by adopting interviews, illustrations and extra editions.

He formed quick, and sometimes erroneous judgments, and fought fiercely for his beliefs. He always advocated international peace and fought vigorously against the social evils of the times. He ran a weekly paper called War Against War during the Boer troubles and sternly condemned the British action in South Africa.

His publications, always startling, covered a variety of subjects and were always vigorous in their denunciation of the evils he opposed. He was well known in America, being familiar with the country. In 1893 he startled two continents by publishing "If Christ Came to Chicago."

Antiquated Laws Blamed for Lack of Titanic Boats

NEW YORK April 16.—The disaster to the Titanic brings to the minds of those who were in London last summer the spirited debate which took place in the British parliament when an effort was made to compel the White Star line to provide more lifeboats on the two new mammoth ships, the Olympic and Titanic.

Horatio Bottomley, representing the South Hackney district, a London di-

(Continued on Page Ten, Column One.)

Seek Parents of the Ten-day Old Baby Abandoned on Doorstep

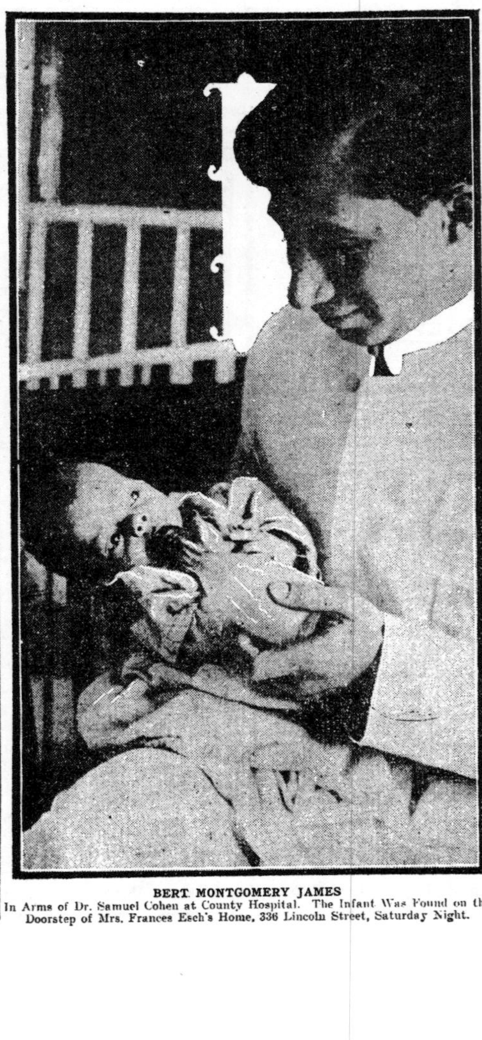

BERT MONTGOMERY JAMES
In Arms of Dr. Samuel Cohen at County Hospital. The Infant Was Found on the Doorstep of Mrs. Frances Esch's Home, 336 Lincoln Street, Saturday Night.

GRAVES OF 1,492 IN ATLANTIC; HOPE FOR THEM IS GONE

(Continued From Page Eight.)

vision, asked the president of the Board of Trade whether the boat capacity of the Olympic, which was then about to make her maiden voyage, was sufficient to take care of all the passengers and crew in the event of an accident.

The reply Bottomley received was that the White Star line had complied with the existing laws, although it was pointed out that those laws were antiquated and dealt with ships up to 10,000 tonnage.

They never have been revised to meet the construction of the mammoth ships. Bottomley pointed out that if the White Star complied with the laws the Olympic could only handle about 600 persons in its lifeboats.

The resolution was pigeonholed.

Isidor Straus Was Oldest of Three Famous Brothers

When but 18 Years Old Was Sent to Europe to Buy Ships for Confederacy.

Isidor Straus, New York merchant and the odest of the three noted Straus brothers, was on board the ill-fated Titantic. The family is an old German one which came to America in 1854.

He was born in Rhenish, Bavaria, in 1845, the son of Lazarus Straus. With his parents and younger brothers he came to the United States when 9 years old. The family settled in Talbotton, Ga., and Isidor was educated there. His business ability was first recognized in 1863, when, at the age of 18, he was sent abroad as assistant to the agent of the Georgia Export and Import company to purchase supplies and steamers for the Confederate states.

After the war he went into business with his father and later went to New York, finally entering the firm of Abraham & Straus, a department store. He was a recognized authority on finance and a noted philanthropist, belonging to many boards of charitable and financial institutions.

He was a member of the fifty-third congress, being chosen at a special election. As bosom friend of William L. Wilson, he was constantly in consultation with him on the formation of the Wilson tariff, and his authoritative knowledge of such matters made him invaluable in the work.

The firm which he founded with his father in 1866, that of L. Straus & Sons, is still in existence and is a leading pottery firm. Nathan Straus, three years his junior, is the American head of the World's Association for the Prevention of Tuberculosis and is at present in Rome at the conference of that body. Oscar Solomon Straus, the youngest son, is the United States ambassador to Turkey, where he has been since 1909. He served previously on Turkish diplomatic missions and was secretary of commerce and labor under Roosevelt. He is the author of many books on government and dipomacy.

Fearful Impact With Ice 'Buckled' Great Ocean Liner

Berg, Eight-Ninths Submerged, Ripped Open Bottom, Leaving Ship Helpless.

WASHINGTON, April 16.—Captain Charles A. McAllister expressed the belief that the mass which sent the Titanic to the bottom of the ocean was a salt water iceberg and not a polar berg of glacial formation. He pointed out that the ratio of ice above water in such an iceberg was only one-ninth of its bulk.

George Uhler, inspector general of the federal steamboat inspection service, said he believed the Titanic plunged into the iceberg with such momentum that the impact buckled her to pieces.

The vessel in all probability, he added, ran over a submerged end of the berg, which ripped open the ship's bottom; that the safety compartments thus quickly filled and the vessel became a helpless mass of twisted steel wedged in a mountain of ice.

Parochial Students at Boulder Stage Crusade Play, Religious Drama, Tonight

Top, Left to Right: Miss Ruth Walsh, Who Takes the Leading Role in the Play, "St. Elizabeth of Thuringia," to Be Given at Boulder Tonight; John Lattora, Leading Man; Miss Anna Stengel, Prominent Member of the Cast, and Mrs. George E. Wilson, Well Known in Boulder Amateur Plays.

"St. Elizabeth's Thuringia" Given Under Direction of Priest.

(Special to The Times.)

BOULDER, Colo., April 16.—After having rehearsed industriously since Christmas the students of Mt. St. Gertrude's academy and of the Sacred Heart Parocial school of this city will present the religious drama, "St. Elizabeth Thuringia," at the Curran Opera house tonight under the direction of Father Antonine Hintenach, O. S. B.

The production will be repeated on Wednesday night. The leading part will be taken by Miss Ruth Walsh, who has won success in former dramatic efforts by the students of the academy.

Mrs. George E. Wilson, who has also taken part in amateur theatricals in this city with success in former years; Miss Eleanor Case and Miss Anna Spengel will play the other leading female roles. The chief male role will be portrayed by John Latorra.

Father Antonine, who has acted as director, has staged this drama on several occasions in the East, where it was played to large houses. Its story has to do with the persecutions that were inflicted upon St. Elizabeth, a German countess, by her ambitous mother-in-law during the absence of her husband at the crusades.

Terrible Suffering by Passengers in Hours of Exposure

NEW YORK, April 16.—The survivors of the Titanic disaster have gone through hardships of exposure and peril which may have left many of them in a serious condition. A dispatch given out at the White Star offices said that those rescued by the Carpathia were picked up from a "small fleet" of lifeboats at 10:30 o'clock Monday morning. It was eight hours before that the Titanic is reported to have gone down.

NEARLY ALL TITANIC CREW MEN OF ENGLISH BIRTH

LONDON, April 16.—Practically all of the Titanic's crew belong in Southampton, where the greatest anxiety prevails as to their fate.

Interviews are published here with experts relative to the possible cause of the disaster. Considerable attention is called to the question as to whether it was possible that suction could have anything to do with it, and it is pointed out that this question came up in the inquiry into the Olympic-Hawke collision. It is considered by some not impossible that the effect of suction near an iceberg might be to draw the vessel out of her course.

Sir Ernest H. Shackleton points out that the scene of the Titanic disaster was fourteen miles south of the supposed possible range of ice fields.

Sir William White, the famous naval constructor, considers that there can be no question of suction in the case of the Titanic because suction, he says, depends upon relative speeds and an iceberg is almost stationary. He thinks that the Titanic simply struck an iceberg.

U. S. INSPECTOR AWAITING ARRIVAL OF RECORDS TO SEE IF LAW WAS VIOLATED

WASHINGTON, April 16.—The federal steamship inspection service is awaiting the arrival of the English records of the Titanic's equipment to see that she complied with the English law with regard to life and other equipment. If the vessel had been of American register it would have been obliged to have lifeboats or liferafts containing 23,470 cubic feet, or accommodations for 2,347 persons.

WOMAN FRACTURES SIX RIBS WHEN BABY CRIES; ANOTHER IS THROWN FROM A HORSE

EATON, Colo., April 16.—Mrs. John W. Wilshire arose at midnight last night when she heard her child crying, walked into an open stairway in the dark and fell to the bottom, fracturing six ribs, dislocating her shoulder and sustaining a bad scalp wound. She is in a critical condition.

Miss Mabel Diking was crossing a railroad track here yesterday, when her horse threw her. She fell on her head and was unconscious for two hours. Displaying great nerve, she mounted her horse as soon as she became conscious and continued her journey.

RANCHER DROPS DEAD.

LONGMONT, Colo., April 16.—John Weese, 70, a wealthy pioneer of this section, dropped dead yesterday afternoon at his ranch, several miles from this city. Heart disease is given as the cause. He leaves a wife, one daughter, Mrs. Lizzie Collar, and one brother, C. C. Weese.

ENGINEER INSTANTLY KILLED

CHEYENNE, Wyo., April 16.—James Brown, engineer of an Oregon Short Line train, was instantly killed near Granger, Wyo., yesterday when he leaned too far from the cab and his head struck a bridge truss.

YOUTH ACCUSED OF ISSUING WORTHLESS CHECKS RELEASED ON BONDS

COLORADO SPRINGS, April 16.—Wilfred Gennerich, who has been in the county jail for three weeks, awaiting trial on a charge of issuing worthless checks, was released yesterday on bonds furnished by his father, Henry W. Gennerich, who came out here from New York in behalf of his son.

The elder Gennerich is a banker in New York and Texas. He has made good all his son's alleged defalcations in Colorado Springs.

He claims his son's fondness for women, and the irresponsible life which he has led has caused his downfall. He will make every effort to get him entirely out of his difficulty here.

POLICE OFFICER MARRIES SOCIETY WOMAN WITHOUT FRIENDS KNOWLEDGE

TRINIDAD, Colo., April 16.—It became known here yesterday that Edward Cookingham, a police officer, and Mrs. Anna Chapman, a well-known society woman here, were married at Raton, N. M., last Wednesday. The wedding took place at the home of Dr. T. B. Ryan, brother of the bride. While they returned to the city Thursday, the secret of the marriage did not become known until yesterday.

ENGINEERS BID TO BOULDER

(Special to The Times.)

UNIVERSITY OF COLORADO, BOULDER, Colo., April 16.—The engineering school faculty of the State university has invited the engineers of Colorado to a meeting to be held here April 20. The gathering is to be under the auspices of the Colorado association of the American Society of Civil Engineers.

The visitors will inspect the engineering departemnt of the university. A scientific program will be given in the afternoon. Among those scheduled to speak are Allison Stocker, president of the Denver Chamber of Commerce and A. D. Parker, vice president of the Colorado & Southern railroad.

COLORADO ALUMNI ORGANIZE

(Special to The Times.)

BOULDER Colo., April 16.—Representatives of various alumni associations of the University of Colorado met here yesterday. Officers of the senate of the central organization were elected as follows: President, Jesse J. Laton, Denver; vice president, F. H. Morton, Greeley; secretary, Miss Carrie Orton, Denver; treasurer, A. A. Paddock, Boulder. These will hold office until June.

GUILTY OF HORSE THEFTS.

(Special to The Times.)

GOLDEN, Coo., April 16.—James Watson, accused of stealing a span of horses from Frank Runge, a resident of the eastern end of Jefferson county, was found guilty of grand larceny by a jury in the district court yesterday afternoon. The usual ten days for stay of sentence was allowed pending the filing of a motion for a new trial.

MAY OIL GREELEY STREETS.

(Special to The Times.)

GREELEY, Colo., April 16.—Work may begin within ten days oiling the business district of Greeley. A petition to this effect has been in circulation for more than a week and will be presented to the city council tonight. If it is acted upon favorably the necessary oil will be telegraphed for tomorrow and work will be started at the earliest possible date.

If you want to get the news—
BUY THE TIMES.

GOLDEN RY. NEAR COMPLETION

Hoisting Plant on Mount Lookout Assures Quick Work on Funicular Road.

(Special to The Times.)

GOLDEN, Colo., April 16.—Construction work on the Lookout Mountain Funicular railroad is being rapidly pushed. A temporary hoisting plant has been installed at the top of the mountain. Work has been begun at the Golden end of the line, and on completion of the roadbed the large permanent hoist will be hauled up by the auxiliary plant. The contractors state that the line will be ready for operation not later than May 15. The road will connect Golden with Mount Lookout park.

COLO. LIBRARY REPLENISHED

(Special to The Times.)

UNIVERSITY OF COLORADO, BOULDER, Colo., April 16.—During the biennial period of 1911-12 over 6,000 volumes were added to the University of Colorado library. This increase is 40 per cent greater than the average of reports from other libraries the same size as the local one. The total number of volumes now in possession of the institution is 62,140. All but 600 of these are catalogued.

STATE U. REGENTS MAY DISCONTINUE BOULDER HOSPITAL

Walkout of Nurses in Defiance of Head Nurse May Cause Radical Action.

(Special to The Times.)

BOULDER, Colo., April 16.—That the walkout of eight nurses at the University hospital yesterday will result in the discontinuance of that institution by the board of regents at their meeting Wednesday was freely predicted today by members of the medical staff of the university who declined to allow their names to be used. Dr. W. P. Harlow, dean of the university medical school, acqnowledged that there was a possibility of such a result, but declared that he would do everything in his power to influence the board of regents to continue the hospital.

"The objection to Miss Elizabeth V. Miller, upon which the nurses left the hospital Sunday," he said, "are wholly unfounded and we intend to back up her administration without any compromise. The nurses are acting very ill-advisedly. Nothing but harm can come to them from what they have done and unless the regents decide Wednesday to convert the present hospital building to other uses, the institution will run along just the same. nder the management of Miss Miller it is in better shape than it ever was before and she has now six additional nurses to take the places of those who left Sunday."

Dr. Harlow declared that the hospital should be maintained as a training school for those medical students who take the first two years of their course in this city, but he said that the whole matter will rest entirely with the regents from whom both he and Miss Miller, as well as the nurses who have walked out, received their appointments.

It was reported today that the real cause of the defection of the nurses was the action of Miss Miller in disciplining Lewis C. House, an interne at the hospital and a member of the Sophomore class of the university for an alleged violation of the rules. House was discharged last Wednesday. The nurses actively aligned themselves on his side and protested against his removal. Miss Miller on the other hand insisted that his course of action was not consistent with the good management of the hospital and she refused absolutely to allow him to return.

CENTRAL MAN FOUND DEAD

Abraham La Caille Discovered at Home With Deep Gash on His Head.

CENTRAL CITY, Colo., April 16.—Abraham La Caille, an old resident and known by many here as Hubert Lacroix, was found dead in bed in his home in this city yesterday. There was a large cut across his head which the coroner believes might have been caused by a fall and which will be closely investigated.

The man was on the streets yesterday afternoon, and with the exception that he was believed to be intoxicated, he was in his usual health.

His wife secured a divorce from him at Cripple Creek and his two children have been in a Denver orphans' home for several years.

If you want to get the news—
BUY THE TIMES.

WHAT THE PLAYERS ARE DOING

The directing members of the Abbey Theater company divided $27,000 profits of their American tour, over and above the salaries they received, when they reached Dublin a few days ago. The nine who received $3,000 were Lady Gregory, William Butler Yeats, Lennox Robinson, Miss Sara Allgood, Arthur Sinclair, Miss Marie ni Shiubhlaigh, J. M. Kerrigan, J. A. O'Rourke and Miss Marie O'Neil.

Minor players, who are known as the juniors, received, in addition to their salaries, their share in $1,800 earned by a benefit performance given in Boston.

Here is one kind of reviewing, and it is from Acton Davies' account of the premiere of "The Rainbow:"

"Any comedy which can make James Kilduff, Corse Payton and John Murray of the Klaw & Erlangerian forces weep so many real pearly tears in the course of the entr'actes that the lobby of the Liberty had to be 'swabbed down' twice during the evening must have something distinctly human and saline to recommend it."

This is equl to Joe Patterson's "made Iago look like a big, good-natured slob."

Where's your taste, men?

"The Concealed Bed," by Graham Moffat, author of "When Bunty Pulls The Strings," had its first American production in St. Paul and Mr. Moffat journeyed all the way from Glasgow to that city to attend the premiere, because of a sentimental interest in the skit.

It was his first bit of writing to get a hearing on the stage, and led to the acceptance of "Bunty."

Mr. Moffat stopped in Chicago for a day, saw a matinee performance of "Bunty" and attended a performance of "Gold" by the Drama players in the evening. He intends to return to this country again in October.

POWDER SMOKE KILLS MINER

VICTOR, Colo., April 16.—Arthur Butcher, a miner working at the Dillon mine, died at 1 o'clock yesterday as the result of inhaling powder smoke while at work in a drift in the mine.

AUTHORIZES DAMAGE SUIT.

SANTA FE, N. M., April 16.—The house passed an act to authorize suit for damages against railroads to be brought in the state courts by nonresidents and an act to prohibit blacklisting.

If you want to get the news—
BUY THE TIMES.

JUDGE READS DUMB SIGNS; GRANTS DIVORCE TO WOMAN UPON EVIDENCE OF FINGERS

GREELEY, Colo., April 16.—To the fact that County Judge G. H. Bradfield undersands the signs used by deaf mutes is due to the fact that Mrs. C. E. Snodgrass secured temporary alimony in the sum of $5 a month yesterday in his court. Snodgrass and his wife are both deaf and she is also a mute.

She sued her husband for divorce, alleging cruelty. Her mother gave most of the testimony before the court as she is able to talk. During the time she was on the stand her daughter kept talking to her in the sign language, refreshing her memory of many domestic incidents.

The court read the signals and an alimony was granted without argument. Mrs. Snodgrass' mother did not tell all of her domestic troubles which her daughter signalled, but the court did not miss any.

BIG DAM DECLARED SAFE.

LOVELAND, Colo., April 16.—After fifty hours' work the large dam at the Boedecker lake, southwest of Loveland, one of the largest irrigation lakes in this district, is considered to be safe. The heavy winds of Saturday and Sunday dashed the waves against the dam and at times the water rose several feet over the dam.

HORSES BOLT; CHILD HURT.

DURANGO, Colo., April 16.—Josephine Deti, the 12-year-old daughter of Mr. and Mrs. James Deti, well-known ranchers of the Florida mesa, is at Mercy hospital at the point of death, the result of a runaway accident at the ranch. She sustained broken legs and several internal injuries.

TEACHERS REAPPOINTED.

LOVELAND, Colo., April 16.—At a meeting of the Loveland school board held yesterday every teacher, with the exception of two who had resigned, was reappointed for next year. R. W. Truscott was appointed superintendent in the place of R. J. Wells.

If you want to get the news—
BUY THE TIMES.

TITANIC DISASTER SPECIAL

10.30 **Boston Evening Transcript** 10.30

EIGHTY-THIRD YEAR—(ESTABLISHED 1830)—No. 91 | TUESDAY, APRIL 16, 1912 | PRICE ONE CENT

THE TITANIC'S SURVIVORS

An Authentic List of Those on Board the Carpathia—Six Hundred Names Already Reported

Second Cabin List Still Coming In—Carpathia Due at New York Thursday—Titanic Foundered in Less Than Four Hours After Hitting Iceberg—Only Boats and Wreckage Strew the Scene

There is no question that the greatest disaster in the history of ocean traffic occurred last Sunday night when the Titanic of the White Star Line, the greatest steamship that ever sailed the sea, shattered herself against an iceberg and sank with, it is feared, 1500 of her passengers and crew in less than four hours. The monstrous modern ships may defy wind and weather, but ice and fog remain unconquered.

Out of nearly 2200 people that the Titanic carried only between 700 and 800 are known to have been saved, and most of these were women and children. They were taken from small boats by the Cunarder Carpathia, which found, when she ended her desperate race against time, only the boats, a sea strewn with the wreckage of the lost ship and the bodies of drowned men and women. Among the 1320 passengers of the giant liner were Isidor Straus, Major Archibald W. Butt, aide to President Taft; George B. Widener and Mrs. Widener of Philadelphia, Mr. and Mrs. Henry S. Harper, William T. Stead, the London journalist, and many more whose names are known on both sides of the Atlantic. The news that few besides women and children were saved has caused the greatest apprehension as to the fate of these.

Although 866 persons are reported to be on the Carpathia, it is apparent that all of them are not passengers, for it was necessary for members of the Titanic's crew to man the boats which set out from the sinking liner's sides. How many of the crew were assigned to each boat under the conditions prevailing is a matter of conjecture. A similarly unsettled matter is the percentage of first-class passengers among those saved. While the names of the survivors so far obtained are largely those of saloon passengers the iron rule "Women first" applies likewise to the second cabin and steerage—a circumstance which may have cost the life of many prominent men above decks. It is natural also that the names of the more obscure survivors would be slower in reaching land.

False news and false hopes and an international belief that the Titanic was practically unsinkable followed the slowly unfolding accounts of her loss in a way without precedent. Eager crowds in a dozen cities in the United States besieged bulletin boards when it became known that the giant liner had really sunk with appalling loss of life, and in New York city hysterical men and women crowded into and about the White Star line offices seeking news of relatives.

Of the foregoing reports concerning the awful tragedy in the ice fields of the Atlantic, two were fraught with hope as the day dawned. The first was that the rescue ship Carpathia carried nearly 900 survivors as against 675 reported to be on board yesterday. The second was the message saying that the Virginian might have others on board whose safety would cut the list of dead.

Captain E. J. Smith, commander of the Titanic, probably went to his grave with his ill-fated vessel without once being able to communicate directly with the agents of his line. Aside from the startling "C D Q" sent by his wireless operator, not one word from him was received up to the time the Titanic sank bow foremost into the ocean. The presumption is that he met his death at his post according to the inflexible tradition of the British merchant service. He and his crew enforced rigidly the unwritten law of the sea—"The Birkenhead drill"—"Women and children first"—is plainly indicated by the preponderance of women among the partial list of survivors that the wireless has given. Although rated one of the ablest commanders since the advent of the modern steamship, Captain Smith's career had been recently marred by ill-fortune. He was in command of the Titanic's sister ship Olympic when that vessel was in collision with the British cruiser Hawke.

All through the night the offices of the White Star line and the newspapers were besieged by scores of persons anxious to learn the fate of relatives or friends on board the Titanic, while a flood of telegrams, cablegrams and telephone messages were received bringing eager inquiries from different parts of the country. Officials of the White Star line had little news to impart. Wireless operators worked through the night trying to send and pick up calls from the scene of the disaster. The wireless was handicapped in the early morning by a thunderstorm which finally silenced wireless transmission for a time.

Gradually the names of the rescued began to come through by wireless by way of Cape Race from the Carpathia and were posted in the Company's offices.

Vice President Franklin, of the International Mercantile Marine, said today that he had heard that the Cunarder Carpathia would arrive here on Thursday evening and that his information was that there were 675 survivors of the Titanic on board. Mr. Franklin said that he did not expect to receive any further wireless messages from the Olympic on this side of the Atlantic and that Captain Haddock of that steamship would soon be in position to send all his wireless reports to the London office.

A cablegram from London, received at the steamship offices in the night, concerning the fate of Sir Cosmo and Lady Duff-Gordon, remained unanswered until this morning, when it was definitely ascertained Sir Cosmo and Lady Duff-Gordon were among the passengers taken from the Titanic and now on board the Carpathia.

Long-distance telephone calls came from Philadelphia regarding the many society folks of that city aboard the Titanic. The name of Mrs. George D. Widener of Elkins Park, was posted as among those on board the Carpathia. The names of her husband, George D. Widener and her son Harry Elkins Widener, did not appear among those saved.

After the first desperate calls by the Titanic for help had been sent flying through space and brought steamers for hundreds of miles around speeding to the rescue what seems to have been an impenetrable wall of silence was raised between her and the anxious world. The giant liner, so far as last night's advices appear, went to her fate without so much as a whisper of what must have been scenes of agonizing tragedy upon her decks.

Along the entire Atlantic coast wireless antennæ were attuned to catch from any source the slightest glimmering of hope that possibly on board the many steamships which went to the assistance of the stricken steamship were other survivors of the sunken vessel. But from none of the ships reported to be at or near the scene of what, viewed in the light of the probabilities, may be recorded as the world's greatest marine horror, came the slightest syllable of encouragement to the anxiously waiting world.

Early last night there was hope that any moment might bring word of relief. But anxiety deepened and many friends and relatives of those who sailed on the Titanic began to despair as hour after hour passed and the night grew old without word from either of the Allan liners, Parisian or Virginian, believed to be, with the exception of the Carpathia, the vessels nearest the Titanic when she made her fateful plunge.

As the Titanic sank before three o'clock in the morning and it was not hoped during the day that the Virginian could reach the scene before 10 A. M., at the earliest, while the Parisian was said to be some distance farther away, it was feared even by the White Star officials, trying their best to calculate differently and yet accurately that they would not have reached the scene to be of service.

The steamer Virginian was finally heard from at 2.15 o'clock this morning. She did not report the presence of any survivors on board, the message from her saying only that she would bring to St. Johns, N. F., such survivors of the Titanic as she "may rescue." The fact that the Virginian was to go out of her course to put into St. Johns on her voyage to Liverpool was taken as a favorable indication, arousing the hope that after all she might have picked up some of the victims of the wreck and was bringing them to port.

The Titanic herself lies buried two miles beneath the ocean's surface, midway between Sable Island and Cape Race. Her position when she struck the iceberg was given as latitude 41.46 north, longitude 50.14 west. According to the Carpathia's advices the liner which struck the iceberg at 10.25 o'clock Sunday night sank at 2.20 o'clock Monday morning, enarly four hours later, in latitude 41.16, longitude 50.14, or not more than half a degree south of the point where the collision occurred. It seems improbable from this thot after the accident the liner made much headway under her own steam.

The exact amount of the property loss was hard to ascertain today. Underwriters stated that they could not say accurately what securities were on board the ship as yet. It was generally estimated, however, that with the cargo, the Titanic would represent a value of aproximately $12,500,000. Of this total, $750,000 was retained by the White Star Company at its own risk and the balance was placed on the insurance market in London, Liverpool, Hamburg and elsewhere.

The officials of the White Star Company say that so far as they know every passenger whose name appeared on the lists cabled to New York yesterday sailed on board the Titanic. There may have been a few who changed their minds at the last moment, but at the offices up to the present no cancellations from or additions to the passenger list have been heard of. As a matter of fact, these would be known only to the purser of the Titanic.

Lord Ashburton and Norman C. Craig, member of Parliament, whose names appeared in some of the published lists of first cabin passengers, did not sail on the Titanic. Lord Ashburton is on his way to America on another steamer. The family of J. Bruce Ismay, managing director of the White Star line, received no direct news from him, but the appearance of his name in the lists of rescued posted by the papers, brought great relief to his friends and relatives.

A wireless despatch received today by the firm of Pears Soap makers and timed 1.20 yesterday said merely, "All well." It was unsigned but was believed to be from Thomas Pears, who, with his wife, was among the Titanic's passengers.

It came via liner Potsdam, but there was no indication as to where it was originally sent from. It may have been despatched before the Titanic sank, but nevertheless it gave welcome relief to the family, who believes that Mr. Pears is aboard one of the steamers which reached the scene of the disaster yesterday.

The underwriters at Lloyds were staggered at the news, but it is declared that the insurance on the lost vessel is so evenly distributed that none of the underwriters are likely to be hard hit. The reassuring cable despatches received yesterday had sent the reinsurance rate down to twenty-five guineas per cent and the underwriters closed up at night hopeful that all was well. When they reopened this morning a little business was done at ninety guineas, but the rate was quickly raised to ninety-five, which is known as a "total loss" rate.

It has been definitely established that Lady Duff-Gordon, who is known in Paris as "Lucille," the name under which she conducted her dressmaking business, sailed on board the Titanic with her husband, Sir Cosmo Duff-Gordon. They appear on the official passenger list as Mr. Morgan and wife.

Robert Bacon, United States ambassador to France, with his wife and daughter, had until a week ago planned to sail on board the Titanic, but in view of the delay in the arrival of Myron T. Herrick, his successor, Mr. Bacon decided to postpone his departure and to leave by the French liner France on Saturday next.

Mrs. G. T. Levis and Miss A. K. Easman, both of New York, now staying at the Hotel Maurice, had engaged passage on the Titanic, but at the last moment transferred to the Olympic, sailing on April 24.

Among those in the second cabin who engaged passages at the last moment at Cherbourg were Mrs. Irvan and Miss Lahmann.

Interference on the part of amateur wireless operators made it difficult for the stations here to get the list of names being sent out by the Carpathia correctly. In several instances the names as picked up have no counterpart in the list of passengers as given out by the White Star line officials, and in other cases the operators were not able to get last names.

DOUBTFUL NAMES

The following list comprises those whose names have probably been transmitted incorrectly. The names, with those corresponding in the official passenger list are as follows:

WIRELESS VERSION:	PROBABLE MEANING:
Abbott, Mrs. Rose	Mrs. N. Aubert
Andrews, Miss K. T.	Mrs. Cornelia I.
Chibinace, Mrs. B.	Mrs. E. B. Chibnall
Douglas, Robert	Mr. or Mrs. W. Douglass or Mrs. F. C. Douglass.
Ellis, Miss	May be Miss Eustis
Kenchen, Miss Emile	Possibly Mrs. F. R. Kenyon
Kimberley, Mr. and Mrs. Ed	Possibly Mr. and Mrs. F. N. Kimball
Kennyman, F. A.	Probably Mr. or Mrs. F. R. Kenyon
Lindstrom, Singrid	Mrs. J. Lindstrom
Mile	Probably Frank D. Millet
Rogerson, Mr. J., Mrs. Arthur, Miss Emily B., Miss Susan P., Master Allison and maid	Practically certain this is Ryerson family of Philadelphia.
Shutter, Miss	Probably Miss E. W. Schutes
Spedden, Mr. and Mrs. J. J.	Probably Mr. and Mrs. Frederick O. Spedden
Williams, Rich N.	Probably N. M. Williams, Jr.
O'Connell, Mrs. Robert	Probably Mrs. R. C. Cornell.

THE BOSTON LIST

Of the Bostonians on board the Titanic the following are definitely accounted for:

A. W. Newell, president of the Fourth National Bank, and his daughters.

Percival W. White, of the firm of Nelson D. White & Co., cotton manufacturers, Winchendon.

Mrs. J. M. Brown of Acton, and her sister, Mrs. E. D. Appleton.

Mrs. Walter G. Stephenson of Haverford, Pa., who was a Miss Eustis of Beacon street.

Mrs. J. Bradley Cummings, wife of J. Bradley Cummings, formerly of this city, but now of New York.

Mrs. Jacques Futrelle.

Miss Elizabeth M. Eustis of 1020 Beacon street, probably figures as Miss Ellis, there being no such name on the first or second-cabin list.

Mr. Frank D. Millett, the artist, is probably Mr. Cornell.

There are still to be accounted for:

Clarence Moore of Washington and Beverly Farms.

J. B. Cummings of New York.

Herbert H. Hillard and Timothy J. McCarthy, buyers for Jordan Marsh Company.

George Q. Clifford, president of the Helcher Last Co. of Stoughton.

Jacques Futrelle, the author, of Scituate.

Mr. and Mrs. E. N. Kimball, president of Hallett & Davis Piano Co.

Walter C. Porter of Worcester, connected with the Porter Last Co.

Rush at North Station

Special Train for Halifax Starts With Difficulty and Is Recalled at Reading

A large number of people went to the North Station last night hoping to get on the special trains that the railroad management had decided to send to Halifax to bring back survivors. Some of them made almost desperate attempts to get on board, though they were informed that no passengers would be taken to Halifax, so that the train had to be stopped twice before it could clear the trainshed. The first train to start was made up of twelve cars, but when it reached Reading the order was cancelled and the train stopped and recalled.

The New Haven-Boston & Maine management had arranged for five special trains, to consist of about twelve cars each, to be sent to Halifax to bring up the passengers from the wrecked steamer Titanic. The first train was to leave Boston at 6.30 and the others should follow at frequent intervals as the White Star Line had announced that it would land its passengers at Halifax about ten o'clock this evening. The run was to be made via Portland, Me.; thence to Lawrence, Worcester, Norwich and New London to New York. At Lawrence a special train connection was provided for passengers for Boston and vicinity.

THE RESCUED

The steamship Carpathia started early today to send by wireless to Cape Race the list of survivors. Great difficulty was experienced in getting many of the names correctly, and more than a score of names as made out here do not appear at all on the Titanic's original passenger list. It is believed that these were passengers who booked passage at the last moment or at Cherbourg. The receipt of the list of the first-cabin survivors required more than six hours effort. Thus far the following passengers of the Titanic have been reported safe on board the Carpathia:

A

Abelson, Hannah
Allen, Miss E. W.
Anderson, Harry
Appleton, Mrs. E. W.
Astor, Mrs. John Jacob, and maid.
Angle, William

B

Ball, Ada R.
Barkworth, A. H.
Barrett, Karl
Bass, Miss Kate
Baxter, Mrs. James
Beane, Edward
Beane, Miss Ethel
Beckwith, Mr. and Mrs. R. T.
Barrett, Karl
Bassina, Miss A.
Behr, Karl H.
Bessette, Miss
Bishop, Mr. and Mrs. D. H.
Blank, Henry
Bonnell, Miss Caroline
Bowen, Miss G. C.
Bowerman, Miss Elsie
Brayton, George A.
Brown, Mrs. J. M.
Brown, Mrs. J. J.
Bryhl, Miss Dagmar
Bystrom, Mrs. Karolina
Bucknell, Mrs. William
Burns, Mrs. G. M.

C

Casebere, Miss D. D.
Calderhead, E. P.
Caldwell, Albert F.
Caldwell, Mrs. Sylvia
Caldwell, Alden G.
Cameron, Miss
Cardell, Mrs. Churchill
Cardeza, Mrs. J. W.
Cardeza, Thomas
Carter, Miss Lucille
Carter, Mrs. William E.
Carter, William E.
Carter, Master William
Case, Howard B.
Cavendish, Mrs. Turrell W. and maid.
Chafee, Mrs. H. F.
Chambers, Mr. and Mrs. N. C.
Chandasen, Mrs. Victorine
Cherry, Miss Gladys
Chevro, Paul
Christy, Mrs. Alice
Christy, Miss Julia
Clarke, Mrs. Walter
Clarke, Mrs. Ada Maria
Collett, Mrs. Stuart
Collyer, Mrs. Charlotte

Dolin, Mrs. Ada
Doling, Miss Elsie
Faunterope, Mrs. Lizzie
Carsiden, Miss Ethel
Hewlett, Miss Mary D.
Harris, George
Herman, Mrs. Jane
Herman, Miss Kate
Herman, Miss Alice
Hold, Miss Annie
Hart, Mrs. Esther
Hart, Miss Eva
Harper, Miss Nina
Hamallainer, Anna and son
Hocking, Mrs. Elizabeth
Hocking, Miss Nellie
Jocobsohn, Mrs. Amy

Collyer, Miss Marjorie
Crosby, E. G.
Crosby, Miss
Cummings, Mrs. John B.

D

Daniel, Robert W.
Daniel, Miss Sarah
Davidson, Mrs. Thornton
Davis, Miss Agnes
Davis, Miss Mary
Davis, John M.
Desette, Miss
Devilliers, Mrs. B.
Dick, Mr. and Mrs. A. A.
Dodge, Mr. and Mrs. Washington and son.
Douglas, Mrs. Fred C.
Douglas, Mrs. Walter
Drauchensted, Alfred
Drew, Mrs. Lulu
Duran, Florentina
Duran, Ascuncion

E

Earnslow, Mrs. Boulton
Emock, Phillip
Endres, Miss Caroline

F

Flynn, J. I.
Fortune, Mrs. Mark
Fortune, Miss Lucille
Fortune, Miss Alice
Francatelli, Miss
Frauenthal, Dr. Henry and Mrs.
Frauenthal, Mr. and Mrs. T. G.
Frolicher, Miss Margaret
Futrelle, Mrs. Jacques

G

Gibson, Mrs. Leonard
Gibson, Miss Dorothy
Goldenburg, Mrs. Samuel
Goldenburg, Miss Ella
Googht, James
Gordon, Sir and Lady Cosmo Duff.
Gracie, Colonel Archibald
Graham, Mr.
Graham, Mrs. William
Graham, Miss Margaret E.
Greenfield, Mrs. Lee D.
Greenfield, Mr. William B.

H

Halversen, Mrs. Alexander
Haraner, Henry
Harder, Mr. and Mrs. George A.
Harper, Henry S. and man servant.
Harper, Mrs. Henry S.
Hawksford, Henry J.
Hays, Mrs. Charles M.
Hays, Miss Margaret
Harris, Mrs. Henry B.
Hippach, Miss Jean
Hippach, Mrs. Ida S.
Hogeboom, Mrs. John C.
Homer, Henry R.
Hoyt, Mr. and Mrs. Fred M.

I

Ismay, J. Bruce

L

Lavory, Miss Bertha
Lesneur, Gustave J.
Leader, Mrs. A. F.
Lines, Mrs. Ernest
Lines, Miss Mary C.
Longley, Miss G. F.

M

Madill, Miss Georgietta A.
Maimy, Miss Roberta
Marschal, Pierre

Keane, Miss Nora
Kelly, Miss Fannie
Laroche, Miss Louise
Leitch, Miss Jessie W.
Lamore, Mrs.
Leuch, Mrs. Alice
Lehman, Miss Bertha
Mellinger, Mrs. Elizabeth and child
Mallet, Mrs. A.
Mallet, Master Andrero
Nye, Mrs. Elizabeth
Philipps, Miss Alice
Pallas, Emilio
Padro, Julian
Parish, Mrs. L.
Portaluppi, Mrs. Emilie
Quick, Mrs. Jane O.
Quick, Miss Wennie O.
Quick, Miss Phyllis O.

Marvin, Mrs. D. W.
Melicard, Madame
Middle, Olivia
Minnihan, Mrs. W. E.
Minnihan, Miss Daisy

N

Newell, Miss Madeleine
Newell, Miss Marjorie
Newsom, Miss Helen

O

Ostby, E. C.
Ostby, Mrs.
Ostby, Miss Helen R.
Omond, Mr. Fiennad

P

Panhart, Miss Nanette
Peuchen, Major Arthur
Potter, Mrs. Thomas, Jr.

R

Ranelt, Miss Apple
Renago, Mrs. Mamam J.
Rheims, Mrs. George
Robert, Mrs. Edward S.
Rolmane, C.
Rosenbaum, Miss Edith
Rothschild, Mrs. Martin
Rothes, Countess of

S

Saalfield, Adolphe
Salaman, Abraham
Schabert, Mrs. Paul
Seegsser, Miss Emma
Serepeca, Miss Augusta
Seward, Frederick
Shadwell, Robert Douglas
Shedell, R. B.
Silvey, Mrs. William D.
Silverthorne, R. Spencer
Simonius, Colonel Alfonso
Slayton, Miss Hilda
Sloper, William T.
Smith, Mrs. P. P.
Smith, Mrs. Lucian P.
Snyder, Mr. and Mrs. John
Spencer, Mrs. W. A., and maid
Steffanson, H. B.
Stehelin, Dr. Max
Stengel, Mr. and Mrs. C. E. H. E.
Stephenson, Mrs.
Stone, Mrs. George M.
Swift, Mrs. Frederick Joel

T

Thayer, Mr. and Mrs. J. B.
Taussig, Miss Ruth
Taylor, Mr. and Mrs. E. Z.
Thor, Miss Ella
Tucker, Gilbert M.
Tucker, Mrs. and maid

W

Ward, Miss Emma
Warren, Mrs. F. M.
White, Mrs. J. Stuart
Wick, Miss Mary
Widener, Mrs. George D. and maid
Willard, Miss Constance
Woolner, Hugh

Y

Young, Miss Marie

Rebouf, Mrs. Lillie
Ridsdale, Mrs. Lucy
Rugg, Miss Emily
Richard, Mr. and Mrs. Emile, [illegible]
Sincock, Miss Maud
Smith, Mrs. Marion
Trout, Miss Edina S.
Weisz, Mrs. Matilda
Webber, Miss Susan
Wright, Miss Marion
Watt, Miss Bessie
Watt, Miss Bertha
West, Mrs., and two children
Wells, Mrs. Addie
Wells, Miss J.
Wells, Ralph
Williams, Charles

DIRECTORY FOR ADVERTISERS WILL BE FOUND TO-DAY ON PAGE 15, COLUMN 7.

THE NEW YORK HERALD.

THE WEATHER. Clearing; slightly warmer. For detailed weather report and forecast see Editorial page.

WHOLE NO. 27,630. *** NEW YORK, TUESDAY, APRIL 16, 1912.—TWENTY-EIGHT PAGES.—BY THE NEW YORK HERALD COMPANY. [COPYRIGHT, 1912, BY THE NEW YORK HERALD COMPANY.] PRICE THREE CENTS.

THE TITANIC SINKS WITH 1,800 PERSONS ON BOARD; ONLY 675 OF HER PASSENGERS SAVED

MRS. JOHN JACOB ASTOR. COPYRIGHT by CAMPBELL STUDIOS

DRAWING OF THE TITANIC ARRANGED TO SHOW THE CHARACTER OF THE DISASTER.

JOHN JACOB ASTOR. KNOEDLER.

FRANK D. MILLET

CAPTAIN ARCHIBALD W. BUTT COPYRIGHT by HARRIS & EWING

ISIDOR STRAUS PHOTO by FALK

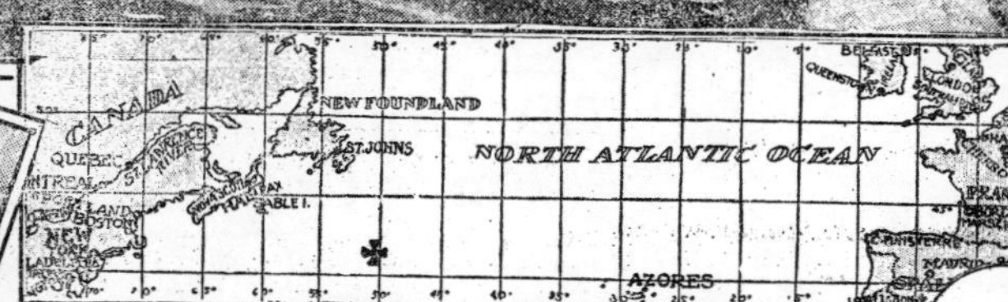

MAP SHOWING LOCATION OF THE TITANIC AT THE TIME OF THE ACCIDENT

J. BRUCE ISMAY

MRS TYRREL W. CAVENDISH PHOTO by MARCEAU

CAPTAIN E. J. SMITH PAUL THOMPSON, PHOTO

WILLIAM T. STEAD COPYRIGHT by DAVIS & SICKEMEYER

CLARENCE MOORE

MRS DANIEL WARNER MARVIN PHOTO by MAROCY

MOST APPALLING DISASTER IN MARINE HISTORY OCCURS WHEN WORLD'S LARGEST STEAMSHIP STRIKES GIGANTIC ICEBERG AT NIGHT

Scores of World's Most Widely Known Persons, Including Colonel John Jacob Astor and His Wife, William T. Stead, Isidor Straus and Mr. and Mrs. George D. Widener Are Among Those Whose Fate Is in Doubt.

In the darkness of night and in water two miles deep the Titanic, newest of the White Star fleet and greatest of all ocean steamships, sank to the bottom of the sea at twenty minutes past two o'clock yesterday morning.

Despatches received late last night from the Cape Race Wireless station in Newfoundland and admissions reluctantly made at the same time by the New York officials of the White Star Company warrant the fear that of the 2,200 persons who were aboard the great vessel when she received her mortal wound in collision with an iceberg more than 1,500 have gone to their death in her shattered hulk, while 675, most of whom are women and children, have been saved.

Should these grim figures be verified, the loss of the Titanic—costliest, most powerful, greatest of all the ocean fleet—while speeding westward on her maiden voyage will take rank in maritime history as the most terrible of all recorded disasters of the sea.

There is as yet no information as to those who are among the saved and the greater number of the unfortunates who must be numbered with the lost. The officers of the White Star Company themselves at the hour of going to press had been able to learn no details of the horror that will carry grief into a thousand American homes, some of them among the proudest in the metropolis.

Women and Children Put Into Boats First.

One point is known from which may be derived a sad satisfaction. In a desperate situation where the salvation of all was not possible the women and children were cared for first. These were sent away in the first of the boats launched from the sinking ship, the only boats apparently which did not share the fate of the mammoth vessel.

America and Britain are spared the horrors that attended the sinking of the French ship, La Bourgogne, in 1898, when the women and children were trampled under foot and cut down with knives amid the mad rush of the panic stricken crew for first places in the ship's boats.

It was learned late last night that the full text of the message from the steamship Olympic reporting the sinking of the Titanic, only a portion of which had been made public earlier in the evening, expressed the opinion that the loss of life would reach 1,800 persons. That despatch said in its concluding sentence:—"Loss likely total 1,800 souls."

It is hoped here that this is an error unless the Titanic had on board more passengers than was reported. The list, as given out, showed 1,310 passengers and a crew of 860, or 2,170 persons in all. Deducting the 670 reported to have been saved and to be bound for New York aboard the Carpathia, of the Cunard line, the loss of life indicated would be 1,495 persons.

The full text of the despatch received from the Olympic is as follows:—

"Carpathia reached Titanic's position at daybreak. Titanic sank about twenty minutes past two o'clock in the morning, in 41.16 north latitude, 50.14 west longitude. All her boats accounted for, containing about 675 souls saved, crew and passengers included. Nearly all saved women and children. Leyland liner Californian remained and searching exact position of disaster. Loss likely 1,800 souls."

By midnight Bowling Green, in front of the White Star line offices, was the parking place of a large number of automobiles of prominent residents of the city, who had driven down town for first hand information. Wealth and society rubbed elbows with poverty in the crowd

FOUND ONLY BOATS AND WRECKAGE WHERE THE TITANIC SANK

MRS. W. E. CARTER. MR. AND MRS. JOHN B. THAYER. MISS E. W. ALLEN. MR. AND MRS. HENRY B. HARRIS.

MR. W. E. CARTER

BENJAMIN GUGGENHEIM. J. CLINCH SMITH. M. J. WHITE. W. A. ROEBLING

that besieged the steamship line officials and both classes were in deep grief.

There were many instances of fashionably gowned women going into hysterics when the hopeful reports of the afternoon were blasted with the news that only 675 persons had probably been saved.

Vincent Astor, only son of Colonel John Jacob Astor, accompanied by A. J. Biddle, of Philadelphia, and Colonel Astor's secretary, were among the crowd at the offices and left with tears in their eyes after a fifteen minute conference with Mr. Franklin. Relatives of Isidor Straus and of other prominent passengers had similar conferences with Mr. Franklin and came away with the same dejection.

Mrs. Robert Guggenheim, Solomon Guggenheim, Louis Rothschild, Benjamin Daniel and Miss Nettie Gerstel arrived in an automobile at the offices of the steamship company early this morning to make inquiry relative to Benjamin Guggenheim, brother of Solomon Guggenheim, who was a passenger on the Titanic.

Mrs. Guggenheim said they were in an uptown restaurant when the cries of "extra" were heard. On learning of the sinking of the Titanic they hastened to the offices of the company. They were told, as were the other inquirers, that no list of the survivors had been received.

The first reports of the disaster, received early yesterday morning, indicated that the Titanic had been in collision with an iceberg not long after ten o'clock Sunday night. It appears, therefore, that this most splendid of modern steam power creations, equipped with every device for the safeguarding of life at sea, remained afloat only a little more than four hours after she sustained the mortal thrust that sent this ten million dollar creation to the bottom of the sea, with her precious freight of human lives, ere ever she had completed her first transatlantic trip.

Of the conditions which made the disaster possible as little definite information is available as is accurate knowledge of its terrible results. It is a natural assumption that such a collision could not happen except in dense fog. The HERALD'S weather service station at Cape Race, N. F., however, reported that at noon yesterday the weather was fair and that a fresh wind was blowing from the west. The temperature was slightly above the freezing point recording three degrees Fahrenheit. The barometer at that time registered 30.20 inches, indicating an absence of fog.

Many of the passengers aboard the giant steamship were men of world-wide prominence. Among these were Colonel and Mrs. John Jacob Astor, Bruce Ismay, W. T. Stead, the famous London journalist, who was on his way to New York to take part in the meeting this week of the Men and Religion Forward Movement; Mr. and Mrs. Isidor Straus, Clarence Moore, the Countess of Rothes, Major Archibald Butt, military secretary to President Taft; Benjamin Guggenheim, the head of vast commercial and financial interests; J. B. Thayer, vice president of the Pennsylvania Railroad; Colonel Washington Roebling, Colonel Archibald Gracie, Mr. and Mrs. Frederick B. Hoyle, F. D. Millet, the artist; Henry B. Harris, theatrical manager; Mr. and Mrs. J. B. Thayer, Mr. and Mrs. George B. Widener, Mr. J. Stuart White, Mr. and Mrs. Henry Harper, Charles M. Hays, president of the Grand Trunk Pacific, of Canada, and many others prominent in the commercial, professional or social life of this and other cities.

Should the present estimates of the fatalities be sustained no maritime disaster in the history of deep sea voyaging approaches in magnitude that of the loss of the Titanic.

The Atlantic went down, in 1873, with a loss of 574 lives. On the day when Sampson's ships destroyed the Spanish fleet at Santiago, La Bourgogne met her fate in collision with another vessel and her victims numbered 571.

These are the nearest approaches to the overwhelming casualty indicated by present advices. Should it prove that other ships, notably the Allan liners, the Parisian and the Virginian, which are known to have been in the vicinity of the Titanic yesterday morning, had rescued others of the passengers, the sweeping extent of the disaster would be materially reduced. This hope remains, though late information does not make it a bright one.

The shock of the later news was made the more acute because during the day hopes had been buoyed up by a series of published despatches reporting that all on board the vessel had been saved and that the Titanic herself was being towed successfully, with every prospect of being able to reach Halifax safely. In the local offices of the White Star Company and of the International Mercantile Marine, of which the White Star is a component part, there was maintained an atmosphere of optimism. P. A. S. Franklin, vice president of the company, said last night that until the bulletin came from Cape Race, at about half-past seven o'clock last night, he and his colleagues had received no definite information of just what had happened, their sole sources of enlightenment until then having been the press despatches.

The Carpathia Picks Up Lost Vessels Life Boats

Spends Hours Searching for Tiny Craft, Tossed About on Ocean's Surface, Since Steamship Went Down in Early Morning.

FEW MEN ARE FOUND AMONG THE SURVIVORS

At the Marconi Wireless Company's offices, at No. 27 William street, it was stated at eleven o'clock last night that the last message that the station had been able to obtain about the Titanic or her passengers had been received at half-past seven o'clock in the evening. The [illegible] received from the steam[illegible] and relayed. It was to [illegible] atter vessel had [illegible] e the Titanic had [illegible] been [illegible] I was engaged in [illegible] sible the life-[illegible]

Life-boats from the [illegible] 's spent hours searching for boats from the Titanic and up to the hour the message was received a total of 675 passengers of the Titanic had been picked up by the boats of the Carpathia, after they had been tossed about on the ocean from midnight.

Of the number of passengers that had been picked up to that hour practically all were women and children. Very few of the men passengers were found in the boats rescued, beyond seamen who manned the Titanic's lifeboats. No statements of passengers nor names of those who had been rescued among the 675 persons had been obtained at half-past seven.

The Titanic's Sister Ship Finds Only Empty Boats

The Olympic, of the White Star Line, Sends Report to Cape Race Confirming Sinking of Other Vessel and Probable Rescue of Women Passengers.

[SPECIAL DESPATCH TO THE HERALD.]

CAPE RACE, N. F., Monday.—The steamship Olympic, of the White Star line, which hastened to the relief of her sister ship as soon as she received word by wireless that the Titanic was in distress, reports that she reached the Titanic's position at daybreak to-day, but found empty boats and wreckage only.

She reported that the Titanic had foundered at about twenty minutes past two o'clock this morning, in latitude 41.16 north and longitude 50.14 west. The message adds that all the Titanic's boats were accounted for, and about six hundred and seventy-five souls saved, crew and passengers, the latter nearly all women and children. There were in all aboard the giant vessel about two thousand two hundred persons.

Should it prove that no other vessel picked up any passengers of the sinking ship, this may mean that few of the men on board have been saved, as the proportion of women and children among the passengers was large. The same facts would also indicate the doom of practically the entire crew of 860 men. In the cabins were 230 women and children, but it is not known how many there were among the 740 third class passengers. In the first cabin there were 128 women and 15 children, and in the second cabin 79 women and 8 children.

The report from the Olmpic states that the Leyland steamship Californian was remaining and searching the vicinity of the disaster. The Carpathia, it was stated, was returning to New York, bringing the survivors, who can hardly be expected to reach this city before Friday morning.

It was officially announced at the White Star line offices at a quarter past eight o'clock last night that "probably a number of lives have been lost in the Titanic disaster." No definite estimate could be made, it was said, until it was positively learned whether the Parisian or Virginian had any of the rescued passengers on board.

The text of the message received from Captain H. J. Haddock, of the Olympic, as made public by Mr. Franklin, vice president of the company, reads:—

"At 2:20 A. M. Titanic foundered. Carpathia proceeding to New York with passengers."

There was reason to believe, however, that the message was considerably longer than the foregoing, and that the White Star officials had not deemed it wise to give out the full text until the reports of loss of life had been confirmed. One of Mr. Franklin's assistants in announcing earlier that the Titanic had gone down said that the Carpathia was proceeding to New York "with survivors."

So far as could be ascertained at the White Star offices it was not known there whether there were any passengers aboard the Virginian and the Parisian.

Some of the survivors who were picked up by the Cunard steamship Carpathia had been afloat for eight hours in the Titanic's lifeboats before they were rescued. It is likely, therefore, that many of those who have escaped death may arrive in this city prostrated as a result of the hardships, exposure and perils to which they have exposed.

Mr. Franklin late last night received a telegram at the local office of the White Star Company announcing that those who were rescued by the Carpathia had been "picked up from a small fleet of lifeboats at half-past ten o'clock Monday morning." It was eight hours before that time that the Titanic is reported to have taken her last plunge into the ocean abyss, where the water is said to be two miles in depth.

In the opinion of Mr. Franklin, the Carpathia will hasten with all possible speed to make this port in order that those survivors suffering worst from exposure or bereavement may be able to obtain the most expert medical attendance.

Mr. Franklin positively refused to give out the full text of the message which he received from Captain Haddock, of the Olympic, reporting the sinking of the Titanic. This attitude led to the belief that the message intimated a loss of life, which the company desired to confirm before spreading alarm.

Mr. Franklin said that Captain Haddock's message was very brief and "neglected to say that all the crew had been saved." It said that the Carpathia had six or seven hundred of the Titanic's passengers aboard, including all the first cabin, and that the vessel should reach New York Friday morning.

Come Direct to New York.

No information had been received from the Virginian or Parisian at the White Star line offices, although it was said "to be known" that many of the Titanic passengers were on board those vessels.

Mr. Franklin said that he had cancelled arrangements for the special trains which they had intended to send to Halifax to bring the rescued passengers to this city by rail, as it was believed that the vessels which had Titanic passengers aboard would steam direct for New York.

Mr. Franklin at half-past eight o'clock conceded that there had been a "horrible loss of life" in the Titanic disaster. He said there was no information to disprove the despatch from Cape Race to the effect that only 675 of the passengers and crew had been rescued. He added that the monetary loss could not be estimated to-night, although he intimated that it would run into the millions.

"We can replace the money," he added, "but not the lives. It is horrible."

"As far as we know," Mr. Franklin continued, "it has been rumored from Halifax that three vessels have passengers on board, namely, the Virginian, the Carpathia and the Parisian. Now we have heard from Captain Haddock, of the Olympic, that the Titanic sank at twenty minutes after two this morning. We have also learned from him that the Carpathia had 675 survivors on board. It is very difficult to learn if the Virginian and the Parisian have any survivors on board. We have asked Captain Haddock and our agent at Halifax to ascertain if there are any passengers aboard the two steamships.

"We very much fear, however, that there has been a great loss of life, but it is impossible for us to give further particulars until we have heard from the Parisian and the Virginian. We have no information that there are any passengers on board these two steamers."

Vast Treasure Also Lost.

Mr. Franklin said there was a sufficient number of lifeboats to take all the passengers from the Titanic. He added that he was confident to-day when he made the statement that "the Titanic was unsinkable" that the steamship was safe and that there would be no loss of life. The first definite news received came in the message from Captain Haddock, he said, and was given to the newspapers at once.

The Titanic was insured at Lloyd's for $5,000,000. No definite information is obtainable as to the amount of valuables on board, but it is generally understood that the vessel took diamonds of great value consigned to dealers. Their estimated value is as high as $5,000,000, but this is admittedly largely conjecture. She also took a large amount of bonds.

HERALD BULLETINS TELL PARIS OF WRECK

News Causes Great Excitement and White Star Offices Are Besieged by Inquirers.

[SPECIAL DESPATCH TO THE HERALD VIA COMMERCIAL CABLE COMPANY'S SYSTEM.]

PARIS, Monday.—News of the accident to the Titanic caused great excitement in Paris early this afternoon. Many persons made inquiries at the White Star Company office and at the HERALD office, in the avenue de l'Opera. When this office closed this evening they went to the HERALD publishing offices, in the Rue Du Louvre, where bulletins were displayed during the evening.

Telephones also were kept busy by persons having relatives or friends on board the steamship.

Much satisfaction was expressed over the early reports that all the passengers were safe.

SEA TWO MILES DEEP WHERE VESSEL SANK

Captain Johnson, Nova Scotia Light Inspector, Estimates Depth from Chart.

[SPECIAL DESPATCH TO THE HERALD.]

HALIFAX, N. S., Monday.—Captain Peter Johnson, inspector of lights for Nova Scotia and one of the most experienced mariners on the coast, said this afternoon he could hardly credit the story that the Titanic struck an iceberg. He held to the view that it was a submerged wreck. It is very rare that a berg is found in latitude 41.46 north as early as this.

Ice, Captain Johnson says, only gets down there in July or August. Where the damage was received he figured out to be 420 miles east southeast of Sable Island or about 400 miles from Halifax, too far south for the ice at this time of the year. The water is very deep at latitude 41.46 north, longitude 50.14 west, and, as he looked at the chart spread before him in the dockyard, he said, it was two miles to the bottom.

Friends of the Victims All Prisoners of Hope

Supreme Confidence of Officers of the White Star Line Reassured Throngs That Rushed to Offices Throughout the Day.

VALUE OF VESSEL IS PLACED AT $8,000,000

Anxious inquirers for news at the offices of the International Mercantile Marine were assured throughout all the hours of yesterday that the Titanic was safe, although ever since twenty minutes past two o'clock yesterday morning she had been beneath the waves.

All officials of the line professed the utmost confidence in her safety. They did not offer any direct communications with the vessel, but presented what purported to be press despatches from different Canadian points, and also a wireless despatch from the master of the Olympic, telling of "the Parisian and the Carpathia coming to the rescue of the ill-fated craft."

Prisoners of hope, indeed, were the friends and relatives who swarmed to the offices in the early part of the day, and some were so reassured that they went away smiling. The offices of the White Star line, which is conducted by the International Mercantile Marine, did not present the usual aspect that offices do when the fate of a vessel is stirring the world, because all who made inquiries soon were convinced by the easy confidence of officers and clerks.

Not Believed at First

No change appeared in the attitude of the officers of the line toward the news at sundown, and the offices still were kept open and not until later in the night did the truth come over the land wires that the vessel had gone down.

When Mr. P. A. S. Franklin, the vice president of the International Mercantile Marine, was informed of press despatches that the Titanic was sinking and later that she had sunk he said he preferred to believe the message sent out by the Allan line that the Titanic was in tow. He declared that he had been endeavoring to get into communication with the wireless operator of the Virginian for further information concerning the Titanic, as no direct word had been obtained.

"How do you account for the lack of wireless communication from the Titanic direct?" Mr. Franklin was asked by a HERALD reporter.

"That is probably due to the fact that her dynamos are out of commission and the secondary batteries used for wireless were not strong enough to carry messages any distance. She may have communicated with the Olympic."

On the matter of insurance of the Titanic Mr. Franklin declined to give definite information. He declared that the company carried insurance of its own and also obtained insurance against total loss at times. As to the amount of this insurance he declined to make any statement, and said he did not know the value of the cargo, nor could he give out any definite information. As far as he knew there was no bullion on board.

The value of the vessel itself he placed at between $7,500,000 and $8,000,000. Throughout the day officers went through the White Star line offices as serenely as though they had absolute evidence that the great steamship was afloat and all on board were safe. Their manner gave the impression that they believed that the steamship blonged to some miraculous armada, proof against the perils of the sea.

Had Chartered Train.

One of the despatches which Mr. Franklin showed was from the agent of the line in Montreal announcing that a press despatch which had been received there announced that the passengers of the Titanic weer being taken off by the Carpathia and the Virginian. He declared that no instructions had been sent to Captain Smith, of the Titanic, because it was considered that in the circumstances instructions from the office would be entirely useless, as aCptain Smith would do the best he could.

Thirty Pullman cars, three dining cars ,ordinary coaches and baggage cars, Mr. Franklin said, were to move for Halifax at five o'clock last night from New Haven, Boston and Portland for the purpose of bringing back the passengers. This calculation provided for the cars reaching Halifax to-morrow morning, and Mr. Franklin then estimated that if the Titanic were six hnudred miles from that port at the time of the colission that she would arrive in Halifax in tow perhaps to-morrow (Wednesday) afternoon.

There was not much of an optimistic nature discerned in the offices of the Marconi Wireless Telegraph Company, at No. 27 William street, where no direct messages had been received from the ill fated vessel during the day. The officers of the International Mercantile Marine commented upon the fact that the Marconi service was not giving much information, but for all that they preserved a calm and hopeful manner.

Was Called Unsinkable.

The first bulletin of the day was given out at eight oclock yesterday morning by Mr. Franklin, who declared to the newspaper men that he was confident that even if the Titanic had struck an iceberg that she was capable of remaining afloat for n indefinite period.

"We place absolute confidence in the Titanic," he said, "we believe that the boat is unsinkable, and although she may have been struck at the bow and have settled in the water, we know that she would remain on the surface. We do not attach any significance to the fact that there are no Marconi messages being received from the vessel. We think this denotes that she is in wireless communication with other steamships or she may have got off all the messages.

Hear of Calm Sea.

The officers received a message from their agent in Montreal purporting to be a press despatch which had come from the Virginian. This stated that at half-past eight o'clock the Titanic was afloat and that she had communicated by wireless with the Virginian and was going under her own power to Halifax.

This message, from whatever source it came, stated that the Virginian had passed boats containing women and children who were passengers of the Titanic. This message spoke of clear weather and a calm sea. It was then reported that the watertight compartments of the Titanic were standing the strain well. Later in the day the following typewritten message was given out at the offices of the steamship line:—

"P. A. S. Franklin, vice president of the International Mercantile Marine Company, said this morning that while no direct message from the Titanic had been received at this office the officials were perfectly satisfied that there was no cause for alarm regarding the safety of the passengers or the ship, as they regard the Titanic as being practically unsinkable. They do not regard the cessation of the ship's wireless messages as denoting anything serious, as this might have been caused by atmospheric disturbances or other causes. The Titanic is well able to withstand almost any exterior damage and could keep afloat indefinitely after being struck.

"The Titanic is now in latitude 41.46 north and longitude 50.14 west. She is being approached from the west by the Olympic, of the White Star line, which they figure will be alongside by eight o'clock P. M. to-day. The Baltic, of the same line, which was east of the Titanic on its way to Europe, has turned back and will probably be alongside of the Titanic by four o'clock P. M. to-day. The Virginian, of the Allan line, eastward bound, is reported as rapidly approaching and should be on the spot by ten o'clock this morning.

Confidence in Steamship.

"The Olympic has just been reported as having been in direct communication with the Titanic.

"Mr. Franklin was most emphatic in his assurances regarding the safety of the passengers and the steamer."

Mr. Franklin called in the reporters to say that no information has come up to that time, to the White Star office in this city, either from the Titanic or the Virginian, but that he was more firmly convinced then than he was earlier in the day that no loss of life will result.

"I am absolutely certain," he said, "that the Titanic cannot be sunk. She has fifteen bulkheads, and not enough of them can be smashed at once to sink the vessel."

Wireless operators at the New York Navy Yard declared yesterday afternoon that no messages concerning the Titanic were received during the day. Last night one operator said that the only message was from the HERALD wireless station when the news was flashed that the Titanic had gone down.

Operators at the United Wireless station at Coney Island said no messages of the disaster were received throughout the day. At the Marconi station at Coney Island it was said before it was known the Titanic had sunk, that no news was received and none was expected until late to-day.

The New York wireless tsations, it was declared, wer eoutside the zone, which must have ben alive with despatches. The z one covered by the Marconi wireless, it was said, was one thousand miles, and no direct communications, it was shown, could have been received from the neighborhood of the Titanic.

MYSTERY IN DELAY---WHOLE WORLD THOUGHT VESSEL SAFE

Left to Right: MR. MURDOCH 1ST OFFICER, TITANIC, MR. J. W. EVANS, MR. ALEXANDER AND CAPTAIN E. J. SMITH, TITANIC. PAUL THOMPSON PHOTO.

CROWD WATCHING HERALD'S FIRST BULLETINS ON THE TITANIC DISASTER.

Complete Passenger List of the Titanic Shows That the Doomed Vessel Carried Some of the Most Prominent Citizens in This Country and Europe

Men and women known well in this country and throughout the world were among the passengers aboard the Titanic.

Colonel John Jacob Astor and his bride, who was Miss Force, were on their way back to this country. Colonel Astor had faced peril before on the sea and at one time the entire nation was concerned about what was believed to be his mysterious disappearance in the Caribbean Sea, aboard his yacht, the Norma. From his yacht, not many months ago, he sent a boat crew to the rescue of a party of yachtsmen, who had been capsized off Newport. Mrs. Astor, then Miss Force, was on board the Norma with her parents and watched the work of rescue.

Major Archibald W. Butt, another of the passengers, was returning on board the Titanic to this country. He is military aid to the President, and as such had gone to Rome to express to the Pope in the name of the President, the pleasure of the American people over the appointment of three American cardinals.

Mr. and Mrs. George D. Widener and Mr. Harry Widener were among the prominent Philadelphia residents on board. Henry Harris, Mr. and Mrs. John B. Thayer, Mrs. J. Stuart White, Miss Marie Young, and the Countess Rothes and Mr. and Mrs. Isadore Straus, were among the Americans well known in social circles who were passengers. The list of first cabin passengers, who embarked at Cherbourg and Southampton, is as follows:—

A.

Adams, Miss E.
Allen, Miss E. W.
Allison, R. J., wife, daughter, son, maid and nurse.
Anderson, Harry.
Andrews, Miss Cornelia I.
Andrews, Thomas.
Appleton, Mrs. E. D.
Artage-Veytia, Raymond.
Arthur, George.
Astor, John Jacob, wife, man servant and maid.
Aubert, Mrs. N. and maid.

B.

Barkworth, O. H.
Baumann, J.
Baxter, Mrs. James.
Baxter, Quigg
Beattie, T.
Beckwith, R. T. and wife.
Behr, K. H.
Bishop, D. H. and wife.
Bjornstrom, H.
Blackwell, Stephen Weart.
Blank, Henry.
Bonnell, Miss Caroline.
Bonnell, Lily.
Borebank, J. J.
Bowen, Miss.
Bowerman, Elsie.
Brady, John B.
Brandeis, E.
Brayton, George.
Brew, Dr. Arthur Jackson.
Brown, Mrs. J. J.
Brown, Mrs. J. H. . . .
Bucknell, Mrs. S. W. and maid.
Butt, Major Archibald.

C.

Calderhead, E. P.
Calley, E. P.
Cardell, Mrs. Churchill.
Cardeza, Mrs J. W. M. and maid.
Cardeza, T. D. M. and man servant.
Carlson, Frank.
Carran, F. M.
Carran, J. P.
Carter, William E., wife and maid.
Carter, Lucille.
Carter, Master.
Case, Howard B.
Vavendish, T. W., wife and maid.
Cheffee, Herbert F., and wife.
Chambers, N. C., and wife.
Cherry, Miss Gladys.
Chevro, Paul.
Chibnall, Mrs. E. M.
Chisholm, Robert.
Clark, Walter M., and wife.
Clifford, George Quincy.
Compton, Mrs. A. T.
Compton, Miss S. W.
Compton, A. T., Jr.
Cornell, Mrs. R. C.
ter.
Crafton, John B.
Crosby, Edward G., wife and daughter.
Cummings, John Bradley, and wife.

D.

Daly, P. D.
Daniel, Robert W.
Davidson, Thornton, and wife.
Devilliers, Mrs. B.
Dick, A. A., and wife.
Dodge, Washington, wife and son.
Douglas, Mrs. F. C.
Douglas, W., wife and maid.

E.

Earnshaw, Mrs. Boulton.
Endres, Miss Caroline.
Vustis, Miss E. M.

F.

Franklin, Mrs. T. T.
Flyn, J. J.
Freeman, B. L.
Fortune, Mark, three daughters and son.
Franklin, T. P.
Frauenthal, T. G.
Frauenthal, Dr. Henry, and wife.
Frelicher, Miss Marguerite.
Futrelle, J., and wife.

G.

Gibson, Mrs. L.
Gibson, Miss D.
Goldenberg, E. L., and wife.
Goldenberg, Mrs. E. L.
Goldschmidt, George B.
Gracie, Colonel Archibald.
Graham, Mr.
Graham, Mrs. William.
Graham, Miss Margaret E.
Greenfield, Mrs. L. D.
Greenfield, W. B.
Gigile, Victor.
Guggenheim, Benjamin.

H.

Harder, George A., and wife.
Harper, Henry Sleeper, wife and man servant.
Harrison, W. H ..
Haven, H.
Hawksford, W. J.
Hays, Charles M., wife, daughter and maid.
Head, Christopher.
Hest, W. F.
Hilliard, Herbert Henry.
Hopkins, W. E.
Hoppach, Mrs. Ida S.
Hippach, Miss Jean.
Hegeboom, Mrs. John C
Helversch, A. O., and wife.
Hoyt, Frederick M., and wife.

I.

Icbam, Miss A. E.
Ismay, Mrs., and man servant.

J.

Jakob, Birnbaum.
Jarvis, John D.
Jenkins, Stephen.
Jenkins, Dr. J. C.
Jones, C. C.
Juliah, H. F.

K

Kano, Nora A.
Kantor, S., and wife.
Karnes, F.
Keano, Daniel.
Kelly, F.
Kent, Edward A.
Kenyon, F. R., and wife.
Kimball, E. N., and wife.
Kirkland, Rev. Charles.
Klaber, Herman.
Kvillner, John Henrik.

L.

Lambert, William S.
Langley, Miss Gretchen F.
Leader, Mrs A.
Lenrnot, Rene.
Lewy, E. G.
Lindstroom, Mrs. J.
Lines, Mrs. Ernest H.
Lines, Miss Mary C.
Linjan, John.
Leyson, Robert W. N.
Laroche, Joseph, and wife.
Laroche, Simonne.
Laroche, Louise.
Lamb, J. J.
Leitch, Jessie.
Lamore, Amelia.
Long, Milton C.
Loring, J. H.

M.

Madill, Miss Georgetta Alexandra.
Maguire, J. E.
Marschal, Pierre.
Marvin, D. W., and wife.
McCaffry, T.
McCarthy, Timothy J
McGough, J. R.
Melody, A.
Meyer, Edgar J., and wife.
Millet, Frank D.
Minahan, Dr. W. E., wife and daughter.
Molsom, H. Markland.
Moore, Clarence, and man servant.
Morgan, Mr., wife and maid.

N.

Natsch, Charles.
Newell, A. W.
Newell, Miss Alice.
Newell, Miss Madeline.
Newsom, Miss Helen.
Nicholson, A. S.

O.

Osthy, E. C.
Asthy, Miss Helen R
Ovies, S.

P.

Parr, M. H. W.
Partner, Austin.
Payne, V.
Pears, Thomas, and wife.
Penasco, Victor, wife and maid.
Peuchen, Major Arthur.
Porter, Walter Chamberlain.
Potter, Mrs. Thomas, Jr.

R.

Reuchlinjg, Jenkheer.
Rheims, George.
Robert, Mrs. Edward S., and maid.
Roebling, W. A., 2d.
Rolmana, C
Rood, Hugh.
Rosenbaum, Miss.
Ress, J. Hugo.
Rothes, Countess, and maid.
Rothschild, M., and wife.
Rowe, Alfred.
Ryerson, Arthur, wife, maid, two daughters and son.
Rosenbaum, Miss.
Ross, J. Hugo.
Rothes, Countess, and maid.
Rothschild, M., and wife.
Rowe, Alfred.
Ryerson, Arthur, wife, maid, two daughters and son.

S.

Saalfeld, Adolph.
Saloman, A. L.
Schabert, Mr.
Seward, Frederick.
Schutes, Miss E. W.
Silverthorne, Mr.
Silvey, William B., and wife.
Simonius, Colonel Alfonse, president of the Swiss Bankverein.
Sloper, William T.
Smart, John M.
Smith, J. Clinch.
Smith, R. W.
Snyder, John, and wife.
Spedden, Frederick C., wife, son and maid nurse.
Spenser, W. A., wife and maid.
Stahelin, Dr. Max.
Stead, W. T.
Stehli, Max Frelicher, and wife.
Stengel, C. E. H. E., and wife.
Stephenson, Mrs. W. B.
Stewart, A. A.
Stone, Mrs. George M., and maid.
Straus, Isidor, wife, man servant and maid.
Sutton, Frederick.
Swift, Mrs. Frederick Joel.

T.

Taussig, Emil, and wife.
Taussig, Ruth.
Taylor, E. S., and wife.
Thayer, J. B., wife and maid.
Thayer, J. B., Jr.
Thorne, G., and wife.
Tucker, G. M., Jr.

U.

Urnchurtu, Mr.

V.

Vanderhoef, Wyckoff.

W.

Walker, W. Anderson.
Warren, F. M., and wife.
Weir, J.
White, M. J.
White, Percival W.
White, Richard F., wife, maid and man servant.
Wick, George D., and wife.
Wick, Miss Mary.
Widener, George D., wife, man servant and maid.
Widener, Harry.
Willard, Miss Constance.
Williams, Duane.
Williams, N. M., Jr.
Woolner, Hugh.
Wright, George.

Y.

Young, Miss Marie.

The second class passengers were:—

A.

Angle, William and wife.
Ashby, John.
Abelson, Samson.
Abelson, Hanna,
Andrew, Edgar.

B.

Bentham, Lillian
Balls, Ada R.
Biss, Kate.
Bateman, Robert J.
Beesley, Lawrence.
Beiker, Mrs. A. O. and three children.
Butler, Reginald.
Beane, Edward.
Beane, Ethel.
Beauchamp, H. J.
De Brito, Jose.
Byles, Rev. Thomas R. D.
Bambridge, Mr.
Bowenur, Solomon.
Brown, Mildred
Baily, Percy.
Botsford, W. Hull.
Berreman, William.
Bryhl, Carl.
Bryhl, Dagmar.
Bystrom, Karolina.
Banfield, Frederick J.

C.

Collender, Erik.
Coleridge, R. C.
Collyer, Harvey.
Collyer, Charlotte.
Collyer, Marjorie.
Corbett, Irene C.
Corey, Mrs. C. P.
Chapman, John H.
Chapman, Elizabeth
Carter, Rev. Ernest C.
Carter, Lillian.
Chirsty, Alice.
Christy, Julia.
Clarke, Charles V.
Clarke, Ada Maria.
Cameron, Clear.
Collender, Erik.
Collett, Stuart.
Chapman, Charles.
Carbines, William.
Cotterill, Harry.
Caldwell, Albert F.
Caldwell, Sylvia.
Caldwell, Alden G.

D.

Von Drachstedt, Baron.
De Carlo, Sebastiani.
Denbury, Herbert.
Drew, James V
Drew, Lulu.
Drew, Marshall.
Davis, Agnes.
Davis, John F.
Duran, Florentine.
Duran, A.
Deacon, Percy.
Davies, Charles.
Dibden, William.
Davis, Mary.
Denton, William J.
Doling, Ada.
Doling, Elsie.
Def, Lena N.

F.

Fox, Stanley.
Fahlstrom, Arnej.
Faunthorpe, Harry.
Faunthorpe, Lizzie.
Fillbrook, Charles.
Fjunk, Annie.
Fynney , Joseph.

G.

Gaskell, Alfred.
Gillespie, William.
Garside, Ethel.
Gilbert, William.
Gale, Harry.
Gale, S.
Gill, John.
Giles, Ralph
Givard, Hans K.
Greenberg, Samuel.
Giles, Frederick
Giles, Edgar.
Gavey, Lawrence.

H.

Hewlett, Mary D.
Harris, Walter.
Harris, George.
Herman, Samuel.
Herman, Jane.
Herman, Kate.
Herman, Alice.
Hold, Stephen.
Hold, Annie.
Hunt, George.
Hickman, Leonard.
Hickman, Stanley.
Hood, Ambrose.
Howard, Benjamin.
Howard, Ellen T
Hart, Esther.
Hart, Eva.
Harper, John.
Harper, Nina.
Hamalainer, Anna and infant.
Hoffman, Mr. and two children.
Hocking, Elizabeth.
Hocking, Nellie.
Hocking, George.
Hodges, Henry P.
Hiltuner, Martha.

I.

Ilett, Bertha.

J.

Jeffert, Clifford..... ...
Jeffery, Ernest. .. ..
Jacobsohn, Sidney S. ..
Jacobsohn, Amy F.
Jenkin, Stephen.
Jenkins, Dr. J. C.
Jarvis, John D.

K.

Kantor, S., and wife.
Keane, Daniel.
Kano, Nora A.
Kirkland, Rev. Charles.
Karnes, F.
Kelly, F.
Kvillner, John Henrik.

L.

Learnot, Rene.
Linjan, John.
Leyson, Robert W. N.
Laroche, Joseph, and wife.
Laroche, Simonne.
Laroche, Louise.
Lamb, J. J.
Leitch, Jessie.
Lamore, Amelia.
Louch, Charles.
Louch, Alice.
Levy, R. F.
Lehman, Bertha.
Lahtigen, William, and wife.

M.

Masgiavacchi, Emilio.
Marshall, Mr.
Marshall, Mrs.
Moraweck, Ernest.
Malachard, Noel.
McCrie, James.
Mellinger, Elizabeth, and child.
Mantvila, Joseph.
Maybery, Frank H.
Myles, Thomas F.
Mack, Mary.
Moudd, Thomas.
Mitchell, Henry.
Mallet, A., and wife.
Mallet, Master A.
Matthews, W. J.
McKane, Peter.
Mellers, William.
Meyer, August.
Milling, Jacob.

N.

Nicholls, Joseph.
Norman, Robert D.
Nye, Elizabeth.
Nasser, Nicolas, and wife.
Nesson, L.

O.

Otter, Richard.
Oxenham, Thomas.

P.

Phillips, Robert.
Phillips, Alice.
Paine, Dr. Alfred.
Pengelly, Frederick.
Pallas, Emilio.
Padro, Julian.
Parker, Clifford.
Parish, Mrs. L.
Ponezil, Martin.
Portaluppi, Emilio.
Pulsaum, Frank.

Q.

Quick, Jane.
Quick, Vera W.
Quick, Phyllis.

R.

Renouf, Peter H.
Rebouf, Lillie.
Ridsdale, Lucy.
Rogers, Harry.
Rugg, Emily.
Emile, Richard.
Rogers, Selina.
Reeves, David.
Reynolds, Miss E.
Richards, Emily.
Richards, William.
Richards, George.

S.

Sweet, George.
Sjostedt, Ernest A.
Smith, Augustus.
Sincock, Maude.
Slemer, Richard J.
Smith, Marion.
Sobey, Hayden.
Stokes, Philip J.
Slayter, H. M.
Sedgwick, F. W.
Sabarp, Percival.
Sinkkenen, Anna.
Stanton, S. Ward.
Swane, George.
Shelley, L. Manita.
Silven, Lillie.
Strant, M. E. I.

T.

Trout, Miss E.
Turpin, William J.
Turpin, Dorothy.
Tooney, Ellen.
Tronpiansky, Moses A.
Tervan, Mrs. A. T.

V.

Veale, James.

W.

Wilkinson, Mrs. George.
Wilkinson, Ada C.
Ware, William J.
Weisz, Leopold.
Weisz, Matilda.
Whendon, Edward.
Ware, John James.
Ware, Florence L.
Webber, Susie.
Wilhelm, Charles.
Wright, Marion.
Watt, Bessie.
Watt, Bertha.
West, E. Arthur.
West, Ada.
West, Constance.
West, Barbara.
Wheeler, Edwin.
Wells, Mrs. Addie.
Wells, Miss J.
Wells, Ralph.
Walcroft, Nellie.
Williams, C.

Y.

Yodis, Miss H.

There were also 740 third class passengers on board.

D.

Drachstedt, Baron von.
De Carlo, Sebastiani.
Denbury, Herbert.
Drew, James V.
Drew, Lulu.
Drew, Marshall.
Davis, Agnes.
Davis, John M.
Duran, Florentina.
Duran, A.
Davis, Mary.
Deacon, Percy.
Davies, Charles.
Dibden, William.
Donton, William J.
Doling, Ada.
Doling, Elsie.
Def, Lena N.

F.

Fox, Stanley.
Fahlstrom, Arnej.
Faunthorpe, Harry.
Faunthorpe, Lizzie.
Fillbrook, Charles.
Fjunk, Annie.
Fynney, Joseph.

G.

Gaskell, Alfred.
Gillespie, William.
Garside, Ethel.
Gilbert, William.
Gale, Harry.
Gale, S.
Gill, John.
Giles, Ralph.
Givard, Hans K.
Greenberg, Samuel.
Giles, Frederick.
Giles, Edgar.
Gavey, Lawrence.

H.

Hewlett, Mary B.
Harris, Walter.
Harris, George.
Herman, Samuel.
Herman, Jane.
Herman, Kate.
Herman, Alice.
Hold, Stephen.
Hold, Annie.
Hunt, George.
Hickman, Leonard.
Hickman, Stanley.
Hood, Ambrose.
Howard, Benjamin.
Howard, Ellen T.
Hart, Benjamin.
Hart, Esther.
Hart, Eva.
Harper, John.
Harper, Nina.
Hamalainer, Anna, and infant.
Hoffman, Mr., and two children.
Hocking, Elizabeth.
Hocking, Nellie.
Hocking, George.
Hodges, Henry P.
Hiltuner, Martha.
Ilett, Bertha.

J.

Jeffert, Clifford.
Jeffery, Ernest.
Jacobsohn, Sidney S.
Jacobsohn, Amy F.
Louch, Charles.

L.

Louch, Alice.
Levy, R. F.
Lehman, Bertha.
Lahtigen, William and wife.

M.

Masgiavacchi, Emilio.
Marshall, Mr.
Marshall, Mrs.
Moraweck, Ernest.
Malachard, Noel.
McCrie, James.
Mellinger, Elizabeth and child.
Mantvila, Joseph.
Maybery, Frank H
Myles, Thomas F.
Mack, Mary.
Moudd, Thomas.
Mitchell, Henry.
Mallet, A. and wife.
Mallet, Master A.
Matthews, W. J.
McKane, Peter.
Mellers, William.
Meyer, August.
Milling, Jacob.

N.

Nicholls, Joseph.
Norman, Robert D.
Nye, Elizabeth.
Nasser, Nicolas and wife.
Nesson, L.

O.

Otter, Richard.
Oxenham, Thomas.

P.

Phillips, Robert.
Phillips, Alice.
Paine, Dr. Alfred.
Pengelly, Frederick.
Pallas, Emilio.
Padro, Julian.
Parker, Clifford.
Parish, Mrs. L.
Ponezil, Martin.
Portaluppi, Emilio.
Pulsaum, Frank.

Q.

Quick, John.
Quick, Vera W
Quick, Phyllis.

R.

Renouf, Peter H.
Rebouf, Lillie.
Ridsdale, Lucy.
Rogers, Harry.
Rugg, Emily.
Richard, Emile.
Rogers, Selina.
Reeves, David.
Reynolds, Miss E.
Richards, Emily.
Richards, George.

S.

Sweet, George.
Sjostedt, Ernest A.
Smith, Augustus.
Sincock, Maude.
Slemer, Richard J.
Smith, Marion.
Sobey, Hayden.
Stokes, Philip J.
Slayter, H M.
Sedgwick, F. W.
Saharp, Percival.
Sinkkonen, Anna.
Stanton, S. Ward.
Swane, George.
Shelley, L. Manita.
Silven, Lillie.
Strant, M. E. I.

T.

Trout, Miss E.
Turpin, William J.
Turpin, Dorothy.
Tooney, Ellen.
Troupiansky, Moses A.
Tervan, Mrs. A T.

V.

Veale, James.

W.

Wilkinson, Mrs. George.
Wilkinson, Ada C.
Ware, William J.
Weisz, Leopold.
Weisz, Matilda.
Wheadon, Edward.
Ware, John James.
Ware, Florence L.
Webber, Sussie.
Wilhelm, Charles.
Wright, Marion.
Watt, Bessie.
Watt, Bertha.
West, E. Arthur.
West, Ada.
West, Constance.
West, Barbara.
Wheeler, Edwin.
Wells, Mrs. Addie.
Wells, Miss J.
Wells, Ralph.
Walcroft, Nellie.
Williams, C.

Y.

Yodis, Miss H.

WOMEN AND CHILDREN SAVED FIRST, DISASTER'S THRILLING TALE

Weeping Throng Besieges White Star Line Offices

Best Information Vouchsafed Is That Newspaper Despatches of 675 Saved Could Not Be Contradicted—Colonel Astor's Son, Taken to Private Room, Emerges in Tears.

EXPECT THE CARPATHIA, WITH SAVED, FRIDAY

An almost interminable stream of excited relatives and friends of those who were known to have been on board the Titanic when she left on her maiden voyage poured into the second floor offices of the White Star line, in the Bowling Green Building, at No. 9 Broadway, last night. Few of those who came were friends or relatives of other than first cabin passengers.

The sight inside and outside the building was unprecedented. Long lines of automobiles stood waiting for weeping men and women, who, seeking some hopeful word that the disaster was of less moment than had been pictured in the late newspaper despatches, had gone to the steamship offices only to be turned away without reassuring messages. The full force of the officers and clerks of the steamship line was deluged with appeals. The employes were unable to answer with any degree of positiveness.

The best information that was forthcoming to those who went to the offices before midnight was that the steamship company could not furnish official contradiction of the newspaper despatches which said that 675 of the 2,200 persons that were on board the Titanic had been saved.

Among the first of those who hurried to the steamship offices to seek authentic information was Vincent Astor, son of Colonel John Jacob Astor. Colonel Astor is known to have been on board with his bride, who was Miss Madeline Force. Mr. Astor was accompanied to the steamship offices by A. J. Biddle, of Philadelphia, and William A. Dobbyn, Colonel Astor's secretary.

Hundreds of other persons were struggling to attain some meagre scrap of information when the Astor party reached the steamship offices and for a long time neither Mr. Astor nor his friends were able to learn anything whatever about the progress of news bulletins that were being received there.

Mr. Astor Emerges, Weeping.

Finally Mr. Astor, Mr. Dobbyn and Mr. Biddle were led upstairs to the private offices of P. A. S. Franklinfi vice president the International Mercailt Marine. They were closeted in Mr. Franklin's office for for more than half an hour. When they left the office at the end of that time young Mr. Astor was weeping and was being supported by his father's secretary and Mr. Dobbyn. They were asked if they received any specific information regarding the fate of Colonel Astor. They refused to answer. Before he entered Mr. Franklin's office Mr. Astor was not weeping and willingly replied to questions that "he had received no news other than what he had read in the nswspapers."

Sylvester Byrne, secretary to Isidor Straus, was another of the throng that besieged the offices. He received no more news than was given to Mr. Astor.

Miss Wheelock, who said she lives at No. 317 Riverside Drive, became hysterical in the offices of the company when she found it was impossible for her to obtain definite information regarding Mr. and Mrs. D. W. Marvin, who live at that address and who she said also were passengers by the Titantic. Mr. and Mrs. Marvin were married recently and were returning to this country from a honeymoon tour of Europe, she said. Mrs. Marvin is Miss Wheeloc's sikster. With a butler and two women friends, neither of whom would identify themselfes, Miss Wheelock remained during all of the evening and a large part of the night pleading with the clerks to assure her of the safety of her relatives. She was one of a hundred whose sobs rose through the din made by the clamoring hundred who were turned away without assurance other than that contained in the message that "675 persons have been saved."

"All at Sea," Says Mr. Franklin.

While the throngs of apprehensive persons were swarming through the steamship offices and in the streets outside, conflicting reports were coming into the offices of the company.

Mr. Franklin at half-past ten o'clock last night made this statement:—

"We have received no word other than that of which I told you before. We have received three messages in all. The first came at fifteen minutes after six o'clock. We do not know whether the Virginian or the Parisian have any passengers on board. We have wired to Captain Haddock, on board the Olympic, asking him if the Virginian or the Parisian have any passengers on board. I do not know where the word came from that said the Virginian was towing the Titanic."

Mr. Franklin was asked if he had any definite information covering the reports that only women and children had been taken from the sinking Titanic.

"I do not know," he said that such is a fact, but it is a matter of courtesy to take the women and children off first. This woudl, of course, include the steerage passengers. We are trying to reach the Virginian and the Parisian by wireless, but we are not likely to do so for some time, as they have low powered wireless apparatus.

"Knowing Captain Smith as I do, however, I would say that, in the event the Titanic went down, Captain Smith would be the last man to leave his ship. Of that you and I can be certain.

"But we are all at sea in this whole matter, and until we receive more definite information we will be unable to make any positive statement. We expect a reply from Captain Haddock of the Olympic, and in that reply we expect the definite information upon which to base a comprehensive statement, and one that will give details. He undoubtedly will tell us everything he knows. I am sure we will learn from him if he knows whether the Virginian and the Parisian have any of the Titanic passengers.

"No Insurance Yesterday."

Soon before midnight the HERALD pressed Mr. Franklin for a specific statement regarding the time the White Star line received messages, wireless or otherwise, conveying any information of whatever character regarding the disaster.

"The first message came between one and two o'clock this afternoon," Mr. Franklin said. "We only made public this evening the messages that we received from Captain Haddock, of the Olympic because we did not consider the messages that we received from other sources as reliable. The first messages that he received discouraged the belief that either the Virginian or th Parisian were carrying any of the Titanic's passengers. We have received more than four messages regarding the disaster.

Mr. Franklin also was pressed to discuss a report that there had been recent, possibly yesterday, a reinsurance of the Titanic.

"Our insurance works automatically," Mr. Franklin answered. "Certainly there was no insurance yesterday. Do you suppose any insurance company would be foolish enough to insure in the circumstances? It is a foregone concluseion that there could have been no insurance yesterday, because the premium would have been too great for the risk."

From the latest advices received at the White Star offices up to midnight, Mr. Franklin said it was expected by him and the other officers that the Carpathia, with the passengers who had been taken from the Titanic, will reach here on Friday. At midnight the Carpathia was 1,080 miles from New York city. A bulletin received at the steamship offices about the same time said that the Olympic was then forty miles from the scene of the disaster.

Awaiting List of Rescued.

As soon as it was possible after it was learned that the rescued passengers are on board the Carpathia, Mr. Franklin said last night, a message was sent by wireless to that steamship requesting that a list of the names of those who had been rescued be sent by wireless immediately to the White Star offices here.

When it became known that this message had been sent and it was likely soon to be answered many of those who, discouraged and fatigued at the long and apparently useless vigil nad given up waiting there came back and at midnight the crowd that a short time before had appeared to be dwindling was swelled and kept growing larger and more vigorous in its demands for information.

Despatches that reached the White star line offices here soon before midnight brought the information that the passengers rescued by the Carpathia were taken on board that vessel from a small fleet of the Titanic's lifeboats that dotted the ocean in the vicinity of the scene of the disaster. They were transferred aboard the Carpathia at half-past ten o'clock in the morning. That was approximately twelve hours after the Titanic is reported to have gone down.

This time of rescue cast gloom over the officers of the company, who still were hoping that the lives of hundreds of the Titanic passengers had been saved by the Virginian and the Parisian, of the Allan line. When they learned the time that the Carpathia had picked up those who have been rescued they figured that neither of the other vessels could have reached the scene in time to have been of material assistance in the work of rescue.

This verdict was not final, however, and was not borne out by an authentic information in either direction. The best estimate of the time in which the Virginia hoped to reached the Titanic when she flashed messages by wireless that she was going to the aid of the Titanic was that she probably would reach the vessel that was in trouble about ten o'clock in the morning.

When it was learned that the Carpathia had taken a course directly for New York city it was decided at the White Star line offices that the reason for this is that, in all probability many of the passengers who were picked up from the lifeboats were found to have been suffering either from exhaustion or exposure, and in many cases undoubtedly from both. Because of this circumstance New York was decided upon as the best place to which to hurry the passengers because here they might receive better and more adequate medical and surgical treatment.

Among the passengers for whom inquiry was made at the White Star offices last night were Mr. and Mrs. Arthur Ryerson, their two daughters and one son, all of Philadelphia. Inquiry for them, which elicited no information as to whether they are among the rescued, was made by Mr. Maidhoff.

Edward Foreman, of this city, also was seeking information regarding his brother, B. L. Foreman, who was a first cabin passenger by the Titanic.

Soon before midnight a brother of Frederick M. Hoyt, commodore of the Larchmont Yacht Club, who was a passenger by the Titantic, made inquiry at the offices of the steamship company, as did Leo Greenfield, of No. 1,239 Madison avenue, whose wife and son were aboard the Titanic.

A young man and woman, who declined to make known their identity, entered the offices of the company just before midnight.

"Is it true that the Titanic has sunk—are the stories in the late afternoon papers true?" he inquired of a clerk.

He was told that the steamship had gone to the bottom.

"My God!" exclaimed the young man, "we are ruined! They are all lost."

The young woman became hysterical.

Captain Smith's Bad Luck Came After 43 Years' Unmarred Record

CAPTAIN SMITH BELIEVED THE TITANIC UNSINKABLE

That Captain Smith believed the Titanic and the Olympic to be absolutely unsinkable is recalled by a man who had a conversation with the veteran commander on a recent voyage of the Olympic.

The talk was concerning the accident in which the British war ship Hawke rammed the Olympic.

"The commander of the Hawke was entirely to blame," commented a young officer who was in the group. "He was 'showing off' his war ship before a throng of passengers and made a miscalculation."

Captain Smith smiled enigmatically at the theory advanced by his subordinate, but made no comment as to this view of the mishap.

"Anyhow," declared Captain Smith, "the Olympic is unsinkable, and the Titanic will be the same when she is put in commission.

"Why," he continued, "either of these vessels could be cut in halves and each half would remain afloat indefinitely. The non-sinkable vessel has been reached in these two wonderful craft.

"I venture to add," concluded Captain Smith, "that even if the engines and boilers of these vessels were to fall through their bottoms the vessels would remain afloat."

Bad luck came to Captain E. J. Smith, commander of the Titanic, after an unbroken career of forty-three years on the sea, during which time he worked up from apprentice to commander of the largest steamship in the world. During all this time, up to last September, when his vessel, the Olympic, crashed into the British cruiser Hawke, in the Solent, he did not figure in a single disaster. Since then, however, misfortune has come thick and fast, for in February the Olympic struck what is believed to have been a submerged wreck and lost a blade from one of her propellers, which made it necessary to put her in dry dock, and last Wednesday the Titanic in leaving Southampton on her maiden voyage narrowly missed being in collision with the New York, of the American line, which had been pulled from her anchorage by suction from the new ocean giant.

For the collision between the Olympic and the Hawke no responsibility was ever placed, but the cause was the great suction caused by the new steamship. Although the British Admiralty Court, after a thorough investigation, exonerated from all blame the officers of the Hawke, and although the Olympic was compelled to go into dry dock at heavy expense to her owners, the company apparently did not seek to place blame on any on board. Not only was Captain Smith retained in command of the Olympic, but he received the further honor of taking the Titanic on her first run.

Retained After Two Mishaps.

It was considered because of Captain Smith's previous excellent career that the officials of the White Star line retained him in its service after the two mishaps to the Olympic, thus violating a deep sea tradition that has been more rigorously maintained by the British merchant marine than by that of any other nation. The rule has been almost invariable among steamship companies to dispense with the services of officers in command of vessels that met with disaster. One reason for this is the insistence of the insurance companies.

Lloyd's keeps in its London office the records of all marine officers, so that when a man is put in command of a vessel his whole career can be immediately inspected.

Whether this "grand old man of the sea" was at fault fer the disaster to the Titanic depended in a great measure on the degree of vigilance used after the delicate instruments all vessels now carry warned of the vessel's proximity to ice.

A few steamship companies, among them the North German Lloyd, have shown leniency toward officers whose previous records were good, and have allowed them a second chance, provided the vessel has not been a total loss.

The White Star line has been among the strictest of the British companies in this regard, as is evidenced in the fate of Captain Inman Sealby, who commanded the Republic when she sank in collision with the Italian line steamship Florida, on January 23, 1909. No blame was attached to Captain Sealby for faulty navigation or bad seamanship in handling the vessel, and all his career he had been with the White Star line without figuring in a wreck. Nevertheless he was dismissed, afterward going to the University of Michigan to study admiralty law.

Captain Smith began his sea career in 1869, when he shipped as apprentice on board the Senator Weber, an American clipper purchased by A. Gibson & Co., of Liverpool. In 1876 he got a commission as fourth officer of the square rigger Lizzie Fennel, and in 1886 was appointed fourth officer of the White Star line's old steamship Celtic, which subsequently was sold to the Thingvalla Company and renamed the America. He attained the rank of captain in 1887, when he took command of the old Republic, later going to the old Baltic. Next he was in command of the freight steamship Cufic, and then of the Runic. Afterward he went to the old Adriatic, then the Celtic, the Brittanic and the Coptic, in the Australian trade.

Commanded All First Voyages.

It was in 1892 that the White Star line bestowed its first great honor on Captain Smith, when it made him commander of its largest steamship, the Majestic, on her maiden voyage. Since that time he has commanded every large steamship of the White Star line on her initial trip. When he was put in command of the Titanic it was reported that he would retire after he had conducted her across the Atlantic and back, but the White Star officials afterward announced that he would have charge of the Titanic until the company built a larger and finer steamship.

Captain Smith had the utmost confidence in the safety of the ocean giants that are now being constructed. In 1907, when he came to New York in command of the Adriatic, on her maiden trip, he said:—

"Shipbuilding is such a perfect art nowadays that absolute disaster, involving the passengers, in inconceivable. Whatever happens, there will be time enough before the vessel sinks to save the life of every person on board. I will go a bit further. I will say that I cannot imagine any condition that would cause the vessel to founder. Modern shipbuilding has gone beyond that.

"When any one asks me how I can best describe my experiences of nearly forty years at sea I merely say, 'Uneventful.' Of course there have been winter gales and storms and fogs and the like, but in all my experience I have never been in an accident of any sort worth speaking about. I have seen but one vessel in distress in all my years at sea, a brig, the crew of which was taken off in a small boat in charge of my third officer. I never saw a wreck and have never been wrecked, nor was I ever in any predicament that threatened to end in a disaster of any sort. You see, I am not very good material for a story.

"The love of the ocean that took me to sea as a boy has never left me. In a way, a certain amount of wonder never leaves me, especially as I observe from the bridge a vessel plunging up and down in the trough of the seas, fighting her way through and over great waves, tumbling, and yet keeping on her keel, and going on and on—I wonder how she does it, how she can keep afloat in such seas, and how she can go on and on safely to port. There is a wild grandeur, too, that appeals to me in the sea. A man never outgrows that."

An officer of the Adriatic who heard part of Captain Smith's remarks put in:—

"Don't forget when you write of the Captain's 'uneventful' life to put in that it is the great captain who doesn't let things happen."

But the iceberg is marked with no cross on the chart. The wise and seasoned mariner can evade rocks and reefs and can pick his way through fogs and storms, but the iceberg brings disaster in spite of all precautions.

Last December, on arriving at New York with the Olympic, a banquet was given to Captain Smith at the Metropolitan Club, and among the guests were General Stewart L. Woodford, Chauncey M. Depew, W. H. Truesdale and W. A. Nash.

Among marine officers who have been dismissed in the past were Captain Wright, of the Norse King, which, with 250 passengers on board, went ashore on the island of Zante in April, 1893. The Norse King was cruising seven miles from shore when a deputation of women passengers begged the captain to go nearer, so they might see the picturesque villages. He obliged them, and his vessel crashed onto a reef. The passengers lived three weeks on Zante, subsisting on dried currants, figs, wild pig and goats' cheese. The Norse King was a total loss, and Captain Wright was dismissed and had his certificate suspended for a year.

Captain Le Horn ended his career by letting his vessel, the China, crash into a reef off Perim Island, in the Red Sea, in 1897, while he was enjoying a birthday dinner provided by Lady Brassey, one of the passengers. He ignored notes sent down by the second officer asking that the course be changed. This disaster led to an order forbidding officers to associate with passengers, which caused four hundred officers to resign.

Who the Persons Were On Board Ill Fated Ship

Colonel John Jacob Astor, Long a Leader in Social Circles, Scion of Famous Astor Family of New York, and Identified with Financial Activities of Metropolis for Years.

Colonel John Jacob Astor, long a leader in New York society, was born at Rhinebeck, N. Y., July 13, 1864, and is a son of Mr. and Mrs. William Astor. He was graduated from Harvard in 1888, and spent the following three years in travel, following which he assumed the management of the family estate, and in 1897 built the Astoria hotel, which has since been consolidated with the Waldorf, becoming the Waldorf-Astoria.

He was made a Colonel on the staff of Governor Levi P. Morton, of New York, in the same year, and at the outbreak of the Spanish-American war in 1898, was commissioned a lieutenant-colonel of the United States Volunteer Infantry.

Although possessed of one of the greatest fortunes in the world and burdened with the care of vast interests, he went to the front for the campaign in Cuba, for which he also presented to the government a mounted battery costing $100,000. As an aide on the staff of Major-General Shafter he saw active service in the attack on, and the capture of Santiago de Cuba.

Colonel Astor is responsible for several valuable inventions, and has written several books. He married Miss Ava Lowle Willing, of Philadelphia, in 1891, and was divorced from her in November, 1909. He married Miss Madeleine Talmage Force, daughter of Mr. and Mrs. W. H. Force, in September of last year, and after a cruise on board their yacht, the Noma, left in January for a trip through Egypt, returning to London in time to take passage on board the Titanic.

Colonel Astor and his son Vincent, with a party of friends on board the yacht Nourmahal, were missing in West Indian waters for two weeks in November, 1910, and revenue cutters and naval vessels were sent out to search for them. They were found in the harbor of San Juan, where they had taken refuge from a storm. Colonel Astor maintains a magnificent town house at No. 840 Fifth avenue and a country estate, Ferncliff, at Rhinebeck, N. Y.

Henry B. Harris, one of the powers in the theatrical world, was born in St. Louis December 1, 1866. His first theatrical experience was in connection with the management of the Howard Athenaeum, in Boston; after which he became a partner in the firm of Rich & Harris, and managed May Irwin, Peter Dailey, Lily Langtry, Amelia Bingham and Robert Edeson. He assumed the management of the Hudson Theatre in 1903 and of the Hackett Theatre in 1906. Among his numerous activities are president of the Henry B. Harris Company, the National Producing Managers of America, director of the Metropolis Theatre Association, director of the Theatre Managers' Association of Greater New York, treasurer of the Actors' Fund of America and trustee of the Hebrew Infant Asylum of New York. He is a thirty-second degree Mason. In October, 1898, he married Miss Irene Wallach, of Wsshington.

Isidor Straus, merchant and philanthropist, was born in Rhenish, Bavaria, February 6, 1845, and was a brother of Nathan and Oscar S. Straus. He came to this country with his parents in 1854 and received an education in several preparatory schools and Washington and Lee University. In 1863 he was sent abroad by a Georgia company to assist in the purchase of steamships and supplies for the Confederacy. With his father, he formed the firm of L. Straus & Sons, importers of pottery, in 1866, and later, with his brother Nathan, became a partner in the firm of R. H. Macy & Co., of New York, in 1888. He was a member of the firm of Abraham & Straus, of Brooklyn; first president of the New York Crockery Board of Trade; director in several banks and financial institutions. He was elected to the Fifty-third Congress in 1893 and became interested in tariff legislation, later becoming a member of several investigating boards and sound money movements, beside having an important part in the construction of the Wilson tariff. He was president of the Educational Alliance, vice president of the J. Hood Wright Hospital of New York, member of the Chamber of Commerce and was on one of the visiting committees of Harvard University.

Mr. Strauss home is at No. 2,754 Broadway. His son, Percy Straus, said last night that Mr. and Mrs. Straus had been travelling in Europe all winter, and that he had heard nothing from them since reciving word that they expected to return on board the Titanic.

Perhaps one of the most celebrated passengers on the Titanic is William T. Stead, of Chicago, noted author and for years editor of the Review of Reviews in London. Mr. Stead is well known in America, having spent several months here in the early 90's, part of which time he occupied gathering material for his book, which later caused a country-wide furore, "If Christ Came to Chicago." The aim of the work was to expose the vice of the Illinois metropolis, and it did so with such elaborate and vivid detail that it immediately became the talk of the country. It all but caused riots in Chicago. Mr. Stead, in reply to all criticisms, said that he stood ready to prove everything he had written.

Previously he had caused a storm in London by publishing a book called "Maiden Tribute of Modern Babylon." This caused court proceedings and resulted in Mr. Stead's severing his connections with the Pall Mall Gazette, of which he was editor. He vigorously assailed the government on many occasions, notably during the Boer War. He was a virile and scholarly writer and his attacks were masterly.

He was born in Northumberland in 1849, the son of a clergyman, and was apprenticed to a merchant. Prosaic business did not appeal to him, however, and he drifted into newspaper work. In 1871 he became editor of the Darlington Northern Echo, under John Morley, and after serving twelve years in second place, was made editor. He was original and established many innovations, notably the interview and extra issues of the Pall Mall Gazette. His first visit to America was in 1893, just after he had finished a sensational vice crusade in London. He received an enthusiastic welcome and was greeted everywhere with warmth, except in Chicago, where his criticism was resented. He wrote many essays and books, which attracted almost worldwide attention. Among his works were "The Truth About Rissue" and the "Americanization of the World."

Jacques Futrelle, who with his wife was on board the Titanic, has recently loomed large in the literary firmament, through a series of magazine articles written by him. He has, however, been well known as a contributor to magazines for several years. He was born in Pike County, Georgia, thirty-seven years ago, and on finishing his education entered newspaper work. He was engaged steadily in it from 1890 to 1902 during part of which time he was on the staff of the HERALD. Some of his books are "Chase of the Golden Plae," and the "Diamond Master." A more recent work was "The High Hand," which has been dramatized, but not yet produced. Mrs. Futrelle is also a writer of considerable note.

Friends of Karl H. Behr, known internationally as a tennis player and all around athlete, were anxiously inquiring as to his fate, last night. The name of K. H. Behr appears on the passenger list of the Titanic, but whether he is the noted athlete it was impossible to ascertain last night.

Mr. Poseph Bruce Ismay, one of the passengers aboard the ill fated steamship, has for many years been President of the International Mercantile Marine Company and chairman of the board and managing director of the White Star Line. He is one of the leading figures in the shipping world, and is very well known

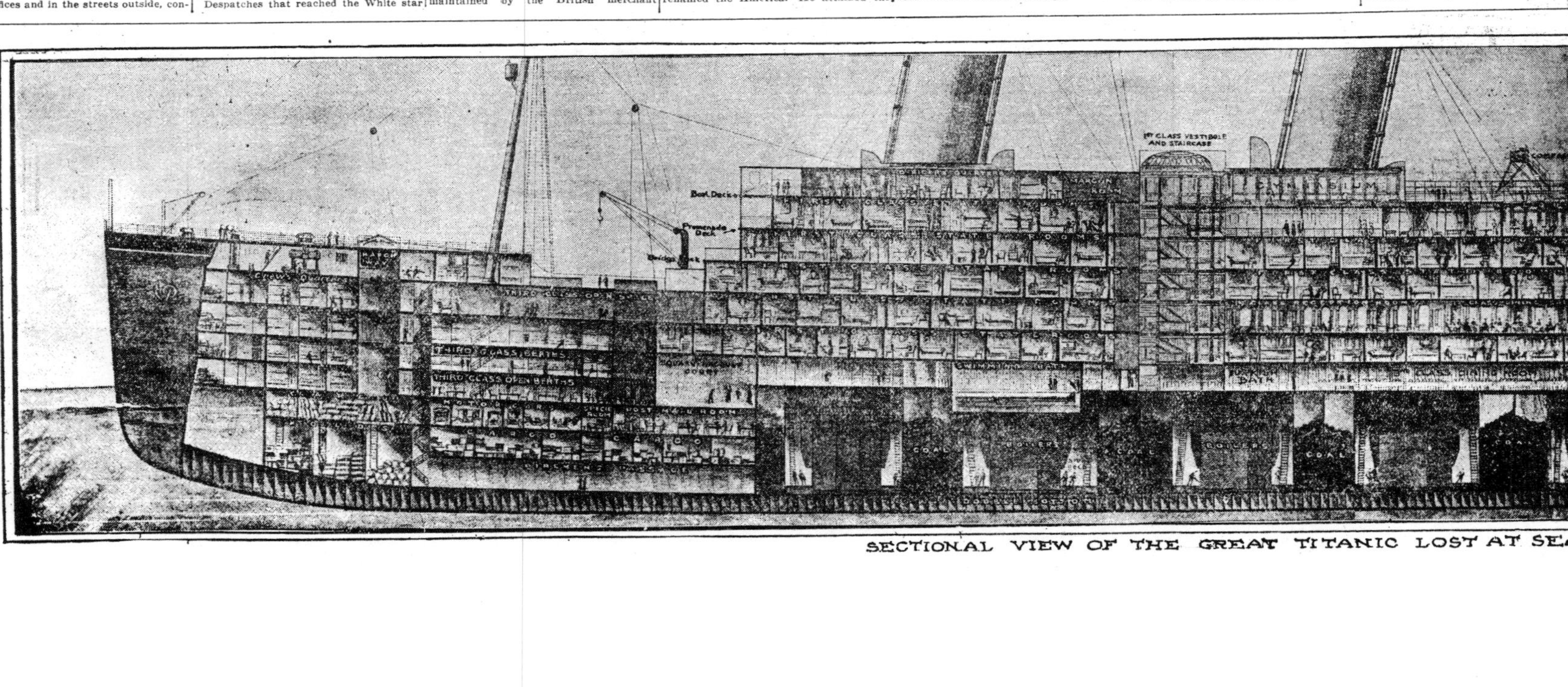

SECTIONAL VIEW OF THE GREAT TITANIC LOST AT SEA

WEEPING CROWDS HERE SEEK NEWS OF FRIENDS IN DISASTER

in American financial circles, having made annual trips to this country for many years. He always has had a strong admiration for this side of the Atlantic, due partly to the fact that he married an American girl, Miss Julia Florence Schieffelin, daughter of George R. Schieffelin, of New York. The marriage was celebrated in 1888 ,and there are four children, two boys and two girls.

Mr. Ismay is a comparatively young man to occupy the important post he has held. Forty-nine years old, he was born in Liverpool, the son of Thomas Henry Ismay, a leading man in the shipping world. He entered the business with his father and rose rapidly to be the head of the great corporation when he was just past forty. He has always been a great exponent of out door sports, especially motoring and golfing. He was last here in 1909.

Another of the distinguished passengers was Norman Carlyle Craig, M. P. He is well known throughout England for his learning and familiarity with economic matters. He was born in 1868 in England, was K. C. in 1909, and entered Parliment in 1910 as a member from the Isle of Thanet. He is a Cambridge graduate and a celebrated sportsman as well as a scholar. He belongs to the Carlton, St. Stephens, Royal Thames Yacht, Royal Temple Yacht, Royal Norfolk and Suffolk Yacht clubs.

Mrs. R. C. Cornell is the wife of Magistrate Cornell and a sister of Mrs. E. D. Appleton, who also was aboard. They went abroad three weeks ago to attend the funeral of their sister, Lady Drummond.

Mrs. J. W. M. Cardeza and her son, Mr. Thomas D. M. Cardeza, wife and son of Mr. Thomas Cardeza, Sr., a retired lawyer, who were aboard, have lived abroad for nearly six years, making yearly visits to Philadelphia. Mr. Cardeza, Jr., is married and lives in Austria-Hungary. They are the cousins of Mrs. Howard J. M. Cardeza, of No. 210 Riverside Drive, New York.

Frederick M. Hoyt, who with Mrs. Hoyt was on board the Titanic, is a prominent broker with offices at No. 45 Broadway. He has a city home at No. 112 East Seventy-third street and a summer dwelling at Stamford, Conn. He is prominent in yachting circles. In 1900 he bought the yacht Isolde and on board her, in 1906, spent his honeymoon. Mrs. Hoyt was Miss Jane Ann Forby, of Amsterdam, N. Y.' Mr. Hoyt belongs to the Yale, Racquette, New York Yacht and Larchmont Yacht clubs. He was rear commodore of the Larchmont Yacht Club in 1901.

Wyckoff Vander Hoef, who was among the passengers is secretary of the Williamsburg City Fire Insurance Company. He is a bachelor, a member of the Excelsior Club, of Brooklyn, the Dykker Heights Golf Club and the Sons of the Revolution. He lives with his parents at No. 109 Jerolamon street, Brooklyn.

Mr. Guggenheim's Family Here

Mr. Benjamin Guggenheim, president of the International Steam Pump Company, who was on board, went to Europe in January on business. Mrs. Guggenheim and three daughters are at their apartment in the Hotel St. Regis.

Dr. Henry W. Frauenthal, of No. 783 Lexington avenue, with his bride and his brother, Isaac G. Frauenthal, a lawyer, was also aboard. Edward F. Fruenthal, a brother, said last night his brother went abroad in March to marry Miss Clara Heinsheimer, of this city, who was in Europe with her family. He received a cable despatch on March 23 saying the marriage had taken place in the south of France. He heard nothing more until he received word that his brothers and Dr. Frauenthal's bride had taken passage aboard the Titanic.

Inquiries at the HERALD office last night first disclosed the presence aboard the Titanic of Miss Edith L. Rosenbaum, a New York woman, now resident in Paris, whose name is not on the passenger list of the ill fated steamship. She is the resident buyer in the French capital of many large American houses and is one of the best known business women in the great cities of Europe. She also is well known as a writer of fashions. Several of her relatives live in New York and their anxiety for her safety led to disclosure of her coming to this country.

Miss Rosenbaum is just recovering from an automobile accident last summer in which she nearly lost her life. She was one of a party which included Ludwig Loewe, of Berlin, who was associated with the Krupp gun factory. The party was making a tour from Paris to Rouen when the car overturned and Mr. Loewe was killed and Miss Rosenbaum severly injured.

The Rev. John Stuart Holden, vicar of St. Paul's, Portman square, London, is another eminent Englishman of the Titanic's passengers who agreed with enthusiasm to aid the men and religion movement in the United States and is on the programme of exercises in New York for next week. He is down for an address on "Men and Boys and the Kingdom of Jesus Christ" to be delieverd in Carnegie Hall next Friday afternoon.

Dr. Holden is surrogate for the diocese of London and honorary chaplain to the Earl of Oberdeen, and is married. He was educated in Liverpool College and Corpus Christi, Cambridge, and first won fame for his eloquence as a mission preacher on the staff of the Church Parochial Mission Society of England in the early years of this century. He has been a prominent delegate to missionary conferences in many parts of the world and is president of the London Missionary School of Medicine.

Mr. and Mrs. George A, Harder, who appear in the passenger list, were returning from their honeymoon. Mr. Harder is a son of Mr. and Mrs. Victor A. Harder, of No. 117 Eighth avenue, Brooklyn. His bride was Miss Dorothy Annan, a daughter of the late Edward Annan, of Brooklyn. They were married January 8 at the home of the bride's sister, Mrs. Eben D. Knowlton, of No. 30 West Eleventh sctreet, Manhattan. Mrs. Harder is a niece of Mrs. Thomas Richardson of the Grosvenor, at Fifth avenue and Tenth street. After the wedding Mr. and Mrs. Harder went abroad with Sydney Whelan and his bride, who was Miss Hortense Harder.

Colonel Archibald Gracie, of Washington, one of the passengers on board the Titanic, is a wealthy confederate officer from Alabama. Mrs. Gracie is the daughter of Danish parents. She is not in Washington. A daughter, Miss Edith Gracie, is here.

Clarence Moore, of Washington, was born in Clarksburg, W. Va., March 1, 1865, and became associated with W. B. Hibbs in the banking and brokerage business in Washington in 1891. He married Miss Mabelle Swift, daughter of E. C. Swift, of Boston. He is well known as a sportsman, having been M. F. H. of the Chevy Chase Club and only recently accepted the position of M. F .H. of the Loudon Hunt, at Leesburg, Va. While in England he purchased fifty couples from the best packs for use in Loudon county. Mr. Moore was a member of the Metropolitan, Alibi and Chevy Chase clubs, of Washington; the New York Yacht Club and the Travellers' Club, of Paris.

Mr. and Mrs. Daniel Warner Marvin, of No. 340 Riverside Drive, were returning on board the Titanic from a honeymoon spent in Europe. Mrs. Marvin before her marriage, March 12, was Miss Mary Graham C. Farquharson, of No. 317 Riverside Drive. Her marriage to Mr. Marvin caused considerable comment, as she and her husband decided to perpetuate a record of the ceremony by having moving pictures taken. Mr. and Mrs. Marvin left for Europe March 13 and had been travelling in Great Britain and on the Continent. Mr. Marvin wrote his father a few days ago that his wife and he would return on board the Titanic.

Edgar J. Meyer is a member of the Stock Exchange house of Eugene Meyer, Jr., & Co., of No. 7 Wall street, and left for Europe about the middle of February on a short vacation trip. He is twenty-nine years old, married, and lives at No. 158 West Eighty-sixth street.

Mrs. Leo D. Greenfield and William B. Greenfield are the wife and son of Leo D. Greenfield, a wealthy furrier, who lives at No. 1,239 Madison avenue. Mr. Greenfield said last night that with his family he went to Europe in January, partly for business and partly for pleasure, and he returned March 29, leaving his wife and son, the latter being twenty-four years old, in Paris. He said they were anxious to remain so they could be on the maiden trip of Titanic.

Dr. Alice Farnham Leader, who was a passenger on board the Titanic, is one of the best known women physicians in New York, where she has been practicing for several years. Accompanied by Mrs. Frederick Swift, of Brooklyn, she went to Europe in the early part of February, and her friends received letters from her last week in which she said she would return on board the Titanic. Her New York city address is No. 430 West 118th street.

Henry Sleeper Harper, who, with Mrs. Harper, was a passenger on board the Titanic, was formerly of the house of Harper Brothers, but retired some years ago. He resides at No. 131 East Twenty-first street and has been in Europe for three months on a pleasure trip. He is forty-five years old.

Edward P. Calderhead, one of the passengers aboard the Titanic, was a buyer for Gimbel Brothers. He lived, with his wife and a seventeen-year-old daughter, at No. 561 West 180th street. A brother-in-law, Harry Pabst, said last night Mrs. Calderhead believed from the early reports that her husband had been saved and he would not tell her the new tidings of the disaster. Mr. Calderhead was forty-five years old and had been a buyer for Gimbel Brothers for ten years.

Harry Anderson, whose name appears in the passenger list, is a broker at No. 63 Broad street, and lives with his wife at No. 317 West Ninety-ninth street. It was said there last night that when Mrs. Anderson heard of the accident she hurried to the White Star line offices and had not returned home up to midnight.

Mrs. Daniel Guggenheim, a niece of Benjamin Guggenheim, a passenger on board the Titanic, was in the audience at the Winter Garden last night when she first learned of the latest reports of the steamship. Quietly she hastened from the theatre to her home.

Leaders in Philadelphia's Social and Financial World Aboard

Relatives of Mr. and Mrs. George D. Widener and Son and Other Prominent Americans Storm Newspaper Offices Seeking News of Disaster.

PHILADELPHIA, Pa., Monday. — Frantic relatives of Philadelphia passengers aboard the Titanic stormed the local newspaper and cable offices to-night and the offices of the White Star line here in an effort to get authentic news of the disaster. At all places it was impossible until late this afternoon, when a wireless message was received at the station at Wanamaker's store that all the passengers had been taken safely off the disabled liner.

Most of the Philadelphia passengers of the Titanic are prominent financially and socially.

They include:—

Mr. and Mrs. George D. Widener, of Lynnewood Hall, Elkins Park, and their son, Harry Elkins Widener.

Mr. and Mrs. John B. Thayer and their son, John B. Thayer, Jr., of Haverford.

Mr. William C. Dulles, of No. 319 South Twelfth street.

Mr. and Mrs. William E. Carter and their son and daughter, William, Jr., and Miss Lucille Carter, of Bryn Mawr.

Mr. and Mrs. Arthur Ryerson, of Haverford, who are hurrying home to attend the funeral of their son, Arthur Larned Ryerson, who was killed last Monday, together with J. Louis Hoffman, another Yale student, in an automobile accident.

Mrs. J. W. M. Cardeza, of Washington lane and Morton street, Germantown, and her son, T. D. M. Cardeza.

Mr. Robert W. Daniel, of the banking firm of Shillard-Smith-Daniel Company, of No. 328 Chestnut street.

Mr. C. Duane Williams and his son, Richard Norris Williams, Jr., formerly residents of this city, who were on their way to visit relatives at Chestnut Hill.

Mrs. Thomas Potter, widow of Colonel Thomas Potter, and her daughter, Mrs. Boulton Earnshaw, of Mount Airy.

It is believed that Mrs. Joseph Pennell, the writer and wife of Joseph Pennell, the artist, is aboard, as letters have been received by Edward Robine, her brother, secretary of the Board of Trustees of the University of Pennsylvania, saying she expected to leave by the Titanic.

Mr. George D. Widener is one of the leading financiers of the country. He is a son of P. A. B. Widener, the traction magnate. Mrs. Widener, before her marriage was Miss Elenor Elkins. The couple went abroad several weeks ago, Mr. Widener for the purpose of inspecting several works of art his father had intended to purchase, and Mrs. Widener to supervise the purchase of a trousseau for her daughter, Miss Eleanor, whose engagement to Fitz Eugene Dixon was announced recently.

John B. Thayer is vice president of the Pennsylvania Railroad Company. His home, Redwood, Haverford, is one of the show places of the country. Prior to her marriage Mrs. Thayer was Miss Marion L. Morris.

William C. Dulles is a widely known banker. He has a country residence at Goshen, N. Y.

Mr. and Mrs. William E. Carter are widely known in social circles. Mrs. Carter was Miss Lucille Polk, of Baltimore.

Mrs. Thomas Potter is a sister-in-law of William Potter, formerly Minister to Italy. Since the death of her husband she has been making a tour through the Holy land with her daughter.

Members of families of several of the passengers of the Titantic last night received wireless messages apparently sent a short time before the steamship struck the iceberg.

MR. W. ROEBLING, 2D, AMONG PASSENGERS

[SPECIAL DESPATCH TO THE HERALD.]

TRENTON, N. J., Monday.—Washington Roebling II., a son of Charles G. Roebling, president of the John A. Roebling Sons Company, the Roebling Construction Company and the New Jersey Wire Cloth Company, who was a passenger on board the Titanic, together with Stephen Blackwell, another Trenton young man, is one of the managers of the Mercer Automobile Works of this city, which manufactures the Mercer car. Mr. Roebling and Mr. Blackwell toured Italy, France and other countries in an automobile.

Mr. Roebling was born in this city and is thirty-one years old. He went to a private school here and attended the Hill Preparatory School at Pottstown, Pa. He is an ardent automobilist and golfer. Two years ago he took part in one of the important automobile races at Savananh, Ga., making second place.

He went through many of the departments in the big Roebling mills, this city, before going to take over part of the management of the Mercer concern. His sisters are Mrs. Richard McCall Cadwallader, of Philadelphia, and Miss Helen Roebling, of this city, whose engagement to C. S. Tyson, a Philadelphia artist, was recently announced.

Mr. Roebling is one of the best known of the younger social set and is exceedingly popular. His mother, now dead, was a Miss Ormsby, of Pittsburg.

H. J. ALLISON, MONTREAL, BANKER, WAS ON BOARD

Hudson J. Allison, who with Mrs. Allison, two children, one and three years old, two maids and a nurse, was a passenger on board the Titanic, is a member of the banking house of Johnston, McConnell & Allison, of London and Montreal. The house is interested in several of the public service corporations of Montreal. Mr. Allison has divided his time between the London and Montreal offices, and engaged passage on board the Titantic because he knew so many of the persons who were going on her maiden voyage.

He is thirty-five years old, a native of Canada, and well known to the financiers of two continents. He owns a large stock farm in Canada to which he had recently sent twenty-five horses from England, and a large estate in England.

MAJOR BUTT AID TO TWO PRESIDENTS

HERALD BUREAU,
No. 1,502 H STREET, N. W.,
WASHINGTON, D. C., Monday.

Major Archibald W. Butt, military aid to the President, is forty-six years old, a native of Georgia and a descendant of an old Colonial family. He was educated at the University of the South, Seewanee, Tenn., and as a young man came to Washington and for several years was well known as a correspondent of various Southern newspapers.

In 1905 he wrote a study of Southern life entitled "The Other Side of the Shield." He was appointed a captain and quartermaster of volunteers in 1900 and commissioned in the permanent establishment the following year. He made a creditable record in the Philippine insurrection and, returning to the United States in 1903, was the youngest officer ever detailed as depot quartermaster at the capital.

When General Funston was placed in command of the second army of Cuban occupation in 1906 he asked for the appointment of Captain Butt as his junior quartermaster.

President Roosevelt about a year before leaving the White House selected Captain Butt as his military aid and became greatly attached to him. When the army officers campained of the rigor of the physical test prescribed by President Roosevelt he proved its feasibility by riding more than one hundred miles in one day with Captain Butt and Surgeon General Rixey, of the navy.

President Taft, who had known Major Butt in the Philippines, asked him to continue as aid to the President. President Taft sent Major Butt with a letter of farewell to Mr. Roosevelt when he left for Africa in 1909. This letter contained a statement that the President owed more to his brother Charles and to Mr. Roosevelt than to any other men in the world. Mr. Roosevelt never forgave the President for naming Charles P. Taft before himself. Despite the estrangement between Mr. Roosevelt and President Taft, Major Butt remained on good terms with both families.

Major Butt's genial nature and magnetic personality commands friends all over the country, and in Washington society he is a popular favorite, while he enjoys a high reputation in the army as an officer and a man.

When travelling with the President, Major Butt is not only his military aid, but performs the duties of secretaries, formerly discharged by such men as Mr. Cortelyou and Mr. Loeb. At White House social functions he makes the introductions. The strain of official duties during the President's last trip to the Pacific coast impaired his health, and he was induced by his personal friend, Frank Millett, the artist, and the President to go to Rome for a rest. While there he was received by the Pope and by the King of Italy. At the White House it is said there is no basis for the story that his mission to the Vatican was to discuss the precedence of American Cardinals at official functions.

MANY NEW ENGLAND RESIDENTS ON BOARD

[SPECIAL DESPATCH TO THE HERALD.]

BOSTON, Mass., Monday.—Among the New England passengers of the Titanic are well known Boston people.

Mrs. Timothy J. McCarthy, whose husband was on board the Titanic, is ill at her home at No. 52 Nelson street, Dorchester, after having heard news of the wreck. With her are her family of five, Miss Annie McCarthy, twenty-two years old; Mildred, twenty; Justin, seventeen; Edmund, fifteen, and Brendon, ten. She told a reporter this morning that Mr, McCarthy, who is fifty-one years old, has been in the employ of Jordan March Company for the last twenty-eight years, having risen to the position of foreign buyer in the stationery department.

He was making his twenty-second ocean trip. Last February he left New York on board the Kronprinz Wilhelm. He visited nearly every large country in Europe except Russia.

Inquiries at the foreign department of Jordan, Marsh & Co., where Herbert H. illiard also is employed, failed to elicit any definite information whether he was on board the Titanic, but the men in charge said it was possible that he was. Mrs. McCarthy has positive information of Mr. McCarthy leaving the other side, and is very sure that Mr. Hilliard also is on board the same vessel.

Both men left for Europe on February 13. Mr. Hilliard is married and family resides at No. 4 0Hichborn street, Brighton. He formerly was employed as a floorwalker in the Boston store, but was promoted to buyer about four years ago. Mr. Hilliard has been in the firm's employ for the last thirty-one years, and has a daughter who is also employed by the company. She was so broken by the first news of the wreck this morning that she was unable to work.

Miss Gretchen N. Longley, of Hudson, N. Y., was another of the Titanic's passengers. She was accompanied by her aunt and guardian, Mrs. Cornelie I. Andrews, also of New York, with whom she was returning from a four or five months' stay in continental Europe, largely in Italy.

Although a New York girl, Miss Longley is very well known about Boston, particularly in social circles, where she has been a familiar figure. Only two years ago she was graduated from the Quincy Mansion School for Girls, at Williston. After leaving the private school Miss Longley decided to acquire her further education through travel instead of college, and the trip abroad was arranged.

At the Quincy Mansion School Miss Longley has many friends, who knew that she was a passenger on board the Titanic.

George L. Clifford, of Stoughton, is a passenger on board the Titanic. He is president of the Belcher Last Company, the largest industry in the town. He hasten on a two months' business trip through England, Germany, France, Russia and Austria. He has a wife and daughter here, the latter Mrs. McArthur.

John F. Maguire, of Brockton, a salesman for the Dunbar Pattern Company, who was on board, left Boston on board the Megantic, February 20, to make a tour of England, Belgium and other parts of Europe. He was accompanied by George Q. Clifford, of Stoughton, and Walter Porter, of Worcester, both shoe manufacturers. Mr. Maguire was two years ago exalted ruler of Brockton Lodge of Elks.

Percival W. White & Son, of Winchendon, are supposed to be passengers on board. Mr. White has a mania for taking "maiden trips" on board new vessels, and he recent went across on board the Olympic to take this trip.

Friends of John R. Dagnino, of John R. Dagnina & Co., wholesale grocers, at No. 102 Commercial street, believe that he is a passenger on board the Titanic. He wrote his children that he would try to catch that steamship, and his daughter is satisfied that he did.

Colonel Astor's Friends in Grave Alarm, Seek News of His Fate

Offices of the Astor Estate Kept Open All Night, While the Secretary and Others Send Wireless and Cable Messages to Ascertain if He Is Among the Lost.

His personal anxiety for his employer, Colonel John Jacob Astor, and for Mrs. Astor, as well as the urgent demands from a thousand relatives and friends of New York's greatest landed proprietor for some news of his fate, kept Mr. W. A. Dobbyn, secretary to Colonel Astor, up all night. The Astor estate offices, No. 23 West Twenty-sixth street, were kept open, with the assistants of Mr. Dobbyn on duty to receive any information that might by chance arrive through some unexpected channel and to reply to the queries which swarmed in by telephone and personal visits all night long.

Here, as in a hundred other cases, the horror stricken relatives and friends of the Titanic's passenger list, with its many noted men and women, turned from the scant and terrifying reports that came by wireless from the Virginian and sought a ray of hope in the remote possibility of escape from death of more than the boatloads of women and children taken off by the Allan line steamship. Whence news of other survivors might come none could surmise, but few were ready to give up all promise of brighter tidings.

Mr. Dobbyn kept informed of every item of news received by the press associations and spent much of the night in the White Star offices. He often was compelled to interrupt his quest for tidings of Colonel and Mrs. Astor to give what news he had and to explain the possibilities of their survival to the constant queries of their friends. These kept increasing in numbers as the night wore on.

The news of the real magnitude of the disaster did not reach the clubs of Fifth avenue and the great hotels until after nine o'clock. Thousands went to their dinners confident after reading the afternoon reports that the worst was over and that their friends and relatives aboard the Titanic were safe. It was another and almost a greater shock to have that feeling of security rudely torn from them and to suddenly face the frightful possibilities of the loss of the greater number aboard the fated steamship.

Companies Here Refuse to Reinsure Baggage

Marine Underwriters Besieged All Day and Premiums of Fifty and Sixty Per Cent Are Offered in Vain.

Heads of marine insurance companies in this city were perturbed last night, on learning of the report that the White Star line steamship Titanic had foundered at sea with the loss of hundreds of passengers. Prominent marine underwriters said they had been besieged all day by persons who were the owners of valuable baggage aboard the Titanic, or had relatives or friends who were bringing such baggage over.

Many of these anxious inquirers offered to pay premiums as high as sixty per cent for reinsurance on such property. The underwriters, however, were alamed at the epots of the accident, and still moe alarmed as the day progressed and no wireless dsaeptches were received directly from the vessel. For this rason, they refused to reinsure either cargo or baggage.

One of the leading marine underwriters in this city, who requested that he should not be quoted, said last night that the White Star line had taken out its insurance on the vessel months ago. Any insurance on the Titanic, he said, had been placd early in January, and that this insurance would continue for a year from that date.

"$5,000,000 Insurance on Vessel."

According to this authority, the insurance on the vessel amounted to about $5,000,000, of which a great deal had been taken in London b ythe Lloyds, but that some of this amount had been assumed in this country.

It was stated by this underwriter, that it would have been impossible for the owners of the vessel to have attempted to reinsure her after the reports came out that she was in trouble. He stated that he had seen all the despatches received by the White Star line during the day, and that the company had been in the dark all the time whether the steamship had been lost or not.

Owners of the cargo, said this authority, had insured themselves, according to immemorial custom. Several of them had reinsured their risks in London yesterday, paying a premium of at least fifty per cent. Underwriters in England, who had no line of insurance on the cargo, had considered the early reports of the accident to the vessel as exaggerated. As a rule, he said, the newspaper accounts of such calamities were pictured worse than they afterward developed, and for this reason many underwriters were willing to take a gambling chance on reinsurance.

Other underwriters, who had heavy lines of insurance, alarmed by the reports, and unwilling to assume the entire risks for which they had become responsible, went to others who had no lines and offered to reinsure for fifty per cent. Many of these offers were accepted abroad.

Sixty Per Cent Refused.

The underwriter said that his office had been beset all day by persons who had valuable baggage on board the Titanic, and who were frantic to have their risks reinsured, offering a premium of sixty per cent. He, however, had been made uneasy by the fact that no direct despatches had come from the vessel, and had refused to take the risks. Life insurance, he added, did not enter into the question.

Mr. Anson W. Hard, a trustee of the Atlantic Mutual Insurance Company, said:—

"I always understood that the White Star line insured its own vessels, as is done by the German lines. A steamship company will sometimes take a large risk and place the remainder of the risk with the insurance concerns. Nearly all of the large steamship companies take a policy of say $400,000 and then reinsure portions of that amount, even without waiting for the reports of an accident.

"Lloyds, of London, are the largest assumers of such insurance risks. No other corporation that I know of is so heavily interested in this class of insurance as that company. A good many prominent men of means form themselves into an association called Lloyds, and each one contributes his proportion of the risk. The foundering of the Titanic is certainly a disaster of tremendous proportions."

BUILDERS THOUGHT SHIP UNSINKABLE

BELFAST, Monday.—A representative of Harland & Wolff, the constructors of the Titanic, said to-day that if the Titanic were sinking the collision must have been of great force. The plating of the vessel, he said, was of the heaviest kind, and even if it were pierced any two of her compartments could be flooded without imperilling the ship.

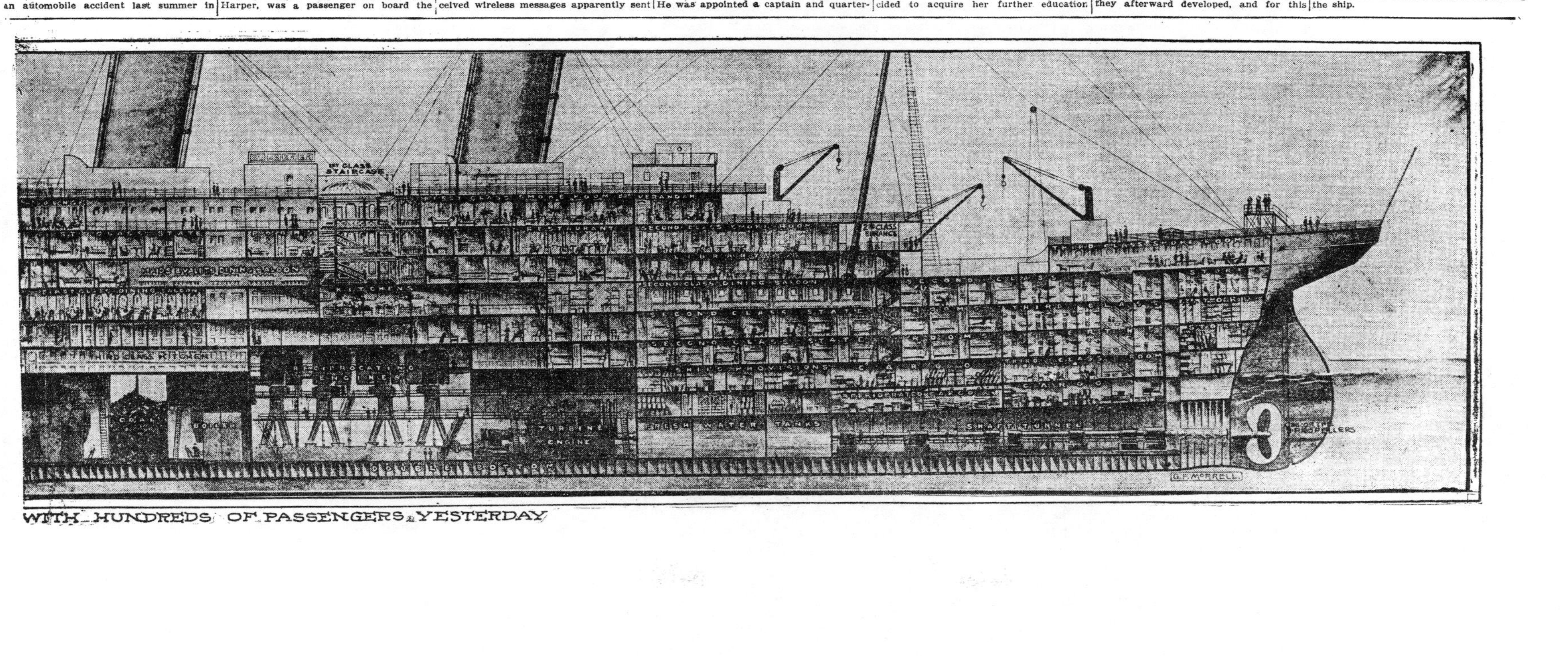

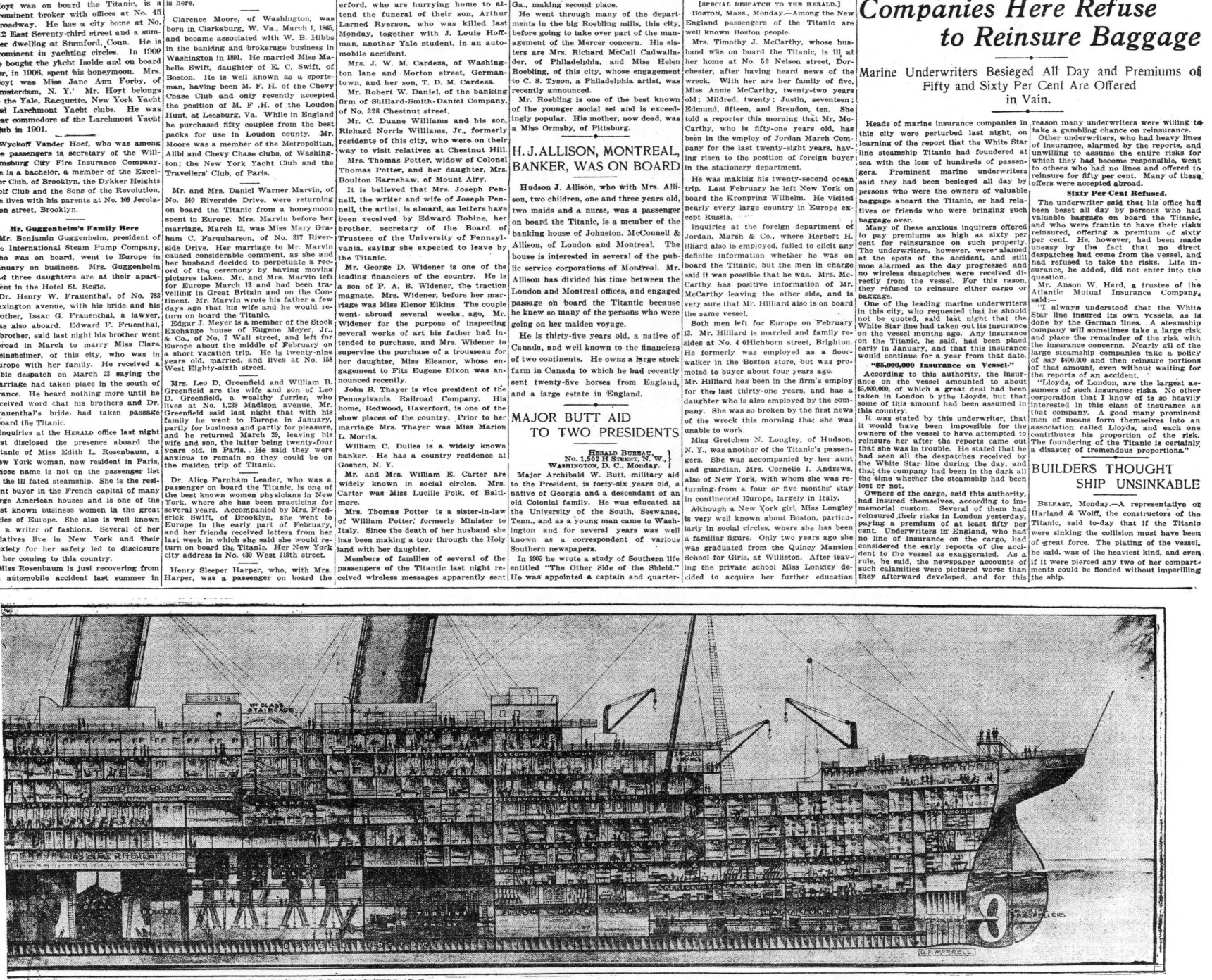

WITH HUNDREDS OF PASSENGERS YESTERDAY

CARPATHIA SPEEDING HERE WITH SURVIVORS, WIRELESS SAYS

Veiled and Silent Icebergs Death Scythes of the Sea

Floating Mountains, Wrapped in Mist, Have Been the Cause of Thousands of Deaths and Always Are the Greatest Fear of Mariners.

DOOM OF THE NARONIC STILL A MYSTERY

Collision with iceergs has always been one of the most deadly of the dangers that confront the mariner. So well recognized is this peril of the Newfoundland Banks, where the Labrador current in the early spring ,and summer months floats southward its ghostly argosy of icy pinnacles detached from the polar ice caps, that the government hydrographic offices and the maritime exchanges spare no pains to collate and disseminate the latest bulletins on the subject.

That the floating iceberg ranks among the most dreaded of sea perils is illustrated by the fact that in cases where vessels have disappeared from the sea, leaving no trace behind to explain their fate, mariners usually incline to the view that they have gone down with all on board after encountering one of these inanimate monsters of the deep.

Such is believed to have been the doom of the fine old sidewheel packet, the steamship Pacific, of the Collins line, which in 1850 was the transatlantic greyhound of her day and wrested the speed supremacy from vessels flying the British flag. The Pacific was a liliputian craft compared with the Titanic of today, but she was the best of her kind when she steamed from this port in 1856, carrying 240 passengers bound for Liverpool.

From that day to this no trace of her has ever been found. Time and again her owners and also the government sent out steamships to hunt for the missing vessel, but not so much as a derelict spar or a bottled scrawl was ever found on which to base a conjecture as to the route by which the Pacific found her way into the port of lost ships.

Fate of the Naronic.

The loss of the White Star ship, the Naronic, is another of the sea's unsolved mysteries which, in lack of any evidence whatever, is generally ascribed to collision with an iceberg. The Naronic was a fine new ship, having been in commission only a year, when, on February 11, 1893, she steamed from Liverpool, eastward bound, with a crew of fifty-four men and a valuable cargo. As passengers she also carried ten wealthy cattle dealers, who were returning from England to America. She never reached any earthly port and was never reported by any other craft. Several bottled messages were picked up months afterward, all of which were pronounced spurious by those best qualified to judge. An exhaustive investigation by the British authorities threw no light upon the mystery. They determined that the vessel was sound and seaworthy in construction and equipment and that her cargo had not been of a character to ignite spontaneously nor to explode readily.

The Arizona, of the Guion line, was one of the blue ribbon flyers of the transatlantic course thirty years ago. She was the pioneer ship of the Guion fleet, then destined to compete with the White Star line in fleetness and accommodations. Her length over all was 464 feet, about one-half the length of the mammoth Titanic, and her gross tonnage was 5,400 tons. She was a big ship for her time.

With passengers and crew to the number of three hundred, she steamed from New York, November 4, 1879, Captain Thomas Jones in command. Among her distinguished saloon passengers were her owner, S. E. Guion, who had with him his sister and two young nieces; J. Pierrepont Edwards, British Vice Consul to New York; J. B. Colgate, banker and yachtsman; L. Coudert, a well known lawyer, any many other distinguished men. The Arizona had been in service only since the previous June and was a favorite ship.

Fearful Crash at Night.

She was steaming at her usual speed at ten minutes past nine o'clock in the evening of Friday, November 7, off the Banks, in latitude 47 degrees north and longitude 53 degrees west. There had been no drop in temperature and none of the other indications of the approach of ice masses. The passengers were diverting themselves in the social hall and in the smoking room when a terrific crash and shock sent them sprawling among the scattered pieces of furniture. The ship had plunged her bows into a mountain of ice and she was stove in as though she had been built of cardboard.

As she slid back from the collision tons of shattered ice blocks fell upon her deck. Fifteen feet of her iron work had been crumpled back, bent, twisted and forced inward, leaving a gaping chasm in her bows, through which the waves were beating. But her collision bulkhead held true and the crippled ship managed to reach the port of St. John's, N. F. When the passengers found that nobody had been hurt and that their danger was not imminent they assembled on the deck and sang in chorus, "Praise God, from Whom All Blessings Flow." The accident was attributed to a faulty and negligent watch.

The Anchor line steamship the City of Rome, another record maker of her time, probably was saved from serious disaster by the fact that the thermometer had given warning of approaching danger from ice. She had a thousand persons aboard and was bound from Glasgow to New York on August 31, 1899, when she struck an iceberg off the Grand Banks of Newfoundland. Captain Hugh Young fortunately had noted the ominous lowering of the temperature some hours before and had reduced to half speed. When the great mass of ice looved up the signal, "Full speed astern," resulted in so slight a contact that the most serious damage sustained were broken bobstays and a crushed figurehead, though the bow of the ship was lifted ten feet as she slid upon the heel of the berg, and she careened sharply to port as she backed off.

Veiled by Fog.

The City of Rome was steaming through dense fog when she struck. An incipient panic among her passengers was allayed promptly, a troop of negro singers contributing valiantly to that end by starting to sing plantation melodies. The passengers afterward adopted resolutions praising the captain, officers and crew for their seamanship, courage and discipline.

The difference etween the experiences of the Arizona and the city of Rome well illustrates the fact that the approach to dangerous ice masses is not always indicated by the thermometer readings. Hydrographic authoritees agree that the temperature test is one that is by no means infallible.

The anchor liner Columbia last August rammed a berg while bound for this port. The fact that she was under very moderate speed probably saved her from more seriuos disaster. The iceberg she encountered, moreover, was almost rotten and the vessel escaped with a smashed bow. Her officers agreed that there had been no drop in the recorded temperatures upto the time the Columbia struck.

The North German Lloyd steamship, the Kronprinz Wilhelm, had a similar mishap in 1907, but the ice she struck was soft. Twenty tons of it dropped upon her deck in shattered masses, but she was not seriously crippled. Perfect discipline prevailed and her compartment bulkheads were closed automatically from the bridge within thirty seconds after the crash.

The Parisian Hits Berg.

The Allan line steamship the Parisian, one of the vessels which was among the first to start to the aid of the Titanic yesterday, had an encounter with ice in May, 1890, while proceeding cautiously at a rate of not more than six miles an hour, off the Newfoundland Banks. Her lookout did not sight the iceberg until it was about forty yards dead ahead. The engines were reversed immediately, but the vessel ran up on a portion of the berg to a distance of about twelve feet. For nearly a minute the Parisian lay almost upon her beam ends, and Captain Ritchie ordered all hands on deck, while the crew stood by ready to lower the boats. The vessel, however, soon settled back into clear water, comparatively uninjured.

The Ethiopia, o fthe Anchor Line, stove in her bows on June 6, 1894, while steaming ahead through a dense fog on her voyage from this port to Glasgow. There was a slight panic on board until the pumps had been sounded and no water was found in the hold.

Fishermen have succumbed in hundreds to the ice peril at sea. Sixty-nine of the seventy-three persons aboard the French brigantine Vaillant were lost when she struck an iceberg and foundered on April 16, 1897. They were fishermen coming from their homes in France to engage in the season's catch off the Banks. Only one of the small boats was ever picked up. It was found long afterward by the French barkentine Victor Eugene. Its four survivors had their arms frozen and their bodies wasted and pinched from hunger which had driven them to cannibalism before their rescue.

In June, 1894, the schooner Rose, Henry Gosse, master, bound for the summer's fishing, hit an iceberg off Partridge Point, north of St. John's, N. F., while sailing through a blanket of fog. She foundered within ten minutes and of the fifty-five members of her fishing crew who were aboard, twelve went down with the schooner. The remaining forty-three managed to clamber upon the berg, which was low and flat. There they were found and rescued by the Irene. Among the lost were two women and two boys.

The unreliability of the thermometer test in some cases was again illustrated by the experience of the new tank ship, the Beacon Light, owned by the Stewart Oil Company, of Liverpool. On May 14, 1890, she was in collision with an iceberg 840 miles east of Nova Scotia. The blow was a glancing one, but it put several ugly punctures in her bottom and stove through her forecastle deck on the starboard side a big hole ten feet square. Her pumps kept her afloat until she made port. Her officers reported that the berg they hit rose ninety feet above the water, and that fifty tons of ice, some of it in huge blocks eight cubic feet in size, crashed down upon the forecastle head.

Although the Beacon Light was a stanch vessel 332 feet long and of 2,107 tons gross, the weight of falling ice sent her over on her beam ends, nearly capsizing her. Captain Elliott and his officers said there had been no change of temperature to warn him of the proximity of ice. The water temperature at midnight had been fifty-four degrees. The vessel struck a short time afterward.

The Moldava, a British tramp, westward bound with a cargo of coal from Cardiff, went down bows first after collision with an iceberg off the Banks, in August, 1896. She was a good vessel, only four years old and of 1,477 tons register. Her collision bulkhead kept her decks above water until her crew of twenty-four men could take to their boats. After thirty-six hours at sea they were picked up by the Anthor line steamship Circassia. There had been no warning of ice. At the moment of collision, according to the testimony, Captain Burnside had been keeping a sharp lookout from the starboard side of the bridge, while Second Officer Wade was peering into the murk from the opposite side.

GREAT STEAMSHIP DISASTERS OF HISTORY

Vessel and Scene.	Lives Lost.
The Atlantic, White Star line, sunk on Mars Head, off Halifax, N. S., in a storm, April 2, 1873	546
The Pomerania, sunk in midnight collision with a bark in the English Channel, November 25, 1878	47
The Naronic, White Star line, lost on the Atlantic and never heard from, February, 1893	74
The Elbe, North German Lloyd line, sunk in collision with the steamship Cathrie, January 30, 1895	330
The Ville de St. Nazaire, French line, burned in a storm off Cape Hatteras, March 7, 1897	40
La Bourgogne, French line, sunk by British steamship Cromartyshire, off Sable Island, July 4, 1898	584
The Norge, foundered at sea, July 3, 1904	750
The General Slocum, excursion vessel, burned near New York Harbor, June 15, 1905	959
The Larchmont, sunk in collision with the schooner Harry Knowlton, off Atlantic coast, February 12, 1907	183
The Berlin, wrecked off Holland coast, February 21, 1907	150
The Aden, sunk off Socotra, on the east coast of Africa, June, 1907	78
The British cruiser Gladiator, sunk in collision with the steamship St. Paul, off the Isle of Wight, April 12, 1908	30
The Ying King, foundered off Hong Kong, July 28, 1908	300
The Folgefouden, sunk at sea, August 23, 1908	70
The Taish, sunk off Etoro Island, Japan, November 6, 1908	150
The San Pablo, sunk off Philippine Islands, November 27, 1908	100
The Republic, White Star line, rammed and sunk by steamship Florida, off Nantucket, all passengers saved, January 24, 1909	6
The Abenton, wrecked off the Spanish coast, February 2, 1911	70
The Koombuna, wrecked April 3, 1911	150
The Asia, ran aground on Finger Island, April 23, 1911	40
The Tucapel, wrecked off the coast of Chili, September 5, 1911	81

MANY HAD ENGAGED PASSAGE FOR RETURN

Lord Ashburton, Governor Dix and Others Had Arranged to Use the Titanic.

There called yesterday at the White Star line offices in the Bowling Green Building, No. 11 Broadway, many citizens of New York and neighboring cities who had engaged passage on board the Titanic for her voyage from this port next Saturday. They expressed disappointment that they were unable to avail themselves of the opportunity of traveling abroad on board the new vessel.

None at that time had any inkling of the true state of affairs and none seemed to think that she was in serious peril. They made arrangements for leaving on board other vessels of the associated lines.

Some of those who were to have been passengers on board the Titanic from New York were Mrs. Potter Palmer, who, however, had already cancelled her passage on account of the death of her brother-in-law, Major General Frederick Dent Grant. Others whose names appeared on the advance list of the Titanic as passengers for the trip from New York were Mrs. J. E. Alexandre, Miss M. C. Alexandre, Lord Ashburton, J. S. Bache, Mrs. Charles T. Barney, Mr. and Mrs. E. J. Berwind, Governor John A. Dix, Mrs. I. Townsend Burden, Comte Stanislas de Vastellani, Mrs. Richard Gambrill, Mrs. James B. Haggin, Mr. and Mrs. John Hays Hammond, Mr. and Mrs. Herman Harjes, Mr. and Mrs. Archer M. Huntington, Miss Kernochan, Alvin W. Krech, Oren Root, Senator Timothy D. Sullivan, Ogden Mills and Mr. nad Mrs. W. D. Sloane.

MRS. JOEL SWIFT'S FAMILY IN GLOOM

Great distress prevailed in the household of Mrs. Frederick Joel Swift, when they learned of the disaster to the Titanic. Mrs. Swift lives at No. 171 Arlington avenue, Brooklyn, and was a passenger aboard the vessel.

Mrs. Swift was widely known in the section of the city where she lived. She had been a widow since 1907, when her husband, who was a builder, died. Mr. Swift was also a Presbyterian minister and superintendent of the Arlington Avenue Presbyterian Sunday School.

No Certain Way to Tell Presence of Dangerous Ice

Many Disasters Have Resulted Despite Usual Precautions Known to Mariners, the Government Hydrographic Service Announces.

THE COLUMBIA WRECK IS AN INSTANCE

According to the men in charge of the United States Hydrographic Service, there is no absolutely sure method of determining the approach, under all conditions, of a vessel into dangerous proximity to floating masses of ice. Many instances of disaster are on record where none of the usual precautions had been neglected, and yet collisions with icebergs had occurred, with serious results.

Lieutenant John Grady, U. S. N., in charge of the branch hydrographic office in the Maritime Exchange Building, said yesterday:—"It is clear from the latitude and longitude named as the point where the Titanic was in collision with the iceberg that the great vessel was following the southern route, which is regarded as the safest of the transatlantic lanes during the season of the year when detached ice is most likely to be encountered. It is fair also to assume, considering the long experience of the captain and officers of the White Star line vessel, that they had neglected none of the precautions which would naturally be observed on the largest and finest vessel in the world, making her maiden voyage with sixteen hundred human lives at stake upon her decks and in her cabins and saloons.

Precaution Sometimes Unavailing.

"On the bridge of a big passenger steamship like the Titanic the system and the discipline are no less perfect than they are on board a warship of the first class. If a dropping temperature or any of the other usual indications of approach to ice had been observable, it is only reasonable to assume that these omens would have been noted in due time. As a matter of fact, we know that collisions have occurred frequently where all such preliminary warnings have failed, despite the utmost vigilance upon the bridge and in the lookout forward. A recent illustration of that fact was the case of the Columbia last August.

"Frequently the temperature of the air falls as ice approaches, but that is not always the case, and it is generally only at an inconsiderable distance from it. The fall of the temperature of the sea water is sometimes a sign of the approximity of ice, although in regions where there is an intermixture of cold and warm currents going on, as at the junction of the Labrador Current and the Gulf Stream, the temperature of the sea has been known to rise as the ice is approached.

"As is set forth in a paper published by the Hydrographic Office, before ice is seen from the deck the ice blink will often indicate its presence. This is readily understood when it is known that it is caused by the reflection of the rays of light from the sun or moon. On a clear day over the ice on the horizon the sky will be much paler or lighter in color and is easily distinguishable from that overhead, so that a sharp lookout should be kept and changes in the color of the sky noted. On a clear day icebergs can be seen at a long distance, owing to their brightness, and at night to their effulgence. During foggy weather they are seen through the fog by their apparent blackness, if such a term can be applied.

Echoes Rid Location of Ice.

"They can also be detected sometimes by the echo from the steam whistle or fog horn. This should b remembered, since, by noting the time between the blasts of a whistle and the reflected sound, the distance of the object in feet may be approximately found by multiplying by 550. Even this test, however, is not always a sure one, for most mariners are familiar with the common phenomenon known as the aberration of sound.

"The presence of icebergs is often made known by the noise of their breaking up and falling to pieces. The crackling of the ice or the alling of plees into the sea makes a noise like breakers or the distant discharge of guns, which may often be heard, though not far away. The appearance of herds of seal or flocks of birds far from land is another common indication of the proximity of ice.

"Here in the Hydrographic office our reports of ice have been rather abnormally frequent during recent months. During the first fifteen days of the present month there have been received from incoming vessels twenty-four such reports, including those of to-day."

Predicted Great Disaster.

Such a disaster as befell the Titanic was predicted by Charles Terry Delaney in a story, "The an on the Bridge," which apepared in the Atlantic Monthly, in May, 1910 .

In this story was outliped the dangers which beset an ocean liner and the hardships of the overworked master. Captain Delaney is a master of long standing and declared that, under regulations which compel the master to remain sleepless and hollow-eyed at his post for impossible periods, the safety of the passengers is more a matter of chance than wise provision.

Without sleep, says the author, no man is fit to have in his hands the destinies of thousands of fellow beings and the fortunes of a huge vessel. "At times," he insists, "the master is no more fit to be left in charge than is a lunatic."

Under the British regulations the master must be upon the bridge at all times during a fog. As the fog often extends from the Banks clear in to New York, it is possible to realize what this means.

"I have seen a mmaster sixty years of age or thereabouts," asserts Delaney, "stand on the bridge fox seventy hours with eyes that were useless through strain and hearing impaired through the constant shrieking of the fog whistle. Is it right to expect such a man to command in case of emergency? In justice to the master and passengers alike should not the command be handed over to the second officer?

"I mean nothing derogatory to any master in what I have said. They know and I know that whatever action they take in an emergency will be taken mechanically and without thought."

Annoyance by Passengers.

Delaney explains of the irritating habit of passengers in playing shuffleboard directly under the bridge while the man above is straining every nerve to discern either by eye or ear floating icebergs and nearing vessels. He refers to weather that, in sailor's parlance, is "one part clear and two parts thick" as the most dangerous of all, on account of the tendency of second officers to cling to their duty on the bridge in order to give the master a rest.

He recounts this experience:—

"A narrow escape happened to me about six years ago, when in charge of a ship carrying a full passenger list, the night being hazy and the ship in the ice track. I kept hanging on until finally, after giving up hope of the weather's clearing, I did decide to call the master and sound the whistle. The responsibility was his, not mine. But before this could be done almost alongside the ship was an iceberg towering up about three hundred feet. The ship passed within twenty feet of it, going at twenty-one knots; had there been a submerged trailer attached to the berg the ship's bottom would have been ripped open. Cold as I was at the time I turned colder still."

After maintaining that considerable speed is justifiable in a fog on account of the increased efficiency in handling a vessel in brisk motion, he speaks thus of the fearful ice risk:—

"But full ahead across the ice track is a different proposition. Under no circumstance is full speed justifiable there. Collision with an iceberg is quite a different matter from collision with a fisherman. Though it is impossible to state with any degree of accuracy the weight of a berg, yet when one remembers that, according to the laws of specifis gravity, only one-ninth of the weight —not height—is above the water, the result of a collision would be greatly in its favor. I once heard a woman passenger ask the master what would happen if our ship struck the iceberg then in view. 'Madam,' he replied, 'the berg would go sailing off as though nothing had happened.'

"All the harm any liner could do an iceberg would be to displace a few tons of ice. Though no one can say with certainty how such fine vessels as the Naronic (White Star line) and Huronic (Allan line) went amissing, yet in nautical circles it is taken for granted that both vessels foundered after collisions with icebergs. Both were bound to the United States during the ice season, and their courses necessitated them cutting across the ice track. I can conscientiously say that in all the time I have followed the sea in liners I have never been with a master who did not slow down in the fog when crossing ice regions."

Evening Telegram First to Tell Real News of the Titanic's Fate

Extra Edition Spreads Tidings of Disaster Throughout the City Soon After White Star Line Officials Admit Vessel Has Sunk.

With characteristic enterprise the Evening Telegram got out an extra edition at ten o'clock last night which gave the people of New York and the surrounding territory the fisrt comprehensive story of the sinking of the Titanic and of the great loss of the life involved. In many parts of the city the news was wholly unexpected and the Telegram carried the first information of the great disaster.

Throughout the day reports had been sent out that all the passengers were safe and that the Titanic was being towed into port. The news that she had gone to the bottom with many hundreds of persons was, therefore, entirely unexpected. Relying upon the accuracy of the reports made yesterday the men in the editorial and mechanical departments of the Evening Telegram quit work at the usual time last evening and started for their homes. It was shortly before nine o'clock when the bulletin from the White Star line offices admitted the great loss of life.

In spite of the fact that every man in the mechanical department and all except one man in the editorial department had left the building, steps were taken to get out an extra. Rush orders were sent to the homes of the men in the editorial and mechanical departments to return at once. They began to arrive within thirty minutes. Within one hour and a quarter after the bulletin first reached the office, and extra edition containing nearly two columns of the latest information was on sale.

The supply of papers was exhausted within a few minutes after they were offered for sale. In the hotels, theatres and clubs the Evening Telegram carried the first authoritative information concerning the great disaster. The demand for the papers was far in excess of the supply. On every side was heard praise and thanks for the energy of the Evening Telegram in relieving the suspense of the people by getting out the extra edition.

Herald the First to Carry News of the Titanic to Philadelphia

Only Out of Town Paper on Stands in Quaker City That Told of Disaster, and Business Men Learned Details Through It.

[SPECIAL DESPATCH TO THE HERALD.]

PHILADELPHIA, Pa., Monday.—The NEW YORK HERALD was the only out of town morning newspaper arriving in Philadelphia this morning with an account of the accident to the Titanic. The other New York papers arriving here had no mention of the accident in the early editions, or at least in the editions that were placed on the news stands of Philadelphia.

Although all of the local newspapers held their telegraph force on duty until nearly five o'clock this morning and got out extra editions, these editions were so poorly circulated that the great majority of Philadelphia business men learned first of the calamity from the HERALD after they arrived at their offices. It was then that the officers of the White Star line here were swamped with inquiries about persons supposed to have taken passage on board the "monster of the deep."

London Goes to Sleep Believing Vessel Safe

Some Newspapers Go to Press Containing Stories That the Titanic Is Proceeding to Halifax Without a Single Fatality.

LONDON, Tuesday.—Some of the London newspapers went to press this morning under the belief that all aboard the Titanic were safe and that the vessel was proceeding for Halifax. These in editorials congratulate all concerned that man's inventive genius has reduced the perils of a sea voyage to a minimum.

Later despatches recording the sinking of the Titanic with loss of life appear only in the very latest editions, and the terrible extent of the disaster will not become known to the British public generally until much later in the day.

All news on the subject still comes exclusively from New York. No wireless communication appears to have been established with this side. A despatch just received from Liverpool says that the White Star line officials have received information from the Olympic of the sinking of the Titanic and of the saving of many of the passengers and crew, and adds that the officers of the company are besieged by friends of the passengers making inquiries.

Writing under the impression that the Titanci was saved, the newspapers call attention to the absence of any dry dock on the American seaboard large enough to acommodate such a vessel and also to the coincidence of accidents happening to the sister ships Olympic and iTtanic.

Exciting scenes were witnessed at Lloyd's Underwriting Rooms yesterday. Insurance losses in the last six months have been heavy in vessels of the biggest class. Since the Olympic collission both the Delhi and Oceana have been wrecked and now comes the disaster to the Titanic When business opened there was a rush to reinsure. Fifty guineas per cent was charged, and this rose rapidly to sixty, but later dropped to twenty-five on the news that the Titanic was being towed to Halifax.

It is understood that there was no specie aboard the vessel, but large insurances had been written on diamonds and other valuables in her cargo.

Up to half-past three this morning the White Star officials at Liverpool had no further news concerning the Titanic. Brief wireless messages from Cape Race have been received, but they are identical with those from New York.

Practically all of the Titanic's crew are from Southampton, where the greatest anxiety prevails as to their fate.

Interviews are published here with experts relative to the possible cause of the disaster. Considerable attention is called to the question as to whether it was possible that suction could have had anything to do with the disaster.

Sir Ernest H. Shackleton points out that the scene o fthe Titanic disaster was fourteen miles south of the supposed possible range of ice fields.

Sir William White, the nited naval constructor, considers that there can be no question of suction in the case of the Titanic, because suction, he says, depends upon relative speeds, and an iceberg is almost stationary. He thinks that the Titanic simply struck an iceberg.

LATEST NEWS BULLETINS FROM LINER TITANIC AND RESCUE BOATS

Chcago, April 17.—2:25 p. m.—Wireless dispatch to Boston from Carpathia, telephoned here, says Carpathia is wiring for help.

* * * * * * *

Wellfleet, Mass., April 17.—The Cunarder Carpathia in communication with the American shore for first time today. She reported that neither John Jacob Astor nor Benjamin Guggenheim was aboard.

* * * * * * *

Boston, April 17.—Following wireless picked up from Carpathia and relayed by Franconia: "Carpathia directly south of Cape Sable. Making thirteen knots. Foggy."

* * * * * * *

Several bodies of victims of the Titanic disaster picked up by Leyland liner Californian.

* * * * * * *

Death list may be greater than 1,312. Cunard lines informed that Carpathia has but 705 survivors on board.

* * * * * * *

Vincent Astor charters tug to hunt for father's body.

* * * * * * *

Navy department orders scout cruisers to meet Carpathia.

* * * * * * *

Cable ship started in effort to pick up possible survivors.

* * * * * * *

Captain of Titanic warned on April 12 of dangerous ice fields.

* * * * * * *

Congress starts inquiry to prevent similar disasters.

* * * * * * *

Chicago Board of Trade plans world movement for patrol vessels.

* * * * * * *

Some Titanic victims may have been saved by fishing smacks.

* * * * * * *

Titanic, after striking, wired: "Not needed; Olympic coming."

* * * * * * *

Wealthy women of New York to provide for steerage passengers.

* * * * * * *

Monetary loss by disaster, $30,000,000.

Revised List of the Drowned of the First Cabin Passengers

Here is a revised list of the first cabin passengers on the Titanic whose names are not mentioned in the list of survivors. In all probability all the following are drowned:

Adams, Miss E.
Allison, H. J., wife, daughter, son, maid and nurse.
Andrews, Miss Cornelia I.
Andrews, Thomas.
Artaga-Veytia, Raymond.
Astor, Colonel John J., and man servant
Aubert, Mrs. N. and maid.
Baumann, J.
Beattie, T.
Birnbaum, Jacob.
Bjornstrom, H.
Blackwell, Stephen Wear.
Bonnell, Lily.
Borebank, J. J.
Brady, John B.
Brandeis, E.
Brew, Dr. Arthur Jackson.
Bucknell, Mrs. S. W., and maid.
Butt, Major Archibald.
Calderhead, E. P.
Carlson, Frank.
Candee, Mrs. C.
Carran, F. M. and J. P.
Caseber, Mrs. H. A.
Cavendish, T. W.
Cahhee, Herbert F.
Chibnall, Mrs. E. M.
Chisholm, Robert.
Clifford, George Quincy.
Colley, E. P.
Compton, Mrs. A. T. and Miss S. W.
Cornell, Mrs. R. C.
Crafton, John B.
Crosby, Edward G.
Cummings, John Bradley, and wife.
Daly, P. D.
Davidson, Thornton.
Dick, A. A., and wife.
Douglas, W.
Dulless, William O.
Eernshew, Mrs. Ernest.
Eustis, Miss E. M.
Eganheim, Mrs. A. F. L.
Evans, Miss E.
Foreman, B. L.
Fortune, Mark.
Franklin, T. P.
Flegenheim, Mrs. A.
Fauenthal, J.
Futrelle, Jacques.
Guggenheim, Benjamin.
Gee, Arthur.
Goldberg, E. L.
Goldenschmidt, George B.
Giglio, Victor.
Harder, George A.
Harrison, W. H.
Haven, H.
Hays, Charles M.
Head, Christopher
Hest, W. F.
Hilliard, Herbert Henry.
Hopkins, W. E.
Holverson, A. O., and wife.
Hoyt, Frederick M.
Icham, Mrs. A. E.
Jones, C. C.
Julian, H. F.
Kent, Edward A.
Kenyon, F. R., and wife.
Kimball, E. N., and wife.
Klaber, Herman.
Lambert, William S.
Lewis, E. G.
Lindstrom, Mrs. J.
Long, Milton C.
Loring, J. H.
McGuire, J. E.
McCaffey, T.
McCarthy, Timothy J.
McGough, J. R.
Melody, A.
Meyer, Edward J., and wife.
Millet, Frank D.
Minahan, Dr. W. E.
Molsom, H. Markland.
Mook, Mrs. P. E.
Moore, Clarence.
Morgan, M. R., and wife.
Natsch, Charles.
Newell, A. W.
Newell, Miss Alice.
Newall, Miss T.
Nicholson, A. S.
Ovies, S.
Parr, M. H. W.
Partner, August.
Payne, V.
Peears, Thomas, and wife.

(Continued on Page 2—Col. 7)

Approximate Statement of Titanic Disaster:

First cabin passengers, 325.
Second cabin passengers, 285.
Third cabin passengers, 858.
Total number of passengers, 1,468.
Members of the crew, 712.
Total passengers and crew, 2,180.
Number of known survivors, 868.
Number who probably perished, 1,312.
Total number of named survivors, 328.

THE tradition of the sea and the honor of sailors demanded that Captain E. J. Smith of the Titanic must go to his death at the bottom of the sea with the ship he commanded—**HE DID.**

BUT no such tradition or honor applied to J. Bruce Ismay the millionaire owner of the ill-fated ship and while 1,300 of the passengers who had paid tribute to his wealth died, he was one of the few men saved.

The Circulation of THE DENVER POST Yesterday Was 65,755

THE DENVER POST

TWO CENTS BY NEWSBOYS. FIVE CENTS ON TRAINS. DENVER, COLORADO, WEDNESDAY, APRIL 17, 1912.—16 PAGES. 3D EDITION.

ALL HOPE IS ABANDONED EXCEPT FOR THOSE PICKED UP BY THE CARPATHIA

COMPANY ADMITS REVISED LIST SHOWS 1,312 ARE DEAD

Rescue Ship Will Reach New York Early Friday Morning With Between 700 or 800 Saved From Disaster.

Vincent Astor Charters Patrol Boat to Go to Scene of Disaster in Search of Father's Body --Cruiser Communicates With Carpathia.

Washington, D. C., April 17.—The scout cruiser Chester won a thrilling race with its sister ship, the Salem, up the New England coast today and at 1 o'clock this afternoon established communication with the Carpathia, which is carrying the Titanic's survivors to New York.

The report sent to the navy department by the Chester indicates that the list of the first and second-class passengers already sent in by the Carpathia was complete and correct, and the Chester has no new names to add to the lists of survivors.

The message follows: "The Carpathia states that the list of first and second-class passengers and crew has been sent to shore. The Chester will relay list of third-class passengers when convenient to the Carpathia. (Signed) BECKER."

New York, April 17.—In faintest touch with the wireless station at Sable island, the Cunard liner Carpathia, with hundreds of survivors of the sunken Titanic on board, was creeping down the coast early this morning, making the best time for this port that foggy conditions would permit.

Speeding up the coast toward the rescue ship and hoping to get within wireless speaking distance of her before very many hours, were the scout cruisers Salem and Chester, ordered by the government at Washington to make all haste possible toward breaking the silence which so far has kept the survivors on the Carpathia from making known to the outside world the thrilling story of the Titanic's last hours afloat and the momentous happenings after she had taken her two-mile plunge to the bottom off the grand banks of Newfoundland early Monday morning.

In New York the White Star line offices received a brief wireless dispatch saying that the Carpathia was 596 miles from the harbor entrance. This should bring her into port probably early Friday morning with between 700 and 800 survivors out of the catastrophe which cost 1,312 lives.

Names of 79 Men Given as Saved.

From the Chester at an early hour this message came:

"Expect to be up with Carpathia within three or four hours."

The injection of the scout cruisers into the situation, indeed, seemed to afford the only hope of opening up communication with the Carpathia until she reached the wireless zone of Nantucket, as she was apparently too far off shore and her wireless apparatus too weak to reach the Sable island station in a way to admit of the ready transmission of messages.

As the lists of saved passengers indicate, the great majority are women. The names of only 79 men rescued have been given in the lists telegraphed from the Carpathia, whereas the names of 249 women appear in the tabulation.

Of the 400 steerage passengers thought to be saved, it is believed that nearly all were women. The men among the passengers seemed largely to have remained to die that the women and children might be saved.

Little hope was entertained that the fishing schooner Dorothy Baird, which was passed by in the vicinity of the Titanic disaster by the freighter Etonian of the Phoenix line, had rescued any of the liner's passengers. Officers of the Etonian thought it probable that the schooner had returned to St. Johns without knowledge of the disaster.

Astor to Search for Father's Body.

The names of John Jacob Astor, Isador Straus, the millionaire merchant; George B. Widener of Philadelphia, Maj. Archibald Butt, aide to President Taft; Francis D. Millet, the American artist; William T. Stead, the London journalist; Benjamin Guggenheim and Col. and Mrs. Washington Roebling are among the more prominent names missing from the list of saved.

Inquiries concerning their fate were being constantly made by callers at the White Star offices and scores of telephone and telegraphic communications were received from all parts of the country. President Taft instructed the company to notify him whenever they heard anything regarding Major Butt.

Vincent Astor, son of Col. John Jacob Astor, after waiting since Monday at the White Star offices for news of his father's fate, has started for Halifax, where he intends to charter a tug and go to the scene of the disaster to search for his father's body.

President Taft has tentatively decided to dispatch two revenue cutters from New York to Sandy Hook to meet the Carpathia and act as an escort into the harbor. The question will be determined at a conference between the president and Secretary MacVeagh of the treasurry department. If convoys are sent out they will be the cutters Seneca and Mohawk, now at New York.

In order that a waiting world might receive the earilest possible information regarding the tragedy, Secretary MacVeagh indicated his willingness to consider the question of sending the revenue cutter Gresham, with newspaper correspondents aboard, from Boston to meet the Carpathia, provided the Cunard line was willing to allow them aboard.

This question was held in abeyance, however, by advices from Deputy Collector of Customs Stewart at New York, stating that the steamship line would not grant the privilege.

100 Coffins Taken to Scene.

The White Star line chartered the cable boat Mackay Bennett and early today she left Halifax at top speed for the scene of the disaster.

One hundred coffins ordered by the White Star line were placed aboard the Mackay Bennett in the gray of the morning. Halifax is stripped of its embalmers and undertakers' clerks. Twenty are

(Continued on Page 2—Col. 3)

WIRELESS NOW SAYS OVER 2,000 ARE DEAD

BULLETIN—NEW YORK, APRIL 17.—The Camperdown wireless station at Halifax today sent the Associated Press the following dispatch: "We are now in communication with the Carpathia and in position to announce unofficially that the Titanic struck an enormous berg and sank. Over 2,000 lost; 700 survivors, mostly women, on Carpathia."

New York, April 17.—The attention of the Camperdown station was at once called to the obvious error in figures, which would give the total of lost and survived at 2,700, whereas the total number of passengers and crew is about 2,200. In reply to this inquiry the following further explanation was received from Halifax:

"The Marconi station reports that nothing authentic regarding lost is known on board the Carpathia, but the steamer Francnian, in relaying the messages from the Carpathia, says that the total number of saved is only 710. There is no list of missing on the Cunarder and only a rough estimate of her total passenger list. There probably will be more than 2,200 on ship, as quite a number boarded her at Cherbourg."

The estimates of 2,200 on board the Titanic have embraced the sailings from all ports, including Cherbourg, as far as the company's officials have been able to learn.

Chinese Save Men First, Not Women

Cleveland, April 17.—Had the Titanic been a Chinese vessel, manned by Chinese sailors, not a woman or child would have been saved, according to Henry Moy Fot, special agent for the Chinese Merchants' Association of America, who was in Cleveland today.

"It is the duty of sailors when a Chinese vessel goes down to save men first, children next and women last," said the agent. "This is on the theory that men are most valuable to the state, that adoptive parents can be found for children and that women without husbands are destitute."

Captain Warned Nearing Icebergs

New York, April 17.—What is believed to be one of the last messages sent from the Titanic before she struck the iceberg was received at the hydrographic office in Washington on April 14 the day preceding the night on which the collision occurred, according to advices received here. The message as given read:

"April 14. German steamer Amerika reported by radio-telegraph passing two large icebergs in latitude 41.27, longitude 50.08. Titanic."

This message indicates that the Titanic had knowledge of ice in her vicinity, as her position when she struck was latitude 41.46, longitude 50.14.

Fate of Maj. Butt Casts Gloom Over Society at Capital

Washington, April 17.—Society is paying a marked tribute to the popularity of Maj. Archibald Butt, U. S. A., whose fate is still in doubt because of the incomplete reports of the Titanic disaster.

On every hand not only is the greatest concern expressed, but several of the leaders in society are cancelling dinners and dances because of the fear that he met death when the big steamship went to the bottom.

Mrs. Richard H. Townsend had issued invitations for a dinner and dance tonight for Mrs. E. R. Thomas of New York, but has recalled them. Several other women had arranged for dinners to precede the dance at Mrs. Townsend's, and these also have canceled the entertainments.

Throughout diplomatic, official and residential circles inquiries were made for Major Butt and for Clarence Moore, whose family is in the greatest distress over the absence of encouraging reports.

Miss Helen Taft and Robert Taft had a half dozen guests at the White house, but anxiety over the probable fate of Major Butt has caused them to cancel all engagements.

MEN ON TITANIC HEROES; DIE CALMLY TO SAVE LOVED ONES

Parting Scenes on Shattered Leviathan Beggar Description--Women and Children Forced to Enter the Lifeboats.

New York, April 17.—Nothing could show more plainly the heroism of the crew and the men passengers who stood by the doomed ship Titanic, facing inevitable death, and sent the women and children away in the lifeboats, than the fact that four women to every man were saved.

That all women passengers were saved from death when the $10,000,000 floating palace sank was the information received here today. It arrived through the medium of a relayed wireless dispatch received by Mrs. J. W. Bonnell of Youngstown, Ohio, who is at the Waldorf.

Mrs. Bonnell came here to meet relatives who sailed on the Titanic. They included a daughter, a niece and Mr. and Mrs. George D. Wick. The latter two were accompanied by their daughter.

The message which she received was sent from the Carpathia via Cape Race and said:

"Women all saved. No trace of George."

This message confirmed the earlier reports of the heroism of the men passengers of the Titanic, who went to certain death that the women might be saved.

It is now a theory that the men who were also saved cast lots and the winners took their places in the boats until filled.

Some would have to be left—that was a certainty. Hundreds, in fact, were left. But to all appearances the men who were left stayed behind deliberately, calmly, stepping aside to let the weaker ones—those to whom they owed protection—take their way to safety.

Final Message of Brave Men.

"Sinking by the head. Have cleared boats and filled them with women and children."

This was the final message these brave men sent the world, for

(Continued on Page 2—Col. 1)

THE KIND OF WEATHER COCK JUSTICE WE GET WITHOUT JUDICIAL RECALL!!

HEROIC ACTS ON TITANIC NEVER SURPASSED IN WORLD'S ANNALS

PARTING SCENES ON DOOMED SHIP BEYOND DESCRIPTION

(Continued From Page One.)

It was directly afterward that their wireless signals sputtered—and then stopped altogether.

The picture that inevitably presents itself, in view of what is known, is of men like John Jacob Astor, master of scores of millions; Benjamin Guggenheim of the famous family of bankers; William T. Stead, veteran journalist; Major Archibald W. Butt, soldier; Washington Roebling, noted engineer—of any or all of these men—stepping aside and bravely, gallantly remaining to die that the place he otherwise might have filled could perhaps be taken by some sabot-shod, shawl-enshrouded, illiterate and penniless peasant woman of Europe.

Thus the stream of woman with toddling infants or babes in arms, perhaps most of them soon to be widowed, filed up from the cabins and over the side and away to life.

They Bravely Remained to Die.

The men—by far the greater part of them—remained to die, millionaire and peasant and man of middle class alike, bravely it must have been, sharing each other's fate and going down to a common grave.

Of the survivors, what? Their story of peril and suffering with the revelation they will furnish of just what happened on board the stricken ocean giant—remains to be told.

From what can be learned, many of those who came through the harrowing scenes of the wreck are in a pitiful state. Most of them had retired and were forced to leave the vessel in their night garments. Then for hours they were buffeted about in the sea of ice. Exposed to the icy blasts of the ocean, they drifted in the small lifeboats and saw the great ocean palace, with its wonderful illumination, slowly sink, carrying with it the husbands, fathers, brothers and sweethearts to whom they had said a hasty farewell.

Officials of the White Star line graphically described what happened when the vessel struck the submerged iceberg, from their intimate knowledge of Captain Smith and the man they knew him to be.

When the ship struck, stopped and vibrated with the terrific pounding of her engines—such engines that were powerless in a path obstructed by nature—Captain Smith's first thought was of the safety of the human lives entrusted to his care. He immediately ordered all hands on deck. That all did not answer the summons; that many of those occupying forward cabins were killed by the impact is regarded as certain.

Moments of Fearful Terror.

Then followed moments of fearful terror—half-clad women and men, too frightened and stunned, probably, to cry out, clinging to each other and shrinking from the spectacle of the towering, specter-like iceberg above them; the gnashing of the detached floes of ice against the sides of the ships; the grinding of the steel prow of the entrapped monster as the reversed engines throbbed frantically to extricate her.

But the crew, if the men performed true to the records which recommended them for service on the new leviathan, alert to the commands of their venerable commander, who stood in his place on the bridge, took their places at the rails to guard against any insane attempts to escape. When it was seen that the vessel might sink, the order came to lower the lifeboats. There was no time to find warm clothes—scarcely time for pitiful farewells.

It was not necessary to invoke the unwritten laws of the sea, of "women first," if man acted in this crisis as he has done from time immemoriable on land and sea. Women and children were taken from husbands and fathers and placed in the boats and lowered away over the towering sides of the doomed ship into impenetrable darkness, with men enough among them only to man the craft.

Heroic Deeds Never Will Be Known.

What deeds of heroism were enacted in this hour of peril will never be known; some of them will be told when the few eye witnesses are brought home by the Carpathia.

Someone probably will tell of the divine devotion of Mrs. Isidore Straus, who is reported as among the missing. It is also reported that Mr. Straus has perished. As the women were given the first opportunity to leave the ship, and as Mrs. Straus is not among the reported rescued, it is inferred by her friends that she preferred death to parting from her husband. Her age was such that even among the women she would be given choice before the younger ones.

How long the boats drifted in the open sea before the Titanic took her fatal plunge cannot be conjectured; indeed, it is not certain that she sank while the crew were yet engaged in lowering the lifeboats.

The mighty plunge came and the horrors of those few brief hours were past for the brave souls aboard—past for the one man who could have fittingly described such a terrible spectacle. That was the venerable William T. Stead, accounted the most famous journalist of the day.

The hours that followed for those tossing about on the swells were hours of intense suffering and anxiety. For hours they strained their eyes for the vessels that they knew had been spoken.

There is but one physician on the Carpathia and women accustomed to the utmost ease and luxury are returning in the steerage scantily clothed, dazed by the ordeal through which they have passed, caring for themselves as best they can.

While lifeboats drifted, the hunt was going on away to the north in the neighborhood of the position first given by the Titanic. Eyes were strained to penetrate the darkness for the first faint glimmer of the lights on the approaching ship, but it was not until day began to break that the smoke of the tall Carpathia appeared on the horizon. The Virginian of the Allan line was the first to catch the "S. O. S." of Operator Phillips on the Titanic, but the Carpathia was miles nearer the scene of the disaster when she turned on her course and steamed toward the Titanic's position. Then came the Parisian, the Virginian, the Baltic and the Olympic.

But all were too late to prevent the appalling wreck. Nature had chosen to mock man's boasts of conquest and achieved her purpose.

Vincent Astor has chartered a tug to go in search of his father's body. This picture shows the use of grappling hooks.

THE TITANIC STRUCK THE ICEBURG WITH AN IMPACT FORCE
OF 13.5000.00 TONS
= TO 37. EXPRESS TRAINS
FIGURES ACCEPTED BY NAVAL EXPERTS
IF THE EMPIRE STATE EXPRESS HAD STRUCK THE SAME OBJECT THE FORCE OF THE IMPACT WOULD BE 367.800 TONS. IT WOULD TAKE 37. OF THESE TO EQUAL THE FORCE OF IMPACT OF THE TITANIC

CUNARD PEOPLE REFUSE TO PERMIT REPORTERS ABOARD THE CARPATHIA

Cruiser Chester in Wireless Touch With Rescue Ship--No New Names to Add to First List of Saved.

(Continued From Page One.)

aboard the cable steamer. The boat will go as far as St. Johns, N. F., and endeavor to find any survivors that may be afloat in lifeboats or on rafts.

It is recalled that when the French liner La Bourgoyne foundered off Sable island in July, 1898, there was evidence that the passengers were afloat on life rafts for several days, and that when the steamer was sent out from Halifax ten days after the disaster by relatives of the missing people, scores of bodies were found floating for miles around where the ship sank.

The dispatch of the relief steamer will also establish the certainty of the sinking of the Titanic, which some people think may be afloat as a derelict.

A thrilling story from St. Johns, N. F., to the effect that the Titanic had dashed upon an iceberg while steaming at a speed of twenty miles an hour had broken in two, and sunk while panic reigned on board, was accepted as one of the many conflicting reports which have been received from time to time, but which have proved groundless.

This version of the sinking of the Titanic was credited to the British steamer Bruce, bound for Sydney, which was reported to have learned the details by wireless. The story ended by stating that more than 1,000 had perished, but that others could have been saved but for the panic on board, the overcrowding and sinking of lifeboats.

Faint Hope That Fishermen Saved Some.

Steamship officials in this city grasped eagerly at every report which brought hope that other survivors of the Titanic than those picked up by the Cunard liner Carpathia had been rescued from the sea off the Newfoundland grand banks.

Of these the most authentic was brought to this port by the captain of the Leyland line freighter Etonian. The commander of this ship today said that he had passed along the route taken by the Titanic and had seen a number of fishing boats in the vicinity of the spot where the great ship foundered. He thought that many of the passengers who could not be taken off in boats probably were able to keep afloat with wreckage and life preservers until they were picked up by the fishing fleet. The fishing boats were headed toward Halifax.

The reason this information was not sent out from the ship before she docked was due to the fact that she does not carry wireless.

The marine department of the Dominion government has notified all government wireless stations along the coast to be on the lookout for messages from steamships which have a bearing on the disaster.

According to naval survey experts there is no possibility that the bodies of the dead ever will be recovered. They will be caught in the whirl of the gulf stream and carried the width of the Atlantic. In the meantime they probably would be eaten by sharks or destroyed by the action of the water.

The Canadian government has more than an ordinary interest in the calamity because, among the missing are a number of personal friends of the Duke of Connaught, governor general of Canada, and Colonel Lowther, the duke's military secretary.

The monetary loss from the sinking of the giant ship is now estimated at $30,000,000. A Paris cable says that Mrs. John Jacob Astor had in her possession $3,000,000 worth of diamonds, which she had purchased before leaving the French capital, and it was not thought likely that she had been able to save any of her jewels in the excitement which attended the sinking of the Titanic after she had crashed into the iceberg.

According to a message relayed from Cape Race, the second wireless operator on the Titanic was saved, as well as four of the ship's officers. This being the case, it would give the Carpathia the services of an additional operator to handle the tremendous wireless business.

All hope was given up today for Col. John Jacob Astor, Maj. Archibald Butt, Isador Straus, William T. Stead, Col. Washington Roebling, George B. Widener, Jacques Futrelle and other notables.

When the Carpathia reaches port she undoubtedly will be greeted by the greatest crowd that ever assembled on the harbor front. In addition to those who know that their relatives or friends are on board, hundreds of others, clinging to the faint hope that their loved ones have been saved, but overlooked in the confusion on the Carpathia will swell the throng. Hundreds of police will handle the crush at the Cunard dock.

The captain of the Carpathia reports she is making all speed possible and has asked that special docking arrangements be made. Orders have been received from Washington to waive all customs regulations and similarly the port officers will not detain the ship at Quarantine. The Carpathia will be given the right of way over all other ships bound in and will proceed directly to her dock at the Cunard piers.

British Majesties Cable Sympathy

New York, April 17.—King George sent the following message to the White Star company:

The queen and I are horrified at the appalling disaster which has happened to the Titanic and at the terrible loss of life. We deeply sympathize with the bereaved relatives and feel for them in their great sorrow with all our hearts. GEORGE R. AND I.

The queen mother, Alexandra, has sent a message of sympathy to the company, in which she says:

It is with feelings of the deepest sorrow that I hear of the terrible disaster to the Titanic and of the awful loss of life. My heart is full of grief and sympathy for the bereaved families of those who have perished.

The Duke of Connaught, governor general of Canada, sent through his military secretary, Lieutenant Colonel Lowther, the following telegram to the White Star company:

Ottawa, Ont., April 17.—I am desired by his royal highness, the governor general of Canada, to send the following message:

"I desire to express to the owners of the Titanic my deep and heartfelt sympathy for the relatives and friends of those who have lost their lives in this terrible catastrophe."

LIEUTENANT COLONEL LOWTHER.

Rome, April 17.—Both Pope Pius and King Victor Emmanuel have expressed their deep sympathy for the victims of the Titanic disaster.

CONGRESS WILL ENACT LAWS FOR SEA TRAVELING

Survivors of Wreck Will Be Called in to Give Testimony.

Washington, April 17.—Immediate and searching investigation of the appalling Titanic disaster will be obtained by congress without a moment's delay.

Introduced by Representative Mott of New York is a resolution providing for an inquiry which will go into every detail of faulty equipment that led up to the disaster and enable congress to provide legislation that will enable it in the future to protect the lives of American citizens taking ship to or from this country, no matter where their embarking place may be.

The resolution will be sent rapidly through the committee on rules, to which it was referred, and by the time the survivors now on board the Carpathia reach New York congress will be in a position to call them before the committee and make full inquiry of them concerning every point that will afford any information.

At the same time Representative Chandler announced that his committee would take action looking to the forcing of steamship companies to provide a sufficent number of lifeboats and rafts to safeguard the lives of all its passengers in the event of such a calamity as befell the Titanic.

Some Tourists Will Come West Instead of Crossing Ocean

That the wreck of the Titanic will not discourage ocean travel to any appreciable extent is the opinion of the majority of railway passenger agents in Denver. On the other hand, there are some who believe that Colorado will receive a large proportion of the tourists who would have gone to Europe this summer were it not for the fear of ocean travel inspired by the terrible disaster.

In discussing the influence of the wreck upon travel, one railroad official said:

"The wreck of the Titanic will have no more effect upon the traveling public than would a fatal wreck on some railroad. It will be talked about with bated breath for a week or so, and then it will be forgotten. If we should hear that there had been a horrible wreck on the Pennsylvania lines today, tomorrow every train would be just as crowded. There may be a few timorous persons who had planned to go to Europe this summer who will be frightened to such an extent by the wreck that they will come to Colorado instead, but their number will be small."

Another railway official said:

"There is no doubt but that the wreck of the Titanic will have some influence upon Colorado tourist travel this season. There are, usually, a great many women who want to take European tours, and women have a dread of ocean travel at best. They will influence their husbands to come to the Western summer resorts instead of going to Europe. I believe, however, that the wreck will have no influence upon the masculine mind, which understands that it will probably be the last wreck of its character in marine history."

At the chamber of commerce it is believed that the wreck will cause many people to come to Colorado for their vacation.

"I believe that this wreck will bring hundreds of people here who otherwise would have gone to Europe. Such a disaster as that carries its horror for many years. The people will not forget it and it will be remembered this summer when tourists are making preparations for travel," said Secretary Deland.

First Cabin Death List Revised by Latest Wireless

(Continued From Page One.)

Penasco, Victor, and wife.
Porter, Walter Chamberlain.
Reuchling, Jonkheer.
Robling, W. A. II.
Rood, Hugh.
Ross, J. Hugo.
Rothschild, W.
Rowe, Alfred.
Ryerson, Arthur, and family.
Schutes, Miss E. W.
Silverthorne, Mr.
Silvey, William B.
Smart, John N.
Smith, J. Clinch.
Smith, Mrs. L. T.
Smith, R. W.
Snyder, John, and wife.
Spedden, Frederick C. and family.
Spenser, W. A.
Stead, W. T.
Stahli, Max Frolicher and wife.
Stengel, C. E., H. E.
Stewart, A. A.
Straus, Isadore, and wife.
Sutton, Frederick.
Taussig, Emil and wife.
Thayer, J. B. Jr.
Thorne, J. and wife.
Tucker, G. M.
Uruchtu, Mr.
Wickhoff, Vanderhoef.
Walker, W. Anderson.
Warren, F. M.
Weir, J.
White, Mrs. J. F., and two servants.
White, M. J.
White, Richard F. and wife.
White, Percival W.
Wick, George D. and wife.
Widener, George D.
Widener, Harry.
Williams, Duane.
Williams, N. M. Jr.
Wright, George.

German Steamer Augsburg Missing

Newport, R. I., April 17.—While the German cruiser Bremen, which arrived here today, was anchored at the harbor of St. Thomas, Danish West Indies, Easter Sunday, a message was received from the admiralty directing the Bremen to proceed with all speed to search for the missing German steamer Augsburg, which had started from New York, Feb. 8, for Africa and which had been reported lost.

The Bremen searched night and day for several days without having discovered any trace of the missing ship. The belief on board the Bremen is that the Augsburg went down with all on board.

SENATOR GUGGENHEIM TO MEET SURVIVORS

Washington, April 17.—Senator and Mrs. Guggenheim departed today for New York to meet the Titanic survivors. The senator's brother, Benjamin Guggenheim, one of the wealthiest men in the world, was on the Titanic.

The family has given up ractically all hope.

Style of life preservers in use aboard the Titanic. There has been no report that they were useful in saving lives.

PANIC ON TITANIC IS REPORT FROM STEAMER BRUCE

When Ship Was Sinking Frenzied Crowd Rushed Madly for Boats.

LIFEBOATS WERE BROKEN

Impact Almost Rent Ship Asunder, Bulkheads Badly. Smashed.

St. Johns, N. F., April 17.—A report is current here, said to have emanated from the steamer Bruce, en route to Sydney, N. S., giving a version of the disaster to the Titanic obtained from other ships.

This version is that when the Titanic struck the berg she was going at a speed of 18 knots. The impact almost rent the ship asunder. It sundered the decks and sides of the bulkheads from the bow nearly to midships and smashing the boat's upper works to pieces.

She struck partially on her bow leaning to the portside and almost turning turtle. Passing over the submerged portion of the iceberg is supposed to have torn the bottom out of her, as the compartments from midships forward quickly flooded and the ship rapidly settled at the head, with a port list and rolling heavily in the trough of the sea.

The surface impact was so terrific that it practically rent the ship from stem to stern.

For a short while sufficient order was maintained to safely launch most of the boats and embark about a thousand persons. When the cry went up that the ship was sinking, a frenzied crowd rushed madly for the boats. As the ship settled into the sea it is said that many of the boats were smashed to pieces in the davits; some were swamped in launching and others went down with the ship.

By this time, the ship was seen to be settling fast and the water had reached the engine rooms. The wireless failed by loss of the motor, and all lights went out all over the ship, adding to the terror and difficulties of handling the boats.

The source of this version, which has the appearance of reliability, gives the number of passengers saved as over 600.

Cincinnati Going to Aid Told It Was Not Needed

New York, April 17. — Captain Schulke of the steamship Cincinnati, which reached port today from Naples, reports that at midnight on April 14 he received a wireless call for help from the stricken Titanic. Although 550 miles away, the Cincinnati headed for the scene of the disaster and would have continued had not another message from the Titanic been received half an hour later: "Olympic coming; not needed."

Although he took the southerly course, Captain Schulke says he saw no icebergs.

JACQUES FUTRELLE, AUTHCR, PERISHED IN TITANIC WRECK

Boston and Vicinity Furnished Dozen Prominent Men as Victims.

BANKERS AMONG LIST

Manager of Kimball Piano Company Probably Among Survivors.

Boston, April 17.—Nearly a dozen Boston men known to have been aboard the Titanic are unaccounted for. Some were accompanied by wives and daughters, all of whom are reported safe on the Carpathia.

Among the missing are A. W. Newell, president of the Fourth National bank, whose two daughters, Madeleine and Marjorie, were rescued, and Jacques Futrelle, the author, whose wife was saved.

Although the names of Mr. and Mrs. E. N. Kimball are not contained in the "saved" list, relatives hope that they are accounted for in the names "Mr. and Mrs. Ed Kimberley" as received by wireless. Mr. Kimball is president of a piano company.

Others living near Boston whose names do not appear among the survivors are George O. Clifford, president of the Belcher Last company of Stoughton; Walter C. Porter of Worcester, also a last manufacturer; Clarence Moore of Washington and Beverly Farms, a well-known sportsman; Herbert H. Hilliard and Timothy J. McCarthy; Percival W. White, cotton manufacturer of Winchenden, and his son, Richard.

Greenport, N. Y., April 17.—It is feared that Mr. and Mrs. Drew, prominent residents here, and Drew's 5-year-old nephew, Marshall Drew, are among the dead of the Titanic's passengers. They were returning from a visit with Mr. Drew's mother, who lives in Constantine, Cornwall, England. They were second cabin passengers.

Yonkers, N. Y., April 17.—Mr. and Mrs. Alexander Robins of this city were passengers on the Titanic, according to their son, Alexander Robins Jr., but the name of neither has appeared in the list of the rescued.

Mr. Robins, a contractor, was a native of Wales.

Newark, N. J., April 17.—C. F. Henry, who with his wife is reported among the saved from the Titanic, is head of a leather firm here.

Henry Blank, also reported saved, is a partner in the manufacturing firm of White, Sizee & Blank of this city.

Other residents of New Jersey listed as Titanic passengers concerning whom nothing has been heard are:

Stephen M. Blackwell of Trenton; Arthur Keefe of East Rahway, Washington A. Roebling II of Trenton, Frank Stanley, Mr. Roebling's chauffeur, and W. A. Walker of East Orange.

St. John, N. B., April 17.—Elmer Young of St. John said that his niece, Miss Emily Young, was a passenger on the Titanic and he could not learn that she was among the survivors. Miss Young is a teacher of music in New York.

Troy, N. Y., April 17.—Among the victims of the wreck of the Titanic are probably Daniel Moran and his sister, Bertha, of this city, who were returning from an extended trip abroad. Their names do not appear among the survivors.

Duluth, Minn., April 17.—A colony of Finlanders coming to settle on land in this vicinity may have perished when the Titanic took her fatal plunge. The colony consisted of 110 persons.

Calumet, Mich., April 17.—Mrs. A. Davis, Joseph Nicholls and John N. Davis of St. Ives, Wales, mother, brother and step-brother of James Nicholls of Calumet, were passengers on the Titanic on their way to visit this country.

The names of Mrs. Davis and Mr. Davis appear among the list of survivors, but Nicholls is probably lost.

Salt Lake City, Utah, April 17.—Mrs. Irene C. Corbett, who was a passenger on the Titanic, is the daughter of Bishop Levi A. Colvin of Provo, Utah. Her name does not appear among the survivors. Her father received a letter from her Tuesday saying she would be home next week.

Gypsy Told Doctor He Would Lose Life in a Sea Disaster

Fon Du Lac, Wis., April 17.—Dr. W. E. Minahan, the Fon du Lac surgeon who met death in the Titanic, was told five years ago by a soothsayer that he would meet his end in a marine disaster. Minahan with a number of friends visited a Gypsy camp and all had their fortunes told. The fortune teller told Dr. Minahan he would die while on a steamer on his second trip abroad.

The physician went to Europe shortly after, spending a year there in medical research. Last January he went again. Friends joked him about the prediction of death made by the fortune teller, but he ridiculed the idea. However, he arranged all his affairs before he went, taking his wife and sister with him.

He carried life insurance to the amount of $100,000 and $50,000 accident insurance. He was one of the foremost surgeons in Wisconsin.

England's Antiquated Laws Shown by Wreck

Parliament Has Never Providedto Protect Patrons of Modern Ships--Disaster May Stop Building of Immense Boats.

That every disaster, such as the sinking of the Titanic, carries in the very horrors that rise out of it an educational lesson is proved by the steps already taken for an overhauling of the navigation rules and the establishment of iron bound regulations for the safeguarding of travelers.

The claim is made that the Titanic carried an insufficient number of lifeboats. Ten million dollars was spent to make the boat the highest triumph in ship building, and a few thousand dollars was grudged for lifeboats to make it the safest craft afloat.

The new rules under which ships will sail to sea should and doubtless will provide for lifeboats that will accommodate all the passengers. And in the event of sudden peril, to ward against confusion and panic, each passenger on purchasing his ticket will find on its face the number of a certain lifeboat to be on davits near the cabin.

Every passenger should, on going aboard, be directed to the boat he or she must take in the event of danger or emergency arising. The crew should be divided into lifeboat sections and drills made imperative. At present the rules contain a drill command, but there is no assurance given by travelers that these are ever held.

Certain it is that the next boat that lifts anchor will be equipped to serve the least as the highest of its patrons, and no man, woman or child be given to the relentless maw of the sea because there is no way of escape.

Thus may the tragedy of a few become the safeguard and blessing of many.

New York, April 17.—Shipping men in New York place responsibility for the fearful loss of life in the Titanic catastrophe upon the antiquated and laxly executed shipping laws of England.

The amazing discovery is made that, as far as the knowledge of so well-informed a person as the British consul general in New York extends, Britain's shipping laws have not been revised or the regulations prescribing protection for life aboard British ships have not been altered to conform with modern ocean transportation since leviathans of the Titanic type have been launched.

The only laws and regulations on the subject are contained in the statute known as the merchant shipping act. At which date parliament enacted this mass of contradictory verbiage into law could not be ascertained.

REGULATIONS BRIEF AND CONFUSING.

The regulations prescribed by the merchant shipping act for safeguarding human life aboard British ships are brief and confusing. Their chief points are:

1—Lifeboats shall be placed under the davits and be ready for use at all times.

2—Masters or owners carrying fewer than the prescribed number of lifeboats must declare at the time of clearance that the boats being carried are actually sufficient to accommodate all persons on board, allowing ten cubic feet for each adult person.

3—If the lifeboats under the davits, in accordance with the table, do not furnish sufficient accommodation for all on board, then additional wood, metal or collapsible or other boats of approved description must be carried or approved life rafts.

4—In addition to the life-saving appliances, ships shall carry not less than one approved life buoy placed under each davit; also approved life belts or similar articles of approved buoyancy suitable for being worn on the person so that there may be at least one for each person.

SHIPS SIZE OF TITANIC OVERLOOKED BY PARLIAMENT.

The most astounding feature of these antiquated regulations is found in the table referred to in paragraph No. 3, above. This table prescribes the exact number of lifeboats to be carried by British ships of various tonnage. It starts with ships of "10,000 tonnage and upward." Vessels of this capacity are required, according to this table, to carry sixteen lifeboats under davits, the boats to have a total cubic foot area of 5,500.

The table then goes down the scale to the lowest tonnage boat. For example, ships of 9,000 tons capacity and upward must carry fourteen lifeboats, with a total cubic foot area of 5,200. Nowhere in the table is there mention of a ship of the Titanic type, whose tonnage capacity is 45,000.

It is significant that the only photographs of the ill-fated Titanic published in the United States have shown eight lifeboats on each side suspended from davits. This number exactly complies with the number prescribed in the regulations in the British consul general's office here for ships of "10,000 tonnage and upward."

Herman Winter, an official of the Cunard line, which also is a British concern, claims that the regulations have been revised recently, requiring an increased capacity for lifeboats of 225 cubic feet for each additional 500 tons of ship capacity above 10,000.

SHOULD HAVE 23,000 CUBIC FEET CAPACITY IN LIFEBOATS.

Under this new regulation, then, the Titanic should have had nearly 23,000 cubic feet capacity in its lifeboats. But the photographs of that ship show the presence of only sixteen lifeboats suspended from the davits.

London, April 17.—Horatio Bottomley, member of parliament from one of the London districts, stated today that the White Star steamer Titanic was equipped with only eighteen lifeboats and two gigs. This life-saving apparatus, Bottomley said, was sufficient to care for only a small percentage of those on board the mammoth ship.

Bottomley has gained considerable prominence in the past few years for his efforts to obtain new maritime laws which will deal with the huge steamships now being constructed. He has always suffered defeat, however, through the strong influences of the shipping trust.

"In my journal, John Bull, in December, I prophesied the catastrophe which has unfortunately befallen the Titanic," said he.

"My criticism was mainly directed to the board of trade regulations. Under these obsolete laws it is actually laid down that tramp steamers, although they do not carry any passengers at all, must have on each side sufficient boats to accommodate the crew—that is, capable of carrying twice as many people as there are on board.

BIGGER THE CROWD, LESS IT IS CARED FOR.

"When a limited number of passengers is carried—not enough to bring them within the emigration act—lifeboats have to be sufficient, but need not be more than just sufficient, for crew and passengers.

"When, however, a great number of passengers is carried, the number of crew and passengers is not taken into account at all when lifeboat accommodation is being reckoned, it being computed on a tonnage basis only.

"Regulations actually set the maximum number of boats legally required 'for ten thousand tons and upward, sixteen boats with cubic capacity of 5,500 feet.' These sixteen boats would each carry about fifty persons.

"I am sorry to say that although it has been stated in the press that the Titanic had boats of a capacity equal to accommodate all on the vessel had she been full, she had on the davits but eighteen lifeboats and two gigs. These would each carry a few more than fifty persons.

"The fact that fewer than this total have been saved is probably accounted for by the unfortunate swamping of one or two of the lifeboats when the leviathan sank.

"Another of the regulations laid down by the board of trade is 'that when ships are divided into efficient watertight compartments to the satisfaction of the board of trade, they shall only be required to carry boats to one-half capacity.' Of course the White Star line claims its vessels are fitted with compartments and are absolutely unsinkable."

The sinking of the Titanic following so closely the wreck of the Delhi, Oceania and other big vessels, has caused consternation among marine underwriters. It will be long before the full effect in insurance of various kinds at Lloyds is known and many underwriters and syndicates may be hard hit.

Several insurance men declined to commit themselves to any definite opinion, but seemed to think there would be a movement in the direction of higher rates of insurance. Asked whether this would prove a setback to the building of huge vessels one member of Lloyds answered that it depended on the details of the disaster given by the survivors.

Instructions have been issued that all Cunard steamships follow the southern routes in order to avoid the icebergs.

Disappointed.

Newlywed (75 years old)—Will you love me dearest when I'm eighty?

Mrs. Newlywed (18 years old)—Why, darling, I thought you had heart disease. —Satire.

"Anonymous" Wants to Know.

If a thing of beauty
Is ALWAYS a joy,
Why does grandma rejoice
When the baby's a boy?
—Chicago Tribune.

Bottom of Titanic Knocked Off by Impact, Theory of Noted Engineers

How the Titanic was wrecked, shown by flashlight photographs of the steamship Navahoe, which was stoved in by a collision with the steamer City of Savannah. The damage to the bow of the Titanic must have been similar to that shown in the photographs.

NEW YORK SOCIETY WOMEN WILL MEET AND AID THE SURVIVORS

Three members of committee of rich New York women who will care for the Titanic'ss steerage passengers when they arrive in New York.

MRS. HERBERT SATTERLEE. MRS. CORNELIUS VANDERBILT SR. MRS. ARTHUR M. DODGE.

New York, April 17.—A committee of thirteen prominent women of this city, headed by Mrs. Nelson Henry, wife of the surveyor of the port of New York, has been formed for the purpose of caring for the surviving steerage passengers of the Titanic on the arrival of the Carpathia in port.

The committee consists of Mrs. Cornelius Vanderbilt Sr., Mrs. Henry F. Dimock, Mrs. Herbert L. Satterlee, Mrs. James Sherman Aldrich, Mrs. Richard Irvin, Mrs. William Church Osborn, Mrs. Edward Kingwood Heitt, Mrs. J. Van Vechten Olcott, Mrs. Henry Whitney Munroe, Mrs. Arthur Murray Dodge and Miss Virginia Potter.

"We do not know how many steerage passengers may have been saved," Mrs. Henry said, "but we fell something should be done for their comfort on their arrival, as there probably will be few of their friends on this side of the ocean to give them adequate care. We wish to give them what financial aid may be necessary to alleviate their sufferings as far as possible and assit the immigration authoritie."

SIDES PROBABLY RIPPED OPEN ALSO

Struck Submerged Part of Berg, Veteran Seaman Believes.

Chicago, April 17.—Capt. Charles Campbell, veteran seaman attached to the government hydrographic office here, said that "longitudinal stress" on the big boat probably caused the sudden sinking when the Titanic struck the iceberg.

"There is no doubt in my mind that longitudinal stress caused the sudden plunge," the captain said. "When the impact occurred, one end of the boat was turned upward, naturally. The rivets of the bottom of the vessel then broke, and, in my opinion, the entire bottom of the boat was severed from the rest of the craft.

"It is a mistaken idea that slow boats are less perilous than fast steamers. Fast ships are much the safer. A slow boat striking the iceberg as in the case of the Titanic, would have met the same fate, and there would have been no difference in the results.

"The Titanic apparently struck the iceberg a mile or more away from the ice that was visible. In large icebergs it is nearly always the case that a large portion of the ice is covered with water. Some section is visible, but a portion a mile or more in length may have been under water. The steamer evidently struck the submerged portion, unmindful of any impending danger."

Ann Arbor, Mich., April 17.—Capt. Inman Sealby, commander of the steamer Republic when it was in collision with the Florida, said that the early arrival of spring probably had indirectly caused the sinking of the Titanic, as ten days later, in ordinary seasons, no ship would have taken the track followed by the Titanic.

"I believe," said Captain Sealby, "that the Titanic hit the submerged part of an iceberg and glanced off, only to have the berg strike the keel of the ship in turn and tear a great hole in the bottom of the vessel.

"Captain Smith was one of the most careful sailors in the world and the Titanic was as safe as man could make it. Ice must have come down in great quantities within the last few days, and it is earlier than usual."

San Francisco, April 17.—That the Titanic was sunk by a lateral tearing and not by a head-on collision is the opinion of Hugo B. Frear, designer of the battleship Oregon and among the experts in naval construction on the Pacific coast.

"The sides of a vessel are the most difficult to protect," said Frear. "They are the most vulnerable spots in a steamship's anatomy, and it is my opinion that the Titanic struck the iceberg from an angle."

Wreck Will Result in New Marine Laws

Captain Smith Could Have Prevented Disaster by Loafing, but Would Have Been Censured, Says Capt. A. B. Benjamin.

"There is one thing certain, had the Titanic stopped where it was in the ice field through which it was undoubtedly plowing before the disaster occurred, nothing could have happened. And yet, if that brave, but unfortunate, man, Captain Smith, had stopped his ship, he would have been blamed and the passengers would have cried out against the vessel as a slow boat."

Arthur B. Benjamin, for years a captain in the Atlantic coastwise service, said this at the Shirley hotel, where he is making a considerable sojourn. "While I have never taken a ship across the Atlantic, I have made the trip to and from Europe a number of times, and I know a good deal about the Atlantic travel lanes.

"No, the iceberg was not unusually far south. I have seen them in much lower latitudes, but it was later in the year, generally in June or July that the bergs get that far down. I cannot account for the berg's presence in those waters at this time of the year.

"My experience has been confined to towing and managing fishing excursions and the like of that, but I have had charge of a number of vessels of the smaller kind, plying up and down the Atlantic coast. I remember once when I ran into an ice field in the gulf off St. Lawrence. There were thousands of small bergs all about when night overtook me and so I stopped my ship dead and waited for daylight. I was nine hours getting through that ice field.

"But nobody can say just how this terrible Titanic disaster occurred. You know it is said that an iceberg floats three-fourths under water. Lots of us who followed the sea were convinced that many rode eleven-twelfths under water, the reason being that many bergs carry imbedded in them tons of rocks from the glacier formations from which they split and float away.

"It may be that this berg which the Titanic ran afoul of didn't show above the surface more than six or eight feet, and thus resembled some of the smaller chunks of ice through which the liner had been pushing. This one, however, was evidently a monster and the ship may have run upon on it and split her plates half her length.

"Of course, this is all conjecture. There is one thing, however, that I cannot understand, and that is how the Titanic's forward bulkheads were stoved in. Had they remained whole there would have been no possibility of the ship's sinking. The berg may have been a quarter of a mile long and, of course, there would have been no way of avoiding it, even if it was discovered, for it would be seen only at close range and a big ship like that under full speed, trying to break a record—oh, well, what's the use talking about it. The dreadful thing has happened and all the good that can come of it now will be an overhauling and amendment of navigation rules, which will, at least, be of benefit to the living."

Titanic's Master Knew Life-Saving Equipment Short

Chicago, April 17.—Capt. Edward J. Smith of the Titanic believed that the steamer was not properly equipped with lifeboats and other live-saving apparatus and protested without success against lack of precaution, according to Glenn Marston, a friend of the captain.

Marston said that while returning from Europe on the Olympic in company with Captain Smith he remarked on the small number of lifeboats carried by such a large passenger steamer. It was then, according to Marston, that Captain Smith spoke of the lifepreserving equipment of the Titanic, then in course of construction, being limited.

Marston quoted Captain Smith as saying he thought the lack of equipment for saving lives was not due to a desire of the owners to save money, but rather because they believed their ships to be safe. Lifeboats were thought to be required, the captain said, only in cases in which passengers were to be brought from other ships in distress or passengers were to be landed. It was the captain's opinion, said Marston, that enough boats and rafts should be carried to insure safety to every passenger in case of an accident.

STRENUOUS TIME AT SABLE ISLAND WIRELESS STATION

Operators Overwhelmed With Messages That Come From Relatives of Passengers.

Halifax, April 17.—Sable Island, so long the terror of trans-Atlantic seamen, is, through the agency of the wireless, the storm center of a great battle for news of the missing passengers and crew of the Titanic.

The wireless station on the lonely sand-driven island, planted in the Atlantic 120 miles southeast of Halifax, is maintained by the Canadian government and is one of the most important of the chain of wireless outposts on the Canadian coast.

It has made the island, known as the graveyard of the Atlantic, the radiating center of news which comes and goes between the passing liners and the shore.

The wireless equipment is powerful within a radius of 300 miles and the business handled runs up to 12,000 to 15,000 messages a year.

The wireless operators at Sable Island are overwhelmed with messages which have come from all quarters from relatives of passengers praying for news, and the strenuous life the wireless men have lived during the last seventy-two hours will not be relieved until the Carpathia gives up her story.

Mrs. Stoiber Rood Sails for America From London Today

Although the repeated appearance of the name of Mrs. J. J. Brown in all the lists of the Titanic's passengers reported saved, has served to allay the fears entertained for her safety by Misses Florence and Helen Tobin, her nieces, who during her absence in Europe have made their home in this city with Mrs. Susan McManus, they are anxiously awaiting some personal message from the Denver woman, confirming the report of her rescue.

Until such tidings are received, the plans of the girls and Mrs. McManus for their tour of Europe have been temporarily abandoned. It had been their intention to start for Montreal immediately and take passage on the Virginian on its next voyage out of that port.

Mrs. Lawrence Brown, daughter-in-law of Mrs. J. J. Brown, who has been at the Adams hotel for several days, has gone to Colorado Springs, where she will remain until definite word concerning the fate of the elder woman is secured.

She received a letter two weeks ago from Miss Helen Brown, her sister-in-law, from Paris, where she has been in school during her mother's tour of Egypt with the John Jacob Astor party. This communication establishes clearly that she had no intention of accompanying her mother on the Titanic's maiden voyage to America. It was written one week before the liner sailed from Southampton, and reads in part as follows:

"I intend to remain in Paris until I have completed my studies. Mother intends to return by the Titanic, and I thought of going, but I decided yesterday that I would remain here until some time in June. I am doing so well with my work that it would be extremely foolish for me to break off just now, when there is no reason for doing so.

"Mamma almost persuaded me to make the return trip with her on this boat, as a great crowd will be aboard. It is the first trip, you know, and there will be much to do away with the monotony of the ordinary trip."

Mrs. Lena Stoiber Rood, whose husband, Hugh R. Rood, is believed to have been lost on the ill-fated liner, will sail for New York today, according to a message received by the firm of MacBeth & May, her attorneys. The Roods at first intended making the return trip to the states together aboard the Titanic, but Mrs. Rood finally decided to remain in London for a few more weeks, and her husband started on the voyage alone. The name of Rood, who was president of the Pacific Coast Creosoting company of Seattle, does not appear in the list of survivors of the disaster.

"I do not know just how the message came from Mrs. Rood," said Attorney May. "I found on my desk a written memorandum stating that a telephone call from some person had been received, stating that Mrs. Rood would sail for New York today. There was some misunderstanding about the name of the person telephoning, and I don't know to whom the communication came directly from London."

The bereavement under which the nation rests is individually felt by Attorney May, whose cousin, E. A. Kent, a prominent architect of Buffalo, N. Y., is believed to have been abroad the Titanic. He has visited in Denver and has many friends here, who anxiously await news of his fate.

MARRIAGE FOLLOWS NEWS OF MAN'S RESCUE

Los Angeles, Cal., April 17.—Miss Sally Bonner, niece of J. Ross Clark, vice president of the Salt Lake railroad, and Harry Innesborden, were married last night after Mr. Clark received a telegram stating that his son, Walter M. Clark, one of the passengers on the Titanic, had been rescued.

During the day the name of Mrs. Clark was among those of the rescued, and fear that her young husband was lost caused the postponement of the wedding. Shortly before 9 o'clock last night Mr. Clark received a private telegram which stated that his son had been rescued, and the wedding followed.

WOMEN IN SILKS AND RAGS TOGETHER AWAIT NEWS

LOVE FOR SISTERS CAUSED DEATH OF MOTHER AND BABES

She Took Steerage Tickets to Have Money to Bring Girls to America.

Chicago, April 17.—Love for her two younger sisters was the cause of the death of Mrs. Alice Johnson, a steerage passenger on the Titanic. She exchanged her second-class tickets and, with the two children, went into the steerage that with the money saved she might bring her sisters to America. The mother, her babies and the two younger women are all believed to have perished.

Oscar W. Johnson, a St. Charles, Ill., business man, was anxiously scanning newspaper accounts of the disaster when a postman brought him a letter mailed by his wife before leaving her parents' home abroad.

Mr. Johnson had sent the money for his wife to purchase a second-class passage for herself and children—Harold, 4 years old, and Eleanor, 1 year old. They had spent the winter in Sweden and were coming home.

In the newspapers he read that practically all women and children of the first and second-class cabins had been saved, and Johnson was horror-stricken when he read his wife's letter.

"At the last moment I decided to exchange the tickets for steerage passage that I might have Marie and Louise with me," said the message.

Marie and Louise Anderson, 16 and 18 years of age, were the girls Mrs. Johnson brought with her. It is feared all were lost and the husband is distracted.

Lady Duff-Gordon and Husband Among Those on Titanic

New York, April 17.—When the first passenger list of the Titanic was published in Monday's papers there was much curiosity over the identity of "Mr. and Mrs. Morgan," who were named as among those on board.

The reporters on duty at the offices of the International Mercantile Marine company thought at first they were meant for Mr. and Mrs. J. Pierpont Morgan, but when J. P. Morgan Jr. appeared to make inquiries he said they were not his father and mother, and he did not know who they could be.

Today the discovery was made that "Mr. and Mrs. Morgan" were Sir Cosmo and Lady Duff-Gordon, who were traveling incognito. Lady Duff-Gordon is the famous London dressmaker and a sister of Mrs. Eleanor Glyn, the author.

Several years ago she established a branch of her business at 17 West Thirty-sixth street, this city. On one occasion she brought over a lot of young English women to show how gowns should be worn.

Last May the customs officers descended upon the establishment and arrested Manager S. J. Duggan on a charge of conspiring to import women's wearing apparel from Europe at less than its true cost.

Sir Cosmo, husband of Lady Duff-Gordon, is the fifth baronet of the name. He was born in 1862, was educated at Eton and was married in 1900. Lady Duff-Gordon was then the widow of James S. Wallace.

MRS. ASTOR HAD GEMS WORTH $3,000,000 ABOARD

Paris, April 17.—It is reported here that Mrs. John Jacob Astor had with her on the Titanic diamonds of the value of 15,000,000 francs, or $3,000,000, which she bought from Cartier, the Paris jeweler.

PATRICIANS WEEP IN PEASANTS' ARMS

Mrs. Guggenheim Faints at Word Husband Is Dead.

BROADWAY MIRTH BECOMES MOCKERY

New York, Bowed With Grief, Gives Up Gayety for Mourning.

New York, April 17.—Hushed by a tragedy to which the annals of the sea offer no parallel, New York has hidden her gaiety behind a countenance of tearful, pallid grief.

Of all the great disasters which have stricken the city with sorrow, none has had the grewsome effect of the sinking, hundreds of miles at sea, of the great Titanic with about two-thirds of her passengers and crew of 2,200 persons.

The flags of all shipping in New York harbor were at halfmast today in honor of the Titanic's dead. This action was taken at the official behest of the maritime exchange, which passed the following resolution under the brief headline, "The Greatest Marine Disaster of Modern Times."

The members of the maritime association of the port of New York express their great regret at the lamentable disaster which has befallen the steamer Titanic, their great sorrow at the deplorable loss of life and property which has evidently accompanied this disaster, and extend to all involved in the great calamity their deep and heartfelt sympathy.

Resolved, That all vessels in the harbor place their flags at halfmast out of respect to the unfortunate dead.

MUTE CROWDS WAIT.

The offices of the White Star line are the focal point for the expression of woe and despair. Since Monday night a multitude of pallid men and women with swollen eyes have stood in front of the stone building at 9 Broadway, waiting for some news of their friends and kin who were aboard the ill-fated liner, and most of whom are known to be resting with the vessel two miles below the surface of the Atlantic.

Fashionably gowned women whose friends rode in the de luxe staterooms of the liner are mingling with and confiding their grief to women in shawls and shabby bonnets whose loved ones embarked in the steerage. There is no word from the steerage passengers. Their names were not printed in the lists.

In front of the newspaper offices are crowds that completely block traffic. Thousands stand too far away to read the bulletins, but the word is passed quickly through the entire throng as a new name appears on the bulletin board as having survived. The streets are veritable seas of newspapers, for editions are being issued from a dozen offices and people are eagerly scanning every new scarehead line.

BROADWAY A MOCKERY.

Tinseled Broadway is a mockery. The theaters are open, but the actors are making dismal attempts to interest small audiences, who are rushing to the streets at regular intervals to secure an "extra."

The lobbies and corridors of the great steamship offices present heartrending scenes. Clerks who have been answering anxious inquiries for the last forty-eight hours are telling sobbing men and women that the ships of their lines have been unable to find more survivors than those aboard the Carpathia and are proceeding to their respective destinations.

Reserve policemen are performing their duty gently. Sobbing, hysterical women are led—sometimes carried—to their waiting limousines or to a place on the curb where they may weep and wait.

The parents of a score of bridal couples who had sailed from the other side on the hapless leviathan are among those who throng lower Broadway. But there was absolutely no news for any one. More than 800 persons are reported on their way to New York on the Carpathia, but in many hours only 250 names of survivors have been received.

A pale little man, who had bitten his lips so that blood trickled down his chin, struggled through the crowd to ask about the fate of his brother, W. Marvin, who was on his honeymoon with his bride. Mrs. Marvin's name was on the list, but not that of her husband. The little man shrieked and fell and was carried to the street.

MRS. GUGGENHEIM FAINTS.

Mrs. Benjamin Guggenheim, wife of the smelter millionaire, became hysterical and fainted when informed by Daniel Guggenheim that her husband's name was not on the list.

"You must do something," she cried, as she rushed at the clerks. "It's a crime; it's a shame."

And she fell in a dead faint in front of the information desk.

Two weeping women inquired in vain for word of Jonkher Reachlin, a director of the Holland-American line.

A Mrs. Rudd of Newark, N. J., when informed that her sister, Mrs. H. E. Stengel of Newark, was safe, pitched forward into a swoon as she was descending the steps to Broadway and was badly bruised about the face.

Mr. Byrnes, secretary of Isidor Straus, returned to his fruitless vigil last night. Neither the name of Mr. nor Mrs. Straus has appeared on the list of survivors.

London, April 17.—Although hope that the list of survivors of the sunken Titanic will be added to has practically been given up, the officers of the White Star line in London, Southampton and Liverpool again were besieged this morning by anxious inquirers.

Some of those who had relatives on board remained at the offices throughout the night, scanning the lists, which, however, proved not to contain any fresh names, but merely corroborations of those given before.

Those who waited in the London offices were mostly women whose husbands had started for America on business or to make new homes there for their families.

Early this morning the White Star company gave out the statement, received from the captain of the Olympic, that neither the Virginian nor the Parisian had survivors on board, and expressing the belief that all those who had been rescued were on board the Carpathia.

RUDELY SURPRISED.

While travelers generally understood the fact that great liners do not carry enough boats to accommodate all the passengers and crew, to the general public the news that all on board the Titanic did not have a chance of saving their lives in this way came as a rude surprise, and there is likely to be considerable agitation in and out of parliament on the subject.

The lord mayor of London today opened a mansion house fund for the relief of the families of the crew of the Titanic and of any others left in needy circumstances in consequence of the disaster.

A memorial service for the victims will be held in St. Paul's cathedral, April 19.

Much indignation is expressed in connection with the publication of the telegrams stating that the Titanic was in tow of the Virginian just after the news of the accident was received. Col. Charles E. Yate, member of parliament for Leicestershire, will ask the president of the board of trade in the house of commons if his attention has been drawn to the publication of the telegrams and whether their origin could be traced.

SEVERELY CRITICIZED.

The electrical control of the bulkheads installed in the Titanic is coming for much criticism. It is stated here that they are a pet idea of Lord Pirrie, who insists on introducing them in ships built at Belfast, despite the condemnation of many well-known contractors who pin their faith to the hydraulic power as being far more reliable. These constructors point out that even a small mishap is liable to render the electrical installation useless.

Wireless cabin aboard the Olympic from which was flashed the S. O. S.

Denver Girl Tells of Shipwreck at Night

Lillian Argall Says Horror of Sinking of the Spokane Is as Vivid Now as When It Occurred.

Only the man or women who has been in a shipwreck can imagine, even faintly the scenes which were enacted on board the Titanic when the giant steamer struck the iceberg that sent her down shortly after midnight on Sunday. The chill terror of unknown disaster that gripped 2,000 hearts as the boat shuddered from the shock of collision and the subsequent emotions endured by the men and women who swarmed the decks of the sinking ship—even the most vivid imagination cannot picture these sufferings without the background of experience.

Three Denver people were in a shipwreck last June the circumstances of which were in some degree similar to those under which the Titanic sank. The steamship Spokane, on which Philip Argall and his two daughters, Lillian and Gladys, set sail for Alaska, ran on a rock two days out from Seattle. The disaster occurred about 11 o'clock at night, the boat sinking after the women and young people had been transferred to lifeboats.

HORRORS OF THAT NIGHT STILL CLING TO HER.

Miss Lillian Argall declares that the horror of that night is as vivid to her today as it was ten months ago.

"We were two days out from Seattle," said Miss Argall. "We had been going through narrows all day long and at a very fast clip, too. All day long the decks were washed by seething waves and the dim outlines of the rocks could be seen looming up on both sides of us, even in the dark. The captain had been delayed at Victoria and was trying to make up for lost time, even though he knew there was danger ahead.

"My sister and I went to our cabin about 10 o'clock and were soon fast asleep. The first thing that I knew after that there was a terrific jar and the engines stopped. I was awakened so suddenly that it took me a few minutes to realize where I was, and then I slipped on a kimono and ran to the door. A man was standing out in the passageway and when he saw me he called out: 'Better go back to bed; it's all right.' I thought I had better wait a few minutes, though, and see if father would come up (he was on the deck below us).

"Sure enough he came running down the passage in a few minutes, his hair fairly standing on end. I knew then that something dreadful had happened. 'Get dressed at once,' he said, 'we've struck a rock and the boat is seriously damaged.'

"I ran back to the cabin and waked my sister and then we got into our clothes. Every few minutes I would go put my head out in the hall and father would fairly drive me back, telling me not to waste time. We finally were ready to go on deck and by the time we got up there nearly all the passengers had gathered there. Most of them were talking quietly, watching the efforts of the pilot to back the boat off the rock, but there was one hysterical woman who was crying and laughing in a terrible way. She was an invalid, just recovering from a serious operation, and she was completely unstrung.

CAPTAIN SIMPLY BLUSTERED AROUND.

"The crew was untrained, most of them Portuguese, with a sprinkling of college boys, who were working their way to Alaska. The captain seemed unable to do anything except bluster around, though finally, when the boat had tilted so from the water she had shipped that the lifebats, which had been on the hurricane deck, were on a level with the upper deck, he gave the order to 'lower the lifeboats.' The men didn't seem to know how to lower the boats at all. They just piled a load of women into the first one and then cut the ropes, letting the boat drop several feet into the water.

"Just as the men at the oars were getting it under way, about thirty of the crew from the boiler rooms burst upon deck and made a leap for the boat, completely upsetting it. The shrieks of the women as they were thrown into the water I shall never forget. Some of them swam around there for twenty minute before they were picked up.

FATHER SHOVED HER INTO BOAT BY SHEER FORCE.

"My sister and I went off in the second boatload. I wanted to stay with father and take my chance with him, but he shoved us into the boat by main force. I grabbed Gladys tightly by the arm so that we wouldn't fall out when they cut the ropes, and for weeks after she bore the print of my fingernails on her arm. There were two sailors trying to row, and they were so frightened they kept pulling the wrong way, so that the boat went around and around. Just then the lights on the ship went out and the women began to shriek at the top of their lungs. They thought it had gone down.

"We hadn't any idea where the land was, but after the boat had been drifting about ten minutes we struck sand, and then we knew we had hit Maud island. We all jumped out on the beach and the boat went back in the direction of the ship. Other boats began to arrive and, as the men finally began to land, there was a terrible confusion, the women calling to their husbands or shrieking out that they must have been drowned.

"SURE ENOUGH, HE WAS IN LAST BOATLOAD."

"Gladys and I were nearly dead with fright, for father was nowhere to be found. As the last boat came in a woman with us turned to me and said: 'Well, if your father isn't on that boat he must be drowned, because they aren't going back any more.' And, sure enough, he crawled out of the boat. He was so exhausted and so relieved to see us that he couldn't say a word.

"Some of the crew came along then and told all of us that the tide was rising so rapidly that if we didn't walk around to the other side of the island we would be drowned. So we picked ourselves up wearily and walked around the island, about a mile and a half. Lots of the people were in their night clothes, without any sign of kimonos or slippers, and the gravel on the beach was so sharp it cut through my shoes.

"We finally reached a point they said was safe, and the men built fires and we all threw ourselves down to rest. The crew went off by themselves and wouldn't even tend the fires. By this time it was daylight and a steamer had sighted our distress signals. It was an English boat and they offered to take us on board for $25 a head. The captain replied: 'No, indeed; his company couldn't afford to pay such a price.' So the boat went on and we waited there, shaking and shivering, until about 11 o'clock, when another boat came along and took us back to Seattle. Nothing ever looked so good to me as the Welcome Arch at the depot when we got back to Denver a few days later. I never want to even see the water again.

LIFEBOATS TOO FEW ON LINERS OF TODAY.

"It didn't affect father that way, though, for he set off for England in October. He had had a much worse experience than we had. After all the lifeboats had left there suddenly came the noise of a terrific explosion and the whole front of the ship was blown up. The men thought the boilers had burst and all dived. They found afterwards that it was the result of the air that had been compressed under the ship as she went down, for the water was quite shallow in that place."

Mr. Argall says that this wreck led him to make some investigations when he crossed the Atlantic, and he found that the Lusitania, on which he crossed, although she could accommodate 3,000 passengers, only carried lifeboats for 600.

"The liners are being built today according to laws which were good enough for the old-time steamers of 5,000 or 10,000 tons," says Mr. Argall, "but not for the leviathans of today. The result of the loss of the Titanic will be that new laws will go into effect in England in a few weeks which will make it impossible for big liners to only carry lifeboats for one-third or one-fourth the number of the passengers."

The wireless station at Cape Saple, where most of the reports from the Carpathia are being received.

MARCONI,

The inventor of wireless telegraphy, which has saved thousands of lives, reading a message.

WIDOW ASKS U. S. TO HELP SAVE HOME

Unless Helped She and Six Daughters Will Become Charges of State.

No more pathetic appeal ever came into the office of M. D. McEniry, chief of the field division of the general land office, than the letter he received from Mrs. Katherine Skalla, living on a 240-acre homestead sixteen miles south of Vona, Kit Carson county, on the Rock Island railroad. She wants leniency from the government so she will not lose her farm and a home for her six daughters.

Mrs. Skalla has a cow and two horses. Forty acres of the farm has been cultivated, but she has no money to buy seed this year, and unless she gets aid at once she will be a charge upon the state with her six daughters, the oldest of whom is 12 years.

The Skallas were doing well until illness came into the family and took away the breadwinner. The husband and father lost his mind and is now in the asylum at Pueblo. When he was taken away from the family the county furnished aid to the Skallas for a short time. The county commissioners, however, soon tired of their work of charity and notified Mrs. Skalla that before she could get any further assistance it must be shown that she had exhausted her own resources.

The distracted woman was told by these commissioners that she would have to sell her cattle before more assistance would be furnished by them. She had one horse and two cows. To be forced to dispose of them meant that the woman and her family could not get to Vona for aid nor plow the forty acres for seed if someone gave it to her. She then appealed to the government.

The Skallas filed on their homestead in 1910, and unless the family is given aid there is no way for them to save it.

FIREMEN TO TEACH SCHOOL PUPILS HOW TO CHECK FLAMES

Thursday Is Fire Prevention Day as Designated by Governor Shafroth.

The campaign of education having for its object united action of citizens of Denver and Colorado in observance of simple rules to minimize danger from fires will be inaugurated tomorrow, which has been set aside by Governor Shafroth as Fire Prevention day. The movement has gained considerable headway in other states, and already officials declare they can see results in a decreased number of fires and less loss.

In the public schools firemen of the local department will talk to the students and explain simple rules which will aid in accomplishing the end desired. The careless use of matches, accumulation of rubbish and prompt alarms when blazes are discovered are the cardinal points which will be emphasized to the youths of the schools, and their co-operation will be asked.

The fire prevention committee of the chamber of commerce has adopted a set of precautions which have the approval of the fire department heads, and which will be distributed generously throughout the city for the information and guidance of citizens. The resolutions read as follows:

"Resolved, That I will make every effort to secure the safest matches for my use.

"That I will make it the rule of my life to see that matches are not left where there is any possibility of their being ignited.

"That I will not throw burned matches carelessly about.

"That I will not use gasoline where there is any fire.

"That I will not permit any rubbish to accumulate in any place that will endanger life or property.

"That I will fully master some plan of action that will be of service in case of fire.

"That I will never start a fire where there is any danger of its spreading.

"I will see that lamps are filled in daylight, without aid of artificial light.

"That coal oil is kept in metal cans and in a safe place.

"That no oily rags are left around the premises over night outside of a good metal receptacle.

"I will promptly turn in the alarm for any fire that comes to my attention, and then will assist in extinguishing it, if my assistance is required.

"I will be very careful about lighted cigars and pipes.

"I will encourage the sane Fourth of July idea."

CACHE LA POUDRE COUPLE OBSERVE GOLDEN WEDDING

Fort Collins, Colo., April 17.—Mr. and Mrs. J. G. Coy, residents of Larimer county for the past fifty years, are celebrating their golden wedding anniversary at the home of their daughter, Mrs. John M. Hoffman, this afternoon.

Mr. Coy is 78 years of age and in spite of his years is still active and manages his farm near this city. Mrs. Coy is 74 years old. They were the parents of ten children, six of whom are still living.

Mr. Coy has twice served as county commissioner and was once candidate for state senator and once for governor.

DEMOCRATS OF JACKSON COUNTY ARE FOR CLARK

Walden, Colo., April 17.—The Jackson county Democratic convention which met at Walden yesterday indorsed Champ Clark for president, but the delegates to the state convention were not instructed. Resolutions were adopted condemning Representative Toovey of the Jackson county district for bolting the part of the Democratic ticket at the last election.

WHO SENT THE LYING WIRELESS MESSAGES OF TITANIC'S SAFETY?

LONDON, April 17.—The London Standard prints this morning the following under the head "A Mystery of the News! Who Sent the Wireless Falsehoods?"

"One of the mysteries in connection with the Titanic disaster which at present is unsolved is the extraordinary series of false messages with which the world was lulled into fancied security on Monday.

"For sixteen hours—until 1 o'clock yesterday morning—right through the editions of the evening papers and earlier editions of the morning a flood of alleged wireless messages was received. They reported that all passengers had been saved; that the Titanic was proceding under her own steam to Halifax; that she could not possibly sink; that twenty boatloads of passengers had been transhipped to the Parisian; that the Parisian and Carpathia were both in attendance; that the Virginia was towing the Titanic toward Cape Race to beach her.

"Then the truth when the dire news came that the Titanic had sunk at 2:30 a. m. This put the possibility of a great disaster forward for the first time. News agencies and correspondents who sent false news messages merely transferred reports given out to them. All praise is due them for their exceptional promptitude, but who sent these wireless messages, and from where were they sent? These are the questions the public will naturally ask."

THE NEW YORK HERALD.

THE WEATHER. Clearing to fair; colder. For detailed weather report and forecast see Editorial page.

WHOLE NO. 27,631. NEW YORK, WEDNESDAY, APRIL 17, 1912.—TWENTY-EIGHT PAGES.—[COPYRIGHT, 1912, BY THE NEW YORK HERALD COMPANY.] PRICE THREE CENTS.

THE TITANIC TORN ASUNDER WHEN SHE STRUCK ICEBERG GOING AT 18-KNOT SPEED

MISS E W ALLEN
LADY COSMO DUFF GORDON
MRS. J. W. M. CARDEZA PHOTO by DAVIS & SANFORD
MRS. WILLIAM E. CARTER
MRS. JOHN JACOB ASTOR PHOTO by AIME DUPONT
MISS MARIE YOUNG PHOTO BY HALLS
MRS. TYRREL W. CAVENDISH & MRS. JOHN B. THAYER
MRS. JACQUES FUTRELLE COPYRIGHT by MARCEAU 1911
MRS. GEORGE D. WIDENER PHOTO by HESTED
MRS. PAUL SCHABERT
MRS. T. D. M. CARDEZA
MRS. DANIEL WARNER MARVIN
MRS. HENRY HARR

ONLY GALLANTRY OF OFFICERS AND CREW SAVED THE 868 WHO ARE ABOARD THE CARPATHIA

Great Ship Thrown Into Darkness as Frantic Work of Loading Women Into the Lifeboats and Male Passengers Left to Their Fate Bid Them Adieu.

CAPTAIN SMITH, COOL TO THE LAST, DIRECTS ORDERS AND REPRESSES PANIC

Vessel Hits Ice with Shock That Crushes Her Forward Part and Almost Capsizes at the Moment of the First Fearful Impact.

[SPECIAL DESPATCH TO THE HERALD.]

St. Johns, N. F., Tuesday.—From the steamship Bruce, bound for Sydney, N. S., come the first detailed reports to-night of the sinking of the Titanic and the appalling scenes attending her end.

The Bruce obtained her story of the disaster from wireless messages picked up from several of the ships which had been in closest touch with the last hours of the mammoth White Star steamship and which were afterward in the zone of communication with the Bruce's apparatus.

When the Titanic struck the mountain of ice that sent her to the ocean bottom within four hours after the impact, she was steaming at the rate of eighteen knots. The shock almost demolished the proud vessel, which her builders had boasted and her captain had believed nothing could master.

Hitting the impenetrable ice mass fairly with her towering bows, the ship was almost rent asunder at the first blow. Her decks were ripped and torn, her sides and bulkheads were split and shattered as with the hammer of some Titan, from the bow to a point almost amidships.

Some of Her Life Boats Crushed.

Her upper works and some of her boats were splintered, while a shower of debris from her spars fell upon the decks like giant hail. Though the ship had struck the monster obstruction head on, as her bow rose clear of the water, smashed to an unrecognizable mass of bent and shivered steel, the vessel listed heavily to port and threatened to turn turtle before the recoil slid of what was left of her proud form back to an even keel.

The Titanic had forced her giant bulk away up on a submerged spur of the iceberg, a phenomenon which is not infrequent in the most disastrous collisions with these ghostlike sentinels of the Banks. In mounting upon the jagged ice spur and in sliding back from her position the ship had torn out many of her bottom plates from the midships section forward to the bow.

As a result her compartments from amidships forward were speedily flooded. She took in water at a rate that defied the efforts of the pumps, and soon began to settle by the head, listing heavily to port and rolling in the trough of the sea as she became gradually disengaged from the ice, many tons of which had fallen upon her upper decks, contributing to the demolition and intricable confusion.

The force of the blow had been so tremendous that the vast ship was started in her every joint, and everything movable throughout her superb equipment of luxurious cabins and saloons was tossed into heaps like discarded junk.

But British seamanship and discipline prevailed, and it did what little might be done as well as dauntless men could do it. Every officer and man leaped to his post, while Captain Smith, megaphone in hand, bellowed his orders over the rolling hulk that an hour before had been the proudest ship in Christendom. Sufficient order was maintained to launch safely most of the boats, the greater number of which had remained seaworthy, despite the ordeal through which they had passed.

THE TITANIC SENT OUT WARNING OF ICEBERGS ONE HOUR BEFORE THE CRASH

[SPECIAL DESPATCH TO THE HERALD.]

BALTIMORE, Md., Tuesday.—A wireless message received by the United States Hydrographic Office here Sunday afternoon indicates that the navigators of the Titanic knew that they were in the midst of dangerous icebergs, and adds to the mystery of the disaster.

The message came from the steamship Amerika, of the Hamburg-American line, and was relayed by the Titanic to one of the shore stations at half-past nine o'clock Sunday night, just one hour before she went to pieces on the iceberg. The message, which was forwarded to the hydrographic offices at Washington, Baltimore, Philadelphia, and probably other sea-coast cities, said:—

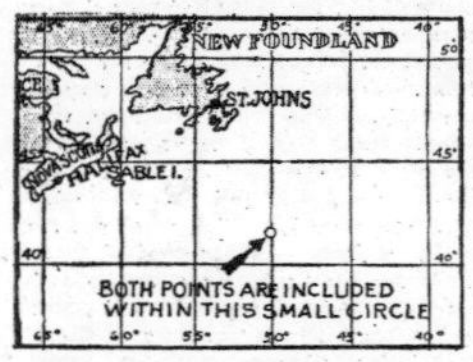

"April 14.—The German steamer Amerika reports by radio-telegraph passing two large icebergs in latitude 41.27, longitude 50.08.—(Titanic, Br. S. S.)

Naval officers here calculate that as the Titanic met her fate in latitude 41.46, longitude 50.14, she may have struck one of the icebergs reported in her own despatch, which had drifted slightly to the north and west. She could not have travelled more than twenty miles from the spot from which she sent the despatch to the spot where she went down.

NATIONS OF WORLD TO MOVE FOR SAFEGUARDING PASSENGERS; ICEBERG PATROL TO BE STARTED

Scarcity of Lifeboats on Board the Ill Fated Ship Aro[...] Legislators in Washington to Necessity of Providing Craft for All, Despite Vessels' Size.

BULKHEADS WILL NEVER SUSTAIN GREAT STEAMSHIPS ENTIRELY, DECLARE EXPER[...]

Pall of Gloom Sweeps Over Country as Many Cities Lea[...] Their Leading Citizens Were Among Those to Go to Bottom with the Giant Vessel.

This work was progressing in a way, the women and children being given the preference in the lifeboats. At first the evidences of panic were wel supressed, though there was many a painful ecene as wives and sisters, sweethearts and mothers parted from their dar ones, whom they were leaving to an unknown fate as they took their allotted places in the boats.

Several times as the compartments rapidly filled, the vessel lurched heavily. Then the cry went up that the ship was sinking and there was a rush for the small boats that for the first time threatened to transform a brave and orderly scene into one of frenzied panic. As the Titanic settled lower under the weight of the rapidly gaining water in her hold it was said that some of her boats were stove in before they could be freed from the davits and that a few were swamped in the effort to launch them.

Darkness Adds to Horror of Scene

Within less than an hour after the doomed queen of the ocean fleets had struck she had settled so fast that the water had flooded her engine rooms and then her wireless apparatus went out of com[...]mission. At the same time the failing of her dynamos extinguish[...] her electric lighting system, and the mammoth craft was plung[...] into Stygian darkness except for such feeble gleams as were afford[...] by the use of torches and lanterns. These served only to empha[...] the horror of the midnight darkness, made more weird by the re[...] tions and shadows cast by the towering masses of arctic pinna[...] surrounding the stricken ship.

In the darkness the work of launching the remaining boats made more difficult, but the Bruce reports that all the boats, or nea[...] all, had cleared the wreck before the Titanic took her final plu[...] into the obscure depths of a grave two thousand fathoms deep.

HOPING AGAINST HOPE, THRONGS AWAIT SURVIVORS

ALL THE TITANIC'S SURVIVORS ABOARD THE CARPATHIA

None of the Other Vessels Near Scene of Disaster Made Rescues.

REVISED LIST GIVES 868 AS TOTAL SAVED

Unconfirmed Report That Charles M. Hays and Jacques Futrelle Are Safe.

FATE OF MANY IS IN DOUBT

Relatives of Colonel Astor and Others Still Cling to Faint Hope.

More appalling with the lapse of time grows the tale of the Titanic's loss.

The few brief messages that came pulsing by wireless out of the ice infested zone, where the white bergs lift their points as the sole monument above the steamship's ocean grave, blasted more hopes than they fostered.

Definite information increased the list of the known saved from the 675 reported yesterday to a total of 868 survivors, including passengers and crew. All these are aboard the Cunard steamship Carpathia. She is, at best, not a fast ship. Her captain reports her steaming cautiously through thick fields of ice, littered with many menacing icebergs. She is taking no chances of a repetition of the horror of Sunday night. At her present rate of progress it is thought that she is not likely to reach this port with her stricken freight of desolated refugees before next Friday morning, or, at the earliest, Thursday night.

None Aboard Other Ships.

In the meantime, the brief illusory hope that other survivors might have been picked up by the Virginian or the Parisian, of the Alen line, was extinguished early in the day. Both these vessels flashed the dispiriting message by wireless that they had none of the Titanic's complement aboard. Each has proceeded on her voyage, the Virginian with United States' mails, which could no longer be delayed except in the most imperative emergency.

By way of London last night came a report, as yet unverified, that two notable rescues had been made by unexpected good fortune.

The despatch said that Charles M. Hays, president of one of the great Canadian railroad systems, and Jacques Futrelle, a well known American novelist and magazine writer, had been picked up by a passing steamship and were on their way to London. Mrs. Futrelle is already known to be among the rescued aboard the Carpathia.

Of the 868 survivors now on board that vessel the names of 326 were received here by wireless up to half-past four o'clock yesterday afternoon, having been relayed from the Olympic, which has now passed on eastward out of the zone of communication. There followed an interval during which nothing was received from the Carpathia, but at half-past nine o'clock last night her wireless apparatus came into communication with the Sable Island station, according to an announcement made at the office of the White Star line in this city, and it was expected that additional names of those rescued and further details of the disaster would soon be forthcoming.

Colonel Astor's Fate in Doubt.

With more than five hundred names of the saved yet to be received, thousands of homes are still left under the pall of a doubt, more harrowing perhaps than the most dreaded of certainties. The imperfect list already received makes it clear that Mrs. John Jacob Astor and her maid are safe aboard the Carpathia.

The fate of Colonel Astor, however, remains in doubt, as does that of Major Archibald Butt, military aid to President Taft; Isidor Straus, the wealthy New York merchant; Benjamin Guggenheim, president of the International Steam Pump Company; William T. Stead, the famous English journalist, and scores of others whose names are well known here and abroad.

The marked predonerance of women and children among those who have been reported as saved indicates that the unwritten law of the sea that gallant men must give place to the weaker woman nd child when death is threatening all 'ke, has not been ignored.

s the Carpathia's grim census of the g and her longer roster of the lost :esses the fear increases that the ›rtion of men among the rescued be pitifully small. By those who the traditions of the sea, stronger g brave men than many a statutory that no British master in the navy e merchant marine may leave his until the last, it is a foregone con- n that Captain Smith went down s post when his splendid charge ›d to her final resting place in the iomed depths off Cape Race. It ught that most, if not all of his t officers, with the exception of whose duty it was to navigate the several lifeboats, have shared the master's fate.

Still Cling to Hope.

With all the revised figures taken into acount there remain 1,341 persons who were aboard the giant ship who are unacounted for and presumably buried in the 1,760 fathoms of water off Cape Race. London, Paris and a hundred other cities here in in Europe are stunned by the news of the tragedy—probably the greatest catastrophe since ships began to breast the deep. So everwhelming is it that people in the various centers hardly began to realize it all until yesterday.

There had been hope in the breasts of those at least who had friends and loved ones aboard the stricken ship that perhaps out of the mysterious space would come word that many had been rescued who were believed to have gone to the bottom; but that last, lingering hope was banished yesterday afternoon and the scenes of grief and hysteria about the offices of the shipping companies here and abroad were almost beyond descripion.

Newspaper offices on two continents were besieged by friends and relatives of those who had shipped on the great vessel. Ticker tapes were watched with more anxiety than has ever before been observed, at least in New York city, and everywhere—in restaurants, hotel lobbies, offices and on street cars—the terrible calamity was the sole topic of conversation.

Mr. Taft Grief Stricken.

President Taft in Washington deplored the accident and joined with those about him in hoping against hope that reports had been exaggerated. He was grief stricken over the probable loss of his military aid, Captain Archibald W. Butt, to whom he had been for years greatly attached. Late in the afternoon he directed the Secretary of the Navy to order the scout cruisers Salem and Chester to start at once to meet the Carpathia and send in by wireless to the government a complete list of the survivors. The Chester was caught by wireless about forty miles off Chesapeake Bay and at four o'clock was steaming northward at twenty knots. Two revenue cutters were also notified to stand in readiness to proceed to the Carpathia if necessary. It is practically taken for granted that both Captain Butt and Mrs. Butt met death in the disaster.

The Sable Island cable ship Minia reported late yesterday afternoon through the wireless station at Halifax, N. S., that she had sighted a great mass of wreckage, but no boats or rafts, from the Titanic. This, for the time being, at least, disposes of the hope that the Minia, which was anchored off Cape Race when the Titanic first called for help, might have picked up some of the Titanic's passengers.

Peril of Ice Fields.

Wherever steamship men gathered there was talk about the danger from icebergs in the northern route at this time of year and of the impossibility of constructing a ship which can withstand a head-on collision with a mountain of ice. Winds and storms of all kinds can be resisted, they agreed, but the one great danger of the ice crag which float down from the Arctic will always be with us, they declared.

"In ordinary circumstances," said A. L. Hopkins, vice president of the Newport News Shipbuilding and Dry Dock Company, "watertight compartments will prevent a ship from sinking, but smashing into an iceberg could produce shattering effects which would render a ship helpless beyond the protection of any design yet known."

Similar sentiment was expressed by prominent ship builders here and abroad. Sympathy was expressed for Captain Smith, one of the most venerable masters of the deep. Persons who have long known him cannot bring themselves to the point of placing blame upon him. His late career had been marred by ill luck, but it was attributed to luck, not lack of skill or ability. He was in command of the Titanic's sister ship, the Olympic, when she was in collision with the cruiser Hawke. Exonerated from all blame in this instance, he was at once placed in charge of the Titanic, the greatest marine structure ever built, and it was his ambition to make an enviable and splendid maiden voyage. All over the civilized world people are anxiously awaiting to hear the actual story of the collision—to know where blame is to be placed and hear the details of the infernal four hours from the time the crash came until the great ship, with her thousand and more of passengers—the élite of two continents—took her plunge into the deep.

President Moves to Stop Mob Rule of Wireless

Mr. Taft, His Cabinet, Army and Navy and Other Experts Confer on Scheme for Worldwide Regulation of Service to Prevent Interference in Times of Disaster.

HERALD BUREAU,
No. 1,502 H STREET, N. W.,
WASHINGTON, D. C., Tuesday.

President Taft presided at a conference at the White House this afternoon to urge the regulation of wireless telegraphy in conformity with international regulations, but found little necessity for argument, for the staggering disaster of the Titanic, coupled with the wireless chaos concerning relief work and accurate reports, was in itself a demonstration which will serve for all time to show that regulation is imperative.

At the conference were the President, Mr. Meyer, Secretary of the Navy; Mr. Stimson, Secretary of War; Mr. Nagel, Secretary of Commerce and Labor; Hutch I. Cone, Engineer in Chief of the Navy; Brigadier General James Allen, Chief Signal Officer of the army, and Messrs. John W. Griggs and James R. Sheffield, of New York, representing the Marconi and other wireless interests.

The conference was arranged for some time ago to give the commercial wireless experts a chance to be heard by the President concerning the advantage or disadvantage of wireless regulation according to the government's ideas. Mr. Griggs has been the champion of the Commercial Wireless Company's interest for several years and his untiring efforts have defeated ratification of the Berlin wireless convention of 1906 in the Senate until about two weeks ago, when the Berlin convention was ratified. If Mr. Griggs had not lost his opposition to regulation of wireless before last night he lost it then. The Titanic disaster has fairly swept off their feet those opposing wireless regulation.

Regulation Now Imperative.

The necessity for regulation to-day stands out so clear that the White House conference found no time to discuss it at all. Instead the discussion was merely general, with admission by all that the chaos in the wireless field was a disgrace to the nation, and that severe penalties should be prescribed for infringements taking place at a great crisis on the seas like the disaster of yesterday.

The President himself had the consequences of this chaos brought home to him in a gruelling and unwelcome fashion to-day when he groped through a maze of wireless messages communicated to the White House from various sources in a vain endeavor to hear news concerning his military aid, Major Butt, on board the ill fated ship. There were upward of a hundred messages received at the White House to-day, but some were incomplete, others were garbled, many were apparently unreliable and few could be relied upon.

From the offices of the White Star line came reports to the President that it was practically impossible to get any reliable information by wireless because of the great number of wireless concerns breaking into the field and because of the work of amateur operators.

Amateurs Break In.

It appears that the disaster to the Titanic had no sooner been flashed over the seas than about every wireless instrument along the coast within range began operations, sending and receiving with no thought of others, so that the net result soon became a hopeless jumble, from which distorted and inaccurate messages were patched up in haphazard fashion and announced to the anxious world.

It is believed here that this chaos was responsible for the messages that were flashed from one end of the civilized world to the other that the Titanic was en route for Halifax under her own steam at six o'clock at night, when as a matter of fact the vessel had been sixteeen hours at the bottom of the sea. This same chaos is held responsible for the reports that passengers were being calmly taken off the ship in the afternoon, when the ship really went down at twenty minutes past two o'clock in the morning. The same chaos is held responsible here for the maze of garbled reports which now are as tragic as they are ludicrous.

Indeed, officials here comment on the fact that the hundreds of lives on board the Titanic were at the mercy of the unscrupulous wireless operators, who might even have called off the vessels that started for her relief by adding to their list of criminal messages one saying that the ship was safe and needed no assistance at all.

"If there ever was a demonstration that regulation of wireless is necessary, this is it," said Hutch J. Cone at the White House to-day just before the wireless conference.

Calls it an Outrage.

"This wireless chaos that places human lives at the mercy of irresponsible operators who are beyond control of the government or any regulation is particularly outrageous at such a time as this. It is precisely what is bound to happen when there is no regulation by law, and it will happen again unless some means of regulation is prescribed."

Mr. Stimson, Secretary of War, reinforced this view as he was leaving the White House.

"This shows unmistakably what happens at a time like this when there is no control of wireless," said he, "and it demonstrates infallibly that regulation of wireless is necessary."

Brigadier General Allen has the same view. He has been fighting for regulation of wireless since 1906, when he signed the Berlin convention as one of the delegates of the United States.

Eugene B. Chamberlain, Commissioner of Navigation, in his annual report sets forth the need for wireless regulation concisely. He says in part:—

"The need for regulation arises primarily from the fact that wireless messages interfere with one another, so that important despatches on public business may be obstructed by the mischievous efforts of a tyro. Land telegraph lines cannot be set in operation anywhere without some official sanction for the erection of poles and stringing of wires, although one wire does not interfere with another. A fine of $1,000 or imprisonment for not more than three years is provided by section 60 of the Penal Code of 1909 for interference with messages over government wires.

"Faking" Distress of Ships.

"The other is common property, and with the cheapest apparatus unrestrained trivial messages can create babel. Again, bogus wireless messages may be sent by the reckless, and some have gone to the criminal length of 'faking' the distress call of a passenger ship at sea."

The Senate has now ratified the Berlin convention, and the United States will be represented at the International Radio Telegraphic Conference to be held at London on June 4, 1912. The question of legislation to regulate wireless in the United States in conformity with the international agreement between nations is now being considered.

Several bills are pending in Congress, and it is believed that the regulations will be made severe enough to guarantee that ships in distress cannot be thrown at the mercy of amateur or irresponsible operators with impunity. Likewise President Taft and government officials expect to see the opposition of commercial wireless companies to effective regulation crumple up before overwhelming public opinion should this opposition manifest itself in the future as it has in the past.

THE HERALD EXHAUSTS ITS DOUBLE SUPPLY

Prints More Than Twice Normal Number of Copies and All Are Quickly Snapped Up.

More than twice the normal daily circulation of the HERALD was exhausted yesterday in an effort to supply the demands of the thousands of readers eager to learn the very last scrap of information that had been gathered by wireless and cable bulletins regarding the greatest marine disaster in the history of the world. Even then the supply was far short of the demand, and every copy of all of the five editions of the paper that were published in quick succession yesterday morning was disposed of without any perceptible lessening of the demand.

Seven full pages of reading matter were devoted by the HERALD yesterday to its recital of the sinking of the Titanic. Praise for the enterprise displayed in the gathering and presentation of the news was forthcoming from every side. Although only a very few of the names could be picked up in the multitude of crossing wireless messages, every edtion of the HERALD except the first contained a part of the list of those of the Titanic's passengers who had been saved and taken on board the Carpathia. As the later editions appeared this list was added to until when the last was issued, soon after four o'clock in the morning, every name that had drifted in over the land wires and over the ocean in wireless messages had been added to the lists.

The almost unprecedented sales of the HERALD yesterday were not confined to any one section of the city or country. From one end of oLng Island and New Jersey to the other through practically all of yesterday, increasing demands for additional copies of this newspaper were received.

Anticipating just such an emergency, twice the usual number of copies were printed, but this double supply was exhausted almost before the last of the papers were off the presses. After eight o'clock in the morning it was almost impossible to obtain a copy of the HERALD within the city limits, but the shortage was felt even earlier in the outlying sections of Queens and Brooklyn and on Staten Island. Similar reports came from upstate districts, Westchester, Connecticut and points in Pennsylvania.

FOUR OFFICERS AND OPERATOR SAVED

Captain Haddock, of the Olympic, Says Only Survivors Are On Board the Carpathia.

CAPE RACE, N. F., Tuesday.—A wireless message to-night from Captain Haddock, of the steamship Olympic, relayed by the Celtic, reads as follows:—

"Please allay rumors that the Virginian has any of the Titanic's passengers. Neither has the Tunisian. I believe that the only survivors are on board the Carpathia. The second, third, fourth and fifth officers and the second Marconi operator are the only officers reported saved."

Families of Prominence Separated by Disaster

Doubly Tragic Are Some of Losses, the Ryersons, Believed Missing, Being on Way to Funeral of Killed Son.

CAREERS OF SOME OF THE TITANIC'S VICTIMS

The fate of Arthur Ryerson, his wife and two daughters, who were passenegrs on board the Titanic and none of whose names appear in the list of those saved, is doubly tragic, because they were hurrying home on account of the violent death ten days ago in Philadelphia of Mr. Ryerson's son, Arthur, who was instantly killed when an automobile in which he was riding with a young man named Hoffman dashed into a telephone pole. Both young men were Harvard students.

The members of the Ryerson family had been touring Europe for a month, when a cablegram reached them that young Arthur had been killed. They felt the blow grievously. Mrs. Ryerson was inconsolable and the father cabled to Philadelphia directing that the burial of his son be delayed until they arrived. Passage was engaged on board the first steamship available. This happened to be the Titanic. Berths were engaged by wire and the family hastened from the Continent and made connections with the great steamship at Southampton.

The Ryersons lived at Haverford, a suburb of Philadelphia. Mr. Ryerson was a brother of Joseph T. Ryerson, of New York city, vice president of the large iron and steel firm of Joseph T. Ryerson & Son, whose offices are at No. 30 Church street, this city, and also of Edward L. Ryerson, chairman of the board of directors of the ig Ryerson concern at Chicago. He was a son of the founder of the Ryerson interests, Joseph T. Ryerson, who started in the iron and steel business in Chicago seventy years ago.

The family was prominent in Philadelphia society. It was their custom to spend the winters in Europe, cruising in the Mediterranean or at the resorts in Italy and in Spain.

Mr. Ryerson was about sixty years old and his wife was a few years his junior. A man servant and a maid of the family also are believed to have lost their lives in the Titanic disaster.

After building up a fortune in New York city in the disinfecting business Emil Taussig, whose home is at No. 777 West End avenue and whose place of business is No. 2 East Forty-second street, decided to go to Germany and found a disinfecting concern there. He left New York three months ago, accomplished the thing he started out to do and, with his wife and daughter, Ruth, started back to America on board the Titanac. The name of Miss Ruth Taussig appears in the list of those rescued, but the father and mother are thought to have gone down with the Titanic.

Mr. Taussig started in business in New York city twenty years ago, with a very modest beginning. His disinfecting business at that time occupied only a part of one room. When he decided to start a concern in Germany Mr. Taussig, desiring to combine business with pleasure, proposed to his wife and daughter that they accompany him. While he was settling the details of the new business the family found time to make a tour of Germany, Italy, England and France. The West Disinfecting Company, at Berlin, is the name of the new Taussig firm.

When the Taussigs started for Europe they closed their home in this city.

Mr. Albert A. Stewart, Eastern representative of the Strobridge Lithographing Company, of Cincinnati, with offices in the Times Building, was returning to New York city from his twenty-ninth trip across the Atlantic when disaster overtook the Titanic. His name is among the first cabin passengers, and no mention of him is made among those saved. Mr. Stewart, who is a man of considerable wealth, is almost as much a resident of Paris as of New York, and is so prominent in France in a business way that he was a member of the Board of Trade of Paris. His family usually spends the winter with him in Europe, and they are at present in Italy, where Mr. Stewart left them when business called him back to America. A native of Gallipolis, Ohio, Mr. Stewart became identified with the Strobridge Lithographing Company early in his life, and was heavily interested in the firm when he came to New York, about thirty years ago, as its Eastern representative. For several years the family has maintained no home in this city, and Mr. Stewart while here has lived at the Hotel Grosvenor, the Knickerbocker and the Plaza. Mrs. Stewart and her daughter have spent most of the time in France.

Mrs. Abraham L. Saloman, of No. 344 West Seventy-second street, torn by the conflicting emotions of grief and hope, late last night was almost prostrated after her long wait for news from the Titanic. Her husband and her daughter, Helen, who is eleven years old, were on board the sunken steamship. When the first news of the Titanic striking the iceberg came Mrs. Saloman was almost distraught. Later came the encouraging tidings that all the passengers were safe and that the vessel was being towed to port, and she felt easier in mind. Next came news of the sinking, with nearly all of her passengers. And now in the later despatches Mr. Saloman's name is given as among the survivors, but the name of the daughter does not appear. Mrs. Saloman is still keeping vigil, hoping against hope that both of those dear to her have escaped. Mr. Saloman is head of the big wholesale stationery firm of Saloman & Co., of No. 345 Broadway. Five weeks ago he went to Europe on a business trip, taking with him his daughter. While abroad he visited England, Germany, France and Austria.

Max Frolicher-Stehli, a Swiss manufacturer, and his wife, who is a sister of Mr. E. J. Stehli, of this city, head of the big silk manufacturing firm of Stehli & Co., with factories in this country and in Europe, were on their way to visit Mr. Stehli and are supposed to have gone down with the Titanic, as the name of neither appears in the list of rescued. He wooed Miss Stehli as Max Frolicher and, according to Swiss custom, assumed his wife's name when he married her. Mr. Frolicher-Stehli is heavily interested in the Stehli concern and is in charge of a silk factory owned by the company at Zurich.

A whole family that somehow escaped the disaster to the Titanic is that of E. C. Ostby, his wife and daughter Helen, who were returning from a two months' tour of Egypt. Mr. Ostby, whose home is in Providence, R. I., is head of the jewelry manufacturing house of Ostby & Barton, whose office is at No. 9 Maiden lane, this city, and which is said to have the largest factory for the making of gold rings in the world, at Providence. He founded the business thirty-five years ago, and the factory now has one thousand employes. The family spends nearly every winter abroad. Mrs. Ostby is a daughter of the late Ashbell P. Fitch, formerly Controller of New York city, and at his death president of the Trust Company of America.

E. S. Taylor, according to those in the office of W. J. Jeandron, No. 172 Fulton street, dealers in carbon brushes, is thought to be an electrical engineer, who was employed there three or four years ago. His present address, it was said, is the Spaulding Building, Portland, Ore. Nothing was known definitely as to whether the E. S. Taylor on the passenger list of the Titanic is the same man as the one formerly employed there.

J. M. Smart, president and general manager of the American Cold Storage and Shipping Company, whose offices are in the Produce Exchange Annex, was supposed to be on board the Titanic, it was said at his office yesterday. No word has been received as to whether he had actually left. Mr. Smart left for London about a month ago to attend the annual meeting of a cold storage company in Southampton. He is on of the largest owners in the concern. He was formerly superintendent of frozen meat transportation from New Zealand and Australia to England. He was accompanied by his counsel, F. K. Seward, whose name appears in the list of those saved from the Titanic and now on board the Carpathia.

Among the supposed victims is Arthur Keefe, of No. 80 Monroe street, Rahway, N. J. Mr. Keefe was returning from a three months' pleasure trip through Ireland and England. Mrs. John C. O'Brien, a sister of Mr. Keefe, received a letter from her brother yesterday in which he stated that he would leave for home on board the Titanic. Several of his friends received postal cards from him to the same effect. Mr. Keefe is well known in Rahway, being a large grocer and a leader in the republican party.

Miss Frances Shepherd, of No. 10 South Twelfth street, Newark, N. J., is a sister of Jonathan Shepherd, third assistant engineer on board the Titanic, who is believed to have gone down with the ship. She had no definite news other than the newspaper reports yesterday.

Word was received yesterday by Ivan Stengel, of No. 1,075 Broad street, Newark, N. J., that his father and mother, Mr. and Mrs. C. E. Henry Stengel, were among those saved from the Titanic. They were returning from a month's Europeon vacation. Mr. Stengel is senior member of the large leather manufacturing firm of Stengel & Rothschild.

Leo D. Greenfield was the recipient of hearty congratulations yesterday when it became known that his wife and his only son, William B. Greenfield, who were first cabin passengers on board the ill fated Titanic, were safe on board the Carpathia. At Mr. Greenfield's residence, No. 1,239 Madison avenue, many friends of the family gathered last evening to await later news from the rescue ship. Mr. Greenfield and his son are furriers, with an establishment at the corner of Fifth avenue and Thirty-second street. Mrs. Greenfield and her son had been abroad on a pleasure trip for the winter.

John Bradley Cumings, a member of the brokerage firm of Cumings & Marckwald, of No. 36 Wall street, was originally from Boston. His home was No. 50 East Sixty-fourth street. He was a member of the Racquet, Metropolitan, Riding and Knollwood Country clubs.

SCARCITY OF LIFEBOATS IS BLAMED FOR TERRIBLE TRAGEDY

CROWD IN FRONT OF THE WHITE STAR OFFICES.

MR. P.A.B. WIDENER WHOSE SON, GEORGE WAS ABOARD THE TITANIC.

COPYRIGHT by POWERS ENG. CO.

Left to Right: MR. DE WITT SELIGMAN, MRS. BENJAMIN GUGGENHEIM AND MRS. DE WITT SELIGMAN ASKING FOR NEWS OF MR. BENJAMIN GUGGENHEIM.

COPYRIGHT by POWERS ENG. CO.

MR LORILLARD SPENCER.

MRS. JOHN M. MARVIN AND MRS. FRANK FARQUARSON WHO INQUIRED FOR NEWS OF MR. AND MRS. DANIEL W. MARVIN.

MR. WILLIAM BARCLAY PARSONS.

Life Boat Scarcity Alone Held Responsible for the Appalling Loss of Life

The Titanic, Under Out of Date British Rules, Was Compelled to Carry Craft for Only 481 Persons.

AMERICA POWERLESS TO COMPEL CHANGE NOW

Enough is already known of the Titanic disaster to establish the repugnant fact that the lives of about two thirds of her complement of passengers and crew were sacrificed for no better reason than that the lifeboat and liferaft equipment provided for this most pretentious of ships was so meagre as to be barely adequate to the needs of the remaining one third aboard her who were actually rescued.

The appalling casualty has brought to public notice the even more disquieting fact that, in thus providing facilities inadequate to such an emergency, the owners of the Titanic were complying fully with British regulations governing the subject, though it is conceded that these admiralty regulations are obsolete and were framed to provide for vessels of a maximum size of 10,000 tons. The Titanic was a 46,000 ton ship, a leviathan such as was not even dreamed of in 1898, when the British regulations now in force were framed.

The Titanic sank into the ocean abyss in a smooth sea. There is nothing to indicate that, had she carried boats and rafts sufficient to have accommodated 2,400 persons, instead of less than one thousand, the Carpathia and the other vessels that were hastening to her relief might not have picked up practically all of the passengers and crew, instead of the remnant of a scant one-third who survived. The Carpathia has reported that every one of the Titanic's lifeboats has been accounted for. There is none missing and, as far as is known, none was lost after having been sent away from the sinking ship.

Fourteen Hundred Helpless.

The appalling fact stands revealed that when the last of the departing lifeboats swung away with the last of the eight hundred who had been chosen to live the Titanic's life saving devices had been exhausted. When those last heartrending farewells had been said from the darkened decks, in midnight gloom and polar cold, the fourteen hundred doomed ones who had been elected for death had no alternative but to leap into the sea clinging to some life belt or buoy, or else to wait in manly fortitude to be swallowed up in the vortex with the sinking ship.

A press association despatch from London yesterday said:—"The apparent fact that the Titanics's boats were not sufficient to accommodate the ship's personnel is causing much comment here, although the papers are chary of discussing the subject. The law does not provide the number of boats the largest ships shall carry. It only applies to those vessels displacing up to 10,000 tons, as it was passed before the present big ships had been designed or built."

In the same despatch from London Alexander Carlisle, lately chief designer for Harland & Wolk, the builders of both the Titanic and the Olympic, made this significant admission:—

"I am of the opinion that the large ships of the present day do not carry anything like a sufficient number of boats, but until the Board of Trade and the governments of other countries require sufficient boats to be carried boat owners cannot afford such extra top weight. As a matter of fact, both the Olympic and the Titanic were fitted with davits designed for and capable of carrying four times the number of boats actually fitted in the ships when they went to sea. Although a large margin was then left, I think I am correct in saying that the Titanic carried fifty per cent more than the number of boats required by the Board of Trade.

Closing Compartments at Night.

"I have little doubt that, sooner or later, when the travelling public is not so fastidious about going up or down stairs, and when they do not require to walk more than half the length of the ship without opening a door, and when the Board of Trade makes it compulsory not to have any watertight compartments open either in the hold or between decks between sunset and sunrise, then an enormous amount of risk at present existing in ships may and can be eliminated.

"If the points as to the closing of the watertight compartments and the carrying of boats are carried out, the public will be fifty per cent safer."

Acting upon the hint of obsolete maritime regulations governing ships flying the British flag, a reporter for the HERALD obtained a copy of those rules. These regulations provide a table setting forth the minimum number of lifeboats to be placed under davits and also the minimum cubic contents of the boats to be so placed upon ships of various dimensions. The largest vessels mentioned directly in this tabulated list are those of a "gross tonnage of 10,000 and upward," a fact that is readily accounted for, as the regulations were formulated in 1892, when few ships were built with a tonnage in excess of that named.

It is specified in the table that for ships of a gross tonnage "10,000 and upward" there shall be caried a minimum of sixteen boats placed under davits, of an aggregate cubic contents of 5,500 feet. The Titanic falls under the classification of Division A, class 1, which includes all "foreign going steamships having passenger certificates under the Merchant Shipping act and for those carrying emigrant passengers, subject to all the provisions of the passenger acts."

For all such craft the rule specifies that they "shall carry boats placed under davits, fit and ready for use and having proper appliances for getting them into the water, inn umber and capacity as presribed by the table in the appendix to these rules. Such boats shall be equipped in the manner required by and shall be of the description defined in the general rules oppended hereto.

Provision for Life Boats.

"If the boats placed under davits in accordance with the table do not furnish sufficient accommodation for al persons on board, then additional wood, metal, collapsible or other boats of approved description (whether placed under davits or otherwise) or approved life rafts shall be carried.

"Such additional boats or rafts shall be of at least such carrying capacity that they and the boats required to be placed under davits by the Table shall provide together in the aggregate, in vessels of 5,000 tons gross and upwards, three fourth, and in vessels of less than 5,000 tons gross one-half more than the minimum cubic contents required by column three of the table."

Supposing that the Titanic complied literally with this rule and did nothing more, the following situation would be revealed:—

The sixteen lifeboats which she is compelled to carry beneath davits would have a necessary minimum capacity of 3,500 cubic feet. Under the three-fourths rule she would have to be equipped with additional life saving devices—boats or rafts—with an additional capacity of 4,125 cubic feet, or a total capacity in all of 9,625 cubic feet.

In paragraph thirty-one of the general rules it is stated that the aggregate passenger carrying capacity of the lifeboats, rafts, &c., shall be determined by dividing the aggregate number of cubic feet by the figure ten. The result of such division in this instance is 962, which represents the entire number of persons for whom life boat and life raft accommodations should have been provided aboard the Titanic under an unmodified interpretation of the British rule now in effect.

Provisions Totally Inadequate.

The fact is, however, that the Titanic did not have to do even that much to comply with a strict interpretation of these obsolete provisions, which, at bes, would have lef more than half her personnel at the mercy of a mortally stricken and fast foundering ship. If the Titanic's has proven one thing more clearly than another, it is that watertight compartments and collision bulkheads are not the infallible safeguards they have popularly been supposed to be, especially against the terrific impact of collision with gigantic icebergs. Yet, so firmly had the bulkhead panacea been implanted in the British mind as long ago as 1808 that, in the "General Rules," paragraph 40, section 12, this vital modification of the foregoing regulations is set forth:—

"When ships of any class are divided into efficient watertight compartments, to the satisfaction of the Board of Trade, they shall only be required to carr additional boats, rafts and buoant apparatus of one half of the capacity required by these rules, but this exemption shall not extend to life jackets or similar approved articles of equal buoyancy suitable to be worn on the person."

Should the Titanic's sponsors have taken advantage of this exemption—and they would have been entirely within their legal rights in doing so—they might have cut down the carrying capacity of their life saving equipment to a minimum of 481 persons, instead of 962.

American Rules Better.

Contrary to the popular notion, the United States regulations for the safeguarding of human life on the high seas are much more modern and stringent than are those of Great Britain. Ships of American register and of 20,000 gross tons must carry a total lifeboat capacity of not less than 12,420 cubic feet, or enough space for 1,242 refugees. The United States rule further provides that for vessels exceeding 20,000 tons there must be provided "an additional boat capacity of 225 cubic feet for each additional 500 gross tons, or fraction thereof. The lost British ship is of 46,000 tons gross. Had she been under the American flag and complying with the American marine requirements her lifeboats would have had a total cubic capicity of 24,120 feet, or ample accommodations for 2,412 persons, which is somewhat in excess of the entire personnel of the Titanic's passengers and crew.

Under the present international working agreement, it is contended, the United States is powerless to enforce its own higher standards upon vessels flying the flag of foreign powers, even though such vessels may find a lion's share of their trade in the carrying of American passengers and cargoes. With Great Britain, France, Germany, Canada and the Netherlands, it was explained yesterday in the local office of the Steamship Inspection Service, the United States has in force reciprocal agreements, under which it binds itself to accept the rules in force in each of those countries as governing the ships flying its flag. They, in turn, vouchsafe to the United States a like guarantee.

To Be Formal Investigation.

At the Britsh Consul's office, yesterday, it was stated that there would be a thorough formal investigation ordered as to the loss of the Titanic and the circumstances connected with the appalling disaster, as soon as they were sure of getting all the facts.

"There is no doubt whatever that the British Board of Trade will order a formal investigation of the circumstances attending this disaster, either here or in England," it was explained. "In every case of loss, stranding, collission or serious damage to a British vessel a formal investigation of this kind is held, and it is to the experience thus acquired that we owe in large measure the splendid volume of laws which make up the British Merchant Shipping Acts.

"Needless to say, the news of the dreadful disaster has caused us great pain, and we sincerely sympathize with the relatives and friends of those who lost their lives, as well as with the company. We hope better news may reach us through the Cunard officers when the Carpathia gets in touch with land."

United States to Act.

That an investigation is contemplated by the United States authorities is indicated by the fact that Mr. Uhler, Supervising Inspector of the Government Inspection service, telegraphed from Washington to the officers of the White Star line, asking immediate information as to the number of lifeboats and life rafts actually carried by the Titanic.

A late despatch from London last night says:—

"According to some experts it would be an impossibility to carry a sufficient number of boats to accommodate all on board the mammoth liners, or if carried that it would be next to impossible to man and provision them. It cannot be doubted however, that the disaster will lead to a strict inquiry by the Board of Trade into this matter and a revision of the regulations.

"This question has already been for some time under discussion by the Advisory Committee, composed of prominent ship owners and the Board of Trade committee, and certain recommendations had been prepared, which have not yet been made public.

"The Titanic was fitted with electrically controlled watertight compartments. Therefore these should have been immediately closed from the bridge unless, as surmised, the collision so damaged the electrical apparatus as to render this impossible, or the vessel's side was torn away by an iceberg."

COMPANIES EVADE LIFEBOAT QUESTION

A point of etiquette was raised by many officials of transatlantic steamship lines yesterday when they were asked to discuss the question of whether it was customary for steamships to carry enough life boats and rafts to take away every person on board in case of disaster.

Inquiry was made at the offices of the International Mercantile Marine Company, which takes in the White Star, Red Star, Atlantic Transport, American, Dominion and Leyland lines, and at the offices of the French, North German Lloyd, Hamburg-American, Cunard and Anchor lines. Officials of all the lines except the French and North German Lloyd companies and the International Mercantile Marine Company asked to be excused from discussing the question of life boats on the ground that anything they might say might be thought indelicate in view of the foundering of the Titanic. International Mercantile Marine officers said the point had already been discussed by their vice president.

At the North German Lloyd offices an official said:—

"Under a rule of the German Admiralty steamships of this line invariably carry enough life boats and rafts to take care of the maximum number of passengers which each steamship is permitted to carry. Each life boat is kept constantly equipped with food, water and nautical instruments and boat drills are held frequently, several on board every steamship on every voyage she makes. Every time one of our steamships arrives at a German port the boats and their equipment are inspected by a German naval o½cer and the steamship's crew called to boat quarters in his presence. German passenger steamships found deficient in the matter of life boats are subject to heavy penalties."

At the offices of the French line it was said:—"Criticism should be directed at the laws defining the duties of steamships in the matter of carrying life boats, and not at the steamship companies."

TO TEST DEVICE FOR FINDING ICEBERGS

Canadian Government to Send Vessel to Fields This Summer on Scientific Mission.

[SPECIAL DESPATCH TO THE HERALD.]

OTTAWA, Ont., Wednesday.—To facilitate experiments with the device for the detection of icebergs invented by Professor Barnes, of McGill University, the Canadian government will send a vessel to the ice fields this season. It is said of the instrument, which is on the lines of a thermometer, that it will immediately detect the presence of an iceberg within an area of five miles.

Experts of the Marine Department here do not hold much hope that any bodies will be washed ashore from the Titanic to the Canadian coast. The Gulf Stream flows rapidly at the point where the ship sank, and victims of the disaster probably will be carried southward. However, orders have been issued to lighthouse keepers to keep a close watch.

The wireless telegraphic service has been instructed by the government to facilitate in every way the sending of messages to the press and public concerning the disaster. A congestion of inquiries is reported, especially from Sable Island. The Duke and Duchess of Connaught are taking a deep personal interest in the disaster, as many of their friends are among the missing.

Congress, Aroused, to Urge Bills for Greater Safety

Sufficient Lifeboats, Strict Regulation of Wireless Use and the Establishment of Safer Winter Routes Are To Be Demanded.

HERALD BUREAU,
No. 1,502 H STREET, N. W.,
WASHINGTON, D. C., Tuesday.

Thoroughly aroused by the unparalleled disaster to the Titanic, both branches of Congress to-day set themselves to finding a means to minimize the danger of such terrible occurrences. It is practically certain that these steps will be taken in Congress as a result of the sinking of the Titanic:—

A complete investigation of the accident by the Committee on the Merchant Marine and Fisheries, with a view to determining the cause and recommending legislation.

The passage of a bill prohibiting foreign vessels from entering American ports unless they are supplied with sufficient lifeboats to accommodate the full complement of the ship in passengers and crew.

The enactment of legislation providing for stringent regulations to prevent interference with wireless messages sent by ships in distress, or, for that matter, at any time, by amateurs and others.

Direction to the Secretary of State to open negotiations with foreign governments with a view to establishing an international patrol to watch for icebergs during the winter season and keep all vessels and land stations informed of their whereabouts.

Representative Oscar W. Underwood, of Alabama, majority leader of the House, in very emphatic language made it plain this afternoon that if he has anything to do with it all vessels using American ports, whether they are under the American or foreign flags, will be required to have sufficient accommodations in the way of live saving apparatus to take off every soul up to the ship's capacity. Such a bill was introduced by Representative Thomas W. Hardwick, of Georgia, a member of the Rules Committee, just before the session of the House ended to-day.

Wireless Bill Now Pending.

There is now pending before the Merchant Marine and Fisheries Committee a bill by Representative Joshua W. Alexander, of Missouri, the chairman, to regulate wireless messages. Here is the paragraph that would be most effective in preventing interference in time of disaster at sea:—

"Section 4.—That for the purpose of preventing or minimizing interference with messages or signals relating to vessels in distress or of naval and military stations by private or commercial stations the President of the United States shall establish from time to time regulations, by designation of wave lengths or otherwise, to govern said private or commercial stations which may be granted licenses by the Secretary of Commerce and Labor in accordance therewith, and such regulations shall have the force and effect of law and be enforced by the Secretary of Commerce and Labor through collectors of customs and other officers of the government as other regulations herein provided for."

This bill will be favorably reported within a short time, according to Mr. Alexander.

It was Representative Luther W. Mott, of New York, who introduced the resolution for an investigation of the accident by the Alexander committee. This resolution is certain to be adopted. Mr. Alexander had this to say about the disaster to the Titanic to-day:—

"From the meagre reports concerning the awful disaster that overtook the Titanic and the resulting loss of life, and the fact that probably less than one fourth of those on board were saved, although four hours intervened from the time she struck the iceberg until she went to the bottom, which would seem to have been ample time for the transfer of the passengers and crew to life boats, it is indicated that the lifeboats provided were wholly insufficient to protect or rescue those on board, and that the failure to provide these life boats was gross negligence and suggests a want of care in the inspection of the vessel.

Will Demand More Boats.

"The disaster also directs attention to the serious defect in the laws if they do not require ships to carry ample life boats for such emergencies as this.

"It also demonstrates that ships of great size are subject to peculiar hazards and that in the event of an accident the results may be most appalling on account of their difficulty of navigation. This was shown before in the accident occurring to the Olympic not long ago in the English Channel and emphasizes the fact that this catastrophe ought to put a stop to the building of such immense ships.

"There is no commercial need for them. They are more liable to accidents than ships of ordinary size that can be handled in an emergency with greater care. The fact, too, that the larger ships carry so many more passengers is an argument against their construction, since in case of their sinking the loss of life is so much greater.

"The press accounts of the difficulty in the transmission of the wireless messages indicate that there should be changes made in the laws regulating wireless telegraphy. It seems that soon after the Titanic struck the iceberg the wireless apparatus was put out of commission. It may be that some other method than that now in use can be devised.

"Certainly it demonstrates that the whole wireless apparatus should be separate in every way from the machinery that operates to keep the vessel in motion, so that the last thing that would be affected by a collision or other disaster would be this method of communication which enables a suffering vessel to communicate with vessels that may come to her aid.

"The Merchant Marine and Fisheries Committee will soon report out a bill to regulate radio-communication. Reports indicate that the receipt of messages from the Titanic was much hampered by the interference of amateurs. Legislation ought to be had to prevent this absolutely in the future.

"As the reports received up to this time are but fragmentary, it is too soon to know just what the conditions were or what legislation may be necessary to protect the safety of lives and property.

"It may become necessary for some action to be taken by international agreement looking to the better protection of sea traffic and regulating the size of ships and enforcing more stringent rules in the adoption of safety appliances and prescribing what routes vessels should travel at certain seasons of the year. Certainly everything should be done that can be to prevent a recurrence of the terrible tragedy that has taken place in the case of the lost Titanic."

Senator Martine, of New Jersey, strongly condemns the White Star line management for having sent the Titanic on the northern route, and will introduce in the Senate tomorrow a resolution requesting the President to confer with the Secretary of Commerce and Labor and open negotiations for an international conference with other maritime nations to agree upon new ocean lanes for travel at the season when danger from ice floes and bergs is greatest, and looking to an agreement as to lifeboats and other safety appliances.

Condemns Great Speed Mania.

"Had the race for speed not impelled the Titanic to take the northern route the dreadful disaster would not have occurred," he said, "and hundreds of homes would have been saved from desolation. But the speed God demanded his sacrifice. Mammon must be satisfied."

On the subject of insuring the safety of passengers at sea, he will urge upon the Senate that there is as great necessity for boiler inspection on board ships as on locomotives, and to see that an adequate number of lifeboats are carried.

BULKHEADS GAVE WAY UNDER GREAT PRESSURE, SAY EXPERTS

'Unsinkable Ship' a Myth, Say Naval Architects

Impact Such as the Titanic Felt Makes Bulkheads of Little Use, Declare Shipbuilders, Who Explain How Rivets Were Snapped and Water Admitted.

CALL FOR WATCHFULNESS AND LOW SPEED

NAVAL architects seen yesterday by reporters for the HERALD agreed that the tradition of the "unsinkable ship" fades into fiction when a mighty ocean steamship at even so called half speed comes into collision with a large iceberg.

So enormous is the mass, so terrific is the force to be absorbed, that when the bow of such a craft as the Titanic crashes into the floating masses, bulkheads are, in their opinion, of scant avail.

The impact is so great that longitudinal girders are forced back, rivets are sheered off as if by some gigantic chisel, and the water will rush in through the seams opened between the steel plates of the sides.

Slow speed through zones of dangers and a sharp lookout for peril are considered by experts who are studying the story of the Titanic as more important than bulkheads and frames of steel. Icebergs vary in size, but usually they are like islands, which may well be considered immovable bodies. To come into collision with them is like trying conclusions with the Battery sea wall. The great bulk of the ocean vessels of to-day gives a momentum which is speedily translated into terms of destruction.

Until some stronger form of building, combined with speed and lightness, can be devised the unsinkable ship is beyond human attainment, in the opinion of such eminent authorities as Francis T. Bowles, formerly chief naval constructor of the United States navy. The shock tears at the rivets which hold the bulkheads to the sides, and if it be strong it will open breaches where transverse walls are attached to the plates.

In the light of revelations made by Lewis Nixon, a noted ship builder of this city; by Professor Cecil H. Peabody, of the Boston Institute of Technology; by David H. Cox, of New York, formerly a constructor in the United States navy, it appears there is no assurance of safety for craft stricken by the ice Titans hurled against them by the cruel north.

It may be that some better way of warning against the white perils of the ocean lanes may be devised, that some instrument more delicate and certain than any yet invented may serve to detect the presence of icebergs at a distance in dark or mist. So far the only actual security against such disasters as that of last Sunday night lies in watchfulness and low speed.

CUSTOMS AND IMMIGRATION BUREAUS WAIVE INSPECTION OF RESCUE SHIP

At the office of William Loeb, Jr., Collector of the Port, it was said yesterday that, acting on instructions from Secretary MacVeagh, the customs authorities here had waived the right to examine passengers' effects when the Carpathia shall arrive here. Customs officials said that such a case has never arisen before.

The passengers who left here on board the Carpathia last week cannot bring anything dutiable into the country and those saved from the Titanic probably have lost all that they had. It was said that the immigration authorities also have waived the right of examination of incoming passengers, so that all those who were saved from the Titanic will be allowed to land immediately. The Carpathia will not be met by a revenue cutter.

Only a limited number of passes to the dock will be issued, the customs authorities said, and no one will be allowed to go on board the incoming rescue ship while she is under steam.

Reporters, as well as relatives and friends, will have to wait until the Carpathia is warped to her pier in the North River before greeting the survivors.

Lewis Nixon Traces Cause of Disaster to the Titanic

Builder of the Oregon Believes Rigid Longitudinals Sheared Off Rivets and Made the Watertight Bulkheads Useless.

"The disaster to the Titanic does not mean the doom of the big ship," said Lewis Nixon, shipbuilder and constructor of the battle ship Oregon, discussing the catastrophe yesterday. "We know how to b[illegible] ships which will weather the greate[illegible] but we do not build them to run [illegible] icebergs and never can. It is [illegible] build an unsinkable ship, but [illegible] good for nothing more than [illegible]

[illegible] is of the opinion that the dis[illegible] Titanic was made possible [illegible] great strength of her longi[illegible]ers, which burst the rivets and [illegible] which the water tight bulk[illegible] attached to the outside skin [illegible]ssel, and made the bulkheads [illegible] The bottom plates, he believed, [illegible] have been sprung throughout [illegible]h of the Titanic, so that the [illegible]ured into every compartment at [illegible] made attempts to close the [illegible]ht compartments of no use.

"[illegible] evident," he said, "that water [illegible] rapidly into the forward com[illegible]nts of the Titanic, sinking her by [illegible]. Had the bulkheads continued [illegible] she would have remained afloat. [illegible]erse bulkheads are made of plating [illegible] to the outside skin or plating [illegible] vessel by steel angles. They are [illegible]hened by vertical and horizontal [illegible], that the bulkheads may with[illegible] the pressure of a bulk of water on [illegible]de or the other. If the pressure be [illegible]eat the bulkheads will bulge out, dis[illegible] the rivets and opening the seams [illegible]e water can pour through into the [illegible] compartment. Or the plates of the [illegible]head may pull away from the out[illegible] plating of the vessel. In either case [illegible] effect would be the same.

Calls Turbines Inferior.

"As the water rises, of course, the pres[illegible] becomes greater, and the rate of [illegible]kage is progressive, so that when the [illegible]ater once begins to gain on the pumps [illegible] continues to gain. Enough of the bulk[illegible]eads probably leaked to bring the ves[illegible]el down by the head to the danger point. As the vessel ran up on the berg, which is easily possible, as the ice formation might have run out like a shelf underneath the surface from the lapping of the seas and the action of the winds on the exposed portion, she may have crushed in her bottom platings for some distance, letting in water from below.

"But there is another factor which probably came into play. While a vessel has transverse frames, or ribs, there are also what are called longitudinals, that is girders running lengthwise. In a vessel as strong as this these longitudinal girders are very rigid, so that instead of curling up as the bow and stern plates were crushed in, they have been forced back far enough to shear rivets and so distort the bulkhead fastenings where they were connected with the girders, thus causing leakage.

"It is easy to criticise construction after a disaster of this kind, and I have no criticism to make of the character or theory of the construction in the case of the Titanic. I have, however, pointed out disadvantages in the turbine engine before this. The turbine has a mighty forward thrust, but when it comes to a sudden reverse, such as would be necessary in a collision, it is far inferior to the old style reciprocating engine. We must not lose sight of the fact that as our ships grow larger they must not grow unweildly. It should be just as easy to handle a large ship as a small one.

Old School Sailor Missing.

"The day of foundering from high seas is past. We build our ships nowadays so that they can weather any sea, but we cannot build them proof against such a collision as this. Another thing that figures is that we don't produce sailors now like we used to. They are not so expert at handling ropes and handling themselves in tackle and rigging. The advent of the motor has brought a dearth of the old school sailor, who was expert with the oar and could man a small boat well. If even a moderate sea was running it would be next to impossible to lower the boats down the side of a vessel so large as the Titanic. The day of motor driven lifeboats is not far away and may be the solution of that problem. Where you will not find one man in fifty who can pull an oar you will find one in twenty men or women who can start a motor and keep it going.

"In this connection I am reminded that one of the German lines recently ordered from us a motor which was to be placed in a lifeboat carried on the highest part of the vessel's superstructure. A dynamo was to be connected with the motor and used to supply the power for the wireless when the main dynamos had gone under. By this arrangement the vessel could send out signals until the last moment, then the lifeboat could be pushed off, carrying those who stayed behind to operate the wireless.

"I once suggested—and was laughed at—having our ships constructed so that a large portion of one of the decks could be detached and launched over the side like a huge raft. This portion could carry the wireless apparatus as well as hundreds of the passengers, and seems a perfectly feasible way of saving many lives in such accidents as this. There is no doubt that in the case of the Titanic many of the lifeboats, especially those carried on the forward decks, were smashed by the impact, and maybe many of the men who could have manned others or worked to preserve the bulkheads were killed in the collision, leaving the crew crippled and the number of available boats greatly reduced."

SHIPS CANNOT STAND SUCH SHOCKS, HE SAYS

Francis T. Bowles, Once Chief Naval Constructor, Declares Unsinkable Vessel Is Impossible.

[SPECIAL DESPATCH TO THE HERALD.]

BOSTON, Mass., Tuesday.—Francis T. Bowels, formerly Chief Naval Constructor of the United States Navy, and head of the Fore River Ship Building Company; Professor Cecil H. Peabody, head of the department of naval architecture of the Massachusetts Institute of Technology, and other prominent experts in naval architecture, interviewed by the HERALD to-day, agreed that the construction of an absolutely unsinkable vessel is beyond human skill. They agree that the Titanic was as safe a vessel as it is possible to construct and as safe in all probability as it will be possible to construct for the next twenty-five years.

Curiously, one suggestion was offered by all, that the only safe thing for commanders to do when their vessels run near icefields is for them to turn about and run the other way. None could suggest any improvement on such a vessel as the Titanic as far as safety devices are concerned.

Mr. Bowles said:—"There is nothing that wil labsolutely prevent the destruction of a ship like the Titanic which runs into a virtually immovable object while going at full speed. The ship may remain afloat after such a shock and she may not. There is nothing known to man that will guarantee that the ship will keep afloat, however. The watertight bulkheads have been proven to be satisfactory safety devices in acidents, except those of the most unusual and looked for nature.

"It seems to me that the Titanic had one chance in a million of sinking, and that it just happened to hit into that chance. As it was, the Titanic probably would have floated after the accident if the impact was not responsible for the immediate disconnection of the machinery and the flooding of compartments, the shells of which were uninjured by the actual collision.

"It is impossible to build a vessel that will be unsinkable under the conditions such as the Titanic is said to have encountered. I should say that the only way to prevent the loss of such a ship and its passengers under the conditions which the Titanic met was for the ship's officers to avoid the icebergs. Captains should not take chances in an ice field. They should turn their ships and run the other way whenever they get in the vicinity of icebergs."

Professor Peabody said:—"There is nothing that can be suggested that will guarantee the safety of a ship that collides with a big iceberg while the ship is going at top speed, just as there is nothing that can be suggested that will guarantee the safety of a ship which runs on a reef. Ships have collided with icebergs and have run on reefs and been saved. The chances are against ships to which such things happen, however."

SAYS NO VESSEL COULD SURVIVE SHOCK

Unsinkable is indeed a relative term applied to a steamship in the opinion of David H. Cox, formerly a na[illegible] constructor in the United States navy, who was seen yesterday at the office of Cox & Stevens, naval architects, at No. 15 William street.

"Ocean assenger steamships," said Mr. Cox, are in these days practically as unsinkable as they can be made without interfering with their operation. On the other hand, no vesel is so strong that when driven at high speed she will withstand the impact with objects as large as an iceberg any more than she could withstand the effect of such a collision with the shore.

"The diseaster which befel the Titanic is such as is likely to happend in the effort to maintain a schedule across the Atlantic. Whether or not htere was a higher rate of speed maintained than conditions warranted can only be determined by investigation. I would not say that vessels of the type of the Titanic are too large, for generally speaking the larger they are the less difficult it is to make them safe against the ordinary dangers of navigation. They certainly have a better means of protecting their passengers with the increase of size and speed.

"The effort to keep up exact schedules, the distinction of keeping up the biggest, fastest regular service from dock to dock, thas they say, is not a step toward safety, but toward insecurity. There is not at present any device which is sufficiently delicate and reliable to detect the presence of an unseen iceberg. There are some very fine and carefully graduated thermometers by which fractions of a degree may be easily ascertained.

Force Is Tremendous.

"Of what good is this, however, when within a quarter of a mile of an iceberg may be a warm current. Theoretitcally, the iceberg is supposed to make the surrounding water colder as the ice dissolves, but in practice the thermometer test is of little use. One of the traditions of the sea is that the presence of an iceberg may be discerned by blowing a whistle and listening intently for the echo from any floating ice mountain which may be in the neighborhood.

"This test is applied when the vessel is going at a low rate of speed. The searchlight is of little avail in foggy weather. As a matter of fact, there is nothing which is of any practical service for detecting icebergs. The only real safety is in going very slowly and in taking no chances in regions where ice is known to exist at this season of the year.

"The iceberg is often enormous. Suppose a vessel approaches at a high rate of speed. The momentum is enormous and that momentum must be absorbed at the impact. The force so suddenly arrested by collision must be taken up and the force is directed to the crushing of the vessel. The bow of the steamer is crumpled up. The first collision bulkhead is broken and perhaps the second and third bulkhead go. The shock has gone through the vessel. It may be the blow so deranged things that the devices for closing the bulkhead doors would not operate. It may have been that the doors could not be closed if they did.

Builders Not to Blame.

"The forward compartments fill. Slowly the vessel begins to go down by the head. The pressure of water on the sides of a vessel has been calculated to a nicety. The bow of the steamship sinking gives a constantly increasing pressure on the bulkhead, which still remains intact. That gives way, the balance is overcome, the pressure increases the resultant strain at last tears away the remaining bulkhead and the vessel sinks to the bottom.

"Judging from what I have read, something like this occurred in the case of the Titanic, which remained afloat for four hours after she was struck. I believe the Titanic was as fine a ship as the intelligence of man could build, and there should be no blame attached to the builders. In these days, when speed is required, vessels cannot be built for the sole purpose of resisting icebergs.

Latest List of Survivors of the Titanic

This list of survivors of first class passengers was issued by P. A. S. Franklin, the vice president, at the office of the White Star line late last night. In making it public Mr. Franklin said that the list had been gone over and checked up by cable with the London office of the company. These survivors are among those known to be aboard the incoming Carpathia.

A

ANDERSON, HARRY.
APPLETON, Mrs. E. D., Bayside, L. I.
ABBOTT, Mrs. ROSE
ALLISON, Master, and nurse.
ANDREWS, Miss CORNELIA I., Newark, Ohio.
ALEN, Miss ELIZABETH WATON
ASTOR, Mrs. JOHN JACOB, and maid.

B

BEHR, KARL H., No. 777 Madison avenue, city.
BESSETTE, Miss.
BUCKNELL, Mrs. WILLIAM
BARKWORTH, Mr. A. H.
BOWERMAN, Miss ELSIE.
BROWN, Mrs. J. M., Boston, Mass.
BURNS, Miss C. M.,
BISHOP, Mr. and Mrs. D. H.
BLANK, HENRY.
BASSINA, Miss A.
BARRETT, KARL.
BAXTER, Mrs. JAMES.
BRAYTON, GEORGE A.
BONNELL, MISS CAROLINE.
BROWN, Mrs. J. J.
BOWEN, Miss. G. C.
BECKWITH, Mr. and Mrs. RICHARD L., Columbus, Ohio.

C

CANDEE, Mr. and Mrs.
CASSEBERE, Miss D. D.
CLARKE, Mrs. WALKER M.
CHIDNALL, Mrs. BOWERMAN.
CROSSBIE, Mrs. E. G., Milwaukee, Wis.
CARTER, Miss LUCILE.
CARTER, Master WILLIAM T.
CARDELL, Mrs. CHURCHILL.
CALDERHEAD, E. P.
CORNELL, Mrs. ROBERT (?), No. 901 Lexington avenue.
CHANDANSON, Miss VICTORINE.
CAVENDISH, Mrs. T. W., and maid.
CHAFFEE, Mrs. H. L.
CARDEZA, THOMAS D. M. and Mrs.
CUMINGS, Mrs. J. BRADLEY, No. 50 East Sixty-fourth street.
CHEVRE, Mr. PAUL.
CHERRY, Miss GLADYS.
CHAMBERS, Mr. and Mrs. N. C.
CARTER, Mr. and Mrs. WILLIAM E.

D

DOUGLASS, Mrs. FREDRICK C.
DE VILLIERS, Mrs. B.
DANIEL, Mr. ROBERT W.
DAVIDSON, Mrs. THORNTON, Montreal, Canada.
DOUGLASS, Mrs. WALTER.
DODGE, Miss SARAH.
DODGE, Mrs. WASHINGTON.
DODGE, Master.
DICK, Mr. and Mrs. A. A.
DANIELL, Mr. H. HAREN.
DRACHENSTEAD, Mr. A.

E

EMMOCK, Mr. PHILIP.
ENDRES, Mrs. CAROLINE.
ELLIS, Miss.
EARNSHAW, Mrs. BOULTON, Philadelphia, Pa.

F

FLEGENHEIM, Miss ANTOINETTE.
FRANCATELLI, Miss.
FLYNN, J. J.
FORTUNE, Miss ALICE.
FORTUNE, Miss ETHEL.
FORTUNE, Mrs. MARK, Winnipeg, Ontario.
FORTUNE, Miss Mabel.
FRAUENTHAL, Dr. and Mrs. HENRY W.
FRAUENTHAL, Mr. and Mrs. I. G.
FROLICHER, Miss MARGARET.
FUTRELLE, Mrs. JACQUES.

G

GRACIE, Colonel ARCHIBALD.
GRAHAM, Mr. and Mrs. WILLIAM G.
GRAHAM, Miss MARGARET.
GORDON, Sir COSMO DUFF.
GORDON, Lady.
GIBSON, Miss DOROTHY.
GOLDENBERG, Mrs. SAMUEL.
GOLDENBERG, Miss ELLA.
GREENFIELD, Mr. G. B.
GREENFIELD, Mrs. LEE.
GREENFIELD, Mr. WM., No. 1,239 Madison avenue.
GIBSON, Mrs. LEONARD D.
GOOGHT, JAMES.

H

HIPPACH, Miss JEAN., Chicago, Ill.
HARRIS, Mrs. HENRY B.
HALVERSON, Mrs. ALEX. M.
HAUSSING, MILO.
HOGEBOOM, Mrs. J. C., Newark, Ohio.
HAWKSFORD, Mr. W. J.
HARPER, Mr. HENRY S., and man servant.
HARPER, Mrs. H. S.
HOYT, Mr. and Mrs. FREDERICK M., No. 112 East Seventy-third street, city.
HORNER, Mr. HENRY R. (Homer?).
HARDER, Mr. and Mrs. GEORGE A.
HAYS, Mrs. CHARLES M., Montreal, Canada.
HIPPACH, Mrs. IDA S., Chicago, Ill.
HAYS, Miss MARGARET, Montreal, Canada.
ISMAY, J. BRUCE.
KIMBALL, Mr. and Mrs. E. N.
KENNYMAN, Mr. F. A.
KENCHEN, Miss EMILE.

L

LONGLEY, Miss GRETCHEN F., Newark, Ohio.
LEADER, Dr. ALICE F., No. 340 West 118th street.
LAVORY, Miss BERTHA.
LINES, Mrs. ERNEST H.
LINES, Miss MARY C.
LINDSTROM, Mrs. SINGIRD.
LESNEUR, Mr. GUSTAVE, Jr.

M

MADILL, Miss GEORGETTE A., St. Louis, Mo.
MELICARD, Mme.
MIDDLE, OLIVIA.
MAIMY, Miss ROBERTA.
MARVIN, Mrs. D. W.
MARECHELL, Mr. PIERRE.
MINAHAN, Miss DAISY, Green Bay, Wis.
MINAHAN, Mrs., Fond-du-Lac, Wis.
NEWELL, Miss ALICE.
NEWELL, Mr. Washington.
NEWSOME, Miss HELEN, Columbus, Ohio.

O

O'CONNELL, Miss R. (may be Mrs. Robert Cornell).
OSTBY, Mr. and Mrs. E. O., Providence, R. I.
OSTBY, Miss HELEN R., Providence, R. I.
OLIVIA, Miss.
OMOND, Mr. Fleunam.
NEWELL, Miss MADELINE.
PANHART, Miss Ninette.
POTTER, Mrs. Thomas, Jr., Chestnut Hill, Philadelphia.
PINCHEN, Major Arthur.
ROGERSON, John.
RENANGO, Mrs. Mamam.
RANELT, Miss Appie.
ROTHCHILD, Mrs. Lord Martin.
ROSENBAUM, Miss Edith.
RHEIMS, Mrs. George.
ROSIBIE, Miss H.
ROTHES, Countess.
ROBERTS, Mrs. EDWARD.
ROLMANE, Mr. C.
RYERSON, Miss SUSAN P.
RYERSON, Miss EMILY.
RYERSON, Mrs. ARTHUR.

S

STONE, Mrs. GEORGE M., Cincinnati.
SEGESSER, Miss EMMA.
SEWARD, Mr. FREDERICK K., the Devonshire, 112th street, Broadway.
SHUTES, Miss E. F.
SLOPER, WILLIAM T., New Gritain, Conn.
SWIFT, Mrs. F. JOEL, 171 Arlington avenue, Brooklyn.
SCHABERT, Mrs. PAUL, Derby, Conn.
SHEDDEL, ROBERT DOUGLASS.
SNYDER, Mr. and Mrs. JOHN.
SEREPECA, Miss AUGUSTA.
SILVERTHORN, R. SPENCER.
SAALFIELD, ADOLPH.
STAHELIN, Mr. MAX.
SIMONIUS, ALFONSIUS.
SMITH, Mrs. Lucien P.
STEPHENSON, Mrs. WALTER B.
SOLOMON, ABRAHAM.
SILVEY, Mrs. WILLIAM B., Superior, Wis.
STENMEL, Mr. and Mrs. O. E. H.
SPENCER, Mrs. W. A., and maid.
SLAYTER, Miss HILDA.
SPEEDEN, Mr. and Mrs. F. O.
STEFFANSON, H. B.
TUCKER, Mrs., and maid.
THAYER, Mr. and Mrs. J. B.
THAYER, J. B., Jr.,
TAUSSIG, Miss RUTH, No. 777 West End avenue, city.
THOR, Miss ELLA.
TAYLOR, Mr. E. K.
TAYLOR, Mrs. E.
TUCKER, GILBERT.

W

WOOLNER, Mr. HUGH W.
WARD, Miss ANNA.
WILLIAMS, RICH. M.
WARREN, Mrs. F. N.
WILSON, Miss HELEN A.
WILLARD, Miss CONSTANCE.
WICKS, Miss Mary, Youngstown, Ohio.
WIDENER, Mrs. GEO. D., and maid.
WHITE, Mrs. J. STEWART.

Y

YOUNG, Miss MARIE.

Second Class Passengers.

A

ANGLE, Mr. WILLIAM.
ABELSON, Mrs. HANNA.

B

BALLS, Mrs. ADA E.
BUSS, Miss KATE.
BECKER, Mrs. A. O. and three children.
BEANLE, Mr. EDWARD.
BEANE, Mrs. ETHEL, Miss ESTELE.
BROWN, Mr. (T. W. S.?).
BROWN, Miss EDITH.
BRENTHAM, LILLIAN W.
BYSTRON, KAROLINA.
BEIGHT, DAGMAR.

C.

CLARK, Mrs. ADA.
CAMERON, Miss.
CALDWELL, ALBERT F.
CALDWELL, Mrs. SYLVAN.
CALDWELL, infant ALDEN.
CARMACION, RENARDE.
COLLYER, Mrs. CHARLOTTE.
COLLYER, Mrs. MARJORIE.
CHRISTY, Mrs. ALICE.
COLLET, STUART.
CHRISTA, MOSS DUCIA?
CHARLES, WILLIAM?
CROFT, MILLIE MALL.

D.

DOLING, Mrs. ELSIE.
DREW, Mrs. LULU.
DAVIS, Mrs. AGNES.
DAVIS, Miss MARY.
DAVIS, JOHN M.
DURAN, FLORENTINE.
DURAN, Miss ASINCION.
DAVIDSON, Miss MARY (?).
DOLING, Ada (?).
DRISCOLL, Mrs. B. (?).
EMCARCION, Mrs. RINALDO.
FAUNTHORPE, Mrs. LIZZIE.
FORNERY, Miss ELLEIN.
GARSIDE, ETHEL.
GERRECIA, Mrs. MARCY.
GENOSESE, Mr. ANGERE.
HART, Mrs. ESTHER.
HART, CHILD. ANNA (?).
HARRIS, GEORGE.
HEWLETT, Mrs. MARY.
HARPER, NINA.
HOLD, Mr. STEPHEN.
HOSENO, Mr. MASABUMI.
HOCKING, Mr. and Mrs. GEORGE.
HOCKING, Miss NELLIE.
HERMAN, Mrs. JANE.
HEALY, NORA.
HANSON, JENNIE.
HAMATAINEN, Mr. W.
HAMATAINEN, Mr. HANNA.

J

JACKSON, Mrs. AMY.

K

KEANE, Miss NORA A.
KELLY, Mrs. F.

L

LEITCH, JESSIE.
LAROCHE, Miss SIMMOME.
LAROCHE, Mrs. JOSEPH.
LAROCHE, Miss LOUISE.
LEHMAN, BERTHA.
LAUCH, Mrs. (ALEXANDER).
LENIORE, AMELIA (ELIZABETH).
LINKKANCE, Miss ANNIE.

M

MELLINGER, ELIZABETH.
MELLINGER, child.
MARSHALL, Mrs. (KATE).
MALLETT, Mr. A.
MALLETT, Mrs.
MANGE, PAULA.
MARE, Mrs. FLORENCE.
MELLOR, Mr. J.
McDEARMONT, Miss LILLIE.
McGOWAN, ANNA.

N

NYE, ELIZABETH.
NASSER, Mrs. (all), Mrs. DELIA.

O

OXENHAM, Thos. (P. J.)
PHILLIPS, ALICE.
PALLAS, Mr. EMILIO.
PADRO, Mr. JULIAN.
PINSKY, ROSA.
PORTALUPPI, EMILIO.
PARSH, Mrs. L.

Q

QUICK, Mrs. JANE.
QUICK, Miss VERA W.
QUICK, Miss PHYLLIS.

R

RIDSDALE, LUCY.
RENOUF, Mrs. LILY.
RUGG, Miss EMILY.
RICHARDS, Mr. EMILE.
RICHARDS, EMILY, two boys and Mr. Jr.
ROGERS, Miss ELIZA.

S

SINCOCK, Miss MAUDE.
SMITH, Miss MARION.
SHELLEG, Mrs. WILLIAM.
SILVEN, LYLLE.

T

TROUTT, Miss E.
TROUTT, Miss CECILIA.

W

WILLIAMS, C. CHARLES.
WEISZ, Mrs. MATHILDA.
WEBBER, Miss SUSIE.
WRIGHT, Miss MARION.
WATT, Mrs. BESSIE.
WATT, Miss BERTHA.
WEST, Mrs.
WEST, Miss CONSTANCE.
WEST, Miss BARBARA.
WELLS, ADDIE.
WELLS, Master.
WELLS, Miss.

The Titanic Was "Sideswiped," Says Architect at Cramps

W. A. Dobson Believes Vessel Attempted to Veer Off After Sighting Iceberg and Had Compartments Ripped Open.

PHILADELPHIA, Pa., Tuesday.—W. A. Dobson, naval architect at Cramps' shipyard here, in discussing the Titanic disaster, says that to make these colossal craft safe it will be necessary to perfect steering appliances. At present he thinks the big boats unmanageable when going at reduced speed.

"The Titanic was literally 'sideswiped' by an iceberg, which ripped open her side, flooded numerous water tight compartments, possibly including the pump engines, and caused her to sink rapidly," said Mr. Dobson. "This is the only explanation I can conceive.

"To me it seems the ship, with the momentum accumulated with her vast bulk and great speed attempted to veer off after sighting a great iceberg. The vessel failed to clear the mass, which caught her side and ripped open a series of compartments, flooding a sufficient section of the ship to cause her to founder with great rapidity.

"There are at least thirty such compartments in a vessel the size of the Titanic. In general there is a minimum requirement that the ship must be so constructed that any two of the compartments could be flooded without bringing a stated deck below the surface of the water.

"Such speed as the Titanic is capable of, combined with her enormous displacement, would cause her to strike an obstacle with great force, certainly with a force sufficient to tear through, even the double hull.

"The watertight compartments honeycomb a ship. That is, they run longituudinally and transversely, cutting the vessel into a series of blocks of both sides of the ship, and with several layers separated by watertight decks. It will thus be seen just how great the damage done by the iceberg must have been to cause the liner to founder.

"When these large vessels, such as the Titanic, are running at a good rate of speed all is well and good. But let them slow down, say to eight or ten knots, and I doubt if they can be managed. There are various ways in which this difficulty might be overcome.

"One way might be to increase the rudder area. The steering appliances of these big ships, I am sure, can so be improved that the vessels could be easily managed no difference what their speed. But such is not the case now. They must have speed to get steerage way."

Luther D. Lovekin, who holds a similar post with the New York Shipbuilding Company, in Camden, thinks the larger the ships the better. He combats the theory that the big vessels are uncontrollable when running slowly.

"The larger they are the better and safe rthey are," said Mr. Lovekin. "And they will build them larger some day than they do now even. Ships 1,200 feet long will be uilt at no distant time. The only thing to limit the size of ships will be the area of harbors.

The larger the vessel the more massive her structure, the better able to withstand shocks and to ride the waves in the most turbulent seas. Large vessels are not unmanageable when going at slow speed."

Vessel Hit Iceberg with Force of 37 Express Trains

Experts Declare That the Titanic in Fatal Crash Had Pressure of 13,500,000 Tons—Say No Steamship Could Have Withstood Strain.

Engineers figured yesterday that when the Titanic hit the ice she struck with a force equal to that of thirty-seven Empire State Express trains travelling at the rate of seventy miles an hour.

With her cargo and passengers, the Titanic had a displacement of about 60,000 tons. Because of the danger of the locality it is thought she proceeded at a speed of about fifteen knots an hour. Figuring on the basis accepted by naval architects and engineers, the Titanic struck the iceberg with an impact force of 13,500,000 tons. If the Empire State Express had struck the same object the force of the impact would be approximately 367,500 tons, it is declared.

Henry J. Gielow, of the firm of Gielow & Orr, naval architects and engineers, of No. 52 Broadway, said yesterday that no ship ever built could withstand such a terrific strain. The force of the blow thought to have been dealt to the bow plates of the Titantic, it is said, in all probability caused her longitudinal plates, from end to end, to shear off and clip every rivet in her sides. This would open up every water tight compartment in the vessel, say experts. If the rivets which held the forward plates of the Titantic could be recovered, it is said, they would be found to have been clipped off as neatly as if the work had been done by a skilled mechanic.

Another possible cause of the rapid sinking of the big steamship advanced by Mr. Gielow's partner, Alexander M. Orr, Jr., is that she grounded on a submerged iceberg, tearing off her keel plates and thus opening up the water tight compartments. Mr. Orr said he had talked with the captains of several ships and that most of them had given this as their version.

Mr. Orr said there were many things which might happen to a ship in collision with a huge iceberg. He likened such a collision to one with a block of granite of the same size as the berg and said that in all of his experience as a designer and builder of ships he has never known of any method of ship construction which could make a vessel strong enough to withstand the force of such a collision.

Society, Mourning for Titanic Victims, Cancels Many Events

Mrs. J. P. Morgan, Jr.'s, Dinner and Dance for Debutante Daughter, One of Largest Affairs of the Season, Abandoned and Many Invitations Recalled.

The gloom that has overspread the city as the result of the Titanic disaster had pronounced effects upon the social events of yesterday. Informal dinners that had been arranged for last evening were abandoned. The tea hour found comparatively few persons at the leading hotels and restaurants, and those who gathered took their refreshment in a perfunctory manner and sought news of friends aboard the ill-fated steamship.

Charity events set for the afternoon and evening were carried out, but the audiences were small. Several women who had engaged tables for the bridge tournament at Sherry's in aid of the Samaritan Home for the Aged sent their checks but did not make personal appearance. Among the latter was Mrs. George Arents, Jr., who sent word that, as friends were among those unaccounted for aboard the Titanic, she could not bring herself to take personal charge of her table.

The most pronounced effect on the events in society was the abandonment by Mrs. J. Pierpont Morgan, Jr., of the dinner and dance she had arranged for last evening at her home for her débutante daughter, Miss Jane N. Morgan. It was to have been the rfist large affair by Mrs. Morgan for her daughter, although several dinners had been given for her during the season.

It was not until the real news of the disaster was brought to Mrs. Morgan during the early afternoon that she took hurried steps to inform those who had been invited, that the dinner and dance had been cancelled. At first it was reported that Boston relatives of Mrs. Morgan were aboard the steamship, and had not been accounted for, but this proved to be untrue. She told her friends that the dance would be so conflicting a note with such general mourning throughout the city, that she had abandoned it.

There was to have been a dinner of forty guests and one hundred and fifty additional had been asked for the dance and supper. It took a greater part of the day to inform them over the telephone and by special messages of her decision.

VINCENT ASTOR IN COLLAPSE AFTER VIGIL

Is Taken to His Home from Offices When Father's Fate Seems Certain.

Following a night and day of nervous tension, without time for sleep and hardly opportunity for refreshment, Vincent Astor, son and heir of Colonel John Jacob Astor, collapsed yesterday afternoon at five o'clock. He was at the office of the Astor estate when he reached the limit of physical endurance. He was hurried to his home, where it was said last evening that there was no alarm over his condition.

Ever since Colonel Astor's son reached manhood and entered college he and his father had been almost constant companions. Rather than have his son separated from him the Colonel took his son with him on his trips, accompanied by a tutor, who prepared him for hi sentrance examination for Harvard, his father's Alma Mater.

The son spent last night at the office of the Astor estate in almost constant communication with the office of the White Star line, the various press associations and the nswspaper offices. He returned home for breakfast and then visited personally the steamship office. The remainder of the day he spent at his father's office. His collapse came when there seemed to be no doubt but that, while Mrs. Astor had been saved, his father had gone down with the steamship.

NAVY OFFICERS FAVOR ICE PATROL SCHEME

Opinion at New York Yard Favorable to the Herald's Idea of Ocean Lookout Service.

The idea of the establishment and maintenance of a patrol where icebergs are often in evidence was termed practicable by officers of the New York Navy Yard consulted yesterday.

"At a time like this," said one officer, "every one feels that any expense is justifiable to eliminate an accident such as befell the Titanic. And it is the expense of the maintenance of a patrol service in the ice fields which has to be considered. Congress complains at the expense of maintaining the cutter service along the coast, and yet these cutters are almost daily making actual rescues. If a patrol were established along the transatlantic lanes I am afraid that soon—after the shock of this disaster has passed— the cry would be raised against that expense.

"But the patrol would be an excellent thing. A fairly good lookout could be kept on ice floes and on the largest icebergs, and steamships could be apprised of their location by wireless messages. However, the real solution is a route further south, where icebergs are fewer."

"It would be a valuable thing to have a patrol to keep track of icebergs," said another officer. "In establishing the present lane for steamships going westward I believe it was thought that the ice floes and the fogs would be largely escaped. But evidently this has not been realized. So I would suggest the longer and safer route and the establishment of a patrol."

"A patrol could keep watch fairly well on the ice floes and fog," said another officer, "and could perhaps keep vessels informed of the larger icebergs and ice fields, but in my opinion the effect would be to confuse captains and to keep the passengers in a constant state of alarm. A vessel's watch and her various instruments must see or feel the iceberg if she plies in seas where there are icebergs."

"A course further south is my idea," said another officer. "This would be the safe way. The voyage would be longer, but the added expense would be less than the expense of maintaining a patrol, if the transatlantic steamship companies paid for the patrol."

HYSTERICAL CROWDS BESIEGE THE WHITE STAR LINE OFFICES

Loss Estimated at from $20,000,000 to $35,000,000

Greatest Amount of Maritime Insurance Must Be Paid by Great Britain and Germany, but America Will Suffer by Loss of Cargo.

AN INCREASE IN THE RATES IS PREDICTED

Marine underwriters in this city were agreed yesterday that the loss of the White Star line steamship Titanic was the greatest in the history of marine insurance. In the opinion of experts the insurance loss ran all the way from $20,000,000 for hull, cargo, baggage and life insurance, to $35,000,000.

This insurance risk is divided, by means of the principle of reinsurance, between the underwriters of this country, Great Britain and Germany. The greatest loss falls naturally upon the British underwriters. Much reinsurance was placed by them in Germany, however, while in this country about ten per cent of the risk on the hull has been underwritten. But Americans, it was stated in Wall street yesterday, probably will have to bear the burden of the insurance risk on the vessel's cargo, which probably will not amount to more than $1,000,000. This figure, however, is exclusive of any diamond shipments, which were insured separately.

According to a prominent Wall street broker, the Titanic carried $3,000,000 in diamonds and a quarter of a million dollars worth of rubber. There were also aboard the vessel many thousand dollars worth of high class securities and specie. The specie has been lost irrevocably, but the bonds and stocks can be duplicated.

Insurance Eagerly Sought.

William A. Prime, vice president of the firm of Willcox, Peck & Hughes, who are agents for many marine insurance companies in this cty, sad:—"The Ttanic was insured on a basis of $1,000,000 deductible average, which means that there must be a loss of not less than $1,000,000 before the insurance companies and underwriters can be called upon to pay anything.

"The vessel, being a total loss, it follows that all of the insurance companies and underwriters will suffer. The sum of insurance placed in excess of $1,000,000, deductible average, was $5,000,000. This amount was spread all over the world, mostly in the large marine insurance companies of the great nations.

"The prsopect of a complete loss of a ship owned by the White Star line was regarded as being so remote that the insurance of such a vessel was eagerly sought for by the major marine insurance companies.

"With respect to the cargo, since the vessel had only 1,500 tons aboard the value of the goods will scarcely exceed $1,250,000. The story that $5,000,000 worth of diamonds were aboard is almost unquestionably wrong. We are fairly certain that there were no securities aboard.

"The value of the ship was $10,000,000 and it really worth it. This loss, coming so close on the recent loss of $5,000,000 in bullion which went down on the Peninsular and Oriental line steamship Oceana in the British Channel, means for many of the insurance companies a serious matter o fbusiness, and will affect the prosperity of most of the marine insurance companies."

American Bankers Interested.

Lloyds, of London, an association of capitalists, who insure the maritime risks of the world, are said to have had the largest risks on the hull and cargo. The nearest approach to a similar organization in this country is the United States Lloyds, of No. 3 South William street.

While the London Lloyd's is more in the nature of an insurance exchange, which may be attended by any man who has an established financial reputation, the American concern, on the contrary, is composed of one hundred members, who not only assume the financial responsibility, but employ attorneys to place the risks. Among the members are M. Orme Wilson, Frank A. Vanderlip, president of the National City Bank; Eugene Kelly, A. Iselin & Co., John Claflin, Flint & Co., Adolph Norden, A. Foster Higgins, J. P. Morgan & Co., Walter P. Bliss, James B. Dickson, Herbert Appleton, J. Ogden Armour, Louis F. Swift, Louis Muller, B. N. Baker and Rufus Woods.

"The object of an association of capitalists," said a representative of the United States Lloyd's yesterday, "in marine insurance is that such insurance differs materially from fire or other forms of insurance. In first risks many policies are issued on one building. But where a shipper is sending, say, $100,000 worth of goods abroad he prefers to have a single policy and then reinsure it with his neighbors, thus distributing the risk.

"Greatest Maritime Loss."

"Personally, I cannot say whether any large amount of the insurance on the hull of the Titanic has been underwritten here, but with regard to the insurance on the cargo it is a different matter. There are about one hundred shippers of consignments. Shippers from abroad who are sending goods to this country would naturally insure their risks in their own country, but the consignees on this side insure their property in this city. Baggage as a rule is not insured. The steamship company is not regarded as being responsible for the risks of the sea, unless negligence can be proved against the company.

"I have no personal knowledge of any large consignment of diamonds to this port aboard the vessel, but if such precious freight was sent the value of it must be left to the imagination. It is impossible to compute it. This also holds good in the case of specie.

"I would regard the loss of the Titanic as the greatest loss in the history of marine insurance. Still, the loss need not cripple any one. Single members of Lloyd's, of London, who took risks too great for them to bear, may be made to suffer. But in the general run the risks have been distributed very widely and the loss will not fall heavily upon any individual firm of underwriters."

An officer of one of the largest marine underwriting houses in the city, at No. 51 Wall street, said he agreed with his associates in regarding the loss of the Titanic as the greatest disaster in marine history. He said he could not recall a greater loss from a financial standpoint. In the case of the Oceana there would be some recovery, but in that of the Titanic the loss was complete.

According to this authority, the value of the vessel had been exaggerated. He did not believe that it had cost the company $10,000,000. In his belief the vessel represented an outlay of not more than $7,500,000. eH said that the insured value was probably $5,000,000, but that it was unlikely that so much insurance had been placed, owing to the reluctance of the underwriters to place so large an amount upon a single vessel.

Insurance Carried Here.

It was stated by this officer that estimates made as to the value of the cargo at $500,000 were far too low. He believed that the cargo was valued at at least $1,000,000. With regard to the insurance on the latter, he expressed the belief that most of it was carried here. He said that there was not a marine underwriter in Nw York city who was not carrying a full line of insurance on the cargo.

Goods sent by British manufacturers to be sold in this country were not, as a rule, hem aintained, sent on the fast steamships of the transatlantic lines. As a rule, such goods were owned by the consignees and represented orders given by houses on this side, who owned the goods when they were afloat, and therefore insured on them for their own benefit. Such freight, being of a high class nature, was able to pay the highest charges.

He also maintained that an estimate of the full value of the cargo was an impossibility, for if there were representatives of leading jewellers aboard they might be carrfying merchandise of a phenomenal value.

As for the matter of baggage, the officer said he would rather insure freight than baggage, since the value of the freight cauld be learned by means of bills of lading, while much of the cargo was a matter of conjecture.

Predicts Raise in Rates.

He did not believe the loss of the steamship with her cargo was a heavy blow to the marine insurance world, since the risks were so widely distributed by means of reinsurance. Underwriters, he said, reinsured their risks from a variety of motives. Some of them were led to this step because they believed they were taking too heavy a responsibility on one steamship. Others, after they had made their contracts, had misgivings as to the nature of the risk, and desired to be relieved of the burden. Others again had the opportunity to reinsure at a lower rate, and saw a profit in such a transaction.

The opinion was expressed that marine insurance risks will undoubtedly be raised on account of the Titanic disaster, especially since this month has been a disastrous one for the underwriters.

According to John E. Gardin, vice president of the National City Bank, only a comparatively small amount of securities was aboard the vessel. "The amount of such securities," said Mr. Gardin, "was unimportant, and that is due to the fact that there is no big movement in securities on at this time. Foreign banks have on deposit here at present securities aggregating $75,000,000 to $100,000,000 in value."

Efforts to learn in the Maiden Lane diamond district if there was a large amount of diamonds aboard the Titanic were futile. At the offices of Ludwig Nissen, No. 182 Broadway, it was said that firm had no consignments aboard. tA the offices of the Jewelers Board of Trade, No. 18 John street, the statement was made that there was no knowledge in the district of shipments approximating $3,000,000 to $5,000,000 in value, although it was admitted that no information would be given out as to the shipments of any firm, since such publication was contrary to practice.

UNITED STATES CANNOT FORCE MORE LIFEBOATS

HERALD BUREAU,
No. 1,502 H STREET, N. W.,
WASHINGTON D. C., Tuesday.

Although the United States government requires that all American vessels carry enough lifeboats and rafts to accommodeate all the passengers and crew, this regulation does not apply to foreign vessels. Since little shipping save that in coastwise commerce flies the American flag, the hundreds of thousand of Americans who go abroad annually enjoy no protection from the American steamboat inspection service.

When it became known in Congress today that the Titanic carried only enough life saving craft for one-half its passengers strong sentiment developed in favor of requiring all foreign ships calling at American ports to carry enough life boats and rafts for the rescue of passengers and crew. Mr. George Uhler, supervising inspector general of the steamboat inspection service to-day declared himself in favor of such action.

"I believe Congress ought to give this subject its most earnest attention. It is too bad such an appalling tragedy should be needed to emphasize the need of vigorous action.

"Just how far Congress ought to go, it is not for me to say. Nor am I attempting to interfere with the jurisdiction of the State Department. But I am firmly convinced the British law which regulates the number of life boats such great vessels shall carry is inadequate, and that Congress ought to take this fact into consideration in determining what attitude ought to be adopted by the United States."

Mr. Uhler, who was one of those who investigated the Slocum disaster, declared that if the Titanic had been subject to the laws governing such craft in the United States she would have been compelled to carry forty-seven large life boats, each with a capacity of forty-eight persons.

The Titanic had only sixteen life boats and four collapsible life craft, with a total capacity for 1,100 persons.

"The Titanic was not amenable to the United States, save to the extent provided for in the Revised Statutes," continued Mr. Uhler. "The law says that the inspection service may compel foreign vessels to observe the laws of their own countries. They are not compelled to ive up to the requirements imposed by the United States on its own steamships.

"The British Board of Trade, under the rulings of which the Titanic operated, provides that a ship of 10,000 tons or more must be equipped with sixteen lifeboats of a minimum cubic capacity of 5,500 feet. Vessels of 20,000 tons must equip themselves with 12,420 cubic feet of lifeboat capacity and steamships which exceed that tonnage must have 225 additional cubic feet of life saving space for each additional 500 tons or fraction thereof.

"Had the Titanic been an American craft, operating under our laws, she would have been compelled to provide a life saving boatage of 23,670 cubic feet, or a capacity for carrying 2,367 persons, more than double the number which were really provided for by the unfortunate steamship.

"The United States does not boat its steamship according to the number of passengers, and neither does any other country. But the United States does require that every vessel must carry enough lifeboats or life rafts to take care of every passenger and every one in the crew.

"A seagoing vessel of between 150 and 200 tons, for example, must have at least 540 cubic feet of lifeboat capacity, or sufficient to take care of 54 persons. Vessels of greater size must regulate their number of lifeboats according to the ratio already mentioned.

"England is one of the countries with which the United States has a reciprocal agreement as to the inspection of passenger carrying craft. We have a similar understanding with France, Germany, the Netherlads, Sweden and Japan. No agreement at all exists between the United States and Italy, Austria or Spain and they, therefore, must observe the same regulations as the American merchant marine.

"In the case with countries with which the United States has no reciprocal understanding, the clearance papers may be refused such vessels as do not observe the law. The same thing can be done with all countries if the present law is changed accordingly."

FATE—OR ECONOMY IN LIFE BOATS.

The Arizona's Iceberg Collision 33 Years Ago Told by Passenger

Guion Line Vessel, One of the First Steel Steamships, Badly Damaged, Backed 220 Miles Into St. John's After Night of Terror.

Recalling a disaster similar to that which overtook the Titanic, and at almost the same spot, thirty-three years ago, R. J. Horner, of R. J. Horner & Co., No. 26 West Thirty-sixth street, yesterday told of his experiences when the Arizona, of the old Guion line, crashed into an iceberg off the Newfoundland coast on the night of November 9, 1879. The bow of the Arizona, which was making her second crossing, was smashed in from the bow to several feet below the water line, but the water tight bulkheads held, the Arizona reversed her engines, and backed to St. Johns, Newfoundland, 220 miles away. With a speed of seventeen knots, steel hull and conveniences which were the marvel of the time the Arizona was the first vessel to be called an "ocean greyhound." She was one of the first of the steel steamships, from which developed such giants as the Titanic and the Olympic.

"I recall distinctly the shock," said Mr. Horner. "It was a clear night, and the iceberg was plainly visible, a great billowy mass of white, on the eastern horizon. It was not the season in which mariners expect icebergs, and the captain thought this was a cloud, until we were too close to stop.

"We struck head on, going at full speed, at nine o'clock. No one had gone to bed, and most of the men were sitting in the smoking room conversing or playing cards. We had only kerosene lamps in those days, and they went out with the first shock. There was a terrific crash and we were thrown from our chairs. The tables and other furniture were broken and we were piled up on the floor. Then came a second crash, as the engines did not stop immediately, and we plunged against the iceberg after the first recoil.

"I ran out on the deck, which was listing sharply. There were 120 passengers aboard, and from the darkness within the vessel came shouts, cries and screams that were terrifying. As I reached the deck I say the great wall of ice stretching above me. The iceberg rose 700 feet above the water, and was at once a majestic and terrifying sight. Tons of ice lay all about the deck, and we knew in a moment what had happened. The bows were bent back upon themselves for thirty-five feet, and the gaping hold filled with all manner of débris. Seven sailors who were in the quarters in the forecastle were injured, but there was no loss of life.

"The women crowwed to the rail, and the darkness and swirling black water added to the terror of the mighty crash. The engines were stopped, and the captain lay too for five hours while the damage was inspected. It was found that we were taking no water, but that it would be impossible to proceed ahead, so the captain decided to back toward St. Johns. We were making seventeen knots when we hit the berg, but it took us all of a day to make the trip to St. Johns backward.

"Two days were required to clear the broken ice and other débris out of the rent in the Arizona's bows. Another similarity to the Titanic disaster was that Stephen Guion, one of the owners of the line, was on board the Arizona at the time."

OSCAR STRAUS HURRIES FROM HOT SPRINGS

Cousin of Major Butt Sends Message to President Taft Inquiring for His Aid.

[SPECIAL DESPATCH TO THE HERALD.]

HOT SPRINGS, Va., Tuesday.—Interest here centres in the Titanic disaster. Many visitors had relatives and friends on board. Despatches have been received at the Homestead, where there is a direct wire to New York, and visitors have crowded there. New York papers of this morning and evening will not reach here till to-morrow. Oscar Straus is cutting short his visit and returning to New York to-night with Mrs. Straus.

Mrs. George Gunton, a cousin of Major Archibald Butt, came down from Gunton Lodge early this morning to send despatches to President Taft.

Mrs. John Topping, of New York, whose sister, Miss Margaret E. Graham, was on board, received telegrams this morning reporting her safe. Others who had relatives on board were Mr. and Mrs. Rawson Wood, of New York, whose cousins, Mr. and Mrs. Frank P. Wood, were passengers, and Mrs. B. Louis Swift, of Chicago, whose sister-in-law, Mrs. Frederick J. Swift, was on board.

WASHINGTON TRIBUTE TO MAJOR BUTT

Engagements Cancelled While Social Leaders Are in Doubt as to His Safety.

HERALD BUREAU,
No. 1,502 H STREET, N. W.,
WASHINGTON, D. C., Tuesday.

Society is paying a marked tribute to the popularity of Major Archibald Butt, U. S. A., whose fate is still in doubt because of the incomplete reports of the Titanic disaster, and on every hand not only is the greatest concern expressed, but several of the leaders in society are cancelling dinners and dances because of the fear that he met death when the big steamship went to the bottom.

Mrs. Richard H. Townsend had issued invitations for a dinner and dance to-morrow night for Mrs. E. R. Thomas, of New York, but to-day recalled them when it seemed almost certain that Major Butt was not among those on board the Carpathia. Several other women had arranged for dinners to precede the dance at Mrs. Townsend's, and these also have cancelled the entertainments.

Throughout diplomatic, official and residential circles inquiry was made during the day for Major Butt and for Mr. Clarence Moore, whose family is in the greatest distress over the absence of encouraging reports.

Should it be definitely known that Mr. Moore and Major Butt are lost it is unlikely that the hunt ball arranged by officials of the Chevy Chase Club for next Friday night will be held. Mr. Moore was one of the most popular officers of the club for many years.

Miss Helen Taft and Mr. Robert Taft have a half dozen guests at the White House, but anxiety over the probable fate of Major Butt has caused them to cancel all engagements.

START WORK TO AID TITANIC VICTIMS

Committee of Fifteen Is Organized at Home of Mrs. Nelson Herrick Henry.

First steps toward the organization of an association for the relief of rescued passengers of the steamship Titanic who may arrive at New York in a destitute condition were taken last night by Mrs. Nelson Herrick Henry, of No. 59 West Ninth street, who formed a committee of fifteen. This body, which will be known as the Organization Committee of the relief committee to aid the steerage passengers of the steamship Titanic, will begin its work at once.

The committee is composed of Mrs. Henry F. Dimock, Mrs. Cornelius Vanderbilt, Sr.; Mrs. Herbert L. Satterlee, Mrs. James Herman Aldrich, Mrs. Richard Irvin, Mrs. William Church Osborn, Mrs. Henry Whitney Munroe, Mrs. Charles B. Alexander, Mrs. Paul Dana, Mrs. Arthur Murray Dodge, Mrs. J. Van Vechten Olcott, Mrs. Edward Hewitt, Miss Eleanor G. Hewitt, Miss Sarah Cooper Hewitt and Miss Virginia Potter.

This committee invites members and volunteer workers, and urges the contribution of money and clothing. The temperoary headquarters will be at No. 59 West Ninth street. Members of other organizations are invited to co-operate with the association.

The organization committee will meet to-morrow afternoon either at the Colony Club or at the home of Mrs. Abram S. Hewitt, No. 9 Lexington avenue. Announcement will be made through the press.

A. S. HOLMES TRAINED IN WHITE STAR LINE

[SPECIAL DESPATCH TO THE HERALD.]

WHEELING, W. Va., Tuesday.—Alfred S. Holmes, ranking officer to Captain Smith on board the Titanic, and who is presumed to have gone down with the vessel, was a brother of Captain Charles Holmes, of Grafton, who is in Wheeling to-day, and who has been captain of several ocean and lake vessels. This morning he received a telegram from New York confirming press despatches of the disaster and informing him of the probable death of his brother.

"I suppose my brother is dead," said Captain Holmes this morning, "because by all established rules of navigation he would be one of the last to leave the ship."

As a boy Alfred S. Holmes was trained for service in an official capacity on White Star line steamships and he had spent most of his life in the service of this company. For several years he was captain of the Egyptian Khedive's yacht during the time he lived in Alexandria, Egypt. Since his return to the White Star line, howeverfi he had been making his home in Liverpool, Ennngland. He supervised the construction of the Titanic.

Throngs of Grief Stricken Women at Steamship Office

Anxious Crowds Besieging White Star Line Headquarters Give Way to Tears or Hysterics When Told of Death or Rescue of Loved Ones on Board the Titanic.

VESSEL TO SEARCH SCENE OF THE DISASTER

The specter of gloom awakened by the tragedy of the Titanic stalked unrestrained in and about the White Star line's offices at No. Broadway yesterday. While thousands thronged Bowling Green anxiously awaiting additional details of the disaster, hundreds of relatives and friends of missing passengers on board the steamship crowded the offices of the steamship company in search of news. Scenes of despair and sorrow were of frequent occurrence throughout the day.

It was a tyying day for all concerned, a day that will live long in the memory of all who participated in its stirring events. Handsomely dressed women sat in their automobiles at the curb, and with saddened faces and tear dimmed eyes awaited the report of their messengers as to the safety and well being of their loved ones. Many burst into tears when told that the names they were searching for did not appear in the latest list of those rescued and went away in blank despair. Others sobbed for joy when they learned that their loved ones were safe and rushed gladly away to spread the joyful tidings.

It was apparent at an early hour yesterday that the offices of the steamship company would be besieged throughout the day by thousands, and the officers of the company requested that the police of the Greenwich street station should give all the aid in their power. Forty policemen, some of the mounted, were detailed for the service and they were on duty throughout the day keeping the crowd from massing in the front offices and in preserving order. Three men guarded the steps leading to the offices and prevented the rank and file from unnecessarily crowding the vestibule leading thereto.

President Taft Anious.

Telegrams of inquiry and telephone calls poured in upon the White Star officers ceaselessly. Chief among these was a telegram from President Taft asking if news had been received of the probable fate of his aid, Major Archibald W. Butt, and if so to notify him without delay. P. A. S. Franklin, vice president of the White Star Company, replied that there was no news of Major Butt, but that if any message was received giving the desired information it would be forwarded to the White House instantly.

After a consultation with several officers of the company Mr. Franklin made the following announcement at ten o'clock last night:—

"The White Star Steamship Company has arranged to have the steamship Mackay Bennett, which was at Halifax, to proceed at once to the scene of the disaster and remain there to search for the bodies of passengers of the Titanic."

A report was received from London that Charles M. Hays, president of the Canadian Pacific Railroad Company, and Jacques Futrelle, the novelist, had been picked up by a passing steamship and now are on their way to London. There was no confirmation of the report available at the offices of the White Star company last night.

Vincent Astor, son of Colonel John Jacob Astor, telephoned to Mr. Franklin several times, asking if news had been received of his father. He was informed that the latest wireless telegrams announced the safety of his step-mother, Mrs. Astor, but in a voice choking with sobs he repeated the question, "But what about my father; haven't you heard from him?" Mr. Franklin could only reply in the negative, and he assured Mr. Astor that if the news he was searching for arrived no time would be lost in apprizing him of the fact.

Sylvester Byrnes, private secretary to Isidor Straus, remained at the offices all night in the hope of getting some reassuring news regarding the fate of Mr. Straus. He left at eight o'clock in the morning and after a few hours returned to keep his fruitless vigil. When the list of survivors sent out at noon failed to show the name of Mr. Straus Mr. Byrnes gave up all hope and sadly took his leave.

A remarkable incident in connection with the sinking of the Titanic was the loss of Mark Fortune, a leading business man of Winnipeg, Manitoba, who, with his wife and daughter, were first class passengers on board. Mr. Fortune was on board a steamship which foundered off Vancouver Island with heavy loss of life twelve years ago. Mr. Fortune escaped, but when he was rescued his hair had turned white. This was his first ocean voyage since that disaster, and a relative who visited the White Star offices in the hope that Mr. Fortune may have been picked up with his wife and daughter, both of whom were rescued, said that Mr. Fortune had repeatedly predicted that the voyage would be fatal to him.

Women in Hysterics.

Two well dressed women, both weeping bitterly, inquired of the clerks if J. McGough, European buyer for Gimble Brothers, of Philadelphia, who was on board the Titanic, had been heard from. When told that his name did not appear on the list of the rescued they became hysterical and, refusing to disclose their identity, ran sobbing into the street.

Accompanied by her brother, De Witt J. Seligman and Mr. and Mrs. Daniel Guggenheim, Mrs. Benjamin Guggenheim, whose husband was a passenger on board the Titanic, visited the White Star offices about noon and tearfully inquired if news of her husband had been received. When told that his name did not appear in the incomplete list of survivors sent in by the Carpathia, she refused to accept that as final, and asked if no other vessels were in search of other survivors. Mrs. Guggenheim was the picture of despair and she wept when, after scanning the revised list of survivors, she failed to find the name of her husband.

On the verge of collapse after a night of worry over the fate of his wife, Magistrate Robert C. Cornell was among the first to reach the White Star offices, and when told that his wife's name was not on the list of survivors, he fell half fainting into a chair. He said that Mrs. Cornell had gone to Southampton several weeks ago to attend the wedding of her sister, who is Lady Hammond. She was accompanied by her sisters, Mrs. E. B. Appleton and Mrs. J. Murray Brown, both of whom appear to have been saved. Magistrate Cornell said that he could not understand how his wife was separated from his sisters, as they occupied the same suite, and he still entertains the hope that she may be with other survivors on board the Carpathia.

Bridal Couples on Board.

Relatives of Mr. and Mrs. George Harder, a bride and bridegroom, of Brooklyn, who were returning home from a bridal tour of Europe, were overjoyed when their names appeared upon the list of survivors rescued by the Carpathia. Mr. Harder is a son of Victor Harder and his wedding with Miss Dorothy Annan in January was a notable event in social circles of Brooklyn.

In a voice choked with emotion, Mrs. Agnes Haran, of No. 446 West Fifty-fifth street, asked for information regarding her mother, Mrs. Mary Mack, of Southampton, who was on board the Titanic. Mrs. Haran said her mother was fifty-seven years old and had been persuaded to make her first voyage to this country by her daughter and other relatives in this city, although she expressed fear of the outcome. The name of Mrs. Mack does not appear on the list of survivors thus far.

A bridal couple among the passengers for whose safety fears are expressed are Mr. and Mrs. D. W. Marvin, of No. 317 Riverside Drive. The name of Mrs. Marvin appears on the list of survivors, but no news of Mr. Marvin has thus far been obtained. At the time of the marriage of the couple the ceremony was photographed by a moving picture operator, this bein the first instance of the kind on record. Mr. and Mrs. H. N. Marvin, the parents of the bridegroom, together with D. G. Carmichael and Miss Carmichael, brother and sister of the bride, were inconsolable when told that the name of Mr. Marvin had not been reported os one of those rescued.

Several relatives of Washington Roebling, 3d, living in Trenton, N. J., spent the day at the White Star offices, hoping to obtain news that the young man had been rescued, but in this they were disappointed. Mr. Roebling is a son of Charles G. Roebling and a grandson of John A. Roebling, a well known bridge builder and founder of the Roebling Steel Works, one of the largest in the country. Mr. Roebling had been abroad for some weeks and joined the Titanic at Southampton.

Daughter Saved, Mother Missing

Mrs. Cahn and two daughters, of No. 777 West End avenue, inquired for news regarding Mr. and Mrs. E. Taussig, who were on board the Titanic with their daughter, Miss Ruth Taussig. The list of survivors issued at noon bore the names of E. Taussig and Miss Ruth Taussig, but the name of Mrs. Taussig did not appear among those saved. Mrs. Cahn and Mrs. Taussig are sisters, and when she learned that her sister's name did not appear on the list of survivors Mrs. Cahn became hysterical.

A handsomely gowned woman seated in a taxicab asked the reporters if the name of Wier appeared on the list of those saved. She refused to reveal her idntity, and when told the name did not appear on the list she collapsed and a physician was called to administer a restorative. The woman then started uptown, with the statement that she would return later. Among the first class passengers on board the Titanic the name of J. Wier appears, but it is believed he went down with the ship.

One heart weighted with the deepest anxiety was lightened when Mrs. Butts, of Newark, N. J., forced her way into the office of the steamship company and asked regarding the safety of Mr. and Mrs. C. F. Stengle, of Newark. On being told that the names were on the list of survivors Mrs. Butts sank upon her knees and voiced a prayer of thankfulness. Men watched her with moistened eyes and a dozen strong hands assisted her to her feet.

H. W. Watson, an engineer of prominence in Buffalo, reached the city early yesterday in quest of news regarding his friends, Mr. and Mrs. Edward Kimberly, both residents of Buffalo, where they are well known socially. The names of the Kimberlys appeared on the list of survivors.

H. E. Sprague, a broker, with offices in Broad street, made anxious inquiries regarding his relative, Miss E. M. Eustis, one of the Titanic's passengers, and when the clerks were unable to find the name upon the list of survivors he left the building in the deepest distress, but hopeful that a later list would declare her safe.

Hears Whole Family Is Saved.

Nathan Vidaver, a lawyer of No. 116 Nassau street, was overjoyed when he learned that his sister, Mrs. Washington Dodge, wife of the assassor of San Francisco, had been rescued. No news regarding Mr. Dodge had been received up to a late hour, and it is believed that he was lost. Mr. Dodge was in public life in San Francisco for more than twenty years, and was one of the most prominent residents of the Pacific coast.

Mrs. Henry Herschell Adams, of No. 806 Madison avenue, was overjoyed when told that her nephew, William E. Carter, his wife and two children had been rescued. Mrs. W. T. Carpenter, mother of a passenger of that name, was prostrated when she learned that there were ne tidings of her son. Mrs. Carpenter is a wealthy woman of Philadelphia, and she came to New York early in the day in the hope of hearing that her son had been saved.

Miss Eleanor Bishop, whose brother, Walter Bishop, was one of the stewards on board the Titanic, scanned the list of survivors in vain for the name of her brother. She expressed the hopse that he might have been assigned to one of the life boats, and that he may have been saved.

There were numerous inquiries from the financial district. Financiers, lawyers, brokers and others having relatives and friends on board the Titanic sent messengers to the White Star offices for the latest bulletins from the Carpathia. The fate of Edgar J. Meyer, vice president of the Braden Copper Company and a brother of Eugene Meyer, Jr., of the stock brokerage firm of Eugene Meyer, Jr., & Co., was repeatedly inquired about. There were inquiries also regarding the safety of Bradley Cumins, of the Stock Exchange firm of Cumins & Marckwald. In neither instance was assuring information forthcoming, the names of neither appearing on the list of survivors. The wife of Edgar J. Mayer, a daughter of Andrew Saks, founder of the firm of Saks & Co., also was on board the Titanic, but her name does not appear among those of persons rescued by the Carpathia.

No News of W. H. Spencer.

Lorillard Spencer, Jr., visited the offices during the afternoon and asked for information regarding his aunt and uncle, Mr. and Mrs. W. H. Spencer, of New York.

Miss Ella Wilhelm, of No. 2,270 Broadway, accompanied by two sisters, asked for news of her brother, Charles Wilhelm, a second cabin passenger. They were unable to get information and the young women wept bitterly when told that there was little probability that he escaped death.

While half crazed men and women thronged the offices below, Mr. Franklin, vice president and general manager of the White Star Company, sat in his private office anxiously awaiting delayed wireless messages from the Carpathia and the Olympic. Several messages were received, but their contents were not immediately made public, and Mr. Franklin explained that he was not prepared to reveal the contents of his code messages without full reflection.

"I did not give out the first message of Captain Haddock, of the Olympic, regarding the disater in full last night," he said, "because it was so discouraging that I felt that it would not be right to alarm the public unnecessarily when there was a bare chance that the news might not be wholly true."

GOVERNMENT PATROL OF ICE FIELDS URGED BY THE HERALD

Another Sacrifice to the "Speed God," Declare Men in Revenue Cutter Service

Vessel Could Not Back Off and Reverse Her Engines, Says Captain Uberroth—Representative Sulzer Asserts Big Steamships Go Ahead in Mad Race Regardless of What Is In Their Path.

HERALD BUREAU,
No. 1,502 H STREET, N. W.,
WASHINGTON, D. C., Tuesday.

'Another sacrifice to the speed-god."

That is what Captain P. H. Uberroth, assistant to the commandant in charge of personnel and operations of the Revenue Cutter Service, thinks of the Titanic calamity. Captain Charles McAllister, engineer in chief of the service, takes a similar view.

"The Titanic," said Captain Uberroth today, "was so big that it was impossible for her officers to avoid collision with an iceberg or other similar object without lights on a dark night. They might sight the iceberg some distance away, perhaps enough to save a smaller vessel, but a ship of the Titanic size would not answer to the helm promptly enough to avoid collision. She could not reverse her engines and back off. Such an attempt would be futile unless the berg was sighted a mile ahead, for going at full speed, approximately twenty miles an hour, she could not be brought to a stop and reversed. She carried tremendous headway with her powerful engines and great size.

"The ocean going travellers of this country do not realize that with increased size and speed of vessels they must be the sacrifice in accidents of thi kind. They are unavoidable. The layman doe not realize this fact, but it preys continuously on the mind of the navigator.

Captains Helpless.

"The captain usually has sleepless nights when he is travelling on forty-four in the spring and early summer, for the floating ice and bergs are the greatest menace of the ocean. The chances are not one in a hundred that he will run directly on a berg, but if you do the captain is practically helpless. He knows his fate in an instant.

"There are many things that may have caused the sinking of the Titanic. It is likely we never will know the real facts, but my opinion is that her bulkheads gave way under the pressure. The larger the bulkheads—that is, the greater area they have to cover—the weaker they are. The traverse water tight bulkheads of the Titanic were necessarily of enormous size. They were made as strong as man could make them, but any hydraulic engineer will acquaint you with the tremendous power of water pressure. If the force of the impact stove in the bow and collision bulkhead the bow would go down. The Titanic's hull was forty feet deep, and the lower her nose sank the greater the pressure. This pressure was increased because with any momentum moving her ahead the bulkhead, being at right angles, met full resistance.

"The iceberg the Titanic struck may have been extremely low in the water. If so the keenest eyed lookout could not detect it on a dark night. A calm sea removed one safeguard against an iceberg. Mariners will tell you that sudden calm water when the sea is rough or choppy will pressage an iceberg before it is visible."

Called Acme of Marine Safety.

Captain McAllister, who is an expert on construction said:—

"The Titanic was believed to be the acme of marine safety. She was of extraordinary heavy and strong construction. I believe she struck the ice with sufficient impact to crush in her bow and forward bulkhead, and perhaps one other.

"In that case many things could happen. It is possible the watertight bulkheads gear refused to work, was thrown out of running order by the force of the collision. Even in that event the Titanic would have been some time sinking because she was credited with being almost unsinkable. Then, too, it is possible that her bulkheads could not withstand the pressure. On our battle ships there is a control lever for all bulkheads that the captain can work from the bridge in anticipation of collision.

"I am confident the berg rammed by the Titanic was not glacier ice, but was one of the shore icebergs formed by the extremely cold winter. It is too early for berg ice. According to Patterson's Nautical Encyclopaedia, if it were shore ice of salt water, nine tenth of its bulk was below water. This would mean that if there were only twenty feet showing above the surface, a small speck compared to the Titanic, the berg would have a total depth of 200 feet, with 180 feet below the surface. Ice conditions are worse this year than they have been for a decade."

"Mad Race for Speed."

"Desire for speed, carelessness of danger—things common to all of the big Atlantic liners—are responsible for the disaster to the Titanic," said Representative Sulzer, of New York city to-day.

"I am convinced," contined Mr. Sulzer, "that there was no excuse for the Titanic's striking an iceberg. I have been in the Arctic regions many times. I have spent days and nights in the fishing smacks on the Newfoundland banks. Vessels that go among icebergs for days and nights at a time seldom if ever hit them. If they do they do not injure themselves badly.

"The reason is simple. In the first place it is absolutely foolish for a vessel to steam at a high rate of speed, at a rate fast enough to cause injury in case she strikes ice—if there is danger of ice being anywhere around. But the big vessels go ahead in their mad race for speed records regardless of who or what is in their path."

DR. FRAUENTHAL SAFE, AGED FATHER LEARNS

Hospital Surgeon, His Bride and Brother, a Lawyer, Are Among Those Rescued.

Samuel Frauenthal, who Monday night was prostrated with grief and anxiety for the safety of his two sons and daughter-in-law, first cabin passengers aboard the Titanic, yesterday celebrated his eighty-sixth birthday at his home, No. 783 Lexington avenue, with much rejoicing. The aged man was informed by a HERALD reporter early in the day that his sons and daughter were safe aboard the Carpathia.

The rescued persons are Dr. Henry W. Frauenthal, physician and surgeon in chief of the Hospital for Deformities and Joint Diseases, in Madison avenue; his wife and his brother, I. Gerry Frauenthal, a lawyer, of New York city. Dr. Frauenthal and his wife were married in Nice, France, March 26, and his brother was his best man. The bride was Miss Clara Heinsheimer, of Nice, who met Dr. Frauenthal when she visited New York some years ago.

With the receipt of the news Monday night that the majority of those aboard the Titanic had perished the members of the Frauenthal family, who had been making extensive preparations to welcome the physician and his bride, were plunged, with thousands of other relatives of the lost ones, into the depths of despair. Dr. Herman C. Frauenthal, of No. 146 West Seventy-second street, another brother of the bridegroom, and chief of clinic and orthopaedic surgeon at the hospital scoured the city for some news of his brother and sister-in-law, stopping occasionally to telephone vague reassurances to his prostrated father. Nothing definite could be obtained, however, until the HERALD informed the family of the brothers' safety, and the octogenarian parent shouted for joy.

Father Shouts for Joy.

"Tell me truly," he said—"tell me truly if they are safe. I cannot stand such another shock." Being assured that his sons and daughter were safe aboard the Cunard steamship when that vessel was last heard from, his face wreathed in smiles and he walked about his son's office with a lively step.

"This is the happiest birthday I have ever had," he confided to the reporter." It is even more pleasant than if nothing whatever had happened and my sons were with me now, as they would have been. Of course I want to have them safely by me before I shall really feel sure. But I know they are safe now. I can feel it."

The tears sparkled in the venerable parent's eyes as his third son shook him warmly by the hand. Numerous friends arrived to offer sympathy, and found congratulations to be in order. Dr. Herman C. Frauenthal said to the HERALD:—"We may seem selfish in our joy, when so many others were dragged to eternity with the stricken vessel, but this reaction must follow the awful night we spent. I had much work to do to-day, but I simply could not trust myself to attempt it.

"The loss, had my brother been drowned, would not have been felt by us, his immediate relatives, alone. The work of the hospital to which he has dedicated his life would suffer, and I am afraid much that is to be done and much that is but half accomplished would never be completed.

Organizer of Hospital.

"I could not begin to enumerate the many lines of work to be picked up by my brother upon his arrival. He and I organized the Deformities and Joint Diseases Hospital five years ago, and I believe the institution is regarded as among the first in the country to-day. Strong in mind and body—he is over six feet in height, as is my brother Gerry—Henry has literally forced the work of the hospital to its present status. I feel proud of him," and with a smile, "almost as proud of him as my father is."

Both physicians are well known in medical circles, and when it was learned Monday evening that the hospital chief and his bride were probably among the missing deep anxiety was felt by his many friends and associates.

Dr. H. C. Frauenthal added that had his brothers and sister-in-law been among the lost ones his father could hardly have survived the shock. Referring to his father he said:—"His whole life's happiness has been centred in the accomplishments and achievements of his sons, and such a blow must indeed have proved too much for him."

I. Gerry Frauenthal was listed among the rescued with "Mrs. Frauenthal." Dr. Frauenthal assured the HERALD that this must be a mistake, or there was but one Mrs. Frauenthal, the wife of the physician, aboard the Titanic.

NINE PHILADELPHIANS AMONG THE MISSING

George D. Widener and His Son, Harry Elkins Widener, Believed To Be Lost.

[SPECIAL DESPATCH TO THE HERALD.]

PHILADELPHIA, Pa., Tuesday. — With every flag in Philadelphia at half mast, business at a standstill, weeping, sorrowful crowds in front of the newspaper offices eagerly devouring every bulletin giving some news of the Titanic, this city, with the rest of the world, is in mourning. Philadelphia has suffered much. The latest lists of the survivors of the terrible accident fail to give the names of nine Philadelphians known to have taken passage on board the Titanic. They are:—

Widener, George D., financier and patron of art.

Widener, Harry Elkins, his son.

Dulles, William C., retired broker.

Williams, C. Duane, retired business man.

Williams, Richard Norris, his son.

McGough, J. R., buyer for Gimbel Brothers.

Calderhead, E. P., buyer for Gimbel Brothers.

Gustave, Louis, valet to T. D. M. Cardeza.

Keeping, Edward, valet to George D. Widener.

Among the passengers rescued appears the name of Mrs. Emma Ward Bucknell. She is the widow of William Bucknell, philanthropist and founder of Bucknell University.

Late this afternoon a cablegram was received from J. Horace Harding, of the firm of Charles D. Barney & Co., that he did not leave on board the Titanic. He and Mrs. Harding have been travelling in Europe with Henry C. Frick.

There are also several persons from Philadelphia or nearby towns passengers on board the Carpathia. They are making arrangements to meet the Carpathia with clothing for their friends on the assumption that the Carpathia passengers, especially the women, probably gave all their surplus clothing to the Titanic sufferers.

In addition there were more than one hundred passengers in the steerage of the Titanic booked for Philadelphia. Of these unfortunates few persons thought until this morning when the dwellers from the Ghetto stormed the local newspaper offices, tears streaming down their faces, asking in broken English for tidings. They came in droves, and whole families were turned away after being informed that the White Star line did not have a list of their steerage passengers.

Along with these poor people suffered P. A. B. Widener, father of George D. Widener. Even this man of millions appealed to the newspaper offices for "something definite." Last night the White Star officials gave him some encouragement. They informed him that John B. Thayer, a close friend of Mr. Widener, had been saved, and therefore it was likely Mr. Widener also was among the survivors. They also informed him that Colonel John Jacob Astor had gone down with the ship, but that Mrs. Astor and Mrs. Widener had been saved. After this information the White Star telephone disconnected.

All night Mr. Widener and his son Joseph E. Widener paced the floor of their beautiful mansion calling up the newspaper offices at regular intervals. At seven o'clock this morning Mr. Widener declared he could stand the suspense no longer and started for New York. Miss Eleanor Widener remains at home. It was on her account that her father and mother went abroad. Recently her engagement was announced to Fitz Eugene Dixon, and Mrs. Widener went to choose her daughter's trousseau. That trousseau to-day lies two miles under the sea.

This bulletin has puzzled many. It purported to come from Robert W. Daniel, a business man of Philadelphia and a passenger on board the Titanic. It was sent to his mother and read:—

"Am safe. We are entering Halifax harbor now."

None of the newspapers had any word of any vessel that had been near the wreck entering the harbor of Halifax at the hour at which the message was received.

Late this evening Edmund Robins, secretary of the University of Pennsylvania, received a cablegram that his sister, Mrs. Joseph Pennell, the writer, had been unable to leave by the Titanic. The cablegram was signed by Robert Underwood Johnson, editor of the Century Magazine, who also was thought to have left by the Titanic.

Mayor Blankenburg and Mr. John Wanamaker are using all means within their power to spread any good news that is received.

SCOUT CRUISERS GO TO MEET THE CARPATHIA

HERALD BUREAU,
No. 1,502 H STREET, N. W.,
WASHINGTON, D. C., Tuesday.

Rush orders were issued by the Navy Department to-day for the swift scout cruisers, the Salem and the Chester to put to sea immediately and intercept the Carpathia, which is slowly coming into New York with survivors from the Titanic. At the same time President Taft has directed that a revenue cutter be sent from New York and one from Boston to meet the incoming steamship. It is expected by this means to shorten the nerve racking hours of delay in getting accurate information of the Titanic's survivors.

The Salem in command of Commander Lloyd H. Chandler, happened to have steam up at Hampton Roads and got under way at about four o'clock this afternoon. The Chester, commanded by Commander Benton C. Decker, left Boston yesterday for Philadelphia. The Navy Department sent a message to the Naval Torpedo station at Newport to get a wireless to the ship, informing her commander to meet the Carpathia instead of coming to Philadelphia.

The two swift scouts, capable of making 26 knots, will proceed full speed, at the same time endeavoring to get accurate wireless reports from the survivors. Both these vessels have powerful wireless sets. The Salem has a slight start in the race, but the Chester is more speedy and may overtake her.

On her trial speed the Salem made 25.95 knots and the Chester 26.52 knots.

The President still hopes that Major Archibald Butt may be on board the Carpathia. The President sent a copy of each telegram received by him to the family of Major Butt at Augusta, Ga., and added hopeful words of his own. It became known this morning that Colonel Archibald Gracia was among those rescued and that he was aboard the Carpathia.

No report has been received concerning Clarence Moore. At the office of Senator Guggenheim and at the Guggenheim home no tidings of any kind had been received from the Senator's brother, Benjamin Guggenheim.

The failure to get news of Major Butt cast a gloom over the White House all day.

The Major's genial nature and amiable qualities were forgotten in thought of Major Butt, army officer and man. Those who knew him best are more anxious than ever to-day, for they say that while there were other lives to save he would have little thought of his own, and that he doubtless sacrificed all thought of personal safety in the great tragedy in which those about him were plunged.

MR. GUGGENHEIM DESPAIRS.

HERALD BUREAU,
No. 1,502 H STREET, N. W.,
WASHINGTON, D. C., Tuesday.

Senator Guggenheim, of Colorado, after a day of anxious waiting and eager hope for some word from his brother, Benjamin Guggenheim, head of the International Pump Company, who was a passenger on board the Titanic this afternoon abandoned hope. Senator Guggenheim was not in the Senate Chamber during the day, and spent only a short time at his office in the capitol.

"My brother had been abroad on a business trip," he said, "and had visited his offices in London and Paris. There was no other member of th efamily with him."

ROUTES OF STEAMSHIPS CHANGED TO AVOID ICEBERGS

To avoid all danger of icebergs the principal transatlantic steamship lines agreed yesterday to use the extreme southerly route. News of the agreement was received at the Cunard offices in this city in the following cable despatch from Liverpool:—

"All lines have agreed eastbound steamships use extreme southerly track, crossing longitude 47 in latitude 40.10, commencing April 16. We have telegraphed Boston. Please instruct Carmania and other steamships. Westbound change, crossing longitude 47 in latitude 41, comes into operation April 25."

Heretofore it has been customary for vessels making the transatlantic crossing in five or six days to use the northern route the year round, despite the danger from icebergs.

News by Wireless to Boy Operator

WILLIE COTTER AND CHARLES WERNER, WIRELESS OPERATORS AWAITING NEWS OF THE TITANIC DISASTER.

Will Cotter Reads Herald Despatches and Is Alert for Tidings Concerning the Titanic.

With receivers clasped tightly to his ears and seated before the wireless apparatus that he made, "Will" Cotter, sixteen years old, received in his home, in Hoboken avenue, Jersey City, the flashes sent from the HERALD's wireless station at the Battery concerning the disaster to the Titanic early Monday morning. Seated beside the young operator was his boon companion, Charles Werner, one year his senior.

Although he has been studying wireless telegraphy for less than a year "Will" was able to read the dots and dashes exactly. A group of friends read the despatches as rapidly as they were received.

"Will" hurried home from school yesterday hoping to catch more news.

To take the HERALD wireless despatches was easy for him. He has taken messages from as far south as Cape Hatteras and north to Cape Cod. He has been able to pick up messages from ships 250 miles at sea.

For his code "Will" has selected his initials "W. C." Half a dozen of his young friends also are interested in wireless and spend their evenings at work with him.

He has a tuning coil, fixed and variable condensors, galene and perikon detector. His sending apparatus consists of a one inch spark coil, telegraph key, sending condensor and a helix. For power he used a storage battery of six volts 60 amperes.

On the wall over the table the young operator keeps the latest shipping charts from the Sunday edition of the HERALD.

The Rev. J. Stuart Holden Was Not on Board Vessel

Delayed by Illness of His Wife, the Herald Learns—Prayers Offered in Churches and in Street for Victims and Their Relatives.

Wherever a prayer was offered or wherever a church door was opened yesterday petitions were lifted to the Throne of Grace for the sufferers from the most terrible catastrophe in modern times. The Roman Catholics and other communions which permit of prayers for the dead offered up petitions for the repose of the souls of the hundreds of men and women who went to a watery grave. All other communions prayed for the thousands of stricken families on two continents.

Especially fervent were the prayers of thanksgiving that the Rev. J. Stuart Holden, vicar of St. Paul's, Portman square West, London, and regal chaplain to the Earl of Aberdeen, was not on board. Dr. Holden engaged passage on board the ill-fated Titanic and cabled to this country his intention of crossing. But just before embarking time it became necessary for his wife to undergo a very serious operation. He cancelled his passage the day before the Titanic left port.

Just as the greatest anxiety was felt for the safety of Dr. Holden, the early passenger lists all having contained his name, a cable message was received by Mr. William R. Moody, of East Northfield, Mass., under whose auspices Dr. Holden was to come to the United States for a month of Bible lectures, that he must either postpone or cancel his trip entirely. Mr. Moody communicated this news to his uncle, Mr. Fleming H. Revell, the book publisher, of No. 158 Fifth avenue, and it was there that the HERALD learned positively that Dr. Holden was not on board the Titanic.

Dr. Holden is as well known here as in England. He was to have spoken at the Men and Religion Movement in Carnegie Hall, conducted a mission the first half of next week in St. Ann's Episcopal Church, Brooklyn, and preached at Princeton, Chicago, Montreal and East Northfield. He expected to spend a month in this country.

At the annual meeting of the Classis of New York yesterday in the Marble Collegiate Church, which takes in the ministers and officers of the Reformed Church, when definite news came that the Carpathia was steaming toward this post with all the survivors on board, those present with one accord put aside all business and went into a season of prayer and meditation.

Instructions were issued from headquarters to all the leaders of the Men and Religion Movement to pray for the afflicted. A great blight has been cast over the entire campaign in this city because W. T. Stead, of London, was on board the Titanic. Up to a late hour last night he had not been accounted for. He was crossing the ocean especially to speak at a big open air mass meeting in Union square next Saturday afternoon and later in Carnegie Hall.

General rejoicing was expressed when a HERALD representative was able to tell the leaders positively that Dr. Holden was not on the Titanic.

"This tragedy has a solemn significance to our movement," said the Rev. B. Guild to a HERALD reporter. "It is going to give a significance to the religious side of our campaign that otherwise might not have been produced.

At a noonday meeting of women at the Fifth Avenue Prebyterian Church yesterday, led by Mrs. John Henry Jowett, wife of the pastor, prayers were offered for the afflicted.

At the closing meeting of the winter conducted yesterday on the stoop of the Sub-treasury by the Rev. Dr. William Wilkinson, Trinity's missioner, known as "the Bishop of Wall street," reolutions were adopted extolling the captain of the Carpathia for his heroism. These were signed by the Rev. Dr. William T. Manning, rector of "old" Trinity, and Henry Clews.

Mr. Wilkinson said:—

"In all the great historic past never has Trinity Parish had a nobler opportunity of doing that for which Jesus Christ appointed it than it has at this hour. To comfort those that mourn, to cheer the sad, to speak to the sorrowful sweetly and helpfully, and this we now do. I scpeak for the church at the head of Wall street, for the rector, for the vestry, for this great daily noon meeting, made up of all sorts and conditions of men, when I say we thank the captain of the Carpathia and his officers, who has just sent his office word that he has more than eight hundred rescued on board his ship and is coming to New York. All hail to him a nd his good ship and help! The friends of the saved will bless him and his fellows. We thank God he could be there.

"To the families of those who have passed from our sphere of action we send word of tender, pure, sweet sympathy, and we commend them to God and to the word of His grace, which will prove sufficient as no human word can. The affluent, the gifted the successful, the known men who had made names in letters, politics, law, commerce and in religion. All came to one end. With their families we sympathize, we condole.

"But the ship's crew—the stewards, the engineers, the firemen, who left happy homes, sweet children and loving wives—to these we turn with feelings no words can express. For them we pray."

As soon as definite news is received arrangements will be made by different communions for memorial services. The delay is due to lack of definite facts. Cardinal Farley went to Washington yesterday to attend a meeting of the trustees of the Catholic University. He was accompanied by Mgr. Michael J. Lavelle, of the Cathedral, and Mgr. James V. Lewis, his secretary. It was said, however, at Catholic diocesan headquarters last night that all the 962 priests of the diocese would remember the victims and their afflicted families in their masses.

BROADWAY MOURNS FOR MR. HARRIS

Friars Dinner Poseponed Until Fate of Theatrical Man is Known.

Fear that Henry B. Harris perished in the Titanic disaster has affected theatrical circles as nothing else in recent years. Little else was talked of yesterday along Broadway than the probable fate of the prominent manager. The news that Mrs. Harris was safe on board the Carpathia cheered their friends somewhat. If they could have heard that her husband also was saved theatrical circles would have had good cause for rejoicing.

Because of the uncertainty as to Mr. Harris, the Friars Club, of which both he and his father, William Harris, are members, announced that a dinner it was to give for David Warfield next Sunday night, has been postponed. It was to be the last of the Friars dinners for the season, and was to be held in the Hotel Astor. Mr. Warfield is a close friend of Mr. Harris, and in view of all the facts the Friars unanimously agreed to put off the entertainment until a date to be set next Monday.

William Harris went to bed early Monday night in the belief that all the Titanic's passengers had been saved. He is advanced in years and has not been very well lately, and with the idea of saving him from worry for another night at least, he was not told of the fate that overtook the great steamship and many of the passengers. Yesterday, however, it was impossible to keep the truth from him longer, and the news that his son's name was not in the list of those saved completely prostrated him; it was even reported during the day that Mr. Harris Sr., had died, but this was quickly denied.

It is a well known fact in theatrical circles thit Henry M. Harris always has been "the apple of his father's eye." He has seen him grow up in the theatrical business until he was one of the largest owners of theatrical property in the city and one of the greatest and gamest producers that the business knows. His father with great wealth always stood behind his son and was ready to back him if he needed it, which he seldom did, in anything he undertook. Henry B. Harris owns the Hudson Theatre and either individually or jointly the Harris, the Fulton, and is interested in the Park. He also had the Walnut Street Theatre in Philadelphia. He has such stars and attractions as Rose Stahl, Elsie Ferguson, Robert Edson, Frank McIntyre in "Snobs;" Ruth St. Denis, "The Country Boy," "The Quaker Girl," one of the most profitable musical plays since "Floradora;" "The Commuters," "The Travelling Salesman," "The Right to Be Happy" and "The Talker."

The future of the Harris theatrical artists if Mr. Harris is among the lost is of great interest to theatrical circles, not only here, but throughout the country.

Suggests Patrol to Warn Ships of Dangerous Ice

Commander Frederick L. Sawyer Outlines to the Herald Idea That Would Prevent Recurrence of Such Sea Tragedies in the North Atlantic as Befell the Titanic.

LOOKOUTS TO DRIFT WITH BERGS AND SIGNAL

While the world is aghast at the tragedy of the Titanic, an officer of the United States Navy has evolved a way to prevent the repetition of the catastrophe by a patrol of the ice infested waters of the Northern Atlantic which will give the mariners a warning against icebergs as the lighthouses mark the dangers of the rocks and shallows.

Commander Frederick L. Sawyer believes than an efficient patrol of the North Atlantic can be maintained so that the danger of a collision with an iceberg can be reduced to a minimum, and the charts of the steamship will show where the danger lies just as they show now where there is an island or an ugly reef. He believes that such a patrol should be international, but until some arrangement can be made to carry it into effect the United States should maintain it.

"The great unsolved problem of navigation," said Commander Sawyer, "is the way to avoid derelicts and icebergs. The maintaining of a sharp lookout, the temperature of the air and the change of the temperature of the water have all been used to detect the presence of icebrgs, and with the sailing vessels of other days they were satisfactory. A ship of the old kind could be handled so she could be stopped or turned about in her own length, but with a vessel like the Titanic, the problem of changing the course to avoid an iceberg after it is sighted is not an easy one.

Nothing Could Witstand Shock.

"No vessel ever has been built that can withstand a collision with an iceberg, and it is beyond the bounds of probability that such a ship will ever be built, for it would be commercially impracticable. So the solution of the problem of avoiding the dangers of icebergs must be along another line than an improvement in the method if construction. I believe it lies in the establishing of an efficient patrol, in the nature of both a patrol and floating light ships.

"The total area of the ice field in the North Atlantic is comparatively small. The pilot charts for the North Atlantic for March, 1912, show that the extreme east and west extent is about 200 miles. To mak this project clear it is only necessary to imagine the area to be a coast line due to volcanic action, with the exception that the ice line would be changing slowly due to the winds and ocean currents.

"The first duty of the patrol would be to define the southern limits of the field, to patrol that line, and when any change is detected to report it. The patrol ships would be in daily communication with the wireless stations on shore, and could issue constant warnings to vessels in the wireless radius. The result of this patrol or survey would be that a vessel like the Titanic or the Mauretania, steaming from New York would arrive at the region of the icebergs inside of two days. At the time of her departure the position of the southern line of the icebergs would be indicated on her charts as accurately as the coast line of an island. If the icebergs had drifted, and in what direction would also be known, so that their positions at the time of passing could be accurately determined, and the course laid accordingly. I believe that with such a patrol the loss of a great ship like the Titanic would be impossible.

Ice Moves Slowly.

"It will be noted that the movement of these ice masses are usually very slow, and often retrograde. The surface exposed to the wind is so small compared with mass under water that any sudden change of drift due to gales is not large. The surface current is usually much greater than the drift of the ice mass by reason of the depth of the ice mass.

"A properly organized patrol would be able to keep all of the vessels equipped with wireless informed of the daily latitude and longitude of the most southerly icebergs, and one or more of the vessels should probably be employed as lightships, drifting with the ice and marking the southern promintories. Lighted buoys, marked with the latitude and longitude so the patrol ships could easily pick them up would be an advantage, so there would never be an error in the notice of the liners of the position of the ice fields. The icebergs usually go in a mass, and if one becomes detached a patrol boat should accompany it and send the wireless warning to all ships.

"This patrol should eventually be international. But as the United States has always kept in the van in the protection of life and commerce on the seas by lightships and all other known methods, this would be an opportune time for the government to make the necessary arrangements and assume the duty.

"The total cost of the service would be less than the interest on the money loss of the Titanic disaster. Five ships—and the modern revenue cutters are admirably equipped for the work—would form an efficient patrol. It is a project that, I believe, should demand the attention of not alone the men engaged in the shipping trade, but of all the people, so they will never be shocked again with a disaster like that which has been visited upon the world this week."

Marine Men Applaud the Herald's Idea of an IcebergPatrol

C. L. Bundy, of the Maritime Exchange, Says the Suggestion Not Only Is Unique and Practical, but Should Receive Prompt Response of the Nations.

Instant and enthusiastic appreciation of the HERALD's suggestion for an international patrol of the ice fields of the upper Atlantic in the dangerous months of floating icebergs was expressed by shipping men yesterday.

"It is an entirely new idea," said C. L. Bundy, superintendent of the Maritime Exchange, "and worthy of thorough investigation and trial. The HERALD is always doing fine things for our maritime interests. If the various governments were to co-operate in establishing such a patrol, the expense would be only a bagatelle for each country.

"Consider what our own government has done in removing wreckage and other dangerous obstructions from the lines of navigation. We were the first to hunt down and remove derelicts and build a derelict destroyer, the Seneca, which destroyed hundreds of obstacles to navigation up and down the coast, under the direction of the Revenue Cutter Service.

"As to the present appearance of ice in the upper Atlantic, it should be said that it is entirely unprecedented. An experienced sea captain whom I know declares that this unheard of ice flow at this early season of the year is undoubtedly due to one of the recent earthquake shocks or some volcanic submarine upheaval dislodging vast fields of ice from the Arctic seas.

"All shipping men know that as a rule icebergs do not begin coming down until the season is well advanced—along in the summer months—July and August. So this untimely appearance of large bodies of ice in the Atlantic 's startlingly new and worthy of investigation as to the causes of the phenomenon. The HERALD's patrol idea could be adjusted to fit the ice season each year. I hope it will be tried and made a succes."

"You may put us down as favoring any idea that will make it safer for ships crossing the Atlantic," was the response to the HERALD's suggestion at the office of the North German Lloyd Steamship Company. "As to whether the proposed patrol suggested by the HERALD could be practically carried out, is a matter to be tried and proved. At present the Hydrographic Office of the government notifies steamship companies of obstructions reported in the pathway of vessels. This notification is sent to the captains of outgoing vessels and also cabled to various home offices, which in turn inform the incoming as well as outgoing steamers on this side.

"When particularly dangerous obstructions to navigation are reported the New York officers try to specially inform the captains of their various incoming and outgoing vessels that are in any ways likely to enter the danger zone. We trust that the HERALD will succeed in its unique and laudable enterprise."

Emil Boaz, the American head of the Hamburg-American company, expressed keen interest in the HERALD's suggestion. "It is something entirely new and of greatest importance to Atlantic shipping if the scheme is properly carried out,' said he. "I most heartily approve of it and will do all I can to help the enterprise along. As to just how the details should be carried out as a metter for the governments who may co-operate to determine.

"I am inclined to think that the United States government, if not America, Canada and England, should be selected to take charge of the patrol work, for the reason that the ice fields are closer to the American coast than to any of the other countries except Canada. If all agreed and a proportionate fund were voted by the various governments it would be easy to decide on a programme for patrolling the ice belts of the Atlantic. By the use of powerful wireless plants all the shipping world, as well as the public at large, would be kept informed daily as to the movement of the ice and where the danger to shipping lies."

PATROL IDEA TO GO 'BEFORE CONGRESS

Representative J. Hampton Moore to Introduce Measure in House at Once.

HERALD BUREAU,
No. 1,502 H STREET, N. W.,
WASHINGTON, D. C., Tuesday.

Influential members of Congress to-day welcomed the proposal of the HERALD that an international patrol be established to locate and report the movements of icebergs and ice fields in the North Atlantic to both ships and land. The practically universal opinion among legislators at Washington to-day was that this would go farthest of anything yest sugegsted to prevent the recurrence of suhc accidents as that which befell the Titanic.

At the HERALD's suggestion, Representative J. Hampton Moore, of Pensylvania, a prominent member of the International Navigation Congress, the Atlantic Deeper Water Ways Association and the Rivers and Harbors Congress, will introduce in the house a resolution directing the Secretary of State to open negotiations at once with foreign governments, with a view to bringing about a conference on this subject and establishing such an international patrol along the steamship lane in the four months of the year, when the ice movement is dangerous to navigation.

Mr. Moore will press the resolution and fully expects that the Committee on Foreign Affairs, of which he is a member, will favorably report it and that the House and Senate will pass it.

Representative William Sulzer, chairman of the Foerign Affairs Committee, looks with favor on the project.

Mr. Moore will bring the subject to the attention of the Twelfth International Navigation Congress on May 23 in Philadelphia. Mr. Moore is a member of the national committee of arrangements for the congress as well as the Philadelphia local committee.

Brigadier General William H. Bixby, chief of engineers of the United States Army, also is a member of this national committee.

SHOCK OF AWFUL DISASTER STAGGERS THE ENTIRE WORLD

Anxious Throng Besieges Herald's Office in Paris

Bulletin Giving Names of Some of the Saved Received at Five o'Clock in the Afternoon—Very Little Reassurance at Office of the White Star Line.

ROBERT BACON CHANGED HIS ARRANGEMENTS

HERALD BUREAU,
No. 49 AVENUE DE L'OPÉRA,
PARIS, Tuesday.

[SPECIAL DESPATCH TO THE HERALD VIA COMMERCIAL CABLE COMPANY'S SYSTEM.]

Pitiful scenes were witnessed at the office of the European edition of the HERALD and at the White Star line office from early this morning until late to-night. Great crowds gathered, the majority being close relatives of persons who had taken passage by the Titanic. The uncertainty created by the contradictory news published in the morning papers was welcomed by hundreds whose loved ones were aboard the ill-fated steamship.

The fact that no lists of the drowned or the saved were received gave rise to hopes which, when more definite news was received as the day wore on, gave way to despair. Scores of women rushed to the HERALD offices early. Time and again one would drop in a faint when informed that no definite news had been received, or when a name which she hoped to see among the list of the saved was not among those incomplete lists at hand.

At the offices of the White Star line, Louis Martin, the Paris manager, personally answered inquiries, but was able to give very little re-assurance. At five o'clock in the afternoon a bulletin giving the names of some of the saved by the Carpathia was received in a message from Liverpool, which obtained the information in a wireless message from Captain Haddock, of the Olympic. When this was posted at the HERALD office the crowd which had been increasing hourly pressed anxiously forward to the windows. Some face would brighten, but there was no good news for the majority of the anxious ones. Similar scenes were repeated during the night.

At the HERALD editorial offices all night long the telephone bell rang and hundreds telegraphed for news. The messages always indicated the fears which prompted them.

An undercurrent of excitement prevails at the Paris hotels. At almost every hostelry frequented by Americans are men and women who each has a personal interest in someone who left on the Titanic.

Robert Bacon, retiring Ambassador, was congratulated by many friends on his escape. He was to have left on Thursday by the Titanic but changed his arrangement. He will take passage by the steamship France on her maiden voyage on April 20. Others who cancelled bookings on the Titanic were Mrs. Charles I. Lewis and Miss Anne K. Eastman, who had paid their passage money but decided to defer their start. Mrs. Hanan was to have left by the Titanic but at the last moment circumstances arose which made her departure impossible. Inquiries have been made all day at Lucile's dressmaking establishment, Lady Duff Gordon's business, concerning the fate of Sir Cosno and Lady Duff Gordon.

HAMBURG-AMERIKA ISSUE AFFECTED

This Is Only Influence of the Titantic Disaster Noticeable on the Berlin Bourse.

[SPECIAL DESPATCH TO THE HERALD VIA COMMERCIAL CABLE COMPANY'S SYSTEM.]

BERLIN, Tuesday.—The bullish tendency at the close of the New York Exchange and excellent news from the German iron market caused the opening to be very firm at the Bourse. Coal and iron issued strong on well founded rumors that the German steel cartel is to be prolonged.

In the shipping section the loss of the Titanic only affected the issue of the Hamburg-American Company, which is the only company having mammoth steamships on the stocks.

THRONG READS NEWS IN HERALD SQUARE

Bulletins Displayed in Front of Herald Building for Vast Crowd that Packs Streets.

Herald square was thronged for hours last night by an eagerly anxious crowd awaiting the latest news regarding the Titanic and her apssengers and crew. It was a cosmopolitan crowd, where the wealthy rubbed elbows with the poor as they stood for hours hoping against hope that the story of the greatest sea disaster of all time would lose some little part of its grimness in the light of the latest news from the survivors.

The HERALD, in anticipation of the crowds, had already arranged to display the bulletins by throwing stereopticon views on a huge sheet which was hung in front of the HERALD Building. In addition, the usual bulletin board on the Broadway side was utilized to post the news as it came from telephone and telegraph. At both places a huge crowd was gathered until far into the night.

It was no morbibdl curious throng which so eagerly grasped at every bit of information that was presented to them. The black bands of mourning and the grief-stricken countenances of some told their own story of the friends and relatives who, perhaps, had gone to their deep sea graves. There were others whose grief was not so deep because it was not so personal, but on every side they were moved by the thought of the lives taken by the giant forces of nature, which once more had proced that tey were far superior to the giant forces of man.

The successive misfortunes of Captain Smith still continued to be a topic of conversation. This was especially noticed when during a lull in the posting of the bulletins a picture of the Titanic was flashed upon the sheet.

After the closing of the theatres there was a notable increase in the size of the crowds. Men and women in evening dress walked down Broadway and stood side by side with the laborer as they watched the bulletins. Chauffeurs were instructed to drive their taxicabs slowly while the persons within got the latest news from the scene of action.

After midnight the crowds gradually began to thin out. Some, however, waited and watched the HERALD presses as they rolled off the great story. When the papers were offered for sale on the streets they were eagerly snapped up by a crowd of no small dimensions, which was unwilling to wait until morning for the complete news.

SOCIAL GAYETIES CHECKED IN HOTELS

Many Persons Living at the St. Regis, Plaza and Similar Places Recall Invitations.

Social gayety in the large hotels came to a standstill yesterday, after news of loss of the Titanic had been received, and many invitations were recalled. The majority of persons living in the hotels either had relatives or friends on board the steamship, and in every case, those interested refused to give up hope.

Colonel John Jacob Astor's name was frequently heard in the lobbies, as he owns two of the largest hotels here, the St. Regis and the Knickerbocker, and is half owner of the Waldorf-Astoria.

Many passengers on board the ship had engaged rooms at the St. Regis, Plaza, Ritz-Carlton, Vanderbilt and Waldorf-Astoria.

SECURITIES MARKET REMAINS UNAFFECTED

Wall Street Feels Titanic Disaster in Sentiment Only—Pall Over District.

The Titanic disaster hung like a pall over the financial district yesterday. Its depressing effect was most noticeable in the stock market. Quotations for securities of all sorts fell and the trading and speculation of the last few days received a sudden check.

While business was not refused, few even of the most hardened brokers displayed any inclination to "drum it up." The known presence on board the ill-fated steamship when she sank of some members of the Stock Exchange and several men intimately associated with it brought the appalling disaster home so closely to Wall street that none seemed to have the heart to continue speculation.

Apart from sentiment there was nothing in connection with the wreck which affected the market for securities. The financial loss, it was known, will be confined to the marine underwriters, principally in England, and to the International Mercantile Marine Company of this country. To the former it is merely an incident of their business, to the latter it means the net loss of about $2,000,000 over the insurance, which will wipe out the company's surplus and leave a slight deficit at the time the company was turning the corner and seemed to be on the high road to paying dividends.

The reports of large quantities of securities in transit from Europe to this country lost on board the steamship, had not the slightest effect on the market. In the first place, if the reports had been true, nothing but some slight inconvenience would have been caused. All the stock certificates and bonds could have been replaced without the loss of a dollar, comparatively speaking. But as a matter of fact the reports were incorrect.

John E. Gardin, vice president of the National City Bank, said:—

"The amount of securities shipped fro mthis country on the Titanic was quite unimportant. That is due to the fact that there is no great movement at this time which would require the shipment of any large quantity of bonds or certificates of stock from Europe to this country."

Miss Booth Going by the Mauretania.

Miss Evangeline Booth, leader of the Salvation Army in this country, who was to leave New York on board the Titanic, of the White Star line, will leave on Wednesday next on board the Mauretania, of the Cunard line. She expects to confer with her father, General Booth, in England, and will be accompanied by William Peart, secretary to the movement.

Pacific Coast Policemen Here.

Police Commissioner Cook and Lieutenant Mattheson, of San Francisco, visited Police Headquarters yesterday and had interviews with Commissioner Waldo and Deputies McKay and Dougherty. The visitors were shown through the building. They are making a study of police conditions here, and will remain a week.

The Plaint of a Benedict.

Memphis News-Scimitar:—
Oft in the stilly night,
Ere slumber's chain has bound me,
I light again the light
And wrap a quilt around me,
And tread alone,
With many a groan,
The stairs with tacks strewn alway,
To calm her fears
Who thinks she "hears
A burglar in the hallway!"

Uncles.

Memphis News-Scimitar:—"Ferdy, old chap, what are 'business relations,' y'know?"

"Why, Clarence, deah fellah, I fawncy that means pawnbrokers."

"Bah Jove! Ferdy, you are deucedly clevah about such things."

NIGHT OF TERROR ON BOARD THE NIAGARA AMID ICEBERGS THAT SUNK THE TITANIC

Panic and Prayer Follow Crash Which Brings Big Steamship Up Standing.

IMPACT HURLS ALL TO FLOORS OF CABINS

Vessel Strains and Trembles in Her Seaway as 1,000 Excited Voyagers See Visions of Death.

NORTH LANE AN ARCTIC FIELD

Three Big Ships Forced to Plough Through Floes Near Graveyard of White Star Giantess.

CAPTAIN JUHAN.

THE NIAGARA, ARROW SHOWS DAMAGED BOW.

Battered by icebergs and floes in the north lane of the Atlantic where the Titanic, of the White Star line, was sunk, a fleet of transatlantic steamships arrived here yesterday with tales of hardship and narrow escapes from sharing the fate met by the White Star steamship.

Passengers on board the Niagara, of the French line, momentarily expected for more than twenty hours that their steamship would go to the bottom.

Men, women and children crowded the deck, many of them praying aloud, while others prepared to take to the lifeboats. In the steerage nine hundred passengers cried out in pitiable appeals or raved over expected death.

Aboard the Niagara were 128 first cabin passengers, in addation to the 900 in the steerage. When they were at dinner last Thursday night there was a terrific crash and the steamship brought up standing, shivering and trembling in her seaway.

Passengers Panic Stricken

Passengers were hurled headlong from their chairs and broken dishes and glass were scattered throughout the dining saloons. The next instant there was a panic among the passengers and they raced screaming and shouting to the decks.

Every one, including the vessel's officers, thought the Niagara was in collision with another steamship. Orders were given to reverse the engines and the big steamship was severely shaken a second time.

Investigation proved that the Niagara had run head on against a large iceberg which rose out of the sea more than one hundred feet. It was reckoned to be seven times that length under the ocean's surface.

Captain Juham, who was at dinner when the accident occurred, immediately took the bridge. A hasty examination of the damage was made and it was found that the steamship had two large holes stove in her bow near the waterline.

"S. O. S." Quickly Answered.

The wireless operator was instructed to send out a distress signal when it was found that the forepeak was making water rapidly.

The "S. O. S." was picked up by the Carmania, of the Cunard line, and she replied that she had hauled her course and was heading for the then supposed sinking vessel.

Subsequent investigation was made and Captain Juham sent a second message to the Carmania that assistance was not needed and he would try to make this port under his own steam.

"I thought we were doomed," said Captain Juham yesterday. "At first I feared we had been in collision with another vessel as I hurried to the bridge. But when I saw it was an iceberg and that we were surrounded by ice as far as we could see through the fog, my fears for the safety of the passengers and the vessel grew. It was a thrilling half hour I spent following the accident. And I breathed a deep sigh of relief when I learned we were not sinking, for I had been in icefloes before and knew the peril of our position.

Iceberg Looms, Crash Follows.

"Late in the afternoon we ran into a dense fog. It was difficult to see far ahead, and we reduced to half speed and picked our way alon.g Had we been going at full speed I am sure our vessel would have gone down.

"We had been plowing through a field of rotten ice for some time when a mist arose, and within the next ten minutes we were completely enveloped in the fog. I never saw like conditions that far south, and all hands were instructed to keep a sharp lookout for icebergs. But we were upon one without an instant's warning, and the crash followed.

"I am sure Captain Smith had a similar experience in practically the same locality when the Titanic went down. He did not expect to come in contact with icebergs so far south, as they were never known to be found there before."

The Niagara battled with the ice throughout the entire night and until late the next afternoon, when she ran into open water.

Night of Grief and Terror.

Not one of the passengers slept during the time the vessel was in the ice, and all kept their clothes on ready to go overside into the lifeboats on short notice. Many of the women and children were hysterical and paced the decks, wringing their hands and crying out in grief and terror.

The greatest excitement prevailed among the steerage passengers. For the most part they were of the Slavonic and Latin races and given to emotional behavior. They begged aloud for the freedom of the vessel, and it was with difficulty that the officers in charge kept them in restraint. They cursed and prayed in turn and either fought those nearest theem or embraced their loved ones.

Perhaps the coolest person aboard the Niagara was Anna Miller, eleven years old, of Newark, N. J., wha has crossed the Atlantic six times. She went among the women and children cheering them with words of assurance and comfort.

Little Girl Leads in Prayer.

When the excitement reached its highest pitch the little girl fell on her knees on the deck and began to pray aloud. She was soon joined by nearly all the women and children and not a few of the men. The child led them in prayer and they answered in concert.

Mrs. Sophie Kistecky, the wife of a hat manufacturer of No. 35 Jefferson street, Manhattan, became hysterical immediately after the vessel struck the iceberg and cried until all danger had passed.

During the entire time she paced the deck with her two children—Albert, four years old, and Marcel, three years old—in her arms and sat weeping in a steamer chair with one of the children on either knee. She could not be induced to go to her stateroom. Nor would she part from the children when other women passengers volunteered to care for them.

Sending the Distress Signal.

Herve aguy, the wireless operator, recounted an interesting story of his experience at the key when he thought the vessel was doomed.

"I little dreamed of the thrills and excitement attending such an experience," he said. "When I got the word from the captain to flash the distress signal my entire body shook with a strange emotion. It was not fright.

"It was the moment, I think, that every operator on board a vessel expects to arrive some day and often wonders what feeling will possess him at that time.

"I went to my key and flashed the three letters 'S. O. S.,' that mean so much in such circumstances. Then came the wait. Every moment seemed an eternity. I waited patiently for several minutes and then sent a second message.

"With every nerve at high tension I kept my eye on the instrument that would reveal to me that our call for aid had been heard.

"I never expect to have another thrill in this world that will equal the one I felt when the instrument began to crack and sizzle and the key ticked off the welcome news that our call had been heard.

Joy Greets Rescue Message.

"I must have been nervous as I wrote the reply. It was from the Carmania and she said she was turning back to stand by us. There was a shout of joy among the apssengers as the word spread over shipboard that our call had been heard and we were sure of aid.

"A strange feeling swept over me as I sat waiting for that message. Below all was excitement and preparation. Some way or another I felt like I should not sit there, apparently not doing anything, while the crew were all at work at the life boats or getting the passengers in readiness to use them. It was a wonderful experience and one that I cannot soon forget."

According to a statement made last night by the French Transatlantic Steamship Company, after Captain Juham had made his report to the company, the ocean lanes in the vicinity where the Titanic went down are absolutely unsafe for any vessel.

The report states that the Niagara passed the first iceberg on April 10 at half-past ten o'clock in the morning. It was about 40 feet high and 115 feet long, in latitude 44.39 north and longitude 46.09 west.

Many Icebergs Sighted.

During the next five hours the vessel sighted many icebergs of all sizes enclosed in heavy packs of ice.

Navigation was extremely dangerous because of the large cakes of ice that were carried over the slushy field by a heavy swell of the sea from the southwest. The report reads in part:—

"All tracks crossing 50 degrees west of Greenwich in a latitude further north than 41.30 are absolutely unsafe for any vessel."

Captain Juham's chart affords a comprehensive explanation of the greatest disaster in marine annuals suffered by the Titanic. The location of the ice floes and icebergs south of the Newfoundland banks is shown in the chart as they were seen by Captain Juham when the Niagara passed through them. The floes were drifting in a strong arctic curent which set to the southward and southwestward.

Three Big Ships in Ice Floes.

Among the other steamships to arrive here yesterday delayed by running into big fields of ice was the Lapland, of the Red Star line, from Antwerp. Captain Doxrud said he encountered the ice on the morning of April 12 and struggled all day and the following night to clear the vessel from her peril.

Captain Pollock, of the George Washington, of the North German Lloyd line, in yesterday from Bremen, also told of encountering long stretches of ice. He said he saw icebergs from fifty to two hundred feet in height and about one thousand feet long. He kept his vessel to the south of the icebergs and avoided damage.

For two days Captain Megin, of the President Lincoln, of the Hamburg-American line, kept his steamship at slow speed in a big field of ice off the Banks. He changed his course twice to avert running into stretches of ice that appeared too solid to break. The weather was clear during the time these three vessels passed through the ice.

Pray for the Titanic's Victims at Cornerstone Laying

Sailor Heroes of Disaster Are Lauded at Exercises at New Home of Seamen's Institute.

Mayor Gaynor and Bishop Greer, with Many Clergymen, Take Part in the Ceremonies.

MAYOR GAYNOR AT THE LAYING OF THE CORNERSTONE OF THE SEAMEN'S CHURCH INSTITUTE

Throughout the ceremonies which marked the laying of the cornerstone of the new twelve story home of the Seamen's Church Institute of New York, at South street and Coenties slip, yesterday afternoon, there was noticeable a touch of sadness among those who are identified with the work for the benefit of countless seafarers.

Few eyes in the room remained dry when the choir of the Church of the Epiphany opened the exercises with the hymn beginning:—

"Eternal Father! strong to save,
Whose arm hath bound the restless wave,
Who bidd'st the mighty ocean deep
It's own appointed limits keep,
Oh, hear us when we cry to Thee
For those in peril on the sea."

The opening prayer, which was composed for the occasion by the Rev. Dr. William R. Huntington, was read by Bishop David H. Greer, after which the Bishop offered a prayer for those who had gone down with the Titanic, and the families who were left to mourn.

The Rev. Dr. Frederick Courtney spoke on "The Sailor," telling of his jovial, care free disposition combined with a courage unknown to most landsmen. Dr. Courtney cited the incidents which must have surrounded the sinking of the Titanic, when the sailors stood back, face to face with death, doing their duty that women and children might be saved.

After an address by Edmund L. Baylies, chairman of the Building Committee, Mayor Gaynor laid the cornerstone, which contained among other things New York newspapers of yesterday morning, in which apeared details of the sinking of the Titanic.

The Rev. Dr. Henry Van Dyke then spoke on "The Landsmen's Dependence Upon the Seamen." He said that while the accident to the Titanic was such an awe inspiring illustration of his subject his words were of little avail he felt that the landsmen owed a debt to the sailors which they could never repay. Dr. Van Dyke then said that the landsmen were in many ways responsible for the kind of men that there were on board the ships, and he asked the question, What kind of men are there on board ships? He answered it with a word painting of the events which must have occurred on board the Titanic that brought tears to the eyes of the two hundred and fifty men and women who heard him.

Dr. Van Dyke said the answer to the question lay in imagining one thousand men standing face to face with their God willing to go down to their death that women and children might be saved. To such men, he said, the landsmen owed the debt which the Seamen's Church Institute was trying to repay.

The ceremonies ended with a prayer by the Rev. Dr. William M. Grosvenor and a benediction pronounced by the Right Rev. Dr. Frederick Burgess, Bishop of Long Island.

BRITISH DINNER POSTPONED

It was announced yesterday that the dinner of the British Schools and Universities Club, which was to have been held to-night at the Hotel Lafayette, had been postponed in view of the disaster to the Titanic and the appalling loss of life.

HEARS NEWS, DROPS DEAD.

BOISSEVAIN, Man., Tuesday.—J. P. Alexander, once a member of the Provincial Parliament, dropped dead to-day when told of the Titanic disaster. He had heart disease.

CITY VOICES SORROW.

New York city's sorrow over the Titanic disaster was expressed officially yesterday by the Board of Aldermen through the adoption of a resolution "joining with the people of the world" in the sorrow felt for those who have been afflicted by the loss of life.

"This, one of the worst calamities in the annals of Christendom," the resolution says, "the most awful in the history of those who go down to the sea in ships has stunned not only this community but the entire land."

SPECIAL MEMORIAL SERVICE.

Memorial services for those who perished on board the Titanic will be held next Sunday morning in the Cathedral of St. John the Divine, on Morningside Heights. There will be special music and prayers for the dead and Bishop David L. Greer will make an address as well as conduot the service. Dean Grosvenor, in announcing the service last night, said persons of all denominations who wished to join in prayer for the victims of the disaster would be welcome.

PREDICTED THE DISASTER.

RACINE, Wis., Tuesday.—"I dread taking this trip to Denmark, for I have a feeling that the vessel will sink or something awful happen to me," said Mrs. Peter C. Hanson, who was among the passengers aboard the Titanic, to her brother, Thomas Howard, of Racine.

Mrs. Hanson, accompanied by her husband, left home last February on a visit to his old home in Denmark. They were on their return voyage aboard the Titanic.

HAD AMERICAN MAIL MEN.

The Titanic carried 3,423 sacks of mail, according to the statement made Wednesday by Postmaster Edward M. Morgan. There were on board three American postal clerks attached to the sea post service. Their names are W. L. Gwynn, O. S. Woodie and J. S. March. There were also two English postal clerks.

FORWARD CRUSADE PUSHED WITH VIGOR

Feared That W. T. Stead and the Rev. Mr. Holden Perished in the Titanic Disaster.

Although shocked by the loss of the Titanic, which, acording to advices, may have taken the lives of two of their principal speakers, the managers of the Men and Religion Forward Movement pushed their arrangements yesterday for their work, including the Christian Conservation Congress, which is to be of a general character, and will be held in Carnegie Hall, beginning April 19 and ending April 24. The men who so far as Fred B. Smith, campaign leader of the movement, knew yesterday were on their way here aboard the Titanic and were to have taken an important part in some of the big meetings of the movement, are William T. Stead and the Rev. J. Stewart Holden, both of London.

R. A. WAITE

According to the letters of acceptance received by Mr. Smith, both men were to leave England by the Titanic, but neither from the list of passengers nor from the list of the rescued have the managers been able to satisfy themselves of the fate of these men, and inquiry at the White Star Line offices threw no light on the uncertainty. Both men are of mature years and in an effort requiring physical power or agility would be apt to be left.

F. B. SMITH

Although the local campaign was pushed with vigor in and about this city yesterday, the opening of the Conservation Congress, which is now as close at hand as Friday, begins to loom up big in the general programme. Included in the various features of the Congress is the mass meeting to be held on the plaza of Union square on Saturday afternoon. William Jennings Bryan will be the principal speaker. His theme will be "The Claims of the Christian Religion on the Men of North America." Bent Brothers' military band will furnish a programme of religious music.

Several delegations from various parts of the country are on their way to New York in special cars. All are to attend the Conservation Congress. As they come, however, they will stop on the way at each town of importance and hold religious meetings explaining the work of the Men and Religion Forward Movement. The delegations include one from Atlanta, headed by W. J. Northern, formerly Governor of Georgia, and from North Carolina, St. Louis, Louisville, Ky., Pittsburg and other places. The cars will be elaborately festooned and marked with signs.

JOHN L. ALEXANDER

Many meetings for boys have been arranged for the rest of the week in Manhattan and the Bronx. A meeting of preparation was held in the Park Hotel yesterday. Prominent in the supervision of this work are John L. Alexander and R. A. Waite.

Mothers' meetings were also held in several places yesterday for the benefit of the boys, at which women spoke who are experts in religious work for boys. One of these meetings was held at the Second Church of the Disciples, No. 595 East 169th street, and another at the Morningside Presbyterian Church, Morningside avenue and 122d street.

MOTHERS HEAR TALK ON BOYS

Three meetings for mothers were held yesterday afternoon in connection with the boys' conference of the Men and Religeion Forward Movment in the "old" First Presbyterian Church, the Second Church of the Disciples of Christ and the Morningside Presbyterian Church. John W. Alexander, formerly national Boy Scout secretary, addressing the meeting in the chapel of the First Church, recommended that boys be organized into Sunday Bible classes in which the boys themselves could be officers, chairmen of committees and so forth. He said the boys would be more interested in such classes than in the present day Sunday school.

THE WEATHER. Rain tonight and probably on Thursday.

THE BROOKLYN DAILY EAGLE

Complete Stock Market

LAST EDITION. Volume 72A No. 107 ★ NEW YORK CITY, WEDNESDAY, APRIL 17, 1912. ★ 28 PAGES THREE CENTS.

NO ADDITIONS TO THE LIST OF THE TITANIC'S SURVIVORS GIVEN BY RESCUE SHIP CARPATHIA TO THE CHESTER

CONGRESS TAKES UP LIFEBOAT PROBLEM

Investigation of Titanic Disaster to Be Followed by Drastic Legislation.

SAFETY FOR ALL ON VESSELS.

New Laws to Require Sufficient Apparatus for Removal of Both Passengers and Crew.

Washington, April 17—A resolution will be introduced in the Senate, probably today, to direct the Commerce Committee or a sub-committee to make a thorough probe of the Titanic tragedy, and to empower the committee to summon witnesses and take any necessary steps.

As a complement to the Congressional investigation, the scope of which has not yet been fully determined, Secretary Nagel of the Department of Commerce and Labor, will take up at once with President Taft the entire subject of safeguarding ocean travel by more stringent American shippping regulations.

The Titanic disaster has aroused Congress, President Taft and the Cabinet to the urgent need for immediate measures of safety for ocean travel. It is believed that laws will be prepared at once in Congress, based on the advice of officials of the Department of Commerce and Labor and American shipping experts, that will insure safety of passengers and crew in cases like the Titanic, where ample time existed for their removal in lifeboats.

No concrete programme of action has yet been outlined. The Congressional investigations announced by Chairmen Alexander and Nelson of the House and Senate committees, will probably result in the summoning also of officials of the White Star Line to state what precautions for safety they are taking on the White Star liners.

"There could be no greater motive for stringent legislation than the fate of the host of passengers whom the lifeboats of the Titanic could not carry to safety," said Representative Alexander. "There could be no more pungent illustration of the necessity of this legislation than is to be found in the stories survivors will be able to tell Congress of the scenes enacted on the wreck in the three hours that passed between the collision with the iceberg and the plunge of the hulk to the bottom."

No accurate information is yet obtainable by government authorities at Washington as to the capacity of the lifesaving apparatus on the Titanic, or the number of lifeboats provided. Several attempts have been made today to secure the exact facts as to the vessel.

Government officials charged with the enforcement of the shipping laws and regulations were engrossed today with the subject of safety and protection for transatlantic travel. It is expected that immediate reforms will be demanded officially by the Government and will be enforced through new laws requiring all vessels entering American ports to carry sufficient emergency apparatus to remove all passengers and crew in time of emergency.

President Taft is taking a keen personal interest in all features of the proposed regulation of passenger vessels; and he will probably send recommendations to Congress containing the suggestions of executive departments for new legislation.

Although several bills pending in Congress to regulate lifesaving apparatus on all vessels clearing American ports, Chairman Alexander of the House committee contemplate drafting a new bill based upon the facts brought out by the Titanic disaster and upon the recommendations and suggestions of officials of the Department of Commerce and Labor.

Government to Regulate Operation of Wireless Plants.

Revenue cutter officials in Washington believe the Titanic disaster will result in insurance companies insisting upon steamships taking a more southerly course across the ocean. The investigations by insurance companies, maritime exchanges and foreign maritime boards are expected to be thorough; but the congressional investigation, because of the power of Congress to compel witnesses to testify, is expected to reveal many important facts.

Chairman Nelson of the State Committee on Commerce stated today that the extent of a congressional investigation cannot be determined at once, but must depend upon the facts reported by survivors and by steamship officials.

Prompt action is to be taken by Congress to report a bill providing strict control of wireless, a subject which was under consideration at a conference yesterday between President Taft and members of the Cabinet. Measures have been pending for some time in the House Committee on Merchant Marine. Interference of amateurs and irresponsible operators with the anxiously awaited messages for the Carpathia and other ships will result in an attempt to secure immediate legislation regulating wireless operation.

This subject has been pending before Congress for several years, and at several hearings juvenile wireless operators were brought here and put on the stand to testify to the highly educational value of their experiments with amateur plants. The sentimental side of the problem and the charges that the government was trying to stifle electrical genius and restrict wireless operations to their own plant and those of certain established companies, undoubtedly prevented an earlier restriction of operations.

FAILS FOR QUARTER MILLION

Wilson and Baillie Company Victims of City Officials' Changed Methods.

The Wilson & Baillie Manufacturing Company, manufacturers of cement pipe, with offices at 26 Court street, and a stone ward at 85 Ninth street, today filed a petition in voluntary bankruptcy in the United States District Court. The schedule shows liabilities of $252,348.87, and assets of $98,830.51.

An officer of the company said this afternoon that the city's methods of dealing with machine-made cement pipe manufacturers was responsible for the failure. Machine-made cement pipe once had a good market in Brooklyn, he said, but the two last city administrations have dealt exclusively with companies producing a certain type of stoneware pipe, and business for the Wilson & Baillie concern gradually fell off, until the directors decided the trade wasn't broad enough to justify continuing business.

Frank B. Johnson, treasurer of the company, and Ellis H. Baillie, secretary, subscribe to a statement, filed with the bankruptcy schedule, to the effect that the directors met at 26 Court sree on Marhc 25, and came o a unanimous decision to file a voluntary bankruptcy petition.

Van Brunt Bergen of Bay Ridge Parkway and Seventy-seventh street is president of the company. H. B. Hubbard, a lawyer at 26 Court street, is counsel. The schedule shows that the company owes Mr. Bergen $9,223 in salary and Mr. Hubbard $26,139 in salary, while the latter is a creditor for about $10,000 as holder of various notes.

The liabilities include $206,817.13 in notes and bills "which ought to be paid by other parties thereto," according to the schedule, and $45,489 in unsecured claims, including dues to the Brooklyn League and other organizationss, and debts due to nearly fifty creditors for salaries, professional services, merchandise, stone and on other accounts. The People's Trust Company is owed $40,000.

The assets include $852.72 in bills and promisory notes, $1,180 in carriages and other vehicles, $29,786 in machinery, tools and other stock, $30,000 in patents and copyrights, $22,992 in other personal property, $11,508 in debts due on open account, and $11 in bank deposits.

GAYNOR FOR PRESIDENT.

Steers Says Mayor Will at Least Get a Complimentary Vote.

Borough President Alfred E. Steers, a delegate to the coming Democratic National Convention at Baltimore, stated today that he would vote to nominate Mayor Gaynor for President. He said he expected all the New York delegates to be for the Mayor, and while he would not predict that Mr. Gaynor would receive the nomination, he said he had been told that such was the plan.

"Do you think Gaynor will be nominated?" he was asked.

"Well, I've been told so. But I know he is to receive a complimentary vote at any rate."

Mr. Steers would not discuss the merits of any other candidates.

"What do you think the Democratic platform ought to contain?" he was asked.

"I think the Democratic party ought to be for a big and efficient Navy, as the best means of preventing war. If the Democratic party wants to cut down the size of the Navy, I am against that."

The Borough President declared that he believed in a "tariff for revenue" plank, and that he was against the recall.

The New York State delegation to the National Convention will have to vote as a unit, according to a resolution adopted at the meeting of the Democratic State Convention which selected the delegates last week. It is practically certain, according to Mr. Steers, that Mayor Gaynor will receive the ninety votes of New York's delegates on the first ballot. Whether the Mayor's name will be withdrawn or not after the first ballot, depends entirely upon conditions at Baltimore.

ALABAMA FOR UNDERWOOD.

Montgomery, Ala., April 17—The Democratic State convention met here today to name twenty-four delegates to the national convention. The delegation will be instructed for Oscar W. Underwood, Alabama's "favorite son."

APPROXIMATE POSITIONS TODAY OF THE CARPATHIA AND THE SCOUT CRUISERS CHESTER AND SALEM

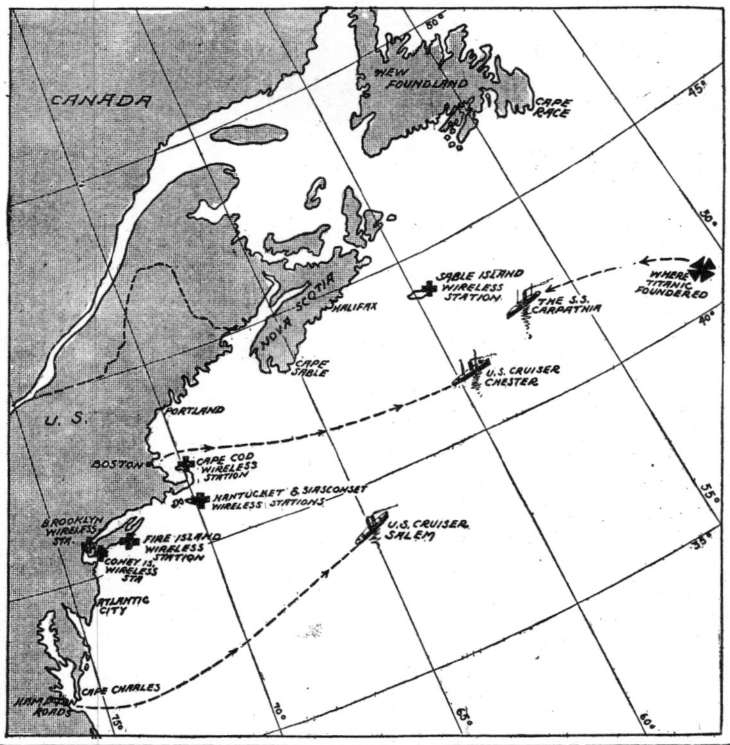

TITANIC'S BULKHEADS PROVED UNRELIABLE

Too Much Reliance Placed Upon Them as a Means of Safety.

FAILED TO WORK IN CRISIS.

Navy Yard Officials Believe Doors to Bulkheads Could Not Be Closed in Time.

Naval experts made assertions today which indicate that the very devices which were intended to render safe the lost Titanic were apparently in large degree responsible for her sinking and that, back of her loss, there is a story of an over-refinement of such safety devices.

At the local Navy Yard the belief is that there is a tendency to place too much reliance on the collision bulkheads as built in the present day mercantile vessels. The traveling public, it was said by Civil Engineer Harris, has been led to believe too strongly that collision bulkheads mean an unsinkable ship.

"There is no such thing as an unsinkable ship," he stated. "But even if bulkheads, rightly constructed, would keep a vessel afloat, the rule is, as regards the transatlantic steamers, there are too many openings for doors and the like in them. Now these doors, or openings, are designed to close simultaneously by a control on the bridge of the ship and, failing this mechanism, there is a float device. If water enters a compartment it rises to a certain height, these floats are lifted by the water and automatically close the doors. At the same time the openings are supposed to be so constructed that they can be shut by hand.

"But it would be almost ridiculous to suppose that, in the moment of such a collision as the Titanic must have met with, the doors could have been closed by hand. There probably would have been too many of them.

Lessons Learned by Naval Constructors.

"We found in our own naval construction some years ago that this was the case. Then why couldn't these other devices have done what they were supposed to do, granting that it would have done any good? In my opinion the trouble was, that to render the safety bulkheads at all of service, they had to be so nicely adjusted—had to have such fine balance and had to fit so perfectly—that the impact of a great collision would have thrown them all out of gear.

"Just imagine that impact. Here was so much inertia meeting an almost immovable body headon. Something had to give. It would be almost a certainty that the bulkheads would buckle. Then what more likely than that there was the rush to close the bulkhead doors from the bridge, the discovery that the mechanism worked there, but that down below decks the doors would close only just so far, or not at all because the hinges on which they swung had been bent out of place, or the bulkhead itself had buckled out of shape?

"Of course there would be a rush then to close the doors by hand, but the result would be the same, and if any doors were closed in this way, so much water would have come in by this time that the vessel would have settled somewhat and other doors which couldn't be closed sufficiently tight, would do the rest.

"In the absence of any definite word as to just what was the force of the collision, or its various other aspects, the advancing of opinions on this point are, of course, mere hazard. But the fact that the Titanic held afloat for about four hours after she had struck the iceberg would seem to indicate that just this thing happened—that they had faith in the collision bulkheads until someone made the discovery that water was seeping through imperfectly closed bulkhead doors and that then, when they tried to close the doors by hand and when the float device should have worked, buckled bulkheads or bent doors, or imperfect alignment of door-hinges and jams, rendered impossible any headway against the inrushing flood."

Novel Passageway on Titanic May Have Aided in Flooding.

Naval Constructor Robert Stocker and two of his associates made substantially the same assertions in regard to the probability of what must have happened to the bulkhead openings. In doing this they pointed out what they termed one very unusual feature of the construction of the Titanic. This they called a center-line passageway, from the fireroom of the ship right up into the bow, so that the fireroom force might get to their quarters directly.

They agreed that it was so unusual that it was improbable it existed.

"Without any plans of the Titanic one can't tell whether or not there was such a passage," said Naval Constructor Stocker, "but Captain Dyson of the Department of Steamboat Inspection at Washington, is said to have seen the plans of the Titanic and, according to what he is credited with saying, the boat did have such a passageway. A pasage from the engineroom right into the bow—the eyes of the ship—is very unusual. If one was there, it would offer exactly the right kind of an opening for the water to get from the bow of a boat struck head-on, into the engineroom, where it would put out the fires and mayhap explode the boilers.

"Even if there were safety doors in this passage, designed to close the bulkhead," the group of naval constructors united in saying, "it would be highly possible, even probable, that the impact of a great collision would throw them out of gear. You simply couldn't do anything with them."

"To my mind," one of the constructors said, "that gives a reason for the Titanic's having gone down as she evidently did. It would seem that she sunk first by the bow. If she did, a passage of this kind would let the water into the vital parts of theboat. Unless the bulkhead doors worked absolutely to perfection in this passage nothing could save her once the water got a chance to get into it."

The Navy Yard officers say, too, that it must be true the Titanic struck the iceberg that gave her the deathblow with tremendous force. It would have made the ship's seams buckle way at the stern they assert. It would be probable that she opened at hundreds of places at once, letting in the water at first gradually and then with a final fierce rush that carried all before it.

$5,000,000 DRY DOCK TO BE BUILT HERE

Foreign Steamship Companies Seek Suitable Site on Brooklyn's Waterfront.

TO FLOAT BIGGEST LINERS.

Loss of Titanic Said to Be a Factor in Locating the Basin Here.

It is the intention of certain foreign steamship companies to construct a monster drydock in the vicinity of Brooklyn if not actually on the Brooklyn water front in the immediate future. The basin will be the largest on this coast and will cost approximately $5,000 000. Although great secrecy is observed regarding the site for the dock, it is quite likely that it will be constructed somewhere along the Brooklyn water front.

The need for a great commercial dry dock is emphasized by the disaster to the Titanic. It is pointed out that if this vessel had been kept afloat and towed to New York Harbor there would have been no means of docking her here. There is not a basin anywhere on this coast large enough to receive a vessel of the monster proportions of the ill-fated White Star liner.

The loss of the Titanic is understood to have had something to do with the determination of the big steamship men to go ahead with a dock at once. Announcements of the location of a site may be expected soon. There is much speculation among the few who know of the plans regarding the location. It was pointed out today by a prominent steamship man that there are only four or five places in this center where a $5,000,000 dock could be located. Two essential requirements are land and a depth of water sufficient to accommodate the largest liners.

The Canadian Government has recognized the shortage of dock facilities on this coast and is now preparing to construct a modern basin. It will cost $5,000,000 and will be located somewhere in the St. Lawrence River. Three sites are now under consideration and the Government has advertised for bids from corporations to operate the enterprise. It is to be a subsidized dock. The Canadian Government will pay a subsidy of three and a half per cent. on the investment for a period of forty years.

At the present time the largest commercial dock in this harbor is at the Morse Iron Works. It is a small affair, relatively, and will only accommodate commercial ships of not more than 12,000 tons. Any vessel larger than this seeking a dock must be sent to Newport News, Va., for the docks of the Newport News Shipbuilding Company.

OREGON DESIGNER'S VIEWS.

San Francisco, April 17—That the Titanic was sunk by a lateral tearing and not by a head-on collision is the opinion of Hugo P. Frear, designer of the battleship Oregon, and among the experts in naval construction on the Pacific Coast.

"The sides of a vessel are the most difficult to protect," said Frear. "They are the most vulnerable spots in a steamship's anatomy, and it is my opinion that the Titanic struck the iceberg from an angle. A head-on collision could scarcely have done the damage necessary to sink the vessel."

CANADIAN STEAMER ASHORE.

Pictou, N. S., April 17—The Government steamer Earl Grey went ashore this morning between Tony River and Cape John, according to a wireless message received here from the Grey. She 's making no water.

The Latest Figures Place the Number of Dead at 1,312 and the Survivors at 868.

FRANCONIA SAYS 700 SAVED

If This Should Prove Correct the Total Number of Dead Would Reach 1,490---Cunarder Steering Slowly Down Coast.

REVISED TABULATION OF TITANIC DEAD AND SURVIVORS.

Number of Lives Lost	1,312
Known Survivors	868
Names of Survivors Transmitted	328
Names of Survivors Not Transmitted	540
Estimated Number of Crew Saved	140
Names of Women and Children That Appear in Tabulations of Survivors	249
Names of Men That Appear in Tabulation of Survivors	79

Nearly all steerage passengers saved are women.

Washington, April 17—The following telegram was received this afternoon by the Navy Department from Commander Decker of the scout cruiser Chester, via Portland, Me.

"Carpathia states that list of first and second class passengers and crew sent to shore. Chester will relay list third-class passengers when convenient to Carpathia."

The message is taken to mean that the list transmitted by wireless from the Carpathia to the station at Cape Race, N. F., through the Olympic contains the names of all the first and second class passengers rescued.

This would make the revised figures of casualties show that 1,312 persons probably perished when the Titanic went down. Of the 868 known survivors the names of 328 have been laboriously transmitted through the powerful wireless apparatus of the Olympic, the Titanic's sister ship, from the Carpathia to the shore.

Besides these, it is estimated that approximately 140 members of the crew were saved, their presence to man the lifeboats being required to insure the safety of the passengers.

An estimate of 400 steerage passengers saved completes the total of 868, which the Carpathia has made known she has on board.

As the lists indicate, the great majority of these are undoubtedly women. The names of only 79 men rescued have been given in the lists telegraphed from the Carpathia, whereas the names of 249 women appear in the tabulations. Of the 400 steerage passengers thought to be saved, it is believed that nearly all were women. The men among the passengers seemed largely to have given up their lives and remained to die that the women and children might be saved.

Franconia Says Only 700 Survivors Are on Carpathia.

If the estimate of the number of survivors of the Titanic disaster now on the Carpathia, as given in a wireless dispatch from the steamer Franconia to the Camperdown station in Nova Scotia prove true, the number of dead will be largely increased. In this dispatch it is said that the number of saved is only 710.

The dispatch reads:

"We are now in communication with Carpathia and in position to announce unofficially that the Titanic struck an enormous berg and sunk; over 2,000 lost; 710 survivors, mostly women, on Carpathia."

The attention of the Camperdown station was at once called to the obvious error in figures, which would give the total of lost and survived at 2,700, whereas the total number of passengers and crew is about 2,200.

In reply to this inquiry the following further explanation was received from Halifax:

"The Marconi station reports that nothing authentic regarding lost is known on board Carpathia, but the steamer Franconia in relaying the messages from the Carpathia says that the total number saved is only 710.

"There is no list of missing on the Cunarder, and only a rough estimate of her total passenger list. There were probably more than 2,200 on ship, as quite a number boarded her at Cherbourg."

The estimates of 2,200 on board the Titanic have embraced the sailings from all ports, including Cherbourg, as far as the company officials have been able to give the information.

At the Cunard Line offices a wireless from the liner Franconia of the Cunard Line was received. The latter boat had established communication with the Carpathia at 6:10 this morning. The Carpathia was then 498 miles east of Ambrose Channel. The message follows:

"The Cunard steamship Franconia established communication by wireless with the steamship Carpathia at 6:10 this morning, New York time. The latter was then 498 miles east of Ambrose Channel and in no need of assistance. She is steaming thirteen knots. She expects to reach New York at 8 p.m. Thursday. She has a total of 705 survivors aboard. The Franconia is relaying personal messages from the Carpathia to Sable Island."

The above is a copy of a Marconi message received from Winfield Thompson of the Boston Globe, who is a passenger on the Franconia.

Carpathia Less Than 600 Miles From New York.

The Cunarder Carpathia was less than 600 miles from New York at noon today, and word was eagerly awaited that would shed further light on the catastrophe of Sunday night.

Sable Island was in brief communication with the rescue ship for a time this morning, but no additional names of survivors were obtained.

Wireless stations along the New England coast were straining to get in communication with the vessel this afternoon, and the scout cruiser Salem was somewhere off Nantucket for the purpose of relaying ashore through her sister cruiser, the Chester, some connected account of the disaster.

At Halifax the cable ship Mackay-Bennett has been fitted out to go to the scene of the disaster. Coffins, ice and embalming materials were loaded aboard in the hope that many bodies may be picked up near the scene of the wreck.

Captain Schulke of the steamship Cincinnati, which reached port today from Naples and Genoa, reports that at midnight on April 14 he received a wireless call for help from the stricken Titanic.

Although 550 miles away, the Cincinnati was headed for the scene of the disaster, and would have continued had not another message from the Titanic been received half an hour later "Olympic coming; not needed." This was followed by silence, and the Cincinnati resumed her course.

Although he took the southerly course, Captain Schulke says he saw no icebergs.

EARLY EFFORTS TO REACH SHIP

In faintest touch with the wireless station at Stable Island and several ships, the Cunard liner Carpathia, with 868 survivors of the sunken Titanic on board,

SCOUT CRUISER SALEM.

was creeping down the coast early this morning, making the best time for this port that foggy conditions along the Atlantic shore line would permit.

Speeding up the coast toward the rescue ship and hoping to get within wireless speaking distance of her before very many hours had passed, were the scout cruisers Salem and Chester, ordered by the government at Washington to make all possible haste in their allotted task in breaking the seal of silence which so far has kept the survivors on the Carpathia from making known to the outside world the thrilling story of the Titanic's last hours afloat and the momentous happenings after she had taken the two-mile plunge to the bottom off the banks of Newfoundland early Monday morning.

From the Chester at an early hour this message came: "Expect to be up with Carpathia within three or four hours."

While the scout cruiser's expectations on this point were not realized, there seemed to be every prospect that through the machinery which the government had set in motion definite word from the Cunarder might be secured within a reasonably short time. The injection of the scout cruisers into the situation, indeed, seemed to afford the only hope of opening up communication with the Carpathia until she reached the wireless zone of Nantucket, as she was apparently too far off shore and her wireless apparatus took weak to reach the Sable Island station in a way to admit of the ready transmission of messages.

Conviction that the Carpathia carried the only key to the details of the Titanic's fate deepened today with the practical elimination of all hope that survivors of the disaster would be found on other vessels. That more than 1,300 persons, passengers and crew, had gone down with the giant liner was the belief that grew into almost a positive conviction as hour after hour passed. Other sources of possible rescue were eliminated and practically the only hope that remained to friends or relatives of the Titanic's passengers was that those they sought might, after all, be found upon the Carpathia when that vessel was able fully to give up the secret she had so tenaciously held since the hour early on Monday when she picked up the floating remnants of the Titanic's cargo of nearly 2,200 souls.

Little Hope of Survivors on Fishing Schooner.

Little hope was entertained today that the fishing schooner Dorothy Baird, which was passed in the vicinity of the Titanic disaster shortly after it occurred by the freighter Etonian of the Phoenix Line, had rescued any of the liner's passengers. Officers of the Etonian though it probable that the schooner had returned to St. John's without knowledge of the disaster.

Officials of the White Star line remained at their offices during the night vainly trying to obtain additional names to the lists of survivors, but efforts to reach the Carpathia by wireless came to nothing. No new names have been added to the list of saved since yesterday, when wireless communication with the Carpathia ceased because the Cunarder had steamed out of her zone of land communication.

The wireless station at Sable Island was in communication for a time this morning with the Carpathia. The Cunarder reported that twenty icebergs were sighted off the banks near the scene where the Titanic sunk, but no details of the disaster were sent.

The wireless station at Halifax reported a violent electrical storm off Sable Island early today, which cut off communication with the Carpathia at that time. Conditions improved as daylight came. And the same station reported that communication with the Carpathia is greatly hampered by the maze of wireless flashes that are being sent out by the fleet of steamers dotting the ocean, all seeking news of the Titanic disaster. Apparently not until the Carpathia gets out of range of these ships will anything filter through.

NO NEWS AT ST. JOHN'S

Hope That Fishing Vessels May Have Been in Vicinity of Disaster Dispelled.

St. John's, N. F., April 17—No details of the sinking of the Titanic have been received in St. John's. The Newfoundland Government officials, wireless operators and newspaper men have maintained a constant watch for any vessel likely to have particulars of the great tragedy.

Some hope has existed that fishing vessels near the scene of the disaster might have information, but up to noon today no fisherman had arrived from the vicinity of the accident. As the Titanic went down at a point 370 miles south of St. John's there has not been sufficient time for any of these fishing craft to reach the harbor here.

The steamer Bruce, which arrived in St. John's harbor at noon on Monday and remained in port until 2 o'clock yesterday afternoon, heard nothing of the tragedy except that her wireless operator reached the operator at the Cape Race wireless station. The Bruce operator received brief bulletins from the Cape Race station telling of the collision with the iceberg and of the rescue of eight hundred or more of the Titanic passengers.

The Bruce was off the coast Sunday night, but heard nothing from the Titanic. The wireless operator on the Bruce closed his office at 11:45 p.m. At 8 o'clock Monday morning when he went on duty again the Cape Race operator notified him that the Titanic had struck an iceberg. The Bruce had no details of the tragedy and was not in communication with any vessel. The operator on the Bruce was unable to use his instrument during his stay in St. John's as the engines were stopped and he had no power to work his apparatus.

MILLET HAD SKETCHES.

New Bedford, Mass., April 17—Frank D. Millet, the artist who was aboard the Titanic and whose name does not appear in the list of survivors, had been engaged to paint the mural decorations for the [illegible] Public Library in this city. Mr. Millet had notified the library trustees [illegible] were complete and [illegible] them back from Europe [illegible]. The artist formerly lived [illegible] a few miles from New Bedford.

SCOUT CRUISER CHESTER.

SEARCH FOR TITANIC DEAD

Cable Ship to Go to Scene of Disaster—100 Coffins Aboard.

Halifax, N. S., Apuril 17—The cable ship Mackay-Bennett, which has been chartered by the White Star Line to go to the scene of the Titanic disaster, was being loaded today preparatory to departure. In the hope that some bodies may be picked up, coffins are being included in the cargo, and several undertakers and embalmers will go along.

The cable ship Minia, which was in the vicinity of the disaster, has arrived here with no survivors on board. It had been hoped that she might have picked up a few stragglers floating on rafts or among the wreckage.

In addition to 100 coffins, the Mackay-Bennet is taking over 100 tons of ice. Long lines of teams were filing down the pier today and the coffins were piled up ten feet high.

The mission of this ship recalls the disaster to the steamer La Bourgogne when a similar vessel was fitted out here to search the sea for dead. At that time more than thirty bodies were found floating in the vicinity of the disaster, although the vessel did not get away from here until a week after the tragedy.

MESSAGE FROM THE OLYMPIC

Loudon Charlton Says That 670 Persons Were Saved, Mostly Women and Children.

On Board the Olympic, at Sea, April 17—The Olympic received news at midnight Sunday that the Titanic had struck ice. She started immediately for the scene, but resumed her course eastward at 5 o'clock in the morning upon hearing that the Titanic had sunk at 2 a.m.

The only details known are that 670 passengers were saved, mostly women and children. All the crew, except those manning the boats, are believed to have been lost, including the principal officers.

This dispatch was sent to the Associated Press by Loudon G. Charlton of New York, a passenger on the Olympic, and is the first word received concerning the disaster from any one outside of official sources. It will be noted that the number of survivors is practically identical with the original dispatches. Later dispatches, however, indicated that 868 persons were saved.

MESSAGES RECEIVED IN BOSTON

Several Vessels and Stations Within Wireless Range of the Carpathia, but Fail to Get Details.

Boston, April 17—Various radiograms received here early today showed that several vessels are within wireless range, either directly or by some relay, with the steamer Carpathia, having on board the survivors of the Titanic.

The outward-bound steamer Franconia was in communication with the Carpathia at 9 a.m.

The scout cruiser Chester stated that she expected to sight the Carpathia at noon.

The scout cruiser Salem announced that she would stop off Nantucket lightship during the forenoon and relay messages from the Chester to shore stations.

A number of outward-bound liners were in the vicinity of the Carpathia during the forenoon.

At 7 o'clock this morning an operator at a local wireless station distinctly heard the signature to a message from the Cunarder Carpathia. The message was not caught.

Several operators, including the wireless man of the scout cruiser Chester, immediately attempted to pick up the Carpathia. Sable Island wireless station then reported the others to hold off until it could communicate with the Cunarder.

At 5:30 o'clock this morning the scout cruiser Chester sent the following message to her sister ship, the Salem, relayed through the Charlestown Navy Yard:

"Increasing speed to 24 knots. As soon as able to reach Carpathia will relay to you. Not able to communicate direct."

The Chester gave her location as latitude 40.36 north, longitude 65.90 west.

RELIEF FUND HERE.

New York Will Follow the Lead of London.

Following the lead of London a relief fund will be opened here for the survivors of the Titanic disaster. The following cable correspondence has passed between the Lord Mayor of London and Mayor Gaynor of this city:

London, Eng., April 17, 1912.
The Mayor, New York:
Opening fund relief sufferers of Titanic distaster. Will warmly welcome your sympathy.
LORD MAYOR OF LONDON.

New York, April 17, 1912.
Lord Mayor of London:
Relief fund Titanic sufferers has our hearty sympathy. Will open one here.
GAYNOR, Mayor New York.

Those who want to contribute to the local relief fund may send their contributions to the Mayor. He will probably appoint a relief committee within a day or two. In the meantime the Mayor has ordered all flags on public buildings half masted as a mark of sorrow and respect.

NARROW ESCAPE OF COL. W. L. OGDEN

Well Known Brooklyn Man Had Planned to Sail on Steamship Titanic.

COULDN'T QUITE MAKE IT.

Fortunate Incident Probably Saved His Life—Saw the Astors.

It was learned today that Colonel Willis L. Ogden, who has just arrived in port, thought for a time of booking passage on the Titanic, but changed his mind at the last moment because had he taken the ship, he would have been obliged to make an exhausting railroad journey of forty-eight hours from Naples to London, and the Titanic would have arrived in New York three days later than Colonel Ogden intended to get here.

Colonel Ogden had not booked his passage, but he had his stateroom picked out on the schedule. He was traveling alone.

"I deliberated on taking the Titanic, but changed my mind when I discovered that it would mean a long railroad journey to London and that the big ship would get into this port three days later than I wanted to get here," said Colonel Ogden today.

"I journeyed from Alexanadria to Naples on the Cedric. At Alexandria Colonel Astor and his wife boarded the Cedric, but I held no conversation with him on the way up and know nothing about his plans to take the Titanic."

JUMPED UNDER SUBWAY TRAIN

A man, who was afterward identified as Samuel Lipson, 29 years old, a painter, living at 61 East 102d street, Manhattan, killed himself this morning by jumping under the wheels of a south-bound local train at the 145th street station of the Broadway branch of the subway. His act horrified a score of women and children who were waiting on the platform. Several cars passed over the man's body before Motorman Hathaway could apply the brakes and bring the train to a halt.

Lipson was killed instantly. His body was taken to the West 152d street police station. In his clothing was found a letter, addressed to him, from Joseph Garfinkel of 1865 Amsterdam avenue. Garfinkel identified the body, but could not assign any reason for Lipson killing himself.

BILL DAHLEN SUSPENDED.

President Lynch of the National League has suspended Bill Dahlen, manager of the Brooklyn Baseball Club, for three days, beginning today, because Bill has had too much tosay regarding the abilities of the umpires in both the New York-Brooklyn and Philadelphia-Brooklyn series. Dahlen's fighting attitude is liked by the fans, but evidently does not meet with the approval of the upper class. The kicks registered by Bill yesterday were in the hands of the fans legitimate, but the umpires must be upheld in their decisions, and consequently the Superba's manager suffers.

Rain played havoc with the baseball schedule today and many games were postponed. The storm hit several sections of the country as well as Greater New York. The local management decided about 2 p.m. to call off the Brooklyn-Philadelphia game, while the New York Americans and the Washingtons also had an idle day. At Cleveland the St. Louis-Cleveland engagement was also postponed; the Philadelphia-Boston conflict in the American league was likewise called off, while at Chicago the Detroit-Chicago contest was put back to a later date because of a mild cloudburst that flooded the grounds.

WIRELESS STATION BUSY.

Eagle Plant in Touch With L. I. Operators—Many Carpathia Calls.

All day long the wireless station in The Eagle office has been in touch with the wireless stations along Long Island and as efforts weer made either to get in touch with the Carpathia or other ships with messages for her the wireless operator in The Eagle heard and recorded the dots and dashes that flew through the air. Every effort to get in the Carpathia was immediately known in The Eagle office through its wireless system.

So many wireless stations have been calling "M P A" through the air that the stations along the south shore of Long Island have been asked to stop. "M P A" is the call of the Carpathia, and with so many stations flashing this call through the air it has only added to the confusion in gettting in communication with the vessel.

Wireless authorities say the wireless system of the Carpathia was intended only for a short radius, eighty-five miles. Because of this short range it has been difficult to get in touch with her.

INSPECT SUBWAY ROUTE.

Chairman Willcox of the Public Service Commission, with his colleagues and engineers, is to take another trip tomorrow to inspect the proposed route of the Union Square-East New York subway line. With the officials will also be the engineers and officers of the Brooklyn Rapid Transit Company. It is stated that the Public Service Commission is a unit on the plan, but it is believed that several sections of subway will be added in lieu of some of the proposed elevated railroad structures. While the commission is said to be agreed on the plan, Chairman Willcox this afternoon stated that the find of the commission was open and that the members wanted to hear all suggestions.

ICEBERGS 70 MILES IN BRETAGNE'S PATH

French Liner Skirted Big Field of Ice in Which Titanic Went Down.

COUNTED FIFTY BIG BERGS.

Ice, Says Captain Mace, Covered the Sea as Far as the Eye Could Reach.

What is pronounced to have been the greatest iceberg field ever seen off the coast of Newfoundland was skirted by the steamship La Bretagne of the French Line, which arrived at this port from Havre today, bringing over 775 passengers. The field was seventy miles in length and probably as wide, and the La Bretagne was five hours in passing along its edge. Scattered among the small ice were between forty and fifty immense bergs, and one of which was as large as a modern hotel building.

The La Bretagne sighted this field on Sunday morning last, in the immediate vicinity of the place where the Titanic struck a berg and went down with more than a thousand persons.

The day, said Captain Mace, commanding the Bretagne, was clear and the air sparkling, when at 7:30 o'clock in the morning, the bergs and small ice came into view on the starboard bow. The ice covered the sea as far as the eye could reach and the great bergs moved up and down rythmically on the undulating billows, the water between being oily in appearance, a condition caused by the bergs shielding the surface from the light breeze. The field had a general southward movement, and the Bretagne was headed in the same direction in order to avoid contact with any of the floating enemies to navigation. From 7:30 o'clock in the morning until after midday the field was alongside the Bretagne, at times some of the bergs being so close as to enable the passengers to make good photographs, many of which were taken.

First Officer Larive said that he counted forty large bergs, while some of the passengers had counted fifty and more. According to the log of the Bretagne, the field was floating from about 50 degrees West Longitude and 47 North Latitude to 51 west Longitude and 42 North Latitude, this being within the radius of the Titanic's fatal collision.

Giuseppe and Ricciotti Garibaldi, grandsons of the Italian Liberator, were passengers on the Bretagne, on their way to their home in the City of Mexico. Each took many good pictures of the ice field and each said that it was many times larger than anything of the sort that they had ever seen.

Miss Mabel Finey of San Francisco, one of the passengers, who has been traveling through the Continent and in Northern Africa, had telegraphed to Southampton for accommodations on the Titanic, but later plans caused her to cancel it.

MAYOR SEES A YOUNG "FAN."

Chats With "Gus" Gelles, Age 14, Buys Him Balls and Glove.

For three-quarters of an hour today Mayor Gaynor forgot the manifold cares of his office and talked baseball with Gustave Gelles, aged 14, of 53 Cannon street.

The Mayor not long since received a long and laboriously written letter from young Gelles. In it he poured out his boy's heart to the man he had heard was the friend of small boys. He told the Mayor that he was very fond of playing baseball, but that he was so very poor that he couldn't afford to get a bat or a ball.

The Mayor wrote back a letter worded as follows:

"My dear boy—Come in here and see me some day, and I will fix you out. Show this letter to the officer at the door.

"Sincerely yours,
"WILLIAM J. GAYNOR."

When the talk was at an end the Mayor shook hands with his small visitor and then assigned Lieutenant "Bill" Kennell to take Gus to a sporting goods store in Nassau street, where the lieutenant purchased for Gus no less than three baseballs and a glove.

PETITIONS IN BANKRUPTCY.

Petitions in bankruptcy were filed today in the United States District Court as follows:

No. 4827, voluntary, by Luke E. Conness, 48 Jackson street, Stapleton, S. I. Liabilities, $10,202, all unsecured; assets, $69.

No. 4828, voluntary, by Wilson & Baillie Manufacturing Company, 26 Court street. Liabilities, $252,348.87; assets, $98,830.51.

No. 4829, voluntary, by Thomas F. Quinlan, Long Island City. Liabilities, $7,662, all unsecured; assets, $130.

JOHN H. BERGEN DEAD.

John H. Bergen, a descendant of the first settlers of Flatbush, died yesterday of pneumonia, after a few days of illness, at his home, 643 Flatbush avenue. He was born 46 years ago in the old Bergen homestead, at Albemarle road and Flatbush avenue, and was the son of Cornelius Bergen. His father died in Flordia about three weeks ago. Mr. Bergen leaves a widow, Helen Prentiss, a daughter and a sister, Mrs. Carr. Funeral services will take place to morrow afternoon at 3:30 o'clock.

SURVIVORS' ROSTER IS NOT LENGTHENED

No Additional Names of Persons Saved From the Titanic Received.

BEHR'S FRIENDS ALARMED.

Tennis Player's Name Does Not Appear Among Those on the Carpathia—May Be Lost.

No additional names of survivors of the Titanic disaster were received in this city up to a late hour this afternoon, although they were being awaited by White Star Line officials, as well as anxious relatives and friends. The list thus far received is that which was published yesterday, and which had been sent from the Carpathia by way of the wireless of the Olympic.

If the report received today from the Franconia by way of Camperdown, Nova Scotia, that there were 710 persons aboard the Carpathia, is correct, there are yet to come some 380 names of survivors, including many of those of steerage or third-class passengers.

Karl H. Behr's Friends Uncertain as to His Fate.

Friends of Karl H. Behr, the famous international tennis player and member of the Crescent Athletic Club, who was returning on the Titanic from a very successful business trip on the other side, are still anxious about his welfare. It was reported yesterday that the Brooklyn man was among those saved, but revised lists today have left off the name among those on the Carpathia. At the White Star Line it was said today that Karl B. Behr was among those saved, and at the same time it was intimated that this information was due to the receipt of a name Karl B. This, it was said, had been interpreted to mean Karl Behr, although it might mean Barrett.

The White Star Line also gave out today the names of ten men and women booked on the Titanic, who appeared on the complete passenger lists cabled to this side, but who did not sail with the steamer. The names are:

Mr. and Mrs. Adelman (probably Mr. and Mrs. Lila).
Miss Nellie Dalcroft.
Mr. George Hart.
Mr. G. Lawrence.
Mr. and Mrs. George H. Turner (probably John H.)
George Turner.
Mrs. S. George Wilkinson.
Miss Ada Wilkinson.

After an all-night "checking-up," it was announced at the office of the White Star Line that they find a number of names given as among those who sailed on the ill-fated vessel, and who they believe are among the survivors on the Carpathia. They say this is the result of clerical work, and has no confirmation by wireless messages. The list follows:

Mrs. J. W. Cardeza.
Howard B. Case.
Mrs. J. C. Crosby.
Mrs. Harriet Crosby (probably).
Mrs. Washington Dodge.

List of Rescued Not Appearing on Cabled Passenger Lists.

After comparing the list of survivors received from the Carpathia with the passenger list as received from London, the officials of the White Star line said today that the following whose names have been received from the Carpathia as having been rescued were not on the cabled passenger lists:

CHARLTON, W. M.
CAMARION, KENARD
DOMORY, MISS ELLEN
LEAHY, MISS NORA
MENDERSON, MISS LETTA
SKELLER, MRS. WILLIAM
TROUT, MISS JESSIE
DANIEL, MISS SARAH
HOLD, MISS J. A.
HOPE, NINA
ANTIONETTE, MISS
MIDDLER, MME. M. OLIVA
MARION, MISS
APPIERANELT, MISS

LIST OF SURVIVORS.

A

ABBOTT, Mrs. ROSE.
ABELSON, HANNA.
ALLEN, Miss E. W.
ANDERSON, HARRY.
ANDREWS, Miss K. T.
ANGLE, Mrs. WILLIAM.
APPLETON, Mrs. E. W.
ASTOR, Mrs. JOHN JACOB, and maid.

B

BALLS, ADA E.
BARKWORTH, A. H.
BATHWORTH, MIAH.
BAXTER, Mrs. JAMES.
BEANE, EDWARD.
BEANE, Mrs. ETHEL.
BECKWITH, Mr. and Mrs. R. T.
BEHR, KARL H.
BISHOP, Mr. and Mrs. D. H.
BISS, Miss KATE.
BLANK, HENRY
BONNELL, Miss CAROLINE.
BOWEN, Miss G. C.
BOWERMAN, Miss ELSIE.
BRAYTON, GEORGE A.
BROWN, Mrs. J. J.
BROWN, Mrs. J. M.
BRYHL, Miss DAGMAR.
BUCKNELL, Mrs. WILLIAM.
BURNS, Mrs. G. M.
BYSTROM, Mrs. KAROLINA.

C

CALDERHEAD, E. P.
CALDWELL, ALBERT F.
CALDWELL, ALDEN G.
CALDWELL, Mrs. SYLVIA.
CAMERON, Miss.
CARDELL, Mrs. CHURCHILL.
CARDEZA, Mrs. J. W.
CARDEZA, THOMAS.
CAMARION, RENARDO.
CARTER, Miss LUCILLE.
CARTER, Master WILLIAM.
CARTER, Mrs. W. E.
CASE, HOWARD B.
CASSEBERE, Miss D. D.
CAVENDISH, Mrs. TURRELL W., and maid.
CHAFFEE, Mrs. H. F.
CHAMBERS, Mr. and Mrs. M. C.
CHARLTON, WILLIAM.
CHERRY, Miss GLADYS.
CHEVRO, PAUL.
CHRISTY, Mrs. ALICE.
CHRISTY, Miss JULIA.
CLARKE, Mrs. ADA MARIE.
COLLETT, Mrs. STUART.
COLLYER, Mrs. CHARLOTTE.
COLLYER, Miss MARJORIE.
CROSBY, Mrs. E. G.
CROSBY, Miss.

D

DANIEL, SARAH.
DANIEL, ROBERT W.
DAVIDSON, Mrs. THORNTON.
DAVIES, JOHN M.
DAVIES, Miss AGNES.
DAVIS, Miss MARY.
DEVILLINES, Mrs. R.
DICK, Mr. and Mrs. A. A.
DODGE, Mr. and Mrs. WASHINGTON, and son.
DOLING, Mrs. ADA
DOLING, Miss ELSIE.
DOUGLAS, FRED C.
DOUGLAS, Mrs. WALTER.
DREW, Mrs. LULU.
DUFF-GORDON, Sir COSMO and Lady.
DURANTE, FLORENTINA.
DURANTE, LENORA ASUNCION.

F

FORTUNE, Mrs. MARK.
FAUNTHORPE, Mrs. LIZZIE.
WLEGENHEIM, Mrs. ANTOINETTE.
FLYNN, J. J.
FORMERY, Miss ELLA
FORTUNE, Miss LUCILLE and Miss ALICE.
FRANCATEL, Miss.
FRAUENTHAL, Dr. and Mrs. HENRY.
FRAUENTHAL, Mr. and Mrs. J. G.
FROELICHER, Miss MARGARET.
FUTRELLE, Mr. and Mrs. JACQUES.

G

GERRCIE, Mrs. MARCY.
GENOVESE, ARGENE.
GIBSON, Miss DOROTHY.
GIBSON, Mrs. LEONARD.
GOLDENBURG, Mrs. SAMUEL.
GOLDENBURG, Miss ELLA.
GOOGHT, JAMES.
GRACIE, Colonel ARCHIBALD.
GRAHAM, Mr.
GRAHAM, Mrs. WILLIAM.
GRAHAM, Miss MARGARET E.
GREENFIELD, Mrs. LEE D.
GREENFIELD, WILLIAM H.
GARSIDE, Miss ETHEL.

H

HAMALANIAN, Mrs. ANNA, and child.
HARNER, HENRY.
HARDER, Mr. and Mrs. GEORGE A.
HARPER, HENRY S.
HARPER, Miss NINA.
HARRIS, GEORGE.
HARRIS, Mrs. HENRY B.
HART, Mrs. ESTHER.
HART, Miss EVA.
HAWSFORD, HENRY J.
HAYS, Mrs CHARLES M., and daughter, MARGARET.
HERMAN, Miss ALICE.
HERMAN, Mrs. JANE.
HERMAN, Mrs. Kate.
HEWLETT, Miss MARY.
HIPPACH, Mrs. IDA S.
HIPPACH, Miss JEAN.
HOCKING, Mrs. ELIZABETH.
HOCKING, Miss NELLIE.
HOGEBOOM, Mrs. JOHN C.
HOLD, Mrs. J. A.
HPE, Miss NINA.
HOYT, Mr. and Mrs. FRED M.

I

ISMAY, J. BRUCE.

J

JACOBSOHN, Mrs. AMY.
JULIET, L.

K

KEANE, Miss NORA.
KELLY, Miss FANNIE.

L

LAMORE, Mrs.
LAROCHE, Miss LOUISE.
LEADER, Mrs. A. F.
LEHMAN, Miss BERTHA.
LEITCH, Miss JESSIE W.
LINES, Mrs. ERNEST.
LINES, Miss MARY C.
LONGLEY, Mrs. G. F.

M

MADILL, Miss GEORGIETTA A.
MAHAN, Mrs.
MALLET, Mrs. A.
MALLETT, Master ANDRERO.
MARSCHAL, PIERRE.
MARVIN, Mrs. D. V.
MELICARD, Madame.
MELLINGER, Mrs. ELIZABETH and child.
MIDDLER, OLIVIA.
MINDERSON, Miss L.
MINNIHAN, Mrs. W. E.
MINNIHAN, Miss DAISY.

N

NEWELL, Miss MADELINE.
NEWELL, Miss MARJORIE.
NEWSOM, Miss HELEN.
NYE, Mrs. ELIZABETH.

O

OMOND, FIENNAD.
OSTBY, Mrs. E. S.
OSTBY, Miss HELEN R.

P

PARISH, Mrs. L.
PENCHEN, Major ARTHUR.
POMERY, Miss ELLEN.
PORTALUPPI, Mrs. EMILIO.
POTTER, Mrs. THOMAS, Jr.

Q

QUICK, Mrs. JANE O.
QUICK, Miss PHYLLIS O.

R

REVOUF, Mrs. LILY
RHEIMS, Mrs. GEORGE
RICHARDSON, Mr. and Mrs. EMILIE
RIGSDALE, Mrs. LUCY
ROBERT, Mrs. EDWARD S.
ROGERS, Mrs. ELIZA
ROGERS, ELINE
ROLMANO, C.
ROSENBAUM, Miss EDITH
ROTHES, Countess of
ROTHSCHILD, Mrs. MARTIN
RUGG, Miss EMILIE

S

SAALFIELD, ADOLPHE
SCHABERT, Mrs. PAUL
SEALEY, Miss NORA
SHELLER, Mrs. WILLIAM
SILVERTHORNE, I. SPENCER
SILVER, Mrs. WILLIAM D.
SIMONIUS, Colonel ALFONSO
SINCOCK, Miss MAUDS
SLOPER, WILLIAM T.
SMITH, Mrs. MARION
SNYDER, Mr. and Mrs. JOHN
SOLOMON, ABRAHAM
SPENCER, Mrs. W. A. and maid.
STEHELIN, Dr. MAX
STENGEL, Mr. and Mrs. C. E. H.
STEWARD, FRED
STONE, Mrs. GEORGE M.
SWIFT, Mrs. FREDERICK JOEL

T

TAUSIG, Miss RUTH
TAYLOR, Mr. and Mrs. E. Z.
THAYER, Mr. and Mrs. J. BB.
THAYER, J. B. Jr.
TOUCH, Miss ALICE
TROUT, Miss EDINA S.
TROUT, Miss JENNIE
TUCKER, GILBERT M.
WARREN, Mrs. F. M.
WEISS, Mrs. MATILDA
WHITE, Mrs. J. STUART
WICK, Miss MARY
WIDENER, Mrs. GEORGE D. and maid.
WILLARD, Miss CONSTANCE

Y

YOUNG, Miss MARIE

THIRD-CLASS PASSENGERS.

The following is a list of the third class steerage passengers who embarked on the Titanic at Southampton:

A

ALLUM, Owen. ALEXANDER, Wm. ADAMS, J. ALFRED, Evan. ALLEN, William.
ABBOTT, Ross and family. ABBING, Anthony. AKS, Leah. AKS, Filly.

B

BRAUND, Lewis. BRAUND, Owen. BADMAN, Emily. BOWEN, David. BEAVEN, W.
BARTON, David. BROCKLEBANK, Wm. BILLIARD, A. and two children. BING, Lee.

C

CAN, Ernest. CREASE, Ernest. COHETT, Gurshon. COUTTS, Winnie and two children. CRIBB, John. CRIBB, Alice C.
CELLOTI, Francesco. CHRISTMANN, Emil. COXON, Daniel. CORN, Harry. CARVER, A. COOK, Jacob. CHIP, Chang.

D

DUGEMIN, Joseph. DEAN, Bertram and family. DORKINGS, Edward. DENNIS, Samuel. DENNIS, William.
DAVIES, John. DOWDELL, E. DAVISON, Thomas. DAVISON, Mary. DAHL, Charles. DRAPKIN, Jennie.

E

EVERETT, Thomas. EMPUEL, Ethel.
ELSBURY, James.

F

FORD, Arthur. FORD, Margaret, and family.
FRANKLIN, Charles. FOO, Choong.

G

GOODWIN, F., and family. GOLDSMITH, Frank, and family.
GREEN, George. GUST, Frank. GARFIRTH, John. GILLINSKI, Leslie.

H

HYMAN, Abraham. HARKNETT, Alice.
HOWARD, May. HARMER, Abraham.

I

ING, Hee.

J

JOHNSON, A., family. JOHNSTONE, W.

K

KEEFE, Arthur. KELLEY, James.

L

LOVELL, John. LOR, William. LOBB, Cordelia. LESTER, James. LITHMAN, Simon. LEONARD, L.
LAM, Ali. LAM, Len. LANG, Fang. LING, Lee. LOCKYER, Edward.

M

MOORE, Leonard. MACKAY, George. MEEK, Annie. MIKALSEN, Sander. MILES, Frank. MILLS, Frederic. MORLEY, William. McNAME, Neal.
McNAMEE, Eileen. MEANWELL, Marian. MEO, Alfonso. MARNER, Simon. MURDLIN, Joseph. MOORE, Belle. MOOR, Meier.

N

NANCARROW, William. NOSWORTHY, Richard.

P

PEDRUZZI, Joseph. PERKIN, John. PEARCE, Ernest.
PEACOCK, Treesteall, and two children. POTCHETT, George. PETERSON, Marius.

R

ROUSE, Richard. RUSH, Alfred. ROGERS, William. REYNOLDS, Harold. ROTH, Sarah.
READ, James. ROBINS, Alexander. ROBINS, Charity. RISIAN, Samuel.

S

SADOWITZ, Harry. SAUNDERCOCK, W. STANLEY, Amy and E. SHELLARK, Fred'k. SAGE, John and family. SAWYER, Frederick. SPINNER, Henry. SHORNEY, Charles.
SIMMONS, John. SEROTA, Maurice. SOMERTON, F. SLOCOVSKI, Selman. SUTCHALL, Henry. SATHER, Simon. STOREY, T. SPECTOR, Woolf.

T

THOMSON, Alex. THEOBALD, Thomas. TOMLIN, Ernest. TURNQUIST, W. THORNEYCROFT, P.
THORNEYCROFT, P. TORBER, Ernest. TREMBISKY, Berk. TILLEY, Edward.

W

WILLIAMS, Harry. WILLIAMS, Leslie. WARE, Frederick. WARREN, Charles.
WISEMAN, Philip. WILKES, Ellen. WEBBER, James. WINDELOV, Einar.

The following is a list of the third class or steerage passengers embarked on the Titanic at Cherbourg:

AKAR, Nourcalain. ASSAD, Said. ATTALA, Malakka. AYONT, Bancura. BACHINI, Zabour. BELMENTOY, Hassef. BADT, Mohamet. BETROS, Yazbeck. BONTOS, Hanna. BACCOS, Boulos. BENROUS, Tannous. CATAVELAS, Vassilios. CARAM, Catherine. CHANNINI, Georges. CHRONOPOLOUS, Demetris. DRAZENOVIC, Josef. DAHER, Shedid. ELIAS, Joseph. ELIAS, Joseph. ELIAS, Hanna. ELIAS, Foofa. GHEORGEFF, Stano. GHEMAT, Emar. GERIOS, Youssef. GERIOS, Youssef. GERIOS, Assaf. CHALIL, Saal. HELENE, Eugene. HANE, Youssef, and two children. HACHINI, Najib. JAMILA, Nicola, and child. JOSEPH, Mary. JEANNAR, Hanna. KHALIL, Labie. KASSEN, Housseln. KARUM, Franz and child. KRIKORIAN, Nichan. KEENI, Fahim. LEMBEROPOLOUS, Peter.

LAKARIAN, Orsen. LATIFE, Marie. MARIA, Joseph. MANTOURA, Moses. MONCARREK, Omine, and two children. MUSTAFA, Nasr. MONSARAK, Hanna. MIKE, Anna. MUSTMANS, Fatima. MARTIN, Johann. MALINOFF, Nicola. NAKLE, Trik. NAKID, Maria. NORMIL, Mansour. ODELE, Catherine. OKTIN, Aurin. RAHIN, Baz. ROUFOUN, Apostolos. SARKIS, Lahowd. SULTAN, Meme. STANKOVIC, Jovan. SAAL, Antoni. SEMAN, Betros. SIRAYAMA, Peter. SAMAAN, Jouseef. SAIDE, Barbara. SAAD, Dibo. SARKIS, Madirossian. THOMAS, John. THOMAS, Charles. THOMAS, Tannous. TUMIN, Thomas, and infant. TAM, Hilton. YASSANI, Daper. USHER, Hadiner. VARTANIAN, David. WAKA, Said. WAZLI, Jousef. WELLER, Abi. YOUSSEF, Brahim. YALSEVAC, Ivan. ZAKARIAN, Mapri.

ENGLISH LAW RECOGNIZED

Titanic's Equipment Approximated That Required by American Laws Governing Shipping.

Eagle Bureau,
608 Fourteenth Street.

Washington, April 17—The United States has reciprocal relations with regard to shipping laws with the following countries: Canada, Denmark, France, Germany, Great Britain, Japan, Netherlands, New South Wales, New Zealand and Norway.

This country establishes reciprocal relations with a foreign country when the shipping laws of that power approximate the laws of the United States. Inspections of such vessels are merely for the purpose of seeing whether they comply with the certificate issued by the country from which they hail. In the case of the Titanic, the United States recognizes the English shipping law as controlling her equipment.

All countries other than those named above have laws which do not approximate ours, and their ships are required, when entering or leaving American ports, to comply with the United States laws regarding equipment.

The lifeboat equipment required by the United States laws would have provided more than sufficient capacity for all the persons aboard the Titanic. It would not, however, have cared for everybody if the ship had been filled to her capacity. While our laws do not require, in the cases of such large steamers, a sufficient number of boats to accommodate everybody when the ship is crowded, they do, however, provide for many more than the British laws.

LIBRARY BIDS OPENED.

11 Received for South Wing of Central Building—Lowest, $170,300.

Deputy Public Works Commissioner Lineburgh today opened bids received on the contract to build the foundations of the south wing of thte central building of Brooklyn's new Public Library, to go up at Eastern Parkway and Flatbush avenue.

Borough President Steers will award the contract within a few days, and it is hoped to have the work of digging begun within six weeks.

Eleven bids were received, the lowest being made by Charles Meads & Co., 165 Broadway, Manhattan, which has done a great deal of work in Brooklyn. This company's bid is $170,300. The estimated cost of the foundations was $200,000, an amount fixed in the calculations of the borough officials.

Public Works Commissioner Pounds and Superintendent Woody of the Bureau of Public Buildings, will examine the bids and will recommend to President Steers the selection of the lowest bidder who has lived up to the qualifications. Besides the Meads bid, four contractors made offers under $200,000. They are: P. J. Carlin, $188,700, and Luke a Burke, $185,000; Northeast Construction Company, $192,000; Benedetto & Egan Construction Company, $191,640.

GILLETT HAS LOW CARD.

Rain Spoils Golf Play for J. F. Shanley Memorial Cup.

(Special to the Eagle.)

Lakewood, N. J., April 17—Rain checked the play in the seniors handicap for the J. F. Shanley Memorial Cup at the Lakewood Country Club this morning.

The card handed in by C. R. Gillett proved the best in the early division. He went out in 47 and came home in 40. His handicap of 4 gave him a net score of 83. H. W. Brown, Phil H. McSweeney, Phil P. Presbery, Garden City; C. A. Spofford, Apawamis, and C. R. Gillett, Wykagyl, are the players who have the smallest allowance on the handicap list.

BANQUET PUT OFF.

The banquet which was to be held Friday evening by the members of the New York Produce Exchange, celebrating the fiftieth anniversary of the chartering of the Exchange, has been postponed indefinitely, but not believed to have been abandoned. The action taken was the result of the appalling Titanic disaster.

INDEX

To Classified Advertisements in Today's Eagle.

UNIFORM SHIP LAWS URGED BY CALDER

Resolution Authorizes President to Call an International Conference.

MORE LIFEBOATS DEMANDED.

Titanic Survivors Will Be Summoned to Appear at a Congressional Investigation.

LIFEBOAT AND PASSENGER CAPACITY OF GREAT LINERS

Figures given out today at the offices of the steamboat inspection service show the inadequate lifeboat equipment of great liners, due to defective international laws.

Vessel.	Passengers and crew.	Capacity boats and rafts.
Amerika	3,434	1,766
Celtic	1,446	1,222
George Washington	3,478	2,911
Kaiserin Auguste Victoria	3,378	2,026
Lusitania	2,889	986
Mauretania	2,972	982
Rotterdam	3,601	1,455
Olympic	3,447	1,171
Cedric	2,094	1,023
Baltic	2,411	1,400

Eagle Bureau,
608 Fourteenth street.

Washington, April 17—Representative William M. Calder of Brooklyn today introduced in the House a resolution which authorizes the President to call an international conference to consider and adopt a uniform system of life saving appliances for all ocean going vessels.

At the present time there is no uniformity of shipping laws among the nations. This country recognizes the laws of certain countries and does not recognize the laws of others.

Mr. Calder's idea is that every ship putting to sea should have a sufficient number of lifeboats to care for all persons aboard, whether passengers or crew.

He held a conference this morning with Assistant Secretary Cable, of the Department of Commerce and Labor, and with J. B. Uhler, inspector general of the steamship inspection service. Both of these officials agreed that the only method of arriving at a uniform international system was through a conference of the nations. Mr. Calder's resolution is as follows:

Be it resolved, That the President of the United States be and hereby is authorized to arrange for a conference with representatives of all the maritime nations of the world and to appoint representatives of the United States thereto for the purpose of considering and establishing a uniform system of inspection of all passenger-carrying vessels, to the end that they shall be equipped with a suitable and sufficient number of lifeboats and other life-saving appliances for the safeguarding of the lives of all persons, including passengers and crews, aboard such vessels.

After a conference with President Taft it was announced today by Secretary of the Treasury Macveagh that no revenue cutters would be ordered to meet the Carpathia unless new conditions should arise.

The two scout cruisers already ordered to meet the Carpathia are much faster boats than the revenue cutters.

STEAMSHIP MEN QUOTED

They Admit Necessity for New Laws to Increase Safety of Transatlantic Travelers.

The steamship company's officers today admitted the necessity of amending the laws under which the big passenger carrying vessels carry lifeboats, liferafts and emergency appliances for the safeguarding of human life.

The reconstruction of the international agreement for the common laws of the big countries can be brought about only through diplomatic channels or in response to a positive demand from Congress.

Vice President Franklin of the White Star line today took the question up and said the demands of the public would be met by the company which sent the ill-starred Titanic out.

White Star Liners Will Carry More Lifeboats in Future.

The following message was sent in to Mr. Franklin early today, for The Eagle, and is responsible for the statement by the official:

"The Brooklyn Daily Eagle desires to ask if the number of lifeboats in commission on the White Star liners is to be increased in view of the lesson of the disaster to the Titanic."

Mr. Franklin answered this letter at his morning interview with the newspapermen. He said: "You may rest assured that this line will now do everything possible to send its ships out in such condition that a repetition of the Titanic disaster will be impossible."

"Is that to be taken as an affirmative reply to our question?" Mr. Franklin was asked for The Eagle.

"It is," he said.

Mr. Franklin today emphasized the absolute and natural feeling of confidence the White Star line officials had felt in the great liner that went down and admitted also that this feeling was entirely unjustified. He repeated that he himself had thought the boat unsinkable and had believed this firmly. He added, with emphasis, that his company would meet the new conditions by every method known to safeguard the lives of the people on the steamships.

International Laws Covering Safety Provisions Need Revision, Say Steamship Men.

The officials in the steamboat inspection service of the United States Government and also those of two of the greatest lines of steamers plying the Atlantic concurred today in urging a revision of the international law regarding the carrying of lifeboats. The United States, Germany, France and Great Britain have approximately the same law. The English law, dispatches from London state today, has not been amended since the day of the 10,000-ton steamer. Not one word of additional English legislation has been passed to provide for the additional burden of human freight carried by the 20,000, 30,000 and 40,000-ton boats.

"The American, English, French and German liners comply with the laws, but the laws are no good."

This is the statement made today to The Eagle at the offices of the steamboat inspection service in the Customs House. The man who made the statement is in a position of authority, but could not be quoted in the absence of Captain Seeley, superintendent of inspectors, the division chief.

O. L. Richard of C. B. Richard & Co., agents for the Lloyd-Italiano Line, said today that the international law covering the lifeboat question should be amended. A. Gipps, general agent for the Holland-American Line, said substantially the same thing. He said:

"If any life-saving apparatus is to be carried it is evident that enough should be carried for all the passengers and the crew. The change desired in the laws, however, can be brought about only through diplomatic channels, as there is no body of any one country empowered to deal fully with the question."

This statement was affirmed at the offices of the steamboat inspection service, where it was explained that the only authority vested in the inspectors at this end of the ocean line was to see that the foreign vessels carried an equipment which coincided with the demands of their own nation.

Titanic Carried All Boats Law Required.

It is pretty evident today that the ill-fated Titanic, whose lifeboats failed so utterly to relieve even the most immediate and pressing need of the passengers, let alone the crew, carried all the lifeboats the law requires.

The London Board of Trade regulations require that a vessel of 10,000 tons shall carry a minimum of sixteen boats.

There are no regulations applying to vessels of greater tonnage, but another rule provides that where boats do not furnish accommodations for all passengers on the steamer additional wood or metal collapsible boats or life rafts shall be carried. The regulations require that the capacity of the boats shall be 5,500 cubic feet. The Titanic's boats, it has been ascertained today, had a capacity of 9,702 each. This would indicate that the Titanic carried nearly double the specified accommodation required by English law, although it leaves open the question whether she complied with the evident intention of the clause which requires "additional wood or metal collapsible boats or life rafts."

It is stated today that the Titanic carried fourteen lifeboats, two cutters, each accommodating sixty-five people and a number of collapsible boats or rafts. An effort was made to secure from the White Star line today the exact number of collapsible boats or rafts carried by the Titanic, but the information was not available.

An analysis of the figures on file with the government steamboat inspection steamboat service, relating to the various big liners that ply back and forth from New York, indicates today that no steamers are carrying an adequate complement of lifeboats, or rafts, although all are complying with the law. The figures indicate that certainly not more than half of the crew and passengers of the big liners could be saved if a catastrophe occurred on one of the big boats when it was carrying anything near its capacity.

The Baltic (23,875 tons), which has a crew and passenger capacity of 2,411, carries twenty-two boats and rafts, with a capacity of about 1,400; the Carpathia (13,603 tons), with a crew and passenger capacity of 2,862, carries eighteen boats and rafts, with a capacity of 1,200; the Cedric (21,034 tons), with a crew and passenger capacity of 2,094, carries twenty boats and rafts, with a capacity of about 1,300; the Kaiser Wilhelm II (19,361 tons), with a crew and passenger capacity of 2,379, carries thirty boats, with a capacity of 1,900; the Mauretania (31,937 tons), with a passenger and crew and capacity of 2,972, carries sixteen lifeboats, exclusive of rafts, capable of holding about 1,000 people.

MEMORIAL SERVICES IN LONDON

London, April 17—Although hope that the list of survivors of the sunken Titanic will be added to has been practically given up, the offices of the White Star line in London, Southampton and Liverpool were again besieged this morning by throngs of anxious inquirers.

Some of those who had relatives on board, in fact, remained at the offices throughout the night, scanning the lists given out during the early hours, which, however, proved not to contain any fresh names, but merely corrections of those given before.

Those who waited in the London offices were mostly women, whose husbands had started for America on business or to make new homes there for their families.

Early this morning the White Star Company gave out the statement received from the captain of the Olympic that neither the Virginian nor the Parisian had survivors on board and expressing the belief that all those who had been rescued were on board the Carpathia.

It still proved a difficult task to make the bereaved relatives believe that those who had left them only a few days ago full of hope would not return, and many of the people waited on.

While travelers generally understand the fact that the great liners do not carry enough boats to accommodate the whole of the passengers and crew, to the general public the news that all on board the Titanic did not have a chance of saving their lives in this way came as a rude surprise, and there is likely to be considerable agitation in and out of Parliament on the subject.

It is now recalled that just prior to the first trip of the Olympic a member of the House of Commons asked Sydney Buxton, president of the Board of Trade, a question as to the number of boats she carried. The President of the Board of Trade replied that the Olympic carried fourteen lifeboats and two ordinary boats, with an aggregate capacity of 9,752 cubic feet, which is in excess of requirements under the statutory rules.

As was pointed out by Alexander Carlisle, the designer of the Titanic and the Olympic, in the course of an interview yesterday, the Titanic was fitted with davits sufficient to carry four times the number of boats actually placed on board.

The Lord Mayor of London today opened a Mansion House Fund for the relief of the families of the crew of the Titanic and of any others left in needy circumstances in consequence of the disaster.

A memorial service for the victims is to be held at St. Paul's Cathedral on April 19.

Much indignation is expressed in connection with the publication of the telegrams stating that the Titanic was in tow of the Virginian just after the news of the accident was received. Colonel Charles E. Yate, Member of Parliament for Leicestershire, will ask the President of the Board of Trade in the House of Commons if his attention has been drawn to the publication of the telegrams and whether their origin could be traced.

The electrical control of the bulkheads installed in the Titanic is coming in for much criticism.

It is stated here that they are a pet idea of Lord Pirrie, who insists on introducing them in ships built at Belfast, despite the condemnation of many well-known constructors, who pin their faith to hydraulic power as being far more reliable. These constructors point out that even a small mishap is liable to render the electric installation useless.

IN MEMORY OF TITANIC'S DEAD

Reference to Tragedy Made at Cornerstone Laying in Manhattan.

References to the Titanic disaster were made at the ceremonies attending the laying of the cornerstone of the Seamen's Church Institute, at South street and Coenties Slip, Manhattan, yesterday. Bishop Charles S. Burch, Bishop Courtney and others spoke feelingly of the tragedy.

The Seamen's Benefit Society subscribed to two rooms in the building at a cost of $100 in memory of the sailors lost on the Titanic.

A MEMORIAL SERMON.

Priest Dwells Upon Preparedness for Death.

Special services for the victims of the Titanic disaster were held last night (Tuesday) in the Church of the Holy Innocents, in Flatbush. The rector, the Rev. William J. Costello, preached a memorial sermon, drawing a lesson of preparedness for death. There was a large congregation.

BISHOP'S DAUGHTER LOST.

Salt Lake City, Utah, April 17—Mrs. Irene C. Corbett, who was a passenger on the Titanic, is the daughter of Bishop Levi A. Colvin of Provo, Utah. Her name does not appear among the survivors. Her father received a letter from her yesterday saying she would be home next week.

HAD PLANNED LUNCH FOR CAPTAIN SMITH

Commander of Titanic Was to Have Been Entertained by Brooklyn Men Tomorrow.

HELD HIM IN HIGH REGARD.

Colonel William Hester Tells of Many Voyages With Ill-Fated Follower of the Sea.

A new touch of tragic interest was added to the story of the sunken Titanic today when it was learned that a pleasant luncheon party had been planned by two prominent Brooklyn men in honor of Captain E. J. Smith, to be held tomorrow. Colonel William Hester and John J. Sinclair, both of whom had sailed many times with Captain Smith and who held him in high regard, had expected to entertain him at noon tomorrow.

Colonel Hester, in speaking of the captain of the ill-fated steamer said:

"I have known Captain Smith a number of years and have crossed with him on the Baltic, Adriatic and Olympic and expected to cross with him again this summer on the Titanic. Except when I was out of town, I always met him when he was in New York and together with an old friend, John J. Sinclair, had expected to lunch with Captain Smith on Thursday (tomorrow). I have visited his home in Southampton and met his wife and daughter.

"Captain Smith had many friends in this city and was a frequent visitor at Glen Cove. Among those who entertained him there was Henry W. J. Bucknall, a fellow Englishman and a friend of long standing.

"Captain Smith had nothing of the old salt in his appearance. He was over six feet in height, well proportioned, fair complexion, and had the appearance of a military or naval officer. His manner was quiet and his address pleasing. It was not necessary for him to be severe in his tone on shipboard to command respect. His whole appearance did that, and as a prominent lady remarked, when introduced to him, 'His countenance inspired confidence.' He was very little in evidence on shipboard, being only where his duty called him. The large circle of friends among ocean travelers that he had was not created by his catering to their society.

"Last fall, on Captain Smith's return to New York after the collision with the Hawk, about one hundred of his friends gave him a dinner at the Metropolitan Club as an expression of their sympathy and confidence in him, at which Chauncey M. Depew spoke, as well as Controller Prendergast, Dr. St. Clair McKelway and Mr. Lawrence of the Lotos Club and others. Captain Smith made a very modest speech thanking his friends for their esteem. Besides good wishes, a purse of several thousand dollars was presented to him."

SHIP FLAGS AT HALF MAST.

Maritime Exchange Passes Resolutions on Titanic Disaster.

Every craft in the harbor today is flying her flag at half mast in memory of the Titanic's dead. The action is in compliance with a resolution adopted at the annual meeting of the Maritime Exchange and offered by Fred B. Dalzell, who referred to the fate of the Titanic as the greatest maritime disaster of modern times. The resolution says:

"Resolved, That the members of the Maritime Association of the Port of New York, assembled in annual meeting, express their great regret at the lamentable disaster which has befallen the steamer Titanic, their great sorrow at the deplorable loss of life and property which has evidently accompanied this disaster, and extend to all involved in the great calamity their deep and heartfelt sympathy; and be it further

"Resolved, That all vessels in the harbor be requested to place their flags at half staff out of respect to the unfortunate dead."

PEACE SOCIETY SYMPATHY.

London, April 17—A meeting of the executives of the British committee for the celebration of the Centenary of Peace, held under the presidency of Earl Grey, today passed the following resolution:

"This committee formed to celebrate the centenary of unbroken peace and friendship between the British Empire and the United States of America desires to convey the expression of its profound and heartfelt sympathy to the families of those who have been lost with the Titanic. In particular it desires to express its solicitude for the safety of William T. Stead, a member of this committee, who was traveling by the vessel on a mission of peace."

HIT WITH A BLACKJACK.

While trying to defend the peanut stand of an Italian friend, Samuel Rochneck, a newsdealer of 204 South Fifth street, was blackjacked early this morning. Later James Farrell, 20 years old, of 872 Driggs avenue, was arrested on a charge of felonious assault and held in $1,500 bail for a hearing tomorrow in the Manhattan avenue police court. The assault occurred at Broadway and Havemeyer street.

GARDEN PARTY POSTPONED.

Mrs. Charles Francis Roe, president of the New York branch of the Army Relief Society, announced today that the annual garden party, which was to have taken place the latter part of May at Governor's Island, has been indefinitely postponed. This action, it was announced, was taken because of the death of General Grant and the Titanic disaster. Many friends of the society were on board the wrecked steamship.

FOURTH AVENUE BILL SIGNED.

(Special to The Eagle.)

Albany, April 17—Governor Dix today signed Senator Cullen's bill to permit the construction of a railroad on Fourth avenue, Brooklyn, with the consent of the local authorities and of the owners of at least half in value of the property on the street, or in lieu of such property owners consent, the consent of the Appellate Division.

POPE SENDS BLESSINGS TO U. S.

Rome, April 17—The Pope today received in farewell private audience Mgr. Giovanni Bonzano, Apostolic Delegate to the United States, who is to leave for America tomorrow morning. The Pontiff gave his last instructions to Mgr. Bonzano and asked him to convey his apostolic blessing to the members of the Catholic Church in America.

SERVICES IN MONTREAL.

Montreal, April 17—Arrangements are being made here for joint memorial services for the victims of the Titanic to be held by the denominations of the various Protestant churches here. A requiem mass will be celebrated by the Roman Catholics in St. James Cathedral. The dates of the services have not yet been fixed.

FRANCE'S REGRETS.

Paris, April 17—The French government today transmitted to Washington and London an official expression of France's regret in connection with the disaster to the Titanic and its condolences with the persons bereaved.

START FUND TO AID POORER PASSENGERS

Women of Greater New York Organize Relief Committee.

MONEY MAY BE SENT TO EAGLE

Great Need Is for Cash and Clothing to Relieve Immediate Distress and Suffering.

Appeals for contributions of money and clothing for the survivors of the Titanic are being sent out today by members of the Women's Relief Committee for the steerage survivors of the Titanic, formed last night by Mrs. Nelson Henry, wife of the Surveyor of the Port. Contributions of money from Brooklyn people may be sent to Miss Clara L. Ogden, of 76 Pierrepont street, or to The Brooklyn Daily Eagle. Due acknowledgment of the contributions will be made in The Eagle. Suitable clothing should be sent to Mrs. Paul Dana, 1A Fifth avenue, Manhattan, for the committee.

Immediate action is requested by the committee because the Carpathia, bearing about 400 of the women and children from the steerage of the Titanic, will reach New York some time tomorrow, and from all accounts, the survivors are in dire distress, lacking clothing and cash.

The Relief Committee met and organized today at the home of Mrs. Abraham S. Hewitt, 9 Lexington avenue, Manhattan. Miss Ogden was placed in charge of the work of the Committee in Brooklyn.

Commissioner of Immigration Williams notified the committee today that it would be called upon to care for 250 of the survivors, because the Bureau of Immigration will not be able to accommodate all of the persons on the Carpathia at Ellis Island. He will cause an investigation to be made into the condition of each immigrant from the Titanic, to determine the needs of the survivors. But, in the meantime, they must be housed and clothed and fed, and the women of New York are invited to co-operate with the Relief Committee for that purpose.

Money Needed at Once and Will Be Carefully Distributed.

"The money contributed will not be distributed recklessly," said Miss Ogden this afternoon, after the meeting of the committee. "Some funds will be required to be expended at once, and the remainder will be carefully distributed. We trust that the generosity of the people whose emotions have been stirred by this tragedy will not be appealed to in vain. And the contributions are needed immediately."

So quickly has the committee worked since it was organized last night that there is already in the hands of the treasurer the sum of $1,110, but this is only a small part of the amount that will be needed. The women have sub-divided themselves into Housing, Entertainment, Finance and Clothing committees.

At noon it was decided to have the entertainment committee, and the first offer of help came from the Liebler Company, which will give a benefit performance of "The Garden of Allah." Then Miss Ada Sterling, the actress, offered to recite "The Lion and the Lamb," for the benefit of the survivors.

At the meeting the Junior League House offered to take care of 70 survivors at the Spencer School. The Association of Working Girls, together with Miss Virginia Potter, will house two hundred, the Day Nursery will look after the children, and ten sisters and ten deaconesses of the Little Sisters of The Poor will be on the dock ready to help in every way possible.

Survivors Will Be Cared For Until They Can Look Out for Themselves.

All of this work will be continued by the committee until such time as the survivors will be able to look after themselves. For instance, many of them are bound for the West to meet relatives, and they will be sent on by the committee. A telegram was sent to President Taft after the meeting to the effect that the women here stood ready to assist the Federal Government in every way possible and also expressing sympathy over the presumed death of his military aide.

The money received thus far by the committee has come from Mrs. Russell Sage, $500; Mrs. J. H. Aldrich, $250; Mrs. Wilbur Fiske, $150; Mrs. Charles Francis Rowe, $50; Mrs. A. M. Dodge, $50, and James H. Aldrich $100. It was also stated that several $10 contributions had been received.

Mrs. E. H. Harriman telephoned that she could not be on hand this morning but that she was ready to help in any way and that she wanted to go on the committees. There is to be another meeting tomorrow at 9 Lexington avenue.

The committees were formed as follows:

Housing—Mrs. E. R. Hewitt, Miss Virginia Potter, Mrs. R. Irving, Mrs. H. Ollesheimer, Mrs. J. H. Price, Mrs. Stafford Morgan, Mrs. Katherine Tweed.

Committee on Entertainment—Mrs. Nelson Henry, Miss Elizabeth Marbury, Miss Anne Morgan, Mrs. Munson Horris, Mrs. J. B. Harrison, Mrs. Richard Irving, Miss Clare Irving and Miss A. Sloane.

Finance—Mrs. Nelson Henry, Mrs. E. H. Harriman, Mrs. C. B. Alexander, Mrs. H. F. Dimock, Mrs. J. H. Aldrich, Mrs. S. D. Ripley.

Clothing—Mrs. Paul Dana, 1A Fifth avenue; Mrs. J. H. Aldrich, 150 West Fifty-ninth street; Miss Grace Bigelow, 29 Gramery Park; Mrs. Henry Dimock, 25 East Sixtieth street; Miss C. M. Stewart, Mrs. A. M. Dodge, and for Brooklyn, Miss Clara Ogden, 76 Pierrepont street.

It was explained that clothing for the sufferers could be sent to any of the last named committee, and it was hoped that warm and suitable garments would be offered.

FUTRELLE MAY BE SAFE.

London, April 17—The list of survivors of the Titanic disaster as given out by the White Star line offices here contains the names of both Mr. and Mrs. Jacques Futrelle of Boston.

Previous lists published here contained the name of Mrs. Futrelle only.

Another new name appearing on the list of second class passengers is that of Miss Finney. The name of Charles M. Hays, president of the Grand Trunk Railway, does not appear on the line's list.

INSTRUCTED FOR TAFT.

New Haven, April 17—Delegates at large to the Republican National Convention at Chicago, elected today are: Charles F. Brooker, J. Henry Roraback, Charles Hopkins Clark and Frank B. Weeks. They are instructed for Taft.

J. STUART HOLDEN NOT ON THE TITANIC

Cable Message Says He Was Detained in London by Wife's Illness.

CANCELED HIS BOOKING.

Rector of St. Paul's Had Engagement to Speak at Conservation Congress and at St. Ann's Church.

Although his name appears among those of the first-cabin passengers aboard the Titanic, the Rev. J. Stuart Holden did not sail from England on the ill-fated ship, according to news received in Brooklyn today. The Rev. Mr. Holden, who is rector of St. Paul's Church in London, apparently canceled his booking at the last minute.

William R. Moody, who is the director of the religious work of the Northfield Foundation at East Northfield, Mass., was to have met Mr. Holden at the dock upon the arrival of the Titanic, but he received a cable message from Mr. Holden, who said that on account of the illness of his wife he would not be able to sail, and asked that his Northfield engagements be canceled. The nature of Mrs. Holden's illness was not given.

Mr. Moody communicated with the Rev. Dr. Cleland B. McAfee, pastor of the Lafayette Avenue Presbyterian Church, to whom he gave the information that Mr. Holden had not sailed for the reasons given. John Polls of 31 South Portland avenue, at the same time, called up The Eagle and gave the information that Mr. Holden was safe, as he had met Mr. Moody on Sunday last, and he told him of the cablegram.

Mr. Holden was engaged by the Men and Religion Forward Movement to deliver one of the addresses at the Conservative Congress, which opens in Carnegie Hall, Manhattan, on Friday morning. At headquarters of the organization in Manhattan the news given out that Mr. Holden had not sailed was confirmed. It was said that a letter had been received there from Mr. Moody, in which he explained that Mr. Holden had sent him a cable message, stating that his wife was too ill for him to take passage on the Titanic.

Mr. Holden was to have opened a mission in St. Ann's Episcopal Church on the Heights on Sunday, which was to continue for several days. It was stated at St. Ann's Church that nothing had been heard from Mr. Holden. An attempt to get Northfield by telephone several times had resulted in the information that the wires were all down.

It was also said that an official of the White Star Line who was connected with St. Bartholomew's Church, in Manhattan, was sure that Mr. Holden was on the Titanic, and a member of the Reformed Church on the Heights, who was in the employ of the White Star Line, had given the Rev. Mr. Cooper, curate of St. Ann's Church, the positive information that the young minister had sailed on the ill-fated vessel. When Mr. Cooper was informed of the news in possession of The Eagle, he was rejoiced and declared that it had lifted a great load from the minds and hearts of the people there.

The Rev. J. Stuart Holden has a high place in the religious world. He has preached for two or three summer vacations in St. Bartholomew's Church, which is one of the wealthiest congregations in the Episcopal denomination. He always attracted large audiences. Mr. Holden was well known in Brooklyn, having preached here a number of terms. He has been one of the attractive speakers of the Christian Workers Conference, which is the principal summer religious event at East Northfield, for a number of years. He has also given a number of addresses in different parts of the country.

In addition to being rector of the influential Church of St. Paul, Mr. Holden was personal chaplain to the Earl of Aberdeen, who is also a well-known religious worker, and who has himself paid visits to Northfield and contributed largely to its work.

CANCELED HIS WILL.

Daniel Heatly Barnes Wrote "Null and Void" Across the Face of It.

Surrogate Ketcham has refused probate to a will of Daniel Heatly Barnes, late of 82 Richmond street. Before he died the testator had written diagonally across the face of the will, which occupied but one page, the folllowing words: "Null and void, Daniel Heatly Barnes, October 30, 1910." This had been written in a large hand with a red pencil.

In his opinion the Surrogate holds that inasmuch as these words were written over the text of the will, and not in the margin, as in a previous case cited as in point, the will was legally canceled. The property, amounting to about $10,000 will not go to the grand nephew, John R. Cave of Bayside, L. I., who had been made the principal legatee.

Objections to the will had been made by a niece, Ada F. DeLaney, who kept house for her uncle at the time of his death. She claims that she had received verbal promises of the estate. The will gave her only $5, and the cancellation of an $800 debt. It also set aside $100 for a cousin, Alice Barnes, who lives in England.

The will was made December 1, 1909, and testator died April 4, 1911.

FLED FROM A SAVINGS BANK.

Michael Rosso Arrested on a Charge of Attempted Forgery.

Michael Rosso, 19 years old, of 114 Watkins street, appeared at the Kings County Savings Bank this morning and, presenting the bankbook of Michael Rocca of 121 South Fourth street, tried to cash a check for $200. The paying teller, John H. Wacke, suspected a forgery and compared the signature of Rocca in the bankbook with that of Rosso on the check. When Rosso saw that he was under suspicion, he ran from the bank and was caught on the street by Policeman Arwecke of the Bedford avenue station. He will be arraigned this afternoon in the Manhattan avenue police court on a charge of attempted forgery. Rosso was visiting Rocca last night.

WOMAN U. S. BUREAU CHIEF.

Taft Names Miss Lathrop as Chief of New Children's Department.

Washington, April 17—Julia C. Lathrop of Chicago, an associate of Jane Addams in the work at Hull House, a member of the Illinois Board of Charity, and a graduate and trustee of Vassar College, was today appointed by President Taft as chief of the new Children's Bureau in the Department of Commerce and Labor.

Miss Lathrop is the first woman to be made a bureau chief under the government.

THE KAISER'S SYMPATHY.

London, April 17—The text of the German Emperor's message of sympathy sent to the White Star line is as follows:

"Achilleion, April 16.

"Deeply grieved by the sad news of the terrible disaster which has befallen your line I send you the expression of my deepest sympathy and also with all those who mourn the loss of relatives and friends.

"WILLIAM, I. R.

CAPT. SMITH KNOWN AT NASSAU

Commander of Titanic Was Frequent Visitor at Glen Cove Club.

(Special to The Eagle.)

Glen Cove, L. I., April 17—Captain Edward J. Smith, commander of the ill-fated steamship Titanic, was very well known among the members of the summer colony here, many of whom had made Transatlantic voyages under his care.

He was a close friend of Mr. and Mrs. Henry W. J. Bucknall of New York and Glen Cove, and last June, during the coronation festivities for King George and Queen Mary, Mr. and Mrs. Bucknall gave a coronation dinner at Lee Head, their Glen Cove estate, at which Captain Smith was the guest of honor. Captain Smith at that time was commander of the steamship Olympic, sister ship of the Titanic.

He has been a frequent guest at the Nassau Country Club for a number of summers past, making his visits between voyages. He was frequently seen on the links, and played a good game of golf. the captain was often seen in company with Mr. Bucknall, Colonel William Hester and Herbert F. Gunnison.

BOY HELD UP BY BOYS.

Lad Attacked on L Stairs and Relieved of $3.

A bold juvenile hold-up, with several boys between the ages of 14 and 16 as the aggressors, and Paul Trauck, 16 years old, of 339 Bridge street, as the victim, occurred at 9 o'clock last night on the stairs leading to the Bridge street station of the Myrtle avenue elevated road.

Shortly before 9 o'clock last night, a cigar dealer on Myrtle avenue gave Trausk $3 and instructed him to go to the ticket agent on the Bridge street station and get it changed into small coins. Trausk had just reached the first landing when the gang of hold-up boys pounced upon him and relieved him of the money.

The boy notified Policeman Dominic O'Connor of the Adams street station and dward Curran of 67½ Lawrence street and Frederick Bradford of 43 Duffield street, both 16 years old, were arrested and taken before Magistrate Fitch in the Adams street court, this morning. Trausk was unable to identify the boys as those who had taken the money and they were discharged.

BOLD DAYLIGHT ROBBERY.

Youth Walks Off With a Large Sum From Beverly Road House.

A daring daylight burglary occurred in Flatbush yesterday afternoon about 3 o'clock. Mr. and Mrs. L. L. Myer, who live at 2215 Beverley Road, reported to the police that about the hour mentioned they missed a silver mesh bag containing a large sum of money that was on their hall rack. The bag was known to be there shortly before 3 o'clock.

Mrs. Arthur E. Delmhurst, who lives next door, was able to give a description of the robbers. She told the police that a young man, wearing a peaked cap and neatly dressed, looking like a butcher's boy or clerk, came to her door about 3 o'clock and asked if a party named Brown lived there. She told him no, but the family living next door might be of that name.

It is supposed that the youth, after leaving Mrs. Delmhurst's door, went to the Myer house, found the coast clear and made off with the bag.

MICHIGAN PEOPLE ON TITANIC.

Detroit, April 17—Mr. and Mrs. D. H. Bishop, whose names are in the list of Titanic survivors, are residents of Dowagiac, Mich. They were returning from a trip to Egypt.

Mrs. Jane O. Quick and her two daughters also saved, are on their way from England to join the husband and father who has been in Detroit for some time.

Mrs. A. Davis and John Davis of Mohawk, Mich., were rescued, but Joseph C. Nichols, a son of Mrs. Davis, probably is lost.

Others known to have been on the steamship and who have not been heard from are:

George Floyd Eitemiller, Detroit; Miss Agnes Sincock, Calumet, Mich.; Alfred Bush, on way from London to join relatives in Detroit, and Alfred, John and Joseph Davies of West Bromwich, England en route to Pontiac, Mich., where a brother resides.

COASTER PLANT SOLD.

Coney Island Amusement Plant Under the Hammer.

The property of the International Giant Coaster Company, at the corner of West Tenth street and Surf avenue, Coney Island, was sold today at foreclosure sale, at the Real Estate Exchange in Montague street, by William H. Smith.

The property includes the coasting structure, the operating plant, the cars and the lease. The coaster was built early last spring on the site of the Loop-the-Loop, and it was opened early in the summer. The Title Guarantee and Trust Company, acting as trustee for the bondholders in the $75,000 mortgage covering the lease, purchased the property.

HAYS NOT SAVED.

An investigation has been made of the report current yesterday that Charles M. Hays, president of the Grand Trunk Railway, was among the survivors of the Titanic.

The name of Mr. Hays does not appear in the list of survivors posted at the White Star offices in either New York or London, and there is no apparent reason for saying that he has been saved. The dispatch in question saying Mr. Hays was among the survivors was first published in Montreal.

Mrs. Charles M. Hays and her daughter Margaret are reported among the survivors on board the Carpathia.

MISS ROSENBAUM RESCUED.

Far Rockaway Young Woman Was Taken From Titanic.

A Far Rockaway young woman, Miss Edith Louise Rosenbaum, daughter of Mr. and Mrs. Harry Rosenbaum of Merrall road, that place, was among the Titanic passengers who were rescued by the Carpathia. Mr. and Mrs. Rosenbaum were distracted from the time they heard of the accident until they received definite assurances that their daughter was safe.

All Monday night the Rosenbaums remained awake in the hope of receiving reassuring news about the rescue of their daughter, but this they did not receive until 8 o'clock yesterday morning.

THE POPE GRIEVED.

Rome, April 17—Both Pope Pius and King Victor Emmanuel have expressed their deep sympathy for the victims of the Titanic disaster and have asked to be informed of the details of the wreck and of the names of the survivors.

Among the passengers were several American citizens who were known personally to the King and the Pope, as they were recently received by them in private audience.

DID NOT SAIL ON TITANIC.

Wausau, Wis., April 17—George Hart, for many years court reporter here, reported to have been a passenger on the Titanic, who was believed to have been lost, was not on board, according to a letter received here, which stated his reservation had been canceled.

ROOSEVELT FIGHT COST $59,126.75

Perkins, Munsey and Cochran Paid $15,000 Each for Manhattan Primaries.

$5,585.64 SPENT FOR TAFT.

Deficiency of $12,500 in the Roosevelt Fund After Campaign Was Over.

Albany, N. Y., April 17—The campaign made at the recent primaries in New York City in behalf of delegates favorable to the nomination of Colonel Roosevelt as President, cost $59,126.75, according to a statement filed with the Secretary of State today by Eton Huntington Hooker, treasurer of the Roosevelt League.

George W. Perkins, Frank A. Munsey and Alexander S. Cochran each contributed $15,000. Other contributors included George Baxter, $5,000; H. L. Stoddard, $2,500; Charles H. Duell, $1,600; E. H. Hooker, A. Foster Higgins and R. P. Perkins, each $1,000, and Byron L. Smith and Oscar Straus, each $500; H. L. Satterlee, $100. The league also received hundreds of dollars in small contributions.

Messrs. Perkins and Munsey contributed $10,000 each prior to the primaries and evidently there was a deficiency on April 9, when the league raised $12,500 more. This money was contributed by Munsey and Perkins, who gave an additional $5,000, and by H. L. Stoddard, who gave $2,500.

The expenses were incurred by office help and in small amounts for campaign purposes.

Ogden L. Mills, treasurer of the New York County Republican Committee, has certified that he received and spent $5,585.64, which was contributed by the Taft National League.

"TONY" DISCUSSES DISASTER.

Eagle Bootblack Is Sure God Is Angry With Mankind.

Tony Gigante, the bootblack of The Eagle Building, is again agitated over the terrible disaster of the loss of the Titanic, and in his agitation he is once more predicting the destruction of the wicked people of the earth. He says that God's anger is manifest. At the time of the San Francisco earthquake Tony talked with much earnestness to an Eagle reporter about the cause of the disaster, and now he is referring to what he said at that time, and in his earnest way, with gesticulations and dialect which shows that he is a thinker, declares that it is just as true today as it ever was. This is what he said at the time of the earthquake:

"The Lord in Heaven is angry with men. He has shown them how to live true and right, and they have not done so. They live wicked and sinful lives. He has told them to love and help each other. They lie, and cheat, and steal, and think only of themselves. He has told men to love their wives and women to love their husbands. They have no respect for marriage, for home, for children, for anything. Most of them do not go to church. Those who go hear nothing of the good. They go on just the same.

"The Lord is angry and He will destroy the bad people in the world. He will begin again with a new world. He has been patient with men, but they get worse and not better. He will kill them all. The rich have robbed the poor. He will kill them, and they cannot take their money with them. All the wicked men and women in the world will be killed. The Lord will burn them up, and He will put new people on the earth, good people, who do as He wants them to.

"It is the same here as in my own country. In Italy, the rich oppress the poor, and there are bad men and women everywhere. The Lord makes Vesuvius to blow up. He sends the fire and the ashes upon them. He will kill them all, and begin all over again.

"The terrible earthquake in San Francisco is but the beginning. It will come to New York and to Brooklyn. It will come everywhere, and the wicked men will be burnt up and killed. I think it will come here this summer, in July or August. All the high buildings will fall down, and the fire will burn them up. The water from the ocean will roll in over the land and everything will be washed clean and new. Then the sun will shine and the Lord will send new people, who are good and who love each other and live as Jesus told men to live."

R. W. SMITH AMONG MISSING.

Tea Exporter of London, Titanic Passenger, Well Known in Brooklyn.

Among the names of the missing appears that of R. W. Smith, who was connected with the well-known tea exporting firm of Reinach-Nephews & Co. of London and who had a great many friends in Brooklyn.

Mr. Smith, as a member of his firm, had made some forty trips across the Atlantic, and his acquaintance in the tea trade was very large. Whenever he came to this city it was his custom to stay at the home of T. G. Matthews, 437 Eastern Parkway. This he had done for twenty-five years. Mr. Matthews said today that he was afraid there was no hope that Mr. Smith might have been rescued.

OHIOANS ON TITANIC.

Gallipolis, Ohio, April 17—Albert A. Stewart of Gallipolis was among the passengers on the Titanic whose name is not found among the survivors on the Carpathia. Mr. Stewart was the New York representative of the Strowbridge Lithographing Company of Cincinnati. He was returning from France, leaving his family on the Continent.

Painesville, O., April 17—Miss Jessie Malletich of Youngstown, who was bringing Emil Nanestnik of Austria to his fatehr here, were second cabin passengers on board the Titanic. Their names are not on the list of those reported as rescued.

ALABAMA IN SEMI-COMMISSION.

The battleship Alabama, which has been undergoing repairs at the Brooklyn Navy Yard for two years, was formally turned over to the Navy Department this morning, when Captain of the Yard L. S. Van Duzer placed the ship in semi-commission.

The Alabama will remain in the yard for a short time, and will then be placed in the reserve fleet at Philadelphia.

FIRE IN A TENEMENT.

A two-alarm fire in the crowded tenement section on Lewis avenue at 3 o'clock this morning caused considerable excitement among the tenants. The efforts of the firemen, however, confined the blaze to the three-story brick unoccupied building at 3 Lewis avenue, owned by William Kestler of 34 Vernon avenue. The loss was $1,000.

BUSINESS BAD; TRIES SUICIDE.

Despondent because of poor business, Samuel Linner, 41 years old, who recently opened a store at 643 East Ninth street, Manhattan, severed an artery in his neck this morning in his store. He was discovered by a customer and later removed to Bellevue Hospital, a prisoner, charged wit hattempted suicide. The surgeons say that he will die.

WOODRUFF DISCUSSES POLITICAL PROBLEMS

Talks About Initiative, Referendum and Recall to Adelphi Academy Alumni.

A GOOD WORD FOR ROOSEVELT

County Leader Sure the Colonel Is Sincere—Wants to Serve the People.

Timothy L. Woodruff, Republican leader of Kings County, spoke on "Political Problems of the Day" at the annual meeting and smoker of the Adelphi Academy Alumni Association, held last night at the University Club, Lafayette avenue and South Oxford street. It was originally intended to have an informal debate between Mr. Woodruff and William M. Ivins, but the latter was unable to be present because of illness, and Mr. Woodruff treated the principles which are dividing the Republican party from a non-partisan point of view.

He pointed out that the party is split on the question as to what form of government is best for the American people, the representative government, as established by the Constitution and under which the nation has prospered for a century and a quarter, or the "pure democracy," which the progressives of the party are urging by their advocacy of the initiative, referendum and recall.

"Now," he said, "the demand is that the people shall have not only a voice in the selection of the candidate of the party, but by the presidential preferential primaries shall select the delegates who are to be sent to the convention. Step by step, they are going farther and farther away from the Constitutional idea of representative government. The initiative and referendum are steps in this same direction which are being taken by the progressives in the Republican party, and also in the Democratic party, if there are progressives in the latter.

"I am not prepared to say that some of these measures are not desirable; nor am I prepared to say that some of them are not necessary. All these measures, and any measure, must be adopted if the people want them, for I believe the people should rule, and the people will rule when they make up their mind to do so."

Mr. Woodruff then took up the matter of direct primaries and said that seven years ago in a speech in Brooklyn he had advocated the reform, but when a bill was introduced in the Legislature in favor of them, after careful study he concluded the direct primaries were not practicable. The recent test of them in this State has proved that they do not accomplish more, if as much, as the old system, and that no more interest is taken in them than in the old primaries. He continued:

"In addition we have learned from the Western States that these primaries can be controlled by men anxious to secure the nomination of a certain man and willing and able to spend money for it; likewise those possessed of good lung power, or the gift of gab, can win the primaries."

Referring to the referendum, he said: "We have had it in this State for the past fifty years, in regard to constitutional amendments, and it has shown that these amendments and laws cannot be understood without much study, and that they are beyond the sphere and interest of the average voter."

The speaker then asserted that he believed Colonel Roosevelt is really sincere in his advocacy of these progressive measures and that the Colonel's only aim is to serve the best interests of the American people. These laws, he said, are likely to become operative, as they have been tried quite successfully in other States, and if the peopel demand them they may have to come here also.

In reference to the recall, he said there was a great deal of error in regard to Colonel Roosevelt's position. He pointed out that Roosevelt favors this only in cases where the courts construe the Constitution too technically and as opposed to the will of the majority of the people. He pointed out that the people ought to have some way of nullifying that decision, and as the machinery of amendment provided by the Constitution is too intricate and slow to accomplish this in a reasonable time, the proposed way would be a remedy.

Dr. Charles H. Levermore also spoke, saying that it would be well for the country if the parties realigned themselves—the progressives of both parties in a radical party and the other elements in a conservative party. The only parties now that have any political gospel, he said, are the freak parties. The Progressive Republicans are urging all these radical doctrines in an effort to dodge the real question of the day, the tariff. The only good thing that has resulted from the radical doctrines of the West is the publicity that legislation and the votes of the legislators in Oregon receive in its own State. This should be the same in all States, he said, but the idea should not be carried to extremes.

At the meeting the following officers of the association were re-elected: President, Parker V. Lawrence; vice president, Howell Topping; treasurer, George A. Anderson; secretary, Kenneth B. Halstead; executive committee, Mortimer W. Byers, Edwin B. Dutcher, William E. Hoshke and Cedric R. Woodward. On the athletic advisory committee were appointed Dr. H. S. Pettit, Mortimer W. Byers, H. H. Romer, R. S. Salter and W. E. Hoshke.

PARIS FASHIONS UP TO DATE.

From the Eagle Paris Bureau, 53 Rue Cambon, through the courtesy of Abraham & Straus.

White serge gown, cerise belt and buttons, batiste collar.

PENNSYLVANIANS MEET.

Movement to Restore Farm Adjoining Penn's Burial Place.

The twelfth annual meeting of the Pennsylvania Society, which was held last evening in the Astor gallery of the Waldorf-Astoria, brought out over two hundred loyal and distinguished sons of the Keystone State. Before the election of officers, which was the important business of the evening, the society adopted a series of amendments to their constitution. Report was made that, through the generous contributions of Colonel Robert M. Thompson, Senator W. A. Clark, Andrew Carnegie, William Guggenheim, George C. Boldt and Henry Phipps, the Pennsylvania Society is enabled to make a contribution of $500 toward the restoration of Jordan's Farm, a tract of land in Buckinghamshire, England, immediately adjoining the burial ground in which the remains of William Penn lie.

The officers and council elected for 1912-1913 are:

William Andrew Clark, president; Robert Mazet, first vice president; Frederick H. Eaton, second vice president; William Uhler Hensel, third vice president; Theodore P. Shonts, fourth vice president; the Rev. Dr. James M. Farrar, chaplain; Barr Ferree, secretary; William Guggenheim, treasurer; Council, Thomas E. Kirby, James Gayley, George C. Boldt.

NOTABLE MILITARY FUNCTION

Co. A of 23d Regiment to Celebrate Semi-Centennial on Friday Night.

One of the great military functions of recent years in Brooklyn will be the semi-centennial celebration of Company A, Twenty-third Infantry, N. G. N. Y., on Friday night. There will be a review and reception tendered to Colonel William Everdell at the armory, Bedford and Atlantic avenues, and hundreds of the present and former members of the crack company of "Ours" will be on hand to greet the colonel and recall the days of auld lang syne.

Colonel Everdell was captain of Company A from January 20, 1862, to July 14, 1862. The company has these charter members living: William Everdell, Benjamin Shepard, Joseph G. Story, James L. Stafford, William H. Marston and Allen I. Ormsbee. The living Civil War veterans are: William Everdell, Benjamin Shepard, Joseph G. Story, Abram Allen, jr.; E. H. Van Ingen, W. T. Sharpe, Willis L. Ogden, Sidney M. Gladwin, Benjamin R. Swan, Joseph J. Swan, Crowell Hadden and Samuel M. Wood.

The company's record is a brilliant one. It saw service in the days of the Civil War and later played a prominent part in quelling the draft riots and the riots of '63, '64 and '70, as well as the Orange riots of '71. It served as well in the railroad riots at Hornellsville, N. Y., in '77; in Buffalo in '92, in the great Brooklyn car strike, and in Albany in 1901. It volunteered three times for service in the Spanish-American War.

The programme of the celebration includes a promenade concert by the Twenty-third Regiment Band, several vocal numbers, a drill and review of the company, followed by dancing.

JONES MEMORIAL UNVEILED.

Imposing Testimonial to Memory of Great Naval Hero.

Washington, April 17—The unveiling of the statue of John Paul Jones in Potomac Park here today brought to a close a movement begun several years ago to provide some appropriate testimonial to the memory of the great naval hero.

It started when a wave of public interest was excited by the discovery in France and removal to America of the remains of the early sea fighter. A setting for the statue included a fountain, pylon and approaches, the whole work costing $50,000.

The memorial consists of a marble pylon of classic design as the background for a colossal bronze figure of the intrepid naval commander of the early days of the republic.

The pylon is a massive rectangular tower about 15 feet in height. It occupies the center of an ornamental fountain, water for which is supplied from the bronze heads of dolphins, on each side of the pylon.

The statue of John Paul Jones stands at the base of the monument in front of the pedestal. It is of heroic proportions, being about 10 feet high. The great naval commander is shown in full uniform, with an expression and pose suggestive of his indomitable will and unconquerable spirit. He has been modeled as though watching a naval engagement.

Most of the dignitaries in Washington were included in the plan to honor the memory of John Paul Jones.

President Taft and General Horace Porter were the only speakers on the programme. George von L. Meyer, Secretary of the Navy, was given the place as presiding officer and to Admiral Dewey was assigned the task of pulling the cords that released the flags about the heroic figure.

The U. S. S. Dolphin and Mayflower anchored in the Potomac just west of the Washington monument were ready for the national salute of twenty-one guns as the admiral of the navy raised his hand and tugged at the cords. Practically all the available military force near Washington, more than 1,000 men were present.

EPIPHANY CHURCH EUCHRE.

Eight Hundred Present at Enjoyable Function.

Last night's euchre and reception for the benefit of the Church of the Epiphany, South Ninth street, at the Knapp Mansion, was very successful. Fully 800 were present. The Rev. Edward A. Duffy and his assistants, Fathers Timothy Murphy and Matthew Flannagan, greeted their parishioners and guests, who included Thomas J. Drennan, Frank V. Kelly, Edward J. Kennedy, Alderman John S. Gaynor, Joseph M. Tully, Edward J. Riegelmann, John J. Bracken, Bart J. Dwyer and Congressman James P. Maher.

The arrangements committee, who worked hard for the success of the affair, included:

Thomas M. James, chairman; John J. Fallon, John T. Rooney, Frank T. Burke, Thomas F. Cahill, Edward J. Donnelly, Walter Miller, Felix McArdle, Walter Pratt, John J. Fallon, jr., Timothy Gleason, James Malloy, James A. Clines, Oakley Morey, Harry Baker and Thomas McKiernan and the Misses Lillian Coleman, Ella Knight, Anastacia Knight, Mary Lynch, Grace Sachlem, Isabel Kent, Winifred Clines, Sarah Sweeney, Viola Hogan, Anna Carman, Jennie Carman, Irene Dwyer, Katharine Clarke, Mary O'Brien and Margaret Struble.

A TALK ON THE TURKS.

The interesting part, excepting the dinner, of the meeting of the "Round Table," the men's organization of the Second Unitarian Church, Clinton and Congress streets, which was held last night, was the talk of Andrew Nicola on "The Young Turk Movement." Although Mr. Nicola, a Turk himself, has been in this country twelve years, he has kept so closely in touch with the advancing "Young Turks" of his own country that he was able to explain in very interesting language the latest moves and their effects. He said that the Turk is influenced by emotion rather than by reason, more markedly, perhaps, than any other people.

MOTHERS IN CONFERENCE.

The mothers of the children of the Second Unitarian Church have been meeting regularly once a month, with Mrs. Caleb Dutton at her home, 115 Montague street. Mrs. Dutton is the wife of the pastor of the church and at these informal meetings, religious subjects are discussed. The subject of yesterday's meeting was "Compulsion and Attraction." Various views were given as to how far a child should be compelled to go to church and how far the parent should depend upon the church attracting the child.

HARD TO BEAR

LIBRARY TRUSTEES HEAR GOOD REPORTS

Brownsville Branch Had Largest Circulation of Books for Month of March.

The board of trustees of the Brooklyn Public Library met last night in the Administration Building, 26 Brevoort place, and it was one of the largest meetings of the year in point of attendance. A letter from Mayor Gaynor was read, announcing the reappointment of R. Ross Appleton and William H. English as trustees for terms of five years each.

Chief Librarian Frank P. Hill reported that the circulation of books for the month of March amounted to 410,659 volumes, an increase of 8,428 over the corresponding month of the preceding year. Brownsville Branch reports the largest circulation, 30,821 volumes, followed by Bushwick Branch with 28,487 volumes. Mr. Hill also reported that the smaller branches—Borough Park, Concord and Sheepshead Bay—show a gratifying increase.

A proposition was recommended to the trustees by Miss Clara Whitehill Hunt, children's librarian, looking to the installation of lantern slides for lectures and instruction in the auditoriums of the Carnegie libraries. The recommendation was referred to the administration committee.

Considerable discussion developed over the question of the payment for repairs to be made to the Montague street branch property, part of which is rented out to business concerns. It was stated that if these repairs were paid from the rental account, the trustees would be establishing a bad precedent, as the Corporation Counsel now claims that all of the money received from rentals should accrue to the credit of the city instead of to the trustees as a corporation. It was finally decided to have the repairs that are to be made to the portion of the building used for library purposes exclusively charged up to the city appropriation, and the repairs to the rented-out portion of the property paid out of the rental account.

Frank L. Babbott, Abner S. Haight and Nathaniel H. Levi were appointed a committee to confer with the Board of Education on the alleged overlapping of the work of the classroom libraries and the public libraries. It is said that well-organized and efficient co-operation between the public library and the public schools which exists in many cities has never been possible in this borough, in so far as work with the elementary schools is concerned. It is felt that the interests of the whole city would be better served if some more effective co-operative plan could be adopted.

Treasurer John W. Devoy reported that there was a balance in the City Appropriation amounting to $324,876.35; in the Directors Fund, $8,447.99, and in the Rental Account, $26,471.01.

THE APOLLO CLUB CONCERT.

Signally Fine in Concerted Work at the Brooklyn Academy.

In one of John Hyatt Brewer's best-arranged programmes a big audience was entertained by the Apollo Club, Mr. Brewer, conductor; Miss Florence Hinkle, soprano, and Miss A. Laura Tolman of Boston, 'cellist, assisting artists, in the third private concert of its thirty-fourth year at the Brooklyn Academy of Music last evening. The club, under the capable drill of Mr. Brewer and by a new arrangement of massing the singers in the center at the very front of the stage, sent out a splendid volume of tone, accurate in attack, and in the pianissimo passages, intimate and moving. It was such a message as one great voice would give out. Flexibility in delivery was notable, which was no light achievement considering the variety in the sentiment of the numbers. Dudley Buck's "The Spring Is Come, Huzza," was a joyful proclamation and Mr. Brewer's composition, "Ocean's Garden," poetically descriptive and finely adapted to words by Longfellow, had in the delivery all the effects of a masterpiece. The men sang it as though inspired and a fitting companion to it was Engelsberg's shimmering "On Upper Langbathsea." Coming esthetically close to the audience were the well-grouped "Fair Maid From the Vale Below," by J. Herbeck, and the following "John Peel," an old English hunting song, arranged for male voices by Mark Andrews. The former was intimate, subdued and was held with finely sustained intonation and delicate light and shade, while the latter came out with such rousing effect, elasticity in every phase, that it had to be repeated. Stormy sweep of winds and murmur of zephyrs were reproduced in mind in Edwin Schultz's "Forest Harps," and abundant humor poured out in Julius Otto's "A Summer Landscape," while applause followed the singing of Osgood's "Rock-a-By-Baby." The old Welsh folksong, "Men of Harlech," was sung with clarion effect; the old war song could not have been better delivered; it had an electric effect. William Armour Thayer at the piano and Albert Reeves Norton at the organ aided in giving as artistic a concert by the club as it has ever been the lot of The Eagle representative to hear.

Miss Hinkle's pure, clear and high soprano voice was heard with pleasure in Spross' "Come Down, Laughing Streamlet," Haille's "In the Moonlight" and Russell's "Sunset," the latter being delivered with such perfect art and poetic effect that she was recalled to sing an encore, which was Spruss' "Will-o'-th'-Wisp." Later Miss Hinkle sang Salter's "Come to the Garden, Love," Arthur Farwell's beautifully written "A Ruined Garden," sung, by the way, with intensely dramatic and passionate effect, and MacFadyen's "Love Is the Wind," followed, in an encore, by Heckscher's "Norse Maiden's Lament." Miss Hinkle was accompanied most sympathetically and with exactness of technique by Sidney Dorlon Lowe, son of Mattie Dorlon Lowe, contralto, formerly a well-known church and concert singer of Brooklyn.

Miss Tolman on the 'cello is a poetic and intimate, rather than a robust, performer. And until her encore was given, her playing on the stage prevented the vibration of the 'cello from being enjoyed on one side of the auditorium. All the delicacy of Popper's "Devotion of the Forest" was brought out by her, and in the same composer's "Tanze" the lilting movement was preserved. Good technique, especially in smoothness of bowing and in perfect harmonics, were notable in Miss Tolman's playing of Goltermann's "Andante," from his "Concerto in E minor," and the "Allegro Molto," from his "Concerto," Op. 65, were numbers that served well to display the qualities in the 'cellist's playing just alluded to. Her encore was played without her written score before her; had she done the same with the programme numbers the effect would have been more telling.

NEW ORGAN USED.

Largely Attended Recital Enjoyed at Glenmore Ave. Presbyterian Church.

A "pure food" supper and organ recital were held last night at the Glenmore Avenue Presbyterian Church, Glenmore avenue and Doscher street, under the auspices of the choir, for the purpose of raising funds for conducting the musical services. A valuable organ was installed in the building last year and last night was the first recital at which the new instrument was used.

Professor Frank Meisner is musical director, and the promulgator of the idea and its most energetic supporter was Mrs. Katherine Richards, wife of Judge Edward A. Richards. The programme included several selections on the violin by Mr. Timorian, an Armenian violinist, who was accompanied by Miss Mildred Iskyan. Miss Ella Lyon, the organist of the church, played two selections and Miss Hazel Hill Carroll sang several soprano solos.

The members of the choir, who acted as a committee of arrangements for the evening, and were responsible to a high degree for the successful outcome of the plan, are:

C. M. Staples, Mrs. George Beck, Mrs. Don Cameron, Mrs. Katherine Richards, Miss Emily Richards, Miss Mabel Weymer, Mrs. H. P. Meigs, Miss Gussie Meymer, Miss Phoebe Bush, Miss Lillian Newbauer, Miss Effie Van Hovenberg, Miss Pauline Meiger, Elliott B. Williams, Arthur Kraft, Samuel Day, Frederick Worriment, F. Lawrence Goldschmidt, Thomas Taylor, Lester Du Val and the director, F. W. Meisner.

"WE, THE PEOPLE."

Dr. Robert W. McLaughlin to Discuss Meaning of the Words.

The Rev. Robert W. McLaughlin, pastor of the Park Slope Congregational Church, will deliver an address at the Logan Club, Sixth avenue and Garfield place, Thursday, April 18, at 8:30 p.m., on the subject: "What the words, 'We, the people,' in the preamble to the Constitution, meant to those who wrote the Constitution, and what they mean today."

Dr. McLaughlin is a thorough student of American history, a deep and clear thinker, and an interesting and convincing speaker, and is thoroughly equipped to deliver an able and instructive address, show the difference between the political requirements of the country during the latter part of the eighteenth century and the first part of the twentieth century, and interpret the words, "We, the people" as they apply to the changed and turbulent political conditions of the present time.

The meeting will be open for discussion, after the address, when the speaker will be pleased to answer any and all questions. Everybody will be welcome, regardless of political belief or affiliation.

MRS. STONEHILL TO SPEAK.

Mrs. Daisy Stonehill, wife of the first pastor of the Knickerbocker Avenue Methodist Episcopal Church, corner of Ralph street, will speak in that church this evening. Mrs. Stonehill comes to the church under the auspices of the Women's Home Missionary Auxiliary. The gathering will be a public one and all members of the church, its friends and the friends of Mrs. Stonehill, are being invited.

Brooklyn Society

Mrs. Irving T. Smith's Bridge; Wicker Creton Trays Prizes.

Another of the fasholnable bridges of the Easter weeks took place yesterday afternoon. Its hostess was Mrs. Irving Thomas Smith. She entertained at her home, 860 St. Mark's avenue, there being nearly a hundred guests.

Twenty-one tables were played. The decorations were magnolias with the diningroom in yellow and white daffodils. The prizes were wicker creton trays for summer piazzas. In the company of the afternoon were:

Mrs. Almet F. Jenks, Mrs. Sylvester L. Blood, Mrs. Edward Hinman, Mrs. William H. Nichols, Jr., Mrs. Alden S. Swan, Mrs. Horatio C. King, Mrs. William L. Moffat, Mrs. George H. Couotts, Mrs. Henry B. Ketcham, Mrs. Walter St. John Benedict, Mrs. James Jourdan, Mrs. Melville H. Bearns, Mrs. William Pohlman Pool, Mrs. William Kenyon, Mrs. William H. Nichols, Mrs. Percy R. Gray.

Mrs. Frederic C. Brown, Mrs. Malcolm Roberts, Mrs. Frank H. Cothren, Mrs. Henry Ingersoll, Mrs. James A. Radcliffe, Mrs. Alfred C. Bedford, Mrs. Clinton Elliott, Mrs. Herman Stutzer, Mrs. Maillard M. Canda, Mrs. John Osborn Polak, Mrs. David Manning, Miss Mary Byrne, Mrs. Walter Perry, Mrs. Russell E. Prentiss, Miss Alice Byrne, Miss Augusta Elliott, Mrs. Frederic C. Truslow, Mrs. Frederick Tuttle, Mrs. George Dunham Provost.

* * *

Mrs. Good's "Italian Girls" Carry St. Teresa's Affair.

"La Delagazione Ausiliaria Delle Signorite" hypnotized the social world last night. There had been many rumors concerning it, and it was freely predicted that the "delagazione" would be Mrs. William H. Good's chief feature in her St. Teresa's Mission dance and card party, and would be even more effective than could possibly be imagined. The rumors were correct, but they were not half enthusiastic enough. The "delagazione" proved as attractive pictorially and so coquettish and pervasive that from the very first movement it made this charity affair the greatest of successes.

The Pouch Gallery was the scene of the St. Teresa's benefit. There was a capital dance, a card party that filled the banquet hall with innumerable tables and offered a very striking array of prizes, ices and frappe served, and this "Ausiliaria" of twenty of the prettiest Brooklyn belles that could be found, each in the most distinctive of Italian costumes. With their wares in flat little baskets, these girls sold flowers. Italian post cards (real ones from Italy), and Italian confectionery. They were the most expert of saleswomen, for they did not attempt to sell at all. They simply posed prettily, and succeeded so well in this that the men present came up and begged them to take money. One of the prettiest of these girls turned in over $30 by herself from her tray of Italian sweetmeats.

The costumes were so illusive and differing—no two being the same—that they are beyond detailed description. Miss Mary Carr, the "delagazione's" chairman and the organizer of the group, was a peasant girl in black, with three rows of blue in the skirt, and a blue headdress. Miss Dorothy Bernard was in red, with a bodice of white. Miss Katherine Murray was a brilliant peasant girl in a festa dress of yellow. Miss Mina Marese, in a flowered gown, made a perfect Italian village maid. Miss Olive Owens, in a Roman scarf headdress and wonderful apron, was a striking figure, as were also Miss Genevieve Markey, Miss Mary Mulqueen of Manhattan, Miss Margaret Carr and Miss Grace Courtney. All these girls were rivaled by Miss Adelaide Moran, Miss Florence Kirwin, Miss Margaret Reilly, Miss Catherine Ughetta, Miss Clara Kent, Miss Anna Catherwood, Miss Marye Ughetta, Miss Olivia Herkimer, Miss Anna Catherwood and Miss Teresa Farrell.

A real peanut cart in the Pouch's big hallway added to the picture. There were two orchestras for dancing. Unfortunately the Bishop could not come for the reception. Otherwise there was nothing lacking, and long before the evening's end the committee announced that the profits would be very large.

In a gown of figured satin in pastel colors on white and lace Mrs. William H. Good presided as general chairwoman of the night. Her aides in receiving were Mrs. William J. Carr in gold embroidered chiffon (Mrs. Carr also presided over the prizes), Miss Virginia O'Connor (the ticket committee chairwoman), Mrs. Philip Brennan (also chairwoman of the Journal), Mrs. John C. Reilly, Mrs. John B. Byrne and Mrs. Luke D. Stapleton. Other "directors" of the night included Mrs. James Shevlin, Miss S. J. Read, Mrs. Frank J. Gallagher, Miss Catherine Carlin, Miss Helen Burns, Miss Harrison, Mrs Edward J. McCrossin, Mrs. Hugh McCrossin, Mrs. Thomas E. Murray, in black satin, steel and jet; Mrs. Curren, Mrs. Martin T. Manton, Mrs. Francis X. Carmody, Mrs. James MacEvitt, in lavender; Mrs. E. J. Byrne, Mrs. E. T. Yates, Miss Hughes, Mrs. James McMahon, Mrs. Girod, Miss Lavalett McCann, Mrs. M. F. McCann, Miss Moore and Miss Kate McAvoy, in black striped velvet.

Eugene O'Connor headed the large floor committee of the evening, his aides being David T. Leahy, Edward J. Byrne, J. Astley Griffin, William J. McConnell, Frank J. Grunning, Edward J. Connolly, John J. Kuhn, Claude M. Becker, Lewis E. A. Drummond, Louis J. Monjo, Frank C. Russell, Frank J. Doherty, John E. O'Connor, Alfred H. Munkenbeck, Charles J. Raleigh, Rodolfo A. Correa, George J. Patterson, Harold J. McNulty, Joseph P. Carlin, C. Stewart Cavanagh, Joseph A. McCann, Reginald J. Meehan.

The personalities of importance, in addition to those above, included, among many others: Judge William J. Carr, Thomas E. Murray, Patrick E. Callahan, Dr. and Mrs. Raymond P. Sullivan, Mr. and Mrs. Edward P. Shallow, Robert O'Connor, Miss Rita O'Keefe, Miss Mary Byrne, in black crepe de chine; James W. Prendergast, Mr. and Mrs. Charles Egan, Mrs. Egan, in blue velvet and crepe de chine; Mrs. Rose Wilding, in white satin; Charles Egan, jr., Mrs. William C. Courtney, in black crepe meteor; Dr. James MacEvitt, Miss Teresa Straukamp, Miss Beatrice McCann, Miss Adelaide McCann, Thomas Murray, Daniel Murray, Edward Carr, Miss Florence Gallagher, in white chiffon and satin; Miss Julia Roach, Edward Keating, William F. Straukamp, Edward J. Byrne, C. Stewart Cavanagh, Harold McNulty, Mr. and Mrs. Martin T. Manton, Mrs. Paul D. Bernard, William J. McConvill, Dr. and Mrs. James S. Waterman, Mrs. Thomas E. Gloucester.

* * *

Miss O'Brien—Mr. Peterkin Have American Beauty Wedding.

The second Easter week of this season is to be decidedly one of weddings, and the long array of these began last night with the marriage of Miss Margaret O'Brien and DeWitt Peterkin. Miss O'Brien is the second of the daughters of Dr. and Mrs. Henry L. O'Brien of 104 Prospect Park West, and Mr. Peterkin the son of Mr. and Mrs. Gilbert C. Peterkin of the Hill. They were married fro mthe bride's home at 8:30 o'clock, the Rev. Emile S. Harper, rector of All Saints Church on the Park Slope, officiating.

The O'Brien house was decorated for this occasion with wild smilax and bride roses, and the very attractive bride of the night wore white satin. Her wedding gown was unusual and distinctive. It was adorned with very beautiful old point lace worn by her mother's mother and her mother's grandmother. That was not all. This bride's costume had, also, an exceedingly pretty bridal veil cap, made from a very old point lace handkerchief.

Miss O'Brien carried white orchids and lilies of the valley and wore a diamond lavalliere, her bridegroom's gift. The seven girls attending her—a maid of honor and six girls who handled the white satin ribbons of the improvised aisle—were all in gowns of white satin and shadow lace and all carried bunches of American Beauties. Miss Gladys O'Brien, her younger sister, was the maid of honor. The six ribbon girls, in the order of their appearance, were Miss Dorothy Moore and Miss Ruth Fairbairn, Miss Agnes Fairbairn and Miss Eileen O'Brien, yet another younger sister; and Miss Elder Potvin of Midland, Ontario, Canada, and Miss Marion Weller. Robert Peterkin, the bridegroom's brother, was best man, and the ushers, as they entered, were Robert Sheldon of Columbus, O., and Edgar Eschman (who is to marry Miss Mildred O'Brien); Ten Broeck Terhune of Manhattan and John T. O'Brien, the bride's brother.

Mrs. O'Brien wore a gown of flesh pink satin draped with a shawl of old black lace.

* * *

Sidney Snyder Marries Miss Elsie Behning.

At the Hotel Savoy, Manhattan, last night, Sidney Snyder of 10 Montgomery place, son of Mrs. Mortimer Snyder, married Miss Elsie Behning, daughter of Mr. and Mrs. Frederick Behning of Graham Court, 116th street and Seventh avenue, Manhattan. This was an attractive bridal, its ceremony solemnized by the Rev. Edgar Tilton of the Collegiate Church of Harlem. Mr. and Mrs. Snyder are to make their home in this borough.

Miss Dora Behning was maid of honor, Miss Marion Lawson and Miss Edith Darling, bridesmaids, and little Miss Pauline Pehning, flower girl. The best man was Raymond Bishop of Philadelphia, and Max Kelly, Harold Ditmars, William Tonk, jr., and Frank Hamilton were ushers.

* * *

Frederick T. Sherman, Jr., Marries in Richmond, Va.

Frederick T. Sherman, jr., son of Frederick T. Sherman, who was for many years a resident of 265 Henry street, and now retired from active affairs, makes his home at Unadilla, N. Y., was a bridegroom of yesterday. Young Mr. Sherman, who with his brother, Arnold Watson Sherman, resides at 18 Monroe place, wedded Miss Elizabeth Fisher, of Richmond, Va., and was married at 6 o'clock in the Monumental Church of that city. Only a small reception followed the large ceremony.

Mrs. James Higginson, of Ivy, Va., was Miss Fisher's matron of honor, and her only attendant. The best man was Arnold W. Sherman, and the ushers Robert Valentine Mathews and Henry E. Mattison, of Brooklyn; William Crump Tucker and John Lightfoot, jr., of Richmond; T. Hayes Gee, of Manhattan, and Edmund Berkeley, of Deering, W. Va.

* * *

Sigma Pi Dances At the St. George.

Sigma Pi "frat" gave an excellent dance last night in the ballroom of the Hotel St. George. Its patronesses were Mrs. H. T. Kneeland, Mrs. William McLoughlin, Mrs. Henry Kusch and Mrs. George Richter.

Among the dancers were Miss Madeleine Pearce in white batiste, embroidered in lavender; Miss Kathleen McLoughlin in white satin, Miss Fanny McLoughlin in flame-colored chiffon over white satin, Miss Alice Ward in blue satin, Miss Edith Wezel in pink satin with a crystal tunic, Miss Elsie Richter in white satin, Miss Margaret Adikes in yellow satin, Miss Anna Adikes in pink satin, Miss Jeanette Nostrand in blue chiffon over blue satin, Miss Kathryn Dunton in turquoise satin, Miss Wahnetah Monroe in pink chiffon over blue satin, Miss Rita Nammack in black satin, Miss Evelyn Merrill in pink satin, Miss Edna Martin in pink satin, Miss Gertrude Evans in nile green satin and Miss Hazel Hooper in green chiffon over white satin. Gerard McLoughlin, Harvey Kneeland, L. Eugene Decker, John Adikes, Robert Luce, Frederick Garngost, Lloyd Bliss, Ronald Boone, William Engels, William Kirk, John Valentine, Kenneth Valentine, Henry Kearsh, Thomas Murray, William McLoughlin, Donald Hardenbrook, James Ouchterloney, Herbert Richter.

WEATHER FORECAST.

Persons desiring information concerning the weather, temperature or other information can secure it by using telephone No. 571 Main, from 8 a.m. to 6 p.m. week days. Nights and Sundays, 6200 Main.

Indications Until 8 P.M. Tomorrow.

Washington, April 17—For Eastern New York: Rain tonight and probably on Thursday; colder in extreme south portion; moderate to variable winds, becoming easterly tonight and increasing.

Local Probabilities.

Rain tonight and probably on Thursday; increasing easterly winds, becoming northwest on Thursday.

General Weather Conditions.

The southwest disturbance has increased in energy and has developed two distince storm centers. One is now in control over Western Tennessee and the other off the Gulf coast. Heavy rains have occurred during the past twenty-four hours ehroughout the Gulf States, east of Texas, in Arkansas and in Eastern Texas. Moderate rains have occurred over the Ohio and Middle Mississippi Valleys and along the entire Atlantic coast. Colder weather prevails over the Southwest, with freezing temperature throughout Kansas and Northern Oklahoma. It is also colder over the Ohio Valley, Lower Lake region, Pennsylvania, New York and the interior of New England. Cloudy, unsettled weather, with fog and rain, and moderate increasing easterly winds, is indicated for this vicinity during the next twenty-four to thirty-six hours, to be followed Thursday night or Friday by clearing and colder, with brisk northwest winds.

	8 a.m. today. Temperature.	Precipitation.		8 a.m. today. Temperature.	Precipitation.
Boston	56	.04	New Orleans	70	1.66
Buffalo	36	...	Cincinnati	50	.42
Manhattan	55	.02	St. Louis	38	.84
Philadelphia	58	...	Chicago	34	...
Washington	64	.04	Duluth	34	...
Charleston	70	...	San Fran'co	50	...

Highest, 70, at New Orleans; lowest, 34, at Duluth.

OFFICIAL TEMPERATURE.

TUESDAY, APRIL 16.

3 p.m.	74	8 p.m.	67
4 p.m.	71	9 p.m.	64
5 p.m.	71	10 p.m.	63
6 p.m.	71	11 p.m.	63
7 p.m.	69	12 (midnight)	62

WEDNESDAY, APRIL 17.

1 a.m.	61	8 a.m.	55
2 a.m.	60	9 a.m.	55
3 a.m.	59	10 a.m.	54
4 a.m.	57	11 a.m.	53
5 a.m.	56	12 (noon)	53
6 a.m.	55	1 p.m.	53
7 a.m.	54	2 p.m.	[illegible]

Average temperature today, 60.
Average temperature a year ago today, 48.

HIGH WATER.

	A.M. Time H.M.	A.M. High Feet	P.M. Time H.M.	P.M. High Feet	Durat'n of Rise H.M.	Durat'n of Fall H.M.
New York	8:10	4.6	8:37	5.3	5:54	6:25
Sandy Hook	8:00	4.7	8:23	5.4	6:08	6:35

BAROMETER, TEMPERATURE AND HUMIDITY.

17 Battery Place, Manhattan.

	8 p.m. yesterday.	8 a.m. today.
Barometer	29.89	29.98
Dry bulb temperature	70	55
Wet bulb temperature	61	48
Relative humidity (p.ct.)	61	59

SUN RISES AND SETS.

April 17. Rises..5:14, Sets..6:37 | April 18. Rises..5:13 Sets..6:38

SHIP NEWS.

Arrived at New York Today.

Prinz August Wilhelm from Kingston.
Hellig Olav from Copenhagen.
Cincinnati from Naples.
La Bretagne from Havre.
Cristobal from Colon.
El Rio from Galveston.
Algonquin from Turk's Island.
Madawaska from Port Spain.
Mohawk from Charleston.
Crown of Navarre from Perth Amboy.

Arrived at Foreign Ports Today.

Algoa Bay—Royal Prince from New York.
Hull—Francisco from New York.

Sailed From Foreign Ports Today.

Barbados—Hungarian Prince for New York.
Liverpool—Atlantian for New York.

FIRE RECORD.

Report of fires and alarms for fire received at office of the Fire Alarm Telegraph Company for twenty-four hours ended at 8 a.m. April 16:

9:46 a.m.—716 Monroe st.
11:22 a.m.—68 Dupont st; damage to building slight.
2:06 p.m.—Washington and Water sts; false alarm.
3:24 p.m.—230 Greene st.
11 a.m.—762A Greene av.
2:40 p.m.—87 Utica av; damage to building slight.
4:12 p.m.—303 Fulton st; damage to building slight.
7:09 p.m.—Lighter, H. B. Hitchcock; slight damage.
10:49 p.m.—Malicious false alarm.
11:37 p.m.—767 Bushwick av; damage to building slight.
2:36 a.m.—Albany and Church avs; malicious false alarm.

A "RAINBOW SOCIAL."

Central Congregational Young People Hold Novel Entertainment.

The "Rainbow Social" given last evening by the young people of the Central Congregational Church on Hancock street, proved a novel entertainment. Colored cards pinned on the players, gave the rainbow effect, as the players moved from table to table. Games played at the tables were "Prince of Wales," "Scrap Book," "Quotations," "That Reminds Me," "Moses" and "Famous Men." General games, such as the peanut and balloon races, spin the platter and camp fire stories—introduced the players for the social evening.

Mr. W. H. Schnitz, as chairman of the committee, arranged the games with the help of Miss Schanz, Miss Tallman, Miss Ralins, Miss King, Miss Lang, George S. Lewis, Mr. York, G. Irving Baily, Mr. Anderson and F. H. Lewis.

HOLD ANNUAL DINNER.

Brotherhood of Marcy Ave. Baptist Church Hears Dr. G. R. Maguire.

The annual dinner of the Brotherhood of the Marcy Avenue Baptist Church was held last evening, and about two hundred were present.

Dr. Gabriel R. Maguire was the speaker of the evening. His subject was, "With an Irishman Through the Jungles of Africa." His address was eloquent and was received with enthusiasm.

The Rev. W. C. P. Rhoades, pastor of the church, spoke briefly, as did the president of the Brotherhood, Don Clyde Kite. It was Mr. Kite's last night as president of the society. The election of officers resulted as follows: Ralph M. Skinner, president; John L. Swan, vice president; Sumner Jones, secretary, and Oscar Stout, treasurer.

THE BROOKLYN DAILY EAGLE

PICTURE AND SPORTING SECTION. ★ NEW YORK CITY, WEDNESDAY, APRIL 17, 1912. PICTURE AND SPORTING SECTION.

MAN

Walks and Talks

By JULIUS CHAMBERS

AMID the horror of the Titanic disaster, now fully known so far as loss of human life is concerned, it is idle to attempt to Talk upon any theme except the sea and its conflict for mastery over man.

When navigation of the deep was confined to the Persian Gulf and the Mediterranean, the smallness of the craft employed therein inspired a wholesome regard for the gods of the winds and of the water. Boreas and his companions and Neptune were propitiated before every embarkation. Not until after the Middle Ages did man give serious attention to domination of the oceans. Likely as not, hardy Phoenicians had ventured outside the Gates of Hercules; somebody must have gone far enough to encounter the Cape Verde or Madeira, and to invent the fairy legend of the "Lost Atlantis." Whether the Norsemen or Columbus first crossed the Atlantic is not vital to the question of ocean navigation. It was a venture sure to be made, sooner or later; and when one stops to remember that little more than 400 years have elapsed since the authenticated first voyage, one comprehends how daring was the undertaking.

Plenty of people are alive today who remember the sailing of the first steamship that made the ocean voyage. My father went to see friends off upon the Collins steamer that sailed from this port and never afterward was seen. That incident had such an effect upon him that he never would cross the ocean. He continued panic-stricken the rest of his life.

This calamity of the present hour is calculated to terrify many people who never have been to sea—much as a railway accident deters the backwoodsman from riding on the cars. When, however, one remembers how many thousands of voyagers cross the acean every year, this terrible percentage of loss is no greater than can be set down to the debit of the railways.

* * *

Until full details of the Titanic disaster are known, speculation regarding the failure of the gigantic ship to keep afloat is idle. It is highly probable that Mr. Ismay, among the saved, knows the absolute facts. He will be within reach of the wireless station on this coast this afternoon, and ought to explain to an anxious public.

As a voyager who has seen many icebergs, my opinion would be that the Titanic ran upon a long slant of a submerged berg, causing the mighty mass to turn partly over, at least sufficiently to break the back of the ship!

It is incredible that mere impact of the bow against a berg of ice would have caused the sinking of the great boat. Shipbuilding certainly has improved since the days of the steamship Arizona! That vessel ran, head on, into a big berg near Cape Race. Her two forward compartments filled with water; but the safety devices worked so well that the Arizona proceeded to St. John's, Newfoundland, under her own steam, and not a passenger was lost.

If water-tight compartments could keep out the sea and prevent loss of ship and human life in 1877, how much more should the same expectation be justified in these days?

Captain Smith himself was authority for the assurance that the modern ocean steamer is unsinkable!

Therefore, the accident that occurred to the Titanic must have been something extraordinary.

To theorize is worse than useless. Her builder was aboard and probably lost no time in joining Captain Smith upon the bridge. They had about three and a half hours to decide upon the extent of the injury. If the machinery intended to operate the water-tight doors failed to work, there was sufficient time to have closed them by hand!

Agan, I say, indications are that the injuries to the great vessel were far more vital than the crushing of her bow. By this time, tomorrow, as players say on the stage, "we shall know all."

* * *

Among the lost are several friends. Especially is this true of Francis D. Millet, artist, special correspondent and all round good fellow. I first knew him in London, when he was starting to the front as a special correspondent in the Russo-Turkish war. That was in 1877; and we did not meet again until 1893, on the battlefield of Gettysburg, when John Russell Young, then fourth vice president of the Reading Railroad, took a party of New York friends to the scene of that three days battle. Henry George, J. I. C. Clarke, General Alexander, Francis D. Millet and others were there. Mr. Millet and I renewed our London acquaintance; we talked much about a mutual friend, whose memory was very dear to both of us, J. A. MacGahan, who had given his life to the salvation of Bulgaria from Turkish misrule.

* * *

William T. Stead, who has perished on the Titanic, I knew when he was editor of the Pall Mall Gazette and was making his crusade for the social purification of London. He was probably best informed man of his day regarding the social and financial conditions of every European government. He was persona grata at every court. One of the greatest prose works in the English language is his "United States of Europe." Any student of contemporaneous affairs on the Continent who hasn't read and digested that volume, is overlooking a storehouse of valuable information. The volume was first published in 1899, but several later editions have brought it up to date.

Mr. Stead was a charming man to meet, despite his propensity to ride his universal peace hobby to the death. In face and figure, I always associated him in my fancy with Socrates! He was only 62 years of age, but he had done the work of a hundred years. His moral sense was acute, although—as is the case with Dr. Charles H. Parkhurst—people did not agree concerning his methods of bringing about reforms. Nothing could swerve him from a course once entered on.

One may be sure he died like a Stoic, probably exhorting those around him to meet their fate as became men.

* * *

Colonel John Jacob Astor was a personal friend of more than fifteen years. His last act, in sending his wife and her maid to safety while he calmly faced inevitable death, is characteristic of a hero and a martyr. He was not of the stuff of which shirkers are made! He would rather have had the humblest woman in the steerage have a place in the boats than pre-empt it himself. He died exactly as those who were at Santiago would have expected him to meet the end.

He died as do the brave.

* * *

Women of the world will do well to moderate the evidence of their criticisms of the male sex.

What a picture of true manhood this picture of strong, healthy men, inspired by unattained ambitions, and aglow with love of life, standing aside to help into boats aged and young women! Let the women critics picture to themselves sturdy old Captain Smith waving farewell to those he had been able to save, and calmly going to the ocean's depths with those who had to die when he did.

Men are not wanting in respect for women!

When a man like Colonel Astor kisses his young bride farewell and surrenders a life that holds for him so many blessings in order that an additional woman may be saved, a lesson is presented that [illegible] silences many a wagging female tongue.

The Destroyer

Out of the night it came, that menace of the seas,
Unmarked by sound and unobserved, its prey of souls to seize;
A pallid shape, dim in the fog, a monster, on it came,
And wallowed in the ocean path, its toll of deaths to claim.

All boasts of modern safeguards, mere affectations were;
Inventive minds it mocked and giant ships seemed dwarfs to her.
That mammoth ship, with armor plate, was but a cockle-shell,
And when its unseen hand reached out, with ease the giant fell.

And then it laughed; it closed its hand; then watched the work it wrought:
The frenzied screams of dying men, sweet music to it brought.
Unmoved it stood, with eager mien, while fifteen hundred souls
Went struggling down for evermore to rest in watery holes.

Its evil deed accomplished, it drew a conquering breath,
And all about the wreckage, a shadow cast—of Death.
The mightiest of giant ships had just obeyed its nod,
And fifteen hundred souls their final voyage made—to God.

F. W. R.

THIS DAY IN HISTORY

APRIL 17.

1741. Samuel Chase, jurist and "Signer," born. "The torch that lighted up the Revolutionary flame in Maryland."

1744. John Page, governor of Virginia, born. Noted for his patriotism and theological learning.

1770. Mahlon Dickerson, statesman, born. Secretary of the Navy under Jackson.

1776. Battle between Lexington and Edward.

1786. Walter Forward, jurist and statesman, born. The ablest judge of his time in Pennsylvania.

1806. William Gilmore Simms, novelist and poet, born.

1813. Susan Fenimore Cooper, author, born. Daughter of James Fenimore Cooper.

1816. Samuel A. Allibone, author, born.

1826. William Lee, publisher, born. Founder of the firm of Lee & Shepard, Boston.

1835. Jonas M. Bundy, editor and author, born. First editor of the Mail and Express, New York.

1837. John Pierpont Morgan, financier, born.

1841. Dr. Harrison Allen, anatomist and naturalist, born. A professor in the University of Pennsylvania.

1842. Charles H. Parkhurst, clergyman and reformer, born.

1848. Louis Charles Elson, musical writer, born. Lecturer in New England Conservatory of Music.

1848. Toledo Blade first issued.

1849. William R. Day, statesman, born. Secretary of State under McKinley.

1853. W. J. McGee, anthropologist and geologist, born. In charge of the Bureau of American Ethnology, Washington, D. C.

1861. Virginia seceded from the Union.

1865. West Point, Miss., captured by the Federals.

1874. Comet discovered by M. Coggia and by Swift.

THEATER TOPICS

Chicago to Have a Theater of Women, by Women and for Women.

GRETE WIESENTHAL'S DEBUT.

Executive Committee of Institute Trustees Considering Endowed Repertory Theater Plan.

The Winter Garden introduced three new dancing acts last evening in its entertainment, which is now so long that the final curtain falls at 12 o'clock on a depleted audience. These are Moon and Morris, a regulation vaudeville "brother" act of dancers; the Texas Tommy Dancers, eight eccentric whirlwinds, and, most important, Grete Wiesenthal, newly brought from Germany, who tried in three dances to express the emotions roused by "The Blue Danube" and other fine music. The rest of the show was the same.

Moon and Morris have achieved a variety of rapid, simultaneous glides, which, when executed in perfect unison, hands in pockets, has a certain amount of amusement in it. The Texas Tommies arouse interest chiefly because one is always fearing one will die of heart failure. They dance in pairs, five minutes at a time, in stage western clothes, five minutes of astonishingly rapid, violent and ungraceful acrobatic dancing, which leaves them exhausted. They were received with great enthusiasm.

Grete Wiesenthal, really about the only artistic thing on the programme, attracted less, partly because she has no place in the tawdry Winter Garden atmosphere, partly because, after all, we have been so used to the best, Duncan, St. Denis and the rest, that Wiesenthal cannot but strike us as an earnest, poetic but really second-rate artist.

She dances before a colorless white sheet, in some rather extraordinary costumes. The first is a tunic of green feathers, a slashed mantle of white feathers, bare, sturdy legs and yellow dancing slippers. The second she dances in a modification of a peasant costume, white blouse, embroidered jacket, very short skirt and flying red hair ribbons. For the Blue Danube, with which she closes, and which is by far the most effective and poetic, Wiesenthal wears a three-quarter length tunic of green, and for the first time lets her lovely hair, which she has worn in trim, Gretchen-like braids, flow and wave over her shoulders.

The dancer seems sincere; she seems to feel emotion which she is trying to portray in motion. She has not the technical, physical excellence of the old school, Pavlova, Genee or the rest, and she has not the emotional background and power of Isadora Duncan, who can give concepts of joy, tragedy, fate almost convincingly in a movement of the body. This dancer is tall, slight, graceful in a girlish way, her face is sweet, and the constant smile not too artificial, but one gathers from watching her that she is always watching herself; there is little of the joyous abandon necessary to carry a dance like the Blue Danube to a climax; even in her brightest, most lyric moods she is a little slow, a little deliberate, calculating effects. Yet, curiously enough, her joy and active happiness is more beautiful and successful than her attempts at tragic emotion.

It must be her sincerity and quietness of method which has charmed Germany. Here, at the fag end of a hard season, we do not need her and cannot, perhaps, appreciate her.

Mrs. Mary Moncure Parker of Chicago is making plans for a woman's theater for that city, which will be owned and operated solely by women. Mrs. Parker is now negotiating for a playhouse in which to launch the project.

A woman will manage the new theater, and according to the plans there will be a woman ticket seller, a woman stage manager, a woman press agent, women scene shifters, women ushers and an orchestra composed of women. The new theater will cater to women, having daily matinees and providing tea and social rooms for patrons.

And now the question arises whether the dramatists, actors and spectators will be women exclusively. If not, then Mrs. Parker is only emulating in a lesser degree the "all women" bills of the vaudeville houses. They had women scene shifters there too—for about thirty minutes on the opening night—and Brooklyn has anticipated Chicago in having women press agents and a woman manager as permanent fixtures. Moreover, Winthrop Ames serves tea at the Little Theater every afternoon, so that Mrs. Parker, if she insists on novelty, can only obtain it by barring out the men altogether.

A matinee performance of "The Rainbow," tendered to the members of the theatrical profession now playing in New York, will be given at the Liberty Theater next Friday afternoon, April 19. Admission is by card only. No tickets will be sold.

The proposal to create an endowed repertory theater in Brooklyn, under the supervision of the Brooklyn Institute, is now being considered by the executive committee of the Institute's board of trustees. The proposal was reported favorably by the Institute council and referred to the trustees. The board placed the matter in the hands of the executive committee, which is now considering the plans.

The repertoire for the first week of the engagement of the French Grand Opera Company, under the direction of Jules Layolle, at the Lyric Theater, will include eight different modern lyric productions, as follows: Monday night, "Trovatore"; Tuesday night, "Faust"; Wednesday matinee, "Mignon"; Wednesday night, "La Favorite"; Thursday night, "Thais"; Friday night, "Manon"; Saturday matinee, "Carmen"; Saturday night, "Lucia."

Caught on the Fly.

A Chicago woman has been jailed for refusing to talk. Any woman who refuses to do that should be allowed full freedom for an indefinite period.

Madero is now having all of the troubles that Diaz had, and a few new ones which have been invented since Diaz abdicated.

An American baseball team has gone to Japan. It will probably capture not only the baseball, but the highball honors of that country.

That Missouri man who has been sentenced to obey his wife six months would probably prefer a straight penitentiary sentence.

One idea of no sort of a good job is that of reading proof on one of those new Chinese revolutionary newspapers.

It takes a pretty lively suffragette to crowd the Dowager Empress of China off the first page these days.

It is not illegal to tip a waiter in Kentucky, but it is probably still legal to shoot them in that state.

A Harvard professor says bread and butter is the ideal food. It is also about the most expensive.

By ROY K. MOULTON.

THE Indignation of the American people over the Titanic tragedy is growing. Like the thunder cloud at sea, first only a speck on the horizon, but with the force of a hurricane back of it sweeping along until the whole sky is overcast; then, breaking forth with a fury that knows no bounds and respects neither the living nor the dead. The Titanic is at the bottom of the sea and so are from 1,500 to 2,000 of her passengers. Many were lost because there were not enough life boats to carry them to safety. One, however, was saved. Regardless of the fact that brave men, noble women and helpless children all around him were doomed to death because the liner upon which they were prisoners had not furnished enough life boats to save them, there was enough room for this one MAN. His name is J. Bruce Ismay—the Reason, he was the millionaire owner of the ship that to make big profits for him failed to protect the lives of its passengers. He is on his way to America, riding in safety and comfort on the gallant Carpathia. But the wireless has been busy and he has been warned of the hurricane of indignation that is sweeping over America. Being a rich and powerful man he has ordered that the Cedric, another of the big ships he owns, stop at sea and take him off the Carpathia and he intends to return to England without setting foot upon American soil. What a fate it would be if the people of England also aro-e in their wrath and warned him not to land in England. Then, as master of all he surveys, he could ride the seas for the rest of his life in the boats he owns that are not safe in time of peril and every time the gale whistles through the rigging or an iceberg looms up in the dark he will see the ghastly forms of the dead at the bottom of the sea, victims of his greed, crooking the fore finger at him and bidding him "Come."

J. Bruce Ismay---Remember the Name---the Benedict Arnold of the Sea.

Latest Reports Say That the Carpathia Will Reach New York At 1 O'clock Tomorrow Morning.

The Circulation of THE DENVER POST Yesterday Was 66,040

THE DENVER POST

TWO CENTS BY NEWSBOYS. FIVE CENTS ON TRAINS. DENVER, COLORADO, THURSDAY, APRIL 18, 1912.—16 PAGES. 3D EDITION.

A Wireless From the Carpathia Says That She Has Only 868 Survivors. This Makes The Dead 1,340.

SURVIVORS GIVE PUBLIC FIRST HARROWING DETAILS OF DISASTER

SHIP'S LIGHTS WENT OUT 4 MINUTES AFTER CRASH

Impact Maimed Many and Members of Crew Asleep in Bow Died Instantly.

Lifeboats Had Terrible Battle With Death in Sea of Ice--Hundreds of Women Ill and Temporarily Insane on Carpathia.

New York, April 18.—The Carpathia has sent ashore the names of 125 third-class passengers and has requested the White Star line to send a ship's officer and fourteen sailors on two tugs to take charge of thirteen Titanic lifeboats at quarantine. This would indicate that only thirteen lifeboats had been found available for rescue work instead of twenty lifeboats as had been approximated.

All hope has been given up that Col. John Jacob Astor, Isidor Straus, Benjamin Guggenheim, George D. Widener, Major Archibald Butt, military aide to President Taft; Henry B. Harris, the theatrical manager, and Charles M. Hays, president of the Grand Trunk railway, have been saved.

The Carpathia's wireless operator sent word this morning that Colonel Astor was not on the Carpathia and he did not know whether Benjamin Guggenheim or Major Butt were aboard.

Carpathia Refuses to Answer Queries From U. S. S. Salem.

The navy department at Washington gave out a dispatch sent by the United States steamship Salem at 8 o'clock corroborating the numerous dispatches declaring that the Carpathia has persistently declined to answer any late message of inquiry, although sometimes acknowledging calls.

The message made remarkable time, having been received in Washington ten minutes after its dispatch from the Salem. It follows:

"U. S. S. Salem, 8 a. m.—Can get no information from Carpathia of any kind, although she is within easy radio communication. She sometimes acknowledges calls but will not admit receipt of messages or make reply. Cannot believe that she has failed to understand the messages I have sent. She is within easy range of the torpedo station (Newport, R. I.), so Salem will sail to Bradford (naval coaling station on Narragansett Bay, R. I.), this afternoon.

"CHANDLER, Commander."

The Cunarder Carpathia, with 868 of the shipwrecked survivors of the sunken Titanic, will dock at 1 o'clock Friday morning, according to General Henry, surveyor of the port of New York. A heavy fog extends afar out.

The wireless report that there are only 705 survivors of the Titanic aboard the Carpathia still persists, but no word, as far as can be learned, has come from the Carpathia within the last twenty-four hours giving the exact number of shipwrecked persons aboard.

THE SEA

By WALTER JUAN DAVIS

I have my habitants and my defenders, too.
But you, O, man, the land was made for you!

In your rash arrogance, you scorn the power of me,
And taunt your ancient enemy, the Sea.

And so, I thousands slay, and slay without a wound,
And welcome all to burial profound.

"Look Out for Iceberg"—Warning "Thanks," Was Titanic's Reply

New York, April 18.—With the arrival in port today of the Allan line steamer Mesaba, which left London on April 6, it was learned that Stanley Adams, the 18-year-old wireless operator, on Sunday last, only three hours before the Titanic collided with the iceberg, sent a warning to the Titanic telling of a great sea of floating ice through which the Mesaba had just passed.

The message flashed by wireless read:

"In latitude 42 to 41.25 north, to longitude 45 to 45.20 west, saw much heavy pack ice and great number of icebergs. Weather clear."

In response to this message the Mesaba received the single word "Thanks" from the Titanic, showing that the warning had been received.

"I sent the warning message to the Titanic about 7:30 p. m. Sunday, about four hours before she crashed into the berg that sank her," said Operator Adams. "At that time she was not in the ice and had a clear course.

"It was then daylight," said Adams. "The Titanic, however, apparently held on her course and entered the ice field that night. It was pitch dark that night and the darkness was made worse by a blue haze that rendered the searchlight powerless."

From figures available at the White Star line offices it is probable that the number of those perished totals 1,312.

Highland Light, Mass., April 18 (via Wireless, 2 a. m.)—The Carpathia is proceeding on her course at about 13 knots an hour with a gale handicapping her. The United States cruisers Chester and Salem are convoying her.

Rescue Ship Battling Gale Will Reach Dock Friday.

The Salem ran alongside and wanted to put provisions aboard. The captain of the Carpathia, replying by wireless said everything was all right aboard, provisions enough to reach New York, which he expected would be late tonight or early Friday morning.

The captain of the Carpathia by wireless said:

"I know for sure that there were no other lives saved except those I have aboard. I have not the body of Col. John Jacob Astor aboard.

"Mrs. Astor is very sick; dangerously ill. Over 100 are sick and in the hospital. When the collision occurred about 200 sailors sleeping in the bow of the Titanic were drowned like rats. After the impact the lights on the Titanic went out in four minutes. The dynamos lasted about the same time, which caused the wireless operator to abandon his calls for help. As his storage batteries were only capable of carrying from 50 to 100 miles the wireless operator was rendered helpless."

Many of the women were hysterical and some in a state of mental collapse. Conditions aboard the Carpathia were described as those which would be unbearable under any other circumstances. The ship's medical supplies were inadequate for the treatment of more than a few of the most serious cases. Passengers gave up their staterooms to the women. The salon is strewn with mattresses.

From the few details that the Carpathia's operator was able to transmit to Wellfleet the sea was perfectly calm when the accident happened. On every side stretched a great white expanse of broken ice and it was through this mass that the Titanic steamed to her doom. From the estimates of the survivors the operator conjectured that the vessel was steaming at the rate of ten miles an hour. Considering the ship's equipment of engines this was approximately at the rate of half her full speed. This indicates that although Captain Smith was hoping to estabish a record on the vessel's maiden trip he had confined his efforts at spurting to unobstructed water and was cognizant of the danger which the captain of the French liner Touraine reports he pointed out to him.

It also indicates that as usual the bulk of the iceberg was below the surface.

Many of Crew Asleep Died Almost Instantly.

The night was dark and a low haze spread over the ocean, making it impossible to discern objects ahead. How many icebergs were shrouded in this mist will never be known. But it is certain that the greatest of them and of the kind that mariners call a "blue bird" stood directly in the path of the Titanic.

Of exactly what orders were given from the bridge there is no report. But the Carpathia's operator said that the survivors had

(Continued on Page 3—Col. 1)

GRAND REVIVAL OF THE BIG MITT—BY WIRELESS!

LATEST BULLETINS OF SURVIVORS NOW ABOARD CARPATHIA

New York bureau says Carpathia admits having body of Astor on board. Thus far captain has denied truth of such report.

* * * * * * *

Passenger on Carpathia wires that rescue ship has only 700 survivors and that 2,000 are lost.

* * * * * * *

Commander of United States cruiser Salem wires Taft that Carpathia refuses to answer his wireless messages.

* * * * * * *

All hope gone for Widener, Butt, Astor, Guggenheim, Hays, Straus and Harris.

* * * * * * *

Nearly 300 sailors sleeping in bow of Titanic drowned like rats when liner struck.

* * * * * * *

Mrs. John Jacob Astor reported dangerously ill; 200 others in hospital on Carpathia, some insane, from disaster.

ISMAY, SAVED BY 'MIRACLE' TO SNEAK BACK TO LONDON

Managing Director of White Star Line, Fearing Public Contempt, Arranges by Wireless to Escape Without Landing.

New York, April 18.—While all waited in suspense today for the arrival of the Carpathia, bearing to shore those rescued from the doomed Titanic, a report became current that J. Bruce Ismay, managing director of the White Star line, had arranged by wireless code with the New York offices of his company to delay the sailing of the Cedric until the Carpathia gets into port that he may return to England without setting foot on United States soil.

If such were his plans, however, they were frustrated, as the Cedric sailed at noon today as per schedule. Unless the Cedric should meet the Carpathia and take Ismay on board, that gentleman will be forced to face the music in the glorious United States of America.

Ismay was one of the first to escape from the Titanic. Along with the women and children, to whom the right of way is given by the unwritten maritime law, the high official of the steamship line made his way to safety.

Around the White Star office it was said he was anxious to get back to London to report to the board of directors.

ANXIOUS TO ESCAPE EXPLAINING DISASTER.

The more plausible reason for the order given by Ismay is that he is anxious to escape the service of a subpoena requiring him to appear before the house committee on merchant marine affairs to testify concerning the number of lifeboats carried by the Titanic.

It had been planned at Washington that the millionaire official of the company—

(Continued on Page 2—Col. 3)

Greater love hath no man than this—that a man lay down his life for his friends.—John XV:XIII.

STATUTE FIXING NUMBER OF LIFEBOATS ANCIENT

Did Not Contemplate Mammoth Liner of Capacity Like Titanic.

Only Sixteen Are Required, With Room for 880 People, Which Is About the Number Rescued.

London, April 18.—The Standard in an editorial says:

"The fierce outcries in America against the board of trade, which sets the standard for all the world in these matters, reveals the fact that leading shipping companies, parliament and navy department here have not yet awakened to the advent of the mammoth liner. It seems incredible, but it is true, that regulations at present in force do not contemplate the existence of a ship of more than 10,000 tons which is not a quarter of the Titanic's register.

"According to these regulations the minimum number of boats of an approved type which must be carried under the davits and ready for instant launching by vessels of 10,000 tons and upwards is sixteen and the total minimum cubic contents of these boats is fixed at 5,500 cubic feet, that is to say, 10 cubic feet for each person.

"This provides for the reception of 880 people which is just about the number that are believed to have been saved and is barely one-third of those on boare the Titanic last Sunday.

"How many passengers who go aboard these huge modern liners have known that if anything happens two out of three or three out of four of them are doomed to perish unless another ship happens to be standing by? They know it now and one result must be a new merchant shipping act with board of trade rules requiring that every ship shall carry sufficient means of taking off the whole of her passengers and crew. It may be said that a steamer like the Titanic cannot be expected to put to sea without at least sixty or seventy rowing boats.

"In that case she will have to carry steam launches and barges like a man-of-war or better still, some portions of her mile long decks must be pontoons which can be detached and used as rafts in an emergency."

Berlin, April 18.—The German regulations in regard to providing boat accommodations for passengers and crew in case of an emergency like the sudden floundering of the Titanic do not call for a seat in a boat for everybody. The largest ships carry about twenty boats.

The newspapers in referring to the Titanic disaster make less criticism in regard to the shortage of boats than in speed craze, to which many ascribe the accident.

It is claimed that if a daily service each way across the Atlantic be adopted the danger of disaster will be lessened as ships will always be in the neighborhood of each other. It is stated that the North German Lloyd, Hamburg-American, Cunard, White Star and French lines are discussing such an arangement.

List of Third-Class Passengers Who Were Taken From Wreck

New York, April 18.—The following third class passengers of the Titanic are reported aboard the Carpathia:

Anguzen, Helena.
Astlund, Selma.
Astlund, Lillian.
Astlund, Felix.
Aksaks, Lily.
Aksaks, Leah.
Abbott, Rosa.
Abelsoph, Akelesep.
Anderson, Edna.
Alderson, ——
Allun, Bednoura.
Abramhamson, Augusta.
Assim, Mariano.
Boklin, Eugene.
Boklin, Latef.
Boklin, Haline.
Boklin, Marie.
Batman, Emily.
Bonikstrom, Maria.
Bradley, Bridget.
Barlson, Einar.
Bridget, Rose.
Bing, Lee.
Charles, John.
Casem, Boyam.
Casem, Nassif.
Churchson, John.
Conto, Neville.
Conto, Minnie.
Connolly, Katie.
Carr, Ellen.
Conto, Will.
Cribb, L. M.
Cubulaket, S.
Devaney, Margaret.
Dianodelman, Delia.
Demueder, Theodore.
Daly, Marsola.
Daly, Charles.
Daly, P. H.
Dean, Mrs. Etta and two children.
Doty, Agnes (or Mrs. Addick).
Eldergrek, L.
Eliazer, Nicola.
Hedvig, Croft.
Hanwakan, ——
Hap, Chang.
Joblom, S.
Krigsene, Joseph.
Kirkora, Krikorean.
Kesorney, Florence.
Kolsbottel, Anna
Kohn, Gus.
Ludgues, Aino.
McKey, Ernest.
Moss, Albert.
McConnack, Thomas.
McGowan, Annie.
McDermott, Delia.
McGaren, John.
McCarthy, Katie.
Messemockes, Anna.
Messemockes, G. D.
Moubarek, Bunos
Muns, Javna.
Malliedel, Bertha.
Maran, Bertha.
Mads n, Koistof.
Merrigan, Maggie.
Mathjoax, Karl.
Muhan, Kirkoean.
Murphy, Nora.
Marlkari, ——
Manman, Hauna.
McKey, Alice.
McGovern, Mary.
Nelson, Demina J.
Nanga, Margaret.
Nelson, Carlo.
Nekett, Mary.
Nickron, John.
Nyhem, Kiree.
O'Leary, Nora.
Omsen, Scurley.
Olsen, Arthur.
Oamb, Nicola.
Osplund, Sanderson.
Person, Ernest.
Patros, Cotrina.
Patros, Nebsa.
Picard, Genoit.
Reibon, Anna.
Sindel, Beatrice.
Sumdian, Johann.
Stanley, Amy.
Schurbint, Jan.
Sulici, Nicola.
Smythe, Paula.
Sap, Jules.
Strinder, Juno.
Shine, Axel.
Sibelrome, Agnes.
Sofia, Anna.
Turkgest, William.
Turkula, Hedwig.
Vartanon, ——
Wicks, Ellen.
Yesberg, Siline.
Yousef, George.
Yousef, Hannah.
Yousef, Marian.
Yousef, Madera.
Zenn, Phillip.

The following list of persons not previously mentioned in the list of persons rescued from the Titanic was given out at the offices of the White Star line:

Miss Antoinette.
Kennard Camarion.
Miss Sarah Daniel.
Miss Nina Hope.
Mme. M. Olivia Middled.
Miss Letta Minderson.
Miss Nora Sedley.
Miss Alice Touch.
Miss Affieramont.
William Charlton.
Miss Ethel Garside.
Miss J. A. Hold.
Mrs. Mohan.
Miss Ethel Pomeroy.
Miss Jessie Troutt.
Mrs. M. Warion (Mrs. F. M. Warren).

These names were added to the list of those saved through the reports which have reached the officials of the White Star company from various sources. None of them has been received by wireless from the Carpathia.

Portland, Maine, April 18.—A list of third-class passengers and crew rescued from the wrecked steamship Titanic by the Carpathia was received by wireless last night. The list follows:

THIRD-CLASS PASSENGERS.

Nora Murphy.
Katie Mullin.
Katie McCarthy.
G. D. Messemeckes.
Anna Messemeckes.
Madera Yusef.
Bunos Moudarck.
Halinan Moudarck.
Gitosa Moudarck.
Mina Musolman.
Sanuca Subulaskat.
Javina Muno.
Kirkoean Muhan.
Delia Dianodelmn.
Karl Mathjoax.
Bertha Maliedell.
Maggie Morrigan.
Bertha Maran.
Kristof Madsen.
Albert Moss.
Mary McGovern.
Ernest McKey.
Alice McKey.
Thomas McCormack.
John Nickaren.
—— Alderson.
Bertha Nelson.
Mary Neket.
Demina K. Nelson.
Yree Nyhem.
Annie McGowan.
Agnes Doyt (or Mrs. A. A. Dick).
Margaret Nanga.
Maggie J. Murphy.
Leonch Eldegrek.
Heuna Manman.
Krikorean Kirora.
Hanwakan (?)
Deliah McDermott.
—— Marlkarl.
John McKaren.
Aing Ludguis.
Helena Angusen.

RAILROAD CHIEF AMONG VICTIMS ON TITANIC

Montreal, April 18.—The Grand Trunk Railway company this morning received the following telegram:

"Mrs. Hays, Mrs. Davidson saved. No news of husband. (Signed) Hays."

This message came from Woods Hole, Mass. This confirms information thus far received to the effect that the president of the Grand Trunk railway is not among the survivors.

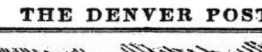

REACHING FOR HIS PREY.

KINGS EXTEND TO AMERICAN PEOPLE THEIR SYMPATHY

George of England and Albert of Belgium First to Cable.

CARDINALS SEND NOTE

Hope Lawmakers Will See Necessity of Greater Security of Ocean Travel.

Washington, April 18.—President Taft has made public cablegrams received from the king and queen of England and the king of Belgium, conveying their sympathies to the American people in the sorrows which have followed the Titanic disaster.

The following was the cablegram from King George, dated at Sandringham:

"The queen and I are anxious to assure you and the American nation of the great sorrow which we experience at the terrible loss of life that has occurred among the American citizens as well as among my own subjects by the foundering of the Titanic. Our two countries are so intimately allied by ties of friendship and brotherhood that any misfortunes which affect the one must necessarily affect the other and on the present terrible occasion they are both equally sufferers.

(Signed) "George, R. and I."

President Taft's reply was as follows:

"In the presence of the appalling disaster to the Titanic the people of the two countries are brought into community of grief through their common bereavement. The American people share in the sorrow of their kinsmen beyond the sea. On behalf of my people, I thank you for your sympathetic message."

(Signed) "William H. Taft."

The message from King Albert of Belgium was as follows:

"I beg your excellency to accept my deepest condolences on the occasion of the frightful catastrophe to the Titanic which has caused such mourning in the American nation."

The president's acknowledgment follows:

"I deeply appreciate your sympathy with my fellow countrymen who have been stricken with affliction through the disaster to the Titanic."

The many expressions of grief to reach President Taft included one signed jointly by the three American cardinals who are here attending the meeting of the trustees of the Catholic University. It said:

"To the president of the United States: The archbishops of the country in joint session with the trustees of the Catholic University of America, beg to offer to the president of the United States their expression of their profound grief at the awful loss of human lives attendant upon the sinking of the steamship Titanic; and at the same time to assure the relatives of the victims of this horrible disaster of our deepest sympathy and condolence.

"They wish also to attest hereby to the hope that the law makers of the country will see in this sad accident the obvious necessity of legal provisions for greater security of ocean travel.

(Signed)
"James, Cardinal Gibbons, Archbishop of Baltimore.
"John, Cardinal Farley, Archbishop of New York.
"William, Cardinal O'Connell, Archbishop of Boston."

The expression of sympathy sent to President Taft by the three American cardinals has been acknowledged by the president in a letter made public today by Cardinal Gibbons:

"My Dear Cardinal Gibbons:

"I have received the written expression by the Roman Catholic archbishops of the country in joint session with the trustees of the Catholic university of their profound grief of the awful loss of human lives in the sinking of the Titanic, and on behalf of the bereaved I beg to express a grateful appreciation of this message of sympathy.

"I note in your communication the valued suggestion as to the necessity for legal provisions for greater security of ocean travel. Sincerely yours,

"WILLIAM H. TAFT."

Stead's Last Visit to U. S. Was 1907

Chicago, April 18.—The last visit of William T. Stead, the London publisher who is believed to have perished in the wreck of the Titanic, was made to Chicago in April, 1907.

At that time he visited many of the acquaintances made in 1893-94, while collecting material for his book "If Christ Came to Chicago." Among places he visited were the Workingmen's exchange saloon owned by Alderman Kenna and the saloon of Hank North in the levee district. He met and interviewed both owners thirteen years before.

On the last visit Mr. Stead was accompanied by his wife and the two showed much interest in the settlement work accomplished by Miss Jane Addams at Hull house.

Titanic Disaster Cast Gloom Over the Mauretania

New York, April 18.—A wireless message from the steamer Mauretania, when 840 miles east of Sandy Hook, to the Cunard company's offices in New York, says that when news was received of the disaster to the Titanic a meeting was called of the passengers, which passed resolutions of sympathy with the surviving passengers. The second cabin also passed similar resolutions.

No concerts were held and the band remained silent. Collections were taken for the seamen's charities and $800 was realized.

Dewey Says Greed Makes Sea Travel Menace to Lives

Washington, April 18.—"I think that every passenger who crosses the north Atlantic takes his life in his hands," said Admiral George Dewey last night. "For myself, I would rather go around the world in a well equipped battleship than make a trip across the north Atlantic in a trans-Atlantic vessel.

"The greed for money-making is so great that it is with the sincerest regret that I observe that human lives are never taken into consideration."

A CROSS SECTION OF THE TITANIC.

(A comparative idea of the vessel's great size.)

If its vast hull were empty, thirty-six full sized replicas of Hudson's famous Half Moon could be laid crosswise in it, under full sail, and still leave 270 feet of unoccupied tapering space at bow and stern; or twenty-eight full sizes replicas of Fulton's Clermont could be piled up like cordwood inside without utilizing 282 feet and 6 inches of tapering space fore and aft, where several more could be stowed away. An ordinary railroad locomotive with tender, and drawing eight Pullman sleepers, could be laid upon the deck, abaft the spot near the captain's bridge, where the artist has cut it in two. From keel to funnel top it is nearly as tall as the 10-story Postal Telegraph building in New York.

TERRIBLE LOSS OF LIFE CHARGED TO NEGLIGENCE

Congress to Begin Immediate Inquiry and Try to Force Officers to Testify.

Stringent Marine Laws Sure to Follow Disaster and Lifeboats Will Be Demanded to Accommodate Passenger List.

Washington, April 18.—Officials of the navy department are suspending judgment on the conduct of officers of the Carpathia, who have treated with scant courtesy requests for information transmitted through the scout cruisers Salem and Chester by government officials, including the president of the United States.

Whether responsibility rests with the captain of the Cunarder or President Ismay of the White Star line, who is reported as a survivor of the Titanic aboard the Carpathia, is a matter of conjecture.

Naval officials indignantly reject an insinuation by the Cunard people that the naval wireless operators are incapable of handling messages with due celerity.

SENATORS DEMAND IMMEDIATE INVESTIGATION.

Senator Smith said he feared his committee would be without jurisdiction to compel Mr. Ismay and other British subjects connected with the International Mercantile Marine to attend its hearing and give testimony.

"We may not have jurisdiction over the individual," said Mr. Smith, "but the American congress is not without jurisdiction over the harbors of the United States. It is for these men who make use of the harbors to meet the public demand for information of this terrible disaster, and to do it now."

Senator Smith said he and several other members of his committee would present this argument to Mr. Ismay and others in the hope they would be willing to accept subpoenas from the sergeant-at-arms of the senate who will accompany them.

Chairman Smith and other members of the committee said no time would be lost in requesting the officials to testify. The senators may go down the harbor on a revenue cutter to intercept the Carpathia. Witnesses will be asked to come to Washington at once.

RESCUED TITANIC OFFICERS TO BE WITNESSES.

Among those who will be summoned to appear beside J. Bruce Ismay will be the second, third, fourth and fifth officers of the Titanic, who are reported to have been saved, and any other officers who may have survived.

An important feature may be the message transmitted through the Titanic April 14, the day of the calamity, from the steamer Amerika to the hydrographic office of the United States navy giving notice of icebergs in the Titanic's vicinity.

Naval officials are of the opinion that one of the icebergs reported by the Amerika through the Titanic was the cause of the Titanic's wreck. These officers were amazed by reports that the Titanic was going ahead at full speed in view of the known presence of danger.

LIFEBOATS DEMANDED FOR PASSENGER LIST.

The bill that was introduced in the senate by Perkins of California and in the house by Sulzer of New York met with enthusiastic approval in both houses. Senators and representatives joined in promises for support to a measure which will put an end to the risk of human life on the altar of corporate greed.

The bill provides that no ship shall be cleared from an American port that is not equipped with sufficient lifebooats to accommodate not only passengers, but crew in case it becomes necessary to abandon the vessel.

Its passage without a dissenting vote seems assured.

"The penitentiary is the place for any one who wilfully sends a ship to sea without proper equipment," is the way Representative Hardwick of Georgia expressed it. Representative Hull of Tennessee pronounced the Titanic disaster the result of "criminal negligence of the worst kind."

In the senate the bill has gone to the commerce committee, of which Knute Nelson of Minnesota is chairman, and in the house to the committee on commerce and fisheries, presided over by Representative Alexander. Members of both committees will confer with the state department and the department of commerce and labor before reporting the bill, so that its final form shall be such as to admit of no opposition.

ARCHIBALD C. BUTT WAS TO HAVE BEEN MARRIED THIS FALL

Was Engaged to Youngest Daughter of Col. John R. Williams.

San Antonio, Tex., April 18.—Major Archibald C. Butt, military aid to President Taft, soon was to wed Miss Williams of Washington, sister-in-law of Joseph Leiter of Chicago and the youngest daughter of Col. John R. Williams, Coast Artillery corps, retired.

This announcement is made here by Brig. Gen. C. Lockwood, U. S. A., retired, now living in San Antonio. He said Major Butt was engaged to Miss Williams, and the wedding was to take place some time next fall, the exact date not having been set. General Lockwood was intensely grieved when the name of Major Butt did not appear in the list of those rescued from the Titanic and while making inquiries of a newspaper here regarding the tidings of Major Butt, he told the story of the major's love affair.

"Major Butt met Miss Williams, my grandniece, soon after he became aide to President Taft," he said. "He was a gentleman and a splendid soldier and she is the most lovable girl in the world. The engagement was kept secret for family reasons, but it was planned to make the announcement some time during the summer. I know that Archie was a passenger upon the Titanic, and as he has not been reported saved, I know he died like a soldier and a man—giving way that others might go to safety."

Laundried.

"All new arrivals are washed," explained the warden of the prison.

"And if they make a fuss?"

"Then they are ironed."—Sacred Heart Review.

PASSENGER SAYS CARPATHIA SAVED BUT 700 PEOPLE

Chicago Man Believes Over 2,000 Perished in Titanic Wreck.

Chicago, April 18.—The following wireless message, date April 17, from a passenger of the Carpathia was received here today:

"Carpathia picked up 700 Titanic, mostly women. Over 2,000 lost. Iceberg continuous mass twenty-five miles. Chicagoans this ship well. 8:35 a. m. Dr. F. H. Blackmarr."

Dr. Blackmarr of Chicago was going to Europe on the Carpathia. His estimate of the number lost is evidently in error as there were not so many as 2,700 on board the Titanic.

New York, April 18.—The Dutch oil tank steamer La Flandre, which came in today from Antwerp, reported an encounter with the ice field on April 11 at 9 o'clock at night in latitude 42.02 and longitude 50.07. In the fog, Captain Claude says, the La Flandre steamed into a large ice field, which became so packed the steamer could not penetrate it.

As far as could be seen from aloft the ice extended in all directions. La Flandre was compelled to put about and steamed for twenty miles to the southward to clear the field. The temperature of the water near the ice pack was 30 degrees.

If the Titanic sank in water registering 30 degrees, those who may have leaped overboard probably survived but a few moments.

Gal-vanism?

There is frequently something about a girl that draws her closer to a man—unless she asks him to remove it.—Judge.

'Women and Children First'

(From The Kansas City Post.)

The next time some littleness of human nature makes you think that the worst of God's work is MAN—think of the sinking of the Titanic—and the order that men gave AND OBEYED—even the least of them—as the great ship wallowed lower and lower and sank into the sea—

"Women and children FIRST!"

There were 2,200 persons and more on that ship—and nearly 1,500—most of them men—went down with her. There was place in the boats for only a third of the Titanic's great passenger list. The men—and there were nearly 1,500 of them—knew when the last one drew away that DEATH had taken command of the TITANIC.

Stronger than the massive ribs and plates of forged steel that made the monster boat's strength; stronger than the tall and shining pinnacles of the white berg whose sharp reefs hidden deep in the sea, tore and twisted the steel of that vessel; stronger than the great master who had taken charge of the sinking ship—were the souls of the men who stood aside that others might be saved.

Looking upon certain death in the icy waters or in the swirling suction that was sure to come as the great ship took its plunge—these men stood firm and steadfast as the last boatload of women and children drew away from the helpless vessel.

"Greater love hath no man than that he shall lay down his life for his friend," the psalmist sang in his wisdom.

Never again think humanity is not worth while. Never again say it to any man.

You may be talking to a hero as great as any who went down on the Titanic—for God has shown he has made them by thousands.

CARPATHIA EXPECTED TO DOCK AT 1 O'CLOCK FRIDAY MORNING

THOUSANDS ARE REFUSED ADMISSION TO LANDING

Rescue Ship, Handicapped by Gale, Is Steaming Slowly Toward New York.

Her Wireless Station Ignores Inquiries From U. S. S. Salem--Messages Tell of Terrible Conditions Aboard.

(Continued From Page One.)

only words of praise for the conduct of Captain Smith and his crew. Captain Smith, it is believed, was on the lookout when the vessel struck. There was no need to sound a muster call for the crew. The crash brought every man to the deck. Neither was there any cause for the enforcement of the law of the sea, that when men disregard the rule of "women and children first" they shall be clubbed back.

The Wellfleet dispatches confirm the supposition that a large number of the crew, peacefully sleeping in the forecastle head, were instantly crushed to death. But how many perished in this manner is a secret of the sea. More than a hundred were killed by the impact and the ripping open of the vessel.

Survivors stated that after they pulled away from the vessel in the lifeboats and looked back only the black outline of the Titanic was visible through the fog. All the lights had been extinguished when the inrush of the water reached the dynamo room.

Lifeboats Escape to Fight Death in Sea of Ice Floes.

The wireless operator managed to utter his cry for help before the electric power gave out. This explained the abrupt ending of his message: "S. O. S. Titanic sinking by the head. Rush assistance"—the last words of his message were too faint to be understood.

The lifeboats escaped the sinking ship, only to fight another life battle against the floating ice. Whether all of them escaped destruction, while drifting among the floes, is not known.

The number of lifeboats picked up by the Carpathia is not definitely known. Neither is it known whether any of the floating bodies were rescued by the Carpathia.

One message received from the Carpathia reports that several lifeboats were picked up more than a mile away from the spot where the Titanic went down.

The crews of the lifeboats warned the survivors that they would be drawn down by the suction of the big ship if they were within a quarter of a mile of her when she went down.

The Titanic went down bow first. Every lifeboat and every raft was crowded with men and women and the decks of the Titanic visible above water, were lined with men who had helped to put the women in the boats.

One message picked up by wireless was from Mrs. John B. Thayer of Philadelphia, wife of the president of the Pennsylvania railroad, saying she and her son, J. B. Thayer Jr. are safe on the Carpathia, but that her husband went down with the Titanic. He is worth about $5,000,000. The news is being kept from Mr. Thayer's mother for fear it will kill her.

Another message was from Mrs. Henry B. Harris, wife of the theatrical manager and read:

"Am safe. Praying that Harry has been picked up by another steamer. Arrive Carpathia.

(Signed) "RENE."

Survivors Believe Loved Ones Left Behind Are Saved.

The very wording of Mrs. Harris' message caused a catch in the throat of those who read it, for in it she revealed her hope that her husband might yet be safe. It is feared that none save those aboard the Carpathia were saved from the Titanic. Mrs. Harris' words show, however, that among the rescued on the ship there lingers the hope that dear ones who were left behind may have been saved.

There was a gathering in the grand salon on Sunday night, attended by men and women of the first cabin in evening clothes. It was a gala night on board the great liner. Many of the women were lowered into lifeboats in their evening gowns, which afforded but scant protection from the chill winds and water.

Guided only by the cries of the distressed survivors, the Carpathia cautiously made her way through the dangerous ice fields, picking up boatload after boatload of frenzied women and children.

Many Women Temporarily Insane From Harrowing Experiences.

Many of the women were rendered temporarily insane by their harrowing experience and are under the care of physicians in the Carpathia's hospital.

Capt. E. J. Smith, commanding the Titanic, was last seen by the survivors standing on the bridge with megaphone in hand. Wireless Operator Phillips did not leave his station. H. S. Bride, the second wireless operator on the Titanic, was placed in one of the boats and is on the Carpathia. It is believed that Phillips, when he realized the ship's doom, compelled Bride to leave the station and make his escape.

The survivors, only a few of whom are able to give connected accounts of what happened before they put off in the lifeboats, pay high tribute to the conduct of Captain Smith and his crew and to the men among the passengers.

The Carpathia's operator said he had tried all Tuesday night to communicate with Sable island, but was unable to do so on account of the storm. The weather cleared somewhat Wednesday, however, and he picked up the Wellfleet station and the scout cruiser Chester, which was dispatched to the scene by the navy department.

As soon as the survivors learned that the Chester had been reached they flooded the station with reassuring messages to friends and relatives. Their messages were sent to the Chester to be relayed by Sable island.

From the fact that this station's communication with the Carpathia was broken off, it is doubted whether the messages filed by the passengers have reached their destination.

CHILEAN STEAMER LOST WITH EIGHTY ABOARD

San Francisco, April 18.—Details of the loss of the Chilean steamer Cachapoal, with eighty lives, on the night of March 31, were brought here last night by the British steamer Queen Helena.

The Cachapoal was manned by British officers and a crew of Chilians and carried thirty passengers. The steamer failed to appear at Payta, Peru, on her regular run from Guayaquil, Ecuador, 250 miles distant, on the morning of March 22, and steamers dispatched in search of her could find no trace.

It is the generally accepted theory, according to officers of the Queen Helena, that the Cachapoal's boilers exploded as they had given her frequent trouble.

SNOW AND RAIN FELL GENERALLY OVER STATE

Reports from all parts of Colorado indicate that the storm last night and today was very general, nearly every section having been visited. At Cripple Creek six inches of snow fell. Snow also fell in northern Colorado, as well as in the far eastern sections.

THE CARPATHIA, FUNERAL CAR OF THE OCEAN

AT 1 O'CLOCK TOMORROW MORNING THE CARPATHIA, CARRYING THE SURVIVORS OF THE GREATEST WRECK IN MODERN MARINE HISTORY, WILL STEAM INTO THE NEW YORK HARBOR. PASSES TO THE DOCK HAVE BEEN ISSUED TO SUCH A THRONG THAT THE SCENE UNDOUBTEDLY WILL BE ONE OF THE MOST HEART-RENDING IN THE HISTORY OF NEW YORK, CITY OF TRAGEDY.

ISMAY, FEARING CENSURE, SNEAKS BACK TO EUROPE

Manager Wires to New York to Hold Cedric Until Carpathia Arrives.

(Continued From Page One.)

who was miraculously preserved while the veteran captain of the Titanic went down with his ship—should be called upon to submit to a grueling investigation. When the first report was flashed to shore that Ismay had gone down to the watery depths with the gallant employes of his company, the story was taken as a matter of course. The law of the sea holds up to universal scorn the member of the crew who saves himself before every passenger's absolute safety is assured. The world did not know that the employers of the crew are held exempt from this inexorable law.

THIS EXEMPTION FORCIBLY RECALLED.

This exemption was forcibly brought to mind when the second message came that Ismay had been saved. Whether he had fought his way into a lifeboat, as the maddened crew of the Burgoyne fought when that ship went down a few years ago, or had been the unwilling victim of the desire of his employes that he be saved, will never be known. Ismay will not tell.

"Some officer had to take charge of the lifeboats," is the shame-faced explanation that the officials in the New York office made.

But why it was not one of the men of sea-faring experience who was assigned to this work no one knows. There were 800 employes on the ship, more or less familiar with the life-saving work. Almost any one of these could have taken charge of the lifeboats, but any one of them who did it and in compensation was spared his life would have been ashamed to live it.

LONDON PAPER IN SARCASTIC COMMENTT.

The London papers have made just one comment on the saving of Mr. Ismay. The Daily Herald, the new labor paper, says:

"One might urge that Mr. Bruce Ismay showed his confidence in the safety of the ship by traveling aboard of her, but Mr. Bruce Ismay, chairman of the White Star line, has been saved."

One of the chief subjects of discussion in London hotels and clubs is Mr. Ismay's escape, there being much wonderment whether he was forced into a boat with the women and children by his employes.

P. A. B. Widener of Philadelphia, a director in the White Star line company, has given up hope of seeing his son, George Widener, again. To some close friends Widener said:

"George went down with the ship, and he went down like a man—fighting to save the women and children."

Then he was asked why, if Ismay were aboard the Carpathia, his son should not also be there.

"Oh, Ismay saved himself," was the answer.

Wireless Riddles Caused by Amateur Sender at Work

S. O. S. . . . — — — . . .

Three dots, three dashes, three dots—it is the wireless cry of peril and call for assistance.

It was the swan song of the ill-fated Titanic, the dreaded "Signal of Sinking."

The wizardry of wireless is more in the public mind today than it was when "Jack" Binns brought help to the rammed Republic and first demonstrated that Marconi's inventive brain had given to the world means of saving hundreds of thousands of lives that without it would be offered as sacrifice to the ocean's toll of death.

Vaguely the methods of telegraphing without wires is known to the public. But the confusion of names and the fragmentary messages which have come from the Carpathia and other ships and stations which relayed from the rescuing craft are not clearly understood. In the beginning, the continental code of the wireless to distinguish from the Morse code of land lines has no spaces between dots and dashes. Also, instead of the sharp, clear-cut clicks of a telegraph sounder there is only a buzz similar to that experienced in telephone communication when electrical disturbances produce what is known technically as "induction."

So much was The Post informed by W. C. Black, superintendent of the Postal lines out of Denver. "Another element that has entered into the situation and will account for indistinct transmission by wireless," said Mr. Black, "is the fact that scores of amateur operators are trying to pick up the Carpathia and the ships that are relaying its messages. That means that the air is heavy with currents, each conflicting to a measurable extent with the other.

"In this medley of buzzing, accurate receiving is almost impossible. Again, the continental code, with its lack of spaces, aids confusion. For instance, D is a dash and two dots, I is two dots and T is one dash. If the receiver gets a dash and two dots it may be D or it may be T-I. Likewise O is three dashes, while M is two dashes and T is one dash, wherefore three dashes, if the current is weakened by disturbances or by interference of other currents, may be M-T or O.

"Suppose an operator gets — . . . — — —, — . or B O N. The rest was not caught, and he makes it Brown, Bowen, or whatever he thinks most probably it should be. Again, take Rood, the name of a Denver man probably lost on the Titanic. In the continental it would be dot-dash-dot, dash-dash-dash, dash-dash-dash, dash-dot-dot. Sit with the operator striving to catch from electrically filled ether something tangible. It may come to him dot-dash, dot-dash-dash-dash, dash, dash, dash, dash-dot, dot. The second letter is J and the third would be J except for the dot. If he missed that the reading would be A J J N E. Is there any doubt that he would immediately write it down A. J. Jones and so give it to the world?"

TITANIC CAN'T SINK, SMITH TOLD FRIEND

New York, April 18.—The night before Captain E. J. Smith of the Titanic left for Europe to take command of the liner he dined with Mr. and Mrs. W. P. Willis of Flushing, L. I.

At the dinner Captain Smith, according to Mr. Willis, was enthusiastic over the prospects of his new command. He said he shared with the designers of the vessel the utmost confidence in her sea-going qualities and told Mr. and Mrs. Willis that it was impossible for her to sink.

He looked forward then to the most successful days of his seafaring and especially dwelt upon the idea that the Titanic's appearance on the Atlantic would mark a high point of safety and comfort in the evolution of ocean travel. He regarded the vessel as one that would keep above the water in the face of the most unexpected trial. Even if a part of the ship should be seriously damaged, he said, there need be no doubt that she would reach port.

Will Bring It Back.

Caller—Is the boss in?
Office Boy—No, sir; he's gone out.
Caller—Will he be back after dinner?
Office Boy—No; that's what he's gone out for.—Judge.

LATE WRECK BULLETINS

White Star line receives revised list first cabin survivors. Elimination of H. B. Cass only change.

Franklin of White Star line says word from Ismay declares he is "stunned, overwhelmed."

National Red Cross will send out country-wide appeal for funds to aid destitute from Titanic.

London, April 18.—Board of trade says 2,208 persons were aboard Titanic when she sank. Vessel carried lifeboats to accommodate 1,178, and had also 48 buoys and 3,560 life belts.

Following made public by White Star line at 3:15 o'clock this afternoon: "Carpathia due at Sandy Hook 9 p. m. Should dock at 11 p. m."

Mrs. Edgar Meyer, Among the Rescued; Name Not Reported

New York, April 18.—A wireless message received yesterday by relatives of Mrs. Edgar Meyer, daughter of the late Andrew Sake, reporting that she is among the survivors on board the Carpathia. Her name was not included in the list of survivors. Her husband, who is vice president of a copper company, was not rescued.

The wireless message from the Carpathia via Halifax is not signed, and reads:

"Leela safe. Well cared for. Edgar missing."

When Vice President Franklin of the White Star line was told the contents of this message, he exclaimed:

"My, gentlemen, I hope that's true. Then perhaps others have been saved."

WRECK NEWS GIVEN WIRELESS MONOPOLY

New York, April 18.—The United Wireless company has sent the following dispatch to all ships and shore stations from New York to Hatteras:

"South Wellfleet, Siasconset, Sagaponack and Sea Gate will handle Carpathia's business exclusively. All other commercial and government stations will cease transmitting while Carpathia's business is being exchanged with above stations. Work other than Carpathia's and business from government ships going to meet Carpathia will not be permitted."

ISIDOR STRAUS' FATE PROSTRATES BROTHER NATHAN

Latter Was Only Delegate From U. S. to Congress for Protection of Infants.

Rome, April 18.—Nathan Straus is dangerously ill here and fears for his recovery are entertained. Mr. Straus collapsed today when he learned that his brother Isidor was among the missing on the Titanic's passenger list. Physicians were summoned immediately and they reported his condition grave.

Nathan Straus, with Mrs. Straus, sailed from New York last August as the representative of the United States government to the international congress for the protection of infants.

He was the only delegate to the congress from the United States and was selected by President Taft because of his signal service in behalf of infants in the United States.

Topeka, Kan., April 18.—The Rev. Ernest Carter and his wife of London were booked for the Titanic's first sailing on their way to Topeka to spend the summer with Mrs. Carter's brother, George Hughes. Mrs. Carter is a daughter of Thomas Hughes, author of "Tom Brown's School Days."

A cablegram from London today announced that they had sailed, and as their names have not appeared in the list of survivors Mrs. Hughes gave up hope of them today.

Wheeling, W. Va., April 18.—Mrs. James A. Hughes, wife of the West Virginia congressman, is reported dying at her home here from shock caused by failure to receive any news from her daughter, who was on board the Titanic.

London, April 18.—To the determination of his wife, Lord Pierre, builder of the Titanic, owes his escape from the disaster that befell that ship.

Despite the fact that he had not yet fully recovered from a recent operation, Lord Pierre arranged to cross on the first trip of the Titanic—the ship which he regarded as the crowning work of his career as a shipbuilder.

Lady Pierre, when she discovered that her husband was obdurate in his intention, canceled all his arrangements.

Brockton, Mass., April 18.—Miss Katherine E. Maguire, aged 50, heartbroken by the news that her nephew, John E. Maguire, was among those probably lost on the Titanic, became violently ill and died within a few minutes. She had been in the best of health.

SEA CHART SHOWS TITANIC WAS CLOSE TO DANGER ZONE

Ice Seen on April 11 South of the Forty-Second Parallel.

Washington, April 18.—For more than a quarter of a century the hydrographic office of the bureau of navigation, navy department, has been publishing a series of charts of the North Atlantic ocean, depicting physical conditions as well as the location of dangers to navigation as reported by incoming ships.

These publications are circulated freely among ship masters and shipping people in return for their news of the sea, the point of contact between the office at Washington and the marine world being a chain of branch hydrographic offices at the principal seaports.

In recent years the collection of marine data has been immensely accelerated by the use of radio-telegraphy, and the hydrographic office is thereby enabled to publish daily memorandum of any important reports of dangers received.

By this means Boston, New York, Philadelphia, Baltimore, Norfolk, etc., daily are put in possession of the accumulated reports of dangerous derelicts and icebergs which have been edited by experts in this line of work.

Shipping companies and shipmasters also are put in possession of the experiences and judgment of a trained staff in the hydrographic office as summarized in a pamphlet entitled "North Atlantic Ice Movements," giving a study of the entire question, with diagrams to show the usual limits of ice for a period of ten years.

The shipping community also is provided from month to month with the pilot chart showing the conditions of ice up to the time of printing, with the weekly hydrographic bulletin giving details in regard to ice and derelicts, and also the daily memorandum summarizing the collected reports of each day.

The April pilot chart issued March 28 showed that in March ice had come as far south as latitude 44 north. The daily memorandum prior to the 13th inst. showed that the trend of ice was to the southward, icebergs being sighted below the 43d parallel on April 7, 8, 9 and 11. On the 9th and 11th it had reached the 42d parallel and on the 11th some of it was seen south of latitude 42.

The Titanic's position was reported to have been latitude 41.16, longitude 50.14, at the time of her disaster.

CAMERAS BARRED AT CARPATHIA'S LANDING

Morgan Jr. Charged With Keeping News From Public to Protect Company.

Officers Deny Rumor That They Knew Titanic Had Gone Down Eight Hours Before It Was Officially Acknowledged.

New York, April 18.—Fearing turbulent scenes when the Carpathia reaches her pier, officials of the Cunard line are making extraordinary arrangements for her return.

There has been a tremendous demand for passes issued to relatives and friends of the survivors. Cunard officials announce that representatives of each individual newspaper and all photographers will be barred from the pier.

Each press association will be permitted to have fifteen representatives on the pier. It was explained that this action was mainly due to the pressure brought to bear upon the officials by J. P. Morgan Jr., who is a director of the White Star line.

The capacity of the pier is 1,200. This number of passes has already been issued by the company to friends and relatives of the survivors. In addition, Surveyor General Henry's office has issued 1,500 pier passes, each good for two persons.

SON SEEKS NEWS OF FATHER AND MOTHER.

The scenes of almost indescribable grief which were witnessed here throughout Wednesday are being re-enacted today by the hundreds who throng Bowling Green park, in front of the White Star line offices, seeking information regarding their relatives or friends on board the Titanic.

As the revised lists of those known to have been rescued and now on board the Cunarder Carpathia, bound for this port, are posted, men and women fight one another for points of vantage.

Women who attempted to smile in the hope of forestalling the fear that had held them for many hours, collapsed entirely as they read the revised lists of the rescued only to learn that the one or ones they sought had not been accounted for.

Many of those who gathered in front of the steamship offices have been keeping a weary vigil for more than forty-eight hours, sleeping little, if any.

Even when the rain came down in torrents last night these hundreds refused to move.

Among those who remained at the steamship offices all during the day and are still there was 23-year-old F. L. Allison of this city. He has been seeking in vain for some news of his father, H. J. Allison, and his mother, who are believed to have perished with the Titanic.

MORGAN CHARGED WITH KEEPING NEWS FROM PUBLIC.

Neither the name of his father nor that of his mother has appeared in any of the lists of survivors. A wireless to this city announced that Allison's youngest brother and his nurse are among the rescued. They are on the Carpathia.

Friends of both Isidor and Mrs. Straus who called at the offices admitted that they had little hope that either of them had been saved. They argued that Mr. Straus, had the occasion called for it, would not have deserted his wife. They probably went down together, their friends declared.

The name of J. P. Morgan Jr. figures prominently in the many rumors afloat here to the effect that the officials of the White Star line knew that the Titanic had sunk eight hours before it was made public by Vice President Franklin of the steamship company.

This has been strenuously denied by Mr. Franklin and other officials of the line, but nothwithstanding these denials, the rumor will not down.

In an interview, Thomas J. Stead said:

"On Tuesday morning a personal friend of mine came into the Cunard offices seeking information about the Titanic disaster. In talking with me he asked:

" 'Didn't you people know of this yesterday?' I told him that we did not, and then he said:

" 'I knew at 10 o'clock yesterday morning that the Titanic had sunk.' "

Mr. Stead denied that Mr. Morgan was the personal friend he referred to.

The U. S. government waived the customs regulations for the Carpathia in view of the fact that she has not touched a foreign port since she left. This was done with the further view of expediting docking.

Thomas J. Stead, assistant to the president of the Cunard line, announced that the speedy Mauretania would probably overtake the Carpathia in New York bay. Chairman Booth of the Cunard line is aboard the Mauretania and he has promised to get all the information from Captain Rostrum possible and flash it ashore.

Dream Kept Man Off Titanic

London, April 18.—How he was prevented from sailing on the Titanic by a dream is related today by J. C. Middleton of Cleveland, vice president of the Canton & Akron railroad. He told friends of the dream ten days before the tragedy and two of these friends have made a signed affidavit to that effect. Mr. Middleton says:

"I was to have sailed on the Titanic, having booked my passage on March 23. On the night of April 3 I experienced this terrible dream. I saw the Titanic go down in midocean and hundreds of people struggling frantically in the water.

"The next night I had the same dream. When I told my wife she immediately importuned me to cancel our passage and I did so after ascertaining that business in America did not necessitate my return at this time."

Thayer, Wife and Son on Carpathia

New York, April 18.—The following statement regarding the rumor that John B. Thayer, second vice president of the Pennsylvania railroad, is not among the survivors of the Titanic on board the Carpathia, was given out today by the Pennsylvania road:

"The Pennsylvania railroad officials most emphatically deny that a personal message of any kind has been received from Mr. J. B. Thayer or any member of his family who are on board the Carpathia bound for New York. The only information regarding Mr. Thayer and his family received by this company has come from the officers of the White Star line, which is that J. B. Thayer, Mrs. Thayer and J. B. Thayer Jr., are among the passengers on board the Carpathia."

Orders Issued to Skirt Ice Fields

New York, April 18.—After a lengthy conference between the officals in this port of the trans-Atlantic Steamship company, instructions were issued to the captains of all vesals at present docked to give the ice fields a wide berth to take an extreme southerly course on their future passages across the Atlantic.

Cablegrams anouncing the agreement were dispatched to the home offices of the companies in Europe and a reply was received from Bremen.

Messages were flashed by liners at present on their way across.

JUDGMENT OF GOD ON ASTOR SAYS PASTOR WHO DENOUNCED MARRIAGE

New Haven, Conn., April 18.—In an interview printed here today George Chalmers Richmond, rector of St. John's Episcopal church, Philadelphia, who preached a red hot sermon last summer when the betrothal of Col. John Jacob Astor and Miss Madeline Force was announced, is quoted as saying it was the hand of providence that sent Colonel Astor to his death on the Titanic. He is quoted as follows:

"The death of Col. John Jacob Astor at sea in the going down of the Titanic preaches a great gospel of God's power to us all. There are forces in life which demand recognition and obedience. Mr. Astor and his crowd of New York and Newport associates have for years paid not the slightest attention to the laws of church or state which have seemed to contravene their personal pleasures or sensual delights.

"But you can't defy God all the time. The day of reckoning comes and comes not in our own way.

"In another world Astor will do penance. Without his millions and bereft of his great estate, which yielded him his means for a continuous carousal, he will begin a new life.

"There are a lot more like Astor in New York and in Newport, but the number is decreasing. The only remedy is to set the moral standards so high that these men will not dare to defy the laws of the country, as these sensualists have done.

"This calamity ought to be a lesson to men like Astor. Our sympathy for the dead causes us to stifle moral judgment for the men of high positions and the courses they should pursue."

Impact of Titanic and Iceberg Equivalent to Combined Fire of Three Dreadnaughts

THE FORCE OF THE COLLISION WAS EQUAL TO THE CONCENTRATED FIRE OF 3 SUCH DREADNAUGHTS AS THE FLORIDA
EQUAL TO 12 30 INCH GUNS FIRED SIMULTANEOUSLY
Gibbons

Washington, April 18.—A graphic comparison of the probable impact o the Titanic against the iceberg that destroyed her with the projectile force of the guns on a modern battleship was made today by Capt. Charles A. McAllister, engineer in chief of the revenue cutter service.

"The impact of the Titanic against the iceberg was probably equivalent to the simultaneous fire of thirty 12-inch projectiles or the concentrated fire of three such dreadnaughts as the Florida," said Captain McAllister.

"The fire of ten 12-inch guns such as the Florida carries is supposed to be sufficient to put any battleship afloat out of business if the projectiles should strike simultaneously. The force of the Titanic striking the iceberg must have been approximately one million foot tons, equivalent to her being struck simultaneously by thirty such projectiles. It is a wonder, in the light of such a comparison, that she floated so long.

"It is inconceivable that the ingenuity of man can ever devise a floating structure to withstand such a terrific collision."

TANGLED SUBMARINE'S CREW NEAR DEATH 200 FEET DOWN

Cable Caught in Hawse Pipe Holds Vessel at Bottom of Ocean--Water Forced Out of Submerging Tanks.

San Francisco, April 18.—Eight members of the crew of the submarine Carp drank champagne on the bottom of the ocean yesterday and then won a toss with death.

A cable caught in a hawse pipe had imprisoned them for an hour and a half at a depth of 200 feet—farther under the waves than a diving vessel ever had gone before. There was no hope of freeing the cable. The only chance lay in using the compressed air in the submarine to force out the twenty-six tons of water in the submerging tanks to give the boat sufficient buoyancy to tear it loose. If the jammed cable still held the men would suffocate.

The compressed air was shot into the tanks. The big steel tube rocked and groaned for an instant, and then was still again. The prisoners looked at the pressure gauge and saw that the vessel was still fast. Lieut. S. B. Smith, in command, ordered the men to run back and forth along the alley of the 144-foot craft, in the hope of starting vibrations than would release the boat. Suddenly the men were thrown on their backs and the pressure gauge fell.

The crew of a barge overhead saw a long fish nose shoot 100 feet into the air, and then the submarine righted itself on the surface. The men were bruised but not seriously injured.

The submarine was drawn under the water by a cable attached to a ten-ton weight at the bottom of the bay in a special government test to determine the pressure-resisting power of the boat at great depth. The Carp's windlass was used in drawing the craft down. The men had orders to remain at the bottom ten minutes. Champagne and sandwiches had been provided, and the men drank a last glass before reversing the windlass to go to the surface.

The windlass would not work, but this contingency had been provided for by a device to cut the cable. The cable was cut, but it was then that the imprisoned men realized that the other cable had caught in the hawse pipe.

COLORADO SPRINGS MAN LEARNS WOMAN RELATIVE ESCAPED

Mrs. Edgar G. Mayer of New York Safe, Husband Drowned, in Titanic Disaster.

Colorado Springs, April 18.—Among the passengers on the Titanic were Mr. and Mrs. Edgar G. Meyer of New York, who are related by marriage to L. C. Levy of Colorado Springs. Mrs. Meyer is among the rescued passengers on board the Carpathia, although Mr. Meyer is reported as missing and is supposed to have gone down with the ship. Mrs. Meyer is a sister of Mrs. Levy. She has been in Colorado Springs a number of times with her husband since they were married three years ago, and is well known here.

According to a wireless telegram sent from the Carpathia to New York and relayed from New York by Western Union to Mr. Levy today, Mrs. Meyer is on the Carpathia without her husband and it is believed that Mr. Meyer was drowned. The message read as follows:

"Lelah aboard Carpathia and cared for. Edgar missing."

The telegram was not signed, but is supposed to have been sent by a brother who lives in New York. Mr. Levy having failed to see the names of Mr. and Mrs. Meyer in the list of the rescued passengers, supposed they both had gone down with the ship.

Mr. Meyer was a prominent bond and stock broker of New York, being a member of the firm of Eugene Meyer & Co., in which Mr. Levy is also largely interested. Before her marriage to Mr. Meyer three years ago Mrs. Meyer was Miss Lelah Saks, a prominent society girl of New York.

Mr. and Mrs. Meyer went to Europe six weeks ago on a pleasure trip and decided almost at the last moment to take passage on the Titantic on their return trip.

Among the passengers on the Carpathia sailing from New York for Europe was Miss Charlotte Tonzalin, a prominent Colorado Springs society girl. She is returning on the Carpathia with its load of rescued passengers and it is believed here that she will postpone her trip abroad and return to Colorado Springs.

BRITAIN TO ENACT LAWS TO PROTECT OCEAN TRAVELERS

London Board of Trade Will Demand Lifeboats to Carry Passenger List.

London, April 18.—As a result of the Titanic disaster legislation will be introduced to invest the Board of Trade with power to compel vessels to carry lifeboats sufficient to hold all of their passengers and crews. The first step will be taken Monday, when the present Board of Trade will be interrogated in parliament.

The fund for the relief of destitute Titanic victims being raised by the lord mayor had been swelled to $25,000 early today, contributions pouring in rapidly.

Mayor Gaynor of New York has cabled the lord mayor his sympathy with the relief fund and stated his intention to start a similar fund in New York.

President Buxton of the Board of Trade will be asked Monday by Col. Iver Phillips, M. P., as to the extent of power that the board possesses to enforce adequate lifeboat equipment. Information was also asked as to the number and capacity of the Titanic's lifeboats when she sailed from Southampton, the number of passengers she was licensed to carry, and the number of passengers and crew she had aboard.

Premier Asquith will be asked by Douglas Hall whether the government is prepared to appoint a commission to inquire into precautions to prevent sea disasters and the efficiency of the Board of Trade regulations.

The necessity and practicability of the use of power of the searchlights on all large passenger vessels also will be taken up.

The Ismay Imrie company today contributed $5,000 to the relief fund.

The Loss of the Arctic

By HENRY WARD BEECHER

It was autumn. Hundreds had wended their way from pilgrimages—from Rome and its treasures of dead art and its glory of living nature; from the side of the Switzer's mountains and from the capitals of various nations—all of them saying in their hearts, we will wait for the September gales to have done with their equinoctial fury, and then we will embark; we will slide across the appeased ocean, and in the gorgeous month of October we will greet our longed for native land and our heart loved homes.

And so the throng streamed along from Berlin, from Paris, from the Orient, converging upon London, still hastening toward the welcome ship and narrowing every day the circle of engagements and preparations. They crowded aboard. Never had the Arctic bore such a host of passengers nor passengers so nearly related to so many of us. The hour was come. The signal ball fell at Greenwich. It was noon also at Liverpool. The anchors were weighed; the great hull swayed to the current; the national colors streamed above, as if themselves instinct with life and national sympathy. The bell strikes; the wheels revolve; the signal gun beats its echoes in upon every structure upon the shore, and the Arctic glides joyfully forth from the Mersey, and turns her prow to the winding channel and begins her homeward run. The pilot stood at the wheel, and men saw him. Death sat upon the prow and no eye beheld him. Whoever stood at the wheel in all the voyage, Death was the pilot that steered the craft, and none knew it. He neither revealed his presence nor whispered his errand.

And so hope was effulgent, and lithe gayety disported itself, and joy was with every guest. Amid all the inconveniences of the voyage there was still that which hushed every murmur, "Home is not far away." And every morning it was still one night nearer home! Eight days had passed. They beheld that distant bank of mist that forever haunts the vast shallows of Newfoundland. Boldly they made it, and, plunging in, its pliant wreaths wrapped them about. They shall never emerge. The last sunslight has flashed from the deck. The last voyage is done to ship and passengers. At noon there came noiselessly stealing from the north that fated instrument of destruction. In that mysterious shroud, that vast atmosphere of mist, both steamers were holding their way with rushing prow and roaring wheels, but invisible.

At a league's distance, unconscious; and at nearer approach, unwarned; within hail, and bearing right toward each other, unseen, unfelt, till in a moment more emerging from the gray mists the ill omened Vesta dealt her deadly hull. She neither reeled nor shivered. Neither comalong the mighty hull. She neither reeled nor shivered. Neither commander nor officers deemed that they had suffered harm. Prompt upon humanity, the brave Luce (let his name be ever spoken with admiration and respect) ordered away his boat with the first officer to inquire if the stranger had suffered harm. As Gourley went over the ship's side, oh, that some good angel had called to the brave commander in the words of Paul on a like occasion, "Except these abide in the ship, ye cannot be saved."

They departed, and with them the hope of the ship, for now the waters, gaining upon the hold, and rising upon the fires revealed the mortal blow. Oh, had now that stern, brave mate, Gourley, been on deck, whom the sailors were wont to mind—had he stood to execute efficiently the commander's will—we may believe that we should not have had to blush for the cowardice and recreancy of the crew, nor weep for the untimely dead. But, apparently, each subordinate officer lost all presence of mind, then courage, and so honor. In a wild scramble that ignoble mob of firemen, engineers, waiters and crew rushed for the boats and abandoned the helpless women, children and men to the mercy of the deep! Four hours there were from the catastrophe of collision to the catastrophe of sinking!

Oh, what a hurial was here! Not as when one is borne from his home among weeping throngs and gently carried to the green fields, and laid peacefully beneath the turf and flowers. No priest stood to pronounce a burial service. It was an ocean grave. The mists alone shrouded the burial place. No spade prepared the grave, no sexton filled up the hollowed earth. Down, down they sank, and the quick returning waters smoothed out every ripple, and left the sea as if it had not been.

Cape Race Earns Her Name, "Terror of the Atlantic"

The terror of the North Atlantic.

So has Cape Race been known from the time that the first sailing vessel was lost in the treacherous Polar current that sweeps and swirls about the gray rocks until the present, when the wreck of the Titanic at a point 400 miles south of the cape, is a disaster that has paralyzed the world.

Dense fogs, huge icebergs, such as gave the Titanic her death blow, northeasterly gales that come with the force of a hurricane, and submerged rocks—these are a few of the difficulties with which navigators plying the North Atlantic route between the old wrold and the new have to deal.

And the worst of all is the Polar current, which flows with the force of a rushing river—sometimes southwest, sometimes northeast—bringing with it in the spring and early summer great mountains of jagged ice that lie sometimes near the coast and sometimes are swept far out to sea, at all times a deadly menace to the safety of ships and steamers of any size or speed, lying as they do with most of their great bulk submerged.

When the icy waters of the Polar current come into contact with the warmer water of the gulf streams a dense fog is raised—a fog that scarcely ever lifts, and that shuts down like an impenetrable, shifting curtain on the ocean for an area of hundreds of miles.

While the route of the Trans-Atlantic lines to and from American ports runs past the cape a hundred miles out at sea, the conditions there are the same—the fogs and icebergs, the current and the gales.

Cape Race itself is inhabited by perhaps 2,000 souls, who make their living by the sea.

"Fishing," says George Harding in "The Menace of Cape Race," in the current number of Harper's Magazine, "is a dependable occupation, but a wreck is the gift of God—an extraordinary, even providential addition to the fruits of toil. It is said that the children of the cape are taught to pray 'God bless papa and mama and send another wreck.'

"In a single month an Atlantic liner, crowded with passengers and four tramp steamers were totally wrecked off the cape within twenty miles of one another."

And now the "Cape of evil name" has added another to its long list of disasters of the sea—the one with which its name shall ever be linked.

"Cape Race and the lost Titanic"—as long as steamers and sailing vessels pass that way whenever people speak of the terrors of the sea, the two names shall go together.

UNDERWRITERS LOSE MILLIONS BY WRECK

One Insured for $250,000; Others for Large Amounts From $50,000 Up.

Astor, Guggenheim and Straus Not Believed to Have Held Many Large Policies--Companies to Pay Promptly.

New York, April 18.—Insurance men declare that John Jacob Astor, Benjamin Guggenheim and Isidor Straus have long been conspicuous as men who do not carry life insurance. If Colonel Astor did carry life insurance, the face value of his policies is unknown, though some believe that his life was insured for hundreds of thousands of dollars.

Eliminating the possibility of heavy insurance upon the lives of Astor, Guggenheim and Straus, accident and life insurance companies of this country and England will have to pay out millions of dollars as the result of the sinking of the Titanic. Practically all the wealthy men reported drowned are believed to have carried heavy insurance, few of which are less than $50,000.

Accident insurance companies lose under what is termed the "double liability" clause because of the nature of the accident, and the present catastrophe will put the insurance underwriters through the severest test in the history of accident insurance. All companies are estimating the aggregate liabilities in case most of the first and second cabin passengers were actually lost.

The Equitable Life Assurance company has announced that its liabilities will exceed $43,000. This estimate is made by the company's officials in view of the very meager reports of the wireless.

The Prudential Insurance company reckons its loss at $95,000, a minimum computation. The Metropolitan Life Insurance company and the Mutual, both of which have many policy-holders among the list of the Titanic's passengers, will not make estimates until further details are known.

All companies announce that claims will be paid without delay.

One of the most heavily insured passengers on board the wrecked vessel was George D. Wick of Youngstown, Ohio. He is said to carry policies that aggregate about $250,000.

MAJOR ARCHIBALD BUTT DIED LIKE A SOLDIER AND GENTLEMAN

That He Was the First to Step Aside and Give His Place to Others Is Belief of Those Who Know Army Life.

(By LOUISE SCHER.)

There has been much speculation among the friends of Archibald Butt, aide to President Taft, and among those persons who are always speculating where a man's bravery is concerned, as to whether Major Butt is really among the lost passengers of the Titanic.

That Major Butt was perhaps the first man to step back and offer his place to others is the belief of every man or woman who knows anything of army life and what its duties involve.

"In the first place," to quote Captain Ray Harrison's opinion, "there isn't a particle of doubt in my mind that Major Butt is dead. He at all times was an officer and second a society man.

CAPT. RAY HARRISON, Denver army officer, who says that Major Butts played the part of a hero.

"Do you remember reading histories of the old days of the army?" questioned Captain Harrison, "when women and men crossed the prairies in schooners? During that time men and women were taken to gold camps by way of the Horn.

"Time and again during this period ships were wrecked and men and women saved by army officers sent to guard them against attacks or dangers of any kind or sort.

"I can remember hearing my father tell of a certain shipwreck which occurred near the Horn—the name has slipped my memory—and in which thirteen United States army officers lost their lives to save a few women. And it has been so since the service began, women first and then the citizens, it's just part of the game. Major Butt went down like an officer and a gentleman.

"There isn't one of us who has a lurking doubt about him. His position as aide to President Taft in its everyday routine entailed countless dangers, or at least from fear of fanatics. Major Butt was an excellent aide. Even when there has been scare after scare, he, before the plain clothes men, was always first where the president's safety was involved."

The opinion voiced by Captain Harrison, who ranks as one of the gallant heroes of the Spanish-American war, he having been the young officer who at the risk of his own life, during the trying days at Daraga Luzon, during a night attack made by Filipinos against American troops, braved untold dangers, risking his own life to save that of his commanding officer and a handful of soldiers who had lost themselves and were cut off from the original force. Captain Harrison, then a lieutenant, had both his arms nearly severed in a hand-to-hand contact with a boloman.

Captain Harrison has recently come to Denver to relieve Capt. J. A. Lockwood as officer in charge of the Denver recruiting office. He is one of the bravest officers of the United States army and has been decorated repeatedly for his acts of bravery during the Spanish-American war.

Hammerstein to Give Benefit for the Relief Fund

London, April 18.—Oscar Hammerstein has offered the lord mayor of London a benefit performance for a relief fund which has been accepted by the lord mayor. Hammerstein's letter follows:

"As one who has crossed the Atlantic over one hundred times, this appalling disaster has affected me in a way no words can express, especially as many of my personal friends are among the lost. I am offering a small tribute to the brave men who gave their lives for duty in placing my opera house and artists at the disposal of your lordship for a performance on behalf of the fund which has been opened at Mansion house for the relief of those whose means of existence has been taken away."

New York, April 18.—A memorable mass meeting will be held Sunday night at a Broadway theater to adopt resolutions of condolence for the families of those who lost their lives on the Titanic and take action looking to international regulation of ocean travel. The meeting will be under the chairmanship of Frederick Towsend Martin, society leader and welfare worker who has been assured of the co-operation of prominent clergymen, city officials and other men of prominence.

Duluth, April 18.—Insufficient lifeboats exist to an alarming degree on the great lakes, according to John Monaghan, government inspector of vessels in Duluth.

"The law does not require passenger vessels to carry lifeboats sufficient in capacity and number to care for all the people on board," he said. "And if a lake boat were in an accident making necessary immediate abandonment, only 25 to 40 per cent of those aboard could be saved."

TITANIC'S BOTTOM RIPPED BY SPINES OF HUGE ICEBERG

Gigantic Steamer, Impaled at First Crash Battled Bravely Against the Monster Until She Went Down.

Vessel Held Helpless On Icy Peaks Until Shattered to Pieces By the Ever-Advancing Mass in Front.

New York, April 18.—An official of the White Star company said last night:

"From the reports that have come it is evident that the Titanic went down after a death grapple with the hidden spines of the icebergs. These spines, sharp and jagged, roweled her bottom, just as the tender side of a greyhound could be roweled by a steel spur.

"The Titanic was so built that she could be turned into thirty water-tight steel boxes within thirty seconds. The device controlling the bulkheads was operated from the bridge. It worked practically instantaneously.

"There is no doubt that in this instance the bulkheads of the Titanic were locked within a few seconds of the first crash. I say first crash, but I believe there were a series of impacts. I believe the ship 'fought' the berg until she went down.

"It is probable that the six-sevenths of the iceberg which was under water projected out a distance of several hundred feet. The Titanic, speeding along at seventeen or eighteen knots, was impaled upon this jagged projection, which held her and at the same time the iceberg approached rapidly and rammed her.

"After the first impact I believe the Titanic was forced back, but this propulsion, combined with the force of her reversed engines, was not sufficient to release her from the clutch of the underwater 'spines.' These spines held the gigantic craft until the ever-advancing mass of ice struck her again.

"All the while the spines were ripping at the Titanic's bottom. Finally they roweled the entire length of the vessel. At the same time the walls of the bulkheads were probably being battered in by huge chunks of ice which were constantly falling.

"The under-water projections at last succeeded in ripping huge holes in the bottom of the vessel. The water rushed in, putting out the fires and flooding the engine and power rooms. This probably cut off power for the wireless apparatus and also plunged the huge craft into pitch darkness."

St. Johns, N. B., April 18.—Three trans-Atlantic liners which arrived here today reported the ice fields off the Newfoundland banks as the worst ever encountered.

The arriving vessels were the Allan liner Corsican from Liverpool, the Hamburg-American liner Pisa from Bremen and the Canadian Pacific liner Montrose from London and Antwerp.

The Corsican reported that she and four other big steamers were all forced to stop in an immense field of ice Thursday night, so thick was the pack and so close were several of the monster icebergs.

The steamer Pisa passed several bergs which were more than two hundred feet high, while even larger bergs were seen to the south and it is believed that it was one of these that the Titanic struck.

WRECK OF TITANIC TOLD IN FICTION BY WILLIAM STEAD

He Was One of Those Lost; Wrote the Story in 1892.

DESCRIBED CORRECTLY

Used Majestic of White Star Line as His Subject.

New York, April 18.—Intimate friends in this country of William T. Stead of London, who up to a late hour today had not been reported among the survivors of the Titanic, recalled a story he wrote in the Christmas extra issue of the Review of Reviews, in London, published in December, 1892, entitled, "From the Old World to the New," a chapter of which tallies in almost every detail with the wreck of the Titanic.

In this chapter, which is called "Coincident and Clairvoyage," Mr. Stead described an encounter with icebergs at sea. His characters are a group of English tourists on their way to the Chicago World's fair. They are crossing the Atlantic on board the Majestic of the White Star line. Suddenly the boat comes upon a great iceberg.

"Hark! What was that?" Mr. Stead here had a voyager ask, and his description of what took place went on:

"There was a sound as if the steamer were crashing through ice and the screws were churning amid ice blocks. Passengers felt their way cautiously to the deck. It was wet and clammy and bitterly cold. Every half minute the fog whistle blew. The crashing of ice against the sides of the ship and clamping of ice under the screws made it difficult to speak so as to be heard.

"Then there came a cry: 'Icebergs on the starboard.'

"The engine bell rang, the engines slowed down in their speed, and the steamer steered a trifle more to the southward, but still kept pounding its way onward. The captain could only see ghostly shadows looming darkly to the northward."

Later in telling of the rescue of castaways in the lifeboats, Mr. Stead wrote:

"Denser and denser grows the fog, but they could see the Majestic right before them, and in another moment they were alongside. Just as they reached the ship they heard a long roar like the reverberation of artillery, and then the water heaved violently and dashed the lifeboat heavily against the side of the Majestic.

"There was a moment of agonizing suspense. No one knew whether the displacement in the iceberg might not lead to a sudden upheaval of the iceberg under the keel of the Majestic. Then the boat's crews were brought safely to deck."

Striking sentences here and there from other writings of Mr. Stead are also recalled in which it might seem that he had some premonition of his fate.

Destructive Theology.

At a certain New England church the pulpit was occupied one Sunday morning by a minister from a neighboring town. A few days later the preacher received a copy of a local paper with the following item marked: "The Rev. —— supplied the pulpit at the Congregational church last Sunday, and the church will now be closed three weeks for repairs."—Judge.

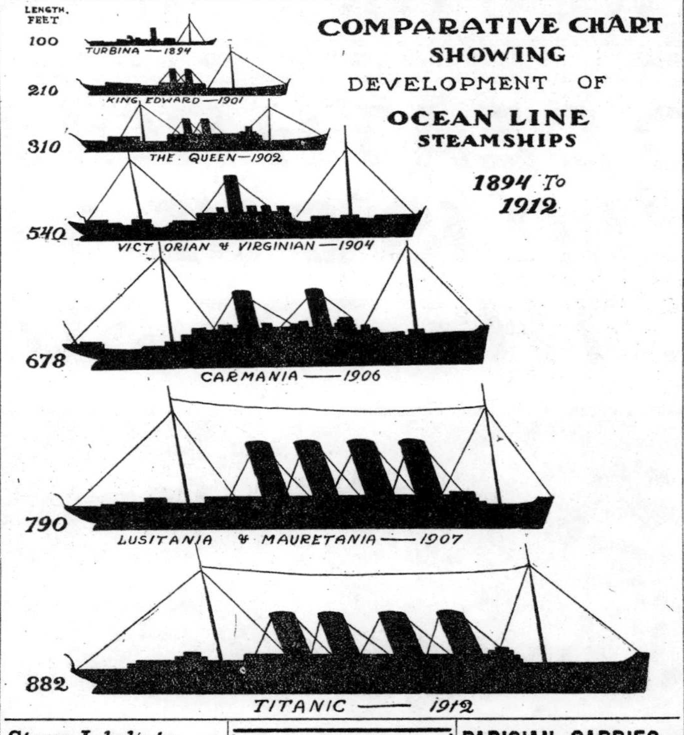

Storm Likely to Last All Night

Conditions Unsettled; Weather Man Not Free With Predictions.

The weather, according to Forecaster F. H. Brandenburg, is like boardinghouse coffee.

Unsettled.

The storm, which "began in the gloaming," the same way that storm did that children "speak pieces" about, will cling to Denver all day and very likely all night. By tomorrow it will be on its way—maybe. Mr. Brandenburg makes no rash promises. He did say that warmer weather was coming, sometime, but on just what date it would arrive he remained silent—because he doesn't know.

The storm is general all over eastern and central Colorado—a regular spring storm. The rain began at 4 o'clock yesterday afternoon and changed to snow at 10 o'clock last night, and the snow has been falling steadily ever since. The total precipitation has been a trifle over half an inch, but the snow has melted rapidly. The lowest temperature was recorded this morning at 5 o'clock, when the thermometer showed 31—one degree below freezing. By noon it had feebly climbed to 34, and there it stayed, and there it will very probably stay until some time tomorrow.

A Large Hairpin Holder.

Mrs. Nagget—I watched your sister fixing her hair the other day, and I must say she's not the most refined person in the world.

Mr. Nagget—You don't approve of her, eh?

Mrs. Nagget—Well, you've never seen me with my mouth full of hairpins.

Mr. Nagget—Of course not. What would you want with so many hairpins?—Catholic Standard and Times.

Bodies Dragged to Bottom, Never Again to Be Seen

Baltimore, April 17.—"The bodies of the victims of the Titanic are at the bottom of the deep, never to leave it," declared Prof. Robert W. Wood of the chair of experimental physics of John Hopkins university.

"At the depth of two miles the pressure of the water is something like 6,000 pounds to the square inch, which is far too great to be overcome by buoyancy ordinarily given drowned bodies by the gases generated in them.

"That the bodies sank to the bottom of the sea there is no question. The Titanic's victims who were not carried down with the boat followed until the very bottom of the sea was reached. There was no such thing as their stopping in their downward course a half mile, a mile, or at any other point."

Hungry for Excitement.

"I jest can't keep thet boy o' mine on the farm," complained Farmer Wayback. "He's jest crazy to see life."

"Has city ideas, eh?" asked the city boarder.

"Yes; he's always wantin' to be over to the railroad station an' see the trains a-comin in."—Catholic Standard and Times.

Butler—There's a man below to see you, sir.

Mayberry—What did you tell him?

Butler—I told him you told me, if it was a lady, to say you were in, and if it was a man, to say you were out.

Mayberry—What did he say then?

Butler—He said to tell you he was a lady.—Harvard Lampoon.

THE SINKING OF THE FRENCH LINE STEAMER, LA BOURGOGNE, JULY 4, 1898

(Drawn by T. Dart Walker From Descriptions Furnished by Survivors.) From Harper's Weekly, July 23, 1898.

BRIDAL PAIR SAFE; GROOM NEPHEW OF DENVER RESIDENT

Mr. and Mrs. Bishop Sailed on Titanic on Return From Wedding Trip.

NO NEWS OF MRS. ROOD

Brother of Mrs. J. J. Brown Goes to New York to Meet the Carpathia.

Dickinson H. Bishop, who, with his bride of three months, was saved from the wreck of the Titanic, is a nephew of J. H. Dickinson, 1580 Cook street, Denver. Bishop lives in Dowagiac, Mich., and is reputed to be wealthy. Immediately after his marriage he and his bride left for a tour of Europe. Upon learning that the Titanic was to sail on a certain date, the couple hastened from Egypt in order to cross the Atlantic in the monster liner on her maiden voyage.

Dickinson has heard no particulars concerning his nephew's adventure. He has been in communication with Mrs. Bishop, the young man's mother, and she is also ignorant of the circumstances.

That Bishop and his bride were saved was announced by the Carpathia when it forwarded its list of Titanic passengers.

Looking through the columns of The Post, Mrs. William G. Lowstuter, wife of Professor Lowstuter of the Iliff School of Theology, learned for the first time that her nephew, Lucian P. Smith of Morgantown, West Virginia, was an board the Titanic. His name, with that of his bride, the daughter of Congressman Hughes of West Virginia, was among the list of the first cabin passengers rescued by the Carpathia. Mr. Smith, 23, and his bride, 19, were returning from their honeymoon trip to the Holy Land.

NO MORE NEWS RECEIVED OF MRS. STOIBER ROOD.

No further communication from Mrs. Lena Stoiber Rood since the cablegram announcing her departure for New York yesterday from Cherbourg, has been received by her attorneys in this city, MacBeth & May, nor have they obtained any information concerning her husband, Hugh R. Rood, save the continued reports that he was among those who went down with the Titanic.

Misses Florence and Helen Tobin, nieces of Mrs. J. J. Brown, who make their home during her absence from Denver with Mrs. Susan McManus, 1420 Pearl street, are expecting some word concerning her from their father, Daniel W. Tobin of Chicago, who has gone to New York to meet and care for his sister upon the arrival of the Carpathia.

Charles M. Hays, vice president and general manager of the Grand Trunk railroad, who is reported among those lost on the Titanic, was a close personal friend of George Ady of the Union Pacific. One dispatch carried a rumor to the effect that Hays had been picked up and the Denver man is hoping that it may prove true.

Another of the reported victims of the ship is Walter W. Clark of Los Angeles, son of J. Ross Clark, vice president of the San Pedro railroad, and a nephew of Senator Clark of Montana. He is well known in this city, where he frequently visited, and many people are eagerly searching the lists of survivors for his name. He was a personal friend of E. B. Erwin, general agent of the San Pedro railroad, and of E. A. Stenbeck of Harris, Winthrop & Co.

WOMAN TELLS STORY OF WRECK IN 1883.

Miss M. L. Dietteman of 2960 Lawrence street has been led by the news of the late disaster to narrate her own thrilling experiences in a shipwreck which occurred Oct. 9, 1883, near the scene of the Titanic's destruction, when she and her uncle, Anton C. Schindelholz, a wealthy cattleman, were voyaging to their old home in Alsace-Lorraine.

The ship was a French liner known as the Herder, one of the first steamships built to carry the increasing passenger traffic across the Atlantic, and was considered a staunch craft. But the fogs off the banks of Newfoundland proved too treacherous for her watchful crew, and midnight, Sunday, the ship went on the rocks. Miss Dietteman describes what followed:

"The shock threw us out of our berths and knocked our staterooms topsy turvy. Dressed only in our sleeping garments we fought our way up the companion way.

"There was no wireless in those days to help us out. For the rest of the night the sailors sent up rockets and fired a cannon carried for that purpose. By daylight we were still in the same plight, as the fog covered us like a blanket.

"The fog cleared sufficiently about 8 o'clock for us to see the mainland, although before that we did not know where we were nor in what direction land was. The lifeboats were cleared away—twelve of them. Just as in the case of the Titanic, the women and children were taken off first. I refused to go until the last boat was almost filled, as I was a strong girl and thought perhaps I could help uncle. They tore me away as I threw my arms about his neck, and then the officers ordered him into the boat with me.

"A rope was tied about my waist and I was lowered over the side onto a rope ladder. The lifeboat swung with the waves and I was told to jump the first time it came directly beneath me. I landed among the women and children in the bottom of the boat."

PARISIAN CARRIES NO SURVIVORS

Halifax, N. S., April 18.—The steamer Parisian, the Allan liner which last Monday was near the scene of the Titanic disaster, and which, it was hoped, had survivors of the Titanic on board, entered Halifax harbor at 7 o'clock last evening.

The Parisian was visited upon her arrival by the port physician, who on landing brought the information that the steamer had no further details of the Titanic disaster.

Captain Haines reported that at 10:30 p. m. (Parisian time) on Sunday night she was in communication with the Titanic, being 150 miles distant. The Titanic was then safe. The operator on the Parisian retired soon after and nothing was known of the disaster until Monday morning.

The weather on Sunday night was clear and starlight. It is the belief that the Titanic struck a low lying iceberg not more than ten feet out of water and seventy feet submerged. With the ship going at high speed, such a berg would rip the bottom open, probably as far as the engine room, and this probably accounts for her going down so quickly after she struck. Had it been a high berg it would have been visible far off.

ITALIANS BOMBARD THE DARDANELLES

London, April 18.—The bombardment of the Dardanelles began today, according to a special dispatch received here from Constantinople. One of the Italian warships has been damaged by a shot from the land batteries.

Athens, Greece, April 18.—Two divisions of Italian war vessels, each comprising a dozen ships, passed Skyro island in the Aegean sea yesterday, sailing to the north.

Widow of Captain Writes Message

London, April 18.—The widow of Captain Smith, the commander of the Titanic, has written a pathetic message which was posted today outside the White Star offices. It reads as follows:

To my poor fellow sufferers: My heart overflows with grief for you all and is laden with sorrow that you are weighted down with this terrible burden that has been thrust upon us. May God be with us and comfort us all.

"Yours in deep sympathy.
"ELEANOR SMITH.

DRUGGED GIRL IS IN SERIOUS CONDITION

Harriet Madiison Assaulted; Marred Escort, Arrested, Denies Guilt.

Suffering from the effects of an assault committed upon her Monday night while she was under the influence of drugs alleged to have been administered by her escort, Harriet Madison, a 16-year-old girl, is in a serious condition in her apartment at the Holland, Eighteenth avenue and Pennsylvania street.

James E. Robinson, a married man and father of two children, is under arrest in connection with the case. He admits having been with Miss Madison Monday night, but denies that he is responsible for her condition.

When she arrived home in a taxicab, in company with Robinson, her clothing was torn and she was in a condition bordering on hysteria.

Simple When You Know.

The secret of real beauty is
As plain as day.
You've merely to accomplish this:
Be born that way.
—Catholic Standard and Times.

WOMEN MUST EXPLAIN WHY THEY ABANDONED MATES IN DEATH

Denver Wives Declare They Would Remain On Sinking Ship In Spite of Romantic Law of the Sea.

(By FRANCES WAYNE.)

Save the women and children and—if needs be—let the men perish!

That is the unwritten law of the sea. A law which re-creates itself from ancient memories and traditions whenever Nature decrees to test the puny strength of man and bring the giant to the level of the pigmy.

This law, or ideal, or inspiration—whatever it may be called—in its strict observance, enriches romance, fires imagination, bows the heart and soul before the heroic and unselfish actions of man. Nine times out of ten its practice makes humanity poor, indeed, and proclaims that those nations which we regard as "heathen" follow the saner, more just way.

By the sinking of the Titanic there are 700 women and children thrown, widowed and orphaned, on the world.

Many of these had no choice. Those in command of foundering ships do not wait to haggle with hysterical and terrorized women, and argue the question of whether they prefer to be saved or to companion their loved ones into the trough of the sea. They are ordered aboard the lifeboats—they obey. Whether they are maids in the service of prominent women or wives and daughters of men of millions and affluence, is not questioned.

When the crew bends to the oars; when the smaller craft slides away from the struggling monster of the deep; when the glare of lights turns into utter darkness, and death folds his hands—then a shuddering world gasps and thinks that, perhaps, there are some ideals not worth following, some laws which should be ignored, or made according to the Chinese code, which holds that the good of all society, and not of the individual, is the thing that is to be considered.

Life is a biting struggle, contend the sages of China. Children, if cared for, will grow into worthy citizens—wherefore, they must be saved in times of peril and the state becomes their mother. Men are necessary to the world's work and human advancement; they, too, must be pushed forward. As for the women—their service in child bearing accomplished, they may be dispensed with.

SOCIETY WOULD HAVE LOST MANY LEADERS.

Had such a rule prevailed when the Titanic's hull was crunched to splinters the wise and strong men would have been gleaned from the crowd; the children would have been shepherded tenderly. The women would have been but memories. Newport and New York society would have had fewer leaders and acolytes had the "heathen" rule been followed on the English ship.

Emil Straus would have been spared to extend his helpful philanthropies and his wisdom would not have been withdrawn from the councils of men of large affairs. The light of William T. Stead, which has shone for many, walking in darkness, would not have been quenched. Archibald Butt, good fellow and brave soldier, would be steaming toward safe harbor, more concerned than ever to prove himself worthy of his country. The genius of Roebling would still be dedicated to the welding of river-separated lands. Jacques Futrelle's merry pen likely would have dipped in a more serious brand of ink. The hundred strong men below and above would have been today planning to make good to the nation for their escape from the terrors of the sea by the service of an undivided heart.

But the widows and orphans are all that remain of that ship's goodly cargo—widows and orphans, and a few men who "somehow" got into the boats.

Perhaps, some day, these widows will explain how it happened that they allowed themselves to be torn away from their husbands instead of going down with them.

DENVER WOMEN EXPLAIN THEIR VIEWS.

Until they speak, we have the opinions of many women who from the comfort of their fireside explain what they would have done in a like emergency and who declare that the price paid by society in the loss of some of the men was too great for any ideal, sentiment or tradition to balance.

These women, some of them pioneers, faced as great perils in crossing a sea of unbroken sand with their young husbands as did the women of the Titanic.

Mrs. John Pierce was a pioneer who, from her bed of illness, declares that such men as were needed to make the world better and easier for all men should have been saved in preference to frivolous women who can be of no service to anyone but shopkeepers. Mrs. Pierce, in pondering the Titanic's fate, recalls how one of her friends, Mrs. George Randolph, was coming across the plains—schooner-wise—with her husband she had just married. Word came of an Indian uprising, and the nearness to the caravan of a bloody band of red men.

"Shoot me, George!" she begged, "and save yourself! The new state needs you and there are other wives to be had."

WOMEN SHOULD ALWAYS BE SAVED.

Mrs. Dewey C. Bailey declares that the action of the men aboard was the most beautiful example of self-sacrifice, self-effacement and wonderful courage that the world knows.

"I believe the women should have been saved, regardless of their frivolity," she declared, "since what humanity needs today is an example in heroism to offset the fearful material agencies that are at work to undermine our ideals. Such disasters as the sinking of the Titanic are like sunlight turned into a dark cellar."

Mrs. Sarah Platt Decker asserts: "If I were a man, regardless of life's calling, I'd hate to have my name in the list of the saved. I believe in the tradition 'women and children first.' As a man, I'd go down proudly."

Mrs. James B. Belford knew this state when it was young and full of hardships.

"At such times," she said, "there is no time to distinguish between classes; to cull the worthy from the ineffective and frivolous. The lives of all are precious, not only to themselves, but to those to whom they belong by family ties. If the immediate good of society is to be taken into consideration the women of that ship should have stood back. If the values of the ideals which swing humanity to high places are not to be lowered or effaced; if they are to continue to be the lights that lead us on and up, then the sacrifice of splendid men was not in vain. I've an idea, though, that the woman who pioneered this country would have gone on the long journey with her man."

ACTION OF MEN IS GREAT IDEAL FOR POSTERITY.

Mrs. J. A. Thatcher, another pioneer, says:

"It is all right. Those men did what all honorable men should do. Women first, regardless of education, ignorance, position. Life is as sweet to the woman in the steerage as to the woman occupying the royal suite. I admire those men for what they have done—but I believe it was only their duty. We've gained some heroes that we needed to set as examples before an indifferent and selfish youth that is growing up in this country. The value of the sacrifice will be known, not today, but in the future."

Mrs. Frank Woodward says: "That was a brave thing for those men to do—a real and splendid thing—though today, flat against the horror as we are, it seems a dreadful waste of splendid material to have such men as Millet, Stead and Astor stand back for ignorant peasant women who are left friendless and destitute. However, we couldn't expect anything but honorable action from our Anglo-Saxon men."

Mrs. James Williams is one of those who would have gone down.

"I'd never let anything part us. He'd go with me or I with him. It is too pitiful for those splendid men, who have earned the esteem of their country by their achievements, to have been called upon to sacrifice their lives for ignorant and frivolous women. Yet, the monument they built for themselves by their heroism will stand forever."

MRS. DODGE WOULD HAVE STAYED ON BOARD.

Mrs. D. C. Dodge explains that "it depends upon conditions. There is some mystery, somewhere, in regard to the women leaving their husbands. There must have been something that made them think their husbands would be saved anyway. I would have remained with the colonel to the end. To be sure, it is difficult today to balance the value of the lives saved with those lost. The example gained is everything. We have been growing reckless of human life, regardless of ideals; we had come to gauge everything by the dollar mark. 'Not what you are, but what you have,' has become the rule of success and popularity. Now we find 'what you are' is all that matters."

Mrs. Felix, president of the Ladies' Pioneer society, believes that this tradition is a wise one in decreeing that the women and children shall be the first to be saved. One life is as precious as another—in her opinion—and the lowly woman may have just as great a destiny to fulfill as has the great man.

Mrs. Fanny D. Hardine, one of Denver's pioneers, says that there are exceptions to all rules and that while, in the main, she believes the tradition to be wise, yet it seems too bad that the lives of great and useful men should be sacrificed for the sake of some poor, wornout immigrant woman who possibly might be turned back at Ellis island and not even allowed to land in this country. "A great man would be justified in saving himself at the expense of such a woman."

DIVINE LIFE MAKES MEN STAY BEHIND.

"There is absolutely no question that, from the social point of view, the lives of some of those men who perished on the Titanic were more valuable to the world than those of some of the women who were saved," states Mrs. Joel Shackelford. "And yet, from the individual standpoint, remembering the immortality of man, that which makes him differ from the animal, he would be violating himself if he did not protect the weaker thing. The spark of the divine in him forbids him to save himself at that cost. That is the reason that this tradition has sprung up and grown stronger with successive ages."

Mrs. J. D. Whitmore thinks that "if there were no time to discriminate in a great emergency, those people should be saved whose lives mean something in the advancement of the world, regardless of sex. In the case of the sinking of the Titanic, however, such discrimination was impossible and therefore the men acted according to inherited instincts in giving way to the women."

"I would not cast this old tradition aside," says Mrs. Henry Hersey, president of the Mothers' Congress. "It would not be fair to the men to put man and woman on exactly the same plane of existence and survival. Men would not be as fine as they are today if they had not borne the greatest burdens of life. The woman is able to do her share and to get along in the world without acts of chivalry from the men, but think how man's nature would be degraded if he were released from this burden.

NO TIME TO SORT OUT SOCIAL DEVELOPERS.

"I suppose this tradition of the sea has grown up from the old idea that all men are physically stronger, and, therefore, better able to care for themselves. This is not true in these days of athletic women, but still we should cling to the old idea. People couldn't be sorted out in a great emergency. Who would determine the potential value of any one human soul?

"For example, some obscure immigrant woman may some day, be the mother of a great statesman, while John Jacob Astor is one of many men who have accumulated fortunes, and who has violated all the decencies of life during the years that he has lived."

Mrs. Henry Sales is another who believes that we must hold to this old tradition.

"The man who saved himself at the expense of a woman could never command any respect from his fellow citizens, and worse than that, he would lose his self-respect," says Mrs. Sales. "That is my opinion looking at the question from an individual viewpoint. And yet, for the sake of the world, I would say that it would be best if some one could be found to set it aside, so that great men should not be sacrificed for a poor woman, who has outlived her usefulness.

MEN MAY BE SAVED FIRST, SOME DAY.

"It may be that some day the women will come to the fore, and demand that the men be saved at their expense. I think that the finest thing I have ever heard of is the case of the woman who stayed with her husband on the Titanic, and went down with him. She deserves to have a monument raised to her memory."

Mrs. E. P. Costigan says that, tradition or no tradition, nothing could ever induce her to leave her husband on a sinking ship, while she herself was being rescued. At the time of a great disaster like the sinking of the Titanic there would be no time for discrimination between the great men and the lowly woman, and that therefore, on the whole, she believes the tradition to be wise.

Mrs. Crawford Hill says: "It is a problem—this going down of the men—which is hard to answer. But their fine chivalry, regardless of position, wealth or attainments, has added to the bright record of tradition. It is pitiable that so many ignorant women should be left to fight for bread, and be saved, at the sacrifice of fine men that the world really can ill afford to spare."

Thus, while men are men, and women are women; while there are ideals to be raised and followed; while there is dependence and courage; while the species continue to be every thing, and the individual nothing in the scheme of nature, we shall have great, and strong and good men go down to sea in ships, after the life boats have drifted away with weak and vain and frivolous, worthless and hapless women and little children.

And when this is not so the sun will have lost its brightness, the flowers their perfume and human nature its humanness.

DIRECTORY FOR ADVERTISERS WILL BE FOUND TO-DAY ON PAGE 15, COLUMN 7.

THE NEW YORK HERALD.

THE WEATHER. Rains, followed by clearing; slightly colder. For detailed weather report and forecast see Editorial page.

WHOLE NO. 27,632. NEW YORK, THURSDAY, APRIL 18, 1912.—TWENTY-SIX PAGES.—[COPYRIGHT, 1912, BY THE NEW YORK HERALD COMPANY.] PRICE THREE CENTS.

THE TITANIC DEATH ROLL 1,312; RESCUE SHIP IS DUE TO-NIGHT WITH ALL THE 705 SURVIVORS

Drawn to Illustrate the Consensus of Views of the Ship Masters Now in This Port on the Events Following the Titanic's Collision with an Iceberg.

(For story see Page 3.)

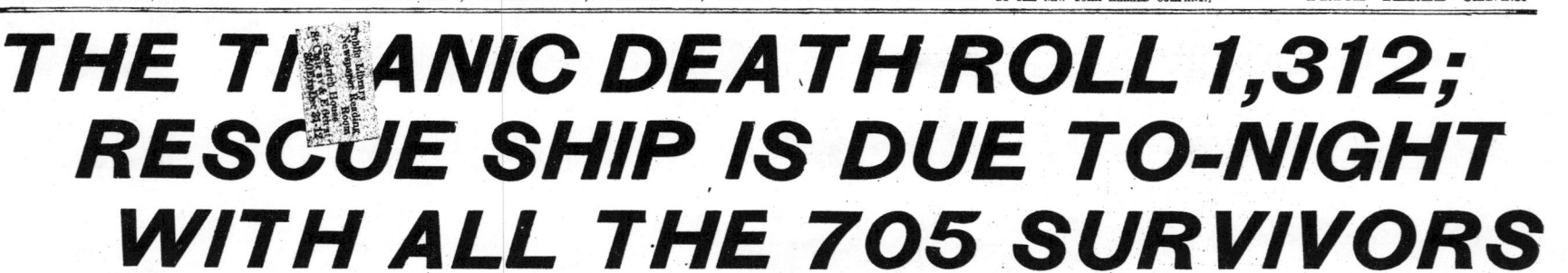

THE CARPATHIA SENDS WIRELESS SAYING SHE HAS REPORTED COMPLETE LIST OF THE SAVED

The Scout Cruiser Chester, Speeding Toward Returning Steamship, Hears Sad News That the Number of Rescued Was at First Exaggerated.

PRESIDENT TAFT SENDS URGENT PLEA, BUT GETS NO TIDINGS OF MAJOR BUTT

Mayor and Government Officials Issue Orders Barring All but Relatives and Close Friends of the Survivors from Pier When Vessel Arrives at New York.

Another day of mingled suspense and despair closed last night with the disheartening probability that the roster of the rescued from the lost Titanic has been closed and that its total may not be more than 705 persons, instead of the 868 indicated yesterday morning.

With every evidence that the grim roll call has been completed on board the Cunard steamship Carpathia, the apparent conclusion is that not more than 379 of the Titanic's first and second cabin passengers, who numbered in all 610, are safe aboard the rescuing vessel, which is now expected to arrive in this port to-night, unless she be delayed by unfavorable weather conditions.

The cabin passengers whose names have not been included in the lists sent ashore by wireless probably must be numbered among the appalling total of 1,312 whose lives were sacrificed when the Titanic, superb in her strength and beauty, but inadequately equipped for the saving of human lives, struck the iceberg that closed her brief career in the gloom and bitter cold of last Sunday night.

The Carpathia Expected To-Night.

The last hope that the number of the saved might be increased with more complete knowledge vanished when the scout cruiser Chester flashed ashore her wireless message yesterday that she had been in communication with the Carpathia and had learned that the rescue ship had no names to add to those already sent ashore by means of the Olympic's relay.

The Carpathia is approaching this port at the rate of about thirteen knots, a speed which, if it be maintained, should bring her to the harbor entrance by about eight o'clock to-night. She was in wireless communication last night with both the scout cruiser Chester and the shore station at Siasconsett. Through the Chester she managed to send slowly ashore the names of those saved from the steerage.

With this evidence that there are none other of the first and second cabin passengers to be reported the final hope seems to have vanished for the lives of Colonel Astor, William T. Stead, Major Archibald Butt, Isidor Straus and the many other notable men for whom suspense has been felt on two continents.

The Cunard line steamship Franconia also established communication by wireless with the Carpathia and received from her a message which included the terse statement:—"She has a total of 705 survivors aboard." Previous statements had been that she carried 868 rescued men, women and children. It is possible that the report received through the Franconia included a count of the rescued passengers only, disregarding the hundred or more of the crew who must have been in the boats which the Carpathia picked up, their presence being necessary to handle the life saving craft.

President Taft tried in vain yesterday through the two naval scout cruisers to get through some definite message concerning the fate of his military aid, Major Butt, and his friends, Mr. Moore and Mr. Millet, the artist.

Captain Chandler, of the Salem, repeatedly tried to elicit some response, adding:—"The President is very anxious. Kindly inform me so I can transmit to him."

UNITED STATES SENATE ORDERS SEARCHING INQUIRY TO PLACE BLAME FOR GREAT SEA HORROR

J. Bruce Ismay, Managing Director of the White Star Line, Surviving Officers of the Titanic and Her Passengers To Be Summoned to Washington and Questioned.

ENTIRE NATION DEMANDS NEW LAW TO STOP MOB RULE OF WIRELESS

Marine Men, Naval Architects and Many Navigators Advocate the Herald's Idea of Iceberg Patrol to Warn Ships of Danger on the Atlantic.

It is evidence of the confusion into which the wireless system has been thrown by the present crisis when it is admitted that up to late last night there had been no response to the President's request. This was the situation despite the fact that he Marconi company had notified its stations at South Wellfleet, Siasconsett, Sagaponack and Sea Gate to handle messages to and from the Carpathia exclusively, and practically all other regular wireless business along the coast was supposed to have been suspended.

In Montreal some credence was given to the unverified report that Mr. Hays, president of the Grand Trunk Railway system, had of Thornton Davidson, a passenger of the Titanic, said he had received a cable despatch to the effect that the Hays party was safe. Judge Davidson, the father of the younger men, also was quoted by a Montreal newspaper as having said that private advices from Mr. Franklin, of the White Star office in New York, had assured him of the rescue of all the passengers from Montreal.

Senate Orders Strict Inquiry.

Prompt steps were taken by the United States Senate yesterday for an immediate and searching investigation by a Congressional committee of the destruction of the Titanic and the attendant loss of human life. Survivors of the disaster soon after their arrival here probably will be summoned to the national capital and subjected to examination as the principal witnesses.

Senator Smith, of Michigan, introduced the resolution for the inquiry, under a request for immediate recognition. After a favorable report from the Committee on Commerce, to which it had been referred, the resolution was adopted by the Senate without discussion.

It directs the Committee on Commerce or a sub-committee

NAVY WIRELESS REACHES THE CARPATHIA; NEARING HOME

therof, to investigate the causes leading to the wreck, and empowers it to summon witnesses and to take testimony "to determine the responsibility therefore, with a view to such legislation as may be necessary to prevent as far as possible any repetition of such disaster."

It instructs the committee to "inquire particularly into the number of lifeboats, life rafts and life preservers and other equipment for the protection of passengers and crew; the number of persons aboard the Titanic, whether passengers or crew, and whether adequate inspections had been made of such vessel, in view of the large number of American passengers travelling over a route commonly regarded as dangerous from icebergs, and whether it is feasible for Congress to take steps looking to an international agreement to secure the protection of sea traffic, including regulation of the size of ships and designation of routes.

Despatches from St. John's, N. F., discredit reports published yesterday to he effect that some of the Titanic's passengers had probably been rescued by fishing schooners cruising in the vicinity. Eperts in the fishing trade said it was highly improbable hat any fishermen were near where the ship went down, especially at this time of the year, and certainly no Nwfoundland vsels.

BAR CURIOUS THRONGS FROM RESCUE SHIP

Anticipating attempts by all sorts of persons to gain admission to the Cunard line piers when the Carpathia arrives bringing the survivors from the Titanic, Mayor Gaynar and Franklin MacVeagh, Secretary of the Treasury, took occasion yesterday to issue orders which they hope will prevent scenes of confusion at the pier and exclude therefrom all persons who should not properly be present.

Mayor Gaynor's order was issued in the form of a communication to Mr. Waldo, the Police Commissioner, and is as follows:—

"SIR:—On the arrival of the Carpathia with the survivers of the Titanic the United States authorities will exclude all photographers from the dock space devoted to the customs service. You will exclude all photographers or picture takers from entrance to the rest of the dock. Also rope off a large space for the protection of these unfortunate people from all approach or interference from photographers or any one else. We owe this to them, and let it be carried out strictly. Very truly, yours,

"WILLIAM J. GAYNOR. Mayor."

No Inspection of Ship.

The order of Secretary MacVeagh was received at the office of William Loeb, Jr., Collector of the Port, late yesterday afternoon. It follows:—

"COLLECTOR OF CUSTOMS, New York:—

"The following statement has been given to the press:—'In order to obviate all possible delays in the landing of the passengers rescued from the Titanic the Secretary of the Treasury has waived all customs regulations in connection with the landing of passengers from the Carpathia and the examination of baggage, and as the scout crusiers Salem and Chester will convey the Carpathia into port there will be no necessity for the despatch of revenue cutters for either customs or convoy purposes.

"There is, however, no obstacle, so far as the government is concerned, to the boarding of the Carpathia by friends of survivors and by representatives of the press, provided the consent of the owners of the Carpathia is obtained. If the authorities of the Cunard line are willing that representatives of the press and relatives should board the Carpathia before her arrival, the department will, upon being so advised by the Cunard company, authorize the use of a cutter for this purpose. But thus far the Cunard company has taken the position that it will be impossible for any one to board the ship prior to her reaching the dock."

It is doubtful if final and definite arrangements for handling the situation which must inevitably transpire with the landing of the Titanic survivors will be complete before this morning. There were several misunderstandings yesterday in relation to the expected arrival of the Carpathia, and many persons who had given over their whole day to seeking passes to the Cunard line piers when the Carpathia shall arrive were told last night that the passes they had taken such pains to get were worthless.

Won't Honor Passes.

All day crowds besieged the office of Colonel Nelson H. Henry, Surveyor of the Port, and the Cunard line offices. At both offices passes were issued to persons able to convince Colonel Henry and the Cunard officials that their presence at the Cunard piers to-day was practically imperative. Each person applying for a pass was compelled to show that he or she was a relative of one of the Titanic's survivors or a close friend of one of them.

Only one pass was alloted against each name on the list of survivors, and none was allowed to those wishing to meet persons on board the Carpathia other than survivors of the Titanic disaster.

Several times it was announced at the Cunard offices that passes issued at Colonel Henry's office would not be honored, and as often it was said at the Surveyor's office that as the federal authorities would be in charge passes given out at the Cunard offices could not be recognized. As a result hundreds of persons attempted to get a pass at each office and by late afternoon confusion reigned in both places.

At each place hundreds of persons wept hysterically when informed that they could get no passes.

Late last night it was announced that H. C. Stuart, Acting Collector of the Port in the absence of Mr. Loeb, who left this city for Panama on April 6, had taken charge over the head of Colonel Henry and would decide to-day on all applications for passes. Later it was announced that Mr. Stuart and the Cunard officials would act in concert and that all passes which it is decided to issue will be in the hands of those who are to receive them by this afternoon.

Orders to the revenue cutters, the Mohawk and the Seneca, both of which lay off Tompkinsville all day in readiness to go out to meet the Carpathia, were sent to them last night through the New York Navy Yard. The commanders of the two cutters were ordered to have their vessels ready to proceed to sea at a moment's notice.

LATEST LIST OF SURVIVORS NOW ON BOARD THE CARPATHIA

According to the latest wireless messages, together with reports from those persons who have received word from the Carpathia, the number of first and second class passengers rescued and who are now believed to be aboard the Carpathia is 379. In the misspelling of names it is thought that several of these names may have been duplicated.

Forty-three names of steerage passengers also were received last night.

From the figures given out at the White Star line offices, No. 9 Broadway, and from other sources the number of missing first cabin passengers is placed at 201 and the missing in the second cabin at 206, a total of 407.

It is reported that of the 710 third class passengers probably 310 lost their lives. It is believed that about 400 steerage passengers have been saved, and 130 of the crew who manned the lifeboats. However, with the many wireless messages sent by the Carpathia's wireless operator, assisted by the second operator from the Titanic, many of the first class passengers have been counted as second and second class as first. It is believed that some of the names of third class pasengers have come through in the second class list.

A

ASTOR, Mrs. JOHN JACOB, and maid, of New York.
ANDERSON, HARRY.
APPLETON, Mrs. E. D., Bayside, L. I.; sister of Mrs. Cornell.
APPERANELT, MISS.
ABBOTT, Mrs. ROSE
ALLISON, Master, and nurse.
ANDREWS, Miss CORNELIA I., Newark, Ohio.
ALLEN, Miss ELIZABETH WALTON.
ANNABILL, MISS GEORGETTA.
ANDREWS, MISS K. T.
ANTOINETTE, MISS.
ARDEN, Mr. GEORGE.

B

BEHR, KARL H., No. 777 Madison avenue, city.
BESSETTE, Miss.
BUCKNELL, Mrs. WILLIAM
BARKWORTH, Mr. A. H.
BOWERMAN, Miss ELSIE.
BROWN, Mrs. J. M., Boston, Mass.
BURNS, Miss C. M.,
BISHOP, Mr. and Mrs. D. H.
BLANK, HENRY.
BASSINA, Miss A.
BARRETT, KARL.
BAXTER, Mrs. JAMES, of Poughkeepsie, N. Y. She was born at sea twenty-four years ago.
BRAYTON, GEORGE A.
BONNELL, Miss ELIZABETH.
BONNELL, Miss CAROLINE.
BROWN, Mr. and Mrs. J. J:
BOWEN, Miss G. C.
BECKWITH, Mr. and Mrs. RICHARD L., Columbus, Ohio.
BATHWORTH, MIAB.
BAYS, MARGARET.
BRAHAM, Mrs.

C

CHARLTON, W. M.
CAMARION, KENNARD D.
CANDEE, Mr. and Mrs.
CASSEBERE, Miss D. D.
CLARKE, Mrs. WALKER M.
CHIDNALL, Mrs. BOWERMAN.
CARTER, Miss LUCILE.
CARTER, Master WILLIAM E.
CARDELL, Mrs. CHURCHILL.
CALDERHEAD, E. P.
CHARLTON, Mr. W. M.
CORNELL, Mrs. ROBERT (?), No. 901 Lexington avenue.
CHANDANSON, Miss VICTORINE.
CAVENDISH, Mr. and Mrs. T. W., and maid.
CHAFFEE, Mrs. H. L.
CARDEZA, THOMAS D. M. and Mrs.
CUMINGS, Mrs. J. BRADLEY, No. 56 East Sixty-fourth street.
CHEVRE, Mr. PAUL.
CHERRY, Miss GLADYS.
CHAMBERS, Mr. and Mrs. N. C.
CARTER, Mr. and Mrs. WILLIAM E.
CARDEZA, MRS. J. W.
CASE, HOWARD B.
CROSBY, MRS. E. G.
CROSSBIE, MRS. (may be Miss).
CLARKE, Mrs. WILLIAM, and baby.

D

DOUGLASS, Mrs. FREDRICK C.
DE VILLIERS, Mrs. B.
DANGER, MARY.
DANIEL, Miss SARAH.
DANIEL, Mr. ROBERT W.
DAVIDSON, Mrs. THORNTON, Montreal, Canada.
DOUGLASS, Mrs. WALTER.
DOUGLAS, Mrs. F. C.
DOUGLAS, Mr. and Mrs.
DODGE, Miss SARAH.
DODGE, Mrs. WASHINGTON, of San Francisco.
DODGE, Master.
DODGE, Miss WASHINGTON.
DICK, Mr. and Mrs. A. A.
DANIELL, Mr. H. HAREN.
DRACHENSTEAD, Mr. A.

E

EMMOCK, Mr. PHILIP.
ENDRES, Mrs. CAROLINE.
ELLIS, Miss.
EARNSHAW, Mrs. BOULTON, Philadelphia, Pa.

F

FLEGENHEIM, Miss ANTOINETTE.
FRANCATELLI, Miss.
FLYNN, J. J.
FORTUNE, Miss ALICE.
FORTUNE, Miss ETHEL.
FORTUNE, Mrs. MARK, Winnipeg, Ontario.
FORTUNE, Miss Mabel.
FRAUENTHAL, Dr. and Mrs. HENRY W.
FRAUENTHAL, Mr. and Mrs. I. G.
FROLICHER, Miss MARGARET.
FUTRELLE, Mrs. JACQUES.
(FUTRELLE, JACQUES, also is reported from London as rescued.

G

GARSIGE, MISS ETHEL.
GRACIE, Colonel ARCHIBALD.
GRAHAM, Mr. and Mrs. WILLIAM G.
GRAHAM, Miss MARGARET.
GORDON, Sir COSMO DUFF.
GORDON, Lady.
GARVAN, ANNA.
GIBSON, Miss DOROTHY.
GOLDENBERG, Mrs. SAMUEL.
GOLDENBERG, Miss ELLA.
GREENFIELD, Mr. G. B.
GREENFIELD, Mrs. LEE.
GREENFIELD, Mr. WM., No. 1,239 Madison avenue.
GIBSON, Mrs. LEONARD D.
GOOGHT, JAMES.

H

HIPPACH, Miss JEAN, Chicago, Ill.
HIPPACH, Mrs. IDA S., Chicago, Ill.
HARRIS, Mrs. HENRY B.
HALVERSON, Mrs. ALEX. M.
HAUSSING, MILO.
HOGEBOOM, Mrs. J. C., Newark, Ohio.
HAWKSFORD, Mr. W. J.
HARPER, Mr. HENRY S., and man servant.
HARPER, Mrs. H. S.
HOLD, Miss J. A.
HOP7, Miss LENA.
HOYT, Mr. and Mrs. FREDERICK M., No. 112 East Seventy-third street, city.
HORNER, Mr. HENRY R. (Homer?).
HARDER, Mr. and Mrs. GEORGE A., of Brooklyn.
HAYS, Mrs. CHARLES M., Montreal, Canada.
HAYS, Miss MARGARET, Montreal, Canada.
HENRY, Mr. and Mrs.

I

ISMAY, J. BRUCE.

K

KIMBALL, Mr. and Mrs. E. N.
KENNYMAN, Mr. F. A.
KENCHEN, Miss EMILE.

L

LEAHY, NORAH.
LONGLEY, Miss GRETCHEN F., Newark, Ohio.
LEADER, Dr. ALICE F., No. 340 West 118th street.
LAVORY, Miss BERTHA.
LINES, Mrs. ERNEST H.
LINES, Miss MARY C.
LINDSTROM, Mrs. SINGIRD.
LESNEUR, Mr. GUSTAVE, Jr.

M

MADILL, Miss GEORGETTE A., St. Louis, Mo.
MAHAN, Mrs.
MELICARD, Mme.
MIDDLE, OLIVIA.
MAIMY, Miss ROBERTA.
MOCK, PHILIP E.
MARVIN, Mr. and Mrs. D. W., of No. 317 Riverside Drive.
MARECHELL, Mr. PIERRE.
MIDDLER, MISS MOLIVA.
MINAHAN, Miss DAISY, Green Bay, Wis.
MEYER, Mrs. EDGAR. (She is the daughter of the late Andrew Saks, of New York).
MINAHAN, Mrs., Fond du Lac, Wis.
MINDERSON, MISS LETTA.

N

NEWELL, Miss ALICE.
NEWELL, Miss MADELINE.
NEWELL, Mr. WASHINGTON.
NEWSOME, Miss HELEN, Columbus, Ohio.

O

O'CONNELL, Miss R. (probably Mrs. Robert C. Cornell, wife of Magistrate Cornell, of this city).
OSTBY, Mr. and Mrs. E. O., Providence, R. I.
OSTBY, Miss HELEN R., Providence, R. I.
OLIVIA, Miss.
OMOND, Mr. FLEUNAM.
OXENHAM, THOMAS, (P. J.).

P

PANHART, Miss NINETTE.
POMORY, Miss Eleen.
POUCH, Miss HELEN.
POTTER, Mrs. THOMAS, Jr., Chestnut Hill, Philadelphia.
PINCHEN, Major ARTHUR.

R

RENANGO, Mrs. MAMAM.
RANELT, Miss APPIE.
ROTHCHILD, Mrs. LORD MARTIN.
ROSENBAUM, Miss EDITH.
ROTHSCHILD, Mrs. MARTIN.
RHEIMS, Mr. and Mrs. GEORGE.
ROSIBIE, Miss H.
ROTHES, Countess.
ROBERTS, Mrs. EDWARD.
ROLMANE, Mr. C.
RYERSON, Miss SUSAN P., Philadelphia.
RYERSON, Miss EMILY, Philadelphia.
RYERSON, Mrs. ARTHUR, Philadelphia.
RYERSON, Master JOHN, Philadelphia.

S

SEALY, Miss NORAH.
STONE, Mrs. GEORGE M., Cincinnati.
SEGESSER, Miss EMMA.
SEWARD, Mr. FREDERICK K., the Devonshire, 112th street, Broadway.
SHUTES, Miss E. F.
SLOPER, WILLIAM T., New Britain, Conn.
SWIFT, Mrs. F. JOEL, 171 Arlington avenue, Brooklyn.
SCHABERT, Mrs. PAUL, Derby, Conn.
SHEDDEL, ROBERT DOUGLASS.
SKELLER, Mr. WILLIAM.
SNYDER, Mr. and Mrs. JOHN.
SEREPECA, Miss AUGUSTA.
SILVERTHORN, R. SPENCER.
SAALFIELD, ADOLF.
STAHELIN, Mr. MAX.
SIMONIUS, ALFONSIUS.
SMITH, Mrs. LUCIEN P.
STEPHENSON, Mrs. WALTER B.
SOLOMON, ABRAHAM.
SILVEY, Mrs. WILLIAM B., Superior, Wis.
STENMEL, Mr. and Mrs. O. E. H.
SPENCER, Mrs. W. A., and maid.
SLAYTER, Miss HILDA.
SPEEDEN, Mr. and Mrs. F. O.
STEFFANSON, H. B.

T

TUCKER, Mrs., and maid.
THAYER, Mr. and Mrs. J. B.
THAYER, J. B., Jr.,
TAUSSIG, Miss RUTH, No. 777 West End avenue, city.
THOR, Miss ELLA.
TAYLOR, Mr. E. K.
TAYLOR, Mrs. E.
TROUT, Miss JESSIE.
TUCKER, GILBERT.

W

WARRIAN, Mrs.
WOOLNER, Mr. HUGH.
WARD, Miss ANNA.
WILLIAMS, RICH. M.
WARREN, Mrs. F. N.
WILSON, Miss HELEN A.
WILLARD, Miss CONSTANCE.
WICK, Mrs. GEORGE.
WICK, Miss MARY, Youngstown, Ohio.
WIDENER, Mrs. GEO. D., and maid, of Philadelphia.
WHITE, Mrs. J. STEWART.

Y

YOUNG, Miss MARIE.

SECOND CLASS PASSENGERS.

A

ANGLE, Mr. and Mrs. WILLIAM.
ABELSON, Mrs. HANNA.

B

BALLS, Mrs. ADA E.
BUSS, Miss KATE.
BECKER, Mrs. A. O., and three children.
BEANE, Mr. EDWARD.
BEANE, Mrs. ETHEL, Miss ESTELLE.
BROWN, Mr. (T. W. S.?).
BROWN, Miss EDITH.
BENTHAM, LILLIAN W.
BYSTRON, KAROLINA.
BEIGHT, DAGMAR.

C

CLARK, Mrs. ADA.
CAMERON, Miss.
CALDWELL, ALBERT F.
CALDWELL, Mrs. SYLVAN.
CALDWELL, infant ALDEN.
CARMACION, Mr. and Mrs.
CARMACION, RENARDE.
COLLYER, Mrs. CHARLOTTE.
COLLYER, Miss MARJORIE.
CHRISTY, Mrs. ALICE.
COLLET, Rev. STUART, son of the Rev. Thomas Collet, of Port Byron.
CHRISTA, Miss JULIA.
CHARLES, WILLIAM.
CROFT, MILLIE MALL.

D

DOLING, Mrs. ELSIE.
DREW, Mrs. LULU.
DAVIS, Mrs. AGNES.
DAVIS, Miss MARY.
DAVIS, JOHN M.
DURAN, FLORENTINE.
DURAN, Miss ASINCION.
DAVIDSON, Miss MARY (?).
DOLING, Ada (?).
DRISCOLL, Mrs. B. (?).

E

EMCARCION, Mrs. RINALDO.

F

FINNEY, Miss. Reported as saved.
FAUNTHORPE, Mrs. LIZZIE.
FORNERY, Miss ELLEIN.

G

GARSIDE, ETHEL.
GERRECIA, Mrs. MARCY.
GENOSESE, Mr. ANGERE.

H

HART, Mrs. ESTHER.
HART, child (ANNA?).
HARRIS, GEORGE.
HEWLETT, Mrs. MARY.
HARPER, NINA.
HOLD, Mr. STEPHEN.
HOLD, Miss ANNA.
HOSENO, Mr. MASABUMI.
HOCKING, Mr. and Mrs. GEORGE.
HOCKING, Miss NELLIE.
HERMAN, Mrs. JANE.
HEALY, NORA.
HANSON, JENNIE.
HAMATAINEN, Mr. W.
HAMATAINEN, Mr. HANNA.

J

JACKSON, Mrs. AMY.

K

KEANE, Miss NORA A.
KELLY, Mrs. F.

L

LEITCH, JESSIE.
LAROCHE, Miss SIMMOME.
LAROCHE, Mrs. JOSEPH.
LAROCHE, Miss LOUISE.
LEHMAN, BERTHA.
LAUCH, Mrs. (ALEXANDER).
LENIORE, AMELIA (ELIZABETH).
LINKKANCE, Miss ANNIE.

M

MELLINGER, ELIZABETH.
MELLINGER, child.
MARSHALL, Mrs. (KATE).
MALLETT, Mr. A.
MALLETT, Mrs.
MANGE, PAULA.
MARE, Mrs. FLORENCE.
MELLOR, Mr. J.
McDEARMONT, Miss LILLIE.
McGOWAN, ANNA.

N

NASSER, Mrs. (all), Mrs. DELIA.
NYE, ELIZABETH.

O

OXENHAM, THOS. (P. J.)

P

PHILLIPS, ALICE.
PALLAS, Mr. EMILIO.
PADRO, Mr. JULIAN.
PINSKY, ROSA.
PORTALUPPI, EMILIO.
PARSH, Mrs. L.
POSOSONS, M. F.

Q

QUICK, Mrs. JANE.
QUICK, Miss VERA W.
QUICK, Miss PHYLLIS.

R

RIDSDALE, LUCY.
RENOUF, Mrs. LILY.
RUGG, Miss EMILY.
RICHARDS, Mr. EMILE.
RICHARDS, EMILY, two boys and Mr. Jr.
ROGERS, Miss ELIZA.

S

SINCOCK, Miss MAUDE.
SMITH, Miss MARION.
SHELLEG, Mrs. WILLIAM.
SILVEN, LYLLE.

T

TROUTT, Miss E.
TROUTT, Miss CECILIA.

W

WILLIAMS, C. CHARLES.
WEISZ, Mrs. MATHILDA.
WEBBER, Miss SUSIE.
WRIGHT, Miss MARION.
WATT, Mrs. BESSIE.
WATT, Miss BERTHA.
WEST, Mrs.
WEST, Miss CONSTANCE.
WEST, Miss BARBARA.
WELLS, ADDIE.
WELLS, Master.
WELLS, Miss.

THIRD CLASS PASSENGERS.

NORA MURPHY.
KATIE MULLIN.
KATIE McCARTHY.
G. D. MESSEMOCKES.
ANNA MESSEMOCKES.
MADERA YUSEF.
BUNOS MOUBARCK.
HALIN MOUBARCK.
GITOSA MOUBARCK.
MINA MUSULMON.
SABUCA SUBULAKET.
JAVNA MANO.
KIRKOEAN MUHAN.
DELIA DIANODELMN.
KARL MATHJOAX.
BERTHA MALLIEDELL.
MAGGIE MERRIGAN.
BERTHA MARAN.
KRISTOF MADSEN.
ALBERT MOSS.
MARY McGOVERN.
ERNEST McKEY.
ALICE McKEY.
THOMAS McCORMACK.
JOHN NICKAREN.
— ADLERSON.
BERTHA NELSON.
YREE NYHEM.
ANNIE McGOWAN.
AGNES DOYT (or Mrs. A. A. DICK).
MARGARET NANGA.
MAGGIE J. MURPHY.
LEONCH ELDEGREK.
HEUNA MANMAN.
KRIKOREAN KIRORA.
HANWAKAN (?)
DELIA McDERMOTT.
MARLKARL (?)
JOHN McKAREN.
AINO LUDGUIS.
HELENA ANGUSEN.
MARY NEKET.
DEMINA J. NELSON.

Reported as Survivors, But Not on Cabled Passenger List.

After comparing the list of survivors received from the Carpathia with the passenger list as received from London, officers of the White Star line said yesterday that the following whose names have been received from the Carpathia as having been rescued were not on the cabled passenger lists:—

CHARLTON, Mr. W. M.,
CAMARION, Mr. KENARD,
POMORY, Miss ELLEN,
LEAHY, Miss NORA,
MENDERSON, Miss LETTA,
SKELLER, Mrs. WILLIAM,
TROUT, Miss JESSIE,
DANIEL, Miss SARAH,
HOLD, Miss J. A.,
HOPE, Miss NINA,
ANTOINETTE, Miss,
MIDDLER, Mme. M. OLIVA,
MAHAN, Mrs.,
APPRIERANELT, Miss,

Revised Report of All First and Second Cabin Passengers Still Missing

Below is a list of the Titanic's first cabin passengers whose names do not appear among those saved:—

A

AUBERT, Mrs. N., and maid.
ALLISON, Mr. H. J.
ALLISON, Mrs., and maid.
ALLISON, Miss.
ANDREWS, Mr. THOMAS.
ARTAGAVEYTIA, Mr. RAMON.
ASTOR, Colonel J. J., and man servant.
ANDERSON, Mr. WALKER.

B

BAXTER, Mrs. JAMES.
BEATTIE, Mr. T.
BRANDIES, Mr. EMIL.
BAUMAN, Mr. J.
BAXTER, Mr., and Mrs. QUIGG.
BIRNBAUM, JACOB.
BJORNSTORM, Mr. H.
BLACKWELL, Mr. STEPHEN WEART, Trenton, N. J.
BONNELL, Miss LILY.
BOREBANK, Mr. J. J.
BRADY, Mr. JOHN B., Pomeroy, Wash.
BREWE, Mr. ARTHUR JACKSON.
BUTT, Major ARCHIBALD W.
CASE, Mr. HOWARD B.
CAVENDISH, Mr. T. W.
CLIFFORD, Mr. GEORGE QUINCY.
COLEY, Mr. E. P., Victoria, B. C.

C

CRAIG, Mr. NORMAN C. K., C. M. P.
CARLSON, Mr. FRANK.
CORRAN, Mr. F. M.
CORRAN, Mr. J. P.
CHAFEE, Mr. H. L.
CHISHOLM, Mr. ROBERT.
COMPTON, Miss S. R.
COMPTON, Mr. and Mrs. A. T.
CORNELL, Mr. R. O.
CORBETT, Mrs. IRENE C., daughter of Bishop Levi A. Colvin, of Provo, Utah. Father received a letter Tuesday saying she would be home this week.
CRAFTON, Mr. JOHN B.
CROSBY, Mr. E. G., Milwaukee, Wis.
CROSBY, Miss HARRIETT, Milwaukee, Wis.
CUMINGS, Mr. JOHN BRADLEY.
CASSEBEER, Mr. and Mrs. H. A.

D

DAVIDSON, Mr. THORNTON, Montreal.
DODGE, Mr. WASHINGTON.
DULLES, Mr. WILLIAM C.
DALY, Mr. P. D.
DOUGLAS, Mr. W. D.
DOUGLAS, Master R., and nurse.

E

EASTMAN, Miss ANNIE K.
EUSTIS, Miss E. M.
EVANS, Miss E.

F

FOREMAN, Mr. B. L.
FORTUNE, Mr. MARK.
FORTUNE, Mr. CHARLES.
FRANKLIN, Mr. T. P.
FUTRELLE, Mr. JACQUES.

G

GEE, Mr. ARTHUR.
GOLDENBERG, Mr. E. L.
GOLDSCHMIDT, Mr. GEORGE B.
GRAHAM, Mr.
GIGLIO, Mr. VICTOR.
GUGGENHEIM, Mr. BENJAMIN.

H

HAYES, Mr. CHARLES M., Montreal.
HEAD, Mr. CHRISTOPHER.
HILIARD, Mr. HERBERT HENRY.
HIPKINS, Mr. W. F.
HOGABOOM, Mr. JOHN C., Newark, Ohio.
HOLDEN, the Rev. J. STUART, M. A.
HOGENHEIM, Mrs. A.
HARRIS, Mr. HENRY B.
HARRISON, Mr. W. H.
HAVEN, Mr. H.
HARP, Mr. and Mrs. CHARLES M.
HARP, Miss MARGARET, and maid.
HUST, Mr. W. F.
HIPKINS, Mrs. W. E.
HALVERSON, Mr. ALEXANDER M.

I

ISHAM, Miss A. E.
IRVAN, Mrs.

J

JULIAN, Mr. H. F.
JAKOB, Mr. BIRNBAUM.
JONES, Mr. C. C.

K

KENT, Mr. EDWARD A. Mr. Kent was a prominent architect, of Buffalo, N. Y., and a nephew of General A. B. Farnham, of Bangor, and a brother of William Kent, of New York.
KLOBER, Mr. HERMAN.

L

LAMBERT-WILLIAMS, Mr. FLETCHER FELLOWES.
LAWRENCE, Mr. ARTHUR.
LEWIS, Mrs. CHARLTON T.
LONG, Mr. MILTON C.
LEVY, Mr. E. G.
LINES, Mr. ERNEST H.
LINDSHOLM, Mr. J.
LORING, Mr. J. H.
LINGREY, Mr. EDWARD.

M

MAGUIRE, Mr. J. E.
MARVIN, Mr. D. W.
McCAFFRY, Mr. T.
McCAFFRY, Mr. T., Jr.
McCARTHY, Mr. TIMOTHY, Jr.
McGOUGH, Mrs. J. R.
MIDDLETON, Hon. J. CONNEN.
MILLETT, Mr. FRANK D.
MINAHAN, Dr., Fond du Lac, Wis.
McGOACH, Mr. J. R.
MAYER, Mr. and Mrs. EDGAR J.
MOLSON, Mr. H. MARKLAND.
MOORE, Mr. CLARENCE, and man servant.
MOOK, Mr. PHILIP E., Derby, Conn.

N

NATSCH, Mr. CHARLES, No. 503 East Seventh street, Flatbush.
NEWELL, Mr. A. W.
NICHOLSON, Mr. A. B.

O

OVIES, Mr. FERNANDO.
ORNOUT, ALFRED T.

P

PARTNER, Mr. M. AUSTIN.
PAYNE, Mr. V.
POND, Miss FLORENCE L., and maid.
PORTER, Mr. WALTER CHAMBERLAIN.
PUFFER, Mr. C. C.
[illegible]R, Mr. M. H. W.
PEARS, Mr. and Mrs. THOMAS.
PENASCO, Mr. and Mrs. VICTOR, and maid.

R

REUCHLIN, Mr. JONKHEER J. G.
ROBERT, Mrs. ELIZABETH WATSON, and maid.
ROEBLING, Mr. WASHINGTON A., 2d, Trenton, N. J.
ROOD, Mr. HUGH R., Seattle, Wash.
ROOS, Mr. J. HUGO, Winnipeg.
RHEIMS, Mr. GEORGE.
ROLMANE, Mr. C.
ROTHSCHILD, Mr. M.
ROWE, Mr. ARTHUR.
RYERSON, Mr. ARTHUR.
REYNOLDS, Miss EDITH. She was engaged to marry H. C. Jones, Secretary to the British Embassy in China.

S

SILVERTHORNE, Mr.
SILVEY, Mr. WILLIAM B., Superior, Wis.
SPADDEN, Master R. DOUGLAS, and nurse.
SPENCER, Mr. W. A.
STEAD, Mr. W. T.
STEHLI, Mr. and Mrs. MAX FROLICHER, Zurich, Switzerland.
STRAUS, Mr. ISIDOR, and man servant.
STRAUS, Mrs. ISIDOR, and maid.
SUTTON, Mr. FREDERICK.
SMART, Mr. JOHN MONTGOMERY, Produce Exchange.
SMITH, Mr. M. J. CLINCH.
SMITH, Mr. R. W.
STENMEL, Mr. C. E. H.
STEWART, Mr. ALBERT A., New York representative of the Strowbridge Lithograph Company.
SMITH, Mr. L. P.

T

TAUSSIG, Mr. and Mrs. EMIL, No. 777 West End avenue.
THAYER, Mr. J. B.
THORNE, Mr. and Mrs. G.

U

URUCHURTU, Mr. M. K.

W

WALKER, Mr. W. ANDERSON.
WARREN, Mr. F. M.
WHITE, Mr. PERCIVAL A.
WHITE, Mr. RICHARD F.
WIDENER, Mr. GEORGE D., and man servant.
WIDENER, Mr. HARRY.
WOOD, Mr. and Mrs. FRANK P.
WYCKOFF, Mr. VAN DER HOF.
WEIR, Mr. JOHN.
WICK, Mr. and Mrs. GEORGE D., Youngstown, Ohio.
WILLIAMS, Mr. DUANE.
WILLIAMS, Mr. R. M., JR.
WRIGHT, Mr. GEORGE.

In the above list should be included:—
Mrs. BUCKNELL'S maid.
Mr. CARDOZA'S man servant.
Mrs. CARDOZA'S maid.
Mrs. CARTER'S maid.
Mrs. DOUGLAS' maid.
Mrs. HAYS' maid.
Mr. ISMAY'S man servant.
COUNTESS ROTHES' maid.
Mrs. ROBERTS' maid.
Mrs. RYERSON'S maid.
Mrs. SPEDDEN'S maid.
Mrs. STONE'S maid.
Mrs. THAYER'S maid.
Mrs. J. S. WHITE'S maid and man.

SECOND CABIN PASSENGERS.

A

ASHBY, JOHN.
ALDWORTH, C.
ANDREW, EDGAR.
ADELMAN, FRANZ.
—, Mrs. LILA.
—, Mrs.
ABELSON, SAMPSON.
ANDREW, FRANK.

B

BYLES, Rev. Thomas.
BEAUCHAMP, H. J.
BEESLEY, LAWRENCE.
BROWN, MILDRED.
BENTHAN, L.
BATEMAN, ROBERT J.
BUTLER, REGINALD.
BOTSFORD, HULL.
BERRIMAN, WILLIAM.
BOWEENER, SOLOMON.
BEACKEN, JAMES H.
BROWN, Mrs. (I. W. S.).
BANFIELD, FREDERICK.
BEIGHT, NARL.
BAILEY, PERCY.
BAMBRIDGE, CHARLES R.
BRAILEY (a musician).
BREICIOUS (a musician).

C

CLARKE, CHARLES.
COREY, Mrs.
CARTER, Rev. ERNEST.
CARTER, Mrs. ERNEST.
COLERIDGE, REGINALD.
CHAPMAN, CHARLES.
CUNNINGHAM, ALFRED.
CAMPBELL, WILLIAM.
COLLYER, HAROLD.
CORBETT, Mrs. IRENE.
CHAPMAN, JOHN R. (or H.).
CHAPMAN, Mrs. ELIZABETH.
CHRISTY, Miss J.
COLANDER, ERIC.
COTTERILL, HARRY.

D

DEACON, PERCY.
DAVIS, CHARLES.
DEFFEN, WILLIAM.
DE BRETO, JOSE.
DALCROFT, Miss NELLIE.
DANBRONY, HERBERT.
DREW, JAMES.
DREW, Master MARSHALL.
DAVID, Master JOHN W.
DAVID, Miss ASINCION.
DOUNTON, WILLIAM J.
DEL VARLO, SABASTIAN.
DEL VARLO, Mrs. Sabastian.

E

EITEMILLER, G. F.
ENANDER, INGBAR.

F

FROST, A.
FYNNERY, Mr.
FOUNTHORPE, HARRY.
FILLBROOK, CHARLES.
FUNK, ANNIE.
FAHELSTROM, AME.
FOX, STANLEY W.

G

GREENBERG, SAMUEL.
GILES, RALPH.
GASKELL, ALFRED.
GILLESPIE, WILLIAM.
GILBERT, WILLIAM.
GALE, HARRY.
GALE, S.
GILL, JOHN.
GILES, EDGAR.
GILES, FRED.
GALE, PHADRUCK.
GARVEY, LAWRENCE.

H

HICKMAN, LEONARD.
HICKMAN, LEWIS.
HICKMAN, STANLEY.
HOOD, AMBROSE.
HODGES, HENRY P.
HART, BENJAMIN.
HARRIS, WALTER.
HARPER, JOHN.
HARBECK, WILLIAM H.
HOFFMAN, Mr.
HOFFMAN, Child.
HOFFMAN, Child.
HERMAN, Mr. SAMUEL.
HERMAN, Miss ALICE.
HERMAN, Miss KATE.
HOWARD, Mr. BENJAMIN.
HOWARD, Mrs. ELLEN T.
HART, Mr. GEORGE.
HALE, REGINALD. Was coming here to resume his position with the Home for the Friendless.
HAMATAINEN, ANNA, and infant son.
HILTUNEN, M.
HUNT, GEORGE.
HENHAM, THOMAS.

I

ELETT, BERTHA.

J

JACOBSON, Mr.
JACOBSON, Mrs.
JACOBSON, SYDNEY.
JEFFREY, Mr. CLIFFORD.
JEFFERY, Mr. ERNEST,
JENKIN, Mr. STEPHEN.
JARVIS, JOHN D.
JULIET, LUICHI.
JACKSON, Mrs. AMY.

K

KARINES, Mrs.
KANTAR, SELNA.
KNIGHT, R.
KEANE, Mr. DANIEL.
KIRKLAND, the Rev. CHARLES.
KARNES, Mrs. F. G.
KEYNALDO, Miss.
KRILLNER, JOHAN HENNIK.

L

LELSON, Mr. ROBERT L. (Larson).
LAWRENCE, Mr. G.
LAROCHE, Mr. JOSEPH.
LAMB, Mr. J. J.
LAMORE, Mrs. AMELIA.
LENGHAM, JOHN.
LEVY, P. J.
LAHTIMEN, Mr. WILLIAM.
LAHTIMEN, Mrs.
LAUCH, CHARLES.

M

MALLETICH, Miss JESSIE; of Painesville, Ohio, was bringing Emil Nanestik, of Austria, to his father in Ohio.
MUDD, THOMAS.
MACK, MARY.
MARSHALL, HENRY.
MELLERS, WILLIAM.
MAYBERG, FRANK H.
MEYER, AUGUST.
MYLES, Mr. THOMAS.
MITCHELL, Mr. HENRY.
MALLETT, Master A.
MATTHEWS, Mr. W. J.
McKANE, Mr. PETER.
MILLING, Mr. JACOB.
MANTVILE, JOSEPH.
MALACHARD, NOLL.
MORAWECK, Dr.
MANGIOVACCLI, EMILIO.
McCRAE, ARTHUR G.

N

NANESTIK, EMIL, of Austria.
NESSEN, ISRAEL.
NICHOLLS, Mr. JOSEPH C.
NORMAN, Mr. ROBERT D.
NASSER, NICHOLAS.

O

OTTEO, Mr. RICHARD.
O'QUICK (see Quick).

P

PHILLIPS, ROBERT.
PONESELL, MARTIN.
PAIN, Dr. ALFRED.
PARKES, FRANK.
PENGELLY, Mr. FREDERICK.
PERNOT, Mr. RENE.
PERUSCHITZ, the Rev.
PARRISH, Mrs. DAVIS.
PARKER, CLIFFORD.
PULBAUM, FRANK.

R

ROGERS, SETINA.
RENOUF, Mr. PETER H.
ROGERS, Mr. Harry.
REEVES, Mr. DAVID.

S

SWORD, HANS K.
STOKES, PHILIP J.
SHARP, PERCIVAL.
SEDGWICK, Mr.
SMITH, AUGUSTUS.
SWEET, GEORGE.
SJOSTEDT, Mr. ERNEST.
SLÆMEN, Mr. RICHARD J.
SOBERG, Mr. HAYDEN.
SLAYTER, Miss H.
SLATTER, Miss H. M.
STANTON, WARD.
SINKONEN, ANNA.

T

TOOMEY, ELLEN.
TURPIN, Mr. WILLIAM J.
TURPIN, Mrs. DOROTHY.
TURNER, Mr. JOHN H.
TURNER, Mrs.
TURNER, Mr. GEORGE.
TROUPEANSKY, MOSES ARON.
TERVAN, Mrs. A.
TRANT, Mrs. JESSE.

V

VEALE, Mr. JAMES.
VON DRACHSTEDT, Baron.

W

WALCROFT, Miss.
WILHELM, CHARLES.
WATSON, EMESS.
WILKINSON, Mrs. S. GEORGE.
WILKINSON, Miss ADA C.
WARE, Mr. WILLIAM C.
WEISZ, Mr. LEOPOLD.
WHEADON, Mr. EDWARD.
WARE, Mr. JOHN JAMES.
WARE, Mrs.
WEST, Mr. E. ARTHUR.
WHEELER, Mr. EDWIN.
WERMAN, SAMUEL.

Y

YROIS, Miss M.

Proud of Husband Who Died a Hero.

[SPECIAL DESPATCH TO THE HERALD.]

CLEVELAND, Ohio, Wednesday.—Mrs. Richard Otter, of Berea, whose husband was a passenger on board the Titanic, rushed to the home of her brother-in-law, William H. Otter, in Cleveland, when she heard of the disaster. She scanned the list of survivors but her husband's name was not there. She was near collapse until she read that men had sacrificed their lives that women and children might live.

"It is hard to lose him," said Mrs. Otter to-day, "but it is fine to think he went as he did. I think it is right the men should stand back.

"It will be a wonderful thing for our son to remember that his father died a hero. My husband was an Englishman and I should want him to meet his end bravely."

TERROR OF THE MIDNIGHT CRASH VIVIDLY DESCRIBED BY EXPERTS

How the Floating Palace Became Ship of Death Is Told by Mariners

Cries of Passengers for Speed, Their Scoffings at the Dangers of the Deep and the Crash That Blotted Out Lives by the Wholesale Pictured.

TRIBUTE TO THE UNMATCHED DISCIPLINE

TWO masters and a first owcer drawing on their own extensive experience and knowledge to supplement the meagre information as to what actually happened, told the story yesterday of the destruction of the Titanic as they visualized the details.. The three accounts have blended into the narrative which is given is given below, and where there were variations th eversion given by the majority has been followed.

Lights gleamed from a thousand ports as the Titanic swept through the southwest swell last Sunday night. The weather was comparatively clear, the air cold and raw. The vessel was going at a reduced speed, little more than half speed in these days when the leviathans of the deep have the swiftness of the wind, a terrific one for the period when smaller craft crept cautiously in the realm of floes.

The rate was eighteen knots an hour, far below what the pulsating engines of the mighty craft were able to attain, yet enough to develop a momentum quickly translatable into terms of destruction.

It was Speed! Speed! Speed!

It may have been that suddenly there came a veil of mist which hid the glacial mountain while the lookout from the crow's nest scanned the sea for signs of peril. What could have brought about this disaster is indeed hard to surmise when all the conditions of wind and weather seem to have been favorable for the observation of peril. Was it that a field of ice was discerned through which it was believed that this new empress of the seas could easily force her way?

On the chance of her quick journey so much depended, for every new fabric which comes from the shipyards to vie for the supremacy of the deep must reduce the record between the Old World and the Ne. The daily pools of the passengers, their talk of the day's runs, their often repeated comparisons of one day's conquest with that of the twenty-four hours before, all reflected the deep interest of this marine Atalanta over the pathways of the sea. If Atalanta should pause by the way she easily might lose this, her maiden race to her suitor, Time.

The salons were aglow, the smoking room had boon companions of the voyage, a few passengers were on deck. It was Sunday night and most of the passengers were in their staterooms and many had gone to bed. The air was still, and the rhythmic beat of propellers was heard from out of the foaming wake.

Floating Palace a Ship of Death.

A slight tremor passed through the hull and then another. Merely the blow of some vagrant floe. There was a stir on board, and in the cheery room where the wreathed smoke rose a man turned to his neighbor and spoke of how in these days steamships are unsinkable, and one may hardly know that the ocean is near unless he look over the side.

Then came the blow of fate. The Titanic hurled herself against a glacial mountain afloat. The terrific impact racked every frame, strained every vaunted barrier of steel, crumpled the bow into a shapeless mass of broken plates.

The momentum of the steamship developed from its 46,000 tons carried her over a hidden ledge of ice at the very base of the towering iceberg. The Titanic listed to port, the forward part slipped from the ledge, as her plates were ripped and torn, and settled once more into the sea.

Masses of ice fell upon the bow and slid over the decks. The floating abode of luxury became a ship of death. The shrieks of the passengers echoed through richly appointed salons and in the bare walls of the steerage.

Becomes Fight For Life.

Decks which had been almost deserted teemed with frantic human beings. The instinct of self preservation, the fight for life against the force of nature drove them from every hidden recess within the hulk of steel. Here were women with jewels worth millions gleaming on their fingers, men who held the destinies of great properties in industries in their power, immigrants who had scarcely more than the pittance required for their entrance into a new land, all leveled into one class as in the twinkling of an eye.

Discipline asserted itself automatically even in the midst of this reign of terror. The blood of the North runs cold and often coldest in time of peril. Below there were men scalded to death in their steel walled pens and others who had been hurled from life by the shattering of plates and the fall of heavy machinery.

The impaot had racked and wrenched the great bulk of the Titanic in every part. The absorbing of the shock of collision cut the rivets from plates and caused the water to seep through yawning seams. The longitudinal girders. driven back by the hammer like blow of the collision, had loosened and started bulkheads, weakening them for the irresistible thrust of the waters yet to come.

Plates at the bottom broken and bent were crumpled upward while the cross beams, which provided stability in the tank space, were made to puncture vital parts, were snapped in two and their broken ends driven up into the tank deck above.

In the Power of the Sea.

By the force of the collision the coal in the bunkers, the cargo in the holds was hurled forward against the bulkheads loosening those barriers of metal all the more. The bulkhead doors had been closed by a hydraulic device after the crash but the whole structure was so weakened that this was of little avail. The engines had been racked by the blow, and wrenched at their fastenings. Live coals were hurled from the doors of the furnace, the boilers swayed.

The engine room was demoralized, and the mighty mechanism, which had only a few minutes before ridden in defiance on the wave, was crippled and helpless in the power of the sea. The collision bulkhead had gone at the bow, and the water was filling the next compartment, causing the vessel to sink by the head.

In every part of the racked and riven hull ruin had spread. The pumps could not be used, for the engine room was demoralized and the powerful machinery intended to protect against disaster only funitioned feebly. Of what aail would have been pumps against the waters which were now making their way where rivets had once held firm but had now been cut off as by chisels?

Facing Doom, Officers Are Calm.

The vessel was doomed. Its proud enginery was humbled and the might which had been Titantic was only human. Man was left to fight his battle for life practically unaided by the powers of the fabric which he had called into being.

Iisting of the vessel to port made the launching of life obats on the opposite side difficult and uncertain. The officers calm, masterful, alert, gave their orders while from the bridge Captain Smith by signal, by word of mouth through the megaphone, directed the preparations for removing the passengers.

It was twenty minutes past ten o'clock when the vessel struck and the next four hours represented to the passengers ages of suspense and anxiety. The horror and confusion of the shock was written on every face and the reassuring words of the officers and the coolness of the captain could not allay the fear which was written on every face. One officer to each boat and four men at the oars was the complement, for insuch emergencies the crews of lifeboats are cut down to the minimum. Discipline prevailed throughout the crew. Sailors and stewards, by command of the officers, stood before the davits.

The rule of the sea, that time honored tradition which has always prescribed that the stronger shall yield the chance for life to the weaker, was observed. The women and children went first to the boats, bidding farewell to husbands and fathers, in obedience to the mandate of the officers.

To all was repeated the story that this was only for a time, that there was hope that the vessel would float, but it was better that the women should first flo.

All Hope Lies In "S. O. S."

The wireless operator had been sending forth into the uncharted regions of the air his call for aid, the continually repeated "S. O. S." which was the hope of all on board. As long as the dynamos of the vessel were working the call was maintained. To all the word was given that, in response to the wireless call, other vessels were hastening to the aid of the Titanic from regions many leagues beyond where the Titanic was surrendering to the foe which the race has known ever since men went down to the sea in ships. a fraction of an inch ETAOI — —

The lights of the salon and cabin were suddenly extinguished, the engine room was flooded and no more could man depend on electricity as his ally. The operator called his final "S. O. S." from the sinking hulk, feebly and slowly, with the power in his storage batteries. All the available boats had been launched, for several had been smashed in the collision or had been stove in the launching. A few of the water tight compartments were still holding when the darkness came.

Neptune Supreme in Night of Terror.

Slowly the Titanic was sinking by the head when the last boats were leaving, and in these were some of the men passengers who, by the chance of fate, the chances of one in three, were able to save their lives. On the bridge stood the commander, waiting for the end of all, while men and crew sought what they could to aid them when Neptune should take the empress of the sea captive to his hidden realm.

Then came the cries of despairing men, the sudden descent, the rush of light wreckage to the surface, following the whirpool of suction.

Here and there in the ice cold waters were victims of this game with destiny clinging to improvised rafts, buoyed by life preservers, seeking to win life in water so cold that within an hour their limbs were benumbed. Beyond were the lifeboats, crowded with fifty or sixty human beings each, waiting for the coming of aid summoned by the wireless call. They were those who were picked up by the Carpathia and are now bound for this port.

It is for them to tell the story of what did actually take place on that dark night of terror, and a few hours will tell how nearly the reality will verify the version which the mariners read in advance from the few details the wireless brought of the sinking of the Titanic to her ocean fate off the banks of Newfoundland.

CRUISER'S NEWS SENT TO MR. TAFT

All Messages from the Chester, Sent to Meet the Carpathia, Relayed to White House.

HERALD BUREAU,
No. 1,502 H STREET, N. W.,
WASHINGTON, D. C., Wednesday.

With the swift scout cruiser Chester, first to get in touch with the Carpathia, having on board survivors of the Titanic, the Navy Department to-day became the medium for information concerning the survivors of the wreck. Bulletins came in at intervals from the Chester and the navy wireless station, but up to a late hour to-night there was no news to contradict the staggering reports that more than a thousand had lost their lives on the Titanic and that the list of survivors already given the world was about complete.

President Taft had all messages relayed to the White House immediately upon their receipt at the Navy Department, hoping against hope that some one of them would give him news of his military aid, Major Archibald W. Butt. But each bulletin was a repetition of disappointment.

Hopes of good news were practically shattered as early as one o'clock in the afternoon, when a telegram was received from Commander Becker, of the Chester, via Portland, Me. This message said:—

"Carpathia states that list of first and second class passengers and crew sent to shore. Chester will relay list third class passengers when convenient to Carpathia."

As the partial list of survivors so far communicated to the shore by the Carpathia did not contain the name of Major Butt and in fact omitted names of many other well known passengers the inevitable conclusion was that they are not aboard the Carpathia and, so far as known, are lost.

The Chester's message sent out by her powerful wireless set was picked up by navy wireless stations all along the coast and relayed to the Navy Department. Thus the unwelcome message came repeated dozens of times, each time bringing home more forcefully to navy officers the horror of the disaster and the discouraging report that no additional passengers had been saved.

A late message to the Navy Department from Newport stated that the Carpathia would reach New York at eleven o'clock to-morrow night.

In order to lose no time in getting important wireless messages from the Chester or Salem the Navy Department ordered that an officer be kept on duty at the Bureau of Operations throughout the night.

The Navy Department's message to the Chester to intercept the Carpathia was picked up by the Chester last night before eight o'clock when the vessel was near the Nantucket Shoals light vessel, and the Chester started to the eastward at top speed. The Salem, which left Hampton Roads at four o'clock yesterday afternoon, will work with the Chester in getting radiograms to the Navy Department, the Salem acting as relay vessel.

JUDGES CITE EACH OTHER.

Chicago Members of the Bench Make Mutual Contempt Charges Over the Democratic Convention.

[SPECIAL DESPATCH TO THE HERALD.]

CHICAGO, Ill., Wednesday.—Judge McKinley, of the Superior Court, and Judge Owens, of the County Court, cited each other to-day to show cause why they should not be punished for contempt. This exchange of judicial greetings grew out of the troubles surrounding the Democratic County Convention, on Monday.

Judge Owens is cited because he ordered the police to smash the doors of the Seventh Regiment Armory, although a copy of Judge McKinley's injunction was nailed on the door. The County Judge cited Judge McKinley for alleged interference with the execution of his orders that Anthony Czarnecki should be allowed to enter the armory and preside as temporary chairman of the convention.

Judge McKinley also cited Herman Schuettler, Assistant Chief of Police; Chief John McWeeny, Sheriff Zimmer, Mr. Czarnecki and others. Judge Owens included in his citation Roger C. Sullivan, National Committeeman; Colonel Daniel Moriarity, commander of the Seventh regiment, and a dozen other anti-Harrison democrats.

THE CARMANIA'S LIST SMALL.

Carrying few passengers, but practically all who had arranged to go to Liverpool on board her before the news came of the Titanic disaster, the Carmania, of the Cunard line, left yesterday.

It was said a few minutes before she left the pier that two first cabin, four second cabin and five third class passengers, who had engaged their passage berore last Sunday, had not come on board. Among the saloon passengers were Mrs. Cornelius Vanderbilt, Sir John and Lady Lynch and the Rev. William Wilkinson and Mrs. Wilkinson.

TO TIE UP MEXICAN RAILROADS.

CEDAR RAPIDS, Iowa, Wednesday.—A strike which will tie up practically every railroad in Mexicow as ordered this afternoon by A. B. Garretson, of Cedar Rapids, president of the Order of Railway Conductors and Brotherhood of Locomotive Engineers.

It will affect six hundred conductors and more than that number of engine drivers. Anti-foreign regulation of operation of lines is one of the primary reasons for the strike. Mr. Garretson said to-night he could not tell how long the strike would be in force.

PHOTOGRAPH OF ICEBERG TAKEN BY CAPTAIN WILLIAM FERRIE WOOD OF THE ETONIAN, BELIEVED TO BE THE BERG AGAINST WHICH THE TITANIC WAS DESTROYED. THE TITANIC DRAWN ALONGSIDE TO SHOW RELATIVE PROPORTIONS

UNITED STATES SENATE ORDERS INQUIRY AT ONCE; PARLIAMENT ALSO WILL ACT

London, Aroused, Is Demanding Revision of Obsolete Rules Governing Life Saving Devices and New Laws Are To Be Forced.

RIGID NEW LAWS EXPECTED AS A RESULT

[SPECIAL DESPATCH TO THE HERALD VIA COMMERCIAL CABLE COMPANY'S SYSTEM.]

HERALD BUREAU,
No. 130 FLEET STREET,
London, Thursday.

England' press and public are stirred by the grim tragedy of the sinking of the Titanic and the loss of thirteen hundred souls, uniting in an imperative demand for greater safeguards for human lives on board ocean steamships. First in importance is the determination that the Board of Trade shall revise the rules designed to meet obsolete conditions, so that every steamship that leaves an English port shall carry enough boats, rafts and other life saving appliances to minimize as far as human foresight and ingenuity can the chance of another disaster like that which has been responsible for thousands of mourners in England and America, and caused the Stars and Stripes and Union Jack to be half masted in expression of common grief.

The cause of the disaster is to be investigated thoroughly by Parliament, and as a result of the discussion and criticism it is expected that measures will be framed that will insure ample life saving devices on board every steamship that leaves ports of both countries. The prevention of interference by reckless amateurs with wireless telegraphy and the passage of a law that will compel all transatlantic steamship companies to send their vessels during the spring season over routes that will make for safety instead of speed.

In England the feeling aroused by the tragedy is as intense as in the United States.

Horatio Bottomley, M. P., has given notice that he will ask Sydney Buxton, President of the Board of Trade, in Parliament to state the exact lifeboat accommodations provided on board the Titanic, and he will ask further whether Mr. Buxton will frame a regulation for the purpose of preventing British passenger steamships for New York during the spring season from taking the northern Atlantic route.

To Question Mr. Buxtra

With a view of establishing crossing records, Fred Hall, M. P. for Dulwich, will ask Mr. Buxton whether the Board of Trade will take steps to compel steamships to carry boats and rafts and other life saving apparatus sufficient to accommodate all on board.

The White Star company stated officially to-day that the Titanic carried more boats than was required by the regulations of the Board of Trade, but it is asserted this means nothing, as the regulations were framed to meet conditions when 10,000 ton vessels, carrying a few hundred passengers, were looked upon as leviathans.

Colonel Yates, M. P., will also ask the Postmaster General to-morrow whether attention has been called to wireless lies that gave now stricken friends of those who perished in the disaster false hopes, and whether the government will trace the origin of these cruel canards. In commenting this morning on the lack of boats the Standard says:—"It seems to be beyond question that those carried by the Titanic were inadequate to save all the passengers and crew in the event of disaster. It is equally certain that the White Star Company more than complied White Star company more than complied conclusion is irresistible that the matter must be considered by maritime authorities with a view to altering the regulations to meet requirements of modern passenger ships.

It is clear, says the Standard, that the question of new regulations is being considered by the United States authorities. The American regulations, however, the Standard holds, do not provide sufficient boatage for the passengers and crew. Only Norway and Swenden have such a rule.

The Standard concludes by stating that official American government records show the total inadequacy of many lines' provisions against the danger which overwhelmed the Titanic.

All papers this morning indorse the declaration of Alexander Carlisle, formerly manager of the Queen's Island Shipbuilding Yard at Belfast, where the Titanic was construoted, that in ships of the future a much smaller number of bulkhead doors should be fitted and should be closed between sunset and sunrise, and that vessels should have increased boat accommodations and life saving appliances.

Indorse Mr. Nixon's View.

English shipbuilding experts generally indorsed the statement by Lewis Nixon that an unsinkable ship has never been built, though it could be built, but would be good for nothing except keeping afloat, and that, instead of adding more lifeboats to a steamship's equipment a detachable raft should be affixed to the vessel's stern.

Lewis oJhnson, engineer of the Thames Iron Works, adocates the adoption of a life saving scheme devised some years ago by Admiral Sartorius, which consists of two steel rafts built on the pontoon principle.

H. J. Duveen, the art dealer, who has crossed the Atlantic more than one hundred times, insists the southern route should be made compulsory at all times and that every steamship should have sufficient boats to carry every one on board.

Fairplay, a shipping journal, discussing this morning the uppermost topic of the day, says:—"It has been many years since ships were commonly built so much upwars of 1,000 tons as to double that tonnage. It has been five years since the Lusitania and the Mauretania, almost as large as the Titanic, were laid down, yet only now are the absurd Board of Trade provisions under revision. During all these years the public has been under the delusion that their safety was properly cared for by law."

Old Regulations.

"It is interesting to nearn that according to the present regulations of the Board of Trade the minimum number of boats of an approved type which must be carried under the davits and ready for instant launching by vessels of 10,000 tons and upward is sixteen. The total minimum cubic contents of these boats is 5,500 cubic feet, ten cubic feet for each person. This provides for saving only 880 people. It is certain that Parliament will speedily pass a law making drastic amendments of the antiquated Board of Trade regulations in order to insure the safety of human lives on board transatlantic liners."

J. Bruce Ismay, Managing Director of the White Star Line, and Other Survivors of the Titanic To Be Called Before Committee and Questioned.

RESOLUTION IS ADOPTED IN RECORD TIME

HERALD BUREAU,
No. 1,502 H STREET, N. W.,
WASHINGTON, D. C., Wednesday.

A searching investigation of the Titanic disaster will be conducted by the Senate Commerce Committee under a resolution passed in record time to-day. J. Bruce Ismay, managing director of the White Star line, will be called before this body, as will other survivors of the disaster. Not only the details of the disaster, but the general policy of the White Star line in regard to speed, construction and safety appliances will be laid bare. The Senate showed quick response to the public surprise and indignation at the meagre life saving equipment of foreign ships now operating in and out of American ports.

The resolution authorizing the inquiry was introduced by Senator William Alden Smith, of Michigan. All rules were suspended to accelerate its adoption. The inquiry may be conducted either by the full committee, of which Senator Nelson, of Minnesota, is chairman, or a sub-committee. The latter course is probable. The Commerce Committee will meet to-morrow and a course of action will have been agreed upon by the time the Carpathia reaches New York.

"I want a through investigation of this disaster such as will disclose the causes leading to it and enable us to place the responsibility where it belongs," said Senator Smith. "Every officer of the ship who survived, the saved of the crew and passengers, the officers and agents of the line will be brought before the committee to give their testimony."

Will be Searching Inquiry.

The resolution follows:—

"Resolved, That the Committee on Commerce or a sub-committee thereof is hereby authorized and directed to investigate the causes leading to the wreck of the White Star liner Titanic, with its attendant loss of life, shocking to the civilized world;

"Resolved, further, That said committee or a sub-committee thereof is hereby empowered to summon witnesses, send for persons and papers and to take such testimony as may be necessary to determine the responsibility therefore, with the view to such legislation as may be necessary to prevent as far as possible any repetition of such a disaster;

"Resolved, further, That the committee shall inquire particularly into the number of lifeboats, life rafts and life preservers and other equipment for the protection of the passengers and crew; the number of persons aboard the Titanic, whether passengers or crew, and whether adequate inspections were made of such vessel in view of the large number of American passengers travelling over a route commonly regarded as dangerous from icebergs; and whether it is feasible for Congress to take steps looking to an international agreement to secure the protection of sea traffic, including regulation of the size of ships and designation of routes.

"Resolved further, that in this report of said committee it shall recommend such legislation as it may deem expedient, and the expense incurred by the investigation shall be paid from the contingent fund of the Senate upon vouchers to be approved by the chairman of said committee.

International in Scope.

The committee is not even confined under the letter of the resolution to restrict its inquiry to the United States, but may broaden it to such an extent as is necessary looking to the international agreement which it is directed to brng about.

Several similar resolutions of investigation are pending in the House and one of them probably will pass in a few days. It is possible that the House may join the Senate and conduct the investigation by a joint committee.

Representative Joshua W. Alexander, of Missouri, chairman of the House Committee on Merchant Marine and Fisheries, announced to-day that in connection with the consideration of the various bills pending before his committee to require proper lifesaving apparatus on board foreign vessels using American ports, survivors of the Titanic wreck would be called to testify as to the equipment of that vessel and to tell the story of the disaster.

THE PARISIAN NOT NEAR SCENE OF WRECK

Captain Heard of the Disaster, but Kept News from All on Board Until Reaching Halifax.

[SPECIAL DESPATCH TO THE HERALD.]

HALIFAX, N. S., Wednesday.—The steamship Parisian arrived here at seven o'clock to-night and brought absolutely no news throwing any light on the Titanic tragedy. Captain Hains said that D. S. Sutherland, the Parisian's wireless operator, was in touch with the Titanic at half-past ten o'clock on Sunday night, when he asked the White Star vessel to relay a message from him via Cape Race to the Allan line in Montreal. It was a business message. He thinks that message the only reason for connecting the name of the Parisian with the Titanic tragedy. Captain Hains did not know of the disaster until four o'clock on Monday morning. The Captain added that no one on board the Parisian except himself and the wireless operator knew of the catastrophe until the ship entered Halifax harbor.

The first intimation the passengers on board the Parisian had that the Titanic had been lost was when the HERALD's correspondent, who boarded the ship at Quarantine, told them about it.

The Parisian was about one hundred and fifty miles east of the place where the Titanic struck when the signals calling for help were sent out, and they were not received by the Parisian because the operators had gone to bed. They had been busy all day to get in touch with the Deutschland, drifting without coal. In the race for this prize, Captain Hains said, were two other ships, the Californian and the Mesaba.

"None of us got her, though," said the captain, "for the prize fell to the Asia, coming from the west.

The tow is following us into the harbor," the captain added.

"The icebergs were very thick," Captain Hains said. "The Carpathia passed us on Sunday night at nine o'clock. We were both avoiding the bergs which were there in hundreds. We exchanged notes on the ice and courses were altered in accordance with information given and received."

Captain Hains heard nothing at all of any survivors, and as he had passed over the scene of the foundering fully twelve hours before the disaster, he could tell nothing of conditions after it occurred. He said the Titanic must have struck a glancing blow which ripped her whole side out.

ALL VESSELS ASKED TO FLY FLAGS HALF MAST

Maritime Association, Deploring the Titanic Disaster, Requests Mark of Respect for Dead.

The Maritime Association of New York at the annual meeting held on Tuesday adopted a resolution requesting all vessels in the harbor to fly their flags at half mast until the Carpathia shall have landed the survivors of the Titanic disaster.

The resolution, offered by Fred B. Dalzell, read:—

"Resolved, that the members of the Maritime Association of the Port of New York, assembled in annual meeting, do express their great regret at the lamentable disaster which has befallen the great steamship Titanic, their great sorrow at the deplorable loss of life and property which has accompanied this disaster, and extend to all involved in the calamity their deep and heartfelt sympathy; and be it further

"Resolved, that all vessels in the harbor be requested to place their flags at half mast out of respect to the unfortunate dead."

WIRELESS ANARCHY TO BE CHECKED AT ONCE BY CONGRESS

WIRELESS TIDINGS BRING DESPAIR AND HOPE TO RELATIVES

Joy Over Rescue of One Dampened by News of Another's Probable Loss.

BONNELL PARTY REPORTED SAFE

Mrs. Edgar J. Meyer, Daughter of the Late Andrew Sax, Also Among Survivors.

HER HUSBAND IS MISSING

Life Stories of Those on Board the Ill-fated Craft Who Went Down or Lived.

Mrs. J. M. Bonnell, of Youngstown, Ohio, who, with her son, is stopping at the Waldorf-Astoria, received a wireless message yesterday from her brother, Henry Wick, a passenger on board the Olympic, saying, "All women aboard."

The message, Mrs. Bonnell says, refers to her daughter, Miss Caroline Bonnell; Miss Elizabeth Bonnell, a relative; Mrs. George D. Wick and her daughter, Miss Natalie Wick. Mrs. Bonnell has been unable to verify the report that Miss Elizabeth Bonnell has been saved.

Miss Caroline Bonnell and Mr. and Mrs. George D. Wick on February 14 left this city on board the Kaiserin Auguste Victoria for a visit to Italy, Paris and London. Mrs. Bonnell and her son came here from Youngstown on Monday to meet Miss Bonnell and her aunt, who is a resident of Birkdale, England.

Mrs. Bonnell had about given up hope of seeing her daughter alive again when the message came yesterday. For the last two days she and her son have been sending messages in the hope of learning if Miss Bonnell was among the survivors on board the Carpathia. Mr. Bonnell said he was unable to confirm the rescue of his aunt. The wireless message that came to Mrs. Bonnell, which was relayed from the Carpathia to the Olympic, was a source of great relief to Mrs. Bonnell, as she has suffered much since the disaster.

That Mrs. Edgar J. Meyer, only daughter of the late Andrew Saks, a dry goods merchant, was rescued was confirmed in a wireless message yesterday from the Carpathia. It read:—"Saks, New York—Leila saved; very well cared for. Edgar missing." Mr. W. A. Saks, of No. 524 Fifth avenue, a brother of Mrs. Meyer, said the message was received at a time when all hope had been given up for the rescue of his sister.

Mr. and Mrs. Meyer were returning to their home, No. 158 West Eighty-sixth street, after a six weeks' visit to European cities. Mr. Meyer was president of the Braden Copper Company, No. 7 Wall street. Hope that Mr. Meyer has been saved is now abandoned by his relatives. The message telling of Mrs. Meyer's rescue came from the Carpathia by way of Halifax.

According to the latest information John V. Drew and his nephew, Marshall Drew, of Greenport, L. I., are believed to be among the Titanic victims. Mrs. Drew was saved. Mr. Drew is one of Greenport's best known business men. He is a soloist in the Baptist church choir. His brother and partner, William J. Drew, is now in New York to meet the Carpathia.

Richard Frazer White, of Brunswick, Me., a senior at Bowdoin College, was a passenger on board the ill-fated Titanic. Mr. White and his father, Percival W. White, left New York on board the Olympic March 23 to go to England and return for the benefit of the elder Mr. White's health.

Percival W. White is a member of the firm of Nelson B. White Company, of Winchendon, Mass., cotton manufacturers. The son's college career has been a brilliant one.

M. Frank K. Hays, of No. 304 West Eighty-third street, has received a wireless despatch from his daughter, Miss Margaret Hays, who was one of the passengers on board the Titanic:—

"All safe and well, on board the Carpathia."

Miss Hays' address in the first lists of survivors was Montreal, Canada, and it was thought she was a daughter of Charles M. Hays. Her father said Miss Hays had not been with the other Hays family, but had been travelling with Mrs. Bouton Earnshaw and Mrs. Thomas Potter, Jr. From the message received Mr. Hays believes there is no doubt that Mrs. Earnshaw and Mrs. Potter are among the survivors.

Mrs. Frederick K. Seward and her three children are overjoyed at the fact of her husband's safety aboard the Carpathia. Mr. Seward, who is a member of the law firm of Curtis, Mallet-Prevost & Colt, of New York city, was in England on business with J. Montgomery Smart, who is reported as being among those who were lost. Mrs. Seward was receiving congratulations of friends all of yesterday.

Mrs. F. Joel Swift, of No. 171 Arlington avenue, Brooklyn, who, with her companion, Dr. Alice F. Leader, of No. 340 West 118th street, was rescued from the Titanic and is now aboard the Carpathia, travelled in South American waters and the Mediteranean before she left England aboard the ill fated vessel. Mrs. Swift is president of the Fortnightly Club and the Woman's Benevolent Association. She is the widow of Frederick Joel Swift, a broker.

Mrs. Swift's sister, Mrs. H. S. Ford, of No. 3 East Sixty-first street, thanked the HERALD yesterday for the paper's verification of the safety of Mrs. Swift and Dr. Leader.

Samuel Ward Stanton, one of the Titanic's passengers, is a noted marine architect and decorator, living at No. 506 West Seventy-second street. He had charge of decorating the Robert Fulton of the Hudson Rived Day Line. Several oil paintings by him are on board the Robert Fulton. Mr. Stanton was once proprietor of the Nautical Gazette. He was born in Newberg, N. Y., fifty years ago. He has a wife, two daughters and a son.

Mrs. W. L. Gwinn, of No. 1,215 Kingsley street, Asbury Park, N. J., received news yesterday that her husband, a United States postal clerk on board the Titanic, had gone down.

Mr. Gwinn was one of the five postal clerks aboard three of whom were in the United States postal service.

Direct news of the safety of Mr. and Mrs. C. E. Henry Stengel, of No. 1,075 Broad street, Newark, was received yesterday afternoon by Ivan Stengel. It was in the form of a relayed wireless message sent to Newark from Halifax and read:—

"Both on Carpathia. Have two automobiles to meet Carpathia. Have some survivors with us. HENRY STENGEL."

It is believed that Miss Daisy Minahan, of Green Bay, Wis., and her mother, whose names appear on the list of rescued, are accompanying the Stengels. R. E. Minahan wired from Green Bay to Mr. Stengel to that effect.

Augustus Smith, twenty-two years old, of No. 59 Halsey street, Newark, was added yesterday to the list of New Jersey passengers aboard the Titanic of whom no word has been received. Mr. Smith, who had crossed the ocean several times, had been in Europe for a year visiting a sister in Paris. He intended to return to Newark a month ago, but deferred his trip in order to make it on the maiden voyage of the Titanic.

W. Hull Botsford, of Orange, N. J., who was connected with the engineering department of the Lackawanna Railroad, went abroad in February last and was a second class passenger on board the Titanic. He is well known in athletic affairs of the Young Men's Christian Association and two years ago was Young Men's Christian Association national lightweight wrestling champion. Mr. Botsford was graduated from Cornell University.

Frederick Myles, of No. 266 Grove street, Jersey City, N. J., received yesterday a telegram from his sister, Miss Gertrude Myles, at Cambridge, Mass., which says:—"Papa left on board the Titanic. Safe on board the Carpathia. All well." Their father, Thomas F. Myles, of Cambridge, has been in the employ of the White Star line for forty-five years.

Miss Bertha Ilett, daughter of Edward Ilett, who is connected with the United States quarantine station at Athenia, near Passaic, N. J., is believed to be among those lost. She was a second cabin passenger and left England to visit her father and friends here. Her name does not appear in the list of those saved.

Among the survivors on board the Carpathia are relatives of the Rev. Dr. James Dallas Steele, of Passaic, N. J. They are Mrs. Edward S. Robert, a cousin; her daughter, Miss Georgett Alexandra Madill, and her niece, Miss Elizabeth Walton Allen, all prominent in St. Louis society. Mrs. Robert is a widow. Her first husband was Judge George A. Madill, of St. Louis. Mr. Robert was a prominent banker in the same city. Accompanied by her daughter and niece, she spent ten months in Surrey, England, for her health.

Sigued Anderson, of No. 193 Morningside avenue, Yonkers, is anxiously awaiting news from his brother, A. T. Harry Anderson, thought to have been on board the Titanic. Harry Anderson is assistant superintendent of D. Saunders' Sons machine shop. He and his wife left here February 1 on a visit to Copenhagen. His brother received a letter last week saying he would leave on board the Titanic, but that his wife would stay in Copenhagen another month.

F. C. Goodwin, who with his wife and six children was on his way from England to make his home in Niagara Falls, N. Y., was on board the Titanic, according to word received by his brother, Thomas Goodwin, of that city, yesterday. The Goodwins were to have left on board the Philadelphia, but cancelled their passage and went aboard the Titanic. Their names do not appear among those rescued by the Carpathia.

In order to cross the ocean on board the world's greatest steamship on her first voyage, Walter C. Porter, senior member of the firm of Samuel Porter & Co., of Worcester, Mass., purposely prolonged his stay in England. His name does not appear among the list of Titanic survivors, and relatives in this city have given up hope that he is saved. He is forty-five years old and has a wife and four children. He went to Liverpool three months ago on a business and pleasure trip.

Edward A. Kent, who is a well known architect at Buffalo, N. Y., and whose brother, William Kent, is an architect in New York city, was a passenger on board the Titanic who is not reported among the rescued. Mr. Kent, who is fifty-eight years old, is a son of the late Henry Kent, of the firm of Flint & Kent, department store proprietors, at Buffalo. He makes his home at the Buffalo Club and is a member of the American Institute of Architects. He designed many of the most important buildings in Buffalo, and also the Board of Trade building in Toronto. He was a delegate to the Berlin convention of architects two years ago, and made many trips abroad. He was returning from a two months' stay on the Continent.

If Milton C. Long, Columbia graduate, went down with the Titanic, and his name does not appear among the list of survivors, it was his second steamship wreck in less than a year. He was a passenger last July on board the steamship Spokane, which was wrecked while making a trip to Alaska, and was among those rescued. He is a son of Judge Charles L. Long, of Springfield, Mass. He was preparing to enter the profession of law.

HANANS NOT ON BOARD.

This cable message was received from Paris yesterday by the HERALD, signed by Mr. and Mrs. John Hanan:—"Were not on board the Titanic. Delayed leaving."

CITY FLAGS AT HALF MAST.

Flags on the City Hall were placed at half mast yesterday by order of Mayor Gaynor as an expression of sympathy for the sufferers in the Titanic disaster. The national State colors, as well as the city flags, were lowered.

WIRELESS MEDDLERS DIREFUL MENACE TO SHIPS IN DISTRESS, SAYS EXPERT

"If there were any ship in distress within twenty miles of New York it is quite possible that she might send out all the 'S O S's' she could and not be able to get one through," said A. P. Andersen, wireless operator on board the steamship Hellig Olav, of the Scandinavian-American line, to a HERALD reporter last night. "The air is so full of messages of all sorts, most of which are quite unnecessary, that often it is impossible to work here at all. That is because there is no regulation of the wireless service here.

"In the English Channel, where there are vastly more ships handled than here, work is easy, because it is regulated. Here anybody may operate a wireless outfit. Amateurs and students go into the business for fun and operators carry on unnecessary private conversations with one another. It means that urgent business messages are often swamped."

Wireless Mob Law Will Be Ended by Senate Bill To Be Reported To-Day

Lack of Order at Present Demonstrated by Appeal of Marconi Company for a Temporary Suspension of All Other Operations—Government Will Establish System of Licenses for Individuals and Companies, with Immediate Revocation Clause.

HERALD BUREAU, No. 1,502 H STREET, N. W., WASHINGTON, D. C., Wednesday.

The HERALD has received a copy of the Senate Commerce Committee's bill for the regulation of wireless telegraphy which will be favorably reported to the Senate to-morrow and passed at an early date. It was introduced by Senator Jonathan Bourne, of Oregon, on February 15 and has been carefully considered not only by the Commerce Committee, but by Administration officials with the purpose of ending the wireless mob law that now prevails over the North Atlantic. To the utter absence of any regulation is due the confusion between rival companies, government wireless and the happy-go-lucky practice of amateurs.

The anguish which this aerial chaos has brought to thousands of homes by preventing coherent communication has aroused a public sentiment which is counted upon to assist speedy enactment of the law. Congress has been dilatory with regard to wireless for the Berlin convention of 1906, which was designed to increase its efficiency among the nations, was ratified only a fortnight ago.

A striking evidence of the lack or order was contained in the appeal which the Marconi Company to-day made to the government and other wireless interests to suspend operations in the hope of permitting its operators to establish unbroken communication with the Carpathia.

Provisions of the Bill.

Section one of the perfected Bourne bill provides for a license to be granted by the Secretary of Commerce and Labor.

No messages by wireless shall be sent or received in interstate commerce except under and in accordance with this license, which is revocable for cause; but a license shall not be required for the transmission of radiograms on behalf of the government. But every government station on land sea shall have special call letters designated. Violations of this section are to be punishable by a fine of not exceeding $500 and the apparatus unlawfully used shall be forfeited to the government.

Section two sets forth that licenses shall be issued only to citizens of the United States or to a company organized under the laws of some State; shall indicate the location and ownership of the station and other particulars by which the apparatus may be identified and its range estimated; shall state the purpose of the station and the wave length used or authorized for use by the station to prevent interference and the hours for which the station is licensed for work. Every license shall provide that the President of United States in time of war or peril may close the station or remove the apparatus or may authorize the use and control of any such station or apparatus by any department of the government upon the payment of just compensation to the owners.

Section Three—The station must at all times be in charge or under the supervision of the person licensed, and the person so licensed shall be a citizen of the United States. Failure to obey any of the regulations or conditions imposed by treaties of the United States shall result in a suspension of license, and the license shall not be renewed for a period of one year thereafter.

It shall be unlawful to employ any unlicensed person or for any unlicensed person to serve in charge of the use and operation of such apparatus, and any person violating this provision shall be guilty of a misdemeanor, and on conviction thereof shall be punished by a fine of not more than $100 or imprisonment for not more than two months or both in the discretion of the Court for each and every such offence; provided that in case of emergency the Secretary of Commerce and Labor may authorize a collector of customs to issue a temporary permit in lieu of a license to the operator on a vessel subject to the radio-ship act of June 24, 1910.

To Prevent Interference.

Section 4—That for the purpose of preventing or minimizing interference with communications between stations in which such apparatus is operated to facilitate radio communication, and to further the prompt receipt of distress signals, said private and commercial stations shall be subject to the regulations of this section. These regulations shall be enforced by the Secretary of Commerce and Labor through the collectors of customs and other officers of the government, as other regulations herein provided for.

Then follows a provision that will authorize the Secretary of Commerce and Labor to waive the provisions of any or all of these regulations when no interference of the kind above mentioned will result. This authority to liberalize the rules looks forward to the further development of the science of radio communication. Temporary licenses may be granted to stations engaged in experiments to develop the science or the apparatus used therein, or to carry on special tests using any amount of power or any wave lengths at such hours and under such conditions as will insure the least interference with the sending or receipt of government or commercial radiograms, or distress signals. Naval and military stations shall be understood to be stations on land.

Regulations of the Bill.

Here are the regulations incorporated in the bill:—

Normal Wave Length.—First, every station shall be required to designate a certain definite wave length as the normal sending and receiving wave length of the station; this wave length shall not exceed six hundred meters or it shall exceed one thousand six hundred meters.

Other Wave Lengths.—Second, in addition to the normal sending wave length all stations, except as provided hereafter in these regulations, may use other sending wave lengths, provided that they do not exceed six hundred meters or that they do exceed one thousand six hundred meters; provided further that the character of the waves emitted conform to the requirements of paragraphs three and four following.

MAYORS URGE NEW LAWS FOR SEA TRAVEL

Mayors of thirty-seven cities in New York State yesterday united in petitioning Congress and the President to take up at once the question of enacting laws to safeguard ocean traffic and make impossible another sea tragedy like the one told in the brief history of the Titanic.

The petition was sent to the President with this message:—

"We unite in urging you to send to Congress a special message recommending the speedy enactment of well considered statutes that will require effectually every passenger vessel leaving a port in the United States to be equipped with such life boats or rafts as shall suffice to receive and float every person on board."

Similar messages were sent to the Senate and the House of Representatives. The signatures were obtained by William P. Capes, secretary of the New York State Conference of Mayors, of No. 105 East Twenty-second street. All the Mayors consulted on the subject signed the petitions with the exception of Mr. Gaynor. In explanation it was said at the City Hall that Mr. Gaynor wished to consider the question more in detail before making a suggestion to Congress.

The Mayors who authorized their signatures are:—John K. Sague, Poughkeepsie; Daniel Sheehan, Elmira; James T. Lennon, Yonkers; John Irving, Binghamton; Louis T. Fick, North Tonawanda; Lynn R. Lewis, Cortland; Otto Pfaff, Oneida; E. J. Hanratta, Watervliet; Alden L. Henry, Gloversville; Robert H. Reed, Lackawanna; Timothy Dasey, Little Falls; Francis M. Hugo, Watertown; Dr. George R. Lunn, Schenectady; James B. McEwan, Albany; Frank J. Baker, Utica; J. J. Bolan, Fulton; Frederick A. Ellison, Corning; Rosslyn M. Cox, Middletown; Stewart E. Townsend, Rome; J. B. Corwin, Newburg; F. H. Waldorf, New Rochelle; Abraham Harrison, Johnstown; Reuben H. Gulvin, Geneva; Peter C. Foley, Olean; F. D. Blodgett, Oneonta; Clarence E. Carruth, Cohoes; Thomas Penney, Rensselaer; W. H. Nearpass, Port Jervis; Louis Van Hoesen, Hudson; W. Irving Griffing, Glens Falls; David D. Long, Oswego; Samuel A. Carlson, Jamestown; Charles Zuckmaier, Tonawanda; Hiram H. Edgerton, Rochester; John Reamer, Ithaca; James J. Moran, Lockport, and George E. W. Van Kennon, Ogdensburg.

With these petitions Mr. Capes sent a letter to the Senate and House of Representatives on behalf of several merchants and steamship proprietors suggesting that a resolution be adopted immediately, pending the enactment of new laws, requiring the publication in newspapers of the life boat capacity of all steamships. Jacob W. Miller, vice president of the New England Steamship Company, is one of those interested in this proposal. The letter states that inasmuch as considerable time must be spent in discussing proposed laws the following measure be adopted forthwith:—

"That no vessel larger than 5,000 gross tonnage shall carry passengers from any port in the United States unless prior to her sailing there shall have been advertised the following facts:—

"The number of passengers that she is entitled lawfully to carry, the number of persons other than passengers that she carries usually and the number of persons for the accommodation of which she is provided with life boats or life rafts."

The communication sets forth that if such information were set forth in advertisements the public would be informed on the risks of travel and the proprietors of steamships would be prompted to provide more life boats.

President Inquires for Major Butt

The following wireless despatch which was being sent from the cruiser Salem to the Carpathia was read at the Brooklyn Navy Yard to-night:—

"President of the United States is very anxious to know if Major Butt, Mr. Millet and Mr. Moore are safe. Please inform me so I can transmit to him.

"CHANDLER."

Up to half-past ten o'clock last night the Salem had received no reply.

GAMBLERS PERISH WITH THE TITANIC

Three and possibly five of a band of professional card sharps and confidence men who were aboard the Titanic are known to be among those who went to the bottom of the ocean with the steamship.

News of the drowning of "Tom" McAuliffe, William Dey and "Peaches" Van Camp was received from George Homer and Ralph Bradley, two New York men, who sent wireless messages to friends in this city yesterday afternoon informing them that they were aboard the Carpathia and that McAuliffe, Dey and Van Camp had gone down with the Titanic.

Another wireless message which was received from Homer and Bradley on board the Carpathia by a well known New York sporting man early last evening said that two others, "Buffalo" Murphy and James Gordon, had not been seen aboard the Carpathia and that they, too, must have been drowned.

That the messages are authentic is not doubted by those who received them, as it is known to the recipients that the gamblers were aboard the Titanic when she left Southampton on April 10. Just before leaving one of the band cabled to a friend in New York that they were about to start, and asked the friend to meet the band at the White Star line pier with two taxicabs.

Many Intended to Take Trip.

When the White Star line officials made known the time of leaving of the Titanic on her first voyage more than a score of New York confidence men and gamblers, known to the police of Scotland Yard as well as New York, made a hurried trip to England. Among them was "Bud" Hauser, who died under mysterious circumstances in his cabin on board the Olympic, of the White Star line, on her arrival in New York on April 10, the date of the steaming of the Titanic.

Hauser, it is asserted, left this country with "Frankie" Dwyer, but when they arrived in Southampton they found such an array of "talent" had engaged passage on board the Titanic that they decided they would have a more profitable field on board one of the earlier boats. At the last moment, it is asserted, Dwyer changed his mind about going on board the Olympic, and it is now believed that he, too, took passage on board the Titanic.

Friends of the men in New York declare that at least three bands of card sharps weer aboard the Titanic when she left. None was booked under his real name, as that is not the custom with ocean gamblers. Usually they book passage under names that have some phonetic relation to the names by which they are known in New York, so that in the event of a mishap their friends will be informed in time to render assistance when they reach their destination.

Expected Easy Picking.

Because of the large number of wealthy persons that it was expected would travel on board the Titanic, McAuliffe, who was the brains of the band, had expressed the belief that the "boobs" would be "easy picking" for the confidence men. Just how much success attended the confidence men up to the time the Titanic struck the iceberg will only be made known when the Carpathia arrives with the survivors.

Efforts to learn something about the relatives of the drowned gamblers were unsuccessful last night. Men of their type seldom speak of their family relations. As a rule they claim to be the sons of wealthy men, but this assertion is so common that little confidence is placed in it. Those who received the messages from Homer and Bradley say they have not the slightest knowledge concerning the families of the men.

$8,000,000 COST IN INSURANCE FOR TITANIC DEATHS

Accident Companies, Under Double Liability Clause, May Have to Pay $3,000,000.

REGULAR POLICIES AT LEAST $5,000,000

Actuaries Already Figuring Sums That Become Due by Loss of Wealthy Men.

QUESTIONS FOR LAWYERS

Opinions Advanced as to the Liability of the Steamship Owners for Damages.

According to P. A. S. Franklin, vice president of the White Star line, that company carried the Titanic on its books at a valuation of $7,500,000, and stands to lose about $3,000,000 with the sinking of the vessel. Lawyers versed in questions affecting the owners of foundered vessels expressed the belief yesterday that the liabilities of the steamship company to the survivors and families of those who perished, owing to the peculiarity of the Titanic disaster, presented many new features and might develop legal precedents in their solution.

Accident insurance authorities said that in the last forty-eight hours the great accident insurance companies had been called upon to issue unusual numbers of new policies as a direct result of the marine catastrophe. While the Titanic affair has stimulated their business, the companies are confronted with the necessity of paying enormouus sums under the "double liability clause" of their policies already issued. This requires the concerns to pay double death benefits in cases where the insured lost their lives when travelling in conveyances propelled by steam or electricity.

Insurance actuaries are busily engaged in figuring the prospective losses they must sustain if most of the well to do or wealthy men who were aboard the Titanic have really perished.

Carried a ig Policy.

It is stated that the estate of Mr. Charles M. Hays, president of the Grand Trunk Railroad, would realize at least $100,000 on the accident policy he carried.

It is estimated that accident claims arising from the disaster may amount to $3,000,000 directly as a consequence of the double liability clause. This is aside from the ordinary life insurance policies that were carried by those who lost their lives, and which have been estimated to amount to at least $5,000,000 additional. Furthermore, the accident insurance concerns may be called upon to pay large sums covering the illness of persons who have lost their health either permanently or temporarily as a result of the shipwreck.

Members of the marine insurance companies learned yesterday that the foreign underwriters had received even smaller premiums than had been reported in taking risks on the Titanic. It had been regarded as a splendid risk from the fact that the vessel had been looked upon as practically unsinkable. Then, moreover, the policies contained a clause that obligated the owners of the vessel to pay a premium of only one per cent, instead of three per cent, in case the owners themselves assumed the first $750,000 of the risk.

Moses H. Grossman, of the firm of House, Grossman & Vorhaus, No. 115 Broadway, who was counsel for the survivors of the General Slocum, when asked yesterday for his opinion respecting the legal liability of the owners of the Titanic to the survivors and families of those who perished, said:—

"Prior to 1884 ship owners were subject to unlimited liability for all accidents. This system of law was found to be too exacting and to discourage shipping, for the reason that owners of many vessels faced financial ruin if, as a result of a single accident, they were required to pay in full the tremendous loss sustained.

Congress Limited Liability.

"The Harter act, passed in 1884 by Congress, sought to encourage ship owners and merchantmen by allowing them to limit their liability as a result of accidents. The Harter act allowed vessels causing the daamge and at fault to become forfeited as a fund for the claimants. In other words, the vessel that was guilty of an act causing the damage was sold and the proceeds or fund resulting therefrom became a sum of money in which all claimants might share. It will, therefore, be seen that a man or corporation owning a number of vessels, while losing one ill fated vessel, would still be permitted to carry on his business with other vessels, limiting his liability to the vessel at fault.

"However the case of the Titanic presents many new features which will, undoubtedly, develop new law in their solution. Few cases are in the records of vessels being entirely lost through purely outside causes. Vessels have struck icebergs before, have run on reefs, have struck submerged derelicts and other obstructions without, however, being totally lost.

"In my opinion, under the American law, the loss of the entire vessel naturally would prevent any limitation of liability, but the English act allows the court to estimate a tonnage valuation just before the accident and fix that amount as the amount which the owners must make up to the creditors or claimants against the vessel. In other words, the owners must establish a fund equal in amount to the sound value of the vessel. It would, therefore, seem that actions instituted in the English courts would result in settlements in favor of the claimants.

Contracts Were English.

"The contract of passage by the travellers on the Titanic were English contracts, the tickets being purchased abroad, and any claim for damage would, necessarily and properly, by litigable in the English courts.

"I am further of the opinion that any insurance which the owners might have on the vessel cannot be reached by claimants as their contract of insurance is a collateral undertaking and its benefit would inure in favor of claimants. There are many claims which would take priority over the claims of the passengers. Salvage, which is sure to be a very large item in this case, would come first, followed by wages due to seamen and those employed in the navigation of the vessel, but if actions were instituted in the English courts, there would have to be provided a very large fund from which claimants might expect their losses to be paid."

WORLD LAWS FOR LIFEBOATS AND SEA SAFEGUARDS URGED

Urges the Hague Tribunal to Adopt World Embracing Rules to Safeguard Travel

Nations' Laws so at Variance, Says Charles von Helmolt, the North German Lloyd Agent, International Board Should Take a Hand.

AID SOCIETY WOULD HOLD DEFICIENT CRAFT

WANTS WORLD'S PEACE COURT TO ADOPT UNIFORM SAFETY RULES FOR STEAMSHIPS

Because the various maritime nations are so widely at variance in their requirements for the safeguarding of steamship passengers at sea, Charles von Helmolt, American representative of the North German Lloyd Steamship Company and formerly its passenger director at Bremen, announced his advocacy of a scheme to have the Hague Tribunal take up the matter immediately and adopt such joint regulations as may insure greater safety and worldwide uniformity.

"With the laws of every nation at variance regarding the safety of passengers on board steamships, I believe the proper solution is to have the Hague Tribunal take up the matter immediately and adopt such joint regulations as would insure as nearly absolute safety as is possible and under which all steamship companies of every nation would be compelled to operate."

This view was expressed yesterday by Charles von Helmolt, general manager for Oelrichs & Co., general agents of the North German Lloyd Steamship Company, and formerly passenger director of the company at Gremen. He continued:—

"It is a matter which demands international agreement. Take for instance a company like the North German Lloyd. It must conform to the maritime laws and regulations of no less than four countries in carrying passengers between New York and Germany. Our steamships have Bremen as a home port and are under the jurisdiction of Germany; by touching at Southampton they come within the regulation and laws of England; at Cherbourg, where passengers from Paris come aboard, the French maritime laws apply and by finally landing in New York there are the American laws to be complied with.

"No company is more anxious to see absolute safety assured all passengers and crew than is the North German Lloyd. This company has not only complied with the letter of the laws, but in every case has even exceeded the legal requirements in providing for the safety of its passengers. Every proposition which has been advanced—no matter by whom—has been carefully and painstakingly investigated and is found to have real worth has been immediately adopted. This is true not only of the North German Lloyd, but of all other steamship lines.

"With the coming of the wireless telegraph, water tight compartments, submarine signals, improved fire fighting apparatus and the other devices of the last ten years, the steamship companies have believed the margin of safety to be practically perfect.

Full Complement Seldom Carried.

"In the case of life boats and life raft equipment it should be remembered that there is seldom a steamship arriving at or departing from New York city that carries its maximum number of passengers. When the season rush begins for Europe in April, May, June and July, the cabin accommodation is filled, but during these months the steerages are practically deserted, for it is at this time that the outdoor construction work of the great companies is being carried on. The foreign labor element is then fully employed. This labor comes over from Europe in the early months of the year, when there is little or no cabin business.

"When the outward bound steerage business increases late in the fall of the year the cabin rush to Europe is over.

"Taking into consideration these facts, the lifeboat and life raft equipment had been considered by the American, German, French and English governments as ample. In most cases the steamship companies have even exceeded the rigid requirements of the various governments, but if it is considered that even this is inadequate all companies would stop at no end to more fully safeguard their passengers as far as is practicable.

"Certainly the safety of human life is vastly of more importance than the settlement of sealing rights or of boundary disputes, which subjects were so skilfully handled at the Dutch capital.

"The Hague Tribunal is peculiarly fitted to deal with this situation. The interests of the various countries are so closely interwoven that it is hard to differentiate between their legal requirements. Thus could the Hague Tribunal formulate recommendations which would carefully cover every point now contained in the laws of the different countries.

Companies Would Co-operate.

"The steamship companies, I know, would gladly co-operate to the fullest extent in carrying out any idea or project which would make for greater safety at sea."

P. A. S. Franklin, resident vice president of the White Star line, refused to add anything to the complete information published by the HERALD yesterday as to the Tinanic's inadequate equipment of life boats and life rafts. He declared, however, as already stated by the HERALD to be the fact, that she was supplied with as many life boats as the British Board of Trade required and a considerable number in excess of that quota.

"Nobody ever imagined that such a disaster could happen," said Mr. Franklin. "We had believed the Titanic to be absolutely safe, and so did Lloyd's when they insured her at the lowest rate."

"But, in view of the lesson taught by this disaster, do you not think a larger number of lifeboats and life rafts should be carried?" he was asked.

"You may rest assured," Mr. Franklin replied, "that whatever improvements over present methods and standards may be found necessary to make every ship absolutely safe will be installed."

Captain Smith Was Dubious.

That Captain Edward J. Smith, master of the Titanic, believed that his ill-starred vessel was inadequately equipped with life saving facilities is the statement made, according to a press association despatch from Chicago by Glenn Marston, of that city. Mr. Marston said that while he was returning from Europe aboard the Olympic, when Captain Smith was in command of that ship, he had commented upon what seemed to him the small number of lifeboats carried by the vessel. The Titanic was then under construction.

"I noticed the small number of boats and rafts aboard for the heavy passenger carrying capacity of the ship and remarked upon it to Captain Smith," said Mr. Marston.

"'Yes,' he replied, 'if the ship should strike a submerged derelict or an iceberg that would cut through into several watertight compartments we have not enough boats or rafts aboard to take care of more than one-third of the passengers. The Titanic, too, is no better equipped. It ought to carry at least double the number of boats and rafts to afford any real protection to the passengers. Besides, there is always danger of some of the boats becoming damaged or swept away before they can be manned.'"

Mr. Marston further quoted Captain Smith as saying he thought the lack of equipment was not due to a desire of the owners to save money, but rather was because they believed the ships to be safe.

"If there has been culpability in this matter," said A. Gips, general agent of the Holland-America line, "the burden of the blame should rest upon the laws and regulations of the various countries and not upon the steamship companies that have complied with those regulations, inadequate as they may now appear in the light of this astounding disaster, the like of which has not been regarded heretofore as possible.

"But the condition now revealed is one that must be faced. There are difficulties in the way of compelling the largest steamships to carry the thirty or forty full sized life boats that would be necessary to afford accommodations for their maximum carrying capacity, a capacity which, by the way, is not often attained in actual cruising experience. But I do not see that these difficulties are necessarily insurmountable.

Listing Affects Boat Launching.

"More space, of course, would have to be devoted to the carrying of boats, and the only place where they can be carried is upon the boat deck, but it might be found feasible to install a double instead of a single row of boats in suitable position for launching from the davits. Unfortunately in cases of collision at sea the mishap is often attended by such a serious list either to starboard or to port that the launching of the entire complement of boats on one side of the vessel becomes a physical impossibility. In the event of danger arising from fire at sea, however, or any other crisis during which the ship maintains an even keel the entire quota of boats would be available.

"There are several types of collapsible lifeboats constructed of canvas and wood which are approved by the highest authorities and which are in general use. When 'nested' these occupy much less space aboard a ship than do the ordinary lifeboats. The more extensive use of some such appliances might overcome the objection raised against lack of room on the boat deck.

"The maritime regulations of Holland in the matter of life boats are more modern and more stringent than are those of Great Britain, though, perhaps, less stringent than are those of the United States. Ships of our line have always gone further than a mere compliance with the regulations. If the Titanic disaster proves that the present standards of safety are too low then the laws should be changed to raise that standard. There is now no body that has power to deal with the international regulation of this matter, but I believe there should be such regulation. It might perhaps be accomplished through regular diplomatic channels."

The New Amsterdam Well Equipped.

Mr. Gips called attention to the fact that in a table printed yesterday a typographical error made it appear that the New Amsterdam, one of the steamships of the Holland-American line carried no life preservers. The fact is that she has no less than 3,447 life preservers, which is more than enough to supply one each to the greatest number of persons she can carry.

O. L. Richards, of C. B. Richards & Co., agents for the Lloyd-Italiano, also admitted frankly the inadequacy of the present requirements. "Those provisions may have been all right in former days," he said, "but we have outgrown them. It looks as though the present outcry might lead to the taking of some sort of efficient international action, and I believe that would be a good thing."

The Legal Aid Society, which has always befriended the seaman and the immigrant, yesterday sent out this announcent:—

"It is generally admitted that the loss of 1,410 lives on board the Titanic was due to gross carelessness. This appalling disaster shows that on board this newest and greatest of all ships there were lifeboats only for one passenger in three. A similar disproportion between the capacity of the lifeboats and the number of passengers prevailed on board the Olympic, her sister ship, which left New York last Saturday under certificate of the United States supervising inspectors of steam vessels setting forth that the steamship had such number of lifeboats and life saving appliances as would best secure the safety of all persons on board. As a matter of fact, the lifeboats of the Olympic are sufficient to hold only a few more than a quarter of the men, women and children on the vessel.

"Had this appalling disaster not happened, the Titanic, like the Olympic, would have been permitted to leave this port with lifeboat accommodations sufficient for about one in four of the number who had booked on board the Titanic, with a certificate of the United States supervising inspectors that sufficient lifeboats and life savnig appliances had been provided to secure the safety of all passengers. Without such a certificate no clearance papers could have been issued by the Collector of the Port to the Olympic or the Titanic.

"Under the revised statutes of the United States the great liners that come into this port—even though they carry the British flag—are subject to the provisions of the United States law and to the rules and regulations of the Board of Supervising Inspectors of the United States.

American Law Ambiguous.

"Unfortunately, the law of the United States on this point is ambiguous. It provides that "all foreign steamers carrying passengers from any port of the United States to any country shall be provided with such number of life boats, floats, rafts and life preservers as will best secure the safety of all persons on board such vessels in case of disaster.' The wording of this law affords the loophole to the United States officials. It includes life preservers in the life saving equipment. The owners of the Titanic will no doubt claim that the steamship had a sufficient number of life preservers on board for all passengers. As a matter of fact, life preservers were inadequate in this disaster, as no human being could live for any length of time in the icy sea.

"Large modern steamships generally do not carry life boats and life rafts sufficient for all persons. The companies take the risk, relying on the theory, which has proven fallacious in the case of the Titanic, that a modern big liner is safe and unsinkable. They stake the lives of passengers and crew on the chance of the unsinkableness of the steamship.

Foresaw a Disaster.

"Among the 1,410 lives reported lost were a large number of seamen and immigrants. The Legal Aid Society, which maintains a Seamen's Branch at No. 1 Broadway and an Immigration Branch at No. 127 Madison avenue, has made it its special duty to see, among other things, that sailors and immigrants are properly protected while on the high sea. It seems the Legal Aid Society has had some prophetic apprehension, for in its last annual report, adopted in February of this year, the matter of lifeboats and life saving appliances on board seagoing vessels was fully considered. In recommending for enactment, House of Representatives bill No. 11,372 the Legal Aid Society advised the Congressional Committee on Merchant Marine and Fisheries to embody in this bill a provision:—

"'That all vessels shall be adequately supplied at the port of departure with boats and crews able numerically and qualified to handle such vessels and man the boats and that all vacancies caused by casualty or desertion be promptly supplied with full complement of qualified seamen.'

"Had this recommendation been acted upon, as it is proposed to do now, the sad result of the disaster that befell the Titanic might have been materially lessened or modified.

"The Legal Aid Society contemplates sending a committee to Washington to urge upon Congress to either have the law changed as to impose more stringent regulations upon all ships leaving American ports or to have new rules and regulations made by the supervising steam vessel inspectors under the existing law in order to make the life boat and other life saving equipment of every ship sufficient for the number of passengers and crew, so that all persons on board a steamship might hope to live afloat for some time, even if the ship went down, as the Titanic did, in an icy but calm sea. The president of the society insists that no clearance papers be issued to any ocean steamship that is not provided with life boats sufficient to hold every human being for the trip for which clearance is sought."

Lives Not Considered, Admiral Dewey Says, in the Greed for Money Making

Declares No Passenger Vessel Should Be Cleared Unless She Has Enough Boats to Care for Great Majority of Passengers—Calls His Experience with Icebergs Worse Than Storming Forts in War.

HERALD BUREAU,
No. 1,502 H STREET, N. W.,
WASHINGTON, D. C., Wednesday.

"I think that every passenger who crosses the North Atlantic takes his life in his hands," said Admiral Dewey today to a HERALD reporter. "For myself, I would rather go around the world in a well equipped man of war than make a trip across the North Atlantic in a transatlantic vessel.

"The greed for money making is so great that it is with the sincerest regret that I observe that human lives are never taken into consideration.

"Let all good Americans exert every energy to have the present laws amended as regards life saving appliances on board every passenger carrying vessel.

"I do not believe that a passenger vessel should be cleared unless she has boats sufficient to float the great majority of her precious cargo in the event of an accident. It is appalling to think that the Olympic when she struck the Hawke, according to reports, had boats sufficient to carry only one out of every six passengers.

"In 1871 when I was commander of the store ship Supply, carrying provisions to the starving French, we sailed from New York on March 2. Not long after, by the temperature, we felt we were in the neighborhood of icebergs, but all the books on the subject indicated that they never had travelled so far south. One night about nine o'clock the first lieutenant, August Kellogg, and I were in the cabin when we heard the officer of the deck give the order, 'Hard up the helm.'

"We knew some danger was imminent, but I never gave icebergs a thought. I feared a collision with another sailing craft. I hurried to the deck, and had the 'pleasure' of gazing on a collection of icebergs about the size of the Capitol. Every soul on board was on deck, and every soul was letting go a rope, and we were like a runaway horse in a crowded thoroughfare.

"Fortunately our craft was about the size of a catboat as compared with a vessel of the dimensions of the unfortunate Titanic, and we spent the rest of the night dodging icebergs. The passage of the forts at New Orleans, the battle at Port Huron and the battle at Manila Bay were not in it as compared with that night dodging icebergs.

"The most unfortunate part of the fatality is that most of the drowned are Americans, and we Americans surely have some rights in the matter. It is very easy to picture an American of the type of Major Archibald Butt, one of God's noblemen, doing all he can to insure the safety of the women and children on board the Titanic, knowing that within a very short time he will face his Creator.

"I sincerely hope Congress will attend to the matter of caring for the lives of passengers aboard our transatlantic vessels. Is there any need for a more striking example?"

W. T. Stead Had Described His Own Fate in a Story

In Tale Written in 1892 Victim of the Titanic Pictures a Collision Between a Steamship of the White Star Line and an Iceberg.

REFERS TO THE ATLANTIC OCEAN AS A GRAVE

Intimate friends in this country of William T. Stead, of London, who up to a late hour last night had not been reported among the survivors of the Titanic, recalled yesterday a story which he himself wrote in the Christmas extra issue of the Review of Reviews, London, published in December, 1892, entitled "From the Old World to the New," a chapter of which tallies in almost every detail with the wreck of the Titanic.

Mr. Stead, for whom all hope has been abandoned, in this chapter, which is called "Coincident and Clairvoyage," describes an encounter with icebergs at sea. His characters are a group of English tourists on their way to the Chicago World's Fair. They are crossing the Atlantic on board the Majestic, of the White Star line. The steamship suddenly comes upon a great iceberg.

The great English writer, long known for his ideas on spiritualism, clairvoyance and mental telepathy, brings all into play in his thrilling story of the high sea, but when he describes the icebergs, fog and conditions of sky and sea and on board the Majestic it would seem that had he been able to send an account of what took place last Sunday evening it could not have been more identical.

"Jack" Compton, a passenger, has the power of automatic writing. Compton rereives a telepathis message from John Thomas, a Scotchman, who is an old friend, that he (Thomas) has been saved in the wreck of the Montrose, which was in collision with an iceberg. The messages continut to come. Meanwhile Mr. Compton has asked the captain of the Majestic to stop at the iceberg on arrival. The old captain scoffs at the idea. But then his own vessel comes within a hair's-breadth of being drecked by an iceberg. He stops. Compton and "the professor" put out in a lifeboat and eventually reach John Thomas, finding him almost dead. They bring him salefly to the Majestic just as it seemed that steamship would go under.

The setting of the story and the descriptions of the icebergs and the wreck tally with the tragedy of Sunday night. The time and place also agree with those of last Sunday's catastrophe. It also was on a vessel of the White Star line, and the captain had under his care just two thousand souls and a cargo worth at least $2,000,000. Perhaps the only difference was that Mr. Stead's mental telepathy has been replaced with wireless telegraphy.

"Then dense cold fog filled theair," wrote Mr. Stead. "You breahed it and swallowed it. On deck all was strained attention. The captain on the bridge kept constant lookout. Every half minute the fog whistle bloomed its great voice into the fog sometimes as from a far away distance they heard the boom of another fog horn. But they could see nothing. At the bows the deck lookout peered into impenetrable midst and the quarter master posted to the leeward and lowered the thermometer in a little canvas bag to test the temperature.'

Describes an Iceberg.

Then Mr. Stead has one of his characters describe one of these terrors of the sea.

"Icebergs are mountains of ice floating about in the sea," he says. "Ice, you know, does not sink in water. The icebergs float just a little above the surface. All the rest is below. These icebergs are born in Greenland. The snow falls on the highland, and as it does not melt and ever more and more snow falls, the great mass presses the lowest snow downward and ever downward to the sea. Thus glaciers are formed, slowly moving solid rivers of frozen and solidified snow. When the glacier pushes its way into the sea, its end breaks off, tumbles over into the water with a noise like thunder and becomes an iceberg. The glaciers are constantly making icebergs. The icebergs drift slowly away into the sea. Sometimes they get cought by frost and are winter bound. When summer comes they drift off again into the current which carries them southward. A whole archipeloga of icebergs will sometimes sail southward right across the ocean route to America.

"It is the greatest danger in the voyage, for the icebergs bring fogs with them, and the fogs hide the icebergs until the steamer is close upon them.

"Imagine a country as big as Ireland without light-houses, fog horns or any other beacons, suddenly towed across the path of the steamer and then enveloped in a dense frost-fog, and then you can imagine what the danger is."

Tells of the Collision.

"Hark! what was that?" Mr. Stead has a voyager ask here. And his descripion of what took place goes on:—

"There was a sound as if the steamer were crashing through ice and the screws were churning away amid the ice blocks. The passengers felt their way cautiously to the dock. It was wet and clammy and bitterly cold. Every half minute the fog whistle blew. The crashing of the flow ice against the sides of the ship and the clamping of the ice under the screws made it difficult to speak so as to be heard."

"Then there came a cry, 'Icebergs on the starboard!'

"The engine bell rang, the engines slowed down in their speed, the steamer steered a trifle more to the southward, but still kept pounding her way onward. The captain could only see ghostly shadows looming darkly to the northward.

"He pointed to a great flotilla of icebergs. Behind the steamer the fog was as thick as a blanket. On the north stretched the dazzling array of icebergs, ever shifting and moving. Now and again a great berg would capsize with a reverberant roar. The captain was cowed. There was something uncanny and awesome about the incident. He had seen icebergs before, but he had seldom had such good luck as to pass clear by the southern edge of a flow and then have a clear sky.

"The Majestic was now once again driving ahead at full speed. All the passengers were on deck eyeing the novel and majestic spectacle."

Later, in telling of the rescue of the castaway in the lifeboat, Mr. Stead writes:—

"Denser and denser grew the fog, but they could see the Majestic right before them. And in another moment they were alongside. Just as they reached the ship they heard a long roar like the reverberation of part of artillerq. And then the water heaved violently and dashed the lifeboat heavily aagainst the side of the Majestic. There was a moment of agonizing suspense. No one knew whether the displacement in the iceberg might not lead to a sudden upheaval of the iceberg under the keel of th Majestic. Then the boat's crew were brought safely to deck."

Striking sentences here and there from other writings of Mr. Stead are also recalled in which it might seem that he had some premonition of his own fate. Especially is this so of a comparison in his book, "How I Know the Dead Return," which has a paragraph beginning, "Let us consider the Atlantic ocean as the grave." Then the autor compares one shore with earth and the other with the Eternal shore.

MRS. GEORGE RHEIMS SAFE.

Mrs. Harry Rheims, head of the millinery house of Leon Rheims & Co., No. 417 Fifth avenue, is puzzled over the list of survivors on board the steamship Carpathia, which gives the names of George Rheims and also of Mrs. George Rheims. Mr. Rheims knew that his brother had engaged passage on board the Titanic, but was not expecting his sister-in-law to come to New York. He sent a cable despatch to Paris, the home of the family, and received a reply from Mrs. George Rheims to the effect that her husband had gone to America, but that she had remained behind.

Captain Sims Condemns Luxury at Cost of Safety

Navy Officer Writes the Herald Urging the Public to Demand More Safety Appliances—Calls Bridge Barge Most Practical.

TO THE EDITOR OF THE HERALD:—

It is stated in the press dispatches of this morning that the disaster to the steamship Titanic demonstrates two things—namely, that no ocean steamship is unsinkable and that a steamship's boats will not carry all of her passengers and crew. It did not require this great sacrifice of life and property to demonstrate either.

The Titanic had, I believe, about thirty transverse bulkheads, but, no matter how many bulkheads there may be, they cannot keep a ship from sinking if her entire side is ripped open by collision with a large ship, as in the case of the Bourgogne, or by an iceberg, as was probably the case with the Titanic. As for the capacity of a steamship's "life boats," catamarans, &c., that can be determined with entire accuracy by a simple inspection.

The truth of the matter is that in case any large passenger steamship sinks, by reason of collision or other fatal damage to her flotability, more than half of her passengers are doomed to death, even in fair weather, and in case there is a bit of a sea running none of the loaded boats can long remain afloat, even if they succeed in getting safely away from the side, and one more will be added to the long list of "the ships that never return."

Most people accept this condition as one of the inevitable perils of the sea, but I believe it can be shown that the terrible loss of life occasioned by such disasters as overtook the Bourgogne and the Titanic and many other ships can be avoided or at least greatly minimized. Moreover, it can be shown that the steamship owners are fully aware of the danger to their passengers; that the laws on the subject of life saving appliances are wholly inadequate; that the steamship companies comply with the law, though they oppose any changes therein, and that they decline to adopt improved appliances because there is no public demand for them, the demand being for high schedule speed and luxurious conditions of travel.

Life Saving Appliance Test.

All of this was clearly brought out by the competition for the Pollok Memorial Prize at the Paris Exposition of 1900. Mr. and Mrs. Anthony Pollok, of Washington, D. C., were lost, with all of the first class passengers, in the Bourgogne disaster. Three of their heirs, Mmes. Parif, Richlieu and Ostheimer, of Paris, offered a prize of 100,000f. for the best means of saving life at sea. More than three thousand appliances were submitted in competition. Being at the time Naval Attaché at the Paris Embassy, I was requested by the Pollok heirs to manage the competition for them. I received and installed all the appliances at the exposition. The authorities of the exposition appointed me a member of the "jury," the judges of the competition. The special jury for this purpose comprised (as I now remember its composition) the directors of the life saving services of Great Britain, France, Russia and some other countries, representatives of the chambers of commerce of London, Paris, Antwerp and a number of other commercial centres and several representatives of steamship associations. The deliberations of the jury brought out the following facts:—

In no case were any large passenger steamships provided with sufficient boats to float, even in smooth water, more than half their passengers and crews.

No passenger steamships carry regular crews for their "life boats." In many cases it was found that there were less men (deck hands—sailors) than there were boats. Moreover, these men are in most cases discharged at the end of each trip and a new crew shipped for the next trip, and in consequence they are often without experience in handling the ship's boat equipment.

There were submitted for competition models of steel boats which, in the opinion of the jury, would safely carry more than sixty passengers, were unsinkable, could not be crushed against the ship in lowering, were suspended from strong built-up davits, were rigged so that one inexperienced man could lower a loaded boat by turning the handle of a winch that could not be turned the wrong way, could be released from the single wire "falls" from which they were suspended by pulling a trigger in the boat on approaching the water, contained water and provisions in watertight compartments and that were fully equipped with oars and sails.

7. These boats were, however, but the secondary means of life saving. The principal appliances, presented by the same competitor, an Englishman, whose name, I believe, was Roper, and to whom the only prize was awarded by the jury, may be briefly described as a barge, or flat boat, about forty feet wide and as long as the width of the ship carrying it. This flat boat was strongly built of steel, had an outer and inner bottom about five feet apart, with numerous cellular compartments between them, a low deck house for the protection of women and children, water tight compartments, containing food, water and blankets, was fitted with sails, &c. The boat was installed in place of and served as the ship's bridge and was so mounted that two men could get it overboard in about three minutes. One turned a winch (that would not turn the wrong way) to lower that end of the boat which was toward the low side of the ship, and another released a friction clamp that permitted it to slide overboard.

Barge Most Successful Appliance.

The details of the appliances for launching were simple (strong automatic launching ways that were lowered in place by the action of the winch that lowered the end of the boat), but could hardly be explained clearly without a sketch. Suffice it to say, however, that not only did the jury consider it practicable and worthy of the only prize given, but there was also submitted by the British expert convincing testimony of the success of a similar boat, or barge, that was fitted to the British man-of-war Prometheus (as I remember the name).

The dimensions of such a boat carried by a steamship of ordinary breadth of beam, the boat being as long as the breadth of beam, would be such that the jury estimated that it would safely support six hundred people in any seaway. Of course the larger the steamship, the greater her beam, the greater the lngth of the boat and the greater its carrying capacity.

If the Titanic had been fitted with three or four of these bridge boats, with the accompanying steel lifeboats above indicated, the rescuing steamship called to her assistance by wireless would have found her 2,200 passengers safely on board of them in not too great discomfort.

Such an equipment would have cost considerably more than the cheap and unseaworthy "lifeboats" and catamarans now provided, but much less than the tennis court, the Turkish baths, Bavarian restaurant and other luxuries.

Why, therefore, are they not provided? The reason is a simple one. It is the same old question of demand and supply and the financial considerations involved in the competition for trade. The steamship companies are not in the passenger carrying business for their health. They naturally take every means to attract custom and to keep down expenses, and they consequently limit their life saving appliances to the minimum required by law. For the same reason they oppose new laws requiring more expensive appliances. Because if, for example, Great Britain forces her shipowners to expend for the purpose thousands of pounds a steamship more than the German law requires the British owner is placed at a great disadvantage in competition.

"Must Keep Down Expenses."

Let me illustrate this point by recounting the substance of a statement made to me in Paris in 1900 by a gentleman interested in a large steamship line. I asked him why his company opposed the introduction of such appliances as that presented by Roper. He replied:—

"If we installed them we would not thereby attract an additional passenger. God knows I would like to see them supplied to all steamships, and we would gladly do so under an international agreement obliging all competitive steamship lines to do the same; that is, to incur the same expense, but, as it is, if we want to stay in the business we must keep down expenses and we must supply what the public wants—that is, speed and luxury.

"We cannot afford expensive life saving gear that other companies do not have to use, and, in the absence of uniform laws on the seubject, we will be obliged to wait until it will pay us to make ocean travel safer—that is, until the travelling public understands the present danger and demands that it be minimized. When the public seeks information as to which are the safest steamship lines there will then be competition as to which line can first get safety appliances installed and as to which can improve them the fastest."

If you are thinking of taking a trip abroad, go on board any of the great transactlantic line steamships and get the following information:—Number of passengers carried? How many boats and catamarans carried and the capacity of each? How many deck hands a boat? Are the deck hands trained men? Are they permanent employees? Are the boats on deck or ready for lowering?

Ask yourself also how long you think the boats would live in a seaway, how you would like to take your chances on a catamaran, and how long you think you could stand exposure in either.

Risk of Sea Travel.

You do not need to be a seaman to get a good idea of the condition of affairs. You will readily understand that every one who crosses the ocean this summer must accept the distinct risk of perishing miserably in case the vessel carrying him sinks from any cause, and, roughly speaking, the larger the steamship the greater the risk in case of collision, because generally the large steamships have a boat capacity for a smaller proportion of their crews than steamships of less size, and the faster the steamship the more the danger, at least until the craze for quick passages abates and eprmits steamships to lay their courses clear of the dangerous ice fields. Men probably will never be able to build ships that will withstand running into, running over or scraping by great masses of ice.

In addition to installing efficient lfe saving appliances, if the great steamship lines should come to an agreement to fix a maximum speed for their vessels of various classes and fix their dates and hours of steaming so that they would cross the ocean in pairs within supporting distances of each other, on routes clear of ice, all danger of ocean travel would practically be eliminated.

The shortest course between New York and the English Channel lies across Nova Scotia and Newfoundland. Consequently, the shortest water route is over seas where navigation is dangerous by reason of fog and ice. It is a notorious fact that the transatlantic steamships are not navigated with due regard to safety; that they steam at practically full speed in the densest fogs. But the companies cannot properly be blamed for this practice, because if the "blue liners" slow down in a fog or take a safe route, clear of ice, the public will take passage on the "green liners," which take the shortest route, and keep up their schedule time, regardless of the risks indicated.

WM. S. SIMS, Captain, U. S. Navy.
NEWPORT, R. I., April 16, 1912.

"ICEBERG PATROL" IDEA MEETS FAVOR AND CONGRESS MAY ACT

Patrol of the Ice Fields Suggested in the Herald Is Urged in Congress

Representatives Alexander, of Missouri, and Levy, of New York, Present Resolutions Calling for International Agreement to Safeguard Ocean Travel.

CONFERENCE OF NATIONS IS PROPOSED

HERALD BUREAU,
No. 1,502 H STREET, N. W.,
WASHINGTON, D. C., Wednesday.

As the horrors of the wreck of the Titanic were realized more fully by members of Congress an avalanche of bills and resolutions proposing investigations and legislation to make ocean steamships safer descended to-day upon the Secretary of the Senate and the Clerk of the House.

Measures proposed to regulate the sending of wireless messages so as to prevent interference by amateurs or commercial companies in time of disasters at sea, to require vessels to have sufficient lifeboats to accommodate both passengers and crew, to establish a more southerly steamship lane and create, by international agreement, a patrol of the North Atlantic ocean during the season of icebergs as advocated in the HERALD.

Two resolutions were introduced in the house embodying the project for an international patrol. One was by Representative Joshua W. Alexander, of Missouri, chairman of the Committee on Merchant Marine and Fisheries, and the other by Representative Jefferson Levy, of New York city.

Urges Nations to Co-operate.

Mr. Alexander's is a joint resolution which will have to be passed by both the House and Senate and signed by the President. There seems to be no doubt that this will be done. It authorizes the President to invite maritime nations to co-operate with the United States in the maintenance of a joint patrol by suitable vessels, to be paid for by the governments principally concerned, just north of the steamship lanes. The patrol is to watch for and report to ships and land stations upon the movements of all icebergs and floes.

Mr. Levy's resolution is as follows:—

"Resolved, That the Secretary of State be and is directed to immediately open negotiations with the maritime nations of the world for the purpose of establishing an international patrol along the steamship lanes of the North Atlantic Ocean and for the purpose of agreeing upon an international wireless regulation, and to make such further regulations compelling the carrying of all modern marine and life saving appliances on ocean going vessels as may be necessary to safeguard life."

Representative John J. Kindred, of New York city, after consultation with Benjamin S. Cable, Assistant Secretary of Commerce and Labor, introduced a bill to strike from section 4,400 of the United States Revised Statutes the proviso exempting foreign vessels from the operation of the American steamboat inspection laws.

"This will settle the matter," said Mr. Kindred, because the American law regarding lifeboats is a splendid one. If the Titanic had followed that law she would have had enough boats to have taken off practically everybody."

Ask President to Call Conference.

There is said to be a question, however, regarding this proposed legislation, due to the fact that the United States has treaties with other maritime nations whereby they undertake to carry out the United States inspection laws in return for the carrying out of their laws by the United States.

Representative William J. Cary, of Wisconsin, in a bill introduced to-day provides a way of meeting this objection. He would make it a requirement that when the United States is prevented by a treaty from enforcing its inspection the captain of the foreign vessel before clearing an American port must notify every passenger and the crew that the American law has not been complied with. This Mr. Cary believes would make the foreign steamship companies provide the necessary lifeboats in order to get business.

Mr. Cary and Representative Cyrus Cline, of Indiana, introduced bills to prevent foreign ships from clearing or entering American ports which have not life saving apparatus adequate to take off both passengers and crew in time of disaster.

Representative Calder, of New York, introduced a resolution authorizing the President to arrange a conference with foreign nations to provide a uniform system of steamship inspection. Representative Alexander, of Missouri, introduced a resolution for a conference looking toward an international agreement on a new steamship lane much further to the south than the present one and out of the iceberg zone.

Favors Imprisonment.

Representative William Sulzer, of New York, chairman of the Foreign Affairs Committee, presented a drastic bill to require proper life saving apparatus aboard all vessels using American ports, both domestic and foreign, and providing ten years in jail at hard labor for a captain violating the law.

Senator Perkins, chairman of the Senate Naval Committee, introduced a bill amending section 4,488 of the Revised Statues to require every ship leaving any port of the United States to be equipped with life boats and life preservers sufficient for every person on board, including the crew. The bill not only applies to ocean ships but to those navigating any lake, bay or sound in the United States. The bill also stipulates that all vessels be provided with seaworthy lifeboats and disengaging apparatus by which the boats can be launched safely when such vessel is under full speed or otherwise. Such disengaging apparatus must permit of one person operating it and release both ends of the boat simultaneously from the tackles.

In the Perkins bill the board of supervising inspectors is authorized to fix and determine by rules and regulations the character of the lifeboats and other safety appliances, the character and capacity of the pumps and other appliances for freeing the ship of water in case of heavy leakage, but shall have no discretion whatever with respect to the number of lifeboats, "such number to be determined solely by the actual capacity of such lifeboats to carry and transport at one time all the passengers and members of the crew on board the vessel, the carrying capacity of such lifeboats to be not less than three cubic feet of displacement for each person."

Severe Penalties Proposed.

It is made unlawful for any vessel to leave from or clear any port of the United States before obtaining from the board of supervising inspectors a certificate specifying the number of passengers and crew on board and verifying that the vessel is fully equipped as provided in the Perkins bill.

Violations of any of the provisions of the law shall be punishable as a felony and subject to sentence at hard labor upon conviction for not more than ten years. Every captain, and in case the owner or charterer is a corporation, every executive officer and resident general agent charged with the control or management, equipment and operation of the vessel shall be deemed particeps criminis.

Any person who knowingly and wilfully manufactures and sells defective life preservers shall be subject to a fine of $2,000 and imprisonment for five years.

NAVAL ARCHITECTS FOR OCEAN PATROL

"If an iceberg patrol is established it should be made an international arrangement," said Edwin B. Sadtler, of No. 50 Church street, a naval architect, yesterday in discussing the suggestion of Commander Frederick L. Sawyer to provide an efficient method for preventing repititions of the Titanic disaster.

"The greater part of the passenger traffic is carried by foreign steamships," said he, "so there is no reason why they should no share the responsibility and expense of the patrol.

"In my opinion the accident to the Titanic was due to the speed mania of the American people. They are crazy for speed and the steamship companies are catering to their wishes. The Titanic officers knew that the ice was afloat. They ought to have gone to the southward instead of keeping on the course where they are most likely to encounter the bergs.

"It is only a matter of some delay for the steamships to take the southerly course, and that idea, if followed out, with the aid of an iceberg patrol, would remove in part the danger of collisions. The officers o fthe steamship were at fault in not demanding that they be permitted to take the safer course.

Favors Ice Patrol.

"The iceberg patrol suggestion is a good one. The patrol vessels should be craft capable of high speed, because if a steamship is in trouble quick action is necessary. There should be laws to punish officers of vessels who are warned regarding the location of icebergs and do not take precaution to avoid them."

Mr. adtler said all steamships needed more life boats. He declared they should be provided with life boats in proportion to the number of passengers they carried and not in proportion to their tonnage.

"It's the duty of the steamship companies to have their vessels follow the safer route," was the statement made at the offices of Theodore E. Ferris, of No. 30 Church street, a naval architect. "It would be well to establish the iceberg patrol, and also take a little more time in making the trips. That would remove much of the danger of collisions in the future with icebergs.

"The suggestion for the patrol as published in the HERALD seems entirely practicable. Let the foreign governments do their share by all means in bearing a part of the expense of the safeguard. It would be well worth the while of all the governments to giv th suggstion considerable thought. There are evidently great possibilities for the future safety of mariners in the proposed project.

"There is not a vessel afloat that has a sufficient number of life boats to insure the safety absolutely of the passengers. Life rafts are as god, if not better, than life boats."

Too Much Speed.

"If the iceberg patrol suggestion is practical it ought to be favored," said Theodore D. Wells, of No. 32 Broadway, a naval architect. "One objection would be in obtaining patrol boats that could stand up under all conditions while on station.

"I believe that there is little likelihood of such an accident as happened to the Titanic occurring freqnently. It seems as though the steamship folk are too fond of making a good showing as recards speed. This feeling always prevails on the maiden trip of a steamship."

APPROVE ICEBERG PATROL SUGGESTION

Continued approval was expressed yesterday of the suggestion published exclusively in the HERALD for an international ice patrol, to warn steamships and the public generally of the movements of dangerous fields of ice. While the New York managers of some of the lines wish to consult their home office before speaking officially, they said they had read the HERALD's editorial on the subject with great satisfaction, and they were highly pleased to read that the big German lines were ready to co-operate with the HERALD in calling attention to the importance of such an enterprise.

Mr. A. Gips, agent of the Holland-American lines, said that he would be only too pleased to have the ice patrol idea developed. "I hear that the companies have ordered their captains to take a more southerly course in future voyages. Still, the ice seems to continue moving in large masses, and it is impossible to do too much to insure the safety of the travelling public. The loss of the Titanic is a calamity beyond words. Everybody is dazed by the horror of it all.

"I have read the HERALD's interviews and editorial on the proposal to police the ice fields of the Northern Atlantic. If the suggestion should be adopted by the government and carried out it would certainly increase the feeling of security for the seagoing public. If those icebergs were stationary or rocky promontories, lighthouses would be erected at once to warn ships of danger. But moving they are all the more dangerous, and the steamships are justified in going further south, even at the expense of prolonging their voyages.

"Safety must be the first consideration in the passenger carrying business. Our captains observe the greatest care to avoid every danger, and we have been particularly fortunate in providing safe transportation for our passengers."

Mr. Edward O. Thomas, general manager of the Uranium line, with steamships between New York and Rotterdam, also approved of the HERALD's articles favoring patrolling the ice fields of the upper Atlantic.

"Of course, I cannot say what ought to be done by the governments. But if the suggestion should be adopted and prove successful it would be a fine thing for the companies and reassure transatlantic travellers. The Titanic disaster is of such magnitude that we hardly know what to do or say. The feeling is not confined to steamship men alone, but to everybody, who will be more than glad if patrolling the ice fields proves successful.

"As to the details, only experts can speak with knowledge and authority. But I can see how a few vessels with properly equipped wireless apparatus, could keep other vessels well informed each day as to the conditions and location of dangerous ice masses. It would insure protection to the big steamships and all other vessels going by that route across the Atlantic. The HERALD is to be congratulated on its public spirited stand for all that benefits our shipping interests and the passenger service generally."

"I think the HERALD's idea is magnificent—splendid! Everything the HERALD has done for shipping has been a success," said Max Straus, of the Russian-American line, owning the Russian Imperial Mail steamships. "We can only be grateful for anything that the HERALD may suggest for making ocean travelling safer. I do not believe the public appreciates how much this calamity affects us. Although the Titanic belonged to a rival line, I feel as if the loss were ours. I did not sleep a wink night before last, and all the other steamship people are crushed by this unspeakable disaster."

"I am glad to hear that the companies have ordered their ships to take the southern course, thus avoiding the ice fields entirely. No expense is too great for the protection of oceangoing business and its passengers. I know the HERALD can succeed in anything it undertakes. Let the good work go on. All hail to the HERALD, I say."

ONCE WEALTHY BARBER MISSING

Arthur White, Once Known as "Soap Wrapper King," Was on Board the Titanic.

Among those reported lost on board the Titanic was an English barber, Arthur White, who was at one time known as "The Soap Wrapper King" in England. Nearly every English newspaper carried his advertisements for soap wrappers, which commanded a high premium, and

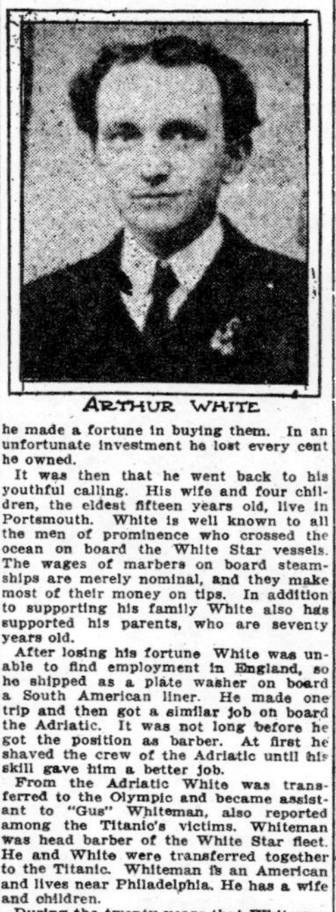

ARTHUR WHITE

he made a fortune in buying them. In an unfortunate investment he lost every cent he owned.

It was then that he went back to his youthful calling. His wife and four children, the eldest fifteen years old, live in Portsmouth. White is well known to all the men of prominence who crossed the ocean on board the White Star vessels. The wages of marbers on board steamships are merely nominal, and they make most of their money on tips. In addition to supporting his family White also has supported his parents, who are seventy years old.

After losing his fortune White was unable to find employment in England, so he shipped as a plate washer on board a South American liner. He made one trip and then got a similar job on board the Adriatic. It was not long before he got the position as barber. At first he shaved the crew of the Adriatic until his skill gave him a better job.

From the Adriatic White was transferred to the Olympic and became assistant to "Gus" Whiteman, also reported among the Titanic's victims. Whiteman was head barber of the White Star fleet. He and White were transferred together to the Titanic. Whiteman is an American and lives near Philadelphia. He has a wife and children.

During the twenty years that Whiteman has been with the steamship company he has shaved most of the prominent men of the day. Mr. J. Pierpont Morgan knew him well and would allow no one else to shave him.

WOMEN TO AID NEEDY IMMIGRANTS

Following a meeting in the home of Mrs. Nelson Herrick Henry, No. 59 West Ninth street, a committee of women will meet the women steerage survivors of the Titanic when the steamship Carpathia arrives on Friday. The women will take a large amount of clothing with them, believing that they will be needed by the rescued ones. Arrangements also have been made with the Commissioner of Immigration to forego the sending of the steerage passengers to Ellis Island.

Rooms have been rented by the committee in different boarding houses, and in the cases of young children whose parents have been drowned it has been decided to send them to day nurseries. In cases of necessity money will be given to the women and every care will be taken of them.

It has been calculated that there are two hundred and fifty women and children from the unfortunate vessel's steerage who will have to be cared for by the committee, which is composed of Mrs. Henry F. Dimock, Mrs. Cornelius Vanderbilt, Sr.; Mrs. Herbert L. Satterlee, Mrs. James Herman Aldrich, Mrs. Richard Irvin, Mrs. William Church Osborn, Mrs. Henry Whitney Munroe, Mrs. Charles B. Alexander, Mrs. Paul Dana, Mrs. Arthur Murray Dodge, Mrs. J. Van Vechten Olcott, Mrs. Edward Hewitt, Miss Eleanor G. Hewitt, Miss Sarah Cooper Hewitt, Miss Virginia Potter, Miss Eleanor Cuyler and Miss Caroline W. Stewart, who is chairman of the clothing committee.

The members of the New York section of the Council of Jewish Women have arranged to meet immediate needs of the women and children among the immigrants saved from the Titanic. A committee of the council will meet the Carpathia and see that clothing, food and shelter are provided for the survivors. Employment also will be found for those who are able to work.

At a special meeting of the Executive Board of the Hebrew Sheltering and Immigrant Aid Society held this afternoon resolutions expressing the sympathy of the society for the sufferers of the Titanic disaster and their friends were adopted and Judge Leon Sanders, president of the society, was authorized to appoint a committee to extend the facilities of the organization to those survivors who are in need of help.

The committee is composed of Joseph Barondess, Leon Kamaiky, J. Saphirstein, J. Massel, Philip Hersh, A. Cooper and Judge Sanders. They will meet the Carpathia upon arrival and co-operate with all other agencies in assisting the surviving immigrants.

The House of Shelter maintained by the society at No. 229-231 East Broadway will be able to care for at least fifty of the survivors.

SACRIFICED SAFETY TO SPEED, DECLARES SECRETARY OF NAVY

Mr. Meyer Believes the Titanic Knew of Danger in Her Path.

QUOTE REPORT SHE SENT TO OFFICIALS

Message Transmitted to Hydrographic Bureau Told of Icebergs in Immediate Vicinity.

WARNINGS ARE PUBLISHED

Information Sent Out from Washington Enables Seamen to Estimate Speed and Direction of Dangerous Obstructions.

HERALD BUREAU,
No. 1,502 H STREET, N. W.,
WASHINGTON, D. C., Wednesday.

That the Titanic not only knew of the danger of ice in her vicinity, but knew specifically of the very ice masses which she struck, is the opinion of Mr. Meyer, Secretary of the Navy, based on data which has come to the Navy Department through the Hydrographic Office.

Mr. Meyer and navy officials are therefore forced to the unwelcome belief that the vessel, to a certain degree at least, sacrificed precaution and safety for speed. Captain John J. Knapp, U. S. N., chief hydrographer, will recommend this week that the transatlantic steamships, during the season of ice movements, take a more southern course.

The Titanic sent out wireless messages warning other vessels of the ice, according to reports received here. "The chances of her getting by safely were twenty to one," naval officers at the Hydrographic Office said to-night, "but in this case the chances were against the steamship, for she struck."

Warnings Are Published.

Commenting on the iceberg peril and the manner in which the Hydrographic Office works to warn ships of the danger, Mr. Meyer said:—

"For more than a quarter of a century the Hydrographic Office of the Bureau of Navigation, Navy Department, has been publishing graphically from month to month a series of charts known as the Pilot Chart of the North Atlantic Ocean, depicting thereon the physical conditions of the ocean and of the atmosphere for the current month, as well as the location of dangers to navigation, as reported by incoming ships. A summary of these dangers and a more detailed description than the space of the Pilot Chart would permit was given in time from week to week on a printed sheet known as the Hydrographic Office Bulletin. These publications were circulated freely among the ship masters and shipping men in return for their news of the sea, the point of contact between the office at Washington and the marine world being a chain of branch hydrographic offices at the principal seaports.

"Practically all the captains in the transatlantic trade co-operate in this work by handing in their information upon arrival in port to branch hydrographic offices. In recent years the collection of marine data has been immensely accelerated by the use of radio-telegraphy, and the Hydrographic Office is thereby enabled to publish daily in a so-called daily memorandum whatever important reports of dangers have been received.

"This sheet is prepared every afternoon and is mailed to the branch Hydrographic Office, and there given publicity to all concerned. By this means Boston, New York, Philadelphia, Baltimore, Norfolk, &c., are put in possession daily of the accumulated reports, edited by experts, of dangerous derelicts and icebergs. Thus in the case of the loss of the Titanic the shipping companies and shipmasters had been put in possession of the experiences and judgment of a trained staff in the Hydrographic Office, as summarized in a pamphlet printed in April, 1909, entitled 'North Atlantic Ice Movements,' giving a study of the entire question with diagrams to show the usual limits of ice for a period of ten years.

News Distributed Quickly.

"More specifically, the shipping community had been provided from month to month with the pilot chart showing the conditions of ice up to the time of printing and with the weekly hydrographic bulletin giving all pertinent details in regard to ice and derelicts and also the daily memorandum summarizing the collected reports of each day.

"In New York the officer in charge of the branch Hydrographic Office has on exhibit on the floor of the Maritime Exchange, as well as in his own office, a large chart of the North Atlantic Ocean, on which is shown the location of the derelicts, ice and other reported dangers. These charts he keeps posted to date. He also informs at once by telephone the various steamship companies of all reported dangers to navigation.

"The officers of these companies and the masters of their vessels, particularly those of outgoing vessels, always have been urged to call at the branch Hydrographic Office to obtain the latest information. Steamship companies also have been urged to keep their ships afloat constantly informed of these dangers by means of wireless telegraphy. Similar action to that above outlined has been taken by the officers in charge of the branch hydrographic offices at the other ports mentioned above.

"Knew Her Danger."

"A trained seaman can and does estimate the probable speed and direction of drift of any dangerous obstruction, so that if he had knowledge of the existence of an iceberg or a derelict in a certain location at a given date he reckons its future position for an interval of a few days.

"The April pilot chart, which was issued March 28, 1912, showed that in March ice had come as far south as latitude 44 deg. north. The daily memorandum prior to the 13th inst. showed that the trend of ice was to the southward, icebergs being sighted below the forty-third parallel on April 7, 8, 9 and 11. On the 9th and 11th it had reached the forty-second parallel, and on the 11th some of it was seen south of latitude 42 deg.

"The daily memorandum of April 15 contains a message from the Amerika, by way of the Titanic and Cape Race, N. F., April 14, 1912, to the Hydrographic Office, Washington, D. C.:—

"'Amerika has passed two large icebergs in 41 deg. 27 min. north, 50 deg. 8 min. West, on the 14th of April.

"KNUTH".

"As the Titanic's position is reported to have been latitude 41 deg. 16 min., longitude 50 deg. 14 min., at the time of her disaster, it is thus seen that the message which she transmitted for the Amerika doubtless relates to the very ice upon which she was wrecked."

STILL HAVE HOPE FOR JOHN WEIR

Friends of Noted Mining Engineer Say He May Not Have Been Aboard the Titanic.

Friends of Colonel John Weir, the world famous mining engineer, who is supposed to have been on board the Titanic, almost gave up hope yesterday when a cable despatch came from his sister in Edinburgh, Scotland, asking for word of him. The name "J. Weir" appears in the list of

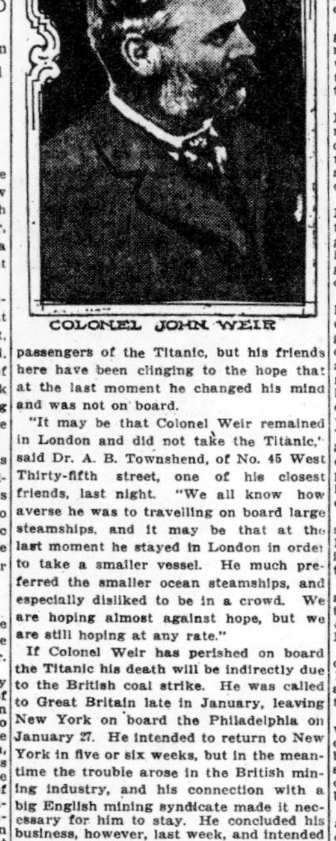

COLONEL JOHN WEIR

passengers of the Titanic, but his friends here have been clinging to the hope that at the last moment he changed his mind and was not on board.

"It may be that Colonel Weir remained in London and did not take the Titanic," said Dr. A. B. Townshend, of No. 45 West Thirty-fifth street, one of his closest friends, last night. "We all know how averse he was to travelling on board large steamships, and it may be that at the last moment he stayed in London in order to take a smaller vessel. He much preferred the smaller ocean steamships, and especially disliked to be in a crowd. We are hoping almost against hope, but we are still hoping at any rate."

If Colonel Weir has perished on board the Titanic his death will be indirectly due to the British coal strike. He was called to Great Britain late in January, leaving New York on board the Philadelphia on January 27. He intended to return to New York in five or six weeks, but in the meantime the trouble arose in the British mining industry, and his connection with a big English mining syndicate made it necessary for him to stay. He concluded his business, however, last week, and intended to take the Philadelphia, which should have arrived last Saturday, but which, because of the coal strike, did not get away. For this reason he engaged passage on board the Titanic.

A week ago Mr. George C. Boldt, manager of the Waldorf-Astoria, received word from Colonel Weir asking him to save his usual room. He had stopped at the Waldorf-Astoria while in New York ever since the hotel opened.

Colonel Weir, though well known in New York, was almost as well known in Bombay, Pekin, St. Petersburg and London, for, as a mining expert, he had been in the employ of half a dozen different governments. In 1899 he went to the Philippines on a mission for the United States government to investigate the coal mining situation on the Island of Mindanao.

MR. P. A. B. WIDENER GIVES UP HOPE

[SPECIAL DESPATCH TO THE HERALD.]

PHILADELPHIA, Pa., Wednesday.—P. A. B. Widener sorrowfully acknowledged this afternoon that he had given up all hope of ever seeing his son and his grandson, George D. Widener, alive. Mr. Widener is a director of the White Star line, and has kept in close touch with the company's offices since the disaster.

"George went down with the ship," Mr. Widener told some close friends, "and he went down like a man—fighting to save the women and children."

"Why shouldn't Mr. Widener be aboard the Carpathia with the survivors if J. Bruce Ismay, head of the White Star line, was saved?" Mr. Widener was asked.

For a moment Mr. Widener forgot his grief, his eyes blazed, rage showed in his face, and with a biting sarcasm he answered:—

"Ismay? Oh, Ismay saved himself."

To persons who knew George D. Widener the fact that his name does not appear among the list of survivors is no surprise. He was a rugged man and full of courage. One night not long ago one of his close friends met him in Fifteenth street. He was carrying a large clothes basket, and beside him trudged a weazened little woman. Mr. Widener had met the woman as she was taking the basket of clothes that she had washed to its owner, and he had taken the burden from her and was carrying it.

Two more persons were added to-day to the list of Philadelphians who took passage on board the Titanic. They are Dr. Arthur Jackson Brewe, an associate of Dr. S. Weir Mitchell, and Frederick Sutton, an importer and president of the Sons of St. George.

Fate of Major Butt and Others Spreads Gloom Over Washington

Chevy Chase Hunt Ball and All Social Gayeties Abandoned Out of Respect to President's Aid and Mr. Clarence Moore.

HERALD BUREAU,
No. 1,502 H STREET, N. W.,
WASHINGTON, D. C., Wednesday.

Announcement was made to-day that the Chevy Chase Hunt ball, which was to have been held next Friday night, has been indefinitely postponed. There will in all probability be no ball this year. The action of the officers, while a direct tribute to Mr. Clarence Moore, many years M. F. H., and Major Archibald W. Butt, who played golf on the club links with President Taft more than any other man, was the result of an anxious wish of every member of the club to show its deepest sympathy for all those who, it is feared, gave their lives in the great sea tragedy last Monday morning.

Society is plunged into the deepest gloom by the failure of more encouraging reports to come from the ships which are now in wireless communication with the Carpathia, on which are the survivors of the wreck.

Invitations for a dinner at the Austro-Hungarian Embassy to-night have been recalled. Ambassador Bryce and others of the British Embassy stayed away from the ceremony of the unveiling of the statue of John Paul Jones on account of the disaster.

While the guests of Miss Helen Taft and Mr. Robert Taft will remain in Washington for the remainder of the week all engagements have been cancelled, and what had been intended as a brilliant programme for their entertainment will be changed to one of the utmost quiet.

Every member of the President's household from the officials and clerks in his offices to the servants of the house are genuinely heartstricken over the almost certain fate of Major Butt. While he was abroad the President's military aid did not fail to remember the attachés of the house with post cards from practically every city he visited and several times a week wrote long letters to the President. The last mail from him was received last Sunday morning. In these letters and cards Major Butt told of the great improvement his trip had been to him and how refreshed he felt to go on with his duties at the White House.

Mr. and Mrs. Joseph Leiter and the Assistant Secretary of the Navy and Mrs. Beekman Winthrop recalled their dinner invitations for to-night because of the sea tragedy.

Mrs. Nicholas Anderson had intended a brilliant dinner and dance at the Country Club in compliment to her son-in-law and daughter, Mr. and Mrs. Philip McMillan, but these were abandoned.

Mr. and Mrs. Nicholas Longworth have cancelled their dinner to-night and the Military Attaché of the French Embassy and Countess De Chambrun have recalled their invitations for to-morrow night.

Mrs. Clarence Moore, wife of Mr. Moore, whose tragic fate seems as assured as that of Major Butt, has secluded herself in her big house in Massachusetts avenue and sees nobody. Mr. and Mrs. Moore are counted among the close friends of the President and Mrs. Taft.

Mr. and Mrs. Perry Belmont postponed a dinner which was to have been given on Saturday in compliment to the Austrian Ambassador and Baroness Hengelmüller.

THE HERALD'S TUG TO MEET RESCUE SHIP

Craft Carrying Reporters and Wireless Apparatus Speeding to Sea for News of Survivors.

ON BOARD THE HERALD TUG WALTER A. LUCKENBACH, OFF NEWPORT, R. I., Wednesday.—Equipped with wireless apparatus in charge of Mr. R. A. Morton, of Brooklyn and Newport, the HERALD tug Walter A. Luckenbach, with a staff of reporters and photographers on board, steamed from here this afternoon to meet the steamship Carpathia off Nantucket.

It is expected that the HERALD tug and the Carpathia will be in communication with each other to-night or early to-morrow morning.

The Luckenbach, which was chartered by the HERALD yesterday, was fitted with a wireless outfit in an hour to-day and as she is steaming out of the harbor messages are being received from stations along the coast and vessels at sea.

Mr. Morton is recognized as one of the leading wireless experts in the United States.

He began a study of wireless telegraphy some years ago, and since has devoted all his time to it. He has written much on the subject for scientific publications. He has an assistant on board the HERALD tug, Mr. O. C. Morse, Jr., of Newport, also a wireless expert.

As the tug is leaving Newport warnings are being sent along the coast of the approach of a northeast gale, which will delay the Carpathias arrival in New York with the survivors of the Titanic.

Gale off Nantucket.

Wireless messages received on board the tug say that it is already blowing heavily off Nantucket and there is a high sea.

As soon as the HERALD tug is at sea calls will be flashed for the Carpathia and all news received will be sent to the HERALD wireless station in New York.

Experts from the naval station at Newport tested the tug's wireless outfit before she put to sea this afternoon, and pronounced it in perfect condition.

The Luckenbach, which is in command of Captain Daley, is one of the most powerful tugs on the coast, and will be able to remain at sea no matter what the weather conditions are.

"The indications are that the coming gale will be one of the hardest we have had this spring," said Captain Daley this afternoon, "but we will make a good run to the point at which we will meet the Carpathia, I am confident."

The HERALD reporters are indebted to the officials of the navy station here for many courtesies, and the naval wireless operators here will be in constant communication with the HERALD tug while she is at sea.

If messages are sent by relatives or friends of the Titanic's survivors to the HERALD tug they will be relayed to the Carpathia.

Word from the scout cruisers Salem and Chester received on board the HERALD tug say they are no wcruising in the path of the Carpathia off Nantucket.

The Chester passed Nantucket Shoals lightship at seven o'clock last night and was making twenty knots. The Salem was close astern of her.

Plea for News of Disaster.

This message for the Carpathia was picked up by the HERALD tug's operators to-day: — "Thousands of relatives and friends craving information that only newspaper men can put together. Were all on board the Titanic transferred to you? Send details of wreck, with names of those lost and condition of survivors, by wireless. It would be a deed of mercy to thousands in terrible suspense."

To the purser of the Baltic a message came from London to-day asking him to send photographs to a London newspaper.

No replies have been received to any of the messages sent to the Carpathia.

The experimental station of the Cloyne House School at Newport was the only station in communication with the scout cruiser Chester between midnight last night and five o'clock this morning. She then became lost to all stations.

Between midnight and five o'clock this morning she was calling the Carpathia every five minutes.

PUT TRINITY HOSPITAL AT VICTIMS' DISPOSAL

Dr. Manning Announces Women and Children of the Steerage Will Be Cared For.

Prayers for the dead in the North Atlantic, for the survivors on board the Carpathia and for all those afflicted by the Titanic disaster were offered in every church yesterday in which there was a service.

"Old" Trinity will not confine her help to prayers alone. The Rev. Dr. William T. Manning, the rector, yesterday notified the Relief Committee of fifteen women who are arranging to care for the women and children of the steerage, that Trinity vestry placed at the disposal of the committee Trinity Hospital, in Varick street, just opposite old St. John's chapel.

The hospital has been closed for the last few years, but was opened during the bitter cold of December as a free lodging place for homeless men. It closed for the season the night before the Titanic went down.

During the five months the "home" was open it gave nineteen thousand lodgings and provided 39,000 meals. Seventy per cent of the men were looking for work, being temporarily out of a job. The hospital is equipped with single cots and other furnishings which will make it an ideal place for these women in a strange country, the majority of whose husbands are at the bottom of the Atlantic.

The eleven o'clock service at Trinity Sunday will be a memorial. St. George's Society will have a memorial service at Trinity at noon Tuesday. This is being arranged by a committee of which Mr. Lloyd B. Sanderson is in charge. It is likely that the British Consulate will attend. Mr. Manning has instructed the vicars of each of Trinity's nine chapels to say daily the prayers for the dead and for those in affliction.

At the Brick Presbyterian Church the Rev. Dr. William P. Merrill dwelt upon the disaster and asked God tenderly to bless all plunged so suddenly into bereavement.

Because of the Titanic wreck the celebration of the sixtieth anniversary of the Episcopal Church of the Incarnation, Madison avenue and Thirty-fifth street, has been postponed from next Sunday to Sunday, April 28. Instead the service this Sunday morning will be a memorial.

"Special memorial services for all those who lost their lives will be held in all the Jewish temples of the country," said Colonel Benjamin Blumenthal, president of the Congregation Rodeph Sholom, Sixty-third street and Lexington avenue, yesterday. Rabbi Rudolph Grossman, of that temple, has already prepared a memorial address for Saturday morning.

In every Catholic church hte dead and the afflicted will be remembered in the daily masses. Mgr. John J. Dunn, in conducting special devotions in honor of St. Anthony at the Church of St. John the Evangelist, prayed and told of the horror which cost two thousand lives.

"The Sorrow of the Sea" will be the subject of the Rev. Dr. Howard Duffield Sunday morning at a memorial service in the old First Presbyterian Church.

Bishop Greer will be at the Cathedral of St. John the Divine Sunday morning and take part in the memorial service which, as already announced, will be held there.

MANY STEAMSHIPS COMING IN TELL OF ICE PERILS IN ATLANTIC

Throngs Still Besiege White Star Line Office

Henry W. Taft and Mrs. Guggenheim Among Those Who Seek News of Survivors—Deny the Carpathia Needs Assistance.

NO WORD RECEIVED FROM J. BRUCE ISMAY

Scenes of inquiry, grief, despair and joy were repeated at the offices of the White Star Line Steamship Company's office in lower Broadway yesterday as men and women, arriving on foot and in automobiles, asked anxiously after their relatives, loved ones and friends who were supposed to have taken passage on board the ill fated Titanic. While many of the inquirers rejoiced when they learned that their relatives were in the list of the rescued, or in the supplementary list issued by the company of persons who had booked passage but were unable to leave at the last moment, despair succeeded hope in the minds of many others, when they were informed that the names of all the first and second class passengers rescued have already been published.

P. A. S. Franklin, resident vice president of the White Star line, said:—

"We have received no message from the Baltic, and there is no doubt in my mind that if she had anybody on board she would have reported it. So far we have received no despatches from the Carpathia, no replies in answer to our inquiries. One message came ashore today, but whether it was in reply to one of our messages or not we do not know. It stated that the Carpathia had sent the first, second and third class passenger lists.

The Carpathia Not in Need.

"It is absolutely untrue that the Carpathia has sent word that she is in need of assistance. She said this morning that she doesn't want any help. This message was relayed by the Salem, but came originally from the Carpathia. Both the Chester and the Salem are proceeding to the Carpathia, which, they say, probably will arrive in this city at about ten o'clock on Thursday night. I presume the Captain means by that he will be at Sandy Hook at eight o'clock at night.

"We are going to have the survivors met by friends and relatives of the first, second and third class passengers. We will offer them every possible facility. They may go to hotels and, in fact, do anything they want to do.

"No, we have received no word from J. Bruce Ismay, the managing director of the line. The Carpathia has apparently two wireless operators, and we know that the wireless operator of the Titanic was saved. The men can work in relays, and thus keep the wireless going day and night."

Mr. Franklin bitterly resented reports that his company had received information of the sinking of the Titanic many hours before it was made public. He again stated emphatically that the company received its first news of the foundering of the steamship at half-past six o'clock on Monday night.

The firm of Saks & Co., of Broadway and Thirty-fourth street, yesterday received a message from Halifax, N. S., stating that Mrs. Edgar L. Meyer, daughter of Andrew Saks, who died several days ago, is safe there and has received good care. As made public, the message reads:—"eLila saved. Well cared for. Edgar missing."

This message was not signed. According to the passenger list, Edgar Meyer was a first class passenger, but no mention is made on the list of Mrs. Meyer.

When Mr. Franklin was told of the receipt of this message he exclaimed:—"Gentlemen, I hope that is true." He added:—"Then, perhaps, others have been saved." He had shown considerable signs of depression during the afternoon, but this message from an outside source brightened him up noticeably.

Mr. Franklin earlier in the day stated that the White Star line had not received any information from the Carpathia or anywhere else in regard to the catastrophe which could be regarded as authentic since nine o'clock on Tuesday morning. He said that the cable steamship Mackay Bennet had left Halifax at half-past ten o'clock yesterday morning for the scene of the wreck. This information, he said, had come to him unofficially, but he believed it to be true; that the vessel was the best one the company could get and that it would make all possible haste to the scene.

Doubts the Californian Story.

Mr. Franklin said he was not inclined to believe that the steamship Californian was headed for Boston with bodies of the Titanic on board. He regarded this report in the nature of an unreliable rumor. He added that he knew nothing of the information cabled from London to the effect that the Olympic was in wireless communication with the other side. The Olympic's regular time of arrival, he said, was next Friday morning, and that she probably would be delayed on account of having waited for the receipt of news from the wreck.

"We place much faith," said Mr. Franklin, "in the message that Captain Rostron has eight hundred survivors on board the Carpathia. This company has communicated with all the wireless stations on the coast in the vicinity, asking them to forward at once any message for the company that might be sent by the Carpathia."

Despite the rain that fell during the greater part of the day, crowds hung about Bowling Green in front of the White Star Line offices, hoping against hope for more cheering news. Eight or ten policemen were stationed on the sidewalks, but their services were not needed. Many non-English speaking persons besieged the offices, making anxious inquiries for friends or relatives.

Among the callers during the forenoon was Henry W. Taft, brother of the President, who stated that he had come to inquire about the fate of Major Butt, the President's military aid; Karl Behr, the tennis player, and Frank D. Millet, artist and war correspondent. Another anxious inquirer was F. L. Allison, whose father and mother, Mr. and Mrs. H. J. Allison, and their other children, Miss Allison and Master Allison, were on board the steamship. Master Allison is the only one of the party reported to have been saved. He appears on the list of the rescued with his nurse. Another inquirer with regard to Mr. Behr, was Mr. W. S. Brewster, a lawyer, who appeared greatly relieved on learning that his friend was aboard the Carpathia.

Mrs. Guggenheim a Visitor.

Mrs. Benjamin Guggenheim, whose husband has not been heard from, appeared again in the company of her brother, Dewitt Seligman. They asked for another interview with Mr. Franklin, and were taken to the office of the vice president of the line. Mrs. Guggenheim showed the effects of a sleepless night and found it difficult to restrain her grief.

Mr. Joseph Eastman, of this city, was overjoyed to learn that his daughter, Miss Annie K. Eastman, and Mrs. Charlton P. Lewis, who had booked passage on board the Titanic from Cherbourg, had cancelled their booking. He received a cable despatch from his daughter, who said that she and her friend would return to this country on board the Olympic on her return voyage.

The Franconia Heard From.

At the Cunard line offices yesterday a wireless message was received from the Steamship Franconia, which established communication with the Carpathia at ten minutes after six o'clock yesterday morning. The Carpathia was then 498 miles east of Ambrose Channel.

The message was:—

"The Cunard line steamship Franconia established communication by wireless with the steamship Carpathia at 6:10 this morning, New York time. The latter was then 498 miles east of Ambrose Channel and in no need of assistance. She is steaming thirteen knots. She expects to reach New York at 8 P. M. Thursday. She has a total of 705 survivors aboard. The Franconia is relaying personal messages from the Carpathia to Sable Island."

Mother's Grief Affects Mind.

A young woman who refused to give her name made inquiry at the White Star offices during the morning for some word of Charles M. Hays and his secretary, V. Payne, who were passengers on board the Titanic. It has been reported that Mrs. Hays has been saved, but the officials were unable to tell the young woman anything concerning the two men. Mr. Hays is general manager of the Grand Trunk Railroad. The young woman said that Mr. Payne's mother, who lives at No. 20 Victoria street, Montreal, had gone out of her mind while awaiting word of her son. She remained in the offices during the greater part of the day, in the hope that some word of cheer might arrive.

At the offices of the Hamburg-American Steamship Company it was announced that they had received a wireless from their steamship, the Cincinnati, which is bound for Bremen, to the effect that the Cincinnati while four hundred miles east of the Titanic on Sunday night received a wireless "S. O. S." call from the Titanic. The message was picked up by the wireless operator on board the Cincinnati at ten minutes after eleven o'clock Sunday night, or about forty minutes after the Titanic crashed into the iceberg. The message called for help and stated that the Titanic was sinking fast.

This was the only message received so far from the Cincinnati, according to the Hamburg-American line's management.

The Cunard Steamship Company has received a letter from the Commissioner of Immigration, William Williams, relative to the reception of the Carpathia. The letter reads:—

"Upon the return to port of the Carpathia the immigration authorities will do whatever in their power lies to facilitate the landing of aliens, who began their voyage on board the Titanic. If any of these have relations or friends to meet them at the pier they will be discharged to the latter. Such of these as do not wish to land at the pier will be brought to Ellis Island and there cared for. At the pier there will be two or three immigration inspectors to take charge of those of the Titanic passengers who may require our assistance.

"It is the present intention of both the Customs and Immigration authorities that no cutter shall board the Carpathia as she comes up the bay. This in order that she may be permitted to reach her pier without any unnecessary delay or interference. Those aliens who are on board the Carpathia for deportation will, if you desire, be cared for at Ellis Island until the Carpathia sails."

Ray of Hope Dispelled.

Hope that fate might have been kind to a few of those on board the Titanic who so far have been unaccounted for, was stimulated when the crew of the Etonion, a freighter that docked on Tuesday night, after preceding the ill fated steamship along the route strewn with icebergs in the Atlantic, reported having seen the three masted schooner Dorothy Baird lying-to within fifty miles of the scene of the disaster.

The crew, however, when questioned, expressed the belief that there was slight probability of any survivors being aboard the schooner, since she is thought to have proceeded to St. John's hours before the Titanic crashed into the iceberg. The crew of the freighter reported that an iceberg extending 200 feet above the ocean and more than a quarter of a mile in length, had been encountered in the Atlantic in the vicinity of the catastrope.

Several relatives of passengers aboard the Titanic were in the White Star offices when a wireless from Captain Haddock, of the Olympic, was read, stating that all the survivors accounted for were on board the Carpathia. This news greatly affected one young man, who was trying to learn something about the fate of his mother. "There is no need of hope now," he exclaimed. "All is lost."

Frederick V. Ridgeway, manager of the steamship department of the White Star line, said the delay in the receipt of messages from the Carpathia might be explained by the fact that the wireless operators on the vessel had been overworked.

THE CONQUEROR.

After Battle for Life Amid Icebergs Steamships Arrive in This Port

Passengers on Board the Bretagne Spend Seven Hours in Prayer When Fog Redoubles the Dangers of the Ice Fields—The Hellig Olav Also Faced Peril, During Which Forty Icebergs Were Passed.

Two steamships that passed through the ice fields off Newfoundland not long before the Titanic was doomed reached this city yesterday.

The vessels are the Bretagne, of the French line, and the Hellig Olav, of the Scandinavian-American line. Each was seven hours working through the unbroken stretch of ice. During their slow progress they were menaced constantly by huge icebergs. Neither heard the call for help sent out by the Titanic's operator, although the Cincinnati, of the Hamburg American line, which also reached this city from the Mediterranean yesterday, and which was to the south of the Bretagne and the Hellig Olav when the Titanic struck, heard the summons and altered her course to go to the Titanic's aid. The Cincinnati met no ice.

The Bretagne entered the ice field about twelve hours before the Titanic, according to the calculations of Captain Mace, her commander, and until she cleared the ice pack proceeded through a sea set thick with towering icebergs and shrouded in heavy fog. From time to time the fog would clear sufficiently to allow of her officers seeing a mile ahead of them and again would settle down so densely that one end of the Bretagne was not visible from the other.

There were times when Captain Mace kept his engines just turning over. His passengers stood the ordeal well for the most part, although some in the third class dressed themselves in their heaviest clothes in anticipation of being ordered to the boats. Others spent the seven hours during which the vessel was in the ice field in prayer.

Captain Mace entered the ice in latitude 41.36, longitude 52.41, and before he was clear of it passed more than forty icebergs. That there were many more in his neighborhood was evident from the sound of one grinding against another, but in the thick fog which surrounded him much of the time he could not estimate their full number.

"The pack ice covered the sea as far as the eye could follow—that is, when we could see it at all," said Captain Mace yesterday. "When we first encountered the pack it was composed of small cakes and lumps, but by the time we were in the thickest of it the floes were of a size which would have injured the Bretagne perhaps mortally had I attempted to drive her through at even moderate speed. We entered the ice at six o'clock Sunday morning and were clear if it by one o'clock in the afternoon. I imagine that the Titanic must have encountered the pack about twelve hours after we did."

The Cincinnati caught the Titanic's distress signal at half-past ten o'clock Sunday night. It ran:—

"C. Q. D. S. O. S. Terrible danger. Rush. Rush."

The Cincinnati which was 540 miles away, at once hauled her course and headed for the Titanic's indicated position, but ceased steaming toward the Titanic when she caught a message sent out by the Olympic three hours later in which the Olympic stated that she was on her way to the Titanic and should arrive beside her many hours in advance of the Cincinnati.

NEVER CAN FIND BODIES, DECLARES SCIENTIST

Pressure of 6,000 Pounds to Square Inch Overcomes Buoyancy, Says Professor Wood.

BALTIMORE, Md., Wednesday. — "The bodies of the victims of the Titanic disaster are at the bottom of the deep, never to leave it," declared Professor Robert W. Wood, of the chair of experimental physics of Johns Hopkins University, to-day.

"It is improbable," he said, "that any will return to the surface, as is the case with bodies drowned in shallow water.

"At the depths of two miles the pressure of the water is something like six thousand pounds to the square inch, which is far too great to be overcome by buoyancy ordinarily given to drowned bodies by the gases generated in time.

"That the bodies sank to the bottom of the sea there is no question. The Titanic's victims who were not carried down with the boat followed until the very bottom of the sea was reached. There was no such thing as their stopping in their downward course.

"Great changes necessarily have been wrought in the vessel itself by the enormous pressure to which it has been subjected. No effect was produced on any portion or compartment or room to whose inside as well as outside walls the water has access. In such instances the pressure from one side neutralized that from the other.

"But wherever there was an airtight or watertight compartment the 6,000 pounds to a square inch pressure of water has crumpled those walls of the vessel as if they were tissue paper."

STARTS FUND FOR SEAMEN.

Calling attention to the probability that the seamen who manned the lifeboats of the Titanic will have only a water soaked suit of clothes, the Rev. George McPherson Hunter, secretary of the American Seamen's Friend Society, yesterday sent out an appeal for funds for them. Mr. Hunter says many of the seamen on board vessels of the White Star line look upon the institute of the American Seamen's Friend Society, No. 507 West street, as their American home. He says the society will receive contributions at No. 76 Wall street.

MAYOR GAYNOR ASKS AID FOR RELIEF FUND

Cable Message from Lord Mayor of London Inviting Co-operation Brings Immediate Response.

Mayor Gaynor yesterday received from the Lord Mayor of London a cable message stating that a fund had been started in London for relief of the sufferers from the Titanic disaster and declaring that assistance would be welcomed. Mayor Gaynor answered:—

"Relief fund for Titanic sufferers has our hearty sympathy. Will open one here."

The Mayor soon afterward issued at City Hall the following notice to the public:—

"TO THE PUBLIC:—No doubt many of the survivors of the crew and passengers of the Titanic and of the survivors of those who lost their lives will be in need of immediate assistance. All those who desire to help may send their contributions to the Mayor's office. A like fund is being raised in London."

GOT THE TITANIC'S "S. O. S."

QUEENSTOWN, Wednesday.—The Caronia, of the Cunard line, which arrived here this evening, reports having received a wireless message from the Titanic at twenty-one minutes to five o'clock (mean time) on Monday morning, saying she had been in collision with an iceberg, was in a sinking condition and would require immediate assistance. The Carona was then 700 miles from the Titanic, and therefore was unable to reach her, but sent messages to other vessels near the scene. The Caronia encountered no ice.

HALT CALIFORNIA DINNER.

Because of the Titanic disaster the California Club has postponed its dinner that was set for April 20 to April 27.

The Titanic Not in Peril, One Steamship Was Told

The Hellig Olav, Reaching Hoboken, Was Receiving Long Wave Messages When "S O S's" Were First Flashed, Says Wireless Operator.

THE OLYMPIC CONSIDERED BIG CRAFT SAFE

First of all the steamships which were in the neighborhood of the ill fated Titanic when she struck the berg which meant her doom, the Hellig Olav, of the Scandinavian-American line, arrived in Hoboken yesterday morning. The wireless operator on board the vessel said that he had not heard the distressed vessel's calls for help, though he had been in communication with the wireless operator on board the Olympic shortly after the accident happened. According to the calculations of Captain L. Holst, in command of the Hellig Olav, his vessel was about four hundred miles from the Titanic at the time of the disaster and was quite close to the Olympic shortly after the Titanic struck.

Captain Holst reported three huge icebergs about six miles from his vessel, when he was at latitude 41.43 north and longitude 49.51 west. These icebergs were sighted between seven and eight o'clock on Saturday evening. About an hour later, after dark, a fourth berg hove in sight, this one much nearer the ship. Captain Holst said that it is quite likely that the iceberg he sighted was the cause of the disaster to the Titanic. The position of the monster ship at the time she met her doom was given as latitude 41.46 north and longitude 50.14 west. The Hellig Olav was about twenty-four hours ahead of the new vessel.

"From ten o'clock on Sunday night until twenty-five minutes after twelve on Monday morning," said A. P. Andersen, wireless operator on board the Hellig Olav, "I was standing by to take the news from the high power land station at Cape Cod. My instrument was adjusted to long wave length work, which means that I would not be able to hear anything from vessels near me. At twenty-five minutes after twelve I switched back to short wave length and almost immediately picked up the Olympic. The wireless operator there asked me right away if I had heard anything about the Titanic. I said 'No.' Then he told me that the Titanic had struck an iceberg. I asked if there was any danger, and the Olympic operator replied that he thought not, that he thought everything was all right. After that I heard him call the Titanic several times, but I did not hear any reply."

Asked as to whether he had received any request to go to the aid of the Titanic, Mr. Andersen said:—"On the contrary, the tone of the message from the Olympic at that time was quite assuring. The Olympic herself was then proceeding full steam toward the Titanic. She was then just about abeam of us.

"That was the last message I had from the Olympic. During the morning I got into touch with the land stations. I asked Cape Cod and Siasconset what news they had, but they could tell me nothing. During the forenoon, however, I heard that a message had been received that the Titanic had gone down, but te operator said that he wished to confirm it. About ten o'clock that night the news was confirmed. I heard it when everybody was being informed.

"While we are at sea we publish a newspaper every two days of the happenings in the world at large. This news is sent out during the night, and this was the news which I was taking during the time that the Titanic must have been sending out her 'S. O. S.'s. We did not publish any newspaper after Saturday."

Captain Holst said that he had not turned in for the last forty-eight hours. He said that at the time he encountered the icebergs which he thinks might have carried destruction to the latest of sea marvels the weather was clear. He said that later there was ice on both sides of his vessel. Speaking of the possibility of learning of the presence of ice during the night Captain Holst said:—

"If the weather is clear the ice can be seen, even if the night is quite dark. If, however, there is fog it is quite possible to run on ice without any indication of it whatever. When there is ice there is often fog."

RAN INTO ICE WHERE THE TITANIC SANK

Grandsons of Garibaldi, Aboard the Bretagne, Take Photographs of Giant Bergs.

During her trip from Havre, France, the steamship Bretagne ran into the iceberg field near where the Titanic sank, and the passengers had an excellent view of about a dozen large icebergs. Among those who were on board when she arrived yesterday were the two grandsons of Garibaldi, the great Italian liberator. Several fine pictures of the icebergs were taken by Ricciotti Garibaldi, who, as is his brother Giuseppe, is an expert photographer.

Ricciotti has taken pictures all over the world and he was very much elated at being able to obtain the pictures of the icebergs. The largest of the icebergs towered several hundred feet in the air. Their presence made the atmosphere very cold. The closest the ship got to any of them was about a mile and a half.

"These icebergs are a great menace to navigation," said Giuseppe Garibaldi, "and our captain, Mons. Mace, did not tarry long in the field where they were. We ran into the icebergs on last Sunday morning about six o'clock. Captain Mace thought that they were dangerous and ran south for about two hours to get to the outer edge of the field.

"The icebergs were visible around us until about noon. There seemed to be a great many of them. Captain Mace said there were more icebergs afloat this year than for a great many years.

"The first news we got of the disaster to the Titanic was a wireless message when we were off Cape Cod on Monday last. The first report said that everyone on board had been saved. On the following day we got another message informing us of the great loss of life among the Titanic's passengers."

CHINESE SAVE MEN FIRST.

CLEVELAND, Ohio, Wednesday.—Had the Titanic been a Chinese vessel, manned by Chinese sailors, not a woman or child would have been saved, according to Henry Moy Fot, special agent for the Chinese Merchants' Association of America, who was in Cleveland to-day.

"It is the duty of Chinese sailors when a Chinese vessel goes down to save men first, children next and women last," said the agent. "This is on the theory that men are most valuable to the State, that adoptive parents can be found for children and that women without husbands are destitute."

HAD ARRANGED LUNCHEON.

Captain E. J. Smith, of the Titanic, was to have been one of a luncheon party arranged for to-day by Colonel William Hester and John J. Sinclair, of Brooklyn. Colonel Hester and Mr. Sinclair had taken passage several times with Captain Smith.

Colonel Hester said yesterday he had been a passenger with Captain Smith when he commanded the Baltic, Adriatic and the Olympic, and expected this summer to take passage on board the Titanic.

"Captain Smith had many friends in this city,' explained Colonel Hester, "and frequently visited Glen Cove, L. I. On every visit there he was either entertained by Mr. Henry W. J. Backnall or others."

THE TUNISIAN AVOIDED ICE

LIVERPOOL, Wednesday.—The Tunisian, of the Allan line, which arrived here to-day, reports that on Saturday at midnight, when 887 miles east of St. John's she sent a message of "good luck" to the Titanic. Later she entered a huge ice field, through which she steamed for twenty-four hours, then stopped all night, eventually turning sixty miles south.

Red Wing Daily Republican.

VOLUME XXVII. NO. 160. RED WING, MINNESOTA, THURSDAY EVENING, APRIL 18, 1912. PRICE TWO CENTS.

GOVERNMENT WILL INVESTIGATE TITANIC DISASTER

NATION AWAITS ARRIVAL OF CARPATHIA; FOG MAY DELAY LANDING TONIGHT

By United Press:

Washington, April 18.—Senator Alden E. Smith, Republican, of Michigan, and his senate committee are instructed to probe the wreck of the Titanic. They conferred with President Taft today and decided to go at once to New York and summon all officers and crew of Titanic and rescued passengers and make a thorough investigation. They will take the Sergeant at Arms of the Senate along with them on the revenue cutter to enforce summons.

Fog Covers Harbor

By United Press:

New York, April 18.—The entrance to the New York City Harbor is covered with a very heavy fog, and the Carpathia may not be able to enter tonight. Undertakers have been ordered to be ready to land bodies, showing that some of the survivors are dead. It is also reported that some of the survivors have been driven insane.

A Ship of Sorrow

By United Press:

New York, April 18.—Vice-President Franklin of the White Star line says that from the advices that have been received at the company's office today by wireless, that the Carpathia is a ship of sorrow. The survivors are wild with grief and cannot tell a connected story of the Titanic disaster.

One hundred of the survivors are in the ship hospital. Two hundred of the Titanic crew were asleep when the crash came. They were killed instantly.

The Titanic was in utter darkness four minutes after the crash.

Searching Inquiry

By United Press:

London, April 18.—Immediate and searching inquiry into the Titanic disaster is promised on the floor of the House of Commons today by president Sidney Buxton of the Board of Trade which controls all sea-going vessels. The postmaster-general Samuel is probing the false stories sent out Monday.

Further particulars of the Titanic disaster will be found on Page 7.

Hayes was Drowned

By United Press:

Montreal, April 18.—A wireless dispatch from Mrs. C. M. Hayes, on board the Carpathia, says that her husband, the president of the Grand Trunk railroad is not on the Carpatia, but was drowned on the Titanic.

ENGAGE ENTIRE HOSPITAL

By United Press:

New York, April 18.—The White Star Line has engaged an entire hospital to care for the injured Titanic victims. Ambulances have been engaged to meet the Carpathia at the dock.

705 SURVIVORS.

By United Press:

New York, April 18.—The Cunard liner Carpathia with 705 survivors of the Titanic disaster on board, is reported to dock here at 9 o'clock tonight.

The Carpathia refuses to answer President Taft's request, through the scout cruiser Chester, for further information of the disaster, and the cruiser has sailed for Bradford.

Despite the fact that the Carpathia will give no details, managing director Ismay of the White Star line who was rescued from the Titanic, is sending code messages from the Carpathia to the White Star officials.

The latest figures show that 705 have been rescued as follows: 381 cabin passengers, 126 steerage passengers, 33 unknown, 165 crew.

The missing number 1514 as follows: first cabin 172, second cabin189, steerage 453 and crew 700.

Many now think that the story of the wreck, when told, will be the worst in marine history, showing that the accident might have been avoided had the Titanic slowed down when in the region of the ice.

The condition of the survivors is unknown. Mayor Gaynor has issued an order that none but representatives of the press associations are to be allowed on the dock when the passengers are being landed, all photographers being barred. The flags are at half mast all over the city, and the municipal lodginghouse is prepared to house the immigrants. Mrs. John Jacob Astor, soon to become a mother, is reported to be in the Carpathia hospital.

MRS ASTOR VERY SICK

By United Press:

New York, April 18.—A message received by wireless from the Carpathia by the Wall Street news bureau says that no lives were saved from the Titanic except those who are on the vessel. John Jacob Astor is among the dead and Mrs. Astor is very sick.

KNEW OF ICEBERGS.

By United Press:

Halifax, N. S., April 18.—The steamer Parisian officials say the Titanic was traveling at a speed of 22 knots an hour when it hit the iceberg. The night was clear and the sea was calm. The Titanic must have known of the presence of icebergs, as it was told by many ships to be on the lookout for them.

STRAUSS AND WIFE MISSING

By United Press:

New York, April 18—A message has been received from the Carpathia stating that neither Isador Strauss nor his wife were saved.

White Star Liner Titanic, Which Collided With an Iceberg While on Her Maiden Voyage.

The Titanic and her sister ship, the Olympic, of the White Star line are the largest ships afloat, being 100 feet longer than their nearest rival. These sea monsters are at the same time floating mansions of luxury. They are 882½ feet long, 92 feet in the beam and 94 feet in depth, with 45,000 tons register and 66,000 tons displacement. With officers and crew numbering 860, the Titanic is capable of carrying 3,000 to 3,500 passengers—cabin and steerage. She was built to be the last word in size, speed, power and sea luxury. The insert in the illustration is Captain E. J. Smith of the Titanic. He also was captain of the Olympic at the time of her collision with the Hawke.

OPERATOR SLEEPS AS CRY FOR HELP COMES

By United Press:

Halifax, N. S., April 18—The wireless operator on the Parisian just went to bed after having worked eighteen hours when the cry for help from the Titanic which was 100 miles away was received.. The Parisian did not know of the disaster for hours, and might have saved many. . . . . .

MANNER BLAMES SPEED ZEAL

Declares Greater Care Would Have Saved Titanic From Ice berg.

Minneapolis, April 18.—John Hogan, who lives at 526 Fifth avenue south, for nine years a sailor on the American line of steamers, believes that the wreck of the Titanic was caused by the zeal of its captain to make a record trip on its maiden voyage.

Hogan, who said he had sailed the same route a hundred times, said that Captain Smith of the Titanic probably had tried to take a short cut between Southampton and New York and had run too far north.

"From all appearances it seems to me that the skipper probably laid his course too far to the north," he said. "They got among the icebergs, knew they were near them, as they would have to know, took a desperate chance to get out, and paid the penalty.

"Any sailor can tell when he is within a mile or more of an iceberg and some one of the men on the Titanic at least must have known of the presence of icebergs.

"It is customary when in that region during the months of April and March, when the ice runs the most frequently, for a man to be in crows'-nest all the time. He usually keeps his cheek turned toward the north to get the first 'feel' of icebergs.

"'A cold wind that comes in a flash and is gone as quick is the sign of the presence of an iceberg. Then the ship usually is backed at full speed to escape it, if it is foggy weather. If clear weather a keen lookout is established. I feel positive that Capt. Smith knew of the presence of icebergs, as this time of year usually sees many there."

BULLETINS

PREPARE TO FORCE ENTRANCE

By United Press:

Constantinople, April 18.—The Italian fleet is reported at the entrance of the Dardanelles preparing to force an entrance and passage to Constantinople. One Italian ship, it is reported, has been lost by contact with a mine.

Charles M. Hayes, Titanic Victim

CANNOT RECOVER BODIES.

Special to The Republican:

Baltimore, April 18.—"The bodies of the victims of the Titanic are at the bottom of the deep never to leave it," said Prof. Wood of the chair of experimental physics of Johns Hopkins university yesterday.

"It is improbable that any of the corpses will ever return to the surface as is the case with bodies drowned in shallow water. At the depth of two miles, the pressure of the water is something like 6,000 pounds to the square inch which is far too great to be overcome by buoyancy ordinarily given drowned bodies by the gases generated in time."

First Candidate to File For Sheriff

THOS. HEISERMAN,

President of the Red Wing City Council who is going into county politics.

BASE BALL XTRA

Rain again today prevented a number of the games in the big leagues from being staged. But one was played on the National circuit and that between St. Louis and Pittsburg. All games in the American Association were postponed.

National.

St. Louis	3
Pittsburg	4

American

New York	☐
Washington	☐
Philadelphia	☐
Boston	☐
Cleveland	☐
Detroit	☐
Chicago	12
St. Louis	7

SECOND DAY OF NEBRASKA CAMPAIGN

Col. Roosevelt Speaks to Large Crowds—Pleased With Reception at Omaha

By United Press:

Auburn, Neb., April 18—Col. Theodore Roosevelt opened his second day's Nebraska campaign by addressing large crowds at Nebraska City and here. Col. Roosevelt was pleased today over the reception tendered him by 12,000 people at Omaha last night.

POLITICIANS BUSY AT WORK

GOSSIP AND SURMISE OF THINGS THAT MAY HAPPEN, BY "CAPITOL OBSERVER."

MEN WHO SEEKOFFICE

National Situation Will Have Marked Effect on Fortunes of Gubernatorial Candidates—All Are Working Hard —St. Paul City Fight—H. H. Dunn May Run for Congress in First District.

Special to The Republican:

St. Paul, April 18.—The national situation is having a bearing upon the state affairs more than one would suppose.

The Eberhart machine long ago decided to cast its fortunes with Taft on the supposition that the president would have delegates enough before the Minnesota convention was held to insure his renomination. But now things are so much in the air that they are beginning to doubt the wisdom of their course and the word has been sent all along the line: "Abandon Taft cause when necessary to secure control," which means that the Eberhart cause is to be placed paramount to all others.

If Caswell and his forces were to control the state convention in May, the one which elects delegates to the national convention, a serious blow to the prestige of the administration would be dealt and they fully realize this. Lee is tied up with the La Follette cause and that makes for more complications. The friends of Senator Bob have not given up hopes and profess to believe that they still have a splendid chance of carrying Minnesota for their man.

In the St. Paul campaign the fight is a bitter one. While Bremer is an acknowledged friend of the breweries and an officer in Schmidt's, his friends claim that it is better so than to be the tool of another brewery. Politicians profess that the fight is for the control of the city between two rival brewery organizations and the fight goes merrily on. It is said that if Bremer is elected the attorney general's office will shut the lid down tight on the underworld.

H. H. Dunn is looked upon to get into the First District congressional fight. It has long been known that the speaker was harboring ambitions along that direction but it had been supposed that he was to stifle them until two years hence. But now it is hinted that the Albert Lea legislator sees a chance to slip into the coveted place and may try conclusions with Sidney Anderson and J. J. McCaughey. Dunn will take a look about the district and will sound sentiment a trifle before he throws his hat into the ring.

Dunn would probably have the almost solid support of Freeborn county for the speaker is unquestionably popular in his home county. True he has some virulent enemies there, but they are mainly of the sort which would help his cause rather than injure it. Dunn is likewise popular in Steel county and is said to possess considerable strength in Mower so that he would start with a good nucleus for a campaign. Things are liable to become interesting yet in the First district.

—Capitol Observer.

WILL SPEAK AT RED WING SOON

Long Prairie Candidate for Gubernatorial Nomination to Tour State in Speaking Campaign.

Hon. William E. Lee, progressive candidate for the nomination for governor on the Republican ticket, expects to speak to the citizens of Red Wing on the issues of the state political campaign which is now pending, in the near future.

He started out in a speech at Wayzata given last evening and next week will be busy in the northern part of the state, speaking at Bemidji and other points.

During his trip into the northern part of the state he will be accompanied by James Manahan. Who will accompany him to Red Wing is not as yet known.

ALLEGED MURDERER CAPTURED

By United Press:

Stockton, Calif., April 18—William Dorr, who is wanted in Lynn, Mass., for the alleged murder of George E. Marsh, the millionaire, was captured today.

YESTERDAY'S NEWS IN DETAIL CLIPPED FROM THIS MORNING'S PAPERS

Today's Latest News by Telegraph Will be Found on the First and Other Pages

CONGRESS PROBES THE CATASTROPHE

BILLS DESIGNED TO PREVENT REPETITION OF TITANIC DISASTER POUR IN.

MARINE TREATIES URGED

Particular Attention Will Be Given to Inadequacy of Life Boats—Propose to Patroll Waterways.

Washington, April 18.—Congress acted swiftly on the Titanic catastrophe. Bills and resolutions designed to prevent repetition of the awful disaster off the Newfoundland banks poured into both houses.

The senate agreed to a resolution directing a thorough investigation by the commerce commission into the cause leading to the wreck, with particular reference to the inadequacy of life boats. This resolution, the first introduced in the senate, presented by Senator Smith of Michigan, who ranks next to the chairman of the commerce committee, was adopted by unanimous consent in one hour and 20 minutes.

Senators Martine of New Jersey and Perkins of California, the latter chairman of the naval affairs committee, also introduced bills.

Senator Martine proposed that the president be advised that the senate would favor treaties with maritime nations to regulate the safety of ocean crafts and their passengers and crew.

Perkins' Resolution.

Senator Perkins' resolution provided for the equipment of steamers with adequate life saving apparatus. It would require that every steamer shall have a sufficient number of seaworthy life boats to carry "at one time every passenger and every member of the crew; that it shall not clear any port without so certifying to the several supervising inspectors who would determine the character of such equipment, but would have no discretion whatever as to the number of life boats, which would be determined solely by the actual capacity to carry all aboard."

The Perkins' resolution even prescribed that the life boats should have not less than three cubic feet of displacement for each person.

The Martine resolution was referred to the foreign relations committee and the Perkins resolution went to the commerce committee.

The house committee on merchant marine will speedily take up the many bills and resolutions which have been introduced bearing on the Titanic disaster.

Representative Alexander of Missouri, chairman of the committee, introduced two resolutions. One would direct the president to invite the maritime nations of the world to appoint members of an international commission to define ship lanes and routes and to minimize the danger of collision at sea.

The other would extend a similar invitation to nations interested in North Atlantic steamship travel to form a commission to arrange for a patrol of North Atlantic waters to warn ships.

Representative Sulzer of New York, chairman of the foreign relations committee, offered a joint resolution identical with the senate resolution introduced by Mr. Perkins. The Perkins-Sulzer provisions would require one life preserver for each person aboard. They would also make it a felony for any captain, executive officer or resident general agent of a corporation actually charged with control, management, operation, equipment or navigation of ocean vessels to knowingly permit a vessel to sail from any port of the United States without full life saving equipment. The penalty would be imprisonment at hard labor for not more than 10 years.

General George Uhler, supervising inspector general of the steamboat inspection service, expressed the view that much good could be accomplished by an international congress to consider life saving appliances. He said that there was no action that his department could take in the Titanic case in view of the fact that the vessel was a foreign craft, complying with the British navigation laws.

FIRST RESULT OF THE COLLISION

ACCORDING TO MARINE AUTHORITIES, THE DAMAGE SUSTAINED HERE MARKED THE BEGINNING OF THE END.

MRS. ELLA WILSON HONORED

BY THE CITIZENS OF HUNNEWELL, KAN.

America's Only Woman Mayor Celebrates First Anniversary of Her Election.

Hunnewell, Kan., April 18. — Great banks of roses and carnations, a reception of her enthusiastic townspeople and hundreds of congratulatory telegrams from suffragists throughout the United States greeted Mrs. Ella Wilson, the only woman mayor in America, when she entered her office today upon the first anniversary of her election as chief executive of Hunnewell. Mrs. Wilson's tenure in office has proved a success and it is

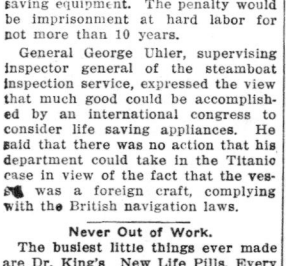

Mrs. Ella Wilson.

confidently stated that if she cares to place her name on the ballot again, at the coming municipal election, she will receive a large majority over any rival who might be put up.

Mrs. Wilson, who is the daughter of a pioneer Presbyterian minister and the wife of a successful business man of Hunnewell, has two sons, one grown and the other just reaching manhood. "I take more pride in my sons than I do in my office," she said today. Her administration of the office of mayor, after an opposing city council, composed of men, had been removed, has instituted a number of reforms, which include the elimination of discrimination in taxation, and the banishment of gamblers, liquor sellers, poolroom keepers and all forms of money-producing vice from the city.

Richards and Grigsby File.

Pierre, S. D., April 18.—The senatorial primary preference petitions of R. O. Richards of Huron and Melvin Grisby of Sioux Falls were filed with the secretary of state, making four republican candidates so far, the others Senator Gamble and Thomas Sterling.

Morgan is Seventy-five.

New York, April 18.—J. Pierpont Morgan is celebrating his seventy-fifth birthday in Aix les Bains, France. According to cablegrams received by members of his firm, he is in excellent health.

TO RECEIVE THE SURVIVORS

ALL FORMALITIES TO BE WAIVED WHEN CARPATHIA TIES UP AT NEW YORK.

REPORTERS ARE BARRED.

Friends and Relatives to Be Admitted to Pier—Boarding of Incoming Liner Forbidden by Cunard Officials.

New York, April 18.—Every effort to facilitate the landing of the Titanic's survivors when the Carpathia docks at her pier on the North river will be made by the immigration and custom authorities, officials of the Cunard line and the New York police. The plans provide for the fullest protection of the survivors and their relatives from interference from curiosity seekers and newspaper representatives until they have left the Cunard pier.

Customs regulations, it was announced, would be suspended and all aliens among the survivors will be immediately discharged by the immigration authorities to their friends and relatives as soon as they leave the ship, although such as may desire will be taken to Ellis Island and cared for.

The Cunard officials announced that they would permit on the pier only friends and relatives of the survivors, who will be admitted by a pass after having established their right to obtain one at the company's offices. No photographers of the press will be admitted, and the police will rope off a large space outside the pier to keep back curious crowds.

Although government officials have signified their willingness to allow newspaper representatives and relatives of the survivors to board the ship from revenue cutters before she reaches the dock, the Cunard officials indicated that this privilege would not be granted. In that event the full story of the great disaster, except such details as may be received by wireless, meanwhile, probably will not be learned until long after the Carpathia has docked.

The Cunard officials stated that they expected that more than 1,000 passes would be issued to relatives of survivors.

The White Star officials announced that arrangements have been made between their company, Commissioner of Immigration Williams and Mayor Gaynor for caring for the third class survivors in the city's municipal lodging houses. Those who are in financial distress or without aid from friends or relatives will be sheltered by the city, it was stated, until they could obtain employment or other relief.

Resents Charge With Blow.

Milwaukee, April 18. — General Joseph B. Doe, former assistant secretary of war in the Cleveland administration, knocked down a lawyer who quarreled with him and was sent to jail and released on bail.

WEATHER FAVORABLE TO CROPS

HEAVY SNOW FILLS THE SOIL WITH MOISTURE.

April's Conditions in Contrast to Those of Several Months Previous.

Washington, April 18.—The weather bureau's crop weather bulletin, just issued, says:

"The weather during April to date has been in marked contrast with the severe conditions that existed during much of the period since the beginning of the year, especially in the districts to the eastward of the Rocky mountains. To the westward of the mountains the weather has been somewhat less favorable during April, but good rains have fallen lately in much of that region and the soil is now generally well saturated with moisture.

"In the winter wheat states west of the Mississippi, the heavy snowfall of the last winter has left the soil well filled with moisture, and the unusual snow covering doubtless proved highly beneficial to the wheat plant during the prevalence of the severe cold. In the winter wheat states east of the Mississippi the snow covering was generally lighter and afforded less protection during the severe cold. The soil is generally well saturated with moisture, and the favorable weather of the last week has rapidly forced vegetation forward in all portions of the belt.

"In the spring wheat region, snowfall was generally less than usual, but good rains during the last week have put the soil in good condition, and the weather was generally favorable for outdoor work."

Woman's Theater Planned.

Chicago, April 18.—Mrs. Mary Moncure Parker is making plans for a woman's theater for Chicago, which will be owned and operated solely by women.

Belgian Aviator Killed.

Versailles, April 18.—Dropping from a great altitude when he lost control of his aeroplane, John Verret, 24, a Belgian aviator, was crushed to death in the wreckage of his machine.

BASE BALL SCORES.

American Association.

All games postponed on account of rain or west grounds.

American League.

All games postponed on account of rain or wet grounds.

National League.

New York, 4; Boston, 1.

Standing of the Clubs.

	Won	Lost	Pct.
St. Louis	4	1	.800
Cincinnati	4	1	.800
Philadelphia	3	2	.600
Boston	3	3	.500
New York	3	3	.500
Brooklyn	2	3	.400
Chicago	1	4	.200
Pittsburg	1	4	.200

DAILY MARKET REPORT.

Twin City Markets.

Minneapolis, April 18.—Wheat, May, \$1.07½; July \$1.09; No. 1 northern, \$1.10; No. 2 northern, \$1.08; No. 1 durum, \$1.10; No. 3 corn, 80c; No. 3 white oats, 56c; barley, malting, \$1.30; No. 2 rye, 89½c; No. 1 flax, \$2.14.

Duluth, April 18.—Wheat, May, \$1.09; July, \$1.09⅜; No. 1 northern, \$1.10; No. 1 durum, \$1.12.

South St. Paul, April 18.—Cattle—Steers, \$5.50@7.00; cows, \$3.50@6.25; calves, \$4.00@6.75; hogs, \$7.65@7.80; sheep and lambs, \$6.00@7.00.

Chicago Live Stock.

Chicago, April 18.—Cattle—Received, 17,000; market steady to shade lower; beeves, \$5.60@8.75; Texas steers, \$4.75@6.10; western steers, \$5.60@7.10; stockers and feeders, \$4.30@6.65; cows and heifers, \$2.65@7.00; calves, \$5.00@8.00.

Hogs — Receipts, 23,000; market steady to strong at yesterday's average; light, \$7.75@8.00; mixed, \$7.65@8.07½; heavy, \$7.70@8.10; rough, \$7.70@7.80; pigs, \$5.00@7.35; bulk of sales, \$7.90@8.05.

Sheep — Receipts, 18,000; market steady to strong; native, \$4.35@6.40; western, \$4.50@6.95; yearlings, \$5.90@7.10; lambs, native, \$5.50@7.85; western, \$6.25@8.20.

Chicago Grain Market.

Chicago, April 18.—Frosts reported all through Nebraska, Kansas, Oklahoma and the north part of Texas, had a bullish effect today on the price of wheat. Moreover, the weather was cold and cloudy northwest, with many places sending word of temperature below freezing. Decreasing stocks at Liverpool counted also against the bear side. No ray of hope appeared from the districts east of the Mississippi, where winter killings were alleged to have wrought such widespread harm. For example, all the way from Peoria to Springfield, Ill., was said to show this morning total failure, only here and there a green field. The opening varied from ⅛c off to ½c up; July started at \$1.06¾ to \$1.07; a gain of ¼c to ½c, touched \$1.06⅝ and then rose to \$1.07¼.

After a trifle more advance, the July option dipped sharply because of a leading firm making heavy sales intended to effect a quick scalp. The close was unsettled with July ⅛@¼c net lower at \$1.06¼@1.06⅝.

Corn turned strong on account of the wet and cold. Shorts scurried to buy and found but little offered. July opened ¼@⅜c to ¾@⅞c higher at 76⅜c to 76⅞c, and mounted to 77c.

The market climbed yet higher, but temporarily fell back after wheat turned weak. Closing prices were nervous with July at 77⅛@77¼c, a net gain of 1⅛c.

A bulge in oats took place as a result of sympathy with corn and wheat. Prospect of additional delay to seeding was a further help to the bulls. July started ¼@⅜c to ⅜@½c dearer at 53⅝c to 53¾c and advanced to 54⅛c.

Her Latest Lover.

"Nell's just crazy over Shakespeare."

"So he's her latest, is he? Where'd she meet him?"

Want ad is a good investment.

GRAIN STORAGE IS ENJOINED

LICHTSTERN, IN AID OF WHEAT CORNER, BRINGS ACTION IN CHICAGO COURT.

ROSENBAUMS ARE SUED

Daring Speculator Devises Tactful Move Against His Opponents in Big Wheat Manipulation Deal.

Chicago, April 18.—Adolph J. Lichtstern, millionaire board of trade operator, made a court move, which grain men say, if successful, will enable the grain man to corner the Chicago wheat market. Warehousemen further declared that if the big operator's legal contentions are upheld, it will mean the loss of thousands of dollars to the big elevator firms.

Lichtstern went before Judge Adelor J. Petit and asked that the J. Rosenbaum Grain company be enjoined from practicing its present business methods with regard to the purchasing and storing of grain in the big warehouses of J. Rosenbaum. He declared in a lengthy bill filed by his attorneys, that the grain firm and the warehouse concern of J. Rosenbaum were operated together, in violation of the supreme court decision, which forbids owners of public warehouses from storing their own grain in their public grain elevators.

He further declared that the defendants have deposited in the Rosenbaum elevators "doctored wheat" of poor quality which is mixed with the better grades of grain of other depositors, thus enabling the elevator people to "grade up" their poor quality holdings.

It is asserted that the Rosenbaums have made pretended sales of grain to brokers, and the brokers in turn have stored the grain in the Rosenbaum elevators, and in reality have simply paid brokers from ⅛ to ¼ cent a bushel commission for their part in the "sale" proceedings.

Warehousemen refused to discuss the matter last night, but it was declared that Lichtstern succeeded in enjoining the warehouse people in this suit others would shortly follow against other warehouse concerns. So wrought up were the big elevator men that one of them is said to have written a letter to the president of the board of trade demanding the discharge of Attorney Robbins, the board's attorney, who represents Lichtstern in the injunction suit.

They declared that the millionaire wheat dealer who has been trying for two years to corner the market, is simply making the present move to keep down the supply of cash wheat in Chicago warehouses. It was stated that Lichtstern now owns practically all of the 12,000,000 or 15,000,000 bushels of cash wheat in Chicago elevators, and if he makes good on his "corner" program he must keep wheat out of the Chicago market. There is warehouse capacity in the city for about 25,000,000 bushels.

SOUTH DAKOTA ELECTION

Annual Wet and Dry Contests Are Held.

Watertown, S. D., April 18.—At the first municipal election under the commission plan, H. A. Wagner was elected mayor without opposition. In a field of twelve candidates for commissioner, three were elected by majorities of all votes cast, while the second election, April 23, will be necessary to choose the fourth. The successful candidates were C. K. Snyder, F. A. Countryman and D. H. Wooley. The next two high men were P. G. Bush and J. C. Southwick, who will be candidates in the second contest. H. S. Fletcher and Frank Bramble were elected members of the board of education without opposition.

The following towns in Watertown territory voted "wet" by the majorities indicated: Castlewood, 46; Clear Lake, 2; Albee, 21; Volga, 9; Lily, 16; Gary, 11; Henry, 10; Turton, 11; South Shore, 45; Altamont, 9; Lake Norden, 6; Nunda, 29; Vienna, 27; Goodwin, 23; Webster, 15; Florence, 30; Estelline, 20; Bryant, 72. Following voted "dry": Revilo, 2; Rockham, 8; Conde, 36; Redfield, 40; Waubay, 14; Hecla, 15; Faulkton, 18.

Pope Instructs Delegate.

Rome, April 18.—The pope received in farewell private audience Mgr. Giovanni Bonzano, apostolic delegate to the United States. The pontiff gave his last instructions to Mgr. Bonzano and asked him to convey his apostolic blessing to the members of the Catholic church in America.

Lucky.

Howell—It costs a good deal to live. Powell—Aren't you glad you are a dead one?—New York Press.

Anything for sale? Advertise it.

Wilson's Suit Case Returned.

Chicago, April 18.—Governor Woodrow Wilson's suit case which was stolen from his rooms in a downtown hotel here ten days ago was found. It was discovered as the result of an anonymous telephone message to the hotel. The message said the case could be found in an areaway between St. Mary's church and the Parish house. A detective was sent to the place and found it. It contained a dress suit, soiled linen and papers. Apparently nothing had been touched.

Anderson Has a Parcels Post Bill.

Washington, April 18.—Representative Sydney Anderson has introduced a bill providing for a parcels post system based on the zone principle which he believes will form the basis for a more general discussion of the parcels post question and eventually lead to the passage of legislation providing this facility. The Anderson bill is designed to meet the objections of rural route merchants to a parcels post by the establishment of a zone system with rates of postage graduated according to distance.

BANGOR DAILY COMMERCIAL.

VOLUME XLI. BANGOR, MAINE, FRIDAY EVENING, APRIL 19, 1912. THREE CENTS.

HER SIDE RIPPED AS BY GIANT CAN OPENER

Titanic Split Open By Berg From Stem to Engine Room---Went Down With Her Band Playing "Nearer My God to Thee," Carrying 1589 Souls Back to Their Maker---745 Survivors, All That Are Living of Ship's Company of 2340, Landed From Carpathia

New York, April 19.--Seven hundred and forty-five persons, mostly women, sick in heart and body, wrote into the annals of maritime history Friday the loss of the finest steamship ever built by man. They were the survivors of the White Star liner Titanic, which sank, bow foremost with 1,595 souls aboard, her captain at the bridge, her colors fllying and her band playing, "Nearer My God To Thee," in 2,000 fathoms of water off the banks of Newfoundland under starlit skies at 2.20 a. m. Monday.

With one voice they told of the splendid heroism of those who remained behind to find a watery grave that they might live.

Capt. Smith died, they say, as a gallant sailor should, after having first placed all the women who would go aboard the lifeboats. There were many who stayed behind to die with their husbands.

From their narratives stand out in bold relief the following:

The Titanic was making 21 knots an hour when she struck the berg.

No one at first thought she would sink.

She remained afloat more than two hours.

The iceberg ripped open her bowels below the water line.

Instant panic was averted by Capt. Smith's terse appeal to his crew: "Be British, my men."

A small number of steerage passengers tried to rush for the liefboats and were held back by the crew and other passengers.

The Titanic turned her nose for the bottom when the last lifeboat was less than 100 yards away, reared her stern high in the air and trembled for a moment before seeking the bed of the sea.

There were two explosions when the inrushing waters reached her boilers.

When she sank there w[as] silence—a moment later the cri[es] and supplications of 1,500 dying men arose in chorus indescribable over the spot where she went down.

For hours the survivors re[mained] in lifeboats over a calm sea i[n] bitter cold, until the Carpathia picked them up.

In the aftermath Friday of the disaster, the personal developments were the testimony of J. Bruce Ismay, managing director of the White Star line before the Senate Investigating committee and the removal of surviving members of the Titanic's cre[w] aboard the Lapland.

The Titanic's Short History

From the facts compiled by the arrival of the steamship, the Titanic story, which began in the fall of 1908, with the White Star line announcing its proposal to eclipse all previous records in ship building with a vessel of staggering dimensions, may be outlined chonologrically as follows:

1909—Keel of the gigantic vessel laid at Harland & Wolff's yards at Belfast.

1911--May 31, the vessel is launched and christened the Titanic.

1912—Completed and fully furnished at an outlay of about $10,000,000.

April 10, noon, starts on the maiden trip from Southampton to New York via Cherbourg.

April 14, sends a routine wireless warning ashore of the presence of icebergs off the Grand Banks of Newfoundland.

April 14, 11.40 p. m., Titanic strikes an iceberg in lat. 41.16 N. long. 50.14 W.

April 14, midnight—Carpathia and other vessels hear Titanic's call for help.

April 15, 12.27 a. m.—Wireless is put out of commission and flashes given that the boat is sinking by the head and that women and children are being put off in life boats.

April 15—About 1 a. m., the first news reached the United States by way of the Allan line offices at Montreal, the Virginian reporting that the Titanic struck an iceberg.

April 15, 2.20 a. m.—Titanic sinks.

April 15, 3 a. m.—Wireless from the Cape Race station direct to the Associated Press gives the first information of a serious disaster.

April 15, 5 a. m.—First survivors picked up from life boats by steamer Carpathia.

April 15, 10 a. m.—No advices.

April 15, noon—Reports current that Titanic is still afloat and all saved.

April 15, 7.30 p. m.—White Star offices admit possible loss of life.

April 16—Carpathia sends by wireless list of survivors, failing to account for about 1300 persons including scores of wealthy and prominent people.

April 17—Hope given up that other vessels have saved any.

April 18—Two days elapsed without slightest description of disaster.

April 18, 9.30—Rescue ship docks at New York with 745 passengsrs and crew confirming the loss of all others and bringing the first details of the Titanic disaster.

Col. Gracie's Story Of Thrilling Escape

Drawn Under in the Vortex of Sinking Ship He Fought Way to Surface and Swam Until He Found Raft

New York, April 19.--Col. Archibald Gracie, who jumped from the topmost deck of the Titanic as she sank and swam about until he found a cork life preserver and then helped to rescue those who had jumped into the water, added Friday to his statement of Thursday night:

"The Titanic was struck by the berg on her port side," Col. Gracie said. "She was ripped from near the middle boat to the bow after the fashion of a can opener opening a box of sardines. The buttons were pressed immediately and the compartments closed as far as possible under the circumstances.

During the intervals between the collision and the sinking of the ship was two hours and 12 minutes time by my watch, which lay open on the dresser. The watch stopped at 2.12 a. m. when I jumped into the water. I was awakened in my cabin at midnight.

"After sinking with the ship it appeared to be as if I was propelled by some great force through the water. This might have been occasioned by explosions under the water. I recall that I was most fearful of being boiled to death. The second officer, who was on the top deck, told me that he had a similar experience when innumerable thoughts of a personal nature, relating to mental telepathy flashed through my brain. I thought of those at home as if my spirit might go to them and say good-bye forever, but for a similar experience in days gone by had occurred in the history of a memory of my wife's family and she was even awake that night, tortured with presentiments.

"Again and again I prayed for deliverance, although I felt sure that the end had come. My great difficulty came in holding my breath until I came to the surface for I knew if I inhaled water I would have suffocated. Under the water I struck out with all my strength for the surface.

"I reached the surface after a time that seemed unending. There was nothing in sight save the ice which dotted the ocean and a large field of wreckage. There were dying men and women all about me, groaning and crying piteously.

FUNNEL FELL NEAR HIM.

"The second officer and J. B. Thayer, Jr., who were swimming near, told me that just before my head appeared above the water, one of the Titanic's funnels separated and fell apart near me, scattering the bodies in the water.

'I saw wreckage everywhere. All that came within my reach I clung to. A great cradle like block of wood floated within my grasp and I grabbed it. It seemed to be sufficiently large to keep me afloat. At this moment, however, I saw an overturned boat a short distance away and swam to it. I caught the arm of a man who grasped me, threw my leg over the boat and rested on it

"On this raft—it was really a collapsible boat, that was called a raft—there were already lying more than 20 men who seemed to belong to the Titanic's crew. Two men, one in the bow, the other in the stern, propelled us through the wreckage with pieces of wood which answered for oars.

(Continued on Third Page).

HOW ASTOR SMUGGLED BOY INTO BOAT AS A GIRL

New York, April 19.—A fine act of heroism by Col. John Jacob Astor was told Friday by George A. Harder, a Brooklyn man, who survived the Titanic disaster:

"When Col. Astor had assisted his tearful young wife and her maid into a lifeboat he tried to put in a young boy, but the sailors refused to let him in, saying that the room was only for the children. Then Col. Astor picked up a woman's hat from the deck and placed it on the boy's head and brought him back to the boat. He said, 'Here, little girl, climb in," and the officers of the ship let the boy through. As the boat lowered away Col. Astor stood on the deck waving good-byes.

COMPLETE TABULATION OF THE PASSENGERS AND CREW

The following tabulation of passengers and crew on board the Titanic together with those saved and lost, has been compiled from the figures in the statement issued by the committee of passengers:

Approximate number of passengers on board: First class, 330; second class, 320; third class, 750. Total passengers, 1,400.

Officers and crew, 940. Total, 2,340.

Number of passengers saved by Carpathia:

First class, 210; second class, 125; third class, 200. Total, 535.

Members of crew saved; Officers, 4; seamen, 39; stewards, 96; firemen, 71. Total, 210.

Total saved, 745.

Total Number perished, 1,595.

First and second cabin passengers, 650.

First and second cabin passengers saved, 335.

Total cabin passengers lost, 315.

PASSENGERS TELL OF CRASH, THEIR ESCAPE AND SINKING OF THE TITANIC

Col. Archibald Gracie's Remarkable Escape---Went Down With Ship---Col. Astor's Conduct---Vivid Tale of Shipwreck and Rescue By An Englishman---Scenes on the Titanic Before She Foundered

How the White Star Liner Titanic, the largest ship afloat, sank off the Grand Banks of Newfoundland on Monday morning last, carrying to their death 1,601 of the 2,340 persons aboard, was told to the world in all its awful details for the first time with the arrival in New York, Thursday night of the Cunard liner Carpathia bearing the exhausted survivors of the catastrophe. Of the great facts that stand out from the chaotic account of the tragedy, these are the most salient:

"The death list has been increased rather than decreased.

"Six persons died after being rescued.

"The list of prominent persons lost stands as previously reported.

"Practically every woman and child, with the exception of those women who refused to leave their husbands, were saved. Among the latter was Mrs. Isidor Straus, wife of the New York millionaire merchant.

The survivors on the life boats saw the lights on the stricken vessel glimmer to the last, heard her band playing and saw the doomed hundreds on her deck and heard their groans and cries when the vessel sank. Accounts vary as to the extent of the disorder on board. Not only was the Titanic tearing through the April night to her doom but she was under orders from the general officers of the line to make all the speed of which she was capable. This was the statement made Thursday night by J. H. Moody, a quartermaster and the helmsmen on the night of the disaster. He said the ship was making 21 knots an hour and the officers were striving to live up to the orders to smash a record.

"It was close to midnight," said Moody, "and I was on the bridge with the second officer, who was in command. Suddenly he shouted, 'Port your helm.' I did so but it was too late. We struck the submerged portion of the berg."

Of the many accounts given by the passengers most of them agre that the shock when the Titanic struck the iceberg, although it ripped her great sides as a giant can-opener would, did not greatly jar the vessel for the blow was a glancing one along her side. The accounts also agree substantially that when the passengers were taken off on the lifeboats there was no serious panic and that many wished to remain on board believing her unsinkable.

The most distressing stories are those of passengers who were in life boats. These tell not only of their own sufferings, but give the harrowing details of how they saw the great hulk of the Titanic plunge to the bottom. As this awful spectacle was witnessed by the group of survivors in the boats, they plainly saw many of those whom they had just left behind leaping from the decks into the water.

J. Bruce Ismay, managing director of the International Mercantile Marine Company, owners of the White Star line, who was among the 70 odd men saved; P. A. S. Franklin, vice president of the White Star line, and U. S. Senator Wm. Alden Smith, chairman of the Senate investigating comimttee, conferred aboard the Carpathia soon after the passengers had come ashore.

After nearly an hour, Senator Smith came out of the cabin and said he had no authority to subpoena witnesses at present, but would begin an investigation into the cause of the loss of the Titanic at the Waldorf-Astoria hotel Friday. He announced that Mr. Ismay had consented to appear at the hearing and that Mr. Franklin and the four surviving officers of the Titanic would appear for examination by the Senate committee. He said that the course the investigation would follow would be determined after the preliminary hearing.

The arrival of the Carpathia brought a vast multitude of people to the Cunard docks. They filled the vast pier sheds and overflowing for blocks, crowded the nearby streets in a dense throng. Through it all the rain fell steadily, adding a funerel aspect to the secne. The landing of the survivors was attended with little excitement, for the crowds stood in awed silence as the groups from the ship passed along. The docking actually began shortly after 9 o'clock and the debarking of passengers was so quickly disposed of owing to the waiving of the usual formalities that practically everything had been finished by 10.30 o'clock. The crowd remained about the pier long after this, however, to get a glimpse of the rescuing steamer and to hear the harrowing stories which were brought back by the ship.

Physicians and nurses went aboard the Carpathia before anyone was allowed to go down the gangway, but soon after the first cabin passengers, women predominating, began descending the incline. Some walked unaided, some were assisted by friends, relatives and nurses and some were on stretchers. Mrs. John Jacob Astor, now a widow, was met by her stepson, Vincent, and her sister, Miss Force. They embraced with tears, hurried to a limousine and drove to the Astor town house.

The two hundred and more steerage passengers did not leave the ship until 11 o'clock. They were in a sad condition. The women were without wraps and the few men there wore very little clothing.

One of the most sensational stories that came from the Carpathia was one that Capt. Smith and the first officer and the chief engineer had shot themselves when they realized that the ship was doomed. These reports could not be confirmed; in fact, they were denied by most of the passengers, although one or two said that they had heard there was some shooting.

The Titanic's four rescued officers were placed on board the Red Star liner Lapland for the night. They refused to talk.

COL. GRACIE PICKED UP AFTER SHIP WENT DOWN

E. Z. Taylor, of Philadelphia, one of the survivors, jumped into the sea a few minutes before the Titanic sank. He told a graphic story as he came from the Carpathia.

"I was eating when the boat struck the iceberg," he said. "There was an awful shock that made the boat tremble from stem to stern. I felt the boat rise and it seemed to me that she was riding over the ice. I ran out on deck and then I could see ice.

"I jumped into the ocean and was picked up by one of the boats. I never expected to see land again. I waited on board the boat until the lights went out. It seemed to me that the discipline on the boat was wonderful."

Col. Archibald Gracie, U. S. A., the last man saved, went down with the vessel, but was picked up. He was met Thursday night by his daughter, who had arrived from Washington, and his son-in-law, Paul H. Fabricius, Col. Gracie told a remarkable story of personal hardship and denied emphatically the reports that there was any panic on board. He praised in the highest terms the behavior of both the passengers and crew and spoke especially of the heroism of the women passengers.

"Mrs. Isidor Strauss," he said, "went to her death because she would not desert her husband. Although he pleaded with her to take her place in the boat, she steadfastly refused; and when the ship settled at the head, the two were engulfed by the wave that swept her.'

Col. Gracie described how he was driven to the topmost deck when the ship settled and how he was the sole survivor after the wave that swept her just before her final plunge, had passed.

"I jumped with the wave," said he, "just as I often have jumped with the breakers at the sea shore; by great good fortune I managed to grasp the brass railing on the deck above and I hung on by might and main. When the ship plunged down I was forced to let go and I was swirled around and around for what seemd to be an interminable time. Eventually I came to the surface to find the sea a mass of tangled wreckage.

"Luckily I was unhurt and casting about managed to seize a wooden grating floating. When I had recovered my breath I discovered a large canvas and cork raft which had floated up. A man whose name I did not learn, was struggling toward it from some wreckage to which he had clung. I cast off and helped him to get on the raft, and we then began the work of rescuing those who had jumped into the sea and were foundering in the water.

"When dawn broke there were 30 of us on the raft, standing knee deep in the icy water and afraid to move lest the cranky craft be overturned. Several unfortunates, benumbed and half dead, besought us to save them and one or two made an effort to reach us but we had to warn them away. Had we made any effort to save we all might have perished.

"The hours that elapsed before we were picked up by the Carpathia were the longest and most terrible that I ever spent. Practically without any sensation of feeling because of the icy water we were almost dropping from fatigue. We were afraid to turn around to look to see whether we were seen by passing craft and when some one who was facing astern passed the word that somethiug that looked like a steamer was coming up the men became hysterical under the strain. The rest of us, too, were nearing the breaking point."

Col. Gracie denied with emphasis that any men were fired upon and said that only once was a revolver discharged.

"This was for the purpose of intimidating some steerage passengers," he said, "who had tumbled into a boat before it was prepared for launching. This shot was fired in the air, and when the foreigners were told that the next would be directed at them, they promptly returned to the deck. There was no confusion and no panic."

Contrary to the general expectation, there was no jarring impact when the vessel struck, according to the army officer. He was in his berth when the vessel dashed into the submerged portion of the berg and was aroused by the jar. He looked at his watch, he said, and found it was just midnight. The ship sunk with him at 2.22 a. m., for his watch stopped at that hour.

Hays Had a Premonition

"Before I returned," said Col. Gracie, "I had a long chat with Chas. M. Hays, president of the Grand Trunk R. R. "One of the last things Mr. Hays said was this:

"'The White Star, the Cunard and the Hamburg-American lines are devoting their attention and ingenuity in vicing one with the other to attain the supremacy in luxurious ships and in making speed records. The time will soon come, when this will be checked by some appalling disaster.' Poor fellow, a few hours later he was dead."

"The conduct of Col. John Jacob Astor was deserving of the highest praise," Col. Gracie said. "The millionaire New Yorker," he said, "devoted all his energies to saving his young bride, nee Miss Force of New York who was in delicate health.

Col. Astor Asked to Go.

"Col. Astor helped us in our efforts to get her in the boat," said Col. Gracie "I lifted her into the boat and as she took her place, Col. Astor requested permission of the second officer to go with her for her own protection.

"'No, sir,' replied the officer, 'not a man shall go on a boat until the women are all off.' Col. Astor then inquired the number of the boat which was being lowered away and turned to the work of clearing the other boats and in reassuring the frightened and nervous women."

NO FALLING OFF IN THE BOOKINGS OF LINERS

New York, April 19.—Demand for transatlantic transportation has shown little or no diminution notwithstanding the disaster to the Titanic. Travelers who had made reservations on the list for her proposed eastward trip on Saturday, have arranged with the International Mercantile Marine Company for accommodations on other steamships. The Lapland sailing on Saturday will take some of those who had booked on the Titanic.

The Cunard liner Mauretania here Friday from Liverpool was practically booked to capacity before the Titanic sank. There have been few cancellations.

THE CUNARD LINER CARPATHIA

Rescue Ship, on Which 745 Survivors of the Titanic Disaster Reached New York Thursday Night

LONDONER ON THE TITANIC TELLS A GRAPHIC STORY

Second Cabin Passenger's Story of the Collision, the Filling of Lifeboats and the Rescue by the Carpathia.

The following account of the disaster was given by Mr. L. Beasley, a Cambridge University man who lives in London. Mr. Beasley was in the second cabin and had not been mentioned in the list of the saved.

"The voyage from Queenstown had been quiet and uneventful; very fine weather was experienced and the sea was quite calm. The wind had been westerly to southwesterly the whole way, but very cold, particularly the last day; in fact after dinner on Sunday evening, it was almost too cold to be out on deck at all. I had been in my berth for about ten minutes when at about 11.15 p. m. I felt a slight jar and then soon after a second one, but not sufficiently large to cause any anxiety to anyone however nervous they may have been. However, the engines stopped immediately afterawrds and my first thought was she had lost a propeller. I went on the top (boat) deck in a dressing gown, and found only a few people there who had come up similarly to inquire why she stopped, but there was no sort of anxiety in the minds of any one. We saw through the smoking room window a game of cards going on, and went in to inquire if they knew anything; it seems they felt more of the jar and looking through the window had seen a huge iceberg go by close to the side of the boat. They thought we had just grazed it with a glancing blow, and the engines had been stopped to see if any damage had been done. No one, of course had any conception that she had been pierced below by part of the submerged iceberg. The game went on without any thought of disaster, and I retired to my cabin to read until we went on again. I never saw any of the players or the onlookers again. A little later, hearing people going up stairs, I went out again and found everyone wanting to know why the engines had stopped.

No doubt many were awakened from sleep by the sudden stopping of a vibration to which they had become accustomed during the four days we had been on board. Naturally with such powerful engines as the Titanic carried, the vibration was very noticeable all the time, and the sudden stopping had something the same effect as the stopping of a loud ticking grandfather's clock in a room.

On going on deck again, I saw there was an undoubted list downward from stern to bow, but knowing nothing of what had occurred, I concluded some of the front compartments had filled and weighed her down. I went down again to put on warmer clothing and as I dressed, heard an order shouted: "All passengers on deck with life belts on." We all walked slowly up with them tied on our clothing, but even then presumed this was a wise precaution the Captain was taking and that we should return in a short time and retire to bed. There was a total absence of any panic or any expressions of alarm, and I suppose this can be accounted for by the exceedingly calm night and the absence of any signs of the accident. The ship was absolutely still and except for a gentle tilt downward which I don't think one person in ten would have noticed at that time, no signs of the approaching disaster were visible. She lay just as if she were waiting the order to go on again when some trifling matter had been adjusted. But in a few moments we saw the covers lifted from the boats, and the crews allotted to them standing by and curling up the ropes which were to lower them by the pully blocks into the water.

"We then began to realize it was more serious than had been supposed and my first thought was to go down and get more clothing and some money but seeing people pouring up the stairs decided me that it was better to cause no confusion to people coming up by doing so. Presently we heard the order:

"All men stand back, away from the boats and all ladies retire to next deck below—the smoking room deck or B deck. The men all stood away and against the end railings of the deck or walking slowly up and down. The boats were swung out and lowered from A deck. When they were to the level of B deck, where all the ladies were collected, the ladies got in quietly with the exception of some who refused to leave their husbands. In some cases they were torn from them and pushed into the boats, but in many instances they were allowed to remain because there was no one to insist they should go.

"Looking over the side one saw boats from aft already in the water slipping quietly away into the darkness, and presently the boats near to me were lowered and with much creaking as the new ropes slipped through the pulley blocks, down the ninety feet which separated them from the water. An officer in uniform came up as one boat went down and shouted 'When you are afloat, row round to the companion ladder and stand by with the other boats for orders.'"

"'Aye, aye, sir' came up the reply but I don't think any boat was able to obey the order, when they were afloat and had the oars at work the condition of the rapidly settling boat was so much more a sight of alarm for those in the boats than those on board, that in common prudence the sailors saw they could do nothing but row from the sinking ship to save at any rate, some lives. They no doubt anticipated that suction from such an enormous vessel would be more than usually dangerous to a crowded boat mostly filled with women. All this time there was no trace of any disorder; no panic or rush to the boats and no scenes of women sobbing hysterically such as one generally pictures as happening at such times. Everyone seemed to realize so slowly that there was imminent danger. When it was realized that we might all be presently in the sea with nothing but our life belts to support us until we were picked up by passing steamers, it was extraordinary how calm everyone was and how completely self-controlled.

"One by one the boats were filled with women and children, lowered and rowed away into the night. Presently the word went around among the men: 'The men are to be put in boats on the starboard side.'

"I was on the port side and most of the men walked across the deck to see if this was so. I remained where I was and presently heard::

"Any more ladies?"

"Looking over the side of the ship, I saw the boat, No. 13, swinging level with B deck, half full of ladies. Again the call was repeated 'Any more ladies?'

"I saw none come on and then one of the crew looked up and said 'Any ladies on your deck, sir?'

"'No,' I replied.

"'Then you had better jump."

"I dropped in and fell in the bottom, as they cried, 'Lower away.' As the boat began to descend two ladies were pushed hurriedly through the crowd on B deck and heaved over into the boat and a baby of ten months passed down after them. Down we went, the crew calling to those lowering which end to keep her level. 'Aft,' 'Stern,' 'both together' until we were some ten feet from the water and here occurred the only anxious moment we had during the whole of our experience from leaving the deck to reaching the Carpathia. Immediately below our boat was the exhaust of the condensers, a huge stream of water pouring all the time from the ship's side just above the water line. It was plain we ought to be smartly away from this not to be swamped by it when we touched water.

"We had no officer aboard nor petty officer or member of the crew to take charge, soon one of the stokers shouted: 'Some one find the pin which releases the boat from the rope and pull it up.'

"No one knew where it was. We felt as well as we could on the floor and sides but found nothing and it was hard to move among so many people we had 60 or 70 on board. Down we went and presently floated with our ropes still holding us, the exhaust washing us away from the side of the vessel and the swell of the sea urging us back again. The resultant of all these forces was a force which carried us parallel to the ship's side and directly under boat 14, which had filled rapidly with men and was coming down on us in a way that threatened to submerge our boat.

"Stop lowering 14' our crew shouted and the crew of 14, now only 20 feet above, shouted the same. But the distance to the top was some 70 feet and the creaking pulleys must have deadened all sound to those above for down she came—75 feet, 10 feet, 5 feet, and a stoker and I reached up and touched her swinging above our heads. The next drop would have brought her on our heads, but just before she dropped another stoker sprang to the ropes with his knife.

"'One,' I heard him say, 'two as his knife cut through the pulley ropes and the next moment the exhaust stream had carried us clear while boat 14 dropped into the water, into the space we had the moment before occupied, our gunwhales almost touching.

"We drifted away easily as the oars were gotten out and headed directly away from the ship. The crew seemed to me to be mostly cooks in white jackets, two to an oar with a stoker at the tiller. There was a certain amount of shouting from one end of the boat to the other and discussion as to which way we should go, but finally it was decided to elect the stoker who was steering, captain, and for all to obey his orders. He went to work at once to get into touch with the other boats calling to them and getting as close as seemed wise; so that when the search boats came in the morning, to look for us, there would be more chance for all to be resened by keeping together. It was now about 1 a. m., a beautiful starlight night with no moon and so not very light. The sea was as calm as a pond, just a gentle heave as the boat dipped up and down in the swell; an ideal night except for the bitter cold for anyone who had to be out in the middle of the Atlantic ocean in an open boat.

"The captain-stoker told us that he had been at sea 26 years and had never yet seen such a calm night on the Atlantic. As we rowed away from the Titanic, we looked back from time to time to watch her, and a more striking spectacle it was not possible for anyone to see. Only the evening before at dinner, I remarked to my neighbor that when we arrived at New York, I should take an opportunity to get a look at her from a distance to realize something of her dimensions. Did not think our desire was so soon to be gratified. In the distance she looked an enormous length, her great bulk outlined in black against the starry sky every port hole and saloon blazing with light. It was impossible to think anything could be wrong with such a leviathian, were it not for that ominous tilt downward in the bows where the water was by now up to the last row of port-holes.

"We were now about two miles from her and all the crew insisted that such a tremendous wave would be formed by suction as she went down that we ought to get as far away as possible. The captain agreed and all lay on their oars and widened the distance between us and the sinking vessel. Presently, about 2 a. m., as near as I can remember, we observed her settling very rapidly, with the bows and the bridge completely under water and concluded it was now only a question of minutes before she went; and so it proved. She slowly tilted straight on end with the stern vertically upwards and as she did so, the lights in the cabin and saloons which had not flickered for a moment since we left, died out, come on again for a single flash and finally went out altogether. At the same time the machinery roared down through the vessel with a rattle and a groaning that could be heard for miles, the weirdest sound surely that could be heard in the middle of the ocean, a thousand miles away from land. But this was not yet quite the end. To our amazement she remained in that upright position for a time which I estimate at five minutes, others in the boat say less, but it was certainly some minutes, while we watched at least 150 feet of the Titanic towering up above the level of the sea and looming black against the sky.

"Then with a quiet slanting dive, she disappeared beneath the waters and our eyes had looked for the last time on the gigantic vessel we had set out on from Southampton last Wednesday. And there was left to us the gently heaving sea, the boat filled to standing room with men and women in every conceivable condition of dress and undress; above the perfect sky of brilliant stars with not a cloud in the sky, all tempered with a bitter cold that made us all long to be one of the crew who toiled away with the oars and kept themselves warm thereby—a curious, deadening bitter cold unilke anything we had felt before.

And then with all these there fell on the ear the most appalling noises a human being ever listened to—the cries of hundreds of our fellow beings struggling in the icy water, crying for help with a cry that we knew could not be answered. We longed to return and pick up some of those swimming, but this would have meant swamping out boat and further loss of the lives of all of us.

"We tried to to sing to keep the women from hearing the cries and rowed hard to get away from the scene of the wreck, but I think the memory of those sounds will be one of the things the rescued will find it difficult to efface from memory. We are all trying hard not to think of it.

"We kept a lookout for lights and several times it was shouted that steamer lights were seen, but they turned out to be either a light from another boat or a star low down on the horizon. About 3 a. m. we saw faint lights showing on the sky and all rejoiced to see what we expected was the coming dawn but afterward watching for half an hour and seeing no change in the light, realized it was the northern lights.

"Presently, low down on the horizon we saw a light which slowly resolved itself into a double light and we watched eagerly to see if the two lights would separate and so prove to be only two of our boats or whether they would remain together in which case we should expect them to be the masthead light and a deck light below, of a rescuing steamer.

"To our joy they moved as one and round we swung the boat and headed for her. The steersman shouted: "Now, boys, sing,' and for the first time the boat broke into song with 'Row for the shore, boys' and for the first time tears came to the eyes of us as we realized that safety was at hand. The song was sung but it was a very poor imitation of the real thing for quivering voices make poor songs. A cheer was given next and that was better—you needn't keep in time for a cheer.

"Our rescuers showed up rapidly and as she swung around we saw her cabins all alight and knew she must be a large steamer. She was now motionless and we had to row to her. Just then day broke, a beautiful quiet dawn with faint pink clouds just above the bottom, and a new moon whose crescent just touched the horizon. "Turn your money over, boys, said our cheery steersman, 'that is if you have any,' he added. We laughed at him for this superstition at such a time, but he countered very neatly by adding, 'Well, I shall never say again that 13 is an unlucky number, boat 13 has been the best friend we ever had.' Certainly the 13 superstition is killed for ever in the minds of those who escaped the Titanic in boat 13. As we neared the Carpathia we saw in the dawning light what we thought was a full rigged schooner standing up near her and presently behind her another all sails set and we said: "They are fisher boats from the Newfoundland banks and have seen the steamer lying-to and are standing by to help.' But in another five minutes the light shone pink on them and we saw they were icebergs towering many feet in the air, huge, glistening masses, deadly white, still, and peaked in a way that had easily suggested a schooner. We glanced round the horizon and there were others wherever the eye could reach. The steamer we had to reach was surrounded by them and we had to make a detour to reach her for between her and us lay another huge berg. We rowed up to the Carpathia about 4.30 and were hoisted or climbed up the ship's sides with very grateful hearts.

"We were received with a welcome that was overwhelming in its warmth and I should like to say her that there is not a member of the Titanic on board who feels capable of expressing in adequate terms his gratitude for the attentions showered upon us by the captain, officers, crew and passengers on board the Carpathia. They were called upon suddenly in mid-ocean to receive, they made every arrangement for so doing. Hot meals, blankets and berths were provided for each as they came on board. Clothing and money was supplied individually by passengers. Berths were given up by men who slept on the smoke room floor or any where else that a corner could be found.

"The ship has sent off hundreds of Marconigrams free of charge to anxious relatives. The catering arrangements in charge of the purser and stewards have been so admirably organized that it would not be possible to be better served had we been regular passengers aboard our own ship.

"The captain has placed all private messages to friends in front of press messages—in fact he has refused to send any press messages, beyond a bare 20 words to a press association and the names of all those saved, placing the needs of the private passengers of the Titanic in front of any 'copy' for the press.

COMMITTEE OF THE SURVIVORS POINTS OUT SHORTCOMINGS

The following statement issued by a committee of the surviving passengers was given the press on the arrival of the Carpathia.

"We, the undersigned surviving passengers from the S. S. Titanic in order to forestall any sensational or exaggerated statements deem it our duty to give to the press a statement of facts which have come to our knowledge and which we believe to be true.

"On Sunday, April 14, 1912, at about 11.40 p. m., on a cold starlit night in a smooth sea and with no moon, the ship struck an iceberg which had been reported to the bridge by lookouts, but early enough to avoid collision. Steps were taken to ascertain the damage and save passengers and ship. Orders were given to put on life belts and the boats were lowered. The ship sank at about 2.20 a. m., Monday and the usual distress signals were sent out by wireless and rockets fired at intervals from the ship. Fortunately the wireless messages were received by the Cunard S. S. Carpathia at about 12 o'clock, midnight, and she arrived on the scene of the disaster at about 4 a. m., Monday.

"The officers and crew of the S. S. Carpathia had been preparing all night for the rescue and comfort of the survivors, and the last mentioned was received on board with the most touching care and kindness, every attention being given to all irrespective of class. The passengers, officers and crew gave up gladly their staterooms, clothing and comforts for our benefit, all honor to them."

"The English board of trade, passenger certificate on Titanic allowed for a total of approximately 3500. The same certificate called for life boat accommodation for approximately 950 in the following boats: 14 large lifeboats, two smaller boats and four collapsible boats. Life preservers were accessible and apparently in sufficient number for all on board.

"The approximate number of passengers carried at the time of collision was:

"First-class—330; second class—320; third class—750; total, 1400.

"Officers and crew, 940. Total, 2340.

"Of the foregoing about the following were rescued by S. S. Carpathia:

"First class, 210; second class, 125; third class, 200; officers, 4; seamen, 30; stewards, 96; firemen, 71—total, 210 of the crew. The total about 745 saved was about 80 per cent. of the maximum capacity of the lifeboats.

"We feel it our duty to call the attention of the public to what we consider the inadequate supply of life saving appliances provided for on modern passenger steamships and recommend that immediate steps be taken to compel passenger steamers to carry sufficient boats to accommodate the maximum number of passengers carried on board. The following facts were observed and should be considered in this connection.

"The insufficiency of lifeboats, rafts, etc.; lack of trained seamen to man same (stokers, stewards, etc., are not efficient boat handlers); not enough officers to carry out emergency orders from the bridge and superintend the launching and control of lifeboats; absence of searchlights.

"The board of trade rules allow for entirely too many people in each boat to permit the same to be properly handled. On the Titanic the boat deck was about 75 feet above water and consequently the passengers were requested to embark before lowering boats, thus endangering the operation and the preventing the taking on of the maximum number the boats would hold. Boats at all times to be properly equipped with provisions, water, lamps, compasses, lights, etc. Life saving boat drills should be more frequent and thoroughly carried out; and officers should be armed at boat drills. Greater reduction in speed in fog and ice, as damage if collision actually occurs is liable to be less. In conclusion, we suggest that an international conference be called to recommend the passage of identical laws providing for the safety of all at sea and we urge the U. S. government to take the initiative as soon as possible.

Note—Although the foregoing was given out as a signed statement by a commitee of passengers, their signatures were omitted attendant upon the confusion when the Carpathia docked.

The Ass'd Press.

WOMAN SURVIVOR TELLS OF THE NIGHT'S HORRORS

New York, April 19—That all possible means were taken to prevent the male passengers on board the Titanic from going away in life boats and allowing only the women and children to be saved is the story told by Miss Lilly Bentham of Rochester, N. Y., a second class passenger who said she saw shots fired at men who endeavored to get away.

Miss Bentham was in a hysterical condition when the Carpathia landed and was unable to give a full account of what happened, but Mrs. W. J. Douton, a fellow passenger, who also comes from Rochester, and who lost her husband, told about what took place.

"I had not been in bed half an hour," said Mrs. Douton, "when the steward rushed down to our cabin and told us to put on our clothes and come up on deck. We were thrown into life boats and packed like sardines. As the men passengers tried to get to the boats they were shot. I don't know who did the shooting. We rowed frantically away from the ship. I arose and saw the ship sinking. The band was playing Nearer My God to Thee. There was a baby in the boat with one of the women. The baby's hands had been cut off. I think it was still alive. The mother did not give it up. During the night while waiting for the Carpathia four of the crew died in the boat and were thrown overboard. It was bitter cold and we had to wait until 8 o'clock in the morning before being taken off the life boats by the Carpathia.

PLENTY OF ROOM SAYS A MAN WHO ESCAPED

New York, April 19.—G. E. H. Stengel of Newark escaped on the lifeboat which carried lights. He believes that a number of persons owe their lives to the forethought of a member of the crew who was quick witted enough to snatch up three green glass lanterns. "These green lights," explained Mr. Stengel, "shining through the darkness, enabled all the boats to keep together in the ice filled waters."

Describing his escape, Mr. Stengel said:

"I put my wife in a boat and as there was plenty of room I followed."

SURVIVORS AT HOTELS

New York, April 19—The hotels in New York found themselves crowded Thursday with the relatives and friends of Titanic sufferers.

One apartment at a large new uptown hotel was occupied by the Earl of Rothes who had every room banked with flowers in preparation for the return of the Countess who was among the Titanic's survivors.

WIRELESSMEN WERE ABOUT TO TURN IN FOR NIGHT

New York, April 19.—How the wireless operator on the Carpathia by putting in an extra ten minutes on duty was a means of saving 745 lives, was told by Dr. J. F. Kemp, the Carpathia's physician, Friday.

"Our wireless operator," said Dr. Kemp, "was about to retire Sunday night, when he said jokingly, 'I guess I'll wait just ten minutes, then turn in.'

"It was in the next ten minutes that the Titanic's call for help came. Had the wireless operator not waited there would have been no survivors."

Dr. Kemp described the iceberg which sank the Titanic as at least 400 feet long and 90 feet high. He said that one of the boats that the Carpathia picked up was filled with stokers from the sunken liner.

"It had just two women aboard," he said. The Carpathia cruised through the ice field near the spot where the Titanic sank and picked up the bodies of three men and one baby.

"On Monday at 8.30 o'clock, in the evening, we held a funeral service on board the Carpathia," continued Dr. Kemp. "At this service there were 30 widows, 20 of whom were under 23 years old and most of them brides of a few weeks or months. They did not know their husbands were among the dead of the disaster. The Californian and the Burmah, the last named a Russian steamer, cruised about the scene of the wreck for sometime in a futile search for the bodies of the victims."

BAND PLAYED TO THE END

New York, April 19.—Mrs. John Murray Brown of Acton, Mass., who with her sisters, Mrs. Robert C. Cornell and Mrs. E. D. Appleton, was saved, was in the last lifeboat to get safely away from the Titanic.

The band played marching from deck to deck and as the ship went under I could still hear the music, Mrs. Brown said.

"The musiciaons were up to their knees in water when I last saw them. My sisters and I were in different boats. We offered assistance to Capt. Smith of the Titanic when the water covered the ship but he refused to get into the boat.

"Mrs. Astor was in the lifeboat with my sister, Mrs. Cornell. I heard Col. Astor tell her he would wait with the men. I saw him on the ship as our boat pulled out. Our boat was almost dragged down by the suction."

CARD. FARLEY BOWED WITH GRIEF, REACHES NEW YORK

New York, April 19—Cardinal Farley, who reached New York from Washington just as the Carpathia was docking, is bowed with grief over the terrible loss of life on board the Titanic. He was especially grieved at the fate of Major Archibald Butt, who went to Rome and saw Pope Pius X. on a special errand for Pres. Taft. Action was taken today by consultors of the diocese to help the distressed in every way possible. It was only because Cardinal Farley was in the capital at a meeting of the trustees of the Catholic university that definite action was not taken before he said. Instructions were drawn up for the clergy to say special prayers for the dead, the physical sufferers, and the afflicted relatives and friends.

The Cardinal expressed especial sympathy over the fate of the third class passengers many of whom he thought, came from his native country.

$10,000 IN RELIEF FUND

New York, April 19.—Before the Carpathia had reached the Cunard line pier Thursday night more than $10,000 in contributions was available for the women's relief fund to care for the destitute steerage passengers, who were for the most part women and children. All were provided with clothing and comfortable homes, and arrangements have been completed to care for them as long as it is necessary. Mrs. S. Hewitt is chairman of the committee having the relief work in charge and she is being assisted by more than 100 women.

Col. Gracie's Story of Thrilling Escape

(Continued From First Page.)

"Presently the raft became so full that it seemed she would sink if more came aboard and the crew, for self-protection, had to refuse to permit others to climb aboard. This was at once the most pathetic and the most horrible scene of all. The piteous cries of those around us still rings in my ears. I will remember them to my dying day.

"'Hold on to what you have, old boy,' we shouted to each man who tried to get aboard. 'One more of you aboard will sink us all."

"And many whom we refused answered, as they went to their death 'good luck and God bless you.'

"All the time we were sustained by the hope of rescue. We saw lights in all directions, rockets were fired in the air. We learned later that the lights and rockets came from one of the lifeboats. And so we passed the night—with the waves washing over us and the raft buried deep in the water under our feet.

NIGHT ONE OF PRAYER.

"Did we pray? We did pray and that night was one of prayer, but at times it seemed they did not rise above the waves.

"Men who had forgotten long ago how to address their Creator recalled the prayers of their childhood and murmured them over and over again. We said the Lord's Prayer again and again together.

"Long before daylight we stood in columns, two deep, back to back, balancing ourselves, fearful to move lest the delicate balanec should be disturbed and all of us thrown again into the water. We were standing and were content to stand and pray, knowing that in that alone lay our hope for rescue. The hand of God seemed to have smoothed the sea and it was calm. An age seemed to have passed when we saw the twinkling light of the Carpathia on the horizon. We knew her and recognized her as our rescuer. With a Marconi operator on the raft, our hopes were confirmed by saying that he, too, knew it was, indeed the Carpathia. While we looked, some one way, one whispered that it was a ship behind us. We dared not turn about to look, so fearful were we that we would disturb the balance.

"The second officer finally ordered one man to look behind, while the others stood still. The slipping of one man would have meant the death probably of all of us. The one man who looked passed the word that there was no ship behind.

SAW FOUR LIFEBOATS.

"When the day broke, four of the Titanic's lifeboats were seen in our port side. The second officer blew his whistle to call attention to our precarious condition and the head boat, towing another, came to our rescue.

"The transfer finally came.

"The second officer was the last man off the raft. Just before he left it, he lifted into a boat the body of a sailor, who had died of cold and exposure, as we prayed. I, with my soggy overcoat, heavy with water, pitched head foremost into the boat, trying my utmost not to disturb the equilibrium of the raft. In this boat I saw several of my companions on the raft. Others had gotten into the other boat.

"Our boat, however, had more than its complement, 65 persons. Fortunately the Carpathia was close. Otherwise, so officers of the Carpathia afterwards told me, all in the boat would have perished in the moderate blow that came up an hour later.

ALL SUFFERED FROM COLD.

"We all suffered from cold, especially those of us who had no hats. It seemed an age before we reached the Carpathia where all were ready for us with medical aid, food and drink to restore us. Nothing can exceed the kindness of the ministering angels who tenderly provided for our needs aboard the Carpathia."

Facts That Stand Out From Wreck Story.

745 Out of a Total On Board of 2340 Are Safe in New York.

1589 Persons Went to the Bottom With the Steamer, Six Died Later.

The Night Was Calm and Starlight. The Berg Was Sighted Too Late.

The Titanic Struck a Quartering Blow and Was Ripped Open for Half Her Enormous Length.

The Shock to the Ship Was Slight and There Was No Panic. Few Really Believed the Ship Would Sink.

Men Refused Places in Uncrowded Lifeboats Because of This Belief.

Stewards in Charge of Some of the Boats Did Not Know How to Row--The Women Took the Oars.

The Passengers' Committee Declares That the Lack of Lifeboats Was the Final Cause of the Great Life Loss.

Col. Gracie said his most serious loss was that of the manuscript on the war of 1812, which he had spent a long time in preparing. He said that he would return to England to duplicate the data which was lost when the Titanic went down.

WAS A BLACK BERG SAYS A WAITER ON THE TITANIC

New York, April 19.—Phillippe, the first Marconi operator, aboard the Titanic, stuck to his post until the last, jumped from the sinking ship, was taken aboard the life raft and died before the rescuers reached him, according to the story told here Friday by Thomas Whitley, who was a waiter in the saloon of the Titanic.

Whitley is in St. Vincent's hospital suffering from a fractured leg and numerous bruises.

Phillippe was on the life boat with me," Whitley said. "He was dead when taken aboard the Carpathia. They tried to revive him with brandy and all that, but it was too late. There were four burials at sea, one sailor, two firemen and Phillipee.

It is believed that Whitley's story clears the doubt surrounding the identity of the fourth man buried from the Carpathia.

It was at first believed that this man was a cabin passenger, but Whitley declares it was Phillipee.

"I helped fill the boats with women," Whitley said. "Collapsible boat No. 2 on the starboard side jammed us. The second officer was hacking at the ropes with a knife. I was being dragged around the deck by that rope when I looked up and saw the boat, with all aboard, turn turtle. In someway I got overboard myself and clung to an oak dresser. I was not more than 60 feet from the steamer when she went down. She went down bow first. I saw all the machinery drop out of her. During the half hour I was in the water I could hear the cries of thousands, it seemed, although there must have been only hundreds. I drifted near a boat rightside up. About 30 men were clinging to her and they refused to let me get aboard. Some one tried to hit me with an oar but I scrambled aboard. There was a bitter panic when it first happened. The officers had to use their revolvers. The chief officer shot one man but three others attempted to get into a boat. The women behaved splendidly as did the firemen.

"It was a black berg we struck and although the night was perfectly clear it was impossible tosee it. I saw a berg like it when we were drifting on the overturned boat."

MRS. JOHN JACOB ASTOR BEARING UP BRAVELY

New York, April 19.—Mrs. John Jacob Astor, whose husband died in the wreck of the Titanic, is being cared for by the family physician at the Astor home and a bulletin issued early Friday says:

"Mrs. Astor is under the care of the family physician. She is not in a critical or dangerous condition at this time."

Mrs. Astor held up bravely until she reached home when she is said to have broken down but quickly rallied.

On landing from the Carpathia, the young bride, widowed by the Titanic's sinking, told members of her family what she could recall of the circumstances of the disaster. Of how Col. Astor met his death she had no definite conception. She recalled, she thought, that in the confusion as she was about to be put into one of the boats the Colonel was standing by her side. After that, as Mr. Biddle recounted her narrative she had no very clear recollection of the happenings until the boats were well clear of the sinking steamer.

Mrs. Astor it appears left in one of the last boats which got away from the ship. It was her belief that all the women who wished to go had then been taken off. Her impression was that the boat in which she left had room for at least 15 more persons. The men for some reason which as she recalled it Friday night, she could not and does not understand, did not seem to be at all anxious to leave the ship. Almost everyone seemed dazed.

"I hope he is alive somewhere. Yes, I cannot think anything else," the young woman said of her husband to her father, as she left the latter to go to the Astor home, according to some who overheard her parting remarks.

The chief steerage steward of the Titanic who came in on the Carpathia says that he saw John Jacob Astor standing by the life ladder as the passengers were being embarked. His wife was beside him, the steward said. The Colonel left her to go to the purser's office for a moment and that was the last seen of him.

BOATS NOT CROWDED AND WOMEN AT THE OARS

New York, April 19—How the Carpathia received the Titanic's passengers is told in detail in a long letter written to the editor of the Herald by Wallace Bradford of San Francisco who was bound for Europe on the Carpathia. He wrote the letter on the morning of the rescue as he watched the Titanic's survivors clustered in nervous groups about the deck. He says:

"Since half past four this morning I have experienced one of those never-to-be-forgotten circumstances that weighs heavily on the soul which shows most awfully what puny things we mortals are.

"I was awakened by unusual noises and jumped and looked out the port hole. The two first boats from the Titanic were in sight. Neither was crowded. This was accounted for later by the fact that it had been impossible to get many to leave the steamer as they would not believe that she was going down. It was a glorious clear morning and a quiet sea. Off to the starboard was a white area of ice plain, from whose even surface rose mammoth forts, castles and pyramids of solid ice.

"As more boats came alongside I noted that all contained a large proportion of women. One of the boats had women at the oars, sometimes two of them handling a single oar.

"Four bodies have been brought aboard. One of them was a fireman who was said to have been shot by one of the officers because he refused to obey orders."

SHOCK WAS SO SLIGHT IT HARDLY AWOKE HER

New York, April 19.—Mrs. Ada Clark, an English woman whose husband was lost said she felt the first crash against the great berg but did not even rise from her berth for half an hour afterward.

"The shock was so slight that it did not disturb me," said Mrs. Clark, "and my husband, who was just preparing to retire, told me to get back to sleep again. Then a stewardess came along and awoke me.

"Everybody on deck, she said, but without any alarm in her voice. There was no confusion in filling the small boats. My husband put me in, kissed me good-bye and commended me to God. Even then we did not believe that the situation was serious. After I got onto the boat two men tried to step in. An officer said that the boat was only for women and they stepped back without a protest.

"I was in my night gown. The cold reached my brain and everybody in the boat was so benumbed that we could not realize what a terrible thing had happened. When somebody said 'it's gone' we sat there without showing any emotion."

COUNTESS TOOK COMMAND AND WOMEN ROWED

New York, April 19.—Miss Alice Farnam Leader, a New York physician, escaped from the Titanic on the same boat which carried the Coutess Rothes.

"The countess is an expert oarswoman," said Dr. Leader, "and thoroughly at home on the water. She practically took command of our boat when it was found that the seamen who had been placed at the oars could not row skilfully. Several of the women took their place at the oars, with the countess and rowed in turns while the weak and unskilled stewards sat quietly in one end of the boat."

18 BOATS AND ONE RAFT

New York, April 19.—John R. Joyce, a banker of Carlsbad, a passenger on the Carpathia said:

"When the Carpathia reached the scene of the wreck we saw 18 boats and one raft on the water. The Carpathia picked them up. Four persons on the raft wer dead. They were buried at sea on our way back to New York. A surviver told me that some of the Titanic's passengers jumped for the life boats, missed them and were immediately drowned then. I heard nothing of Major Butt."

"How did Mr. Ismay get out?" Mr. Joyce was asked.

In reply Mr. Joyce said:

"Well he got into a life boat. On the Carpathia he went to a stateroom without saying a word. There was some criticism regarding him on the boat but he was not criticised severely. Survivors said that everybody would have been saved if there had been enough boats.

MRS. HAYS HURRIES TO HOME IN MONTREAL

New York, April 19.—Upon the arrival of the Carpathia, Mrs. Chas. M. Hays, wife of the president of the Grand Trunk railway, who went down with the ill-fated Titanic, and her two daughters, Mrs. Thornton Davidson and Miss Margaret Hays, were met by relatives at the pier and taken to the Grand Central Station where they left for Montreal on a special train. Dr. J. Alexander Hutchinson of Montreal, her family physician, accompanied Mrs. Hays on the special train.

WAS THE FIRST WOMAN IN THE FIRST BOAT

New York, April 19.—Mrs. Dickenson Bishop of Detroit declared Friday that she was the first woman in the first boat.

"We floated around a half mile or so from the scene of the disaster for four hours before we were picked up by the Carpathia," she said. "I was in bed when the crash came. There was not much alarm but I decided to dress and go on deck. By the time I was dressed, everything seemed quiet and I lay down in my berth again, assured that there was no danger. I rose again at the summons of a stewardess. There were very few passengers on the deck when I reached there. There was no panic and the discipline of the Titanic's crew was perfect. My husband joined me on the Carpathia and we knelt together and thanked God for our preservation."

CAKE OF ICE SAVED HIM

New York, April 19.—A huge cake of ice was the means of aiding Emile Portaluppi of Ariogabo, Italy, in escaping death when the Titanic went down. Portaluppi, a second class passenger, was awakened by the explosion of one of the boilers of the ship. He hurried to the deck, strapped a life preserver around him and following the example of others, leaped into the sea. With the aid of the preserver and by holding to the cake of ice he managed to keep afloat. He was seen by one of the life boats and picked up. There were 33 other people in the boat when he was hauled aboard.

ASTOR REFUSED LIFE BELT

New York, April 19.—Col. John Jacob Astor refused to take a life belt when it was presented to him by one of the waiters of the Titanic. This is the story told by one of the survivors to Wm. David, a saloon passenger of the Carpathia.

"He was approached by a frantic waiter," said David, "and urged to put on a life preserver. Col. Astor waved the waiter away by saying: 'Pooh, this is nothing. There is no need of life belts.' This was the last seen of Mr. Astor.

"J. Bruce Ismay was pulled on board the Carpathia from a life boat. He was clad in pajamas. He collapsed upon reaching the deck and was in a semi-conscious condition for sometime afterwards."

MANY OF SURVIVORS ARE TAKEN TO THE HOSPITALS

New York, April 19.—The survivors of the Titanic, taken to hospitals on their arrival here are generally reported Friday morning to be improving. The following are the names of those taken to hospitals:

St. Luke's

Deane, Mrs. Etta, of London, Eng.
Deane, Bertram, a son.
Deane, Eliza, two months old, daughter of Mrs. Deane.
Johnson, Mrs. Alice, 27 years old of No. 215 West 3rd street, St. Charles, Ills.; shock.
Johnson, Eleanor, one year old, daughter of Mrs. Johnson.
Johnson, Harold, four years old, son of Mrs. Johnson.
Nelson, Mrs. Thelma of St. Charles, Ills.
Thorneycroft, Flirry, 32, of London, Eng., shock.

St. Vincent's

Ashlyus, Mrs. Selina, steerage, and two daughters, one 7 and one 5 years.
McIntyre, Wm., 21 years, coaltrimmer, Southampton.
Thompson, John, 42 years old, fireman, fracture of left arm.
Whitley, Thomas, 21 years, waiter in first saloon, fracture of right leg and a number of bruises.

Mount Sinai

Parish, Mrs. Thomas, Butte, Mont., injury to foot and shock.
Shelley, Mrs. Butte, Mont., shock.
Sudenham.
Balls, Mrs. Ada E., Jacksonville, Fla., shock (she accompanied the Rev. Rob't J. Bateman, who was drowned.)
Jarman, Mrs., New York City, severe cold, bronchitis, shock.

SERVICES FOR THE DEAD IN ST. PAUL'S, LONDON

London, April 19.—Pitiable scenes were again witnessed at the White Star offices in London Friday morning. One woman who had kept vigil throughout the day and most of the night since the first news of the disaster came, found in the list posted at the office the name she had been waiting for and rushed into the street shrieking "He is saved."

Memorial services for the dead were held at noon in St. Paul's cathedral and these were attended by the members of the cabinet and the diplomatic corps. Among them were Ambassador Whitelaw Reid and Mrs. Reid and other distinguished personages. The White Star company and the International Mercantile Marine Co. were also represented.

A memorial service is to be held in St. Patrick's Cathedral, Dublin, on Sunday.

The lord mayor and sheriffs were present at the service at St. Paul's. Many thousands wer unable to gain admission to the cathedral. The whole congregation stood while a military band played "The Dead March" from Saul. Hundreds of men and women broke down and sobs were noticeable throughout the edifice.

The designer of the Titanic who was among the congregation was so affected that he fainted and had to be carried out.

FOR GOV'T CONTROL OF WIRELESS TELEGRAPH

Washington, April 19.—The government's inability to get early information regarding the loss of the Titanic, through the wireless outfits of the scout cruisers Chester and Salem, or the naval shore stations, has confirmed the Navy department in its decison to press for legislation by Congress which will enable the government to assert control over wireless telegraph whether personal or corporate, which may seek to restrain or interfere with the government officials as this.

Sec'y Meyer who was one of the parties to the conference recently held at the White House on the subject of wireless control, is giving the subject much attention either from the Navy department or the department of Commerce and a bill will soon emerge which it is hoped will be accepted by Congress as a basis for its action.

J. BRUCE ISMAY WILL TESTIFY AT HEARING

Managing Director of White Star Line to Tell Federal Committee of the Great Disaster

New York, April 19.—J. Bruce Ismay, managing director of the International Mercantile Marine, and the four surviving officers of the Titanic, will appear Friday before the United States investigating committee at the Waldorf-Astiria to give their version of the marine disaster which has shocked the entire country.

Senator Wm. Alden Smith of Michigan, chairman of the committee and Senator Newlands of Nevada was in conference Thursday night for two hours with Mr. Ismay and P. A. S. Franklin, vice president of the International Mercantile Marine Co.

Senator Smith said that Mr. Ismay had made a very frank statement but that he wished that the public should "hear Mr. Ismay's story from his own lips, before the Senate investigating committee."

Chas. C. Burlingame of the law firm of Burlingame, Montgomery and Behr, will appear as counsel for Mr. Ismay and the International Marine Co. Mr. Burlingame hurried to the Cunard pier and conferred with Mr. Ismay in his state room before the members of the Senate committee were received on board the Carpathia.

"The White Star line welcomes any governmental inquiry," Mr. Franklin said, "and the United States Senate investigation cannot be too broad for us, and if it results in the adoption of any measures calculated to prevent the recurrence of such a disaster as the Titanic loss the White Star line will be only too thankful that such has been the outcome. Mr. Ismay will not shirk his duty, nor will any other officer of the company. All the information the Senate comimttees seeks will be cheerfully afforded and we will cooperate in every way possible with the committee."

Sec'y of Commerce and Labor Nagel, who accompanied Senators Smith and Newlands to New York will be present at the hearing Friday.

PASSENGER ON CARPATHIA TELLS OF RESCUE

A passenger on the Carpathia made the following statement:

"I was awakened at about half past twelve at night by a commotion on the decks which seemed unusual but there was no excitement. As the boat was moving, I paid little attention to it and went to sleep again.

"At 3 o'clock I again awakened. I noticed that the boat had stopped. I went to the deck. The Carpathia had changed her course. Lifeboats were sighted and began to arrive—and soon, one by one, they drew up to our side. There were 16 in all and the transferring of the passengers was most pitiable. The adults were assisted in climbing the rope ladders by ropes adjusted to their waists. The little children and babies were hoisted to the deck in bags. Some of the boats were crowded, a few were not half full. This, I could not understand. Some people were in full evening dress; others were in their night clothes and wrapped in blankets.

"These, with immigrants in all sorts of shapes, were hurried into the saloon, indiscriminately for a hot breakfast. They had been in the open boats for four or five hours in the most biting air I ever experienced. There were husbands without wives, wives without husbands; parents without children and children without parents. But there was no demonstration. No sobs, they seemed to be stunned. Immediately after breakfast divine services were held in the saloon. One woman died in the lifeboats; three others died after reaching our decks. Their bodies were buried at sea at 5 o'clock that afternoon. None of the rescued had any clothing except what they had on, and a relief committee was formed and our passengers contributed enough for their immediate needs.

"When her lifeboats pushed away from the steamer, the steamer was brilliantly lighted, the band was playing, and the captain was standing on the bridge giving directions. The bow was well submerged and the keel rose high above the water. Suddenly the boat seemed to break in two. The next moment everything disappeared. The survivors were so close to the sinking steamer that they feared the lifeboats would be drawn into the vortex. There were preparations for a brilliant party to be given on board the next evening. On our way back to New York we steamed along the edge of a field of ice which seemed limitless. As far as the eye could see to the north there was no blue water. At one time I counted 13 icebergs."

The statement was signed by Samuel Godenberg, chairman and a committee of some 25 passengers.

MESSAGE NOT NEEDED ON LIFE SAVING LAWS

Washington, April 19.--Pres. Taft will not send a special message to Congress urging legislation to strengthen the present laws regulating supervision of steamships clearing from American ports.

The President believes Congress needs no such suggestion since the Titanic disaster, and moreover he is of the belief that existing laws are adequate if strictly enforced.

Under agreement with Great Britain the certificate of the Titanic that she had met with the requirements of the British board of trade as to life saving equipment would have been accepted in New York and the Titanic would have been allowed to clear again for England.

The disaster, however, will undoubtedly bring about a new agreement between the United States and Great Britain and with other nations in the same class.

In the opinion of officials here the regulations of the United States as applied to vessels sailing under the American flag or the flags of nations not in the agreement, are strict enough to compel the carrying of life saving equipment sufficient to take care of every passenger and every member of the crew An act of Congress nullifying the existing agreement would make it necessary for officials of the department of commerce and labor to refuse a certificate from any steamer unless the requirements of this country were met as well. Such action by Congress was regarded as probable here Friday.

EXPLOSION OF BOILERS FINISHED THE TITANIC

How the Titanic sank is told by Chas. P. Hurd, a staff correspondent of the New York Evening World, who was a passenger on the Carpathia and who Wednesday night furnished that paper with his account.

He gives the number of lives lost as 1700. He praises highly the courage of the crew hundreds of whom gave their lives with a heroism which equalled but could not exceed that of John Jacob Astor, Henry B. Harris, Jacques Futrelle and others in the long list of first cabin passengers.

It was the explosion of the boilers, according to Mr. Hurd's account which finally finished the Titanic's career.

The bulkhead system, though probably working, proved only to delay the ship's sinking. The position of the ship's wound on the starboard quarter admitted icy water, according to Hurd's story, which caused the boilers to explode and these explosions broke the ship in two. The ship's string band gathered in the saloon near the end, the narrative says, and played "Nearer, My God to Thee." The crash against the iceberg which had been sighted at only a quarter mile distance came almost simultaneously with the click of the levers operated from the bridge, which stopped the engines and closed the watertight doors. Captain Smith was on the bridge a moment later, summoned all on board to put on life preservers and ordered lifeboats lowered. The first boats had more male passengers, as the men were the first to reach the deck. When the rush of frightened men and women and crying children to the decks began, the "women first" rule was rigidly enforced.

Officers drew revolvers but in most cases there was no use for them. Revolver shots heard shortly before the Titanic went down caused many rumors, one that Captain Smith had shot himself, another that first officer Murdock had ended his life, but members of the crew discredit these rumors. Captain Smith last seen on the bridge, just before the ship sank, leaping only after the decks had been washed away. What became of the men with the life preservers was a question asked by many since the disaster.

Many of those with life preservers were seen to go down despite the preservers, and dead bodies floated on the surface as the last boats moved away.

Mrs. Isidor Straus refused to leave her husband's side and both perished together.

Harold Cotton, Marconi operator on the Carpathia, did not go to bed at his usual time Sunday night, and as a result caught the first message of the Titanic's plight which was responsible for the saving of hundreds of rescued, who were landed in New York Thursday night. It was testified to by several survivors that the Titanic was going 23 knots an hour when she dashed into the iceberg.

WAS A CONTINENT OF ICE

New York, April 19.—Hugh Wellner, a son of Thomas Wellner, R. A., of London, says there were two explosions before the Titanic made her dive into the sea. Wellner believes he was the last person to leave the Titanic. To a friend he said:

"We saw what seemed to be a continent of ice. The iceberg, which we struck, I have learned, was very much higher than the bridge of the Titanic. Because of some atmospheric conditions, however, the mountain of ice could not be seen until the Titanic was close to it. It was not thought at first that the big liner had been dealt a dangerous blow. Everybody took things comparatively easy at first.

"Not long after the ship struck there came the first big explosion. Then came, a moment later, a second explosion. It was this second explosion that did the most damage. It blew away the funnels and tore a big hole in the steamer's side and the boat rocked from the explosion as if she was an egg shell. The Titanic careened to one side and passengers making for the boats were spilled into the water. The ship filled rapidly and as it was evident she would have to go, I jumped into a boat as it swung down the side."

WILL USE SOUTHERN COURSE

The North German Lloyd announced the information Thursday afternoon that they have instructed the commanders of all their steamships both at New York and at Bremen to take a course two degrees south of the regular southerly sailing lane until further orders.

THE SAVED AND THE MISSING

One of the survivors of the Titanic disaster is Augustus H. Weikman, ship's barber. He is a resident of Palmyra, near Mount Holly, N. Y., and is one of the largest property owners of the town. Relatives and neighbors were sympathizing with Mrs. Weikman Thursday when [illegible] received from her husband via Halifax, that he was safe.

A wireless message was received at Philadelphia from James R. McGough, a Titanic passenger, by his wife stating that he was safe. McGough's name was on the missing list. He is a buyer for a department store of Philadelphia.

A wireless telegram from the Carpathia was received at St. Louis, Thursday, from Spencer V. Silverthorne, a survivor of the Titanic. It read:

"Safe; notify wife."

There was some question as to the identity of Silverthorne in the survivors' list as received early in the week. The name in the list was R. Spencer Silverthorn.

"Father lost. No hope," was the terse wireless message received at Philadelphia, Thursday, from Richard Norris Williams who, with his father, C. Duane Williams, was a passenger on the Titanic. The elder Mr. Williams, who was an attorney, formerly lived in Philadelphia. With his son he was on his way here from Switzerland to visit relatives. After the death of his wife in 1890 Mr. Williams made [illegible] home abroad.

Miss Helen R. Ostby of Providence was taken at once from the deck to a New York hotel. She was informed by friends that the name of her father, E. C. Ostby, had been telegraphed from the Carpathia as among those saved. She at once said that she had not seen her father on board the Carpathia, and she could not believe he was aboard without her knowing it. The only explanation was that a mistake was made in the wireless transmission of the names.

Dr. Henry F. Bauenthal and his wife of New York city were the first persons off the Carpathia. They were driven off quickly in an automobile without having spoken to anyone. They were followed off the ship by a man who said he was James Googht of Philadelphia. Googht said that it was exactly 2.20 a. m. on the 15th when the liner sank. He says he was thrown bodily into a small boat and it was 5 o'clock that morning when they were picked up by the Carpathia. Googht was met by two brothers and a sister and after he had made this short statement, he was driven away.

LIFE BOAT SCARCITY ALONE HELD RESPONSIBLE FOR THE APPALLING LOSS OF LIFE

The Titanic, Under Out of Date British Rules, Was Compelled to Carry Craft for Only 481 Persons; America Powerless

Enough is already known of the Titanic disaster to establish the repugnant fact that the lives of about two-thirds of her complement of passengers and crew were sacrificed for no better reason than that the lifeboat and liferaft equipment provided for this most pretentious of ships was so meagre as to be barely adequate to the needs of the remaining one-third aboard her who were actually rescued, says the New York Herald.

The appalling casualty has brought to public notice the even more disquieting fact that, in thus providing facilities inadequate to such an emergency, the owners of the Titanic were complying fully with British regulations governing the subject, though it is conceded that these admiralty regulations are obsolete and were framed to provide for vessels of a maximum size of 10,000 tons. The Titanic was a 46.000 ton ship, a leviathan such as was not even dreamed of in 1898, when the British regulations now in force were framed.

The Titanic sank into the ocean abyss in a smooth sea. There is nothing to indicate that had she carried boats and rafts sufficient to have accommodated 2,400 persons, instead of less than one thousand, the Carpathia and the other vessels that were hastening to her relief might not have picked up practically all of the passengers and crew, instead of the remnant of a scant one-third who survived. The Carpathia has reported that every one of the Titanic's lifeboats has been accounted for.

Thirteen Hundred Helpless

The appalling fact stands revealed that when the last of the departing lifeboats swung away with the last of those who had been chosen to live the Titanic's life saving devices had been exhausted. When those last heartrending farewells had been said from the darkened decks, in midnight gloom and polar cold, the 1,300 doomed ones who had been elected for death had no alternative but to leap into the sea clinging to some life belt or buoy, or else to wait in manly fortitude to be swallowed up in the vortex with the sinking ship.

A press association despatch from London Tuesday said: "The apparent fact that the Titanic's boats were not sufficient to accommodate the ship's personnel is causing much comment here, although the papers are chary of discussing the subject. The law does not provide the number of boats the largest ships shall carry. It applies only to those vessels displacing up to 10,000 tons, is it was passed before the present big ships had been designed or built."

In the same despatch from London Alexander Carlisle, lately chief designer for Harland & Wolf, the builders of both the Titanic and the Olympic, made this significant admission:

"I am of the opinion that the large ships of the present day do not carry anyhing like a sufficient number of boats, but until the board of trade and the governments of other countries require sufficient boats to be carried boat owners cannot afford such extra top weight. As a matter of fact, both the Olympic and the Titanic were fitted with davits designed for and capable of carrying four times the number of boats actually fitted in the ships when they went to sea. Although a large margin was then left. I think I am correct in saying that the Titanic carried 50 per cent. more than the number of boats required by the board of trade.

Closing Compartments at Night

"I have little doubt that, sooner or later, when the traveling public is not so fastidious about going up or down stairs, and when they do not require to walk more than half the length of the ship without opening a door, and when the board of trade makes it compulsory not to have any watertight compartments open either in the hold or between decks between sunset and sunrise, then an enormous amount of risk at present existing in ships may and can be eliminated.

"If the points as to the closing of the watertight compartments and the carrying of boats are carried out, the public will be 50 per cent safer."

Acting upon the hint of obsolete maritime regulations governing ships flying the British flag, a reporter obtained a copy of those rules. These regulations provide a table setting forth the minimum number of lifeboats to be placed under davits and also the minimum cubic contents of the boats to be so placed upon ships of various dimensions. The largest vessels mentioned directly in this tabulated list are those of a "gross tonnage of 10,000 and upward," a fact that is readily accounted for, as the regulations were formulated in 1898, when few ships were built with a tonnage in excess of that named.

It is specified in the table that for ships of a gross tonnage "10.000 and upward" there shall be carried a minimum of 16 boats placed under davits, of an aggregate cubic contents of 5.500 feet. The Titanic falls under the classification of Division A, class 1, which includes all "foreign going steamships having passenger certificates under the 'Merchant Shipping act and for those carrying emigrant passengers, subject to all the provisions of the passenger acts."

For all such craft the rule specifies that they "shall carry boats placed under davits, fit and ready for use and having proper appliances for getting them into the water, in number and capacity as prescribed by the table in the appendix to these rules. Such boats shall be equipped in the manner required by and shall be of the description defined in the general rules appended hereto.

Provision for Life Boats

"If the boats placed under davits in accordance with the table do not furnish sufficient accommodation for all persons on board, then additional wood, metal, collapsible or other boats of approved description (whether placed under davits or otherwise) or approved life rafts shall be carried.

"Such additional boats or rafts shall be of at least such carrying capacity that they and the boats required to be placed under davits by the table shall provide together in the aggregate, in vessels of 5,000 tons gross and upward, three-fourth and in vessels of less than 5,000 tons one-half more than the minimum cubic contents required by column three of the table."

Supposing that the Titanic complied literally with this rule and did nothing more, the following situation would be revealed:

The 16 lifeboats which she is compelled to carry beneath davits would have a necessary minimum capacity of 3,500 cubic feet. Under the three-fourths rule she would have to be equipped with additional life saving devices—boats or rafts—with an additional capacity of 4.125 cubic feet, or a total capacity in all of 9,625 cubic feet.

In paragraph 31 of the general rules it is stated that the aggregate passenger carrying capacity of the lifeboats, rafts, etc., shall be determined by dividing the aggregate number of cubic feet by the figure ten. The result of such division in this instance is 962, which represents the entire number of persons for whom lifeboat and life raft accommodations should have been provided aboard the Titanic under an unmodified interpretation of the British rule now in effect.

Provisions Totally Inadequate

The fact is, however, that the Titanic did not have to do even that much to comply with a strict interpretation of these obsolete provisions, which at best would have left more than half her personnel at the mercy of a mortally stricken and fast foundering ship. If the Titanic's loss has proven one thing more clearly than another it is that watertight compartments and collision bulkheads are not the infallible safeguards they have popularly been supposed to be, especially against the terrific impact of collision with gigantic icebergs. Yet so firmly had the bulkhead panacea been implanted in the British mind as long ago as 1898 that in the "General Rules," paragraph 40, section 12, this vital modification of the foregoing regulations is set forth:

"When ships of any class are divided into efficient watertight compartments, to the satisfaction of the board of trade they shall only be required to carry additional boats, rafts and buoyant apparatus of one-half of the capacity required by these rules, but this exemption shall not extend to life jackets or similar approved articles of equal buoyancy suitable to be worn on the person."

Should the Titanic's sponsors have taken advantage of this exemption—and they would have been entirely within their legal rights in doing so—they might have cut down the carrying capacity of their life saving equipment to a minimum of 481 persons, instead of 962.

Contrary to the popular notion, the United States regulations for the safeguarding of human life on the high seas are much more modern and stringent than are those of Great Britain. Ships of American register and of 20,000 gross tons must carry a a total lifeboat capacity of not less than 12,420 cubic feet, or enough space for 1,242 refugees. The United States rule further provides that for vessels exceeding 20,000 tons there must be provided "an additional boat capacity of 225 cubic feet for each additional 500 gross tons or fraction thereof." The lost British ship is of 46,000 tons gross. Had she been under the American flag and complying with the American marine requirements her lifeboats would have had a total cubic capacity of 24,120 feet, or ample accommodations for 2,412 persons, which is somewhat in excess of the entire personnel of the Titanic's passengers and crew.

Under the present international working agreement, it is contended, the United States is powerless to enforce its own higher standards upon vessels flying the flag of foreign powers, even thought such vessels may find a lion's share of their trade in the carrying of American passengers and cargoes. With Great Britain, France, Germany, Canada and the Netherlands, it was explained recently in the local office of the Steamhsip Inspection Service, the United States has in force reciprocal agreements, under which it binds itself to accept the rules in force in each of those countries as governing the ships flying its flag. They, in turn, vouchsafe to the United States a like guarantee.

PRESIDENT TAFT SENT FAST SCOUT CRUISERS TO MEET THE CARPATHIA HOPING TO LEARN DEFINITE NEWS OF MAJOR ARCHIBALD BUTT

SCOUT CRUISER CHESTER

PRESIDENT TAFT AND HIS FAVORITE AID, MAJOR BUTT

SCOUT CRUISER SALEM

President Taft was deeply grieved at the news that Major Archibald Butt was probably lost on the Titanic, and so long as there was hope that he would be reported as saved the President was eager for the latest information concerning survivors. When it became known that the wireless apparatus on the Carpathia was unable to send messages to a great distance President Taft ordered the scout cruisers Chester and Salem to proceed eastward to meet the Cunard liner bringing in the hundreds rescued from the Titanic's boats. The Chester and Salem were at sea, but were reached by wireless and were told what they were to do. Major Butt had been with President Taft on all of his many trips, and the two men had become fast friends. Major Butt went to Europe ostensibly for a rest, but it is understood that he carried a confidential message from President Taft to Pope Pius X. Major Butt was unmarried.

SHORTAGE OF LIFEBOATS "APPALLING," SAYS DEWEY

Old Fighter Tells of His Own Thrilling Experience in a Field of Icebergs.

In a statement about the Titanic and general danger in ocean voyages, Admiral Dewey at Washington, said Wednesday:

"I think that every passenger who crosses the North Atlantic takes his life in his hands every time. For myself, I would rather go around the world in a well-equipped man-of-war than make a trip across the North Atlantic in a trans-Atlantic vessel. The greed for money-making is so great that it is with the sincerest regret that I observe that human lives are never taken into consideration.

"Let all good Americans exert every energy to have the present laws amended as regard life-saving appliances on every passenger-carrying vessel. I do not believe that a passenger vessel should be cleared unless she has boats sufficient to float the great majority of its precious cargo in the event of an accident.

"It is appalling to think that the Olympic, when she struck the Hawke, according to reports, had boats sufficient to carry only one out of every six passengers.

"In 1871, when I was commander of the ship Supply, carrying provisions to the starving French, we sailed from New York on March 2. Not long after, by the temperature, we felt we were in the neighborhood of icebergs, but all the books on the subject indicated that they never had traveled so far south.

"One night about 9 o'clock, the first lieutenant, Augustus Kellogg, and I were in the cabin, when we heard the officer of the deck give the order 'hard up the helm.' We knew some danger was imminent, but I never gave icebergs a thought. I feared a collision with another sailing craft. I hurried to the deck, and had the pleasure of gazing on a collection of icebergs, about the size of the Capitol.

"Every soul on board was on deck, and every soul was letting go a rope, and we were like a runaway horse in a crowded thoroughfare.

"Fortunately, our craft was about the size of a catboat as compared with a vessel of the dimensions of the unfortunate Titanic, and we spent the rest of the night dodging icebergs.

"The passage of the forts at New Orleans, the battle of the Port Hudson and the battle of Manila Bay weren't in it as compared with that night dodging icebergs.

"The most unfortunate part of the fatality is that most of the drowned are Americans, and we Americans surely have some rights in the matter.

"It is very easy to picture an American of the type of Major Archibald Butt, one of God's noblemen, doing all he can to insure the safety of the women and children aboard the Titanic, knowing that within a very short time he will face his Creator.

TO PROBE CRUEL HOAX OF "ALL SAVED" WIRES

Carpathia's Captain's: "Titanic Sunk; 800 Saved," Message Muzzled, Is the Report—Government Begins Inquiry.

The mystery of why the news of the sinking of the Titanic and the consequent appalling loss of life was suppressed in transmission from Cape Race, Newfoundland, for 24 hours and why the actual messages that were being flashed across the sea by the Olympic, Carpathia, Virginian and other vessels were garbled and held back from an anxious and apprehensive world is occupying the attention of steamship and financial circles, and is likely to be taken up in other quarters that were heavily hit by the Titanic's loss.

It was learned at the Cunard offices that the two messages from the Carpathia, which did not reach the officials of the Cunard line until Wednesday morning had been sent to Cape Race at 7 o'clock, Monday morning.

Both were flashes from Capt. Rostron of the Carpathia and told that the Titanic had gone down and that only about 800 survivors of the crash had been picked up.

The Cunard people suggest that it is more than likely that the Olympic relayed the Carpathia's messages to shore. If the Olympic did not hold them back the White Star people must have received them almost a day before the Cunard line received them, in which case they must have been deliberately suppressed, marine men argue.

Who Held Up Message?

Both these messages are dated Monday morning and had been relayed from Cape Race Island. They should have been despatched from Sable Island to New York via the Postal Telegraph Co. No explanation has been made of why they were not sent on. No explanation has been made to establish who held up the vastly important messages.

That there has been an extraordinary and unaccountable censorship which has resulted in the stifling of the news of the disaster is halfway admitted by the Cunard officials. It is also stated in steamship circles that there must have been an extraordinary misreading of messages by officials of the International Mercantile Marine in the White Star line offices.

The text of the despatch from the liner Olympic upon which the White Star officials based their assurance that all on board the Titanic were saved is still withheld. An admittedly garbled text of this message was given out.

The skipper of the Olympic was made to say that the Parisian had picked up 20 boatloads of Titanic's passengers and that the Virginian and Carpathia were standing by.

World Waits Solution of Mystery

It is being asked all over the world how the Olympic could have misread the brief wireless despatch of the Carpathia which told that the Titanic had struck an iceberg and gone down; how she could have misread that the Virginian and the Parisian were taking part in a rescue when they were still many miles from the scene of the disaster.

Furthermore, it is urged by those familiar with the workings of wireless messages at sea that the Olympic must have picked up the Carpathia's messages Monday morning and read them accurately.

In view of all this it seems more than probable, marine men insist, that there has been cruel jugglery and garbling of messages in high circles. The whole world is asking why the White Star people did not get more accurate information from the Carpathia.

MAJOR BUTT MADE HIS WILL IN FEAR OF DEATH

Mysteriously Warned That He Might Die on His Trip to and From Europe.

A mysterious warning that he would meet death on his trip abroad came to Major Archibald Butt before he left Washington.

Six weeks ago, when the Major determined on a European trip to regain his health, a premonition that he might not return alive caused him to make his will. He called his lawyer and closed up his affairs, preparing for death.

President Taft and other friends of the missing officer hoped against hope Wednesday that the scout cruiser Salem, speeding toward the Carpathia, would report Major Butt alive and well, but the conviction was general that he went down to death with the Titanic, after the women and children had been put into the boats.

GEM WORN BY FRANCE'S QUEEN LOST AND FOUND

Pin Was Dropped Year Ago by Mons. Garnier in Lake Ronkonkoma Hotel.

Lost nearly a year, a diamond and ruby cravat pin once the property of Marie Antoinette, Queen of France, has been found in a crevice in the Hotel Petit Trianon, at Lake Ronkonkoma, Long Island, where Mons. Ulysses Garnier, of Paris, missed it after removing his automobile coat. William K. Vanderbilt, Jr., into whose possession the pin has been given, sent a cable message recently to Mons. Garnier notifying him of the recovery of the treasured pin.

The diamond contained in the pin was worn by Marie Antoinette as an earring. During the visit of Mons. Garnier to New York a year ago he went on an automobile ride through Long Island with a party, of which Mr. Vanderbilt was a member. They went by way of the Motor Parkway. The next morning Mons. Garnier missed the pin. He was not certain whether he had lost it while inspecting the Motor Parkway or had dropped it to the floor of the hotel while he was removing his coat.

When a search of the hotel rooms failed to reveal the treasure it was supposed that it had been lost on the Parkway. Because of the historic value of the pin Mr. Vanderbilt instructed the foreman of the Parkway to have his men search the highway. They did, but in vain.

The pin was found while the hotel was undergoing alterations.

NOTICE!

The time for becoming parties to the common law assignment of Linwood C. Tyler is extended to May 1, 1912.

Signed
F. MARION SIMPSON,
FREDERICK H. PARKHURST,
Assignees of Linwood C. Tyler.
apr15 MWF 3t

INQUIRY INTO WRECK BY THE FEDERAL COMMITTEE

Ismay Tells How He Left the Ship

One of the Boats Was Being Filled. There Were no More Women. No Passenger Were Ready 'I Got in As It Was Lowered

New York, April 19.—The story of how the Titanic met its fate was told Friday to the U. S. Senate Investigating committee on the Titanic disaster by J. Bruce Ismay, managing director of the White Star line. The details of the story were drawn out by Senator William Alder Smith, chairman of the special subcommittee, charged with the examination of witnesses and Senator Newlands, the other senator who came to New York to conduct the inquiry.

Mr. Ismay was accompanied by P. A. S. Franklin, vice president, and Emerson T. Parvin, secretary of the International Mercantile Marine Co. Besides the committee, Rep. Hughes of West Virginia, whose daughter, Mrs. Lucien P. Smith, was saved, and whose son-in-law was lost, was present. Another inspector was Trueman H. Newberry, former assistant secretary of the navy.

When asked the circumstances under which he left the boat, Mr. Ismay replied almost in a whisper:

"One of the boats was being filled. Officers called out to know if there were any more women to go. There were none. No passengers were ready. As the boat was being lowered I got into it."

Adjusting his cuffs Mr. Ismay was overcome when he took the stand. He gave his age as 50. In response to a few formal question, he said he sailed as a voluntary passenger on the Titanic.

Senator Smith began to ask the witness to detail his experience on the Titanic. Mr. Ismav interrupted, but Senator Smith continued. Mr. Ismay said he desired to express his sincere regret at the catastrophe and to welcome the fullest investigation.

"Please tell us all the circumstances surrounding your voyage," said Senator Smith.

"First, I wish to say that I court the fullest inquiry," said Mr. Ismay. "This awful catastrophe I must say at the outset, I greatly deplore. We have nothing to conceal, nothing to hide.

"The boat left Belfast, I think, on the first of April. She arrived at Southampton on Wednesday, April 3rd, I think. She sailed on Wednesday, April 10, leaving Southampton at 12 o'clock, noon. That evening the Titanic reached Cherbourg, having run at about 68 revolutions. We arrived at Queenstown Thursday noon. The Titanic was then running at 70 revolutions. The first day I think we made about 467 miles. The next day we increased the speed to 72 revolutions and I think we ran 519 miles. The next day we increased to 75 revolutions and ran about 546 to 549 miles.

"The accident took place on Sunday night. The exact time I do not know, because I was asleep. The ship sank, I am told at 2.30.

"I understand you have been told the Titanic was running at full speed. It never had run at full speed. She was built to go 80 revolutions and had never been speeded up to that. We had all her boilers working and it was our intention to speed the boat up to the full quota on Tuesday, but the catastrophe came to prevent it."

Although he came on a "voluntary trip," Mr. Ismay said his purpose was to see how the ship worked and in what manner she could be improved upon. A representative of the builders, Mr. Andrews, was on board, Mr. Ismay said.

"Did he survive?" asked Mr. Smith.

"Unfortunately, no."

Mr. Ismay said it was arranged between himself and Capt. Smith of the Titanic not to arrive at New York lightship before 7 a. m. Wednesday.

"There would have been no advantage in arriving earlier," he said.

"During your voyage did you know you were in the vicinity of ice?" Sen. Smith asked.

"I knew some had been reported," replied the witness.

He said the ship was not in proximity of icebergs Saturday or Sunday although he knew the ship would be in the proximity of ice on Sunday night. The witness said he knew nothing of the American and the Titanic talking by wireless about icebergs.

Sen. Smith asked if he sought to send a wireless message from the Titanic after she struck. He said he did not.

According to Mr. Ismay, he said he heard the captain give the order to lower the boats.

"I then left the bridge," added the official.

He said he saw the boats lowered and filled. In his own boat were four members of the crew and 45 passengers.

"Was there any jostling by men to get in the boats?" asked Mr. Smith.

"I saw none."

"How were the women selected?"

"We picked the women and children as they stood nearest the rails."

Rep. Hughes handed Senator Smith a note and then the chairman told Mr. Ismay it was reported the second lifeboat left without its full complement of oarsmen and from 11.30 to 12.30 women were forced to row the boat.

"I know nothing about it."

Mr. Ismay was asked how long he remained on the injured ship.

"That would be hard to estimate," he responded. "Porbably an hour and a quarter."

Then Senator Smith asked the circumstances under which he left the boat.

"The boat was being filled," began Mr. Ismay. "The officers called out to know if there were any more women to go. There were none. No passengers were on the deck. As the boat was being lowered I stepped into it."

"The ship was sinking?" asked Senator Smith.

"The boat was sinking," almost whispered Mr. Ismay.

"Was there any attempt to lower the boats of the Carpathia to take on passengers after you went aboard her?" asked Senator Smith.

"There were no passengers there to take on," said Mr. Ismay.

"How long were you in this lifeboat?"

"About four hours."

"How many lifeboats were there on the Titanic?"

"Twenty altogether, I think," said Mr. Ismay, "16 collapsible and four wooden boats."

Whether the boats were taken on board the Carpathia or not he did not know.

"Were all the lifeboats leaving the Titanic accounted for?"

"I think so; I've been told so, but I do not know it of my own knowledge."

"Did you see the Titanic sink?" Mr. Smith asked.

"I did not see the Titanic go down," Mr. Ismay said, shaking his head mournfully. "I did not want to see her go down. I was rowing the lifeboat all the time until we were picked up. I turned back only once after we left the vessel. I saw her green light and never turned back again. I did not want to see the end."

"After you left Capt. Smith on the bridge did you see him again?"

"I did not."

"Did you have any message from him?"

"None."

"How many wireless operators were there on the Titanic?"

"I presume there were two," said Mr. Ismay. "One is always on watch."

"Did they survive?"

"I have been told one did but I do not know whether it is true or not."

Mr. Ismay said he would have known if there had been an explosion on board but that there was none.

In response to a question the witness estimated the speed of the ship when she struck at 21 knots.

Sen. Smith, skipping to another question at the suggestion of Rep. Hughes, asked the witness if he had anything to do with selecting the crew for his lifeboat.

"I did not," was the response.

"Can you tell us," Sen. Smith asked, "anything about the inspection certificate that was issued for the Titanic before she sailed?"

"I know that the government had issued her a certificate."

Turning to the construction of the ship Mr. Ismay declared that the ship was especially constructed so that with any two of the larger compartments in the ship full of water she would still float.

"If the ship had struck head on, she would in all human probability be afloat today," he added.

"Did you attempt to interfere with the working of the wireless on the Carpathia?" he was asked.

"The captain will probably tell you I was not out of my room from the time I got into it until last night," was the reply.

"As a final question, Mr. Ismay was asked what he had on when he got into the lifeboat.

"A pair of slippers, a pair of pajamas, a suit of clothes and an overcoat," he replied.

Mr. Ismay was asked to hold himself in readiness during the day for another call before the committee. Sen. Smith said it was desired to hear the captain of the Carpathia in the meantime.

Magnificent Bravery of Men Who Stayed Behind

Women Clung to Husbands and Only Left The Ship When Forced to Leap---Scenes to Make Us Proud of American Manhood

New York, April 19.—The magnificent bravery displayed by the men on the Titanic in the hour of death is the principal topic upon which the survivors will talk. The women who escaped mourn the loss of the men and say that there were no scenes enacted to make mankind feel anything else than proud of the courage shown.

"Mrs. Colin Cooper Campbell, a passenger on the Carpathia, tells how Mrs. H. B. Harris, wife of the theatrical manager, who was lost, struggled against leaving her husband and, with Mrs D. Thorne, remained on deck until the men forced them to jump into a collapsible boat, the last to leave the ship.

The men told Mrs. Harris and Mrs. Thorne that they wanted them to go; that the Titanic, they believed, would have a better chance if all who could leave her would do so," says Mrs. Campbell.

"Mrs. Harris told me that all the men were brave beyond anything. When her collapsible life boat had gone about a hundred yards from the Titanic, not more, the Titanic sank. She saw a crowd of men and knew her husband was one of them, rush toward the stern in an effort to save themselves when the boat began to sink. The band was playing. There were waves, but no suction.

"All the men stood back. The men were ordered to go below; women to the upper deck. The men went below without a word.

"The theory grew that although the Titanic was badly injured she would float indefinitely. Some men and women even went back to bed. Other men smoked on the deck. Among many men and women there was a strong preference displayed to stay on the Titanic. Many women did not go into the life boats until they were ordered and even then they told me, they expected to be called back to the Titanic after a while.

"The whole talk of the women after they boarded the Carpathia was that so many men had sacrificed themselves. 'My life is finished,' said one survivor to me, and these useful men staid back without a murmur.'

"Two hundred stokers with blackened faces and almost without clothes came from below and saw a lifeboat. Two men jumped in and started to lower it. The captain called: 'Go back in your place every one of you.'

"And everyone of those men turned back without a word. They said they thought all the women had been put off.

"The men saved were not cowards. The women repeatedly said they felt that more men should have been given a chance.

"One of the stewards, the last to leave the Titanic, told us that at the last, when the passengers realized the Titanic really was sinking and that there was no escape, there was painful excitement, but that there was no time to make place for any one else."

FEW CELEBRITIES IN THE LIST OF SAVED

One of the best known of the Titanic's survivors yet reported is J. Bruce Ismay.

Mr. Ismay succeeded Clement A. Griscom as president of the International Mercantile Marine company on Feb. 23, 1904. Before that he was managing director of the White Star line. He was born at Liverpool Dec. 12, 1862, and is the eldest son of the late Thomas Henry Ismay, who was the head of the old firm of Ismay, Imrie & Co., the pioneers of the modern steamship business and founders of the White Star line. His fleet operated not only on the North Atlantic, but between England and Australia and from San Francisco to the Orient.

J. Bruce Ismay was educated at Elstree and Harrow, and then joined his father in business. He soon became one of the leading steamship men in the world and succeeded his father as the head of the old firm. After the formation of the White Star line he came to New York city and was for several years the agent of that company here. In 1888 he married Julia Florence, daughter of George R. Schieffelin of New York and has two sons and two daughters. He returned to England in 1890 and became a partner in the firm of Ismay, Imrie & Co. and on the death of his father in 1899, he became chairman of the White Star company.

Since he was elected president of the International Mercantile Marine he has divided his time between his home near Liverpool and New York city and nearly always has made a trip across the ocean when a new vessel has come here making the first passage on that vessel. He is a patron of many sports and his favorite recreations are shooting, motoring and playing golf.

THE WEATHER

FAIR TONIGHT

Washington, April 19.—For Southern New England—Fair tonight and Saturday. Moderate to brisk westerly winds.

For Northern New England—Fair tonight and Saturday; moderate to brisk westerly winds.

Boston, April 19.—For Boston and vicinity.—Fair and continued cold tonight and Saturday; moderate westerly winds.

Unsettled weather conditions still prevail in all northeastern portions of the country, and light to moderate rains have been reported in those districts and also in the far west and southern plains states. The only clear weather is in the southwestern states and near the Gulf coast. The disturbance that was over the Lake region yesterday has moved northeastward and is now central at Sydney, C. B., 29.38 inches. It is somewhat colder in eastern sections and slightly warmer in western portions of the country. In New England the temperature ranges from 32 at Greenville, Maine, to 40 at Boston and Nantucket, Mass. In New York at 8 a. m. it was 44; Washington, 46; St. Louis, 44; Chicago, 40; St. Paul, 40; Kansas City, 44; San Francisco 46.

THE DAY ON WALL STREET.

Details of Trading With Prices and Volume of Business

	April 19. Opening.	April 18. Closing.
Amal. Copper	82⅞	83⅜
Am. Beet Sugar	65½	65⅝
Am. Cotton Oil	52⅜	52½
Am. Smelt. & Refining	84½	84⅜
Atch., Top. & Santa Fe	108⅝	108⅝
Baltimore & Ohio	107¼	107⅞
Canadian Pacific	251½	252¼
Chesa. & Ohio	79½	79⅜
Chi., Mil. & St. Paul	110⅜	110½
Colo. Fuel & Iron	29⅜	30⅝
Interborough-Met.	19⅝	20
Inter.-Met. pfd.	58	58⅝
Missouri Pacific	43¼	43¼
New York Cetnral	119	119⅝
Northern Pacific	120⅝	121
Reading	164⅛	165¼
Rock Island	28	29¼
Southern Pacific	112⅜	112⅞
Southern Railway	29⅜	29⅜
Union Pacific	171½	171⅞
U. S. Steel	70⅝	71

Wall St., 10.10 a. m.—Without exception prices tended downwards at Friday's opening. The greatest weakness was in the coppers, New York Central, Baltimore & Ohio, American Can, Colo. Fuel and International Harvester. Dealings were light.

11 a. m.—Trading came almost to a full stop after the opening and the market dragged along with few exchanges of note save for some of the inactive issues, including Bethlehem Steel pfd., which gained 2½. Other specialties made gains, but the movement in the active issues was unimportant. There was another sensational rise in the stock of the Marconi Wireless Co. on the "Curb."

Noon—Stagnation of the like of which the market has not witnessed in many weeks, prevailed during the morning session of the stock market. Dealings were so light as to have absolutely no significance and the movement was altogether perfunctory. The financial community was still underl the spell of the great maritime tragedy and there was seemingly no disposition to trade for either side of the account. Bonds were easier.

Noon Quotations

New York, April 19.

	Noon.
Amalgamated Copper	82⅜
American Car & Foundry	60⅛
American Locomotive	43⅛
American Smelting & Refining	85
American Sugar Refining	127b
Anaconda Mining Co.	32⅜
Atchison	108⅜
Baltimore & Ohio	107¼
Brooklyn Rapid Transit	[illegible]
Canadian Pacific	255½
Cenertl Leather	26¼
Chicago, Mil. & St. Paul	110½
Chicago & North Western	143
Colorado & Southern	44b
Consolidated Gas	143¾
Delaware & Hudson	170
Denver & Rio Grande	23
Erie	36⅜
General Electric	170
Illinois Central	130
Louisville & Nashville	159⅜
Missouri Pacific	43½
National Lead	57
New York Central	119¼
Norfolk & Western	112½
North American	83⅜
Northern Pacific	121
Pennsylvania	124⅞
People's Gas	108⅝
Reading	164⅝
Republic Iron & Steel	23⅜
Rock Island Co. pfd.	56⅜
Southern Pacific	112⅜
Southern Railway	29⅝
Texas & Pacific	24b
Union Pacific	171⅛
United States Steel	70⅝
United States Steel pfd.	112½
Wabash pfd.	21½
Western Union	83½
Westinghouse Elec. & Mfg. Co.	75b

Call Money Easier

New York, April 19.—Noon—Money on call easier at 2¾; prime mercantile paper 4¼ to 4½ per cent.; exchanges, $303,391,375; balances, $10,485,807.

Cotton Opened Steady

New York, April 19.—Cotton futures opened steady. May, 11.34; June offered at 11.40; July, 11.47; Aug., 11.51; Sept., 11.50 b; Oct., 11.58; Nov., 11.61 b; Dec., 11.64; Jan., 11.63; Feb., offered 11.64; March, 11.70 bid.

WANTS PAPAL RECOGNITION

Countess Spottiswood-Mackin, Who Has Visited in Bangor, Wants Title Confirmed

Many Bangor people will be interested in the following despatch to the St. Louis Globe-Democrat concerning Countess Spottiswood-Mackin, formerly of St. Louis, and who is now in Rome endeavoring to obtain recognition of her title as a papal princess. The countess is an aunt of Mrs. Edwin G. Merrill of New York, formerly a resident of this city, and is most happily remembered here, having been entertained on different occasions at the former Merrill residence on Union street. The despatch says:

Countess Spottiswood-Mackin, formerly Miss Sally Britton of St. Louis, is in Rome, determined to obtain recognition of her title as a papal princess with all the privileges of her rank. She is to spend a month in Count Antonelli's apartments in the Palazza Rosticuocoi, the residence of the Pope's two sisters, who are her friends.

The title "princess" was conferred on her five years ago, but she never used it and was officially registered as "Countess." There has been a great delay in reaching a settlement of the case, and the countess says if her patience is exhausted she will take the matter directly to the Pope.

Mrs. Mackin was created a countess by the late Pope Leo XIII., and was decorated by the present Pope with the cross of the papal order, Pro Ecclesi et Pontifice. Although she is entitled to a seat in the tribunal of the Roman nobility at all solemn pontifical functions, an over-zealous attendant denied her admittance at the November consistory on the ground an American could not be a Roman noble-woman. The countess complained and was told her right to sit in the tribune was not included in her patent of nobility.

According to the countess she was notified five years ago, by Mgr. Marini, under-secretary of briefs, that the Pope had promoted her to be a princess with a seat in the tribuna of Roman nobility among her privileges. This letter was filed, but during the delays attending the drawing up of the patent of nobility, the Pope abolished the office of secretariate of briefs. The matter was left in abeyance until last year, when the countess decided after experiences at the consistory that she would insist upon her title being confirmed.

SIX LIVES LOST IN THE MISSISSIPPI FLOOD

Greenville, Miss., April 19.—Six lives are known to have been lost by the breaking of the Mississippi river levee at Beulah, Miss., Wednesday night. All of the victims were negroes who lived near the crevasse. It is believed here that many more persons have perished. Twenty houses in the direct path of the loosened water were swept away and more than a hundred persons were rescued from housetops and trees.

Win or Lose

10 Per Cent.

—ON—

WATER RATES

Last day to pay without the fine,

Saturday, April 20th

Office open day and night.

W. I. BROWN, Collector

NERVOUS PEOPLE MUST CURE THEMSELVES

The First Step Is to Stop the Cause of the Trouble, Then Build Up the Strength of the Disordered Nerves.

The first thing to do in nervous debility is to stop the cause of the trouble, if possible, whether it is irregular living, worry, or whatever it may be. Then the nerves must be given special nourishment and the blood must be kept pure and rich. This is the mission of Dr. Williams' Pink Pills and this is why the pills have been used with such great success in nervous troubles that did not yield to ordinary methods of treatment.

Nervous exhaustion early shows itself in the decreased activity of the organs that normally cast out the waste products of the body. The kidneys, skin and bowels are deprived of some of their energy and a part of the poisonous waste materials, which they readily pass off during health are turned back into the blood.

The result is plain. The blood, filled with impurities, is unable to give even its usual amount of nourishment to the nerves and a general breakdown follows. This is the explanation of the depressed and irritable feeling, pallor, loss of spirits, headaches, shortness of breath and poor digestion of the nervous sufferer.

The tonic treatment for nervous troubles, by building up the blood and supplying it with added oxygen, burns up and casts off the impurities and gives to the nerves the elements they need. In no other way can these elements be conveyed to the nervs xcept through the blood.

Mr. George B. Fox of No. 416 Seyburn avenue, Detroit, Mich., says: "I am glad to acknowledge what Dr. Williams' Pink Pills for Pale People did for me. Through overwork I became a sufferer from nervous prostration and, although I was under the doctor's care, I was sick for five years. I was very nervous and had frequent headaches—almost daily. I was dizzy-headed and saw rings and specks floating around in the air. I never slept well. My appetite was poor and I lost twenty pounds in weight. I was troubled with constipation. I had a bad cough and was examined for tuberculosis by two specialists. They told me that my lungs were sound but that I was a nervous wreck. A friend advised me to try Dr. Williams' Pink Pills for Pale People and a short trial convinced me that they were doing me good, so I continued using them and was restored to good health again. I keep the pills in the house now and if any of the family are in need of a tonic I give them Dr. Williams' Pink Pills for Pale People. I can highly recommend them to the public and have done so to a good many shopmates who have been benefited by them."

Those who are interested in the treatment which cured this case can obtain further information by writing for the booklet, "Nervous Disorders," which we send free on request.

Dr. Williams' Pink Pills are also recommended for sick headache, sleeplessness, nervous exhaustion, nervous dyspepsia, neuralgia, sciatica, St. Vitus' dance and locomotor ataxia. They are guaranteed to be free from opiates or harmful drugs.

They are for sale by all druggists, or will be sent, postpaid, on receipt of price, 50 cents per box; six boxes for $2.50, by the Dr. Williams Medicine Company, Schenectady, N. Y.

THIEVES ARE ABOUT

Police Say Bangor People Should Take Precautions Now

FAHEY MAKES A HAUL

Catches One With the Goods Friday After a Chase—Contents of Missing Suitcase Found.

Bangor people should be especially [illegible] about going away from home [illegible]t seeing that their doors and win[illegible] are securely locked just now as [illegible] number of tramps have drifted [illegible]wn recently, according to state[illegible] made by the police Friday. The[illegible]ve been congregating on lower [illegible]gton street for some time past, [illegible]ers say, and many of them have [illegible] various residences about the [illegible]ging for food.

[illegible] police have been especially watch[illegible] for cases of petty thieving for some [illegible] past. On Friday morning at 7.45 o'clock Deputy Chief of Police Fahey was walking down State street on his way to City Hall, when he saw two suspicious-looking characters standing at the corner of State and Essex streets. The deputy stopped in front of the Essex street pharmacy to see what was up, and presently one of the men ascended the steps of Dr. J. F. Starrett's home on State street, took an umbrella which was standing there, and started off with it before the officer's eyes, he says.

The man started up Essex street, turned down Penobscot and back Pine and was arrested by Deputy Fahey at the corner of that thoroughfare and State street. At police headquarters he gave his name as Joseph Allen and his home as Lynn, Mass. He claimed to have arrived in Bangor Thursday with $12, which, he said, he earned by sawing wood at Brownville. The police are skeptical of this statement, however, and say that his hands show no evidence of his having sawed wood or of his having done other work recently. The man who was talking with Allen when the officer first saw them, made his escape.

Earl Mann of Boston complained to the police Thursday evening of the loss of his suit case at the Union station. He set it down while he went to the telegraph office to send a wire and when he returned to where he left it, it had disappeared, he said. Early Friday the police found a portion of its contents, some pajamas, letters and papers, back of some Broad street stores. The suitcase itself was not recovered, however. Mr. Mann was particularly annoyed over the disappearance of some papers he wished to refer to in a business conference he was to have held here Friday. He admitted his carelessness in leaving the suitcase unprotected in the station waiting room.

As Friday was a court holiday, Patriots' day, those who were arrested Thursday night will not be brought before Judge Harding until Saturday morning. The cells at the police station were fairly well filled up by Friday afternoon, most of the arrests having been made for intoxication.

BAPTIST INSTITUTE ENDS

Combining of Baptists and Free Baptists Considered in Closing Session at Waterville.

The closing session of the Maine Baptist Institute, Colby college, and the Maine Baptist Missionary convention, co-operating, was held, Thursday, in the Baptist church at Waterville.

Rev. S. C. Whitcomb of Bangor, secretary of the Free Baptist State association, conducted the devotional service at 8.30 a. m. In order to accommodate some of the speakers, the order of the program was changed. Rev. I. B. Mower, who was to have spoken at 11 o'clock, on the Outlook, spoke at 9 o'clock, instead. Mr. Mower referred to the need of studying the community in which churches exist for the purpose of learning the religious needs and discovering how best to meet them. He pointed out the opportunity that is presenting itself of combining the Baptist and Free Baptist interests so as to give more efficient service. Rev. S. C. Whitcomb, Rev. T. J. Ramsdell, Rev. A. W. Bradeen and Prof. A. W. Anthony, participated in the discussion which followed.

Under the title, The Real Value of Foreign Missions, Dr. Anthony reiterated that their real value is the spiritual uplift that arises from the presence of a Christian minister in a heathen community.

The next topic on the program was the Best Current Literature, in which was discussed Sociology and the Church. The speakers were Rev. F. L. Wilkins, D. D., of Portland, and Rev. H. B. Hutchins, pastor of the Bates street church, Lewiston. Dr. Wilkins stated that the Bible is the book among all others that touches every phase of life. Rev. H. B. Hutchins reviewed the writings of Prof. Rauschenbusch and Dean Shaller Matthews. Closing prayer was offered by Rev. C. E. Owen, D. D., of Waterville.

In the afternoon, at 1.30, a meeting of the joint committee of conference and co-operation of the Baptists and Free Baptists was held. Those present were Rev. S. C. Whitcomb of Bangor, Rev. M. C. Miner, Gardiner; Rev. F. S. Hartley, Waterville. Prof. A. W. Anthony, Lewiston; and Rev. Mr. Tetley of the Free Baptists; Rev. J. K. Wilson, D. D., of Portland; Rev. T. J. Ramsdell, Caribou; Rev. F. H. Pratt, Waldoboro; Rev. I. B. Mower, Waterville; Rev. H. G. Clark, Perham, representing the Baptists. The committee organized with Rev. I. B. Mower, chairman, and Rev. F. S. Hartley, clerk. The committee proceeded to discuss the matter of re-districting the state so that the denominations might better co-operate, and discussed the legal aspects of the matter of union involved. The question of combining the annual report of the two denominations was considered. These matters were referred to sub-committees for further consideration. These committees will report at a meeting of the joint committee to be held in October, at the time of the state conventions of the churches.

ELLSWORTH NEWSOF A DAY

Ellsworth, April 19.

At the Supreme Judicial court Friday morning the Whiting vs. Whiting case for the recovery of bonds to the extent of $8,000 was brought up for trial but after a little testimony was introduced the case was taken from the jury and sent to the law court. In the afternoon and evening, the Gamong vs. Henderson case was on trial and is to be continued on Saturday. There was no session of court Friday it being Patriots' day and a legal holiday.

Work has begun on the extension of the post office in this city. Conners Bros. of Lowell, Mass., who have taken the contract to build the extension, have men here surveying the lot and making plans.

Miss Georgia Foster, who is employed as teacher at East Corinth academy arrived in this city Friday for a short visit with her parents, Mr. and Mrs. Austin Foster.

The regular meeting of the Thursday club was held Thursday afternoon at the Congregational chapel.

Mrs. J. A. Peters and Mrs. R. E. Mason spent Thursday in Bangor, the guests of relatives and friends.

A county road meeting will be held at the courthouse in this city Saturday, April 20, at 1.30 p. m.

The tickets for the conferring of the degree of chivalry by Canton lodge of Bangor at Hancock hall, Wednesday evening, April 24, will go on sale at the W. R. Parker clothing store Saturday afternoon at 2 o'clock. Dancing will follow.

Harry Achorn of Boston is spending a few days with relatives and friends in this city.

Herbert Foster, who is employed at Bangor, is visiting his parents, Mr. and Mrs. Austin Foster, in this city.

WILLIMANTIC

Will Gilman of Guilford was in town at his farm Saturday.

George Beasey started his drive out of the Davis stream Monday.

Annie Weston and daughter Marie, and son, Merton, were at Guilford Center, visiting relatives last week.

Mr. and Mrs. John Sears were at Guilford over Sunday, the guests of Mr. and Mrs. C. M. Small.

Merton, the little son of Mr. and Mrs. Irving Weston, burned his hand very badly last week in a cup of hot tea.

Ed Copeland and family of Monson were in town Saturday, the guests of O. L. Coffin.

TITANIC WAS WARNED OF ICEBERGS IN TRACK

Allan Liner Got News of Catastrophe Early Monday From Both Baltic aud Olympic in Suppressed Messages

With one expedition leaving Halifax, N. S., Thursday to search for the Titanic dead and another already on the way, the Allan steamship Parisian crept through the fog to her dock Thursday night bearing the first big authentic news known of the stupendous tragedy of the sea, says a despatch from Halifax to the N. Y. Evening World.

The great glaring fact, as given by Donald Sutherland, the wireless operator of the Parisian, was his unqualified statement to The World correspondent that the night of the disaster, judged from the position of the Parisian, which he estimates to have been about 50 miles southwest of the Titanic at the time she was struck, the weather was remarkably clear. In all the course through the day no fog had been encountered.

Sutherland says that while he has no positive information he is sure the warnings that he and other wireless operators sent out must have reached the Titanic. He said:

"On Sunday, the 14th, I was at my instrument until 10 o'clock at night. The Masaba of the Atlantic Transport line was ahead of us. The Californian was about 50 miles in our rear and the Titanic was following the California at a distance, I judge, of 75 to 100 miles. The Mesaba was passing me warning messages about the unusual icy condition of the court and warned me of the presence of big bergs. I passed the information to the Californian. I sent this message repeatedly: 'Running into ice—very thick—and big bergs.'"

Sure Titanic Was Warned

"I assume, although I do not know, for I did not talk directly to the Titanic, that the Californian passed to the Titanic the messages I had sent and which I had myself previously received from the Mesaba.

"I left my instrument at exactly 10 o'clock. I was ordered to do so by Capt. Hains because I had been up many hours in an effort to get a ship to go to the aid of the tank steamship, Deutschland, which I had heard was in distress. The Deutschland had no wireless so I could not get into direct communication with her, but our information was that she was pretty far to the south, and Capt. Hains was heading in that direction as fast as he could go.

"Next morning when we were 50 miles farther south of our course than the Parisian had ever before gone when we were on our way to Halifax, but of course had to dig southward to escape the ice line, I got a wireless from the Aisan stating that she had picked up the Deutschland, and so we have come on.

"I received a query on the night of the disaster from Capt. Haddock of the Olympic, the Titanic's sister ship, travelling east, as to the condition of the ice and I sent to him the same message that I had relayed from the Mesaba to the Californian.

Was Far From Usual Ice Line

"Certainly the Titanic when struck was far south of what the chart defines as the 'ice line.' She was fully 75 to 100 miles south of it."

"You could see 15 miles.

"At 10 o'clock that night we were approximately a hundred and fifty miles southwest of the Titanic. Under the captain's orders I turned in about 10 o'clock.

"By the time I got up we had left the ice pack and had headed westward. Of course in a little while I got out of touch with the Mesaba. I knew the Californian had followed us and I presumed the big Titanic had followed the same course and had passed us both.

"My thoughts had reverted to that unusually big fleet of icebergs and I was wondering how it was with the other fellows when I got from the Carpathia the shocking news about the Titanic. It staggered me. I could hardly believe it. Even yet it seems unreal, but soon I got confirmation of the dreadful news from the Baltic and the Olympic. It was all over then and there was no need of our turning back.

Kept News From Passengers

"After a conference with Capt. Hains it was decided that our passengers should be kept in ignorance of the disaster until we got to port.

"What was the message you received from the Baltic?" Sutherland was asked.

"I can't tell you that. Well, it's a professional secret. The message was intended for the Captain's ears alone."

"You understand that it isn't only the newspapers who are interested—that behind the newspapers are thousands of people directly concerned, and hundreds of thousands of people who are wondering how this accident could happen?"

"The Carpathia," answered Sutherland, "has been in touch with Sable Island all morning. Why don't you ask her?"

"The Carpathia will not answer. She will give out nothing despite the fact that her captain and officers are besieged undoubtedly with the pleadings of survivors to get m[illegible] [illegible]d the officers in New York, [illegible] [illegible]ed by frantic relatives and [illegible] [illegible]sking for news of some kind."

Sutherland smiled, not in an amused but a serious sort of way, and answered:

"I'm sorry, but these are professional secrets and I cannot honorably divulge them."

"If the World got for you a release from the Marconi company would you then tell us what these messages were?"

"No, I couldn't tell you even then."

Heard From the Baltic, Too

"From what other ship than the Carpathia did you get news of the Titanic's loss?"

"The Olympic and the Baltic."

"Were their messages of the same private nature?"

"They were absolutely."

"Could Capt. Hains release you?"

"No: he couldn't and he wouldn't."

Operator Sutherland was the chum of Jack Phillips, the chief wireless operator of the Titanic, who is among the missing.

The Mackay-Bennett cable ship of the Commercial Cable company, chartered by the White Star Steamship company, left late Wednesday at 4 o'clock to seek the Titanic dead. She carried a doctor in the remote possibility of finding living survivors, but she also carried an undertaker and 110 coffins.

Thursday another cable ship, the Minia, of the Direct United States Cable company, which only Wednesday arrived from St. Pierre, Miquelon, will put out to follow the Mackay-Bennett in this solemn, gruesome venture. She also will carry coffins, an undertaker and tons of ice. And both ships will carry scrap iron. And both will carry parsons. The meaning of these two last facts must be only too poignantly clear.

GATHERING OF THE THRONG TO MEET THE CARPATHIA

Friends and Relatives of the Saved and the Missing at Pier to Meet the Rescue Ship.

In a drizzling rain 250 policemen gathered early Thursday night at the Cunard line piers at West 14th street and North river preparatory to handling the crowds. Inspector McCluskey was in charge of the squad and ropes, dotted with green lights, were stretched for 75 yards in front of the piers to hold back the throng. No one without special permits was allowed beyond these ropes. As early as 8 o'clock automobiles in which veiled women and silent men were seated began arriving and at 8.30 a small crowd had already entered the great steel and concrete structure which covers the piers. A small hotel across the way had been converted into headquarters for the newspaper and press associations and a meeting place for those who had been bereaved or had relatives aboard the Carpathia. Although there was no rule for silence, everyone talked in whispers and there were those who had hoped against hope that some dear one was alive, although the list of survivors had failed to show their names.

The police regulations were made rigid as the evening wore on. All traffic on West street directly in front of the piers was diverted to 14th street on the north and at 13th street on the south. Another line was drawn on east at 11th avenue. Thus the block immediately in front of the piers was made private for those immediately concerned in the tragedy. Shortly before 8 o'clock news came that the Carpathia was passing the Statue of Liberty. At that hour more than 50 automobiles were parking in front of the piers.

The early arrival of the Carpathia at quarantine surprised even the customs officials, 150 of whom were on the pier under the direction of Gen. Nelson P. Henry, surveyor of the port, who came to facilitate the landing of the survivors.

Five hundred friends and relatives had gathered inside the pier sheds at 8.30 o'clock, taking up their positions under the customs alphabetical arrangement, each one under the initial of the name of the survivor expected. The Carpathia at this time was a quarter of a mile down the Hudson and drawing near the docks. A stream of people was filling into the pier entrance and automobiles continued to take their places.

A committee from the New York Stock Exchange brought to the pier shortly before the Carpathia arrived $20,000 in cash to be distributed among those most in need of assistance. This money was raised on the Exchange of popular subscription and brought to the pier in an oblong box.

A committee composed of R. H. Thomas, president of the Exchange; Charles Kloblock, H. N. Barruch, Charles Halsdoner and J. Carlisle had the funds in charge.

Surveyor Henry assigned to their use the little customs house on the pier. Several Red Cross nurses and a dozen physicians arrived upon the pier and two ambulances form St. Vincent's hospital stood outside.

The Pennsylvania Railroad Co. had a special train waiting at their station at 34th street and a number of taxicabs to convey survivors desiring to go to Philadelphia to their friends.

An apartment for Mr. Ismay had been secured at the Ritz-Charlton hotel.

J. Pierpont Morgan, Jr., put in an appearance as the boat was about to dock. Representatives of the Widener and Thayer families of Philadelphia were also early arrivals, having chartered a special train over the Pennsylvania railroad.

There were a thousand persons in the shed at 8.45 o'clock, many of whom were weeping. Outside the automobiles kept piling up.

The Carpathia was off the end of the pier ready to dock at five minutes to 9 o'clock.

The pilot of a tug boat engaged to assist in warping her in announced that she could not dock until the lifeboats were taken off.

A large number of Sisters of Charity from the various hospitals arrived in a number of automobiles. A commissioner of immigration was present to expedite the landing of a number of steerage passengers.

Belated friends of the survivors continued to arrive in large numbers.

HOW WIDENER AND RYERSON WENT TO THEIR DEATHS

New York, April 19—Geo. D. Widener, the wealthy Philadelphian, and Arthur L. Ryerson, of New York, went to their death like men, is the statement made by Mrs. Ryerson to her brother-in-law, E. S. Ryerson, who resides at the St. Regis. She says that when the women were put into the life boats they saw Mr. Ryerson and Mr. Widener standing behind the rail of the Titanic, both waving their arms, throwing kisses and calling farewell to their wives and children. They believed there were boats enough for all. Mrs. Ryerson having her two daughters, Susan and Emily B. and a young son, John B., in the same boat with her.

Milady's Toilet Table

By Mme. D'MILLE

Of all home treatments for the hair, the therox dry shampoo seems to be the most satisfactory by far. There is something about it totally different from any other treatment, and the hair responds so quickly. Put four ounces of powdered orris root (or a cupful of corn meal) in a fruit jar and add the contents of a small original package of therox, shaking well together. Sprinkle a little on the head and brush thoroughly. It makes the hair wavy, glossy and lustrous.

To have a fair and lovely skin, to retain the attraction of youth, to keep the complexion clear and beautiful—the face, neck and forearms should be massaged every morning with a solution made by dissolving a small original package of mayatone in a half-pint witch hazel. Use this instead of powder. It does not rub off nor show. Mayatone reduces large pores, eradicates dark and muddy spots, and leaves the skin smoth, soft and satinlike.

Sometimes a sore may be slow in healing. In cases like this Mother's Salve is good to use, for it is autiseptic as well as healing and tends to prevent blood poisoning. It quickly heals cuts, burns, scalds, etc., and will also cure chaps, cold sores, pimples and skin eruptions when not caused by constitutional trouble.

No woman need be humiliated by wild hairs or fuzzy growths. They will vanish quickly if delatone paste is applied. Mix enough powdered delatone with water to cover the hairy surface; apply and after two or three minutes rub off, wash the skin, and the hairs will be gone.

HAYS A RAILROAD GENIUS

Born in Illinois, But Went to Canada to Manage Grand Trunk.

Charles Melville Hays, president of the Grand Trunk and the Grand Trunk Pacific railways, was described by Sir Wilfrid Laurier at a dinner of the Canadian Club of New York at the Hotel Astor last year as "beyond question the greatest railroad genius in Canada, as an executive genius ranking second only to the late Edward H. Harriman." He was returning aboard the Titanic with his wife and son-in-law and daughter, Mr. and Mrs. Thornton Davidson of Montreal.

Mr. Hays was born at Rock Island, Ill., in 1856. At 17 he became a clerk for the Atlantic and Pacific railroad in St. Louis. In 1877 he was made secretary to the general manager of the Missouri Pacific and after nine years he was assistant general manager of that road. In 1887 he was appointed general manager of the Wabash, St. Louis and Pacific and was soon promoted to the general managership of the Wabash Western. When the Wabash lines were consolidated he became vice-president and general manager. At that time he was a director of many other middle western traffic lines. He left the Wabash in 1896 to become general manager of the Grand Trunk at Montreal. In his five years at that post he reorganized the Central Vermont Railway Company, a subsidiary of the Grand Trunk; completed the Victoria Jubilee open span double track bridge across the St. Lawrence at Montreal and the single span steel arch bridge replacing the old suspension bridge at Niagara Falls. Under his management the Grand Trunk was double tracked for 878 miles, making it at that time the longest stretch of continuous double track under one management in the world.

When Collis P. Huntington died the Southern Pacific got Mr. Hays as president. He removed to San Francisco on January 1, 1901, but in the fall of the same year he resigned and returned to the Grand Trunk as vice-president and general manager. He conceived in 1902 the project of the Grand Trunk Pacific Railway, the building of which, made possible by laws passed at the instance of Sir Wilfrid Laurier and the government, is still going on. This will be the only transcontinental railroad wholly within Canada, extending from Moncton, N. B., to Prince Rupert, B. C., a distance of 3,600 miles. It will cross the Rocky Mountains with a maximum grade of only 21 feet to the mile.

Mr. Hays was elected to the presidency and a directorship of the Grand Trunk Railway Company on January 1, 1910, also to the presidency of all the subsidiary lines, with a total mileage of about 14,000. Mr. Mays was in full charge of the Grand Trunk's affairs in America, the directors of the company and most of its 54,000 stockholders being in England.

Among the companies of which Mr. Hays was president are the New England Elevator Company, the Portland Elevator Company, the Ctnadian Express Company, the St. Clair Tunnel Company, the Montreal Warehousing Company and the International Bridge Company.

Mr. Hays was married to Clara J. Gregg of St. Louis in 1881

PRES. TAFT HAD NO HOPE THAT MAJ. BUTT WAS SAFE

Pres. Taft told visitors late Thursday that he had never expected to hear of the rescue of Major Butt, his military aide, after the first shocking news of the Titanic disaster reached land.

"I never had any idea that Archie was saved at all," said the President. "As soon as I heard that 1,200 people went down, I knew he went down, too. He was a soldier and was on deck where he belonged."

RYAN WINS THE 16TH MARATHON

Andrew Sockalexis, Old Town Indian, Second—Ryan Breaks the Record.

Boston, April 19.—Mike J. Ryan, the Irish-American A. C. of New York, won the Boston Athletic association's 16th annual run Friday and qualified for the American Olympic team at Stockholm. Ryan established a new record of 2 hours, 21 minutes, 18 1-5 seconds. The old record was made in 1910 by Demar of 2:21; 39 3-5 seconds.

Andrew Sockalexis, the Old Town Indian, was second.

Ryan was looked upon as a strong contender for marathon honors this year, in the light of past performances, especiallly his winning of the London Harrod race last summer.

The bid of Sockalexis for first place which he missed my 34 seconds, was the feature of the record finish. The Old Town Indian, running under the colors of the North Dorchester A. C., came through the field on the home stretch like a whirlwind and would probably have caught Ryan in another time. The times of the first ten men follow:

M. J. Ryan, Irish American, New York, 2:21:18 1-5; A. Sockalexis, North Dorchester, Mass., 2:21:52 3-5; F. J. Madden, North Dorchester, 2:23:34; T. H. Lilley, North Dorchester, 2:23:50 4-5; Fritz Corlson, Minneapolis, 2:25:38 1-5; J. C. Karlson, Minneapolis, 2:25:50; H. F. Jenson, Pastime A. C., New York, 2:26:07; R. F. Piggott, unatached, 2:26:48 4-8; Edwin Fabre, National A. A., Montreal, 2:26:20; William Galwin, Yonkers, 2:26:50.

Boston, April 19.—More than a hundred of the hardiest and swiftest long distance runners in the country assembled in Ashland Center Friday, 25 miles outside of Boston, for the 16th renewal of the Boston Athletic association's marathon run and a possible chance of representing this country in the Olympic games at Stockholm.

The road from Ashland into this city, over which Clarence De Mar established the record last year of two hours, 21 minutes, 39 3-5 seconds, was not at its best Friday, because of Thursday's northeaster.

Because of his record run of last spring followed by his victory in the Marathon to Brockton in the fall De Mar was given assurance of a place on the American Olympic team without going through Friday's test.

The favorites in the field were Edward Gabree of Montreal, Sidney Hatch of Chicago, Wm. Calvin of Yonkers, Joseph Forshaw of St. Louis, Andrew A. Sockalexis of Old Town, Me., and North Dorchester, Mass., Wm. J. Hackett of Brookline and Festus Madden of North Dorchester.

The race was scheduled to start at noon as usual.

When the participants faced the starter just before noon a morning shower had turned the first five miles into Framingham into a mass of slippery mud, while the remainder of the course had an oil finish that gave almost as bad footing.

Sparson of Leicester and Saklad of North Dorchester set the pace in the first mile, running side by side from the start, through the village of Ashland and then on over the gently rolling road towards Framingham.

Granacopolis of Yonkers, Arequette and Hermequetewa and Tellyumptewa, three Carlisle Indians, were running along side of the veteran Sammy Melor of Yonkers.

The little hill a mile outside of Ashland was taken with a rush and like a pack of eager hounds the runners swung around the corner on top of the hill and sighted the first timing place at South Framingham.

Just before reaching Framingham depot Sparson dropped back into the ruck and Saklad found himself leading the field.

Silva was second and then came the three Indians Arequette, Tellnymptewa and Hermequatewa.

Saklad's time at South Framingham depot was 12; 22, 18, something more than a minute behind Caffrey's record, but better than Demar's time last year.

After leaving the five mile point at South Framingham the runners had level ground for the next five miles into Natick and the pace became very fast.

Gallagher of Yale dashed through the field and was the leader at Natick square which he reached at 12; 43:10 about a minute behind Welton's record. Close to his heles ran Tellnymptewa and Hermequatewa while Clifton Horne of Haverhill and Saklad were within challenging distance.

The road continued level for a mile out of Natick and then the first rise was encountered. At the top of the hill sits Wellesley college and the lightly clad runners received a warm greeting and a parting cheer from several hundred white jacketed and bareheaded college girls.

Gallagher maintained his lead into Wellesley, which he reached at 1:00:20, a full minute ahead of the record held by Lee. Telnymptemwa Cleary of North Dorchester and Hermequatewa were running close behind.

The half-way point was passed just out of Wellesley and for the next three miles it was down hill with a decided dip, approaching Charles river at Newton Lower Falls, 14 miles from the start.

Despite the slippery road the pace continued very fast and the runners fairly flew across the bridge over the Charles, sped up the little incline for the first sharp turn in to Washington street and then headed for the next timing place at the turn into the Commonwealth avenue boulevard, 16 miles from the start. The running through Washington street was also uncertain and again the sidewalks proved more attractive than the street.

A big crowd had gathered at the Woodland Park hotel. Gallagher continued in the lead, still running ahead of the record.

The first stiff climb of the course came at the turn into the boulevard, but Gallagher took the mile hill with true Yale grit and pulled out nearly a hundred yards from his trailers.

From the top of Braeburn hill the course was gradually down grade again for two miles and then came the second and last big hill, to the reservoir. Here Gallagher put on more steam and came dashing down the other side of the hill, minutes ahead of Demar's record of last year.

Gallagher passed Lake street, five miles from the finish, at 1; 51; 30, four minutes ahead of the record.

The runners passed Lake street thus: Gallagher, Cleary, Ryan, Fabre, Silva, Smith, Mermequatewa, Root.

On the run in on Beacon street Gallagher was overhauled and at Coolidge corner, three miles from the finish, Hermequatewa had a slight lead.

WHITE STAR PEOPLE TRY TO MUZZLE MEN OF CREW

Instructions From Ismay to Keep Them Quiet and Smuggle Them Out of Country at Once.

New York, April 19.—Incensed by the few stray bits of information given out Thursday night by the members of the crew of the ill-fated Titanic officials of the White Star line Friday kept the men thoroughly under cover so that no trace of their whereabouts could be discovered until late in the morning when it was found that a portion of them had been transferred aboard the Red Star liner Lapland where they were held incommunicado.

The four surviving officers of the Titanic, when they arrived on the Carpathia were quickly transferred to the Red Star liner where they remained until they were summoned to appear before the Senate investigating committee. These officers had been instructed to refuse to answer any questions, except those propounded by the committee of inquiry.

It developed Friday that J. Bruce Ismay, managing director of the Mercantile Marine Co. had instructed Vice Pres. Franklin of the same company to segregate the Titanic's men as soon as they arrived on the Carpathia. Mr. Ismay urged Mr. Franklin to take every effort to smuggle the men into seclusion as soon as they landed at the pier and to make speedy preparations to get them out of the country.

TITANIC'S SURVIVORS TO SHOW APPRECIATION

New York, April 19.—A committee of the Titanic survivors agreed Friday morning to meet later in the day aboard the Carpathia to draft a set of resolutions thanking the officers and crew of the Carpathia for their services and assistance in saving their lives. They will present to Capt. Rostrom of the Carpathia a tall silver loving cup as a token of their appreciation.

PLAY BALL FOR SUFFERERS

New York, April 19.—Pres. John T. Brush of the New York National Baseball club announced Friday that the Giants would play an exhibition game with the New York American League club next Sunday afternoon, April 21, at the Polo Grounds for the benefit of the Titanic survivors. The game will be called at 3 p. m.

MR. CARNEGIE WANTS TO KNOW

Along with a gift of $5,000 which Andrew Carnegie made Thursday to the relief fund for the Titanic disaster sufferers, the following correspondence between the retired ironmaster and Mayor Gaynor was made public:

New York, April 18, 1912.

Dear Mayor: What was the Titanic doing up among the icebergs when she had the whole Atlantic ocean south open and free?

This is the root of the matter. Passenger steamers should be compelled to keep far south below the range of icebergs at all seasons. Lifeboats are secondary to this vital requirement.

"Yours,
Andrew Carnegie.

April 18, 1912.

Dear Mr. Carnegie: As usual you hit the nail exactly on the head. They had no business up there among the icebergs, and being there should have stopped. The question of lifeboats is a secondary one. I thank you exceedingly for your generous check of $5,000 for the sufferers.

Sincerely yours,
W. J. Gaynor, Mayor.

PRES. FALLIERES SENDS HIS PROFOUND SYMPATHY

The White House Thursday night made public the following cable message from Pres. Fallieres of France:

"Your profound affliction I have heard of the Titanic's awful catastrophe, which brings mourning to so many American families and I have it at heart to extend most sincere condolences. I wish to tell your excellency how much I share in your anguish about the fate of your aide and friend, Major Butt."

In reply Pres. Taft paid touching tribute to Major Butt.

"I am grateful," he cabled, "for your references to my friend and aide, Major Butt. Soldier that he was, with rescue only possible for part of the company, I know that he felt his place to be on the ship as she went down."

"BE BRITISH" SLOGAN OF DEATH SHIP

Rallying Cry Called From the Bridge By Capt. Smith—Member of Crew Tells of Heroic Self Sacrifice

New York, April 19.—But for the unparalleled self-sacrifice and heroism of Captain Smith and the Titanics' officers, the sea would have claimed an even greater toll when the gigantic ship went down. From the bridge Captain Smith called through his megaphone, "Be British," and that became the rallying cry of officers and crew.

Such was the graphic description of the conduct of men responsible for the saving of human souls in the smitten Titanic, as told Friday by John Johnson, a member of the crew, who took an oar in a lifeboat. He gave his version of how the ship struck the iceberg and went down; how officers and male passengers stood unafraid upon the deck awaiting the inevitable hour; how the lifeboats were lowered and how husbands and wives said their last farewells.

"When the crash came," he said, "the Titanic was going 23 knots an hour. She ripped herself clear, there was no panic. Everything was quiet. When the boats were lowered there were many who refused to go. One of the most pathetic scenes was the refusal of Mrs. Isidor Straus to leave her husband. She remained with him to the last.

"When the first signal was given to lower the boats, some of the crew pressed forward. It was then that the rallying cry came through the megaphone from the bridge, 'Be British, my men.' It was Captain Smith's voice. Every man obeyed the command and faced about calmly.

"They knew there was no hope and as the big, strong, English seamen assisted the women and children into the boats, they gave no sign that they realized that Captain Smith's words, 'Be British' had sealed their fate. They remained at their posts and died like men."

When J. Bruce Ismay, president of the International Mercantile Marine company, stepped into the last lifeboat, Johnson said, there were no women left on the deck. He was forced into the boat by officers of the ship and this was done, Johnson said, just as the boat was being lowered.

FACTS ABOUT PASSENGERS ON ILL-FATED TITANIC

Many Returning From Pleasure Trips and One Honeymoon Couple Aboard.

Here are some facts about the passengers on the Titanic whose residence and business is known. Some of the names appear in the list of those rescued, but many of them, especially of the men, are among the missing.

Howard B. Case, formerly of Rochester, N. Y., has been living in Ascot, England, for several years, as London manager of the Vacuum Oil Company.

W. D. Douglas, who was traveling with his wife and a maid, is from Minneapolis, and is director of the Quaker Oats Company, and a cousin of James H. Douglas, president of the company, who lives in Chicago. Mr. Douglas' two sons are in Mineapolis.

Thomas Andrews, Jr., a director of the shipbuilding firm of Harland & Wolff, was accompanied by a number of mechanics who were watching the workings of the latest ship from their yards. His home was in Belfast, Ireland.

Mrs. Ida S. Hippach, and her 15-years-old daughter, Jean, are the wife and daughter of L. A. Hippach, a wealthy glass dealer of Chicago. Mr. and Mrs. Hippach lost two sons in the Iroquois theatre fire in Chicago.

John B. Brady has been a resident of Pomery, Wash., and president of the Pomery State bank.

Mrs. George N. Stone of Cincinnati is the widow of the former president of the Cincinnati Bell Telephone Company. She was returning from a year in Europe and Egypt.

Mr. and Mrs. Richard L. Beckwith, and Mrs. Beckwith's daughter, Miss Helen Newsome of Columbus, Ohio, were returning from a pleasure trip to Europe. Mrs. Beckwith is a daughter of William Munypeny of Columbus, and a cousin of Gov. Judson Harmon.

F. P. Colley of Victoria, British Columbia, has been employed as a land surveyor by the British Columbia government.

Hugh R. Rood made his home in Seattle, Wash., where he was vice president and general manager of the Pacific Creosotin company. His wife and her maid, who were with him in Europe, were to sail for America on another steamer.

Mr. and Mrs. John P. Snyder, prominent in society in Milwaukee, left for Europe in January, on a honeymoon trip, and were on their way home.

John E. Maguire was a salesman for the Dunbar Pattern company of Brockton, Mass.

George Q. Clifford was connected with the Belcher Last company of Stoughton, Mass.

Walter C. Porter was a last manufacturer of Worcester, Mass.

Mr. and Mrs. Edgar Meyer were on the passenger list of the Titanic. Mrs. Meyer is the daughter of the late Andrew Saks and niece of Isidor Saks, of Saks & Co., New York city.

Emil Brandeis lived in Omaha, Neb., where he was a member of the merchant firm of J. E. Brandeis & Son.

Dr. Washington Dodge of San Francisco, who was accompanied by his wife and child, was widely known as an authority on taxation.

Frederick M. Hoyt has been one of the best known yachtsmen along the Massachusetts coast. He made his summer home at Marblehead, Mass. He was a member of the New York, the Corinthian and the Eastern Yacht clubs.

Mr. and Mrs. Tyrrell Cavendish were on their way from London, where they make their home. Mrs. Cavendish is a daughter of Henry Siegel of New York city and a niece of Ferdinand Siegel of Chicago.

Percival W. White, a Massachusetts cotton manufacturer, made his home in Brunswick, Me. His son, Richard F. White, who accompanied him, was a senior at Bowdoin college.

Walter M. Clark is the son of J. Ross Clark, vice president of the San Pedro, Los Angeles & Salt Lake railroad, and a nephew of Senator W. A. Clark of Montana.

Miss Georgette Madill is a 15-year-old heiress of St. Louis, with an allowance of $7,500 a year to pay for clothing and education. She is the principal heir to the estate of the late Judge George Madill, a prominent banker of St. Louis. She is the daughter of Mrs. Edward S. Robert, who was the widow of Judge Madill. Mrs. Robert and her niece, Miss Elizabeth W. Allen, were also on the Titanic.

Mrs. J. C. Hogaboom is a resident of Newark, Ohio, and was accompanied by a cousin, Miss Gretchen Longley, and an aunt, Miss K. Andrews.

Milton C. Long lived in Springfield, Mass. His father is Judge Charles L. Long of that city. He was a graduate of Columbia university.

Erwin G. Lewy lived at 5,826 South Park avenue, Chicago, and was the treasurer of Lewy Brothers, jewelers.

Col. Jacob Weir of North Berwick, Scotland, was on his way to visit his son, H. W. Weir, a traveling salesman of Goshen, Ind.

George Hart, a son of Mr. and Mrs. Alfred Hart of Appleton, Wis., was for many years court reporter at Wausau, Wis. He was returning from a year's visit in Europe.

George J. Graham was a buyer for the Eaton company of Canada.

Herbert Henry Hilliard, a buyer for Jordan Marsh company of Boston, was on his way home from a purchasing trip to Europe.

Timothy J. McCarthy, Jr., was another buyer for Jordan, Marsh.

R. Spencer Silverthorn had been abroad on a purchasing trip for B. Nugent & Brothers, a dry goods firm of St. Louis.

SHE CHOSE TO DIE WITH HER HUSBAND

Friends of Mrs. Isador Straus Think She Clung to Him on the Titanic.

Friends of the Strauss family still continued Thursday their ceaseless vigil at the White Star offices for news of Mr. and Mrs. Isador Strauss. Neither Mr. Strauss nor his wife is mentioned in the list of survivors wirelessed from the Carpathia, but as only half the names are given in the first list hope is still maintained.

The absence of Mrs. Strauss' name from among those of the women saved is believed by some of her friends to mean that when the terrible moment came for her to leave her husband to certain death she chose to stay and die with him.

Mr. and Mrs. Oscar Strauss who were at Hot Springs, Va., cut their visit short at once on hearing of the disaster. They arrived in New York Wednesday morning and went at once to the White Star offices. But no more encouragement could be given them there than was obtained Tuesday by Herbert Straus or Sylvester Byrnes, Isador Straus' private secretary, who remained at the offices through day and night.

Mr. Straus, who is one of New York's leading merchants and philanthropists is a member of the firms of R. H. Macy & Co., and Abraham & Straus.

CALIFORNIAN HAS NO SURVIVORS OR BODIES

Boston, April 19.—The Leland liner Californian, which arrived Friday from London had neither survivors nor bodies from the Titanic aboard.

"We arrived at the scene of the disaster" said Capt. Stanley Lord, "just in time to see the last boat filled with survivors being hauled aboard the Carpathia. We circled the waters about the sunken craft for three hours, but saw no sign of the three life boats which we now understand are still missing. There was no sign of life among the wreckage."

Capt. Lord said he received a wireless from the Virginian at 5.30 a. m., Monday telling of the Titanic disaster. The Californian was then north of the scene. Intervening were great masses of ice including a number of large bergs and it was such difficult manoeuvring that it took three hours to reach the wreckage.

REFUSED TO LEAVE SHIP WITHOUT HER PET DOG

New York, April 19.—A narrative of the disaster to the Titanic is prepared by one of the stewards of the Carpathia, containing the following:

"One of the earlier boats to arrive was seen to contain a woman tenderly clasping a pet Pomeranian. When assisted to the rope ladder and while the rope was being fastened around her she emphatically refused to give up for a second the dog which was evidently so much to her."

The steward further says that a survivor told him that one woman declined to leave the Titanic because they would not take off a pet dog belonging to her.

MRS. ASTOR IS VERY ILL

New York, April 19.—The following statement was issued later Friday at the office of the Astor estate:

"Mrs. Astor is very ill and under the care of a physician. It will be impossible for her to be interviewed or to give out any statement."

CITY EDITION EXTRA

The Globe

AND Commercial Advertiser. EST'D 1797.

NEW YORK'S OLDEST NEWSPAPER.

CITY EDITION EXTRA

115TH YEAR. NUMBER 178. VOLUME 115. NEW YORK, FRIDAY, APRIL 19, 1912. ONE CENT.

TITANIC INQUIRY ON; LOSS OF 1,595 LIVES DUE TO SPEED MANIA

Last Hours of the Giant Liner Filled With Unprecedented Scenes of Self-Sacrifice and Heroism---Astor Put His Wife in the Boat and Then Made Way for a Woman---Mr. and Mrs. Straus, the One Refusing to Be Saved Without the Other, Went Down Clasped in Each Other's Arms---Band Played "Nearer, My God, to Thee," as Ship Sank.

There was nothing to conceal. From the moment she struck the iceberg until the arrival of her passengers in New York, the story of the Titanic was an unparalleled record of self-sacrifice and devotion.

In the last grave stress, when it became known beyond doubt that she must sink, those who could not go because honor demanded way for women and children awaited unafraid on her decks the inevitable hour.

These were men.

With the arrival of the Carpathia with 745 human souls from the smitten Titanic the story of the fateful disaster upon the Grand Banks became an open book of heroism. It told of John Jacob Astor clamly waving farewell to his bride, who is soon to be a mother; of Isidor Straus and his aged wife, who refused to leave him, standing clasped in each other's arms while the ship went down; of heroic faithfulness of crew and officers; of a self-sacrifice of men and women that surpasses all understanding.

SANG "NEARER, MY GOD, TO THEE."

And the Titanic sank with the band playing "Nearer, My God, to Thee," while the musicians stood knee deep in the water that mounted over the decks; with every man of her crew standing to his post and with her captain on her bridge until the sea swept him away.

An explosion which rent the ship literally in twain brought the catastrophe to a close. As the icy water reached the boilers they blew up and the vessel dived prow foremost. Her after part threw the crowd of men into the air like a swarm of bees.

The Titanic struck the berg at 11.40 Sunday night. She was going at top speed at the time, probably twenty-one knots. She sank at 2.20, an hour and three-quarters after the crash. The watch in the pocket of Col. Archibald Gracie, said to be the last of the survivors to leave the ship, stopped at 2.22, when he was washed into the water off the upper deck by the engulfing wave.

The men who were saved, most of them at any rate, were taken in the boats to help man them, or jumped overboard and were picked up afterward.

The berg was discovered before the Titanic struck it by the lookout, who notified Quartermaster Moody to port his helm. Moody obeyed, but it was too late.

A group of men at cards in the smoking room sent one of their number to look out of the window, and when he came back with the announcement that the boat had grazed an iceberg the party went on with the game until the order came to put on life belts and gather at the boats.

There was no confusion when the ship struck. There was no confusion while her crew and the men among the passengers were lowering the boats and loading them with women. There was no panic when the last boat left and those who had not gone in it stayed behind to face certain death. Of the 1,595 who went down there was hardly one whom the supreme test found wanting.

Nor was that heroism confined to any class or kind. There was no breed nor birth in the courage that made all men equal that night. Peasant and merchant prince acted and died heroes of an equal stamp.

LIKE A GREAT CAN OPENER.

When the shock came most of the 2,340 passengers and crew were asleep. Many were not awakened by the blow to the stricken leviathan. The ice, entering the port bow of the ship, gouged out her side like a gigantic can opener.

At first it was thought that she was not dangerously damaged. Passengers who had rushed on deck were told by officers to return to their staterooms, only to be roused hastily a few moments later when it was discovered the giant vessel was sinking by the head.

At no time was there unnecessary disorder. The passengers gathered on the boat deck. On the starboard side men were permitted to join their wives. To port only women and children were gathered. Capt. Smith stood on the bridge shouting commands.

Hardly a passenger thought the ship was sinking. Hardly a man of them dreamed that in one hour and three-quarters death would have claimed two-thirds of all on board.

Some considered the lowering of boats unnecessary.

HOW ISIDOR STRAUS DIED.

Isidor Straus stood on Deck B. He was half clad. By his side was his wife. A boat was being lowered. An officer tried to help Mrs. Straus to it. She refused to leave her husband. He pleaded with her to go, but he pleaded in vain.

G. N. Stengel of Newark was there. He was among the rescued, and he drew the picture as the Carpathia arrived.

"Mrs. Straus clung to her aged husband," he said. "An officer seized her and tried to carry her to a waiting boat, but she would not go. Then sailors stroye to tear her from the man whose life partner she had been for more than a score of years, but she clung desparately to him. Finally they gave it up. The last thing I saw as we pulled away in the boats was the woman in whose gentle heart was a heroism greater than I have ever witnessed, standing clasped in her husbands arms while the water mounted about them."

Not far from the woman who would not let her husband meet death alone, Col. Astor stood supporting the figure of his young bride.

A boat was being filled with women. Col. Astor helped his wife to a place in it. The boat was not filled, and there seemed no more women near it. Quietly the colonel turned to the second officer, who was superintending the loading.

"May I go with my wife? She is not well." he asked.

ASTOR GAVE UP HIS PLACE.

The officer nodded. The man of millions got into the boat. The crew were about to cast off the falls. Suddenly the colonel sprang to his feet, shouting to them to wait. He had seen a woman running toward the boat. Leaping over the rail, he helped her to the place he had occupied.

Mrs. Astor screamed and tried to climb from the boat. The colonel restrained her. He bent

(Continued on Second Page.)

SENATORS OPEN INVESTIGATION AT THE WALDORF

J. Bruce Ismay, Managing Director of the White Star Line, on Hand to Testify as to Why Titanic Was Going at Full Speed When Crash Came — Vice-President Franklin Will Be Asked to Explain Bulletins Disproved by Event.

Fortified by the facts gathered in th[illegible] to the [illegible] ship last night, the Senate sub-committee to investigate the Titanic catastrophe began its inquiry at the Waldorf-Astoria at 11 o'clock this morning.

Witnesses summoned to tell the story of the disaster were on hand before the scheduled hour and the investigators expressed a confidence that all who had material information would co-operate with them in giving the truth an official record.

Among the witnesses at the hotel were J. Bruce Ismay, managing director of the White Star Line, who was among the seventy-nine men surviving; four officers of the Titanic, Captain Rostron, of the Carpathia, Vice-President Franklin of the White Star Line, who is expected to make some explanation of the contusion and contradiction of news that was the rule at his offices before the Carpathia arrived, and a number of the rescued passengers, who have retained sufficient grip on their nerves to testify.

It was apparent from the begining of the investigation that the question of speed would loom large, as from all sources it has been established that the Titanic was under full head of steam when she ran down the iceberg. Captain Smith, and the first officer who stood on the bridge when the crash came, are both dead and so cannot repeat the orders which guided tha engineer, but it is believed that Ismay may be able to throw considerable light on the point, as he is supposed to have been in constant touch with the captain.

Senator William Alden Smith, chairman of the committee, had a twenty minute conference with Vice-President Franklin and Ismay as soon as the senators were put on board the Carpathia last night. His questions to-day were framed as a result of that talk last night.

The hearings will be held as far as possible in this city, where most of the important witnesses can be easily reached, and after that will be tranferred to Washington, when it comes to the stage where experts begin to testify regarding modern ship construction. Senators Smith and Newlands of Nevada were the only ones who made the trip to the Carpathia last night, but they consider the visit a most important one and gathered direct information among the harrowing scenes on the dock that will be invaluable to them in pressing the inquiry.

It was declared to-day that the disposition of all concerned was to help the committee by frank and full recitals. No subpoenas were necessary to gather the witnesses though the senators were prepared with them had they been required.

The investigation in this country will be carried on at the same time the Board of Trade inquiry in Great Britain is under way. The Senate sub-committee consists of Senators Smith, Newlands, Perkins of California, Bourne of Oregon, Burton of Ohio, Simmons of North Carolina, and Fletcher of Florida.

The night was dark, two warnings to look out for icebergs had been received by the Titanic's captain, yet the newest giantess of the sea was ploughing through the ice fields at the rate of twenty-one knots an hour—a speed which can be equalled by not more than six liners of the great ocean fleet.

Every ounce of steam was crowded on. General officers of the line—J. Bruce Ismay, managing director, was on board—had given orders to push her to the limit, and the ship's officers were striving to live up to that order, and win speed honors for their line by smashing previous records.

This is the story told by J. H. Moody, a quartermaster of the ship, and the man who was at the helm on that fatal night. It is corroborated by the tales of survivors among the passengers and crew.

"We were crowding her to the limit," said the helmsman. "Every

(Continued on Sixteenth Page.)

HOW THE GREAT TITANIC RACED TO DESTRUCTION

(Continued From First Page.)

and tenderly patted her shoulder.

"The ladies first, dear heart," he was heard to say.

Then, quietly, he saluted the second officer and turned to help in lowering more boats.

Some survivors say they last saw Major Archie Butt playing a soldier's part at the steerage passageway. With an iron bar he drove back men who were pressing forward and crowding back women. He held that gate until all the women and children were on deck an had their chance to escape.

In many cases when husbands and wives were parted the women did not know that the parting was for all time.

"We did not know the ship was going down," sobbed one woman at the Carpathia's pier, where the rescued were disembarked. "We did not know we were leaving our husbands and fathers forever. We thought they would follow us in more boats. But there were no more boats."

In other cases, heartrending farewells were said under the flare of the rockets which were sent up to light the departure of the boats.

THEY SAVED THE BABY.

H. J. Allison, his wife Lorraine; a daughter of three years, and a ten-month baby were asleep when the giant ship struck. Katy Andrews, a nurse, was in the cabin with the baby. She instantly dressed it and hurried on deck. Officers seized her and hurried her into a lifeboat. The next moment she was being pulled away from the sinking ship with the Allison baby in her arms.

Mr. and Mrs. Allison, who were in a stateroom with Lorraine, startled by the crash, hastily dressed and ran to the cabin occupied by the nurse and baby only to find it empty. Without hesitation both started out to find the nurse and child, not knowing that they were already being pulled away from the ship. Carrying little Lorraine in his arms, his wife clinging to him, Mr. Allison dashed about the ship. And all the time the boats were being filled and sent away. The last one had gone while the Allisons still hunted for the child which arrived safe on the Carpathia last night. But the father and mother and the little sister stayed with the Titanic forever.

There were many stories of the final parting between Col. Astor and his bride, and in all the man who for years headed society in New York made a sacrifice such as few could have made with more fearless heroism.

ASTOR AND BUTT TOGETHER.

"Col. Astor and Major Archibald Butt died together on the bridge of the ill fated ship," said Dr. Wshington Dodge of San Francisco, one of the survivors.

"I saw them standing there side by side. I was in one of the last boats, and I could not mistake them. Earlier during the desparate struggle to get the boats cleared I had seen them both at work quieting passengers and helping the officers maintain order.

"A few minutes before the last I saw Col. Astor help his wife, who appeared ill, into a boat, and I saw him wave his hand to her and smile as the boat pulled away."

Three of the lifeboats were lost or swamped in launching, spilling their passengers into the sea. A life raft was launched with thirty-five persons on it, many of them men, but before the Carpathia arrived in reach nine of these had been washed away, and six had died from exposure on it and their bodies were held there by the survivors.

"I saw Col. Astor helping his wife into one of the lifeboats," declared Miss Margaret Hays. "I saw her beg him to come, and I saw him shake his head. But as the boat pulled away in the darkness he leaned over the side and threw kisses to her.

"It was fully half an hour before the real condition of the ship was discovered by the officers," said Edward Wheelton, chief steward of the Titanic. "If they had known sooner that she could not last more than two hours, we might have saved time in launching the boats at once, which would have enabled us to load them to better advantage. Some were over and some underloaded."

Miss Slater, one of the passengers, said she saw Col. Astor light a cigarette during the work of getting the boats away from the Titanic.

STEAD AND ASTOR ON RAFT.

As the big ship took her final plunge those in the last lifeboats to leave her, saw a broken life raft with two men clinging to it. One of the men some survivors say was Col. Astor, the other was thought to be William T. Stead, the journalist. When he had done all he could for others, when his courage and self-sacrifice had saved the lives of comrades in distress, Astor had died fighting grimly for the life he had gladly risked in the course of honor. Mr. Dodge's story places him on the bridge with Major Butt, but those who tell of seeing him on the raft say the icy water chilled him and Stead to unconsciousness and that they lost hold and slipped away to death.

Henry B. Harris, whose wife was saved, stood heroically with the crew and officers in the work of rescue. When last seen he was helping lower the last boat t oleave the doomed vessel. He stayed behind with the others to wait the fate of those who could not go.

SAVED BY A CHANCE.

That the entire list of souls on the Titanic was not lost was due to a freak of chance. Harold Cooton, wireless officer of the Carpathia, had been off duty Sunday night. Near midnight he thought he would look over the wireless room. Merely to test the air conditions he placed the cap to his ear. Instantly he froze to the spot. We had caught the first wild call of the Titanic for help.

It was the scene as the boats got away from the foundering liner that stands up sharp above the other tatters of the appalling tragedy.

The band was on the upper deck when the ship struck. Instantly the leader struck up a snatch of a popular song. Falling in line the band marched from deck to deck, while the passengers fled to the boats, and the great liner sagged lower and lower at the bows.

As the crisis drew near the catchy songs changed to selections from opera, and then, when tragedy loomed certain, when the inevitable cast the shadow of doom, and when fate demanded the lives of two-thirds of those aboard that the other third might live, the music pealed off into the solemn strains which at sea mean that the mercy of God is the only hope. The band still played "Nearer, My God, to Thee," when the ship went down.

On board the funeral ship Carpathia were seventy widows, the handiwork of the lack of boats on the Titanic. But if the Titanic was short of boats, her crew were not short of bravery.

Mrs. E. Z. Taylor of Philadelphia said she was handed a life preserver by a steward. She asked him why he did not put one on.

"Maybe there will not be enough to go around," he answered.

One of the boats was loaded with women and lowered, but the crew had neglected to put the plug in a drainage hole in the bottom of the craft. It put out from the ship and soon sank with all hands, according to Mrs. Taylor.

WOMEN ROWED FOR HOURS.

One woman survivor said she was in the boat which Mr. Harris helped lower. "There were no men in the boat," she said, "and an English woman and I rowed for four hours. We were a long way from the ship when she went down, but there was no wind and we could hear the screams of passengers as they jumped into the sea."

George Brayton of Los Angeles told a dramatic story of the heroism of Capt. Smith. When the captain was washed from the sinking vessel he swam to a baby that was struggling, held up by a mass of wreckage. Grasping the child, he struck out for a lifeboat, reached it, handed it to the officer in charge of the boat, and refusing assistance swam back toward where the stern of his ship was settling forever.

Brayton told of how there were a series of explosions as the ill-fated ship sank. Before she had disappeared he said she had broken in two.

"I was in the water two hours," Brayton continued. "I was finally picked up by a lifeboat containing twenty-two passengers. When I got aboard I took an oar, but it was hard to row, for nearly every stroke hit a body."

Six-year-old Nana Harper, daughter of the Rev. John Harper, the evangelist, who was lost, arrived on the Carpathia with her aunt, Miss Jessie Leitch. The child did not know that she would never see her father again.

"When we were awakened by the sound of the collision we were told to go to deck A, said Miss Leitch. "Dr. Harper picked up little Nana and kissed her. I think now he knew it was for the last time. But we did not know. We never saw him again. We were put in a boat. When the Carpathia picked us up we thought we would find Dr. Harper in one of the other lifeboats, but we found there were no lifeboats for the men they were only for the women."

Officers of the Carpathia explained that the reason some meagre details of the Titanic disaster were not wirlessed from the Carpathia was because of the large number of personal messages sent by survivors to their relatives.

Harold Bride, one of the wireless operators from the Titanic, relieved the regular Carpathia operator. He sent 119 personal messages yesterday and fifty the day before.

Bride told the officers of the Carpathia that the operators on the Salem were so poor that he could not afford to waste time working with them.

Capt. Rostron of the Carpathia says that he cannot remember receiving any message from Capt. Chandler of the Salem or any one else in the name of the President. He said that if such a message had been received all other business would have been suspended until it was answered.

SHIP'S BARBER SAYS HE URGED ASTOR TO JUMP

Latter Refused, Declaring That the Boat Could Not Sink—Shook Hands With His Adviser.

Alfred Whitman, barber on the Titanic, says he was standing beside Col. John Jacob Astor when the doomed ship started to sink.

"I had shaved Col. Astor in the afternoon," said Whitman. "When the ship struck I rushed on deck. The first impulse of everybody was to discount any danger. A number of people returned to their state rooms. But I am an old seaman. I felt from the first we were doomed. I saw how things were going. I watched the women being put into the boats. And then I realized that the last boat had pushed off. I went and hunted for a life preserver and found one and put it on. I came back and stood on the first deck by the rail. I felt some man standing very close to me and I looked up and it was Col. Astor.

"I am going to jump, colonel," I said. "She is going down fast."

"You are a fool if you jump," answered Colonel Astor. "This ship may settle but she can't sink. Besides, there are several more rafts on board."

"There are no more rafts and she's going fast," I said. "For God's sake, I am an old hand at the sea; take my advice and get a life preserver and jump."

"I am not going to jump," said the colonel. "I tell you you are a fool; there must be another raft."

"There's no other raft," I repeated. "Will you shake hands? It's each man for himself now and not much chance for any of us."

The colonel put out his hand and we shook hands and I jumped. I swam as far as I could from the sinking ship. The water was horribly cold, and I do not know how long I was in it. I was unconscious when I was picked up."

U. S. SENATE BEGINS PROBING THE HORROR

(Continued From First Page.)

ounce of steam was crowded on, and she was under orders from the general officers of the line to make all the speed of which she was capable.

"We had made 565 miles that day, and were tearing along at the rate of twenty-one knots when we struck the iceberg. The officers were striving to live up to the orders to smash a record."

This agrees with the opinion of many experts, who pointed out the fact that if the bottom or sides had not been ripped off the boat the airtight compartments would have kept the boat afloat. As the wreck occurred every one of the compartments was torn open, and none of them was "airtight." In discussing the wreck itself, the second officer said:

"I was asleep in my cabin when the berg was struck. It foundered about two hours and a half later. We struck the "black" side of the berg, not head on but crashed into it with our side.

"First Officer Merdock was on watch, and Capt. Smith was on the bridge. The speed at the time was full, forward. The first boat that left the Titanic carried very few. One of the later ones carried seventy-eight persons. Men who jumped overboard attempted to clamber into the later boats, but were beaten off; the boats were already overloaded."

The second officer of the Titanic, when interviewed on the dock, said that the consensus of opinion of those members of the crew that were saved was that the wreck of the giant of the seas was caused by responsible officials who were attempting to make a record trip. He said that the Titanic struck the berg with its side and ripped the plates off the whole side.

The captain of the Titanic had received two warnings of the "icebergs ahead," yet, according to these stories of the ship's officers who survived, the warning had been disregarded and the only thought was of speed.

On April 12 the first iceberg warning was sent to the Titanic by the French liner La Touraine. The Titanic's captain acknowledged the message with thanks. The second warning was sent out on April 14 by the Parisian. It is not known positively that the Titanic received this warning. On the same day, however, she did get a warning message from the Amerika. The Hydrographic Office in Washington has records showing that the navigators of the Titanic were aware that they were in the vicinity of icebergs. The record under the heading "Ice Reports" is as follows:

"April 14.—The German steamer Amerika reported by radio-telegraph passing two large icebergs in latitude 41 degrees, 27 minutes; longitude 50 degrees 8 minutes—Titanic (Br. S. S.)"

Mariners express the belief that had the Titanic been going at a moderate speed when she hit the iceberg the damage would not have amounted to disaster. Passengers who described the accident declare that the Titanic ran on to the iceberg, so great was her speed. At first some of the passengers thought they had run on to a sand bank. The ship hung on this iceberg, and after the bilge was ripped away the plates buckled.

THOUGHT SHIP STRUCK LARGE CAKE OF ICE

C. H. Romacue of Georgetown, Ky., a Titanic survivor, said, after landing, that there was no great panic on the ship. He was in the smoking room of the liner with a Mr. Case. They had just met on the deck where they were viewing the ice field and were chilled. A highball was suggested, and they were seated in the smoking room with their drinks before them when the crash came.

Mr. Romacue said that as the vessel had been crunching its way through the floes all night long, he at first thought that she had struck a floating cake somewhat larger than the others and that had caused her to stagger. A few moments later, however, she sagged badly forward and the highball was tossed from the table. The lights began to get dimmer, and there was a cry, "We're going down."

He said there was little excitement after the first rush was over. The cry of "All women and children first" came from male passengers on all sides.

Mr. Romacue said the lifeboat into which he climbed got about a mile and a half from the scene of the wreck before the gigantic liner took the final plunge. In the boat that he was nothing was felt of the suction.

Frank Chance Arrested.

Chicago, April 19.—Frank L. Chance, manager of the Chicago National League Baseball team, was arrested last night for driving a "smoking" automobile.

HELP WANTED—MALE.
Advertisements Under This Classification 10 Cents Per Line.

EXPERIENCED SALESMEN for retail business. Long hours, hard work but splendid chance for advancement. State age, experience, name of last three employers with length of service. Promotion, Box 1, Globe.

SALESMEN.—Quick money on the side selling A1 apple orchard securities; new features; farm to consumer; 94 miles to New York, etc. MT. TOM FRUIT CO., 32 Broadway.

SALESMAN by 5th Ave. publishing house; permanent travelling position, to follow up leads secured through correspondence; proposition pays $100 weekly and over, according to ability; only salesmen of exceptional ability and strong closers with good references considered; travelling expenses advanced; call 9 to 3. SCHNEIDER, sales manager, 251 5th Ave.

SALESMEN for trade and direct in cities and suburbs; indispensable appliance used universally; new; no competition; quick sales; territory protected. SWEET MFG. CO., 47 W. 34th St.

SALESMAN, specialty, to call upon stationery, drug, novelty and 5c. and 10c. stores around New York with well known line of sheet music; commissions paid; $7.50 and $10 an order; salesmen of fair ability can earn $75 weekly, with opportunity after ability is demonstrated to be given out-of-town territory; good opportunity for right man. Call after 11 o'clock. Mr. Iris, care Shapiro, 39th St. and B'way.

SALESMAN—High-grade salesman, having personal acquaintance with automobile owners, can make permanent connection; others not wanted. United Auto Owners' Protective Association, 1 West 34th St.

WANTED—Hustling salesman for necessary telephone and office specialities, on commission. Some capital required. Territory given. Room 1116, 66 Broadway.

SALESMEN and Managers.—We manufacture radio reflectors for incandescent lamps; retail for 15 cents; only one of its [illegible]; 100 per cent. profit; absolutely new [illegible] territory. Room 1008, 116 Nassau St.

UNIFORM SALESMAN.—A well-known concern desires the services of an experienced uniform salesman to solicit contracts for hotels, apartment houses and yachts; applications strictly confidential. L. C., Box 205, Globe uptown.

SALESMEN—Six bright salesmen for specialty; high-class proposition; liberal commission; bankers and merchants all prospective purchasers; splendid opportunity for advancement. J. A. Stivers, 257 Broadway.

AGENTS, BROKERS, SALESMEN — We assure men's wages against loss from accident, illness; pay monthly indemnity; death benefit any cause; costs $1 monthly; assets over $200,000; right men, $50 weekly. New York State Reserve Fund, 150 Nassau St., New York.

SALESMEN wanted to demonstrate high class hornless phonograph; liberal commission compensation. Sonora Phonograph Co., 78 Reade St.

AGENTS wanted to sell our cut-rate photograph coupons in New York or nearby towns; best ever issued; you can add to your income in spare time or make it a regular business; call or write for information. De Youngs', Cor. Broadway and 17th St., N. Y.

MAN, good, wanted to represent a life insurance company that makes a specialty of temperance risks; new and attractive features; low rates and liberal contract. Apply S. WILSON, Room 502, 253 Broadway, New York.

SALESMAN—Wanted, high class specialty salesman; restricted territory guaranteed; reference and bonds required. Apply 10-4, Money Weight Scales Co., room 1105, 225 5th Ave.

YOUNG MEN
To join the best Hospital Corps in the N. Y. National Guard; applicants must be of good character and physique; over 18 years of age; uniforms and equipment free; reviews and dancing monthly; camp this summer with pay; first aid and military sanitation instruction; athletic and social advantages; Christians preferred. Apply 1st Class Sergeant J. E. Heaney, Surgeon's room, at Armory, 94th St. and Park Ave., Monday and Friday evenings.

SALESMAN—Can you create the atmosphere and connect? Enough said. Room 408, 302 Broadway.

SALESMEN—A business house of long standing desires to engage the services of a few bright young men for their soliciting department. Apply 92 Pine St., near Front.

SALESMEN wanted everywhere for the MUFLETUCH, the latest office appliance; indispensable article; low price; large commissions. The Mufletuch Co., Room 1415, 150 Nassau St., N. Y. City.

SALESMEN—A large corporation with branch offices in the leading cities and an extensive advertising line desires to add to its selling force two first class salesmen; if you feel you can make good after being shown how, call on Sales Manager, 134 W. 29th St., 10th floor.

ACTIVE, intelligent men will find good opportunity as special representatives for The Germania Life Insurance Co. Large commission, opportunity for advancement. No salary. Call 11-1 A. M. H. Abeles, District Manager, 50 Union Square.

CASUALTY AGENTS—The National of Detroit wants producers; to such will give managers; $1 buys $20 to $60 monthly benefits; $200,000 capital. Room 604, 84 William St.

A1 SALESMAN of good appearance investigate one of the best propositions; experience not necessary; steady position; apply between 11 and 1. Mr. Dalton, 9 E. 26th St., room 226.

SALESMEN (4) for outside positions, to assist sales manager; $25 weekly; expense money advanced; city and road work; want men with some salesman's ability who are willing to work six hours daily under instructions. Apply room 702, Mr. Burditt, 45 W. 34th St.

SALESMAN, good appearance and well recommended, to sell low priced best chemical dry fire extinguisher on market; moderate drawing account; high commission; only live wires need apply, afternoons, 3 to 5. Firex, 163 Pearl St.

FOUNTAIN PENS are legitimate merchandise and sell like wildfire; agents' profits enormous, yet not ashamed to face customers again; you have same opportunity; now is the time; $2 brings dozen samples goldine, German silver and pearl fountain pens, which tell a better story than a bushel circulars. PEERLESS PEN CO., largest manufacturers, 212 Broadway, New York.

SALESMEN—Real estate men with record of past success to sell entirely new proposition; New Jersey; excellent opportunity for energetic men; liberal commissions; apply mornings. MEYER, 234 5th Ave.

HELP WANTED.—FEMALE.
Advertisements Under This Classification 10 Cents Per Line.

A FEW refined young ladies accustomed to mingling in good society to interview prominent artists; no canvassers need apply. Room 212, 56 Pine St.

SITUATIONS WANTED—MALE.

CARETAKER wants private house for summer months—West End Ave., Riverside Drive, near 92d St. Call or address COSSEY, 2485 Broadway.

CARETAKER wants private house for summer months—West End Av., Riverside Drive, near 92d St. Call or address Cossey, 2485 Broadway.

YOUNG ENGLISHMAN seeks situation as coachman; has lived with best of families; can furnish best of references; age 30; country preferred. HARRY FINN, 541 46th St., Brooklyn.

BOOKKEEPING—ACCOUNTING.
Bookkeeping, $2.50 up per week. Auditing, $5.00 up per month. C. P. A., care Globe.

PORTER, 25 years old, wishes position in private house. Salary $8 a week. JOSEPH YURIK, 335 E. 70th St., city.

Certified Advertisements

12 W. 31st Street — The Globe — Telephone 8000 Cortlandt

NOTE—The integrity of every advertiser under this heading is thoroughly investigated before the advertisement is accepted. All applicants for space in the CERTIFIED columns must abide by this rule. If you need capital in your business, if you have money to invest, if you have property for sale, if you require high-class employees, or if you are seeking a good position, we can assist you through a CERTIFIED advertisement. Call at CERTIFIED Department office, 12 West 31st Street, or phone for our representative to call on you —8000 Cortlandt.

EMPLOYER & EMPLOYEE

TEN YEARS WITH ONE OF NEW YORK'S LARGEST CORPORATIONS.

Bright and capable young man, fifteen years of wide and varied business experience, speaks and writes French fluently, of very good executive ability and capable of assuming responsible duties, will make good in any capacity, seeks opening with concern requiring the above qualifications. Address G 658 THE GLOBE.

EXPERT WOMAN STENOGRAPHER SEEKS POSITION.

Bright business woman, well educated, ten years' experience, also Court experience, desires position with brokerage or other reliable firm. Address G 634 THE GLOBE.

CLEAN, CLEAR HEADED YOUNG MAN WITH GRIT, ENERGY AND ABILITY.

Backed up by four years' Daily and Trade Journal experience, wants position in publishing house; holds necessary qualifications for position of trust; highest credentials. G 652 THE GLOBE.

GRADUATE CHEMIST.

Expert in making up formulas of salable articles such as polishes, toilet preparations, disinfectants, enamels, inks, etc., would make connection with good concern. Have own equipped laboratory for general analytical and research work; processes studied and reported on. Best of references furnished. Address G 643 THE GLOBE.

QUALIFIED IN SECRETARIAL DUTIES.

Young woman stenographer, several years' real estate, insurance and commercial experience, familiar with secretarial requirements, desires position. Downtown preferred. Address G 654 THE GLOBE.

WILL DO DESIGNING OR DRAUGHTING IN SPARE TIME.

Structural and mechanical engineer holding responsible position with large company, wishes to dispose of spare time profitably. Address G 662 THE GLOBE.

ASSISTANT MANAGER SEEKS POSITION.

Young man (33) wants position in executive or confidential capacity; familiar with accounts, systems, costs, etc.; expert stenographer; seeks connection with responsible concern. Address G 632 THE GLOBE.

HE DESIRES POSITION AS OFFICE MANAGER'S ASSISTANT OR SALESMAN.

Gentleman experienced along above lines desires to make a change by securing connection with some high grade concern. References on file assure us that a firm securing his services will obtain a satisfactory representative. G 667 THE GLOBE.

BOOKS BALANCED—AUDITS.

Let me be your auditor. I'll balance your books, improve your accounting system and will make periodical audits. The cost of this service makes it worth investigating. Address G 300 THE GLOBE.

BRIGHT YOUNG COLORED MAN, NEAT APPEARANCE, DESIRES OFFICE POSITION.

Young light colored man (18), energetic and experienced in office work, desires office position. Good penman. Will start on small salary, with advancement. Address G 452 THE GLOBE.

EXPERT PUBLIC ACCOUNTANT SEEKS CONNECTION.

Public accountant must seek new position on account of dull times; wants executive position; 27 years old; university graduate; 13 years' business experience; best references. Address G 701 THE GLOBE.

EXPERIENCED CHAUFFEUR AND MOTOR BOAT ENGINEER WANTS POSITION.

Careful driver, thoroughly good mechanic. Had charge of private yacht last cruise of season. Address G 517 THE GLOBE.

INVESTMENT OPPORTUNITIES

TO CLOSE AN ESTATE.

I WILL SELL FINE BUILDING LOTS IN QUEENS BOROUGH AT BARGAIN PRICES. ADDRESS EXECUTOR, G 653 THE GLOBE.

AN EXCELLENT OPPORTUNITY FOR INVESTMENT WITH OR WITHOUT SERVICES.

New York Corporation, manufacturing complete and profitable line DRUG SPECIALTIES and TOILET PREPARATIONS, having $10,000 paid-in capital, will issue $10,000 7 per cent. preferred stock (no more), to take care increasing business. Active interest and Treasurership given right party taking total issue. Address G 665 THE GLOBE.

$15,000,000 PAID IN CLAIMS

By the largest and oldest company. Time has money value. Protect it with health and accident policy. Monthly payments of $1.00 and up insure benefits from $10.00 to $25.00 weekly. Address G 700 THE GLOBE.

AN UNUSUAL OPPORTUNITY TO BUY A BUNGALOW.

Five-room Bungalow on 64x100 ft. plot fronting on Lake, $1200. Three-room Bungalow on large plot, $500.00. Location, Lake Lackawanna, Lake stocked with trout, woods filled with game in abundance, ideal location, desirable social conditions. Write for maps and free R. R. tickets. Address G 666 THE GLOBE.

ACTIVE PARTNER OR PARTNERS WANTED BY CONCERN MANUFACTURING AUTOMOBILE STRUCTURES. LARGE NET PROFITS MADE.

A Corporation manufacturing Automobile Structures which can be universally adopted by motor manufacturers and owners desires active partner who must be experienced and capable business men of character and integrity and must invest from $15,000 to $20,000, which sum will be fully secured by either one-half interest in voting trust or controlling interest by agreement. The investment and services will return large profits. The present members of this company are men of the highest standing and are connected with some of the largest moneyed interests in the country. Address G 668 THE GLOBE.

PARTNER WANTED IN AN ESTABLISHED MANUFACTURING COMPANY.

An opportunity is offered to a man of integrity to buy part interest of retiring partner in company with established trade, manufacturing mostly patented articles. Would be required to invest from $5,000 to $10,000. Searching investigation solicited. Address G 657 THE GLOBE.

WORTH YOUR ATTENTION.

An income of a few thousand dollars a year can be secured for $1,100 in easy payments by a plan in which your own money, amply secured, under your own control, produces your own income, and you get it all. Address Income, G 307 THE GLOBE.

MISCELLANEOUS.

PLAYER BARGAINS.

EVERY MAKE AND IN GUARANTEED CONDITION. SEND FOR LIST AND PRICES WITH TERMS. TEL-ELECTRIC COMPANY, 299 FIFTH AVE., COR. 31ST ST., N. Y. CITY.

VERY FINE HARDMAN PIANO.

COST $500. OUR SPECIAL PRICE TO QUICK BUYER $250. TEL-ELECTRIC COMPANY, 299 FIFTH AVE., COR. 31ST ST., N. Y. CITY.

EFFICIENT BOOKKEEPING.

Expert accountant will keep books for small firm or individual at moderate cost. Regular weekly calls. Also special audits and installation of systems. Address G 663 THE GLOBE.

FOR RENT, FURNISHED, AT UPPER MONTCLAIR.

Fully furnished ten room house; all modern conveniences; high location, exceptional view; garage; select neighborhood; to Oct. 1st, at $100.00 per month. Address G 659 THE GLOBE.

CAN YOU BEAT THIS PRICE FOR LETTERHEADS?

Two thousand water-marked bonds, $3.50; five thousand, $7.50. Other work proportionately. Phone Stuyvesant 449 for samples of Lithographic Stationery. Address Custer Press, 201 E. 13th St.

Towering Iceberg Is Fleeting Monument to 1,500 Heroes Who Died That Women and Children Might Be Saved

New York, April 19.—In response to telegrams from the Kansas City Post and The Denver Post, William Randolph Hearst today sent the following message:

"Kansas City Post, Kansas City, Mo.
"Denver Post, Denver, Colo.

"In the middle of the North Atlantic a giant iceberg lifts its white cliffs 500 feet in the air. It towers like a mighty monument above the graves of 1,500 heroes, who died that the women and children might be saved.

"Soon this monument will dissolve and disappear, as, sooner or later in the lapse of years, all monuments disintegrate and disappear. But the memory of the noble deeds of these brave and self-sacrificing men should live forever.

"Swept without need, without heed, without reckoning or reason, into a disaster which meant inevitable death, these heroes thought not of their own safety, not of their own lives, but only of the lives and safety of the weak women and little children confided to their care.

"Husbands embraced their wives, fathers kissed their children goodby, and the men who were leaving wives and children desolate far away at home labored to save the wives and children of companions in misfortune.

"Then, when the dear ones, the dependent ones, had been sent to safety in the lifeboats and had drifted away into the dark night, these true men, calm and courageous, stood alone on the deck of the doomed ship and went down to death and to glory.

"Who would not choose so glorious a death? Who would not rather die a hero than live a coward?

"These men have died as men should die. They performed their obligation to their fellow-men, their duty to God.

"So may God reward them, and may men remember them, and may the memory of them remain forever a noble record of heroism for humanity, a splendid inspiration to future deeds of duty and devotion.

"WILLIAM RANDOLPH HEARST."

MRS. J. J. BROWN OF DENVER IS HEROINE OF THE TITANIC

Thrown Into Lifeboat, She Seizes Oars and Rows With All Her Might Until She Falls Exhausted--Two Hours After Rescue She Is in Hospital Nursing the Sufferers.

Though on Verge of Nervous Collapse, She Refuses to Leave Ship Until Her Charges Are All Cared For--Gives Thrilling Version of the Great Disaster and the Rescue.

New York, April 19, 1912.—To The Denver Post, Denver, Colo.—"Tell my Denver friends I'm safe," said Mrs. James J. Brown, to a Post reporter who found her in the Carpathia's hospital, nursing 100 hysterical women that were unable to get off the ship.

"Tell them I'm crazy with grief, but that it isn't my own grief, for my daughter Helen is safe in Paris, thank God!"

These were the first words that came from the brave little woman to the outside world that was clamoring for news of the Titanic's dead.

Mrs. Brown has a story of hardship and privation which few on board the rescue boat Carpathia can equal. She looks the picture of health, but in the course of the interview it became evident that the strain was too much to bear and that a nervous breakdown could only be forestalled a few hours.

Mrs. Genevieve Spinner of 36 West Forty-sixth street and Daniel Fuller Tobin of 434 Fifth avenue, New York, were the only friends to meet Mrs. Brown. They pleaded with her to leave the ship and not stay on it over night. Mrs. Spinner was hysterical.

Will Continue to Nurse Sick and Dying Until She Is Exhausted.

To all their appeals Mrs. Brown replied that from the minute she was safely on board the Carpathia to the present time she had nursed the sick and dying, and would continue to do so until she dropped.

"I was saved," she cried. "God knows I can do little enough to save these poor souls around me that are out of their senses. You that have escaped this will never know what a hell it has been. Every baby of a tender age has died. Think of it! Right here in this room a score of little babies have died of insufficient medical treatment, and their mothers have cried hideously for three days. How can you expect me to leave these suffering people when my own life has been spared? Tomorrow morning I'll leave—and not before. Oh, if you only knew—and I can't tell you about it. It is beyond my power of speech."

She was asked to tell exactly how she was saved and finally rescued. Between sobs and cries, which necessitated the presence of the ship's assistant surgeon, she said:

"I was walking on the promenade deck with Mr. G. A. Brayton of Los Angeles, the member of our party who jumped overboard and

(Continued on Page 6—Col. 1)

Ismay Crowded Into Lifeboat Leaving Women and Babes to Die

The story of how J. Bruce Ismay saved his life is now known.

When the third lifeboat was lowered into the sea he claimed to be an able seaman and demanded the privilege of rowing one of the boats.

Shortly after he took his seat a woman, hugging an infant to her breast, appealed for aid and the dying spark of manhood in Ismay flickered up for the last time when he got out of the boat and made room for her.

He crowded into the next boat lowered, however, and, although there were hundreds of women and children still unprovided for, he rowed away to safety.

Is it better to be a living Ismay or a dead Astor? They were both millionaires.

UNCLE SAM—"HERE'S WHERE I CALL A HALT!"

ISMAY, IN SCARED WHISPER, TELLS HOW HE ESCAPED

WRECK INCIDENTS

One woman laughed as she landed at the Cunard pier last night. Her male escort remarked: "My God! Don't laugh in a place like this."

* * *

The wireless operator on the Carpathia had a "hunch" to work ten minutes overtime on Sunday night. This "hunch" saved 745 lives.

* * *

Charles Dahl, an Australian, lost in the sinking ship every cent he had in the world. He jumped into the sea garbed only in his night robe.

* * *

Four sailors in one lifeboat were frozen to death. They were found with their lifeless hands still clutching the oars.

* * *

When a semblance of a panic ensued on board the Titanic, Captain Smith shouted through his megaphone, "Be British!" and the excitement was quelled.

'There Were No Women on Deck, and as Boat Was Lowered I Got Into It,' Reply to Senate Committee Probers.

London, April 19.—While memorial services for Titanic's dead were being held in St. Paul's cathedral Alan Berguine, a member of parliament, demanded that England join with the United States in a rigid investigation of the disaster. He said that on Monday in parliament he would ask Premier Asquith to have the British government join with the United States in an inquiry.

New York, April 19.—The story of how the Titanic met its fate was told today to the United States senate committee investigating into the Titanic disaster by J. Bruce Ismay, managing director of the White Star line.

When asked the circumstances under which he left the boat, Mr. Ismay replied almost in a whisper:

"One of the boats was being filled. Officers called out to know if there were any more women to go. There were none. No passengers were on the deck. As the boat was being lowered, I got into it."

The details of the story were drawn out by Senator William Alden Smith, chairman of the special sub-committee charged with the examination of witnesses, and Senator Newlands, the other senator who came to New York to conduct the inquiry.

Mr. Ismay was accompanied by P. A. S. Franklin, vice president, and Emerson E. Parvin, secretary, of the International Mercantile Marine. Besides the committee, Representative Hughes of West Virginia, whose daughter, Mrs. Lucien P. Smith, was saved and whose son-in-law was lost, was present. Another spectator was Truman H. Newberry, former assistant secretary of the navy.

Adjusting his cuffs, Mr. Ismay was visibly nervous when he took the stand. He gave his age as 50 years. In response to a few formal questions, he said he

(Continued on Page 7—Col. 1.)

WRECK INCIDENTS

Ten members of the social set of Madrid, Spain, perished with the Titanic. One of them was worth $5,000,000.

* * *

Society women row lifeboats. One of them promptly took the oars when one of the crew was found to be drunk.

* * *

Ismay, chief of the White Star line, is treated like royalty aboard the Carpathia. He's telling all about it now to Uncle Sam.

* * *

Colonel Astor had planned marine highway that would have made wreck of the Titanic impossible.

* * *

Physician survivor says: "It seemed as if all the devils of hell had been let loose when people realized ship was sinking."

* * *

Assistant wireless operator: "I caught a burly stoker stealing Phillips' safety belt and shot him to death."

WORD PICTURES OF SAVED SHOW HOW 1,595 PERISHED

Women Refused to Believe Ship Was Sinking Until Last Few Minutes, Then Panic Ensued --Boats Were Badly Managed, in Some Cases Sent Away With No Men to Swing the Oars

'Seemed as All the Devils of Hell Were Let Loose,' Physician's Impression--Men Attempting to Rush Boats Were Shot Down--Strong Men Die From Exposure in Boats.

NEW YORK, April 19.—With all its tragic details the complete story of the Titanic disaster, the world's greatest sea horror, was told here today by the survivors, who arrived last night on the Carpathia of the Cunard line.

After striking an iceberg that towered 150 feet above water line the Titanic sank slowly. As the inrush of icy water reached the engine rooms the boilers exploded, sending up showers of live flame, sparks and smoke that caused the four great funnels of the ship to resemble craters of active volcanoes.

It is believed that the explosion broke the ship's back, for she sank at once in water two miles deep. She carried down with her leading men of America and England among the total of 1,595 passengers lost.

Included in the list of those who perished are Col. John Jacob Astor, Maj. Archibald Butt, the latter aide-de-camp to President Taft. Both unflinchingly met their fate. Eye-witnesses say they were heroes.

Astor fought men to allow the women to reach the lifeboats.

Butt, worn out by his gallantry and heroism throughout the terrible ordeal, stood close by Astor as the great vessel plunged to the depths.

Captain Smith Did Not Realize Collision Was So Serious.

As the ship went down the band was playing "Nearer My God to Thee." Captain Smith stood upon the bridge. The last glimpse of the ship by those in lifeboats was accompanied by strains of the orchestra. The Titanic went down on her nose. As she took the final plunge her stern rose high in the air, she left the sea covered with struggling men. The water and air were bitter cold and they could not survive the exposure. There were some cries, but these soon died away and nothing more was heard. The narratives of the various survivors gathered into a consecutive story, makes one of the most thrilling tales of modern life. It is a story filled with heroism unparalleled, bravery and heroism performed by American business men.

They were men of millions who had everything to live for, and yet in that crisis at sea, they worked, coolly and steadfastly to save

(Continued on Page 8—Col. 1)

'Be British!' Was Command That Made Heroes of Sailors

New York, April 19.—But for the unparalleled self-sacrifice and heroism of Captain Smith and the Titanic's officers, the sea would have claimed an even greater toll when the ship went down. From the bridge Captain Smith called through his megaphone, "Be British," and that became the rallying cry of officers and crew.

Such was the graphic description of the conduct of the men responsible for the saving of human souls on the smitten Titanic, as told today by John Johnson, a member of the crew, who took an oar in a lifeboat.

MRS. ISIDOR STRAUS

Unknown because her identity was sunk in the name of a husband who was known from one end of the land to the other for his philanthropy. Now in the hour of death she eclipses the well earned honors of her husband and stands forth from the horrors of the Titanic disaster as a woman "with a love that surpasseth understanding." Many times she was urged to save her life by getting into the boats which were being lowered, but to all entreaty she replied, "I will live with my husband or die with him." And there she stood on the deck of the giant of the sea when the death rattle was in his throat and the life of one of the world's noblewomen was blotted out. Here in Colorado we honor brave and loving women more than in any other place in the world and in Denver a tablet should be erected to the memory of this woman, by the women of the state. What an inspiration it would be to the invalids at the National Jewish Hospital to see that flowers ever bloomed around a tablet which commemorated the love of this woman. All over the world we have statues erected in memory of the bravery of men, but how few are erected to the love of women.

I hold it truth with him who sings
To one clear harp in divers tones,
That men may rise on stepping stones
Of their dead selves to higher things.—In Memoriam.

The Circulation of THE DENVER POST Yesterday Was 85,469

THE DENVER POST

TWO CENTS BY NEWSBOYS. FIVE CENTS ON TRAINS. DENVER, COLORADO, FRIDAY, APRIL 19, 1912.—24 PAGES 3D EDITION.

RECRUIT MILITIA FOR MEXICAN WAR, ORDER

Chase Receives Command to Have Guard Up to Full Strength.

Spanish War Veterans Take First Steps to Form Regiment for Service If Intervention Comes.

"Recruit all departments of state militia to their fullest capacity," was the order which Adjutant General Chase has been given by the war department. The war department, fearful of immediate necessity for intervention in Mexico, is taking steps to have ready as strong a force as possible.

The Colorado departments, in every branch, will offer the war department at least 3,200 men, three-fifths of whom are ready to mobilize at any designated spot upon an instant's notice. It will not be necessary for them to come to Denver in order to start.

All members of the Colorado National guard carry full equipment, and Adjutant General Chase believes his soldiers are ready for any emergency which they may have to encounter.

The Colorado militia is looked upon as one of the best trained and equipped militias in the country. That fact, and because of Colorado's proximity to Mexico the Colorado guard is likely to be the first troops ordered to the front. General Chase has furnished the war department full information concerning the Colorado National guard and has intimated the entire readiness of every member of the guard to place his services at the disposal of the government.

The United States government has been in constant communication with adjutant generals for several weeks. It would seem that all plans and details of mobilization for an invasion of Mexico have been well made. General Chase said that he would not be surprised to receive an order from Washington at any minute of the day dispatching the Colorado guard to some southern point.

GUARDSMEN WELL DRILLED.

The Colorado guard consists of every department of military service, including cavalry, infantry and artillery. The various companies have been undergoing vigorous drill tests for several weeks. Recruits are being added constantly, and the emergency message from Washington, received today, will add zest to the appeal for volunteers.

Nearly every member of the national guard has made arrangements to take part in the intervention. There are only a few whose family and business duties are of such a nature as to make it imperative for them to stay at home.

General Chase, guided by figures from Washington, had previously estimated that not more than 10,000 of the members of the Colorado guard would be summoned by the first order. The latest order from Washington, however, would lead the general to believe that the entire strength of the Colorado guard will be called upon to serve.

The additions to the roll of the guard, occasioned by the increase in recruits, will not diminish the efficiency of the troops' equipment, as General Chase declares that he has more equipment per man than is provided for by regulations of the war department. Recruits will be drilled as rapidly as they come in and put in condition to stand the campaign in Mexico, be it short or long. The hike of officers, taken a week ago, demonstrated to the satisfaction of General Chase that his staff is well fit for any ordeal its members may have to meet.

SPANISH VETERANS READY.

Spanish war veterans in Colorado have taken the first steps toward forming a regiment to offer its services to the government in case of war with Mexico. At a meeting last night of the Serpents, a secret society of Spanish war veterans, 300 ex-soldiers made plans for service. It is expected that veterans from nearly every Colorado town will join the organization.

At the meeting last night, the election of Colonel James Bulger was ratified. Colonel Bulger served in the Volunteers and the regular cavalry, commanded a company of Philippine scouts, and also held commissions in twelve foreign armies. He commanded Madero's second column, and was wounded twice at the capture of San Rosalis, Mexico.

Robert F. Silvers of the county treasurer's office, was elected lieutenant colonel.

Thomas Boutwell, assistant superintendent of the Denver mint, was elected senior major. The election of S. R. Cleaver at a former meeting was ratified by a unanimous vote. He was elected regimental adjutant, with the rank of captain. T. B. Callahan was elected captain.

Edward Wurst, soldier from the famous fighting Seventh cavalry, was elected to a captaincy. Frank W. Hartley was elected first lieutenant, and will be attached to regimental headquarters. Herbert W. Jones and William Hamilton were elected second lieutenants. Dr. L. B. Sandall of Grand Junction was elected assistant surgeon with the rank of captain.

TITANIC SURVIVORS LADEN WITH GRIEF HEAR BURIAL CHANT

"I am the resurrection and the life."

Never, perhaps, were these words from the Episcopal burial service read with such solemnity and under such gruesome and distressing circumstances as when they were uttered by the captain of the Carpathia, on the occasion of the burial of some unfortunate victim of the Titanic disaster, picked up from the flotsam, after the big ship went down, only to succumb later to the effects of exposure and the shocking terror of it all.

One may imagine how those 700 and odd, half-clad, fright dazed, grief-crazed huddling survivors of the wreck gathered on deck with the pity-stricken sympathetic passengers of the Carpathia and, mid groans and weeping, listened to the grave and, perhaps, quavering tone of the captain as he read the solemn service.

Resting on a wide grating before him, lies the still form, shrouded in stout tarpaulin in which the ship's sailmaker has taken some strong retaining stitches. Weights, strips of lead, are sewn securely into the canvas at the feet and such floral offerings as the ship affords are secured upon the breast.

No funeral service imaginable, sad as all such functions always are, could be surrounded and overshadowed by so dense an atmosphere of gloom, hopefulness, despair. There, with eyes staring stonily as those of the corpse itself, were the wives and mothers bereft; the children orphaned, and the Carpathia passengers, their eyes wet, their hearts wrung with pity.

The long service concluded, a dirge comes wailing from the ship's band. Slowly one end of the grating, the other end of which extends over the deck rail, is lifted and eased gently downward toward the water. The corpse slides slowly down and into the deep, feet foremost, and with scarcely a splash, disappears beneath the waves.

The closing words of the impressive service which is always read at funerals at sea are:

"Forasmuch as it hath pleased Almighty God, in His wise providence, to take out of this world the soul of our deceased brother, we therefore commit his body to the deep, looking for the general resurrection in the last day, and the life of the world to come, through our Lord, Jesus Christ; at whose second coming, in the glorious majesty, to judge the world, the sea shall give up her dead; and the corruptible bodies of those who sleep in Him shall be changed, and made like unto His glorious body; according to the mighty working whereby He is able to subdue all things unto Himself. Amen."

ALL THIRD-CLASS APPROPRIATIONS TO BE PAID BY STATE

Secretary Pearce Has Been Making Investigation of State Finances.

"NO CAUSE FOR ALARM"

But Rhoady Kenehan Says He's Got a Say Coming About the Revenue.

"I have taken a little time to size up the financial condition of the state," says Secretary of State James B. Pearce, "and it looks to me as though all of the third class appropriations made by the eighteenth general assembly will be paid. I do not think there is any cause for alarm."

State Auditor M. A. Leddy has about reached the same conclusion, and it is expected that Gov. Shafroth, shortly, will issue a statement in reply to some of the heavy criticism with which the administration has been bombarded.

In the background—for the present—is Treasurer Roady Kenehan, who recently declared that he didn't know whether all of the first class appropriations could be paid. Furthermore, Kenehan announced, he will not register a single warrant in excess of the revenue, even if he is ordered so to do by the highest court in the land.

It is noted, however, that the state treasurer already has paid out 25 per cent of the third class appropriations and that the heads of the institutions who demanded the money were given to understand that another 25 per cent shortly would be forthcoming.

Secretary Pearce says that in his department he has practiced economy and that, by the strict enforcement of the new requirements of the statutes, he has been able to collect a considerable sum which otherwise would not have been paid to the state.

On March 1, Pearce had one half of his biennial appropriation left. The clerks have been worked overtime without extra pay, and the receipts for the month of April, this year, were in excess of those for the same month last year.

In the months of December, and the first three months of 1912, there was an increase of $29,000 in receipts, in the office of the secretary of state, over the month of December, 1910, and the first three months in 1911. Still the office is handicapped by the lack of funds with which to publish the defunct corporations and to prosecute officers of corporations who have violated the statute in regard to the filing of annual reports.

"But I know more about th' revenue of the state than th' whole bunch av thim," says Kenehan, "and whin they have had their say, thin I'll have mine."

AUTO OWNERS LOSE 3 DAMAGE SUITS

Three verdicts have been rendered by juries in the district court against automobile owners within two days, aggregating $6,750.75. The first was in favor of John Hipp, an attorney, against T. T. Cornforth for $2,000. Then Jacob Strock recovered a verdict against Mrs. Anna De Remer for $4,175.75, and Friday morning the jury in the case of Joseph Bitterley against the Denver Cab and Omnibus company brought in a verdict for $575.

In the Hipp and Strock cases each of the injured men was riding a bicycle when struck by the automobiles. Bitterley was on his way from the depot to his home in a taxicab when the cab struck a street car at Broadway and Colfax avenue and threw him through a window of the cab, badly injuring his face and ear, hands and shoulder. He convinced the jury that it was the driver's fault and not that of the car crew.

HALTED!

BY HAL COFFMAN

THUS A BOB-TAIL FLUSH BEATS A PAT STRAIGHT

The government, believing that it has the lumber trust, coal land grabbers, the fake irrigationists, salted mine experts, counterfeiters and a score of other law violators in Colorado, on the run, has started a campaign against the men who are selling palming wax, marked cards, loaded dice and other gambling paraphernalia used to fleece the unwary.

The first arrests in this campaign to be waged by the postoffice inspectors of the Denver district were made today, when Postoffice Inspector Williamson and Deputy United States Marshal Jefferds took two brothers, M. E. and L. A. Hill, into custody at Salida, on the charge of using the mails to defraud, because they sold loaded dice, and cards so marked for the use of the gambler that it would be impossible for him to lose.

The Hills have been operating at Salida for several years under the name of G. L. Lee & Co., and a large part of the business they transacted were sales resulting from advertising their goods in publications out of the state. For $2.60 they agreed to send a deck of cards and some loaded dice that would make the intelligent player a small fortune in a short time if he followed instructions.

The palming wax is used to enable the faker to "cop chips" while handling the stacks, while the "holdout" cards can be slipped up the sleeve, or, by the use of a special apparatus advertised by the Hills, secreted under a table and used when it is desired to fill out a flush. They had cards marked for suit and size. Sets of cards were marked both ways to make sure the dealer knew what his opponent had in his hand.

Colorado fake card dealers—and they are numerous—according to the inspectors, have been immune, because it has always been the theory of federal prosecutors that when a man advertised to sell fake dice and marked cards, the man who bought the goods and answered the advertisement got what he asked for, and there was no fraud. Had he sent good cards and good dice when he advertised marked cards and loaded dice, he would have been guilty of using the mails to defraud, was the argument of former prosecutors.

United States District Attorney Harry E. Kelly does not take this view of the case and believes that a man should be punished if he uses the mails for an illegal purpose. The Colorado federal authorities are hopeful of a successful campaign in this state against the men who sell marked cards and loaded dice, because the federal courts of Illinois have sent several men to prison in the past two years on the same charge.

PLATFORMISTS QUIT CITIZENS' MEETING; SPLIT OVER OFFICES

Keating Faction Opposes Arnold and Chance to Heal Breach Is Small.

NO TIME TO LOSE NOW

Friends of Arnold Will Confer and Decide Upon Plan for City Campaign.

ARNOLD MEETINGS.

Tonight—Eighth Ward Arnold club, 1643 Adams; Central Arnold club, 1890 Lafayette; Second Ward club, 435 West Colfax avenue.

Saturday night—Tenth Ward club, Houston hall, 1080 Broadway; Fourteenth Ward club, 574 High street.

Disagreement over certain changes in the Citizens municipal ticket to be proposed to the independent voters of Denver caused the Platform Democratic committee of five to leave the other two committees, from the Progressive Republicans and Citizens respectively, in the conference Thursday evening.

The triple alliance had spent a week trying to agree upon a ticket that would be acceptable to all interested—one that would appeal to the voters by its personnel. Some in the joint conference were disposed to get together by a give-and-take process. Several appeared to want to play the game of political intrigue rather than to meet the requirements of a patient waiting public.

Influences from the outside insinuated themselves. These were subtle and effective as well as ingenious. Bitternesses were engendered. Platform Democrats today charge bad faith on the part of the Citizens and Progressive Republicans. Denial of this is made by the latter. Charge is also made that Edward Keating, who dominated the Citizens conferees, made a combination with the Progressive Republicans and named certain of the nominees over protests.

KEATING OPPOSED ARNOLD FROM THE START.

Keating was opposed to Arnold from the start. His influence among the Citizens and Progressives conferees was such as to at least justify strong suspicion. In fact, some of the candidates named on the ticket with Arnold are known to have been out talking against him. That Arnold was the only logical man with whom to defeat the bi-partisan corporation machine all realized and agreed. They were forced to nominate him. There was reason to believe that there was enough patriotism in the conferees to turn out a ticket that would appeal to the vast throng of voters in Denver and be elected.

PLAYED POLITICS IN CONFERENCE CHARGE.

Itch for office, together with a desire to play machine politics for spoils, was seemingly the first consideration of some. There is also a well defined belief now that the motive which actuated several in the conference was to force a rupture and thereby tend to break up the movement to overthrow machine rule. There are those even who declare that underground wires lead from machine headquarters to the conference.

If proof of this serious charge is wanted, those who make it say they are ready to submit it. Opposition to Arnold, manifest in Keating hostility, seemingly found expression in a combination to load the ticket up with candidates who are not acceptable—particularly those who had been cast for assessor, clerk and recorder. These nominees are known to be hostile to Arnold.

The split came after vain attempts on the part of the Platform Democrats to have the nominees for assessor, clerk and recorder changed for others more acceptable. In fact, the platformists say they presented names but they were voted down by the Citizens-Progressive element. There was nothing else to do, say the Platformists, but to walk out of the conference, leaving the other conferees to continue their deliberations.

Friends of Arnold, prominent citizens and men and women who are standing against machine politics and want to see Denver freed from corporation misrule, will gather today in conference to determine upon what shall now be done with reference to naming a strong set of nominees for municipal offices and providing ways and means to elect it. No further time will be wasted. The plan, furthermore, is to select a campaign committee for the contest.

The Citizens and Progressives will also meet tonight and determine their course. There is hardly any chance of the triple alliance getting together again. It would be useless, say the Paltformists. Both the Citizens and Progressive conferees are likely to issue a statement tonight, detailing their story of the causes that led up to the rupture. One thing seems to be apparent. Either the Progressives have been unconsciously led to intriguing or they have been too credulous.

HEARST AND SULLIVAN IN FINAL CLASH

Battle for Delegates Feature of Illinois Democractic Meet.

PARTY SEES VICTORY

Republican Convention Gets Surprise When Fred Busse Seeks Place.

Chicago, April 19.—Interest in the two state conventions being held today, the Republican at Springfield and the Democratic at Peoria, centers in the contest in the latter meeting between the Hearst-Harrison and the Roger Sullivan factions. Indorsement of national candidates was settled definitely at the primaries, and Roosevelt and Clark will have the Illinois delegates in their respective conventions.

Sullivan won the first battle of the Democratic convention when the state committee, by a vote of 21 to 3, seated 334 of that leader's delegates from Cook county and gave the followers of W. R. Hearst and Mayor Carter Harrison but seventy and those from districts where Sullivan admits he has no strength.

Democrats of Illinois believe the state ticket has a chance this year in the anticipated landslide, and a bitter clash between factions is inevitable in making the slate. Another clash is expected in the committee on credentials, which will judge each contestant individually, whereas the state committee only invalidated the Seventh armory convention of the Harrisonites by declaring it illegal.

Fred Busse, former poastmaster and mayor of Chicago, created some excitement in the Republican convention by announcing himself a candidate as delegate-at-large to the national convention. Busse is an avowed Taft man, and the word has gone out that only Roosevelt supporters may expect places on the delegation. The platform will commend the administration of President Taft, favor the election of United States senators by the people, amendment of the Sherman law, indorse the initiative and referendum, and will denounce "jack pot" and bipartisan rule of legislatures.

Reports from Nebraska are that the result will be close. Managers of the different candidates are each claiming victory. Five parties are in the field—Republican, Democratic, Socialist, Prohibitionist and People's Independent. The largest vote in years is predicted by political wiseacres.

NEVER COUNT YOUR CHICKENS BEFORE YOU LOOK INTO THE INCUBATOR

Drawn for The Denver Post by 'Bud' Fisher

Three Boiler Explosions Helped to Rend Big Ship Asunder

First Boat Picked Up Had Men Only in It

Carried but 18 Passengers, Others Were Loaded Until Not Another Pound Could Be Taken Aboard.

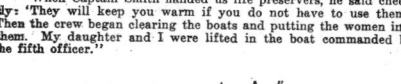

A STEWARD from the Carpathia told the story of the rescue of the Titanic's passengers and crew to a group of his mates.

"It was between quarter after and half after one o'clock on ship's time Monday morning," he said, "when all the stewards were mustered and Chief Steward Hughes told us that a wireless had just come in that the Titanic had hit an iceberg and probably would need help. He urged us to turn right in and get things ready for a ship's load of people. The Carpathia turned in the direction the wireless had called from.

"We got hot coffee ready and laid out blankets and made sandwiches and everything like that. It seemed as if every passenger on the boat knew about the trouble and turned out. Captain Rostrom had shut off the hot water all over the ship and turned every ounce of heat into steam and the old boat was as excited as any of us.

"After we got things ready we went out on deck. It was a glorious morning, no swell in the sea, but bitter cold. The ship's lights were on full blast and we were there in the middle of a sea of ice—the finest sight I ever saw.

"Just as it was about half day and dark we came upon a boat. There were eighteen men in it and it was in charge of an officer. There were no women in the boat and it was not more than one-third filled. All of the men were able to come up the Jacob's ladder on the Carpathia, which we threw over the port side. Every one of them was given a hooker of brandy or as much hot black coffee as he wanted. After they were all on board we pulled up their boat.

"It was a bright morning by now and all around the Carpathia here and there, about a quarter of a mile apart, were more boats. These were fuller than the first and there were women in all of them. The women were hoisted up in bo'sun's chairs and the men who could do so climbed the Jacob's ladder. Some of them, however, had to be hauled up, especially the firemen. There was a whole watch of firemen saved. They were nearly naked. They had jumped overboard and swam after the boats, it turned out, and they were almost frozen stiff.

"The women were dressed, and the funny thing about it is only five of them had to be taken to the hospital. Both the men's hospitals were filled—twenty-four beds in all. We got twelve boatloads, I think, inside of a little more than an hour. Then between quarter after and half past eight we got the last two boats, crowded to the guards, and almost all women."

Ten Minutes Overtime By Operator Saves 745 Lives

Was Ready to Retire Sunday Night, Decided to Wait, Would Have Been No Survivors If He Had Not.

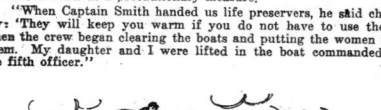

NOW the wireless operator on the Carpathia, by putting in an extra ten minutes on duty was a means of saving 745 lives, was told by Dr. J. F. Kemp, the Carpathia's physician, today.

"Our wireless operator," said Dr. Kemp, "was about to retire Sunday night when he said, jokingly: 'I guess I'll wait just ten minutes, then turn in.'

"It was in the next ten minutes that the Titanic's call for help came. Had the wireless man not waited there would have been no survivors."

Dr. Kemp described the iceberg that sank the Titanic as at least 400 feet long and 90 feet high. He declared that one of the boats that the Carpathia picked up was filled with stockers from the sunken liner. "It had just two women aboard," he said. The doctor declared that the Carpathia cruised twice through the ice field near the spot where the Titanic sank and picked up the bodies of three men and one baby.

"On Monday at 8:30 in the evening we held a funeral service on board the Carpathia," continued Dr. Kemp. "At this service there were thirty widows, twenty of whom were under 23 years of age, and most of them brides of a few weeks or months. They did not know their husbands were among the dead. The Californian and the Burmah, the last named a Russian steamer, cruised about the scene of the wreck for some time in futile search for the bodies of the victims.

"Mrs. John Jacob Astor," the doctor continued, "had to be carried aboard. She had to be taken into a cabin and given medical attention. She was more completely attired, however, than many of the women who were rescued."

Mrs. Alexander T. Compton and her daughter, Miss Alice Compton, of New Orleans, two of the Titanic's rescued reached New York prostrated over the loss of Mrs. Compton's son, Alexander, who went down with the big liner.

"We waved good bye to my son," said Mrs. Compton. "We did not realize the great danger but thought we were only being sent out in the boats as a precautionary measure.

"When Captain Smith handed us life preservers, he said cheerily: 'They will keep you warm if you do not have to use them.' Then the crew began clearing the boats and putting the women into them. My daughter and I were lifted in the boat commanded by the fifth officer."

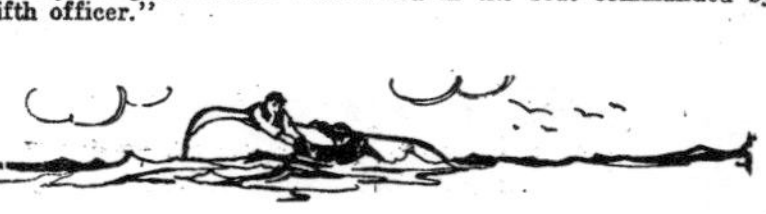

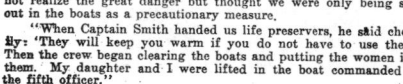

IN THE HOLLOW OF HIS HAND

Many Women Killed in Staterooms Is Belief

Philadelphian Saw None but Men on Deck When He Stepped Into Boat--Thought All Women Were Saved.

MANY of the survivors assert positively that not a woman was to be seen on any of the decks at the time the officers of the Titanic gave the word for the men to enter the lifeboats. It is therefore believed many of those who lost their lives must have been killed in their cabins, as the survivors also say that everyone had ample time to dress.

E. Z. Taylor of Philadelphia says he was awakened at 12:10 o'clock by his watch by a dull, grinding crash that rocked the boat, but was not sufficiently hard to throw him from his berth.

"I knew instantly," he said, "that we had struck something, but was not frightened. We had plenty of time to dress, for when the ship struck it was 12:10, and she didn't sink until 2:30 by my time.

"I saw the iceberg we struck and it was fully eighty feet high above the water. It seems to me that when we struck it we passed over part of it and under part, as if below the floor and ceiling of a room.

"Everybody rushed to the decks, but it did not at first appear that we were facing a horrible danger, and those not fully dressed retired to attire themselves to face the cold, which was terrible.

"The sea was as smooth as glass and there was little trouble, as far as I could see, in launching the boats when the word was given out that we were sinking.

"The rule in loading the boats was 'women first,' and we thought all the women on board were in the boats first. At last, when not a woman was to be seen on the decks, the officers ordered the men to the boats. I dropped into one containing Mrs. Astor and several other women whose names I do not know. We were four and one-half hours on the water, but the Carpathia picked us up. The thoughts of those who had gone down and from the cold that bit into our flesh like knives we were half crazed.

"I can say with assurance that I do not believe over 500 persons have been saved from the wreck."

Large Number of Crew Saved by Swimming

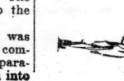

IN AN interesting story Miss Margaret Hays of New York, a survivor of the Titanic, gave one version of the manner in which Colonel Astor met his death.

"Colonel Astor, with his wife, came on deck as I was being assisted into a lifeboat," said Miss Hays, "and both got into another boat. Colonel Astor had his arms about his wife and assisted her into the boat. At the time there were no women waiting to get into the boats and the ship's officer at that point invited Colonel Astor to get into the boat with his wife. The colonel, after looking around and seeing no women, got into the boat and his wife threw her arms about him.

"The boat in which Colonel Astor and wife were sitting was about to be lowered when a woman came running out of the companion way. Raising his hand Colonel Astor stopped the preparations to lower his boat and stepped out and assisted the woman into the seat he had occupied. Mrs. Astor cried out and wanted to get out of the boat with her husband, but the colonel patted her on the back and said something in a low tone of voice.

"As the boat was being lowered I heard him say: 'The ladies will have to go first.'"

Another version of the deaths of John Jacob Astor and William T. Stead was told by Philip Mock, who, with his sister, Mrs. Paul Schabert, were among the survivors.

"Many men were hanging on to rafts in the sea" said Mr. Mock. "William T. Stead, the author, and Col. John Jacob Astor clung to a raft. Their feet became frozen and they were compelled to release their hold. Both were drowned."

According to a surgeon of the New York hospital who went aboard the Carpathia after she docked four bodies were buried at sea from that steamship.

The chief steward of the Carpathia explained the large number of the crew saved by saying that the majority of them had jumped from the Titanic and were picked up by the boats.

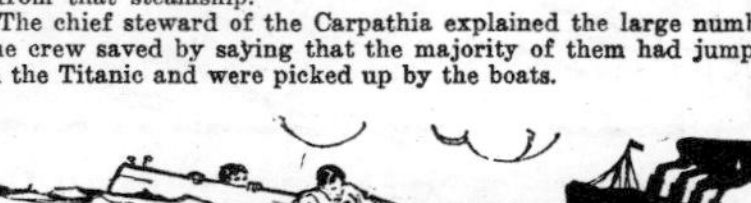

Ismay Hidden From Reporter by Captain

Man Seeking Interview Threatened With Arrest by Rostrom, Who Refused to Answer Questions.

REPRESENTATIVE of the International News Service managed to get aboard the Carpathia and made his way to the bridge, where he had an interview with Captain Rostrom as to why the news of the wreck and the condition of the survivors had been withheld. The following was the interview:

"But you have not given out the news, and we have waited a week. Will you let me get it now?"

"You stay on this bridge with me, or I will put you in irons."

"Did you save the bodies that the Carpathia either did pick up or might have picked up?"

"What do you mean?"

"I mean that of thirty-five put in one lifeboat at 2:20 in the morning only sixteen were found alive when she was picked up. At that time there were three dead bodies in the boat."

"I won't talk to you, and I want you to stay here where I can watch you."

"Captain Rostrom, do you realize that this is the most gigantic story in the history of the sea, and the world will not accept your whims in giving it the information it awaits?"

"I realize, sir, that you came aboard this boat in spite of orders from a thousand sources, and I won't be catechised or criticised by you."

"Captain, I want to see Mr. Bruce Ismay. The American people would like to hear from him."

"You be quiet. You can't see anybody, I tell you."

"Is John Jacob Astor, Maj. Archibald Butt, William T. Stead, Artist Millet, Isador Straus or Mrs. Isador Straus or Benjamin Guggenheim aboard this ship?"

"I think not."

"Do you still refuse to let me see Mr. Ismay?"

"I will let you see no one."

After this he paced the bridge like a man suffering from a great load of anxiety, and in spite of the general opinion that he was the master of his ship, seemed conscious of the fact that he had subordinated his position, advisedly or otherwise, to more powerful influences.

Panic Terrible Just Before Vessel Sank

'Seemed as If All the Devils of Hell Had Been Let Loose,' When People Realized Worst, Says Doctor.

DR. HENRY W. FRAUENTHAL of New York declared all of the women on board the Titanic were thought to have been safely lowered to the boats before the order for the men to take them came.

"When the ship first struck," he said, "none of us dreamed of the danger we faced. All who had been asleep, after the first rush to the decks, returned to their cabins to dress.

"When the word came that we were sinking and the lifeboats were ordered over the side, the panic was fearful. From all sides came shrieks and groans and cries, and it seemed as if all the devils of hell had been let loose.

"Just now I am so thankful to be alive that my appreciation of the horror is dulled. I am only afraid that when I recover from the first shock it will all come back to me again, and I would rather have gone down with the boat, I think, than have to live over again, even in my imagination, the last few minutes of that fearful night.

"I would rather have stayed, too, than know that women went down with the Titanic, but I swear we thought every woman on the ship had been placed safely in the boats. It was 'Women first' with all of the men, and at last it seemed as if the decks had been cleared of them, for not one was to be seen save those already lowered. Then the officers ordered the men to leave the sinking vessel and we left for the boats, not knowing, any one of us, I think, how many of our fellow men we were leaving behind as prey to death."

Another of the survivors who would have embraced death more happily than safety was Mrs. A. O. Horveson, whose husband, who was connected with the Peabody company, went down with the Titanic.

With her husband, Mrs. Horveson had been in Buenos Ayres on a three months' pleasure and business trip, and, returning by way of England, had thought it would be great fun to help the Titanic make her maiden trip.

"We were so happy," she cried with tears streaming down her face. "We had thought it such a lark to come back home on the Titanic.

"But now there is nothing, nothing left. Oh, I can't stand it."

Oscar Johansen of Detroit:

"I was awakened in the steerage of the Titanic by a grinding, tearing thump. I ran to the deck and reached the salon, and there found the band playing some popular air. The officers were assuring the people that there was no danger. They told me to go back into the steerage and tell the people who knew my tongue that the accident was nothing. I went back. An hour afterward the Titanic sank. I jumped off and came to the surface of the water beside a collapsible lifeboat. There was no one in it. I hung to the boat for two hours and a half, and then I was picked up. The last thing I saw was a man who had been pointed out to me as Major Butt standing on the forward deck, that was already under water."

Jane Smith, one of the English nurses employed by J. W. Allison of Ontario, who brought "Baby" Smith through the Titanic disaster, came down the gangplank with the 9-months-old baby boy wrapped in her arms. He was all that was left of a family of father, mother and two children. The other child was a girl, 3 years old. Miss Smith said:

"It was shortly before midnight when I went into the room where the baby was sleeping, to see if he was all right.

"I had just gotten into the room when I felt a slight rasping shock. The machinery suddenly stopped.

"I ran to Mr. Allison's stateroom near by and awakened him and Mrs. Allison. The three of us went on deck. At first we saw nothing unusual. Mr. Allison made light of his wife's fears."

Iceberg Was Higher Than the Bridge of the Ship

Atmospheric Conditions Prevented Officers From Seeing It Until It Was Too Late to Prevent the Collision.

HUGH WOLLNER, a son of Thomas Wollner, R. A., of London, says there were two explosions before the Titanic sank. He believes he was the last person to leave the Titanic. To a friend he said:

"We saw what seemed to be a continent of ice. The iceberg which we struck, I have learned, was much higher than the bridge of the Titanic. Because of some atmospheric conditions, however, it could not be seen until the Titanic was close to it. It was not thought at first that the ship had been dealt a dangerous blow. Everybody took things comparatively easy. Some of the men were in the gymnasium taking exercise before turning in. For some minutes after the Titanic struck those men continued with their exercises not knowing what was passing above.

"Not long after the ship struck there came the first big explosion, then, a moment later, the second. It was this second explosion that did the most damage. It blew away the funnels and tore a big hole in the steamer's side and caused the ship to rock as if she were an eggshell.

"The Titanic careened to one side and passengers making for the boats were spilled into the water. The ship filled rapidly and I jumped into a boat as it swung down the side.'"

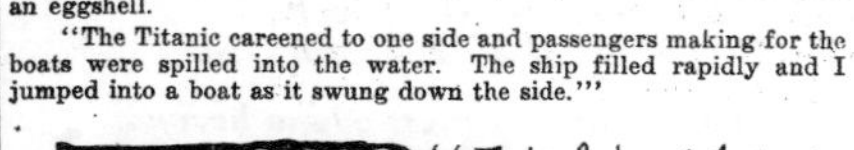

Captain Smith, Washed From Bridge, Swims Back to Ship

Women Row Lifeboats When Men Are Exhausted

Frenzied Scenes Enacted as Lifeboats Are Rapidly Driven From Proximity of Sinking Titanic.

MISSES CAROLINE and Lily Bonnell of Youngstown said:

"We were asleep in our berths when the Titanic crashed into the iceberg. We immediately rushed on deck, only stopping to throw on a coat over our nightgowns. The night was bright and starlit. We could see the crowds of passengers falling down the stairways, while the officers sought to reassure them of their safety. Major Butt and Colonel Astor stood by the lifeboats bravely and helped the women. They did not think the boat was going to sink.

"The Titanic kept settling lower and lower, however. Then word came that the engine room was flooded.

"There was some shooting. They would not allow those half-crazed men to get into the boats. I was in one of the lifeboats. After we were lowered away the men in our boat started to row.

"I looked back to the Titanic and could see the big ship settling. She seemed already to be only half her former height. The officer in charge of our lifeboat kept urging the men at the oars to row harder. Some of the oarsmen fell exhausted. Then we women took turns at the oars.

"We must have been about a mile away from the Titanic when she went under.

"There was a big wave. The sea was calm otherwise and I asked a sailor what it was. He said: 'The Titanic has sunk!'

"It was bitterly cold. We half-dressed women suffered intensely until we were picked up."

According to one of the first passengers ashore the Titanic struck the iceberg at 11:41 p. m. Sunday night and went down at 2:20 Monday morning. The Carpathia reported at the scene at 4:40. She picked up nineteen lifeboats.

J. B. Thayer of Philadelphia said:

"The Titanic struck about midnight as near as I can guess. It rode upon the ice, hesitated for a few seconds and then slipped off with a tremendous crash and broke in the middle. The manning of the lifeboats immediately began.

"Bruce Ismay manned one of the boats as a sailor, but he had no sooner taken his seat at one of the oars when he jumped up again and gave his place to a woman. Then Ismay, with an oar in his hands, got into a second lifeboat. About twenty minutes afterward our lifeboat pulled away. Then the Titanic sank."

Margaret Hayes of 384 West Eighty-third street, New York, said:

"**I first came to my senses in one of the lifeboats. My first realization was that I was holding in my arms a 2-year-old girl. I don't know the name or identity of the child. She was almost naked. I kept her with me and will closely guard my little ward given to me by Providence.**"

Mrs. Cornelius P. Anderson of Hudson, N. Y., said:

"The ship struck with a terrible crash. It dazed me. The next thing I knew was when I found myself in a lifeboat about a mile away from the Titanic. As I looked back I was horrified to see people jumping off the big boat. The great vessel sank lower and lower, and finally went down with a great plunge. We felt the sea rise up beneath us and we were carried yards away on the crest of the great wave. We suffered terribly from the cold until the Carpathia rescued us."

Four Buried at Sea While Survivors Throng the Deck

New York, April 19.—Services for the burial of the dead at sea were read over the bodies of four men on the Carpathia Monday afternoon by Father Roger Anderson of the Episcopal Order of the Holy Cross. During the services the Titanic survivors and passengers of the Carpathia thronged the deck.

G. Wikeman, the Titanic's barber, was treated for bruises. He declared that he was blown into the water by the second explosion on the Titanic after her collision with the iceberg.

A passenger who was picked up in a drowning condition caused grim amusement on the Carpathia by demanding a bath as soon as the doctors were through with him.

Hundreds of delegates to the Men and Religion congress, who were to have listened to an address by William T. Stead, the English journalist, lost in the Titanic disaster, today joined in memorial services for Mr. Stead at Carnegie hall. William J. Bryan, who is to be the principal speaker tonight, will pay a tribute to the distinguished journalist.

More Than $10,000 for Rescued Women Raised on Carpathia

New York, April 19.—Before the Carpathia reached the Cunard Line pier last night, more than $10,000 in contributions was available for the women's relief fund to care for the destitute steerage passengers, who were chiefly women and children. All were provided with clothing and comfortably houses and arrangements have been completed to care for them as long as is necessary.

Mrs. Abram S. Hewitt, chairman, is being assisted by more than 100 women. The pasengers were removed to the Junior League house, the Swiss Benevolent home, the Margaret Louisa home, the Municipal lodging house and the St. Vincent de Paul home.

London, April 19.—The fund being raised by Lord Mayor Crosby for the survivors has reached $150,000. Those who hoped that the Curnarder Olympic had picked up some of the survivors of the Titanic were disappointed. The Olympic was too far away to reach the scene in time.

HEROES OF THE TITANIC

By JEAN HOOPER PAGE

The master of millions and pauper's son
At last stood side by side,
But the broadcloth coat and the corduroy
Held the hearts of men that died.

The master of millions, proud lord of the earth,
And the lowly son of the sod,
Are after all but brothers of flesh,
In the eyes of a wonderful God.

Both came from the mystic land beyond,
Both found their graves in the sea.
So the master of millions and pauper's son
Are one in eternity.

One of the most pathetic scenes was gray-headed Isador Straus, with his arms wrapped about his wife, standing on the deck calmly waiting for death to claim them.

Tragedy Followed 'Captain's Day' Aboard New Steamship

After First Shock There Was Utter Silence—Not One Passenger Thought Titanic Would Sink in 45 Minutes.

F. H. FLYNN of Philadelphia, said:

"There is just one way to describe the suddenness of the tragedy that lurked over the sea in the calm of last Sunday night—it came as unheralded as the proverbial thunderbolt out of a clear sky.

"The crash of impact came, and after the first shock there was quiet. The engines were not even running, but the doom of the Titanic was sealed. We did not know it, though, because there was not one among us who had so lately been listening to the strains of waltz music—it was Captain's day aboard ship—who realized the danger confronting us.

"The band, playing 'Nearer, My God, to Thee,' told passengers and crew that the greatest tragedy of the sea would be written in the early morning."

C. H. Roumaine, Georgetown, Ky., said: "I had just retired for the night when the Titanic crashed into its doom. The jar was so slight that not much attention was paid to it. Going on deck, I was told there was not the slightest danger, the vessel having struck only a fishing smack or something of the kind. Forty-five minutes afterward we were told the vessel was sinking.

"No confusion was apparent among the passengers. Men, women and children were gathered together on deck. All of us thought there was no question but that our lives would be saved. Men stood as if to let the women and children take their places on the boats. The men who remained behind were confident the Titanic would float for hours. I was commissioned to row one of the first boats that left the ship. We passed out of sight of the Titanic before she sank, but I distinctly heard the explosion of her boilers."

Women, Thinly Clad, Suffered From the Cold

Frenchman Puts Boys In Lifeboat, Then He Calmly Waits Death as the Ship Sinks.

INTENSE sufferings of the Titanic's passengers when taken off the lifeboats by the Carpathia were graphically told by John Kuhl of Omaha, Neb., who was a passenger on the latter vessel.

Many of the women, he said, were scantily clad and all were suffering from the cold. Four died on the Carpathia as a result of the exposure.

"In spite of the suffering and crowded condition of the boats," said Mr. Kuhl, "the utmost heroism was displayed by all the unfortunates. When they were lifted to the deck of the Carpathia many of the women broke down completely and there were many touching scenes. Many of the women were incoherent and several were almost insane."

Of all the heroes who went to their death when the Titanic dived to its ocean grave, none, in the opinion of Miss Hilda Slater, a passenger in the last boat put off, deserved greater credit than the members of the vessels orchestra. According to Miss Slater the orchestra played until the last. When the vessel took its final plunge the strains of a lively air mingled gruesomely with the cries of those who realized that they were face to face with death. She added:

"**There were many touching scenes as the boats put off. I saw Col. John Jacob Astor hand his young wife into a boat tenderly and then ask an officer whether he might also go. When permission was refused he stepped back and coolly took out his cigarette case. 'Goodbye, dearie,' he called gayly as he lighted a cigarette and leaned over the rail. 'I'll join you later.'**

"Another man, a Frenchman, I think, approached one of the boats about to be lowered. He had with him two beautiful little boys. An officer waved him back sternly. 'Bless you,' he said, 'I don't want to go, but for God's sake take the boys. Their mother is waiting for them in New York.' The boys were taken aboard."

The Titanic was sinking. Captain E. J. Smith stood on the bridge of the mightiest vessel ever constructed by man. It had been intrusted to his care and he was found waiting. Deeper settled the ocean liner until he was in the grasp of the waves. A roller washed him overboard, but he swam back to his station, and when she took her final plunge he was still standing there.

Boats In Bad Shape, Leaked, and 2 Sank

Band Played 'Nearer My God to Thee" Until Instruments Were Choked Off by Swirling Water.

HENRY STENGEL of Newark, N. J., had ordered two automobiles to meet him. He had several hysterical survivors in his care.

"I have no praise for anything connected with the rescue of the Titanic survivors," he said. "There were holes in the lifeboats uncalked. I have a clear recollection that when the lifeboat in which I came off was leaving the Titanic, a band was playing aboard the big ship.

"We suffered dreadfully. There was no food, no water and no light aboard any of the lifeboats and, from what I could learn, none of the lifeboats was in good shape. I saw with my own eyes two lifeboats loaded with passengers go down. I can only attribute this to the bad condition of the boats."

Mrs. Ida S. Hippatch of Chicago and her daughter, Jean, two of the survivors, were met at the pier by Mrs. Hippatch's son, John Hippatch. The mother was in a serious state of collapse and was taken to the Hotel Imperial.

Mrs. A. A. Dick, who was saved with her husband, said:

"There was the wildest excitement after the ship struck. The crew first ran to the rails to prevent any one from jumping overboard. I was standing near the first two boats that were launched. At first a few men struggled to gain seats, but when they saw us women they calmed down and put us aboard the boats. Their bravery was wonderful. The lowering of our boat into the sea was a terrible experience. The boats with the rescued passengers lay in the vicinity of the foundering vessel for about an hour. We had been assured by the captain that she could not sink, but she began to settle and our oarsmen made frantic efforts to pull far enough away so that we could not be drawn down with the Titanic in her vortex.

"The marine band did nobly. An air was struck up soon after the crash came, and as we were lowered away we were cheered by the strains of music. After we had reached the water and until we were 200 yards away we could hear the music on board. Even when the giant vessel had lowered to the point where it was seen that she must go down this music kept up. The last I remember of the Titanic was hearing the strains of 'Nearer My God to Thee.' There was a great sound of rushing water and the vessel sank beneath the waves. I know that these musicians stopped playing that hymn only when their instruments were choked off by the swirling water that closed about their heads when they went to heroes' graves."

Passenger Saw Berg Mile Ahead Before Ship Hit It

Top Protruded 80 Feet Out of Water, but Submerged Part Was Struck by the Liner, He Says.

CAPTAIN SMITH is a hero, says Mrs. John Murray Brown of Acton, Mass., who, with her sisters, Mrs. Robert C. Cornell and Mrs. E. D. Appleton, was saved in the last lifeboat to get safely away.

"The band played, marching from deck to deck," Mrs. Brown said. "The musicians were up to their knees in water when I last saw them. We offered assistance to Captain Smith of the Titanic when the water covered the ship, but he refused to get into the boat.

"Mrs. Astor was in the lifeboat with my sister Mrs. Cornell. I heard Colonel Astor tell her he would wait with the men."

E. W. Beane, a second cabin passenger, was picked up after swimming in the icy water for twenty minutes. He jumped into the sea after the boats were lowered.

"I heard a shot fired," said Beane, "just before I jumped. Afterwards I was told a steerage passenger had been shot while trying to leap into a lifeboat filled with women and children."

H. B. Steffenson of New York, another survivor who leaped into the sea and was picked up, declared that he saw the iceberg before the collision.

"It seemed to me that the berg, a mile away, I should say, was about eighty feet out of the water. The ice that showed clear of the water was not what we struck. After the collision I saw ice all over the sea. When we hit the berg we seemed to slide upon it. I could feel the boat jumping and pounding and I realized that we were on the ice, but I thought we would weather it. I only saw the captain once after the collision. He was telling the men to get the women and children into the boats.

"I thought then that it was only for precaution and it was long after the boats had left that I felt the steamer sinking. I waited on the upper deck until about 2 o'clock. I took a look below and saw that the Titanic was doomed. Then I jumped into the ocean and within five minutes I was picked up."

Mr. Steffenson also described the discipline upon the boat as perfect. Many women as well as men, he said, declined to leave the Titanic, believing she was safe.

Mrs. Cornelia Andrews of Hudson, N. Y. was one of the first to put into a lifeboat.

"I saw the Titanic sink," she said. "I saw her blow up. Our little boat was a mile away when the end came, but the night was oclear and the ship loomed up plainly even at that distance. As our boat put off I saw Mr. and Mrs. Astor standing on the deck. As we pulled away they waved their hands and smiled at us. We were in the open boat for about four hours before we were picked up."

Many Wives Scorned Death to Stay at Husbands' Side

GREATEST ASTOR OF THEM ALL

John Jacob Astor—born a millionaire, died a hero.

He is dead, cut off in the prime of life, but had he lived the allotted three score and ten he could not have brought more glory to the name of Astor than he did by going down with the Titanic.

From early youth his every impulse has been misconstrued because of his great wealth, and he would have gone to an unhonored and unremembered grave had it not been for the opportunity that cost him his life. Now when the name of Astor is mentioned, it will be the John Jacob who went down with the Titanic that will first come to the mind; not the Astor who made the great fortune, not the Astors who added to its greatness, but John Jacob Astor, the hero.

He stood on the deck of the ill-fated ship while she settled deeper and deeper, and when she took the final plunge that carried her to a grave two miles below the surface of the ocean, there stood John Jacob Astor, with his hand at a salute. There were no applauding multitudes; there was no sham about it. John Jacob Astor, hero, just died.

Hymn They Learned at Mother's Knee Rang in Ears of the Dying

NEARER, MY GOD, TO THEE.

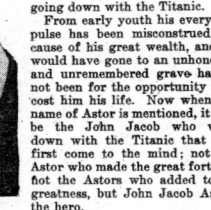

There is something in music that makes men brave.

In 1776 the men with the fife and drum led the charge up to the cannon's mouth, playing "Yankee Doodle."

In 1898 the band belonging to the First Colorado volunteers led the charge that resulted in the fall of Manila, and during the rain of bullets played "Hot Time."

In 1912 while the Titanic was making her last struggle against a sea that was sure to conquer, the band of the vessel stood on the deck playing "Nearer, My God, to Thee."

There could be no greater bravery than this.

MR. AND MRS. STRAUS GO DOWN WITH ARMS ENTWINED

One Woman Refused to Leave Brother and Thereby Saved His Life--Wife Tells of Last Few Minutes With Husband.

New York, April 19.—A picture of Mr. and Mrs Isidor Straus clinging to each other after the last boat was gone was revealed by Mrs. Schabert of Dary, Conn., who, with her brother was rescued. Mrs. Schabert had stateroom twenty-eight on the starboard side amidships.

"It was a grazing but not a great one, it seemed to me, that awakened me," she said. When I went on deck I said to a steward 'Are we going down?' He answered, calmly, 'Madam, I guess we are!'

"An officer on the bridge or near it was shouting, the life boats were being got ready 'Women and children first.'

"They tried to get me away from my brother and put me in a boat. I refused to go without him. Finally my brother stood alone in our part of the ship. A boat was just leaving that had room for two more passengers. The officers in charge said to me:

"Well, if you won't leave your brother, he may come, too.'

"We got into the boat and so, by hesitating, I saved my brother's life.

"Mrs. Straus had a chance to be saved, but she refused to leave her husband. As our boat moved away from the ship, the last boat of all, we could plainly see Mr. and Mrs. Straus standing near the rail with their arms around each other.

"The lights of the Titanic were all burning and the band was playing. To me the most affecting episode of the whole disaster was that final glimpse of this elderly couple awaiting the end together."

Three sailors of the Titanic, who were standing near Mrs. Schabert, spoke up at this moment to say:

"You know the Titanic just crawled up on that iceberg and broke in two."

Mrs. Edward Meyer said: "It was a clear night. When the ship struck we were in our cabin. My husband went out on the deck to see what was the trouble. He came down and said we had hit an iceberg but that it did not amount to much. I said I was nervous and we went on deck for a walk. He said that the accident was of no importance. It would only delay our arrival.

"I was afraid and made my husband promise if there was trouble he would not make me leave him. He walked around the deck awhile, an officer came up and cried 'All women into the lifeboats.'

"We went down into the cabin and did not part, he helped me put on warm things. I got into a boat, but there were no sailors aboard. We called to the ship that there were no men in the boat. They sent a sailor down.

"An English girl and I rowed for four hours and a half. Then we were picked up at 6 o'clock in the morning. We were well away from the steamer when it went down.

"There were about 70 widows on the Carpathia and all were wonderfully brave. The captain of the Carpathia and the passengers did all they could for us. Mrs. Harris says my husband and Mr. Harris and Mr. Douglas lowered the last boat load full of women. All three were perfectly calm."

"I knew that Major Butt had gone down; he was a soldier and was on deck, where he belonged." So said President Taft, but only the women survivors know how well he did his duty as he stood, revolver in hand, and held the frantic men at bay while the women got into the boats.

Lady Duff Gordon Tells of Sinking of Great Liner

Titanic Gave a Curious Shiver, the Stern Shot 100 Feet in the Air, Then Sea Was Filled With Screaming Souls.

LADY DUFF GORDON dictated the following: I was asleep. The night was perfectly clear. I was awakened by a long grinding sort of shock. It was not a tremendous crash, but more as though someone had drawn a giant finger all along the side of the boat. I awakened my husband and told him that I thought that we had struck something.

There was no excitement that I could hear. My husband went on deck and told me that we had hit a big iceberg but there seemed to be no danger. We were not assured of this, however, and Sir Cosmo went upstairs again. He came back to me and said: "You had better put your clothes on, because I heard them give orders to strip the boats."

We each put on a life preserver and over mine I threw some heavy furs. I took a few trinkets and we went up to the decks. There was no excitement at that time. The ship had listed slightly to port and was down a little at the head. As we stood there, one of the officers came rushing up and said: "The women and children are to go in the boats."

No one apparently thought there was any danger. We watched a number of women and children and some men going into the lifeboats. At last one of the officers came to me and said: "Lady Gordon, you had better go in one of the boats." I said to my husband: "Well, we might as well take the boat, although I think it will be only a little pleasure excursion until morning." The boat was the twelfth or thirteenth to be launched. It was the captain's special boat. There was still no excitement. Five stokers got in and two Americans, A. L. Salomon, whose address is No. 245 Broadway, New York City, and C. W. Stengel of Newark. Besides these there were two of the crew, Sir Cosmo, myself and a Miss Frank, an English girl.

There were a number of other passengers, mostly men, standing nearby and they joked with us because we were going out on the ocean. "The ship can't sink," said one of them. "You will get your death of cold out there in the ice."

We were slung off and the stokers began to row us away. For two hours we cruised around. It did not seem to be very cold. There was no excitement aboard the Titanic. We were probably a mile away.

Suddenly I clutched the sides of the lifeboat. I had seen the Titanic give a curious shiver.

Almost immediately we heard several pistol shots and a great screaming arise from the decks. Then the boat's stern lifted in the air and there was a tremendous explosion. After this the Titanic dropped back again. The awful screaming continued. Two minutes after this there was another great explosion. The whole forward part of the great liner dropped down under the waves. The stern rose a hundred feet almost perpendicularly. The boat stood up like an enormous black finger against the sky. Little figures hung to the point of the finger and dropped into the water. The screaming was agonizing. I never heard such a continued chorus of utter despair and agony.

The great prow of the Titanic slowly sank as though a great hand was pushing it gently down under the waves. As it went the screaming of the poor souls left on board seemed to grow louder. It took the Titanic perhaps two minutes to sink after the last explosion. It went down slowly without a ripple. We had heard of the danger of suction when one of these great liners sinks. There was no such thing about the sinking of the Titanic. The amazing part of it all to me as I sat there in the boat looking at this monster being destroyed was that it all could be accomplished so gently.

Then began the real agonies of the night. Up to that time no one in our boat, and I imagine no one on any of the other boats, had really thought that the Titanic was going to sink. For a moment an awful silence seemed to hang over all, and then from the water all about where the Titanic had been arose a bedlam of shrieks and cries. There were men and women clinging to the bits of wreckage in the icy water.

It was at least an hour before the last shrieks died out. I remember the very last cry was that a man who had been calling loudly: "My God! My God!" He cried monotonously in a dull, hopeless way. For an entire hour there had been an awful chorus of shrieks, gradually dying into a hopeless moan until this last cry that I speak of. Then all was silent.

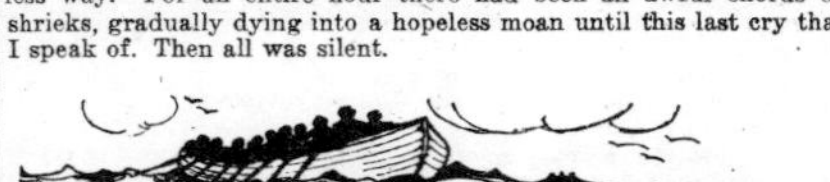

Raft Being Lowered Tilts Sweeps Occupants Into Sea

Women in Boats Offered Up Prayers and Gazed Longingly and Reverently at the Approaching Rescue Ships.

HEROISM of the English sailors who went down with the Titanic was the one thing which most impressed Paul Cheveret, the Canadian sculptor, who left the steamship in one of the first lifeboats lowered. He said there was no sign of cowardice among the male passengers of the crew.

"I was off the Titanic before there was any real panic," Mr. Cheveret said. "I will take my hat off to the English seamen who went down with their ship and to the men who manned the lifeboats. Every one of them was a man. It was a difficult matter to force some of those who were rescued into the lifeboats. I was literally thrown into the third boat lowered."

Mrs. J. C. Hogeboom of Cleveland, Ohio, said:

"I was lifted into a lifeboat when I came up on the deck in answer to the call of 'All passengers on deck.' Then I must have fainted for I remember nothing until several hours later.

"When the Carpathia came in sight I offered up a prayer of thanksgiving. My fellow passengers stopped their meditations, gazing longingly and reverently at the approaching vessel."

Mrs. William F. Warden, Portland, Ore.:

"The Titanic sank while her passengers fully believed that she would limp into port. When the first shock came I had no idea that the lives of the thousands aboard were in danger. I saw one of the life rafts which had been lowered over the side tilt and half of its human freight swept into the sea. Excitement was much more apparent among the passengers of the first class than of the steerage."

Probably there was no survivor who suffered like this man Johansen. For hours he was battered around in a sea of ice while he clung to a plank, but his faith never failed and he was rescued.

BUTT AN HONOR TO HIS UNIFORM

Archibald Butt is dead.

The man who was so proud of the uniform he wore for Uncle Sam died a death that will make the nations of the world respect that uniform; the man so chivalrous in the grand places of the world stood with death staring him in the face and was still chivalrous.

There he stood on the deck of the sinking Titanic, watching the lifeboats loaded and with a bravery unequaled, forcing crazy men to stand back and make room for the women and children.

Every man who wears the uniform of the United States, whether on sea or land, must feel his heart swell with pride when he reads the story of Archibald Butt. The captain of the ship stood on the bridge of his pride and waited for the summons of death that would come with the final plunge of the vessel, while Archibald Butt was down on the deck working with a desperation that death alone knows to save life. Not his life, but the lives of the women in the first, second and third cabins, and in the steerage.

Self-preservation is the first law of cowards, and Archibald Butt was no coward.

PITIFUL tales were related by some of the steerage passengers of the Titanic as they came off the Carpathia, few of the passengers were met by relatives or friends, and a majority were taken in charge by charitable persons. A thrilling story was told by Ellen Shine, a 20-year-old girl from County Cork, Ireland, who came here to visit a brother. Those who were able to get out of bed," said Miss Shine, "rushed to the upper decks where they were met by the members of the crew, who endeavored to keep them in the steerage quarters. The women, however, rushed by these men, knocking them down and finally reached the upper decks. When informed that the boat was sinking, most of them fell to their knees and began to pray. I saw one of the lifeboats and made for it. In it were four men from the steerage. They were ordered out by an officer and refused to leave. And then one of the officers jumped into the boat, and, drawing a revolver, shot the four men dead. Their bodies were picked out from the bottom of the boat and thrown into the ocean."

A pathetic incident of the steerage was the placing of seven children—four girls and three boys—into one of the lifeboats. Their parents were lost. Two of the little ones, whose names could not be learned, were taken to hospitals. One has scarlet fever and the other meningitis.

August Wennerstrom, a Swede, spied a collapsing boat behind one of the smokestacks as the vessel was sinking. With three other men he managed to tear it from its lashings and the four jumped overboard with it. The boat overturned four times, but each time they managed to right it, and finally all of them were saved by the Carpathia. While drifting about Wennerstrom said he saw at least 200 men in the water, who were drowned.

MRS. MAY FUTRELLE, whose husband, Jacques Futrelle, the novelist, went down with the ship, was met here by her daughter, Miss Virginia Futrelle, who was brought to New York from the Convent of Notre Dame in Baltimore.

Miss Futrelle had been told that her father had been picked up by another steamer. Mrs. Charles Copeland of Boston, a sister of the writer, who also met Mrs. Futrelle, was under the same impression. Miss Futrelle and Mrs. Copeland, with a party of friends, awaited at a hotel the arrival of Mrs. Futrelle from the dock.

"I am so happy that father is safe too," declared Miss Futrelle as her mother clasped her in her arms.

It was some time before Mrs. Futrelle could compose herself.

"Where is Jack?" Mrs. Copeland asked.

Mrs. Futrelle, afraid to let her daughter know the truth, said: "Oh, he is on another ship."

Mrs. Copeland, however, guessed the truth and became hysterical. Miss Futrelle also broke down.

"Jack died like a hero," Mrs. Futrelle said, when the party became composed. "He was in the smoking room when the crash came—the noise of the smash was terrific—and I was going to bed. I was hurled from my feet by the impact. I hardly found myself when Jack came rushing into the state room.

"'The boat is going down, get dressed at once,' he shouted. When we reached the deck everything was in the wildest confusion. The screams of women and the shrill orders of the officers were drowned intermittently by the tremendous vibrations of the Titanic's deep bass fog horn. The behavior of the men was magnificent. They stood back without murmuring and urged the women and children into the lifeboats. A few cowards tried to scramble into the boats, but they were quickly thrown back by the others. Let me say now that the only men who were saved were those who sneaked into the lifeboats or were picked up after the Titanic sunk.

"I did not want to leave Jack, but he assured me that there were boats enough for all and that he would be rescued later.

"'Hurry up, May! You're keeping the others waiting,' were his last words as he lifted me into a lifeboat and kissed me goodbye. I was in one of the last lifeboats to leave the ship. We had not put out many minutes when the Titanic disappeared. I almost thought when I saw her sink beneath the water that I could see Jack standing where I had left him and waving at me."

Mrs. Futrelle said she saw the parting of Col. John Jacob Astor and his young bride. Mrs. Astor was frantic. Her husband had to jump into the lifeboat four times and tell her that he would be rescued later. After the fourth time, Mrs. Futrelle said he jumped back on the deck of the sinking ship and the lifeboat bearing his bride made off.

500 Police Unable to Prevent Riots When Boat Landed at Pier

Silence of Air Made Capt. Rostron Shudder

Realized Seriousness of Titanic's Condition After First Frantic Appeal and His Operator's Failure to Get Answer.

(By R. H. ROSTRON.)

(Captain of the Cunard Steamship Carpathia, Rescuer of the Titanic Survivors.)

I cannot yet make a connected statement. I have gone through so much since I received aboard my ship the first distress call of the Titanic that a complete narrative is impossible. I was between fifty and sixty miles away from the Titanic when the wireless sang into the ears of my operator the first call for help. The operator said that we received only one call. The silence after the frantic appeal for relief was ominous to me. Our Marconi sent out rays that scraped the sky in vain, but there was no response whatever to any of our inquiries. I swung the Carpathia around straight to the position the poor Titanic's first aerogram said she occupied. Our engines were put at top speed.

Silence of the Air Was Ominous.

The silence of the air so far as the Titanic was concerned made me shudder as we sped on our way to the rescue. I realized what it meant. On and on we sped. Our stokers never worked harder. When the first faint daylight came and I knew we were still miles from the spot of the tragedy, I felt as if we should arrive too late to be of any service.

When, however, after full daylight we sighted the first lifeboat filled with women and children and eight or ten strong-armed and brave-hearted men of the Titanic's crew, I realized that we could at least save a few human lives.

"I was too busy for the next hour or so to recall now just what occurred. My mind was wholly set upon saving the lives of the people who crowded the boats.

The sea was calm. There was scarcely a ripple upon its face. Great ice floes were crunching down from the north.

In the distance several icebergs shimmered like mirrors. Why the lifeboats were not crushed by the swiftly moving ice floes I could not understand. The sixteen boats seemed at first nearly all full of women.

'God Checked Further Murder.'

I remember that it occurred to me that the good God had stretched out His mighty hand and had checked further murder by His elements.

We got aboard the Carpathia every human being in the sixteen lifeboats of the Titanic. Every officer and member of our crew stood by like the brave and loyal lads they are and did his full duty. My mind is in no condition now to tell you much more of what I heard and felt during the two hours' work of rescue.

We took aboard 745 women and children who were alive, but some of them were unconscious. We also dragged to the decks of the Carpathia four members of the Titanic's crew who had been tolled off to man the lifeboats and were stark dead. They had been frozen to death. Their strong, horny fingers still clutched the oars that they had been desperately pulling. We buried these men in sailor's graves only yesterday from the deck of the Carpathia.

I am told that it was reported to President Taft by Captain Chanler of the scout cruiser Salem, that the Carpathia had received Wednesday night wireless messages from the commander of the Salem asking, in the name of the president, if Major Butt, John Jacob Astor, Frank Millet, Clarence Moore and Isidor Straus were aboard his vessel.

Never Received President's Message.

Upon my word as a man—upon my honor as a sailor—I cannot remember receiving any such message from Captain Chanler or anybody else in the name of the president or any other person. Had such a message been referred to me I immediately would have ordered that all other business of the wireless be sidetracked until the answer could have been sent to the president that none of his friends of whom he had inquired was aboard the Carpathia.

It is possible that the Carpathia's wireless operator refused to answer messages, even from the president of the United States, received after Wednesday night, as he had then been at his post more than seventy-two hours without rest. But he never reported such a message to me—and I do not blame him.

Thinks Shooting Story a Lie.

After I reached the Cunard pier I was asked as to the truth of reports that some passengers, and particularly some men passengers, on the Titanic were kept back from the lifeboats at the muzzle of the pistol and that two well-known men were shot. Of course, I was not there. I did not see the ship go down. But from the survivors who came aboard my ship I heard no such story.

I do not give the least credence to that report. If I had to write about it I would denounce it as an abominable lie. The Carpathia was amply provisioned for the passengers rescued, and likewise there was abundant and comfortable sleeping room for the unexpected increase of her passenger list by bringing into requisition the big lounges in the salons.

I thank the people who have congratulated me, but I am not entitled to any more credit than would have been due any other man of the sea had the opportunity for the service my ship rendered been afforded others. I thank Almighty God that I was within wireless hailing distance and that I got there in time to pick up every one of the survivors of the Titanic wreck.

Cardinal Farley Bowed With Grief Over Loss of Life

New York, April 19.—Cardinal Farley, who reached New York from Washington just as the Carpathia was docking, is bowed with grief over the terrible loss of life on board the Titanic. He was especially grieved at the fate of Major Archibald Butt, who went to Rome and saw Pope Pius X on a special errand for President Taft.

Action was taken by Consul Teors of the diocese to help the distressed in every way possible.

Instructions were drawn up for the clergy to say special prayers for the dead, the physical sufferers and the afflicted relatives and friends.

The cardinal expressed especial sympathy over the fate of the third-class passengers, many of whom, he thought, came from his native country.

Make Ships Stay South of Bergs, Says Carnegie

New York, April 19.—Dear Mayor: What was the Titanic doing up among the ice when she had the whole Atlantic ocean south, open and free? This is the root of the matter. Passenger steamships should be compelled to go far south below the range of icebergs at all seasons.

Lifeboats are secondary to this vital requirement. Yours,

ANDREW CARNEGIE.

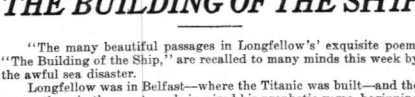

Colonel Astor said: "Goodby, dearie," to his bride he had placed in a lifeboat, lighted a cigarette and perished with the boat.

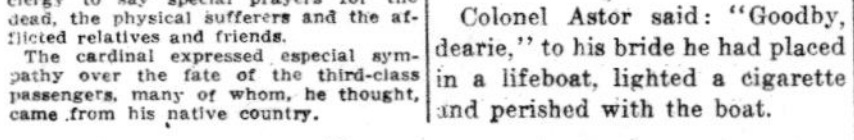

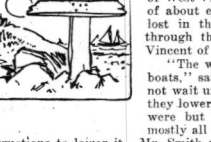

Many of the survivors say that the last they saw of the Titanic showed John Jacob Astor standing in the stern, apparently making no effort to save his life. When the final plunge came he was standing at attention and saluting his Maker.

Drunken Sailor Only Man In Mrs. Astor's Boat

J. Bruce Ismay Was There, Too, but He Didn't Count--Owner Was Treated Like Some King.

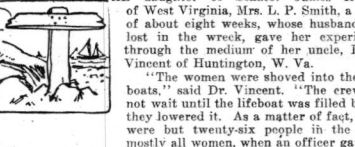

THE daughter of Senator James Hughes of West Virginia, Mrs. L. P. Smith, a bride of about eight weeks, whose husband was lost in the wreck, gave her experiences through the medium of her uncle, Dr. J. Vincent of Huntington, W. Va.

"The women were shoved into the lifeboats," said Dr. Vincent. "The crew did not wait until the lifeboat was filled before they lowered it. As a matter of fact, there were but twenty-six people in the boat, mostly all women, when an officer gave instructions to lower it. Mr. Smith was standing alongside the boat when it was lowered. There was plenty of room for more people to get into the lifeboat, its capacity being fifty.

"Mrs. Smith implored Captain Smith to allow her husband in the boat but her repeated appeals were ignored.

"This lifeboat was permitted to be lowered with but one sailor in it and he was drunk. His condition was such that he could not row the boat and therefore the women had to do the best they could in rowing about in the icy waters.

Mrs. Smith was in the third boat that was launched and in that boat was Mrs. John Jacob Astor.

"My niece saw Mr. Ismay leaving the boat. He was attended by several of the crew, and every assistance was given him to get into the boats. And when the Carpathia finally came along and rescued the shipwrecked, some of the crew of the Carpathia, together with men of the Titanic, actually carried Mr. Ismay to spacious rooms that had been set aside for him. As soon as Mr. Ismay had been placed in this stateroom a sign was placed on the door: 'Please don't knock.'

"Mrs. Smith bore up bravely on the pier but shortly after she had been in her hotel room she became exhausted and retired very early."

Her father, Senator Hughes, with Dr. Vincent and other relatives was here to meet her.

THE BUILDING OF THE SHIP

"The many beautiful passages in Longfellow's' exquisite poem, "The Building of the Ship," are recalled to many minds this week by the awful sea disaster.

Longfellow was in Belfast—where the Titanic was built—and the scenes there in the great yards inspired his prophetic verse, beginning with:

"Build me straight, Oh, worthy master!"

As the great ship grew in size the poet exclaims:

"Ah, what a wondrous thing it is!"

The lines that follow suggest the disaster of last Monday morning:

"And the trembling maiden held her breath
At the tales of that awful, pitiless sea,
With all its terror and mystery—
The dim, dark sea, so like unto Death
That divides, and yet unites, mankind."

The following lines will give an idea of the labor connected with the building of a ship, and the launching of the Titanic:

"Day after day the vessel grew . . .
Horned aloft, the shadowy hulk . . .
All is finished, and at length . .
The bride of the gray old sea" . . .

is ready for her maiden voyage. As "she leaps into the ocean's arms," Captain Smith watching her launching—as he did—might have said with the poet:

"How beautiful she is! How fair! Nowhere in her grand construction "are the signs of doubt.'"

Then when the crash came, Captain Smith, supreme in his confidence of the unsinkable character of his beloved vessel, might have quoted Longfellow with:

"Fear not each sudden sound and shock, to
Sail on, nor fear to breast the sea."

The famous poem closes with words expressing the sentiment of the entire world:

"Our hearts, our hopes, are all with thee;
Our hearts, our hopes, our prayers, our tears,
Our faith triumphant o'er our fears,
Are all with thee—are all with thee!"

Baby In Life Boat Both Hands Cut Off

Woman Declares That Widener and Ryerson Went to Death Like Men, Throwing Kisses to Loved Ones.

PETER D. DALY of New York jumped from the deck of the Titanic after it was announced that there were only boats enough for the women and children. As he saw the ship settling gradually he swam away with all his might to prevent being carried down with the suction of the sinking liner. "For six hours I beat the water with hands and feet to keep warm," he said. "Then I was picked up by one of the Carpathia's boats. I was numb with the cold after a fight which I can scarcely bear to discuss.

"There was no violent impact when the vessel collided with the ice. I rushed to the deck from my cabin, got a life preserver, and when things began to look serious threw myself into the water. The boat had already begun to settle."

Mrs. W. J. Douton, a fellow passenger, comes from Rochester.

"I had not been in bed half an hour," said Mrs. Douton, "when the steward rushed down to our cabin and told us to put on our clothes and come on deck. We were thrown into lifeboats. As soon as the men passengers tried to get to the boats they were shot at.

"There was a baby in the boat with one of the women. The baby's hands had been cut off.. I think it was still alive. The mother did not give it up. During the night, when waiting for the Carpathia, four of the crew died in the boat and were thrown overboard. It was bitter cold and we had to wait until 8 o'clock in the morning before we were rescued."

George D. Widener, the wealthy Philadelphian, and Arthur L. Ryerson of New York went to their deaths like men, is the statement by Mrs. Ryerson to her brother-in-law, E. S. Ryerson, who resides here. She says that when the women were put into the lifeboats she saw Mr. Ryerson and Mr. Widener standing behind the rail of the Titanic, both waving their arms, throwing kisses and calling farewell. Mrs. Ryerson and her two daughters, Susan and Emily B., and a young son, John B., were in the boat with her.

SAID Mrs. Washington Dodge, wife of the assessor of San Francisco:

"On Sunday evening I retired early. My husband remained in the smoking room. I fell asleep. I don't know how long I had been sleeping when I was awakened by a shock. It was not a severe one. It did not worry me. It was so slight that I remained in bed and in a few minutes fell asleep again. Then my husband came down and awakened me. He said there had been an accident but that it was slight. I then got up and dressed and went up on deck. I heard persons laughing, and my husband and I agreed that the accident had not been a serious one. We did not know at this time that the Titanic had struck an iceberg. After remaining on deck a short time I returned to my room and again retired. Then my husband came in and said:

"'Ruth, the accident is rather a serious one. You had better come up on deck at once.'

"I did so. I dressed hastily and then put on my fur cloak. My 4-year-old son, Washington Dodge Jr., was with me. When we got up to deck A, the top deck, I saw them manning the lifeboats.

"Even at this time I did not have the slightest idea that the Titanic would sink. I asked my husband if he was not coming with our son and myself. He replied that he would remain. I urged him to come with us. He said:

"'We men must take care of the women and children first. After that has been done I shall follow. I do not believe the boat is going to sink.'

"So thoroughly did I believe that the Titanic was not in danger that I did not kiss my husband goodby. Had I suspected that she would sink I would not have left unless he went with us.

"Our boat went about 200 yards away from the ship. There she lay to while we watched the boat.

"At this time I began to grow thoroughly alarmed for the safety of my husband. We saw the Titanic gradually settling. It was pitch dark, but her side lights were still burning and we could tell by them how she was sinking.

Sides Split Open at Explosion of Boilers

Women Refused to Believe Immense Boat Could Sink and Many Remained Aboard Rather Than Enter Lifeboats.

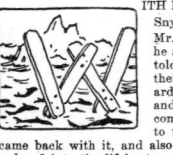

WITH his bride of eight weeks, John Pillsbury Snyder went to a hotel when they landed. Mr. Snyder said that when the crash came, he and his wife went to the deck, but were told there was no danger and returned to their stateroom. Shortly afterward a steward told them they had better go on deck, and they obeyed. Mrs. Snyder, however, complained of the cold and again returned to the stateroom for heavier clothing, and came back with it, and also her jewel case. Then the people were ordered into the lifeboats.

"But the women," continued Mr. Snyder, "after looking over the rail into the water, refused to change their seeming safe position for the more precarious one in a lifeboat. An officer pleaded, then ordered them into the boat. But still they refused to go."

Mr. Snyder said that he and his wife were in the first boat launched, which was full. There was no excitement, only the moaning and quiet sobbing of the women and once in a while an exclamation from a man. He could see the deck plainly and it appeared remarkable to him that nobody was wearing a life preserver. Gradually the lifeboat floated away until it was fully 500 yards from the Titanic. Then came a loud explosion followed closely by two others not so resonant.

With the first explosion Mr. Snyder said the sides of the stricken ship bulged out and by the bright starlight he could see the nose of the liner dip into the sea. The stern of the boat was raised high into the air, two propellers glistened above the water and the Titanic sank.

Charles Williams, the racquet coach at Harrow, England, who is the professional champion of the world and was coming to New York to defend his title, said he was in the smoking room when the boat struck. He rushed out, saw the iceberg, which seemed to loom above the deck over 100 feet. It broke amidship and floated away. He jumped from the boat deck on the starboard side as far away from the steamer as possible. He was nine hours in the small boat, standing in water to his knees. He said the sailors conducted themselves admirably.

CHURCHES WILL PRAY FOR SOULS OF DEAD

Father Hugh L. McMenamin, at Request of The Post, Suggests Supplication Expressing Catholic Faith.

In all the Catholic churches of Denver on Sunday morning, prayers will be offered for the repose of the souls of the victims of the Titanic wreck. This custom is followed universally in the wake of great disasters because of the belief of Catholics in an intermediate state in the after life, from which prayer is efficacious in obtaining deliverance.

At the request of The Post, Father McMenamin, rector of the Immaculate Conception cathedral, has written the following prayer, which conveys the idea of the Catholic belief in the efficacy of prayers for the departed:

(By Father H. L. McMenamin.)

Let us pray. O God, the Creator and Redeemer of all the faithful, hear our supplications and through Thy infinite love and mercy graciously grant to the souls of Thy servants departed the remission of all their sins, by which they may have deserved the severity of Thy divine justice and punishment in the world to come.

Vouchsafe to them grace and mercy before Thy divine tribunal, and let them attain to everlasting rest and happiness through the infinite merits of Jesus Christ.

Grant, O Lord, we beseech Thee, that whilst we lament the tragic departure of our brothers and sisters, Thy servants, out of this life, we may bear in mind that we are most certainly to follow them. Give us grace to make ready for that last hour by a devout and holy life, and protect us against a sudden and unprovided death.

Teach us how to watch and pray that when Thy summons comes we may go forth to meet the Bridegroom and enter with Him into life everlasting.

Almighty and most merciful Father, who knowest the weakness of our nature, bow down thine ear in pity upon Thy servants, upon whom Thou hast laid the heavy burden of sorrow. Take away out of their hearts the spirit of rebellion and teach them to see Thy good and gracious purpose working in all the trials which Thou doest send upon them. Grant that they may not languish in fruitless or unavailing grief nor sorrow as those who have no hope, but through their tears look meekly up to Thee, the God of all consolation.

Through Jesus Christ, our Lord. Amen.

CHRONOLOGY OF THE TITANIC FROM TIME KEEL WAS LAID

New York, April 19.—From the facts completed by the arrival of the rescue ship the Titanic's story, which began in the fall of 1908, when the White Star line announced its proposal to eclipse all previous records in shipbuilding with a vessel of staggering dimensions, may be outlined chronologicaly as follows:

1909—Keel of the gigantic vessel laid at Harland & Wolff yards at Belfast.

1911—May 31 the vessel is launched and christened the Titanic.

1912—Completed and fully furnished at an outlay of about $10,000,000.

April 10—Noon, starts on the maiden trip from Southampton to New York via Cherbourg.

April 14—Sends a routine wireless warning ashore of the presence of icebergs off the Grand Banks of Newfoundland.

April 14—11:40 p. m., Titanic strikes an iceberg in latitude 41.16 north, longitude 50.14 west.

April 14—Midnight, Carpathia and other vessels hear Titanic's call for help.

April 15—12:27 a. m., Titanic's wireless is put out of commission and flashes given that the boat is sinking by the head and women and children are being put off in lifeboats.

April 15—About 1 a. m. the first news reached the United States by way of the Allan line offices at Montreal. The Virginian reported that the Titanic struck an iceberg.

April 15—2:20 a. m., Titanic sinks.

April 15—3 a. m., wireless from the Cape Race station directed to the Associated Press gives the first information of a serious disaster.

April 15—5 a. m.,—First survivors picked up from lifeboats by steamer Carpathia.

April 15—3 a. m. to 10 a. m.—No advices.

April 15—Noon—Reports current Titanic still is afloat and that all are saved.

April 15—7:30 p. m.—White Star line offices admit a probable great loss of life.

April 16—Carpathia sends by wireless list of survivors, failing to account for about 1,300 persons, including scores of wealthy and prominent people.

April 17—Hope given up that other vessels have saved any.

April 18—Two days elapsed without slightest description of disaster.

April 18—9:30 p. m.—Rescue ship docks at New York with 745 passengers and crew, confirming the loss of all others and bringing the first details of the Titanic disaster.

Operator Sticks to Key at Cost of His Life; Saves 745

DENVER WOMAN HEROINE; CARES FOR THE RESCUED

Mrs. J. J. Brown, Two Hours After Rescue, Goes Into Ship Hospital and Nurses the Saved Women and Babies.

(Continued From Page One.)

remained in the icy sea four hours, just as the terrible shock came. Mr. W. H. Haven of New York had just said to us, 'What a pleasure to travel like this,' when the ship gave a terrible lurch, mounted in the air, settled and settled again.

"In the twinkle of an eye Mr. Haven was gone, and Mr. Brayton and I lay stunned on the deck. For the next few minutes I don't know what I did. I have a recollection of running to my room in the awful darkness, grasping what jewels I had and hurrying out on the deck. Mr. Brayton had jumped overboard with a life preserver and then I was alone—helpless, unable to move or say a thing.

"Someone said 'Women first, quick!' and I was literally thrown into a lifeboat and lowered to the foaming ocean.

Rowed for Seven Hours and a Half Until Her Head Was Sick.

"There in that lifeboat, with a sailor at my side, I rowed for all my might for seven and a half hours. I rowed until my head was sick, until I thought I was dead. Fifteen more could have been saved in our boat.

"I owe my life to my exercise. Two women died at my side of exposure, while my blood was at a boiling point. You can imagine the shouting and crying that went up when the Carpathia came to us out of the misty daylight. Some of the thankful hearts in our boat grasped and kissed one another until they were too weak to lift a hand. Others wanted to die, and persisted in jumping overboard.

"Just as the Carpathia swung alongside of us, I lost my remaining strength and fell exhausted. Two hours after that I was in the ship's hospital, nursing the hysterical. Don't ask me how I did it—I don't know myself. Here in this little gloomy room I have been for three days and nights, working with every bit of strength in my body.

"Dying mothers, sweethearts and little children separated in an instant from their dearest ones on earth have whispered messages in my ears to those who will ask for them. I have prayed earnestly that God would spare that painful anxiety, but suppose that one of those grief-stricken relatives should come on board to ask about those who were saved, and I should not be here? Now can you blame me for staying—for staying and telling them that I have made the last hours of their mothers, of their wives, peaceful ones?

"No; there was no distinction of race, color or name."

Goes Into Hysterics Recalling Events of That Terrible Night.

Mrs. Brown broke down here, and the sight made Mrs. Spinner faint. The two women were so hysterical that they were removed to an adjoining room where medical aid was summoned. In half an hour Mrs. Brown was able to speak again. She walked into the ship's hospital without assistance and held a cup of water to the lips of a steerage passenger in the corner.

"Poor creature," she whispered. "She has lost her four children and a husband, and both her feet have been frozen. I have nursed her night and day. She was rescued in our boat."

Outside the hospital, on the mammoth double-decked pier, heartrending scenes were being enacted. The custom officials were powerless to keep back a man when he saw his wife. Men acted like animals until they sighted the face they were waiting for, and women literally tore their hats and cloaks to pieces. It is pitiable and pathetic beyond description. Mrs. Brown did not want to see it.

"I can hear them," she said. "I know what it is."

"Did you nurse Mrs. John Jacob Astor?" she was asked, to which she replied:

"I nursed the poor girl up to the hour before the boat docked. If she lives it will be through the wonderful work of doctors in New York and nothing else. Mrs. Astor was scantily dressed when the disaster came unannounced, and her sufferings from exposure were terrible.

Expects to Raise Fund of $10,000 for Relatives of Those Who Perished.

"You can tell my dear ones in Denver that I have collected $7,000 for the dead, and before I leave the Carpathia in the morning I expect to have it raised to $10,000. This money will go to my patients' relatives and toward the burial of those that died in this little room."

She turned to Mrs. Spinner, Mr. Tobin and the reporter.

"I think I had better be left alone now," she suggested. "I feel weak and there is much work yet to be done before I leave here for good. Come for me tomorrow, and I will go to the Ritz Carlton, where I will stay until I feel like a big, strong woman again. Be sure to tell Denver that my Helen is safe, and is attending school in Paris and that I am sick at heart but alive and safe."

Mrs. Brown was an eyewitness at the sinking of the Titanic. Only a bare 200 yards intervened between the little boat which bore her to safety and the monster which went down with 1,600.

She said that she could easily bear the shock of the whole disaster if she could only get her mind off the sight of seeing the 500 people huddled together on the deck at the stern of the boat thrown amidst the wildest confusion in the air, to fall helpless victims to the suction of the ship as she foundered.

Mrs. Brown is the most idealized woman on board the Carpathia. No other woman rowed a stroke, and she was the only survivor who was physically and mentally able to sacrifice life and effort to the lives of the sick and mangled on board.

Captain Rostron of the Carpathia was first asked where to find Mrs. Brown after the big ship had reached her port.

"In the hospital," he shouted, "and no persuasion on earth can make her leave it."

MEMORIAL SERVICES FOR TITANIC DEAD

The protestant churches of Denver will probably unite in a memorial service for the victims of the Titanic disaster next Sunday. The Ministerial Alliance has made no plans but this idea is being followed in other cities throughout the country.

"It is likely that we will have a joint memorial service," says the Rev. Thomas S. Young, secretary of the Alliance. "We have not arranged anything but we cannot let this great catastrophe pass without some concerted prayer for those who are gone."

THURSDAY ANNIVERSARY OF FRISCO EARTHQUAKE

Six years ago yesterday—on April 18, 1906—the world shuddered at the news of an appalling disaster as it is shuddering today as the bulletins tell the story of death and destruction aboard the Titanic.

On April 18, 1906, came the earthquake, quickly followed by flames, that destroyed the city of San Francisco, killing thousand, rendering 300,000 people homeless, and destroying property to the value of $400,000,000.

On April 18, 19012, the waiting world was only beginning to get the details of the most terrible ocean disaster of centuries.

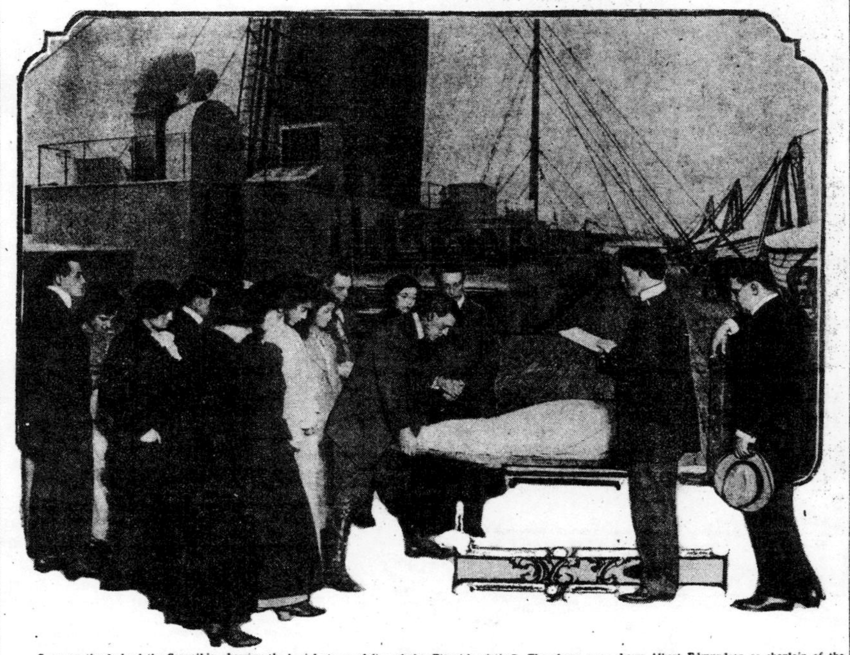

Scene on the deck of the Carpathia, showing the burial at sea of five of the Titanic's victims. The above scene shows Albert Edmundson as chaplain of the Carpathia reading the burial service, and survivors of the ill-fated ship attending the ceremonies.

Story of Mrs. Brown's Girlhood and Marriage Like Romance

Great Aim Was to Make Father Comfortable--Doing for Others Has Been Keynote of Her Life Since.

(By ELIZABETH KELLY.)

In the most gigantic story in the history of the sea the name of Mrs. James J. Brown of Denver figures.

The listening world that hangs upon the stories of heroism that are drifting from the wreckage of the once magnificent Titanic is hearing today how the Denver woman gave up her splendid health and vitality to those who were less strong in the face of shipwreck.

Quite naturally does the tragedy of a wreck at sea, the miracle of preservation, and the aftermath of heroism, fit in with the life story of Margaret Tobin Brown. Fiction has been written and given fame to its creator when it was founded on vastly less romantic stories than hers.

Fraught with dramatic interest, bristling with romance, the story of haw the wealthy globe-trotter's destiny was carved out from nothing reads like the vagaries of the novelist's imagination.

It is a story that Mrs. Brown tells herself. It is no betrayal of confidence. It is a story that is the key to the genuineness of the woman's nature.

REARED IN TOWN MADE FAMOUS BY MARK TWAIN.

Long years ago, in the small town of Hannibal, Mo.—which perhaps no one would ever have heard of had not Mark Twain immortalized it by spending the days of his common school education there—Margaret Tobin dreamed her dreams. Her father was a laborer but gave to his family a wealth of devotion that made up in a measure for the lack of material wealth. Margaret was a splendidly healthy girl, a prepossessing miss who lived in a little world of her own. Her air-castle was built about the stooping shoulders of her father.

"I longed to be rich enough to give him a home so that he would not have to work," Mrs. Brown has since told her friends. "I used to think that the zenith of happiness would be to have my father come to his home after a pleasant day and find his slippers warmed and waiting for him. It was a little thing to want, I thought. Of course we could have had his slippers ready for him in those days, you will say, but father was too tired when his work was done to enjoy any comfort. His life was bounded by working and sleeping."

It was toward what the world would call a successful marriage that Margaret Tobin looked in those days to bring to her father the things of which she dreamed. Women did not enter the professions then, even had she had the means of securing the requisite education.

When she was a little more than 16 years old an older brother decided to come West. He had read the stories of fabulous wealth that the Colorado mountains were yielding to those who knocked at the door of the treasure house. He saw in Colorado a chance to make a fortune.

Margaret Tobin accompanied her brother to the new country. In his cabin in Leadville she cooked his meals, made him as comfortable as she could and in her leisure dreamed on. There were men about her who had made the "stake" that the brother still struggled for. But there were more men in the vicinity who were still prospecting. One of these was James J. Brown—just plain "Jim" Brown in thos days who didn't own a "boiled" shirt even for Sunday wear. His fortune was just a little less certain than that of the Tobin family. He admired the buxon Missouri girl with the lustrous brown eyes and the even rows of white teeth. He told her so and she listened.

"I wanted a rich man," Mrs. Brown laughingly said in telling the story many years later, "but I loved Jim Brown. I thought about how I wanted comfort for my father and how I had determined to stay single until a man presented himself who could give to the tired old man the things I longed for for him.

"Jim was as poor as we were, and had no better chance in life. I struggled hard with myself those days. I loved Jim, but he was poor. Finally I decided that I'd be better off with a poor man whom I loved than with a wealthy one whose money had attracted me.

"So I married Jim Brown.

"I gave up cooking for my brother and moved to Jim's cabin, where the work was just as hard."

SIX WEEKS LATER HE MADE RICH STRIKE.

Six weeks after that James J. Brown had made the strike in the Little Jonny mine that brought him immense wealth. From that time on Mrs. Brown has had ease and comfort. She was able to give to her father the home that she had wanted him to have, to do for the less fortunate members of her family and to give to the two children who came to bless her home the education that she had craved in her youth and acquired later in life. The daughter, Helen, a very studious and well-read girl, is now a student in the Sarbonne at Paris. Her admission there is evidence of her mental caliber.

Mrs. Brown is seldom in Denver any more. Most of her life is spent in travel, this last trip having consumed three years.

Her own story of how she preferred to remain on the Carpathia, even after it had docked, so long as she could be of any assistance to those whose health had broken under the horror of shipwreck, is consistent with her life. Her philanthropies always have been numerous. It is toward those situated as was her father until the Little Jonny gave up its treasure that her interest is especially directed.

Two Close Friends of a Denver Man Among the Dead

To A. B. Parker, second vice president of the Colorado & Southern railway, the wreck of the Titanic and the dreadful loss of life that went with it is personal in its grief and anguish.

"Two of the men who went down I knew well. Arthur Ryerson and J. B. Thayer of Philadelphia, and Col. Archibald Gracie, who survives, and myself were boys together in Elizabeth, N. J., until our ways separated when we left home for schools," said Mr. Parker.

"I was particularly interested in the fate of the Ryerson family. Their oldest son was killed in an automobile accident Easter Monday while with a young cousin of mine, Lewis Hoffman, in Philadelphia, and they were coming home on the Titanic for the burial service.

"I have not heard the details of Archie Gracie's escape, but, knowing him as I do, I am confident he took a man's chance. Archie was not the sort to seek safety until the women and children were secure. He would have gone as gallantly to death as did Astor, Widener, Butt and others had not Providence intervened to spare his life.

"Mr. Thayer was vice president of the Pennsylvania railway system, in charge of traffic, and by his wife's family, the Morrises, was related to nearly all the prominent society folk of Philadelphia. If the Ryersons went down with the sunken ship while journeying home on their errand of sorrow it will be tragedy added to tragedy. I am hopeful that some of them, if not all, will be named in the list of survivors."

A boatload of women survivors in the open sea. The Titanic as it appeared when forced up against the iceberg which wrecked it is shown in the background.

TITANIC SURVIVORS ISSUE A STATEMENT

Praise Officers and Crew of Carpathia for Aid to Injured After Rescue From Ocean.

NEW YORK, April 19.—The following statement issued by a committee of the surviving passengers was given to the press on the arrival of the Carpathia:

"We, the undersigned surviving passengers of the Titanic, in order to forestall any sensational or exaggerated statements, deem it our duty to give the press a statement of facts which have come to our knowledge, and which we believe to be true:

"On Sunday, April 14, 1912, at about 11:40 p. m., on a cold, starlight night, in a smooth sea, and with no moon, the ship struck an iceberg which had been reported to the bridge by lookouts but not early enough to avoid collision.

"Steps were taken to ascertain the damage and save passengers and ship. Orders were given to put on life belts and the boats were lowered. The ship sank at about 2:20 a. m., Monday, and the usual distress signals were sent out by wireless and rockets at intervals from the ship. Fortunately, the wireless message was received by the Cunard's Carpathia at about midnight, and she arrived on the scene of the disaster at about 4 a. m., Monday.

"The officers and crew of the steamship Carpathia had been preparing all night for the rescue and comfort of the survivors, and last mentioned were received on board with the most touching care and kindness, every care being given, irrespective of class. The passengers, officers and crew gave up gladly their staterooms, clothing and comforts for our benefit, all honor to them.

"The English board of trade passengers' certificate on board the Titanic showed approximately 3,500. The same certificate called for lifeboat accommodations for approximately 950, in the following boats:

"Fourteen large lifeboats, two smaller boats and four collapsible boats.

"Life preservers were accessible and apparently in sufficient number for all on board.

"The approximate number of passengers carried at the time of the collision was:

"First class, 330; second class, 320; third class, 750. Total, 1,400. Officers and crew, 940. Total, 2,340.

"Of the foregoing about the following were rescued by the steamship Carpathia: First class, 210; second class, 125; third class, 200; officers, 4; seamen, 39; stewards, 96; firemen, 71. Total, 210 of the crew.

"The total saved, about 745, was about 80 per cent of the maximum capacity of the lifeboats.

"We feel it our duty to call the attention of the public to what we consider the inadequate supply of lifesaving appliances provided for on modern passenger steamships, and recommend that immediate steps be taken to compel passenger steamers to carry sufficient boats to accommodate the maximum number of people carried on board. The following facts were observed and should be considered in this connection:

"The insufficiency of lifeboats, rafts, etc.; lack of trained seamen to man same (stokers, stewards, etc., are not efficient boat handlers); not enough officers to carry out emergency orders on the bridge to superintend the launching and control of lifeboats; absence of searchlights.

"The board of trade rules allow for entirely too many people in each boat to permit the same to be properly handled. On the Titanic the boat deck was about 75 feet above water, and consequently the passengers were required to embark before lowering boats, thus endangering the operation and preventing the taking on of the maximum number the boats would hold. Boats at all times to be properly equipped with provisions, water, lamps, compasses, lights, etc. Lifesaving boat drills should be more frequent and thoroughly carried out, and officers should be armed at boat drills.

"Great reduction in speed in fog and ice, as damage, if collision actually occurs, is liable to be less.

"In conclusion, we suggest that an international conference be called to recommend the passage of identical laws providing for the safety of all at sea, and we urge the United States government to take the initiative as soon as possible."

Although the foregoing was given out as a signed statement by a committee of passengers, their signatures were omitted attendant upon the confusion when the Carpathia docked.

A passenger on the Carpathia made the following statement:

"I was awakened at about half past 12 at night by a commotion on the decks, which seemed unusual, but there was no excitement. As the boat was moving, I paid little attention to it and went to sleep again. About 3 o'clock I again awakened. I noticed that the boat had stopped. I went to the deck. The Carpathia had changed her course. Lifeboats were sighted and began to arrive and soon, one by one, they drew up to our side.

"There were sixteen in all, and the transferring of the passengers was most pitiable. The adults were assisted in climbing the rope ladders by ropes adjusted to their waists. The little children and babies were hoisted to the deck in bags. Some of the boats were crowded; a few were not half full. This I could not understand.

"Some people were in full evening dress. Others were in their nightclothes, and were wrapped in blankets. These with immigrants in all sorts of shapes were hurried into the saloon for a hot breakfast. They had been in the open boats for four or five hours, in the most biting air I ever experienced. There were husbands without wives, wives without husbands, parents without children and children without parents. But there was no demonstration. No sobs—scarcely a word spoken. They seemed to be stunned.

Frantic Men Who Tried to Rush Lifeboats Are Shot Dead

ISMAY PUT ON THE GRILL; TELLS HOW HE GOT AWAY

Senate Investigators Demand Specific Replies--Witness Says He Courts Fullest Inquiry Into the Disaster.

(Continued From Page One.)

sailed as a voluntary passenger on the Titanic.

Senator Smith began to ask the witness to detail his experience on the Titanic. Mr. Ismay interrupted, but Senator Smith continued. Then Mr. Ismay said he desired to express his sincere grief at the disaster and to welcome the fullest inquiry.

COMMITTEE INSISTS ON DEFINITE ANSWERS.

"Kindly tell the committee all the circumstances surrounding your voyage," said Senator Smith. "Tell us as succinctly as possible, beginning with your boarding the vessel at Liverpool, your place on the ship and as many circumstances as possible to help this committee."

"First, I wish to say that I court the fullest inquiry," said Mr. Ismay. "This awful catastrophe. I must say at the outset, I greatly deplore. We have nothing to conceal, nothing to hide.

"The boat left Belfast, I think, on the first of April. She underwent her trials safely and arrived at Southampton on Wednesday, April 3, I think. We sailed on Wednesday, April 10, leaving Southampton at 12 o'clock noon. That evening the Titanic reached Cherbougr, having run at about sixty-eight revolutions.

"We arrived at Queenstown Thursday noon. The Titanic was then running at 70 revolutions. The first day I think we made about 467 miles. The next day we increased the speed to 72 revolutions and I think we made 519 miles. The next day we increased to 75 revolutions and ran about 546 or 549 miles.

DENIES TITANIC WAS RUNNING FULL SPEED.

"The accident took place on Sunday night. The exact time I do not know because I was asleep. The ship sank. I am told, at 2:30.

"I understand you have been told the Titanic was running at full speed. It never had run at full speed.

"She was built to go 80 revolutions and had never been speeded up to that. We never had all her boilers working. It was our intention to speed the boat up to her full quota on Tuesday, but the catastrophe came to prevent it."

Although he came on a "voluntary trip," Mr. Ismay said his purpose was to see in what manner she could be improved upon. A report of the builder, Mr. Andrew, was on board, Mr. Ismay said.

"Did he survive?" asked Mr. Smith.

"Unfortunately, no."

Mr. Ismay said it was arranged between him and Captain Smith of the Titantic not to arrive at New York lightship before 5 a. m. Wednesday.

"There would have been no advantage in arriving earlier," he added.

"Was there any attempt to lower the boats of the Carpathia to take on passengers after you went aboard her?" asked Senator Smith.

"There were no passengers to take on," said Mr. Ismay.

IN LIFEBOAT ABOUT FOUR HOURS.

"In your lifeboat what course did she take?" the senator asked.

"We saw a light and headed for it," said Mr. Ismay.

"How long were you in this lifeboat?"

"About four hours."

"Were there any other lifeboats that you saw?"

"Yes, we hailed one," he said.

He said he saw no life rafts in the sea.

"How many lifeboats were on the Titanic?"

"Twenty altogether, I think," replied Mr. Ismay; "sixteen collapsible and four wooden boats."

"Were all the lifeboats that left the Titanic accounted for?"

"I think so; I've been told so, but I do not know of my own knowledge."

"It has been suggested," Senator Smith continued, "that two of the lifeboats sank as soon as lowered. Do you know anything about that?"

HE DID NOT SEE SHIP SINK.

"I do not. I never heard of it and I think all the lifeboats were accounted for."

"Did you see the Titanic sink?"

"I did not see the Titanic go down," Mr. Ismay said, shaking his head mournfully. "I did not want to see her go down. I was rowing in the life boat all the time until we were picked up. I turned back once after we left the vessel. I saw her green light and never turned back again. I did not want to see the end."

"Was there confusion apparent on the Titanic when you looked back?"

"I did not see any," Mr. Ismay replied.

"All I saw was the green light the last time I looked."

"After you left Captain Smith on the bridge did you see him again?"

"I did not."

"Did you have any message from him?"

"None."

"How many wireless operators were there on the Titantic?"

"I presume there were two," said Mr. Ismay. "One is always on watch."

"Did they survive?"

"I have been told one did, but I do not know whether it is true."

"Were any of the crew enlisted men in the English navy?"

"I do not know."

Mr. Ismay said he would have known if there had been an explosion on board but there was none.

In response to a question, the witness estimated the speed of the ship when she struck at 21 knots.

DENIES PICKING LIFEBOAT CREW.

Senator Smith asked the witness if he had anything to do with selecting the crew for his lifeboat.

"I did not," was the snappy reply.

"No rafts were on board because I presume they are not regarded as suitable," the witness said, "replying to a question.

"Can you tell us," Senator Smith asked, "anything about the inspection certificate that was issued for the Titanic before she sailed?"

"I know that the government inspection was thorough or the boat never could have sailed."

"Do you know whether the Titanic had its proper number of lifeboats?"

"Yes, she had; I think there were twenty boats altogether."

"Do you know whether the boat you were in was a Titanic lifeboat, or one that had been taken from some other White Star ship?"

"I did not notice the name on the oar or the boat, but I am sure it was a new lifeboat."

Turning to the construction of the ship Mr. Ismay declared the ship was especially constructed so that, with any two of the larger compartments full of water, she still would float.

"If the ship had struck head-on she probably would be afloat today," he added.

"Did any of the collapsible boats sink?"

"No, sir."

"Did you attempt to interfere with the working of the wireless on the Carpathia?"

"The captain probably will tell you I was not out of my room from the time I got into it until last night," was the reply.

As the final question to his examination, Mr. Ismay was asked what he had on when he got into the lifeboat.

"A pair of slippers, a pair of pajamas, a suit of clothes and an overcoat," he replied.

Mr. Ismay was asked to hold himself in readiness during the day for another call before the committee. Senator Smith announced it was desired to hear the captain of the Carpathia in the meantime.

Robert Hutchins, a survivor, a quartermaster on the Titanic, says that all the lifeboats on board the ill-fated vessel except two got away. One was swamped and the other, a collapsible boat, failed to open and passengers clung to it in the water, using it as a buoy.

The government's inability to get early information regarding the loss of the Titanic through the wireless outfits of the scout cruisers Chester and Salem or the naval shore stations, has confirmed the navy department in its decision to press for legislation which will enable the government to assert control over all agencies, whether private or corporate, which may seek to restrain or interfere with the government officials in such cases.

Secretary Meyer, who was one of the parties to the conference recently on the subject of wireless control, is giving the subject much attention and either from the navy department or the department of commerce and labor a bill soon will emerge which, it is hoped will be accepted by congress as a basis for action.

President Taft will not send a special message to congress urging legislation to strengthen the present laws regulating supervision of steamship clearing from American ports. The president believes congress needs no such suggestion since the Titanic disaster.

Under agreement with Great Britain, the certificate of the Titanic that she had met with the requirements of the British board of trade would have been accepted in New York and the Titanic would have been allowed to clear again. The regulations of the United States, as applied to vessels that sail under the American flag or under the flags of nations not in the agreement are strict enough to compel the carrying of life saving equipment sufficient to take care of every passenger and every member of the crew.

An act of congress nullifying the existing agreement would make it impossible for officials of the department of commerce and labor to accept a certificate from any board of trade or similar organization unless the requirements of this country were met as well. Such action by congress was regarded as probable here today.

Men supporting a woman survivor of the Titanic on coming down the gang plank of the Carpathia in New York. Posed by F. T. Charlton (on the left), Lena Allen and Selmar Romaine.

Rescued Who Perished Thrown From Lifeboats

Fearing to Weight Boats With Dead Bodies, Officers in Charge Threw Them Into Sea.

GHAVEN of Indianapolis said the Titanic was going at high speed when she struck, and that the helmsman apparently had seen the danger and put the helm over, for the boat veered to port, and struck the iceberg a glancing blow. This ripped off a large section of the plates on the starboard side and the water began to pour in.

"There was a great rush for the lifeboats as soon as it was known there was any real danger. So precipitate was this rush, that many, in apparent frenzy, jumped into the sea.

"A remarkable thing was that the lights continued to burn, although the Titanic settled lower and lower. When we were at some distance from the sinking ship, and could still see the figures of hundreds of persons on the deck at the railings, there were several explosions.

"More persons went overboard. Presently, the Titanic buckled amidships, and we could see persons sliding off into the water, both fore and aft. Then the boat settled somewhat by the bow, the lights went out and that was the last we saw of the Titanic.

"The temperature must have been below freezing, and neither men nor women in my boat were warmly clad. Several of them died. The officer in charge of the lifeboat decided it was better to bury the bodies. They were weighted so they would sink, and were put overboard. We also could see similar burials taking place from other lifeboats that were all around us.

"Of course, at that time we did not know the Carpathia was near."

Titanic Disaster Told In Figures

PASSENGERS ABOARD.	
First class	330
Second class	320
Third class	750
Total	1,400
Officers and crew	940
Grand total	2,340
SAVED BY CARPATHIA.	
First class	210
Second class	125
Third class	200
Total	535
Members of crew saved	210
Grand total saved	745
Subsequently died	6
Total lives lost	1,601

BISHOP M'GOVERN TAKEN TO HOSPITAL

Cheyenne, Wyo., April 19.—Bishop Patrick McGovern, who Wednesday was officially consecrated bishop of the diocese of Cheyenne, yesterday was taken to St. Joseph's hospital in Denver, suffering with a nervous breakdown due, it is thought, to the severe strain under which the bishop has been for several weeks.

His health has been poor for some time and the work and excitement incident to his being promoted to the position of bishop of this diocese have left him in a serious condition.

Ismay's Craven Acts Verified by Woman

Seized Seat In Lifeboat and Picked Crew to Row Him; She Says--He Keeps Mouth Shut About Episode.

New York, April 19.—"For God's sake get me something to eat. I'm starved. I don't care what it costs or what it is; bring it to me."

These were the first words uttered by J. Bruce Ismay, managing director of the White Star steamship line, when he set his foot on the deck of the Carpathia, after being "miraculously" preserved from shipwreck.

This statement, vouched for by an officer of the Carpathia, who requested that his name be withheld, is the keynote to the attitude of the millionaire ship owner who made his way to safety in one of the first lifeboats lowered.

"Mr. Ismay reached the Carpathia in about the tenth boat," said the officer. "I did not know who he was, but afterward I heard others of the crew discussing his desire to get something to eat the minute he put his foot on the rescue boat. The steward who waited on him, McGuire of London, says Ismay came dashing into the dining room and, throwing himself into a chair, gave his order for food, supplemented by a request that it be hurried."

Safely Seated He Picked Crew.

According to Mrs. W. J. Cardeza of Philadelphia, who told her story after she had arrived at the Ritz-Carlton with T. D. M. Cardeza, J. Bruce Ismay was not only safely seated in a lifeboat before it was filled, but he also selected the crew that rowed the boat.

According to Mrs. Cardeza, Mr. Ismay knew that Mr. Cardeza was an expert oarsman and he beckoned him into the boat. Mr. Cardeza manned an oar until Mr. Ismay's boat was picked up about two hours later.

Mrs. William Bucknell of Philadelphia, after telling of taking an oar in a lifeboat and rowing "till her hands were blistered," said:

"After being taken aboard the Carpathia, J. Bruce Ismay went to a cabin and remained closeted until waited upon by a committee of the survivors, who demanded that they be permitted to see him. He then appeared. One of the questions that was put to him was as to what the White Star and the International Merchant Marine companies intended doing in the way of reparation. To this Mr. Ismay replied that the company would do all in its power to make a partial repayment for the suffering of the survivors. Further than this he would say nothing."

Ismay's Lawyer Makes Statement.

Before receiving the senate investigating committee in his stateroom on the Carpathia, Ismay conferred with his lawyer, Charles C. Burlingham, who will appear for the International Mercantile Marine company at the investigation, and P. A. S. Franklin, vice president of the company, who went with the attorney to confer with Ismay, made this statement as he left the boat:

The White Star line welcomes any government inquiry, and the United States senate investigation cannot be too broad for us, and if it results in the adoption of any measures calculated to prevent the recurrence of such a disaster as the Titanic loss, the White Star line will be only too thankful. Mr. Ismay will not shirk his duty, nor will any other officer of the company. All the information the senate committee seeks will be cheerfully offered, and we will cooperate in every way possible with the committee.

Senator Smith said:

Mr. Ismay's recital to us of what happened is very, very interesting. It tends to show that the newspaper reports of this awful calamity received up to date, however wild and alarming they appear to have been, have not exaggerated the exact situation that developed when the disaster occurred.

All of the lifeboats that were used to rescue the Titanic's passengers have been saved, brought here on board the same steamer that brought the survivors, and will be used by the senate investigating committee.

Mr. Franklin, however, did not carry to the world Mr. Ismay's explanation of how he happened to be among the few men saved and one of the very first of the passengers to find his way to a lifeboat.

Senator William Alden Smith of Michigan, chairman of the senate committee, and Senator Francis G. Newlands of Nevada were in conference for two hours last night with Ismay and Franklin, but declined to give out Ismay's statement. Senator Smith said that the ship official had been frank, but that he preferred that the public "hear Mr. Ismay's statement from his own lips when he appears before the senate investigating committee."

Secretary of Commerce and Labor Nagel accompanied the senators to New York, and will be present at the hearing at the Waldorf-Astoria today.

Ismay left the Carpathia at about 11:15 o'clock last night, and went to the Cunard offices at the rear of the dock. Detectives guarded him, and only a limited number of newspaper men were permitted to see him. He was dapper in a fresh, new suit, with a Scotch cap. A statement prepared by him was read by one of the officers of the White Star line. One of the newspaper men followed with a question.

"On what boat did you leave the Titanic?" he asked.

"What do you mean? I don't know what you mean," Ismay replied.

The question was repeated.

"I left on a boat leaving from the center."

He was asked what the number of the boat was, and answered:

"The last one. I left on the starboard forward collapsible—the last boat to leave."

Will Welcome Full Inquiry.

He said regarding the collision that the Titanic hit the iceberg a glancing blow, and that she slid off, and that, in his opinion, and in the opinion of experts, she tore out a large part of her keel. He then went on to state as follows:

In the presence and under the shadow of a catastrophe so overwhelming, my feelings are too deep for expression in words. I have only to say that the White Star line, its officers and employes will do everything possible to alleviate the suffering and sorrows of the survivors and the relatives and friends of those on her who perished. The Titanic was the last word in shipbuilding. Every regulation described by the British board of trade had been rigidly complied with. The master, officers and crew were the most experienced and skillful in the British service.

I am informed that a committee of the United States senate has been appointed to investigate the circumstances of the accident. I heartily welcome the most complete and exhaustive inquiry and any aid that I or my associates or builders or navigators can render is at the service of the public and the governments of both the United States and Great Britain. Under these circumstances I must respectfully defer making a statement at this time.

One of the wealthy women among the first cabin passengers saved $750,000 in jewels by wearing them all of the time according to the insurance agreement. This shows her horrified condition as she escaped from the sinking vessel. Posed by Louise Valentine, leading woman in "Graustark."

Guggenheim Had $50,000 Insurance Written in Denver

Meyer Harrison, of Joseph H. Harrison & Company, representative of the Pennsylvania Mutual Insurance company, said today that when Benjamin Guggenheim was in Denver several years ago he took out a $50,000 insurance policy with the local firm. That amount was the limit that a person could take in one company at that time.

Two years ago Colonel Astor, Mr. Harrison was told recently in New York, paid cash for a $2,000,000 policy.

Actors Pose for Pictures of Wreck

Pictures in this issue of The Post of scenes aboard the Titanic and Carpathia and on the pier in New York were posed after telegraphic descriptions by members of the "Graustark" company, now playing at the Tabor Grand, on the stage of that theater, by courtesy of Manager Fred Andrews of the players, and Manager Peter McCourt of the theater, and the members of the company.

The thespians entered readily into the plan of The Post to depict graphically what its correspondents have written thrillingly. Among the players who posed were Miss Louise Valentine, Frank Charlton, Miss Lena Arland, Miss Ann Bert, Harry Hearn, Fred McQuirk, Paul White, Owen Williamson, Albert Edmundson and Selmar Romaine, who will be seen in the reproductions of photographs taken early this morning. The pictures were carefully posed by these experienced actors to depict as accurately as possible the stories told by the survivors.

Three panic stricken Italians who were third class passengers dashed for the lifeboats when the crash came. They were shot down by the ship's officers.

Wives were torn from their husband's arms by the ship's officers to get the women into the lifeboats, according to the press dispatches. This picture shows one of the heart-breaking scenes of this character.

Newburyport Morning Herald.

ESTABLISHED IN 1793, DAILY IN 1832
ONE HUNDRED AND TWENTIETH YEAR

NEWBURYPORT, MASSACHUSETTS, FRIDAY, APRIL 19, 1912

VOLUME CXX. NUMBER 94
PRICE ONE CENT; THREE DOLLARS A YEAR

BAND PLAYED TILL END!

Titanic Sacrifice to Speed God—Hurled Through Water at 21 Knot Clip "TO SMASH A RECORD"

LIST OF FAMOUS MEN LOST CORRECT

Astor, Butts, Hays, Stead, Straus and Others Went to Their Doom Unafraid--Six Die After Rescue

(Associated Press Despatch.)

NEW YORK, April 18—How the White Star liner Titanic, the largest ship afloat, sank off the Grand Banks of Newfoundland on Monday morning last carrying to death 1601 of the 2340 persons aboard, was told to the world in all its awful details for the first time tonight, with the arrival in New York of the Cunarder liner Carpathia, bringing the exhausted survivors of the catastrophe.

Of the great facts that stand out of the chaotic accounts of the tragedy these are the most salient:

(Continued on Page Four.)

Numbers of the Lost and Saved

(Associated Press Despatch.)

NEW YORK, APRIL 18—THE FOLLOWING TABULATION OF THE PASSENGERS AND CREW ON BOARD THE TITANIC, TOGETHER WITH THOSE SAVED AND LOST HAS BEEN COMPILED, IN A STATEMENT ISSUED BY A COMMITTEE OF PASSENGERS.

APPROXIMATE NUMBER OF PASSENGERS ON BOARD:

FIRST CLASS	330
SECOND CLASS	320
THIRD CLASS	750
Total Passengers	1400
OFFICERS & CREW	940
Total	2340

NUMBER OF PASSENGERS SAVED BY CARPATHIA:

FIRST CLASS	210
SECOND CLASS	125
THIRD CLASS	200
TOTAL	535

MEMBERS OF CREW SAVED:

OFFICERS	4
SEAMEN	39
STEWARDS	96
FIREMEN	71
TOTAL	210

TOTAL NUMBER SAVED ....745 TOTAL NUMBER PERISHED 1595

EXTRA COMING GET IT!

STORIES OF SAVED RECEIVED TO 4 A.M.

Death of Captain Smith Graphically Described--Sea Strewn With Frozen Bodies

(Associated Press Despatch.)

NEW YORK, April 19, 3:30 a. m. —George A. Draden (on the passenger list George Drayton) told of how Capt. Smith met his death. "I saw Capt. Smith, while I was in the water. He was standing on the deck all alone. Once he was swept down by a wave, but managed to get to his feet. Then as the boat sank he was again knocked down by a wave and disappeared from view."

Mrs. Churchill Candee of Washington, D. C., was taken from the Carpathia with both her legs broken. She was hurried in an ambulance to a hospital. Mrs. Candee said she was injured while getting into a lifeboat.

(MEN TAKEN FROM WATER)

Most of the men saved, she declared, were picked up from the water, having plunged overboard after the lifeboats had been launched. "Major Archibald Butts and Col. John Jacob Astor died like heroes," said Mrs. Candee. Before she could tell more of the end, however, she was hurried away.

Simon Senecal, a Montreal merchant, who was a passenger on the Carpathia, said that after the Carpathia had rescued boat-loads of women, a life-raft was seen on which were about 24 persons.

(WATER THICK WITH BODIES)

"One half of these were dead," said Mr. Senecal. "One of the Carpathia's boats went to the raft and took off the living, leaving the dead. The water was thick with bodies. The crew of the Carpathia in their work of rescue came across numerous bodies floating in the water. I know of seven instances of persons, who had been rescued, dying on board the Carpathia and being buried at sea."

(ORCHESTRA WAS HEROIC)

Of all the heroes who went to their doom when the Titanic dived to its ocean grave none, in the opinion of Miss Helen Slater, a passenger in the last boat to put off, deserved greater credit than the members of the vessel's orchestra. According to Miss Slater, the orchestra played until the last. When the vessel took its final plunge, the strains of a lively air mingled grewsomely with the cries

(Continued on Page Four.)

HERALD EXTRAS

IN CASE OF IMPORTANT NEWS during the day on the "Titanic Story" extra editions of the Morning Herald will be published

Owing to the Holiday The Herald will be the only local paper published today

Look For The Herald Extras

The Weather

Probabilities.

Today rain, followed by clearing; Saturday fair, not much change in temperature; brisk, variable winds, becoming westerly.

Midnight Conditions.

The thermometer at the Herald office at midnight registered 38 degrees, wind north and cloudy.

Miniature Almanac.

Sun rises	4:57
Sun sets	6:30
Length of day	13:33
Day's increase	4:29
High tide	12:15 a. m., 12:45 p. m.
Light Auto Lamps	7:00

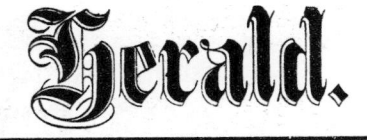

LIST OF LOST

(Continued from Page One.)

The death list has increased rather that diminished.

Six died after being rescued.

The list of prominent persons lost stand as previously reported.

Practically every woman and child, with the exception of those women who refused to leave their husbands, were saved. Among the latter was Mrs. Isidore Straus, wife of the New York millionaire banker.

The survivors in the lifeboats saw the lights of the stricken vessel glimmer to the last, heard the band playing and saw the doomed hundreds on her decks and heard their groans and cries when the vessel sank. Accounts vary as to the extent of disorder on board.

Under Orders to Speed Up.

"Not only was the Titanic carried through the April night to her doom, but she was under orders from the general officers of the line to make all the speed of which she was capable." This was the statement made tonight by J. H. Moody, a quartermaster and helmsman.

"On the night of the disaster," he said, "the ship was making 21 knots an hour and the officers were striving to live up to the orders to smash a record.

"Port Your Helm!"

"It was close to midnight," said Moody, "and I was on the bridge with the second officer, who was in command. Suddenly he shouted, 'Port your helm!' I did so, but it was too late. We struck the submerged portion of the berg."

Of the many accounts given by the passengers most of them agree that the shock, when the Titanic struck the iceberg, although it ripped her great sides as a giant can-opener would, did not greatly jar the vessel, for the blow was a glancing one along her side.

The accounts also agree substantially that when the passengers were taken off on the lifeboats that there was no serious panic and that many wished to remain on board believing her to be unsinkable.

Hulk Stood on End.

The most distressing stories are those of passengers who were in the lifeboats. These tell, not only of their own sufferings, but give harrowing details of how they saw the great hulk of the Titanic stand on end, stern uppermost before plunging to the bottom.

As this awful spectacle was witnessed by groups of survivors in the boats, they plainly saw many of those whom they had just left behind leaping from the decks into the water.

J. Bruce Ismay, managing director of the International Merchantile Marine Co., and owner of the White Star line, who was among the 70 odd men saved, P. A. S. Franklin, vice president of the White Line, and U. S. Senator William Alden Smith, chairman of the senate investigating committee, conferred aboard the Carpathia soon after the passengers had come ashore tonight.

DEATHS.

FELLOWS—In this city, April 18, 1912, Mary W. Fellows, aged 97 years, 1 month.

Mrs. John Jacob Astor, the Most Interesting Widow In America.

Mrs. John Jacob Astor, through the death of her husband in the Titanic disaster, becomes one of the world's wealthiest widows and easily the most talked of American woman. She is in her twenty-first year, tall, graceful and has brown hair. Her late husband's estate is valued at $100,000,000 Before her marriage to Colonel Astor in September last Mrs. Astor was Miss Madeleine Talmage Force. She is a daughter of William H. Force, head of a New York shipping firm.

A Dismal Scene.

The arrival of the Carpathia brought a vast multitude of people to the Cunarder's decks. They filled the vast pier shed, and overflowing for blocks, crowded nearby streets in dense throngs. Throughout it all the rain fell steadily, adding a funeral aspect to the scene.

The landing of the survivors was attended with little excitement, for the crowd stood in awed silence as groups from the ship passed along.

The docking actually began shortly after 9 o'clock and the debarking of the passengers was so quickly disposed of, owing to the waiving of the usual formalities, that practically everything had been finished by 10:30 o'clock. Crowds remained about the piers long after this to get glimpses of the steamer and to listen to the harrowing accounts of the disaster.

Physicians and nurses went aboard the Carpathia before anyone was allowed to go down the gangway, but soon after the first cabin passengers (women predominating) began descending the incline. Some walked unaided, some were assisted by their friends, relatives and nurses and some on stretchers.

Mrs. John Jacob Astor, now a widow, was met by her stepson, Vincent, and her sister, Miss Force. They hurried to a limousine and drove to the Astor town house.

The second and third class passengers did not leave the ship until 11 o'clock. They were in a sad condition. The women are without wraps and the few men wore very little clothing.

MRS. ASTOR'S STORY

(Associated Press Despatch.)

NEW YORK, April 18—Although utterly exhausted by her exposure Mrs. John Jacob Astor was said tonight by Nicholas Biddle, a trustee of the Astor estate, to be in no danger whatever. Her physician had given orders, however, that neither Mrs. Astor nor her maid, who was saved with her, be permitted to talk about the disaster.

On landing from the Carpathia the young bride, widowed by the Titanic sinking, told members of her family what she could recall of the circumstances of the disaster. Of how Col. Astor met his death she had no definite conception.

She recalled that in the confusion, as she was about to be put into one of the boats, the colonel was standing by her side. After that, as Mr. Biddle recounted her narrative, she had no very clear recollection of the happenings until the boat was well clear of the sinking steamer.

Mrs. Astor, it appeared, left in one of the large boats which got away from the ship. It was her belief that all the women to go had then been taken off. Her impression was that the boat in which she left had room for 15 more persons.

The men for some reason, as she recalled it tonight, she could not and does not now understand, did not seem to be at all anxious to leave the hip. Almost every one seemed dazed.

PARISIAN MISSED S. O. S. CALL OPERATOR HAD GONE TO BED

Titanic's Appeal For Help Unheard by Allan Liner—Cable Ship to Make Search For Bodies

HALIFAX, N. S., April 18—The Allan liner Parisian, came up last night when the weather cleared. Capt Hains can tell nothing of the Titanic disaster. He had no intimation of it till Monday morning about 4 o'clock, when he received the news from the Osian, that had taken in tow the disabled Deutschland, which the Parisian also had been trying to pick up. The only communication the Parisian had with the Titanic was on Sunday night at 10.30, when the Parisian was in touch with her about 150 miles off and had asked her to relay a message to the Allen Line in Montreal. This message was accepted and doubtless was forwarded. The Parisian's operator then went to bed and when the fateful call for help came from the Titanic not long afterward it fell on space so far as the Parisian was concerned, and the Allen liner knew nothing of the awful affair till a couple of house after it was all over, and when she was fully 150 miles west from the scene of its occurrence. which she had passed twelve hours before.

"The ships nearest to the disaster—and they were very much closer—were the Californian and the Carpathia,' said Capt. Hains. "There weer icebergs in hundreds, and when we met the Carpathia some time before we told them of the course we had come and they did the same thing for us, so that both gained."

Many cross messages were obtained afterward bearing on the disaster, but none of these were mentioned by the Parisian's master, for he said it would be a violation of the rules.

"They would add nothing, however, to what you have in the newspapers that you give me," added the captain, who declined to make any comment on the loss of the Titanic other than to say the liner could not have struck head on but sideways, inflicting much more terrible damage than the mere smashing of the forward bulkheads.

It is a remarkable thing that the only men on the Parisian who knew of the accident to the Titanic were the captain and the Marconi operator. None of the officers besides these two and not a single passenger knew that the Titanic was lost till they entered Halifax harbor and learned the tragic news. After landing passengers and cargo the Parisian proceeded to St. John.

The cable ship Minna has just arrived here. Her captain says that the wireless operator on board had received messages on Monday which told of the sinking of the Titanic.

The Minna passed 150 miles north of the scene of the wreck on her way here.

The White Star Line has charted the cable ship Mackay-Bennett to go to the scene of the wreck and look for bodies. The ship sailed from here yesterday afternoon. She will remain at sea ten days or more.

The Mackay-Bennett carries a wireless outfit and news of the finding of bodies that can be identified will be flashed to the White Star officials in New York.

Half a dozen small boats equipped with grappling irons and nets were taken for use in combing the sea for bodies.

The belief that many bodies may be found is based upon the success of a similar expedition after the wreck of the French liner La Bourgogne, which was sunk in collision off this port. Scores of bodies were picked up at sea for two weeks after that disaster.

Capt. Larnbener of the cable ship before sailing said:

"We are under charter of the White Star Company. Just as soon as any body is found and identified a wireless message will be sent to the White Star Company in New York."

WILLIAM BALCH WINS SILVER CUP IN BOWLING CONTEST AT DALTON CLUB

The bowling at the Dalton club last night for the silver cup presented by Laurence P. Dodge, contested for by the twelve having the best attendance records during the past season, resulted in the cup going to William Balch, with a handicap of 52. His total for five strings was 560. Harry Noyes, with a total of 549 and ex-Alderman Russell, with a total of 533 were the next best bowlers. Walter B. Rogers had the highest single string of 124. Three men, Jacoby, John H. Balch, Jr. and Foss were tied for sixth position at 493. Leroy Berry, the scratch man, was last, bowling far below his usual form. A collation followed the bowling. The summary:

	Handicap	1	2	3	4	5	Total
Harry Noyes	55	110	110	89	95	90	549
W. Balch	52	107	88	112	89	112	560
Russell	58	81	102	92	102	98	533
A. Berry	98	106	84	76	83	78	525
W. B. Rogers	8	124	102	89	95	106	524
Jacoby	26	94	92	93	87	101	493
J. H. Balch Jr.	49	77	85	103	91	88	493
Foss	52	82	98	100	67	94	493
Patten	71	86	80	86	86	79	488
M. B. Noyes	20	91	106	80	93	89	479
G. B. Hatch	59	80	86	86	87	79	477
Leroy Berry (scratch)		95	95	83	81	83	437

WORKING FOR THE GOOD OF THE ORDER

Deputy Supreme Governor Colburn of Pilgrim Fathers Here in Interest of Order

C. E. Colburn of Swampscott, Deputy Supreme Governor of the United Order of Pilgrim Fathers, is spending some time in this city in the interest of the order, and is working to secure an influx of new members. A fine entertainment has been arranged for the evening of Friday, April 26th, at which Supreme Governor George F. Bradstreet of Malden and Supreme Secretary Crary of Lawrence will be the speakers. There will also be orchestral and vocal music, readings, etc., and light refreshments will be provided. The event will take place at Phoenix hall.

CHANGE MEETING DATE.

The regular weekly prayer meeting of the Washington Street Methodist church has been changed from Wednesday to Friday evening. Rev. Howard Adair of Boston University the newly appointed pastor will be present and lead the meeting.

Baseball Results

American League.
Chicago 12, St. Louis 7.

National League.
Pittsburgh 4, St. Louis 3.

All other games postponed on account of rain.

World's Most Costly Carpet.

A carpet, which took three years in the making, is one of the treasures of the Gaekwar of Baroda. The carpet is only ten feet by six feet in size, but it is woven from strings of pure pearls, with a center and corner circles of diamonds. The magnificent fabric cost £200,000 ($1,000,000), and is guarded in the Mabarajah's treasure room.

What Fleet Street Wants.

The Newsboy—"Yus. lady, the only thing wot'll do us much good now is a good 'orrible murder reg'lar once a week!"—London Opinion.

MUSICALE AT THE ST. PAUL'S

Delnightful Program Rendered Under Auspices of Newburyport Musical Club

NUMBERS HEARTILY ENCORED

A delightful musicale under the auspices of the Newburyport Musical club was given at St. Paul's parish hall last evening and those present were given a rare treat. The numbers called for many encores. The artists were Carolyn Belcher, violinist; Caroline A. Hooker, soprano; accompanists, Gertrude Belcher and Louise Walker. Following is the program:

Violin solo, "Allegro Molto Apassionata"(Eiml Bernard) from suite for violin and pianoforte

Songs:
(a) "La Colomba" (Kurt Schindler)
(b) "Valzer de Musetta" La Boheme, (Puccini)

Violin solos:
(a) "EnBateau" (Debussy)
(b) "Hungarian Dance"... (Brahms-Joachim)

Song, "Ah fors' lui," La Traviata, (Verdi)

Violin solos:
(a) "Intermezzo" (Paula Szalit)
(b) "Vaggsang" (Tor Aulin)
(c) "Rondo" (Wieniawski

Songs:
(a) "Yesterday and Today" (Spross)
(b) "'Twas April" (Nevin)

Violin solo. Two movements from "Sonata in F Major" (Handel)

The executive committee who were in charge of the arrangements consisted of the following: Miss Laura Legate, Miss Abby Sawyer, Miss Alice Cummings, Miss Elsa Castelhun and Mrs. George Learned.

DUMMER TO PLAY BOSTON LATIN ON SATURDAY

The Dummer Academy nine will play against the strong Boston Latin school of Boston Saturday afternoon at South Byfield. Worcester will do the twirling.

The academy boys have put in a hard week's practice, and should show a great deal more speed than they did with St. John's "prep" of Danvers last week. A large crowd of local boys will witness the game.

ORPHEUM THEATRE CLOSED

The Orpheum theatre, which for the past two months has been running a stock company and musical comedy, closed its doors to the public yesterday afternoon. Whether it will start up again in the near future is not known.

RUNNING TIME TO PLUM ISLAND

Friday, April 19—Cars leave Market square for the Island at 7 and 11 a. m.; 1, 4 and 8 p. m.

Saturday, April 20—Cars leave Market square at 7 and 11 a. m.; 1, 4 and 8 p. m.

Sunday, April 21—Cars leave the square every haif hour from 9:30 a. m. to 5:30 p. m. fri.&sat.

G. A. R. VETERAN ILL

Warren Merrill, the G. A. R. veteran, has been confined to his home on Merrimac street with illness for the past eight weeks.

FIND TRUE BILLS AGAINST ETTOR ANDGROVANNALTI

Indicted for Conspiracy to Intimidate and Accessory Before the Fact to Murder

J. J. BREEN HELD FOR TRIAL

SalvatoreB runo Indicted for Assault With Intent to Murder Two Police Officers

Joseph J. Ettor and Artura Giovannitti, both of New York, who figured prominently as leaders in the recent Lawrence strike, were indicted by the grand jury for accessory before the fact to murder, yesterday afternoon in a partial report rendered at the afternoon session of the Superior court. A number of other important indictments were handed in, among them being John J. Breen, ex-school committeeman of Lawrence, held for intent to injure by unlawful storage of dynamite.

The morning session of court opened at 9:30, Judge Brown presiding. The following cases called were disposed of as follows:

Teeley Haggas, violating city ordinance, case filed Mary Talgier, Lawra Kowash, for the same offence, had their cases filed also.

Pedro Lassordro of Methuen, for lewdness, was fined $5.

Filemino Di Angelo, assault and battery, fined $5.

Sarah Alice, disturbance, filed.

Joanna Radsicilowicz, for intimidation, case given to the jury at noon. Several witnesses were called in this case to testify and they required the services of an interpreter.

Afternoon Session.

The afternoon session began at 2:30 and the jury returned a verdict of guilty inthe case of Frank Antefarnaro of Lawrence, charged with intimidation. He was given a fine of $100.

In the case of Richard E. Cox of Methuen, for neglect of family, the defendant pleaded guilty. He was given his freedom on condition that he pay three dollars to his wife each week.

The cas eof Mary B for assault and battery on one Lillian McGuire, was then called and was given to the jury at 4:45. A sealed verdict will be brought in Monday morning.

The grand jury then presented the following indictments:

Conspiracy to intimidation on Jan. 24, Joseph J. Ettor, 22 counts; Artura Giovannitti, 22 counts and Ettor Gianinni, 22 counts.

Conspiracy to intimidate, Jan. 30, Ettor Gianinni, 22 counts.

Accessory before the fact to murder, Joseph J. Ettor, Artura Giovannitti.

Intent to injure by unlawful storage of dynamite, John J. Breen of Lawrence.

Salvatore Bruno was indicted for an assault with intent to murder two metropolitan police officers on Feb. 26.

No bill was presented against Gildo Mazzeretta on accessory to assault with intent to murder.

Ettor Gianinni was arraigned yesterday afternoon and pleaded not guilty. He was placed under $500 bonds which had not been furnished at the close of court.

Truly Considerate.

Marie—"Is your husband considerate?" Alice—"So much so he doesn't come home at night for fear he'll wake me up."—The Sphinx.

STORIES OF SAVED

(Continued from Page One.)

of those who realized that they were face to face with Death.

(HOW ASTOR AND STEAD DIED)

One version of the death of John Jacob Astor and William T. Stead was told by Phillip Mock who, with his sister, Mrs. Paul Schabert, were among the survivors. "Many men were hanging onto rafts in the sea," said Mr. Mock. "William T. Stead, the author, and Col. John Jacob Astor clung to a raft. Their feet became frozen and they were finally compelled to release their hold. Both were drowned."

According to surgeons of the New York hospital, who were sent aboard the Carpathia after she docked, four bodies were buried at sea.

DICKENS NIGHT ENJOYED AT SOCIAL ROOMS OF THE BELLEVILLE CHURCH

At the Belleville social rooms last evening the A, B, C, D, E, and F's of the parish held a very pleasant Dickens social and all the famous characters including Bill Sykes, Mr. Pickwick and others were personated in a capable manner. Various tableaux, solos, duets and recitations made up the evening's entertainment.

BEST SINGLE STRING

"Doc" Williams and Harry Cole, who have been tied for the best single string record of 137 during the past bowling season at the Dalton club, had a roll-off last evening.

Williams scored 109 and Cole 84 on the one string bowled, the former thereby being acknowledged as the champion.

AGED RESIDENT DEAD

Miss Mary Fellows, aged 97 years, one of the oldest residents of the city, passed away at her home, 50 Federal street, yesterday forenoon. She was born in Ipswich, but had lived in this city for many years.

DIRECTORY FOR ADVERTISERS WILL BE FOUND TO-DAY ON PAGE 15, COLUMN 7.

THE NEW YORK HERALD.

THE WEATHER. Partly cloudy, followed by clearing; slightly warmer. For detailed weather report and forecast see Editorial page.

WHOLE NO. 27,633. NEW YORK, FRIDAY, APRIL 19, 1912.—TWENTY-FOUR PAGES.—[COPYRIGHT, 1912, BY THE NEW YORK HERALD COMPANY.] PRICE THREE CENTS.

THE TITANIC'S CAPTAIN SHOT HIMSELF AS THE SHIP WENT DOWN, WITH BAND PLAYING

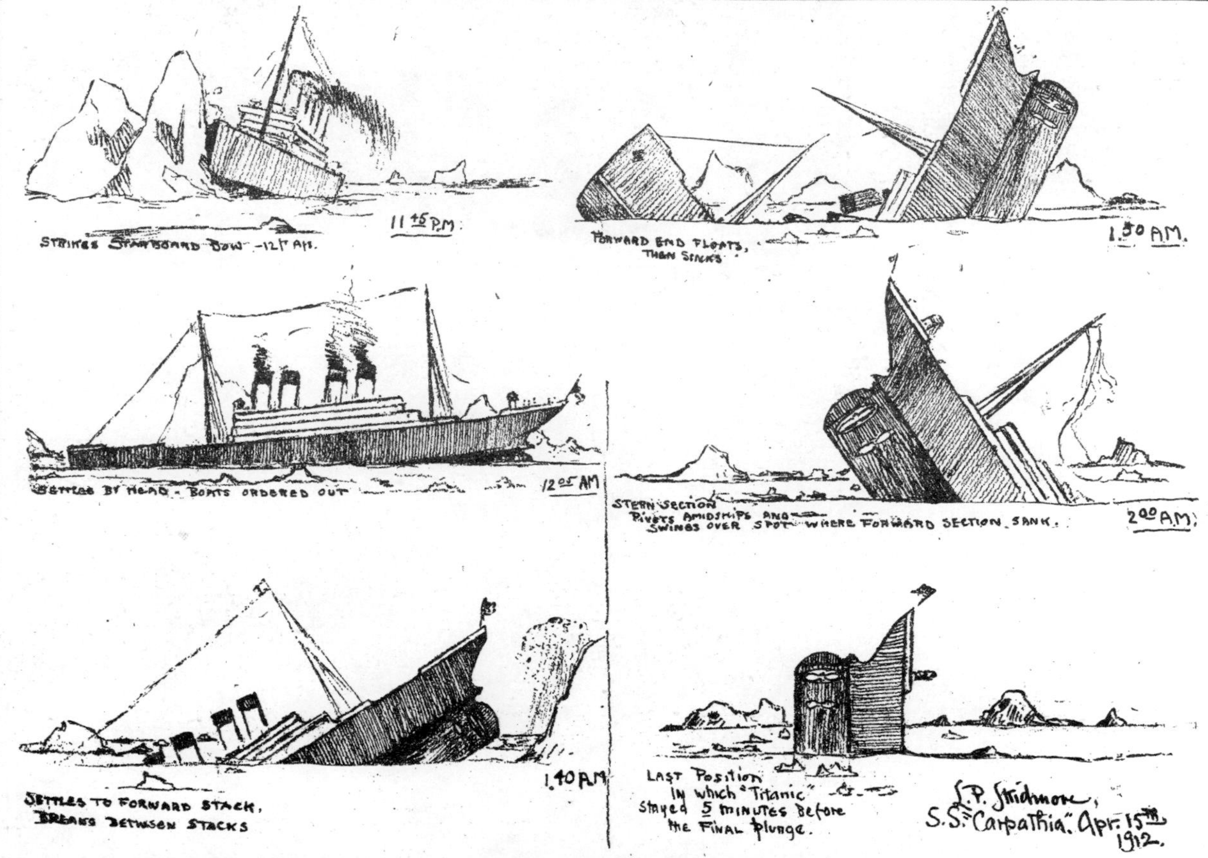

DRAWN BY PASSENGER ON BOARD THE ILL-FATED TITANIC FROM SKTECHES MADE THE MORNING OF THE WRECK.

The Carpathia Reaches This Port with 745 Survivors and Tales of Horror and Rare Heroism of Men and Women.

COLONEL ASTOR DIES AT SIDE OF MAJOR BUTT

Henry B. Harris Gallantly Left Boat for Women—Mrs. Isidor Straus Refused to Leave Husband Behind and Save Her Life.

LIFTING BABE INTO LIFEBOAT WAS CAPTAIN SMITH'S LAST ACT

Vast Throngs of Weeping Relatives of Victims at Pier When Rescue Ship Arrives Freighted with the Survivors.

FREIGHTED with her argosy of woe, disaster and death, bringing glad reunion to some, but misery unutterable to many, the Carpathia, with the survivors of the lost Titanic aboard, came back to a grief stricken city and nation at nine o'clock last night.

The story she brought home was one to crush the heart with its pathos, but at the same time to thrill it with pride in the manly and womanly fortitude displayed in the face of the most awful peril and inevitable death.

As the Titanic went down, according to the story of those who were among the last to leave her wounded hulk, the ship's band was playing. Captain Smith stood to his post calm, resolute, efficient to the last, and when all had been done that mortal man could do for the two thousand lives intrusted to his care he raised his revolver and shot himself while standing on the bridge.

Captain Fought to End Life.

The passenger who told this story of the captain's end said that he made two attempts upon his life before he succeeded, fellow officers wresting his weapon from his hand the first time as he stood in the ship's library. He then broke away and, standing at his post on the bridge, discharged the revolver into his mouth. The chief engineer, it is said, also committed suicide.

Henry B. Harris, the theatrical manager, of this city, was one of the men who showed superb courage in the crisis. When the lifeboats were first being filled, and before there was any panic or extraordinary excitement, he had been assisted into one of them at the side of his wife before the boat was lowered away.

"Women first!" shouted one of the ship's officers. Mr. Harris glanced up and saw that the remark was addressed to him.

"All right," he replied, cooly. "Goodby, my dear," he said as he kissed his wife, pressed her a moment to his breast and then climbed back to the Titanic's deck.

The night was clear and the majestic ship was steaming at a rate of eighteen knots when she struck the iceberg that sent her to the ocean bottom two thousand fathoms deep. Her hull rose on a shelf of the berg, just as has been surmised, and in so doing and in the subsequent recoil her bottom plates and her port side were badly torn and shattered, but there was no such terrific shock from the impact as might have been supposed, according to the preponderance of the evidence.

The captain and officers at once reassured the passengers, believing that there was no immediate danger. Under his encouragement many of them went back to their staterooms, and not a few calmly returned to their berths. That is said to account for the fact that many of the women were not even on deck when the imminence of their danger was realized, and scores of them were drowned in their staterooms, like rats in a trap.

Three Explosions in Boiler Room.

About one hour before the ship plunged to the bottom there were three separate explosions from the boiler rooms as the vessel filled. These were at intervals of about fifteen minutes. Until then there had been no panic and but little disorder. From that moment, however, there was a different scene. The rush for the remaining boats became a stampede.

The officers had to assert their authority by force, and three foreigners from the steerage who tried to force their way in among the women and children were shot down without mercy.

Robert Daniel, a Philadelphia passenger, tells of terrible scenes at this period of the disaster. He says men fought and bit and struck one another like madmen, and exhibits wounds upon his face to prove the assertion. Mr. Daniel says that he was picked up naked from the ice cold water and almost perished from exposure before he was rescued. He and others say that the Titanic's bow was completely torn away by the impact with the berg.

Narratives of survivors do not bear out the supposition that the final hours upon the vessel's decks were passed in darkness. They say the electric lighting plant held out until the last, and that even as they watched the ship sink from their places in the floating lifeboats her lights were gleaming in long rows as she plunged under by the head. Just before she sank, some of the refugees say, the ship broke in two abaft the engine room after the boiler explosions had occurred.

Colonel Astor a Hero.

As brought to this port last night, the total death list is placed at 1,601 and the total number of those saved at 745, the ship having had aboard, in all, 2,340 persons.

Colonel Astor was another of the heroes of the awful night. Efforts were made to persuade him to take a place in one of the lifeboats. He emphatically refused to do so until every woman and child on board had been provided for, not excepting the women members of the ship's company.

One of the passengers, describing the consummate courage of Colonel Astor's bearing, said:—

"He led Mrs. Astor to the side of the ship and helped her into the lifeboat to which she had been assigned. I saw that she protested and said that she would remain and take her chances with him. But Colonel Astor quietly insisted and tried to reassure her in a few words. As she took her place in the boat, her eyes fixed upon him, Colonel Astor smiled, touched his cap and when the boat moved away safely from the ship's side he turned back to his place among the men."

When Mrs. Astor arrived on the Carpathia last night she was still clinging to the futile hope that by some good fortune her husband had been rescued by some other vessel after her parting from him.

William T. Stead, the famous English journalist, was so little alarmed that he calmly discussed with one of the passengers the probable height of the iceberg after the Titanic had shot into it. According to this passenger, who was among those taken off in the boats, Mr. Stead, believing there was not the slightest danger of the vessel foundering, returned to his stateroom and presumably died there.

Into the last lifeboat that was launched from the ship Captain Smith, with own hands, lifted an infant into a seat beside its mother. As the gallant officer performed this final act of humanity several who were already in the boat tried to force the captain to join them, but he turned away resolutely toward the bridge.

Before the last of the boats got away, according to some of the passengers' narratives, there were more than fifty shots fired upon the decks by officers or others in the effort to maintain the discipline that until then had been well preserved.

Officers of the Carpathia report that when they reached the scene of the Titanic's wreck there were fifty bodies or more floating in the sea. Only one mishap attended the transfer of the rescued from the lifeboats to the decks of the Carpathia after they had been afloat in the open boats from eight to ten hours. One large collapsible lifeboat, in which were thirteen persons, turned turtle just as they were about to save it and all in it were lost.

No Scenes of Brutality.

Mrs. Churchill Candee, of Washington, said that she was standing close beside Mr. and Mrs. Isidor Straus when the lifeboats were being lowered. Mrs. Straus was urged to take her place in one of them, but she resolutely refused to leave her husband's side.

News Points of the Sinking of the Titanic

How Hundreds Were Saved Through Heroism and Others Went Down to Death.

The Titanic slid onto the narrow ledge of an iceberg, hung there for a brief moment and fell back into the water. Her three boilers then exploded and she began to sink.

The last thing Captain Smith did before he shot and killed himself on the bridge was to place a baby in a lifeboat.

The band on board the Titantic went down with the mighty craft playing "Nearer, My God, to Thee."

Mrs. Isidor Straus was partly dragged into a lifeboat. She refused to leave her husband to die alone, crawled back to him and died in his arms, a tragic heroine of the sea.

Henry B. Harris was placed in a lifeboat, saw a woman and child who must have died, left his place and lifted them into the boat and then went down to his death.

Colonel John Jacob Astor refused to accept a life belt, helped a dozen women and children into lifeboats, refused to get into one himself and was seen to die.

Two lifeboats were lowered almost on end and capsized as soon as they struck the water, survivors assert. All of the women and children who had been placed in them slid into the water and were drowned. The boats were found by the Carpathia floating bottom side up.

Three men were shot to death by men who prevented them from pushing women and children out of the way to save themselves. The men who did the shooting died.

More than one hundred of the Titanic's passengers were blown to atoms by the force of the explosion of her boilers. A hundred others were maimed and tossed into the water.

Passengers declare they saw Chief Officer Wilde shoot himself and that his body fell into the sea.

Officers stood at the lifeboats, revolvers in hand, enforcing the rule of the sea:—"Women and children first."

R. W. Daniels, a banker, of Philadelphia, declares four boats were launched with women and children that were not accounted for in the lists of those survivors brought in by the Carpathia.

Mrs. Candee and many other survivors agreed that they had witnessed no scenes of brutality over the departure of the boats. There was no fighting, they said, and order and discipline were well maintained up to the time the last of the lifeboats dropped away.

Of the men who were among the rescued, many of the survivors said, the majority had been picked out of the water and some of them afterward died from exposure. Three were burried at sea the day after the disaster and two more on the following day. Others gave a somewhat different version of the reason why men were among the women and children brought safely to shore, while hundreds of other women were lost. These say that at first the panic had been allayed by the officers' assurances that there was no immediate danger. Many of them had returned to their staterooms and had gone to bed. They were not on deck when some of the lifeboats received their quota of passengers and were sent away.

Passengers denied reports that there had been explosions immediately following the collision with the iceberg. The only explosion that occurred, they say, was that of the boilers about half an hour after the shock, when the engine rooms had filled with water.

If a desperate naval battle had been fought in New York waters and the city awaited the coming of the dead and wounded from the scene of action, West street could hardly have presented a more realistic picture of war's horrors than that of which the Chelsea piers were the centre and a frenzied mob of twenty thousand persons were the setting.

Weeping Throng at Pier.

The uniforms of two hundred nurses and Red Cross attaches mingled in the picture with the trim garbs of the ambulance surgeons and the chaste costumes of sad faced sisters of charity. Ten score city policemen guarded the roped cordon, lighted up at intervals with green lanterns, whereby the guardians of the city's peace kept back at a distance of seventy-five feet the throng that kept pressing over eagerly toward the pier as the Carpathia was warped into her berth.

Within the shelter of the pier sheds were huddled nearly a thousand of the friends and relatives of the rescued and the lost. To them had been issued special passes. Many of them were weeping and sobbing without restraint.

Outside, in the murk and drizzle of the forbidding night, stood ominous lines of ambulances, to which nearly all the hospitals in the city had contributed their quota. There were black, funereal vehicles from the shops of the undertakers, too, conveying their own grim message, and the city Coroners were there, ready to do their work.

While the long lines of wounded were being tenderly borne ashore at pier 54, where the Carpathia was berthed, the adjoining pier 56 had been converted into an improvised hospital ward, to which the injured were taken for treatment. There were installed all the suggestive paraphernalia of cots, stretchers, operating tables and surgical appliances, while skilled nurses with deft fingers were preparing bandages for ready use.

It was, in truth, a wartime scene, relieved only by one lighter touch. Parked outside the enclosed space in West street, among the ambulances and death wagons, were sixty or more trimly uphol-

HEARTRENDING SCENES AS THE CARPATHIA LANDS HER RESCUED

SURVIVING PASSENGERS OF THE TITANIC ON BOARD THE CARPATHIA, THE CALIFORNIAN STANDING BY.

THE TITANIC'S BOATS FILLED WITH RESCUED.

stered automobiles. In these many of the scions of New York's best known families had gone to the "front" bent on their sad missions of condolence or succor.

Major Butt Calm to Last.

Throughout the entire section of which the new Chelsea piers are the focus ordinary street traffic was wholly suspended and held rigidly in check by Inspector McClusky's lines of police reserves, who stood like sentinels guarding the reservation selected for some great field hospital.

In one of the handsomest of the waiting automobiles Vincent Astor, the son of Colonel John Jacob Astor, had arrived. When Mrs. Astor was carried ashore, apparently grievously ill, she was hurried into the machine with the young man and driven away under the escort of physicians and nurses. Several of the rescued said that as they left the sinking ship they had seen Colonel Astor and Major Butt, the military aid of the President, standing together on the deck of the doomed ship. Mrs. Astor had been forced into one of the lifeboats in a condition of almost complete prostration, but she revived in time to look up from the lifeboat as it swung away from the Titanic. She saw several men struggling in the water near by and cried out, urging that the boat put back and pick them up.

Almost at the same moment Mrs. Astor, who until then had supposed her husband had been rescued also, thought she saw him still standing on deck. Again she cried out, stretching her arms toward him, but other passengers in the boat insisted that it pull away in time to escape the danger from suction when the leviathan should go down. With a cry Mrs. Astor fell forward in a faint.

Senators Go Aboard.

Members of the Senatorial Investigating Committee went aboard the Carpathia as soon as she was berthed. They found J. Bruce Ismay in the hands of a physician and surgeon. After two conferences, each of which lasted half an hour, Senator Smith and his colleagues succeeded in exacting from Mr. Ismay his personal promise that he will attend to-day a session of the federal subcommittee to be held at the Waldorf-Astoria.

Mr. Ismay said that he left the ship in the last of the lifeboats that got away and did not see the Titanic sink. The latest evidence is to the effect that the great empress of the seas struck the iceberg at fifty minutes past eleven o'clock Sunday night, instead of at twenty minutes past ten, and that she sank about two and one-half hours later.

Five of those rescued died afterward from exposure and the hardships they had undergone. Two hundred members of the crew were among the saved, as was also the third officer.

THE TITANIC'S LIFE BOATS ON BOARD THE CARPATHIA

TITANIC SEAMEN AND RESCUED PASSENGER ON BOARD THE CARPATHIA.

With such energy did representatives of the federal government begin their task of inquiry that for a time it looked as though an impromptu race had developed between the Carpathia and the Congressional Limited from Washington, to see which could reach New York city first. Acting upon a decision taken only half an hour before, the members of the Senatorial committee, to whom the investigation of the Titanic disaster had been intrusted on Wednesday, took the fast train in the hope of reaching this city in time to board the rescue ship and there lose no time in serving subpoenas upon such witnesses as they might desire to summon to the capital.

For that purpose the committeemen brought with them the sergeant-at-arms of the Senate and one of his deputies. On the arrival of Senator Smith, of Michigan, and his colleagues on the Congressional Limited they established headquarters at the Waldorf-Astoria and lost no time in getting down to business.

Notice had been served previously in due form upon the White Star officers in New York that the federal committee would demand especially the presence of J. Bruce Ismay and other officers of the company, as well as survivors of the Titanic's crew.

After J. Bruce Ismay.

There had been widely published a report earlier in the day to the effect that Mr. Ismay had arranged to be transferred to the outbound steamship Cedric, without coming to New York at all. For that reason the committee asked of the company's officers an absolute assurance that Mr. Ismay would be produced.

"Will Mr. Ismay appear voluntarily before the Senate investigating committee?" P. A. S. Franklin, vice president of the White Star company, was asked late in the afternoon.

"So far as I know, he will," Mr. Franklin replied. "I cannot speak for him, of course, but I can say that everybody connected with the White Star line will aid the committee in every possible way."

Mr. Franklin added that the company probably would issue a formal statement to-day, following the immediate investigation to be made under its own auspices.

Up to the time of the Carpathia's actual arrival at her pier the sphinxlike slience observed by her wireless operators, so far as regarded any details of the Titanic's death blow and the scenes that followed it, had been unbroken. So strict was the censorship that had been apparently imposed by persons high in authority that scores of messages of eager inquiry were unanswered, if not ignored.

President Taft, almost prostrated by the probable death of his military aid, Major Butt, and other close friends, was no more fortunate than the most obscure inquirer. To the scout cruisers Salem and Chester the funeral ship, steaming slowly over fog blanketed seas, heavily freighted with her cargo of suffering, agony and despair, yielded no word of information. Silent as death itself she plodded on through slanting rain and darkening skies, refusing to break the seal upon her grim story until she had brought it in all its unspeakable horror back to the home port.

Scout Cruisers Baffled.

Early in the chill, dispiriting day—a day throughout all the hours of which leaden and weeping skies seemed in sympathy with the gloomy event—this significant silence from the ship whose progress an impatient world was watching was interpreted as the worst of omens. It had prepared the city and the country in some measure for revelations that followed.

The fast scout vessels of the navy abandoned the futile effort to glean some details before the noon hour. Early in the morning the commander of the Salem sent to Washington a wireless report by way of the Brooklyn Navy Yard in which he said:—

"Can get no information from Carpathia of any kind. Although she is within easy radio communication, and sometimes acknowledges calls, she will not admit receipt of message or make reply. Cannot believe that she has failed to understand the messages I have sent. She is within easy range of the torpedo station (Newport, R. I.), so the Salem will go to Bradford (naval coaling station in Narragansett Bay) this afternoon."

To the homecoming refugees New York extended a great city's welcoming arms. It opened its hospitals and its relief stations. It clipped the red tape of all its immigration and customs regulations and it extended alike its sheltering arms and its open purse to the suffering and the destitute. Within a few hours its citizens had contributed $35,000 to two relief funds.

Relief Comes Promptly.

In response to the Mayor's appeal $24,547 was sent to his office, the largest single contribution being $10,000 from J. P. Morgan & Co. Andrew Carnegie forwarded his check for $5,000. The Women's Relief Committee, of which Mrs. Nelson Herrick Henry is chairman, raised nearly $10,000.

Nearly every hospital in the city had volunteered to care for the ill and injured to the extent of their capacity. Battalions of physicians, surgeons and trained nurses were at the pier ready for duty and eager to be set to work. Fifteen members of the Women's Relief Committee met the stricken, forlorn and destitute steerage passengers as they were disembarked and sent them to snug lodgings in the care of sympathetic friends. It was a night of dire need and unspeakable sadness, but it was a night when the Good Samaritan was something more than a Scriptural legend.

Not long before the Carpathia arrived a committee from the New York Stock Exchange brought to the pier $20,000 in cash to be distributed among those most in need of immediate assistance. The money had been raised by popular subscription within a few hours, and it was taken to the Cunard pier unostentatiously in a big box and in bills of various convenient denominations. The committee was composed of E. H. Thomas, president of the Exchange; Charles Nobloch, H. N. Baruch, Charles Holsdoner and J. Carlisle. Surveyor Henry assigned to their use the little branch customs pavilion on the pier.

In the huge Pennsylvania Railroad station a special train stood waiting to carry immediately to their friends in Philadelphia such of the survivors as might desire to go there.

BAND PLAYED BEFORE THE TITANIC SUNK

Some of the crew at the pier said that difficulty was experienced in lowering the lifeboats from the davits. They said there was a patent device that should have released the boats quickly, but the men seemed to be unfamiliar with the davits and much time was consumed before the first lifeboat was lowered to the sea. This device was said to be a recent invention.

They said that following the crash with the iceberg there was gerat confusion on the Titanic and officers and crew hastened among the terrified passengers trying to allay their fears.

The band was quickly summoned and ragtime airs were played. The music seemed to have little effect on the passengers. When it was seen that the Titanic was doomed and that many of the men, women and children would go down with the ship, the band played "Nearer My God to Thee."

Colonel Gracie, Last Man Saved, Had Gone Down with the Titanic

Army Officer Tells of Mrs. Straus Refusing to Leave Her Husband—Both Ingulfed by Sea That Swept Deck as the Steamship Sank.

Colonel Archibald Gracie, U. S. A., the last man saved, went down with the vessel but was picked up. He was met last night by his daughter, who had arrived from Washington, and his son-in-law, Paul N. Fabricius.

Colonel Gracie told a remarkable story of personal hardship and denied emphatically the reports that there had been any panic on board. He praised in the highest terms the behavior of both the passengers and crew and paid a high tribute to the heroism of the women passengers.

"Mrs. Isidor Straus," he said, "went to her death because she would not desert her husband. Although he pleaded with her to take her place in the boat she steadfastly refused, and when the ship settled at the head the two were engulfed by the sea that swept her."

Colonel Gracie told of how he was driven to the topmost deck when the ship settled and was the sole survivor after the sea that swept her just before her final plunge had passed.

"I jumped with the sea," said he, "just as I often have jumped with the breakers at the seashore. By great good fortune I managed to grasp the brass railing on the deck above, and I hung on by might and main. When the ship plunged down I was forced to let go and I was swirled around and around for what seemed to be an interminable time. Eventually I came to the surface to find the sea a mass of tangled wreckage.

"Luckily I was unhurt, and casting about managed to seize a wooden grating floating near by. When I had recovered my breath I discovered a larger canvas and cork life raft which had floated up. A man whose name I did not learn was struggling toward it from some wreckage to which he had clung. I cast off and helped him to get on to the raft and we then began the work of rescuing those who had jumped into the sea and were floundering in the water.

"When dawn broke there were thirty of us on the raft, standing knee deep in the icy water and afraid to move lest the cranky craft be overturned. Several unfortunates, benumbed and half dead, besought us to save them and one or two made an effort to reach us, but we had to warn them away. Had we made any effort to save them we all might have perished.

"The hours that elapsed before we were picked up by the Carpathia were the longest and most terrible that I ever spent. Practically without any sensation of feeling because of the icy water, we were almost dropping from fatigue. We were afraid to turn around to see whether we were seen by passing craft, and when some one who was facing astern passed the word that something that looked like a steamship was coming up, one of the men became hysterical under the strain. The rest of us, too, were nearing the breaking point."

Colonel Gracie denied with emphasis that any men were fired upon and declared that only once was a revolver discharged.

"This was for the purpose of intimidating some of the steerage passengers," he said, "who had tumbled into a boat before it was prepared for launching. This shot was fired in the air, and when the foreigners were told that the next would be directed at them they promptly returned to the deck. There was no confusion and no panic."

Contrary to the general expectation, there was no jarring impact when the vessel struck, according to the army officer. He was in his berth when the vessel smashed into the submerged portion of the berg and was aroused by the jar.

"Before I retired," said Colonel Gracie, "I had a long chat with Charles H. Hays, president of the Grand Trunk Railroad. One of the last things Mr. Hays said was this:—'The White Star, the Cunard and the Hamburg-American lines are devoting their attention and ingenuity in vieing one with the other to attain the supremacy in luxurious ships and in making speed records. The time will soon come when this will be checked by some appalling disaster.' Poor fellow, a few hours later he was dead!"

"The conduct of Colonel John Jacob Astor was deserving of the highest praise," Colonel Gracie declared. "Colonel Astor," he said, "devoted all his energies to saving his young bride. He helped us in our efforts to get her into the boat. I lifted her into the boat, and as she took her place Colonel Astor requested permission of the second officer to go with her for her own protection.

"'No, sir,' replied the officer, 'not a man shall go on a boat until the women are all off.' Colonel Astor then inquired the number of the boat, which was being lowered away, and turned to the work of clearing the other boats and in reassuring the frightened and nervous women."

PASSENGERS TELL THRILLING TALES OF HEROISM AND HORROR

"I Left in Last Boat" Is Mr. Ismay's Statement

Was Awakened by Crash, Says Head of White Star Line, Who Declares He Did Not See Vessel Sink.

HE ASSERTS THERE WAS NO DISORDER

J. Bruce Ismay described to a HERALD reporter how the catastrophe occurred.

"I was asleep in my cabin," said Mr. Ismay, "when the crash came. It woke me instantly. I experienced a sensation as if the big liner were sliding up on something.

"We struck a glancing blow, not head on, as some persons have supposed. The iceberg, so great was the force of the blow, tore the ship's plates half way back, I think, although I cannot say definitely. There was absolutely no disorder.

"I left in the last boat. I did not see the Titanic sink. I cannot remember how far away the lifeboat in which I was had been rowed from the ship when she sank."

Mr. Ismay began his interview by reading a prepared statement, to this effect:—

"In the presence and under the shadow of so overwhelming a tragedy I am overcome with feelings too deep for words. The White Star line will do everything humanely possible to alleviate the sufferings of the survivors and of the relatives of those who were lost.

"The Titanic was the last word in ship building. Every British regulation had been complied with and her masters, officers and crew were the most experienced and skillful in the British service.

"I am informed that a committee of the United States Senate has been appointed to investigate the accident. I heartily welcome a most complete and exhaustive inquiry as the company has absolutely nothing to conceal and any aid that my associates or myself, our ship builders or navigators can render will be at the service of both the United States and the British governments."

"How soon did she sink after she struck?" Mr. Ismay was asked.

"Let me see, it was two hours and twenty-five minutes, I think. Yes, that is right."

"In other words, there would have been ample time to have taken everybody off if there had been enough life boats?" he was asked.

"I do not want to talk about that now," was the reply.

"Did you go off in the first boat?" some one asked.

"What do you mean?"

"Were you in the first boat that left the ship?"

"No," he replied, slowly and firmly, "I was not. I was in the last boat. It was one of the forward boats."

"Did the captain tell you to get in the boat?"

"No."

"What was the captain doing when you last saw him?"

"He was standing on the bridge."

"It is not true that he committed suicide?"

"No, I heard nothing of it."

Mr. Ismay was asked to explain the delay in the sending of news of the wreck from the Carpathia. He said:—

"I can't say anything about that now except that I sent the first telegram announcing what had happened to Mr. Franklin about eleven o'clock on the morning that we were picked up. I am told that that telegram did not reach its destination here until yesterday."

In response to requests for more details Mr. Ismay said:—

"I must refuse to say more until tomorrow, when I appear before the Congresional committee."

Says Mr. Ismay on Being Saved Demanded Food at Any Cost

Officer of the Carpathia Declares White Star Line Chief Reached That Ship in About the Tenth Lifeboat.

"For God's sake get me something to eat. I'm starved. I don't care what it costs or what it is. Bring it to me."

This was the first statement made by J. Bruce Ismay, directing head of the White Star line, one of the few men rescued from the Titanic, a few minutes after he was landed on board the Carpathia. It is vouched for by an officer of the Carpathia who requested that his name be withheld. This officer gave to the HERALD one of the most complete stories of what happened aboard the Carpathia from the time she received the Titanic's appeal for assistance until she landed the survivors at the Cunard line pier.

"Mr. Ismay reached the Carpathia in about the tenth lifeboat," said the officer. "I didn't know who he was, but afterward I heard the others of the crew discussing his desire to get something to eat the minute he put his foot on deck. The steward who waited on him, McGuire, from London, says Mr. Ismay came dashing into the dining room and throwing himself in a chair, said:—'Hurry, for God's sake, and get me something to eat; I'm starved. I don't care what it costs or what it is; bring it to me.'

"McGuire brought Mr. Ismay a load of stuff and when he had finished it, he handed McGuire a two dollar bill. 'Your money is no good on this ship,' McGuire told him. 'Take it,' insisted Mr. Ishmay, shoving the bill in McGunre's hand.' I am well able to afford it. I will see to it that the boys of the Carpathia are well rewarded for this night's work.' This promise started McGuire making inquiries as to the identity of the man he had waited on. Then we learned that he was Mr. Ismay. I did not see Mr. Ismay after the first few hours. He must have kept to his cabin.

"The Carpathia received her first appeal from the Titanic about midnight. According to an officer of the Titanic, that vessel struck the iceberg at twenty minutes to twelve o'clock and went down for keeps at nineteen minutes after two o'clock. I turned in on Sundaly night a few minutes after twelve o'clock. I hadn't closed my eyes before a friend of the chief steward told me that Captain Rostron had ordered the chief steward to get out 3,000 blankets and to make preparations to care for that many extra persons. I jumped into my clothes and was informed of the plight of the Titanic. By that time the Carpathia was going at full speed in the direction of the Litanic."

"The entire crew of the Carpathia were assembled on deck and were told of what had happened. The chief steward, Harry Hughes, told them what was expected of them.

"'Every man to his post and let him do his full duty like a true Englishman,' he said. 'If the situation calls for it, let us add another glorious page to British history.'

"After that every man saluted and went to his post. There was no confusion. Everything was in readiness for the reception of the survivors before two o'clock. Only one or two of the passengers were on deck, one of them, Mr. Beachler, having been awakened by a friend, and the other because of inability to sleep. Many of the Carpathia's passengers slept all through the morning up to ten o'clock, and had no idea of what was going on.

"We reached the scene of the collision about four o'clock. All was black and still, but the mountain of ice just ahead told the story. A flare from one of the lifeboats some distance away was the first sign of life. We answered with a rocket, and then there was nothing to do but wait for daylight.

Saved in Evening Dress.

"The first lifeboat reached the Carpathia about half-past five o'clock in the morning, and the last of the sixteen boats was unloaded before nine o'clock. Some of the lifeboats were only half filled, the first one having but two men and eleven women, when it had accommodations for at least forty. There were few men in the boats. The women were the gamest lot I have ever seen. Some of the men and women were in evening clothes, and others among those saved had nothing on but night clothes and raincoats.

"As soon as they were landed on the Carpathia many of the women became hysterical, but on the whole they behaved splendidly. Men and women appeared to be stunned all day Monday, the full force of the disaster not reaching them until Tuesday night. After being wrapped up in blankets and filled with brandy and hot coffee, their first thoughts were for their husbands and those at home. Most of them imagined that their husbands had been picked up by other vessels and they began ooding the wireless rooms with messages. We knew that those who were not on board the Carpathia had gone down to death, and this belief was confirmed Monday afternoon when we received a wire from Mr. Marconi himself asking why no news had been sent.

"We knew that if any other vessel could by any chance have picked them up it would have communicated with land. After a while, when the survivors failed to get any answer to their queries, they grew so restless that Captain Rostron posted a notice that all private messages had been sent and that the wireless had not been used to give information to the press, as had been charged. Little by little it began to dawn on the women on board, and most of them guessed the worst before they reached here. I saw Mrs. John Jacob Astor when she was taken from the lifeboat. She was calm and collected. She kept to her stateroom all the time, leaving it only to attend a meeting of the survivors on Tuesday afternoon.

DOUBT OVER WHAT PERISHING ENDURED

Survivors having told the story of the wreck of the Titanic and also the sufferings of those who perished, there still remained a question to be answered regarding those who may have floated out to sea on spars or rafts. How long could they endure the low temperature which prevailed and how long could they live partly submerged, in the ice filled water about the place of the wreck?

Easy as this question seemed to be for a medical man to answer, from the layman's point of view, there were few specialists in the city who cared to talk on the subject, some frankly admitting that they did not know, others that they would have to consult authorities and make some experiments before they would venture an opinion on the subject. The only professional man who had some definite and interesting opinions on the subject was Dr. James J. Walsh, of No. 110 West Seventy-fourth street, and he was able to speak upon the subject because it has presented itself to him in some of the articles he has written on questions touching the one brought up by this accident.

From all the answers it is plain that here is a new subject for the scientists to pursue. It is a subject for the physiologist, no the general practitioner. Yet even the physiologists could not answer the question, but they gave reasons. How long a person can live in water of a temperature of thirty or forty degrees depends upon a number of conditions, they said—the vitality of the individual to begin with, how active he is in the water, that is, whether he struggles or attempts to swim, and also whether or not he retains full consciousness.

In persons who have fainted the respiration required is very low, and they could be brought back to life again after submerison for o much longer period than those who did not faint. The nature of the accident, in the opinion of those who discussed it yesterday, was such that, although there was reason for them to faint before they fell into the sea, there is every reason to believe that the shock of the plunge into the water resuscitated them again.

In the case of drowning, when the air has been shut off from the lungs, which is what happens, for a period of say five minutes, the heart does not recover. In the human body, however, according to the explanations given by the physiologists, there is a constant struggle to ward off the effects of both cold and heat. A man may live in a temperature as high as one hundred and twenty degrees, but the temperature of his body does not rise above niety-eight degrees. He also can live in very low temperature, as explorers have proved, but the temperature of the body does not change. How long they can resist these unnatural conditions from without depends upon the vitality of the individual, and that is the reason which the physicians gave why they could not answer the question definitely.

From these deductions it becomes plain that if the stories which were told by the survivors last night are to be supplemented by individual survivors on rafts and spars hereafter, it will depend upon how strong the sufferers were to resist the cold that prevailed. That it was cold one of the survivors answered like this, last night:—

"It was so cold that we almost perished."

BAND PLAYED 'NEARER, MY GOD, AS THE TITANIC SANK, CRIES OF LOST MINGLING WITH MUSIC

Miss May Birkhead, of the Carpathia, Tells of Finding of Survivors.

NO PANIC AT FIRST

Women Believed They Were Leaving Husbands Only for a Short Time in Lifeboats.

MISS MAY BIRKHEAD

Raft of Chairs Carried Twenty-Seven and Nineteen Lost Before Big Vessel Came.

AN ANGEL FROM HEAVEN

Mental and Physical Suffering in a Night of Horror Continues After Rescue Is Accomplished.

BY MAY R. BIRKHEAD, ONE OF THE CARPATHIA'S EYE WITNESSES.

It was half-past four on the morning of Monday, April 15, when I was awakened by much rushing around of hasty footsteps on deck above, just over my head. I got out and on deck by five and was greeted with a most beautiful sight of icebergs on every side—some of much greater dimensions than the ship, and then some baby ones—all beautiful white in the calm sea and glittering sun, a most impressive view, but one that turned from gorgeous beauty to sickening pangs when I learned the great disaster one had caused.

The sea was dotted with tiny lifeboats from the Titanic, and much to my amazement there was one at our side and our sailors were pulling the passengers up onto our deck with ropes. Some were so cold it was impossible for them to climb the ladders, and had to be put in bags to be hauled up. Then I heard one, then another woman calling for her husband—husbands who have never yet appeared.

One gentleman (Titanic passenger) told me that he was in the smoking room of the Titanic at quarter to twelve when he felt the shock of the big ship as if it had run against something, but he thought little of it—in fact, he thought so little of it that he went to his room to retire. He was ready for bed, but hearing increasing noises he dressed with his room mates, who had been awakened by the jar but thought nothing of it, and went out to see what it was all about, having no idea that anything serious had happened.

Realized Danger Slowly.

They went on deck and found that boats were being lowered. This was before the extent of the catastrophe was even guessed. The seamen were really having difficulty filling the lifeboats, because no one had any idea that the ship would sink. A lifeboat was being lowered only about half filled, and as there were no more women close around these men got in as it was swung off the ship and out to sea. They received orders from the captain to row out until the lowest row of lights were hidden by the waves from observers in the boat.

Mrs. —ark, of Los Angeles, told me that she had just gotten into her bed when she felt this sudden jar and heard the engine's immediate stop with a deathlike stillness. Thinking the engine was panting, she listened to hear it take up again. At that moment she looked at her window, the Titanic having huge windows instead of portholes, and instead of seeing the blackness of the night she saw a perfectly white background. She got up very calmly and not at all frightened and went to the window, and as far as she could see she saw this huge white thing. She had no thought of an iceberg—the thing was so huge she thought it a tremendous ship with its white bow at the window. She then went to her bathroom, climbed up on her tub and put her head out the porthole and there was nothing to be seen, which shows the rapidity with which the ship must have passed the huge white thing after it was hit.

Side and Bottom Torn.

From this account it evidently hit the ship a little to the side of the front and then scraped along tearing the bottom and side entirely out. After looking out this porthole this woman started back to bed, thinking the damage would be easily and soon repaired, but just then the steward came and told her to put on a life preserver and warm clothes and go out on deck. She did so, not at all willingly, as she had such explicit confidence in the Titanic and much preferred risking her life to that ship instead of a small lifeboat. This seems to have been the general feeling. Nobody believed the boat could sink, as it had been pronounced absolutely non-sinkable by the Board of Trade of the English government.

There was absolutely no panic in getting into the lifeboats. The women, of course, were put in first. They kissed their husbands goodby, thinking they were going out to sea for a short time only by way of precaution and would return as soon as the ship was righted. This woman whom I speak of was so perfectly sure of returning that she scarcely had a thought of her husband coming, too, and he did not offer to come. After her boat was put out at sea she could see that they had to row rapidly to get away from the ship. She realized then and only then that the ship was sinking and the suction would be great and they would have to row fast to get away from it.

In the meantime some of the men had grown frightened, and not being allowed to get into the lifeboats until the women were saved had jumped from the ship and were swimming for the lifeboats. The women who had left husbands, on seeing this, wanted to go back for them, but others wanted to row hard to get away from being sucked in by the ship with their own lives.

There were only sixteen lifeboats—not nearly enough to accommodate half the passengers, so at the very best there must have been some heartsickening scenes among the men, when they discovered there was nothing in which they could put to sea. They simply had to go down with the ship.

Made Raft of Chairs.

There was one bunch of twenty-five men and two women who made a raft of chairs and any pieces of wood that they could find. Only eight of these souls reached the Carpathia.

One of the women died from the cold and exposure. The other woman reached the Carpthia almost frozen to death. She had only her nightgown and a coat to cover her and had been standing in that icy water up to her knees for five hours.

There were 710 persons rescued by this ship, four or five of whom died since we turned toward New York. Besides the sixteen lifeboats there were two canvas collapsible boats, one of which reached us among the first of the boats. The other cannot be accounted for. Supposedly it was either capsized, was lost or picked up by another ship later in the day.

The Carpathia must have been anchored very near the actual spot of the sinking of the Titanic, as there was much débris floating around us and we were very close to a number of icebergs.

Not One Vestige of Wreck.

Not one vestige of the Titanic could be seen when the Carpathia came into sight of the lifeboats at dawn—not even one mast sticking up as might have been expected. That nonsinkable boat was entirely out of view in just those two and one-half hours.

I had it from the wireless operator on board the Carpathia that he received the "C. Q. D." message at twenty minutes after eleven o'clock New York time, and the marvellous part of it is that in five more minutes he would not have received the message at all, as he was just going to bed and was ready to turn off the instrument.

Mr. Ismay "Pitiable Sight."

Among the rescued ones who came on board the Carpathia was the president of the White Star line, Mr. Ismay, who naturally feels the loss most keenly, and a pitiable sight he was—hatless, as they all were, but with Romeo slippers and pajamas on and an overcoat.

I am told that the lookout of the Titanic, who is on board the Carpathia, now says he signalled the bridge that icebergs were ahead, and there was no response. It was alleged that there was no officer on the bridge at the time, but this is not authentic and scarcely seems possible. I am also told that Captain Smith, of the Titanic shot himself with a pistol as the ship was going down.

On the other hand, I have heard it contradicted, and it is said he went down with the ship, as did the second officer. The second officer, Lightoller by name, had the most wonderful escape of which I have yet heard. He actually went down with the ship and was blown out by an explosion, which occurred after the ship had sunk with tremendous force. After going down the second time he was blown near a raft of men, and as he was being pulled on the raft he was struck by some funnel part of the ship which had been blown out and was knocked off the raft. Then he was pulled on again and is here to tell the tale.

From all I can gather the truth of the Titanic seems to be that it was not completed. It seems that the workmen were pushed very hard to start her on the day she was booked and consequently left numerous little things undone. For instance, the lifeboats were not supplied as they should have been with food and brandy and such necessities, and one can realize what horror might have been added to the already too great disaster had our ship not received the "C Q D" message, it being the only ship that did receive the message. Those people would have been left to drift the seas in hunger and to reach their death through starvation.

Cries for Help Harrowing.

These poor souls say after leaving the Titanic in the lifeboats that the cries for help of those left to go down were the most harrowing. They will never forget them as long as they live if they live for a thousand years, and some can't sleep at night for hearing those awful cries.

Here Is Our Estimate.

Those saved from the Titanic by the Carpathia were:—

First class	220
Second class	120
Third class	160
Crew	210
Total	710

The total crew on board the Titanic was 900.

Circled About the Scene.

I am told the band was playing as the big ship went down, and when last heard it was playing "Nearer, my God, to Thee."

Sir Duff Gordon with his wife, Lady Duff Gordon, and her maid and two oarsmen were among the first to be taken on board the Carpathia from a small boat containing only those five persons. They seemed to have had really the easiest time of all with life.

Survivors Watch New Boats.

There are several children on board, who have lost their parents—one baby of eleven months with a nurse, who coming on board the Carpathia with the first boat, watched with eagerness and sorrow for each incoming boat, but to na avali. The parents had gone down.

There is a woman in the second class cabin who lost seven children out of ten, and there are many other losses quite as horrible. Such a loss of life has never before been known on the sea and who is to be blamed can scarcely be told. All seems to have been done that could have been on board the Titanic after she started to sink. The explicit confidence of her passengers seems to have been their undoing. I have not yet found anyone among these rescued ones who was frightened when they started out to sea in the small boats or who had a thought of its being anything but a temporary arrangement.

The work of the crew on board the Carpathia in rescuing was most noble and remarkable, and these four days that the ship has been over crowded with its 710 extra passengers, could not have been better handled. The stewards have worked with undying strength—although one was overcome with so much work and died and was put to his grave at sea.

Every cabin has been filled and women and children sleeping on the floors in the dining saloon, library and smoking rooms. The passengers of the Carpathia have divided their clothes with the shipwrecked ones until they have at least kept warm. 'Tis true that many women have had to appear on deck in kimonas and some in underclothes with a coat thrown over them, but their lives have been spared and they have not thought of dress. Some children were entirely without clothes in the second cabin, but the women have joined together and made warm clothes out of the blankets belonging to the Carpathia and with needles and thread they could pick up from passenger to passenger.

Passengers Saved.

Among other notable passengers rescued we have Mrs. J. J. Astor, Mr. Astor having been lost with the majority. Mrs. Astor has been ill ever since she came on board, and many others have not so far been able to recover the dreadful loss.

After we got the Titanic's passengers on board our ship it was a question as to where we should take them. Some said the Olympic would come out and meet us and take them on to New York, but others said they would die if they had to be lowered again into small boats to be taken up by another, so we finally turned toward New York, delaying the Carpathia's passengers eight days in reaching Gibraltar.

These subscriptions were taken up on board the Carpathia on Monday:—

Mrs. William Bucknell	$250.00
Mrs. Walter Clark	200.00
Mr. Washington Dodge	150.00
Mr. Richard Beckwith	100.00
Mrs. George N. Stone	100.00
Mrs. Leo D. Greenfield and Mr. William B. Greenfield	100.00
Mr. E. N. Kimball, Jr.	100.00
Dr. H. W. Frauenthal	100.00
Mr. Robert W. Daniel	200.00
Mr. F. C. Spedden	100.00
Mr. J. J. Brown	100.00
Mrs. E. E. Lines	5.00
Mr. Frederick H. Seward	20.00
Mrs. C. Williams	50.00

Other subscriptions were made by Mr. Charles Whilem, Mr. G. L. Longley Hudson, Mrs. Edward S. Robert, Miss Georgetta Matill, Miss Elizabeth W. Allen and Mr. Harry Anderson.

One woman who was in the first lifeboat told me that when the order first came for her to get into it she declined, saying:—"I do not believe the Titanic is in danger. I will stay here with my husband."

To that the officer replied:—

"Madam, if you do not obey orders you will spread confusion among the other ladies of the ship. You owe it to yourself and to everybody on board to do as you are told in this matter."

Then the woman obeyed, taking her place.

Five women saved their pet dogs, carrying them in their arms. Another woman saved a little pig, which she said was her mascot. Though her husband is an Englishman and she lives in England she is an American and was on her way to visit her folk here. How she cared for the pig aboard ship I do not know, but she carried it up the side of the ship in a big bag. I did not mind the dogs so much, but it seemed to me to be too much when a pig was saved and human beings went to death.

Mrs. Isidor Straus was drowned because she would not leave her husband. A person who was standing beside the aged couple on the deck of the Titanic heard Mr. Straus say to his wife:—"Get into the lifeboat." To that she replied. "I will not leave you. I will get into the boat only if you will."

Mr. Straus refused to make a move toward the boat. They must have died together.

The attitude of Mrs. Straus seemed to typify that of the other women who were saved. They went into the boats because they obeyed, and I heard several of them express regret that they had not been allowed to remain and drown with their husbands.

Though most of the women were overcome by the disaster when they realized its enormity, that was not invariably the case. One woman whose husband was drowned never mentioned him, but never ceased to bewail the loss of her jewels, which she repeatedly assured all who would listen to her were worth $30,000.

All night the people in the lifeboats sang, according to Lord Duff-Gordon. This was in part to keep their ears and minds closed to the awful cries for help which came from the Titanic when it became clear that the ship was going down.

A steward who was saved told me that when he went to one of the first cabin passengers—a woman—and told her to dress and put on a life preserver, she merely laughed.

"If that little bump is all that has happened, I'll stay right here," she said.

"Madam," replied the steward, "my orders are from the captain to tell you to dress and put on a life preserver."

"My orders to myself are to get back into bed and go to sleep again," said the woman. And she did. She paid for that with her life.

A woman from Wisconsin said that she was not called at all, and if she had not heard Mrs. Astor out in the passageway crying she would have remained in her stateroom.

One first class passenger, after all the lifeboats had put out, heard several stokers saying that they knew where there was a collapsible boat, which they proposed to put overboard. So the passenger kept close to the stokers, and, sure enough, they launched the boat. He got it with them and was saved. These same stokers yesterday decided to put some cheer into the dreary atmosphere on board the Carpathia, so they took an accordion and several tin pans, and gave a burlesque entertainment. That served to dispel some of the gloom.

"Two French cildren, three and five years old, were brought aboard the Carpathia without their father, who was lost. They could not speak to us, and it was not known at first whether they were speechless from cold or could not speak English. "Spoken to finally by a Frenchman, they answered in their native tongue, and were soon crying for their father. Women in the boat with them comforted them as best they could.

"In the boat with Mrs. John Jacob Astor, who wanted to put back toward the Titanic to rescue men who after plunging overboard were struggling to same themselves, were other women who wanted to keep going forward. Mrs. Astor was inclined to return to the men, her own husband had been left behind, and she was urged to offer the oarsmen any amount of her wealth if they would put back; but the will of those who were opposed prevailed and the oarsmen rowed onward.

Mrs. Astor was ill aboard the Titanic, but she bore up well in the lifeboat. She was taken aboard the Carpathia in negligee costume. The captain of the Carpathia gave up his cabin to her and she was made perfectly comfortable. She did not leave it until New York was reached. All of the rescued women were made as comfortable as possible, passengers aboard the Carpathia either giving up their staterooms entirely to them or else sharing them.

Mental Suffering Terrific.

"Many of the survivors of the Titanic, especially women, as may be expected, were in a violent state of excitement when rescued, and one woman appeared to have lost her mind entirely. She seemed to be beyond recovery. She appeared to be in possession of her mental faculties when the rescue was being made; her husband was among the missing and she scanned every lifeboat for him. When the last lifeboat had come alongside the Carpathia and he was not among the passengers, then it was that her mind gave away. She became suddenly frantic, and all efforts of women and men to quiet her were in vain. The mental suffering of many others from shock was severe.

One Man Took All Blankets.

All of the men in the lifeboats, except one, conducted themselves most commendably. They worked well and rowed hard. The exception was a man who absolutely refused to work at all. There was but one other man in the boat with him. This beast (I wish I could tell you his name) not only refused to work, but took for himself all blankets in the boat, the women having to go without and shiver and also row.

One of the women in the boat finally told this man that she would shoot him if he did not give up the blankets and work. The display of a pistol had the desired effect.

Only two of the Carpathia's passengers knew at two o'clock in the morning that the Carpathia was rushing to the aid of those aboard the doomed Titanic. They were awakened by the rushing around of the crew making ready for the work that was ahead of them, and went out on deck and asked what it all meant. They were told that nothing at all was the matter, but they were convinced that something unusual and of great moment had happened. Just by accident it was learned at five o'clock what was going on.

Major Arthur Penshen, of Canada, owes his life to the fact that he is a yachtsman. His story was one of the most interesting of those told aboard the Carpathia. When the boats were putting out from the Titanic Captain Smith noticed that one of the places for oarsmen was vacant. The sailor whose place that was was not at hand. Captain Smith, addressing the men passengers asked:—"Can any of you men handle an oar?"

There was silence for a moment, and then Major Penshen, stepping forward, said, "I am a yachtsman, Captain, and am familiar with small boats too."

"Get aboard," ordered Captain Smith.

Major Penshen jumped to a rope which hung over the side and hand over hand made his way to the lifeboat beloww. He rowed all night, aand when he came on board the Carpathia his hands were a mass of blisters.

Lord Duff Gordon, one of those who was saved, said that the last thing that he did before entering the lifeboat was to put his pistol in his pohcket, thinking that there might be trouble and he would need it.

The sea was practically calm when the rescue was made, and all during that time that the rescue was being made, but shortly afterward a storm swept over the sea and, according to seamen, a lifeboat could not have gone fifty feet in it.

Lord Gordon wanted a picture of the men who had rowed him; he wanted it with the men in their life preservers, but some of the rescued women could not bear the sight of a life preserver, and out of deference none was brought out. Lord Gordon gave to each of the men a check, which he called a "fiver," probably five pounds sterling.

Miss May R. Birkhead is from Louisiana, Mo. She is a niece of Judge Virgil Rule, of St. Louis, Mo., and well known in social circles in that city. She was on the way to Europe for a six months' trip in company with her aunt, Miss Sue E. Rule, of Louisiana, Mo. Though there was no necessity for it, Miss Birkhead earned the money for her trip to Europe herself by making art shirt waists. She is a friend of the family of Speaker Champ Clark, who began his law career in her home town. Just previous to starting on board the Carpathia, Miss Birkhead had visited at the home of the Clarks in Washington for six weeks.

HEARS COLONEL ASTOR REFUSED LIFE BELT

"Colonel Astor was walking the deck at the time the Titanic struck the iseberg." said William David, assistant saloon steward on board the Carpathia, in reciting incidents which had been repeated to him by surviving passengers.

"He was approached by a frantic waiter, I was told, and urged to put on a life belt. The waiter had several life belts in his hand. Colonel Astor waved the waiter away.

"'Pooh,' he said, 'this is nothing. There is no need of life belts,' and that was the last seen of Colonel Astor.

"J. Bruce Ismay was pulled on board the Carpathia from a lifeboat. He was clad only in pajamas. He collapsed completely upon reaching the deck and was semi-conscious ever since."

Mr. David was emphatic in his statement that failure to realize the extent of the damage to the Titanic on the part of the passengers of the doomed vessel was responsible in great part for the large loss of life. He described the terrible suffering of the survivors and the manner in which it affected the passengers and crew of the Carpathia. An assistant steward lost his mind upon seeing one of the Titanic's rescued firemen expire after being lifted to the deck of the Carpathia.

"At midnight on Sunday," said Mr. David, "the men on the Carpathia received the word that the Titanic was sinking. They laughed at the idea, and it was not until fifteen minutes after twelve that the real situation occurred to them. Instantly torches, electric apparatus and other signal devices were prepared on the decks, masts and bridge of the Carpathia and provisions placed in all boats. Blankets and robes were placed in alleyways and gangways. All available men were put on the lookout and al equipped with powerfu glasses.

Ligh Lifeboat Torch.

"The first light—a blue light—was sighted, and it was found to be the torch on one of the Titanic's lifeboats, the only one having a light. It was for a time thought that the illumination was from the head mast light of the sinking Titanic. Everyone on board believed that they were seeing the Titanic gradually going to her grave.

"But this lifeboat was positively recognized soon before three o'clock Monday morning. It was picked up and found to contain only fifteen persons, while it could have easily accommodated sixty. It had on board one entire family, one sailor and five firemen.

"We found the Titanic's lifeboats within three or four miles of one another. All passengers rescued were lifted to the deck of the Carpathia by means of the jacket ropes. All were too exhausted to climb the rope ladders which were lowered. Mrs. Astor was lifted to the deck in this manner. The Carpathia picked up twenty-two boats. There were from thirty to forty persons in each.

Mrs. Rothschild (Mr. David could not tell which Mrs. Rothschild) carried a little Pomeranian when taken on board. Her husband was not saved.

"Surviving passengers told me that when two firemen attempted to board a lifeboat when the Titanic was sinking the ocer of the boat shouted to them that they would swamp it because it was already overcrowded. The firemen are quoted as saying:—'All right, Jerry.' After which they went out of sight in the icy water. I was told that the Titanic's officers directed the filling of the lifeboats with drawn revolvers and that only two shots were fired and those by the second officer, who meant to intimidate several of the crew fighting to escape from the sinking ship.

Captain Smith Saved, Leaps Into Sea.

"The Titanic went down slowly. When the bridge was on a level with the water Captain Smith, who had remained on the bridge, was picked up by two sailors, I was told, and dragged on board a floating raft. He had no sooner been taken on board than he leaped into the sea. It was not until the boilers of the Titanic burst that she sank fast. She went down bow first.

"It was the belief on board the Carpathia that the steerage passengers were 'battened' below. The gangways, it is thought, were strapped shut. To my knowledge, only fifty steerage passengers escaped.

"The male passengers of the Titanic thought the collision not serious, so far as I have learned, and hundreds refused to heed the warnings of the crew, just as Colonel Astor had. The women, however, were instantly panic stricken. That is why so many escaped, although there were many instances where the men gave the women the preference in the rush for boats, and in consequence were lost. There were 46 stewards saved.

"Two maids attempted to board life boat No. 11 with morocco bags containing their mistresses' valuables. The maids were saved, the bags were lost, as were their mistresses.

Ten Survivors Die.

"The shrieks and cries of the women and men picked up in lifeboats by the Carpathia were horrible. The women were clothed only in night robes and wrappers. The men were in their night garments. One was lifted on board entirely nude. All the passengers who could bear nuorishment were taken into the dining rooms and cabins by Captain Ralston and given foods and stimulants. Passengers of the Carpathia gave up their berths and state rooms to the survivors. Theer was a subscription taken up and up to Wednesday the amount contributed totalied $15,000.

"On Monday, five survivors died; on Tuesday, three, and on Wednesday, two. They were buried at sea. All the survivors declare that Mr. Ismay was brave and showed his worth throughout the whole terrible affair."

ONLY 705 WERE SAVED

In a report to the health officers of the port by the surgeons of the Carpathia a complete list of the survivors was stated.

Of the officers and crew of the Titanic 210 were saved and 202 of the first class passengers, 115 of the second class and 178 of the streerage were rescued.

In all, 705 were saved from the Titanic.

SUFFERINGS IN FROZEN ATLANTIC DESCRIBED BY SURVIVORS

J. Bruce Ismay Promises to Face Senate Inquiry

United States Senators Compelled to Stand Around While Company's Representatives Decide if Questioning of Line's Head Will Be Permitted.

LIFEBOATS TO BE AT THE INVESTIGATION

J. Bruice Ismay, managing director of the White Star line, who was saved from the Titanic, was in the care of physicians on board the Carpathia when seen by the subcommittee of the Investigating Committee of the United States Senate. Mr. Ismay was visited by United States Senators William Alden Smith and Francis G. Newlands, who compose the subcommittee. After two conferences, each of which lasted half an hour, Senators Smith and Newlands got from Mr. Ismay his promise to attend to-day a session of the subcommittee at the Waldorf-Aastoria. The meeting probably will be in the afternoon.

The Senate Committee, accomanied by the sergeant and assistant sergeant at arms of the Senate reached the Pennsylvania railroad station at nine o'clock. They went immediately to the Carpathia. For half an hour the Senators were compelled to wander aimlessly on the long pier. They asked officer after officer of the steamship company for directions. Each man they approached told them they would have to speak to another officer. Finally the ship was found, just having been made fast and the Senators went on board.

Senators Have Long Wait.

They asked to see P. A. S. Franklin, vice president of the White Star line, and after another long delay reached him.

They explained their mission and said they desired to interview Mr. Ismay. They were told that was impossible because Mr. Ismay was ill and under the care of a physician. They insisted, however, and were compelled to explain what questions they desired to address to Mr. Ismay. Mr. Franklin, the Senators said, then refused to conduct the sub-committee to Mr. Ismay until he had conferred with the steamship company's lawyers.

Mr. Burlingham, one of the lawyers, was on the pier. He and Mr. Franklin went into conference. They talked for half an hour, during which time Senators Smith and Newlands were compelled to wait. At its close the Senators were led to a stateroom directly across from the one in which they had been waiting. There they saw Mr. Ismay. The doors to the cabin in which the interview took place were closed. They remained talking to Mr. Ismay for half an hour.

What was said in the conference the Senators declared they did not desire to divulge, at least until Mr. Ismay had an opportunity to talk to the newspaper men. Mr. Ismay promised to see the reporters immediately after the Senators left.

Mr. Ismay's Story "Interesting."

"All we care to say of what we have learned," Senator Smith said as he was leaving the Carpathia, "is that Mr. Ismay's recital to us of what happened is very, very interesting. It tends to show that the newspaper reports of this awful calamity received up to date, however wild and alarming they may appear to have been, certainly have not exaggerated the exact situation that developed when the disaster occurred.

"All the lifeboats that were used to rescue those few of the Titanic passengers who did survive have been saved, brought here on board the same steamer that brought the survivors, and will be used by the Senate investigating committee."

Calmness Marked First Moments, Says Mr. Beasley

London Man Declares Shocks of Collision Were so Slight Few Realized Danger—Card Players Continued On and Went Down.

Here is the account of Mr. Beasley, of London:—"I had been in my berth for about ten minutes when at about fifteen minutes after eleven o'clock I felt a slight jar and then soon after a second one, but not sufficiently large to cause any anxiety to any one, however nervous he may have been.

"However, the engines stopped immediately afterward and I first thought 'she has lost a propeller.' I went up on the top (boat) deck in a dressing gown and found only a few people there, who had come up similarly to inquire why we had stopped, but there was no sort of anxiety in the minds of any one.

"We saw through the smoking room window a game of cards going on and went in to inquire if they knew anything; it seems they felt more of the jar, and, looking through the window, had seen a huge iceberg go by close to the side of the boat. They thought we had just grazed it with a glancing blow and the engines had been stopped to see if any damage had been done. No one, of course, had any conception that she had been pierced below by part of the submerged iceberg.

Game of Cards Undisturbed.

"The game went on without any thought of disaster and I retired to my cabin to read until we went on again. I never saw any of the players or the onlookers again. A little later, hearing people going upstairs, I went out again and found every one wanting to know why the engines had stopped.

"On going on deck again I saw that there was an undoubted list downward from stern to bow, but, knowing nothing of what had happened, concluded some of the front compartments had filled and weighed her own. I went own again to put on warmer clothing, and as I dressed heard an order shouted:—'All passengers on deck with life belts on.'

"We all walked slowly up with them tied on over our clothing, but even then presumed this was a wise precaution the captain was taking, and that we should return in a short time and retire to bed. There was a total absence of any panic or any expressions of alarm, and I suppose this can be accounted for by the exceedingly calm night and the absence of any signs of the accident.

"The ship was absolutely still, and except for a gentle tilt downward, which I don't think one person in ten would have noticed at that time, no signs of the approaching disaster were visible. She lay just as if she were waiting the order to go on again when some trifling matter had been adjusted. But in a few moments we saw the covers lifted from the boats, and the crews alloted to them standing by and curling up the ropes which were to lower them by the pulley blocks into the water.

Realization Came Slowly.

"We then began to realize it was more serious than it had been supposed and my first thought was to go down and get more clothing and some money, but seeing people pouring up the stairs decided it was better to cause no confusion to people coming up by doing so. Presently we heard the order:—'All men stand back away from the boats and all women retire to next deck below'—the smoking room deck or B deck.

"The men all stood away and remained in absolute silence leaning against the end railings of the deck or pacing slowly up and down. The boats were swung out and lowered from A deck. When they were to the level of B deck where all the women were collected, the women got in quietly with the exception of some who refused to leave their husbands. In some cases they were torn from them and pushed into the boats, but in many instances they were allowed to remain because there was no one to insist they should go.

'Looking over the side one saw boats from aft already in the water slipping quietly away into the darkness, and presently the boats near me were lowered, and with much creaking, as the new ropes slipped through the pulley blocks down the ninety feet which separated them from the water.

"One by one the boats were filled with women and children, lowered and rowed away into the night. Presently the word went round among the men, 'the men are to be put in boats on the starboard side.' I was on the port side, and most of the men walked across the deck to see if this was so. I remained where I was, and presently heard the call:—

No More Women, He Jumped.

" 'Any more women-'

"Looking over the side of the ship I saw the boat No. 13 swinging level with B deck, half full of women. Again the call was repeated:—

" 'Any more women?'

"I saw none come on and then one of the crew looked up and said:—

" 'Any women on your deck, sir?'

" 'No,' I replied.

" 'Then you had better jump.'

"I dropped in and fell in the bottom, as they cried 'lower away' as the boat began to descend, two women were pushed hurriedly through the crowd on B deck, and heaved over into the boat and a baby of ten months passed down after them. Down we went, the crew calling to those lowering each end to keep her level 'aft,' 'stern,' 'both together,' until we weer some ten feet from the water, and hre occurred the only anxious moment we had during the whole of our experience.

Trouble in Launching.

"Immediately below our boat was the exhaust of the condensers, a huge stream of water pouring out all the time. Down we went and presently floated, with our ropes still holding us, the exhaust washing us away from the side of the vessel and the swell of the sea urging us back against the side again. The resultant of all these forces was a force which carried us parallel to the ship's side and directly under boat 14, which had filled rapidly with men and was coming down on us in a way that threatened to submerge our boat.

"Just before she dropped a stoker sprang to the ropes with his knife.

" 'One,' I heard him say; 'two,' as his knife cut through the pulley ropes, and in a moment the exhaust stream had carried us clear, while boat No. 14 dropped into the water, into the space we had the moment before occupied, our gunwales almost touching.

"We drifted away easily as the oars were got out, and headed directly away from the ship. The crew seemed to me to be mostly cooks in white jackets, two to an oar, with a stoker at the tiller.

It was decided to elect the stoker who was steering captain, and for all to obey his orders. He set to work at once to get into touch with the other boats, calling to them and getting as close as seemed wise, so that when the search boats came in the morning to look for us there would be more chance for all to be rescued by keeping together.

WOMAN SURVIVOR HEARD SHOOTING

Mrs. A. A. Dick Says She Could See Men Leaping from Ship That Was Sinking.

One of the most comprehensive and connected stories of the disaster was that recounted by Mrs. A. A. Dick, wife of a merchant in Calgary, Canada.

"We were awakened in our cabin on hearing the crash. Together with my husband I made my way to one of the decks and learned that the steamship had struck an iceberg. We could see the iceberg. The night was clear and the sky was filled with stars.

"We were indifferent about leaving the steamship as we did not believe it was going to sink. We put off in the third boat. We had not gone far when we realized the big liner was sinking. Then, at a safe distance, away from the possibility of suction, we saw one deck after another sink from view. We could see men jumping into the water and could hear terrifying screams and shouts of distress.

"We heard several rounds of shots echoing across the water and learned afterward that many men were shot down as the last boat put away. There were three men shot in the steerage by the second or third officer, we understand. As the steamship went down the band was up forward and we could faintly hear the start of 'Nearer My God to Thee.'

"There was no evidence of panic while we were on board and I first laughed at the idea of the Titanic sinking. We were in the open boat for more than six hours, but had bread and water with us. We thought aid was never coming and we suffered some from the cold."

COPYRIGHT BY CLINEDINST MRS. LUCIEN SMITH

MASTER WASHINGTON DODGE

MRS. WASHINGTON DODGE PHOTO BY LALLIE CHARLES

MRS. E. W. APPLETON

COPYRIGHT 1910 BY MARCEAU MRS. S. L. GOLDENBERG

DR. ALICE F. LEADER

The Californian Found No Bodies

BOSTON, Mass., Thursday.—A message just received from Captain Lord, of the steamship Californian, of the Leyland line, says:—

"Arrived scene the Titanic disaster half-past eight A. M. 15th. All survivors then aboard the Carpathia. Have not and did not see any bodies.

"(Signed) LORD, Captain."

Mr. Taft's Tribute To Major Butt

WASHINGTON, D. C., Thursday.—President Taft told visitors late to-day that he never had expected to hear of the rescue of Major Butt, his military aid, after the first shocking news of the disaster.

"I never had any idea that Archie was saved at all," said the President. "As soon as I heard that 1,200 went down I knew he went down, too. He was a soldier and was on deck where he belonged."

Scores Returned to Sleep, Dying in First Cabin Staterooms

Shock When the Titanic Struck the Ice Scarcely Felt—Many Passengers Dressed, and Calmed by the Ship's Officers Sought Their Berths.

Testimony of half a dozen of the Titanic passengers given to a HERALD reporter immediately after they left the Carpathia last night at the Cunard pier goes to show that the Titanic struck an ice field that stretched away for more than fifty miles over the surface of the ocean. The shock was scarcely felt. Many of the passengers felt a slight jar and rushed out on deck. They saw only blackness ahead. The ship's lights still were burning. There was nothing to indicate they soon were to be victims of the biggest sea tragedy in the history of the world.

As nearly as these passengers can remember the Titanic, sliding through the water at no more speed than had been maintained consistently during all the trip, slid gracefully a few feet out of the water, with just the slightest tremble. She rolled slightly. Then she pitched. The shock, scarcely noticeable to those on board, drew out on deck a few loungers who were in the salons and the smoking room. They looked out over the waters. Officers and petty officers were hurrying about. There was no destruction within the ship, at least not in sight of the passengers. There was no panic. Everything that could be seen tended to alleviate what little fear had crept into the minds of those passengers who were more apprehensive than the regular travellers who cross the ocean at this season of the year and who were used to their ships experiencing small quivers.

Returned to Sleep and to Die.

Not one person aboard the Titanic, unless possibly those of the crew who were working far below, knew the extent of the injuries she had sustained. Many of the passengers had taken time to dress, so sure were they that there was no danger. They came out on deck, looked the situation over and were unable to see the slightest sign that the Titanic had been torn open beneath the water line.

A Mrs. Dorothy ——, whose last name could not be remembered by Captain C. F. Crain, of the United States Army, to whom she told her story on board the Carpathia as soon as she was lifted out of one of the lifeboats more dead than alive from exhaustion and from excitement and shock, declared that she herself had dressed. Her fears were calmed by the officers of the Titanic, who said there was no danger, and she went back to sleep satisfied also of her safety from the results of her own observation. Dozens of other persons went through the same performance, but they went to sleep when they returned to their staterooms, and when the Titanic settled within four hours after she had been struck they were drowned like rats in traps in their first cabin passengers' quarters.

The night was remarkably clear, according to the hasty explanations dropped to the weeping relatives by the long line of Titanic's rescued as they walked from the piers. The big ship was the scene of gayety half an hour before the shock came, and the orchestra was playing.

When the shock was over, when the passengers' fear had been partly calmed and most of them had returned to their staterooms or to the card games in which they were engaged before the quiver was felt, there came surging through the first cabin quarters a report that seemed to have drifted in from nowhere and without reason that the ship was sinking.

How this word crept from outside the limit of the officers themselves no one seems now to know. Immediately the crew began to man the boats.

No Man Shoved Women Aside.

For the men who were passengers on board the Titanic, those passengers who could be questioned last night declared positively and in the strongest terms that not one man attempted to push a woman aside or to advance his own chances for being rescued. The boats were filled with those who could get into them. Some men were permitted to enter the boats only because so many women had retired to their rooms and were asleep that all the women in sight already had been placed on board the lifeboats. Eighteen lifeboats were loaded with those who were to survive. One life raft was manned and loaded to its full capacity.

The Carpathia was steaming along the edge of the great field of ice at little less than her normal speed, going carefully, her commander knowing the danger that confronted him in the darkness of the night if his ship slipped up over the edge of the great field. Suddenly, the Carpathia passengers estimated it was about half-past ten o'clock or eleven o'clock, the "S. O. S." signal was received by the wireless operator on board the Carpathia.

The Carpathia was sent ahead, her passengers all on deck and hanging over the rail. The night was bitterly cold and all the wraps carried by the passengers were being used by her freezing passengers as they gathered to aid in the work of rescue.

Hour after hour passed and still the Carpathia plunged ahead, regardless of danger that had kept her back during all of the earlier part of the trip. The ice field she had been fearing she had run into within a short time after leaving New York and it had been in evidence almost continuously during her trip up to the point where the Titanic's distress signal floated in out of the night.

Sight a Life Boat.

Suddenly a shout went up from the deck of the Carpathia. In the far-off swelling surface of the ocean appeared a speck. It grew into a flame. Those on board the rescue ship realized that it was not the Titanic they were sighting. The speck grew too slowly and remained always too small. Finally the speck was recognized as a light. It seemed almost on the water. The light grew to be a flame. As she raced rocket after rocket was sent heavenward from the Carpathia.

Finally a sound came over the water. The Carpathia was running close to the first of the eighteen lifeboats. The crew of the second lifeboat refused to come on board the Carpathia, but manned their oars again and rowed away. In half an hour, just as the last load of the remaining seventeen boats filled with shivering, hysteric, grief stricken and in many cases unconscious women and nearly exhausted men, was climbing over the bulging sides of the Carpathia the lifeboat that had disappeared came bobbing over the waves again. It had transferred the survivors from a life raft which could not reach the side of the Carpathia and those survivors were taken on board the ship.

Men Stood Back, Expecting Rescue.

A few spars, a box or two, some small pieces of wreckage was all of the Titanic that was beheld by the persons on board the Carpathia that had rushed to the rescue. It was just breaking day as the rescue work was completed.

So exhausted were the survivors that scarcely any of them were able to tell their story of what actually had happened until late in the afternoon of Monday. It seemed impossible aboard the Carpathia to obtain a complete story of the tragedy.

Few of the Titanic's passengers were hurt on board that great vessel. Their sufferings were caused chiefly by exposure, shock and grief. The women had stepped into the lifeboat after kissing their husbands goodby. The men stood back, expecting that their rescue would be only a little delayed. More boats were to be launched, they thought, and as soon as rescue, being summoned even then by the wireless apparatus on board the Titanic, was at hand they, too, would be taken on board the relief ships.

As they stood, thinking of this, the great Titanic even then was settling. They overlooked the danger. The women in the lifeboats saw their loved ones plunge to death. The survivors' boats were bobbing about in the waves all within a radius of half a mile of the great Titanic, when, with a roar and burst of spray, she settled and passed out of sight.

See the Carpathia's Rockets.

Then began one of the most torturous experiences for the helpless women in the drifting lifeboats that human beings ever were compelled to endure. It was black night. Fortunately several of the men and some of the petty officers who had manned the lifeboats had a few matches in their pockets. Torches were improvised from letters and scraps of papers found in their pockets.

It was not until the first rocket the struggling occupants of the lifeboats saw shoot heavenward from the Carpathia that the first of the torches was applied with a match and its filmy blaze shot up as high as was possible when one of the men was held on the shoulders of five others, standing up, and waved the flaming bit of papers until it burned down to his finger tips. The desolate groups, huddled together in the tossing and rolling tiny craft, could not tell whether their torch had been seen by the ship that was firing the rockets. They waited fifteen minutes and the operation was repeated.

Then the huge hulk of the Carpathia took form in the gray of the breaking morning and she swept swiftly down into the centre of the widely separated fleet of lifeboats with their human freight. They had been for approximately eight hours in the open, with the waves sending spray and at intervals whole barrelsful of water in upon them. They were drenched and the severe cold was freezing their clothing to their bodies.

Four Dead in Lifeboats.

Only a few of them were able to walk. The Carpathia's sailors, unable to drag on board their own craft those who were lying unconscious on the bottom of the lifeboats, went after them and the unconscious ones were lifted up to other sailors standing on the Carpathia's ladders.

Everything that could be done for the survivors was done on the Carpathia. Several of them had been cut and bruised in their attempts to get into the lifeboats and by falling from exhaustion during the awful ordeal they were compelled to pass through while waiting for the Carpathia to come to their relief. These received surgical care. The others were placed in bed and few if any of them was able during the rest of the voyage to go on deck.

Only four dead were taken on board the Carpathia from the lifeboats, as nearly as could be learned from the distracted throng that issued from the Cunard line's piers within five minutes after the first passenger walked down the Carpathia's gangplank last night. Those who came in the first batch of survivors, to be greeted by relatives and friends knew of none of the survivors from the wreck who had died while on board the Carpathia in the trip to New York.

SILENCE ENJOINED ON MANY SURVIVORS

Officers of the Titanic Taken from the Carpathia Secretly by Third Class Passengers' Gangway.

Mrs. Antoinette Fliggenheim, who would not give her address, but friends who met her at the pier said she was Philadelphia, made the statement that a paper was passed among the surviving passengers of the Titanic before the Carpathia reached here, praying the survivors not to make a statement of any details.

She said she felt in duty bound to carry out this agreement. Like many others who were hurried off the pier as soon as the rescue ship arrived, she preserved her reticence and would say nothing more than the night was clear and the sea smooth.

Many other passengers who were approached by reporters declined to say a word and dismissed the interviews with a sweep of the hand. Not one in ten would submit to questioning.

The officers of the Titanic were smuggled off a gangway where the third class passengers disembarked.

NO NEWS OF FATHER, YOUNG WOMAN FAINTS

She Visits Cunard Pier and Is Told Parent's Name Does Not Appear on List.

At eleven o'clock last night a young woman, fashionably dressed, arrived at the Cunard line pier and made inquiry for Timothy McCarthy, and said tha the was her father and had left England on board the Titanic, in the second cabin.

An official of the ship looked over the passenger list, but could find no such name upon it. The young woman, however, would not be convinced, and after wandering about the pier for half an hour, pleading with officials she collapsed. She was carried to the street, where she revived, and went home in a cab. Her name could not be learned.

7 CHILDREN GO TO HOSPITAL

Just before mid-night seven children, said to have been steerage passengers on board the Titanic, were carried off the Carpathia by an ambulance surgeon and hurried to a hospital. They were said to be suffering from measles, which they had contracted before the Titanic was wrecked.

The surgeon in charge said that two of the children were very seriously ill, due to their exposure in the open boat.

Thrilling Race to Rescue Survivors from Ice Field

Fred Beachler, Employe of the Herald, Who Was Passenger on Board the Carpathia, Gives Vivid Description of Finding Boats Where the Titanic Went Down.

Fred Beachler, of No. 131 Manhattan avenue, for fifteen years a compositor on the HERALD, was a passenger aboard the Carpathia. He gave this description of the rescue of the Titanic's passengers:—

"The Carpathia left New York at noon on Thursday, April 11, for her regular Mediterranean cruise, taking the northerly course and almost immediately ran into cold weather, which continued, but with a smooth sea, until the evening of Sunday.

"It was about midnight by the ship's clock when we got the Titanic operator's message stating that the great steamship had struck an iceberk and was in danger.

Captain Rostron, of the Carpathia, at once gave orders for full steam and set out for the distressed Titanic, the Carpathia at that time being about eighty miles distant. Before reaching the scene we got the word that the Titanic was badly ripped along the starboard side and soon afterward learned of the great ship going down. It was about three o'clock when we reached the place where the wreck occurred, and we could plainly see the huge, dark iceberg which she had struck. Just as dawn was breaking the first boat from the Titanic came alongside the Carpathia and our officers and crew brought the passengers on board, removed the life preservers, wrapped the rescued in blankets, gave them stimulants and did everything possible for their comfort. The weather then was clear, but very cold, and the sea smootn.

Praise for Officers and Men.

"It may as well be said here that the officers and men of the Carpathia deserve the highest praise for their splendid work throughout the trying night, and also for their continuous work day and night until our return to New York. They worked not only unceasingly, but were cool and courteous at all times and gave the same attention and care to the poorest steerage passenger that was given to those in the first and second cabin.

"It seemed nearly an hour from the time of arrival of the first life boat until another came up, but from then on they came more frequently and by eight o'clock the sixteenth and last to be picked up by us arrived, with a total of about 720 survivors.

"The first boats to put off the Titanic contained mostly women and children, and many of the women helped at the oars. At first rope was dipped in pitch and burned in some of the boats to give their location, while men burned paper in other boats. Some of the boats were well filled, while others were but half full.

"Bruce Ismay, president of the White Star line, was the last to leave the boat in which he reached the Carpathia.

"All the rescued seemed remarkably calm, some women laughing while being put on board, but, once safe, many of them went into hysterics, but were quieted and looked after by our stewardess. Many of the arrivals were fully dressed, while others had very little clothing.

See Many Icebergs.

"Since daylight we could see countless icebergs all about us, some of them of mountainous size and fantastic shape, and an endless field of ice stretched away to one side as far as we could see. A conservative estimate would be fully one hundred miles of the floes. It was at once a most awe inspiring and grand spectacle, and the oldest mariners and greatest Atlantic travellers on board the Carpathia unite in saying they never beheld its like before nor expect to see its equal again.

"It was not unlike the beautiful harbor of Rio Janeiro, with its famed fantastic shaped peaks, except that this was on a grander scale.

"The large black iceberg which caused the disaster stood out like the Rock of Gibraltar, but close by also were Old Sugarloaf and Hunchback, the beautiful peaks of the Brazilian harbor, but now presented to us in huge ice mountains.

"The Californian, of the Leyland line, having come alongside us about eight o'clock we exchanged signals and soon after steamed for New York, a distance of more than one thousand miles, while the Californian remained.

The Carpathia in Danger.

"The Carpathia had been in a dangerous position during the whole night, both from icebergs and high pressure on boilers because of the forced run we were making, but none of the passengers knew this at the time. As a matter of fact few of them left their staterooms until after daylight, and some did not learn of the Titanic disaster until all the lifeboats were in.

"Two of the rescued from the Titanic died from shock and exposure before they reached the Carpathia and another died a few minutes after being taken on board. The dead were W. H. Hoyte, first cabin; Abraham Hormer, third class, and S. C. Sirbert, steward, and they were buried at sea the morning of April 15, latitude 41 deg. 14 min. north, longitude 51 deg. 24 min. west. P. Lyon, able seaman, died and was buried at sea the following morning.

"It was not until noon of Monday that we cleared the last of the ice and Monday night a dense fog came up and continued until the following morning, then a strong wind, a heavy sea, a thunderstorm and a dense fog Tuesday night caused some uneasiness among the more unnerved, the fog continuing all of Tuesday.

"The second cabin dining room had been turned into a hospital to care for the injured, and the first, second and third class dining rooms were used for sleeping rooms at night for women, while the smoking rooms were set aside for men. All available space was used, some sleeping in chairs and some on the floor, while a few found rest in the bathrooms.

"One of the most seriously injured was a woman who had lost both her children. Her limbs had been severely torn, but she was very patient.

"In talks with surviving officers and passengers of the Titanic the time given from the striking of the iceberg until the ship sank varies, but I learn from a reliable source, my informant being an officer of the Titanic, that she struck at twenty minutes of twelve by the ship's clock (twenty minutes to one, New York time); that the forward starboard side was ripped open about half the length of the vessel, and that great pieces of ice fell over her bow. It was nineteen minutes past two when the vessel disappeared with a report of two explosions.

Captain Rescued Child.

"I also learn on the same reliable authority, verified by others, that Captain Smith, of the Titanic, was in the water with a child in his arms, which he succeeded in placing in one of the boats. He was begged to come on board himself, but refused and turned back as though to aid others, and was not seen again.

"There was little excitement, according to my informant, when the passengers were told to get up and dress and go to the upper decks, as none of the crew or passengers thought the great boat would sink, and those who had put off in the small boats felt reassured when they saw the lights from the Carpathia. But many failed to get overboard before the ship sank, and their screams could be heard by those who had left the vessel as the great mass went to the bottom.

"One of the most remarkanie escapes was that of an American barber from Philadelphia, the only American employed aboard. He was blown off as the boilers exploded and was injured, but was rescued after being in the icy water three hours. He has made 750 ocean trips, but says he is through now.

"About the first news we got told of Colonel Astor's death.

"Mr. and Mrs. William Carter, Miss and Master Carter, of New York, had spent the last year in England and were returning. They were made comfortable by Chief Steward Hughes, of the Carpathia. The Carter valet and a chauffeur were lost.

"A boy of the ship's crew jumped for an overturned boat on which a number of men were clinging, but fell into the water. He swam for the boat, but was struck on the head with an oar by one of the men. He caught hold of the man's leg and threatened to pull him into the water if he repeated the blow, and was permitted to get aboard.

"Among the rescued was a Japanese and four Chinese. Two small dogs, one being a handsome chowchow, were also saved and taken care of.

Meeting of Survivors.

"On Tuesday afternoon a meeting was called of the uninjured survivors in the main saloon for the purpose of devising means of assisting the more unfortunate, many of whom had lost relatives and all their personal belongings, and thanking Divine Providence for their deliverance. The meeting was called to order and Mr. Goldenberg was elected chairman. Resolutions were then passed thanking the officers, surgeons, passengers and crew of the Carpathia for their splendid services in aiding the rescued and like resolutions for the admirable work done by the officers, surgeons and crew of the Titanic.

"A committee was then appointed to raise funds on board the Carpathia to relieve the immediate wants of the destitute and assist them in reaching their destinations and also to present a loving cup to the officers of the Carpathia and also a loving cup to the surviving officers of the Titanic.

"Mr. I. G. Frauenthal, of New York, was made chairman of the Committee on Subscriptions.

"A committee, consisting of Mrs. J. J. Brown, Mrs. William Bucknell and Mrs. George Stone, was appointed to look after the destitute.

"Mr. Murdock, first officer of the Titanic, sacrificed his life in seeing all the lifeboats away from the ship, and his display of coolness is indescribable.

"The spectacle on board the Carpathia on the return trip to New York at times was heartrending, while at other times those in board were quite cheerful.

"A number of whales were sighted as the Carpathia was clearing the last of the ice, one large one being close by, and all were spouting like geysers."

ACTS OF BRAVERY TOLD BY SURVIVORS

Henry B. Harris Gave His Place in a Lifeboat to a Woman and Perished.

Acts of bravery and cowardice, many more of the former than the latter, were told by survivors of the Titanic as they straggled from the Carpathia on the Cunard line pier last night.

Here for the first time were heard those stories of suffering and peril, of anguish and terror, told by weeping relatives and friends. These were the tales from the deep for which millions have waited since Monday night, when the first authentic information concerning the Titanic was flashed around the world.

The survivors when they landed were warmly clad in blankets, heavy overcoats, shawls and capes. These garments were the property of persons on board the Carpathia, voyagers who had left this port bound for the Continent on business and pleasure.

Order on the pier was excellent and marked by efficient behavior of the government's officers and the employes of the Cunard line.

One of the first of the Titanic survivors to step upon the pier was Dr. Henry W. Frauenthal, of this city. With him was Mr. Frauenthal, his bride of six weeks, whom he had married this winter in Nice. The physician and his wife were surrounded by friends and relatives, who were far more unstrung than the two survivors. Others who surrounded the group seeking information from the physician were told by him that the line would make a statement.

He was advised by friends also not to speak. Dr. Frauenthal, however, said that he and his wife had retired to their stateroom on Sunday night when the crash was first felt. Hurriedly they stepped on deck, found the officers and crew struggling with other passengers to bring about some semblance of odrer, and then in their turn were pushed or thrown into the lifeboats.

Heartrending, indeed, was the story of rescue told to her friends by Mrs. Henry B. Harris, who with her husband was returning from abroad on the Titanic after an eight weeks' pleasure trip on the Continent. Mr. Harris was one of the best known theatrical managers in the country.

The two had just retired to their first cabin suite when the crash came, Mrs. Harris told friends and relatives. Alarmed they hastened to the main deck just as the first of the lifeboats were being lowered into the icy sea. A steward pushed Mrs. Harris into the boat, her husband followed, but the steward shouted:—

"Women and children first."

Mr. Harris rose in his seat and gave way to a woman. His last words to his wife were:—

"That's right, my dear. Goodbye, I must take my medicine."

The wife tried vainly to follow, but the boat was lowered and in the subsequent crush, either during the lowering or in the first struggle, Mrs. Harris broke her right arm at the elbow. She was met at the pier last night by William Harris, Jr., her brother in law and Mr. and Mrs. Max Steur.

TOURING CLUB SENDS CARS.

News of the approach of the Carpathia reached the Touring Club of America, Broadway and Seventy-sixth street, last evening as the club's secretary, Frederick H. Elliott, was about to leave for the day. He immediately informed the New York headquarters of several well known cars, who offered to send automobiles to the vessel's pier to aid in removing the survivors.

The steamship officials were informed of the offer and at once replied that they would be glad of such assistance. A score of cars were hastily gathered under the Touring Club's pennant and sent to the pier.

PURSES OF THE NATION ARE OPEN TO AID THE SUFFERERS

$35,000 Raised in a Day as Country Rushes to Aid of the Needy Survivors

J. P. Morgan & Co. Send $10,000 and Andrew Carnegie $5,000 to Fund Being Raised by Mayor Gaynor.

WOMEN TO HAVE CHARGE OF IMMIGRANTS

NEW YORK city, deeply touched by the great ocean tragedy and desiring to relieve the sufferings of the needy who were rescued from aboard the Titanic, yesterday opened wide its purse.

It was announced in Washington that an appeal to the nation would be made by the American Red Cross Society in aid of the steerage passengers.

For the survivors on board the Carpathia almost $35,000 was raised in a day. Of this amount $24,547 was subscribed to the fund started by Mayor Gaynor. Almost $10,000 was obtained through the committee of New York women, who will have complete charge of the steerage passengers.

Waiting for them with words of sympathy, and prepared to provide lodging and all things necessary to their physical well being, the steerage passengers found this committee of women. The need was great, for the majority of steerage passengers had no one to meet them, a surprisingly small number of persons having made inquiries at the White Star offices concerning third class passengers.

Nearly every hospital in the city volunteered its services, and many hotels as well as individuals offered to give accommodations to those saved from the Titanic.

The funds being collected in New York city will be disbursed by the American Red Cross Society and the committee of women, which will act together. Mr. Jacob H. Schiff will have charge of the funds collected through the Mayor's office.

J. P. MORGAN & CO. HEAD RELIEF FUND

Philadelphia Joins in Humane Work Started by Mayor Gaynor and Sends $2,000.

Quick response was made yesterday to the appeal of Mayor Gaynor for funds for the relief of the Titanic's survivors. Up to last night $24,547.47 had been received. The largest check was for $10,000 and was from J. Pierpont Morgan & Co. The next largest was for $5,000, received from Andrew Carnegie.

New York was not alone in giving aid. Mayor Gaynor received a telegram from Mayor Rudolph Blankenburg, of Philadelphia, as follows:—

"The Citizens' Permanent Relief Committee has sent you through Drexel & Co. $2,000, to be used for the immediate relief of the immigrants rescued from the steamship Titanic. Please transmit the money to the proper committee organized for the relief of the sufferers. An appeal for contributions has been issued, and we shall be glad to co-operate with you in whatever measure may be deemed advisable."

The first mail brought to the Mayor's office $7,500. One of the first to arrive at the Mayor's office was Michael J. Drummond, Commissioner of Charities, who conferred with the Mayor on the relief work. Mr. Drummond offered for the use of the Titanic survivors the Municipal Lodging House, which has ample restaurant facilities, and provision was made to feed all survivors as long as they desire to remain at the lodging house.

Robert W. De Forest, chairman of the Emergency Relief Committee of the American Red Cross, arrived at the Mayor's office soon before noon, as did the Rev. Dr. Edward O. Divine, of the Charity Organization Society, and W. Frank Persons, of the American Red Cross.

The Emergency Relief Committee, of which Mr. De Forest is the head, will adopt a relief system and submit it to the Mayor for approval. The relief fund, it was said, would be turned over to Jacob H. Schiff, who is treasurer of the Red Cross Society.

Mayor Gaynor sent the following message to Mr. Schiff:—

"I have arranged that funds coming in for the relief of the Titanic crew and passengers are to be distributed by the Emergency Committee of the American National Red Cross, and as contributions come in I shall therefore mail them to you as treasurer of the Red Cross Society."

Mr. Schiff replied, stating:—

"I shall be pleased to act in compliance with your desires."

Included in contributions received at the Mayor's office yesterday were the following:—

J. Pierpont Morgan & Co.	$10,000
Philadelphia Relief Committee	2,000
Lewis Cass Ledyard	1,000
Andrew Carnegie	5,000
Morimura Aria & Co.	200
Seth Low	100
M. Guggenheim Sons	1,000
Mrs. Emerson McMillen	250
Miss Maude McMillen	250
John E. McGoran (by cable from Paris)	100
John Vanderbilt	10
S. Heilbroner	10
Ephraim Karelson	25
"A Sympathizer"	5
George Surand	100
F. W. Simonberger	50
Fred Butterfield & Co.	100
M. and C. Mayer	100
George F. Baker	1,000
M. Kurzman & Sons	100
Robert W. De Forest	100
Farmers' Loan and Trust Company	100
A. G. Hyde & Sons	100
Adrian Iselin, Jr.	100
Ross Schofield Company	100
Henry A. Dows	2
Bella C. Landauer	20
Fairchild Bros. & Foster	100
C. E. Wadbrook	5
Samuel A. Salvage	20
Michael A. Freedo	1
William J. Gaynor	100
T. G. Sellew	50
Henry L. Calman	25
J. M. B.	1
Carl Pelz	10
C. C. M. Hoeg	25
Clarence H. Eagle	10
W. B. Symmes	5
Frank DuBois	100
Burlington, Montgomery & Beecher	250
W. H. Newman	100
Wm. A. Read & Co.	1,000
Middleton S. Burrill	250
Cash (anonymous)	3.47
Browning & Co.	10
Henry Wollman	10
George F. Baker, Jr.	250
Crossman & Sielcken	500

The Mayor was advised that the dinner of local school boards, which was to have taken place at the Hotel Astor last night, and that of the Produce Exchange, set for to-night at the Waldorf-Astoria, and that of the Interborough Women Teachers, for Saturday night at the Waldorf-Astoria, have been postponed, the last named until May 11. Mayor Gaynor was to speak at all these dinners.

THROW HOSPITALS OPEN TO RECEIVE SURVIVORS

Offers of Physicians, Nurses, Ambulances and Beds Made in All Parts of the City.

Almost every hospital in New York yesterday offered accommodations for the survivors of the Titanic. St. Luke's Hospital offered to the White Star line, through Mrs. W. A. Bastedo, of No. 57 West Fifty-eighth street, a newly completed ward containing between thirty and forty beds. Mrs. Bastedo's husband is Dr. W. A. Bastedo. She is a member of the Relief Committee of which Mrs. Nelson Henry is chairman and was in charge of the nurses which met the Carpathia. The offer also included the sending of ambulances and physicians and nurses to the pier and clothing for fifty persons. The offer was accepted on the part of the company by Mr. Franklin, the vice president.

St. Vincent's Hospital announced it had accommodations for 120, New York Hospital for 12, Bellevue for 120 and the Flower Hospital for 20. At the New York Hospital it was announced that two ambulances were available. The staff at St. Vincent's put itself at the disposal of the White Star Company and the women's relief committee.

If called upon Charities Commissioner Drummond announced he was ready to send the ferryboat Thomas S. Brennan, equipped as a hospital ship, to the Cunard pier.

At the J. Hood Wright Hospital it was said they would attend to all the patients possible. At the Harlem Hospital it was announced that they would accept all the patients within the district covered by the hospital.

There are two private rooms and four ward beds available at the Washington Heights Hospital, and at Mount Sinai Hospital it was said that they would be glad to care for patients. The Volunteer Hospital offered several physicians and nurses. The Hudson Street Hospital announced it was prepared to send two ambulances and three or more physicians.

Hotels offered to care for survivors. An offer from the Holly, Arlington and Earl hotels came from D. H. Knott, of No. 103 Waverly place, who said he would provide accommodations for one hundred and provide them with food and lodging in the three hotels named. One woman living in Fiftieth street, just off Fifth avenue, offered to put her home at the disposal of the survivors.

NEW YORK WOMEN TO COMFORT NEEDY

Steerage Passengers Will Be Well Provided For by Committee Headed by Mrs. Henry.

Women of New York came forward and asserted that it was their right to care for the destitute steerage passengers of the Titanic. The relief committee formed Tuesday by Mrs. Nelson Herrick Henry, wife of the Surveyor of the Port, is the recognized official relief body for the immediate care of the unfortunates. Headquarters will be opened and a definite programme outlined for the care of the immigrants.

Besides its work of caring for the immigrants at the pier the New York Women's Relief Committee to Aid Titanic Sufferers already has raised almost $10,000.

William Williams, United States Immigration Commissioner, after consulting with General Henry, Surveyor of the Port, yesterday issued orders making the women's committee the guardians of the immigrants. Quarters at the Cunard pier were assigned to the committee, fifteen members of which, together with ten interpreters, ten Sisters of Charity and ten nurses, were allowed to see the steerage passengers.

Final preparations for relief of the immigrants were made yesterday at a meeting of the committee at the home of Mrs. Abram S. Hewitt, No. 9 Lexington avenue. Mrs. Henry was chairman.

The housing committee arranged to divide the survivors into groups, one to include the unmarried men, another the married men and women and another the women and children. These were to be taken to the lodgings. Their names will be obtained and a report made to Mrs. Henry and to the Commissioner of Immigration.

Aid was forthcoming from a men's auxiliary committee to care for the men. This committee was announced as Alexander Haddon, of the State Prison Commission; John D. Price, Murray Young, Everet J. Wendell, Frederick Weeks and D. T. Upjohn, the latter the superintendent of the All Night Mission in the Bowery.

The Clothing Committee had arranged to have emergency bundles on hand at the pier, each bundle including stockings, underwear and a long cape or shawl. Later in the day the committee found donations of clothing so numerous that no more could be used.

Mrs. Shepard Morgan, in charge of the work of providing places for the survivors, had so many offers that she had difficulty in selecting the ones to be used. St. Vincent de Paul Hospital offered accommodations for one hundred, and the Municipal Lodging House announced it could care for a similar number. The Junior League Home offered accommodations for sixty, the Welcome Home for twenty, the Salvation Army Girls' Home twenty, and the Salvation Army Training School thirty.

Mrs. Frederick W. Vanderbilt agreed to provide all the vehicles required to transport the survivors.

Among the women at the meeting were Mrs. Frederick W. Vanderbilt, Miss Eleanor Hewitt, Miss Sarah Hewitt, Mrs. Charles G. Ayres, Mrs. Charles B. Alexander, Mrs. Richard Irvin, Mrs. Stewart L. Woodford, Mrs. A. M. Dodge, Mrs. Van Vechten Olcott, Mrs. Nelson Burr, Miss Virginia Potter, Miss Flora Bigelow, Miss Lota Robinson, Miss Winifred Holt, Mrs. Shepard Morgan, Miss Anne Morgan, Miss Elizabeth Marbury, Mrs. Gilbert H. Montagne, Mrs. Edward R. Hewitt, Mrs. Paul Dana, Mrs. Herman Aldrich and Mrs. Ollisheimer.

After the meeting Mrs. Henry said:—"It is our purpose to show that representative American women of the city rose to the situation, and we will continue our work until the unfortunate newcomers are established in their new land."

GIRLS SHUN CANDY TO AID SURVIVORS

Pupils in the City Normal College, Numbering 2,216, Contribute Their Pin Money.

Setting a splendid example in self-denial for the great army of school children in this country and abroad, more than two thousand two hundred girls in the Normal College of the City of New York are foregoing candies and matinees that their spending money may swell the fund being raised to aid poor survivors of the Titanic.

On the desk of the dean, Miss Annie E. Hickinbottom, rests a pasteboard box and into this the girls of the college, at Park avenue and Sixty-eighth street, keep a stream of money flowing almost constantly all day. A HERALD reporter who peeped into the treasure box yesterday saw money of every denomination, from pennies to $5 bank notes. The same sight can be witnessed at the three annexes of the college, at Seventy-seventh street and Amsterdam avenue, having 240 pupils; Ninety-third street and Amsterdam avenue, with 268 pupils, and in 108th street near Amsterdam avenue, having 608 pupils.

In the college proper there are twelve hundred pupils, and these were all assembled in chapel when Miss Viola Foster, president of the student council, arose and asked for permission to speak. The nature of her proposed talk was known to the dean and the request was granted. There were tears in the eyes of scores of girls and dainty kerchiefs were everywhre visible as the story of the world's worst marine disaster was recited. Miss Foster pictured the suffering which the poverty stricken steerage passengers must endure unless substantial assistance was received immediately upon their arrival and she pleaded that her college mates lend a helping hand.

With the inherent sympathy of the sex every pupil arose when the dean called for a rising vote on the question of a voluntary contribution. The news was communicated quickly to the annexes, and each has vied with the others in making noteworthy the first fund to be raised by school children in this country or Europe for the unfortunate third class passengers.

Presidents of the various classes acted as missionaries and preached the gospel of self-abnegation to their classmates. Girls who were known to have ample spending money were among the first to announce that they would deny themselves usual luxuries in the way of candy and matinees. The other girls became imbued with the spirit. Before the hour for the opening of classes girls were at the office of the dean, and after the close of studies the rush to leave the building was halted by the long line of depositors who had offerings for the relief fund.

To expedite matters Miss Hickinbottom announced to the girls that they could give their donations to the class presidents. These girls will assemble to-day and make the final offering before the fund is closed. The dean showed the way for the teachers by making a contribution, and now every teacher in the college and the three annexes is enrolled among the contributors to the fund.

The funds in the college and annexes will be closed this afternoon and the money counted. The entire amount will be turned over to the president of the college, who will forward a check to Mrs. Nelson M. Henry, of No. 59 West Ninth street, chairman of the committee of prominent New York women raising funds for the poor survivors. With the check will be enclosed a copy of the resolutions of sympathy adopted by the 2,216 girls. These will be signed by Miss Foster and Miss Martha Guiri, president of the class presidents.

$20,000 AT PIER FROM THE STOCK EXCHANGE

Relief Committee Meets Survivors with Ready Cash to Relieve Their Immediate Needs.

With more than $20,000, contributed by the members of the New York Stock Exchange for the relief of the arriving survivors of the Titanic disaster, a committee of five members, consisting of Ransom H. Thomas, president of the Stock Exchange; C. E. Knoblauch, J. F. Carlisle, H. N. Baruch and C. P. Holzderher, was at the pier last night to give assistance in any possible manner.

The suggestion for the raising of the fund met with such quick response that the larger part of the amount was turned over to George W. Ely, secretary of the Exchange, soon after the closing hours. Realizing that time was precious, many of the contributors gave actual cash, while in other instances, the relief committee was supplied with certified checks, that the work might be entirely unhampered by any delay.

It was realized by the committee that many of the rescued passengers of the Titanic who arrived on board the Carpathia last night, while ordinarily wealthy, would be temporarily as poor as the most obscure of the steerage survivors. This, it was recognized, would especially be the case with those whose homes were distant from this city, or who had no relatives or friends to meet them at the pier.

For this reason the committee went prepared to turn over actual cash to those who were in need of it, either for the provision of transportation to their homes, for shelter and sustenance until communications could be made arranging for funds, or for the many contingencies arising which could not be foreseen.

Special attention was directed by the committee to those who were in the second cabin list. These, it was said, were in many cases persons of moderate means who could ill afford to be forced to provide themselves with new clothes, conveniences and other necessities.

In addition to the money which was disbursed to the survivors, the committee made provisions for the care of as many of the rescued as they could arrange for at the various hotels in the city. Still others were assisted in locating their friends and sending messages of reassurance to their families, while transportation was provided for many to other cities.

Three other members of the relief committee who assisted in obtaining the fund were J. H. Griesel, Leopold Newborg and Seymour Cromwell. These were not able to reach the pier.

PATERSON TO AID.

[SPECIAL DESPATCH TO THE HERALD.]

Mayor Andrew F. McBride, of Paterson, N. J., yesterday issued a proclamation to the people of Paterson calling special attention to the disaster and extending an invitation to the citizens to contribute to the funds started by Mayor Gaynor and the Lord Mayor of London. Mayor McBride will receive contributions at his office. Special services in the Paterson churches next Sunday will take the form of a memorial to those who lost their lives.

CLOTHING IS SENT FROM THE WALDORF

Friends and relatives of survivors of the Titanic stopping at the Waldorf-Astoria sent clothing to the Cunard dock last night to supply those in need. Their general contributions, including dresses, stockings, shoes and underwear, were augmented by contributions by many disinterested persons. Those articles were sent in a van.

The hotel management supplied steamer rugs and blankets. Many articles were carried to the pier in twenty taxicabs despatched from the Waldorf-Astoria. In these cabs friends and relatives of the survivors went to the dock. They carried articles of clothing for those in whom they were personally interested. The general contributions were for distribution among the steerage passengers as well as the first and second cabin passengers.

BENEFIT PERFORMANCE AT CENTURY THEATRE

For the benefit of the destitute survivors Liebler & Co. have arranged a special performance of "The Garden of Allah" at the Century Theatre Monday afternoon, April 29. By arrangement with the Women's Relief Committee the entire proceeds will go to that body. The offer was accepted by the entertainment committee of the relief committee, consisting of Mrs. Nelson H. Henry, Mrs. Hunson Morris, Mrs. J. Borden Harriman and Miss Anne Morgan.

Another offer of a special benefit performance was received by Mayor Gaynor from Mr. Dixie Hines, director of the commemoration performance of Hamlet to be given at Wallack's Theatre next Tuesday afternoon in honor of the birthday anniversary of Shakespeare. Mr. Hines, in behalf of the company, offered to repeat the performance.

GERMAN HOSPITAL WILL AID

William M. Condon, superintendent of the German Hospital, at Wyckoff and St. Nicholas avenues, Brooklyn, notified the officers of the Cunard and White Star lines yesterday afternoon that wards in that institution would be thrown open to survivors in case there was an overflow in the Manhattan hospitals. Mr. Condon said the hospital would send ambulances to the pier if they were needed.

RED CROSS TO GIVE AID.

WASHINGTON, D. C., Thursday.—After a conference at the White House to-day between Mr. Nagel, Secretary of Commerce and Labor; C. D. Hilles, secretary to President Taft, and Miss Mabel Boardman, active head of the American Red Cross, it was announced that an appeal to the people of the United States probably would be sent broadcast to-day by the Red Cross. Funds will be asked to aid the destitute rescued from the Titanic.

MR. CARNEGIE SENDS $5,000 AND BLAMES COMPANY FOR USING ICEBERG ROUTE

2 East Ninety-First Street,
New York, April 18, 1912.

Dear Mayor:—

What was the Titanic doing up among the ice when when she had the whole Atlantic Ocean south open and free? This is the root of the matter. Passenger steamships should be compelled to keep far south below the range of icebergs at all seasons. Lifeboats are secondary to this vital requirement. Yours,

ANDREW CARNEGIE.

Office of the Mayor.
April 18, 1912.

Dear Mr. Carnegie:—

As usual, you hit the nail exactly on the head. They had no business up there among the icebergs, and, being there, they should have stopped. The question of lifeboats is a secondary one. I thank you exceedingly for your generous check of $5,000 for the sufferers.

Sincerely yours,
W. J. GAYNOR, Mayor.

Andrew Carnegie, Esq.,
2 East Ninety-first street,
New York city.

The Carpathia Leaves Her Course to Dodge Inquiry

Vessel Speeding Toward New York with Rescued Leaves Usual Steamship Path and Risks Fog Perils to Avoid Being Spoken by Despatch Boats.

SILENT TO PLEAS FOR NEWS OF COLONEL ASTOR

[SPECIAL DESPATCH TO THE HERALD.]

NEWPORT, R. I., Thursday.—New mysteries were added to the story of the Titanic by the conduct of the Carpathia in the early hours of her first close touch with the shore. Wednesday night and early to-day she declined to give her position by wireless to anybody, even to the naval inquirers.

She swung far to the southward of the steamship lanes in passing Nantucket Lightship, and gave evidence of an effort to avoid imparting any information except that officially demanded by White Star officials ashore. Communication with them was almost entirely by code.

The Carpathia was due off the Nantucket Lightship at six o'clock this morning, and if she had held to her shortest course to New York or to the regular steamship lane westward at this time of year she should have passed within seven miles of the lightship. She passed at least twenty and probably more miles to the southward of the light about six o'clock.

The strength increasing and decreasing of her wireless code messages as picked up at the lightship indicated that on code instructions from shore she had swung wide of the coast to avoid interception and any communication by megaphone with the Titanic's passengers whom she carried. This not only delayed appreciably her arrival in New York, but held her apparently in position where she became an earlier victim of the fog in which she seems now enveloped and which she would have longer escaped had she taken the shorter course.

Despatch Boat in Gale.

The HERALD despatch boat, Walter A. Luckenbach, an ocean going tug, was equipped with the best wireless apparatus quickly available in Newport on Wednesday afternoon. It was installed on board the Luckenbach within an hour and an expert placed in charge.

The Luckenbach put to sea on Wednesday evening in the teeth of a northeast gale with storm signals flying from the Newport Naval Station. She made her way steadily all night through rain and bucking a heavy swell from the fast rising wind.

All other vessels sought harbor. The Luckenbach made Nantucket Lightship before daylight and stood by for wireless talk with the operator on board. She then proceeded due south to the furthest point from which she might keep the lightship in sight and extend her range of observation an equal distance to the southward. A sudden and brief clearing of the sky made her range of view about fifteen miles altogether.

From the time the Luckenbach left Newport she was in touch with the wireless messages to and from the Carpathia between seven and twelve o'clock on Wednesday night. Several messages, nearly all of them in code, passed between Siasconset and the Carpathia.

Several messages of condolence and sympathy for Mrs. Astor, Mrs. Widener and others on board the Carpathia were sent rom Siasconsett. One message repeatedly asked if Colonel John Jacob Astor were on board. This was not answered until eight o'clock this morning. The personal chatter of the wireless operator of the steamship Governor Cobb, returning from Cuba to Boston, describing his personal experiences for the benefit of the operators aboard Merchant and Miners' line steamships, seriously interrupted every message to or from the Carpathia for several hours and the Governor Cobb operator paid no attention to the pleading of operators with important business to desist.

Admits Strict Censorship.

At ten o'clock last night, when a perfect deluge of wireless requests for news of various persons and several official ones for her position sent to the Carpathia had been picked up by the Luckenbach, a peremptory reply came from the Cunard steamship. It said that her operator had orders not to give out information of any kind unless signed by the Captain.

Shortly after this the scout cruiser Salem sent a list of third cabin passengers of the Titanic to the Newport Naval Station. During the following houre the Salem repeatedly sought from the Carpathia news of her position. At 5 o'clock this morning Commander Chandler, of the Salem, evidently amazed and offended, sent the following message to the Newport Station addressed to the Secretary of the Navy:—

"I have been unable to obtain any information from the Carpathia, although she is in easy working distance. Cannot believe she has misunderstood my messages. Shall proceed to Bradford to coal. "CHANDLER."

The only message not in code effecting the Carpathia which was sent while she was in the Nantucket lightship radius was to the White Star Company, in New York, giving insistent orders that two special tugs should be sent out to meet her. This was interpreted to mean that some of her passengers may be taken off before she goes to her dock.

The Luckenbach's wireless and that on board the lightship, both seeking to locate the Carpathia by the strength of her calls, were unable to do so, and it was not until nine o'clock that the diminishing sound waves proved that she had done as it was feared she would—dodged away from the Nantucket lightship and the numerous important messages to passengers carried by the Luckenbach which awaited her there.

Lying near the Nantucket Lightship from early this morning until a quarter-past nine o'clock, when the Carpathia was forty miles further along on her way to New York, was an ocean tug in the employ of another newspaper. It was equipped with a dynamo and fairly powerful wireless apparatus. It hung close to the lightship except for trips to the eastward, and during the stay of the HERALD despatch boat in that vicinity the latter was always from half a mile to twelve miles nearer the Carpathia's actual position as she passed far to the southward of both tugs.

When the two tugs at the same time realized from the Carpathia's sound waves that she had passed and was going westward it was after nine o'clock, and the highest strength of the Carpathia's messages on examination of the record proved to have been about six o'clock.

As the Carpathia was moving at a steady gait of thirteen knots she was about forty miles nearer New York when the fact that she had passed was positively established at the lightship wireless station.

During her stay and also on her trip from Newpotr to the lightship this other newspaper boat afforded the naval wireless and other operators listening considerable amusement by the imaginary news she incorporated in frequent messages by wireless to the newspaper by which she was employed.

One of the early ones was:—"The Carpathia is now 250 miles east of Cape Cod."

Cape Cod has an area which eliminates it from definite points of nautical measurements. Also a schol boy need only have taken the hour of the generally known position of the Carpathia on Monday night, multiplied the number of intervening hours by 13, the number of knots, subtracted it from 576, the Carpathia's Monday night distance from Ambrose Channel lightship, and if he didn't get 250 he would have gone to the foot of his class.

The parting fling of the imaginary wireless service was sent just after the newspaper boat dashed away at full speed after the Carpathia, which was going faster and which was forty miles in the lead.

This message read:—"The Carpathia will reach New York early to-night."

SENATE PASSES BILL UNIFYING LAWS OF SEA

Provisions for Reward for Assistance and Salvage Included in Measures Legalizing Convention.

HERALD BUREAU,
No. 1,502 H STREET, N. W.,
WASHINGTON, D. C., Thursday.

The Senate this afternoon passed a bill carrying into effect the provisions of a convention for the unification of certain rules with respect to assistance and salvage at sea. The bill was introduced by Senator Burton, of Ohio, and was reported out favorably by the Committee on Foreign Relations without amendment.

It is provided first that the right to remuneration for assistance or salvage services shall not be affected by common ownership of the vessels rendering and receiving such assistance or salvage services.

The bill, in its second section, provides "that the master or person in charge of a vessel shall, so far as he can do so without serious danger to his own vessel, crew or passengers, render assistance to every person who is found at sea in danger of being lost, and if he fails to do so he shall, upon conviction, be liable to a fine of not to exceed $1,000 or imprisonment for a period of not to exceed two years, or both."

Section three provides "that salvors of human life, who have taken part in the services rendered on the occasion of the accident giving rise to salvage, are entitled to a fair share of the remuneration awarded to the salvors of the vessels, her cargo, and accessories."

Suits for remuneration must be brought within two years unless the court in which the suit is brought shall be satisfied that during such period there has been no reasonable opportunity of arresting the assisted or salved vessel. The act excludes ships of war and government ships appropriated exclusively to a public servant. The act is to take effect July 1, 1912.

THE CARPATHIA'S WIRELESS INADEQUATE

Guglielmo Marconi Says Steamship Owners Practice Too Much Economy in Fitting Out Vessels.

Owners of the big passenger steamship lines practise too much economy, declared Guglielmo Marconi, inventor of the Marconi system of wireless telegraphy, yesterday. Mr. Marconi was speaking on the Titanic disaster at the fourth annual luncheon of the League for Political Education at the Hotel Astor.

If it had been the Carpathia, for instance, which struck the iceburg instead of the Titantic, in all probability not a life would have been saved, he said. The Carpathia, according to Mr. Marconi, is fitted with a small, old fashioned wireless station that cannot send or receive messages at a distance much greater than one hundred miles.

Mr. Marconi said that wireless telegraphy saved the lives of the survivors who are coming into New York on board the Carpathia and that, considering the apparatus which the Carpathia carries, the wireless had worked well. But, he added, because of the inadequacy of the apparatus little news has been receievd.

All yesterday morning, he asserted, the Marconi stations were transmitting messages from survivors to their relatives in various parts of the country and it was apparent that the operator on board the Carpathia was sending out little else.

Laws governing life saving apparatus were responsible for the great loss of life, in Mr. Marconi's opinion, and he urged the immediate passage of a bill which would remedy this. Mr. Marconi had nothing to say concerning the interference of amateurs at the time when the first communications were established on the land and the steamships.

Mr. Thomas A. Edison, who was to have been present at the luncheon, was unable to attend.

PREPARING TO PAY LOST MONEY ORDERS

Thousands of Dollars' Worth Carried on Board the Titanic Will Be Redeemed Eventually.

HERALD BUREAU,
No. 1,502 H STREET, N. W.,
WASHINGTON, D. C., Thursday.

The Post Office Department to-day issued the following regarding the loss of mail on board the Titanic:—

"Among the millions of pieces of mail matter carried on board the lost steamship Titanic there were doubtless thousands of dollars' worth of international money orders, together with descriptive lists of such orders. It is assumed that many of the remitters of those orders will communicate with the payees in this country concerning them, and that these payees in turn will take up the matter through their respective postmasters.

"It is the earnest desire of the department that in all such cases postmasters give careful attention to the inquiries made and promptly report the facts to the Third Assistant Postmaster General (division of money orders), to the end that every effort may be made to insure early payment of the intended beneficiaries."

REVISED FIGURES NOW PLACE THE TOTAL DEATH ROLL AT 1,595

MRS. STRAUS DIED WITH HER HUSBAND, FAMILY IS TOLD

Son Receives Wireless from J. A. Badenoch, a Friend, Aboard the Carpathia.

CALL AGED COUPLE "MARTYRS OF WRECK"

Miss Funk, a Missionary, Returning After Five Years in India, Was Aboard the Titanic.

ALL THE LAND MOURNS

Among the Survivors and Missing Are Persons from Almost Every Large City in the Country.

The fact that Mr. and Mrs. Isidor Straus are among the victims of the Titanic disaster was established yesterday, when Herbert Nathan Straus, son of the distinguished New York man, received a wireless message from J. A. Badenoch, head buyer of the grocery department of R. H. Macy & Co., who is aboard the Carpathia. Mr. Badenoch stated that Mr. and Mrs. Straus were not among the survivors.

The message was handed to members of the Straus family, who were in the private office of R. H. Macy & Co., hoping against hope. Since the first news of the disaster the sons and daughters of Mr. and Mrs. Straus had spent most of the time in the private office of Macy's, directing that all messages and revised passenger lists be sent to them. The terrible suspense cast a gloom over the entire store.

Mr. Herbert Straus would not discuss the death of his parents. He said:—"The wireless despatch from Mr. Badenoch seems to leave no loop hole for hope. It is conclusive proof that my father and mother were martyrs of the wreck. We have waited long and patiently for some news, and now what we have received is most disheartening."

The Rev. Charles L. Kirland, listed among the lost, is believed to be the father of Henry W. Kirkland, of Bangor, Me. He was on his way home after a visit of two months in Scotland.

"Father lost. No hope" was the terse wireless message received in Philadelphia yesterday from Richard Norris Williams, who, with his father, C. Duane Williams, was a passenger. The elder Mr. Williams, who was an attorney, formerly lived in the Quaker City. With his son he was on his way from Switzerland to visit relatives. After the death of his wife, in 1890, Mr. Williams made his home abroad.

Miss Annie Funk, thirty-eight years old, a Methodist Episcopal missionary in India and daughter of James Funk, of Boyertown, Pa., is believed to have perished. She was a second class cabin passenger and her name is not on the list of survivors. She was returning on her first furlough in five years.

Among the first cabin passengers whose name does not appear on the list of those rescued by the Carpathia is S. Ward Stanton, a well known marine artist and editor of Master, Mate and Pilot, a nautical magazine. Mr. Stanton was returning on board the Titanic from a visit to the Alhambra in Spain and the famous art galleries of Paris, to which he had gone to study for a series of marine paintings and which were to be placed in the salons of the new Hudson River steamer the Washington Irving, of the Hudson Rier Day Line.

Cable advices received from Paris confirm the report that George Rosenshine, a retired member of the firm of Rosenshine Sons Company, feather manufacturers at No. 19 East Twenty-second street, was a passenger on board the steamship Titanic. Albert Rosenshine, a brother, received a cablegram with this information from Louis Weber, a friend, now in Paris. The Messrs. Rosenshine retired on February 17. The company was then incorporated, several nephews being still connected with it. A short time after he retired George Rosenshine left for Europe. His brother Albert received several letters from him, in one of which he declared it was his intention to return on board the Titanic. Mr. Rosenshine's name does not appear on the Titanic's list, and it is supposed he went aboard at the last moment.

Among those believed to have gone down with the Titanic is George B. Goldschmidt, of New York, a brother of Edward Goldschmidt, a lawyer, who formerly lived in Hackensack. The brothers had law offices at No. 307 West Seventy-eighth street. The name of George B. Goldschmidt has not once appeared among those who may have escaped, and his relatives have abandoned hope.

Among George Goldschmidt's best seafaring friends was Captain Smith, of the ill-fated Titanic.

W. E. Hipkins, it was positively stated last night, was one of the Titanic victims. He was one of the heads of the weighing machine firm of Avery & Co., of Birmingham, England, and lived with his sister in the suburb of Edgbaston. Mr. Hipkins was coming to this country on one of his occasional business visits and had anticipated a brief stay with Thomas W. Wilby, a writer, of No. 249 West Seventy-sixth street. Mr. Hipkins was a widower, his wife having died two years ago. He was prominently connected with the foundation of a commercial chair in the University of Birmingham, was a collector of Napoleonic relics and a man of recognized culture.

NO NEWS OF MR. HAYS.

MONTREAL, Canada, Thursday.—The Grand Trunk Railway Company this morning received the following telegram:—

"Mrs. Hays, Mrs. Davidson, saved. No news of husband. HAYS."

This message came from Wood's Hole, Massachusetts. This confirms information thus for received to the effect that the president of the Grand Trunk Railway is not among the survivors.

GERMAN LLOYD CHANGES.

The North German Lloyd announced yesterday afternoon that they have instructed the commanders of all their steamships, both here and at Bremen, to take a course two degrees south of the regular southerly steaming lane until further orders.

LATEST LIST OF SURVIVORS NOW ON BOARD THE CARPATHIA

Number of First and Second Class Passengers Aboard the Carpathia Placed at 379.

White Star officials gave out early last night a revised list of first class passengers on the Titanic, who were rescued by the Carpathia. This list shows 209 survivors, counting maids and men servants of the passengers. This shows a total of 337 first and second class passengers brought in by the Carpathia.

In the revised list appears the name of a Miss O'Connell, who had been hitherto identified, by conjecture, as Mrs. Cornell, wife of Magistrate Cornell.

In addition there are eighty-three third class passengers among the survivors, according to the White Star Company's figures.

FIRST CLASS PASSENGERS.

A

ANDERSON, Harry.
APPLETON, Mrs. E. W.
ABBOTT, Mrs. Rose.
ALLISON, Master, and nurse.
ANDREWS, Miss K. T. (Miss Cornelia I.?).
ALLEN, Miss E. W.
ASTOR, Mrs. John Jacob, and maid.
AUBERT, Mrs. N.
BARRATT, Karl Behr (Behr?)
BESSETTE, Miss.
BUCKNELL, Mrs. William.
BARTHWORTH, Mr. A. H. (Bathworth?)

B

BOWERMAN, Miss E.
BROWN, Mrs. J. J.
BURNS, Miss G. M. (Mrs.)
BISHOP, Mr. and Mrs. D.
BLANK, H.
BASSINA, Miss A.
BAXTER, Mrs. James (Brayton).
BAYTON, George A. (Brayton).
BONNELL, Miss C.
BROWN, Mrs. J. M.
BOWAN, Miss G. C.
BECKWITH, Mr. and Mrs. R. L.

C

CARDEZA, Mrs. J. R.
CASSEBERE, Miss D. D.
CLARKE, Mrs. W. M.
CHIBINACE, Mrs. B. (Chibnall?).
CROSSBIE, Miss E. G. (Mrs. E. G. Crosby?).
CROSBY, Mrs. (Miss?).
CROSBY, Miss H.
CARTER, Miss Lucille.
CARTER, Master William.
CANDER, Mrs. Churchill (Cardell?).
CALDERHEAD, N. P. (E. P.?).
CHANDANSON, Miss Victorine.
CAVINDISH, Mrs. TURRELL and maid (Mrs. T. W.?)
CHAFFEE, Mrs. H. L. (H. I.?).
CARDEZA, Thomas.
CUMMINGS, Mrs. J.
CHEVRE, Paul.
CHERRY, Miss Gladys.
CHAMBERS, Mr. and Mrs. B. C. (N. C.?).
CARTER, Mr. and Mrs. W. E.

D

DAILY, P. D.
DOUGLASS, Mrs. FRED C.
DE VIELLIEN, Mme. (Mrs. B. De Villiers?).
DANIEL, ROBERT W.
DAVIDSON, Mrs. THORNTON.
DOUGLASS, Mrs. WALTER.
DODGE, Miss SARAH.
DODGE, WASHINGTON.
DODGE, Mrs. WASHINGTON and son.
DICK, Mr. and Mrs. (A. A.?).
DANIELL, Mr. H. HAREN (see Haren).

E

ENDRES, Miss CAROLINA (Mrs. ?).
ELLIS, Miss.
EARNSHAW, Miss BOULTON (Mrs. ?).

F

FLEGNHEIM, Miss ANTOINETTE (Flagenheim?).
FRANCATELLI, Miss.
FLYNN, J. N. (J. I. ?).
FORTUNE, Miss ALICE.
FORTUNE, Miss LUCILLE.
FORTUNE, Mrs. MARK.
FORTUNE, Miss MABEL.
FRAUENTHAL, Mr. and Mrs. HENRY (Dr.?).
FRAUENTHAL, Mr. and Mrs. J. G. (Mrs. T. G.?)
FROLICHER, Miss MARGARET.
FUTRELLE, Mrs. JACQUES.

G

GRACIE, Colonel ARTHUR (Archibald?).
GRAHAM, Mr. and Mrs. WILLIAM.
GRAHAM, Miss.
GORDON, Sir COSMO DUFF.
GORDON, Lady.
GIBSON, Miss DOROTHY.
GOLDENBERG, Mrs. SAMUEL.
GOLDENBERG, Miss ELLA.
GREENFIELD, Mrs. LEE D. (L. P.?).
GREENFIELD, Mr. WILLIAM.
GIBSON, Mrs. LEONARD.
GOOHT, JAMES.

H

HAREN, Mr. H. (H. Haven?).
HIPACK, Mrs. IDA S. (Hippach?).
HIPACK, Miss JEAN (Hippach?).
HARRIS, Mrs. L. Y. B. (H. B.?).
HALVERSON, Mrs. ALEX (or Malverson).
HOGIBOOM, Mrs. I. C. (J. C.?).
HAWKSFORD, Mr. W. J.
HARPER, Mr. HENRY S., and man servant.
HARPER, Mrs. H. S.
HOYT, Mr. and Mrs. FRED.
HOMER, Mrs. HENRY.
HARDER, Mr. and Mrs. GEORGE.
HAYS, Mrs. CHARLES M. and maid.
HAYS, Miss MARGARET.

I

ISMAY, J. BRUCE.

K

KIMBALL, Mr. and Mrs.
KENNYMAN, Mr. F. A.
KENCHEN, Miss EMILE.

L

LONGLEY, Miss G. F.
LEADER, Mrs. F. A.
LAVORY, Miss BERTHA.
LINES, Mrs. ERNEST.
LINDSTROM, Mrs. SINGIRD
LINES, Miss MARY C.
LESNEUR, Mr. GUSTAV J.

M

MADILL, Miss GEORGETTE A.
MELICARD, Mme.
MAIMY, Miss ROBERTA.
MARTIN, Mrs. D. W. (Marvin?).
MARECHELL, Mr. PIERCE.
MINAHAN, Mrs.
MINAHAN, Miss DAISY.
MOCK, Mr. PHILIP E.

N

NEWELL, Mrs. MARJORIE (Miss Alice?).
NEWELL, Mrs. MADELINE (Miss?)
NEWSOM, Miss HELEN.

O

O'CONNELL, Miss R.
OSTBY, Mr. and Mrs. (E. C.?).
OLIVIA, Miss.
OSTBY, Miss HELEN.
OMOND, Mr. FIEUNAM.

P

POTTER, Mrs. THOMAS, Jr.
PENCHEN, Major ARTHUR.

R

ROGERSON, JOHN (?).
RENAGO, Mrs. MAMAM J. (Ronge).
RANELT, Miss APPIE.
ROTSCHILD, Mrs. LORD MARTIN.
ROSENBAUM, Miss EDITH.
RHEIMS, Mrs. GEO. (Mr.?)
ROTHES, Countess.
ROBERTS, Mrs. EDNA (Edward S?).
ROLMANE, Mr. C.
RYERSON, Mrs. SUSAN P.
RYERSON, Miss EMILY.
RYERSON, Mrs. ARTHUR.

S

STONE, Mrs. GEORGE N. (M?).
SEGESSER, Miss EMMA.
STEWARD, Mr. FRED K. (Seward?).
SHUTTER, Miss (E. W. Shutes?).
SLOPER, WILLIAM T.

LATEST FIGURES SHOWING THOSE RESCUED AND LOST

At the White Star line offices last night it was said that it was estimated that there were 2,340 persons aboard the Titanic, distributed as follows:—

First class passengers	330
Second class	320
Third class	750
Officers and crew	940

The number reported rescued is 705 and is estimated to be as follows:—

First class passengers	210
Second class	125
Third class (estimated)	200
Officers and crew (estimated)	210
Total originally on board	2,340
Total rescued	745
Total lost	1,595

SWIFT, Mrs. F. JOEL.
SCHABER, Mrs. PAUL.
SHEDDEL, ROBERT DOUGLASS (Spedden?).
SNYDER, Mr. and Mrs. JOHN.
SEREPECA, Miss AUGUSTA.
SILVERTHORN, V. SPENCER.
SAALFELD, ADOLF.
STACKLIEHN, Mr. MAX (Stahelin?).
SIMONIUS, ALFONSIUS.
SMITH, Mrs. LUCIEN P.
STEPHENSON, Mrs. WALTER P. (W. B.?).
SALOMON, ABRAHAM (Mrs. A. L.?).
SILVEY, Mrs. WILLIAM B.
STENGEL, Mr. and Mrs. HELERY (C. E. H. Stenmel?).
SPENCER, Mrs. W. A., and maid.
SLAYTER, Miss HILDA.
SPEDDEN, Mr. and Mrs. J. O. (F. O. Speeden?).
STEFFANSON, H. B.

T

TUCKER, Mrs., and maid.
THAYER, Mr. and Mrs. J. B.
THAYER, Mr. J. B., Jr.
TAUSSIG, Miss RUTH.
TAUSSIG, Mr. E.
THOR, Miss ELLA.
TAYLOR, E. Z.
TAYLOR, Mrs. E.
TUCKER, GILBERT (G. M., Jr.?).

W

WOOLNER, Mr. HY.
WARD, Miss ANNA.
WILLIAMS, RICH M., Jr.
WARREN, Mrs. F. M.
WILSON, Miss HELEN A.
WILLARD, Miss.
WICKS, Miss MARY.
WIDENER, Mrs. GEORGE D., and maid.
WHITE, Mrs. J. STEWART.

Y

YOUNG, Miss MARIE.

SECOND CLASS PASSENGERS.

A

ANGLE, Mr. WILLIAM.
ABELSOM, Mrs. HANNA.

B

BALLS, Mrs. ADA E.
BUSS, Miss KATE.
BECKER, Mrs. A. O., and three children.
BEALE, Mr. EDWARD (Beane).
BEANE, Miss ETHEL.
BROWN, Mr. T. W. G.
BROWN, Miss EDITH.
BENTHAM, LILLIAN W.
BOYSTRON, KAROLINA.
BEIGHT (Bright), DAGMAR.

C

CLARK, Mrs. ADA.
CAMERON, Miss.
CALDWELL, ALBERT F.
CALDWELL, Mrs. SYLVAN.
CALDWELL, Infant ALDEN.
COLLYER, Mrs. CHARLOTTE.
COLLYER, Miss MARJORIE.
CHRISTY, ALICE.
COLLET, STUART (Mrs.).
CHRISTY, JULIA.
CHARLES, WILLIAM.

D

DOLING, Miss ELSIE.
DOLING, Mrs. ADA.
DREW, Mrs. LULU.
DAVIES, Mrs. AGNES (Davis).
DAVIS, Miss MARY.
DAVIS, JOHN M.
DUVAN, FLORENTINE.
DUVAN, Miss A.
DAVIDSON, Miss MARY.
DRISCOLL, Mrs. B.

F

FAUNTHROPE, Mrs. ELIZ. (Lizzie).
FORMERY, Miss ELEIN (Mr. Fynnery).

G

GARSIDE, ETHEL.
GERRCAI, Mrs. MARCY.
GENOVESE, Mr. ANGERE.

H

HART, Mrs. (Esther).
HART, child (Eva?).
HARRIS, GEORGE.
HEWLETT, Mrs. MARY.
HARPER, NINA.
HELD, Miss ANNA (Mrs. Stephen).
HOSENE, Mrs. MASSABUMI.
HOCKING, Mrs. ELIAS (Eliza).
HOCKING, Miss NELLIE.
HERMAN, Mrs. JANE.
HERMAN, Miss KATE.
HERMAN, Miss ALICE.
HEALY, NORA (?).
HANSON, JENNIE (?).
HAMALAMIAN, Mrs. ANNA. (Hamatalanen, Anna).
HAMALAMIAN, Mrs. HANN. (infant son).

J

JACKSON, Mrs. AMY (Mrs. Jacobson).

K

KEANE, Miss NORA A.
KELLY, Mrs. F. (Miss Fannie).

L

LEITCH, JESSIE.
LA ROCHE, Mr. JULIET (Joseph) or Mrs.
LA ROCHE, Miss SIMMONE.
LA ROCHE, Miss LOUISE.
LEHMAN, BERTHA.
LAUCH, Mrs. (ALEX.).
LENORE, Mrs. ELIZABETH (Amelia), (Laniore).
LINKKANCA, Miss ANNIE.

M

MELLINGER, ELIZABETH.
MELLINGER, child.
MARSHALL, Miss KATE.
MALLETT, Mr. A.
MALLETT, Mrs.
MALLETT, Master R. E.
MANGE, PAUL A.
MELLOR, Mr. J. (Mellers, William).
McDEARMONT, Miss LILLIE.
McGOWAN, ANNA.
MARION, Mrs.
MARE, Mrs. FLORENCE (Mrs. Ware).

N

NVE, ELIZABETH.
NASERAEL, Mrs. ADELIA (Israel Nessen).

O

OXENHAM, PERCY J. (Thomas).

P

PHILLIPS, ALICE.
PALLAS, Mr. EMILIO.
PADRO, Mr. JULIAN.
PINSKY, ROSA.
PORTALUPPI, EMILIO (Mrs.).
PARSH, Mrs. L. (Mrs. Davis Parrish).

Q

QUICK, Mrs. JANE.
QUICK, Miss VERA W.
QUICK, Miss PHYLLIS.

R

RENALDO, Mrs. ENCARNAVCION.
RIDSDALE, LUCY.
RENOUF, Mrs. LILY.
RUGG, Miss EMILY.
RICHARDS, EMILY.
RICHARDS, Miss EMILY.
RICHARDS, Mr. Jr.
RICHARDS, Mr. EMILE, two boys, and Mr., Jr.
ROGERS, Miss ELIZA.
SINCOCK, Miss MAUDE.

S

SMITH, Miss MARION.
SKELLERY, Mrs. WILLIAM (Shelly, Mrs. Imanitia?).
SILIVANA, SYNLI (Silven Lylie?).

T

TOUCH, Miss ALICE.
TROUT, Miss EDINA S.
TROUT, Miss CECILIA.
TROUT, Mrs. JESSIE (Trant, Mrs. Jessie?).

W

WILLIAMS, CHARLES C.
WEISSE, Mrs. MATHILDA (Mrs. Leopold?).
WEBBER, Miss SUSIE.
WRIGHT, Miss MARION.
WATT, Mrs. BESSIE.
WATT, Miss BERTHA.
WEST, Mrs.
WEST, Miss CONSTANCE.
WEST, Miss BARBARA.
WELLS, ADDIE.
WELLS, Master.
WELLS, Miss.
WARE, Mrs. FLORENCE (Mare?).
WALCROFT, MILLIE.
WARION, Mrs. (Marion?).

THIRD CLASS PASSENGERS.

NORA MURPHY.
KATIE MULLIN.
KATIE McCARTHY.
G. D. MESSEMOCKES.
ANNA MESSEMOCKES.
MADERA YUSEF.
BUNOS MOUBARCK.
HALIN MOUBARCK.
GITOSA MOUBARCK.
MINA MUSULMON.
SABUCA SUBULAKET.
JAVNA MANO.
KIRKOEAN MUHAN.
DELIA DIANODELMN.
KARL MATHJOAX.
BERTHA MALLIEDELL.
MAGGIE MERRIGAN.
BERTHA MARAN.
KRISTOF MADSEN.
ALBERT MOSS.
MARY McGOVERN.
ERNEST McKEY.
ALICE McKEY.
THOMAS McCORMACK.
JOHN NICKAREN.
— ADLERSON.
BERTHA NELSON.
YREE NYHEM.
ANNIE McGOWAN.
AGNES DOYT (or Mrs. A. A. DICK).
MARGARET NANGA.
MAGGIE J. MURPHY.
LEONCH ELDEGREK.
HEUNA MANMAN.
KRIKOREAN KIRORA.
HANWAKAN (?)
DELIA McDERMOTT.
MARLKARL (?)
JOHN McKAREN.
AINO LUDGUIS.
HELENA ANGUSEN.
MARY NEKET.
DEMINA J. NELSON.
ANNA KOLSBOTTEL.
NORA O'LEARY.
ARTHUR OLSEN.
COTERINA PATROS.
GENOIT PICARD.
NOBESA PATROS.
ERNEST PERSON.
NARAS ROTH.
ANNA REIBON.
JOHN CHURCHSSON.
NICOLA SULICI.
JUHO STRINDER.
JAN SCHURBINT.
JULES SAP.
ANNA SOFIA.
S. JOBLOM.
BEIERIGE SINDE.
ROSE SIBELROME.
AGNES SIBELROME.
AMY STANLEY.
JOHAN SUMDIAN.
PALIA SMYTHE.
AXEL SHINE.
FLORENCE KESORNY.
CROFT HEDVIG.
HEDVIG TURKULA.
WILLIAM TURKGEST.
VARTAUON.
ELLEN WICKS.
SILINE YESBURG.
HANNA YOUSEF.
GEORGE YOUSEF.
MARIAN YOUSEF.
SCURLY OUMSON.
PHILLIP ZENN.
NICOLA ELIASE.
NICOLA OANB.
AUGUST ABRIHAMSON.
BEDNOURA ALOUN.
MARIANA ASSIM.
CARLO NELSON.
CANDERSON OSPLUMD.
JOHN CHARLES.
ROSA ABBOTT.
EDNA ANDERSON.
SELMA ASTLUND.
FELIX ASTLUND.
LILLIAN ASTLUND.
AKLESEP ABELSEPH.
LEAK AKSAKS.
LEE BING.
MARIE BOKLIN.
EUGENE BOKLIN.
HALINE BOKLIN.
LATEFE BOKLIN.
FILLY AKSAKS.
NASSIF CASEM.
BOYAM CASEM.
EMILY BATMAN.
MARIA BOCKSTROM.
DANIEL BUCKLEY.
BRIDGET BRADLEY.
CHING HIP.
EINARE BARLSON.
BEATRICE SANDE.
GUS COHN.
L. M. CRIBB.
MINNIE CONTO.
NEVELLE CONTO.
WILL CONTO.
KATIE CONNOLLY.
ELLEN CARR.
THEODORE DEMUEDER.
JOSEPH KRIGESNE.
P. D. DALY.
CHARLES DALY.
MARSOLA DALY.
Mrs. ETTIE DEAN and two children.
MARGARET DEVANEY.
CHOENSEN, John.
LARE, Elleonch.
MARRIGAN, Margaret.
MARSON, Adele.
MATHYO, Karl.
MUN, Hannah.
NEKET, Hobla.
NELSON, Helmina J.
NYHAN, Anna.
ONGULEN, Helena.
SUBMAKET, Fituasa.

Revised Report of All First and Second Cabin Passengers Still Missing

Below is a list of the Titanic's first cabin passengers whose names do not appear among those saved:—

A

AUBERT, Mrs. N., and maid.
ALLISON, Mr. H. J.
ALLISON, Mrs., and maid.
ALLISON, Miss.
ANDREWS, Mr. THOMAS.
ARTAGAVEYTIA, Mr. RAMON.
ASTOR, Colonel J. J., and man servant.
ANDERSON, Mr. WALKER.

B

BAXTER, Mrs. JAMES.
BEATTIE, Mr. T.
BRANDIES, Mr. EMIL.
BAUMAN, Mr. J.
BAXTER, Mr., and Mrs. QUIGG.
BIRNBAUM, JACOB.
BJORNSTORM, Mr. H.
BLACKWELL, Mr. STEPHEN WEART, Trenton, N. J.
BONNELL, Miss LILY.
BOREBANK, Mr. J. J.
BRADY, Mr. JOHN B., Pomeroy, Wash.
BREWE, Mr. ARTHUR JACKSON.
BUTT, Major ARCHIBALD W.
CASE, Mr. HOWARD B.
CAVENDISH, Mr. T. W.
CLIFFORD, Mr. GEORGE QUINCY.
COLEY, Mr. E. P., Victoria, B. C.

C

CRAIG, Mr. NORMAN C. K., C. M. P.
CARLSON, Mr. FRANK.
CORRAN, Mr. F. M.
CORRAN, Mr. J. P.
CHAFEE, Mr. H. L.
CHISHOLM, Mr. ROBERT.
COMPTON, Miss S. R.
COMPTON, Mr. and Mrs. A. T.
CORNELL, Mr. R. O.
CORBETT, Mrs. IRENE C., daughter of Bishop Levi A. Colvin, of Provo, Utah. Father received a letter Tuesday saying she would be home this week.
CRAFTON, Mr. JOHN B.
CROSBY, Mr. E. G., Milwaukee, Wis.
CROSBY, Miss HARRIETT, Milwaukee, Wis.
CUMINGS, Mr. JOHN BRADLEY.
CASSEBEER, Mr. and Mrs. H. A.

D

DAVIDSON, Mr. THORNTON, Montreal.
DODGE, Mr. WASHINGTON.
DULLES, Mr. WILLIAM C.
DALY, Mr. P. D.
DOUGLAS, Mr. W. D.
DOUGLAS, Master R., and nurse.

E

EASTMAN, Miss ANNIE K.
EUSTIS, Miss E. M.
EVANS, Miss E.

F

FOREMAN, Mr. B. L.
FORTUNE, Mr. MARK.
FORTUNE, Mr. CHARLES.
FRANKLIN, Mr. T. P.
FUTRELLE, Mr. JACQUES.

G

GEE, Mr. ARTHUR.
GOLDENBERG, Mr. E. L.
GOLDSCHMIDT, Mr. GEORGE B.
GRAHAM, Mr.
GIGLIO, Mr. VICTOR.
GUGGENHEIM, Mr. BENJAMIN.

H

HAYS, Mr. CHARLES M., Montreal.
HEAD, Mr. CHRISTOPHER.
HILIARD, Mr. HERBERT HENRY.
HIPKINS, Mr. W. F.
HOGABOOM, Mr. JOHN C., Newark, Ohio.
HOLDEN, the Rev. J. STUART, M. A.
HOGENHEIM, Mrs. A.
HARRIS, Mr. HENRY B.
HARRISON, Mr. W. H.
HAVEN, Mr. H.
HARP, Mr. and Mrs. CHARLES M.
HARP, Miss MARGARET, and maid.
HUST, Mr. W. F.
HIPKINS, Mrs. W. E.
HALVERSON, Mr. ALEXANDER M.

I

ISHAM, Miss A. E.
IRVAN, Mrs.

J

JULIAN, Mr. H. F.
JAKOB, Mr. BIRNBAUM.
JONES, Mr. C. C.

K

KENT, Mr. EDWARD A. Mr. Kent was a prominent architect, of Buffalo, N. Y., and a nephew of General A. B. Farnham, of Bangor, and a brother of William Kent, of New York.
KLOBER, Mr. HERMAN.

L

LAMBERT-WILLIAMS, Mr. FLETCHER FELLOWES.
LAWRENCE, Mr. ARTHUR.
LEWIS, Mrs. CHARLTON T.
LONG, Mr. MILTON C.
LEVY, Mr. E. G.
LINES, Mr. ERNEST H.
LINDSHOLM, Mr. J.
LORING, Mr. J. H.
LINGREY, Mr. EDWARD.

M

MAGUIRE, Mr. J. E.
MARVIN, Mr. D. W.
McCAFFRY, Mr. T.
McCAFFRY, Mr. T., Jr.
McCARTHY, Mr. TIMOTHY, Jr.
McGOUGH, Mrs. J. R.
MIDDLETON, Hon. J. CONNEN.
MILLETT, Mr. FRANK D.
MINAHAN, Dr., Fond du Lac, Wis.
McGOACH, Mr. J. R.
MEYER, E. J.
MOLSON, Mr. H. MARKLAND.
MOORE, Mr. CLARENCE, and man servant.
MOOK, Mr. PHILIP E., Derby, Conn.

N

NATSCH, Mr. CHARLES, No. 503 East Seventh street, Flatbush.
NEWELL, Mr. A. W.
NICHOLSON, Mr. A. B.

O

OVIES, Mr. FERNANDO.
ORNOUT, Mr. ALFRED T.

P

PARTNER, Mr. M. AUSTIN.
PAYNE, Mr. V.
POND, Miss FLORENCE L., and maid.
PORTER, Mr. WALTER CHAMBERLAIN.
PUFFER, Mr. C. C.
R, Mr. M. H. W.
PEARS, Mr. and Mrs. THOMAS.
PENASCO, Mr. and Mrs. VICTOR, and maid.

R

REUCHLIN, Mr. JONKHEER J. G.
ROBERT, Mrs. ELIZABETH WATSON, and maid.
ROEBLING, Mr. WASHINGTON A., 2d, Trenton, N. J.
ROOD, Mr. HUGH R., Seattle, Wash.
ROOS, Mr. J. HUGO, Winnipeg.
RHEIMS, Mr. GEORGE.
ROLMANE, Mr. C.
ROTHSCHILD, Mr. M.
ROWE, Mr. ARTHUR.
RYERSON, Mr. ARTHUR.
REYNOLDS, Miss EDITH. She was engaged to marry H. C. Jones, Secretary to the British Embassy in China.

S

SILVERTHORNE, Mr.
SILVEY, Mr. WILLIAM B., Superior, Wis.
SPADDEN, Master R. DOUGLAS, and nurse.
SPENCER, Mr. W. A.
STEAD, Mr. W. T.
STEHLI, Mr. and Mrs. MAX FROLICHER, Zurich, Switzerland.
STRAUS, Mr. ISIDOR, and man servant.
STRAUS, Mrs. ISIDOR, and maid.
SUTTON, Mr. FREDERICK.
SMART, Mr. JOHN MONTGOMERY, Produce Exchange.
SMITH, Mr. M. J. CLINCH.
SMITH, Mr. R. W.
STENMEL, Mr. C. E. H.
STEWART, Mr. ALBERT A., New York representative of the Strowbridge Lithograph Company.
SMITH, Mr. L. P.

T

TAUSSIG, Mr. and Mrs. EMIL, No. 777 West End avenue.
THAYER, Mr. J. B.
THORNE, Mr. and Mrs. G.

U

URUCHURTU, Mr. M. K.

W

WALKER, Mr. W. ANDERSON.
WARREN, Mr. F. M.
WHITE, Mr. PERCIVAL A.
WHITE, Mr. RICHARD F.
WIDENER, Mr. GEORGE D., and man servant.
WIDENER, Mr. HARRY.
WOOD, Mr. and Mrs. FRANK P.
WYCKOFF, Mr. VAN DER HOF.
WEIR, Mr. JOHN.
WICK, Mr. and Mrs. GEORGE D., Youngstown, Ohio.
WILLIAMS, Mr. DUANE.
WILLIAMS, Mr. R. M., JR.
WRIGHT, Mr. GEORGE.

In the above list should be included:—
Mrs. BUCKNELL'S maid.
Mr. CARDOZA'S man servant.
Mrs. CARDOZA'S maid.
Mrs. CARTER'S maid.
Mrs. DOUGLAS' maid.
Mrs. HAYS' maid.
Mr. ISMAY'S man servant.
COUNTESS ROTHES' maid.
Mrs. ROBERTS' maid.
Mrs. RYERSON'S maid.
Mrs. SPEDDEN'S maid.
Mrs. STONE'S maid.
Mrs. THAYER'S maid.
Mrs. J. S. WHITE'S maid and man.

SECOND CABIN PASSENGERS.

A

ASHBY, JOHN.
ALDWORTH, C.
ANDREW, EDGAR.
ADELMAN, FRANZ.
—, Mrs. LILA.
—, Mrs.
ABELSON, SAMPSON.
ANDREW, FRANK.

B

BYLES, Rev. Thomas.
BEAUCHAMP, H. J.
BEESLEY, LAWRENCE.
BROWN, MILDRED.
BENTHAN, L.
BATEMAN, ROBERT J.
BUTLER, REGINALD.
BOTSFORD, HULL.
BERRIMAN, WILLIAM.
BOWEENER, SOLOMON.
BEACKEN, JAMES H.
BROWN, Mrs. (I. W. S.).
BANFIELD, FREDERICK.
BEIGHT, NARL.
BAILEY, PERCY.
BAMBRIDGE, CHARLES R.
BRAILEY (a musician).
BREICIOUS (a musician).

C

CLARKE, CHARLES.
COREY, Mrs.
CARTER, Rev. ERNEST.
CARTER, Mrs. ERNEST.
COLERIDGE, REGINALD.
CHAPMAN, CHARLES.
CUNNINGHAM, ALFRED.
CAMPBELL, WILLIAM.
COLLYER, HAROLD.
CORBETT, Mrs. IRENE.
CHAPMAN, JOHN R. (or H.).
CHAPMAN, Mrs. ELIZABETH.
CHRISTY, Miss J.
COLANDER, ERIC.
COTTERILL, HARRY.

D

DEACON, PERCY.
DAVIS, CHARLES.
DEFFEN, WILLIAM.
DE BRETO, JOSE.
DALCROFT, Miss NELLIE.
DANBRONY, HERBERT.
DREW, JAMES.
DREW, Master MARSHALL.
DAVID, Master JOHN W.
DAVID, Miss ASINCION.
DOUNTON, WILLIAM J.
DEL VARLO, SABASTIAN.
DEL VARLO, Mrs. Sabastian.

E

EITEMILLER, G. F.
ENANDER, INGRAR.

F

FROST, A.
FYNNERY, Mr.
FOUNTHORPE, HARRY.
FILLBROOK, CHARLES.
FUNK, ANNIE.
FAHELSTROM, AME.
FOX, STANLEY W.

G

GREENBERG, SAMUEL.
GILES, RALPH.
GASKELL, ALFRED.
GILLESPIE, WILLIAM.
GILBERT, WILLIAM.
GALE, HARRY.
GALE, S.
GILL, JOHN.
GILES, EDGAR.
GILES, FRED.
GALE, PHADRUCK.
GARVEY, LAWRENCE.

H

HICKMAN, LEONARD.
HICKMAN, LEWIS.
HICKMAN, STANLEY.
HOOD, AMBROSE.
HODGES, HENRY P.
HART, BENJAMIN.
HARRIS, WALTER.
HARPER, JOHN.
HARBECK, WILLIAM H.
HOFFMAN, Mr.
HOFFMAN, Child.
HOFFMAN, Child.
HERMAN, Mr. SAMUEL.
HERMAN, Miss ALICE.
HERMAN, Miss KATE.
HOWARD, Mr. BENJAMIN.
HOWARD, Mrs. ELLEN T.
HART, Mr. GEORGE.
HALE, REGINALD. Was coming here to resume his position with the Home for the Friendless.
HAMATAINEN, ANNA, and infant son.
HILTUNEN, M.
HUNT, GEORGE.
HENHAM, THOMAS.

I

ILETT, BERTHA.

J

JACOBSON, Mr.
JACOBSON, Mrs.
JACOBSON, SYDNEY.
JEFFREY, Mr. CLIFFORD.
JEFFERY, Mr. ERNEST.
JENKIN, Mr. STEPHEN.
JARVIS, JOHN D.
JULIET, LUICHI.
JACKSON, Mrs. AMY.

K

KARINES, Mrs.
KANTAR, SELNA.
KANTAR, Mrs.
KNIGHT, R.
KEANE, Mr. DANIEL.
KIRKLAND, the Rev. CHARLES.
KARNES, Mrs. F. G.
KEYNALDO, Miss.
KRILLNER, JOHAN HENNIK.

L

LEYSON, Mr. ROBERT W. N. (Larson?).
LAWRENCE, Mr. G.
LAROCHE, Mr. JOSEPH.
LAMB, Mr. J. J.
LAMORE, Mrs. AMELIA.
LENGHAM, JOHN.
LEVY, P. J.
LAHTIMEN, Mr. WILLIAM.
LAHTIMEN, Mrs.
LAUCH, CHARLES.

M

MALLETICH, Miss JESSIE; of Painesville, Ohio, was bringing Emil Nanestik, of Austria, to his father in Ohio.
MUDD, THOMAS.
MACK, MARY.
MARSHALL, HENRY.
MELLERS, WILLIAM.
MAYBERG, FRANK H.
MEYER, AUGUST.
MYLES, Mr. THOMAS.
MITCHELL, Mr. HENRY.
MALLETT, Master A.
MATTHEWS, Mr. W. J.
McKANE, Mr. PETER.
MILLING, Mr. JACOB.
MANTVILE, JOSEPH.
MALACHARD, NOLL.
MORAWECK, Dr.
MANGIOVACCLI, EMILIO.
McCRAE, ARTHUR G.

N

NANESTIK, EMIL, of Austria
NESSEN, ISRAEL.
NICHOLLS, Mr. JOSEPH C.
NORMAN, Mr. ROBERT D.
NASSER, NICHOLAS.

O

OTTEO, Mr. RICHARD.
O'QUICK (see Quick).

P

PHILLIPS, ROBERT.
PONESELL, MARTIN.
PAIN, Dr. ALFRED.
PARKES, FRANK.
PENGELLY, Mr. FREDERICK.
PERNOT, Mr. RENE.
PERUSCHITZ, the Rev.
PARRISH, Mrs. DAVIS.
PARKER, CLIFFORD.
PULBAUM, FRANK.

R

ROGERS, SETINA.
RENOUF, Mr. PETER H.
ROGERS, Mr. Harry.
REEVES, Mr. DAVID.

S

SWORD, HANS K.
STOKES, PHILIP J.
SHARP, PERCIVAL.
SEDGWICK, Mr.
SMITH, AUGUSTUS.
SWEET, GEORGE.
SJOSTEDT, Mr. ERNEST.
SLEMEN, Mr. RICHARD J.
SOBERG, Mr. HAYDLN.
SLAYTER, Miss H.
SLATTER, Miss H. M.
STANTON, WARD.
SINKKONEN, ANNA.

T

TOOMEY, ELLEN.
TURPIN, Mr. WILLIAM J.
TURPIN, Mrs. DOROTHY.
TURNER, Mr. JOHN H.
TURNER, Mrs.
TURNER, Mr. GEORGE.
TROUPEANSKY, MOSES AARON.
TERVAN, Mrs. A.
TRANT, Mrs. JESSE.

V

VEALE, Mr. JAMES.
VON DRACHSTEDT, Baron.

W

WALCROFT, Miss.
WILHELM, CHARLES.
WATSON, EMESS.
WILKINSON, Mrs. S. GEORGE.
WILKINSON, Miss ADA C.
WARE, Mr. WILLIAM C.
WEISZ, Mr. LEOPOLD.
WHEADON, Mr. EDWARD.
WARE, Mr. JOHN JAMES.
WARE, Mrs.
WEST, Mr. E. ARTHUR.
WHEELER, Mr. EDWIN.
WERMAN, SAMUEL.

Y

YROIS, Miss H.

POLICE SWEPT ASIDE AS FRANTIC THRONG SEES WOUNDED

Wan and Eager, Victims Watch for City Lights

Passengers Peer Over Rail as the Carpathia Dashes by Tugs at Sandy Hook and the Quarantine Station.

RIDES LOW, IS PLAINLY A SHIP OF SORROW

With wan and eager faces peering over the rail to get a first view of the lights of the harbor, the Carpathia with the survivors of the ill-fated Titanic came up the bay early last evening. The women and handful of men who had witnessed and been a part of the greatest maritime tragedy of the ages were entering the port under circumstances far different from what they had expected when taking passage on board the ship which represented achievement of the ship builders and many of them had no idea how great the loss of life had been in that collision off the Newfoundland coast.

The Carpathia, with the red funnel and black band, the distinguishing mark of the Cunard line, was seen off the Sandy Hook lightship just before seven o'clock. There she took her pilot aboard and steamed up the channel toward the pier, where the anxious thousands were awaiting some details of the great catastrophe.

A swarm of tugs were at her heels, but the Carpathia, though small in comparison with the ocean greyhounds of the present day, was able to pull away from the fleet which had tried to get the first authentic news of the disaster.

The deck of the steamship was illumined by the flashes of lightning from the clouds that gathered as the relief ship started through Ambrose Channel and then by the flashlights of the photographers on board of a dozen of the mosquito fleet that was pursuing her. As soon as the Carpathia appeared in the channel Dr. Joseph J. O'Connell, Health Officer of the port, put out for her in the Governor Flower, the boarding tug.

Takes Aboard Health Officer.

Everything had been facilitated, and she hardly slackened her speed as Dr. O'Connell climbed up her side. It was arranged that he should remain aboard and make the perfunctory inspection required by law before she arrived at her pier, while his own tug followed to take him back to the station.

At the Quarantine Station there was another fleet of tugs, and one after another of the photographers touched off the flashlights, the faces of the passengers of the Carpathia and those rescued from the Titanic showing in the momentary flash. As the tugs pulled alongside the attempts to communicate with the captain or other officers of the Carpathia, her passengers or any of the survivors were of little avail. The seas were running too high to allow the fleet of tugs to approach nearer than five hundred yards, and a brisk southeast wind whirled the words shouted through megaphones away into nothing.

The HERALD tug, however, managed to ask the men on the bridge of the Carpathia regarding the condition of Mrs. John Jacob Astor, Mrs. Widener, Mrs. Marvin and others of the survivors, who were reported to be in a critical condition as a result of their terrible experiences, but from the bridge it was said that nothing was known there regarding the condition of any individual passengers.

"Are any ill?" was asked.

"Yes," was the reply.

But this was the only information which could be obtained, and the Carpathia started briskly up the Ambrose Channel, quickly leaving the tugs behind.

Although a pouring rain was falling and the gathering darkness was punctuated by lightning flashes the rail of the Carpathia was crowded and the wan and terrified look on many of the faces made it easy to distinguish between the survivors of the Titanic's terrible disaster and the regular passengers of the Carpathia.

Baptism of Terror Enduring.

The eagerness with which they hailed the little squadron of tug boats, the pilot boat, the lightship and the distant lights of Sandy Hook, Coney Island and the Ambrose Channel was testimony to the fact that their baptism of terror had not ended when the Carpathia picked them from the icy waters above the Titanic's grave on Monday afternoon.

Their days of agony, packed like animals on a vessel but little fitted to carry such a crowd, ill, sick at heart, torn with anxiety over their relatives at home and with grief over the dear ones whom they had left twelve hundred miles out in a lonely ocean grave, had only served to emphasize a thousandfold the terror of darkness, panic and death on that awful Sunday night in mid-ocean.

Few of the conveniences necessary to care for 700 injured, ill, half crazed women were available on board the Carpathia. There was no room to house them properly, and the survivors, after three days in a rough sea, with every motion of the deck awakening in their breasts the terror which will never die, welcomed the sight of land and home with a fervor which they had never felt before.

Yet there were no expressions of joy, no glad hailing of the lights of New York nor pleasant thoughts of the loved faces soon to be greeted at the pier. Never has New York seen a homecoming like it. Silently the Carpathia steamed up the harbor bearing her load of human agony to the piers which had expected to receive it the day before as a load of human joy and triumph over the mastery of the seas.

Vessel Rides Low in Water.

It was plain that the Carpathia was overcrowded. She rode low in the water and her movements were deliberate. Every stateroom was illuminated and every deck filled, and even in the fast falling darkness the steamship had the appearance of having been converted hastily from an excursion palace into an emergency hospital.

Numbers of the eager passengers, doubtless some of those who were rescued from the disaster, made attempts to communicate with the tugs. They leaned far opt over the rail and shouted tidings or greetings, but their words were whisked away by the sharp south wind and were unintelligible.

The tugs stood in as close to the Carpathia as they dared and searchlights were played on the deck. Everything possible had been done to expedite her passage to her pier, the pilot was waiting in a small boat, and it required only a few minutes for him to clamber up the side, elbow his way through the crowded decks and saloons and take his place on the bridge. Then the vessel was off, with the fleet of tugs folowing.

CARDINALS ADOPT RESOLUTIONS OF GRIEF

Archbishops of Country in Joint Session Express Sympathy for All Sufferers.

Cardinal Farley reached home from Washington late last night bowed with grief over the terrible loss of life on board the Titanic. He arrived just at the time the Carpathia was docking. He heard through a HERALD reporter a brief account of the dead, the dying and the ill on board.

Action will be taken this morning by consultors of the diocese to help the distressed in every way possible, and instructions will be drawn up for the clergy to say special prayers for all the dead, the physical sufferers and the afflicted relatives and friends. It was only because Cardinal Farley was in the capital at a meeting of the Trustees of the Catholic University that definite action was not taken before.

The Cardinal was especially sympathetic over the fate of the third class passengers, who, though unknown to the world, were sturdy people. Many of them came from his native country.

Cardinal Farley also was especially grieved over the fate of Major Archibald Butt, who went to Rome to see Pope Pius X. on a special errand for President Taft which vitally concerned the three American members of the Sacred College.

The Cardinal had his private secretary give a HERALD reporter a copy of the resolutions Cardinals Gibbons, Farley and O'Connell and the archbishops of the country adopted and sent to President Taft expressing their grief over the Titanic horror. These were signed by the three Cardinals and read:—

"The archbishops of the country, in joint session with the Trustees of the Catholic University of America, beg to offer to the President of the United States the expression of their profound grief at the awful loss of human lives attendant upon the sinking of the steamship Titanic, and at the same time to assure the relatives of the victims of this horrible disaster of our deepest sympathy and condolence.

"They wish also to attest hereby to the hope that the lawmakers of the country will see in this sad accident the obvious necessity of legal provisions for the greater security of ocean travel."

This session was the first occasion on which the three Cardinals have been together since Cardinals Farley and O'Connell were elevated. The New York Cardinal spoke of the incident as unique.

WOULD MAKE OWNERS CRIMINALLY LIABLE

Representative Sulzer Cites the Slocum Disaster to Prove Need for Drastic Action by Congress.

HERALD BUREAU,
No. 1,502 H STREET, N. W.,
WASHINGTON, D. C. Thursday.

More bills for the protection of human life at sea were reported favorably to the House and Senate to-day. The committees gave them swift consideration after the disaster to the Titanic aroused the public to the needs of better life saving equipment on foreign ships, regulation of wireless and an iceberg patrol.

Representative Alexander, of the Committee on Merchant Marine, favors an investigation by that body as a means of determining what legislation is required for the safeguarding of transatlantic travel. Some of the House leaders favor an investigation by a joint committee of the Senate and the House.

Representative Sulzer, of New York, who introduced a bill to compel ocean steamships to carry an adequate number of lifeboats and rafts, said to-day:—

"This investigation business is only throwing dust into the people's eyes. The question at issue was inquired into after the destruction of the Slocum in New York harbor eight years ago. What we want to do is to make steamship owners criminally liable for failing to equip their vessels properly for the saving of life. Make it a felony and send some of those criminally negligent to jail and we will not have any more disasters. My bill contains strict penal provisions to be enforced against masters and owners who permit vessels to go to sea without ample life saving equipment. I shall make every effort to have this bill reported and passed."

Representative Alexander's joint resolution providing for the international agreement of the lane routes to be followed by transatlantic steamships was reported favorably to the House. It authorizes the President to invite maritime nations to co-operate with the United States to this end.

CRIPPLES TO GREET TITANIC SURVIVOR

Dr. Frauenthal, the Founder of Joint Disease Hospital, To Be Welcomed by Sixty Patients.

Sixty almost helpless cripples, twenty-six of them children, in the Hospital for Deformities and Joint Diseases, at No. 1,919 Madison avenue, will to-day welcome the return of Dr. Henry W. Frauenthal, of No. 783 Lexington avenue, the director and founder. The children have been praying for Dr. Frauenthal's safe return since the first news of the Titanic disaster.

When a message was received late yesterday afternoon from Dr. Frauenthal, stating that he, his bride and his brother, Isaac Frauenthal, were safe on the Carpathia, the patients told Miss S. A. Barden, the superintendent, that they would like to make some demonstration.

When in the city Dr. Frauenthal visits the hospital between nine and ten o'clock each day. It has been assumed that he will follow his custom, and the patients will be taken in wheeled chairs to the verandas to watch for his approach, which they will greet with cheers and the waving of handkerchiefs. An informal reception inside the hospital will follow.

Dr. Frauenthal, who founded the hospital five years ago and who has been very successful in the treatment of difficult cases, recently married Miss Clara Heinsheimer, of New York city and Far Rockaway. The wedding took place in Nice, France, on March 26.

ALL FLAGS HALF MAST.

HERALD BUREAU,
No. 1,502 H STREET, N. W.,
WASHINGTON, D. C., Thursday.

President Taft has ordered that all government flags be half masted to-morrow as a mark of national mourning for the Titanic's disaster. The order was issued late this afternoon and forthwith transmitted to all government departments.

THERE WERE NOT ENOUGH LIFEBOATS, SAYS COMMITTEE OF SURVIVORS

THE following statement, issued by a committee of the surviving passengers, was given to the press on the arrival of the Carpathia:—

"We, the undersigned surviving passengers from the steamship Titanic, in order to forestall any sensational or exaggerated statements, deem it our duty to give to the press a statement of facts which have come to our knowledge and which we believe to be true.

"On Sunday, April 14, 1912, at about twenty minutes to twelve P. M., on a cold, starlit night, in a smooth sea and with no moon, the ship struck an iceberg which had been reported to the bridge by lookouts, but not early enough to avoid collision. Steps were taken to ascertain the damage and save passengers and ship. Orders were given to put on life belts and the boats were lowered.

"The ship sank at about twenty minutes past two A. M. Monday, and the usual distress signals were sent out by wireless and rockets fired at intervals from the ship. Fortunately the wireless message was received by the Cunard steamship Carpathia at about twelve o'clock midnight, and she arrived on the scene of the disaster at about four A. M. Monday.

Tender Care for Rescued.

"The officers and crew of the steamship Carpathia had been preparing all night for the rescue and comfort of the survivors, and the last mentioned were received on board with the most touching care and kindness, every attention being given to all, irrespective of class. The passengers, officers and crew gave up gladly their staterooms, clothing and comforts for our benefit, all honor to them.

"The English Board of Trade passengers' certificate on board the Titanic allowed for a total of approximately 3,500. The same certificate called for lifeboat accommodation for approximately 950 in the following boats:—Fourteen large lifeboats, two smaller boats and four collapsible boats. Life preservers were accessible and apparently in sufficient number for all on board.

"The approximate number of passengers carried at the time of the collision was:—

"First class, 330; second class, 320; third class, 750; total, 1,400; officers and crew, 940. Total, 2,340.

"Of the foregoing about the following were rescued by the steamship Carpathia:—

"First class, 210; second class, 125; third class, 200; officers, 4; seamen, 39; stewards, 96; firemen, 71. Total, 210 of the crew. The total saved, about 745, was about eighty per cent of the maximum capacity of the lifeboats.

"Not Enough Lifeboats."

"We feel it our duty to call the attention of the public to what we consider the inadequate supply of life saving appliances provided for on modern passenger steamships, and recommend that immediate steps be taken to compel passenger steamers to carry sufficient boats to accommodate the maximum number of persons carried on board. The following facts were observed and should be considered in this connection:—

"The insufficiency of lifeboats, rafts, &c.; lack of trained seamen to man the same (stokers, stewards, &c., are not efficient boat handlers); not enough officers to carry out emergency orders on the bridge and superintend the launching and control of lifeboats; absence of searchlights.

"The Board of Trade rules allow for entirely too many persons in each boat to permit the same to be properly handled. On the Titanic the boat deck was about seventy-five feet above water, and consequently the passengers were required to embark before lowering boats, thus endangering the operation and preventing the taking on of the maximum number the boats would hold. Boats at all times to be properly equipped with provisions, water, lamps, compasses, lights, &c. Life saving boat drills should be more frequent and thoroughly carried out, and officers should be armed at boat drills.

Greater reduction in speed in fog and ice, as damage, if collision actually occurs, is less. In conclusion, we suggest that an international conference be called to recommend the passage of identical laws providing for the safety of all at sea, and we urge the United States government to take the initiative as soon as possible."

The statement was signed by Samuel Goldenberg, chairman, and a committee of twenty-five.

Mrs. Astor Visits Ill Father, Then Proceeds to Her Own Home

Young Widow of Colonel John Jacob Astor Among the First to Leave the Carpathia—Not in State of Collapse, as Reported.

The report that Mrs. John Jacob Astor was in a state of complete collapse and was a patient in the steamship's hospital proved to be untrue shortly after the Carpathia had been warped into her dock. The young widow of Colonel Astor was among the first to leave the vessel. She walked down the gang plank unassisted, and followed by her maid, who also was among the fortunate few to escape from the sinking craft.

Mrs. William H. Force, her mother; Miss Katherine E. Force, her sister, and Mr. William Vincent Astor, the only son of Colonel Astor, had arrived early at the pier armed with the necessary credentials to pass them through the lines of police to the spot set aside for the waiting relatives.

Young Mr. Astor was the first to pick out his stepmother as she descended the gangplank. He, however, obeyed the rules obliging relatives to keep their positions until the survivors had sought them out under the initials of their family names. For a few moments Mrs. Astor looked helplessly about until Mr. Astor was able to reach her side.

Then it appeared as if the last fragment of endurance had fled when the young widow fell into her mother's arms. No words were spoken. Mr. Astor led the way through the throng of waiting relatives to an automobile.

Mrs. Astor, it is reported, did not know that Colonel Astor was dead until she entered her stepson's automobile. She had been led to believe that he and others on board when she went away in a lifeboat had been rescued later and were on board another vessel.

Her first words to Vincent Astor when she met him at the pier were, "Have you any word of Jack?"

Mrs. Astor reached her home at eleven o'clock. Vincent Astor sat with the chauffeur. Inside the machine were Mrs. Astor's maid and Mr. Nicholas Biddle, a trustee of the Astor estate. Mrs. Astor walked from the car to the residence assisted by Mr. Biddle. She seemed to be very weak.

Dr. R. B. Kimball, of No. 135 East Fifty-second street, was waiting at the Astor residence for Mrs. Astor and her maid. In a few minutes he returned to the street and met a HERALD reporter. He was smiling.

"Mrs. Astor is in excellent health," said Dr. Kimball. "The ordeal she went through must be taken into consideration. It was enough to rack the nerves of the strongest person. I believe with a few days' rest in familiar surroundings Mrs. Astor will be herself again. She needs a complete rest.

"Her condition has not been impaired by the accident as far as I can ascertain at the present time. A more than superficial examination of the brave woman convinces me that she will suffer no ill effects. I will not visit her again until some time in the morning, and I see no reason why I should be called to prescribe for her before that time."

Women Rowed Lifeboats, Says an Eyewitness

Mr. Wallace Bradford Writes from Aboard the Carpathia to the Herald as the Survivors Are Being Taken on Deck.

Mr. Wallace Bradford, of San Francisco, a passenger aboard the Carpathia, gave the following thrilling account of the rescue of the Titanic's passengers in a letter addressed to the editor of the HERALD:—

"Monday Noon, April 15.—Since half-past four this morning I have experienced one of those never to be forgotten circumstances that weighs heavy on my soul and which shows most awfully what puny things we mortals are. Long before this reaches you the news will be flashed that the Titanic has gone down and that our steamer, the Carpathia, caught the wireless message when seventy-five miles away, and so far we have picked up twenty boats estimated to contain about 750 people.

"None of us can tell just how many, as they have been hustled to various staterooms and to the dining saloon to be warmed up. I was awakened by unusual noises and imagined that I smelled smoke. I jumped up and looked out of my port hole, and my eyes must have bulged when I saw a huge iceberg looming up like a rock off shore. It was not white, and I was positive that it was a rock, and the thought flashed through my mind, how in the world can we be near a rock when we are four days out from New York in a southerly direction and in midocean?

"When I got out on deck the first man I encountered told me that the Titanic had gone down and we were rescuing the passengers. The first two boats from the doomed vessel were in sight making toward us. Neither of them was crowded. This was accounted for later by the fact that it was impossible to get many to leave the steamer, as they would not believe that she was going down. It was a glorious, clear morning and a quiet sea. Off to the starboard was a white area of ice plain, from whose even surface rose mammoth forts, castles and pyramids of solid ice almost as real as though they had been placed theer by the hand of man.

"Our steamer was hove to about two and a half miles from the edge of this huge iceberg. The Titanic struck about 11:30 P. M. and did not go down until two o'clock. Many of the passengers were in evening dress when they came aboard our ship, and most of these were in a most bedraggled condition. Near me as I write is a girl about eighteen years old in a fancy dress costume of bright colors, while in another seat nearby is a woman in a white dress trimmed with lace and covered with jaunty blue flowers.

Women at the Oars.

"As the boats came alongside after the first two all of them contained a very large proportion of women. In fact, one of the boats had women at the oars, one in particular containing, as near as I could estimate, about forty-five women and only about six men. In this boat two women were handling one of the oars. All of the engineers went down with the steamer. Four bodies have been brought aboard. One is that of a fireman, who is said to have been shot by one of the officers because he refused to obey orders. Soon after I got on deck I could, with the aid of my glasses, count seven boats headed our way and they continued to come up to half past eight o'clock. Some were in sight for a long time and moved very slowly, showing plainly that the oars were being handled by amateurs or by women.

"No baggage of any kind was brought by the survivors. In fact, the only piece of baggage that reached the Carpathia from the Titanic is a small closed trunk about twenty-four inches square, evidently the property of an Irish female immigrant. While some seemed fully dressed, many of the men having their overcoats and the women sealskin and other coats, others came just as they had jumped from their berths, clothed in their pajamas and bath robes.

Suffer from the Cold.

"It was a beautiful clear morning, but extremely cold, and the sufferings that those in the boats had endured for the three to four hours that they were afloat was plainly shown by their condition. Rope ladders were lowered over the sides for those that could climb aboard and canvas bags were sent down for the women and children, their being a large number of both babies and half grown children in the boats. The children were taken from the mothers and deposited in the bags and hoisted to the decks, while the anxious mothers watched eagerly for the moment when they were received by the men on deck and hurried to the dining saloon.

"We cruised about until about two P. M. and were headed for New York. Our captain has just told me that he is going to New York unless he receives wireless orders otherwise. I was standing near the second officer of the Titanic, who is the senior surviving officer, when he was questioning some of his crew, who had come aboard. They agreed that eighteen boats had reached the Carpathia. Three of the men said that one of the Titanic's boats had not been cut away, and the officer asserted that that left only one boat not accounted for.

Washington Dodge Missed.

"I soon discovered that Washington Dodge, City and County Assessor of San Francisco, and his wife and four-year-old boy were passengers on board the Titanic. Several of the boats have come in, but only Mrs. Dodge and the little boy have so far arrived on our steamer. Mr. Dodge's friends in San Francisco will understand that he is th elast one in the world to leave a ship while there are any women and children that have not been put into the boats.

Soon after writing this I discovered that Mr. Dodge had got aboard, having come in one of the last boats that left the ship, and it was a good deal of satisfaction to me to turn over my stateroom to them. Before we started for New York the steamer California, a freight boat, arrived and communicated for fifteen or twenty minutes with our boat with the aid of a megaphone, she evidently agreeing with our captain to stay there and cruise about in the hopes of picking up more people. No more floating palaces for me. I'll take my chances on a moderate sized boat with a limited number of people.

"There are two darling little French twins who left Europe with their father, their mother having died, who have finally landed on our steamer, the father having gone down with the Titanic. The children were brought aboard in their night clothes, but have been rigged out by some of our passengers so that they now present a neat appearance. The wireless operator caught the S. O. S. from the Titanic when he was supposed to be off duty, it being his hours for sleep. We did not see anything of the steamer and the only evidence that she had gone down was a very limited amount of wreckage which floated by our steamer about two hours after we had hove to. You can imagine that the taking on of seven hundred new passengers in a steamer of the size of the Carpathia has demoralized to some extent the sleeping accommodations, but it is simply astonishing what fine work the culinery department of the steamer has done.

"The meals are served in almost as good shape as they were before the Titanic's passengers came aboard and everybody connected with the ship, from the captain to the scullery boys, is doing his utmost to handle the passengers which overcrowded the steamer. Beds have been made up on the tables in the dining saloons and the women, who have not been able to find berths in the staterooms, are occupying these beds, while the men who were occupying berths on the Carpathia have turned them over to the rescued passengers and are sleeping in the hallways and smoking rooms of the steamer.

"A young man told me of his fearful experience. After the last boat left about fifty men who were near one of the collapsible boats on the upper deck, which up to that time they had been unable to open, finally succeeded in pulling up the movable sides, but before they could cut her loose, the bow of the Titanic sank beneath the surface and they went down with her, but as the stern of the Titanic sunk the bow came above the surface of the water and they managed to cut loose and float off.

"Dead Cast Overboard."

"Of something like fifty men who left the steamer on that raft, or collapsible boat, only seventeen managed to reach the Carpathia. As one after another succumbed to the bitter cold, they were dropped overboard in order to lighten the weight of the raft, as those that were on the raft were standing in water up to their knees for nearly four hours.

"I have talked with many of the survivors, both men and women, and all agreed that the discipline aboard the Titanic after she struck was first class in every respect. The officers were armed with their revolvers and in the sternest manner commanded that none but women should be put in the boats, with the exception of from four to six men who could handle oars. The women passengers were formed into line and marched to the stairway, the officers telling them that there was no immediate danger and that they were to be put into the boats as a matter of precaution and that they would all probably be taken back when the captain was satisfied that the damage to the steamer would not cause her to sink.

"There are from fifteen to twenty-five women aboard, most of them being young brides, who were forced to leave their husbands and go into the boats. Among these is Mrs. John Jacob Astor, of New York. She has kept to her cabin since she has come aboard the Carpathia. I listened this morning to the story of the quartermaster of the Titanic, who was at the wheel when the steamer struck. He said that the man in the crow's nest reported an iceberg ahead, but as the icebergs take on the color of their surroundings, and as the water was very dark at the time, he said that it was not likely that the lookout could have seen the iceberg much more than a quarter of a mile away, and that if the iceberg was a quarter of a mile away when he reported it the steamer would be up with the iceberg in less than two minutes, and going at the speed she was it was impossible to check her headway enough to avoid a collision in so short a time.

"This seems a reasonable statement, as many of the passengers have told me that the iceberg struck the steamship up near the bow, but on the side and not full on. Some of the passengers say that the only evidence that they saw of an iceberg anywhere near the ship was several tons of crushed ice on her forward deck, while a very intelligent English woman has told me that she plainly saw the huge iceberg that the steamer struck and that it had two elevations resembling the towers of a cathedral. The case of this woman is a sad one, as she told me that her husband had sold his business in England and that he and she and their eight-year-old daughter were on their way to Fayette, Idaho.

Saw Boat Loads Drown; Says Captain Was a Hero

Robert Daniel, of Philadelphia, Tells of Terrible Battle in Dark, When Passengers Seemed to Go Insane After the Titanic Crashed Into Iceberg.

TWO LIFEBOATS WERE DRAWN DOWN BY WRECK

Robert Daniel, of Philadelphia, carried from the Carpathia Mrs. Lucian P. Smith, daughter of Representative Hughes, in a fainting condition. Mrs. Smith had been rescued by the Carpathia. She was hurriedly taken from the pier by her father.

Mr. Daniel said:—"I had just left the music room and disrobed and was in my bunk when there was a terrific crash. The boat quivered, and the lights went out. In the darkness I rushed on deck almost naked. There seemed to be thousands fighting and shouting in the dark, and then they got the storage batteries going and that gave us a little light.

"Captain Smith is the biggest hero I ever saw. He stood on the bridge and shouted through a megaphone, trying to make himself heard. The crew obeyed his orders as well as could be expected.

"Five minutes after the crash everybody seemed to have gone insane. Men and women fought, bit and scratched to be in line for the lifeboats. Look at my black eye and cut chin. I got those in the fight.

Saw Men Praying.

"Then Captain Smith seemed to get some order and the passengers were sent to the fore and aft of the big boat. There was a frightful grinding noise throughout.

"I saw men praying as I struggled to get to the rail. Curses and prayers filled the air. Women who had been in the music room, where a concert had been in progress, were still dressed in evening attire and wearing diamonds. Other women had just got to their bunks and were dressed in flimsy night attire. All rushed with one object—to get to the lifeboats.

"Captain Smith remained on the bridge, trying to make himself heard. He was still shouting when I last saw him. As the passengers got into the boats the women were thrown in if they did not move fast enough. An officer jumped on to command and the boats were swung from their davits and down into the water.

"Hundreds, it seems, did not wait for the lifeboats. They could see there was no chance for them, and they jumped overboard."

"What happened to you?" Daniel was asked.

Went Over Side of Boat.

"Oh, I can't tell you what happened. I hardly know myself," he returned. "I was naked. I grabbed something and uttered one prayer. Then I went over the side of the boat—over the side of the boat."

At this point Daniel was so overcome that he had to be led to a rail, where he rested for a few minutes.

"Let me smoke a cigar before I go on," he said.

"After waiting for an interminable time with a collapsible boat in my hands," he continued, "I felt the Titanic sinking under my feet. I could feel her going under at the bows. The storage batteries furnishing the light again gave out and there was darkness. I tried to wait awhile, but I suddenly found myself leaping from the rail away up in the air and it felt an eternity before I hit the water. When I came up I felt that I was been drawn in by the suction, and when I felt a cake of ice near I clung to it.

"I was naked. For five hours I battled with ice cakes, and when I saw other boats near I almost gave up."

Describing his trip in the Carpathia, Daniel said:—

"I did not see Bruce Ismay on board the Carpathia. If my understanding of Captain Smith is correct, I know Smith never would have permitted a man to enter one of those lifeboats.

"I recall, when I got aboard the Carpathia that Mrs. John Jacob Astor was assigned to a cabin given to her by one of the passengers of the Carpathia. I did not see Mrs. Astor since Monday morning, but I know she was in care of a ship's surgeon."

Asked if he knew there had been any shooting on board the Titanic in the panic, Daniel said he heard nothing of the sort, but added it might have been somebody was shot and he would not know it in the pandemonium.

Mr. Daniel in his narrative said:—

"I saw Mrs. Smith on board the Carpathia. She is a daughter of Representative Hughes. Her husband was lost."

Describing the horrible pounding and knocking he heard in the last hours of the Titanic's struggle to keep afloat, Mr. Daniel said he thought some part of the monster vessel's machinery had given out and was pounding against the bottom or sides of the big craft. He said he did not think the vessel remained close enough to the iceberg to have been pounding against the ice.

Mr. Daniel was asked about the condition of the survivors when picked up from the lifeboats.

Several in Boats Frozen.

"Horrible," was his reply.

"Every one of the persons rescued was on the open sea for hours," he said. "We had not a bite to eat. The wind, coming over the sea of ice and the great bergs, chilled us to the marrow of our bones. One or two of the persons in the boats were frozen, I think, to death.

"The Titanic struck the berg at twenty minutes after ten o'clock. We could tell from the first she was sinking. The whole front part of the steamer, it seemed, was torn away.

"We knew from the first there was no hope. We were doomed. We were confident of that. The vessel gradually went down. The bow entered the water first. When I got into the boat I saw a throng of insane, struggling persons at the rail of the doomed ship.

"I know two or three lifeboats were drawn under the wrecked steamer and were lost. Each was filled with passengers.

"Many passengers, I am confident, were in the bow of the vessel when that part sank. Why they did not go, or were not allowed to go, to another part of the steamer I don't know.

"It was not possible for us to save personal property. I had several things in my stateroom that I would have very much liked to have saved. When the crash came—it seemed as if the whole thing was over in a minute—the passengers were apparently insane. Many of the women, fearing death in many forms, collapsed. Perhaps they died where they lay."

Mr. Daniel was among the first to appear on the gangway of the steamer. He was exhausted and assisted Mrs. Smith. Reaching the bottom of the gangway, he surrendered the fainting woman to her father, Representative Hughes.

Removing a tattered derby that had been given to him by a passenger on board the Carpathia, he said:—

"I did the best I could."

He reeled and was caught by several men who had gathered about him.

Told to Watch for Ice, Says Man at the Wheel

Robert Hichens, Quartermaster, Tells of Receiving Instructions to Keep a Lookout for Small Floes—Crash Comes Few Seconds After Warning Gong Sounds.

NO NEED OF WEAPONS TO ENFORCE RULE OF SEA

From Robert Hichens, quartermaster at the wheel of the Titanic when the great vessel crashed into the iceberg, and then in command of one of the boats which left the steamship before it went down, have come details of the terrible hight at sea which could have been known to perhaps no other person. And standing out in memory of this young Cornishman are shrieks and groans that went up from the dark hulk of the giant steamship before she sank.

Hichens, a type of young Englishman who follows the sea, had for years been on the troop ship Dongolo, running to Bombay, and thought himself fortunate when he obtained his berth as quartermaster of the Titanic, the greatest and largest of all steamships. He told a HERALD reporter in their sequence the events of the night and morning of April 14 and 15.

It was in his boat that Mrs. John Jacob Astor took her place, after Colonel Astor had kissed her goodbye, and handed her a flask of brandy, then taking his place in the line of men, some of whom realized even then that the steamship was doomed. And his last sight as his boat was lowered was of Captain Smith, standing on the bridge, giving his orders as calmly as if he were directing her entrance into a harbor.

No Need of Revolvers.

He told of how the officers stood with revolvers drawn, to enforce, if the emergency should arise, that rule of the sea of women first, but how the emergency did not arise, and the men stood back or helped the women to their seats. In the way of a seaman he told the story of the night spent in the little boat, comforting as best he could the women who did not realize as he did that some of them had looked upon their loved ones for the last time.

"My watch was from eight to twelve o'clock," said Hichens last night. "From eight to ten o'clock I was the stand-by man, and from ten to twelve I had the wheel. When I was at the stand-by it was very dark, and while it was not foggy there was a haze. I cannot say about the weather conditions after ten, for I went into the wheelhouse, which is inclosed.

"The second officer was the junior watch officer from eight to ten, and at eight o'clock he sent me to the carpenter with orders for him to look after the fresh water, as it was going to freeze. The thermometer then read 31½ degrees, but so far as could be seen there was no ice in sight. The next order was from the second officer for the deck engineer to turn the steam on in the wheelhouse, as it was getting much colder. Then the second officer, Mr. Loetheller, told me to telephone the lookout in the crow's nest.

Told to Keep Lookout for Ice.

"'Tell them,' he said, 'to keep a sharp and strict lookout for small ice until daylight and to pass the word along to the other lookout men.'

"I took the wheel at ten o'clock, and Mr. Murdock, the first officer, took the watch. It was twenty minutes to twelve and I was steering when there were the three gongs from the lookout, which indicated that some object was ahead. Almost instantly, it could not have been more than four or five seconds, when the lookout men called down on the telephone:—'Iceberg ahead!' Hardly had the words come to me when there was a crash.

"I ain't likely to forget, sir, how the crash came. There was a light grating on the port bow, then a heavy crash on the starboard side. I could hear the engines stop, and the lever closing the water tight emergency doors.

"Mr. Murdock was the senior officer of the watch, and with him on the bridge were Mr. Buxtell, the fourth officer, and Mr. Moody, the sixth officer. The Titanic listed, perhaps five degrees, to the starboard, and then began to settle in the water. I stood attention at the wheel from the time of the crash until twenty minutes after twelve, and had no chance to see what the captain did.

CRIES OF LOST MINGLED WITH MUSIC OF SINKING BAND

Crowds Become Frantic at Sight of Wounded

Police Lines at Pier Are Swept Away When Survivors Are Carried Off the Carpathia on Cots.

MRS. CORNELL WAS FIRST TO COME ASHORE

At eight o'clock last night automobiles and carriages containing relatives and friends of the survivors began arriving at the pier. When the Carpathia was sighted coming up the river at quarter to nine o'clock there were more than five hundred automobiles and other vehicles parked within the police lines.

Significant were the frequent arrival of ambulances and automobile trucks from all the big department stores. The latter were filled with cots and invalid chairs. Right of way was the rule for the ambulances and they were permitted to park directly alongside the pier entrance.

From St. Vincent's Hospital arrived twelve black robed Sisters to nurse the injured and all the ambulances of the institution except one. The full surgical staff of the hospital also was in attendance. Ambulances and surgeons were on hand from St. Luke's Hospital, Bellevue, Roosevelt and Flower hospitals and a great number of physicians who had volunteered their services.

The Sisters of Charity found work to do before the arrival of the Carpathia. Women in the throng awaiting relatives became hysterical with dread and anxiety and the black robed Sisters put their arms about them, comforted them and administered restoratives.

Commander Eva Booth, of the Salvation Army, with fifty assistants, who meet all incoming vessels to minister to immigrants, were allowed within the police lines, but they were turned back at the entrance of the Cunard pier and only Miss Booth and three of her party were admitted.

$20,000 in Cash at Pier.

Among those on the pier were six members of the New York Stock Exchange, with $20,000, which had been collected on the floor of the Exchange to-day. They had instructions to use the money among the steerage passengers in any way they saw fit.

The women of the relief committee to look after the steerage passengers arrived in motor coaches provided to take the sufferers to hospitals or shelters. Gimbel Brothers sent all their delivery wagons to the pier, laden with first aid appliances and cots, and placed them at the disposal of the women's relief committee. In addition the firm announced they would provide quarters for two hundred sufferers over night in their store.

Relatives and friends of the survivors had reached the pier before half past eight o'clock, but for another half hour automobiles arrived containing physicians and nurses, and loaded with first aid appliances. The surgeons and nurses were in working attire, the women in white gowns and caps, the surgeons in white duck trousers and jackets.

A party of four surgeons and ten nurses arrived in three automobile buses, and as they hurried to the pier one of them said they had been sent by Mrs. William K. Vanderbilt.

In spite of the number of physicians that had reached the pier at half past eight o'clock, it was found there was a dearth of nurses, and hurried calls were sent out to all the city institutions and private hospitals and nurses' exchanges. In response to these calls nurses began arriving in taxicabs and automobiles, and before the Carpathia was warped in there were more than two hundred nurses waiting to go on board.

The Wounded Carried Off.

Piers Nos. 52 and 56, adjoining that at which the Carpathia was made fast, were turned over to the hospital corps. Cots were placed in rows and tables were provided, at which surgeons and nurses hurriedly prepared bandages.

At half-past nine o'clock the throng pressing against the police lines gave a shout of horror as a line of sailors bearing the wounded on cots emerged from Pier 54 and went to Pier 56, the temporary hospital. It was the first intimation that the Carpathia was discharging her passengers.

At that hour there were more than twenty thousand persons pressing against the roped-off inclosure in West street. The throng stretched as far back as Ninth avenue. Much confusion was caused by the number of persons who had been admitted within the police lines. All those who had arrived in automobiles had been admitted inside the ropes without question, and many of these were found later to be only curious persons. When they tried to press forward toward the pier entrance the strong arm squad was kept busy.

Police Swept Aside.

Before the Carpathia was warped into her berth she stood off for some time in the fairway. A report spread through the watching throng that the delay was caused by an effort to get such of the crew of the Titanic as were aboard off under cover of darkness before the Senate Committee went aboard the vessel.

The Rev. William D. Carter, pastor of the Madison Avenue Reformed Church, was at the pier with a private ambulance awaiting Miss Sylvia Caldwell, one of the survivors. She is one of the church's foreign mission workers. Miss Caldwell will be taken directly to the Presbyterian Hospital.

The Salvation Army notified the Cunard line officers that its barracks in Fourteenth and Fifteenth streets would be open for steerage passengers.

Just as the first passengers were coming ashore Vincent Astor, Craig Biddle and William A. Dobbyn, secretary to Colonel Astor, arrived with a physician, two nurses and a private ambulance to take charge of Mrs. Astor. They were escorted through the crowd by three policemen.

Outside Pier No. 54 a throng of foreigners awaiting news of relatives and friends in the steerage had been buffeted about by the police all night. But when the first line of injured emerged their emotions overcame them and, with a concerted rush they swept the police aside and forced an entrance to the pier.

Mrs. Cornell First on Shore.

One of the first passengers to leave the vessel was Mrs. Robert C. Cornell, wife of the city magistrate. She was met by her husband and hurried to her home, at No. 901 Lexington avenue. Mrs. Cornell was practically the first apssenger aboard the Titanic to step outside the pier. She had told the story of the wreck to her husband quickly during the walk up the pier. As she stepped into the street Inspector McClusky was compelled to fight chauffeurs aside to get to the Cornell automobile. She said to her husband:—

"It was the most ungodly thing I ever have heard of or ever hope to encounter. The survivors on board the Carpathia seemed to be insane. Every one was good to us, but oh, the scene and the awful experiences I have been compelled to undergo during and since that awful night of terror almost drives me mad!"

After saying this much her husband lifted her into the automobile and would not let her talk further. Mrs. Cornell appeared greatly distraught. Evidently she had been rescued in her night attire, as she wore a cheap skirt, a jacket and a wrap that did not fit her.

Washington Dodge, of San Francisco, with Mrs. Dodge and their three year old son, were among the first to leave the pier. Mr. Dodge said the Titanic struck at twenty minutes after one o'clock in the morning and sank an hour later. He said that she went down before all the lifeboats were launched.

"Good order prevailed at first," he said. "Later, when every one realized that the ship was sinking, the men became as wild as the women. After we had gone over with the lifeboat, I heard as many as fifty shots fired, which was evidence to me that there had been scenes of dreadful fighting aboard."

Mr. Dodge said that as the lifeboat pulled away from the Titanic he saw Colonel Astor and Major Butt standing together upon the upper deck.

Vincent Astor assisted his physician and the nurses to carry his stepmother to an automobile. He then drove rapidly away and refused to say whether he was taking Mrs. Astor to her home or a hospital. It was learned from passengers aboard the Carpathia that Mrs. Astor was seriously ill.

Mrs. J. B. Thayer, wife of the vice president of the Pennsylvania Railroad Company, and her son, J. B. Thayer, Jr., were among the earliest to leave the pier. Mr. Thayer, who accompanied his wife and son, is among the missing. Mrs. Thayer was carried from the deck of the Carpathia to an automobile.

Mrs. Straus Clung to Husband.

The first ambulance to leave the pier conveyed Mrs. Churchill Candee, of Washington, D. C., to New York Hospital. Mrs. Candee wah placed in the first lifeboat to leave the Titanic, but some frantic women leaped into the boat from the deck of the steamship and broke both her legs.

"I was standing near Mrs. Isador Strauss on deck," said Mrs. Candee, "and she was asked to get into the lifeboat, but she refused, saying she would stay with her husband. I heard shots before the Titanic went down but we were too far away to see any fighting on deck. Most of the men who were rescued were picked up out o fthe water, and many of these died from xposure."

A pathetic group that forced a way through the crowd was made up of Miss Fritzie Stengel, a survivor, her two brothers and her mother. The girl, who was in a state of collapse and meanly clad in borrowed attire, was supported by her brothers. She had her arms about their necks and they literally carried her along. The mother, weeping, followed behind. Mrs. Stengel said:—

"My poor child is unnerved by the awful experience she has gone through. From the little she has told me it is horrible beyond comprehension. She is unable to tell anything coherently."

The group pased through the police lines and as they merged into the great throng in Thirteenth street the curious moved aside and made a path for them.

PROTESTANT MEN TO AID SURVIVORS

The Titanic Disaster Is Chief Topic at Union Institute and Inter-Church Conference.

In Carnegie Hall last night at a union institute and interchurch conference for the Protestant men of Manhattan and the Bronx a collection was taken up for the Titanic sufferers on board the Carpathia. This was done at the suggestion of Fred B. Smith, who frequently referred to the greatest tragedy of modern times during the evening.

Mr. Smith had been in Washington during the day endeavoring to fill the place of William T. Stead, whose body there is every reason to suppose is at the bottom of the Atlantic. Mr. Smith was not willing to announce whom he had obtained, hoping against hope that Mr. Stead might still be alive.

The great English author was to have spoken on "World Peace" on Saturday afternoon at an open air service in Union square, crossing the ocean especially for the purpose. He was also expected to speak next Tuesday night in the Fifth Avenue Presbyterian Church.

Fred B. Smith presided last night and among the speakers were Raymond Robbins and John L. Alexander, the boy scout specialists; H. F. La Flamme and the Rev. Dr. W. E. Bierdewolf. Each man told of the institutes held in different centres of Manhattan and the Bronx during the last few nights.

The staff of the Academy of Political Science, Columbia University, entertained the members of the Social Service Department of the Men and Religion Movement at dinner in the Hotel Astor last evening. James G. Cannon, president of the Fourth National Bank, gave a dinner to the other leaders at the Manhattan Hotel last night. Mr. Cannon is chairman of the National Committee of Ninety-seven.

To-night a convention for "older boys" will be held in the Episcopal Church of Zion and St. Timothy, at which Mornay Williams and Mr. Alexander will speak on "Together or Not Together." The National Conservation Congress will open to-morrow.

WORKS 2 YEARS ON MEMORIAL MODELS

Lorado Taft Has Finished Preliminary Task Connected with Washington Statue of Columbus.

After two years of work Lorado Taft, the Chicago sculptor, has completed the models for the sculptural feature of the Columbus memorial, which is to be erected, in Georgia marble, on the plaza in front of the Union Station, in Washington. The plan for erecting an imposing Columbus memorial, says Popular Mechanics, was started by the Knights of Columbus several years ago, and Congress later encouraged the idea by appropriating $100,000.

The memorial consists of a semicircular fountain adorned with a great statue of Columbus and other appropriate figures. It will be 70 feet wide and 65 feet high. One of the principal features, rising at the rear of the fountain, is a shaft 45 feet in height, surmounted by a globe representing the world. It forms the background of the statue of Columbus, who is represented as standing on the prow of a ship. At the stem of the ship is a beautiful figure typifying "The Spirit of Discovery." The great basin of the fountain is located immediately beneath this figure.

LATITUDE 41.46 NORTH, LONGITUDE 50.14 WEST.

WHERE MANHOOD PERISHED NOT.

Gloom Over the Provence, Carrying Myron T. Herrick

New Ambassador from America Reaches Paris, Praising French Vessel—Icebergs 300 Feet High Were Sighted on Voyage.

SPEED AND NORTHERN ROUTE CONDEMNED

[SPECIAL DESPATCH TO THE HERALD VIA COMMERCIAL CABLE COMPANY'S SYSTEM.]

HERALD BUREAU, No. 49 AVENUE DE L'OPERA, PARIS, Thursday.

Mr. Myron T. Herrick, the new American Ambassador, arrived to-day by the Provence. To the HERALD correspondent Mr. Herrick spoke in high praise of the Provence, its seagoing qualities, comfort, cuisine and the courteous attention to passengers. Although Mr. Herrick has been an annual visitor to Europe for many years, this is the first time he has travelled on board a French line steamship.

Gloom, however, was cast over the ship toward the end of the voyage by the news of the tragedy on board the Titanic. The Provence was in communication by wireless with the ill fated vessel on Saturday and Sunday.

PARIS, Thursday.—Myron T. Herrick, the newly appointed United States Ambassador to France, who arrived here this afternoon, said the Provence encountered a series of icebergs. The Provence had been advised by the Niagara of the presence of icebergs, and these were sighted at six o'clock on Saturday evening. They had evidently moved swiftly. The icebergs numbered twelve, and they were about fifteen miles away from the Provence. Some of them were 900 feet long and 300 feet high.

According to other passengers the Titanic was warned by the Provence, the Niagara and another vessel that icebergs were in her path.

French shipping circles think that the lesson learned from the disaster to the Titanic should be the necessity for an international agreement to put a stop to the absurd competition for speed between Europe and New York, which leads the commanders of transatlantic steamships unconsciously to take chances that prudence would forbid. There is also a conviction among shipping men that the speed of steamships should be reduced off Newfoundland.

In the meantime the French Transatlantic line has given orders to the captains of its steamships to take a more southerly course.

The father of Paul Chevre, who is among the passengers rescued, has received a wireless despatch from his son on board the Carpathia saying that he is among those saved, and that he expects to reach New York to-night. Paul Chevre is a sculptor of considerable attainments, who is on his way to Canada to attend the unveiling of his statue of Sir Wilfrid Laurier.

AMBASSADORIAL MAIL LOST

[SPECIAL DESPATCH TO THE HERALD VIA COMMERCIAL CABLE COMPANY'S SYSTEM.]

CONSTANTINOPLE, Thursday.—It was learned here to-day that pouch No. 14, containing the American Ambassadorial despatches and mail, and also the quarterly accounts of the United States guard ship Scorpion were on board the Titanic and consequently were lost.

THE BALTIC TURNED BACK.

LIVERPOOL, Thursday.—The White Star Company here has received a wireless from the Baltic, saying:—"At eight minutes after eleven (New York time) Sunday night received wireless 'C. D. Q.' from the Titanic, 253 miles east of her position. Immediately turned back and steamed 134 miles in her direction, when, hearing from the Carpathia that assistance was no longer required, we continued our course to Liverpool."

BELGIANS AMONG LOST.

BRUSSELS, Thursday.—Ten of the steerage passengers on board the Titanic were natives of Dendermonde, about sixteen miles from Ghent, where they left many relatives, who are very anxious as to their fate.

PORTUGUESE SENATE ACTS.

LISBON, Portugal, Thursday. The Portuguese Senate this morning adopted unanimously a resolution expressing the sympathy of the government and people of Portugal with the victims of the Titanic disaster.

LEGAL AID SOCIETY TO DEMAND NEW LAWS

Immediate action was taken yesterday by the Legal Aid Society demanding amendment to the laws governing the requirements for life saving appliances on board steamships plying in American ports. The initiative was taken by J. Augustus Johnson, chairman of the Seaman's Branch Committee of the society, who addressed letters to the Department of Commerce and Labor and to the chairman of the Committee on Merchant Marine and Fisheries at Washington.

Mr. Johnson, who during the last twenty years has championed many laws affecting the welfare of the seamen, said last night:—

"It seems to me the thing most needed is an immediate amendment to the law, which now leaves it to the discretion of the steamboat inspector as to the number of lifeboats and other appliances required. This law should be changed to make it mandatory upon owners to furnish a certain number of lifeboats for every one hundred passengers.

"Before we can expect to make any great progress in the direction of more safety we must get a reciprocal agreement between this country, Great Britain, France and Germany. Every ship entering American ports should be required to carry enough boats for all the passengers and crew.

"This is the time, of course, when every one is suggesting improvements in the existing laws. As yet we shall take no definite steps until we have seen what other persons are suggesting. Then we shall make an effort to embody in our scheme the desirable points which have been neglected by other official bodies.

"Until I get an exact line of the condition aboard the Titanic and Carpathia we shall go slow. The situation is one which demands serious thought and immediate and persistent action."

In addition to these propositions the Legal Aid Society is considering the formation of a special bureau which will prevent the issuance of clearance papers to any ship that has not the number of lifeboats required by the American law. No definite steps, however, have been taken in this direction.

CANADA FAVORS ICEBERG PATROL

[SPECIAL DESPATCH TO THE HERALD.]

OTTAWA, Ont., Thursday.—In measures for the preservation of life on the ocean the Canadian government will co-operate with that of the United States. The appalling disaster to the Titanic brought to the attention of the Department of Marine a situation of a seriousness never before realized.

There are upward of fifteen transatlantic steamships running to Canadian ports, and while, when in Canadian waters, they are under the jurisdiction of the Dominion authorities, the fact that they were licensed and inspected by the British Board of Trade was accepted as a sufficient guarantee. The inadequacy of this provision, however, is now apparent, and it is proposed to establish in Canada a separate and rigid inspection, calling for an adequate number of life boats, wireless telegraphic equipment on board all ships and proper life saving equipment of all kinds.

As a large part of the track of icebergs is in Canadian waters or where Canadian vessels navigate, the government here will also join in the proposed international iceberg patrol, as outlined by the HERALD.

DISTRESS CALLS TO HAVE RIGHT OF WAY

HERALD BUREAU, No. 1,502 H STREET, N. W., WASHINGTON, D. C., Thursday.

The Senate wireless bill to be presented to-morrow by Senator Bourne, of Oregon, will insure the right of way for distress calls. The Committee on Commerce to-day authorized Senator Bourne to report his bill to regulate radio communication with the amendment providing priority for signals of distress.

As stated in the HERALD to-day, the bill, introduced February 15, has been carefully considered not only by the Senate Committee on Commerce, but also by the administration and by those engaged in seeking an international means of putting an end to piracy of the air by amateur operators and others making wireless service useless at times when it may be needed most.

The important amendment is included in the Bourne bill as section nine, and is entitled "Right of Way for Distress Signals." It reads:—

"All stations are required to give absolute priority to signal and radiograms relating to ships in distress; to cease all sending on hearing a distress signal, and, except when engaged in answering or aiding the ship in distress, to refrain from sending until all signals and radiograms relating thereto are completed."

Save for this important amendment, which brings the bill fully within the demands that have been raised since the loss of the Titanic over the aerial confusion due to the failure or refusal of operators to cease sending immaterial messages while the "S. O. S." calls were going out, the Bourne bill which will be reported is practically as outlined in the HERALD.

It is specified that failure to preserve secrecy of radiograms shall result in revocation of an operator's license by the Secretary of Commerce and Labor.

Another amendment made is as to the time when the act shall become operative. As first drawn it was to become effective January 1, 1913, but this has been stricken out, and by to-day's committee amendment the act is to be effective ninety days from its passage.

The House Committee on Merchant Marine to-day favorably reported a bill restricting the operations of amateur wireless operators to wave lengths not exceeding two hundred meters. This bill, if enacted into law, will eliminate interference of which all wireless companies complain. as a two hundred metre wave length will not transmit a message more than two miles.

The Carpathia Welcomed in Heavy Thunderstorm

Men Aboard the Herald Tugboat See Passengers Leave the Rail When the Titanic's Lifeboats, Stored on Deck, Are Lowered Into the Hudson River.

LIGHTNING FLASHES REVEAL NURSES AT WORK

The Carpathia was met off Fort Wadsworth by the Fred B. Dalzell, Jr., a tug chartered by the HERALD, as the Cunarder was steaming at a thirteen knot speed toward the Narrows at eight o'clock last night. Only about fifty persons leaned over the port rail of the vessel to watch the little tug as she crept within twenty feet of the steamship. Flashes of lightning lit the air, showing distinctly every part of the Carpathia as she ploughed through a heavy sea in a downpour of rain, accompanied by thunder and lightning.

The Governor Flower, with a staff of physicians and surgeons, met the Carpathia soon afterward a little to the north of the fort. At first it seemed that the rescue ship was not going to check her speed for the medical staff to board her. Several toots from the Governor Flower were signalled to the incoming vessel, and she slackened her speed to about six knots. Then the physicians hurried up the side.

The Governor Flower remained as escort until well within the Narrows, when she left the Carpathia. Many passengers looked over the side of the Carpathia to watch the physicians as they boarded the steamship.

The HERALD tug, which had put out from Quarantine when the Carpathia was sighted about five miles away, steamed at the port side of the steamship for several miles, until a Staten Island ferryboat compelled the tug to change its course. The flashes of lightning that lit up the Carpathia showed an unusual amount of activity aboard.

Nurses Busy Aboard Ship.

Women dressed in the garb of nurses were seen to hurry about from one stateroom to another. A passenger in the stern of the vessel called to the HERALD tug:—

"Who are you?"

"THE NEW YORK HERALD," a reporter shouted through a megaphone.

For the next fifteen minutes a driving rain forced the passengers on the promenade deck to seek shelter, and from cover they watched the flashlights that were being set off by a HERALD photographer on board the tug.

Not a whistle was sounded as the steamship passed through the Narrows, only the short, muffled blasts of the Dalzell signalling to other craft breaking the stillness. Occasional roars of thunder took the place of the usual whistles that are to be heard in the harbor.

Many tugs went to meet the Carpathia as she neared Bedloe's Island, photographers flashlights being set off aboard each one of them. As the Carpathia passed the Batery, a ferryboat crossed her bow and several others steamed astern. The HERALD tug followed in the wake of the Carpathia. She decreased her speed to about five knots an hour when the ferry line section of the Hudson River was reached.

Off the Cunard line pier the great rescue ship stoped her engines and several tugs atached lines to her bow and stern. She was about midstream. It was half-past eight o'clock when this position was reached. There was a long delay and many of the pasengers could be seen hurrying about aboard the vessel.

A fleet of tugs had now reached the Carpathia and a handful of passengers watched the preparations for guiding the big steamer to her pier.

The reason for the long delay was seen about nine o'clock, when seamen had gathered at the port side on the upper deck. The ropes holding the lifeboats to the davits were unfastened, the boats swung over the side of the Carpathia and slowly the men began to lower them. They were the boats that had been used to rescue the men, women and children who survived the Titanic's plunge to the ocean bottom.

As the HERALD tug drifted in toward the Carpathia the name Titanic was plainly discerned on the bow of the little life craft. Four of the Titanic's boats were lowered from the davits and the work seemed painfully slow. On the port side three more were dropped into the water. The other boats were piled in the stern of the Carpathia, on the upper deck.

Guard for the Titanic's Boats.

Seamen were in the boats as they were being lowered to the river. The tug John Nichols, in charge of Captain Richard Wray, towed the life craft to the south end of the Cunard pier, wheer they were moored. A police launch from Harbor A, with a squad of policemen aboard, steamed to the pier and a watch was placed upon the boats.

As the last of the lifeboats was being lowered into the water, the HERALD tug crept in cautiously toward the Carpathia. The commands of the officers of the Carpathia and the shouts of the seamen were the only noises to break the stillness, save for an occasional signal from a tug that had gone too close to another.

It was noticed that the passengers who were looking over the rail of the vessel went inside as the boats were being hoisted from the davits. It seemed that the sight of the Titanic's boats had unnerved them.

Soon after nine o'clock a warning blast from the whistle of the John Nichols told the captains of the numerous tugs that the Carpathia was about to swing into her pier. At a snail's pace the big vessel swung about and her bow pointed toward the wharf. A small tug barely missed being run down by the Carpathia, but a burst of speed carried her across the bow in safety.

The Carpathia, bow on, was warped into her dock. It was expected by those on the pier facing the river front that the vessel would dock at right angles to the pier, for they were seen to hustle toward the north side of the wharf as the Carpathia was being swung in that direction.

Surgeons and nurses were standing on the river front part of the pier, and they picked up their bags and blankets when they saw that the steamship would make fast on the side. They hurried inside the pier and were seen to run through the gathering.

More than fifty persons, men and women, stood on the forward deck on board the Carpathia and watched the seamen and tugs as they skilfully guided the giant vessel to her pier. One woman, holding a child, appeared to be in tears. Many were seen to be crying on the promenade deck as the hawsers from the Carpathia were being made fast.

Woman Stricken at Pier.

From the HERALD tug, which nearly scraped the port side of the vessel, a woman was seen being carried to a stateroom by a man. A nurse hurried in after her.

The Carpathia was little more than a half hour steaming from the Narrows to midstream in the Hudson River. After the Governor Flower had sent the surgeons aboard, the rescue ship increased her speed to about thirteen knots, holding it until a little past the Battery. She easily outdistanced the tugs that shot out from the darkness o meet her.

The HERALD tugboat, which was in charge of Captains Al Brady and Al Eneas, was the first tugboat to meet the Carpathia off Fort Wadsworth. The HERALD tugboat had been waiting at Quarantine and sped out to meet the rescue vessel when the lights in the distance indicated that the Carpathia was approaching. So rough was the water that seas broke over the bow of the tugboat.

SAYS THE OLYMPIC GAVE FIRST NEWS

BOSTON, Mass., Thursday.—John H. Thomas, manager of the Boston office of the International Mercantile Marine Company, said to-day:—

"The first authentic news of the disaster received by the company was in the form of a message from Captain Haddock, of the Olympic, relayed from the Carpathia via Cape Race, to the effect that the Titanic had foundered at twenty minutes past two o'clock on Monday morning and that the Carpathia was on the way to New York with about 675 survivors.

"This message was received by Mr. Franklin about half-past six o'clock on Monday evening, and the news was immediately thereafter given to the press. It was also telephoned by Mr. Franklin to the manager of the Boston office and given to the press here about twenty minutes after seven o'clock.

"This was the first and only message received by the company with definite news that the ship had actually foundered. The only messages since received were those relayed by the Olympic from the Carpathia giving the names of the rescued passengers. These messages continued until the Carpathia lost communication with the Olympic, on Tuesday evening, and none has since been received."

COLONEL ASTOR AND MAJOR ARCHIBALD BUTT DIED HEROICALLY

The Titanic Disaster Greatest Newspaper Test

Every Facility Known to the Science of Modern News Gathering Pushed to Limit by the Herald in Serving Hundreds of Thousands of Anxious Readers.

PICKET PATROL ALONG ENTIRE NORTH COAST

Millions of newspaper readers who have been eagerly devouring every word about the greatest sea tragedy of all time have little or no idea of the tremendous efforts that have been made by the press of the entire country to keep them acquainted with every additional detail of the thrilling story.

Every important newspaper in the country has kept its telegraph operators at their posts night and day since the report of this disaster was verified, an additional paragraph of one or two lines being sufficient to warrant getting out extras.

Special writers, reporters, artists and photographers have been flocking to this city since Monday night, when the real fate of the giant steamship became known for the first time. Several hundred skilled newspaper men have been scouring the Atlantic seaboard for three days in the hope of picking up some detail of the disaster. An army of reporters waited patiently at Sandy Hook for the first sight of the steamship Carpathia, all the great metropolitan dailies and many of the newspapers in cities within a radius of one hundred miles having their own special tugs at the scene. Recognized as one of the greatest stories of the age, no expense has been spared to get it, and no sacrifice on the part of the newspaper men has been too great to make sure that every angle of the heart breaking tragedy has been properly covered.

The Herald in the Lead.

The preparations by the local papers for getting the story were as complete as the resourcefulness of men skilled in handling news of world wide import could make them. Aside from the question of expense, the distribution of men and the arrangements for wire service, there was endless detail to be overcome before the news gathering machine could be set in motion. This included obtaining passes and cards of identification admitting the workers to piers, police stations, hospitals and the other places where news details of a big disaster are to be found.

The story of how the HERALD set about the thrilling tale for its host of subscribers will give the reader some idea of the lengths to which the up-to-the-second newspaper goes to lay the news of the world on the breakfast table.

The first flash telling of the accident to the Titanic reached this office just before midnight on Sunday night. Through its own wireless telegraph station maintained at the HERALD's ship news office at the Battery the HERALD learned some time before its contemporaries that the mishap was a serious one. There was nothing in the additional information to indicate that the Titanic had received her death wound, but enough was learned to make it clear that one of the big stories of the year was being enacted out there in the ice-strewn waste off the shores of Newfoundland.

Wireless Worked to Limit.

Less than a minute after verification of the crash had been received wireless messages were on their way to every HERALD correspondent along the Atlantic seaboard between this city and St. Johns directing them to keep a sharp lookout for all steamships making a landing at their ports and to hold themselves in readiness for instantaneous action of any kind.

One of the earliest bits of information that drifted in from the scene of the collision a few hours later was that steamships were rushing to the aid of the injured vessel and that in all probability the survivors would be taken to Halifax. This message was not cold before the HERALD's correspondent at Boston had received instructions to take the first train to Halifax with photographers and a corps of assistants.

He had reached Bangor when he was intercepted with a message directing him to return to Providence, as the White Star line officials had decided to bring the survivors to this city on the Carpathia. At Providence he was joined by a member of the HERALD staff sent from this city. The ocean going tug Walter A. Luckenbach was chartered by the HERALD, and, after being equipped with a wireless outfit, started from Newport with reporters and photographers on board.

Despatch to Mr. Stead.

Early Monday morning, when it was still believed that the Titanic was afloat, wireless messages were sent to W. T. Stead, who had contributed many special articles to the HERALD; Jacques Futrelle, author of detective stories, who had once been a member of the HERALD staff; John R. Phillips, wireless operator on the ill-fated steamship, and others who had had business relations with the HERALD at some time or other. They were directed to spare no expense in getting the story for this paper, and up to the time the news that the vessel had gone to the bottom was received the men handling the news in the office were confident that graphic stories of the accident would be forthcoming from the gifted writers.

With the arrival of the direful news on Monday night preparations already made were doubled all along the line until there was no possible avenue of information left uncovered.

In addition to the tug Luckenbach, which had been scouring the coast for the Carpathia, another tug with a complete staff of writers, artists and photographers was sent to Sandy Hook on Tuesday morning and remained there until the Carpathia came up the bay with its cargo of suffering and misery.

On board the Carpathia, gathering in every detail for the HERALD readers were Frederick C. Bechler, formerly employed in the HERALD composing room, and Miss May Birckhead, a woman writer who has made frequent contributions to the paper. Both were well qualified from every angle to furnish all the incidents of the horrifying tragedy.

A third tug met the Carpathia near Quarantine and kept in her wake for the purpose of picking up any fragment of news that might drift over the side of the vessel, while a fourth tug occupied a point of vantage in the North River near the Cunard Line pier for the purpose of enabling a staff of photographers to get pictures of the scenes that attended the docking of the big ocean ambulance.

HERALD reporters were stationed on the pier, at the hospitals, at police stations, at the morgue, at all the big hotels and in the immense crowd that thronged the street in front of the Cunard line piers. Each of these men knew just where to reach a telephone and had instructions to send in every scrap of news, no matter how unimportant it might be.

As this flood of news poured into the office, men at the desks whipped it into shape, the work being divided to insure speed as well as accuracy. All reports were duplicated, the duplicate sheet being turned over to the man who later in the evening summarized the entire story in a general introduction. That's the way the HERALD covered the story of the Titanic disaster.

THE CARPATHIA.

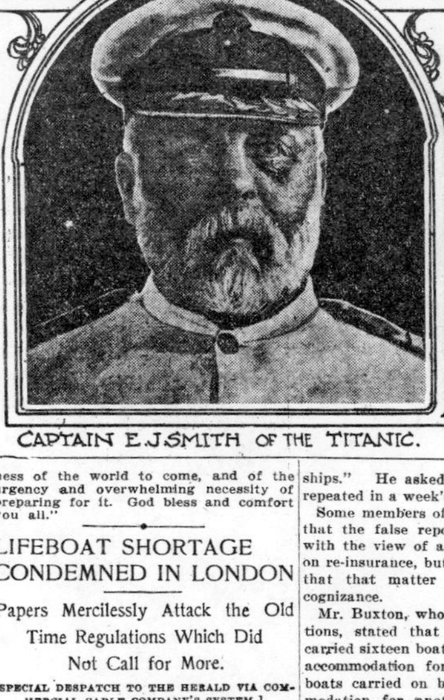

CAPTAIN E.J.SMITH OF THE TITANIC.

CAPTAIN R.H.ROSTROM OF THE CARPATHIA.

THRILLING TALE OF RESCUE BY MRS. CRAIN

Colonel Astor Saved Boy as Boats Were Loading — Caring for Suffering Survivors.

Captain Smith, of the Titanic, was still at dinner when his vessel received the blow that sent her to the bottom, according to Captain Charles Frederich Crain, of the Twenty-seventh Regiment of Infantry, United States Army, who was a passenger aboard the rescue ship Carpathia, and obtained his information from several of the survivors.

"It had been a gay trip out, the rescued passengers told me," continued Captain Crain, "with dinner parties, dancing and concerts. It seemed more like a picnic party than an ordinary voyage of a transatlantic steamship.

"None of the passengers with whom I talked told me anything about any great crash. So far as I could learn all they had felt was a comparatively slight shock.

"Mr. aHrper, of No. 21 Gramercy Park, was one of my informants. Mr. Harper was put in one of the boats with his wife because he was an invalid. According to his story, and to that of others with whom I talked, there was absolutely no confusion on board the doomed ship up to the time they left her.

Colonel Astor Saves Boy.

"Another of the survivors with whom I talked was a boy about fourteen years of age. He told me a remarkable story of his rescue through the intervention of Colonel John Jacob Astor. He said he had tried to get into one of the lifeboats with his mother, but that the sailors had pushed him back and said:—'You're not a girl. You can't get in there. Stand back.'"

"Colonel Astor, who was assisting women into the boat, picked up from the deck a girl's hat, and jamming it on the boy's head, said:—'There, my boy, you're a girl now. Go ahead.'"

The only thing of which any of the survivors with whom I talked complained in connection with the work of rescue was the difficulty experienced in getting the boats away from the sinking ship fter they had been lowered.

"This was due to a new arrangement in connection with the ropes with which the boats are lowered. The sailors did not understand it. It was a new contrivance placed on board the Titanic for the first time. The result was that as the boats touched the water the crew could not detach the lines and eventually had to cut them.

Even Women Used Oars.

"The intention of the officers of the Titanic was to place four sailors in each boat, but this could ont be carried out in every case, with the result that in several of the boats passengers themselves had to take oars. In some instances, women were forced to row.

"Mr. Harper told me he was in his cabin at the time the ship struck. He felt the shock, but it was not severe enough for him to be alarmed. However, he dressed and went to one of the upper decks, where he remained for about ten minutes.

"Then he noticed the passengers coming down from another deck who told him as they passed that they had been ordered to put on life preservers. Mr. Harper went back to his cabin, aroused his wife, and after both had put on life belts they went to the upper deck. There they found the women and children being put into the boats, and Mrs. Harper was sent with them, and, her husband, being an invalid, was permitted to accompany her.

"The boat in which the Harpers were experienced no trouble beyond that mention in disconnecting the tackle. It was rowed away from the Titanic and the occupants watched the great ship sink.

Sank Gradually Before Plunge.

"It was twenty minutes past three A. M. on Monday when she plunged head first out of sight. Her lights had been burning almost until the last. She had sunk gradually until the water reached high enough to extinguish the fires and stop the lights. Soon after that she took the fatal plunge.

"The last boat that left the wreck had only seven passengers in it, but it was one of the smallest boats. However, it could have held more and Mr. Harper is convinced that many women must have been left on board.

"As a matter of fact there was no great rush to get into the boats, he said, because very few of the passengers realized the gravity of the accident. They had a natural disinclination and fear to entrust themselves to the little craft. As a matter of fact, many of them felt safer aboard the big ship. None believed she would sink.

"The shock was so mild, one of the women survivors told me, that after she had dressed and had gone on deck she thought so little of it that she went back to her cabin and remained there until her husband went for her. Another played several games of bridge after the crash.

DUKE OF CONNAUGHT SENDS HIS SYMPATHY

OTTAWA, Ont., Thursday.—The Duke of Connaught to-day sent the following message to President Taft at Washington:—

"I have delayed telegraphing to you in the hope that Major Butt might still be among the saved, but fear there is now no hope. Accept the expression of my deepest sympathy on this gallant officer's tragic end and the loss to yourself of a devoted member of your staff. I also take this opportunity of assuring you of my heartfelt sympathy with the United States in the loss of so many of its citizens through the awful catastrophe of the sinking of the Titanic. ARTHUR."

PRESIDENT STIRRED BY SHIP'S SILENCE

The Carpathia's Refusal to Reply to Inquiries Astound Mr. Taft and Mr. Meyer.

HERALD BUREAU,
No. 1,502 H STREET, N. W.,
WASHINGTON, D. C., Thursday.

President Taft, Secretary Meyer and officials here are astounded to-day over the refusal of the Carpathia to make any reply to the persistent wireless inquiries conveyed to that vessel by the scout cruisers Chester and Salem concerning the Titanic's survivors.

The inexplicable silence of the Carpathia's wireless except to reply to commercial companies' messages, authorized by the censor aboard that ship, stands out prominently to-day as another instance of lack of wireless control which, in this great crisis, left all important messages unanswered.

Commander Chandler, in command of the Salem, which was sent out specially by the government to get news for officials here and the thousands anxiously awaiting news of the survivors, sent this radiogram to the Navy Department this morning:—

"Can get no information of any kind from the Carpathia. Although she is within easy radio communication she sometimes acknowledges calls, but will not admit receipt of messages or make reply. Cannot believe that she has failed to understand the messages I have sent to her. She is within easy range of torpedo stations, so Salem will go to Bradford this afternoon."

When this message was shown to Secretry Meyer there was no concealing the fact that the Secretary was deeply incensed. He had ordered Commander Chandler to obtain if possible information concerning Major Butt for the President.

In earlier messages to the Department Commander Chandler tells of vainly trying to get some report from the Carpathia. The Salem, after giving up the task, steamed for Newport, arriving there at three o'cloc this afternoon.

MEETS MOTHER AT PIER; BELIEVED HER LOST

Mrs. Kelly Was Carrying $8,000 to Start Son in Business, but He Forgets That.

After having believed since Tuesday morning that his mother, Mrs. F. Kelly, had perished with the Titanic, James Kelly discovered her name among a revised list of survivors published in the Evening Telegram last night and hurried to the Cunard pier to meet her.

Mrs. Kelly was on her way to the United States for the first time, bringing with her $8,000 so that her son could purchase the Chester Lunch, at No. 130 West Thirty-sixth street, and start in business for himself. It was all the money that she had in the world, and it was this sum which was to set her son up in business. He forgot the money when he saw his mother's name among those saved. He could only rejoice at his good fortune.

"My mother is saved!" he cried while tears of joy streamed down his face. "I don't know whether she lost the money or not, and I don't care so long as I have her."

POPE EXPRESSES GRIEF FOR TRAGEDY

ROME, Thursday.—The Osservatore Romano publishes the following official communication:—

"The Pope has learned with deep regret that among the victims of the ruthless disaster to the Titanic, which has so profoundly grieved him, was Major Butt, returning from a visit to Rome. Major Butt had been the bearer of an autograph letter from the President of the United States to the Pontiff, and now, on returning home, had an autograph letter from the Pontiff to the President, together with an answer from Cardinal Merry del Val, the Papal secretary, to a letter addressed to him by the President.

"The Pontiff, while expressing to President Taft his profound sympathy and sorrow for all, hastened to ask for news respecting the fate of Major Butt. President Taft immediately answered, expressing to the Pope his profound gratitude for the interest and sympathy shown by the Pope toward sufferers and adding that unfortunately, there was no hope that Major Butt had been saved."

PRESIDENT OF FRANCE SENDS CONDOLENCE

WASHINGTON, D. C., Thursday.—The White House to-night made public the following cable message from President Fallières of France:—

'With profound affliction have I heard of the Titanic's awful catastrophe, which brings mourning to so many American families, and I have it at heart to extend to you my most sincere condolence. I wish to tell Your Excellency how much I share in your anguish about the fate of your aid and friend, Major Butt."

In reply President Taft paid a touching tribute to Major Butt.

"I am grateful," he cabled, "for your reference to my friend and aid, Major Butt. Soldier that he was, with rescue only possible for part of the company, I know that he felt his place to be on the ship as she went down."

GENERAL BOOTH GRIEVES.

The following cable despatch came last night from General William Booth, head of the Salvation Army at London:—

"My heart is moved by the fearful calamity which has befallen the world in the loss of the Titanic—moved with sorrow for the dead, among whom are some of my long tried friends; moved with sympathy for the living, whose loss can never be repaired, and moved in its deepest sources of feeling concerning that sudden and awful summons into the presence of God. I pray that it may speak to the multitude of the reality and nearness of the world to come, and of the urgency and overwhelming necessity of preparing for it. God bless and comfort you all."

LIFEBOAT SHORTAGE CONDEMNED IN LONDON

Papers Mercilessly Attack the Old Time Regulations Which Did Not Call for More.

[SPECIAL DESPATCH TO THE HERALD VIA COMMERCIAL CABLE COMPANY'S SYSTEM.]

HERALD BUREAU,
No. 130 FLEET STREET,
London, Friday.

Commenting on Mr. Sydney Buxton's speech and the report of the Merchants' Shipping Advisory Committee, made public last night, in which the committee advocates more wireless and raft facilities, but recommends only an addition of eight lifeboats to vessels of a tonnage of 45,000 and upward, the English newspapers mercilessly attack the Board of Trade for what is called "criminal somnolence."

The Daily News:—"Mr. Buxton is loath to make changes in this time of panic, but public opinion will insist that every ship must be provided with lifeboat accommodations for every person carried."

The Standard:—"The loss of life could have been prevented if the Titanic had not been disgracefully undersupplied with lifeboats."

The Morning Post:—"The Titanic did not carry enough boats under its davits, and here the responsibility rests with the Board of Trade."

The Morning Leader:—"That the Titanic could have carried more boats is shown by the fact that provision for them on the davits was actually made. Those davits hung empty. This brings home the hideous responsibility of delay to the department."

The Daily Mail:—"In France there must be boat accommodation for all passengers. In Germany the number of boats carried by liners is much larger than in the British merchant marine. The Board of Trade is behind the age. This matter is of the first importance, involving the safety of human life."

The Daily Express:—"All great shipping companies, irrespective of ationality, seem to be equally open to criticism for the lack of lifeboats."

The Daily Telegraph:—"The disparity between the carrying capacity of a liner and the carrying capacity of lifeboats raises a question which the government must not be allowed to shirk. A searching inquiry is demanded."

London, Friday.—The Morning Post learns that several technical experts and others are about to leave England for the Nnited States to assist in the inquiry into the Titanic disaster. The experts will give evidence as to the construction of the steamship. It is understood that she evidence taken in the United States will be utilized for the inquiry subsequently to be held in England.

The relief fund here now totals nearly $200,000. Of this amount the London Corporation and Lord Mount Stephen have contributed $5,000 each, and the American Ambassador, Whitelaw Reid, $2.500.

A searching inquiry into matters concerning the catastrophe to the Titanic appertaining to their respective departments was promised in the House of Commons this afternoon by both Sydney Buxton, President of the Board of Trade, and Herbert L. Samuel, Postmaster General.

The Postmaster General declared that he had already taken up the subject of the false reports which had been published. He continued:—

"I am making inquiries as to whether the wireless messages from ships holding my license for wireless telegraphy on which the reports were represented to be founded were in fact sent from those ships." He asked that the question be repeated in a week's time.

Some members of the House suggested that the false reports had been spread with the view of affecting the premiums on re-insurance, but Mr. Samuel declared that that matter was not within his cognizance.

Mr. Buxton, who was plied with questions, stated that the Titanic actually carried sixteen boats on her davits, giving accommodation for 990 persons. Other boats carried on board provided accommodation for another 188, making together a total of 1,178. In addition there were forty-eight life buoys and 3,560 life belts. The actual number of passengers and crew on board the Titanic was 2,208.

Mr. Buxton was apologetic when explaining the inadequacy of the Board of Trade regulations in regard to shipping. A committee, he said, had been appointed last year to consider the necessary revisions of the regulations, but the increased provision of boats recommended by that committee was not considered altogether adequate, so the matter was referred back for further consideration. He continued:—

"I want the House clearly to understand that up to the present it has never been suggested by a responsible expert authority that every vessel, however large and however well equipped with waterright compartments, should necessarily carry lifeboats adequate to accommodate all on board. The present disaster, however, has created a new situation which will need to be most carefully considered not in a panic but in the light of all the information which the inquiry will disclose."

Mr. Buxton said that he was not prepared at present to express an opinion whether British passenger steamships should be prevented from taking the northern route during the spring months. This and other questions were to be submitted to a searching inquiry. He was also afraid that the Board of Trade had no power to prevent racing for records across the Atlantic. He continued:—

"I c an assure the House that there will be no delay in conection with the inquiry into the disaster. We fully recognize the great resposibility that the Board of Trade bears in the matter, but I do urge that it is far better that we should give a little more time and come to a really satisfactory conclusion rather than act too rapidly, which might possibly lead to greater evils."

Asked if the German-American lines carried nearly double the number of boats required by the British Board of Trade regulations Mr. Buxton replied, "I do not think so."

Horatio Bottomley moved the adjournment of the House to "call attention to the failure of the Board of Trade to provide adequate protection for the lives of passengers on ocean liners."

The Speaker admitted the propriety of Mr. Bottomley's motion, but pointed out that a full discussion of the subject could occur on the civil service estimates to-night, so that an adjournment was not necessary.

Meanwhile announcements are appearing in increasing numbers in the newspapers that the transatlantic steamships are ordering lifeboats nearly doubling the present capacity.

The disaster has apparently had no effect on bookings except for the preference now shown for the smaller and slower ships, some of the prospective travellers transferring from the mammoths.

At the meeting of the Grand Trunk Railway, of Canada, the chairman, A. W. Smithers, feelingly referred to the probability that Charles M. Hays, the president, had been drowned.

The relief funds being raised here amount already to $125,000.

The House of Commons resumed the debate on Mr. Bottomley's motion in the evening, but no fresh light was thrown on the situation. rM. Bottomley wanted the condition attached to he cerificaes of seamships that they should not use the northern route at certain seasons.

Mr. Buxton explained that the delay in providing new regulations was due to the fact that experiments were being made with respect to life saving and the Board of Trade was anxious not to act without full knowledge.

Andrew Bonar Law, leader of the opposition, agreed with Mr. Buxton that it would be inadvisable to act under the influence of a panic, and the subject was dropped.

The widow of Captain Smith, the commander of the Titanic, has written a pathetic message, which was posted to-day outside the White Star offices. It reads:—

"To My Poor Fellow Sufferers:—My heart overflows with grief for you all and is laden with sorrow that you are weighed down with this terrible burden that has been thrust upon us. May God be with us and comfort us all.

"Yours in deep sympathy,
"ELEANOR SMITH."

The Herald Besieged by Telephone for Tidings of Ship's Victims

Thousands of Relatives and Friends of Those Aboard the Titanic, in Voices Filled with Anguish, Seek Information of Their Loved Ones' Fate.

In their hour of anguish thousands of relatives and friends of the men and women whose names were numbered among the passengers on board the Titanic have turned to the HERALD for information. From the hour when the first report of the accident flashed over the wires requests for news of missing loved ones have come in an endless stream into the HERALD office.

All day the telephone wires leading into the office have borne the queries of anxious voices of men and women. Witn nightfall there came no surcease in the number of messages seeking a ray of hope for those who took passage on board the Titanic.

The calls came not only from persons in or near New York city. Hundreds of them have come daily from towns and cities hundreds of miles away. Probably never before in history has a grief stricken people turned in such numbers to a newspaper to give them immediately the benefits of its facilities for gathering the news.

And to these men and women, whose voices over the telephone speak the anguish in their hearts, the HERALD has supplied all the information that it is possible for human ingenuity to gather.

No sooner has a wireless operator on the Carpathia or some other ship far out at sea flashed a message to land than it has been at the disposal of all who turned to the HERALD for the latest scrap of news. Hundreds of times a day the list of survivors, carefully edited and checked to eliminate so far as possible all errors, has been consulted at the request of some inquiring voice.

While many persons called at the HERALD office to learn whether any news of the incidents connected with the sinking of the Titanic has been received, the great majority of the inquiries are for light on the fate of a loved one.

After the fate of the Titanic became known on Monday night many persons who had relatives or friends on board the big White Star craft called up the office regularly at half hour or hour intervals all night. It was not until nearly two o'clock Tuesday morning that the names of any of the survivors on the Carpathia were obtained.

As the list of those who had been rescued from the lifeboats lengthened the calls for information grew in number and increased in frequency. Before daylight came the news that the HERALD was able to supply had brought happiness to the hearts of scores who before had been plunged in gloom. But to hundreds of other inquiries the reply that went back over the wire carried little to lighten the heart.

Overcome by long hours of mental torture and physical fatigue many persons who had remained up the first night after the receipt of the news of the sinking of the Titanic were forced to seek rest Tuesday night. But before retiring they took the precaution to give the HERALD their home telephone numbers, with the request that they be called in case definite information came of missing ones. These requests were complied with whenever possible.

Inquiries to the HERALD office by telephone show that relatives and friends of those on board the Titanic, whose homes were in other cities, have flocked to New York. In this city they believed it would be possible to obtain quicker information of those they sought, and scores of inquiring ones from distant points kept in constant communication with the HERALD.

Many of the calls to the office resulted from errors in the first published lists of the survivors. Unfortunately some of the names as first sent ashore from the Carpathia brought mingled hope and dread, for, while they bore resemblance to the true name, they left an element of doubt that tore the heart strings of those who breathlessly scanned the list.

It was to straighten out if possible these errors of the first list that the HERALD was called upon many times each hour. Women whose voices betrayed the tragedy that had come into their lives asked if the HERALD did not think that a certain name might not be that of a husband. And as the answer went back the wire seemed charged with the agonizing strain under which she labored as the reply cheered or plunged her deeper into doubt.

Hundreds of the calls came from children seeking some word of the fate that had overtaken a parent. As with bated breath they asked their questions, distance could not conceal the fact that they had been visualizing the scenes on the sinking Titanic, in which loved ones had been actors.

Because of the prominence in financial, social and educational circles and in the professions of many of the first cabin passengers, thousands of the calls over the HERALD telephone wires have come from persons equally prominent.

Business associates of men who directed the affairs of great estates and corporations, and whose names were known the world over, have sought the latest information possessed by the HERALD. Persons in all walks of life have called to learn the fate of Colonel John Jacob Astor. Thousands of inquiries asked for news of Mr. Isidor Straus, and, while many of these seekers after information had never met Mr. Straus, the regret that a life so useful to the community should be snuffed out so needlessly was expressed by all.

Major Archibald W. Butt, Dr. William T. Stead, Mr. George D. Widener, Mr. Frank D. Millett, Mr. Benjamin Guggenheim and Mr. Washington A. Roebling, 2d, were others on board the Titanic whose fate has elicited score of inquiries.

Not a club of prominence in the city but has had brought home to its members the awfulness of the disaster, and from these clubs there has come to the HERALD an endless stream of requests for the latest news. Often the request has been for some word of a member whose name was missing from the list of survivors.

Every one connected with the stage has anxiously awaited definite news as to the fate of Mr. Henry B. Harris, and actors and producers, men whose names are known throughout theatredom, have depended upon the HERALD to keep them informed. Actors have jumped to the telephone between acts to call up this office and learn if anything new has been heard about Mr. Harris.

In hotel lobbies throughout the city the one topic of conversation has been the sinking of the Titanic, and additional information has been eagerly sought. At all hours of the day and night the big hotels of the city have been in telephone communication with the HERALD, asking for news of a passenger or general information concerning the wreck.

WASHINGTON, GRIEVING, HALTS ENTERTAINMENTS

Major Butt's and Clarence Moore's Loss Throws Pall Over the Capital.

HERALD BUREAU,
No. 1,502 H STREET, N. W.,
WASHINGTON, D. C., Thursday.

Society continues to manifest its sympathy for those who lost relatives in the Titanic disaster. Several important social events were cancelled to-day. Chief of these was the Society Circus, which had been arranged for the evenings of April 27 and 28 in the hall of the Riding Club of Washington.

The circus was to have been a complete reproduction of the "turns," which are offered in professional performances and some of the most prominent men and women in society were rehearsing for the event. Mr. Clarence Moore was a prominent member of the Riding Club, which had given the majority of the performers, and the entertainment was cancelled to-day when it became evident that both Mr. Moore and Major Archibald W. Butt, military aid to the President, were among those lost at sea.

It was learned to-day that both Major Butt and Mr. Moore were returning to Washington before their intended date in order to be present and participate in the Chevy Chase Hunt ball to-morrow night. It has been postponed.

THE WEATHER.
Rain late tonight or on Sunday; warmer tonight.

THE BROOKLYN DAILY EAGLE

Complete Stock Market

LAST EDITION. Volume 72A No. 110 ★ NEW YORK CITY, SATURDAY, APRIL 20, 1912. ★ 26 PAGES. THREE CENTS.

REMARKABLE PHOTOGRAPH OF SURVIVORS IN HALF-EMPTY LIFEBOAT OF TITANIC

(Copyright, 1912, Brooklyn Daily Eagle.)

This picture was taken from the deck of the Carpathia by Lewis P. Skidmore, of Brooklyn, as the White Star Liner's boats approached the rescue ship.

THE most remarkable photograph of any incident connected with the Titanic disaster was taken by Lewis P. Skidmore, of 381 Vanderbilt avenue, an instructor at Pratt Institute.

The photograph shows one of the Titanic lifeboats approaching the rescue ship Carpathia early Sunday morning. The picture is not only remarkable as a bit of first-hand evidence, caught by the camera, showing just how these lifeboats filled with survivors looked, but, carefully studied, it presents many remarkable details.

It indicates that there was plenty of room left in the boats which put off from the sinking vessel and that, all the women and children having been saved, many of the brave men who gave up their lives were needlessly sacrificed. They could have been taken into the boats, and why they were not is an interesting question. One naturally asks whether the other boats were no more filled than this one, which held much less than half the number of passengers it had capacity for.

The photograph outlines the figures of just twenty passengers, although all of the boat did not get in the picture. The lifeboat could have held seventy-five. It will be observed at a glance that fifteen or twenty more unfortunates could have been stowed away in the bow of the craft and that there are large gaps in the middle and at the rear where there are no passengers. The space where the figure holding the second oar appears at once suggests that five or six other survivors might have found ample room there. Behind the third oar there also seems to have been a lot of room wasted.

MORE STRIKING TITANIC PICTURES IN SUNDAY'S EAGLE.

The Eagle will print tomorrow two more remarkable photographs by Lewis P. Skidmore, taken from the deck of the Carpathia.

One is a picture of the monster iceberg which sent the Titanic to the bottom. The mountain of ice has been thoroughly identified by the survivors.

The other photograph shows a second boat load of survivors just about to be taken on board the Carpathia.

In the bow of the boat is shown the figure of a solitary man, evidently a sailor who is making ready to fend the boat off as she approaches the sides of the Cunarder. The second figure at the oar seems to be that of a woman and the other oarsmen look like women, too.

Photograph Demonstrates Sea Was Calm.

The picture disposes of the stories that after the wreck a wind sprang up and that the sea was rough. The evidence of Mr. Skidmore's camera shows that the sea was comparatively calm.

One of the women is bare-headed and wears a fur coat. A number have on life preservers strapped around their waists and several display attitudes of great weariness. There are just three oarsmen to propel the large craft.

Mr. Skidmore, who took the picture, was on a vacation with his wife and they had booked passage on the Carpathia for England. He was up at an early hour and hearing a disturbance he learned that a boat containing survivors from the Titanic was drawing near. Seizing a camera he ran up on deck and snapped several pictures, of which this is one.

When Mr. Skidmore reached the deck in New York he was met by a friend of his named Leeming. He embarked again yesterday on the Carpathia with Mrs. Skidmore, having spent the intervening time between the arrival of the ship and its departure for England in fitting out several survivors with shirts and collars.

HUNDREDS PERISH AS DIKES BREAK

Nearly All of Boliver County, Mississippi is Under Water.

200 DROWNED THERE

Fifteen More Are Known to Have Been Lost Near Benoit.

MOST OF VICTIMS NEGROES.

Many Whites Also Swept Away. Loss of Life May Be Greater Than Indicated.

Jackson, Miss., April 20—Reports reached here today that 200 persons have been drowned in Bolivar County, Miss., by the flood that swept through that section when the river dikes broke near Beulah. Bolivar County is covered with water and efforts to verify the report are meeting with many obstacles.

The reports declare many white persons were swept away by the deluge, although it is said the majority of the victims were negroes, who failed to reach high ground in time to get out of the flood's path.

Governor Earl Brewer was advised there are 6,000 refugees in camp at Cleveland and that the food supply will last less than twenty-four hours.

Greenville, Miss., April 20—Fifteen persons are known to have been drowned during last night near Benoit in the flood that came from the levee break between Benoit and Beulah, Miss. Unverified reports of other and more extensive loss of life are being received here today. Because of the extent of the present flood river observers express the opinion that the loss of life in this section of the delta will reach 200.

WATERS STILL RISING.

Louisiana Town Inundated—Rescue Work in Mississippi.

Tallulah, La., April 20—Water from the Dog Tail crevasse in the Missippi River continues to rise today with no sign of abatement. Every section of the town is inundated by water from two to ten feet deep. An appeal has been made to the flood relief committee at New Orleans for motorboats to be used in carrying relief to those marooned in the interior of Madiison parish.

Rosedale, Miss., April 20—Rescue work continued today with an increased force of workers, boats going further inland and bringing out many residents who were marooned by the break in the Mississippi levee at Beulah, Miss.

CHINAMAN MURDERED

Coney Island Has a Tong Mystery in the Death of Fong Lee.

Coney Island has one of those strange Oriental murder mysteries which defy the efforts of Caucasian police to unravel. The victim was an On Leong Tong man, and the On Leong Tongs and Hep Sing Tongs have had many bitter disputes in the past in which the revolver has figured as the favorite arbiter of all difficulties.

Fong Lee, a Chinese of 35 years, is the dead man, and he kept a laundry at Sea Breeze avenue, near Fifth street, Coney Island.

William Pictoria of 93 Park place, one of Fong's customers, went to the laundry at 8 o'clock this morning. He walked in and called to Fong, but there was no response.

Pictoria glanced behind the counter and saw the dead body of Lee. It was stretched on the floor with a bullet wound just over the heart. The arms were folded. Everything in the place was in its usual order.

Pictoria notified the police of the Coney Island station and Lieutenant Kennedy had an ambulance summoned from the Coney Island Hospital. Dr. Overend came with it. He examined the body and said Fong had been dead about five hours.

Detectives under Captain of Detectives Deevy searched carefully through the three rooms of Lee's shack for some clew which might throw light on the tragedy. They thought they had found it when they came upon a revolver in Fong's bedroom but investigation soon sowed that all the cartridges in it were intact. So they gave up the theory that the man might have killed himself.

The detectives are sure that Fong was a victim of a tong feud. These feuds are generally started by quarrels over gambling privileges but their various ramifications and the secretiveness of the Orientals are such as to baffle Mr. Waldo's best men.

BUTT'S FATE SHOCKS ROOSEVELT

Washington, April 20—Captain McCoy of the general staff of the Army today received a telegram from Colonel Roosevelt as follows:

"Am deeply shocked and grieved about poor Archie Butt. If there is any news about him, pray let me know."

Captain McCoy was military aide of the former President.

"CY" SEYMOUR MAKES A HIT.

In Fact, Many Hits, When Ball Player Captures Alleged Burglar.

"Cy" Seymour, the one-time Giant and now playing with the Baltimore International League team, this morning turned a badly battered up young man over to Patrolman Brady of the Highbridge station, charging him with being in the ballplayer's apartments, on the fourth floor of 904 Ogden avenue, the Bronx. The young man appeared to be pleased with the appearance of the patrolman and crouched away from Seymour whenever the latter approached him. Seymour appeared peevish when told he would have to appear against the man, and complained that he had not thought of throwing the stranger out of the window, which would have saved him much inconvenience.

The young man told the police he was Adolph Siegle, 31 years old, a haberdasher of 3 West 116th street, but he was locked up, charged with burglary. Seymour told the police that he was in bed when a watchdog barked and awoke him. Seymour got out of bed, and, he claims, found Siegle prowling around in his room. Seymour grappled with him and there was a fight, in which Siegle gave up. Then Seymour backed the man in a corner, told him to stand there, and he left the room to dress. Seymour had the young man so frightened that he never moved, and when the ballplayer erturned fully dressed willingly accompanied him to the street, where they found the policeman. Siegle's right eye was closed, there was a black and blue mark under his left eye, his nose was badly swollen, and his clothing showed the result of having fought with the ballplayer.

When searched the man had a copy of a Sunday newspaper in his pocket which told of the operations of the "Arson" gang.

FOR INTERNATIONAL TREATIES

Washington, April 20—The Senate Committee on Foreign Relations today agreed to recommend to the Senate the adoption of the amended Martine resolution looking to an international co-operation in the regulation of ocean traffic.

It advises the President the Senate would favor treaties with the maritime powers regulating speed, routes and life-saving and wireless equipment.

Searchlights were especially recommended.

BRIDE-TO-BE SAVED.

San Diego, Cal., April 20—S. G. Willis of this city received a telegram today from Miss Buss of Kent, England, who was a passenger on the Titanic, saying she had been rescued and was on her way to San Diego to be married to Willis, according to their agreement.

NUPTIALS AND REQUIEM

Mass for Priest Lost in Titanic Disaster Follows Brother's Wedding.

There was a wedding this morning that was not all joy, at St. Paul's Church, Congress and Court streets. William E. Byles, of 124 Pacific street, was married to Isabelle C. Russell, of 119 Pacific street, by the Rev. Dr. William F. McGinnis. The wedding was to have been performed by the bridegroom's brother, the Rev. Thomas R. D. Byles, but the latter was one of the victims of the Titanic disaster, and from all accounts one of the heroes of the awful calamity. It is said that he administered the last rites to all that asked his services, and helped also to save many people from death.

After the low nuptial mass today, a solemn high requiem mass was celebrated for the lost priest, who hailed from Ongar, Essex County, England. The mass was sung by the Rev. M. G. Flannery, the rector of the church, assisted by the Rev. John Patterson, and the Rev. Father Ford. The eulogy was pronounced by the Rev. Dr. McGinnis.

The church was packed and among the other priests noticed in the church was the Rev. Father Chidwick, formerly chaplain of the U. S. S. Maine. Many members of the Cathedral Club attended the strange double service.

HITS CHILD; SPEEDS AWAY.

A speeding automobile knocked down Sadie Cully, a girl of 12, of 189 North Fourth street, at Driggs and Metropolitan avenues last night. The chauffeur, who was alone in the car, stopped his machine and picked the girl up.

The girl was severely hurt. A crowd quickly gathered and black looks were bent on the chauffeur. Seeing it, he jumped into his car, opened the speed clutch and disappeared at a rapid pace along Driggs avenue.

When Policeman Boehling of the Bedford avenue station reached the scene the automobile was still in view. Boehling got on a crosstown car and attempted a pursuit, but it was useless, and the car was soon lost to sight. From passengers on the car, Boehling obtained a number, which he believes to be the correct number of the car. The police are keeping that number to themselves and have detectives out trying to find the car. They think they will have little difficulty in locating both the owner and the chauffeur.

Sadie Cully had several ribs broken and was generally cut and bruised. She was taken to the Eastern District Hospital.

PRAYERS BY CATHOLICS.

Pastors Will Ask Parishioners to Remember Titanic Dead.

In the Roman Catholic Churches of Brooklyn and Long Island tomorrow the prayers of the congregations will be asked for the repose of the souls of those who perished in the Titanic disaster.

The Dev. James J. Coan, chancellor of the diocese, stated today that no general order or directions had been sent out to the rectors, but that each one would undoubtedly request the members of his flock to offer prayers for the victims.

In the New York Archdiocese Cardinal Farley has directed that the prayers of the faithful be requested at the services tomorrow. On Monday requiem mass will be said in the churches throughout the archdiocese.

MARCONI CAPITAL INCREASED.

Stock Declines After the Sensational Rise of Yesterday.

Trenton, N. J., April 20—The Marconi Wireless Telegraph Company filed with the Secretary of State today a certificate increasing its capital stock from $1,622,500 to $10,000,000.

CALL OF WARNING WAS NOT TAKEN ON THE TITANIC

Later Wireless Man Heard Message That Icebergs Were Near.

SAID HE WAS BUSY

Steamer Frankfurt's Inquiry Was Answered by Demand to Stop Interfering.

WAS NEARER THAN CARPATHIA

Origin of False Messages From the Rescue Ship Denied by Operator Cottam at Inquiry.

Harold Bride, one of the wireless operators of the Titanic, gave testimony to the Senate Investigating Committee at the Waldorf-Astoria today, which showed that the German steamship Frankfurt had been apparently nearer to the Titanic when it sent its first C. Q. D. signals through the air, and that the response had been not an answer that the boat would steam instantly to the rescue, but an inquiry as to what was the matter.

Bride said that his lost chief, Phillips, was authority for the statement that the Frankfurt was nearer than the Carpathia.

"He believed it was nearer," the witness said, "from the strength of the wireless current. After the first answer from the Carpathia there was a wait of about twenty minutes and then the wireless operator of the Frankfurt asked what was the matter. Phillips told him he was a fool—to cut out, and to stop interfering with his communication."

Bride said they did not learn the position of the Frankfurt and did not send any explanation as requesaed.

"The C. Q. D., with the position of the Titanic, should have been enough for any operator who knew his business. We hadn't time for explanations," declared the witness.

Call of Warning Not Answered.

Almost equally sensational was another portion of Bride's testimony when he was questioned about his knowledge and that of Phillips as to messages which told the Titanic's officers of ice in her vicinity.

He told that at 4:30 o'clock on Sunday afternoon the steamship California had tried to "raise" the Titanic by wireless, but no attention had been paid because they were "busy."

It wasn't until more than five hours before the disaster that they got the message which the California had been trying to give them in the afternoon. Then it was being sent to the Baltic and was picked up by the air. It told the Baltic that three large icebergs were ahead of the ship.

"Did you give this message about ice to Captain Smith?" questioned Senator Smith.

"I gave it to the officer on watch. I don't remember who it was," said Bride.

Baltic Got First Details.

Endeavor to get at all the facts of the Titanic disaster was approached by the special investigating committee of the United States Senate at the Waldorf-Astoria today from the point of the origin of the false news of the catastrophe and the assertions that efforts had been made by those most interested to conceal the truth, even to the extent of giving orders to that effect.

It was established positively at the beginning of the session, the second day of the investigation, that the Baltic of the White Star Line, had known the full details of the disaster at 10:30 o'clock Monday morning—had known that the vessel had sunk; that the Carpathia had only about 700 survivors aboard and that probably no more had been saved. This came from the first witness of the day, Cottam, the youthful wireless operator of the Carpathia.

The news that the White Star line officers knew early Monday morning that the Titanic had sunk was printed exclusively in The Eagle on Thursday.

With Harold Bride, the crippled surviving wireless man of the lost Titanic, and Guglielmo Marconi, the inventor, present when the Senators commenced anew their inquest, in addition to Cottam, it was made quite manifest that most of the day's inquiry would be devoted to the facts they might disclose.

Bride, with both feet swathed in bandages, but still with a boyish smile continuously on his face, was carried into the room where the grill was resumed, in a great invalid chair and was placed in a deep upholstered chair, with his feet stretched across two other chairs.

Carpathia Wireless Operator the First Witness.

Harold T. Cottam, wireless operator of the Carpathia, called as the first witness, was reminded at the beginning of the questioning by Senator Smith of the testimony he had given at the session

THE DAILY GRAPHIC
TITANIC
IN MEMORIAM NUMBER
ONE PENNY

HOW THE TITANIC MET WITH DISASTER ON HER MAIDEN VOYAGE.

The Titanic sailed from Southampton on Wednesday, April 10th, and she struck the iceberg on Sunday, April 14th, at 10.25 p.m. (American time), in the neighbourhood of the Newfoundland banks to the south of Cape Race. After the collision the Titanic sent out wireless appeals for immediate assistance, which were recorded on the Virginian, the Baltic, the Carpathia, and her sister ship the Olympic. All these vessels proceeded at once to the scene of the disaster, but apparently only the Carpathia was in time to render assistance. Our diagram illustrates the position of the Titanic at the time of the catastrophe, and shows the locality of the first boats to receive the distress signals. Inset portraits (left): Lord Pirrie, chairman of Messrs. Harland and Wolff, the builders of the Titanic; (right) Captain Smith, the commander of the Titanic, who went down with the ship.

THE CUNARD LINER CARPATHIA WHICH RESCUED THE SURVIVORS OF THE DISASTER.

THE OCEAN GRAVE OF THE TITANIC.

LOST LINER'S TRAGEDY.

THE SAILING AND— THE END.

ICE, THE FOE.

SHOCK THAT RENT THE SHIP.

THE BRAVE DEAD.

WOMEN SAVED BY MEN'S SACRIFICE.

THE NOBLE ELEMENT IN THE OCEAN TRAGEDY.

No element of tragedy seems to have failed to contribute its share to the overwhelming catastrophe of the Titanic. The forces of nature shook themselves free from the chains with which Man would bind them, burst in all their power from the limits in which he has sought to confine them, and dealt him a blow that has sent mourning through two nations. His last word in ship construction, equipped with every last device making for safety, or for aid in case of need, met at her maiden issue with the sea a challenge that broke her utterly and took her in toll with over twelve hundred of the lives she carried.

The magnitude of such a disaster leaves the mind as incapable of expressing the emotions aroused in it as its agencies were powerless to avert the catastrophe. For years we take our eager, heedless way, demanding more and more of life, increasingly impatient of its hindrances to our pleasure and our business, increasingly bold and cunning in overcoming them, and never pausing but to congratulate ourselves upon our triumphs. Every now and then comes some cataclysmic reminder that, if it is not possible to go too far and too fast, it is very possible to congratulate ourselves too well. For a brief moment we are brought to a full stop.

We trust the relatives of those who have perished may find some solace in the thought that though they have been called upon to suffer a grief almost unendurable to bear, they suffer it amidst that deepest sympathy which only when we are brought to face the realities of life can be aroused. For us, as for them, moreover, there is heartening thought in one thing that can be read into the disaster from the facts that have come to light. It is terribly clear that scenes of most dreadful horror must have taken place in the few hours between the Titanic's striking and her disappearance. And it is clear, from the fact that women and children form by far the greater majority of the saved, that in this dire emergency the imperilled rose to supreme heights of courage and devotion. Millionaire and steerage emigrant alike were called upon: alike they have presented us with that most inspiring of all spectacles—the inherent nobility of mankind.

The largest ship in the world went to sea from Southampton harbour on the tenth of April, 1912.

People spoke of the tenth of April as a great day in the history of shipping, and they said this they gave utterance to a truth more awful than could be conceived by living man.

It was a great day also in the history of Southampton, for many fathers of families had found employment on the Titanic, many women's faces were lightened because the shadow of need and poverty had been banished from their homes.

It was a day that no one who stood upon the quayside will ever forget. We who saw it saw a sight that will be unforgettable until our eyes are turned to dust.

We saw the start of the mightiest vessel in the world upon her solitary and uncompleted voyage. She was named Titanic and she has been Titanic in her sorrow. We saw her, the mightiest, finest product of human brains in the matter of ships to sail the sea, a gigantic vessel that realised in her being a floating city of treasured glories, riches, and luxury, as she first ploughed the grey fields of the ocean.

And her displacement of water, the foam, and the rush of her passage, was so tremendous that the stern ropes of another mighty liner parted and the New York, but for the ready aid of holding tugs, would have swung out aimlessly into the fairway.

THE HAPPY START.

We paused in our cheering then, chilled to a sudden silence at this first evidence of the great ship's untested powers for evil as for good. And our cheering now is hushed into sobbing, for within a week of her majestic passage from Southampton Harbour, the displacement of the Titanic has been so tremendous that she has drenched the bosom of the world in an ocean of tears.

Those of us who had come to wish the vessel "Good speed"—in the dark wisdom of Providence to wish "God speed" and "a fair journey" to those loved ones who were going out upon the longest and loneliest voyage in Eternity—were up "by times" on that pleasant Wednesday morning, long before the stroke of noon when we knew Captain Smith would climb into his lofty perch on the navigating bridge and give the order to "let go" from the Trafalgar landing stage.

The air was busy with chatter, with "good bye for the present" and good wishes. We lived that morning in an atmosphere of pride. All these happy-faced Southampton women were proud that their men had entered into service on the greatest vessel ever built by man. They prattled of the Titanic with a sort of suggestion of proprietorship.

Rumours and legends and tales of her glories and luxuries and powers were bandied about in every street in Southampton. She was a caravanserai of marvels: a mighty treasure house of beauty and luxurious ease. In the phrase of the people, she was "the last word." The phrases of the people are often true, because they are double edged.

Another phrase sticks now in the puzzle of a darkening mind: "They're breaking all records this time." And so they were. It had been determined that the Titanic should excel in luxury and equipment her sister vessel, the Olympic, which had sailed for New York a week before. And in a sort of desperate endeavour to achieve this we who had come to take a temporary parting from dear ones and friends were shown a new and latest marvel on the promenade deck of the Titanic. It was called the Café Parisien. Its walls were covered with a delicate trellis work around which trailed cool foliage. We looked at the soft-cushioned chairs, we regarded the comfort of the whole scene, and, feeling the suggestive atmosphere of the place, thought of those who would be taking coffee there after dinner with music lulling every sense, melting into the gentle roll and rhythm of the open sea. What a place in which to dream!—perhaps if one were young to hold a little romantic dalliance—what a place in which to forget the trials and harass of the world! What a place in which to sleep!

Some of us looked into the private suites that were to cost a mere trifle of £870 a voyage, and here we found snug dining-rooms, bedrooms that looked in themselves like little enchanted palaces of slumberous rest, and private promenade decks. Let us note that everyone spoke of "dining-rooms" and "bedrooms." The word "cabin" would have been an anachronism in this floating citadel of luxurious beauty. We examined the delicate glass and napery, the flowers and the fruit, the baths and the playing-courts, and the innumerable mechanical appliances that seemed to make personal effort or discomfort the only human impossibility on board.

There was one thing that no one looking even for a brief half-hour on this cushioned lap of luxury ever thought of giving a cursory glance or a thought. No one looked at the boats.

Punctually at noon Captain E. J. Smith, a typical figure of an English sailor as we knew him and imagined him in tougher, pre-Titanic days, took up his post of captainship on the navigating bridge. And as the bells sounded, the cheers of the multitudes went upward and hands and handkerchiefs were waved from quay and ship's side, and kisses were blown across and last familiar greetings exchanged.

So she went away with her human freight of two thousand two hundred and eight souls. We cheered to the last and waved our salutations, and that night I think there was not an unhappy woman in all Southampton. And to-night—who is to count the tear-stained faces or to cast a reckoning over the travail of these broken hearts, some here, some two thousand miles away, but all united beyond the cleavage of the pitiless seas, by the sacred companionship of sorrow!

WHAT WE THOUGHT—

So the Titanic went her away, and we went ours, and thought perhaps little about her, save thoughts of remembered joy in her strength and beauty, until on Tuesday morning came the news that smote upon our hearts with the thunder of doom. These were, of course, the first indefinite rumblings that woke fear in every human breast.

She had struck an iceberg; she had been rent; but she was unsinkable. She was heading slowly for shore, a great giant wounded thing in the wake of the Virginian. How our hopes died down until it seemed that the heart was burnt into a heap of dead cold ashes, only to rise, Phœnix-like, in jubilant and hopeful expectancy. Human lips have sobbed out strange prayers before to-day, but what volume of prayer went up to heaven in thankfulness to the Lord of Hosts who had brought the new wonder of wireless telegraphy out of the slow womb of time.

We thought of that unforgettable message speeding through the viewless air that is marked upon the chart sheets S.O.S. We picked up the common phrase of the operator and repeated to ourselves: "Save Our Souls," and thanked Providence for their salvation.

We pictured the scene. The lonely operator, composed with that old English valiance that has turned the blood of history into wine, calmly tapping out the cry of help. We saw the realization of that message in the operator's cabin on other vessels. We saw the wonderful chain composed of those three words, stronger than stone or iron or tempered steel, stronger than wind or sea, suddenly dragging all the vessels within the sphere of hearing away from their allotted course, and sending them on the great adventure of succour and mercy. We pictured them racing along the railless roads of the open sea, rushing with insensate speed towards the spot of the catastrophe. We had leisure to imagine the scene, because we were told there had been a great deliverance; because we felt that man had fought his battle with the ocean and had won.

Then we knew that we had lost.

—AND WHAT WE LEARNT.

All the world knows how slowly those confessions of defeat came in upon us, how slowly the last flicker of an expiring hope was beaten down within our breasts, with what dilatory hands the veils were drawn from the implacable face of doom. Gradually the hush laid hold upon us, gradually a realisation of what had happened sank into our souls.

We knew that nothing but a miserable residue of the great human freightage had been saved to us. We knew that the enchanted floating palace, conceived by the brain of man and wrought by his hands, with all its mighty scheme of luxurious ease, health, and comfort, lay somewhere tangled in an old sea forest, two miles beneath the quiet surface of the sea. Little more do we know as I write. We can only hear the sobbing of the women at the street corners of Southampton, and find in them an eternal echo of the cheers with which we sent the Titanic out on her first, her last, her only voyage.

We know that among these women are many mothers. We know with thankfulness that though their faces are dark with sorrow they are untouched with the lightest shadow of shame. For though man has been beaten once again in his old fight with the sea, yet he has done one thing with all the glory and splendour of a victory.

He has taken the last gift of God and used it well. He has died as we all would die—for others.

Picturing that last dark awful moment, the last order of the captain, the last farewells—so different from these we exchanged at Southampton—the last tears and the last high human courage, all our sorrow is tempered by the thought that the women are alive to us and the children, and that the men died as we would have had them die, as we should like to have died ourselves had God steeled our hearts with a similar courage.

Knowing this, as we peer into the dark picture of that yet unrecorded scene, so deep with human anguish and yet so lighted with human grandeur, we may learn to endure the sobbings of the women and the cries of the fatherless that come up to us in every surge of the immemorial sea. Knowing this, we may take comfort in the great cry of a great poet in a sea-washed island that had born so many poets, and acclaim with him that:—

Nothing is here for tears, nothing to wail,
Or knock the breast, no weakness, no contempt,
Dispraise or blame, nothing but well and fair,
And what may quiet us in a death so noble.

THE COMMANDER OF THE TITANIC AND THE BOWS OF HIS SHIP.

The portrait of Captain Smith was taken on board the Titanic on the day of the vessel's departure from Southampton. He was in command of the Olympic, the Titanic's sister ship, when, on her maiden voyage, she collided with H.M.S. Hawke.

SOME OF THE TITANIC'S NOTABLE PASSENGERS.

Lady Duff-Gordon ("Lucile").—She is known to be saved.
(Photographed by Bassano, Old Bond Street.)

Mr. and Mrs. Daniel Marvin, who were returning to New York from their honeymoon. Mr. Marvin is only nineteen years of age, and his bride is a year younger. Their parents are prominent New York people. Mrs. Marvin was saved. (Photographed at the Dover Street Studios.)

Mrs. J. J. Astor, wife of Colonel J. J. Astor, the well-known millionaire.—She is known to be saved.

Mr. Isidor Straus, formerly a member of the United States Congress, and a partner in the New York firm of L. Straus and Son.

Mr. James Carleton Young, a prominent citizen of Minneapolis.

Mr. Cardeza, a partner in the firm of Cardeza Brothers, of Rio de Janeiro and New York.—Known to be saved.

Mrs. F. J. Swift, a New York society hostess—Known to be saved.

Mr. J. J. Borebank, a well-known Californian horticulturist.

Major Archibald W. Butt, aide-de-camp to President Taft.

Mr. Charles Williams, the racquets champion, who was on his way to New York to meet G. Standing.

Mr. C. M. Hays, the president of the Grand Trunk Railway.

Mrs. H. B. Harris, daughter-in-law of an American theatre owner.—Known to be saved.

Mrs. C. E. H. Stengel, an American society hostess and wife of a well-known racehorse owner.—Known to be saved.

Miss Margaret Graham, a well-known Californian actress.—Known to be saved.

Mrs. G. M. Stone, well known in American society.—Known to be saved.

SOME OF THE TITANIC'S NOTABLE PASSENGERS.

Mr. Herbert Parsons, formerly Congressman for New York City.

Mr. Francis M. Warren, formerly United States Senator for Wyoming.

Mr. W. Van der Hoef, a prominent citizen of Minneapolis.

Mr. P. Marechal, a well-known resident of Washington.—Known to be saved.

Miss E. M. Eustis, well known in New York society.—Known to be saved.

Mrs. J. Snyder, well known in New York society.

Mrs. Figler, well known in New York society.

Mrs. Ettlinger, well known in New York society.

Mr. Christopher Head, ex-Mayor of Chelsea.

Colonel Archibald Gracie, a large cotton grower, of Jefferson County, Arkansas.

Mr. George Eastman.

Mr. J. H. Ross, a professor of Wisconsin University.

The Countess of Rothes.—Known to be saved. (Photographed by Lafayette, Bond Street.)

Miss Gladys Cherry, daughter of Lady Emily Cherry.—Known to be saved. (Photographed by Kate Pragnell.)

Mrs. F. M. Hoyt, wife of an ex-Governor of Washington.—Known to be saved.

Mrs. W. E. Carter, of Pennsylvania.

FEATURES WHICH CONTRIBUTED TO THE SPLENDOURS OF THE TITANIC.

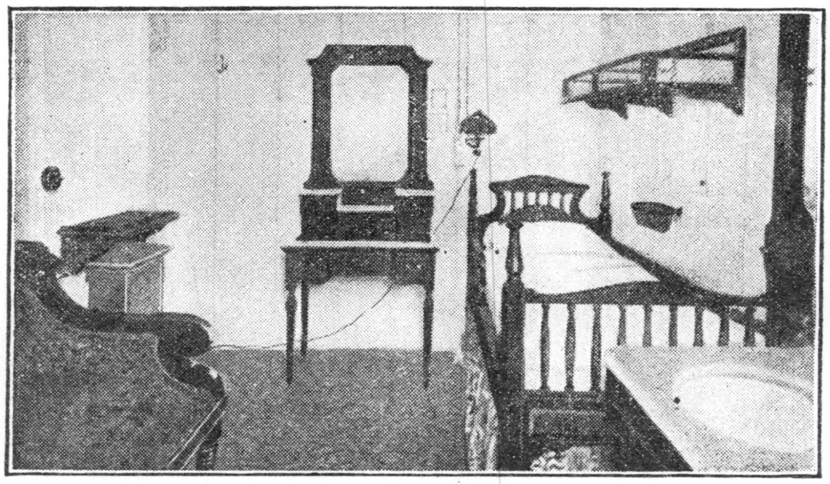

A SINGLE BERTH STATE-ROOM.

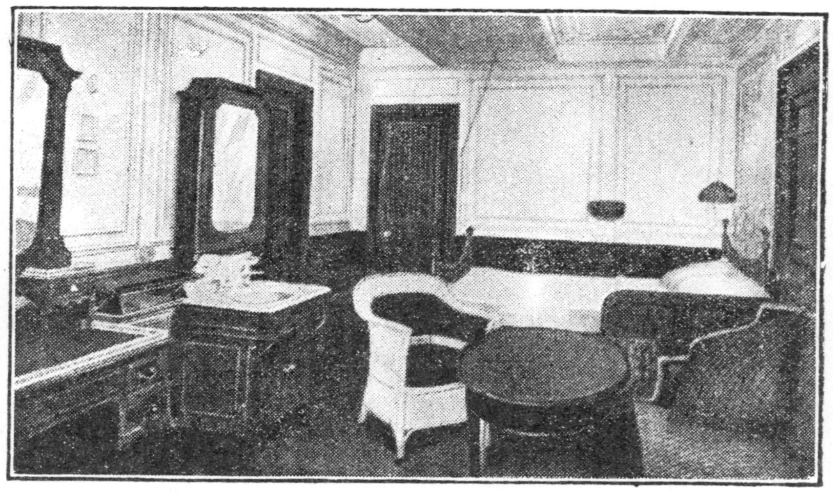

A DECK STATE ROOM.

THE SWIMMING BATH, A POPULAR FEATURE WHICH IS POSSESSED BY VERY FEW VESSELS AFLOAT.

THE TURKISH BATH COOLING ROOM, WHICH, WITH ITS SUGGESTION OF THE "MYSTERIOUS EAST," IS ONE OF THE SHIP'S MOST INTERESTING ROOMS.

THE VERANDAH CAFE ADJOINING THE SMOKE ROOM. IT IS SURROUNDED BY GREEN TRELLIS-WORK, OVER WHICH GROW CLIMBING PLANTS.

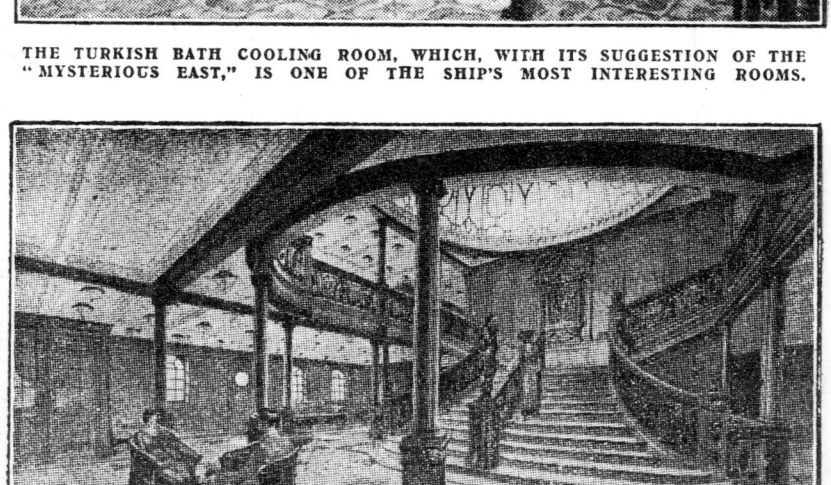

THE MAIN STAIRCASE FROM THE GREAT HALL.—FROM THIS HALL LIFTS GO UP AND DOWN TO EVERY FLOOR OF THE SHIP.

THE GEORGIAN SMOKE ROOM, PANELLED IN THE FINEST MAHOGANY AND RELIEVED EVERYWHERE WITH MOTHER-O'-PEARL INLAID WORK.

THE RESTAURANT. DECORATED IN LOUIS XVI. STYLE, AND PANELLED FROM FLOOR TO CEILING IN FRENCH WALNUT.

HER FIRST AND LAST VOYAGE: THE TITANIC PASSING UP THE SOLENT ON WEDNESDAY, APRIL 10th, ON HER DEPARTURE FROM SOUTHAMPTON.

THE OCEAN GRAVE OF THE TITANIC.

WORLD-WIDE HELP.

FUNDS FOR THE RELIEF OF SUFFERERS.

MANSION HOUSE FUND.

KING AND QUEEN AMONG THE SUBSCRIBERS.

Widespread distress will inevitably follow upon a disaster of such magnitude as the sinking of the Titanic, and all the money which can be collected will be required to alleviate the suffering.

The Lord Mayor (Sir T. B. Crosby) on Wednesday opened a Mansion House Fund, and below we publish a letter from Sir Thomas in which he appeals to the generosity of the nation.

Among the first to contribute to the fund were their Majesties, Queen Alexandra, and the Princess Royal. These donations were as follows:—

The King	**500 gns.**
The Queen	**250 gns.**
Queen Alexandra	**£200**
The Princess Royal	**£100**

By Thursday night the Fund amounted to over £25,000, and each succeeding post brought further donations to swell the total. The larger of the first subscriptions included the following:—

Shipping Federation...	£2,100	Baring Bros. and Co., Ltd.	525
Messrs. Morgan, Grenfell and Co.	2,000	Messrs. Baker, Mason, and Co.	500
Corporation of London	1,050	Messrs. Brown, Shipley, and Co.	500
Messrs. Speyer Bros...	1,050	Messrs. Emile Erlanger and Co.	500
Lord Mount Stephen...	1,000	Messrs. Glyn, Mills, Currie and Co.	500
Sir William Nelson .	1,000	Messrs. George Kitchin and Co.	500
Mr. Edward C. Grenfell	1,000	The American Ambassador (Mr. Whitelaw Reid)	500
Messrs. N. M. Rothschild and Sons	525	Messrs. C. Hambro and Son	500
Canadian Agency, Ltd.	525	Royal Mail Steam Packet Co.	500
Messrs. J. Henry Schroder and Co. ...	525	Union Castle Mail Steamship Co.	500
Messrs. Lazard Bros. and Co.	525		
Messrs. Sperling and Co.	525		
Messrs. Stocken and Concasson	525		
Donald Currie and Co.	525		

THE LORD MAYOR'S APPEAL.

The Lord Mayor's letter is in the following terms:—

To THE EDITOR OF THE DAILY GRAPHIC.

Sir,—I desire, by your courtesy, to intimate that I have to-day opened a fund at the Mansion House for the immediate aid and permanent relief of the widows, orphans, and dependent relatives of those—whether they be crew or passengers—who have lost their lives in this great national calamity, and to invite the ever-generous assistance of the benevolent public in attempting to relieve, in some degree, the distress which has been occasioned in many hundreds of families by a disaster fortunately unparalleled in the history of ocean navigation.

In taking this step I feel sure that I am promptly responding to the wishes of those who urge that the keen sympathy, universally and unstintedly entertained for those who have thus suddenly been plunged into misery and distress, should assume some practical shape for the future advantage of the bereaved families.

Of the real extent of the calamity it is too soon to expect reliable details. Some time must necessarily elapse before information can be obtained as to the number of those lost and their wives and families and their circumstances, but sufficient is known to make it evident that a very large sum will be required to adequately provide for those in distress, apart from their claims under the Workmen's Compensation Act.

In raising a Mansion House Fund, I am assured of the hearty and active co-operation of the Mayor of Southampton, to whose town the great bulk of the crew and their families belonged, and of others who are raising subscriptions, and I should especially welcome the assistance of the London and Provincial Press in making known the existence of the fund, and, if possible, in collecting, acknowledging and remitting donations in response to this appeal.

Donations may be sent to the Mansion House or to the Bank of England, where an account, "The Titanic Disaster Fund," has been opened.—Your obedient servant,

THOMAS BOOR CROSBY,
Lord Mayor.

The Mansion House, April 17th, 1912.

THE TITANIC'S OPERATORS.

Mr. J. G. Phillips, the chief wireless operator on the Titanic, was a young man of twenty-five. He was the son of Mr. G. A. Phillips, a well-known Godalming tradesman. He received his training as a telegraphist in the Godalming post-office, and seven years ago joined the Marconi School at Liverpool.

Since then Mr. Phillips had acted as wireless operator on the Teutonic, Mauretania, Lusitania, and Oceanic. He was transferred from the Oceanic to the Titanic for her maiden voyage.

The second Marconi operator, who is reported saved, is Mr. Harold Sydney Bride, of Shortlands, Bromley. He has been with the Marconi Company for twelve months, and is twenty-two years of age and unmarried.

PERIL OF THE BERG.

FLOATING ICE-FIELDS THAT HARASS THE NAVIGATOR.

WHAT CAN BE DONE?

It was the misfortune of the Titanic to begin her career at a moment when the North Atlantic was exceptionally dotted with icefields and icebergs. There is a season for Atlantic ice, as for everything else. It opens with the month of April. It closes with the month of August. Anywhere within this period you may have much ice or little.

One ice season is never just like another. The present has opened badly from the navigator's point of view. For reasons which are difficult to dogmatise about, but which probably are the result of climatic eccentricity, the ice has come down in the very early days of April, driven irresistibly by currents to the warmer waters into which it is ultimately to disappear.

It is curious that, just as the Atlantic now appears at the beginning of the season to be at its worst so far as ice is concerned, it was at the end of last season that the ice danger was most marked.

On August 6th of last year the Anchor Line steamer Columbia arrived at New York with her bow plates crushed in for a distance of fifteen feet. It is said that her port anchor, which was lost, was left on the iceberg into which she crashed. She had a narrow escape. On August 15th the Donaldson liner Saturnia struck on a ledge of an iceberg when 170 miles from East Belle Isle. She got safely across the Atlantic to Glasgow, but she was making water.

What can ships do to avoid such peril? Primarily there is only one thing—namely, to keep a vigilant look-out.

It is, of course, the practice of Atlantic liners to adapt their routes to the ice season, but ice has sometimes got down as far south as the Azores, and sometimes so near to our shores as the Fastnet. Hence it is impossible to locate this peril and say that a particular part of the North Atlantic is always ice-free. Still, there are some things in the way of limitations, these, again, depending upon the general character of the season.

It used to be believed that an infallible indication of the proximity of icebergs was afforded by the sea surface temperature. That notion is exploded. You may, it appears, get within quite a reasonable distance of a berg and the water will give no indication of it, neither will the air. That, at all events, is what the text-book writers say.

It is stated, again, that the whiteness of the ice gives off during the night an indication of its presence known as "ice-blink." That may possibly help the navigator, but it is clear that to the watchful eyes on the Titanic it was of little or no use.

We may safely assume that on this splendid ship everything was done that could have been done by human agency to keep her out of danger. Yet this uncharted peril, this libertine of the ocean, could not be seen till it was too late.

Will science, which has already done so much to secure safe navigation, some day come to our aid in this matter?

NOTABLE TRIBUTES.

MESSAGES FROM THE KING AND THE KAISER.

PREMIER'S ELOQUENCE.

It is fitting that a disaster so tremendous as the sinking of the Titanic should have called forth notable tributes of grief and sympathy.

Chief among these are the messages of the King. To the White Star Line he telegraphed:—

The Queen and I are horrified at the appalling disaster which has happened to the Titanic and at the terrible loss of life.

We deeply sympathise with the bereaved relations, and feel for them in their great sorrow with all our hearts. GEORGE R. and I.

His Majesty's feeling message to President Taft was worded as follows:—

The Queen and I are anxious to assure you and the American nation of the great sorrow which we experience at the terrible loss of life that has occurred among the American citizens and my own subjects by the foundering of the Titanic.

Our two countries are so intimately allied by ties of friendship and brotherhood that any misfortune which affects the one must necessarily affect the other, and on the present heartrending occasion they are both equally sufferers.

(Signed) GEORGE R. and I.

Queen Alexandra telegraphed to the White Star Line:—

It is with feelings of the deepest sorrow that I hear of the terrible disaster to the Titanic and of the awful loss of life.

My heart is full of grief and sympathy for the bereaved families of those who have perished.

The Kaiser sent the following telegram to the White Star Line:—

Deeply grieved at the sad news of the terrible disaster which befell your line. I send expression of deepest sympathy also with all those who mourn the loss of relatives and friends.

WILLIAM I.R.

President Fallières also sent telegrams of condolence to King George and President Taft.

In the House of Commons members listened with bared heads while Mr. Asquith made a touching reference to the disaster. Amid solemn silence the Prime Minister said:—

"I am afraid we must brace ourselves to confront one of those terrible events in the order of Providence which baffle foresight, appal the imagination, and make us realise the inadequacy of words to do justice to what we feel.

"We cannot say more at this moment than to give necessarily imperfect expression to our sense of admiration that the best traditions of the sea seem to have been observed in the willing sacrifice which offered the first chance of safety to those who were least able to help themselves, and to award the warm and heartfelt sympathy of the whole nation to those who find themselves suddenly bereft of their nearest and dearest, in the desolation of their homes."

SENDER OF THE 'S. O. S.' SIGNAL FOR HELP.

Mr. G. G. Phillips, the Marconi wireless operator on board the Titanic, whose signal, "S.O.S.," was received by liners hundreds of miles away. (Photographed by Jennie Stedman.)

DOOMED SHIP'S FAREWELL.

LAST MESSAGES FROM THE TITANIC BEFORE SHE SANK.

'MANY THANKS: GOOD-BYE.'

Tragic interest attaches to some of the messages which several liners report having received from the Titanic, for they were among the last sent out by the liner before going to her doom.

The French liner Touraine, which arrived at Havre on Monday, mentions that Captain Smith, of the Titanic, was apprised of the presence of the ice, and replied thanking the Touraine's captain.

At midnight on Wednesday, the 10th, when in latitude 44.58 north, and longitude 50.40 west, the Touraine entered an ice-field. Speed was reduced in order to avoid collisions, and at one o'clock in the morning she left the ice behind. The ice was very low-lying. At six in the morning of the same day the Touraine ran alongside the edge of another ice-field, past which she steamed until 6.45. Two icebergs were seen.

The Touraine, on Friday, the 12th, was in communication all the afternoon and until nine o'clock in the evening with the Titanic. Captain Caussin, the commander of the Touraine, signalled the position of the ice floes to the Titanic's commander, who replied thanking him.

"GOOD LUCK" AND "GOOD BYE."

The Cunard liner Caronia, which put into Queenstown from New York on Wednesday, reported that on Monday, at 4.39 a.m., she received from the Titanic a message stating that the White Star liner had been in collision with an iceberg, was in a sinking condition, and required immediate assistance. Being about 700 miles distant from the Titanic Captain Barr knew that the Caronia could not reach the White Star liner in time to render help.

Another ship, the Tunisian, of the Allan Line, on arriving at Liverpool on Wednesday from Canada reported that on Saturday midnight she spoke the Titanic by wireless, sending the message: "Good luck!" To this the reply came: "Many thanks, good-bye."

The Tunisian, when 887 miles east of St. John's, entered a huge icefield, through which she carefully picked her way for twenty-four hours, then stopped all night, and eventually turned sixty miles south. No fewer than 200 icebergs were seen. The commander was on the bridge for a thirty-six hours' spell.

CUNARD LINER'S ESCAPE.

The perils of the icebergs are clearly shown in reports made by the captains of other ships.

This time of the year is the most perilous to vessels in the Atlantic, owing to the break-up of the Arctic ice and the floating of immense bergs southward. A great ice-field, the length of which was estimated at seventy miles, with a breadth of about thirty-five miles, had been obstructing the West-bound Transatlantic sea-lane off the Newfoundland Grand Banks for more than a week past.

The Cunard liner Carmania, which arrived at New York on Sunday last, ran through the pack on Thursday, the 11th. She was in grave danger for a time, and had to stop frequently because of fog. The passengers sighted twenty-five icebergs, one cluster a hundred feet away. The liner had to feel her way through an ice-lane for hours.

A French liner, the Niagara, was less lucky, and had two holes knocked in her bottom and several plates bent.

The Canadian Pacific liner Empress of Britain, which arrived at Liverpool from Halifax on Sunday, encountered an ice-field a hundred miles in extent, with enormous bergs, and steered a wide course, which delayed the vessel. This was on Tuesday, the 9th inst, when the vessel was three days out from Halifax.

The extent of the ice was regarded as phenomenal, and the bergs appeared to be joined to the ice-field, which appeared as an enormous white line on the horizon.

One full-rigged ship and one fishing smack are imprisoned in the floes.

ICEBERGS' DEATH TOLL.

Icebergs are often hidden, either in the water or by fog. Frequently the only indication of their presence is a fall in temperature. Only one-eighth of an iceberg is above water, so the bulk of one with a peak of 150ft. is immense. Two thousand million tons is the estimated weight of a berg once seen by Admiral Markham.

The death toll of the Atlantic icebergs is great. A bad year was 1909, when many vessels were lost or damaged, and in 1903 no fewer than twenty steamers were seriously damaged and two lost.

FEATS OF WIRELESS.

Perhaps the most famous "wireless" rescue was that of the Republic, which was in collision in January, 1909, with the Florida. The wireless "C.Q.D." message—"Come quick, danger"—was sent out by the Republic's operator, Jack Binn, and was picked up by the Baltic and the Loraine, which went to the sinking ship's assistance.

In 1904 the Kroonland, an Atlantic liner, broke one of her shafts some eighty miles out. Communication by wireless was at once set up between Crookhaven Station and the disabled liner, and over one hundred messages were cleared, the majority being to friends of the passengers in different parts of the world, and others summoning assistance, which was speedily rendered. For twenty-four hours the operators were busily engaged, and the liner was ultimately enabled to continue upon her voyage.

THE OCEAN GRAVE OF THE TITANIC.

THE LINER DE LUXE.

SPLENDOUR THAT NOW LIES IN THE DEPTHS.

A MILLION AND A HALF.

RESTAURANT, RACQUET COURT AND PARISIAN CAFE.

Sister to the Olympic, the Titanic was the last word in ocean liners and the largest ship in the world. Her fittings were the most luxurious of any vessel afloat, including a restaurant, furnished in the Louis XVI. style, a reception-room of Jacobean style, and a squash racquet court.

The Titanic's displacement was 46,328 tons, 1,004 tons more than that of the Olympic. She cost over a million and a half. She was built by Messrs. Harland and Wolff at Belfast, and launched on May 31st, 1911. Her building took over a year, and her fitting-out nearly another year.

Some idea of the Titanic's enormous size may be gauged from the following figures:—

Total length, 882ft. 9in.
Breadth, 92½ft.
Height from keel to navigating bridge, 104ft.
Gross tonnage, 45,000.
Load draft, 34½ft.
Displacement, 60,000 tons.
Indicated horse-power of reciprocating engines, 30,000.
Shaft horse-power of turbine engine, 16,000.
Speed, 21 knots.

She carried ten decks, of which seven were passenger decks. The bridge deck extended over a length of 550ft. amidships, while the promenade and boat-decks were also over 500ft. long.

For first-class passengers there were thirty suite rooms on the bridge deck, and thirty-nine on the shelter deck, so arranged that they could be let in groups to form suites, including bedrooms, with baths, etc., with communicating doors. In all, the first-class accommodation comprised nearly 370 rooms, 100 of which were single-berth rooms.

The Titanic was a floating town with accommodation for a population of over 3,000 people, made up as follows:—

Saloon passengers	750
Second-class passengers	500
Steerage passengers	1,100
Crew	800
Total	3,150

ENORMOUS FOOD STORES.

To feed this community she carried the following stores:—

Fresh meat	75,000lb.	Sweetbreads	1,000lb.
Fresh fish	11,000lb.	Coffee	2,200lb.
Salt fish	4,000lb.	Tea	800lb.
Bacon and ham	7,500lb.	Sugar	10,000lb.
Fresh butter	6,000lb.	Jams	1,120lb.
Poultry	8,000 head.	Flour	200 barrels.
Fresh eggs	40,000	Potatoes	40 tons.
Sausages	2,500lb.	Apples	180 boxes.

The ship was fitted with electrically-controlled watertight doors, and those giving communication between the various boiler-rooms and engine-rooms were arranged, as usual in White Star Line steamers, on the "drop system." They were of Messrs. Harland and Wolff's special design, of massive construction, and provided with oil cataracts.

Each door, according to the official description, was held in the open position by a friction clutch, which could instantly be released by means of a powerful electric magnet controlled from the captain's bridge, so that in the event of accident the captain, by simply moving an electric switch, could instantly close the doors throughout, thus, it was believed, practically making the vessel unsinkable.

As a further precaution, floats were provided beneath the floor level, which, in the event of water accidentally entering any of the compartments, would automatically lift and thereby close the doors opening into that compartment if they had not already been dropped by those in charge of the vessel.

The lifeboats attached to the liner were 30ft. long, and mounted on special davits on the boat deck. For purposes of wireless telegraphy the Titanic had two masts 205ft. above the average draught-line.

UNPARALLELED LUXURY.

Among the features of the Titanic may be mentioned the first-class promenades on the three top decks, which were exceptionally fine. In keeping with the public rooms were the large and beautiful first-class state-rooms, perhaps the most striking of these being the suite rooms decorated in different styles and periods, including the following:—Louis Seize, Empire, Adams, Italian Renaissance, Louis Quinze, Louis Quatorze, Georgian, Regence, Queen Anne, Modern Dutch, Old Dutch.

The second and third-class accommodation was also on a scale of unparalleled luxury for those classes.

The Titanic's special features were the two promenade deck suites, with private promenades about fifty feet long—an absolutely novel feature—and the open-air Parisian café which adjoined the restaurant. The rates for these two suites during the busy season was to be £870 each.

The following is the official account of the Titanic's first-class dining saloon:—

"It is an immense room decorated in a style peculiarly English, reminiscent of early Jacobean times; but instead of the sombre oak of the sixteenth and seventeenth centuries, it is painted a soft, rich white, which, with the coved and richly-moulded ceilings and the spacious character of the apartment, would satisfy the most æsthetic critic.

"The furniture is of oak designed to harmonise with its surroundings.

SURVIVORS' THRILLING STORIES.

"NEARER MY GOD TO THEE" PLAYED BY ORCHESTRA AS TITANIC SETTLED.

Mr. W. C. Chambers, one of the Titanic's survivors, interviewed by a Central News reporter, said the Titanic struck the iceberg head on.

The passengers came running out on deck, but believing that the ship could not sink, and being assured that this was so by the liner's officers, they went back to their state-rooms again.

After about two hours, however, the alarm was sent round, and the passengers started to enter the lifeboats. There was nothing in the way of a panic at first, as everybody believed there were plenty of lifeboats to go around.

After the lifeboat in which he was seated had gone about four hundred yards from the ship they saw the Titanic begin to settle down very quickly. It was then that there was a rush for the remaining boats, and one was swamped.

The Titanic sank head first.

So far as his own boat was concerned, she created no suction. No shots were fired. There was nothing of that kind.

Of those who were rescued from the Titanic seven were subsequently buried at sea, four being sailors and three passengers. Two rescued women had gone insane.

As the liner continued to gradually recede into the trough of the sea the passengers marched towards the stern. The orchestra belonging to the first cabin assembled on deck as the liner was going down and played "Nearer my God to Thee."

Mr. and Mrs. Isidor Straus were drowned together, Mrs. Straus refusing to leave her husband's side. They went to their deaths together, standing arm in arm on the first cabin deck of the Titanic.

Mr. C. H. Stengel, a first-class passenger, said that when the Titanic struck the iceberg the impact was terrific, and great blocks of ice were thrown on the deck, killing a number of people. The stern of the vessel rose in the air, and people ran shrieking from their berths below.

Women and children, some of the former naturally hysterical, having been rapidly separated from husbands, brothers, and fathers, were quickly placed in boats by the sailors, who, like their officers, it was stated, were heard by some survivors to threaten that they would shoot if male passengers attempted to get into the boats ahead of the women.

Mr. Stengel added that a number of men threw themselves into the sea when they saw that there was no chance of their reaching the boats. He himself dropped overboard, caught hold of the gunwale of a boat, and was pulled in because there were not enough sailors to handle her. In some of the boats women were shrieking for their husbands, others were weeping, but many bravely took a turn with the oars.

Mrs. Dickinson Bishop, of Detroit, Mich., said:—"I was in my bed when the crash came. I got up and dressed quickly, but being assured that there was no danger I went back to bed. There were few people on deck when I got there, and there was little or no panic.

Mr. Robert Davill, of Richmond, Virginia, said:—"I jumped overboard, and I reckon that over a thousand did likewise. I swam about in the icy water for an hour before being picked up by a boat. At that moment I saw the Titanic take her final plunge. It was awful.

"Colonel Astor has gone down. So has Major Butt and Mr. W. T. Stead. I believe they jumped into the sea.

"I was in a state of collapse when picked up, and there are scores of survivors seriously ill.

"Captain Smith stuck to the bridge and behaved like a hero."

William Jones, a fireman, of Southampton, who was making his first trip, said that when the Titanic sank four of her lifeboats were swamped. He also declared that her boilers exploded, and that ice from the berg falling on her decks killed many people.

Mrs. Andrews, an elderly lady, interviewed by the Exchange representative, said the crash occurred at 11.35 p.m. on Sunday night. The women and children got off in the lifeboats at 12.45 a.m. The Titanic sank at 2 a.m., and the Carpathia picked up the boats at 8.30 a.m.

A WIRELESS CABIN ON AN ATLANTIC LINER.

Appalling as is the loss of life the death-roll would have been much longer but for the wireless telegraph. This picture shows a typical Marconi cabin on a large Atlantic liner, a cabin similar to that from which the signal "S.O.S." was despatched immediately after the Titanic had struck the iceberg.

SOME OF THE MISSING

MEN FAMOUS ON BOTH SIDES OF THE ATLANTIC.

CAPTAINS OF INDUSTRY.

Among those well-known passengers on the Titanic who have not been heard of are the following:—

Colonel John Jacob Astor.—Eldest son of Mr. William Astor, who had five children, four daughters and one son. His father was an uncle of Mr. William Waldorf Astor, and great-uncle of Mr. Waldorf Astor, M.P. Colonel Astor, who was born in 1864, served in the Spanish-American war, and presented a mountain battery to the Government for use in the campaign. His surviving sisters are Mrs. George Ogilvie Hay, of London, and Mrs. Orme Wilson. The dead body of Colonel John Jacob Astor—whose marriage last year created a considerable sensation—is to be searched for. His young wife is among those saved.

Famous Financier.

Mr. Benjamin Guggenheim.—A member of the famous Guggenheim family of capitalists, associates of Mr. Pierpont Morgan, and world-famous in connection with Alaskan development and copper production.

Major Archibald Butt.—Aide-de-Camp to President Taft, returning to Washington after visiting the Pope.

Mr. George D. Widener. Well-known Philadelphia capitalist, and son of Peter A. Widener, who bought Rembrandt's "The Mill" for £100,000. Some of the exhibits in the London Museum, recently opened, were presented by Mrs. George Widener, who has been visiting London with her husband.

Twice Wrecked.

Mr. C. M. Hays.—President of the Grand Trunk Railway, and one of the best-known railwaymen in Canada. He, with Mrs. Hays and Miss Hays, both on board, had recently been on a short visit to London. Mr. Hays had also been shipwrecked in the Pacific Ocean.

Mr. J. B. Thayer.—President of the Pennsylvania Railroad.

Mr. Washington Roebling. Millionaire president and director of John A. Roebling's Sons Company, iron and steel wire and wire-rope manufacturers. He directed the construction of Brooklyn Bridge.

Steamship Director.

Jonkheer von Reuchlin.—Joint managing director of the Holland America Line.

Mr. Frank D. Millet.—An American artist, who has a house at Broadway, Worcestershire.

Mr. Isidor Straus.—Member of Congress. He lives in Broadway, New York, is a merchant, a member of the firm of L. Straus and Sons, and director of various banks.

Mr. C. Clarence Jones.—New York stockbroker, who has been visiting European capitals in connection with the purchase of American Embassy sites.

Mr. J. Futrelle.—The noted story writer, author of "The Thinking Machine."

Mr. W. T. Stead.

Mr. W. T. Stead.—Editor of the "Review of Reviews," on his way to attend the convention to close the "Man and Religion Forward Movement," which has been operating in America for some months with the object of inducing business men to take an active part in religious movements. Several messages were sent to Mr. W. T. Stead in the hope that as a practised journalist he might be able to give a reliable account of the disaster, but no reply has been received.

Mr. Thomas Andrews, Jun.—Managing director of Messrs. Harland and Wolff, builders of the Titanic.

Mr. Christopher Head.—Former Mayor of Chelsea, who was much interested in art matters and took a prominent part in the discussions at the Mansion House regarding the King Edward Memorial.

SOME OF THE SAVED.

LADY DUFF-GORDON, COUNTESS OF ROTHES, WHITE STAR CHAIRMAN.

The Titanic's saved include:—

Lady Duff-Gordon—who carries on the famous firm of "Madame Lucile"—and her husband, Sir Cosmo Duff-Gordon. They sailed incognito as Mr. and Mrs. Morgan.

The Countess of Rothes.—On her way to New York to join her husband. They have planned a trip through the States to the West, returning via Canada. The Earl has been some months on the American Continent, as it is his intention to settle down there fruit farming.

Mr. Ryerson.—Who was making the journey from England to attend the funeral of a daughter in Philadelphia.

Mr. J. B. Ismay.—Chairman and managing director of the White Star Line, and president of the International Mercantile Marine Company. He was carrying out his usual custom of sailing on the maiden voyage of the company's liners.

Also among the saved are Mr. and Mrs. Henry S. Harper. He is a grandson of the founder of the famous publishing house.

THE GREATEST OF ALL SHIPS AND THE GREATEST OF ALL SHIPPI

A SECTIONAL VIEW OF THE TITANIC. HER HUGE HULL WAS DIVIDED INTO THIRTY WATER-TIGHT COMPARTMENTS, WHICH, IT WAS CLAIMED, RENDERED HER "PRACTIC TWENTY-ONE KNOTS AN HOUR. (Drawn by F. G. M

ONE OF THE PERILS OF THE NORTH ATLANTIC: A HUGE ICEBERG, THREE HUNDRED FEET HIGH ABOVE THE WATER LINE AND TWO THOUSAND FEET HIGH OVER ALL. THE HIGHEST POINT ABOVE WATER IS PRACTICALLY EQUAL TO THE HEIGHT OF ST. PAUL'S CATHEDRAL, OF WHICH A SILHOUETTE IS GIVEN FOR THE PURPOSE OF COMPARISON. (From a photograph by Mr. Sandon Perkins, F.R.G.S., in the possession of the Royal Geographical Society.)

[. . .]G DISASTERS. THE TITANIC AND THE PERILS OF THE ATLANTIC.

[. . .] "UNSINKABLE." SHE CONTAINED ELEVEN STEEL DECKS, AND WAS PROVIDED WITH TRIPLE SCREWS DRIVEN BY ENGINES OF 50,000 HORSE-POWER. HER SPEED WAS ABOUT [. . .]
[. . . f]rom materials supplied by Messrs. Harland and Wolff, the builders.)

ANOTHER OF THE ATLANTIC DANGERS: A MONSTER ICEBERG PHOTOGRAPHED FROM THE DECK OF A WHALER. IT IS PROBABLE THAT THE BERG WITH WHICH THE TITANIC COLLIDED HAD DRIFTED DOWN FROM GREENLAND THROUGH THE COLD WATER OF THE NORTH AMERICAN COAST UNDER CONDITIONS WHICH WOULD CAUSE THE TOP TO MELT MORE QUICKLY THAN THE SUBMERGED PART.

(From a photograph by Mr. Sandon Perkins, F.R.G.S., in the possession of the Royal Geographical Society.)

FAMOUS WRECKS OF BYGONE DAYS: SOME HISTORIC DISASTERS AT SEA—

THE STELLA, WRECKED ON THE CASQUETS, NEAR ALDERNEY, ON MARCH 28th, 1899. SEVENTY-FIVE LIVES WERE LOST.

THE DRUMMOND CASTLE, WRECKED OFF USHANT ON THE HOMEWARD VOYAGE FROM SOUTH AFRICA ON JUNE 17th, 1896; NEARLY 250 LIVES WERE LOST. ONLY ONE PASSENGER AND TWO MEMBERS OF THE CREW WERE SAVED. SHE WAS THE FIRST CASTLE LINER LOST IN THE HISTORY OF THE COMPANY.

(Reproduced from "The Graphic.")

—RECALLED BY THE DISASTER WHICH HAS OVERTAKEN THE TITANIC.

THE BERLIN, WRECKED ON THE BREAKWATER AT THE HOOK OF HOLLAND ON FEBRUARY 21st, 1907, WITH A LOSS OF ABOUT 140 LIVES. THE PICTURE SHOWS THE BERLIN BREAKING IN HALF AND THE FORE-PART FALLING INTO THE WATER BEFORE THE EYES OF THOSE ON BOARD THE CLACTON (ON THE RIGHT). A HUNDRED PERSONS WENT DOWN WITH THIS PART OF THE VESSEL. PRINCE HENRY OF THE NETHERLANDS ASSISTED IN THE RESCUE WORK.

THE FOUNDERING OF THE ELBE OFFFF LOWESTOFT ON JANUARY 30th, 1895. NEARLY 400 LIVES WERE LOST.—THE LAST BOAT TO LEAVE THE SHIP.

THE SINKING OF THE BOURGOYNE THROUGH COLLISION OFF THE COAST OF NOVA SCOTIA ON JUNE 4th, 1898. NEARLY 500 LIVES WERE LOST.

—and the "Daily Graphic.")

A LINER THREADING HER WAY THROUGH A FIELD OF ICE IN THE NORTH ATLANTIC.

In this sketch a "Daily Graphic" artist has re-constructed from telegraphic descriptions the scene in the North Atlantic when a liner encounters one of the dreaded ice fields. The Carmania, which arrived at New York, reports that she ran through a field seventy miles in length. The passengers state that twenty-five bergs were sighted in one cluster, and that some of them were no further than a hundred feet away from the vessel. The liner had to feel her way through the ice lane for hours. She finally put about, and steering south avoided further danger.

THE HOURS OF AWFUL SUSPENSE IN LONDON.

Relatives and friends of passengers on the Titanic studying the lists of the saved, and leaving the White Star Line offices at Oceanic House, Cockspur Street, after making anxious inquiries for news

BREAKING THE NEWS OF THE TITANIC'S LOSS WITH OVER TWELVE HUNDRED LIVES TO LONDON.

Consternation reigned in London when the news of the Titanic's awful fate became known. All day long the City and West End offices of the White Star Company, over which the White Star flag floated at half-mast, were besieged by anxious relations and friends of those who sailed in the liner. The photograph on the left shows the flag at half-mast over Oceanic House, Cockspur Street. At the top, on the right, the scene inside the Cockspur Street offices is depicted, and below an anxious crowd is seen outside the City offices of the company.

THE ALLAN LINER VIRGINIAN, THE FIRST VESSEL TO RECEIVE THE TITANIC'S WIRELESS MESSAGE OF DISTRESS. UNFORTUNATELY SHE ARRIVED TOO LATE TO BE OF SERVICE.

Mr. Guggenheim, one of the millionaire passengers.

Colonel May.

Mr. W. T. Sloper, a prominent business man of Seattle.—Known to be saved.

Mr. E. W. King, chief clerk to the Titanic's purser.

AN ARTIST'S IMPRESSION OF THE DISASTER.

THE AWFUL NEWS AT LLOYD'S.

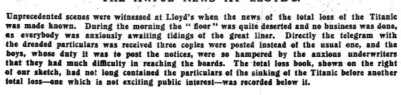

Unprecedented scenes were witnessed at Lloyd's when the news of the total loss of the Titanic was made known. During the morning the "floor" was quite deserted and no business was done, as everybody was anxiously awaiting tidings of the great liner. Directly the telegram with the dreaded particulars was received three copies were posted instead of the usual one, and the boys, whose duty it was to post the notices, were so hampered by the anxious underwriters that they had much difficulty in reaching the boards. The total loss book, shown on the right of our sketch, had not long contained the particulars of the sinking of the Titanic before another total loss—one which is not exciting public interest—was recorded below it.

Colonel J. J. Astor, the famous millionaire.—His wife is among the saved.

Senator Carter, of the United States.

Mr. W. T. Stead, editor of the "Review of Reviews."

Master Harry Widener, son of the traction magnate who recently bought Rembrandt's "The Mill."

Master Spedden, son of Mr. John Spedden, of New York.

Mr. Harry Rogers, of Tavistock.

Mr. Thomas Andrews.

Mrs. W. D. Douglas, well known in American society.—Known to be saved.

THE AGONISING WAIT FOR THE LIST OF THE LOST AT SOUTHAMPTON.

The majority of the Titanic's crew belonged to Southampton, and day after day the relations swarmed round the offices of the White Star Company in Canute Road anxiously awaiting tidings. As hour after hour passed and no list of the lost, or additions to the list of the saved were forthcoming, the distress of the people was pitiable to witness. The company erected a great board in readiness to receive the list as soon as it should come, and though repeatedly told that delay was inevitable, nothing could persuade the sufferers to leave this board. ("Daily Graphic" photograph.)

THE ICEBERG ABOVE AND BELOW THE WATER.

The iceberg is one of those dangers to shipping against which the ingenuity of man cannot guard. It often rises from 150 to 300 feet above the sea level, and seven or eight times as much lies under the surface of the water.

THE UPPER DECK OF THE TITANIC.

A view showing some of the lifeboats by which many of the survivors left the ship. Most of the boats were filled with women and children, and all these boats have been accounted for.

("Daily Graphic" photograph.)

MANSION HOUSE FUND OPENED FOR THE WIDOWS AND CHILDREN OF TITANIC SAILORS.

The Lord Mayor very promptly opened a fund at the Mansion House for the relief of the widows and orphans of those sailors of the Titanic who have gone down in the ship. In this picture the Lord Mayor's servants are seen fixing a public collecting box outside the Mansion House. The King and Queen, and Queen Alexandra were among the first to send donations to the fund.

THE FINANCIAL SIDE OF THE GREAT DISASTER: EXCITEMENT AT LLOYD'S CONTINUES.

The underwriters at Lloyd's will suffer financially by the loss of the Titanic, which was insured for a million pounds. The state of excitement, which was so very acute on Tuesday, continued in a more modified form on Wednesday, and during the business hours the entrance to the "house" at the back of the Royal Exchange was the scene of a great deal of activity. Our photograph shows the constant stream of underwriters entering and leaving the building, or standing in little groups discussing the terrible event.

THE CHEFS OF THE LOST TITANIC: VISITORS TO THE WHITE STAR OFFICES.

The centre pictures show above the Titanic's chef and his assistants, and below is a view of one of the ship's kitchens. On the left is a picture showing the Right Hon. Alexander Montgomery Carlisle, the designer of the Titanic, leaving the White Star office. On the right is a picture of two ladies waiting at the office for fuller details.

THE TITANIC'S PASSENGERS TAKING THEIR LAST LOOK AT HOME.

A photograph taken as the boat was leaving Southampton on April 10th, showing, on the deck, some of the passengers who are probably among the missing.

THE SCENE ROUND THE FATEFUL BOARD AT SOUTHAMPTON.

The board erected by the White Star Company outside their Southampton offices was watched day after day by the crowd of grief-stricken wives and other relatives of the Titanic's crew. One list of members of the crew known to be on the Carpathia was posted, but it only contained about half a dozen names. ("Daily Graphic" photograph.)

Printed and Published by the Proprietors, Messrs. H. R. BAINES and Company, Ltd., at Tallis House, Whitefriars in the City of London.—Saturday, April 20, 1912.

THE WEATHER.
Cloudy Sunday; probably showers on Sunday night.

THE BROOKLYN DAILY EAGLE

The Eagle is the Only Paper in Brooklyn that prints the Associated Press News and the complete Stock Market Reports.

6 SECTIONS. Volume 72A No. 111 ★ NEW YORK CITY, SUNDAY, APRIL 21, 1912. ★ 70 PAGES. THREE CENTS.

DISASTER STORY OF WIRELESS MEN SHOCKS LISTENERS

Iceberg Warning Unanswered and Steamer Inquiry Ignored.

PRECIOUS TIME LOST

White Star Liner Baltic Was Informed of the Catastrophe Last Monday Morning.

WASHINGTON HEARING MONDAY

Ismay and Titanic Crew Are Held in This Country by Senate Committee Subpenas.

At yesterday's session of the Senate Investigating Committee in the Waldorf-Astoria the following startling facts were brought out about the loss of the Titanic:

Harold S. Bride, the second wireless operator on the Titanic, refused an "iceberg warning" from the steamship Californian, at about 5 p.m. on Sunday. He "picked it up" later as it was being sent to the steamship Baltic, and delivered it to the officer on the bridge.

Chief Operator Phillips on the Titanic sent out a "C Q D" after the Titanic had struck the iceberg, and the first answer he received was from the Frankfurt of the North German Lloyd Line. Phillips told his assistant that the Frankfurt was the nearest vessel, judging from the "strength of the current."

About twenty minutes later the Frankfurt operator asked by wireless: "What is the matter?"

Phillips by that time was in commuunication with the Carpathia, and he told the Frankfurt operator he was "a fool" and to stop interfering with his connections.

News of Disaster Refused to Frankfurt by Titanic Wireless Man.

The Titanic's operator refused to send the news that his ship had hit an iceberg and was sinking to the Frankfurt, and no more was heard from the German liner.

Captain Smith of the Titanic asked for the Frankfurt's position, but his wireless operators were unabl- to tell him.

Second Operator Bride told the investigating committee that the "C. Q. D." as sent out, wit hthe position of the ship, was enough information for the Frankfurt, and that is the reason further information was refused. He added they were depending on the Carpathia, whose position they knew, for assistance.

It was figured out that during the time the "C. Q. D." calls were being sent out the officers of the Titanic were telling the passengers there was no danger, and that many passengers thereupon refused to embark in the lifeboats.

Bride testified that Captain Smith jumped from the bridge as the ship went down, and did not shoot himself, as had been reported.

Bride, the second wireless operator, is 21 years old. Phillips, who died on a lifeboat before reaching the Carpathia, was 24 years old. Bride did not answer a question of Senator Smith as to whether the regulations permitted such an exercise of discretion as to refuse the Frankfurt's demand for information.

Hearing in Washington Checks Ismay's Plans to Return to England.

The hearing will be resumed tomorrow morning at 10:30, in Washington, D. C.

Twenty sailors from the Titanic, all the surviving passengers who could be served with subpenas, J. Bruce Ismay, managing director of the White Star Line; the four surviving officers of the Titanic and many other witnesses will be required to appear before the committee.

Ismay and the sailors were served with subpenas yesterday, although they are English subjects, and the plans of the White Star officials to ship the crew and Ismay to England were checked by the prompt action of Senator William Alden Smith of Michigan, chairman of the Senate Investigating Committee, who insists that they give their testimony in the United States before going back to England. That Ismay wanted to get away was confirmed by Senator Smith in a formal statement.

Senator Smith said that he had received scores of messages from the survivors and others in all parts of the United States, offering to testify at the hearing.

Mr. Ismay and Vice President Franklin of the White Star Line refused to make any formal statements at the close of yesterday's hearing, asserting that as they were under subpena to testify, "it might be unfair to the Senate Committee to make any statements."

Mr. Ismay stated, however, that he would attend the hearing in Washington without protest.

"The Senate Committee has been ab-

Continued on Page 5.

THE ICEBERG WHICH SUNK THE TITANIC

This picture is probably the only one taken of the iceberg which was responsible for the sinking of the Titanic. Various statements were made about the iceberg, among them being that it was 160 feet above water.

The picture was taken by Lewis P. Skidmore of 381 Vanderbilt avenue, an instructor at Pratt Institute, who was a passenger on the Carpathia, and who took the remarkable picture of the lifeboat published in yesterday's Eagle. The iceberg was snapped on the spot after the Carpathia had steamed to the scene of the wreck and officers of the Titanic had pointed it out. It was positively identified, not only by the officers rescued, but by several passengers.

It will be observed that the berg was very symetrical in its proportions. It was about as long as the ill-starred liner. It is said that only one-eighth of an iceberg shows above the surface of the water, and it is not improbable that the Titanic struck a floating mountain 1,200 feet in height.

As to the appearance of the iceberg Mr. Skidmore's statement is that "it looked like an immense dirgible balloon about to rise from the water.'"

At the time the picture was taken the bits of wreckage from the Titanic were still floating near the spot where the giant vessel went down. The iceberg was taken at close range and its identity was clearly established by a number of witnesses before Mr. Skidmore snapped the shutter.

Mr. Skidmore was a guest of Thomas L. Leeming of Brooklyn during the period the Carpathia was in port. When the Cunarder put back to England on Friday afternoon after landing the Titanic survivors, Mr. Skidmore resumes on his interrupted vacation.

PRENDERGAST WILL STUMP FOR COLONEL

To Begin Roosevelt Speaking Tour in New Hampshire Tomorrow.

MASSACHUSETTS IS NEXT.

Controller Will Follow President Taft in Each Place Where Latter Speaks.

Jubilant over Colonel Roosevelt's success in the Nebraska and Oregon primaries, Controller William A. Prendergast, who was the first of the prominent Republicans in this city to advocate the Colonel for the Presidency, will invade New Hampshire tomorrow on a speaking tour on behalf of the Roosevelt candidacy.

The latter part of the week will be devoted by Mr. Prendergast to touring the principal cities and manufacturing towns of Massachusetts.

Apparently, President Taft is beginning to realize that the situation has become a critical one. He in person will make a tour of Massachusetts this week to argue his own cause for a renomination. Whatever good impression he makes during his speech-making tour, the Roosevelt forces will try to dissipate through the medium of Controller Prendergast, who is recognized as one of the most finished platform speakers in New York State.

The militant Rough Rider will leave the fate of these two New England States largely in the hands of Mr. Prendergast. He is of the opinion that the Controller can make an equally effective impression on the Republican voting population as if he spoke from the platform himself. Colonel Roosevelt will confine his activities mainly to the Southern tier of States, to break up the instructed delegations for President Taft. Already five of the twenty-one delegates of South Carolina have broken away from their instructions and announced that they will vote for Colonel Roosevelt in the national convention.

Roosevelt at Work in Solid South.

Colonel Roosevelt left Arkansas last nuight, and will pass through all the Southern States with North Carolina as his objective point. His campaign managers claim that before he leaves the South, President Taft will have additional cause for anxiety.

To give him more time to attend to the South, Colonel Roosevelt has called upon Controller Prendergast to look after his interests in the New England States. The Presidential preferential primary will be held in New Hampshire next Tuesday. Mr. Prendergast will make his principal speech in Nashua, on Monday evening. He will utilize his time between his arrival and the hour at which he is scheduled to speak at Nashua in making a flying automobile trip to adjoining towns to convince the Republican voters that the salvation of the party lies in the renomination of Colonel Roosevelt.

The itinerary of the Massachusetts trip has not yet been laid out for Mr. Prendergast by the Roosevelt campaign managers.

Controller to Spend Two Full Days in Massacuhsetts.

The present arrangement is to have the Controller spend two solid days on a speech-making tour in that State. The primaries will be held on Tuesday, April 23.

Controller Prendergast's tour of Massachusetts will be guided entirely by President Taft's trip through the State. Mr. Prendergast will speak in every city, town and hamlet visited by the President. The progressive platform advocated by Colonel Roosevelt will be the keynote of every one of Mr. Prendergast's speeches, and at the same time he will draw a sharp contrast with the policies advocated by Mr. Taft.

So that Mr. Prendergast may be well informed on the speeches which President Taft will make, it is the present plan of the Roosevelt committee not to have him begin his tour of Massachusetts until Friday. He will leave New York immediately after the Board of Estimate meeting on Thursday. This will leave him Friday and Saturday to carry out the itinerary of the committee, and if the time is too short, he may also spend Monday in completing his tour of the State.

MRS. J. J. ASTOR IMPROVES.

Mrs. John Jacob Astor was reported much improved last night by her physician, Dr. Reuel B. Kimball. He says that at present there is no apparent danger as a result of her experiences in the Titanic disaster.

DR. J. BION BOGART WEDS

Mrs. Marion Corbit Ricketts, Bride of Prominent Brooklyn Surgeon.

Dr. J. Bion Bogert of 463 Clinton avenue, one of the best?known surgeons in this city and prominent socially in Brooklyn, was married quietly in Plymouth Church last night to Mrs. Marion Corbit Ricketts of Chicago.

The Rev. Dr. Newell Dwight Hillis, pastor of Plymouth Church, performed the ceremony at 6:30 o'clock in the presence of a few relatives and friends of Dr. Bogart and his bride, including a sister of Mrs. Ricketts and a brother of Dr. Bogart.

Dr. Bogart is a widower. His first wife was Maud Lewis. Mrs. Ricketts is a widow and is a member of a prominent Chicago family.

Dr. Bogart was graduated from New York University in 1884. He is a member of the Crescent, Hamilton and Dyker Heights Golf clubs and of the Kings County Medical Society, the Surgical Society and the Physicians Mutual Aid Society, and has been associated with the surgical staffs at the Kings County, Methodist Episcopal and Bushwick hospitals.

WIRELESS REPORTS ORDERED.

Naval Secretary Anxious to Learn Conditions During Carpathia's Trip.

Washington, April 20—Special reports on the wireless conditions in the Atlantic at the time the Carpathia was bringing in the survivors of the Titanic disaster were today requested by the Secretary of the Navy from the commanders of the scout cruisers Chester and Salem, which had been ordered by the President to get into communication with the Carpathia and get any available news.

The Secretary especially wishes to learn how much interference was prevalent at the time and, if possible, from whence it came. The radio experts of the Navy Department are determined to get at the bottom of the failure of the Carpathia to answer the President's message asking whether Major Butt and the other Americans were safe.

According to very careful measurements made by Captain Knapp, chief hydrographer of the Navy, the decision of the Transatlantic steamship companies to accept his suggestion to change the great sea routes 180 miles further south, in the interest of safety of passengers, results in lengthening the distance from Ambrose Channel Lightship, at the entrance to New York Harbor, to Bishop's Rock, off the Scilly Islands, on the English coast, by precisely 133 nautical miles for the southern route east-bound and 138 miles west-bound.

The exact distances are: Southern route, east-bound, old 2,996, new 3,129; southern route, west-bound, old 2,953, new 3,091 miles. This means that at 22 knots average speed it will take the liners a trifle over six hours more to cover the Transatlantic course.

QUARREL MAY END FATALLY.

John Blake in Serious Condition. Three Men Arrested.

As a result of a saloon quarrel, John Blake, 47 years old, having no known home, was attacked last night by three men outside of a saloon on the corner of Rockaway avenue and Hull street, and sustained a fracture of the skull. He was removed to the Bushwick Hospital in an unconscious state, and at a late hour had not regained sensibility. Dr. Krite, who responded to the ambulance call, said the man was in a very dangerous condition and would probably die.

The three men who are believed to have attacked Blake were arrested later in the evening by Detectives Kavangh, Connelly and Conroy of the Ralph avenue precinct on a charge of felonious assault to await the outcome of the man's injuries. The men gave their names as Louis Pauline, 29 years old, of 42 Somers street, a glassworker; Grover Gillespie, 27 years old, of 1324 Herkimer street, a laborer, and John Dowling, 28 years old, of 1309 Herkimer street.

PUNCHED BY UMPIRE DAHLEN HITS BACK

Lively Fisticuffs Between Rigler and Brooklyn Manager End Giants' Game.

BOSS EBBETS THEN GETS HOT.

Wires President Lynch of National League Demanding That Umpire Be "Severely Punished."

About seventeen thousand folk, largely from Brooklyn, saw New York beat the Brooklyn Superbas yesterday afternoon by 4 to 3, at Brush Stadium, Manhattan, in a game that was more full of real thrills than the modern generation of fans can hope to see in several seasons. The game wound up in an exchange of fisticuffs by Manager Dahlen of the Brooklyn team and Umpire Rigler.

Nothing short of a dogfight in a barbershop could have produced so much excite-

Manager Bill Dahlen.

ment in a short time. From three thousand versions, the following has been culled as approximating to the majority opinion:

Brooklyn most unexpectedly made a rally in the first half of the ninth inning by making three runs off Tesreau, who had been making the Superbas look foolish up to that point. In New York's half of the ninth Herzog was thrown out by Smith. Groh singled. Wilson, who came to bat next, had succeeded Meyers in the ninth because the Indian had kicked himself out of the game. Wilson is a right handed hitter, and he hit a hard, straight ball from Nap Rucker with force sufficient to send it into the second tier of the grand stand seats. If it was fair it was a home run. If it was foul it was a strike. Umpire Rigler, who was working behind the bat and had jurisdiction over the swat said it was fair.

Fought Regardless of the Rules.

Manager William Dahlen of the Superbas rushed up to the umpire and asked heatedly why a ball at least six feet foul should be called fair. The perturbed Dahlen had no time to work his vocabulary up to the exploding point and was merely gesticulating and uttering general words of inquiry and condemnation, when the aggrieved umpire struck him upon the right cheek.

The manager promptly took a life-sized punch at the aggressor. He landed somewhere above the waist and a bout that would have gladdened the heart of the Boxing Commission was well under way when Wilbert Robinson, the veteran catcher, who is coaching the New York pitchers, projected his 250-pound form into the fray.

The umpire picked his way through the dense masses of fans, who had rushed joyously to the field, and Dahlen trotted off with his team. Some said the peppery Dahlen had been nimble enough to deliver a couple of stout blows before the huge Robinson butted in, but he declared afterward that he did no more than counter with a well meant right and then stood on guard.

President Charles H. Ebbets of the Brooklyn club was one of those who became involved in the turmoil on the field and had some trouble reaching the clubhouse. When he got there he announced that he had been in a position to see the ball that caused the trouble and that it was undoubtedly foul. He added:

"Players are suspended for a whole season for hitting umpires, and I have telegraphed President Lynch of the National League demanding that a severe penalty be imposed upon Umpire Rigler for hitting Manager Dahlen when there was no occasion for such an attack. There is no chance to protest the game, because the calling of a foul or a fair ball is a matter of judgment entirely within the hands of the umpire, but the discipline of the league demands that Rigler be penalized for his inexcusable display of temper. From my position in the stand I could see that Wilson's hit landed in the upper stand foul by a number of feet, and Rigler should have been able to see that."

THREE KILLED IN TORNADO

Oklahoma City, Denver, Pueblo, Col., and Other Places Hard Hit by Storms.

Oklahoma City, Okla., April 20—Three persons are known to have been killed, at least a score injured and many farmhouses and village dwelling were wrecked late today, when a tornado which forbed in the vicinity of Yukon, near Oklahoma City, swept in a northeasterly direction through the counties of Oklahoma and Logan.

Hoisington, Kan., April 20—Fifteen persons were injured, four probably fatally, at Bison, a town of 400 inhabitants, 24 miles west of here, when a tornado struck the place today. Many oof the houses were blown down, a large elevator was destroyed and a number of freight cars were hurled over a quarter of a mile. The path of the storm was three hundred yards wide.

Denver, Col., April 20—Several persons are reported to have been killed and others injured in a tornado which struck Bison, in Rush County, Kan., today, according to advices received here. Much property damage is reported also.

Pueblo, Co., April 20—The Missouri Pacific offices here received a dispatch saying four persons were killed and several houses blown down by a tornado at Bison.

No particulars are obtainable, the wires being blown down.

Oklahoma City, Okla., April 20—Fifty houses were demolished at the town of Hennessy. Mrs. Mary Holmes and another woman whose name cannot be ascertained, were killed.

At Perry, one man was killed and twenty persons reported to have been injured, several of whom probably will die. Twenty-five buildings, including a stone business structure and a school house were completely wrecked. Numerous buildings were unroofed, and according to passengers who arrived in Guthrie to-night, aboard a Santa Fe train, residents of the little town are panic stricken.

Near Yukon, a school house was demolished. All of the children have been accounted for except one, James Beasly.

GAFFNEY DIES INHOSPITAL.

Hicks Street Man Shot His Infant Child and Himself.

Benjamin Gaffney, a saloon keeper of the firm of Gaffney & Mahon, of 582 Hicks street, who was removed to the Long Island College Hospital Friday after an insane shooting affair in his apartments of 566 Hicks street, died last night as a result of a fracture of his spine. Gaffney had been watching over his seven weeks old baby, Thomas, who had been dangerously ill since birth, and brooding over this he is believed to have become insane.

While in his apartments Friday afternoon he suddenly lost control of himself and began shooting, later turning the revolver upon himself. In the shooting the baby over which he ad been brooding was killed outrigt, and his wife, Ellen, miraculously escaped. Gaffney fired a number of shots and finally jumped out of a second-story window, sustaining a fracture of the spine.

The lower portion of his body became paralyzed, and all day yesterday the doctors at the hospital entertained no hope of his recovery. He was 29 years old.

BURIED 500 FEET UNDER THE STREET

Three Laborers Caught Far Down in Acqueduct Shaft.

ONE KILLED; TWO INJURED.

Myrtle and South Portland Avenues Scene of Excitement as Rescues Are Made.

One man was buried alive and two others passed through a terrible experience 500 feet down in the bowels of the earth at North Portland and Myrtle avenues last night.

The men were at work at the foot of a narrow shaft where connections will be made with the Catskill Aqueduct system.

The circumstances under which the men were caught by a sudden rush of tons of earth, the great crowd pressing around the mouth of the pit and the manner in which the rescuers worked to free the imprisoned suggested a mine disaster on a small scale.

By the light of lanterns a band of volunteers descended in hoisting buckets and dug away for three-quarters of an hour to free the two who stood almost entirely covered by dirt and to recover the body of the man who was dead.

The man killed was George Vonloskey, a laborer of 64 Box street. The two survivors, who passed through an experience which would turn the heads of most men gray, are Capia Curchile of 1139 Greenpoint avenue and Edward Wrange of 135 Ryerson street. Both were removed to the Cumberland Street Hospital suffering from internal injuries and shock.

Vanloskey, at the bottom of the 25-foot wide shaft, was shoveling dirt up to his comrades who stood on a wooden platform [illegible] feet above. Suddenly and without warning a side of the shaft gave way with a roar and an avalanche of earth cascaded down on the three. Vanloskey was completely buried. Curchile was pinned fast to the waist and only Wrange's head remained free. He kept his arms locked over his head in the effort to fend of a further fall.

The shrieks of the men were heard faintly high above, and the rescuers, approaching the opening, peered down and saw the two who were just visible in the gathering dusk. They called to them to keep up their courage. Lights were brought and the shaft was illuminated. Then men went down in the hoisting buckets, which are used to haul the dirt to the surface.

A great crowd gathered, and it was necessary to call upon the police of the Classon avenue station to keep them back. Work had to be carried on slowly on account of the danger of a further fall of earth.

A hearty cheer arose as first one and then another of the injured men was hoisted above and hurried away in an ambulance.

What caused the dirt to slide is something of a mystery.

SERVICES ON WARSHIPS.

Memorial for Titanic Victims on All Vessels in Home Ports.

London, April 20—The British Admiralty has ordered that divine services on all warships in home ports tomorrow shall take the form of a memorial service for the victims of the steamer Titanic.

During the services the flags on all the ships will flutter at half-mast in respect for the "officers and men of all ranks in the British mercantile marine and others who were drowned, and for their good seamanlike behaviour after the accident."

The services in all the churches will be of a memorial character, with the singing of "Nearer, My God to Thee," as the special feature.

LAND CLAIMS REJECTED.

Juneau, Alaska, April 20—The Juneau Land Office has notified the claimants of the three so-calld "Dick Ryan Land Claims," on Controllr Bay, Alaska, that their filings have been rejected. These are the claims that led to the Congressional inquiry last October in which the forged "Dick to Dick" letter figured.

Unusual Ice Fields In Steamship Lanes

Wireless Warns Transatlantic Liners of Dangers. Hydrographic Office Tabulates Reports of Passing Vessels and Spreads Them Broadcast.

Eagle Bureau,
608 Fourteenth street.

Washington, April 20—The year 1912 appears to be exceptionally productive of ice in the North-Atlantic steamship lanes. It may break a record, although it has not done so as yet. There have been a number of years when no ice whatever was reported within several hundred miles of the point where the Titanic was lost. On the other hand, there have been years when bergs were found far South of that point.

In these days of wireless telegraphy there is not the least excuse for the captain of a trans-Atlantic vessel leaving port without the very latest knowledge of ice conditions. Further than that, he may keep his chart up to date from day to day through reports received from other vessels.

In the United States, the Hydrographic office of the Navy Department is the clearing house' for information as to ice conditions in the North Atlantic. Its service in this respect is as complete as modern science will permit. Furthermore, this service is as the disposal of every mariner who chooses to seek it. The Hydrographic Office not only supplies information free to the merchant marine, and issues charts at a nominal cost, but it also encourages and urges mariners to avail themselves of it. It issues three publications which are of direct interest to the commanders of Trans-Atlantic vessels.

Weekly Bulletin Contains Latest Advices of Conditions.

One is a monthly chart, upon which is indicated late information as to winds, currents, ice, derelicts, and other features of ocean travel. Then there is a weekly bulletin, containing even more recent data, from which a ship's captain can correct his monthly chart. Supplementing this is a daily bulletin. This contains reports as fresh as those in a daily newspaper. It is available to mariners at the Hydrographic offices and maritime exchanges in every port where large ships clear.

Furthermore, a large chart which is corrected daily and hourly is kept at each of the hydrographic offices. Thus, at the Maritime Exchange in New York, a captain whose vessel is about to put to sea can go to the office and find on the chart the very latest information as to ice and other condition along the course he is to follow. The Hydrographic Office invites him to do so, and if he does not avail himself of the opportunity it is his own fault.

The information which the Hydrographic Office utilizes for the preparation of this data, so far as it covers the North Atlantic steamship routes, is largely obtained from merchants vessels, because there are seldom any naval ships in that vicinity. A vessel at sea will, for instance, transmit by wireless the information that it has sighted icebergs or field ice at a certain point of longitude and latitude. This wireless message may either be received directly ashore or be relayed by other vessels. When it comes ashore the Hydrographic Office in Washington receives an immediate bulletin. This bulletin is included in its daily memorandum. It is also telegraphed in turn to all ports where ships may clear. Thus, if Boston receives a report of ice at sea, the Hydrographic Office will at once be notified and within a short time the information will be available for mariners at New York, Philadelphia and other points. It will also be recorded on the charts which are kept at all ports. Supplementing this wireless service, are bulletins brought in by vessels when they arrive at port. Their information is often several days old, but is sometimes very valuable, nevertheless.

Wireless Covers Every Part of Ocean in Danger Zone.

The use of wireless telegraphy leaves very few conditions in the North Atlantic steamship lanes unknown for as long a period as twenty-four hours. Not only does the Hydrographic Office supply actual information, but it also furnishes charts and data which indicate with a good deal of accuracy what the mariner may expect to find during certain months of the year, even in the absence of actual reports. The science of hydrography has become exact. English and German charts of the North Atlantic tally very closely with those issued by the United States. With regard to the indication of ice conditions, however, there is one difference. The American charts show only ice that has been actually reported during the month previous to their publication. The English and German charts indicate the average extent of the ice fields for that particular month, without reference to the most recent data.

While it now looks as though the North Atlantic steamship routes would be filled with fields of ice and bergs for the next two or three months, such conditions may, of course, change with very little warning. Changes, however, will be kept track of by the Hydrographic office and no captain can have any excuse for leaving the port of New York or other ports without full information concerning them. The April ice for 1912 is now about as far south as it has ever been reported in any other year. In 1903 icebergs were reported as far south as the fortieth parallel and by June of that year they had reached to the thirty ninth. The year 1905 was another when the April ice went very far south, almost reaching the fortieth-parallel. In 1899 bergs and field ice were reported as far south as the forty-first degree of latitude. There have been years when the ice did not come within several hundred miles of the point where the Titanic encountered it. In 1908, for instance, there was no ice below the forty-fourth parallel. In 1901 nothing was reported below the forty-sixth parallel, and such ice as there was hugged closely to the shores of Newfoundland. The same is the case in 1902, except for a small field of ice sighted at the forty-third parallel.

No Way of Forecasting Ice Conditions.

There is no regularity concerning the amount of ice which may be found in the steamship lanes in any given year. The source from which it comes is the Arctic. If the Hydrographic office had any means of getting information from the Arctic region, it might be possible to forecast the spring and summer ice conditions of the North Atlantic. But in the absence of such data there is no way of telling how much ice is coming down from the north until it has arrived.

The iceberg or field ice which a trans-Atlantic liner may sight is not necessarily of recent birth. It may be several years old, this depending entirely upon what sort of a passage it has had on the way south. Nearly all of the bergs which appear annually in the North Atlantic originate in Western Greenland, although a few may come from the Spitzbergen Sea and some from Hudson Bay. They reach the North Atlantic by way of the Labrador current, which flows southward. This drift is subject to many stoppages and mishaps. Only a small proportion of the icebergs released by the Arctic glaciers reach the North Atlantic. Many of them go aground in the ...tic Basin and break up there. Others ...me stranded on the shores of Labra... Many disappear entirely at sea, due ...aking up. The remainder which ...he trip from the north in safety ...ly reach the Grand Bank of Newf...and, and these are the ones which menace to navigation. The av... of the Labrador current is from ten to thirty-six miles per day and this is approximately the speed of the icebergs which are carried with it. They are little affected by winds, because so much of their bulk is beneath the surface of the water.

If an iceberg released in Western Greenland should have an uninterrupted journey southward it would reach the steamship lanes in four or five months, allowing for a drift of ten miles a day. But not all, in fact, only a few of the bergs have a clear passage. Most of those liberated on the west coast of Greenland are out of the strong sweep of the southerly current and often take several months to find their way out of Davis Strait. By the time they reached the steamship lanes they may be two or three years old. Field ice often obstructs their passage.

Icebergs Rare Below Fortieth Parallel

Icebergs are not often found below the fortieth parallel. At that point they melt and break up rather rapidly under the influence of the Gulf Stream. There are isolated exceptions to this general rule, however. Bergs have been sighted as much as 1,000 miles south of the point where the Titanic is lost, although they are rare exceptions. The disintegration of an iceberg may be due to several causes. They are frozen at a very low temperature, so that when their surface is exposed to a thawing temperature the tension of the exterior and the interior is very different. This often causes them to burst. Then, too, during the daytime water which is made by melting finds its way into the crevices of icebergs, expands and splits them like a wedge. If these processes did not go on large bergs would probably remain intact for several years before they melted and would always be present in the trans-Atlantic routes. Instances are on record where masses of ice actually have drifted across the ocean and reached European waters.

Field ice is less of a menace to trans-Atlantic vessels, although it is often thick enough to inflict serious damage. That which finds its way into the steamship lanes may come from the Arctic or from the shores of Newfoundland. The Arctic ice is apt to be heavier and is usually several seasons old. It is also very apt to contain what are known as growlers, small fragments of icebergs which have mingled with the pack. Growlers are regarded as very dangerous because they only expose a small surface, while their bulk may be great enough to crush in the hull of a ship.

In a recent publication the Hydrographic Office says, concerning ice indications:

"Ice Blink" Gives Indication of Presence of Peril.

"Before ice is seen from deck the ice blink will often indicate its presence. This is readily understood when it is known that it is caused by the reflection of the rays of light from the sun or moon. On a clear day over the ice on the horizon the sky will be much paler or lighter in color and is easily distinguishable from that overhead, so that a sharp lookout should be kept and changes in the color of the sky noted.

"On a clear day icebergs can be seen at a long distance, owing to their brightness, and at night to their effulgence. During foggy weather they are seen through the fog by their apparent blackness, if such a term can be applied.

"They can also be detected by the echo from the steam whistle or foghorn. This should be remembered, since, by noting the time between the blast of a whistle and the reflected sound, the distance of the object in feet may be approximately found by multiplying by 550.

"The presence of icebergs is often made known by the noise of their breaking up and falling to pieces. The cracking of the ice or the falling of pieces into the sea makes a noise like breakers or a distant discharge of guns, which may be heard at a short distance.

"The absence of swell or wave motion in a fresh breeze is a sign that there is land or ice on the weather side.

"The appearance of herds of seal or flocks of birds far from land is an indication of the proximity of ice.

"The temperature of the air falls as ice is approached, especially on the leeward side; but generally only at an inconsiderable distance from it. The fall of the temperature of sea water is sometimes a sign of the proximity of ice, although in regions where there is an intermixture of cold and warm currents going on, as at the junction of the Labrador Current and the Gulf Stream, the temperature of the sea has been known to rise as the ice is approached. If a berg be grounded, water flowing past it will be lowered in temperature and thus give an indication of its presence. Change of temperature may therefore serve as a warning, and frequent observations, both of the temperature of the air and the sea, should be taken and considered."

BRAINERD.

MILITARY FIELD MASS PLANS

Programme for Annual Religious Event at Navy Yard Being Prepared.

Since the first announcement of the arrangements for the military field mass, which is annually held on the parade grounds of the Marine Barracks at the Brooklyn Navy Yard on Memorial Sunday, May 26, under the auspices of Gloucester Naval Camp No. 5, United Spanish War Veterans, assisted by the Long Island Chapter of the K. of C., many requests for information from military, patriotic and fraternal organizations have been received by Chairman John Daly of the mass committee. In order to complete all of the many details connected with the erection of stands, streets of formation, assembly and approach to the Navy Yard entrances by military bodies and the public, the committee has decided to hold weekly meetings in the Veterans Room, Borough Hall, during the remainder of the month of April and all of the month of May.

Invitations will be sent to the President, Governor, Mayor, Borough Presidents and all federal and city officials, as well as officers of the Army, Navy and Marine Corps and officers of the National Guard regiments of Brooklyn.

From assurances received by the committee the provisional battalions from the Brooklyn regiments will be much larger than in former years, as also will be the detachments from the U. S. Regular Army, Navy Marine Corps, the Sixty-ninth Regiment of Manhattan, the Irish Volunteers, the uniformed detachments from the police and fire departments, U. S. Letter Carriers, Street Cleaning Department, U. S. Customs Benevolent Association, Naval Posts, United Spanish War Veterans of New York State and New Jersey, U. S. Volunteer Life Saving Corps, Uniformed Rank Knights of Columbus, First New York Regiment, C. B. L. Knights of Columbus councils, C. B. L. councils, Ancient Order of Hibernians, Foresters of America, uniformed cadet organizations, and Ladies Auxiliary of the United Spanish War Veterans.

Invitations will also be sent to the Thirteenth Regiment Coast Artillery and the Manhattan Rifles of New York and other organizations who have never as yet participated in the annual services.

A choir of 150 voices assisting at the mass will be under the direction of Arthur S. Somers, and there will be orchestra and piano interpretations of selection from the masses of Gounod and Haydn.

Captain Alfred A. Mitchell, of Gloucester Camp, who has been elected Grand Marshal of the parade, which precedes the ceremonies in the yard, has appointed Captain Robert N. Mackin of Gloucester Camp; Lieutenant William Macauley and Past Commander William J. Keating, of the Fourteenth Regiment Camp, and Past Commander John Fitzgerald, of Major-General George F. Elliott Camp as Assistant Marshals.

SPECIMEN OF GIGANTIC ICEBERG WHICH OCCASIONALLY GETS INTO LINE OF OCEAN STEAMSHIPS

GHOSTLIKE BERGS ONE OF SEA'S PERILS

Majestic and Beautiful Under Sunshine, but Deathdealing in Mist.

MANY SHIPS THEIR VICTIMS.

Derelicts Are as Dangerous as Icebergs, but Cutter Seneca Disposes of Them in Time.

Icebergs and derelicts are two of the greatest dangers to the great modern steamship; the two things, barring a tremendous storm or a boiler explosion, which can seriously cripple or sink a liner. What an iceberg can do has just received its greatest known exemplar in the loss of the Titanic, though these stupendous masses of floating ice have always been known as a great peril in the northern seas.

When one considers that bergs have been seen a quarter of a mile long and fully 500 feet high, and that scientists say that what one sees of a berg above the water is only one-eighth or less of the total bulk, it can be imagined what a danger they are. Very pretty they are, floating high and white, glistening and sparkling over the blue water in the sunshine of a clear day, very majestic and beautiful. But let there be, says the old sailor, a fog; a dull drawn or thick twilight, a dark night unlit by moon or stars, or thick with mist, and they are no longer things to admire; they are destroyers, treacherous in their silence and elusiveness, more terrible than rock or shoal, for rock and shoal can be charted, but who can chart these silent, ghastly nomads of the sea?

There is a case on record, however, in which such an iceberg, after being a destroyed became a savior. In May, 1885, the British bark Sunderland was nosing her way through an ice field. Captain Harry Turner, then a mate, said he "smelt ice," as the sailors say, and before he really knew of it or had time to reverse, a monster iceberg loomed up before them—a high, white dully glistening wall. The impact of the ship was so great that the bow was stove in clean to the heel of the foremast, and was instantly a total wreck. The longboats were put into a sea full of big bergs which threatened every moment to smash the frail craft. Finally it was suggested they land on the very berg which had caused the disaster, and which seemed to be fairly solid. This was done, a tent for the women was pitched, an alcohol stove was got going, food was brought on the ice and prepared, and the survivors made themselves as comfortable as possible. They were ten days on this berg, which was described as being fully a hundred feet high. As it drifted southward it began to melt, and to become so honeycombed as to be unsafe, so that the little party began to be very anxious. Finally they were sighted by the steamship Nottingham bound for Liverpool, and everyone saved.

Careful Owners and Captains Go Out of Way to Escape the Bergs.

But every vessel does not have such luck, nor can count upon it. Many vessels such as the steamship Astoria, in 1906, went 200 miles out of her course to avoid bergs, and it is said that the late Colonel Astor always gave his yacht captain full power to change his course at will to keep out of danger, a precaution which, had the Titanic taken it, would have saved his life together with the other hundreds. It was in 1906 that the steamship Anglo-Peruvian was sunk by a large berg, but fortunately the drifting survivors were saved by the steamhip Mohawk. In May, 1909, the steamship Mongolian was lost in a like manner. The extent of the dangerous berg field in the winter and early spring may be gauged by the experience of the steamship Oronsa, which, in 1906, sailed through 300 miles full of these ice mountains.

These icebergs originate in the great icefields of the polar regions and are supposed to be sections of enormous glaciers, which, as they reach the sea in their slow movement, break off and float away to become the menace of the seas. The so-called "northern lane" is never free from them, even in summer. They have been seen as far south as the New England coast. Generally they last till they meet the warmer water on our coasts, and then melt rather quickly. For this reason the "southern lane," which does not lead up north off the Banks, is much safer, even in summer, and this latest experience should make it plain that it is in winter the only comparatively safe route. The "northern lane" is never free from hazard.

There is in existence an instrument for detecting icebergs, with which most modern vessels are equipped; but at the best it can only forewarn at a short distance, and must leave everything to the captain's judgment and good sense quite as much as the old method of "smelling" the ice. The instrument is called the marine thermometer, which, hung over the bow some five feet under the water, records any variation in the temperature of the water to a thousandth of a degree centigrade. The very high resistance of a metal wire makes this delicate detection possible, and magnifies it so upon the instrument that it can be easily observed. Readings can be taken every half minute. It is true that it is a crude test and valueless unless properly heeded, but it is better than nothing in dealing with these slow, silent, often unseen, monsters.

Derelicts Are as Dangerous as Icebergs.

Hand in hand with the arctic iceberg as the great destroyer at sea is the derelict, which is bound to no climate or temperature or sea, but is a vagabond and a wanderer on the face of the water; no vessel knows where to look for derelicts; they are at the mercy of wave and wind and the ship is at their mercy.

The derelict is an abandoned ship, waterlogged and helpless, which cannot sink, yet drifts half-sunken through the seas, a constant menace to navigation. There can be no indication of them unless they are seen in time to steer clear of them. Most of them are wrecked lumber schooners, which were abandoned by the crew because they were unseaworthy, yet, waterlogged, lie half above the water. The region in the Atlantic where they most abound makes a gigantic triangle, corresponding roughly with the area washed by the Gulf Stream, one angle at the Nantucket Shoals of Massachusetts: another off the Irish coast, and the third off the Azores. It can be seen the area they are likely to be found in is fairly large.

It is the custom for any ship meeting a derelict to note its position in the log and to report it generally among the maritime profession; so, by observing a derelict in its various positions during a number of years, unless it is lost sight of or destroyed, experts can "get on to its curves," so to speak, and chart the ocean currents which are washing it about, and thus warn mariners of its probable position at any time. But there is no good derelict but a dead derelict, and it is the duty of any ship, with the power, to sink or otherwise destroy such a menace.

Formerly it was left to the individual vessel to do what opportunity or strength permitted, but that was felt to be dangerous and too haphazard; so a few years ago a boat was built, to belong to the revenue cutter service of the United States, designed especially to kill derelicts, and sent to patrol the seas, hunt down the derelict in its lair and kill it. The boat had special marks and flags, known all over the sea, whereby any ship meeting her could signal the latest news, position, characteristics, etc., of any derelict she might meet.

This boat is the cutter Seneca, which was put in commission in November, 1908, and has been patrolling the seas ever since, from Bermuda to Sable Island. Besides all the other modern improvements which make her safe, swift-sailing, etc., she mounts four six-pounder rapid-firing guns and carries stores of gun-cotton and powder for destroying strays.

There are various ways of disposing of derelicts. To blow up a wooden ship is dangerous, particularly if laden with lumber, for that breaks up one derelict into many menaces, for floating timbers, spars, etc., are often as dangerous as a whole vessel. The best way to dispose of one, if it is possible, is to tow her ashore and beach her. Burning is of no use, for one can burn only to the water's edge, and the charred hulk and burnt, floating timbers are still perilous. Sometimes, however, a few well-directed shots below the waterline will sink her completely and so end her. An iron or steel vessel, particularly if with heavy cargoes, can be shot or blown to pieces with carefully placed mines of gun-cotton without any danger of making the matter worse.

So, with the Seneca hawksnawing through the seas, and the position of all derelicts carefully charted and posted, this second great menace has been made much less formidable.

No Light to Penetrate the Fog Has Yet Been Found.

Another great menace, the fog, has not as yet been guarded against. Ships still collide in the fog, and seem likely to collide for some time to come. The only remedy or safeguard is extreme caution and efficient signals of every sort. The sinking of the Republic and the damage to the Florida is the best recent illustration of what running at high sped in the fog can do, and the need of great caution. The many frequent foggy mornings in New York, with the many petty accidents which oftentimes are not far removed from serious ones, show what little can be done against the element which blinds man's eyes and muffles his ears so that he cannot save himself till disaster is upon him.

The peril from rocks and shoals can be and is to large measure, being prevented. The charts of our seas are good and growing better steadily. It is seldom that a vessel comes to grief on a rock or shoal which proves to be absolutely unknown. Most often it was overlooked on the chart, or the reckoning was wrong, and the ship, while in fancied security, struck the dangerous place thought so far away. Here, as in other things, the danger cannot be absolutely done away with, as no sea danger can be done away with, but rocks and shoals are stationary, can be charted accurately, and ships can tell their position with a good deal of accuracy, so that this form of shipwreck ought to grow less common.

The last and greatest danger to the ship at sea is the tempest. Nothing can guard against that. No safeguard can be invented, no ship made so strong and stanch as to be confident it can defeat the hurricane. Ships will always go down in storms as long as there are ships, and as long as the sea holds its power. "They who go down into the sea in ships, and do a mighty business in great waters" can only trust and hope; they can never be sure. For the sea is the sea, and her power is infinite.

So there are the great dangers to navigation: The iceberg, the derelict, the fog, the shoal or rock and the tempest. Some can be partially guarded against. And the greatest of these, and the most untamable, is the tempest.

ARMY AND NAVY UNION.

The department commander, accompanied by Aids Freeman and Gledhill, will visit Colonel J. J. Astor Garrison, Jersey City, on Wednesday evening, to muster in a number of recruits and make arrangements for memorial services in honor of Colonel Astor, for whom the garrison is named.

General Nelson A. Miles Garrison will meet Monday evening in Room 2, Borough Hall.

George A. Custer Garrison will meet Wednesday evening in Room 2, Borough Hall.

The grand marshal of the Memorial Day parade assures the comrades that this will be the largest parade ever held by this organization.

John Cornell of General Lawton Garrison, Newburg, N. Y., Past Commander Roach of Shields Garrison, New Rochelle, and Arthur J. Williams of Sedgwick Garrison, West Point, attended headquarters night, together with the garrison commanders of New York City, making it one of the largest gatherings of the year.

Chief Kenlon of the New York Fire Department has granted permission for William McKinley Garrison, Fire Veterans, to parade in the Army and Navy Union Division on Memorial Day in Fire Department uniform.

CHADWICK—PRICE.

Charles Chadwick of Brooklyn, son of Mr. and Mrs. Charles N. Chadwick, was married on Wednesday afternoon to Miss Winifred Allender Price, daughter of Mr. and Mrs. Ernest Melville Price of New Haven, Conn. The marriage took place at the home of the bride, Canner street, New Haven, the Rev. Edward M. Chapman officiating. Mr. Chadwick has a summer home at Old Lyme, near New Haven, and spends much of his time there.

MARINE DISASTERS OF RECENT YEARS

Atlantic and Bourgogne Were Lost Near Titanic's Grave.

FORMER RAN ON THE ROCKS.

Latter Struck British Ship—Hundreds of Lives Lost, but Not So Many as on Titanic.

In view of the terrible loss of life on the Titanic, the marine disasters of the past seem small in comparison. A little over thirty years ago the White Star liner Atlantic went on the rocks near Meaghers Island while trying to make a course for Halifax, N. S. The Atlantic left Liverpool for New York on Saturday, March 28, 1873. Her passenger list numbered 931 persons, which was considered phenomenally large for that day. The ship encountered, after leaving the English coast, a series of fierce equinoctial gales, which seriously interfered with her progress. These conditions continued until the 31st, when Captain Williams decided to change his course and run for Halifax.

The captain, not apprehensive of special danger, retired at midnight of the date last given. He gave instructions to the officer on watch to call him at 3 o'clock. Knowing that the ship was now approaching a dangerous coast, his purpose was to have the vessel lie off shore until daylight. But, apparently, Captain Williams had been at fault in his calculations, for when 3 o'clock came it required no human voice to rouse him from his slumbers. The cry "breakers ahead" resounded through the ship, and the Atlantic, the pride and favorite of ocean travelers, was driven upon the rocks with all the force of her engines. The ship was hard and fast and the sea, lashed by the cruel wind, was washing over her. The boats on the port side were swept away by the force of the waves, and the vessel then heeled over, rendering those on the starboard side entirely useless. The officers of the Atlantic, who were now on deck, advised the passengers to secure themselves to the rigging, as their only protection from the wild waves which were sweeping the decks in rapid succession.

The consternation among the passengers, after being aroused from their slumbers, by the ship striking upon the rocks with full force, was something absolutely indescribable. At first they could not realize what had happened. Some thought that the boiler had exploded; others that the ship had struck an iceberg. Hundreds of the steerage passengers were drowned in their berths, while among those who succeeded in gaining the decks scores were swept away by the waves. To add to the consternation among the passengers, the foreboom broke loose, and swinging to and fro, crushed all who came within its terrible sweep. Some of these terror-stricken human beings, driven frantic by their surroundings, plunged into the sea and were seen no more. Only one means of escape was available. At a distance of 150 feet from the wreck there was a high rock. To this point the seamen contrived to carry five lines, which afforded a frail and dangerous means of communication with the ship. Between the rock and the shore was a farther distance of 100 yards. This distance was bridged by Mr. Brady, the third officer, and two quartermasters carried a rope by swimming. About 200 persons were reported to have made the passage from the wreck to the rock by means of the life lines thus established. But only fifty succeeded in making the more perilous passage from the rock to the shore.

Boats Propelled Through Raging Surf by Heroic Men.

At break of day a boat put off from shore, but was not able to render much assistance, because of the violence of the surf. Mr. Brady, having got on shore, succeeded in procuring three large boats, and with these many were rescued from the rock and from the rigging of the Atlantic. One of the narrowest escapes was that of Mr. Firth, the chief officer. With thirty-two passengers, one of whom was a woman, he had taken refuge in the mizzen rigging. By degrees the number lessened—some were rescued by the boats, others were washed away by the sea. Finally, Mr. Firth, the woman and a boy only remained. The sea had now risen until the boats could no longer reach the wreck. The boy was washed off, and after a courageous effort, swimming skillfully and steadily, reached one of the boats and was pulled in. Mr. Firth then caught hold of the unfortunate woman and lashed her to the mast as a final resource, though neither for him nor for her did there seem any hope.

The terrible position of the first officer of the Atlantic and the woman in the rigging was observed in the village of Prospect on the main land, opposite Meaghers Island, where the fated ship went ashore. The Rev. William J. Ancient, a clergyman of the Church of England, bravely put out in a small boat with the purpose of rescuing them. He succeeded in getting a footing in the main rigging, from which he threw a rope to Mr. Firth, who fastened it to his body and plunged into the sea and was hauled on board the boat. It was found to be unnecessary to make any further effort to save the woman, for she had frozen to death.

Captain Williams remained on the deck of the vessel through all these heart-rending scenes. He issued his orders with perfect composure, and it was not until his hands and feet were frozen that he consented to go ashore in one of the boats. The Court of inquiry severely censured him for not using the lead and for not keeping a sharp lookout when approaching a dangerous and treacherous coast. In consideration of his bravery and devotion after the disaster occurred, his certificate was only suspended for two years. Of the 931 passengers on board the Atlantic, 481, including 295 women and children, perished.

The Rev. Mr. Ancient, who showed so much intrepidity in not only saving lives but also by spurring on others to do the same, was presented with a gold watch by the Canadian Government and a similar presentation was made by citizens of Chicago. He died at Halifax July 20, 1908, at the age of 74.

On the morning of July 4, 1898, the French Line steamship Bourgogne was sunk in a collision with the Cromartyshire. The disaster occurred sixty miles south of Sable Island, off the coast of Nova Scotia, and in the same region where the Atlantic and, more recently, the Titanic, catastrophes occurred. Of the 734 souls on board, about 535 were drowned, including 206 of the 217 first and second class passengers. All the first cabin passengers were lost, and of the 300 women passengers on the fated vessel but one was saved.

The disaster occurred at 5 o'clock in the morning. A dense fog prevailed when the steamship struck the steamship Cromartyshire. Descriptions of what immediately followed the collision state that in an instant the deck of the liner was transformed into an inferno. Women, who obstructed the way of strong men on their way to the boats, were struck down with knives. The steerage had contained many Italians, and it seemed that in facing death a thirst for blood came upon them. Right and left their weapons flashed and trampled bodies marked their course. The officers who had to face these conditions died like brave men, but it was impossbile for them to control their mad passengers and madder crew. One raft, on which forty women had been placed, had been made fast to the side of the ship. It was dragged down when the ship went under. Not a man would stop to cut the line and give the women life.

When the ship had gone down the very few boats which floated were surrounded by drowning passengers. Some women caught hold of the lines of one cockleshell, not endangering the occupants of the boat, but merely enabling the women to keep their heads above water. The fiends in the boat cut the rope, and so made certain the death of these poor, struggling human creatures. In other instances men who were struggling to keep themselves above water by clutching the gunwales of the lifeboats, were beaten off by oars and boathooks.

The British ship which had been in collision stood by, and for hours kept up the work of rescue. Then she was towed into Halifax. Marvelous was the endurance of those who remained in the water for hours before being rescued. The officers of the Bourgogne, every man of them, went down with their ship. One of them came to the surface and was saved.

Among the Bourgogne's passengers who perished were a number of New York City merchants and business men. There were artists and engineers from this vicinity, and their untimely death carried the deepest grief into many households. The brutality shown by the second class passengers and the crew of the lost ship made the disaster specially harrowing.

In the record of marine disasters during the past forty years the nearest approach to that of the Titanic in the loss of life was the burning of the excursion steamer General Slocum on the morning of June 15, 1904. The list of fatalities on this occasion, as made up by the police, totaled 1,031, which included 78 from Brooklyn. Next to the Grand Republic, the Slocum was the largest excursion steamer doing business in New York Harbor. She was carrying, on the occasion of the catastrophe, a Sunday school excursion from the East Side of Manhattan, and when proceeding up the East River fire broke out and swept the boat with such rapidity that the loss of life was appalling.

Disasters to Atlantic liners during recent years have been caused by collision and by going ashore. They have been exempt from accidents caused by fire. Even in the face of the terrible disaster to the Titanic, it must be admitted that, considering the number of people transported, the loss of life, or injury to passengers, has been very small.

SPIRIT PICTURE SHOWN WITH STEAD

"George Washington" Also Photographed With Author Who Was Drowned in Titanic Disaster.

BELIEVED IN DR. SLADE.

Shipwreck Victim Was Exceedingly Popular in the World of Letters.

By J. H. Johnson.

A photograph of William T. Stead with a so-called "spirit" photograph looking over his right shoulder was presented to me by Mr. Stead at his office in London in 1902. He showed me several others, one notably interesting to me, an American, Mr. Stead's photograph, with George Washington's spirit picture in the background.

The "spirit" of Washington stood out much clearer than the one he gave me. There was no mistaking it for anyone else, and I longed to own it instead of the one he had given me. When I suggested that I should greatly like to own the Washington picture, he exclaimed: "Oh, no, I could not part with that," and he began asking questions about his New York friends, ending by inviting myself and wife to dinner at the house of his married daughter on the following day.

A short time before this there had been an exposure in New York of a "spirit photo" taker. It was complete and perfect, leaving no doubt in the minds of average men and women that it was a trick of the operator. I asked Mr. Stead at this second interview if he did not think it possible that he had been deceived as well as some New Yorkers, but he could not see how such a thing was possible, as he watched the man too closely.

I asked him if he had ever heard of Dr. Slade of New York.

"Oh, yes, indeed, and had met him in London." "You may remember that his greatest feat was in having the initials of spirit friends appear 'in letters of blood, as he called it, on his fat, white forearm and wrist?" Mr. Stead remembered that.

Could Do the Same Trick as Dr. Slade.

I then remarked that more than thirty years ago I had learned sleight-of-hand and my friends thought I was an expert performer. When I went to see Dr. Slade I was nonplussed over it, but said nothing, and handed him his $5 fee. I then went home, thinking it all over, and at the end of twenty-four hours I could do the trick as cleverly as he had done it.

The next Saturday I went to see Dr. Slade a second time, taking a friend with me, to whom I explained just how the trick was done. I told him just how to act during the interview, and the result was there was nothing done. At last I said to the doctor: "Dr. Slade, last Saturday you swindled me out of $5, and I now demand the return of that money."

He said he never would return it, and then taking out my watch I said: "Dr. Slade, it is now half-past 10 o'clock. Here is my business card, and if you send me the $5 before 12 o'clock that will end the trouble between us, but if you do not, I shall go down to the District Attorney's office at once, and have you indicted as an impostor. Good morning."

Just a quarter before 12 o'clock a man came into my place of business and handed me an envelope with a five-dollar bill in it, saying: "Dr. Slade sends you this."

After telling this to Mr. Stead I said: "If I had been in Slade's place, and been an honest man, I would have gone to jail before giving up that money, and while Mr. Stead said, "So would I," I felt that he was unconvinced of Slade's rascality.

Knew Many Famous Men.

Mr. Stead on this occasion and two other occasions, when I called at his office, was full of inquiries about my acquaintance with Horace Greeley, Charles A. Dana, Robert G. Ingersoll and Walt Whitman. I am sure he spoke of Whitman every time I met him, and seemed as familiar with "Leaves of Grass" as the most earnest admirer of Walt could desire.

Mr. Stead had the gift of making everyone feel that he was his particular friend, in whom he felt interested, and I question if he did not have a larger acquaintance among the literary men of his day than any other writer. Perhaps he will be missed by more friends than any other person who lost his life on the Titanic. Peace to his ashes!

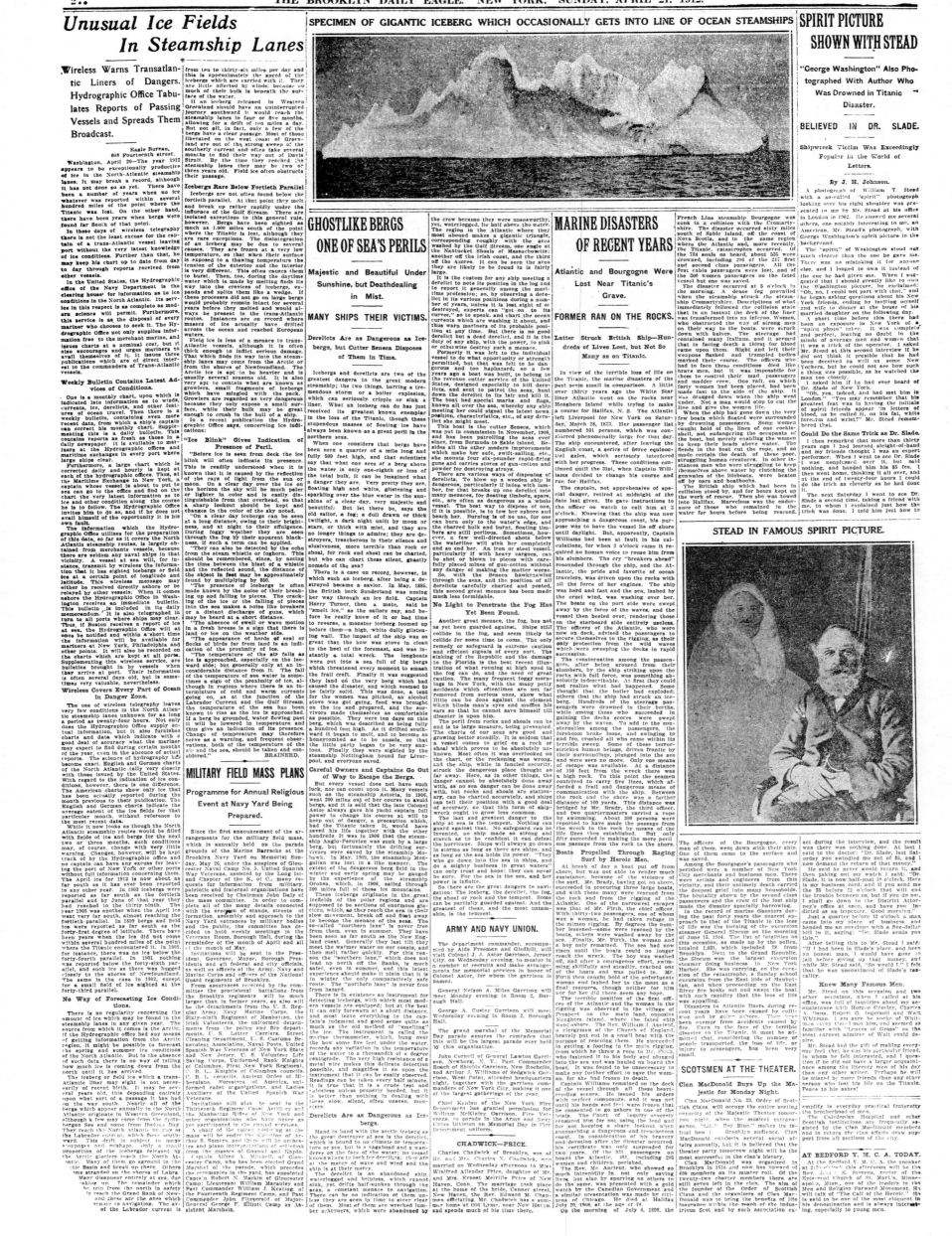

STEAD IN FAMOUS SPIRIT PICTURE.

SCOTSMEN AT THE THEATER.

Clan MacDonald Buys Up the Majestic for Monday Night.

Clan MacDonald No. 33, Order of Scottish Clans, will occupy the entire seating capacity of the Majestic Theater tomorrow night, when the musical extravaganza, "Little Boy Blue," makes its initial bow to Brooklyn audience. Clan MacDonald conducts several social affairs annually, but it is believed that the theater party tomorrow night will be the most successful in the clan's history.

Clan MacDonald was organized in Brooklyn in 1878 and now has upward of 400 members on its muster roll. Of the twenty-two charter members there are still seven left in the clan. The aim of the founder of the Order of Scottish Clans and the organizers of Clan MacDonald was to bring the benefits of life insurance within the reach of the industrious Scot and by such association exemplify in everyday practical fraternity the brotherhood of man.

The Caledonian Hospital and other Scottish institutions are frequently assisted by the Clan MacDonald members and in return the clan affairs draw support from all sections of the city.

AT BEDFORD Y. M. C. A. TODAY.

At the Bedford Y. M. C. A. the speaker at 3:30 o'clock this afternoon will be the Rev. J... E. Stevens, rector of the Episcopal Church of St. Mark's, Minneapolis, Minn., one of the leaders in the Men and Religion Forward Movement. He will talk of "The Call of the Heroic." He is said to be one of the most eloquent in his denomination and is always interesting, especially to young men.

The Iceberg Specter That Comes Out of the North

Uncle Sam Knows All About the Source of the Floating Mountains That Break Up His Vessels and Has Laid Many Plans as to Their Avoidance.

By William Atherton Du Puy.

THAT her ocean-plowing titans might not break themselves to pieces upon the ice derelicts that come out of the Far North, the Federal Government has for years been studying the problem of avoiding those dangers of the deep. It has traced the iceberg to its origin, has followed its toboggan down the slopes of Greenland, watched it plunge with a mighty splash into the icy ocean, followed it in its erratic drift of two thousand miles to the south, and there witnessed its final melting in the warm waters of the Gulf Stream. For years past it has traced an imaginary line off the coast of Newfoundland which represents the point of danger for ocean traffic. To all navigators, the Federal Government has extended a warning of the constant danger of coming within this line, particularly at just this season of the year.

"The speed demon is responsible for another great tragedy," said Captain John J. Knapp, Chief Hydrographer of the Navy Department, when the Titanic broke herself to pieces on an iceberg last Sunday night. "It is the business of this office to warn navigators of the dangers of the seas. For years we have been issuing maps and warnings to all the steamship companies showing them just where there is ice and where death accompanies whoever puts to sea in ships. These warnings have not been heeded, and now the greatest marine tragedy in history has resulted. This tragedy took place within the region that we have been marking as unsafe for years. The steamship companies have been regularly running the gauntlet of the known dangers of these icefields that they might cut a few hours off the time of making the transatlantic trip. By but slightly lengthening their journey they might have made it entirely safe. The Federal Government has given its warnings in vain.

Origin of Icebergs.

It is this hydrographic office of the Government that is the great authority upon icebergs. Particularly has this office made a study of the icebergs and the ice fields of the North Atlantic Ocean. Here it has found much of fascination, because the conditions are such in this region as to breed the greatest icebergs that the world knows. Greenland is the mother of these monsters.

All the interior of Greenland dips toward her western shore. Beginning at the water's edge, the elevation of Greenland rises steadily until it has reached a height of 10,000 feet. This entire mass is covered by a huge sheet of ice formed from compressed snow, and is in reality one enormous glacier, which gradually creeps downward to the sea. Along the coast of Greenland there is a fringe of islands, which stick up like the teeth of a saw and tear great rifts in this descending glacier. The weight of the trillions of tons of ice crowds the nose of the glacier between these promontories and into the sea. There is a thousand miles of waterfront that thus converts itself into an iceberg manufacturing machine.

After the glacier is thrust between two of these promontories and into the waters of the Atlantic Ocean it projects itself until its very weight breaks it off. Then a huge block of this glacier drops into the ocean and becomes an unattached floating mountain of ice. An iceberg has here been born. In the language of the experts of the hydrographic office, this process is called "calving."

The size of the pieces set adrift in this way vary greatly. In the Arctic an iceberg would be considered an average specimen if its perpendicular walls were a hundred feet high and its spires and pinnacles reached to two or three hundred feet in height and the length and breadth of which was two or three city blocks. The Capitol Building at Washington would be about the size of the portion of an ordinary Greenland iceberg which may be seen above the water. The portion of the iceberg that is submerged is eight or nine times as great as that which appears above the water. Many authors give the depth under water as being eight or nine times the height above. This is incorrect, however, as measurements above and below water should be with reference to mass and not to height. It is even possible to have a berg as high out of water as it is deep below the surface, for, if we imagine a large, solid lump of any regular shape which has a very small, high pinnacle in its center, the height above water can easily be equal to the depth below.

How Icebergs Travel.

Icebergs are made the year around, but are bred more rapidly in the summertime in that the glaciers move faster at that season of the year. When once set adrift on the western shore of Greenland the iceberg soon finds itself in the Labrador current, and in this southbound stream of the waters of the north it begins its journey to the southward and toward its ultimate dissolution. This is not an unobstructed drift, but one attended with many stoppages and mishaps. Many icebergs run aground in the Arctic basin and there break up. Others reach the shores of Labrador, where they flounder along the coast for a season or two before they go to pieces. Others stick, reach the open seas without hitch, and in this way make a much more rapid drift to the south. These are the icebergs that go farthest, because less time is expended in the trip and less opportunity for melting is, therefore, to be had. These are the icebergs that stick their noses even into the warm waters of the Gulf Stream and that offer themselves to any transatlantic liner which wants to convert itself into a battering ram. The Labrador current upon the bosom of which rides great fields of the most imposing icebergs that the world ever knows, passes to the southward along the coasts of Baffin Bay and Labrador, and although its currents are in places very slow, it makes an average headway of twenty miles a day. It pours into the Atlantic enormous masses of water, for which compensation is derived from the warm streams of the Atlantic and the the east Greenland currents that are sucked around Cape Farewell and furnish the only warming influence that comes to the west coast of Greenland.

The life of the average iceberg is two or three years. From the time of calving to the time of dissolution in the warm Atlantic the successful iceberg travels a maximum of two thousand miles. There are usually many delays and it is the second or third season before the iceberg finally gets into the open Atlantic and melts. The sheets of surface ice that cover these northern waters through the greater part of the year materially delay the progress of the iceberg. So vast is the bulk of the berg that is below water and so strong is the pull of the current upon it, however, that it is no uncommon thing to see an iceberg steadily advancing in a frozen sea and plowing its way through ice that is four or five feet thick. Many of those sturdy vessels that have explored far northern waters have taken advantage of the drifts of an iceberg to the south, have moored their ships in its wake and have been towed many miles to the southward. Thus have they gained passage through ice that it would have been impossible for them to break.

Iceberg Treachery Known to All Sailors.

This association with an iceberg is, however, one of the most dangerous of all affiliations. The stuff of which these huge bodies is made is the brittlest imaginable and it is a matter of wonder what small things may upon occasion cause it to break to pieces. The blow of an ax will at times split a huge iceberg, the report of a gun by concussion may cause it to break to pieces. The men o fthe North who know the treachery of icebergs approach them with great caution when it becomes necessary to get water from them or to anchor to them. Along the coast of Labrador in July and August when it is packed with birds the noise of the rupture of these great ice masses is often deafening and the experienced give them a wide berth.

When the process of melting is going on the water from the surface which is caused by the heat of the sun finds its way into the crevasses and at night freezes again. In the freezing process it expands and, acting like a wedge, forces the berg into fragments. This process greatly aids in the final breaking up of an iceberg. There are on record instances of icebergs that have been so formed as to leave no crevasses and so fortunate as to strike no obstructions during their trip toward the open and that have drifted almost to the Azores.

These stately derelicts of the far north assume such fantastic shapes as to remind one of crystal palaces of the imagination. Some approximate regular geometric figures, while others are crowned with spires, domes, minarets, while yet others are pierced by deep indentations or caves. Small cataracts precipitate themselves from the large bergs, while icicles hang in clusters from every projecting lodge. It is no uncommon sight to see one of these crystal palaces of the north suddenly change its center of gravity, turn turtle, dip its mighty crest and reappear another creature. Often the bergs are so nicely balanced that the slightest melting of their surfaces causes a shifting of the center of gravity and a turning of the mass as a piece of ice is often seen to turn over in a pitcher. Vessels that are very near these icebergs when they turn over or break to pieces are in great danger of being crushed or capsized. Even falling pieces from a tall iceberg may break a ship in two. Portions of an iceberg under water may project far from its apparent mass and a vessel may crash into this to its destruction. All these are but lesser dangers as compared with the result of running head-on into one of these ice monsters.

The iceberg is but one form of the danger that lurks in the cold waters of the north. Field ice is little less to be dreaded than are the solitary monster chunks of that material. Field ice forms upon the surfaces of northern bodies of water and along the shores of such inhospitable lands as Labrador. This ice grows thicker year after year until it is fifteen or twenty feet deep. Then, some summer, a great area of it becomes detached from the shore and begins drifting. It may be taken up by some such influence as the Labrador current and borne on along. This current is prone to do strange things with the field ice. The current may strike but one portion of the ice while the rest of it remains in sluggish waters. This will start the entire piece whirling. Winds may accentuate this motion. Smaller icebergs become a part of the mass and are liberated to the southward. These are known as growlers, and are among the most dangerous of the ice masses that interfere with traffic to the north. A growler, a low, dark indigo-colored mass, is just barely awash, and with a rounded top like a whale's back, is difficult to discern and may cause the death of any ship. Great masses of this field ice works steadily to the south and is augmented by other areas that it breaks loose from the Labrador coast. The whole moves on at an average rate of ten miles a day until it reaches Belle Isle, between the middle of January and the middle of February.

Many strange experiences have been recorded in the North in connection with the drift of this field ice. The greatest journey ever made by white men as a part of such a drift was accomplished by Captain Tyson in 1871. He and a part of nineteen others were separated from the United States survey ship in latitude 78 degrees north. Being unable to regain the ship, they remained on the floe and accomplished one of the most wonderful journeys on record. They drifted 1,500 miles on this ice barge, which ground and broke and reunited itself continually beneath them. As they came further south, they saw the ice that kept them afloat gradually melting beneath them. Every day for six months they seemed to be near the inevitable end. Finally, the Tigris, a sealing steamer from Newfoundland, picked them up near the Strait of Belle Isle, in latitude 53 degrees north.

Off Belle Isle these areas of field ice find their way south in the Gulf Stream, where they are often to be seen in all manner of shapes. Usually these ice areas are white, covered with snow, and visible at a long distance. They are full of hummocks, uneven blocks piled high upon each other or stood on end, and the whole mass forms an impenetrable field, which is dangerous to any craft.

Locating Ice Is Done in Many Ways.

Old seadogs of the North have many methods by which they are able to sense the presence of icebergs. Before ice is seen from the deck of a ship what is known as a "blink" is detected by the old mariner and indicates the presence of danger. This blink is a sort of flare of light in the sky and comes from the fact that the ice refracts either moonlight or sunlight. When in the region where there is a possibility of encountering ice the navigator always keeps his eye out for the blink. On a clear day icebergs can be seen at a long distance, owing to their brightness, and at night because of their effulgence. Seen through a fog they can be made out because of an apparent blackness. When in a region suspected of harboring icebergs the whistle or foghorn of the ship is often sounded, and great care is exercised to determine whether or not there is an echo. When this echo is heard it indicates that there is some object which throws back the sound.

The distance of that object from the ship may even be figured by the time which elapses between the blowing of the whistle and the hearing of the echo. Sound travels 1,100 miles a second, and upon this basis of determining the difference between the ship and the iceberg the time in seconds would be multiplied by 550. The presence of icebergs is often made known by the noise of their breaking up and falling to pieces. The cracking of the ice or the falling of pieces into the sea makes a noise like breakers or a distant discharge of guns. The absence of swell of wave motion in a fresh breeze is a sign that there is land or ice on the weather side.

The appearance of herds of seal or flocks of birds far from land is an indication of the proximity of ice. The temperature of air falls as ice is approached, especially on the leeward side, but generally at an inconsiderable distance from the object endangered. The fall of the temperature of sea water is sometimes a sign of the nearness of ice. The ability of old seamen of the North to determine the nearness of an iceberg by the mere fan of a cold breeze often seems almost superhuman.

"Taking passage on a transatlantic liner at this season of the year and crossing over by the northern route," said Captain Commandant E. P. Bertholf of the Revenue Cutter Service, "is like getting into a cab and ordering it driven up a street that you know to be studded with bombs. If you get through this sort of street, you congratulate your cabby. If you strike a bomb, it is all over, and the public has no epithet vile enough to apply to your stupidity and the enemy's lack of skill. Yet the public is demanding, and the steamship companies are furnishing just such risks every time a vessel hurries across the Atlantic under full steam by the Northern route. Both the public and the steamship people refuse to avoid danger by taking the longer route. One great tragedy has resulted from this policy, and others will result unless the warning is heeded."

PEARY'S SHIP ROOSEVELT FIGHTING THE ICE.

MONSTER ICEBERG IN PATH OF STEAMSHIPS.

There Is Eight Times as Much Under Water.

REVENUE CUTTER CAUGHT IN THE ICE.

One of the Many Dangers Experienced by Uncle Sam's Sea Rovers in the Far North.

TITANIC WAS LAST WORD IN STEAMSHIP CONSTRUCTION.

But Watertight Bulkheads Failed to Save Her.

WHY THE BULKHEADS FAILED ON TITANIC

Construction, Thought to Make Ships Unsinkable, Proved Critically Weak.

KNEW ICE WAS NEAR.

No Instruments Needed to Tell Presence of Floating Reefs of Crystal.

In the construction of modern transatlantic liners no feature of safety has been more implicitly relied upon than the watertight bulkhead. Bulkheads are partitions separating the compartments of a ship. They are transverse and longitudinal. The former divide the ship into several great compartments and the latter subdivide them. The name "collision bulkhead" is also applied to this part of a great ship's construction, indicating that they were expected to be serviceable in just such an accident as has just occurred. With thirty watertight bulkheads how was it possible for the Titanic to founder?

The White Star liner Titanic had thirty of these watertight compartments. They were of steel construction and had doors opening from one compartment to another. The opening and closing of these doors was a part of the electrical equipment of the great ship. Captain Smith has frequently been quoted as having unbounded confidence in the impossibility of his ship foundering. It was believed by everybody that if the bulkheads at the bow of the Titanic were stove in the other watertight compartments would keep the craft afloat. But the damage seems to have been of such a sweeping character that these bulkheads appear to have played no part whatever in the preservation of the vessel after the accident occurred.

Many instances are on record of vessels having their bow bulkheads very badly damaged, but by reason of the other watertight compartments have remained afloat until picked up and towed into port. From the evidence so far at hand it seems that the Titanic must have struck the iceberg on the side and thus exposed a number of her compartments to the incoming sea. Another theory is that she ran up on the ice floe, and that by a tremendous strain she was damaged beyond any hope of remedy. None of the testimony so far given makes mention of attempts to pump. This would either indicate that the damage was so great that pumping was seen to be useless, or that the machinery of the ship needed for pumping was entirely out of commission. One fact stands out prominently in the terrible story of the loss of the Titanic, which is that the latest inventions of the shipbuilders for the prevention of accidents are not infallible.

Disaster May Bring Out Many Protective Devices for Ships at Sea.

Results of last Monday's disaster will no doubt stimulate the introduction of other inventions to accurately determine the nearness of ice in the ocean lanes traversed by the Atlantic liners. The presence of icebergs in such enormous quantities as have been met with this season, can be told by even the most casual observer. A very decided fall in the temperature is immediately felt when the ocean travelers get into the region where the bergs are most numerous. Tourists speak of the sensation caused by coming into the ice field as similar to opening the cover of a well-filled icebox. Those who have related their experiences on the day before the Titanic went down all refer to the atmosphere being cold, notwithstanding the fact that the sun was bright. A number declare that they were satisfied that there were great icebergs in the neighborhood. They did not need any mechanical devices to tell them that such was the case.

The lesson of the founding of the Titanic is a terribly expensive one, but it will, undoubtedly, bear fruit in greater precautions being taken to protect vessels from similar experiences. There can be no doubt that there will be a speed limit set for ships running in zones where ice is likely to be encountered, and the equipment as regards searchlights will be carefully looked after in all cases.

As an indication that the owners of ocean steamships are progressive in the matter of the adoption of precautionary measures for the protection of passengers they carry, it may be mentioned that the Pacific Mail Steamship Company has recently decided to equip the vessels of its line with the submarine signal receiving apparatus. This is an invention of recent application for communicating atmospheric conditions and other information under water to vessels at sea. Signaling stations have been established in the United States, Canada and other countries. Over 800 ships of various lines have been supplied with this new invention, and it is expected that it will prove of great service to navigators in warning them of fogs, of icebergs, of derelicts which may be expected in the route they may be taking.

LECTURE ON THE CANAL.

Frederick Monsen to Tell of Its Wonders for Benefit of Norwegian Hospital.

When Frederick Monsen, the explorer and lecturer, gave his lecture, "The Panama Canal Today," before the Brooklyn Institute of Arts and Sciences, last winter, a large number were deprived of the opportunity of hearing him, owing to the limited seating capacity of the music hall. For this reason, Mr. Monsen has consented to repeat this lecture, with its colored stereopticon and motion pictures, on Thursday evening, May 2, at the Young Men's Christian Association Hall.

Through Mr. Monsen's generosity, the proceeds of the lecture will go toward securing a very much needed automobile ambulance service for the Norwegian Hospital in Bay Ridge. This is one of the largest, if not the largest, ambulance district in Brooklyn.

ATLANTIC CITY VISITORS.

Atlantic City, April 20—Mrs. A. L. Gorman and her daughter, Miss Miriam Gorman, who have been spending the April days since Easter by the sea, will return early next week to their home in Jamaica.

Mr. and Mrs. A. Maltbie, Miss C. Maltbie, W. A. England, Miss L. England and Dr. and Mrs. B. S. Van Zile of Brooklyn, made up a motor party that spent the week-end at the Seaside House.

John B. Schlechting of Brooklyn is a guest at Hotel Shelburne during a brief visit by the waves.

Mrs. T. H. Heffron and Mrs. J. Mettler of Brooklyn are visitors enjoying the balmy spring days down by the sea, with apartments at Hotel Dennis.

Mrs. L. G. Gumbride of Brooklyn has apartments at the Traymore during a short stay by the sea.

The Misses Anna E. Harvey, Grace E. Mills, Alma Louthard, Jeannette Wheldon, Ella F. Biedeman and N. Louise Roethgun of Brooklyn are spending the week-end at the Glaslyn-Chatham.

William T. Morrison of Brooklyn is a visitor at the Grand Atlantic Hotel during a short stay.

Mrs. E. H. Smith of Brooklyn has apartments at the Hotel Runnymede.

Mr. and Mrs. W. J. Cosgrove are Seaside House guests from Brooklyn over the week-end.

Miss E. Fearon of Brooklyn is spending the week-end at the Avoca.

Mr. and Mrs. C. H. Bruell are Brooklynites resting at the Beechwood.

Mrs. K. M. Dillon of Brooklyn has apartments at the Westminster.

J. T. Canfield of Brooklyn is at the Seaside House.

Mrs. H. P. Alsgood and Mrs. G. B. Goodwin are Brooklyn matrons enjoying the spring days at Hotel Traymore.

Mrs. John W. Duncan of Brooklyn has apartments at Hotel Dennis.

Mrs. M. R. Cameron of Brooklyn joined friends at the Beechwood during the week.

Mrs. B. Schefer and Mrs. L. V. Nichols of Brooklyn are resting by the sea.

H. R. Byard of Brooklyn is at Hotel Edgewater for the week.

"THIRD ORDER" REUNION.

The members of the Third Order of St. Francis attached to the Church of Our Lady of Peace, Carroll street and Fourth avenue, are working for the success of their reunion, which will take place at the Imperial, April 29. The aim of this reunion is to make the Third Order of St. Francis better known and to help a worthy cause.

WIRELESS FOR WESTERN UNION

The Western Union Telegraph Company has entered into traffic arrangements with the Marconi company, whereby the Western Union offices will receive and deliver marconigrams to and from Europe. The agreement provides for the extension of the United States to Hawaii, China, Japan and the Philippines, thus giving the Western Union company a wireless trans-Pacific service.

COPPER RANGE WAGE INCREASE

Houghton, Mich., April 20—An increase in wages back to the old scale in effect in 1907, has been announced by the Cooper Range Company. This action benefits 3,000 men. It is expected that increases will also be announced in a few days by the Wolverine, Mohawk and Quincy companies.

THE BOAT DECK OF THE TITANIC.

Showing the Lifeboats Hanging From Davits.

A "STUNT" PARTY.

Given Thursday by the Women of the Fifth Avenue Baptist Church.

Thursday night the Women's Bible Class of the Fifth Avenue Baptist Church, Manhattan, held a "Stunt" party, at which the members entertained or furnished evidence of their ability in other directions. The result was that Miss C. C. Bickel furnished excellent examples of achievements in millinery, Mrs. Walter Woodward made some choice candy, Miss Lillian Walker a ham cooked in a fireless cooker, Miss Elsie Hirst, luscious black walnut creams, Mrs. Price a nut loaf, Mrs. Santry a delicious cake a nut loaf, Mrs. Santry a foamy loaf of bread, Mrs. Robert Walker an orange marmalade, Miss Lena Walker a delicious cake and Mrs. Conklin and Mrs. Julia Loughlin tempting layer cakes. Miss Pettus and Miss Emma Blake also made candy. The table where they were displayed and from which they were afterward eaten was decorated artistically by Miss Smith with hand-made and hand-painted butterflies and two water colors of flowers.

Miss Reda Jarnageux presided gracefully over the entertainment which followed the reception. Miss Madeleine Lodgewick gave a monologue, Miss Isabelle Pettus told of her experiences as a lawyer, Miss M. H. Crocker read some original rhymes, Miss Lydia Walker recited, Miss Martha Pettus sang a soprano solo, and three mere men, John Elder, William B. Green and the Rev. Dr. Addison Moore related their experiences in their various lines. A pleasant addition to the programme was the piano playing of Miss Eleanor Fields, niece of Miss Bickel. Although but 12 years old, she played Godard's "Cinquieme Valse," a Polonaise in A, by Chopin, and afterward the "Polonaise op. 53," by Chopin. She displayed wonderful technique and deep feeling for one so young.

GRANT BIRTHDAY DINNER.

Twenty-third Annual Event of Grant Post and Union League Club.

The twenty-third annual dinner commemorating the birth of General U. S. Grant, under the auspices of the Union League Club, the U. S. Grant Post No. 327, G. A. R., and the Associate Society of U. S. Grant Post, will be given at the Union League Club, Bedford avenue and Dean street, on Saturday evening, at 6:30 o'clock. The committee has acceptances from the following speakers: Philip P. Campbell, Representative from Kansas; William M. Calder, Representative from Brooklyn; the Rev. R. W. McLaughlin, Pastor of Park Congregational Church. There will be other prominent speakers.

Charles K. Buckley, past commander, is chairman of the dinner committee, and C. B. French secretary and treasurer.

WIRELESS MESSAGES AVERT SEA HORRORS

Bring Aid in Time of Peril and Same Life and Property.

DAY OF MISSING SHIPS PASSES

Call of the Wireless Pierces the Air, and Help Is Soon Forthcoming.

The day in which a ship went to her doom through fire or ice alone, shut in by her little circle of horizon, with no one in the world knowing or being able to come to her help—that day is well past, and will soon, with perfected wireless, be done with. Some of the greatest tragedies of the past have those of the missing ships—the ships which went down so suddenly as a result of collision or storm that no one was left to tell of it. Month after month the ship was posted as overdue, until the time-limit turned it to "missing."

Today all ships of any importance carry wireless, and with the recent Marconi improvements, the time is not far off when no ship can meet disaster without the world knowing of it, and every craft in the neighborhood hurrying to save her. With the saving of the passengers of the Republic a new era in marine tragedies began.

The "missing" ship has always been surrounded with romance and tragedy. The most famous missing ship in our country's history is probably that on which Aaron Burr's daughter embarked from the South to come to New York in the first quarter of the last century. It was never heard of, and for days and months, the disappointed, broken old man walked the Battery in the faint hope that the bark was going to turn up and bring his daughter to him.

The suspense and anguish in the case of a missing ship is almost greater than when a ship is definitely known to be lost, for in the latter case the anguish, though sharp, is soon over and certainly always tends to lessen grief. In the case of a missing ship, the anxiety, despair and the hope deferred which "maketh sick the heart," may drag for weeks, sometimes months. In the old days, where a sailing ship was at the mercy of the winds, there could be no certainty, sometimes for the greater part of the year, that she was really lost. Even the modern steamers can take surprisingly long and not be lost after all.

Perhaps the most interesting case of a modern steamship mysteriously missing is that of the French liner La Gascogne, which took sixteen days, twice her schedule, to sail from Havre to New York in February, 1894. As she was a large vessel, with many people on board, and as eight days went by without a word being heard, there was much anxiety. Finally one night she was seen slowly and painfully nosing her way up past Sandy Hook, and the suspense was at an end. She had had four breakdowns. After a first break in a piston-rod had been repaired after a fashion, another, more serious, occurred. The ship had to lie hove to with sea anchors out while the break was repaired. A day or two later, in a heavy cyclone, the machinery, which seemed to be growing more fragile, broke down again, and again for the fourth time, but repairs were pluckily made, and in spite of almost complete discouragement the captain and the engineer, who were almost broken down with their experience, brought her safely in. The greeting at the dock was fitting, for La Gascogne had fought the doom, not of the wrecked, but of the missing ships, and come triumphant out of the great void.

Another famous mystery is that of the Waratah, the 9,300 twin screw liner which disappeared between Durban and Cape Town in 1909. In that case there were sufficient circumstances remembered about the boat to make the mystery perhaps not entirely inexplicable. It was remembered that she had had a list to one side or another most of the time; in painting the boat the paint ran through the seams; it was said the davits of the lifeboats were rusted in. The Waratah was what is known as "dead" in the water; could not ride head to the seas; pitcher and rolled badly enough to empty water out of a stateroom bathtub, and was very slow in recovering when she dipped her bows. Nothing was ever known, but these reasons were accepted by most naval experts as the probable explanation of her loss. Had she had wireless we might have known.

The Republic of the White Star Line was rammed off Nantucket early on Janurary 23, 1909, by the Florida, which was damaged not badly enough to be sunk, but too badly to give aid to the other ship. Jack Binns, the wireless operator, who became famous over night, stuck to his post and raked the sea with wireless appeals for aid, since it was known the Republic must sink in a few hours.

The Baltic, poking her slow way through the same dense fog that had destroyed the Republic, heard the appeal and made full speed ahead, taking every risk, through the fog, circled all day about the Republic without finding her, and at night caught sight of the signal rockets, stood by, and saved everybody on board except the few who were killed in the collision. The Republic sunk a little later, a few hours after. The world rang with the achievement, recognizing for the first time that the wireless was the only thing to save vessels in such a position. The loss of the Titanic has emphasized this. Without the summons which sent the Olympic, Virginian and Carpathia hastening to the spot the loss of life might have been much greater for many of the crowded lifeboats mi[illegible] never have been heard of more. Had Titanic been able to keep afloat seven hours, as everyone took as [illegible]ter of course, there would have [illegible] loss of life, except those w[illegible] drowned in the hold at the f[illegible] And the glory would have be[illegible] now, to the wireless.

DISASTER STORY OF WIRELESS MEN SHOCKS LISTENERS

Continued From Page 1.

solutely fair," said Mr. Ismay, "and I have absolutely no criticism to make of its conduct of the hearing."

Mr. Ismay denied the story attributed to Mrs. J. G. Ryerson of Philadelphia, one of the passengers on the Titanic, that he had shown her a Marconigram telling of icebergs in the path of the ship, and had asserted that the steamer would get steam up on a couple of more boilers and put on more speed so as to get past the ice field.

Mrs. Ryerson is stopping at the Hotel Belmont in Manhattan and is confined to her room with illness. Senator Smith personally directed that she be served with a subpena, "not abruptly," by a subordinate of the Senate Committee yesterday afternoon, and she will be asked to testify about the story she is reported to have told.

Timothy Woodruff to Testify Regarding Suppressed News.

A subpena has been issued for Timothy L. Woodruff of Brooklyn, who will be a witness at the hearing in Washington. Woodruff will be asked to tell at what time the directors of the Union Typewriter Company were informed on Monday of the probable loss of the Titanic.

Woodruff will tell the committee that about 10:30 on Monday he and the other directors of the typewriter company in a directors' meeting, were informed by the White Star Line officials that the Titanic was sinking and probably would go down in about half an hour. The news of the loss of the Titanic was not given out to the public and the press until about 7 o'clock on Monday evening.

Harold Cottam, the wireless operator of the Carpathia, the rescue ship, told the committee yesterday that about 10:30 o'clock on Monday morning he sent a wireless message to the Baltic, of the White Star Line, telling of the sinking of the Titanic. The Baltic is believed to have been in direct communication with Cape Race, so that it is expected to prove the White Star Line officials in New York City knew before noon that the Titanic had gone beneath the waves, and suppressed the information.

The White Star Line seemed very anxious to hurry the members of the Titanic's crew who were rescued away to England, and the hearing yesterday morning was delayed for nearly an hour while Senator Smith argued with representatives of the line that the crew should be examined in this country, forthwith.

The twenty-five surviving sailors of the Titanic who were at the Waldorf-Astoria were kept under constant surveillance by detectives employed by the committee, and a select twenty, who had been talking, in the hearing of the detectives were served with subpenas.

Astonishing Stories Expected From Sailors.

Senator Smith intimated during the day that some of these sailors would tell astonishing stories of the wreck, and in the afternoon he gave out a list of the men under subpena.

Mrs. John Jacob Astor, Mrs. George D. Widener and practically all the other prominent Americans on board the Titanic, will be called upon to testify.

Herbert John Pitman, the Titanic's third officer, was the only witness at the session of the hearing which began at about 4 o'clock yesterday afternoon. He was asked if the log of the Titanic had been saved, and said that he did not know.

Senator Smith then read the following list of those officially connected with the Titanic or the White Star Line who have been subpenaed to appear at Washington tomorrow morning:

J. Bruce Ismay, managing director of the White Star Line; P. A. S. Franklin, vice president of the line; Harold Bride, second wireless operator on the Titanic; H. T. Cottam, wireless operator on the Carpathia; C. H. Lightolier, second officer of the Titanic; H. J. Pitman, third officer; J. G. Boxhall, fourth officer, and H. G. Lowe, fifth officer, and the following members of the Titanic's crew: W. Perkins, T. Archer, W. H. Taylor, W. Bryce, E. Bully, S. Heming, F. O. Evans T. Jones, Frank Osman, G. Moore, A. Cunningham, A. Oliver, F. Fleet, G. A. Hoog, A. Crawford, W. Burke, E. Wheelton, F. Clench, Frederick Ray, G. Crow, C. Andrews, J. Widgery, H. Etches, G. W. Rowe, John Collins, A. J. Bright, G. Symons, J. Hardy and Albert Haines.

Cold chills crept up and down the backs of the listeners to the testimony of Harold S. Bride, the second wireless operator of the Titanic, when he told of the sending out of the dread "C. Q. D." from the stricken ship, and of the refusal of Chief Operator Phillips to send details of the collision with an iceberg to the freighter Frankfort of the North German Lloyd, which Phillips told him was "probably the nearest vessel."

Frankfurt Was the Nearest Steamer.

Instead of sending a line saying the Titanic had hit an iceberg and was sinking, Brire testified Phillips had hotly retorted to the Frankfurt's request for information that the operator was "a fool," and told him in the same message to stop interferring with the Titanic's communications.

None of the listeners, apparently, had any knowledge of the distance the Frankfurt was from the Titanic when the "C. Q. D." was sent out, and Bride was emphatic in his declaraiton that the Frankfurt did not send her position.

But his statement that the Frankfurt was possibly "the nearest ship," and as indicated in the palned question of one of the investigating committee, might have been twenty miles nearer the Titanic than the Carpathia, shocked the listeners more than any of the testimony brought out so far.

Men groaned on hearing of the momentary anger of Phillips, and thought of what "might have been," if instead of using up precious moments in sending out a message calling the Frankfurt's operator a fool and telling him to shut up, the Titanic had taken the same time to flash a short line saying the ship had hit an iceberg and was sinking.

They looked at the unfortunate Bride, a beardless youngster of 21, with broken ankles and sprained back, and thought of the other young man, Phillips, his chief, only 24, with the hot ardor and impulses of youth and shook their heads. These two men stood between the Titanic and death, and while they did good work, and summoned the Carpathia, one of them had been angry at the most critical time in the marine history of the world.

Smith Tries to Soften Shock of Bride's Testimony.

Senator Smith, the chairman of the committee, evidently realized the shocking effect of Bride's testimony, and he sought to soothe the feelings of the listeners, and to let Bride explain the actions of his dead chief. He took the words from Bride's mouth and put them in language which would sound more reasonable.

"You did not want to interrupt your sending to the Carpathia, whose position you knew, and which you knew was coming to your assistance at full speed, to send messages to the Frankfurt, which apparently was very slow in understanding you and whose position you did not know? Or, in other words, you were working on the Carpathia as a certainty, rather than taking a chance on sending messages to the Frankfurt, as an uncertainty? Is that right?" asked the Senator.

"Yes, sir," responded the operator.

"We depended on the Carpathia," he added, "because she was the best thing going. We used common sense, and the Frankfurt's operator did not."

Over and over again, to the almost agonized questions of the committee as to why a bulletin of the facts of the collision had not been sent to the Frankfurt, Bride stoutly responded that the "C. Q. D." should have been enough to bring any ship to the rescue immediately.

He seemed indignant that the Frankfurt had waited "quite a bit, about twenty minutes, sir," before asking for information, and defended his chief. He maintained that the distress signal which was accompanied by the exact latitude and longitude of the Titanic should have forced the German liner to head at once for the Titanic, and said that he and Phillips "expressed very uncomplimentary opinions" about the Frankfurt when her only response twenty minutes later was to ask for information.

He was asked if he knew whether the Frankfurt's operator understood English, and he replied that the knowledge was not necessary, as the "C. Q. D.' was the code signal for distress and call for assistance in any language in the world.

Marconi, the inventor of the wireless apparatus, explained the significance of "C. Q. D." to the committee at this point. He said that 'C. .' meant "all station, attention," and "D." meant "in distress" or "in danger," and that it was an arbitrary code grouping of letters, the significance of which was generally understood.

Bride was asked, in a shocked voice by Senator Smith, if his instructions allowed such a wide use of discretion as to permit of a disregard of a request for specific information, and the sending of a reply such as was sent to the Frankfurt. He maintained that the C. Q. D. first sent, was enough.

After all, the listeners concluded, the Frankfurt may have been too far away to have arrived in time to rescue the 2,340 souls on the Titanic. That will be brought out by subsequent investigation, when the Frankfurt can be reached. They hoped it was so.

Bride was taken into the hearing in a wheel chair and was placed in a large upholstered seat, wit hhis ankles swathed in bandages on pillows, in another chair, and gave his testimony, half reclining, while his fingers locked and interlocked, and Marconi sat next to him, patting him on the shoulder occasionally to encourage him.

He delivered his answers in a very low voice, which was inaudible ten feet away. He said he had received but four pounds ten shillings a month and his board on the ship, and had learned his business at a telegrapher's training school. He had made six voyages across the Atlantic before this trip, and that was all his practical experience amounted to.

Carpathia Operator's Long Vigil.

He had been preceded by Harold Cottam, the wireless operator on the Carpathia, who testified to serving long hours for small pay, and to the "providential" fact that he had the wireless receiver to his ear as he undressed, and so caught the Titanic's "C. Q. D."

Cottam denied having sent a message that the Titanic was being towed into Halifax and that all her operators had been saved, and said he had been continuously in sole charge of his instrument all day Sunday, all night Sunday night, all Monday, Monday night, Tuesday, Tuesday night, and not relieved until Bride came to his help on Wednesday.

He said Mr. Ismay had not tried to interfere with the messages he sent out from the Carpathia. Cottam also denied any interference from Ismay or that he had sent out any false reports that the Titanic was being towed into port. The origin of this rumor will be looked into by the committee.

Bride began his story with telling of his training and his work for the White Star Line before his assignment to the Titanic.

"I kept a watch every six hours," he said. "During that time I was constantly at the instrument. I went to Belfast to join the Titanic, and was on board during her speed tests. We were testing the apparatus during the speed tests, and these trials lasted about a month as far as I know."

Bride then described the Marconi apparatus on board the Titanic, and said it was of the latest and most approved type, and that about 250 telegrams had been sent up to the time the Titanic struck the iceberg. He said he had been told that Mr. Ismay was on board during the trial tests, but that he had not met the manager at that time. During the tests many messages were sent to the White Star offices at Southampton and Belfast to the general effect that the trial of the speed of the ship was very satisfactory.

"Did you send any message for Mr. Ismay after leaving Southampton on this voyage, or receive any for him?" asked Senator Smith.

"I don't know, sir; there were so many messages."

"Did he come to the wireless offices?"

"I don't know, sir."

"Did he send any word to you either before or after the wreck while you were on the Titanic?"

"No sir."

"Can you recall whether Mr. Ismay or the captain received any messages from the White Star officers on Sunday regarding the speed of the ship or her course?"

"No, sir. No such messages were received. I should have delivered them."

No Orders Regarding Speed on Course

"You are ready to testify neither the captain nor any officers received any direction about the speed or the course the ship was to take by wireless on Sunday?"

"Yes, sir."

This line was taken by the committee to attempt to determine the responsibilifor the 21½-knot speed the Titanic was making when the iceberg was struck.

"Were you on duty when the wireless warning was received from the Amerika regarding icebergs?"

"No such message was received to my knowledge. Mr. Phillips might have received it, but he did not tell me."

Bride then told of receiving an "unofficial" message from the steamship Californian, telling of three large icebergs, on Sunday evening.

Too Busy to Take Direct Ice Warning

"In the first place, the Californian had called me with an 'ice report' about 5 o'clock. I was rather busy, and I did not take it. They did not call me again, but transmitted it to the Baltic. I took it down as it was transmitted to the Baltic—about half an hour afterward. I was doing some writing at the time, sir, writing some accounts on the table. I continued to work on the accounts for about thirty minutes. Then I took the report she sent to the Baltic. It was an 'ice report,' so I knew it was the same she had for me. I acknowledged it direct to the Californian. It was that the Californian had passed three large icebergs and gave their latitude and longitude.

"I wrote it on a slip of paper and handed it to the officer on the bridge."

"Did you make a record of it?"

"No, sir. If we made a record of all these messages we could not begin to make up our accounts."

Bride said he did not recall the name of the officer on the bridgeto whom he gave the warning.

"Did you receive any other communications regarding icebergs that afternoon or evening?"

"No, sir."

Bride's Story of the Wreck.

Bride then got down to the story of the wreck.

"At the time of the collision I was in bed, sir, in the room adjoining the apparatus. I had retired about 8 o'clock. I woke up of my own accord. I got up about five minutes to 12, ship's time. I got up because I had promised to relieve Mr. Phillips earlier than usual. I did not know of the collision, then.

"I asked Mr. Phillips how he was getting on. He said he had a big batch of telegrams for Cape Race that he had just finished."

"This was after the collision?"

"After the collission. I returned to the bedroom and got dressed."

"Didn't Mr. Phillips tell you of the collision?"

"Not until after I was dressed. Then he told me we had got damaged in some way and he thought she'd have to go back to Harlan & Wolf's (meaning the builders of the Titanic).

"The captain came in and said he wanted to send a distress call, and Phillips said, 'yes, sir, at once.' Then he sent out 'C Q D-N G Y' about half a dozen times. 'C Q D is the recognized distress cal. 'N G Y' is the code call of the Titanic."

Marconi then explained the code calls.

"We received a reply in about three or four minutes," continued Bride. "I did not get it. Mr. Phillips had the receivers to his ear. He told me to go to the captain, who was on the boat deck, and report the Frankfurt. The captain wanted to know where the Frankfurt was and I told him we'd get that as soon as we could. I went back, and Mr. Phillips was writing the position of the boat then. The next boat was the Carpathia. She sent her latitude and longitude and said she had turned around and was steaming at full speed toward the Tianic. I took that to the captain; he was on the wheelhouse, on the bridge. The captain asked what other ships had answered, and he Carpathia and the Titanic, and the operator continued to exchange messages. The Olympic answered also. After the Olympic we didn't get any replies.

"Mr. Phillips went out to see how they were getting on, and I took the 'phone."

"Did you receive any further messages from the Frankfurt?"

"We had sent our position in the sea and never received a reply. He told us to 'stand by,' meaning to wait his answer. He meant he was coming back again. Mr. Phillips told me, pudging from the clearness of the signals, the Frankfurt was the nearer. Mr. Phillips was of the opinion when the Frankfurt received our position and our 'C. Q. D' he would take it to the bridge and take further steps, but apparently he did not. The captain (Smith) asked for their position and he was told we could not answer."

"Did any officer of the Titanic express the hope that the Frankfurt would come first to their relief?"

"No, sir. The Frankfurt called up a considerable period after and asked what was the matter. About twenty minutes after. He merely inquired, sir."

"Mr. Phillips responded in a bit of a hurry, sir. He told him he was a fool."

"Did he preface that word with anything more serevere?"

"No, sir. Mr. Phillips asked for the position of the Frankfurt when we received her first response, and he received 'Stand by.'"

Expressed Uncomplimentary Opinions of Frankfurt Operator.

"We expressed our opinion of the operator of the Frankfurt, sir. It was very uncomplimentary.

"We realized then what had happened to the ship. We told him to keep out of it. Not to interfere with his instrument because we knew the Carpathia was the best thing going and we told him not to interfere with our communications. He didn't seem to realize the position we were in and we had made it very clear to him."

Bride then testified over and over again about the urgency of the "C. D. D." and its sufficiency, in defending Phillips for not sending details to tre Frankfurt.

Bride then told of his own efforts to save himself as the ship went down. He said that a number of men were trying to launch a boat when it was washed over by a wave, and he clung to it.

When he found himself in the water, the boat was upturned, over him. Asked how long he remained under the boat, he replied, with a wan smile:

"It seemed an eternity, sir."

Later, he gave an estimate of from three-quarters of an hour to an hour for the time he was under the boat. He said he finally got from under and swam to the boat and was pulled up to the top.

"Was there and suction when the Titanic went down?" he was asked.

"I was swimming about 100 feet away when she sank," he replied, "and I didn't feel any suction."

Saw Captain Jump From Bridge.

He said that he saw Captain Smith of the Titanic jump from the bridge as the ship sank.

"Then the captain did not abandon the ship before she went down?"

"No, sir. The water was all over forward when he jumped."

Bride said that his chief, Phillips, was picked up on the upturned lifeboat, and that about forty men were on it. He said that dozens of men were in the water about the lifeboat, but they could not be taken aboard. Phillips, he said, died on the lifeboat before it was picked up by the Carpathia.

With the conclusion of Bride's story the session adjourned. It was resumed about 4 o'clock, when Senator Smith announced no further testimony would be taken and it would be resumed in Washington on Monday.

It is believed the adjournment to Washington was taken to allow the committee to acquire wider federal jurisdiction.

Senator Smith Explains Course of Committee.

Senator Smith, after the hearing adjourned, made a statement to the press in which he explained the course the committee had pursued during the inquiry at New York, and touched on the immediate steps to be taken at the Washington hearing, which will begin Monday. He said:

"The object of the committee in coming to New York coincidental with the arrival of the Carpathia was prompted by the desire to avail itself of first hand information from the active participants in this sad affair. Our course has been guided solely by this purpose—to obtain accurate information without delay.

"We were told that some of the officers of the Titanic who were British subjects and resided in England desired and intended to return to their homes immediately upon arrival at this port. We concluded that it would be most unfortunate if we were to be deprived of their testimony for any indefinite period, and their removal beyond the jurisdiction of our authority might complicate and possibly defeat our purpose.

"We went directly to the Carpathia upon her arrival; were received courteously by the captain and officers of the ship; were accorded a prompt interview with the managing director and vice president of the White Star line. We satisfied ourselves that their promise to appear insured their presence at the hearing and have not been called upon to use more drastic means to accomplish this result.

"Mr. Ismay intended to return to England forthwith, but at our request has remained here, as have the other officers and members of the crew.

"It was found necessary to take the testimony of the captain of the Carpathia immediately that he might not be further inconvenienced in his departure with his ship after his most creditable conduct, worthy of the highest praise. We felt that it would not be an evidence of our appreciation to detain him and his ship and passengers after he had brought the survivors of the Titanic voluntarily to this port. We examined the second officer because he was in command during the hours immediately preceding the collision and we thought it wise to take his testimony immediately.

"Mr. Bride, the wireless telegrapher on the Titanic who survived, had been injured and was unable to be conveniently moved from New York. As his testimony and the testimony of the wireless operator of the Carpathia were so intimately related, we concluded to take the testimony of both forthwith and in order that we might beyond peradventure have the statement of Mr. Ismay formally on record, we decided to take his testimony immediately. All were notified of the fact that we had not finished with them and they were requested to remain.

"After conferring with our associates we concluded to exercise our authority and formally subpoenae these officers, together with about twenty men of the ship's crew and take the further testimony at least for the time being at Washington, where the entire sub-committee could be present.

"In summoning the surviving passengers, many of whom were distressed, some quite ill and others injured, we have thought it wise to proceed with care and consideration for their physical and mental condition. Many of them have already been subpoenaed, but returns have not yet been made and I am unable to give a list of those subpoenaed to the press.

"I want to acknowledge our debt of gratitude to the representatives of the press for their marked consideration and courtesy and to assure them that everything that has transpired has been entirely in their presence and that this course will be pursued so far as I am concerned in the future hearings before the committee."

SURVIVORS ASK ASSISTANCE.

Penniless Victims of Titanic Wreck Apply at White Star Offices.

P. S. A. Franklin, vice president of the White Star Line, did not appear at the executive offices of the company yesterday, owing to the fact that he had to attend the investigation proceedings held at the Waldorf-Astoria Hotel.

During the day several survivors of the wrecked Titanic appeared at the offices of the company, looking for assistance. In all these instances the people applying for aid had been rendered penniless by the sinking of the Titanic.

In the afternoon Mrs. Florence Ware, a good-looking young Englishwoman, who was a passenger in the second class in the Titanic, visited the offices of the company, seeking aid. Her husband, who was coming to America with her, was drowned in the wreck. Florence Ware and his wife lived in Bristol, England. After having accumulated about a thousand dollars the couple decided to come to America and go in business at New Britain, Conn. Ware being a carpenter by trade, it was his intention to engage in the contracting carpenter business on a small scale. When the couple sailed for this country Ware carried with him about a thousand dollars in gold. In the excitement he forgot to give his wife the money when she got into the lifeboat, and as a result, when Ware perished, the savings of a lifetime went to the bottom of the Atlantic with him.

The White Star Line provided her with a railroad ticket to New Britain, Conn., where Mrs. Ware intends to remain for a time at the home of her brother-in-law, Charles Ware of 186 South Main street.

An official of the company informed Mrs. Ware that when she got ready to go back to England the company would cheerfully furnish her with passage.

CHICAGO FUND APPEAL.

Chicago, April 20—Mayor Harrison today issued another appeal for contributions to the Titanic relief fund following receipt of a cablegram from the Lord Mayor of London declaring that any financial aid given the sufferers by Chicago would be appreciated.

HOISTING TITANIC SURVIVORS FROM A LIFEBOAT TO THE CARPATHIA.

LITTLE BOYS SAW TITANIC MEN SHOT

Officers Used Revolvers on Those Too Eager to Reach Boats.

YOUNGSTERS' THRILLING TALE

"Jack" Thayer and William Carter Saved—Tell of Their Terrible Experience.

Philadelphia, April 20—Seventeen-year-old John B. Thayer, Jr., and William T. Carter, 10 years old, two small survivors of the Titanic wreck, told thrilling stories to-day of the disaster and the scenes that accompanied it. Master Carter seemed to remember most vividly the shooting of men who tried to get into the lifeboats with the women.

"The men were separate from the women," he said, "and the little boys and all the girls were with the women. The officers threatened to shoot any man who disobeyed and attempted to board a lifeboat.

"Once in a while a man would try to break through and there would be some shooting, for officers armed with gleaming revolvers stood guard over the men passengers. Once a lot of men got through and there was a lot of shooting. Several of the men fell to the deck. One stood still for a long time. His whole jaw was shot away. Then he fell to the deck. Just then it came time for mother and I to get aboard a boat and I saw no more of the shooting, but I could hear it at intervals."

Young Carter's mother and father and sister were also saved.

Jack Thayer's Father Lost in Disaster.

"Jack" Thayer, as he is known among his playmates, and his mother were saved, but his father, John B. Thayer, second vice president of the Pennsylvania Railroad, was lost. The shock of the tragic death of her husband and the horrible experiences to which she was subjected have laid Mrs. Thayer on a bed of sickness and grave fears are entertained for her recovery.

Jack tells a graphic story of being hurried from his berth to the deck, together with his mother and father, after hastily throwing about them what clothes they could find easily.

"I saw women all around me refusing to leave their husbands when the order came that the men must remain aboard while the women were taken off. Mother was one of them. She took me by the arm and endeavored to drag father to the man in charge of the lifeboat we were near.

"Father was in bed and mother and myself were about to get into bed when the boat struck. There was no great shock. I was on my feet at the time and I do not think it was enough to throw anyone down. I put on an overcoat.

Youngster Lost Track of His Father and Mother.

"Father and mother went ahead and I followed. They went down on 'B' deck and a crowd got in front of me and I was not able to catch them and lost sight of them.

"On the starboard side the boats were getting away quickly. Some boats were already off in a distance.

"The list to the port had been growing greater all the time. About this time the people began jumping from the stern. I thought of jumping myself, but was afraid of being stunned on hitting the water.

"Finally I jumped out feet first. I was clear of the ship; went down, and as I came up I was pushed away from the ship by some force. I came up facing the ship and one of the funnels seemed to be lifted off and fell toward me, about fifteen yards away, with a mass of sparks and steam coming out of it.

"I saw the ship in a sort of a red glare, and it seemed to me that she broke in two just in front of the third funnel. I was sucked down and as I came up my hands touched the cork fender of an overturned boat. I looked up and saw some men on the top and asked them to give me a hand. One of them helped me up. In a short time the bottom was covered with about 25 or 30 men.

"The assistant wireless operator was right next to me, holding on to me and kneeling in the water.

"We had the second officer, Mr. Lightholder, on board. He had an officer's whistle and whistled for the boat in the distance to come up and take us off. It took about an hour and a half for the boats to draw near. Two boats came up. The first took half and the other took the balance, including myself."

Late this afternoon it was reported that Mrs. George D. Widener, who lost her husband and son, was very low and was not expected to recover from the terrific shock. Grave fears are also entertained for the recovery of P. A. B. Widener, the father and grandfather of the lost Wideners. He has lain for hours at his country home, Elkins Park, in a state of stupor as a result of the death of his favorite son and grandson.

SUICIDE DUE TO DISASTER.

Santa Monico, aCl., April 20—The body of Mrs. M. U. Schuler, said to have been wealthy and from St. Louis, Mo., was found in the ocean here today. She had jumped to her death some time last night.

According to friends, Mrs. Schuler was much affected by the Titanic disaster, and it is believed her mind gave way.

THE NEW YORK HERALD.

NEW YORK, SUNDAY, APRIL 21, 1912.—120 PAGES.— BY THE NEW YORK HERALD COMPANY. [COPYRIGHT, 1912.] PRICE FIVE CENTS.

LOOKOUTS' WARNINGS OF ICEBERGS THRICE DISREGARDED WITHIN HALF HOUR OF CRASH DECLARES STEWARD, THE TITANIC'S CRY FOR HELP IGNORED, SAYS OPERATOR

Thomas Whiteley, Tells of Hearing Men Who Were in Crows Nest Express Indignation Because Mr. Murdock, the First Officer, Repeatedly Refused to Act on Their Report of Danger.

"NO WONDER MR. MURDOCK SHOT HIMSELF," SAID SAILOR WHO TOLD OF ICE AHEAD

Conversation of Two Men Who Saw Mountain of Ice That Caused the Disaster Overheard in Lifeboat by Man Now in St. Vincent's Hospital.

TO PLACE BLAME FOR FALSE MESSAGES

Senators Demand Full Explanation for Word to World That "All Aboard Are Safe" Hours After Vessel Had Gone to the Bottom—The Baltic Had Full Story, Committee Hears.

THAT three warnings were given to the officer on the bridge of the Titanic that icebergs were ahead, less than half an hour before the fatal crash was the declaration made last night by Thomas Whiteley, a first saloon steward aboard the vessel, who now lies in St. Vincent's Hospital with frozen and lacerated feet.

Mr. Whitney also says he understands that the first officer of the Titanic, Mr. Murdock, did shoot himself after the crash. This has been rumored, but never verified.

Mr. Whiteley does not attempt to explain why the warnings were ignored or why the speed of the vessel was not reduced or her course changed, but he is positive, he asserts that the first officer was warned distinctly three times. The warnings came from the two men in the crows' nest, Mr. Whiteley said, and the fact that their warning was unheeded caused the lookouts much indignation and much astonishment.

After being thrown from the Titanic while helping to lift women and children into the small boats, Mr. Whiteley finally swam to a small boat and was helped in. It was while there that he heard a conversation between the two lookouts, neither of whom he recalled having seen before, but who, he is confident, were on board the steamship.

WONDERED AT INDIFFERENCE OF OFFICER.

The two men talked freely in his hearing and expressed wonderment that their attempts to get the officer to slow up or take other precautionary methods to avoid the bergs had failed. Mr. Whiteley says he carefully marked every word they uttered.

"I don't recall the exact words of the men, but I am certain of the sentiment they expressed. They were very indignant. I was particularly astounded when I heard one of them say:—

"'No wonder Mr. Murdock shot himself.'"

Asked if he knew how the reports from the crows' nest to the first officer were made, whether in person or by telephone, the steward said he did nott know, but his idea was that it was done by bells—three bells meaning danger or straight ahead, two bells starboard and one bell port. "My only information is that I heard one of the two men say that he had reported to the first officer that he saw an iceberg."

"I heard one of them say," said he last night, in the hospital, "that at a quarter after eleven o'clock on Sunday, about twenty-five minutes before the great ship struck the berg, that he had told First Officer Murdock that he believed he had seen an iceberg. He said he was not certain, but that he saw the outline of something which he thought must be a berg. A short time later, the lookout said, he noticed what he thought was another mountain of ice. Again he called the attention of the first officer to it.

"A third time he saw something in the moonlight which he felt certain was an iceberg. The air was cool and there were indications to his mind that there were bergs in the neighborhood. A third time he reported to the first officer that he had seen an iceberg. This time, as I recall it, he did not say merely that he fancied he saw one, but that he actually had seen one.

"His words to the officer, as I remember them, were:—

"'I saw the iceberg. It was very large and to me it looked black, or rather a dark gray instead of white.'"

Mr. Whiteley is not in a serious condition and will be out soon. He is a man above the average intelligence and seems to be very certain of what he says. He was helping to pass women and children into the small boats when he was whipped overboard. It was only after considerable manoeuvering that he was able to get to a rowboat. He tells an interesting story about a small boat dubbed the "money boat."

"It was reported," said Mr. Whitehead, "that the chief occupant was a wealthy American, who had with him his wife and two valets. In addition there was in the boat seven fireman and coal trimmers. It was stated that the crew were to receive £5 each upon reaching safety, and it was true, I believe, for I saw an order for £5 given to one of the men by the reputed millionnaire. It was an ordinary piece of paper, made out to the Coutts Bank, of England."

Determined to fix the responsibility for the false messages sent out last Monday, announcing the safety of the Titanic hours after she had sunk off Newfoundland, and to ascertain every fact connected with the fatal crash, the Senate Committee investigating the disaster will continue exhaustive hearings in Washington and will cross examine not only all surviving officers of the vessel, but many American passengers. It is likely that Mrs. John Jacob Astor will be a witness.

The hearing was continued in this city yesterday, but late in the afternoon was adjourned until to-morrow in the national capital. There came a sensation yesterday when Harold T. Cottam, wireless operator of the Carpathia, testified that nothing had been flashed from his vessel which could have formed the basis for the alleged wireless despatch made public last Monday, stating that the Titanic was safe and was being towed to Halifax by the Virginian.

SEEKS SOURCE OF FALSE NEWS.

These despatches were presumably sent from the Carpathia, and they gave a great solace to the thousands who had relatives and friends aboard the vessel, and whose oonly information was that the great craft had struck an iceberg and was badly but not dangerously injured.

Senator Smith, chairman of the committee, laid great stress upon this point and made it clear that his purpose in pursuing the particular line of inquiry was to show that for some reason misinformation was circulated at a time when the truth should have been told.

Mystery from the start has surrounded the source of these reassuring messages—messages which convinced the entire world that the great vessel was safe, and it is the purpose of the committee to run them down. Particular attention will be paid to the despatch received from the White Star line on Monday by Representative Hughes, of Wes Virginia, stating that the Titanic was being towed to Halifax and that here passengers were safe.

Two of the most interesting developments of the day were the disclosure that the Baltic, of the White Star line, learned all the details of the disaster by wireless Monday morning from the Carpahia and that the Frankfort, a freighter, was in communication by wireless with the Titanic just after she hammed the ice crag, and that instead of steaming to the aid of the wrecked vessel she continued. She was bound from Galveston to Bremen.

SAYS THE "C. Q. D." WAS NOT HEEDED.

It was just after Harold Bride, assistant wireless operator of the Titanic, had afished his C. Q. D. signal, calling for immediate assistance, that he received reply from the Frankfort, which, Bride believes, was much nearer than the -pathia. The operator of the Frankfort did not reply to the satisfaction of Titanic's operator, and, knowing the Carpathia, a larger vessel ,to be not a distance away, Mr. Bride gave up trying to communicate with the Frank- d called upon the Carpathia to come at once.

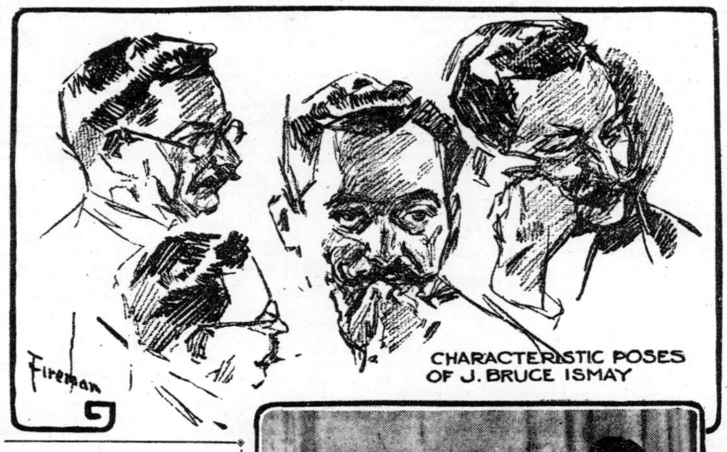

CHARACTERISTIC POSES OF J. BRUCE ISMAY

England's Grief Voiced in Dirge by Hall Caine

[SPECIAL CABLE TO THE HERALD.]

HERALD BUREAU, No. 130 FLEET STREET, LONDON, Saturday.

Hall Caine has written the following poem, entitled "The Titanic," which will be sung to the tune of "O God, Our Help in Ages Past," at a great memorial service in the City Temple to-morrow night:—

THE TITANIC.

Lord of the everlasting hills,
God of the boundless sea,
Help us through all the shocks of fate
To keep our faith in thee.

When nature's unrelenting arm
Sweeps us like withes away,
Maker of man, be thou our strength
And our eternal stay

When blind insenate heartless force
Puts out our passing breath,
Make us to see thy guiding light
In darkness and in death.

Beneath the roll of soundless waves,
Our best and bravest lie,
Give us to feel their spirits live
Immortal in the sky.

We are thy children frail and small,
Formed of the lowly sod;
Comfort our bruised and bleeding souls,
Father and Lord and God.

H. BRIDE H. T. COTTAM

Says Uncle Sam Cannot Hold British Seamen

Marconi Official Protests Against Detention of Wireless Man as Witness.

Can the United States government hold British seamen not charged with any crime and compel them to remain in this countryand givetestimony?

This question was raised yesterday afternoon by Frederick Sammis, chief engineer of theMarconi Company of America.

The burden of Mr. Sammis' complaint was that the company was forced to keep H. T. Cottam, the Marconi operator of the Carpathia, in New York when the vessel left New York on Friday, and put in his place the operator of the Mauritania, which steams next Thursday. If Cottam cannot be sent out with the Mauretania because his presence is desired in Washington the Marconi company will be put to some inconvenience.

"They cannot hold a British seaman and force him to leave his ship," said Mr. Sammis to a HERALD reporter. "The British Consulate may e counted upon to look after that. These men have signed for a voyage, and it is not completed until they return to the point of embarking."

He was asked if any complaint had been made to the British Ambassador at Washington, or if any protest had been received from the British Embassy. He said there had not, so far as he knew. He appeared to be very indignant, however.

ASKED ABOUT BRICK TRUST.

Head of the Brockaway Company Testifies at Inquiry Before Magistrate.

Edward B. Brockaway, president of the Brockaway Brick Company, at Fishkill Landing, N. Y., was questioned yesterday by Assistant District Attorney Ellison in the investigation being conducted before Magistrate Freschi, in Tombs Police Court, into the business methods of the Greater New York Brick Company. Mr. Brockaway is a director of the corporation.

"Our total output of brick is consigned to the Greater New York company, "Mr. Brockaway said. "I don't know who in the office of the company fixes the price of brick, but I presume it is State Senator John B. Rose, its president. The brick we consign to the company is sold at the prices fixed by it."

The hearing will be continued next Tuesday.

'Keep Your Mouth Shut; Big Money for You,' Was Message to Hide News

Hold Story for 'Four Figures,' Marconi Official Also Warned the Carpathia Operator, While Anxious World Waited Details of Disaster.

While the world was waiting three days for information concerning the fate of the Titanic, for part of the time at least, details concerning the disaster were being withheld by the wireless operator of the steamship Carpathia aunder specfic orders from T. W. Sammis, chief engineer of the Marconi Wireless Company of America, who had arrangefor the sale of the story.

This was admitted yesterday by Mr. Sammis, who defended his action. He said he was justified in getting for the wireless operators the largest amount he could for the details of the sinking of the ship, the rescue of the passengers and the other information the world had waited for.

The first information concerning the loss of the Titanic came Monday evening, and it was known at that time the survivors were on board the Carpathia. About midnight the first of the list of survivors began to come by wireless, and from that time until Thursday night, when the rescue ship arrived in port, the world waited and waited in vain for the details of how the "unsinkable ship" had gone down.

Three messages were sent to the Carpathia telling the operator to send out no news concerning the disaster. Two of these were unsigned, and the last one had the signature of Mr. Sammis.

"Keep Mouth Shut; Big Money."

The first message was unsigned, and it is said it was sent as a list of names of survivors were being forwarded. It read:—

"Keep your mouth shut. Hold story. Big money for you."

The messages from the Carpathia to the Marconi office concerning this matter were not available, but there was evidently some communication, for the second unsigned message followed after an interval. This message read:—

"If you are wise, hold story. The Marconi company wil ltake care of you."

The third and last message was addressed to "Marconi officer, the Carpathia and the Titanic," and signed "S. M. Sammis," chief engineer of the Marconi Company of America. This one read:—

"Stop. Say nothing. Hold your story for dollars in four figures. Mr. Marconi agreeing. Will meet you at dock."

Mr. Sammis was at the Waldorf-Astoria yesterday at the hearing before the subcommittee of the United States Senate, and he was asked about the message.

Mr. Sammis Resents Criticism.

"It is reported," he was told, "that a message was sent by you to the wireless operator on the Carpathia in which you gave the orders or at least said to him not to give out any details of the sinking of the Titanic, as you had arranged for four figures."

"Well?" he said in a defiant way.

"Did you sen such a message?"

"Maybe. What of it?" he replied.

"It would be interesting to know if you actually sent such a message."

"Yes, I sent the message, but whose business is it?" Mr. Sammis asked with some heat.

"Perhaps it was no one's business," he was told, "but it is interesting to know that when the world was horror stricken over the disaster and waiting for the news, that there were persons preparing to capitalize the suspense and had arranged for 'four figures.'"

"Do you blame me for this," retorted Mr. Sammis, as he backed up against the wall. "Do you blame me for getting the highest price I could for the operator for the story he had to tell about the collision and the rescue. I though I was doing a good turn for him, and I can't see how it is the business of anyone."

It is not unlikely that the sending of these messages with the apparent result that no details of the disaster came from the relief ship will form part of the inquiry that is being made by a sub-committee of the Senate. Part of this inquiry has been directed as to why a message from President Taft asking for information about Major Archibald W. Butt was unanswered, and it is not unlikely that in view of the message from Mr. Sammis that this will be taken up again.

Navy Likely to Have Records.

While these messages were intercepted by more than one wireless receiving station, there is one place where the Senate Committee could undoubtedly get copies of them. The New York Navy Yard has a powerful receiving station, and has what is known as an "intercepted message" book. These messages are considered confidential and are never given out, but the book would undoubtedly be at the disposal of the nivestigating committee.

Senator Smith said yesterday that the authorities in Washington knew on Thursday long before the Carpathia arrived, that the White Star line was contemplating the return of part of the Titanic crew to England by the steamship Cedric, and this information undoubtedly came from a government station.

John W. Griggs, one time Attorney General of the United States and Governor of New Jersey, is president of the Marconi Wireless Company of America. He said last night he had not heard that the chief engineer of the company was marketing the information of the disaster.

"This is a matter which will be looked into," he said. "I know nothing about it, had not heard of it before, and, of course, cannot say what will be done until it is brought to my attention in an official way."

Man at the Key Aboard the Titanic Called the Frankfort's Operator "A Fool" When the Call for Help Failed to Bring Promise of Aid, Witness Tells Senators.

CLUNG TO THE CARPATHIA, SAYS WITNESS, ALTHOUGH OTHER VESSEL SEEMED NEARER

Mrs. John Jacob Astor and Other Prominent American Women Will Be Called to Tell Investigators Their Version of the Disaster.

MR. ISMAY IS NOT PERMITTED TO GO HOME

Sergeant at Arms of Senate Technically in Charge of White Star Lins Officers and Seamen, Who Are Notified to Testify in Washington.

WITH J. Bruce Ismay and P. A. S. Franklin, of the White Star line, and forty other witnesses, mostly officers and seamen from the Titanic, technically in the custody of the sergeant-at-arms of the Senate. the investigation in New York of the loss of the Titanic was brought to an end yesterday afternoon by the sub-committee of the United States Senate.

In Washington to-morrow morning Senators William Alden Smith, of Michigan, chairman, and the full committee will take up the work anew and will press the inquiry with vigor.

Witnesses who have been served with the Senate's summons include Harold Thomas Cottam, wireless operator of the Carpathia; Harold Bride, Jr., wireless operator of the lost ship; five of the Titanic's officers and thirty of her surviving seamen and firemen.

Daniel M. Ransdell, Sergeant-at-Arms of the Senate, will produce the witnesses in Washington before the full membership of the investigating committee. Mr. Ismay will be cross-examined, each of the Senators being armed with the testimony given by others who were present on board the vessel when she struck.

When the men on the Titanic, British seamen, have been heard under oath by the committee they will be allowed to return to their homs. The Senate committee will then turn its attention without delay to the accounts of the wreck by American survivors.

To Call Mrs. Astor Before Committee.

That Mrs. John Jacob Astor will be called seems certain. Other women will be heard, among them Mrs. L. P. Smith, daughter of Representative James A. Hughes, of West Virginia. Like Mrs. Astor, she lost her husband in the wreck because he insisted on staying behind and allowing the women and children to go first.

Almost all the men who escaped—the Americans who manned the boats or who, like Colonel Archibald Gracie, of Washington, went down with the ship and managed later to stramble aboard an upturned lifeboat—will be called as witnesses.

"We must hear the Englishmen first," said Senator Smith a few minutes before he and Senator Newlands left early this morning for Washington, "because they need to get back home as soon as possible. We will be able to get the Americans whenever we want them."

It has been suggested to Senator Smith that the British government might offer objections to the keeping of British seamen in this country in the circumstances.

"I am proceeding," said Mr. Smith, "just as if there was not the slightest possibility of such a protest. Should one come we will deal with it at that time."

The committee has in mind the drafting of important legislation as the result of its hearing. Regulation of the use of the air by wireless operators, so as to prevent interference in times of wrecks at sea, is one law seems certain to be enacted. Another is legislation requiring not only American but all foreign vessels using American ports to be equipped with enough lifeboats to take off every passenger and every one of the crew if need be. Patrol of the steamship lanes for icebergs is another.

TO INVESTIGATE FALSE MESSAGES.

It is not unlikely that the committee will recommend and Congress enact a law requiring ships, at least those under American registry, to carry two wireless operators, so that one may be on duty while the other sleeps. The President is likely to be asked by a joint resolution of Congress to open negotiations with foreign Powers to establish a new and much more southerly steamship lane across the Atlantic by international agreement.

It developed to-day that the Senate Committee intends to make one of the most important features of its work an examination into the false messages that were given out last Monday, when it was said that the Titanic had struck an iceberg but that she was in tow of the Virginian, which was taking her to Halifax and that all on board were safe. At that time the ship had been at the bottom of the ocean many hours and more than 1,500 drowned.

One of these announcements was made to Representative Hughes. Anxious about his daughter he telegraphed to the White Star office from his home in Huntington, W. Va. esterday at the inquiry Senator Smith produced a reply, which Representative Hughes received, at a quarter to nine o'clock Monday night, announcing that all the passengers and crew were safe and that the Titanic was being towed to Halifax, where she was due Tuesday.

OPERATOR DENIES SENDING FALSE REPORT.

"Did you at any time send any message or pick up any message or hear of any message which could be used as the basis for such a telegram as that?" demanded Senator Smith of Harold T. Cottam, the Carpathia's wireless operator.

"No, sir, I did not, sir."

This emphatic reply summed up the testimony of Cottam lasting for nearly an hour on this point. Senator Smith insisted on going over the ground many times and of making sure that Cottam had given no excuse for the false news from the White Star line.

"I sent the real news of the sinking of the Titanic in a message to the Baltic at ten o'clock Monday morning," said the operator.

But it remained for Harold Bride, the junior wireless operator of the Titanic, to surprise the committee. He went down with the ship, rose again and got on the same raft with Colonel Gracie. His ankles are injured badly, one being broken, and his back is wrenched. He was taken in a wheeled chair to the Waldorf-Astoria, where the investigation was held. Guglielmo Marconi, inventor of wireless telegraphy and head of the Marconi companies of America and Europe, assisted him.

During the time the two operators gave their testimony before the committee, and particularly when Senator Smith was seeking to find out just what messages, if any, had been sent and received by Mr. Ismay either on board the Titanic or the Carpathia the managing director of the White Star line pulled his chair closer and sat with his face within three feet of the witnesses.

SAYS THE "C. Q. D." WAS IGNORED.

The Frankfort, of the North German Lloyd line, according to Mr. Bride, was first to answer the "C. Q. D." call of the sinking Titanic, but she did not respond. Instead, her operator asked questions and Phillips, the senior operator of the Titanic, told him he was "a fool" and to "keep out of it."

"Phillips preferred to hang on to a certainty in the shape of the Carpathia, which was coming full speed for us, than wait to answer questions from the Frankfort, even though the force of her sending seemed to indicate she was much nearer," said Bride.

"When we sent out our 'C. Q. D.' signal we could say nothing stronger," he added. "She should have responded at once, but we never heard from her again nor saw her."

Bride said that when he was on duty about five o'clock last Sunday night on board the Titanic the Californian tried to get him in order to give an ice report, but he did not answer because he was writing out a record. A half hour

THE PART THE WIRELESS PLAYED IS TOLD BY MEN AT THE KEY

later, he said, he heard the Californian giving the same ice report to the Baltic and he took it. The California, he said, reported that she had passed three large icebergs and gave their exact position, which Bride could not remember yesterday. He reported this information to the officer on the bridge of the Titanic, he testified.

Never Reported "All Safe," Says Wireless Operator

H. T. Cottam Tells Senate Investigating Committee He Did Not Send Message Reported Given Out by White Star Officers.

Harold Thomas Cottam, wireless operator of the Carpathia, was recalled to the witness stand by the committee of the United States Senate which is investigating the sinking of the Titanic when the inquiry was resumed at the Waldorf-Astoria yesterday morning. Senator Smith, of Michigan, chairman of the committee, asked the operator to tell more about messages he received and sent on the night of the tragedy.

"The last message we received from the Titanic," said Cottam, "was that we must hurry, as they were sinking."

"I sent word by direction of the Captain of the Carpathia that they get their lifeboats ready, that we had ours ready and were making all possible speed toward the Titanic."

"Did you receive any communication either from the Marconi coast stations or any other station or any officer of the White Star line from the time of the wreck until you reached New York?" asked Senator Smith.

"I was in communication with some ship nearly all of the time."

"Were you in communication with any officer of the White Star line?"

"I got one or two official messages by way of the Baltic, but I cannot tell whether they were signed or what they were about now."

"Did you receive any message indicating a desire that the true state of things be kept as confidential?"

"No, sir. I informed the Baltic about half-past ten o'clock Monday morning, the day after the wreck, that the Titanic had sunk and that we had the survivors. I gave all the details. She was steaming toward the scene of the wreck, but I do not know how far away she was at the time. I told the Baltic that we were returning to New York with the survivors."

"Never Reported All Safe."

"Did you say anything then or at any other time about Halifax?"

"No, sir—yes, sir. I believe I did mention Halifox once. I believe I told the Baltic that we were bound for Halifax. The captain hald told me that and then changed his mind—I mean the captain of the Carpathia."

"Did you at any time on Monday send a message to the Baltic or anywhere else that all the passengers and crew were safe and that the Titanic was being towed to Halifax?"

"No, sir."

"Or anythting resembling that?"

"No, sir."

"Then I am to understand that you did not in any way attempt to withhold the exact facts about the sinking of the Titanic?"

"That is right, sir."

"Did you pick up or hear of any message at any time on Monday or Tuesday from any source whatever indicating a rumor about Halifax?"

"No, sir."

"Your only message mentioning Halifax was the first you sent to the Baltic, which you have told us about?"

"Yes, sir, except that I may have sent that same message to other ships."

"You were not instructed by anybody not to send the full details of the actual conditions?"

"No."

"Did you send any communication indefinite enough to be construed so as to indicate that the Titanic was being towed to Halifax?"

"No, sir."

Worked Till He Fell Asleep.

"Such a message would have been false, would it not?"

"Yes, sir."

"You know that of your own knowledge that it would have been false?"

"Yes, sir."

"If the White Star line sent the following telegram:—

" 'New York, April 15, 1912.

" 'James A. Hughes, Huntington, W. Va.:—

" 'Titanic proceeding to Halifax. Passengers probably land there Tuesday. All safe. (Signed) White Star Line.'

"The information contained therein did not come from you, did it?"

"No, sir," emphatically.

This telegram, it is said, was received by Representative Hughes at a quarter to nine P. M. at Huntington. He was present at the hearing yesterday. Mr. Hughes is the father of Mrs. L. P. Smith, who was saved from the wreck and whose husband stayed and was drowned. Senator Smith, when he asked the question, had the telegram in his hand and read from it.

"Nor did such information come from any other operator on board the Carpathia?" insisted Senator Smith.

"No, sir."

"You were at your instrument all the time Sunday night, all day Monday, Monday night, all day Tuesday, and fell asleep a while Tuesday night, awaking at dawn. Is that correct?"

"Yes, sir."

"When did Mr. Bride, the operator of the Titanic, relieve you?"

"I think it was Wednesday afternoon, about five o'clock, sir."

Mr. Ismay Listens Attentively.

Senator Smith went over this ground again and again to show that Cottam was at his post all the time and would have known if any messages were going through the air within the radius of the wireless instrument of the Carpathia.

During this part of Cottam's testimony Mr. Ismay sat so close to him that he could have touched him by reaching out with his hand. Guglielmo Marconi, head of the British and American Marconi companies, sat directly behind. Both were listening intently.

"Bride could not walk or even stand on account of the injuries he had received in the wreck," continued Cottam.

"What was Bride's mental condition when he relieved you? Was he lucid?" asked Senator Smith.

"No, he was not lucid. He was all right."

The operator's little slip broke for a moment the tension of the inquiry.

"I understand that you say he was all right?" asked Senator Smith.

"Yes, sir."

"If Bride had sent any messages about the safety of the passengers you would have known it, would you not?"

"Yes. I was in charge and remained in the room with him."

"Did he send any such message?"

"No, sir."

"Did anybody talk to you in New York after you got back about any messages of this nature?" asked Senator Smith.

"Yes. Somebody asked me if I had sent a message telling that the Titanic was going to Halifax and that everybody was safe. I do not remember who it was, but I think it was a reporter. I told him 'No.' "

Describes the Titanic's Wireless.

Senator Smith led Cottam back to the point when he got his first message from the Titanic. He said it was this:—

"C Q D, old man. It is a distress call."

"Why did he call you 'old man.'?"

"I guess it was a compliment to me. I did not give that part of it to the captain."

Harold S. Bride, twenty-two years old, the junior wireless operator of the Titanic, who got on an upturned lifeboat after the ship had sunk and was saved, had been sitting some distance away in an easy chair, one of his feet bandaged above the ankle. Mr. Marconi assisted in drawing his chair up to the table when Senator Smith called for him.

Bride looked even more of a boy than Cottam. He said his experience as a wireless operator at sea had been confined to three voyages to this country and two to Brazil. Each time he was the only operator on board except in one instance, when he was junior operator on board the Lusitania.

The wireless set on board the Titanic, he said, was of the latest type, with a carrying power of four hundred miles by day and a practically limitless power at night. He said it had been tested on the trial trip.

"No Speed Orders."

"Were you pretty busy on the Sunday of the accident—last Sunday?" asked Senator Smith.

"Yes, up to the time she struck the ice we had sent 250 commercial messages on the whole trip and many were sent on Sunday."

"Did you ever send or receive any message by or to Mr. Ismay while aboard the ship relating to her speed?"

"Yes, when the ship was going from Belfast to Southampton. I cannot recall anything about the messages, just which way they went or what they said, except that the general idea of them was that the trial speed had been very favorable."

"Did he send or receive any messages through you after you left Southampton?"

"No, sir; I think not. Not to my knowledge."

"Did he send or receive any through Phillips?"

"I can't say, sir."

"Did he send any after the collision?"

"No."

"Did he send or receive any last Sunday?"

"I can't recall."

"Did the captain receive any official message regarding the speed of the ship?"

"No."

"Did you hear Phillips say anything about any such message?"

"No, sir."

"Did the captain or any other officer of the ship send any message to the White Star officials or any one of them about the speed of the ship or the weather or her position?"

"No. The captain only exchanged compliments with the captain of the Baltic and mentioned the good weather."

Gets Report of Icebergs.

"Have you any knowledge of a message from the Amerika about icebergs?"

"No, sir; I know nothing about that, although Mr. Phillips may have received such a message and not told me. Late Sunday afternoon, I think about five o'clock, I received a message from a ship whose call was M W L—I think it was the Californian—saying she had passed three large icebergs and giving their position."

Frederick Semis, engineer of the American Marconi Company, told the committee that M W L was the call of the Californian.

"She was transmitting the ice report to the Baltic when I took it," explained Bride. "She had tried to get me about twenty or thirty minutes before to give me the ice report, but I was busy making out a record and I did not take it. Later when I heard it going to the Baltic I knew it was the same that was intended for me, so I took it and gave it to the officer on the bridge. It was not official, however, for it was not intended for me.

"This was my first information about any icebergs. I confirmed it with the Californian before losing her. She gave the latitude and longitude of the icebergs, but I cannot recall it. The captain was not on the bridge and I did not take it to him. I do not know who the officer was on the bridge to whom I gave it.

I relieved Phillips for dinner between seven and half-past seven P. M. Sunday. When he came back I went to bed. That was about eight o'clock. I was in bed when the collision came. It did not awake me. I awoke a little while later, I think about five minutes to twelve, because I had promised to relieve Phillips a little earlier than usual that night. We took six hour watches, turn about. I went from the adjoining cabin into the operating room without dressing and asked Phillips how he was getting on. He said he had just finished a big batch of telegrams for Cape Race. I went back and got dressed.

"When I came out a few minutes later Phillips said the ship had been damaged in some way and might have to go back to where she was built in Ireland. I took the watch and he went into the other cabin. Pretty soon the Captain came in and said to me, 'You had better get assistance.'

The Carpathia Answers.

"Mr. Phillips heard him from the other room and came in to where we were. He asked the Captain if it was a distress call he wanted sent. The Captain said 'Yes,' and Phillips went to the instrument and started sending the 'C. Q. D.' immediately."

At this point Senator Smith had Mr. Marconi explain just what "C. Q. D." means. He said that it was the original distress call of the Marconi companies. Since it was established, he said, the Berlin convention has adopted "S. O. S." as the distress call, but the Marconi operators all over the world still use the "C. Q. D." usually and that signal is better known everywhere by operators of all companies than is the "S. O. S." signal.

" 'C Q' means 'all stations,' " he explained, "and the 'D' means danger. Thus literally the call means 'All stations take notice, danger.' There is another signal, 'D D D,' which means all stations shut up except the two who are talking. This is known as the 'silence signal.' "

Continuing his story, Bride said that Phillips got a reply almost immediately from the Frankfort and gave her our position. Phillips sent me to tell the captain, who had gone outside, that we were in touch with the Frankfort. He was on the boat deck. He told me to get the Frankfort's position and I said I would as soon as possible. I went back and found that the Carpathia had also answered. Phillips thought that the Frankfort was nearer from the force of the signal, but he was not sure. He gave the Carpathia our position and in a few minutes the Carpathia's operator had obtained his position from the bridge and sent it to us with the statement that the Carpathia had reversed her course and was steaming at full speed toward the Titanic's position.

"I went out and found the captain in the wheelhouse on the bridge and told him about the Carpathia. He came back with me to the operating room and worked out roughly the difference between the position of the Titanic and the Carpathia. After that he went outside again. I took the telephone receiver and Phillips went out to see what was going on.

Blames the Frankfort.

"When Phillips gave the Frankfort our position her operator told us to wait for him. 'Stand by' was what he said. But apparently the Frankfort's operator or her captain did not take the steps we expected to result from the 'C. Q. D.' Twenty minutes after we first got the Frankfort we got in touch with her again and the operator asked, 'What is the matter with you.' Phillips replied, 'You're a fool! Keep out!' and did not tell him. Phillips and I both knew that the signal we had sent was sufficient to make any ship come toward us as fast as possible without asking questions. He should have given us the Frankfort's position and he did not.

"Meantime the Olympic told us she was coming. We thought the best thing to do was to hang on to the Carpathia and not take chances with the Frankfort. We did not want to lose time answering questions."

"Did you ever learn the position of the Frankfort?" asked Senator Smith.

"No, sir. She had told us to stand by and that meant that she wanted us to wait until she could give us her position. We thought the Frankfort operator derelict in his duty and that the Frankfort was not doing what she should have done when she got our distress signal. We realized then what had happened to the Titanic, and decided that we would stick to the Carpathia as the best chance. Any operator in the world knows the meaning of 'C. Q. D.' It means 'Come at once!' It was the strongest thing we could have said."

"How do you know the other operator got it correctly?" asked Senator Smith.

Says Operator Knew Signal.

"Because Phillips sent it himself very slowly and repeated it many times."

"Did you ever see the Frankfort thereafter?"

"No, sir."

Senator Smith wanted to know why in such an emergency Phillips did not reply that the Titanic was sinking and the lives of passengers and crew were in danger.

"It takes time to send messages. If that operator had understood his business no such thing would have been necessary. He didn't know his position. That's all."

"Do you mean to say that in such times he would not answer a simple question like 'What is the matter with you?' "

"We didn't know for sure whether the Frankfort was nearer."

"Was your object in not answering the somewhat tardy message of the Frankfort that you wanted to hold to a certainty?"

"That was just it."

"If the Frankfort had been twenty miles nearer to you than the Carpathia would you have thought the same?"

"We would have used our judgment. We had told the Frankfort all that we could in that distress signal and the giving of our position."

Here Mr. Marconi was questioned again. He said he thought the Frankfort was fitted with the German Marconi wireless system and the operator beyond all doubt must have known the meaning of "C Q D."

"There can be absolutely no doubt about that," said the inventor of wireless telegraphy. "Under the regulations which the operator must have known that call was amply sufficient to bring instant relief."

"Could not the Frankfort have heard everything you were saying to the Carpathia and her reply?" asked Senator Smith of Bride.

"Certainly she could if her operator was on the job. Phillips thought that if he could not understand our first call he could not get anything else."

"Did he get the message about his being a fool?"

"I don't think so. It was sent too fast for him," was the reply of Bride.

"You evidently haven't much of an opinion of that operator." Bride shrugged his shoulder as he said, "He should have understood."

Senator Smith led the witness to tell of the final scenes before he left the ship.

"You sent one message after putting on a life belt?"

"Yes, 'C Q D M G Y,' which meant 'Waiting for some one to answer.' "

"That was the last you saw of your apparatus?"

"Yes."

The witness said that he then went out on deck and saw many persons looking for life belts. There were no big lifeboats left, but one collapsible boat above the officers' quarters, he said. He verified the testimony of Charles W. Lightoller in regard to the way this boat was got away.

"It was washed over the side of the ship. I grabbed it and went down with it. I came up under the overturned boat."

Finally the boat was righted, he said, and he clambered into it. Men floating in the water with life belts on also were pulled in. Phillips, the senior wireless operator, was one of these. He died from exposure on the way to the Carpathia.

"Were there any other dead men in this boat?" he was asked.

"There was a man lying aft who they said was dead. In all there were thirty-five or forty men in this boat, but no women."

"Did you see Mr. Ismay at any time?"

"I did not."

In response to a question as to when he last saw Captain Smith the witness said:—

"I saw him when he went overboard from the bridge. He jumped overboard as we were trying to launch the collapsible lifeboat."

"How long was this before the ship went down?"

"About five minutes."

"Did the Captain have on a life belt?"

"Not when I last saw him."

"Tell the last you saw of the ship."

"She was then practically under water. The bridge was submerged. The stern came out of the water and she slipped down fore and aft."

"The Captain went with his vessel?"

"Practically so, sir."

"Was there any suction?"

"No, sir. I was possibly 150 feet from the Titanic when she sank and I was swimming at the time. I felt practically no suction at all."

Senator Smith stated that he appreciated the fact the witness was not well and thanked him for his uncomplaining and manly attitude.

"I will not press you further to-day, but I will ask you to hold yourself subject to the call of the committee and be ready to respond when we want you again."

It was almost four o'clock when the committee resumed the hearing in the afternoon. Senator Smith asked, if Charles W. Lightoller, the second officer of the Titanic, was in the room. It was announced that he had gone out to buy a pair of shoes.

H. J. Pittman, third officer, was called. He said his home was in Somersetshire, England.

He was asked if the ship's log had been preserved, and replied that so far as he knew it had gone down with the ship.

Senator Smith then announced that the hearing was closed for the day.

MRS. ASTOR AND OTHER AMERICAN WOMEN TO BE CALLED BY SENATE COMMITTEE

Hearings before the investigating committee of the United States Senate will be resumed in Washington to-morrow, when J. Bruce Ismay and P. A. S. Franklin will be called to the stand. The four surviving officers of the Titanic also will be called to testify.

Mrs. John Jacob Astor, Mrs. George D. Widener, Mrs. J. B. Thayer, Colonel Archibald Gracie and a score of others among the American survivors also will be requested to appear and give their version of the disaster.

Twenty-eight of the crew have been subpoenaed and are under arrest and in the care of E. L. Cornelius, assistant sergeant-at-arms of the Senate, to be produced at Monday's hearings.

The Marconi operators, H. T. Cottam and Harold Bride, have been instructed to hold themselves in readiness to give additional testimony in Washington.

The four surviving officers of the Titanic are C. H. Lightoller, second officer; H. J. Pittman, third officer; J. G. Roxhall, fourth officer, and H. G. Lowe, fifth officer.

Twenty-eight of the Titanic's crew, who had expected to leave New York on board the Lapland for England, have been required to remain.

BRITISH EMBASSY RECEIVES PROTEST

HERALD BUREAU,
No. 1,502 H STREET, N. W.,
WASHINGTON, D. C., Saturday.

That the action of the Senate committee of inquiry in questioning British subjects and demanding their attendance here to give information about the Titanic disaster may involve the governments of Great Britain and the United States was indicated here to-day by reports that protest had been made to the British Embassy against the committee's action in recalling from the steamship Lapland the wireless operator and fifteen of the Titanic's crew. The British Embassy does not deny that the protest has been received, but refers all inquiries to the American Department of State.

Huntington Wilson, Assistant Secretaary of State, said to-night that no word had reached the department from the British Embassy on the subject to-day, but the reports indicate that the protest has only just been made, so that it will be Monday at the earliest before any official action by the Embassy may be expected.

Bullets and Fists Kept Frenzied Mob from Trampling Women on Steerage Deck

Hungarian Physician Aboard the Carpathia Learns from Foreign Survivors Tale of Horror as Armed Stokers Emerge from Bowels of Vessel and Fight Sailors and Petty Officers, Who Drive Them Back from Swarming Into the Lifeboats.

Humble heroes who went to their deaths aboard the Titanic fighting a frenzied mob of armed brutes attempting to crowd women and children from the lifeboats were the British sailors and petty officers of the Titanic stationed on the steerage deck. Up from the stoke hole, a blackened frantic crew surged upon the steerage passengers, when the icy flood rushed in about the boilers far below and carried the alarm to the scores that fed them.

Armed with the tools of their trade, stoking bars, shovels, ashpan hoes and levelers, the stokers and coal passers stormed the line of steadfast sailormen guarding the boats then coming down the sides from the upper decks and loading into them as they were halted at the steerage deck the women and children there. Under the onslaught of these mad ruffians order already dearly bought was again driven out. Manhood met brutehood undaunted, however, an honest fists faced iron bars, winning at last the battle for death with honor.

No tale of the final hour of the great steamship exceeds in horror that pieced together by Dr. Lengyl Arpad, a Hungarian and steerage physician of the Carpathia, from the stories he gleaned as he bent over the bruised, the scalded and the frostbitten men and women who had been rescued from the steerage of the Titanic. He told it to the HERALD with all the smiles gone from his chubby jovial face.

Where Shots Were Fired.

His account cleared up many statements of cabin passengers which have seemed contradictory, told where the shots that were fired came from, and explained the shrieking which many had attributed to the doomed and drowning.

"There was great fright in the steerage from the moment the ship struck the ice, all of the passengers told me," Dr. Arpad said. "Some who had been on deck said that just before the crash, they heard the lookout on the forward mast just above them shout out a warning.

"Piling up to their deck, shouting and crying, dragging their bundles, the men and women were at first beyond control. Sailors went among them telling them tha ship had struck the ice, but was not in danger, and they grew calmer. Just as the boats began to come down from the upper deck, the steamship listed heavily to starboard, and the steerage passengers were piled up against the rail. This renewed their terror and they fought to extricate themselves.

"Despair took possesion of them because the first and second boats lowered past them were not stopped at that deck and neither was half filled. They said there were not more than fifteen in the first boat and probably eighteen in the second, though each would have held fifty. They seem from their accounts to have been perfectly frantic, believing they were being deserted when the petty officers and sailors came along to take charge of loading the boats.

"When the first boat was stopped at the steerage deck everyone surged forward to get into it, the men forcing themselves to the front and none of them, so far as they told me, thinking of anything but his own safety and his precious bundles. One woman rescued could talk of nothing bu the 'beautiful goose liver and cheese' they had torn from her. The first boat stopped was filled with men before the sailors could interfere. They had a battle to drag out the men and let the women take their places. Many of the women had enormous bundles on their heads or in their arms and they fought like demons to keep them.

"Every boat that came down after the first two and which was not already full was stopped at the steerage deck, they told me, but those who went off in the last to leace declared that there were still hundreds crowding at the rail, shrieking and praying and screaming, many of them completely mad with fright.

Stokers Fight Sailors.

"This great panic seems to have begun when the stokers rushed up from below and tried to beat a path through the steerage men and women and through the sailors and officers to get into the boats. They had their iron bars and shovels and they struck down all who stood in their way.

"The first to come up from the depths of the ship was an engine oiler. From what he is reported to have said I think perhaps the steam fittings were broken, and many were scalded to death when the Titanic listed. He said he had to dash through a narrow place beside a broken pipe and his back was frightfully scalded.

"Right at his heels came the stokers. The officers had pistols, but they could not use them at first for fear of killing the women and children. The sailors fought with their fists and many of them took the stoke bars and shovels from the stokers and used them to beat back the others. Then it seems, from what the survivors told me, the officers thought of firing in the air.

"One of the stokers, a Chinese, managed to slip into a boat, an officer saw him just as the boat was lowered and shot at him. Those in that boat with whom I talked said the bullet did not hit the stoker and the officer seemed afraid to shoot again for fear of hitting others.

"Many of the coal passers and stokers who had been driven back from the boats went to the rail and whenever a boat was filled and lowered several of them jumped overboard and swam toward it trying to climb aboard. Several of the patients I had said that men who swam to the sides of their boats were pulled in or climbed in.

"Dozens of the cabin passengers were witnesses of some of the frightful scenes on the steerage deck. The steerage survivors told me that often the women from the upper decks were the only cool persons in the life boats and they tried to quiet the steerage women who were nearly all half crazy.

"Only a few of the steerage passengers rescured wore life preservers and none of them remembered orders to put them on. It may have been because they did not understand English.

Women Cry for Husbands.

"The first cry of nearly every woman when we got her to the deck of the Carpathia was:—

"'Where is my husband?' or 'Where is my father?' Mothers and daughters, who had escaped on different lifeboats, greeted each other with heartrendering cries. Others not so fortunate looked across the sea for hours, watching and praying for sight of their loved ones. Many were under the impression that other passengers had been rescued by other steamships and would be found in New York.

"A pretty Spanish girl, a bride of a few weeks, had to be restrained by force from jumping overboard when she found that her husband was not on board the Carpathia.

"Mrs. Astor and her maid did not leave their cabin until Thursday. Mrs. Astor was very ill at first.

"Mr. Ismay was not acressible to any one but the captain. He remained in his cabin."

Captain of the Titanic's Sister Ship Denies That He Sent Messages of Hope

Commander of the Olympic, Which Has Reached Plymouth and Cherbourg, Says She Altered Course and Sped Toward Scene of Disaster Until He Heard Vessel Had Sunk and Survivors Were on Board the Carpathia.

[SPECIAL DESPATCH TO THE HERALD VIA COMMERCIAL CABLE COMPANY'S SYSTEM.]

CHERBOURG, Saturday.—Never has the harbor of Cherbourg seen so sad a landing as that of the passengers of the Olympic, which arrived at half-past one o'clock this afternoon, her crossing from Plymouth having been delayed by mist.

Every one on board the huge vessel, whose flags were flying at half mast, seemed plunged in mourning. Consternation was written on the faces of the passengers and crew as they read in the European edition of the HERALD, for which there was a wild scramble, the latest news of the catastrophe to the Titanic.

It was about a quarter to twelve o'clock on Sunday night, said several of the passengers, that the Olympic's wireless operator received the first call for help from the Titanic. The calls continued until twenty minutes after midnight. Immediately upon receiving the first call Captain Haddock decided to change his course and steam toward the Titanic, which was 390 miles away.

Hurried to Rescue.

The Olympic steamed at full speed. The crew (above all, the stokers) worked like Trojans, never slackening a moment or taking the slightest rest. The Olympic had steamed about fifty miles in the direction of the Titanic when she received a message from the Carpathia saying the Titanic had sunk, that the Carpathia had picked up the survivors and that the Olympic's help was useless.

Captain Grief Stricken.

Captain Haddock was grief stricken and thereupon decided to continue on his original course. It will thus be seen that it is untrue that the Olympic passed several hours at the scene of the wreck.

It was only at luncheon time on Monday that the news of the disaster, which at first was kept secret, was made known to the passengers. Every one broke into tears, and since then not a smile has been seen on any face. The orchestra no longer played, and the voyage, which began gayly, ended in mourning. Among the crew the deepest sadness prevails.

Many passengers and sailors expressed dissatisfaction at the life saving arrangements. All sorts of rumors were current and it was even stated that the Olympic's crew would refuse to accompany her on her next trip unless steps were taken to remedy this on the voyage.

Subscriptions were opened in behalf of the victims of the catastrophe and £1,400 ($7,000) was quickly collected. Subscriptions also have been opened at Cherbourg among those concerned with the transatlantic traffic.

Captain Haddock was greatly surprised to learn that the loss of the Titanic was caused by an iceberg. A few days before, when he passed the region where the Titanic sank, he saw no ice, and on the return journey he naturally took a more southerly course and avoided the dangerous section.

NEWS HELD BACK, PASSENGERS SAY

[SPECIAL DESPATCH TO THE HERALD VIA COMMERCIAL CABLE COMPANY'S SYSTEM.]

HERALD BUREAU,
No. 130 FLEET STREET,
LONDON, Saturday.

[illegible] the Olympic, sister ship of the [illegible] reached Plymouth this mornnig [illegible] Haddock emphatically denied that he had sent any messages to New York announcing the safety of the Titanic's passengers or that the Titanic was being towed to Halifax by the Virginian. These messages did not originate on board the Olympic, he said, nor were the retransmitted by the Olympic's operator. Captain Haddock added that when he heard from the Carpathia on Monday of the extent of the disaster he at once sent a message to New York informing the White Star officials of the loss of the Titanic and the number of lives saved.

As the captain was in possession of this information at nine o'clock on Monday morning, according to stories told by the passengers, it is evident that the news of the disaster was withheld for many hours from relatives and friends of those who were drowned. The Olympic's passengers are emphatic in expressing hope that those responsible for withholding the news of the tragedy for a whole day should be exposed and if possible made to suffer for their strange conduct.

The Herald in Demand.

Immediately the tenders got alongside the Olympic the newsboys were besieged for copies of the European edition of the HERALD. The passengers and crew seemed more intent on reading the details of the Titanic's fate than paying attention to disembarking.

"We are thankful that the voyage is over," said Mr. E. Marshall Fox, European representative of the United States Steel Corporation. "The suspense and anxiety were terrible, and then the knowledge that so many men, women and children were lost is frightful. The passengers and crew were struck dumb by the enormity of the disaster. When word was passed around that it probably would be necessary for the Olympic's passengers to make room for the rescued all hands displayed eagerness to do everything possible. Then came the order for boat practice, but this was not necessary, as later in the day (Monday) a wireless message from New York told us of the futility of our mission, and once again the Olympic turned toward England.

"Later in the day we got in touch with the Carpathia. She told us that 675 persons had been saved. We knew then the terrible magnitude of the calamity.

"As soon as we knew the full extent of the idsaster the first class passengers elected a committee to organize a fund for the relief of the sufferers. This body included Lord Asburton, Lord Leitrim, Mons. Claude Casimir Perier, the Right Rev. Robert Hugh Benson, Mr. F. L. Hine, President of the First National Bank of New York; Mr. A. H. Wiggin, vice president of the Chase National Bank; Honorable Cyril Ward, Mr. Edmund Jackson, of Liverpool, and myself. Our appeal realized more than $6,000. We also made a collection among the second class passengers, stewards and stewardesses, enough to make the total about $7,500. This money was handed to the captain.

Americans Offer Aid.

The Right Rev. R. H. Benson said the first message received by the Olympic was from the Titanic saying she was sinking.

"That was just after Sunday midnight," said he. "The message added that the passengers already had taken to the boats; also that two ships were standing by. We were told that we were to take over the Baltic's mail for England and that the Baltic would return to New York with the Titanic's passengers. It was also stated that the Carpathia and another vessel in addition to the Baltic were cruising around the scene, but this was not borne out by what we have read since reaching Plymouth." The arrival of the Olympic boat train in London was delayed more than an hour owing to a hot box.

The American managers in London, Messrs. Frohman, Enrlanger Hammerstein and other were among the first to offer to give benefits for the fund to help the poor survivors. The King and Queen probably will attend a matinee for the sufferers at the London Opera House.

Mrs. Astor, the mother of Vincent Astor, has decided to proceed to New York to be with her son. She will leave London at the earliest possible moment.

FLAGS HALF MASTED THROUGHOUT CITY

In Financial District, in Harbor, Through Fifth Avenue and Elsewhere Colors Droop.

More flags appeared at half mast yesterday in this city than since the first news of the Titanic disaster. Mayor Gaynor, on the confirmation of the sad tidings, ordered flags on the City Hall and on all municipal buildings to be lowered.

Although no official proclamation has been issued citizens generally are expressing their sorrow by placing flags at half mast on their places of business and dwellings. The Wall street banks and the offices of the great financial firms exhibited the sign of mourning, and in the narrow side streets where importing houses are situated the drooping colors could be seen from scores of windows. The foreign consulates observed the same signs, and in many of the large establishments of the lower city the English ensigns were also shown.

The colors were at half mast on all vessels in the harbor, and over the entrance of every pier the squares of bunting had also been drawn down on their halyards to half the usual height.

Fifth avenue, with flags lowered on the tops of the high buildings, disclosed a national calamity, and in the residences of the upper city and in Riverside Drive were the same evidences of sorrow. All this was an expression of grief which was entirely spontaneous in every quarter of the city.

UNION CLUB MOURNS FIVE OF ITS MEMBERS

Black Bordered Announcements Name Messrs. Astor, Moore, Smith Spencer and Thayer.

Posted in the entrance of the Union Club Friday were four framed announcements in heavy black borders of the death of members of the club on the Titanic. They read:—

"Died April 15, 1912:—John Jacob Astor; elected February 13, 1889. Clarence Moore; elected November 9, 1911. J. Clinch Smith; elected March 11, 1891. W. Augustus Spencer; elected April 8, 1885. John B. Thayer; elected January 9, 1907."

STORE TO AID RELIEF FUND

Announcement was made last night that one per cent of the total receipts next week of J. L. Kesner & Co.'s department store, Sixth avenue, Twenty-second and Twenty-third streets, will be devoted to the relief of those who have suffered through the Titanic disaster. The money so donated will be expended where it is most needed.

NEW TALES OF HEROISM AND HORROR GIVEN BY SURVIVORS

Lawyers See Basis for Big Claims on White Star Line

Element of Gross Negligence, Experts Say, Might Remove Cases in the Titanic Disaster from Usual Limitations of Admiralty Law.

MR. ISMAY'S ATTITUDE TO CAPTAIN AN ISSUE

Admiralty lawyers in this city believe the courts would be likely to uphold claims against the owners of the Titanic for loss of life and property.

In ordinary circumstances claimants for damages would have to prove that the vessel was unseaworthy when she left the last port and that owners had not exercised due care in the selection of officers. If they cannot prove this they must be content with what money could be obtained from the sale of the damaged vessel after the accident. In the case of the Titanic only a few lifeboats remain.

It would be difficult to prove under English laws that the floating palace was unseaworthy, because these statutes are very favorable to ship owners. If, however, gross negligence, such as running at full speed through dangerous ice fields, could be proven, there is a prospect of obtaining damages from the company without reference to the shattered hulk of the Titanic.

The International-Mercantile Marine is incorporated in the State of New Jersey. It has many American stockholders. J. Pierpont Morgan and other American financiers are interested in its affairs. It is the holding company which controls the White Star and other ocean steamship lines. The Titanic, however was under the British flag and her lifeboat equipment, which served to save only one-third of those on board, was sufficient to meet the requirements of the English laws.

United States Law in Case.

There is a section of the United States Statutes which is especially applicable to the case of the Titanic. It is:—

"That if the owner of any vessel transporting merchandise or property to and from any port of the United States of America shall exercise due diligence to make the said vessel seaworthy and properly manned, equipped and supplied, neither the vessel, her owners, agent nor charterers shall be held responsible for danger or loss arising from the damages of the sea, or other navigable waters, acts of God or public enemies, or the inherent defect, quality or vice of the thing carried or seizure made by legal officers, or from loss resulting from any act or omission of the shipper or owner of the goods, his agent or representative, or from saving or attempting to save life or property at sea or for any deviation in rendering such service."

Silas B. Axtell, counsel in charge of the Seamen's Branch of the Legal Aid Society, at No. 1 Broadway, where many interesting admiralty cases are considered, said yesterday that the question of the liability of the owners of the Titanic presented many interesting legal aspects.

Lifeboat Equipment an Issue.

"Under the United States law," said Mr. Axtell, "the provision is made that no vessel is required to carry more lifeboats than are required for the use of the number of passengers and of the crew on board, or in other words, the steamboat inspectors have authority to insist upon a place in a lifeboat being made for every person on board.

"The English regulations do not require this much, yet for all that there is a question as to whether or not any vessel may be considered seaworthy which is not provided with appliances for saving the lives of passengers and crew. If it had been established, for instance, that her pumps were inadequate, and that the fact were known when she left port, or the bulkhead doors could not be closed, she was in no sense seaworthy under even the British law. The company is liable under the admiralty law, which is in reality the common law, provided that the Titanic were seaworthy on leaving, but only to the extent of her value after the accident.

The Merida and the Admiral Farragut came into collision several years ago. The Merida was a total loss and the Farragut, although much damaged, was sold for $105,000. Her value was divided among those who had sustained losses from the Merida. The claims aggregated $800,000 to $900,000.

"If it can be shown that the owners of the Titanic failed to exercise reasonable caution and that a high rate of speed was maintained when warning of icebergs in the vicinity had been given there is an element of negligence which might be so strong that the courts would award damages."

Thinks Company Is Liable.

"It seems to me," said Mr. B. B. Coyne, of Abbott & Coyne, admiralty lawyers, at No. 29 Broadway, "that the White Star line is liable, and now the question is, Will it begin a proceeding to limit liability? If that be successful all that can be levied upon are the few lifeboats of the Titanic, which are all that remains of her. This would leave only a few hundred dollars to be divided among the passengers and the owners of the property which was lost. It would seem to me, however, that the Limitation act would not be applicable if negligence were established.

"The fact that Mr. Ismay, the managing director, was on board is to be considered especially if it were established, as I notice a passenger is quoted as saying, that he had actually given directions to the captain to increase speed in a region of icebergs. If Mr. Ismay gave the order to go faster it could not be pleaded that the captain did not have to obey.

"Theoretically he was absolute master, but with the prospect of being removed from command on his arrival in New York if he did not obey the managing director it could hardly have been expected that he would have declined to obey. It is certainly an act of the grossest negligence to go through ice fields at full speed.

Wants Senate Records Public.

Mr. Coyne said that it would be of great benefit if the testimony now being taken by a committee for the information of the Senate could by law be made a public record, as it contained much valuable testimony which otherwise would be lost in a legal sense.

There were on board several husbands and wives who died together. Both Mr. Coyne and Mr. Axtell say that in such shipwrecks husband and wife are considered as having died at the same time. The old presumption of the English law, the man being stronger would live longer in the water, is not recognized. If any one interested in the wills of persons dying in such circumstances should make a claim on the basis that one or the other died first the litigant must bear the burden of the proof and establish his view to the satisfaction of court and jury.

VICTIMS' LEGAL DEATH EASILY TO BE PROVED

Lawyers Believe Little Trouble Will Be Had in Establishment by Heirs of Death Claims.

Prominent lawyers yesterday expressed the belief that the heirs and relatives of those who went down with the Titanic would have little trouble in establishing the legal death of the lost. The question has caused much discussion in view of the fact that men like Colonel Astor and George B. Widener left large estates. The death of these men must be proved legally before the various heirs can come into the possession of these estates.

Clark L. Jordan, of No. 154 Nassau street, yesterday explained the law on this subject.

"It is not so much a question of law," said Mr. Jordan, "as it is a question of common sense. All the conditions, such as the cold water, the position a man was in when the vessel went down, must be considered. Say, for instance, that a man was last seen on the deck of the Titanic as she was going down. In such a case the presumption, I think, would be that he met instant death through the force of the suction caused by the sinking of the vessel. If, on the contrary, as the vessel was sinking that man was last seen in the act of jumping from the vessel, then the legal proof of death wouldn't be so complete. This is especially true in case there should have been any wreckage or other thing to which he might cling. In the latter case it would be necessary to wait a reasonable time before the death could be proved. Death would be presumed in law if in all human probability he couldn't survive and if he is not heard from within a reasonable time. The length of time is not important, provided there was imminent danger at the moment the man was last seen. In the last analysis, each case must be decided in accordance with the individual circumstances surrounding it."

"Under the common law," said T. Louis Britt, of No. 271 Broadway, "there seems to be no presumption of death—that is, life is presumed to exist until the contrary is affirmatively proven. Under the statutory law, and under the law of this State, a person who is absent seven years without having had communication with those with whom he might naturally be supposed to communicate—when there is nothing present to explain this absence—is legally presumed to be dead.

"For the presumption of death to arise, however, no stated period is absolutely necessary when it can be affirmatively shown that the person whose death is in question was, when last heard of, known incurable disease, or known to be in the presence of imminent danger. It has been held many times that in case a person was known to have embarked on a certain vessel and no tidings of that vessel were received after the longest period of time within which it would require to make the particular voyage embarked upon had elapsed, that person might legally be presumed to be dead.

"In the case of the Titanic, when persons were known to be passengers on that vessel, and sufficient time had elapsed to preclude the possibility of a rescue by any other vessel than the one which saved some of them, there is no question that they may be legally regarded as dead. There is no presumption of priority of death of those who died in the same disaster. That question is left to the affirmative proof of the person seeking to establish the fact."

Frederick Allen, general solicitor of the Mutual Life Insurance Company, expressed the opinion that all life insurance companies would be very liberal in their names of passengers supposed to have requirements of those who attempt to prove death claims on policies in the been lost on the Titanic.

"All the proof that the Mutual expects to require," said Mr. Allen, "is proof that the particular person in question was a passenger on the Titanic when the ship left Southampton, and that that person was not among the list of those rescued. We intend to aid the beneficiaries in every way that we can."

Survivor's Cries Weak, Dog's Bark Causes Rescue of Boatload

Rigel, Whose Master Sank with the Titanic, Guides the Carpathia's Captain to Suffering Passengers Hidden Under Rescue Ship's Bow.

Not the least among the heroes of the Titanic disaster was Rigel, a big black Newfoundland dog, belonging to the first officer, who went down with his ship. But for Rigel the fourth boat picked up might have been run down by the Carpathia. For three hours he swam in the icy water where the Titanic went down, evidently looking for his master, and was instrumental in guiding the boatload of survivors to the gangway of the Carpathia.

Jonas Briggs, a seaman aboard the Carpathia, now has Rigel and told the story of the dog's heroism. The Carpathia was moving slowly about, looking for boats, rafts or anything which might be afloat. Exhausted with their efforts, weak from lack of food and exposure to the cutting wind, and terror stricken, the men and women in the fourth boat had drifted under the Carpathia's starboard bow. They were dangerously close to the steamship, but too weak to shout a warning loud enough to reach the bridge.

The boat might not have been seen were it not for the sharp barking of Rigel, who was swimming ahead of the craft, and valiantly announcing his position. The barks attracted the attention of Captain Rostron and he went to the starboard end of the bridge to see where they came from and saw the boat. He immediately ordered the engines stopped and the boat came alongside the starboard gangway.

Care was taken to take Rigel aboard, but he appeared little affected by his long trip through the ice cold water. He stood by the rail and barked until Captain Rostron called Briggs and had him take the dog below.

RESOLUTION FOR MARINE TREATIES PASSES IN SENATE

Senator Martine's Measure to Regulate Speed and Course of Vessels Adopted.

OFFER DEFENCE FOR J. BRUCE ISMAY

Mr. McCumber Declares It Is Unfair to Place Blame Before There Is a Fair Trial.

MATTER GOES TO PRESIDENT

England, France and Germany To Be Asked to Participate in International Agreement.

HERALD BUREAU,
No. 1,502 H STREET, N. W.,
WASHINGTON, D. C., Saturday.

By unanimous vote the Senate to-day passed the Martine resolution, introduced on Wednesday, calling for negotiation of treaties with other maritime nations regulating the speed and course of vessels engaged in ocean traffic and insuring the safety of passengers and crews.

This morning the Senate Committee on Foreign Relations made a few changes in the wording of the Martine resolution and reported it favorably at the opening of this afternoon's session.

Following is the text of the resolution as passed:—

"Resolved, That the President of the United States be, and he is hereby, advised that the Senate would favor treaties with England, France, Germany and other maritime governments to regulate the course and speed of all vessels engaged in the carrying of passengers at sea, to determine the number of life boats, rafts, searchlights and wireless apparatus to be carried by such vessels, and to assure the use of such other equipment as shall be adequate to secure the safety of such vessels, passengers and crews."

Senator McCumber, of North Dakota, after declaring the resolution "the proper, orderly and just method of approaching the subject that is now engrossing the attention of the whole world," turned on those now condemning J. Bruce Ismay, the White Star line and the lack of life saving accommodations with the declaration that it was unfitting to condemn any one without proper trial, and he asserted that the American people are more to blame for the catastrophe than any one else, because of the prevailing American spirit of conducting everything in the spirit of sport and seeking everlastingly to break all known records.

Lays Blame on Law.

Senator Lodge declared:—"The blame rests on the law for not compelling ships to carry sufficient lifeboats. The Titanic carried all the boats the law required. She had a certificate from the British Board of Trade. The lack is proper legislation. The purpose of this act is, by treaty, to get proper legislation."

Senator Martine said the sole purpose of the resolution was to establish world safety for passengers and crew.

Mr. McCumber said:—

"Yesterday, Mr. President, one of the survivors of that terrible catastrophe, upon a rather flimsy report, in my opinion, was tried, convicted, sentenced and executed in the Senate of the United States."

"I, as a Senator of the United States and as an American citizen, desire to register my protest against the trial of any one connected with the running of that boat, from the officers of the company to the lowest man and seaman who sailed thereon, without a fair, honest and full consideration.

"The Lord knows, Mr. President, that the habit of accusing and trying and condemning public men without a hearing and without a trial is bad enough, but when the feeling of the entire civilized world is wrought up to such an extent that it is rather eager for a victim upon whom it may expend its wrath I say that then, above all times, we should hold in abeyance our judgment to ascertain whether or not there has been any guilt in connection with the operation of this vessel.

"Mr. President, my own view is that the American people are more to blame for this catastrophe than any one or any other body. We of late years have conducted almost all of our enterprises with the spirit of the sport rather than with the spirit of the man of sober judgment.

"We seek always to build greater vessels than someone else has constructed; we seek and encourage people to push those vessels to the very last test of endurance and speed. When the Lusitania was successful and made her maiden trip the whole country was filled with laudation and praise.

Refers to Aviation.

"There is no evidence that her equipment was any greater or any better than was that of the Titanic's we had in this boat; there is no evidence that she did not take practically the same route that was taken by the Titanic, and if the Titanic had been successful for weeks we would have heard of nothing, Mr. President, but the wonderful achievement and the record that she had made. This desire for notoriety to exceed, to excell everything else in speed and in size has so diverted our judgment from the ordinary in life to the one idea of excelling in everything that we forget ourselves.

"In the matter of aviation, while we all know that all the feats that are performed could be done from one to two hundred feet above the surface of the earth, yet we, as a people, are constantly demanding that we shall have some one that will go one, two or three thousand feet up into the skies, and when he comes down we decorate him and the papers are filled with laudations of the wonderful achievement. Acting under that spirit, he attempts the next day to go higher, and the following day be bury a mass of flesh with laudation, and we call for another victim of the American spirit of contest and the desire to excell.

"So, Mr. President, it seems to me that it is most unjust to condemn any one connected with this affair until at least there has been a hearing."

CLOTHING DISTRIBUTION.

The HERALD inadvertently said in a news yesterday that clothing had been distributed to some of the survivors of the Titanic wreck at the Seamen's Church Institute. The distribution of the clothing was made at the American Seamen's Friend Society's Institute, at No. 507 West street.

THE LAPLAND TAKES THE TITANIC'S MAIL

Red Star Line Ship Also Has Many of Wrecked Vessel's Crew on Board When She Steams.

One hundred and fifty of the Titanic's seamen and all the mail, numbering 1,927 sacks, which was to have gone aboard that vessel yesterday, left this city yesterday on board the Lapland, of the Red Star line. J. Bruce Ismay arranged to go home on board the Lapland when the Carpathia arrived Thursday night, but has remained here at the request of the Senate Committee which is investigating the Titanic disaster.

All the survivors of the Titanic's crew were not on board because many of them have been summoned to appear before the investigating committee. One man, one of the Titanic's quartermasters, returned to this city by the pilot boat after the Lapland got away. His return was requested by wireless.

None of the Titanic's seamen leaving on board the Lapland yesterday would discuss the Titanic disaster. The men said they had their orders from the office of the White Star line.

Governor Dix and Mrs. Dix were among the Lapland's passengers. Governor Dix said he was going abroad to enjoy the first vacation he has had since he became Governor.

THE VICTORIAN KEPT NEWS.

HALIFAX, N. S., Saturday.—Not one of the 1,424 passengers on board the Allan line steamship Victorian knew of the Titanic catastrophe until they reached here to-day. The Victorian steamed from Liverpool April 12.

The reason given for keeping back the information was fear of causing uneasiness. The news was received by the Victorian eight hours after it occurred. The persons who knew of the message were the wireless operator and Captain Edmund Outram. The news was received from the Carpathia, via the Baltic, on Monday.

Captain Outram said no bodies or wreckage were sighted, although a lookout was kept. Captain Outram said he had to go very far south to avoid collision with icebergs.

MEMORIAL RESOLUTIONS.

The Executive Committee of the National Committee for the Celebration of the One Hundredth Anniversary of Peace yesterday and adopted memorial resolutions on the death of those who went down with the steamship Titanic. Five of the most conspicuous members of the committee were among those who were lost. They were Colonel John Jacob Astor, William T. Stead, Charles M. Hays, Isidor Straus and Francis D. Millet. The resolutions were signed by Andrew Carnegie, chairman.

COMPANY ASSISTS WOMEN SURVIVORS

Free Passage Promised to the Destitute Who Desire to Return to England.

Bereft of her husband, $900 in currency and all her household effects and personal property when the Titanic sank, Mrs. Florence Ware, of Bristol, England, one of the survivors of the disaster, appeared at the offices of the White Star Steamship Company, at No. 9 Broadway, and appealed for aid yesterday. She was accompanied by a relative from New Britain, Conn., and when the facts of her case were made known she was provided with ample funds to meet all her wants and the assurance that she would be returned to her home free of charge.

Mrs. Ware said her husband, John J. Ware, had resolved to go into the contracting business in New Britain, and to that end he had sold out his business in Bristol and taken passage on board the Titanic with his wife. In the hold were their household effects, while in Mr. Ware's pocket was $900 with which to start life anew in the country to which he and his wife were strangers.

"We were asleep when the ship struck the iceberg," said Mrs. Ware. "We realized that there might be danger and we both dressed and went on deck. We heard the cry, 'Ladies first in the boats' and my husband suggested that I enter one of them. We went to the boat deck and an officer took my arm and placed me in a boat which then was well filled. It was the second boat to leave the ship, I believe, and I saw only two men in it, a steward and fireman."

Mrs. Ware said her husband refused to enter the boat, although there was ample room for him at the time, he saying he would come later. The last she saw of Mr. Ware was when he was walking toward a group of women. She said she observed no signs of panic and that at the time she left the Titanic no one believed that the steamship was sinking. She heard no shooting.

Although revised lists of the survivors have been printed repeatedly numerous persons continue to inquire at the White Star offices for information regarding missing relatives and friends who were known to have been aboard the Titanic. Several inqiries were made regarding the identity of "R. Knight," which name appeared in the list of second cabin passengers, bt who evidently was drowned

Friends of a Mrs. Rose Knight sought in vain to ascertain if there was any record to show that "R. Knight" and Mrs. Rose Knight were one and the same. The clerks consilted the list of names sent from the Southampton office of the company, but there was nothing to show that the person designated as "R. Knight" was a woman. Efforts will be made to learn the truth, but as no woman answering to the name of Knight was rescued her friends are convinced that she was lost in the disaster.

A pathetic search for some information regarding the death of Charles H. Chapman, an exporter of this city, has been instituted by his two sons, Charles H. and Ralph Chapman, of No. 1,321 Plimpton avenue, New York. The young men posted photographs of their missing father in the White Star offices yesterday, to which was appended the request that if any second class passenger on board the Titanic could give any information regarding the missing man it would be appreciated by his sons.

SPECIAL TITANIC SECTION

THE NEW YORK HERALD.

SPECIAL TITANIC SECTION

THIRD SECTION.—16 PAGES.—PART ONE. NEW YORK, SUNDAY, APRIL 21, 1912.— PRICE FIVE CENTS.

THE FOUNDERING of the TITANIC

Record of the Greatest Tragedy in the History of the Seas; Tales of Heroism and of Sacrifice; Its Place in History and Its Lessons for Mankind.

NEVER was ill starred voyage more auspiciously begun than when the Titanic, newly crowned empress of the seas, steamed majestically out of the port of Southampton at noon on Wednesday, April 10, bound for New York.

The new White Star ship represented the apotheosis of human achievement in marine construction. For more than a decade the great steamship lines, competing keenly in their rivalry for supremacy in the transatlantic carrying trade, had been taxing the resourcefulness of designers, engineers and shipbuilders to evolve vessels ever larger, more powerful, speedier, more luxurious than their predecessors. In comparison with these recent mammoth creations the ocean greyhounds of a scant generation ago seemed as inferior, as obsolete, as the sun dial in comparison with the chronometer or the stagecoach beside the Twentieth Century Limited.

Steamship companies had found that it paid to provide not only the speediest but the best transit facilities across the sea. They vied with one another to make the ocean cruise—once on a time, in the primitive past, regarded as a hardship—a beautiful dream of unalloyed pleasure and relaxation. The modern voyager of ample means must have at command while afloat, as well as ashore, all the comforts and elegancies of the most pretentious of metropolitan hotels. He must have his electric elevators, his sun parlors and palm gardens, his squash and tennis courts on deck, his swimming tank and a thousand and one attractions never dreamed of a generation ago as salt water accessories.

But time, too, was more precious than ever before. It is a fast and busy age as well as a luxury loving era. Often the very men who will pay the highest price for a cabin de luxe on the finest and latest of ocean flyers will pay it the more willingly if her whirling turbines are of such power as will promise them the gain of an extra business day in New York or London or Paris at the end of the voyage.

THOUGHT PROBLEM SOLVED IN THE TITANIC.

Here, then, was the problem upon which designer and constructor have focussed their genius and skill—to combine in one superb marine creation the maximum of attainable size, power, speed and luxurious accommodation consistent with the ever vital factor of safety.

The Titanic was universally acclaimed to be the solution of that problem. No consideration of expense had weighed an atom in the thoroughness of her construction, the perfection of her design or the palatial elegance of her appointments and furnishing. She was literally a huge and magnificent oceangoing hotel, stanch and true in every frame, rib and joint, equipped with all the most approved of modern safety devices—so it was then thought—and with the most lavish extravagancies. Life in her brilliant saloons and along her smooth, holystoned decks was to be "a thing of beauty and a joy forever."

"Build me true, oh, worthy master,
Stanch and strong, a goodly vessel."

The Titanic had fulfilled the poetic appeal. Had she not her collision bulkheads, her double bottom? Was not the vast expanse of her hull honeycombed with lateral and transverse watertight compartments? She was to be the mistress of the seas, superior in the pride of her strength to all the obsolete perils of grim old Ocean. She was "unsinkable," so her builders proudly announced when they slid her towering bulk down the ways at Belfast, while the people cheered as the hand of a fair maid baptized her with wine, proclaiming her the empress of all the fleets of this or any other age.

Captain Smith, premier officer of the White Star squadrons, tried and true seaman, a veteran of the bridge and quarterdeck, believed what her builders said. "You might drop her engines clear through her bottom and still her severed parts would float," he is said to have proclaimed.

LATITUDE 41.46 NORTH, LONGITUDE 50.14 WEST.

WHERE MANHOOD PERISHED NOT.

ALL RIVALS DWARFED BY COLOSSAL SHIP

And so it was only her due that as the Titanic steamed out of the harbor bound on her maiden voyage a thousand "godspeeds" were wafted after her, while every other vessel that she passed, the greatest of them dwarfed by her colossal proportions, paid homage to the new queen regnant with the blasts of their whistles and the shrieking of steam sirens.

Attired as she was for her first triumphal progress, the acknowledged sovereign represented an expenditure of something like $10,000,000. As steady as the Rock of Gibraltar, as impressively huge in bulk and strength, and seemingly no less invulnerable, the proud ship swept out to sea. Her bunting fluttered merrily above her boat deck, on which happy throngs were promenading and waving handkerchiefs at an elevation above the water as great as is the roof of a high building above the street.

From the forward bridge, fully ninety feet above the sea, peered out the benign face of the ship's master, cool of aspect, deliberate of action, impressive in that quality of confidence that is bred only of long experience in command.

From far below the bridge sounded the strains of the ship's orchestra, playing blithely a favorite air from "The Chocolate Soldier." All went as merry as a wedding bell. Indeed, among that gay ship's company were two score or more at least for whom the wedding bells had sounded in truth not many days before. Some were on their honeymoon tours. Others were returning to their motherland after having passed the weeks of the honeymoon, like Colonel John Jacob Astor and his young bride, amid the diversions of Egypt or other Old World countries.

What daring flight of imagination would have ventured the prediction that within the span of six days that stately ship, humbled, shattered and torn asunder, would lie two thousand fathoms deep at the bottom of the Atlantic, that the benign face that peered from the bridge would be set in the rigor of death and that the happy bevy of voyaging brides would be sorrowing widows?

The ship's company was of a character befitting the greatest of all vessels and worthy of the occasion of her maiden voyage. Though the major part of her passengers were Americans returning from abroad, there were enrolled upon her cabin lists some of the most distinguished names of England, as well as of the younger nation. Among the men were leaders in the world of commerce, finance, literature, art and the learned professions. Many of the women were socially prominent in two hemispheres. Their names are familiar to the newspaper readers of the last week.

One of the most notable was William T. Stead. Few names are more widely known to the world of contemporary literature and journalism than that of the brilliant editor of the Review of Reviews. He was on his way to America to take part in the Men and Religion Forward Movement and was to have delivered an address in Union square last Thursday from the platform with William Jennings Bryan as his chief associate. Other distinguished Englishmen were Norman C. Craig, M. P.; J. Bruce Ismay, managing director of the White Star line, who had taken the trip as a volunteer passenger to see how the greatest vessel ever built by man would conduct herself, and Thomas Andrews, a representative of the firm of Harland & Wolff, of Belfast, the ship's builders.

DISTINGUISHED MEN AND WOMEN VOYAGERS.

From homes in the United States, to which they were returning, were Colonel and Mrs. John Jacob Astor, Mr. and Mrs. Isidor Straus, Mr. and Mrs. George D. Widener, of Philadelphia; Major Archibald W. Butt, military aid to President Taft; Benjamin Guggenheim, Clarence Moore, Mr. and Mrs. Henry S. Harper; Washington A. Roebling, of Trenton, N. J., and a grandson of the builder of the Brooklyn Bridge; Jacques Futrelle, a writer of successful fiction and formerly a member of the HERALD staff, who was accompanied by his wife, also an accomplished writer; Colonel Archibald Gracie, U. S. A.; Francis D. Millet, head of the American Academy at Rome and formerly a HERALD correspondent in the Russo-Turkish war; J. B. Thayer, one of the vice presidents of the Pennsylvania Railroad, with whom were his wife and son, and many other well known persons.

In a distinguished party from Montreal, Quebec, was Charles M. Hays, president of the Canadian Grand Trunk Railway, who was accompanied by Mrs. Hays. Other prominent women who were on board the Titanic were Lady Duff Gordon, Countess Rothes and Mrs. William Bucknell, widow of the founder of Bucknell University.

When the mammoth ship touched at Cherbourg and later at Queenstown she was again the object of a port ovation, the smaller craft doing obeisance while thousands gazed in wonder at her stupendous proportions. After taking aboard some additional passengers at each port the Titanic headed her towering bow toward the open sea and the race for a record on her maiden voyage was begun. There were aboard the vessel then 2,340 persons. Of these 330 were first cabin passengers, 320 were in the second cabin, 750 were rated third class and the officers and crew numbered 940 men.

NEW BURST OF SPEED EACH DAY.

The Titanic left Queenstown at midday Thursday, April 11. According to the testimony of Mr. Ismay given later before the Senate investigating committee, she made 484 miles as her first day's run, her powerful new engines turning over at the rate of seventy revolutions. On the second day out, according to the same authority, the speed was hit up to seventy-three revolutions and the run for the day was bulletined as 519 miles. Still further increasing the speed, the rate of revolution of the engines was raised to seventy-five and the day's run was 549 miles, the best yet scheduled.

According to the evidence of the managing director of the White Star company, the ship had not yet been speeded to her capacity. She was capable, he said, of turning over about seventy-eight revolutions. Had the weather conditions been propitious, he admitted, it was intended to press the great racer to the full limit of her speed on Monday. But for the Titanic Monday never came.

Until Sunday, April 14, the voyage had been a delightful but uneventful one. The passengers had passed the time in the usual diversions of ocean travellers, amusing themselves in the luxurious saloons, promenading on the boat deck, lolling at their ease in steamer chairs and making pools on the daily runs of the steamship. The smoking rooms and card rooms had been as well patronized as usual, and a party of several notorious professional gamblers had begun reaping their usual easy harvest.

As early as Sunday afternoon the officers of the Titanic must have known that they were approaching dangerous ice fields of the kind that are a perennial menace to the safety of steamships following the regular transatlantic lanes off the Great Banks of Newfoundland.

AN UNHEEDED WARNING.

On Sunday afternoon the Titanic's wireless operator forwarded to the Hydrographic offices in Washington, Baltimore, Philadelphia and elsewhere the following despatch:—

"April 14.—The German steamship Amerika (Hamburg-American line) reports by radio-telegraph passing two large icebergs in latitude 41.27, longitude 50.08.—Titanic, Br. S. S."

Naval officers calculated afterward that it was not improbable the Titanic received her death blow in contact with one of the very icebergs of the immediate presence of which the warning of the Amerika had informed her.

The location in which the White Star giantess struck was given as latitude 41.16 and longitude 50.14. This theory would be consistent with the supposition that there had been a slight drift of the ice masses toward the northwestward after they had been sighted by the Amerika.

ALL SERENELY CONFIDENT.

Despite this warning, the Titanic was forging ahead Sunday night at her usual speed—from twenty-one to twenty-five knots. It was a clear and starlit night, though without the moon. Objects at sea were clearly visible at a considerable distance. No pall of baffling fog or mist hung over the dreaded Banks, as it so often does to obscure the path of speeding ships.

The officers felt confident that even though one of these ghostly sentinels of the sea were sighted the great ship could be brought under control in ample time to evade it.

The passengers, some of them keeping late hours in the pastimes of the smoking and card rooms, while many others had already retired for the night to their staterooms, rested serenely confident in the belief that in their temporary quarters in the most magnificent vessel ever built by man they were as safe as they could be in front of their own firesides at home.

SPEEDING FOR A RECORD.

Captain Smith had retired to the captain's quarters, and at half-past eleven o'clock First Officer Murdock was in command of the bridge, while Quartermaster J. H. Moody was at the wheel. The latter testified before the Senatorial committee that the Titanic at the time was making twenty-one knots, or about twenty-six miles an hour.

The officers were under orders, he said, to keep up the speed in the hope of making a record passage to New York. This order was being executed in spite of the foreknowledge that dangerous icebergs were adrift in the Titanic's path, although she had laid her course well in the southern lanes established for westbound vessels.

It was twenty minutes to twelve o'clock when the lookout in the crow's nest away aloft on the Titantic's foremast sighted ice ahead and cried the warning. The helm was put over, but vessels of the enormous size and tremendous momentum of the new White Star ship are not easily manoeuvred within a short time or distance. The warning had come to late.

CRASHES AT FULL SPEED.

With her tremendous speed practically unchecked, the leviathan struck the tremendous mass of ice. Its exposed top towered a hundred feet above the water—higher than the upper deck and the bridge of the big ship—while its unseen mass beneath the water, as is always the case with floating ice, was not less than three times the bulk of its visible area.

(CONTINUED ON PAGE TWO.)

THE TITANIC, DEFYING PERILS, SPED EVER FASTER TO OCEAN TOMB

So Much Confidence Was Felt There Was No Terror in Vessel's Shock.

CONTINUED CARD GAME.

(CONTINUED FROM PAGE ONE.)

The blow was a glancing one, the result of the Titanic having partially answered her helm at the moment of the impact, but the bow and the starboard side were "sidewiped" by the iceberg and worse damage than what was visible had been wrought beneath the surface.

Most icebergs that have been exposed to the action of the seas for a considerable time have their surfaces just above the waterline cut away by wave action, much as sand is washed out by breakers. This frequently leaves below the surface of the water projecting shelves or spurs of ice of vast proportions.

Upon such a shelf, it is supposed, the Titanic grated her bottom plates, ripping them out and permitting tons of water to rush into more than one of her compartments from the midship sections forward.

NO TERROR IN SHOCK.

The shock of the collision was by no means the terrifying sensation that might be supposed. The Titanic had received a mortal wound, but at first there was little external evidence to show it. Many slept soundly through the experience and were not aroused until the steward summoned them to the decks, with life belts adjusted, ready for the worst.

One woman turned over in her berth and glanced out of the window in time to see the ship, which was still moving fast, glide swiftly past some great, weird ex-se of whiteness that gave out a chill- breath. She had never seen an ice-g in her life and wondered what this ange object was that had become so e a neighbor of their gallant vessel.

he men in the smoking room who were in their game of cards sent one of r number to a window to see what happened. He stuck his poker hand of cards into the side pocket of his coat, glanced out the window and remarked that she had "only grazed an iceberg." Then the enthusiasts went on with their game, but it was not for long. The game was never finished and most of those who were in it never will play another.

DEVOID OF PANIC.

It is significant of the implicit confidence the passengers felt in the Titanic's invulnerable strength that there was an entire absence of panic at the time of the collision. Many of them have said that the stoppage of the engines disturbed them more than did the grating of the ship over the shelf of jagged ice. They did not know that it was cutting through to the vessel's vitals.

Even the stoppage of the ryhthmic throb of the engines, as one of the survivors said, had little more effect upon his peace of mind than would the stopping in the night of a loudly ticking clock.

ptain Smith had appeared upon the ge the moment after his ship had felt blow of fate. He took prompt steps scertain the probable extent of the ies received. The rush of water into forward compartments was ominous gh to warrant the most conservative se, though it was by no means clear et that the Titanic was a doomed ship.

The veteran shipmaster did not hesitate. Hoping for the best, he prepared for the worst. He issued the order:—

"All passengers on deck with the lifebelts on!"

FIRST DANGER WARNING.

The ship's stewards carried the order through the vessel, and to many a sleeping passenger the ominous message presaging disaster was the first intimation of danger.

"Stand by to clear away the lifeboats!" was the next order that rang out from the bridge. Officers and seamen knew their posts. In times of a crisis such as this various subordinate officers are assigned under the ship's system of discipline to take command of each of the lifeboats and life rafts, with a sufficient number of seamen to man them. All sprang to their posts. The discipline was perfect. There was as yet no disorder and little alarm.

Meantime the captain had directed J. G. Phillips, the wireless operator, to be ready to send out immediately the "S. O. S." signal, the seaman's call of distress. The captain was having an inspection made to determine the extent of the damage done below the waterline. It was about ten minutes later, Harold Bride, the surviving assistant wireless operator of the Titanic says, when Captain Smith returned and ordered Mr. Phillips to send out the call for help at once.

BLUE SPARKS CALL HELP.

The key in the operator's room crashed and the blue spark flashed as the message went vibrating out over the broad Atlantic that the Titanic had struck ice and was sinking by the head. The Carpathia, of the Cunard line, eastward bound, heard the call, answered it and instantly put about and hurried to the rescue.

The two ships remained in wireless communication, Mr. Phillips giving explicit directions as to the Titanic's position, while the Carpathia flashed back messages of encouragement. This continued until about half-past twelve o'clock, when the Titanic's wireless went out of commission. Its last sputtering cry to the straining Carpathia was the grim call:—

"Engine rooms flooded. Taking passengers off in boats. Hurry! Hurry!"

The Carpathia is not one of the ocean greyhounds. Her normal speed is hardly more than half that of the Titanic, but she was pressing forward as fast as her engines could drive her, despite the perils of a vast field of ice extending over a sea area of more than fifty miles. Her master, Captain Arthur H. Rostron, realized now that hundreds of human lives depended alone upon him and his vessel, and he never slackened his speed.

MANNING THE LIFE BOATS.

Upon the broad decks of the Titanic in the meantime an almost phlegmatic calm had yielded to some degree of trepidation, but not to panic. Officers passed the word that danger was by no means imminent; that the passengers were to be taken off in the boats as a precautionary measure, and that help was expected to arrive soon.

Of the many narratives of what occurred at this stage of the disaster one of the most intelligent and graphic is that told by Mr. L. Beasley, a Cambridge University man, who was one of the second cabin survivors.

"The pulsing of the engines had ceased," said he, "and the steamship lay just as though she were awaiting the order to go on again after some trifling matter had been adjusted. But in a few minutes we saw the canvas covers being lifted from the lifeboats and the crews allotted to each standing by, ready to lower them to the water.

"Presently we heard the order, 'All men stand back and all women retire to the deck below.' That was the smoking room deck, or the B deck. The men stood away and remained in absolute silence, leaning against the rail or pacing up and down the deck slowly. Many of them lighted cigars or cigarettes and began to smoke.

LOADING THE BOATS.

"The boats were swung out and lowered from the A deck above. The women were marshalled quietly in lines along the B deck, and when the boats were lowered down to the level of the latter the women were assisted to climb into them.

"As each of the boats was filled with its quota of passengers and a sufficient number of seamen to handle the sweeps the word was given and it was carefully lowered down to the dark surface of the water.

"Most of the women took their places in the boats without protest, though some refused to leave their husbands. In a few instances I saw gentle violence used to force them into the boats. I think most of those who were leaving their husbands or other relatives at that time believed the parting was not to be for long.

"As I look back upon those moments it seems to me remarkable how slowly the realization dawned upon us that we were standing face to face with imminent death. During all this time there was no disorder, no unseemly panic, no frenzied rushing at the boats. There were pathetic partings between those who were to go and those others who were to stay, but there was no hysterical sobbing or protest either among the women or the men."

PERIL NOT REALIZED.

So slowly did many of the passengers concede the peril of their position that scores of them deliberately elected to remain upon the Titanic rather than entrust themselves to the small boats and what seemed to them the danger of descent to the sea sixty or seventy feet below them.

Several of the earliest boats launched were sent away for this reason with many less than the number they were able to carry. Others were sent away with several men in them after no women had appeared ready to respond to the call.

When the last of the too meagre equipment of lifeboats was ready to be lowered away the situation had changed. The Titanic, which all the time had been perceptibly settling by the head, was now getting much lower in the water. Everybody at last began to realize that the mighty craft in which they had placed such unbounded confidence was about to fail them. There was no disguising the fact longer that the incomparable Titanic was about to sink.

FALSE SECURITY VANISHES.

With the horror of that certainty staring them in the face, the remaining passengers learned that the entire life saving equipment of this most pretentious of vessels was only sufficient to rescue from her doomed hulk about one-third of those who had entrusted their lives to this "unsinkable" empress of the sea. They had been self-hypnotized into a sense of false security.

At last the awful truth had penetrated their minds that death must be portion of the majority, death in the darkness of a wintry sea studded with its ice monuments like the marble shafts in some vast cemetery.

In that hour, when cherished illusions of possible safety had all but vanished, manhood and womanhood aboard the Titanic rose to their sublimest heights. It was in that crisis of the direst extremity that brave women deliberately rejected life and chose rather to remain and die with the men whom they loved.

DEATH FAILS TO PART THEM.

"I will not leave my husband," said Mrs. Isidor Straus. "We are old; we can best die together," and she turned from those who would have forced her into one of the boats and clung to the man who had been the partner of her sorrows and joys. Thus they stood hand in hand and heart to heart, comforting each other until the sea claimed them, united in death as they had been through a long life.

"Greater love hath no man than this, that he give up his life for his friends."

Miss Elizabeth Evans fulfilled this final test of affection laid down by the Divine Master. The girl was the niece of the wife of Magistrate Cornell, of this city. She was placed in the same boat with many other women. As it was about to be lowered away it was found that the craft contained one more than its full quota of passengers.

The grim question arose as to which of them should surrender her place and her chance of safety. Beside Miss Evans sat Mrs. J. J. Brown, of Denver, the mother of several children. Miss Evans was the first to volunteer to yield to another.

GIRL STEPS BACK TO DOOM.

"Your need is greater than mine," said she, turning toward Mrs. Brown. "You have children who need you, and I have none."

So saying she rose from the boat and stepped back upon the deck. The girl found no later refuge and was one of those who went down with the ship. She was twenty-five years old and was beloved by all who knew her.

It was in that same hour that Colonel John Jacob Astor, Major Archibald W. Butt, the President's military aid and hundreds of men less well known gave illustrious examples of what Kipling has called "the gentleman unafraid." Looking death squarely in the face, they met it without flinching.

Many survivors have told how Major Butt, with coat stripped off, stood beside the boats when the rush for them had begun in the last few minutes of frenzy and gave what aid a gentleman and a soldier might to the officers of the ship. With a revolver in one hand and a belaying pin in the other he stood on guard ready to strike down or to shoot the first man who attempted to dispute the precedence of women and children in the boats.

COLONEL ASTOR'S BRAVERY.

Many of the survivors have told of the gallant conduct of Colonel Astor. After helping his bride to dress and calming her fears he led her to the line where the women were waiting their turn to embark.

Mrs. Astor protested that she would not leave him aboard the sinking ship. He reassured her, telling her that he would hope to join her in a short time, and then insisted that she take the place allotted her in the lifeboat. She did so.

The boat was lowered away, after Colonel Astor had pressed a goodby kiss upon his bride's lips. Peering over the side of the ship, he watched until the boat had started safely away from the Titanic's towering side.

Then drawing himself up in a soldierly attitude, he touched his cap in military salute to his bride and stepped back to his place among the men.

Washington Roebling, young scion of a wealthy New Jersey family and grandson of the builder of the Brooklyn Bridge, was another who exemplified the highest traditions of manhood. When one of the last of the boats was being filled he gallantly escorted to the ship's side Miss Margaret Graham, her mother and a governess and helped them into the boat.

A NONCHALANT GOODBY.

Smilingly Mr. Roebling bade them a nonchalant farewell and wished them a safe journey. Then, as thoroughly self-possessed as though he were at the wheel of his familiar automobile, he lifted his cap, lighted a cigarette and stepped back to await his doom.

Almost overcome with emotion, Daniel Guggenheim, eldest of a family of brothers who represent mining and manufacturing interests in America aggregating many millions in value, told on Friday how bravely his younger brother, Benjamin, went down on board the doomed ship.

One of the Titanic's stewards, Johnson by name, had called upon the widow of Benjamin Guggenheim at the Hotel St. Regis, where the family make their home. He had delivered to the sorrowing widow the last message from her husband.

"When Mr. Guggenheim realized that there was grave danger," said the room steward, "he advised his secretary, who also died, to dress fully and he himself did the same. Mr. Guggenheim, who was cool and collected as he was pulling on his outer garments, said to the steward:—

PREPARED TO DIE BRAVELY.

"I think there is grave doubt that the men will get off safely. I am willing to remain and play the man's game, if there are not enough boats for more than the women and children. I won't die here like a beast. I'll meet my end as a man."

There was a pause and then Mr. Guggenheim continued:—

"Tell my wife, Johnson, if it should happen that my secretary and I both go down and you are saved, tell her I played the game out straight and to the end. No woman shall be left aboard this ship because Ben Guggenheim was a coward.

"Tell her that my last thoughts will be of her and of our girls, but that my duty now is to these unfortunate women and children on this ship. Tell her I will meet whatever fate is in store for me, knowing she will approve of what I do."

In telling the story the room steward said that the last he saw of Mr. Guggenheim was when he stood fully dressed upon the upper deck talking calmly with Colonel Astor and Major Butt.

"AN AWFUL CRIME."

Tears filled the eyes of his elder brother as Daniel Guggenheim said:—

"It comes hard to me, the oldest of seven, seven who have grown up together with never a death among us till now. But my grief is little compared with that of his three daughters and his wife, who were devotedly happy in their home life.

"According to the room steward, my brother afterward went to the forward end of the Titanic. I know not how he died, but his death, and the death of those fifteen hundred and more brave souls is a frightful price to pay for safety on our seas. This is an awful crime, but it is best to suspend our judgment until after the pending investigation has been made by both governments.

"We surely can afford to tax foreign vessels with the price of safety at any cost. Let there be provided for our American travellers by sea more safety, less luxury and less speed. Let there be smaller dividends and larger profits in the saving of lives of human beings."

Benjamin Guggenheim, who went down with the ship, was a graduate of Columbia University. He married a daughter of James W. Seligman. Several months ago he was called to Europe on business concerning the International Pump Company, of which he was president. In arranging for his return to America he had booked passage for the Mauretania, and wrote that he would come on board that ship. At the last moment he decided to return home aboard the Titanic.

GAVE LIFE FOR THE WEAK.

Henry B. Harris, a well known New York theatrical manager, was another who willingly surrendered his one chance of rescue in favor of the weaker women and children. In one of the boats, which was not filled rapidly, he had been helped into a seat beside his wife. One of the ship's officers, seeing him there, cried out:—

"Women and children first!"

"That's right," said Mr. Harris. Then he turned to his wife, kissed her lightly and said:—

"Goodby, my dear; I must take my medicine with the rest."

He resumed his place upon the ship's deck, joined the other men and shared their fate.

Incidents of like cool fortitude might easily be multiplied. There is one, however, that is worthy of the best traditions of the sea and that will shine forever in marine history. There are few episodes either in history or fiction that depict a finer fortitude than was displayed by the ship's band on board the Titanic.

Soon after Captain Smith realized that there was grave danger of the ship foundering and of panic preceding that catastrophe, he ordered that the ship's musicians should play an impromptu programme of lively music, in the hope that it might tend in some measure to hold in check the peril of a frenzied rush upon the boats.

LIVELY AIRS PLAYED.

No soldiers ever obeyed a military order more promptly or loyally. The members of the musical organization, which is composed of the ship's stewards, lined up with their instruments and played one air after another in excellent harmony and rhythm.

They ran through much of the repertoire, including such rollocking strains as "Turkey in the Straw" and even "Alexander's Ragtime Band." They recognized the fact that lively music was wanted in

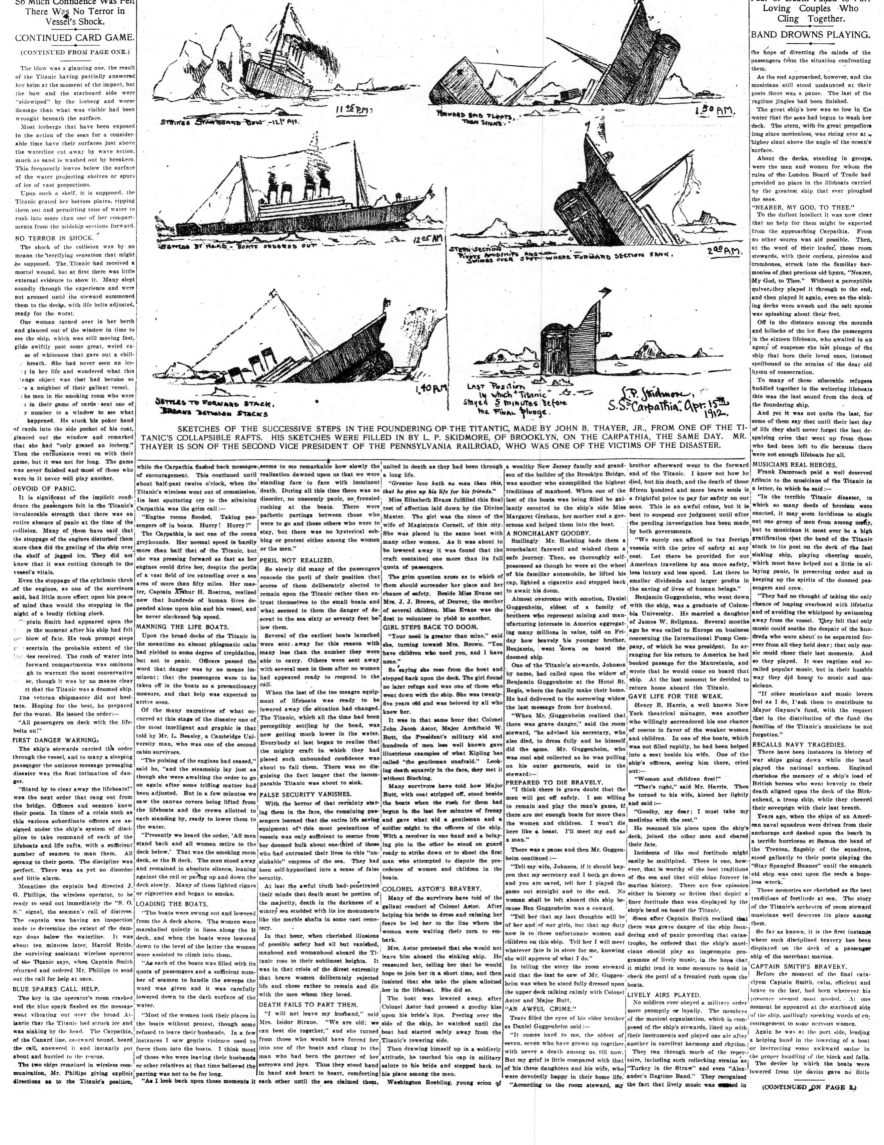

SKETCHES OF THE SUCCESSIVE STEPS IN THE FOUNDERING OF THE TITANTIC, MADE BY JOHN B. THAYER, JR., FROM ONE OF THE TITANIC'S COLLAPSIBLE RAFTS. HIS SKETCHES WERE FILLED IN BY L. P. SKIDMORE, OF BROOKLYN, ON THE CARPATHIA, THE SAME DAY. MR. THAYER IS SON OF THE SECOND VICE PRESIDENT OF THE PENNSYLVANIA RAILROAD, WHO WAS ONE OF THE VICTIMS OF THE DISASTER.

Fear of Death Failed to Part Loving Couples Who Cling Together.

BAND DROWNS PLAYING.

the hope of diverting the minds of the passengers from the situation confronting them.

As the end approached, however, and the musicians still stood undaunted at their posts there was a pause. The last of the ragtime jingles had been finished.

The great ship's bow was so low in the water that the seas had begun to wash her deck. The stern, with its great propellors long since motionless, was rising ever at a higher slant above the angle of the ocean's surface.

About the decks, standing in groups, were the men and women for whom the rules of the London Board of Trade had provided no place in the lifeboats carried by the greatest ship that ever ploughed the seas.

"NEARER, MY GOD, TO THEE."

To the dullest intellect it was now clear that no help for them might be expected from the approaching Carpathia. From no other source was aid possible. Then, at the word of their leader, those room stewards, with their cornets, piccolos and trombones, struck into the familiar harmonies of that precious old hymn, "Nearer, My God, to Thee." Without a perceptible quiver they played it through to the end, and then played it again, even as the sinking decks were awash and the salt spume was splashing about their feet.

Off in the distance among the mounds and hillocks of the ice floes the passengers in the sixteen lifeboats, who awaited in an agony of suspense the last plunge of the ship that bore their loved ones, listened spellbound to the strains of the dear old hymn of consecration.

To many of these miserable refugees huddled together in the weltering lifeboats this was the last sound from the deck of the foundering ship.

And yet it was not quite the last, for some of them say that until their last day of life they shall never forget the last despairing cries that went up from those who had been left to die because there were not enough lifeboats for all.

MUSICIANS REAL HEROES.

Frank Damrosch paid a well deserved tribute to the musicians of the Titanic in a letter, in which he said:—

"In the terrible Titanic disaster, in which so many deeds of heroism were enacted, it may seem invidious to single out one group of men from among many, but to musicians it must ever be a high gratification that the band of the Titanic stuck to its post on the deck of the fast sinking ship, playing cheering music, which must have helped not a little in allaying panic, in preserving order and in keeping up the spirits of the doomed passengers and crew.

"They had no thought of taking the only chance of leaping overboard with lifebelts and of avoiding the whirlpool by swimming away from the vessel. They felt that only music could soothe the despair of the hundreds who were about to be separated forever from all they held dear; that only music could cheer their last moments. And so they played. It was ragtime and so-called popular music, but in their humble way they did honor to music and musicians.

"If other musicians and music lovers feel as I do, I ask them to contribute to Mayor Gaynor's fund, with the request that in the distribution of the fund the families of the Titanic's musicians be not forgotten."

RECALLS NAVY TRAGEDIES.

There have been instances in history of war ships going down while the band played the national anthem. England cherishes the memory of a ship's load of British heroes who went bravely to their death aligned upon the deck of the Birkenhead, a troop ship, while they cheered their sovereign with their last breath.

Years ago, when the ships of an American naval squadron were driven from their anchorage and dashed upon the beach in a terrific hurricane at Samoa the band of the Trenton, flagship of the squadron, stood gallantly to their posts playing the "Star Spangled Banner" until the staunch old ship was cast upon the reefs a hopeless wreck.

These memories are cherished as the best traditions of fortitude at sea. The story of the Titanic's orchestra of room steward musicians well deserves its place among them.

So far as known, it is the first instance where such disciplined bravery has been displayed on the deck of a passenger ship of the merchant marine.

CAPTAIN SMITH'S BRAVERY.

Before the moment of the final cataclysm Captain Smith, calm, efficient and brave to the last, had been wherever his presence seemed most needed. At one moment he appeared at the starboard side of the ship, smilingly speaking words of encouragement to some nervous women.

Again he was at the port side, lending a helping hand in the lowering of a boat or instructing some awkward sailor in the proper handling of the block and falls. The device by which the boats were lowered from the davits gave no little

(CONTINUED ON PAGE 3.)

SUBLIME HEROISM IN MEN AND WOMEN AT DOOR OF ICY CEMETERY

THE TITANIC.

THE LAST OF THE TITANIC.

CAPTAIN E. J. SMITH of THE TITANIC.

(CONTINUED FROM PAGE TWO.)

trouble. It appeared that many of the sailors were unfamiliar with its operation, perhaps because the great ship was on her maiden voyage and they had not yet been sufficiently schooled in the lifeboat drills which many of the transatlantic steamship companies make an important feature of their organization and discipline at sea.

In at least two instances the clumsy lowering of the lifeboats cost a heavy toll of human lives. Each of these boats had been filled with its full quota of fifty persons.

LIVES LOST AT START.

While the boats were being lowered rapidly, the rope running freely through the pulley blocks, the stern tackle jammed, with the inevitable result that the boats were suspended at a height of fully fifty feet above the sea and their passengers were thrown out and drowned within sight of those who stood upon the deck.

Such mishaps have been so common in ocean disasters that steamship companies which pride themselves especially upon their safeguarding of human life spare no pains to have men in the ship's company thoroughly schooled in the art of lowering and subsequently of handling the lifeboats and life rafts.

On one occasion, when a group of the ship's seamen showed a momentary disposition to charge upon one of the boats, Captain Smith confronted them with flashing eyes. Raising his arms above his head, he cried:—

"Stand back, men, and prove once more that Englishmen know how to die."

The sailors quailed before the master's rebuke and thereafter they stood to their posts, as he did, until the awful end.

So far as is known the last act of Captain Smith in behalf of the passengers committed to his charge was to seize a child who had become parted from her parents or guardians and lift her gently into the last of the lifeboats that was swung from the davits before the Titanic sank.

AT HIS POST TO THE END.

As to how the gallant captain of this greatest of ships met his own fate there have been conflicting reports. One of these was to the effect that after all had been done that mortal man could do he stood at his post on the bridge and shot himself.

This was a rumor that passed current from lip to lip in the excitement and confusion that attended the arrival of the survivors of the wreck aboard the Carpathia. Careful inquiry later failed utterly to substantiate its truth.

Other survivors who went overboard protected only by lifebelts and who afterward made their way to a half submerged liferaft, said that as they were tossed about in the surging waves in the outer rim of the maelstrom caused by the sinking ship they caught a glimpse of a uniformed officer whom they believed to be Captain Smith. He rose to the surface for a moment, they say, but was soon swept away out of their sight.

Whether either or neither of these stories be well founded, certain it is that the captain of the Titanic faced his death like a gallant man and went down into the depths with his ship.

A MARVEL OF FATE.

First Officer Murdock shared the fate of his captain. The third officer of the ship, Robert H. Lightroller, also remained at his post after having done yeoman service up to the last. He, too, went down when the Titanic made her final plunge into her ocean grave.

By one of those marvellous chances which seem to defy all physical laws, he survived the mad whirl of waters and the resistless suction of the sinking ship and rose again to the surface, where he was pulled aboard one of the liferafts and back to life.

Mr. Lightroller was one of the witnesses who was examined in the first day's session held by the Senatorial Investigating Committee at the Waldorf-Astoria.

Under the questioning of Senator Smith, chairman of the committee, the third officer gave his answers in the frank, bluff manner of a seaman.

"At about what time did you leave the ship?" asked Senator Smith.

"I didn't leave the ship," replied the officer, with just a touch of justifiable pride in his tone. "The ship left me."

ESCAPES OCEAN TOMB.

At least one other man had an equally remarkable experience in going down with the ship and yet living to tell the tale. That man is Colonel Archibald Gracie, U. S. A. He told an extraordinary story of personal hardship and praised in the highest terms both the passengers and crew. Colonel Gracie also paid high tribute to the bravery of many of the women in the first and second cabins.

"Mrs. Isidor Straus," he said, "went to her death because she would not desert her husband. Although he pleaded with her to take her place in the boat she steadfastly refused, and when the ship settled at the head the two were engulfed by the sea that swept her."

Colonel Gracie told of how he was driven to the topmost deck when the ship settled and was the sole survivor after the sea that swept her just before her final plunge had passed.

"I jumped with the sea," said he, "just as I often have jumped with the breakers at the seashore. By great good fortune I managed to grasp the brass railing on the deck above, and I hung on by might and main. When the ship plunged down I was forced to let go and I was swirled around and around for what seemed to be an interminable time. Eventually I came to the surface to find the sea a mass of tangled wreckage.

REFUGE ON A RAFT.

"Luckily I was unhurt, and casting about managed to seize a wooden grating floating near by. When I had recovered my breath I discovered a larger canvas and cork life raft which had floated up. A man whose name I did not learn was struggling toward it from some wreckage to which he had clung. I cast off and helped him to get onto the raft, and we then began the work of rescuing those who had jumped into the sea and were floundering in the water.

"When dawn broke there were thirty of us on the raft, standing knee deep in the icy water and afraid to move lest the cranky craft be overturned. Several unfortunates, benumbed and half dead, besought us to save them and one or two made an effort to reach us, but if we had made an effort to save them we all might have perished.

"The hours that elapsed before we were picked up by the Carpathia were the longest and most terrible that I ever spent. Practically without any sensation of feeling because of the icy water, we were almost dropping from fatigue.

HYSTERICAL UNDER STRAIN.

"We were afraid to turn around to see whether we were seen by passing craft, and when some one who was facing astern passed the word that something that looked like a steamship was coming up one of the men became hysterical under the strain. The rest of us, too, were nearing the breaking point."

Colonel Gracie denied with emphasis that any men were fired upon and declared that only once was a revolver discharged.

"This was for the purpose of intimidating some of the steerage passengers," he said, "who had tumbled into a boat before it was prepared for launching. This shot was fired in the air, and when the foreigners were told that the next would be directed at them they promptly returned to the deck. There was no confusion and no panic.

"Before I retired,' said Colonel Gracie, "I had a long chat with Charles H. Hays, president of the Grand Trunk Railroad. One of the last things Mr. Hays said was this:—'The White Star, the Cunard and the Hamburg-American lines are devoting their attention and ingenuity in vying one with the other to attain the supremacy in luxurious ships and in making speed records. The time will soon come when this will be checked by some appalling disaster.' Poor fellow, a few hours later he was dead!

FEARED BOILING DEATH.

"After sinking with the ship," said Colonel Gracie, "it appeared to me as if I was propelled by some great force through the water. It might have been occasioned by an explosion under the water. I recall I was fearful most about being boiled to death. A similar feeling was described to me by the second officer, who had nearly the same experience. Innumerable thoughts of a personal nature relating to mental telepathy passed through my brain. I thought of those at home as if my spirit might go to them and say goodby forever.

"I prayed for deliverance, though sure my last hour had come. Meantime I was striking out with all my strength, swimming under water. Reaching the surface, no ship was in sight, but there was a large field of wreckage.

"Finally the raft became so full that it seemed she would sink beneath the sea, and for self-preservation the crew had to decline to take more aboard.

"This was the most pathetic and horrible of scenes, with the air all round us rent with screams which the survivors will not forget to their dying days.

HEROES SINK TO DEATH.

"'Hold on to what you have, old boy!' one of the crew would cry. 'One more of you aboard would sink us all.'

"'Good luck, and God bless you,' was the magnificent reply of some unknown hero.

"All the time we were buoyed up by the hope of rescue. We saw light in several directions, but particularly in front, where a green light shone and rockets were fired from what after all was only one of the Titanic's lifeboats.

"So we passed the night, with the water washing over us up to our waists.

"How we did pray for the coming of day, and some of the men of this rough crew thought of their God and all of us repeated over and over the Lord's Prayer. Before the break of day most of us were standing on our feet, balancing ourselves in columns two deep and back to back, fearful all the while lest a sudden lurch might overturn the raft and the air beneath might escape. The slightest wind would have caused our destruction.

"We saw the lights of the Carpathia in the distance. We knew it to be her from our Marconi man, who happened to be with us.

"Word was passed that there was also a ship behind, and the second officer bade us all be still while one looked, for the slipping of one man meant death for all.

LIFEBOAT TO THE RESCUE.

"But when day broke, O glorious scene! Four of the Titanic's lifeboats appeared on our port side and the second officer's whistle called attention to our precarious condition, and the head lifeboat towing another came to our rescue.

"Then followed a dangerous but successful transfer. The second officer, waiting till the last, helping to lift the corpse of one of the crew from the raft.

"I, with my soggy overcoat and clothing heavy with water, had gone head foremost into the boat, careful not to disturb the equilibrium of the raft. In this boat to which we were transferred I saw some of the men who had been with me on the raft, while others got onto the second boat.

"Our boat, however, now had more than its complement, sixty-five persons. Fortunately the Carpathia was not a great distance away, otherwise, so officers of the Carpathia said, we would have sunk when a moderate blow came up one hour later.

"We all suffered from cold, especially those of us with no hats. It seemed an interminable time before we reached the Carpathia, where all were ready for us with first aid to the injured and warm potations to restore our much fatigued bodies. Nothing can exceed the kindness we all received from the hands of the ministering angels who welcomed us on board the Carpathia.

"Such was my personal experience, relating only what I myself saw and what I did. I have nothing but praise for all concerned."

A GRAPHIC DESCRIPTION.

Mr. Lawrence Beasley, of London, was one of the men who was told to jump into a vacant place in a lifeboat at a time when there were no more women in sight who were willing to go. He afterward gave a graphic description of the sinking of the Titanic in the calm sea of a starlight night as he witnessed it from the lifeboat which had carried him to safety. Mr. Beasley said:—

"The captain stoker told us that he had been at sea twenty-six years and had never yet seen such a calm night on the Atlantic. As we rowed away from the Titanic we looked back from time to time to watch her, and a more striking spectacle it was not possible for any one to see.

"We were now about two miles from her and all the crew insisted that such a tremendous wave would be formed by suction as she went down that we ought to get as far away as possible. The captain agreed and all lay on their oars and widened the distance between us and the sinking vessel.

"Presently, about two o'clock, as near as I can remember, we observed her settling very rapidly, with the bows and the bridge completely under water, and concluded it was now only a question of minutes before she went, and so it proved.

"She slowly tilted straight on end with the stern vertically upward, and as she did the lights in the cabins and saloons, which had not flickered for a moment since we left, died out, came on again for a single flash and finally went altogether.

WEIRD SOUNDS OF DEATH.

"At the same time the machinery roared down through the vessel with a rattle and a groaning that could be heard for miles, the weirdest sound surely that could be heard in the middle of the ocean, a thousand miles away from land. But this was not quite the end.

"To our amazement she remained in that upright position for a time, which I estimate as five minutes—others in the boat say less—but it was certainly some minutes while we watched at least one hundred and fifty feet of the Titanic towering above the level of the sea and looming black against the sky.

"Then, with a quiet slanting dive, she disappeared beneath the waters and our eyes had looked for the last time on the gigantic vessel we had set out on from Southampton last Wednesday.

"And then there fell on the ear the most appalling noise that human being ever listened to—the cries of hundreds of our fellow beings struggling in the ice cold water, crying for help with a cry that we knew could not be answered. We longed to return and pick up some of those swimming, but this would have meant swamping our boat and further loss of the lives of all of us.

AWAITING RESCUE SHIP.

"We kept a lookout for lights, and several times it was shouted that ship lights were seen, but they turned out to be either a light from another boat or a star low down on the horizon. About three o'clock we saw faint lights showing on the sky and all rejoiced to see what we expected was the coming of dawn but after watching for half an hour and seeing no change in the intensity of the light realized it was the northern lights.

"Presently low down on the horizon we saw a light which slowly resolved itself into a double light and we watched eagerly to see if the two lights would separate or whether they would remain together in which case we should expect them to be the masthead light and a deck light below of a rescuing steamship.

"To our joy they moved as one, and round we swung the boat and headed for her. The steersman shouted, 'Now, boys, into song with "Row for the Shore, Boys," ' and for the first time tears came to the eyes of us all as we realized that safety was at hand."

ESCAPED CAPTAIN'S FATE.

J. Bruce Ismay, managing director of the White Star company, did not share the fate of the Titanic's captain. He found a place in one of the lifeboats, which he said was the tenth to be sent away from the sinking ship.

After Mr. Ismay reached New York he was subjected to a searching inquiry by members of the Senatorial investigating committee. He said that in the boat in which he made his escape the only other men were four of the crew who were handling the oars, and one of them, a quartermaster, was in command of the boat. His other companions were forty women and children.

Mr. Ismay said he had given no commands to Captain Smith concerning the movements of the ship or the speed to be maintained. He asserted that the Titanic at the time of the disaster was on the extreme southern route charted for west bound ships. He knew that ice had been reported in the vicinity, but had heard nothing concerning the wireless message relayed by the Titanic from the Amerika reporting icebergs in that precise latitude.

MR. ISMAY'S FIRST ICEBERG.

Until he made his escape in one of the lifeboats, Mr. Ismay said, he had never seen an iceberg in his life. The managing director added, in reply to further questions, that he had not consulted with Captain Smith concerning the danger of encountering icebergs at the speed which the Titanic was then maintaining, as that was a matter entirely outside of his province.

It was twenty minutes after two o'clock on Monday morning, April 15, when the Titanic, with a final shiver, plunged to the bottom of the Atlantic in water two thousand fathoms deep and nearly a thousand miles from the nearest shore. Some time before this final act in the sea tragedy the horror stricken refugees in the little fleet of waiting lifeboats heard the muffled report of three sharp explosions at intervals of a few minutes.

These reverberations marked the successive bursting of the great ship's compartment bulkheads as the sea finally plunged its waters into her vitals at the rate of a thousand tons a second.

Men who observed closely the last scene in this most harrowing of all ocean dramas said that this series of explosions, together with the heavy strain placed upon the Titanic's midship section by the gradual lifting of her bow, broke her fairly into two great sections amidships.

VIVID SKETCHES OF SHIP.

The various phases of her foundering were graphically illustrated in a series of sketches made by John B. Thayer, Jr., son of one of the vice presidents of the Pennsylvania Railroad, who was rescued from death by clinging to one of the collapsible rafts, although his father, less fortunate, was among the lost.

Mr. Thayer's sketches, as filled in by L. P. Skidmore, of Brooklyn, a passenger on board the Carpathia, were reproduced in the HERALD of last Friday. They show most vividly the utter demolition, the complete collapse of this marvellous creation of man's skill in marine construction.

All that is left of the proud empress of the seas, with her boasted water tight compartments, her lavish appointments, her sun parlors, palm gardens, golf links and tennis courts, lies buried so deep in the ocean that scientists say there is little hope that any of the bodies coffined in her gilded saloons will ever rise to the surface.

Of the 2,340 persons who came out with her from Southampton Water amid the merry waving of handkerchiefs and the tribute of steam whistles paid to the queen of the ocean fleet, all but 745 have shared the death of the newly crowned sovereign of the seas, whose first triumphal progress ended in chaos and death before ever she reached a Western port.

Mr. Wm. Harris to Continue Theatrical Enterprises Left by Son, Henry B. Harris

Policies of Noted Producer, Who Perished in the Titanic Disaster, Will Be Followed.

WHAT is to be the future of the theatrical enterprises of Henry B. Harris?

This question was widely discussed in Broadway last week by men and also by women who had known Mr. Harris as among the leading theatrical producers in America. Only those who are intimate with the friendships which exist in the world of the stage can understand the sorrow and shock to fellow members in the profession caused by the news that Mr. Harris was among the passengers on board the Titanic who perished at sea. The discussion as to his theatrical affairs extended beyond the limits of theatrical circles and among playgoers, who in the last twelve years had come to look upon an attraction of Mr. Harris' as possessing distinct features.

Careful investigation among business associates and personal friends of Mr. Harris has led to the conclusion that the enterprises which had their beginning in the imagination of Mr. Harris will be carried on according to the original designs under the direction of the manager's father, Mr. William Harris. It is no reflection on the abilities of the younger man to say his father ever was his adviser and supporter and that no small degree of the success of the son was due to his policy of constant consultation with his father.

MR. HENRY B HARRIS
PHOTO BY WHITE

Mr. William Harris was conversant with every phase of the younger man's business. Broad as the business ramifications of the son appear to be, they by no means eclipse Mr. William Harris' enterprises. In view, also, of the fact that the elder man has been in charge of the affairs of his son during the last eight weeks, while the latter with his wife was abroad on a vacation, it is asserted on good authority that Mr. William Harris will retain his place indefinitely, supervising the arrangements for this season's attractions and carrying out those that the son had projected for next season.

What degree of love and admiration

"The Lion and the Mouse" Among Famous Successes—Others Had Rejected It.

Henry B. Harris had for his father may best be shown by recalling one of this season's most interesting incidents. This was the dedication last autumn of the Harris Theatre in West Forty-second street, which was previously called the Hackett. Miss Rose Stahl began her season there in "Maggie Pepper," and the audience was a brilliant one. On the programme appeared these words:—

> In gratitude to my father, whose influence has shaped my career, I dedicate this theatre.
> HENRY B. HARRIS.

Mr. Henry B. Harris was born "in the business," an incident to which he often proudly referred in after years. At that time his father was appearing in a song and dance act at DeBarr's Opera House in St. Louis with Mr. William Carroll as his partner. In the theatres of the Middle West Master Harris first obtained a glimpse of theatrical life. When seven years old he sold song books in the gallery of a theatre in St. Louis.

In every way that a boy might be useful around a playhouse, both in the front and at the back, Master Harris held positions, which for the greater part yielded commissions that allowed him to increase

(CONTINUED ON PAGE FOUR.)

STIRRING PICTURES OF VITAL EPISODES IN TITANIC TRAGEDY

CAPTAIN A. H. ROSTRUN OF THE CARPATHIA.

THE ICEBERG WHICH CAUSED THE DISASTER PHOTOGRAPHED FROM THE CARPATHIA.

THE CARPATHIA.

LIFE BOAT UNDER SAIL APPROACHING THE CARPATHIA

FOUR OF THE TITANIC'S LIFEBOATS ALONGSIDE THE CARPATHIA. UNLOADING SURVIVORS.

LIFE PRESERVERS USED BY SURVIVORS HEAPED ON THE DECK OF THE CARPATHIA

J. BRUCE ISMAY (↓) WITH OTHER SURVIVORS IN LIFE BOAT ALONGSIDE THE CARPATHIA

SURVIVORS IN LIFE BOATS ON WAY TO THE CARPATHIA.

SURVIVORS WAITING TO BE HOISTED ON BOARD THE CARPATHIA.

HENRY B. HARRIS, VICTIM

(CONTINUED FROM PAGE THREE.)

his savings in proportion to his work and ability.

When seventeen years old he left the theatrical business to enter a commercial house in Boston, and there eight years later he accepted a position as assistant treasurer of the Columbia Theatre at a salary of $24 a week. Three years later found him the business manager of the playhouse, which was under the control of Messrs. Charles Frohman, Isaac B. Rich and William Harris. Next the younger Harris, in association with Mr. Charles J. Rich, son of the manager, established a stock company at Howard's Athenæum, Boston.

First Play a Success.

It was in 1894 that Mr. Harris made his first strike as an individual manager and producer, purchasing for $2,500 an interest in "The Widow Jones," with Miss May Irwin as star. The share was sold by the elder Mr. Rich, and the other owner was Mr. William Harris. Thus was first established the business association between father and son. At the end of the first season young Mr. Harris had cleared more than $12,000 as his share of the profits.

But success did not come without its failures, and seven years later, or in 1901, Mr. Harris had lost his earnings as a producer, and then became the business manager for the Frohman, Harris and Rich companies. His success in this post led to an offer from Miss Amelia Bingham to go with her as her business manager in "The Climbers," in which he obtained an interest, and from this point forward his career was successful, artistically and financially.

Mr. Harris was a believer with his father in American drama for Americans. Following his connection with Miss Bingham, he placed Mr. Robert Edeson under contract to star, and then engaged Mr. Augustus Thomas, the playwright, to dramatize Mr. Richard Harding Davis' "Soldiers of Fortune." This all-American combination was highly successful, and was followed by the engagement of other American actors and actresses to star under his management. Mr. George G. Heye, the real estate man, became jointly interested with Mr. Harris in the building of the beautiful Hudson Theatre in West Forty-fourth street. Subsequently Mr. Harris became the sole owner. The theatre was opened in 1903 with Miss Ethel Barrymore in "Cousin Kate."

His Noted Productions.

His next great success came two years later, in 1905, when, after trying to dispose of the play elsewhere, Mr. Charles Klein handed to Mr. Harris the manuscript of "The Lion and the Mouse." It was an instantaneous hit, running in New York for more than a year, and elsewhere presented by several companies for two or three seasons. In a recent article in a weekly publication Mr. Harris stated that his profits from "The Lion and the Mouse" exceeded a quarter of a million dollars. He stated further that a producer who succeeds in placing before the public one play they will support can more than pay his losses on eight unsuccessful productions.

Following "The Lion and the Mouse" came Mr. James Forbes' play "The Chorus Lady," in which Miss Rose Stahl, for her impersonation of Maggie O'Brien, is known from coast to coast.

It is stated that when Miss Stahl made her first appearance in the play in New York the theatre at which she played was under lease to some other manager than Mr. Harris. After the first two weeks of the run, looking around unsuccessfully for a playhouse in which to present his star, Mr. Harris negotiated for the purchase of the Hackett Theatre in Forty-second street. Here Miss Stahl played "The Chorus Lady" for two seasons.

To mention each of these early successful productions would be interesting, for they are still fresh in the minds of the American playgoer. In 1908 Mr. Harris had so far extended his business that he had six acknowledged stars under contract and eleven plays on tour. Mr. Edeson, in "Strongheart," was one of these. Miss Elsie Ferguson, in "Such a Little Queen," was another.

Had Share of Failures.

Predictions made by other managers that Mr. Harris' good fortune could not continue seemed to have some basis, when, two years ago, according to his own statements in the article referred to, he produced thirteen successive failures. Last season he was more successful, although his interest in the Folies Bergère, in West Forty-sixth street, proved expensive. After seven months the Folies Bergère project was abandoned and Mr. Harris took over exclusively the lease of the playhouse, renaming it the Fulton.

In the season now drawing to a close Mr. Harris made several productions. Some have been failures, others successes. The ratio is less than that specified by Mr. Harris.

Among them were Mr. Frank McIntyre in "Snobs," at the Hudson Theatre; Miss Elsie Ferguson in "The First Lady in the Land," at the Gaiety and later the Fulton; Miss Rose Stahl in "Maggie Pepper," at the Harris; Mr. Robert Edeson in "The Cave Man," at the Fulton; "The Quaker Girl," with Mr. Clifton Crawford, at the Park; Miss Dorothy Donnelly and Mr. Edmund Breese in "The Right To Be Happy," at the Hudson, and Mr. Edgar Selwyn in "The Arab," at the Lyceum and later at the Astor. "The Talker" is now at the Harris. Besides these Mr. Harris presented on the road this season three companies playing Mr. Selwyn's "The Country Boy," one company in "The Travelling Salesman" and one presenting "The Commuters." Miss Ruth St. Denis, the dancer, was under his direction.

A friend of Mr. Harris related yesterday an incident of the manager's faith in his judgment and his companies once he was convinced that success would come, even if it were delayed. One of his stars appearing this season on the road without much encouragement from the public wrote to Mr. Harris asking that the tour be abandoned because it appeared to be a financial loss. Mr. Harris replied:—

"Cannot think of giving up. Perhaps they aren't coming to see you now, but they will. We'll get it all back."

Leaves Large Estate.

To estimate the value of the estate left by Mr. Harris was too difficult during the last week. It is known that he had interests outside of the theatrical business. As to some of his theatrical holdings, however, the chief ones, aside from his ownership of the rights of more than thirty-five plays, were the Hudson and Harris theatres, which he owned outright. He held the lease to the Fulton and to the Grand Opera House, in New Haven, which in turn had been sublet. He also held the lease of the Walnut Street Theatre, Philadelphia. It is generally believed that Mr. Harris was interested in the Park Theatre, but this is incorrect, the playhouse being controlled by Messrs. Frank McKee and William Harris. With these men Mr. Harris was interested in "The Quaker Girl," the attraction at the Park, which has been the musical comedy hit of the present season in New York.

Two companies of "The Quaker Girl" will be presented on the road next season, and Mr. Harris, before leaving for Europe, arranged that Mr. Clifton Crawford would be starred in another musical comedy. Some other tentative projects for the coming season are two companies in "The Talker" and the production of new plays by Messrs. Edgar Selwyn, George Broadhurst, Mrs. Marion Fairfax and other playwrights.

Captain Polack Points Out Dangers of the Deep

"IT is not a question of who a man is, but what he is! It is a matter that only his God and he can decide," said Captain Polack, of the North German Lloyd steamship George Washington.

"Who can say what we should have done under such awful circumstances?" Captain Polack said in answer to a question. "Might we not have all proven to be cowards? Is it not in the realm of possibility that we should have lived up to the laws of nature and striven to save ourselves?

"Precedent, the laws of humanity and our own consciences forbid, so we try to face the inevitable with the best hearts that we can muster."

"Supposing that your ship was in a collision, what is the first thing that you would do?"

In answer Captain Polack stepped on the working bridge and pressed a button.

Gongs rang through the great ship and men sprang from nowhere! They crawled from hatches, crept from alleys, appeared as ghosts. Swarms and swarms of men, tumbling over one another to get to their respective places by the boats.

Clang! Clang!! Clang!!!

On the bridge tiny red lights showed one by one as the water tight compartments closed!

Still more men! They manned the falls—stood by.

Stewards—stewardesses — stokers — all waited.

A superb exhibition of discipline!

"We are steaming in a few hours," Captain Polack said, "and you must forgive, for we have so much to do.—Yes?"

Clang!

They vanished as mysteriously as they had come until the decks were empty and the yawning hatches stared up to a dimly starred sky.

"On the sea we use the force of arms, if necessary," Captain Polack continued, "until the boats can be got away. After that"—— he hesitated, and a grim look settled on his face. "After that each man must prepare to meet his God in his own way. But you can picture to yourself the feelings that riot in the minds of those for whom there is no chance. The ship is in darkness, shall we say; fog grips everything in its clammy embrace, and as we wait for the end that never seems to come we can hear out there"—the skipper's arm moved slowly in a semicircle—"the faint and still fainter calls of goodby from those whose time to die has not yet come.

"We roll heavily in the sea; the surface is well below us yet, and we feel the gradually increasing sluggishness of the hull under us as the water pours through the gaping rents. Lower and lower. We officers that are left try to pacify every one, but they"—— Ach! The forceful quiet in which Captain Polack had been speaking vanished; he jumped up. "What would you expect? The water seethes and bubbles, wetting some man to his knees, and he screams in the human fear of death. That scream unleashes the hell that an apathy has controlled and men are no longer men but animals, tearing each other, shrieking for the help that cannot come.

"But the greater part rush from side to side, huddling away from the death that crawls steadily nearer, climbing over one another like ants, swarming up the standing rigging, if there is any, calling ceaselessly with the voices of beasts.

"The ship scarcely lifts to the seas now, and there comes that indescribable horror of the knowledge that it really is the end.

"From somewhere below comes a muffled report, the ship quivers as the last bulkhead that kept her afloat bursts, and then, to the laughter of madmen, the wailings of helpless souls, curses, fiendish screams and the final crash of seas, she goes down."

CAPTAIN CHARLES POLACK

Silence in the skipper's quarters, broken only by the creaking of derricks and the rattle of donkey engines fore and aft hoisting in the last of the cargo.

"Yes," he said then, "it is more terrible than even all one can imagine. But in life one is in death, and one can but try to do one's best."

FAMOUS PERSONS WHO WENT TO HEROIC DEATH; LIST OF MISSING

MR. CHARLES M. HAYS

MR. FRANK D. MILLET

MR. JACQUES FUTRELLE

MR. W. T. STEAD

MR. JOHN JACOB ASTOR

MAJOR ARCHIBALD W. BUTT

MR ISIDOR STRAUS

PERSONS OF WORLD WIDE FAME LOST IN THE FOUNDERING OF THE TITANIC

MRS. ISIDOR STRAUS

Below is a list of the Titanic's first cabin passengers whose names do not appear among those saved:—

A

AUBERT, Mrs. N., and maid.
ALLISON, Mr. H. J.
ALLISON, Mrs., and maid.
ALLISON, Miss.
ANDREWS, Mr. THOMAS.
ARTAGAVEYTIA, Mr. RAMON.
ASTOR, Colonel J. J., and man servant.
ANDERSON, Mr. WALKER.

B

BAXTER, Mrs. JAMES.
BEATTIE, Mr. T.
BRANDIES, Mr. EMIL.
BAUMAN, Mr. J.
BAXTER, Mr., and Mrs. QUIGG.
BIRNBAUM, JACOB.
BJORNSTORM, Mr. H.
BLACKWELL, Mr. STEPHEN WEART, Trenton, N. J.
BONNELL, Miss LILY.
BOREBANK, Mr. J. J.
BRADY, Mr. JOHN B., Pomeroy, Wash.
BREWE, Mr. ARTHUR JACKSON.
BUTT, Major ARCHIBALD W.
CASE, Mr. HOWARD B.
CAVENDISH, Mr. T. W.
CLIFFORD, Mr. GEORGE QUINCY.
COLEY, Mr. E. P., Victoria, B. C.

C

CRAIG, Mr. NORMAN C. K., C. M. P.
CARLSON, Mr. FRANK.
CORRAN, Mr. F. M.
CORRAN, Mr. J. P.
CHAFEE, Mr. H. L.
CHISHOLM, Mr. ROBERT.
COMPTON, Miss S. R.
COMPTON, Mr. and Mrs. A. T.
CORNELL, Mr. R. O.
CORBETT, Mrs. IRENE C., daughter of Bishop Levi A. Colvin, of Provo, Utah. Father received a letter Tuesday saying she would be home this week.
CRAFTON, Mr. JOHN B.
CROSBY, Mr. E. G., Milwaukee, Wis.
CROSBY, Miss HARRIETT, Milwaukee, Wis.
CUMINGS, Mr. JOHN BRADLEY.
CASSEBEER, Mr. and Mrs. H. A.

D

DAVIDSON, Mr. THORNTON, Montreal.
DODGE, Mr. WASHINGTON.
DULLES, Mr. WILLIAM C.
DALY, Mr. P. D.
DOUGLAS, Mr. W. D.
DOUGLAS, Master R., and nurse.

E

EASTMAN, Miss ANNIE K.
EUSTIS, Miss E. M.
EVANS, Miss E.

F

FOREMAN, Mr. B. L.
FORTUNE, Mr. MARK.
FORTUNE, Mr. CHARLES.
FRANKLIN, Mr. T. P.
FUTRELLE, Mr. JACQUES.

G

GEE, Mr. ARTHUR.
GOLDENBERG, Mr. E. L.
GO!)SCHMIDT, Mr. GEORGE B.
GRAHAM, Mr.
GIGLIO, Mr. VICTOR.
GUGGENHEIM, Mr. BENJAMIN.

H

HAYS, Mr. CHARLES M., Montreal.
HEAD, Mr. CHRISTOPHER.
HILIARD, Mr. HERBERT HENRY.
HIPKINS, Mr. W. F.
HOGABOOM, Mr. JOHN C., Newark, Ohio.
HOLDEN, the Rev. J. STUART, M. A.
HOGENHEIM, Mrs. A.
HARRIS, Mr. HENRY B.
HARRISON, Mr. W. H.
HAVEN, Mr. H.
HARP, Mr. and Mrs. CHARLES M.
HARP, Miss MARGARET, and maid.
HUST, Mr. W. F.
HIPKINS, Mrs. W. E.
HALVERSON, Mr. ALEXANDER M.

I

ISHAM, Miss A. E.
IRVAN, Mrs.

J

JULIAN, Mr. H. F.
JAKOB, Mr. BIRNBAUM.
JONES, Mr. C. C.

K

KENT, Mr. EDWARD A. Mr. Kent was a prominent architect, of Buffalo, N. Y., and a nephew of General A. B. Farnham, of Bangor, and a brother of William Kent, of New York.
KLOBER, Mr. HERMAN.

L

LAMBERT-WILLIAMS, Mr. FLETCHER FELLOWES.
LAWRENCE, Mr. ARTHUR.
LEWIS, Mrs. CHARLTON T.
LONG, Mr. MILTON C.
LEVY, Mr. E. G.
LINES, Mr. ERNEST H.
LINDSHOLM, Mr. J.
LORING, Mr. J. H.
LINGREY, Mr. EDWARD.

M

MAGUIRE, Mr. J. E.
MARVIN, Mr. D. W.
McCAFFRY, Mr. T.
McCAFFRY, Mr. T., Jr.
McCARTHY, Mr. TIMOTHY, Jr.
McGOUGH, Mrs. J. R.
MIDDLETON, Hon. J. CONNEN.
MILLETT, Mr. FRANK D.
MINAHAN, Dr., Fond du Lac, Wis.
McGOACH, Mr. J. R.
MEYER, E. J.
MOLSON, Mr. H. MARKLAND.
MOORE, Mr. CLARENCE, and man servant.

N

NATSCH, Mr. CHARLES, No. 503 East Seventh street, Flatbush.
NEWELL, Mr. A. W.
NICHOLSON, Mr. A. B.

O

OVIES, Mr. FERNANDO.
ORNOUT, Mr. ALFRED T.

P

PARTNER, Mr. M. AUSTIN.
PAYNE, Mr. V.
POND, Miss FLORENCE L., and maid.
PORTER, Mr. WALTER CHAMBERLAIN.
PUFFER, Mr. C. C.
:R, Mr. M. H. W.
PEARS, Mr. and Mrs. THOMAS.
PENASCO, Mr. and Mrs. VICTOR, and maid.

R

REUCHLIN, Mr. JONKHEER J. G.
ROBERT, Mrs. ELIZABETH WATSON, and maid.
ROEBLING, Mr. WASHINGTON A., 2d, Trenton, N. J.
ROOD, Mr. HUGH R., Seattle, Wash.
ROOS, Mr. J. HUGO, Winnipeg.
RHEIMS, Mr. GEORGE.
ROLMANE, Mr. C.
ROTHSCHILD, Mr. M.
ROWE, Mr. ARTHUR.
RYERSON, Mr. ARTHUR.
REYNOLDS, Miss EDITH. She was engaged to marry H. C. Jones, Secretary to the British Embassy in China.

S

SILVERTHORNE, Mr.
SILVEY, Mr. WILLIAM B., Superior, Wis.
SPADDEN, Master R. DOUGLAS, and nurse.
SPENCER, Mr. W. A.
STEAD, Mr. W. T.
STEHLI, Mr. and Mrs. MAX FROLICHER, Zurich, Switzerland.
STRAUS, Mr. ISIDOR, and man servant.
STRAUS, Mrs. ISIDOR, and maid.
SUTTON, Mr. FREDERICK.
SMART, Mr. JOHN MONTGOMERY, Produce Exchange.
SMITH, Mr. M. J. CLINCH.
SMITH, Mr. R. W.
STENMEL, Mr. C. E. H.
STEWART, Mr. ALBERT A., New York representative of the Strowbridge Lithograph Company.
SMITH, Mr. L. P.

T

TAUSSIG, Mr. and Mrs. EMIL, No. 777 West End avenue.
THAYER, Mr. J. B.
THORNE, Mr. and Mrs. G.

U

URUCHURTU, Mr. M. K.

W

WALKER, Mr. W. ANDERSON.
WARREN, Mr. F. M.
WHITE, Mr. PERCIVAL A.
WHITE, Mr. RICHARD F.
WIDENER, Mr. GEORGE D., and man servant.
WIDENER, Mr. HARRY.
WOOD, Mr. and Mrs. FRANK P.
WYCKOFF, Mr. VAN DER HOF.
WEIR, Mr. JOHN.
WICK, Mr. and Mrs. GEORGE D., Youngstown, Ohio.
WILLIAMS, Mr. DUANE.
WILLIAMS, Mr. R. M., JR.
WRIGHT, Mr. GEORGE.
In the above list should be included:—
Mrs. BUCKNELL'S maid.
Mr. CARDOZA'S man servant.
Mrs. CARDOZA'S maid.
Mrs. CARTER'S maid.
Mrs. DOUGLAS' maid.
Mrs. HAYS' maid.
Mr. ISMAY'S man servant.
COUNTESS ROTHES' maid.
Mrs. ROBERTS' maid.
Mrs. RYERSON'S maid.
Mrs. SPEDDEN'S maid.
Mrs. STONE'S maid.
Mrs. THAYER'S maid.
Mrs. J. S. WHITE'S maid and man.

SECOND CABIN PASSENGERS.

A

ASHBY, JOHN.
ALDWORTH, C.
ANDREW, EDGAR.
ADELMAN, FRANZ.
—, Mrs. LILA.
—, Mrs.
ABELSON, SAMPSON.
ANDREW, FRANK.

B

BYLES, Rev. Thomas.
BEAUCHAMP, H. J.
BEESLEY, LAWRENCE.
BROWN, MILDRED.
BENTHAN, L.
BATEMAN, ROBERT J.
BUTLER, REGINALD.
BOTSFORD, HULL.
BERRIMAN, WILLIAM.
BOWEENER, SOLOMON.
BEACKEN, JAMES H.
BROWN, Mrs. (I. W. S.).
BANFIELD, FREDERICK.
BEIGHT, NARL.
BAILEY, PERCY.
BAMBRIDGE, CHARLES R.
BRAILEY (a musician).
BREICIOUS (a musician).

C

CLARKE, CHARLES.
COREY, Mrs.
CARTER, Rev. ERNEST.
CARTER, Mrs. ERNEST.
COLERIDGE, REGINALD.
CHAPMAN, CHARLES.
CUNNINGHAM, ALFRED.
CAMPBELL, WILLIAM.
COLLYER, HAROLD.
CORBETT, Mrs. IRENE.
CHAPMAN, JOHN R. (or H.).
CHAPMAN, Mrs. ELIZABETH.
CHRISTY, Miss J.
COLANDER, ERIC.
COTTERILL, HARRY.

D

DEACON, PERCY.
DAVIS, CHARLES.
DEFFEN, WILLIAM.
DE BRETO, JOSE.
DALCROFT, Miss NELLIE.
DANBRONY, HERBERT.
DREW, JAMES.
DREW, Master MARSHALL.
DAVID, Master JOHN W.
DAVID, Miss ASINCION.
DOUNTON, WILLIAM J.
DEL VARLO, SABASTIAN.
DEL VARLO, Mrs. Sabastian.

E

EITEMILLER, G. F.
ENANDER, INGRAR.

F

FROST, A.
FYNNERY, Mr.
FOUNTHORPE, HARRY.
FILLBROOK, CHARLES.
FUNK, ANNIE.
FAHELSTROM, AME.
FOX, STANLEY W.

G

GREENBERG, SAMUEL.
GILES, RALPH.
GASKELL, ALFRED.
GILLESPIE, WILLIAM.
GILBERT, WILLIAM.
GALE, HARRY.
GALE, S.
GILL, JOHN.
GILES, EDGAR.
GILES, FRED.
GALE, PHADRUCK.
GARVEY, LAWRENCE.

H

HICKMAN, LEONARD.
HICKMAN, LEWIS.
HICKMAN, STANLEY.
HOOD, AMBROSE.
HODGES, HENRY P.
HART, BENJAMIN.
HARRIS, WALTER.
HARPER, JOHN.
HARBECK, WILLIAM H.
HOFFMAN, Mr.
HOFFMAN, Child.
HOFFMAN, Child.
HERMAN, Mr. SAMUEL.
HERMAN, Miss ALICE.
HERMAN, Miss KATE.
HOWARD, Mr. BENJAMIN.
HOWARD, Mrs. ELLEN T.
HART, Mr. GEORGE.
HALE, REGINALD. Was coming here to resume his position with the Home for the Friendless.
HAMATAINEN, ANNA, and infant son.
HILTUNEN, M.
HUNT, GEORGE.
HENHAM, THOMAS.

I

ILETT, BERTHA.

J

JACOBSON, Mr.
JACOBSON, Mrs.
JACOBSON, SYDNEY.
JEFFREY, Mr. CLIFFORD.
JEFFERY, Mr. ERNEST.
JENKIN, Mr. STEPHEN.
JARVIS, JOHN D.
JULIET, LUICHI.
JACKSON, Mrs. AMY.

K

KARINES, Mrs.
KANTAR, SELNA.
KANTAR, Mrs.
KNIGHT, R.
KEANE, Mr. DANIEL.
KIRKLAND, the Rev. CHARLES.
KARNES, Mrs. F. G.
KEYNALDO, Miss.
KRILLNER, JOHAN HENNIK.

L

LEYSON, Mr. ROBERT W. N. (Larson?).
LAWRENCE, Mr. G.
LAROCHE, Mr. JOSEPH.
LAMB, Mr. J. J.
LAMORE, Mrs. AMELIA.
LENGHAM, JOHN.
LEVY, P. J.
LAHTIMEN, Mr. WILLIAM.
LAHTIMEN, Mrs.
LAUCH, CHARLES.

M

MALLETICH, Miss JESSIE; of Painesville, Ohio, was bringing Emil Nanestik, of Austria, to his father in Ohio.
MUDD, THOMAS.
MACK, MARY.
MARSHALL, HENRY.
MELLERS, WILLIAM.
MAYBERG, FRANK H.
MEYER, AUGUST.
MYLES, Mr. THOMAS.
MITCHELL, Mr. HENRY.
MALLETT, Master A.
MATTHEWS, Mr. W. J.
McKANE, Mr. PETER.
MILLING, Mr. JACOB.
MANTVILE, JOSEPH.
MALACHARD, NOLL.
MORAWECK, Dr.
MANGIOVACCLI, EMILIO.
McCRAE, ARTHUR G.

N

NANESTIK, EMIL, of Austria.
NESSEN, ISRAEL.
NICHOLLS, Mr. JOSEPH C.
NORMAN, Mr. ROBERT D.
NASSER, NICHOLAS.

O

OTTEO, Mr. RICHARD.
O'QUICK (see Quick).

P

PHILLIPS, ROBERT.
PONESELL, MARTIN.
PAIN, Dr. ALFRED.
PARKES, FRANK.
PENGELLY, Mr. FREDERICK.
PERNOT, Mr. RENE.
PERUSCHITZ, the Rev.
PARRISH, Mrs. DAVIS.
PARKER, CLIFFORD.
PULBAUM, FRANK.

R

ROGERS, SETINA.
RENOUF, Mr. PETER H.
ROGERS, Mr. Harry.
REEVES, Mr. DAVID.

S

SWORD, HANS K.
STOKES, PHILIP J.
SHARP, PERCIVAL.
SEDGWICK, Mr.
SMITH, AUGUSTUS.
SWEET, GEORGE.
SJOSTEDT, Mr. ERNEST.
SLEMEN, Mr. RICHARD J.
SOBERG, Mr. HAYD: N.
SLAYTER, Miss H.
SLATTER, Miss H. M.
STANTON, WARD.
SINKKONEN, ANNA.

T

TOOMEY, ELLEN.
TURPIN, Mr. WILLIAM J.
TURPIN, Mrs. DOROTHY.
TURNER, Mr. JOHN H.
TURNER, Mrs.
TURNER, Mr. GEORGE.
TROUPEANSKY, MOSES AARON.
TERVAN, Mrs. A.
TRANT, Mrs. JESSE.

V

VEALE, Mr. JAMES.
VON DRACHSTEDT, Baron.

W

WALCROFT, Miss.
WILHELM, CHARLES.
WATSON, EMESS.
WILKINSON, Mrs. S. GEORGE.
WILKINSON, Miss ADA C.
WARE, Mr. WILLIAM C.
WEISZ, Mr. LEOPOLD.
WHEADON, Mr. EDWARD.
WARE, Mr. JOHN JAMES.
WARE, Mrs.
WEST, Mr. E. ARTHUR.
WHEELER, Mr. EDWIN.
WERMAN, SAMUEL.

Y

YROIS, Miss H.

COMPLETE LIST OF SURVIVORS

FIRST CLASS PASSENGERS.

A

ANDERSON, Harry.
APPLETON, Mrs. E. W.
ABBOTT, Mrs. Rose.
ALLISON, Master, and nurse.
ANDREWS, Miss K. T. (Miss Cornelia I.?).
ALLEN, Miss E. W.
ASTOR, Mrs. John Jacob, and maid.
AUBERT, Mrs. N.

B

BARRATT, Karl Behr (Behr?)
BESSETTE, Miss.
BUCKNELL, Mrs. William.
BARTHWORTH, Mr. A. H. (Bathworth?)
BOWERMAN, Miss E.
BROWN, Mrs. J. J.
BURNS, Miss G. M. (Mrs.)
BISHOP, Mr. and Mrs. D.
BLANK, H.
BASSINA, Miss A.
BAXTER, Mrs. James (Brayton).
BAYTON, George A. (Brayton).
BONNELL, Miss C.
BROWN, Mrs. J. M.
BOWEN, Miss G. C.
BECKWITH, Mr. and Mrs. R. L.

C

CARDEZA, Mrs. J. R.
CASSEBERE, Miss D. D.
CLARKE, Mrs. W. M.
CHIBINACE, Mrs. B. (Chibnall?).
CROSSBIE, Miss E. G. (Mrs. E. G. Crosby?).
CROSBY, Mrs. (Miss?).
CROSBY, Miss H.
CARTER, Miss Lucille.
CARTER, Master William.
CANDER, Mrs. Churchill (Cardell?).
CALDERHEAD, N. P. (E. P.?).
CHANDANSON, Miss Victorine.
CAVINDISH, Mrs. TURRELL, and maid (Mrs. T. W.?)
CHAFFEE, Mrs. H. L. (H. I.?).
CARDEZA, Thomas.
CUMMINGS, Mrs. J.
CHEVRE, Paul.
CHERRY, Miss Gladys.
CHAMBERS, Mr. and Mrs. B. C. (N. C.?).
CARTER, Mr. and Mrs. W. E.

D

DAILY, P. D.
DOUGLASS, Mrs. FRED C.
DE VIELLIEN, Mme. (Mrs. B. De Villiers?).
DANIEL, ROBERT W.
DAVIDSON, Mrs. THORNTON.
DOUGLASS, Mrs. WALTER.
DODGE, Miss SARAH.
DODGE, WASHINGTON.
DODGE, Mrs. WASHINGTON and son.
DICK, Mr. and Mrs. (A. A.?).
DANIELL, Mr. H. HAREN (see Haren).

E

ENDRES, Miss CAROLINA (Mrs. ?).
ELLIS, Miss.
EARNSHAW, Miss BOULTON (Mrs. ?).

F

FLEGNHEIM, Miss ANTOINETTE (Flagenheim?).
FRANCATELLI, Miss.
FLYNN, J. N. (J. I. ?).
FORTUNE, Miss ALICE.
FORTUNE, Miss LUCILLE.
FORTUNE, Mrs. MARK.
FORTUNE, Miss MABEL.
FRAUENTHAL, Mr. and Mrs. HENRY (Dr.?).
FRAUENTHAL, Mr. and Mrs. J. G. (Mrs. T. G.?)
FROLICHER, Miss MARGARET.
FUTRELLE, Mrs. JACQUES.

G

GRACIE, Colonel ARTHUR (Archibald?).
GRAHAM, Mr. and Mrs. WILLIAM.
GRAHAM, Miss.
GORDON, Sir COSMO DUFF.
GORDON, Lady.
GIBSON, Miss DOROTHY.
GIBSON, GRENVILLE.
GOLDENBERG, Mrs. SAMUEL.
GOLDENBERG, Miss ELLA.
GREENFIELD, Mrs. LEE D. (L. P.?).
GREENFIELD, Mr. WILLIAM.
GIBSON, Mrs. LEONARD.
GOOHT, JAMES.

H

HAREN, Mr. H. (H. Haven?).
HIPACK, Mrs. IDA S. (Hippach?).
HIPACK, Miss JEAN (Hippach?).
HARRIS, Mrs. L. Y. B. (H. B.?).
HALVERSON, Mrs. ALEX (or Malverson).
HOGIBOOM, Mrs. I. C. (J. C.?).
HAWKSFORD, Mr. W. J.
HARPER, Mr. HENRY S., and man servant.
HARPER, Mrs. H. S.
HOYT, Mr. and Mrs. ::ED.
HOMER, Mrs. HENRY.
HARDER, Mr. and Mrs. GEORGE.
HAYS, Mrs. CHARLES M. and maid.
HAYS, Miss MARGARET.

I

ISMAY, J. BRUCE.

K

KIMBALL, Mr. and Mrs.
KENNYMAN, Mr. F. A.
KENCHEN, Miss EMILE.

L

LONGLEY, Miss G. F.
LEADER, Mrs. F. A.
LAVORY, Miss BERTHA.
LINES, Mrs. ERNEST.
LINES, Miss MARY C.
LINDSTROM, Mrs. SINGIRD
LESNEUR, Mr. GUSTAV J.

M

MADILL, Miss GEORGETTE A.
MELICARD, Mme.
MAIMY, Miss ROBERTA.
MARTIN, Mrs. D. W. (Marvin?).
MARECHELL, Mr. PIERCE.
MINAHAN, Mrs.
MINAHAN, Miss DAISY.
MOCK, Mr. PHILIP E.

N

NEWELL, Mrs. MARJORIE (Miss Alice?).
NEWELL, Mrs. MADELINE (Miss?)
NEWSOM, Miss HELEN.

O

O'CONNELL, Miss R.
OSTBY, Mr. and Mrs. (E. C.?).
OLIVIA, Miss.
OSTBY, Miss HELEN.
OMOND, Mr. FIEUNAM.

P

POTTER, Mrs. THOMAS, Jr.
PENCHEN, Major ARTHUR.
PENASCO, Mrs. JOSEPH.

R

ROGERSON, JOHN (?).
RANELT, Miss APPIE.
ROTSCHILD, Mrs. LORD MARTIN.
ROSENBAUM, Miss EDITH.
RHEIMS, Mrs. GEO. (Mr.?)
ROTHES, Countess.
ROBERTS, Mrs. EDNA (Edward S?).
ROLMANE, Mr. C.
RYERSON, Mrs. SUSAN P.
RYERSON, Miss EMILY.
RYERSON, Mrs. ARTHUR.

S

STONE, Mrs. GEORGE N. (M?).
SEGESSER, Miss EMMA.
STEWARD, Mr. FRED K. (Seward?).
SHUTTER, Miss (E. W. Shutes?).
SLOPER, WILLIAM T.
SWIFT, Mrs. F. JOEL.
SCHABER, Mrs. PAUL.
SHEDDEL, ROBERT DOUGLASS (Spedden?).
SNYDER, Mr. and Mrs. JOHN.
SEREPECA, Miss AUGUSTA.
SILVERTHORN, V. SPENCER.
SAALFELD, ADOLF.
STACKLIEHN, Mr. MAX (Stahelin?).
SIMONIUS, ALFONSIUS.
SMITH, Mrs. LUCIEN P.
STEPHENSON, Mrs. WALTER P. (W. B.?).
SALOMON, ABRAHAM (Mrs. A. L.?).
SILVEY, Mrs. WILLIAM B.
STENGEL, Mr. and Mrs. HELERY (C. E. H. Stenmel?).
SPENCER, Mrs. W. A., maid.
SLAYTER, Miss HILDA.
SPEDDEN, Mr. and Mrs. J. O. (F. O. Speeden?).
STEFFANSON, H. B.

T

TUCKER, Mrs., and maid.
THAYER, Mr. and Mrs. J. B.
THAYER, Mr. J. B., Jr.
TAUSSIG, Miss RUTH.
TAUSSIG, Mr. E.
THOR, Miss ELLA.
TAYLOR, E. Z.
TAYLOR, Mrs. E.
TUCKER, GILBERT (G. M., Jr.?).

W

WOOLNER, Mr. HY.
WARD, Miss ANNA.
WILLIAMS, RICH M., Jr.
WARREN, Mrs. F. M.
WILSON, Miss HELEN A.
WILLARD, Miss.
WICKS, Miss MARY.
WIDENER, Mrs. GEORGE D., and maid.
WHITE, Mrs. J. STEWART.

Y

YOUNG, Miss MARIE.

SECOND CLASS PASSENGERS.

A

ANGLE, Mr. WILLIAM.
ABELSOM, Mrs. HANNA.

B

BALLS, Mrs. ADA E.
BUSS, Miss KATE.
BECKER, Mrs. A. O., and three children.
BEALE, Mr. EDWARD (Beane).
BEANE, Miss ETHEL.
BROWN, Mr. T. W. G.
BROWN, Miss EDITH.
BENTHAM, LILLIAN W.
BOYSTRON, KAROLINA.
BEIGHT (Bright), DAGMAR.

C

CLARK, Mrs. ADA.
CAMERON, Miss.
CALDWELL, ALBERT F.
CALDWELL, Mrs. SYLVAN.
CALDWELL, Infant ALDEN.
COLLYER, Mrs. CHARLOTTE.
COLLYER, Miss MARJORIE.
CHRISTY, ALICE.
COLLET, STUART (Mrs.).
CHRISTY, JULIA.
CHARLES, WILLIAM.

D

DOLING, Miss ELSIE.
DOLING, Mrs. ADA.
DREW, Mrs. LULU.
DAVIES, Mrs. AGNES (Davis).
DAVIS, Miss MARY.
DAVIS, JOHN M.
DUVAN, FLORENTINE.
DUVAN, Miss A.
DAVIDSON, Miss MARY.
DRISCOLL, Mrs. B.

F

FAUNTHROPE, Mrs. ELIZ. (Lizzie).
FORMERY, Miss ELEIN (Mr. Fynnery).

G

GARSIDE, ETHEL.
GERRCAI, Mrs. MARCY.
GENOVESE, Mr. ANGERE.

H

HART, Mrs. (Esther).
HART, child (Eva?).
HARRIS, GEORGE.
HEWLETT, Mrs. MARY.
HARPER, NINA.
HELD, Miss ANNA (Mrs. Stephen).
HOSENE, Mrs. MASSABUMI.
HOCKING, Mrs. ELIAS (Eliza).
HOCKING, Miss NELLIE.
HERMAN, Mrs. JANE.
HERMAN, Miss KATE.
HERMAN, Miss ALICE.
HEALY, NORA (?).
HANSON, JENNIE (?).
HAMALAMIAN, Mrs. ANNA. (Hamatalanen, Anna).
HAMALAMIAN, Mrs. HANN. (infant son).

J

JACKSON, Mrs. AMY (Mrs. Jacobson).

K

KEANE, Miss NORA A.
KELLY, Mrs. F. (Miss Fannie).

L

LEITCH, JESSIE.
LA ROCHE, Mr. JULIET (Joseph) or Mrs.
LA ROCHE, Miss SIMMONE.
LA ROCHE, Miss LOUISE.
LEHMAN, BERTHA.
LAUCH, Mrs. (ALEX.).
LENORE, Mrs. ELIZABETH (Amelia), (Laniore).
LINKKANCA, Miss ANNIE.

M

MELLINGER, ELIZABETH.
MELLINGER, child.
MARSHALL, Miss KATE.
MALLETT, Mr. A.
MALLETT, Mrs.
MALLETT, Master R. E.
MANGE, PAUL A.
MELLOR, Mr. J. (Mellers, William).
McDEARMONT, Miss LILLIE.
McGOWAN, ANNA.
MARION, Mrs.
MARE, Mrs. FLORENCE (Mrs. Ware).

N

NVE, ELIZABETH.
NASERAEL, Mrs. ADELIA (Israel Nessen).

O

OXENHAM, PERCY J. (Thomas).

P

PHILLIPS, ALICE.
PALLAS, Mr. EMILIO.
PADRO, Mr. JULIAN.
PINSKY, ROSA.
PORTALUPPI, EMILIO (Mrs.).
PARSH, Mrs. L. (Mrs. Davis Parrish).

Q

QUICK, Mrs. JANE.
QUICK, Miss VERA W.
QUICK, Miss PHYLLIS.

R

RENALDO, Mrs. ENCARNAVCION.
RIDSDALE, LUCY.

(CONTINUED ON PAGE SIX.)

CAPT. SMITH'S DEATH ON TITANIC ADDS ANOTHER TO HERO LIST

Marine History Full of Tales of the Heroic Bravery of the Men on the Bridge.

DEATH WITH HONOR

WHEN Captain E. J. Smith, commander of the ill-fated Titanic, went down to death with that vessel and its priceless cargo of lives last Monday morning, one more name was added to the long roll of marine heroes who have subscribed to the unwritten law of the seas—that the captain shall not desert his ship while another human being remains on board. As old as the seas themselves, this tradition has come down through the ages, the sublime courage and devotion to duty of these rulers of the sea serving to relieve many of the sombre tragedies of the deep.

Somewhere in the tangled mass of wreckage—only one short week ago the proudest steamship afloat—now lying under three miles of water off the treacherous Newfoundland coast, rests the body of the grizzled veteran, and those who know him are confident that his face bears a peaceful expression.

Standing on the bridge as the mighty pile of steel and iron sank to its final cradle, the awful moments before the waters closed over him gave him plenty of time to realize that his career of almost half a century had reached a fitting close. To go down with his vessel is the supreme test of courage for every true sailor, and few are the instances where commanders have lacked of that courage.

No braver or more resourceful body of men could be picked out than the men in charge of the great ocean steamships. With thousands of lives and millions in property entrusted to their care every trip, they have to have the mental and physical equipment to meet every emergency. Few men are called upon to shoulder such tremendous responsibilities, and they are pretty near perfect in every department before they are given the chance by the big steamship companies. In addition to [illegible]ing long apprenticeship in every [illegible] of the operating service, the cap[illegible] to have a thorough knowledge of [illegible] under his command.

[illegible] to be a man of many parts, [illegible] at home in the first cabin or the engine room, in the smoking room or explaining the nautical terms to some of his fair passengers. Most of the time the captain moves back and forth among his charges, resplendent in a well fitting uniform of blue and gold, smiling, affable and the picture of jollity. Underneath this amiable, pleasant weather exterior is the ability to give orders and enforce discipline when the occasion demands it. Until something happens on board the ocean steamship few persons pay much attention to the man in charge of the vessel, but the minute anything goes wrong all eyes are turned in his direction. His every word becomes fraught with the greatest importance. It is then that the passengers realize that their lives are in his keeping.

Next to the boasted stability of the Titanic, the passengers put most of their confidence in Captain Smith, a man of the widest possible experience in handling giant vessels, a man who had weathered the ocean storms of forty-three years.

Following the awful blow which shattered the steel clad steamship as if she had been a wooden scow, one can imagine the terror stricken passengers crowding about that stalwart form begging him for some word of reassurance. One can see him directing the work of lowering the women and children to safety and then taking his place on the bridge and giving orders to the end. No one knew better than Captain Smith that the Titanic had received her death wound and that in a few hours she would be resting on the bottom, but he stuck to his post and went down with flying colors.

Strange as it may seem, there are many men who envy him his tragic end. These are men who formerly commanded ocean steamships or large vessels of some sort and who forfeited their master certificates for some error of judgment, the commander of a steamship rarely getting a chance to make more than one mistake. These men are to be found in small villages in England, Germany, Holland France and down Long Island way, sorrowing their lives away in solitude because of the miscalculation which cost them their right to command a ship. Any one of these gray bearded, heartbroken mariners would gladly exchange places with the commander of the Titanic. In many instances captains of vessels that have met with some mishap have committed suicide on the spot, not waiting for the inevitable suspension that was almost certain to follow. Captain Smith was one of the few commanders who had been given more than one chance, his splendid record being instrumental in keeping him in the service of the White Star line even after the Olympic, sister ship of the Titanic, had been in collision with the Hawke, a British war ship.

Marine history records many cases of commanders going down with their vessels, but none that should cause a greater thrill of pride to an American than that of Commander William L. Herndon, U. S. N., who stood on the bridge of the steamship Central America, of the Pacific Mail line, when she went down in midocean on September 18, 1857. A member of a family noted for its courage, father-in-law of President Arthur, he had the rank of lieutenant in the navy, a leave of absence permitting him to engage in the mercantile service. As is invariably the case, Lieutenant Herndon had plenty of opportunity to save himself, but he chose to go down with his vessel and the rest of her ill fated passengers.

Tales of the sea always bring to mind the unexampled courage of Sir George Tryon, Vice Admiral of the British navy, who went down with the flagship Victoria when that vessel was rammed by the ironclad Camperdown during the manoeuvres off the coast of Tripoli, Friday, June 23, 1893. The Victoria sank almost immediately, going down bow first and turning completely over before she disappeared from view. Between four and five hundred of the crew, officers and men, went down with her, and the last seen of Vice Admiral Tryon he was on the bridge directing the men under him.

A story dear to the heart of the British sailor is that Vice Admiral Tryon saluted the colors just as the swirling waters shut out his form forever. He was one of the prominent figures of the, British navy and his death caused profound regret throughout Europe.

Captain Louis Deloncle, commander of the French line steamship Bourgogne when that vessel went to the bottom with 535 souls on July 4, 1898, is another hero whose courage will always be remembered. It was especially noteworthy in his case because of the alleged cowardly manner in which many of the men under him behaved. Following a collision with the steamship Cromartyshire about sixty miles south of Sable Island the Bourgogne went down not far from the spot now occupied by the Titanic.

In the confusion which followed the crash it was charged that many of the crew lost their heads and beat the women and children away from the lifeboats in their efforts to get to safety. About two hundred passengers were saved and many of them testified to seeing members of the crew using their knives on women and children. This charge had corroboration when the sea gave up the bodies of women who had been hacked to pieces. Members of the crew who reached this city and who were given anything but a cordial reception denied the charges of cowardice and shifted the blame to some of the male steerage passengers. This sea tragedy furnished one of the most grewsome chapters in marine history—one of the few cases in which a crew has been charged with cowardice. But every one of the rescued passengers had words of praise for Captain Deloncle. He was the last to be seen on the doomed vessel. He stood with arms folded on his chest as his ship sank. The Bourgogne's cargo was worth $300,000, and its loss was considered a great one at that time. The cargo that went down with the Titanic was worth at least $10,000,000, which shows how the value of cargoes has increased in the last fourteen years.

Captain Von Goessel, of the steamship Elbe, of the North German Lloyd line, was on the bridge of that vessel when she went down with 330 passengers, following a collision with the steamship Crathie, off the coast of England, January 30, 1895.

One of the greatest disasters of recent years was the sinking of the Norge, a Danish emigrant steamship, on Wednesday, June 29, 1904. Of the 800 passengers only twenty-seven were saved when the vessel went to the bottom a short time after going to pieces on the Rockall rocks in the North Atlantic. Captain J. V. Gundel went down with his ship.

Captain Griffith was in command of the Mohegan when she sank off the English coast October 14, 1898. He had plenty of opportunity to save himself, but elected to

Famous Cases of Sea Captains Who Went to Death with Their Gallant Vessels.

THE UNWRITTEN LAW

go down with the 160 passengers who perished. When the Berlin, the Great Western Railway Company's steamship, went down in a storm off the Hook of Holland, February 21, 1907, the figure of Captain Precious, clinging to the rigging, was the last thing discernible to the watchers on shore.

Captain H. Brunswig went to his cabin and killed himself as soon as he made certain that all the passengers had been rescued from the Prinzessin Victoria Luise, of the Hamburg-American line, which ran on the rocks near Port Royal, Jamaica, on Sunday, December 16, 1906. The ship had left this city a few days earlier for a winter cruise and had many prominent persons on board. Captain Brunswig feared that his mistake would cost him his certificate and decided to take no chances on an adverse verdict. His employers had every faith in his judgment, and it was almost certain that he could have cleared himself, but the dread of suspension and subsequent loneliness were too strong to stay his hand.

A bullet through the head ended the long career of Captain Giuseppe Paradi, commander of the Italian steamship Sirio, wrecked on the rocks near Hormigas Island, August 2, 1906. Three hundred persons were drowned, and before he ended his life Captain Paradi admitted to those about him that his miscalculation had caused the disaster. He was sixty-two years old and had been in charge of vessels for more than forty years.

Many are the instances in which the commander of a steamship has been retired to private life following a mishap to his vessel, the most recent case being that of Captain Inman Sealby, who was in command of the steamship Republic, of the White Star line, when it was rammed by the steamship Florida, of the Lloyd Italiano line, off Nantucket early on the morning of Saturday, January 23, 1909. The collision occurred during a dense fog. Six lives were lost in the accident. The Republic's passengers were transferred to the Florida and later retransferred to the steamship Baltic, this hazardous feat in a rough sea being accomplished without a single mishap.

The Republic kept afloat until the following night and then went to the bottom, Captain Sealby and some of the officers remaining on deck until a few minutes before the ship took its final plunge. Captain Sealby wept bitterly as the lifeboat bore him away from the sinking vessel. It was generally conceded that his seamanship had not been at fault and that he was not to blame for the collision, but he was dismissed from the service of the company. The fact that he is now, at the age of fifty, studying admiralty law in the University of Michigan shows the pluck and determination of the man.

A record of fifty years at sea was brought to a pathetic close when Captain Frederick Watkins, one of the most popular commanders, lost his certificate after the grounding of his vessel, the City of Paris, of the American line, on the British coast. No lives were lost, but the vessel was badly damaged before it was floated. The accident occurred on May 21, 1899, and in the investigation which followed Captain Watkins assumed entire responsibility for the error of judgment. It was his first mistake, but it finished his career.

Captain Le Horn's career came to an end when the steamship China, one of the biggest vessels of the Peninsular and Oriental company, went aground on an island in the Red Sea in 1897. The inquiry which followed disclosed the fact that Captain Le Horn had been helping Lady Brassey, a passenger, to celebrate her birthday. One of his subordinates said he had written several notes to his superior warning him of the ship's danger and that Captain Le Horn had ignored the warnings until it was [illegible] late. After this incident many steamship companies ordered the commanders and officers of vessels to drop all social intercourse with passengers and attend strictly to business.

THE NEWSPAPERS' PART IN TITANIC WRECK.

NOT the least interesting feature of the grim sea tragedy which has plunged a large share of the world in grief was the manner in which the newspapers of the country, especially the great metropolitan dailies, gathered every scrap of information concerning the greatest ocean disaster of all time. To-day, for the first time in a week, thousands of newspaper makers are trying to catch up with the sleep lost since Monday night, the time when the awful truth about the fate of the Titanic became known.

For five days the men on the staffs of the local papers have been on duty the greater part of the time, stealing away for a few minutes to get a hurried meal or a few winks of sleep, and this same condition of affairs, in smaller proportion, existed in most of the newspaper offices throughout the country. Experts in handling big news stories say that no happening of the last twenty-five years made such great demands on the strength and resourcefulness of the men who serve the reading public with its daily history. Certainly no event has ever caused a greater demand for special stories of every character, the requests reaching this city from all parts of the United States and Canada. Newspapers in small cities and towns, publications that have never before had special stories, spent large sums of money to the end that their subscribers might have the benefit of a graphic description by skilled writers.

Men with half a century of newspaper experience behind them are unanimous in the opinion that the story of the sinking of the ill-fated Titanic was one of the biggest and most important that the newspapers are ever called upon to handle. These are the men who handled the news of the Brooklyn Theatre fire, the Johnstown flood, the Martinique disaster, the Iroquois Theatre fire, the San Francisco earthquake, the burning of the steamboat General Slocum and other catastrophes attended by great loss of life and property.

In putting the Titanic's tragic tale ahead of all these famous disasters they point out the fact that they affected but one section of the world or country, while the sinking of the White Star line giantess claimed more than fifteen hundred victims from all parts of the world and sent the messenger of grief to millions of hearts on both sides of the Atlantic. In the noble band of martyrs that went to the bottom in the shattered hulk of the Titanic were a score of men and women whose names have been well known in all parts of the world for years, owners of immense fortunes, captains of industry, merchant princes, authors, artists and men prominent in the higher professions. The pomp and ceremony which marked the launching of the monster vessel, the dramatic circumstances surrounding the collision and the superb courage of the passengers were just a few of the things which made the wreck of the Titanic a happening which touched the high water mark in tragic events.

Any incident connected with the maiden trip of the world's greatest steamship would have been worthy of record by the newspapers, the local papers having made extensive arrangements to get the news of her first voyage long before she weighed anchor on what proved to be her first and last trip. When the first flash last Sunday night warned the telegraph operators in newspaper offices throughout the land that the Titnaic had met with a mishap the men behind the pencils and typewriting machines got ready to round up a big story, but when the announcement of her sinking was verified every editor, reporter, artist and photographer realized that the busiest hours of their careers were at hand. They guessed right, for the week just closed has been one of the hardest in the history of the newspaper business.

Beginning Monday night, newspapers outside of the metropolis began beseeching the local papers and press associations to send them every word and to let no detail go by that might add to the completeness of the story. Tuesday these outside papers started whole staffs toward this city in order that their own men should be on the scene when the Carpathia arrived with its cargo of grief and misery. At least five hundred reporters, photographers and artists came from Baltimore, Boston, Philadelphia, Chicago, Cincinnati, St. Louis, Cleveland, Buffalo, Rochester, Syracuse, Utica, Albany, Montreal, Ottawa, Winnipeg and points as far off as Minnesota to supplement the army of men who gathered in the details and pictures for the local papers.

Many of these out of town men brought along their own telegraph operators in order that nothing should prevent their papers from having the best of service. On arriving here these men had to obtain credentials from the federal, municipal and police departments before they could get to work, a task that entailed considerable hustling on their part. Scores of reporters lived in ocean-going tugs along the coast for the better part of last week, every one of them willing to risk his life if necessary in order to get any additional scrap of information to his paper. An army of photographers found little to do, this being one of the few stories in which they failed to circumvent the elaborate preparations made to thwart them. Outside of getting photographs of the Carpathia as she came up the North River or of snapping an occasional survivor they did not get a chance at the scenes on the piers, all of which would have made prize pictures.

In this respect the HERALD was fortunate in getting sketches made by a Titanic survivor and photographs taken by officers of the steamship Carpathia, the HERALD having more authentic pictures of the scenes attending the sinking of the vessel and subsequent rescue of the survivors than any other paper in the country. A faint idea of the confidence placed in the HERALD's news and picture gathering organization by other papers throughout the United States is shown by the fact that more than two hundred prominent dailies arranged to get the HERALD's complete story and many of the pictures.

Something like 1,500,000 words went out of the HERALD's telegraph department from Sunday night to Friday morning, this figure being a record that was not exceeded during the stirring times that attended the Spanish-American War. The Carpathia docked at nine o'clock Thursday night and an hour later duplicates of the HERALD's picture equipment were on the way to scores of cities. More than two hundred afternoon papers were enabled to beat their competitors yesterday owing to the promptness of the HERALD's service, and from most of these publications came heartiest congratulations on the praiseworthy achievement.

Four oceangoing tugs, some of them equipped with wireless apparatus, plied the waters between here and Newport, reinforcing the HERALD's land organization of skilled newspaper men. Correspondents at all points along the Atlantic seaboard between this city and St. John's had been on duty constantly since verification of the dreadful news was received Monday night. No source, no matter how small, that might furnish an additional detail of news had been overlooked, and the result was a more complete story of the disaster than appeared in any newspaper.

All the local papers made heroic efforts to keep up with shifting scenes in the tragedy, but through the medium of its own wireless telegraph station and its other resources the HERALD was enabled to keep several laps ahead of its competitors during the week, the thorough presentation of the details and accompanying photographs Thursday morning being regarded by experienced newsgatherers as one of the most notable feats of modern journalism.

To the millions of readers who have no idea of the manner in which a metropolitan newspaper is made, the editorial department of the HERALD on Thursday night would have furnished an object lesson of the tremendous amount of brains and energy required to whip a story of worldwide interest into shape. In all its long history the HERALD office never has known such a busy night, yet with all the nerve racking, heartbreaking pressure of the race with time there was no trace of confusion. The human machine—the machine that has played an honorable part in the events of the last seventy years and more—never worked more smoothly, albeit it has never before been keyed up to such dizzy speed.

Three hours before the Carpathia was warped into her berth on West street the men who were to receive the avalanche of news from the men outside on the firing line were at their posts. From the time the Carpathia reached Sandy Hook the news began to filter in over the wires and telephones, the tide of detail rising steadily until it reached its flood about ten o'clock, remaining at that altitude until long after a new day was born. Reporters who had been stationed at every point in the territory between here and the scene of the disaster either reported in person or got in touch with the office by wire.

By half-past nine the newsgathering machine was going at top speed. Every inch of space in the big room was occupied, the exception being the passageways left open for the copy boys to carry out their instructions. Men worn out by long vigil, faces white and tense under the strain, but eyes a-glisten at the thought of participating in the preparation of such an epoch making story, bent low over their typewriting machines, the steady click of hundreds of flying fingers against the keyboards harmonizing with the clicking of scores of telegraph instruments in an adjoining room.

Sheet after sheet, freighted with the tragic tale of the sea, was passed on to the city editor, to be transferred by him to one of his subordinates, the work being distributed to insure accuracy as well as speed. All this eye dazzling speed, and not a trace of disorder! Directions issued in a conversational tone, and none of the uproar and noise that might very well be a part of such a night. Upstairs in the composing room and down in the press department there was the same orderly condition of affairs. One, two, three four editions were sent away with the story of the century, and then as the morning began to gray the men who prepared it filed out into Herald square and home.

FATHER REPORTED SAVED, GIRL SAYS HE PERISHED

Miss Helen R. Ostby was taken at once from the pier to a hotel. She was informed by friends that the name of her father, E. C. Ostby, had been telegraphed from the Carpathia as among those saved. She at once declared that she had not seen her father on board the Carpathia, and she could not believe he had been aboard without her knowing it. The only explanation was that a mistake had been made in the wireless transmission of the names.

COMPLETE LIST OF SURVIVORS

(CONTINUED FROM PAGE FIVE.)

RENOUF, Mrs. LILY.
RUGG, Miss EMILY.
RICHARDS, EMILY.
RICHARDS, Miss EMILY.
RICHARDS, Mr. Jr.
RICHARDS, Mr. EMILE, two boys, and Mr., Jr.
ROGERS, Miss ELIZA.
SINCOCK, Miss MAUDE.

S

SMITH, Miss MARION.
SKELLERY, Mrs. WILLIAM (Shelly, Mrs. Imanitia?).
SILIVANA, SYNLI (Silven Lylie?).

T

TOUCH, Miss ALICE.
TROUT, Miss EDINA S.
TROUT, Miss CECILIA.
TROUT, Mrs. JESSIE (Trant, Mrs. Jessie?).

W

WILLIAMS, CHARLES C.
WEISSE, Mrs. MATHILDA (Mrs. Leopold?).
WEBBER, Miss SUSIE.
WRIGHT, Miss MARION.
WATT, Mrs. BESSIE.
WATT, Miss BERTHA.
WEST, Mrs.
WEST, Miss CONSTANCE.
WEST, Miss BARBARA.
WELLS, ADDIE.
WELLS, Master.
WELLS, Miss.
WARE, Mrs. FLORENCE (Mare?).
WALCROFT, MILLIE.
WARION, Mrs. (Marion?).

THIRD CLASS PASSENGERS.

NORA MURPHY.
KATIE MULLIN.
KATIE McCARTHY.
G. D. MESSEMOCKES.
ANNA MESSEMOCKES.
MADERA YUSEF.
BUNOS MOUBARCK.
HALIN MOUBARCK.
GITOSA MOUBARCK.
MINA MUSULMON.
SABUCA SUBULAKET.
JAVNA MANO.
KIRKOEAN MUHAN.
DELIA DIANODELMN.
KARL MATHJOAX.
BERTHA MALLIEDELL.
MAGGIE MERRIGAN.
BERTHA MARAN.
KRISTOF MADSEN.
ALBERT MOSS.
MARY McGOVERN.
ERNEST McKEY.
ALICE McKEY.
THOMAS McCORMACK.
JOHN NICKAREN.
— ADLERSON.
BERTHA NELSON.
YREE NYHEM.
ANNIE McGOWAN.
AGNES DOYT (or Mrs. A. A. DICK).
MARGARET NANGA.
MAGGIE J. MURPHY.
LEONCH ELDEGREK.
HEUNA MANMAN.
KRIKOREAN KIRORA.
HANWAKAN (?)
DELIA McDERMOTT.
MARLKARL (?)
JOHN McKAREN.
AINO LUDGUIS.
HELENA ANGUSEN.
MARY NEKET.
DEMINA J. NELSON.
ANNA KOLSBOTTEL.
NORA O'LEARY.
ARTHUR OLSEN.
COTERINA PATROS.
GENOIT PICARD.
NOBESA PATROS.
ERNEST PERSON.
NARAS ROTH.
ANNA REIBON.
JOHN CHURCHSSON.
NICOLA SULICI.
JUHO STRINDER.
JAN SCHURBINT.
JULES SAP.
ANNA SOFIA.
S. JOBLOM.
BEIERICE SINDE.
ROSE SIBELROME.
AGNES SIBELROME.
AMY STANLEY.
JOHAN SUMDIAN.
PALIA SMYTHE.
AXEL SHINE.
FLORENCE KESORNY.
CROFT HEDVIG.
HEDVIG TURKULA.
WILLIAM TURKGEST.
VARTAUON.
ELLEN WICKS.
SILINE YESBURG.
HANNA YOUSEF.
GEORGE YOUSEF.
MARIAN YOUSEF.
SCURLY OUMSON.
PHILLIP ZENN.
NICOLA ELIASE.
NICOLA OANB.
AUGUST ABRIHAMSON.
BEDNOURA ALOUN.
MARIANA ASSIM.
CARLO NELSON.
CANDERSON OSPLUMD.
JOHN CHARLES.
ROSA ABBOTT.
EDNA ANDERSON.
SELMA ASTLUND.
FELIX ASTLUND.
LILLIAN ASTLUND.
AKLESEP ABELSEPH.
LEAK AKSAKS.
LEE BING.
MARIE BOKLIN.
EUGENE BOKLIN.
HALINE BOKLIN.
LATEFE BOKLIN.
FILLY AKSAKS.
NASSIF CASEM.
BOYAM CASEM.
EMILY BATMAN.
MARIA BOCKSTROM.
DANIEL BUCKLEY.
BRIDGET BRADLEY.
CHING HIP.
EINARE BARLSON.
BEATRICE SANDE.
GUS COHN.
L. M. CRIBB.
MINNIE CONTO.
NEVELLE CONTO.
WILL CONTO.
KATIE CONNOLLY.
ELLEN CARR.
THEODORE DEMUEDER.
JOSEPH KRIGESNE.
P. D. DALY.
CHARLES DALY.
MARSOLA DALY.
Mrs. ETTIE DEAN and two children.
MARGARET DEVANEY.
CHOENSEN, John.
LARE, Elleonch.
MARRIGAN, Margaret.
MARSON, Adele.
MATHYO, Karl.
MUN, Hannah.
NEKET, Hobia.
NELSON, Helmina J.
NYHAN, Anna.
ONGULEN, Helena.
SUBMAKET, Fituasa.

UNSINKABLE SHIP IMPOSSIBLE, SAYS NAVAL DESIGNER LEWIS NIXON

All That Can Be Done Is to Minimize the Loss of Life and Property.

WARNING SIGNALS

By LEWIS NIXON,
Naval Architect and Designer of the Battle Ship Oregon.

LEWIS NIXON. ALMAN PHOTO

DRAWN AT THE SUGGESTION OF MR. LEWIS NIXON TO ILLUSTRATE HIS IDEA OF A FLOATING DECK HOUSE

IN the face of such a calamity as the Titanic disaster the early discussion of material detail might seem heartless, were it not that such discussion may lead to saving precious lives in the future.

Here was a vessel presumed, and I think rightly so, to be the perfection of the naval architect's art, yet sunk in a few hours by an accident common to North Atlantic navigation.

At this writing we have not learned just how the impact occurred, but as she sank by the head it is to be presumed that the damage was done forward, most probably by a head-on collision. The ice of a berg, by wind and wave action, is often eaten in from the top, so that under water ledges may have projected.

At any rate, the integrity of the bulkheads forward was destroyed, so that the openings made through the collision let in enough water to let the vessel's head sink below the danger point. Longitudinal girders, which in such a vessel are of great rigidity, may, instead of buckling, have been forced rearward in such a way as to cause leaking in the bulkheads nearest the bow. A crushing in of the bottom may have contributed to the same end.

However, we know the great mass of metal ran into an incomparably greater mass of solid ice, so great that as compared with the vessel it was the same as hitting a reef, and opened to the sea enough compartments to sink the Titanic.

The Unsinkable Ship.

An unsinkable ship is possible, but it would be of little use except for flotation. It may be said that vessels can not be built to withstand such an accident.

We might very greatly subdivide the forward compartments, where much space is lost at best, making the forward end, while amply strong for navigation purposes, of such construction that it would collapse and take up some of the energy of impact; then tie this to very much stronger sections farther aft. Many such plans will be proposed by those who do not realize the momentum of a great vessel which will snap great cables like ribbons, when the motion of the vessel is not perceptible to the eye.

So, if the results can be avoided, the proper plan is to avoid the accident, and if an accident is unavoidable, to minimize the loss of life and property.

The introduction of wireless telegraphy on board ships has greatly minimized the risk of seagoing. In the lines of regular travel assistance is usually obtainable within a few hours. I still think that the risk of collision with ships is greater than with icebergs.

The wireless telegraph apparatus will doubtless be supplemented by a small apparatus greatly differing in tension from the main apparatus, which will act as a feeler up to, say, fifteen to twenty miles, so that vessels which are close together can know of one another's presence and proceed with caution.

Perhaps international support may be given to a project to station vessels in the North Atlantic that will be in touch with one another all the way across over a fairly wide area. Certainly there could be means of warning vessels of the probable location of icebergs during certain seasons by an international patrol. Carriage on the ocean will double within the next twenty-five years, and while we cannot think of the ocean as crowded, the chances of collisions of all kinds will be increased.

Most large vessels now have the submerged bell signals. Sounds are quickly communicated by water, as every one knows who has had two stones struck together while diving. The direction in which lies the bell making the sound is accurately determined by a receiving apparatus acting on the principle that when we hear a sound exactly the same in each ear we are facing its origin.

Above water the eophone will very accurately pick up the echo of its own ship's whistle from another vessel or an iceberg, so undoubtedly a means of making an underwater noise that would be echoed from an iceberg will be found.

Searchlights on the bow for discovering icebergs are proposed, but I do not believe much in them as they would not show far enough ahead and would be practically useless in thick weather.

However, it may be that some ray development may be found whose beams would penetrate a fog or mist. This would greatly aid navigation in fogs, especially in crowded harbors.

Here is what I consider a practical suggestion to the radio experts. Would it not be possible to develop a generator whose rays, acting on a special needle on another vessel, will turn it in the direction of their length, and so point it directly toward the vessel from which they flow?

The Question of Lifeboats.

An adequate supply of lifeboats should be rigidly enforced. It is stated that Captain Smith, of the Titanic, had criticised the boat equipment of his vessel, and the designer is quoted as saying that there were many empty davits. If space was provided for more boats and they were refused, some one of course is very much to blame.

No more difficult problem confronts the designer than the stowage of boats. And there is not only the question of stowage but, perhaps even more important, the risks of smashing by waves and of getting passengers into the boats. Then the number of seamen in the deck force capable of lowering, releasing and managing the boats must be considered.

The seaman of to-day is not the seaman of the days of the sailing vessel. I do not mean to belittle the seamen of the modern steamship. They are a particularly capable set of men, but their duties have grown to be different from what they were in sailing days. The modern seaman must be a good mechanic, a pipe fitter, a man capable of cleaning decks and polishing brass, but he is not accustomed to launching a lifeboat under necessity nor of handling it in a high sea. In the old times scarcely a sailor but had been through a wreck and knew what it was to launch boats when life was at stake. To-day I believe such men are fairly exceptional.

The Board of Trade is a competent body, and it aims to strike a fair, just mean in the matter of safety devices. Probably, however, too much reliance has been placed upon lessons of past disasters where boats were used to transfer passengers to some waiting vessel.

I find some criticism for saying that the question of boats was in a measure sentimental. This might be much misunderstood taken by itself. The statement was intended to indicate that the sentiment calling for more boats might mislead. There has been but little improvement in lifeboats and in boat handling since the day of Noah. So merely a greater number of boats is not what is needed, unless they can be efficiently used.

When we think of the great skill required in the handling of boats in any sort of sea, the difficulty and the necessary time of lowering, the possibility of accidents from smashing against the great, tall, sheer sides of a modern passenger vessel, we find great risk in the use of boats. This is no argument against carrying as many boats as can be handled with efficiency. I am convinced that it will be found a great length of time was required to get the boats of the Titanic in the water even in a calm sea.

The ordinary life raft in the ocean is far from a comfortable craft, but in the case of such vessels as the Titanic they could be made very large, and it would not be necessary for men to be chilled to death in the water from hanging onto the raft.

United States laws require boats, rafts, life belts and other devices sufficient for every one on board ship. In deep sea navigation this means that when the boat capacity is exhausted the required remaining flotation is provided by life rafts. On rivers life preservers are largely depended upon, and in some cases small planks are counted as life preservers. On the sea, however, there should be no dependence upon life belts, though, of course, an ample number should be provided.

Boats Not Efficient.

The ordinary person thinks of a lifeboat as a craft easily handled by four or five men, when, as a matter of fact, a steamship's lifeboat is as bulky as some of the old caravels. They must be suspended from davits, and it requires not only skill and knowledge but constant drilling to insure their reaching the water in safety.

We hear that much space on promenade decks might be utilized for lifeboats and that they might be stowed one within another like a lot of pans, but these are the ideas of the uninitiated. The lifeboats have air compartments to make them unsinkable and are heavy, strong and seaworthy—too heavy to be handled in such a manner. Even after escaping the perils of lowering and disengaging and dropping they require expert handling in a heavy sea. As I said before, the modern merchant vessel does not develop the seamen of the days of sailing craft, though the fishing and coasting fleets furnish splendid nurseries for capable seamen.

In our life saving service we are gradually supplementing oar propulsion by motors. When men pull out to a wreck in a heavy sea and wind they have pretty much everything taken out of them and are in no condition for their work of rescue, but with the motor lifeboats they can drive out to sea and be in full strength when they arrive at the wreck.

In the future I believe that lifeboats will be built very similar to the coast life saving craft, not of very great power, however, for they will also be equipped with oars and a sail.

In addition to this there should be a large pontoon raft, built as a part of the vessel. It could be used as a café or cardroom in pleasant weather. It would be practically a large detachable compartment, wide as the vessel and fifty or sixty feet in length. It would, of course, be air tight and communication from the inside to the top, which could be part of the upper deck, would be by means of hatchways.

The pontoon would have a small rail about the deck and one or two masts for signals and for wirless apparatus. The wireless could be operated by a small dynamo and a gas engine. This would also serve for lighting and heating purposes, and although the raft could not be made exactly comfortable it would make possible innumerable little conveniences.

Of course lighting should not depend upon the dynamo, for accidents to machinery are always possible, and in the dark a panic might ensue. When persons can see what is going on about them they are much less likely to lose their heads.

Adequate Supply of Lifeboats Should Be Enforced by Navigation Laws.

A NEW LIFE RAFT

Quantities of concentrated food and drink could be stowed in the raft at all times, just as is done now in lifeboats. I do not think that it would be possible to propel the raft itself by a motor, but it could be towed by the motor lifeboats. If it was constructed at the very stern of the vessel, the somewhat pointed stern would be the bow of the raft once it was in the water.

On the top of the raft, which would be in appearance considerably like one of the old "cheese box" gunboats used in the civil war, could be lashed one or two lifeboats and some rafts of the two-cylinder type—catamarans. They could be fitted with small motors and the propeller would be situated between the two cylinders.

It would be imperative that the pontoon raft should be launched by hand. Enormous levers would be used to lift it and slide it over the side. The launching would entail a few very uncomfortable moments for the refugees inside the raft, as it would necessarily plunge into the water sideways and shoot some distance below the surface, unless the side from which it was launched was settling close to the sea. When occasion arose all the passengers and crew possible would be crowded into the launch. In a calm sea such as it is now reported the Titanic sank in, it would be possible for the survivors to go above on the deck. The ability to launch the raft by hand power is absolutely necessary, for when a vessel is wrecked you cannot depend upon the boilers or the engine.

Larger lifeboats could also be used, and it would be possible to have them entirely roofed over and airtight. They could be swung outward and lowered by means of derricks and the passengers put in them before they were lowered. If a sea dashed over them they would not be swamped or the occupants drowned. Ports in the bow would enable a man to steer, and they should certainly be equipped with motors as well as oars. There are far more persons nowadays who can start and run an engine, especially a gas engine, than can pull an oar. Of course, if these boats depend upon power for lifting and lowering the power might be cut off, and there must be supplementary hand operated apparatus for the purpose.

Big Vessels Not Dangerous.

I can find no argument in this accident against the greater size of vessels. In fact, my judgment is that a designer can put more safety into a larger vessel than he can into a small one. The larger vessel is locally much stronger than a smaller one.

It is true that the momentum of such an enormous mass is tremendous almost beyond conception, but so is the power controlling it. It may be that the turbine system, which has sufficient power for ordinary manoeuvring, cannot be exerted to its fullest extent in backing. This power, being only possible of utilization in forward propulsion, may not be the best. It should be so modified as to allow the full power of the engines to be used in reversing.

The transmission from full speed ahead to full speed astern is very quickly accomplished by our men-of-war, but we shall have much authentic light thrown upon this power in a modern turbine vessel if any of the survivors among the officers were on the bridge at the time of sighting the iceberg.

It has been suggested that brakes, in the form of monster wings under water, which would be projected from the sides of a vessel, might be used, but I consider this impracticable. They would be unwieldy and the strain on them would be terrific. A light racing shell is stopped by the action of the sweeps in the water on this principle, but if the sweeps are turned with the blades perpendicular to the surface of the water, the tough wood is splintered. A shell only weighs about 160 pounds, and the men in it might aggregate about 1,440 pounds. Now try to calculate the strain on wings of the greatest toughness on a vessel the size of the Titanic. It would be difficult to get material to stand the strain.

The plunging of the vessel into darkness, the crippling of the wireless plant and the after results of flooding the boiler rooms or dynamo rooms far down in the vessel must be avoided. It would be a capital idea to maintain a supplementary plant far above the water line, amidships, which would supply electricity for lighting and wireless operation. All that would be necessary is a gas engine or even a gasolene engine and a dynamo and motor. A small plant, which would not take up too much room, could be made to supply power for two or three days.

It is to be hoped that adequate life saving equipment will be insisted upon by the government. Of course the Titanic carried the equipment required by the Board of Trade, but the fact that inadequacy of such equipment caused the loss of many lives will cause drastic action in the changing of rules.

Let us hope, too, that there be a let up in the tremendous pressure put upon the managers of shipping lines to be lax in enforcing proper precautions.

A little more patience on the part of the travelling public would add very much to their safety on the sea. When the fog or bad weather is over and a landing is made a few hours late grumblings and threats to take another line in future are all felt, and the tremendous pressure brought on the management forces men to take risks that otherwise their better judgment would cause them to avoid. In future when the captain takes measures to safeguard those intrusted to his care let the traveller commend instead of blame.

It is quite possible for all vessels to avoid the dangerous northerly passage in the season when icebergs are a menace by taking the southern course, but it means a longer time for the passage, and hundreds of passengers would forsake the vessels which went by the longer route.

MAJOR ARCHIBALD BUTT, THE ADMIRABLE CRICHTON

Officer Mourned by President Taft Was a Man of Many Parts and Friends.

SOLDIER TO THE LAST

MAJOR ARCHIBALD W. BUTT'S RESIDENCE, No 2000 G STREET N.W. WASHINGTON, D.C.

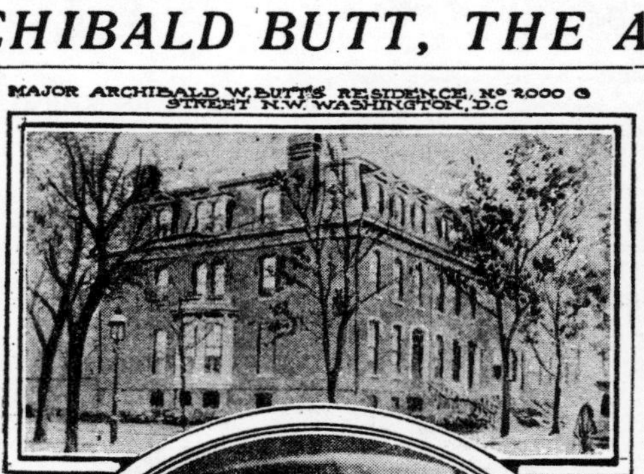

MAJOR ARCHIBALD W. BUTT

"ARCHIE" BUTT'S epitaph was written by President Taft even before the White House had received confirmation of his loss in the Titanic disaster.

"When I heard that the Titanic had sunk with twelve hundred souls," said the President—and his face showed his sorrow—"I knew that Major Butt had not been saved. He was a soldier and remained on deck, where duty told him he belonged."

The President's faith in his military aid was seconded by all of "Archie" Butt's friends, who include such extremes as Cardinal Gibbons and "Ty" Cobb, Mr. Roosevelt and Andrew Carnegie. With inspiring unanimity those who knew him best declared that he must be lost, for to him marine peril would mean not only "women and children first," but "other men first."

To the American public Major Archibald Willingham Butt, U. S. A., was a debonair attaché of the President. Always doing the right thing, always saying the right thing, he went wherever the President went, now swinging across the country on a political trip, dashing over to New York for a great public dinner, attending a baseball game or playing golf at Chevy Chase. The soldierly uniformed figure of the President's military aid was a reminder of official formality of the office held by the most democratic of men.

Major Butt was more than this. An "Admirable Crichton" he was, remarkably combining the best qualities of military aid and secretary, intimate and adviser.

Born in Georgia, of an old Southern family, "Archie" Butt was educated at the University of the South, at Sewanee, Tenn., where they put a Delta Tau Delta pin on his waistcoat. Under sail of his full name, Archibald Willingham Butt, he came to Washington as a newspaper correspondent early in the nineties and fired the Southern heart with despatches to a syndicate of publications south of Mason and Dixon's line. Commissioned as a captain and quartermaster of volunteers in 1900, he was taken into the permanent establishment the following year and creditably served three years in the Philippines, returning to the post of depot quartermaster at Washington, a billet usually accorded officers much older in the army. General Funston took him to Cuba with the army of pacification in 1906, and he was recalled in 1908 to become military aid to President Roosevelt, whose attention had been first attracted to him by one of his stories, "Both Sides of the Shield," which dealt with Southern life.

President Roosevelt found in Major Butt not only a keen sportsman, ever ready for a horseback ride, tennis on the White House court or a long tramp through the rain, but also a man of shrewd judgment of public affairs and a sound taste in literature. Mrs. Roosevelt and the other members of the family were devoted to "Archie," as he was known to them all.

When Mr. Taft, who had known Major Butt in the Philippines, became President he asked him to continue as military aid, and during the present administration this office has assumed importance it never before held.

While Presidents McKinley and Roosevelt had military aids, they were not requested to travel on Presidential journeys. Major Butt accompanied President Taft from the beginning of his administration, discharging the duties which in previous administrations were intrusted to men of the calibre of Lamont, Cortelyou and Loeb.

Upon Major Butt during President Taft's first transcontinental tour largely devolved the arduous duty of supervising the programme apportioning the President's time, controlling the great numbers of persons who demanded interviews with him, &c. Any weakness on the part of the manager of a Presidential trip is certain to result in disaster. The more successful the manager the more positive is he in control of his President.

Major Butt had to see that the President took proper care of himself, protected his voice and got plenty of rest.

"I have four bosses," said Mr. Taft, dejectedly, one night on a Southern trip, when Major Butt interrupted his conversation with several newspaper correspondents to say it was bedtime. "And Archie is the hardest," he added. Who the others were he did not say. Probably Mrs. Taft, Charles P. and Henry W. Taft, his brothers.

Major Butt's training as a newspaper correspondent stood him in good stead during his service with President Taft. He had a quick news sense. He always noted the little incidents, the "human interest" episodes which would satisfy the public's interest in the doings of the President. Their publication often did much to increase the popularity of the administration.

Major Butt's counsel was valuable in the direction of the social side of the administration. While the average man is somewhat disposed to regard this as a carpet knight's job, it should be remembered that much of the good relation among nations depends on official social intercourse. The spectacle of any army officer studying tables of precedent or seating arrangements for a state banquet may not appear impressive, but dislocation of precedence may offend an Ambassador and provoke his government. Ententes have been accelerated by harmonious dinners.

Under Major Butt's direction the four great evening receptions at the White House during the official season were changed from hopeless crushes into dignified and enjoyable levees. At these affairs, as well as at musicales and smaller receptions in the White House, Major Butt stood opposite the President and Mrs. Taft and announced the guests as they arrived in the Blue Room. His accuracy in the pronunciation of names was remarkable.

Nothing could be further from the truth than the idea that Major Butt enjoyed, as military aid to the President, a social sinecure. His duty was probably more exacting than that of any officer of the service, despite its non-military character. He seldom had any time that he could call his own. He could make no social engagement without the proviso that he might have to break it should his services be required at the White House.

In fact, Major Butt's health was so impaired during his last transcontinental trip with the President that he went under the physician's care until induced by the President and his warm personal friend, Frank Millett, the artist, to take the trip to Rome, from which he was returning on the Titanic when he met his death.

Major Butt gave to his duties as aid to the President the same painstaking study that he would have given to a military problem. He knew to a nicety how to meet the perplexing situations constantly arising about the President. As a result he made friends with the host of diplomatists and officials with whom he came into contact. The abandonment of social functions by embassies and legations in Washington was a recognition of the national disaster, but in each instance there was a personal pang due to the loss of Major Butt.

The intimate glimpse which was vouchsafed Major Butt of the history of two administrations he carefully recorded. Two volumes he constantly worked on, one an official record of the President's doings day by day, his journeys, receptions, &c. The other was Major Butt's own observations of what he had seen and heard, and this may, by his direction, be published many years hence.

To Major Butt's genius for friendship thousands of persons in this country are bearing witness. A characteristic of his rapid rise in the official world was that his friends of yesterday were his friends of to-day—and to-morrow.

THE FORTUNE TELLER.

"THE fallacy and infallibility of fortune tellers is not always to be relied on," said one of the chief officers of the steamship George Washington when the matter of superstitions, vague fears and forebodings was brought up.

"I have been going to sea for a great many years and in the natural course of things a lot of the traditions of the sea have been rubbed in. There is one incident in particular that was strange. Last year in Bremenhaven my wife and I with our two daughters went to a fair—a cattle fair it was—and the outlying grounds were filled with gypsy camps. For the fun of the thing we decided to have the future read. Oh, so old a crone! She was eighty if a day, and as her dim eyes peered into the hollow of my palm I could not help laughing.

Shaking with palsy she looked up, and there was a peculiar expression in her wavering stare.

"You may laugh," she quavered. "They always do laugh, but on the sea lies your work, and next year the greatest ship in the world will sink—sink—sink!"

And still I laughed.

She thrust my hand aside and began to cry—

"I have told you too much! I see too much! Sadness—death—sinking — sinking!"

My wife and I left the crazy-quilt tent—still laughing.

THE WEATHER.
Rain tonight; Tuesday clearing and colder.

THE BROOKLYN DAILY EAGLE

Complete Stock Market

LAST EDITION. Volume 72A No. 112 ★ NEW YORK CITY. MONDAY, APRIL 22, 1912. ★ 26 PAGES. THREE CENTS.

ENGINEERS REFUSE ARBITRATION PLAN

Were Asked to Join With Railway Managers in Petition to Congress.

FOR INCREASE ON FREIGHT.

Committees in Session, and Crisis in Situation Is Expected This Afternoon.

Both committees of railroad engineers and managers went into conferences in Manhattan, this morning for the purpose of adjusting the differences between the engineers and railroads and if possible to prevent a strike. The committee of Brotherhood of Locomotive Engineers, with Grand Chief Warren S. Stone, was in conference at the Broadway Central Hotel, while the railroad managers' committee had a similar conference at 50 Church street.

Mr. Stone left the committee room this morning for a few minutes and went to the lobby of the hotel, where he said his committee was awaiting the answer of the railroad committee, of which J. C. Stuart is chairman. He said there was nothing particular to say just at that moment and that at present the whole situation seemed to be in the hands of the railroad managers committee.

"Of course we are waiting their answer and expect to be promptly advised of their decision at any moment," said Mr. Stone.

It was said that if a strike is ordered it would take about three hours to send out the strike order and that it would be twenty-four hours before the strike was in operation. If the strike order goes out, according to a member of the committee, the engineers at the time on run will be permitted to finish the run before going out on strike.

Engineers Decline Offer for a Truce and Mediation.

That all efforts for arbitration are outside of any further consideration now, is clearly shown by a statement of Chief Stone that a man prominent in politics and in the Government service called on the general committee of the engineers and also consulted with Mr. Stone five times last night in an effort to get them to call a truce and join with the railway managers in going before Congress for a general petition for an increase in freight rates.

This prominent intermediary, whose name Mr. Stone gave with the request that the name be not published or his official position be made known, came from a conference with President Brown of the New York Central Railroad, according to Mr. Stone, and through Mr. Brown said he had authority to speak for all of the railroad presidents.

Mr. Stone, representing the engineers committee, replied to the representative of the railroads, that they could not consider any such proposition and that the men refused to join with the railroads as suggested and go before the Interstate Commerce Commission.

This would appear to be the end of the attempt for mediation or arbitration, as Mr. Stone says the next move must come from the railroad managers.

It was reported that Judge Martin A. Knapp, a member of the Department of Labor in Washington, joined Commissioner Neill at the Manhattan Hotel today, ready to do what might present itself to bring about a settlement. Both expect to see Mr. Stone today.

Later Commissioner Neill, Judge Knapp and Mr. Stone left the Broadway Central Hotel and went to the National Arts Club, where they were in conference.

Railroads That Will Be Affected in Case of Strike.

There are the fifty railroads lying east of Chicago and north of the Ohio River which will be affected if a strike is called today by the Brotherhood of Locomotive Engineers:

Baltimore and Ohio, Bessemer and Lake Erie, Boston and Albany, Boston and Maine, Buffalo, Rochester and Pittsburgh, Buffalo and Susquehanna, Central New England, Chicago, Indianapolis and Louisville, Chicago, Terre aHute and Southeastern, Chicago, Indiana and Southern, Cincinnati Northern, Cincinnati, Hamilton and Dayton, Cleveland, Cincinnati, Chicago and St. Louis, Coal and Coke, Delaware and Hudson, Delaware and Hudson, Delaware, Lackawanna and Western, Detroit, Toledo and Ironton, Dunkirk, Allegheny Valley and Pittsburgh, Erie, Grand Rapids and Indiana, Hocking Valley, Indiana Harbor Belt, Indianapolis Union, Kanawha and Michigan, Lake Erie and Western, Lake Erie, Alliance and Wheeling, Lake Shore and Michigan Southern, Lehigh Valley, Long Island, Maine Central, Michigan Central, New York Central and Hudson River, New York, Chicago and St. Louis, New York, New Haven and Hartford, New York, Ontario and Western, New York, Philadelphia and Norfolk, New York, Susquehanna and Western, New Jersey and New York, Pennsylvania Lines, East, Pennsylvania Lines, West, Pere Marquette, Pittsburgh and Lake Erie, Reading System, Toledo and Ohio Central, Toledo, St. Louis and Western, Vandalia Lines, Western Maryland, Wheeling and Lake Erie, West Side Belt Line, Wabash Pittsburgh Terminal.

NO BUTT MISSION TO POPE.

White House Denial That Major Carried Letter From Taft.

Eagle Bureau,
608 Fourteenth Street.

Washington, April 22—The story that Major Archie Butt went to Europe to carry an important message to the Pope from President Taft was denied at the White House this morning.

A message of sympathy was received at the White House this morning and referred to the statement that Major Butt had a mission abroad. Secretary Hilles, on behalf of the President, replied as follows:

"The President feels Major Butt's loss keenly and is only consoled by the knowledge that he gave up his life as a soldier and a man.

"There is absolutely no truth in the report that Major Butt was on a mission to Rome. The sole object of the visit was to get the benefit of the long sea voyage, and in order to add to the interest of his trip, the President gave him a number of formal notes of introduction to personages in Rome, whom he knew. None of the letters contained more than a formal introduction."

WARNING OF A STORM.

The Eagle Weather Bureau has received the following special from Washington: "Southwest storm warning, 10 a.m., Delaware Breakwater to Eastport. Disturbance over Great Lakes moving eastward, will cause brisk and probably high southerly winds this afternoon and tonight, shifting to westerly Tuesday. Rain and foggy this afternoon and tonight; clearing Tuesday."

MAYOR'S BROAD HINT.

How He Answered Colonel Roosevelt's Moneyless Message of Sympathy.

Mayor Gaynor's dry response to the message of sympathy for those afflicted by the loss of the Titanic sent to him by Theodore Roosevelt, became known today. Roosevelt sent a brief message to the Mayor expressing sorrow at the disaster and extending his sympathy to the sufferers. The Mayor has received many such messages, from prominent perons, but Roosevelt's was one of the few given to the press, owing to the prominence of the sender. The Mayor's answer, however, was not made public at the time. In effect, it was as follows:

"Your message of sympathy duly received and much appreciated. I am glad to be able to inform you that the relief fund is still growing."

Roosevelt did not contribute to the Mayor's relief fund for the Titanic sufferers. Most of the other sympathizers who wrote to him did. The Mayor has not heard from Roosevelt since.

LOWELL STRIKE ENDS.

Lowell, Mass., April 22—More than 14,000 employes in six Lowell cotton mills returned to work today, ending the strike which began four weeks ago. The operatives receive a wage increase of 10 per cent and other concessions.

SISTERS DROWN.

Lansing, Mich., April 22—Cecil and Josephine Richardson, sisters, 21 and 26 years old, were drowned yesterday when the canoe in which they were riding with Frank Eidman was capsized in the swift current.

HOLD TWO-THIRDS OF C. I. AND B. STOCK

Lawyers Title Insurance and Trust Co. Make Announcement.

WILL BUY SHARES AT $100 PAR

No Explanation of Deal Forthcoming From Men in Position to Talk.

The Lawyer's Title Insurance and Trust Company today makes the announcement that it has in its control two-thirds of the shares outstanding of the Coney Island and Brooklyn Railroad Company.

The company further states that it is prepared to pay $100 a share, or par value for all of the remaining stock.

Circulars to the above effect were sent to the minority stockholders on Saturday and today are being sent to banks and trust companies.

The stock of the company was recently bid for by George Prentics & Co., at $75 a share.

Little information was forthcoming today as to who is buying the stock of the Coney Island and Brooklyn Company. Men in position to know what is going on and who undoubtedly have received some information say they know nothing of what is going on.

President Slaughter W. Huff, of the Coney Island and Brooklyn Company said today that the minority stockholders now had a chance to dispose of their holdings at par. He would make no comment on who is buying the stock.

For the Brooklyn Rapid Transit Company it was said today that the stock is being held in "friendly hands," and that the corporation could secure the holdings at any time. The inference given was that the transaction is being steered by the B. R. T. and is with their knowledge.

Men in touch with the Coney Island and Brooklyn situation however, say today that the B. R. T. has no line into the grou of men who are buying the Coney Iseland and Brooklyn. It is stated that a big anti-B. R. T. movement is being organized.

The general feeling is that the New York influences which have been fighting the B. R. T. know considerably more of the transaction than the Brady group. The opinion is being offered today that when the present situation clears away it will be found that men antagonistic to the B. R. T., or at least strictly neutral in regard to its politices, have carried the war into the heart of the Brady company's territory.

MAYOR'S FUND NOW $81,571.88

$10,299.13 Received Today From Sympathizers With Victims of Titanic.

The contributions to Mayor Gaynor's relief fund for the Titanic sufferers was swelled this morning by $10,299.13 in cash and checks. The Mayor's fund now reaches a total of $81,571.88. Through W. A. Magee, the Mayor of Pittsburg, a fund of $1,788 was raised, which was received at the City Hall this morning. Mayor Carter Harrison of Chicago sent a check on behalf of citizens there for $289.75. James G. Wentz of Manhattan sent two checks each for $50, which he requested the Mayor to forward to Charles W. Lighttoller, the second officer of the Titanic and Harold S. Bride, second wireless operator on the liner.

Mrs. John W. Mackay and Johnson & Higgins each sent their check for $1,000 to the fund. The following is a list of the other principal contributions: Schuyler L. Parsons, $500; the Gorham Company, $500; Brooklyn Lodge of Elks, No. 22, $500; the Metropolitan Tobacco Company, $250; Ethel Zabriskie, $250; the Standard Paint Company, $200; Edward R. Bacon, $250; Free Sons of Israel, $175. The following contributed $100: W. H. Schofield, W. C. Brown, Centaur Company, William Hall Walker, Herman A. H. Lebus, L. Lemieux, E. Naumburg & Co., Mrs. Charles H. Duell, Gertrude D. Walker, Andrew Mount, A. D. Bendheim, Fleitman & Co., Otto T. Bannard, Greene, Tweed & Co., George M. Landers, Hotel Bossert of Brooklyn, Louis Martin, Louis N. Kramer, Marc Edlitz & Company.

Scores of other contributions ranging from 25 cents to $50 were also received by the Mayor. It is expected that before nightfall that the fund will reach the $100,000 mark.

H. C. McEldowney, who sent the check for Mayor Magee on behalf of the Pittsburg contributors declares that the $1,788 was raised in one day.

SERVICES IN BRITAIN.

London, April 22—In all the Catholic churches in the United Kingdom services were held today in memory of the victims of the Titanic disaster.

Westminster Cathedral was thronged. A catafalque draped with purple had been erected before the high altar. Cardinal Bourne officiated and gave absolution.

FRONT VIEW OF THE MONSTER ICEBERG WHICH SENT TITANIC TO THE BOTTOM.

The Eagle prints today the last of the series of five remarkable photographs taken from the deck of the Carpathia by Lewis P. Skidmore, instructor of art in the Pratt Institute of Brooklyn. This photograph shows a front view of the iceberg which sunk the Titanic. A side view of the same monster was printed in The Eagle yesterday.

After picking up the survivors in the lifeboats at daybreak Monday morning, the Carpathia, under full steam, headed for the scene of the wreck of the Titanic. It was hoped that more survivors would be rescued from rafts or wreckage. None was found.

At the spot where the vessel had foundered was the gigantic iceberg which had destroyed the steamer. It was identified by officers and crew. Mr. Skidmore took several photographs of the mountain of ice. He spoke of the great icefloe, which stretched away like a huge gray blanket on the surface of the sea. This covering of ice is distinctly shown in The Eagle photograph.

TITANIC LOOKOUT ASLEEP.

Sailor Also Says Members of Crew Were Drunk.

Cleveland, O., April 22—Lewis Klein, the Hungarian who claims to have been a member of the crew of the Titanic, is under arrest here under a technical charge of mutiny; pending the arrival of a subpena of the Senate investigating committee. He was arrested by direction of Senator William Alden Smith.

Klein's story, interpreted by the Austrian vice consul here, is that the lookout in the crow's nest of the Titanic was asleep when the collision occurred and that members of the crew were drunk from champagne that had been given to them by stewards serving the late dinner party aboard.

Klein asserts that he rang the alarm bell which apprised the third officer, who had just ascended the bridge after dining, of the danger ahead.

DERRICK BREAKS, MAN KILLED

Horse Also Killed in Street in Front of New Municipal Building.

Frank Walsh, a bricklayer, was almost instantly killed today when the beam on one of the cranes used in hoisting the large blocks of granite used in making up the columns at the Centre street front of the new Municipal Building in Manhattan broke and a thirty foot section crashed down upon the platform where he was working. The section then fell to the street and killed a horse attached to a dray owned by Donovan Bros., of 614 Union street, Brooklyn. Another workman, S. Freeman, of 1517 Charles street, the Bronx, was almost thrown to the street, 40 feet below, by Walsh's body striking him.

The accident happened just as the hoisting of the 50 ton section of one of the columns was started. Donovan Bros. had trucked the block underneath the column and the tackle was placed on it. Just as the work of hoisting it was commenced, there was a tremendous crash, and the beam of the crane, which is 70 feet in length, broke off about about 40 feet from its base.

Walsh and Freemen were working on a platform near the top of the column, and the falling section hit Walsh in its descent. He was mangled almost beyond recognintion, but was still living and was immediately lowered to the street in a sling, where Father Evers of St. Andrew's Roman Catholic Church gave him the last rites of the church. The priest had just completed his function when Dr. Worthheim in an ambulance from the Hudson street hospital drew up and pronounced Walsh dead. Walsh's age is unknown. He lived on East 149th street, between Bergen and Brooks avenues.

HUNDREDS STILL MAROONED.

Rescue Parties Scouring Inundated Country for Refugees.

New Orleans, April 22—Hundreds of persons still are marooned on flating housetops and rafts in the flooded sections of Northwestern Mississppi, according to official reports received here today.

Rescue parties have employed motorboats and launches to scour the inundated country for refugees. There has been intense suffering among the flood's prisoners.

FOR POSTAL CLERKS' FAMILIES

Congress May Appropriate $10,000 Each for Those of Titanic Victims.

Washington, April 22—Resolutions authorizing $10,000 appropriations for the families of each of the three postal clerks who lost their lives on the Titanic were introduced in the House today by Representative Reilly of Connecticut.

The three men were Oscar S. Woody of North Carolina, John S. March and William M. Gwynn of Brooklyn.

They were all United States clerks, and Gwynn had exchanged trips from another vessel in order to reach New York in time to be present for an operation to be performed on his wife.

KILLED WITH BASEBALL BAT.

Archangello Palmerri of Brooklyn Had His Skull Broken in a Fight.

Archangello Palmerri, 22 years old, a dealer in coal and wood, at 235 Forty-eighth street, Brooklyn ,and who, the police claim, was struck over the head with a baseball bat at the corner of Canal and Chrystie streets, Manhattan, last evening, by an unidentified man, died before daybreak this morning in Gouverneur Hospital, as the result of his injuries. The surgeons said the man's skull had been fractured.

All that the police know about the assault was gathered from residents of the neighborhood, who told them that Palmerri had been seen in an altercation with a man at the corner, and had been struck over the head with a baseball bat by the one he was quarreling with. The assailant disappeared before Patrolman Cray of the Clinton street station, who was summoned, could reach the corner.

PORCUPINE STOCKS BREAK REINHARDT

Bank Calls $100,000 Loan, and Curb Broker's Offices Are Closed.

BIG DROP IN SHARES; NO BIDS.

Reinhardt's Liabilities Are Estimated at $400,000, With Value of Assets Unknown.

The brokerage offices of J. Thomas Reinhardt, one of the largest curb brokers in this city, at 38 Broad street, Manhattan, were closed today and a sign on the door stated that business would be temporarily suspended until the return of Mr. Reinhardt from London, where he is at present engaged in establishing a new branch of his business, opened only three weeks ago. Simultaneously with the closing of the New York office dispatches from Boston were received in this city stating that his branch office there had been closed and that a notice on the door said that the intrinsic value of the firm's assets would enable a full payment eventually of all claims.

Reinhardt was a curb broker, dealing principally in Porcupine stocks and recently much interested in Marconi Wireless stock. He had branches in Toronto and Montreal, Canada, as well as in New York, Boston and London.

Immediately following the closing of the offices in Manhattan, which was done by the local manager, Mr. Freeman, the New York Curb Association announced the suspension of Reinhardt from the privileges of the association and it has notified the other members to close out whatever contracts they may have with Reinhardt in the regular way.

Loan of $100,000 on Porcupine Stocks Was Called.

A loan of $100,000, the collateral for which was principally in Porcupine stock, was called on Reinhardt by a Wall street bank last Saturday and the call was repeated this morning. It was following the second call that the managers of the local office decided to close the doors of the firm. Although the outward and apparent reason for the closing was the calling of the loan, it is believed generally on the Street that Reinhardt had been caught in the Marconi Wireless stock crash of Saturday.

Reinhardt's liabilities are estimated to be about $400,000, and the assets are principally in the Porcupine stocks and Porcupine properties. In these he was a specialist and promoted them on the curb. They include Porcupine Central, which was started at 40 cents a share and went as high as $5 9-16; Porcupine Northern, which started at 50 cents and went as high as $1 11-16, and Porcupine Southern, which started at 60 cents and went as high as $2 3-16. The Porcupine stocks were Cobalt stocks, in which Julian Hawthorne and others were interested and in connection with which they were indicted.

Operating with these stocks last fall Reinhardt engineered a successful squeeze of shorts, which resulted in some suspensions. He had a conflict with the new Curb Association in reference to the listing of these stocks, and made charges against certain brokers who refused to make good on their contracts because of certain irregularities.

When Reinhardt opened the London branch he devoted it to Marconi Wiredess stock. This stock broke sensationally last Saturday, closing 160 points lower, and the opening quotes on it this morning were 175-200 old stock, and subsequently were quoted 190-195. The new stock is quoted at 11½-11⅝.

Porcupine Offered at a Big Drop. Without Bids.

There seems to be no one connected with the local office able to give any more detailed information regarding conditions than that given on the notice, except for the simple statement to the effect that "the suspension was said to be due to the calling of cetrain large loans in Porcupine stocks which the firm was not in a position to meet at the present time." It was announced at the office late today that a detailed statement of the assets and liabilities of the firm would be given out later. The members of the local office, it was stated, are now at work on such a report.

The stocks in which the Reinhardt firm was interested were dull this morning when the curb market opened. Porcupine Central was without a bid. Saturday it was quoted at $5.50. Porcupine Southern, which sold on Saturday at $2, was offered at 50 cents a share today, and there were no bids. Porcupine Northern, quoted Saturday at $1.50, was also offered today for 50 cents a share.

PRENDERGAST OFF FOR NASHUA

Controller Prendergast left on the noon train today for Nashua, N. H., where he will deliver a speech this evening in behalf of Colonel Roosevelt. The preferential presidential primaries in New Hampshire take place tomorrow.

Friday and Saturday Mr. Prendergast will spend in a speechmaking tour of Massachusetts, where the preferential presidential primariess will be held the following Tuesday. The controller will return from New Hampshire tomorrow morning.

LET CHILD FREEZE TO DEATH.

Negro Father Pleads Guilty to Manslaughter in Queens Court.

David Jenkins, a negro, of Flushing, today pleaded guilty to a charge of manslaughter, before Judge Humphrey, in the Queens County Court. Jenkins was left in charge of his home by his wife last winter, while she was doing washing.

As she left the house one morning his wife gave him 25 cents to buy coal and wood, so as to keep their one-year-old child warm. Instead of doing as he was told, Jenkins went to a nearby liquor emporium and played pinochle with the money.

When the wife returned she found the child dead on the floor, having frozen to death in the cold. Jenkins was this morning arraigned, and pleaded guilty to the charge. He was remanded for sentence.

$40,000 THEATER LEASE.

New Halsey Theater Rented Out at This Figure by T. A. Clarke Co.

It was announced today that the new Halsey Theater, now being erected by the Thomas Clarke Company, has been leased to the Benedict Amusement Company at an annual rental of $40,000 a year. The house is to be ready within a few months and will run on the same plan as the DeKalb Theater, with vaudeville and moving pictures.

The deal has been completed and the contracts signed. Thirty thousand dollars has already been placed in the hands of the builders and $10,000 more will be forthcoming as soon as the theater is ready for occupancy.

CUTS HUSBAND OFF WITH $1.

Mrs. Jarashow Leaves Spouse Small Share of $20,000 Estate.

One dollar out of a $20,000 estate was left by Mrs. Mary Jarashow to her husband, Israel Jarashow of 7711 Nineteenth avenue. Mrs. Jarashow, whose will was filed for probate today, died March 27, 1912. She left $500 each to her grandchildren, Sophie, Samuel, Henry and Mary Stamm of 1029 Herkimer street, and the residue to her sons, Nathan and Benjamin Jarashow, of 110 Vernon avenue, Long Island City, who are also made executors.

The will, which was made October 10, 1911, gives no reason for the small bequest to the husband.

EVERGLADES CANALS OPEN.

Gulf to Atlantic Waterway First of System of Channels to Be Completed.

Tallahassee, Fla., April 22—Official opening of the Everglades drainage canals, which are being constructed for the purpose of reclaiming the Everglades of Florida, began today.

The Gulf-to-Atlantic Canal is the first of a system of five great channels begun two years ago to reclaim four million acres of Everglades land. This territory resembles a great saucer, irregular in shape, 160 miles long by 60 miles wide.

It contains Lake Okechobee, the second largest body of fresh water situated wholly within the confines of the United States. The four main canals, aggregating 203 miles in length, are expected to transform this vest swamp into one of the most productive areas in the country. The contracts provide that the channels shall be completed before July 1, 1913.

Cost of draining the Everglades will not exceed $1 per acre. Title to the land is held by the State.

ST. LOUIS TERMINAL CO. TRUST

Supreme Court Rules It Operates in Violation of Sherman Law.

Washington, April 22—The Terminal Railroad Association of St. Louis and fourteen railroads entering that city and owning the terminal company, were today held by the Supreme Court of the United States to be a combination operated in violation of the Sherman antitrust law to control transportation across the Mississippi River at St. Louis.

Justice Lurton announced the decision. He said it was not contended that every terminal company in every city was a violation of the Sherman law. It might be a facility instead of a restraint on interstate commerce.

SAW TWO BOATS SINK.

Carpathia Passengers Say About Sixty Passengers Were in Them.

Toledo, O., April 22—Mrs. Barbara Posan and her sister-in-law, Mrs. Florin Posan, with their children, who were passengers on the rescue ship Carpathia, bound for Hungary, arrived home yesterday, suffering from the nervous strain under which they passed last week.

The women tell a story of the women of the steerage taking off their skirts and giving them to the women passengers rescued off the Titanic.

The Posan women declare they saw two boats filled with women on Monday, near where the Titanic sank. There were about sixty women in the two boats; they said none of them was able to steer the lifeboats. Soon they saw both boats capsize and all were drowned.

STEAMERS COLLIDE OFF CAPE HATTERAS

Cretan, of Merchants and Miners Line, and Iroquois, of Clyde Line, Damaged.

PROBABLY IN NO DANGER.

Reports State That Neither Ship Is in Serious Situation—No Fatalities Reported.

Norfolk, Va., April 22—The steamer Cretan of the Merchants and Miners Line, bound from Jacksonville and Savannah to Baltimore, is making her way slowly up the coast, seriously damaged above the waterline, as a result of a collision during thick weather early today off Hatteras, with the Clyde Line steamer Iroquois, from New York, for Charleston and Jacksonville.

The Savannah Line steamer City of Montgomery was standing by the Cretan to give assistance if needed. Both steamers carried passengers.

News of the collision reached here over the United States Weather Bureau's Sea Coast Telegraph Line from Cape Hatteras station, via Cape Henry. It stated the Cretan was in no immediate danger, but gave no information concerning the whereabouts of the Iroquois. It is thought the Iroquois perhaps sustained little damage, and has proceeded on her voyage southward. No fatalities were reported.

The Cretan, 1,650 ton vessel, is heading for Norfolk. Details of the accident are lacking.

Baltimore, April 22—Wireless advices to the Merchants and Miners Line offices here are to the effect that neither the Cretan nor the Iroquois, which were in collision early today, was seriously damaged.

The Cretan was not leaking and is proceeding to Baltimore unassisted, having notified the steamer City of Montgomery, which stood by for a time, that no aid was required.

Charleston, S. C., April 22—The wireless station here was speaking this morning with the Clyde line steamer Iroquois, but no details of the collision with the Cretan was given. The Iroquois reported herself all right and said she would dock at 7 o'clock tonight. The station expects other reports.

MASSACRE IN FEZ.

Many French Soldiers and Citizens and Jews Slain.

Paris, April 22—The revolution in Fez, the Moroccan capital, in which the populace and a large number of mutinous Moorish soldiers participated, developed into a veritable massacre, accompanied by many atrocities, according to a wireless dispatch received this morning from Fez at the Foreign office.

It is now known that 15 French officers and 40 soldiers were killed in the fighting, while 13 civilians, all of them French citizens, were massacred in their homes or in the streets. Besides these, four French officers and 70 soldiers were wounded and 100 Jews were slain and a large number wounded and mutilated.

The greatest misery prevails in the Jewish quarter of the city.

Elaborate measures have been taken by the commander of the French troops to prevent further outbreaks.

The French government explains that the absence of detailed news from Fez is due to the fact that four or five telegraphers stationed there, as well as those attached to the wireless station, were massacred at their post of duty where they remained heroically through the revolt, sending official dispatches.

BETTING ON ELECTION.

Big Wagers Made and Others Waiting to Be Taken Up.

Several political bets in anticipation of the coming Presidential campaign have already been recorded at Schum's, on Fulton street. A number of small bets on the nomination of Wilson, Clark and Harmon by the Democrats have been made, but the "big money" is up on the Republican situation. One man has bet $500 that Taft will be renominated. Another has a standing offer, not yet accepted, of $5,000 at even money that the next President will be a Republican. A third offer of $1,000 to $500 that Roosevelt will not be the Republican nominee has not yet been covered.

REASSURING NEWS BASED ON RUMORS

Franklin Says He Had No Authentic Reports of Titanic's Safety.

"HOLD CEDRIC"—ISMAY.

Message Said It Was "Not Desirable" to Send Titanic Sailors Back on That Steamer.

NO WIRELESS CENSORSHIP.

Denial of Any Intention to Spirit Away Titanic Sailors Because of the Senate Investigation.

Washington April 22—Vice President P. A. S. Franklin of the International Mercantile Marine Company told the Senate Investigating Committee today, how he had asked to have the earlier reports of the Titanic disaster held up to avoid unnecessary alarm.

He denied any knowledge of the message addressed to Representative Hughes of West Virginia about the ship being towed to Halifax and gave other details.

Bit by bit he contributed to the evidence the Senate is seeking to throw light on the catastrophe that sank the Titanic, the pride of the seas, sent almost 1,600 people to their death and plunged the world into mourning.

The inquiry took place in the luxurious caucus room of the Senate, regarded as perhaps the handsomest legislative hearing room in the world.

In its center sat the sub-committee, with William Alden Smith of Michigan presiding.

Jammed about the long table which the committee occupied were witnesses and spectators. Among them were Senators and representatives and their wives; Baron von Hengelmuller, the Austrian ambassador and other representatives of the diplomatic and official circles, newspaper correspondents and a large number of women, mostly drawn from the national gathering of the daughters of the American Revolution.

The hearing overshadowed all other Congressional proceedings.

No Facts on Which to Base Reassuring Statements.

After denying that officials of the White Star Line had any knowledge of a misleading telegram to Mr. Hughes, it was acknowledged by Mr. Franklin that he has issued reassuring statements when he had no facts on which to base them. Mr. Franklin was the first witness.

The witness read from a great sheaf of wireless telegrams received Monday morning. None of them contained any information of value, but it was upon this data that the line issued its statements in an effort, Mr. Franklin said, to reassure inquirers.

Later, when the news came, he said he sent immediately for the reporters and proceeded to begin reading reading to them the long Marconigram from the Carpathia giving the gruesome news in considerable detail.

"I began to read," said Mr. Franklin, "'Titanic went down this morning at 2:20 a.m,. and then I looked up. There was not a reporter in the room. They were all racing for 'phones to get the news out to the world."

The White Star people considered the Titanic absolutely unsinkable, and that there had been loss of life never entered their minds. Mr. Franklin denied that he attempted any censorship of the wireless.

Mr. Franklin said the cost of the Titanic was $7,500,000.

He said that Ismay had sent a telegram to him asking that the Cedric be held because he considered it "most desirable" that members of the Titanic crew be sent back on that steamer. He also declared his intention of sailing on that ship himself.

Mr. Franklin denied that the White Star Company had any intention to spirit away from the country any Titanic officers or crew, or that the plans to return the survivors of the crew were prompted by any desire to suppress the facts.

He said that nothing the officers or crew could tell could affect what might be told by surviving passengers.

TODAY'S TESTIMONY.

There had been a long delay before the first witness took the stand. Mr. Ismay, seated at the end of the long table, chatted intermittently with J. P. Kierlein, one of the officials of the White Star Line. Incessantly he drew upon a sheet of paper he had acquired from the press table. Always the sketch was that of the White Star flag, such a flag as was flown at the peak of the Titanic when it sailed to its doom.

Just as the hearing was opened Senator Smith said:

"The inquiry we are making is in obedience to a direction by the Senate and is for the purpose of ascertaining the important facts connected with the unfortunate loss of the Titanic.

"We are not at all concerned about the convenience of visitors upon the hearing. We are concerned primarily to [illegible]tain the truth, and I desire to warn [illegible] person, here solely by sufferance [illegible] committee and not for entertai[illegible] that any expression of any charac[illegible] not be permitted. Any violatio[illegible] will result in changing these

AT LEAST 35 DEAD IN TORNADO ZONE

List of Fatalities Expected to Be Increased When Communication Is Restored.

MANY HOUSES DESTROYED.

Two Distinct Storms in Ceneral and Southern Illinois and Northwestern Indiana.

Chicago, April 22—The tornado which late yesterday swept over central and southern Illinois and northwestern Indiana, killed at least thirty-five persons and injured nearly 200 others, according to advices received here early today.

Miles of telegraph and telephone wires were blown down, farmhouses were demolished in the path of the storm, and it is probable that the death list will be increased when communication is restored with all points over which the tornado passed.

While there is no means of estimating the damage by the storm, it is certain to run into hundreds of thousands of dollars.

At Bush, a village in Williamson County, the greatest loss of life occurred, eighteen persons having been killed and more than forty injured. Nearly every dwelling in the village was either destroyed or damaged. Most of the dead were foreigners who worked in the coal mines near Bush.

At Morocco, Ind., nine persons lost their lives by being crushed in the collapse of their houses.

At Grant Park, Ill., half a dozen persons were injured and damage amounting to more than $100,000 was caused by the tornado.

The family of Nelson Hulse, at Campus, a village near Reddick, was almost wiped out. Hulse, his wife and oldest daughter, were killed and two other children were severely injured. Trolley lines throughout the storm-swept district suffered heavy damage on account of the destruction of the poles.

The loss of life in the towns which are in communication with the outside world follows:

Bush—18 dead, 40 injured.
Willisville—5 dead, 40 injured.
Campus—3 dead, 6 injured.
Morocco—9 dead, 12 injured.

The St. Louis, Iron Mountain and Southern Railroad shops at Bush were demolished and many residences destroyed.

Four persons were injured, one probably fatally, just north of Murpheysboro. Heavy property damage, but no loss of life was reported at Duquoin.

Residents of the stricken area declare there were two distinct storms, one striking at 5:30 and the other shortly before 7.

All of the south and east part of Grant Park, Ill., near Kankakee, was destroyed. Six persons were so severely injured as to require medical attention. A German church was demolished, and other buildings were blown down in Grant Park.

SEC. MEYER TO REVIEW

Navy Department Head Will Inspect Naval Militia Here on on Wednesday Evening.

Secretary of the Navy Meyer, as the guest and reviewing officer at the joint exercises of the First and Second Battalion of the Naval Militia, on Wednesday evening, will see one of the finest indoor exhibitions by citizen sailors ever given in the United States. The review will be held in the armory of the Second Battalion of Brooklyn, at Fifty-seventh street and the Bay.

The First Battalion of Manhattan will be commanded by Commander Russell Raynor, and the Second Battalion by Commander Kingsley L. Martin. Both battalions, when united, will be in command of Commodore Forshem. The following programme will be carried out:

Infantry drill by the First Battalion, light artillery drill by the Second Battalion, signal work by Second Battalion, boat drill by the Second Battalion.

The individual battalion exhibitions will be preceded by a review of both commands by Secretary Meyer.

One of the features of this review will be the first appearance of the new band of the Second Battalion, under direction of Bandmaster Shannon of the Twenty-third Regiment, who, in addition to leading the band of the big Bedford avenue regiment, has undertaken to develop the naval band. The musicians, twenty-one in number, will wear the marine band regulation full-dress uniform of red coat and blue trousers.

The boat drill of the Second Battalion promises to be one of the best displays of the evening. In this will be illustrated the "rule of the road" for both steam and sailing vessels, with the aid of four miniature ships, two with sail and two with steam. The first part of this drill will be given over to the sailing craft, after which two launches will come out and exemplify the working of the "road" rule for steam vessels.

The exercises will begin at 8:30 o'clock.

PARIS FASHIONS UP TO DATE.

From The Eagle Paris Bureau, 53 Rue Cambon, through the courtesy of Abraham & Straus.

Evening gown of white embroidered chiffon, with charmeuse skirt; black velvet flower.

STOP! LOOK! LISTEN!

HEROIN FIENDS LOOT DRUG STORE

Force Entrance to East New York Pharmacy; Get $200 Worth of Loot.

WORKED IN GLARE OF LIGHT.

Got No Heroin, but Secured Money, Stamps, Cigars and Candies. Pharmacist Has a Clew.

That the "heroin gang" had committed another burglary in the East New York section became known today, when it was learned that the pharmacy of Harry Balzhiser, at 2040 Fulton street, near Saratoga avenue, had been robbed early Saturday morning. About $200 worth of loot was taken by the burglars, and it is estimated they must have been at work nearly three hours. They ransacked the shelves and lockers for cocaine and heroin, but did not obtain any of the latter, as Druggist Balzhiser kept none in stock.

A large number of robberies of drug stores in the East New York and Bushwick sections have been reported to the police recently, and all are attributed to the members of the same gang who are slaves to the heroin habit. Three drug stores on Knickerbocker avenue were robbed in one night not long ago, and the operations of the gang have extended into Brownsville, where a druggist on Eastern parkway only a few weeks ago was held up in his store in day light by two frenzied youths who demanded to be supplied with heroin.

About a week ago, two young men called at Balzhiser's store and asked to be sold some heroin. Balzhiser refused to serve them and they raised such a row that he went to the telephone to call up police headquarters. The two men then went outside and waved their fists in the door at him, threatening to "get even." Mr. Balzhiser observed the pair looking intently in the window some days after that and sizing up the arrangements of the store.

Burglars Worked in Glare of Pharmacy Light.

A light was left burning in the store all Friday night, but that did not deter the burglars. They entered by forcing an iron grating over one of the windows in the rear, breaking the window and unfastening the catch.

Mrs. Rathjen, who lives over the drug store, heard a noise, she thought, about daybreak, in the rear of the store and, getting out of bed, went downstairs and pounded on the door leading to the hall from the compounding department of the store. She did not get any response, and although she listened for some minutes, she did not hear a sound. She went upstairs again and soon after heard the noises repeated. She went down to the front of the building and waited from about 5 o'clock until 5:30 before she saw a policeman. When the policeman entered the building the burglars had vanished.

They took with them about $50 worth of cigars, leaving all the five-cent brands, and having smoked while they were at work. They had also rifled the candy case and eaten some maraschino cherries during their stay. They took the most expensive candies, $20 worth of postage stamps, and a lot of perfumery and drugs. They left many bottles of drugs and essences scattered about the floor.

The last thing they did was to break open the coin box of the telephone pay station in a booth. This set off an alarm, which was not transmitted to the telephone company, as they had cut the wires, but the alarm evidently scared them off. They dropped about $8 in small change from the coin box on the floor and made their escape. They took about $30 from the telephone box, according to the telephone company.

A reward has been offered for the arrest and conviction of the thieves.

TALKS OF MISSION WORK.

David J. Ranney, leader of a mission at 131 Bowery, Manhattan, spoke last night before the members of St. Paul's Congregational Church, Sterling place and New York avenue, on "From the Bottom Up." He recounted incidents of his own career before his conversion and described the present sordid conditions among Bowery characters as he found them. His mission work, he said, was progressing slowly, but the results are daily becoming more gratifying.

BROOKLYNITES SAIL.

Several Brooklynites will sail for Europe on the Barbarossa of the North German Lloyd line tomorrow. They include Miss Katherine Huephel, Mrs. Bertha Schwalb and Eugene Sontag. On the Anchor Line California, sailing last Saturday, was Miss Sarah Todd of Brooklyn.

OWENS ASSOCIATION ELECTS.

Republican Club of 14th A. D. Chooses Officers for Year.

The annual meeting of the George A. Owens Republican Association, the representative organization of the Fourteenth Assembly District, was held on Saturday night at the clubhouse in South First street, with John T. Branigan in the chair. Reports of the various committees were presented and accepted. That of the secretary-treasurer showed there was a substantial sum in th treasury. The following officers were elected:

John T. Branigan, president; William Prange, vice president; William H. Knapp, secretary-treasurer; trustees, Henry Lissner, Arthur A. Higgins and F. McLoughlin; lecturer, George Thomas.

Ex-Senator George A. Owens, the executive member of the district and standard bearer of the association, was called upon for a few remarks, during the course of which he said:

"The year now ended has been a most successful one. I am informed by the secretary that we have taken in two hundred new members and that we now have sixteen applications under consideration. Our treasury is in better shape than it ever was and we are ready now to enter into the coming campaign with vigor."

MRS. BOOTH ON PRISON WORK.

Head of Prison League Tells of Remarkable Results Achieved.

Mrs. Ballington Booth, head of the Volunteer Prison League of the Volunteers of America, was the speaker last night at the regular service of the First Baptist Church, Lee avenue and Keap street. Mrs. Booth is known as the "Little Mother" by inmates of our State Prisons and she told last night something of the work of the League, and also cited some stories of the reformed lives of some of the men who have come under her influence.

Mrs. Booth began by saying that when she announced to her friends that she was going to help those inside prison walls, they laughed at her and tried to discourage her by saying that there was no more unsympathetic and unresponsive crowd than a gang of State prisoners, but she has found after seventeen years that it is just the reverse. "Now," said Mrs. Booth, "I have more personal, warm friends in men who have served time in State Prison than anywhere else. Many times the world outside is the unresponsive field even to the message of the preachers, because they are prosperous, and only turn to the church and its teachings when they are in need, but the men in prison are just the reverse."

Mrs. Booth went on to say that the Volunteer Prison League was formed in Sing Sing with about sixty men and that within a few short months, the number was 600, and that now in all the prisons in the United States there are 75,000 members. Prison officers all over the country are begging Mrs. Booth to start a branch in their prison, a fact which Mrs. Booth says proves its efficacy in starting the men on the right road. In a prison in Tennessee there have been enrolled 450 men since February. Here Mrs. Booth cited cases where a term in prison was the best thing that could happen to a man. She told of the good that her homes for discharged prisoners have done all over the country, and said that within ten years 20,000 men have come to these homes straight from prison and of this number 75 per cent. have made good; 20 per cent. are doubtful and only 5 per cent. have found their way back into prison.

UNION BANK SUITS.

Stockholders Engage Counsel to Defend Actions by State Banking Department.

From recent developments it appears that the State Banking Department will have a long, hard legal battle to collect assessments on the Union Bank stock held by the stockholders, against 500 of whom suits were brought by State Superintendent George C. Van Tuyl, jr., a short time ago. It became known last night that a committee of stockholders, headed by James J. Farrell, had been formed and that they had retained the law firm of J. Stewart and Leroy W. Ross to defend them against the suits begun by the Banking Department.

The subpenas in these suits were turned over to Sheriff Charles B. Law for service and deputies have been searching the city since then for the deefndants. Some of them are now in other States while others are reported in Europe.

The procedure planned by the State Department was to serve the summonses and if no answer was made to take judgment by default. The twenty days given for the filing of answers will expire in a few days and in several cases Ross and Ross have already demanded copies of the complaint, indicating clearly that the suits will be defended.

It was declared last night that the banking officials had made little headway in collecting from the stockholders and that it was expected that months would pass before the suits were brought to trial.

Leroy W. Ross admitted last night that his firm had been retained to look after the interests of the stockholders of the defunct bank.

MEMORY OF DEAD PHYSICIANS HONORED

Kings County Medical Society Holds Service for Thirty Deceased Members.

EARNEST TRIBUTES PAID.

The Rev. Dr. McAfee Says the Doctor Leads Most Sacrificial of Lives.

At the memorial services held yesterday afternoon at the library building of the Medical Society of the County of Kings, 1313 Bedford avenue, the Rev. Dr. Cleland B. McAfee, pastor of the Lafayette Avenue Presbyterian Church, called attention to the striking change in the nature of the large advertisements during the last ten years, which change Dr. McAfee declared was traceable directly to the medical profession.

"Ten years ago," said Dr. McAfee, "eight out of ten of the large advertisements we saw every day, were for patent medicines: today eight out of ten of the advertisements we see in the daily newspapers are for health foods."

The memorial services were held in honor of the physicians and surgeons who have died during the past fifteen months. The list was a long one containing thirty names, the longest in the history of the society, and contained the names of men who had become famous in the field of medicine. Dr. E. H. Bartley, president of the Medical Society of the County of Kings presided, and the roll of the honored dead was read by Dr. William Schroeder, the chairman of the historical committee of the society.

A Clergyman's Tribute to the Dead Physicians.

The Rev. Dr. McAfee's address was in the nature of a layman's tribute to those who had been called from the medical profession to their eternal reward. He said that the grief and sorrow over the death of a physician is not felt alone in his family circle, or in a gathering such as the one yesterday, but there are many who felt they have lost the friend on whom they most depended. He said the physician is mourned in many groups, some that gather around breakfast tables, dinner tables, in homes and in clubs; of these griefs the deceased's family and his more intimate associates were not aware, but they were none the less sincere.

"The members of the medical profession are the largest givers to social uses of capital without interest, of any class or profession on earth, and I do not except the ministry, either. The ministers are supposed to be on call at all times when needed, and theirs is not a labor for recompense. The troubles that the doctors cure are as nothing to the troubles they prevent. Most of our doctors lead the sacrificial life, and many of them do so because they do not know it."

Dr. McAfee spoke feelingly of the life of the late Dr. Reynolds, one of his parishioners, who, when he suspected that he was afflicted with tuberculosis, denied himself the comforts of domestic life and remained a bachelor, giving all of his time until his death, to the work of preventing the spread of tuberculosis.

Dr. McAfee called attention to another case of a young physician of his acquaintance who saved a woman's life through an operation—"a woman, whose life when measured in the value of lives, was worth nothing to anyone except to her child. I was present when this operation was performed, and knew from the nature of it that her body was filled with the most virulent of poisons. Her life was saved; she regained her health; but, alas, there must have been some slight rent in the physician's glove; some minute abrasion of his skin, for blood poisoning set in, and he died. Is it not true that we can say of such men as was said of the Great Physician, 'He saved others, Himself He could not save?'"

Young and Old Represented Among the Dead.

In reading the roll of deceased members of the society Dr. Schroeder called attention to the age, the number of years of practice and the class of practice of each physician, also giving a short sketch of their activities as best known to the medical world. The years of service these men had given to the public ranged from that of Dr. Agrippa Nelson Bell, aged 91, who had practiced medicine for sixty-nine years, to that of Dr. Henry Lockwood Finley, aged 27, who had practiced but four years.

In speaking of Dr. Bell, Dr. Schroeder said that it was rarely that the physician came in for prominent mention in local history, but Dr. Bell's work in New Utrecht, during the yellow fever epidemic in 1856 had given him three pages in Mrs. Bleecker Bang's history of that section. The death of Dr. Hermann Philip Bender, killed by an automobile, was feelingly referred to, as was also the service of thirty years rendered the police force as its surgeon, by Dr. Charles H. Terry. The complete list of deceased physicians follows:

Joseph Hill Hunt, M. S., M. D., Eugene P. Hickok, B. S., M. D., James Youngs Tuthill, M. D, James William Dodd Hancock, M. D., Elbert Goodman Van Orsdell, M. D., John Wilkinson Van Deusen, M. D., Sewell Matheson, B. S., M. D., John Randolph Quinn, M. D.; Hermann Philip Bender, M. D.; William Blythe Lane, M. D. Benjamin Edson, M. D., Henry Lockwood Finley, M. D., Agrippa Nelson Bell, A. M., M. D., John Franklin Davis, M. D., Charles H. Terry, M. D., Ralph Melville Mead, M. D., Frederick Henry Colton, A. M., M. D.; W. Vincent Dee, M. D.; Francis Watson Bowron, M. D., Harold Flagg Jewett, M. D., Edward H. Pollock, jr., M. D., Walter Howard Muchmore, M. D.; Thomas Henry Wilde, M. D., Edwin Augustus Lewis, A. M., M. D., Charles Eddy, M. D., Richard Morris Wyckoff, A. M., M. D., William Fenton Millington, M. D., Frank Baldwin, M. D., Leon Millard Fleming, M. D., Victor Seymour Pier, M. D.

BOYS IN CONCERT.

German-American Chorus in Fine Singing Festival.

At the Palm Garden on Hamburg avenue yesterday afternoon a large gathering of interested parents and friends listened to an excellent entertainment given by the German-American Boys Chorus. The boys sang splendidly and were warmly applauded.

The soloists and directors were: Ernst Scharpf, Otto Triebig, Mrs. Noack-Fique, D. A. Knabenchor and B. Maskos.

The officers and committees were:

John M. Bauer, president; George Schuettinger, vice president; H. A. Hahn, correspnding secretary; John Sarter, financial secretary; A. Carl, treasurer; Ernst Scharpf, Benno K. Maskos, Otto Triebig, directors.

Arrangement Committee—Hermann A. Hahn, Adolph Carl, William Fuchs, A. Hoeckle, William Soehl, J. Sarter, G. Schaefer, H. Rudolph, J. Pieroth, L. Streit, B. Schnell, John M. Bauer, ex-officio.

Reception Committee—B. Schnell, Max Altenkirch, G. Doerschuck, Arnold Greiner, Gustav Heil, Fr. Jaeck, Bernhard Klein, Fred Rath, J. Schreiner, Valentine Stehlin, J. Bauer, T. Buss, Peter Grimm, W. Haug, J. Jager, A. Lindemann, Karl Ruefer, J. Schmidt, R. Stutzmann, Ernst Behrens, Aug. Dreyer, L. Gaissert, H. Hartmann, Adam Yungblut, L. Petery, Henry Roemhild, Fr. Schmalz, F. Wendler, Charles Balzner, J. Geyer, T. Hunger, Hy. Hoffman, John Kikel, Mr. Popp, H. Schneller, W. Stenniger, Jacob Winkler, Ed. Winkopp.

Finance Committee—Adolph Carl, Gregor Schaefer, Louis Streit, D. Schaaf, J. Geyer, H. Rudolpf, Albert Heil, Herman Hahn, Charles Wagner.

Press Committee—John M. Bauer, John Roehner, John Ernst, Benno Maskos, Ernst Scharpf, O. Triebig, E. Kampermann, E. Meinhardt.

UNITY CLUB ELECTION.

Montague D. Cohn Chosen President at Annual Meeting.

Yesterday afternoon the sixteenth annual meeting of the Unity Club was held in the assembly room of the clubhouse, Franklin avenue, opposite Hancock street. The report of the retiring president, Louis Newman, showed that the club has passed through a most successful year in its history. The financial condition today is excellent, a very substantial surplus being in the treasury.

Announcement was made of the annual dinner, to be held Thursday evening at the clubhouse, and of the annual Children's Day entertainment, to be held Saturday afternoon, May 11.

The election of officers resulted as follows: President, Montague D. Cohn; vice president, Julius Strauss; treasurer, Simon Levy; corresponding secretary, Jacob Levine; recording secretary, J. W. Kahn; the directors elected for a term of two years are Louis Newman, Bertram N. Manne, Joseph Matthias and Max Karlsruher.

"A REGIMENT OF TWO."

St. Bernard Dramatic Society to Present Play Wednesday Night.

The St. Bernard Dramatic Society, connected with St. Bernard's R. C. Church, Hicks and Rapelye streets, of which the Rev. James J. Kunz is pastor, will present, for the benefit of the church, a three-act farcial comedy entitled "A Regiment of Two," on Wednesday evening, at Prospect Hall.

The play was chosen by the coach, Joseph A. Finegan, as a suitable one to bring out the splendid acting for which the society is known. It has for the past five years produced successes and has made for itself a name as one of the leading dramatic societies in Brooklyn. The evening programme will be opened with a selection by the entire society. This will be followed by the play, the cast being:

Arthur Sewall, Frank Rickert; Reginald Dudley, William Cobb; Ira Wilton, August Rickert; Jim Buckner, eGorge Kestler; Barry Brentworth, Joseph Rickert; Conrad Melger, Michael Galvin; Eliza Wilton, Mary Gibbons; Grace Sewall, Frances Dilberger; Laura Wilton, Loretta Madigan; Lena, Mrs. August Rickert.

BAND CONCERT FOR CHURCH.

On Thursday evening, April 25, the Thirteenth Regiment band of sixty musicians will give a concert in the auditorium of the Bedford Branch Y. M. C. A. The proceeds are for the building fund of the Bethlehem German Evangelical Church, 595 East Seventh street. The congregation is five years old, and in that time it has outgrown its present building. The church has purchased a new site and expects to build this summer.

The band will be assisted at the concert by the following soloists: Hans Elleson, tenor; Miss Mabel Schoemaker, soprano; Miss Olga Venino, contralto; Signor Joseph F. Fonzo, flute.

Brooklyn Society

Miss Owens' Song Recital Was an Event of Yesterday.

In the studio of S. Constantino Yost, Carnegie Hall, Manhattan, Miss Olive Carey Owens gave the most attractive of song recitals yesterday afternoon, taking the entire programme of twelve numbers herself. Miss Owens wore a gown of white satin and poinsettias. Tea followed the music, with Miss Ethel Gentsch at the tea table.

Brooklyn and Manhattan were about equally represented at this musicale of considerably over a hundred guests. Among those from Brooklyn were Mrs. George Brewster Bretz, Miss Margaret Bretz, Judge and Mrs. Luke D. Stapleton, Miss Katherine Murray, Miss Mary Carr, Mr. and Mrs. Charles G. Balmanno, Judge and Mrs. William J. Carr, Mr. and Mrs. Charles Egan, Miss Katherine Ughetta, Jerome Ughetta and his fiancee, Miss Marie Brinkman of Newark; Joseph Murray, Miss Margaret Carr, Charles Egan, jr.; Mr. and Mrs. Richard L. Walsh, Miss Marye Ughetta, Miss Marguerite Keating, William Carr, Mrs. J. C. Reilly, Daniel Murray, Mr. and Mrs. Franklin Tomlin, Peo Ughetta, Dr. and Mrs. Raymond P. Sullivan, Miss Genevieve Markey, Miss Nina Maresi, Miss Margaret Reilly, Miss Clara Kent.

Miss Owens' numbers included selections from Bizet, Leoncavello, Ponchielli and Verdi, the "Ballatella" from I. Pagliacci, "Ritorna Vincitor" from "Aida," the air of "Michaela," from "Carmen," and "Suicidis," from "La Gioconda." She gave two songs of MacDowell, "The Myrtle" and "The Blue Bell"; Debussy's "Romance," Huntington Woodman's "The Pine" and the "Little Fish Song" of Arensky's; Dell' Acqua's "Villanelle," a Serenade of Burgmen and Carey's "Pastorale."

• • •

Mr. Wheelock—Miss Giese Married Saturday Afternoon.

William E. Wheelock of the Heights, a son of the late A. D. Wheelock of Joralemon street, who was one of the important figures of the old Brooklyn City Government of a generation ago, and brother of Miss Laura Wheelock, Miss Clara Wheelock, Mrs. Henry W. Beebe and Mrs. Robert P. Vidaud, married for the second time Saturday afternoon. The ceremony was a very quiet and simple one. Only near relatives were present; there were no attendants on bridegroom and bride and no reception followed. The wedding took place in the Spencer Memorial Church (the old Second Presbyterian at the corner of Remsen and Clinton streets, the famous Dr. Van Dyke's pulpit for a long time). The Rev. Louis Van Den Burg officiated.

Mr. Wheelock married Miss Esther Giese, daughter of the late Rev. Dr. E. F. Giese and sister of Mrs. Clyde D. Gray of 394 East Twenty-first street. Miss Giese was formerly of the Packer staff and has been prominent in the field of feminine education. She finally left Packer and studied at Berlin. Upon her return she became vice principal of a school for girls at Washington, Conn.

Mr. Wheelock has for some time resided at 75A Willow street and he will bring his bride there. Dexter Wheelock, whose engagement was announced a short time ago, is his son.

• • •

St. Mary's Cleared Just $2,400 By Substitute for Garden Party.

The last of the great garden parties of Brooklyn, famous in their day for raising funds for charity and full of social charm, vanished and became permanent and settled local history last Friday when the Ladies Aid Association of St. Mary's Hospital gave a musicale instead. This proved a distinct success as a substitute. Yesterday it was definitely stated that $2,400 had been netted, with several more promised contributions to come in.

The Ladies Aid of St. Mary's was the final organization to attempt these garden parties, and, for the past ten years each succeeding one has been more difficult to pull through with any degree of success. Mrs. John H. Delaney had the musicale of Friday in hand. The talent comprised Miss Edna Nally and Miss Vera Kelly (violin and piano duet), Mrs. Richard Asterly, with Miss McNicoll accompanying (contralto solo), William Stewart Larkin (piano solos), Miss Angela Harker (soprano solo, Mrs. Lahey her accompanist), James Byrne (baritone solos) and Miss Catherine Armstrong (piano solo).

DR. GRENFELL'S LAST TALK.

Labrador Missionary Interests Large Crowd at Bedford Church.

Dr. W. B. Grenfell, widely known for the missionary work he has been doing among the deep sea fishers of Labrador, spoke in the Bedford Presbyterian Church last evening. Dr. Grenfell is in this country for the purpose of raising funds for the continuation of his work, and his lecture last night was the last. Standing room was at a premium when the Rev. Dr. S. Edward Young, the pastor, introduced him. The lecture was finely illustrated. Especially interesting were the views of the dangerous ice-floes and gigantic icebergs, pictures taken in the region where the Titanic went down.

Dr. Grenfell spoke of Labrador as "a place where there is no nervous prosperity." The people among whom he was working were high-principled, resourceful and honest folks, though uneducated. Speaking of their homes, he told of how he and his corps of volunteer workers had erected a mill, in order that the people might secure cheap lumber and build larger houses, thereby providing better ventilation.

The lecturer paid a high tribute to the men and women who are helping him in his work. Illustrative of these, he described a Princeton graduate, a minister, who worked as an engineer during the week; a Boston schoolteacher, who for the past two years has spent her summers in Labrador, teaching in one of the schools; of a young physician, who gave volunteer service, and many other college men.

Among the many interesting pictures shown were those of the boats donated by the student bodies of Harvard, Yale and Princeton. Another boat is now building. "Funds for it had been raised," said Dr. Grenfell, "by a young man at the University of Pennsylvania, and he was now in Labrador, superintending its construction." Another picture was of a hospital building erected with funds provided by a professor at Williams College, who had been marooned on the Labrador coast and cared for by the fishermen.

Speaking of the co-operative store, which has been in operation for a number of years, Dr. Grenfell said that it had been as powerful an agency as the church in assisting the people to live better lives. He expected the same results from the new Y. M. C. A. Building, now being erected, which, it was hoped, would do away with saloons.

After the offering had been taken up, many gathered around Dr. Grenfell to wish him well.

DISCUSSED SOCIALISM.

An interesting meeting took place yesterday afternoon in the gymnasium of Trinity Club, at 157 Montague street. The Fellowship is a group of people gathered together by Bouck White, whose endeavor is to relate the economic and spiritual ideals of Socialism. The meeting was opened by Mr. White's reading from the Old Testament the story of Moses, and his repudiation on coming of age of the principles of the ruling class, and placing himself with the people.

This Mr. White took as his theme, exhorting all to come out and class themselves with the workers, like the leaders of all ages. He cited the Man of Nazareth, and told at length the story of John Ball, Wendell Phillips and others.

The struggle of the middle classmen in their social climbing he uncovered. Mr. White held out the efficient help they could be to the world were they boldly to class themselves with the working people, thus clearing the way of an utterly useless class, and uniting with the producing classes of the world.

Mr. White's appeal was strong and forceful, and after more music the meeting was thrown open to questions and discussion.

This developed the many sides of Socialism, material, economic, industrial, ethical, spiritual, in a very illuminating manner.

These open meetings take place every Sunday afternoon at 157 Montague street, at 2:30 o'clock. Bouck White presiding, and everyone welcome.

MEMORIAL TO W. T. STEAD.

A memorial service to William T. Stead, the noted writer and advocate of peace, who lost his life on the Titanic, will be held in Carnegie Hall, Seventh avenue and Fifty-second street, Manhattan, at 8 o'clock tonight. The speakers will be Dr. J. A. McDonald, editor of the Toronto Globe, who was a personal friend of Mr. Stead and who will give Mr. Stead's message of peace obtained from him in an interview, and the Rev. Dr. Newell Dwight Hillis, pastor of Plymouth Church.

MACCABEE EXAMINER DEAD.

Port Huron, Mich., April 22—Dr. Talbot Sleneau, great medical examiner of the Knights of the Modern Maccabees, is dead at his home here after a long illness. He was 66 years of age.

THE BROOKLYN DAILY EAGLE

PICTURE AND SERMON SECTION. ★ NEW YORK CITY, MONDAY, APRIL 22, 1912. PICTURE AND SERMON SECTION.

ALLEGORICAL PICTURES OF THE TITANIC DISASTER

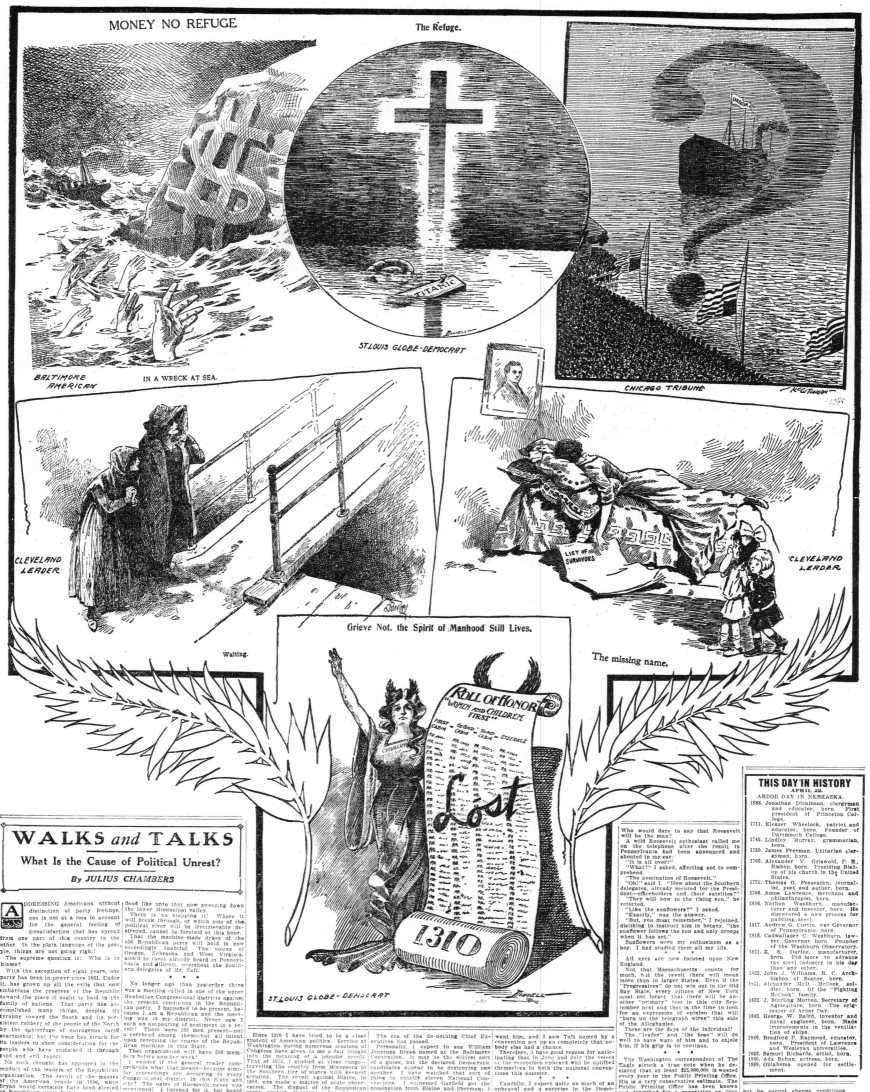

MONEY NO REFUGE

The Refuge.

IN A WRECK AT SEA.

Waiting.

The missing name.

Grieve Not, the Spirit of Manhood Still Lives.

WALKS and TALKS

What Is the Cause of Political Unrest?

By JULIUS CHAMBERS

ADDRESSING Americans without distinction of party feelings, one is not at a loss to account for the general feeling of dissatisfaction that has spread from one part of this country to the other. In the plain language of the people, things are not going right!

The supreme question is: Who is to blame?

With the exception of eight years, one party has been in power since 1861. Under it, has grown up all the evils that now embarrass the progress of the Republic toward the place it ought to hold in the family of nations. That party has accomplished many things, despite its tyranny toward the South and its persistent robbery of the people of the North by the subterfuge of outrageous tariff enactments; but the hour has struck for its leaders to show consideration for the people who have sustained it through good and evil report.

No such thought has appeared in the conduct of the leaders of the Republican organization. The revolt of the masses of the American people in 1896, when Bryan would certainly have been elected by Republican votes had it not been for his heresies on the money question and the millions of money that Chairman Hanna poured into the "doubtful states," has been growing until it has become a flood like unto that now sweeping down the lower Mississippi valley.

There is no stopping it! Where it will break through, or which side of the political river will be irretrievably destroyed, cannot be foretold at this hour.

That the machine-made dykes of the old Republican party will hold is now exceedingly doubtful. The voices of Oregon, Nebraska and West Virginia, added to those already heard in Pennsylvania and Illinois, overshout the Southern delegates of Mr. Taft.

* * *

No longer ago than yesterday there was a meeting called in one of the upper Manhattan Congressional districts against the present conditions in the Republican party. I happened to be present, because I am a Republican and the meeting was in my district. Never saw I such an outpouring of sentiment in a revolt! There were 160 men present—not a sorehead among them—but all intent upon reversing the course of the Republican machine in this State.

That organization will have 300 members before another week!

I wonder if the general reader comprehends what that means—because similar proceedings are occurring in every Congressional district in this State and city? The name of Roosevelt never was mentioned! I listened for it, but heard it not.

The revolt is deeper than Roosevelt or any individual man. That is the serious phase of the situation, so far as President Taft is concerned.

Since 1870 I have tried to be a close student of American politics. Service at Washington during numerous sessions of Congress have given to me a fair insight into the meaning of a popular revolt. That of 1872, I studied at close range—traveling the country from Minnesota to the Southern tier of states with keenest scrutiny. The revolt against Blaine, in 1884, was made a matter of acute observation. The disgust of the Republican party against Harrison—when his do-nothing administration was contrasted with that of Cleveland—was followed through fourteen States. Harrison went down, just as Taft may go [illegible] because he was a do-nothing.

The era of the do-nothing Chief Executives has passed.

Personally, I expect to see William Jennings Bryan named at the Baltimore Convention. It may be the wildest sort of a guess, but the declared Democratic candidates appear to be destroying one another. I have watched that sort of thing in exactly eleven National Conventions. I witnessed Garfield get the nomination from Blaine and Sherman; I saw Harrison succeed when Blaine wrote the foolish "Florence letter"; I heard Bryan win a nomination by a clever speech; watched McKinley's second nomination forced by Mark Hanna upon a convention at Philadelphia that did not want him, and I saw Taft named by a convention set up so completely that nobody else had a chance.

Therefore, I have good reason for anticipating that in June and July the voices of the heretofore unheard will be uplifted themselves in both the national conventions this summer.

* * *

Candidly, I expect quite as much of an upheaval and a surprise in the Democratic National Convention at Baltimore as in that of the Republicans, previously assembled at Chicago.

If President Taft be not named on the first ballot, the betting ought to be 20 to 1 that he will not be the candidate.

Who would dare to say that Roosevelt will be the man?

A wild Roosevelt enthusiast called me on the telephone after the result in Pennsylvania had been announced and shouted in my ear:

"It is all over!"

"What?" I asked, affecting not to comprehend.

"The nomination of Roosevelt."

"Oh!" said I. "How about the Southern delegates, already secured for the President—officeholders and their satelites?"

"They will bow to the rising sun," he retorted.

"Like the sunflowers?" I asked.

"Exactly," was the answer.

"But, you must remember," I rejoined, disliking to instruct him in botany, "the sunflower follows the sun and only droops when it has set."

Sunflowers were my enthusiasm as a boy. I had studied them all my life.

* * *

All eyes are now focused upon New England.

Not that Massachusetts counts for much, but the revolt there will mean more than in larger States. Even if the "Progressives" do not win out in the Old Bay State, every citizen of New York must not forget that there will be another "primary" test in this city September next and that is the time to look for an expression of opinion that will "burn up the telegraph wires" this side of the Alleghanies.

These are the days of the individual!

The "leader" and "the boss" will do well to have ware of him and to cajole him, if his grip is to continue.

* * *

The Washington correspondent of The Eagle struck a true note when he declared that at least $25,000,000 is wasted every year in the Public Printing Office. His is a very conservative estimate. The Public Printing Office has been known and described for a generation as "the Botany Bay" for appointments. I have heard a score of Congressmen so designate it.

The present Public Printer is a fine chap. I know him well and respect [illegible]im; but he cannot change conditions have existed for a generation.

The conduct of Congress was fo[illegible] by the ancient Greeks when th[illegible] scribed the conduct of the woman who tried to hold water [illegible]

THIS DAY IN HISTORY

APRIL 22.

ARBOR DAY IN NEBRASKA.

1688. Jonathan Dickinson, clergyman and educator, born. First president of Princeton College.
1711. Eleazer Wheelock, patriot and educator, born. Founder of Dartmouth College.
1745. Lindley Murray, grammarian, born.
1759. James Freeman, Unitarian clergyman, born.
1766. Alexander V. Griswold, P. E., Bishop, born. Presiding Bishop of his church in the United States.
1771. Thomas G. Fessenden, journalist, poet and author, born.
1786. Amos Lawrence, merchant and philanthropist, born.
1816. Nathan Washburn, manufacturer and inventor, born. He discovered a new process for puddling steel.
1817. Andrew G. Curtin, war Governor of Pennsylvania, born.
1818. Cadwallader C. Washburn, lawyer, Governor, born. Founder of the Washburn Observatory.
1821. Z. S. Durfee, manufacturer, born. Did more to advance the steel industry in his day than any other.
1822. John J. Williams, R. C. Archbishop of Boston, born.
1831. Alexander McD. McCook, soldier, born. Of the "Fighting McCook" family.
1832. J. Sterling Morton, Secretary of Agriculture, born. The originator of Arbor Day.
1843. George W. Baird, inventor and naval engineer, born. Made improvements in the ventilation of ships.
1846. Bradford P. Raymond, educator, born. President of Lawrence and Wesleyan universities.
1853. Samuel Richards, artist, born.
1860. Ada Rehan, actress, born.
1889. Oklahoma opened for settlement.

Dr. Hillis and Dr. L. M. Clarke on Titanic Disaster

Lessons of the Great Disaster;

by

The Rev. Dr. Newell Dwight Hillis.

SINCE the memorial services immediately after the death of President McKinley, no more sympathetic audience has assembled in Plymouth than that which filled the spacious auditorium at the morning service yesterday. The services opened with Chopin's "Funeral March," played by the fine organist, Arthur Depew; the choir sang appropriate anthems and Dr. Newell Dwight Hillis gave a notable treatment of the Titanic disaster. The last hymn played by the band of the Titanic, "Nearer, My God, to Thee," was sung, and after the benediction the entire audience stood in profound attention while Mr. Depew played General Horatio C. King's "Funeral March." The scene was most impressive, and there was scarcely a dry eye in the house. It will be a lasting memory.

Dr. Hillis' subject was "Lessons From the Disaster." The texts were Psalms xlvi and Isaiah xl. He said:

Plainly the writer of these words conceived of our earth as a huge ship bearing its human freight across the seas of time. Our modern scientists also often liken our world to a steamer sheathed in plates of granite, riveted by the right hand of omnipotence, whose volcanic fires drive it along the gulf stream of God's providence. The astronomers make the voyage seem more wonderful by saying that the round trip of the world's ship consumes 365 days in its journey of 600,000,000 miles. In December it seems as if the ship is journeying away forever from light and warmth into the region of blackness and Arctic winter, but obedient to the touch of the captain at the helm, it curves in its flight, and returns, never a second late with its harvest cargo on the 21st of September. What a wondrous voyage is this, of a ship that returns without a sail torn, a rivet started or a plate sprung. Man is a passenger who can only stand upon the deck and breathe the air, and rejoice at the summer clime into which the ship is sailing, and trust the captain who keeps the light upon the prow and determines the course, and will bring the ship into the desired haven. Verily, God alone is great! His power is absolute, He is fully equal to all man's emergencies. He weighs the mountains in scales, and the hills in the balance; the sea also is His, and He holdeth it in the hollow of His hand. All they who sink into the sea, therefore, rest in the right hand of Omnipotence. But the child that is in the Father's hand can never be far from his Father's heart. Ruling the land, to the sea also He saith, "Thus far and no farther—here stay thy proud waves." God calleth the storms back to the hollow of His hand, as the bird returns to its nest. Whether man's grave, therefore, be on the hillsides, billowy with dead, on on the sea, billowy with waves, the soul is in God's hands, and nothing evil can befall this divine child, before death or afterward. Therefore, though the earth be removed and though the mountains be carried into the midst of the sea, we will not fear!

Victory Over Sorrow.

The sinking of the Titanic hath spread a shadow across the sun, and darkened the whole world. But the people already have lingered too long upon details that are beginning to poison the mind and sap confidence and courage. The investigation of the disaster belongs to Congress and Parliament; the meting out of penalties is for the courts; the analysis of causes and the discovery of remedies is for experts. Those who have lost their dead will henceforth look with altered eyes upon an altered world. Theirs is a sorrow that will never cease until the separation ceases. The whole world is sympathetic, to their grief, and their sorrow is our sorrow. For today the American and English people have but one heart, and that heart is very sore. But meanwhile, commerce must go forward, the ships must needs whiten the sea, and we must exchange our goods or bear starvation and suffering. The multitudes who behold the scene now discover a new illustration of the principle that without shedding of blood there is no remission of sin, or ignorance or folly. The law of social progress through individual sacrifice is reinforced. One boat strikes the rock, and then the buoy is set up, that fleets henceforth may be saved. One pilgrim eats the poisoned fruit and dies, but henceforth the chemist converts that poison into medicine for man's pain. One workman is scalded by the steam, but taught thereby, the steam begins to pound the piston, and carry man's burdens. The soldier dies that the slaves may be free. One ship goes too near the Arctics, after a winter of excessive cold, and henceforth the fleets will understand that if there is little ice after the warm winters, that there is much ice pushed southward after excessive winters. And henceforth the fleets will sail on in happiness and safety, during centuries of time. Be the reasons what they may, man will not learn until he must learn. Ours is a world where the soil dies that the vegetable may live, where the vegetable dies that the animal may live, where the low animal dies that man may grow, where the blood dies that thought may live, where thought is converted into affection and affection is transmitted into aspiration and character. Every Magna Charta of liberty is witnessed in the life blood of those who win it. Scientists tell us that even the song of the lark began in a cry of pain, just as immortality began on Calvary. Those who gave up their lives in the north seas last week have bought exemption from peril for innumerable fleets, and safeguarded millions who shall cross the seas, in happiness and in peace. Blessed are the dead who die in the Lord —yea, saith the Spirit, for their works do follow them, and their names shall live forever more.

The New Racial Unity Ushered In by Trade and Commerce.

1. The loss of the Titanic has brought a sudden revelation of the new interdependence of England and America and Canada. Who could have realized that the warp and woof of civilization was made up of racial threads so diverse and apparently separate? While we have been busy here and there, God has been making the world one, through trade. Agriculturists tell us that the honey bees carry the pollen from field to field and fertilize our seed for shock and sheaf. Not otherwise these editors, bankers, merchants, railroad men, authors, pass swiftly from continent to continent, fertilizing the rich fields of civilization. Here is the great editor who was due for an oration this afternoon in Carnegie Hall, and planning to return to England on Tuesday. Here is the great French author coming with his drama and his books. Here is the noble railway president, Charles M. Hays, architect of new States and a builder of the Commonwealth. Here is the merchant, our honored Mr. Straus, the manufacturer, and Mr. Guggenheim; the diplomat, representing our President, Major Butt; here is the financier, Mr. Astor, with any others, interested in enterprises at concerned the food, the raiment, property and the commercial inter- of multitudes on both sides of the Invention has made the world smal' lantic has become a narrow rib- liver. Men step from London to k as our fathers crossed the street from house to house. The world is become one Eden garden, one market place, one little public square, where all the races meet, jostle, trade, converse, as brothers. God has not given any one nation all the good things. The fruits, the grains, the minerals are so distributed between the zones and the continents that men must meet as brothers exchange their goods, develop respect, confidence and good will. God gave the tea to China, the coffee to Brazil, the sugar to Cuba, the olive and the fig to Italy, and England and the United States each have their special gift in nature. Thus also God broke up man into men, and gave to the German his scientific industry, to the Frenchman his artistic impulse, to the Dutchman his self-reliance, to England her power of colonization, and to this great western people their victory over the forces of nature. The time has come for every Chinese wall to go down. The world is the Father's house, and all the races are brothers. What injures England injures the United States. What weakens our people and their higher life, injures the mother land. We are one today in our heartbreak, but we have long been one in the necessities of trade, manufacturing, finance. When two nations stand weeping over the same scene, they ought not to turn away from the acre where they have given their beloved unto God, and on the morrow sharpen the sword or build a battleship against one another. Today we have a common sorrow, and henceforth and forever we should hold in common the great heritage of liberty and obedience to law, with our common watchwords of liberty, equality, opportunity, intelligence and integrity, that make our nations great.

The Heroism of the Titanic a New Tonic to the Youth of the Nation.

II. There has been that in the heroism of many who gave up their lives for what they believed to be their duty, that has become a powerful tonic to the manhood of our nation. Our people will never be the same again. The heroism of some men and women has entered chemically into the very constitution of the American soul. Many who have been tempted toward laxity, and were in danger of yielding to fear and moral cowardice, have been kindled by the brave conduct of these noble souls, awakened to realize their moral flabbiness, and have girded up their soul in a high resolve that shall never be relaxed. When tomorrow comes, the American life will begin on a new level. Merchants will have a higher standard of honor, working people will take more self-respect to their task, editors, authors, actors, moral teachers, realize anew that every hour is a testing time, and every day a battlefield, and that every man is either a coward or a hero. The philosophy of the event is that God lifts the people through occasional dramatic events. He lifts up Achilles, and all the Greeks, looking up, climb toward the hero's level. What is Switzerland save William Tell's dramatic deed, multiplied and reappearing in the universal life. What is Germany, save Martin Luther, braving a thousand soldiers with spears, and alone, with his back to the wall, exclaiming, "I cannot and I will not retract. I can do no other. God help me." What is brave little Holland, save William the Silent's dramatic deed, lifted up and made glorious for the Dutch people. When God wants to usher in a new epoch for the race, He lifts up a great soul, prepares him for the emergency, thrusts him into a great crisis, and then makes him equal to the dramatic moment, and henceforth young people and children look up to that brave soul that died for duty, and looking, their fear is changed to courage, their weakness to loyalty, until through emulation they take on the likeness of the man they admire and love. When long time hath passed, succeeding generations will see that that moment of pain and testing on the Titanic was the great opportunity. Take it all in all, the best thing that ever happened to William McKinley was his unique suffering, for he bore himself as a man in the hour of his assassination, and engraved his image on every human heart. Lincoln was fortunate in the manner of his taking off—shed no tears for happy Lincoln. And now that they understand, these noble souls that died, and realize the meaning of the event, they must first of all and above all thank God that they did not die peacefully in their beds, through commonplace diseases, but that God lifted them up, and gave them strength to do a splendid deed, and make their names a kind of moral lighthouse, flashing beams for others out into the dark night, and the yeasty sea. Henceforth young soldier boys will take the name of Major Butt upon their lips, and use him as a standard of bravery. Henceforth the name of Astor with his millions will shine with lustre unquenchable. Henceforth all railway men can point to a name, the name of Hays, with solemn, glorious pride. Henceforth the very name of editor hath added sanctity, through William Stead.

A Noble Jewish Name.

And what shall I say of Mr. and Mrs. Straus, save that marriage henceforth hath a double sanctity. They have taught the young how to love and the old how to die. In the old Hebrew Apocrypha, when the young husband and wife knelt down on their marriage night, the boy asked God for good fortune and favor, and closed his tender prayer with this petition, "And grant that we may grow old together." A Jewess herself, Mrs. Straus must have had that prayer in mind. When her husband would not go, while women were left, and sailors tried to pull her away, she made her answer, "We have grown old together, and together we will meet the end." God, bless the name of Straus, henceforth, to all American and English homes. Great souls did valiant deeds while the Titanic was sinking. It is a proverb that nothing is so fascinating as stories of eloquence and heroism. Some of the things that were achieved last week by brave men and women, henceforth will be told by soldiers around the camp fire, by parents to their children on wintry nights. These deeds will find a place in dramatic literature, and lend lustre to the history of heroism. Achievements like these are rounds in the ladder up which young hearts climb hand over hand to the heights of character and manhood. Already God hath overruled this event so that the whole American people have been baptized into a new birth of courage, fortitude, devotion to duty, loyalty to the highest ideals. God who gave to these men and women rich gifts through beauty, health, success, wealth, and to others modest prosperity only as sailor or deck hand, reserved His last, best gift by counting them worthy to stand at a critical moment in face of peril, to flame out a higher standard for the uplift of their whole generation. Tears therefor, for the living. Immeasurable sympathy for their dear ones left. But congratulation and shouts and high acclaim unto these who have lent new lustre to the name of hero, and who shall henceforth have a place forever in the calendar of glorious names.

A Revelation of an Inexpugnable Religious Faith in Man.

III. The scenes incident to the sinking of the Titanic tell us that man is incurably religious. Trust in God is a quality that is stained in fast colors in the very structure of man's soul. There is one faculty that cannot be taken out without destroying the constitution of man—the religious faculty. If you release the needle it must needs point to the Pole. When the deep things in the human heart speak, their voice is eloquent with trust in God, their heavenly Father. So long as the man is strong and prosperous, has honors and friends, he may think himself independent of the Divine Being above himself. When he is sick he can buy his physicians, when he is weary he can buy travel and leisure, when he is lonely he can buy friends and companions, when he is tired he can purchase amusement and recreation. But the moment that man comes into deep waters he has a revelation of values. When Colonel Gracie came up after the sinking of the Titanic, he says that he made his way to a sunken raft. The submerged little reed was under water often. But every man, without regard to nationality, broke into instant prayer. There were many voices, but they all had one signification—their sole hope was in God. There were no millionaires, for millions fell away like leaves; there were no poor. Men were neither wise nor ignorant, they were simply human souls on a sinking raft, and the night was black, and the waves yeasty with foam, and the grave where the Titanic lay was silent under them, and the stars were silent over them! But as they prayed each man by that inner light saw an invisible Friend walking across the waves. Henceforth these need no books on Apologetics to prove there is a God. This noble man who has written his story tells us that God heard the prayers of some, by giving them death, and heard the prayers of others equally by keeping them in life, but God alone is great! Do you not recall the memoirs of the War Secretary, and how after the Battle of Bull Run, when Washington was in suspense, and Lincoln set apart a day of prayer, one of the first men to enter the church was a leading infidel and the noisest atheist that Washington knew? "I was surprised to see you there," said the Secretary, on going out into the street. "Ah, the country is in a tight place," answered the atheist, "and there is no one to whom we can go, except to God!" Oh, all ye young hearts! bethink yourself of this, the God you need when you stand upon the sea in a sinking raft, looking toward death, is the God that you need when you stand on the solid rock, and look toward life! In this hour when these were praying on their little raft, there were no fading leaves called gold or office or honor. In that moment the evanescent, transient, temporary things dissolved like smoke, and the big, permanent things stood out, God, truth, purity, love, and oh, how happy those who were good friends with God, their conscience and their record. How worthless the thick clay that we load ourselves down with, and the mists that some pursue. It is for us to reflect that the fleeting things belong to the earth and are temporary, and the permanent things belong to the inner fidelities of righteousness, and love to man and God.

The Invisible Light Upon the Vessel's Prow.

IV. This dramatic event has lent new meaning to the hope of immortality. It has become easy to believe in this hour that there is another and a better life. It was as if God had sifted the world to find souls equal to devotion to duty, that they might flame their heroism and their faith out for the redemption of their generation. Sometimes artists have an exhibition, and the judges select and sift thousands of canvases to find a view worthy of immortal recognition. Do the judges then proceed to destroy into nothingness these treasures they have secured? Scientists ransack the world for an occasional flashing sapphire or ruby. Having found it, do they fling it into the depths of the sea? Not a drop on the crest of any wave can be destroyed. Not an atom of the universe can be annihilated. There is not one molecule of matter less today than there was in the dawn of creation. But the human soul, as it stood upon the deck of the Titanic, can leave the body and step from star to star, and weigh their masses and search out their movements. The soul it is that is deeper than sea, the soul has heights of heroism beyond the tops of the mountains; it is the soul, made in God's image, whose love glows like a sun. It is the soul that writes the songs and invents the tools and conceives the laws and achieves the liberties. It is the soul that is made for God, and is restless until it finds rest in Him. It is the soul that rides like a star through the sky, glowing and sparkling with ten thousand effects. The whole round world is but a little teacup, and the ocean itself a spoonful of water; but the soul—all the centuries live in man's imagination, all words subsist in man's thought, all the realms are concealed in man's dreams, and because the soul is God's child, and God is eternal, the soul is eternal also. Little minds will say, "I do not believe in a God who will let the Titanic sink." The careless, superficial thoughts will indict the throne of God with heartlessness, injustice and cruelty, just as Athenians indicted God when Socrates was poisoned, never dreaming that it was the greatest good fortune that God ever gave to Socrates. Byron mourned above Dante's grave because he held heartbreak at bay; but if God blessed Dante in his palace, He quadrupled His gifts when He exiled Dante therefrom. Happy the patriot who can identify himself by martyrdom to the cause of liberty. Happy blind Homer, and sightless Milton! Happy imprisoned Galileo and this burning Huss! Thrice happy all these heroes and martyrs, chosen to be kings of suffering, that they may later be kings of influence and immortal renown! They knelt down to receive their crown of cruel thorns and drink the cup of pain, but rising up, lo! the angel of immortal remembrance stood beside them! Lo! instead of thorns they are crowned with stars, and shall shine forever and ever, both in man's earth and in God's heaven.

Sixty Little Bellboys.

Great is the power of the modern press, and wonderful the pages they have spread out before the American people. Often in crossing the ocean I have made friends with some little bellboy, and knowing there must have been many on the Titanic I have searched every paper with lighted candles, but searching I have found only one little scant sentence saying there was sixty bellboys between 12 and 14 years of age, who were ordered by the steward to take their seats in the diningroom to keep out of the way of the passengers on deck. Think of it! Old men had had their chance at life, but no one seems to have thought of these little boys. Their parents must have been poor, and the little boys must have found it necessary to help the mother at home. They had climbed the steps only, on the front porch of the palace of life. With their tender years they were still on life's portico, never having crossed the palace threshold. The great halls and gallery in the halls of life, where maturity and occupation and travel bring their treasures—ah, they were never to know marriage, love, office, or honors. But what if there is much hard work to do beyond? What if death is but a little river separating the rich fields of God? What if their young hands pick up tools there, and write books and songs and paint pictures, and pursue their ambitions, just as here, only under friendlier skies! This morning in my dreams, waking, I saw these boys going up the happy hills of God. With laughter and with shouts they ran from one flowering bush to another. And in my dream, too, I saw one little boy's face cloud with the thought of his sorrowing mother, and gathering an armful of roses made red by heaven's beauty, he hurried to the battlements and looked down, and saw the little mother, that with such tender love, had stitched the white braid upon his little blue uniform, saw her with her face lying in England's grass, and with dry sobs moaning only one word,—"God—God—God." And flinging down his flowers I saw them fall upon his mother's wounds, and heal her hurt. And rising up she whispered, "I shall go to him, but he shall not return to me." So Rachel, weeping for her children, was comforted. God of our fathers, bless all smitten families this day. Comfort the comfortless! Grant solemn joy and pride to those who henceforth bear a name made lustrous by their dead! For one moment let the door of heaven be opened, that we may see that those who have entered into Thy presence are chiefly thankful for that which has broken our heart. And beholding them as they go up to Thy throne to have their hard question answered, grant us happiness through their knowledge that the golden chain that bound them to the feet of God never once was broken.

Interesting Religious News.

There were some remarkable gifts in the Episcopal churches of Brooklyn on Easter Sunday which have just been made public. In the Church of the Messiah, the Rev. Dr. St. Clair Hester, rector, $2,500 was asked and $3,500 received; Grace Church on the Heights, the Rev. Dr. C. J. F. Wrigley, rector, the gifts amounted to $8,100; the Church of the Holy Trinity, the Rev. John Howard Melish, rector, $3,500; Christ Church, Bedford avenue, the Rev. William Sheafe Chase, rector, $3,300; St. Peter's, State street, the Rev. Dr. W. G. McCready, rector, $2,500.

The Northern Baptist Convention will meet in Des Moines, Iowa, May 22 to 29. Altogether there will be twenty-four sessions, presenting all phases of work, chapel car, Sunday school, women's mission endeavor, missions, laymen's work, missionary labor in foreign fields, the Baptist Laymen's Missionary Movement, a Brotherhood Council, publication, social service, community extension, etc. The Rev. Dr. James A. Francis of the Clarendon Street Church, Boston, will conduct two devotional services each day. An entire evening has been assigned to Baptist men. The list of speakers at the convention includes the names of many prominent men, coming from all parts of the Northern and Western States. On Sunday, May 5, previous to these gatherings, the anniversary of the Rochester Theological Seminary will be held in that city. Many prominent men will make addresses. The annual sermon will be preached by the Rev. Dr. Thomas S. Barbour of Boston, in the First Baptist Church.

One of the most important sessions of the Conservation Congress in the Men and Religion Forward Movement will be that of Wednesday morning at 10 o'clock in Carnegie Hall, Manhattan. The theme will be "Christian Unity." The chairman will be Bishop E. R. Hendrix, Kansas City, Mo. The secretary is President Ira Landrith of Belmont College, Nashville, Tenn., both of whom will make brief addresses. Other short speeches will be made by Bishop W. F. McDowell of the Methodist Episcopal Church, Chicago; Bishop William M. Bell of the United Brethren Church, Los Angeles, Cal.; the Rev. Dr. Nehemiah Boynton, moderator of the National Council of Congregational Churches and pastor of the Clinton Avenue Congregational Church, Brooklyn; William Jennings Bryan; the Rev. L. B. Wolf of the Foreign Mission Society of the Lutheran Church, Baltimore; the Rev. Dr. John F. Carson, moderator of the General Assembly of the Presbyterian Church, and pastor of the Central Presbyterian Church, Brooklyn; the Rev. Dr. Randolph McKim, president of the House of Deputies of the Protestant Episcopal Church, Washington, D. C.; J. A. Patten of the Committee on Unity of Methodist Episcopal Church, Chattanooga, Tenn.; the Rev. Peter Ainslie of Baltimore, and the Rev. Dr. Howard B. Grose, editor of Missions, Boston.

The first international conference of the King's Daughters and Sons will be held in Louisville May 10 to May 14. The order, which has spread to all countries of the world during the twenty-six years of its existence, will enter upon its second epoch. The founders provided that when the order should have grown enough to warrant such a step, a general conference should be held.

Deep Calling to Deep;

by

Dr. L. Mason Clarke.

DR. L. MASON CLARKE, pastor of the First Presbyterian Church, preached a remarkable sermon yesterday morning on the Titanic disaster. The subject was "Deep Calling Unto Deep." During the service the congregation stood while Organist Woodman played the Dead March from "Saul," and it was most impressive. The church was draped with flags of the two nations in mourning. Dr. Clarke's text was Psalm xlii:7: "Deep calleth unto deep." Dr. Clarke said:

There is only one subject for us this morning. The awful and the glorious week has ended at last. The start being heart-breaking, despairing and inspiring days have slowly dragged themselves out to their close. Human nature cannot forever stand such an intensity of strain. The incredible has happened once more. Once more the "impossible" has become the dreadful reality. One colossal tragedy has engaged the attention of the world. Everything else has been made little in its towering presence. A drama has been enacted with the ocean for a stage and all the continents for an audience.

Furthermore, an hitherto unmatched chapter has been added to human annals. The long and terrible record of the sea has been surpassed beyond the bounds either of belief or fear. The ocean, as if hungry for another trial of its strength with man, has seemed to wait in sullen confidence, until it could meet the best that human skill and power have been able to create, and then with one swift, unerring blow has crashed into ruin man's boast of mastery of the deep. The empress of the sea, the superlative of science and of experience, found her challenge accepted and has ended her maiden voyage in a mammoth grave.

Lo, all our power of yesterday
Is one with Nineveh and Tyre.
Lord God of Hosts, be with us yet
Lest we forget.

Then, again, when did so many diverse elements ever before conspire on such a scale to complete such a spectacle? When did irony and pathos, power and weakness, wealth and helplessness, obscurity and magnanimity ever before so mingle together in a democracy of woe—in an aristocracy of heroism?

Irony? The Titanic! Invincible, invisible. Pathos? That needless waste of life! That victory and that defeat of science, side by side. The human heart cannot utter its grief and "has no language but to cry." 'Out of the depths have we cried unto Thee, O God!" indeed.

But, on the other hand, there was a greater victory last Sunday night than that which was won by the sea. Human nature scored again in its immemorial battle with Nature. Crushed by a pitiless power, man once more showed himself far mightier than the power which crushed him. The ocean triumphed after its dumb, blind, passionless manner. Human nature triumphed with intelligent chivalry and magnificent self-sacrifice. The victory of the sea has only added one new horror to its ancient treachery. The victory of human nature has heartened a world of men in the midst of all their grief.

To whom, then, can we go but unto God? For the sea is His and He made it. He holds it all in the hollow of His hand. It is the chosen symbol of His mercy, though it seems to mock all thought of mercy. It is the image of His boundless love, though it has seemed to laugh at every suggestion of such love.

God of Nature, indeed! Is He as merciless as the sea? God of Love! Where was He last Sunday night, when His children were being drowned by hundreds upon hundreds? What sign of Himself did He give, this God of mercy and of love? What single feature of the entire scene was different, by as much as one jot, from what it would have been if there were no God at all? You who say that you find all the God you need in Nature, be honest with yourselves today and recognize both sets of facts. Do you think He was evident in that freezing sea of anguish?

But now, when you turn to the other aspect of the tragedy and ask for some sign of God, you see it! See it in that high consecration of human nature, in that heroic courage, in love refusing to be torn from love, in the quiet standing back of the many for the sake of the few who could be saved—in that record of manhood and womanhood which has so few saints upon it, thank God! There, in human nature, you find the only evidence there is that God trod those waves in majesty; but what immortal evidence it is! If you look for signs of God, my friends, look for them in the godlike spirit that men and women and boys and girls reveal in such a time of crisis. Yes, "deep does call unto deep," and up from those two miles of watery depths come the voices that speak to the deeps of our own souls, for all God's waves and billows have gone over us, every one.

Now, it is wonderful how this venerable Book speaks to all our moods and reflects all our own experiences, be those moods and experiences what they may. Where, for example, could you find a more felicitous word than this which makes our text? The psalmist knew nothing of the sea. The Jews were no sailormen upon the deep. To them it was a barrier and a boundary; never an invitation, never an opportunity. And really here is a marvel —that the Bible, which is a landsman's book, makes such a wonderful use of the sea all through its pages.

One text is very interesting, and its beautiful metaphor touches the heart of sorrow with exquisite grace and tenderness. Our psalmist was an exile, who was longing to come home again. He was up among the foothills of Hermon, lonely, desolate and sick at heart. Banished from the temple of his fathers, in a strange land, he yearned for the holy hill of Zion. He seems to have seen a deer running from its pursuers, and hot and trembling, stopping for an instant to drink from one of the mountain streams, in order to dash on again, and it awakens the song that is in his own mind. "As the hart panteth after the water brooks so panteth my soul after thee, O God." One disaster after another has overtaken him. His foes are pursuing him and continually sneer at his misery, saying "Where is thy God?"

And mark the beauty of the metaphor. He is in the depths himself, and as he listens he hears the noise of the mountain streams pouring in cataracts down the sides of Hermon, and the scene is harmonious with his feelings. "Deep calleth unto deep," he says. One torrent calls to another, from opposite sides of the valley, as they all rush down to swell the central current. "Deep calleth unto deep"—for all thy waves and thy billows have gone over me. And so the deeps without speak to the deeps within, and thus this exile, who never knew the ocean, gives us the very thought we need as we hear this latest cry from the greatest sorrow of the sea.

Let me first emphasize that word "deep." Not of superficial things are we summoned to think. Today we are down among the great elementals of the soul and of human life. The foundations have been uncovered and they speak to the foundations of our very being. All lesser concerns are eclipsed. Every minor interest is hushed. There is one profound cry from the deeps to the deeps and we would try to interpret it to our minds.

First, and nothing less than first, there is the deep of sorrow calling to the deep of sympathy. Before any other question arises or any other thought is named, we must listen to that cry from more than a thousand homes, broken, bereft and crushed. How everything else gives way to this! How it witnesses to the silent love of the human heart! And how the world uncovers in the presence of such elemental grief. Can you think of anything which so emphasises the oneness of our humanity as a tragedy like this? Differences of wealth and station pass away like cobwebs in the fire. Education and ignorance now know only the brotherhood and sisterhood of the human heart. Rank and birth are all on the one level of humanity. Down below all these accidents of fortune and of surface distinctions, there is the unity of human nature, and sorrow calls out to the sympathy of all confident of its answer. Here at least we are one. Sorrow's crown of sorrow is matched by sympathy's crown of sympathy. And when was there ever before in history a quicker response to this cry from the deep?

Is it not worth our while to abate our criticisms and our indignation long enough to see just the real grandeur of human nature in the lurid light of such an event? "Let love clasp grief lest both be drowned." Let the splendor of human affection light up this darkness. Let the agony measure the divineness of the human nature which is capable of such agony. For the mark of rank in nature is capacity for pain. And sympathy calls out to sorrow as deep calls to deep, for, O God, by these things, men, after all, do live.

But there is another cry from the deep to the deep. It is a strong clear call to realize again the supremacy of human life. And I can but think we needed this lesson, though it comes to us at such a frightful cost. There out on the sea, under the traditions of the service of the greatest sea-power of history, there where the discipline of generations asserts its high and holy creed again, that the fittest place for a man to die is where he dies for men—there where millions of treasure are not thought of in the presence of even one human life—out of the deep of that event comes to us the call that we in our unperilous ease reconsider our valuation of life. Heve we not thought more of comfort than of safety? Have we not provided or demanded luxuries at the sacrifice of the simplest essentials for safeguarding life itself? In this race of our times, this fancied need of risking all for speed and for profits, and of putting elegance of appointments before the sturdy plainness of simple necessities, have we not forgotten something for which no subsequent heroism can compensate? Oh, how that rich, magnificent Titanic, drives this lesson home as she speaks out of her deep grave! Everything for luxury. So little for safety. Everything to minister to elegant comfort in the hour when no danger was near, and so terribly little, so pitifully little to save life when the danger came.

"Wise after the event," you say. But we should have been wise before the event. That condition is a symptom of our time. I tell you, we all have sinned, for this depreciation of life marks the whole scheme and structure of our generation. We kill men easily, selfishly, unthinkingly. Lord God of Hosts how we forget!

We have forgotten the words of Jesus, What shall a man give in exchange for his life? The Master was not speaking of losing the soul, but the life! We have lost His sense of the infinite value of life as life. And now out of the heart of this awful calamity flashes the lightning of that truth we knew before but a truth we had meanly thrust away from us. How abundant the means of enjoyment. How scant the means of saving life itself. And how miserable is all that costly luxury, so impotent to save, and how precious those few cheap and simple boats that alone remain of the most perfect ship, we are told, that ever gave herself to the ocean. God grant that this cry from the deep may be heeded in the deep of the conscience of this age.

Then there is a third voice that calls from deep to deep, and it is a voice of infinite sacredness and tenderness. It is the voice of majesty and might—the divinest voice of man, the very echo of the voice of God. See those wives refusing to be torn from their husbands. See those venerable two—known to many of us. Hebrews in religion and race, son and daughter of the Highest in devotion and character—see them standing by the rail clasped together in that last embrace as the ship goes down! I can only wonder if the great words of their Hebrew scriptures did not flash across their minds in that great moment. "Love is strong as death. Many waters can not quench it. Neither can the floods drown it. Lovely and pleasant in their lives and in their death they were not divided."

I call that sublime. There is dignity joined with supreme devotion. Oh, it is majesty, it is the height of heights, it is the finest human nature can do to interpret the nature of God. If now you ask for any sign of God's presence in that scene, my answer is you find it there. Nor do we forget the others who were torn asunder by force. When, all told, has there been on such a scale a more brilliant and vivid expression of love—yes, of love divine, than on that Sunday night?

"Deep calleth unto deep." We ask ourselves how we should have behaved in such an hour. We wonder whether we should have been cowardly or brave. Could we have met such a death with such calmness and such heroism? These are foolish questions to ask, because the only answer that can be given is the answer that only such a moment can reveal. But we can do this: We can dedicate ourselves to duty again. We can consecrate ourselves again to the wonder and mystery of love in our homes. Every household ought to be made more sacred by this revelation. Every man of us, every woman, ought to feel that we have had a breath from Almighty God upon us, and it is the breath of the new creation—the breath of life, of eternal life, of the kind of life God lives.

"A very flame of the Lord is love. Many waters can not quench it. Neither can the floods drown it. If a man would give all the substance of his house for it, he would be utterly contemned."

Last of all, there is a fourth call of the deep to the deep. It comes to us from those scenes of simple, passionate prayer. It comes to us from the music of that land playing "Nearer, My God, to Thee," as the great ship went to its wide and unguarded grave. What a moment that must have been, as the music lingered on the air after that deep, deep grave was closed forever and forever. "Nearer, My God, to Thee." It is the deepest cry of the human heart, answered by the deepest that is in the heart of God. It is man's need of religion. It is religion as the answer of man's need. Oh, men and women, how this tears away our superficial skepticism, our petty unbeliefs, our miserable indifference to God, which our easy prosperity and safety seem to foster. How it dwarfs all our wretched discussions of endless dogmas and our ceaseless wranglings over the unessentials of religion. How it emphasizes the big simplification and the deep unshaken need of us all for God!

Was that prayer for them alone? Was it not also for every one of us who have had the foundations of our souls laid open by the stroke of this astounding blow? Are we going to be the same as we were before? Can we have lived through this past week and be no better men and women in our different ways and walks? Shall we soon forget it all and go on our course as if this voice of God had not spoken with such emphasis? Good God, forbid it. But with sobered hearts let us go forth to sympathize and to save and to live and to love, until we behold the new heaven and the new earth, and the sea shall be no more!

Father of mercies and God of all comfort, nearer to thee, nearer to thee.

Calamity's Lessons;

by

The Rev. W. E. Thompson, Ph.D

THE REV. W. E. THOMPSON, Ph.D., pastor of Embury Memorial M. E. Church, Lewis avenue and Decatur street, preached yesterday morning on "Calamity's Lessons," a sermon suggested by the great disaster. The text was: Psalm lvii:1, "In the shadow of thy wings will I make my refuge until these calamities be overpast." Dr. Thompson said:

That terrible disaster of the sea with which our thoughts have been so largely occupied during this past week, the sinking of the monster steamship, Titanic, with the loss of over sixteen hundred lives, is a calamity that has brought forth the expression of deepest sorrow and sympathy not only from those who had relatives and friends on board, but also from the people in general, both at home and abroad. Such things as this give us pause in the midst of our busy lives, and make us to ponder over questions to which otherwise we might give little, perhaps too little, thought.

Terrible earthquakes, devastating floods and hurricanes, great holocausts of fire, and woeful tragedies of the sea, as they occur from time to time, all raise in the minds of many people the question so often impossible for them to satisfactorily answer—as to why, if there be a God of infinite love for man and unlimted power over all natural forces, He should allow such awful catastrophes to happen.

Job, out of the midst of his afflictions, sought to find the answer, but, after showing him the insufficiency of the human mind ever to have planned all the wonders of creation, with their wonderful construction and adaptations, or to have established the laws by which the universe in its different realms is governed, God clearly demonstrated to him that it was not to be expected, nor indeed possible, that the all-sufficient, infinite mind of the Creator and Ruler of the universe should be fathomed in all its purposes and plans by the limited finite mind of man. This is a lesson we too need to learn. With all our boasted knowledge there are some things beyond our ken.

That God could prevent physical calamities by the interposition of supernatural power we firmly believe; and that this He has done time and again when by so doing He might further some great moral end which He had in view. That some great moral purpose of good might eventually be carried out by not interposing and allowing such disasters to occur, is equally credible. Who knows but that a part of such purpose may be to teach men lessons concerning their relations toward God and their fellowmen that shall eventually be conducive to the highest welfare of life on earth and more certain and careful preparation for the life that is beyond?

One of the lessons this calamity has impressed upon us is that of the danger of allowing the mercenary spirit to gain the mastery and dull the sense of moral obligation. This terrible disaster has brought to general notice the fact that while there is a southern route of comparative safety, rival steamship companies in order to shorten the time of passage and thus save expense and attract a larger patronage, have been sending their ships by a shorter northern route that is known to be dangerous at this time of year, and thus for the sake of financial gain it seems as though they have disregarded their moral obligation for the greatest possible safety of their patrons and placed the lives of thousands intrusted to their care in jeopardy. The Titanic was traveling by this route, and though warned of the special danger in the great icefield through which some ships moved very slowly and which some went around by going miles out of their intended course, her captain, probably trusting in her great size and strength for safety and desiring to make her first a record trip that would attract large business to her owners, took the risk he had no moral right to take with so many lives intrusted to his care, whatever his instructions may have been before leaving port, and sent her ploughing through the zone of danger at great speed with the result that she did make a record—which, please God, shall never be equaled by any other.

And if this terrible loss of life shall result, as it undoubtedly will, in the passage of laws that shall so curb this spirit as to make it subservient to adequate provision for the safety of every seagoing traveler of the future and the avoidance of such unnecessary risks and dangers, then those sixteen hundred of the Titanic's lost, whom we so sincerely mourn, will not have died in vain, but under God, will be the martyrs through whose death will come such safeguards and restrictions of ocean travel as shall in coming days give the world less cause to mourn.

Another lesson is that of man's insufficiency and the sin of overconfidence in ourselves and our achievements. Because God has allowed us to make use of the laws of life and growth in nature for our sustenance, and discover earth's treasures for our enrichment, and harness its forces for our service, and make the seas our highway, men have been wont to become impressed with a sense of their own greatness and self sufficiency and to forget, or at least ignore, their dependence upon and duties toward God the great Creator, Who "upholdeth all things by the might of His power" and "in Whom we live, move and have our being."

In Wednesday's issue of The Brooklyn Daily Eagle Nelson Harding has a picture entitled "Man," that is a sermon in itself. As you look upon it you see first of all a great white iceberg; above and beyond it a threatening sky; below and around it an angry sea. You wonder why it was entitled "Man," but as you look again, more closely, you see the reason why, for in the foreground, in the midst of the dark waters, you discover a man with one arm clinging for support to a piece of broken mast and the other lifted aloft as in an effort of defense, while over him towers a massive wave of thousands of tons of water just about to break upon him and bury him from sight forever. It is to me a wonderful picture and I have never heard or seen a stronger sermon on "the insufficiency of man" than this preaches.

How weak and small and utterly helpless we feel as we imagine ourselves struggling against a power like that! Yet that represents only one of countless waves and bergs that are only a small part of the great forces of nature under God's control. If these then are so appalling in their strength, how infinitely mighty must be the God who created and controls them all. Suppose God should let loose upon us the earth's internal fires; suppose He should release the ocean from its bounds; suppose He should allow to cease in their operation the laws that govern the movements of the planets in their courses or suspend for a moment only the law of cohesion whereby material things are held together—what dire calamity and terrible destruction it would mean. God gives us just a faint suggestion of it in the fires and floods and earthquakes that come to us from time to time, and making us realize our helplessness before them, teach us to realize the truth of the Scriptures where they say that "our sufficiency is not of ourselves, but of God."

Captain Smith was a navigator of large experience and acknowledged ability and had a ship which he declared and believed to be "unsinkable." His overconfidence, undoubtedly, led him to take a risk that otherwise he would have avoided and thus contributed toward his disaster. May it be a warning to all of us who are sailing out on life's great sea that we trust not overmuch in our own strength or goodness nor even in the best that the world has to give us for protection against the dangers that threaten our moral and spiritual welfare; but may we, avoiding all unnecessary risks by keeping as much as possible away from evil influences and associations, seek the help and guidance of Christ, the Master Pilot of our souls, and thus make sure to avoid making moral shipwreck of our lives and make sure of reaching the soul's harbor in heaven at last.

This disaster has done much also to inforce the lesson of universal brotherhood and the duty of love and sympathy and helpfulness for all mankind. Not only have the great nations been bound together by this calamity with a bond of common sympathy and sorrow and cooperation in raising of funds for the relief of the sufferers, but in the passage of some mutual agreement concerning requirements and restrictions of transportation, they will take still another step toward international peace and harmony and help toward the recognition of the fact that "God hath made of one blood all nations" and that all men everywhere are brothers.

Another lesson that has been emphasized is that taught and exemplified by Jesus Christ Himself: The duty and glory of self-sacrifice for others. All honor be to those heroic men who remained on the sinking ship and gave up their chance of life that the women and helpless children might be saved! Mr. Harding has in another picture suggested the erection of a monument in memory of these self-sacrificing heroes with the inscription on it: "They saved the women and children." Such examples of self-sacrifice for others' welfare are very wholesome and worthy of emulation in a larger degree by those who make a practice of exploiting children or depriving others of their rights or endangering others' lives, for the sake of personal gain. May they by this striking example of unselfish consideration of the welfare and rights of others, suffer the rebuke they so sorely need.

The last lesson I would notice in connection with this sad event is that of the uncertainty of life and the need of being ever prepared for death. So certain were the passengers of the Titanic that she could not sink that they were slow to realize their danger, and many at first refused to enter the lifeboats and did so eventually only under great persuasion. How glad they must be now, and were soon afterward, when they saw the great ship sinking, that they had yielded to persuasion and taken the only way of safety even when they did not realize its especial need.

May these and other lessons that come with equal force be so impressed upon the world by this great disaster that out of our great affliction there may come, as some measure at least of compensation, blessings that shall make for the higher welfare of mankind in the relations of this life and a more general preparedness for the life that is to come. May each one of us commit ourselves to the guiding and keeping power of Almighty God, saying in the words of our text: "In the shadow of Thy wings I will make my refuge until these calamities be overpast."

Dr. C. H. Parkhurst's Strong Words--Men and Religion

A Horrible Marine Massacre;

by

The Rev. Dr. Charles H. Parkhurst.

YESTERDAY morning the Rev. Dr. Charles H. Parkhurst, pastor of the Madison Square Presbyterian Church, Manhattan, preached a scathing sermon, arraigning what he deemed to be the conditions—"life sacrificed to luxury"—which brought about the Titanic disaster. He spoke in cutting terms of what he called a "horrible marine massacre." His text was taken from Ezekiel vii:19: "Their silver and their gold shall not be able to deliver them." Dr. Parkhurst said:

There are depths in the human spirit that are rarely, if ever, fathomed; depths that are like the hiddenmost places in the sea, to which no light comes, and into which no voice enters.

But vast possibilities of thought, feeling and presentiment are in those secret chambers, and we learn to know it right well whenever there occurs at the entrance-way into the soul a disturbance so disquieting and so upheaving as to carry the knowledge of ourselves down into recesses more profound than those in which the ordinary tenor of our experience is maintained.

With the very substance of our being shot through with sudden and appalling disquietude, we learn to suspect how immense are the containings of our natures, and find ourselves expanding to more than common grasp upon the meaning of the life we are living and the import of the relations in which we are held.

The impact upon us of any event which produces deep penetration is certain to work in us seriousness and even solemnity of thought. The gayeties of life all lie at the surface. Whatever takes massive hold upon us never flows off through channels of mirth and hilarity. The real man is a serious man, serious not in the sense of tristeful and lachrymose, but serious with that thoughtfulness and gravity certain to ensue when whatever is deeply real in us has been reached and pierced, and we have been thereby stimulated to large appreciation of whatsoever has come to us through the avenue of word or of event.

This last week, since Tuesday morning, has been a serious one, serious not only for the bereaved, but serious for the city, the country and the world. The very complexion of the town has altered itself. What has occurred has reflected itself in the faces and spirit of the people. That has been due in part to sympathy with those who have suffered; both with those who have perished and with those who almost wish that they might have perished.

But it is due also to the fact of having been imaginatively the witnesses to so appalling a tragedy. We have been sobered by it, for it has cut down into the very fabric of our souls, and we have been shaken by it. It has pierced us to a point deeper than that where we ordinarily live. It has bored down into the understratum of our being. It has operated upon us as an earthquake sometimes works in cutting down deep crevasses, opening broad abysses into the substance of the underground, showing us to ourselves in those unfamiliar and mysterious places in our being where we can grow bigger thoughts and thoughts not so easily spoken as those which vegetate in the mind's and heart's shallower furrows.

Different temperaments have, of course, seized upon different aspects of this unparalleled tragedy. No one has been left exactly as he was before. The quickening of thought, incident to the terrific surprise, has entered into every heart in its own special way, and has started or has prolonged in each some particular line of contemplation or widened some special area of vision. Each of you know your own. I am going to tell you mine, and I am going to cut as close to the line of truth and to the nerve of the sensitive heart as I know how; for if this event is treated as it ought to be, it is going to produce some searchings of heart that will modify to a degree the attitude of the general mind toward certain vital questions of individual and public life.

The picture that has hung before my eyes ever since last Tuesday morning has been that of the glassy, glaring eyes of the victims staring meaningless at the gilded furnishings of this sunken palace of the sea; dead helplessness wrapped in priceless luxury: jewels, valued in seven figures, become the strange playthings of the queer creatures that sport in the dark depths. Everything for existence, nothing for life. Grand men, charming women, beautiful babies, all become horrible in the midst of the glittering splendor of a ten-million-dollar casket.

And there was no need of it. It is just so much sacrifice laid upon the accursed altar of the dollar. The boat had no business to be running on that line. We are told that the authorities of the several companies are arranging now to put their crafts on a more southerly route. There is no more occasion for the southerly route than there was a week ago. They knew that the ice was there in very excessive quantities. They dared it. They would dare it now, but they do not dare the public. There is no doing anything with the public when the public has come to its own. Even the great moneyed directors of Great Britain are puny things as against the sentiment of the people as sentiment is now stirred.

It is cheaper to run by the short route. There is more money in it for the stockholders, and the great, strong multi-millionaires are working for dividends. Capable men they are, and very godly some of them, but they want money and as much as they can get, and this is what has come of it. And we can be righteously gratified that the company is mulcted in a pretty heavy sum, so large as to reduce immediate dividends to microscopic proportions. It is a lesson, a lesson all around, to the effect that commercialism when pushed beyond a certain pace breaks down and results in stringency and poverty, and that action when crowded produces reaction that wipes out the results of action. Running by the northerly route save coal. The coal is saved and starting a little mine of its own down there under the sea somewhere between Sable Island and Cape Race.

Then there is the matter of the insufficiency of lifeboats. It is true that government does not require an equipment of that kind adequate for the carriage of more than about half the number of passengers: but the government would require it if the people demanded it. And if neither government nor people demanded it the steamship companies would furnish it, if the individual members of those companies, stanch, wealthy, godly men, most of them, laid as much stress on the value of human life as they do on what they receive in passage money. Willing to risk loss of life rather than diminish net gains by expending dollars on expedients for preventing the loss of life. More commercialism. Lives against ducats. More worship of the golden calf. Worshipping God in the sanctuary and worshipping mammon in the steamship business.

The grim humor of it all as it lies in the steamer people's minds was displayed to me in a way that struck home when, some years ago, I was standing on deck talking with the captain. Our position was such as to give us a view of the lifeboats, and other life-saving appliances. I said to him, "Are there boats enough there to take off all the passengers in case of wreck?" "Hardly," said he. "But what would you do in such case?" I asked. "We would take off as many as we could and land them; then come back after the rest," he added, with a semi-chuckle.

The boat that landed the 700 survivors Friday morning is not going back for the rest. The rest will stay where they are. The cold-bloodedness, the fiendish heartlessness, the devilishness that was in that captain's tone of voice I have never forgotten, though his cruel and inhuman word was spoken twenty-five years ago. It showed me that the stanch, good men that administer the business cherish toward the people whose names are on the passenger list somewhat the feeling that they do toward a cattle cargo, only with an added tincture of geniality, seeing that men, women and children are more valuable than cattle for purposes of transportation.

Steamship management alleges the difficulties that are in the way of furnishing adequate means of rescue. Of course, it alleges difficulties. Undoubtedly there is a difficulty in the way of utilizing for life-saving equipment space that will pay better when occupied by passengers that tender anywhere from a hundred to four hundred dollars for the trip. Lifeboats and liferafts don't pay passage money. Men do, and they pay in advance, and if they drown on the way the dollars are in the company's strong box, ready to be served out as dividends.

It is business that these good steamship men are doing. And business means crowding people up to the point where increase of tension means reactionary exasperation that renders further crowding pecuniarily injudicious. It is worked in the same way that the rack used to be worked in seasons of persecution, which was twisted till there was danger that the agony would prove fatal, and then was relaxed a notch or two to enable the victim to recover consciousness. That is what business means, and it means it on land as well as at sea.

The policy of corporate evasion of improvements on the ground of difficulties involved is one that is quite familiar to us. We have learned to understand it here in New York. We have encountered it in the matter of public utilities in the hands of corporations. Improvements that have been urged by the people have been strenuously resisted on account of the impossibility of executing them or on the ground that it would be financially ruinous to the company; until popular pressure becomes so intense that the demand had to be yielded to or the company go out of business, whereupon it appeared that what was insisted upon was altogether practicable and involved no fatal abatement of net income.

Now, my friends, I have utilized this absolutely unnecessary disaster, this utterly fiendish disaster, as my text this morning, not because I have taken a brief against the steamship companies in general nor against the White Star Line in particular, which has served me faithfully as good many times; that is to say, it never happened to drown me, but I have used the event because it is tremendously in the general mind at the moment and on the public nerve, and because it is the terrific and ghastly illustration of what things come to when men throw God out at the door and take a golden calf in at the window.

And I have used it not because in its spirit there is anything in it out of the ordinary, but because it exhibits on a monstrous scale what is everywhere apparent in both the larger and smaller areas of human experience and purpose—everything for existence and nothing for life, everything brought down to the hard, cold, glittering, metallic basis of the dollar.

And I am impelled to this not by any motive of anger. The occasion is too tremendous to admit the intrusion of any passion so paltry; but by indignation that is hot and holy. For all this sorrow, this horrible slaughter, this parting of loved ones, tragic rending of families, separation of husbands and wives, fathers and children, lovers and brides, at the moment of the ship's immersion was totally without reason.

We can conceive no severer punishment that could be inflicted upon the guilty parties or sharper warning that could be given to other parties equally guilty, but whose ships happen never to have met with such disaster—no severer punishment, nor sharper warning than to be compelled to read and daily to reread the harrowing details of those two hours running from midnight to 2 in the morning.

We will not be angry with them: rather do we pity them, for if their hearts have not been hardened to the consistency of the metal in which they deal, the perusal of the ghastly record, the contemplation of the vivid drama of men leaping to their death, bidding speechless and long goodbys to their loved ones and all to the accompaniment of the infernal music of the orchestra, must be to them a kind of foretaste of the tortures of the damned. Yes, we pity them, for unless their hearts are clean gone, burnt to a crisp, these days are to them days of remorse, of gnawings of soul, of writhings in the flames of convicted conscience.

It is not that these directors, these men of fine repute, of standing in the State and in the Church (I had occasion at one time to have correspondence with the board, and I can testify to the fine strain of character evinced by the terms of their communication), it is not that they have not sometimes reflected upon the risks they were taking, upon the way in which they were jesting with awful possibilities, and using men and women and homes as pawns with which to play their game of financial accumulation.

They have thought about it. They have known that there were liabilities of disaster and of wreckage in mid-ocean against which no provision, no certain infallible provision, could be made, and that means of survival in such case were so limited that half or two-thirds of their patrons, men, women and dear little children, were liable to become victims of the deep and food for the fishes. They knew it all, have known it all these years past. Their guilt is no momentary guilt, but a long-drawn-out guilt, only now by this horrible marine massacre their guilt is brought home to them.

They have consciences, but consciences get worn, and there is no hammer like a hammer of gold for beating down the keenness of conscience to a blunt edge. And in that lies the supreme significance of this event. And the disaster will prove a wasted and a superfluous one unless it shall be interpreted with a wider reference than to the dulled consciences and extravagant criminality of those immediately responsible.

For it seems as though Providence, or nature, or whoever or whatever is ultimately accountable for this tragedy, had held back the event, had withheld the lesson, till there was ready for the occasion a craft sufficiently mammoth in its proportions, and sufficiently regal in all the overwrought elegance of its furnishings and appurtenances, to strike home to the heart of the entire world the lessson of the moral leanness that is wrought by the appetite for gold, the moral debauchery that is nursed in the lap of luxury.

Returning to that in a moment, I want to say parenthetically that without recalling a word of the excoriation just visited upon the steamship authorities, they are not the only ones to whom censure belongs. The whole traveling public is in the guilt. Whether those who never go upon the sea are aware of the careless and risky conditions upon which steamships are run I cannot say, but those who do go are aware, and if we had unanimously risen to our obligation as protestors, the steamship management would have yielded, would have had to yield, and fifteen hundred of our friends would not now be sleeping at the bottom of the north Atlantic.

We are a regardless, a careless and a risk-taking people. We put matters in the hands of a few and then leave them there instead of looking after them ourselves after putting them there. We treat as though not part of our concern things that are part of our concern. We assume that once put a man in a position of accountability he will act fully up to the level of his accountability, and he will not, not one time out of ten. We appoint inspectors. We had inspectors to secure the safety of the Triangle shirtwaist factory and it was stated after the fire, after a couple of hundred girls had been roasted and trampled to death—girls that had as much right to live and be protected as you and I have—that there were at least 200 respects in which building requirements had been violated. Inspectors do not inspect, and they are not going to do so till the public inspects the inspectors. We cannot be part of a community and get away from the responsibility that community entails.

So as relates to this disaster—and here I am preaching to myself more than to most—it is not only the privilege but the obligation of every traveler who goes upon the sea and pays to be taken across alive, to make a demand upon the authorities that every reasonable condition shall be met upon which the attainment of that result shall be accomplished without being thrown out into the water and dropped to the bottom of the sea when half way over. We are a community and cannot in justice to ourselves or to our contemporaries evade the responsibility pertaining to us all in our communal capacity.

We may thereby make ourselves a nuisance to those who have been specifically appointed to the work and who would prefer to do the work in their own way without supervision; which means that they would prefer to do only as much of the work as they find to be to their convenience. But in times like our own, in the midst of all our careless and mercenary administration that we know so much about and that obtains both on land and upon sea, it is our duty to make of ourselves a nuisance, and it should be welcomed by us as a privilege rather than as an obligation.

And now to come back for a moment, for I must not hold you much longer, the two sore spots, which really run into each other and which constitute the disease that is gnawing into our civilization are love of money and passion for luxury.

Those two combined are what sank the Titanic, and sent fifteen hundred souls prematurely to their final account. The passengers wanted to cross the Atlantic in a palace, and in order to satisfy them and to win the spoils that would come by satisfying them, the ship's management ordered the construction of a boat that would sacrifice the security of passengers to the gratification of their fantastic tastes, and ran the boat at a latitude, at a rate of speed and under conditions of peculiar danger of which ample warning had been given, in order to gratify that silly passion for haste that comes with money, with the love of money and with a consequent surfeit of physical convenience, ploughing through ice at the rate of 21½ knots an hour with the captain off of the bridge and banqueting down in the saloon, we are informed, in company with the official head of the line. That is the entire story. Money was the fundamental factor in the entire business.

And it is the same passion that is gnawing into the moral vitals of the times. It is draining the rich natural juices of our humanness. It is subordinating the imperishable to the perishable. It is working its diabolical work of commercialism. It is reducing all commodities, the immaterial as well as the material, to the standard of dollars and cents—pounds, shillings and pence. It is impregnating our civilization with the same virus that converted the twelfth disciple into a Judas who could appreciate only the money value of the ointment with which Mary anointed the feet of her Lord, and who figured out the worth of the Son of God at thirty pieces of silver.

Under the blight of such an atmosphere there can be little profound philosophy, or fine art, or choice ethics, or beautiful and tender piety, any more than there can be more than an occasional flower blooming on the Desert of Sahara.

The charm of this horror, if I can put those two words so close together, is that it brongs us face to face—with a directness we cannot possibly slink away from—brings us face to face with the sordid temper of the times under a form of manifestation so repulsive as to work universal contempt and with a vastness of proportions that makes it visible clear around the world.

There is one spot of brightness, only one; one rift in the awful cloud through which sifts a bit of light that puts a goodbye touch of glory on the sinking Titanic, when magnanimity, which nevertheless slumbers somewhere in every human soul, awoke and laid upon the tragedy in its closing act an aspect of solemn and ineffable grandure. What had been horrible only, became thus transfigured. And if the event goes down in history as a fruit of the meanest passion of the soul, it will also stand forth as exponent of that which is finest and closest of kin to the sacrificial passion of our Lord, demonstrating that when under the baptism of a great crisis the heart of man comes to itself, values range themselves before it in due order, chivalrous death is felt to be grander than cowardly life, and the ties of love to bind with a tenacity not to be broken by the allurements of a beautiful world that is left behind.

THE TITANIC'S DEAD.

BY FREDERICK F. SHANNON.

[Most of the saved are women and children.—Wireless message.]

What wondrous soul-grandeurs the words relate!
Deeds worthy of great heroes of old,
High darings these of men of splendid mold,
Who plucked half the sting from Death, and straight
Into the swirling blackness sank. Nor fate,
Nor fear, nor dark, nor deep, nor ice could steal
The deathless strength of Love their souls reveal,
When swift Death spake and said: "O Men, die great!"
Valiantly through that shuddering gloom,
When woman's agony and childhood's tears
Answered the Sea's call for human toll,
These sons of God, within their liquid tomb,
Made Death conceal his face behind Death's Tears,
As they said: "We're men of Titanic soul!"

PRESBYTERIAN PROSPECTS.

At General Assemblies of the Southern and United Presbyterians, to be held next month, the question of consolidation of these bodies will be presented. Already general committees on the proposition exist, and periodicals of both bodies are expressing hopes for union. As its name implies, the first is the great Presbyterian body of the Southern States, and the latter is a Northern body, strongest in and around Pittsburg. Their respective memberships are 175,000 and 135,000.

Students in Union Theological Seminary, Richmond, which is controlled by Southern Presbyterians, have recently issued an open letter to ministers, officers and members of their church, asking why it is that so many Presbyterian churches in the South show little or no growth, and that the body as a whole reaches so few men and does so little. The students refer solely to evangelism. In missions Southern Presbyterians have just passed the $500,000 mark in annual gifts to foreign missions last year, and in home missions, all phases, they increased last year $15,000, making a total of $126,000.

In line with others in the same church the laymen have just held a meeting in Chattanooga, and have issued a formal appeal for a campaign to begin now and end March 31, 1913, to add 50,000 to Southern Presbyterian membership and raise benevolences to $1,500,000. Appeal is also made for 250 volunteer laymen to give part or all of their time during this year to push the plan.

The Patriot's Vision;

by

The Rev. J. C. Welwood.

CHAPLAIN J. C. WELWOOD, rector of the Church of the Holy Spirit, Brooklyn, as chaplain of the New York Commandery of the Naval and Military Order of the Spanish-American War, preached before that body in the Cathedral of St. John the Divine, Manhattan, yesterday afternoon. It was the occasion of the anniversary of the beginning of the war with Spain, and was the annual memorial service. This commandery has 465 members and is the largest of the thirteen commanderies in the State. Colonel Hull of Governors Island is the commander. Chaplain Welwood saw service in the battles of El Caney and San Juan Hill. He has served as chaplain for eight years. With him in the chancel were the Rev. Henry A. F. Hoyt of Philadelphia, chaplain in chief, and other members of the order who were chaplains in the war. The subject of the sermon was "The Patriot's Vision." The text was from Revelation xv:4, "For all nations shall come and worship before thee." Chaplain Welwood said:

This revelation of St. John the Divine may be intended for a vision of heaven, but it is equally applicable to those beatific characters that will ultimately bless the nations while still upon the earth. He, indeed, is weak in faith who halts before a vision of heaven on earth for all the nations of men. If the American eagle must spread its wings, let it be as the harbinger to all people that the destiny of nations is an affair of the ever living God and not subject to the caprice of men. If the American nation would pause long enough to observe the trend which its history reveals, it would see that it is leading all nations to come and worship before God.

Along with those men who fell in battle or from disease in the Spanish War, in whose memory we meet here, we all had a vision when we offered our lives for our country. It was not the vision, "My country, right or wrong." It was a vision of "My country, right," and, because right, a vision of thrilling inspiration because our country would always be right. We men of '98 did not analyze our vision. But we were under its spell. By faith we saw results. Let us revive that vision this afternoon and we shall behold in its center of effulgence a spiritual destiny produced by spiritual forces. This is our subject, "The Patriot's Vision," and it will reveal the mightiest force in a nation. This spiritual force has three manifestations to which I would call your attention.

I. Observe, in the first place, the manifestation of this mighty spiritual force in our political history. Our conception of force has been too material. We have grown up in the error that marred the philosophy of Carlyle, whose only hero was the man of brute strength. In dynamite and guncotton and smokeless powder and war and "the arm of the law" and the overworked appetite for material wealth and control of the markets, we have enthroned the reign of force. Competing with all these, a finer energy has been at work in the material world, compared with which these are but crude and dangerous playthings. All through the history of force, from its first display in muscle down through water and wind power and steam, it has been becoming progressively finer, and the finer the mightier, till now, indescribable and impalpable in its fineness, electricity crowns the labors of the past. What will be the next powerful agent discovered, no one knows; but we do know that it must be still finer and mightier or it will not be accepted. The steps of its progress are on the highway to spirit force, finer and greater than all. He puts himself out of court who denies that the trend of force is spiritual.

From the beginning of our national history there has been a subconscious recognition of a spiritual control. Recall a few of the principles and deeds of our brief history of which we are proud. Notice how they are operations of the spirit. Those were seeds of the spirit that were planted with the Declaration of Independence. Free-born, and, in privilege, equal-born, our basic principle. Justice and right and merit in our foundation. Our national conscience has been uneasy in contemplating our wars or our diplomatic aggressions prompted by greed for territory. Our two wars with England, our Civil War, the Spanish-American War were holy wars. In the last century, our freeing the slaves was a spiritual act. Our giving them the suffrage, grave blunder that it was, was an impulse of the heart. At the close of the Civil War, when one great general treated another great general with magnanimity, he had the enthusiastic approval of his countrymen. We have opposed the partition of conquered nations whenever we had a voice. We returned a large unused indemnity to China. We have protested in no uncertain tones against foreign outrages as far as international relations would permit. Our spiritual conscience rejoiced when an American President took the initiative in ending a destructive war. We are in the van of the universal peace movement. We have shown a patience with the Cuban Republic that astonishes the world. We have abrogated a treaty with a friendly nation because we draw no distinction in matters of religion. We have unselfishly wrought miracles in the Far East. In making our laws, we have shown a spiritual prompting in our care for the rights of the individual. When the guilty have been unpunished or have delayed the action of justice, in the enormous majority of cases it has resulted from our fear of punishing the innocent. In the opening of this century we face a throng of new propositions of government. Direct primaries, the initiative, the referendum and the recall may all be wise or unwise, but the motive that prompts them is to secure ideal, fair, uncorrupt laws and legislators and to continue along the same line of government by the people laid out by our fathers.

This proud record has been achieved by a spiritual force. A power outside of us has been molding us toward righeousness. There are national creeds as well as theological creeds. If American civilization is to live—and it will live—it must acknowledge the creed of its history and the first article of that creed is, "I believe in God the Father Almighty." We may not have the name of God in the Constitution, but we have His abiding presence as the throbbing heart of the great republic. There is no other alternative to a spiritual force. Civilization is not wet clay for a man to model his experiments in. It is alive and walking the sunlit paths to God. It does not grow like the Tower of Babel, expecting to reach heaven, keeping its foundation on the material earth. Its ascent is by a ladder let down from heaven, such as Jacob saw. The vision of heaven must come first.

II. Brotherhood—Another manifestation in which this mighty spiritual force will assert itself will be found in the compulsion of all men to recognize the universal brotherhood of mankind.

The day was when at the mention of brotherhood men bristled with hostility as violent as many do today at the suggestion of Socialism. But in all up-to-date nations the principle commands the profoundest respect. In approaching this problem America is setting the pace for the world in at least one respect, in proclaiming that only by recognizing the family tie can humanity accomplish its destiny; only by being animated by this master principle, that there is a flaw in the title of wealth as long as a particle of injustice attaches to it.

Observe how God's spirit, as the mightiest force in the nation, has nurtured the growth of brotherhood among men. What importance He has bestowed upon discovery and invention. We converse with each other a thousand miles apart. We communicate with friends in the middle of the ocean. We can hurry to each other by burrowing in the earth or by whirling on its surface with the speed of incarnate beings or cleave the seas a small city at a time, or vie with Aurora in driving our chariots above the clouds. The inventor's laboratory has crowded us together so closely that we are one big family. Our civilization is one great "Get-Together Club." Society is inextricably aand fraternally interrelated. Men compete with each other in contributing millions to alleviate the pains of the body, to train the intellect or to inspire the soul.

Everywhere, all over the world, irrespective of its particular form of government, the State is giving effect to these principles by its enactment of beneficent legislation in the form of old age pensions and stricter liability laws, to cite but two striking instances. Society is a stupendous, all-embracing spider's web. The slightest disturbance at any one point reports itself at the center. The day shows signs of breaking when we shall rejoice with them that rejoice and weep with them that weep.

This has not been the gracious handiwork of brute force. No rancorous bomb uplifts in this way. No poisonous arrow has inoculated civilization thus with the energy of blessed growth. No overreaching commercial greed has wrought such beauty. Civilization has not thus unaided lifted itself by its own bootstraps. A power without it is modeling society in love. The heart of God devised it. The hand of the Almighty has let down to struggling humanity golden chains from the throne on high. The dying patriot could describe no fine details, but with the vision before him he plunged to death impelled by the audacious faith that his country stood for the truth of human brotherhood.

III. A third manifestation of this mightiest force in a nation is in the prominence attaching to the individual. If your vision is true, you are peopling the future with a nobler race of men. The individual is giving promise of fulfilling your vision. His cultivation now holds the center of the stage. In the great ship of state he may be only a bolt or a lever or one link in a chain. But the honest shipbuilder is as careful of the detail as he is of the grand plan. Now the methods of any enterprise are crude and unnatural that are not immune from danger to the welfare of the individual. Dangerous occupations have no place in a perfect civilization. Either the business is illigitimate or the methods are inadequate. In the erection of a great bridge like those across the East River, in rearing to dizzy heights the steel structure of an office building, the method employed is incomplete and intolerable if, among the estimates of the cost of the building, must be included that of how many men will have to be sacrificed in executing the plans. Because that estimate must be made before a battle is evidence that war has no natural place among the forces of progress. The same indifference to the welfare of the individual obtains when he is squeezed to death by competition or crushed under that Juggernaut substitute for competition to which our newest financial sages refer when they speak of co-operation. But the individual is arousing himself and arising above the level where he may be charged up to profit and loss like pigiron, pulley blocks and ammunition. The magnificent and progressive force of the spirit is calling in a thousand ways for the individual to awake. The ease of transportation and communication is opening up capacious avenues of knowledge. Cheapness of worthy publications and opportunities for instruction in unemployed moments are making the individual an expert. Ready access to market quotations and information on the problem of immigration and foreign importations give him a speaking acquaintance with the whole world. The average business man is thus enabled to be and compelled to be far more alert than his predecessor of fifty years ago. He is more self-centered and self-poised and self-controlled. To be a successful lawyer or physician or minister or teacher, the individual must show, and does show, incomparably more acumen than his father had to exhibit. The strenuous methods of business life require a stronger race of men, and future conditions will have in store a still severer test. The individual is responding to the test. Conditions are calling out the man, the larger man, the completer man. That the Spirit of God is at work as the mightiest force in this nation is seen in the development of the individual, the average man, who is learning to be unsatisfied unless climbing to increasingly higher levels of character and achievement.

This is the Patriot's Vision of the trend of the spirit, the mightiest force in the nation. Every indication of national history in politics, every sign shown in the study of brotherhood and the individual points to the truth of the vision. It seems to dispense with the profession with which you are or have been connected Yes, and only the pessimist clings to the old slogan that, as long as governments continue, we must be prepared for war. If this were a material universe, under the domination of material forces, then warfare would never cease. But it is a universe throbbing with life of the spirit. The accomplished vision may be a long way off, but, though the mills of God grind slowly, they grind exceedingly sure, as well as small. The future holds two things as inexorably sure as the revolution of the earth on its axis. One is that the progress of civilization is under the influence of a spiritual force and the other is that that force will never cease to operate, but rather will continue inflexible to shape our national course until we satisfy the demands of a perfect ideal. The soldier and sailor have been and still are as important factors in civilization as the merchant, but their profession is the most self-sacrificing of all and most noble in its sacrifice because they offer not only their lives, but, in the evolution of the spirit, they offer also their livelihood and all that they have, on the altar of their country. At present we must continue to maintain our army and navy. We may have another war. High international courts of arbitration cannot yet look with unprejudiced eye. Nevertheless, our vision is true. It is practical, certain of realization, the aim of destiny, the glorious consummation, for the kingdoms of this world are determined upon in the mind of God to become one kingdom of justice and righteousness. Then shall the prophecy of the text be verified and all nations shall come and worship before God.

DR. ABBOTT IN CHICAGO.

Noted Preacher Pays Tribute to Titanic Heroes.

Chicago, April 22—Dr. Lyman Abbott of New York said in an address here, last night, that the dead who lost their lives in the Titanic wreck are living now and can never die.

"When that great ship went down," he said, "and men with courageous hearts and smiling lips bade adieu to the women and children whom they put into the boats for safety, and the musicians played 'Nearer, My God, to Thee,' am I to believe that these men were only a more differentiated type of machinery with a little more subtle force than the steam motor which took them down under the sea?

"Death is a launching. It sets the freed spirit upon its native element."

One hundred dollars was subscribed at a church meeting, yesterday, for the orphaned daughter of the Rev. John Harper of London, England, who was on his way to America in the Titanic to take charge of the Moody church of Chicago.

Men and Religion.

Addresses by

Former Governor Northern,
Booker T. Washington,
Bishop W. F. Anderson,
Dr. A. L. Phillips, and
President Frank Strong.

CARNEGIE HALL was filled with interested audiences yesterday afternoon and last evening at the eighth and ninth sessions of the Christian Conservation Congress of the Men and Religion Forward Movement. In the afternoon the meeting opened with devotions and greetings by the Rev. Dr. J. S. Wardell Stafford, fraternal delegate of the Wesleyan Church, Great Britain, to the Methodist Episcopal Church General Conference. The first address was made by former Governor Northen of Atlanta, Ga. His subject was, "The Church in Relation to the Negro Problem."

The Governor declared that the negro question is "not a sectional but a national problem" and "that it is moving North and very fast." Speaking as one who had had thirty years' experience with domestic slavery and who for twenty-five years had been doing all in his power to redeem his State from crime and violence he denounced lynching in soothing terms and white complicity in negro immorality in terms just the reverse. He then went on to enter a plea for the killing of sectional prejudice, and for charity on the part of the nation for the South which is "dealing with a problem never faced by any nation before in the history of the world." He also said:

"The problem of the negro home is the problem of good morals. Living as many of them do they cannot be kept morally clean. This makes the women of the negro home an easy prey to immoral and degenerate white men. What has constructive Christianity ever done up to this good day in any of the states, to remedy this dreadful sin? Every mulatto mingling in our social system is a living evidence of the meanness of some degenerate white man, who has helped to destroy the home of some defenceless and ignorant negro. Count them as they meet you in the street, or serve you in your homes, and see the enormity of this dreadful sin.

"I make no kind of defence of the criminal lawlessness of mobs. Let me say in this presence, as I have repeatedly said all over the South, every member of a mob that does violence to human life by lynching or burning the body of a human being is a murderer and should be punished to the full extent of the law. And every beast in human form that criminally outrages the purity of our womanhood deserves the extremest penalty of the law, as administered by the courts and never by the criminal lawlessness of mobs. There can be no place anywhere for mobs in our Christian civilization."

To indicate that the white man has helped to create the conditions which now must be solved, the Governor said:

"In my thirty years experience with domestic slavery I never saw or heard of a drunken negro. Now the bane of the negro in the South and the curse of the community life is found in idleness and vagrancy and crime by drunken negroes. Georgia led all the states at the South in statutory prohibition of the manufacture and sale of whisky. This action was taken because of the tendency on the part of negroes toward all the evils that come from drink. During these thirty years I never saw or heard of a case of tuberculosis? White people had tuberculosis, but negroes, seldom if ever. Now the negroes of Georgia and the South are dying three to one as compared with the whites. The negro problem is the American adjustment of the relations which should exist between the white people and the negro people of a common soil, whose welfare, in the last analysis, is the common weal. In all the history of the world's civilization no nation on earth has had to settle anything like this American problem. We must give the negro the Gospel just as we give it to the backward peoples of the earth."

Booker T. Washington, president of Tuskegee Institute, took up the same subject. He said among other things:

"The negro problem is to a very considerable extent the problem of rural life everywhere. So long, too, as the negro in the rural districts is fed upon the old wornout theological dogmas, instead of getting from the pulpit inspiration and direction in practical work of community building, connecting religion with every practical and progressive movement for the improvement of the home and community life, so long will he forsake the land and flee to the city. If we would save the negro, 82 per cent. of whom live in the country, he must be taught that when the Bible says 'The earth is full of thy riches,' it means that the earth is full of corn, potatoes, cotton, chickens and cows, that these riches should be gotten out by the hand of men and turned into beautiful church buildings and a righteous, useful living.

"From a money point of view, it is much cheaper to keep men from falling than to lift them up after they are down."

Congressman Richmond P. Pearson spoke on "The Church in Relation to Temperance."

At the evening service the devotions were led by President William T. Slocum of Colorado College, Colorado Springs. Greetings from the Southern Presbyterian Church were given by the Rev. Dr. A. L. Phillips, General Secretary of the Brotherhood, Richmond, Va. In the course of his address he said:

"We looked to the Men and Religion Forward Movement with expectancy not unmingled with doubt and hesitation. With glad hearts we acknowledge our enormous debt to this movement for bringing us face to face with the very serious problems that stand before the Church, for new visions of the possibilities of Bible study; for strengthening our convictions of the duty of evangelizing all men of whatever nation or race on the face of the earth; the deepening of our concern for the salvation of men through personal persuasion; for a tremendous awakening to the transforming power of the Gospel when released upon our complex social conditions; and finally for the deposit of an efficient programme of Christian service of men and boys for men and boys.

"In many of our most populous centers the religious leaders, with a few notable exceptions, have scarcely learned that there is a 'boy problem.' The dire necessity of maintaining our Anglo-Saxon civilization in vast regions cannot excuse the neglect of social evils that are gnawing at its very heart. Our social complacency has been severely jarred. There are signs of an irritated social conscience. There is an appalling need of both a firing up and a firing out. In our cities and their adjacent territory where the campaigns have been held, our religious life can never flow easily in its ancient channels. We must have broader thinking, deeper passion, large embraces and more intense application. We have seen something of the almighty power of the Spirit of God working through a united church, and we have yielded to the joyful influences of a bond of peace. We have been brought full many a day's journey toward the place of the melting pot where God in Christ through the supernatural power of the Holy Spirit shall transform the men of America into the Brotherhood of Christ."

"The Church" was the subject of Bishop William F. Anderson of the Methodist Episcopal Church, resident at Chattanooga, Tenn., who spoke in part as follows:

"The Church of today must be aggressive spirit. It is in strong competition with other influences which strive for the mastery of the modern world. The Church is not an end within itself. An organization existing in and for itself must not regard itself as the Church of Jesus Christ. Neither God nor man can approve an institution of such spirit. The Church, like its Lord, must become the servant of humanity. Like Him it must go about doing good. Like the true disciple, it must lose its life in order that it may find it.

"A present-day leader defines the institutional church as a 'Church of organized kindnesses to the individual.' That is a happy phrasing of the true mission of the true Church of Jesus Christ. Its mission we have come to see is to the whole man. It includes the betterment of his physical, his intellectual, his social environment. It especially emphasizes the development of his moral and spiritual nature. The old-time distinction between secular and sacred has lost its force in our modern thinking. We regard everything as sacred which relates itself directly or remotely to the well-being of mankind. But the individual is only the unit of society. He must be builded into an organization for the conservation of the great fact of salvation. The Kingdom of God is the Scripture term most frequently used. It is the most comprehensive term descriptive of the redemptive influences. It is larger than any one branch of the Church; larger than all branches of the Church combined, for the movement of the Spirit of God in human affairs is in larger circles than human conception or human organization. The waters of the river of God's love are not confined to the channels which men dig. They flow co-extensively with the stream of human life."

"The Church in Relation to University and College Students" was the subject treated by President Frank Strong, LL.D., of the University of Kansas. He made a strong address, in the course of which he said:

"The life which Christians share in common is the essence of Christianity. It manifests itself in many different forms. Christianity is, however, greater than any single manifestation of its life. It is greater than the Church, its organized form. Nevertheless, the Church is the chief exponent of Christianity. Modern aspirations for universal high and noble living have come recently through the development of historic Christianity, whose organized instrument is the Church. The Church, therefore, is mainly responsible for the crystalization, the world over, of human hopes, a vague defining of the world demand, that all the relations of life shall be so adjusted that every man shall have a fair chance for the development of the best in his own life and for doing the best service for the generation in which he lives.

"Have the university and college any necessary relation to this world demand, this coming of the Kingdom of God? They ought to have some definite relation to the Church, for they themselves are in their modern development a result of the Christian movement. Christianity and the Book which is its greatest exponent have invariably been in every age a tremendous intellectual stimulus and have led to great intellectual development. The university also has been an instrument inseparable from the growth of the civilization out of which our present world visions have come. The university has had an almost determining influence on the moral and religious development of Christianity, and there must be the strongest possible alliance and co-operation between the Church and the university. While the Christian Church has recognized this in connection with its own schools it has been strangely blind to its duty toward education controlled by the state. Education is going largely into the hand of the municipality, of the state. The growth of public high schools and public universities is vastly more rapid than that of private high schools and universities. The number of young people from the Christian denominations in public universities is very large, largely exceeding, in some states, the number of the same denomination in the denominational college. In America the Church cannot get along without the public universities. This larger vision is born of a true interpretation of the Gospel's significance of the life of men.

"The number of young men fitting themselves for the ministry has declined partly at least because of this attitude of the church toward a large body of our ablest young people now in state institutions whose moral and spiritual life is as strong and pure and wholesome as that of the young people in any other class of institutions. It is a matter of great importance, therefore, that the ministry of the Christian church be recruited from those that have had as large and varied an intellectual experience as possible.

"Colleges and universities must be held for Christ. The Christian Church must put aside the prejudices of sect, must cease to demand of the growing generations now in our colleges the same modes of religious expression that were adequate for our fathers. The church must prove itself to the young as an organization that is full of a Christian democracy, that is aflame with the purpose to make all life square with the teachings of the Lord and Master of us all."

DIRECTORY FOR ADVERTISERS WILL BE FOUND TO-DAY ON PAGE 11, COLUMN 7.

THE NEW YORK HERALD.

THE WEATHER. Rain, followed by clearing; stationary temperature. For detailed weather report and forecast see Editorial page.

WHOLE NO. 27,636. NEW YOR NDAY, APRIL 22, 1912.—TWENTY PAGES.—[COPYRIGHT, 1912, BY THE NEW YORK HERALD COMPANY.] ✻✻✻ PRICE THREE CENTS.

SIXTY-FOUR BODIES ' THE TITANIC VICTIMS RECOVERED; "I GAVE NO ORDERS TO CAPTAIN," SAYS J. BRUCE ISMAY; MRS. ASTOR TELLS HER STORY OF THE DISASTER

ADRIFT 7 HOURS IN OPEN BOAT, TAKES TURN AT OARS, BAILS, AND RESCUES DROWNING MAN

HERE is Mrs. John Jacob Astor's story of the sinkingg of fthe Titanic and the scenes attending her rescue.

She did not tell it at any one time, but bit by bit, as her strength permitted, since she landed from the rescuing steamship Carpathia last Thursday night. Her physicians forbade her talking very much at any one time—in fact, they would have preferred that she say nothing until she was strong, but that was too much to ask aftter the experiences of that awful night, and little by little she has related the facts that go to make up the history of the foundering of the White Star steamship.

To her mother and father, Mr. and Mrs. W. H. Force; to her sister, Miss Katherine Force, and her physician, Dr. Reuel B. Kimball, it is known that she has told of being awakened from sleep by the shock and of being reassured by Colonel Astor, of the preparations for leaving the ship, of his loving solicitude for her as she left in the lifeboat, one of the last to leave the foundering ship; of his promise to rejoin her in the morning.

She has told how she saw the Titanic take her final plunge and of how half a score of drowning men were pulled into the boat, some of them only to die before they were taken on board the rescuing steamship.

HER EXPERIENCE FULL OF PATHOS.

Mrs. Astor's experience was as tragic as any of the women whose stories have been heard, and more so than most of them. If it is lacking in details it is because no one has cared to question her or risk adding to her grief, which is of the deepest kind.

It is well known that Colonel and Mrs. Astor were returning from a trip to Europe and to Egypt. It was a sort of delayed honeymoon journey, as they had taken no other lengthy trip since their marriage in Newport last Septetmber. They crossed to Europe on board the Olympic, and on both trips they were fellow passengers with J. Bruce Ismay, one of Colonel Astor's close friends. In fact, on the way to Europe Mr. Ismay is known to have given up his own suite in order that Mrs. Astor might, perhaps, be more comfortable there than in the one that had been reserved for them. When they got on board the Titanic at Liverpool they were glad to find that Mr. Ismay was to be a fellow traveller again.

The Astor party consisted of Colonel and Mrs. Astor, a trained nurse for Mrs. Astor and her French maid; the Colonel's valet, Rollins, who had been with him for fifteen years or more, and the chauffeur. Then there was Kitty, Colonel Astor's favorite Airedale terrier, that had travelled all over the world with him. The two had been inseparable companions for years, and they were not to be saparated, for Kitty went down on board the Titantic with her master.

Pathetically Mrs. Astor told of how Kitty got lost in Egypt on the trip up the Nile. She wandered away from Colonel Astor's side one day at a landing and went sightseeing on her own account. Colonel Astor was greatly distressed by the loss of the dog. He spent a great deal of time looking for her, and when he had to give up and start up the Nile again he employed scores of natives to look for her, promising a handsome reward for her return. Nothing was heard of Kitty until on the return trip when on passing another dahabea.

Colonel Astor spied Kitty making herself at home on board. The Astor boat was stopped and Kitty found her master with joyous barks. Kitty wore a collar with her own and Colonel Astor's names and "No. 840 Fifth avenue, New York city," engraved on it. She went on board the wrong dahabeah, evidently looking for her master after being lost for a time, and a party of wealthy Americans who had chartered the boat for a Nile trip quickly knew to whom she belonged and were looking for Colonel Astor's dahabeah to return her. After that a closer waatch was kept of Kitty on board the Titanic. She slept in Colonel Astor's room.

ASTOR SUITE WAS FINEST ON THE SHIP.

The Astor suite was one of the finest on the great ship. Mrs. Astor's nurse occupied a room near her own, for she had not been at all well on the trip through Europe and Egypt and needed constant cart. The nurse was among the passengers in the first cabin, although few of her fellow travellers knew it tor knew that Mrs. Astor's health was so delicate that she needed the attention of a nurse.

Mrs. Astor spent a good deal of the time in her room and was hardly off the one deck until the accident. Colonel Astor and she took frequent walks and he romped with Kitty a great deal. He was interested in the maiden performance of the new Titanic, for anything mechanical interested him, and he frequently consulted the log and heard from Captain Smith and Mr. Ismay of how the great ship was behaving.

But no unusual incident marked the voyage until the collision that sent her to the bottom. Colonel and Mrs. Astor had both retired when the great ship struck. Whether he was awakened by the shock or not Mrs. Astor has not said, but, at any rate, he went to his wife's bedside and awakened her.

Gently he told her that something was wrong and that he thought she had better get up and dress. He dressed before she did and said he would go and find out the extent of the ship's injury.

But all the time he was getting ready he was reassuring his wife, saying not to be afraid, that the Titanic could not sink.

Loud talking in the companionways near Mrs. Astor's room, the cries of stewards awakening the passengers alarmed her, but she remained calm, as she had the utmost faith in Colonel Astor's knowldege of ships and the ways of the sea. He said he would go and see Captain Smith and find out just what had happened.

When he went back his face was graver than it had been, but still he was sure there was no danger. Mrs. Astor did not know at the time, but since she has come to believe that her husband musthave known that the Titanic and all her passengers were in peril.

The Colonel told his wife that the Titanic had struck a submerged iceberg and was apparently resting on it. He assisted her in the final details of dressing, but without hurry, and his calmness encouraged her greatly.

Mrs. Astor did not have all of her jewelry with her. Of course, she had her engagement ring, a magnificent oblong diamond, and a string of superb pearls. Colonel Astor stood by as his wife took these from a jewel case and put them on, along with other less important pieces, a beautiful pin, among other things that he had given her.

When she was ready they went to another deck, probably the boat deck. There were a few other persons there at the time. All put on lif preservrs. This contradicts th report that Colonel Astor would not or did not at least take this precaution. He saw particularly that his wife's belt was adjusted properly.

His solicitude for Mrs. Astor was then shown in another way. She shrank from the cold and he noticed it. He said:—

"You are not dressed warmly enough, my dear. That suit you have on is too light," and then he noticed that she had put on one of the lightest costumes in her wardrobe. Colonel Astor then ordered Rollins, the valet, to return to their suite and get one of Mrs. Astor's heaviest dresses.

The faithful Rollins quickly returned with the garment, and there in the cold of the deck Mrs. Astor changed her gown, putting on the heavier dress. The nurse and the maid and Colonel Astor all assisted her in this operation.

The life preserver was adgain adjusted and also a fur coat was made up of several different kinds of fur and put over all. By that time most of the boats had been lowered with their human freight, and Mrs. Astor was told to get into one. She did so. She thinks it was the last or next to the last craft that left the Titanic. She is of this opinion because other boats were bobbing far out in the dim starlight and she saw no others nearer to the foundering ship.

Emphatically she denied the report that Colonel Astor got into or made any move to enter the lifeboat in which she was. He was the calmest man on the Titanic's deck, so far as she could see. He said:—

"The sea is calm and you will be all right. You are in good hands and I will meet you in the morning."

The boat was launched and got away without accident.

CARRYING COFFIN UP GANGPLANK

CAPTAIN F.H. LARDNER

THE MACKAY-BENNETT

Bodies on Board the Mackay-Bennett Can Be Identified Is Belief; Many Others Found and Buried at Sea

Three Huge Icebergs Seen in Vicinity of Disaster, Says Report to St. Johns, N. F.—Men and Women Drowned in Night Clothes Offered No Clews to Identity—Other Vessels Tell of Seeing Floating Victims and Wreckage.

[SPECIAL DESPATCH TO THE HERALD.]

ST. JOHNS, N. F., Sunday.—Sixty-four bodies of victims of the Titanic disaster, which it is believed can be identified, have been recovered by the cable steamship Mackay-Bennett, which went to the scene of the sinking under orders from the White Star line officials to search for bodies and stay until recalled.

The report of the Mackay-Bennett, which was received here to-night, says that many other bodies were found, but were without marks of identification and in such condition that they were buried at sea. None of the names of those, if any, who had been identified could be obtained through the Cape Race wireless telegraph station. Dense fog, it is said, has delayed the search for the victims by the Mackay-Bennett.

Messages were sent from the Mackay-Bennett yesterday saying the steamships Rhein and Bremen, of the North German Lloyd line, had passed by wreckage and bodies. No mention was made by either of these vessels as to whether any of the bodies had been picked up by them.

Many of those bodies which may have been found and which were unidentifiable were probably those of sailors who were crushed when the Titantic struck the iceberg, and others, it is understood, were those of men and women who were drowned in their night clothes, making identification almost impossible.

Three huge icebergs were approximately ten miles from the spot where the majority of bodies were found floating.

WIRELESS GIVES FIRST NEWS OF THE LOCATION OF BODIES

Messages from the Cable Ship Mackay-Bennett Said They Were Seen by Other Vessels and Work of Recovery Was Under Way.

Wireless messages were received here yesterday from the cable ship Mackay-Bennett, which is at the scene of the Titanic disaster, saying that it had heard that the steamship Rhein, of the North German Lloyd line, in passing in the lane taken by the Titanic had seen bodies and wreckage afloat in the vicinity of three big icebergs.

The messages were addressed to J. Bruce Ismay and were dated April 20. The Mackay-Bennett received orders last Wednesday to proceed to the point where the Titanic foundered and stay there until further orders to search for bodies. The messages came by way of Cape Race. The first runs:—

"The steamship Rhein reports passing wreckage and bodies 42.1 north, 49.13 west, eight miles east of three big icebergs. Now making for that position and expect to arrive at eight o'clock to-night. MACKAY-BENNETT."

The second message reads:—

"Received further information from the steamship Bremen and arrived on ground at eight o'clock P. M. Start operations to-morrow. Have been considerably delayed on passage by dense fog. MACKAY-BENNETT."

The White Star line offices were open until nine o'clock Few persons went to the White Star line offices yesterday. The messages from the Mackay-Bennett were placed on the bulletin board. In the offices also were photographs of one of the men lost in the wreck, of whom relatives ask for information, hoping he still may be alive.

That bodies had been seen by the steamships was surprising to many persons yesterday, as it was thought that through the tremendous suction of the big vessel the drowned would never come to the surface. It also was said that the bodies of those seen by the Bremen and the Rhein may possibly be those who dropped dead through cold and exertion in the lifeboats.

WILL TEST AT SEA INSTRUMENT FOR DETECTION OF ICEBERGS

Professor Howard Barnes, of McGill University, Hopes by the Device to Convey Warnings to Captain's Bridge.

[SPECIAL DESPATCH TO THE HERALD.]

HALIFAX, N. S., Sunday.—The orders under which the Mackay-Bennett steamed were to report first to New York and then to Halifax. The range of the Mackay-Bennett's wireless is one hundred and fifty miles by day and fifty miles more at night. The scene of the disaster is some three hundred and forty miles from Cape Race, which would therefore have to be reached by relay message. The distance to Sable Island is considerably more than four hundred miles.

A wireless message, direct from the steamship Bremen, by way of Sable Island and Camperdown stations, confirmed to-night the reports that many bodies were located in the vicinity of the disaster. The message read:—

"The steamer Bremen, bound for New York, and the steaamer Rhein passed on Saaturday afternoon in 42.00 north laatitude and 49.20 west longitude in the neighborhood of three large icebergs. Sighted numerous pieces of wreckage and a great number of human bodies with life preservers on floating in the sea. Sighted and spoke the cable steamer Mackay-Bennett on the way to recover the floating bodies.

(Signed.) "CAPTAIN PRAGER."

The Canadian Pacific steamship Empress of Ireland steamed from Halifax for Liverpool at seven o'clock Saturday evening and will pass not far from the grounds over which the cable ship is cruising. It is probable there will be communication between the two ships and the Mackay-Bennett may relay via the Empress of Ireland, which should be within close speaking distance to-morrow morning.

Professor Howard Barnes, of the science department of McGill University, Montreal, will go on board the Royal George, leaving in a few days, to test an instrument which he says will instantly show any changes in the temperature of the water on an indicator at the bridge. He calls it a pyrometer, and says that by means of it the presence of an iceberg would be instantly revealed by a lowering of temperature in the water.

The mechanism consists of a coil of platinum in the water connected by wire with the vessel. The changes in temperature are indicated by the resistance shown in the platinum to an electric current passing through it.

White Star Director Denies That He Issued Any Commands Whatever About Speed of Ship or Interfered with Control of Vessel in Any Way Either Before or After Fatal Crash.

HELPED PUT WOMEN AND CHILDREN IN BOATS; ENTERED LAST THAT LEFT SHIP

No Other Passengers, Men or Women, Near as He and Mr. Carter Got Into Collapsible Craft Containing Thirty or Forty Persons, He Declares in Statement.

READY TO TELL THE SENATE ALL HE KNOWS

Asserts Idea of Unsinkable Ships Has Been Proved a Myth and That All Vessels Must in Future for Safety's Sake Carry Lifeboats Enough for Every Soul on Board and Men to Handle Them.

J. BRUCE ISMAY, head of the International Mercantile Marine, last night issued a statement refuting the charges which have been made against his conduct. It is apparent from the tone of his remarks that he has been deeply stirred by the accusations that he was seeking a speed record for the Titanic; that he gave orders to speed ahead when told he was among icebergs, and that he was making arrangements to rush back to Europe to avoid testifying before the Senate committee. He said:—

"When I appeared before the Senate Committee Friday morning I supposed the purpose of the inquiry was to ascertain the cause of the sinking of the Titanic, with a view to determining whether additional legislation was required to prevent the recurrence of so horrible a disaster.

"I welcomed such inquiry and appeared voluntarily, without subpoena, and answered all questions put to me by the members of the committee to the best of my ability, with complete frankness and without reserve. I did not suppose the question of my personal conduct was the subject of the inquiry, although I was ready to tell everything I did on the night of the collision.

"As I have been subpoenaed to attend before the committee in Washington to-morrow I should prefer to make no public statement out of respect for the committee, but I do not think that courtesy requires me to be silent in the face of the untrue statements made in some of the newspapers.

GAVE NO ORDERS, HE SAYS.

"When I went on board the Titanic at Southampton on April 10 it was my intention to return by her. I had no intention of remaining in the United States at that time. I came merely to observe the new vessel, as I had done in the case of other vessels of our lines.

"During the voyage I was a passenger and exercised no greater rights or privileges than any other passenger. I was not consulted by the commander about the ship, her course, speed, navigation or her conduct at sea. All these matters were under the exclusive control of the captain. I saw Captain Smith only casually, as other passengers did. I was never in his room; I was never on the bridge until after the accident; I did not sit at his table in the saloon; I had not visited the engine room nor gone through the ship, and did not go, or attempt to go, to any part of the ship to which any other first cabin passenger did not have access.

"It is absolutely and unqualifiedly false that I ever said that I wished that the Titanic should make a speed record or should increase her daily runs. I deny absolutely having said to any person that we would increase our speed in order to get out of the ice zone or any words to that effect.

"As I have already testified, at no time did the Titanic during the voyage attain her full speed. It was not expected that she would reach New York before Wednesday morning. If she had been pressed she could probably have arrived Tuesday evening.

"The statement that the White Star line would receive an additional sum by way of bounty or otherwise for attaining a certain speed is absolutely untrue. The White Star line receives from the British government a fixed compensation of £70,000 per annum for carrying the mails, without regard to the speed of any of its vessels, and no additional sum is paid on account of any increase in speed.

"I was never consultted by Captain Smith or by any other person nor did I ever make any suggestion whatsoever to any human being about the course of the ship.

INSTRUCTIONS OF CAPTAINS ARE SPECIFIC.

"The Titanic, as I am informed, was on the southernmost westbound track of transatlantic steamships. The tracks, or lanes, were designated many years ago by agreement of all the important steamship lines, and all captains of the White Star line are required to navigate their vessels as closely as possible on these tracks, subject to the following standing instructions:—

"'Commanders must distinctly understand that the issue of these regulations does not in any way relieve them from responsibility for the safe and efficient navigation of their respective vessels, and they are also enjoined to remember that they must run no risk which might by any possibility result in accident to their ships. It is to be hoped that they will ever bear in mind that the safety of the lives andproperty intrusted to their care is he ruling principle that should govern them in the navigation of their vessels, and that no supposed gain in expedition or saving of time on the voyage is to be purchased at the risk of accident. The company desires to maintain for its vessels a reputation for safety, and only looks for such speed on the various voyages as is consistent with safe and prudent navigation.

"'Commanders are reminded that the steamers are to a great extent uninsured and that their own livelihood, as well as the company's success, depends upon immunity from accident; no precaution which insures safe navigation is to be considered excessive.'

"The only information I ever received on the ship that other vessels had sighted ice was by a wireless message received from the Baltic, which I have already testified to. This was handed to me by Captain Smith without any remark as he was passing me on the passenger deck on the afternoon of Sunday, April 14. I read the telegram casually and put it in my pocket. At about ten minutes past seven, while I was sitting in the smoking room, Captain Smith came in and asked me to give him the message received from the Baltic, in order to post it for the information of the officers. I handed it to him and nothing further was said by either of us. I did not speak to any of the other officers on the subject.

"If the information I received had aroused any apprehension in my mind—which it did not—I should not have ventured to make any suggestion to a commander of Captain Smith's experience. The responsibility for the navigation of the ship rested solely with him.

DID NOT DINE WITH THE CAP TAIN.

"It has been stated that Captain Smith and I were having a dinner party in one of the saloons from half-past seven to half-past ten Sunday night and that at the time of the collision Captain Smith was sitting with me in the saloon.

"Both of these statements are absolutely false. I did not dine with the captain, nor did I see him during the evening of April 14. The doctor dined with me in the restaurant at half-past seven, and I went directly to my stateroom and went to bed at about half-past ten. I was asleep when the collision occurred. I felt a jar, went out into the passageway without dressing, met a steward, asked him what was the maatter, and he said he did not know. I returned to my room. I felt the ship slow down, put on an overcoat over my pajamas and went up on the bridge deck and on the bridge.

"I asked Captain Smith what was the matter, and he said we had struck

SENATE COMMITTEE TO ASK WHY WARNINGS WERE DISREGARDED

ice. I asked him whether he thought it was serious, and he said he did. On returning to my room I met the chief engineer and asked him whether he thought the damage serious, and he said he thought it was.

"I then returned to my room and put on a suit of clothes. I had been in my overcoat and pajamas up to this time. I then went back to the boat deck and heard Captain Smith give the order to clear the boats. I helped in this work for nearly two hours, as far as I can judge. I worked at the starboard boats helping women and children into the boats and lowering them over the side. I did nothing with regard to the boats on the port side.

"By that time every wooden lifeboat on the starboard side had been lowered away and I found that they were engaged in getting out the forward collapsible boat on the starboard side. I assisted in this work, and all the women that were on this deck were helped into the boat. They were all, I tnink, third class passengers.

NO PASSENGERS LEFT FOR BOAT.

"As the boat was going over the side Mr. Carter, a passenger, and myself got in. At that time there was not a woman on the boat deck, nor any passenger of any class, so far as we could see or hear. The boat had between thirty-five and forty in it, I should think, most of them women.

"There were perhaps four or five men, and it was afterward discovered that there were four Chinamen concealed under the thwarts in the bottom of the boat. The distance that the boat had to be lowered into the water was, I should estimate, about twenty feet. Mr. Carter and I did not get into the boat until after they had begun to lower it away. When the boat reached the water I helped row it, pushing the oar from me as I sat. This is the explanation of the fact that my back was to the sinking steamer.

"The boat would have accommodated certainly six or more passengers in addition if there had been any on the boat deck to go. These facts can be substantiated by Mr. W. E. Carter, of Philadelphia, who got in at the time that I did and was rowing the boat with me. I hope I need not say that neither Mr. Carter nor myself would for one moment have thought of getting into the boat if there had been any women there to go on it, nor should I have done so if I had thought that by remaining on the ship I could have been of the slightest further assistance.

"It is impossible for me to answer every false statement, rumor or invention that has appeared in the newspapers. I am prepared to answer any questions that may be asked by the committee of the Senate or any other responsible persons. I shall, therefore, make no further statement of this kind, except to explain the messages that I sent from the Carpathia.

KNEW NOTHING OF SENATE INQUIRY.

"These messages have been completely misunderstood. An inference has been drawn from them that I was anxious to avoid the Senate committee's inquiry, which it was intended to hold in New York. As a matter of fact, when despatching these messages I had not the slightest idea that any inquiry was contemplated, and I had no information regarding it until the arrival of the Carpathia at the Cunard dock in New York on Thursday night, when I was informed by Senators Smih and Newlands of the appoinment of the special committee to the inquiry.

"The only purpose I had in sending these messages was to express my desire to have the crew returned to their homes in England for their own benefit at the earliest possible moment, and I also was naturally anxious to return to my family, but left the matter of my return entirely to our representatives in New York.

"I deeply regret that I am compelled to make any personal statement when my whole thought is on the horror of the disaster. In building the Titanic it was the hope of my associates and myself that we had built a vessel which could not be destroyed by the perils of the sea or the dangers of navigation. The event has proved the futility of that hope.

"The present legal requirements have proved inadequate. They must be changed. But whether they are changed or not this awful experience has taught the steamship owners of the world that too much reliance has been placed on water tight compartments and on wireless telegraphy, and that they must equip every vessel with life boats and rafts sufficient to provide for every soul on board. and with sufficient men to handle them."

SAW BERG AHEAD, REVERSED ENGINES.

The White Star line gave out yesterday a copy of the cable report of the disaster which was sent to the Liverpool office on April 19 and posted at Lloyds on the following day. It follows:—

"Until arrival Carpathia, 9:30 P. M., April 18, 1912, no statement whatever as to facts of collision. Carpathia wireless short distance type and wholly occupied transmitting names passengers. Master Carpathia and officers Titanic testifying to-day before United States Senate sub-committee, New York. Facts substantially as follows:—

"Titanic followed strictly southernmost track westbound, changing course at corner 47 meridian 42 latitude, thence south 86 degrees west true. All officers watch perished except Fourth Officer Boxhall, who was working observations in chart room and making rounds.

"Night perfectly clear; starlight; no wind; sea calm. Had encountered no ice previously. Proceeding with vigilant lookout full speed, but reduced consumption probably twenty-one to twenty-two knots. Engineers all perished.

"At 11:45 P. M., April 14, ship sighted low lying berg direct ahead. First officer starboarded helm, reversed full speed and closed all compartments. Struck berg bluff starboard bow. Slight jar, but grinding sound, evidently opening several compartments starboard side. Boats cleared, filled with women and children, lowered and sent off under responsible persons.

"Ship sank bow first 2:20 A. M. All boats away except one collapsible. Carpathia rescued survivors 4 A. M. Discipline perfect."

MR. ISMAY WON'T QUIT UNDER FIRE

Tells Counsel and Associates He Will Remain in America Until Investigation Is Over.

J. Parker Kirlin, who is associated with Charles C. Burlingham as counsel for the White Star line, emphatically denied last night a report that J. Bruce Ismay was preparing to start for England immediately following the conclusion of his testimony before the United States Senate committee. Mr. Kirlin said that his statement was fully confirmed by a conversation which took place last Saturday afternoon between Mr. Ismay, Mr. Kirlin, Mr. Burlingham and P. A. S. Franklin, vice president of the White Star line.

In this conversation Mr. Ismay was advised that if he considered it necessary immediately to return to England there were no legal obstacles in his way. Mr. Ismay said:—

"I want to settle that question right now, once and for all. I am not going back to England until this investigation is finished. I have absolutely nothing to conceal. I will help the investigating committee to the best of my ability.

"There are thousands in this country who are holding me up to scorn. Under such conditions I will not leave the country. So long as I am a target I shall remain to be fired at.

"I will make use of no legal loopholes to get away. When it becomes necessary for me to go to England I shall stand ready at the first call. I am in this investigation to stay, and I shall still be standing in the open after those who are criticising me have fired their last shot."

"DEAD" MAN APPEARS.

Rockport, Mass., Sunday.—Among those reported lost on board the Titanic was Niles Sigurd, who was coming from Sweden to visit his uncle, Captain Carl Green, of this town. Captain Green was grieving at the death of his nephew when he appeared. Niles Sigurd had booked aboard the Titanic, but missed her at the last minute and followed on board the Cymric.

CAPTAIN SEALBY PRAISES MR. ISMAY

Retired Commander of the Republic, Sunk in Collision, Suggests Preventive Measures.

[SPECIAL DESPATCH TO THE HERALD.]

Ann Arbor, Mich., Sunday.—When Captain Isman Sealby, who commanded the Republic, of the White Star line, when she was rammed by the Florida, and who now is a University of Michigan student, was asked for an expression on the Titanic disaster he said—

For twenty-five years I served under an Ismay, father and son, and during that period I never saw anything which would have led me for a minute to anticipate anything but the best of conduct in J. Bruce Ismay at all times and in all circumstances.

"The world—especially the shipbuilders themselves—knew that one half the passengers cannot be taken care of with the present small number of lifeboats. The question is, does the public want the added protection with the increased cost?

"I would recommend, first that the commanders of the North Atlantic steamships be ordered by their owners to go south of the ice track and always to travel slowly in a fog.

"Second, the government should hold owners of ships responsible for seeing that these orders are carried out to the letter at all times, any failure of which would result in the withdrawal of their passenger carrying license.

"Third, the people of the country should hold their Representatives in Congress responsible or liable for the ship owners carrying out these provisions, failing which the Representatives themselves should be compelled to resign their seats.

"I should say, further, that for the benefit and safety of the public, which demands both speed and safety, the structuural alterations of steamships and the carrying out of the requirements would mean additional cost to ship owners, and this additional cost would have to be met by the public. A passage that could be bought now for $50 would cost $150."

Missouri Girl Tells How She Scored 'Beat' on the Titanic Story for the Herald

Miss May R. Birkhead Wrote While Mending Coats and Aiding Survivors.

OUTSTRIPS A RIVAL

Knew Western Editor Was Aboard, so Got Sketches and Pictures Before Others Could Obtain Them.

Many persons—newspaper readers as well as newspaper publishers—have inquired of the Herald as to how it obtained some of the exclusive features which marked the notable issue of Friday, April 19, containing the report of the sinking of the Titanic as related by the survivors of the wreck and the passengers of the rescuing vessel, the Carpathia. A considerable part of this friendly curiosity centred upon the intensely interesting and illuminating series of sketches made by a survivor to illustrate the various stages of the disaster, and filled in the same day by an artist passenger on board the Carpathia, and the photographs of the rescue work at sea published on the second page of that day's paper.

"And how did you get a young woman to write four columns of matter to appear in the paper, which must have been printed about one o'clock, when the Carpathia did not discharge her passengers until about ten o'clock?" was asked.

Singularly, all these incidents noted are related, and the history of that part of the Herald's most comprehensive account of the distster shows how the long arm of circumstances reaches out to half way around the world to work out its purpose.

The series of events concerning this world "beat" began a year ago, when a Herald reporter enjoying a period of leisure in Missouri, thought to improve an opportunity by preparing a story upon the early days of Champ Clark, then becoming a more conspicuous figure in national affairs. He heard that Mrs. Laura E. Birkhead, a widow, living in Louisiana, Mo., was a close frend of the Clark family, her husband having been a chum of the Speaker in boyhood and early manhood. He called on Mrs. Birkhead, and while getting the information he sought met the daughter of the family, Miss May R. Birkhead—slender, dark eyed, level browed—and learned incidentally that she had added to her store of pin money by making shirt waists. Those of her friends who saw them wanted some like them, and insisted upon paying for the products of her skill.

The reporter came back to New York and Miss Birkhead continued to make shirt waists, her fame spreading beyond the confines of Louisiana, Mo., so that she received orders from as far as St. Louis and Chicago. Her personal bank account went up amazingly, so a short time ago she decided to accompany her aunt on a European trip, insisting upon paying her own way. Passage was engaged aboard the Carpathia, and when Miss Birkhead and her aunt reached New York the Herald published an interesting story of the independent Missouri girl who was travelling abroad on the fruit of her own enterprise.

So on Thursday, April 11, the Carpathia steamed out of port, and Miss Birkhead with her.

When the News Broke.

At fifteen minutes before one o'clock on the morning of Monday, April 15, the first bulletin suggesting the Titanic disaster reached the Herald office. A few minutes later came confirmation enough to show that an event that would interest the world was in progress. Immediately the department of the Herald having to do directly with the matter began to put the news gathering machinery into operation. Instructions were sent to correspondents all along the North Atlantic coast; preparations were made to charter vessels at Halifax, Boston, Providence and New York, and reporters and photographers were started for Nova Scotia.

And the wireless messages were sent to half a dozen persons on board the Titanic, some to the Baltic, the Virginian, the Olympic and to the Carpathia.

Three persons were addressed on board the Carpathia as probably being willing to respond. The presence of Miss Birkhead was recalled and her first message read—"Wireless all operator can take on Titanic."

Later when it became known that the Carpathia had picked up the survivors of the wreck additional wireless messages were sent to the persons aboard with whom the Herald sought to get into communication, among them, of course, Miss Birkhead, but the winged words found no resting place and can pass into the limbo of forgotten things. The uncertainty of wireless was taken into consideration, and each day a new set of messages was sent out in the hope that if one failed another would find the mark. Of all the messages, so far as can be learned, only the first brief one to Miss Birkhead reached the operator of the Carpathia. He transcribed it, addressed the envelope to "Major Birkhead" and put it aside for delivery. There it remained until it was uncovered from a pile of papers on Thursday afternoon, when a steward was commissioned to take it and search for "Major Birkhead." On such narrow bridges does fortune walk.

It chanced that Miss Birkhead heard of the inquiry that was being made for the Major and claimed the wireless message.

Miss Birkhead Got Busy.

The Carpathia was then less than eight hours from her pier. Miss Birkhead knew that an editor connected with a Western paper was on board as a passenger and that he had been working in the interest of a New York paper, but, nothing daunted, she took up her commission from the Herald and began to make up for lost time. She heard that sketches had been made of the progress of the disaster and her first care was to insure that the possessor would undertake to deliver them to the Herald in her company. She also knew that photographs had been made of the survivors and the lifeboats, and she sought out the possessor of those valuable films and made similar arrangements about their disposition. Then she began to write.

"I was so much interrupted that I thought I never should get anything done and that when I had done it it would be such a jumble that it wouldn't be of any use to anybody," said Miss Birkhead afterward. "I never even had a chance to read it over. While I had been lying in my berth during the nights after we picked up the passengers I had been writing the story in my mind, but I never thought that the call to produce it would come when it did. I had, however, made some notes of the things I did not want to forget so I should be able to tell them to mother when I got back. You know we are going to be away for at least six months, and it is so easy to forget things in such a long time.

"The captain had given orders that private messages of survivors to their friends were to take precedence of press messages, and, though I inquired repeatedly, I found that it was impossible to get anything through. So I just had to write the things down as they came to me and trust that it would come out all right in the end.

MISS • MAY BIRKHEAD — COPYRIGHT BY THE NEW YORK HERALD

Story Writing Interrupted.

"First one person would come to me to have something done, and then another. A little thirteen-year-old English girl was trying to mend a tear in a coat for one of the physicians, and she came to me because she could not get it right. I showed her how, but I had done nearly half of the work before I gave it up.

"Then a woman came in to borrow some ink. I hadn't any ink, but my aunt had a fountain pen. We lent her that, and soon she was back again in the cabin in worse trouble than before. The pen, poor thing, leaked, and the woman's fingers were all stained. She was nearly ready to go on shore, and at such a time as that something had to be done about the fingers. So I took some manicure powder and cleaned the fingers and began to write on my Herald story just where I had left off.

"Then when we got nearer to port I had another anxiety. Tug after tug loomed up, and I expected at any time to hear my name called out on a megaphone and to have to throw overboard what I had to somebody from the Herald. I carried what I had already written in an envelope in my shirt waist, and had a block ready to tie it fo to weight it. When anything hove in sight I would go to the side and listen and then go back to write some more to add to the story already in my envelope.

"We got nearer and nearer to New York, and several tugs had been unable to approach us, and so it seemed that I would have to depend on my own efforts to get to the Herald office as best I could. Everybody said that we wouldn't be able to get a taxicab and that we never would get there in time.

"A little German woman, who couldn't speak any English, had promised to come with me to the Herald office. She had taken some photographs, too, but she got separated from us in the hurry when the passengers began to go off. I had to go along without her, but everything came out right in the end. The Herald was waiting for me at the pier. There was a taxicab waiting there, too. When it was all over naturally I was tired, but there was nobody prouder than I to find the Herald had every paper 'beaten to death.'"

Reaches the Herald Office.

It was precisely ten o'clock when Miss Birkhead walked up the steps of the Herald office with the party she had corralled. The sketches of the sinking of the Titanic and two rolls of undeveloped films were on their way to the art department in a very few minutes. Miss Birkhead turned over what she had written of her story and began the dictation of the remainder to a stenographer.

After the work was ended Miss Birkhead went to the Hotel Martha Washington, where Mrs. Champ Clark and her daughter, Miss Genevieve Clark, were waiting for her, and the party stayed talking till four o'clock next morning. Miss Birkhead had visited the Clark family in Washington for six weeks before she started to go to Europe, and Mrs. Clark and her daughter, Miss Genevieve Clark, came to New York on Thursday night to meet her.

Mrs. Clark takes pride in the share she has had in the bringing up of Miss Birkhead. Here is something she said:—

"I am proud to know her and proud to think that she has come out as I thought she would. With my own children, as well as with the young folk growing up around me, I always insisted that they should be able to help themselves, and that when emergencies arise their self-reliance should be sufficiently developed for them to meet the exigencies.

"I believe I shall take Miss Birkhead as a text for something I want to say at the Dolly Madison breakfast in Washington. I believe in women getting out and doing something more than spending their time at 'pink teas,' and I believe the case in point of a Missouri girl who got out and 'showed them' has its moral."

Bride Who Was Rescued from Death Finds She Is Destitute Widow

MRS. ARGENIA DEL CARLO AND SISTER OF SAN RAFFAELE HOME

Mrs. Del Carlo, Who Was on Her Way to Chicago with Husband, Who Had Savings of Years, Now Cared for by, Charity.

Few of the Titanic's survivors are in as sad plight as Mrs. Argenia Genovesi Del Carlo, a second cabin passenger from Lucca, Italy. Married a little more than three months ago in Tuscany to Sebastiano Del Carlo, she left with her husband to take up her residence in Chicago, where, employed as a carpenter, he had lived for nine years, and had arranged to provide a comfortable home. He perished after placing her in a lifeboat.

Mrs. Del Carlo saved nothing except the clothing she wore. Her husband carried all their money, $2,500. She is being cared for by the Rev. Father Moretto and the sisters of the San Raffaele Society, No. 10 Charlton street.

Mrs. Del Carlo's parents are in Italy. Her two sisters live in Fresno, Cal. When her husband emigrated to the United States ten years ago he promised to return for her when he had made sufficient money to get married. On last Christmas they were married. Good wishes and presents were showered upon them as they started for their home in the wonderland of America.

Father Moretto has communicated by telegraph with the woman's sisters in Fresno, and whether she will return to her parents in Italy or join her sisters in the West depends on whether the latter can defray the expenses of a transcontinental trip.

"I did not want to go without my husband," said the woman yesterday when relating her story to an interpreter, "but he kissed me and said 'Do not be afraid, Argenia, I shall come later.' We went away and I did not know my husband was dead until I came here from the hospital."

Senate Inquiry Resumed in Washington To-Day

Investigators Seek Light on Story That the Titanic's Officers Ignored Warning of Icebergs Half Hour Before the Crash.

CHAIRMAN LAUDS WORK OF CAPTAIN ROSTRON

Herald Bureau,
No. 1,502 H Street, N. W.,
Washington, D. C., Sunday.

Why three warnings of icebergs ahead, given to the first officer on the bridge of the Titanic within half an hour before she struck, were ignored will be one of the first points the Senate committee investigating the disaster will take up when its sessions are reopened here at ten o'clock to-morrow morning.

The statement of Thomas Whiteley, a first saloon steward aboard the Titanic, who told a Herald reporter of a conversation he overheard in a lifeboat between the two men who had been in the crow's nest, brings a new and startling feature into the investigation. Thirty of the crew of the Titanic are here, technically in the custody of the Sergeant at Arms of the Senate. Whiteley, who is in St. Vincent's Hospital in New York, doubtless will be brought here in the hope that the men who were on lookout duty and survived may be here. If he can identify them their testimony will be taken to throw light on the discipline aboard the vessel.

Harold Bride, Jr., the Titanic's second wireless operator, who was under examination when the committee suspended its sessions in the Waldorf-Astoria in New York on Saturday afternoon, will be a witness here to-day, as will Harold Thomas Cottam, the wireless operator of the Carpathia.

Seek to Solve Wireless Mystery.

The committee is not yet satisfied with what progress it has made in clearing up the mystery of the wireless despatches which were sent out last Monday announcing that the Titanic was in tow of the Virginian. Another point the committee wishes to clear up is the statement, published exclusively in Sunday's Herald, that T. W. Sammis, chief engineer of the Marconi Wireless Telegraph Company of America, had warned the wireless operator aboard the Carpathia to withhold details of the disaster, as he had arranged to sell his story for "dollars in four figures." The Senate Committee is anxious to know what bearing this fact may have on the refusal of the Carpathia's o perator to furnish the Salem with information especially requested by President Taft.

With J. Bruce Ismay, P. A. S. Franklin, five officers and thirty of the crew of the Titanic here to-night, it is expected that to-morrow's session of the inquiry before the full Senate committee will develop many interesting facts. The big marble conference room in the Senate office building will be used for the first time to-morrow.

It is the earnest desire of Senator Smith, chairman of the committee, to finish with all of these men of the Titanic at the earliest moment practicable and permit them to return to their homes. He said officials of the White Star line had given the assurance that any of the men subject to their command would be produced whenever the committee needed them, but he preferred finally to complete the taking of testimony at this time.

Asked if he had heard of any protest from the British Embassy over the detention of the British seamen he said he had not.

Major Arthur Peuchen, of Toronto, Canada, who was pressed into service in rowing one of the Titanic's lifeboats when no seaman was at hand at the time of the boat being lowered into the water, will also be in Washington to-morrow.

Senator Smith sent a wire to the editor of the Toronto Globe asking if Major Peuchen would appear. He received a reply before leaving New York last night saying Major Peuchen had left Toronto for Washington.

Lauds Work of Captain Rostron.

After a quiet Sunday devoted to resting up from his nerve racking experiences of the last three days Senator Smith discussed to-night the impression made upon him by the tales of the Titanic's survivors. He was deeply impressed with the testimony given by Captain Arthur Henry Rostron, of the Carpathia, who told of the rescue.

"Wasn't it splendid?" he declared with deep feeling. "I was talking with one of the women passengers, who declared that on reaching the Carpathia there was hot coffee already prepared. I asked if she knew when it had been prepared, and she did not. I then told her the order was given immediately upon the receipt of the distress signal from the Titanic.

"And that was not all. There were blankets ready for those who had been in the icy waters and exposed to the early morning air and hot cloths for the babies.

Not a single precaution had been overlooked or omitted by this most efficient captain. Every man knew his place, the doctors were assigned to the different dining saloons and told to improvise hospitals and get everything in readiness. The lifeboats were made ready to pick up any survivors who might still be afloat in the water. Every man on board knew his place. When dawn was breaking and as the last preparations on board the rescue ship were made the first lifeboat came alongside.

"And then after the survivors were all picked up and cared for what a noble heart and a clean, manly soul it was that dictated the holding of religious services! Keeping himself on the alert, Captain Rostron manoeuvred his ship to cover the whole scene of the disaster, while prayers of thanksgiving went up from the living and the ship's bell tolled its requiem for the dead.

"Captain Rostron is not only a sailor; he is a soldier and has served his government in the field. The discipline he maintained on shipboard shows that he is a man who measures up to the highest traditions of the sea. His conduct of the rescue shows that he is not only an efficient seaman, but one of nature's noblemen.

His earnest denial that he had been in any way responsible for indifference to a message sent by President Taft and his shocked surprise that he could have been thought guilty of such a thing impressed me as being the expression of an honest man. When he had finished his testimony and was preparing to return to his ship to resume the voyage which had been so sadly interrupted I could not find words to express all I felt, but we looked each other in the eye, and I think he understood."

As Senator Smith talked his eyes filled with tears, the first that had come to them in all his harrowing experiences on the docks last Thursday night, and in his able conduct of the investigation, and the Herald reporter was reminded of the lines of Kipling's ballad:—

"For there is neither east nor west,
Border, nor breed, nor birth,
When two strong men stand face to face,
Though they come from the ends of the earth."

Impressed by Wireless Operator.

The gripping story of Harold Bride, the Marconi man on the Titanic, who told of how he and Phillips had stuck to their post until the deck containing the wireless room was awash, because the captain had not given them permission to desert their duties, deeply moved Senator Smith.

"As that young boy sat there and told in a simple, unemotional way his narrative of the disaster," he said, "I thought of the heroism he had displayed, and although I was insistent upon getting his testimony and resisted numerous appeals that he be permitted to leave the stand I felt a deep compassion for his injuries and was filled with emotion.

"His last few words were dramatic in the extreme. 'I stayed at the key while Phillips went out and took a look,' said young Bride. 'He came back and I asked him how it looked. He said that it looked bad, that we had better put on our lifebelts. I then took up my lifebelt and put it on and put what money I had in my pocket. Phillips stepped in and adjusted his lifebelt. All the lifeboats were stripped. There was one boat left—a collapsible boat. Phillips said it was useless to send any more, as we were sinking. That was about four minutes before she went down. We started out on deck when a woman and her husband staggered in and she fell in a faint. Phillips got her a glass of water and then led her out of the room.'

"Wasn't that superb?" ejaculated Senator Smith, in rehearsing Bride's story. "I then asked him, 'Did you then leave the ship?' He answered, 'No, sir; the captain had not told us we could. But later we saw him and he said for us to look out for ourselves.'

"Bride then jumped into the water, came up under the overturned collapsible boat, but was finally rescued.

Inadequte Boat Equipment.

"What most impressed me about the testimony," said Senator Smith in conclusion, "was that it showed that if there had been enough lifeboats practically all the 1,500 lives that were forfeited would have been saved.

"There was nothing in the testimony to show that any man sought by reason of his position or his money to secure a place in the lifeboats. All became one in level. John Jacob Astor did not say 'I am John Jacob Astor, and demand a place, but he placed his wife in the boat and returned to the men.

"Major Archibald W. Butt did not declare himself the military aide of President Taft and ask to be rescued; but he cheered and encouraged those who were leaving and went down with the ship."

SAYS COMPANY KNEW OF DISASTER EARLY

Alexander Arthur Gordon, R. N. R., a retired engineer, who has been in the White Star line service for seventeen years and who occupies an apartment with Port Captain W. M. Smith at No. 938 Hudson street, Hoboken, confirmed the report yesterday that he had received the first official news that the Titanic was sinking at half-past three o'clock Monday morning. The message was given to Mr. Gordon by the White Star line, he says, with the understanding that he was to find Captain Smith and give it to him.

"I knew of the serious condition of the Titanic on Monday morning at half-past three o'clock," said Mr. Gordon, "and I can give no reason why the true state of affairs was kept from the public for so long. Captain Smith, of the White Star line, shares quarters with us here and the message I received was for him. I was in bed when the telephone rang at half-past two o'clock and I hopped up and answered it. A voice asked for Captain Smith, and when I said he was not in the man hung up the receiver. The telephone rang again at half-past three and again I answered. A voice informed me that the White Star line was talking and that they wanted Captain Smith at once. I told them he was away for the night. I told them who I was and they asked me to find the Captain at once and tell him that the Titanic was down by the head, sinking fast and that the passengers were being taken off in boats.

"Immediately I started telephoning for Captain Smith, and while I was trying to find him Mr. Ridgeway, of the White Star company, called me up and told me to tell Captain Smith to report at the office immediately. I finally got in communication with the Captain in Brooklyn and gave him the message."

THE TITANIC'S MEN GO TO WASHINGTON

In care of E. L. Cornelius, assistant sergeant-at-arms of the Senate, the four surviving officers and twenty-eight of the crew of the Titanic started for Washington yesterday afternoon.

J. Bruce Ismay left by the same train. P. A. S. Franklin, vice president of the White Star line, who probably will be called to the stand to-day, went by a later train.

J. Parker Kirlin, who is associated with Charles C. Burlingham as counsel for the White Star line, took the half-past twelve o'clock train this morning for Washington. He said that Mr. Burlingham would remain here.

Senators William Alden Smith and Francis G. Newlands, who conducted the first sessions of the investigation as representatives of the Senate committee, arrived in Washington early yesterday.

Daniel M. Ransdell, sergeant-at-arms of the Senate, remained in this city until five o'clock yesterday afternoon.

"No subpoenas have been issued," Captain Ransdell said, "other than for those persons named yesterday. The government, of course, will pay all travelling and maintenance expenses of witnesses summoned to Washington.

"Mrs. John Jacob Astor, Mrs. George D. Widener, Mrs. J. B. Thayer, Colonel Archibald Gracie and others prominently named in the list of survivors probably will be requested to appear and give their versions of the disaster. The progress of the investigation will determine what other persons will be called."

FIND THIRTY MILES OF ICE IN PATH THE TITANIC FOLLOWED

SENT NO FALSE WORD, SAYS CAPTAIN OF THE VIRGINIAN

Commander of Allan Line Vessel Unable to Account for Report of Towing the Titanic.

SPED TOWARD SCENE ON GETTING SIGNAL

Advised by the Californian to Resume Course When the Carpathia Made Rescues.

PASSED NEAR SHIP'S GRAVE

Saw No Wreckage, but Many Icebergs, He Reports on Reaching Liverpool.

(From Yesterday's Evening Telegram.)
[SPECIAL DESPATCH TO THE EVENING TELEGRAM VIA COMMERCIAL CABLE COMPANY'S SYSTEM.]

LIVERPOOL, Sunday.—Captain Gambell, of the Allen line steamship Virginian, which arrived here to-day, reports that he received a wireless message from Cape Race at forty minutes after twelve o'clock on Monday morning saying that the Titanic had struck an iceberg and wanted immediate assistance. Captain Gambell altered his course to go to her aid. He was in communication with the steamships Californian, Carpathia, Frankfurt and Baltic. The Californian replied:—

"Can see the Carpathia taking passengers aboard from boats."

At ten o'clock in the evening, he said, he received a message from the Carpathia, saying:—"Turn back. Everything O. K. Have eight hundred on board. Return to your northern track."

Captain Gambell then proceeded eastward, and when he later sighted a field of close-packed ice he changed his course to avoid it.

Captain Gambell says he can throw no light on the false messages to the effect that the Virginian had the Titanic in tow and that other steamships were standing by.

He says he passed the place where the Titanic disappeared at a distance of six or seven miles, but saw no boats or wreckage. Captain Gambell said he lost 160 miles in trying to reach the Titanic.

SAYS THE FRANKFURT WENT TO RESCUE

BREMEN, Sunday.—The North German Lloyd Steamship Company has issued the following statement after having taken under advisement the statement made by Harold S. Bride, the assistant wireless operator of the Titanic, regarding the steamer Frankfurt:—

"We sent a wireless message to the Frankfurt and have just received the following reply:—'The steamer Frankfurt turned north immediately after getting the signal of distress, and arrived at ten minutes to eleven at the scene of the disaster. The distance was 140 miles. We found the steamers Birma, Virginian and Carpathia there. 'HATTORF.'"

Captain Hattorf is commander of the Frankfurt. According to the testimony of Bride before the Senate investigating committee, the first reply to the Titanic's call for help was received from the Frankfurt.

"We sent the C Q D," said Bride, "and the Frankfurt answered. We sent our position and the Frankfurt replied, 'Stand by.' About twenty minutes later the Frankfurt asked 'What's the matter?' We answered, 'You're a fool; stand off and don't interfere.'"

Bride went on to testify that they had asked for the position of the Frankfurt and that the only answer was "Stand by."

FRANCE TO CO-OPERATE ON SAFETY MEASURE

HERALD BUREAU,
No. 1,502 H STREET, N. W.,
WASHINGTON, D. C., Sunday.

Mons. Jusserand, the French Ambassador, called on Senator Smith this afternoon and extended congratulations on the good already accomplished by the inquiry into the Titanic wreck. He said that the French government stood ready to aid and co-operate in every way possible to insure the greater safety of transatlantic travel.

An international marine conference similar to that of 1889 in Washington will be held undoubtedly within a short time. Resolutions have been reported favorably in Congress authorizing the President to invite the maritime nations to participate. Those most active in urging the conference have been gratified at the news from Berlin that the German government was favorable to the idea. The statement of the French Ambassador has caused further satisfaction.

In discussing means to bring about greater safety to passengers and crews Senator Smith and Ambassador Jusserand dwelt upon these points:—

First, more life boats, such as will be adequate to accommodate every person on board.

Second, the adoption of a more southerly route for ships to avoid icebergs.

Third, a requirement that two wireless operators shall be carried on each vessel.

When the wireless conference meets in London in June such a regulation will be pressed for adoption. The narrative of Harold T. Cottam, the wireless operator on board the Carpathia, which revealed how he came within a moment or two of missing the C. Q. D. signal of the Titanic, will be quoted to emphasize the need of having an operator on duty constantly.

BRAZIL SENDS SYMPATHY.

[BY MEXICAN CABLE TO THE HERALD.]

RIO JANEIRO, via GALVESTON, Texas, Sunday.—The Chamber of Deputies to-day adopted a resolution of condolence for the loss of the Titanic and sent it to the governments of the United States and Great Britain.

ICEBERG FIELD SKETCHED WHERE THE TITANIC SANK

ICEBERGS SKETCHED BY AN OFFICER OF THE SAVOIE ON APRIL 18 (THREE DAYS AFTER DISASTER) IN RUN OF THIRTY MILES, ALMOST ON THE SPOT WHERE THE TITANIC SANK—BERG IN LOWER LEFT HAND CORNER IS SUPPOSED BY THE SAVOIE'S OFFICERS TO BE THE ONE THE WHITE STAR STEAMSHIP STRUCK.

The Savoie, French Steamship, Passes Through Vast Flotilla Where Disaster Occurred.

NO TRACE OF WRECK

Passing over the scene of the wreck of the Titanic on Wednesday morning, three days after the disaster, the steamship Savoie, of the Compangie Générale Transatlantique, which arrived at New York yesterday, encountered a field of icebergs and "growlers" thirty miles wide and extending north and south for hundreds of miles. The great berg upon which the Titanic struck, distinguished from the others by its two pinnacles, was seen four miles south of the spot where the wreck occurred, its drift being little more than a mile a day.

News of the disaster had been received by the passengers of the Savoie on Monday, together with the warning that a dangerous field of icebergs lay directly in the path of the steamship. Signs of ice were observed by a distinct lowering of the temperature on Tuesday night and early on Wednesday morning, the Savoie entered the ice zone at quarter speed.

Passengers crowded the decks for hours, and at about noon the position of the ship was latitude 41 degrees 33 minutes north and longitude 52 degrees 20 minutes west, almost the precise spot where the Titanic foundered. The sea was searched in every direction for possible survivors floating upon rafts or for bodies or wreckage, but not a sign of the disaster was visible.

"We searched the sea for miles with our glasses, but saw nothing but icebergs and floating ice," said an officer of the Savoie, who sketched the scene for the HERALD. "We counted thirty-five icebergs all grouped within a radius of four miles, some being unusually large, and several larger than any of the crew of the Savoie ever had seen before. One of these, a two-pinnacled berg one hundred feet or more high, was especially beautiful, but we did not realize until we reached New York that it was this berg in all probability that gave the Titanic her death wound. It had drifted only four miles in three days, but we were told that the drift of the bergs in the latitude where the Titanic sank was quite slow, because of their tremendous bulk under the surface.

"From the description of the iceberg given by one of the survivors to the HERALD we are sure that the berg we saw to the southward of our course was the one which sank the Titanic. Scores of photographs were taken of the larger ones we passed, but the two pinnacled berg was too far away for that. The Savoie wormed her way through the flotilla. Then we went forward at full headway, leaving the icebergs in our wake. The line extended as far as we could see on both the northern and southern horizons and, illuminated by the rays of the setting sun, formed a spectacle of grandeur seldom witnessed on the high seas."

Officers of the Savoie said the number of bergs crossing the southern route of the transatlantic lines was remarkable for this season and that in extent and size of the bergs it was unparalleled. During the passage through the flotilla several of the smaller bergs came into collision with each other with the result that all of them were badly ground. The crash was plainly heard at a distance of two miles when one of the smaller bergs was split in half, each portion tumbling about at a lively rate until its floating equilibrium had been restored.

Officers of all transatlantic lines regard the bergs as a menace to navigation, but none is able to say just how long they will continue to float out of the frozen north. Those encountered by the Savoie ranged in color from milk white to sapphire, but all indicated that they would hold their own against the elements until the Gulf Stream and warmer latitudes of the south were encountered.

Lady Rothes Describes the Horror of Survivors' Chase of Phantom Light

"Rowing, Rowing Toward Beacon That Disappeared in the Night," She Says.

Distinguished Woman Who Helped Pull Lifeboat Pays Tribute to Captain Smith.

COUNTESS OF ROTHES

"The pitiful sadness of our rowing, rowing toward the lights of a ship that disappeared. We in boat No. 8 saw some tramp steamer's mast head lights, and then we saw the glow of red as she swung toward us for a few minutes. Then darkness and despair."

Lady Rothes yesterday, at the Ritz Carlton, told of her experiences on board the Titanic.

"I went to bed at half-past seven," she said, "and my cousin, Miss Gladys Cherry, who shared my room—No. 77 on deck B.—also retired. It was bitterly cold. I was awakened by a slight jar and then a grating noise. I turned on the light and saw that it was 11:46, and I wondered at the sudden quiet. Gladys had not been awakened and I called her and asked did she not think it strange that the engines had stopped. As I opened our cabin door I saw a steward. He said we had struck some ice. Our fur coats over our night gowns were all the clothes we had. My cousin asked the chief steward if there was any danger and he answered, 'Oh, no, we have just grazed some ice and it does not amount to anything.'

The Call for Lifebelts.

"As we hurried along Lambert Williams came up and explained that the watertight compartments must surely hold. Just then an officer hurried by.

"'Will you all get lifebelts on! Dress warmly and come up to A deck!' Quite stunned by the order, we all went. As I was going in to our stateroom my maid said water was pouring into the racquet court. I gave her some brandy, tied on her lifebelt and told her to go straight up on deck. We had to ask a steward where our lifebelts could be found. The man said he was sure they were unnecessary until we told him we had been ordered to do so.

"We dressed as warmly as we could and went up to A deck. Mr. Brown, the purser, touched his hat as we passed, saying:—'It is quite all right; don't hurry!' What a lovely night it was! I stood close to Mrs. Astor. She was waiting under the starboard ports of the library and her husband got a chair for her. She was quite calm. The last I saw of Colonel Astor was when he still stood by his wife, trying to comfort her.

"Captain Smith stood shoulder to shoulder with me as I got into the life boat, and his last words were to the lone seaman—Tom Jones—'Row straight for those ship lights over there; leave your passengers on board of her and return as soon as you can.' Captain Smith's whole attitude was one of great calmness and courage, and I am sure he thought that the ship—whose lights we could plainly see—would pick us up and that our life boats would be able to do double duty in ferrying passengers to the help that gleamed so near.

"There were two stewards in boat No. 8 with us and thirty-one women. The name of the steward was Crawford. We were lowered quietly to the water, and when we had pushed off from the Titanic's side I asked the seaman is he would care to have me take the tiller, as I knew something about boats. He said, 'Certainly, lady.' I climbed aft into the stern sheets and asked my cousin to help me.

"The first impression I had as we left the ship was that above all things we must not lose our self-control. We had no officer to take command of our boat, and the little seaman had to assume all the responsibility. He did it nobly, alternately cheering us with words of encouragement, then rowing doggedly. Then Signora de Satode Penasco began to scream for her husband. It was too horrible. I left the tiller to my cousin and slipped down beside her to be of what comfort I could. Poor woman! Her sobs tore our hearts and her moans were unspeakable in their sadness. Miss Cherry stayed at the tiller of our boat until the Carpathia picked us up.

"The most awful part of the whole thing was seeing the rows of portholes vanishing one by one. Several of us—and Tom Jones—wanted to row back and see if there was not some chance of rescuing any one that had possibly survived, but the majority in the boat ruled, that we had no right to risk their lives on the bare chance of finding any one alive after the final plunge. They also said that the captain's own orders had been to 'row for those ship lights over there,' and that we who wished to try for others who might be drowning had no business to interfere with his orders. Of course that settled the matter, and we rowed on.

"Indeed, I saw—we all saw— a ship's lights not more than three miles away!"

Turning to Lord Rothes, Lady Rothes said:—"I am a fair judge of distances, am I not?" He answered, "Yes, you are."

The Lights Disappear.

Continuing, Lady Rothes said:—

"For three hours we pulled steadily for the two masthead lights that showed brilliantly in the darkness. For a few minutes we saw the ship's port light, then it vanished, and the masthead lights got dimmer on the horizon until they, too, disappeared.

"A Mrs. Smith did yeoman service. She rowed for five hours with Tom Jones without taking a rest. Really, she was magnificent, not only in her attitude, but in the whole souled way in which she worked.

"Mrs. Pearson also rowed, and my maid, Roberta Maloni, rowed the last half of the night.

"I did not know Mr. Ismay by sight, until one night at dinner in the restaurant he came in late, and some one pointed him out to me as being the managing director of the line. There was no excitement of any kind, save that once the third class passengers became obsteperous, but it was instantly put down.

"When the awful end came, I tried my best to keep the Spanish woman from hearing the agonizing sounds of distress. They seemed to continue forever, although it could not have been more than ten minutes until the silence of a lonely sea dropped down. The indescribable loneliness, the ghastliness of our feelings never can be told. We tried to keep in touch with the other boats by shouting, and succeeded fairly well. Our boat was the furthest away because we had chased the phantom lights for three hours. Yes, I rowed for three hours."

Roberta Maloni, the maid, said:—

"I was not at all frightened. Everybody was saying as we left the ship that 'she was good for twelve hours yet' and I was too numb to realize the terror of it all until we were safe on board the Carpathia."

"Brave men, all that stood back so that women should have at least a chance to live!" said Lady Rothes. "Their memories should be held sacred in the mind of the world forever."

TOUCH OF PITY, ALL AKIN.

Louis Kappel, a Newark restaurant waiter, who shipped as a steward on board the Carpathia, has high praise for the work of the Carpathia's officers, crew and passengers in caring for the passengers of the Titanic. He says that long before the Carpathia reached the scene of disaster she had been transformed into a hospital ship, and that after the rescues had been made the wealthy first cabin passengers of the Carpathia acted as stewards and stewardesses and vied with each other in caring for the survivors. Most of the rescued women, he says, wore only nightgowns, kimonos or other light clothing and were suffering intensely from cold and hunger.

SHIP'S SURGEON DIED AS HE WISHED

Dr. O'Loughlin Was Famed for His Kindness to Passengers and Crew.

DR. WILLIAM FRANCIS NORMAN O'LOUGHLIN

PHOTO by BRADLEY

In accounts printed about the Titanic and the bravery of her officers little has been said of one who probably was the most widely known and best beloved by all classes. He was Dr. William Francis Norman O'Loughlin, senior surgeon of the White Star line, who perished with the ship.

During the forty years Dr. O'Loughlin had been a surgeon aboard ships of that line he gained the close friendship of innumerable men and women of prominence. Known as one of the most upright and kindly men, he also was regarded as a leader in his profession and a student of the highest order.

Survivors say they saw Dr. O'Loughlin on Deck D going from one to another of the frightened passengers soothing them and aiding them in getting into the lifeboats. As the last lifeboat left the vessel he was seen standing in a companionway beside the chief steward, the purser and another officer, swinging a life belt. He was heard to say:—

"I don't think I'll need to put this on."

He was in the companionway when the vessel went down.

From those who knew him well, statements were obtained yesterday regarding the fine character of the friend all were mourning. All agreed he was one of the kindest men they ever had met. Many incidents showing his unselfishness were related. One of the friends said:—

"He was the strongest personal friend of every officer and seaman he ever left a port with, and he was a most thorough officer. He would give his last dollar to charity, and was never known to speak ill of any one. He was the most tender hearted man I ever met."

One of Dr. O'Loughlin's intimate friends in the profession was Dr. Edward C. Titus, medical director of the White Star line. He said:—

"Dr. O'Loughlin was undoubtedly the finest man that I have ever known. Kind at all times, his work among the persons he met endeared him forever to them. Always ready to answer a call for aid at all hours of the day and night, he would go into the steerage to attend an ill mother or child, and they would receive as much consideration from him as the wealthiest and mightiest on board.

"He was one of the best read men I ever met. Dr. O'Loughlin was always doing some charitable act. Of his income I believe it will be found that he left little, having distributed most of it among the poor. There is no doubt that he died as he wished. Once recently I said to him that as he was getting on in years he ought to make a will and leave directions for his burial, as he had no kith or kin. He replied that the only way he wanted to be buried was to be placed in a sack and buried at sea."

Dr. O'Loughlin was a native of Ireland. Left an orphan he was raised and educated by an uncle. He studied at Trinity College, Dublin, and the Royal College of Surgeons in Dublin. When twenty-one years old he went to sea because of ill health and followed the sea continuously thereafter. Prior to being transferred to the Titanic he was surgeon on board the Olympic.

There will be a solemn mass of requiem for Dr. O'Loughlin in St. Patrick's Cathedral to-morrow morning at ten o'clock.

SUCTION OF SHIP SAVED HIS LIFE

Peter Dallas Daly, a survivor of the Titanic disaster, who is at the Hotel Victoria, asserts that the suction from the ship as she made her final plunge to the bottom of the ocean is responsible for his rescue from the water later by a collapsible boat.

"There was a suction created as the Titanic sank," said Mr. Daly. "It drove me through the water more than one hundred feet.

"I remained on board the Titanic talking with Howard B. Case, who went down with the ship, never to return. Mr. Case displayed remarkable courage and was absolutely indifferent to our danger. We were on the starboard side of the Titanic and saw many persons enter the lifeboats. I saw a man, whose name I do not care to mention, forcibly enter the second boat that was lowered from the starboard side, regardless of the order to allow the women and children to enter the lifeboats first. This man now says he left in one of the last boats.

"There is the exact time that the Titanic sank," declared Mr. Daly, as he pointed to the dial of a watch which he drew from his pocket." The watch had stopped at 2:20:40. "I set that watch by the ship's clock just before I went to bed, which was nine o'clock that night."

Mr. Daly will start to his home in Lima, Peru, on Thursday.

PRAISE THE HERALD AS LEADING ALL OTHER JOURNALS IN NEWS OF THE TITANIC'S FATE

[SPECIAL DESPATCH TO THE HERALD.]

PITTSFIELD, Mass., Sunday.—There was a tremendous demand for the NEW YORK HERALD to-day throughout the Berkshire region. Newsdealers here were unable to supply the demand and the same was true in the smaller resort towns. Ever since last Monday morning, when the HERALD beat all the other New York newspapers with the news that the Titanic was calling for help, discriminating readers in this section have praised its enterprise. They say it has led all the other newspapers in its comprehensive and interesting presentation of the greatest news story in a generation.

MEN WHO HELPED BUILD HER STUCK

Survivors Have High Praise for Thomas Andrews, Jr., Representative of the Constructors.

THOMAS ANDREWS, JR.

Among the representatives of Harland & Wolff, builders of the Titanic, who were aboard the steamship was Thomas Andrews, Jr., member of the Board of Directors, who had been in charge of designing the vessel and had superintended her construction. Mr. Cummings, another director, who built the engines and was regarded as one of the leading engine builders of the world, was aboard with ten master mechanics. According to the testimony of passengers, all these men stuck to their posts and lost their lives.

James M. Montgomery, of this city, a relative of Mr. Andrews, said yesterday:—

"On the night of the arrival of the Carpathia I interviewed the second, third and fourth officers, who assured me that Mr. Andrews had assisted in the launching of the lifeboats, and the last they saw of him was on deck A throwing chairs overboard to passengers who were struggling in the water. He did not even try to save himself, thinking only of the others.

Tried to Avert Panic.

"Several of the survivors stated that after the vessel struck the iceberg Mr. Andrews repeatedly went to the engine room to ascertain the damage and report to Captain Smith. It was he who called the passengers together and in deliberate tones told them to be calm, to return to their staterooms, don their life preservers and come back to the deck. He went from lifeboat to lifeboat, assisting in launching the craft, being familiar with the tackle and everything connected with the boats. He did everything possible to avert a panic and save lives.

"Mr. Andrews entered the employ of the Harland & Wolff Shipbuilding Company when sixteen years old and worked his way through the various departments. He finally became a director of the company in charge of designing and was familiar with every detail of the construction of the Titanic. He was accustomed to go on the first trip with most of the steamships of the line with master mechanics from the yard. He was the special representative of the builders and stood by his post to the last. He was thirty-eight years old and leaves a widow and a young daughter."

These statements regarding Mr. Andrews were borne out by Albert A. Dick, of Calgary, Alberta, who, with his wife, was a passenger aboard the Titanic.

"It is against my own desire to make any statement on this matter," said Mr. Dick yesterday, "but I wish to say a few words through the medium of the HERALD on account of incorrect quotations of words attributed to my wife. Many things she is supposed to have said she never did say.

"With regard to Mr. Andrews, he knew that he would lose his life, and yet he behaved so nobly that his heroism is worthy of the greatest praise, as he certainly knew the danger we were in, yet voluntarily sacrificed his life. At the time of the accident my wife and I were in our berths. We dressed and went on deck. The Captain and Mr. Andrews went down to investigate the damage. I saw them coming up from the bottom of the vessel looking anxious a few minutes afterward.

"We were standing on the hurricane deck when Mr. Andrews came up and calmly and earnestly told all to go to their cabins and put on the life belts which they would find on the tops of the wardrobes and get back on deck quickly. We followed out these instructions, and I helped a few women. Several persons were manning the boats and placing water and food in them.

"The first boat was lowered in an orderly manner, the passengers not displaying any anxiety to get into it. After the first boat was lowered the order was issued not to let the men get in. My wife refused to leave me as boat after boat went down, but as the sixth boat was being lowered and as she still refused to leave me the officers pushed us in together.

Expected to Return to Vessel.

"So far as I could perceive, everything was as orderly as could be. Real difficulty was experienced in getting the women to enter the boats. A woman in our boat told me that J. Bruce Ismay behaved with remarkable coolness, and that she had been placed in by his own hands.

"So far as concerns the large proportion of the crew of the Titanic having been rescued, I must say that those men in the boat in which we found ourselves were confident of going back to the Titanic again. I counted the lights from the front and the rear of the boat, and soon perceived that she was going down. I know from men whose word I can believe that long after the boats had left the vessel the men who had remained aboard the Titanic were smoking cigars and thinking of no real danger.

"One young Englishman shook hands with them and jumped overboard. I noticed that the stern stayed up a few minutes longer than the bow. It is not true that the lights went out soon after the accident, for I noticed that the lights were not extinguished until five or ten minutes before the vessel actually went down."

WAIFS OF THE SEA STILL A MYSTERY

Apparently happy in their surroundings and grateful for every little attention the two little waifs who were found in the lifeboat of the Titanic in which Miss Margaret Hays was placed are spending their time in play at the home of Mr. Frank K. Hays, No. 304 West Eighty-third street, not in the least concerned over the fact that their identity is still a mystery. They call each other Louis and Lola, but do not seem to know any other names.

Mons. Etienne Lanel, the French Consul General, has spoken with the little fellows, but found their pronunciation a dialect of French that suggested they might have come from Switzerland or some place where the language is not spoken purely by nurses and other servants who might have had the care of the boys.

The Consul General will send out inquiries everywhere that French is spoken in hopes of attracting the attention of parents or relatives of the boys who may recognize the descriptions and pictures.

The youngsters, who are about two and a half years and three and a half years old, are winning the hearts of their protectors and all who meet them, and are in excellent health. They like to play with toy boats and miniature automobiles. They also like to ride in automobiles and enjoyed a long ride about the city yesterday with Mr. Hays and his daughter.

THOUSANDS ATTEND MEMORIAL SERVICES FOR THE VICTIMS

CHURCH THRONGS PRAY FOR DEAD OF THE TITANIC

Scenes of Deep Emotion at Memorial Services Throughout the City.

MANY CONGREGATIONS MOURN FOR MEMBERS

Parents of Drowned Youth Recite Prayers with Rabbi at Carnegie Hall.

PASTORS POINT LESSONS

See in Christianity the Source of Heroism and Self-Sacrifice of Vessel's Victims.

In every place of public worship in New York city and in many cities throughout the country prayers were offered yesterday for the Titanic's dead. Special memorial services were held in many churches, but the manifestation of the public's grief was general wherever persons gathered together to pray.

Many congregations in this city had intimate cause to mourn in the loss of those who had worshipped among them. But the expression of sorrow was no less keen among those who felt only the common grief which the disaster has caused throughout the world.

The pitch of emotion to which last Monday's tragedy has wrought the public was shown by many unrestrained demonstrations of grief. None seemed ashamed to withhold the tribute of tears. In the Cathedral of St. John the Divine a man fainted as Bishop Greer preached. In Trinity sobs were audible in the great church throughout Dr. Manning's address. In the Free Synagogue, in Carnegie Hall, the congregation wept when the parents of Benjamin Forman, a young banker, who died aboard the Titanic, stood up to recite with the rabbi the beautiful prayer of the Talmud for those who have passed.

Prayers in Catholic Churches.

One thousand persons with tear stained faces left the Church of St. Catherine of Genoa, in West 153d street, after an impromptu memorial service of striking simplicity and impressiveness. The Catholic ritual does not provide for requiem services on Sunday, and yesterday the announcement was made at all masses throughout the dioceses that the ritualistic prayer for the dead would be read at the end of mass, and that to-day, at nine o'clock, a solemn mass of requiem would be celebrated in all Catholic churches.

The Rev. P. A. McCorry, pastor of St. Catherine's, turned to the congregation after mass and spoke of the Titanic disaster. After sketching the story of the wreck and lauding the heroism of those who died he spoke of the solace the Christian world should find in the fact that those who went down to death were singing "Nearer, My God, to Thee."

"Let us hope," he said, "that the Infinite Father regarded the singing of those sacred words, a profession of faith, not complete, but ample under the terrible conditions."

Then he repeated slowly the words of the hymn and asked that his hearers join in singing it. Led by the choir the entire congregation stood up and sang the hymn with deep emotion. At the end tears were streaming from the eyes of every one in the edifice.

Churches All Thronged.

In all the churches an unusual attendance testified to the public's recognition of the occasion as an opportunity to participate in the office of mourning. Hundreds were turned away from the Cathedral of St. John the Divine, from St. Thomas' Protestant Episcopal Church and many other places where special memorial services had been announced. The tenor of all the sermons was in praise of the heroism of the men who faced death calmly that their wives and children might be saved, but there was denunciation too for the neglect that caused avoidable loss of life and demand for laws to safeguard the public against official short-sightedness and greed.

At St. Bartholomew's, where Mr. P. A. S. Franklin, of the White Star line, is a pewholder, the Rev. Dr. Leighton Parks, without mentioning him by name, referred to him in his remarks, saying he was sure the congregation felt the most profound sympathy and respect for their friend and brother in the heavy load of labors and anxieties that had come upon him in the last week.

Dr. Parks took his text from Corinthians, "Quit ye like men, be strong." He spoke of the shipwrecks mentioned in Holy Writ, showing that in each case those on board sought to sacrifice some one. No shipload of persons of ancient Greece or Rome would have thought of giving preference to women and children in time of danger. That men did so to-day was because Christianity had been leavening society and changing its standards for nineteen hundred years.

Tribute to Womanhood.

Speaking of the sacrifice of the men aboard the Titanic, he said the women did not ask for the sacrifice, but it was made. "Those women who go shrieking about for their 'rights' want something very different," he said. "Put the world on a basis merely of 'rights' and you put it on an inclined plane where it will never stop until it has gone down to the lowest level of barbarism and bestiality.

"These men gave up their lives in love, and in so doing they helped to pay the debt we all owe to the mothers who bore and suckled us, to the sweethearts that have kept us pure, to the wives and friends, who have suffered and sacrificed themselves for us."

Twenty classmates of Major Archibald W. Butt at the University of the South, Sewaneee, Tenn., attended a memorial service for him yesterday in St. Mark's Church, Second avenue and Tenth street, where the Rev. W. N. Guthrie, a classmate, preached the sermon. After the service a committee consisting of Dr. John P. H. Hutchin, Beverly Wrenn, T. Channing Moore, Robert B. Elliott and W. M. Puckette, was appointed to draw up resolutions of sympathy and send them to Major Butt's family.

Sees God's Judgment.

Oscar Straus and his son and daughter attended the memorial service in the Church of the Divine Paternity, where many of the congregation had lost friends in the disaster. Dr. Frank Oliver Hall, the pastor, said:—"Considering all the theories that might be advanced—the truth of the matter is there is some of God's judgment in the accidents that we make by our own heedlessness and ignorance. It is that judgment that says we must take the consequences of our greed for gold and for speed records. If God had placed His hand under that ship and sent it back to shore safely we would be depending upon miracles for safety in our ocean travel instead of depending upon not violating the natural laws that God has set up."

In Trinity Church Dr. Manning at the close of his sermon read three prayers; the first for the survivors, the second for the dead, the third for the families and friends of the dead. In his remarks Dr. Manning said:—"In times of great disaster like this, we realize that God is our comfort and our strength. Think of that tenderness, that spirit of self-sacrifice which caused the men aboard the Titanic to step aside and make way for the women and children. Such tenderness is the greatest message we have from the Cross. Before Christ laid down His life to save others such a spirit was unknown in the world."

Services in Carnegie Hall.

At the service of the Free Synagogue in Carnegie Hall Abraham I. Elkus spoke of the loss of the Titanic and said:—"It will be a long time before the world will forget the quiet and manly heroism of Isidor Straus and the wifely devotion of Mrs. Straus, who refused to be saved without him with whom she had lived most happily for forty years."

Rabbi Emil G. Hirsch, of Chicago, said in his address:—"The Jew knows how to live—as is clearly shown all about us in this work-a-day world. It goes without saying he knows how to die. A moment like that which the world witnessed the other day, with many a home wreathed in sombre mourning and many a heart weighed down in sorrow, shows us that the Jew knows how to die."

At the Madison Avenue Reformed Church the Rev. William Carter preached a memorial sermon, proclaiming the heroism of the passengers and crew and denouncing the man who, as head of all the fleet, took to the lifeboat and left the vessel and passengers to their fate. The collection, amounting to $400, was turned over to the Women's Relief Committee. After service the congregation adopted resolutions asking the government to join with other governments to place the blame for the accident.

At the Church of the Incarnation an anniversary service to commemorate the founding of the church eighty years ago was postponed for a service of requiem.

Makes for Brotherhood.

The Rev. Junius B. Remensnyder, pastor of St. James' Lutheran Church, preached from the text, "Thy way is in the sea and thy path in the deep waters and thy footsteps are not known." He said the lessons of such crucial tests was that in eliciting world wide expressions of sympathy they banish prejudices, belittle jealousies and reveal the essential brotherhood of the race.

In St. Andrew's Episcopal Church the processional hymn was omitted and the choir entered to the strains of Chopin's Funeral March. The Rev. Dr. George R. Vandewater preached a memorial sermon in which he paid high tribute to Captain Smith, of the Titanic, who had been his friend.

At a memorial service in the Messiah Swedish Lutheran Church, in the Bronx, it was announced that of one hundred Swedes aboard the Titanic only a few were saved. Prayers for the victims were offered.

Before his sermon at the Fifth Avenue Presbyterian Church the Rev. G. A. Johnston Ross, of Montreal, read a resolution of sympathy for all those bereaved through the Titanic disaster.

TRIBUTE TO ARTHUR RYERSON

[SPECIAL DESPATCH TO THE HERALD.]

ALBANY, N. Y., Sunday.—Bishop Doane preached at All Saints' Cathedral to-day upon the lessons of the Titanic disaster. He paid especial tribute to Arthur Ryerson, late of Cooperstown, who was a member of the General Board of Missions of the Albany diocese. Continuing, the Bishop said:—

"Here are men striving and struggling with the one single end in view of getting money, more and more money, for investment and luxurious expenditure, instead of taking time to build up character and life along high and noble lines—and in a moment, in a twinklinfi of an eye, this moey they have spent their lives in gaining is swept away and gone."

SPEED TO BLAME, SAYS W. J. BRYAN

LEWIS NIXON · RABBI J. SILVERMAN · WILLIAM JENNINGS BRYAN · SCENE AT MEMORIAL SERVICE BROADWAY THEATRE

Race Not to the Swift, He Declares at Memorial Service in Broadway Theatre.

NEW LAWS ARE URGED

Resolutions Presented by Lewis Nixon Demanding More Stringent Regulations Are Adopted.

Urging that salutary laws be enacted to prevent as far as possible the wanton sacrifice of lives at sea, William J. Bryan, Frederick Townsend Martin, Rabbi Joseph Silverman, the Rev. David G. Wylie, Lewis Nixon and other speakers made addresses at the Titanic memorial services in the Broadway Theatre yesterday afternoon. Resolutions favoring stringent laws to safeguard the travelling public on the high seas were adopted. The stage was decorated with American and British flags, both draped with crêpe.

On the stage besides the speakers were the Duchess de Chaulnes, Mrs. Gouverneur Kortright, Miss Lota Robinson, the Rev. H. M. Warren, Captain Wendell Fenton, J. F. Chaplin, Mr. and Mrs. Ormond Smith, Dr. L. L. Seaman and the Rev. Thomas R. Slicer. These resolutions, introduced by Lewis Nixon, were adopted:—

"Resolved, That we urge the immediate adoption and drastic enactment of laws that will require all vessels leaving our ports to install adequate and efficient lifesaving appliances to take care of every person in the boats, and that wireless operators be carried in such numbers as to provide for having an operator always on duty ready to receive and send messages, and that compelling penalties be exacted for failure to answer calls of distress, or to send misleading or false messages, or not to observe special precautions prescribed when warned of danger; and be it further.

"Resolved, That this assemblage, with a deep sense of appreciation of the services to mankind of Guglielmo Marconi, affirm its appreciation of the debt which the entire world owes him."

Mr. Bryan said:—

"This great disaster has shown us the men and women who needed only this emergency to prove them heroes, who were capable of facing death and standing back, saying, 'Before me.' It is easy to be polite when there is no danger, but it is a great trial when death awaits. We should be proud of the bravery and manliness of those who gave way so that others might be saved, while they themselves went down to death."

Mr. Bryan paid a high tribute to the devotion of Mr. and Mrs. Isidor Straus, as well as to the scores of other brave men and women who died because honor and duty could dictate no other course. He declared that without the sacrifice of human lives no great good for humanity can be accomplished. He predicted that the wireless system will be made more effective immediately, and that the disaster will check the mania for speed and luxury and provide more life boats on board steamships. "Ship owners," he said, "must learn that the race is not to the swift, but to those who can carry the lights of life all the way without extinguishing them."

The Rev. Joseph Silverman, of the Temple Emanu-El, said:

"God is not responsible for the Titanic disaster. The blame must lay with those who violated the immutable laws of God. The iceberg had a right to be where it was, but the Titanic, out of its course, had not the right to be in the position that was to engulf it.

"Those responsible for the steamship being out of its course are responsible for the disaster. Those fifteen hundred died martyrs because of the errors of men so that these errors might be corrected. Our consolation is that hard as it was to pay the price, the pice is well paid. This disaster will point the way to a greater civilization and a more enduring humanity."

Dr. David G. Wylie paid a tribute to Mr. Marconi, whom he termed an uncrowned king and the wireless operators, his lieutenants, and said it was criminal not to provide life boats, rafts, preservers and other life saving apparatus for all on board sea going vessels. He urged the enactment of laws to compel ship owners to provide adequately for the safety of those in their charge.

Miss Alice Preston sang Gounod's "Ave Maria," accompanied on the violin by Nahan Franco. Benediction was pronounced by the Rev. H. M. Warren.

SAYS TRAGEDY HAS ENNOBLED MANKIND

Colonel Astor's Pastor Declares Heroism of Those Who Died Was a Sublime Chapter in History.

"Be thou faithful unto death and I will give thee a crown of life," is the text the Rev. Dr. Ernest M. Stires, the rector, took for his sermon yesterday morning in St. Thomas' Episcopal Church. He "justified the ways of God to man," warned of other great tragedies which were sure to happen if man did not pay obedience to the laws of nature.

He paid a tribute to Colonel John Jacob Astor, Major Archibald W. Butt, Arthur Ryerson, of Philadelphia; Mr. and Mrs. Isidor Straus, Mr. Benjamin Guggenheim, Mr. M. J. Clinch Smith, of Chicago, and "those unknown who had no great traditions back of them, but all of whom were known to God."

There was one vacant pew in the crowded church. It was the pew of Colonel John Jacob Astor. There was no mourning on it. There was no explanation. It was a silent explanation of itself.

An offering was taken for the Titanic survivors, and the plates were piled with money.

"There were four women I knew on that boat," said Mr. Stires. "They all returned. There were four men I knew. They did not return.

"I speak of Colonel John Jacob Astor for a reason. His brother was a parishioner here, with a pew in this church. Often have I seen him there by her side in the family pew. He was a pewholder here. He learned how to endure in the Spanish-American War.

"At the last he could look death in the face. He died a brave man. Friends, it is a good epitaph. And brave men the world over will not withhold from him this estimate.

"I speak of Major Butt, a childhood friend of the dearest member of my household and my own friend twenty years. Not in any one of those twenty years have I failed to have a cheery visit from Archie. Much has been said about his character; there has been none too much. He was a soldier, a Christian, a gentleman. This country, the world to-day, is richer because of his life.

"Mr. Ryerson for years was president of St. Luke's Hospital, Chicago, and for fifteen years he was a lay member of the Episcopal Board of Missions, making the trip back and forth once a month to New York to devote himself to this work. He was a true husband, a noble father, a splendid churchman.

"You know the sad errand that was bringing him and his family home. His oldest son had been killed in an accident. And yet you can see the quiet smile of Mr. Ryerson as he put his wife, three children and other women and children into a lifeboat and said 'Farewell.'

"I thank God for the compensation that is coming to us. We do not have to go back to the old times for an example of heroism.

"I speak of Mr. and Mrs. Straus. You see them standing. The picture tells the story. They stood there representing the best and noblest of their race. I speak of Miss Edith Evans, who got out of a lifeboat and gave her seat to a mother because she had children. I speak of Mr. Smith, whom I married fifteen years ago.

"Surely here are lessons awakening the deepest sympathy, inspiring in us the noblest chivalry. They were 'faithful unto death.'

"No more sublime chapter in the world's history was ever written than that which was written last week. The world is a better place. All mankind and womankind is nobler. Faith in human nature is stronger."

SEAMEN ATTEND MEMORIAL SERVICE

The Right Rev. Charles S. Burch Preaches to Mariners on the Titanic Disaster.

Memorial services for the passengers and crew of the Titanic were held last night in the Church of the Holy Comforter, known as the Seamen's Church Institute, at Houston and West street. The congregation was composed principally of seamen and a relief fund for the families of the crew was collected.

The right Rev. Charles Summer Burch delivered the sermon. He said in part:—

"A world bows to-night in sorrow for the greatest marine disaster in its history. The tragedy makes us feel so pitiably small in the great scheme of things that we cannot fully appreciate it. Thousands are staggering to-night under a weight of grief almost too great to bear. Why in all God's providence did it happen we cannot fathom. We ask our hearts, but there is no response. We seek for a reason in this terrible catastrophe, but can only find a lesson. We can only reverently hope that out of the disaster will come some blessing.

"It has brought us to a closer approach of a finer ideal of great sacrifice. The wonderful spectacle a week ago to-night proves that there are real men alive today, and that a majority of them, when it comes to a test, will bear the burdens of the weak.

There are few cowards to-day despite the cry of the pessimist. We do not need any stronger exemplification of this than the story of the Titanic last Sunday night. There we found that man still lives up to the ideal of 'women and children first.'

"Neither must we forget the beautiful heroism of that band of musicians who played 'Nearer, My God, to Thee' in the face of death. What a joy and comfort it must have been to those men in the last moments of their lives. We must not forget the brave women who would not leave the side of their husband, brother, father, or whatever the case might be.

"Nine weeks ago I was called to this church to confirm a class of seamen. In the number was Thomas B. Clark, an able seaman. Little did we think then that a watery grave awaited him so soon. But he went down with the Titanic, proving himself one of God's faithful soldiers to the end. May his soul rest in peace."

The seamen present chorused a loud "Amen" to this tribute.

NO PROTEST MADE TO GREAT BRITAIN

HERALD BUREAU,
No. 1,502 H STREET, N. W.,
WASHINGTON, D. C., Sunday.

Prepared to face the Senate Committee of inquiry into the Titanic disaster thirty of her crew arrived in Washington to-night at fifty-five minutes after seven o'clock. Thirty-five minutes later J. Bruce Ismay, P. A. S. Franklin, vice president of the White Star line, who also have been summoned to reappear before the committee, arrived. The men were taken by Charles W. Lightoller, second officer of the Titanic, to the Continental Hotel, near the Capitol. Mr. Ismay and his party went to the Willard Hotel.

In the party were C. C. Burlinghame, attorney for the White Star line, and his son, a member of the law firm.

At the Union Station, Mr. Ismay was asked:—"Is it true that you or any official of the White Star line has made a protest to the British Embassy or any representative of the British government against the holding of the Titanic's officers or crew in this country?"

"No," said Mr. Ismay. "We have made no protest. We are here to co-operate in every way we can with the United States government in the inquiry and the whole truth will be told."

80 SEAMEN HEAR SERMON ON WRECK

Sailors from the Celtic Listen to the Rev. O. S. Roche Decry Speed Craze.

Eighty seamen from the Celtic, of the White Star line, attended services yesterday morning in St. Peter's Protestant Episcopal church and heard the rector, the Rev. Olin S. Roche, deliver a sermon on the Titanic disaster. Wearing their ship uniform, the seamen attracted much attention. Two women survivors were in the congregation.

"There should be a readjustment of the steamship routes," said the Rev. Mr. Roche. "The shortest route is not the safest route. The world is rich enough in money and vessels so that the steamships can travel in pairs. This arrangement would at least lessen the chance of mishaps.

"Very much of this mad haste and rushing about is unnecessary. Those that go about quietly seem to accomplish just as much. In this city one can hardly walk a block without witnessing some kind of accident. The chauffeur, the careless smoker, all figure in the accidents. It is time that we began to think of the sanctity of human life."

The rector closed by paying a tribute to the heroes aboard the Titanic.

SAYS LOOKOUT WAS ASLEEP ON WATCH

Sailor Charges That Officers Were at a Banquet When Ship Headed for Iceberg.

[SPECIAL DESPATCH TO THE HERALD.]

CLEVELAND, Ohio, Sunday.—Telling a story of lax discipline on board the Titanic, Luis Klein, a sailor who was rescued by the Carpathia, is held here under arrest until he can be taken to Washington to testify in the Senate inquiry.

The man when questioned by Huge E. Varge, the Austrian Vice Consul, said:—

"The night the ship went down," said Klein, "I was doing patrol duty on the promenade deck, starboard side. I took the watch half past nine o'clock and was to have kept it for six hours.

"There was a ball following a banquet of some kind going on down below and the captain and the officers were there with many of the passengers. I thought the company was connected with it somehow.

"After the party, the stewards served the champaigne and other wines that were left over to the crew. I knew that many of them were drunk.

"A passenger standing at the rail of a sudden saw something dead ahead, or maybe a little bit to starboard.

"'Look quick,' he said, 'see the hill over there.' I followed his arm as he pointed, and I saw it was a big iceberg.

"I ran for the bridge. The third officer saw me coming and yelled to me. I ran for the spart with the crew's nest on it and shouted to the lookout I knew was up there to give the alarm.

"Not a word did I hear, so I started up. It was less than a minute before I left the promenade deck that I got to the top of the spar and found the lookout sound asleep. I rang the alarm bell myself."

PRAYERS FOR THE DEAD WITH THE TITANIC

All the Catholic Churches in the Diocese to Hold Special Mass To-Day.

Cardinal Farley was present at solemn high mass in St. Patrick's Cathedral yesterday when the regular prayers for the dead of the Catholic Church were recited for those who had lost their lives aboard the Titanic. Mgr. Hayes read the announcement that a special requiem mass would be offered up for the victims at nine o'clock this morning in every church of the diocese.

Following the special requiem mass in the Cathedral a high mass of requiem will be sung at ten o'clock for the repose of the soul of Dr. William Francis Norman O'Loughlin, who was chief surgeon aboard the Titanic.

The Rev. Charles L. Slattery, rector of Grace Church, will officiate at a memorial service at half-past twelve o'clock noon on Wednesday.

In the Church of the Transfiguration, better known as "The Little Church Around the Corner," the Rev. George C. Houghton will offer a requiem mass at eleven o'clock this morning.

Requiem masses will be offered this morning at eight o'clock and at half-past nine o'clock in the Episcopal Church of St. Mary the Virgin.

BROOKLYN PASTORS EXTOL DEAD HEROES

Clergy of All Sects and Denominations Praise Bravery of Those Who Lost Their Lives.

Hardly a Brooklyn congregation left its church yesterday morning without a vivid impression of the Titanic disaster. Minister, priest, and rabbi were one in expressing their sorrow for those who lost their lives and extending sympathy and condolence to those whose loved ones perished.

Praise for the men who resigned their chances of being saved in favor of women and children was the key note of many a sermon. In more than one prominent church the sermon of the day was given over exclusively to a discussion of the disaster, the remainder of the service being a memorial for those who lost their lives in the disaster. At all of the morning masses in the Catholic churches prayers for the dead were requested from pulpits and mention of the shipwreck was made later in the sermons.

At Plymouth Church the Rev. Newell Dwight Hillis spoke at length upon the heroism of Major Butt and Colonel Astor. At the Central Congregational Church the Rev. Dr. S. Parkes Cadman paid a tribute to Anglo-Saxon manhood—the self-sacrifice of those who lost their lives that the weaker might be saved.

SONS OF ISRAEL AID.

Resolutions of sympathy for the Titanic sufferers and a contribution of $50 were voted at the convention of the Independent Order of the Free Sons of Israel yesterday in the Murray Hill Lyceum. Six hundred delegates were present from all parts of the country. Mayor Gaynor has promised to address the convention to-day, when the sessions will be ended.

Thousands Attend Service in Episcopal Cathedral

BISHOP DAVID H. GREER AT MEMORIAL SERVICE FOR THE VICTIMS OF THE TITANIC IN THE CATHEDRAL OF ST JOHN THE DIVINE

Church on Morningside Heights Is Decked in Mourning and Impressive Music and Prayers Mark Tribute to the Titanic's Victims.

Most impressive of the many notable services that have been held in the new Cathedral of St. John the Divine, on Morningside Heights was that of yesterday in memory of the 1,595 victims of the Titanic disaster.

The great edifice was decked in mourning. Reading desk and pulpit were swathed in purple. On either side of the arch of the chancel massive American and British flags were intertwined and from them hung great streamers of crêpe. In the niches of the choir gallery stood anchors of purple immortelles. The dazzling whiteness of the marble altar was sobered by a screen of Jerusalem palms against which stood a row of lilies.

Many of the early arrivals were gowned in mourning, and later as the church filled the general sombreness of attire was in marked contrast with the usual aspect of the Sunday morning throng.

Fully five thousand persons sought admission to the service, and long before eleven o'clock hundreds were turned away. A solemn requiem service had been prepared by Bishop Greer, with special prayers for the victims and survivors and their families and friends.

The choir and clergy entered to the strains of Mendelssohn's Funeral March, and after the processional hymn a hush of awe fell upon the great congregation as the Bishop's voice was heard reciting the words, "I am the resurrection and the life. * * * They asked life of Thee and Thou gavest them a long life, even forever and forever." Then followed the reading of the psalm, "Lord Thou Hast Been Our Refuge," from the Episcopal burial service, and after the recitation of the lesser litany the congregation knelt while the "De Profundis" was chanted.

Bishop Greer's sermon stirred his hearers deeply and many wiped away tears as he spoke of the sacrificial bravery of the victims—greater far, he declared, than the bravery of men who die on battlefields—and made touching reference to the grief of the bereaved survivors. Bishop Greer touched only once on other aspects of the disaster, but then his words were measured and firm when he said at the outset of his sermon:—"This is certainly not the occasion or the service in which to try to show in what way that disaster on the sea might have been avoided. That time will come. It must come, and come soon. For the public conscience has been stirred by that great disaster, as well as the public heart, and full inquiry must be made into the causes of it. And great will be our blame, criminal will it be, if, when we know them, we fail to do what we can to remedy or remove them."

After the sermon communion service was held and fully one thousand persons approached the altar. The service ended with the singing of Gounod's Resurrection anthem, and, omitting the recessional hymn, the choir and clergy left the cathedral in silence.

Women Leads the Survivors by Her All Abiding Faith

Resolutions of Thanksgiving Adopted Aboard the Carpathia Are Changed to Include Gratitude to "Him from Whom All Blessings Flow."

At a meeting of the survivors, where resolutions were drawn up thanking the captain of the Carpathia, the passengers and all who had help save their lives, the chairman said we wanted every one to feel perfectly free to add to or take from or to make any suggestion whatever before they were formally adopted. The meetin was in the dining salon aboard the Carpathia. There was a general chorus of "They are all right," "Go ahead" and "We will all sign them."

It seemed as if the original copy would be final when a little woman rose. She explained in a low tone that she did not want to appear to be criticising but said she felt that, after all they had experienced, some reference to God and gratitude to the Giver of All should be recorded. The woman was Mrs. F. W. Ryerson.

There was a sudden stillness. As she spoke her timidity seemed to lessen and she proceeded to uggest that instead of beginning as they did, the resolutions should start.

"Whereas in the mercy of Almighty God it has pleased Him to spare our lives."——

Immediately every head waas bowed in the gathering of men and women of many faiths. The silence and the bowed heads was recorder as an unanimous vote for the suggestion. While every rescued man and woman looked on the chairman wrote in:—"Whereas in the mercy of Almighty God it has pleased Him to spare our lives, we do humbly render thanks to our Father in Heaven and to all who have assisted in our rescue."——

Then silently the survivors walked up and signed their names.

This story was told by a woman who was present.

HIS PRAYERS ANSWERED.

A few hours before the Titanic went down the Rev. Charles A. Brown, rector of All Saints' Protestant Episcopal Church, Bayside, L. I., prayed for the safe return of two members of his congregation, Mrs. Robert C. Cornell, wife of Magistrate Cornell, and her sister, Mrs. Edward D. Appleton. Yesterday from the same pulpit Dr. Brown spoke feelingly of the safe return of his parishioners.

"We thank God to-day for the safe return of those for whom last Sunday we offered our prayers that they might be conducted in safety through the perils of the great deep," said Dr. Brown.

"Whatever we may feel about the carrying companies of the world," he said, "whatever we may say about the ship being steered where it ought not to have been, and however we may join in the cry that one great vice of our time is the ever growing spirit of record breaking and record making, one inevitable thing remains for our most serious consideration, and that is death."

GRAPHIC STORIES ARE TOLD BY THOSE WHO FACED DEATH

SUNDAY DOES NOT HALT THE RELIEF WORK OF WOMEN

Committee Keeps Headquarters Open and Continues to Dispense Aid.

MAY COMPLETE ITS WORK TO-DAY

Though yesterday was Sunday work for the relief of the Titanic sufferers went right ahead. The Women's Relief Committee kept its headquarters, room No. 6,007 Metropolitan Building, open for two hours in the afternoon, with Miss Virginia Potter in charge, and additional survivors were provided with clothing, transportation to their homes and funds to last for thirty days. The cases cared for at headquarters are in addition to the survivors who were taken in charge at the pier on the night the Carpathia arrived. The work of providing for the latter has been completed except in a few instances where the survivors are still undecided as to where they will go.

The Women's Relief Committee expects to complete its work of furnishing temporary relief either to-day or to-morrow, when its headquarters will be closed and all its records, together with the balance of the money in the Women's Fund, will be turned over to the Red Cross Emergency Relief Committee, with headquarters in room No. 11, the Arcade, Metropolitan Building. This organization will then begin its work of providing permanent help for those made dependent by the disaster.

Heavy additions to the Mayor's list of contributions are expected to-day, two days' mail coming together. One certain addition will be the sum of $9,425.25 from the Yankee-Giant ball game at the Polo Ground yesterday. Saturday evening the two funds had passed the $100,000 mark. It is predicted that they will reach $150,000 to-day. All this money and much more will be needed by the committee.

In the list of subscriptions received at the Mayor's office $500 credited to William C. Demorest should be credited to the Pilgrims of the United States, of which society Mr. Demorest is treasurer. The error was caused by the check being signed by Mr. Demorest.

The special performance of "Hamlet" for the benefit of the Titanic sufferers, which is to be a repetition of the performance to be given to-morrow afternoon at Wallack's Theatre in celebration of Shakespeare's birthday, will probably take place at Wallack's next Friday afternoon. Mayor Gaynor has written to Mr. Dixie Hines, the director, accepting the company's offer.

The Imperial Order of Daughters of the Empire met at the Hotel Victoria Saturday and passed resolutions of sympathy with the Titanic sufferers and took steps to give assistance in the individual cases that had come under their notice.

Mrs. J. Herman Aldrich, chairman of the Finance Committee of the Women's Relief Committee, has given out the following additional list of contributions:—

Anonymous	30.00
Mrs. C. A. Fuller	5.00
Mrs. Emilie Mazoyen	5.00
Mrs. J. Milton Goetchius	10.00
Mrs. Ferris J. Meigs	10.00
Mrs. E. Brokaw Fischer	50.00
Mrs. Francis Blake	3.00
Mr. George R. Bornheim	50.00
Mr. F. Pasquali	1.00
Mr. Arthur L. Cahn	50.00
Mrs. Kate E. Brush	10.00
Mrs. Alexander S. Porter, Jr.	50.00
Mrs. James E. Munson	5.00
Mrs. W. A. M. Burden	250.00
Mrs. B. Phelps	10.00
Mr. William Hall Penfold	50.00
Mr. Edmund Penfold	50.00
Miss N. K. Lane	10.00
Miss Helen L. Doas	20.00
Mrs. Roza I. Odell	10.00
Mrs. Charles Potter Kling	50.00
Mrs. Frederic Bronson	25.00
Mrs. John Pells	10.00
Mrs. Augustus E. W. Painter	100.00
Mrs. Zella C. Wheeler	25.00
Mrs. Benjamin Brewster	100.00
Mrs. H. O. Chapman	100.00
Mr. Stephen H. Olin	25.00
Miss Augusta Borland Greene	25.00
Miss Caroline M. Merrall	25.00
Mr. James A. Hill	10.00
Mr. Edgar Josephson	2.00
Miss Rachel Noe	10.00
Mr. Francis S. Tilley	5.00
Mr. F. R. Lefferts	50.00
Mr. D. H. Tenney (for 3 Tenneys)	30.00
Mrs. J. J. McCook	10.00
Miss C. Talmage	1.25
Mr. Hiram S. Levine	5.00
Dr. and Mrs. Caroll Dunham	100.00
Mrs. Prescott Lawrence	100.00
Miss Elizabeth Stewart Hamilton	100.00
Henry Egers & Co	10.00
Miss Martha R. White	5.00
Mrs. Louis M. Greer	40.00
Isaac Rosenfield	25.00
Miss Cecelia D. Jonbings	25.00
Mrs. H. H. Curtis	10.00
Mrs. A. Erlanger	100.00
Mrs. Ralph Wolf	5.00
Mrs. Howland Russell	15.00
Mrs. Helen Jennings Silver	10.00
Mrs. Howard Van Sinderen	10.00
Miss Priscilla P. Middleton	5.00
Mrs. Ella A. Tieman	50.00
Mrs. B. C. Megie	5.00
Mr. and Mrs. Ralph Pulitzer	1,000.00
An English Girl	2.00
Eunice F. Faulkner	5.00
Miss E. K. Chamberlayne	5.00
Miss Nettie G. Naumberg	20.00
Mrs. Eleanor Garrigue Ferguson	5.00
Mrs. Geraldyn Redmond	200.00
A. A. C.	5.00
Miss Kate S. Mulford	25.00
Mrs. Henry Fairfield Osborn	50.00
Emma C. Sebring, St. Agath's School	50.00
Mrs. Elizabeth H. Phillips	1.00
Littlefield & Littlefield	75.00
Mrs. Isaac N. Seligman	100.00
A Friend	2.00
E. N. E.	10.00
Miss Marie Strohmeyer	10.00
Mrs. Helen E. Bradbury	10.00
Miss Nora A. Smith	5.00
Mrs. Eugene D. Hawkins	10.00
Mrs. John Duncan Emmet	10.00
Mrs. William Douglas Sloane	1,000.00
Mrs. James Douglas	250.00
Mrs. Eliza C. Tappan	10.00
E. N. T.	1.00
K. T.	5.00
Dr. Emil Schill	5.00
Dr. R. F. Amend	25.00
Mrs. J. A. Moore	200.00
Mrs. de Herozing	5.00
Miss N. Rhoades	25.00
Miss R. Rhoades	25.00
Mrs. Lyman Rhoades, Jr.	5.00
Mrs. S. B. Jackson	15.00
Insurance Friends	61.70
Mrs. Isidor Norman	200.00
Mrs. Bernhard M. Beskow	25.00
Mrs. Caroline A. Gattle	25.00
R. G. R.	2.00
Miss Lota R. Robinson	5.00
Dr. E. L. Keyes	50.00
Mr. James H. Ripley	5.00
Mrs. Henry A. Alexander	100.00
Miss Eleanor Butler Aldrich	25.00
Mrs. Francis Roche	250.00
Mr. A. S. Alcaide, Lucas T. Valdivieso and Carlos McCormick	25.00
Mr. S. R. Bertron	100.00

Flags of Two Nations Must Come Down to Make Way for the Week's Washing

BRITISH AND AMERICAN FLAGS FLYING FROM MRS. M. T. SMITH'S APARTMENT. LIEUTENANT ALEXANDER A GORDON HAULING DOWN THE BRITISH AND AMERICAN FLAGS

Alexander Arthur Gordon, Retired Officer of the White Star Line, Angered When House Owner Objects to American and British Colors Being Hung Afoul of Her Clotheslines.

A controversy over British and American flags floating at half staff from the rear of a fashionable apartment at No. 938 Hudson street, Hoboken, threatened to cause serious complications yesterday when Mrs. M. T. Smith, who rents the apartment, was ordered to take them down by Mrs. A. Weller, of No. 936 Hudson street, the owner of the building.

Captain William Smith, superintendent of the White Star line docks, and Alexander Arthur Gordon, a retired engineer officer of the White Star line, also reside in the Smith apartment. Mr. Gordon's brother-in-law, Robert C. Hesketh, was second engineer on board the Titanic and was lost. The disaster came home to Captain Smith and Mr. Gordon and they have had the British and American flags floating at half mast as a mark of respect.

Yesterday morning Mrs. Weller called Mrs. Smith on the telephone and demanded that the flags be taken in. According to Mr. Gordon, she gave no reason for making the demand and although the flags were his property he refused to take them down. Mrs. Smith, not wishing any serious trouble, took them down under protest. Mr. Gordon became indignant and communicated with officials in Hoboken to see if there was any law by which he could keep the flags flying. An agreement was finally reached whereby Mrs. Weller permitted Mr. Gordon to have his flags flying yesterday afternoon, but he will have to take them in to-day. Mr. Gordon can see no reason why the flags should not fly at all times and he says the matter is not ended.

When asked her reason for ordering the flags down Mrs. Weller said to a HERALD reporter:—"I ordered them down because they were interfering with the clothes line on the floor below. I cannot understand this man. He seems to have a mania for flags. I have no objection to the flags, but what good can they do hanging from the rear of the house over the garden? Yesterday when the woman in the apartment below was hanging some clothes on the line I noticed that the flags interfered with the line and she was inconvenienced. It is my duty to look after all the tenants and see that they get a fair deal.

"I recall one occasion—Mr. Gordon's son's birthday—when he insisted on hanging out a big flag. The son was in England, but the flag had to be out just the same. He may have the flags out to-day, but they must come in to-morrow—it's wash day."

When told of the reason given by Mrs. Weller for ordering the flags down Mr. Gordon was even more indignant. "The idea of letting a clothes line interfere with a mark of respect on such an occasion! It shows lack of thought and is disrespectful," said he. "There certainly must be some other reason. I refused to take the flags down this morning and they would have remained up had not Mrs. Smith wished to avoid trouble. As it was they were only taken down under protest. I lost my brother-in-law in the Titanic disaster, and even if I had not I would have put out the flags as a mark of respect to the other dead. I have no flag mania any more than the thousands of people in New York who are flying flags to-day. I am flying the British naval reserve flag because I am an officer in the reserve service and as such have a right to do so."

Mrs. Archer Huntington	75.00
Mrs. A. Murray Young	100.00
Miss Charlotte Pendleton	5.00
Mr. Richard Mortimer	200.00
Mr. James Goldmark	10.00
Mrs. Mary L. Harrison	5.00
Miss A. L. Livingston	5.00
Mrs. Dunham Jones Crain	20.00
Mrs. Thomas H. Rodman, Jr.	5.00
Mrs. Benjamin Nicoll	20.00
Mrs. Charles Hanson Towne	5.00
Mr. Robert Rogers	50.00
Mr. William Mason	10.00
Cash	5.00
Brooklyn Committee, through Miss Clara L. Ogden	1,035.68
Mr. Charles J. Chapman	5.00
Mrs. John R. MacNeille	10.00
Mrs. Henry Dwight Chapin	5.00
Miss Ida Kissay	5.00
A friend	2.00
Mr. John Howell	15.00
Mrs. Henry B. Wilson	10.00
Mrs. A. M. F.	5.00
J. N. G.	1.00
A few young Swiss fellows	2.00
Mrs. G. Harrison Smith	10.00
Mrs. George William Douglas	25.00
Mr. M. Goldman	5.00
E. B. B.	2.00
A sympathizer	1.00
Mrs. Augustine J. Wilson	15.00
Mrs. Newbold LeRoy Edgar	50.00
Miss Jessie A. Mather	5.00
Mrs. Julius R. Wolff	10.00
Mrs. J. Augustus Johnson	25.00
Mrs. Carl C. Weaver	2.00
Alcuin Preparatory School	38.00
William Harris Douglas	100.00
Deacons' Fund, Fifth Avenue Presbyterian Church, through L. L. Hopkins	100.00
A. X.	20.30
Mrs. George C. Clark	10.00
Mrs. D. C. Clark	10.00
Mrs. S. P. Blagden	10.00
Alexander L. Brodhead	5.00
Hudgins & Dumas	100.00
Miss Marguerite E. Coombe	5.00
Mrs. Thomas Gorton Coombe	50.00
Mrs. John E. Padden	10.00
W. M. B.	5.00
Mrs. George Rathbone Dyer	25.00
Anonymous	1.00
Mrs. Margaret W. Miner	25.00
Mrs. Margaret W. Miner's employes	20.30
Anonymous	50.00
Mrs. H. W. Cannon	100.00
Mrs. Douglas Robinson	50.00
Mrs. Henry Parish, Jr.	25.00
Yours in Sympathy	1.00
A Mite for the Titanic Passengers	2.00
Mrs. Snowden Andrews Fahnestock	25.00
Mrs. Samuel R. Bertron	100.00
Mr. Louis Hirsch	10.00
Mr. and Mrs. J. Crawford McCreery	50.00
Mrs. Henry M. Toch	10.00
G.	2.00
Mrs. William Brock Shoemaker	25.00
Mr. John Love	10.00
Mr. A. A. Booth	500.00
Mrs. Levi P. Morton	1,000.00
Mr. R. Percy Eccles, of Liverpool, through H. Hentz & Co	100.00
Mrs. F. Ernest Hagemeyer	50.00
Mrs. Philip Le Boutillier	5.00
Mrs. Charles E. Benner	5.00
Margaret J. Becker	50.00
C. W. C.	5.00
Mrs. T. J. Evans	20.00
Mrs. G. Hunter Brown	10.00
Mrs. George Bullock	5.00
Mrs. Jane E. Cox	30.00
Elizabeth S. Morris	5.00
Countess de Langier-Villars	200.00
Mrs. Henry R. Mallory	25.00
Mrs. B. W. Strawbridge	50.00
Mrs. William P. Draper	25.00
Mrs. Charles Corkler	10.00
Mrs. Victor C. Thorne	10.00
Mrs. Florence S. Brezee	5.00
Mr. Charles Newman	15.00
School girls of Rosemary Hall	426.30
Miss Ruetz Rees and Miss Lowndes	75.00

TOLD TO 'KEEP OUT' NAVY MAN CHARGES

Wireless Operator Aboard Cruiser Declares the Carpathia's Man Ignored President's Request.

[SPECIAL DESPATCH TO THE HERALD.]

PHILADELPHIA, Pa., Sunday.—That the Carpathia had not only refused to give the United States scout cruiser Chester information concerning the Titanic, but had told her wireless men to "keep out," was the statement made to-day by Frank Gaffney, chief operator of the Chester, now at League Island.

The refusal to answer, Gaffney declared, was after the Carpathia had been informed that President Taft was anxious to learn the fate of Major Butt and other prominent persons. Commander Decker, who was in charge of the cruiser, said the statements made by Harold Bride, that the navy operators were "wretched" was absurd.

The Chester, it is said, continued to flash quesaions to the Carpathia until the operators aboard the latter were compelled to answer because the high power of the navy's aparatus made the reading of messages to other points impossible.

"We made an effort to learn about Major Butt," said Gaffney, "and the only reply we got was 'keep out.'"

Gaffney declared that he and Frank Blackstock, the other operator aboard the Chester, probably would be witnesses before the Senate committee.

Gaffney declared that the operators on board the Carpathia left them under the impression that all had been saved. He said that at one time they did answer when inquiries were made for Major Butt by saying "He is not here."

One of the officers on board the Chester said this afternoon:—

"The operators of the Carpathia ignored everything that Gaffney and Blackstock sent or asked. Gaffney has been a wireless operator for more than six years, while Blackstock has been one for about three or four years. The former is capable of sending about forty-five words a minute and to say that they are slow and wretched is absurd."

GIRLS SAVED YOUTH.

Thomas McCormick, nineteen years old, of No. 36 West Twentieth street, Bayonne, N. J., who was a passenger on the Titanic, and is a patient in St. Vincent's Hospital, this city, suffering from exposure, says hat his life was saved by two sisters, Kate and Mary Murphy, who picked him up from the water, dragging him into a lifeboat and sitting on him after sailors manning the boat had struck him on the head and tried to drive him from clinging to the sides of the boat.

McCormick lives with his sister, Mrs. Catherine Evers, and was returning from a visit to relatives in Ireland. Two cousins, John and Philip Kiernan, of Grove and Second streets, Jersey City, went down with the Titanic.

WIRELESS REFORM IS NOW DEMANDED

Operators Overworked and Underpaid, Say Experts—Should Be Two on Every Vessel.

Wireless operators are unanimous in the opinion that one operator on a vessel, as in the case of Harold Thomas Cottam, who intercepted the Titanic's distress signal aboard the Carpathia, is overworked. They say there should be at least two wireless operators on every vessel to insure the safety of the passengers. It was only by chance that Cottam caught the message of the Titanic as he was preparing for bed.

Guglielmo Marconi, before the Senate Committee testified that when the wireless operator went to bed no wireless signals were received aboard ship. He gave it as his opinion that there should be two operators to relieve each other every twelve hours. This would keep a man at the instrument all the time. He said the only objection was that the ship owners did not want to stand the additional cost. Wireless men aboard English vessels get $20 a month and board. On the American vessels they get $30 a month.

W. J. J. Cusack, an expert telegrapher, whose brother has been employed for years as a wireless operator, said last night that not long ago his brother was abed when the Princess Irene sent wireless messages for aid and that it was within the zone of his instrument and he would have heard the message had he been awake. The injured ship was only a short distance away.

"The low salaries paid by the wireless and steamship companies," said Mr. Cusack, "is accounted for because so many men just go for the trip, considering it a vacation. They don't stay long in the service. Then again, to account for the youth of so many of the operators, they are mostly amateurs, who in school vacations obtain positions for the amusement. A girl was employed for a few trips on a coastwise steamship.

"The law to license wireless operators is now in effect, but this does not keep out amateurs. In fact they are better qualified to pass the examination than the practical man, because of its technical character.

"It's my belief the time has come when two operators must accompany every vessel, and keep a sharp watch all during the day and night for signals of any kind.

"A device for receiving in a visible or oral form may some day be thought of, whereby the signal may be seen or heard by passengers, and the operator, should he not be near, called to his post. At present the operator to hear the wave impulses must have the receiver on his head. This receiver is similar to that used by telephone operators, with a cup to fit the ear."

GIVES NEW LIGHT ON MARCONIGRAMS

Wireless Manager Denies His Company Tried to Suppress the Titanic News.

HAD ASKED FOR DETAILS

Mr. Sammis Admits Sending "Dollars" Message, but Says It Went Later Than Reported.

J. Bottomley, general manager of the Marconi Company of America, in a letter, and T. W. Sammis, chief engineer of the company, in an interview, assert that an injustice has been done the company and Mr. Sammis personally by the publication in the HERALD yesterday of the marconigrams sent to the wireless operators of the Carpathia and the Titanic, in which they were told to "Say nothing. Hold your story for dollars in four figures."

No question is raised that the marconigrams printed in the HERALD were not sent to the operators, but they assert that the messages were sent on Thursday, the last one when the Carpathia was steaming up the bay, and for that reason there could have been no suppression of news. The article in the HERALD did not mention the time the messages were sent because it did not have that fact in its possession, and Messrs. Bottomley and Sammis complain on that score alone.

The HERALD, with this article, as with all others, tried to ascertain all the facts before publishing it. When Mr. Sammis talked with a HERALD reporter at the Waldorf-Astoria he made no mention of the time when the wireless message, which he admitted sending, was sent. If any inference was to be drawn from the interview with Mr. Sammis it was that the message was sent at an earlier time than Thursday night, and this interview was in the presence of at least two persons besides the reporter obtaining it, and was confirmed by one of them after it had been written out and before it was published.

Mr. Griggs Surprised.

Early on Saturday evening a HERALD reporter talked with John W. Griggs, one time Attorney General of the United States and now president of the Marconi Company of America. He was told that Mr. Sammis had sent a wireless message to the Marconi operator on board the Carpathia, advising him not to give out the details of the Titanic disaster, but to hold for four figures.

Mr. Griggs declared it was the first information he had received that any such message had been sent. Inasmuch as the last of the wireless messages to the operators said that Mr. Marconi had agreed to the sale of the article, the inventor was seen Saturday night in his apartments in the Holland House. He declared it was the first he had heard of it, and said he had not agreed to the sale of any article, but on the contrary had been of the opinion that it would have been much better to give out the news of the disaster.

Because it has been willing at all times to give all the sides of any question, the HERALD publishes the letter of Mr. Bottomley, in which he denies the sending of the messages was for the purpose of suppressing the news, and asserts that the company endeavored to get the details of the disaster. The letter follows:—

Calls Article Unjust.

TO THE EDITOR OF THE HERALD:—

The article in your issue of this morning under the heading, "'Keep Your Mouth Shut; Big Money for You,' Was Message to Hide News," was a grave injustice to the Marconi company, and calls for immediate correction. Dealing with stolen wireless messages, with no mention of dates or other informing circumstances, it is not difficult to create a false and injurious impression; and such an impression is certainly sought to be conveyed by the assertion that any of the messages you quote was sent at a time when the sending of news from the Carpathia could be influenced, or that any of the messages was intended to suppress the sending of such news.

The quoted messages to the wireless operator on the Carpathia were sent about eight o'clock on Thursday evening when the Carpathia was coming up the bay, and not as you intimate on any of the early days following the Titanic disaster. They referred to an opportunity for the operators, after they had landed from the ship that evening and their duties to the public, to the Carpathia and to the Marconi company had been fully discharged, to sell to a newspaper narratives of their personal experiences, a thing they had a complete right to do, for these narratives were their own personal property. Who will begrudge these unfortunate and hard working men the remuneration they thus received, or because of it charge them with previous neglect of duty?

Asked for Information.

As to obtaining information of the Titanic disaster for the public, everything possible was done by the Marconi company, as will be seen when it is remembered that everything transmitted from a ship is under the control of its commander. I personally sent the following message to the operator on board the Carpathia:—

"Send earliest possible moment at least five hundred words reliable for public, our office. Remember Jack Binns.
MARCONI COMPANY,
"J. Bottomley, General Manager."

And this was followed by others to the ship and to the various land stations, but without effect.

My company depends on the transmission of messages for its support, and it is not reasonable to suppose it would for any reason cut off such a wonderful source as the first four days of the week offered.

J. BOTTOMLEY,
General Manager of the Marconi Company, 254 West 132d street, New York.
April 21, 1912.

Mr. Sammis Explains.

Mr. Sammis called up the HERALD office on the telephone last night and said an injustice had been done him in the story. He admitted that he was talking with a HERALD reporter at the time he gave the interview in the Waldorf-Astoria, but said he did not know he was "talking with a reporter for a paper which had in its possession stolen messages." Neither did he deny the accuracy of the interview.

As a matter of fact the rumor that the wireless operators had received a message instructing them not to give out details of the disaster had been current since the Carpathia arrived Thursday night, and when Mr. Sammis was asked about such a message he admitted the sending without offering any explanation about the time, although he knew he was talking with a reporter who was seeking information for the purpose of publication.

Mr. Sammis said that the letter of Mr. Bottomley explained his reason for asserting that the publication of the article in the HERALD had done him an injustice.

Herald Readers Give Views of Sea Disaster

Many Suggestions Are Offered to Prevent Repetition of the Titanic Tragedy—Some Criticise Conduct of Vessel's Officers.

TO THE EDITOR OF THE HERALD:—

From the horror of the Titanic's fateful plunge comes the suggestion from Adolph Graut, whose relative, Benjamin Guggenheim, was drowned, that hereafter the scheme of construction be changed so that, for instance, the main deck, the second deck, and, possibly, the third deck, be made with a honeycomb cellular contruction such that if the keel and all the cabins below were flooded, these decks, or even one, having sufficient displacement would act as a huge raft on which humanity might easily be safeguarded until help arrived.

By this device it would be impossible to sink the boat, regardless of the vertical water tight compartments. The suggestion is given for what it is worth in the interest of humanity.

GEORGE MARTIN HUSS.
NEW YORK, April 19, 1912.

"REMEMBER THE TITANIC."

TO THE EDITOR OF THE HERALD:—

The loss of life in the recent sinking of the Titanic is the human sacrifice made upon the Altar of Greed belonging to a few financial magnates. "Remember the Titanic" can now be substituted for "Remember the Maine."

The fact that the Titanic was the largest vessel in the world, on her maiden voyage, with a notable passenger list, an example of modern marine engineering, and the fact that this "unsinkable" craft should be the one to sink to the bottom of the sea, seems beyond comprehension. The whole world is astonished at the catastrophe.

Such a great loss of human life has been brought home to all of us for a purpose. It is time to call a halt; time to look conditions squarely in the face. How has all the luxury of the Titanic—squash courts, tennis courts, swimming pools, sun parlors and gymnasiums—compensated for the loss of lives on this vessel?

Of what avail were all these luxuries when the ship was foundering and lives were being sacrificed? * * *

Let us hope that the terrible lesson taught will cause the desire for fast travelling to cease, and men to become more conscientious regarding the lives of others entrusted to their care.

E. T. HYNES.
WASHINGTON, D. C., April 19, 1912.

NEED FOR SEARCHLIGHTS.

TO THE EDITOR OF THE HERALD:—

I read the account of how Hichens, quartermaster of the Titanic, who was at the wheel when the great vessel crashed into the iceberg, was ordered to tell the lookout in the crow's nest to keep a sharp eye out for small ice. Then, again, we read that the vessel was going along at twenty-one knots.

What a situation—a vessel that could not be stopped within half a mile ploughing along at this rate with a lookout or so peering out into the darkness, 2,340 persons in the hands of a few men who were relying on their seeing all danger ahead.

The public will not be satisfied to cross the ocean in the future unless everything possible for their safety on the sea is done. But is it? I say no! It is possible to see far ahead with powerful searchlights. Why are they not used? If the companies refuse to install them let them be compelled to do so by law.

Strange that in this country there has to be a great national calamity before there is a reform. Shall we wait before there is a terrible automobile accident before there is any attempt to stop the speeding in and about New York city? I think so. * * *

IRVING BROKAW,
No. 985 FIFTH AVENUE, NEW YORK, April 19, 1912.

FOR A HEROES' MONUMENT

TO THE EDITOR OF THE HERALD:—

I am a deep sympathizer with the families of those who lost relatives and friends in the Titanic disaster.

I want to be the first to head the list with a subscription for a monument to the memory of those brave men who sacrificed their lives for humanity. I suggest that this be erected in New York, near where the Carpathia docked and landed those who were rescued.

You are privileged to head the list with two hundred dollars ($200) in my name and call on me at any time for that amount.

I do not feel that history can show one instance, from the beginning of the world to the present time, where so many men in the various walks of life have displayed such courage, resigning themselves inevitably to the sacrifice of their own lives to save women and children, and in many instances their servants.

CHARLES M. FAULKNER.
BALTIMORE, April 19, 1912.

THE COASTWISE LINES.

TO THE EDITOR OF THE HERALD:—

Now that the protection to those who travel by water is being brought to the front, owing to this dreadful disaster to the Titanic, let us get to work at home and give our coastwise steamships a little attention. At this season of year, when the tourists are returning from Jacksonville, Fla., to their Northern homes, the stateroom accommodations on these vessels are readily taken, but the desire to take advantage of every dollar in sight exists and the settees are used for sleeping accommodations, much to the discomfort of all concerned. In case of an accident the chances of taking care of so many passengers, it seems to me, would be slender.

C. B. HARRIS.
NEW YORK, April 19, 1912.

THE WIRELESS QUESTION

TO THE EDITOR OF THE HERALD:—

All papers lay special emphasis on the few lifeboats carried by transatlantic ships, but they fail to bring out forcibly the fact that one wireless operator cannot work twenty-four hours a day.

For example, according to the wireless operator of the Parisian they were only fifty miles southwest of the Titanic at the time of the disaster.

The operator states that he went to bed at ten o'clock. Had there been a second operator on duty on the Parisian when the Titanic struck it would have been possible for the Parisian to have reached the doomed vessel in time to have saved many lives.

All familiar with wireless know that messages carry further at night than in the daytime, and as vessels are in more danger at night than in daytime, would it not be wise to require all passenger steamships to have a night as well as a day operator?

G. R. GUILD,
First Lieutenant Signal Corps, U. S. A.
FORT WOOD, N. Y., April 18, 1912.

A SAFETY SUGGESTION.

TO THE EDITOR OF THE HERALD:—

I have been a reader of the HERALD all my life, and I cannot remember of any horror that can compare with the Titanic's loss and the hundreds of poor souls that went down with her, and would like to make a suggestion through your paper for the safety of ocean travel. It may sound foolish to some, but I am sure can do no great harm.

Arrange the sailing time of two, three or four vessels, and have them keep a distance of ten, fifteen, twenty or twenty-five miles apart, so that they would sail in company all the way across. This can be arranged without any trouble, as all vessels are now equipped with wireless; and just imagine the feeling of safety that all would have, knowing that help was within reach at all times.

READER.
NEW YORK, April 17, 1912.

OTHER SEA DISASTERS.

TO THE EDITOR OF THE HERALD:—

As a reader of the HERALD for more than thirty years, I am prompted to make a suggestion and a request. In the issue of the NEW YORK HERALD of Tuesday, April 16, on page 4, you publish a list of great steamship disasters of history. In this you have omitted the Arctic and other losses intervening between the Arctic and the Atlantic, which you have listed. Why not print the complete list for the benefit of your readers?

T. F. McGREW.
SCRANTON, Pa., April 17, 1912.

AN ALIEN'S SUGGESTION.

TO THE EDITOR OF THE HERALD:—

The heroes belong to mankind. That is why I, a foreigner, suggest that you create a public fund, in order to build a monument to memoralize Mr. and Mrs. Straus, Colonel Astor and Major Butt. Such a memorial will honor the United States and be a lesson to its future citizens.

FOREIGNER.
NEW YORK, April 19, 1912.

SELF-PRESERVATION.

TO THE EDITOR OF THE HERALD:—

In the appalling disaster to the Titanic J. Bruce Ismay played the true part of his nationality—self-preservation. The lifeboat for his. He was not taking any chances as the line manager should have done, at least, for women, for whom some Englishmen have little regard.

CELTIC.
NEW YORK, April 19, 1912.

LESSON FOR AMERICANS.

TO THE EDITOR OF THE HERALD:—

One lesson of the Titanic disaster is the need for Americans to see their own country first before risking their lives on alien steamships. It's no wonder American shipping cannot compete with undermanned floating coffins.

GREEN STAR.
NEW YORK, April 19, 1912.

THE TRUE AMERICAN.

TO THE EDITOR OF THE HERALD:—

Let us be glad that J. Bruce Ismay and Lord Duff-Gordon are not Americans.

Colonel Astor showed the calibre of the true American, in contrast to that of the Englishmen.

MADELINE BURTON.
NEW YORK, April 19, 1912.

TRIBUTE TO THE HEROES.

TO THE EDITOR OF THE HERALD:—

Why not raise a monument to the memory of those "who died that others might live"?

S. P. LIPPINCOTT.
WYNCOTE, Pa., April 19, 1912.

Newburyport Morning Herald.

ESTABLISHED IN 1793, DAILY IN 1832
ONE HUNDRED AND TWENTIETH YEAR

NEWBURYPORT, MASSACHUSETTS, TUESDAY, APRIL 23, 1912

VOLUME CXX. NUMBER 97
PRICE ONE CENT; THREE DOLLARS A YEAR

UNKNOWN STEAMER REFUSED TO GO TO AID OF THE TITANIC

Only Five Miles Away When Liner Struck Iceberg, But Failed to Respond to Frantic Signals

OFFICER'S TESTIMONY AT HEARING MONDAY

Body of G. W. Widener Believed to Have Been Recovered; List of Names of 25 Bodies Received

(Associated Press Despatch.)

WASHINGTON, April 22—With succor only five miles away the huge White Star liner Titanic slid into her watery grave carrying with her more than 1600 of her passengers and crew, while an unidentified steamer which might have saved all failed or refused to see the frantic signals flashed to her for aid.

This phase of the disaster was brought out today before the senate investigating committee when J. E. Boxhall; fourth officer of the Titanic described his unsuccessful efforts to attract the stranger's attention.

This steamer, according to Boxhall, could not have been more than five miles away and was stee-ing toward the Titanic. So close was she that from the bridge Boxhall plainly saw her masthead light and then her red side light. Both with rockets and with the Morse electric signals did the young officer hail the stranger.

Captain Smith and several others near the bridge declared at the time their belief that the vessel had seen them and was signalling in reply. Boxhall failed to see such replies, however, and in any case the steamer kept on her course obliquely past the Titanic without offering aid.

This and the declaration by P. A. S. Franklin, vice president of the White Star liner, that there was not sufficient lifeboats aboard the Titanic to care for the ship's company at one time were easily the features of the hearing.

RECOVERS THE BODY OF GEORGE D. WIDENER

Cable Steamer Sends List of 25 Names of Bodies So Far Recovered

(Associated Press Despatch.)

NEW YORK, April 22—The first list of names of bodies recovered from the Titanic disaster by the cable steamer Mackay-Bennett was received here tonight in a wireless message to the White Star Line offices.

The list of 25 names contain none of several of the most prominent men perished unless it be that of "George W. Widen" as sent by wireless, refers, as is believed, to George D. Widener of Philadelphia.

The regular passenger list of the Titanic did not mention Widen, which apparently establishes the identification of the body as that of Mr. Widener, son of P. A. D. Widener of Philadelphia, one of the victims of the tragedy.

Most of the bodies so far recovered were passengers from the steerage. Only one woman's body has so far been recovered.

DEATHS.

BOWDEN—In this city, April 22, 1912, Miss Frances E. Bowden. Funeral services from her late residence, 8 Coffin's court, Thursday, April 25, at 2:30 p. m. Relatives and friends invited. Burial private.

BROWN—In Albany, Me., April 19, 1912, Minnie B. wife of Eubert P. Brown and daughter of Stephen W. and Lydia B. Gale of this city, aged 35 years, 8 months. Funeral from the residence of her parents, 4 Kent street, Tuesday, April 23d, at 2 p. m. Relatives and friends invited.

ROOSEVELT MEN TALKED IN RAIN LAST EVENING

Despite Conditions Market Square Held Many Hearers at Rally of Progressives

CONG. GARDNER WAS TARGET

Speaker Donnells Says His Side Is Fighting Against Abuse and Not Argument

Quite a large number of citizens, with a good sprinkling of the fair sex, gathered in the rain last evening at Market square and listened to the following Roosevelt advocates, who spoke from an automobile, Senator A. L. Nason of Haverhill, Rep. G. P. Webster of Boxford and S. H. Donnells of Peabody, candidate for delegate. Each speaker fired some hot shot at Congressman A. P. Gardner.

The auto, with some red fire burning and containing a cornetist who played some lively airs, hove in sight shortly after 9 o'clock and for nearly an hour the speakers talked on the issues of the campaign from a progressive outlook.

Attacked Taft Machine.

Mr. Donnells was especially vehement in his attacks on the Taft machine. He said that he had read in the newspapers that the Republican bosses were now returning home from Washington to look after matters here, and that Mr. Gardner had been in charge of the Taft campaign for several weeks in this state, and that the congressman had been forced into the campaign because he realized the great probabilities of a defeat for the bosses in Massachusetts.

"The only way the bosses are trying to get in contact with the common citizens is to open a suite of rooms in Boston and have their henchmen issue a string of abuse at Roosevelt and open the money barrel," said Mr. Donnell.

(Continued on Page Four.)

"THE IMPORTANCE OF BEING EARNEST" TO BE PRESENTED TONIGHT

"The Importance of Being Earnest," a three-act play, will be presented at Music hall this evening by a local cast under the auspices of the Woman's club. It is to be the annual guest night of the club and an evening of keen enjoyment is anticipated by the members and their friends.

HERALDINGS

Mrs. Fred Schuman of Springfield, formerly of this city, is the guest of her mother Mrs. Daniel Wallace at her home on Hancock street.

Thomas Houlihan of Worcester has returned home after spending the past week as the guest of his cousin Miss Mary Shea at her home on Middle street.

Daniel J. Casey has returned home after enjoying a few days with his brother, Andrew Casey of Boston.

A number of new trees have been set out on Middle street by Supt. Kelley and his men.

Edward O'Connell Esq., of Boston is visiting his parents at their home in this city.

Miss Mae Houlihan of this city has returned home after spending the past few days with her sister in Somerville.

TAFT RALLY TO BE HELD HERE MONDAY NIGHT

Ex-Gov. Bates, Rep. Cavanaugh, Herbert Parker and Others to Be the Speakers

PLAN OF CAMPAIGN ANNOUNCED

"Watch Us Boost the Hat," Will Be the Slogan from Now On by Campaigners

The executive committee of the Taft organization in the sixth congressional district announces a plan of campaign for the closing of the week which shows an active and energetic program, including each day and every evening and extending from one end of the district to the other.

Many prominent speakers will be heard and the citizens in every city, town and community in the district will be given an opportunity to greet James F. Ingraham of Peabody, Mayor Isaac C. Patch of Gloucester, William W. Coolide of Salem and Alfred E. Lunt of Beverly, the delegate and alternate delegates pledged to President Taft. The four gentlemen have been flitting back and forth over the district during the past few weeks, giving the voters a chance to size them up, but this week they will know no rest, being called upon to speak in every noon and corner of the district as well as in the cities and towns. They will be assisted in spreading the gospel of Taft and a second term by an imposing array of prominent speakers.

The slogan of the Taft campaigners during the week will be "Watch Us Boost the Hat." Every automobile bearing the speakers in their speed-defying runs through the district will be supplied with literature showing Roosevelt's labor record during the seven years of his administration, his connection with the Harvester, Steel and other corporate interests and the achievements of the Taft administration which will be distributed at every stopping point.

In-door rallies will be held in all of the cities and several of the towns, but out-door rallies will be equally as popular and the blare of trumpets and roll of drums will be heard and the reflections of red fire will be seen from one end of the district to the other as the campaigners hit up the hot pace they have set for themselves in committing themselves to an arduous week of disillusionizing and enlightenment of the voters.

The campaign will be brought to a close next week Monday night with a rally in City hall, when the speakers will be ex-Gov. John L. Bates, Rep. James F. Cavanaugh, Herbert Parker and others who will not only appear in this city, but also in Haverhill, where another rally will be held.

FUNERAL NOTICE.

Members of Quascacunquen Lodge No. 39, I. O. O. F. are hereby notified to attend the funeral of Bro. Joshua L. Chase, at his home, 25 Forrester street, Tuesday afternoon, April 23, at 1:30.

WALTER BRYANT, N. G.
WILLIAM H. WELCH, Secretary.

MISS FRANCES E. BOWDEN DEAD

Miss Frances E. Bowden died at her home, 8 Coffin's court, yesterday noon after a long illness. She leaves one sister, Mrs. Albert L. Woodman of this city. Miss Bowden was a member of the Central church.

LECTURE ON CHRISTIAN SCIENCE

By Judge Clifford P. Smith, C. S. B., in Griffin hall, Thursday evening, 8 o'clock. All are welcome.

TEMPORARY HALT IN A STRIKE OF R. R. ENGINEERS

Federal Government Tenders Its "Friendly Offices" at a Most Critical Stage

EMPLOYEES' DEMANDS REFUSED

Trouble May Tie Up 52 Per Cent. of Railroad Traffic of the Entire Country

(Associated Press Despatch.)

NEW YORK, April 22—Tender of "friendly offices" of the representatives of the Federal government called at least a temporary halt tonight to a strike by the railroad engineers in all the territory east of Chicago and north of the Potomac river, in which it is estimated that 52 per cent. of the railroad traffic of the entire country is conducted.

The offer of mediation followed immediately the refusal by the management of the 50 railroads concerned to concede the engineers' demands for an increase in wages of 18 per cent., and the announcement by Chief Warren S. Stone of the Brotherhood of Locomotive Engineers that in consequence of the refusal an engineer' strike would go into effect before another 36 hours had elapsed.

Knowing that the situation had reached a critical stage, Martin A. Knapp, presiding justice of the U. S. Commerce Court and Charles P. Neill, U. S. commissioner of labor, hurried to this city from Washington and as soon as the decisive break between the engineers and railroads occurred, they addressed a letter to both Chief Stone and J. C. Stuart, chairman of the conference committee of railroad managers, explaining that a grave situation had arisen and that a sense of duty impelled them to tender their "friendly offices" to the disputants in the hope that some means might be found of adjusting the matter in controversy without the calamity of a "general strike."

HOLD SUPPER TOMORROW EVENING IN AID OF HOMEOPATHIC HOSPITAL

Strong individual efforts have been made to dispose of the three hundred tickets for the excellent supper and dance in support of the Homeopathic hospital, which will be held in the Unitarian Parish hall Wednesday evening from 6 to 8 o'clock. Musical selections will be rendered by the Philharmonic orchestra, while Kimball's well-known musicians will furnish music for dancing from 8 to 12.

The Homeopathic hospital is doing splendid work, as scores will willingly testify, but is greatly hampered from lack of funds.

The Ladies' Auxiliary has been indefatigable in raising funds, and is ambitious of doing more as there is need for all the financial as well as other assistance they can give.

In a few years it is hoped that the hospital will be well endowed and self-supporting.

With an excellent supper, thrilling music and dancing, all the tickets will doubtless be sold to the many supporters of a worthy institution.

EXHIBITION OF SCHOOL DRAWINGS

Remarkable Display of Children's Artistic Work to Be Seen at High School Hall

MISS MURPHY'S PUPILS SHOW GREAT ABILITY

The exhibition of the drawing and the paper cutting work of our public schools now open in the High school ascembly hall is the finest yet seen in this city.

The display is well mounted on large uniform sheets of a neutral brown cardboard, and shows that chief attribute of beauty, unity in variety, like drawings being in every case grouped together.

Miss Florence Murphy is to be complimented on the progress made from year to year by the classes under her competent supervision.

DORR IS INDICTED FOR MURDER AT SUPERIOR COURT

Grand Jury Sitting Here Brought in Report Yesterday Afternoon on Lynn Mystery; Other Cases

ALLEGED MURDERER OF WOMAN IS ARRAIGNED

Trial of Orlando Antonio of Lawrence, Charged With Assault to Murder, to Begin Here Today

William A. Dorr was indicted by the grand jury at Superior court here yesterday charged with the murder of George E. Marsh, the wealthy soap manufacturer of Lynn, whose body was found bullet-riddled on Lynn marshes Saturday morning, April 30.

Jeshph Caruso of Lawrence, who was charged with the murder of Annie Lopezzi, was arraigned at the afternoon session and pleaded not guilty. He was held without bail.

The case of Orlando Antonio, charged with assault to murder, was called for trial in the afternoon, but no witnesses were present and the case will be resumed this morning.

The morning session opened at 10 o'clock, Judge Brown presiding, and the following cases came up for disposition:

John Swarie, Lawrence, intimidation, pleaded guilty, fined $50.

William Freiberg, Lawrence, intimidation, pleaded guilty, fined $100.

Henry Ezetais, Lawrence, intimidation, pleaded guilty, fined $50.

Vaclavas Backauslas, Lawrence, assault and battery on Edith Baree, during strike, held on same charge on person unknown, fined $10 on each charge.

Mike Sarbig, Lawrence, intimidation, pleaded guilty, fined $50.

Pasquale Megliazzi, Lawrence, disturbing peace, pleaded guilty, fined $5.

Vincenzo, Lawrence, intimidation, pleaded guilty, fined $25.

David Ambrose, Lawrence, rioting, pleaded guilty and was fined $15.

Nicholas Nebano, Lawrence, for carrying a loaded revolver, pleaded guilty and was fined $50.

George Thompson of Andover, assault and battery, pleaded guilty and was fined $25.

Hugh Callahan of Andover, held on two charges, assault and battery, and for disturbance of the peace, was fined after pleading guilty, for the first offence $25, and for the second charge, $10.

James Callahan, Andover, assault, pleaded guilty and was fined $25.

The cases of Salvatori Privatari for malicious mischief and Dominico Campiano were called, the defendants not appearing.

The case of Hebib Zalapat of Lawrence, for assault and battery, was given to the jury at 11:30.

Afternoon Session.

The afternoon session session began at 2 o'clock and the first case called was that of Michael Ramsey of Andover on the charge of cruelty to animals. He pleaded guilty and was fined $50, which he paid.

At 3:10 the jury on the Zalapat case returned a verdict of not guilty.

The case of Annie Weizenheck of Lawrence, charged with intimidation, was then called and occupied nearly the entire afternoon session. A number of witnesses testified and at the conclusion of the evidence Judge Brown took the case from the jury and it was placed on file.

Grand Jury Report.

The grand jury then made their final report, and presented the following indictments:

William A. Dorr, murder; William Driscoll and Guy Stewart, both of Lynn, breaking and entering. The jury was then excused until the second Monday in July, when they will report at Salem.

The following, charged with conspiracy, and who were indicted last week were arraigned and pleaded not guilty, Gildo Mozzaretta, William Yater, Thomas Halliday. These men are under $1000 bonds each.

Baseball Results

American League.
St. Louis 7, Detroit 4.
All other games were postponed on account of rain.

National League.
Cincinnati 9, St. Louis 6.
All other games were postponed on account of rain.

New England League.
Haverhill 4, Fall River 3.
All other games were postponed on account of rain.

The Weather

Probabilities.

Today clearing and cooler; Wednesday fair, brisk west winds.

Midnight Conditions.

The thermometer at the Herald office at midnight registered 56 degrees, wind southwest and cloudy.

Miniature Almanac.

Sun rises	4:51
Sun sets	6:35
Length of day	13:44
Day's increase	4:40
High tide....3:30 a. m., 4 p. m.	
Light Auto Lamps	7:05

PROTEST AGAINST THE NEGLECT OF AMERICAN MERCHANT MARINE

A protest against the neglect of the American merchant marine is embodied in the following statement:

We, citizens of the United States, passengers on the steamship, "Bluecher" to the number of 101, have now sailed together from New York around South America and return, covering some twenty thousand miles. We have visited many foreign ports, including Buenos Aires, with a commerce second only to New York in the Western Hemisphere, Rio de Janeiro, the beautiful, Montevideo, Valparaiso, Santos—all great and to be greater.

But at all places and at all times we have looked in vain for a merchant steam vessel carrying the flag of the United States. What is the reason? It apears to be the provisions of our laws, which prevent the acquisition of foreign-built vessels for American registry in foreign trade. This law, enacted for the up-building of American shipyards, has not resulted in the building of American ships for foreign trade. The cost of American-built ships, in comparison with those of foreign build, is prohibitive. They have not been built, and in consequence our flag has practically disappeared from the high seas.

Nothing is more conducive to acquaintance between nations, and intercourse and friendship between their citizens, than the constant sight of their respective flags.

Most of the Latin American people (and there are 50,000,000 of them) are friendly. They are eager to deal with us; but we persist in remaining strangers. At present, to reach New York comfortably, an Argentinian usually goes to Genoa or Liverpool. Naturally, he rarely continues to New York. London and Paris, England and France, his acquaintances and friends supply all wants.

This is the message we would convey to our friends and especially to those who shape the policies of our country.

Remove the prohibition upon the American registration of foreign-built ships for foreign trade.

Let us buy cheap ships abroad, let them be officered by American citizens and let them carry our flag to the people who want to see us, and who are ready and eager to know and trade with us. By this simple process we shall take nothing from our shipyards that they now enjoy, since they do not build ships for foreign trade; we shall add to our merchant marine and our foreign and domestic trade; we shall lay the foundation of a naval organization of the greatest value in case of war with a foreign nation; and we shall establish a real bond between the Americas of the Western Hemisphere that will be of vast, mutual and permanent benefit.

The early opening of the Panama Canal makes this subject of transcendent importance at this time.

On board S. S. "Bluecher," April, 1912.

MAY PRACTICE TOGETHER

If proper arrangements can be made the baseball teams representing the local High school and Dummer Academy will practice together during the week days.

J. Bruce Ismay, White Star Line Head, Before the Senate Committee Probing Titanic Disaster.

Copyright, 1912, by American Press Association.

The committee of United States senators, of which William Alden Smith of Michigan is chairman, had J. Bruce Ismay, managing director of the White Star line, before it as the first witness in the inquiry into the Titanic catastrophe. The hearings will be held in New York as far as possible and later will be transferred to Washington, where expert testimony will be heard regarding modern ship construction. The arrow points to Mr. Ismay. At the left is Philip A. S. Franklin, vice president of the White Star line. Mr. Franklin, Captain Rostrom of the Carpathia and the four surviving officers of the Titanic were also witnesses

CRITICIZES TAFT LEADERS.

Matthew Hale, the manager of the Roosevelt campaign in Massachusetts, issued a statement today, in which he sharply criticized the methods which the Taft leaders are employing in this State.

Manager Hale said: "The machine now has its back to the wall. It leaders realize that it looks virtually certain that Col. Roosevelt will carry Massachusetts and that the cause of the people will triumph over the cause of the machine.

"The Taft men are desperate. They are resorting to the anonymous circular and the 'gag.' The State is being flooded with unsigned political literature teeming with false statements. To these no responsible man apparently dares to put his name. They are doing this in open defiance of the laws of this State, which not only prohibit this kind of cowardly campaigning, but make the offenders liable to a jail sentence.

"In certain sections of the State, particularly the towns, no provision has been made for registration for the primaries.

"The Taft men would narrow the contest down to as few voters as possible, with the hope that the machine-controlled men may be able to dominate the coming primaries.

"In some cities they have provided that the voting shall be done in a single poling place, instead of by precincts. This is another method by which they would make it as hard as possible for the voters to avail themselves of their right of franchise.

"The machine has from the outset been fighting a free expression of the preference of the rank and file of the voters of the Republican party at the coming presidential primaries. Its leaders fought the primary bill from the start. The surely can't be charged with being inconsistent in this respect.

"But their fight is a hopeless one. The great majority of the rank and file of the party in this State, I feel confident, will stand with the Republicans of Maine, Illinois, Pennsylvania and other States, and vote for the nomination of Col. Roosevelt and the defeat of the machine.

"The voters of this State realize that they do not have to be enrolled in either party to go into the coming primaries and cast their ballots for Theodore Roosevelt.

"The machine may do its worst. The people are aroused to the situation. They have confidence in Col. Roosevelt as a man who really knows their needs and who accomplishes things. From the outset the members of the Roosevelt committee felt that President Taft could not be elected if nominated. It is safe to say that a large majority of the voters of this State now feel this way. They realize also that Taft cannot now even be nominated and that Col Roosevelt not only can be nominated but elected."

(Signed) MATTHEW HALE.

A BIG FASHION NUMBER.

"Summer Fashions" will be the title of the Big Fashion Number edited by May Manton, to be given with New York Sunday World of May 5th. The demand for the special number will be great, so it is advisable to order from your newsdealer in advance. The big sixteen page Joke Book will be given next Sunday (April 28th) as usual, and another Joke Book will be given with the Fashion Number on May 6th. These Joke Books given with the Sunday World has made the biggest hit of anything since the introduction of color pages in newspapers nearly twenty years ago.

OCCUPYING FAMOUS HOUSE AT HAMPTON FALLS

The Misses Mace of Newburyport are occupying the old Gen. Moulton house at Hampton Falls which is one of the homes in this section wealthy in history and which had during the past few years been allowed to go into a partial state of dilapidation. The house has lately been remodelled.
—Portsmouth Times.

The Stock Market

Closing quotations for April 22, 1912, furnished by F. S. Moseley & Co., 50 Congress street, Boston:

	Bid	Asked
First Nat'l Bank	102	108
Merchants Nat'l Bank	32⅛	35
Ocean Nat'l Bank	65	68
Newb'yp't Gas & E.		195
Boston & Maine RR.	100¼	100½
N. Y., N. H. & H. RR.	136½	137
Amalgamated	82¼	82⅜
Am. Tel. & Tel. Co.	145¾	146
Am. Woolen pfd.	90½	91¼
N. E. Tel. & Tel. Co.	145¾	146
Mass. Electric com.	20	21
Mass. Electric pfd.	80½	81½
Mass. Gas pfd.	96	97
Mergenthaler Lino.	217	221
New York Central	118½	118⅞
Pennsylvania RR.	124¾	125
United Fruit	185	186
United Shoe com.	51	51¾
United Shoe pfd.	28⅞	29¼
U. S. Steel com.	70⅜	70½
U. S. Steel pfd.	112⅜	112½

CENTRAL CHURCH.

WEDNESDAY, 6.15 p. m., supper for S. S. teachers and officers (10 cts) followed at 6.45 by the normal Bible class, taking up next Sunday's lesson.

7.45 p. m. Regular weekly prayer meeting. Subject: "Has the Church Outgrown the Prayer Meeting?" Col. 4:2-3; Matt. 18:15-20; Heb. 10:19-25.

THURSDAY, 3 p. m. Regular monthly meeting of the King's Daughters in the parlor.

8. p. m. Parish meeting in the vestry. This is the most important meeting of the Parish during the year. Appropriations for the year beginning May 1, 1912, will be made and the matter of selling a strip of our land to the city for street purposes will be discussed along with other important matters.

Both of the Thursday meetings were postponed from last week because of the rain.

THURSDAY, FRIDAY and SATURDAY. The Ladies' Circle will hold a Rummage Sale in the Foster Smith store on Water street. Will those who have articles to give notify Mrs. W. H. Noyes, Mrs. C. C. Henry or Mrs. M. L. Kimball. The articles will be called for on Wednesday.

FRIDAY, 3 p. m. Ladies' Prayer Meeting with Mrs. Meader.

FRIDAY, 7 p. m. Meeting of the Boy Scouts in the Social Rooms. Every boy is invited.

CITY HONORS OLDEST MAN

(Continued from page 1).

Garibaldi, its great leader sand Gambetta did wonderful things for France. Japan, China and the Central American countries have moved forward to Republican forms of government.

David Hancock was born in Massachusetts and his boyhood was spent in New Hampshire and Vermont and afterwards he was a steamboat captain on the Connecticut river for many years. He came to Red Wing in 1854. Nine years before that date the Northwest territory had been carved out of an area purchased from France. He came here while Minnesota was still a territory and four years before it became a state. Here he has lived—a true, loyal citizen. He drove stage for a while—how far back that seems—then steamboated on the Mississippi and at the call of his country enlisted in the Third Minnesota regiment and served during the Civil war. He defended the Constitution of the United States which some one has said "is to liberty what grammar is to language." Then he came home and in the years that have followed he has been the industrious, unassuming, upright, gentleman. He has given us an example of what a true, worthy man can be. His modesty and simplicity of character are a priceless heritage to the youth of Red Wing and to posterity.

Letters, which will be more fully noticed tomorrow, were then read by President Neill.

A quartet, composed of Misses Helen Park, Florence Johnson, Clifford Sutherland and Elias Magnussen, tenderly rendered "Annie Laurie."

Major Bowler.

The next speaker was Maj. James Bowler of St. Paul, an old comrade of Capt. Hancock in the Civil war. He said he had risen from a sick bed, against the advice of his family, in order to be here at this time. "I wanted to come down to Red Wing," he said, "and look into the face of my old friend, "Uncle Dave," something of that spirit of kindliness and resignation that is found in the face of the men who have served their country. I do not know where it was born, this spirit of resignation and peace but I think it comes from that comradeship which was found in the common experiences of men who stepped forth, when a nation was in peril, to save the flag and to free men.

"That is the only event of this kind that I ever helped to celebrate. To live a hundred years is to have done an unusual thing, especially when one is still vigorous. I am glad to be here and extend my congratulations to my dear old friend, David Hancock."

Rev. J. T. Fulton.

Rev. J. T. Fulton said that it was certainly a notable occasion which brought together so many of the veterans of the civil war to rejoice with the rest of the people in this city, who are younger, over the centennial of a man whose life has been such an honorable and manly one. The chief event of that life was its participation in the great struggle of the sixties.

"The last survivor of the war of 1812, Daniel F. Bacon, died at Freedom, N. Y., in 1869. There are still those who survive who fought in the Mexican war. And now the time has come when those who shared in the marches and camp life of the Civil war are growing feeble. Their hearts are united by a common purpose and common experience. They have learned that life's blessedness is found in doing one's duty, stern though it may be. The shadows are falling upon them as they are upon the fine old gentleman whom we delight to honor. May they have the sweet consciousness that they will soon be going home to the 'Father's house' into the light."

"Before many years, you veterans, who wear the brown button, will have passed from earth. What shall we have left? A memory, monuments, headstones, the old flag, this great country, the constitution, liberty, freedom, a united and happy people. Isn't this worth fighting for?

"We are all proud to have known this grand old veteran whom this entire community honors and loves today."

A solo was given by Miss Florence Swanstrom.

Rev. Dr. S. Arthur Cook.

Rev. Dr. S. Arthur Cook, in his remarks, dwelt on the character of David Hancock. He was one of the men who had "lived by the side of the road and been a friend to man." He talked more particularly to the young people and assured the veterans that the heart of young Red Wing beat true to the great principles for which Mr. Hancock and his comrades suffered and fought. "The tread of coming millions who would love and be true to freedom was the asset of posterity made possible by the heroic deeds of such men as we honor at his centennial celebration."

He closed with a beautiful reflection upon the peace, grandeur and dignity of old age. It is God's badge of knighthood.

Rev. C. C. Rollit.

The next speaker was Rev. C. C. Rollit of Minneapolis, who said he had traveled 353 miles from Iowa to Red Wing to be at this event. He alluded to what wah transpired in the one hundred years that David Hancock had lived. When he was born the preparations were being made for the war of 1812; when he was two years old Stephenson invented the first locomotive; when he was seven years old the first steamboat crossed the ocean; at 35, the first telegraphic message was sent. Dickens, Thackery, Tennyson, Longfellow, had not any of them given their priceless treasures to the world of literature. How rich the world has been made by the achievements of the past 100 years!

"And yet we honor this man, our esteemed and beloved friend, not for the large part he has played or his century has played, but most of all because he has lived a true, kindly life. If any man in Red Wing has the respect, confidence and love of a whole community it is David Hancock. He has the great consciousness of a life well lived and the promise that 'at eventide it shall be light.'"

"Uncle Dave" Plays on the Fife.

It was at the close of Rev. Mr. Rollit's remarks that Uncle Dave arose from his chair and played the old familiar tunes on his fife. The whole audience rose spontaneously and gave tribute to the old hero as he once more stirred the hearts of all who heard it. After he sat down he played another tune and did not manifest any weariness because of his splendid effort.

Mosher Talks.

After the quartet had given another selection Comrade Mosher of Zumbrota, who had just returned from California, extended his congratulations and told the audience that "Uncle Dave" was the oldest drum major now living, who served in the Civil war.

Presents Flag.

In behalf of the Commercial club, Jens K. Grondahl, the president, presented Mr. Hancock with a beautiful silken flag. He spoke of the long span of life that had been given the aged veteran. Only one man in 150,000 ever passes the century mark. The Commercial club desired to give some token of their veneration, love and devotion to him and they felt that "Old Glory" would be the one thing he would prize most. When he was born it had 17 stars, when he went forth to fight for the flag it had 31 and now, at his one hundredth anniversary, it had 48. He closed by presenting the flag to the grand old man of Red Wing. The centennarian took the flag pole in his hands and waved the beautiful banner vigorously. The band played the "Star Spangled Banner" and the audience arose.

Lucius F. Hancock of Wyoming thanked those who had the celebration in charge and the people of Red Wing generally for their interest in and kindness to his father.

The quartet closed the program with "Tenting on the Old Camp Ground."

After the exercises were finished many went forward and snook hands with Mr. Hancock and this closed the public celebration of his birthday. He was conveyed to his home in an auto.

GRAND AND PETIT JURORS ARE DRAWN

Eight Men from Red Wing Selected to Serve at Session of Grand Jury.

Of a list of 72 names drawn by Clerk of Court C. S. Dana, Sheriff P. J. Lundquist and Justice of the Peace S. H. Haynes for the grand jury of twenty-four members, eight are residents of Red Wing. They are: Henry Adler, S. L. Morley, Geo. F. Gross, Peter Nelson, Sr., John Rockvam, R. Hesselberg, Elmer Hyde and G. A. Constantine. Others drawn to serve on the grand jury are: Amos Scofield, Roscoe; Wm. Fanslow, Hay Creek; Orin Parker, Goodhue village; C. W. Gress, city of Cannon Falls, Martin Casey, Belle Creek; Nels Anderson, Cannon Falls town; T. T. Comstock, Cherry Grove; August Sauter, Florence; L. L. Cornwall, Pine Island village; D. Boland, Welch; Cornelius Erstad, Minneola; John G. Nelson, Cannon Falls town; E. R. Rosen, Kenyon town; C. Danielson, Cannon Falls city; Nels Merison, Belle Creek.

Petit Jurors—N. H. Featherstone, R. Kolbe, John Munson, East Seventh street, Gotlieb Seebach, Harry Nordholm and Louis Hallenberger, Red Wing; S. O. Swanson, Minneola; Elner O. Overby, Cherry Grove; Magnus Olson, Cannon Falls city; H. C. Vonwold, Holden; F. F. Lohman, Kenyon village; Otto Ness, Featherstone; Frank Tillman, Welch; Delmar Brynildson, Vasa; G. O. Mogren, Kenyon village; S. E. Kyllo, Wanamingo; Richard Miller, Leon; Iver Kase, Warsaw; A. B. Haugsland, Belle Creek; Otto Andrist, Pine Island village; F. E. Tate, Cannon Falls town; John Langsdorf, Zumbrota town; O. T. Hallgren, Cannon Falls town.

Card of Thanks.

On behalf of the committee in charge of the celebration of David Hancock's one hundredth birthday, I desire to thank those who took part in the program, the ladies of the W. R. C., members of Co. L, Captain John N. Loye, and all who helped make the event a success.

—S. W. Park.

TITANIC PROBE STILL GOES ON

SENATE COMMITTEE QUESTIONS WITNESSES IN REGARD TO OCEAN HORROR.

BODIES IDENTIFIED

The Identity of Several New Bodies Has Been Learned—Cable Ship Will Continue Search for Victims of the Greatest Disaster in Marine History.

By United Press:

Rotterdam, April 23.—The captain of the steamer Birma, arriving in this port today, says that he was only 100 miles from the Titanic and heard the calls for help. He tried to reach her but was stopped by icebergs until it was too late.

RECOVERS BODIES.

By United Press:

New York, April 23.—The White Star line has a wireless message from the cableship Mackay-Bennett which is stationed at the scene of the Titanic wreck that she has recovered seventy bodies of which forty-two have been identified.

The ship will remain until she recovers one hundred and then she will proceed to Halifax.

MORE BODIES IDENTIFIED

By United Press:

New York, April 23. — The following are new names of the dead from the Titanic: Mrs. Mack, Mrs. N. McNamee, Catavelas Vasselics, W. Vear, Mrs. Madagan, William Sage, James Farrell, Henry D. Hansen, James Kelly, Mauretz Dahl, Rev. Mr. Hale, W. D. Douglass. All of these were passengers, except four who were members of the crew.

MOVES TO SMALLER ROOM.

By United Press:

Washington, April 23. — Senator Smith of the esnate committee which is investigating the Titanic disaster, moved to a smaller room and 500 women shrieked and fought for admission today.

Third Officer Herbert J. Pittman of the Titanic was the first witness called.

In his testimony Pittman told of the wreck, how he was in a life-boat near the scene, and how the moans and cries of the dying could be heard for an hour.

Many of the women who were present wept and even the senators wiped their eyes. Pittman said that Ismay asked that the women and children be placed in the life-boats first. He said that Captain Smith gave all the orders.

Pittman told of the loading of the boats with women and children he said that he was later ordered by Murdock, the first officer, to go in one of the boats to take charge of it. He then shook hands with him and never saw him again.

He continued his testimony by saying there were forty people in his boat, and he thought they could have rescued a dozen more, and he wanted to do so but the passengers objected, fearing it would swamp the boat, so he did nothing, although he heard cries for help and prayers and moaning for an hour.

Pittman did not think that the boilers exploded although he heard four different explosions. He thought they were caused by the bursting of the bulkheads.

People of India.

There are in India about 250,000,000 people who are supported by agriculture, 50,000,000 supported by industries, 8,000,000 supported by commerce, 3,000,000 supported by professions, and the balance are dependents.

Advertise in want column.

ALLEN GANG FORMALLY ARRAIGNED FOR MURDER

SIX OF THE GANG ARE TO BE TRIED IN SAME ROOM WHERE CRIME WAS COMMITTED.

By United Press:

Hillsville, Va., April 23.—Six members of the Allen gang were formally arraigned for murder today, in the same room where the crime was committed. Floyd Allen will be tried first. All spectators were searched for weapons.

BIBLICAL PLAGUE TO BE WIPED OUT

French Scientist Discovers Method for the Quick Extermination of the Locust.

By United Press:

Paris, April 23.—One of the Biblical plagues of Egypt will shortly be wiped out by modern science, according to a paper read before the French Academy of Sciences here, by Dr. Roux.

A French scientist, M. Deresme, has discovered a method whereby swarms of locusts can be quickly banished. The remedy is a microbe, fatal to locusts, a microbe easily "cultivated" in a laboratory and just as easily "turned upon" the insects. The manner of doing this is extremely simple. All one has to do is to apply the microbe to one locust. This locust will carry the microbe along with it, infecting thousands of others as it hops or flies along. It quickly dies and (after the habit of the locusts) is eaten by the others. These in turn become infected and die; and so on.

After having watched the effect of the remedy in Mexico for some time, the Argentine government commissioned M. Deresme to try his hand in an infested district of that country. In eight days the pests were gone.

YESTERDAY'S NEWS IN DETAIL CLIPPED FROM THIS MORNING'S PAPERS

Today's Latest News by Telegraph Will be Found on the First and Other Pages

ENGINEERS' STRIKE IS POSTPONED

OFFER OF MEDIATION BY GOVERNMENT ACCEPTED BY UNIONS.

SITUATION IS AT A CRISIS

Walkout on Fifty of Eastern Roads, Affecting Thirty-four Thousand Engineers Had Been Called.

New York, April 23.—The tender of the "friendly offices" of representatives of the federal government called a temporary halt to a strike of railroad engineers in all the territory east of Chicago and north of the Potomac river in which it is estimated that 52 per cent of the railway traffic of the entire country is handled.

The mediation of federal officials came immediately after the refusal of the managers of 50 railroads concerned, to concede the engineers' demands for an 18 per cent increase in wages, when Chief Warren Stone of the Brotherhood of Locomotive Engineers had announced, that in view of this refusal, a strike of engineers would go into effect within 36 hours.

Mediation Offered.

Knowing the situation had reached a critical stage, Martin A. Knapp, presiding justice of the United States commerce court and Charles P. Neill, United States commissioner of labor hurried here from Washington and as soon as the decisive break occurred they addressed a letter to both Chief Stone and to J. C. Stuart, chairman of the conference committee of railroad managers, declaring that a grave situation has arisen and that the sense of duty impelled them to tender their "friendly offices to the contending parties in the hope that some means may be found to adjust the matters in dispute without the calamity of a general strike."

Although Chief Stone had a few minutes before declared that his 49 associates on the engineers committee would proceed to their headquarters to prepare for a strike within 36 hours, the committee was so impressed with the letter of Messrs. Knapp and Neill that it was decided to accept the proposal for mediation.

Chairman Stuart of the railroad committee received an identical letter from Messrs. Knapp and Neill but would not comment on what position the railroads would take as to the tender of mediation. He immediately ordered a meeting of the committee, however, to consider the proposal.

The railroads affected by the strike crisis are:

Baltimore & Ohio; Bessemer & Lake Erie; Boston & Albany; Boston & Maine; Buffalo, Rochester & Pittsburg; Buffalo & Susquehanna; Central New England; Chicago, Indianapolis & Louisville; Chicago, Terre Haute & Southeastern; Chicago, Indiana & Southern; Cincinnati, Northern; Cincinnati, Hamilton & Dayton; Cleveland, Cincinnati, Chicago & St. Louis; Coal & Coke; Delaware & Hudson; Delaware, Lackawanna & Western; Detroit, Toledo & Ironton; Dunkirk, Allegheny Valley & Pittsburg; Erie; Grand Rapids & Indiana; Hocking Valley; Indiana Harbor Belt; Indianapolis Union; Kanawha & Michigan; Lake Erie and Western; Lake Erie, Alliance & Wheeling; Lake Shore & Michigan Southern; Lehigh Valley; Long Island; Maine Central; Michigan Central; New York Central & Hudson River; New York, Chicago & St. Louis; New York, New Haven & Hartford; New York, Ontario & Western; New York, Philadelphia & Norfolk; New York, Susquehanna & Western; New Jersey & New York; Pennsylvania Lines east; Pennsylvania lines west; Pere Marquette; Pittsburg & Lake Erie; Reading system; Toledo & Ohio Central; Toledo, St. Louis & Western; Vandalia lines; Western Maryland; Wheeling & Lake Erie; West Side Belt line; Wabash; Pittsburg terminal.

Three Lines Unaffected.

The list includes practically all but three of the railroads in the territory roughly described as east of Chicago and north of the Potomac river. The three exceptions are the Central Railroad of New Jersey, whose contract with the engineers does not expire until June 1 and the Central Vermont and Rutland railroads in Vermont, which have a separate agreement with the men employed so that the result will be their taking up the wage question directly with the men.

It is declared by Stone that 34,000 men will be affected by a strike order. Of these 25,700 are members of the Brotherhood of Locomotive Engineers, and about 6,500 are in the Brotherhood of Firemen and Enginemen, who, the engineers declare, will join the strike. The rest are non-union men who, Chief Stone said, have joined in the strike vote passed by the brotherhood.

BUD FISHER A BENEDICT

Creator of Mutt and Jeff Deliberately Disregards Mutt's Advice.

New York, April 23.—"Bud" Fisher, the cartoonist, has become a benedict. Despite the fact that he has for some time been fully aware of the marital troubles of a close friend of his, one Mutt, he deliberately embarked on the sea of matrimony via the elopement route.

The young woman is Miss Pauline Welch, a pretty blonde vaudeville actress.

EXPEDITION FOR ASTOR'S BODY

MILLION DOLLARS WOULD BE SPENT TO FIND IT.

Millionaire Was About to Change Will So as to Provide for An Expected Heir.

New York, April 23.—Vincent Astor admits for the first time since the sinking of the Titanic that he had lost all hope of seeing his father alive. Time in which survivors afloat on wreckage might keep up a spark of life is long past. Every ship that passed over the floes of broken ice, bearing bodies of the dead on the face of the sea, have been heard from.

Mr. Astor did not know whether he would send an expedition out from Halifax in search for his father's body. Such an expedition will probably be sent, but the details of the plans are yet to be worked out.

At the offices of the Astor estate there was intense activity in making arrangements. While no reward has been offered for the recovery of Colonel Astor's body, it is known that a million dollars will be freely spent in an effort to find it. The size of the reward for the recovery of the body by outsiders may be guessed at from this information.

The managers of the estate have been in conference with the Marine engineers and have retained several to go with the expedition.

From those in the confidence of young Mr. Astor and from the managers of the estate, it was learned that the last trip of Colonel Astor, which caused him to engage passage on the Titanic, was due to his desire to make changes in his will in anticipation of the birth of his new heir in about two months, the contingency of which he had been made certain.

He had already prepared a will which covered the fact of his marriage to Madeline Force. But for some reason not clear he wished to make more definite the proportion of the estate which was to go to the expected heir.

The coming to New York of Mrs. Ava Willing Astor, who divorced Colonel Astor, and her daughter, Muriel, is not believed to have anything to do with the partitioning of the estate, except so far as it affects Muriel Astor.

There are reasons why it might be more convenient for the purpose of disposing of so vast a fortune that the heirs should all be in the country.

72 LIVES LOST IN SUNDAY STORM

SECTIONS OF ILLINOIS AND INDIANA DEVASTATED—100 FAMILIES HOMELESS.

NEARLY 200 ARE INJURED

Damage to Property Estimated at Between $500,000 and $2,000,000—Bush, Ill., Reduced to Ruins.

St. Louis, April 23.—Latest reports from the storm-swept territory of southwestern Illinois told of more than 72 dead, 200 injured and property damage estimated at between $500,000 and $2,000,000.

Bush, a village of 600 in the northwestern corner of Williamson county, suffered heaviest. The two storms which wrought havoc in central and southern Illinois Sunday evening met at Bush, at 6 p. m., one coming from the northwest and the other from the southeast.

Fifteen persons were killed, three died of injuries and a hundred more are suffering injuries as the result of the storm. The two storms met at a velocity of 75 miles an hour and in a few minutes, Bush was in ruins. The property of the Western Coal & Mining company was destroyed as was the postoffice, general department store, hotels, restaurants and 40 dwellings. Thirty-five other dwellings were partially wrecked. In addition to the dead and injured accounted for, 15 persons are missing.

Thirteen persons, a family of eight and five boarders, sought refuge in a cistern. The house was blown over, covering the opening of the cistern and the 13 were not rescued until late yesterday.

Traffic on the Herrin, St. Louis and Benton divisions of the St. Louis, Iron Mountain and Southern railroad will be tied up for a few days because of the wrecking of 60 freight cars on the main line near Bush.

Family Wiped Out.

J. W. Campbell was section foreman at Bush. With his wife and six children he was sitting in the section house when the storm demolished it, killing the occupants instantly. One son, 16 years old, was in Benton when the storm broke and escaped injury.

A cow was picked up in a Bush street, carried 100 yards by the wind and landed safely on the railroad tracks. Guards have been placed around the general store to prevent looting and the contents are being distributed to survivors.

A trainload of injured were taken from Bush to Murphysboro, where three died. They have not been identified. Seventeen persons are reported dead at Marion, but the count has not been verified. A two-year-old child was killed by the storm in Hamilton county, where the wind left a path of ruin 40 yards wide. Three are reported dead at Murphysboro and five are seriously injured.

Three Dead at Willsville.

Willsville reported three dead and 20 injured. In the district within 12 miles east of Bush, eight are known to be dead and 30 injured. Seventy-five families are homeless and destitute in southwestern Illinois and an appeal has been sent to the state. In the meantime, officials of the St. Louis, Iron Mountain and Southern railway, led by W. E. Merrifield, division superintendent, are looking after the rescuing of survivors.

William Gambill and his two daughters were killed at Freeman in Williamson county. Gambill was crushed by a falling barn. The two women were carried 100 feet into the air. A son and farm hand are believed to be fatally injured.

Kankakee Loss is Heavy.

Kankakee, Ill.—Damage amounting to $500,000 resulted from Sunday evening's storm in this section of Illinois. Reports from Grand Park show that 4 residences and buildings were demolished there.

Levees Being Strengthened.

New Orleans, April 23.—Reassuring reports concerning the levees of the Mississippi river which remain intact were received at the offices of the United States army engineers here from inspectors stationed at all weak points south of Vicksburg. Another hard fight against high waters is ahead, however, and Captain C. O. Sherrill, chief of the government engineers, began concentrating his forces in the vicinity of the Red River landing, about 40 miles south of Natchez.

Fifteen Killed in Alabama.

Birmingham, April 23.—A tornado swept Adamsville, Hinckney City, Judgtown, Brookside and several other mining towns in this district. Incomplete reports say twelve to fifteen persons were killed and several hurt.

CARL HAYDEN

Carl Hayden, new congressman-at-large from Arizona, is getting acquainted with his official duties rapidly and watching over the interests of the new state.

SHIP IGNORED TITANIC SIGNALS

FOURTH OFFICER SAYS HE CLEARLY SAW LIGHTS.

Shown Ismay Planned Early Flight for Himself and Crew from the Country.

Washington, April 23.—With succor only five miles away, the Titanic slid into its watery grave, carrying with it more than 1,600 of its passengers and crew, while an unidentified steamer that might have saved all failed or refused to see the frantic signals flashed to it for aid. This phase of the tragic disaster was brought out before the senate investigating committee when J. B. Boxhall, fourth officer of the Titanic, told of his unsuccessful attempts to attract the stranger's attention.

This ship, according to Boxhall, could not have been more than five miles away and was steaming toward the Titanic. So close was it that from the bridge Boxhall plainly saw its masthead lights and side lights. Both with rockets and with the Morse electric signal did the young officer hail the stranger. Capt. Smith and several others in the vicinity of the bridge the vessel had seen them and was signaled at the time their belief that nalling in reply. Boxhall failed to see the replies, however, and in any case the steamer kept on its course obliquely past the Titanic without extending aid.

This, and the declaration by P. A. S. Franklin, vice president of the White Star line, that there were not sufficient lifeboats aboard the Titanic to care for the ship's company at one time were the features of the hearing.

The official was quizzed throughout the morning session on the messages exchanged between the Carpathia and himself after the ship had started for New York with the Titanic's survivors aboard. Among the survivors was J. Bruce Ismay, managing director of the line.

Among the wireless telegrams read into the record was one from Mr. Ismay urging that the steamship Cedric be held until the Carpathia arrived with its sorry burden. He declared he believed it most desirable that the survivors of the Titanic's crew be rushed out of the country as quickly as possible. He also, the message said, would sail on the Cedric and asked that clothing be ready at the pier for him when the Carpathia docked. The senate's subpoenas blocked the plan.

HOME BURNS; FOUR DEAD

Canadian Farmer's Three Children and Hired Man Perish.

Prince Albert, April 23.—Four persons were burned to death in a fire which destroyed the residence of Robert Adamson, a farmer three miles west of Shelbrook. The dead are, Hazel Naimo, aged eight, Cecil, aged six, Horace, aged 3, John Ruhlban, the hired man.

The details of the fire indicate that Mr. Adamson who slept down stairs got up and started the fire in the cook stove. He called the hired man who answered and then went down to the barn. A few minutes later, on hearing screams, he ran back to find the house in flames. He succeeded in getting a ladder up to the upstairs window and pulled at the bed clothes but could not find the children.

In the meantime, Mrs. Adamson who was severely burned about the arms, called to the hired man to throw the children out of the window, but getting no response, she attempted to get out of the door but was unable to open it and had to escape by the window with the baby in her arms.

25 BODIES ARE IDENTIFIED

LIST IS SENT INTO THE OFFICES OF WHITE STAR LINE NEW YORK.

NOTABLE NAMES MISSING

One Garbled Name Believed to Be That of George D. Widener—Another Ship Goes Out to Search.

New York, April 23.—The first list of names of bodies recovered from the Titanic disaster by the cable steamer Mackay-Bennett was received here through wireless messages to the White Star line offices.

The list of 25 names contain none of several of the most prominent men who perished unless it be that "Geo. W. Widen" as sent by wireless refer as is believed probable to George D. Widener of Philadelphia.

The original passenger lists of the Titanic do not mention "Widen," which apparently established the identity of the body as that of Mr. Widener, son of P. A. B. Widener, one of the directors of the White Star line who, together with his son, Harry, was lost.

The list as received at the White Star line offices is as follows:

Bodies Identified.

L. A. Hoffman.
Mrs. Alexander Robbins.
Wm. H. Harbeck.
Malcolm Johnson.
A. J. Halverson.
H. W. Ashe.
Leslie Williams.
Leslie Galinski.
A. H. Hayter.
Jerry Monroe.
Frederick Sutton.
J. S. Gill.
Ernest E. Tomlin.
George Rosenshire.
N. Marriott.
John H. Chapman.
W. Colbine.
H. Greenberg.
Simon Sother.
N. Colas Rasher.
—— Shea.
George W. Widen.
Ramon Artagaveytia.
Nihil Schedig.
R. B. Att.
Steward No. 76.
Yosite Drazenoul.

A number of the 25 names in the list do not check up with the Titanic's passenger list, which leads to the belief that a number of the bodies recovered are members of the Titanic's crew.

Names Much Garbled.

The White Star officials studied without success in interpreting the meaning of some of the spellings, and came to the conclusion that many of them were badly garbled because of the fact that the list had been relayed. It came via the steamer La Conia to the Cape Race wireless station and was sent by cable to New York. Telegraph operators acquainted with both Morse and continental code speculated as to whether the names of Maj. Archibald Butt and Col. John Jacob Astor were intended in two instances, but they could come to no decision, that appeared trustworthy in such a case.

In the list as it came the following combination appeared:

"Nihil Schedig R. B. Att, which operators believe might have been intended for Major Archibald Butt's name.

Similar speculation developed over the name "N. Colas Rasher," a name which the White Star line could not account for and which telegraph operators thought might be Col. Astor's.

The White Star line dispatched a combination in an effort to clear up such questionable interpretations.

According to a message from Troy, N. Y., A. J. Halverson, whose body has been recovered, was the foreign representative of Cluett, Peabody & Co., of that city. He was returning with his wife from South America, having gone to Europe for a brief visit. They postponed their departure to take the Titanic. Mrs. Halverson was saved.

Another Ship Sent for Bodies.

Halifax, N. S.—Rush orders were received here to prepare another to go in search of the dead. The cable ship Minia was chartered and local undertakers placed 150 coffins on board, while 100 tons of ice were stored away in the holds.

A quantity of iron was also placed on board to be used in burying the unidentified. The Minia is under orders to meet the steamer Mackay-Bennett. Rev. Hind will be transferred to the Minia and the Mackay-Bennett then will proceed to port with the dead.

Gossip.

If a report is said to be a matter of common knowledge it's a sign it can't be proved.—Washington Post.

THE WEATHER.
Fair and warmer tonight and Thursday.

THE BROOKLYN DAILY EAGLE

Complete Stock Market

LAST EDITION. Volume 72A No. 114 ★ NEW YORK CITY, WEDNESDAY, APRIL 24, 1912. ★ 28 PAGES. THREE CENTS.

WOODRUFF MAY DROP MR. TAFT

Leader Admits Ardent Admiration for Colonel Roosevelt.

HE SEES PRENDERGAST

Won't Discuss Prospect of Somersault, but His Words Are Significant.

BUSINESS INTERESTS SAFE

Should Roosevelt Be Republican Presidential Candidate, Woodruff Is Sure.

WOODRUFF ON ROOSEVELT.

There is no more ardent admirer of Colonel Roosevelt in this country than I am. That does not mean that I am in favor of his nomination as against President Taft. I am doing everything I can and shall do everything I can for the nomination of Taft.

If Roosevelt should be nominated I don't think there would be the slightest danger to the business interests of this country. Such talk is silly and I have told this to hundreds of people with whom I have discussed the Presidential situation.

You can tell this to anybody you please.

Timothy L. Woodruff, the county leader of the Republican organization in Kings County, made the foregoing statements yesterday during a conference which he held with Controller Prendergast. The last part of Mr. Woodruff's statement is regarded as significant. The friends of Colonel Roosevelt are inclined to believe that it is only a question of time when Mr. Woodruff and the Kings County delegation to the national convention will come out automatically—that is the way they express it—in favor of Colonel Roosevelt to lead the national fight of the Republican organization.

The defection of Sheriff Law and his frank proclamation that he regards Col. Roosevelt as the logical Presidential candidate of the Republican organization came as a distinct surprise and shock to the Taft leaders in Brooklyn. But they will probably be more amazed when they learn that immediately after Mr. Law made his announcement, Mr. Woodruff sought a conference with Controller Prendergast during which the presidentia lsituation was freely discussed.

Woodruff Sought Out Conference With Prendergast.

It is not sufficiently clear yet, why Mr. Woodruff, who has been one of President Taft's strongest partisans in Brooklyn, should indirectly seek Controller Prendergast's opinions on the Presidential outlook. Mr. Prendergast is the original Roosevelt man of prominence in Kings County and is also one of the delegates to the national convention.

Controller Prendergast declines to give his impressions of the motive which caused Mr. Woodruff to seek a conference with him and discuss national politics. Nevertheless the general impression is that the support of the Old Guard in this State toward President's Taft renomination is bound by a very slender thread. That thread can be broken any time if any situation arises to indicate that the Roosevelt forces may control the Chicago convention. The friends of the Colonel are beginning to believe that Mr. Woodruff is preparing himself for a political somersault to mount the Roosevelt bandwagon.

Mr. Woodruff, however, is not yet prepared to make any such admission. He frankly acknowledged that he and Controller Prendergast had gone over the national political situation.

Woodruff Says He Has Greatest Admiration for Roosevelt.

"I talked as a Taft man and the Controller as a supporter of Colonel Roosevelt," said Mr. Woodruff.

"I have the greatest admiration for the Colonel, but I am still for Taft," he continued smilingly.

"We also talked on a few patronage matters," he continued.

Mr. Woodruff then spoke reminiscently of the debate which he had with the late Senator McCarren, during which he took up the defense of Colonel Roosevelt that he, as President, was not responsible for the panic of 1907.

"I must look up the copies of my speech in that debate," said Mr. Woodoruff. "If I remember rightly I think Colonel Roosevelt has cribbed some of the arguments I used at that time."

Mr. Prendergast, it was learned, made no promises to Mr. Woodruff on the patronage question. The Controller recognizes him as the leader of the county organization and he suggested to Mr. Woodroff that it might be a good idea to send the man whom he has in mind to the Finance Department, so that he, as the appointing power, can look them over and pass upon their qualifications.

Law's Defection Only Beginning of Revolt, Say Roosevelt Men.

Sheriff Law's advocacy of Colonel Roosevelt's nomination means, according to those who are acquainted with the situation in Brooklyn that Jacob W. Holzman, his law partner and a delegate to the National convention, will vote for Colonel Roosevelt. The defection of Mr. Law, the friends of Colonel Roosevelt say, is only the beginning of revolt against the plan of the county leaders to support President Taft for a renomination. A prominent supporter of the Colonel said today that he could give the names of a number of other delegates from Kings County to the national convention who will break away from the Taft programme in the course of the next few days.

Though Controller Prendergast maintained a discreet silence, and referred all inquiries to Mr. Woodruff, it is understood that the Kings County leader and State Chairman William Barnes, jr., are not the enthusiastic Taft supporters that they were in the beginning of the campaign. The results in Pennsylvania, Illinois, Nebraska and Oregon have rather disturbed Mr. Barnes. His statement of yesterday that he had 83 delegates to the national convention sewed up for Taft is described as nothing but a bluff by the Roosevelt people.

While they refused to give the names friends of Roosevelt said today that there were a number of delegates to the national convention from the western and eastern tier of counties in this State, who are being counted on by Mr. Barnes as Taft delegates, but who will really vote for the Colonel. That statement, as far as the delegates from the eastern tier of counties is concerned, was confirmed yesterday by a former Governor of this State.

TWO STRIKES PUZZLE.

President Taft may be able to prevent the great strike which threatens to tie up the railroads, but can he settle the colossal strike now paralyzing the Republican Party?

GIRLS IN HIGH HEELS WORK AS FARMERS

Adelphi Students in Kindergarten Teaching Tackle Spade and Hoe.

ARE ADMIRINGLY WATCHED.

Plant Vegetables and Flowers, but Are Not Oversanguine as to Results.

Thirty-five young women of Adelphi College this morning tried to prove that close fitting skirts and high heeled shoes are not a drawback to gardening and farming.

These young women, bedecked in such a way that every young man passing by, found it excusable to waste his employer's time in watching, created some excitement at the corner of Gates and Franklin avenues. In tow of Miss E. V. Gaines, their teacher, the girls marched to thes pacious garden, which is owned by Mrs. Post, who graciously allowed the use of the plot for the purpose.

These girls have been studying in the laboratory, the scientific end of gardening, but the present day interest in this field led to an experiment today in the practical end of planting seeds.

The girls are of the Kindergarten Normal Class and some day will be teaching other youngsters how to create a pretty garden, or useful vegetable plot in their back yards. The brigade today was fully equipped with shovel, rake and hoe and their progress almost looked like a suffragette parade in London.

For two hours and a half the girls turned sod, planted seeds and placed pegs in their own spaces assigned to them. Each girl had a plot of six and a half feet by four feet for vegetables, and in front of this was a space of one and a half feet for flowers. It is still a little early for the flowers and today only onions, lettuce, carrots, beets and radishes were planted. Next week beans are to be planted and the following week will come the flowers.

This is not the only Adelphi class that is to have actual experience in gardening, for the senior class is also to take up the subject. They are studying the heredity of plants, under the guidance of Mrs. Walter Weil.

Miss Gaines today was hoping that the experiment would prove successful, but she looked dubiously at the high heels, the hobble skirts and the "near ballroom" regalia amid the sod.

BURGLAR TRIPPED ON STAIRS.

Fled Empty-Handed From Home of Dr. Frederick H. Bruce.

Dr. and Mrs. Frederick H. Bruce were about to retire shortly after midnight last Saturday after a reception held in their home at 296 Sixth avenue, when they were startled by the noise of some one tripping on the stairs. Doctor Bruce rushed to the basement in time to see a desperate-looking man dart through a rear door. The intruder escaped empty-handed in First street. The case was reported to the Bergen street station, but Doctor Bruce was unable to give a description of the burglar.

STEEL TRUST SUIT EXAMINER.

Trenton, N. J., April 24—Announcement was made here today that Henry P. Brown of Philadelphia has been appointed examiner to take testimony in the proceeding instituted by the United States Government for the dissolution of the United States Steel Corporation and some of its subsidiary concerns.

FRANKFURT REACHED SCENE TOO LATE

Commander Got First Wireless C. Q. D. Sent by Doomed Titanic.

DESCRIBES FATAL ICEBERG.

Huge Mass Showed Effect of Collision When Frankfurt Arrived at Spot of Disaster.

Bremerhaven, April 24—The North German Line steamer Frankfurt, which, according to her commander, Captain Hattorff, was the first vessel to receive the Titanic's appeal for help, arrived here today.

Captain Hattorff reports that he sighted the iceberg which sunk the White Star steamer, bearing evidences of the collision, shortly before arriving on the scene of the catastrophe. The Frankfurt on receiving the appeal for help immediately headed at the utmost speed in the direction of the Titanic. The German vessel made thirteen and one-half knots, though normally her speed was only twelve, but she did not reach the scene of the disaster until 10 o'clock Monday morning.

Captain Hattorff states that his first message from the Titanic was received at 12:10 o'clock Monday morning. It asked him to communicate the Frankfurt's position which was immediately done. The Titanic then communicated her own position as 41.54 latitude, 50.24 longitude and stated that she was fast in the ice and urgently needed assistance.

The Frankfurt was then 140 nautical miles distant. Captain Hattorff informed the Titanic that the Frankfurt would reach her at 11 o'clock.

Got C. Q. D. at 12:15 A.M. on Monday.

Hattorff reports that at 12:15 a.m. the distress signal "C Q D" was received from the Titanic, and that at 1:05 the Titanic reported that her passengers were being loaded into lifeboats. Wireless communication with the Titanic was interrupted at 1:15 and Captain Hattorff believes that the White Star ship then sank.

The Frankfurt, steaming at top speed, reached the scene of the disaster at 10 o'clock in the morning, passing on the way three great icebergs, seventeen smaller ones and great ice fields of from 10 to 30 miles in extent. The greatest iceberg was 120 feet high and 900 feet long.

The Frankfurt, with the Russian steamer Birma, the Allan liner Virginian and the Cunard steamship Carpathia, cruised among the icebergs searching for the victims of the catastrophe, but without success. The Carpathia's officers said, according to Captain Hattroff, that they had picked up twenty-two boats and that two other were missing. As a further search was useless and as the captain wished to escape from the labyrinth of ice, the Frankfurt resumed her course at noon.

The foregoing facts were taken from the official report of Captain Hattorff to the North German Lloyd Steamship Company.

Iceberg Showed Effects of Collision.

Captain Hattorff described to a correspondent the iceberg which the Frankfurt passed about an hour before reaching the scene of the disaster and which he believes sunk the Titanic. At one place the mass of ice was darkly colored and badly splintered this evidently being the point of impact. The weather was clear and the wind was blowing about five miles an hour.

The officers of the Frankfurt believe that the Titanic before the accident must have passed big ice fields which should have caused her officers to take precautions.

The Frankfurt on leaving the scene had to steam an hour to the southward to emerge from the ice before she could turn her course to the eastward.

$5,000 DEPOSITED

To Pay Arbuckle Estate Claims. $1,500,000 for Inheritance Tax.

In order to pay all claims against the John Arbuckle estate, the two sisters of the late coffee and sugar millionaire, Miss Christina Arbuckle and Mrs. Catherine A. Jamison, who are the only heirs, have deposited $5,000 with the Brooklyn Trust Company. A further deposit of $1,500,000 in bonds and other securities has been made at the same place to pay the State inheritance tax as soon as the amount can be ascertained.

No schedule of the value of the estate has yet been filed in the administration department of the surrogate's office, beyond an affidavit by William N. Dykman, of Dykman, Oeland & Kuhn, attorneys for the Arbuckle heirs, in which he states on information and belief that the amount is "over $1,000,000."

According to affidavits by the two sisters John Arbuckle owned the following real property in this State: The residence at 315 Clinton avenue, and one-third interest in the Arbuckle building at 367 Fulton street; the Hotel Margaret, on Columbia Heights, and the Sunnyside apartments at 780 Park avenue, Manhattan.

TITANIC MEMORIAL IN PARIS.

Paris, April 24—Myron T. Herrick, United States Ambassador to France; Sir Francis Bertie, the British Ambassador, and several representatives of the French Government, with a large number of prominent personages, attended today a special requiem mass which was celebrated at the Madeleine for the victims of the Titanic disaster. The ceremony was under the auspices of the French Red Cross Society.

There was a touching scene as the entire congregation joined in the singing of "Nearer, My God, to Thee."

THE WIRELESS DISTRESS CALLS.

C Q D — IN CONTINENTAL CODE
—·—· ——·— —··

S O S — IN MORSE CODE
··· · · ···

S O S — IN CONTINENTAL CODE
··· ——— ···

"C. Q. D." and "S. O. S." are the signals used by vessels in case of distress and when aid is needed. The former is the call that is employed by the Marconi company and on foreign ships, the international or continental code being used in forming the characters. This is slightly different from the Morse code, in that spaces in the combination of characters are not used. "S. O. S." is the American code for signals. It came into use after the Republic disaster, when the United and other wireless companies were formed in this country.

Operator Phillips of the Titanic first sent out the "C. Q. D." call, but later, under orders from Captain Smith, he sent out the Morse call of "S. O. S."

THE SENATE COMMITTEE HEARING ON THE TITANIC DISASTER.

This picture was taken yesterday, at Washington, and shows the following persons, as numbered: No. 1, Senator Perkins of California; No. 2, Senator W. Afl Smith (chairman), of Michigan; No. 3, Senator Newlands of Nevada; No. 4, Senator Fletcher of Florida, and No. 5, Bruce Ismay, Managing Director of the White Star Line. All the men setting near Mr. Ismay, along the side of the room, are White Star officials.

NON-PARTY VOTES SOUGHT BY COLONEL

Taft Manager Says Roosevelt Bids for Democratic and Other Support at Primaries

QUOTES NEWSPAPER AD.

Early Morning Cabinet Conference Considers Hot Shot Which Taft Is to Fire at Roosevelt.

Eagle Bureau,
608 Fourteenth Street.

Washington, April 24—In a statement issued this afternoon William B. McKinley, director of the National Taft Bureau, charges that the Massachusetts Roosevelt Committee caused a paid advertisement to be printed in a Springfield newspaper Monday, April 22, as follows:

Remember, you don't have to be enrolled in any party to vote at this primary."

"What does it mean?" says the McKinley statement. "It means that Theodore Roosevelt is making a paid bid for the votes of Democrats, Socialists and Prohibitionists to defeat President Taft, who is asking for Republican votes for his renomination. Here, openly, is the evidence that he has done the same thing secretly all over the United States."

Mr. McKinley charges that in all the primaries held thus far Colonel Roosevelt has received the votes of large numbers of Democrats.

At a conference at the White House, that began at 8 o'clock last night, and came to an end at 2:20 o'clock this morning, consideration was given the political speeches to be delivered in Massachusetts tomorrow by President Taft. It was the desire of the President and his advisers to make these speeches "bullet proof," as most of them will be aimed at Theodore Roosevelt and recent caustic remarks of his concerning the policies of the administration.

The President has finally decided, after a good deal of persuasion, to go after Colonel Roosevelt, and the Taft people are seeing to it that the President's speeches are so framed that there shall be no "come back."

For many weeks now the President's friends have been trying to induce him to reply to the personal attacks made by the former President. He resisted the importunities in this regard on the ground that it was not befitting a person occupying the presidential office to engage in personal controversy in the course of a political campaign.

A crisis having been reached in the Taft candidacy, the President has at last awakened to a realization that he must either speak out now, or take a chance of losing the nomination. Mr. Taft's friends declare that after the delivery of his speeches in Massachusetts the prostrate political form of Colonel Roosevelt will be found lying outside the ring.

WOMAN KILLS CHILD AND SELF

Mrs. Kangas Became Despondent Brooding Over Titanic Disaster.

Believed to have become despondent by constantly brooding over the fate of the Titanic victims, Mrs. Ella Kangas of 762 Thirty-ninth street, yesterday afternoon put her 9-year-old daughter Helen to bed and then waiting until she was asleep followed her, after attaching a gas tube to the jet above the bed and turning on the gas. When found at 6 o'clock by her husband, Andrew, one end of the gas tube was in her mouth and the bedclothes had been pulled over her own and her daughter's head. Both had been dead for several hours when found.

Yesterday morning when Kangas, who is a carpenter, left for Coney Island, where he is employed, his wife appeared to be in excellent spirits. He kissed both his wife and daughter, telling them that he would probably get home late in the afternoon. On reaching the street, he said, each waved to him from the front window.

Kangas said that his daughter had had spinal meningitis when 13 months old and had never been able to talk as a consequence. She was very bright, however, and made an excellent record at Public School 131, where she was a pupil. She never had been very well and her mother worried a great deal about her. Kangas thinks that this fact, together with her taking to heart the sinking of the Titanic was largely responsible for her act.

It was shortly before 6 o'clock when Kangas returned home.

He smelled gas, and fearing the worst called a policeman and the two went upstairs and discovered the bodies.

Kangas said that his wife must have planned her death and that of the child, as she had gone to a store earlier in the day to purchase the gas tube.

The two bodies will be buried in Greenwood Cemetery in the same grave tomorrow.

FALLS 50 FEET OFF BUILDING.

Anthony Dougherty of Brooklyn Will Probably Die From Injuries.

Crowds of passengers of the New York Central Railroad and many pedestrians at Forty-second street and Vanderbilt avenue, Manhattan, saw a man fall from the top of a new building of the Grand Central Terminal near that corner this afternoon to an areaway fifty feet below. The man was Anthony Dougherty, 35 years old, of Vanderbilt and Myrtle avenues, Brooklyn, employed by the contractors putting up the new building. He was removed to the Flower Hospital, where it was said his injuries would probably result in his death.

Dougherty was setting a stone on the cornice of the building, and in stepping from one stone to another stumbled and pitched headlong to the ground.

REINHARDT ASSETS $25,000.

Judge Mayer today appointed Benjamin W. B. Brown as receiver for J. Thomas Reinhardt, stock broker, at 38 Broad street, Manhattan, with a bond of $5,000. The liabilities, the creditors state, possibly amount to several hundred thousand dollars and they say that the assets are in the neighborhood of $25,000.

FOUR MEN BEAT AGED WOMAN

Mrs. Mary Carney Brutally Assaulted by Burglars in Her Flat.

Mrs. Mary Carney of Eighth avenue and Fifteenth street, is today in a serious condition at the home of her son-in-law, Joseph Garvey, in Eighth avenue, suffering from the effects of a beating she received at the hands of four men in her own home on Monday night.

Mrs. Carney, who is nearly 60 years old, lives on the top floor of the apartment house at Eighth avenue and Fifteenth street and was alone during the early part of Monday evening when a loud knock came at her door. She opened it and four men rushed in. They beat her about the head and body and then ransacked the apartment.

Although it is believed that robbery was the motive of the men, a member of the family stated today that so far they had not missed anything of value from the flat.

Mrs. Carney was taken to the Methodist Episcopal Hospital and attended and afterward removed to her son-in-law's home.

FATHER OF TOT'S COURTS HERE

Dr. A. S. Orne Will Stay in Brooklyn for a While to Study Conditions.

Dr. A. S. Orne, "Father of Children's Courts," was a visitor to Judge Ryan's Children's Court this morning after having completed over 300,000 miles of traveling in the interests of delinquent children in every city in the United States.

Dr. Orne arrived in Brooklyn last night and is stopping for a time at 487 Pacific street. He is here trying to interest the authorities in the erection of houses of correction for the borough, and will canvass the condition of poor children, investigate the social conditions, and inspect the charitable and correctional institutions of Brooklyn.

Dr. Orne claims to have been the one to interest Judge Tuttle, of Chicago, and Judge Lindsay of Denver, the first two Judges to realize the benefit of children's courts, in that subject. Back in 1901, he said, he first approached Judge Lindsay, trying to get him to organize a children's court in Denver. Five years later one was started there. Since that time he has seen the idea developd in every State in he Union except North Carolina. He hopes soon to see that State also adopt it.

MARONEY HELD IN $1,500 BAIL

Brooklyn Policeman to Be Tried on Charge of Petty Larceny.

Patrolman John Maroney, 31 years old, of 1653 Eighty-first street, Brooklyn, attached to them Leonard street station, Manhattan, who was arrested on Sunday night by Captain Rohrig, his commanding officer, on the charge of petty larceny, was held in $1,500 bail for trial in Special Sessions when arraigned before Magistrate Freschi in the Tombs Court today.

The specific charge made against the patrolman by Captain Rohrig was that Maroney abstracted a golf cap and a pair of sleeve buttons from a showcase in front of 96 Warren street, a few minutes previous to his arrest. The captain said that he found a cap and a pair of sleeve buttons, together with the lock and a bunch of skeleton keys, in the patrolman's pocket. The cap and buttons, the captain said, were identified by Edward Jones, owner of the store.

BOMBS THROWN AT SOLDIERS.

Lisbon, April 24—Many soldiers and civilians were killed today at Villa Nova de Gaia, a suburbffi of Oporto, when the strikers threw a number of bombs into the ranks of the infantry, who replied with volleys of rifle shot.

OLYMPIC DESERTED BY PART OF CREW

Feared That Collapsible Lifeboats on Titanic's Sister Ship Were Unseaworthy.

300 MEN REFUSE TO SAIL.

Tried to Get Seamen to Join Them. Departure of White Star Liner Delayed.

Southampton, England, April 24—Three hundred of the firemen and greasers belonging to the crew of the Olympic struck five minutes before the White Star liner was due to sail today for New York.

The men deserted the ship in a body. They gave as their reason for striking that the collapsible lifeboats installed on the vessel were unseaworthy.

A deputation of men employed in the engine room of the Olympic waited on the officers of the ship and on Commander Clarke, the chief of the emigration office in Southampton, to whom they declared that the collapsible craft on the Olympic were flimsy.

They refused to sail unless wooden lifeboats were substituted for the collapsible ones, and also demanded that two additional seamen be signed, one for each boat.

Commander Clarke argued with the men, explaining that it was impossible to procure wooden lifeboats in time. He assured them that he had previously officially examined all the collapsible boats and was perfectly satisfied with them.

Commander Clarke offered to take the Olympic to the Cowes Roads and allow any of the crew to select any boat or boats on board, and he would prove by demonstration that they were absolutely safe.

The men refused to be convinced by Commander Clarke and left the ship in a body. They attempted to get all the seamen, also, to leave the liner, but this move was checkmated by the White Star officials, who removed all the gangways.

By pressing into service all the available engineroom hands on the other White Star and American liners in port, the Olympic was able to leave the dock just before 2 o'clock this afternoon and proceed down Southampton waters, where she awaits a fresh batch of firemen and greasers.

One of the strikers alleged that he put his thumb through the canvas of one of the new collapsible boats.

The White Star officials declared that the requisite complement of firemen, greasers and crew is aboard the Olympic and that the vessel will shortly proceed on her voyage.

The Olympic has 1,400 passengers on board.

ISMAY ORDERED TO GET AWAY FROM LIFEBOAT

Fifth Officer Says Director Interfered With Lowering of Craft.

HAD ONLY ONE DRILL

Witness Declares He Left His Reckoning of Ship's Position on Table.

INTERFERENCE IS RESENTED.

Smith Will Not Tolerate Any Further Attempt by Anyone to Shape Course of Committee.

Washington, April 24—J. Bruce Ismay, the chief official of the steamship line which owned the ill-fated Titanic, was ordered away from one of the ship's lifeboats while it was being lowered, because, in his excitement, he was interfering with the ship's officers.

Langauge too objectionable to be repeated aloud in the Senate inquiry into the Titanic disaster was used by Harold G. Lowe, the fifth officer of the ship.

Lowe dramatically recited to the Senate investigating committee how he, not knowing that he was talking to the head of the company which employed him, had told Ismay to "Get to —— out of here so that I can work," while Lowe and other sailors were trying to lower the first lifeboat on the starboard side of the Titanic.

Lowe declared that Ismay was not trying to get into the boat, but that he was very much excited and interfering with the proper lowering of the boat.

"This man (Ismay)," said Lowe, "was greatly excited. He was hollering 'lower' away, lower away, lower away," and I swore at him to order him back."

Lowe said that Ismay went back and made no reply to him. Lowe also testified that he never would have known the man was Ismay if he had not met a steward on board the Carpathia who told him what he had done and asked him why he "swore at Ismay."

Senator William Alden Smith, the chairman, announced after a meeting with his colleagues that the British witnesses would be called as rapidly as possible before any more passengers were examined.

Frederick Fleet, lookout on the Titanic, was recalled as the first witness of the day.

Senator Burton asked:

"When you were in the Titanic were your eyes examined?"

"Yes."

"How often?"

"Frequently."

"Can you distinguish colors?"

"Yes, sir."

"Did you, when in the Titanic's crow's nest, see a light?"

Saw No Light Until He Got Into Lifeboat.

"No. I saw no light until I got in the lifeboat. Then I saw a bright light on the forward bow. I don't know what it was. Mr. Lightoller saw it before we got off the Titanic, and told us to pull

J. BRUCE ISMAY AND P. A. S. FRANKLIN ON WAY TO INQUIRY IN WASHINGTON

INSTALLING NEW LIFEBOATS ON ONE OF THE CUNARDERS.

toward it. Finally is disappeared. We never made out what it was."

"When you have binoculars, what share of time do you have the glasses to your eyes while on the lookout?"

"If we fancy we see anything on the horizon," said Fleet, "then we use the glasses to make sure."

Senator Fletcher asked Fleet if he had helped in the loading of the boats.

"Yes, sir."

"Had you ever had any experience in loading and lowering lifeboats?"

"All of us do in the White Star."

He said he saw no lifeboats loaded other than No. 6, the boat in which he pulled away with about thirty passengers.

"Were there any women left on the decks who did not get in the boat?"

"No, sir; I saw none."

"Did you call for them?"

"Yes, sir."

The witness said that there were a number of men on the decks, but that none of them sought or even asked to be taken on.

Fleet told of the appearance in the boat of a stowaway, who had hidden beneath a seat. The man, an Italian, was of no assistance because of an injured arm. His boat, Fleet said, asked for and got another man from a lifeboat to which they tied up.

"Did you hear any cries for help?" asked Senator Smith.

"Yes, but they were very faint."

"Did you go back to help."

Quartermaster Refused Call for Help From Sinking Ship.

"No, sir; some of the passengers wanted to, but the quartermaster, who was in command, ordered us to keep on rowing."

"How far were you from the Titanic when it sank?"

"Oh, it must have been a mile."

"As to your experience in trying to estimate how far the Titanic was from the iceberg when you sighted it, I should say you did not have any judgment of distance," Senator Smith commented.

"No more, I haven't," Fleet answered, and then was excused.

Senator Smith then arose and formally announced that he wanted to meet an inquiry that had arisen as to the purposes of the committee.

"It is to get all of the facts attending this catastrophe," he said. "The surviving officers and men of this ship are not shipbuilders, and if we can get from them what they know it is all that we can expect. Now, a word as to the plan. It is the intention of the committee to inquire of all subjects of Great Britain who may be in this country, and who may know anything of the disaster, and to hold them here until we have leraned all that we can.

"This course will be pursued until the committee conclude they have obtained all accessible and useful information to a proper understanding of this disaster.

Meddlesome Attempt to Influence Course of Committee.

"Now a word about the difficulty. To the credit of most of the officers and members of the crew, we have experienced little difficulty in securing such witnesses as we thought necessary, but from the beginning until now there has been a voluntary, gratuitous, meddlesome attempt upon the part of certain persons to influence the course of the committee and to shape its procedure.

"Misrepresentations have been made, I have heard. I have not, however, read the newspapers because I did not wish to be prejudiced.

"The representatives of the press have all co-operated in every possible way to lighten the burdens of the committee.

"The committee will not tolerate any further attempt on the part of anyone to shape its course. We shall proceed in our own way and the judgment of our efforts well may be withheld until those who criticise our course may have opportunity to examine the official record."

As Senator Smith delivered this announcement he spoke emphatically and punctuated his remarks by pounding the table with his fists. Afterward he did not give any detailed explanation of what actuated him to make the statement.

Fifth Officer Tells of Lifeboats.

Harold G. Lowe, fifth officer of the Titanic, was the next witness. He told of his early experiences, from the time he ran away to sea at 14 and shipped on a schooner. He knocked around the world on sailing ships, then took up steamers, and about fifteen months ago joined the White Star Line.

Until he shipped on the Titanic, he said, he never before had been in the North Atlantic.

"You were present at the test of the Titanic in Belfast harbor?" asked Stnator Smith.

"Yes, sir."

"What did you do?"

"I looked to the lifeboats. With Mr. Moody and Mr. Boxhall, I looked over the lifeboats, examined them carefully, and found everything in them except that in one a dipper was missing."

As to the collapsible boats, Lowe said he could not remember precisely what was found.

"We did find that there were plenty of oars, with extra oars for each boat," he said.

The witness said that while it had been plannned to hold a lifeboat drill April 1, it was postponed because there was a breeze. In fact, the witness said, it was almost "squally."

The witness declartd there had been no test for speed on the Titanic. He believed the Titanic was capable of making from 24 to 25 knots an hour.

"Have you any idea yourself the speed the Titanic made on her trial trip?" the Senator continued.

"I do not know exactly," Lowe replied, "but I believe it was between 20 and 20½ knots."

"How many revolutions did that speed require?"

"I can't tell exactly, because the revolutions had not been entirely worked out when the ship went down."

"Was there any representative of the British Board of Trade on the Titanic during the trip?"

"Not that I know of."

Only One Drill Held.

The witness said that before the Titanic sailed on her maiden and last voyage one drill of the crew was held. He could not remember whether it was held at Belfast or in the harbor at Southampton. He hesitated, also, when asked his especial station, and did not know whether any other officers were at their stations on the starboard side of the ship, where his station was located.

"I was a complete stranger in the ship," he said, in extenuation. Later he remembered that the test was held at Southampton. He was in charge of one of the two boats lowered there. The entire drill, he said, consisted in rowing bout the harbor for a half hour.

"Now, Mr. Lowe," the Senator con-ed, "no other drill took place after until the accident?"

drill took place after that."

there no fire drill—no alarm, a uiring the presence of each man place?"

lways is fire drill when we rill. There was a fire drill previous to the general drill at Southampton."

"Are you quite sure you had that fire drill?"

"Let me see——," said Lowe. "I don't want to be telling a story—I may be confusing her with some of the other ships."

Lowe thought for a long time and then said: "We will annul that, because I am not sure."

"Well," said the Senator, "we will not annul that and I want your best answer."

Steward F. Dent Ray.

This is the steward who waited on Major Archibald Butt aboard the Titanic and who was called to the White House by President Taft.

"Well, I'm here to help you all I can and I don't remember."

"Then that is what you want us to understand. You do not remember?"

"Yes."

Lowe said that most of the officers of the Titanic at the beginning were strangers to each other.

"Did you ever hear of ice in the vicinity of Newfoundland?"

"No, sir."

"Did you ever hear of an iceberg?" inquired Senator Smith in surprise.

"Yes, sir. Off Cape Horn."

This one, Lowe said, was the only one he had seen in his career until he saw a number at dawn the day following the collision.

Icebergs Were in Titanic Course.

"Were they in the course of the Titanic?"

"Yes sir; they must have been, for they were all around the horizon."

The biggest, he said, was at least 100 feet high. This was from four to five miles away and all were within a radius of six miles.

The Secretary of the Treasury, Franklin MacVeagh, arrived at the committee room during Lowe's examination and sat at the committee table near the chairman throughout the morning session.

"Was the ship on its true course at the time of the collision?" the Senator asked.

"I was in bed, but from the position on the chart, I believe she was on the track," said Lowe.

"Was the Titanic on the north track or the south track?"

"I think she was on the north track, sir."

"What makes you think so?"

"The general run of things."

Lowe said he was not on duty the Sunday night of the accident after 8:30 o'clock. From 6 to 8 that night he was working a dead reckoning for the ship at 8 o'clock. This he reported to the captain.

"Personally?"

Left Paper of Ship's Position on Table.

"No, I put it on his table with a weight on it."

"Wasn't it important?"

"Well, in the general run of things, not so important," said Lowe.

"You mean that the position of the ship was not important?" continued the senator. "Wasn't that to be a part of the ship's log?"

"Oh, yes: I'm not saying it wasn't important for this one voyage. In the event of accident it would be important."

Senator Smith asked the witness flatly if he could give the position of the ship at 8 o'clock on that night.

"No, sir."

"I want you to think hard. If we could get the position at that hour we could figure the speed of the ship by [illegible] elapsed time between then and the time of the collision."

"The speed of the ship on that day was a fraction below 21 knots an hour," said the witness, reading from a memorandum.

Senator Smith criticised the methods employed by the officer in ascertaining the position of the ship. Lowe said he had figured it on the speed of the vessel between noon and 8 o'clock. The chairman questioned the accuracy of such a method, and held that the revolutions of the engines should have been the basis.

"Did you see the captain after 8 o'clock that night?"

"Yes, just after I got out of bed."

"What time?"

"As near as I can judge it was about 12 o'clock."

"After the accident?"

"It must have been, but the impact didn't awaken me."

"Are you a temperate man, Mr. Lowe?"

"I am sir. I say it without fear of contradiction."

"I am glad to hear that because I have just had passed up to me a note which says it was reported from a reputable man that you were drinking the night of the wreck," said Senator Smith.

"Me drinking!" Lowe exclaimed excitedly. "Impossible—that's rubbish—I am a total abstainer."

Lowe pointed out on a deck chart the quarters of all the officers and the chart was filed with the committee.

The witness repeated that he did not know when he was awakened. He said he dressed hurriedly and went on deck and found people with lifebelts on and the boats being prepared.

"I could feel by my feet that something was wrong," he said. "The vessel was tipping and was about 15 degrees by the head."

"Did anyone awaken you?"

"I was not aroused that I know of, but Boxhall told me afterward that he had come into the room and told me we'd struck an iceberg. I don't remember that. I must not have been awake."

Lowe said that when he did get out on deck he began working at the lifeboats.

"I was working the boats under First Officer Murdock," he continued. "Boat No. 5 was the first one we lowered."

"How many officers were helping you on that boat?"

"I should say about ten, two at each end, two in the boat, and others at the ropes."

"Who got in that boat?"

Ordered Ismay Away From Boat.

"I don't know, but there is a man here and had I not been here I would not have known that I ordered Mr. Ismay away from the boat.

"A steward met me on the Carpathia. He said to me 'What did you say to Ismay that night on the deck?' I said I did not know that I had said anything to Mr. Ismay. I said I didn't know Mr. Ismay. I didn't know him. Well, the steward on the Carpathia said I had used very strong language to Mr. Ismay.

"Shall I repeat it?" asked Lowe. "If you want me to I will—if not, I won't."

"I happened to talk to Ismay because he appeared to be getting excited. He was saying, excitedly, Lower, lower away, lower away.' "

At this juncture Chairman Smith asked Ismay about the language, and Mr. Ismay suggested that the objectionable language be written down to see if it was appropriate. This was done. After Chairman Smith had read what Lowe had written, he said: "Then you said this to Mr. Ismay?" not mentioning the objectionable word, but showing it to the witness. "Why did you say it?"

Ismay Did Not Try to Get In Boat.

"Because he, in his anxiety to get the boat lowered," Lowe replied, "was interfering with our work. He was interferring with me, and I wanted him to get back so that we could work. He was not trying to get in the boat. Finally I turned to him and said: 'If you will get to hell out of here we can get this boat away.' "

"Did he step back?"

"Yes."

"Did Mr. Ismay make any reply?"

"No, he did not."

"How many men were in the boat?"

"I'm not sure, sir, but I should say about ten."

"How many men were put into the boat for the purpose of manning her?"

"Five, sir."

The witness did not know whether there was any officer aboard. He said that possibly Mr. Pitman was in that boat or No. 3.

"Were there any male passengers?"

"I think so, because we could find no more women."

In response to questions Lowe said the gear on the davits worked perfectly and the launching of the lifeboat was altogether successful. There was no trouble, he said.

"That's why I spoke as I did to Mr. Ismay," explained the witness.

Senator Smith asked Lowe if in his opinion the lifeboat before it was lowered was loaded to its proper capacity.

Lowe tried to avoid making a direct answer. He complained that the chairman was "pulling him up." Senator Smith insisted upon an answer.

"Yes, sir," said Lowe, finally, "I think it was properly loaded for lowering."

"What is the official quota for such a lifeboat?"

"It is 65.5."

"You mean——"

65 Is Official Quota for Lifeboats.

"That it can carry 65 adults and, say, a boy or a girl."

"Then you wish the committee to nunderstand that a lifeboat under British regulations could not be lowered with safety with new tackle and equipment containing more than 50 people?"

"The dangers are if you overcrowd the boat it will buckle up from the two ends," said Lowe. "The 65.5 is a floating capacity. If you load from the deck to the lower, I should not like to put more than fifty in a lifeboat."

"Mr. Boxhall has stated that his lifeboat contained only twenty-three people when lowered," suggested Senator Smith. "That was not full capacity, was it?"

"Well, he was not in charge of that boat, was he?" replied Mr. Lowe.

"If Officer Lightoller said that boats on the portside were not loaded with more than thirty-five people because of safety, those boats were not loaded to their full capacity, were they?"

"Well," answered Lowe, "that is a matter of personal judgment—some men might think differently about what would be safe."

"All right. What became of lifeboat No. 5?"

"It was lowered and I saw it pull away."

Senator Smith then referred to Third Officer Pitman's testimony yesterday, in which he said there were thirty-five persons in lifeboat No. 5. That being the case, he asked why Pittman could not have gone to the rescue of the drowning whose cries he heard plainly but did not heed.

"Wouldn't he have been able to accommodate thirty more people safely in that lifeboat?" demanded Senator Smith.

"No, sir," said Lowe. "Had he attempted to rescue those in the water he would have endangered the lives of those with him.

"I want to say a word about that danger," Lowe continued. "I heard Major Peuchen say on the stand that the sailors could not row. Sailors and boatmen are different. Many sailors may be at sea for years, and never go in a rowboat. They are different callings. That is the reason that a great many of the sailors could not row."

PIERREPONT ESTATE IS NEARLY $2,000,000

Report of Transfer Tax Appraiser Is Filed With Surrogate.

PORTRAIT VALUED AT $30,000.

It Is Stuart's Painting of Washington, Willed to Son, Robert Low Pierrepont.

An estate of nearly $2,000,000 was left by Henry E. Pierrepont, who died November 7, 1911. The report of State Transfer Tax Appraiser John J. Bridges was filed in the office of Surrogate Ketcham today.

The Gilbert Stuart portrait of George Washington, which was specifically bequeathed to a son, Robert Low Pierrepont, is valued at $30,000, and a portrait of Abraham Lincoln, left to another son, is estimated at $500. The same value is set on a Giroux painting called "Sunset in the Alps," which was left to a daughter.

The residence at 216 Columbia Heights is appraised at $23,500, and real estate at 1 Pierrepont place, of which the decedent owned one-third, at $130,000. In the estate is also included several parcels of land along Furman street and some under water at the Wall street ferry. In St. Lawrence County Mr. Pierrepont owned 90 parcels of real estate, remnants of land bought by his garndfather, William Constable, in 1790. That land is left to a son, Robert Low Pierrepont, and the land in Brooklyn and parcels in Franklin County are left principally to a brother, John Jay Pierrepont.

The total amount of the real property is valued at $146,635.38, and the remainder of the total of $1,848,528.96 consists of bonds and stocks in a number of corporations. The bulk of the estate was left to the five children, Anne P. Luquer of 321 West Eightieth street, Ellen P. Moffat of 12 East Sixty-sixth street, Robert Low Pierrepont of 140 Columbia Heights, Rutherford S. Pierrepont of 216 Columbia Heights, and Seth Low Pierrepont of 2019 Massachusetts avenue, Washington, D. C. The children get $324,173.43 each.

BISHOP'S ANNIVERSARY.

Rt. Rev. C. E. McDonnell Consecrated Twenty Years Ago Tomorrow.

The Right Rev. Charles Edward McDonnell, Bishop of the Roman Catholic Diocese of Brooklyn, will celebrate tomorrow the twentieth anniversary of his consecration.

In accordance with the wishes of the Bishop, the commemoration of the anniversary will be of the quietst possible kind. In the morning he will pontificate at mass of thanksgiving at St. James Procathedral, after which he will confirm a large class of children. It is probable that during the day most of the Brooklyn rectors will call at the Bishop's house to pay their respects, but there will be no general reception.

DR. CLARKE WILL REMAIN.

Pastor of First Presbyterian Church Decides Not to Leave Brooklyn.

Althougih it is not known what church it was that wanted the Rev. Dr. L. Mason Clarke, pastor of the First Presbyterian Church, as its pastor, or where it was located, because he contented himself with saying that he had been considering a call elsewhere, but had gotten through with the consideration, it is known that a proposition came to the eminent pastor, but he has resolved that he will remain in Brooklyn.

A meeting of the trustees of the church was held and the matter of the proposal to Dr. Clarke was taken up and after consultation with him the trustees and the people were rejoiced to receive the assurance that he would continue his pastorate with the First Presbyterian Church.

BANKRUPTCY PETITION.

Carmine Dezego of 923 Kent avenue, a paper manufacturer at 110-116 Classon avenue, today filed a petition (No. 3840) in voluntary bankruptcy in the United States District Court. Liabilities, $35,-580.28; assets, $1,525.

INDEX

To Classified Advertisements in Today's Eagle.

CLEAN TAFT SWEEP IN NEW HAMPSHIRE

Roosevelt Leaders Do Not Expect to Send a Single Delegate From State.

RHODE ISLAND FOR PRESIDENT

Strong Fight in Missouri for Control of Convention—Roosevelt Leads in Kansas Primaries.

Concord, N. H., April 24—A revision of the figures in yesterday's Republican primary election for delegates to the State and district conventions on April 30 was attempted today by both the Taft and Roosevelt campaign managers, but in each political camp the figures only served to emphasize the victory of the President.

Many little towns far to the north and in other obscure regions were still to be heard from today. The figures at the Roosevelt headquarters stand: Taft, 409; Roosevelt, 224, with 178 delegates to be reported.

Roosevelt leaders admitted today that they did not expect to have a New Hampshire delegate to the Chicago convention.

No Taft Opposition in Rhode Island.

Providence, R. I., April 24—No opposition to the election of delegates favoring the renomination of President Taft was developed today in either the State or the three district conventions to select Rhode Island's representatives to the Republican National convention.

The programme for today's State and district conventions had been arranged in detail by the State Central Committee.

Congressman George H. Utter of Westerly was the convention chairman. In addressing the delegates, Mr. Utter declared that "the Theodore Roosevelt we stood by two years ago is not the Theodore Roosevelt of today. Knowing the things that we know now, the time has come for the American people to say that while we had an idol, we have no idol now. Reference to President Taft was greeted with prolonged cheers.

Resolutions instructing the delegates to Chicago to support President Taft's candidacy for the nomination "until released," were adopted, after which the following delegates at large were chosen without opposition:

U. S. Senator Henry F. Lippitt, R. H. I. Goddard, jr., and Robert A. Rice of Providence, and George R. Lawton of Tiverton.

Hot Fight in Missouri.

St. Louis, Mo., April 24—After spending a large part of the night in caucuses, leaders of the Taft and Roosevelt forces in Missouri awoke here this morning prepared to wage later in the day a stubborn battle for the State Committee's appointment of temporary chairman of tomorow's convention. Both sides admitted that this appointment would be a long step toward the victory which each declares it will win.

Roosevelt Leads in Kansas.

Topeka, Kas., April 24—Primaries or conventions in thirteen Kansas counties yesterday added a total of 155 to the list of delegates to the Republican State convention instructed for Colonel Roosevelt.

According to a list compiled to date, Colonel Roosevelt now has a total of 398 delegates to the State Convention and President Taft has 92. To control the convention 450 votes are necessary.

Taft Looks Like Winner in Iowa.

Cedar Rapids, Ia., April 24—The situation prior to the opening of the Republican State convention here today was construed by Taft adherents to point to the selection of Taft delegates-at-large to the national convention and by Cummins suppporters to mean that the Senator's managers had plans for taking control of the permanent organization, which would develop later.

The district conventions for the Second, Fourth and Eleventh districts were held during the morning. Cummins was conceded the four delegates from the Fourth and Eleventh districts, while the Second was considered as a certainty for Taft.

REMEMBERING THE MUSICIANS

Women Arrange Benefit Concerts for Families of Men Who Played as Titanic Sank.

Women of Brooklyn and Manhattan have undertaken arrangements for concerts for the benefit of the families of the musicians aboard the Titanic, who played until the ship went down, and who are counted among the real heroes of the disaster. The musicians were not paid employes of the steamship company, but depended upon subscriptions taken up among the passengers at the end of the trip.

In Manhattan there will be a concert next Saturday evening, April 27, at the Regneas Studio, 133 West Eightieth street. The committee in charge of this event includes Mrs. George Chapman, Mrs. R. Walter Leigh, Miss Provan, Miss De Pina, Mrs. Joseph Regneas, Mrs. Charles L. Sicard, Mrs. Solomon M. Stroock and Mrs. D. B. Van Emburgh. The committee has set the minimum price of a ticket at $2.50, but "will welcome larger contributions." Tickets may be had from Mrs. Chapman of 605 West 111th street, Manhattan, or Mrs. Charles L. Sicard, formerly of Brooklyn, now of 329 West Seventy-seventh street, Manhattan.

In Brooklyn a concert is being arranged by Miss Lotta Davidson, violinist, to take place at the Washington Avenue Baptist Church on the evening of May 1. The use of this church has been donated for the benefit concert, and the following artists have donated their services: Miss Alice Ralph, soprano; Miss Lotta Davidson, violinist; W. Paulding DeNike, 'cellist; Livingston Chapman, baritone, and Miss Eva McHaye and Arthur Rowe Pollock, accompanists. The tickets are $1 each, and subscriptions and applications should be made to Miss Lotta Davidson, 693 Bushwick avenue.

There were eight men in the Titanic's band, five of them comprising the saloon orchestra, and the other three the deck band. Bandmaster Hartley, who led them, is credited by his confreres on the other ocean steamers with having believed that music could always prevent a panic. It is believed that when he learned of the peril of the Titanic he gathered his men about him on the deck, explained to them what he wanted, and then, aided by their magnificent courage, made possible the wonderful stories told by survivors of music that did not cease while the great ship was sinking.

Two of the band—"Jock" Hume and Fred Clarke—came from Scotland. Hume, according to the ship's musicians who knew him, was to have been married on his return from the Titanic's maiden trip. He was on the Olympic when she crashed into the British cruiser Hawke, and was then begged, they say, by his aged mother to give up following the sea. Herbert Taylor and George Woodward of the saloon orchestra, both came from England, the latter from Leeds. He was unmarried, but Taylor left a widow.

Those who knew the three who constituted the deck band and who are known to have joined Hartley when the call came for music remember them only by their last names. They were Brailey, Krins and Breicoux, said to have been Irish, German and French, respectively.

MITCHEL IN OPPOSITION

Will Probably Be Against Findings of McAneny Subway Committee.

John Purroy Mitchel, it was said in Manhattan today, will oppose the findings of the McAneny subway committee when the report on the dual subway plan is submitted to the Board of Estimate. Mr. Mitchel has had several conferences recently with Borough President McAneny. He has gone over the situation with some care, and, according to the information today, is prepared to oppose the settlement which has been reached.

Mr. Mitchel could not be reached today. Mr. McAneny said:

"I have discussed the settlement that has been reached with Mr. Mitchel. I do not know whether or not he will object or make any minority report to the findings of the committee. I do not think it would make a great deal of difference one way or the other. The people have agreed to the plan and the Board of Estimate will support it."

Today's information is to the effect that Mr. Mitchel will probably prepare a minority opinion. It is said the President of the Board of Aldermen has gone over with careful scrutiny the report of the City Club and believes its objections to the contract with the Interborough Company are well founded.

Borough President McAneny has been working every morning this week at home preparing his report and trying to get it ready for presentation to the Board of Estimate. It will not be ready, however, in time for tomorrow's meeting.

"ONLY ONE GREAT CHURCH"

Bishop Hendrix Declares Denominationalism Ought to Go Out of Existence.

"The Men and Religion Congress goes out of existence tonight, and denominationalism ought to go out of existence with it."

This startling declaration was made by Bishop E. R. Hendrix of the Methodist Episcopal Church, one of the best known men in the country, at the closing morning session of the Christian Conservation Congress of the Men and Religion Forward Movement in Carnegie Hall, in Manhattan today. The themes of the morning were "Bible Study" and "Christian Unity," and on the former the consensus of opinion was that the great need of America today was the re-establishment of the family altar, that having been in the days gone by one of the bulwarks of the nation.

In discussing "Christian Unity," Bishop Hendrix said that the chorus of sectarianism was like the croaking of a bunch of frogs in a pond. "If you drain the pond," said Bishop Hendrix, "all you will find is two big frogs singing a duet of self-sacrifice. The denominations should be as self-sacrificing as the doctors. A doctor aims to cure a man, and when he is cured the man has nothing more to do with the doctor. The work of the denominations should be the same, and they should get together in such a way that there would be only one great church working for the one aim of bringing in the kingdom of God."

Both the reports on "Bible Study" and "Church Unity" were comprehensive and carefully prepared documents covering many points. This afternoon two of the prominent speakers will be John D. Rockefeller, jr., and the Rev. Dr. Nehemiah Boynton of Brooklyn, moderator of the National Council of the Congregational Church. A union meeting of the Men and Religion Congress and the Manhattan Congregational Ministers Association was a feature of the morning session, but the principal addresses will be made this afternoon. There will be a meeting tonight, when the sermon will be delivered by the Rev. Dr. J. H. Jowett, pastor of the Fifth Avenue Presbyterian Church. Dr. Boynton is also announced to make an address.

HELD UP AT DOOR OF HOME.

John Orlus of 265 Wythe Avenue Robbed—Stephen Seideck Arrested.

John Orlus of 265 Wythe avenue was held up and robbed by a masked man at that address about 4 o'clock this morning. As he reached the door a revolver was thrust in front of him and he heard a demand for his money. He surrendered a gold watch worth $65 and $43 in cash.

Policeman James McConville of the Bedford avenue station captured a man, who later described himself as Stephen Seideck, 22 years old, living at the same address as that given by Orlus.

Seideck pleaded not guilty to charges of assault and robbery when arraigned before Magistrate Voorhees, in the Manhattan avenue police court, and was held in $2,000 bail for the Grand Jury.

TWO ELEPHANTS AT AUCTION.

Jess and Jib May Be Put on the Block for Luna Park Debt.

Sheriff Julius Harburger of Manhattan is planning a new role for himself, to meet with the requirements of circumstances arising out of an attachment made today. In possession of the Sheriff are two perfectly sound, well-trained elephants, which must be sold at public auction unless a claim of $1,125 owing to Margaret J. Drake is paid within the next two days by the Luna Park Company. The Sheriff in the event of the claim not being paid intends to prepare himself as the auctioneer.

Mrs. Drake was awarded $1,125 for personal damages last November, and a writ of attachment was taken out by her lawyer and given to the Sheriff of Kings County to serve. He minutely examined Luna Park and then returned the writ to the attorney "no property." The two elephants, Jess and Jib, owned by the company, were found at Hippodrome today and attached.

It is the intention of the Sheriff to hold matters in abeyance for two days, and then if the claim is not satisfied he will advertise them for public auction.

HARVESTER TRUST AGREEMENT

Washington, April 24—Some agreement between the Government and the International Harvester Company, relating to the dissolution of that corporation, has been reached, according to statements here today. Its nature is not divulged and officials decline to discuss the matter at this time.

FALLERT MARRIAGE SURPRISES FRIENDS

Granddaughter of Brewer Weds at Sixteen, Edward C. Waller.

ARE NOW ON HONEYMOON.

Bridegroom Said to Be Descendant of Edward Waller, the Poet, and Is Wealthy.

Henrietta Virginia Fallert, the granddaughter of Joseph Fallert, who founded the Fallert Breweries, and Edward C. Waller, said to be a direct descendant of Sir Edward Waller, the versifier, were married either yesterday or Saturday.

They did not elope. The girl's mother established this fact today, when she was seen at 55 Patchen avenue. She was asked if she had given her consent to the wedding.

"Yes," she said, "I did." Then she added that she was afraid if she hadn't given her consent the young people would have run away.

Henrietta V. Fallert.

Waller is 28 and is said to be well fixed in business, and Miss Fallert is 16, fetching, and very independent.

It was pretty hard today to find out just where the descent of the bard and the grandchild of the brewer had been married. A letter written in to The Eagle said that the wedding had been in Atlantic City and that Mr. and Mrs. Waller had gone on a trip through New York State and Canada in a touring car. But at Miss Fallert's house it was said the wedding had been somewhere in Ridgewood and that the couple had gone to Atlantic City.

Miss Fallert lived up to yesterday with her mother and sisters at 55 Patchen avenue. Waller lived with his mother at 96 Sterling place. Waller met Miss Fallert a year ago.

The mother and father of Waller said this afternoon they knew of the wedding and knew beforehand it was to take place. Mr. Waller is the head of the Waller Lighterage Company, with offices at 29 Broadway, Manhattan. His son is in business with him. He said Edward C. Waller would be back in town on Friday.

A CONFIRMED BAD BOY.

Joseph Is Only 15, but Seems Bent on Burglary.

Joseph Kilkovich, 15 years old, of 564 Driggs avenue, was sentenced to the House of Refuge for two years, this morning, by Judge Ryan, in the Children's Court, having been found guilty of burglary. It was his fourth conviction for a like offense. On his first conviction sentence was suspended, on his second he was committed to the Catholic Protectory for a year and a half, and he spent two years at the Brooklyn Disciplinary Training School for the third offense.

Joseph was arrested March 16, charged with having broken into the store of James Eagan at 80 and 82 Grand street on March 12 and stealing over $60 worth of lead pipe.

At the trial this morning, several boys, all much younger than Joseph, testified that they were mixed up in the robbery, but no complaint was made against them.

LAW ON SHIPS' WIRELESS.

Should Be in Good Order and Should Carry 100 Miles.

It is pointed out by lawyers familiar with Federal statutes that if the vessels which were in the vicinity of the Titanic when she struck the iceberg had been equipped with wireless apparatus "in good working order," as provided by the laws of the United States, the Titanic might have been reached by some of these ships before her plunge to the bottom.

Dispatches from Boston and Portland indicate that the Leyland steamship Californian, the freight steamship Lena, the tramp steamship Kelvindale and other ships were at points ranging from twenty to thirty miles from the ill-fated White Star liner.

The law, which went into effect on July 1, last, reads as follows: "It shall be unlawful for any ocean-going steamer of the United States, or of any foreign country, carrying passengers and carrying fifty or more persons, including passengers and crew, to leave or attempt to leave any port of the United States unless such steamer shall be equipped with an efficient apparatus for radio-communication, in good working order, in charge of a person skilled in the use of such apparatus, which apparatus shall be capable of transmitting and receiving messages over a distance of at least 100 miles, night or day: Provided, that the provisions of this act shall not apply only between ports less than 200 miles apart."

CHINESE CRUISER COMPLETED.

Philadelphia, April 24—The first Chinese war vessel ever built in the United States, the Fei Hung, is ready for launching at the yard of the New York Shipbuilding Company, at Camden, N. J., on the Delaware River. The vessel will take its initial plunge on a day to be set by the Chinese Government. The Fei Hung is a steel-armored vessel, 330, feet long and is expected to have a speed of 20 knots an hour. Two other cruisers similar to the Fei Hung are being built in England.

JUDGMENT AGAINST VALENTINE

A judgment for $4,034.87 has been rendered against Benjamin E. Valentine, the former Brooklyn lawyer, against whom a conviction for forgery has been sustained by the Court of Appeals by a jury in the Supreme Court. The plaintiffs are the owners of the Bay Dredging and Construction Company, for whom Marcus B. Campbell acted as attorney.

THE NEW YORK HERALD.

NEW YORK, WEDNESDAY, APRIL 24, 1912.—TWENTY-FOUR PAGES.—[COPYRIGHT, 1912, BY THE NEW YORK HERALD COMPANY.] PRICE THREE CENTS.

MEXICAN BANDITS PUT AMERICANS TO THE TORTURE

Refugees Reaching Galveston Tell of Horrors Inflicted by Guerillas Before They Fled.

ONE VICTIM BEHEADED BY THE DESPERADOES

Woman Bound Hand and Foot and Her Feet Bastinadoed While Husband and Son Stand By.

WHOLE TOWN IS DESERTED

Roving Bands of Marauders, Unrestrained by Government, Laying Waste Entire Districts.

[SPECIAL DESPATCH TO THE HERALD.]

GALVESTON, Texas, Tuesday.—Fleeing from the awful tortures inflicted upon them in a land of almost unrestrained brigandage, assassination and all but unbelievable cruelty, forty-seven passengers, all but one American citizens, reached here to-day on board the steamship Texas. In their flight they left everything they possessed.

When the little band of refugees, who tell stories of the women of their families being tortured in sight of men relatives, looting and the beheading of American citizens, began their flight they left behind them, practically uninhabited, the town of Sanburn, which they had formed in the State of Vera Cruz, on the Vera Cruz and Isthmus Railway, twenty-three miles northwest of Santa Lucretia.

One of the worst of the stories of the cruelties practised on a woman was told by John T. McGee, a wealthy planter who went to Mexico to live two years ago. As a result of her terrible experience the woman now is in a critical condition in a hospital at Mexico City.

Brigandage Unrestrained.

"The Mexican government," said Mr. McGee, "is not able to restrain or to quiet the brigands, and desperadoes who are roaming through the inland country. Many Americans believe the Madero forces so dislike the Americans that they would rather permit the brigandage than try to stop it.

"A week before I left Sanburn the desperadoes in that section rode up to the home of a Mr. Shay, whose family were neighbors of mine. They demanded money and guns. Mr. Shay gave them one gun and $12 in cash, telling them that was all he had. For the time the bandits seemed to be satisfied. They rode away, but returned to the Shay home some time later and made new demands. Mr. Shay was persistent in his assertion that he had previously given them all the money and arms he had.

The bandits thereupon drove Mr. Shay and his son out, took Mrs. Shay, bound her hand and foot and then began beating her feet. To stop the torture Mr. Shay and his son finally produced $800 in cash and four more guns and gave them to the bandits. The bandits went away after giving Mrs. Shay a final beating. When she was taken to the hospital at Mexico City it was found that nearly every bone in her feet had been broken.

An American Killed.

The murder of an American named Wait was related by N. H. Ish, another of the refugees. The man who was killed was one of his neighbors. According to Mr. Ish, the brigands went to the Wait home and made a demand for money.

"When their demands were not satisfied," said Mr. Ish, "the desperadoes drew their machetes and beheaded Mr. Wait. Then they herded his cattle together and drove them off. There are many instances similar to this one. Every one of the eleven families who lived with me in the little town of Sanburn were forced to flee for their lives. We knew if we stayed longer we would be killed or tortured."

Another of the men who came in on board the Texas told of the desolation that is spreading through the country because of the flight of planters and farmers who have been driven out by the depredations of organized bands of thieves.

"The bandits are in such large numbers," one of them said, "and so scattered over the interior that to resist them is useless. No matter how well armed we might have been, the Americans in those States were so terrorized that they were compelled to give up everything they had.

"No matter where you go so long as it is not in the heart of the largest cities deserted farms and the ruins of homes may be seen. The only reason we are here is that we were able to escape from two brigands when they held us up in the mountain pass."

Mr. McGee lost more than $20,000, in addition to his farms and other property. Mr. Ish lost all of his money also, as well as his lands and other belongings.

"Before leaving," said Mr. McGee, "we filed claims for damages with the American Consul in Mexico City."

ANTI-MADERO PLOTTERS THRUST INTO PRISON

President Sends Armed Squads Out to Arrest Conspirators, One of Them a Supposed Friend.

[BY MEXICAN CABLE TO THE HERALD.]

MEXICO CITY, Mexico, via GALVESTON, Texas, Tuesday.—Political conspirators are being summarily dealt with by the Madero government, which not only has two revolutions on its hands but has unearthed several plots in the capital itself which threatened to lead to uprisings.

The latest plot was nipped in the bud last midnight when Elfredo Robles Dominguez and three others were seized by armed squads at their homes and thrust into prison. Surprise was occasioned by the arrest of Senor Dominguez, for he had been known as a personal friend and supporter of President Madero, and was formerly chief of police, an office usually filled by some trusted friend of the President.

Senor Dominguez was charged with engaging in a plot to put Vasquez Gomez in the palace, but members of the prisoner's family say his arrest was due to malice.

It is announced here that Orozco, leader of the northern rebels, has severed relations with Gomez, who had been regarded as the choice of the rebels for president. It is stated that emisaries of Orozco, now here, have opened negotiations with another prospective candidate.

The government continues to gather volunteers, many of whom are being sent to the front daily. A Spanish newspaper has printed an attack on the organization of a military company by Americans, charging that it was formed to aid an American army of invasion and suggesting that Article 33 of the constiution for the expulsion of pericious foreigners be applied to some members of the company.

Mr. Hudson, vice president of the National Railways, reports that a passenger train was fired upon south of Azumba and a bridge burned by Zapata rebels, who have returned to that district. No passengers were killed. The train service beetweent the capital and Cuernavaca is extremely uncertain.

Consul General Shanklin, who has been in the United States, is expected to return to-morow. nI the last two months more than seven thousand American residents have registered at his office.

"INTERVENTION MEANS FIFTY YEARS OF WAR"

HERALD BUREAU,
No. 1,502 H STREET, N. W.,
WASHINGTON, D. C., Tuesday.

"Intervention in Mexico means fifty years of war," according to a statement made at the War Department to-day by Brigadier General Anson Mills, U. S. A. (retired), who is one of the Mexican Boundary Commissioners of the United States and has been in touch almost constantly with developments on the boundary and in the interior of Mexico.

General Mills told army officers of the General Staff to-day that there was no reason whatever for the United States to think of intervening in Mexico and that the immediate consequences of such action would mean prolonged complications which few persons here have ever dreamt of.

"Let the Mexicans fight it out," is the slogan of General Mills. "Let them fight as we were allowed to fight during the civil war. Think of what would have happened if some foreign power had attempted to intervene in our war.

"If our army should invade Mexican soil it would be fifty years before it would come out. It would mean 250,000 men in the field and even then it would be an endless process to subdue the country. We might take Mexico City with 50,000 troops, but what good would that do? President Madero has Mexico City now, but there is still fighting in Mexico.

"Americans are not in danger and I should feel safer in many of the Mexican cities to-day than in many places in the United States. There never was a time when the rights of Americans were getting more consideration under like conditions than at the present time in Mexico. While this vague talk of Americans being endangered is going on in the United States these Americans themselves are getting a thousand times more protection than the Mexicans themselves. In many instances Americans legitimately imprisoned for crimes are let out of jail simply because they are Americans.

MEXICAN REBELS WILL FORCE DECISIVE BATTLE

[SPECIAL DESPATCH TO THE HERALD.]

ESCALON, Mexico, Tuesday.—The exact position of the rebel columns which are daily expecting an attack from the south became definitely known do-day for the first time. The outposts now extend to Zavalza, a small village nine miles south of here, but scouting parties have advanced to a point ten miles beyond.

The rebels are now holding their position in two divisions. Generals Fernandez and Argumendo are at Rellano, eleven miles north of here, while Generals Campa and Murillo are at Asuncion, half way between here and Rellano. There are two thousand men, mostly cavalry, in each of these commands. The garrison, here, with a thousand men, is under command of Colonel José Flores Alatorre.

General Salazar has a reserve force of fifteen hundred men at Jimenez, while at Santa Rosalia there are a thousand more, and it is estimated that the force at Chihuahua is about twelve hundred. These with the eight hundred men now at Juarez make up the entire rebel strength.

General Salazar, who went to Chihuahua several days ago for the final conference of the liberal chiefs, has returned to Jimenez and preparations for a battle are being made. It has been definitely decided that no advance shall be made by the rebels until the government forces show positively that they do not mean to advance. Generals Orozco and Salazar are anxious that the battle shall be waged in the vicinity of Rellano.

FIVE WIVES CLAIM HIM.

Man Arrested in Portland (Ore.) Accused of Many Bigamous Marriages.

[SPECIAL DESPATCH TO THE HERALD.]

PORTLAND, Ore., Tuesday.—With five women ready to testify against him, George E. Carr, accused of many bigamous marriages under many aliases, was arrested here last night and will be taken to Spokane for trial.

Among other victims, it is alleged, he married Ernestine Levert, in 1910. She is the daughter of a wealthy sugar merchant of Baton Rouge, La. They met on her father's plantation and eloped. Three months later, it is alleged, he deserted her in Portland.

GRANITE STATE'S EIGHT DELEGATES ARE FOR MR. TAFT

President Sweeps New Hampshire Primary Elections After Fierce Day's Fighting.

CRUSHING BLOW TO THE BASS MACHINE

Roosevelt Men Badly Beaten and Will Fall More Than One Hundred Behind in Convention.

TEST FOR BOTH SIDES

Result Regarded as Indicating How Massachusetts Will Go in Next Week's Balloting.

Line Up of Delegates to Date

INCLUDING NEW HAMPSHIRE.

Republican.

Taft	391
Roosevelt	201
La Follette	36
Cummins	6
Unclassified	2
Total number delegates in Republican National Convention	1,078
Needed to nominate (a majority)	540
Needed to give Taft majority	149
Needed to give Roosevelt jority	239
Yet to be elected	450

[SPECIAL DESPATCH TO THE HERALD.]

CONCORD, N. H., Tuesday.—Sweeping victory and complete control of the State Convention seem assured from reports received up to midnight from the State-wide primary elections. This means that the State's eight delegates will be for Taft. The Taft managers are jubilant over the outlook and say that if there was a steady drift away from the President, as possibly indicated by the primary results in Pennsylvania, Illinois, Nebraska and Oregon, the drift has been checked and henceforth the stock of the President will see a distinct rise.

General H. M. Baker, chairman of the Taft League, said:—

"The returns received up to eleven o'clock to-night show that President Taft has carried the State and both Congressional districts by substantial majorities. The victory is complete."

Reports from more than half the State were received here at midnight and they pointed to almost certain defeat of Theodore Roosevelt. His supporters practically admitted that they had gone down to a crushing defeat, but said they would make some gains as the returns came in from the country sections.

At eight o'clock this evening the Roosevelt men practically gave up hope. They said they were at a loss to understand why the State had not followed the footsteps of Maine, her neighbor, which recently was carried for Roosevelt. Governor Robert B. Bass, one of the original "seven little Governors" who came out for Mr. Roosevelt, is partially responsible for the Roosevelt defeat. He antagonized the organization and was fought by it.

By six o'clock this afternoon returns had come in from several of the cities and towns, and they showed that Mr. Taft had made an extraordinary run. Manchester, one of the largest cities in the State, went solidly for the President, giving him its ninety-eight delegates.

Dover went for Mr. Taft, giving him twenty-two delegates. Berlin did not elect a single Roosevelt delegate. Keene elected twelve Taft and four Roosevelt men. Portsmouth, where the Roosevelt forces have made their fight against the President on the question of the abolition of the navy yard, was solid for Taft. Laconia elected six Taft and four Roosevelt delegates. Franklin stood six for Roosevel tand four for the President. In Concord, the capital of the State, every ward but two went for Mr. Taft.

Taft managers have been very active here during the last few days, and they are exultant over the result as shown by the early returns. Particularly eager were they to carry the State, because of the nearness of the Massachusetts primaries, which, in many quarters, are recognized as the crucial test in the fight between the President and the erstwhile President for control of the Chicago convention. The Roosevelt managers had exerted every possible energy to swing this State into line with Pennsylvania, Illinois, Nebraska and Oregon, and they were predicting as late as this afternoon that the erstwhile President would score a notable victory. His failure to do so leads many of the republicans here to believe that the tide which came his way ten days ago has suddenly receded, and they express the belief that from now on the President will steadily gain ground.

One of the latest tables prepared shows that 202 of the 290 cities and towns gave Taft 380 delegates and Roosevelt 234 out of a total of 811 in the State Convention.

Governor Bass' home town, Peterboro, went 116 for Taft, 105 for Roosevelt.

The town of Cornish, in which lives Winston Churchill, the novelist, and an enthusiastic Roosevelt worker, went for Taft by a majority of 20.

(For Other Political News See Page 6.)

THE TITANIC LOOKOUT BLAMES LACK OF GLASSES IN CROW'S NEST FOR WRECK; SAYS VESSEL NEVER SLACKENED SPEED

THE TITANIC DISASTER HEARING IN WASHINGTON. HARRIS & EWING PHOTO
1 SENATOR PERKINS, 2 SENATOR W. A. SMITH, 3 SENATOR NEWLANDS, 4 SENATOR FLETCHER, 5 MR. ISMAY.

Seaman Who Sighted Iceberg Declares Binoculars Would Have Given Ample Warning.

HALF FILLED BOATS WOULDN'T AID DYING

Third Officer Tells of Dreadful Cries That Filled Air for Hour After Ship Sank.

HERALD BUREAU,
No. 1,502 H STREET, N. W.,
WASHINGTON, D. C., Tuesday.

If the testimony of Frederick Fleet, the lookout in the crow's nest of the Titanic at the time she struck the iceberg, is to be believed, the superb ship with her sixteen hundred lives was sacrificed for the lack of one pair of binoculars at the place where they would have done the most good at a moment of crisis.

Fleet testified before the Senatorial investigating committee that if he or his mate in the crow's nest had been equipped with a glass they would have sighted the iceberg much sooner than they did and could have reported it to the officers on the bridge in time to have enabled them to swing the great ship safely past the obstruction.

It was customary, he said, for the lookouts to have a glass, and during the four years he had held that post on the Oceanic, one of the other large ships of the White Star line, he had always had one. Before the Titanic left Southampton he had asked Second Officer Lightoller for a glass and had been told there was none for him and his mates to use.

Fleet, who is a typical English cockney of the type that drop their H's, is an experienced seaman twenty-five years old. At ten o'clock on the night of Sunday, April 14, he and his mate, Lee, went on duty in the crow's nest, relieving Symonds and Jewel at that post. The latter, having received the order before they went on watch to keep a sharp lookout for small ice, passed the word to that effect to their successors, Fleet and Lee, who then took their task in the responsible place of observation.

Tells of Reporting Iceberg.

"We did keep a sharp lookout," said Fleet. "It was nearly at the end of our two hours' watch, and when we were about to be relieved, that I saw and reported the thing we hit. It looked to me like a black mass, and I immediately made a report to the bridge to that effect."

"What did you report?"

"I reported an iceberg straight ahead. As soon as I saw it I pushed the button ringing three bells on the bridge, which meant that I had seen something ahead. I then seized the telephone transmitter, which is right at hand in the crow's nest, and communicated with the bridge. A voice from the bridge—I don't know what officer it was—asked after a very brief delay:—'What did you see?'

" 'An iceberg ahead,' " I said.

" 'Thank you,' " said the voice from the bridge."

Senator Smith tried hard to have the witness estimate how much time approximately had elapsed after he gave this warning and before the Titanic struck the iceberg. Fleet said he could not possibly venture an opinion on that point, and when the committee chairman pressed him further, he retorted:—"I'm no good 'and at guessin' "

The room was painfully silent, and so tensely was the seaman holding the attention of his auditors that his reply did not even cause a smile. Replying to further questions, the lookout went on:—

"When we got up to the berg it looked to me to be rising out of the water about ten feet higher than the forecastle head, which would make it about sixty feet above the sea. When I had first sighted the black mass it appeared to me no bigger than those two tables," pointing to the tables used by the committee and counsel, which together represent an area of about ten square feet.

Says Vessel Did Not Stop.

"After I gave the signal and reported the iceberg the ship did not stop. It ran right on past the mass, but while I was telephoning the report to the bridge my mate, Lee, was watching out ahead. I think he and I saw the thing about the same time. He was keeping his eyes on it and he saw that the wheel was being swung over hard a-starboard and that the ship had begun to start to port.

"She hit the ice about twenty feet back from the starboard bow, I should think. I felt only a slight jar—just a grinding noise. It didn't harm me at all. I thought it was a narrow shave.

"On this ship we lookout men had nothing but our own eyes—no glass whatever. On the run from Belfast to Southampton we had one pair of glasses for the whole six men in the team of lookouts, who went on watch turn and turn about, but from the time we left Southampton until the accident we had no glass at all. I asked Mr. Lightoller to let us have a glass, but he said there was none for us. We had one glass for the team on the Oceanic while I was on lookout duty on that ship, but it was a very poor one."

"If you had had a glass like you had on the Oceanic," said Senator Smith in a serious tone, "and like you had on the Titanic from B'fast to Southampton, could you have seen the iceberg sooner?"

"We'd have seen it a bit sooner, sir, soon enough to have got out of the way."

The witness said he knew First Officer Murdock, who was on duty on the bridge, had a pair of glasses, as he saw him use them, but he was equally sure there were no extra lookout men on duty in the eyes of the ship or at any point forward of the bridge except the two men stationed in the crow's nest.

"What are your wages, Mr. Fleet?" asked the examiner.

"Five pounds a month, sir, and five shillings lookout money additional."

Life Boats Scantly Filled.

Cumulative testimony was heard to-day which indicates that, meagre as was the provision made aboard the Titanic for lifeboats and life raftsfi many more lives might have been saved if even these inadequate facilities had been more efficiently utilized.

Witnesses described in detail the loading and departure of four of the regular largest size lifeboats, two from the starboard and two from the port side of the deck. Each of these was capable of holding safely sixty persons. The evidence was to the effect that they were sent away with half or less than half that number aboard and not one of them returned, after it was evident that the foundering ship was doomed to go to the bottom soon.

Lifeboat No. 6, on the port side of the ship, went off with only thirty persons in it. Quartermaster Hitchins had it in charge. One of his passengers was Major Arthur Godfrey Peuchen, of Toronto, an officer of the Canadian Militia, who was the principal witness of the afternoon session, and who was permitted aboard, he said, because he was an accomplished yachtsman and capable of doing a man's work in the craft.

Major Peuchen told with much feeling how one of the officers aboard the sinking ship had tried with a whistle to recall some of the lifeboats after it became evident that many were doomed to a certain death if they could not get off from the Titanic. Hitchins, the quartermaster, he said, heard the call and explained to them what it meant.

Many of the women in the bow, who had left their husbands or other dear ones on the Titanic's decks, implored Hitchins to return and fill the boat at least to something like its quota. He refused to do so. "It is our lives now or theirs," said the man in command of the lifeboat.

This boat, Major Peuchen said, was not more than five-eighths of a mile from the wreck when the ship took her final plunge, and for what seemed like an hour they could hear the heartrending moans and cries of those who were making a hopeless fight for their lives within easy earshot. Again they pleaded with the quartermaster to try to pick up some of the survivors, but he refused, saying:—

"It is no use; there's only a lot of stiffs there now."

The Canadian officer said he had been at odds already with Hichins, who too-

FINDS WIFE KILLED HERSELF AND CHILD

Husband Frantic When He Discovers Daughter, Clasping Doll, and Mother, Holding Her, in Death.

Attired in her wedding gown, and with her only child, a girl of nine years, clasped in her arms, Mrs. Ella Kanges, forty-six years of age, wife of Andrew Kanges, committed suicide with illuminating gas in their home, No. 762 Thirty-ninth street, Brooklyn, late yesterday. Mr. Kanges found their bodies on his return from work last night.

Although his wife had been suffering from acute rheumatism for several months, she had never appeared despondent. The husband was overcome on finding the bodies.

His first warning that something was wrong was when he missed his little girl's welcome on the steps of his home, where she had always greeted him with a hug and a kiss. His daughter had been dear to him, partly because she had been afflicted from childhood with deafness following an attack of spinal meningitis.

At first Mr. Kanges believed his wife had gone out, but fumes of gas in the hallway caused him to hurry to her bedroom, where he found she had the end of a rubber tube from a gas jet in her mouth.

Frantically he shattered the windows in the room and turned off the gas. Neighbors heard his cries for help and rushed in. Dr. Ackerman, a surgeon who was called from the Norwegian Hospital, said both Mrs. Kanges and the girl were dead.

As her mother clasped her child in her arms in death, so did the child hold to her own breast a large doll, which her father had given her on her ninth birthday recently.

Their daughter's delicate health had been a strong tie between Mrs. Kanges and her husband, and he had many times remarked that his wife neglected herself so that she could devote all of her time to the child.

Neighbors said they heard Mrs. Kanges in her apartments at four o'clock, shortly after she had called the child from her play. Mr. Kanges is a carpenter.

VESSEL AVOIDS ICEBERGS.

Course of the Kroonland Changed After the Titanic Disaster.

On account of news of the Titanic disaster the captain of the Kroonland, of the Red Star line, changed the course of the vessel and ended the voyage here last night without having sighted an iceberg.

Among the twenty first cabin passengers was Jean de Buisseret, fourteen years old, whose father was formerly Belgian Minister to the United States. He is to visit friends in the Belgian Legation at Washington. There was also Miss Jeanne Chaillot, an actress, of Brussels; Judge W. S. Andrews, Mr. and Mrs. W. S. Boody and Miss Winifred Boody, Miss Sylvia Dechene, Professor Caspar Schieler, H. S. Wallis and Miss Marian Wilson.

Two Sea Waifs Identified by Scars on Baby's Body

Mme. Navratil, of Nice, Certain That Little French Boys Rescued from the Titanic Are Her Children, Who Were Kidnapped by Father, Known on Board as Mr. Hoffman.

[SPECIAL DESPATCH TO THE HERALD VIA COMMERCIAL CABLE COMPANY'S SYSTEM.]

NICE, Tuesday.—Mme. Navratil to-day gave out a few details which may help to identify her youngest baby, who is believed to be one of the two little French boys, survivors of the Titanic disaster. The child had been suffering from eruptions, dut to milk alimentation. The eruptions were behind the ear and near the umbilicus. If they have disappeared they certainly have left scars. Mme. Navratil is more than ever convinced that the two children who escaped from the wreck are hers.

Mons. Navratil had a large tailoring establishment in the rue de France, at Nice, and left here on the night of April 7. Thus he had time to proceed to Cherbourg and embark on board the Titanic.

SAY MONS. NAVRATIL FLED WITH CHILDREN

Paris Despatch Says Father Disappeared with Little Ones During Divorce Proceedings.

[SPECIAL DESPATCH TO THE HERALD VIA COMMERCIAL CABLE COMPANY'S SYSTEM.]

HERALD BUREAU,
No. 49 AVENUE DE L'OPERA,
Paris, Wednesday.

Excelsior this morning says that Mme. Navratil was born in South America of Italian parents, and that she was married in London several years ago to Mons. Navratil, who was of Hungarian origin. The couple, Excelsior goes on to say, went to live at Nice, where Mme. Navratil started a women's tailoring establishment. They soon quarrelled and a divorce case is now in progress. Recently the husband was fined for having taken the children away from the mother. On Easter Day he disappeared, taking the children with him.

In the meantime he had sold his business and his wife believes he had about 40,000f. ($8,000) in his possession. Notwithstanding her search the woman could find no trace of her husband. On reading of the Titanic disaster she felt certain that her husband was on board, because he had often expressed a desire to go to the United States. Mme. Navratil thinks her husband assumed the name of Hoffman to hide his tracks.

FOSTER MOTHER FINDS SCARS ON BABY

Mme. Navratil's Description Tallies Exactly with Boy's Rescued from Shipwreck.

Identification of the Titanic's two waifs was made positive last night when the description given by Mme. Navratil of certain marks on the body of the younger boy was found to tally exactly with the personal appearance of the child, who at the time the cable despatch was received from Nice was sleeping contentedly in the temporary home he has found with Miss Margaret Hays, No. 304 West Eighty-third street.

The "milk crust" marks were found exactly as indicated, one behind the right ear and the other near the umbilicus. Moreover, the remainder of the description fits the two boys precisely. The elder is the darker and also the thinner of the two. "Lolo's" hair is a golden brown and the curls in front are lighter than those at the back of his head.

"There can no longer be any doubt that Mme. Navratil is the mother of the children," said Miss Hays last night. "The description of the 'milk crust' marks is one that only a mother would make. We noticed these marks as soon as I brought the boys to my home, and we even called in our family physician to make an examination. His diagnosis was precisely that given in the HERALD's despatch, that the trouble was due to milk alimentation.

"We kept the existence of the marks a secret for just this purpose, knowing that if a parent could describe them identification would be positive."

The White Star line yesterday afternoon received an unsigned cable despatch which said she was on her way to this country to claim the two children. The message, dated Liverpool, said that the sender was the mother of the boys.

What pitiful story is behind this woman's frantic journey is not known. It is surmised, however, that the woman's children were on board the Titanic and went down with her.

Still another chapter is being added to the story, however, for last night a despatch was received from Centreville, Iowa, saying:—"Frank Lefebre to-night started for New York to try to identify the two French children thrown from the Titanic into a lifeboat. His wife and four children were on board the Titanic, coming to meet him after he had been in this country a year making money to pay their passage."

Before the second HERALD's cable despatch was received Miss Hays had by talking with the elder of the boys obtained almost positive confirmation of Mme. Navratil's contention. Shortly after they arose she casually asked:—

"Que sais-tu de Nice?" (What do you know about Nice?)

The answer came without hesitation:—

"Maman est á Nice." (Mamma is in Nice.)

Mr. Lawrence Beasley, a young Englishman, who was a first cabin passenger on board the Titanic and who became casually acquainted with the second cabin passenger who was known as Hoffman, called at the Hays home yesterday and positively identified the two children as those whom he had seen with Hoffman.

PASSENGER AND CREW TELL SENATORS OF TITANIC'S LAST HOUR

a wrap from one of the women, brandy from another and insisted upon letting the woman row at the oars while he held the tiller. Hitchins had asserted his authority gruffly and had not permitted one of the women to hold the tiller, which she could easily have done on a night when the sea was as quiet as a mill pond, thus permitting Hitchins to help Major Peuchen at the oars.

The Canadian, whose evidence was given in a very temperate vein, summarized his opinion of the man from whom he had to take orders in this way:—

"I don't think he was qualified to be a quartermaster."

Major Peuchen Tells of Crash.

Major Peuchen is an experienced sailor, who for years has had his own yacht and knows how to run it. This witness described the shock following the impact with the iceberg as little more than the sensation following a heavy wave striking the ship's side. He wondered at it because it was such a phenomenally calm night he knew a large wave was impossible. When he first noticed that the ship had begun to show a list to port he was standing with Charles M. Hays, president of the Canadian Grand Trunk Railway, who was one of those lost.

Mr. Hays observed the list also and said to the Major, "You can't sink this ship. No matter what she has struck she is good for eight or ten hours, and by that time help will come."

Major Peuchen was confident that from the time the Titanic struck until he left the ship no general alarm had been sounded and no messengers sent through the cabins and staterooms to arouse the passengers who had retired. Friends of his afterward told him on board the Carpathia that they would have been lost had it not been that their rooms were near to those of Colonel and Mrs. Astor, and that Mrs. Astor came and aroused them and told them to dress.

When the witness was asked if he thought the accident might have been prevented if the lookout had been equipped with a glass, Major Peuchen replied:—

"I think a glass would have helped us, but I think that if we had had a searchlight in operation we would have saved the ship."

Criticises Vessel's Discipline.

Summarizing his opinion of the state of discipline shown by the Titanic's crew, Major Peuchen said:—

"Among officers and men whom I saw lowering and filling the boats the discipline could not have been better, but it seemed to me there were too few of them. I was surprised not to see more men at their stations, and I was surprised also that more men were not put into the boats at times when there were no women and children to respond to the invitation.

"I do not criticise Captain Smith, but I do criticise the policy and methods pursued by the company, for I feel sure in this case caution would have averted the terrible calamity. I have been credited with saying many things absolutely untrue. I wish to state that I have not said any personal or unkind things about Captain Smith."

Women Help to Man Oars.

Major Peuchen said the life boat he was in was equipped with everything required. Some of the boats, he heard, were not sufficiently equipped with food. When he got on the Carpathia he examined several lifeboats and found they had lights, hardtack and water.

"Did the women row in the boats?"

"Yes, and they were very plucky about it, too. They worked with a will. One helped me until she became ill from the hard work and was forced to cease."

"Dou you know who those women were?"

Major Peuchen said Miss E. A. Norton, of Acton Lane, London; Mrs. Walter Clark, of Los Angeles; Mrs. Lucien B. Smith, Huntingdon, W. Va.; Mrs. Cavendish, New York; Mrs. Walter Douglas, Minneapolis, and Mr. and Mrs. G. B. Burnham, of Denver, were among others in the boat, many of whom handled oars.

Third Officer's Story.

Herbert J. Pitman, third officer of the Titanic, who was the first witness of the day, told a story that brought tears to many eyes. He admitted that the lifeboat he commanded might have saved additional lives, as it was not filled to its normal capacity. It contained more men of the crew also than it should have carried.

The third officer was at his regular station, which is lifeboat No. 5, the second which was sent away from the starboard side of the Titanic. First Officer Murdock, who was superintending the embarking of the passengers on that side of the ship, had told him to go ahead with the boat. Mr. J. Bruce Ismay, with a dressing gown over his pajamas, had also appeared and told Mr. Pitman there was no time to lose. Mr. Pitman, who said he did not then know who Mr. Ismay was, told the managing director that he would take his orders from the commander.

His boat got away with five of the crew aboard in addition to himself and with five men passeengers.

There were approximately thirty-five women passengers. The boat was capable of carrying sixty. Mr. Pitman expressed the opinion, however, that loading lifeboats from the rail at a height of seventy feet above the sea is a dangerous expedient, and that to have put more persons into boats that had to be let down after having been filled would not have been prudent. The usual method, he said, is to fill the boats after they have been floated, especially in calm weather.

Harrowing Cries of the Drowning.

Mr. Pitman saw no persons in the water and heard no cries until after the ship sank. When that occurred their boat had drifted to a distance of not more than four or five hundred yards from the Titanic. Then there arose a harrowing chorus of moans and cries of distress that lasted, the witness thought, fully an hour, and, gradually becoming feebler, finally died away.

At this period the officer begged the examiner to spare him the further recital of what occurred, but Senator Smith, painful as it might be, insisted upon getting at the facts.

The third officer said he decided to take the boat back nearer to where the Titanic had sunk. He gave the order to do so and his men at the oars had started to obey when many of the passengers in his boat protested that it would be madness to risk it. He was in command of the craft, but he yielded to their protests and for an hour they lay there motionless, listening to the dying cries of their fellows.

Lifeboat No. 7, which lay a long time in company with his boat, he thought had not more than thirty or thirty-five persons aboard, of its quota of sixty.

Skeptical of Detecting Icebergs.

The same witness, although he holds a master's certificate, showed much skepticism or ignorance when he was catechised upon the manual issued by the Hydrographic Office concerning the recognized methods of determining the approach of icebergs. He said he had no faith in the tests made by thermometer readings either of the temperature of the water or the atmosphere, as indicating the approach of ice. He took no stock in the echo tests as employed by the sounding of the steam whistle from time to time, and said that the Titanic's whistle had not been sounded after she had received notice that she was approaching an ice zone.

The fact that ice had been reported was mentioned in the officers' mess and one of the officers had remarked that they might reach the ice in Mr. Murdock's watch on the bridge. Mr. Pitman said, however, that the conversation did not particularly interest him, as he was going off duty at the time.

The vessel's speed was not slackened at all because of her approach to the ice. It was not customary to do so, the third officer said. The custom was to depend upon "picking up" the reported iceberg from the bridge or the lookouts in time to avoid them.

No General Alarm for Passengers.

When the witness was asked whether a general alarm was sent among the passengers' staterooms after the vessel struck, he said he did not know as that was in the province of the stewards or victualling department. Mr. Pitman was out on deck and about his duties soon after the accident, but he had not heard any such alarm sounded.

This witness incidentally confirmed the accuracy of the sketches published by the HERALD last Friday illustrating how the Titanic sank. He watched her go down as a close observer and he noted the fact that just before the big ship took her final plunge her stern rose perpendicularly and remained in that position until the last phase, when she went under.

MAN IN CROW'S NEST TELLS OF SIGHTING ICE

Notified Officer on Bridge Immediately, He Says—Had Not Usual Equipment of Binoculars.

HERALD BUREAU,
No. 1,502 H STREET, N. W.,
WASHINGTON, D. C., Tuesday.

Frederick Fleet, first person on the Titanic to see the iceberg which sent her to the bottom of the ocean, told his story to the Senate Investigating Committee this afternoon. He "picked up" the berg from his place in the crow's nest many feet above the deck, and instantly warned First Officer Murdock on the bridge, who ported the helm, but failed to clear the obstruction.

Fleet is a stolid English lad—a typical man of the sea. He was for four years a lookout on the Oceanic. He did not easily comprehend the questions of Senator Smith and several times, when asked about distances and figures, said:—"I am no 'and at guessin', sir."

"Was there any other officers or employe stationed at a higher point on the Titanic than you were?" asked Senator Smith.

"You were the outlook?"

"Yes, sir."

"Can you tell who was on the forward part of the Titanic Sunday night when you took your position in the crow's nest?"

"There was nobody."

"Who was on the bridge?"

"Mr. Murdock and, I think, the third officer, Mr. Pitman."

"Who was with you on the watch?"

"Lee."

"What, if anything, did Simonds and Jewell, whom you relieved at ten o'clock, say to you when you relieved them of the watch?"

"They told us to keep a sharp lookout for small ice. I said, 'All right.' "

"Did you keep a sharp lookout for ice?"

Warns Bridge of the Ice.

"Yes, sir. I reported an iceberg right ahead—black mass. It was just after seven bells. My two hour watch was nearly over. I had done the best part of the watch up in the nest."

Fleet could not tell just how long it was before the ship struck that he reported the ice, but he said it was only a few minutes. The berg seemed about as large as two tables in the hearing room put together. This would have made it about thirty feet in diameter. It kept growing larger, he said.

"Did it impress you as serious?" insisted Senator Smith.

"I reported it as soon as ever I seen it," he replied somewhat resentfully.

"I struck three bells first. Then I went straight to the telephone and rang them up on the bridge. I got an answer straight away, 'What did I see?' I told him an iceberg right ahead. He said:—'Thank you.' I remained in the crow's nest until I got relief, and Lee remained in the nest. We were there about a quarter of an hour to twenty minutes after."

"How large did the iceberg get to be finally when it struck the ship?"

"When we were alongside it was a little bit higher than the forecastle head, about sixty feet high."

Says Vessel Did Not Stop.

"Do you know whether the ship was stopped after you gave that telephone signal?"

"No, no; she did not stop at all. She did not stop until she passed the iceberg."

"Do you know whether her engines were reversed?"

"Well, she started to go to port while I was at the telephone. The wheel was put to starboard."

"How do you know that?"

"My mate saw it and told me. He told me he could see the bow coming around. We had been making straight for it. The iceberg struck the ship on the starboard bow, just before the foremast, about twenty feet from the stern."

"Was there much of a jar to the ship?"

"No, sir; just a slight grinding noise. Not sufficient to disturb us in our position in the crow's nest."

"Did it alarm you seriously when it struck?"

"No, sir. I thought it was a narrow shave."

"Did any of this ice break on the decks?"

"Yes; some on the forecastle light and some on the weather deck. Only where she rubbed up against it."

Had No Spyglasses.

"Are you given glasses of any kind?"

"We had none this time; we had nothing at all, only our own eyes to look out."

"On the Oceanic you had glasses, had you not?"

"Yes, sir."

"Each of you?"

"There is one pair in the nest."

"Did you make any request for glasses on the Titanic?"

"We asked them in Southampton, and they said there was none for us."

"Whom did you ask?"

"We asked Mr. Lightoller, the second officer."

"Did you make the request yourself?"

"No, the station lookout men did, Hogg and Evans."

"How do you know they made it?"

"Because they told us."

"Where did they tell you—after leaving Southampton?"

"In Southampton and afterward."

"You expected glasses?"

"We had a pair from Belfast to Southampton."

"Suppose you had had glasses such as you had on the Oceanic or such as you had between Belfast and Southampton, could you have seen this black object a greater distance?"

"We could have seen it a bit sooner."

"How much sooner?"

"Well, enough to get out of the way."

"Did you and your mates discuss with one another the fact that you had no glasses?"

"We discussed it all together between us."

"Did you express surprise or regret that you had none?"

"I do not know what you mean."

"Were you disappointed that you had no glasses?"

"Yes, sir."

"Do you know whether the officer on the bridge had glasses?"

"Yes, sir."

"Who was on the bow of that boat, if any one, Sunday evening, forward of the bridge?"

"There was nobody forward of it. We were the only ones that were forward—up in the nest."

Fleet explained that glasses were an aid in seeing at night just as in the daytime.

THIRD OFFICER TELLS STORY OF THE CRASH

HERALD BUREAU,
No. 1,502 H STREET, N. W.,
WASHINGTON, D. C., Tuesday.

Joseph G. Boxhall, fourth officer of the Titanic, was taken ill with pleurisy here to-day and was temporarily excused as a witness before the Senate Investigating committee. The announcement was made by William Alden Smith, chairman, at the opening of the morning session, which, it was expected, would open with a continuation of the fourth officer's story.

Mr. Boxhall has been complaining of a pain in his chest since the Carpathia reached New York. His hpysician here says it is the result of exposure, but he will probably be well in a few days.

Third Officer Takes Stand.

The first witness was Herbert John Pitman, of Somerset, England, third officer of the Titanic. He is thirty-four years old and has had seventeen years' sea experience. He said he held a master's certificate from the British Board of Trade.

Senator Smith asked:—"Were you on the bridge during Saturday or Sunday preceding the accident?"

"Oh, yes," replied Mr. Pitman. "Part of the time, sir."

"During that time did you see any icebergs or any field ice?"

"No ice at all, sir."

"Did you hear anything about any ice on Saturday?"

"No, sir."

"Did you hear anything about a wireless message from the California?"

"No, sir. I heard something about a wireless message from some ship, or it may have been Saturday night. I am not sure. I was not on watch. Mr. Boxhall put the position of the iceberg on the chart. I saw the mark there. He just simply made a cross and wrote 'Ice' in front of it."

"This was Sunday?"

"It may have been Saturday night."

"Did you have any talk with Mr. Boxhall or Mr. Murdock or Mr. Lowe regarding the proximity of the Titanic to ice?"

"I did not, sir."

"Did you have any talk with the Captain about it?"

"It was not in my place to talk to the Captain about such things."

"Did you notice any change in the temperature of the weather?"

"Yes. That would not denote anything at all, sir."

"You do not think that would denote anything?"

"No, because in this country and in our own country we will probably want no clothes on at all and the next day we will want overcoats, winter clothes; and that is not due to ice."

"Have you ever been up to the Grand Banks before in the month of April?"

"I never have, sir."

"Have you ever seen any ice in that part of the sea, the North Atlantic?"

"One small berg."

"Where?"

"I cannot recollect exactly where it was, sir."

At this point Senator Smith referred to the manual of the United States Hydrographic Office.

"As a matter of fact do you not know that before ice is seen at all from the deck of a ship the ice will often indicate its presence; does not the reflection of the rays from the sun or the moon tell some definite story about the proximity of ice?" asked Senator Smith.

Denies Means of Detecting Ice.

"It may do so in the arctic region, but never in the Atlantic Ocean."

"Never in the North Atlantic Ocean?"

"There is not sufficient ice there to cause that."

"On a clear day, over the ice on the horizon is it not true that the sky is much paler or lighter in color and distinguishable from that overhead?"

"No, sir."

"During foggy weather are not icebergs seen through the fog by their apparent blackness?"

"That may be so; I have never seen them, though."

"Are there any other signs known to mariners by which icebergs may be discovered or their proximity known?"

"I do not think there are any signs at all, sir."

"Is it not a fact there is an echo in the vicinity of icebergs?"

"I never heard of it, sir."

"One moment. From the steam whistle or fog horn?"

"I never experienced it."

"Do you know how the proximity of an iceberg can be tested mathematically?"

"No, sir."

"Did you ever hear of it?"

"No, sir. As regards the temperature of the water, it is absolutely useless."

"In your opinion?"

"I have proven it."

"Has anybody ever told you that knowing the time between the blast of a whistle at sea and the reflected sound the distance in feet may be found by multiplying a certain numeral."

"No."

"And none of these signs were familiar to you?"

"None whatever."

"Do you know of your own knowledge whether any tests of the temperature of that water were made on board the Titanic?"

"They are made every two hours. We usually have a canvas bucket which they lower into the water. But we did not have time to make one. They were using a tin."

Scenes Night of Crash.

"What were the hours of your watch Sunday night of the accident?"

"I was on the bridge from six to eight o'clock P. M."

"Whenever you went to the bridge, from six to eight o'clock, do you recall having seen the Captain?"

"I saw him once."

"Did you hear anything about the wireless from the California on the question of icebergs?"

"I did not."

"No one mentioned that to you?"

"No, sir."

"Did you have any conversation with the Captain on Sunday?"

"None whatever."

"Who was the officer of the watch from ten o'clock on?"

"Mr. Murdock."

"Was he keeping a special lookout?"

"Yes. Because he was warned. Second Officer Lightoller passed the word along to him. I had heard some one mention it."

"Mention it before the collision or since?"

"Oh, since."

"Exactly. What did you do after you left the watch at eight o'clock on Sunday evening?"

"Went to bed."

"Between six and eight o'clock did you take any observation?"

"Yes; we took stellar observations, and also observations for compass deviation."

"Do you know how those observations located the ship?"

"Yes; right on the track."

"And at that time the speed of the ship was about twenty-one and one-half knots per hour?"

"Yes, sir."

"Did you regard that as pretty good speed?"

"No; nothing to what we expected her to do. We thought it quite possible she should reach twenty-four knots."

"Were you trying to reach twenty-four knots?"

"No; we had to study the coal. We had not the coal to do it."

"You did not talk over the matter of ice with your fellow officers?"

"We were just remarking that we should be in the vicinity of ice in Mr. Murdock's watch, which began at ten o'clock."

"And you expected ice at that time?"

"Well, we might see it."

"Were you all in accord on that?"

"I had nothing to say in the matter. I was not interested in it."

"I understand, you retired to your berth after taking the observation. When did you next appear outside of your berth?"

"About ten minutes to twelve or a quarter to twelve, sir."

"What occasion was there for rising at this time?"

Awakened by Crash.

"The collision woke me up. There was a sound that I thought seemed like the ship coming to anchor, the chains running out over the windlass. It gave just a little vibration. I was about half awake and about half asleep. It did not quite awaken me. I wondered where we were anchoring. I lay in bed a while after the impact, maybe three or four minutes. I got up and walked on deck without dressing.

"I had a look around and I could not see anything, could not hear any noise, so I went back to the room and sat down and lit my pipe, thought that nothing had really happened, that perhaps it might have been a dream or something like that. A few minutes afterward I thought I had better start dressing, as it was near my watch, so I started dressing and when partly dressed Mr. Boxhall came in and said the mail room—there was water in the mail room.

"I said, 'What happened?' He said, 'We struck an iceberg.' So I put a coat on and went on deck and saw the men uncovering the boats and clearing them away. I walked along to the after end of the boat deck and met Mr. Moody, the sixth officer. I asked him if he had seen the iceberg. He said 'No, but there is some ice on the forward wall deck.' So, to satisfy my curiosity, I went there myself.

"I saw a little ice there. I went further to the forecastle head to see if there was any damage there. I could not see any at all. On my return, before emerging from under the forecastle head, I saw a crowd of firemen coming out with their bags—bags of clothing. I said:—'What is the matter?' They said:—'The water is coming into our place.' I said:—'That is funny.' I looked down No. 1 hatch then and saw the water flowing over the hatch. I then immediately went to the boat deck and assisted in getting boats uncovered and ready for swinging out. I stood by No. 5 boat. They would not allow the sailors to get anything, as they had thought we should get it again in the morning.

Tells of Mr. Ismay.

"In the act of clearing away this boat a man said to me that was dressed in a dressing gown, with slippers on, he said to me very quietly, 'There is no time to waste.' I thought he did not know anything about it at all. So we carried on our work in the usual way."

"Do you know who that was?"

"I did not then."

"Do you now?"

"I do now."

"Who was it?"

"Mr. Ismay. I did not know who is was then; I had never seen the man in my life before. So I continued on getting this boat uncovered and swinging out. It struck me at the time, the easy way the boat went out, the great improvement the modern davits were on the old fashioned davits. I had about five or six men there, and the boat was out in about two minutes.

"Then this man in the dressing gown said, 'We had better get afloat with women and children.' So I said, 'Await the commander's orders,' to which he replied, 'Very well,' or something like that. It then dawned on me that it might be Mr. Ismay, judging by the description I had had given me. I went along to the bridge and saw Captain Smith, and I told him that I thought it was Mr. Ismay that wished me to get the boat away with women and children in it. So he said, 'Go ahead; carry on.'

"I came along and brought in my boat. I stood on it and said, 'Come along, ladies.'

Mr. Ismay Assists Women.

"There was a big crowd. Mr. Ismay helped to get them along—assisted in every way. We got the boat nearly full, and I shouted out for any more ladies. None were to be seen, so I allowed a few men to get in it. Then I jumped on the ship again. So Murdock said, 'You go away in this boat, old man, and hang around the after gangway.'

"I did not like the idea of going away at all, because I thought we were better off on the ship. I filled my boat easily. We had about forty. I should say about half a dozen men there. There would not have been so many men there had there been a woman around, but there was none.

"Murdock shook hands goodby and said, 'Good luck with you.'

"We then cast the boat off and pulled away some safe distance from the ship. It was an hour before I realized she would go down—an hour after we got into the water. I quite thought we would have to return to the ship again, perhaps at daylight. My idea was if any wind sprang up we should drift away from the ship and have a job to get back again."

"Did you see the Titanic go down?"

"Yes."

"Describe how she sank."

"Judging by what I could see from a distance she gradually disappeared until the forecastle head was submerged to the bridge, then she turned right on end and went down perpendicularly."

"I heard four reports. They sounded like the report of a big gun in the distance. I assumed it was bulkheads going. I heard people say the boilers exploded, but I have my doubts about that. I do not see why boilers should burst, because there was no steam there. They should have been stopped about two hours and a half. The fires had not been fed, so there was very little steam there."

"Did you see any people in the water?"

"None."

Dreadful Cries of the Drowning.

"Did you hear any cries of distress?"

"Oh, yes, crying, shouting, moaning from the water after the ship disappeared; no noises before. I may have been four or five hundred yards away."

"Did you attempt to get near them?"

"As soon as she disappeared I said, 'Now, men, we will pull toward the wreck.' Every one in my boat said it was a bad idea, because we had far better to save what few we had in my boat than to go back to the scene of the wreck and be swamped by the crowds that were there."

"As a matter of fact, do you not know your boat would have accommodated twenty or twenty-five more people?"

"My boat would have accommodated a few more, yes. Certainly."

"I said:—'We may be able to pick up a few more.' "

"Who demurred to that?"

"The whole crowd in my boat, a great number of them did."

"Women?"

"I could not discriminate whether women or men. They said it was rather a mad idea."

"You were in command; they ought to obey your orders?"

"So they did. The men commenced pulling toward the ship, and then I decided I would not pull back."

Shudders at Memory of It.

"How many of those cries were there? Was it a chorus?"

"I would rather you did not speak about that."

"I would like to know how you were impressed by it?"

"Well, I cannot very well describe it. I would rather you would not speak of it."

"I realize that it is not a pleasant theme, and yet I would like to know whether these cries were general and in chorus or desultory and occasional?"

"There was a continual moan for about an hour."

"And you lay in the vicinity of that scene for about an hour?"

"Oh, yes; we were in the vicinity of the wreck the whole time."

"Did this anguish or these cries of distress die away?"

"Yes, they died away gradually. I would rather that you would have left that out altogether."

"I know you would, but I must know what efforts you made to save the lives of passengers and crew under your charge. If that is all the effort you made, say so."

"That is all, sir—that is all the effort I made."

Left Mr. Ismay on Deck.

"You spoke of the services of Mr. Ismay with the women and children—assisting in loading and so forth."

"Yes."

"Did you leave Mr. Ismay on the deck when you were lowered?"

"Mr. Ismay was on the deck when I was lowered; yes. The next I saw of him was coming on the Carpathia."

"You did not see him after you were lowered to the water?"

"Not until morning."

"And you say he was dressed, or partially dressed; that he had a dressing gown on?"

"It struck me that he had a dressing gown and pajamas on."

"Was No. 7 boat lowered at the same time yours was lowered?

"Two or thre minutes previously."

"Can you say whether Mr. Ismay was in boat No. 7?"

"I know he was not, for he came off from a collapsible boat."

Mr. Pitman said he saw a white light about three or five miles away and pulled toward it, but as it seemed to go away he stopped. He did not know whether it was another ship, but he thought so.

EXPLAINS MONEY GIFT TO LIFEBOAT CREW

Newark Survivor Says Sir Duff-Gordon Donated It to Remedy Their Lax Discipline.

C. E. Henry Stengel, of No. 109 Lincoln Park, Newark, who with his wife was among those saved from the wreck of the Titanic, denies emphatically that any one in the lifeboat in which he and Sir Duff-Gordon and Lady Gordon were passengers offered or gave any money to men of the crew. He declares that the statement made before the Senate investigating committee that "an American millionaire" paid his way to safety is absolutely untrue.

"After we had been away from the ship an hour or more," says Mr. Stengel, "the men of the crew acted badly. They didn't want to row or help keep the boat afloat or properly directed. They stopped to smoke cigarettes, and in other ways misbehaved. I had to kick one of them who sought to protect himself from the cold with the skirts of the women.

"To encourage them to do better both Sir Duff-Gordon and Lady Gordon told them they would be rewarded when the boat was picked up if they would do the work properly, and keep a sharp lookout for a rescue ship. Their promises had the desired effect, and when we were taken aboard the Carpathia Sir Duff-Gordon gave them orders on his London bank. The amounts I did not know. It is an outrage to impute to Sir Duff-Gordon any but manly and courageous actions."

THE HELLIG OLAV FAR OFF.

A. E. Johnston, of Johnston & Co., which represents the Scandinavian-American line in this city, denied yesterday reports that the steamship Hellig Olav, of his line, was the vessel that might have been only five miles from the sinking Titanic after striking the iceberg which foundered her. He cited the steamship charts showing the Titanic 1,284 miles east of Ambrose Channel at fifteen minutes after two o'clock the afternoon preceding the disaster, while the Hellig Olav was reported as 735 miles east at twenty-five minutes after three o'clock.

DENIES VESSEL WAS NEAR.

[SPECIAL DESPATCH TO THE HERALD.]

TORONTO, Ont., Tuesday.—Dr. F. C. Quitzrua, a medical graduate of Berlin University, formerly a resident of Hanover, Germany, who arrived in Toronto yesterday, was a passenger aboard the Mount Temple, a Canadian Pacific vessel, which reached St. John from Antwerp on Friday last. He said that the wireless operator of the Mount Temple informed him that they were the first to get the Titanic's "C Q D" and that they were only about forty miles from her at the time. The Mount Temple makes ordinarily about eleven knots.

Captain Moore, of the Mount Temple, has wired from St. John to the Star here a denial of Dr. Quitzrua's story.

MAKES PATHETIC APPEAL.

Mrs. Charles Natsch, of No. 503 East Seventh street, Flatbush, has made a pathetic appeal to survivors of the Titanic to tell her something concerning the last moments of her husband, Charles Natsch, who was returning from a business trip to Europe. In all the stories of Titanic survivors no mention has been made of Mr. Natsch.

Since the disaster Mrs. Natsch's condition has been extremely pitiful. She has been partly prostrated and relatives and neighbors have aided her to care for her three children.

"If I could only get some word concerning my husband's last hours it would be some comfort," said Mrs. Natsch.

THE RHEIN NEARS PORT.

BALTIMORE, Md., Tuesday.—A wireless despatch from Captain Madsen, of the steamship Rhein, to the local agents of the steamship company reports that he was four hundred miles from Cape Henry, Va., at noon to-day. The vessel is due here about noon Thursday. No bodies from the Titanic wreck were reported on board the Rhein.

The Corsican Hit No Iceberg.

MONTREAL, Canada., Tuesday.—The Allan line officials to-day denied a report that the steamship Corsican had struck an iceberg while on her way from St. John, N. B., to Liverpool. This report came from St. Johns, N. F., but on communication with that place the steamship officials were informed that while the Corsican saw ice off the Grand Banks she avoided it.

Youngest Survivor of the Titanic Gleeful with Foster Parents

COPYRIGHT BY PAUL THOMPSON

BABY ALLISON AND NURSE ANDREWS OF MONTREAL WHO WERE SAVED FROM THE TITANIC WRECK,—THE BABY IS THE ONLY SURVIVOR OF THE ALLISON FAMILY

Boy, Eleven Months Old, Saved When Parents Went Down with Wreck, Becomes Centre of Much Attention and Smiles Happily.

Although Travers J. Allison, eleven months old, did not realize it yesterday, much interest was centred in his case. He is probably the most youthful survivor of the Titanic disaster. One would never think he had undergone such an experience to see him smiling and chuckling under the care of foster-parents at the Manhattan Hotel. He is the son of Mr. and Mrs. Hudson J. Allison, of Montreal. Mr. Hudson was a capitalist in that city and had various interests. When the Titanic went down the Allisons were on board, with two other children, a chauffeur and a maid.

During the rush and panic when lifeboats were lowered the Allison baby was found on the deck and taken aboard the next to the last lifeboat that went over the sides. It is doubtful if another person in the wrecked party received more care and attention than he. He did not seem to be any worse for his experience yesterday and smiled heartily when his picture was taken.

Relatives and Friends of Victims Hurry to Meet Funeral Ship

The Mackay-Bennett, Bearing Bodies Recovered from the Titanic Disaster, to Arrive at Halifax Friday Night or Saturday Morning.

Of the seventy-seven identified dead on board the cable steamship the Mackay-Bennett, forty-two, it was said yesterday in the offices of the White Star line, have been checked off with the passenger list.

The Mackay-Bennett, with her cargo of bodies, will arrive at Halifax either on Friday night or Saturday morning. Many of the relatives and friends of those who perished already have left New York to meet the funeral ship.

The Mackay-Bennett, which will be relieved by the Minia, was not heard from after ten o'clock yesterday morning, and it is presumed that she is making a thorough search for miles around the scene of the sinking of the Titanic, until she has recovered one hundred bodies. It was declared that the bodies of Major Butt and Colonel Astor were not among those identified on board the funeral ship. There is still a little doubt as to some names.

Mrs. N. McNamee is one of these. It is presumed that this is Eileen McNamee, a steerage passenger from Ireland. There is no Catavelas Vasilios, but on the passenger list there appear a Thomas and a Peter Vasilios. tI is not possible to say which of these two has been found. The name of William Sage does not appear. It is thought he was the son of John Sage. Both father and son were among the lost. There is no W. Vear, as sent in the wireless message list, and it is taken to mean W. J. Ware, a second class passenger.

On the passenger list there is no Mrs. A. Robins, but there is a Charity Robins, a third class passenger. The lists have no mention of H. Greenberg, but there is a Samuel Greenberg on the list of second class passengers.

The list of identified dead follows:—

A

ASHE, H. W. (steward).
ARTAGAVEYTIA, RAMON.
ATT, H. B. (may be Major Butt).

B

BUTT, W. (sailor).

C

CHAPMAN, JOHN H.
CORBINE, W.

D

DOUGLAS, W. D.
DAHL, MAURITZ.
DRAZNOVIC, JOSEF.

F

FARRELL, JAMES.

G

GILINSKI, LESLIE.
GILL, JOHN.
GREENBERG, H.

H

HALE, REGINALD.
HANSEN, HENRY D.
HINCKLEY, G., hospital attendant.
HAYTER, A., steward.
HOFFMAN, LOUIS M.
HOLVERSON, A. J.
HAMBECK, W. H.

J

JOHNNSON, MALCOLM.

K

KELLY, JAMES.

M

MONGAN or MANGON, MARY.
MACK, Mrs. MARY.
McNAMEE, Mrs. N.
MORROSE, JERRY.
MARRIOTT, H.

N

NIHHLSHEDDD.
NASSER, NICOLAS.

R

RICE, J. R., assistant purser.
ROBINS, Mrs. ALEXANDER.
ROSENSHIRE, GEORGE S.

S

SAGE, WILLIAM.
SOTHER, SIMON.
SUTTON, FREDERICK.
SHEA, ——.
STEWARD 76.

T

TOMLIN, ERNEST P.

V

VASSILIOS, CATAVELAS.
VEAR, W.

W

WIDEN, GEORGE (may be George D. Widener).
WILLIAMS, NESLIE.

That the name E. Colas Rasher, as received by wireless, does not mean Colonel John Jacob Astor, was ascertained yesterday when Mrs. Nicolas Nasser told the White Star officials that the name undoubtedly meant that the body of her husband had been recovered.

William H. Harbeck, Titanic Victim, a Seattle Man.

[SPECIAL DESPATCH TO THE HERALD.]

SEATTLE, Wash., Tuesday.—William H. Harbeck, of Seattle, whose name appeared on the list of the bodies recovered by the Mackay-Bennett, was a moving picture operator, who travelled extensively. Harbeck had written to his wife that he was coming to America on board the Titanic, but as his name did not appear on the passenger list she hoped he had changed his mind.

New Haven Friends of James Kelly Believe His Body Is Found.

[SPECIAL DESPATCH TO THE HERALD.]

NEW HAVEN, Conn., Tuesday.—The James Keely, whose body was picked up at sea and whose name appears in to-day's list of the Titanic's victims, probably was James Kelly, who was on his way here to join relatives. He was in the steerage.

IDENTIFY BODY OF MR. GEORGE D. WIDENER

Mr. P. A. B. Widener Receives Message from Mr. Mackay Making Identification Sure.

[SPECIAL DESPATCH TO THE HERALD.]

PHILADELPHIA, Pa., Tuesday.—Mr. P. A. B. Widener, a director of the International Mercantile Marine Company, received a message to-day from Mr. Clarence Mackay which establishes the identity of the body of Mr. George D. Widener, Mr. P. A. B. Widener's son. The name of George Widen appeared in the list last night. Captain Chase, commander of P. A. B. Widener's yacht; George D. Widener, Jr., and George W. Elkins left New York for Halifax to get the body and bring it to Philadelphia for burial.

Fred Sutton, mentioned in the list, is undoubtedly Frederick Sutton, of this city. He was sixty-one years old and had been visiting his brother and sister in England.

MRS. E. R. KENYON SAVED.

Mr. and Mrs. E. R. Kenyon, who were on board the Titanic, were not mentioned in the passenger list of the White Star line or among the victims of the disaster. A member of the family writes to the HERALD that Mrs. Kenyon was put into one of the last lifeboats by her husband, who is a well known steel man in Pittsburg. He went down with the Titanic. Mrs. Kenyon helped at the oars for five hours. Her name figured on the list of survivors as Mrs. Kenneyman.

COMPANIES RUSH TO PLACE LIFEBOATS ON THEIR VESSELS

$8,000 ADDED TO THE TITANIC FUND BY MANY GIVERS

Mrs. Florence A. V. Twombly Sends a Check for $1,000 to Committee.

TOTAL AMOUNT IS NOW $96,565

Contributions Come to City Hall from Distant Points as Well as Nearby Towns.

HERALD FUND SWELLS

More than $8,000 was added yesterday to the Mayor's relief fund for the Titanic survivors and their families. The total received at City Hall is $96,565. Many small contributions came from nearby towns and distant cities. Murrell Alte, an Indianapolis newsboy, sent $1, which he said was all he possessed. Mrs. Florence A. V. Twombly sent a check for $1,000. The contributions, not made anonymously, of $5 or more, were:—

E. T. H. Talmage	200.00
E. W. Kridel	5.00
James B. Dickson	100.00
First Presbyterian Church of Rockport	30.00
Irving Swan Brown	10.00
Slatington Baptist Church	10.00
John Innes Kane	500.00
Gertrude L. Kemmerer	50.00
Walter E. Ives	20.00
Celestino de Marco	20.00
S. Stroock & Co.	50.00
L. H. Clarke	10.00
Max H. Schwarcz & Co.	100.00
Paris, Allen & Co.	100.00
Syrian-American Club of New York and the Lebanon League of Progress	307.45
Morris Hermann & Co.	50.00
Benjamin Lowenstein	25.00
J. R. Rattenbury, for Becher Memorial Congregational Church	10.00
Klauber Brothers & Co.	50.00
Collection received by Trinity Baptist Church of Brooklyn	41.00
Employes of the Pictorial Review and American Fashion Companies	109.20
S. L. Van Wezel	50.00
Emanuel Schorsch	25.00
F. Prosser Son	25.00
West Side Club of the D. Y. N. T. House	10.00
Collection of Bulkeley High School of New London, Conn.	15.84
Arnold & Zeiss	500.00
Congregation worshipping with corps of cadets at United States Military Academy, West Point	15.75
W. N. Davey	100.00
St. Thomas Church New Windsor on Hudson	17.62
Miss Rhinelander	250.00
S. N. Rice	100.00
Herbert Weil	5.00
E. R. Richter	5.00
Apeda Studio	10.00
Sol Freidus	10.00
Franklin Riker	10.00
Collection at Union Memorial Service at Methodist Episcopal Church of Cold Spring	30.63
Charles M. Higgins & Co.	100.00
Tower Mfg. & Novelty Co.	50.00
Herman Brand	20.00
Florence H. Lynch	5.00
Roethlisberger & Co.	50.00
William A. Martin	100.00
Charles C. Cluff	10.00
Goodfriend Brothers	25.00
W. A. Openhym	25.00
Harry M. Lasker	100.00
Herman Boker & Co.	100.00
A Friend	10.00
Marienthal & Martin	46.25
Cash	10.00
Townsend Scudder	25.00
Arthur Stern	25.00
A. J. Prager	10.00
David Stern	10.00
Augusta MacMannus	5.00
Boys' United Club	10.00
Frederick Gerken	100.00
St. Michael's Episcopal Church of Bristol, R. I.	45.00
National Meter Company	100.00
D. A. Mock	5.00
E. J. LaPlace	5.00
C. H. Tenney	250.00
Palestine Lodge, 204, F. & A. M.	25.00
James M. Phyfe & Co.	100.00
George F. Handel	10.00
Mrs. Moss Blosveren	20.00
The Misses Hendricks	50.00
Mrs. Joshua S. Brush	25.00
Harmon W. Hendricks	50.00
Mrs. Silas W. Stein	10.00
Mildred M. Meyer	10.00
John T. Lockman	25.00
Ladenburg, Thalmann & Co.	250.00
Urban H. Broughton	400.00
Young Friends' Lodge, No. 147, I. O. B. A.	25.00
S. Herzog Embroidery Works	5.00
Florence A. V. Twombly	1,000.00
Students and instructors, Townsend Harris Hall	78.50
Samuel Elliott	25.00
Nederland Israelitish Sick Fund	10.00
Harriet E. Ostrander	10.00
Ostralenker Y. M. B. A.	10.00

Mrs. Nelson H. Henry's committee, organized to relieve the sufferings of the Titanic survivors, is more than $1,000 in purse as the result of a Hungarian dinner and cabaret show at the Café Boulevard last night. Among those who entertained at dinner were General and Mrs. Henry, Mrs. Chauncey Olcott, Charles H. Steinway, president of the Steinway Piano Company; Mlle. Yolanda Mero and Ernest Yuchs. Mr. Steinway arranged the cabaret show, in which Miss Ruth St. Denis was one of the volunteers.

PERMANENT RELIEF FOR DEPENDENT ONES

"The Red Cross Committee intends to stand in the shoes of the fathers and breadwinners who went down on board the Titanic," declared Robert W. de Forest, chairman of the Red Cross Tmergency Relief Committee, yesterday. "To look after the widows and orphans of the Titanic disaster will be our main work, because the work of furnishing relief to the men survivors and single women is being done satisfactorily by the Women's Relief Committee, whose activities cannot be too highly praised.

"Of course, we do not know just how adequately we are going to be able to take care of these dependents. It will all depend on the amount of money at our command. We cannot make definite allowance to families until we know how large the fund is going to be. In the meantime we are cataloging each individual case and will be in readiness when the time comes for us to act.

"The same system will be employed that was used by this committee in caring for the victims of the Triangle fire. Guardians for children will be appointed and permanent funds assigned to them—enough, we hope, to provide for their support and for their education.

"Steps will be taken soon to co-operate with the English committee, so that no duplications of relief will be made and no impositions practised on either committee.

The Women's Relief Committee will conclude its work Thursday evening and its headquarters will be closed. All remaining survivors wishing help must apply Thursday morning. Its records will be turned over to Mr. Williams, Commissioner of Immigration, to whom the committee was accountable, and the remainder of its funds, after authorization by the full committee, probably will be turned over to the Red Cross Committee."

$305 SENT TO HERALD FOR TITANIC SUFFERERS

Contributions amounting to $306 were received yesterday by the HERALD for the aid of the Titanic survivors and the families of those lost at sea. These funds will be distributed where needed most through the Red Cross Society. The amounts sent to the HERALD were:—

J. Howard Wright	$250
Rosenthal & Grotta	25
Mrs. Louis Kaufman	5
S. Sawyer	5
Mr. Marshall	5
C. Gaconnier	2
J. Buxton	5
Miss M. Brown	2
Miss R. Crone	2
Miss H. Brill	2
Miss A. Beuler	2

MR. CARUSO WILL AID.

Largest of the benefit performances that have been arranged for the families that have suffered loss through the Titanic disaster will take place next Monday night at the Metropolitan Opera House. Seats will be placed on sale this morning at the box office.

Mr. Enrico Caruso will be the feature of the programme, having volunteered to sing in English "The Lost Chord," to the accompaniment of the orchestra of the Philharmonic Society, conducted by Mr. Frank Damrosch. Mr. W. Bourke Cockran will deliver the principal address and the Executive Committee of the benefit will present to Mr. Marconi a gold tablet which is being made by Prince Paul Troubetskoy.

Builders' Drawings of the Titanic Show Thirty-Two Lifeboats, but Steamship Carried Only Sixteen on Her Fatal Voyage

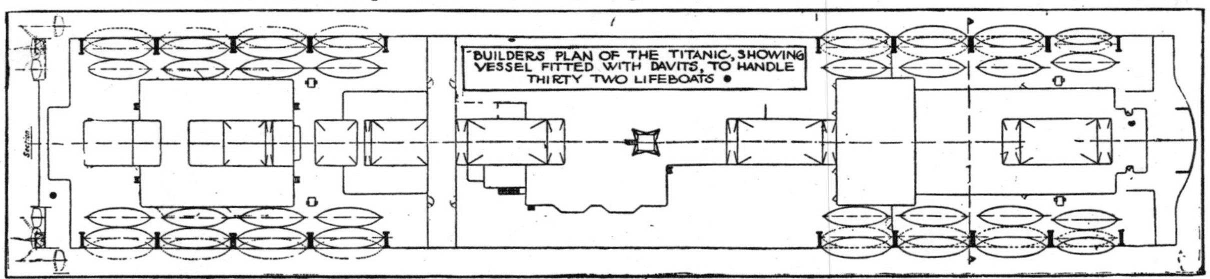

BUILDERS PLAN OF THE TITANIC, SHOWING VESSEL FITTED WITH DAVITS, TO HANDLE THIRTY TWO LIFEBOATS

Original Plans of the Titanic Prove She Had Only Half Her Full Complement.

HAD SIXTEEN DAVITS

Expert in Describing Her to to Underwriters Two Years Ago Outlined Safety Appliances.

That provision was made for thirty-two lifeboats in the construction of the Titanic is shown by the drawings of the builders. These drawings show sixteen sets of davits, which would accommodate double that number of lifeboats.

There were only sixteen lifeboats on board the Titanic. Thirteen of these were picked up by the Carpathia and three were capsized.

The plans for davits called for and accepted in the original orders for the Titanic and Olympic were prepared by Axel Welin, and he read a paper to a gathering of ship builders and underwriters at Glasgow on May 25, 1910, describing in full the things that were necessary for the saving of human life on shipboard.

"The deck plans of the two greatest ships, the Titanic and Olympic," said Mr. Welin, "called for thirty-two boats, and Messrs. Harland & Wolff, of Belfast, Ireland, have authorized the placing of the boats. Each vessel will be fitted with double acting davits and will carry sixteen sets of boats—that is to say, the specifications call for thirty-two lifeboats. We have arranged frames that provide for the manipulation of either davit arm without blocking the ease of manipulation. The drawing that shows the number of boats that we have ordered to supply davits for is herewith given, and they should contain more than sixteen hundred souls."

The drawings published in the HERALD to-day are reproduced from those which Mr. Welin refered to in his address.

Mr. Hoppin, of the White Star line, was surprised when the drawings in possession of the HERALD were shown him yesterday. He said there were no copies of the Titanic's plans in the White Star offices here.

"The davit people had the contract for supplying the Titanic with davits," said Mr. Hoppin, "but I am frank to say that the Olympic's outlay of boats is quite different from the plan of Harland & Wolff that you now show me as the Titanic's. This is the first thing of its kind that I have seen, and indeed it is the first of its kind extant, for we have been asked many times for plans of the boat arrangements and have been able to give none because we had none here."

SHOWING A DOUBLE ROW OF LIFEBOATS ON THE TITANIC

STEAMSHIPS ADD TO LIFEBOAT SUPPLY

Owners in Rush Buy Up Available Boats in City and Order Many More.

Principal steamship lines are making all speed in the matter of equipping their vessels with enough lifeboats and rafts to take care of every person on board. It was learned yesterday that more than one hundred boats and rafts had been purchased in this city within the week.

The Cunard line has purchased twelve lifeboats and twelve rafts from one firm, Davis Kahnweiler's Sons, of No 260 Front street, and has directed the firm to continue building boats and rafts to the full extent of its facilities until advised that the Cunard line has as many as it requires.

Other boat building firms in the city and in New Jersey reported they had sold every boat and raft they had on hand and have more orders than they can fill.

The Mauretania, of the Cunard line, which leaves her pier this morning, will carry fifteen additonal lifeboats.

The Rotterdam, of the Holland-America line, which steamed from Hoboken yesterday, carried twenty large lifeboats, each capable of carrying seventy persons in an emergency. She took also four collapsible lifeboats and three rafts.

With Boats for 3,000, the Olympic Will Start from England To-Day

Steamship Carries Sixteen Regular and Forty-Four Collapsible Life Craft, and Will Proceed Along the Forty-First Parallel of North Latitude—More Than Two Hundred Saloon Passengers Will Make the Voyage.

[SPECIAL DESPATCH TO THE HERALD VIA COMMERCIAL CABLE COMPANY'S SYSTEM.]

HERALD BUREAU,
No. 130 FLEET STREET,
LONDON, Tuesday.

The Olympic, which leaves Southampton to-morrow for New York, will carry sixteen lifeboats and forty-four collapsible boats, enough for more than three thousand persons. The Titanic carried sixteen lifeboats and four collapsible boats, only enough for 1,178 persons.

The Olympic's route will be along the Forty-first parallel of north latitude.

Aboard the Olympic will be more than two hundred saloon passengers, among whom are the Duke of Sutherland, the Comte de Sibour, Major C. E. Polloch, Lieutenant Colonel G. M. W. Macdonough, Major George L. Gross, Commander R. R. Belknap and Mrs. George E. Belknap.

Mrs. Carter, who, with her husband, the Rev. E. E. Carter, went down with the Titanic, was the daughter of Thomas Hughes, author of "Tom Browne's School Days."

American Society, London, will hold a memorial service Friday at St. Margaret's, adjoining Westminster Abbey, for the late Howard B. E. Case, one of the Titanic victims, formerly president of the society. The American Ambassador and all employes of the Vacuum Oil Company will attend.

At the Carlton Club many friends are in mourning over the death by drowning of Tyrell William Cavendish, a member of the famous English family, of which Lord Waterpark is the head. Mr. Cavendish married in December, 1906, Miss Julia Siegel, daughter of Henry Siegel, of New York. Two sons survive.

full patronage of their American clientele ths summer.

The Shipping Gazette says:—"The red hot, hasty, ill informed investigation of the loss of the Titanic in the United States has done more than anything else to enlighten us as to the real character of this disaster."

The Evening Standard declares:—"America has struck too soon, but has succeeded in hurrying us on."

These two half hearted indorsements stand out as the only favorable English criticisms of the Senate committee's inquiry, which is designed to protect American lives by compelling foreign steamships to adopt proper safeguards.

The Titanic disaster still holds first place in the public mind. The newspapers publish at great length the thrilling details of the evidence given before the Senatorial committee, while the extraordinary flow of money to the relief funds is proof of the wide-felt sympathy. The total fund, including that in New York, is approaching $1,000,000. Perhaps the most noteworthy is the Daily Mail fund, which has been contributed exclusively by women, and already amounts to $120,000. The Lord Mayor's fund has reached $545,000 and the Dail Telegraph's $87,775.

The fund at Southampton amounts to $72,700 and that at Liverpool to $64,500. Many special performances have been arranged at various music halls and theatres for the benefit of the sufferers.

The famous retired steamship commander, Captain McKay, who, during forty years in service made 800 Atlantic voyages without the loss of a single life, in an interview says that no blame, in his opinion, attaches to Captain Smith, the commander of the Titanic. The disaster, however, points to the necessity of following a more southerly route, which he says he always advocated.

"If the existing lane of routes," continues Captain McKay, "were charted another thirty or forty miles further to the south the boats would enjoy clearer weather and less liability of meeting icebergs, and add less than an hour to the time of crossing. I used to think that vessels of 15,000 to 20,000 tons were too unwieldy; new 55,000 is talked of. It is time to call a halt and consider the question of safety."

Shipbuilding firms are overloaded with sudden orders for lifeboats from all sides and are unable to supply the demand.

WANTS MORE BOATS ON ARMY TRANSPORTS

HERALD BUREAU,
No. 1,502 H STREET, N. W.,
WASHINGTON, D. C., Tuesday.

H. L. Stimson, Secretary of War, has called for a report on the lifeboat provisions on the transports of the army. It is admitted no adequate provision is made to accommodate anything like the number of passengers which transports carry, and War Department ocials anticipate that the law may be changed to make it mandatory to have life boat accommodations for all. Anyway, Mr. Stimson thinks this precaution should be taken.

In the navy about sixty-five per cent of the officers and crew can find places in the lifeboats, the other thirty-five per cent depending upon liferafts, hurriedly constructed, and other means to insure their safety. Navy officers, however, do not anticipate any change in thes regulations because of the Titanic disaster.

Secretary Meyer explained that the battle ships in the navy are nearly always in fleet or squadron formation, so there would be likelihood in losing men in case of accident to any one ship Then, too, by their profession, navy men are paid for the risk they take at sea, and in case of war a ship stripped for action carries only two lifeboats.

THE LEYLAND 20 MILES OFF.

BOSTON, Mass., Tuesday.—The Leyland steamship California was less than twenty miles from the Titanic when the latter vessel sunk. Captain Lord, of the Californian, said to-night that had he but known of the Titanic's plight all the passengers could have been saved. That his ship was the steamship reported to have passed within five miles of the sinking Titanic and to have disregarded signals for help, Capain Lord denied positively. "I figure that we were from seventeen to nineteen miles distant from the Titanic that night," he said.

Cabinet in Late Night Meeting

President Summons Secretaries to a Conference—May Be the Archibald Case.

HERALD BUREAU,
No. 1,502 H STREET, N. W.,
WASHINGTON, D. C., Tuesday.

President Taft to-night called the members of the Cabinet to a meeting, the purpose of which was not divulged, but the importance of which became known when the members remained at the White House long past midnight. At nine o'clock Mr. Nagel, Secretary of Commerce and Labor, was excused, and he hurried away on a train for St. Louis. His mission was not divulged.

Rumors of all sorts were flying thick and fast around the Presidential offices when it became known that the important all night session of the Cabinet was on.

There is a report that the Cabinet was called to consider the charges pending against Associate Judge Robert W. Archibald, of the Commerce Court. This matter has reached a head in the House.

A resolution directing the President "if not incompatible with public interest" to "transmit to Congress a copy of any charges filed against Judge Archibald, now under fire of accusation in connection with a deal with the Erie Railroad, was introduced in the House this morning by Representative Norris, the Nebraska Roosevelt insurgent. The resolution was referred to the Committee on the Judiciary. The House is likely to pass it and it may come up to-morrow.

The resolution also directs that copies of all affidavits, photographs and evidence filed with the Department of Justice be transmitted to the House.

Judge Archbald is alleged to have been negotiating with the Erie for the purchase from the road of "culm banks," piles of refuse coal, afterward found to have value. It was the alleged intention of Judge Archbald and his associates to sell the culm banks to an electric railroad in Pennsylvania. The alleged impropriety lies in the fact that, as a member of the commerce court, Judge Archbald is called upon to pass upon questions in which the Erie is involved.

TITANIC LOSS IN COURT.

Long Island Railroad Must Substitute Director's Name for J. B. Thayer, Who Was Lost.

One of the first legal complications to arise from the sinking of the Titanic came up yesterday in the Special Term of the Queens County Supreme Court, in Long Island City, before Justice Crane, in an action by the Long Island Railroad to obtain the appointment of commissioners to condemn a strip of land at Dunton, in Queens borough, belonging to J. K. O. Sherwood, for the use of freight terminals at Jamaica.

Frank E. Haff, secretary of the Long Island Railroad Company, testified that one of the directors of the railroad who had signed the papers for the improvement was J. B. Thayer, who was a victim of the Titanic.

It will be necessary to make another director a party to the action. Justice Crane decided that the hearing could continue and the directors of the railroad should make the necessary substitution.

STRAUS MEETING DRAWS THRONG OF 20,000 PERSONS

Police Forces to Disperse Vast Crowd at Memorial to Titanic Victims.

BATTLE AT DOORS OF EAST SIDE HALL

Admirers of Mr. and Mrs. Isidor Straus Pack Streets for Blocks to Pay Tribute to Them.

RESERVES ARE CALLED OUT

Promoters Forced to Abandon Services Because of Vast Number Who Seek to Gain Admittance.

The sympathy aroused on the lower east side over the tragic and heroic deaths of Mr. and Mrs. Isidor Straus almost caused a panic and a riot last night, when twenty thousand persons gathered in front of the Educational Alliance Building, No. 197 East Broadway, and tried to force their way into the building to hear a memorial talk on the life of Mr. Straus and the death of Mr. and Mrs. Straus by the Rev. Hirsch Maslinsky, rabbi of the People's Synagogue.

The seating capacity of the auditorium of the building is only 750. The time set for the address was eight o'clock, but as early as five o'clock the streets were crowded for four blocks each way. Mr. Straus had been president of the Educational Alliance League for twenty years, and many of the persons in the throng were personally acquainted with him.

As the hour for the memorial exercises approached the crowd became impatient and, forcing the doors, packed the auditorium in two or three minutes. Those who could not get in kept pushing and crowding and finally the situation became so acute that the reserves from three police stations were called. The meeting was abandoned and the police began to disperse the throngs. On the Jefferson street side of the building many women were jammed against an iron railing, three feet high. The pressure on this fence became so great that it broke. It fell against the building wall and bridged the gap over a seven foot areaway, thereby saving many of the women and children from serious injury.

HOLD MEMORIAL SERVICE IN TRINITY

White Star Officials Attend Impressive Ceremonies—Tribute to Work of W. T. Stead.

Memorial services for the victims of the Titanic disaster were held by the St. George's Society in Trinity Church yesterday.

Officials of the White Star Steamship Company, survivors of the disaster and many notables, including Lord Eustace Percy, secretary of the British Embassy in Washington; W. Cortenay Bennett, Consul General, and Mr. Broderick, Vice Consul at New York, attended. The services were under the auspices of Henry W. Bucknall, president of St. George's Society, and he was assisted by L. B. Sanderson, past president.

There were present all the vicars and curates of the nine chapels of Trinty Parish.

In front of the church, above the entrance, hung two large British and American flags, entwined with black and purple. The pulpit was similarly draped. There was no sermon or eulogy, the regular funeral service of the church being held.

A memorial service for W. T. Stead was held in the Fifth Avenue Presbyterian Church last evening, at which Mornay Williams paid a tribute to the life work of Mr. Stead. It was announced several weeks ago that Mr. Stead was to deliver an address in the church last night, but his death prevented. The service concluded with the singing of the hymn "Nearer, My God, to Thee."

A memorial service for Henry B. Harris will be held in the Hudson Theatre, of which he was the manager, next Sunday evening. The programme, which will include addresses by several well known theatrical men, will be announced to-morrow.

At a meeting of Commonwealth Council, No. 542, Royal Arcanum, held in Masonic Temple, Brooklyn, resolutions were adopted expressing sympathy for the brave men and women of the Titanic disaster. The resolutions urged the enactment of laws and regulations compelling all steamship companies to provide adequate life saving equipment.

The Board of Trustees of teh American Scenic and Historic Preservation Society inaugurated yesterday a movement to erect a memorial tablet, mural monument or sculpture in Battery place or some other suitable location to the memory of the victims of the Titanic disaster. The society will head the movement with a substantial contribution, if the project meets with public favor, the remainder to be contributed by the public at large. The proposed tablet, it is estimated, will cost $5,000. A suitable design is now being prepared.

ARRANGE MEMORIAL TO DR. O'LOUGHLIN

Friends of the Titanic's Physician Consider Building Hospital Laboratory in His Name.

In a movement for the endowment of a pathological laboratory at St. Vincent's Hospital in memory of Dr. William Francis Norman O'Loughlin, ship's physician of the Titanic, who was lost when she went down, a meeting was held at the hospital yesterday at which it was agreed that a committee should be appointed to carry out the idea. The names of the committee will be made known to-day or to-morrow.

The idea originated with a friend of the physician, a foundress of the hospital, who desired that her name be withheld.

Dr. O'Loughlin was in the service of the White Star line forty years and had sent many patients to St. Vincent's Hospital.

Henry B. Harris' Will Discovered

Testament of Theatrical Manager Who Went Down with the Titanic Soon To Be Filed.

The will of Henry B. Harris, theatrical manager, who perished in the Titanic disaster, was found yesterday among the papers in his office safe in the Hudson Theatre, of which he was lessee and manager. The instrument, which disposes of an estate approximating $1,000,000 in value, will be filed for probate within a few days.

It was reported that Mr. Harris left the whole of his estate, including valuable unexpired contracts, leaseholds, rights to plays and other property, to Mrs. Harris. This, however, was denied by Max D. Steuer, attorney for the estate, of No. 115 Broadway. Mr. Steuer refused to discuss the provisions of the will until it was filed for probate early next week.

While there is no evidence that the body of Mr. Harris was recovered among those picked up by the steamship Mackay-Bennett, which is now on its way to Halifax, the family of the dead manager are hopeful that it may have been recovered, and no steps to probate his will are to be taken until all hope of recovery of his body has been dissipated.

NO SCARE, INSIST LONDON HOTEL MEN

Their American Trade Will Be as Good as Ever, Assert Managers of Famous Houses.

[SPECIAL DESPATCH TO THE HERALD VIA COMMERCIAL CABLE COMPANY'S SYSTEM.]

HERALD BUREAU,
No. 130 FLEET STREET,
LONDON, Tuesday.

Hotel proprietors in London indignantly repudiate statements in the yellow English press that Americans are frightened by the Titanic disaster and are cancelling reservations. The managers of the Ritz-Carlton, the Savoy, the Cecil and other famous hotels say that, naturally, there will be a slight falling off, but that they expect a

Total Insurance Loss $15,000,000

Hartford Underwriters Give Estimate of Policies To Be Paid for the Titanic Wreck.

[SPECIAL DESPATCH TO THE HERALD.]

HARTFORD, Conn., Tuesday.—Mr. Dunham, president of the Travelers Insurance Company, to-night says that the total risk of the Travelers on the lives of those who were on board the Titanic was $1,100,000. The total loss of the company through the disaster is about $350,000, of which $90,000 was reinsured in a reinsurance company, he says. Thus the Travelers net loss as far as known is less than $400,000.

The largest loss by any individual death resulting from the wreck that will affect the Travelers is the casualty insurance of John B. Thayer, second vice president of the Pennsylvania Railroad Company. Mr. Thayer's family will receive $120,000, all from the Travelers, as Mr. Thayer carried insurance for $60,000, which doubles under the policy contracts when life is lost by accident to common carriers. Mr. Thayer had paid premiums since 1907.

Insurance men here are generally agreed that the losses on the Titanic will amount to $15,000,000. This includes life, accident and marine insurance. Two-thirds of the loss will fall upon the marine insurance companies. All the marine insurance is carried abroad, the insurance underwriters say, but the risk is distributed largely in this country by reinsurance.

THE WEATHER:
Fair tonight; Friday, probably showers by night; warmer.

THE BROOKLYN DAILY EAGLE

Complete Stock Market

LAST EDITION. Volume 72A No. 115 ★ NEW YORK CITY, THURSDAY, APRIL 25, 1912. ★ 26 PAGES. THREE CENTS.

TAFT SAYS T. R. DISTORTED FACTS

Misstated His Conduct and Actions in White House.

NOT A "SQUARE DEAL."

President Evinces Much Indignation in His First Answer to Roosevelt's Criticisms.

TIME TO SPEAK PLAINLY.

Believes People Should Not Choose Colonel Because of His Doctrines and Appeal to Class Hatred.

Springfield, Mass., April 25—President Taft made his answer heer today to the criticism that Colonel oRosevelt has made of him and his administration.

In a speech that bristled with indignation, in which he named Colonel Roosevelt over and over again, Mr. Taft told a crowd that filled Springfield's public square how he believed Mr. Roosevelt had not given him a "square deal," and how he had "misstated" and "distorted" the facts concerning Mr. Taft's conduct and atcions in the White House.

The President replied in some detail to many of the charges that Colonel Roosevelt has made against him since the present campaign began.

He took pains to make plain Mr. Roosevelt's knowledge and complete agreement with many of the actions and policies of the present Administration which lately he has condemned and denounced.

The President declared that after the Columbus speech of Colonel Roosevelt he found the country unresponsive, and he shifted his method of campaign from a declaration of "principles" and proposals of reform to a series of attacks upon the Administration.

Why Taft Believes People Should Not Choose Roosevelt.

Mr. Roosevelt's doctrine of the recall of judges and the recall of decisions, his willingness to disregard the "wise custom" that forbids a third term whether consecutive or not, his appeal to "class hatred and prejudice," and his "absolute failure" to put forth any concrete propositions for true reform and true progress, Mr. Taft said, all combined to make him believe that the American people should not choose Mr. Roosevelt to sit again in the White House.

Mr. Taft began his speech by declaring that he spoke plainly only because he believed it time for him to do so. He brought in Colonel Roosevelt's name only because events had forced him to use it.

"In 1908 Theodore Roosevelt recommended to the people of the United States that I, then the Secretary of War, be nominated by the Republican party and be elected. He labored hard and long to bring this result about, and he succeeded. I have felt the deepest gratitude to him.

Never Disloyal to Friendship He Owes to Roosevelt.

"Neither in thought nor word nor action have I been disloyal to the friendship I owe Theodore Roosevelt. When the time came for this campaign to begin I let the people know that I would like to have my administration approved by their giving me another term. At that time Theodore Roosevelt said he was not a candidate and that it would be a calamity if he were nominated. Since then he has changed his mind."

So far as he personally was concerned, the President said, he never would have attacked Colonel Roosevelt, nor had a quarrel with him. "So far," said he, "as personal ambition is concerned, so far as personal feeling is concerned, I would never answer his charges.

"But I cannot act for myself. I represent a cause. I represent an element of the Republican party that believes in constitutional government and its preservatio; that believes in wise progress under the guarantee of the Constitution.

"By misstatements throughout the country he has led many people to believe charges made against me and my administration."

KAISER CALLS MEETING.

First Step in Arranging International Conference on Ocean Traffic Regulations.

Berlin, April 25—The calling of an international conference to discuss the subject of the improvement of lifesaving facilities on board passenger steamers is regarded as a practical certainty. The initiative taken by Germany in the matter has aroused the greatest interest among the other powers and the suggestion has been received everywhere with sympathy.

A preliminary step toward the conference was taken today upon the Emperor's instigation by the calling of a meeting for May 6 to be held at the Department of the Interior under the presidency of the Secretary of State. The meeting is to be attended by department officials, representatives of the trans-Atlantic shipping companies, shipbuilders, marine associations, etc.

Questions to be considered include lifesaving equipment, ocean routes, wireless telegraphy, bulkheads and speed.

NEGRO GUILTY OF CONSPIRACY

Convicted After a Trial Covering Four Days.

John M. Atkins, a negro, living at 1339 Forty-fifth street, and one of the directors and officers of the Metropolitan Mercantile and Realty Company, was found guilty of conspiracy today before County Judge Moore after a four days' trial.

Some months ago there was considerable notoriety given to the dealings of the above named company, the charge being made that its officers were engaged in swindling operations in which persons of color were inveigled out of their savings. Atkins, with others of the company, when arrested, was indicted for conspiracy.

The chage against Atkins is that as a representative of the realty company, he was guilty of selling to one Robert Stewart a piece of property in Rahway, N. J., which the company did not own. Following the conviction this morning Atkins was remanded for sentence on Monday next.

Only Photograph of Wireless Operator J. G. Phillips of the Titanic.

The Eagle prints today the first photograph ever published in the United States of John George Phillips, the gallant wireless operator of the Titanic who was lost when the vessel was sunk. Everybody is familiar with the thrilling story of how Phillips stuck to his post and kept sending the S. O. S. distress call until the water rose in the sending room and the motor was stopped. He did not even stop when a frenzied stoker crept up behind him and attempted to steal his life preserver.

Young Phillips was only 26 years old. He had worked for the Marconi Wireless Company for six years and had operated all over the world. The Marconi people speak in terms of high praise of Phillips. An official of the company, in speaking of him, said:

"His installation on the Titanic possessed a range of about 500 miles under all conditions. Usually, however, it would convey messages a much greater distance.

"Mr. Phillips took day and night turns with his assistant at the apparatus, so that it was never for a moment left unwatched.

"The equipment of the wireless cabin on the Titanic contained all the latest improvements, and was the best of its kind in existence.

"The old danger signal was 'C.Q.D.' and the operators used to speak of it as 'Come quick, danger.' Now they have got a phrase for the new 'S.O.S.' message. They speak of it as 'Save our souls.'

"The 'C.Q.D.' signal was abandoned because it was possible to confuse it with others. 'S.O.S.' in the Morse code is three dots, three dashes, three dots. There is nothing else like that in all the Morse language.

"Any operator would suspend all commercial business immediately that danger signal spelled out its dots and dashes, and he would immediately endeavor to get in touch with possible rescuers.

"The message sent out by the Titanic would travel about a thousand miles. The ship was fitted with the 5KW Marconi sets with a range of about 500 miles, but at night the electric waves would travel twice this distance."

HIS SON LYNCHED; HE APPEALS TO TAFT

Hoefner Wants Justice for Slayers of Union Course Youth.

WAS HANGED BY MOB.

Father Sure Henry Was Innocent of Charge of Murder in Montana.

BOY DID NOT RUN AWAY.

Went to Seek Fortune Three Weeks Ago—Body Returned to Parents in Coffin.

John H. Hoefner of 1231 Atlantic avenue, whose 19-year-old son Henry was lynched by a masked mob in Montana, is going to write to the President of the United States appealing for justice. He says that his boy was innocent and that he was brutally murdered.

"I am going to gather my family around me tonight," he said, as he looked up from a bolt of cloth he was cutting in his tailor shop, and his eyes filled with tears. "I have a daughter who is a stenographer and I'll have her write the letter. I shall ask for justice. We are all entitled to that. The only thing I am uncertain about is how to address the letter. I suppose you say 'Your Honor.'

Henry Hoefner left home on April 3. His father says that he did not run away, as newspaper accounts have already stated, but that he went away from Brooklyn with the full knowledge of the family to work on his uncle's ranch in Montana. In Forsythe, Montana, he was thrown into jail on an accusation of murder, and at 2 o'clock in the morning a mob stormed the jail, took him out and hanged him. His body was found dangling from a tree.

"There has never been a stain on my family—never," said the elder Hoefner today. "I have five children living and Henry was as good a boy as you could find anywhere. It is simply impossible that he should have done this thing. He was never a bad-tempered boy, always minded his mother and father, came home early at night and didn't drink.

Boy Belonged to Cadet Corps of St. Peter's Lutheran Church.

"Henry was baptized and confirmed in St. Peter's Lutheran Church on Bedford avenue. He was a member of the Cadet Corps there. The whole family were members of that church. I came here in 1870, raised my family and built up my business. Never in all that time was there one blot on the family history, and now this thing comes.

"The boy left school when he was 16 and for three years he worked hard in machine shops. His employers all speak well of him. In April he took his own money and went West. His uncle, Henry Fitter, who is personally known to the Governor of Montana, has a big ranch there, and he had said that he would be glad to take the boy. So Henry, who had become tired of working in a machine srop, left us.

"Last week I got a telegram from the sheriff of Forsythe, telling me that the boy had been locked up in jail on suspicion of murder. I telegraphed to the sheriff that the boy's uncle, Henry Fitter, would go to Forsythe to look after him and sent word also to Mr. Fitter.

Got Message From Montana Coroner Saying Youth Was Dead.

"Within twenty-four hours I received word from the coroner of Forsythe that the boy was dead. I don't remember just what that telegram said, except that it notified me of his death. I have the two telegrams at home in Union Course where I live.

Sure Son Was Innocent.

"The boy never had a gun and I am as sure as I stand here that he is innocent."

According to the dispatch from Sheriff McMullin of Forsythe, the boy was accused of killing Mrs. Maud Merrill, wife of a wealthy ranchman of Joppa after Hoefner had been surprised in the act of stealing. It was said that young Hoefner, armed with an automatic revolver, opened fire on the woman and her 11-year-old son.

A gang of ranchmen surrounded the Merrill home and after a desperate fight captured the Brooklyn boy, when his ammunition was exhausted. The mob which took him from the jail after overpowering the sheriff and the guards numbered two hundred.

CAN'T ABANDON A "NAGGER."

Husband Who Suffers From That Must Secure Legal Relief.

That a man cannot abandon his wife simply because she "nags" him was thte position taken by Supreme Court Justice Marean today in the trial of the suit for a separation brought by Mrs. Amelia Kahler against William Kahler, a flour salesman. Justice Marean granted Mrs. Kehler a separation with $10 a week, but only with the understanding that she must keep away from Kahler. If she does not obey she will lose her alimony.

Mrs. Kahler's attorney said that the action was brought because Kahler abandoned his wife some time ago. Mr. Kahler's lawyer said that he did leave her, but it was because Mrs. Kahler was constantly "nagging" him and he couldn't live in peace and comfort.

"A man has to stand such treatment from his wife," put in Justice Marean. "He can't abandon her simply because she 'nags' him."

It was evident that the husband was equally desirous with the wife for a separation—and, perhaps, more so, for Mrs. Kahler said she dearly loved her husband still.

Mrs. Kahler lives at 58 Sackett street, and Kahler said he lived at Lyndhurst, N. J. The latter said on the witness stand that his wife "raised a row" so many times that he had to move away from Brooklyn. This Mrs. Kahler denied.

THE MACKAY-BENNETT.

Which Is Conveying 205 Victims of Titanic Disaster to Halifax.

HOLDUP MAN TRIES TO ROB A CASHIER

Nervy Attempt by Thief in Office at Lexington Avenue and Broadway.

IS OUTWITTED AND CAUGHT.

J. E. Janson Dodges Pointed Pistol, Jumps Through Window and Gives the Alarm.

A daring attempt at holdup and robbery, followed by a chase by a policeman and 500 men and boys, who succeeded in capturing the man charged with the crime, furnished excitement about noon today for the business district in the vicinity of Broadway and Lexington avenue.

A young man entered the offices of the Colonial Life Insurance Company, on the second floor at 1262 Broadway, and pointed a gun at the cashier, J. G. Janson. "Hands up!" he said, in a nickel novel style.

Instead of obeying the command, the cashier, who is 22 and nervy, ducked his head to one side, slid from his stool, made a short run in a crouching position to the window and took a flying leap through the open window and out of sight.

The would-be robber was astonished and stood stock still until, from below, he heard sounds which indicated that the cashier had given the alarm. Then he turned and ran down stairs and out into the street.

Had the robber held up Janson a few minutes earlier he woud have found the cashier with $1,000 in bills in his hands, as Janson said later that he was about to take that amount from the safe and count it.

When Janson disappeared through the open window he landed on the roof of the rear extension of Postoffice Station S, which occupies the ground floor at the Broadway address. Janson dropped from the roof by hanging by his hands. Then he went into Station S, told his story, and went through to Broadway in search of a policeman.

By this time the man with the gun in his hand had reached the sidewalk. He ran toward Greene avenue. The police say that he still had a pistol with him at that time.

Great Crowd Chases Holdup Man and He Is Finally Caught.

The crowd took up the pursuit. The man turned into Greene avenue, ran through to Patchen avenue, Lexington avenue, Reid avenue, back to Greene avenue and along Stuyvesant avenue. On the way, the police say, he tossed the gun aside.

By this time Policeman Elmer Dunlap, who was leading the chase, got near enough to make the pursued man hear what he had to say.

"Stop!" Dunlap shouted. "If you don't I'll blow your head off."

The man stopped at once and Dunlap arrested him and took him to the Ralph avenue police station, where he described himself as Fred Diener, 31 years old, a piano tuner, of 244 Stockton street. He was locked up on a charge of attempted robbery and felonious assault. In one pocket was found a cloth mask, the only convicting trace of evidence obtained by the police.

Cashier Janson lives at 520A Decatur street. He is a son of Louis Janson, who is manager of the Colonial Life Insurance Company. Young Janson said that when the man with the gun leveled the weapon at his face he could look straight down the barrel and see that it was loaded.

"I don't know why I jumped," Janson said. "I only know that I jumped. Maybe I was too scared to keep still with that gun aimed at my head."

The police are looking for a man they believe was Diener's confederate. The elder Janson was in the insurance offices a few moments before his son was held up. A young man approached the window and fumbled in his pockets as though after insurance papers. At the same time his glance took in the whole office and he was able to see who was there. Janson, senior, says he became suspicious and said to the stranger:

"You don't want to pay any insurance here."

"Oh," replied the stranger. "This is the Colonial, isn't it? I thought it was the Metropolitan. I've made a mistake."

The Metropolitan Life Insurance offices are a few doors away from the Colonial's. The police believe the first man came in to look the field over for Diener.

When the prisoner was more closely searched, another mask was discovered upon him fitted with leather straps to hold it firmly over the face.

When questioned by reporters the prisoner denied being in the Colonial Fire Insurance office. He said that he carried the masks "just for fun," and when asked what he had done with "the revolved" he replied: "I didn't have one."

Lieutenant Londergan of the Ralph avenue police station asked him, "Were you there?" and in some confusion he replied, irreleventiy, "I wasn't the one."

About 2:30 o'clock this afternoon a citizen telephoned to the Ralph avenue station and informed the police that a person who ran fast past the house at 892 Greene avenue had thrown a revolver into the areaway at that address.

The holdup occurred three doors from a pool room, where six men held up a crowd of men last winter and took from them about $500.

WHITEWASH PUZZLE

Now that President Taft is exposing the Roosevelt "Please-don't-prosecute" letters, who can the Harvester Trust; also what will the harvest be?
(Find answer in the picture.)

ENGINEERS GROW RESTLESS.

Believe Railroad Managers Are Parleying for Higher Freight Rates.

Little progress has been made today in the controversy between the Brotherhood of Locomotive Engineers and the railroad officials toward a settlement of the threatened strike. The delay of the managers of the railroads in coming forward with a proposition has impressed the engineers with the belief that they are more interested in the question of getting increased freight rates than they are about the demands of their employes or the difficulties that may ensue from a strike.

Warren S. Stone, who is directing the situation for the engineers, has been notified by Commissioner Neill and Judge Knapp to appear with his committee of fifty for a conference this afternoon at the Manhattan Hotel.

"Our men are getting restless," said Chief Stone today, "and if it appears the railways are using mediation as a cloak to secure their kind of arbitration they will discover that we, too, have something to say about arbitration, what kind of arbitration and how these matters shall be arbitrated. We shal! insist upon mediation until there is no further prospect of success from that source, and we do not intend that the railways shall drag this thing along to secure a big commission and the hope that thereby they may force the Interstate Commerce Commission to grant them increased rates."

ANYONE LOST A SMALL BOY?

Isaac Shesechtman, 8 Years Old, Asks Policeman to Find His Home.

Patrolman Bunn of the Bedford avenue police station was approached this morning by a small boy at the corner of South Fourth and Roebling streets, who confessed that he "didn't know how to get home." The boy said his name was Isaac Shesechtman, 8 years old, but he couldn't remember the name of the street where he lived. Bunn took the boy to the station house. The police of the station had been unable up to this afternoon to find trace of his home or of anyone who had lost a boy.

SOLDIERS OFF FOR DELHI, LA.

Negro Lynched There, and Race Troubles Are Feared.

Monroe, La., April 25—Company I of the Louisiana National Guard left here this morning for Delhi, thirty miles east, where serious trouble between whites and negroes developed last night. One negro was lynched and further disorder is anticipated.

GUNS AT FORTS SILENCED.

Infantry Drills at Florida Garrisons May Mean March to Border.

Pensacola, Fla., April 25—All of the mortars and heavy guns at Forts Pickens and McKee have been put out of commission, and the soldiers here and at Fort Barrancas, instead of ordinary artillery drills, are being put through infantry tactics.

They go through skirmishes and extended order drills two hours or more every day. Long marches along the beach are included in the programme.

It is the general opinion that preparations are being made to take the field on short notice, similar to the movement to the Mexican border some months ago.

Charlotte, N. C., April 25—W. W. Boyce, in charge of the foreign mission councils of the Associate Reformed Presbyterian Church of the South, today wired the twelve missionaries in Mexico under this denomination to return at once to America, on account of the extreme danger to their lives, as reported to him in combination with the Mexican trouble.

AGREEMENT SOON IN COAL DISPUTE

Sub-Committee's Recomendations Will Be Acted Upon May 2.

10 PER CENT. RAISE REPORTED

Approval of Proposed Agreement Will Have to Be Ratified by the Miners.

Philadelphia, April 25—Confirmation of the report that the anthracite miners and operators had reached an agreement in settlement of their dispute as to wages and hours of labor was had today when the office of President Baer in this city gave out the following:

"George F. Baer, the chairman of the operators committee, has issued a call for a meeting of the general committee of operators' and miners' representatives in New York on Thursday, May 2, at 2 p.m., to receive and act upon the report of the sub-committee appointed by the general committee to suggest a method of settling differences; the sub-committee having unanimously submitted a recommendation of terms and conditions looking to an adjustment of all differences.

"The terms and conditions of this report, however, will not be made public until after the meeting of the general committee on the second of May."

The report that the sub-committee of anthracite miners and operators had reached an agreement in New York and that the new pact includes a 10 per cent. increase in wages, was received with satisfaction in all parts of the anthracite regions.

The new working arrangement will be presented to the full committee of ten operators and ten miners on May 2. If this committee approves it the proposed agreement will have to be ratified by the miners before it can be put into effect. This probably will be done at a convention of delegates from the three anthracite districts.

According to the reported agreement the miners are conceded a 10 per cent. increase in wages. They asked for 20 per cent.

The board of conciliation created by the anthracite coal strike commission after the strike of 1902, with some modifications, is continued.

The miners asked for a "more convenient and uniform system of adjusting local grievances."

The sliding scale by which the men were given an increase of 1 per cent. when the price of coal was advanced 5 cents a ton above the $4.50 basis at tidewater, is abolished.

A four-year agreement is reported. The miners asked for a one year arrangement.

Nothing has yet been made public regarding the demand for a reduction of hours, recognition of the union or the minor demands.

The sub-committee has been meeting almost daily since April 11. It is expected that if the agreement is ratified by the miners the 170,000 men who have been idle since April 1 will have returned to work by May 10.

It is possible that the executive committee of the three anthracite districts, headed by National President John White, may order the workers back at an earlier date and trust to the convention to endorse their course.

The announcement of the plan of settlement of the anthracite difficulty was accompanied today by lively speculation in Wall Street in Reading and Lehigh Valley stocks, two important "coalers." Reading sold at its highest price since March, 1910, when it reached 172¼. Its high record was 173⅜ in 1909. As recently as 1904 the stock sold at $40 a share.

HAD NO LICENSE FOR SHOWS.

Five Men Fined for Exhibiting Moving Pictures at Coney Island.

Magistrate Dodd, in the Coney Island court, today, found five men guilty of running moving picture shows without a license and fined each $5. They were Peter Ecounoupoly, proprietor of a resort at the Bowery and Henderson's walk; Herman Wacke of Surf avenue and West Twelfth street, Thomas Mavrutkas of the Mardi Gras Hotel, at Surf avenue and the West End station; Benjamin Weissberger, Surf avenue, near West Eighth street, and Samuel Dicker of Surf avenue and West Eighth street. They all claimed that they were putting on shows as part of their hotel and liquor business, and that as such no license other than their State license was needed.

The magistrate held that the men were voilating the city ordinance which requires that anyone putting on a show to attract patrons to his establishment must take out a common show license.

When the season is fully open about thirty-five other Coney Island resorts will be affected by this decision.

WITH 205 BODIES, SHIP IS INBOUND

Mackay-Bennett Finds Remains Extending Over Many Miles.

ONLY 43 IDENTIFIED.

Message Confirms Identification of George D. Widener's Body.

MAY HAVE MAJOR BUTT'S.

"Death" Ship Has Been Drifting About in Fog, and Is Now Returning to Halifax.

Two hundred and five bodies of the victims of the Titanic disaster, according to dispatches received in the city today, have been picked up at sea by the cable steamer Mackay-Bennett and are being brought to Halifax, N. S.

The captain of the Mackay-Bennett confirms the identification of the body of George D. Widener, son of P. A. B. Widener of Philadelphia, and gives the further information that the majority of the bodies will never come to the surface of the sea.

The White Star Line has received a new wireless list of identified dead from the Mackay-Bennett in response to a request by the company's officers, who desired to check off the names contained in the first list sent Monday. Today's list confirms all names in the first wireless with but one exception.

In the first message there appeared the name of "Nihilschedig Rbatt." In the check-off list this name is separated into "Nahil Schedig," and "L. Butt." After an examination of all the passenger lists the officials have been able to find only one "Butt," that being Archibald W. Butt," President Taft's military aide. There is, also, a "W. Butt" mentioned in the wireless from the Mackay-Bennett, but it is stated that this is the body of a member of the crew. In consequence the opinion is advanced that "L. Butt" may be "Major Butt."

Of the 205 bodies recovered by the Mackay-Bennett and now being brought to Halifax, only 43 have been identified, leaving 162 unidentified dead on board.

Steamer Drifting in the Fog Since Noon Yesterday.

Captain Lardner of the Mackay-Bennett sends word through the Cape Race (N. F.) wireless station that the steamer has been drifting in a fog since noon yesterday. He does not indicate when he will reach Halifax. Bodies are floating upon the sea many miles east and west in latitude 41.35 north and longitude 48.37 west, says the wireless from the "death ship."

The following dispatch was received today by the White Star Line through the Cape Race (N. F.) wireless station.

"Drifting in dense fog since noon yesterday. Total picked up, 205. We brought away all embalming fluid to be had in Halifax—enough for 70.

"With a week's fine weather I think we would pretty well clean up relics of the disaster. It is my opinion that the majority will never come to the surface."

Another wireless dispatch from the Mackay-Bennett received today states:

"Bodies are in latitude 41.35 north, longitude 48.37 west, extending many miles east and west. Mail ships should give this a wide berth. Medical opinion is death has been instantaneous in all cases owing to pressure when bodies were drawn drown in vortex."

The fact that the Mackay-Bennett has been able to communicate by wireless with the Cape Race (N. F.) station shows that she is laying her course toward Halifax, as she was without the zone of the Cape Race station for several days and was only able to get into touch with land through other steamers relaying her messages.

No comment was made by the White Star officials here, nor were the movements of the Mackey-Bennett given out. It was said yesterday, however, that the ship had been instructed to return to Halfax at once with the bodies recovered, while the Minia was told to continue the search.

Reports of the finding of the bodies and the identification of the following have been confirmed:

W. H. Marriortt, Mrs. A. Robins, Louis M. Hoffman, George Rosenshire, John H. Chapman, W. Carbines, H. G. Reenberg, Ramon Artagaveytia, Simon Sather, H. W. Ashe, W. H. Harbeck, Malcolm Johanson, A. O. Holverdon, Nicholas Nasser, Nahil Scheidid, L. Butt, — Shea, Leslie Williams, A. Haytor, Jean Monros, Steward 76, George D. Widener, Leslie Gilinski, J. H. Gill, Ernest P. Tomlin, Yosip Drazencui, Mrs. Mack, Mrs. N. McNamee, Catavolas Cassilios, W. Vear, Mary Mangan, William Sago, James Farrell, Henry D. Hansen, James Kelly, Mauritz Adahl, Reg. Hall, W. D. Douglas, J. R. Rice, G. Henckley, Hospital attendant; W. Butt.

SHOPKEEPERS ARE FINED.

25 Storekeepers Penalized for Selling at Short Weights.

Twenty-five shopkeepers were fined from $25 to $100 each in the Fourth District Municipal Court today by Justice Meagher on charges of selling short weight. There were 50 cases called altogether, but half were adjourned or disposed of in some other manner. All of the actions were brought by the Corporation Counsel and represented every variety of charge possible under the short weight law. Some were accused of having "fast" scales, others were charged with selling produce by liquid measure, which should have been sold by dry measure, and still others were up for selling at little as one ounce under weight.

The excuses offered by the defendants were many and varied. Some alleged ignorance of the law, others said the short weight was given by clerks in their absence, while still others declared they had just purchased their stores and had not yet had time to test their scales to see if they were accurate.

The Fourth District Municipal Court has been set aside especially to short weight cases and during the month disposed of more than [illegible] cases.

Newburyport Morning Herald.

ESTABLISHED IN 1793, DAILY IN 1832
ONE HUNDRED AND TWENTIETH YEAR

NEWBURYPORT, MASSACHUSETTS, THURSDAY, APRIL 25, 1912

VOLUME CXX. NUMBER 99
PRICE ONE CENT; THREE DOLLARS A YEAR

WOULD NOT ALLOW SEN. SCHOFIELD TO HAVE THE FLOOR

President Greenwood of Senate Refuses to Recognize Ipswich Man in Debate

SEN. NASON GIVEN PREFERENCE

Bill Relative to Expense of Maintaining Bridges Over Merrimac Postponed to May 2nd

By E. W. PRESCOTT
Special State House Correspondent For the Herald.

STATE HOUSE, BOSTON, April 25—The bill relative to the expense of maintaining the so-called chain bridge and the Essex-Merrimac bridge over the Merrimac river at Deer Island, between Newburyport and Amesbury, was yesterday postponed in the senate until May 2nd.

Senator Bennett of Saugus, who moved postponement, said that he desired an opportunity of looking into the bill and ascertaining if it met with the approbation of Newburyport. He said that he remembered the fight of last year or the year before on this matter, when he said the city of Newburyport had opposed bearing any more of the burden of maintaining these bridges.

Senator Schofield of Ipswich said that he was not opposed to a postponement for consideration of the matter, but preferred that a day be specified rather than placing the matter on the table, which was Senator Bennett's original motion. Mr. Schofield said that the bill was satisfactory to Newburyport and Amesbury and there was no reason for such delay, but he was only too glad to give the senator from Saugus any neces-

(Continued on Page Four.)

EQUALLY ANXIOUS FOR A SETTLEMENT

Railway Managers and Engineers Are Sincere in Endeavors to End Trouble

CONFERENCE HELD YESTERDAY

(Associated Press Despatch.)
NEW YORK, April 24—U. S. Commissioner of Labor Charles P. Neill and the sub-committee of railroad managers were in conference all day long over the proposition by Commissioner Neill and Justice Martin A. Knapp of the U. S. Commerce Court, that their "kindly offices" be made use of in adjusting the wage controversy, which has threatened a strike by the engineers on practically all railroads east of Chicago and north of the Potomac river.

"I want to say," the commissioner said in the course of an interview tonight, "that the railway managers are sincere and so are the engineers. Both sides are equally anxious for a settlement."

As to what progress was made in a conference with representatives today, Mr. Neill was reticent, insisting that an informal discussion of negotiations might tend to embarrass the work.

EYESIGHT WILL BE SAVED

Charles Allen, the young son of Alvah Allen, manager of the Western Union Telegraph Co., who was injured in the eye on Tuesday, is getting along finely at the Anna Jaques hospital. It is expected that the sight of his right eye, the one injured, will be saved.

PRIVATE DANCING PARTY FOR BENEFIT OF TEAM

A private dancing party for the benefit of the High school athletic association will be held in Music hall, Friday evening, May 17, and the invitations will be out in a few days.

HOMEOPATHIC HOSPITAL WILL BE BENEFITED

Tidy Sum Raised by Ladies' Aid Society's Successful Supper and Dance

AFFAIR HELD LAST EVENING

Nearly 350 Persons Enjoyed Banquet at Fraternity Hall; Members Who Assisted

The Ladies' Aid Society of the Homeopathic Hospital association held a highly successful supper and dance last evening at Fraternity hall, and as a reward of the untiring efforts of the efficient committee in charge of the event, will net a tidy sum of money, which will be added to the funds of an institution that is accomplishing much in a humanitarian sense in this city.

It is estimated that nearly 350 persons sat down to the sumptuous supper, served between 6 and 8 o'clock, while the Philharmonic orchestra, Miss Elise Biron, leader, of Amesbury, discoursed sweet music in a pleasing manner.

In the evening from 8 until midnight the main hall was thronged with merry dancers, who whiled the happy hours away, their enjoyment being multiplied by the fact that all

(Continued on Page Four.)

WARD SIX STUDENTS TO GIVE EXHIBITION OF THEIR WORK FRIDAY

On Friday afternoon and evening the Belleville Parent-Teachers' association will hold an exhibition at the Currier school of the work in drawing, penmanship, manual training, cooking and sewing of the Curtis, Currier and Moultonville school pupils. Prizes will be given for the best individual exhibits in each department. In the afternoon the exhibition hours will be from 3 to 5 o'clock. Cake, icecream and candy will be on sale both afternoon and evening, and a very small admission fee will be charged.

In the evening the regular business meeting of the society will be held and a short musical program rendered.

The public is cordially invited to be present.

Advertise in the Herald.

COL. BRYAN MAY ENTER THE RING

Nebraskan Would Like Another Try If Roosevelt Is Nominated

SO SAYS WASHINGTON REPORT

(Associated Press Despatch.)
WASHINGTON, April 24—The visit of William J. Bryan to Washington yesterday and his talk with the various party leaders here, particularly in the senate, was followed today by a widespread discussion of the possibility of the Nebraskan again being the Democratic candidate for president.

Mr. Byran frankly told interviewers that he was not a candidate for the nomination in any sense of the word, and that it was difficult for him to conceive of any circumstance under which he might be a candidate.

Despite these public utterances some Democratic senators were inclined today to the belief that under certain conditions Mr. Bryan would not decline the nomination.

In short the impression left was that if Col. Theodore Roosevelt should be the Republican nominee, Mr. Bryan would like once more to take the field against him.

REV. AND MRS. ALEXANDER DIXON PRESENTED WITH RUG BY THEIR FRIENDS

The members of the official board and their wives of the Washington Street M. E. church paid an unexpected call on Mr. and Mrs. Alexander Dixon at their hospitable home on Washington street last evening.

When the welcome guests had assembled they showed their regard for the city missionary and his wife by presenting them a handsome Axminster rug, General Secretary Bumpus of the Y. M. C. A. making the presentation speech in behalf of the church members.

Refreshments were served and a pleasant evening ensued.

FUNERAL OF MRS. BECKMAN

The funeral of Mrs. Frances Beckman was held at 2:30 p. m. yesterday from the Advent church, Seabrook, N. H. Rev. Alexander Dixon of this city officiated. Interment will be at Danvers, where the body will be taken today by Undertaker Elliott.

Mr. and Mrs. Mahar of Seabrook sang "Lead Kindly Light" and "The Christian's Good-night."

LECTURE ON CHRISTIAN SCIENCE Thursday evening, at 8 o'clock in Griffin hall. Public cordially invited. *

VICTIMS OF AUTO ACCIDENT ARE RESTING WELL

Horrigan Operated Upon at the Hospital Yesterday for Fractured Skull

DUPRAY WAS BADLY INJURED

Fountain Replaced Upon Its Base Yesterday; Machine Not Yet Claimed

Michael Horrigan of Arlington Heights, who was injured in the automobile accident at the Upper Green, Newbury, early yesterday morning, was operated upon yesterday forenoon at the Anna Jaques hospital. Late last evening Mr. Horrigan was reported to have stood the operation well, was very comfortable and strong hopes are being held out for his recovery. He is suffering from a fractured skull.

Wilbur Dupray, of Ipswich, owner of the car, also sustained severe injuries, and he also is doing well.

The other occupants of the car at the time of the accident sustained only minor injuries, and left for their homes yesterday.

The fountain, which had been knocked out of place by the impact of the machine, was put back in position, while the shattered automobile was taken in charge of by George Little, who lives nearby.

TAFT INDORSED BY IOWA REPUBLICANS; HAS 16 DELEGATES

(Associated Press Despatch.)
CEDAR RAPIDS, Iowa, April 24—President Taft was endorsed by Iowa Republicans in their state and conressional convention here today, four delegates-at-large to the National Convention were instructed to vote for him, his list of Iowa delegates to the National Convention increased to 16 and the "favorite" son presidential candidacy of the United States Senator Albert B. Cummins was rejected, President Taft having a majority of 41 votes.

All Iowa districts have now chosen delegates. Counting four delegates-at-large, President Taft's strength is 16. Senator Cummins has 10 delegates.

Baseball Results

American League.
Washington 5, Boston 2.
Chicago 6, Cleveland 1.
Philadelphia 7, New York 0.
St. Louis 9, Detroit 5.

National League.
Boston 3, Brooklyn 1 (8 innings, darkness).
New York 11, Philadelphia 4. (7 innings, darkness).

New England League.
Worcester 5, Lynn 3.
Brockton 5, Haverhill 2.
Lawrence 6, Fall River 0.

PASSENGERS ON 'MOUNT TEMPLE' SAW LINER SINK

Steamer, Believed to Have Been Near Titanic at Time of Disaster, Arrives at St. John, N. B.

WITNESS TO APPEAR BEFORE COMMITTEE

Dramatic Story Told by Fifth Officer Lowe of Part Played by Him in Saving Survivors of Wreck

(Associated Press Despatch.)
WASHINGTON, April 24—Harold G. Lowe, fifth officer of the sunken Titanic told the senate investigating committee today of his part in the struggle by the survivors for life after the catastrophe.

His testimony showed that with a volunteer crew he rescued more men from the water; saved a sinking collapsable lifeboat by towing it astern of his and took off 20 men and one woman from the bottom of an overturned boat. Every one of these under his charge he landed safely on the Carpathia. From first to last Lowe's recital demonstrated that he played the man.

Ordered away in charge of lifeboat No. 14, he packed it to its fullest capacity on the top deck and fearing that some might attempt to jump into it while it was descending, kept up a fusillade with his revolver. Once afloat he took charge of a flotilla of small craft, which was eventually picked up by the rescue ship without the loss of a life.

Saw Steamer Sink.

Competing in interest with the day's testimony was the interchange of telegrams between Senator Smith, chairman, and the acting premier of Canada, George E. Foster. The latter mentioned the docking of the steamer Mount Temple at St. John, New Brunswick, with passengers aboard who professed to have seen the Titanic sink.

It was believed that the Mount Temple was the ship which was only five miles from the White Star liner when she went to the bottom.

Senator Smith has requested that the depositions of the officers and crew of the Mount Temple be sent to him.

In addition he accepted the offer made by Dr. E. C. Quitzman of Toronto to appear before the committee. Dr. Quitzman was one of the passengers who say that they saw the Titanic sink.

CAPTAIN DENIES RUMOR

(Associated Press Despatch.)
ST. JOHN, N. B., April 24—The rumor that the steamer Mount Temple was within five miles of the Titanic when she sank and without heeding signals of distress steamed away, is indignantly denied by Capt. Moore, who was in command of the vessel.

LOCAL HIGH TO PLAY PINKERTON ACADEMY NINE HERE SATURDAY

The High school baseball team will play its opening game at the Fair grounds Saturday afternoon when it lines up against the Pinkerton Academy nine. The latter school has been represented by a crack team for the past five years and the game should be an interesting one as the locals are in fine form and are anxiously awaiting the opening contest.

Coach Southwell has been working the team hard for the past two weeks and the boys have shown much improvement.

Gorwaiz will undoubtedly do the twirling, and much is expected of him in the coming games, as his work in practice has been snappy, with a variety of "benders" in the curve line, and as to speed—he has it, with good control.

Betts is scheduled to occupy the backstop position, and he works well with Gorwaiz.

A number of candidates are out for the outfield, but as yet no choice has been made.

The Weather

Probabilities.
Today fair; Friday increasing cloudiness, probably followed by showers, warmer, moderate west winds.

Midnight Conditions.
The thermometer at the Herald office at midnight registered 50 degrees, wind west and clear.

Miniature Almanac.

Sun rises	4:48
Sun sets	6:37
Length of day	13:49
Day's increase	4:45
High tide	5:45 a. m., 6:15 p. m.
Light Auto Lamps	7:07

The Business of Getting Ahead

No. XIX—The Cigarmaker Gets His First Lesson in Advertising.

"See that man who went out as you came in?" said the advertising agent. "He thinks he wants to start an advertising campaign. Somebody told him to come to me for advice. However, like all the new ones, he thinks he knows just about what kind of advertising will bring in the money for him, and because I told him a few honest facts he doesn't mean ever to come back. On the whole, though, I think he has enough sense to realize that there may be some truth in what I told him—especially when he comes to realize that my opposing his ideas indicates that it wasn't only his money that interests me—and he may be back in a week's time for a second lesson.

"Honestly, though, isn't it amazing what follies wise men will commit when it comes to advertising. Men who will analyze an ordinary business proposition until they classify every bone in its makeup will jump at conclusions on advertising questions like—oh, like anything foolish you have a mind to name.

"Now, that man is a cigarmaker, who has built up a very considerable business by making a really good 5-cent cigar and by making it a pleasure for people to come into his shop. His customers tell their friends, and they tell others. Now he wants to reach out and build his business faster by advertising.

"He said to me: 'I want an ad that will attract attention—big, black type—something they can't miss—like "Wilson's great little cigar—5—cents—best in the city. Try one." '

"Can you beat it? Something to attract attention. It takes me back to the old days when we used to see 'Stop, Look and Listen' at the top of any old advertisement.

"Want to know what I told him? Just a few rudimentary facts. He'll get further along with the next lesson. I said: 'Sure, you're right about attracting attention, but you want to attract favorable attention. A boy shouting on the street attracts attention, but you don't rush up and pay him money when you hear him. You want to attract interest as well as attention. Your shout must say something interesting about your goods. Sunny Jim attracted a lot of attention, but it didn't succeed as an advertising device, because it had no real connection with the cereal it was meant to advertise.

" 'Watch the news headlines in the papers. What has experience taught the editor who wants people to read a particular story? Prominence as to type, all right, but not necessarily spread across the page. A phrasing of the top line so that the reader is impressed that here is something that is bound to interest him. If the event is of great intrinsic importance, a simple, direct statement of fact. If it is one of those oddities of human experience that make half of the news, the headline must bring out that oddity. The people who read the news are the same people you want to read your advertisement. Take a leaf out of the editor's experience and put something into your advertisement headline that is bound to catch their interest as well as their attention. Look at the question from the reader's viewpoint. It isn't what you want him to read that should determine the wording of the headline and of the advertisement itself. It's what you can tell him that he wants to read.

"I could have told him a lot more, but I wanted that point to have time to sink in. Yes, I think he'll come back, because, after all, he's a sensible man, and sensible men are influenced by sense."

THEATER TOPICS

Dr. M. Baumfeld Will Resume Management of Irving Place Theater in October.

TO GIVE HIGH CLASS PLAYS

Lilliput Land at Wallack's Yesterday, When the Kiddies Shone in "Disraeli."

Dr. M. Baumfeld, who managed the Irving Place Theater some years ago, is going to try his luck again this fall, undeterred by the fact that the friends of Gustav Amberg, the retiring manager, are working hard to give him a successful benefit. The new director's plans are explained in the following announcement:

"Please take notice, that on October 1, 1912, I assume again the management of the German, 'Irving Place Theater,' and that I have engaged as my first guest Miss Leopoldine Konstantin, who appeared in the leading part of 'Sumurun' in the past season and who is one of the most eminent members of the German theater in Berlin; also Rudolf Schildkraut, formerly a member of the German theater in Berlin, and one of the foremost living German actors.

"I am pleased to inform you that I have been able to procure during the few days, which were available for this purpose, a number of plays for the next season which have never been produced in New York heretofore. Among them, plays of Herman Bahr, Arthur Schnitzler, Frank Molnar (writer of 'The Devil'), Karl Hauptmann (brother of Gerhard Hauptmann, who traveled America a few years ago), and Frank Wedekind. I will also produce the 'Volksfein,' by Ibsen, who as far as I know, has not been seen in this city at all, or at least not for many years. I intend to produce the following classical plays: 'Faust,' first part, staged in an especially artistic way; furthermore, 'Sappho' and 'Des Meeres und der Liebe Wellen,' by Grillparzer.

"It would be most important for me if you state that this is another and absolutely serious attempt to raise the German Theater in New York once more to the high artistic standard which it has had heretofore, an attempt which can be successful only if it attracts the patronage of the many Americans who are studying the German language, and who are increasing in number from year to year. In order to make it possible for the students of all high schools, colleges and universities in New York to see the classical plays which they read in school, produced in their original language, special matinees at very reduced prices will be arranged for them according to an agreement which I am going to make with the principals of the various institutions."

Those who saw the performance of "Disraeli" yesterday afternoon might have thought themselves in Lilliput land. The cast was composed entirely of children under 16 years of age, and the performance was for the benefit of St. Mary's Free Hospital for Children. It seemed hardly possible to believe that these little folks who stalked, strutted or skipped across the stage as their role would have it, were children and not a troup of skilled dwarf actors. The spirit of the time and tenseness of the action were well sustained throughout. George Tobin was in gait and gesture an exact copy of what George Arliss had made out of the part of Lord Beaconsfield. Thomas B. Carnahan, jr., with a head of yellow curls, was most delightful and blase as Lord Brooke and in a later scene showed his skill by playing the old gardener with a real brogue and much honest disgust at the audacity of the peacocks. The tiny footman, with his reverential bows, was most amusing and played his part with unflinching dignity. The girls were all very pretty and did much to help the play along. Ruth Wells was Dutchess of Glastonbury, and Hazel Turney a charming Lady Clarissa. Madeleine Chieffo did very good work in impersonating Mrs. Travers, the spy. There was much spontaneous applause and the general opinion was that one had enjoyed it "more than the grownups performance."

The members of the cast to appear in "Patience" May 6 at the Lyric Theater are rehearsing daily under the stage direction of William J. Wilson. For musical director Clarence Rogerson has been engaged. The run of "Patience" will be confined to four weeks time, and on June 3 "The Pirates of Penzance" will be revived in conformity with the plan to give permanency to this organization and supply a repertoire of favorite light operas.

Bert Levy, the artist entertainer, who appears at the Bushwick Theater the coming week, is the latest vaudeville celebrity to become enmeshed in the dragnet of the so-called legitimate stage. He will be one of A. H. Woods' stars next season, having been fitted by Willard Holcomb with a medium becoming his peculiar talents.

The announcement of the dates of the all-star gambol of the Lambs Club, which opens at the Manhattan Opera House on May 27, indicates that it is due in Brooklyn on the afternoon of Thursday, May 30. The performance here will be given at the Montauk. The complete route follows: Tuesday, May 28, matinee, National Theater, Washington; Tuesday, May 28, evening, Academy of Music, Baltimore; Wednesday, May 29, matinee, Apollo Theater, Atlantic City; Wednesday, May 29, evening, Hammerstein Opera House, Philadelphia; Thursday, May 30, matinee, Montauk Theater, Brooklyn; Thursday, May 30, evening, Hyperion Theater, New Haven; Friday, May 31, matinee, Providence Opera House, Providence; Friday, May 31, evening, Boston Theater, Boston.

Though a woman does well to marry outside the profession I should advise the layman to think twice before he marries an actress. If she retires from the stage she is apt to find life a little dull with her work taken away from her. If she continues to act her husband may feel neglected. Of course, there is the exceptional man who feels himself honored by the honors that come to the woman who bears his name. He looks at his wife and realizes that, if, in spite of all temptations and the pettiness of the world, she has kept herself fine, all the flattering attentions she receives add to his happiness, for a man is bound to take pride in his possessions, says Mary Mannering in McCall's Magazine for May.

People outside of the theater often wonder how a husband can sit in the audience and calmly watch another man make love to his wife. Of course, to people who are on the stage this is all in the day's work and they never give it a second thought. As a general thing people who are playing opposite each other are more apt to feel antagonistic than affectionate. I know perfectly well that there is nothing personal about a man's lovemaking on the stage, and when he kisses me, it is the same as though he were kissing a chair. People scarcely every really kiss on the lips, anyway. Of course, when a man is supposed to kiss you he doesn't kiss you behind the ear, but it isn't necessary for their lips to meet.

But far from taking lovemaking on the stage seriously I am afraid that if the two players were thinking of each other instead of their scene they would be apt to burst out laughing. A man can look very ridiculous a few inches away when he is appearing very romantic from across the footlights. I don't believe that actors and actresses fall in love with each other on the stage—in the wings, they may, perhaps, but not in front of the audience. There they have other work in hand.

BATTERMAN TROPHY

Trophy for the One-mile Relay, donated by Henry Batterman, to be contested for at the games to be held next Wednesday at the Forty-seventh Regiment Armory.

ECHOES OF THE TITANIC DISASTER

P. A. S. Franklin and J. Bruce Ismay of the White Star Line, leaving the Senate Office Building, where the Titanic hearings are being held. The second man from the left is Franklin and the man at the extreme right of the picture is Ismay.

Senator William Alden Smith of Michigan, the chairman of the Titanic Investigating Committee, arriving at the Senate Office Building.

Some of the Survivors of the Crew of the Titanic, walking about the streets of Washington. Some of them will probably be called as witnesses by the Committee.

Mrs. Lumsdon's 'Theodora' In Institute Museum

"THEODORA"

From a painting by Mrs. Christine Lumsdon, member of Executive Committee of the Brooklyn Institute Department of Fine Arts. This painting is now hanging in the Institute Museum Art Galleries.

The Yarn of the G. O. P.

(After the Yarn of the Nancy Bell.)

'Twas on the beach near Sagamore,
Which once was Oyster Bay,
I spied alone on an Outlook stone
A grizzled old man one day.

His eyes were stary, his teeth were large,
And fierce and large was he,
And I heard this fellow, with a gutteral bellow,
Grunt in a terrible key:

"I'm Big Bill Taft, and La Follette, too,
And the Boss of the G. O. P.,
And the candidates from several States,
And Charlie Hughes, too, you see."

And he waved the Big Stick, and tore his wool,
'Till I really felt afraid,
For I couldn't help thinking the man had been drinking,
And so I calmly said:

"Oh, wonderful man, 'tis little I know
Of doings of men like thee,
But it gets my goat (if you'll but note),
However you can be,

At once Bill Taft and La Follette, too,
And the Boss of the G. O. P.,
The candidates from several States,
And Charlie Hughes, too, you see."

So he gave a swing with that Big Stick thing,
Which is a trick he often used,
And having let out a bellow and shout,
He told me how he had cruised.

" 'Twas in the good ship G. O. P.,
We sailed on the waters of state,
But on Tariffs and Trusts the old ship busts;
'Twas a perfectly terrible fate.

"An' purty nigh all the party was lost,
There was many a hundred of soul,
But only a few of the G. O. P. crew,
Said 'Here' to the muster roll.

"There was Big Bill Taft and La Follette, too,
And the Boss of the G. O. P.,
And candidates from several States,
And Charlie Hughes, too, you see.

"For a time we'd neither votes nor food,
Till a-hungry we did feel,
So we drawed a lot an' accordin' shot
La Follette for our first meal.

"Then we settled on Charlie Hughes,
And a delicate dish he made,
Then the candidates from several States
The rest of our appetites stayed.

"The next to go was the Boss so brave,
Of the good ship G. O. P.,
And we made the most of him on toast,
Did Big Bill Taft and me.

"Then only me and Big Bill was left,
And the delicate question which
Of us two goes to the kettle arose,
And we argued it out as sich:

"For I loved Big Bill as a brother, I did,
And Big Bill he worshipped me,
But we'd both be blowed if we'd either be stowed
In the other chap's hold, you see.

"Said he, 'Dear Ted, to murder me,
Were a foolish thing to do,
For don't you see, you can't cook me,
While I can, and will, cook you.'

"He heated some water and put in some liars,
And chucked in my fakers, too,
And said, 'Now Teddy, I'm just about ready,
To make you into a stew.'

" 'Big Bill,' says I, 'the popular demand
Which I am pleased to mention,
Is that you get ready, to become part of Teddy,
For I'm going to the Chicago convention.

"Said he, 'Dear Ted, just take a whiff,
And please mark the odor well;
'Twill soothing be if I let you see
How nature fakish you'll smell.'

"And he stirred it round and round and round,
And sniffed at the foaming froth,
When I up with his heels and smothered his squeals,
In the scum of the boiling broth.

"And I eat Big Bill in a month or so,
And as I eatin' be,
The last of his hide I almost died,
For a vessel in sight I see.

D. N. R.

"An' I never talk, and never swing
The Big Stick in the same old way,
But I sit alone on this Outlook stone,
And mumble this song all day:

"Oh I'm Big Bill Taft, and La Follette, too,
And the Boss of the G. O. P.,
The candidates from several States
And Charlie Hughes, too, you see."

SIX GREAT CONSPIRACIES

NO. 4—THE GUNPOWDER PLOT.

The Roman Catholics had expected great favors and indulgences on the accession of James, both as he was descended from Mary, whose life they believed to have been sacrificed to their cause, and as he himself, in his early youth, was imagined to have shown some partiality toward them.

Very soon they discovered their mistake, and were at once surprised and enraged to find James, on all occasions, express his intention of strictly executing the laws enacted against them and of persevering in all the rigorous measures of Elizabeth. Catesby, a gentleman of good parts and of an ancient family, first thought of a most extraordinary method of revenge, and he expressed his intention to Percy, a descendant of the illustrious house of Northumberland. "In vain," said Percy, "would you put an end to the King's life. He has children."

"To serve any good purpose we must destroy at one blow the King, the royal family, the Lords, the Commons, and bury all our enemies in one common ruin. Happily, they are all assembled at the meeting of Parliament, and afford us the opportunity of glorious and useful revenge. Great preparations will not be required. A few of us combining may run a mine below the hall in which they meet, and choosing the very moment when the King harangues both houses, consign over to destruction these determined foes to all piety and religion."

Percy was charmed with this project of Catesby's, and they agreed to communicate the matter to a few more, and among the rest to Thomas Winter, whom they sent over to Flanders in quest of Fawkes, an officer in the Spanish service, with whose zeal and courage they were all thoroughly familiar.

All this passed in the spring and summer of the year 1604, when the conspirators hired a house in Percy's name, adjoining to that in which Parliament was to assemble. Toward the end of that year they began their operations.

They soon pierced the wall, three yards in thickness, but on approaching the other side they were somewhat startled at hearing a noise which they knew not how to account for. Upon inquiry they found that it came from the vault below the House of Lords; that a magazine of coals had been kept there, and that as the coals were selling off, the vault would be let to the highest bidder. The opportunity was immediately seized; the place was hired by Percy; thirty-six barrels of powder was lodged in it, the hole coverel up with faggots and bullets; the doors of the cellar boldly flung open, and everybody admitted, as if it contained nothing dangerous.

The day (November 5, 1605), so long wished for, now approached, on which the Parliament was appointed to assemble. The dreadful secret, though communicated to about twenty persons, had been religiously kept, during the space of nearly a year and a half. No remorse, no pity, no fear of punishment, no hope of reward had as yet induced any conspirator, either to abandon the enterprise or make a discovery of it. But the betrayal was unwittingly made after all by one in the plot, who tried to deter Lord Monteagle from attending the opening session of Parliament, by sending him a mysterious message of warning. Lord Monteagle showed the letter to Lord Salisbury, Secretary of State, who attached little importance to it, but who laid it before the King.

The Scotch Solomon read it with more anxiety and was shrewd enough, by some expressions in the missive, to order an investigation of the vaults underneath the Parliamentary Houses. The gunpowder was discovered and Fawkes was found in the place, with matches for the firing of it on his person. Being put to the rack, he disclosed the names of his accomplices. They were seized, tried and executed, or killed while resisting arrest. Among those executed, besides Fawkes, were Sirs Edward Digby, Rockwood, Winter and Garnet, a Jesuit.

NO. 5—THEFT OF THE CROWN JEWELS.

There never were such profligate times in England as under Charles the Second. His court was surrounded by some of the worst vagabonds in the realm though they were classed as "lords and ladies" of the court, who passed their time drinking, gambling, indulging in vicious conversation and committing every kind of profligate excess.

It has been a fashion to call Charles the Second the "Merry Monarch," and there were so many "merry" things transpiring during his reign that he was well entitled to the nickname. That Charles was an unprincipled and dissolute monarch no historian has attempted to gainsay, and although his crimes were many, some of them were never susceptible of proof.

In the latter class was his part in the attempt of the adventurer known as Colonel Blood to steal the crown jewels of England from the Tower of London. It is supposed he fell in with a scheme advanced by Blood to seize the jewels and divide with the King the proceeds of their sale abroad.

The fact that Blood, though caught, was pardoned by Charles and rewarded for a crime that would have cost any common thief his head, gives color to the theory of the King's connivance in the attempt.

Blood was well suited to such an undertaking. He had been an adventurer all his life, and as a soldier of fortune had been involved in daring escapades in various countries. He first came into notice in an attempt to seize Dublin Castle and the person of the Duke of Ormond, lord lieutenant of Ireland, in 1663. Escaping, he fled to Holland. He returned about 1664, going to London, where he joined the fanatical religious band known as the "Fifth monarchy men" who, led by Thomas Venner, a former Boston cooper, attempted to overthrow King cooper, attempted to overthrow King Charles by force of arms.

Blood saved his neck when Venner and his men lost theirs, and was next in view in Scotland, fighting with the Covenanters in the Pentland. Changing his religious views or his allegiance when convenient, he engaged in other exploits, and in the year 1671 he again appeared in London. Disguised as a clergyman, and accompanied by a woman, he visited the tower to see the crown jewels, kept then as now, in a small room devoted to their display. Their value was very great. Although the tower had many guards, there was but one old man in the jewel room.

With this attendant Blood scraped an acquaintance. His supposed wife, feigning illness, the old keeper, Talbot Edwards, who was near eighty, secured medicine for her from his wife. Blood next day returned to thank the old man and bring a present of gloves for Mrs. Edwards. He then said he had a son he wished to marry off, and the old man, having a daughter, an understanding was arrived at that the son should call.

Blood soon came again with some friends, to whom he wished to show the jewels. Under his clergyman's dress he carried arms. His companions were also armed. They seized the old man when his back was turned, and, throwing a cloak over his head, gagged and bound him. On his resisting, they stabbed him. They then seized the crown, the jeweled orb representing the world, and the scepter. The latter was so long that they were obliged to file it, and break it into two parts before concealing it.

The work took so long they were interrupted by the old man's son, who was returning from a journey, and was accompanied by a friend. The thieves dashed out of the tower, fired at a guard at the gate, and made their way to the street, where horses were waiting for them.

Young Edwards and his friend gave chase, caught Blood, and after a fight threw him down. The crown falling from under his cloak rolled into a ditch. Blood's companions were also taken. A ruby from the scepter was found in the pocket of one of them. Little harm had been done except to the old keeper, who had been wounded beyond recovery.

King Charles affected to consider the affair as a joke. He sent to the tower for Blood, who had been locked up, and not only pardoned him, but rewarded him with money and gave him a pension equal to $2,500 a year. None of his accomplices were punished, and Blood became one of the most assiduous courtiers at King Charles' court, to the great disgust of all honest men.

TOMORROW—PONTIAC'S CONSPIRACY.

A LILLIPUTIAN WEDDING.

A lilliputian wedding was the attraction in Greenpoint last evening at the Union Baptist Church on Noble street. Mrs. Elmer S. Chatfield did the coaching and made all the costumes. Lincoln Jones was the minister; Robert Hawley the bridegroom and Miss Dorothy R. Sperick the bride. All were very "cute."

Mrs. Chatfield, who is president of the Mission Gleaners of the church, was complimented very highly by the pastor.

FUNNY BIRDS

Bird with the high hat: "Goodness, where am I?"

"Hoot mon, dina ye ken Scotland when ye see it?"

OVERHEARD IN UGANDA.

"Gee, but they have grownsnobbish since they moved into that historic mansion!"

THE REPUBLICAN IS A MEMBER OF THE UNITED PRESS ASSOCIATION AND RECEIVES ITS TELEGRAPHIC NEWS REPORTS.

Red Wing Daily Republican.

VOLUME XXVII. NO. 167. RED WING, MINNESOTA, FRIDAY EVENING, APRIL 26, 1912. PRICE TWO CENTS.

TAFT DONS HIS FIGHTING TOGS

PRESIDENT OPENS WIDE HIS WELL-TRAINED GUNS UPON COL. ROOSEVELT.

REMARKS SPECIFIC

"Is This Square Deal." He Asks His Audiences—Claims Roosevelt Broke His Promises—Cites Reasons Why He Does Not Believe in Third Term—Enthusiastically Received.

Special to The Republican:

Boston, Mass., April 26.—The speech of President Wm. H. Taft last evening in this city, in which he donned his fighting clothes and attacked Theodore Roosevelt for his insincerity and lack of fairness, has caused much comment here today. It is regarded as the parting of the ways between "Theodore and Will" and the Taft supporters believe it is the marking of the high tide in the Roosevelt movement. They contend that Massachusetts will stand by the president and that now that Roosevelt's unfairness has so clearly been exposed, the enthusiasm for his candidacy will rapidly decrease.

The Massachusetts primaries will be held Tuesday. Meantime Roosevelt is to travel through the state and his answer to President Taft is eagerly awaited both by his political friends and opponents.

TO TAKE AMERICANS FROM MEXICAN COAST

Army Transport Leaves San Francisco to Help Care for Americans.

By United Press:

Washington, April 26.—The army transport Buford will leave San Francisco tonight for ports on the west Mexican coast for the purpose of taking aboard the Americans in these ports and surrounding country.

PLEASANT EVENING AT TRINITY CHURCH

Young People's Society Furnishes Musical and Literary Program.

Nearly one hundred members and friends of the Young People's society of Trinity church enjoyed a social time last evening at the church.

The program was a pleasing one. Enoch Johnson and Randall Weber in their violin and clarinet duet and the orchestra selections were all highly appreciated. The orchestra is composed of Sigurd Hjermstad, Randall Weber, Enoch Johnson and Misses Ione Tripp and Nora Hjermstad. Two solos were contributed by Clifford Sutherland.

Prof. E. O. Kaasa gave an interesting talk on "Teutonic Mythology."

A special business meeting will be held next Friday evening.

PANAMA DREDGES ALONG MISSISSIPPI

Railway Head Invokes Aid of Speaker Clark and Congress to Avert Future Floods.

Special to The Republican:

St. Louis, April 26.—B. F. Yoakum, chairman of the board of the St. Louis & San Francisco Railroad company, makes the timely suggestion that dredging material now becoming idle at Panama be utilized to prevent a repetition of the Mississippi Valley flooding.

Champ Clark, speaker of the house of representatives, has been asked to take the matter up, and Representative Randall of Louisiana is in favor of the project. He is now in New Orleans attending the National Dredging congress.

Mr. Yoakum's suggestion is being cordially indorsed in the Mississippi valley, where such widespread disaster has just been wrought.

Secretary Fischer recently proposed to use the Panama organization and machinery in Alaska, but those familiar with conditions declare that dredging and levee building machinery would not be of as much service there as picks and dynamite.

It is expected that Mr. Yoakum's proposal will shortly be formally laid before the Washington legislature for favorable action.

CAPT. AMUNDSEN GALLANT TO FRIEND

Explorer Names Highest Southern Polar Peak After an American Woman.

New York, April 26.—A tall mountain near the south pole, the tallest and in the words of Amundsen, the most beautiful in the south pole range, is to bear the name of an American woman.

It is to be known as Mount Ruth Gade, and the woman honored is Mrs. Ruth Gade, whose husband, John A. Gade, is an architect here.

When he was last in this country Amundsen was a guest at the home of Gade, from whom he received a substantial contribution for his expedition.

"When I come very close to the pole," he said on departing, "I shall look around for something very beautiful and name it for Mrs. Gade."

Gade has received a long personal letter from Amundsen, stating he had carried out his promise.

MANY TESTIFY OF TITANIC LOSS

FURTHER ACCOUNTS FROM PASSENGERS AND CREW OF AWFUL OCEAN TRAGEDY.

COMMITTEE LISTENS

Babies and Children Thrown into Boats—Boats Too Crowded—Word Sent of Danger—Bodies of Astor, Strauss and Hayes Among Those Recovered.

By United Press:

Washington, April 26.—F. O. Evans, Titanic sailor, told the Chairman Smith of the investigating committee that some women drowned because they could not jump across three feet of space from the rail to the swinging life-boats. Babies and children were thrown into boats. Captain Stanley Lord and Wireless Operator Evans of California are on their way here from Boston to testify. Albert Haines in charge of boats with fifty passengers, said he was unable to row the boat because of the crowd. They could not rescue the drowning in the water.

Ernest Gill, sailor on the California, said he saw rockets from the Titanic but did not steam to assistance till seven hours later. Samuel Henning of the Titanic crew testified that Mr. Andrews, one of the builders of the Titanic, sent word to the crew after the vessel struck that she was sinking and they had only half an hour in which to escape.

RECOVER ASTOR AND STRAUSS.

By United Press:

New York, April 26.—That the bodies of John Jacob Astor and Isador Strauss have been recovered and identified, and have been embalmed on the cable ship Mackay-Bennett, is declared in an official wireless dispatch to the White Star line today.

HAYES' BODY RECOVERED.

By United Press:

Toronto, April 26.—A wireless dispatch says the cable ship Minia in searching for Titanic victims recovered the body of Charles M. Hayes, president of the Grand Trunk railroad.

DISCHARGES PASSENGERS.

By United Press:

Portsmouth, England, April 26.—Because of the strike of 50 deck hands, on the Olympic who refused to work with non-union firemen, the steamer put back to Southampton and discharged the passengers who were on board for two days.

AUTHORITIES ON CHARITY MISSION

Mrs. Marith Boe, Not Insane But Poverty Stricken—Red Wing Officials Assist Woman.

Not insane but poverty-stricken and suffering from worry over the welfare of herself and six children, was the decision reached by Judge Axel Haller and a board of physicians after examining Mrs. Marith Boe, who was said to be acting queerly and believed to be insane. The investigation was conducted at the woman's home, eight miles from Cannon Falls. Judge Haller, Sheriff P. J. Lundquist, County Attorney Wm. M. Ericson of this city and Dr. A. T. Conley and Dr. Ed. Conley of Cannon Falls were present.

The hearing brought out the fact that the woman's husband, Ole Boe, is serving a sentence of sixty days in the county jail for non-support of his wife and family and that while Mrs. Boe is rather odd she is not insane. She has six children, two of whom are being cared for in an orphan asylum in Iowa. A boy and girl aged 10 and 12 years respectively, are attending school and live with the mother, while two older children are working for their board on a farm near Cannon Falls. The authorities found a well-kept house and the children neat and clean. With a mortgage on the little two-acre farm and the future dark for her, Mrs. Boe worried considerably and this led to the belief that she was not of sound mind.

The trip made by the authorities was converted into a mission of charity. The judge, county attorney and sheriff, unknown to each other, opened their purses and gave her some money. While the hearing was being conducted, Sheriff Lundquist and the driver of the rig saw that there was wood to be sawed and split and they got busy with the saw and ax and provided plenty for the stove. The two physicians also furnished the woman with financial aid. She is now receiving county assistance.

Team Experts of the Men and Religion Movement Who Conducted Campaign Throughout the Country.

The men and religion forward movement, a campaign in the interest of the churches that has been conducted throughout the country for six months, is to be brought to a close with a national Christian conservation congress to be held in New York April 19-24. The speakers will number fifty, and the list includes five bishops of three different denominations. The campaign leader was Fred B. Smith of New York. Included in the list of team experts were (1) J. A. Whitmore, (2) Rev. Charles Stelzle, (3) Rev. W. R. Lone, (4) Rev. David Russell, (5) C. R. Drum. Mr. Smith is No. 6 in the group.

OFFICIAL RETURNS ON AMENDMENTS

		1st WARD		2nd WARD		3rd WARD		4th WARD		TOTAL	Necessary to carry	Short 60%	Over 60%
		1 Pre.	2 Pre.	1 Pre.	2 Pre.	1 Pre.	2 Pre.	1 Pre.	2 Pre.				
NO. 1.— Local Option.	Yes	73	53	110	164	75	72	97	151	795	1,004	209	
	No	136	82	110	77	109	98	96	98	806			
NO. 2— License Fee.	Yes	85	50	122	164	80	83	100	164	848	1,004	156	
	No	125	82	106	78	115	95	94	86	781			
NO. 3— Fiscal Year.	Yes	169	97	195	214	138	139	156	217	1,325	1,004		321
	No	34	27	29	24	47	32	32	28	224			
NO. 4— Initiative and Referendum.	Yes	146	80	175	215	120	126	132	200	1,165	1,004		161
	No	54	43	46	24	59	37	52	47	362			
NO. 5— Recall.	Yes	142	75	164	202	117	129	133	197	1,159	1,004		155
	No	59	46	53	35	60	38	53	45	389			

Blank votes were cast as follows: Amendment No. 1, 72; No. 2, 44; No. 3, 95; No. 4, 117; No. 5, 125.

1,673 votes were cast. This number was used as a basis in computing the vote necessary to carry the amendments.

GEN. F. D. GRANT BURIED WITH FITTING HONORS

PRESIDENT TAFT AND MILITARY OFFICERS PRESENT AT WEST POINT FUNERAL.

By United Press:

New York, April 26.—With all honor due to his rank, the body of Major General F. D. Grant was taken to the cemetery at West Point from Governor's Island today. President Taft, Vice President Sherman and high officials of the army attended the funeral. Minute guns were fired by the battery. The body was escorted to the boat by a battalion of infantry and G. A. R. post. At West Point the cadets received the body at the dock.

NEW TYPE OF SHOE FOR SOLDIER BOYS

Washington, April 26. — Experiments to abolish corns from the feet of Uncle Sam's soldier boys are being made by direction of Secretary of War Stimson.

A new type of shoe for the military service is being developed, in the interests of increased efficiency and comfort of the soldiers.

An "Army Shoe Board" has been ordered to convene at Fort Leavenworth, Kansas, where preliminary tests with various types of shoes have been held. An order has been placed with the shoe factory to make 100 pairs of the new experimental type for the test demonstrations. Maj. William J. Glasgow has been assigned to superintend the manufacture.

Slight alterations to the broad shape of the toes of the present army shoes are recommended in the experimental shoes. Less oil in the leather is another innovation to be tried.

The shoes will be made in three styles, for garrison and marching service, and tried out upon members of the Seventh infantry. A march of 112 miles will be the final supreme test of the new shoes.

Matinee at Auditorium—There will be a matinee at the Auditorium tomorrow at which a regular program of moving pictures and vaudeville will be presented.

ROOSEVELT TO ANSWER TAFT

COLONEL PLEASED THAT HE GAINED MAJORITY OF MISSOURI DELEGATES.

HE IS BUSY WRITING

At Outlook Office Today Preparing Speeches to Be Delivered in Massachusetts Before the Primaries to Be Held on Tuesday—Issue Pleases Him.

By United Press:

New York, April 26.—Roosevelt was delighted at receipt of message from the Missouri state convention. He is at the Outlook office today very busy preparing speeches to be delivered in Massachusetts before the primary Tuesday. He will answer Taft's attack, and his friends say the issue pleases him.

By United Press:

St. Louis, April 26.—Colonel Theodore Roosevelt got eight delegates-at-large, each with half a vote, at the state convention which adjourned at daylight after an all night fight.

This gives him sixteen delegates in the state, while Taft gets ten. Two are yet to be selected at the district convention. A test vote in the state convention gave Roosevelt 663 votes and Taft 322. The Taft men are to hold a rump convention today to send a contesting delegation to Chicago.

BANKER SEES A BUMPER CROP

J. M. Wheeler Says Conditions Point to Big Year for Farmers—Bank Clearings Show Gain.

Special to The Republican:

St. Paul, April 26.—Bank clearings for the week ending today amounted to $9,562,442.24 as against $9,344,409.51, for the corresponding week of 1911, an increase of $218,032.73. Every day of the week except last Saturday, showed an increase over the corresponding day of last year.

"Crop conditions throughout the Northwest," said J. W. Wheeler, vice president of the Capital National bank, "are better than they have been for fifteen years. Seeding has been done nearly two weeks earlier and the recent rains will bring the grain right along.

"There was a shortage of fall plowing in North Dakota and in some parts of Minnesota, but so many farmers own traction plows that this can be largely remedied. At present there is nothing in the way of a bumper crop for the entire Northwest.'"

NEBRASKA CYCLONE INJURES PASSENGERS

Strikes Union Pacific Passenger Train and Throws Cars from Track.

By United Press:

Omaha, Neb., April 26.—Twenty-eight persons were injured, James Davis perhaps fatally, when a cyclone struck a Union Pacific passenger train near North Loup, Neb., today, throwing the cars from the track. Telegraph wires are down.

FOR SURVIVORS OF THE TITANIC

Concert in New York Monday Evening for Benefit of Ocean Tragedy Sufferers.

By United Press:

New York, April 26.—A concert, the proceeds of which will be used as the foundation for an annuity for the needy survivors of the Titanic disaster, will be given Monday night at the Metropolitan opera house. The patrons will be President and Mrs. Taft and the Duke and Duchess of Connaught. They will be unable to attend, however.

On the program will be Caruso, Nordica and the Walter Damrose orchestra. Prominent New York society people are in charge of the plans for the concert.

CANADA AIDS THE TITANIC INQUIRY--205 BODIES ARE FOUND

Canada Co-operates with Senators in the Titanic Inquiry; Sends Witnesses

Captain and Wireless Operator of the Steamship Mount Tempie Are on Way to Washington to Explain Failure to Go to Sinking Vessel's Aid.

MR. ISMAY WAS NOT IN LAST BOAT, SEAMAN WITNESS TELLS COMMITTEE

Mr. Marconi Admits He Permitted Wireless Operator of the Carpathia to Sell His Story to Newspaper, but Denies He Tried to Keep News from the Public.

HERALD BUREAU,
No. 1,502 H STREET, N. W.,
WASHINGTON, D. C., Thursday.

With the stories of a dozen more witnesses, the grim outlines of the Titanic tragic story became clearer to-day. It is now fairly well established that "the light that failed" the survivors of the White Star liner was the Canadian Pacific Railway Company's steamship Mount Temple, whose master heard the Titanic's distress call, but was prevented from reaching the scene of her sinking by the heavy ice that rimmed about her burial ground. Canada has joined the United States in an effort to determine the Mount Temple's part in the doings of that Monday morning.

The Acting Prime Minister of Canada telegraphed Senator William Alden Smith, chairman of the Senate Investigating Committee, saying the captain and wireless operator of the Mount Temple were on their way to Washington.

The captain's statement that he put about on getting the Titanic's "C Q D," but his inability to sight the Titanic's survivors was told in telegrams published in the HERALD to-day.

Explains the Frankfurt Incident.

Senator Smith questioned to-day Harold T. Cottam, the Carpathia's operator, for the purpose of ascertaining whether the Titanic had rebuffed the steamship Frankfurt when it may have been even closer to the Titanic than the Carpathia.

The Titanic's wireless men shot their "C Q D's" into the air at the moment of the collisions and were so angered at the Frankfurt's tardy "What the matter?" twenty minutes later that they shot back "You're a fool, keep out."

Cottam, in full sympathy with Bride, the Titanic's crippled operator, who helped him on the Carpathia's weary voyage into port, stoutly declared this was the only answer fit for a ship which would ask "What's the matter?" after her wireless caught the "C Q D."

"Suppose," said Senator Smith, slowly, "it should turn out that the Frankfurt was nearer than the Carpathia and that answer of the wireless operator prevented or discouraged the Frankfurt from coming to the Titanic when that ship might have arrived an hour or longer before the Carpathia?"

"I do not think she was nearer than the Carpathia," replied Cottam.

Senator Smith:—"You do not know anything about that?"

Cottam:—"Only by the strength of the signals, that is all."

Senator Smith:—"Your information does not agree with mine."

Records of Ice Warnings.

The inquiry is winding itself around the actions of the other ships in that part of the North Atlantic at the time of the Titanic disaster, with special regard to the reception aboard the Titanic of the warnings of ice which their wireless was busy transmitting to all who would read.

The Titanic's officers have testified that these warnings were posted in the chart room. Senate subpoenas have been served at Boston on the captain and wireless operator of the steamship Californian. They are bringing to the committee the ship's log and wireless register in order that the committee may know the exact phrasing of the ice warning which the Titanic caught as it was being flashed from the Californian to the Baltic. The Titanic did not get it when it was offered direct.

The committee's work was accelerated to-day. Senator Smith publicly contradicted the rumors of committee friction based on dissatisfaction with his extensive questioning of witnesses. Among the seamen of the Titanic who were brought here there was great anxiety to get away, which found expression on their visit to the British Embassy yesterday. No official action was taken, but as one seaman witness, Louis Klein, who had charged there was intoxication on board the Titanic, had disappeared, there were fears that others might become restive. Accordingly, each member of the subcommittee personally examined several witnesses, and much of the detailed story of the four hours of the great ship's death struggle became known.

Women Halted Aid to Drowning.

Alfred Olliver, quartermaster on the Titanic, told Senator Burton that nearly all of the women in his boat objected to going back to the sinking ship after Mr. Pitman, the officer in charge of the boat, gave the order to go back in the hope of rendering aid to others.

"Did you hear Pitman give an order to go back to the ship?" Senator Burton asked.

"Yes, sir."

"What happened?"

"The women passengers implored him not to go, because they reckoned it was not safe."

"How far were you away from the ship then?"

"I should say about three hundred yards."

"Did Pitman, then, countermand the order?"

"Yes, sir; he did not go."

"Did only a few of the passengers on board object to his going back, or did they all object?"

"They very nearly all objected."

"Did any ask him to go back?"

"No, sir; not as I know of."

"Would it have been safe to go back?"

"To my idea, sir, no."

"Why not?"

"I reckon it would have been endangering the lives of the people we had in the boat already."

"In what way; being sucked down or persons trying to climb on?"

"Both, sir."

"Which would have been the more serious of the two?"

"The suction, as I thought, sir."

Mr. Marconi Testifies.

All the public hearing to-day was devoted to wireless. Mr. Guglielmo Marconi was closely questioned as to his connection with the "Keep your mouth shut" telegrams sent to Bride, the Titanic's operator, and Cottam, the Carpathia's operator, advising them they would get "four figures" for their story.

Senator Smith read into the records the full text of three messages sent to the Carpathia as she came up New York harbor, and these fully sustain the HERALD's publication of the facts regarding this effort to corner news in which all the world was interested.

More than this, Senator Smith's action showed that not only was the name of T. W. Sammis, chief engineer of the American-Marconi Company, attached to one, but that another was signed "Mr. Marconi." The latter repeatedly in his testimony denied he had sent or authorized such messages, but admitted he had given permission for both wireless men to sell the story of their experiences. He denied he thus expected to gain exclusive news for any one or that he had any desire to suppress the sending of information from the Carpathia as she was coming from the scene of the disaster to New York.

Senator Smith asked a comprehensive question as to whether any person connected with the White Star company had asked Mr. Marconi or any one associated with him to transmit to the wireless operator of either the Titanic or the Carpathia any message enjoining silence as to the time or manner of the Titanic disaster. Mr. Marconi returned an equally comprehensive denial.

An interesting feature of the testimony was the statement of Edward John Buley, a seaman of the Titanic, that J. Bruce Ismay was not in the last lifeboat that left the sinking vessel. Buley was one of the men who manned the last boat.

MR. MARCONI TELLS HOW NEWS WAS SOLD

Declares Intention Was Not to Suppress It, but Merely to Get Money for Operators.

HERALD BUREAU,
No. 1,502 H STREET, N. W.,
WASHINGTON, D. C., Thursday.

Mr. Marconi said when he took the stand that the Canadian Pacific Railway Company's steamship, the Mount Temple, reported to have been within sight of the Titanic at the hour of disaster, had wireless capable of communicating two hundred miles by day and five to six hundred miles by night under the best circumstances. He did not know the range of the Frankfurt's wireless, but believed it was efficient.

Senator Smith sought to determine what connection, if any, Mr. Marconi had with messages sent to Bride and Cottam on the Carpathia to keep their mouths shut and to hold the story of the disaster for "four figures." By Senator Smith:—

Q. Did you have any communication with the Carpathia, directly or through the coast or ship station, Sunday, Monday, Tuesday, Wednesday, Thursday, up to the time of the arrival of the Carpathia in New York? A. I had no direct communication with the Carpathia. I telephoned to Mr. Bottomley at my office at frequent intervals. I got no information except, I think, it was on Monday evening. The information was that the Titanic had sunk with a very heavy loss of life.

Q. That was the first information you received from any officer of your company anywhere? A. Anywhere.

Mr. Marconi said that at two o'clock Friday morning Cottam telephoned to him at the Holland House, saying he had been offered money by a newspaper for his story and asking permission to sell it. Mr. Marconi permitted it.

By Senator Smith:—

Q. Did you send a wireless to the operator on the Carpathia and ask him to meet you and Sammis at the Strand Hotel, No. 502 West Fourteenth street, saying, "Keep your mouth shut?" A. No, sir; I did not.

Navy's Record of Wireless.

"I am going to read to you the following and ask whether you know anything about any fact or circumstances connected with it. This is from the commanding officer of the Florida to the Secretary of the Navy, dated April 22 and reading as follows:—

"'On the evening of the steamship Carpathia's arrival in New York the four following radiograms were intercepted by the chief operator, J. R. Simpson, chief electrician, United States Navy. They appear to me to be significant enough to be brought to the attention of the department:—

"Seagate to Carpathia, 8:12 P. M.—'Say, old man, Marconi company taking good care of you. Keep your mouth shut and hold your story. It is fixed for you so you will get big money. Now please do your best to clear.'

"That was 8:12 P. M. Then follows this one:—'8:30 P. M.—To Marconi officer, Carpathia and Titanic:—Arranged for your exclusive story for dollars in four figures, Mr. Marconi agreeing. Say nothing until you see me. T. W. Sammis.'

"9:00 P. M., from Seagate to Carpathia operator:—'Go to Strand Hotel, 502 West Fourteenth street, to meet Mr. Marconi. C.'

"9:33 P. M., from Seagate to Carpathia.—A personal to operator Carpathia:—'Meet Mr. Marconi and Sammis at Strand Hotel, 502 West Fourteenth street. Keep your mouth shut. (sig) Mr. Marconi.'"

Q. What can you say about that, Mr. Marconi? A. I do not know anything whatever about any of those messages. They are not the phraseology which I would have approved of if I had passed them. I should, however, say that I told Mr. Sammis or Mr. Bottomley—I do not remember which—that I, as an officer of the British company, would not prohibit or prevent these operators making anything which they reasonably could make out of their selling their story of the wreck. I was anxious that, if possible, they might make some small amount of money out of the information they had.

Q. Is that the custom of your company? A. It is not a custom. It is the thing that is done.

Q. Is it a habit? A. No, it is not a habit. It is done on very special occasions. I think it was done on the occasion of a former wreck, the Republic. I think Binns was allowed to make a statement to the press for money.

Q. Mr. Marconi, do you wish the committee to understand that you approve that method? A. I was in favor or at least I approved or consented to his getting something out of this story.

Q. I know, but let me ask you:—With the right to exact compensation for an exclusive story, detailing the horrors of the greatest sea disaster that ever occurred in the history of the world, do you mean that an operator under your company's direction shall have the right to prevent the public from knowing of that calamity except through the exclusive appropriation of the facts by the operator who is cognizant of them? A. I say not at all. I gave no instructions in regard to withholding any information, and I gave no advice or instructions in regard to any exclusive story to anybody. The only thing I did say or did authorize was that if he was offered payment for a story of the disaster he was permitted, so far as the English company went, to take that money.

Q. Did you expect the operator to syndicate this information or to give it exclusively to one newspaper? A. I did not expect him to give it exclusively.

Bride Got $500 for Story.

Q. Do you know how much they got? A. I was told that Bride got $500 from the New York Times.

Q. Was it expected, or did any officer of your company receive any portion of it, within your knowledge? A. No; I do not believe any one did receive any portion of it. I do not care whether it was through the New York Times or any other newspaper, but I was very anxious that the public should have the news of this disaster as quickly and as accurately as possible. I should also state that this message signed by Mr. Sammis, and mentioning the four figures, was, I believe from the information before the committee, transmitted when the ship was practically entering New York Harbor. It was not transmitted when the ship was days out and it was a long way from shore. I am not expressing any opinion of the message except the fact I did not authorize it, and I might also say that I do not like it.

Operator Cottam's Story.

Harold Thomas Cottam, the Carpathia's wireless operator, repeated much of the testimony he gave in New York last week. He told how he got the Titanic's "C Q D."

Senator Smith asked if he had been in communication with the Mount Temple, the Canadian Pacific steamship, one of whose passengers has declared he was within sight of the Titanic at the hour of disaster. A. I had a communication with the Mount Temple about half-past ten and gave him good night.

Q. Did you know the position of the Mount Temple? A. No, sir.

Q. How did you happen to get in communication with him? A. I called the Parisian and I didn't get a reply, and the Mount Temple gave me "Good night" soon as I had called the Parisian.

Q. Did any of these ships with whom you were in touch around half-past ten on that Sunday evening at all say anything to you about ice? A. In the afternoon I heard the Parisian and one of the other ships talking about ice.

Q. What other one? A. I don't know whether that was the Californian or not.

Message to the Frankfurt.

Q. You heard Mr. Bride testify in New York that after sending the C Q D call from the Titanic and it was picked up by the Frankfurt the Frankfurt operator waited about twenty minutes before replying, and then said:—"What is the matter?" Whereupon Bride said to him, "You are a fool. Keep out." A. Yes, sir.

Q. You heard Bride testify to that? A. Yes, I heard it.

Q. From anything you know, was there any rivalry between the operators on the Frankfurt, under that system, and the operator on the Titanic? A. No, sir. There ought to be no rivalry. The C Q D call ought to be quite sufficient for any man who understands the English language, or the German language, for that matter. It is a universal call, the C Q D call.

Q. Under the regulations of the Berlin Convention, the Frankfurt was obliged to give her position, was she not, upon receipt of this C Q D call? A. If he had used any common sense he would have done it.

Q. How is that, Mr. Marconi? A. They are obliged to give the best assistance possible. I suppose that would include that.

Messages to the Mount Temple.

Senator Smith to C. W. Ham:—Q. Do you remember whether the Mount Temple replied to the C Q D call of the Titanic that night? A. I do not think so; I did not hear her.

Q. The Captain says they did. The Captain says the Mount Temple replied to the C Q D call of the Titanic? A. I heard nothing from the Mount Temple.

Q. I want to know whether you picked up any message from the Mount Temple that night in addition to these other ships' messages that you have spoken of. A. No, sir. If the Mount Temple had replied I should have been bound to have heard it, because there was not a sound in the air, and this communication of the Titanic was all that was going.

Q. When you got this message from the Titanic the Carpathia was about fifty-eight miles from the Titanic's position? A. Yes, sir, about fifty-eight or sixty miles.

Q. Why did the operator of the Titanic tell this other operator he was a fool and to keep out? Was it because he had not responded? A. Because if he had not have done it he would have been a nuisance, as we were in good satisfactory communication; and as he could not get satisfactory communication with the Frankfurt he would have tried elsewhere then.

Q. What would you have told him if you had been the operator on the Titanic? A. I should have told him the same.

Q. Regardless of whether he was a Marconi operator or a German independent operator? A. It does not matter what system. I don't care. When a man takes twenty minutes to answer in a case like that, when two hours is between life and death, it is about the only fit thing you can call him.

Q. You know that is a pretty big responsibility for you to exercise, not knowing the ship's position. As a matter of fact, suppose it should turn out that the Frankfurt was nearer than the Carpathia to the Titanic, and that the answer of the wireless operator prevented the Frankfurt or discouraged the Frankfurt from coming to the Titanic, when that ship might have arrived an hour or longer before the Carpathia? A. I do not think she was nearer. I do not think she was nearer than the Carpathia.

Senator Newlands:—Q. While the conversation was going on between the Titanic and the Olympic and the Carpathia and the Frankfurt, could the Frankfurt have heard all these messages? A. Yes. If she heard the first message from the ship she ought to have heard all the communications from all the others. Apparently she was not on watch.

Senator Newlands—Q. She could get direct details just as the other vessels to whom they were specially directed would receive them? A. Yes sir. I got the message and she ought to have done so, as apparently she was closer. Apparently she was closer and she ought to have had it if I got it.

Q. I want to get into your mind the fact that there are people who were on the Mount Temple who say they saw the lights of the Titanic when it went down and there are people on the Titanic who say they saw the lights of a boat ahead when the Titanic was sinking, and in that situation it is no time to be flippant or discourteous in such a responsible position as you hold. A. I was not flippant. Nobody was flippant with the Mount Temple. The Mount Temple was off watch.

Tells of Mr. Ismay's Conduct.

Senator Burton examined three of the Titanic's crew, including Quartermaster George T. Rowe, who was in charge of the lifeboat that conveyed J. Bruce Ismay to the Carpathia. Rowe and possibly the two other witnesses will be called to testify before the full committee to-morrow. All three were positive they saw a light on the horizon as the lifeboats pulled away from the sinking ship. They steered for it.

Rowe's testimony concerning the actions of Mr. Ismay bears out in many respects the testimony of Mr. Ismay himself. Rowe said there were no women present when Mr. Ismay entered the boat, and that just prior to this the call for "More women—are there any more women?" was repeated.

Mr. Ismay did not once interfere with the running of the boat, Rowe said.

A new feature in the investigation was brought out when Senator Burton was told by one of the witnesses of a note sent by Captain Smith, of the Titanic, to the engineer. The seaman who carried the note said it was handed to him by Captain Smith a few minutes after the collision. He did not read it, as it was folded with one corner of the folded paper turned down.

When the engineer opened it, he said emphatically:—

"Tell Captain Smith I will do this as soon as I can," whereupon the seaman delivered his verbal order, and thought no more of it.

The inference was plain, that message referred to some precautionary measure, which Captain Smith believed necessary, in view of the ship's condition, as it was not given until after the preliminary investigation of the damage by the collision had been made.

Children Forego Candy and Soda to Swell the Titanic Relief Fund

MISS IRENE EBLING. MISS KATHARINE SMITH. MISS CLEO ROBERTSON.

MISS ADELE STRAUSS. MISS PEARL ALTMAN. MISS LILLIAN GROSSMAN.

Inspired by Six Young Alumnae of Public School No. 90 a Score of Them Deny Themselves and Send $26.50 for Survivors.

Because six young women set an example of self-denial which was quickly emulated by a score of children, residents of the Washington Heights section, the HERALD's fund for the relief of Titanic survivors has been swelled by the receipt yesterday of a check for $26.50. The money was sent in the name of the Alumnae Association of Public School No. 90 and represents pennies and nickels the children otherwise would have invested in ice cream soda and candy.

The idea of abstaining from ice cream and candy was originated on Tuesday by one of the young women. The period during which the fund was to be accumulated ended yesterday, and immediately afterward the fruits of their denial reached the HERALD office in the shape of the check. With it came the message that they wished they "could send a thousand times the amount of the check." The young women who carried out the campaign with the aid of the children are the Misses Cleo Robertson, Irene Ebling, Adele Strauss, Pearl Altman, Lillian Grossman and Katharine Smith.

From Rosenthal and Grotta the HERALD received yesterday an addition of $25 to a former contribution, making a total contribution of $50.

SEEK MYSTERIOUS WITNESS IN THIS CITY

Acting on information that first was laid before Senator Smith, who is conducting the Senate investigation into the sinking of the steamship Titanic, secret service agents searched this city last night for a man who is expected to give testimony more sensational than any yet divulged. Senator Smith regarded the information placed in his hands so important that he refused to reveal the nature of it.

In every quarter last night the greatest secrecy was thrown about the efforts of Senator Smith and the local secret service men to locate the mysterious witness. It is known, however, that, while the witness was not located last night, the men engaged in the search reported they expected to find him to-day.

THE SAVOIE BOATS AMPLE.

No additional life saving devices were necessary on board the Savoie, of the French line, which left New York yesterday morning for Havre, for her equipment of twenty lifeboats and ten life rafts is sufficient for about half as many more persons as the boat carries. On board her was Mons. Pierre Marechal, the son of General Marechal, of the French army. Mons. Marechal was among the survivors of the Titanic disaster. He intended to stay in this country for a month, but his experience caused him to cut short the time.

WHEELS STOP FOR MR. HAYS

[SPECIAL DESPATCH TO THE HERALD.]

NEW LONDON, Conn., Thursday.—Several hundred persons took part to-day in the land and water memorial service to Charles M. Hays, president of the Grand Trunk Railroad, who lost his life in the Titanic disaster. Every wheel on the railway system stopped for the brief service, which was held aboard the steamship New London. Many flowers were strewn on the water.

PASSENGERS ANGRY AT CHERBOURG DELAY

[SPECIAL DESPATCH TO THE HERALD VIA COMMERCIAL CABLE COMPANY'S SYSTEM.]

CHERBOURG, Thursday.—The 310 passengers who arrived here yesterday by special train to embark on board the Olympic are still waiting. The lack of news concerning the delay is causing discontent among the passengers, who criticise the company severely. From yesterday afternoon to this afternoon at five o'clock the company has sent no word to its agency here saying when the Olympic might be expected.

Many of the passengers are all the more discontented because the absence of definite news prevents them from engaging passage by other lines. If the delay is likely to be prolonged they would, they say, proceed to Havre or Liverpool and catch steamships leaving those places.

Among the passengers who are particularly desirous of reaching home are Mr. and Mrs. Strawbridge, Miss G. T. Perkins and her friend, Mrs. G. T. Earl. Miss Perkins was in Paris when she learned by cable that her home in New York and all its contents had been destroyed by fire. She hastened to obtain passage on board the Olympic and is distressed at her enforced delay.

Senate's Titanic Inquiry a Bullying Inquisition, Is Verdict of British Press

Senator Smith, Who Is Made Centre of Attack, Is Accused of Using Disaster as Means of Getting Into the Limelight and Winning Votes.

THE OLYMPIC TO RESUME VOYAGE TO-DAY

[SPECIAL DESPATCH TO THE HERALD VIA COMMERCIAL CABLE COMPANY'S SYSTEM.]

HERALD BUREAU,
No. 130 FLEET STREET,
London, Friday.

The British press this morning again hotly attacks the Senate Titanic inquiry, but the fiercest criticism is reserved for Senator Smith. Even the Morning Leader, which sounds the only friendly note, saying that the investigation is justified by the loss of so many leading Americans, adds that "certainly no one would accuse Senator Smith of the highest dignity."

The Mail says:—"Senator Smith is a past master in the art of butting in. He is a republican. Champ Clark, who invites laughter by his landlubber questions, is conspicuous for his childishness. Little good can be achieved by an investigation along these lines."

The Daily Express says:—"There is no need to suppose because Senator Smith is an asinine American that the inquiry is purposeless."

The Morning Post:—"A schoolboy would blush at Smith's ignorance. He has an eye on his public and his press and intends to make the Titanic and our dead serve to catch votes."

The Standard, denouncing the proceedings of the Smith committee, says:—"There must be an unsparing inquiry, but as the Titanic was a British ship, with a British crew, it will be held in this country. The Michigan Senator is less qualified as an investigator than the average individual to be picked up in the average American street car."

In brief the London press looks upon the inquiry as being in bad taste, regards the investigators unqualified for such duty and the holding of British witnesses as an infraction of international law.

To quote the Standard again:—"The unhappy survivors of the catastrophe have been subjected to a process of browbeating, baiting and bullying which must be trying enough to men whose nerves can hardly have recovered from the terrible ordeal through which they have passed."

"Senator Smith not only treats the officers and staff of the White Star Company as if they were prisoners on trial, but remorselessly insists on specific replies to questions, some of which are irrevelant and others painful."

There is no question that these criticisms of the Senate committee and its chairman have aroused a feeling of resentment against America and sympathy with the officials of the White Star line.

MONS. HOFFMAN IS FOUND IN PARIS

[SPECIAL DESPATCH TO THE HERALD VIA COMMERCIAL CABLE COMPANY'S SYSTEM.]

HERALD BUREAU,
No. 49 AVENUE DE L'OPERA,
PARIS, Thursday.

The HERALD's correspondent has found Mons. and Mme. Hoffman, Mons. Navratil's friends, who reside in the Rue de la Chaussé d'Antin, Paris. Mons. Hoffman, who was thought to have been on board the Titanic in charge of the two Navratil children, who were rescued, declares he was well aware of the disagreement which had arisen between his friends, Mons. and Mme. Navratil, at Nice. He says that during the Easter holidays Mons. Navratil called him to Nice with the hope that he would purchase his business, which Mons. Navratil was anxious to dispose of.

Mons. Hoffman went to Nice, but decided not to purchase the business. Mons. Navratil then asked him to stop at Nice and look after the business a few days while he took the two children, who were in his custody, to relatives in Hungary.

Mons. Navratil left and did not return. As Mons. Hoffman had his own affairs to attend to in Paris he was forced to leave at the end of eight days. Since then he has not heard of Mons. Navratil and is firmly convinced that he embarked on board the Titanic with the two children. He does not believe Mons. Navratil went to Hungary, nor does he believe that the father, who was passionately fond of the children, would place them in the care of some one else to cross the Atlantic.

Moreover, Mons. Hoffman says Mons. Navratil had often spoken of going to America with the children. Mons. Hoffman is sure the man travelling with the children under the name of Hoffman was Mons. Navratil.

Mother Sends Photographs of Children to French Consul.

Mons. Etienne Lanel, French Consul General, yesterday received a cable despatch from Mme. Navratil, of Nice, France, advising him that she was mailing photographs of her two children, survivors of the Titanic, now at the home of Miss Margaret Hays, No. 304 West Eighty-third street. From this it is assumed that Mme. Navratil will not come to this country, but that the two boys will be returned to Nice through the agency of the French diplomatic officials.

Rudolph Navratil, nephew of the man who was carrying away his children, yesterday visited Miss Hays' home and saw the children. He asserted that Michel, the older of the two, bore a marked resemblance to the father.

EXPECT THE OLYMPIC TO STEAM TO-DAY

SOUTHAMPTON, Thursday.—The White Star officials said late to-night that a new crew had been shipped without recourse to the strikers, and that the Olympic probably would steam at daybreak.

The strikers were satisfied to-day of the seaworthiness of the Berthon boats by a practical demonstration, but they then demanded that the company should dismiss the firemen who had remained aboard when the strikers quit the ship. This the company refused to do.

CANADA GIVES $10,000.

[SPECIAL DESPATCH TO THE HERALD.]

OTTAWA, Ont., Thursday.—For the relief of relatives of the victims of the Titanic disaster the government of Canada to-day made a grant of $10,000.

IN TWO PARTS—PART I

HARPER'S WEEKLY

A JOURNAL OF CIVILIZATION

VOL. LVI. New York, April 27, 1912 No. 2888

SOME OF THE PITIFUL SEVEN HUNDRED

A BOATLOAD OF THE "TITANIC'S" SURVIVORS JUST BEFORE THEY WERE SUCCORED BY THE "CARPATHIA"

THE "TITANIC" DISASTER

A DETAILED AND EXCLUSIVE NARRATIVE BY ONE OF THE SURVIVORS, ILLUSTRATED WITH PHOTOGRAPHS TAKEN BY PASSENGERS ABOARD THE "CARPATHIA"

OUT OF THE JAWS OF DEATH

THE TRUE STORY OF THE DISASTER

WHAT REALLY HAPPENED WHEN THE "TITANIC" SANK, TOLD BY ONE OF THE SURVIVORS AND RECORDED EXCLUSIVELY FOR "HARPER'S WEEKLY"

By WILLIAM INGLIS

SAVED from the wreck of the *Titanic* in a way so casual as to seem miraculous, Henry Sleeper Harper told me, soon after he came ashore, the following astonishing story of his experiences—a story probably unique in the history of maritime narratives. A keen and competent observer, this narrator, who never loses his mental balance, has been familiar with the sea since boyhood, and often crossed the Atlantic. His story was told in response to a few questions. Things he had not actually seen and heard he would neither affirm nor deny. Here is his narrative:

I was fast asleep when the *Titanic* struck, for I had been kept in my stateroom by tonsilitis ever since coming aboard the ship. Our stateroom was pretty well forward on the starboard side and was perhaps

A handful of survivors nearing the "Carpathia." They are wearing life-preservers

thirty feet or more above the water. I remember that the sea was quite smooth when we went to sleep. As to how fast the ship was going I have no knowledge.

I am inclined to believe the statements of many passengers that the *Titanic* was going at the pace of twenty-three knots an hour when she ran over the submerged edge of the berg that ripped a long gash in her bottom and sank her. My first knowledge about it was that of being awakened by a grinding sound that seemed to come from far below our deck. It was not a loud crash; it was felt almost as much as heard. But years before I had been in a ship that ran over a reef and was sunk, and I remembered that the impact and thrill then were so slight that I thought we were simply running over a fishing-smack that bumped and scraped under our keel. So the moment I was awakened by the noise and heard the same sort of sound I sat up in bed and looked out of the nearest port.

I saw an iceberg only a few feet away, apparently racing aft at high speed and crumbling as it went. I knew right away what that meant.

"Get dressed quickly," I told my wife. "We must go on deck."

"Wait," she replied. "I'll ask Mrs. —— across the way if she has heard any word."

"You haven't a moment for talk," I insisted. "Get dressed—at once."

She dressed much faster than I did, for I was pretty weak from my sickness, and she hurried to the stateroom of the ship's doctor.

"I wish you'd speak to my husband," she said. "He insists upon going on deck and he won't mind me."

The doctor came in and ordered me to undress and go back to bed. He said he was sure there was nothing serious.

"Damn it, man," I told him, "this ship has hit an iceberg! How can you say there's nothing serious?"

I'm sorry now that I cussed him out, but it made me hot to hear him make little of such a grave danger.

"Well, stay here awhile," he said, "and I'll see what's up." He was gone only a few moments, and then popped his head in at my door.

"They tell me the trunks are floating around in the hold," he said. "You may as well go on deck."

So I put on my overcoat and my wife put on her fur coat and we started up. I suppose this was a quarter of an hour after the ship struck, for we were completely dressed as if we were going ashore—shoes all laced up and tied, and all that sort of thing.

We walked very slowly up the steps of the big stairways, for I was pretty weak, and when we got to the next deck above I sat down on a lounge and rested five or six minutes. Then we climbed up to the next deck, and so on. At last we got up to the gymnasium, which was on the top deck, and I sat down beside my wife. Men and women were standing about in groups talking. I have heard some talk since about excitement, but I saw none then. Everybody seemed confident that the ship was all right. She certainly *seemed* all right. The engines had been stopped soon after we struck and by this time she had slowly lost headway and was standing still. The sea was quiet, a flat calm, but all the ship's lights were lit and there was not a suggestion of excitement anywhere. A few people were talking about the life-boats, but they were laughed at.

"Life-boats!" said a woman near me. "What do they need of life-boats? This ship could smash a hundred icebergs and not feel it. Ridiculous!"

After a little time, word was passed among the passengers that we'd better go back to bed.

"The ship will be delayed two hours," the stewards said, "and then go on to New York."

At this a great many people went away from our neighborhood. Whether they went back to bed or not I don't know; but I can't remember seeing their faces again. They dropped away a few at a time—casually drifted off. Funny thing to remember how they scattered here and there—two or three crossing over from one group to another and two or three going from that group to still another. They all seemed curious, not a bit anxious. The reassurance that the ship would be delayed only two hours seemed to satisfy the curiosity of most of them, though, and the crowds soon dwindled. However, there were still a few dozens of us left, in our neighborhood, on the upper deck.

Perhaps a quarter of an hour later word was passed that we'd better put on life-preservers. Some people put on the life-belts and others laughed at them. Then came a long wait. I was surprised that there was no officer in sight to direct people where to go or to warn them or reassure them. We were left to ourselves. It was rather like a stupid picnic where you don't know anybody and wonder how soon you can get away from such a boresome place. I couldn't help wondering what had become of all the fine sea discipline I had heard and read about so much. I said to myself: These steamship men are hotel-keepers rather than sailor-men. They hear there are icebergs ahead, and instead of swinging out of their way they simply turn on more steam as a hotel man would do with a cold-wave coming, and then go plunging right into the iceberg. They hit an iceberg and then tell their guests they'd better go back to bed. I was pretty sore by that time, and I think any one would be who knows anything about seafaring.

Not long after the passengers began telling one another that we were ordered to put on life-preservers, stewards came around our neighborhood and began calling out: "All women to go to the lower deck!" Some women went. Others were escorted down the companionway by their husbands. I take it that they

Four boat-loads of the "Titanic's" passengers at the "Carpathia's" side

all understood, as we certainly did, that the women were to be kept together there ready to be sent off in the first boats if it should become necessary to abandon the ship. My wife and I said nothing to each other, but simply sat still and waited.

Presently a number of stewards and other men of the ship's company began to fuss with the tackle of a couple of life-boats near where we were on the upper deck. I say "fuss" with them, but I might as well say "make a mess of them." They seemed quite unused to handling boat gear. They took away a section of the deck rail near each boat and then climbed into the boat and hoisted away on the falls so as to swing the boat clear on the davits and let her down so that the gunwale was flush with the deck. We passengers still remaining on the deck gathered around and watched the men at work. Very slowly, and stumbling here and there, the people began to get in. It was like stepping down, say, from this table to the chair alongside. We took a look at both boats. My wife thought the one farther off was better because there would be hardly a dozen people left to go in it after

One of the "Titanic's" collapsible life-boats with its human freight

Copyright by Underwood & Underwood

Telling their experiences—a group of the rescued aboard the "Carpathia"

Copyright by International News Service

The deck of the "Carpathia" crowded with "Titanic" survivors

SOME OF THOSE WHO RETURNED

THE SINKING

AS THE MORTALLY WOUNDED LINER NEARED THE LAST MOMENTS OF HER DEATH-STRUGGLE, THE INRUSH OF
ARTIST DEPICTS HER AS SHE APPEARED TO THE HORRIFIED SURVIVORS IN THE LIFE-BOATS JUST BEFORE SHE
OF THE WHITE STAR MANAGEMENT) OR PERISHED AFTERWARD FROM EXPOSURE AND SHOCK. 705 PERSONS SURV

DRAWN FROM DESCRIPTIONS

THE "TITANIC"

ER TO HER FORWARD COMPARTMENTS DEPRESSED HER BOW, LEAVING HER STERN CLEAR OF THE WATER. OUR HER FINAL PLUNGE. 1,635 PERSONS WENT TO THEIR DEATH WITH HER (ACCORDING TO THE OFFICIAL ESTIMATE THE DISASTER, ACCORDING TO THE MOST TRUSTWORTHY FIGURES AVAILABLE AS THE "WEEKLY" GOES TO PRESS

EYE-WITNESSES BY L. A. SHAFER

the big boat beside us was filled. I looked them both over, saw that the farther boat had no water-tight compartments in it while the one near had; so I said: "No; let's take this. It will float longest."

With that I handed my wife down into the nearer, bigger boat, and she comfortably seated herself on a thwart. Other women and other men climbed aboard. An old dragoman of mine who had come with me from Alexandria—because he wanted "to see the country all the crazy Americans came from," as he explained it—made his way into the unfamiliar boat and settled himself. He made himself quite at home. Four or five stokers or some such men came along and jumped into the boat at the forward end. The sailor who seemed to be in charge of the boat laughed a little.

"Huh!" he said; "I suppose I ought to go and get my gun and stop this." But he did not go and get any gun, and neither did he order the stokers out. Everybody seemed to take what was happening as a matter of course and there wasn't a word of comment.

I stepped in and sat down among the stokers. There was no one in sight on the decks. I had on my arm a little brown Pekingese spaniel we had picked up in Paris and named Sun Yat Sen in honor of his country's first President. The little dog kept very quiet. I found out, after boarding the *Carpathia*, that several dogs had been rescued in the same way in the early boats. There seemed to be lots of room, and nobody made any objection. The sailor who seemed to be in charge ordered, "Lower away!" The gang at each end of the boat began to pay out the boat-falls, so that our life-boat went down, first by the head, then by the stern, in a series of jerks. Lower by machinery? Not an inch—so far as I saw. It was all done by hand, and very clumsily done. If there had been any sea running, I feel sure our boat would have been smashed against the ship's side. A boat that had descended fifteen or twenty feet was hailed by a man on the upper deck—a second-class passenger, an Australian going out to America to see his mother, it transpired later. He leaned out over the edge and called: "Hey! Will you take me in that boat?"

"No," said the man who seemed to be in charge.

"But you've lots of room in your boat," the man on deck insisted.

"Yes," replied the sailor, "but we're too far down now for you to jump in. You'd hurt yourself."

"Yes; but I can slide down the ropes," the passenger answered.

"Very well. Come on," the sailor agreed. Whereupon the crew ceased lowering, and the passenger twined arms and legs around the falls, slid down to the boat, said, "Thanks," and sat down. More lowering by fits and starts, and at last our boat was afloat. Then we had more trouble—they didn't know how to cast loose the tackle. They fussed and fiddled, and the life-boat grated up against the ship's black hull for minutes. Just imagine how we'd have pounded to pieces if there had been any sort of a sea running!

Some of the "Titanic's" life-boats on the deck of the "Carpathia"

Somehow or other they got her clear at last, and the four men at the oars began to row. And such rowing! You've seen the young man who hires a boat on Central Park lake on Sunday and tries to show off? Well, about like that—skying the oar on every recover, burying the blade on the pull or missing it altogether. There was only one man in the four who knew how to row. The steering was worse. The four oarsmen paddled as briskly as they could, and our boat, with, say, some forty people in it, began to move away from the ship, slowly but not surely. For the man at the tiller would pull it toward himself for a while and send her around to port, or push the tiller away and swerve her around to starboard.

"Ow!" he exclaimed; "let's get on. There'll be a big wave when she goes under—ow! a terrible big wave!—so let's get out of her way!"

But the poor fellow was so anxious to escape from the neighborhood of the *Titanic* that he kept steering in half-circles or worse. At last he headed the boat clear around so that her bow was pointed straight toward the ship. I couldn't stand that.

"Here!" I cried, "do you want to run the ship down? I guess you may have steered with a wheel, but surely you've never handled a tiller. Shove the tiller the opposite to the way you want to go, and you'll be all right."

He got her straightened out then, and our poor crew paddled very slowly away from the *Titanic*. I suppose by this time it must have been about one o'clock in the morning. There was a very little bit of the moon in the sky—the last quarter, I suppose. The water was smooth as a lake, not a piece of ice anywhere except the big iceberg that had wrecked us, far astern; and at every stroke of the oars great glares of greenish-yellow phosphorescent light would swirl aft from the blades and drip in globules like fire from the oars as they swung forward. The phosphorescence was so brilliant that it almost dazzled us at first. I have never seen it so fine.

In the foreground may be seen one of the frail craft that bore the few hundred survivors to safety

As we drew away from the *Titanic* she was brightly lighted as ever and not a sound came from her. I have heard since coming ashore about rioting and shooting, but throughout the whole incident I did not hear a shot fired or a loud voice. Of course, there may have been something like this as the later boats were loaded, but there was nothing like it in our vicinity. We seemed deserted on our part of the deck before launching our life-boat, and I guess whatever violence there was happened on the lower deck to which the women were ordered some time before we left.

Nor did I see much of a list in the ship's body as I looked at her from the boat. She seemed a little down by the head, but as we moved away from her she looked like a great mountain of strength that would last forever. Her lights were all burning, as it seemed to us, and she made a wonderful picture. The air was so clear that we could see plainly such details as her rails and bits of the rigging, standing out like lines in an engraving. We were lying off perhaps a quarter of a mile from her when I heard several bursts of cheering. I suppose that was when the people on board received the news by wireless that other ships were hurrying to the rescue.

After an hour or more—I had no way of seeing the exact time, but it seemed very long—the lights of the *Titanic* suddenly went out and we began to think her end could not be very far away. I have heard a lot of talk about explosions in the *Titanic;* that her boilers blew up and tore her body apart. I certainly heard nothing that sounded like an explosion. I did hear a great roar mingled with hissing coming from the direction of the ship. I supposed that this was caused by the sea-water rising in the hull high enough to put out the fires under the boilers. Water thus heated would hardly make boilers explode, I should think. No one in our boat said a word, but I feel sure the seriousness of the situation began to depress everybody. Very slowly the giant black hull began to diminish against the sky-line. It was a frightful thing to feel that the ship was going, faster and faster, and that we could do nothing for the people on her. Not a sound came from the ship until the very last, and then

Captain R. H. Rostron, of the "Carpathia," who rescued the "Titanic's" survivors and brought them safely into port

The scene at the Cunard Line pier, New York, as the "Carpathia" was docking

"Titanic" survivors leaving the pier after the arrival of the "Carpathia"

WHEN THE "CARPATHIA" CAME IN

there rose in the air a sort of wild maniacal chorus, a mingling of cries and yells in which I could distinguish voices of different tones. Many of the people, I fear, had gone mad as they felt the ship settle for her final plunge to the depths. No one gave any command, but our crew began to row as hard as they could away from the awful sounds, and then in the twinkling of an eye we were all alone on the dark sea. There was no talking in our boat, nothing but the rattling of the oars in the rowlocks. But the air still resounded with the long-drawn wail of agony that rose from the ship. These were the most awful moments in the whole experience. Bravery was shown by the people in every phase of the emergency; but flesh and blood could not withstand that gasping cry of horror as the sea rose to them. After a time our boat passed out of reach of the cry and we were alone indeed.

One sailor called to another: "Did you put the plugs in the bottom of this boat before she was launched?"

"Well," the other replied, meditating, "I'm sure I put in one plug an' I *hope* I put in both, for I don't feel any water about our feet."

Either the men didn't know where to look or they couldn't grope their way among the passengers to find out; but we found out later that both plugs were in place. After a long silence some one cried out that there was a green light dead ahead.

"Must be the starboard light of a fishing-smack," another voice answered. I felt pretty sure it couldn't be, since very few fishermen will waste their money on kerosene for side-lights; but our crew made for the green light just the same. When we got a mile nearer to the light we found that it was the reflection of the stars shining on the side of an iceberg. A wind was blowing off the ice that seemed to bite as it struck us, it was so cold. No picture I have ever seen gives a fair idea of the size and the menace of a berg. This one looked fearful, and seemed to breathe out the threat of death. Nevertheless no one in our boat was frozen. We were all well wrapped up and we sat so close together that we kept one another comfortably warm. As the wind freshened up to what would be a good sailing breeze, the sea rose with it, and we began to pitch and roll.

They say it was a little before four o'clock in the morning when the *Carpathia* came in sight. Her lights looked very low and dim at first, but within a short time after we sighted her she came up near us and stopped. I remember thinking how tiny she looked, all picked out against the sky by her rows of lights, compared with the great bulk of the *Titanic* which we had seen all lighted up only a few hours before. Within a few minutes the sun began to show its edge above the horizon and soon rose clear of the sea. I never saw a finer sight than that ship which had raced through fifty miles of field ice and bergs to come to our rescue. I saw some of the bergs later, and they looked as big as the pyramids.

The little life-boats began racing toward the *Carpathia* as fast as their crews could row. They couldn't do much more than paddle, but soon they came alongside. Presently our boat came up to where they had a chair rigged to a whip and let down for our people, one by one. The third person to leave our boat—a woman of substantial size—was stepping forward to take her place in the chair when, to the utter amazement of everybody, another woman, clad only in nightgown and kimono, sprang from nowhere and sat up on the floor of the boat.

"Look at that horrible woman!" she cried, pointing at the astonished lady in the chair. "Horrible! She stepped on my stomach. Horrible creature!"

The unhappy woman in the kimono had been lying for all of the four hours on the floor of the life-boat, either unconscious or too frightened to speak. She was next up in the chair after her oppressor.

When it finally came my turn to go up I found myself hoisted aloft quickly. A pair of hands was thrust out to keep me from bumping my head against the ship as I ascended. At the deck one man seized me to hold me up, while another wrapped a blanket, warmed in advance, completely around me. A third man assisted me into a room where a cup of hot coffee and a big drink of brandy were served to me—the whole process from the moment of lifting me out of the chair taking about half a minute.

It seems to me now as if I should remember these details as long as I live. And, of course, all I saw and heard was a very small part of all the happenings of that awful night.

The ship toward which the eyes of the world were turned for four days—the "Carpathia" passing Fire Island on her way to New York with her tragic cargo of rescued "Titanic" survivors

The "Carpathia" docking, with two of the "Titanic's" life-boats in the foreground

A near view of the side of the "Carpathia" as she passed Sandy Hook, the "Titanic" survivors crowding to the rail for the first glimpse of the harbor which 1600 of their comrades will never see

Red Wing Daily Republican.

VOLUME XXVII. NO. 169. | RED WING, MINNESOTA, SATURDAY EVENING, APRIL 27, 1912. | PRICE TWO CENTS.

ORATORS WHO WIN PRIZES

SEVEN RED WING SEMINARY STUDENTS CONTEST IN FLIGHTS OF ELOQUENCE.

ALL DO GOOD WORK

Estenson, Thompson and Weeks Win the Three Prizes While Toipcs of Day Are Ably Handled by the Entire Number — Thought and Delivery Both Excellent.

The annual oratorical contest at the Red Wing seminary, under the auspices of the Alumni association, by whom the three prizes are offered, occurred last evening at the seminary chapel.

Prof. George H. Ellingson presided as chairman and the judges on thought and composition were: Prof. C. M. Melom, University of Minnesota, Minneapolis; Rev. H. N. Bakke, Cando, N. D.; Attorney N. T. Moen, Fergus Falls. The judges on delivery were: Prof. F. M. Rarig, University of Minnesota; Judge Albert Johnson and Robert Putnam.

The exercises of the evening began with a trombone solo by A. Grinde, and during the program the Seminary quartet also rendered a selection.

There were seven orations given, each with much earnestness and power and the productions were noticeable for the thoughtful and able way in which they were stated.

E. Espelien spoke on "An Unfortunate People," and told the pathetic story of the crushing tyranny of Russia which so heavily burdened the brave, earnest but seemingly helpless people of Finland. He called upon free America to protect against Russia's inhumanity and interfere, if necessary in behalf of the liberty-loving people who had done so much for humanity in the past history of Europe.

A National Problem.

In his oration, "A National Problem," E. Estenson gave a very lucid and able consideration of the question of the control of "Big Business." He said the present situation was one of distrust and chaos and well nigh intolerable to the business welfare. The Sherman law was good as far as it went but its proper interpretation and enforcement was difficult because its meaning was too vague. What it needed, he contended, was an addition that should define what unreasonable restraint of trade was and with this the law should be fully and persistently enforced. There was need of an industrial commission that should furnish the expert administration necessary to make it effective.

Albert Anderson spoke on "An Opportunity of the Christian Church," and called specific attention to the great changes going on in China and the need and splendid opportunity there was for American missionaries to go in and possess the land for the church and for Christianity, if they were properly supported by the Christian people of this country. There was an intellectual awakening in the Orient and now was the time to make Christian influence potentially felt.

Ole Aune in the familiar theme, "American Ideals," drew a picture of the possibilities of American civilization dominated by Christian ideals and the tremendous responsibility that rested upon our shoulders for the progress and prosperity of the whole world. It was an earnest presentation of the subject.

In his oration on "The White Slave Trade," Arthur Thompson depicted the growth and horrors of the awful traffic and in vivid and plain language appealed for a crusade against it that should result in its extermination. Mr. Thompson's delivery was very forceful and he held the closest attention of his audience.

Our International Duties.

"Our International Duties, Past and Present," was well handled by Ole Olson. He gave a graphic history of the Monroe doctrine and the many times it had been a means of protecting the countries of Central and South America when they were threatened by European countries with invasion and conquest. He pointed to the Orient and thought that America should extend to the new republic of China all the moral support possible in protecting its integrity and life against the scheming designs of Russia, Japan and Great Britain.

Anfin Weeks, in the closing oration given, spoke of "American Opportunities in China," and in an eloquent manner depicted the friendly relations which existed between the republic of the West and the new republic of the East and showed what opportunities were opening for us as a nation to increase our trade, our influence and our Christian civilization in the heart of the Orient.

The decision of the judges gave the first prize to E. Estenson, the second to Arthur Thompson, and the third to Anfin Weeks.

Brief remarks of congratulations for the excellent orations delivered and the pleasure of listening to them were given by Prof. Rarig of the university, Judge Johnson and Robert Putnam.

HARRY K. THAW TO HAVE HEARING

Question of His Release from Asylum to Be Decided on May 6.

By United Press:

New Rochelle; N. Y., April 27.—Following a brief hearing before Supreme Court Justice Martin J. Keugh, it was announced that the question of the release of Harry K. Thaw from Mattewan insane asylum would be definitely disposed of on May 6. Justice Keogh said that at that time without a jury, he would take up the question and dispose of it. Thaw was in court today. His hair is grey. He wore glasses and an old suit of clothes. He has grown heavy since he was placed in the asylum. He weighs 200 pounds.

BASE BALL

National.

Cincinnati	4
Pittsburg	23
Philadelphia	Rain
Brooklyn	
New York	Rain
Boston	
Chicago	9
St. Louis	0

American

St. Louis	2
Cleveland	3
Boston	6
Philadelphia	5
New York	0
Washington	5
Detroit	0
Chicago	2

American Assn.

Minneapolis	2
Indianapolis	1
St. Paul	5
Louisville	1
Milwaukee	4
Toledo	6
Kansas City	2
Columbus	3

Cable Steamship Mackay-Bennett and Her Crew, Which Picked Up Many Bodies of Titanic Victims.

The cable steamship Mackay-Bennett picked up a number of bodies of victims near the scene of the sinking of the Titanic. Those of the bodies which it was believed could be identified were brought to shore The others, without marks of identification, were buried at sea. Many wore life preservers and apparently died after terrible sufferings in the cold sea. The arrow indicates Captain F H. Lardner of the Mackay-Bennett.

BUYS WHISKEY FOR INDIANS

CHAS. J. SWANSON, FRANK LAWRENCE AND FRED ANDERSON ARE ORDERED TO JAIL.

TRIO STEAL LUMBER

Swanson Furnished Fire Water to Indian and Is Held to Grand Jury—Redskin Drew Forty Days and Anderson, who Engineered Lumber Theft Must Serve 60 Days in Jail.

Frank Lawrence, an Indian from the Prairie Island reservation, was sentenced to 40 days in the county jail on a drunk charge; Fred. Anderson, better known as "Chicken Fred," drew 60 days for stealing lumber from the Red Wing Advertising company and endeavoring to sell it to the Red Wing Manufacturing company, and Chas. John Swanson was bound over to await the action of the grand jury for furnishing whiskey to the Indian. The trio was committed to the county jail this morning by Justice Haynes.

Another Indian, John Hoffman, escaped punishment as he was innocently drawn into the affair, by taking Lawrence's word and hauling the lumber from the city market to the Red Wing Manufacturing company's plant. He was permitted to return to the reservation last evening.

Much Fire-water.

The trio sent to jail were all intoxicated when placed under arrest by Officers Tebbe and Jansen late yesterday afternoon. Seven bottles of whiskey, purchased by Swanson, decorated the table in justice court. At first Lawrence refused to say who purchased the liquor for him but finally admitted that Swanson provided it. The Indian told the court that if he were to tell the truth he feared that the guilty party would kill him. He was assured protection and finally pointed out Swanson as the guilty man.

Fred. Anderson, engineered the theft of the lumber. With Lawrence acting as interpreter, John Hoffman, an aged Indian, was led to believe that Anderson owned it and he agreed to haul it away for him. The police saw that the trio had been pretty active during the afternoon and put an end to the operations just as Anderson went into the furniture company's office to offer the lumber for sale.

Chas. J. Swanson claimed that he gave the liquor to Lawrence, when the latter told him that his boy on the reservation was sick and needed a stimulant. He had five other bottles of fire water in his possession and said that he made the large purchase, because he was about to go out on the farm for several months and needed a good supply. Lawrence admitted that Swanson had furnished him considerable liquor at other times.

Swanson's case will be considered by the grand jury, which convenes in June. Lawrence begged to be let off with a fine and told the court that he would try to leave liquor alone in the future. The county attorney and Chief Severson would not consent to anything but a jail sentence so the court gave him 40 days.

HAMLINE UNIVERSITY HAS NEW PRESIDENT

Dr. Samuel F. Kerfoot of Mitchell, S. D., to Be Successor of Dr. Bridgman.

Rev. S. A. Cook returned last evening from St. Paul where he attended a meeting of the board of trustees of Hamline University of which he is a member.

Dr. Cook says that the prospect for the coming year at Hamline is very auspicious.

The new president selected by the board is Dr. Samuel F. Kerfoot who for the past four years has been the president of Dakota Wesleyan university at Mitchell, S. D. He is an alumnus of Hamline and of Drew Theological seminary at Madison, N. J. He was for eight years pastor of the Central Methodist church at Winona.

Dr. Kerfoot has been very successful in his college work. He is a man a little more than 40 years old and has recognized qualities of leadership and is very likable. He has accepted the position and begins his work at Hamline on Sept. 1.

KILLD HIS FATHER WHO REFUSED TO BUY AUTO

YOUNG MAN AND SISTER ARRESTED IN IOWA CHARGED WITH MURDER.

By United Press:

Des Moines, Ia., Apr. 27.—Ray Wayman, 19 years old, accompanied by his sister, Mabel, 13 years of age, was arrested here today, charged with the murder of their father, John Wayman, aged 55, at his home near Wick, Iowa. The girl says she was forced to accompany her brother. The crime was committed, she says, because the elder Wayman refused to buy an automobile for the son. When young Wayman was arrested he was trying to pass a check for $400 to buy a machine.

MINNESOTA COLLEGE SECURES $25,000.00

Minneapolis, April 27.—Having obtained subscriptions for $18,000, a condition placed upon the promise of a donation of $6,000, Minnesota college, Harvard and Delaware streets, has received a check for the latter amount from James J. Hill. The offer was made to members of the faculty two years ago.

Minnesota college, which is owned by the Minnesota conference of the Swedish Lutheran church, was organized Oct. 4, 1904. At that time there was not one cent in the institution. Today its property is valued at $102,000 and it has an enrollment of 472 students. Its faculty numbers twenty and there are eight departments.

Although the subscription to the $18,000 is representative of the entire Swedish Lutheran people of not only Minneapolis but of the northwest, much credit is due to C. L. Johnson, vice president of the C. A. Smith Lumber company, a member of the board of directors. Other instruments insecuring the necessary amount were Calvin G. Goodrich, C. A. Smith, B. F. Nelson, C. C. Webber, E. G. Dahl, F. G. Broogberg, Professor T. E. Verner, Rev. E. O. Stone of Minneapolis: J. W. Carlson and Dr. E. M. Lundholm of St. Paul and John Ogren of Stillwater.

NEARS HALIFAX BRINGING 189 TITANIC DEAD

Mackay-Bennett on Its Way Home Approaching Nova Scotia.

FRIENDS AWAIT SHIP'S ARRIVAL

Preparations Being Made for the Tenderest Care of Unfortunate.

VINCENT ASTOR ON SPECIAL TRAIN

Lonely, He Speeds to Halifax to Take Father's Body to New York.

By United Press:

Halifax, N. S., April 27.—With 189 bodies aboard the steamer Mackay-Bennett is on its way here. She may not dock until Monday. The Mayflower curling rink will be turned into a morgue. The undertakers are ready to prepare the bodies before relatives are admitted to see them. The prominent dead are to be taken to New York on a special train.

THREE MORE WITNESSES.

By United Press:

Washington, April 27.—Three more important witnesses were summoned today in the Titanic investigation. They were: H. Sammis, chief engineer and manager of the Marconi New York wireless office; Harold Bride, operator on the Titanic, and J. A. Hosey. Captain James H. Moore of the steamer Mount Temple took the stand and said his wireless operator told him of the Titanic's calls for help and how he tried to reach the Titanic but was prevented by icebergs until it was too late. Moore said he passed a schooner whose light might have been seen by the Titanic and also passed a small tramp steamer.

IMMEDIATE RESULT.

By United Press:

Washington, April 27.—Senator Smith, chairman of the senate committee investigating the Titanic disaster, said today that the immediate result of the investigation will be framing of a law forcing all steamers to carry two wireless operators so one will be on duty at all times, also regulations providing that the operators be mature men of judgment.

FUNERAL TRAIN OF JOHN JACOB ASTOR

Vincent Astor Speeds to Halifax on Special Train for Body of His Father.

By United Press:

Portland, Maine, April 27.—Aboard the Astor funeral train enroute from New York to Halifax, Vincent Astor, alone in his sorrow today, hurried northward to Halifax on a special train to receive the body of his father, Colonel John Jacob Astor. One friend and a valet accompanied him. The Astor body is to be placed aboard a private car and hurried to New York by special train as soon as the steamer Mackay-Bennett lands.

MAKES NO COMMENT ON 'TEDDY'S' ATTACK

President Reads Roosevelt's Speech But Does Not Reply—To Speak at Philadelphia Tonight.

By United Press:

South Orange, N. J., April 27. — President Taft slept late this morning at the home of Clarence H. Kelsey.

At breakfast he read Roosevelt's speech attacking him, but made no comment. He expects to answer Roosevelt at Trenton this afternoon or at Philadelphia tonight.

Taft is to speak in Boston Monday night in reply to Roosevelt who speaks there tonight.

RED WING DAILY REPUBLICAN

Entered at the Postoffice at Red Wing, Minnesota as Second-class matter.

Tams Bixby, President. N. Halvorson, Treasurer. Jens K. Grondahl, Secretary.

Red Wing Printing Company

Republican Building, Third St. Red Wing, Minn

SUBSCRIPTION RATES

One Year...... $5.00 Three Months......$1.25 Delivered by carrier in the city, per week... 10c
Six Months..... 2.50 One Month.... .... .45 Morning Rural edition on rural routes, year.. $3

The Republican is a member of the United Press Association and receives its telegraph news.

OUR SALOON POLICY.

The Republican has been requested to define its position on the liquor business in Red Wing. While any-one who has read our editorials ought not to find it necessary to ask this, it is an easy matter to recapitulate briefly what this paper believes should be the saloon policy in Red Wing:

1. A $1,000 license.

2. A strict enforcement of the laws of the state and of the ordinances of the city, governing the liquor business.

3. A patrol limit within the boundaries of which should be conducted all the retail liquor establishments.

4. The absence of brewery control from the city government.

5. Due respect on the part of those interested in the liquor business for the opinion of others.

The Republican does not believe that prohibition would be practical or desirable in this community at present for reasons which have been reiterated from time to time, and that in order to avoid that issue the liquor interests should make reasonable concessions and conduct the business in such a way as to arouse the least public disapproval.

DESTRUCTIVE CONFLAGRATIONS

$50,000 FIRE IN NEW ROCKFORD, N. D.

It Is Believed That Incendiaries Are Responsible for $50,000 Blaze.

New Rockford, N. D., April 27.—An entire block of buildings was wiped out by fire and incendiaries are believed to be responsible for the blaze. The total loss is about $50,000.

The fire had gained a big headway before it was discovered. The losses in every instance but two, are total, the owners of two places being successful in removing the stock and fixtures before the fire reached the buildings.

The city's fire fighting force was inadequate when it came to fighting the blaze. The places destroyed are Mrs. Tottners Millinery store; the Wiemals building; the Hays and Adams Hardware store, Ellsworth paint shop; Johnson-Allair land office; Lenox building; Davis hotel; Mulzey Hardware store; Morrisey's confectionery store and the Herman Smith tailoring shop.

The old court house building was occupied by three of the firms. The fire started in the courthouse building, which, on two previous occasions, has been set on fire.

Fire Menaces a Maine Town.

Brunswick, Me.—More than a dozen buildings, including two churches, the water tower and shops of the aine Central railroad, the sheds of a coal firm and a dozen dwelling houses were destroyed by a fire which for a time threatened to wipe out the town. The losses total upwards of $100,000. For three hours the flames were beyond control, until help arrived from Bath, Topsham, Lewiston, and Portland.

Among the burned buildings are St. John's Catholic church and parochial school and St. Paul's Episcopal church.

Winnipeg Has Big Fire.

Winnipeg.—Fire destroyed Brown and Rutherford's lumber mills in this city. The warehouses, drying plant, lumber piles, stables and offices were all consumed. A high wind rendered the fire a hard one for the firemen to fight. The loss is estimated at $250,-000.

THAW WANTS OUT.

Begins Another Action to Secure Release From Mattewan.

New Rochelle, N. Y., April 27. — With greater zeal than ever, Harry K. Thaw, through his attorney. Clarence J. Shean, today began another fight for liberty, when an inquiry into the present mental state of Stanford White's slayer was opened here by Justice Keogh. The proceeding is similar to several that Thaw has instituted since his acquittal on the ground of insanity.

Olympic Abandons Her Trip.

Southampton, April 27.—The voyage of the Olympic has been abandoned and the liner has returned to port.

DR. STRATTON D. BROOKS

Dr. Brooks has resigned the superintendency of the Boston schools to become president of the Oklahoma State university at a reduced salary because it has been his life's ambition to build up a great university.

HALIFAX IS IN FUNERAL GARB

AWAITING ARRIVAL OF THE MACKAY-BENNETT.

Relatives and Friends of Dead Waiting to Identify the Bodies.

Halifax, April 27.—Halifax is waiting in funeral garb the arrival of the cable ship Mackay-Bennett with its cargo of dead from the Titanic. Hotels are crowded with the bereaved and every train brings additional relatives of victims. When the floating morgue will arrive is uncertain.

Among those here are Capt. Richard Roberts, of Col. John Jacob Astor's yacht, seeking his late employer's body, which had been identified; Wallach, brother-in-law of Henry B. Harris, whose body has not been reported; George B. Widener, Jr., and party, who await the body of the Philadelphia capitalist and H. G. Kelley, vice president of the Grand Trunk railway, whose president Charles M. Hays, is among the recovered dead.

Maurice Rothschild of New York, seeks the bodies of Mr. and Mrs. Isidor Straus and Benjamin Guggenheim; Joseph Richardson of Philadelphia hopes to find the body of Second Vice President Thayer of the Pennsylvania; Karl G. Roebling of Trenton, N. J., is ready to identify the body of Washington A. Roebling of engineering fame, R. A. Fortune of Montreal will claim the body of Mark Fortune, and Charles Fortune. No inquiries concerning the body of William T. Stead, the English journalist, had been received here. If recovered it will be held pending instructions from England. J. W. Ragsdale, United States consul here, is prepared to take charge of the body of Major Archibald Butt, although he has received no instruction from Washington. It is understood, however, that Major Winship, an intimate friend of Major Butt, will arrive before the Mackay-Bennett docks.

An express company will transport the dead from here free of charge, and the White Star line will see to it that bodies of victims who lived in England or on the continent are sent where relatives designate.

It is doubtful whether messages from the funeral ship mean that all bodies so far recovered will be brought to port. Some from the steerage may have been sunk after being picked up; others may have been so mutilated as to render bringing them to land inexpedient.

The body of W. H. Harrison, private secretary to J. Bruce Ismay, which has been recovered, will be sent to Liverpool, under instructions received by the White Star lin agents.

Read the wants.

The Number Forty In the Bible.

The rain that produced the flood fell for forty days and forty nights, and after it ceased it was forty days before Noah opened the ark. Moses was forty days on the mountain fasting, and the spies spent forty days investigating matters in Canaan before making their report. Elijah fasted forty days in the wilderness, and Jonah gave the people of Nineveh forty days in which to repent. The forty days' fast of Jesus is known to all readers of the New Testament.

She Can, That's a Fact.

Boyce—Why does a woman give so much attention to dress? Is it because she wants to attract men or because she desires to outshine her sister women? Mrs. Boyce—Can't a woman do two things at once?—Exchange.

First Photographs Showing Arrival of Titanic Survivors and the Rescue Ship at New York.

Scenes on the Cunard line pier at New York when the rescue ship brought into port the survivors of the Titanic tragedy were indescribably pathetic. For hours the pier echoed with the shrieks of men and women suffering from their experience of the few days previous. The photograph of the Carpathia shows three of the ill fated Titanic's lifeboats being lowered from her side.

Latest In Fashion

Helps and Hints to the Careful Dressers

New York, April 27.—Fussy taffeta frocks and suits of this and other silks are a feature notable wherever the well dressed assemble. Changeables are a veritable craze and are used not only for frocks and hats and their trimmings but for bags, linings, scarfs and coats.

The new Quaker Bag is long saddle bag style with rings in the centre to close, it is out not only in ilks but in English Morocco. This bag opens at both ends where gilt frames and secure fastenings hold it for the closings downward in carrying. One end holds the purse and the other the vanity fittings, between the two, in the center, are the rings and chain for carrying. In leather this style costs $10; in moire less, while in white pique trimmed with lace and fringe it can be made at a very moderate figure.

Hand embroidered Quaker collars and cuffs edged with Irish or Cluny lace are fashionably worn, and frills of hemstitched lawn or fine net finish most of the three quarter sleeves that are popular for both tailored frocks and coats. These ruffles can be bought with rubber ribbon fitting them to the arm which saves sewing in. Macrame lace for waist trimmings in bands and collars and cuff shapes is well endorsed and is most often used with decidedly contrasting textures. A waist of fine Brussels net will be dressed up with the heavy lace, or it will relieve the flat look of taffeta or satin. Girdles of velvet ribbon that tie once and have the ends weighted with fringe or other danglers, and similar contraptions of silk or satin are universally worn. Very fancy belts of leather in two colors or soft crushable styles are also desirable additions now that the shirt waist season is upon us.

New Waists.

Severely tailored shirt waists in washable silk are in excellent vogue. These have soft close fitting collars of the material closed with links to match those in the turned back cuff of similar shape which finishes the sleeve. White satin shirt wists made after the same fashion are quite practical also since these wash perfectly in lukewarm soapy water and are ironed on the wrong side when nearly dry after the same method as the regulation "wash silks."

Whip Cords and Serges.

Whip cords and serges are the materials most employed for wool tailor-made attire and every woman who can compass it is having as many white serge costumes as her purse or needs permit. These are so useful and becoming if well selected that their popularity is easily understood. Wool fringe is used considerably as a trimming but discreetly. If it follows the overskirt lines that run in the fashionable diagonal on the skirt the lapels and sleeve cuffs are apt to want it, and be finished in broadcloth or ribbed facings of silk, wool or cotton corduroy or terry cloth. Figured pongee printed in dull tones of red or blue makes effective revers and sleeve facings.

White Skirt and Colored Coat.

A white skirt worn with a colored coat is one of the present fads and coats of this sort are apt to be built either on Blazer or Norfolk lines. Blue coats are first favorites, but black and other tones are permissible if preferred. The dark coat usually has white facings and buttons and is often outlined with heavy cording which is one of the late wrinkles.

—Lucy Carter.

The above designs are by The McCall Company, New York, Designers and Makers of McCall Patterns.

WIND RAZES HOME.

Dock Machinery Wrecked and Several Are Injured at Duluth.

Duluth.—A heavy wind swept the city doing much damage to homes in the suburbs and demolishing the residence of G. W. Palmer, an eight-room building. The dock machinery of the Great Lakes Coal and Dock company on the bay was wrecked, entailing a loss of $50,000. Several persons were slightly injured. Ships in the harbor were buffeted, but none injured.

Chicagoan Killed by Train.

La Crosse, Wis., April 27—B. N Robinson, a civil engineer of Chicago, was instantly killed near Trempealeau by a passenger train on the Chicago, Burlington and Quincy railroad while directing construction work.

Pioneer Banker Passes.

Kansas City, April 27.—Howard M. Holden, a pioneer banker, died here aged 75 years. Before coming here he was in the banking business at Washington, town, and had served as a member of the Iowa legislature.

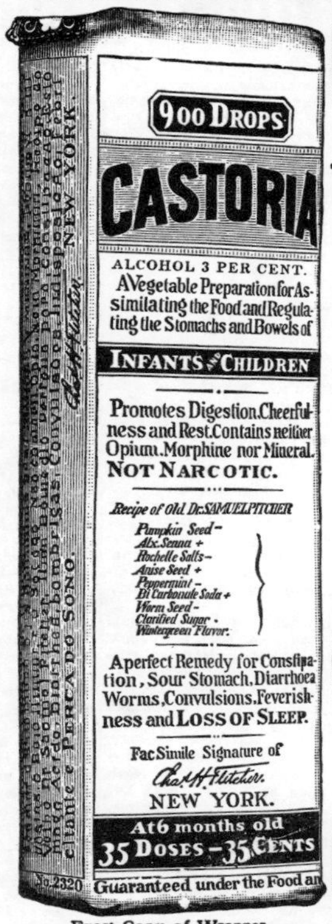

Newburyport's White Plague Fight

BY EDITH S. DOLE

Recording Secretary Newburyport Anti-Tuberculosis Association.

(ANNUAL REPORT)

In submitting the following report to this association and to the public at large it may be well to state that the executive and medical boards, with the visiting nurse, have done the work that has come before them without much publicity or announcement of details. This his been necessary because of the nature of the work. No physician publishes the list of his patients and their ills, neither have the various boards of this association felt it considerate to continually bring before the public many of the pathetic and interesting cases they had to consider, for the greater part of the work has had to do with conditions in the home and this, necessarilly, must be of a private nature. No one knows but those who have done the work how much time and earnest thought have been given to individual cases, to the spending of the money intrusted to our care in order to obtain the best possible results and to impress upon unthinking ones the necessity of caring for themselves and conformity to the laws of hygiene.

At the annual meeting held April 20, 1911 the revised constitution was adopted by a unanimous vote. The president elected at that meeting, Mr. Charles W. Moseley, finding it imposible to continue the duties of that office owing to his business interests outside the city, declined and the office has since been filled by the first and second vice presidents.

Since the beginning of the financial year there have been 13 meetings of the executive board, 2 of the executive board and church representatives and 5 of the executive and medical boards.

On May 4th, Miss Margaret Weir, the visiting nurse engaged by the association for the period of six months, returned from her studies in Cambridge and Boston, reported for duty, received instructions and on May 10th, began her work among the patients.

In July 600 annual reports were compiled—as in the previous year—under the direction of Miss Edith M. Howe of the executive board. These were sent to the National, State and various organizations through the country.

The special day on which everyone so disposed was given an opportunity to contribute to the support of the association and in return receive an equivalent for the money so given occurred on September 16th, and like that of last year was called "Candy Day."

Nearly eight hundred pounds of home made candy was contributed and sold and this, supplemented by the sale of pencils stamped with the association's name and small tablets of paper, brought the total receipts of the day to $789.00

On October 17th, a joint meeting of the Executive and Medical Boards was called to consider the advisability of continuing the services of the visiting nurse—the period for which she had first been engaged having expired. The sentiment of all the physicians on the board was, that her work in seeking out, bringing to the notice of the physicians and the board and helping to care for in the most practical way patients afflicted or suspected of being afflicted with tuberculosis, was too valuable to be lost and they recommended that she be reengaged for another six months at $75 per month. This was done and in November she began systematic work in the schools in connection with Dr. Shaw, the School Physician.

By the work of the Corresponding Secretary the list of members has been newly catalogued greatly facilitating the collection of dues and enabling the church representatives to keep in touch with the members of their parishes.

In November the contract to again conduct a sale of Red Cross Seals was signed by Mrs. Joshua Hale and these were placed in some of the stores of the city with the result that $70 worth were sold, netting $54 to the association.

The annual State Conference of Anti Tuberculosis Societies was held in Boston, March 22 to which Miss Margaret Cushing was sent as delegate. These conferences are always interesting and helpful, this year the session on Fresh Air in Public Schools being particularly so.

As in the past two years meetings for the examinations and instruction of patients have been held in the class room on Essex Street, Drs. Nason, Hurd and Noyes being in attendance, with Miss Weir as assistant.

Dr. Frank W. Snow, city physician, has been ever ready with advice and help and has greatly assisted Miss Weir in her work about the city. To all these and to Dr. Robert Hamilton for free bactereodical examinations do we owe our sincere thanks.

Two of our Honorary members have been called from earth during the past year, Dr. Francis A. Howe and Dr. John F. Young. Both had given the best years of their lives to heal the sick and comfort the dying and both were deeply interested in whatever pertained to the welfare of man. We shall long hold them in loving remembrance.

We have no words with which to express our thanks to the press, to the city officials, to the churches of all denominations, to the members of the medical profession and to the public for the encouragement given to us during the past year.

This work means the true brotherhood of man and should be one of grand cooperation.

Every sum, no matter how small, helps someone, every word of encouragement or act of kindness helps along to some less fortunate than ourselves. us in our work and all these we pass

Report of Miss Caroline M. Moulton Treasurer.

April 15, 1911.

To cash		balance	$622.23
"	"	from patients	50.00
"	"	rebate	5.20
"	"	fees 1911	278.00
"	"	fees 1912	304.50
"	"	interest	10.99
"	"	donation	412.96
"	"	Candy day receipts	904.93
"	"	Red Cross seals	70.00
"	"	returned	20.00
"	"	from Savings Bank	400.00
			$3078.81

Additional funds Newburyport Five Cent Savings Bank	$ 457.20
Institution for Savings	1061.20
Wm. E. Chase fund	218.64
	$1737.04

By Cash		paid for board	$899.21
"	"	advertising	8.13
"	"	rent	84.00
"	"	milk	47.32
"	"	janitor	23.20
"	"	nurses supplies	43.69
By Cash		supplies	232,36
"	"	nurse	729.10
"	"	postage	12.24
"	"	express	4.65
"	"	carpenter	15.43
"	"	carfare	27.55
"	"	medicine	23.23
"	"	class room	3.82
"	"	candy day	115.93
"	"	printing	37.70
"	"	fuel	35.40
"	"	tent	17.30
"	"	rail road	34.50
"	"	Red Cross seals	14.00
"	"	money advanced	20.00
"	"	deposited in savings Bank	345.00
			$2773.76
April 15, 1912 Cash Bal.			305.05
			$3078.81

ANOTHER SOCIALIST PRAISES BOY SCOUTS

S. J. Duncan-Clark,, editorial writer for the Louisville Herald, who is one of the leading socialists in Kentucky, does not agree with his socialist colleagues who denounce the boy scout movement. In an editorial in the Herald, entitled "How Much For Your Boy," he discusses the principles of the scout movement and commends every one of them. He writes about the scout movement as follows: "This is primarily a boy's organization, led by men who know and believe in the boy. It seeks to get at boy nature from within by encouraging every instinct that is good, giving to activity occupations that are absorbing and wholesome, cultivating the sense of chivalry, unselfish comradeship and helpfulness, promoting the ambition to achieve and to create. Here is the spirit of the Boy Scout Movement, originated by General Baden-Powell, recently a visitor to Louisville, and under the splendid and inspiring direction locally of Admiral Watson.

"Let us say here that the Boy Scout movement is not a military movement. It has been misrepresented as such. Drill has been eliminated as an essential feature. No weapons are carried, real or imitation. The boys are scouts of peace and not of war; the lore they learn is that of useful effort; the games they play are designed to impress the thought of social responsibility of cooperation and mutual aid. The summer camp is one of the most excellent adjuncts of the movement. Under wise and careful, but sympathetic supervision, the boys discover the delights of the open world, practice the arts of woodcraft, grow chummy with Nature and her myriad progeny. They learn to be resourceful, to fit means to an end, to find a way or make it."

Not Those Two.

Sillicus—"Do you think a man can afford to indulge in two luxuries at the same time?" Cynicus—"Not if they happen to be a wife and a champagne supper appetite."

World Has Little Use for Them.

The spirit of the snob sends a vast number of people to the place where human rubbish is tipped.

Doubly [illegible].

The mother of little Helen was one of twins. As the twin sisters lived quite a way apart, Helen did not see her aunt until she was about two years old. On first seeing her she was greatly puzzled over the resemblance of her mother and aunt, and after looking bewilderedly from one to the other finally exclaimed, "More mamma."

New York . . Letter . .

NEW YORK, April 27—Industrial and commercial New York is taking particular interest in what seems to be a case of "lese majeste" as the result of the testimony of a former subject of the Kaiser to the effect that European business methods, particularly those of Germany, which have long been held up by "industrial efficiency engineers" as models for this country to copy are after all in many respects far behind those in use here. That the greater efficiency in the methods of production and manufacture followed by foreign nations is largely imaginary is the cheering conculsion reached by Hans Mendelson, a native of the land of the Kaiser but now an American citizen, who has just completed an elaborate comparison of the methods employed in the two countries. "Neither German farming nor German manufacturing is by any means the model of efficiency so many people think, "says Herr Mendelson. "The low wages are unquestionably a temptation for a great waste of human labor. Many of the factories are antiquated. The technical supervision of the details of the factory processes is not so careful as here. Take the beet sugar industry for example, since it is common to both countries and involves both agriculture and manufacturing. It is true that Germany can produce sugar more cheaply than the United States, and that the removal of the tariff duty probably would result in the wiping out of the industry on this side of the Atlantic. But this difference is due, partly to the lower prices paid for the raw material, and partly to the abundance of hand labor and the low wages paid for it in Europe, and not to the superiority of German machinery and manufacturing methods, as is often claimed. In fact I found the American factories more fully equipped with up to date machinery than those in Germany. In the West expensive automatic unloading devices are in use at all the factories. Such machinery is unknown in Germany. The technical supervision and detailed cost-accounting systems followed in the United States are not to be found in Europe. Americans have been lectured so much about their inferior methods by so called efficiency engineers that they are prone to believe that they have fallen behind their foreign competitors in some way, but my observation is that their manufacturing methods in many respects really are superior to those followed abroad."

* * *

That more than anything else New York, to become a modern reproduction of ancient Rome, needs an up to date Nero to fiddle at its burning is indicated by the report of the fire losses in this city during the past twelve months. To what an alarming extent property is being wiped out here by conflagration is indicated by the report which shows that these losses aggregated for the period the enormous sum of $12,470,000 or more than $1,000,000 a month. More significant still is the fact that this figure represents an increase of nearly fifty percent over the total of $8,591,000 for the preceding year. At this rate of increase the end of the present decade, that is the year 1920, would show an annual fire loss of about $200,000,000. The most important factor in this great increase seems to exist in the city's larger buildings, since although the loss for 1911 far exceeded that of 1910 the fires in the last year were less by 537 than in 1910 while the average loss from each fire in 1911 was $855 as against $596 in 1910. As usual carelessness with lighted matches accounted for a large number of fires, 1366 in all. Lighted cigars or cigarettes caused 970 fires and carelessness with lighted candles 509. To handle the work of protection the city now has 4420 uniformed officers and men and 560 civilian employes in various bureaus. Perhaps the best idea of what the fire fighting problem as it now exists in New York really amounts to is found in the estimate of the money needed for the maintenance of the Fire Department this year. It is $8,537,000.

* * *

The golf ball has now been added to the list of deadly weapons and now that the season is beginning it behooves golfers throughout the country to take a warning from the fate of a local golfer and to refrain from too much curiosity as to how a golf ball is made. Of course many persons who have intercepted the flight of the "gutty" with various portions of their anatomy have for years considered it a deadly weapon. But in these cases it was merely a missile and not inherently dangerous. Now, however, it has been discovered that the golf ball must also be classed as an explosive. This unexpected state of affairs was brought to light here because of the curiosity of a golfer to discover what sort of a liquid center the ball with which he had been playing contained. As the easiest manner of finding out he was proceeding to vivisect it with his pocket knife, when it suddenly exploded, the liquid center entering one of his eyes. As a result, it is feared that he may lose his sight although this will not be known until he emerges from the dark room to which the accident will confine him for several weeks. Just what the liquid center of the ball which caused it to burst consisted of no one seems to know although the effect was that of an acid of caustic which burned the eye in quest[illegible] Whether golfers carrying a half [illegible] en balls through the city streets [illegible] be arrested under the concealed w[illegible] on law remains to be seen, but [illegible] that they have entered the cate[illegible] of explosives the game may take [illegible] new feature of sportiness.

* * *

A feature of metropolitan [illegible] which for years has gradually [illegible] disappearing is soon to suffer [illegible] plete extinction. New York's [illegible] horse car is to go. The city has h[illegible] this statement made a number [illegible] somehow, by this fact. times before but there seems t[illegible] no room for incredulity in this [illegible] since the information comes from [illegible] highest transit official in the cit[illegible] is not so many years since these h[illegible] drawn cars bumped about in [illegible] heart of the financial district.

(Continued on page 7).

Two French Babies and a Swedish Boy Who Were Left Orphans by the Titanic Catastrophe.

Photos copyright, 1912, by American Press Association.

Among the Titanic survivors are two bright French children and a Swedish boy who were left orphans by t[illegible] disaster. The parents of the French boys were among those who lost their lives. The older, Louis, is four years o[illegible] and the younger, Zolo, is three. Both have brown hair, brown eyes, rosy faces and perfect teeth. They cannot t[illegible] anything definite about themselves. They are being given a home by Miss Margaret Hayes of 304 West Eighty-thi[illegible] street, New York. The Swedish boy is Sven Svenson, fourteen years old. His father was lost in the wreck, and [illegible] mother died a year ago.

"Man's Brightest Hope for Future Cannot Exceed Reality of Present,"---Judge Smit[illegible]

Christian Science declares that man's brighest hope for a better life in the hereafter cannot exceed what is in fact the present reality of life; that mortal existence is a state of ignorance and false belief based on a material sense of things; that the actuality is a condition of purity, completeness, joy, harmony, and goodness—a perfect state of mental and spiritual activity, a consciousness free from error or evil; an eternal identity determined by Mind or Spirit, not by matter. And Christian Science declares that this true selfhood must be attained, and can be attained, by gaining a demonstrable understanding of reality; by getting and using a scientific knowledge of the truth of being; by comprehending in its true import and following the example of him who came that we might have life, and have it abundantly.

Taking human life from birth, Jesus the Christ ascended progressively to the Life which is divine. Having the understanding of Truth he grappled with and overcame one after another, the errors which fetter and belittle the life seen in this world, until he rose above it and passed beyond the range of mortal vision. With the knowledge of Spirit he outgrew the belief of life in matter until every mortal or human element vanished. Nor did he do this as though it were possible for him alone. On the contrary, his declared purpose was to be the "way," or wayshower for all men; to enlighten the world; to be the door by which any man might enter in and be saved.

Although immediate and lasting benefits resulted to the world from the ministry of Christ Jesus, the absolute truth which he taught was soon adulterated in human belief, so that the religion which took his name failed to bear the very fruits by which he said his system should be known. His religion differed from all others not only in doctrine but in results, and by its fruits it was to be known or identified. The distinctive feature of the religion founded by Christ Jesus was its saving quality, and this was a present salvation from all evil—from sin, disease, and death. In fine his Christianity was as broad as human need, and the truth of it alone was proved by demonstration.

In the course of time, however, the understanding of true Christianity became diluted and demonstration failed accordingly, until a consistency between theory and practice was obtained by modifying the scope of Christian salvation. A distinction was made between moral disorder and physical, and the healing of the latter was left outside the Christian ministry. The Master of St. Peter said, "went about doing good, and healing all that were oppressed of the devil;" but this distinction, which was in no wise authorized by Christ Jesus, left half of the works of the devil to a profession which did not pretend to have a remedy for evil and did not deal with disease on that basis. Consequently even the nature of evil ceased to be comprehended; and for fifteen centuries before the discovery of Christian Science Christendom suffered disease, death, and certain other forms of evil as though there were no divine remedy for it, while faith looked hence for a better life which might be gained, it was hoped, by death.

This was the scene upon which Christian Science entered. Some persons are not disposed to consider this Science seriously because it was not discovered by either a physical scientist or a doctor of divinity. But St. John, for instance, was not graduated from a theological school, and there is no reason why the vision of spiritual reality should come to those scientists whose researches are confined to the elements, properties, and phenomena of matter. It is more reasonable to expect that understanding will come to those who are gaining the Mind of Christ.

For these reasons there is nothing abnormal in the fact that the world has gained a great accession of actual knowledge through Mary Baker Eddy. Mrs. Eddy was brought up in the atmosphere of piety and devoutness that prevaded a New England home of nearly a century ago. From childhood she was a profound student of Scriptures. She was compassionate, helpful, spiritual; she was a Christian in the true sense of that name. She had become accustomed to ponder the larger problems of human affairs. She had grown in the love for God and neighbor until her desire and aspiration were to heal and to save. She had turned away from matter to Spirit with an unusual degree of understanding. In these circumstances, the normal operation of divine law enabled Mrs. Eddy to discern the true nature of God and His universe, including man, and to penetrate the mystery of evil. The discovery of Christian Science declared the one divine Principle of the universe, separated the error from the truth in human thought, and furnished the scientific method by which the belief in evil can be overcome and abolished.

The attitude of existing churches toward her message made it necessary for Mrs. Eddy to found a new church; but the Church of Christ, Scientist, has gained members only as those who have come to Christian Science have gained a better life. Surely there is no cause for offense in this. It is the object of all churches, and none of them need feel a loss when a man finds in Christian Science what he could not, or even did not, find elsewhere.

Mrs. Eddy never sought a personal following. Throughout her work as the leader of a great religious movement she consistently turned the attention of Christian Scientists away from herself to the message from God to men which was spoken through her. Her aim and hope, as she often said, were to "quicken and increase the beneficial effects of Christianity" (Science and Health, page 367; Miscellaneous Writings, page 207). The spiritual vitality of her message is proved by what it has already accomplished; but this is only a foretaste of the benefits that will accure to humanity as this Science is more widely understood and practised.

For ages humanity has accepted evil as a fearful reality, never doubting that the wretched havoc following as the consequence of this belief was in some manner ordained by an actual power. Intelligent truth-seekers have sometimes perceived more or less clearly that the government of the universe could not possibly be divided between two opposite and antagonistic powers; and sometimes they have inquired how evil can exist in spite of divine and infinite Love; but no explanation consistent with the goodness of God has ever been furnished by scholastic theology. So Christendom has taken its choice between evil as an independent and actual power and a concept of God which includes evil as His agent. In either view the resistance to evil has been vitiated by the admission of its reality; for no effort which concedes the truth of evil can ever overcome it; it can be abolished only with the understanding which dispels it as illusion or error. Therefore although Chrsit Jesus plainly taught the utter omnipotence and the absolute goodness of God and the consequent unreality and nothingness of evil, the adulteration or dilution of his instruction has postponed for centuries the fruition of his work.

Jesus often spoke of healing as casting out devils; and once he said, "If I with the finger of God cast out devils, no doubt the kingdom of God is come upon you" (Luke 11:14-22). Also when he sent forth the seventy disciples, he told them when they were received in any city to "heal the sick that are therein, and say unto them, The kingdom of God is come nigh unto you" (Luke 10:1-12). The kingdom of God comes upon the human mind when the belief in evil is cast out; and Jesus always dealt with both moral and physical disorder upon this basis. In his teaching and practice both were removed by the finger or power of God; and he expressly repudiated the practice of trying to cast them out by any other means or power. He asked, "How can Satan cast out Satan?"

In this as in everything Christian Science adopts the Christ method, and for these reasons there is a radical difference between Christian Science healing and the results of drugs, hypnotism, suggestion, or any material method. Christian Science cures by means of the finger of God; by means of the power of Truth. Faith in drugs, hypnotism, or suggestion employs one phase of matter or mortal mind to work against another. Christian Science is truly educational; it develops the knowledge and love of Spirit, or God. Material means and methods inculcate faith in matter and magnify the knowledge of material theories.

Sin, disease, and death are different phases of matter or materiality; they are particular results of the general belief in error. Actual and permanent changes for the better are gained only as the mentality is loosed from the mesmerism of error. The primary subject of actual healing is not the physical body but false belief. Genuine health of body can only result from health of mind or thought. Science therefore, heals by the renewing or correcting of the consciousness; by putting off the "old man" with his sins and sickness [illegible] putting on the "new man" whic[illegible] flects God is rightness and whole[illegible] Drugs, suggestion and hypnotis[illegible] not cure at all. They may alle[illegible] but in the final analysis they [illegible] shift the old man from one beli[illegible] another; they merely exhibit di[illegible] ent phases of mortal mind; and [illegible] times the last state is worse tha[illegible] first.

Our Saviour and Wayshower [illegible] "He that hath seen me hath see[illegible] Father." Evidently he did not [illegible] that he was God, for he also [illegible] "My Father is greater than I," "[illegible] of mine own self do nothing." saying, "He that hath seen me [illegible] seen the Father," must have [illegible] that the nature of God must be [illegible] in man. The real man is exactly [illegible] God; he is the expression of [illegible] qualities. Good only being real, [illegible] whole man remains when the [illegible] in evil has been eliminated.

Man did not produce himself; [illegible] is not a state of self-existence. [illegible] exhibits life as the effect of a [illegible] cause. He manifests intelli[illegible] by reason of his relation to an in[illegible] gent Principle. So it is with eve[illegible] tual quality and faculty; it is [illegible] found in the real man because [illegible] flects the action and being of [illegible] All that is good belongs to yo[illegible] to me as our inalienable birthr[illegible] All that we may honestyl pra[illegible] is already ours by reason of ou[illegible] lation to the divine Father. M[illegible] the receiving of God's giving a[illegible] is infinite good.

(From Address of Judge Cl[illegible] P. Smith, C. S. B., Thursday ni[illegible]

Mrs. David Beach Starting on Her New York to Chicago Walk

Photo by American Press Association.

TO test her theory of the nutritive value of raw food Mrs. David Beach, a musician, is making her way on foot from New York to Chicago, attended by an automobile bearing her maid and the newspaper men and photographers who are to keep the records of her trip of approximately 1,000 miles. Her daily bill of fare will consist, for the most part, of wheat, raisins and nuts. She will eat no meat, and none of her food will be cooked. She will follow the railroad routes as closely as possible, taking the highway, however. She expects to be examined by physicians in the different cities—among which are Albany, Buffalo, Cleveland and Toledo—through which she passes, who will take note of her physical fitness. The examinations will have to do with weight, pulse, blood pressure and temperature. With good fortune Mrs. Beach hopes to reach Chicago by June 1. Edward Payson Weston, the veteran pedestrian, has coached her for her task and expresses confidence in her ability to perform it.

A King's Ransom Lost In the Destruction of the Titanic

THE terrific loss of life in the sinking of the Titanic, which makes the disaster the most memorable in the history of the sea, causes the money loss, to the general public, to seem an insignificant consideration. Yet the iceberg which sent the giant liner to the bottom destroyed property of probably more value than that represented in the Spanish armada destroyed by Elizabeth's ships and the gale which aided them. The Titanic was the largest ship ever built and in its luxurious appointments exceeded any vessel afloat. She was valued at $7,500,000, and the jewels and other personal effects of her passengers are estimated to have been worth $5,000,000 more. She was a fifteen story floating palace, built for an average speed of twenty-one knots. Two of her suits cost each $4,350 for a single trip. She was 882½ feet long, 105 feet high, measured from the bottom of the keel to the top of the captain's house, and had a displacement of 66,000 tons. The survivors owe their lives to the Carpathia, of the Cunard line, which was the first ship to reach the scene of the disaster.

ELECTRIC SPARKS

Every Spring bonnet has its day.

Goodby, Boies Penrose! Take keer o' yourself!

We wait the announcement that China has adopted the state-wide primary.

Judging by Ill., results, that suit

Francisco I. Madero promises to put an end to the Mexican revolution in two months. He reminds us of a baseball manager before the season starts.

Chicago woman has sued a beauty doctor for $50,000 for spoiling her complexion. Just think of any girl with $50,000 worth of beauty seeking the services of a beauty doctor.

ROBERT MARION LA FOLLETTE

EARLIEST in the field among "Progressive" Republican candidates was Robert Marion La Follette, senior senator from Wisconsin. His personality as a fighter and "mixer" is sufficiently indicated by the nickname of "Battle Bob," by which he is known among his constituents, a sobriquet which he earned early in his political career. He has been thrice governor of Wisconsin and has served in two congresses as representative. He was elected senator for the term 1905-11 and re-elected for the 1911-17 term. He led the movement to nominate all candidates by direct vote. Prominent among his supporters for the 1912 presidential nomination is Gifford Pinchot, who was the close friend and adviser of President Roosevelt during the latter part of his administration. Senator La Follette received twenty-five votes for the nomination in the last Republican national convention.

Scene of the Republican Convention

THE CHICAGO COLISEUM

THE building in which the delegates to the Republican national convention will assemble on June 18—the Chicago Coliseum—is on part of the ground occupied by the world's fair of 1893. It is in Wabash avenue, near Fifteenth street, a few blocks south of the hotel center. It was erected in 1900 on the site of the Libby prison exhibit, and was dedicated by President McKinley. The stone wall and turreted gate which stood in front of the old building are seen at the main entrance. It is 300 feet long, 150 feet wide and has a seating capacity of 10,000 people, which can be somewhat increased on occasion. It has an immense steel arched roof and has no posts to obstruct the view. A great balcony runs around the four sides of the hall. There are twenty exits, many windows and a glass roof.

The number of delegates will be 1,074, an increase of 94 since 1908. This is due to the reapportionment by congress, which increased the size of the house of representatives from 391 to 433 members or 436 with the representation from the new states of Arizona and New Mexico.

The distribution of delegates will be as follows:

Alabama, 24; Arizona, 6; Arkansas, 18; California, 26; Colorado, 12; Connecticut, 14; Delaware, 6; Florida, 12; Georgia, 28; Idaho, 8; Illinois, 58; Indiana, 30; Iowa, 26; Kansas, 20; Kentucky, 26; Louisiana, 20; Maine, 12; Maryland, 16; Massachusetts, 36; Michigan, 30; Minnesota, 24; Mississippi, 20; Missouri, 36; Montana, 8; Nebraska, 16; Nevada, 6; New Hampshire, 8; New Jersey, 28; New Mexico, 8; New York, 90; North Carolina, 24; North Dakota, 10; Ohio, 48; Oklahoma, 20; Oregon, 10; Pennsylvania, 76; Rhode Island, 10; South Carolina, 18; South Dakota, 10; Tennessee, 24; Texas, 40; Utah, 8; Vermont, 8; Virginia, 24; Washington, 14; West Virginia, 16; Wisconsin, 26; Wyoming, 6.

Alaska, District of Columbia, Hawaii, Philippines and Porto Rico 2 each.

BOY SCOUTS WORK FOR LOCAL OPTION

The boy scouts of Stoughton, Wisconsin, under the Rev. J. G. Wade their scout master, carried on a campaign recently agaisnt the sale of intoxicating liquors in that town. They made an appeal to all voters interested in the welfare of boys who fought against saloons in their city. The city went dry at the election.

case stolen from Governor Wilson, must have contained most of his Illinois supporters.

It seems to be an inalienable right of the "minority" to make a contest in every district where it is beaten.

FACTS ABOUT THE PRIMARY

(Continued from Page Five.)

party enrollment requirement.

No Enrollment Needed

But when the presidental preference primary was created it was argued that there might be many unenrolled persons who would wish to participate in the primary. Accordingly the law was drawn so as to allow registered voters who were not previously enrolled to participate in either party's vote without enrollment.

This phase of the matter is likely to complicate the result, as in other states where such latitude is allowed charges of fraud and "cross-voting" have been frequent.

The Ballots

When the voter designates which ballot he desires he will receive it and discover at once a number of "groups" of candidates for delegates-at-large. There are eight of these to be elected. The "groups" are formed of delegates whose names were grouped on the petitions by which they were proposed for the ballot. On the Republican ballot there is a Taft group of eight and a Roosevelt group of the same number and one group of one whose name was proposed on a separate petition. He is pledged to Taft.

On the Democratic ballot is one group of seven pledged to Governor Foss and no less than eight "groups" of one each, some for Foss, three for primary preference, one for Wilson and one unpledged. The Democratic voters will not be able to find a full delegation under any one group but must choose one of the independent candidates to fill his slate.

For alternate delegates-at-large, the voter will find on the Republican ticket two full groups and on the Democratic ballot one full group and three single names.

Next in order come the district delegates from the Sixth Congressional district. There are two Taft and two Roosevelt delegates. There are four Democratic candidates, only one of whom is pledged to Governor Foss. There is a full set of alternates on the Republican ballot but only one on the Democratic so the voter will have to fill in one name or let a place go by default.

Last on the ballot comes the space for the expression of preference for president. It is worthy of note that Governor Foss, who has many delegates pledged to him, has no place on the preferential ballot. Champ Clark and Woodrow Wilson contest the Democratic vote, William Howard Taft, Theodore Roosevelt and Robert Marion La Follettee, the Republican. There is no candidate for vice-presidency.

INTERNATIONAL EXHIBITION OF BOY SCOUTS IN 1914

An international exhibition of the boy scouts of the world will be held in Burlingham, England, in 1914. Lieutenant General Sir Robert S. S. Baden-Powell in the course of his visit to this country held a conference with Colin H. Livingstone, President of the Boy Scouts of America and several scout leaders in regard to having many troops of boy scouts sent from the different cities in this country to Burlingham to participate in the exhibition. It is likely that many troops will be sent. That exhibition, however, will include boys from Canada, Australia, Japan, China, India, Russia, Germany, France, Norway, Sweden and Denmark. The international exhibition will last about two weeks and in that time the boys of the world will display their skill in camping, handicraft work, in public service. The boy scouts will make all displays of their work in fire brigade, bridge building, ambulance corps and the like. There will also be athletic games.

SCOUT TRAINING LASTS THROUGH ONES LIFE

J. B. Leonard, scout master of a troop of Boy Scouts in Coatesville, Pa., believes that the training which the boy gets through activities have an influence upon them for the remainder of their lives. "Scout activities," he says, "provide ample and varied outlets for the surplus energy which may be found in every boy.

"Contact with nature develops the religious instinct of the boy and trains him to be a strong moral man. Scout Laws have a wonderful effect on the boy's after life. If he is encouraged to be thrifty in boyhood, he seldom slips on that point in manhood. The same principle applies to honor, loyalty, service, brotherhood, kindness and the like. The outdoor life develops a clean, healthy body in which an unclean mind is very rare. The boy is transformed from a rowdy to a gentleman. A scout who has had much experience in camping trips is generally cheerful, philosophical and energetic. Various kinds of manual work trains the will as well as the hand.

BOY SCOUTS HAVE FUN AND DO GOOD TURN

The Pioneer Scout of St. Paul tells of this good turn done by the boy scouts: "You all know how sloppy the streets are when the snow and ice begin to melt. You also know how much fun it is to play in the running water and to dam it up with sticks and mud. Well, these Scouts instead of damming up the water cut channels for it to run off the streets into the sewer. One place where the sidewalk had been flooded for a quarter of a block was quickly drained. These Scou htj tssda amus etaoini These Scouts had just as much fun as the boys on the next street who obstructed the water so that passersby had to wade through or walk around the block, and they were doing a real service to the community. If you're going to play in the water anyway, Scouts, you might just as well do some good while you are doing it."

THE CAMP FIRE GIRLS ARE BUSY

The national headquarters of the Camp Fire Girls of America have been established in No. 118 E. 28th Street, New York City. Miss G Sebellov, who as a student in Col bia University made a specialit psychology and social service been elected Secretary of the org zation. Miss L. Halstead is As ant Secretary and Miss E. W. B is Office Secretary.

An esteemed Virginian conte ary sings the praises of sassafra with a warmth of eloquence, th sufficient to convince any one when a boy never had to drink quarts" of it a day, in the spring top off at night with a heapin' spoonful of sulphur and molass

Woodrow Wilson asks the Democratic nomination on the strength of pr ises of what he will do if made president, rather than on his record as an ecutive, for until he became governor of New Jersey last year he had b known only as an educator. He was highly esteemed as president Princeton university, and is considered a man of advanced ideas concern government and legislation, and a deep thinker. He has been expounding theories in all parts of the country.

Former leader of the minority in congress, and now speaker of the h Champ Clark has plenty of record on which to base his candidacy fo Democratic nomination, and his boomers are taking every advantage Mr. Clark has been active in congress for so many years that his positi most questions is well known to the public. Missouri is for him strong the retirement of Joseph Folk in his favor.

Red Wing Daily Republican.

VOLUME XXVII. NO. 170. RED WING, MINNESOTA, MONDAY EVENING, APRIL 29, 1912. PRICE TWO CENTS.

BIG TIME HERE BY U. C. T. BOYS

PROGRAM OUTLINED PROMISES CONVENTION WILL BE A HUMMER.

MEET JUNE 6, 7 AND 8

Rochester, Duluth, Albert Lea and Other Bands in Attendance—Big Steamboat Excursion—Uniform of U. C. T.—Preliminary Banquet — Best Meeting in This Jurisdiction.

There will be plenty of doings and they will all be done up brown in connection with the U. C. T. convention, when the plans for the gathering are all completed. At the U. C. T. meeting, Saturday evening, different features of the program were gone over and everything points to a successful consummation of the plans which have been so well laid. It was decided that the last meeting in May, which wil be the last regular meeting before the convention, will take the form of a 6 o'clock banquet. At that time the finishing touches will be put to all the arrangements and everything made ready to go off according to schedule when the boys press the button on the coming day of the big show.

The U. C. T. boys will wear a uniform during the convention. It will consist of white duck trousers, blue serge coats, blue neckties, white canvass shoes and white caps.

Gustave Doerr was elected to fill a vacancy on the executive committee.

The members were all in fine humor over the splendid prospects for the most successful U. C. T. gathering ever held within this jurisdiction.

Excursion and Music.

One of the features of the forthcoming U. C. T. convention will be the two steamboat excursions—afternoon and evening—the jolliest and largest excursions which have gone out of Red Wing. The local council has secured the steamer Frontenac and barge for an outing, Saturday, June 8. This craft is large enough to accommodate at least 2,500 people and it is anticipated that this excursion will be one of the gala events of the convention.

There will be music galore for the convention in Red Wing. The famous Rochester band has accepted an invitation to be present and it will attract a great deal of attention because of the known excellence of this musical organization. Outside of the big cities there is probably no band in the entire Northwest that includes so many musical artists as the Rochester band and the U. C. T. should be heartily congratulated in getting the band to Red Wing. Except for the desire to be neighborly and accommodating it would have been impossible to have obtained the services of the Rochester band.

Other splendid bands are also coming to help swell the volume of music during the festive season of June 6, 7 and 8. Duluth will be on hand with the best band north of the Twin cities. Albert Lea, proud of her musicians, will take them along to the convention and the Twin city delegations will, presumably be accompanied by their bands. Other cities, also, are expected to do likewise and it would not be surprising if a half a dozen first-class bandse were to fill in the air with patriotic music during the convention.

SAMUEL TURNER DIES IN VASA

Goodhue County Pioneer Called by Death at the Age of 93 Years—Funeral on Tuesday.

Samuel Turner, one of the pioneer settlers of Goodhue county, died at his home in Vasa at 9:20 o'clock Saturday evening. He has been confined to his bed for the past two or three years but had suffered little and until recently his mental faculties were alert. He was born in the province of Smoland, Sweden, Sept. 8, 1819. Coming to this country in 1863 he bought a farm in Vasa, where he has lived since that time.

Mr. Turner's wife died about seven years ago. He is survived by four daughters and one son. The daughters are Mrs. O. N. Nelson and Mrs. H. J. Lundell, Vasa, and Mrs. F. A. Carlson and Mrs. P. J. Lundquist of this city. The son, John S. Turner, resides on the old homestead in Vasa.

The funeral will be held Tuesday afternoon, with services conducted at 1 o'clock at the family residence and later at the Swedish Lutheran church at Vasa, by Rev. B. Modine.

HON. WM. E. LEE WILL SPEAK HERE

Candidate for Governor to Deliver an Address Thursday Evening.

Hon. Wm. E. Lee, of Long Prairie, will deliver an address at the Armory Thursday evening. Mr. Lee is opposing the machine which has Governor Eberhart for its standard bearer and is making a campaign in favor of the house cleaning necessary in Minnesota politics. He is a splendid gentleman and a man of much experience. Although he is not a brilliant orator, he is a clear and forceful speaker who has practical ideas, high ideals, and a backbone to stand for what he thinks right. All should turn out and hear him.

WILL HURRY INVESTIGATION

SEN. SMITH ANNOUNCES THAT ONLY A FEW PASSENGERS WILL BE CALLED.

BUTT BURNED PAPERS

Woman Says Major Burned What She Believes to Have Been Diplomatic Papers, Just Before Boat Sank—Cable Ship to Land Tuesday Morning with Dead Bodies.

By United Press:

Washington, April 29.—To hurry the report and legislation, Senator Smith announced that the Titanic investigators would summon but half a dozen passengers as witnesses.

William Marconi while on the stand told of the sending of messages and said that the operators on the Carpathia sent many messages for survivors to friends ashore, but he gave no orders to suppress the report of the disaster.

President Greiggs of the Marconi company said that he would submit the copies of all messages sent and received from the Carpathia.

BURNS DIPLOMATIC PAPERS.

By United Press:

Binghampton, N. Y., April 29.—Mrs. H. A. Casselber, a Titanic survivor, said today that before the last lifeboat left the Titanic, Major Archibald Butt went to his state room and burned many papers which she thought were diplomatic papers.

She is to appear before the senate investigating committee.

SHIP TO LAND TUESDAY.

By United Press:

Halifax, April 29.—The cable ship, Mackay-Bennett, with the bodies of 225 Titanic victims, will not reach here before 9 o'clock Tuesday morning. Hundreds of relatives of the dead fill the hotels here awaiting the arrival of the ship.

"UNIVERSITY WEEK" TO BE HELD HERE

Notable and Varied Program of Instruction and Entertainment, June 10-15.

The local committee, consisting of F. W. Putnam, Dr. M. W. Smith and Superintendent C. C. Swain, having in charge the arrangements for university week, met Saturday evening in conference with Prof. Quigley of the state university, in this city.

The week will be held from June 10 to 15, inclusive, and will be crowded full of instruction and entertainment for all classes of people. During the day there will be agricultural, domestic and business programs, a boys' camp, that will include at least forty boys from the rural districts of the county, will be maintained in the city.

On Monday evening, June 10, at the Auditorium Dr. Burton of the state university will lecture. On Tuesday evening, June 11, Manuel I. Flagg of the Minnesota Art association will give an illustrated lecture on "Art in Common Things."

Wednesday evening, June 12, the University Dramatic club will present the "Merchant of Venice;" Thursday evening, June 13, A. W. Rankin will lecture on "How Minnesota Educates Her People; Friday evening of that week, Dean Frankforter of the university will talk about the "Gyroscope and Liquid Air;" Saturday evening there will be a concert by the University Glee club.

J. Bruce Ismay, White Star Line Head, Before the Senate Committee Probing Titanic Disaster.

Copyright, 1912, by American Press Association.

The committee of United States senators, of which William Alden Smith of Michigan is chairman, had J. Bruce Ismay, managing director of the White Star line, before it as the first witness in the inquiry into the Titanic catastrophe. The hearings will be held in New York as far as possible and later will be transferred to Washington, where expert testimony will be heard regarding modern ship construction. The arrow points to Mr. Ismay. At the left is Philip A. S. Franklin, vice president of the White Star line. Mr. Franklin, Captain Rostrom of the Carpathia and the four surviving officers of the Titanic were also witnesses.

Mexicans Love for Americans Is Measured by Cry "Let it be War"

Former Red Wing Man Tells of Situation in Mexico.

Says Revolution Is Not as Bad as Intervention of U. S. Would Be.

Reports That Americans Have Been Massacred Is Not True.

In a letter dated April 3 to a friend here, John Anderson, formerly of this city and now living at Tampico, Mexico, gives some interesting sidelights on the revolution there. He says that everything near Tampico is still quiet and continues: "I am inclined to think that this revolution is not as bad as American newspapers are trying to make it. Most of the reports about Americans being murdered, and their property destroyed, are stretched a good deal, and some of them are absolutely untrue, but God help us who are here if the United States intervenes. There are plenty of ships here, all right, but another thing is to get aboard in time. I do not think I would wait until the last minute. But I sincerely hope that everything will be settled without war."

Mr. Anderson encloses a translation of an article which is clipped from the Mexican paper "Gil Blas," showing as he says: "How much these people love Americans." The article from the Mexican paper reads as follows:

"It is no longer time to cherish illusions. We will have war with the United States, to judge from the latest news from New York.

"Then let it be war. We shall prepare ourselves for it without loss of time and call it, as the children of Islam call it: A Holy War.

"Face to face with a foreign enemy, who insults before attacking us; who spits on us before wounding us; who mocks us before proceeding to conquer, it is our duty to wipe out at a single stroke all of our internal differences. Madero may govern badly but he is a Mexican.....we believe a good Mexican. We must rally round him, for he is our flag and from now on require of him but one thing, that he do not weaken nor bend nor yield as long as there is one of us, his defenders, still alive.

"Mexicans, of all parties, creeds and classes, this is the supreme moment in our history. Let there be not a single traitor, not a single coward, not a single one who thinks of self.

"Do you believe that the yankees will conquer us?

"It is a lie. They can not conquer us with half a million men. Many will come, hundreds of thousands; but in fear they will come because they have seen how Mexicans can fight and how die. They will come filled with fear because they come to commit a contemptible act.

"They will come filled with fear because they know that when our bayonets are all gone, when our powder is exhausted, we will fight with teeth and nails and poison their water as if for dogs.

"This is why they will be afraid and why they will be vanquished.

"We must strengthen the government.

"Soldiers? There will be no lack of these. There will be a million men if we need them.

"But the upkeep of an army costs much money. To maintain ours on a war footing, we propose the immediate creation of a great national fund, easily to be raised by having every Mexican set aside 5 per cent of his income or salary.

"We place the immediate realization of this idea in the hands of the Social Defense league, of the political parties, of the press of all complexions, of all classes of society, of the clergy, commerce and industry, of men, women and children. The daily assistance of three millions of Mexicans will make a world-wide triumph of the holy war of Mexico against the land-eating vulture of the North. Now is the time, Mexicans. Race against race; right against might; loyalty against the lie, that is the holy war."

GIVES AUTHORITY TO COMMISSION

By United Press:

Washington, April 29.—The supreme court today gave the Interstate Commerce commission authority to regulate commerce in Alaska, holding that Alaska is a territory and not a district.

PIANO RECITALS AT LADIES' SEMINARY

Miss Grindeland This Evening, Miss Groth's Excellent Work and Recitals to Follow.

This evening the third in the series of graduation recitals at the Lutheran Ladies' seminary will be given by Miss Evelyn Grindeland, assisted by Miss Ella Christiansen and Miss Anette Berkstrand. The second of these recitals was given last Friday evening by Miss Henrietta Groth, assisted by Miss Grindeland. The program that evening consisted of selections from Raff, Mason, B. Chopin, Tschaikowsky and Liszt. Miss Groth gave a very pleasing and intelligent interpretation of the different masters and her recital was much appreciated by the i nvited friends who were present.

The recitals which are to follow by the graduates of the musical department this year are: Miss Lorna Stone, Monday evening, May 6; Miss Mabel Tweed, Friday, May 10; Miss Ruth Olson, Monday, May 13; Miss Ruth Landeck, Monday, May 20; Miss Lillian Seebach, post-graduate, Friday, May 24; Miss Clara Allen, post-graduate, Tuesday, June 4.

TEDDY AND TAFT IN VERBAL DUEL

PRESIDENT AND COLONEL ASSAIL EACH OTHER IN MOST BITTER MANNER.

ON EVE OF PRIMARIES

Outcome Is of Utmost Importance to the Republican Candidates—Taft Denies Roosevelt's Statements in Regard to Harvester Trust Prosecution.

By United Press:

Boston, April 29.—President Taft and Colonel Roosevelt in special trains crossed each other's trails in a whirlwind campaign for votes in tomorrow's primaries. There has been the hottest verbal duel ever seen in the Eastern states.

Meanwhile speakers for Champ Clark and Woodrow Wilson are fighting hard for votes.

It is admitted that the result is all-important to the Republican candidates, particularly Taft.

CONTINUES ATTACK.

By United Press:

Providence, R. I., April 29.—President Taft in speaking here continued his attack on Colonel Roosevelt.

He said that he was not in America when Roosevelt and his cabinet decided to protect the Harvester trust at Lynn.

Colonel Roosevelt said he would answer Taft's statement later in the day.

STATEMENT BY ROOSEVELT.

By United Press:

Havre Hill, Mass., April 29.—Col. Roosevelt issued a statement saying that he was certain that Taft was at the cabinet meeting when the Harvester case was considered, despite Taft's denial.

Roosevelt attempts to prove that Taft was there by statements from Bonaparte, Cortelyou and others. He asserts he talked over the entire matter with Taft and he approved the delay in the prosecution and even if Taft did not approve, Roosevelt says he has had over three years as president and has done nothing against the Harvester trust till now on the eve of the Massachusetts primaries.

UPHOLDS TARIFF BOARD.

By United Press:

Attelboro, Mass., April 29.—President Taft desisted in his attack on Colonel Roosevelt here and told the mill hands that he wanted the employers' liability laws. He also claimed that the Payne-Aldrich tariff had made prosperity for the mill towns. Taft's throat is in a bad condition.

TO BEGIN SUIT TO DISSOLVE TRUST

Action to Be Brought Against Harvester Company at St. Paul Tomorrow.

By United Press:

Washington, April 29.—The suit to dissolve the International Harvester company will be brought in the federal court at St. Paul tomorrow, according to the announcement of the department of justice today. This action was decided upon yesterday.

The Taft and Roosevelt speeches precipitated the action.

SAIL TO RESCUE OF AMERICAN REFUGEES

Torpedo Boat Destroyers Go to Mexican West Coast to Watch Japanese Fishermen.

By United Press:

San Diego, April 29.—The torpedo boat destroyers, Preble and Perry, are racing from here to the Mexican west coast, probably to Magdalena bay to watch the Japanese fishermen.

The transport Buford sailed from San Francisco during a storm to the rescue of the American refugees in Mexico.

CHAMP CLARK IS CHOICE IN COLORADO

Secures a Solid Delegation from the Western State to the Baltimore Convention.

Colorado Springs, Colo., April 29.—Champ Clark was nominated by the Democratic state convention here this afternoon, having six-sevenths of the delegates. A solid Clark delegation will be sent to the Baltimore convention.

FAMOUS AMERICAN INDIANS

BY ALBERT PAYSON TERHUNE

MOSES.

A huge chief, dressed like a frontier dandy, and bearing a startling resemblance to Henry Ward Beecher, was one of the foremost Indians of the great Northwest not many years ago. He kept the government guessing, worried the settlers and managed to win important favors from both. Some historians say he was a worthy and noble man. Others describe him as one of the cleverest, most consummate hypocrites unhung. He was one of the few Indians who understood "grafting" as thoroughly as does any ward politician and who was by nature a money maker as well as a warrior. Again, unlike most of his people, he was a humorist and a mimic.

A Warlike Career.

His Indian name was Sulktash-Kosha ("Half Sun"), but the white men nicknamed him "Moses," and the nickname stuck. He was war chief of the Oki-no-Ka-Ne tribe (a branch of the Nez Perces "nation") and was later chosen chief of many other wandering bands. In early years Moses led his braves through a series of bloody wars against the Sioux and won for himself local fame as a fearless soldier as well as for almost superhuman cunning. In 1858, when the wave of white emigration was rolling rapidly westward, Moses did his best to beat back the tide of civilization. With his savage forces he met a detachment of troops under Gen. George Wright in a fierce battle at the Yakima River. This was one of the deadliest combats ever waged between white men and savages.

It was after the Yakima River battle that Moses's whole character seemed to change. He saw clearly that the Indians could make no headway against the government; that the old free warlike days were at an end. Some native chiefs continued to wage hopeless campaigns against the troops and soon or late were killed, driven far from their homes or caught. Other chiefs meekly consented to lead their tribes to one of the reservations and there to lose power and freedom as "wards of the government."

Neither of these two courses appealed to Moses's taste. He set his wily brain to work at finding some pleasanter means of solving the Indian problem. And soon his plans were made. He declared himself the friend of the local Indian agent and asked only to be allowed to settle down with his people to a quiet life of hunting and farming. He let it be known that he and his tribes were more than ready to meet Uncle Sam half way on any reasonable proposition. His sense of humor and his powers as a comic actor helped to do away with suspicions that such a brain harbored plots of a serious nature.

It was hard to treat a man of this sort in the stern fashion accorded to "hostiles." Yet the government did not care to have the chief and his great following at large as a possible menace to settlers. So he was told to move with his people to the Yakima Reservation. Moses answered that he would be very glad indeed to go on a reservation, but that the one selected for him was already full of savage Indians who would not treat him well. So he begged to be allowed to settle upon a Columbia River tract that was of no use to white men but would make a fine home for his followers. There, he said, he and the braves would raise vegetables, grain, etc., and be model farmers.

This rural picture so delighted the government that his request was at last actually granted. Instead of being pacfied off to some already crowded reservation he was allowed to settle on the rich tract of Columbia River land. There he promptly made a more comfortable living by renting out the prairie pastures (on which he had told the authorities he wanted to raise crops) as grazing ground to cattlemen. By this means alone he yearly pocketed a rich sum. And there were other means of the same sort whereby he was able to make goodly quantities of money. Thus he spent his declining days, honored and trusted by the government.

A Clever Escape.

But before he succeeded in bending Uncle Sam so skillfully to his wishes, there were one or two times when Moses needed all his ready wit to save his life. For instance, when Chief Joseph of the Nez-Perces began his terrible war against the government, Moses (perhaps foreseeing the result of the conflict) loudly refused to let his people join their relatives, the Nez-Perces. Yet rumors soon arose that he and braves of his were waging secret war on white settlers. Moses indignantly denied this, and succeeded in convincing the agents that he was innocent. Then an entire white family named Perkins on the Columbia River were murdered and their house and barns burned. "Friendly" Indians accused Moses and his men. Again Moses denied the charge and even offered to help find the slayers. But public opinion was for once too strong for him. He was arrested, put in irons and imprisoned at Yakima City. Gen. Howard, Agent Wilbur and other officials who believed in Moses, were hastily summoned and had the old chief set free. Then, by a final diplomatic stroke, he secured the special reservation he had so long wanted, and retired to a life of ease and profit.

(Copyright.)

Two French Babies and a Swedish Boy Who Were Left Orphans by the Titanic Catastrophe.

Photos copyright, 1912, by American Press Association.

Among the Titanic survivors are two bright French children and a Swedish boy who were left orphans by the disaster. The parents of the French boys were among those who lost their lives. The older, Louis, is four years old, and the younger, Zolo, is three. Both have brown hair, brown eyes, rosy faces and perfect teeth. They cannot tell anything definite about themselves. They are being given a home by Miss Margaret Hayes of 304 West Eighty-third street, New York. The Swedish boy is Sven Svenson, fourteen years old. His father was lost in the wreck, and his mother died a year ago.

BASE BALL SCORES.

AMERICAN ASSOCIATION.

Minneapolis, 11; Indianapolis, 2.
Louisville, 5; St. Paul, 4.
Kansas City, 11; Columbus, 9.

Standing of the Clubs.

	Won	Lost	Pct
Columbus	12	4	.750
Minneapolis	9	5	.634
St. Paul	9	6	.600
Toledo	9	6	.600
Kansas City	7	8	.467
Louisville	5	8	.385
Milwaukee	5	9	.357
Indianapolis	2	12	.143

AMERICAN LEAGUE.

Chicago, 9; Detroit, 5.

Standing of the Clubs.

	Won	Lost	Pct.
Chicago	10	3	.750
Boston	8	3	.727
Philadelphia	6	5	.545
Washington	6	5	.545
Cleveland	6	6	.500
Detroit	5	9	.357
St. Louis	5	8	.385
New York	2	9	.182

NATIONAL LEAGUE.

Cincinnati, 3; Pittsburg, 2.
Chicago at St. Louis; rain.

Standing of the Clubs.

	Won	Lost	Pct.
Cincinnati	9	3	.750
New York	8	3	.727
Boston	6	6	.500
Chicago	5	6	.455
St. Louis	5	7	.417
Pittsburg	5	7	.417
Philadelphia	4	6	.400
Brooklyn	3	7	.300

THE MARKETS.

Twin City Markets.

Minneapolis, April 29.—Wheat, May, \$1.14¼; July, \$1.15¾; No. 1 northern, No. 1 durum, \$1.09½; No. 1 \$1.16¾; No. 2 northern, \$1.14¾; corn, 80c; No. 3 white oats, 55½c; barley, malting, \$1.30; No. 2 rye, 90c; No. 1 flax, \$2.15.

Duluth, April 29.—Wheat, May, \$1.16; July, \$1.16⅛; No. 1 northern, \$1.17; No. 1 durum, \$1.12½.

South St. Paul, April 29.—Cattle—Steers, \$6.35@7.50; cows, \$4@6.25; calves, \$4@6.75; hogs, \$7.50@7.70.

CHICAGO LIVE STOCK.

Chicago, April 29.—Cattle—Receipts 200; market steady; beeves, \$5.70@8.90; Texas steers, \$5.25@7.25; western steers, \$5.65@7.65; stockers and feeders, \$4.30@6.80; cows and heifers, \$2.70@7.50; calves, \$5@8. Hogs—Receipts, 9,000; market dull at Friday's average; light, \$7.50@7.90; mixed, \$7.55@8.05; heavy, \$7.55@8.05; rough, \$7.55@7.75; pigs, \$4.90@7.15; bulk of sales, \$7.80@8. Sheep—Receipts, 1,000; market slow at Friday's close; native, \$4.75@7.25; western, \$5@7.50; yearlings, \$6.25@8; lambs, native, \$6@9; western, \$6.25@9.60.

CHICAGO GRAIN MARKET.

Chicago, April 29.—Probable showers tonight or Sunday throughout Kansas and Nebraska checked the buying fever today in wheat. The fact, however, that the weather map showed no rain had fallen in either state during the last twenty-four hours caused a display of strength at the outset. Besides there were continued damage reports from Kansas, indicating that no surplus yield might be expected to come from that commonwealth as an offset to the losses in territory further east. On the other hand the English markets were not following the advance here except to a small extent and seemed to be giving more attention to statements that the Dardanelles would be opened Monday. The opening here was ¼@⅜c lower to ⅜@½c up. July started at \$1.12⅜@1.13, varying from ¼@⅜c lower to ¼@⅜c advance and declined to \$1.12¼.

Steadiness to a degree unusual of late developed in the corn trade. There was not much demand but neither was there much pressure to sell. July opened ⅛c off to a shade up at 77½c to 77⅝@77¾c and appeared inclined to keep within those limits.

Lost anything? Advertise it.

MONUMENT FOR TITANIC MEN

MOVEMENT STARTED BY PRESIDENT'S WIFE.

Hopes Smallness of Amount Solicited Will Enable Others to Contribute.

Washington, April 29.—Mrs. Taft has made the first contribution to the fund being raised among the women of the United States to be used in erecting a monument to the men on the Titanic who gave their lives that women passengers might be saved. Mrs. Taft enclosed the contribution in a letter as follows:

"It gives me pleasure to start the women's Titanic memorial fund by giving the first dollar. I am glad to do this in gratitude to the chivalry of American manhood, and I am sure that every woman will feel that the smallness of the contribution solicited will enable her to do the same.

"Helen H. Taft."

It is expected that a very large sum will be raised, and that the dedication may be held within a year. The tribute will probably be in the form of a memorial arch, giving to the national capital the one thing of beauty which it now lacks.

Tens of thousands of letters will be sent to women members of women's clubs, fraternal orders, labor unions, literary and social organizations. There are approximately 28,000 women's clubs in the United States, and every one of these will be reached.

No contributions will be accepted from men. The memorial will be the result of contributions from women only.

Mormons Bar Swedish.

Grand Junction, Col., April 29.—To offset the edict issued in Sweden last year barring all Mormons, the Mormon board of school directors at Gateway has issued an order to exclude all Swedish children from the Gateway schools.

Had Too Much Gin.

Wilkesbarre, Pa., April 29.—Joseph Gourkas is dead at Daryea, as a result of his attempt to win a \$25 wager by drinking twenty-five glasses of gin. He dropped dead as the sixteenth glass was being poured out.

You will look a good while before you find a better medicine for coughs and colds than Chamberlain's Cough Remedy. Try it when you have a cough or cold, and you are certain to be pleased with the prompt cure which it will effect. For sale by all dealers.

Minneapolis Unitarian Church Burns.

Minneapolis, April 29.—Seven firemen were injured, two of them seriously, and the lives of a score of others endangered in a fire that badly wrecked the First Unitarian church, causing an estimated loss of about \$20,000. The accident to the firemen happened after the fire was practically extinguished, when part of the roof collapsed, tearing through the balcony floor and carrying the fire fighters to the balcony below, where they were covered with timbers, slate and debris.

Mayor Robert Dollar Passes.

Santa Monica, Cal., April 29.—Major Robert Dollar, 70 years old, prominent in Grand Army circles, died here. He at one time was attorney general of Dakota territory.

Norwegian Ship Helpless.

San Francisco, April 29.—The government wireless station on Yerba Bueno island picked up a message from the Norwegian steamer Admiralen that she had dropped her rudder 25 miles north of Humboldt and was unmanageable. The Admiralen is bound for Alaska from Sandefjrd, Norway, her port of registry. The Admiralen is a small iron vessel, built in 1869, and registering 1,517 tons gross. The steamer J. H. Chancellor, bound from this port for Eureka, started to her assistance.

GIRL SUED BY CARUSO.

Italian Tenor Wants \$12,000 Damages for Defamation of Character.

Milan, April 29.—Counsel for Signorina Canelli, the young woman who lost her suit against Enrico Caruso, the operatic tenor, has taken an appeal from that judgment. Counsel for Caruso has now entered a counter claim for \$12,000, which, it is claimed, the singer spent for the young woman's trousseau and also moral damages for defamation of character.

Midnight in the Ozarks

and yet sleepless, Hiram Scranton of Clay City, Ill., coughed and coughed. He was in the mountains on the advice of five doctors, who said he had consumption, but found no help in the climate, and started home. Hearing of Dr. King's New Discovery, he began to use it. "I believe it saved my life," he writes, "for it made a new man of me, so that I can now do good work again." For all lung diseases, coughs, colds, la grippe, asthma, croup, whooping cough, hay fever, hemorrhages, hoarseness or quinsy, it's the best known remedy. Price 50c. and \$1. Trial bottle free. Guaranteed by Sylvander's drug store.

Read the wants.

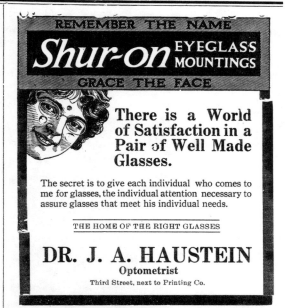

Red Wing Daily Republican.

VOLUME XXVII. NO. 171. RED WING, MINNESOTA, TUESDAY EVENING, APRIL 30, 1912. PRICE TWO CENTS.

SHIP ARRIVES IN PORT WITH DEAD

CABLESHIP MACKAY - BENNETT LANDS WITH 190 TITANIC VICTIMS ON BOARD.

MANY BURIED AT SEA

Because of Impossible Identification 116 Other Bodies Were Buried in the Ocean — Church Bells Toll While Flags Were Hung at Half Staff—Bodies Cared For.

By United Press:

Halifax, April 30.—The cableship Mackey-Bennett docked here at 9:40 o'clock this morning, while church bells tolled and flags were hung at half staff. The people hushed their voices and were kept back by soldiers from the dock.

One hundred coffins had been piled on docks while thirty undertakers were on hand ready to care for the dead. Rows of dead were laid out, some in canvas, while others were laid naked on the deck of the ship.

The officers of the ship said that 116 bodies had been picked up but were buried at sea because identification was impossible. On the ship there were 190 bodies, two of which were women.

As soon as the steamer had docked two rows of sailors were stretched from the ship to the shore and the bodies were passed along this row at the rate of one a minute to the undertakers who placed them in coffins and had them carried to the morgue in ambulances.

CAPTAIN MAKES STATEMENT.

By United Press:

Halifax, April 30.—Captain Ladner of the Mackay-Bennett gave out a statement of the cruise. He said it became necessary to bury many bodies at sea because they had been badly mutilated by the ice and he had embalming fluid on deck for only 70 and it was impossible to keep the rest.

IDENTIFIES ASTOR'S BODY.

By United Press:

Halifax, April 30.—The body of John Jacob Astor has been identified by the captain of his yacht. A body which is thought to be Widener, the Philadelphia millionaire, was buried at sea.

Many bodies on deck had been frozen in the ice for days, and were greatly discolored by the salt water and cannot be identified as many faces are distorted. The ship captains think that few more bodies will be recovered as a storm has driven them eastward into the Gulf stream.

SAYS OFFICIALS KNEW OF DISASTER MONDAY

Witness in the Titanic Investigation States That Officers of Company Were Informed of Wreck.

By United Press:

Washington, April 30.—F. B. Dunn of Beechhurst, Long Island, told Senator Smith's Titanic investigators today that a mysterious stranger whose father is a Western Union operator in New York told him of the Titanic disaster which was known by the White Star officials on receipt of a telegram at eight o'clock Monday morning.

This statement is denied by Vice President Franklin and Senator Smith is demanding an investigation by the Western Union officials.

Fourth Officer Boxhall of the Titanic said that J. W. Andrews ,one of the builders of the ship, told Captain Smith that the vessel would sink in an hour after she struck the iceberg. J. Bruce Ismay to be examined again this afternoon.

DESTRUCTION OF TRUST IS ASKED

Petition Was Filed by the Government in the Federal Court This Morning.

By United Press:

St. Paul, Minn., April 30.—The destruction of the International Harvester trust and its seven subsidiaries is asked for by the government in a petition which was filed in the federal court this morning.

Eighteen directors are named as individual defendants. The petition says that the concern violates both the criminal and civil provisions in the Sherman anti-trust law.

Interesting Pictures of Former Days

Few Red Wing people would recognize this picture although the woman and the child have lived here later in life. The woman is Mrs. L. Hazlett, formerly of this city and now residing at Rochester. The child is her son, H. M. Hazlett, engineer on the Chicago Great Western.

TEN KILLED AND SCORE INJURED BY TORNADO

STORM SWEEPS SECTION OF LOUISIANA DOING MUCH DAMAGE—BUILDINGS WRECKED.

By United Press:

Gilbert, La., April 30.—Ten persons are reported killed and a score injured by a tornado which swept three parishes in Louisiana this morning. A score of buildings were wrecked.

MAKE COLLECTION OF OLD WEAPONS

Arms of Philippine Tribes and From the Spanish Islands to Be Installed in Academy.

Washington, April 30.—A collection of weapons of the Philippine tribes is to be made and installed at the West Point Military academy. Old weapons of the Spaniards of the islands will also be included.

General Barry, superintendent of the West Point academy, has asked congress to appropriate $750 to buy certain styles of weapons, which have become scarce in the islands and owned only by private collectors.

The directors of the Philippine constabulary will superintend the collection of the Filipino weapons, which, it is planned, will represent the military history and evolution of even the most savage tribes.

REV. KNICKERBOCKER WILL GIVE ADDRESS

Closing Meeting of Series at the Y. W. C. A. to Be Held This Evening.

This evening at 8:15 o'clock the last in the series of membership talks which have been given this winter by different professional and business men of the city will be held at the Y. W. C. A. rooms. Rev. A. E. Knickerbocker will give an address on "The Art of Finding Contentment."

The Bible class will convene at 7:15.

There will be no meeting of the millinery class this evening as Mrs. Dryden has been called away from the city.

CHRISTEN SPEED CRAFT THE "U. C. T."

Edwin Anderson Will Name His Fast Boat for the United Commercial Travelers.

Edwin Anderson's new speed boat, which will be equipped with 86 horsepower engines, will be called the "U. C. T.," and the United Commercial Travelers in convention here in June will have an opportunity of taking a trip on the Mississippi in the fastest boat on the upper river if the boat comes up to the expectations of the owner.

The boat, designed by Mr. Anderson, is a twenty-footer and he believes that she will maintain a speed of about thirty miles an hour. The owner says he knows of no more suitable name for the craft than the "U. C. T."

SENDS CHEER TO 'UNCLE DAVE'

A. L. LARPENTEUR, ST. PAUL'S OLDEST SETTLER, WRITES INTERESTING LETTER.

TELLS OF EARLY DAYS

Came to St. Paul, Passing Up Mississippi by Red Wing in 1843—Has Lived in Capital City Ever Since—Early Scenes in Which He Took Part—Congratulates Hancock.

A. L. Larpenteur, the venerable Minnesota pioneer, who came up the Mississippi river in 1843 and located at St. Paul, writes the following exceedingly interesting personal letter to The Republican in reference to the Hancock centennial and the early history of Minnesota.

The letter is in his own handwriting and while he is nearly ninety years of age, it is written in a very clear legible manner and would do credit to a much younger man both in its legibility and contents.

The letter follows:

"Some kind friend has been thoughtful enough to send me a copy of your valued paper giving me an account of the centennial anniversary of the veteran David Hancock of your city and the celebration that was held in his honor by the people of Red Wing.

"Please convey to them my most grateful thanks. Had I known of it I should have been present on that occasion as I have often wished to visit your city, where in days gone by I had many friends. Most of them, alas! have paid the debt to our mortality.

"On the sixteenth of May, I shall have reached my ninetieth milestone and nearly seventy years of that time has been spent right here in St. Paul.

Passed Red Wing in 1843.

"Passing your port on the little steamer, Otter, in 1843, I soon arrived at St. Paul Landing. In 1846 Wisconsin sent this territory adrift and in 1847 a few of us early settlers laid out the town. We left off the 'landing' and called it St. Paul.

"In 1848 the United States government had completed its surveys and established a land office at the Fals of St. Croix, Wisconsin. At that time Gen. Sibley and I went to the land office and entered our lands. The quarter section which I entered was the land upon which our present beautiful state capitol is located and for which I paid one dollar and twenty-five cents an acre. I made a little money on the transaction. I held the land some five years and then sold sixty acres of it to Phillip Beaupre for two dollars and fifty cents an acre. In this I doubled my money and thought I was doing well.

"On August 26, 1848, on our return from the land sale at St. Croix Falls sixty-one of us met in Stillwater and held a convention. We signed a petition and forwarded it to the acting governor of Wisconsin asking him for permission to have an election for the purpose of choosing a delegate to congress in order to begin proceedings for the organization of the new territory of Minnesota. The request was granted and Gen. H. H. Sibley was the first congressional delegate chosen. Of the 61 members of that convention at Stillwater I am the only one now living.

Congratulates "Uncle Dave."

"Now 'Uncle Dave,' stay with us as long as you can! I am 'wid you.' You have been a good boy. So have I tried to be. The good Lord has work yet for us to do.

"Minnesota! Thou art dear to me. I knew you when you were in your swaddling clothes. I helped to nurse you into greatness! I knew you when you did not have one dollar's worth of taxable property. I have lived to see you have more money in your school fund than Thomas Jefferson paid Napoleon Bonaparte for the Louisiana purchase. You have done well for a country that was thought of at first as only fit for the Indians and the buffalos!"

Mr. Larpenteur signs his name to this valuable historical letter as secretary of the Minnesota Old Settlers' association.

An Anxious Query.

A certain New York restaurant has become famous for its high prices. At the entrance a man just leaving, having paid his bill, was recently overheard to ask the waiter, "I say, do you charge anything for going out?"

TOBACCO IN MINNESOTA.

TOBACCO FIELD AT WABASHA.

It has been demonstrated that tobacco can be raised successfully in this section. Over in Pierce county, Wisconsin, some farmers have raised quite a little of the weed. This illustration shows a tobacco field at Wabasha. Why don't Goodhue county farmers also try the experiment? Tobacco is usually a very profitable crop.

WAGE CAMPAIGN FOR FINANCES

Y. W. C. A. DIRECTORS DISCUSS PLANS AND ELECT OFFICERS FOR THE YEAR.

OUT TO RAISE MONEY

Confident of Success — Turn to Business Men for Help in Carrying on Their Work—All the Old Officers Re-elected—Prospects Bright For Next Year.

The Young Women's Christian association of this city will carry on a campaign among the business men and friends of the work, beginning tomorrow, and continuing the next few days, to raise sufficient funds with which to carry on the association work during the coming year.

At the first meeting of the association year, held last Saturday afternoon, the board of directors unanimously re-elected Mrs. C. E. Sheldon as president for the ensuing year; Mrs. O. O. Stageberg, first vice president; Mrs. G. E. Gates, second vice president; Gena Lundquist, treasurer; Miss Anna Fridell, recording secretary.

The directors planned a finance campaign to be instituted on May 1. They hope and expect to raise sufficient funds to carry on the work for an entire year.

During the last year they raised the money which was needed for the expenses of conducting the work as they went along and it was not altogether satisfactory. It is true that the responses were generous and the association made a fine showing at the end of the year. Every debt was paid and there was money in the credit of the society in the bank. But on general principles it was a sort of a hand-to-mouth way of doing things that does not give the best results. It puts altogether too much constant stress on the money side of the proposition and detracts from the larger and more important work that is to be done in many different directions.

For this reason the association is going out this next week, beginning tomorrow, to appeal to the business men and citizens for a sufficient support to put the work on its feet securely and comfortably at the very outset of the new working year. It is the systematic and business-like way of doing things. Heretofore only a few business men have been asked to help. They responded promptly and well. Now the ladies are going to give all the merchants and other business men the privilege of helping in this work. It is a privilege and no doubt it will be considered as such. The work is one of prevention and protection in behalf of the sisters, and daughters of the men who will be asked to contribute. It is wholly undenominational in its character but grandly and devotedly inter-denominational. It asks and receives the endorsement and encouragement of many churches and its influence is reciprocal upon these institutions. If it seeks their help it stimulates and incites in return a deeper and more earnest interest in the church itself.

From every point of view, socially, intellectually, morally and spiritually, it uplifts and broadens the life of each member.

It has a place, distinct and useful in the community and is an asset that brightens, dignifies and ennobles and makes Red Wing a better and more desirable city in which to live.

The ladies will hold another meeting this afternoon and the directors will go out tomorrow among the business men seeking substantial financial aid. They have already proved and established the value of their association work and they are confident that there will be a prompt and liberal response.

BULLETINS

SHIP STRIKES TORPEDO.

By United Press:

London, April 30.—It is reported from Constantinople that the American ship, Texas, was struck by a torpedo at the entrance of the Gulf of Smyrna and demolished. Her crew of fifty went down with the ship.

The boat is reported to be a steamer owned by the Texas Oil company.

TEXAS NOT AMERICAN BOAT.

By United Press:

London, April 30.—The Texas, the small steamer of the Archipelago American Co., was not owned by Americans and it is now reported that seventy-seven men are missing out of a crew of 140.

MISS FALCK TO WED FOREST FIRE HERO

Joseph P. Halm, Deputy Supervisor of National Forest to Be Married at Cannon Falls May 4.

Joseph P. Halm, deputy supervisor of the Coeur d'Alene National forest, who figured prominently in the news of two continents in August, 1910, when he and his band of 85 volunteers were given up as lost in the forest fires of Northern Idaho which cost several hundred lives and destroyed millions of dollars' worth of property, is to be married to Miss Grace Falck of Cannon Falls on May 4. The ceremony will be performed at the home of the bride's parents.

The marriage will be the culmination of a romance begun four years ago when Miss Falck and Mr. Halm were students at Washington state college, Pullman. Halm was the greatest all-round athlete of his time in the inter-mountain and Pacific coast country, being the brightest star of the baseball, football and track teams at the college.

Soon after being graduated from the college he entered the United States forestry service and was stationed in the Coeur d'Alene forest, where he was mentioned for bravery in leading 85 men to safety near Missoula, Montana, when every avenue of escape appeared to be cut off by fire.

Miss Grace Falck is the daughter of Mr. and Mrs. O. Falck, prominent residents of Cannon Falls. She is well known in Red Wing, where she has visited friends frequently. Invitations have been received by a number of Red Wing friends to attend the wedding.

PRINTS $6,000,000 IN WAR NOTES

By United Press:

Geneva, April 30.—Anticipating the possibility of war breaking out in Europe, the Swiss National bank has just finished printing $6,000,000 worth of twenty franc "war" notes. This action was taken in accordance with a federal law which permits such an emergency circulation "in extraordinary circumstances," and upon the report of one of the bank's directors, who recently made a careful investigation of the relations existing among the Great Powers. The notes are now stored in the cellars of the bank's headquarters at Zurich, and will not be issued unless war is actually declared. The lowest bank-note at present is fifty francs.

CONFIDENT OF WINNING MASS.

TAFT AND ROOSEVELT FORCES SURE OF THE MASSACHUSETTS PRIMARIES.

IS IN ANANIAS CLUB

Colonel Says President Is Telling Untruth When He Says That He Was Not at the Cabinet Meeting When the Harvester Trust Case Was Discussed.

By United Press:

Boston, Mass., April 30.—Chilling rain falling, both Taft and Roosevelt men are confident of a victory but all politicians admit that the situation is quite unique and hard to guess the result.

ATTACKS TAFT.

By United Press:

New York, April 30.—Colonel Theodore Roosevelt issued a formal statement attacking President Taft in connection with the International Harvester trust matter to the effect that the president is not telling the truth when he said he was not present at the cabinet meeting which discussed the side-tracking of the prosecution of the Harvester trust.

RE-ELECT HANISCH CEMETERY SUPT.

Annual Meeting of Cemetery Board Held Last Evening—Chas. Beckman Chosen President.

Herman Hanisch was re-elected superintendent of city cemeteries at a salary of $1,100 per year at the annual meeting of the cemetery board held at the city hall last evening.

The officers of the board elected are: Chas. Beckman, president, and C. A. Betcher, vice president.

Superintendent Hanisch reported that the ornamental fence at Oakwood is nearing completion and that the hedge along the northeast line of Block N would be set in by the first of the coming week. Bills to the amount of $2.55 were allowed when adjournment was taken.

Louis Hallenberger, C. F. Hjermstad, Chas. A. Betcher and Andrew Lindgren of the board were present.

INSURGENT WOODMEN START INJUNCTION

Will Try to Restrain Head Camp from Putting Into Force the Advanced Rates.

By United Press:

Des Moines, Ia., April 30.—The law committee of the Insurgent Woodmen of America started an injunction suit in the state courts here to restrain the head camp from putting into force the advance in rates. A similar action will be brought in Illinois.

GREAT BATTLE IS EXPECTED HOURLY

General Orozco and His Rebels Are Preparing for a Clash with the Federals.

By United Press:

El Paso, Texas, April 30.—General Orozco's rebels and the federals are expected to fight a decisive battle near Torreon today or tomorrow, and aeroplanes are to be used on both sides.

ENTERTAINMENT OF HIGH ORDER

Miss Evelyn Grindeland Pleases Many at Lutheran Ladies' Seminary.

Miss Evelyn Grindeland's recital at the Lutheran Ladies' seminary last evening proved a success. Her selection of musical numbers gave ample opportunity to display her fine powers of interpretation, from the soft, gentle lays of "Elsa's Dream and Lohengrin's Reproof," by Wagner-Liszt, to the brilliant technique exhibited in Grieg's "Aus dem Carneval."

The vocal numbers by Miss Anette Berkstrand won a generous applause. She has a rich mezzo voice, and further numbers from her in the future will be anxiously awaited by those who heard her last evening.

Miss Ella Christiansen in her reading, "Renting a Baby," did exceptionally well.

The Stock Market

Closing quotations for April 29, 1912, furnished by F. S. Moseley & Co., 50 Congress street, Boston:

	Bid	Asked
First Nat'l Bank	102	108
Merchants Nat'l Bank	32⅛	35
Ocean Nat'l Bank...	65	68
Newb'yp't Gas & E...		195
Boston & Maine RR..	100	100½
N. Y., N. H. & H. RR.	137½	138
Amalgamated	84	84⅛
Am. Tel. & Tel. Co...	146⅝	146⅞
Am. Woolen pfd....	90½	91
N. E. Tel. & Tel. Co. .	—	155
Mass. Electric com...	20	21
Mass. Electric pfd. .	81	81½
Mass. Gas pfd.......	97	—
Mergenthaler Lino. . .	218¾	220
New York Central . .	119⅞	120⅛
Pennsylvania RR....	125¼	125⅜
United Fruit	187⅞	189
United Shoe com....	51	51½
United Shoe pfd.....	29	29½
U. S. Steel com......	71¾	72
U. S. Steel pfd......	113	113¼

Do not fail to vote at the Presidential primaries today. Polls open in Newburyport from 6 a. m. to 3 p. m.

GREAT SINGER'S GENEROSITY

Among the stories told by Arthur Pougin of Malibran, the great singer, is one of her stay in Venice. She was to give six performances at one theater there, when Gallo, the director of the Teatro Emeronito, being on the eve of bankruptcy, begged her to give two at his theater, promising her £120 for each. She consented, but when Gallo went to take her the second payment, he entered saying: "Here is the sum we agreed on." "What sum?" she replied with an air of surprise. "Oh, the £120 for yesterday's performance." "I don't want your money. Take it all away and spend it on your children. You shall kiss me and we'll be quits." Did the good fellow believe his ears? His two performances had brought him in £400 in round figures, had saved him from bankruptcy, and to crown his joy, he kissed Mme. Malibran. This magnanimity to a poor Venetian was received publicly by a frantic ovation, and crystalized in verse, while the theater was renamed Malibran.

Do not fail to vote at the Presidential primaries today. Polls open in Newburyport from 6 a. m. to 3 p. m.

PROGRAM FOR "TWELFTH NIGHT" ARRANGED FOR NEXT THURSDAY NIGHT

The programs for the "Twelfth Night" have arrived and the Parent-Teachers' association feel sure that those who have planned to attend will be more than satisfied. The entertainment is to be given at City hall, Thursday evening, May 2nd.

The New Haven Evening Register says of Mrs. Rice:

"Mrs. Elizabeth Pooler Rice, who is a great favorite in the literary circles of Boston as a Shakespearean scholar and a reciter of the plays of Shakespeare, gave in the Yale University Extension Course last evening at College Street hall a, recital of "Twelfth Night." The play, as all William Shakespeare's famous play of lovers of Shakespeare know, is a genuine comedy and Mrs. Rice left upon that large audience present a vivid impression of its beauties and its charms."

The program will be as follows:

Overture, "Lustspiel" (Keler Bela) .... The Trio
Mandolin solo, "Blue Bells of Scotland" Air Varie (Farmer).... .... Eleanore Soule Hayden
Art I "Twelfth Night" (Shakespeare) .....Elizabeth Pooler-Rice
Operatic selections:
With chimes and xylophone
(a) Sextet from Lucia di Lammermoor (Donizette)
(b) "Miserere" (Il Trovatore).. (Verdi)
(c) "Anvil Chorus" (Il Trovatore) (Verdi)
.... The Trio
Violin solo, "Nordische Sage" (Bohm)....Edwin Byron Powell
Act 2, "Twelfth Night" ....Elizabeth Pooler-Rice
Chimes solo, "Sweet Afton" ......
Act 3, "Twelfth Night"........ ....Elizabeth Pooler-Rice
Xylophone solo, "The Mocking Bird" (Stobbe) .... Eleanore Soule Hayden
Act 4, "Twelfth Night" ....Elizabeth Pooler-Rice
Selections, with chimes:
(a) Barcarolle ......(Offenbach)
(b) "Chapel in the Mountains" (Wilson) .... The Trio
Finale, "Cavalry March," with xylophone (Spindler)....The Trio

Do not fail to vote at the Presidential primaries today. Polls open in Newburyport from 6 a. m. to 3 p. m.

WEST NEWBURY

Lucy Moseley, one of whose legs was broken by bumping into an apple tree while sliding on her sled in February, is now able to walk almost as readily as ever, although her leg is still somewhat stiffened, the fracture being near the ankle.

At a recent meeting of the Merrimack Cemetery association, Frederick W. Stickney was chosen to membership in the board of trustees, to fill the vacancy caused by the death of William H. Loring; Robert L. Smith was chosen to fill the vacancy caused by the retirement of James A. Chase; Romulus Jaques was chosen to fill the vacancy caused by the retirement of Francis D. Chase. This makes the board of trustees consist of G. D. Whittier, C. D. Ordway, A. P. Chase, S. W. Giddings, F. W. Stickney, R. Jaques and R. L. Smith. At a meeting of the board of trustees Cyrus D. Ordway was chosen president and treasurer; George D. Whittier, superintendent and custodian of funded lots; D. E. N. Carleton, secretary. It was voted to burn over the grass in the cemetery next Saturday.

Do not fail to vote at the Presidential primaries today. Polls open in Newburyport from 6 a. m. to 3 p. m.

OSLER'S CURE FOR GOUT

Since his proposition the man should be chloroformed at sixty, Dr. William Osler has been regarded more or less as a grim monster by many people, says "One Who Knows Him." In reality Dr. Osler is a mild-mannered man, with a fund of genuine humor, as witness the following cure for gout which he once recommended to a friend:

"First, pick a handkerchief from the pocket of a spinster who never wished to wed; second, wash the handkerchief in an honest miller's pond; third, dry it on the hedge of a person who has never been covetous; fourth, send it to the shop of a physician who never killed a patient; fifth, mark it with a lawyer's ink who never cheated a client; and, sixth, apply it, hot, to the gout-tormented part. A speedy cure must follow."

Do not fail to vote at the Presidential primaries today. Polls open in Newburyport from 6 a. m. to 3 p. m.

WORK WITH BOY SCOUTS BEST YEAR OF HIS LIFE

R. A. Garrison, scout commissioner of the Boy Scouts of America in Dowagiac, Michigan, has worked with boy scouts for a year. He is so pleased with the development of the boys in that time under the stimulus of scout activities that he feels the year has been the most successful in his life. Writing to James E. West, Chief Scout Executive of the Boy Scouts of America, he says, "It does me good to see the cases where moral difficulty has been controlled by the efforts of the organization. Makes one feel that you are really living to believe that you have been of service to the fellows. On the whole I believe that the past year has been my best year, the best year I ever lived—but I want to have a better one. Colonel Roosevelt stopped five minutes in our town yesterday—he greeted the fellows in such a way as made them all very happy indeed."

Cable Steamship Mackay-Bennett and Her Crew, Which Picked Up Many Bodies of Titanic Victims.

The cable steamship Mackay-Bennett picked up a number of bodies of victims near the scene of the sinking of the Titanic. Those of the bodies which it was believed could be identified were brought to shore. The others, without marks of identification, were buried at sea. Many wore life preservers and apparently died after terrible sufferings in the cold sea. The arrow indicates Captain F. H. Lardner of the Mackay-Bennett.

MAY FESTIVAL TO BE GIVEN IN AID OF SUSAN BABSON SWASEY HOME

The Maypole dance will be one of the main features at the May festival to be given this week in aid of the Susan Babson Swasey Home. The dance will be under the supervision of Mrs. L. M. Brown, assisted by Mrs. Fred E. Smith and Mrs. Jerome Hardy.

The young people who are to take part are:

Elizabeth Pearson, Abigail Thompson, Vora Conant, Catherine Pearson, Elizabeth Hopkinson, Elizabeth Little,, Dorothy Andrews, Olga Froelich, Pauline Froelich, Ruth Hoyt, Mildred Pinkham, Paul Lunt, Philip Pearson, Arthur Berry, Steven Berry, Milton Thompson, Charles Huntington, Russell Holt, Craig Fisher, Frederick Toppan, Milton Conant, Malcolm Ayers.

Other features have been arranged for that will lend to the attractiveness of the festival: "Rebekah at the Well" will be in charge of Miss Emma Bell, with Jean Pearson and Jessie Foley as attendants, assisted by Mrs. William Moulton and Miss Eva Smith.

In the flower dance the following misses will take part:

Charlotte Osgood, Katherine Cole, Nancy Little, Dorothy Brown, Elizabeth Littlefield, Blanche Luddington, Marion Coffin, Marion Stickney, Eleanor Stickney, Inez Dame, Helen Toppan, Mildred Noyes.

The tea room committee is Mrs. Charles F. A. Walcott, chairman, Mrs. Arthur W. Moody. Miss Caroline Balch will pour and the assistants are Katherine Cole, Helen Toppan, Blanche Luddington, Marion Coffin, Mildred Noyes, Nancy Little.

The ice cream will be presided over by Miss McKenzie, chairman; Mrs. George P. Tilton, Mrs. Samuel March, Mrs. Life Griffin.

HERALDINGS

The organ which was used in the Prospect street church has been purchased by the Peoples Methodist Society and will be installed in a few days.

Albert E. Read, organist at the Central church has resigned his position.

A number of local boys have joined the Parker River Motorcycle Club.

John Donlan of Lynn is visiting his parents on Federal street for a few days.

Mr. and Mrs. Thomas O'Brien of East Boston have taken up their residence in this city on Collins street.

Collections will be taken up in the churches of this city for the Anna Jaques Hospital next Sunday. These collections are taken up every year.

The gymnasium class of Miss Mabel Rogers will give a private dancing party in Griffin hall next Saturday evening. Invitations have been issued for the event.

Mrs. R. Jacoby of Orange street has returned home after spending the past month with relatives in New York.

Beatrice Perry who attends at Quincy Mansion spent the week end with her parents in this city.

Herbert Noyes has purchased a new White gasoline auto.

Warren Frost demonstrator for the Rambler Automobile Co .is spending a few days with his parents in this city.

The High School baseball team will play their old rivals, Salem High, next Saturday afternoon.

Do not fail to vote at the Presidential primaries today. Polls open in Newburyport from 6 a. m. to 3 p. m.

ELECTRIC SPARKS

Now it remains for the Senate to tell Lorimer to take his hat and go, as Illinois, his own state has so spoken.

Of New York's "big four," Elihu Root is a good 3.99.

A CURIOUS PUNISHMENT

The Dutch settlers in the early days of what is now New York city administered a curious punishment to disorderly persons. In the records of the coloney there appears the following item:

"Oct. 14, 1638, for drawing his knife upon a person, Guysbert van Regerslard is sentenced to throw himself three times from the sailyard of the yacht Hope and to receive from each sailor three lashes at the ringing of the bell."

Those Dutchmen were believers in the efficacy of cold water and counter irritation to cool the angry passions. The bell was rung every morning and evening to call persons to and from their labors and at 9 o'clock at night to announce the hour for going to bed. Guysbert, therefore,, received not only three duckings, but also three lashings, and doutbless ever after that kept his knife in its sheath when his temper was bad. The bellringer was a notable man. He was the court messenger, the grave digger, the chorister, and sometimes the schoolmaster. When the minister was absent he read a sermon to the congregation.—Harper's.

Do not fail to vote at the Presidential primaries today. Polls open in Newburyport from 6 a. m. to 3 p. m.

MAN AND THE MAMMOTH

The skeleton of a mammoth discovered in the department of Pas de Calais, France, measures 49½ feet in length. The head is well preserved, with finely enameled molars of the true Siberian type, thus furnishing one more proof that the whole country was once a land of ice and snow. At a dinner given recently on a sandbar in the Danube an attempt was made to convey an idea of the food consumed by man in the time of the mammoth. Cabbage soup cooked over hot stones, horse ham, roast pork with boiled millet, and turnips cooked in hot ashes composed the bill of fare. The dessert was dried pears and honey.—Harper's Weekly.

J. Bruce Ismay and P. A. S. Franklin, White Star Officials, Witnesses at Senate Titanic Inquiry.

Copyright, 1912, by American Press Association.

This photograph of J. Bruce Ismay, managing director of the White Star line; Philip A. S. Franklin, vice president of the line, other officials of the company and private detectives who are guarding Mr. Ismay was taken as the party was descending the steps of the senate office building at Washington, where they had attended a session of the senate Titanic committee. The cross indicates Mr. Ismay, the arrow Mr. Franklin.

DANGER FROM FOREST FIRES.

It is important at this season to call the attention of land owners to the danger from forest fires. Most of our large fires have occurred between the time when the snow goes off and the green growth gets well started. Winds are often high and unless rains are frequent the ground dries out quickly.

Many people take this season of the year to burn brush and rubbish. About 20 per cent. of the fires last spring were due to this cause. It should be remembered that no person is permitted to burn brush in or near woodland without the permission of the town forest fire warden.

It is extremely dangerous to leave slash and cut brushes along the railroad lines. Every year the railroads clear their right of way of inflammable material, but to insure safety a wider strip should be cleaned. If at this time land owners would co-operate with the railroad companies in clearing brush where cuttings have been made along the tracks, a great many fires would be prevented.

In nearly every town there are some heavy slashings along the most frequented roads awaiting the lighted match or cigar from a passing vehicle. Town selectmen and timberland owners would do well to clear the brush for a few feet along the roads where timber cutting has left an inflammable slash.

A little forethought and attention to such matters would lessen the fire danger materially and reduce the expense which the towns and the state bear in fighting forest fires.

HOOKED PERFECT

A few nights ago an old family friend was calling at the apartment of Gen. George Pennington Borden, U. S. A., retired. The general and his friends were conversing on military tactics when Mrs. Borden entered the room and with the brief explanation, after greeting the guest, "Maids busy," indicated to the majestic warrior that he was to fasten those two buttons at the back of her blouse which defy the most agile feminine contortions. Meekly the veteran arose, murmuring, "How are the mighty fallen! What rights are left to men when a brigadier general of the United States army must button a blouse in the back? How can I pose as a military tactician when I can be driven into a corner by a simple wave of a feminine hand?"

Despite his wail, the struggle was soon over, and the gallant soldier was rewarded with the information: "You did that very well."

"Thank you, my dear," said the general mournfully. "I am glad to have my humble talents recognized."

THE "SPANISH PRISONER."

At Last Seems to Have Struck Retribution—Famous Swindlers in Hands of Police

In spite of repeated warnings issued by the police authorities, the international swindlers working what is known as the 'Spanish prisoner' fraud continue their ingenious activity, sometimes meeting with success, but on other occasions, as the latest instance shows, having success snatched from them just as it was within their reach.

The other day a German subject arrived at El Escorial from abroad bringing with him the sum of $2000. He had been beguiled by the persuasive eloquence of the swindlers and was attracted by the lure of a vast sum of money supposed to be buried in the vicinity of the Escorial. He was simple enough to believe that by handling over the $2000 he would obtain information as to the whereabouts of the buried treasure.

The guileless Teuton was met at the station by a couple of Spaniards and the trio adjourned to a hostelry for the purpose of clinching the bargain. Unfortunately for the plans of the Spaniards, fortunately for their victim, the civil guard had all the threads of the little plot in their hands. Seated round a little table discussing a bottle of wine and the alluring fortune, the Spaniards and their prospective victim were surprised by the entrance of an officer, and the colloquy came to an abrupt termination.

Realizing that the game was up, the two Spaniards jumped out of a window and fell into the clutches of a civil guard. The Teuton, fearful of losing his money and misunderstanding the true state of affairs, also jumped out of the window. The swindlers, the German and the proprietor of the hostelry are now under detention. This ingenious "Spanish prisoner" fraud has been going on for years, but no amount of publicity seems sufficient to put a stop to it.

Pretty nearly everything in the Republican party that the Colonel is criticising was happening all the time he was bossing it, a fact that would be somewhat embarrassing to anybody else.

	clear	frosted
15 watts	.50	.53
20 watts	.50	.53
25 watts	.50	.53
40 watts	.55	.59
60 watts	.75	.80
100 watts	1.10	1.17
150 watts	1.65	1.75
250 watts	2.30	2.45

Newburyport Morning Herald.

ESTABLISHED IN 1793, DAILY IN 1832
ONE HUNDRED AND TWENTIETH YEAR

NEWBURYPORT, MASSACHUSETTS, FRIDAY, MAY 3, 1912

VOLUME CXX, NUMBER 106
PRICE ONE CENT; THREE DOLLARS A YEAR

REPUBLICANS ARE TO PETITION FOR RECOUNT OF VOTE

To Go Over Ballots Again to Get at True Figures For Taft Delegates at Large

NINE NAMES ON THE BALLOT CONFUSING

President's Managers Hope to show That Number Thrown Out if Counted Would Have Elected the Taft Ticket

(Associated Press Despatch.)

BOSTON, May 2—A petition has been filed with the Boston board of election commissioners by Chairman Herman Hormel of the Republican state committee, asking for a recount of the vote cast at the Tuesday primaries for the Republican delegates at large in every ward in Boston except ward 7.

Tomorrow similar petitions will be filed asking for recounts of the vote for the Republican delegates at large throughout the state.

The Taft managers hope that the recount will show that the number of ballots thrown out because of nine crosses marked for ex-Senator Seiberlich and the regular Taft ticket headed by Senator Crane would have been sufficient if counted to have elected the Taft ticket for delegates at large.

The voters were allowed to vote for eight only, but the proximity of the name of Seiberlich, also pledged for Taft to the regular ticket, resulted in many invalidating their ballots by marking all nine names.

TO REST IN OAK HILL

The body of Lewis Talcott Wasson, who died in Colorado Springs on April 25, was brought to this city yesterday afternoon, in charge of H. F. Lunt, undertaker, and placed in the Daniel Smith tomb in Oak Hill cemetery.

SUDDEN DEATH OF OLIVER B. MERRILL EARLY YESTERDAY

Summons Came While at Work in His Garden; Expired Almost Immediately

WAS PUBLIC SPIRITED CITIZEN

Was Teacher in Brown High and Consolidated High Here for Thirty Years

One of Newburyport's leading and most highly esteemed citizens, Oliver B. Merrill, passed away very suddenly yesterday forenoon at his home on Monroe street.

He was born in Newburyport and his ancestors were of old Newbury stock. He was 76 years and three months old.

Death came to Mr. Merrill while engaged in trimming a grape-vine at the rear of the house. Having a faint spell from the exertion he came down the ladder and sat down to rest.

He sank rapidly and Mrs. Merrill summoned medical aid with the assistance of a neighbor. Dr. Worcester soon arrived, but Mr. Merrill had expired.

The cause given was heart trouble. Wednesday he was down town looking after a civil service examination in his official capacity as secretary of the local board of examiners.

The deceased was educated in the public schools here, attended Amherst in 1860, was appointed assistant master at the Brown High school. He taught school for 30 years, being assistant at the High school when the consolidation was effected.

He resigned in 1892 and retired to private life. He served in the legislature in 1893 and 1894 and from 1895 was a prominent member of the school committee for several years, and because of his educational training he was influential in its affairs.

Much concerning the history of

(Continued on Page Four.)

WITNESSES WERE REFRACTORY AT TITANIC HEARING

Committee Endeavoring to Learn If News of Disaster was Received in the Morning

EXAMINATION HELD IN PRIVATE

Telegram Confirming Sinking Said to Have Been Received Hours Before Made Public

(Associated Press Despatch.)

NEW YORK, May 2—Testimony taken today by Senator Smith of Michigan, chairman of the senate committee investigating the Titanic disaster, did not reveal any facts tending to confirm the report that news of the Titanic's sinking, which the White Star Line made public on Monday evening, April 15, had reached New York earlier that morning.

To determine this question was the principal object of Senator Smith's visit to New York, and he had before him today in private hearing John Bottomly, vice president of the American Marconi Co.; E. J. Dunn, a New York merchant who had testified in Washington that he had been informed by the son of a Western Union operator that a message had been received in New York on Monday morning telling of the Titanic's fate, and the operator himself, who returned to the city today, Mr. Smith said, after having been absent since Sunday night.

The two witnesses were disposced to be recalcitrant, the senator said, and their examination very unsatisfactory. He said he would call the operator again, when he hoped to obtain more definite information.

THAT AUTO FIRE TRUCK

Will the city council vote to buy that much talked of auto chemical truck at the meeting Monday night? This question is being debated by many of our citizens who are interested in the matter.

It will come up for consideration for the fourth time and the members who are in favor of the purchase claim that they are gaining strength and think they will have enough votes to pass the order at the next meeting.

Advertise in the Herald.

"TWELFTH NIGHT" AT CITY HALL ABLY PRESENTED

Given Under Auspices of Parent-Teachers' Association of the High and Kelley Schools

ASSISTED BY THE HAYDN TRIO

Every Number Enthusiastically Received; Proceeds for Benefit of the Two Schools

The musicale given at City hall last evening by the Parent-Teachers' association of the High and Kelley school districts for the benefit of said schools was of a high order and deserving of a packed house, whereas the audience was rather slim though warmly appreciative.

The Haydn Trio are finished artists each in his line, and in perfect accord and their selections were most happy.

The Shakespearean reader, Mrs. Elizabeth Pooler-Rice, had the commanding grace, beauty and majesty of one of Shakespeare's own heroines, a full voice and the requisite culture to dare to read a Shakespeare play.

Every number on the program was enthusiastically received by the audience. "Twelfth Night" was given charmingly.

The programs for the "Twelfth Night" have arrived and the Parent-Teachers' association feel sure that those who have planned to attend will be more than satisfied. The entertainment is to be given at City hall, Thursday evening, May 2nd.

The New Haven Evening Register says of Mrs. Rice:

"Mrs. Elizabeth Pooler Rice, who

(Continued on Page Four.)

VOTE REVISION BY THE ASSOCIATED PRESS SAYS TAFT'S LEAD IS 4235

A revision by the Associated Press of the vote for the principal Republican candidates at the primaries of Tuesday, including several missing towns, gave the following:

Presidential Preference.

La Follette 2005
Roosevelt 81,854
Taft 86,089

Delegates at Large.

Baxter (heading Roosevelt group) 84,834
Crane (heading Taft group) 76,854

A partial tabulation of the town clerk returns for other delegates at large shows very little variation from the leaders of the groups.

IN NEW LOCATION

The American Express Co. has removed their office to 18 State street.

WOULD COST STATE $4800 YEARLY TO MAINTAIN BRIDGE

So Stated Commissioner Kimball Yesterday at Hearing on Maintainence of Local Bridge by Commonwealth

HIGHWAY COMMISSION REPORT SUBMITTED

Mayor Burke Speaking in Favor Said That River or Sea Had Little if Any Commercial Value to City

By E. W. PRESCOTT
Special State House Correspondent For the Herald.

STATE HOUSE, Boston, May 3—The House committee on Ways and Means gave a hearing yesterday on the petition of Mayor Robert E. Burke of the city of Newburyport, and others, for legislation to provide that the expense of maintaining and operating the Newburyport bridge over the Merrimac river shall be borne by the Commonwealth. This petition was given a hearing on Jan. 15th by the committee on Roads and Bridges from whom it was given a favorable report and subsequently referred to Ways and Means.

Commissioner Kimball in Favor.

Representative Fowle of Newburyport, who is in charge of the bill, presented Mr. Kimball, chairman of the county commissioners of Essex county, who said that the Newburyport bridge over the Merrimac river between the city of Newburyport and the town of Salisbury, is on the through road from Boston to the beaches in Maine and the mountains in New Hampshire. He said that people traveling over this bridge can come direct from Salem, Lynn, Marblehead and Essex over the state highway. "In every sense of the word," he said, "this bridge is a state highway. The state highway has been constructed by the Commonwealth on both sides of this bridge, and in my mind the bridge is as much a state highway as the highways on either side of it."

Mr. Kimball said that when this bridge was first constructed it was a toll bridge, and that after forty years it was to revert to the state. He claimed that for 12 months or more this bridge actually belonged to the state, but that some individual from down country or out country had sought legislation to push the burden of maintaining and operating this bridge upon the community in which it was located, because they foresaw an added expense was to fall upon the Commonwealth. He told the committee that this bridge could be maintained by the state at a cost of about $4800 a year, and that Newburyport's portion of maintaining and operating said bridge would be reduced from 60 per cent. to 25 per cent.

Highway Commission Report.

Representative Washburn, chairman of the committee, read a report made by the highway commission, relative to the taking over and maintaining bridges, as follows:

(Continued on Page Four.)

The Weather

Probabilities.

Today fair; Saturday probably continued fair, light north to northeast winds.

Midnight Conditions.

The thermometer at the Herald office at midnight registered 47 degrees, wind northwest and clear.

Miniature Almanac.

Sun rises 4:36
Sun sets 6:46
Length of day 14:10
Day's increase 5:06
High tide...12:15 a. m., 12:45 p. m.
Light Auto Lamps 7:16

Memorial Suggested For Mrs. Isidor Straus, Who Refused to Part From Her Husband on the Titanic.

"Whither thou goest, I will go; where thou diest, will I die, and there will I be buried."

A movement has been started for the erection of a memorial to Mrs. Isidor Straus, whose noble sense of duty when she went to her death by her husband's side on the Titanic so splendidly illustrated the fidelity and tenderness of love. This quotation from the book of Ruth has been suggested for the memorial: "And Ruth said, entreat me not to leave thee or to return from following after thee: for whither thou goest, I will go; and where thou lodgest, I will lodge: thy people shall be my people, and thy God my God: where thou diest, will I die, and there will I be buried."

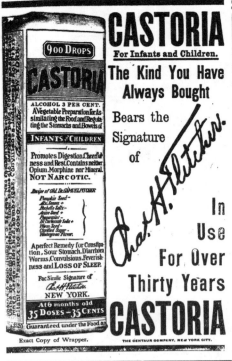

...UP OF YALE, ONE OF PEARY PARTY DROWNS

...r Canoe overturns in Long ...nd Sound and Two Lose Lives Before Help Comes

...RWICK, Conn., April 30—...e Borup of New York city, who ...ith Peary in his successful dash ... north pole, and Samuel Win... Case of Norwich, Ct., both grad... students of Yale university, drowned in Long Island sound ...y afternoon, when their pow... ...oe was suddenly overturned by ...vy sea.

... Cases have a summer cottage ...ecent Beach. Young Case, in ...any with Borup, went there Saturday night to spend yesterday. Early yesterday morning they started out in their canoe, headed for New London. They were not seen again until about 5 o'clock, when Harry Gardner, who is a quarry owner at Millstone, saw the canoe suddenly capsize. He immediately put out in a fast power boat. He at first saw one man clinging to the overturned craft, but before he could reach the scene, which was a half-hour's run from shore, the body had disappeared.

A coat and cap were found floating in the water. Mr. Gardner searched for sight of the bodies for some time and then went back to shore. An organized search then began among many power boat owners, but at a late hour last night neither body had been receovered.

MUCH LIKE LEGAL EXECUTION

How Two Women, Justly Incensed, Did Away With the Disturber of Their Rest

A north side family gave a "big" dinner recently and left a good part of it on the table until the next morning. In the night Mr. Rat smelled the good things left on the table, sunk his teeth into the butter, scratched the oyster dressing out on the table and then, getting his feet well soaked in the cranberry sauce, seemed to delight in leaving his red tracks all over the white table cloth.

The next night the two women members of the family were in the house alone. They heard the rat industriously gnawing his way through the kitchen floor. He finished the job and spent the greater part of the night exploring the dining room and kitchen, as he could be plainly heard in the stillness.

When sleep became impossible the two women, in spite of their natural fear of rats, got out of bed and chased the rat back down the hole he had gnawed in the floor. Then they laid a piece of wood over the opening. But the rat was persistent. He pushed the wood away and began his nightly scampering. The two women got out of bed again, and, placing a sadiron over the hole, they vowed vengeance on the disturber of their rest. With all points of egress in the shape of doors closed, there was no hope of escape for the rat.

After a chase of half an hour the rat finally took refuge in the kindling box behind the stove. A sewing board was placed over the box and the rat was a captive. But that did not end matters. The next problem was the execution. Tired out, the two women sat down to reflect. They thought of hot water to scald the enemy to death. But they decided it was too cruel. So they dressed, got a wash tub, placed kindling box and all in the tub and carried the tub out under the hydrant. The water was turned on and the kindling box was held down under water. And thus the rat died. The story merely explains the screams that came from the house mentioned. Of course the neighbors knew the trouble when they saw the rat the next morning, but they didn't know what to think of it until the situation was explained..—Indianapolis News.

RAMP AND ESCALATOR

Where large numbers of persons are compelled to pass and repass, the elementary "ramp" offers some advantages, as regards safety and simplicity, over a stairway. The stairway is peculiarly dangerous to human life and limb under crowded conditions, and the effort required in ascent brings about a pronounced check in the movement of large bodies of persons in motion, which has been assumed to be absent from the ramp. A return has, therefore, been made to the inclined plane, or "ramp," as the means of access to or egress from several modern railway stations, the depth of which below the general surface has been too great for convenient stairways, and yet too small to develop the advantages of elevators.

The traveling public, brought to and landed at low levels in these stations, is confronted by exists extending upwards upon the ancient method of the inclined plane, involving physical effort and personal fatigue in the ascent to the level of the streets.

The descent of the same form of planes is also accompanied by some fatigue accompanying the motion of descending angular inclines. For such conditions the moving stairway appears to afford advantageous relief, both as regard to convenience of the passengers and the removal of congestion. The capacity of an escalator in the movement of people is very considerable. Such an appliance having a width of only 40 inches will carry upwards of 10,000 persons per hour.—Cassier's Magazine.

The Stock Market

Closing quotations for May 2, 1912, furnished by F. S. Moseley & Co., 50 Congress street, Boston:

	Bid	Asked
First Nat'l Bank	102	108
Merchants Nat'l Bank	32⅛	35
Ocean Nat'l Bank...	65	68
Newb'yp't Gas & E...		195
Boston & Maine RR.	99¾	100
N. Y., N. H. & H. RR.	137	137¾
Amalgamated	82⅞	83
Am. Tel. & Tel. Co. ..	146⅜	146⅝
Am. Woolen pfd....	90¾	91
N. E. Tel. & Tel. Co. .	152	155
Mass. Electric com..	20	21
Mass. Electric pfd..	80	81
Mass. Gas pfd......	97	97½
Mergenthaler Lino. ..	218	220
New York Central ..	119¾	120¼
Pennsylvania RR....	126	126⅛
United Fruit	189½	190
United Shoe com....	50¾	51¼
United Shoe pfd.....	29¼	29½
U. S. Steel com......	71½	71⅝
U. S. Steel pfd......	112¾	113

BYFIELD

Rennie Rogers is confined to the house with the grippe.

Mr. and Mrs. Walter Bodell sailed for England on the Laconia from Boston Tuesday morning.

Elmer H. Humphreys has nearly finishing the overhauling of the automobile he purchased last fall.

John Culivan has moved from his Lunt street home to Newburyport.

John Dickie has erected temporary living quarters at his place on the Downfall road, and has hired Thomas Brookings to assist him in the building of his bungalow.

G. Roy Tarbox has sold his apple crop to a Boston firm.

A number of motor boat owners have launched their boats at the slip for the season.

The Sons of Veterans have closed a contract with Porter, Rogers & Co. of Newburyport for baseball uniforms. An agent will meet the members at Junior O. U. A. M. hall next Monday night.

THE OMNIPOTENT SEX

(Boston Post)

In New York the street commissioner has promised and ordered the route of the proposed suffragist parade to be put in spick and span condition. There shall be neither dust nor mud to mar the cleanliness of the skirts of the paraders—that is to say, of those who may prefer to wear skirts.

What demonstration of mere men ever elicited such unasked-for consideration from municipal authority? It is an unprecedented concession to the masterfulness of the organization which is thus favored. What can they not get if they go after it in the right way?

The streets here in Boston occasionally need cleaning for the general comfort. Perhaps a suffrage parade might bring as happy result as is promised in New York.

PRESIDENTIAL NOMINATION RACE

STANDING OF CONTESTANTS TODAY

REPUBLICAN

Number of delegates 1078
Majority necessary for choice 540

For Taft	
ALABAMA	21
DISTRICT OF COLUMBIA	2
CONNECTICUT	14
COLORADO	10
DELAWARE	6
FLORIDA	12
KANSAS	4
NORTH CAROLINA	8
GEORGIA	26
ILLINOIS	2
INDIANA	20
OWA	16
*KENTUCKY	23
LOUISIANA	14
MICHIGAN	16
MASSACHUSETTS	26
MISSISSIPPI	19
MISSOURI	8
NEW HAMPSHIRE	8
NEVADA	6
NEW MEXICO	7
NEW YORK (estimated)	83
OKLAHOMA	4
PENNSYLVANIA	9
PHILIPPINES	2
RHODE ISLAND	10
SOUTH CAROLINA	20
TENNESSEE	15
VERMONT	6
VIRGINIA	24
HAWAII	6
Total for Taft	439

VERMONT 4 Unpledged

For Roosevelt	
NEW MEXICO	1
ILLINOIS (estimated)	56
GEORGIA	2
OKLAHOMA	14
INDIANA	10
*KENTUCKY	3
MAINE	12
MICHIGAN	6
MISSOURI	24
MASSACHUSETTS	10
MISSISSIPPI	5
NEBRASKA	16
NEW YORK (estimated)	7
NORTH CAROLINA	6
OREGON	10
PENNSYLVANIA	67
VERMONT	2
WEST VIRGINIA	14
Total for Roosevelt	269

For La Follette	
NO. DAKOTA	10
WISCONSIN	26
Total for La Follette	36

For Cummins	
IOWA (three districts)	10

* Six seats in Kentucky contested by Taft and Roosevelt.

DEMOCRATIC

Number of delegates 1094
Two-thirds necessary for choice 730

The Democrats allow six delegates each to territorial possessions. Republicans allow two each except to Hawaii, which has six.

For Clark	
ILLINOIS (estimated)	58
ALASKA	6
COLORADO	58
MASSACHUSETTS	20
OREGON	10
MAINE	1
MISSOURI	36
KANSAS	20
OKLAHOMA (one half)	10
PENNSYLVANIA	2
WISCONSIN	6
NEBRASKA	16
Total for Clark	243

For Harmon	
MAINE	4
PENNSYLVANIA	2
Total for Harmon	6

For Wilson	
DELAWARE	6
OKLAHOMA	10
MAINE	5
PENNSYLVANIA	76
WISCONSIN	19
OREGON (3 in doubt)	10
Total for Wilson	126

For Marshall	
INDIANA	26

For Burke	
NORTH DAKOTA	10

For Underwood	
ALABAMA	24

The Stock Market

Closing quotations for May 6, 1912, furnished by F. S. Moseley & Co., 50 Congress street, Boston:

	Bid	Asked
First Nat'l Bank	102	108
Merchants Nat'l Bank	32⅛	35
Ocean Nat'l Bank...	65	68
Newb'yp't Gas & E...		195
Boston & Maine RR.	99¼	99¾
N. Y., N. H. & H. RR.	137	137¾
Amalgamated	80⅞	81
Am. Tel. & Tel. Co..	145¼	145⅜
Am. Woolen pfd	90½	91
N. E. Tel. & Tel. Co..	153	155
Mass. Electric com..	19	19½
Mass. Electric pfd..	79½	80½
Mass. Gas pfd......	97	97½
Mergenthaler Lino ..	217	218½
New York Central ..	117½	117¾
Pennsylvania RR....	123¼	123½
United Fruit	188½	189
United Shoe com....	50	50¾
United Shoe pfd.....	29	29½
U. S. Steel Com......	65½	65⅝
U. S. Steel pfd......	110⅜	110⅝
Am. Sugar com.....	127½	128¼
Am. Sugar pfd......	121	121½

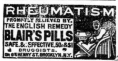

IS SURE OF OBITUARY

ONE REASON WHY MR. SPARROWGRASS LIVES IN COUNTRY

There Are Others, of Course, But This One Is Paramount—Sort of a Letter of Recommendation To St. Peter

One argument against the rush to the cities is the city obituary column. I have known men to lead long, useful and honorable lives in the city and get only four or five lines at last, whereas if they had stayed on the farm the country papers awould have given them columns.

We don't have porcelain bathtubs up here in the hills. Steam heaters and janitors are scarce. There's a good deal of snow ,too, and no delicatessen around the corner. But there is always the satisfaction of knowing that the local paper will print a fine piece about us when our turn comes to be shoveled on, as Shakespeare puts it.

I may have to raise my own turnips instead of paying a market gardener three prices to raise them for me, and a grocer six prices for bringing them to me. I may work hard in the sunlight and the air of the fields when I might be lolling in the gaslight and the dust of a factory. I may have to send my children a mile to school instead of two miles to a sweatshop; and perhaps there is a Plymouth Rock rooster on the premises instead of one of them things your newspaper calls pianoletups. I admit the country's disadvantages freely. But when the vale of tears is done with me and I am laid to rest under the pine trees in the old family lot, I know there will be a generous write-up by Editor Green in the Backwoods Weekly Guide, Joyville and Passaic county papers please copy.

I shall not go out like a common critter of the pasture, without a letter of recommendation to St. Peter. There will be a long article right down the middle of the first page and Lemuel Green will spread himself to make it a first-class job. He will tell the neighbors all the good things in my history that the neighbors can think up to tell him; how I was industrious, sober, honest, patient under trial, kind in propriety a loving son, a devoted husband, a fond father, a faithful friend, a man true to principle and spotless in character, a worthy citizen, whose loss is a severe blow to all. Would there were more of my kind.

He will recall my public deeds and private virtues; the time I ran for sheriff on the Prohibition ticket; the poor families I helped shelter the year the dam broke, and the time I carried water to save the Widow Garwin's cottage from the flames and caught my last cold. No matter how lowly my life has been, I shall go out in style and good order, and a loving hand will write "The End" after my own has dropped the pen. You see Mr. Editor, the country still has something the city can't offer.—"Simon Sparrowgrass" in Newark News.

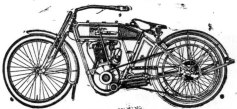

The Astor Home In New York and Those Most Interested In Colonel John Jacob Astor's Will.

Photo of Mrs Ava Willing Astor copyright, 1912, by American Press Association.

WEST NEWBURY

The grass in the Merrimack cemetery was burned over last Saturday, under the direction of the following corps of fire-fighters, who worked valiantly to prevent the flames from damaging the abutting property: George D. Whittier (superintendent of the cemetery), Cyrus D. Ordway, (president of the association), Robert L. Smith, Ambros P. Chase, David E. N. Carleton and Herbert N. Carleton. There was need of the most rigid supervision to guard against injury to the posts of the fence surrounding the yard and to young trees in an adjoiningfield the cemeteryis bordered with woods at a short distance from its boundaries, ni which disastrous fires have repeatedly occurred in previous years, although they have escaped such damage so far this season.

A novel entertainment takes place in West Newbury town hall this Tuesday evening. There will be a full brass band and a regiment of militia. The scene will be laid on a Southern plantation and will be enlivened with singing by a chorus of "chocolate beauties.". Candy and popped corn will be served.

ESSEX COUNTY

Tsouklaus, the Peabody greek who murdered a fellow countryman Friday is to be defended on the ground of insanity.

Mrs. Aurelia Provencher of Haverhill, keeper of a lodging house, was found dead in her room, probably a victim of heart disease.

Yesterday afternoon the White Plague Reliex exposition, a sort of fair for the benefit of the anti-tuberculosis campaign ,was opened in the state armory at Lynn.

An auto driven by Charles Brown, and occupied by Miss Belle Lane of Riverside, was struck by a locomotive on a grade crossing in Gloucester. The machine was smashed, but neither occupant was injured.

While at her desk in the West Gloucester school, Miss Elsie McComisky was struck in the shoulder by a stray bullet, which came through one of the windows.

A Lawrence milkman, Ohannas Ozarian, was fined $10 for using unsealed milk bottles.

Mrs. Margaret J. Reardon of Salem lost a foot yesterday morning when she attempted to cross the tracks in Salem depot in front of a Boston-bound train. She will be a cripple for life.

The fact that his assailant used the small blade of his stout jackknife is largely responsible for the fact that Stephen Pulen of Salem is alive. He was stabbed twice in the abdomen by John Quateione.

Schooner Evolution of Liverpool, N. S. while coming up Salem harbor hit the middle ground and hung fast till released by a tug and the rising tide.

A tribute to the memory of Major Archibald Butt was paid in the Washington Street Church Beverly, Sunday.

ADVERTISED LETTERS MAY 6, '12

The following unclaimed letters are at the post office:

F. Brown, Summer street; W. J. Corffin, Mf. Degel Water street; L. W. Denno, 12 Essex street; Harry Jornson; E. W. Noyes; Ralo Veter, 27 Oliver street; Chas. T. Rose, Gen. Del.; Miss Demello, 306 South Lee street; Mrs. Geo. Lawrence, 2047 E. 90th street; Miss C. A. Pritchard, money back flour; Mrs. Thos. Rand, 168 Water street; Miss Annie Smith, Wolfe Tavern.

Responsibilities of Citizenship.

The duties of citizens are not fulfilled so long as there is a single hovel in a city; a man, woman, or child sweated, or a hungry, uncared-for child in their midst.—Exchange.

Begin at Home.

Everybody wants to reform somebody else, but the citizen's first duty to the state is to reform himself.

FORMER TAX COLLECTOR OF WENHAM RELEASED FROM COUNTY JAIL

Salem, May 6—The county commissioners this noon granted the petition of Fred P. Stanton, formerly tax collector of Wenham, who was serving a two-year sentence for larceny of town funds, and released him on probation.

His term would have expired Aug. 28, and the application for probation was approved by the probation officer and district attorney.

M. L. Sullivan and Jackson & Jackson appeared for the petitioners.

A petition was presented, signed by 105 residents of Wenham and Hamilton, for Stanton's release; also a release from liability signed by the selectmen. In addition there was a letter from Rev. Walter A. Eaton, a former pastor of the Wenham church, recommending Stanton's release.

B. Hammond Tracey, Arthur C. Cummings, H. L. Colby and Charles E. Beard, who is Stanton's father-in-law, testified in behalf of Stanton. It was brought about that the reason for asking the release is that the family is in needy circumstances; that while his oldest daughter is carrying on the store, she is near a breakdown.

M. Porter Perkins and Arthur C. Prince testified in opposition, taking the ground that Stanton's sentence of two years was not an excessive one considering his offense.

COLONIAL THEATRE, BOSTON

At the Colonial Theatre next week opening May 13th, Mrs. Geo. W. Cohan will present himself and his own company in the great revival of his music play, "45 Minutes from Broadway" in which the famous author-actor-playwright-composer and producer will be seen in the role of "Kid" Burns.

Mr. Cohan's Kid Burns comes nearer, it is said, to a stage realization of the genuine Bowery type than has heretofore been visualized. In the author's hands, the peculiar, past understanding vocabulary of Burns, his slangy philosophy, but really sincere at heart, is brought out and individualiezd as never before, and the revival of the piece has been one of the surprise hits of the season in New York where Mr. Cohan and his splendid company, which includes Miss Sallie Fisher, have just completed a two months' run of it.

Mr. Cohan believes in never doing things by halves. Therefore, when he presents himself it will be with a surrounding that includes his enire company, production and scenery, as well as the orchestra from his own theatre.

Of almost equal importance as Mr. Cohan's appearance in this revival is that of Miss Sallie Fisher, who has created a sensation by her conception of the part of Mary.

"45 Minutes from Broadway" will be seen at the Colonial exactly as it was presented at the Geo. M. Cohan Theatre in New York. With a promise like this amusement-seekers can rest assured that the play will be presented as it never was before, and it is safe to predict that there will be sufficient people take advantage of it to fill the theatre to the capacity point at every performance during his Colonial engagement which includes Wednesday and Saturday matinees.

Professions Taught Free of Charge.

There is just one country in the world where the highest education is free and that country, surprising as it may seem to those who read this, is Chili. There every profession is taught in the most modern methods by the best authorities with no charge whatever to natives.

AGRICULTURAL REVOLUTION IN THE CULTURE OF SUGAR BEET

WASHINGTON, May 18—I believe we are on the eve of an agricultural revolution in this country. It will be a bloodless revolution and one wholly beneficial to the country at large—a revolution in farming methods. This will not be brought about by wonderful inventions of farming machinery or the discovery of new agricultural ideas. It will simply result from the application of a principle accidentally discovered in Europe a century ago. This principle has really revolutionized agriculture in Europe. It has doubled and trebled the yield per acre in the five staple crops of wheat, corn, oats, barley and potatoes during the past sixty years. I refer to scientific rotation in connection with the culture of the sugar beet.

The culture of sugar beets in Europe was started by Napoleon, when, after ten years of experimentation, his scientists discovered that by growing sugar beets on the land every fourth year, the yield of all other crops grown during the three remaining years, was increased from forty to one hundred percent. At that time European fields were at their lowest stage of productivity and economists were in despair because of their growing inability to feed the increasing population. At the same time that Napoleon decided to prohibit the importation of sugar from the British colonies, he issued a decree appropriating a million francs ($200,000) with which to teach beet sugar culture and manufacturing methods to farmers and manufacturers and in two years' time he had 334 factories in operation.

After Napoleon's downfall, the Cossacks stabled their horses in the French beet sugar factories and all but two suspended operations. But the farmers had learned how greatly the culture of sugar beets increased their yields of other crops and as soon as political conditions became more settled the industry revived in France and from there spread over all Europe.

Today, as a result, of the beneficent culture of these tubers, the "worn-out" soil of Europe is twice as productive per acre as out own rich Western lands.

America has lagged behind Europe in learning this important agricultural lesson. But now the farmers of the West and Middle West are realizing its value. I have gathered reports from hundreds of these farmers showing their yields in the staple crops before and after rotation with the sugar beet. The figures are startling. They indicate that if the average American farmer followed the lead of his beet-raising brethren, the production of our fields would be increased over 100 percent. Our crops in the five staples would show an increased value of $3,817,603,000 annually. This stupendous sum may arouse skepticism, but it is simply a deduction from cold figures.

Here are the results of my inquiries, averaged. They show the average yield per acre in bushels before and after the culture of beets:

	Before	After	P.C.In.
Wheat	28.88	43.07	49.1
Corn	41.6	53.1	27.6
Oats	40.9	60.6	48.1
Barley	38.97	59.4	52
Potatoes	151.97	222.2	46

The farmers who kept reports enabling them to furnish the required information were all high-class men. Even before they cultivated the beet, their yields showed a productivity far above the average in the United States. They were producing yearly 50 percent more wheat per acre than the average farmer, 60 percent more corn, 25 percent more oats, 60 percent more barley and 50 percent more potatoes.

The sugar beet is in itself a valable crop, in addition to its aid to the productivity of the farm generally. Many beet farmers report a greater profit per acre from beets than from any other crop. The farmer sells his beets to the beet sugar factory at a price fixed before he plants his seed, thus making him independent of the speculator. The beet tops and the pulp left over after the sugar has been extracted from the beet, make excellent fattening fodder for the stock. So nothing is lost to the farmer.

I believe we are about to enter upon an era of wonderful agricultural development with the sugar beet as a basis. As soon as European governments realized the value of the sugar beet they forced its development by heavy export bounties on beet sugar and heavy protective tariffs against sugar grown in foreign countries under the cheapest labor in the world the sugar beet industry will in a comparatively few years reach proportions comparable to those it has attained in Europe.

New York . . Letter . .

NEW YORK, May 18—As a result of the introduction of a new system of collecting taxes, New York is now enjoying the unique spectacle of a mad scramble among her many millionaires to see who shall be first to turn into the city the money due on their large holdings. Heretofore, particularly among the more wealthy the annual city tax has been an item to be sworn off if possible or failing this to be paid at the last possible moment. But by the new system Father Knickerbocker has succeeded in hitting the ultra-wealthy in their most sensitive point, that is the pocket book, and as a result has had them actually begging for an opportunity to discharge their obligation in this connection to the city. The new system is so simple that it is surprising that it has not been tried before. It consists merely in making taxes payable in two instalments, six months apart, with a provisio that there will be a rebate at the rate of four percent a year on the second instalment provided it is paid with the first. As this amount to more than one percent on the whole tax for a year, a figure considerably in excess of the tax rate, the result is that the largest property owners are making every effort to get their money into the hands of the city as rapidly as possible. On the first day of tax collections under the new system a line nearly a sixth of a mile long obstructed the sidewalk in front of the collector's office and of the $150,000,000 due it is estimated that more than twenty million dollars were paid in. How different this situation was from the old one under which delays and repudiations until the last moment were the chief feature is indicated by the fact that in spite of every effort it was impossible for the city officials to check up and deposit more than one-fourth of this amount. Ten million dollars in collections were received during the first two hours after the opening of the office and so great was the rush that the clerical force numbering seventy-five was literally swamped. Altogether if the first day collections under the new plan is an indivation of its efficiency, it will not only be continued in this city but doubtless copied widely throughout the country.

* * * * * *

The latest tabulation of figures at this port serves sharply to accentuate one of the changes in the vast tide of immigration that flows into the United States from Europe every year which has puzzled and alarmed students of this subject of late. More than four-fifths of all the immigrants arriving here fifty years ago came from countries of northern Europe with Germany in the lead whereas at present an equal prepondenance comes from southern Europe with the Slavonic races and Italy supplying fully three-fourths of the total. Many studies have been made and many theories advanced to account for the change. The latest of these is put forward by an expert who has just returned from a prolonged study of economic conditions in northern Europe. While it seems somewhat startling at first blush, agricultural authorities here agree that it is well founded. This observer asserts in short that the responsibility for changing the currents of European immigration so remarkably rests with no more formidable an agent than the sugar beet which he points out has revolutionized the agriculture of Germany and to a great extent of all northern Europe. "The reason the Germans and their neighbors formerly came flocking over here," he says, "was because their fields couldn't produce enough to feed them. Since that time they have trebled their grain yield per acre through systematic use of the sugar beet in rotation with other crops, and, as this enables them to live comfortably and even properously at home, naturally they have stopped seeking new countries. The sugar beet industry is not adapted to southern Europe and consequently there has been no such agricultural improvement there and the people of these countries are crossing the Atlantic in steadily increasing numbers. While the knowledge of these facts may not help us much in changing the character of our immigration, we may at least profit by encouraging the cultivation of the humble beet stimulate our declining agricultural production so that we will be able to feed our rapidly increasing population for a long time to come."

* * * * * *

Chinatown is in deep mourning because of the loss of its most sacred dragon, said to be the second largest in the country. It was not, however, a modern St. George but merely a fire which brought about its untimely end. Neither was the dragon a real one but an enormous creation cunningly made from papier mache and various kinds of Oriental cloths cunningly lighted from within which the Chinese in this city have been accustomed to carry in the street parade in connection with the New Years celebration. Unfortunately for them the dragon was quietly reposing in the basement of a building in the shopping district awaiting the next parade and when this building was attacked by fire the pungent smoke from the stack of josh sticks, Chinese incense and other inflammable substances dear to the Celestial nostril because of the pungency was so thick as to render any attempt at rescue impossible. Only the great dragon in San Francisco exceeded the lost one in size, it is stated, but it is understood that before the next Chinese New Year rolls around there will be a new dragon larger than any yet heard of.

* * * * * *

From now on visitors to the tomb of General Grant on Riverside Drive will behold the latest material evidence that the Yellow Peril is a figment of the alarmist. This evidence is in the form of 2500 cherry trees and a large bronze tablet commemorating the gift to the city of New York through Dr. Jokichi Takamine of Japan. The ceremony attending the interment of the Yellow Peril was unique in the annals of the city. In the presence of members of the Japanese legation at Washington, the Governor General of Korea and many Japanese of note, to say nothing of the usual throng of New Yorkers, thirteen diminutive kindergarten girls, armed with small shovels, planted the last 13 of the 2500 trees. During the ceremony was played the music of "Sakurá, Sakura," the Japanese cherry tree song. The small agriculturists and guarantors of peace with Nippon concluded their part of the program with a solemn Japanese folk dance. Park Commissioner Stover declared it to be the intention of the city to have the cherry tree orchard called Sakura Park to be dedicated next September if the city fathers agree.

Mme. Marcelle Navratil, Who Came From France For Her Children, the "Waifs of the Titanic."

Copyright, 1912, by American Press Association.

Mme. Marcelle Navratil, mother of the two children rescued from the Titanic and brought to New York without anybody knowing at first who they were, recently came to this country from her home in Nice and claimed them. The boys, Edmund, aged two, and Michel, four, were delighted to see their mother. Her husband, from whom she was living apart, had stolen the children and was bringing them to this country. He went down with the Titanic.

CAMERA HERO SAVED TRAIN

Spoiled Films an Ill Reward for Act That Deserved Better Things of Fortune.

The slave of the camera was dozing in the smoking car when a half dozen shots rang out in the night air.

The train slackened. There were more shots.

"Train robbers!" shrieked a pallid passenger as he crawled under the seat.

The camera man grasped his black box and tripod, and, running to the car platform, sprang off into the darkness.

The robbers, most of them, were grouped about the express car. There was much money in the express safe. The company said not over $17, but it must have been thousands. Anyway, the robbers were determined to get it, whatever it was. They had done a lot of wild shooting and several persons had been hurt. Now they had shoved a stick of dynamite into the car and were just about to ignite the fuse.

Suddenly a blinding glare filled the air with dazzling fire.

With a wild shriek the robbers fled to the woods.

The flashlight of the camera man had saved the train.

When they found him he was crouched before a train hand's lantern, weeping bitterly.

"Something went wrong with the dum thing," he moaned. "The film's spoiled!"

Blunders of Royal Authors.

Royal authors sometimes need a deal of editing. A glaring instance is Frederick the Great, whose spelling and punctuation astounded Carlyle, says the London Chronicle. "A steure" for "a cette heure" was a specimen of the former, "and as for punctuation, he never could understand the mystery of it; he merely scatters a few commas and dashes as if they were shaken out of a pepper box upon his page and so leaves it."

How, asks Carlyle, can such slovenliness be explained in a king who "would have ordered arrest for the smallest speck of mud on a man's buff belt, indignant that any pipe clayed portion of a man should not be perfectly pipe clayed?" He can only conclude that Frederick really cared little about literature after all. Also "he never minded snuff upon his own chin, not even upon his waistcoat and breeches." "I am a king and above grammar," said another monarch.

Floating Cannery.

A new phase of scientific management has been put into operation out on our progressive Pacific coast by the conversion of the good old ship Glory of the Seas into a floating cannery of salmon. There is the whole proceedings right on one floating spot—catching, cleaning, cooking, canning, boxing and then, when the hold is full of the season's pack of cases, a tow of the factory into port and the market.

DICKENS AS HE WAS IN 1839

Interesting Description of Great Writer Published in the Knickerbocker of That Year.

In person he is a little above the standard height, though not tall. His figure is slight, without being meagre, and is well proportioned. The face, that first object of physical interest, is peculiar, though not remarkable. An ample forehead is displayed under a quantity of light hair, worn in a mass on one side rather jauntily, and this is the only semblance of dandyism in his appearance. His brow is marked, and his eye, though not large, is bright and expressive. The most regular feature is the nose, which may be called handsome; an epithet not applicable to his lips, which are too large. Taken altogether, the countenance, which is pale without sickliness, is in repose extremely agreeable and indicative of great refinement and intelligence.

Mr. Dickens' manners and conversation, except perhaps in the perfect abandon among his familiars, have no exhibition of particular wit, much less of humor. He is mild in the tones of his voice, and quiescent, evincing habitual attention to etiquette and the conventionalisms of polished circles. His society is much sought after, and, possibly to avoid the invitations pressed upon him, he does not reside in London, but with a lovely wife and two charming children occupies a retreat in the vicinity. He is about 26 years of age, but does not look more than 23 or 24. Mr. Dickens is entirely self-made, and rose from an humble station by virtue of his moral worth, his genius and his industry.—From the Knickerbocker, August, 1839.

Are Learning Right Ways.

An English lady, long resident in Tokyo, once wrote to a friend that the impulse of her Japanese maids is always to sew on cuffs frills and other similar things topsy turvy and inside out. Since the publication of such reports the art of needlework has been greatly improved in Japan. Several of the English methods have been taught with great success, if only to judge by the lovely drawn thread work sold in great quantities in Great Britain.

SORRY FOR HIS WRONGDOING

"Mr. Win'" Unhappy Because He Once Did Ill Deeds at Old Man Winter's Behest.

Once 'pon a time Mister Win' wuz sleepin', still an' peaceable, dreamin' 'bout de time w'en he useter blow de blossoms an' talk ter de li'l chilluns as dey played under de trees; but Ole Man Winter, he come 'long an' waked him up, an' tol' him dat he wuz in need er comp'ny, kase he had a long ways ter go, an' Mister Win' riz up an' went wid him, an' Ole Man Winter say ter him:

"You see dat steeple yander?"

Mister Win' make answer dat he sho' do, an' den Ole Man Winter say:

"All right. Des whirl in an' blow it down fer me, kaze I got a grudge ag'in it. Blow it down!" An' down come de steeple.

Den he make Mister Win' take de roof off de po' man's house, whar de li'l' chilluns wuz sleepin', an' blow de fire out what kep' 'em warm; an' w'en dat come ter pass Mister Win' he git mighty sorry, an' tol' Mister Winter no mo' er dat fer him; an' he gone off a-grievin' ter hisse'f f'um dat day ter dis you kin hear him cryin', an' cryin', des lak he had de breakin' er de heart.—Atlanta Constitution.

Power of Two Words.

"I will," is a projectile that hits the mark; a power that moves mountains.—Henry Wood.

Disconcerted by Sneeze.

The world has now well-nigh forgotten M. Vivier, the once famous French-horn player, who was so unnerved by the late Lord Houghton's blowing his nose at a critical moment of his performance that he threw up all his London engagements. "Ah," he would say after this, "the English have terrible noses. They remind you of the day of judgment."

ONE CENT EVERYWHERE

LOS ANGELES EVENING HERALD
AN INDEPENDENT NEWSPAPER

SECTION 2 WANTADS

VOL. XXXVIII. PRICE 1 CENT. TUESDAY, MAY 28, 1912. PRICE 1 CENT. NO. 210.

U. S. PROBE SAYS BRITISH BOARD AT FAULT FOR TITANIC LOSS

Poor Regulations and Poor Inspection of Ship Laid at Their Door

SCORED BY SENATOR SMITH

Five Hundred Lives Sacrificed Through Careless Loading of Lifeboats

RECOMMENDATION FOR PROTECTION ON SHIPS

The senate Titanic investigation committee recommends that passenger ships:

Carry two searchlights.
Wireless on duty 24 hours.
Lifeboats to accommodate all.
Assignment to boats before sailing.
An international agreement.

WASHINGTON, D. C., May 28.—Five hundred lives were needlessly sacrificed through the careless loading of the Titanic's boats, the ship was poorly equipped and poorly inspected and responsibility for this rests with the British board of trade, according to the report of the Titanic investigating committee and the speech of William Alden Smith, its chairman, in the senate today.

Responsibility for the Titanic disaster and the loss of more than 1000 lives that resulted from it was laid directly at the door of the British trade board by Smith. Captain Smith, who went down with the Titanic, was mentioned in passing as a "dauntless hero whose willingness to die in expiation of his mistakes is evidence of his fitness to live."

The British board of trade was bitterly scored by Senator Smith for the alleged laxity of its regulations and its hasty inspection of the Titanic before that ship sailed on its maiden and final voyage.

CAUSES OF DISASTER

Two main causes are given in the report which Smith presented following his speech as the cause of the disaster. They are:

1.—Indifference to danger in the face of warning displayed by Captain Smith.

2.—The increase in speed of the Titanic in spite of the warnings of icebergs it had received from other vessels.

Although pointing out the rashness of Captain Smith, Senator Smith declared that he was no more to blame than others connected with the company to which the Titanic belonged who were on board the ship. This clause obviously referred to J. Bruce Ismay, managing director of the White Star line, although Senator Smith refrained from mentioning Ismay's name.

Smith declared that insufficient tests were made of the Titanic's boilers, bulkheads, gearing equipment, life-saving and signal devices, and that the officers and members of the crew were strangers to one another, and many of them unfamiliar with their duties.

Smith paid a tribute to the actions of the wireless operators of the Titanic and the rescue ship Carpathia for the faithful performance of their duties. He praised Captain Rostron of the Carpathia, saying that he should be made to realize the debt of gratitude this nation owes him.

COMMITTEE SUGGESTIONS

The report of the Titanic committee presented to the senate by Chairman Smith showed that the committee had found that additional legislation was necessary for the safety of travelers at sea.

It recommended that each steamship carrying 100 or more passengers should have two electric searchlights, wireless operators on duty twenty-four hours per day and that the reciprocal arrangements between the United States and other countries be terminated.

The commmittee urged that the statutes be amended so as to definitely require a sufficient number of lifeboats to accommodate every passenger and member of the crew of each ship; that four members of the crew, skilled in the handling of boats, be assigned to every boat, and that the assignment of the passengers and crew to lifeboats be made before sailing.

Captain Lord of the Californian is denounced by the committee, concluding that the captain and his officers saw the distress signals of the Titanic and did not heed them. The report says the Californian might have saved all the lost passengers and crew of the ship that went down.

$1,000,000 State Bonds to Be Sold to Highest Bidder

Treasurer E. D. Roberts Diagnoses of California Documents at Auction in Capitol Today

SACRAMENTO, May 28.—One million dollars in state bonds, voted by the people under the Basin act at the general election in 1910, will be sold to the highest bidder by State Treasurer E. D. Roberts at auction today.

The bonds are very desirable, and an effort was made by one of the leading bond firms to have the bonds sold in a single block of $1,000,000/ but to insure competitive bidding and to give the smaller brokers an opportunity to take part in the bidding, State Treasurer Roberts will offer the issue in smaller lots, or eight parcels in all.

BODY FOUND IN BAY STILL UNIDENTIFIED

Mystery surrounding the identity of the man whose body was found in San Pedro harbor May 19 became much deeper today when Detective Bruce Boyd learned that James W. Grundy is alive and in the northern part of the state.

Detective Boyd also stated that after having a long talk with William H. Rein of Detroit the latter had declared he was positive the body was not that of his father, Bernard Rein.

RAINS IN NORTH BRING CHERRY MARKET SHORTAGE

Los Angeles cherry consumers will have to quit eating the fruit for the next few days. This does not signify that an abnormal price range has been established or that some mystifying epidemic has effaced the California cherry crop for which the consuming public has been patiently waiting for several months. The real cause of the shortage is that recent rains in the northern section of the state in the vicinity of Sacramento, from which this city derives the bulk of its annual cherry supply, have made picking and shipping of the fruit practically impossible, and as a natural result prices on all varieties have already recorded a slight elevation.

Wholesaler to retailer quotations today were on a range from 8 cents upward per pound.

UNWRITTEN LAW TO BE DOUBLE SLAYER'S DEFENSE

SAN DIEGO, May 28.—Bert G. Lewis must stand trial for slaying G. H. Toliver, the aged inventor, and his wife. A coroner's jury after hearing the grewsome details of the double crime as told by neighbors who were attracted to the scene by the shooting and the officers who later made the arrest, brought in a verdict yesterday that Toliver came to his death from ten gunshot wounds and a dagger thrust, that Mrs. Toliver died from two wounds and that the crimes were committed by Bert G. Lewis.

According to officials, the unwritten law will be the slayer's defense.

MRS. CLARK TO MANAGE ESTATE OF TITANIC VICTIM

Mrs. Virginia Clark, widow of Walter Miller Clark, who last saw her husband standing at the rail of the Titanic when she left in a lifeboat, will have the management of her late husband's estate, together with Henry C. Lee. The two have been appointed executors of the estate by Judge Rives of the probate court. Young Clark's father, J. Ross Clark, has been appointed guardian of his 2-year-old grandson, J. Ross Clark II. The child will inherit about $40,000. Clark's estate is valued at $78,310 and consists mostly of stocks.

GETS RIGHT TO TRANSFER PIPE LINE FRANCHISE

The city council today granted to F. E. Fitzpatrick the right to transfer to the General Pipe Line company the franchise recently voted to him by the council for a pipe line through the city from the Midway oil fields to the Los Angeles harbor.

BELLUS WINS STOCK SUIT

By virtue of a decision of the district court of appeals affirming a decision of the superior court, M. L. Bellus will receive $10,000 from D. L. Peters as compensation for 40,000 shares of stock of the Orange County Gas company, which, the plaintiff charges, Peters converted to his own use.

$10,000 LOSS IN BROADWAY GEM STORE FIRE

Firemen Fight an Early Morning Blaze in Cellar of Brock & Co.

VALUABLE GOODS BURN

Silverware and Silk Jewelry Cases Destroyed; Discovered by Watchman

Valuable silverware, costly jewel cases and a large stock of stationery were destroyed early this morning when a smoldering fire broke out in the basement of the jewelry store of Brock & Company on Broadway near Fifth street. The fire is believed to be of a spontaneous nature. The loss was estimated this morning by D. T. Dunsmore, an officer of the company, at between $8000 and $10,000. The loss was fully covered by insurance.

The fire was discovered about 3 o'clock this morning by William Houghton, the watchman, who summoned the fire department and then led the way into the basement. About one-third of the cellar was smoldering and sm-'-- was rising in dense clouds. Ventilation was effected by opening basement entrances and then a squad of firemen equiped with oxygen helmets descended. Lines of hose were forced into the cellar and the smoldering mass saturated. The blaze was out within thirty minute- of the time the firemen arrived.

In that portion of the basement where the blaze started, was stored a large amount of silverware, velvet and silk cases in which jewels are delivered to purchasers and stationery of first quality. The mass was declared to be a total loss.

The store was opened for business at the usual hour this morning, the fire not having damaged the building.

ATTORNEY SEES VICTORY IN LEMON RATE FIGHT

Declaring that the citrus shippers of California will finally win over the railroads in the $1 lemon rate case to be argued before the commerce court at Washington, June 4, and that the $375,000 trust fund created by the shippers will be repaid to them within a very short time afterward, A. F. Call, attorney for the Citrus Protective league, is preparing to go to Washington to represent the growers and shippers.

BOY WHO BROKE PAROLE CANNOT WED SAYS COURT

Raymond Bruce, 17 years old, a ward of the juvenile court who recently violated his probation by taking an automobile joy ride which ended in a collision, will not be allowed to marry Miss Irene Klencey on June 5 and escape punishment for his misdeeds. Judge Wilbur refused permission to the couple yesterday for the marriage. He has not yet decided what Bruce's punishment shall be.

CITY TOO POOR TO RAISE SALARIES OF POLICEMEN

Because the city's finances are not in a condition to permit it, the city council has declined to increase the standard of salaries of the police department. The men are getting from $83,33 to $102 a month. The new scale requested by the police would make the city pay from $100 to $120 a month.

MRS. WHIPPLE NAMED NEW PICTUHE CENSOR

Mayor Alexander sent to the city council today his appointment of Mrs. Charles H. Whipple to succeed Ralph Daniels as a member of the motion picture censoring commission. Daniels had resigned. Confirmation will be made next Tuesday.

WIDOW WHIPS POLITICIAN

EVERETT, Wash., May 28.—"Now I've got you," shouted Mrs. Emily J. Russell, a widow of Oakland, Cal., as she horsewhipped Schuyler Duryee, a pioneer citizen, lawyer and candidate for city commissioner in the election to be held June 4.

Duryee's back was cut and his body bruised before he could get the whip away from the infuriated woman.

P. T. DELEGATES OFF TO MOTHERS' CONGRESS

Snapshot by The Evening Herald Photographer This Morning of P.-T. A. Delegates Just Before Leaving for the Congress of Mothers in Pomona. Mrs. H. N. Rowell of Berkeley, Candidate for President, Is Shown on the Left; Mrs. Thomas F. Salsburg of Berkeley in Center and Mrs. Figg-Hablyn of Santa Barbara in Foreground on Right

Special Trains for Pomona of Those Interested in Free Text Book Debates

About two hundred members of the Southern California Parent-Teacher association left for Pomona this morning to attend a two-day meeting of the California congress of mothers.

The principal features of this convention will be the election of officers and a discussion of constitutional amendments, with a closing program tomorrow in which State Senator W. H. Shanahan and County Superintendent of Schools Mark Keppel will discuss the free text book bill.

The election of officers is expected to be practically without contest, since the southern delegates have agreed almost as a whole to support Mrs. H. N. Rowell of Berkeley for the state presidency. Mrs. A. L. Hamilton of Pasadena, who is now president, has not definitely withdrawn her name from the list of candidates, although she is said to favor the transferring of the executive power to the north of the state. It is said by many of Mrs. Hamilton's friends that she will withdraw her name tomorrow morning if it is placed in nomination at the primaries this afternoon.

Other women prominently mentioned and in fact meeting with general approval from the Southern California delegates, who are a controlling faction in the situation, are: Mrs. E. N. Strong of Long Beach as first vice president; Mrs. W. H. Marston of Berkeley, second vice president; Mrs. L. B. Avery, San Jose, recording secretary; Mrs. F. W. Pierson of Berkeley, corresponding secretary; Mrs. P. T. Anderson, Los Angeles, financial secretary; Mrs. A. L. Colby, Los Angeles, treasurer; Mrs. George B. Bird, Stockton, parliamentarian, and Mrs. Leo McLaughlin. Pasadena, as auditor. The historian will be some Pomona woman to be chosen by the delegates of the hostess city.

Among the amendments to be considered is one providing a two year term for state officers so that at alternate conventions to association work can be done without time b wasted on lobbying. Other amendments include the dropping of directors meetings, as at present required, further working out of the district organization with Los Angeles county to be known as the first district. This will be brought about by action upon Mrs. Harry Huston's amendment to section 2, article 5 of the constitution.

Three cars full of delegates, including several from the north, with Mrs. Rowell, Mrs. Thomas A. Seabury of Berkeley and Mrs. H. F. Herrington of Oakland, left the Arcade station this morning at 9 o'clock and the train was augmented at Shorb station by another car of delegates representing the Pasadena, Alhambra, San Gabriel and other districts of that locality.

Another large delegation will leave here tomorrow morning especially for the purpose of hearing the text book debate.

D. A. R. REGENT JUST ELECTED RESIGNS

Mrs. Harrison Purdon, newly elected regent of Eschscholtzia Chapter D. A. R., has resigned from the office before her installation. At the meeting of the board of directors held this afternoon at the home of Mrs. Enoch Pepper, Rampart apartments, a note by special messenger was received in which Mrs. Purdon declared that circumstances over which she had no control prevented her accepting the office.

The board may either appoint the incoming vice regent, Mrs. Frank Young, to the regency or it may appoint some other candidate. Mrs. Englehoff Rundle has been mentioned for the place.

Eight new members were received into the chapter this afternoon and other routine business was arranged. The installation of officers will take place next Tuesday afternoon at Ebell clubhouse. Mrs. Young, who is now in the east, may return in time for that event although her formal acceptance of the office of vice regent expressed no certainty of that.

FLOUR MAN SUED BY WIFE FOR $150 MONTH ALIMONY

Alleging cruelty and abuse, Mrs. Nicholas Koss is suing her husband, who is a retired flour dealer formerly of Minneapolis, for separate maintenance. Koss is said to be worth $50,000.

Mrs. Koss is 25 years her husband's junior, and on February 17, she alleges, Koss tried to kill her, shooting at her and stabbing her. Koss is now on parole from the insanity court.

Mrs. Koss wants $150 a month for her support, $500 attorney's fees and $100 costs.

WOMEN BY LIGHT OF MOON TRAP BURGLARS IN STORE

Occupants of Apartment Watch Thieves Enter Store, Then Call Police

MAY APPEAR IN COURT

Officers, Imitating Joy Riders, Drice Up in Auto and Overpower Men

Police officials may boast the efficiency of the department but it is nevertheless true that great credit is due the West Sixth street "women's auxiliary" for the capture early today of a burglar and his alleged accomplice, who br :e into the grocery store of R. W. Hite, 829 West Sixth street. When the men were arraigned in police court they were confronted by the women who watched them at work.

About 1:30 o'clock this morning two young men sauntered west on Sixth street until the store was reached. One of them pointed toward a window and an instant lated he pried it open while his companion took his position in front.

The moonlight was very bright and it chanced that some of the women in nearby buildings were awake. They watched the alleged burglar climb in and a few minutes later telephoned to central stattion.

An automobile carrying L. A. Blaisdell, T. W. Miller and Harry Henderson was sent from the police station, and so as not to alarm the burglar they drove recklessly, pretending they were joy riders. They drove a few feet past the store, then Blaisdell stopped the machine and leaped out, pinning the arms of the alleged lookout behind him so quickly he did not know what had happened. Miller and Henderson then concealed themselves near the open window and when the man inside emerged they seized him.

The pair gave the names of Oliver Wentworth and L. C. Bullock.

MINNESOTA PROFESSOR TO LECTURE ON DRAMA

Dr. Richard Burton of the University of Minnesota will lecture at Cumnock hall in July, giving a series of talks on modern drama. He will speak on eight subjects: Scandinavian drama, Ibsen and Strindberg, French drama, Maeterlinck and Rostand, the Irish school—Synge, Lady Gregory and Yeats—English drama, Pinero, Jones and Wilde; American drama, Moodey, Mackaye and others; poetic drama, Phillips, Masefield and Peabody; Galesworth and his school and George Bernard Shaw.

POLICEMAN RISKS HIS LIFE TO SAVE BOY

Walter Smith, a messenger boy living at 340 Bodie street, was saved from serious injury yesterday afternoon by the presence of mind of Traffic Officer Johnson, who signaled the motorman of a car at Fourth and Spring streets to stop instantly when he saw the boy fall from his bicycle with his feet under the car. The officer then hurried to the boy and drew him to safety.

Smith was taken to the receiving hospital, where it was learned that his ankle had been sprained.

POLICE BAFFLED BY SLAYING OF JAPANESE

Although several persons saw the men as they departed from the restaurant, the detectives have no clew to the identity of the two Japanese who last night shot and killed Tokuzo Tamura, sometimes called George Tamura, in the establishment conducted by Y. Imamura at 135 North Central avenue.

A good description of the men was given the police, but their names have not been learned.

TITANIC PROBERS BLAME CAPTAIN OF CALIFORNIAN

Also Arraign Commander of Lost Liner in Finding Made Public by Sen. Smith in the Senate Yesterday

SCORE THE BRITISH BOARD OF TRADE

(Associated Press Despatch.)

WASHINGTON, May 28—Blame for the Titanic disaster is chargeable directly to the failure of the dead Captain Smith to heed repeated warnings of icebergs ahead, but responsibility for unnecessary loss of life must be shared by Captain Lord of the steamship Californian, through his disregard of distress signals. This is the finding of the Titanic, as prepared in a comprehensive speech delivered by William Alden Smith, of Michigan, Chairman of the Committee.

Senator Smith declared that responsibility also rests upon the British Board of Trade, "to whose laxity of regulation, and hasty inspection, the world is largely indebted for the awful fatality." In denouncing Captain Lord, of the Californian, the Senator said the Titanic's distress signals were plainly seen from the deck of his vessel a short distance away.

America will leave to England the chastisement of those guilty asserted the Senator, and he quoted British law to show that Captain Lord might be prosecuted for a misdemeanor.

Other conclusions presented, in brief, were as follows:

Before the Titanic departed on her maiden voyage there were no sufficient tests of boilers, bulkheads, equipment or signal devices.

Officers and crew were strangers to each other not familiar with the ship's implements or tools, and no drill or station practice took place and no helpful discipline prevailed.

The speed of the Titanic was 24 miles an hour at time of the accident, although officers of the Titanic had been advised of the presence of icebergs by the steamships Baltic, Amerika and Californian.

Passengers were not advised of danger, although President Ismay of the White Star Line, who was taking the vessel's maiden voyage, was informed. No general alarm was given nor any organized system of safety undertaken.

Of the 1,324 passengers and 899 members of the crew on board, there was room in the lifeboats for only 1,176 persons and because of lack of orderly discipline the boats took off only 704 persons, 12 being rescued from the water.

Officers of the White Star Line "battled with the truth" after receiving information from their Montreal office Monday morning following the accident.

Senator Smith condemned "antiquated shipping laws and overripe administrative boards" and asked that all nations act together in shipping reforms. "New laws," he said, "will best testify our affection for the dead."

Captain Rostron, of the rescue ship Carpathia was praised by Senator Smith and he urged that Congress recognize his valor.

At the outset, Senator Smith defended the course of his committee in holding British subjects to secure their testimony without delay, and briefly answered criticism of his lack of nautical knowledge.

"Our course was simple and plain—to gather the facts relating to this disaster while they were still vivid realities," he said. "Questions of diverse citizenship gave way to the universal desire for the simple truth. It was of paramount importance that we should act quickly to avoid jurisdictional confusion and organized opposition at home or abroad. We, of course, recognized that the ship was under a foreign flag; but the lives of many of our own countrymen had been sacrificed and the safety of many had been put in grave peril, and it was vital that the entire matter should be reviewed before an American tribunal if legislative action was to be taken for future guidance.

"Without any pretension to experience or special knowledge of nautical affairs, nevertheless I am of the opinion that very few important facts which were susceptible of being known escaped our scrutiny. Energy is often more desirable than learning, and the inquisition serves a useful purpose to the State.

"In the construction of the Titanic," continued the Senator, "no limit of cost circumscribed their endeavor and when this vessel took its place at the head of the line every modern improvement in shipbuilding was supposed to have been realized; so confident were they that both owner and builder were eager to go upon the trial trip.

"When the crisis came a state of absolute unpreparedness stupified both passengers and crew and, in their despair, the ship went down, carrying as needless a sacrifice of noble women and brave men as ever clustered about the Judgment Seat in any single moment of passing time.

"We shall leave to the honest judgment of England and its painstaking chastisement of the British Board of Trade, to whose laxity of regulation and hasty inspection the world is largely indebted for this awful fatality. Of contributing causes there were very many. In the face of warning signals, speed was increased and messages of danger seemed to stimulate her to action rather than to persuade her to fear.

"The Titanic rushed onward on her true course—one recognized as appropriate and agreed upon by mariners as the international highway for westbound vessels, yet dangerous at this season of the year, when the Labrador current may be bearing vast masses of ice across the track of ships—scores of these towering glaciers planted themselves in the very pathway of this ship and were so large and so numerous that, in the absence of fog, they should have been easily discernible by the lookout, if, as he says in his testimony, he had been supplied with glasses.

"Capt. Smith knew the sea and his clear eye and steady hand had often guided his ship through dangerous paths; for 40 years storms sought in vain to vex him or menace his craft. His indifference to danger was one of the direct and contributing causes of this unnecessary tragedy, while his own willingness to die was the expiating evidence of his fitness to live; those of us who knew him well—not in anger, but in sorrow—file one specific charge against him, overconfidence and neglect to heed the oft-repeated warnings of his friends; but, in his horrible dismay, when his brain was afire with honest retribution, we can still see, in his manly bearing and his tender solicitude for the safety of women and little children, some traces of his lofty spirit.

"The mystery of his indifference to danger, when other and less pretentious vessels doubled their lookout or stopped their engines, finds no reasonable hypothesis in conjecture or speculation; science in shipbuilding was supposed to have attained perfection and to have spoken her last word; mastery of the ocean had at last been achieved; but overconfidence seems to have dulled the faculties usually so alert. With the atmosphere literally charged with warning signals and wireless messages registering their last appeal, the stokers in the engine room fed their fires with fresh fuel, registering in that dangerous place her fastest speed.

"Nature gave a warning of approaching peril so significant that pasengers in stateroom and steerage shut out the chill and spoke to one another of the sudden cold. Sailors off the Grand Banks know the importance of the thermometer, which is almost as necessary to their safety as is the compass. Even the quartermaster, Hichens, who regularly took the temperature of the water from the sea, said: 'It suddenly became bitter cold' and added that the first order received by him from Second Officer Lightoller at 8 o'clock Sunday evening was 'to take his compliments down to the ship's carpenter and inform him to look to his fresh water, that it was about to freeze.'"

Senator Smith declared that the command of the officer of the watch to avert the disaster actually exposed the most vulnerable part of the Titanic to the ice when the shock came.

"Distracted by the sudden appearance of danger," said the speaker, "he sharply turned aside the prow, the part best prepared to resist collision, exposing the temple to the blow; at the turn of the bilge the steel encasement yielded to a glancing blow so slight that the impact was not felt in many parts of the ship, although representing an energy of more than a million foot tons, said to be the equivalent of the combined broadsides of 20 of the largest guns in our battleship fleet at the same moment, with a blow so deadly many of the passengers and crew did not even know of the collision until tardily advised of the danger by anxious friends, and even then official statements were clothed in such confident assurances of safety as to arouse no fear.

Senator Smith said that the awful force of the impact must have indicated to master and builder that the ship was doomed. He commented caustically upon the failure of the ships officers immediately to give general alarm or to establish some orderly routine. Concerning the conduct of the ship's officers he said:

"Haphazard, they rushed by one another, on staircase and in hallway, while men of self control gathered here and there about the decks, helplessly staring at one another or giving encouragement to those less courageous than themselves. Lifebelts were finally adjusted to all and the lifeboats were cleared away, and although strangely insufficient in number, were only partially loaded and in all instances unprovided with compasses and only three of them had lamps. They were manned so badly that, in the absence of prompt relief, they would have fallen easy victims to the advancing ice floe, nearly 30 miles in width and rising 16 feet above the surface of the water. Their danger would have been as great as if they had remained on the deck of the broken hull, and if the sea had risen these toy targets with over 700 exhausted people would have been helplessly tossed about upon the waves without food or water.

"One witness swore that two of the three stewards in her boat admitted that they had never had an oar in their hands before and did not even know what the oarlock was for. The lifeboats were filled so indifferently and lowered so quickly that, according to the uncontradicted evidence, nearly 500 people were needlessly sacrificed to want of orderly discipline in loading the few that were provided. And yet it is said by some well-meaning persons that the best of discipline prevailed. If this is discipline what would have been disorder?

"Among the passengers were many strong men who had been accustomed to command, whose lives had marked every avenue of endeavor, and whose business experience and military training especially fitted them for such an emergency. These were rudely silenced and forbidden to speak, as was the president of this company, by junior officers, a few of whom, I regret to say, availed themselves of the first opportunity to leave the ship. Some of the men, to whom had been intrusted the care of passengers, never reported to their official stations, and quickly deserted the ship with a recklessness and indifference to the responsibilities of their positions as culpable and amazing as it is impossible to believe. And some of these men say they 'laid by' in their partially filled lifeboats and listened to the cries of distress 'until the noise quited down' and surveyed from a safe distance the unselfish men and women and faithful fellow officers and seamen, whose heroism lightens up this tragedy and recalls the noblest traditions of the sea."

Tributes to the valor of Phillips and Bride, the wireless operators on the Titanic, were paid by Senator Smith. He said that the final exit of the Phillips boy was "not so swift as to prevent him from pausing long enough to pass a cup of water to a fainting woman." The senator showed that had not the underpaid wireless operator on the Carpathia prepared for bed with his receiver still on his head the Titanic's distress signals never would have been received by the rescue ship.

"When the world weeps together over a common loss," said Senator Smith, "all nations should take steps wisely to regulate wireless telegraphy and see that operators are fairly paid." He condemned the "reign of silence" concerning the details of the disaster. In condemning the failure of the Californian to learn all about the disaster before the Titanic sank, and go to her rescue, Senator Smith said:

"The steamship Californian was within easy reach of this ship for nearly four hours after all the facts were known to Operator Cottam. The captain of the Carpathia says he gave explicit directions that all official messeges should be immediately sent through other ships, and messages of passengers should be given preference. According to Binns, the inspector, the apparatus on the Californian was practically new and easily tuned to carry every detail of that calamity to the coast stations at Cape Sable and Cape Race, and should have done so.

"The course taken was singularly in accord with the reticence of the officials of the White Star Co., who knew at 2.30 Monday morning," said the Senator, "what was supposed to have occurred, and yet, at 7.51 Monday evening a message from their own office, officially signed, containing the positive assurance of the safety of the passengers, was sent to a half-crazed father at Huntington, W. Va., nearly two hours after their admitted familiarity with the details of the disaster. It is little wonder that we have not been able to fix with definiteness the author of this falsehood."

Senator Smith reviewed the testimony of Captain Lord, showing that the Californian came within four miles of the doomed vessel and that he went to his room to lie down while signal rockets were being fired.

"Failure of Captain Lord to arouse the wireless operator on his ship, who easily could have ascertained the name of the vessel in distress and reached her in time to avert loss of life," said Senator Smith, places a tremendous responsibility upon this officer from which it will be difficult for him to escape.

"Contrast, if you will, the conduct of the captain of the Carpathia in this emergency and imagine what must be the consolation of that thoughtful and sympathic mariner, who rescued the shipwrecked and left the people of the world his debtor as his ship sailed for distant seas a few days ago. By his utter self-effacement and his own indifference to peril by his promptness and his knightly sympathy, he rendered a great service to humanity. He should be made to realize the debt of gratitude this Nation owes to him, while the book of good deeds, which had so often been famaliar with his unaffected valor, would henceforth carry the name of Capt. Rostron to the remotest period of time.

"The lessons of this hour," said Senator Smith in conclusion, "are, indeed, fruitless and its precepts ill-conceived if rules of action do not follow hard upon the day of reckoning. Obsolute and antiquated shipping laws should no longer encumber the parliamentary records of any Government, and overripe administrative boards should be pruned of dead branches and less sterile precepts taught and applied."

Senator Smith recommended that lanes of travel should be more carefully defined, strength of ships' bows increased, life saving equipment bettered, and discipline and practice made an exaction. He said bouys should be carried to mark temporarily the place of the ship's burial in case of accident; and men of strength and spirit there must be, won back to a calling already demoralized and decadent.

"But 10 per cent of the men before the mast in our merchant marine are natives or naturalized Americans," he said. "Even England, that 20 years ago had barely 7000 Orientals on her merchant ships, now carries over 70,000 of that alien race. Americans must re-enlist in this service, they must become the soldiers of the sea, and, whether in the lookout, on the deck or at the wheel, whether able or common seamen they should be better paid for their labor and more highly honored in their calling; their rights must be respected, and their work carefully performed; harsh and severe restraining statutes must be repealed, and a new dignity given this important field of labor."

SCHOOL CHILDREN KEEPING BRIGHT THE MEMORY OF BRAVE DEEDS

The school children of this city will this afternoon hold patriotic exercises in the several grades throughout the city. The annual custom is looked forward to with great pleasure by both pupil and teacher, and the many programs are arranged with care and long study by those who participate.

Details from the local Post will visit the schools and the remarks by the veterans to the children are always a feature of the exercises. Following are the exercises to be given at the Kelley and Jackman schools today. The programs of the other schools and grades will be published in tomorrow morning's Herald.

KELLEY SCHOOL

Eighth Grade

1. Recitation—The Vanishing Army—Katherine Duggan, Barbara Chambers, Katherine Cashman, Ida Stanton, Marion Chesterman.

Sixth Grade

2. Vocal Duet—The Spot of Earth—Harold De Courcy, Sidney Harris.
3. Nellie Decorations—May Nelson.
4. Address at Gettysburg—Louis Balch.
5. Recitation—Together—Gladys Dummer.

Fifth Grade

6. Exercise—Leslie Harris, Pauline Wilkinson, Grace Warren, Hazel Randall, Olive Noyes, Anna Brooks, Mary Ananian, Ruth Richardson, Amanda Guptill, Christine Nealey, Edith Shepperson, Margaret Ogasapian, Eleanor French.
7. Recitation—Flowers for the Brave—Andrew Arnesen.

Sixth Grade

Song and Dialogue—The Patriotic Calendar—Hannah Lynch, Mildred Hatch, Mary Barth, Lillian Buzzell, Eleanor Dow, Kathryn Ayers, Dorothy Eaton, Eva Norman, Grace Randall, Beatrice Shepperson, Julia Lynch.

Ninth Grade

9. Song—American Hymn—May Dawson, Mary Doyle, Annie Doyle, Helen Bartlett, Lawrence Clarkson, Willard Grant.

Fifth Grade

10. Flag Drill—Avan Gulian, William Paul, Leslie Harris, Harold Golden, Emery Cleaves, Harold Kay, George Kalashian, Allan Clarkson, Louis Ginsberg, Abraham Hirsch, Douglas Eaton, Barton Titcomb, Jacob Deamond, Paul Lunt, Donald Lovejoy, Clifford Swaine.
11. Ode for Memorial Day—Dorothy Keefe.
12. Recitation—Hurrah for Old New England—Harold DeCourcey.
13. The Spirit of a Great Nation—Belva Chase.
14. Early American Heroes—Helen Pond, Dorothy Hughes, Richard Greaton, Elmer Barry, Harold DeCourcey, Isabel Beckman, Jeremiah Duggan, Sidney Harris, Leland Sibley, William Groves, John Mayes, Philip Pearson, Lula Cronin, Charles Estabrooks, George Nice, Weston Heywood, George Jackman, George Tenney, Mildred Philips, Elizabeth Toggerson.
15. Hymn—Fifth Grade.
16. Reading—Music in Camp—Jennie Miller; musical accompaniment, Lurline Mullins.
17. Recitation—Both Blue and Gray—Anthony Towle.

JACKMAN SCHOOL

Room J.

Singing—American Hymn.
Memorial Day—Marion Johnson.
The Meaning of the Day—Edw. Wright.
The Origin of the Day—Malcolm Jones.
Singing—Memorial Day.
To Their Memory—Muriel Richardson.
A Soldier's Offering—Rachel Hunter.
Strew with Flowers—Marion Piper, Hazel Phinney, Marion Ireland.
Singing—E'er Fadeless Be Their Glory.
Patriotism—School.
That Starry Flag of Ours—Elizabeth O'Connor.
The Flag Goes By—Henry Stillman.
Singing—Star Spangled Banner.
The Banner Betsy Made—Eleanor Walton.
When the Northern Band Plays Dixie—Elliott Knight.
Suwanee River—School.
Decoration Day—Jessie Felch.
Roll Call—Roland Woodwell.
Battle Prayer—School.
Address at Gettysburg—School.

Rooms E and F—Sixth Grade

Song—The Lord's Prayer—Room F.
Recitation — Decoration Day—Pauline Watts.
Recitation—Wm. Glover.
Song—Battle Hymn of the Republic—Rooms E and F.
Recitation — Our Tribute—Henry Thompson.
Recitation — Driving Home the Cows—Mildred Thurlow.
Song—Flag of the Free—Room E.
Choosing the Flowers—Room E. Ada Chase, Pauline Watts, Evalyn Meinerth, Dorothy Wilson, Dorice Nutting, Dorothy Shafner, Elvira Ilsley.
Song—God Ever Glorious—Rooms E and F.
Recitation—Wreaths and Flowers—Elvira Ilsley.
Recitation—The Love of Country—John Henry.
Song—How They So Softly Rest—Room F.
Recitation—Bringing Flowers—Dorothy Wilson.
Recitation—Grace Tibbetts.
Song—Bringing Flowers—Room E.
Recitation—The Flag Is Passing By—Isadore Goldsmith.
Recitation—Ector Lathram.
Song—The Star Spangled Banner—Rooms E and F.
Recitation—The Blue and the Gray—Wilfred Kneeland.
Lincoln's Speech at Gettysburg—Rooms E and F.
Song—The Battle Cry of Freedom—Rooms E and F.
Recitation—Caro'ine Barth.
Exercise—Evalyn Wright, Ethel Landford, Gladys Lang, Dorothy Shafner, Doris Nutting.
Song—Our Fatherland—Room F.
Recitation—The Soldier's Flag—Hazel Hudson, Raymond Whitley.
Recitation—The Ship of State—Charlotte Gould.
Song—Just Before the Battle, Mother—Room F.
The Roll Call—Howard Knapp, Gordon Ingalls, James Erskine, Joseph Moulton, Isidore Goldsmith, Stuart Sanders.
Song—America—Rooms E and F.

Eighth Grade

Singing—Maryland.
Recitation—Decoration Day—Dan Brenan.
Recitation—The Flag Goes By—Norman Carver.
Singing—Battle Hymn.
Reading—The History of Our Flag—Joseph Williams.
Reading—Sheridan's Ride—Clarence Wheeler.
Singing—Star Spangled Banner.
Reading—The Blue and the Gray—Dorothy Thurlow.
Reading—Driving Home the Cows—Cora Welch.
Singing—Columbia, the Gem of the Ocean.
Recitation—The Bride of the Battery B—Edith Colby.
Recitation—Song of the Union—Earl Lieber.
Singing—Rally Round the Flag.
Recitation—The American Flag—Jessie Foley.
Recitation—We Honor Our Country—Carlton Brown.
Singing—Suwanee River.
Recitation—Our National Banner—Max Distelman.
Singing—America.

Ninth Grade

Singing—American Hymn—The School.
Recitation—The National Flag—Abel Brudno.
Recitation—When the Northern Bands Played Dixie—Thomas Bell.
Singing—Dixie—School.
Recitation—New England's Dead Viola Pyfrom.
Singing—The Nation's Heroes—School.
Recitation—Hymn for the Nation Edith Hardy.
Recitation — The Roll Call—Joseph Kendell.
Singing—Memorial Day—School.
Recitation — The Battlefield—Eleanor Plummer.
Recitation—What Makes a Nation?—Raymond Abbott.
Singing—Columbia, the Gem of the Ocean—School.
Recitation—The Gettysburg Address—Daniel Nichols.
Recitation—Song of the Battleflag—Florence Perkins.
Singing—Star Spangled Banner—School.
Recitation — Women of the War Marion Nutter.
Recitation — Keenan's Charge—Samuel Stratton.
Singing—Decoration Day — The School.
Recitation—Flower of Liberty—Laura Little.
Singing—America—School.

BURGESS WINS A LICENSE TO WORK HYDRO AEROPLANE

MARBLEHEAD, June 5—The first aviator's license to be granted in New England to an operator of a hydro aeroplane was won before most of the residents of the town were awake this morning by W. Starling Burgess, one of the pioneers in flight in New England and president and designer of the Burgess Company and Curtis. This is the second aviator's license for which tests have been made in New England, Norman Prince of the Back Bay making his tests in a biplane during a rainstorm at the 1911 Harvard-Boston aero meet.

Prof. R. W. Wilson of the department of astronomy at Harvard, recently appointed New England representative of the Aero Club of America to succeed the late Prof. Rotch, officially observed the tests, which were made in a regular model Burgess hydro-aeroplane. The course was marked out by a buoy and a stake boat just outside the entrance to the harbor and, at 4.30 this morning, the ascent was made.

Burgess flew to a height of 300 feet and then completed the necessary three figure eights. The final test, that of gliding to the water with engine cut off, was successfully completed, the distance from the designated point to the point of contact with the water being but 114 feet, according to the measurements of Prof. Wilson with his sextant.

John Gray and H. L. Hattemer, two of the pupils at the Burgess school, also planned to qualify for their licenses, but a sharp wind sprang up just before they were ready and it was necessary to postpone their flights.

Pads and Pencils Also.

PILGRIM FATHERS.

George Whitfield Colony 68, at its meeting Friday evening, June 7, will have initiation at 9 o'clock. The doors will be thrown open for the public installation of officers. The work will be done by the Waverly degree staff of Somerville. Nathan Crary, Supreme Secretary, will be present.

DEATHS.

MERRILL—In this city, June 5th, 1912, Warren Merrill, aged 86 years, 11 months. Funeral services will be held at his late home, 240 Merrimac street, Friday, June 7th, at 2:30 o'clock p. m. Relatives and friends invited to attend. Burial private.

DISCUSS PLANS ON PURCHASE OF A PLAYGROUND

Project of Filling in Water Front For Field Considered to be Too Expensive

SEVERAL PLACES CONSIDERED

Committee to Look Over Lot Adjoining the Kent Street Landing

The committee on public playgrounds was scheduled to meet at City Hall at 7.30 last evening but it was nearly half an hour before enough members put in an appearance to make a quorom.

The members discussed the matter in an informal manner and did not take any action during the evening.

The project of filling in the water front at lower end of the city at some time in the future was discussed, but in the opinion of those present it would cost a fortune to erect cement bulkheads and do the other necessary work.

President Bass advocated the Kent street park as being a good location for a playground for all of the children both at the north and south ends of Newburyport.

Alderman Perkins said that the city should have two base-ball fields one at each section of the city for the use of the boys.

Mayor Burke stated that it would be a good plan to have a permanent playground as it would cost less in the end than to appropriate money year after year for rentals.

The land near the Towle Silver factory from Littlefield's wharf to the silver factory owned by Cornelius F. Creeden was advocated as an ideal place to purchase but economy made it impossible to pay out any money this year for that purpose.

The fact was brought out that it was very difficult to secure proper fields within the city limits for the use of the children, the proprietors either asking too much for their property or did not care to sell.

President Bass made the suggestion that a committee be appointed to confer with Mr. Creeden and see what his property could be secured for. This land consisting of several acres adjoins the Kent street landing and in the opinion of several members it is a very desirable lot.

Several of the ladies, expected to attend the meeting who are interested in the children's welfare, but other duties prevented them from being present.

Mr. Bass said that the boys had taken much of the equipment from the old playground but that the police had recovered much of this.

Some criticism of one of the instructors at the playgrounds last year was indulged in and it was stated that the young people in certain cases acted about as they pleased.

The members present besides the mayor were President Bass, Alderman Perkins and Councilman Thurlow.

Your Contribution will Help Swell the Fund.

GETTING INTO FORM AT THE RED TOP QUARTERS

(Associated Press Despatch.)

RED TOP, Conn., June 5—The Harvard varsity eight went over the four mile course on the Thames this afternoon on a time row, but no time was given out by the coaches. Coach Wray said, however, that the time was very good.

The varsity crew had a snappy two mile row with the freshmen eight at the start, the latter crew then dropping out while the varsity finished the whole course.

Remember the Cause. Buy.

MORAL FORCE.

The world stands on ideas and not on iron or cotton, and the iron of iron, the fire of fire, the ether and source of all the elements, is moral force.—Emerson.

Captain A. H. Rostron of the Carpathia and Loving Cup Given Him by Titanic Survivors.

Photo copyright, 1912, by American Press Association.

Captain Arthur Henry Rostron of the Cunard liner Carpathia, the Titanic rescue ship, was presented a silver loving cup inscribed with declarations of thanks by a committee of survivors of the disaster. Three hundred and twenty medals were also presented, gold and silver ones for the officers, stewards and engineers and bronze ones for every member of the crew. The presentation was made upon the recent visit of the Carpathia to New York, which was her first return to this side since she brought in the Titanic survivors. Mrs. J. J. Brown, shown at Captain Rostron's side, came from Denver for the occasion.

Communication

CONDITIONS AT KELLEY SCHOOL

To the Editor of the Herald:

Although the article on the conditions at the Kelley school, by Dr. Abbie Noyes Little is to a great extent too true, there are two or three statements which may be misleading.

First—The statement that there is only one outside door, is incorrect. There are two entrances, each large enough for four children to march abreast, that are always used in assembling or dismissing the school.

Second—The statement that "At present conditions at the Kelley school are so bad that is is not unusual for parents to take their children from it and send them to private schools" is true in three cases this year; but in the meantime we have had fifteen come to us from the private schools in the city. We also have seven non resident pupils.

Third—There has been but one epidemic of any disease other than the ordinary children's diseases such as whooping cough and measles since I have been connected with the school.

I refer to the cases of diphtheria two years ago.

I. H. Johnson.

DEAD AVIATOR'S PLANS ARE TO BE CARRIED OUT BY BROTHER ORVILLE

NEW YORK, June 5—Unless the wishes of Orville Wright are overruled by the board of directors of the Wright company the secret plans of the late Wilbur Wright, father of aviation, to make aerial navigation as safe and practical as travel by an ocean liner or a railway passenger train, will be carried out by Orville Wright and Alexander Ogilvie, the English aviator who assisted Orvill Wright in making experiments at Kill Devil Hill, N. C., with a motorless glider.

LAND 450 AMERICAN MARINES FOR GUARD DUTY ON CUBAN SOIL

CAIMANERA, Cuba, June 5—Four hundred and fifty American marines under command of Col. Lucas were landed this morning at Deseo Point, close to Caimanera, from which point they proceeded by train for Guantanamo City. The announced purpose of the movement is to guard American property and not for intervention.

Six negroes attempting to escape were today shot and killed by Federals in the wholesale arrest of the blacks at Guanaja, in the province of Pinar del Rio, on charges of conspiracy. One hundred and twenty-six negroes were brought to Havana and jailed.

AVIATION MEET AT SQUANTUM

Plans for the third annual Boston Aviation meet which is to be held from June 29 to July 7 at the Harvard Field, Squantum, under the direction of William A. P. Willard are being rapidly pushed forward. Already 10 aviators have been signed to fly, and at least 15 of the world's greatest aviators will enter the contests.

The field at Squantum is now being put into shape for the meet. For the past week several surveyors have **been laying out the grounds which this year will be entirely different** from that of the past two seasons. The ground is all staked off and a gang of several hundred workmen began Monday to lay out the field according to the plans of Manager Willard.

The getaway will be at right angles with the one used at the previous meets. The getaway will be nearly a half mile long and 150 feet wide. It will be constructed as a gravel road and when finished will be covered with oil and other preparations to make it firm.

On one side of the getaway will be constructed a row of hangars to accommodate at least 20 machines. These hangars will be built of wood and the backs of them will be of wire so that the spectators will have a chance to view the machines at close range. This is the first time in the East that hangars have been constructed in this manner. At meets where this plan has been worked, the people have been able to watch the mechanicians tune up the machine and to view the aviators while at work preparatory to flight.

Below the hangars on the same side of the getaway the administration house will be erected. This will be used as the headquarters for the officials of the meet. A huge grandstand, which will seat 10,000 people, is to be started at once a short distance from the administration building. The grandstand will be built so that every seat will be desirable to spectators.

The automobile space will be located opposite the hangars and the grandstand. Room for over 5000 cars has been provided for. These cars will line up on the getaway and the park room for the machines will be nearly perfect. A separate road to the field for automobiles will be provided.

One of the chief attractions will be Lincoln Beachy, who was easily the star of last year's meet. Aviator Beachy has, since his last appearance in Boston, become one of the most daring and thrilling aviators in the country. His performance last year was the talk of the meet and since that time he has added much to his reputation. Last August he established an altitude record at Chicago of 11,474 feet. This record was recently broken again by a foreign aviator.

The other aviators who have sent their contracts to Manager Willard are Hugh A. Robinson, William Hoff, Charles F. Walsh, Charles Whitmer, Beckwith Havens, George W. Beatty and Frank Coffyn. During the coming week it is expected that the word will be received from as many more aviators and that the total number who will compete probably will be over 15.

Several foreigners have signified their intention of coming to Boston to participate in the events. Negotiations are pending with two operators of the Wright biplanes and their entries are expected every day. Beside the men, plans are being formulated to have three women aviators fly at the meet. Miss Blanche Scott, Miss Matilde Moisant and Miss Harriet Quimby are the ones whom Manager Willard hopes to secure to enter the meet.

Home-made Candy Is the Best.

SICK MAN WATCHES AUTO KILL BOY AND DIES FROM THE SHOCK

NEW YORK, June 5—Henry Logan, convalescing from pneumonia was seated in a reclining chair at the window of his home, 446 East 179th street, at the corner of Park avenue, yesterday, watching small boys playing in the street.

Down the avenue came an automobile truck, owned by Gimbel Bros. and driven by Albert Olsen. The boys, who were chasing each other back and forth across the avenue, ran in front of the truck. One misjudged the distance. The truck knocked him down and both wheels passed over his body, killing him.

Logan's wife was at the front door of their home. She saw the accident and was about to go to the boy when there came a shriek from her husband's room. She ran upstairs. As she entered she saw Logan rise from his chair, stagger across the room and with a shriek fall lifeless on the bed.

Olsen was arrested, but after the police learned that he was not responsible for the accident the chauffeur was paroled in custody of a lawyer.

FIRE SOON EXTINGUISHED

Hose 1 was called to the home of John Thurlow, 2½ Atkinson street yesterday morning at 11.17 and when the firemen arrived they discovered a small blaze on the ell of the roof and it was soon extinguished.

The fire was discovered by John Cashman and he with a number of companions, practically had the fire extinguished when the firemen arrived.

"Candy Day" has Arrived.

B. U. DEGREE CONFERRED

Miss Mabel L. Page of this city was among the graduates from the College of Liberal Arts, Boston University, who received degrees at the commencement exercises held in Tremont Temple, Boston, yesterday morning.

WITHHOLDS NAME OF PERSON WHO CUT HIS THROAT

HAVERHILL, June 5—Nelson Bassett of South Groveland is at the Haverhill City hospital with two razor slashes on his throat, one of them having penetrated the outer covering of the jugular vein on the right side.

The wounds, he alleges, were made by a would-be murderer early this morning at his home at South Groveland. Bassett is in a critical condition, while the Haverhill and Groveland police are in quest of people who might know something of the details. It was theorized by the police from the nature of the wounds that Bassett had attempted suicide, but no trace of the weapon with which the deed was committed could be found, and Bassett's attitude afterward at the hospital caused the police officials to set to work on the attempted murder theory.

Buy Early and Often.

UNITED STATES SEN. GEO. S. NIXON PASSES AWAY AT WASHINGTON

(Associated Press Despatch.)

WASHINGTON, June 5—United States Senator George S. Nixon of Nevada died at 10 o'clock tonight. Senator Nixon had been at the Episcopal Eye, Ear and Throat hospital since last Tuesday when an operation for nasal catarrh was performed. Spinal meningitis developed and the senator's condition soon became critical.

He was 52 years of age and a native of California, going to Nevada early in life.

From ten cents up to $

FUNERAL OF INFANT

The funeral of Winifred Rogers, infant son of Mr. and Mrs. Clarence Rogers of Byfield was held at the home of the parents in Byfield yesterday afternoon, Rev. Earl Hanna pastor of the Byfield M. E. church officiating. The interment was in the South Byfield cemetery.

Buy Early and Often.

Baseball Results

American League

At Detroit—Detroit 8, Boston 6.

At Cleveland—Cleveland 7, New York 0.

At Chicago—Washington 8, Chicago 4.

At St. Louis—St. Louis 13, Philadelphia 1.

National League

At Boston—Pittsburgh 7, Boston 5.

At Philadelphia—St. Louis 8, Philadelphia 5.

At Brooklyn—Brooklyn 4, Chicago 3.

At New York—New York 22, Cincinnati 10.

New England League.

Lynn 4, Lawrence 1.

New Bedford 13, Worcester 7.

Brockton 12, Fall River 7.

Haverhill 7, Lowell 6.

THE STANDING

American League

	W.	L.	Pts.W.
Chicago	30	15	.675
BOSTON	26	17	.605
Detroit	24	21	.533
Philadelphia	19	19	.500
Washington	23	21	.523
Cleveland	21	20	.514
New York	13	26	.333
St. Louis	13	30	.302

National League

	W.	L.	Pts.W.
New York	32	7	.821
Cincinnati	26	18	.592
Chicago	22	18	.550
Pittsburgh	20	19	.513
St. Louis	21	25	.457
Philadelphia	16	21	.432
Brooklyn	13	25	.342
BOSTON	13	30	.302

"Candy Day," Don't Forget.

BROUGHT HERE FOR BURIAL

The remains of William P. Ellery were brought here for burial on the 11.35 train from Keene, N. H., yesterday forenoon by Undertaker McKinney.

Committal services were held at the grave by Rev. Alexander Dixon. There were a large number of kindred and friends present and the floral tributes were very beautiful.

Interment was in the Highland cemetery.

Home-made Candy Is the Best.

FUNERAL OF W. W. DOW

The funeral of Warren W. Dow was held at his home in Seabrook, N. H. Rev. Mr. Savage, pastor of the Line church officiating. The pall bearers were Willis Brown, Willie Davis, Charles Bragg and Lester Fellows. The interment was in Elmwood cemetery, Seabrook, N. H.